RAND McNALLY

GOODE'S
WORLD ATLAS

20TH EDITION

John C. Hudson	Edward B. Espenshade, Jr.
EDITOR	EDITOR EMERITUS

CONTENTS

Goode's World Atlas

Copyright © 2000 by Rand McNally & Company; Fifth printing, Revised
Copyright © 1922, 1923, 1932, 1933, 1937, 1939, 1943, 1946, 1949, 1954, 1957, 1960, 1964, 1970, 1974, 1978, 1982, 1986, 1990, 1995 by Rand McNally & Company
Formerly *Goode's School Atlas*
Made in U.S.A.

Library of Congress Catalog Card Number 99-38535

Cover Photo: Dolomite Range
in northern Italy

Regional Maps [66–244]

CONTENTS, *continued*

Geographical Tables and Indexes [245–372]

INTRODUCTION

This is the twentieth edition of the Rand McNally *Goode's World Atlas*, which was first published more than seventy years ago. The name of Dr. J. Paul Goode, the original editor and distinguished cartographer who designed the early editions, has been retained to affirm the high standards that all those who have participated in the preparation of the atlas during these years have sought to attain.

Through the years, general-reference map coverage has been expanded; the number of thematic maps has been increased and their subject range broadened; and systematic improvements in symbolism, cartographic presentation, and map production and printing have been incorporated.

The twentieth edition continues this tradition. New maps include world forest regions and products, oceanic environments, three new ocean-floor maps, and eight new political maps. For the United States and Canada new or extensively revised maps of the grain trade, agricultural regions, and population density have been included.

Thematic maps, statistics, graphs, and various tables have been revised to incorporate the latest available data. The list of source materials and the index to thematic topics (subject index) have been revised. These additions and other revisions reflect the editors' and publisher's commitment to increasing the usefulness and quality of each edition of the Rand McNally *Goode's World Atlas*, thus maintaining it as a standard among world atlases.

Sources

Every effort was made to assemble the latest and most authentic source materials to use in this edition. In the general physical-political maps, data from national and state surveys, recent military maps, and hydrographic charts were utilized. Source materials for the specialized maps were even more varied (see the partial list of sources at the end of the atlas). They included published and unpublished documents in the form of maps, descriptions in articles and books, statistics, and correspondence with outside experts. Appreciation and thanks are expressed to the various agencies and organizations that cooperated. Noteworthy among them are: the United Nations (for demographic and economic statistics); the Food and Agriculture Organization of the United Nations (for production statistics on livestock, crops, and forest products and for statistics on world trade); the Office of the Geographer, Department of State (for the map, Surface Transport Facilities and other items); the Division of Foreign Agriculture, U.S. Department of Agriculture (for information on crop and livestock distribution); various branches of the national military establishment; the National Oceanic and Atmospheric Administration (for information on temperature, wind pressure, and ocean currents); the Maritime Commission and the Department of Commerce (for statistics on ocean trade); the American Geographical Society (for permission to use the Miller cylindrical projection); the University of Chicago Press (for permission to use **Goode's** Homolosine equal-area projection); the McGraw-Hill Book Co. (for permission to use Glenn Trewartha's map of climatic regions); the Association of American Geographers (for permission to use Richard Murphy's map of landforms); and publications of the World Bank (for nutrition, health, and economic information).

Additional data sources consulted include: *World Oil* (for oil and gas data); International Labor Organization (for labor statistics); and the International Road Federation (for transportation data). The United Nations High Commissioner for refugees provided data for the refugees map.

Acknowledgments

The variety and complexity of problems involved in the preparation of a world atlas make the participation of specialists highly desirable. Of those who have contributed over the years the editors especially acknowledge: A. W. Küchler, Department of Geography, University of Kansas; Richard E. Murphy, late professor of geography, University of New Mexico; Erwin Raisz, late cartographer, Cambridge, Massachusetts; Glenn T. Trewartha, late professor of geography, University of Wisconsin; Derwent Whittlesey, late professor of geography, Harvard University; and Bogdan Zaborski, professor emeritus of geography, University of Ottawa.

The editors thank the entire Cartographic and Design staff of Rand McNally & Company for their continued outstanding contributions. We particularly appreciate the many years of valuable input we have received from Pat Healy and Jon Leverenz; the support of Dennis DeCock; and the help and dedication of Robert Argersinger, Greg Babiak, Brian Cantwell, Marzee Eckhoff, Winifred Farbman, Susan Hudson, Elizabeth Hunt, Jill Stift, and Barbara Strassheim. Ryan Baxter and Jeffrey Gray, Northwestern University, provided invaluable assistance in the preparation of several new maps in this edition.

With this edition, John C. Hudson, Professor of Geography at Northwestern University, assumes the editorship of *Goode's World Atlas* and Edward B. Espenshade, Jr., becomes editor emeritus. Professor Espenshade's tenure as editor, which spanned more than five decades, saw the innovation of most of the features that have made *Goode's World Atlas* the leading atlas in its field. He will continue to serve as an editorial advisor and as a source of inspiration for all who participate in the production of *Goode's*.

John C. Hudson
Edward B. Espenshade, Jr.

Geography and Maps

Geography is the science of location on the earth's surface. Its subject matter includes people, landforms, climate, and all other physical and human phenomena that make up the world's environments and give unique character to diverse places. Geographers construct maps that depict these patterns in order to better understand and explain them. Cartography is the branch of geography that focuses on the theory, methods, and techniques of mapping. Images derived from remote sensing, such as from an orbiting satellite, are now used routinely in mapping. The new technology has simultaneously produced more data for the mapmaker and a higher level and standard of accuracy for the map.

Geographic Education

For several decades geography instruction has been organized around five themes: location, place, human/environment interaction, movement, and regions. More recently, Geography for Life: National Geography Standards (National Geographic Research & Exploration, 1994) has provided a detailed list of objectives in geographic education.

The subject matter of geography is recognized as having six essential elements, beginning with the importance of understanding the **World in Spatial Terms**. Every geographically informed person should know how to use maps in studying the people, places, and environments of the Earth. **Places and Regions** are the localities, both small and large, with which individuals, groups, and whole cultures are identified. These human-defined regions stand apart from the ecosystems of the earth that are understood to be the result of complex **Physical Systems**. Human and physical regions come together in the study of **Human Settlements**, which focuses on the distribution of people, rates of demographic change, patterns of economic activity, and the network of connections and transactions that makes the systems function. Beyond these themes are broader issues of concern focusing on **Environment and Society**. Humans modify and affect their environments just as natural systems influence human activities. Resources are not fixed but rather are the subject of human appraisal as to their value, whether for use or for preservation. The **Uses of Geography** also include interpreting the past and planning for the future as well as interpreting the present.

Organization of the Atlas

Goode's World Atlas consists of three parts, beginning with *World Thematic Maps*, portraying the distribution of climatic regions, resources, landforms, and other major worldwide features. The second part is the *Regional Maps* section and main body of the atlas. It provides detailed reference maps for all inhabited land areas on a continent-by-continent basis. Thematic maps of the continents are also contained in this part. The third part contains a series of geographical tables, a glossary of geographical terms, the index of place names, a subject index, and a list of sources. The tables provide comparative data on a wide variety of topics. The index provides the locations of places named on the regional reference maps.

Cartographic Communication

To communicate information through a map, cartographers must assemble the geographic data, use their personal perception of the world to select the relevant information, and apply graphic techniques to produce the map. Readers must then be able to interpret the mapped data and relate it to their own experience and need for information. Thus, the success of any map depends on both the cartographer's and the map reader's knowledge and perception of the world and on their common understanding of a map's purpose and limitations.

The ability to understand maps and related imagery depends first on the reader's skill at recognizing how a curved, three-dimensional world is symbolized on a flat, two-dimensional map. Normally, we view the world horizontally (that is, our line of vision parallels the horizon), at the eye level about five and one-half to six feet above ground. Images appear directly in front and to either side of us, with our eyes encompassing all details as nonselectively as a camera. Less frequently, when we are atop a high platform or in an airplane, we view the world obliquely, as shown in *Figure 1*, in which both vertical and horizontal facets of objects can be seen. And only those persons at very high altitudes will view the world at a vertical angle (*Figure 2*). Yet maps are based on our ability to visualize the world from an overhead, or vertical, perspective.

A map differs from a purely vertical photograph in two important respects. First, in contrast to the single focal point of a photograph, a map is created as if the viewer were directly overhead at all points (*See Figure 3*). Second, just as our brains select from the myriad items in our field of vision those objects of interest or importance to us, so each map presents only those details necessary for a particular purpose-a map is not an inventory of all that is visible. Selectivity is one of a map's most important and useful characteristics.

Skill in reading maps is basically a matter of practice, but a fundamental grasp of cartographic principles and the symbols, scales, and projections commonly employed in creating maps is essential to comprehensive map use.

Map Data

When creating a map, the cartographer must select the objects to be shown, evaluate their relative importance, and find some way to simplify their form. The combined process is called *cartographic generalization*. In attempting to generalize data, the cartographer is limited by the purpose of the map, its scale, the methods to produce it, and the accuracy of the data.

Figure 1. Oblique aerial photograph of New York City.

Figure 2. High-altitude vertical photograph of New York City area.

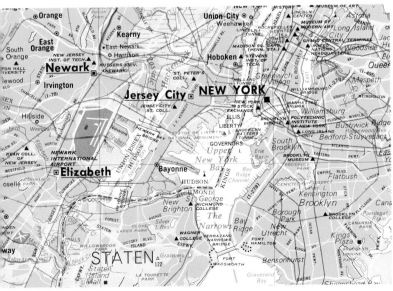

Figure 3. Map of New York City and environs.

Cartographic generalization consists of simplification, classification, symbolization, and induction.

Simplification involves omitting details that will clutter the map and confuse the reader. The degree of simplification depends on the purpose and scale of the map. If the cartographer is creating a detailed map of Canada and merely wants to show the location of the United States, he or she can draw a simplified outline of the country. However, if the map requires a precise identification of the states in New England and the Great Lakes region, the mapmaker will have to draw a more detailed outline, still being careful not to distract the reader from the main features of the Canadian map.

Classification of data is a way of reducing the information to a form that can be easily presented on a map. For example, portraying precise urban populations in the United States would require using as many different symbols as there are cities. Instead, the cartographer groups cities into population categories and assigns a distinct symbol to each one. With the help of a legend, the reader can easily decode the classifications.

Symbolization of information depends largely on the nature of the original data. Information can be *nominal* (showing differences in kind, such as land versus water, grassland versus forest); or *ordinal* (showing relative differences in quantities as well as kind, such as *major* versus *minor* ore deposits); or *interval* (degrees of temperature, inches of rainfall) or *ratio* (population densities), both expressing quantitative details about the data being mapped.

Cartographers use various shapes, colors, or patterns to symbolize these categories of data, and the particular nature of the information being communicated often determines how it is symbolized. Population density, for example, can be shown by the use of small dots or different intensities of color. However, if nominal data is being portrayed—for instance, the desert and fertile areas of Egypt—the mapmaker may want to use a different method of symbolizing the data, perhaps pattern symbols. The color, size, and style of type used for the different elements on a map are also important to symbolization.

Induction is the term cartographers use to describe the process whereby more information is represented on a map than is actually supplied by the original data. For instance, in creating a rainfall map, a cartographer may start with precise rainfall records for relatively few points on the map. After deciding the interval categories into which the data will be divided (e.g., thirty inches or more, fifteen to thirty inches, under fifteen inches), the mapmaker infers from the particular data points that nearby places receive the same or nearly the same amount of rainfall and draws the lines that distinguish the various rainfall regions accordingly. Obviously, generalizations arrived at through induction can never be as precise as the real-world patterns they represent. The map will only tell the reader that all the cities in a given area received about the same amount of rainfall; it will not tell exactly how much rain fell in any particular city in any particular time period.

Cartographers must also be aware of the map reader's perceptual limitations and preferences. During the past two decades, numerous experiments have helped determine how much information readers actually glean from a map and how symbols, colors, and shapes are recognized and interpreted. As a result, cartographers now have a better idea of what kind of rectangle to use; what type of layout or lettering suggests qualities such as power, stability, movement; and what colors are most appropriate.

Map Scale

Since part or all of the earth's surface may be portrayed on a single page of an atlas, the reader's first question should be: What is the relation of map size to the area represented? This proportional relationship is known as the *scale* of a map.

Scale is expressed as a ratio between the distance or area on the map and the same distance or area on the earth. The map scale is commonly represented in three ways: (1) as a simple fraction or ratio called the representative fraction, or RF; (2) as a written statement of map distance in relation to earth distance; and (3) as a graphic representation or a bar scale. All three forms of scale for distances are expressed on Maps A–D.

The RF is usually written as 1:62,500 (as in Map A), where 1 always refers to a unit of distance on the map. The ratio means that 1 centimeter or 1 millimeter or 1 foot on the map represents 62,500 centimeters or millimeters or feet on the earth's surface. The units of measure on both sides of the ratio must always be the same.

Maps may also include a *written statement* expressing distances in terms more familiar to the reader. In Map A the scale 1:62,500 is expressed as being (approximately) 1 inch to 1 mile; that is, 1 inch on the map represents roughly 1 mile on the earth's surface.

The *graphic scale* for distances is usually a bar scale, as shown in Maps A–D. A bar scale is normally subdivided, enabling the reader to measure distance directly on the map.

An *area scale* can also be used, in which one unit of area (square inches, square centimeters) is proportional to the same square units on the earth. The scale may be expressed as either $1:62,500^2$ or 1 to the square of 62,500. Area scales are used when the transformation of the globe to the flat map has been made so that areas are represented in true relation to their respective area on the earth.

When comparing map scales, it is helpful to remember that the *larger* the scale (see Map A) the smaller the area represented and the greater the amount of detail that a map can include. The *smaller* the scale (see Maps B, C, D) the larger the area covered and the less detail that can be presented.

Large-scale maps are useful when readers need such detailed information as the location of roadways, major buildings, city plans, and the like. On a smaller scale, the reader is able to place cities in relation to one another and recognize other prominent features of the region. At the smallest scale, the reader can get a broad view of several states and an idea of the total area. Finer details cannot be shown.

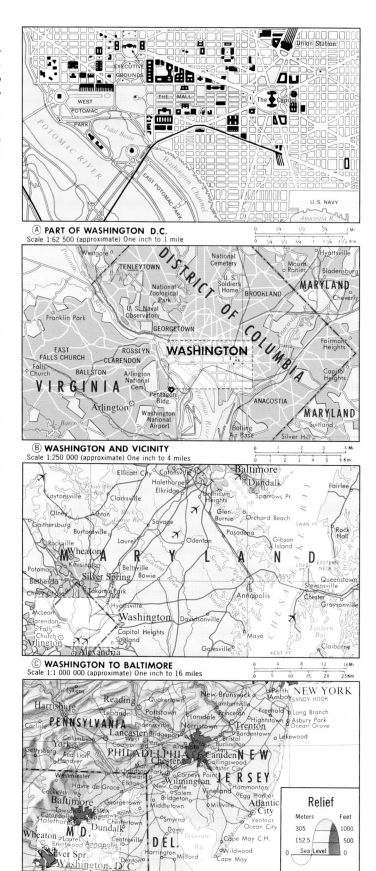

Ⓐ PART OF WASHINGTON D.C.
Scale 1:62 500 (approximate) One inch to 1 mile

Ⓑ WASHINGTON AND VICINITY
Scale 1:250 000 (approximate) One inch to 4 miles

Ⓒ WASHINGTON TO BALTIMORE
Scale 1:1 000 000 (approximate) One inch to 16 miles

Ⓓ WASHINGTON TO NEW YORK
Scale 1:4 000 000 one inch to 64 miles. Conic Projection

Map Projections

Every cartographer is faced with the problem of transforming the curved surface of the earth onto a flat plane with a minimum of distortion. The systematic transformation of locations on the earth (spherical surface) to locations on a map (flat surface) is called projection.

It is not possible to represent on a flat map the spatial relationships of angle, distance, direction, and area that only a globe can show faithfully. As a result, projection systems inevitably involve some distortion. On large-scale maps representing a few square miles, the distortion is generally negligible. But on maps depicting large countries, continents, or the entire world, the amount of distortion can be significant. Some maps of the Western Hemisphere, because of their projection, incorrectly portray Canada and Alaska as larger than the United States and Mexico, while South America looks considerably smaller than its northern neighbors.

One of the more practical ways map readers can become aware of projection distortions and learn how to make allowances for them is to compare the projection grid of a flat map with the grid of a globe. Some important characteristics of the globe grid are found listed on page xi.

There are an infinite number of possible map projections, all of which distort one or more of the characteristics of the globe in varying degrees. The projection system that a cartographer chooses depends on the size and location of the area being projected and the purpose of the map. In this atlas, most of the maps are drawn on projections that give a consistent area scale; good land and ocean shape; parallels that are parallel; and as consistent a linear scale as possible throughout the projection.

The transformation process is actually a mathematical one, but to aid in visualizing this process, it is helpful to consider the earth reduced to the scale of the intended map and then projected onto a simple geometric shape—a cylinder, cone, or plane. These geometric forms are then flattened to two dimensions to produce cylindrical, conic, and plane projections (see Figures 4, 5, and 6). Some of the projection systems used in this atlas are described on the following pages. By comparing these systems with the characteristics of a globe grid, readers can gain a clearer understanding of map distortion.

Mercator: This transformation—bearing the name of a famous sixteenth century cartographer—is conformal; that is, land masses are represented in their true shapes. Thus, for every point on the map, the angles shown are correct in every direction within a limited area. To achieve this, the projection increases latitudinal and longitudinal distances away from the equator. As a result, land *shapes* are correct, but their *areas* are distorted. The farther away from the equator, the greater the area distortion. For example, on a Mercator map, Alaska appears far larger than Mexico, whereas in fact Mexico's land area is greater. The Mercator projection is used in nautical navigation, because a line connecting any two points gives the compass direction between them. (See Figure 4.)

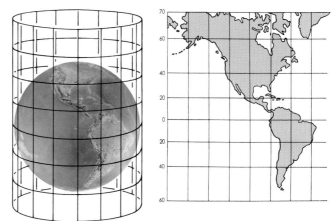

Figure 4. Mercator Projection (right), based upon the projection of the globe onto a cylinder.

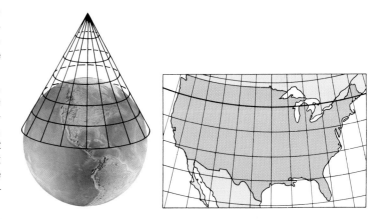

Figure 5. Projection of the globe onto a cone and a resultant Conic Projection.

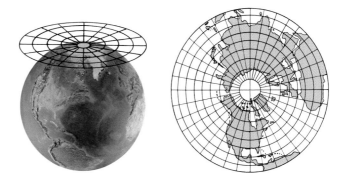

Figure 6. Lambert Equal-Area Projection (right), which assumes the projection of the globe onto a plane surface.

Conic: In this transformation—a globe projected onto a tangent cone—meridians of longitude appear as straight lines, and lines of latitude appear as parallel arcs. The parallel of tangency (that is, where the cone is presumed to touch the globe) is called a standard parallel. In this projection, distortion increases in bands away from the standard parallel. Conic projections are helpful in depicting middle-latitude areas of east-west extension. (See Figure 5.)

Lambert Equal Area *(polar case):* This projection assumes a plane touching the globe at a single point. It shows true distances close to the center (the tangent point) but increasingly distorted ones away from it. The equal-area quality (showing land areas in their correct proportion) is maintained throughout; but in regions away from the center, distortion of shape increases. (See Figure 6.)

Miller Cylindrical: O. M. Miller suggested a modification to the Mercator projection to lessen the severe area distortion in the higher latitudes. The Miller projection is neither conformal nor equal-area. Thus, while shapes are less accurate than on the Mercator, the exaggeration of *size* of areas has been somewhat decreased. The Miller cylindrical is useful for showing the entire world in a rectangular format. (See Figure 7.)

Mollweide Homolographic: The Mollweide is an equal-area projection; the least distorted areas are ovals centered just above and below the center of the projection. Distance distortions increase toward the edges of the map. The Mollweide is used for world-distribution maps where a pleasing oval look is desired along with the equal-area quality. It is one of the bases used in the Goode's Interrupted Homolosine projection. (See Figure 8.)

Sinusoidal, or Sanson-Flamsteed: In this equal-area projection the scale is the same along all parallels and the central meridian. Distortion of shapes is less along the two main axes of the projection but increases markedly toward the edges. Maps depicting areas such as South America or Africa can make good use of the Sinusoidal's favorable characteristics by situating the land masses along the central meridian, where the shapes will be virtually undistorted. The Sinusoidal is also one of the bases used in the Goode's Interrupted Homolosine. (See Figure 9.)

Goode's Interrupted Homolosine: An equal-area projection, Goode's is composed of the Sinusoidal grid from the equator to about 40° N and 40° S latitudes; beyond these latitudes, the Mollweide is used. This grid is interrupted so that land masses can be projected with a minimum of shape distortion by positioning each section on a separate central meridian. Thus, the shapes as well as the sizes of land masses are represented with a high degree of fidelity. Oceans can also be positioned in this manner. (See Figure 10.)

Robinson: This projection was designed for Rand McNally to present an uninterrupted and visually correct map of the earth. It maintains overall shape and area relationships without extreme distortion and is widely used in classrooms and textbooks. (See Figure 11.)

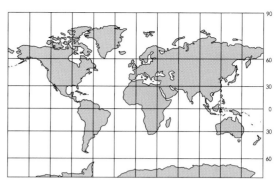

Figure 7. Miller Cylindrical Projection.

Figure 8. Mollweide Homolographic Projection.

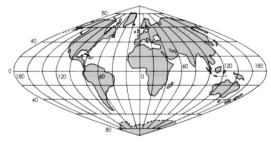

Figure 9. Sinusoidal Projection.

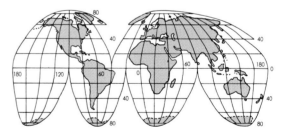

Figure 10. Goode's Interrupted Homolosine Projection.

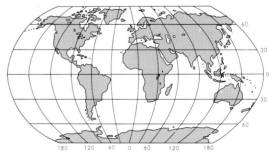

Figure 11. Robinson Projection.

Bonne: This equal-area transformation is mathematically related to the Sinusoidal. Distances are true along all parallels and the central meridian. Farther out from the central meridian, however, the increasing obliqueness of the grid's angles distorts shape and distance. This limits the area that can be usefully projected. Bonne projections, like conics, are best employed for relatively small areas in middle latitudes. (See Figure 12.)

Conic with Two Standard Parallels: The linear scale of this projection is consistent along two standard parallels instead of only one as in the simple conic. Since the spacing of the other parallels is reduced somewhat between the standard parallels and progressively enlarged beyond them, the projection does not exhibit the equal-area property. Careful selection of the standard parallels, however, provides good representation of limited areas. Like the Bonne projection, this system is widely used for areas in middle latitudes. (See Figure 13.)

Polyconic: In this system, the globe is projected onto a series of strips taken from tangent cones. Parallels are nonconcentric circles, and each is divided equally by the meridians, as on the globe. While distances along the straight central meridian are true, they are increasingly exaggerated along the curving meridians. Likewise, general representation of areas and shapes is good near the central meridian but progressively distorted away from it. Polyconic projections are used for middle-latitude areas to minimize all distortions and were employed for large-scale topographic maps. (See Figure 14.)

Lambert Conformal Conic: This conformal transformation system usually employs two standard parallels. Distortion increases away from the standard parallels, being greatest at the edges of the map. It is useful for projecting elongated east-west areas in the middle latitudes and is ideal for depicting the forty-eight contiguous states. It is also widely used for aeronautical and meteorological charts. (See Figure 15.)

Lambert Equal Area *(oblique and polar cases):* This equal-area projection can be centered at any point on the earth's surface, perpendicular to a line drawn through the globe. It maintains correct angles to all points on the map from its center (point of tangency), but distances become progressively distorted toward the edges. It is most useful for roughly circular areas or areas whose dimensions are nearly equal in two perpendicular directions.

The two most common forms of the Lambert projection are the oblique and the polar, shown in Figures 6 and 16. Although the meridians and parallels for the forms are different, the distortion characteristics are the same.

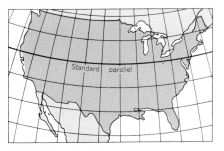

Figure 12.
Bonne Projection.

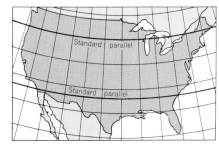

Figure 13.
Conic Projection with Two Standard Parallels.

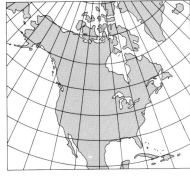

Figure 14.
Polyconic Projection.

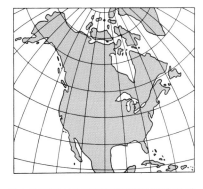

Figure 15.
Lambert Conformal Conic Projection.

Figure 16.
Lambert Equal-Area Projection (oblique case).

Important characteristics of the globe grid

1. All meridians of longitude are equal in length and meet at the Poles.
2. All lines of latitude are parallel and equally spaced on meridians.
3. The length, or circumference, of the parallels of latitude decreases as one moves from the equator to the Poles. For instance, the circumference of the parallel at 60° latitude is one-half the circumference of the equator.
4. Meridians of longitude are equally spaced on each parallel, but the distance between them decreases toward the Poles.
5. All parallels and meridians meet at right angles.

EDWARD B. ESPENSHADE, JR.
JOHN C. HUDSON

THE SEASONS
(NORTHERN HEMISPHERE)

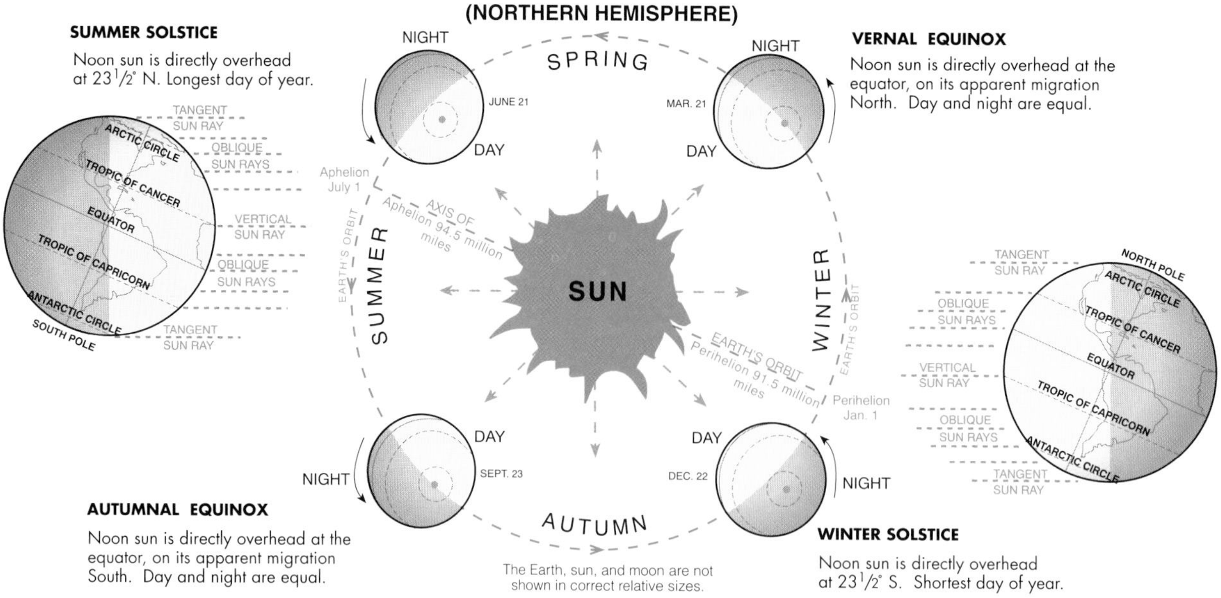

SPRING

SUMMER

WINTER

AUTUMN

SUMMER SOLSTICE
Noon sun is directly overhead at 23$\frac{1}{2}$° N. Longest day of year.

NIGHT
DAY
JUNE 21

TANGENT SUN RAY
ARCTIC CIRCLE
OBLIQUE SUN RAYS
TROPIC OF CANCER
EQUATOR
VERTICAL SUN RAY
TROPIC OF CAPRICORN
OBLIQUE SUN RAYS
ANTARCTIC CIRCLE
SOUTH POLE
TANGENT SUN RAY

VERNAL EQUINOX
Noon sun is directly overhead at the equator, on its apparent migration North. Day and night are equal.

NIGHT
DAY
MAR. 21

Aphelion July 1
AXIS OF EARTH'S ORBIT
Aphelion 94.5 million miles
EARTH'S ORBIT

SUN

EARTH'S ORBIT
Perihelion 91.5 million miles
Perihelion Jan. 1

TANGENT SUN RAY
NORTH POLE
ARCTIC CIRCLE
OBLIQUE SUN RAYS
TROPIC OF CANCER
EQUATOR
VERTICAL SUN RAY
TROPIC OF CAPRICORN
OBLIQUE SUN RAYS
ANTARCTIC CIRCLE
TANGENT SUN RAY

DAY
SEPT. 23
NIGHT

DAY
DEC. 22
NIGHT

AUTUMNAL EQUINOX
Noon sun is directly overhead at the equator, on its apparent migration South. Day and night are equal.

The Earth, sun, and moon are not shown in correct relative sizes.

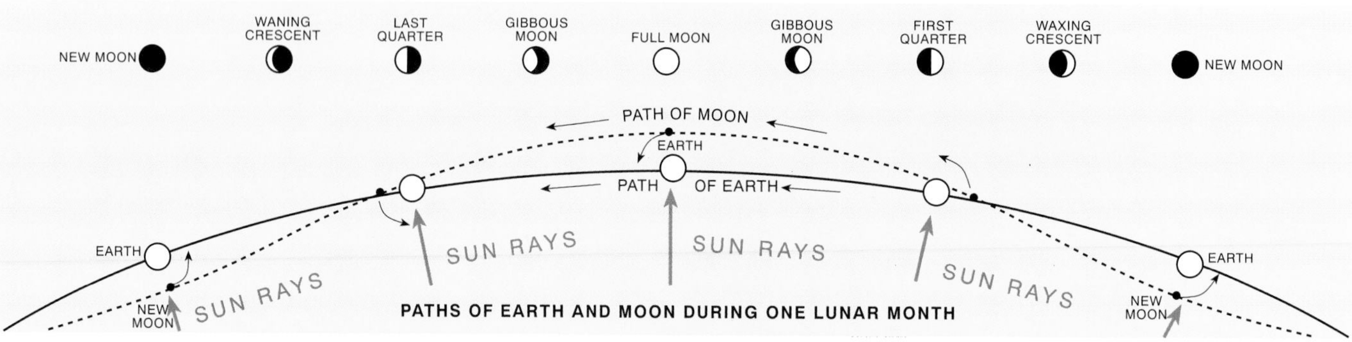

WINTER SOLSTICE
Noon sun is directly overhead at 23$\frac{1}{2}$° S. Shortest day of year.

NEW MOON | WANING CRESCENT | LAST QUARTER | GIBBOUS MOON | FULL MOON | GIBBOUS MOON | FIRST QUARTER | WAXING CRESCENT | NEW MOON

PATH OF MOON
EARTH
PATH OF EARTH
SUN RAYS   SUN RAYS   SUN RAYS   SUN RAYS
EARTH
NEW MOON
EARTH
NEW MOON

PATHS OF EARTH AND MOON DURING ONE LUNAR MONTH

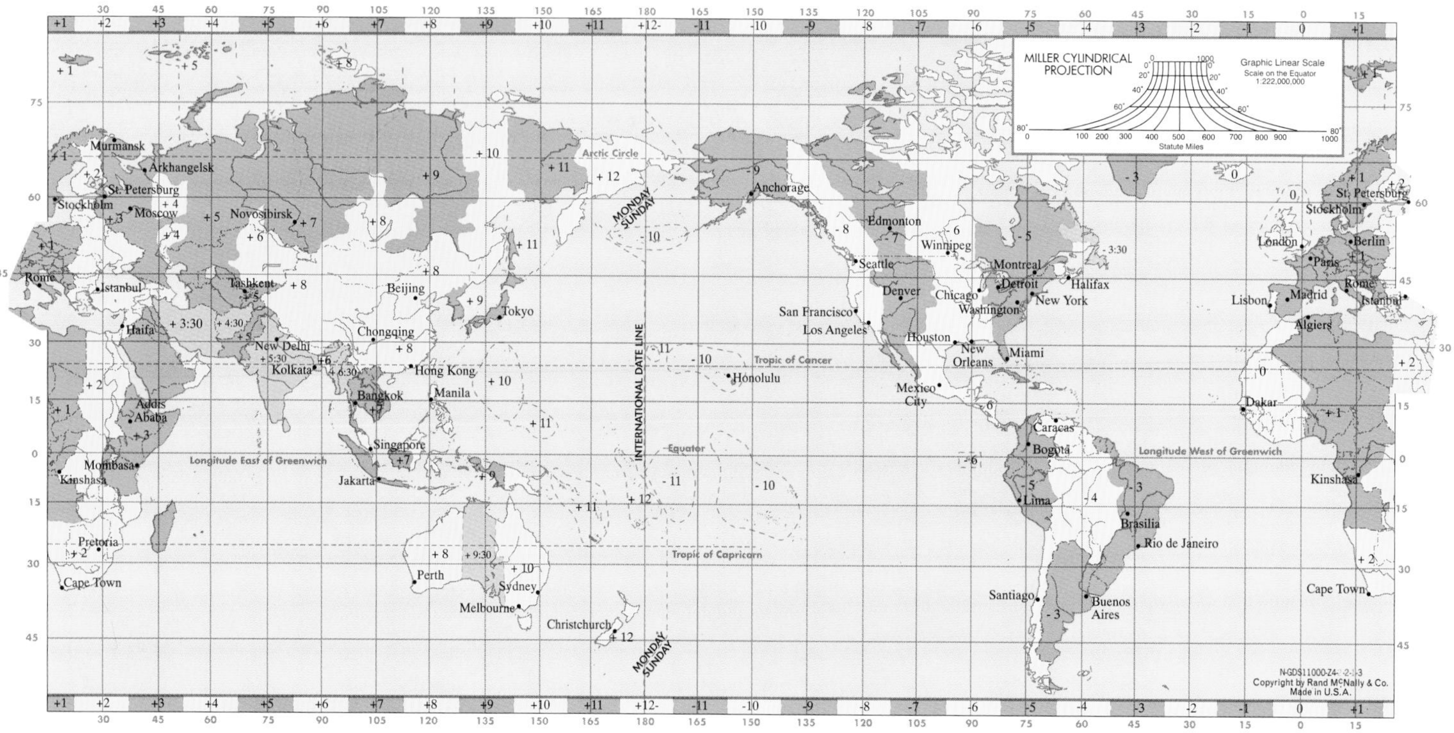

MILLER CYLINDRICAL PROJECTION
Graphic Linear Scale
Scale on the Equator
1:222,000,000
Statute Miles

Time Zones

The surface of the earth is divided into 24 time zones. Each zone represents 15° of longitude or one hour of time. The time of the initial, or zero, zone is based on the central meridian of Greenwich and is adopted eastward and westward for a distance of 7½° of longitude. Each of the zones in turn is designated by a number representing the hours (+or-) by which its standard time differs from Greenwich mean time. These standard time zones are indicated by bands of orange and yellow. Areas which have a fractional deviation from standard time are shown in an intermediate color. The irregularities in the zones and the fractional deviations are due to political and economic factors.

(After U.S. Defense Mapping Agency)

WORLD THEMATIC MAPS

This section of the atlas consists of more than sixty thematic maps presenting world patterns and distributions. Together with accompanying graphs, these maps communicate basic information on mineral resources, agricultural products, trade, transportation, and other selected aspects of the natural and cultural geographical environment.

A thematic map uses symbols to show certain characteristics of, generally, one class of geographical information. This "theme" of a thematic map is presented upon a background of basic locational information–coastline, country boundaries, major drainage, etc. The map's primary concern is to communicate visually basic impressions of the distribution of the theme. For instance, on page 47 the distribution of cattle shown by point symbols impresses the reader with relative densities–the distribution of cattle is much more uniform throughout the United States than it is in China, and cattle are more numerous in the United States than in China.

Although it is possible to use a thematic map to obtain exact values of a quantity or commodity, it is not the purpose intended, any more than a thematic map is intended to be used to give precise distances from New York to Moscow. If one seeks precise statistics for each country, he may consult the bar graphs accompanying the maps or statistical tables such as those following page 244.

The map on this page is an example of a special class of thematic maps called cartograms. The cartogram assigns to a named earth region an area based on some value other than land surface area. In the cartogram below, and in all others appearing in this atlas, the areas assigned are proportional to their countries' populations. The result of mapping on this base is a meaningful way of portraying distributions such as natural increase which are causally related to existing size of population. On the other hand, natural increase is not causally related to earth area. In the thematic maps in this atlas, relative earth sizes have been considered when presenting the distributions.

Real and hypothetical geographical distributions are practically limitless but can be classed into point, line, area, or volume information relative to a specific location or area in the world. The thematic map, in communicating these fundamental classes of information, utilizes point, line, and area symbols. The symbols may be employed to show qualitative differences (difference in kind) of a certain category of information and may also show quantitative differences in the information (differences in amount). For example, the natural-vegetation map (page 24) was based upon information gathered by many observations over a period of time. It utilizes area symbols (color and pattern) to show the difference in the kind of vegetation as well as the extent. Quantitative factual information was shown on the annual-precipitation map, page 20, by means of isohyets (lines connecting points of equal rainfall). Also, area symbols were employed to show the intervals between the lines. In each of these thematic maps, there is one primary theme, or subject; the map communicates the information far better than volumes of words and tables could.

One of the most important aspects of the thematic-map section is use of the different maps to show comparisons and relationships among the distributions of various types of geographical information. For example, the relationship of dense population (page 30) to areas of intensive subsistence agriculture (page 38) and to manufacturing (page 55) is an important geographic concept.

The statistics communicated by the maps and graphs in this section are intended to give an idea of the relative importance of countries in the distributions mapped. The maps are not intended to take the place of statistical reference works. No single year affords a realistic base for production, trade, and certain economic and demographic statistics. Therefore, averages of data for three or four years have been used. Together with the maps, the averages and percentages provide the student with a realistic idea of the importance of specific areas.

POPULATION

Note: Size of each country is proportional to population.

Tints indicate rate of natural increase.

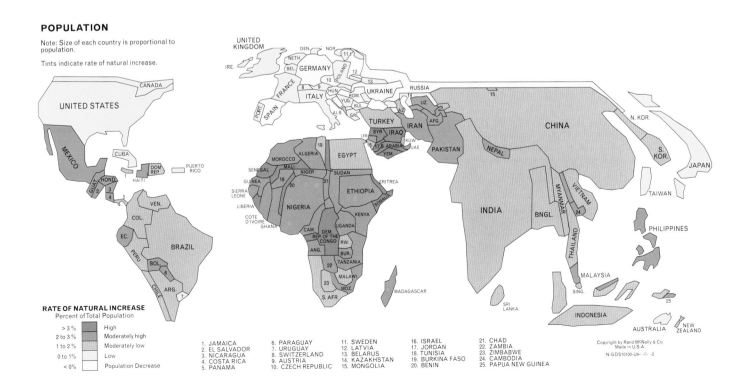

RATE OF NATURAL INCREASE
Percent of Total Population

> 3 %	High
2 to 3 %	Moderately high
1 to 2 %	Moderately low
0 to 1 %	Low
< 0%	Population Decrease

1. JAMAICA
2. EL SALVADOR
3. NICARAGUA
4. COSTA RICA
5. PANAMA

6. PARAGUAY
7. URUGUAY
8. SWITZERLAND
9. AUSTRIA
10. CZECH REPUBLIC

11. SWEDEN
12. LATVIA
13. BELARUS
14. KAZAKHSTAN
15. MONGOLIA

16. ISRAEL
17. JORDAN
18. TUNISIA
19. BURKINA FASO
20. BENIN

21. CHAD
22. ZAMBIA
23. ZIMBABWE
24. CAMBODIA
25. PAPUA NEW GUINEA

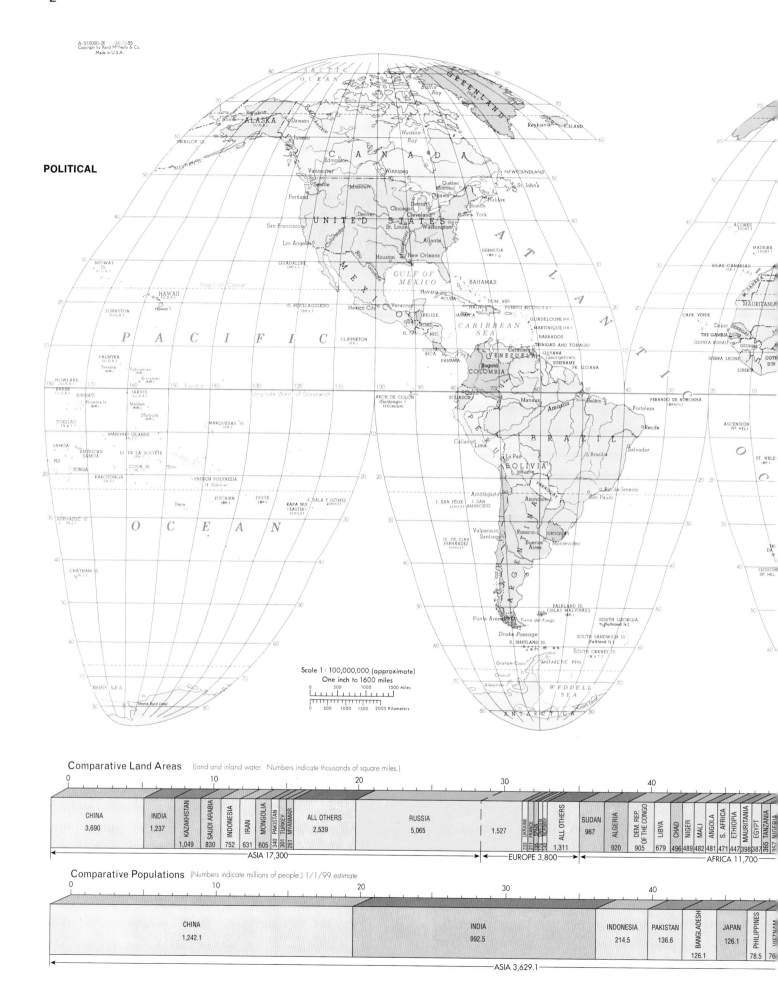

2

POLITICAL

Scale 1 : 100,000,000 (approximate)
One inch to 1600 miles

Comparative Land Areas (land and inland water. Numbers indicate thousands of square miles.)

| CHINA 3,690 | INDIA 1,237 | KAZAKHSTAN 1,049 | SAUDI ARABIA 830 | INDONESIA 752 | IRAN 631 | MONGOLIA 605 | PAKISTAN 340 | TURKEY 301 | MYANMAR 261 | ALL OTHERS 2,539 | RUSSIA 5,065 | 1,527 | UKRAINE 233 | FRANCE 211 | SPAIN 195 | SWEDEN 174 | NORWAY 125 | ALL OTHERS 1,311 | SUDAN 967 | ALGERIA 920 | DEM. REP. OF THE CONGO 905 | LIBYA 679 | CHAD 496 | NIGER 489 | MALI 482 | ANGOLA 481 | S. AFRICA 471 | ETHIOPIA 447 | MAURITANIA 398 | EGYPT 387 | TANZANIA 365 | NIGERIA 357 |

ASIA 17,300 — EUROPE 3,800 — AFRICA 11,700

Comparative Populations (Numbers indicate millions of people.) 1/1/99 estimate

| CHINA 1,242.1 | INDIA 992.5 | INDONESIA 214.5 | PAKISTAN 136.6 | BANGLADESH 126.1 | JAPAN 126.1 | PHILIPPINES 78.5 | VIETNAM 76 |

ASIA 3,629.1

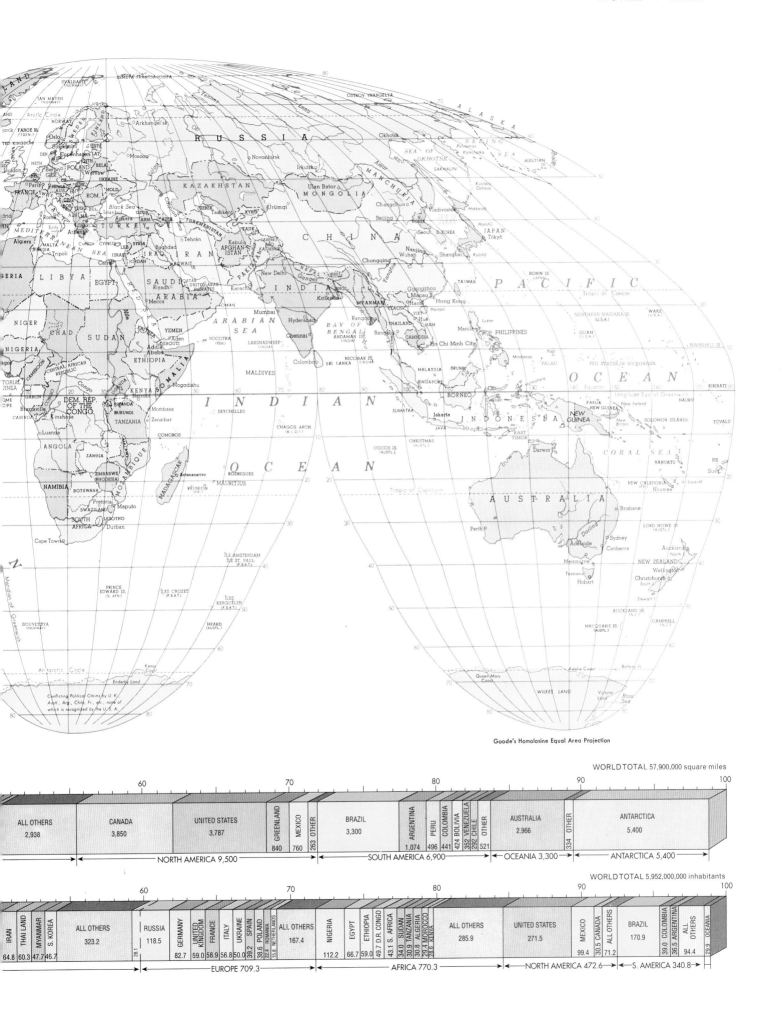

Goode's Homolosine Equal Area Projection

WORLD TOTAL 57,900,000 square miles

| ALL OTHERS 2,938 | CANADA 3,850 | UNITED STATES 3,787 | GREENLAND 840 | MEXICO 760 | OTHER 263 | BRAZIL 3,300 | ARGENTINA 1,074 | PERU 496 | COLOMBIA 441 | BOLIVIA 424 | VENEZUELA 352 | CHILE 292 | OTHER 521 | AUSTRALIA 2,966 | OTHER 334 | ANTARCTICA 5,400 |

← NORTH AMERICA 9,500 → ← SOUTH AMERICA 6,900 → ← OCEANIA 3,300 → ← ANTARCTICA 5,400 →

WORLD TOTAL 5,952,000,000 inhabitants

| IRAN 64.8 | THAILAND 60.3 | MYANMAR 47.7 | S. KOREA 46.7 | ALL OTHERS 323.2 | RUSSIA 118.5 | 28.1 | GERMANY 82.7 | UNITED KINGDOM 59.0 | FRANCE 58.9 | ITALY 56.8 | UKRAINE 50.0 | SPAIN 39.2 | POLAND 38.6 | ROMANIA 22.4 | NETHERLANDS 15.8 | ALL OTHERS 167.4 | NIGERIA 112.2 | EGYPT 66.7 | ETHIOPIA 59.0 | D.R. CONGO 49.7 | S. AFRICA 43.1 | SUDAN 34.0 | TANZANIA 30.9 | ALGERIA 30.8 | MOROCCO 29.4 | KENYA 28.6 | ALL OTHERS 285.9 | UNITED STATES 271.5 | MEXICO 99.4 | CANADA 30.5 | ALL OTHERS 71.2 | BRAZIL 170.9 | COLOMBIA 39.0 | ARGENTINA 36.5 | ALL OTHERS 94.4 | OCEANIA 29.9 |

← EUROPE 709.3 → ← AFRICA 770.3 → ← NORTH AMERICA 472.6 → ← S. AMERICA 340.8 →

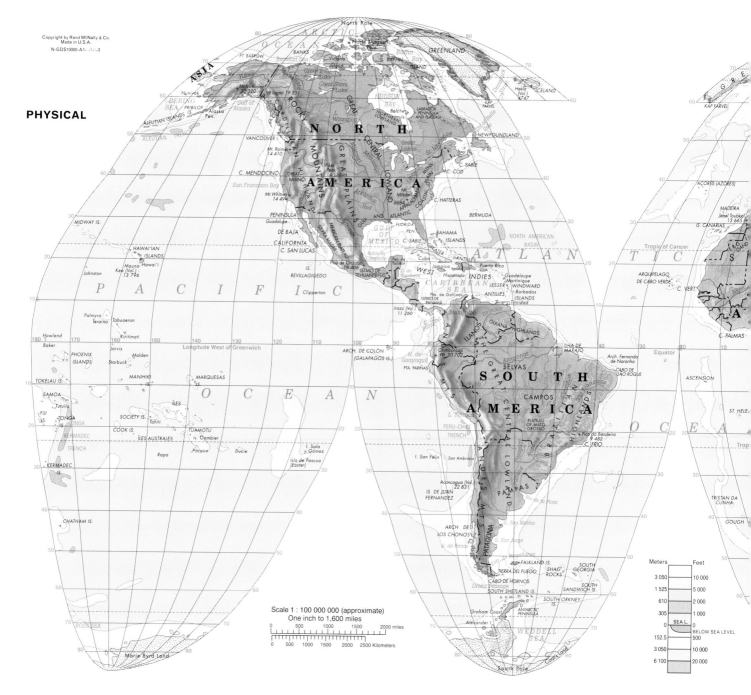

PHYSICAL

Land Elevations in Profile

Ocean Depths in Profile

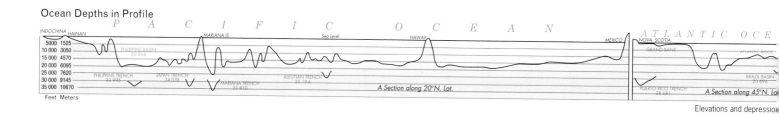

For Glossary of Foreign Geographical Terms see page 260

Goode's Homolosine Equal Area Projection

EUROPE	ASIA	OCEANIA

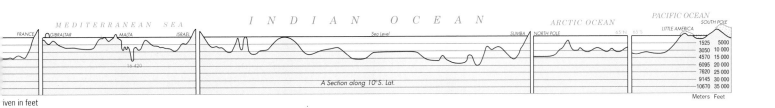

A Section along 10° S. Lat.

iven in feet

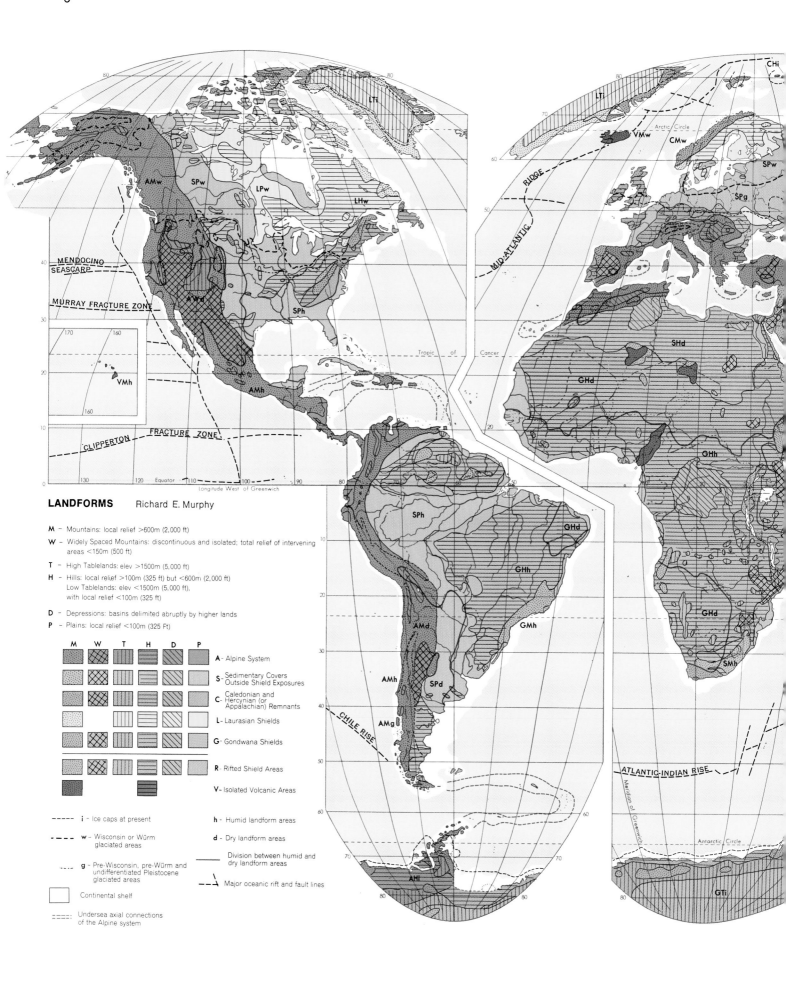

LANDFORMS   Richard E. Murphy

M – Mountains: local relief >600m (2,000 ft)

W – Widely Spaced Mountains: discontinuous and isolated; total relief of intervening areas <150m (500 ft)

T – High Tablelands: elev >1500m (5,000 ft)

H – Hills: local relief >100m (325 ft) but <600m (2,000 ft)
Low Tablelands: elev <1500m (5,000 ft), with local relief <100m (325 ft)

D – Depressions: basins delimited abruptly by higher lands

P – Plains: local relief <100m (325 Ft)

A - Alpine System

S - Sedimentary Covers Outside Shield Exposures

C - Caledonian and Hercynian (or Appalachian) Remnants

L - Laurasian Shields

G - Gondwana Shields

R - Rifted Shield Areas

V - Isolated Volcanic Areas

i - Ice caps at present

w - Wisconsin or Würm glaciated areas

g - Pre-Wisconsin, pre-Würm and undifferentiated Pleistocene glaciated areas

Continental shelf

Undersea axial connections of the Alpine system

h - Humid landform areas

d - Dry landform areas

Division between humid and dry landform areas

Major oceanic rift and fault lines

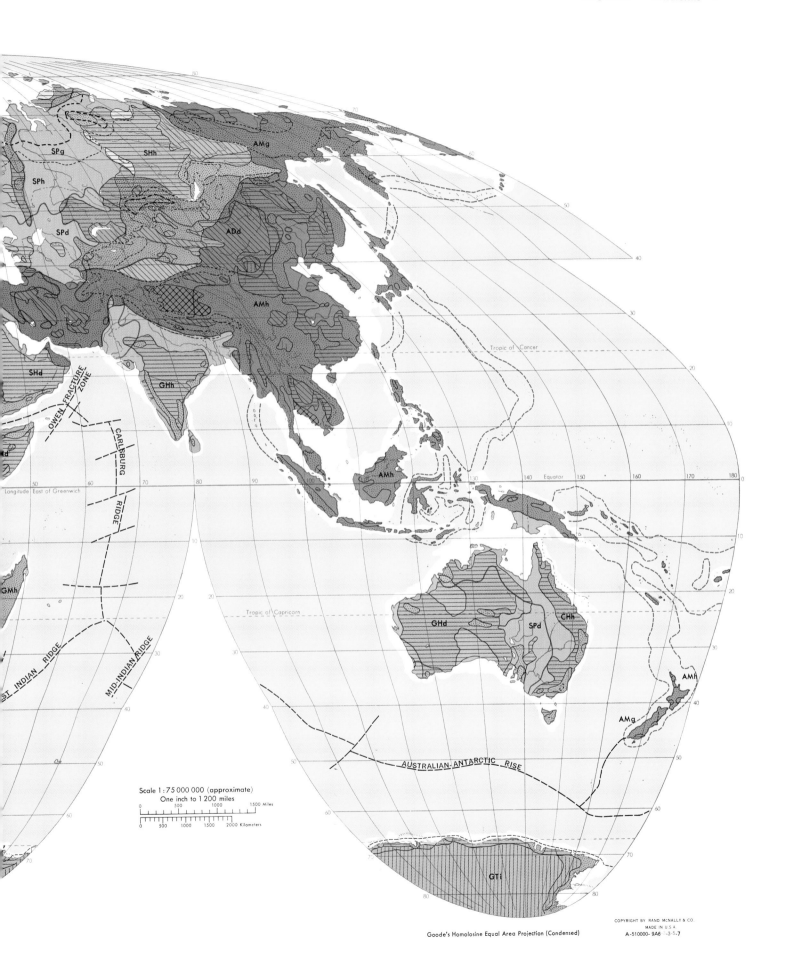

SPg

SPh

SHh

AMg

SPd

ADd

AMh

SHd

OWEN FRACTURE ZONE

CARLSBURG RIDGE

GHh

AMh

GMh

WEST INDIAN RIDGE

MID-INDIAN RIDGE

Longitude East of Greenwich

Tropic of Cancer

Equator

Tropic of Capricorn

GHd

SPd

CHh

AMh

AMg

AUSTRALIAN-ANTARCTIC RISE

GTi

Scale 1:75 000 000 (approximate)
One inch to 1 200 miles

0   500   1000   1500 Miles

0   500   1000   1500   2000 Kilometers

Goode's Homolosine Equal Area Projection (Condensed)

CONTINENTAL DRIFT

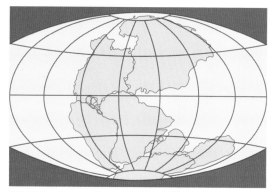

225 million years ago the supercontinent of Pangaea exists and Panthalassa forms the ancestral ocean. Tethys Sea separates Eurasia and Africa.

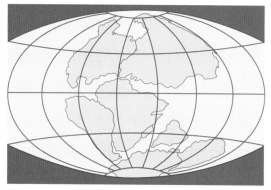

180 million years ago Pangaea splits, Laurasia drifts north. Gondwanaland breaks into South America/Africa, India, and Australia/Antarctica.

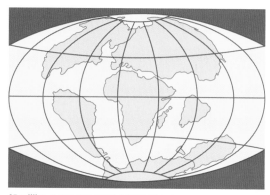

65 million years ago ocean basins take shape as South America and India move from Africa and the Tethys Sea closes to form the Mediterranean Sea.

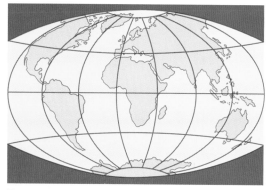

The present day: India has merged with Asia, Australia is free of Antarctica, and North America is free of Eurasia.

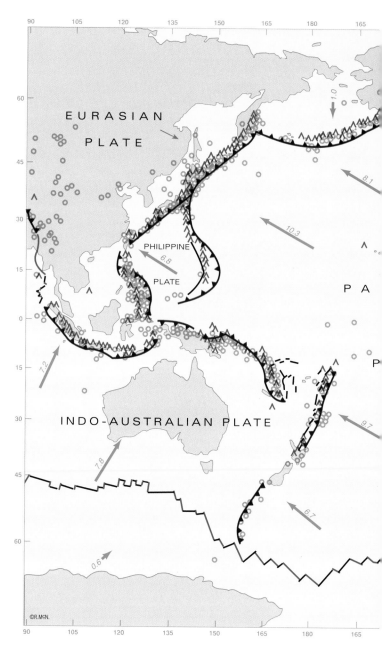

PLATE TECTONICS

Types of plate boundaries

Divergent: magma emerges from the earth's mantle at the mid-ocean ridges forming new crust and forcing the plates to spread apart at the ridges.

Convergent: plates collide at subduction zones where the denser plate is forced back into the earth's mantle forming deep ocean trenches.

Transform: plates slide past one another producing faults and fracture zones.

Other map symbols

→ Direction of plate movement

6.7 Length of arrow is proportional to the amount of plate movement (number indicates centimeters of movement per year)

○ Earthquake of magnitude 7.5 and above (from 10 A.D. to the present)

∧ Volcano (eruption since 1900)

✳ Selected hot spots

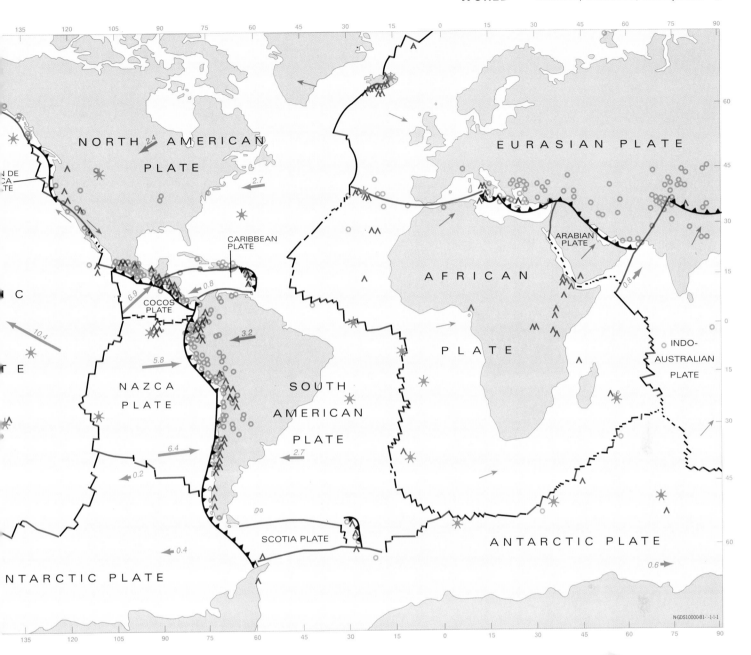

NORTH AMERICAN PLATE

DE CA TE

CARIBBEAN PLATE

COCOS PLATE

C E

NAZCA PLATE

SOUTH AMERICAN PLATE

SCOTIA PLATE

NTARCTIC PLATE

EURASIAN PLATE

ARABIAN PLATE

AFRICAN PLATE

INDO-AUSTRALIAN PLATE

ANTARCTIC PLATE

NGDS10000-81- -1-1-1

The plate tectonic theory describes the movement of the earth's surface and subsurface and explains why surface features are where they are.

Stated concisely, the theory presumes the lithosphere - the outside crust and uppermost mantle of the earth - is divided into about a dozen major rigid plates and several smaller platelets that move relative to one another. The position and names of the plates are shown on the map above.

The motor that drives the plates is found deep in the mantle. The theory states that because of temperature differences in the mantle, slow convection currents circulate there. Where two molten currents converge and move upward, they separate, causing the crustal plates to bulge and move apart in mid-ocean regions. Transverse fractures disrupt these broad regions. Lava wells up at these points to cause volcanic activity and to form ridges. The plates grow larger by accretion along these mid-ocean ridges, cause vast regions of the crust to move apart, and force the plates to collide with one another. As the plates do so, they are destroyed at subduction zones, where the plates are consumed downward, back into the earth's mantle, forming deep ocean trenches. The diagrams to the right illustrate the processes.

Most of the earth's volcanic and seismic activities

occur where plates slide past each other at transform boundaries or collide along subduction zones. The friction and heat caused by the grinding motion of the subducted plates causes rock to liquify and rise to the surface as volcanoes and eventually form vast mountain ranges. Strong and deep earthquakes are common here.

Volcanoes and earthquakes also occur at random locations around the earth known as "hot spots". Hot rock from deep in the mantle rises to the surface creating some of the earth's tallest mountains. As the lithospheric plates move slowly over these stationary plumes of magma, island chains (such as the Hawaiian Islands) are formed.

The overall result of tectonic movement is that the crustal plates move slowly and inexorably as relatively rigid entitles, carrying the continents along with them. The history of this continental drifting is illustrated in the four maps to the left. It began with a single landmass called the supercontinent of Pangaea and the ancestral sea, the Panthalassa Ocean. Pangaea first split into a northern landmass called Laurasia and a southern block called Gondwanaland and subsequently into the continents we map today. The map of the future will be significantly different as the continents continue to drift.

Subduction Zone

Ocean Ridge Zone

15° 0° 15° 30° 45° 60° 75° 90° 105° 120° 135° 150°

Barents Sea

Norwegian Basin

Arctic Circle

Ob'

Yenisey

Lena

NORWAY SWEDEN FINLAND

North Sea

DEN. Baltic Sea EST. LAT. LITH. BELARUS

Moscow

RUSSIA

Sea of Okhotsk

Okhotsk Basin

GERMANY POLAND

EUROPE UKRAINE

AUS.

ROMANIA

KAZAKHSTAN

Volga

MONGOLIA

ozero Baykal

SAKHALIN

Amur

Nor

Pa

Black Sea

Aral Sea

Balqash kölï

ASIA

Istanbul

GREECE TURKEY

UZBEKISTAN

KYRGYZSTAN

Beijing

NORTH KOREA Seoul SOUTH KOREA JAPAN

Japan Basin

Kuril Trench

Mediterranean Sea

SYRIA Tehrān

TURKMENISTAN TAJIKISTAN

CHINA

Huang

Yellow Sea

Tokyo

Japan Trench

Izu Trench

Mid

Cairo

IRAQ IRAN

AFGHANISTAN

Yangtze

Shanghai

East China Sea

Ryukyu Trench

Tropic of Cancer

EGYPT

SAUDI ARABIA

Nile

Red Sea

PAKISTAN

Indus

Delhi

NEPAL Ganges BNGL.

Karachi

Kolkata Dhaka

T'aipei

TAIWAN

Hong Kong

Philippine Sea

South China Sea

Philippine Basin

South-Honshu Ridge

Kyushu-Palau Ridge

Mariana Trench

NORTHERN MARIANA ISLANDS (U.S.)

East Marian Basin

SUDAN

YEMEN

OMAN

Arabian Sea

Arabian Basin

INDIA

Mumbai

Bay of Bengal

Chennai

MYANMAR LAOS

THAILAND

ANDAMAN ISLANDS (India)

Bangkok

CAMB.

VIETNAM

Andaman Basin

South China Basin

Manila

PHILIPPINES

PALAU

Eauripik Rise

CAROLINE ISLANDS

FEDERATED ST OF MICRONE

AFRICA

ERITREA

ETHIOPIA

SOMALIA

Carlsberg Ridge

MALDIVES

NICOBAR ISLANDS (India)

SRI LANKA

SUMATRA

Sunda Shelf

Ho Chi Minh City

BRUNEI

MALAYSIA

SINGAPORE

Sulu Basin

Celebes Basin

West Caroline Basin

East Caroline Basin

MELA

UGANDA KENYA

Equator Nairobi

Somali Basin

SEYCHELLES

Mascarene Plateau

Chagos-Laccadive Plateau

MID-INDIAN RIDGE

BORNEO

CELEBES

Jakarta

INDONESIA

JAVA

NEW GUINEA

Bismarck Sea

PAPUA NEW GUINEA

Solomon Basin

Lake Victoria

TANZANIA

MALAWI

COMOROS

Mascarene Basin

INDIAN

Mid-Indian Basin

Ninety East Ridge

COCOS ISLANDS (Austl.)

CHRISTMAS ISLAND (Austl.)

Java Trench

EAST TIMOR

Darwin

Arafura Shelf

Gulf of Carpentaria

Coral Sea Basin

ZAMBIA

ZIMBABWE

MOZAMBIQUE

Mozambique Channel

MADAGASCAR

REUNION (Fr.) MAURITIUS

OCEAN

Wharton Basin

North Australian Basin

AUSTRALIA

Cor

SOUTH AFRICA

Johannesburg

Mozambique Plateau

Madagascar Basin

Madagascar Plateau

MID-INDIAN RIDGE

Southwest Indian Ridge

Broken Ridge

Perth Basin

Perth

Darling

Bris

Tropic of Capricorn

Agulhas Basin

PRINCE EDWARD ISLANDS (S. Afr.)

ÎLE AMSTERDAM (Fr.)

ÎLE ST. PAUL (Fr.)

Crozet Basin

Great Australian Bight

South Australian Basin

South Tasman Rise

Melbourne

Sydney

Tas S

Atlantic-Indian Ridge

ÎLES CROZET (Fr.)

ÎLES KERGUELEN (Fr.)

Kerguelen Plateau

Southeast Indian Ridge

SOUTHERN

TASMANIA

Tas Bas

Atlantic-Indian Basin

HEARD ISLAND (Austl.)

South Indian Basin

OCEAN

South Magnetic Pole

Antarctic Circle

ANTARCTICA

15° 0° 15° 30° 45° 60° 75° 90° 105° 120° 135° 150°

Scale 1:72 000 000 at 40° latitu

Chukchi Sea
Anadyr
Bering Strait
UNITED STATES
Anchorage
Mackenzie
GREENLAND (Denmark)
Arctic Circle
Labrador Sea
Irminger Basin
Bering Sea
Aléutian Basin
ALEUTIAN ISLANDS
Gulf of Alaska
Aleutian Trench
Gulf of Alaska Seamount Province
Prince Rupert
CANADA
NORTH AMERICA
Hudson Bay
Labrador Basin
NEWFOUNDLAND
Emperor Seamounts
PACIFIC
Seattle
Columbia
Missouri
Chicago
New York
Washington
ATLANTIC OCEAN
North American Basin
OCEAN
Mendocino Fracture Zone
San Francisco
UNITED STATES
Mississippi
BERMUDA (Br.)
Blake Plateau
Musicians Seamounts
Murray Fracture Zone
Los Angeles
New Orleans
Gulf of Mexico
Mexico Basin
BAHAMAS
Tropic of Cancer
Mountains
Hawaiian Ridge
Honolulu
HAWAIIAN ISLANDS
Molokai Fracture Zone
MEXICO
Mexico City
Campeche Bank
Havana
CUBA
HAITI
DOM. REP.
Christmas Ridge
UNITED STATES
Clarion Fracture Zone
Middle America Trench
BELIZE
GUAT. HOND.
Caribbean Sea
Venezuelan Basin
Central Pacific Basin
Clipperton Fracture Zone
Guatemala Basin
NIC.
COSTA RICA
PANAMA
VENEZUELA
MARSHALL ISLANDS
POLYNESIA
Colón Ridge
Cocos Ridge
Panama Basin
Bogotá
COLOMBIA
NAURU
KIRIBATI
LINE ISLANDS
GALAPAGOS ISLANDS (Ec.)
Equator
ECUADOR
SOUTH
SOLOMON ISLANDS
PHOENIX ISLANDS
TOKELAU (N.Z.)
COOK ISLANDS
PERU
BRAZIL
AMERICA
TUVALU
Lima
SANTA CRUZ ISLANDS
WALLIS and FUTUNA
SAMOA
Peru-Chile Trench
North Fiji Basin
AMER. SAMOA
Tuamotu Ridge
FRENCH POLYNESIA
Peru Basin
NEW HEBRIDES
FIJI
NIUE (N.Z.)
TAHITI
Sala y Gomez Ridge
Nazca Ridge
New Hebrides Trench
South Fiji Basin
TONGA
Austral Seamounts
PITCAIRN (Br.)
EAST PACIFIC RISE
Tropic of Capricorn
BOLIVIA
NORFOLK ISLAND (Aust.)
Lau Ridge
Tonga Ridge
Tonga Trench
EASTER ISLAND (Chile)
New Caledonia Basin
Kermadec Ridge
Kermadec Trench
Louisville Ridge
Southwest Pacific Basin
ARCHIPIÉLAGO JUAN FERNANDEZ (Chile)
Santiago
CHILE
ARGENTINA
Auckland
NEW ZEALAND
NORTH ISLAND
Chatham Rise
Chile Rise
Peru-Chile Trench
Bounty Trough
BOUNTY ISLANDS
PACIFIC
Argentine Basin
Campbell Plateau
ANTIPODES ISLANDS
FALKLAND ISLANDS (Br.)
Scotia Ridge
CAMPBELL ISLAND
OCEAN
Southwest Pacific Basin
SOUTH SHETLAND ISLANDS (Br.)
Balleny Basin
Pacific-Antarctic Ridge
Southeast Pacific Basin
Antarctic Circle
Atlantic-Indian Basin
Ross Sea
Amundsen Sea
Antarctic Peninsula
Weddell Sea

© Rand McNally & Co.
N-GDS14700-A2----4

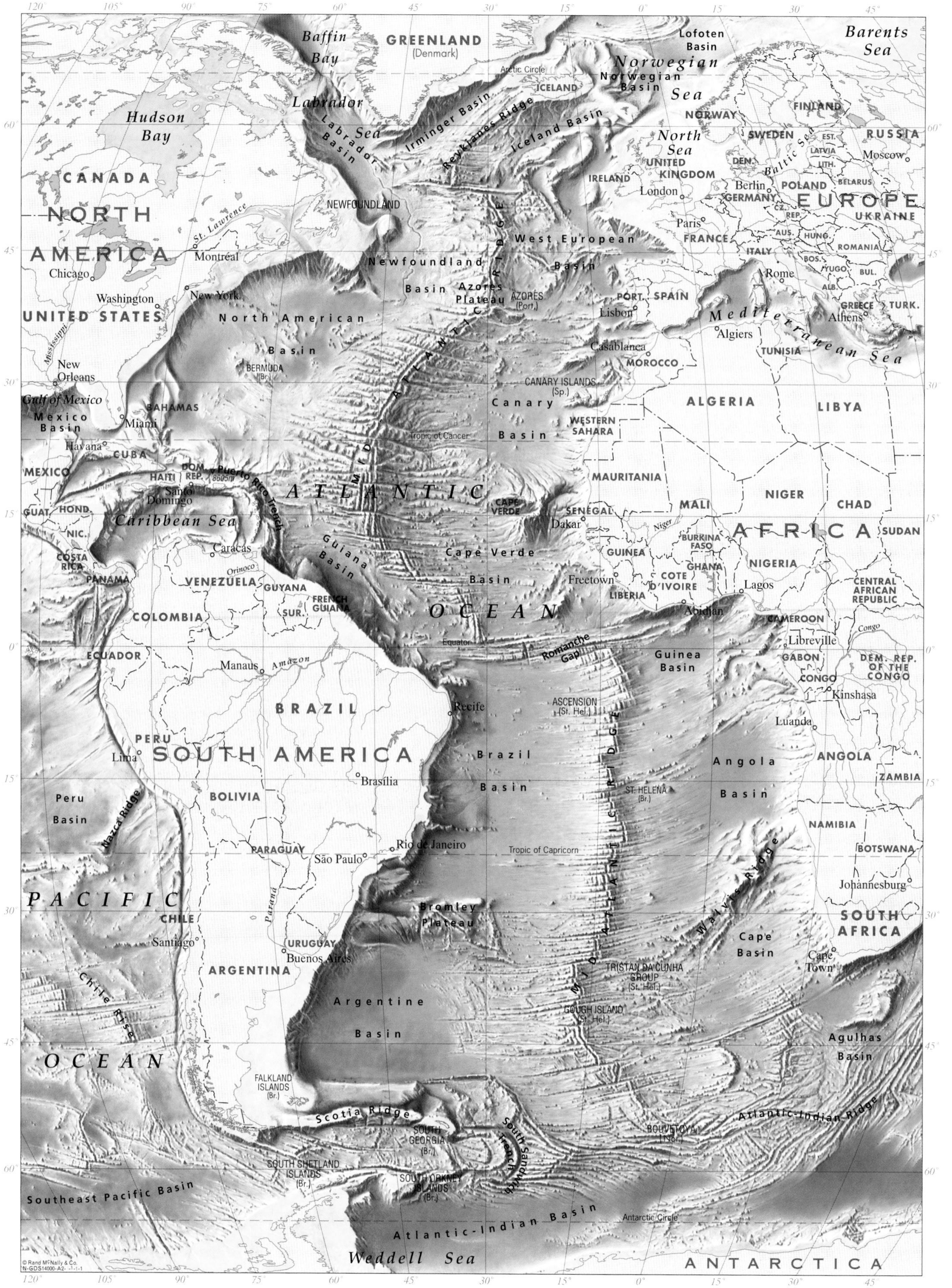

Baffin Bay

GREENLAND (Denmark)

Lofoten Basin

Barents Sea

Arctic Circle

Norwegian Basin

Norwegian Sea

Labrador Sea

Irminger Basin

Reykjanes Ridge

ICELAND

Iceland Basin

NORWAY

SWEDEN

FINLAND

RUSSIA

Hudson Bay

CANADA

NORTH AMERICA

Labrador Basin

NEWFOUNDLAND

North Sea

DEN.

Baltic Sea

LATVIA

LITH.

Moscow

St. Lawrence

Montreal

UNITED KINGDOM

IRELAND

London

Berlin

POLAND

BELARUS

GERMANY

CZ.

UKRAINE

Chicago

New York

Newfoundland

West European Basin

Paris

FRANCE

AUS.

HUNG.

ROMANIA

Washington

North American Basin

BERMUDA (Br.)

Azores Plateau

AZORES (Port.)

ITALY

Rome

YUGO.

BUL.

ALB.

GREECE

TURK.

UNITED STATES

Lisbon

SPAIN

PORT.

Mediterranean Sea

Athens

Mississippi

Casablanca

Algiers

TUNISIA

New Orleans

Gulf of Mexico

Mexico Basin

BAHAMAS

Miami

Tropic of Cancer

CANARY ISLANDS (Sp.)

Canary Basin

MOROCCO

WESTERN SAHARA

ALGERIA

LIBYA

Havana

CUBA

HAITI

DOM. REP.

Puerto Rico 8605 m

Santo Domingo

Puerto Rico Trench

ATLANTIC

MAURITANIA

MALI

NIGER

CHAD

SUDAN

MEXICO

GUAT.

HOND.

NIC.

Caribbean Sea

CAPE VERDE

SENEGAL

Dakar

GUINEA

BURKINA FASO

NIGERIA

AFRICA

Caracas

Guiana Basin

Cape Verde Basin

GHANA

COSTA RICA

PANAMA

Orinoco

VENEZUELA

GUYANA

SUR.

FRENCH GUIANA

OCEAN

Freetown

LIBERIA

COTE D'IVOIRE

Lagos

CAMEROON

CENTRAL AFRICAN REPUBLIC

Abidjan

COLOMBIA

ECUADOR

Equator

Romanche Gap

Guinea Basin

Libreville

GABON

DEM. REP. OF THE CONGO

Congo

Manaus

Amazon

Ascension (St. Hel.)

Kinshasa

BRAZIL

Recife

Brazil Basin

Luanda

PERU

Lima

SOUTH AMERICA

Brasília

ST. HELENA (Br.)

Angola

ANGOLA

ZAMBIA

Peru Basin

BOLIVIA

Tropic of Capricorn

Angola Basin

NAMIBIA

Nazca Ridge

PARAGUAY

Rio de Janeiro

São Paulo

Paraná

MID-ATLANTIC RIDGE

Walvis Ridge

BOTSWANA

Johannesburg

PACIFIC

CHILE

Santiago

URUGUAY

Bromley Plateau

TRISTAN DA CUNHA GROUP (St. Hel.)

St. Helena

Cape Basin

SOUTH AFRICA

Cape Town

ARGENTINA

Buenos Aires

GOUGH ISLAND (St. Hel.)

Chile Rise

Argentine Basin

Agulhas Basin

OCEAN

FALKLAND ISLANDS (Br.)

Scotia Ridge

SOUTH GEORGIA (Br.)

South Sandwich Trench

BOUVETØYA

Atlantic-Indian Ridge

SOUTH SHETLAND ISLANDS (Br.)

SOUTH ORKNEY ISLANDS (Br.)

Southeast Pacific Basin

Atlantic-Indian Basin

Antarctic Circle

Weddell Sea

ANTARCTICA

© Rand McNally & Co.
N-GDS14000-A2-

Scale 1:72 000 000 at 40° latitude. ROBINSON PROJECTION

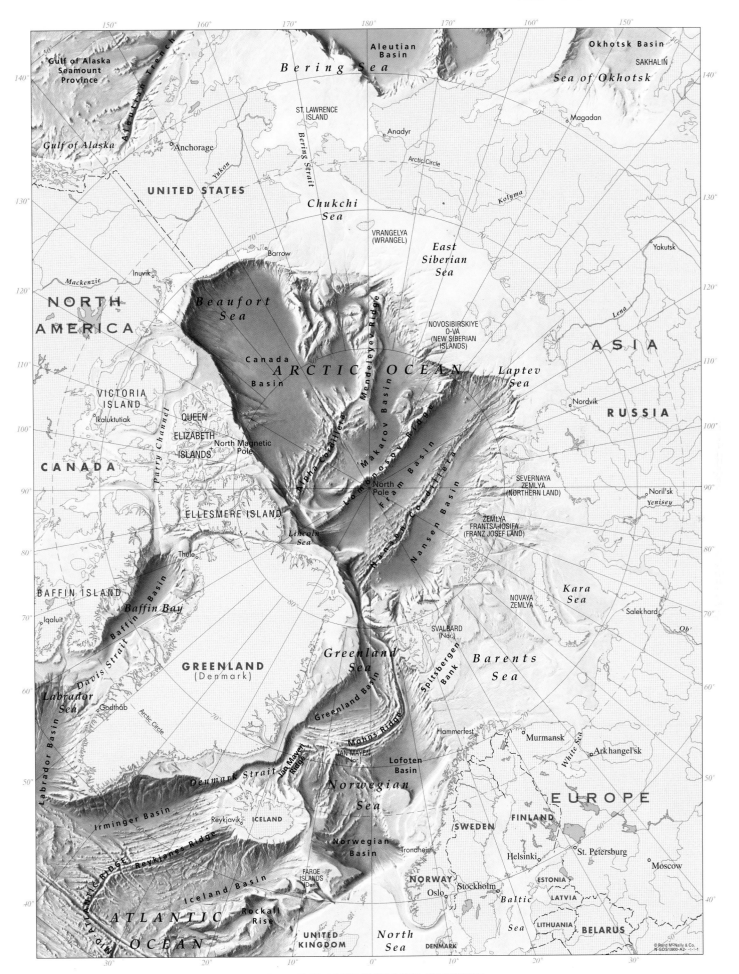

14

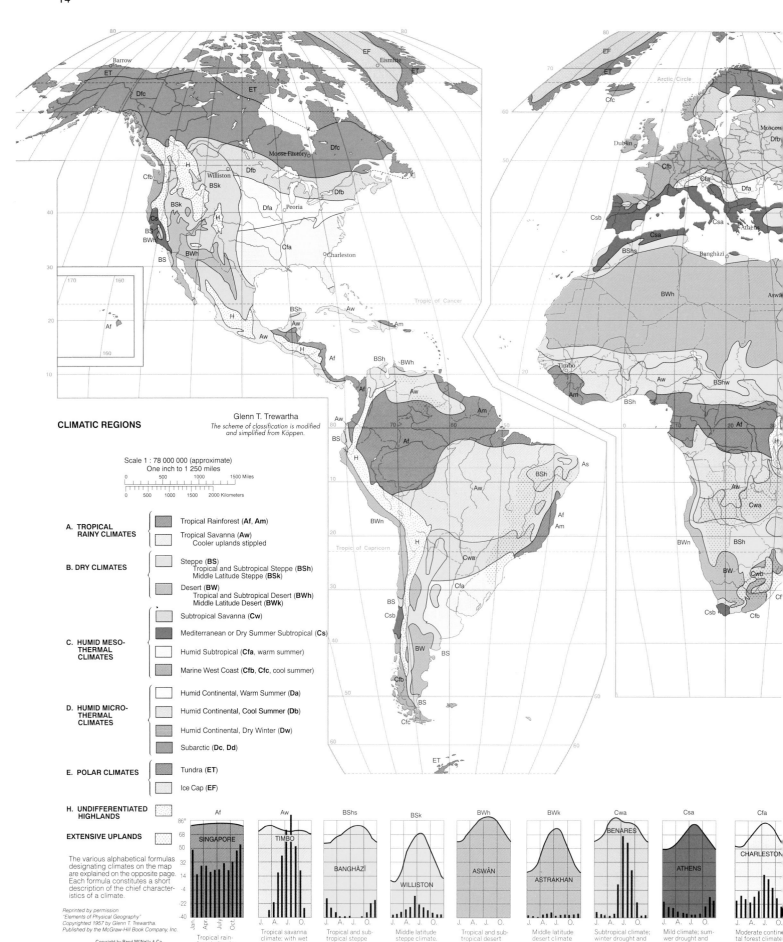

CLIMATIC REGIONS

Glenn T. Trewartha
*The scheme of classification is modified
and simplified from Köppen.*

Scale 1 : 78 000 000 (approximate)
One inch to 1 250 miles

0   500   1000   1500 Miles

0   500   1000   1500   2000 Kilometers

A. TROPICAL RAINY CLIMATES
- Tropical Rainforest (**Af, Am**)
- Tropical Savanna (**Aw**) Cooler uplands stippled

B. DRY CLIMATES
- Steppe (**BS**) Tropical and Subtropical Steppe (**BSh**) Middle Latitude Steppe (**BSk**)
- Desert (**BW**) Tropical and Subtropical Desert (**BWh**) Middle Latitude Desert (**BWk**)

C. HUMID MESO-THERMAL CLIMATES
- Subtropical Savanna (**Cw**)
- Mediterranean or Dry Summer Subtropical (**Cs**)
- Humid Subtropical (**Cfa**, warm summer)
- Marine West Coast (**Cfb, Cfc**, cool summer)

D. HUMID MICRO-THERMAL CLIMATES
- Humid Continental, Warm Summer (**Da**)
- Humid Continental, Cool Summer (**Db**)
- Humid Continental, Dry Winter (**Dw**)
- Subarctic (**Dc, Dd**)

E. POLAR CLIMATES
- Tundra (**ET**)
- Ice Cap (**EF**)

H. UNDIFFERENTIATED HIGHLANDS

EXTENSIVE UPLANDS

The various alphabetical formulas designating climates on the map are explained on the opposite page. Each formula constitutes a short description of the chief character-istics of a climate.

*Reprinted by permission
"Elements of Physical Geography"
Copyrighted 1957 by Glenn T. Trewartha.
Published by the McGraw-Hill Book Company, Inc.*

Copyright by Rand McNally & Co.
Made in U.S.A.
N-GDS10000-C1-·-1-·-2

Af	Aw	BShs	BSk	BWh	BWk	Cwa	Csa	Cfa
SINGAPORE	TIMBO	BANGHĀZĪ	WILLISTON	ASWÂN	ASTRAKHAN	BENARES	ATHENS	CHARLESTON
Tropical rain-forest climate	Tropical savanna climate; with wet and dry seasons	Tropical and sub-tropical steppe climate	Middle latitude steppe climate.	Tropical and sub-tropical desert climate	Middle latitude desert climate	Subtropical climate; winter drought and summer rain	Mild climate; sum-wer drought and winter rain	Moderate conti-tal forest climate mild winters

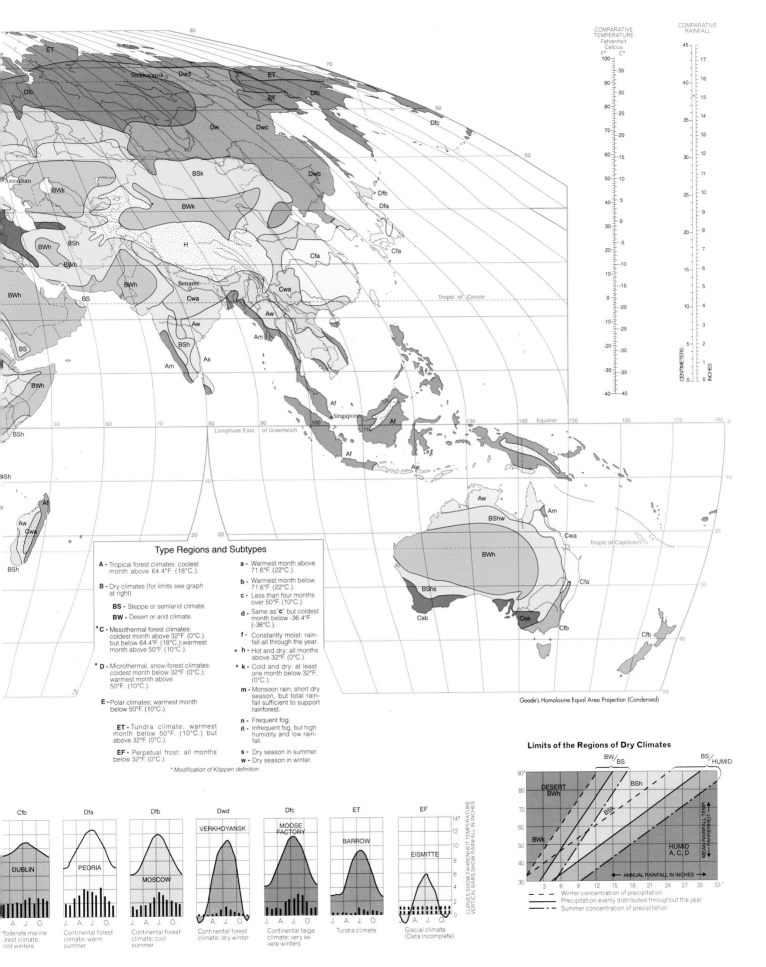

COMPARATIVE TEMPERATURE
Fahrenheit
Celcius
F° C°

COMPARATIVE RAINFALL

Type Regions and Subtypes

A - Tropical forest climates: coolest month above 64.4°F. (18°C.).

B - Dry climates (for limits see graph at right)

    BS - Steppe or semiarid climate.

    BW - Desert or arid climate.

*C - Mesothermal forest climates: coldest month above 32°F. (0°C.). but below 64.4°F. (18°C.);warmest month above 50°F. (10°C.).

*D - Microthermal, snow-forest climates: coldest month below 32°F. (0°C.); warmest month above 50°F. (10°C.).

E - Polar climates; warmest month below 50°F. (10°C.).

    ET - Tundra climate: warmest month below 50°F. (10°C.) but above 32°F. (0°C.).

    EF - Perpetual frost: all months below 32°F. (0°C.).

a - Warmest month above 71.6°F. (22°C.).

b - Warmest month below 71.6°F. (22°C.).

c - Less than four months over 50°F. (10°C.).

d - Same as"c" but coldest month below -36.4°F (-38°C.).

f - Constantly moist: rainfall all through the year.

* h - Hot and dry: all months above 32°F. (0°C.).

* k - Cold and dry: at least one month below 32°F. (0°C.).

m - Monsoon rain; short dry season, but total rainfall sufficient to support rainforest.

n - Frequent fog.

ń - Infrequent fog, but high humidity and low rainfall.

s - Dry season in summer.

w - Dry season in winter.

* Modification of Köppen definition

Goode's Homolosine Equal Area Projection (Condensed)

Limits of the Regions of Dry Climates

BW/BS BS/HUMID

DESERT BWh

BSh

BSk

BWk

HUMID A, C, D

MEAN RAINFALL TEMP FAHRENHEIT

ANNUAL RAINFALL IN INCHES

- — Winter concentration of precipitation
- —— Precipitation evenly distributed throughout the year
- —·— Summer concentration of precipitation

CURVES SHOW FAHRENHEIT TEMPERATURE
VERTICAL BARS SHOW RAINFALL IN INCHES

Cfb
DUBLIN
Moderate marine forest climate; mild winters

Dfa
PEORIA
Continental forest climate; warm summer

Dfb
MOSCOW
Continental forest climate; cool summer

Dwd
VERKHOYANSK
Continental forest climate; dry winter

Dfc
MOOSE FACTORY
Continental taiga climate; very severe winters

ET
BARROW
Tundra climate

EF
EISMITTE
Glacial climate (Data Incomplete)

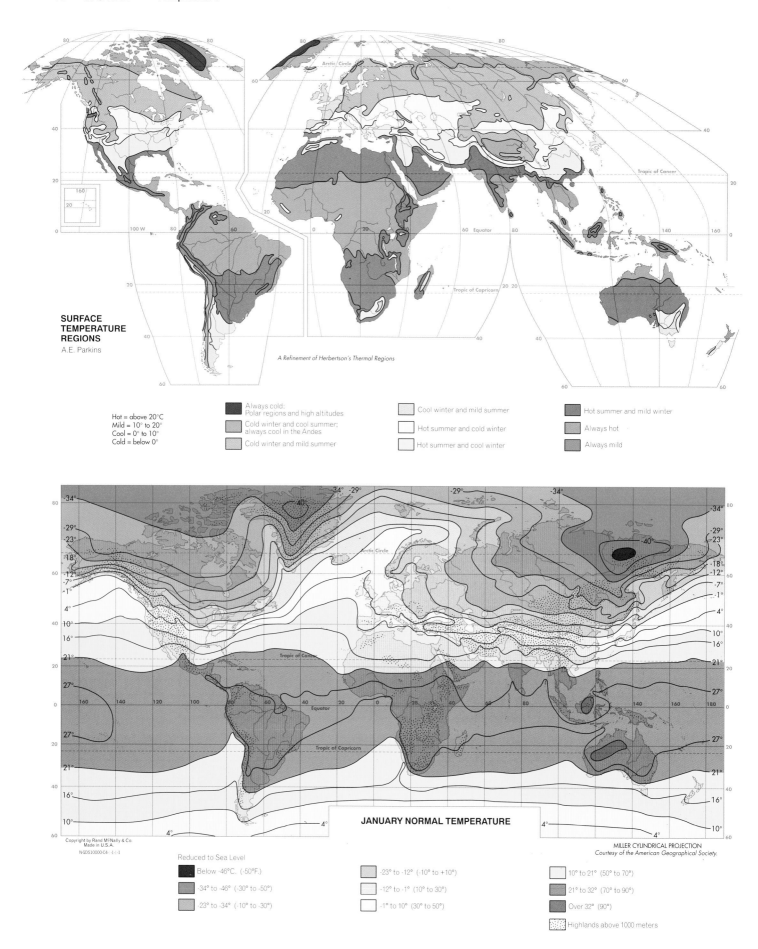

**SURFACE
TEMPERATURE
REGIONS**
A.E. Parkins

A Refinement of Herbertson's Thermal Regions

Hot = above 20°C
Mild = 10° to 20°
Cool = 0° to 10°
Cold = below 0°

Always cold; Polar regions and high altitudes	
Cold winter and cool summer; always cool in the Andes	
Cold winter and mild summer	
Cool winter and mild summer	
Hot summer and cold winter	
Hot summer and cool winter	
Hot summer and mild winter	
Always hot	
Always mild	

JANUARY NORMAL TEMPERATURE

MILLER CYLINDRICAL PROJECTION
Courtesy of the American Geographical Society.

Reduced to Sea Level

Below -46°C. (-50°F.)	
-34° to -46° (-30° to -50°)	
-23° to -34° (-10° to -30°)	
-23° to -12° (-10° to +10°)	
-12° to -1° (10° to 30°)	
-1° to 10° (30° to 50°)	
10° to 21° (50° to 70°)	
21° to 32° (70° to 90°)	
Over 32° (90°)	
Highlands above 1000 meters	

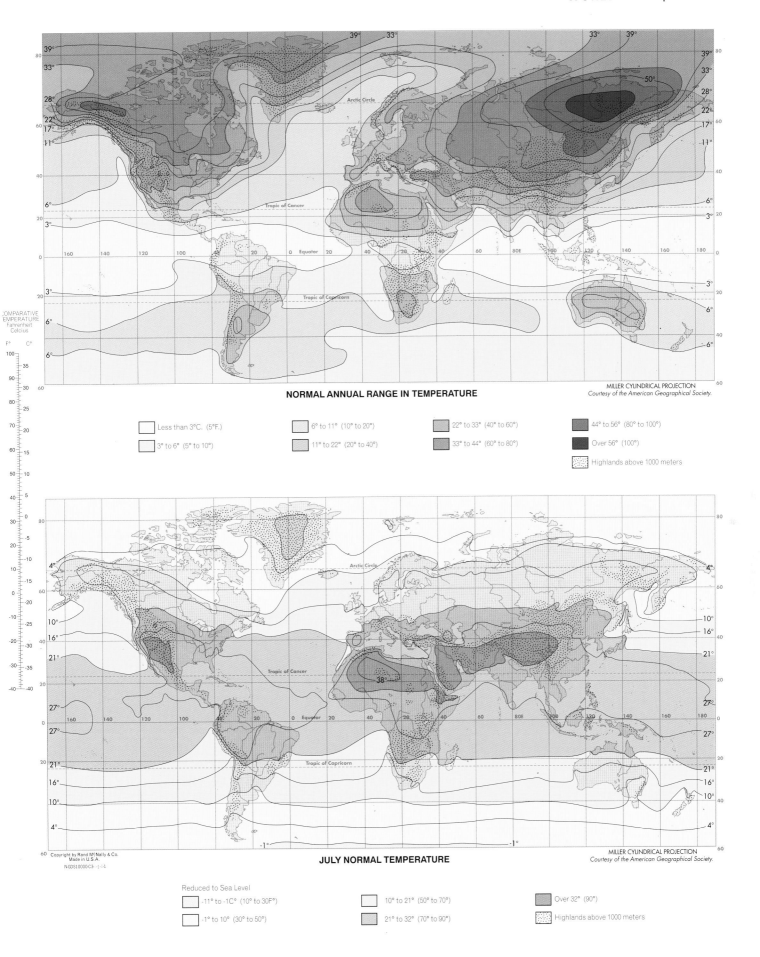

NORMAL ANNUAL RANGE IN TEMPERATURE

MILLER CYLINDRICAL PROJECTION
Courtesy of the American Geographical Society.

COMPARATIVE
TEMPERATURE
Fahrenheit
Celcius

	Less than 3°C. (5°F.)		6° to 11° (10° to 20°)		22° to 33° (40° to 60°)		44° to 56° (80° to 100°)
	3° to 6° (5° to 10°)		11° to 22° (20° to 40°)		33° to 44° (60° to 80°)		Over 56° (100°)
							Highlands above 1000 meters

JULY NORMAL TEMPERATURE

MILLER CYLINDRICAL PROJECTION
Courtesy of the American Geographical Society.

Reduced to Sea Level

| | -11° to -1C° (10° to 30F°) | | 10° to 21° (50° to 70°) | | Over 32° (90°) |
| | -1° to 10° (30° to 50°) | | 21° to 32° (70° to 90°) | | Highlands above 1000 meters |

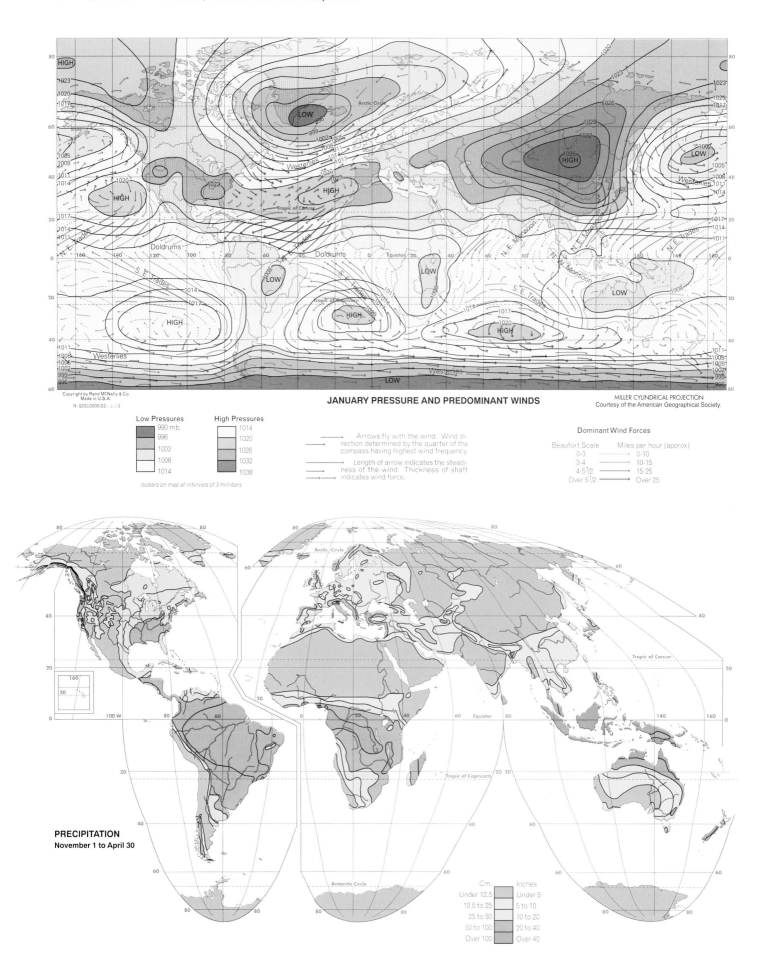

Copyright by Rand McNally & Co.
Made in U.S.A.
N·GDS10000-D2-

JANUARY PRESSURE AND PREDOMINANT WINDS

MILLER CYLINDRICAL PROJECTION
Courtesy of the American Geographical Society.

Low Pressures
990 mb.
996
1002
1008
1014

High Pressures
1014
1020
1026
1032
1038

Isobars on map at intervals of 3 millibars

Arrows fly with the wind. Wind direction determined by the quarter of the compass having highest wind frequency.

Length of arrow indicates the steadiness of the wind. Thickness of shaft indicates wind force.

Dominant Wind Forces

Beaufort Scale	Miles per hour (approx)
0-3	0-10
3-4	10-15
4-5½	15-25
Over 5½	Over 25

PRECIPITATION
November 1 to April 30

Cm.
Under 12.5
12.5 to 25
25 to 50
50 to 100
Over 100

Inches
Under 5
5 to 10
10 to 20
20 to 40
Over 40

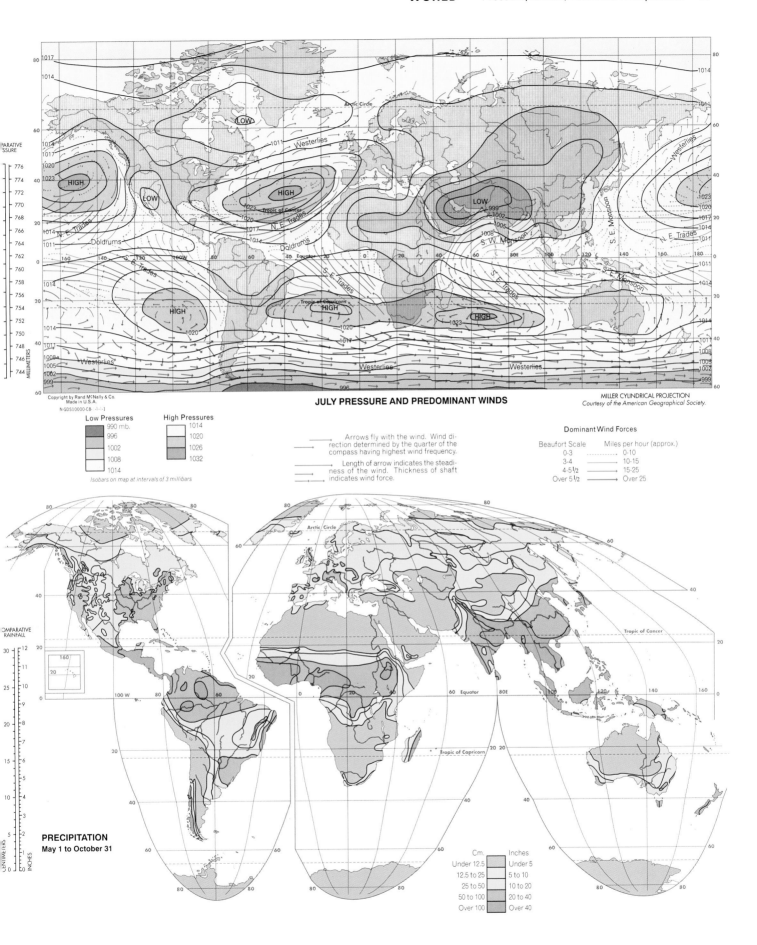

JULY PRESSURE AND PREDOMINANT WINDS

MILLER CYLINDRICAL PROJECTION
Courtesy of the American Geographical Society.

Copyright by Rand McNally & Co.
Made in U.S.A.
N-GDS10000-CB -1-:-1

COMPARATIVE PRESSURE

MILLIMETERS
776
774
772
770
768
766
764
762
760
758
756
754
752
750
748
746
744

Low Pressures
990 mb.
996
1002
1008
1014

High Pressures
1014
1020
1026
1032

Isobars on map at intervals of 3 millibars

Arrows fly with the wind. Wind direction determined by the quarter of the compass having highest wind frequency.

Length of arrow indicates the steadiness of the wind. Thickness of shaft indicates wind force.

Dominant Wind Forces

Beaufort Scale	Miles per hour (approx.)
0-3	0-10
3-4	10-15
4-5½	15-25
Over 5½	Over 25

PRECIPITATION
May 1 to October 31

COMPARATIVE RAINFALL

CENTIMETERS	INCHES
30	12
	11
	10
25	9
	8
20	7
	6
15	5
	4
10	3
5	2
	1
0	0

Cm.	Inches
Under 12.5	Under 5
12.5 to 25	5 to 10
25 to 50	10 to 20
50 to 100	20 to 40
Over 100	Over 40

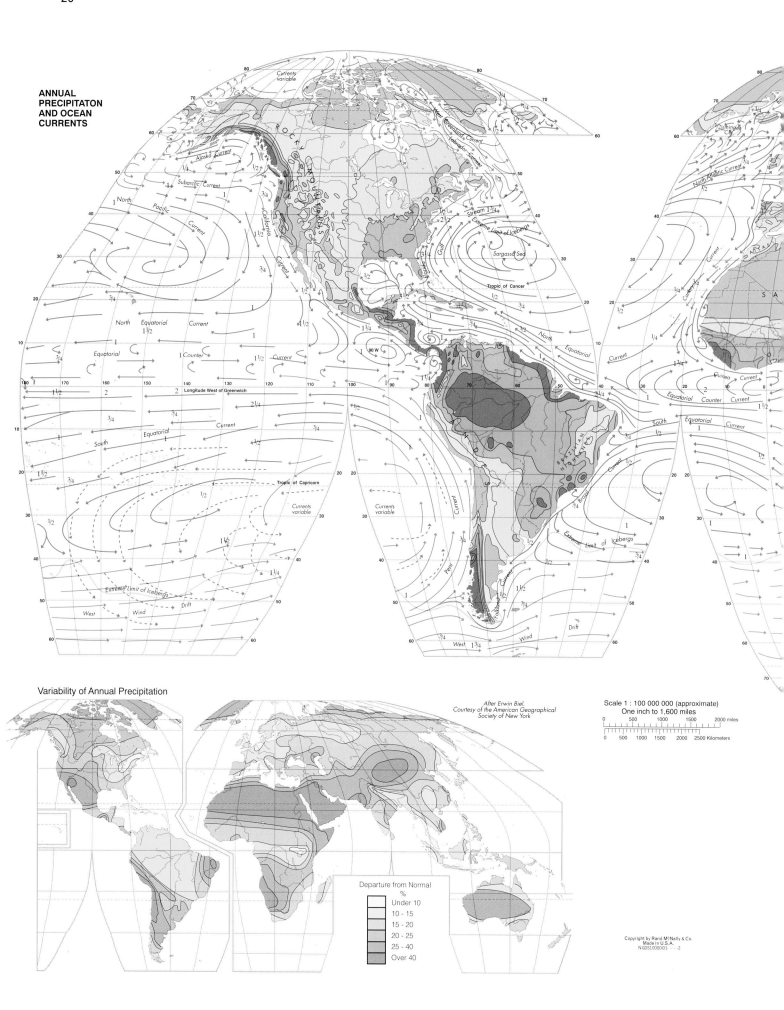

**ANNUAL
PRECIPITATON
AND OCEAN
CURRENTS**

Variability of Annual Precipitation

After Erwin Biel.
Courtesy of the American Geographical
Society of New York

Scale 1 : 100 000 000 (approximate)
One inch to 1,600 miles

Departure from Normal
%
Under 10
10 - 15
15 - 20
20 - 25
25 - 40
Over 40

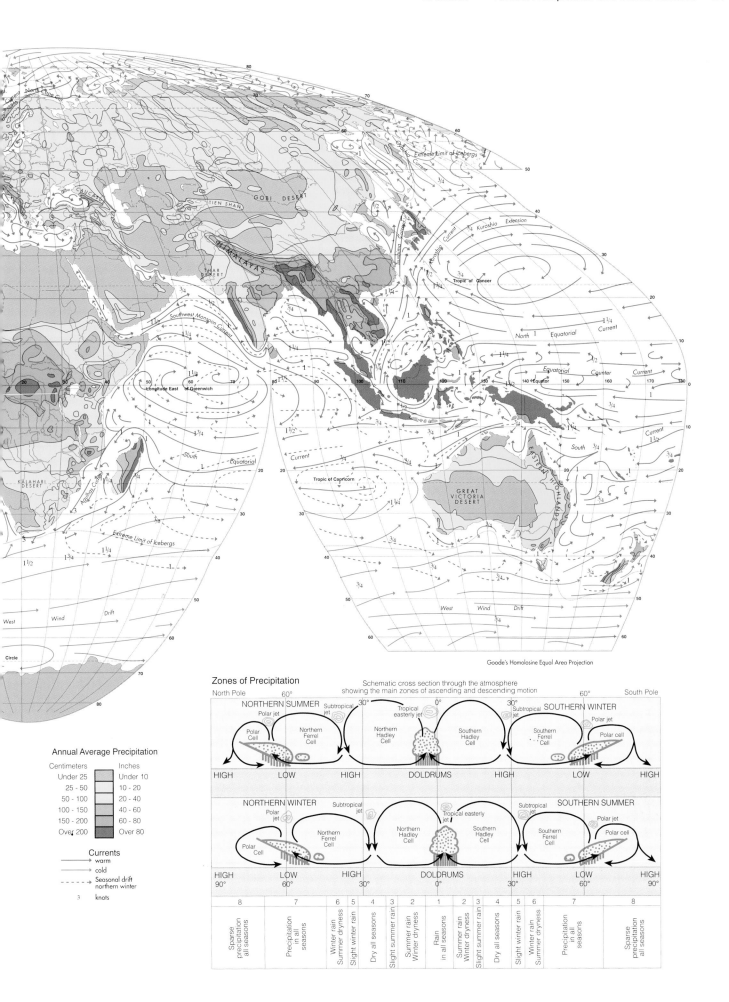

Goode's Homolosine Equal Area Projection

Zones of Precipitation

Schematic cross section through the atmosphere
showing the main zones of ascending and descending motion

Annual Average Precipitation

Centimeters	Inches
Under 25	Under 10
25 - 50	10 - 20
50 - 100	20 - 40
100 - 150	40 - 60
150 - 200	60 - 80
Over 200	Over 80

Currents

→ warm
→ cold
--→ Seasonal drift
    northern winter
3   knots

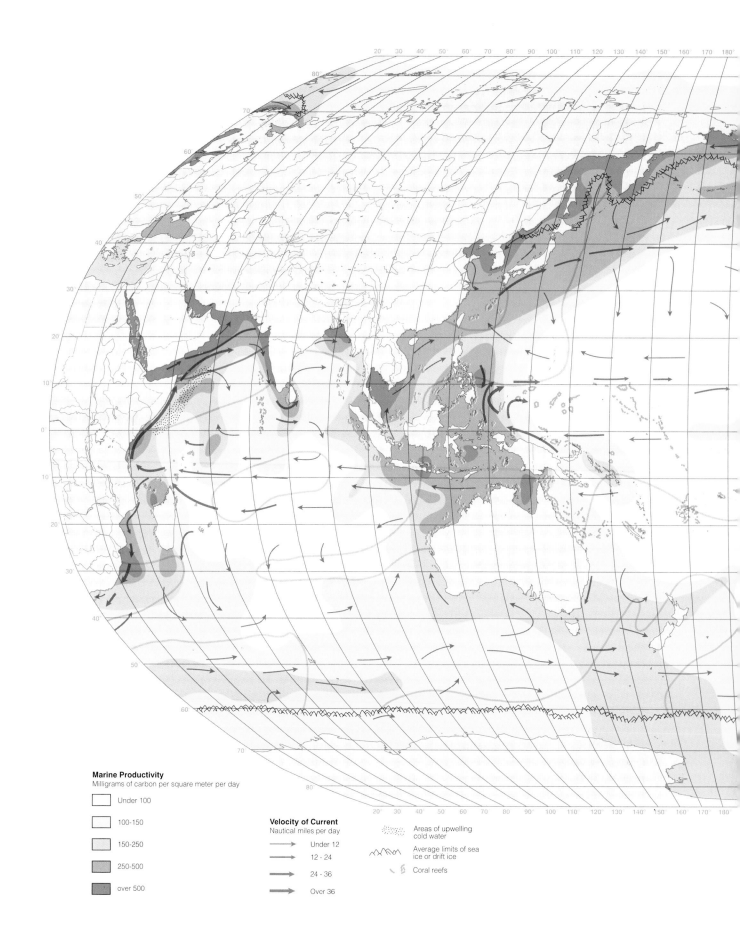

Marine Productivity
Milligrams of carbon per square meter per day

- Under 100
- 100-150
- 150-250
- 250-500
- over 500

Velocity of Current
Nautical miles per day

- Under 12
- 12 - 24
- 24 - 36
- Over 36

- Areas of upwelling cold water
- Average limits of sea ice or drift ice
- Coral reefs

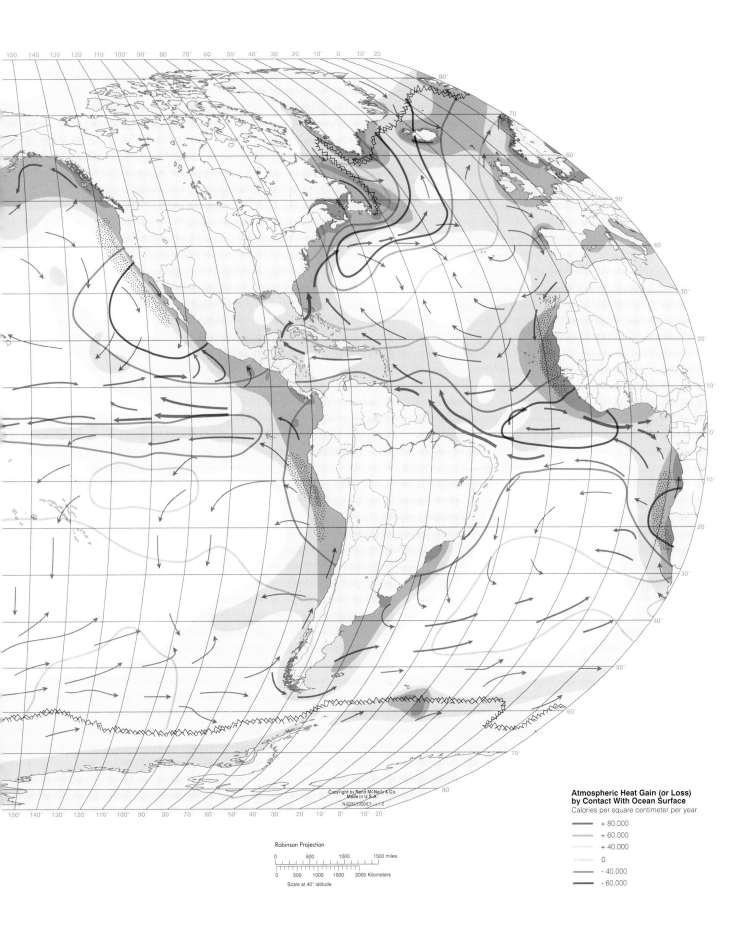

Atmospheric Heat Gain (or Loss)
by Contact With Ocean Surface
Calories per square centimeter per year

+ 80,000
+ 60,000
+ 40,000
0
- 40,000
- 60,000

Robinson Projection

0   500   1000   1500 miles

0   500   1000   1500   2000 Kilometers

Scale at 40° latitude

Copyright by Rand McNally & Co.
Made in U.S.A.

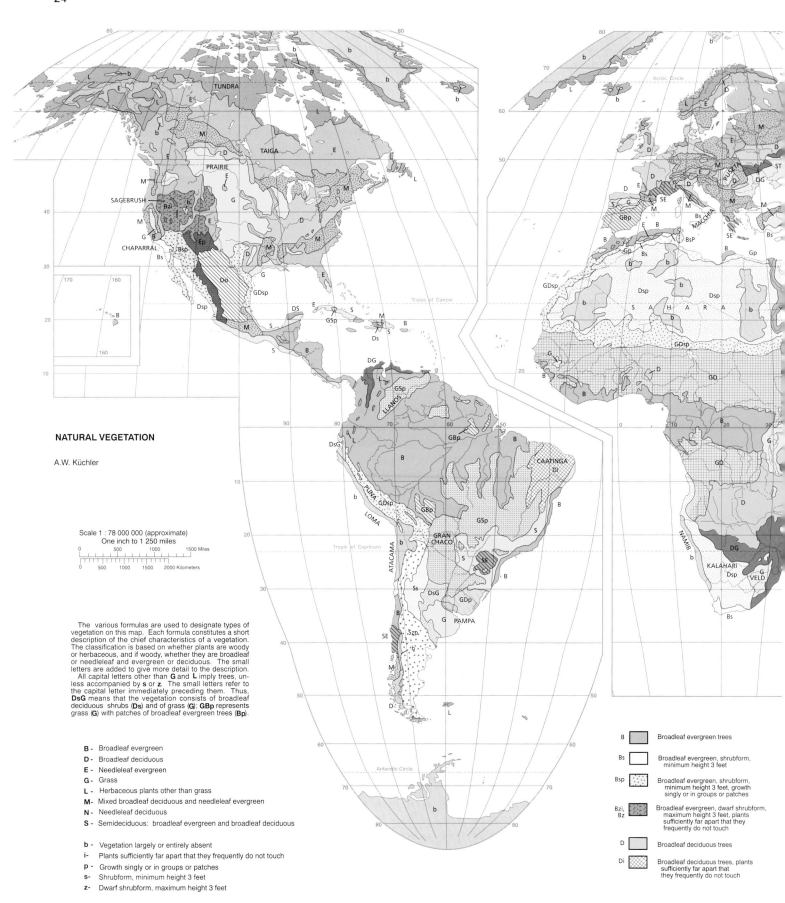

NATURAL VEGETATION

A.W. Küchler

Scale 1 : 78 000 000 (approximate)
One inch to 1 250 miles

0   500   1000   1500 Miles

0   500   1000   1500   2000 Kilometers

The various formulas are used to designate types of
vegetation on this map. Each formula constitutes a short
description of the chief characteristics of a vegetation.
The classification is based on whether plants are woody
or herbaceous, and if woody, whether they are broadleaf
or needleleaf and evergreen or deciduous. The small
letters are added to give more detail to the description.
All capital letters other than **G** and **L** imply trees, un-
less accompanied by **s** or **z**. The small letters refer to
the capital letter immediately preceding them. Thus,
DsG means that the vegetation consists of broadleaf
deciduous shrubs (**Ds**) and of grass (**G**); **GBp** represents
grass (**G**) with patches of broadleaf evergreen trees (**Bp**).

B - Broadleaf evergreen
D - Broadleaf deciduous
E - Needleleaf evergreen
G - Grass
L - Herbaceous plants other than grass
M - Mixed broadleaf deciduous and needleleaf evergreen
N - Needleleaf deciduous
S - Semideciduous: broadleaf evergreen and broadleaf deciduous

b - Vegetation largely or entirely absent
i - Plants sufficiently far apart that they frequently do not touch
p - Growth singly or in groups or patches
s - Shrubform, minimum height 3 feet
z - Dwarf shrubform, maximum height 3 feet

B	Broadleaf evergreen trees
Bs	Broadleaf evergreen, shrubform, minimum height 3 feet
Bsp	Broadleaf evergreen, shrubform, minimum height 3 feet, growth singly or in groups or patches
Bzi, Bz	Broadleaf evergreen, dwarf shrubform, maximum height 3 feet, plants sufficiently far apart that they frequently do not touch
D	Broadleaf deciduous trees
Di	Broadleaf deciduous trees, plants sufficiently far apart that they frequently do not touch

Goode's Homolosine Equal Area Projection (Condensed)

Symbol	Description
	Broadleaf deciduous, shrubform, minimum height 3 feet
	Broadleaf deciduous, shrubform, minimum height 3 feet, plants sufficiently far apart that they frequently do not touch
	Broadleaf deciduous, shrubform, minimum height 3 feet, growth singly or in groups or patches
	Broadleaf deciduous, dwarf shrubform, maximum height 3 feet, growth singly or in groups or patches
	Broadleaf deciduous, shrubform, minimum height 3 feet Grass and other herbaceous plants
	Broadleaf deciduous trees Grass and other herbaceous plants
	Broadleaf deciduous trees Broadleaf evergreen, shrubform, minimum height 3 feet
E	Needleleaf evergreen trees
Ep	Needleleaf evergreen trees, growth singly or in groups or patches
G	Grass and other herbaceous plants
Gp	Grass and other herbaceous plants, growth singly or in groups or patches
GBp	Grass and other herbaceous plants Broadleaf evergreen trees, growth singly or in groups or patches
GD	Grass and other herbaceous plants Broadleaf deciduous trees
GDp	Grass and other herbaceous plants Broadleaf deciduous trees, growth singly or in groups or patches
GDsp	Grass and other herbaceous plants Broadleaf deciduous, shrubform, minimum height 3 feet, growth singly or in groups or patches
GSp	Grass and other herbaceous plants Semideciduous: broadleaf evergreen and broadleaf deciduous trees, growth singly or in groups or patches
L	Herbaceous plants other than grass
M	Mixed: broadleaf deciduous and needleleaf evergreen trees
N	Needleleaf deciduous trees
ND	Needleleaf deciduous trees Broadleaf deciduous trees
S	Semideciduous: broadleaf evergreen and broadleaf deciduous trees
Ss	Semideciduous: broadleaf evergreen and broadleaf deciduous, shrubform, minimum height 3 feet
SsG	Semideciduous: broadleaf evergreen and broadleaf deciduous, shrubform, minimum height 3 feet Grass and other herbaceous plants
Szp	Semideciduous: broadleaf evergreen and broadleaf deciduous, dwarf shrubform, maximum height 3 feet, growth singly or in groups or patches
SE	Semideciduous: broadleaf evergreen and broadleaf deciduous trees Needleleaf evergreen trees
b	Vegetation largely or entirely absent

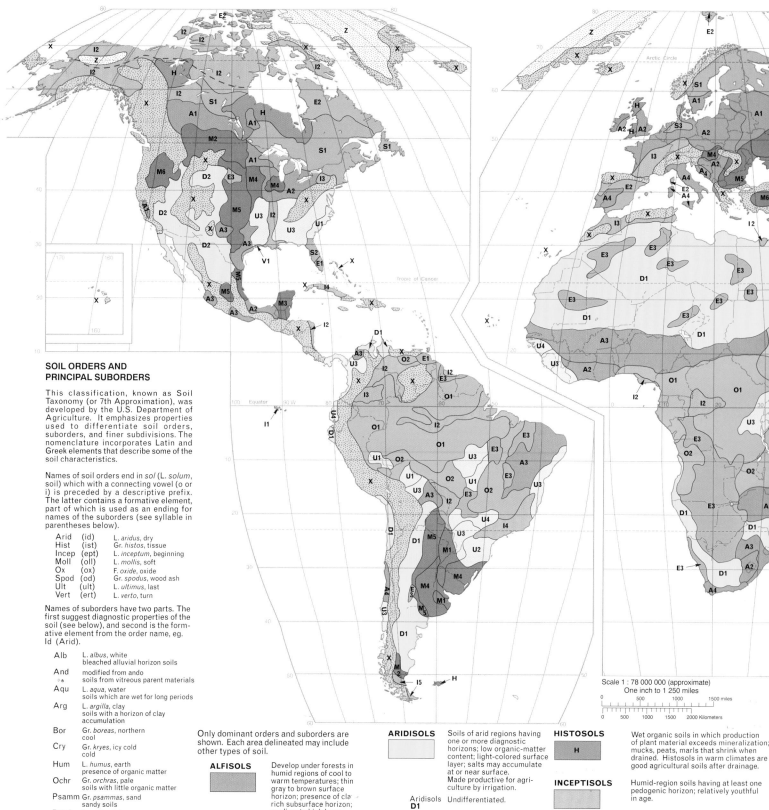

26

SOIL ORDERS AND PRINCIPAL SUBORDERS

This classification, known as Soil Taxonomy (or 7th Approximation), was developed by the U.S. Department of Agriculture. It emphasizes properties used to differentiate soil orders, suborders, and finer subdivisions. The nomenclature incorporates Latin and Greek elements that describe some of the soil characteristics.

Names of soil orders end in *sol* (L. *solum*, soil) which with a connecting vowel (o or i) is preceded by a descriptive prefix. The latter contains a formative element, part of which is used as an ending for names of the suborders (see syllable in parentheses below).

Arid	(id)	L. *aridus*, dry
Hist	(ist)	Gr. *histos*, tissue
Incep	(ept)	L. *inceptum*, beginning
Moll	(oll)	L. *mollis*, soft
Ox	(ox)	F. *oxide*, oxide
Spod	(od)	Gr. *spodus*, wood ash
Ult	(ult)	L. *ultimus*, last
Vert	(ert)	L. *verto*, turn

Names of suborders have two parts. The first suggest diagnostic properties of the soil (see below), and second is the formative element from the order name, eg. Id (Arid).

Alb	L. *albus*, white; bleached alluvial horizon soils
And	modified from ando; soils from vitreous parent materials
Aqu	L. *aqua*, water; soils which are wet for long periods
Arg	L. *argilla*, clay; soils with a horizon of clay accumulation
Bor	Gr. *boreas*, northern cool
Cry	Gr. *kryes*, icy cold cold
Hum	L. *humus*, earth; presence of organic matter
Ochr	Gr. *orchras*, pale; soils with little organic matter
Psamm	Gr. *psammas*, sand sandy soils
Rend	from Rendzina; high carbonate content
Torr	L. *torridus*, hot and dry; soils of very dry climate
Ud	L. *udus*, humid; soils of humid climate
Umbr	L. *umbra*, shade; dark color reflecting relatively high organic matter
Ust	L. *ustus*, burnt; soils of dry climates with summer rains
Xer	Gr. *xeros*, dry; soils of dry climates with winter rains

Only dominant orders and suborders are shown. Each area delineated may include other types of soil.

ALFISOLS

Develop under forests in humid regions of cool to warm temperatures; thin gray to brown surface horizon; presence of clay rich subsurface horizon; medium to high base saturation; adequate moisture supply most of year. Generally fertile agricultural soils.

Boralfs **A1** — Well-drained soils of boreal and subalpine forests.

Udalfs **A2** — Humid, well-drained, highly fertile soils of warm-summer climates.

Ustalfs **A3** — Reddish-brown forest and grassland soils of warm, subhumid to semiarid climates.

Xeralfs **A4** — Reddish soils lacking moisture during summer in Mediterranean climate zones.

ARIDISOLS

Soils of arid regions having one or more diagnostic horizons; low organic-matter content; light-colored surface layer; salts may accumulate at or near surface. Made productive for agriculture by irrigation.

Aridisols **D1** — Undifferentiated.

Argids **D2** — Presence of clay horizon.

ENTISOLS

Soils lacking pedogenic horizons; varied in nature.

Aquents **E1** — Seasonally or perenially wet; bluish or gray and mottled.

Orthents **E2** — Soils thinning due to erosion or where no sedimentation occurs.

Psamments **E3** — Sandy texture in all layers below surface; form on dune sands.

HISTOSOLS

Wet organic soils in which production of plant material exceeds mineralization; mucks, peats, marls that shrink when drained. Histosols in warm climates are good agricultural soils after drainage.

INCEPTISOLS

Humid-region soils having at least one pedogenic horizon; relatively youthful in age.

Andepts **I1** — Soils formed on recent volcanic ash; high organic-matter content.

Aquepts **I2** — Humid region soils developed on river floodplains. Cryaquepts are tundra soils on permafrost.

Ochrepts **I3** — Thin, light-colored surface horizons; little organic-matter content.

Tropepts **I4** — Brownish or reddish soils of tropical environments.

Umbrepts **I5** — Dark-colored surface layer; high organic-matter content; hilly to mountainous topography.

Scale 1 : 78 000 000 (approximate)
One inch to 1 250 miles

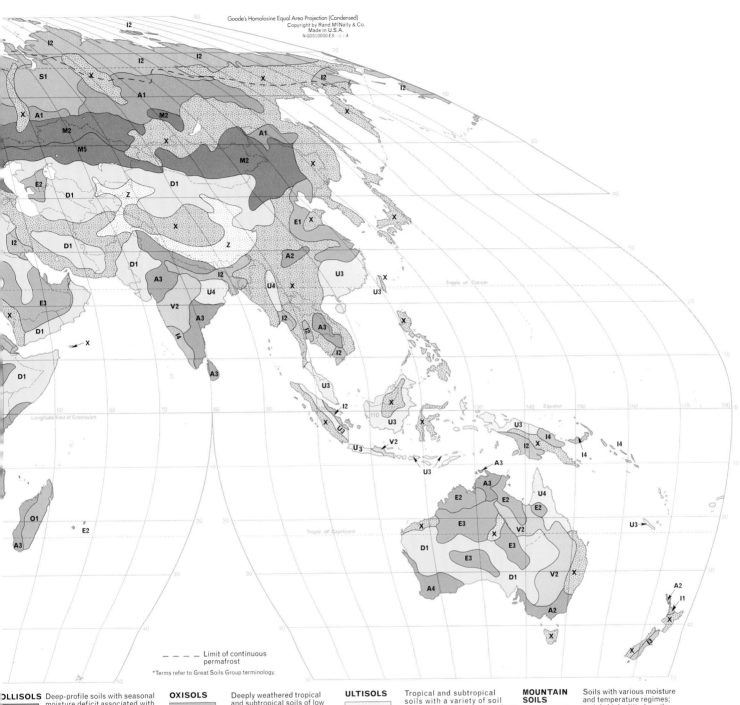

Goode's Homolosine Equal Area Projection (Condensed)
Copyright by Rand McNally & Co.
Made in U.S.A.
N-GDS10000-E3--1-:4

– – – – Limit of continuous
permafrost

*Terms refer to Great Soils Group terminology.

OLLISOLS Deep-profile soils with seasonal moisture deficit associated with grasslands; dark brown to black upper layer; may have subsurface horizon of calcium accumulation; high base saturation. Very productive for grain crops.

Albolls
M1 — Soils with a grayish subsurface horizon over clay layer and a fluctuating water table.

Borolls
M2 — Well-drained, fertile grassland soils of cool summers and cold winters.

Rendolls
M3 — Formed on calcareous limestones.

Udolls
M4 — Freely drained soils of humid regions with warm summers; excellent agricultural soils.

Ustolls
M5 — Fertile agricultural soils of subhumid climates.

Xerolls
M6 — Pronounced soil-moisture deficit during high-sun season; associated with Mediterranean climates.

OXISOLS Deeply weathered tropical and subtropical soils of low natural fertility; low base saturation; limited ability to hold soil nutrients against leaching; presence of plinthite (laterite) layers. Generally unsuited to large-scale agricultural production.

Orthox
O1 — Hot and nearly always moist; associated with tropical rainforests.

Ustox
O2 — Hot to warm forest and savanna soils with a drier season of low soil-moisture availability.

SPODOSOLS Soils of moist climates ranging from subtropical to cold conditions; include a spodic subsurface horizon incorporating active organic matter beneath a light-colored, leached, sandy horizon. Generally marginal for agriculture.

Spodo-sols
S1 — Undifferentiated, mostly in high latitudes.

Aquods
S2 — Seasonally wet developed on sandy parent material.

Humods
S3 — Considerable organic matter present in subsurface horizon.

Orthods
S4 — Subsurface accumulations of iron, aluminum, and organic matter.

ULTISOLS Tropical and subtropical soils with a variety of soil moisture regimes; subsurface clay horizon; low base saturation; very old soils characterized by long weathering of clay minerals; low ability to hold nutrients against leaching. Often marginal for agriculture.

Aquults
U1 — Seasonally wet with mottled, gray subsurface horizon.

Humults
U2 — Dark soils with high organic-matter content, warm temperatures.

Udults
U3 — Low organic-matter content and temperate to hot conditions.

Ustults
U4 — Seasonally dry, warm to hot conditions.

VERTISOLS Dark tropical and subtropical soils developed on heavy clays; deep shrinkage cracks appear during dry season which become filled with loose surface materials that absorb moisture and swell during wet season. Generally fertile and well suited to crop production.

Uderts
V1 — Generally moist with limited period for shrinkage cracks to develop.

Usterts
V2 — Over three months of shrinkage-crack formation.

MOUNTAIN SOILS Soils with various moisture and temperature regimes; mainly high altitude soils forming on steep slopes; soils vary greatly within a short distance.

X

Z — Areas with little or no soils.

APPROXIMATE CORRELATION WITH OTHER SOIL CLASSIFICATION SYSTEMS

Soil Taxonomy	Great Soil Groups (former U.S. system)	Canadian system
Udalfs	Gray-brown Podzolic	Luvisolic Gray-Brown
Ustalfs	Reddish Chestnut; Red and Yellow Podzolic	
Aridisols	Desert and Reddish Desert Solonetz, Solonchak	
Entisols	Lithosols	Regosolic
Histosols	Bog	Organic
Inceptisol		Brunisolic
Orthents	Lithosols	
Aquepts	Humic Gley	Gleysolic
Cryaquept	Tundra	Cryosolic
Boralfs		Luvisolic Gray; Solonetzic
Borolls	Chernozem Chestnut Brown	Chernozemic, Solonetzic
Rendolls	Rendzina	
Udolls	Prairie	
Ustolls	Brown	
Oxisols	Latosols	
Humod		Humic Podzolic
Orthods	Podzols	Podzolic
Udults	Red and Yellow Podzolic Reddish Brown Lateritic	
Vertisols	Rendzina	

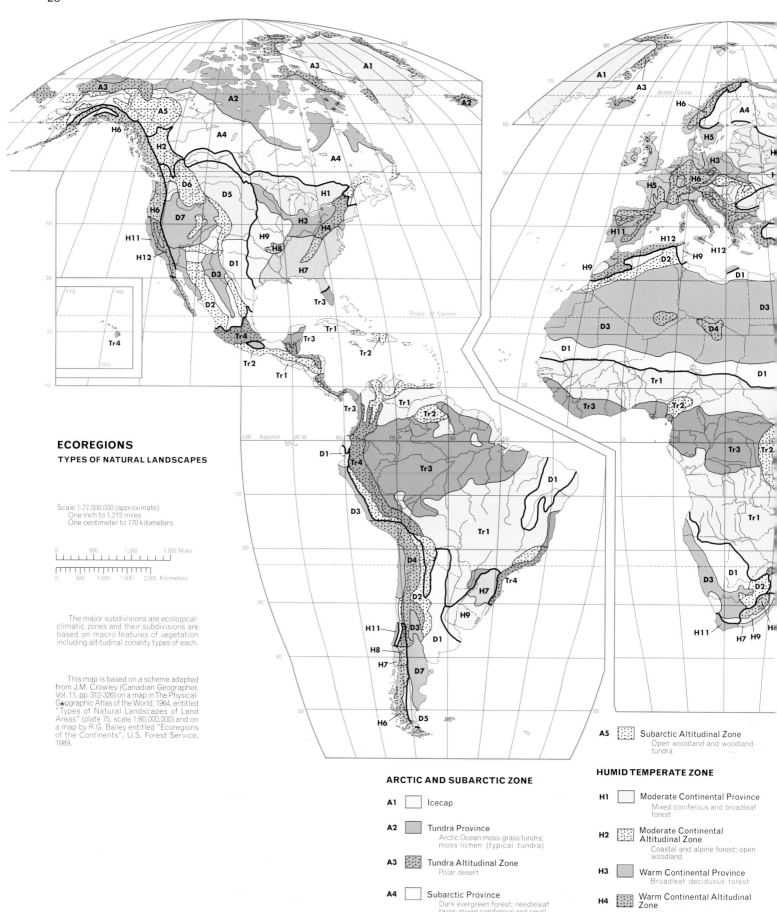

ECOREGIONS

TYPES OF NATURAL LANDSCAPES

Scale 1:77,000,000 (approximate)
One inch to 1,213 miles
One centimeter to 770 kilometers

| 0 | 500 | 1,000 | 1,500 Miles |

| 0 | 500 | 1,000 | 1,500 | 2,000 Kilometers |

The major subdivisions are ecological-
climatic zones and their subdivisions are
based on macro-features of vegetation
including altitudinal zonality types of each.

This map is based on a scheme adapted
from J.M. Crowley (Canadian Geographer,
Vol. 11, pp. 312-326) on a map in The Physical-
Geographic Atlas of the World, 1964, entitled
"Types of Natural Landscapes of Land
Areas" (plate 75, scale 1:80,000,000) and on
a map by R.G. Bailey entitled "Ecoregions
of the Continents", U.S. Forest Service,
1989.

A5 Subarctic Altitudinal Zone
Open woodland and woodland-
tundra

ARCTIC AND SUBARCTIC ZONE

A1 Icecap

A2 Tundra Province
Arctic Ocean moss-grass tundra;
moss-lichen (typical tundra)

A3 Tundra Altitudinal Zone
Polar desert

A4 Subarctic Province
Dark evergreen forest; needleleaf
taiga; mixed coniferous and small-
leafed forest

HUMID TEMPERATE ZONE

H1 Moderate Continental Province
Mixed coniferous and broadleaf
forest

H2 Moderate Continental
Altitudinal Zone
Coastal and alpine forest; open
woodland

H3 Warm Continental Province
Broadleaf deciduous forest

H4 Warm Continental Altitudinal
Zone
Upland broadleaf and alpine
needleleaf forest

Copyright by Rand McNally & Co.
Made in U.S.A.
N-GDS10000-E5-1- -:-:-4

H5		Marine Province
		Lowland, west-coastal humid forest

H6		Marine Altitudinal Zone
		Humid coastal and alpine coniferous forest

H7		Humid Subtropical Province
		Broadleaf evergreen and broadleaf deciduous forest

H8		Humid Subtropical Altitudinal Zone
		Upland, subtropical broadleaf forest

H9		Prairie Province

H10		Prairie Altitudinal Zone
		Upland mixed prairie and woodland

H11		Mediterranean Province
		Sclerophyll woodland, shrub, and steppe

H12		Mediterranean Altitudinal Zone
		Upland shrub and steppe

DRY AND DESERT ZONE

D1		Tropical/Subtropical Steppe Province
		Dry steppe, desert shrub, semi-desert savanna

D2		Tropical/Subtropical Steppe Altitudinal Zone
		Upland steppe and desert shrub

D3		Tropical/Subtropical Desert Province
		Hot, lowland desert at subtropical and coastal locations

D4		Tropical/Subtropical Desert Altitudinal Zone
		Desert shrub

D5		Temperate Steppe Province
		Medium to short steppe grassland

D6		Temperate Steppe Altitudinal Zone
		Alpine meadow and coniferous woodland

D7		Temperate Desert Province
		Midlatitude rainshadow desert

D8		Temperate Desert Altitudinal Zone
		Extreme continental desert-steppe

HUMID TROPICAL ZONE

Tr1		Savanna Province
		Seasonally dry forest, open woodland, tall grass

Tr2		Savanna Altitudinal Zone
		Open woodland-steppe

Tr3		Rainforest Province
		Constantly humid, broadleaf evergreen forest

Tr4		Rainforest Altitudinal Zone
		Broadleaf evergreen and subtropical deciduous forest

POPULATION DENSITY

Population

Per. Sq. Km.	Per. Sq. Mile
Uninhabited	Uninhabited
Under 1	Under 2
1-10	2-25
10-25	25-60
25-50	60-125
50-100	125-250
Over 100	Over 250

□ Metropolitan areas over 2,000,000 population
○ Metropolitan areas 1,000,000 to 2,000,000 population

Some cities are identified by initial letter only.

Scale 1 : 78 000 000 (approximate)
One inch to 1 250 miles

0 500 1000 1500 miles

0 500 1000 1500 2000 Kilometers

Goode's Homolosine Equal Area Projection (Condensed)

Population Density
per square kilometer (per square mile)

	of Total Area		of Cultivated Land
AUSTRALIA	2 (6)		37 (95)
RUSSIA	9 (23)		113 (293)
ARGENTINA	12 (32)		127 (328)
BRAZIL	19 (49)		247 (639)
UNITED STATES	27 (70)		150 (388)
EGYPT	60 (155)		1,840 (4,764)
FRANCE	107 (276)		299 (776)
CHINA	127 (328)		895 (2,318)
GERMANY	229 (594)		678 (1,756)
UNITED KINGDOM	239 (620)		952 (2,467)
INDIA	295 (764)		557 (1,442)
JAPAN	333 (862)		2,900 (7,51

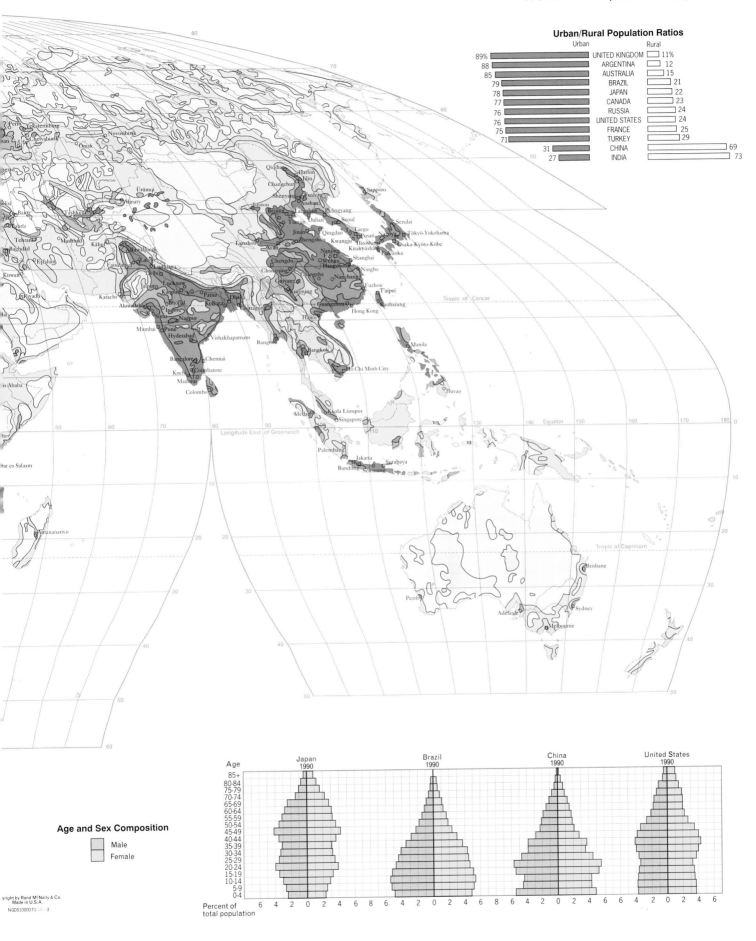

Urban/Rural Population Ratios

Urban		Rural
89%	UNITED KINGDOM	11%
88	ARGENTINA	12
85	AUSTRALIA	15
79	BRAZIL	21
78	JAPAN	22
77	CANADA	23
76	RUSSIA	24
76	UNITED STATES	24
75	FRANCE	25
71	TURKEY	29
31	CHINA	69
27	INDIA	73

Age and Sex Composition

Male
Female

Japan 1990 · Brazil 1990 · China 1990 · United States 1990

Age: 85+, 80-84, 75-79, 70-74, 65-69, 60-64, 55-59, 50-54, 45-49, 40-44, 35-39, 30-34, 25-29, 20-24, 15-19, 10-14, 5-9, 0-4

Percent of total population

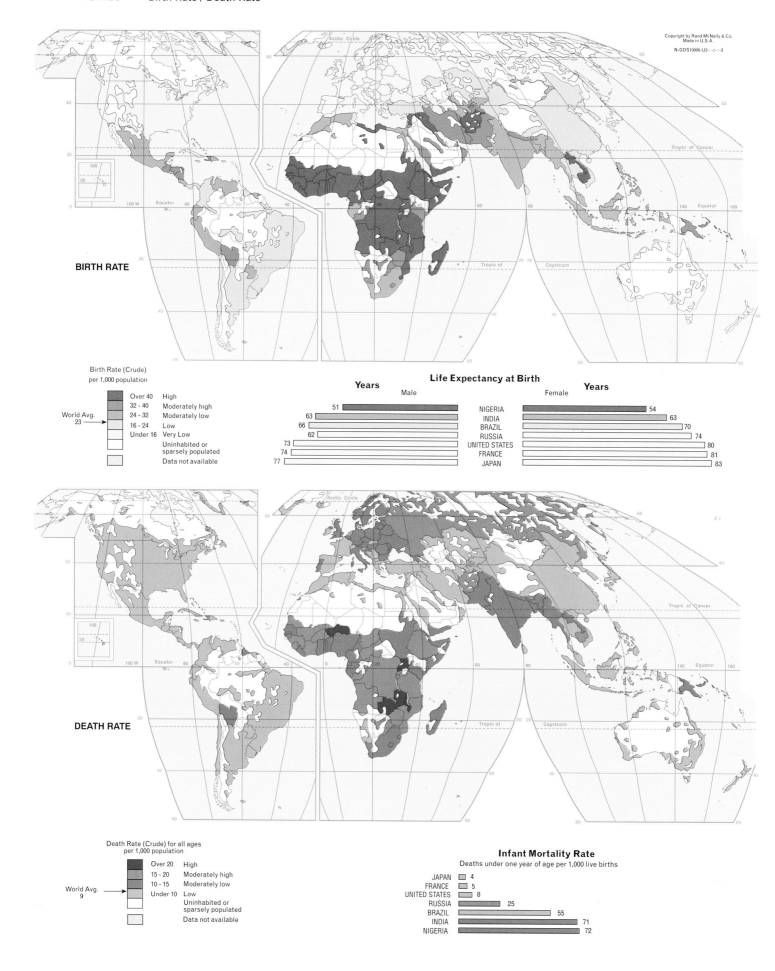

Copyright by Rand McNally & Co.
Made in U.S.A.
N-GDS10000-U2--2-1-3

BIRTH RATE

Birth Rate (Crude)
per 1,000 population

Over 40	High
32 - 40	Moderately high
24 - 32	Moderately low
16 - 24	Low
Under 16	Very Low
	Uninhabited or sparsely populated
	Data not available

World Avg.
23 →

Life Expectancy at Birth

Years   Male   Female   Years

Male		Female
51	NIGERIA	54
63	INDIA	63
66	BRAZIL	70
62	RUSSIA	74
73	UNITED STATES	80
74	FRANCE	81
77	JAPAN	83

DEATH RATE

Death Rate (Crude) for all ages
per 1,000 population

Over 20	High
15 - 20	Moderately high
10 - 15	Moderately low
Under 10	Low
	Uninhabited or sparsely populated
	Data not available

World Avg.
9 →

Infant Mortality Rate

Deaths under one year of age per 1,000 live births

JAPAN	4
FRANCE	5
UNITED STATES	8
RUSSIA	25
BRAZIL	55
INDIA	71
NIGERIA	72

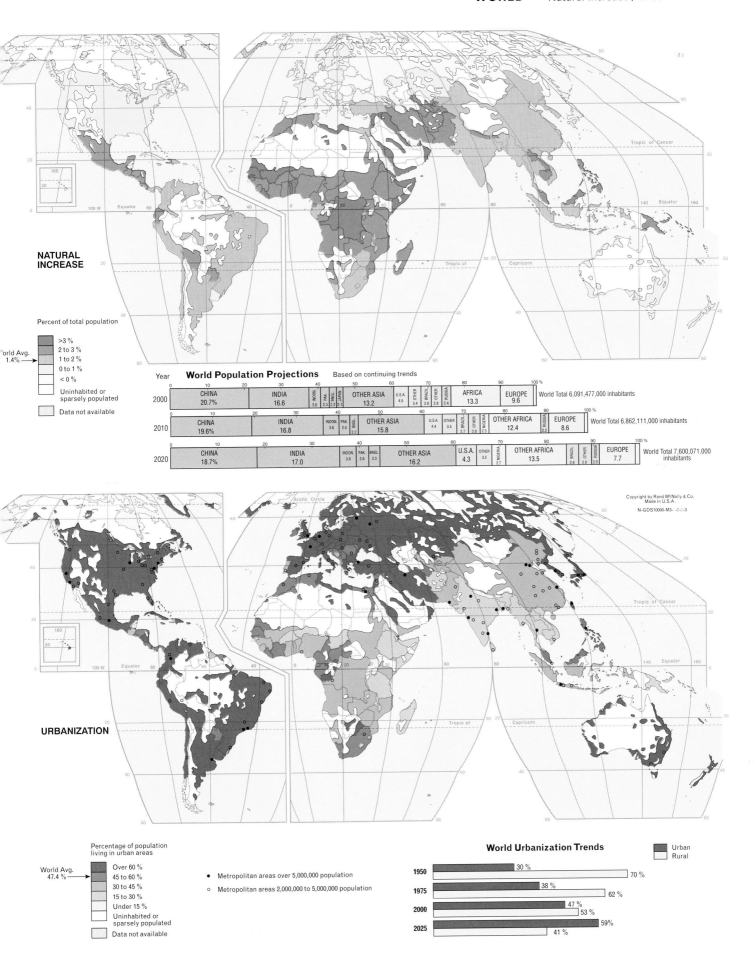

NATURAL INCREASE

Percent of total population

World Avg.
1.4% →

- >3 %
- 2 to 3 %
- 1 to 2 %
- 0 to 1 %
- < 0 %
- Uninhabited or sparsely populated
- Data not available

World Population Projections   Based on continuing trends

Year		
2000	CHINA 20.7% / INDIA 16.6 / INDON. 3.6 / PAK. 2.3 / BNGL 2.2 / JAPAN 2.1 / OTHER ASIA 13.2 / U.S.A. 4.5 / OTHER 3.4 / BRAZIL 2.8 / OTHER 2.8 / RUSSIA 2.4 / AFRICA 13.3 / EUROPE 9.6	World Total 6,091,477,000 inhabitants
2010	CHINA 19.6% / INDIA 16.8 / INDON. 3.6 / PAK. 2.5 / BNGL / OTHER ASIA 15.8 / U.S.A. 4.4 / OTHER 3.5 / BRAZIL 2.7 / OTHER 2.8 / NIGERIA 2.3 / OTHER AFRICA 12.4 / RUSSIA 2.2 / EUROPE 8.6	World Total 6,862,111,000 inhabitants
2020	CHINA 18.7% / INDIA 17.0 / INDON. 3.8 / PAK. 2.6 / BNGL 2.3 / OTHER ASIA 16.2 / U.S.A. 4.3 / OTHER 3.5 / NIGERIA 2.7 / OTHER AFRICA 13.5 / BRAZIL 2.6 / OTHER 2.8 / RUSSIA 2.0 / EUROPE 7.7	World Total 7,600,071,000 inhabitants

Copyright by Rand McNally & Co.
Made in U.S.A.
N-GDS10000-M3- -2-/-3

URBANIZATION

Percentage of population living in urban areas

World Avg.
47.4 % →

- Over 60 %
- 45 to 60 %
- 30 to 45 %
- 15 to 30 %
- Under 15 %
- Uninhabited or sparsely populated
- Data not available

- ● Metropolitan areas over 5,000,000 population
- ○ Metropolitan areas 2,000,000 to 5,000,000 population

World Urbanization Trends   ■ Urban   □ Rural

1950	30 %	70 %
1975	38 %	62 %
2000	47 %	53 %
2025	59%	41 %

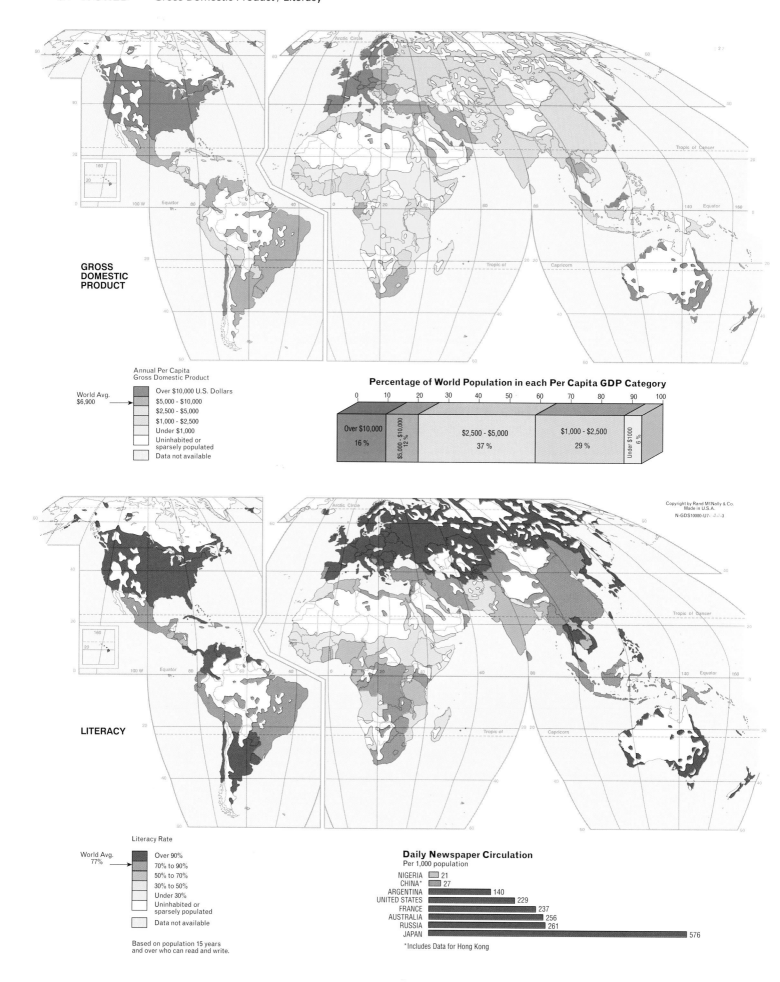

GROSS DOMESTIC PRODUCT

Annual Per Capita
Gross Domestic Product

World Avg.
$6,900

- Over $10,000 U.S. Dollars
- $5,000 - $10,000
- $2,500 - $5,000
- $1,000 - $2,500
- Under $1,000
- Uninhabited or sparsely populated
- Data not available

Percentage of World Population in each Per Capita GDP Category

Over $10,000 16 %	$5,000 - $10,000 12 %	$2,500 - $5,000 37 %	$1,000 - $2,500 29 %	Under $1000 6 %

LITERACY

Copyright by Rand M?Nally & Co.
Made in U.S.A.
N-GDS10000-U7- -2-?-3

Literacy Rate

World Avg.
77%

- Over 90%
- 70% to 90%
- 50% to 70%
- 30% to 50%
- Under 30%
- Uninhabited or sparsely populated
- Data not available

Based on population 15 years
and over who can read and write.

Daily Newspaper Circulation
Per 1,000 population

NIGERIA	21
CHINA*	27
ARGENTINA	140
UNITED STATES	229
FRANCE	237
AUSTRALIA	256
RUSSIA	261
JAPAN	576

* Includes Data for Hong Kong

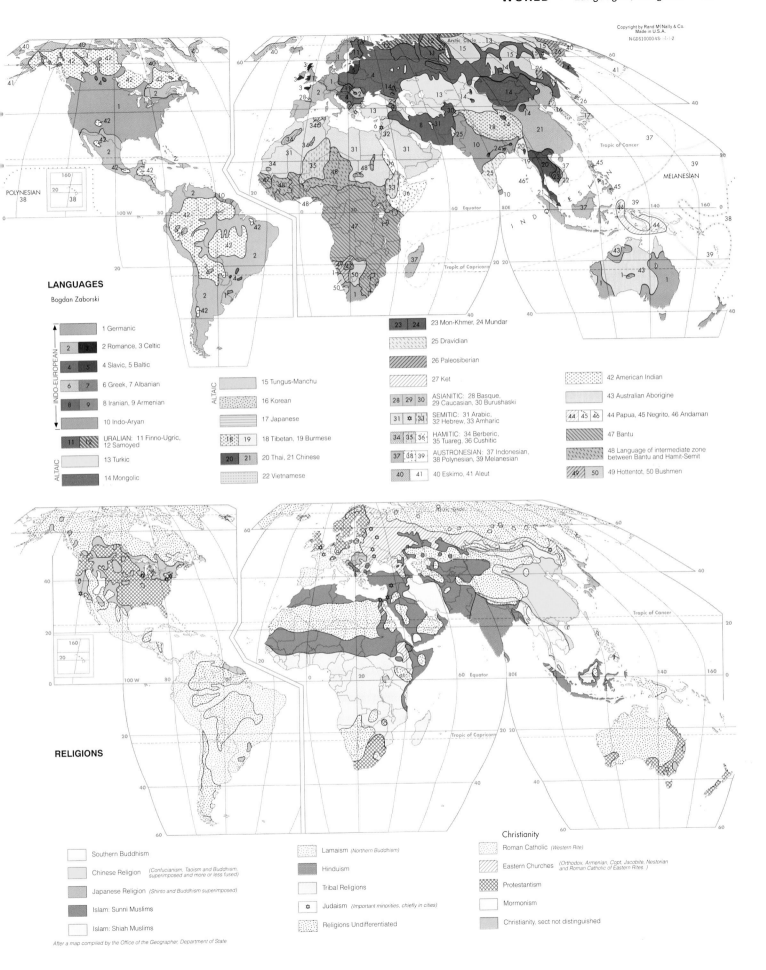

Copyright by Rand M{c}Nally & Co.
Made in U.S.A.
NGDS10000-VS- -I-I--2

LANGUAGES

Bogdan Zaborski

POLYNESIAN 38

MELANESIAN

INDO-EUROPEAN

| 1 Germanic |
| 2 Romance, 3 Celtic |
| 4 Slavic, 5 Baltic |
| 6 Greek, 7 Albanian |
| 8 Iranian, 9 Armenian |
| 10 Indo-Aryan |

URALIAN: 11 Finno-Ugric, 12 Samoyed

ALTAIC

13 Turkic

14 Mongolic

15 Tungus-Manchu

16 Korean

17 Japanese

18 Tibetan, 19 Burmese

20 Thai, 21 Chinese

22 Vietnamese

23 Mon-Khmer, 24 Mundar

25 Dravidian

26 Paleosiberian

27 Ket

ASIANITIC: 28 Basque, 29 Caucasian, 30 Burushaski

SEMITIC: 31 Arabic, 32 Hebrew, 33 Amharic

HAMITIC: 34 Berberic, 35 Tuareg, 36 Cushitic

AUSTRONESIAN: 37 Indonesian, 38 Polynesian, 39 Melanesian

40 Eskimo, 41 Aleut

42 American Indian

43 Australian Aborigine

44 Papua, 45 Negrito, 46 Andaman

47 Bantu

48 Language of intermediate zone between Bantu and Hamit-Semit

49 Hottentot, 50 Bushmen

RELIGIONS

Southern Buddhism

Chinese Religion *(Confucianism, Taoism and Buddhism, superimposed and more or less fused)*

Japanese Religion *(Shinto and Buddhism superimposed)*

Islam: Sunni Muslims

Islam: Shiah Muslims

Lamaism *(Northern Buddhism)*

Hinduism

Tribal Religions

✿ Judaism *(Important minorities, chiefly in cities)*

Religions Undifferentiated

Christianity

Roman Catholic *(Western Rite)*

Eastern Churches *(Orthodox, Armenian, Copt, Jacobite, Nestorian and Roman Catholic of Eastern Rites.)*

Protestantism

Mormonism

Christianity, sect not distinguished

After a map compiled by the Office of the Geographer, Department of State

CALORIE SUPPLY

Note: Size of each country is proportional to population.

Calorie supply per capita
(percentage of requirements*)

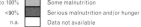

≥120%	Well above requirements
110 to 120%	Above requirements
100 to 110%	Adequate nutrition
90 to 100%	Some malnutrition
<90%	Serious malnutrition and/or hunger
n.a.	Data not available

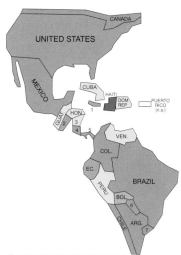

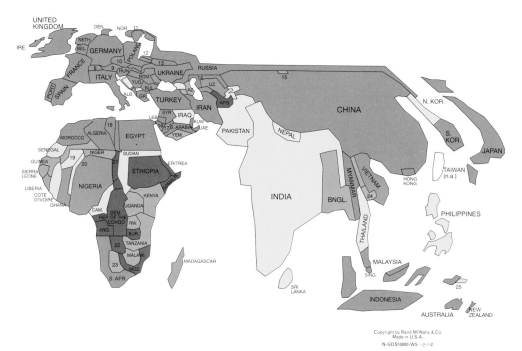

*Requirements estimated on the basis of
physiological needs for normal activity with
consideration of environmental temperature,
body weight, and age and sex distribution of
the population in various countries.
Estimates are for 1994-6.

Copyright by Rand McNally & Co.
Made in U.S.A.
N-GDS10000-W5- -:-:-2

1. JAMAICA	6. PARAGUAY	11. SWEDEN	16. ISRAEL	21. CHAD
2. EL SALVADOR	7. URUGUAY	12. LATVIA	17. JORDAN	22. ZAMBIA
3. NICARAGUA	8. SWITZERLAND	13. BELARUS	18. TUNISIA	23. ZIMBABWE
4. COSTA RICA	9. AUSTRIA	14. KAZAKHSTAN	19. BURKINA FASO	24. CAMBODIA
5. PANAMA	10. CZECH REPUBLIC	15. MONGOLIA	20. BENIN	25. PAPUA NEW GUINEA

PROTEIN CONSUMPTION, 1996

Note: Size of each country is proportional to population.

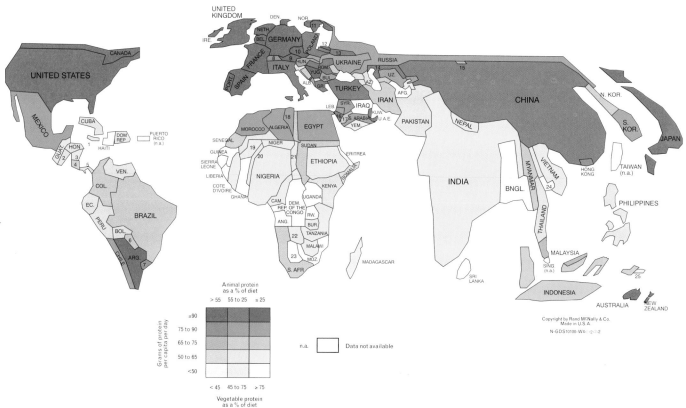

Animal protein
as a % of diet

> 55   55 to 25   ≤ 25

Grams of protein
per capita per day

≥90
75 to 90
65 to 75
50 to 65
<50

< 45   45 to 75   ≥ 75

Vegetable protein
as a % of diet

n.a.   Data not available

Copyright by Rand McNally & Co.
Made in U.S.A.
N-GDS10100-W4- -:-:-2

PHYSICIANS

Note: Size of each country is proportional to population.

Population per Physician

- Less than 1,000
- 1,000 to 6,000
- 6,000 to 18,000
- Greater than 18,000

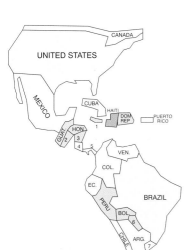

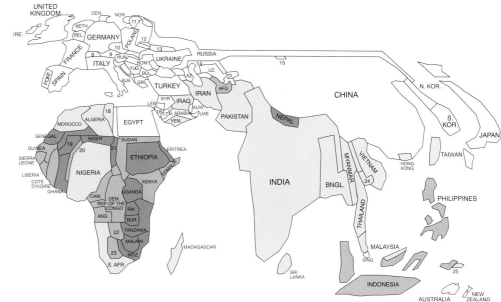

Copyright by Rand McNally & Co.
Made in U.S.A.

N-GDS10000-W3- -2-2-2

1. JAMAICA	6. PARAGUAY	11. SWEDEN
2. EL SALVADOR	7. URUGUAY	12. LATVIA
3. NICARAGUA	8. SWITZERLAND	13. BELARUS
4. COSTA RICA	9. AUSTRIA	14. KAZAKHSTAN
5. PANAMA	10. CZECH REPUBLIC	15. MONGOLIA

16. ISRAEL	21. CHAD
17. JORDAN	22. ZAMBIA
18. TUNISIA	23. ZIMBABWE
19. BURKINA FASO	24. CAMBODIA
20. BENIN	25. PAPUA NEW GUINEA

LIFE EXPECTANCY

Note: Size of each country is proportional to population.

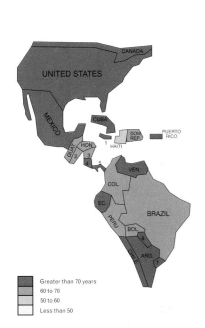

Greater than 70 years
60 to 70
50 to 60
Less than 50

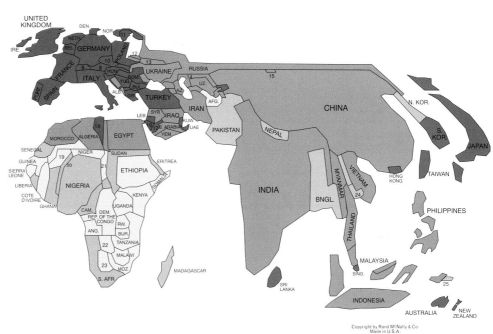

Copyright by Rand McNally & Co.
Made in U.S.A.

Life Expectancy at Birth

LOW INCOME*	55 years
LOWER-MIDDLE INCOME*	69
UPPER-MIDDLE INCOME*	71
HIGH INCOME*	76

*as defined by the World Bank

MAJOR AGRICULTURAL REGIONS

Derwent Whittlesey

Scale 1 : 75 000 000 (approximate)
One inch to 1 200 miles

A	Nomadic Herding
B	Livestock Ranching
C	Shifting Cultivation
D	Rudimental Sedentary Cultivation
E	Intensive Subsistence Tillage, Rice Dominant
F	Intensive Subsistence Tillage, Rice Unimportant
G	Plantation Agriculture
H	Mediterranean Agriculture
I	Crop Farming, Grain or Cotton Dominant
J	Commercial Livestock and Crop Farming
K	Subsistence Crop and Livestock Farming
L	Dairy Farming
M	Specialized Horticulture
X	Non-Agricultural Areas

Goode's Homolosine Equal Area Projection (Condensed)

(Revision of Agricultural Regions by Whittlesey, Annals Assoc. Am. Geographers, 1936)

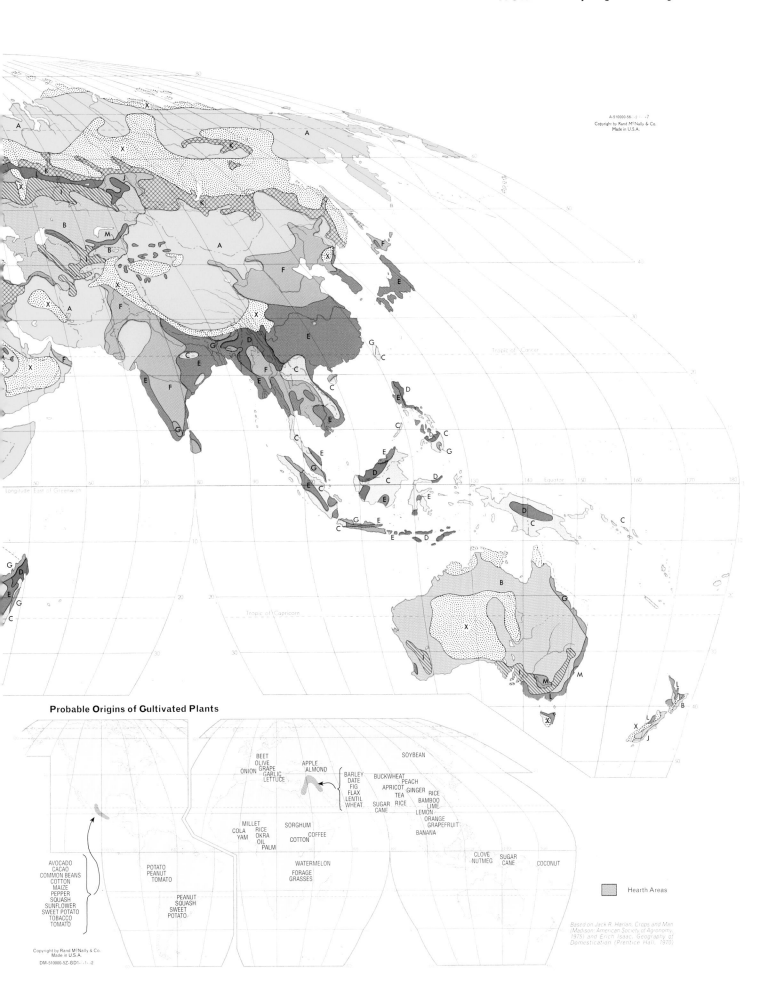

Probable Origins of Cultivated Plants

SOYBEAN

BEET
OLIVE
GRAPE
ONION GARLIC
LETTUCE

APPLE
ALMOND

BARLEY
DATE
FIG
FLAX
LENTIL
WHEAT

BUCKWHEAT
PEACH
APRICOT GINGER
TEA RICE
SUGAR RICE BAMBOO
CANE LIME
LEMON
ORANGE
GRAPEFRUIT
BANANA

MILLET
COLA RICE
YAM OKRA
OIL
PALM

SORGHUM
COFFEE
COTTON

WATERMELON
FORAGE
GRASSES

CLOVE
NUTMEG SUGAR
CANE COCONUT

AVOCADO
CACAO
COMMON BEANS
COTTON
MAIZE
PEPPER
SQUASH
SUNFLOWER
SWEET POTATO
TOBACCO
TOMATO

POTATO
PEANUT
TOMATO

PEANUT
SQUASH
SWEET
POTATO

Hearth Areas

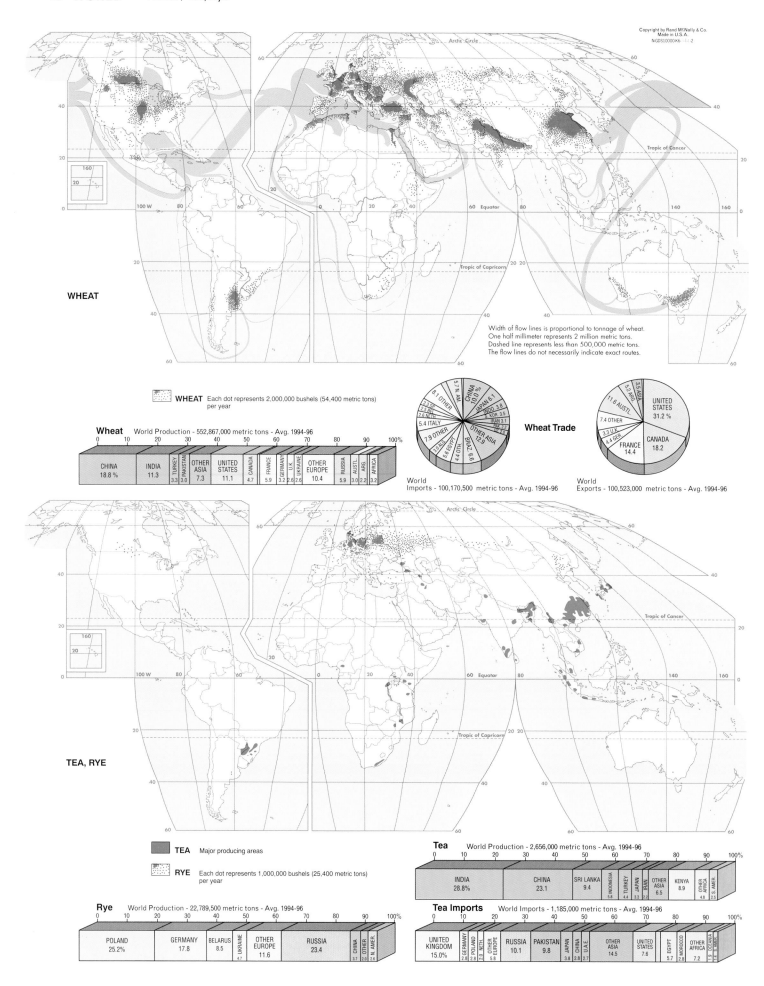

Copyright by Rand McNally & Co.
Made in U.S.A.
NGDS10000-K6-⸳⸳-⸳-⸳-2

WHEAT

Width of flow lines is proportional to tonnage of wheat.
One half millimeter represents 2 million metric tons.
Dashed line represents less than 500,000 metric tons.
The flow lines do not necessarily indicate exact routes.

WHEAT Each dot represents 2,000,000 bushels (54,400 metric tons) per year

Wheat World Production - 552,867,000 metric tons - Avg. 1994-96

| CHINA 18.8% | INDIA 11.3 | TURKEY 3.3 | PAKISTAN 3.0 | OTHER ASIA 7.3 | UNITED STATES 11.1 | CANADA 4.7 | FRANCE 5.9 | GERMANY 3.2 | U.K. 2.6 | UKRAINE 2.6 | OTHER EUROPE 10.4 | RUSSIA 5.9 | AUSTL. 3.0 | ARG. 2.2 | AFRICA 3.2 |

Wheat Trade

World Imports - 100,170,500 metric tons - Avg. 1994-96
CHINA 10.0%, JAPAN 6.1, INDO. 3.8, S. KOR. 3.5, IRAN 3.1, PAK. 2.2, OTHER ASIA 12.9, BRAZ. 6.6, HI/O 4.4, EGYPT 5.6, ALG. 3.0, 7.9 OTHER, 5.4 ITALY, 2.6 NETH., 2.5 BEL., 2.3 SP., 8.1 OTHER, 5.7 N. AM.

World Exports - 100,523,000 metric tons - Avg. 1994-96
UNITED STATES 31.2%, CANADA 18.2, FRANCE 14.4, 4.4 GER, 3.3 U.K., 7.4 OTHER, 11.6 AUSTL, 5.2 ARG., 3.5 ASIA

TEA, RYE

TEA Major producing areas

RYE Each dot represents 1,000,000 bushels (25,400 metric tons) per year

Tea World Production - 2,656,000 metric tons - Avg. 1994-96

| INDIA 28.8% | CHINA 23.1 | SRI LANKA 9.4 | INDONESIA 5.8 | TURKEY 4.4 | JAPAN 3.3 | IRAN 2.2 | OTHER ASIA 6.5 | KENYA 8.9 | OTHER AFRICA 4.8 | S. AMER. 2.5 |

Tea Imports World Imports - 1,185,000 metric tons - Avg. 1994-96

| UNITED KINGDOM 15.0% | GERMANY 2.8 | POLAND 2.0 | NETH. 1.8 | OTHER EUROPE 5.8 | RUSSIA 10.1 | PAKISTAN 9.8 | JAPAN 3.8 | CHINA 2.8 | U.A.E. 2.7 | OTHER ASIA 14.5 | UNITED STATES 7.6 | EGYPT 5.7 | MOROCCO 4.9 | OTHER AFRICA 7.2 | OCEANIA 1.9 | S. AMER. 1.7 |

Rye World Production - 22,789,500 metric tons - Avg. 1994-96

| POLAND 25.2% | GERMANY 17.8 | BELARUS 8.5 | UKRAINE 4.7 | OTHER EUROPE 11.6 | RUSSIA 23.4 | CHINA 3.7 | OTHER 2.6 | N. AMER. 2.6 |

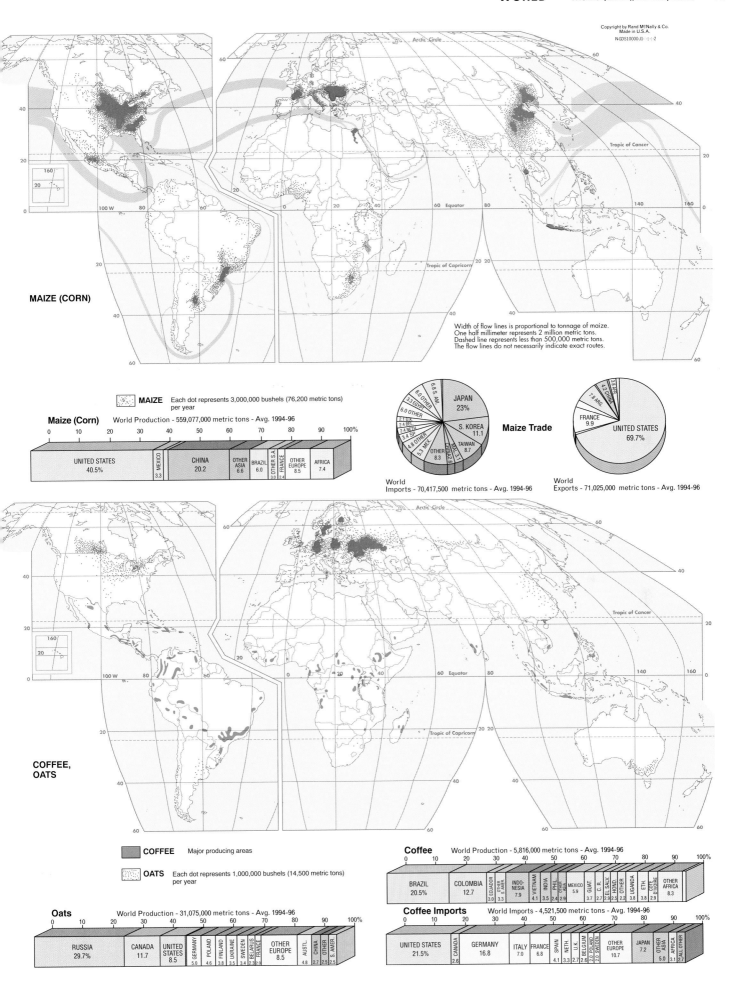

MAIZE (CORN)

Width of flow lines is proportional to tonnage of maize.
One half millimeter represents 2 million metric tons.
Dashed line represents less than 500,000 metric tons.
The flow lines do not necessarily indicate exact routes.

MAIZE Each dot represents 3,000,000 bushels (76,200 metric tons) per year

Maize (Corn) World Production - 559,077,000 metric tons - Avg. 1994-96

0	10	20	30	40	50	60	70	80	90	100%

UNITED STATES 40.5%	MEXICO 3.3	CHINA 20.2	OTHER ASIA 6.6	BRAZIL 6.0	OTHER S.A. 3.0	FRANCE 2.4	OTHER EUROPE 8.5	AFRICA 7.4

Maize Trade

World Imports - 70,417,500 metric tons - Avg. 1994-96

(Pie chart: JAPAN 23%, S. KOREA 11.1, TAIWAN 8.7, OTHER 8.3, 4.8 MEX, 5.3, 3.4 SP, 2.4 BEL, 2.1 U.K., 6.0 OTHER, 3.3 EGYPT, 6.0 OTHER, 6.8 S. AM.)

World Exports - 71,025,000 metric tons - Avg. 1994-96

(Pie chart: UNITED STATES 69.7%, FRANCE 9.9, 7.8 CHINA, 4.2, 3.8 ARG.)

COFFEE, OATS

COFFEE Major producing areas

OATS Each dot represents 1,000,000 bushels (14,500 metric tons) per year

Coffee World Production - 5,816,000 metric tons - Avg. 1994-96

0	10	20	30	40	50	60	70	80	90	100%

BRAZIL 20.5%	COLOMBIA 12.7	ECUADOR 3.0	OTHER S. AMER. 3.3	INDO-NESIA 7.9	VIETNAM 4.1	INDIA 3.5	OTHER ASIA 2.4	MEXICO 5.9	GUAT. 3.7	C. R. 2.7	EL SALV. 2.5	HOND. 2.2	OTHER 3.8	UGANDA 2.6	ETH 3.8	COTE D'IVOIRE 2.9	OTHER AFRICA 8.3

Coffee Imports World Imports - 4,521,500 metric tons - Avg. 1994-96

0	10	20	30	40	50	60	70	80	90	100%

UNITED STATES 21.5%	CANADA 2.6	GERMANY 16.8	ITALY 7.0	FRANCE 6.8	SPAIN 4.1	NETH. 3.3	U.K. 2.7	BELGIUM 2.6	POLAND 2.0	SWEDEN 2.0	OTHER EUROPE 10.7	JAPAN 7.2	OTHER ASIA 5.0	AFRICA 3.1	ALL OTHER 2.7

Oats World Production - 31,075,000 metric tons - Avg. 1994-96

0	10	20	30	40	50	60	70	80	90	100%

RUSSIA 29.7%	CANADA 11.7	UNITED STATES 8.5	GERMANY 5.0	POLAND 4.6	FINLAND 3.8	UKRAINE 3.5	SWEDEN 3.4	BELARUS 2.9	FRANCE 2.9	OTHER EUROPE 8.5	AUSTL. 4.8	CHINA 2.7	OTHER 2.5	S. AMER. 2.5

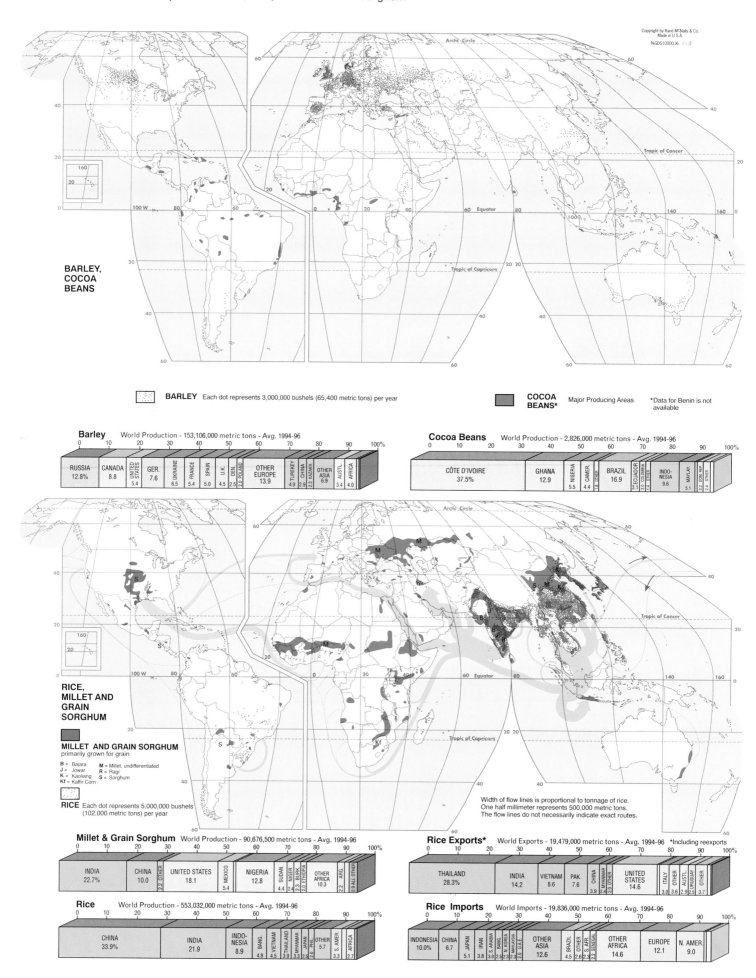

Copyright by Rand McNally & Co.
Made in U.S.A.
NGDS10000-J6

BARLEY, COCOA BEANS

BARLEY Each dot represents 3,000,000 bushels (65,400 metric tons) per year

COCOA BEANS* Major Producing Areas *Data for Benin is not available

Barley World Production - 153,106,000 metric tons - Avg. 1994-96

| | 0 | 10 | 20 | 30 | 40 | 50 | 60 | 70 | 80 | 90 | 100% |

| RUSSIA 12.8% | CANADA 8.8 | UNITED STATES 5.4 | GER. 7.6 | UKRAINE 6.5 | FRANCE 5.4 | SPAIN 5.0 | U.K. 4.5 | DEN. 2.5 | POLAND 2.0 | OTHER EUROPE 13.9 | TURKEY 4.9 | CHINA 2.9 | KAZAKH. 2.3 | OTHER ASIA 6.9 | AUSTL. 3.4 | AFRICA 4.0 |

Cocoa Beans World Production - 2,826,000 metric tons - Avg. 1994-96

| CÔTE D'IVOIRE 37.5% | GHANA 12.9 | NIGERIA 5.5 | CAMER. 4.4 | OTHER 1.6 | BRAZIL 16.9 | ECUADOR 3.1 | COLOMBIA 2.0 | OTHER 1.4 | INDO-NESIA 9.6 | MALAY. 5.1 | DOM. REP. 2.2 | OTHER 2.4 |

RICE, MILLET AND GRAIN SORGHUM

MILLET AND GRAIN SORGHUM
primarily grown for grain

B = Bajara   M = Millet, undifferentiated
J = Jowar   R = Ragi
K = Kaoliang S = Sorghum
Kf = Kaffir Corn

RICE Each dot represents 5,000,000 bushels (102,000 metric tons) per year

Width of flow lines is proportional to tonnage of rice. One half millimeter represents 500,000 metric tons. The flow lines do not necessarily indicate exact routes.

Millet & Grain Sorghum World Production - 90,676,500 metric tons - Avg. 1994-96

| INDIA 22.7% | CHINA 10.0 | OTHER 2.2 | UNITED STATES 18.1 | MEXICO 5.4 | NIGERIA 12.8 | SUDAN 4.4 | NIGER 2.3 | BURK. 2.0 | ETHIOPIA 2.0 | OTHER AFRICA 10.3 | ARG. 2.2 | ALL OTHER 2.9 |

Rice World Production - 553,032,000 metric tons - Avg. 1994-96

| CHINA 33.9% | INDIA 21.9 | INDO-NESIA 8.9 | BANG. 4.8 | VIETNAM 4.5 | THAILAND 3.9 | MYANMAR 3.3 | JAPAN 2.0 | OTHER 5.7 | S. AMER. 3.3 | AFRICA 2.7 |

Rice Exports* World Exports - 19,479,000 metric tons - Avg. 1994-96 *Including reexports

| THAILAND 28.3% | INDIA 14.2 | VIETNAM 8.6 | PAK. 7.6 | CHINA 3.9 | MYANMAR 2.4 | OTHER | UNITED STATES 14.6 | ITALY 3.0 | OTHER 3.6 | AUSTL. 2.9 | OTHER 3.7 |

Rice Imports World Imports - 19,836,000 metric tons - Avg. 1994-96

| INDONESIA 10.0% | CHINA 6.7 | JAPAN 5.1 | IRAN 3.8 | S. ARABIA 3.0 | BANG. 2.3 | N. KOREA 2.3 | MALAYSIA 2.0 | U.A.E. | OTHER ASIA 12.6 | BRAZIL 4.5 | OTHER 2.6 | S. AFR. 2.3 | SENEGAL 2.2 | OTHER AFRICA 14.6 | EUROPE 12.1 | N. AMER. 9.0 |

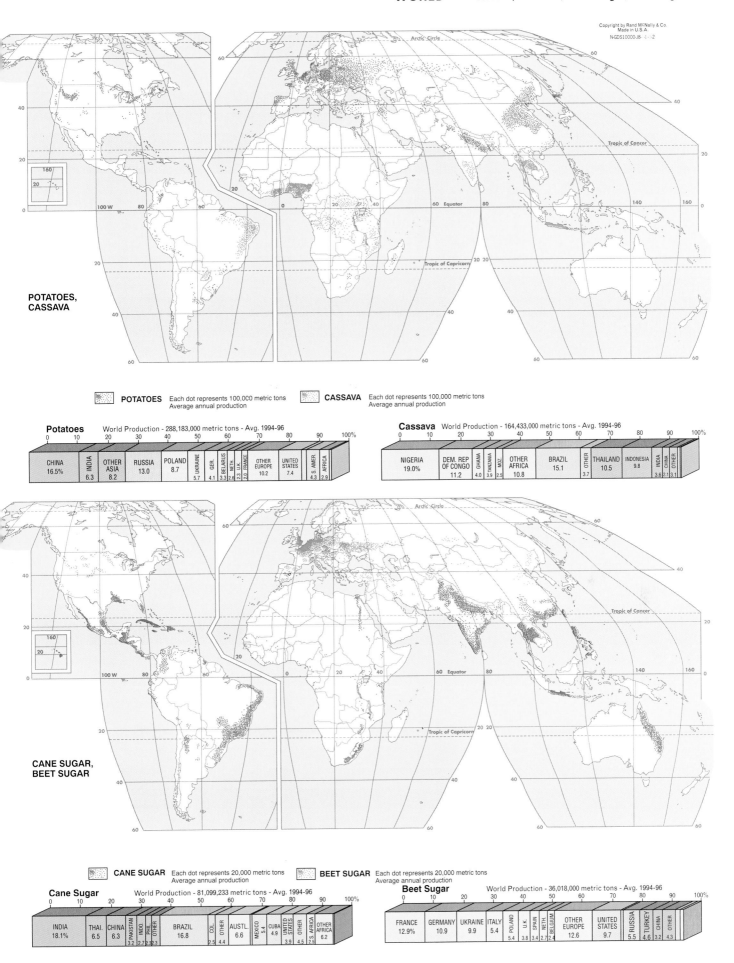

**POTATOES,
CASSAVA**

POTATOES Each dot represents 100,000 metric tons
Average annual production

CASSAVA Each dot represents 100,000 metric tons
Average annual production

Potatoes World Production - 288,183,000 metric tons - Avg. 1994-96

CHINA 16.5%	INDIA 6.3	OTHER ASIA 8.2	RUSSIA 13.0	POLAND 8.7	UKRAINE 5.7	GER. 4.1	BELARUS 3.3	NETH. 2.3	U.K. 2.0	FRANCE	OTHER EUROPE 10.2	UNITED STATES 7.4	S. AMER. 4.3	AFRICA 2.9

Cassava World Production - 164,433,000 metric tons - Avg. 1994-96

NIGERIA 19.0%	DEM. REP OF CONGO 11.2	GHANA 4.0	TANZANIA 3.9	MOZ. 2.5	OTHER AFRICA 10.8	BRAZIL 15.1	OTHER 3.7	THAILAND 10.5	INDONESIA 9.8	INDIA 3.6	CHINA 2.1	OTHER 3.1

**CANE SUGAR,
BEET SUGAR**

CANE SUGAR Each dot represents 20,000 metric tons
Average annual production

BEET SUGAR Each dot represents 20,000 metric tons
Average annual production

Cane Sugar World Production - 81,099,233 metric tons - Avg. 1994-96

INDIA 18.1%	THAI. 6.5	CHINA 6.3	PAKISTAN 3.2	INDO 2.7	PHIL 2.3	OTHER	BRAZIL 16.8	COL 2.5	OTHER 4.4	AUSTL. 6.6	MEXICO 5.4	CUBA 4.9	UNITED STATES 3.9	OTHER 4.5	S. AFRICA 2.5	OTHER AFRICA 6.2

Beet Sugar World Production - 36,018,000 metric tons - Avg. 1994-96

FRANCE 12.9%	GERMANY 10.9	UKRAINE 9.9	ITALY 5.4	POLAND 5.4	U.K. 3.8	SPAIN 3.4	NETH. 2.7	BELGIUM 2.4	OTHER EUROPE 12.6	UNITED STATES 9.7	RUSSIA 5.5	TURKEY 4.6	CHINA 4.3	OTHER

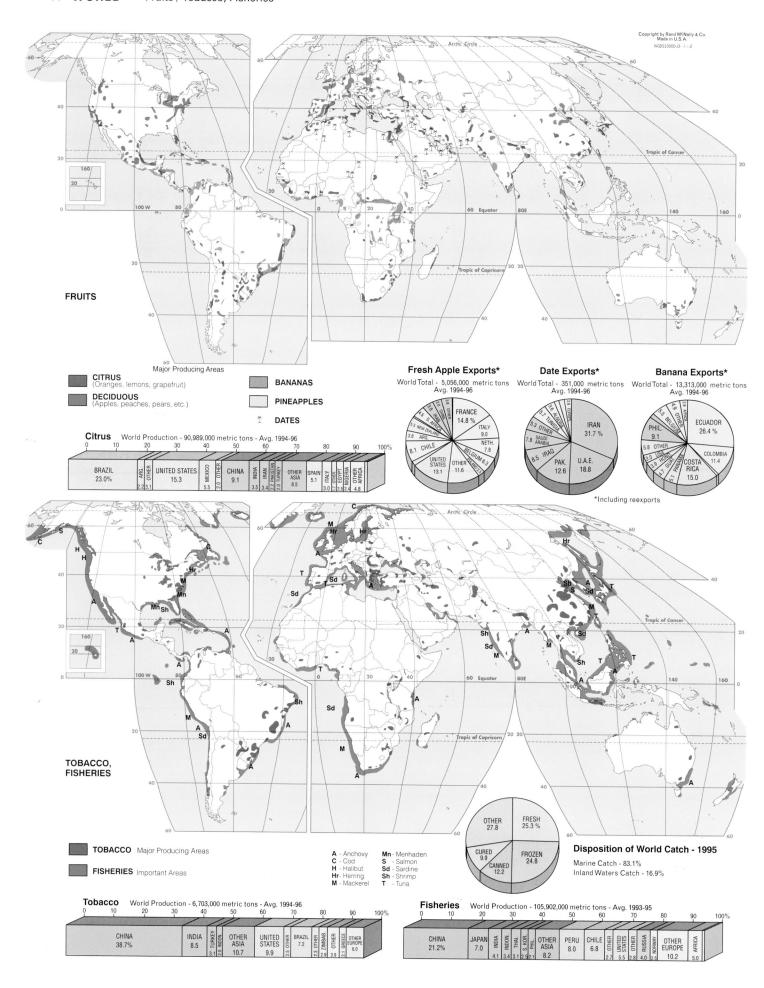

FRUITS

CITRUS
(Oranges, lemons, grapefruit)

DECIDUOUS
(Apples, peaches, pears, etc.)

BANANAS

PINEAPPLES

DATES

Major Producing Areas

Fresh Apple Exports*
World Total - 5,056,000 metric tons
Avg. 1994-96

FRANCE 14.8 %
ITALY 9.0
NETH. 7.8
BELGIUM 6.3
OTHER 11.6
UNITED STATES 13.1
CHILE 8.1
ARG. 3.8
NEW ZEALAND 5.3
IRAN 2.2
S. AFRICA 3.8
OTHER 3.8

Date Exports*
World Total - 351,000 metric tons
Avg. 1994-96

IRAN 31.7 %
U.A.E. 18.8
PAK. 12.6
IRAQ 8.5
SAUDI ARABIA 7.8
OTHER 5.3
TUNISIA 5.7
ALGERIA 3.8
OTHER 2.8

Banana Exports*
World Total - 13,313,000 metric tons
Avg. 1994-96

ECUADOR 26.4 %
COLOMBIA 11.4
COSTA RICA 15.0
PANAMA 5.1
HOND. 4.7
GUAT. 3.9
USA 3.0
OTHER 5.8
PHIL. 9.1
BELGIUM 6.5
OTHER 4.9
ARG. 2.8

*Including reexports

Citrus World Production - 90,989,000 metric tons - Avg. 1994-96

| BRAZIL 23.0% | ARG. 2.2 | OTHER 3.1 | UNITED STATES 15.3 | MEXICO 5.5 | CHINA 9.1 | INDIA 3.5 | IRAN 3.4 | PAKISTAN 2.2 | TURKEY 2.0 | OTHER ASIA 8.5 | SPAIN 5.1 | ITALY 3.0 | EGYPT 2.5 | NIGERIA 6.3 | OTHER AFRICA 4.8 |

TOBACCO, FISHERIES

TOBACCO Major Producing Areas

FISHERIES Important Areas

A - Anchovy
C - Cod
H - Halibut
Hr - Herring
M - Mackerel
Mn - Menhaden
S - Salmon
Sd - Sardine
Sh - Shrimp
T - Tuna

OTHER 27.8
FRESH 25.3 %
CURED 9.9
CANNED 12.2
FROZEN 24.8

Disposition of World Catch - 1995

Marine Catch - 83.1%
Inland Waters Catch - 16.9%

Tobacco World Production - 6,703,000 metric tons - Avg. 1994-96

| CHINA 38.7% | INDIA 8.5 | TURKEY 3.1 | INDON. 2.0 | OTHER ASIA 10.7 | UNITED STATES 9.9 | OTHER 2.5 | BRAZIL 7.2 | ZIMBABWE 2.3 | OTHER 2.9 | GREECE 2.1 | OTHER EUROPE 6.0 |

Fisheries World Production - 105,902,000 metric tons - Avg. 1993-95

| CHINA 21.2% | JAPAN 7.0 | INDIA 4.1 | INDON. 3.4 | THAI. 3.1 | S. KOR. 2.5 | PHIL. 2.1 | OTHER ASIA 8.2 | PERU 8.0 | CHILE 6.8 | OTHER 2.7 | UNITED STATES 5.5 | OTHER 2.8 | RUSSIA 4.0 | NORWAY 2.1 | OTHER EUROPE 10.2 | AFRICA 5.0 |

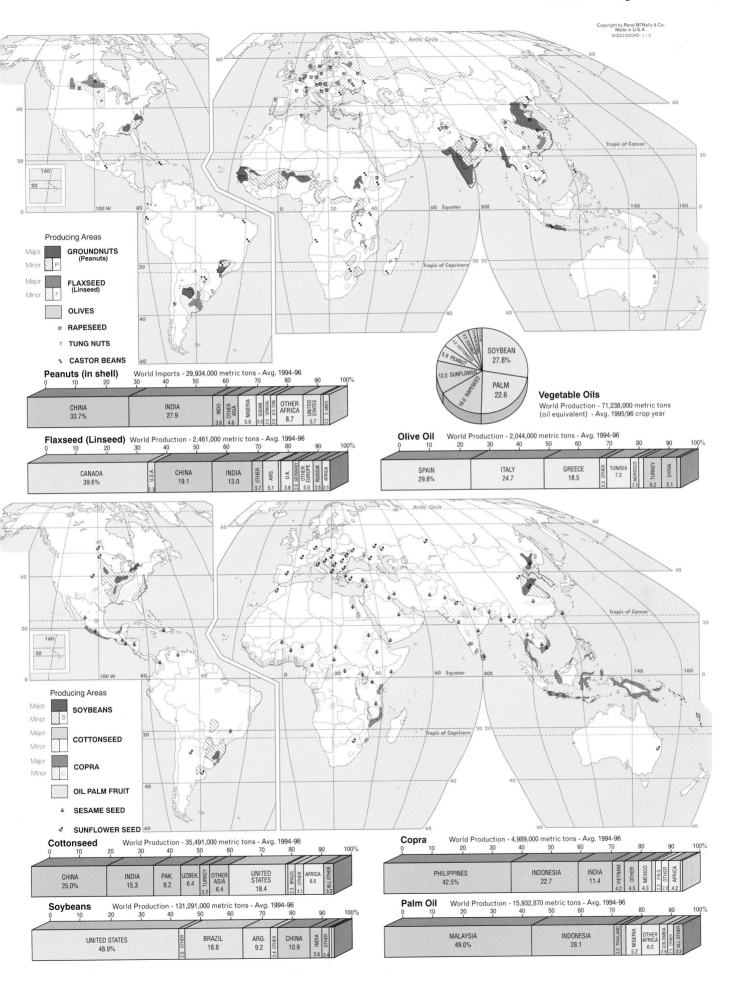

Producing Areas

Major		GROUNDNUTS (Peanuts)
Minor	P	
Major		FLAXSEED (Linseed)
Minor	F	
		OLIVES
ⴲ		RAPESEED
T		TUNG NUTS
∴		CASTOR BEANS

Vegetable Oils

SOYBEAN 27.8%
PALM 22.6
16.0 RAPESEED
12.5 SUNFLOWER
5.9 PEANUT
5.4 COTTONSEED
4.3 COCONUT

World Production - 71,238,000 metric tons
(oil equivalent) - Avg. 1995/96 crop year

Peanuts (in shell) World Imports - 29,934,000 metric tons - Avg. 1994-96

| CHINA 33.7% | INDIA 27.9 | INDO. 3.6 | OTHER ASIA 4.6 | NIGERIA 5.9 | SUDAN 2.5 | SENEGAL 2.0 | D.R. CON. | OTHER AFRICA 8.7 | UNITED STATES 5.7 | S. AMER. 2.2 |

Flaxseed (Linseed) World Production - 2,461,000 metric tons - Avg. 1994-96

| CANADA 39.6% | U.S.A. 2.3 | CHINA 19.1 | INDIA 13.0 | OTHER 3.7 | ARG. 5.1 | U.K. 3.8 | GERMANY 2.0 | OTHER EUROPE 5.0 | RUSSIA 2.5 | AFRICA 2.5 |

Olive Oil World Production - 2,044,000 metric tons - Avg. 1994-96

| SPAIN 29.8% | ITALY 24.7 | GREECE 18.5 | OTHER 2.3 | TUNISIA 7.3 | MOROCCO 2.5 | TURKEY 6.2 | SYRIA 5.1 |

Producing Areas

Major		SOYBEANS
Minor	S	
Major		COTTONSEED
Minor		
Major		COPRA
Minor	C	
		OIL PALM FRUIT
⬇		SESAME SEED
⤳		SUNFLOWER SEED

Cottonseed World Production - 35,491,000 metric tons - Avg. 1994-96

| CHINA 25.0% | INDIA 15.3 | PAK. 9.2 | UZBEK. 6.4 | TURKEY 3.2 | OTHER ASIA 6.4 | UNITED STATES 18.4 | BRAZIL 2.3 | OTHER 3.1 | AFRICA 6.5 | ALL OTHER 3.3 |

Copra World Production - 4,989,000 metric tons - Avg. 1994-96

| PHILIPPINES 42.5% | INDONESIA 22.7 | INDIA 11.4 | VIETNAM 4.2 | OTHER 4.5 | MEXICO 4.3 | PNG 2.3 | OTHER 2.0 | AFRICA 4.2 |

Soybeans World Production - 131,291,000 metric tons - Avg. 1994-96

| UNITED STATES 48.9% | OTHER 2.0 | BRAZIL 18.8 | ARG. 9.2 | OTHER 2.4 | CHINA 10.9 | INDIA 3.6 | OTHER 2.4 |

Palm Oil World Production - 15,932,870 metric tons - Avg. 1994-96

| MALAYSIA 49.0% | INDONESIA 28.1 | THAILAND 2.2 | NIGERIA 5.2 | OTHER AFRICA 6.0 | COLOMBIA 2.1 | OTHER | ALL OTHER 3.2 |

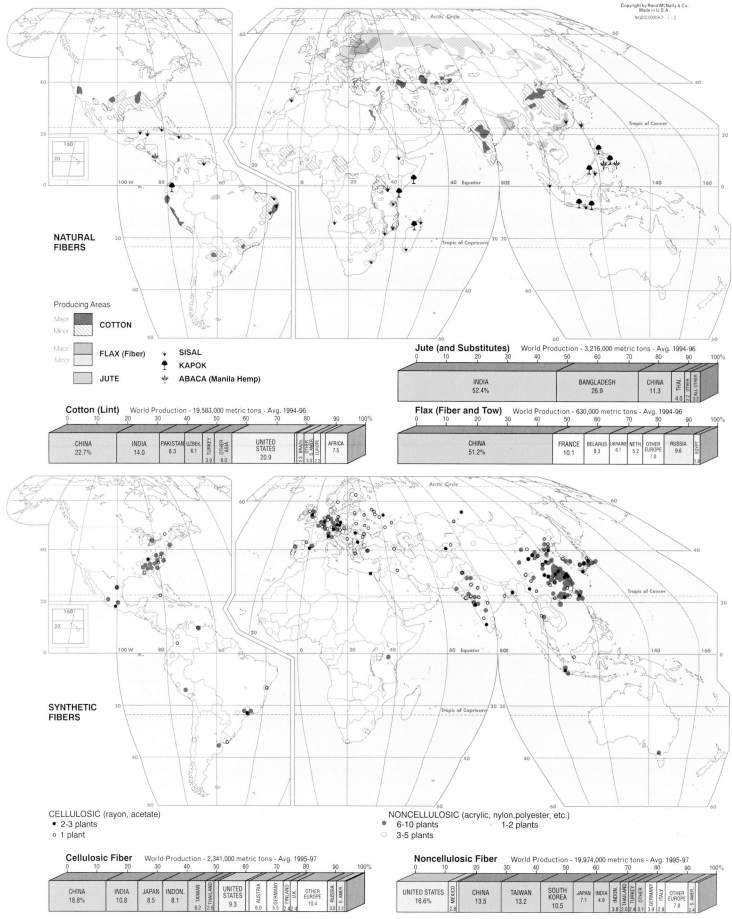

NATURAL FIBERS

Producing Areas

Major / Minor	COTTON
Major / Minor	FLAX (Fiber)
	JUTE

SISAL
KAPOK
ABACA (Manila Hemp)

Jute (and Substitutes) World Production - 3,216,000 metric tons - Avg. 1994-96

INDIA 52.4%	BANGLADESH 26.9	CHINA 11.3	THAI. 4.0	OTHER 2.2	ALL OTHER 3.2

Cotton (Lint) World Production - 19,583,000 metric tons - Avg. 1994-96

CHINA 22.7%	INDIA 14.0	PAKISTAN 8.3	UZBEK. 6.1	TURKEY 3.9	OTHER ASIA 6.0	UNITED STATES 20.9	BRAZIL 2.3	OTHER S. AMER 3.3	EUROPE 2.2	AFRICA 7.5

Flax (Fiber and Tow) World Production - 630,000 metric tons - Avg. 1994-96

CHINA 51.2%	FRANCE 10.1	BELARUS 8.3	UKRAINE 6.1	NETH. 5.2	OTHER EUROPE 7.0	RUSSIA 9.6	EGYPT 1.9

SYNTHETIC FIBERS

CELLULOSIC (rayon, acetate)
● 2-3 plants
○ 1 plant

NONCELLULOSIC (acrylic, nylon, polyester, etc.)
● 6-10 plants   × 1-2 plants
○ 3-5 plants

Cellulosic Fiber World Production - 2,341,000 metric tons - Avg. 1995-97

CHINA 18.8%	INDIA 10.8	JAPAN 8.5	INDON. 8.1	TAIWAN 6.2	THAILAND 2.6	UNITED STATES 9.3	AUSTRIA 6.0	GERMANY 5.5	FINLAND 2.4	U.K. 2.4	OTHER EUROPE 10.4	RUSSIA 3.5	S. AMER. 2.2

Noncellulosic Fiber World Production - 19,974,000 metric tons - Avg. 1995-97

UNITED STATES 16.6%	MEXICO 2.8	CHINA 13.5	TAIWAN 13.2	SOUTH KOREA 10.5	JAPAN 7.1	INDIA 4.9	INDON. 3.8	THAILAND 2.6	TURKEY 2.4	OTHER 3.1	GERMANY 3.9	ITALY 2.8	OTHER EUROPE 7.8	S. AMER. 2.4

Copyright by Rand McNally & Co.
Made in U.S.A.
N-GDS10000-HI - -1-1-2

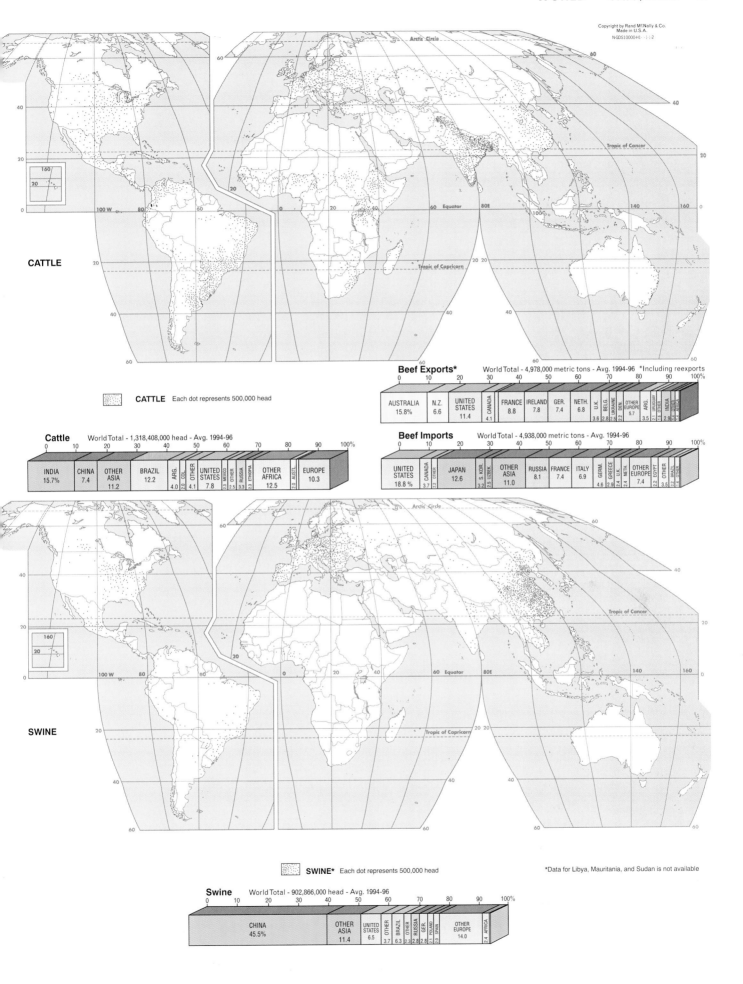

CATTLE

CATTLE Each dot represents 500,000 head

Cattle
World Total - 1,318,408,000 head - Avg. 1994-96

0	10	20	30	40	50	60	70	80	90	100%

| INDIA 15.7% | CHINA 7.4 | OTHER ASIA 11.2 | BRAZIL 12.2 | ARG. 4.0 | COL 2.0 | OTHER 4.1 | UNITED STATES 7.8 | MEXICO 2.5 | OTHER 2.5 | RUSSIA 3.3 | ETHIOPIA 2.3 | OTHER AFRICA 12.5 | AUSTL 2.0 | EUROPE 10.3 |

Beef Exports*
World Total - 4,978,000 metric tons - Avg. 1994-96   *Including reexports

0	10	20	30	40	50	60	70	80	90	100%

| AUSTRALIA 15.8% | N.Z. 6.6 | UNITED STATES 11.4 | CANADA 4.1 | FRANCE 8.8 | IRELAND 7.8 | GER. 7.4 | NETH. 6.8 | U.K. 3.6 | BELG. 2.8 | UKRAINE 2.5 | DEN. 2.2 | OTHER EUROPE 5.7 | ARG. 3.5 | URUGUAY 2.1 | INDIA 2.9 | OTHER 1.4 | AFRICA 1.4 |

Beef Imports
World Total - 4,938,000 metric tons - Avg. 1994-96

0	10	20	30	40	50	60	70	80	90	100%

| UNITED STATES 18.8% | CANADA 3.7 | JAPAN 12.6 | S. KOR. 3.2 | UZBEK. 2.5 | OTHER ASIA 11.0 | RUSSIA 8.1 | FRANCE 7.4 | ITALY 6.9 | GERM. 4.6 | GREECE 2.9 | U.K. 2.4 | NETH. 2.4 | OTHER EUROPE 7.4 | EGYPT 2.2 | OTHER 3.5 | BRAZIL 1.4 | OTHER 1.6 |

SWINE

SWINE* Each dot represents 500,000 head

*Data for Libya, Mauritania, and Sudan is not available

Swine
World Total - 902,866,000 head - Avg. 1994-96

0	10	20	30	40	50	60	70	80	90	100%

| CHINA 45.5% | OTHER ASIA 11.4 | UNITED STATES 6.5 | OTHER 3.7 | BRAZIL 6.3 | OTHER 2.3 | RUSSIA 2.8 | GER. 2.8 | POLAND 2.0 | SPAIN 2.0 | OTHER EUROPE 14.0 | AFRICA 2.4 |

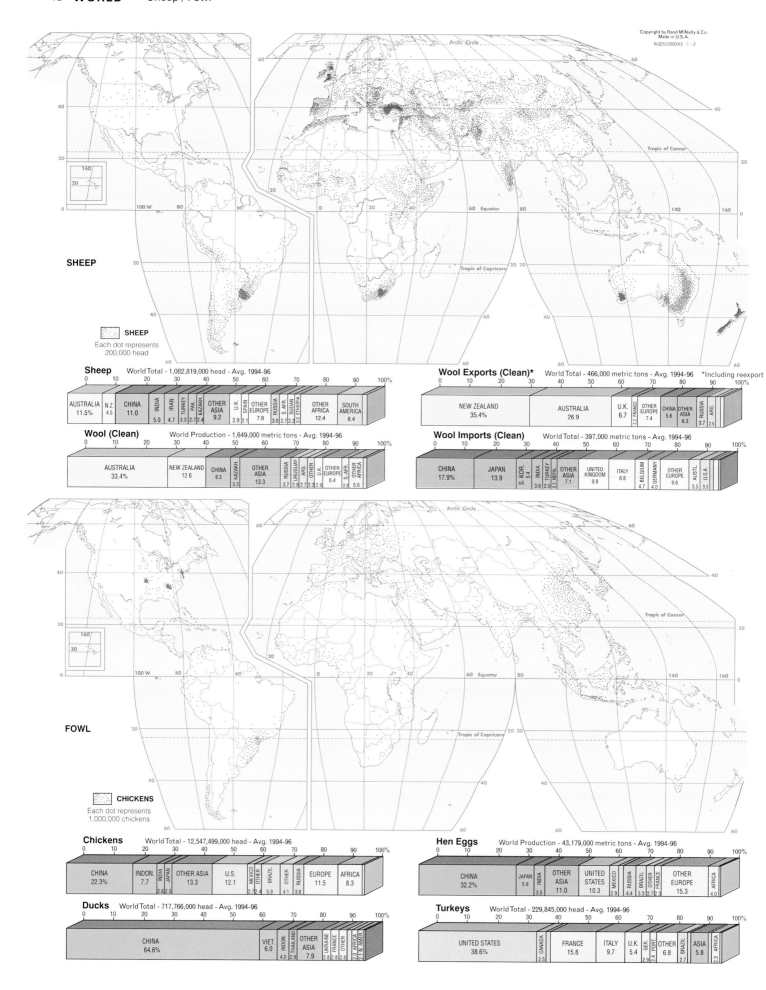

Copyright by Rand McNally & Co.
Made in U.S.A.
NGDS10000H3 -1-:-2

SHEEP

☐ **SHEEP**
Each dot represents
200,000 head

Sheep World Total - 1,082,819,000 head - Avg. 1994-96

AUSTRALIA 11.5%	N.Z. 4.5	CHINA 11.0	INDIA 5.0	IRAN 4.7	TURKEY 3.3	PAK. 2.7	KAZAKH 2.4	OTHER ASIA 9.2	U.K. 3.9	SPAIN 2.1	OTHER EUROPE 7.6	RUSSIA 3.0	S. AFR. 2.7	SUDAN 2.2	ETHIOPIA 2.0	OTHER AFRICA 12.4	SOUTH AMERICA 8.4

Wool (Clean) World Production - 1,649,000 metric tons - Avg. 1994-96

AUSTRALIA 33.4%	NEW ZEALAND 12.6	CHINA 8.3	KAZAKH 3.3	OTHER ASIA 13.3	RUSSIA 3.7	URUGUAY 2.9	ARG 2.7	OTHER 2.3	U.K. 2.9	OTHER EUROPE 6.4	S. AFR. 2.2	OTHER AFRICA 5.0

Wool Exports (Clean)* World Total - 466,000 metric tons - Avg. 1994-96   *Including reexport

NEW ZEALAND 35.4%	AUSTRALIA 26.9	U.K. 6.7	FRANCE 2.2	OTHER EUROPE 7.4	CHINA 5.6	OTHER ASIA 6.3	RUSSIA 3.7	ARG 2.5

Wool Imports (Clean) World Total - 397,000 metric tons - Avg. 1994-96

CHINA 17.9%	JAPAN 13.9	S. KOR. 5.4	INDIA 3.6	TURKEY 2.5	NEPAL 2.1	OTHER ASIA 7.1	UNITED KINGDOM 9.8	ITALY 8.8	BELGIUM 4.7	GERMANY 4.0	OTHER EUROPE 9.6	AUSTL. 3.5	U.S.A. 3.3

FOWL

☐ **CHICKENS**
Each dot represents
1,000,000 chickens

Chickens World Total - 12,547,499,000 head - Avg. 1994-96

CHINA 22.3%	INDON. 7.7	INDIA 2.6	JAPAN 2.5	OTHER ASIA 13.3	U.S. 12.1	MEXICO 2.7	OTHER 2.4	BRAZIL 5.9	OTHER 4.1	RUSSIA 3.8	EUROPE 11.5	AFRICA 8.3

Ducks World Total - 717,766,000 head - Avg. 1994-96

CHINA 64.6%	VIET. 6.0	INDON. 4.0	THAILAND 2.9	OTHER ASIA 7.9	UKRAINE 2.8	FRANCE 2.8	OTHER 2.8	AFRICA 2.0	N. AMER. 2.1

Hen Eggs World Production - 43,179,000 metric tons - Avg. 1994-96

CHINA 32.2%	JAPAN 5.9	INDIA 3.5	OTHER ASIA 11.0	UNITED STATES 10.3	MEXICO 2.9	RUSSIA 4.4	BRAZIL 3.3	FRANCE 2.7	OTHER EUROPE 15.3	AFRICA 4.0

Turkeys World Total - 229,845,000 head - Avg. 1994-96

UNITED STATES 38.6%	CANADA 2.5	FRANCE 15.8	ITALY 9.7	U.K. 5.4	GER. 2.9	PORT. 2.4	OTHER 6.8	BRAZIL 2.7	ASIA 5.8	AFRICA 2.3

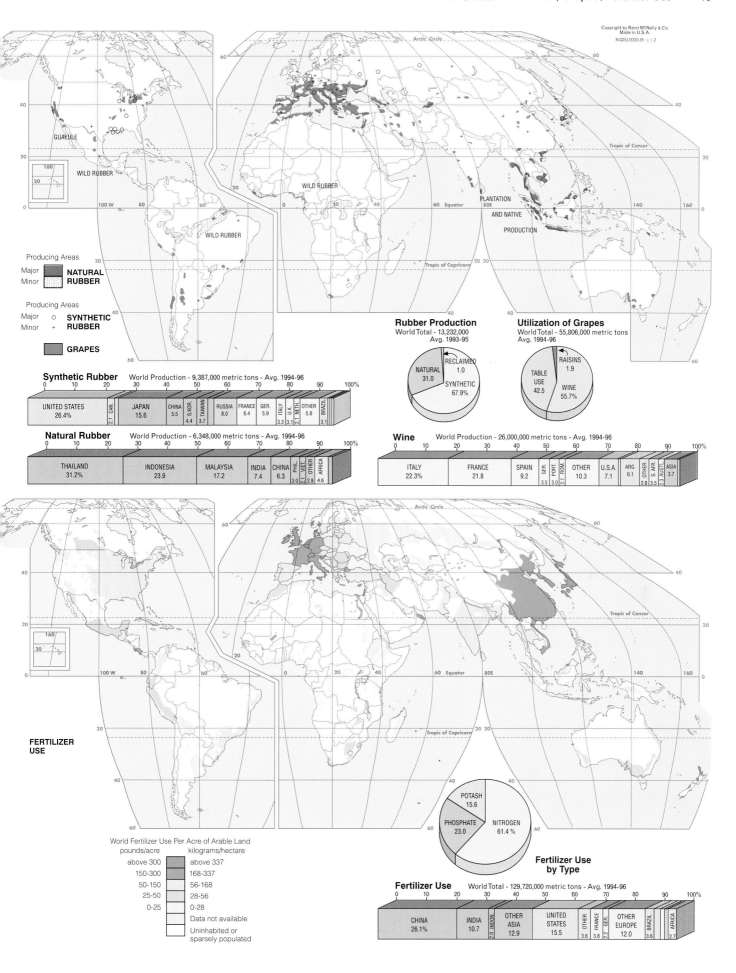

GUAYULE

WILD RUBBER

WILD RUBBER

WILD RUBBER

PLANTATION
AND NATIVE
PRODUCTION

Producing Areas
Major / Minor — **NATURAL RUBBER**

Producing Areas
Major ○ / Minor + — **SYNTHETIC RUBBER**

GRAPES

Rubber Production
World Total - 13,232,000
Avg. 1993-95

- NATURAL 31.0
- RECLAIMED 1.0
- SYNTHETIC 67.9%

Utilization of Grapes
World Total - 55,806,000 metric tons
Avg. 1994-96

- RAISINS 1.9
- TABLE USE 42.5
- WINE 55.7%

Synthetic Rubber
World Production - 9,387,000 metric tons - Avg. 1994-96

| UNITED STATES 26.4% | CAN. 2.1 | JAPAN 15.6 | CHINA 5.5 | S.KOR. 4.4 | TAIWAN 3.7 | RUSSIA 8.0 | FRANCE 6.4 | GER. 5.9 | ITALY 3.3 | U.K. 3.1 | NETH. 2.1 | OTHER 5.8 | BRAZIL 3.1 |

Natural Rubber
World Production - 6,348,000 metric tons - Avg. 1994-96

| THAILAND 31.2% | INDONESIA 23.9 | MALAYSIA 17.2 | INDIA 7.4 | CHINA 6.3 | PHIL. 3.0 | VIET. 2.1 | OTHER 2.8 | AFRICA 4.6 |

Wine
World Production - 26,000,000 metric tons - Avg. 1994-96

| ITALY 22.3% | FRANCE 21.8 | SPAIN 9.2 | GER. 3.5 | PORT. 3.0 | ROM. 2.1 | OTHER 10.3 | U.S.A. 7.1 | ARG. 6.1 | OTHER 2.8 | S. AFR. 3.5 | AUSTL. 2.3 | ASIA 3.7 |

FERTILIZER USE

Fertilizer Use by Type

- POTASH 15.6
- PHOSPHATE 23.0
- NITROGEN 61.4 %

World Fertilizer Use Per Acre of Arable Land

pounds/acre	kilograms/hectare
above 300	above 337
150-300	168-337
50-150	56-168
25-50	28-56
0-25	0-28
Data not available	
Uninhabited or sparsely populated	

Fertilizer Use
World Total - 129,720,000 metric tons - Avg. 1994-96

| CHINA 26.1% | INDIA 10.7 | INDON. 2.0 | OTHER ASIA 12.9 | UNITED STATES 15.5 | OTHER 3.6 | FRANCE 3.8 | GER. 2.2 | OTHER EUROPE 12.0 | BRAZIL 3.6 | AFRICA 2.7 |

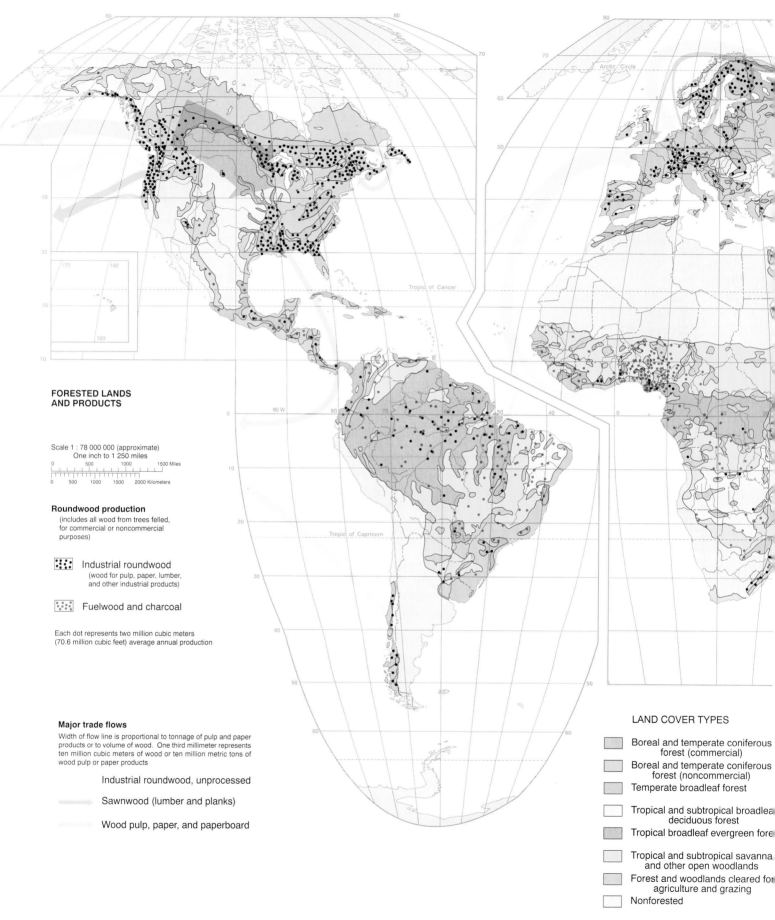

**FORESTED LANDS
AND PRODUCTS**

Scale 1 : 78 000 000 (approximate)
One inch to 1 250 miles

0   500   1000   1500 Miles

0   500   1000   1500   2000 Kilometers

Roundwood production
(includes all wood from trees felled,
for commercial or noncommercial
purposes)

Industrial roundwood
(wood for pulp, paper, lumber,
and other industrial products)

Fuelwood and charcoal

Each dot represents two million cubic meters
(70.6 million cubic feet) average annual production

Major trade flows
Width of flow line is proportional to tonnage of pulp and paper
products or to volume of wood. One third millimeter represents
ten million cubic meters of wood or ten million metric tons of
wood pulp or paper products

Industrial roundwood, unprocessed

Sawnwood (lumber and planks)

Wood pulp, paper, and paperboard

LAND COVER TYPES

Boreal and temperate coniferous
forest (commercial)

Boreal and temperate coniferous
forest (noncommercial)

Temperate broadleaf forest

Tropical and subtropical broadlea
deciduous forest

Tropical broadleaf evergreen fore

Tropical and subtropical savanna
and other open woodlands

Forest and woodlands cleared fo
agriculture and grazing

Nonforested

Wood Production

FUELWOOD AND CHARCOAL 55.1 %

SAWLOGS AND VENEER LOGS 27.6

INDUSTRIAL 44.9%

12.6 PULPWOOD

4.7 OTHER

Tropic of Cancer

Tropic of Capricorn

Longitude East of Greenwich

Equator

Goode's Homolosine Equal Area Projection (Condensed)

Wood Cut (Roundwood)   World Total - 3,335,611,000 metric tons - Avg. 1994-96

0	10	20	30	40	50	60	70	80	90	100%

| UNITED STATES 15.0% | CANADA 5.6 | OTHER 2.1 | CHINA 9.2 | INDIA 8.9 | INDO. 5.9 | OTHER ASIA 10.7 | BRAZIL 6.6 | OTHER 3.1 | NIGERIA 3.3 | OTHER AFRICA 13.8 | RUSSIA 3.3 | EUROPE 10.8 |

Wood Pulp & Pulp Products Exports*   World Total - 32,860,000 metric tons - Avg. 1994-96

0	10	20	30	40	50	60	70	80	90	100%

| CANADA 32.0% | UNITED STATES 20.0 | SWEDEN 8.2 | FINLAND 4.4 | PORTUGAL 3.1 | SPAIN 2.0 | OTHER EUROPE 7.8 | BRAZIL 6.4 | CHILE 4.9 | RUSSIA 3.3 | N.Z. 2.0 | AFRICA 2.6 | ASIA 2.5 |

* Including reexports

Lumber Imports (Sawn Wood)   World Total - 108,360,000 metric tons - Avg. 1994-96

0	10	20	30	40	50	60	70	80	90	100%

| UNITED STATES 38.2% | OTHER 3.1 | JAPAN 10.5 | THAI 2.5 | OTHER ASIA 7.8 | U.K. 6.2 | ITALY 5.7 | GERMANY 5.0 | NETH 3.2 | FRANCE 2.8 | OTHER EUROPE 10.4 | EGYPT 2.2 | OTHER 2.2 |

Lumber Exports (Sawn Wood)*   World Total - 110,108,000 metric tons - Avg. 1994-96

0	10	20	30	40	50	60	70	80	90	100%

| CANADA 43.8% | UNITED STATES 6.6 | SWEDEN 9.8 | FINLAND 6.5 | AUSTRIA 4.0 | OTHER EUROPE 12.3 | RUSSIA 4.9 | MALAY 3.9 | S. AMER. 2.5 | OTHER 3.0 | ALL OTHER 2.3 |

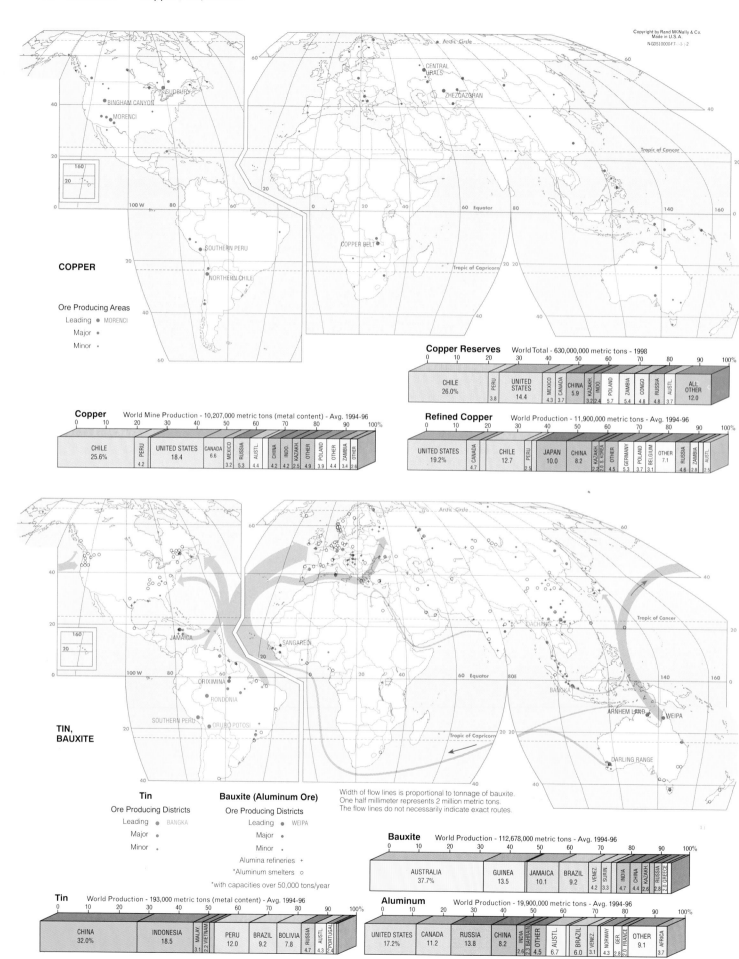

Copyright by Rand McNally & Co.
Made in U.S.A.
NGDS10000-F7- -1- -2

COPPER

Ore Producing Areas

Leading ● MORENCI

Major ●

Minor ·

BINGHAM CANYON
MORENCI
SUDBURY
CENTRAL URALS
ZHEZOAZGHAN
SOUTHERN PERU
NORTHERN CHILE
COPPER BELT

Copper World Mine Production - 10,207,000 metric tons (metal content) - Avg. 1994-96

0	10	20	30	40	50	60	70	80	90	100%

| CHILE 25.6% | PERU 4.2 | UNITED STATES 18.4 | CANADA 6.6 | MEXICO 3.2 | RUSSIA 5.3 | AUSTL. 4.4 | CHINA 4.2 | INDO. 4.2 | KAZAKH. 2.5 | OTHER 4.9 | POLAND 3.9 | ZAMBIA 3.4 | OTHER 2.6 |

Copper Reserves World Total - 630,000,000 metric tons - 1998

0	10	20	30	40	50	60	70	80	90	100%

| CHILE 26.0% | PERU 3.8 | UNITED STATES 14.4 | MEXICO 4.3 | CANADA 3.7 | CHINA 5.9 | KAZAKH. 3.2 | INDO. 2.4 | POLAND 5.7 | ZAMBIA 5.4 | CONGO 4.8 | RUSSIA 4.8 | AUSTL. 3.5 | ALL OTHER 12.0 |

Refined Copper World Production - 11,900,000 metric tons - Avg. 1994-96

0	10	20	30	40	50	60	70	80	90	100%

| UNITED STATES 19.2% | CANADA 4.7 | CHILE 12.7 | PERU 2.5 | JAPAN 10.0 | CHINA 8.2 | KAZAKH. 2.0 | S. KOREA 4.5 | GERMANY 5.3 | POLAND 3.7 | BELGIUM 3.1 | OTHER 7.1 | RUSSIA 4.6 | ZAMBIA 2.8 | AUSTL. 2.5 |

TIN, BAUXITE

JAMAICA
SANGAREDI
DACHANG
ORIXIMINA
RONDONIA
SOUTHERN PERU
ORURO POTOSI
BANGKA
ARNHEM LAND
WEIPA
DARLING RANGE

Width of flow lines is proportional to tonnage of bauxite.
One half millimeter represents 2 million metric tons.
The flow lines do not necessarily indicate exact routes.

Tin
Ore Producing Districts

Leading ● BANGKA

Major ●

Minor ·

Bauxite (Aluminum Ore)
Ore Producing Districts

Leading ● WEIPA

Major ●

Minor ·

Alumina refineries +

*Aluminum smelters ○

*with capacities over 50,000 tons/year

Bauxite World Production - 112,678,000 metric tons - Avg. 1994-96

0	10	20	30	40	50	60	70	80	90	100%

| AUSTRALIA 37.7% | GUINEA 13.5 | JAMAICA 10.1 | BRAZIL 9.2 | VENEZ. 4.2 | SURIN. 3.3 | INDIA 4.7 | CHINA 4.4 | KAZAKH. 2.6 | RUSSIA 2.8 | GREECE 2.0 |

Tin World Production - 193,000 metric tons (metal content) - Avg. 1994-96

0	10	20	30	40	50	60	70	80	90	100%

| CHINA 32.0% | INDONESIA 18.5 | MALAY. 3.1 | VIETNAM 2.2 | PERU 12.0 | BRAZIL 9.2 | BOLIVIA 7.8 | RUSSIA 4.7 | AUSTL. 4.3 | PORTUGAL 2.4 |

Aluminum World Production - 19,900,000 metric tons - Avg. 1994-96

0	10	20	30	40	50	60	70	80	90	100%

| UNITED STATES 17.2% | CANADA 11.2 | RUSSIA 13.8 | CHINA 8.2 | INDIA 2.6 | BAHRAIN 2.3 | OTHER 4.5 | AUSTL. 6.7 | BRAZIL 6.0 | VENEZ. 3.1 | NORWAY 4.3 | GER. 2.8 | FRANCE 2.0 | OTHER 9.1 | AFRICA 3.7 |

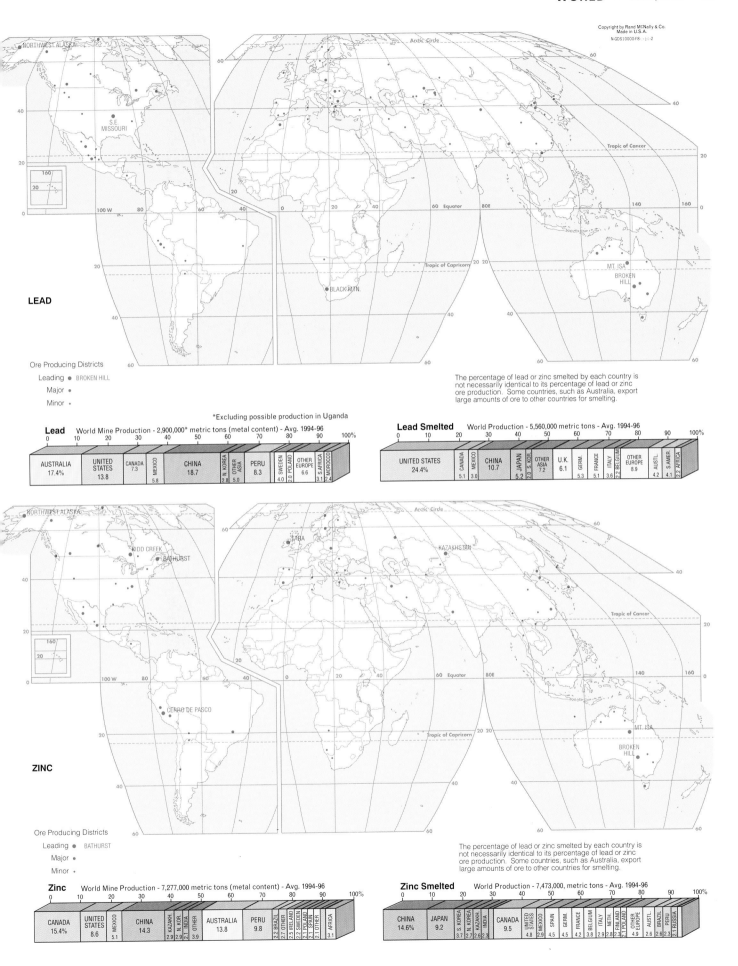

LEAD

Ore Producing Districts

Leading ● BROKEN HILL

Major ●

Minor ·

The percentage of lead or zinc smelted by each country is not necessarily identical to its percentage of lead or zinc ore production. Some countries, such as Australia, export large amounts of ore to other countries for smelting.

*Excluding possible production in Uganda

Lead World Mine Production - 2,900,000* metric tons (metal content) - Avg. 1994-96

0	10	20	30	40	50	60	70	80	90	100%

| AUSTRALIA 17.4% | UNITED STATES 13.8 | CANADA 7.3 | MEXICO 5.8 | CHINA 18.7 | N. KOREA 2.8 | OTHER ASIA 5.0 | PERU 8.3 | SWEDEN 4.0 | POLAND 2.0 | OTHER EUROPE 6.6 | S.AFRICA 3.1 | MOROCCO 2.4 |

Lead Smelted World Production - 5,560,000 metric tons - Avg. 1994-96

0	10	20	30	40	50	60	70	80	90	100%

| UNITED STATES 24.4% | CANADA 5.1 | MEXICO 3.0 | CHINA 10.7 | JAPAN 5.2 | S. KOR. 2.0 | OTHER ASIA 7.2 | U.K. 6.1 | GERM. 5.3 | FRANCE 5.1 | ITALY 3.6 | BELGIUM 2.2 | OTHER EUROPE 8.9 | AUSTL. 4.2 | S.AMER. 4.1 | AFRICA 2.2 |

ZINC

Ore Producing Districts

Leading ● BATHURST

Major ●

Minor ·

The percentage of lead or zinc smelted by each country is not necessarily identical to its percentage of lead or zinc ore production. Some countries, such as Australia, export large amounts of ore to other countries for smelting.

Zinc World Mine Production - 7,277,000 metric tons (metal content) - Avg. 1994-96

0	10	20	30	40	50	60	70	80	90	100%

| CANADA 15.4% | UNITED STATES 8.6 | MEXICO 5.1 | CHINA 14.3 | KAZAKH. 2.9 | N. KOR. 2.9 | INDIA 2.1 | OTHER 3.9 | AUSTRALIA 13.8 | PERU 9.8 | BRAZIL 2.2 | OTHER 2.7 | IRELAND 2.5 | SWEDEN 2.2 | POLAND 2.1 | SPAIN 2.1 | OTHER 2.1 | AFRICA 3.1 |

Zinc Smelted World Production - 7,473,000, metric tons - Avg. 1994-96

0	10	20	30	40	50	60	70	80	90	100%

| CHINA 14.6% | JAPAN 9.2 | S. KOREA 3.7 | N. KOREA 2.7 | KAZAKH. 2.6 | INDIA 2.3 | CANADA 9.5 | UNITED STATES 4.8 | MEXICO 2.9 | SPAIN 4.5 | GERM. 4.5 | FRANCE 3.8 | BELGIUM 2.9 | ITALY 2.8 | NETH. 2.3 | FINLAND | POLAND | OTHER EUROPE | AUSTL. | BRAZIL 2.3 | PERU 2.3 | RUSSIA 2.1 |

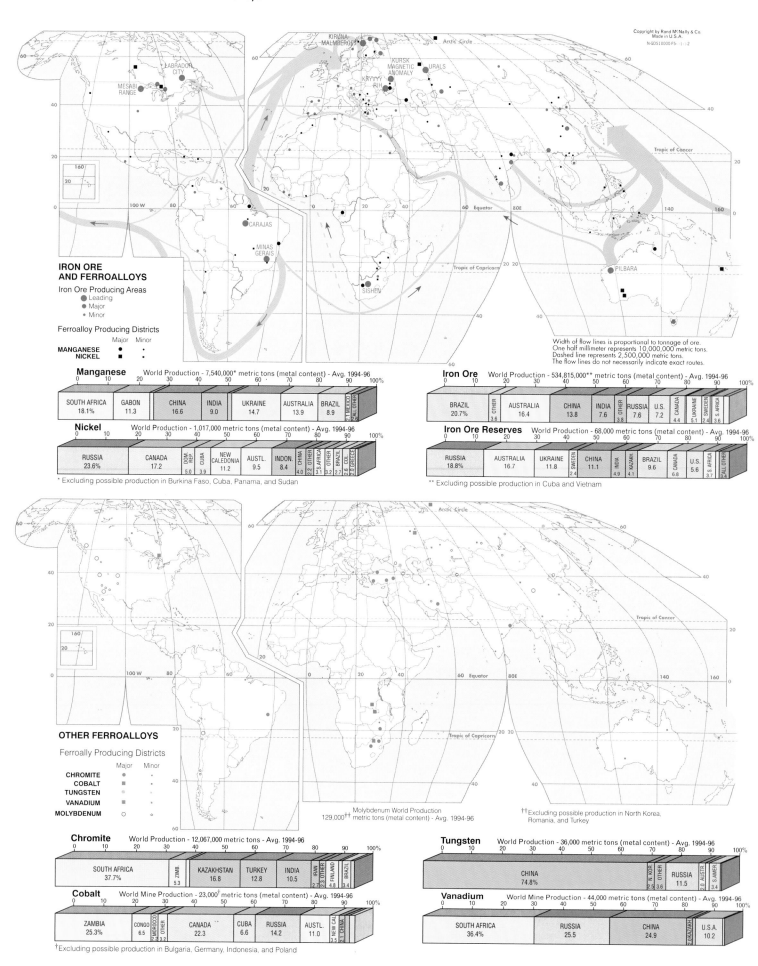

IRON ORE AND FERROALLOYS

Iron Ore Producing Areas
- ● Leading
- ● Major
- • Minor

Ferroalloy Producing Districts

	Major	Minor
MANGANESE	●	•
NICKEL	■	•

Width of flow lines is proportional to tonnage of ore.
One half millimeter represents 10,000,000 metric tons.
Dashed line represents 2,500,000 metric tons.
The flow lines do not necessarily indicate exact routes.

Manganese   World Production - 7,540,000* metric tons (metal content) - Avg. 1994-96

SOUTH AFRICA 18.1%	GABON 11.3	CHINA 16.6	INDIA 9.0	UKRAINE 14.7	AUSTRALIA 13.9	BRAZIL 8.9	MEXICO 2.1	ALL OTHER

Nickel   World Production - 1,017,000 metric tons (metal content) - Avg. 1994-96

RUSSIA 23.6%	CANADA 17.2	DOM. REP. 5.0	CUBA 3.9	NEW CALEDONIA 11.2	AUSTL. 9.5	INDON. 8.4	CHINA 4.0	S. AFRICA 3.1	OTHER 3.2	BRAZIL 2.7	COL 2.6	GREECE 2.0

* Excluding possible production in Burkina Faso, Cuba, Panama, and Sudan

Iron Ore   World Production - 534,815,000** metric tons (metal content) - Avg. 1994-96

BRAZIL 20.7%	OTHER 3.6	AUSTRALIA 16.4	CHINA 13.8	INDIA 7.6	OTHER 3.8	RUSSIA 7.6	U.S. 7.2	CANADA 4.4	UKRAINE 5.1	SWEDEN 2.4	S. AFRICA 3.6

Iron Ore Reserves   World Production - 68,000 metric tons (metal content) - Avg. 1994-96

RUSSIA 18.8%	AUSTRALIA 16.7	UKRAINE 11.8	SWEDEN 2.4	CHINA 11.1	INDIA 4.9	KAZAKH. 4.1	BRAZIL 9.6	CANADA 6.8	U.S. 5.6	S. AFRICA 3.7	ALL OTHER 3.4

** Excluding possible production in Cuba and Vietnam

OTHER FERROALLOYS

Ferroally Producing Districts

	Major	Minor
CHROMITE	●	•
COBALT	■	•
TUNGSTEN		
VANADIUM	■	•
MOLYBDENUM	○	○

Molybdenum World Production
129,000†† metric tons (metal content) - Avg. 1994-96

††Excluding possible production in North Korea, Romania, and Turkey

Chromite   World Production - 12,067,000 metric tons - Avg. 1994-96

SOUTH AFRICA 37.7%	ZIMB. 5.3	KAZAKHSTAN 16.8	TURKEY 12.8	INDIA 10.5	IRAN 2.3	OTHER 4.1	FINLAND 4.8	BRAZIL 3.4

Cobalt   World Mine Production - 23,000† metric tons (metal content) - Avg. 1994-96

ZAMBIA 25.3%	CONGO 6.5	MOROCCO 2.3	OTHER 3.2	CANADA 22.3	CUBA 6.6	RUSSIA 14.2	AUSTL. 11.0	NEW CAL 3.5	CHINA 2.1

†Excluding possible production in Bulgaria, Germany, Indonesia, and Poland

Tungsten   World Production - 36,000 metric tons (metal content) - Avg. 1994-96

CHINA 74.8%	N. KOR. 3.6	OTHER	RUSSIA 11.5	AUSTR. 2.0	S. AMER. 3.4

Vanadium   World Mine Production - 44,000 metric tons (metal content) - Avg. 1994-96

SOUTH AFRICA 36.4%	RUSSIA 25.5	CHINA 24.9	KAZAKH. 2.0	U.S.A. 10.2

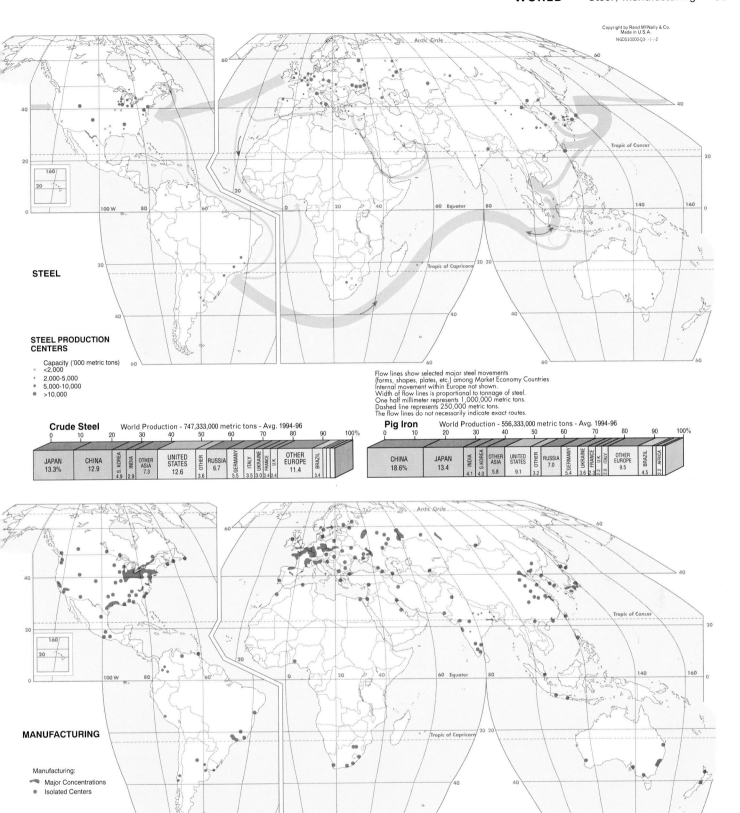

STEEL

STEEL PRODUCTION CENTERS

Capacity ('000 metric tons)
× <2,000
· 2,000-5,000
· 5,000-10,000
● >10,000

Flow lines show selected major steel movements
(forms, shapes, plates, etc.) among Market Economy Countries
Internal movement within Europe not shown.
Width of flow lines is proportional to tonnage of steel.
One half millimeter represents 1,000,000 metric tons.
Dashed line represents 250,000 metric tons.
The flow lines do not necessarily indicate exact routes.

Crude Steel   World Production - 747,333,000 metric tons - Avg. 1994-96

0	10	20	30	40	50	60	70	80	90	100%

JAPAN 13.3% | CHINA 12.9 | S. KOREA 4.9 | INDIA 2.9 | OTHER ASIA 7.3 | UNITED STATES 12.6 | OTHER 3.6 | RUSSIA 6.7 | GERMANY 5.5 | ITALY 3.5 | UKRAINE 3.0 | FRANCE 2.4 | U.K. 2.4 | OTHER EUROPE 11.4 | BRAZIL 3.4

Pig Iron   World Production - 556,333,000 metric tons - Avg. 1994-96

0	10	20	30	40	50	60	70	80	90	100%

CHINA 18.6% | JAPAN 13.4 | INDIA 4.1 | S. KOREA 4.0 | OTHER ASIA 5.8 | UNITED STATES 9.1 | OTHER 3.2 | RUSSIA 7.0 | GERMANY 5.4 | UKRAINE 3.6 | FRANCE 2.2 | U.K. 2.0 | ITALY | OTHER EUROPE 9.5 | BRAZIL 4.5 | AFRICA 2.2

MANUFACTURING

Manufacturing:
∼ Major Concentrations
● Isolated Centers

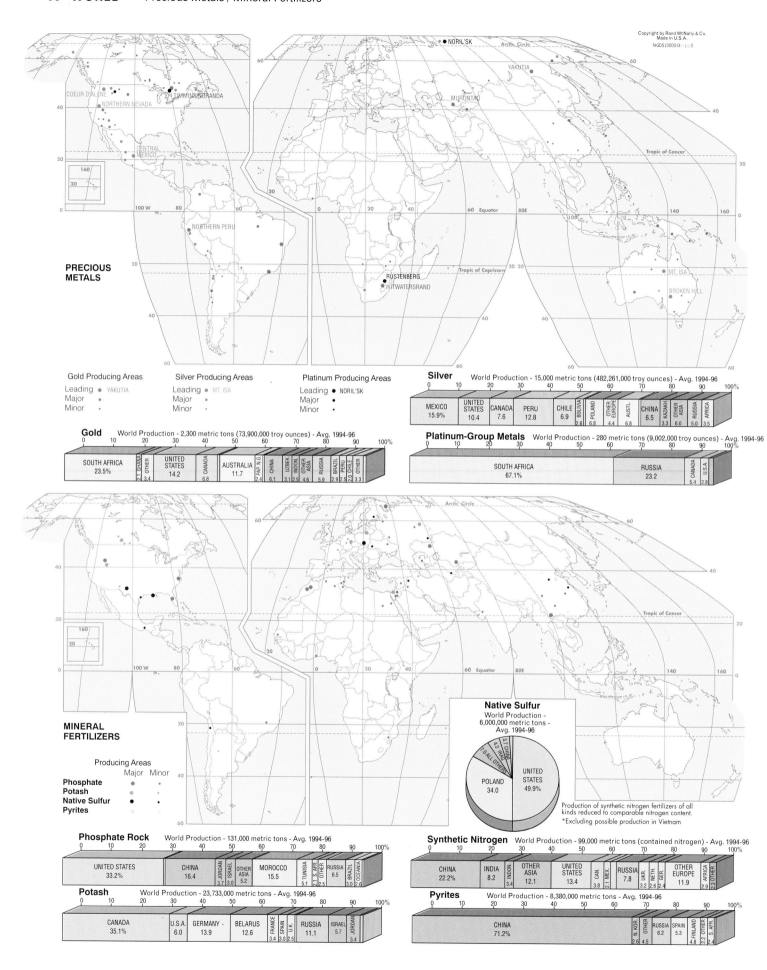

Copyright by Rand McNally & Co.
Made in U.S.A.
NGDS100004-3- -|-|-2

NORIL'SK
YAKUTIA
MURUNTAU
COEUR D'ALENE
TIMMINS/NORANDA
NORTHERN NEVADA
CENTRAL MEXICO
NORTHERN PERU
RUSTENBERG
WITWATERSRAND
MT. ISA
BROKEN HILL

PRECIOUS METALS

Gold Producing Areas
Leading ● YAKUTIA
Major ●
Minor ·

Silver Producing Areas
Leading ● MT. ISA
Major ●
Minor ·

Platinum Producing Areas
Leading ● NORIL'SK
Major ●
Minor ·

Silver
World Production - 15,000 metric tons (482,261,000 troy ounces) - Avg. 1994-96

| MEXICO 15.9% | UNITED STATES 10.4 | CANADA 7.6 | PERU 12.8 | CHILE 6.9 | BOLIVIA 2.6 | POLAND 6.8 | OTHER EUROPE 4.4 | AUSTL. 6.8 | CHINA 6.5 | KAZAKH 3.3 | OTHER ASIA 6.0 | RUSSIA 5.0 | AFRICA 3.5 |

Gold
World Production - 2,300 metric tons (73,900,000 troy ounces) - Avg. 1994-96

| SOUTH AFRICA 23.5% | GHANA 2.1 | OTHER 3.4 | UNITED STATES 14.2 | CANADA 6.8 | AUSTRALIA 11.7 | PAP. N.G. 2.4 | CHINA 6.1 | UZBEK. 3.1 | INDON. 2.5 | OTHER ASIA 4.6 | RUSSIA 5.9 | BRAZIL 2.9 | PERU 2.0 | CHILE 2.6 | OTHER 3.3 |

Platinum-Group Metals
World Production - 280 metric tons (9,002,000 troy ounces) - Avg. 1994-96

| SOUTH AFRICA 67.1% | RUSSIA 23.2 | CANADA 5.4 | U.S.A. 2.8 |

MINERAL FERTILIZERS

Producing Areas
             Major   Minor
Phosphate   ●   ·
Potash   ●   ·
Native Sulfur ●   ·
Pyrites   ●   ·

Native Sulfur
World Production - 6,000,000 metric tons - Avg. 1994-96

UNITED STATES 49.9%
POLAND 34.0
7.0 ALL OTHERS
4.2 IRAQ
3.7 CHINA

Production of synthetic nitrogen fertilizers of all kinds reduced to comparable nitrogen content.
*Excluding possible production in Vietnam

Phosphate Rock
World Production - 131,000 metric tons - Avg. 1994-96

| UNITED STATES 33.2% | CHINA 16.4 | JORDAN 3.7 | ISRAEL 3.0 | OTHER ASIA 5.2 | MOROCCO 15.5 | TUNISIA 2.1 | S. AFR 2.1 | OTHER 2.1 | RUSSIA 6.5 | BRAZIL 3.0 | OCEANIA 2.0 |

Potash
World Production - 23,733,000 metric tons - Avg. 1994-96

| CANADA 35.1% | U.S.A. 6.0 | GERMANY 13.9 | BELARUS 12.6 | FRANCE 3.4 | SPAIN 3.0 | U.K. 2.5 | RUSSIA 11.1 | ISRAEL 5.7 | JORDAN 3.4 |

Synthetic Nitrogen
World Production - 99,000 metric tons (contained nitrogen) - Avg. 1994-96

| CHINA 22.2% | INDIA 8.2 | INDON. 3.4 | OTHER ASIA 12.1 | UNITED STATES 13.4 | CAN. 3.8 | MEX. 2.1 | RUSSIA 7.8 | UKR. 3.2 | NETH. 2.6 | GER. 2.4 | OTHER EUROPE 11.9 | AFRICA 2.9 | OTHER 2.3 |

Pyrites
World Production - 8,380,000 metric tons - Avg. 1994-96

| CHINA 71.2% | N. KOR 2.6 | OTHER 4.5 | RUSSIA 6.2 | SPAIN 5.3 | FINLAND 4.8 | OTHER 2.2 | S. AFR 2.4 |

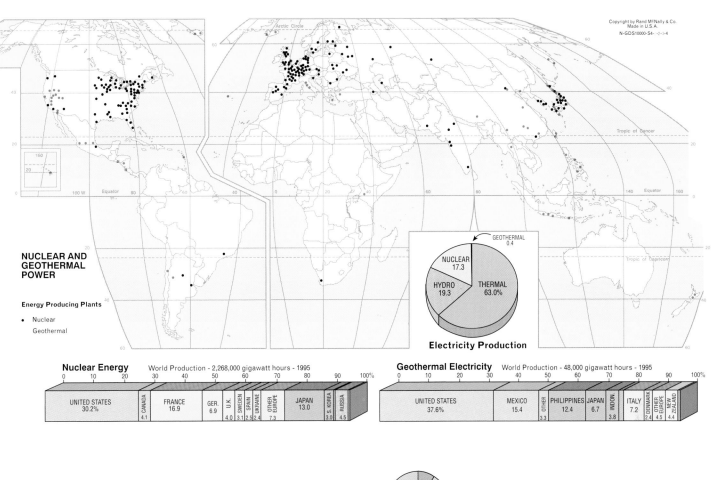

NUCLEAR AND GEOTHERMAL POWER

Energy Producing Plants

● Nuclear

Geothermal

Electricity Production

GEOTHERMAL 0.4
NUCLEAR 17.3
HYDRO 19.3
THERMAL 63.0%

Nuclear Energy
World Production - 2,268,000 gigawatt hours - 1995

0	10	20	30	40	50	60	70	80	90	100%

| UNITED STATES 30.2% | CANADA 4.1 | FRANCE 16.9 | GER. 6.9 | U.K. 4.0 | SWEDEN 3.1 | SPAIN 2.5 | UKRAINE 2.4 | OTHER EUROPE 7.3 | JAPAN 13.0 | S. KOREA 3.0 | RUSSIA 4.5 |

Geothermal Electricity
World Production - 48,000 gigawatt hours - 1995

0	10	20	30	40	50	60	70	80	90	100%

| UNITED STATES 37.6% | MEXICO 15.4 | OTHER 3.3 | PHILIPPINES 12.4 | JAPAN 6.7 | INDON. 3.8 | ITALY 7.2 | DENMARK 2.4 | OTHER EUROPE 4.5 | NEW ZEALAND 4.4 |

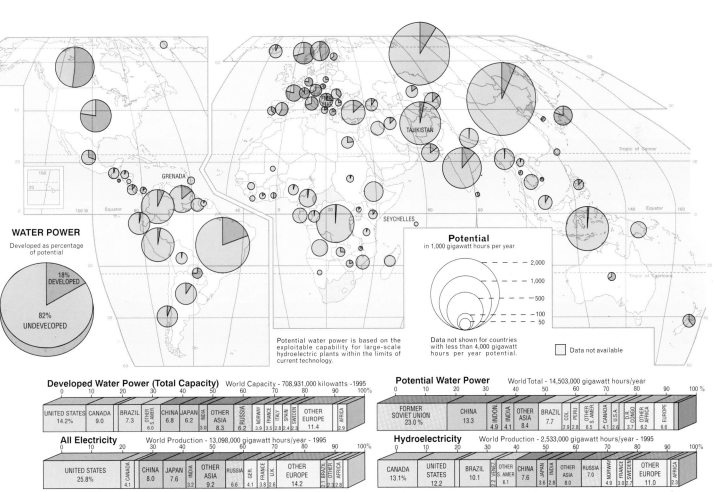

WATER POWER

Developed as percentage of potential

18% DEVELOPED
82% UNDEVELOPED

Potential
in 1,000 gigawatt hours per year

— 2,000
— 1,000
— 500
— 100
— 50

Data not shown for countries with less than 4,000 gigawatt hours per year potential.

Data not available

Potential water power is based on the exploitable capability for large-scale hydroelectric plants within the limits of current technology.

Developed Water Power (Total Capacity)
World Capacity - 708,931,000 kilowatts -1995

0	10	20	30	40	50	60	70	80	90	100%

| UNITED STATES 14.2% | CANADA 9.0 | BRAZIL 7.3 | OTHER S. AMER. 6.0 | CHINA 6.8 | JAPAN 6.2 | INDIA 3.0 | OTHER ASIA 8.3 | RUSSIA 5.2 | NORWAY 3.9 | FRANCE 3.5 | ITALY 2.8 | SPAIN 2.4 | SWEDEN 2.3 | OTHER EUROPE 11.4 | AFRICA 2.9 |

Potential Water Power
World Total - 14,503,000 gigawatt hours/year

0	10	20	30	40	50	60	70	80	90	100%

| FORMER SOVIET UNION 23.0 % | CHINA 13.3 | INDON. 4.9 | INDIA 4.1 | OTHER ASIA 8.4 | BRAZIL 7.7 | COL 2.9 | PERU 2.8 | OTHER S. AMER. 6.5 | CANADA 4.1 | U.S.A. 2.6 | D.R. CONGO 3.7 | OTHER AFRICA 6.6 | EUROPE 6.6 |

All Electricity
World Production - 13,098,000 gigawatt hours/year - 1995

0	10	20	30	40	50	60	70	80	90	100%

| UNITED STATES 25.8% | CANADA 4.1 | CHINA 8.0 | JAPAN 7.6 | INDIA 3.2 | OTHER ASIA 9.2 | RUSSIA 6.6 | GER. 4.1 | FRANCE 3.8 | U.K. 2.6 | OTHER EUROPE 14.2 | BRAZIL 2.1 | OTHER 2.3 | AFRICA 2.8 |

Hydroelectricity
World Production - 2,533,000 gigawatt hours/year - 1995

0	10	20	30	40	50	60	70	80	90	100%

| CANADA 13.1% | UNITED STATES 12.2 | BRAZIL 10.1 | VENEZ. 2.2 | OTHER S. AMER. 6.1 | CHINA 7.6 | JAPAN 3.6 | INDIA 2.8 | OTHER ASIA 8.0 | RUSSIA 7.0 | NORWAY 4.9 | FRANCE 3.0 | SWEDEN 2.7 | OTHER EUROPE 11.0 | AFRICA 2.3 |

58

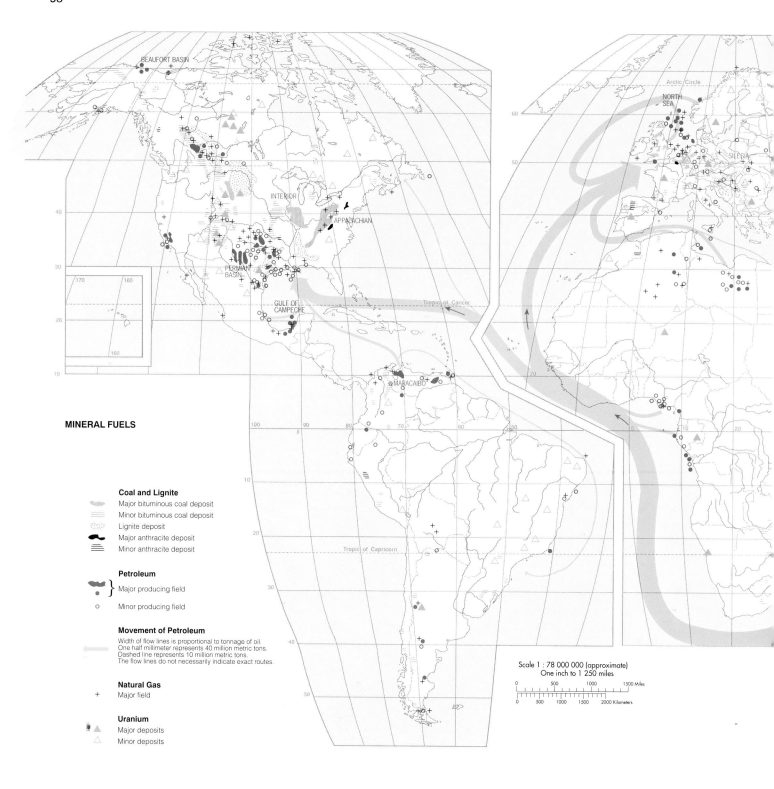

BEAUFORT BASIN

NORTH SEA

Arctic Circle

SILESIA

INTERIOR

APPALACHIAN

PERMIAN BASIN

GULF OF CAMPECHE

Tropic of Cancer

MARACAIBO

Tropic of Capricorn

MINERAL FUELS

Coal and Lignite

▨ Major bituminous coal deposit

▤ Minor bituminous coal deposit

▨ Lignite deposit

▬ Major anthracite deposit

▤ Minor anthracite deposit

Petroleum

◖ ⬤ } Major producing field

○ Minor producing field

Movement of Petroleum

Width of flow lines is proportional to tonnage of oil.
One half millimeter represents 40 million metric tons.
Dashed line represents 10 million metric tons.
The flow lines do not necessarily indicate exact routes.

Natural Gas

+ Major field

Uranium

▲ Major deposits

△ Minor deposits

Scale 1 : 78 000 000 (approximate)
One inch to 1 250 miles

0   500   1000   1500 Miles

0   500   1000   1500   2000 Kilometers

Coal World Production - 4,645,332,000* metric tons - Avg. 1994-96

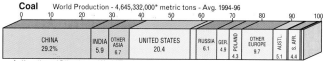

| CHINA 29.2% | INDIA 5.9 | OTHER ASIA 6.7 | UNITED STATES 20.4 | RUSSIA 6.1 | GER. 4.9 | POLAND 4.3 | OTHER EUROPE 9.7 | AUSTL. 5.1 | S. AFR. 4.4 |

Anthracite and Bituminous: World Total - 3,745,599,000 metric tons

Coal Reserves World Total - 1,035,786,456,000* metric tons - 1998

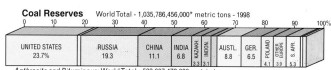

| UNITED STATES 23.7% | RUSSIA 19.3 | CHINA 11.1 | INDIA 6.8 | KAZAKH. 3.3 | INDON. 3.1 | AUSTL. 8.8 | GER. 6.5 | OTHER EUROPE 4.1 | POLAND 3.9 | S. AFR. 5.3 |

Anthracite and Bituminous: World Total - 523,607,472,000 metric tons
* Includes anthracite, subanthracite, bituminous, subbituminous, lignite, and brown coal

Petroleum World Production - 3,100,472,000** metric tons (22,797,544,000 barrels) - Avg. 1994-96

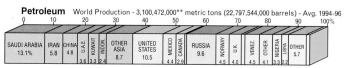

| SAUDI ARABIA 13.1% | IRAN 5.8 | CHINA 4.8 | U.A.E. 3.6 | KUWAIT 3.3 | INDON. 2.4 | OTHER ASIA 8.7 | UNITED STATES 10.5 | MEXICO 4.4 | CANADA 2.9 | RUSSIA 9.6 | NORWAY 4.5 | U.K. 4.0 | VENEZ. 4.5 | OTHER 4.1 | NIGERIA 3.3 | LIBYA 2.2 | OTHER 5.7 |

Petroleum Reserves World Total - 157,769,452,000** metric tons (1,160,069,500,000 barrels) - 1997

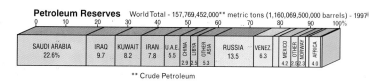

| SAUDI ARABIA 22.6% | IRAQ 9.7 | KUWAIT 8.2 | IRAN 7.8 | U.A.E. 5.5 | CHINA 2.9 | LIBYA 2.5 | OTHER ASIA 5.3 | RUSSIA 13.5 | VENEZ. 6.3 | MEXICO 4.2 | OTHER 2.5 | NORWAY 2.3 | AFRICA 4.0 |

** Crude Petroleum

WESTERN SIBERIA

KUZNETSK

EKIBASTUZ

KARAGANDA

VOLGA-URALS

-ETSK

TENGIZ

KIRKUK

PERSIAN GULF FIELDS

GHAWAR

SONGLIAO BASIN

DATONG

BOHAI BASIN

SHANXI

SHAANXI

Tropic of Cancer

70

60

50

40

30

20

10

Equator

Longitude East of Greenwich

Equator

Tropic of Capricorn

Goode's Homolosine Equal Area Projection (Condensed)

N-GDS10000-F1- -1- -:- -2

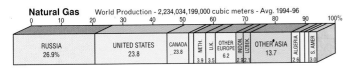

Natural Gas   World Production - 2,234,034,199,000 cubic meters - Avg. 1994-96

| 0 | 10 | 20 | 30 | 40 | 50 | 60 | 70 | 80 | 90 | 100% |

| RUSSIA 26.9% | UNITED STATES 23.8 | CANADA 23.8 | NETH. 3.9 | U.K. 3.5 | OTHER EUROPE 6.2 | INDON. 2.9 | UZBEK. 2.1 | OTHER ASIA 13.7 | ALGERIA 2.6 | S. AMER. 3.0 |

Natural Gas Reserves   World Total - 140,074,431,000 cubic meters - 1997

| 0 | 10 | 20 | 30 | 40 | 50 | 60 | 70 | 80 | 90 | 100% |

| RUSSIA 34.4% | IRAN 15.0 | QATAR 5.1 | U.A.E. 4.1 | S. ARAB. 3.8 | IRAQ 2.4 | TURKMEN. 2.0 | OTHER ASIA 11.2 | U.S.A. 3.4 | N. AMER. 2.7 | VEN. 2.9 | ALGERIA 2.6 | NIGERIA 2.1 | EUROPE 4.7 |

Uranium   World Production - 33,653 metric tons - Avg. 1994-96

| 0 | 10 | 20 | 30 | 40 | 50 | 60 | 70 | 80 | 90 | 100% |

| CANADA 31.5% | U.S.A. 6.0 | AUSTRALIA 10.8 | NIGER 9.2 | NAMIBIA 6.3 | S. AFR. 4.5 | OTHER 1.9 | RUSSIA 7.2 | UZBEK. 5.1 | KAZAKH. 5.0 | OTHER 2.2 | UKRAINE 3.0 | FRANCE 3.0 | OTHER 4.0 |

Uranium Reserves   World Total - 3,414,000 metric tons - 1997

| 0 | 10 | 20 | 30 | 40 | 50 | 60 | 70 | 80 | 90 | 100% |

| AUSTRALIA 20.9% | KAZAKHSTAN 17.6 | UZBEK. 2.5 | OTHER ASIA 5.9 | UNITED STATES 10.6 | CANADA 9.7 | SOUTH AFRICA 9.7 | NAMIBIA 9.7 | NIGER 2.0 | BRAZIL 4.7 | RUSSIA 4.2 | UKRAINE 3.5 | OTHER 3.9 |

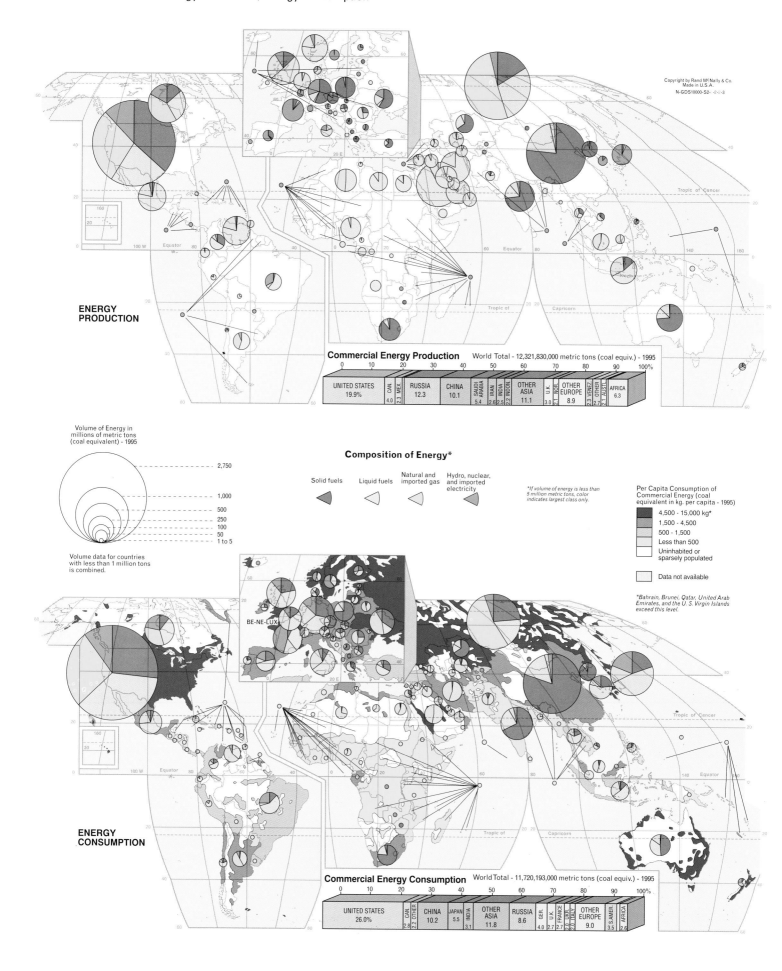

ENERGY PRODUCTION

Commercial Energy Production World Total - 12,321,830,000 metric tons (coal equiv.) - 1995

0	10	20	30	40	50	60	70	80	90	100%

| UNITED STATES 19.9% | CAN. 4.0 | MEX 2.3 | RUSSIA 12.3 | CHINA 10.1 | SAUDI ARABIA 5.4 | IRAN 2.6 | INDIA 2.5 | INDON 2.2 | OTHER ASIA 11.1 | U.K. 3.0 | NOR 2.1 | OTHER EUROPE 8.9 | VENEZ 2.3 | OTHER 2.7 | AUSTL 2.1 | AFRICA 6.3 |

Volume of Energy in millions of metric tons (coal equivalent) - 1995

- 2,750
- 1,000
- 500
- 250
- 100
- 50
- 1 to 5

Volume data for countries with less than 1 million tons is combined.

Composition of Energy*

Solid fuels   Liquid fuels   Natural and imported gas   Hydro, nuclear, and imported electricity

If volume of energy is less than 5 million metric tons, color indicates largest class only.

Per Capita Consumption of Commercial Energy (coal equivalent in kg. per capita - 1995)

- 4,500 - 15,000 kg*
- 1,500 - 4,500
- 500 - 1,500
- Less than 500
- Uninhabited or sparsely populated
- Data not available

Bahrain, Brunei, Qatar, United Arab Emirates, and the U. S. Virgin Islands exceed this level.

BE-NE-LUX

ENERGY CONSUMPTION

Commercial Energy Consumption World Total - 11,720,193,000 metric tons (coal equiv.) - 1995

0	10	20	30	40	50	60	70	80	90	100%

| UNITED STATES 26.0% | CAN. 2.8 | OTHER 2.2 | CHINA 10.2 | JAPAN 5.5 | INDIA 3.1 | OTHER ASIA 11.8 | RUSSIA 8.6 | GER. 4.0 | U.K. 2.7 | FRANCE 2.7 | ITALY 2.0 | UKR 2.0 | OTHER EUROPE 9.0 | S. AMER. 3.5 | AFRICA 2.6 |

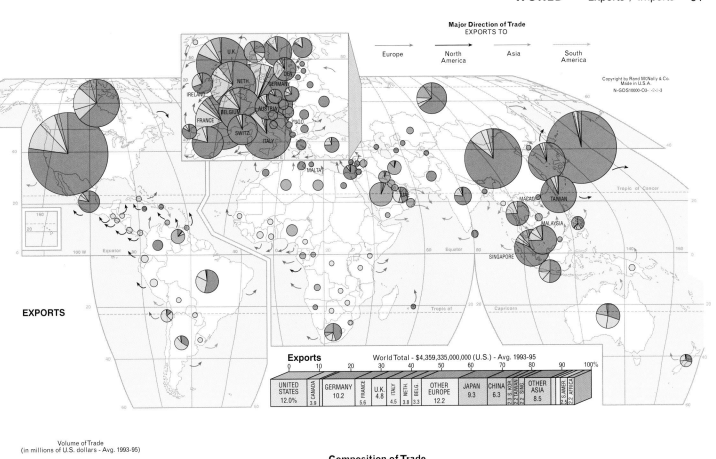

Major Direction of Trade
EXPORTS TO

Europe   North America   Asia   South America

EXPORTS

Exports   World Total - $4,359,335,000,000 (U.S.) - Avg. 1993-95

UNITED STATES 12.0%	CANADA 3.9	GERMANY 10.2	FRANCE 5.6	U.K. 4.8	ITALY 4.5	NETH. 3.8	BELG. 3.3	OTHER EUROPE 12.2	JAPAN 9.3	CHINA 6.3	S. KOR. 2.3	TAIWAN 2.7	SING.	OTHER ASIA 8.5	S. AMER.	AFRICA 2.2

Volume of Trade
(in millions of U.S. dollars - Avg. 1993-95)

500,000
200,000
100,000
50,000
20,000
10,000
500 - 2,000

If volume of trade is less than 10 billion dollars, color indicates major class only. If no symbol is shown, volume of trade is less than 500 million dollars.

Composition of Trade

Manufactured Articles   Food, Beverages, & Tobacco   Raw Materials   Fuel & Related Products   All other or undifferentiated

Major Direction of Trade
IMPORTS FROM

Europe   North America   Asia   South America

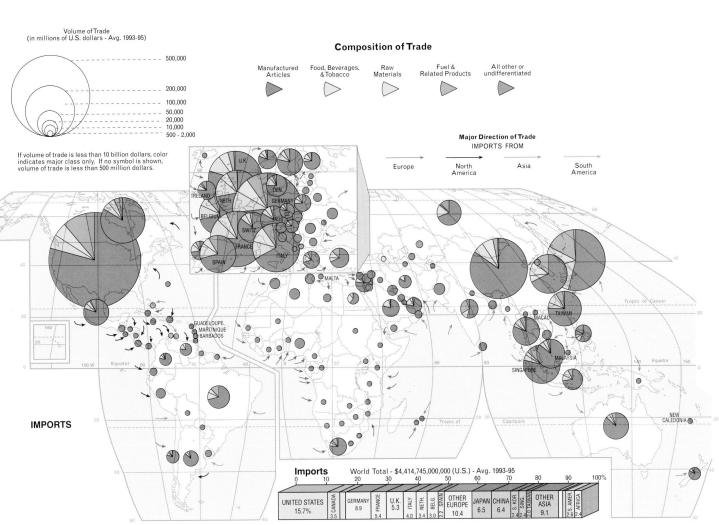

IMPORTS

Imports   World Total - $4,414,745,000,000 (U.S.) - Avg. 1993-95

UNITED STATES 15.7%	CANADA 3.5	GERMANY 8.9	FRANCE 5.4	U.K. 5.3	ITALY 4.0	NETH. 3.4	BELG. 3.0	SPAIN 2.2	OTHER EUROPE 10.4	JAPAN 6.5	CHINA 6.4	S. KOR. 2.4	SING. 2.4	TAIWAN 2.0	OTHER ASIA 9.1	S. AMER. 2.6	AFRICA 2.4

LAND AND OCEAN
TRANSPORTATION

Vehicles   Per kilometer (mile) of motorable road

INDIA	2.3 (3.7)
CHINA	6.1 (9.7)
RUSSIA	25.3 (40.7)
ARGENTINA	27.7 (44.6)
UNITED STATES	30.3 (48.8)
FRANCE	31.7 (51.1)
UNITED KINGDOM	73.5 (118.3)

Persons per Vehicle

UNITED STATES	1.3
FRANCE	2.0
UNITED KINGDOM	2.2
ARGENTINA	5.5
RUSSIA	6.4
INDIA	179.1
CHINA	184.6

Inland Waterways   Thousands of kilometers (miles)

UNITED KINGDOM	3.2 (2.0)
ARGENTINA	11.0 (6.8)
FRANCE	14.9 (9.3)
INDIA	16.2 (10.1)
UNITED STATES	41.0 (25.5)
RUSSIA	101.0 (62.8)
CHINA	110.6 (68.7)

Railroads and Motorable Roads
Kilometers per 100 square kilometers
(miles per 100 square miles)

Railroads
Motorable Roads
(excluding city street

RUSSIA	0.9 (1.5)
	5.4 (8.7)
ARGENTINA	1.2 (2.0)
	7.8 (12.5)
CHINA	0.6 (0.9)
	11.1 (17.8)
INDIA	1.9 (3.1)
	63.6 (102.3)
UNITED STATES	1.9 (3.0)
	64.0 (103.0)
UNITED KINGDOM	6.8 (10.9)
	149.3 (240.3
FRANCE	5.9 (9.5)
	167.5 (2

Copyright by Rand McNally & Co.
Made in U.S.A.
NGDS10000-R3- -1-1-2

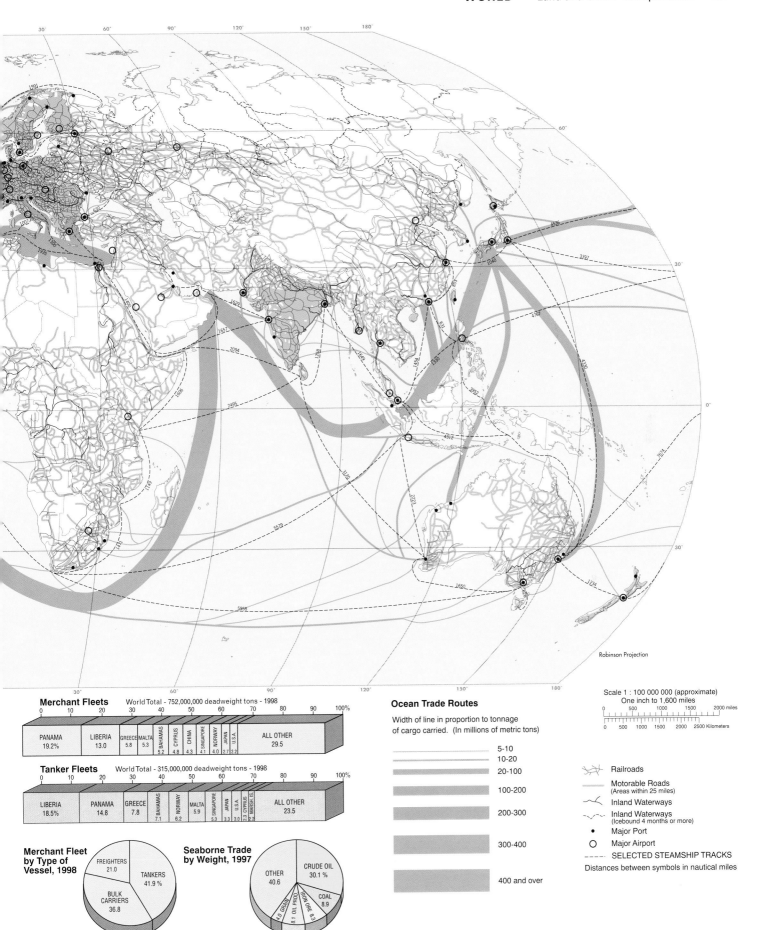

Robinson Projection

Merchant Fleets   World Total - 752,000,000 deadweight tons - 1998

| | 0 | 10 | 20 | 30 | 40 | 50 | 60 | 70 | 80 | 90 | 100% |

| PANAMA 19.2% | LIBERIA 13.0 | GREECE 5.8 | MALTA 5.3 | BAHAMAS 5.2 | CYPRUS 4.8 | CHINA 4.3 | SINGAPORE 4.1 | NORWAY 4.0 | JAPAN 2.7 | U.S.A. 2.2 | ALL OTHER 29.5 |

Tanker Fleets   World Total - 315,000,000 deadweight tons - 1998

| | 0 | 10 | 20 | 30 | 40 | 50 | 60 | 70 | 80 | 90 | 100% |

| LIBERIA 18.5% | PANAMA 14.8 | GREECE 7.8 | BAHAMAS 7.1 | NORWAY 6.2 | MALTA 5.9 | SINGAPORE 5.3 | JAPAN 3.3 | U.S.A. 3.0 | CYPRUS 2.3 | MARSH. IS. 2.2 | ALL OTHER 23.5 |

Merchant Fleet by Type of Vessel, 1998

FREIGHTERS 21.0
TANKERS 41.9 %
BULK CARRIERS 36.8

World Total - 752,000,000 deadweight tons - 1998

Seaborne Trade by Weight, 1997

OTHER 40.6
CRUDE OIL 30.1 %
COAL 8.9
IRON ORE 8.3
OIL PROD. 8.1
GRAIN 4.0

World Total - 5,074,000,000 metric tons - 1997

Ocean Trade Routes

Width of line in proportion to tonnage
of cargo carried. (In millions of metric tons)

- 5-10
- 10-20
- 20-100
- 100-200
- 200-300
- 300-400
- 400 and over

Scale 1 : 100 000 000 (approximate)
One inch to 1,600 miles

0   500   1000   1500   2000 miles

0   500   1000   1500   2000   2500 Kilometers

Railroads

Motorable Roads
(Areas within 25 miles)

Inland Waterways

Inland Waterways
(Icebound 4 months or more)

• Major Port

O Major Airport

----- SELECTED STEAMSHIP TRACKS

Distances between symbols in nautical miles

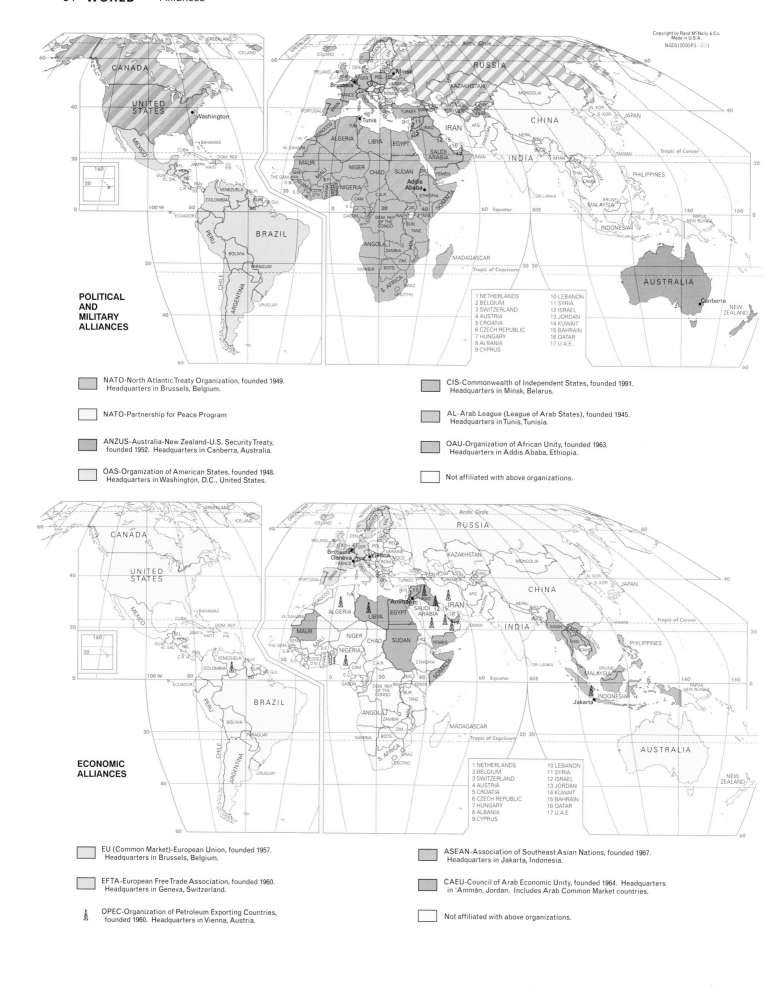

Copyright by Rand McNally & Co.
Made in U.S.A.
N-GDS10000-P3- -2-2-1

POLITICAL AND MILITARY ALLIANCES

1 NETHERLANDS	10 LEBANON
2 BELGIUM	11 SYRIA
3 SWITZERLAND	12 ISRAEL
4 AUSTRIA	13 JORDAN
5 CROATIA	14 KUWAIT
6 CZECH REPUBLIC	15 BAHRAIN
7 HUNGARY	16 QATAR
8 ALBANIA	17 U.A.E.
9 CYPRUS	

NATO-North Atlantic Treaty Organization, founded 1949. Headquarters in Brussels, Belgium.

NATO-Partnership for Peace Program

ANZUS-Australia-New Zealand-U.S. Security Treaty, founded 1952. Headquarters in Canberra, Australia.

OAS-Organization of American States, founded 1948. Headquarters in Washington, D.C., United States.

CIS-Commonwealth of Independent States, founded 1991. Headquarters in Minsk, Belarus.

AL-Arab League (League of Arab States), founded 1945. Headquarters in Tunis, Tunisia.

OAU-Organization of African Unity, founded 1963. Headquarters in Addis Ababa, Ethiopia.

Not affiliated with above organizations.

ECONOMIC ALLIANCES

1 NETHERLANDS	10 LEBANON
2 BELGIUM	11 SYRIA
3 SWITZERLAND	12 ISRAEL
4 AUSTRIA	13 JORDAN
5 CROATIA	14 KUWAIT
6 CZECH REPUBLIC	15 BAHRAIN
7 HUNGARY	16 QATAR
8 ALBANIA	17 U.A.E.
9 CYPRUS	

EU (Common Market)-European Union, founded 1957. Headquarters in Brussels, Belgium.

EFTA-European Free Trade Association, founded 1960. Headquarters in Geneva, Switzerland.

OPEC-Organization of Petroleum Exporting Countries, founded 1960. Headquarters in Vienna, Austria.

ASEAN-Association of Southeast Asian Nations, founded 1967. Headquarters in Jakarta, Indonesia.

CAEU-Council of Arab Economic Unity, founded 1964. Headquarters in 'Ammān, Jordan. Includes Arab Common Market countries.

Not affiliated with above organizations.

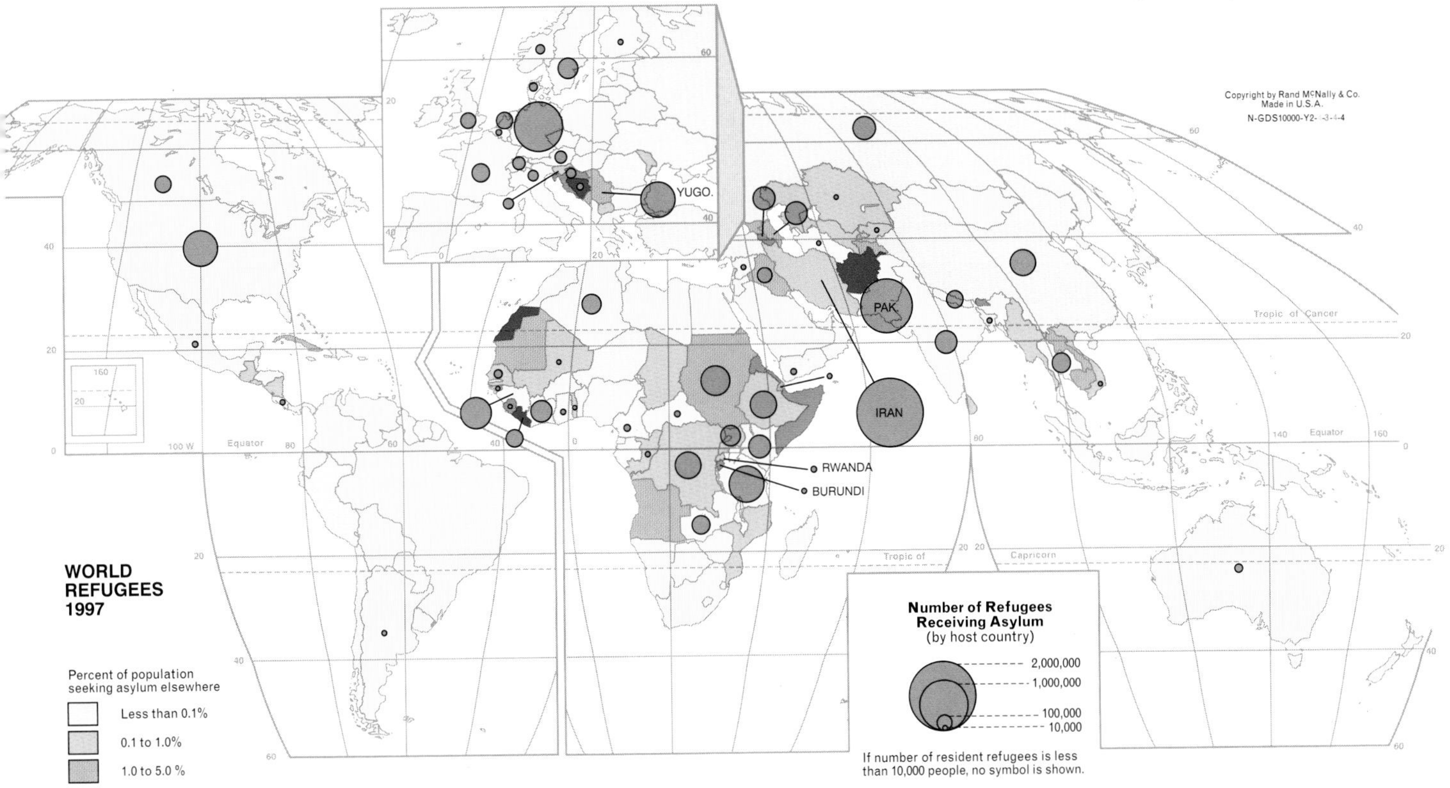

YUGO.

PAK

IRAN

RWANDA

BURUNDI

WORLD REFUGEES 1997

Percent of population seeking asylum elsewhere

Less than 0.1%

0.1 to 1.0%

1.0 to 5.0 %

5.0 to 10.0%

Greater than 10.0%

Excludes countries fled by 1,000 or fewer refugees. The origin of refugees is not always known and/or consistently reported by a number of countries.

Number of Refugees Receiving Asylum
(by host country)

2,000,000

1,000,000

100,000

10,000

If number of resident refugees is less than 10,000 people, no symbol is shown.

Refugee Population (by Host Country)

World Total - 11,975,500 - 1997

0	10	20	30	40	50	60	70	80	90	100%

| IRAN 16.6% | PAKISTAN 10.0 | CHINA 2.4 | AZER. 2.0 | OTHER ASIA 8.5 | GER. 8.8 | YUGO. 4.6 | OTHER EUROPE 9.2 | TANZ. 4.8 | GUINEA 3.6 | SUDAN 3.1 | ETH. 2.7 | D.R.CON. 2.5 | OTHER AFRICA 12.4 | U.S.A. 4.6 | RUSSIA 2.0 |

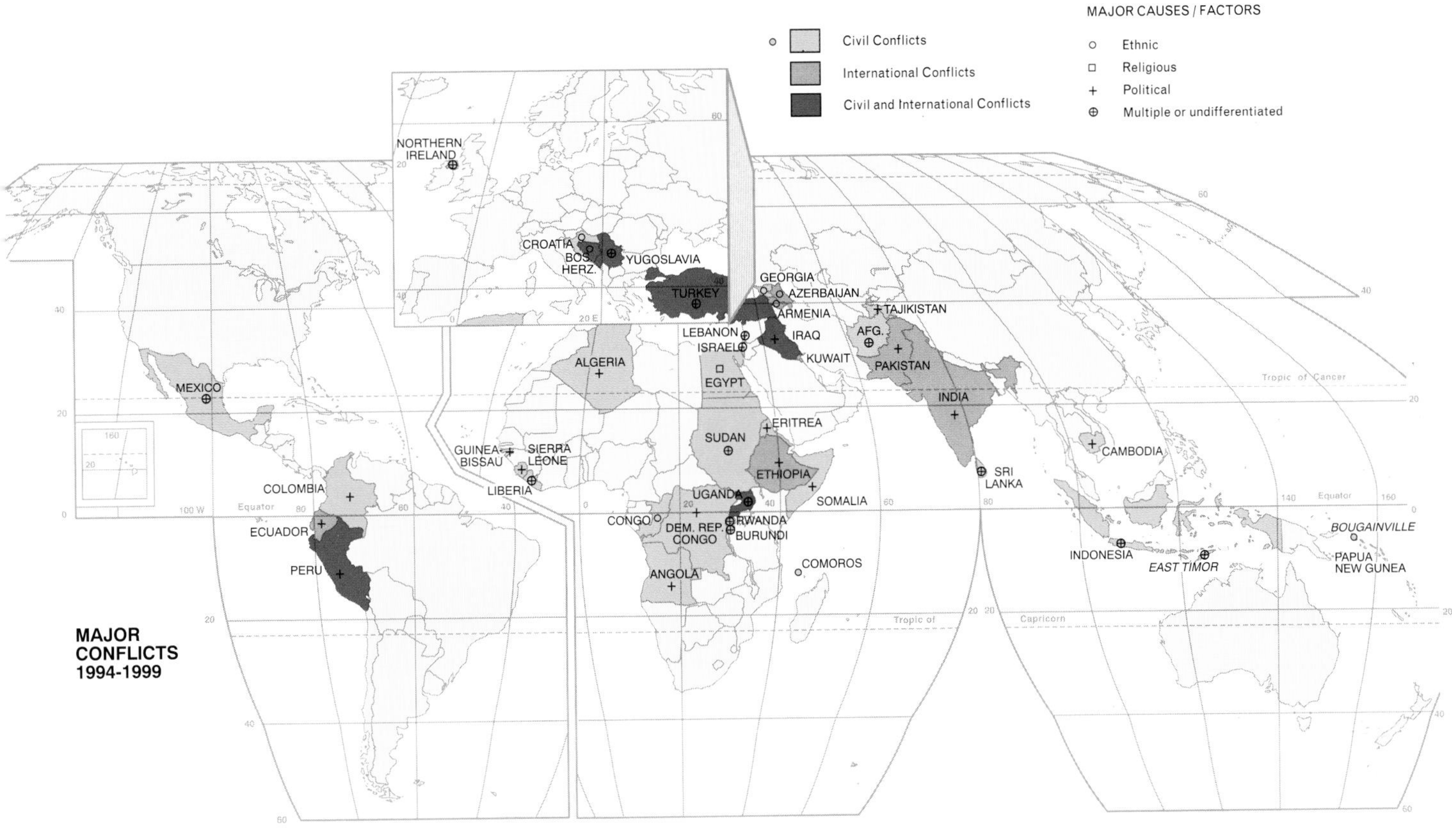

Civil Conflicts

International Conflicts

Civil and International Conflicts

MAJOR CAUSES / FACTORS

○ Ethnic

□ Religious

+ Political

⊕ Multiple or undifferentiated

NORTHERN IRELAND

CROATIA
BOS. HERZ.
YUGOSLAVIA

TURKEY

GEORGIA
AZERBAIJAN
ARMENIA

TAJIKISTAN

LEBANON
ISRAEL
IRAQ
KUWAIT

AFG.

PAKISTAN

ALGERIA

EGYPT

INDIA

MEXICO

GUINEA-BISSAU
SIERRA LEONE
LIBERIA

SUDAN

ERITREA

ETHIOPIA

SOMALIA

SRI LANKA

CAMBODIA

COLOMBIA

ECUADOR

PERU

CONGO
DEM. REP. CONGO

UGANDA
RWANDA
BURUNDI

COMOROS

BOUGAINVILLE

INDONESIA

EAST TIMOR

PAPUA NEW GUNEA

ANGOLA

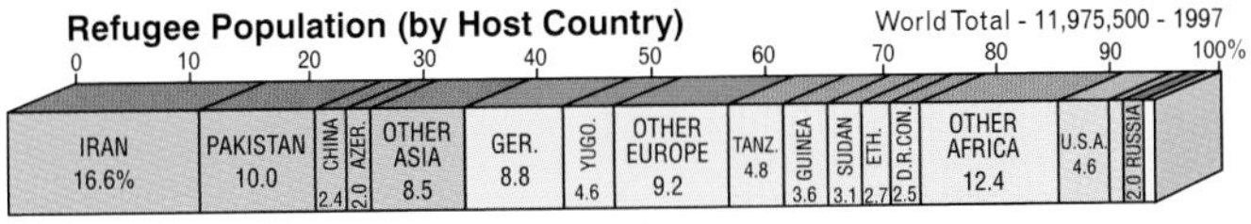

MAJOR CONFLICTS 1994-1999

REGIONAL MAPS

Basic continental and regional coverage of the world's land areas is provided by the following section of physical-political reference maps. The section falls into a continental arrangement: North America, South America, Europe, Asia, Australia, and Africa. Introducing each regional reference-map section are basic thematic maps.

To aid the student in acquiring concepts of the relative sizes of continents and of some of the countries and regions, uniform scales for comparable areas were used so far as possible. Continental maps are at a uniform scale of 1:40,000,000. In addition, most of the world is covered by a series of regional maps at scales of 1:16,000,000 and 1:12,000,000.

Maps at 1:10,000,000 provide even greater detail for parts of Europe, Africa, and Asia. The United States, parts of Canada, and much of Europe are mapped at 1:4,000,000. Ninety-two urbanized areas are shown at 1:1,000,000.

Many of the symbols used are self-explanatory. A complete legend below provides a key to the symbols on the reference maps in this atlas.

General elevation above sea level is shown by layer tints for altitudinal zones, each of which has a different hue and is defined by generalized contour lines. A legend is given on each map, reflecting this color gradation.

The surface configuration is represented by hill-shading, which gives the three-dimensional impression of landforms. This terrain representation is superimposed on the layer tints to convey a realistic and readily visualized impression of the surface. The combination of altitudinal tints and hill-shading best shows elevation, relief, steepness of slope, and ruggedness of terrain.

If the world used one alphabet and one language, no particular difficulty would arise in understanding place-names. However, some of the people of the world, the Chinese and the Japanese, for example, use nonalphabetic languages. Their symbols are transliterated into the Roman alphabet. In this atlas a "local-name" policy generally was used for naming cities and towns and local topographic and water features; however, for a few major cities and other well known features, Anglicized names were preferred. In these instances, local names may also be given in parentheses - for instance Moscow (Moskva), Vienna (Wien), Naples (Napoli). In countries where more than one official language is used, a name is in the dominant local language. The generic parts of local names for topographic and water features are self-explanatory in many cases because of the associated map symbols or type styles. A list of foreign generic names is given in the Glossary.

Place-names on the reference maps are listed in the Pronouncing Index, which is a distinctive feature of *Goode's World Atlas.*

Physical-Political Reference Map Legend

Cultural Features

Political Boundaries

International (over water) (Demarcated, Undemarcated, and Administrative)

Disputed de facto

Claim Boundary

Indefinite or Undefined

Secondary, State, Provincial, etc. (over water)

Parks, Indian Reservations

City Limits — Urbanized Areas

Neighborhoods, Sections of City

Populated Places

- ◉ 1,000,000 and over
- ◎ 250,000 to 1,000,000
- ⊙ 100,000 to 250,000
- • 25,000 to 100,000
- ○ 0 to 25,000

TŌKYŌ National Capitals

Boise Secondary Capitals

Note: On maps at 1:20,000,000 and smaller the town symbols do not follow the specific population classification shown above. On all maps, type size indicates the relative importance of the city.

Transportation

Railroads

Railroads On 1:1,000,000 scale maps

Railroad Ferries

Roads

Major / Other On 1:1,000,000 scale maps

Major / Other On 1:4,000,000 scale maps

On other scale maps

Caravan Routes

✈ Airports

Other Cultural Features

Dams

Pipelines

▲ Points of Interest

Ruins

Land Features

- △ Peaks, Spot Heights
- = Passes
- Sand
- Contours

Water Features

Lakes and Reservoirs

Fresh Water

Fresh Water: Intermittent

Salt Water

Salt Water: Intermittent

Other Water Features

Salt Basins, Flats

Swamps

Ice Caps and Glaciers

Rivers

Intermittent Rivers

Aqueducts and Canals

Ship Channels

Falls

Rapids

Springs

△ Water Depths

Fishing Banks

Sand Bars

Reefs

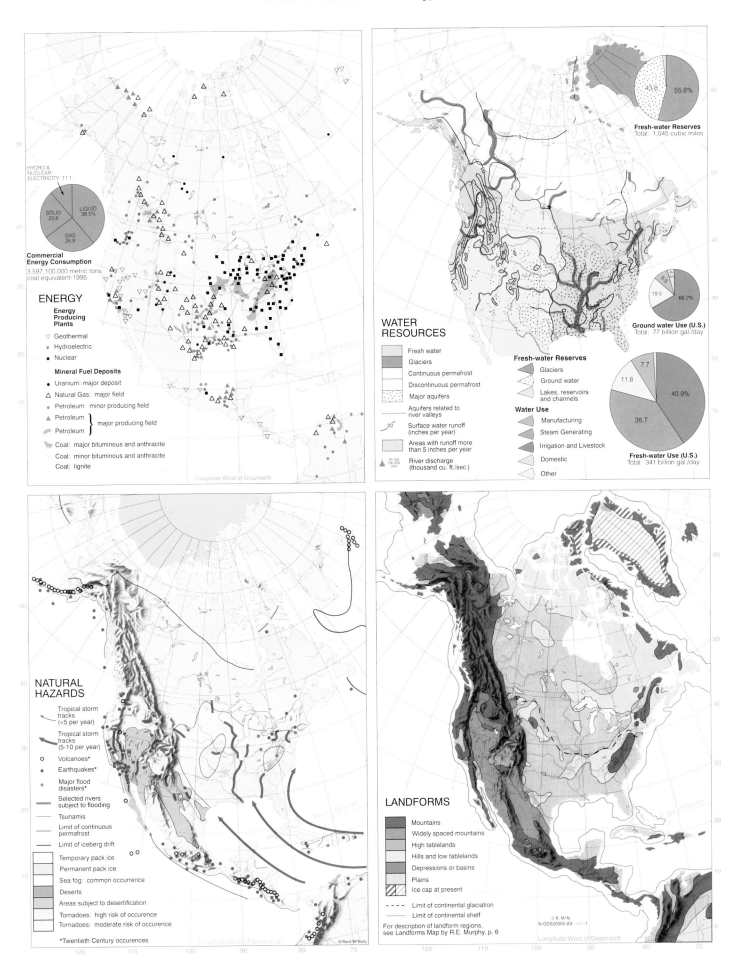

ENERGY

HYDRO &
NUCLEAR
ELECTRICITY 11.1

SOLID
23.6

LIQUID
38.5%

GAS
26.8

**Commercial
Energy Consumption**
3,597,100,000 metric tons
coal equivalent-1995

**Energy
Producing
Plants**

▽ Geothermal
• Hydroelectric
■ Nuclear

Mineral Fuel Deposits

• Uranium: major deposit
△ Natural Gas: major field
△ Petroleum: minor producing field
▲ Petroleum
◣ Petroleum } major producing field

Coal: major bituminous and anthracite
Coal: minor bituminous and anthracite
Coal: lignite

Longitude West of Greenwich

WATER RESOURCES

Fresh water
Glaciers
Continuous permafrost
Discontinuous permafrost
Major aquifers
Aquifers related to
river valleys
—20— Surface water runoff
(inches per year)
Areas with runoff more
than 5 inches per year
River discharge
(thousand cu. ft./sec.)

Fresh-water Reserves
◣ Glaciers
◁ Ground water
◁ Lakes, reservoirs
and channels

Water Use
◣ Manufacturing
◣ Steam Generating
◣ Irrigation and Livestock
◁ Domestic
◁ Other

43.0   55.8%
Fresh-water Reserves
Total: 1,045 cubic miles

4.3
9.8
19.5   66.2%
Ground water Use (U.S.)
Total: 77 billion gal./day

7.7
11.8   40.9%
38.7
Fresh-water Use (U.S.)
Total: 341 billion gal./day

NATURAL HAZARDS

Tropical storm
tracks
(<5 per year)
Tropical storm
tracks
(5-10 per year)
○ Volcanoes*
• Earthquakes*
• Major flood
disasters*
Selected rivers
subject to flooding
Tsunamis
Limit of continuous
permafrost
Limit of iceberg drift

Temporary pack ice
Permanent pack ice
Sea fog: common occurrence
Deserts
Areas subject to desertification
Tornadoes: high risk of occurence
Tornadoes: moderate risk of occurence

*Twentieth Century occurences

© Rand McNally

LANDFORMS

Mountains
Widely spaced mountains
High tablelands
Hills and low tablelands
Depressions or basins
Plains
Ice cap at present

- - - Limit of continental glaciation
—— Limit of continental shelf

For description of landform regions,
see Landforms Map by R.E. Murphy, p. 6

© R. McN.
N-GDS20000-A3- -1-1-1

Longitude West of Greenwich

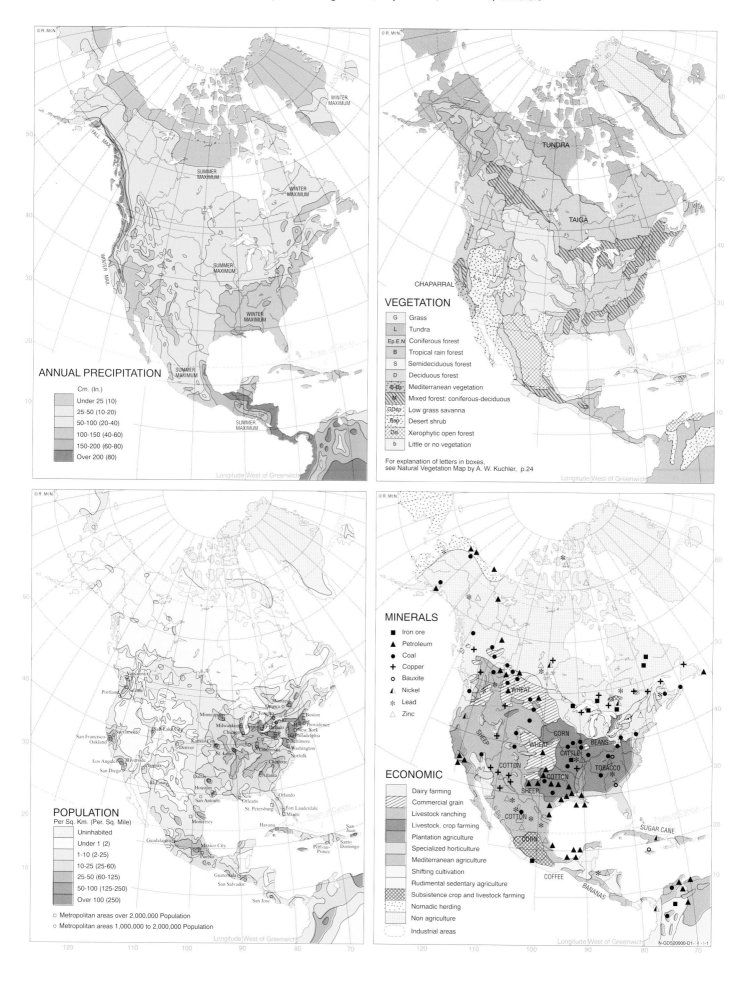

ANNUAL PRECIPITATION

Cm. (In.)
- Under 25 (10)
- 25-50 (10-20)
- 50-100 (20-40)
- 100-150 (40-60)
- 150-200 (60-80)
- Over 200 (80)

VEGETATION

G	Grass
L	Tundra
Ep.E.N	Coniferous forest
B	Tropical rain forest
S	Semideciduous forest
D	Deciduous forest
B-Bs	Mediterranean vegetation
M	Mixed forest: coniferous-deciduous
GDsp	Low grass savanna
Bsp	Desert shrub
Ds	Xerophytic open forest
b	Little or no vegetation

For explanation of letters in boxes,
see Natural Vegetation Map by A. W. Kuchler, p.24

POPULATION

Per Sq. Km. (Per. Sq. Mile)
- Uninhabited
- Under 1 (2)
- 1-10 (2-25)
- 10-25 (25-60)
- 25-50 (60-125)
- 50-100 (125-250)
- Over 100 (250)

☐ Metropolitan areas over 2,000,000 Population
○ Metropolitan areas 1,000,000 to 2,000,000 Population

MINERALS

- ■ Iron ore
- ▲ Petroleum
- ● Coal
- ✛ Copper
- ○ Bauxite
- ◮ Nickel
- ✳ Lead
- △ Zinc

ECONOMIC

- Dairy farming
- Commercial grain
- Livestock ranching
- Livestock, crop farming
- Plantation agriculture
- Specialized horticulture
- Mediterranean agriculture
- Shifting cultivation
- Rudimental sedentary agriculture
- Subsistence crop and livestock farming
- Nomadic herding
- Non agriculture
- Industrial areas

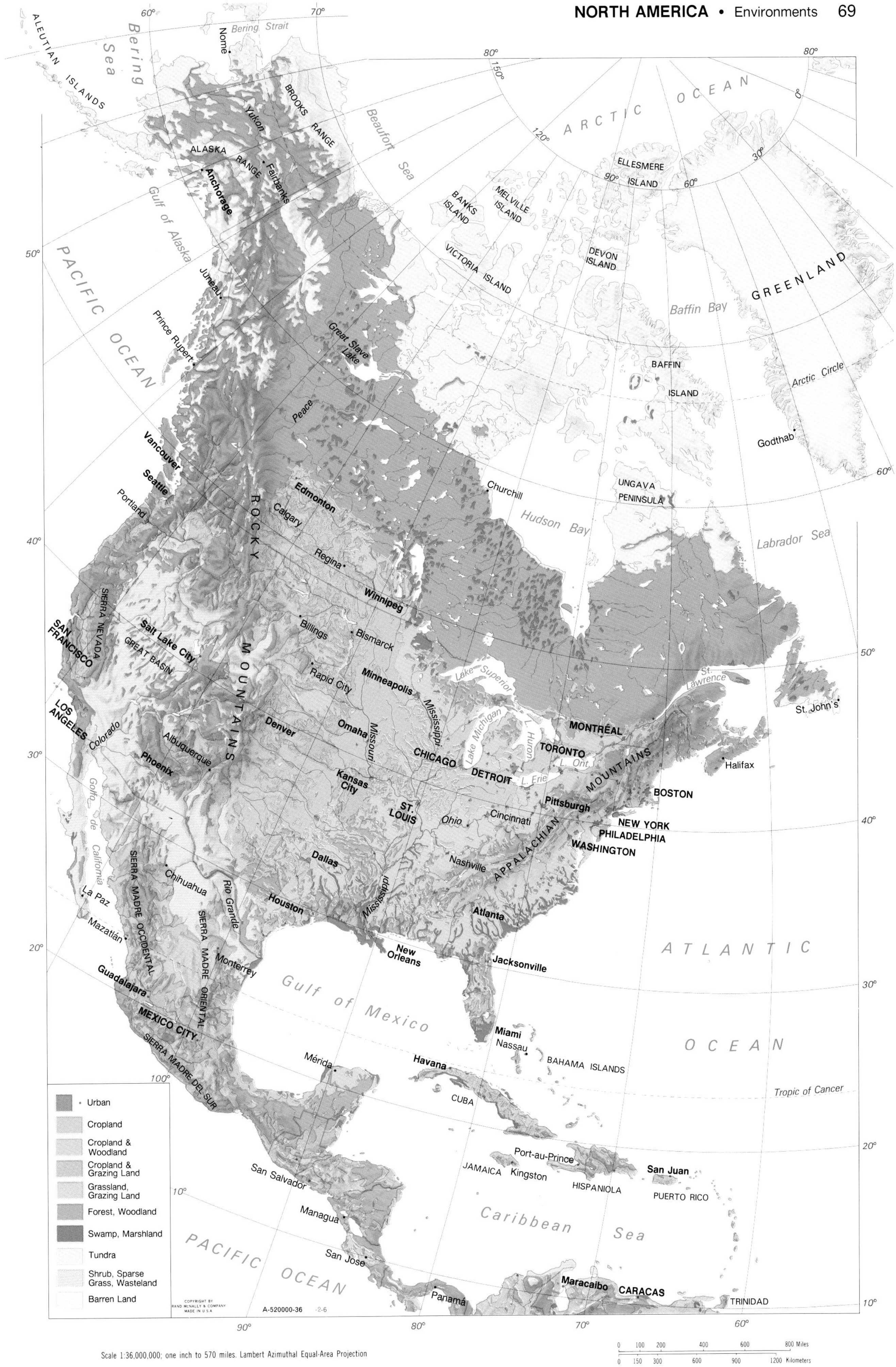

Legend

- Urban
- Cropland
- Cropland & Woodland
- Cropland & Grazing Land
- Grassland, Grazing Land
- Forest, Woodland
- Swamp, Marshland
- Tundra
- Shrub, Sparse Grass, Wasteland
- Barren Land

Scale 1:36,000,000; one inch to 570 miles. Lambert Azimuthal Equal-Area Projection

0 100 200 400 600 800 Miles
0 150 300 600 900 1200 Kilometers

COPYRIGHT BY
RAND McNALLY & COMPANY
MADE IN U.S.A.
A-520000-36   -2-6

Water bodies and regions

ARCTIC OCEAN
PACIFIC OCEAN
ATLANTIC OCEAN
Bering Sea
Bering Strait
Beaufort Sea
Gulf of Alaska
Baffin Bay
Labrador Sea
Hudson Bay
Gulf of Mexico
Caribbean Sea
Golfo de California
GREENLAND
Arctic Circle
Tropic of Cancer

Islands and land regions

ALEUTIAN ISLANDS
BANKS ISLAND
MELVILLE ISLAND
VICTORIA ISLAND
DEVON ISLAND
ELLESMERE ISLAND
BAFFIN ISLAND
UNGAVA PENINSULA
BAHAMA ISLANDS
CUBA
JAMAICA
HISPANIOLA
PUERTO RICO
TRINIDAD

Mountain ranges and physical features

BROOKS RANGE
ALASKA RANGE
ROCKY MOUNTAINS
SIERRA NEVADA
GREAT BASIN
SIERRA MADRE OCCIDENTAL
SIERRA MADRE ORIENTAL
SIERRA MADRE DEL SUR
APPALACHIAN MOUNTAINS

Rivers and lakes

Yukon
Peace
Great Slave Lake
Mississippi
Missouri
Ohio
Colorado
Rio Grande
St. Lawrence
Lake Superior
Lake Michigan
Lake Huron
L. Ont.
L. Erie

Cities

Nome
Anchorage
Fairbanks
Juneau
Prince Rupert
Vancouver
Seattle
Portland
San Francisco
Los Angeles
Salt Lake City
Phoenix
Albuquerque
Denver
Edmonton
Calgary
Regina
Winnipeg
Billings
Bismarck
Rapid City
Minneapolis
Omaha
Kansas City
St. Louis
Dallas
Houston
New Orleans
Chicago
Detroit
Cincinnati
Nashville
Atlanta
Jacksonville
Miami
Pittsburgh
Boston
New York
Philadelphia
Washington
Montréal
Toronto
Halifax
St. John's
Churchill
Godthab
Chihuahua
Monterrey
Mazatlán
La Paz
Guadalajara
Mexico City
Mérida
Havana
Nassau
Port-au-Prince
Kingston
San Juan
San Salvador
Managua
San Jose
Panamá
Maracaibo
Caracas

PHYSIOGRAPHIC DIVISIONS

1 Pacific Mountain System
2 Intermontane Plateaus
3 Rocky Mountain System
4 Interior Plains
5 Ozark-Ouachita Highlands
6 Gulf-Atlantic Plain
7 Appalachian Highlands
8 Laurentian Upland (Canadian Shield)
9 Hudson Bay Lowland

Scale 1:12 000 000; One inch to 190 miles.   POLYCONIC PROJECTION

0 25 50 75 100   200   300   400   500 Miles
0   50   200   400   600   800 Kilometers

lowland

Beach lines

Dunes

Albany R. sand

Moose R.

L. Nipigon

C L A Y   B E L T

ANTICOSTI I.

Gaspe

GASPE PA.

C. BRETON I.

PR. EDWARD I.

NOVA SCOTIA

Halifax

St. Lawrence R.

Saguenay R.

L. St. John

PARC DES LAURENTIDES

GRENVILLE FAULT ZONE

St. Maurice R.

Quebec

Ottawa R.

Gatineau R.

ALGONQUIN PARK

Pem

Ottawa

Montreal

Bay of Fundy

St. John R.

AROOSTOOK PLAIN

WHITE MTS.

Portland

Portsmouth

Concord

Merrimac R.

Boston

Cape Cod

Nantucket I.

Providence

LONG ISLAND

New York

Trenton

Philadelphia

Wilm.

Baltimore

C. May

Delaware Bay

Washington

Potomac R.

Dover

L. Superior

SUPERIOR UPLAND

KEWENAW PA.

602

PORCUPINE MTS.

HURON MTS.

Sault Ste Marie

GOGEBIC RA.

MENOMINEE RA.

CUESTA

L. Huron

581

L. Michigan

581

NIAGARA CUESTA

MAGNESIAN CUESTA

DRUMLINS

Milwaukee

Madison

Lansing

Detroit

St. Clair

Toledo

Cleveland

Akron

L. Erie

572

Erie

Buffalo

Niagara Falls

Toronto

L. Ontario

246

Ham.

MOHAWK SC.

Syr.

Roch.

ADIRONDACK MTS.

GREEN MTS.

CONNECTICUT R.

Hudson R.

POCONO PLAT.

ALLEGHENY FRONT

G R E A T   V A L L E Y

Pittsburgh

Columbus

Ohio R.

DRIFTLESS AREA

BARABOO RA.

MILITARY RA.

Dubuque

NIAGARA ESC.

Chicago

KANKAKEE R.

MAUMEE LAKE PLAIN

Wabash R.

Peoria

Springfield

Indianapolis

Dayton

Cincinnati

OLD DRIFT FLATS

D R I F T   P L A I N S

P R A I R I E S

Des Moines R.

Illinois R.

Mississippi R.

St. Louis

L. of the Ozarks

OZARK PLATEAU

SALEM UPLAND

ST. FRANCIS KNOBS

BOSTON MTS.

Springf.

White R.

Hot Spr.

OUACHITA MTS.

Little Rock

GRAND PRAIRIE

YAZOO BASIN

TENSAS BASIN

Mon.

Shrev.

Red R.

WOLD

PINE FLATS

ATCHAFALAYA DELTA

Baton Rouge

New Orleans

St. Louis

Evansville

Louisville

BLUEGRASS HILLS

MOULDRAUGS HILLS

WESTERN COALFIELDS

DRIPPING SPRINGS

KNOBS

Cumberland R.

NASHVILLE BASIN

Nashville

HIGHLAND RIM

C U M B E R L A N D   P L A T E A U

Chattanooga

Tennessee R.

Charleston

Kanawha R.

PINE RIDGE

BIG STONE RIDGE

GREAT SMOKY MTS.

B L U E   R I D G E

Knoxville

Asheville

Birmingham

TALLAPOOSA UPLAND

COOSA R.

P I E D M O N T

Atlanta

Augusta

Columbia

Charlotte

Raleigh

Richmond

Roanoke

Roanoke R.

James R.

Norfolk

C. Charles

C. Henry

Albemarle Sound

Dismal Swamp

Pamlico Sound

C. Hatteras

C. Lookout

Neuse R.

Pee Dee R.

C. Fear

Cape Fear R.

Charleston

Savannah

Altamaha R.

Ocmulgee R.

Oconee R.

F A L L   L I N E

PINE HILLS

MIDLAND SLOPE

C O A S T A L   P L A I N

JACKSON PLAIN

PONTOTOC RIDGE

FLATWOODS

LITTLE

Memphis

JACKSON PRAIRIE

RIPLEY ESC.

RED HILLS

Jackson

Selma

Montg.

Columbus

Mobile

Pensacola

Biloxi

DOUGHERTY PLAIN

TIFTON UPLAND

LIME SINK REGION

FLATWOODS

Jacksonville

St. Aug.

St. Johns R.

Tampa

St. Petersburg

HIGH PINE LANDS

PINE LANDS

BIG CYPRESS SWAMP

THE EVERGLADES

Okeechobee

Palm Beach

Miami

Key West

PHYSIOGRAPHY
BY ERWIN RAISZ

LITHOLOGY AND STRUCTURE

Unconsolidated deposits: alluvium, sands, playa deposits, etc.

Essentially horizontal sedimentary rocks; many partially unconsolidated.

Slightly to moderately tilted, older sedimentary rocks.

Steeply folded or faulted, sedimentary rocks

Volcanics; largely lava flows.

Metamorphic and intrusive igneous rocks; structure complex.

Limits of continental glaciation.

LANDFORMS

PLATEAUS

HILLS

MOUNTAINS

MESAS

CUESTAS

FOLDED MOUNTAINS

BASIN RANGES

VOLCANO AND LAVA

SAND

SINKS

MORAINES

DRUMLINS

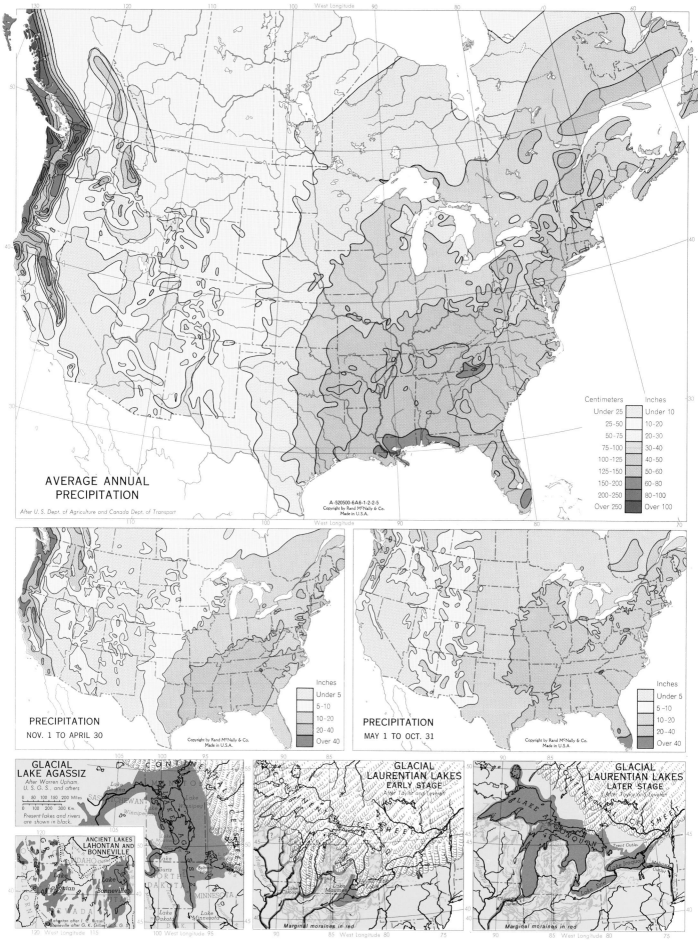

AVERAGE ANNUAL PRECIPITATION

After U. S. Dept. of Agriculture and Canada Dept. of Transport

A-520500-6A6-1-2-2-5
Copyright by Rand McNally & Co.
Made in U.S.A.

Centimeters	Inches
Under 25	Under 10
25–50	10–20
50–75	20–30
75–100	30–40
100–125	40–50
125–150	50–60
150–200	60–80
200–250	80–100
Over 250	Over 100

PRECIPITATION
NOV. 1 TO APRIL 30

Copyright by Rand McNally & Co.
Made in U.S.A.

Inches
Under 5
5–10
10–20
20–40
Over 40

PRECIPITATION
MAY 1 TO OCT. 31

Copyright by Rand McNally & Co.
Made in U.S.A.

Inches
Under 5
5–10
10–20
20–40
Over 40

GLACIAL LAKE AGASSIZ

*After Warren Upham,
U. S. G. S., and others*

0 50 100 150 200 Miles
0 100 200 300 Km.

*Present lakes and rivers
are shown in black.*

ANCIENT LAKES LAHONTAN AND BONNEVILLE

*Lahontan after I. C. Russell
Bonneville after G. K. Gilbert, U. S. G. S.*

GLACIAL LAURENTIAN LAKES
EARLY STAGE
After Taylor and Leverett

Marginal moraines in red

GLACIAL LAURENTIAN LAKES
LATER STAGE
After Taylor and Leverett

Marginal moraines in red

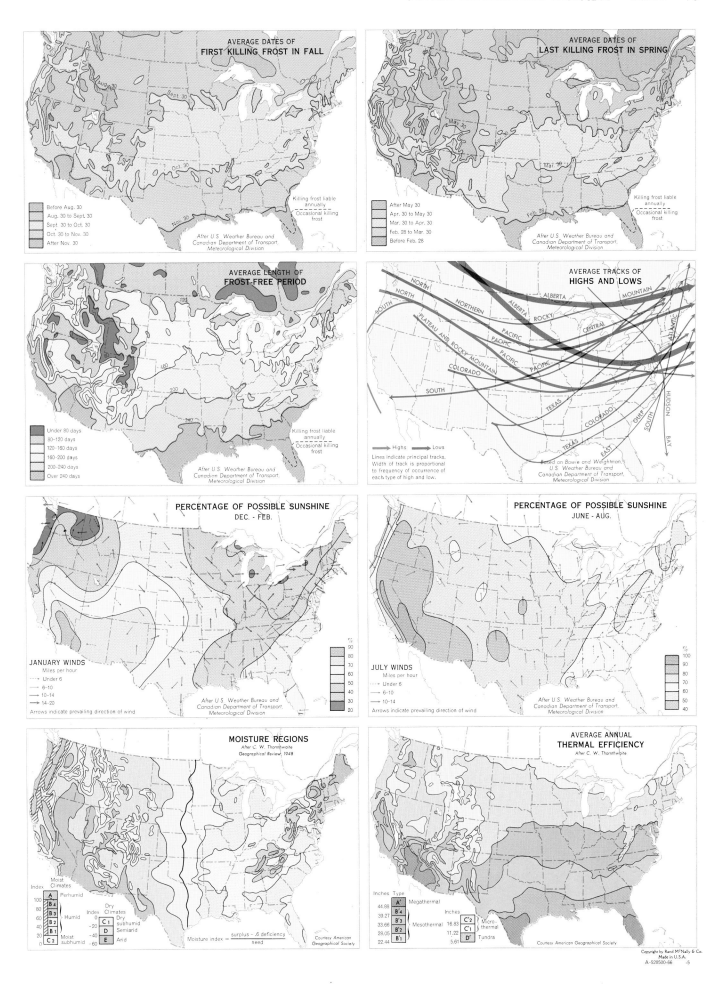

AVERAGE DATES OF
FIRST KILLING FROST IN FALL

Before Aug. 30
Aug. 30 to Sept. 30
Sept. 30 to Oct. 30
Oct. 30 to Nov. 30
After Nov. 30

Killing frost liable
annually

Occasional killing
frost

After U.S. Weather Bureau and
Canadian Department of Transport,
Meteorological Division

AVERAGE DATES OF
LAST KILLING FROST IN SPRING

After May 30
Apr. 30 to May 30
Mar. 30 to Apr. 30
Feb. 28 to Mar. 30
Before Feb. 28

Killing frost liable
annually

Occasional killing
frost

After U.S. Weather Bureau and
Canadian Department of Transport,
Meteorological Division

AVERAGE LENGTH OF
FROST-FREE PERIOD

Under 80 days
80–120 days
120–160 days
160–200 days
200–240 days
Over 240 days

Killing frost liable
annually

Occasional killing
frost

After U.S. Weather Bureau and
Canadian Department of Transport,
Meteorological Division

AVERAGE TRACKS OF
HIGHS AND LOWS

Highs   Lows

Lines indicate principal tracks,
Width of track is proportional
to frequency of occurrence of
each type of high and low.

Based on Bowie and Weightman,
U.S. Weather Bureau and
Canadian Department of Transport,
Meteorological Division

PERCENTAGE OF POSSIBLE SUNSHINE
DEC. - FEB.

JANUARY WINDS
Miles per hour
Under 6
6–10
10–14
14–20
Arrows indicate prevailing direction of wind

%
90
80
70
60
50
40
30
20

After U.S. Weather Bureau and
Canadian Department of Transport,
Meteorological Division

PERCENTAGE OF POSSIBLE SUNSHINE
JUNE - AUG.

JULY WINDS
Miles per hour
Under 6
6–10
10–14
Arrows indicate prevailing direction of wind

%
100
90
80
70
60
50
40

After U.S. Weather Bureau and
Canadian Department of Transport,
Meteorological Division

MOISTURE REGIONS
After C. W. Thornthwaite
Geographical Review, 1948

Index Moist
Climates
100 A   Perhumid
80   B4
60   B3 Humid
40   B2
20   B1
0   C2 Moist
subhumid

Index Dry
Climates
C1   Dry
0   subhumid
-20 D   Semiarid
-40
-60 E   Arid

Moisture index = surplus − .6 deficiency / need

Courtesy American
Geographical Society

AVERAGE ANNUAL
THERMAL EFFICIENCY
After C. W. Thornthwaite

Inches Type
44.88   A'   Megathermal
39.27   B'4
33.66   B'3 Mesothermal
28.05   B'2
22.44   B'1

Inches
16.83   C'2 Micro-
11.22   C'1 thermal
5.61   D'   Tundra

Courtesy American Geographical Society

74

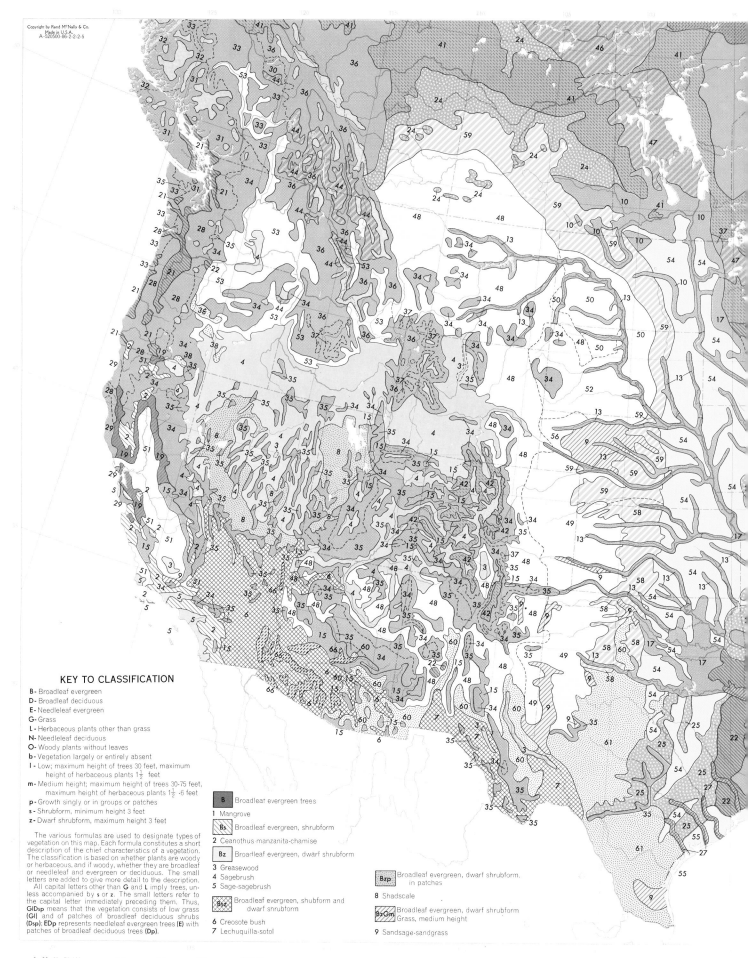

KEY TO CLASSIFICATION

B - Broadleaf evergreen
D - Broadleaf deciduous
E - Needleleaf evergreen
G - Grass
L - Herbaceous plants other than grass
N - Needleleaf deciduous
O - Woody plants without leaves
b - Vegetation largely or entirely absent
l - Low; maximum height of trees 30 feet, maximum
   height of herbaceous plants 1½ feet
m - Medium height; maximum height of trees 30-75 feet,
   maximum height of herbaceous plants 1½ -6 feet
p - Growth singly or in groups or patches
s - Shrubform, minimum height 3 feet
z - Dwarf shrubform, maximum height 3 feet

The various formulas are used to designate types of
vegetation on this map. Each formula constitutes a short
description of the chief characteristics of a vegetation.
The classification is based on whether plants are woody
or herbaceous, and if woody, whether they are broadleaf
or needleleaf and evergreen or deciduous. The small
letters are added to give more detail to the description.

All capital letters other than **G** and **L** imply trees, un-
less accompanied by **s** or **z**. The small letters refer to
the capital letter immediately preceding them. Thus,
GlDsp means that the vegetation consists of low grass
(Gl) and of patches of broadleaf deciduous shrubs
(Dsp); EDp represents needleleaf evergreen trees (E) with
patches of broadleaf deciduous trees (Dp).

B	Broadleaf evergreen trees
1	Mangrove
Bs	Broadleaf evergreen, shrubform
2	Ceanothus manzanita-chamise
Bz	Broadleaf evergreen, dwarf shrubform
3	Greasewood
4	Sagebrush
5	Sage-sagebrush
Bsz	Broadleaf evergreen, shubform and dwarf shrubform
6	Creosote bush
7	Lechuquilla-sotol

Bzp	Broadleaf evergreen, dwarf shrubform, in patches
8	Shadscale
BzGm	Broadleaf evergreen, dwarf shrubform Grass, medium height
9	Sandsage-sandgrass

0 25 50 75 100   200   300   400   500 Miles

0 50 100   200   400   600   800 Kilometers

Scale 1 : 14 000 000;   One inch to 220 m

NATURAL VEGETATION

BY A. W. KÜCHLER

Based on "A Physiognomic Classification of Vegetation"
Annals of the Assoc. of American Geographers, Vol. 39, September, 1949

	D	Broadleaf deciduous trees
10 Aspen-oak
11 Beech-maple
12 Beech-tulip tree-maple-basswood
13 Cottonwood-willow
14 Maple-basswood
15 Oak
16 Oak-ash-maple
17 Oak-hickory
18 Oak-tulip tree

DB Broadleaf deciduous trees
Broadleaf evergreen trees

19 Oak-madrone

DE Broadleaf deciduous trees
Needleleaf evergreen trees

20 Maple-yellow birch-hemlock-pine
21 Oak-Douglas fir
22 Oak-pine
23 Maple-beech-hemlock

D Broadleaf deciduous trees
Gmp Grass, medium height, in patches

24 Aspen-needle grass-wheat grass
25 Oak-hickory-bluestem

DN Broadleaf deciduous trees
Needleleaf deciduous trees

26 Bay trees-bald cypress
27 Tupelo-gum-bald cypress

E Needleleaf evergreen trees

28 Douglas fir
29 Douglas fir-redwood
30 Hemlock-arbor vitae
31 Hemlock-arbor vitae-Douglas fir
32 Hemlock-arbor vitae-fir
33 Hemlock-spruce
34 Pine
35 Pine-juniper
36 Pine-spruce
37 Spruce-fir

Esp Needleleaf evergreen, shrubform,
in patches

38 Juniper

EDp Needleleaf evergreen trees
Broadleaf deciduous trees, in patches

39 Douglas fir-pine-aspen
40 Pine-spruce-birch
41 Spruce-aspen
42 Spruce-fir-aspen
43 Spruce-poplar-birch

EN Needleleaf evergreen trees
Needleleaf deciduous trees

44 Hemlock-arbor vitae-Douglas fir-larch
45 Pine-bald cypress
46 Pine-spruce-larch
47 Spruce-larch

Gl Grass, low

48 Grama grass
49 Grama grass-buffalo grass
50 Grama grass-needle grass
51 Needle grass-blue grass
52 Wheat grass
53 Wheat grass-blue grass

Gm Grass, medium height

54 Bluestem
55 Broom grass-water grass
56 Marsh grass
57 Saw grass

Gml Grass, medium and low height

58 Bluestem-bunch grass
59 Needle grass-wheat grass

Gl Grass, low
Dsp Broadleaf deciduous, shrubform, in patches
60 Bunch grass-oak

Gm Grass, medium height
Dsp Broadleaf deciduous, shrubform, in patches
61 Mesquite grass-mesquite

L Herbaceous plants other than grass

62 Lichens, etc.

LEp Herbaceous plants other than grass
Needleleaf evergreen trees, in patches
63 Lichens-spruce

LEp Herbaceous plants other than grass
Np Needleleaf evergreen trees, in patches
Needleleaf deciduous trees, in patches
64 Lichens-spruce-larch

N Needleleaf deciduous trees

65 Bald cypress

Op Woody plants without leaves, in patches
66 Palo verde-cacti-ocotillo

b Vegetation largely or entirely absent

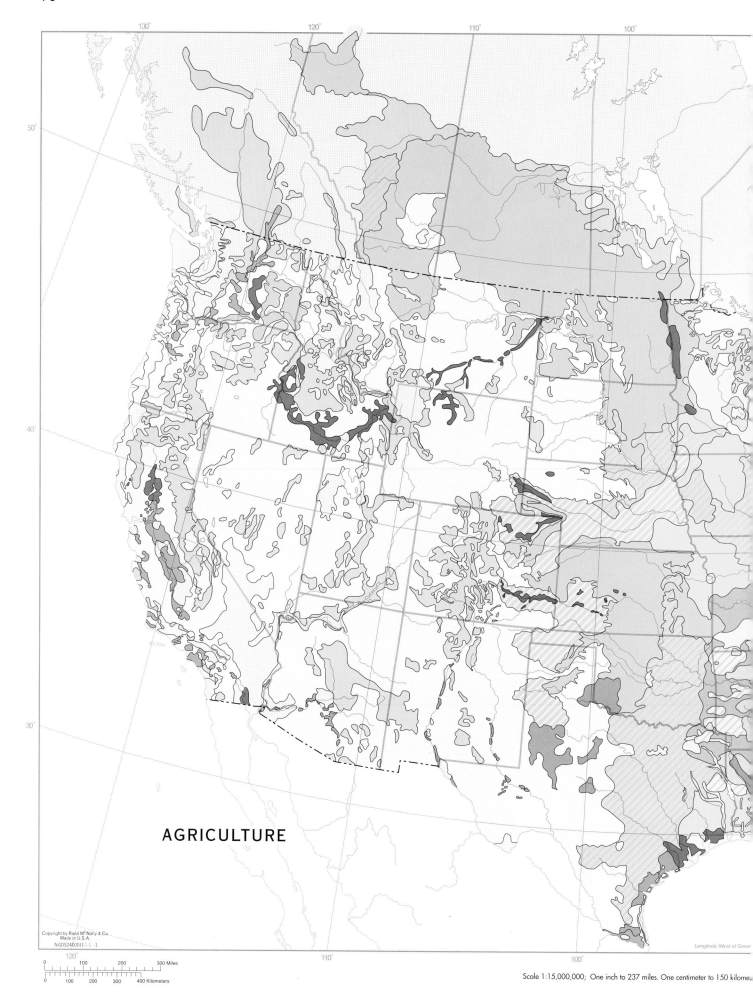

AGRICULTURE

0   100   200   300 Miles

0   100   200   300   400 Kilometers

Scale 1:15,000,000; One inch to 237 miles. One centimeter to 150 kilome.

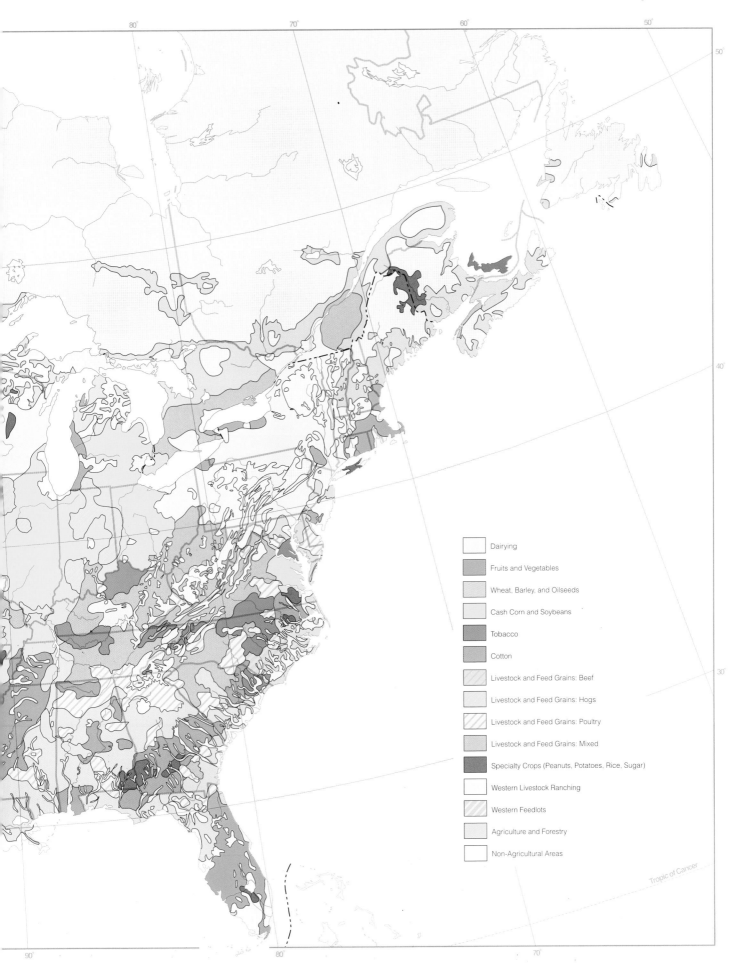

Dairying

Fruits and Vegetables

Wheat, Barley, and Oilseeds

Cash Corn and Soybeans

Tobacco

Cotton

Livestock and Feed Grains: Beef

Livestock and Feed Grains: Hogs

Livestock and Feed Grains: Poultry

Livestock and Feed Grains: Mixed

Specialty Crops (Peanuts, Potatoes, Rice, Sugar)

Western Livestock Ranching

Western Feedlots

Agriculture and Forestry

Non-Agricultural Areas

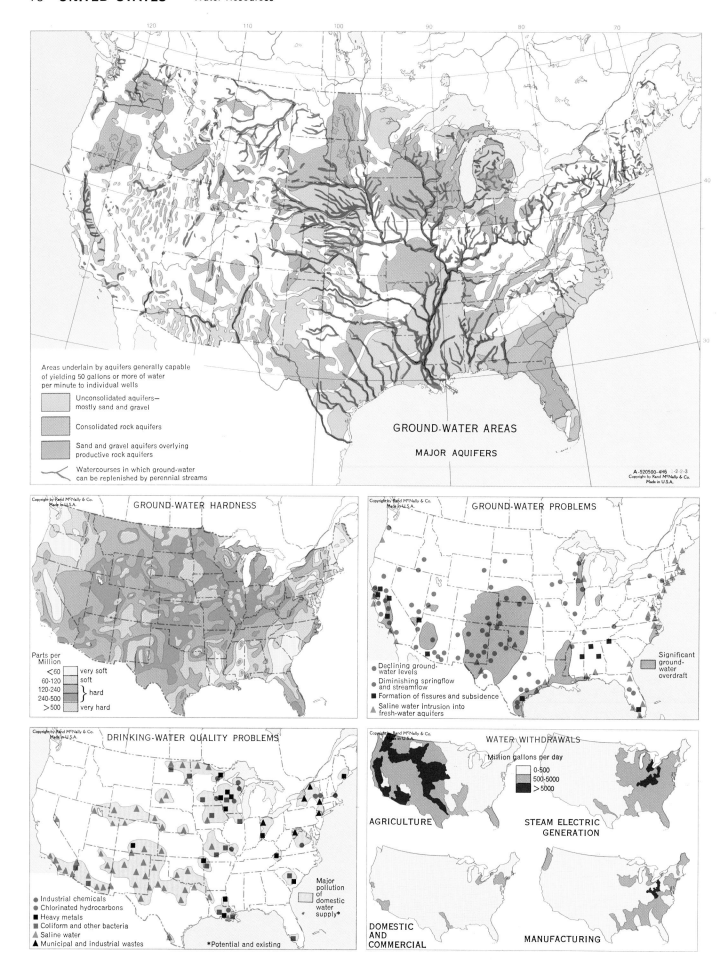

GROUND-WATER AREAS

MAJOR AQUIFERS

Areas underlain by aquifers generally capable
of yielding 50 gallons or more of water
per minute to individual wells

Unconsolidated aquifers—
mostly sand and gravel

Consolidated rock aquifers

Sand and gravel aquifers overlying
productive rock aquifers

Watercourses in which ground-water
can be replenished by perennial streams

A-520500-4H6 -2-2-3
Copyright by Rand McNally & Co.
Made in U.S.A.

GROUND-WATER HARDNESS

Parts per
Million
<60   very soft
60-120   soft
120-240   } hard
240-500
>500   very hard

GROUND-WATER PROBLEMS

● Declining ground-
  water levels
● Diminishing springflow
  and streamflow
■ Formation of fissures and subsidence
▲ Saline water intrusion into
  fresh-water aquifers

Significant
ground-
water
overdraft

DRINKING-WATER QUALITY PROBLEMS

● Industrial chemicals
● Chlorinated hydrocarbons
■ Heavy metals
■ Coliform and other bacteria
▲ Saline water
▲ Municipal and industrial wastes

Major
pollution
of
domestic
water
supply*

*Potential and existing

WATER WITHDRAWALS

Million gallons per day
0-500
500-5000
>5000

AGRICULTURE

STEAM ELECTRIC
GENERATION

DOMESTIC
AND
COMMERCIAL

MANUFACTURING

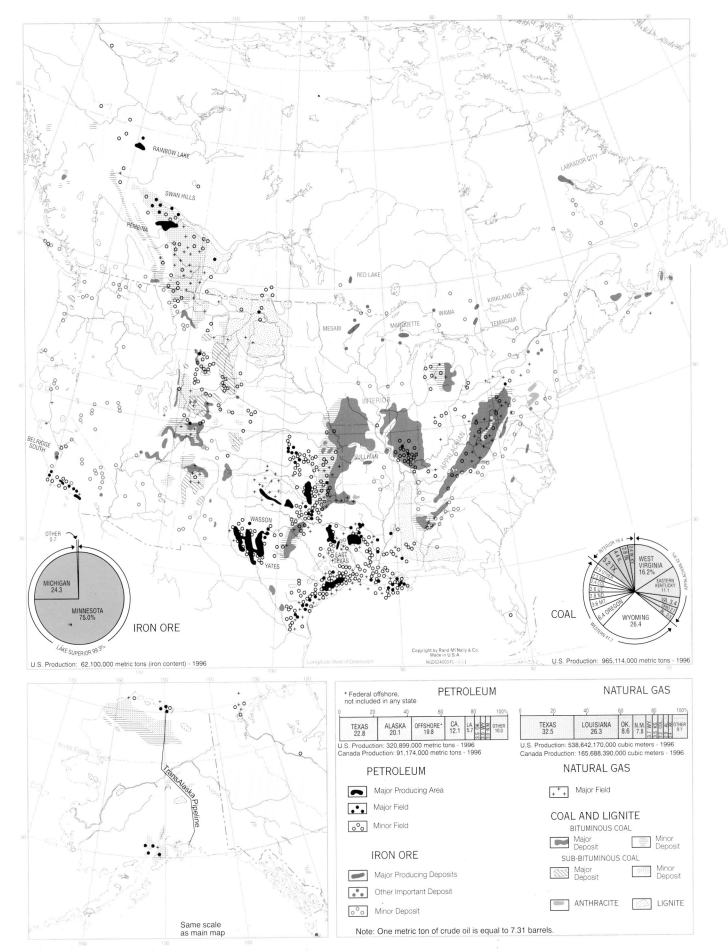

RAINBOW LAKE

SWAN HILLS

PEMBINA

LABRADOR CITY

RED LAKE

KIRKLAND LAKE

MESABI

MARQUETTE

WAWA

TEMAGAMI

INTERIOR

BELRIDGE SOUTH

SULLIVAN

APPALACHIAN

WASSON

EAST TEXAS

YATES

OTHER 0.7

MICHIGAN 24.3

MINNESOTA 75.0%

LAKE SUPERIOR 99.3%

IRON ORE

U.S. Production: 62,100,000 metric tons (iron content) - 1996

Copyright by Rand McNally & Co.
Made in U.S.A.
NGDS24000-F1-·-7-1-1

Longitude West of Greenwich

INTERIOR 16.4

24 W.V.

4.4 IL

2.8 W.V.

5.2 TX

2.9 OTHER

2.3 IN

2.4 CO

2.6 UT

2.8 ND

3.6 MT

6.4 OREGON

APPALACHIAN 40.9%

WEST VIRGINIA 16.2%

EASTERN KENTUCKY 11.1

VA. 3.4

OHIO 2.7

AL. 2.3

WYOMING 26.4

WESTERN 41.7

COAL

U.S. Production: 965,114,000 metric tons - 1996

TransAlaska Pipeline

Arctic Circle

Same scale
as main map

Scale 1:29,000,000; One inch to 457 miles.   ALBERS CONIC PROJECTION

* Federal offshore,
not included in any state

PETROLEUM

0	20	40	60	80	100%

TEXAS 22.8	ALASKA 20.1	OFFSHORE* 19.8	CA. 12.1	LA. 5.7	3.5 OK	OTHER 10.0

U.S. Production: 320,899,000 metric tons - 1996
Canada Production: 91,174,000 metric tons - 1996

NATURAL GAS

0	20	40	60	80	100%

TEXAS 32.5	LOUISIANA 26.3	OK. 8.6	N.M. 7.8	3.7 WY	3.5 KS	2.6 CO	OTHER 9.1

U.S. Production: 538,642,170,000 cubic meters - 1996
Canada Production: 165,688,390,000 cubic meters - 1996

PETROLEUM

Major Producing Area

Major Field

Minor Field

IRON ORE

Major Producing Deposits

Other Important Deposit

Minor Deposit

NATURAL GAS

Major Field

COAL AND LIGNITE

BITUMINOUS COAL

Major Deposit   Minor Deposit

SUB-BITUMINOUS COAL

Major Deposit   Minor Deposit

ANTHRACITE   LIGNITE

Note: One metric ton of crude oil is equal to 7.31 barrels.

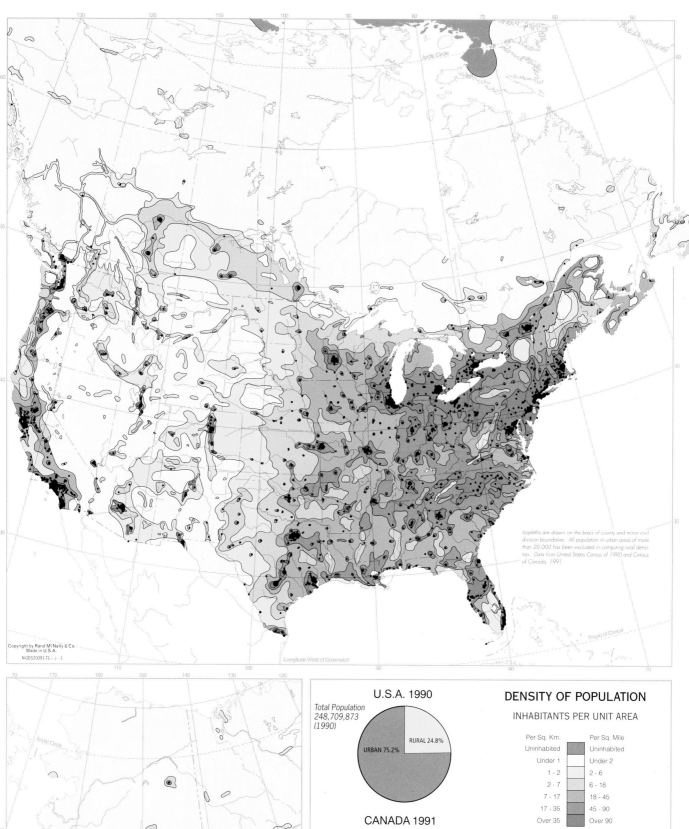

Isopleths are drawn on the basis of county and minor civil division boundaries. All population in urban areas of more than 20,000 has been excluded in computing rural densities. Data from United States Census of 1990 and Census of Canada, 1991

Copyright by Rand McNally & Co.
Made in U.S.A.
N-GDS20091-T1-|-:-|- -:-1

Longitude West of Greenwich

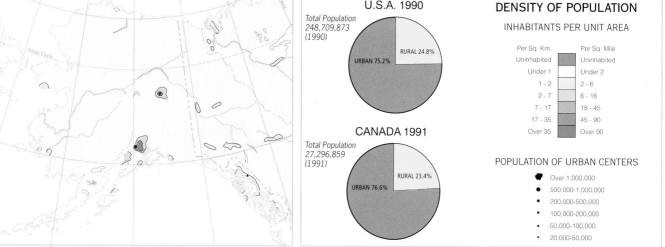

U.S.A. 1990

Total Population
248,709,873
(1990)

URBAN 75.2%   RURAL 24.8%

CANADA 1991

Total Population
27,296,859
(1991)

URBAN 76.6%   RURAL 23.4%

DENSITY OF POPULATION

INHABITANTS PER UNIT AREA

Per Sq. Km.	Per Sq. Mile
Uninhabited	Uninhabited
Under 1	Under 2
1 - 2	2 - 6
2 - 7	6 - 18
7 - 17	18 - 45
17 - 35	45 - 90
Over 35	Over 90

POPULATION OF URBAN CENTERS

- Over 1,000,000
- 500,000-1,000,000
- 200,000-500,000
- 100,000-200,000
- 50,000-100,000
- 20,000-50,000

Scale 1:29,000,000; One inch to 457 miles.   ALBERS CONIC PROJECTION

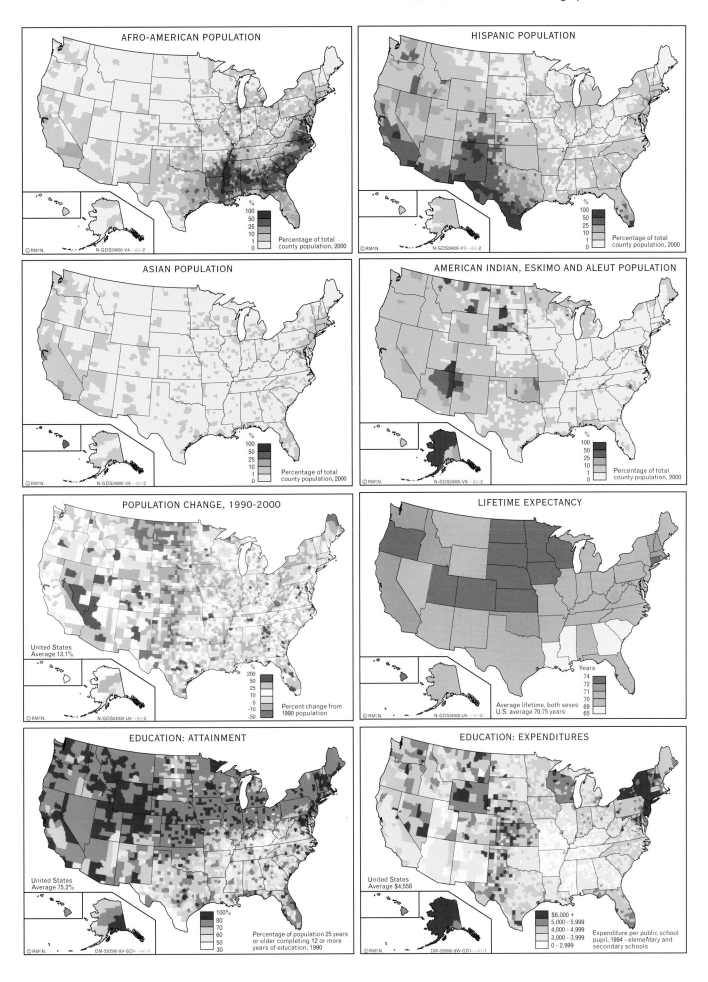

AFRO-AMERICAN POPULATION

%
100
50
25
10
1
0
Percentage of total
county population, 2000

HISPANIC POPULATION

%
100
50
25
10
1
0
Percentage of total
county population, 2000

ASIAN POPULATION

%
100
50
25
10
1
0
Percentage of total
county population, 2000

AMERICAN INDIAN, ESKIMO AND ALEUT POPULATION

%
100
50
25
10
1
0
Percentage of total
county population, 2000

POPULATION CHANGE, 1990-2000

United States
Average 13.1%

%
200
50
25
10
0
-10
-50
Percent change from
1990 population

LIFETIME EXPECTANCY

Years
74
72
71
70
69
65
Average lifetime, both sexes
U.S. average 70.75 years

EDUCATION: ATTAINMENT

United States
Average 75.2%

100%
80
70
60
50
30
Percentage of population 25 years
or older completing 12 or more
years of education, 1990

EDUCATION: EXPENDITURES

United States
Average $4,558

$6,000 +
5,000 - 5,999
4,000 - 4,999
3,000 - 3,999
0 - 2,999
Expenditure per public school
pupil, 1994 - elementary and
secondary schools

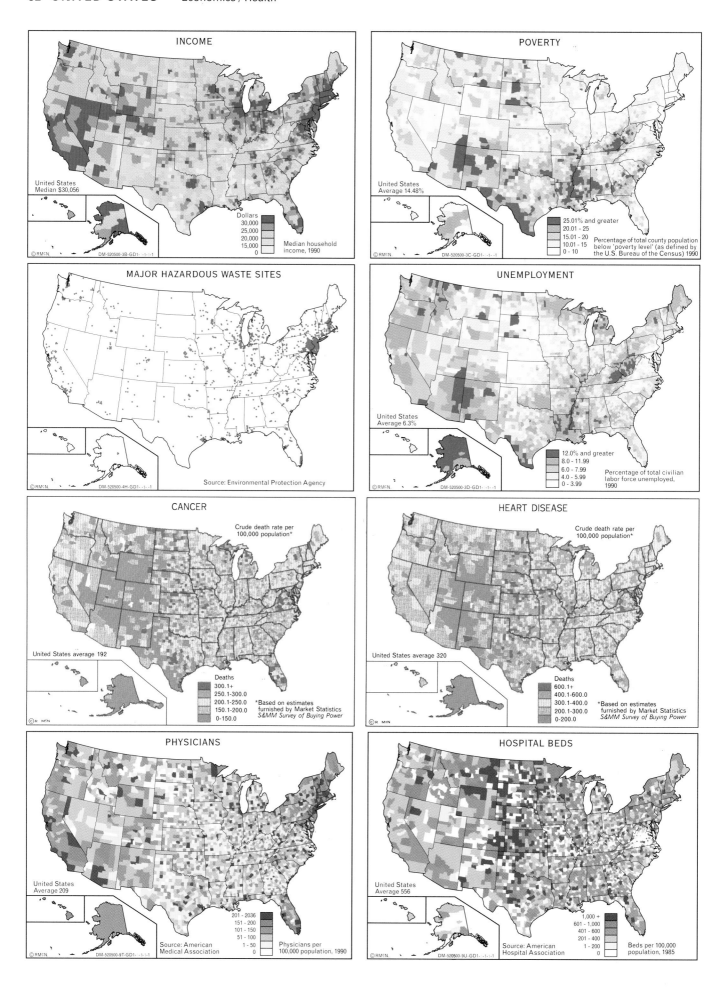

INCOME

United States
Median $30,056

Dollars
30,000
25,000
20,000
15,000
0

Median household
income, 1990

© RMcN. DM-520500-3B-GD1- -1- -1-1

POVERTY

United States
Average 14.48%

25.01% and greater
20.01 - 25
15.01 - 20
10.01 - 15
0 - 10

Percentage of total county population
below 'poverty level' (as defined by
the U.S. Bureau of the Census) 1990

© RMcN. DM-520500-3C-GD1- -1- -1

MAJOR HAZARDOUS WASTE SITES

Source: Environmental Protection Agency

© RMcN. DM-520500-4H-GD1- -1- -1

UNEMPLOYMENT

United States
Average 6.3%

12.0% and greater
8.0 - 11.99
6.0 - 7.99
4.0 - 5.99
0 - 3.99

Percentage of total civilian
labor force unemployed,
1990

© RMcN. DM-520500-3D-GD1- -1- -1

CANCER

Crude death rate per
100,000 population*

United States average 192

Deaths
300.1+
250.1-300.0
200.1-250.0
150.1-200.0
0-150.0

*Based on estimates
furnished by Market Statistics
S&MM Survey of Buying Power

© R McN

HEART DISEASE

Crude death rate per
100,000 population*

United States average 320

Deaths
600.1+
400.1-600.0
300.1-400.0
200.1-300.0
0-200.0

*Based on estimates
furnished by Market Statistics
S&MM Survey of Buying Power

© R McN

PHYSICIANS

United States
Average 209

201 - 2036
151 - 200
101 - 150
51 - 100
1 - 50
0

Physicians per
100,000 population, 1990

Source: American
Medical Association

© RMcN. DM-520500-9T-GD1- -1- -1-1

HOSPITAL BEDS

United States
Average 556

1,000 +
601 - 1,000
401 - 600
201 - 400
1 - 200
0

Beds per 100,000
population, 1985

Source: American
Hospital Association

© RMcN. DM-520500-9U-GD1- -1- -1-1

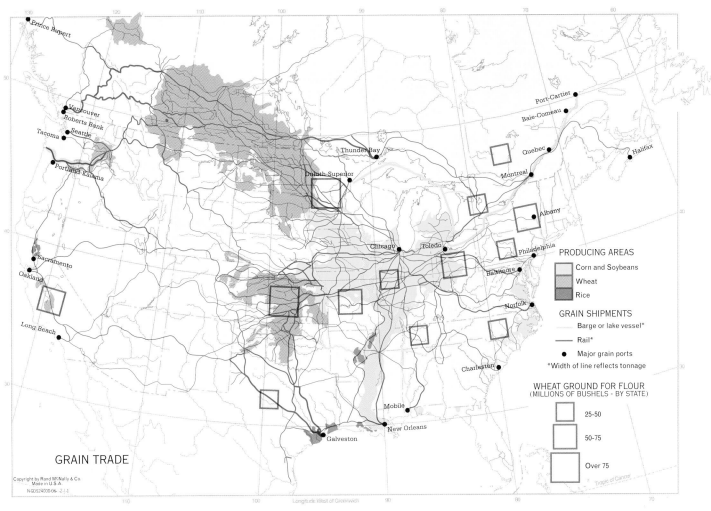

GRAIN TRADE

PRODUCING AREAS
- Corn and Soybeans
- Wheat
- Rice

GRAIN SHIPMENTS
- Barge or lake vessel*
- Rail*
- Major grain ports
*Width of line reflects tonnage

WHEAT GROUND FOR FLOUR
(MILLIONS OF BUSHELS - BY STATE)
- 25-50
- 50-75
- Over 75

Copyright by Rand McNally & Co.
Made in U.S.A.
N-GDS24000-06- -2-I-I

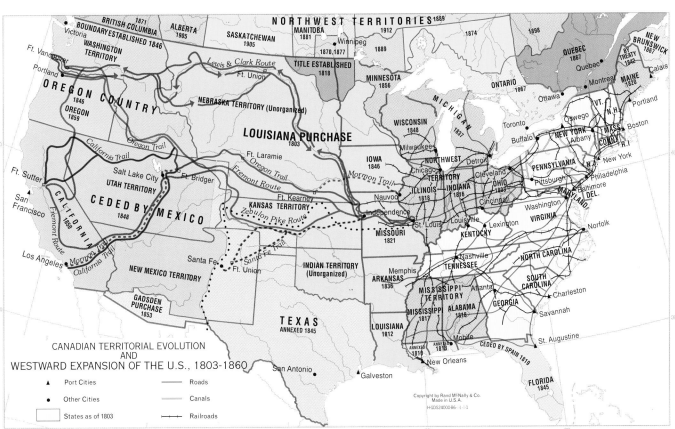

CANADIAN TERRITORIAL EVOLUTION
AND
WESTWARD EXPANSION OF THE U.S., 1803-1860

- ▲ Port Cities
- ● Other Cities
- ☐ States as of 1803
- —— Roads
- —— Canals
- ┼┼ Railroads

Copyright by Rand McNally & Co.
Made in U.S.A.
H-GDS24000-86- -I-I-I

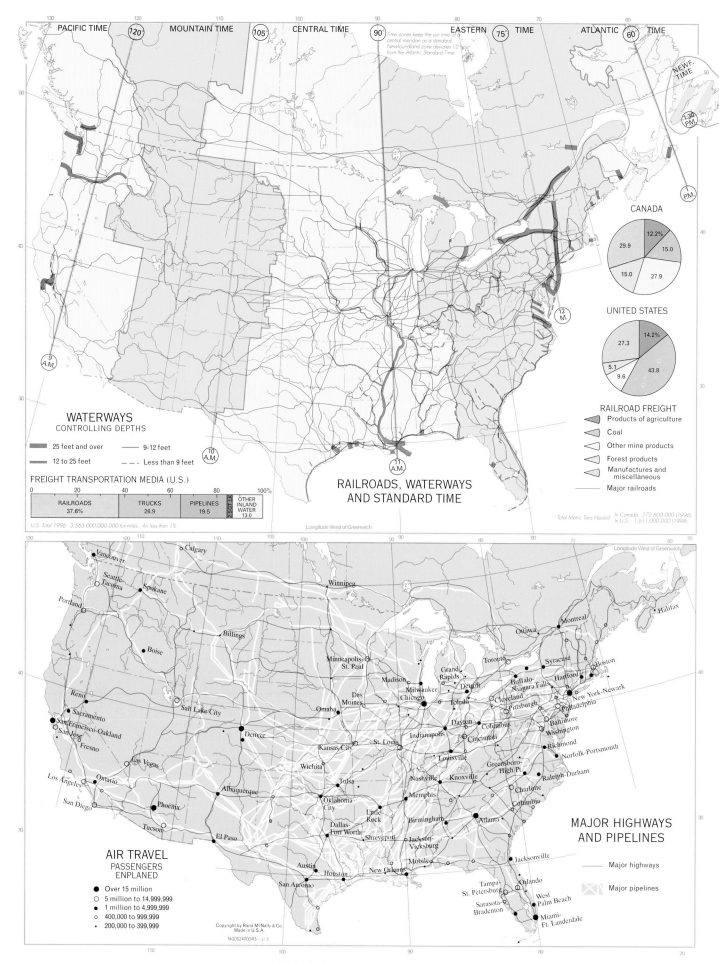

PACIFIC TIME ⑫⓪ MOUNTAIN TIME ⑩⑤ CENTRAL TIME ⑨⓪ Time zones keep the sun time of a EASTERN ⑦⑤ TIME ATLANTIC ⑥⓪ TIME
central meridian as a standard.
Newfoundland zone deviates 1/2 hour
from the Atlantic Standard Time

NEWF. TIME

1:30 P.M.

1 P.M.

12 M.

CANADA

12.2%
29.9   15.0
15.0   27.9

UNITED STATES

14.2%
27.3   43.8
5.1
9.6

WATERWAYS
CONTROLLING DEPTHS

— 25 feet and over   — 9-12 feet
— 12 to 25 feet   --- Less than 9 feet

FREIGHT TRANSPORTATION MEDIA (U.S.)

0	20	40	60	80	100%
RAILROADS 37.6%		TRUCKS 26.9		PIPELINES 19.5	2.5 GT UK / OTHER INLAND WATER 13.0

U.S. Total 1996 - 3,563,000,000,000 ton-miles. Air less than 1%

RAILROADS, WATERWAYS
AND STANDARD TIME

RAILROAD FREIGHT
◤ Products of agriculture
◤ Coal
◤ Other mine products
◤ Forest products
◤ Manufactures and miscellaneous
— Major railroads

Total Metric Tons Hauled   In Canada - 272,600,000 (1996)
In U.S. - 1,611,000,000 (1998)

Longitude West of Greenwich

Longitude West of Greenwich

AIR TRAVEL
PASSENGERS ENPLANED

● Over 15 million
○ 5 million to 14,999,999
• 1 million to 4,999,999
○ 400,000 to 999,999
· 200,000 to 399,999

MAJOR HIGHWAYS
AND PIPELINES

— Major highways
⊠ Major pipelines

Copyright by Rand McNally & Co.
Made in U.S.A.

NGDS24000-R3- -|-|-

Scale 1:29,000,000; One inch to 457 miles.   ALBERS CONIC PROJECTION

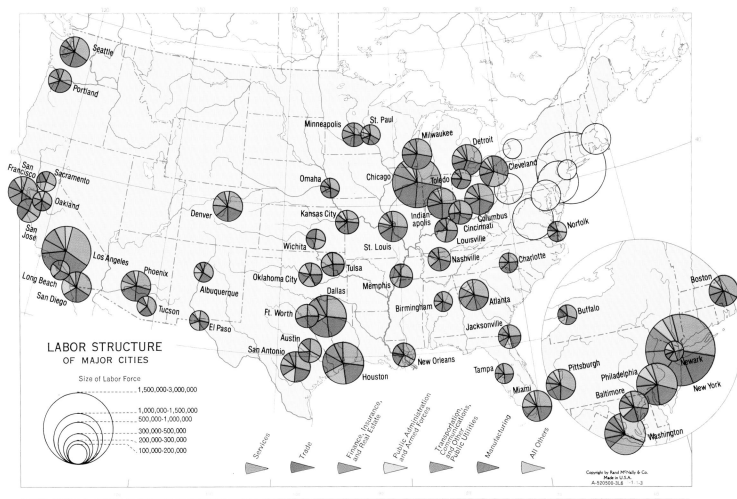

LABOR STRUCTURE
OF MAJOR CITIES

Size of Labor Force

- 1,500,000-3,000,000
- 1,000,000-1,500,000
- 500,000-1,000,000
- 300,000-500,000
- 200,000-300,000
- 100,000-200,000

Services

Trade

Finance, Insurance, and Real Estate

Public Administration and Armed Forces

Transportation, Communications, and Other Public Utilities

Manufacturing

All Others

Copyright by Rand McNally & Co.
Made in U.S.A.
A-520500-3L6   -1 -1 -3

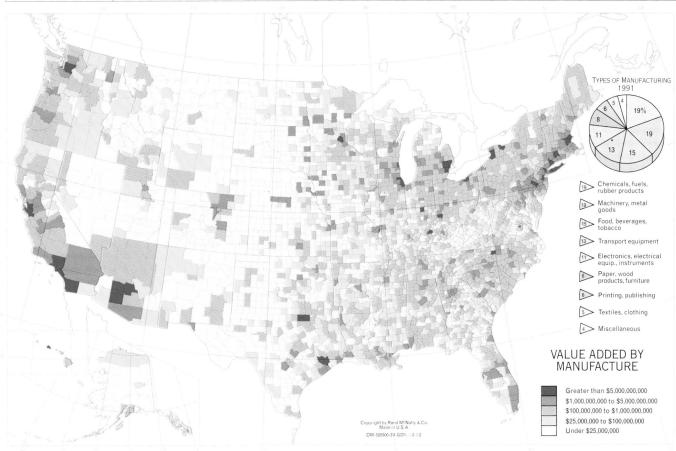

TYPES OF MANUFACTURING
1991

19%

19

15

13

11

8

6

5

4

- 19 Chemicals, fuels, rubber products
- 19 Machinery, metal goods
- 15 Food, beverages, tobacco
- 13 Transport equipment
- 11 Electronics, electrical equip., instruments
- 8 Paper, wood products, furniture
- 6 Printing, publishing
- 5 Textiles, clothing
- 4 Miscellaneous

VALUE ADDED BY MANUFACTURE

- Greater than $5,000,000,000
- $1,000,000,000 to $5,000,000,000
- $100,000,000 to $1,000,000,000
- $25,000,000 to $100,000,000
- Under $25,000,000

Copyright by Rand McNally & Co.
Made in U.S.A.
DM-520500-3V-GD1- -2-9-2

Scale 1:12,000,000.

One inch to 190 miles.
One centimeter to 120 kilometers.

Albers Conic Projection

0   50   100   200   300   400 Miles

0 50 100 150 200   300   400   500   600 Kilometers

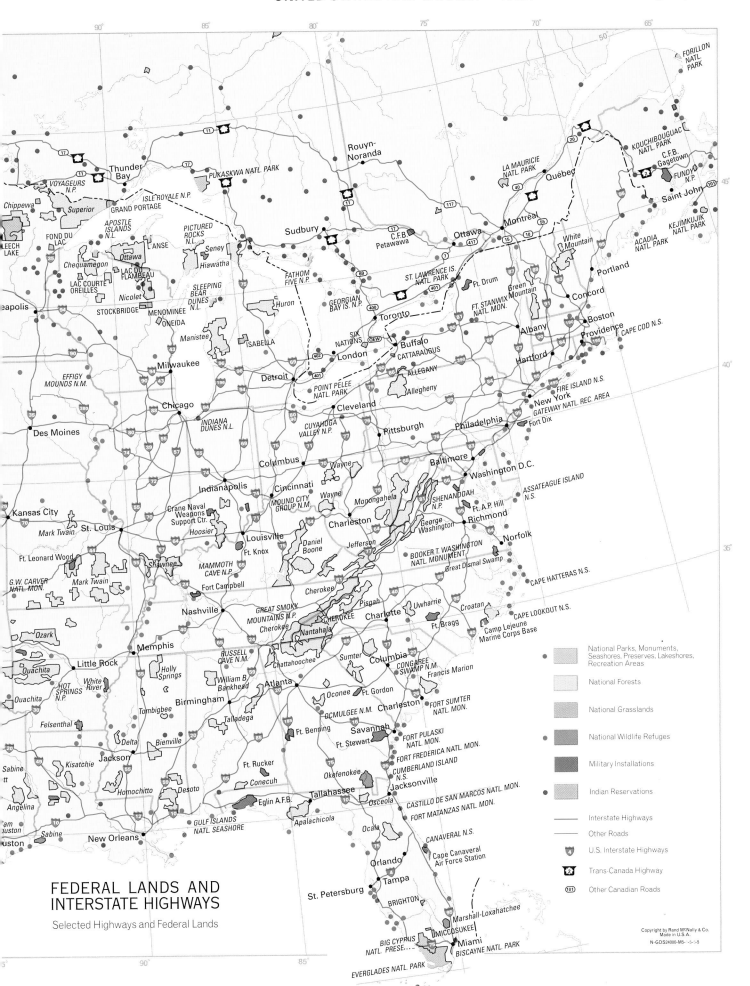

FEDERAL LANDS AND INTERSTATE HIGHWAYS

Selected Highways and Federal Lands

	National Parks, Monuments, Seashores, Preserves, Lakeshores, Recreation Areas
	National Forests
	National Grasslands
	National Wildlife Refuges
	Military Installations
	Indian Reservations
	Interstate Highways
	Other Roads
	U.S. Interstate Highways
	Trans-Canada Highway
	Other Canadian Roads

Copyright by Rand McNally & Co.
Made in U.S.A.

N-GDS24000-M5- -5- -5

Scale 1:40 000 000; one inch to 630 miles. Lambert's Azimuthal Equal-Area Projection
Elevations and depressions are given in feet

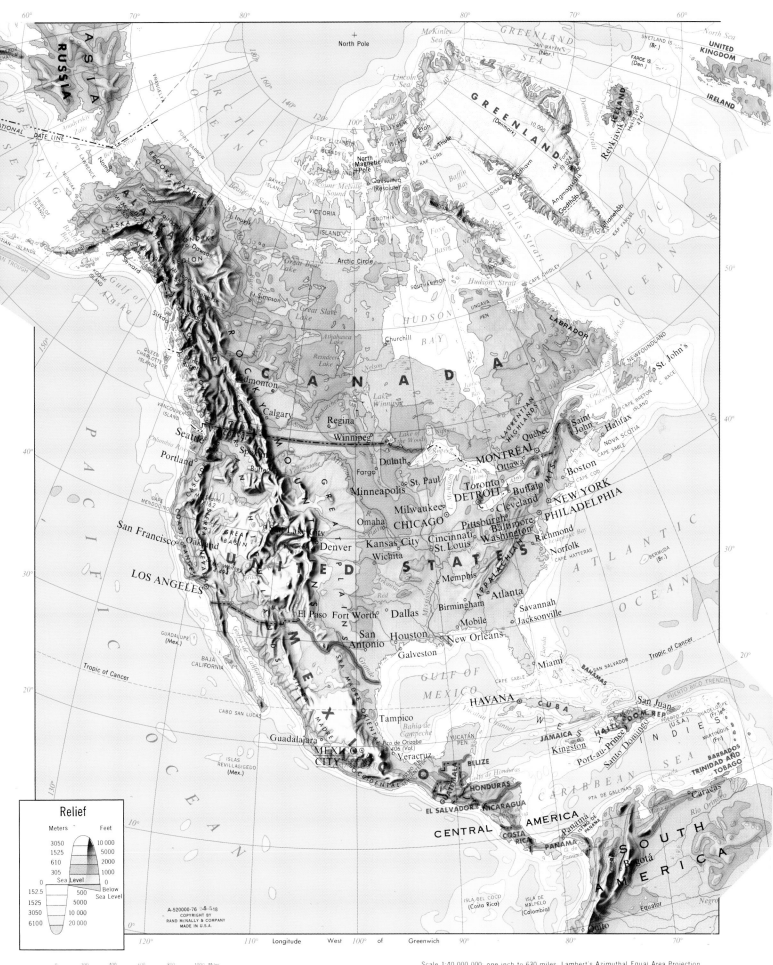

RUSSIA
ASIA
BERING SEA
NATIONAL DATE LINE
BROOKS RANGE
ALASKA
Nome
Fairbanks
Anchorage
ALASKA
Gulf of Alaska
KODIAK GRAND
Seward
ALEUTIAN ISLANDS
ALEUTIAN TROUGH
PRIBILOF ISLANDS
NUNIVAK
ST. LAWRENCE
POINT BARROW
Beaufort Sea
Inuvik
KLONDIKE REGION
Dawson
ARCTIC OCEAN
WRANGELIA
North Pole
North Magnetic Pole
Qausuittuq (Resolute)
ELLESMERE
QUEEN ELIZABETH ISLANDS
PARRY ISLANDS
Viscount Melville Sound
BANKS ISLAND
VICTORIA ISLAND
PRINCE OF WALES ISLAND
SOMERSET
BOOTHIA PEN
McKinley Sea
Lincoln Sea
Etah
Thule
KAP YORK
GREENLAND (Denmark)
10,000
Mt. Forel
Kangerlussuaq
Godhavn
DISKO
Godthåb
Angmagssalik
Julianehåb
KAP FARVEL
GREENLAND SEA
JAN MAYEN (Nor.)
SHETLAND IS. (Br.)
FAROE IS. (Den.)
ICELAND
Reykjavík
Hekla (Vol.) 4747
Denmark Strait
North Sea
UNITED KINGDOM
IRELAND
Arctic Circle
Great Bear Lake
El Simpson
Great Slave Lake
Athabasca Lake
Reindeer Lake
CANADA
Edmonton
ROCKY
Calgary
Regina
Winnipeg
Lake Winnipeg
Nelson R.
Saskatchewan R.
Lake of the Woods
Churchill
HUDSON BAY
SOUTHAMPTON
FOXE BASIN
BAFFIN ISLAND
Baffin Bay
Davis Strait
UNGAVA
Ungava Bay
LABRADOR
CAPE CHIDLEY
ATLANTIC OCEAN
NEWFOUNDLAND
St. John's
C. RACE
HUDSON STRAIT
Hudson Strait
QUEEN CHARLOTTE ISLANDS
VANCOUVER ISLAND
Vancouver
Seattle
Spokane
Portland
Columbia River
COAST RANGES
CAPE MENDOCINO
San Francisco
Oakland
SIERRA NEVADA
Mt. Shasta 162
LOS ANGELES
GUADALUPE (Mex.)
Tropic of Cancer
BAJA CALIFORNIA
ISLAS REVILLAGIGEDO (Mex.)
CABO SAN LUCAS
Mt. Whitney 14,494
GREAT BASIN
Lake City
Denver
UNITED STATES
Butte
Yellowstone
Helena
MOUNTAINS
GREAT PLAINS
Duluth
Fargo
Minneapolis
St. Paul
Milwaukee
CHICAGO
Omaha
Platte R.
Kansas City
St. Louis
Wichita
Arkansas R.
Red R.
Memphis
El Paso
Fort Worth
Dallas
San Antonio
Houston
Galveston
New Orleans
Mobile
Birmingham
Atlanta
Savannah
Jacksonville
Miami
DETROIT
Cleveland
Buffalo
Toronto
Ottawa
MONTRÉAL
Québec
Saint John
Halifax
NOVA SCOTIA
CAPE BRETON ISLAND
CAPE SABLE
Boston
CAPE COD
NEW YORK
PHILADELPHIA
Washington
Baltimore
Pittsburgh
Cincinnati
Richmond
Norfolk
CAPE HATTERAS
APPALACHIAN MTS.
LAURENTIAN HIGHLANDS
Gulf of St. Lawrence
BERMUDA (Br.)
ATLANTIC OCEAN
PACIFIC OCEAN
MEXICO
SIERRA MADRE ORIENTAL
SIERRA MADRE OCCIDENTAL
Guadalajara
MEXICO CITY
Tampico
Veracruz
Pico de Orizaba 18,406 (Vol.)
Bahía de Campeche
YUCATÁN PEN.
GULF OF MEXICO
HAVANA
CUBA
CAPE SABLE
Yucatan Channel
BAHAMAS
SAN SALVADOR
Tropic of Cancer
San Juan
PUERTO RICO (U.S.A.)
PUERTO RICO TRENCH
GUADELOUPE (Fr.)
MARTINIQUE (Fr.)
BARBADOS
TRINIDAD AND TOBAGO
HAITI
DOM. REP.
JAMAICA
Kingston
Port-au-Prince
Santo Domingo
WEST INDIES
CARIBBEAN SEA
GUATEMALA
BELIZE
HONDURAS
EL SALVADOR
NICARAGUA
COSTA RICA
PANAMA
G. de Panamá
ISTMO DE PANAMÁ
CENTRAL AMERICA
PTA DE GALLINAS
Caracas
Rio Orinoco
SOUTH AMERICA
Bogotá
Equator
Quito
Negro
ISLA DEL COCO (Costa Rica)
ISLA DE MALPELO (Colombia)

A-520000-76
COPYRIGHT BY
RAND MCNALLY & COMPANY
MADE IN U.S.A.

Relief

Meters		Feet
3050		10 000
1525		5000
610		2000
305		1000
	Sea Level	0
152.5		500 Below
1525		5000 Sea Level
3050		10 000
6100		20 000

| | 200 | 400 | 600 | 800 | 1000 Miles |
| 400 | | 800 | 1200 | 1600 Kilometers |

Scale 1:40 000 000: one inch to 630 miles. Lambert's Azimuthal Equal Area Projection
Elevations and depressions are given in feet

Longitude West 100° of Greenwich

Continued on pages 104-105

Scale 1: 12 000 000; one inch to 190 miles. Conic Projection

Elevations and depressions are given in feet

Longitude West of Greenwich

QUEBEC

Same scale as
main map

NEWFOUNDLAND
AND
LABRADOR

CAPE BAULD

C. ST. JOHN

Gulf of
St. Lawrence
GROS MORNE
NAT'L PARK
Deer Lake
Corner Brook
Stephenville
Botwood
Grand Falls
Windsor
Gander
Bonavista

NEWFOUNDLAND
St.
George's
Channel-Port-aux-Basques
Grand Bank
Burin
St. Pierre and Miquelon (Fr.)

Twillingate

Trinity

St. John's

CAPE RAY
CAPE NORTH
CAPE BRETON
ISLAND

ATLANTIC OCEAN

MELVILLE
PENINSULA

Foxe
Basin

Arctic Circle

BAFFIN

ISLAND

Cumberland Sound

A   U   T

Foxe
Channel

SOUTHAMPTON
ISLAND

Iqaluit

Frobisher Bay

HALL
PEN.

EVERETT
MTS.

RESOLUTION

HUDSON

BAY

All islands within bays and straits
lie within Nunavut.

Hudson
Strait

Ungava
Bay

TORNGAT
MTS.

Hebron

Nain

PENINSULE

D'UNGAVA

NEWFOUNDLAND AND LABRADOR

MEALY MTS.

Hopedale
Makkovik
Rigolet

Cartwright

Battle Harbour

Happy
Valley-
Goose Bay

L   A   B   R   A   D   O   R

Churchill Falls

Hamilton Inlet

C. ST. ANTHONY

LONG RANGE MTS.

GROS MORNE
NAT'L PARK

Corner Brook
Stephenville
St. George's

Schefferville

Lac
Bienville

Caniapiscau

Q   U   E   B   E   C

MTS.
OTISH

R. aux Outardes

Sept-Îles

ÎLE D'ANTICOSTI

ONTARIO

Fort Severn

James
Bay

Chisasibi

La Grande

Eastmain

Nichicun

Lac Mistassini

Gulf of
St. Lawrence

ÎLES DE LA MADELEINE

CHIC-CHOCS
MTS.

Gaspé

PEI.
PRINCE EDWARD
NAT'L PARK

NEW
BRUNSWICK

NOVA SCOTIA

Halifax

Saint John

MAINE

Québec
Lévis

MONTRÉAL

Ottawa

TORONTO

Lake Ontario

NEW YORK

PENNSYLVANIA

ATLANTIC
OCEAN

BOSTON

VERMONT
NEW HAMPSHIRE
MASS.
CONN.
R.I.

Albany

40,000 SQ MI
AREA
0   100   200
Miles

0 25 50 75 100   200   300   400   500 Miles
0   100   200   400   600   800 Kilometers

A-520200-26 · 10·9·23
COPYRIGHT BY
RAND MCNALLY & COMPANY
MADE IN U.S.A.

Continued on pages 106-107

Scale 1: 12 000 000; one inch to 190 miles. Conic Projection

Elevations and depressions are given in feet

Longitude West of Greenwich

Scale 1:4 000 000; one inch to 64 miles. Conic Projection

Elevations and depressions are given in feet.

Longitude West of Greenwich

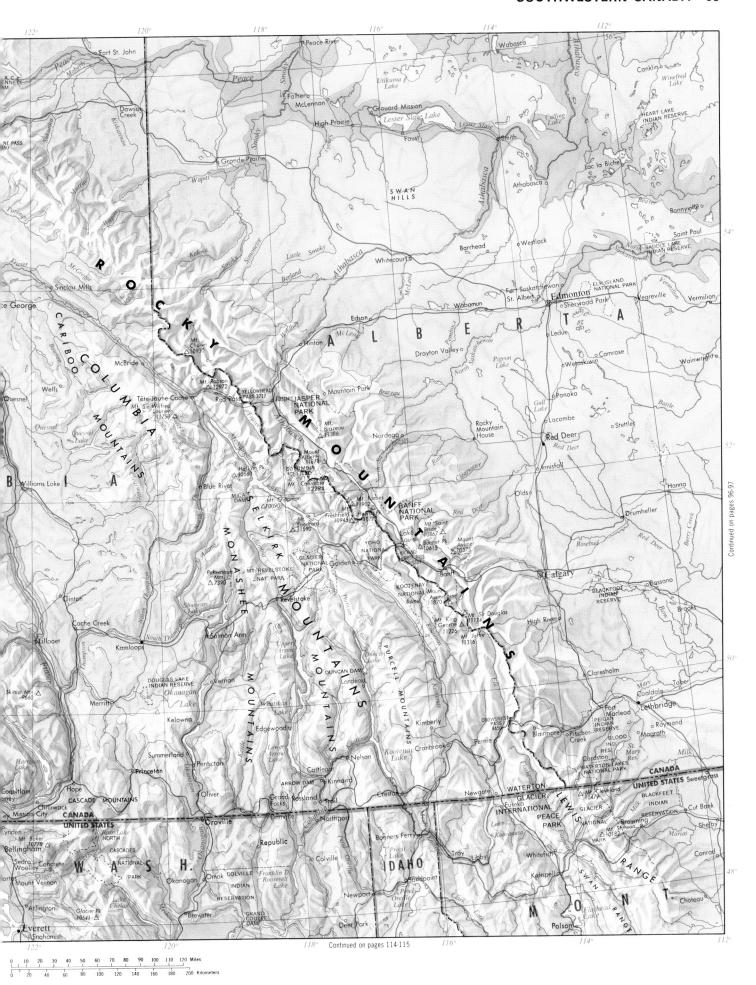

Continued on pages 96-97

Continued on pages 114-115

0 10 20 30 40 50 60 70 80 90 100 110 120 Miles

0   20   40   60   80   100   120   140   160   180   200 Kilometers

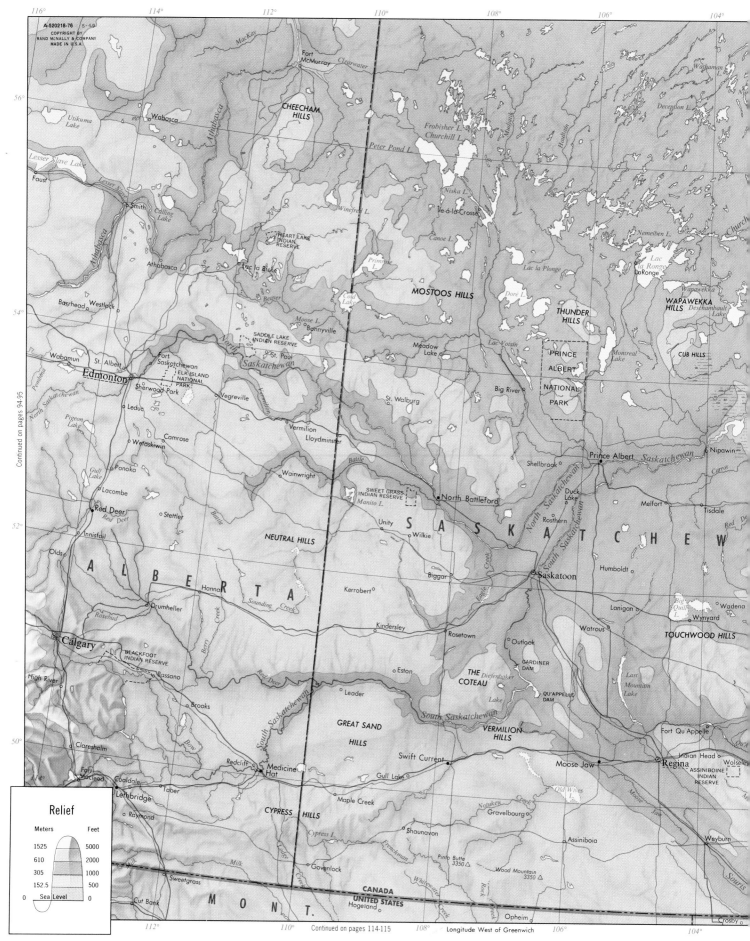

A-520218-76   5-49
COPYRIGHT BY
RAND McNALLY & COMPANY
MADE IN U.S.A.

116°   114°   112°   110°   108°   106°   104°

56°

54°

52°

50°

Continued on pages 94-95

Relief

Meters		Feet
1525		5000
610		2000
305		1000
152.5		500
0	Sea Level	0

MacKay
Fort McMurray   Clearwater
CHEECHAM HILLS
Athabasca
Utikuma Lake   Wabasca   Frobisher L.   Churchill L.   Deception L.
Peter Pond L.   Wathaman L.
Lesser Slave Lake   Lesser Slave   Winefred L.   Île-à-la-Crosse   Niska L.
Faust   Calling Lake   Primrose L.   Canoe L.   Nemeiben L.
Smith   HEART LAKE INDIAN RESERVE   Lac la Plonge   Lac la Ronge   LaRonge
Athabasca   Lac la Biche   Cold Lake   MOSTOOS HILLS   Doré L.   Wapawekka L.
Barrhead   Westlock   Beaver   Moose L.   Bonnyville   Meadow Lake   Lac Voisin   THUNDER HILLS   WAPAWEKKA HILLS   Deschambault Lake
Wabamun   St. Albert   SADDLE LAKE INDIAN RESERVE   St. Paul   PRINCE   Montreal Lake   CUB HILLS
Edmonton   Fort Saskatchewan   North   Saskatchewan   St. Walburg   Big River   ALBERT
Sherwood Park   ELK ISLAND NATIONAL PARK   Vegreville   NATIONAL
Ledue   Vermilion   PARK
Pigeon Lake   Camrose   Vermilion   Lloydminster   Prince Albert   Saskatchewan   Nipawin
Wetaskiwin   Shellbrook   Carrot
Ponoka   Wainwright   Battle   Rosthern   Melfort   Tisdale
Gull Lake   Duck Lake   Red De
Lacombe   Battle   SWEET GRASS INDIAN RESERVE   North Battleford   SASKATCHEWAN
Red Deer   Manito L.   Unity   Wilkie   Humboldt
Innisfail   Stettler   NEUTRAL HILLS   Big Quill L.
Olds   ALBERTA   Hanna   Biggar   Saskatoon   Lanigan   Wadena
Drumheller   Kerrobert   Watrous   Wynyard   TOUCHWOOD HILLS
Calgary   Rosebud   Sounding Creek   Kindersley   Rosetown   Outlook   GARDINER DAM   Last Mountain Lake
BLACKFOOT INDIAN RESERVE   Berry Creek   Eston   THE COTEAU   Diefenbaker   QU'APPELLE DAM
High River   Bassano   Red Deer   Leader   GARDINER DAM
Brooks   South Saskatchewan   GREAT SAND HILLS   South Saskatchewan   Fort Qu'Appelle
Claresholm   Bow   VERMILION HILLS
Redcliff   Swift Current   Moose Jaw   Regina   Wolseley
Fort Macleod   Medicine Hat   Gull Lake   Old Wives L.   Indian Head   ASSINIBOINE INDIAN RESERVE
Coaldale   Taber   Maple Creek   Gravelbourg
Lethbridge   Raymond   CYPRESS HILLS   Notukeu   Cr   Weyburn
Cypress L.   Shaunavon   Assiniboia
Pinto Butte 3350△   Wood Mountain 3350△
Milk   Govenlock   Frenchman   Whitemud
Sweetgrass   CANADA   Opheim   Crosby
Cut Bank   MONT.   UNITED STATES   Hogeland   South

112°   110°   Continued on pages 114-115   108°   Longitude West of Greenwich   106°   104°

Scale 1:4 000 000; one inch to 64 miles. Conic Projection
Elevations and depressions are given in feet.

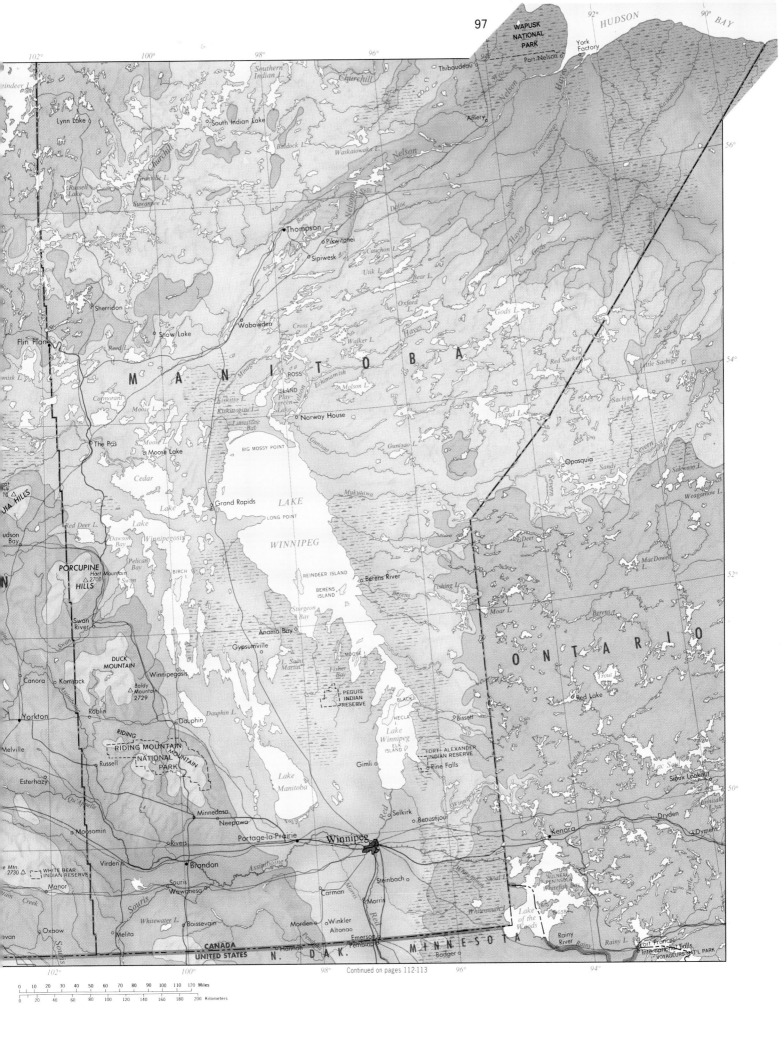

HUDSON BAY

WAPUSK NATIONAL PARK

York Factory

Port Nelson

Thibaudeau

Amery

Reindeer L.

Lynn Lake

South Indian Lake

Southern Indian L.

Churchill

Nelson

Baldock L.

Waskaiowaka L.

Granville L.

Russell Lake

Suwannee L.

Churchill

Burntwood

Thompson

Pikwitonei

Sipiwesk

Split L.

Daloe

Gods

Hayes

Sherridon

Cross L.

Walker L.

Utik L.

Bear L.

Cauchon L.

Oxford L.

Gods L.

Snow Lake

Wabowden

Hayes

Red Sucker L.

Flin Flon

Reed L.

ROSS

Echimamish

Molson L.

Island L.

Sachigo

Cormorant

Kiskitto L.

Kiskinogisu L.

Play-green Lake

ISLAND

Norway House

Nelson

Little Sachigo

The Pas

S. Moose L.

Moose Lake

Limestone Bay

Gunisao

Gunisao L.

Opasquia

Sandy

Salawaso L.

Cedar Lake

Big Mossy Point

LAKE

Grand Rapids

LONG POINT

Mukutawa

Severn

Weagamow L.

Lake Winnipegosis

Dawson Bay

WINNIPEG

PORCUPINE HILLS

Hart Mountain 2700

Pelican Bay

Swan L.

BIRCH L.

Reindeer Island

Berens River

Deer L.

MacDowell L.

Berens

Fishing L.

Berens R.

Swan River

BERENS ISLAND

Sturgeon Bay

Moar L.

ONTARIO

Canora

Kamsack

Winnipegosis

Anama Bay

Gypsumville

L. St. Martin

Fisher Bay

MOOSE I.

Trout L.

Red Lake

Yorkton

Baldy Mountain 2729

Roblin

Dauphin L.

PEGUIS INDIAN RESERVE

BLACK I.

Dauphin

HECLA I.

Bissett

Melville

RIDING MOUNTAIN

Lake Winnipeg

ELK ISLAND

FORT ALEXANDER INDIAN RESERVE

Sioux Lookout

RIDING MOUNTAIN NATIONAL PARK

Russell

Gimli

Pine Falls

Lac Seul

Esterhazy

Ou'Appelle

Lake Manitoba

Selkirk

English

Dryden

Minnedosa

Neepawa

Beausejour

Kenora

Dymehi

Moosomin

Rivers

Portage-la-Prairie

Winnipeg

Mo. Mtn. 2730

WHITE BEAR INDIAN RESERVE

Virden

Brandon

Assiniboine

Steinbach

Whitemouth L.

Whitefish

Manor

Souris

Wawanesa

Carman

Morris

Lake of the Woods

Rainy L.

Oxbow

Melita

Whitewater L.

Boissevain

Morden

Winkler

Altona

Emerson

Rainy River

Fort Frances

Souris Creek

CANADA

UNITED STATES

N. DAK.

Hannah

Pembina

Badger L.

MINNESOTA

International Falls

VOYAGEURS NAT'L PARK

Continued on pages 112-113

102° 100° 98° 96° 94° 92° 90°

56° 54° 52° 50°

0 10 20 30 40 50 60 70 80 90 100 110 120 Miles

0 20 40 60 80 100 120 140 160 180 200 Kilometers

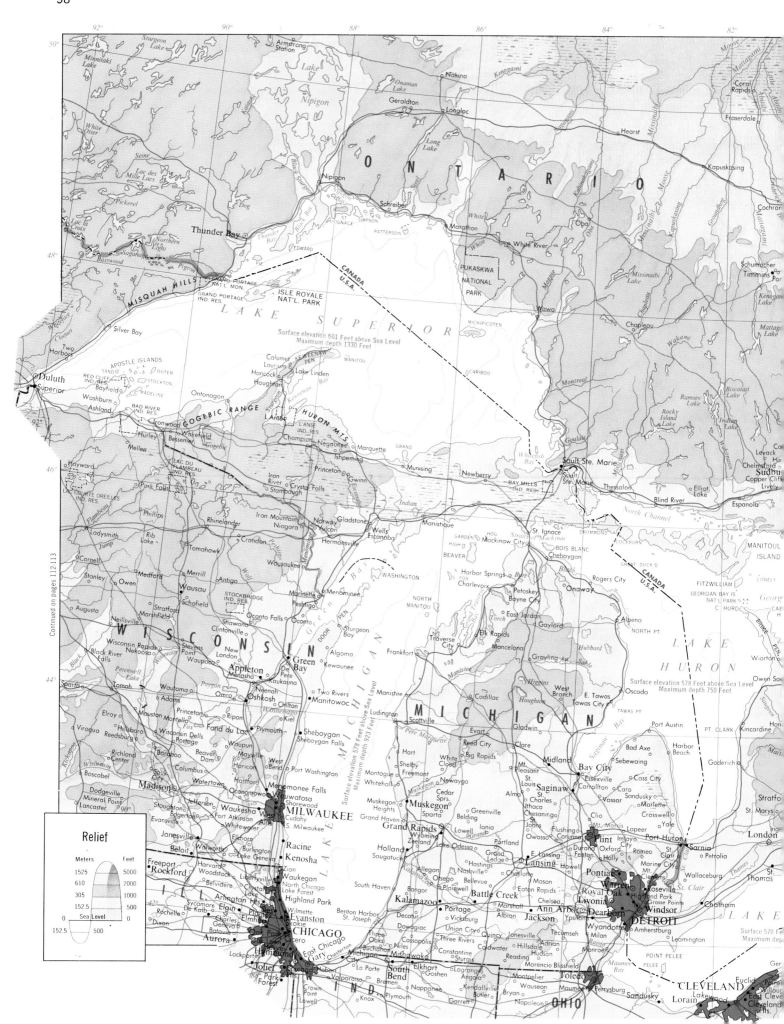

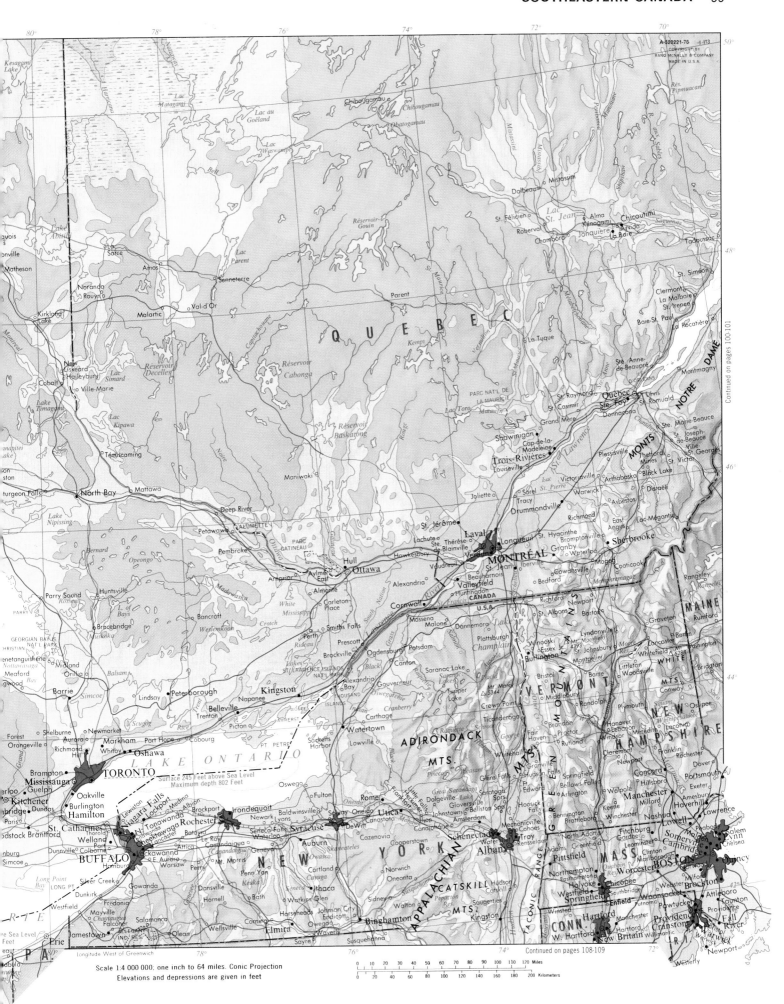

Continued on pages 100-101

Continued on pages 108-109

Scale 1:4 000 000; one inch to 64 miles. Conic Projection
Elevations and depressions are given in feet

Longitude West of Greenwich

0 10 20 30 40 50 60 70 80 90 100 110 120 Miles
0 20 40 60 80 100 120 140 160 180 200 Kilometers

LAKE ONTARIO
Surface 245 Feet above Sea Level
Maximum depth 802 Feet

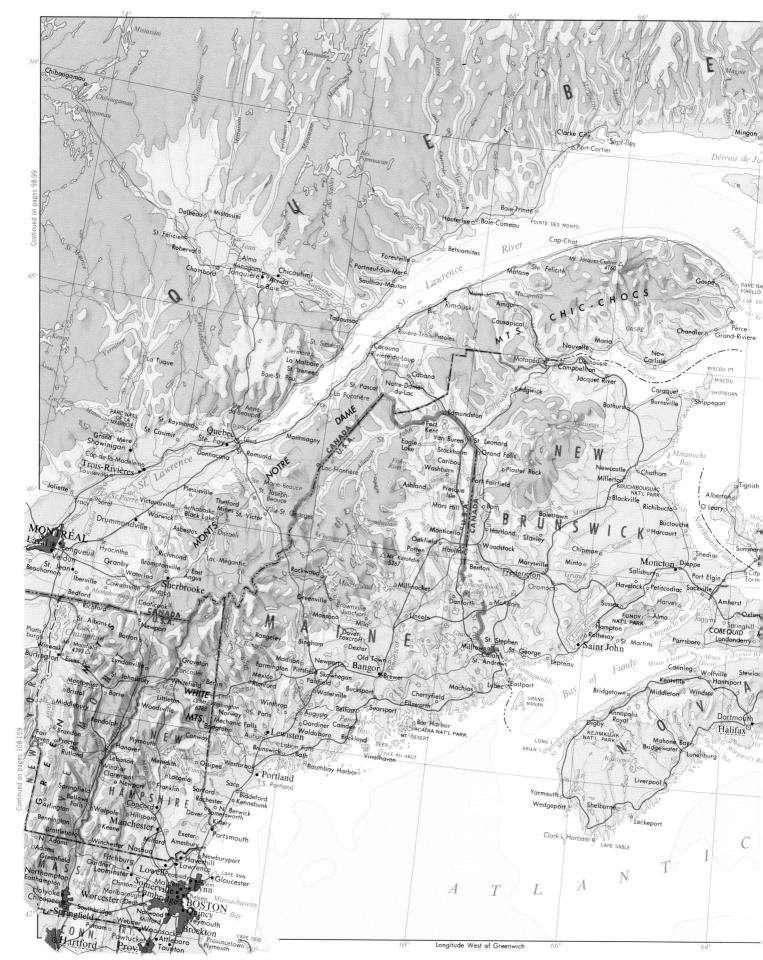

Continued on pages 98-99

Continued on pages 108-109

Longitude West of Greenwich

Scale 1:4 000 000; one inch to 64 miles. Conic Projection

Elevations and depressions are given in feet

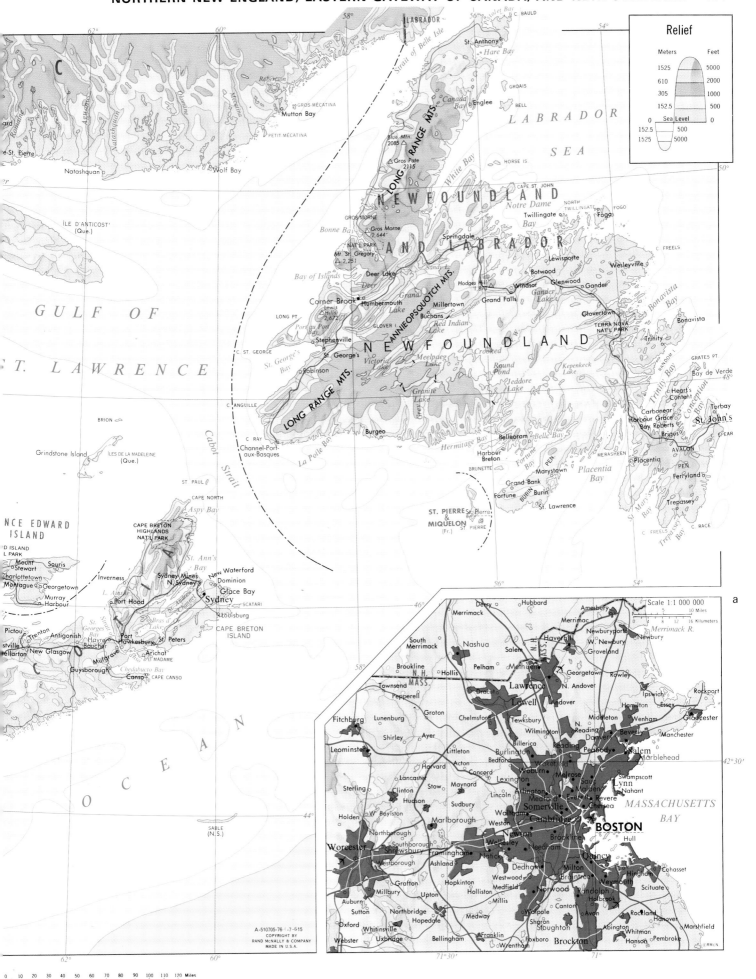

a — MONTRÉAL

Laurentides, L'Épiphanie, L'Assomption, St-Sulpice, Verchères, St. JÉRÔME, Ste. Anne-des-Plaines, Mascouche, Repentigny, Charlemagne, Dalesville, St. Canut, St. Janvier, Terrebonne, Brownsburg, Ste. Scholastique, Bois-des-Filion, Varennes, Lachute, Ste. Thérèse-de-Blainville, Rosemère, PTE.-AUX-TREMBLES, St. Philippe-d'Argenteuil, St. Benoît, Deux-Montagnes, St. Augustin, MONTRÉAL NORD, ANJOU, Boucherville, Île Fortune, St. André-Est, St. Placide, St. Eustache, ST. LÉONARD, St. Joseph-du-Lac, LAVAL, Mont-Royal, St. Bruno, ST. HUBERT, Rigaud, Hudson Hts., Oka, Deux Montagnes, ST. LAURENT, OUTREMONT, St. Lambert, Greenfield Park, Trés-St-Rédempteur, Hudson, Como-Est, Lac des Deux Montagnes, Westmount, VERDUN, Chambly, St. Lazare-de-Vaudreuil, Pte-Claire, Dorval, LACHINE, Brossard, Vaudreuil, Beaconsfield, Dorion-Vaudreuil, Île Perrot, LA SALLE, La Prairie, Ste. Justine-de-Newton, St. Clet, Léry, Caughnawaga, St. Dominique, Pte.-des-Cascades, Maple Grove, Mercier, St. Isidore-de-Laprairie, Coteau-du-Lac, Les Cèdres, Chateauguay, Dolson, St. Philippe-de-Laprairie, L'Acadie, Coteau-Landing, St. Constant, Rivière-Beaudette, VALLEYFIELD, St. Timothée, St. Louis-de-Gonzague, Beauharnois, St. Rémi, St. Michel-de-Napierville, St. Édouard-de-Napierville, St. Stanislas-de-Kostka, Howick, Napierville, Ste. Barbe, St. Anicet, Ste. Martine, Aubrey, St. Valentin, Ormstown, Barrington

b — QUÉBEC

St. Féréol, ÎLE AUX GRUES, Beaupré, Ste. Anne-de-Beaupré, St. Joachim-de-Montmorency, Cap-St. Ignace, Stoneham, Lac-Beauport, Château Richer, St. François, MONTMAGNY, Valcartier-Village, L'Ange-Gardien, ÎLE D'ORLÉANS, St. Pierre d'Orléans, Ste. Famille, Berthier, Ste. Pierre-Montmagny, CHARLESBOURG, Beauport, St. Jean, St. Laurent d'Orléans, St. Vallier, St. François-Montmagny, Loretteville, QUÉBEC, St. Pétronille, St. Michel, Ste. Euphémie, Ancienne-Lorette, STE. FOY, Sillery, Lévis, La Durantaye, St. Raphaël, Armagh, St. Augustin-de-Québec, Cap-Rouge, St. David, Beaumont, Neuville, Charny, St. Romuald d'Etchemin, Carrier, St. Gervais, St. Nérée, St. Nicolas, St. Jean-Chrysostome, St. Henri, St. Philémon, St. Antoine-de-Tilly, St. Étienne-de-Lauzon, Breakeyville, Honfleur, St. Lazare, St. Apollinaire, Ste. Claire, St. Damien-de-Buckland, St. Lambert-de-Lévis, St. Isidore-Dorchester, Buckland

c — OTTAWA

Alcove, Wakefield, McGregor L., Perkins, Montebello, PARC DE LA GATINEAU, Papineauville, Plaisance, Alfred, Chelsea, Masson, Thurso, Buckingham, Wendover, Plantagenet, Templeton, Angers, Rockland, Bourget, Curran, Pointe-Gatineau, Gatineau, Orleans, Cumberland, HULL, Rockcliffe Park, Vanier, St. Isidore-de-Prescott, Aylmer, OTTAWA, Navan, Deschênes, Ramsayville, Bear Brook, Bells Corners, Leitrim, Vars, Limoges, Casselman, Stittsville, Embrun, Maxville, Manotick, Russell, Moose Creek, Richmond, Metcalfe, Crysler, Monkland, Vernon, Morewood, Avonmore, N. Gower, Osgoode, Finch, Newington

d — TORONTO / Hamilton

Orangeville, Nobleton, Bolton, King City, RICHMOND HILL, MARKHAM, Alton, Caledon, Inglewood, Vaughan, Hillsburgh, Erin, Bramalea, Snelgrove, BRAMPTON, Rockwood, Georgetown, Acton, Norval, GUELPH, Streetsville, Milton, MISSISSAUGA, Port Credit, LAKE ONTARIO, Oakville, Freelton, Sheffield, Waterdown, BURLINGTON, St. George, Dundas, Hamilton Hbr., Hamilton, Niagara-on-the-Lake, Youngstown, Lynden, Winona, Welland Canal, BRANTFORD, Stoney Creek, Grimsby, Lincoln, Lewiston, Cainsville, Mt. Hope, Twenty Mile Cr., ST. CATHARINES, NEW YORK, Thorold

e — CALGARY

Ghost Lake, Bow, Balzac, Kathryn, Keoma, STONY IND. RES., Cochrane, McDonald L., Morley, Delacour, Dalroy, Conrich, Lyalta, CALGARY, Chestermere, Elbow, Jumpingpound, Bragg Creek, SARCEE IND. RES., Shepard, Langdon, Priddis, Indus, Lloyd L., Dalemead

f — WINNIPEG

Delta Beach, Argyle, Stonewall, Warren, Lockport, Reaburn, Marquette, Grosse Isle, Stony Mountain, Gonor, Poplar Point, Meadows, High Bluff, St. Eustache, Rosser, Gordon, Birds Hill, PORTAGE LA PRAIRIE, Fortier, Pigeon Lake, St. François Xavier, WINNIPEG, Newton, Oakville, Elie, Dacotah, Springstein, Prairie Grove, Grande Pointe, Oak Bluff, Fannystelle, Starbuck, Culross, Sanford, La Salle, St. Adolphe

g — EDMONTON

ALEXANDER IND. RES., Morinville, Cardiff, Bruderheim, Rivière Qui Barre, Sandy L., Carbondale, Duagh, Fort Saskatchewan, Josephburg, Calahoo, Namao, Villeneuve, Sturgeon R., St. Albert, Oliver, Big L., Cannell, ELK ISLAND NAT'L PARK, Stony Plain, EDMONTON, Clover Bar, Bremner, Spruce Grove, Ardrossan, Sherwood Park, STONY PLAIN IND. RES., Uncas, N. Cooking Lake, Devon, Hercules, Cooking Lake, Ellerslie, Looma, Nisku, Beaumont, Saunders, Buford, Calmar, Leduc, New Sarepta, Miquelon L.

RELIEF

Meters	Feet
3 050	10 000
1 525	5 000
610	2 000
305	1 000
152.5	500
0 Sea Level	0
152.5	500

A-520055-76 -7 -43

Scale 1:1 000 000; One inch to 16 miles.
Elevations and depressions are given in feet.

Miles: 0 2 4 6 8 10 12 14 16 18 20 22 24
Kilometers: 0 4 8 12 16 20 24 28 32 36 40

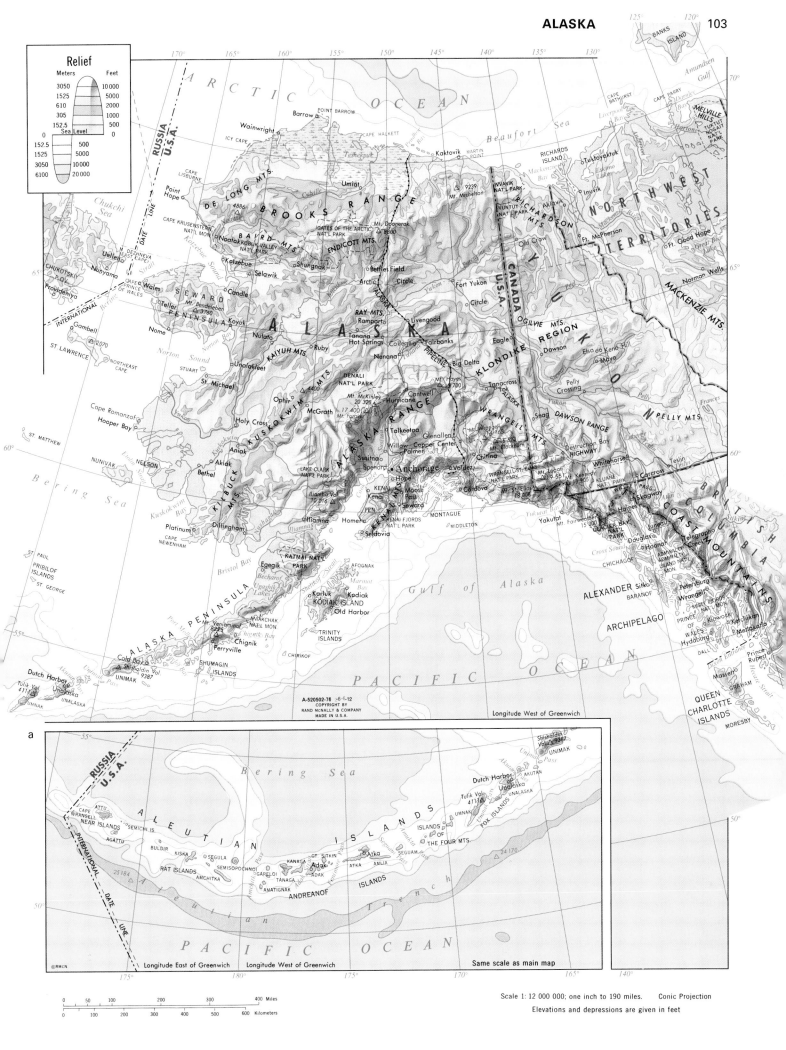

Relief

Meters		Feet
3050		10 000
1525		5000
610		2000
305		1000
152.5		500
0	Sea Level	0
152.5		500
1525		5000
3050		10 000
6100		20 000

ARCTIC OCEAN

Beaufort Sea

RUSSIA
U.S.A.

Amundsen Gulf

NORTHWEST TERRITORIES

DE LONG MTS.
BROOKS RANGE
BAIRD MTS.
ENDICOTT MTS.
RICHARDSON MTS.

Chukchi Sea

SEWARD PENINSULA

ALASKA

YUKON

KLONDIKE REGION

OGILVIE MTS.

MACKENZIE MTS.

Norton Sound

KAIYUH MTS.

RAY MTS.

Bering Strait

KUSKOKWIM MTS.

DENALI NAT'L PARK

ALASKA RANGE

WRANGELL MTS.

DAWSON RANGE

PELLY MTS.

KILBUCK MTS.

Bering Sea

KENAI PEN.

Anchorage

WRANGELL-ST. ELIAS NAT'L PARK

GLACIER BAY NAT'L PARK

COAST MOUNTAINS

BRITISH COLUMBIA

ALASKA PENINSULA

KATMAI NAT'L PARK

KODIAK ISLAND

Gulf of Alaska

ALEXANDER ARCHIPELAGO

QUEEN CHARLOTTE ISLANDS

PACIFIC OCEAN

A-520502-76
COPYRIGHT BY
RAND MCNALLY & COMPANY
MADE IN U.S.A.

Longitude West of Greenwich

a

RUSSIA
U.S.A.

Bering Sea

ALEUTIAN ISLANDS

NEAR ISLANDS

RAT ISLANDS

ANDREANOF ISLANDS

FOX ISLANDS

ISLANDS OF THE FOUR MTS.

UNIMAK

Dutch Harbor

Aleutian Trench

PACIFIC OCEAN

INTERNATIONAL DATE LINE

Longitude East of Greenwich   Longitude West of Greenwich   Same scale as main map

Scale 1: 12 000 000; one inch to 190 miles.   Conic Projection
Elevations and depressions are given in feet

Continued on pages 90-91

Scale 1:12 000 000; one inch to 190 miles. Polyconic Projection

Elevations and depressions are given in feet

A-520500-26   -810-20
COPYRIGHT BY
RAND McNALLY & COMPANY
MADE IN U.S.A.

Scale 1: 36 000 000

Scale 1: 36 000 000
One inch to 570 miles

Scale 1: 3 400 000

Same scale as main map

GULF OF MEXICO

ATLANTIC OCEAN

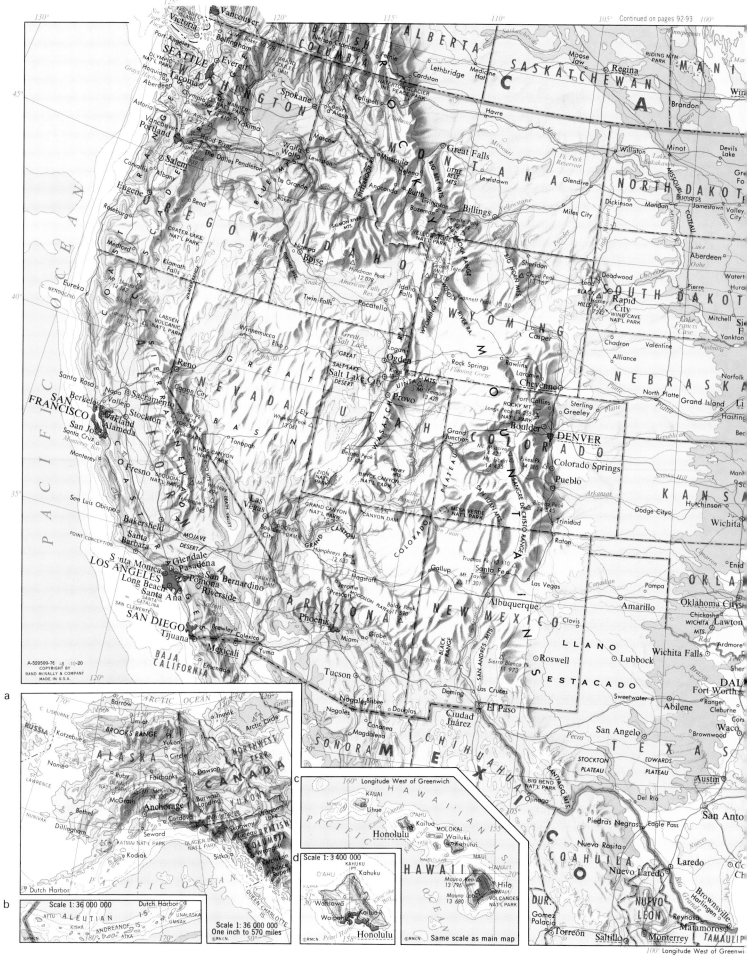

Continued on pages 92-93

a

b

Scale 1: 36 000 000

Scale 1: 36 000 000
One inch to 570 miles

c

Longitude West of Greenwich

d

Scale 1: 3 400 000

Same scale as main map

Honolulu

100° Longitude West of Greenwi

Scale 1:12 000 000; one inch to 190 miles. Polyconic Projectio

Elevations and depressions are given in feet

Continued on pages 98-99

Relief

Meters		Feet
1525		5000
610		2000
305		1000
152.5		500
0	Sea Level	
152.5		500
1525		5000
3050		10 000

A-520596-76
COPYRIGHT BY
RAND McNALLY & COMPANY
MADE IN U.S.A.

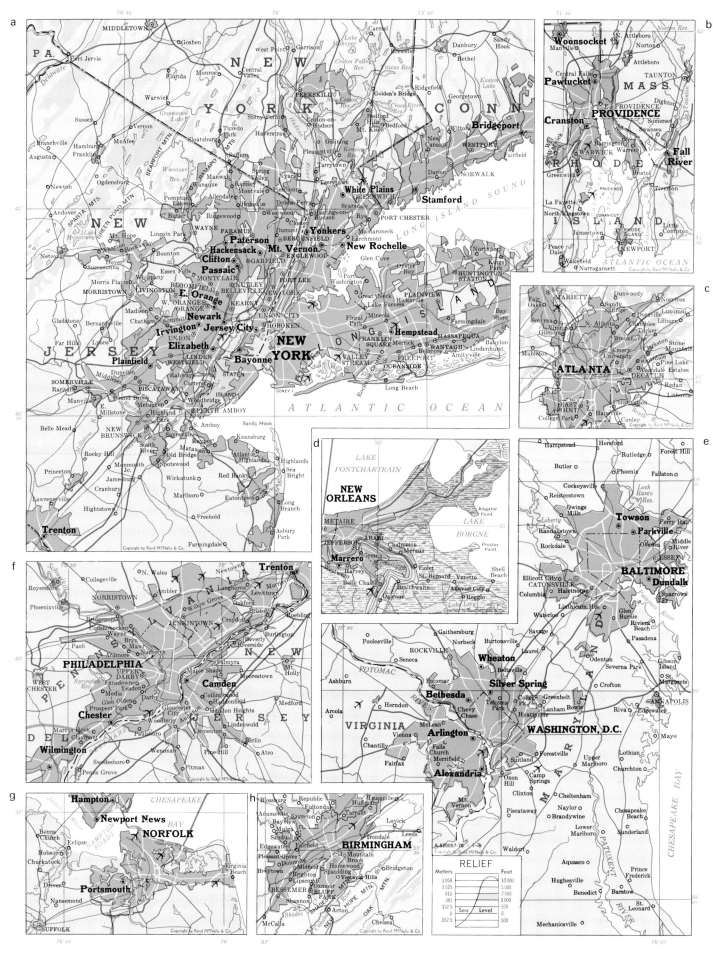

Scale 1:1 000 000; One inch to 16 miles.
Elevations and depressions are given in feet.

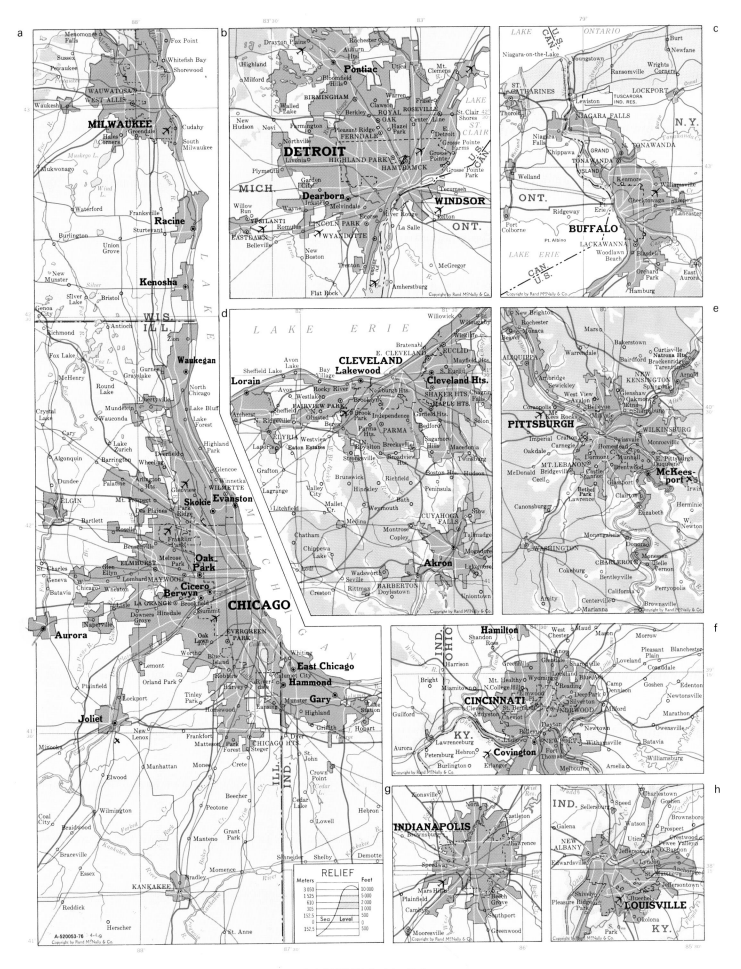

RELIEF

Meters		Feet
3 050		10 000
1 525		5 000
610		2 000
305		1 000
152.5		500
0	Sea Level	0
152.5		500

Scale 1:1 000 000; One inch to 16 miles.
Elevations and depressions are given in feet.

0 2 4 6 8 10 12 14 16 18 20 22 24 Miles
0 4 8 12 16 20 24 28 32 36 40 Kilometers

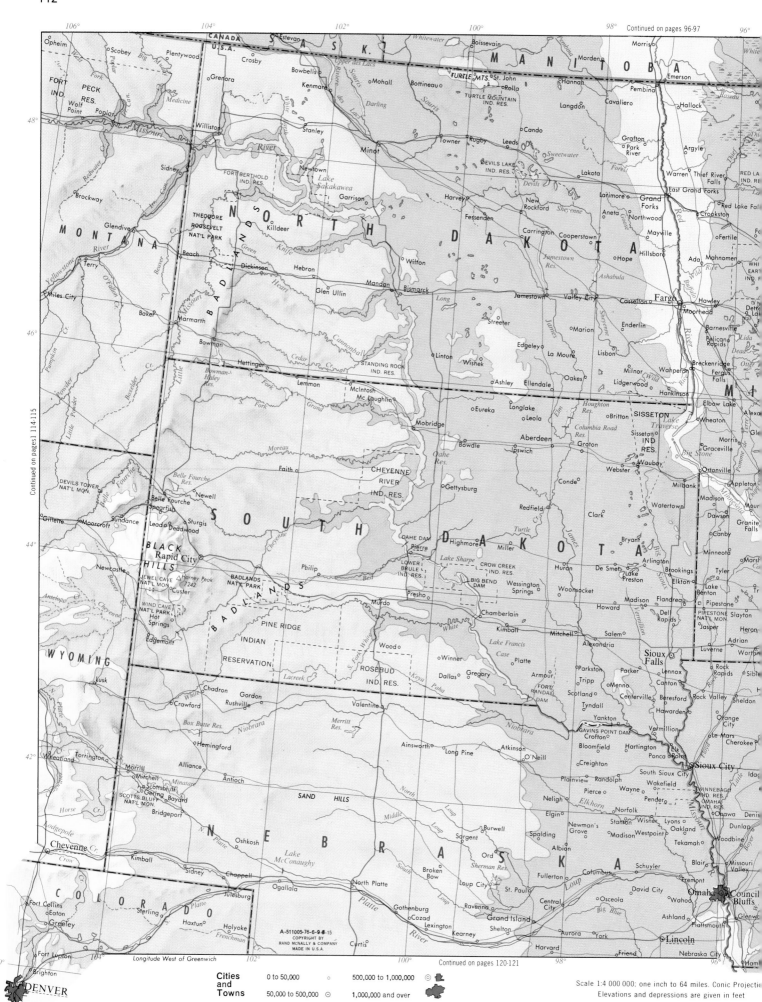

CANADA

S A S K.

MANITOBA

Continued on pages 96-97

MONTANA

NORTH DAKOTA

SOUTH DAKOTA

WYOMING

NEBRASKA

COLORADO

Continued on pages 114-115

Continued on pages 120-121

Longitude West of Greenwich

A-511005-76-6-9-8-15
COPYRIGHT BY
RAND McNALLY & COMPANY
MADE IN U.S.A.

DENVER

Cities
and
Towns

0 to 50,000

50,000 to 500,000

500,000 to 1,000,000

1,000,000 and over

Scale 1:4 000 000; one inch to 64 miles. Conic Projection
Elevations and depressions are given in feet

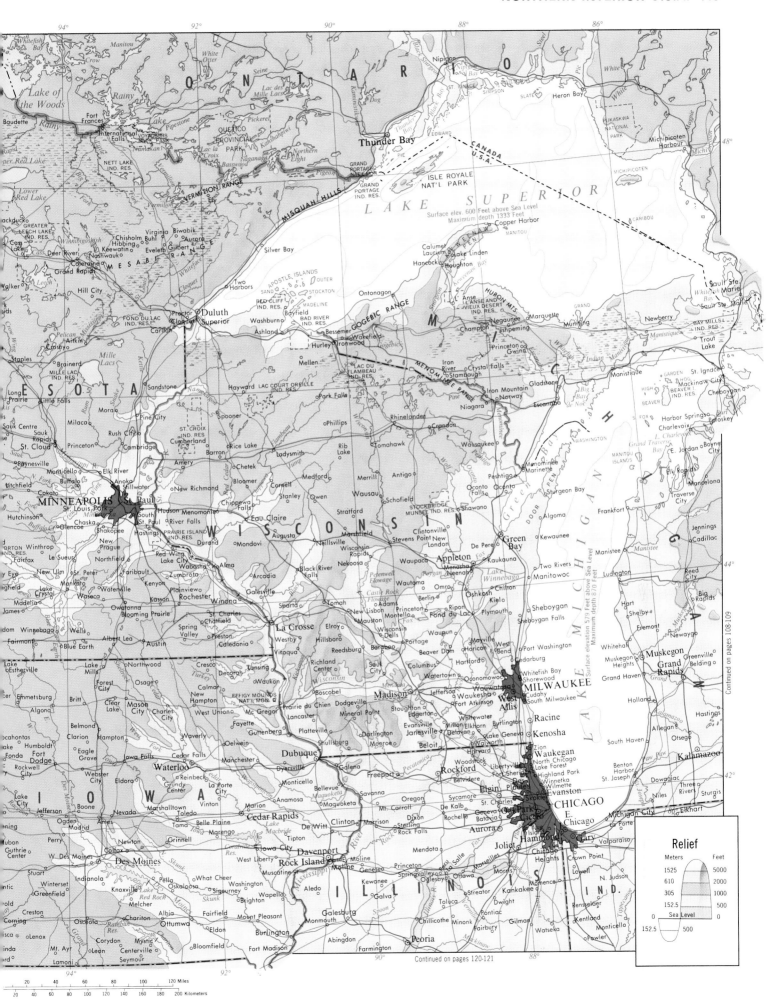

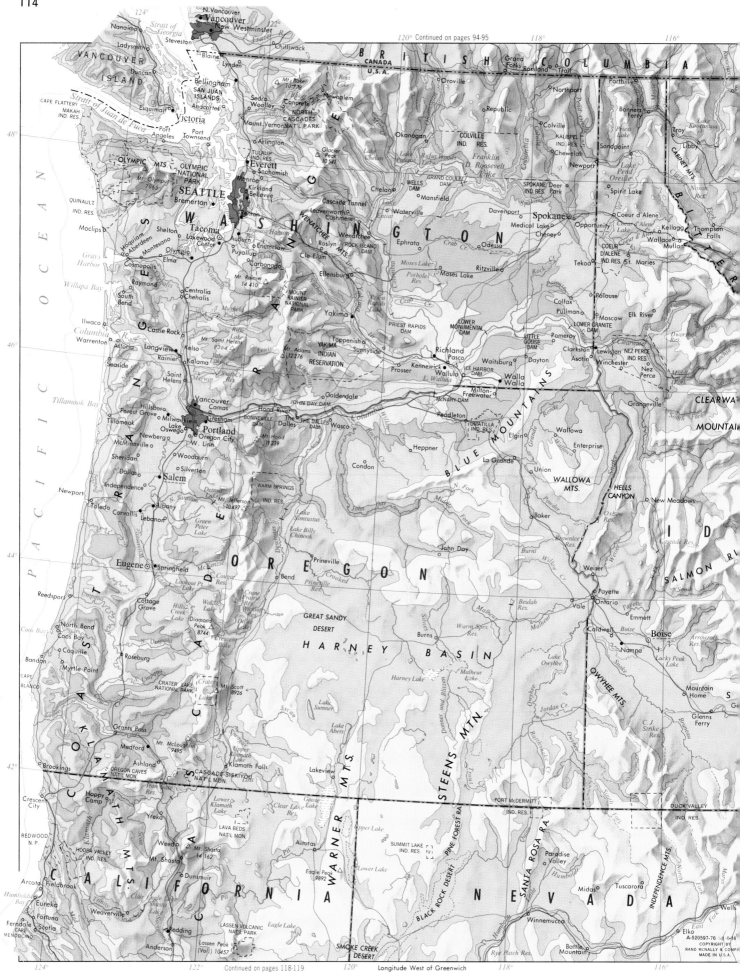

120° Continued on pages 94-95

Continued on pages 118-119

Longitude West of Greenwich

A-520597-76 -8-6-14
COPYRIGHT BY
RAND McNALLY & COMPANY
MADE IN U.S.A.

Scale 1: 4,000 000; one inch to 64 miles. Conic Projection
Elevations and depressions are given in feet

Continued on pages 96-97

Continued on pages 112-113

Continued on pages 118-119

ALBERTA
SASKATCHEWAN
CANADA
U.S.A.
N. DAK.

MONTANA

WYOMING

UTAH
COLO.

IDAHO

GREAT
SALT LAKE
DESERT

YELLOWSTONE
NATIONAL
PARK

Relief

Meters		Feet
3050		10000
1525		5000
610		2000
305		1000
152.5		500
0	Sea Level	0
1525		500

20 40 60 80 100 120 Miles
20 40 60 80 100 120 140 160 180 200 Kilometers

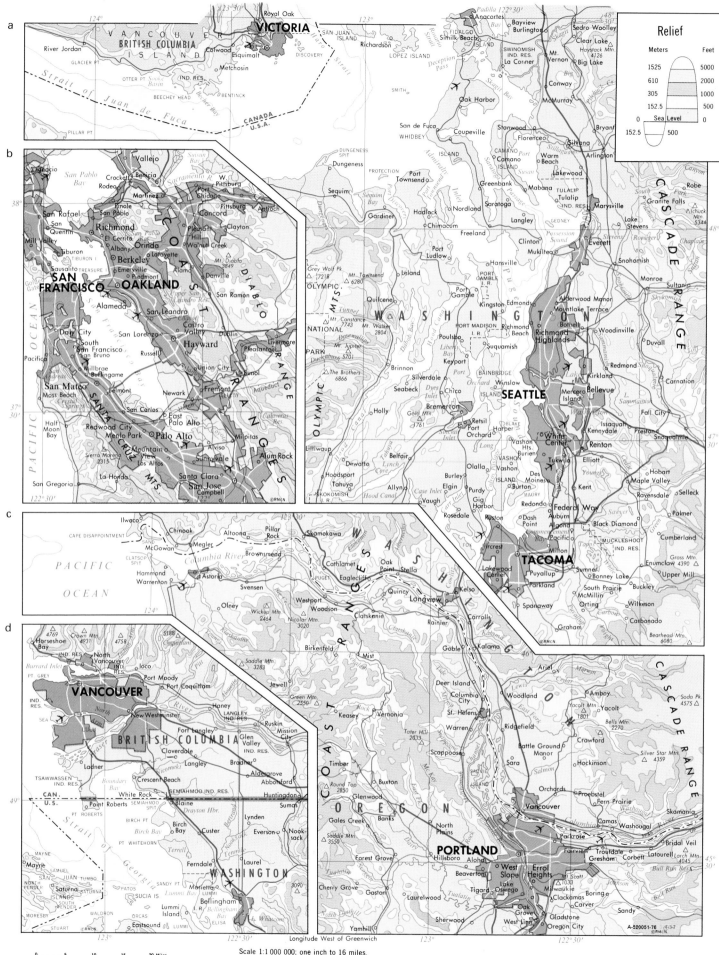

Relief

Meters		Feet
1525		5000
610		2000
305		1000
152.5		500
0	Sea Level	0
152.5		500

Longitude West of Greenwich

Scale 1:1 000 000; one inch to 16 miles.
Elevations and depressions are given in feet.

0   5   10   15   20 Miles
0 4 8 12 16 20 24 28 32 Kilometers

A-520051-76   4-3-7

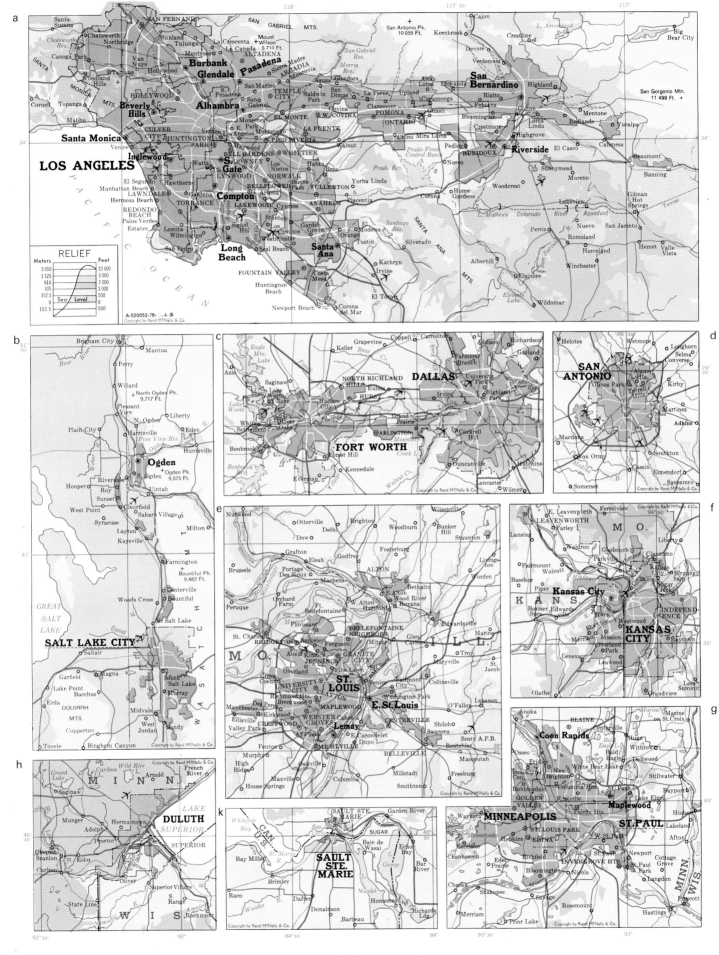

a

Santa
Susana
Chatsworth Northridge
Canoga Park
Woodland
Hills
Tarzana
Van
Nuys
Hollywood
Burbank
Glendale **Pasadena**
Cornell
Topanga
Malibu
Beverly
Hills
HOLLYWOOD
Santa Monica
Venice
Inglewood
LOS ANGELES
Manhattan Beach
El Segundo
Hawthorne
Hermosa Beach
REDONDO
BEACH
Palos Verdes
Estates
San Pedro
Compton
TORRANCE
Lomita
Wilmington
San Pedro
Long
Beach
Seal Beach
Santa
Ana
FOUNTAIN VALLEY
Huntington
Beach
Newport Beach
Corona
del Mar

San Fernando
ALTADENA
La Crescenta
La Canada
Mount Wilson
5 710 Ft.
SAN GABRIEL MTS.
San Antonio Pk.
10 059 Ft.
Keenbrook
Cajon
L. Arrowhead
Crestline
Devore
Verdemont
Big
Bear
City

RELIEF
Meters   Feet
3 050   10 000
1 525   5 000
610   2 000
305   1 000
152.5   500
Sea Level
152.5   500

A-520052-76-   -4-   Copyright by Rand McNally & Co.

San Bernardino
Highland
Rialto
Fontana
Colton
Loma
Linda
Redlands
Mentone
Yucaipa
Beaumont
Banning
Riverside
RUBIDOUX
El Casco
Cahmesa
Sunnymead
Moreno
Woodcrest
Perris
Nuevo
San Jacinto
Lakeview
Gilman
Hot
Springs
Hemet
Valle
Vista
Homeland
Romoland
Winchester
Elsinore
Wildomar
Corona del Mar
San Gorgonio Mtn.
11 499 Ft. +

b
Brigham City
Mantua
Perry
Willard
North Ogden Pk.
9,717 Ft.
Pleasant
View
N. Ogden
Liberty
Eden
Harrisville
Huntsville
Ogden
Ogden Pk.
9,575 Ft.
Riverdale
Roy
Sunset
Uintah
Clearfield
Sahara Village
Layton
Kaysville
Farmington
Bountiful Pk.
9,482 Ft.
Centerville
Bountiful
Woods Cross
N. Salt Lake
GREAT
SALT
LAKE
SALT LAKE CITY
Saltair
Garfield
Magna
Lake Point
Bacchus
Erda
South
Salt Lake
Murray
OQUIRRH
MTS.
Midvale
Sandy
Copperton
West
Jordan
Tooele
Bingham Canyon

c
Eagle
Mtn.
Lake
Coppell
Carrollton
Keller
Grapevine
Addison
Richardson
Garland
Azle
Saginaw
NORTH RICHLAND
HILLS
Farmers
Branch
DALLAS
University
Park
Lake
Worth
Village
Haltom
City
Euless
HURST
Irving
Highland
Park
White
Settlement
River
Oaks
FORT WORTH
Grand
Prairie
Cockrell Hill
Benbrook
ARLINGTON
Mountain
Creek L.
Forest Hill
Everman
Kennedale
Duncanville
Lancaster
Wilmer

d
Helotes
Wetmore
Longhorn
Selma
Converse
SAN
ANTONIO
Alamo
Hts.
Kirby
Olmos Park
Terrell
Hills
Macdona
Martinez
Adkins
Von Ormy
Cassin
Elmendorf
Saspamco
Somerset

e
Nutwood
Otterville
Brighton
Wilsonville
Delhi
Woodburn
Bunker
Hill
Dow
Fosterburg
Staunton
Grafton
Elsah
Godfrey
Livings-
ton
Brussels
Portage
Des Sioux
Machens
ALTON
Bethalto
Peruque
Orchard
Farm
Ft.
Bellefontaine
E. Alton
Wood River
Roxana
Worden
St. Charles
Florissant
W. Alton
Hartford
Edwardsville
BELLEFONTAINE
NEIGHBORS
Marine
BRIDGETON
Berkeley
Mitchell
Glen
Carbon
Troy
Aimo
Kinlock
Ferguson
GRANITE
CITY
Maryville
St.
Jacob
UNIVERSITY
CITY
Overland
Pine Lawn
Venice
Fairmont
City
Collinsville
O'Fallon
Des Peres
Richmond Hts.
ST.
LOUIS
Washington Park
Lebanon
Manchester
Kirkwood
Brentwood
MAPLEWOOD
E. ST. LOUIS
Ellisville
Valley Park
CRESTWOOD
WEBSTER
GROVES
Cahokia
CENTREVILLE
Shiloh
Swansea
Fenton
AFFTON
Carondelet
Dupo
Scott A.F.B.
Mascoutah
Murphy
MEHLVILLE
BELLEVILLE
High
Ridge
Oakville
Maxville
Millstadt
Freeburg
House
Springs
Columbia
Smithton

f
E. Leavenworth
Ferrelview
LEAVENWORTH
Farley
M O.
Lansing
Waldron
Gladstone
Liberty
Fairmount
Wolcott
Parkville
Claycomo
Basehor
Piper
Kansas City
N.
Kansas
City
Birming-
ham
Edwards-
ville
R. Turner
Sugar
Creek
KANS.
Bonner
Springs
Westwood
INDEPEND-
ENCE
Shawnee
Merriam
KANSAS
CITY
Mission
Overland
Park
Raytown
Lenexa
Leawood
Olathe
Grandview
Lees
Summit

g
Anoka
BLAINE
Marine
on St.Croix
Osseo
Centerville
Hugo
Withrow
Fridley
Bald
Eagle
New
Brighton
White Bear Lake
Stillwater
Coon Rapids
Brooklyn
Center
Robbinsdale
Columbia Hts.
Bayport
Lake Elmo
GOLDEN
VALLEY
Roseville
St. Paul
Maplewood
Afton
Falcon Hts.
MINNEAPOLIS
ST. LOUIS PARK
ST. PAUL
Wayzata
Hopkins
EDINA
W. St. Paul
Lakeland
Excelsior
Chanhassen
Eden
Prairie
Richfield
INVERGROVE HTS.
Newport
Cottage
Grove
Chaska
Bloomington
Nicols
St. Paul
Park
Langdon
Shakopee
Savage
Rosemount
MINN.
WIS.
Chaska
Merriam
Prior Lake
Hastings
Prescott

h
Wild Rice
L.
Caribou
Arnold
French
River
M   I   N   N.
Grand
Lake
Saginaw
Munger
Hermantown
LAKE
Adolph
DULUTH
SUPERIOR
Cloquet
Scanlon
Esko
Proctor
Superior
Carlton
Oliver
Superior Village
S.
Range
State Line
Rockmont
W   I   S.

k
SAULT STE.
MARIE
Garden River
Whitefish
Bay
CAN.
U.S.
Soo Locks
SUGAR
Baie de
Wasai
Echo
Bay
Bay Mills
St. Mary's R.
GEORGE
Bar
River
Brimley
Nicolet
Raco
Dafter
Waiska R.
Homestead
Richards
Ldg.
Donaldson
Barbeau

0 2 4 6 8 10 12 14 16 18 20 22 24   Miles
0 4 8 12 16 20 24 28 32 36 40   Kilometers

118

Continued on pages 114-115

Scale 1:4 000 000; one inch to 64 miles. Conic Projection
Elevations and depressions are given in feet

A-520599-76 -8 -8-21
COPYRIGHT BY
RAND McNALLY & COMPANY
MADE IN U.S.A.

Longitude West of Greenwich

Scale 1:1 000 000

SAN DIEGO

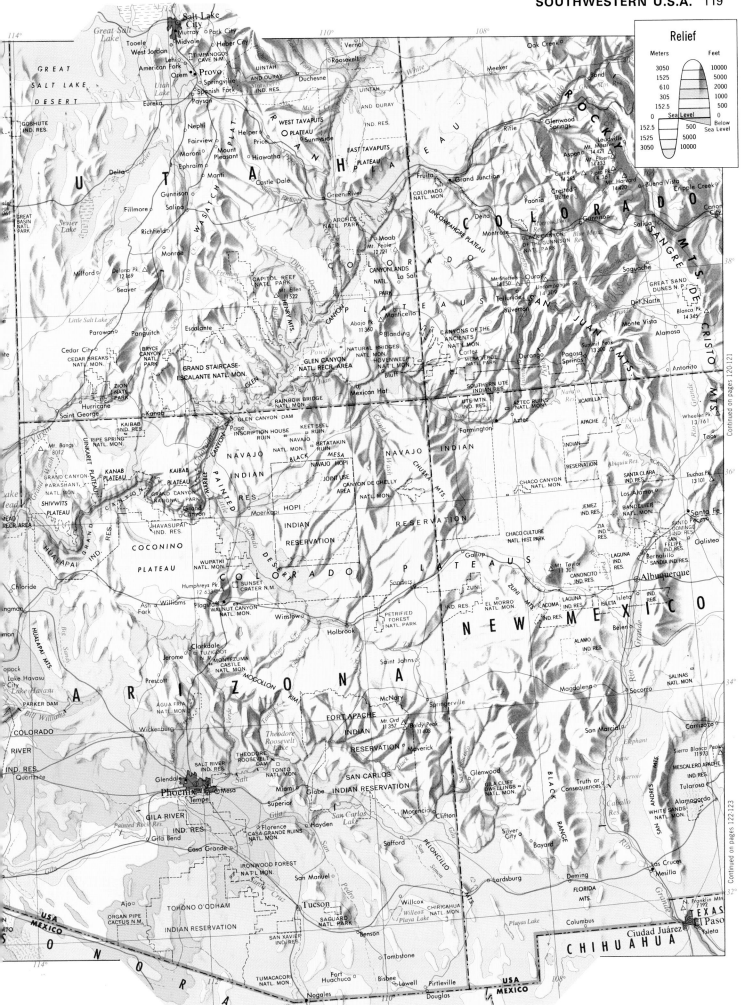

Continued on pages 120-121

Continued on pages 122-123

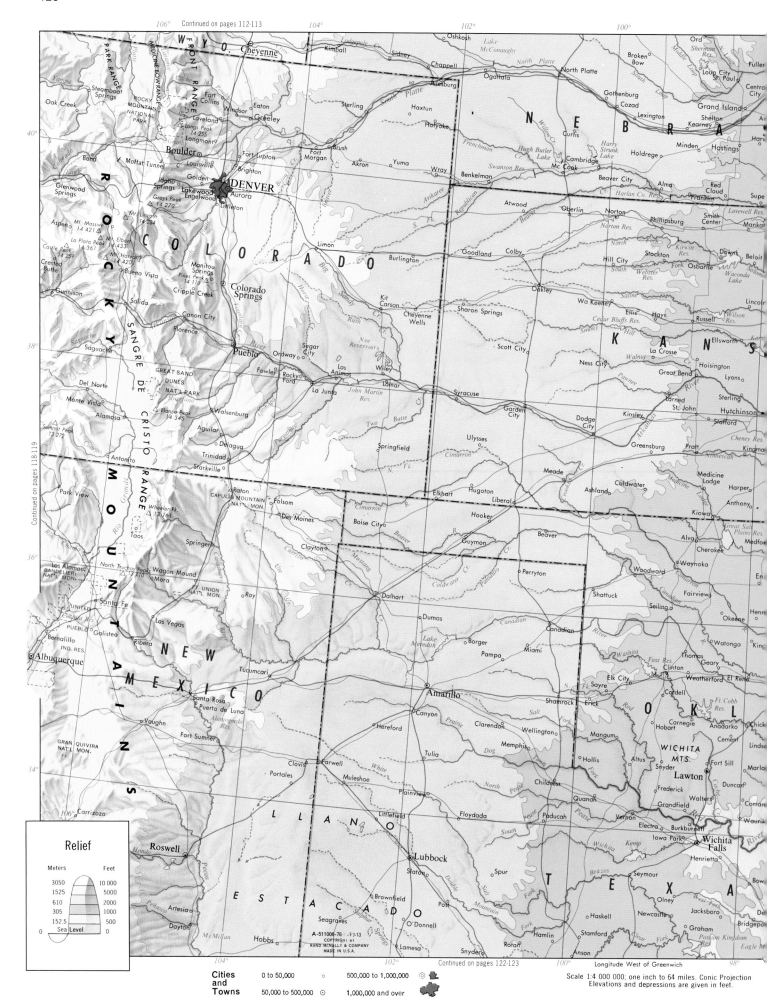

Continued on pages 112-113 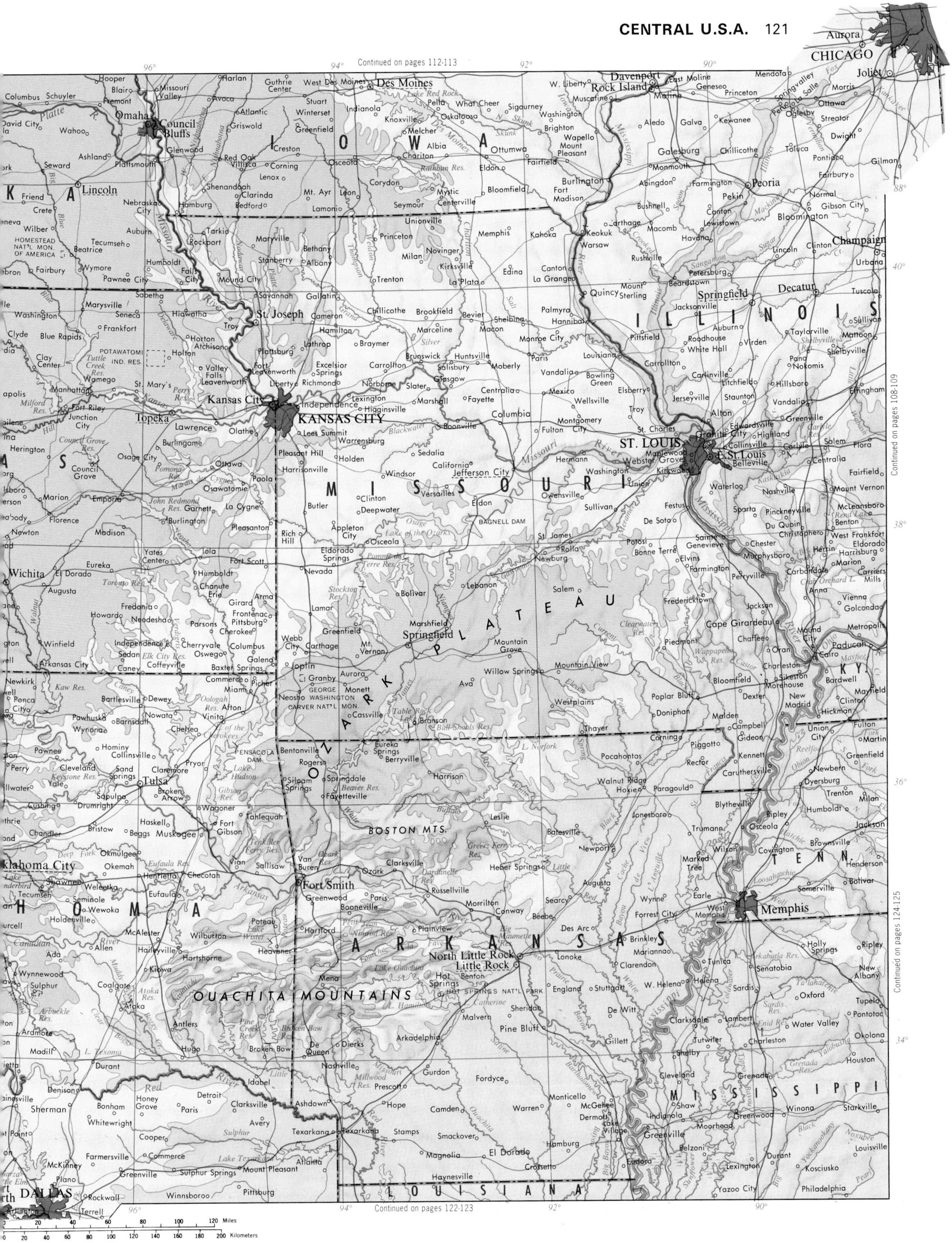
Continued on pages 108-109
Continued on pages 124-125
Continued on pages 122-123

CHICAGO

IOWA

ILLINOIS

MISSOURI

KANSAS

OKLAHOMA

ARKANSAS

OZARK PLATEAU

BOSTON MTS.

OUACHITA MOUNTAINS

LOUISIANA

MISSISSIPPI

TENN.

KY.

KANSAS CITY

ST. LOUIS

Memphis

DALLAS

Miles
0   20   40   60   80   100   120 Miles
0   20   40   60   80   100 120 140 160 180 200 Kilometers

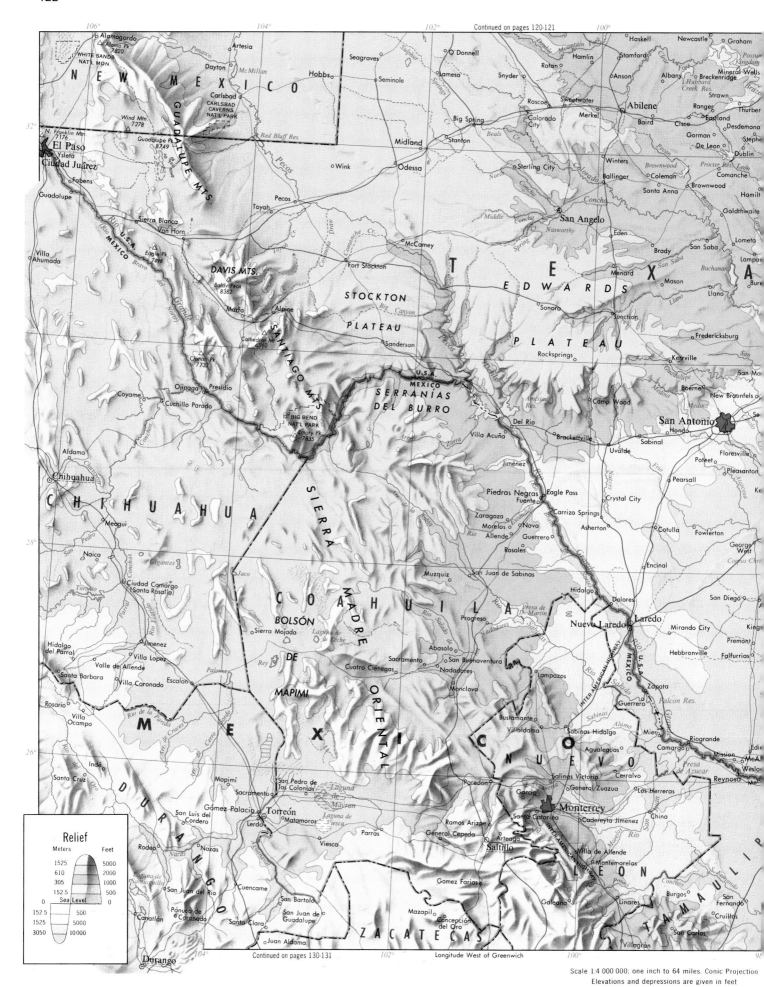

Continued on pages 120-121

NEW MEXICO

WHITE SANDS NAT'L MON.

CHIHUAHUA

COAHUILA

SIERRA MADRE DE ORIENTAL

DURANGO

ZACATECAS

NUEVO LEÓN

TAMAULIPAS

TEXAS

EDWARDS PLATEAU

STOCKTON PLATEAU

DAVIS MTS.

GUADALUPE MTS.

SANTIAGO MTS.

SERRANÍAS DEL BURRO

BOLSÓN DE MAPIMÍ

MEXICO

El Paso
Ciudad Juárez
Ysleta
Fabens
Guadalupe
Villa Ahumada

Alamogordo
Alamo Pk. 7820
N. Franklin Mtn. 7176
Wind Mtn. 7278
Guadalupe Pk. 8749

Carlsbad
CARLSBAD CAVERNS NAT'L PARK
Red Bluff Res.
Artesia
Dayton
McMillan
Seagraves
Seminole
Lamesa
O'Donnell
Snyder
Hobbs

Haskell
Newcastle
Graham
Hamlin
Stamford
Rotan
Anson
Mineral Wells
Strawn
Albany
Breckenridge
Roscoe
Merkel
Abilene
Baird
Ranger
Eastland
Thurber
Cisco
Gorman
Desdemona
De Leon
Stephe
Dublin
Sweetwater
Colorado City
Winters
Coleman
Comanche
Ballinger
Santa Anna
Brownwood
Hamilt
Goldthwaite
Lometa
Comanche

Wink
Odessa
Midland
Stanton
Big Spring
Sterling City
San Angelo
Eden
Brady
San Saba
Lampas
Menard
Mason
Bur
Llano
Buchanan

Pecos
Toyah
Van Horn
Sierra Blanca
Eagle Pk. 7496
Baldy Peak 8382
Marfa
Alpine
Cathedral Mt. 6860
Chinati Pk. 7730
Fort Stockton
McCamey
Sonora
Junction
Fredericksburg
Kerrville
Rocksprings
Camp Wood
Boerne
New Braunfels
San Ma
San
Sanderson

BIG BEND NAT'L PARK
Emory Pk. 7835
Ojinaga
Presidio
Coyame
Cuchillo Parado
Aldama
Chihuahua
Meoqui
Naica
Ciudad Camargo (Santa Rosalía)
Jimenez
Valle de Allende
Santa Barbara
Hidalgo del Parral
Villa Lopez
Rosario
Villa Ocampo
Indé
Santa Cruz
Hidalgo
Escalón
Villa Coronado
Jaco
Gigantes
Sierra Mojada
Laguna de la Leche
Rey
Laguna de Palomas
Mapimí
Sacramento
Gómez Palacio
San Luis del Cordero
Torreón
Lerdo
Matamoros
Rodeo
Nazas
Cuencame
San Juan del Rio
Canatlán
Durango
Juan Aldama
San Bartolo
San Juan de Guadalupe
Santa Clara
Pánuco de Coronado
Mazapil
Concepción del Oro
Villagrán

Del Rio
Villa Acuña
Jiménez
Piedras Negras
Fuente
Eagle Pass
Zaragoza
Nava
Morelos
Allende
Guerrero
Rosales
Muzquiz
San Juan de Sabinas
Progreso
Abasolo
Sacramento
San Buenaventura
Nadadores
Monclova
Cuatro Ciénegas
Presa de D. Martin
Hidalgo
Dolores
Nuevo Laredo
Laredo
Lampazos
Bustamante
Villaldama
Sabinas Hidalgo
Mier
Camargo
Agualeguas
Cerralvo
Los Herreras
Salinas Victoria
General Zuazua
García
Monterrey
Santa Catarina
Ramos Arizpe
Cadereyta Jimenez
China
Saltillo
Arteaga
Montemorelos
Villa de Allende
General Cepeda
Gómez Farías
Galeana
Linares
Burgos
San Fernando
San Carlos

Crystal City
Uvalde
Sabinal
Hondo
San Antonio
Floresville
Poteet
Pleasanton
Pearsall
Ke
Carrizo Springs
Asherton
Cotulla
Fowlerton
Encinal
George West
Corpus Chr
San Diego
Mirando City
Premont
Hebbronville
Falfurrias
Zapata
Guerrero
Falcon Res.
Riogrande
Mission
McA
Wesla
Reynosa
Presa de Azucar
Edi

Brackettville
Amistad Res.

Rio Grande
Rio Bravo del Norte
Pecos
Concho
Colorado
Inter-American Highway

DURANGO

Longitude West of Greenwich

Continued on pages 130-131

Relief

Meters	Feet
1525	5000
610	2000
305	1000
152.5	500
0 Sea Level	0
152.5	500
1525	5000
3050	10000

Scale 1:4 000 000; one inch to 64 miles. Conic Projection
Elevations and depressions are given in feet

106° 104° 102° 100° 98° 32° 28° 26°

Continued on pages 120-121

Continued on pages 124-125

a

Scale 1:1 000 000
0   5   10 Miles
0 4 8 12 16 Kilometers

©RMCN

A-511007-76
COPYRIGHT BY
RAND McNALLY & COMPANY
MADE IN U.S.A.

Cities
and
Towns

0 to 50,000
50,000 to 500,000
500,000 to 1,000,000
1,000,000 and over

0   20   40   60   80   100   120 Miles
0 20 40 60 80 100 120 140 160 180 200 Kilometers

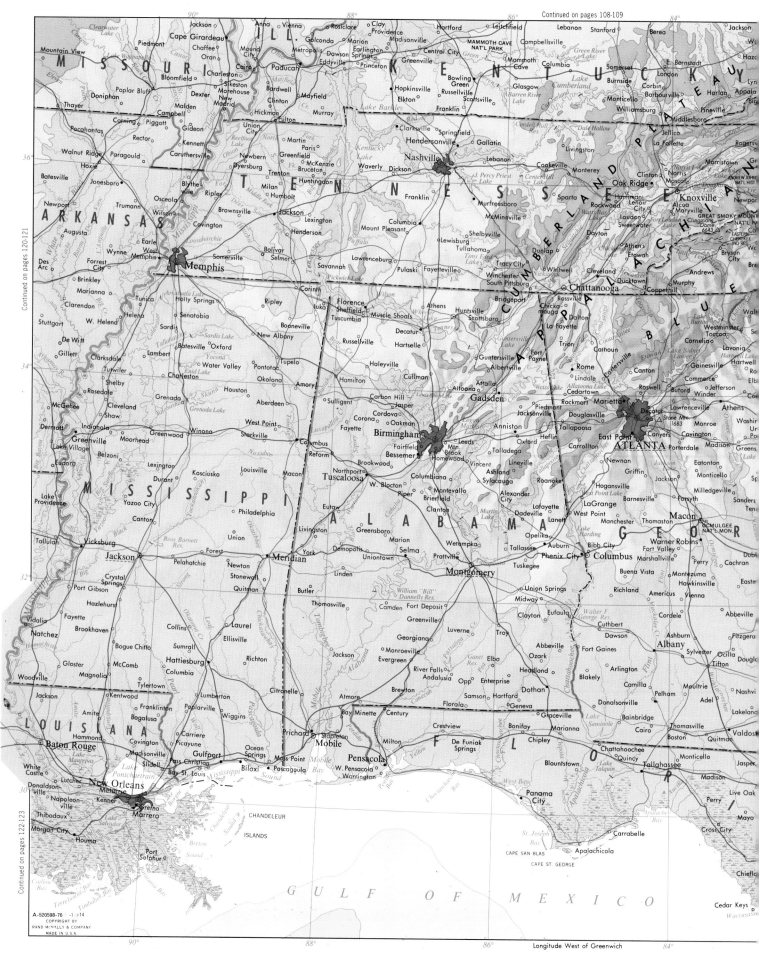

Continued on pages 108-109

Continued on pages 120-121

Continued on pages 122-123

GULF OF MEXICO

Longitude West of Greenwich

Scale 1:4 000 000; one inch to 64 miles. Conic Projection
Elevations and depressions are given in feet

Relief

Meters		Feet
1525		5000
610		2000
305		1000
152.5		500
	Sea Level	
152.5		500
1525		5000

Same scale as main map

a

©RMCN.

0   20   40   60   80   100   120 Miles
0   20   40   60   80   100 120 140 160 180 200 Kilometers

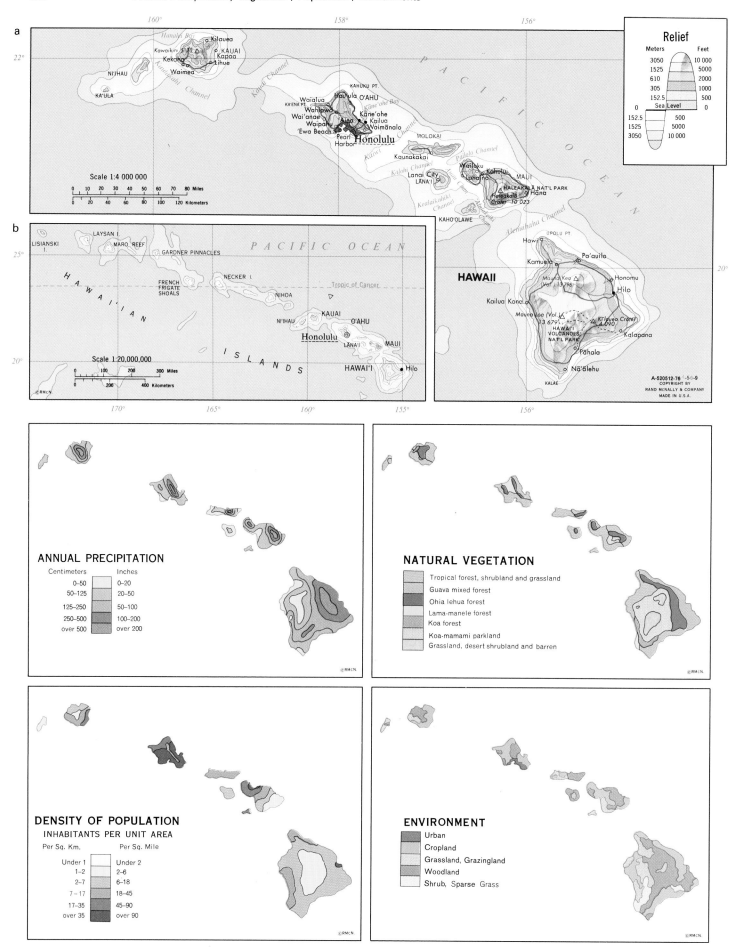

Relief

Meters		Feet
3050		10 000
1525		5000
610		2000
305		1000
152.5		500
	Sea Level	
0		0
152.5		500
1525		5000
3050		10 000

Scale 1:4 000 000

HAWAII

A-520512-76
COPYRIGHT BY
RAND McNALLY & COMPANY
MADE IN U.S.A.

Scale 1:20,000,000

©RMcN.

ANNUAL PRECIPITATION

Centimeters	Inches
0–50	0–20
50–125	20–50
125–250	50–100
250–500	100–200
over 500	over 200

©RMcN.

NATURAL VEGETATION

Tropical forest, shrubland and grassland
Guava mixed forest
Ohia lehua forest
Lama-manele forest
Koa forest
Koa-mamami parkland
Grassland, desert shrubland and barren

©RMcN.

DENSITY OF POPULATION
INHABITANTS PER UNIT AREA

Per Sq. Km.	Per Sq. Mile
Under 1	Under 2
1–2	2–6
2–7	6–18
7–17	18–45
17–35	45–90
over 35	over 90

©RMcN.

ENVIRONMENT

Urban
Cropland
Grassland, Grazingland
Woodland
Shrub, Sparse Grass

©RMcN.

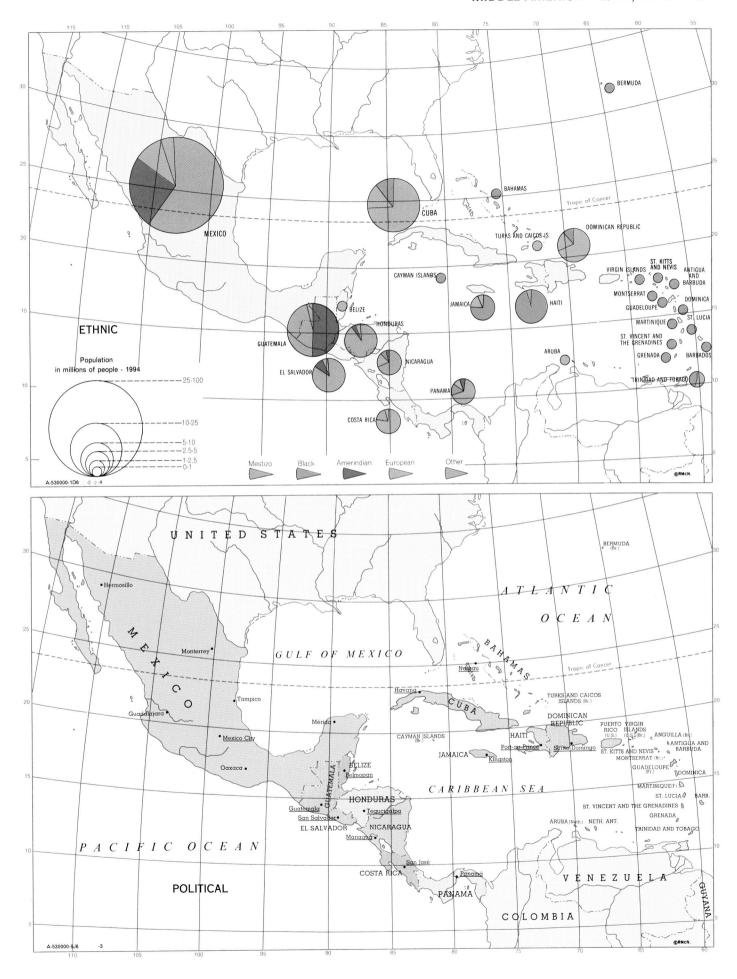

ETHNIC

Population
in millions of people - 1994

- - - - - 25-100
- - - - - 10-25
- - - - - 5-10
- - - - - 2.5-5
- - - - - 1-2.5
- - - - - 0-1

A-530000-1D6   2 -2 -4

Mestizo   Black   Amerindian   European   Other

MEXICO
BERMUDA
BAHAMAS
Tropic of Cancer
CUBA
DOMINICAN REPUBLIC
TURKS AND CAICOS IS.
VIRGIN ISLANDS
ST. KITTS AND NEVIS
ANTIGUA AND BARBUDA
CAYMAN ISLANDS
MONTSERRAT
GUADELOUPE
DOMINICA
BELIZE
JAMAICA
HAITI
ST. LUCIA
HONDURAS
MARTINIQUE
ST. VINCENT AND THE GRENADINES
GUATEMALA
NICARAGUA
ARUBA
GRENADA
BARBADOS
EL SALVADOR
PANAMA
TRINIDAD AND TOBAGO
COSTA RICA

©RMcN.

POLITICAL

UNITED STATES
• Hermosillo
MEXICO
• Monterrey
GULF OF MEXICO
Tropic of Cancer
BERMUDA (Br.)
ATLANTIC OCEAN
BAHAMAS
Guadalajara •
• Tampico
Nassau
• Mexico City
Mérida •
Havana
CUBA
TURKS AND CAICOS ISLANDS (Br.)
DOMINICAN REPUBLIC
PUERTO RICO (U.S.)
VIRGIN ISLANDS (U.S.) (Br.)
ANGUILLA (Br.)
Oaxaca •
CAYMAN ISLANDS (Br.)
HAITI
Santo Domingo
ST. KITTS AND NEVIS
ANTIGUA AND BARBUDA
MONTSERRAT (Br.)
BELIZE
JAMAICA
Port-au-Prince
Belmopan
Kingston
GUADELOUPE (Fr.)
DOMINICA
GUATEMALA
HONDURAS
CARIBBEAN SEA
MARTINIQUE (Fr.)
Guatemala
Tegucigalpa
ST. LUCIA
BARB.
San Salvador
EL SALVADOR
NICARAGUA
ST. VINCENT AND THE GRENADINES
Managua
ARUBA (Neth.)
NETH. ANT.
GRENADA
PACIFIC OCEAN
San José
TRINIDAD AND TOBAGO
COSTA RICA
Panamá
VENEZUELA
GUYANA
PANAMA
COLOMBIA

A-530000-5J6   -3

©RMcN.

Scale 1:16 000 000; one inch to 250 miles. Polyconic Projection
Elevations and depressions are given in feet

b

ATLANTIC OCEAN

Arecibo   San Juan
Aguadilla   Bayamón   CABEZAS DE   ST. THOMAS   TORTOLA
PTA. HIGUERO   Utuado   Fajardo   SAN JUAN   (U.S.A.)   (Br.)
CULEBRA   Charlotte   ST. JOHN
Mayagüez   PUERTO RICO   Caguas   Amalie   (U.S.A.)
(U.S.A.)   Cayey   Vieques
Coamo   Humacao   VIEQUES
CABO ROJO
Ponce   Salinas   Guayama   Christiansted

CARIBBEAN   SEA   SAINT CROIX
(U.S.A.)

© RMCN
Scale 1:4 000 000
0 10 20 30   40 Miles
0 10 20 30 40 50 60 Kilometers

c
LITTLE
HANS LOLLICK
64°50'
OUTER BRASS   HANS LOLLICK
INNER BRASS   PICARA PT
STORMY PT   THATCH CAY   GRASS
ST ▲ THOMAS   CAY
Crown Mt (U.S.A.)
1558   Charlotte Amalie   18°
(St. Thomas)   20'
WATER   FLAMINGO PT   St. Thomas   Nadir
© RMCN   Harbor   Scale 1:500 000

W. VIRGINIA   Richmond
VIRGINIA   Roanoke
Norfolk
35°
NORTH CAROLINA   CAPE HATTERAS
MT MITCHELL   Charlotte
6684
SOUTH   Wilmington   CAPE FEAR
Columbia
CAROLINA   Charleston
Augusta
GEORGIA   Savannah

BERMUDA
(Br.)

Tallahassee   Jacksonville
St. Augustine
Ocala   CAPE CANAVERAL
Tampa
Tampa Bay
W. Palm
Beach
MIAMI   Lake
Okeechobee
CAPE SABLE
Key West
FLORIDA KEYS

NORTH AMERICAN

BASIN

GRAND BAHAMA
GREAT ABACO
BAHAMAS   ELEUTHERA
Nassau
CAT   20°
ANDROS   SAN SALVADOR (WATLING)

HAVANA   Guanabacoa   Matanzas
Marianao   Cárdenas
ar del Río   Santa Clara
CUBA   Sancti Spíritus   Nuevitas
Cienfuegos   Ciego
Trinidad   de Ávila   Camagüey
ISLA   Holguín
DE LA   PUNTA
JUVENTUD   Manzanillo   MAISÍ
SIERRA MAESTRA   Cap-Haïtien   Puerto Plata
GRAND CAYMAN   Guantánamo   Santiago de los
(Br.)   C. CRUZ   Santiago   Gonaïves   Caballeros   C. SAMANÁ
de Cuba   ÎLE DE LA   El Norte   Sánchez   C. ENGAÑO
Montego Bay   GONÂVE   Pédro   Mayagüez
Mt. Denham   HAÏTI   417   DOMINICAN   San Juan
3236   Port Antonio   Port-au-Prince   REPUBLIC   Ponce   Charlotte Amalie
Spanish Town   Santo Domingo   PUERTO RICO   SAINT CROIX
JAMAICA   Kingston   HISPANIOLA   (U.S.A.)   (U.S.A.)

ACKLINS
GT INAGUA
CAICOS
TURKS

PUERTO RICO   TRENCH
∇ 28 374

VIRGIN IS
ST. THOMAS   ANGUILLA
(Br.)
BARBUDA
ST. KITTS AND NEVIS   ANTIGUA
MONTSERRAT   AND
(Br.)   BARBUDA
V. Soufrière   Pointe-à-Pitre
4813   GUADELOUPE
Basse Terre   (Fr.)
DOMINICA

ATLANTIC   OCEAN

GREATER   ANTILLES

WEST   INDIES   LESSER   ANTILLES

MARTINIQUE (Fr.)
Fort-de-France   15°

ST. LUCIA
ST. VINCENT   BARBADOS
AND THE
GRENADINES   Bridgetown
Kingstown

GRENADA

TOBAGO
TRINIDAD AND TOBAGO
PUNTA DE GALLINAS   ARUBA   SAN ROMÁN   Port of Spain
PENÍNSULA   (Neth.)   CURAÇAO BONAIRE
DE GUAJIRA   (Neth.)   ISLA LA   Trinidad
Golfo de   PEN. DE   Willemstad   TORTUGA
Santa Marta   Venezuela   PARAGUANÁ   ISLA DE
Barranquilla   Ciénaga   Coro   MARGARITA   Carúpano   10°
AMERICA   Cartagena   Soledad   Maracaibo   Puerto   La Guaira   CARACAS   Cumaná
Cabimas   San Felipe   Cabello   Maracay   Puerto   Maturín
Bluefields   Lago de   Barquisimeto   Valencia   la Cruz
Maracaibo
Limón   Trujillo   El Tigre   Morawhanna
San José   Golfo de los   Colón   PANAMÁ   Lorica   Sincelejo   Mompós   Valera   Guanare   Calabozo   Orinoco
RICA   Mosquitos   Portobelo   ISTMO   Magangué   Mérida   Puerto de   San Fernando   Ciudad Guayana
Cartago   Golfo   PANAMA   Montería   Nutrias   de Apure   Río   Ciudad Bolívar
Anton   del Darién   CORDILLERA DE MÉRIDA   Cerro Bolívar
Panamá   Cúcuta   San Cristóbal   VENEZUELA
David   Santiago   Barrancabermeja   Pamplona   Apure
PEN. DE   Golfo de   Bucaramanga   Cerro Neblina
Coiba   AZUERO   Panamá   7800   GUYANA
Medellín   Meta
Sonsón   Tunja
Manizales   COLOMBIA   San Fernando   SERRA PACARAIMA
Pereira   de Atabapo
Armenia   BOGOTÁ
Ibagué   Girardot   Villavicencio
ISLA DE   Buenaventura   Cali   Palmira   Guaviare   BRAZIL
MALPELO   Guaviare
(Colombia)

Longitude West of Greenwich

Continued on pages 142-143

Relief
Meters   Feet
3050   10000
1525   5000
610   2000
305   1000
152.5   500
0   Sea Level   0
152.5   500
1525   5000
3050   10000
6100   20000

0 50 100   200   300   400   500 Miles
0   100   200   400   600   800 Kilometers

Cities   0 to 50,000   500,000 to 1,000,000
and
Towns   50,000 to 500,000   1,000,000 and over

Continued on pages 122-123

106°   104°   102°   100°

24°

Río San Dimas   Durango   Miguel Auza   o Juan Aldama   o Gruñidora   N U E V O   o Hidalgo   o Jiméne
El Salto   o   Nieves   o Ascensión   Aramberri   Padilla
Nombre de Dios   o   o Río Grande   L E O N   Zaragoza
Pánuco   Mezquital   Chalchihuites   10 100   Sombrerete   Vanegas   Cedral   Peña Nevado   Ciudad Victoria
Siqueros   Cancordia   Santa María   11 700   Catorce   La Paz   Doctor Arroyo   13 300   Miquihuana   T A M A U L I P A
Pueblo   de Ocotán   Matehuala   Jaumave   Llera   Xicotencatl

22°

N A Y A R I T

SINALOA   Rosario   Escuinapa   Huajicori   o   Acaponeta   Tecuala   San Felipe   Rosamorada   Ruiz   Tuxpan

SIERRA   DE   NAYARIT

Tepic   San Blas   Jalisco   Sta. María del Oro   Compostela   San Pedro   Lagunillas   San Pedro

PACIFIC   OCEAN

Acapulco

Scale 1:4 000 000; one inch to 64 miles. Conic Projection
Elevations and depressions are given in feet

Relief

Meters   Feet
3050   10 000
1525   5000
610   2000
305   1000
152.5   500
0   Sea Level   0
152.5   500
1525   5000
3050   10 000

A-531695-76   6-15
COPYRIGHT BY
RAND McNALLY & COMPANY
MADE IN U.S.A.

104°   102°   100°
Longitude West of Greenwich

Cities and Towns
0 to 50,000   o   500,000 to 1,000,000   ◎
50,000 to 500,000   ⊙   1,000,000 and over

Continued on pages 132-133

132

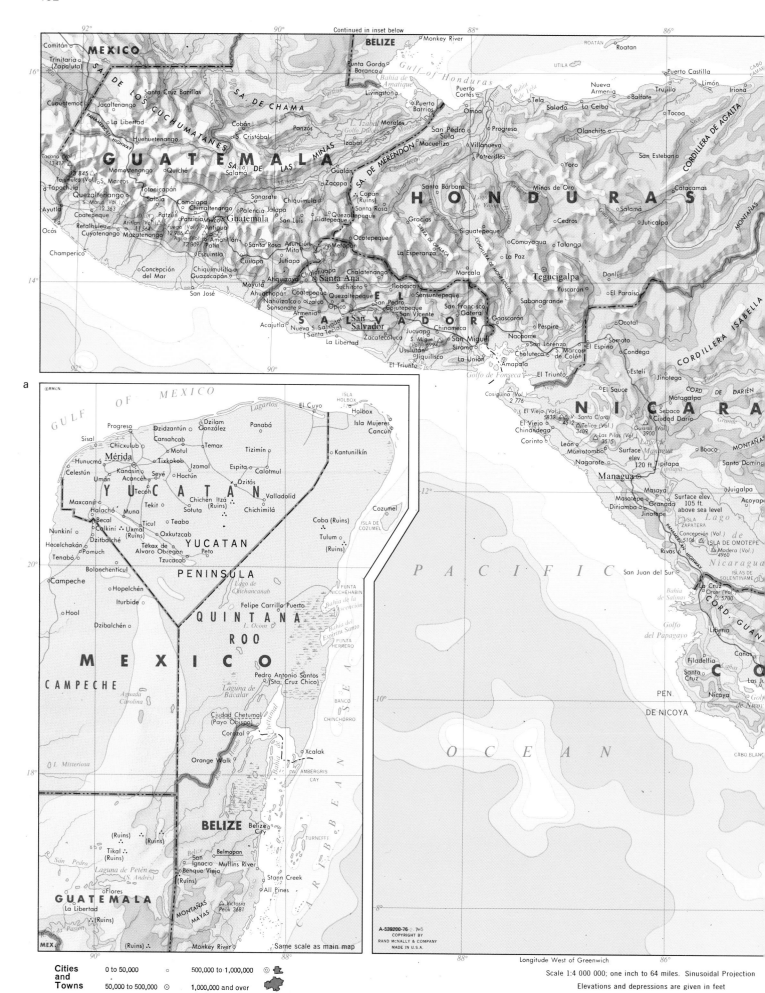

a ©RMcN.

MEXICO

BELIZE

GUATEMALA

HONDURAS

EL SALVADOR

NICARA

YUCATAN

QUINTANA ROO

MEXICO

CAMPECHE

PENINSULA

BELIZE

GUATEMALA

PACIFIC OCEAN

CARIBBEAN SEA

GULF OF MEXICO

Same scale as main map

Cities and Towns

0 to 50,000	○	500,000 to 1,000,000	◉
50,000 to 500,000	⊙	1,000,000 and over	

Longitude West of Greenwich

Scale 1:4 000 000; one inch to 64 miles. Sinusoidal Projection

Elevations and depressions are given in feet

Longitude West of Greenwich

Relief

Meters		Feet
3050		10 000
1525		5000
610		2000
305		1000
152.5		500
	Sea Level	
152.5		500
1525		5000
3050		10 000

b

PUNTA PATUCA

Cabo Gracias a Dios

CAYOS MISKITO

Puerto Cabezas

Lone Star   Laguna Caratá

Huaunta   Laguna Huaunta

Prinzapolca

C A R I B B E A N

Laguna las Perlas

ISLA DE PROVIDENCIA
(Colombia)

Rama

SAN ANDRÉS
(Colombia)

Bluefields   ISLA DE LA CIERVO

LITTLE CORN

CAYOS DE ESE

S E A

PUNTA MICO

GREAT CORN
(Nicaragua)

CAYOS DE ALBUQUERQUE
(Colombia)

Río Punta Gorda

Bahía
de San Juan
del Norte

San Juan del Norte
(Greytown)

L E E W A R D

ANGUILLA
(Br.)

ST. MARTIN
(Neth. and Fr.)

ST BARTHÉLEMY
(Fr.)

Codrington   BARBUDA

SABA
(Neth.)

ST. EUSTATIUS
(Neth.)   ST KITTS

Mt. Misery
3792   Basseterre
Charlestown   ST. KITTS AND NEVIS
Nevis Peak   St. Johns
3596
NEVIS   Boggy Peak   ANTIGUA
1319   AND
REDONDA   BARBUDA

MONTSERRAT
(Br.)
Plymouth   Chances Pk.
3000

Guadeloupe Passage

POINTE DE
LA GRANDE VIGIE
GRANDE TERRE
Ste. Rose   Le Moule   DÉSIRADE
(Fr.)
Pointe-à-Pitre   PETITE TERRE
BASSE TERRE   Ste. Anne   (Fr.)
Soufrière   GUADELOUPE
4813   Capesterre   (Fr.)
Basse Terre   MARIE GALANTE
LES SAINTES IS   Grand Bourg

I   Portsmouth   Morne Diablotins
S   4747
L   St. Joseph   DOMINICA
A   Roseau
N   Dominica Channel
D
S   Mt. Pelée (Vol.)   Trinité
4583   Pitons du Carbet
St. Pierre   3960
Fort-de-France   Le François
MARTINIQUE
Le Marin   (Fr.)
POINTE D'ENFER
St. Lucia Channel

C   Castries
A   Morne Gimie
R   3117   ST. LUCIA
I   Soufrière
B
B   St. Vincent Passage
E
A   Soufrière
N   4048
ST. VINCENT
S   Kingstown   AND THE
E   GRENADINES
A   BEQUIA

W   MUSTIQUE
I
N   CANOUAN
D
W   CARRIACOU
A
R   Mt. St. Catherine
D   2757
St.   Grenville
George's   GRENADA

©RMcN   THE GRENADINES

NORTH POINT
BARBADOS
Mt. Hillaby
1115   Bathsheba
Bridgetown
SOUTH POINT

A T L A N T I C   O C E A N

Same scale as main map

San Ramón   Guápiles   Cairo   Matina
Alajuela   Heredia
San José   Irazú Vol.   Turrialba
Cartago   Paraíso   Límón

Parrita   Quepos
Cerro Chirripó
12 530
PUNTA QUEPOS   San Isidro   Cerro Kámuk
11 696
Bahía   Buenos Aires   Cerro Echandi
de   10 394
Coronada   Puerto Cortés
ISLA DE CAÑO   PENÍNSULA   Boquete
Puerto Jiménez   Volcán Barú
DE OSA   11 401
CABO MATAPALO   Golfito
Concepción   C. de Santa
La Cuesta   Catalina
David   5249
Puerto Armuelles   SERRANÍA
Horconcitos   DE TABASARA
Bahía Charco   Remedios
de Azul   Las Palmas
PUNTA BURICA   Soná   Río de Jesús   Chitré
Santiago   Los Santos

PUNTA CAHUITA

Golfo
de los Mosquitos

Bocas del Toro
Bahía de Almirante

Almirante   PUNTA CHIRIQUI

Guabito

Laguna   ESCUDO
de Chiriquí   DE VERAGUAS
Chiriquí Grande

C. Negro 4429

PANAMÁ
Peñonomé   Bejuco
Antón   PUNTA CHAME
Natá   Río Hato
Aguadulce   ISLA DE SAN JOSÉ
ISLA DE SAN JOSE   Golfo
de Parita

Golfo   Golfo de Panamá

PENÍNSULA

DE AZUERO

Chitré   Las Tablas
PUNTA MALA

ISLA COIBA

ISLA CEBACO

ISLA JICARÓN   PUNTA MARIATO

PUNTA MANZANILLO   Nombre   El
de Dios   Porvenir   PUNTA SAN BLAS
Portobelo   Mandinga   Golfo de San Blas
Colón
Gatún   Silver City   C. Brewster   CORD. DE SAN BLAS
North Gamboa   Chepo   3018
Lago   Chepo
Gatún   Balboa Heights
Balboa   Panamá
Chorrera   Bahía de Panamá

ISTMO DE PANAMÁ

P   A   N   A   M   Á

ARCHIPIÉLAGO
DE LAS PERLAS   San Miguel
ISLA
DEL REY
Bahía
San Miguel   La Palma

SERRANÍA DEL DARIÉN

CABO
TIBURÓN

PUNTA GARACHINE   Garachiné   El Real

COLOMBIA

0 20 40 60 80 100 120 Miles
0 20 40 60 80 100 120 140 160 180 200 Kilometers

134

GULF

OF

MEXICO

FLORIDA

SANIBEL

Naples
*the Big Cypress
Swamp*
SEMINOLE
IND. RES.

Delray Beach

Fort Lauderdale
Dania

CAPE ROMANO

Everglades
TEN THOUSAND
ISLANDS

MIAMI
Miami Beach

EVERGLADES

EVERGLADES
NATIONAL PARK

Homestead
*Biscayne
Bay*

CAPE SABLE

*Whitewater
Bay*

Florida Bay

KEY
LARGO

MARQUESAS
KEYS

DRY TORTUGAS

PINE IS

FLORIDA KEYS

Key
West

Straits of Florida

Tropic of Cancer

HAVANA
CIUDAD DE
LA HABANA
Marianao
Regla
Guanabacoa

Bahia de Matanzas

CAYO BLANCOS

ARCHIPIELAGO DE SABANA

CAYO

Santa Fé
Nueva Gerona
ISLA DE LA
JUVENTUD

ISLAS DE MANGLES
ARCHIPIELAGO DE
LOS CANARREOS

CAYOS DE
JUAN LUIS

CAYO LARGO

BANCO
XAGUA

BANCO JARDINES

Santaren Channel

Nicholas Channel

Cienfuegos
*Bahia
Cienfuegos*

Palmira
Rodas
Cruces

VILLA CLARA

Santa
Clara
Camajuaní
Zulueta
Placetas

Remedios
Caibarién

Fomento
SIERRA DE
TRINIDAD
Trinidad
Casilda

SANCTI
SPIRITUS
Sancti
Spiritus

Morón
CIEGO DE
AVILA
Ciego de Ávila

Tunas de Zaza

Júcaro

CAMAGÜEY

Camagüey

LAS
TUNAS

Victoria de
las Tunas

CAYOS
ANA MARIA

CAYOS CINCO BALAS

CAYOS
DE LAS DOCE LEGUAS

LABERINTO DE LAS
DOCE LEGUAS

GOLFO DE
GUACANAYABO

Campechuela

Santa Cruz
del Sur

Guayabal

Manzanillo

GRAN

Niquero
Pico Ojo del Toro
1748

SIERRA

CABO
CRUZ

LITTLE CAYMAN

CAYMAN BRAC
(Br.)

CAYMAN ISLANDS

George Town

GRAND CAYMAN

CARIBBEAN

SEA

JAMAICA

Montego Bay
Lucea

Falmouth
St. Ann's Bay

SOUTH NEGRIL PT.
Savanna la Mar

Black River

May Pen

Mt. Denham

Spanish

Longitude West of Greenwich

Relief

Meters		Feet
3050		10 000
1525		5000
610		2000
305		1000
152.5		500
0	Sea Level	0
152.5		500
1525		5000
3050		10 000
6100		20 000

Cities and Towns

| 0 to 50,000 | ○ | 500,000 to 1,000,000 | ◎ |
| 50,000 to 500,000 | ⊙ | 1,000,000 and over | |

Scale 1:4 000 000; one inch to 64 miles. Conic Projection

Elevations and depressions are given in feet.

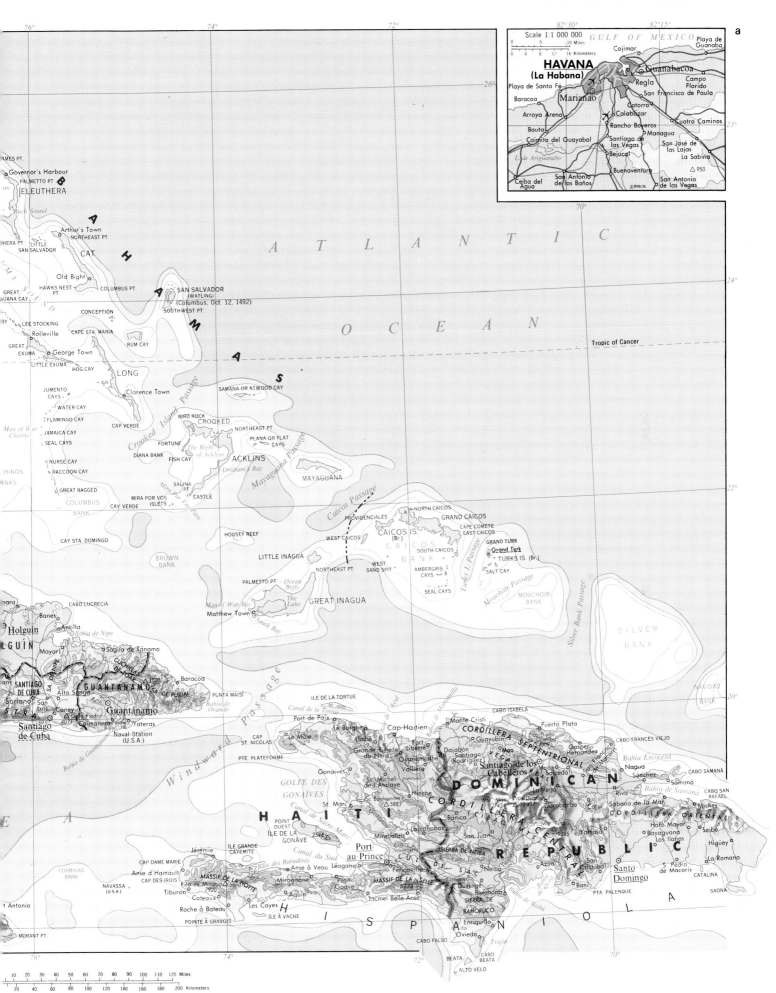

HAVANA
(La Habana)

Scale 1:1 000 000

GULF OF MEXICO

Playa de Guanabo
Cojimar
Playa de Santa Fé
Baracoa
Marianao
Guanabacoa
Regla
Campo Florido
San Francisco de Paula
Cotorro
Arroya Arena
Calabazar
Rancho Boyeros
Cuatro Caminos
Managua
Bauta
Caimito del Guayabal
Santiago de las Vegas
Bejucal
San José de las Lajas
La Sabina
Ceiba del Agua
San Antonio de los Baños
Buenaventura
San Antonio de las Vegas
L. de Ariguanabo
△ 950
©RMcN.

A T L A N T I C

O C E A N

Tropic of Cancer

ATMES PT.
Governor's Harbour
PALMETTO PT.
ELEUTHERA
HERA PT.
LITTLE SAN SALVADOR
Arthur's Town
NORTHEAST PT.
CAT
Old Bight
HAWKS NEST PT.
COLUMBUS PT.
SAN SALVADOR (WATLING)
(Columbus, Oct. 12, 1492)
SOUTHWEST PT.
CONCEPTIÓN
CAPE STA MARIA
LEE STOCKING
Rolleville
RUM CAY
GREAT GUANA CAY
GREAT EXUMA
George Town
LITTLE EXUMA
HOG CAY
LONG
Clarence Town
JUMENTO CAYS
WATER CAY
FLAMINGO CAY
CAP VERDE
SAMANA OR ATWOOD CAY
JAMAICA CAY
CROOKED
BIRD ROCK
NORTHEAST PT.
Man of War Channel
SEAL CAYS
FORTUNE
PLANA OR FLAT CAYS
NURSE CAY
DIANA BANK
FISH CAY
The Bight of Acklins
RACCOON CAY
ACKLINS
GREAT RAGGED
SALINA PT.
CASTLE
MAYAGUANA
COLUMBUS BANK
MIRA POR VOS ISLETS
CAY VERDE
Mira por Vos Pass.
CAY STA. DOMINGO
HOGSTY REEF
Caicos Passage
PROVIDENCIALES
NORTH CAICOS
GRAND CAICOS
CAPE COMETE
EAST CAICOS
WEST CAICOS
CAICOS IS. (Br.)
SOUTH CAICOS
GRAND TURK
BROWN BANK
LITTLE INAGUA
CAICOS BANK
Grand Turk
TURKS IS. (Br.)
AMBERGRIS CAYS
SALT CAY
PALMETTO PT.
Ocean Bight
NORTHEAST PT.
WEST SAND SPIT
SEAL CAYS
MOUCHOIR BANK
Man of War Bay
The Lake
GREAT INAGUA
Matthew Town
South Bay
Mouchoir Passage
Silver Bank Passage
SILVER BANK
CABO LUCRECIA
NAVIDAD BANK
Holguin
Banes
Antilla
Bahia de Nipe
HOLGUÍN
Mayari
Sagua de Tánamo
CUCHILLAS DE TOA
△ 3100
Baracoa
SANTIAGO DE CUBA
GUANTÁNAMO
SA. DE PURIAL
PUNTA MAISÍ
ILE DE LA TORTUE
CABO ISABELA
Alto Songo
Soriano
Caney
San Luis
Guantánamo
SIERRA
SA. DE
Yateras
Naval Station (U.S.A.)
Santiago de Cuba
Bahia de Ovando
Port de Paix
Le Borgne
Cap-Haïtien
Monte Cristi
Puerto Plata
CORDILLERA SEPTENTRIONAL
CABO FRANCÉS VIEJO
Canal de la Tortue
CAP ST. NICOLAS
Le Môle
Guayubín
Pico Diego de Ocampo
Gaspar Hernández
PTE. PLATEFORME
Grande Rivière du Nord
Fort Liberté
Dajabón
Santiago Rodríguez
Santiago de los Caballeros
Nagua
CABO SAMANA
Gonaïves
Ouanaminthe
Vallière
La Vega
Moca
Solcedo
Sánchez
Bahia Escocesa
Windward Passage
Bahia de Guantánamo
GOLFE DES GONAÏVES
St-Michel-de-l'Atalaye
Hinche
DOMINICAN
Riva
Bahia de Samaná
CABO SAN RAFAEL
St. Marc
Pico Duarte △ 10,417
Jarabacoa
Bonao
Cotuí
Sabana de la Mar
Miches
Mte. Tina △ 3087
CORDILLERA ORIENTAL
Pic Boonhomme △ 5883
CORDILLERA CENTRAL
POINT OUEST
ILE DE LA GONÂVE
△ 2546
Mirebalais
Lascahobas
Banica
San Juan
Jarabacoa
Hato Mayor
Bayaguana
Los Llanos
Seibo
HAITI
Jérémie
ILE GRANDE CAYEMITE
Canal du Sud
Port-au-Prince
Pétionville
SIERRA DE NEIBA
Lago Enriquillo
Neiba
REPUBLIC
San Cristóbal
Higüey
La Romana
CAP DAME MARIE
Anse d'Hainault
CAP DES IROIS
MASSIF DE LA HOTTE
Pico de Macaya △ 7920
Miragoâne
Anse à Veau
Petit Goâve
Léogane
MASSIF DE LA SELLE △ 8773
Duvergé
Barahona
San Pedro de Macorís
CATALINA
Santo Domingo
Bani
PTA. PALENQUE
H I S P A N I O L A
Tiburon
Coteaux
Aquin
Les Cayes
ILE À VACHE
Jacmel
Belle-Anse
SIERRA DE BAHORUCO
SAONA
FORMIGAS BANK
NAVASSA (U.S.A.)
San Antonio
Roche à Bateau
POINTE À GRAVOIS
CABO FALSO
Oviedo
Enriquillo
Bahia de Neiba
MORANT PT.
BEATA
CABO BEATA
ALTO VELO
Trujín

10 20 30 40 50 60 70 80 90 100 110 120 Miles
20 40 60 80 100 120 140 160 180 200 Kilometers

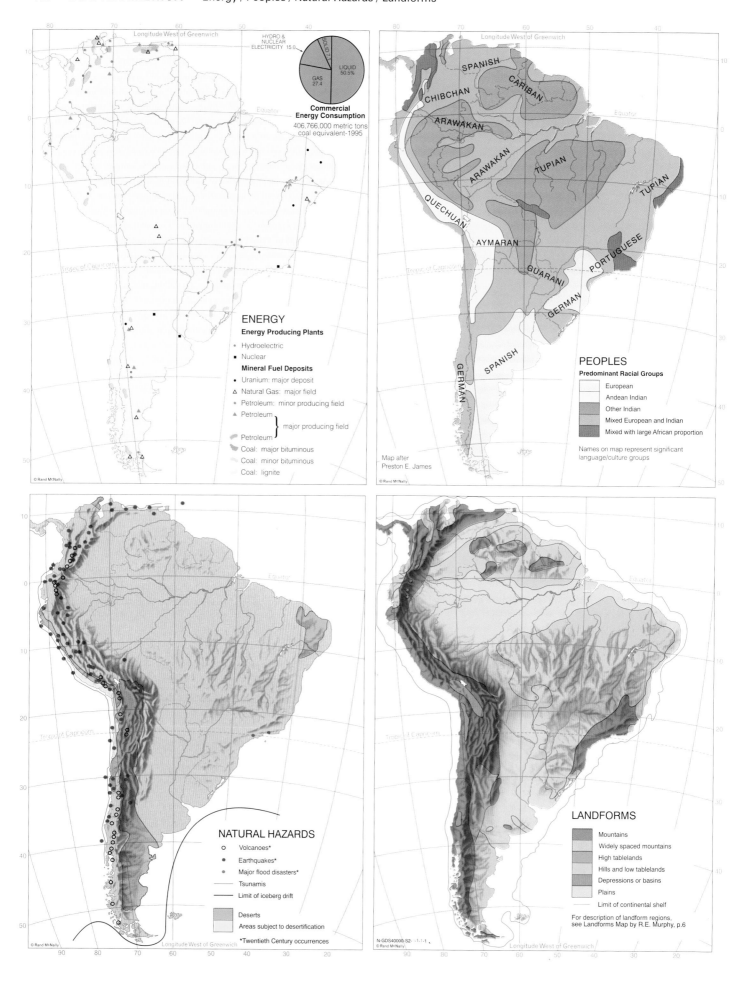

ENERGY

Energy Producing Plants

- Hydroelectric
- Nuclear

Mineral Fuel Deposits

- Uranium: major deposit
- Natural Gas: major field
- Petroleum: minor producing field
- Petroleum
- Petroleum } major producing field
- Coal: major bituminous
- Coal: minor bituminous
- Coal: lignite

HYDRO & NUCLEAR ELECTRICITY 15.0
SOLID 7.1
LIQUID 50.5%
GAS 27.4

Commercial Energy Consumption
406,766,000 metric tons coal equivalent-1995

© Rand McNally

PEOPLES

Predominant Racial Groups

- European
- Andean Indian
- Other Indian
- Mixed European and Indian
- Mixed with large African proportion

Names on map represent significant language/culture groups

Map after Preston E. James

© Rand McNally

SPANISH
CHIBCHAN
CARIBAN
ARAWAKAN
ARAWAKAN
QUECHUAN
TUPIAN
TUPIAN
AYMARAN
GUARANI
PORTUGUESE
GERMAN
SPANISH
GERMAN

NATURAL HAZARDS

- ○ Volcanoes*
- ● Earthquakes*
- ● Major flood disasters*
- Tsunamis
- Limit of iceberg drift
- Deserts
- Areas subject to desertification

*Twentieth Century occurrences

© Rand McNally

LANDFORMS

- Mountains
- Widely spaced mountains
- High tablelands
- Hills and low tablelands
- Depressions or basins
- Plains
- Limit of continental shelf

For description of landform regions, see Landforms Map by R.E. Murphy, p.6

N-GDS40000-S2- -1-1-1
© Rand McNally

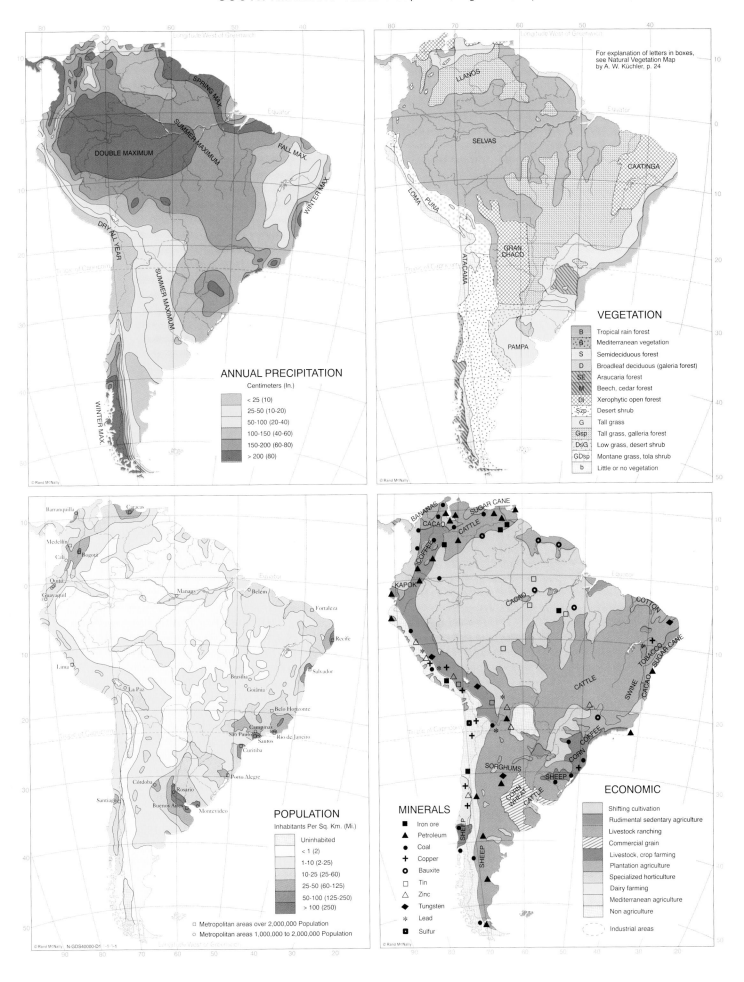

ANNUAL PRECIPITATION

Centimeters (In.)

- < 25 (10)
- 25-50 (10-20)
- 50-100 (20-40)
- 100-150 (40-60)
- 150-200 (60-80)
- > 200 (80)

SPRING MAX.
SUMMER MAXIMUM
FALL MAX.
DOUBLE MAXIMUM
DRY ALL YEAR
WINTER MAX.
SUMMER MAXIMUM
WINTER MAX.

VEGETATION

For explanation of letters in boxes, see Natural Vegetation Map by A. W. Küchler, p. 24

B	Tropical rain forest
B̃	Mediterranean vegetation
S	Semideciduous forest
D	Broadleaf deciduous (galeria forest)
SE	Araucaria forest
M	Beech, cedar forest
Dl	Xerophytic open forest
Szp	Desert shrub
G	Tall grass
Gsp	Tall grass, galleria forest
DsG	Low grass, desert shrub
GDsp	Montane grass, tola shrub
b	Little or no vegetation

LLANOS
SELVAS
CAATINGA
LOMA
PUNA
ATACAMA
GRAN CHACO
PAMPA

POPULATION

Inhabitants Per Sq. Km. (Mi.)

- Uninhabited
- < 1 (2)
- 1-10 (2-25)
- 10-25 (25-60)
- 25-50 (60-125)
- 50-100 (125-250)
- > 100 (250)

□ Metropolitan areas over 2,000,000 Population
○ Metropolitan areas 1,000,000 to 2,000,000 Population

MINERALS

- ■ Iron ore
- ▲ Petroleum
- ● Coal
- + Copper
- ◉ Bauxite
- □ Tin
- △ Zinc
- ◆ Tungsten
- ✳ Lead
- ▪ Sulfur

ECONOMIC

- Shifting cultivation
- Rudimental sedentary agriculture
- Livestock ranching
- Commercial grain
- Livestock, crop farming
- Plantation agriculture
- Specialized horticulture
- Dairy farming
- Mediterranean agriculture
- Non agriculture
- Industrial areas

HAVANA

C U B A

Bahía de Campeche

PEN. DE YUCATÁN

Gulf of Honduras

Yucatán Channel

JAMAICA

HISPANIOLA

San Juan
PUERTO RICO (U.S.A.)

PUERTO RICO TRENCH

W E S T   I N D I E S

C A R I B B E A N   S E A

GUADELOUPE (Fr.)

MARTINIQUE (Fr.)

BARBADOS

TRINIDAD AND TOBAGO
Port of Spain

NORTH AMERICAN BASIN

Tropic of Cancer

A T L A N T I C   O C E A N

CENTRAL

AMERICA

Lago de Nicaragua

ISLA DEL COCO (Costa Rica)

Panamá
IST. DE PAN.

Golfo del Darién

Golfo de Panamá

ISLA DE MALPELO (Colombia)

PUNTA DE GALLINAS

Barranquilla
Cartagena

Maracaibo
La Guaira
Valencia CARACAS
Mérida
VENEZUELA
Ciudad Bolívar
Cerro Icutú △7800

Orinoco

Georgetown

Paramaribo

Cayenne

GUYANA

SURINAME **FR. GUIANA**

Península de Venezuela

Medellín
BOGOTÁ
Nevado del Tolima 17 110

Boa Vista do Rio Branco

COLOMBIA

Guaviare

Río Branco

GUIANA HIGHLANDS

ILHA DE MARAJÓ

Equator

ROCEDOS SÃO PEDRO E SÃO PAULO (Brazil)

Quito
Cotopaxi 19 347
ECUADOR
Guayaquil Chimborazo 20 704

Putumayo
Japurá

Negro

Manaus (Manáos)

Amazon (Amazonas)

Belém (Pará)

São Luís (Maranhão)

ARQUIPÉLAGO DE COLÓN (GALÁPAGOS ISLANDS) (Ec.)

ARCHIPIÉLAGO DE COLÓN

Golfo de Guayaquil

Iquitos
Leticia

Solimões

Juruá
Purús

Madeira

Tapajós

Xingu

Tocantins

Fortaleza (Ceará)

ARQUIPÉLAGO DE FERNANDO DE NORONHA (Brazil)

Chiclayo
Trujillo
Nevs Huascarán 22 133

Porto Velho
Rio Branco

B R A Z I L

Teresina

SERRA DO PIAUÍ

CABO DE SÃO ROQUE

Natal
João Pessoa (Paraíba)
RECIFE (Pernambuco)
Maceió

P E R U

LIMA
Callao
Cusco

Arequipa
Mollendo

CHAPADA DE MATO GROSSO

Cuiabá

Brasília

Diamantina

Salto Paulo Afonso

Salvador (Bahia)

Volcán Misti

La Paz
Nev Illimani 20 741
BOLIVIA
Sucre
Potosí

Lago de Titicaca

Belo Horizonte

Pico da Bandeira 9482

Vitória

São Francisco

BRAZILIAN HIGHLANDS

SERRA DO ESPINHAÇO

Iquique

Antofagasta

Tropic of Capricorn

ISLA DE SAN FÉLIX ISLA DE SAN AMBROSIO (Chile)

DESIERTO DE ATACAMA

Salta
Tucumán

GRAN CHACO

PARAGUAY

Asunción

SÃO PAULO

Santos

CABO FRIO

RIO DE JANEIRO

Paraná

Iguassú Falls

PERU-CHILE TRENCH

Cerro Azul

Copiapó

Cerro Aconcagua 22 835

Bermejo

Corrientes

Salado

Florianópolis

Coquimbo

Valparaíso
SANTIAGO
Mendoza

Córdoba
Rosario
Santa Fe
Salto
BUENOS AIRES
La Plata

URUGUAY
Rio Grande

Porto Alegre

MONTEVIDEO

Río de la Plata

Concepción

PAMPAS

Colorado

Bahía Blanca

A T L A N T I C   O C E A N

Valdivia

Viedma

Golfo San Matías

P A C I F I C   O C E A N

Puerto Montt
ISLA DE CHILOÉ

A R G E N T I N A

ARCHIPIÉLAGO DE LOS CHONOS

Monte Valentin 314

Chubut

Comodoro Rivadavia

Golfo San Jorge

A N D E S

WELLINGTON

HANOVER

DESOLACIÓN

Punta Arenas
Mt. Sarmiento 8100

Río Gallegos

Stanley

FALKLAND IS. (ISLAS MALVINAS) (Br.)

Estrecho de Magallanes

TIERRA DEL FUEGO

ISLA DE LOS ESTADOS

CABO DE HORNOS (CAPE HORN)

D r a k e   P a s s a g e

SOUTH SHETLAND ISLANDS

SOUTH GEORGIA (Br.)

SOUTH ORKNEY IS. (Br.)

SOUTH SANDWICH ISLANDS (Br.)

SOUTH SANDWICH TRENCH

JOINVILLE

JAMES ROSS

ANTARCTIC PENINSULA

Antarctic Circle

A-540000-26 -4-7-16
COPYRIGHT BY
RAND MCNALLY & COMPANY
MADE IN U.S.A.

40,000 SQ MI	

AREA

0   300   600
Miles

0   200   400   600   800   1000 Miles
0   400   800   1200   1600 Kilometers

Scale 1:40 000 000, one inch to 630 miles. Lambert's Azimuthal. Equal Area Projection
Elevations and depressions are given in feet

Urban

Cropland

Cropland & Woodland

Cropland & Grazing Land

Grassland, Grazing Land

Forest, Woodland

Swamp, Marshland

Shrub, Sparse Grass, Wasteland

Barren Land

Scale 1:36,000,000; one inch to 570 miles   Lambert Azimuthal Equal-Area Projection

0   100   200   400   600   800 Miles

0   150   300   600   900   1200 Kilometers

A-540000-36
COPYRIGHT BY
RAND McNALLY & COMPANY
MADE IN U.S.A.

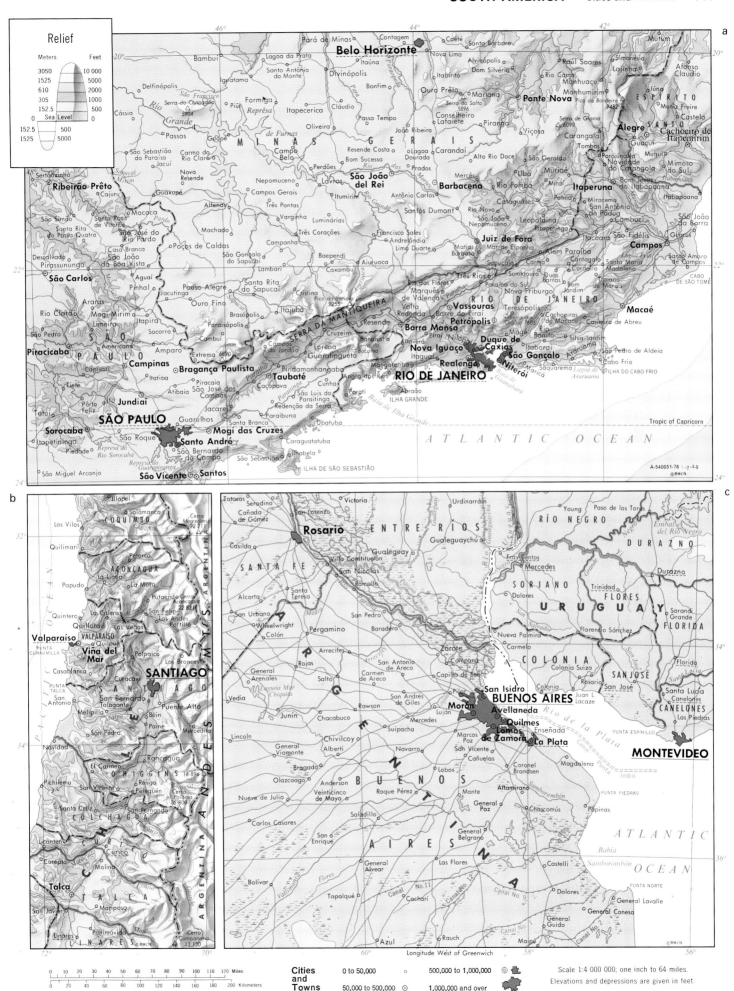

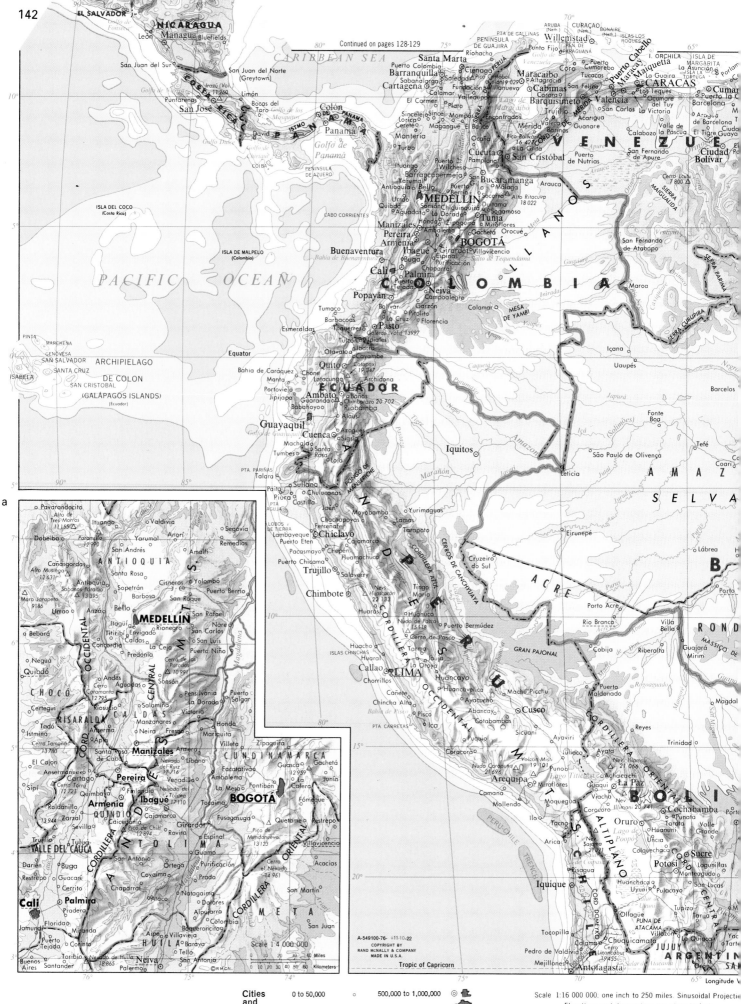

142

Continued on pages 128-129

CARIBBEAN SEA

PACIFIC OCEAN

EL SALVADOR
NICARAGUA
León   Managua   Bluefields
San Juan del Sur   San Juan del Norte (Greytown)
Irazú (Vol.) 11 260
Puntarenas   Limón   Bocas del Toro
San José   David   ISTMO
COSTA RICA
PANAMA
Colón   Panamá
Golfo de Panamá
COIBA
PENINSULA DE AZUERO

ISLA DEL COCO (Costa Rica)

ISLA DE MALPELO (Colombia)

PINTA
MARCHENA
GENOVESA
SAN SALVADOR   SANTA CRUZ
ISABELA   SAN CRISTOBAL
ARCHIPIELAGO DE COLON
(GALÁPAGOS ISLANDS)
(Ecuador)

Equator

ARUBA (Neth)   CURAÇAO (Neth)   BONAIRE (Neth)   ISLAS LOS ROQUES
PTA. DE GALLINAS   PENINSULA DE GUAJIRA
Willemstad   Punto Fijo
Riohacha   Maracaibo   Coro   Cumarebo   Puerto Cabello   Maiquetía   CARACAS
Santa Marta   CÚCUTA   Maracay   La Guaira   Teques
Barranquilla   Ciénaga   Pico Cristóbal Colón   Cabimas   San Felipe   Valencia   La Victoria
Puerto Colombia   Soledad   Barquisimeto   Ocumare del Tuy   Barcelona
Cartagena   Sabanalarga   Fundación   Villanueva   San Carlos   Valle de la Pascua   El Tigre
El Carmen   Plato   Valledupar   Trujillo   Acarigua   Guanare   Calabozo
Calamar   Mérida   Barinas
Sincelejo   Magangué   El Banco   Pico Bolívar   San Fernando de Apure   Ciudad Bolívar
Lorica   Cereté   Mompós   Alto Ritacuva 18 022   Puerto de Nutrias
Montería   Ocaña   Cúcuta   Pamplona   San Cristóbal   Arauca
Turbo   Ituango   Bucaramanga   Málaga
Barrancabermeja   San
Urrao   Yarumal   Puerto   Duitama   Socorro
MEDELLÍN   Bello   La Grita   Maroa
Antioquia   Sonsón   Chiquinquirá   Gachetá   Orocué
Quibdó   Aguadas   La Dorada   Tunja
Manizales   Honda   Ambalema   Zipaquirá   Miraflores
Pereira   BOGOTÁ
Armenia   Ibagué   Girardot   Villavicencio
Buenaventura   Buga   Espinal   Salto de Tequendama
Cali   Palmira   Chaparral
COLOMBIA   San Fernando de Atabapo
Popayán   Puerto Tejada   Neiva
Bolívar   Campoalegre
Tumaco   Garzón   Calamar
Barbacoas   Pitalito   MESA DE YAMBI
Taquerres   Florencia
Esmeraldas   Pasto   Icana
Tulcán   Ipiales   Uaupés
Otavalo   Ibarra   Cayambe
Quito   Cotopaxi 19 347   Archidona

ECUADOR
Latacunga   Baños
Manta   Ambato   Chimborazo 20 702
Portoviejo   Guaranda   Riobamba
Jipijapa   Babahoyo   Alausí
Guayaquil   Cuenca   Azogues
Machala   Sigsig
Santa Rosa
Tumbes   Loja

São Paulo de Olivença

AMAZ
SELVA

Fonte Boa
Tefé

Talara   PTA PARIÑAS
Paita   PONGO DE MANSERICHE   Iquitos
Piura   Castilla
Sullana   Leticia
Chulucanas
PTA AGUJA
LOBOS DE TIERRA   Jaén   Moyobamba   Yurimaguas
Chiclayo   Chachapoyas   Lamas   Eirunepé
Ferreñafe   Cajamarca   Tarapoto   Lábrea
Lambayeque   Cutervo
Puerto Eten
Pacasmayo   Chepén   Huamachuco   ACRE
Puerto Chicama   Cruzeiro do Sul
Salaverry   Tingo María
Trujillo   Huánuco
Chimbote   Huascarán 22 133   Porto Acre
Huaraz   Nudo de Pasco   Porto Acre
Huacho   15 118   Puerto Bermúdez   Río Branco   Villa Bella
ISLAS CHINCHAS   Cerro de Pasco   Cobija   Riberalta   Guajará Mirim
Hvaral   Tarma   GRAN PAJONAL
Callao   La Oroya   MASSIÇO DE
Chorrillos   LIMA   Huancayo
Cañete   Jauja   Puerto Maldonado
Chincha Alta   Huancavelica   Machu Picchu   RONDÔ
Bahía de Pisco   Ayacucho
Pisco   Abancay   Cusco
PTA CARRETAS   Ica   Cotabambas
Puquio   Sicuani   Reyes
Coracora   Ayaviri   Trinidad
Nudo Coropuna 21 696   Juliaca
Volcán Mishi 19 101   Puno   Ayata
Arequipa   Lago Titicaca   Achacachi
Camaná   Guaqui   Miraflores   Nev. Illampu 21 066
Mollendo   Viacha   LA PAZ
Moquegua   Corocoro   Illimani 20 741   Cochabamba
Ilo   BOLIVIA   Tarata
Tacna   Nev. Sajama 21 066   Oruro   Punata
Arica   Colquechaca   Valle Grande
ALTIPLANO   Huanuni
Pisagua   Lago de Poopó   Uncía
Iquique   Huanchaca   Potosí   Sucre
Huancané   Uyuni   Pulacayo   Lagunillas
PUNA DE ATACAMA   Monteagudo
Tocopilla   Ollague   San Lucas
Calama   Chuquicamata 19 455   Tupiza
Pedro de Valdivia   Uyuni   Quiaca
Mejillones   Tarija
Antofagasta   JUJUY
ARGENTINA

Tropic of Capricorn

SIERRA PARIMA
SERRA CURUPIRA
SIERRA MAGUALIDA
Cerro Icutu 7 800

LLANOS

Meta
Orinoco
Guaviare
Inírida
Vaupés
Caquetá
Putumayo
Napo
Marañón
Amazonas
Juruá
Purus

a

Pavarandocito   Alto de Tres Morros 11 155   Ituango
Dabeiba   Valdivia   Segovia
Paramillo 12 990   Yarumal   Anorí
San Andrés   Amalfi   Remedios
Cañasgordas   ANTIOQUIA
Alto Musinga 12 631   Santa Rosa   Yolombó
Antioquia   Sopetrán   Cisneros
Maro Jarapeto 9186   Sabanas-Páramo 13 395   Barbosa   Puerto Berrío
Urrao   Anzá   Bello   San Roque
Bebará   ITAGÜÍ   San Rafael
Neguá   MEDELLÍN   Nare   Rionegro
Quibdó   Titiribí   Envigado   San Carlos
Concordia   Caldas   San Luis
CHOCÓ   Andes   La Ceja   Puerto Niño
Cerro Caramanta 12 795   Aguadas   Cerro de los Paredes 10 991
Certegui   Fredonia   Sonsón   Puerto Salgar
Tadó   Riosucio   Pensilvania
RISARALDA   Salamina   La Dorada
Istmina   Anserma   CALDAS   Victoria
Cerro Tamaná 13 780   Neira   Manzanares   Honda
Tadó   Fresno   Mariquita   Zipaquirá
Apía   Santa Rosa de Cabal   CUNDINAMARCA
El Cajón   Nevado del Ruiz 17 716   Libano   Guasca   Gachetá
Anserma   Facatativá   La Calera   Junín
Cartago   MANIZALES   Venadillo   Ambalema
Cerro Torrá 12 721   Finlandia   Nevado de Tolima 17 110   La Mesa   Fontibón
Sipí   Quimbaya   PEREIRA   Totaima   BOGOTÁ   Fómeque
Roldanillo   Cajamarca   Fusagasugá
QUINDÍO   ARMENIA   IBAGUÉ   Girardot   Quetame   Restrepo
Zarzal   13 944   Caicedonia   Pico de Chili 16 894   Rovira   Espinal   Villavicencio
Sevilla   Pico de Mendanueva 13 123
Tuluá   TOLIMA   Guamo   Acacías
VALLE DEL CAUCA   CORDILLERA   San Antonio   Órtega   Purificación
Darién   Buga   Coyaima   Prado   San Martín
Restrepo   Guacarí   Cerro el Nevado 14 961
Cerrito   Chaparral   Natagaima   Dolores
CALI   PALMIRA   Pradera   Ataco   Alpujarra   Colombia   META
Jamundí   Florida   Miranda   Baraya
Puerto Tejada   Corinto   Aipe   Villavieja   San Juan
Buenos Aires   Toribío   Nevado de Huila 18 865   HUILA
Santander   Neiva   San Antonio
Palmero

OCCIDENTAL   CENTRAL   ORIENTAL   MTS.   ANDES   CORDILLERA

CABO CORRIENTES
Bahía de Buenaventura
Golfo de Guayaquil
Bahía de Caráquez

Scale 1:4 000 000
0   10   20   30   40 Miles
0   10   20   30   40   50   60 Kilometers
© R MCN.

A-549100-76-   *11-10-22
COPYRIGHT BY
RAND MCNALLY & COMPANY
MADE IN U.S.A.

Scale 1:16 000 000; one inch to 250 miles. Sinusoidal Projection
Elevations and depressions are given in feet

Longitude

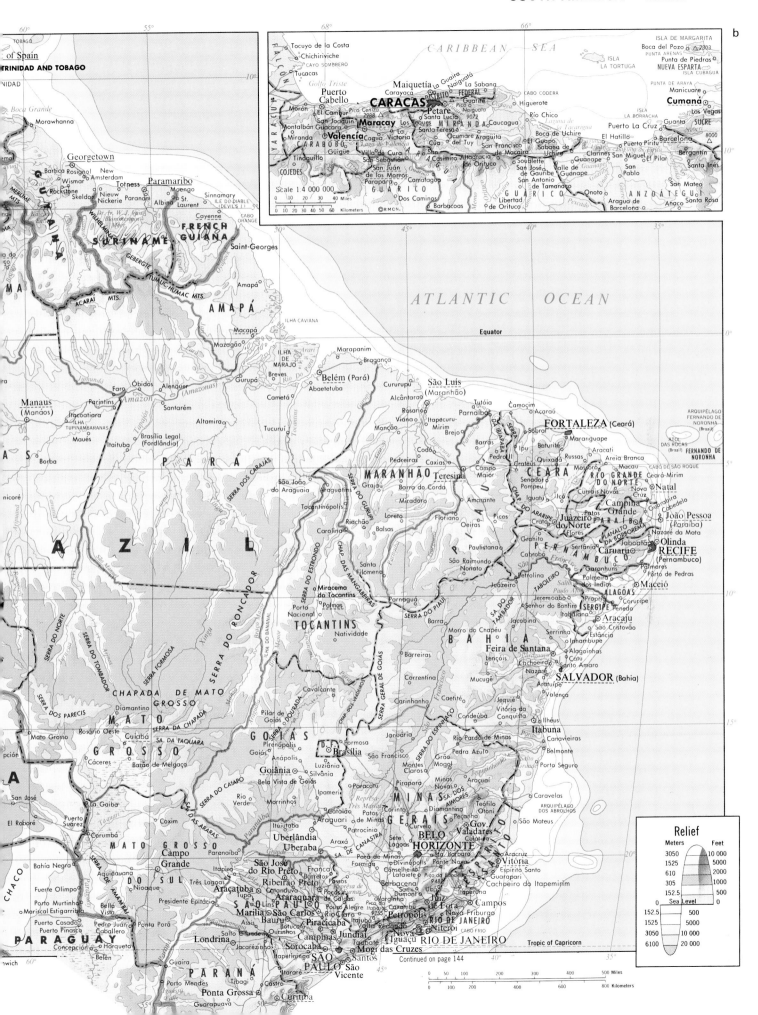

b

Inset map (top right):

CARIBBEAN SEA

ISLA DE MARGARITA
Boca del Pozo △2303
PUNTA ARENAS
Punta de Piedras
NUEVA ESPARTA
ISLA CUBAGUA

Tocuyo de la Costa
Chichiriviche
Cayo Sombrero
Tucacas

FALCÓN
Golfo Triste

La Guaira
Maiquetía
Carayaca
Naiguatá
Sabana
Caraballeda

ISLA
LA TORTUGA

CABO CODERA

Manicuare
PUNTA DE ARAYA
Cumaná
SUCRE
△8000

Puerto
Cabello
Morón
El Cambur
Montalbán Guacara
Miranda
CARABOBO

CARACAS
Pico Ceniza
7988 △
Petare
Santa Lucía
9072 △
Los Teques
Maracay
La
Victoria
Valencia
Villa de Cura

DISTRITO
FEDERAL
Guatire
San José
Santa Teresa
Ocumare
del Tuy
San Sebastián

MIRANDA
Higuerote
Río Chico

Caucagua
Araguita
San Francisco
de Macaira

Boca de Uchire
El Guapo
Sabana de
Uchire
Clarines
Guanape

Puerto La Cruz
El Hatillo
Guanta
Puerto Píritu
Barcelona

Las Vegas

Santa Inés

GUÁRICO

Tinaquillo
Güigüe
Lago de Valencia
Cagua
San Joaquín
COJEDES

Scale 1:4 000 000
0   10   20   30   40 Miles
0 10 20 30 40 50 60 Kilometers
©R.M.C.N.

San Juan
de los Morros
Parapara
Camatagua
Dos Caminos

San Casimiro
Altagracia
de Orituco
Soublette
San Juan
de Gauribe
Guanare
Libertad
de Orituco
Barbacoas

San Antonio
de Tamanaco
Onoto
Aragua de
Barcelona

San Miguel
San
Pablo
El Pilar
Santa Rosa

GUÁRICO

ANZOÁTEGUI
Anaco

Main map labels:

Gulf of Spain
TRINIDAD AND TOBAGO
NIDAD
TRINIDAD

Boca Grande

Morawhanna

Georgetown

Bartica Rosignol
New
Amsterdam
Wismar
Nieuw
Rockstone
Skeldon
Nickerie Paranam
Albina
St.
Laurent

Totness
Paramaribo
Moengo
Sinnamary
ILE DU DIABLE
(DEVIL'S I.)

GUYANA

MERUME
MTS.

Kaieteur
Falls

WILHELMINA
GEBERGTE

SURINAME
FRENCH
GUIANA
Cayenne
CABO
ORANGE

Saint-Georges

TUMUC-HUMAC MTS.
ACARAÍ MTS.

AMAPÁ

Amapá

Macapá
Mazagão
ILHA CAVIANA

ILHA
DE
MARAJO

Marapanim
Bragança

Breves
Belém (Pará)
Cururupu
São Luís
(Maranhão)
Alcântara

Gurupá
Abaetetuba
Cametá
Rosário
Tutóia
Čamoçim
Acaraú

Faro
Óbidos
Alenquer
(Amazonas)
Santarém

Manaus
(Manáos)
Itacoatiara
ILHA
TUPINAMBARANAS
Parintins
Amazon

Viana
Itapecuru-
Mirim
Monção
Brejo
Parnaíba
Barras

Sobral
Baturité
FORTALEZA (Ceará)
Maranguape
Ipu
Russas
Aracati
Areia Branca

Altamira
Tucuruí

PARÁ

Brasília
Legal
(Fordlândia)
Itaituba
Maués
Borba

São João
do Araguaia
Araguatins

SERRA DOS CARAJÁS
SERRA DO GURUPI

MARANHÃO
Teresina
Grajaú
Barra do Corda

Codó
Caxias
Pedreiras
Campo
Maior
Pompeu
Senador
Crateús
Quixadá
Mostoro
CEARÁ
RIO GRANDE
DO NORTE
Ceará-Mirim
Natal
Currais Novos
Nova
Cruz

B
R
A
Z
I
L

SERRA DO RONCADOR

Tocantinópolis
Miradoro
Amarante
Picos
Iguatu
Içó
Patos
Campina
Grande
PARAÍBA
João Pessoa
(Paraíba)
Cabedelo
Nazaré da Mata

Riachão
Loreto
Carolina
Balsas
Floriano
Oeiras
Paulistana
Crato
Juazeiro
do Norte
Flores
Granito
Sertânia
PLANALTO
DA BORBOREMA
Caruaru
Olinda
RECIFE
(Pernambuco)

Santa
Filomena
São Raimundo
Nonato
Cabrobó
PERNAMBUCO
Garanhuns
Palmeira
dos Índios
Pôrto de Pedras

CHAP. DAS MANGABEIRAS
SERRA DO ESTRONDO

Miracema
do Tocantins
Palmas
Porto
Nacional

SERRA DO PIAUÍ
P
I
A
U
Í

Parnaguá
Barra
Juazeiro
Petrolina
Jeremoabo
TABOLEIRO
Propriá
ALAGOAS
Penedo
Maceió
Coruripe

Natividade
TOCANTINS
Barra

Remanso
SERRA DO TOMBADOR
Senhor do Bonfim
SERGIPE
Itabaiana
Aracaju
São Cristóvão
Estância
Inhambupe

B   A   H   I   A
Morro do Chapéu
Jacobina
Serrinha

Barreiras
Feira de Santana
Alagoinhas
Catu
Santo Amaro

CHAPADA DE MATO
GROSSO
Diamantino

SERRA FORMOSA
SERRA DO TOMBADOR

SERRA DOS PARECIS

Rosário Oeste
Cuiabá
SA. DA TAQUARA

GOIÁS

Correntina
Lençóis
Mucugê
Nazaré
Cachoeira
SALVADOR (Bahia)

MATO
GROSSO

Cáceres
Barão de Melgaço

Pilar de
Goiás
SERRA DA CHAPADA
Goiás
SERRA DO CAIAPÓ

Cavalcante
Januária
Carinhanha
Caetité
Condeúba
Vitória da
Conquista
Jequié
Ilhéus

Itabuna

Canavieiras

San José
La Gaiba

Rio
Verde
Morrinhos

Formosa
D.F.
Brasília
São Francisco
Montes
Claros
Pedra Azul
Grão
Mogol
Araçuaí
Belmonte

El Roboré

Diamantino
Bela Vista de Goiás
Ipameri
Paracatu
Pirapora
MINAS
NOVAS DOS
AIMORÉS
Diamantina
Teófilo
Otoni
Caravelas

Puerto
Suárez
Corumbá
Coxim

Anápolis
Luziânia
Silvânia
Goiânia
Pirenópolis

Catalão
Araguari
de Minas
Curvelo
Sete
Lagoas
Sta. Bárbara
Gov.
Valadares
Colatina
Pecanha
São Mateus

Bahía Negra
MATO
GROSSO

Campo
Grande
Paranaíba
Uberlândia
Uberaba
Araxá
SA. DA CANASTRA
Pará de Minas
Divinópolis
BELO
HORIZONTE
Conselheiro
Lafaiete
Barbacena
Ponte Nova
Vitória
Espírito Santo
Guarapari
Cachoeiro de Itapemirim
ARQUIPÉLAGO
DOS ABROLHOS

Aquidauana
DO
SUL
Itaporã
Franca
Barretos
Ribeirão Prêto
Poços
de Caldas
São
9488 △
Caxambu
Juiz
de Fora
Nova Friburgo
Campos
CABO FRIO

Fuerte Olimpo
Nioaque
São José
do Rio Prêto
Catanduva
Pouso Alegre
Itatiaia
9235 △
Petrópolis

Porto Murtinho
Três Lagoas
Presidente
Epitácio
Tupã
Araçatuba
Bauru
Lins
Rio Claro
Campinas
Jundiaí
Nova
Iguaçu
RIO DE JANEIRO
Niterói

Mariscal Estigarribia
Puerto Casado
Bella
Vista
Pedro Juan
Caballero
Marília
São Carlos
Piracicaba
Taubaté

Puerto Pinasco
Ponta Porã
Assis
SÃO PAULO
Sorocaba
Mogi das Cruzes

PARAGUAY
Londrina
Jacarèzinho
SÃO
PAULO
São
Vicente
Santos

PARANÁ
Guaíra
Itararé
Tibagi
Castro
Concepción
Belén
Porto Mendes
Ponta Grossa
Curitiba
Guarapuava

Tropic of Capricorn

Continued on page 144

ATLANTIC OCEAN

Equator

ARQUIPÉLAGO
FERNANDO DE
NORONHA
(Brazil)
ATOL
DAS ROCAS
(Brazil)
FERNANDO DE
NORONHA
CABO DE SÃO ROQUE

Relief legend:

Relief		
Meters		Feet
3050		10 000
1525		5000
610		2000
305		1000
152.5		500
0	Sea Level	
152.5		500
1525		5000
3050		10 000
6100		20 000

Scale bar:
0   50   100   200   300   400   500 Miles
0   100   200   400   600   800 Kilometers

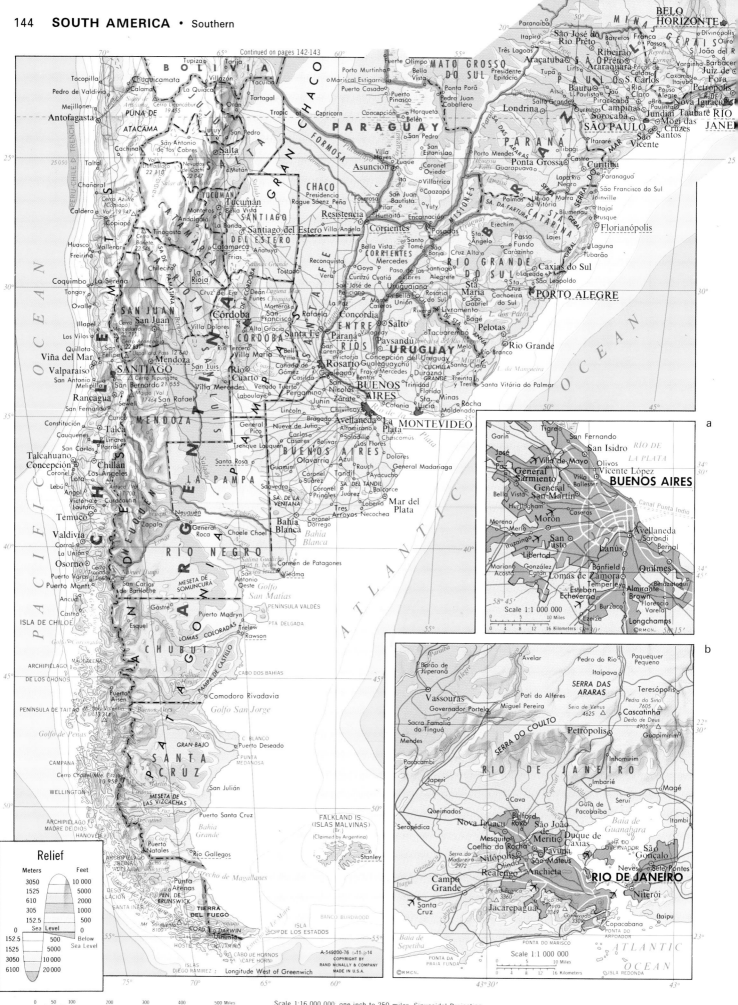

Continued on pages 142-143

BOLIVIA

PARAGUAY

B R A Z I L

MINAS GERAIS

BELO HORIZONTE

São José do Rio Prêto

Franca

São Paulo

PARANÁ

Curitiba

RIO GRANDE DO SUL

PORTO ALEGRE

URUGUAY

MONTEVIDEO

A R G E N T I N A

CHILE

BUENOS AIRES

Córdoba

Santiago

Valparaíso

Mendoza

LA PAMPA

RÍO NEGRO

CHUBUT

SANTA CRUZ

TIERRA DEL FUEGO

PACIFIC OCEAN

ATLANTIC OCEAN

FALKLAND IS. (ISLAS MALVINAS) (Br.) (Claimed by Argentina)
Stanley

CABO DE HORNOS (CAPE HORN)

a

BUENOS AIRES

RIO DE LA PLATA

Scale 1:1 000 000

0   4   8   12   16 Kilometers

b

RIO DE JANEIRO

SERRA DAS ARARAS

Petrópolis

Nova Iguaçu

Niterói

Baía de Guanabara

ATLANTIC OCEAN

Scale 1:1 000 000

0   4   8   12   16 Kilometers

Relief

Meters	Feet
3050	10 000
1525	5000
610	2000
305	1000
152.5	500
0	Sea Level
152.5	500
1525	5000
3050	10 000
6100	20 000

Sea Level

Below Sea Level

0   50 100   200   300   400   500 Miles

0   100   200   400   600   800 Kilometers

A-549200-76   -11- ⊕ -14
COPYRIGHT BY
RAND McNALLY & COMPANY
MADE IN U.S.A.

©RMCN.

Scale 1:16 000 000, one inch to 250 miles. Sinusoidal Projection
Elevations and depressions are given in feet

Longitude West of Greenwich

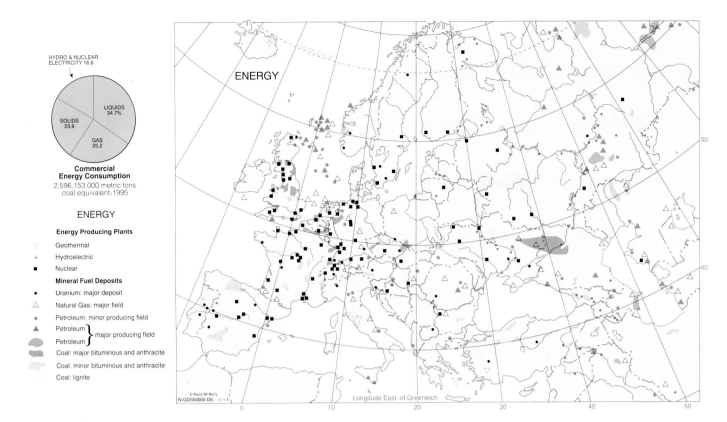

HYDRO & NUCLEAR
ELECTRICITY 16.6

LIQUIDS
34.7%

SOLIDS
23.6

GAS
25.2

**Commercial
Energy Consumption**
2,596,153,000 metric tons
coal equivalent-1995

ENERGY

Energy Producing Plants

▽   Geothermal

·   Hydroelectric

■   Nuclear

Mineral Fuel Deposits

·   Uranium: major deposit

△   Natural Gas: major field

●   Petroleum: minor producing field

▲   Petroleum }
   Petroleum } major producing field

   Coal: major bituminous and anthracite

   Coal: minor bituminous and anthracite

   Coal: lignite

ENERGY

Longitude East of Greenwich

© Rand McNally
N-GDS50000-D5- -:-1-1

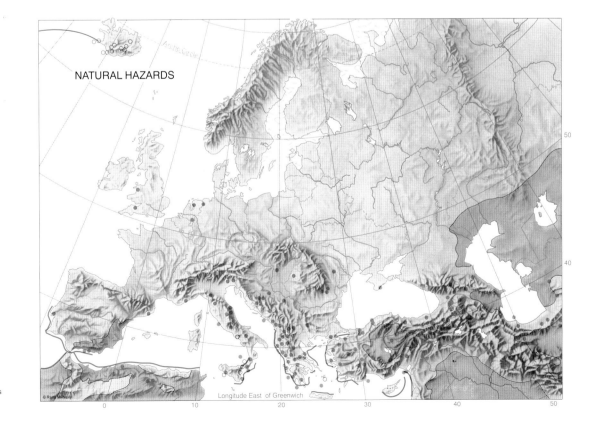

NATURAL HAZARDS

NATURAL HAZARDS

○   Volcanoes*

·   Earthquakes*

·   Major flood disasters*

   Tsunamis

   Limit of iceburg drift

   Temporary pack ice

   Areas subject to desertification

*Twentieth Century occurrences

Longitude East of Greenwich

© Rand McNally

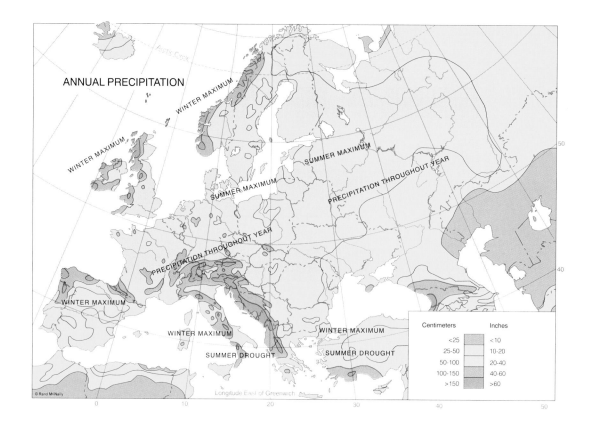

ANNUAL PRECIPITATION

Centimeters	Inches
<25	<10
25-50	10-20
50-100	20-40
100-150	40-60
>150	>60

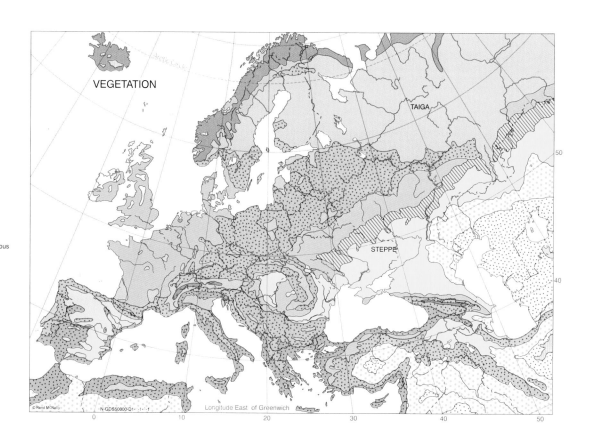

VEGETATION

E	Coniferous forest
B,Bs	Mediterranean vegetation
M	Mixed forest: coniferous-deciduous
S	Semi-deciduous forest
D	Deciduous forest
DG	Wooded steppe
G	Grass (steppe)
Gp	Short grass
Dsp	Desert shrub
L	Heath and moor
L	Alpine vegetation, tundra
b	Little or no vegetation

For explanation of letters in boxes,
see Natural Vegetation Map
by A. W. Kuchler, p. 24

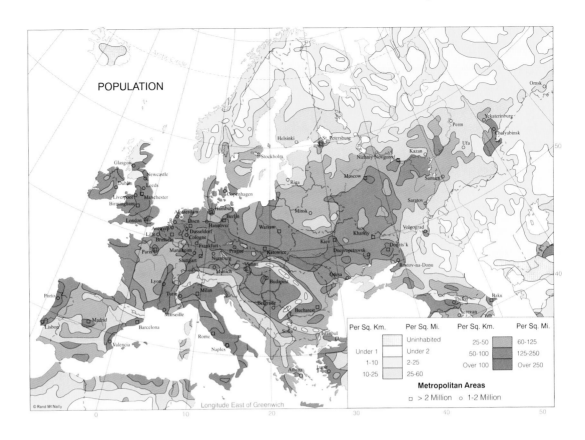

POPULATION

Per Sq. Km.	Per Sq. Mi.	Per Sq. Km.	Per Sq. Mi.
Uninhabited	Uninhabited	25-50	60-125
Under 1	Under 2	50-100	125-250
1-10	2-25	Over 100	Over 250
10-25	25-60		

Metropolitan Areas

☐ > 2 Million   ○ 1-2 Million

Longitude East of Greenwich

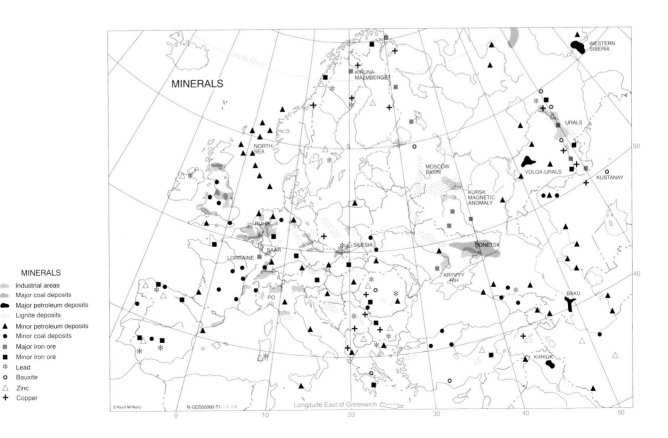

MINERALS

- Industrial areas
- Major coal deposits
- Major petroleum deposits
- Lignite deposits
- ▲ Minor petroleum deposits
- ● Minor coal deposits
- ■ Major iron ore
- ■ Minor iron ore
- ✳ Lead
- ○ Bauxite
- △ Zinc
- ✛ Copper

Longitude East of Greenwich

Urban

Cropland

Cropland & Woodland

Cropland & Grazing Land

Grassland, Grazing Land

Forest, Woodland

Swamp, Marshland

Tundra

Shrub, Sparse Grass;
Wasteland (pattern)

Barren Land

Oasis

ATLANTIC

OCEAN

North
Sea

Reykjavik

Narvik

Trondheim

Bergen

Oslo

Göteborg

Copenhagen

Stockholm

Helsinki

ST.
PETERSBURG

Tallinn

Riga

Gulf of Bothnia

Baltic Sea

Kaliningrad

Vilnius

Minsk

Glasgow

Belfast

MANCHESTER

Dublin

Amsterdam

Hamburg

Elbe

BERLIN

Oder

Warsaw

Prip

LONDON

Antwerp

Essen

Leipzig

Brest

Frankfurt

Prague

Kraków

L'viv

PARIS

Seine

Loire

Strasbourg

Rhine

Danube

Munich

VIENNA

CARPATHIANS

Zürich

Lyon

A   L   P   S

MILAN

BUDAPEST

Tisza

Bay of Biscay

A Coruña

Bordeaux

Garonne

Bilbao

Rhône

Zagreb

Sava

Venice

Belgrade

Bucharest

Duero

PYRENEES

Marseille

Genoa

Adriatic
Sea

Danube

Sofia

Lisbon

MADRID

Ebro

BARCELONA

CORSICA

ROME

Tirane

Tanger

Sevilla

SARDINIA

ISLAS BALEARES

Naples

Tyrrhenian Sea

Aegean
Sea

Casablanca

Oran

Algiers

Palermo

Athens

ATLAS   MOUNTAINS

Tunis

SICILY

M e d i t e r r a n e a n   S e a

MALTA

CRETE

Longitude West of Greenwich   0°   Longitude East of Greenwich

Scale 1: 16,000,000; one inch to 250 miles. Conic Projection

0   50 100   200   300   400   500 Miles

0   100   200   400   600   800 Kilometers

White Sea

Nar'yan-Mar

Pechora

Ob'

Novosibirsk

Irtysh

Archangelsk

Omsk

U R A L S

YEKATERINBURG

Perm

Karaganda

Kirov

Vologda

Ufa

Balqash

Volga

Kama

Kazan

Magnitogorsk

Nizhniy
Novgorod

Orsk

Oyzylorda

MOSCOW

Samara

Syr Darya

Tula

Volga

Aral
Sea

KYZYL-KUM
(DESERT)

Saratov

Ural

DEPRESSION

40°

VOLGOGRAD

CASPIAN

Amu Dar'ya

Kharkiv

Don

Kiev

Volga

Astrakhan'

KARA-KUM (DESERT)

Dnipropetrovs'k

Donets'k

MANYCH DEPRESSION

Dnieper

C a s p i a n

S e a

Odesa

Krasnodar

Ashgabat

C A U C A S U S

BAKU

Black Sea

TBILISI

Yerevan

ELBURZ MTS.

ISTANBUL

TEHRAN

DASHT-E KAVIR

Ankara

30°

TOROS

AĞRI

Kerman

Tigris

ZAGROS

Nicosia

Euphrates

Baghdad

MOUNTAINS

CYPRUS

Beirut

Abadan

150

Arctic Circle

Nord Cape

ICELAND

Lava
Ice

ATLANTIC OCEAN

NORTH SEA

LAPPLAND

Kiruna

Drift and Drift sand

Northern Muskeg LOWLAND

Granite Upland

Elongated Lakes

Moraines

Gulf of Bothnia

BALTIC SEA

Gulf of Finland

Helsinki

Stockholm

Gotland

Öland

Southern Driftland

Skåne Plain

Copenhagen

Kiel

BALTIC LAKE PLAINS

Mazurian Lakes

Mazovian Plain

Berlin

Warsaw

Łódź

Lublin Plateau

Silesian Plain

SUDETES

ORE MTS

Bohemian FOR.

Prague

Bohemian Basin

Moravian Hills

Cracow

Galician Basin

Podolian

Shetland Is.

Orkney Is.

NW. HIGH'LDS

GRAMPIAN MTS

SO. HIGHLANDS

PENNINE CHAIN

Cleveland Hills

WELSH HIGHLANDS

Snowdon

Chiltern Hills

London

N. Downs

S. Downs

Dartmoor

Exmoor

Limit of Glaciation

English Channel

Amsterdam

NETHERLANDS

The Hague

Rhine R.

Flandrian Plain

Ardenne

Eifel

Hunsruck

Taunus

Vogelsbg

Rhön

Thuringian For.

ARMORICAN MASSIVE

PARIS BASIN

Paris

CHAMPAGNE LOWL'D

Lorrain Basin

Vosges

Black Forest

Schwabian Jura

Fran. Jura

LOIRE BASIN

Loire R.

MORVAN PLAT.

LANGRES PLAT.

CENTRAL MASSIVE

JURA

SWISS

BAVARIAN BASIN

Austrian Plain

Vienna

Little Alföld

Budapest

HUNGARIAN BASIN (Alföld)

Transylvanian Basin

Cluj

Bay of Biscay

Bordeaux

Garonne R.

AQUITANIAN LOWL'D

Landes

Dunes

CAUSSES PLAT.

CEVENNES

Lyons

PO VALLEY

Milan

Turin

Po R.

Genoa

Venice

Trieste

Riviera

Monaco

Marseilles

KARST

DINARIC ALPS

KAPELA

VELEBIT

ABRUZZI

ADRIATIC SEA

WALLACHIAN PLAIN

Danube R.

Bucharest

Danubian Plateau

Belgrade

Sava R.

Zagreb

Papuk

BALKAN RA.

ANTIBALKANS

Niš

Sofia

Rila

RODOPE MTS.

CANTABRIAN Mts.

Douro R.

LEON

OLD CASTILIAN BASIN

Guadarrama

Ebro R.

EBRO BASIN

CATALAN Mts.

Barcelona

Costa Brava

Lisbon

Tagus R.

NEW CAST.

Madrid

S. de Gredos

Toledo

Valencia

Balearic Islands

CORSICA

SARDINIA

VOLCANIC BELT

Rome

M. Gargano

MURGE PLAT.

APULIAN V.

Naples

Vesuvius

TYRRHENIAN SEA

Lipari Volcanoes

Palermo

SICILY

Etna

CALABRIAN

IONIAN SEA

VINDUS Mts.

Athens

S. MORENA

ANDALUSIAN LOWL'D

Guadiana R.

S. Nevada

Strait of Gibraltar

Tangier

MEDITERRANEAN

Rabat

COASTAL PLAIN

RIF ATLAS

MOROCCO MESETA

MIDDLE ATLAS

MOULOUYA BASIN

HIGH PLATEAUS

SAHARAN ATLAS

HIGH ATLAS

TELL ATLAS

Oran

Algiers

Bône

Tunis

Sousse

TUNISIAN ATLAS

JEB. AURES

Biskra

Malta

CRETE

Scale 1:16 000 000; one inch to 250 miles. Conic Projection
Elevations and depressions are given in feet.

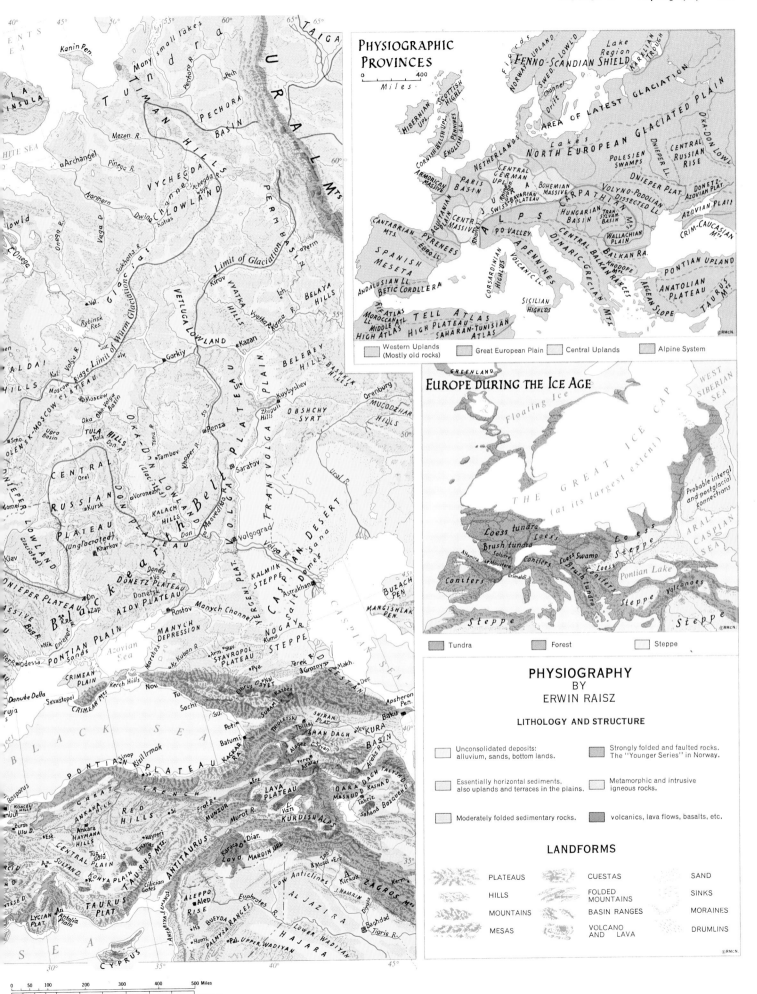

PHYSIOGRAPHIC PROVINCES

Miles 0 — 400

Western Uplands (Mostly old rocks) | Great European Plain | Central Uplands | Alpine System

EUROPE DURING THE ICE AGE

Tundra | Forest | Steppe

PHYSIOGRAPHY
BY
ERWIN RAISZ

LITHOLOGY AND STRUCTURE

Unconsolidated deposits: alluvium, sands, bottom lands.

Strongly folded and faulted rocks. The "Younger Series" in Norway.

Essentially horizontal sediments, also uplands and terraces in the plains.

Metamorphic and intrusive igneous rocks.

Moderately folded sedimentary rocks.

volcanics, lava flows, basalts, etc.

LANDFORMS

PLATEAUS | CUESTAS | SAND
HILLS | FOLDED MOUNTAINS | SINKS
MOUNTAINS | BASIN RANGES | MORAINES
MESAS | VOLCANO AND LAVA | DRUMLINS

EUROPE LANGUAGES
BY
BOGDAN ZABORSKI

Scale 1:16,500,000; one inch to 260 miles Conic Projection

| 0 | 100 | 200 | 300 | 400 | 500 | 600 Miles |

| 0 | 200 | 400 | 600 | 800 | 1000 Kilometers |

B-550000-1C6-1-1-1-4
COPYRIGHT BY
RAND McNALLY & COMPANY
MADE IN U.S.A.

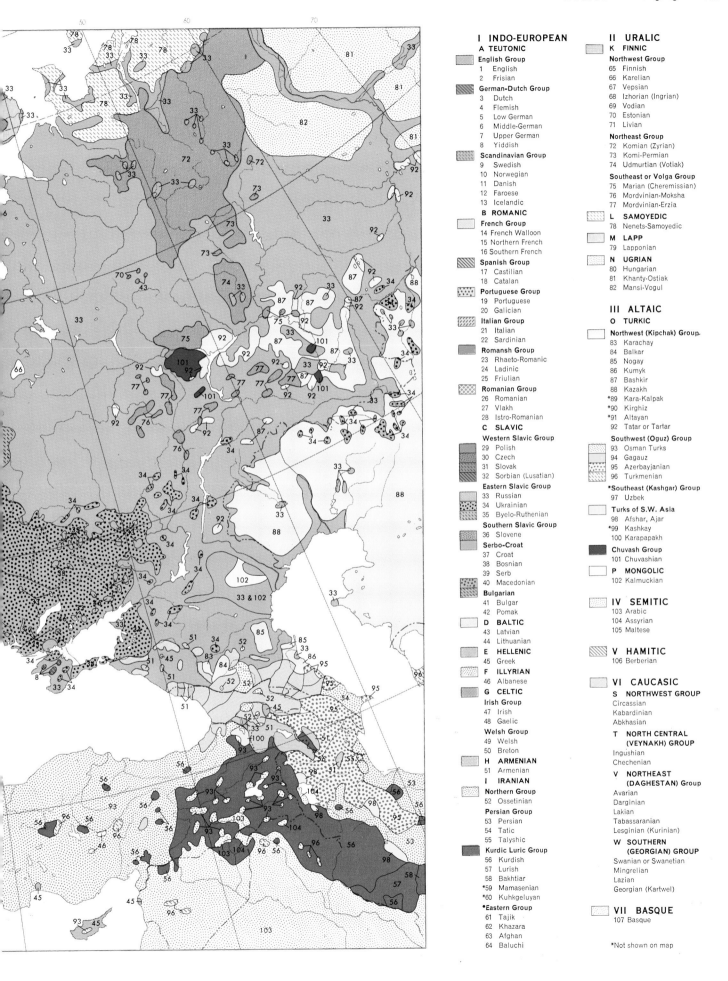

I INDO-EUROPEAN
A TEUTONIC
English Group
1 English
2 Frisian
German-Dutch Group
3 Dutch
4 Flemish
5 Low German
6 Middle-German
7 Upper German
8 Yiddish
Scandinavian Group
9 Swedish
10 Norwegian
11 Danish
12 Faroese
13 Icelandic
B ROMANIC
French Group
14 French Walloon
15 Northern French
16 Southern French
Spanish Group
17 Castilian
18 Catalan
Portuguese Group
19 Portuguese
20 Galician
Italian Group
21 Italian
22 Sardinian
Romansh Group
23 Rhaeto-Romanic
24 Ladinic
25 Friulian
Romanian Group
26 Romanian
27 Vlakh
28 Istro-Romanian
C SLAVIC
Western Slavic Group
29 Polish
30 Czech
31 Slovak
32 Sorbian (Lusatian)
Eastern Slavic Group
33 Russian
34 Ukrainian
35 Byelo-Ruthenian
Southern Slavic Group
36 Slovene
Serbo-Croat
37 Croat
38 Bosnian
39 Serb
40 Macedonian
Bulgarian
41 Bulgar
42 Pomak
D BALTIC
43 Latvian
44 Lithuanian
E HELLENIC
45 Greek
F ILLYRIAN
46 Albanese
G CELTIC
Irish Group
47 Irish
48 Gaelic
Welsh Group
49 Welsh
50 Breton
H ARMENIAN
51 Armenian
I IRANIAN
Northern Group
52 Ossetinian
Persian Group
53 Persian
54 Tatic
55 Talyshic
Kurdic Luric Group
56 Kurdish
57 Lurish
58 Bakhtiar
*59 Mamasenian
*60 Kuhkgeluyan
*Eastern Group
61 Tajik
62 Khazara
63 Afghan
64 Baluchi

II URALIC
K FINNIC
Northwest Group
65 Finnish
66 Karelian
67 Vepsian
68 Izhorian (Ingrian)
69 Vodian
70 Estonian
71 Livian
Northeast Group
72 Komian (Zyrian)
73 Komi-Permian
74 Udmurtian (Votiak)
Southeast or Volga Group
75 Marian (Cheremissian)
76 Mordvinian-Moksha
77 Mordvinian-Erzia
L SAMOYEDIC
78 Nenets-Samoyedic
M LAPP
79 Lapponian
N UGRIAN
80 Hungarian
81 Khanty-Ostiak
82 Mansi-Vogul

III ALTAIC
O TURKIC
Northwest (Kipchak) Group
83 Karachay
84 Balkar
85 Nogay
86 Kumyk
87 Bashkir
88 Kazakh
*89 Kara-Kalpak
*90 Kirghiz
*91 Altayan
92 Tatar or Tartar
Southwest (Oguz) Group
93 Osman Turks
94 Gagauz
95 Azerbayjanian
96 Turkmenian
*Southeast (Kashgar) Group
97 Uzbek
Turks of S.W. Asia
98 Afshar, Ajar
*99 Kashkay
100 Karapapakh
Chuvash Group
101 Chuvashian
P MONGOLIC
102 Kalmuckian

IV SEMITIC
103 Arabic
104 Assyrian
105 Maltese

V HAMITIC
106 Berberian

VI CAUCASIC
S NORTHWEST GROUP
Circassian
Kabardinian
Abkhasian
**T NORTH CENTRAL
(VEYNAKH) GROUP**
Ingushian
Chechenian
**V NORTHEAST
(DAGHESTAN) Group**
Avarian
Darginian
Lakian
Tabassaranian
Lesginian (Kurinian)
**W SOUTHERN
(GEORGIAN) GROUP**
Swanian or Swanetian
Mingrelian
Lazian
Georgian (Kartwel)

VII BASQUE
107 Basque

*Not shown on map

Scale 1: 16 000 000; one inch to 250 miles. Conic Projection

Elevations and depressions are given in feet

Continued on pages 194-195

Relief

Meters		Feet
3050		10 000
1525		5000
610		2000
305		1000
152.5		500
0	Sea Level	0
152.5		Below
1525	500	Sea Level
3050	5000	
	10 000	

Scale 1: 16 000 000; one inch to 250 miles. Conic Projection
Elevations and depressions are given in feet

Longitude West of Greenwich   Longitude East of Greenwich

Continued on pages 230-231

| 0 | 50 | 100 | 200 | 300 | 400 | 500 Miles |
| 0 | 100 | 200 | 400 | 600 | 800 Kilometers |

Continued on pages 184-185

Continued on pages 198-199

A-519697-76 J5-15-34
COPYRIGHT BY
RAND MCNALLY & COMPANY
MADE IN U.S.A.

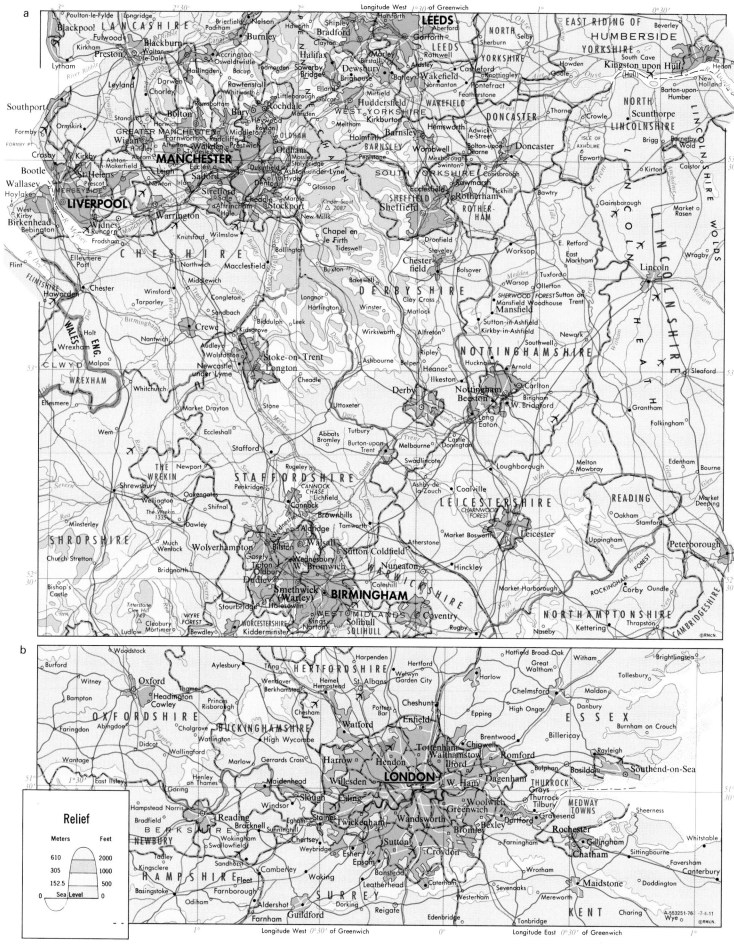

a

LANCASHIRE

Blackpool! Longridge Poulton-le-Fylde
Fulwood
Kirkham Brierfield Nelson
Preston Walton- Padiham Haworth Shipley Horsforth **LEEDS** NORTH Beverley
Lytham le-Dale Accrington Burnley Bradford Aberford EAST RIDING OF
Haslingden Oswaldtwistle Todmorden Halifax Morley Garforth HUMBERSIDE
Leyland Darwen Blackburn Sowerby Dewsbury Rothwell LEEDS Sherburn Selby YORKSHIRE Kingston upon Hull
Chorley Rawtenstall Whitworth Bridge Brighouse Batley Wakefield Castleford (Hull) South Cave New
Southport Ramsbottom Littleborough Elland Mirfield Normanton Knottingley Goole Howden Holland
Ormskirk Standish Bury Rochdale Golcar Huddersfield WAKEFIELD Pontefract Featherstone Thorne NORTH Hedon
Formby Horwich Heywood Marsden Kirkburton WEST YORKSHIRE Crowle Scunthorpe LINCOLNSHIRE
Crosby Kirkby GREATER MANCHESTER Farnworth Middleton Royton Meltham Holmfirth Barnsley Hemsworth Adwick DONCASTER Brigg Barton-upon-Humber
Wigan Radcliffe Prestwich OLDHAM le-Street Bolton-upon-Dearne Barnetby Barnetby le Wold
Bootle St Helens Ashton- Atherton Tyldesley Walkden Penistone BARNSLEY Wombwell Doncaster Epworth ISLE OF
Wallasey Prescot in-Makerfield Leigh **MANCHESTER** Salford Oldham Mossley Mexborough Swinton Kirton
Hoylake Newton Eccles Stalybridge SOUTH YORKSHIRE Conisbrough Caistor
West Birkenhead MERSEYSIDE Stretford Ashton-under-Lyne Ecclesfield Rawmarsh Tickhill Market
Kirby Bebington **LIVERPOOL** Sale Denton Hyde SHEFFIELD ROTHER- Bawtry Gainsborough Rasen
Widnes Altrincham Marble Glossop HAM
Runcorn Cheadle Sheffield
Warrington Stockport New Mills Dronfield
Frodsham Knutsford Wilmslow Chapel en Staveley Worksop E. Retford Wragby
le Frith Bolsover East Lincoln
Ellesmere Northwich Tideswell Chesterfield Markham LINCOLN
Flint Port Macclesfield Buxton WOLDS
Chester CHESHIRE Bakewell DERBYSHIRE Tuxford
Hawarden Middlewich Clay Cross Ollerton Sutton on
WALES Tarporley Congleton Winster Matlock SHERWOOD FOREST Trent Sleaford
Holt Winsford Biddulph Leek Wirksworth Mansfield Woodhouse Mansfield Newark
Wrexham Sandbach Longnor Hartington Ashbourne Alfreton Sutton-in-Ashfield
WREXHAM Crewe Kidsgrove Belper Ripley Kirkby-in-Ashfield Southwell H
Ellesmere Nantwich Audley Stone Hucknall NOTTINGHAMSHIRE
Wolstanton Stoke-on-Trent Heanor Arnold Grantham
Malpas Newcastle Longton Derby Ilkeston Nottingham Carlton
under Lyme Beeston W. Bridgford Bingham E Sleaford
Whitchurch Market Drayton Uttoxeter Long Folkingham
Wem Eccleshall Cheadle Eaton
Stafford Abbots Tutbury Castle Melton
Bromley Burton-upon Melbourne Donington Mowbray
THE Stone Trent Swadlincote Loughborough Bourne
Newport WREKIN Rugeley Swadlincote Edenham
Shrewsbury STAFFORDSHIRE CANNOCK Lichfield Ashby-de- Coalville LEICESTERSHIRE Uppingham Market
Penkridge CHASE la-Zouch Deeping
Wellington Oakengates Cannock Charnwood READING
The Wrekin Shifnal Brownhills FOREST
Minsterley 1335 Dawley Aldridge Tamworth Oakham Stamford Market
SHROPSHIRE Walsall Sutton Coldfield Market Bosworth Leicester Deeping
Much Wolverhampton Bilston Atherstone Peterborough
Church Stretton Wenlock Gosley Wednesbury Nuneaton Uppingham
Bishop's Bridgnorth Tipton W. Bromwich WARWICKSHIRE Hinckley NORTHAMPTONSHIRE
Castle Oldbury Coleshill Market Harborough ROCKINGHAM Corby Oundle
Titterstone Dudley WEST MIDLANDS FOREST Kettering Thrapston
Clee Hill WYRE Smethwick BIRMINGHAM Coventry CAMBRIDGESHIRE
1749 FOREST Stourbridge (Warley) Solihull Naseby
Cleobury Halesowen WORCESTERSHIRE Kings SOLIHULL Rugby ©RMcN
Ludlow Mortimer Bewdley Norton
Kidderminster

b

Woodstock Harpenden HERTFORDSHIRE Hatfield Broad Oak Brightlingsea
Burford Aylesbury Tring Hertford Great Witham
Witney Oxford Wendover Hemel St Albans Welwyn Harlow Waltham Tollesbury
Bampton Headington Hempstead Garden City ESSEX Maldon
Cowley Princes Chesham Potters High Ongar Danbury Burnham on Crouch
OXFORDSHIRE Risborough BUCKINGHAMSHIRE Cheshunt Epping Chelmsford
Faringdon Abingdon Chalgrove Watford Enfield Billericay
Watlington High Wycombe Brentwood Basildon Rayleigh
Wantage Didcot Marlow Gerrards Cross Harrow Tottenham Romford Southend-on-Sea
East Ilsley Wallingford Henley Maidenhead Hendon Walthamstow Ilford Bulphan Grays
Goring on Thames Willesden **LONDON** Dagenham THURROCK
Hampstead Norris Slough Ealing W. Ham Woolwich Thurrock Tilbury MEDWAY Sheerness
Bradfield Reading Windsor Staines Twickenham Greenwich Grays TOWNS
Egham Wandsworth Bexley Dartford Gravesend Rochester
BERKSHIRE Bracknell Chertsey Sutton Bromley Farningham Gillingham Whitstable
NEWBURY Wokingham Weybridge Esher Croydon Chatham Faversham
Swallowfield Sunninghill Epsom Banstead Wrotham Sittingbourne
Tadley Camberley Weybridge Caterham Sevenoaks Maidstone Canterbury
Kingsclere Sandhurst Waking Leatherhead Mereworth Doddington
HAMPSHIRE Fleet Farnborough SURREY Dorking Westerham KENT Charing
Basingstoke Aldershot Guildford Reigate Edenbridge Wye
Odiham Farnham Tonbridge A-553251-76 -7-4-11
©RMcN

Relief

Meters		Feet
610		2000
305		1000
152.5		500
0	Sea Level	0

Scale 1:1 000 000; one inch to 16 miles.
Elevations and depressions are given in feet.

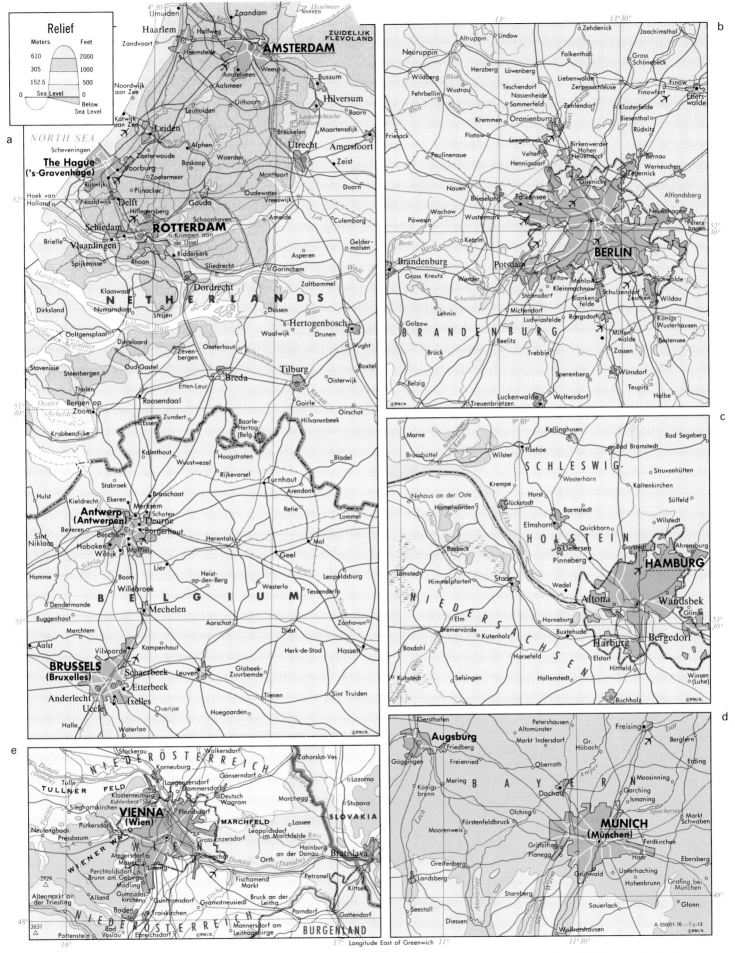

Relief

Meters	Feet
610	2000
305	1000
152.5	500
0 Sea Level	0
	Below Sea Level

a

NORTH SEA

IJmuiden Zaandam *ZUIDELIJK FLEVOLAND*
Haarlem Halfweg *MARKEN* *IJsselmeer*
Zandvoort **AMSTERDAM**
Heemstede Amstelveen Weesp Bussum
Noordwijk Aalsmeer Uithoorn *Loosdrechtse Plassen* Hilversum
aan Zee Leimuiden Baarn
Katwijk Leiden Breukelen Maartensdijk
aan Zee Alphen Woerden Utrecht Amersfoort
Scheveningen Zoeterwoude Boskoop Zeist
The Hague Voorburg Zoetermeer Montfoort Doorn
('s-Gravenhage) Rijswijk Pijnacker Oudewater Vreeswijk
Hoek van Naaldwijk Delft Gouda *Lek* Culemborg
Holland Hillegersberg Schoonhoven Gelder-malsen
Brielle **ROTTERDAM** Krimpen aan Ameide *Waal*
Schiedam de IJssel Asperen
Vlaardingen Ridderkerk Gorinchem Zaltbommel
Spijkenisse Rhoon Sliedrecht
Haringvliet *NETHERLANDS* Dordrecht Dussen *Maas* 's-Hertogenbosch
Dirksland Klaaswaal Drunen Vught
Numansdorp Strijen *Hollands Diep* Waalwijk Boxtel
Ooltgensplaat Zeven-bergen Oosterhout *Wilhelmina* Oisterwijk
Stavenisse Steenbergen Oud Gastel Tilburg *Kanaal*
Dinteloord Breda Etten-Leur Goirle
Bergen op Roosendaal Oirschot
Zoom Zundert Baarle- Hilvarenbeek
Krabbendijke Essen Hertog Bladel
Kalmthout (Belg.) Hoogstraten
Wuustwezel Rijkevorsel Turnhout
Staekroek Arendonk Retie
Kieldrecht Ekeren Schoten Mol
Sint Merksem Deurne Geel
Niklaas **Antwerp** Borgerhout Herentals
Beveren (Antwerpen) Berchem
Hoboken Mortsel Lier Heist- Leopoldsburg
Hamme Wilrijk op-den-Berg Lommel
Boom Westerlo Tessenderlo
Willebroek *B E L G I U M* Diest Hasselt
Dendermonde Mechelen Aarschot Zonhoven
Buggenhout Merchtem Herk-de-Stad
Aalst Kampenhout Diest
Vilvoorde Glabbeek- Sint Truiden
BRUSSELS Schaerbeek Leuven Zuurbemde
(Bruxelles) Etterbeek Tienen
Anderlecht Ixelles Overijse
Uccle Hoegaarden
Halle Waterloo

b

Altruppin Lindow Zehdenick Joachimsthal
Neuruppin Herzberg Löwenberg Falkenthal Gross Schönebeck
Wildberg Wustrau Teschendorf Liebenwalde Finow
Fehrbellin Nassenheide Zerpenschleuse Finowfurt Ebers-walde
Kremmen Sommerfeld Zehlendorf Klosterfelde Rüdnitz
Flatow Oranienburg Birkenwerder Biesenthal
Friesack Leegebruch Hohen Bernau
Paulinenaue Velten Neuendorf Werneuchen
Nauen Hennigsdorf Glienicke Zepernick
Brieselang Falkensee Neuenhagen
Wachow *Havel* Altlandsberg
Päwesin Wustermark Peters-hagen
Ketzin **BERLIN**
Beetz *Havel*
Brandenburg Potsdam Teltow Mahlow Eichwalde
Gross Kreutz Werder Stahnsdorf Kleinmachnow Schulzendorf Wildau
Schwielowsee Blanken- Zeuthen
Golzow Michendorf felde Königs
Lehnin Ludwigsfelde Rangsdorf Wusterhausen
B R A N D E N B U R G Beelitz Mitten- Bestensee
Brück Zossen walde
Belzig Trebbin Sperenberg Wünsdorf
Luckenwalde Woltersdorf Teupitz
Treuenbrietzen Halbe

c

Marne Kellinghusen Bad Segeberg
Nord-Ostsee Wilster Bad Bramstedt
Brunsbüttel Kanal Itzehoe *SCHLESWIG-* Struvenhütten
Krempe Westerhörn Kaltenkirchen
Nehaus an der Oste Glückstadt Horst Barmstedt Sülfeld
Hamelwörden *Elbe* Quickborn Wilstedt
Elmshorn *H O L S T E I N*
Basbeck *Oste* Uetersen Garstedt Ahrensburg
Himmelpforten Pinneberg **HAMBURG**
N I E D E R S A C H S E N Stade Wedel Altona Wandsbek
Lamstedt Horneburg Glinde
Elm Buxtehude *53° 30'*
Bremervörde **Harburg** Bergedorf
Basdahl Kutenholz Hittfeld Winsen (Luhe)
Harsefeld Elstorf Hollenstedt
Kuhstedt Selsingen Buchholz

d

Gersthofen Petershausen Freising *Isar*
Augsburg Altomünster Berglern
Friedberg Markt Indersdorf
Göggingen Freienried Oberroth Gr. Höbach Moosinning
B A Y E R N Garching Erding
Königs- Mering Dachau Ismaning
brunn Olching *Amper*
Fürstenfeldbruck Speichersee
Moorenweis **MUNICH** Markt Schwaben
Gräfelfing (München) Feldkirchen
Greifenberg Planegg Haar
Landsberg Unterhaching Ebersberg
Grünwald Hohenbrunn Grafing bei München
Starnberg Sauerlach Glonn
Seestall Diessen Wolfratshausen

e

Stockerau Wolkersdorf Zahorská-Ves
N I E D E R Ö S T E R R E I C H
Donau Korneuburg Gänserndorf Lozorno
(Danube) Tulln Langenzersdorf Deutsch Stupava
TULLNER Klosterneuburg Stammersdorf Wagram Marchegg
FELD Kahlenberg 1584 Floridsdorf *SLOVAKIA*
Sieghartskirchen **VIENNA** Lassee
Neulengbach (Wien) *MARCHFELD*
Purkersdorf Gross-Enzersdorf Leopoldsdorf
Pressbaum *W I E N* im Marchfelde *Russ*
Perchtoldsdorf Schwechat **Bratislava**
2929 Atzgersdorf Orth Petronell
WIENER WALD Liesing an der Donau (Danube)
Brunn am Gebirge Fischamend Kittsee
Altenmarkt an Mödling Markt
der Triesting Gumpoldskirchen Bruck an der
Alland Baden *Fischa* Leitha Parndorf
3631 Guntramsdorf Gramatneusiedl Gattendorf
Pottenstein Traiskirchen Mannersdorf am
N I E D E R Ö S T E R R E I C H Leithagebirge *BURGENLAND*
Bad Vöslau Ebreichsdorf

16° *17° Longitude East of Greenwich 11°* *11° 30'*

Scale 1:1 000 000; one inch to 16 miles.
Elevations and depressions are given in feet.
A-550051-76 -7-5-13

0 5 10 15 20 Miles
0 4 8 12 16 20 24 28 32 Kilometers

Continued on pages 180-181

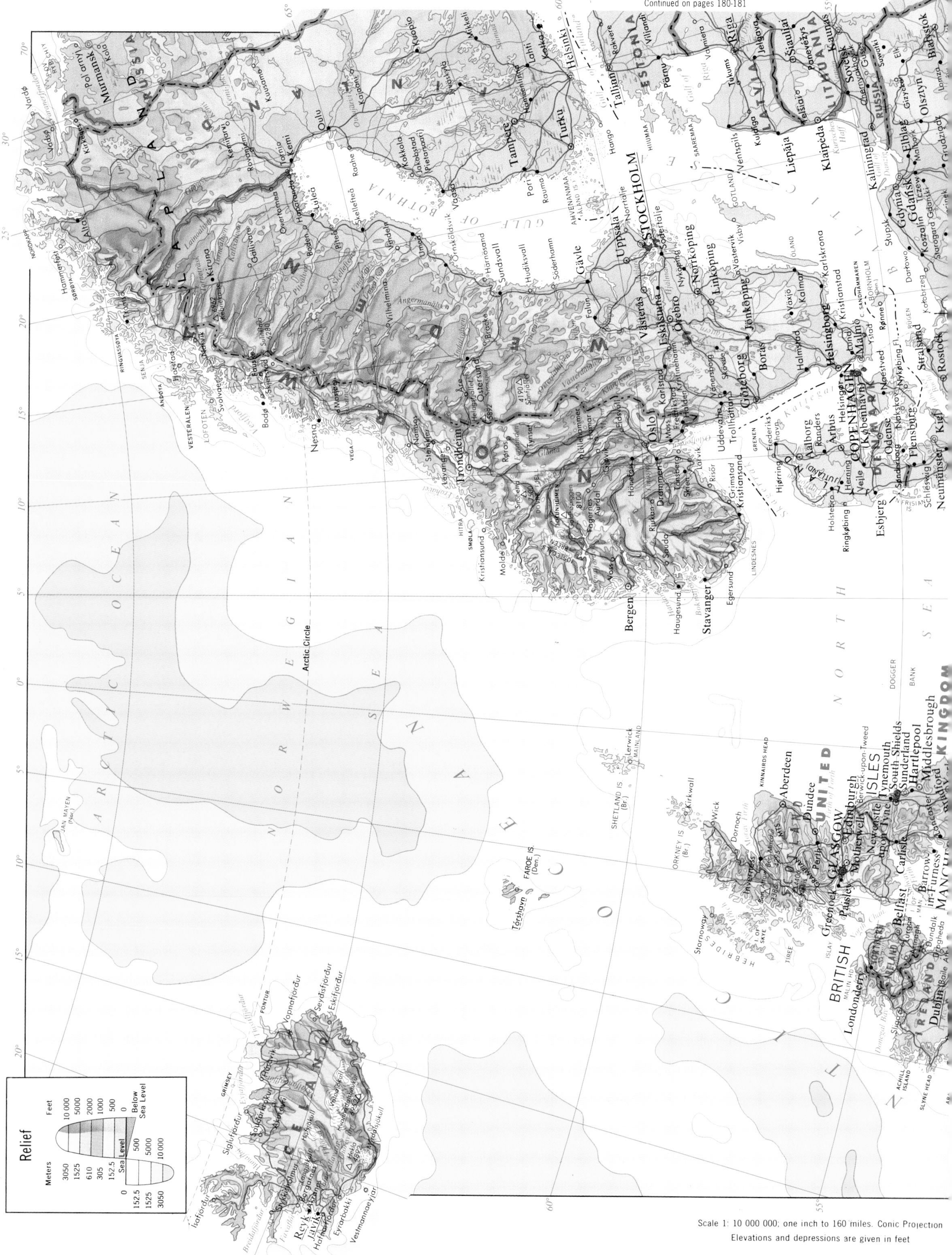

BELARUS

RUSSIA
Murmansk
Vadsø
Nordkapp
Hammerfest
Alta
Kirkenes
Kola
Pol'arnyy

LAPLAND

FINLAND

Oulu
Kemi
Tornio
Kokkola
(Pietarsaari)
Raahe
Kuusamo
Kuopio
Mikkeli
Lahti
Tampere
Turku
Helsinki
Pori
Rauma
Hanko

Kiruna
Gällivare
Boden
Luleå
Piteå
Skellefteå
Umeå
Örnsköldsvik
Härnösand
Sundsvall
Hudiksvall
Söderhamn
Gävle

S W E D E N

Östersund
Sundsvall
Falun
Uppsala
STOCKHOLM
Södertälje
Västerås
Eskilstuna
Örebro
Norrköping
Linköping
Jönköping
Visby
GOTLAND
ÖLAND
Kalmar
Karlskrona
Kristianstad
Växjö
Borås
Göteborg
Skövde
Trollhättan
Uddevalla
Halmstad
Helsingborg
Lund
Malmö
Ystad

GULF OF BOTHNIA
AHVENANMAA
(ÅLAND)
Norrtälje
HIIUMAA
SAAREMAA

ESTONIA
Tallinn
Pärnu
Viljandi

LATVIA
Riga
Ventspils
Liepāja
Jelgava
Valmiera

LITHUANIA
Šiauliai
Panevėžys
Kaunas
Klaipėda
Sovetsk

RUSSIA
Kaliningrad

Gdynia
Gdańsk
Słupsk
Koszalin
Szczecin
Stargard

N O R W A Y
Trondheim
Namsos
Mo i Rana
Bodø
Narvik
Harstad
Svolvær
LOFOTEN
VESTERÅLEN
ANDØYA
SENJA
Tromsø
Molde
Kristiansund
Ålesund
Bergen
Haugesund
Stavanger
Egersund
Kristiansand
Arendal
Grimstad
Oslo
Drammen
Moss
Fredrikstad
Hamar
Lillehammer
Røros
LINDESNES

DENMARK
COPENHAGEN
(København)
Helsingør
Roskilde
Næstved
Nykøbing
Odense
Kolding
Esbjerg
Herning
Vejle
Århus
Randers
Ålborg
Frederikshavn
Hjørring
Holstebro
Ringkøbing
Bornholm
Rønne
JUTLAND

KATTEGAT
SKAGERRAK

Flensburg
Kiel
Neumünster
Rostock
Stralsund
Schleswig
RÜGEN

ICELAND
Reykjavík
Ísafjörður
Siglufjörður
Akureyri
Seyðisfjörður
Eskifjörður
Vopnafjörður
Höfn
Vestmannaeyjar
GRÍMSEY

FAROE IS.
(Den.)
Tórshavn

ATLANTIC OCEAN
ARCTIC OCEAN
NORWEGIAN SEA
NORTH SEA
Arctic Circle
JAN MAYEN
(Nor.)
DOGGER BANK

SHETLAND IS.
(Br.)
Lerwick
MAINLAND

ORKNEY IS.
(Br.)
Kirkwall

UNITED KINGDOM
Aberdeen
Dundee
Edinburgh
Glasgow
Greenock
Paisley
Motherwell
Newcastle upon Tyne
Sunderland
South Shields
Tynemouth
Hartlepool
Middlesbrough
Carlisle
Barrow-in-Furness
Wick
Dornoch
HEBRIDES
Stornoway
ISLE OF SKYE
TIREE
ISLAY

BRITISH ISLES

IRELAND
Belfast
Londonderry
Dublin
Sligo
ACHILL ISLAND

Relief

Meters	Feet
3050	10 000
1525	5000
610	2000
305	1000
152.5	500
0	Sea Level

Below Sea Level

152.5	500
1525	5000
3050	10 000

Scale 1: 10 000 000; one inch to 160 miles. Conic Projection
Elevations and depressions are given in feet

SCALE

| 0 | 50 | 100 | 150 | 200 | 250 | 300 Miles |

| 0 | 100 | 200 | 300 | 400 | 500 Kilometers |

ATLANTIC
OCEAN

BAY OF BISCAY

FRANCE

PARIS

SPAIN

MADRID

BARCELONA

LISBON

PORTUGAL

CORDILLERA CANTABRICA

PYRENEES

ANDORRA

SIERRA MORENA

SIERRA NEVADA

BALEARS (Sp.)

MENORCA

MALLORCA

EIVISSA

FORMENTERA

CORSICA
(Fr.)

SARDINIA
(It.)

LIGURIAN SEA

GERMANY

SWITZERLAND

AUSTRIA

MILAN

TURIN

GENOA

ROME
(Roma)

NAPLES
(Napoli)

VATICAN CITY

SAN MARINO

TYRRHENIAN
SEA

M E D I T E R

Algiers
(El Djazaïr)

MOROCCO

ALGERIA

TUNISIA

ATLAS MOUNTAINS

SAHARAN ATLAS

MOYEN ATLAS

HAUT ATLAS

MONTS DES KSOUR

MONTS DES OULAD NAIL

GRAND ERG OCCIDENTAL

GRAND ERG ORIENTAL

Tripoli (Ṭarābulus)

T A R Ā B U L U
(TRIPOLITANIA)

SICILY

Palermo

MALTA

Rabat

Tunis

Constantine

Oran
(Wahran)

Casablanca

Continued on pages 160-161

FRANKFURT

MANNHEIM

STUTTGART

MUNICH

PRAGUE
(Praha)

Relief

Meters		Feet
3050		10000
1525		5000
610		2000
305		1000
152.5		500
0	Sea Level	0
152.5		500
1525	Below Sea Level	5000
3050		10000

A-558300-76
COPYRIGHT BY
RAND McNALLY & COMPANY
MADE IN U.S.A.

Longitude West of Greenwich 0° Longitude East of Greenwich

Scale 1:10 000 000; one inch to 160 miles. Bonne's Projection
Elevations and depressions are given in feet

a

Same scale as main map

ATLANTIC

SHETLAND

St. Magnus Bay
ISLANDS
(Br.)
YELL

FOULA

MAINLAND

Lerwick

SUMBURGH HD.

OCEAN

FAIR
ISLAND

WESTRAY
ROUSAY
N. RONALDSAY
SANDAY
STRONSAY
ORKNEY
Kirkwall
(MAINLAND)
ISLANDS
(Br.)
HOY
S. RONALDSAY

Thurso
Pentland Firth
DUNCANSBY HD.
SCOTLAND

©RMcN.

ATLANTIC

OCEAN

Longitude West of Greenwich

Scale 1: 4 000 000; one inch to 64 miles. Conic Projection
Elevations and depressions are given in feet

Relief

Meters		Feet
610		2000
305		1000
152.5		500
0	Sea Level	0
152.5		500
1525		5000

Below
Sea Level

A-559700-76- -9- 717
COPYRIGHT BY
RAND McNALLY & COMPANY
MADE IN U.S.A.

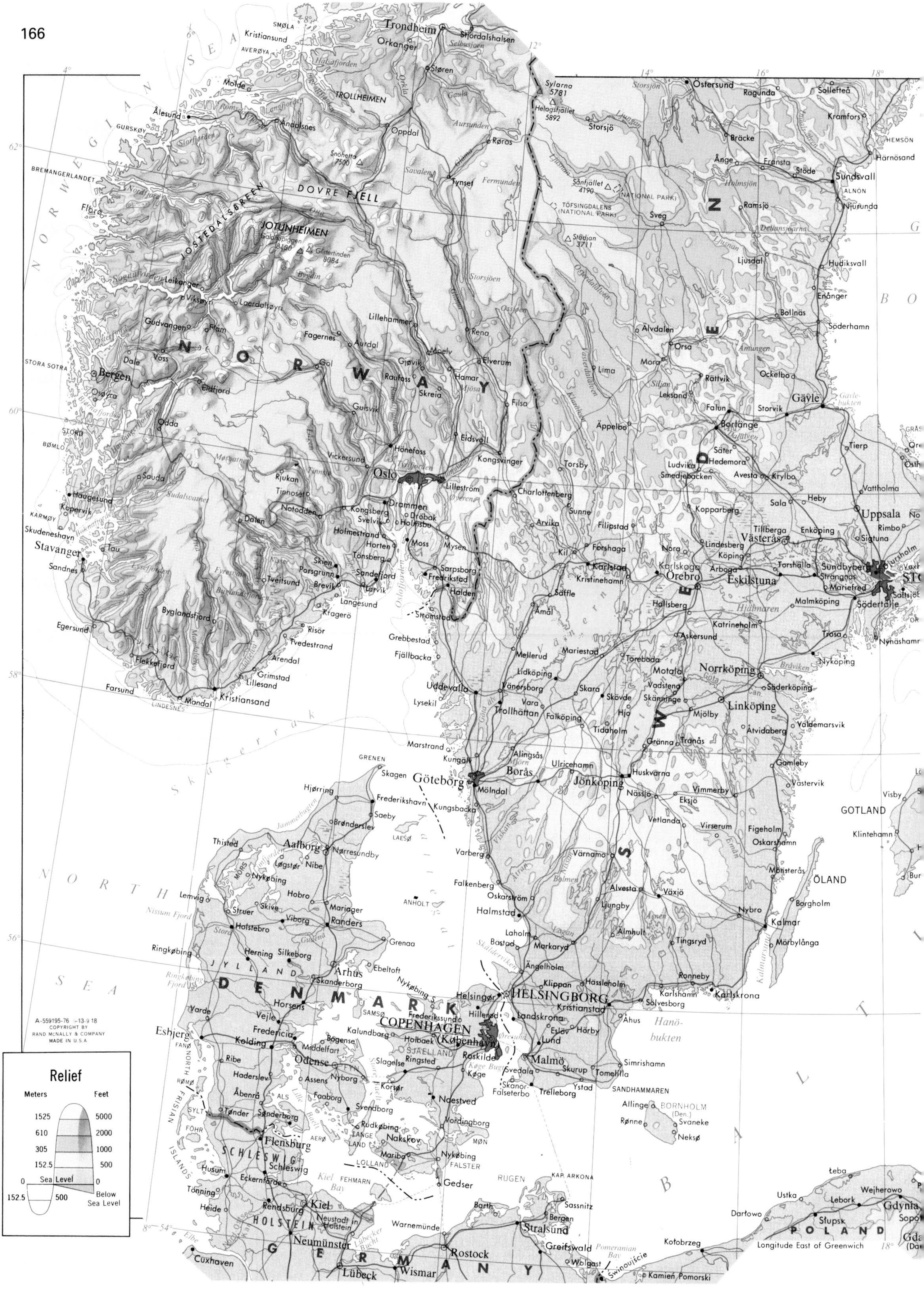

NORWEGIAN SEA

SMØLA
Kristiansund
AVERØYA
Trondheim
Stjørdalshalsen
Orkanger
Selbusjøen
Støren
Haltafjorden
Molde
Andalsnes
Ålesund
TROLLHEIMEN
Gaula
Orkla
Sylarna 5781
Helagsfjället 5892
Storsjö
Östersund
Ragunda
Sollefteå
Kramfors
HEMSÖN
GURSKØY
Slartfjorden
Oppdal
Røros
Fermundsjø
Sånfjället
(NATIONAL PARK)
Ånge
Bräcke
Fränsta
Stöde
Sundsvall
ALNON
Härnösand
BREMANGERLANDET
Snøhetta 7500
Tynset
TØFSINGDALENS (NATIONAL PARK)
Sveg
Ramsjö
Njurunda
DOVRE FJELL
Savalen
Flora
Aursunden
Storsjön
Holmsjön
Städjan 3711
Älvdalen
Ljusdal
Enånger
Hudiksvall

JOTUNHEIMEN
Galdhøpiggen 8106
Glittertinden 8084
JOSTEDALSBREEN
Leikanger
Lillehammer
Rena
Lima
Mora
Orsa
Bollnäs
Söderhamn
Sognefjorden
Viksøyri
Lærdalsøyri
Fagernes
Gjøvik
Amungen
Rättvik
Leksand
Gävle
Gudvangen
Aurdal
Moely
Elverum
Filsa
Äppelbo
Siljan
Falun
Storvik
Flåm
Gol
Raufoss
Hamar
Hjøsa
Ludvika
Smedjebacken
Säter
Hedemora
Avesta
Krylbo
Tierp
Dale
Voss
NORWAY
Hønefoss
Eidsvoll
Kongsvinger
Torsby
Kopparberg
Sala
Heby
Vattholma
Bergen
Eidfjord
Gulsvik
Oslo
Lillestrøm
Øyeren
Charlottenberg
Sunne
Filipstad
Nora
Lindesberg
Köping
Arboga
Torshälla
Sundbyberg
Uppsala
Osøyra
STORA SOTRA
Odda
Rjukan
Drammen
Drøbak
Holmestrand
Arvika
Kil
Forshaga
Karlstad
Karlskoga
Västerås
Eskilstuna
Strängnäs
Mariefred
STOCKHOLM
BØMLO
Sauda
Tinnoset
Notodden
Kongsberg
Holmsbu
Mysen
Kristinehamn
Örebro
Hallsberg
Malmköping
Södertälje
Haugesund
Kopervik
Dalen
Skien
Porsgrunn
Horten
Tønsberg
Moss
Sarpsborg
Fredrikstad
Halden
Säffle
Åmål
Askersund
Katrineholm
Trosa
Nynäshamn
Skudeneshavn
Tveitsund
Brevik
Larvik
Sandefjord
KARMØY
Langesund
Stavanger
Sandnes
Kragerø
Risør
Strömstad
Grebbestad
Mellerud
Mariestad
Töreboda
Söderköping
Nyköping
Egersund
Byglandsfjord
Tvedestrand
Arendal
Fjällbacka
Vänersborg
Skara
Skövde
Skänninge
Motala
Vadstena
Norrköping
Bråviken
Flekkefjord
Grimstad
Lillesand
Uddevalla
Lysekil
Vänersborg
Vara
Hjo
Mjölby
Linköping
Valdemarsvik
Farsund
Mandal
Kristiansand
LINDESNES
Marstrand
Kungälv
Trollhättan
Falköping
Tidaholm
Gränna
Tranås
Åtvidaberg
Gamleby
SKAGERRAK
Alingsås
Ulricehamn
Huskvarna
Vimmerby
Västervik
GRENEN
Skagen
Göteborg
Mölndal
Borås
Jönköping
Nässjö
Eksjö
Visby
GOTLAND
Hjørring
Frederikshavn
Kungsbacka
Vetlanda
Virserum
Figeholm
Klintehamn
Saeby
LAESØ
Varberg
Värnamo
Oskarshamn
Brønderslev
Falkenberg
Alvesta
Växjö
Mönsterås
ÖLAND
Thisted
Aalborg
Nørresundby
Nibe
Løgstør
Nykøbing
Oskarström
Ljungby
Nybro
Borgholm
Lemvig
Hobro
Halmstad
Kalmar
Struer
Skive
Viborg
Mariager
ANHOLT
Bolmen
Laholm
Almhult
Tingsryd
Mörbylånga
Ringkøbing
Holstebro
Randers
Grenaa
Bastad
Markaryd
Ronneby
Herning
Silkeborg
Ebeltoft
Ängelholm
Karlshamn
Karlskrona
JYLLAND
Skanderborg
Nykøbing S.
Klippan
Hässleholm
Sölvesborg
Århus
Helsingør
HELSINGBORG
Kristianstad
Åhus
Varde
Horsens
Vejle
Landskrona
Eslöv
Härby
Hanöbukten
DENMARK
Esbjerg
Fredericia
Hillerød
Frederikssund
Lund
Malmö
Simrishamn
Kolding
Middelfart
Bøgense
COPENHAGEN (København)
Roskilde
Svedala
Skurup
Tomelilla
FANØ
Ribe
Odense
Assens
Nyborg
SJÆLLAND
Holbæk
Ringsted
Köge
Skanör
Falsterbo
Trelleborg
Ystad
SANDHAMMAREN
Haderslev
Åbenrå
ALS
Faaborg
Svendborg
Korsør
Slagelse
Køge Bugt
Allinge
BORNHOLM (Den.)
Rønne
Svaneke
Nekso
RØMØ
Tønder
Sønderborg
AERØ
Rudkøbing
LANGELAND
Nakskov
Næstved
Vordingborg
MØN
SYLT
FØHR
FRISIAN ISLANDS
Flensburg
SCHLESWIG
Schleswig
LOLLAND
Maribo
Nykøbing FALSTER
Gedser
Husum
Eckernförde
Kiel Bay
FEHMARN
Barth
RUGEN
KAP ARKONA
Sassnitz
Tønning
Heide
Rendsburg
Kiel
Neustadt in Holstein
Warnemünde
Stralsund
Greifswald
Świnoujście
Kamień Pomorski
Kołobrzeg
HOLSTEIN
Neumünster
Lübeck
Lübecker Bucht
Rostock
Pomeranian Bay
Wolgast
POLAND
Cuxhaven
Elbe
Wismar
Greifswald
Ustka
Darłowo
Łeba
Lębork
Wejherowo
Gdynia
Sopot
NORTH SEA

BALTIC SEA

Relief

Meters		Feet
1525		5000
610		2000
305		1000
152.5		500
0	Sea Level	
152.5		500 Below Sea Level

Longitude East of Greenwich

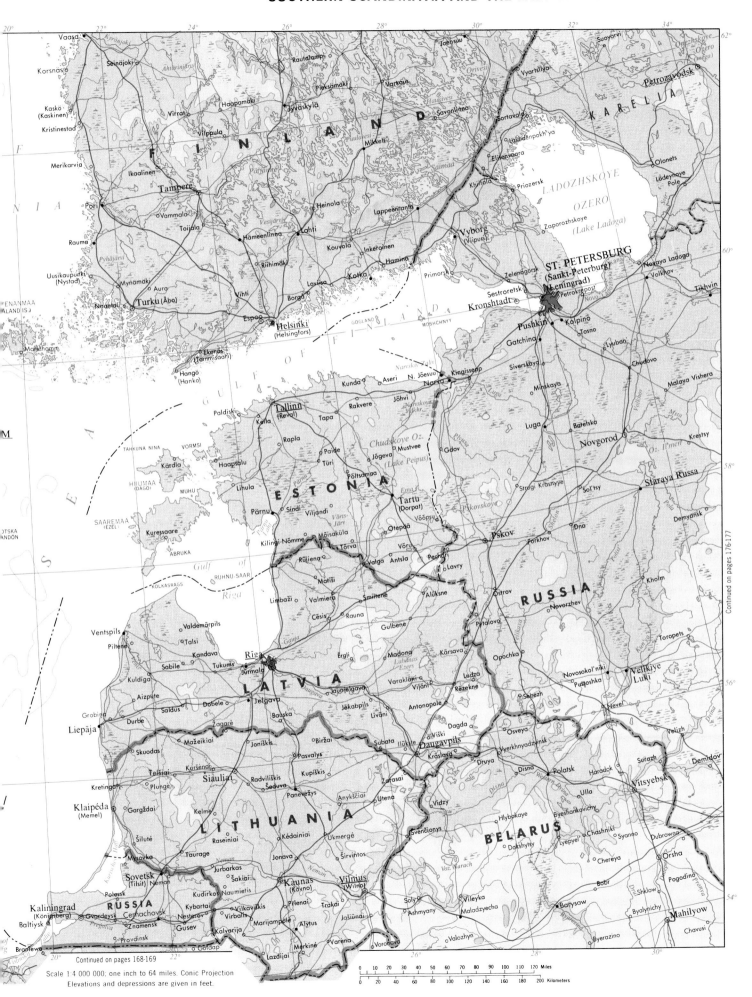

Continued on pages 176-177

Continued on pages 168-169

Scale 1:4 000 000; one inch to 64 miles. Conic Projection
Elevations and depressions are given in feet.

Continued on pages 166-167

NORTH SEA

DENMARK

Flensburg Sønderborg Svendborg Rudkøbing Nakskov Nykøbing FALSTER Gedser

SCHLESWIG Schleswig Eckernförde Rendsburg Kiel Neustadt Lübecker Bucht Sassnitz RÜGEN Bergen

Husum Tønning Heide HOLSTEIN Kiel-Canal Itzehoe Bad Oldesloe Lübeck Rostock Stralsund Barth Greifswald Wolgast

Cuxhaven Stade Elmshorn HAMBURG Schwerin Wismar Güstrow Demmin Anklam Świnoujście Kamień Pomorski Trzebiatów Kosza

Wilhelmshaven Bremerhaven Lüneburg MECKLENBURG Waren Neubrandenburg Pasewalk Gryfice Biatogard Świdwin

Delfzijl Emden Leer Oldenburg Bremen Delmenhorst Verden LÜNEBURGER HEIDE Ludwigslust Parchim Müritz Neustrelitz Prenzlau Ueckermünde Szczecin (Stettin) Stargard Szczeciński

NETHERLANDS Groningen Meppel Lingen Nienburg Celle Uelzen Salzwedel Wittenberge Perleberg Templin Zehdenick Angermünde Pyrzyce Choszczno

AMSTERDAM Zwolle Deventer Apeldoorn Utrecht Almelo Nordhorn Rheine Osnabrück Minden Hannover Wolfsburg Stendal Rathenow Oranienburg Eberswalde Bernau Strausberg Gorzów Wlkp.

Arnhem Enschede Gronau Bielefeld Herford Detmold Hameln Hildesheim Braunschweig Helmstedt Magdeburg Gardelegen Genthin Brandenburg Potsdam BERLIN Fürstenwalde Frankfurt an der Oder Poznań

's-Hertogenbosch Kleve Münster Gütersloh Paderborn Einbeck Northeim Göttingen Halberstadt Quedlinburg Stassfurt Bernburg Zerbst Dessau Wittenberg Lübben Cottbus Guben Zielona Góra

Eindhoven Duisburg ESSEN Dortmund Hamm Soest Lippstadt Kassel Nordhausen Eisleben Halle Bitterfeld Delitzsch Senftenberg Spremberg Żary Żagań Głogów Nowa Sól

DÜSSELDORF Bochum Hagen Gummersbach Marburg an der Lahn Eschwege Mühlhausen Merseburg Leipzig Grimma Riesa Grossenhain Kamenz Bolesławiec

Mönchengladbach Wuppertal Solingen Siegen Wetzlar Giessen THÜRINGEN Eisenach Gotha Erfurt Weimar Jena Gera Altenburg Meerane Döbeln Meissen Dresden Bautzen Görlitz Legnica

COLOGNE (Köln) Aachen Bonn Siegburg WESTERWALD Neuwied Koblenz HESSEN Fulda Meiningen Suhl Saalfeld Crimmitschau Zwickau Chemnitz Freiberg Pirna Sebnitz Liberec Jelenia Góra Wałbrzych

Liège Verviers Malmédy EIFEL Mayen Andernach Limburg an der Lahn Hildburghausen Reichenbach Greiz Plauen Aue Annaberg-Buchholz Teplice Ústí nad Labem Česká Lípa Litoměřice Trutnov Náchod

LUXEMBOURG Trier RHEINLAND Wiesbaden FRANKFURT AM MAIN Hanau Aschaffenburg Würzburg Schweinfurt Bad Kissingen Coburg Sonneberg Hof Kulmbach Marktredwitz Cheb Karlovy Vary Chomutov Most Kladno PRAGUE (Praha) Hradec Králové

Thionville Mainz Darmstadt Bensheim ODENWALD Worms MANNHEIM Heidelberg Bamberg Bayreuth Weiden Amberg Plzeň Beroun Pardubice

Metz Kaiserslautern Ludwigshafen Speyer Heilbronn Erlangen Fürth Nürnberg Schwandorf Nýřany Rokycany Příbram CZECH REPUBLIC

Nancy Saarbrücken Neustadt Landau Karlsruhe Bruchsal Ansbach Rothenburg Schwäbisch Hall Weissenburg Neumarkt Regensburg Domažlice Klatovy Strakonice Písek Tábor Jihlava Brno

Strasbourg Baden-Baden Pforzheim STUTTGART Esslingen Aalen Nördlingen Neuburg Ingolstadt Straubing Deggendorf Passau České Budějovice Třeboň Znojmo

FRANCE Colmar Offenburg Tübingen Reutlingen Ulm Neu-Ulm Günzburg Augsburg Landshut BAYERN (BAVARIA) Linz St. Pölten VIENNA (Wien)

Freiburg Villingen-Schwenningen Rottweil Balingen Sigmaringen Biberach Memmingen Landsberg Dachau Freising Mühldorf Braunau Ried Wels Amstetten

Mulhouse Belfort Lörrach Schaffhausen Konstanz Ravensburg Kempten Kaufbeuren Weilheim MUNICH (München) Rosenheim Traunstein Salzburg Bad Ischl Gmunden Steyr Waidhofen

Basel Baden Winterthur Sankt Gallen Lindau Bregenz Immenstadt Garmisch-Partenkirchen Bad Tölz Bad Reichenhall Wiener-Neustadt Neunkirchen

Zürich LIECHTENSTEIN Feldkirch Bludenz Innsbruck Kufstein Schwaz ALPS Bad Ischl Murzzuschlag Graz

Bern Luzern Chur Arlberg Tunnel Brenner Pass HOHE TAUERN NIEDERE TAUERN Leoben Szombathely Fürstenfeld

SWITZERLAND Interlaken St. Moritz RHAETIAN ALPS DOLOMITES Lienz Spittal Villach Klagenfurt Maribor

Geneva (Genève) BERNER ALPEN GOTTHARD PASS Bolzano Merano Bressanone CARNIC ALPS KARAWANKEN SLOVENIA CROATIA Udine Trento

Continued on pages 170-171

Continued on pages 174-175

Longitude East of Greenwich

Scale 1:4 000 000, one inch to 64 miles. Conic Projection
Elevations and depressions are given in feet.

Continued on pages 166-167

Continued on pages 176-177

Relief

Meters		Feet
3050		10 000
1525		5000
610		2000
305		1000
152.5		500
Sea Level		0
		Below Sea Level

RUSSIA
LITHUANIA
BELARUS
UKRAINE
POLAND
SLOVAKIA
HUNGARY
ROMANIA
MOLDOVA
TRANSYLVANIA
GALICIA
CARPATHIAN MOUNTAINS
RUTHENIA
MASURIA
MOLDAVIA
BUKOVINA

Kaliningrad (Königsberg)
Sovetsk (Tilsit)
Kaunas (Kovno)
Vilnius
Minsk
Gdynia
Sopot
Gdańsk (Danzig)
Elbląg
Olsztyn
Toruń
Bydgoszcz
WARSAW (Warszawa)
Łódź
Kraków
Katowice
Lublin
Białystok
Hrodna
Brest
Pinsk
Luts'k
Rivne
L'viv
Ternopil'
Ivano-Frankivs'k
Chernivtsi
Uzhhorod
Mukacheve
Košice
BUDAPEST
Debrecen
Oradea
Cluj-Napoca
Târgu Mureş
Sibiu
Braşov
Miskolc
Satu Mare
Baia Mare
Bălţi
Iaşi
Bacău

Gulf of Danzig

HIGH TATRA MTS.
NIZKE TATRY
JABLUNKOV PASS
DUKLA PASS
GÓRY ŚWIĘTOKRZYSKIE

| 0 10 20 30 40 50 60 70 80 90 100 110 120 Miles |
| 0 20 40 60 80 100 120 140 160 180 200 Kilometers |

170

Continued on pages 164-165

Relief

Meters		Feet
3050		10 000
1525		5000
610		2000
305		1000
152.5		500
0	Sea Level	0
152.5		500
1525		5000

UNITED KINGDOM

Honiton · Dorchester · Southampton · Worthing · Hove · Folkestone · Dover · Dunkerque · Calais · Roeselare · Gent · Aalst · Mechelen
Exeter · Poole · Ryde · Portsmouth · Chichester · Brighton · Lewes · Hastings · Ieper · Anderlecht · BRUSSELS
Launceston · Exmouth · Cowes · Newport · ISLE OF WIGHT · Bexhill · Eastbourne · Boulogne-sur-Mer · St. Omer · Armentières · Lille · Tourcoing · Roubaix · Nivelles · BELGIU
Plymouth · Torquay (Torbay) · Weymouth · Bournemouth · Étaples · Berck · Béthune · Bruay-en-Artois · Valenciennes · Mons · Nam
Dartmouth · START POINT · St. Valéry-sur-Somme · Crécy-en-Ponthieu · Arras · Douai · Denain · Hautmont · Maubeuge · Charleroi · Dinant

CHANNEL

Dieppe · Abbeville · Albert · Bapaume-en-Artois · Péronne · Cambrai · Fourmies · Hirson · Revin · Nouzon
Le Tréport · PICARDIE · Amiens · Corbie · Roye · Guise · St. Quentin · Charleville-Mézières · Sedan · ARD

ENGLISH · Fécamp · Neufchâtel-en-Bray · Montdidier · Laon · Rethel · ARGONNE
Bolbec · Yvetot · Compiègne · Chauny · Soissons · Vouziers
C. DE LA HAGUE · ALDERNEY · PTE DE BARFLEUR · Le Havre · Beauvais · Meru · Creil · Reims
GUERNSEY · SARK · Cherbourg · Baie de la Seine · Honfleur · Pont-Audemer · Rouen · Aisne · Châlons-sur-Marne
St. Peter Port · CHANNEL ISLANDS (Br.) · Valognes · Trouville · Elbeuf · Louviers · Gisors · Pontoise · Château-Thierry · Épernay · CHAMPAGN · Bar-le-Du
JERSEY · St. Helier · Catentan · Bayeux · Caen · Lisieux · Vernon · Mantes-la-Jolie · Argenteuil · St-Denis · Meaux · Marne · Vitry-le-François · Arcis-sur-Aube · Joinville

St. Pol-de-Léon · Golfe de St. Malo · St. Malo · Granville · NORMANDIE · Évreux · St. Germain-en-Laye · Versailles · Boulogne-Billancourt · Clichy · PARIS · Melun · Corbeil-Essonnes · Romilly-sur-Seine · Aube · Troyes · Chaumont
Morlaix · Guingamp · St. Brieuc · Dinard · Avranches · Flers · Argentan · L'Aigle · Dreux · Rambouillet · Chartres · Étampes · Montereau-faut-Yonne · Seine
I. D'OUESSANT · Landerneau · MTS D'ARRÉE · Lamballe · Dinan · COLLINES DE NORMANDIE · COLLINES DU PERCHE · Fontainebleau · Joigny · Sens
Brest · Carhaix-Plouguer · Fougères · Alençon · Nogent-le-Rotrou · Pithiviers · Nemours · MONTBARD · PLAT
Douarnenez · BRETAGNE · Pontivy · Vitré · Montfort · Orléans · Montargis · Auxerre · MORVAN · Dijon
PTE DU RAZ · Quimper · Audierne · Rennes · Laval · Le Mans · Vendôme · Gien · Briare · Clamecy · Avallon · CÔTE D'OR
Pont l'Abbé · Concarneau · Ploërmel · Château-Gontier · Sablé-sur-Sarthe · Châteaudun · Loire · SOLOGNE · Cosne-sur-Loire · Montbard · Béa
ILES DE GLÉNAN · Lorient · ILE DE GROIX · Redon · Sarthe · La Flèche · Château-Renault · Blois · Romorantin-Lanthenay · FRANCE · Autun · Le Creusot
Hennebont · Vannes · Châteaubriant · Angers · Trélazé · Tours · Amboise · Cher · Vierzon · Mehun-sur-Yèvre · Nevers · Chalon-sur-Saône
Quiberon · BELLE-ÎLE · St. Nazaire · Loire · Saumur · Chinon · Loches · Issoudun · St. Florent-sur-Cher · Bourges · Digoin · Paray-le-Monial · Cluny · Mo
ÎLE DE NOIRMOUTIER · Pornic · Nantes · Cholet · Chemillé · Loudun · Descartes · Châteauroux · St. Amand-Mont-Rond · Moulins · Montceau
Le Lac de Grand Lieu · Thouars · HAUTEURS DE GÂTINE · Châtellerault · Vienne · Creuse · Argenton-sur-Creuse · Commentry
ÎLE D'YEU · Bressuire · Poitiers · Le Blanc · Montluçon · Guéret · Vichy · Roanne · Villefranche
La Roche-sur-Yon · Fontenay-le-Comte · Parthenay · Montmorillon · Riom · Thiers · MTS DU FOREST · Tarare
Les Sables-d'Olonne · Luçon · Ruffec · Confolens · Aubusson · Clermont-Ferrand · Villeurbanne
PERTUIS BRETON · ÎLE DE RÉ · La Rochelle · Surgères · St. Junien · Limoges · Ussel · Bort-les-Orgues · Issoire · Ambert · Montbrison · St. Chamond · Rive-de-Gier · Outlins
BAY OF BISCAY · Rochefort · St. Jean-d'Angely · PLATEAUX DU LIMOUSIN · Puy de Sancy 6185 · Firminy · St. Étienne
ÎLE D'OLÉRON · Marennes · Saintes · Charente · Angoulême · Brive-la-Gaillarde · Tulle · AUVERGNE · MASSIF · Murat · Le Puy · Annonay · Yssingeaux · Romans
La Tremblade · Cognac · Barbezieux · St. Yrieix-la-Perche · Argentat · Plomb du Cantal 6076 · St. Flour · Valenc
Royan · Jonzac · Périgueux · Coutras · CENTRAL · Aurillac · Mt. Mézenc 5751 · Privas · Aubenas · Le Teil
Gironde · Blaye-et-Ste. Luce · Libourne · Dordogne · Salat-la-Caneda · Langogne · Bagnols-sur-Cèze · Or
Blanquefort · Mérignac · Pessac · Bègles · Bordeaux · Bergerac · Figeac · Mende · Alès
Bassin d'Arcachon · Arcachon · La Réole · Decazeville · Aubin · Carpent
Arcachon · La Teste-de-Buch · Langon · Marmande · Lot · Cahors · Villefranche-de-Rouergue · Rodez · Millau · CÉVENNES · La Grand Combe · Avignon
Étang de Cazaux · Tonneins · Villeneuve-sur-Lot · Aubin · Bagnols-sur-Ceze · Nîmes · Tar
LANDES · Labouheyre · Étang de Biscarosse · Agen · Moissac · Gaillac · St. Affrique · Vigan · Beaucaire
Mont-de-Marsan · Nérac · Condom · Castelsarrasin · Montauban · Albi · Castres · Lodève · Montpellier · Lunel · Arles
GASCOGNE · Dax · Aire-sur-l'Adour · Verdun · Carmaux · Bédarieux · Miramas
Biarritz · Bayonne · Salies-de-Béarn · Orthez · Auch · Muret · Toulouse · Baziège · Castelnaudary · Pézenas · Béziers · Sète · Martig
Irún · St. Jean-de-Luz · Pau · Tarbes · St. Gaudens · Pamiers · Limoux · Agde · Golfe du L
Oloron-Ste. Marie · Lourdes · Bagnères-de-Bigorre · St. Girons · Foix · Carcassonne · Sigean · Narbonne
Rondesvalles · Louvins · Bagnères-de-Luchon · Tarascon · Quillan · Rivesaltes · ME
Pamplona · PYRÉNÉES · Pico de Aneta 11007 · Ax-les-Thermes · Perpignan
SPAIN · Jaca · Mt. Perdido 11168 · ANDORRA · Prades · Céret · Port Vendres
Tafalla · Bolaña · Andorra · C. DE CREUS

Longitude West of Greenwich · Longitude East of Greenwich

Continued on pages 172-173

A-550900-76 9-76-14
COPYRIGHT BY
RAND McNALLY & COMPANY
MADE IN U.S.A.

a

Miramas · Équilles
St. Chamas · Aix-en-Provence
Istres · Berre-l'Étang · Rognac · Gardanne · Simiane
Étang de Berre · Marignane · St. Victoret
Port-de-Bouc · Lavéra · Châteauneuf · L'Estaque · Allauch
La Couronne · Carro · Sausset-les-Pins · Carry-le-Rouet · La Penne-sur-Huveaune
Marseille · Mazargues
Golfe du Lion · La Madrague · COL DE LA GINESTE 1073

Scale 1:1 000 000

MEDITERRANEAN SEA

0 ... 16 Kilometers

©RMcN.

Scale 1:4 000 000; one inch to 64 miles. Conic Projection
Elevations and depressions are given in feet

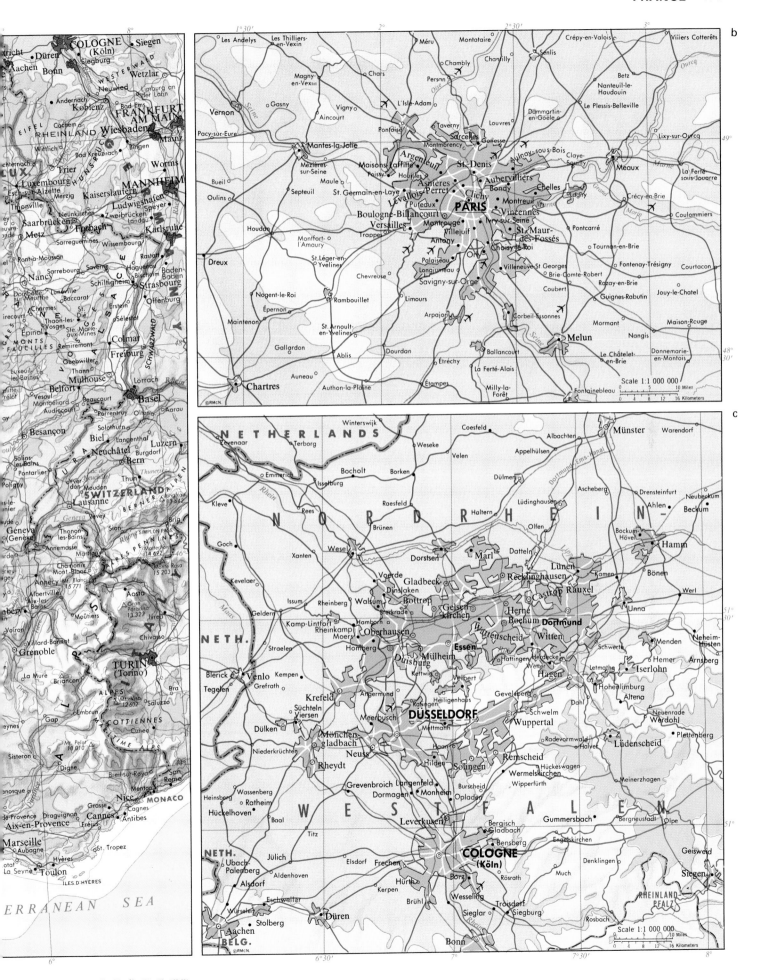

BAY OF BISCAY

CABO ORTEGAL
Aviño
Ferrol
A Coruña
Puentedeume
Laxe
Carballo
CABO DE FISTERRA
Corcubión
Muras
Muxía
Noia
Santiago de
Compostela
Santa Uxía
Pontevedra
Marín
Vigo
Redondela
Ponteareas
La Guardia
Tui
Valença

Vivero
Ribadeo
Luarca
CABO DE PEÑAS
Pravia
Avilés
Gijón
Ribadesella
Santander
Santoña
Laredo
Bermeo Donostia-
San Sebastián
Biarritz
Bay
Oviedo
Pola de Siero
Mieres
Llanes
Torrelavega
Castro-
Urdiales
Portugalete
Bilbao
St. Jean-d
Irun
Orreagal

ASTURIAS
CORDILLERA CANTABRICA
BASQUE PROVINCES
Reinosa
Bergara
Eibar
Tolosa
Vitoria
Pamplona
Tafalla

Cangas
de Narcea
Vilablino
La Vecilla
de Curueño
La Robla
Cistierna
Miranda de Ebro
Haro
Logroño
Santo Domingo
de la Calzada
Arnedo
Ejea
Tudela

A Fonsagrada
Lugo
Becerreá
Sarria
Villafranca
del Bierzo
Ponferrada
Astorga
León
Carrión de los
Condes
Burgos
Briviesca
Soria
Cervera del
Río Alhama
Calahorra
Alfaro

Arzúa
A Estrada
Lalín
Chantada
Monforte de Lemos
Quiroga
O Barco de
Valdeorras
Viana do
Bolo
Benavente
Villalpando
Medina de
Ríoseco
Palencia
Aranda de Duero
Lerma
Burgo de
Osma
Almazán
Tarazona
Borja
Alag

Carballiño
Ourense
Allariz
Bande
Xinzo de Limia
Verín
Vinhais
Bragança
Zamora
Toro
Valladolid
Peñafiel
Cuéllar
Medina del
Campo
Cega
Peñaranda
Monzón
7605
La Almunia de
Doña Godina

Caminha
Montalegre
Chaves
Mirandela
Miranda do Douro
Fermoselle
Nava del Rey
Segovia
S. Ildefonso
o la Granja
Sigüenza
Molina de
Aragón

TRAS-OS-MONTES
SA. DE LA CABRERA
SA. DE LA CULEBRA
SIERRA DE GUADARRAMA
IBÉRICO

GALICIA
MINHO
Braga
Guimarães
Vila Real
Porto
(Oporto)
Peñafiel
Vila Nova de Gaia
Matosinhos
(Leixões)
Esposende
Póvoa de Varzim
Vila do Conde
Barcelos
Fafe
Amarante
Lamego
Peso da Régua
Vila Nova
de Foz Côa
Ledesma
Salamanca
de Bracamonte
Alba de
Tormes
Ávila
S. Lorenzo
de El Escorial
Cebreros
MADRID
Colmenar
Viejo
Guadalajara
Brihuega
Henares
Embalse de
Buendía

Ovar
Castro Daire
Albergaria-
a-Velha
Aveiro
Ilhavo
Viseu
Mangualde
Trancoso
Pinhel
Guarda
Ciudad Rodrigo
Béjar
Hervás
SA. DE GATA
Arenas
de S. Pedro
Candeleda
Talavera
de la Reina
Huete
Cuenca
SA. DE CUENCA

BEIRA
CABO MONDEGO
Coimbra
Figueira da Foz
Soure
Lousã
Fundão
Covilhã
SA. DA ESTRELA
Estrela
6539
Plasencia
Navalmoral
de la Mata
La Puebla
de Montalbán
Toledo
Navahermosa
Mora
Corral de Almaguer
Embalse
de Alarcón

Marinha Grande
Leiria
Fátima
Caldas
da Rainha
FARILHÕES
BERLENGA
CABO CARVOEIRO
Peniche
Nazaré
Ferreira
do Zêzere
Serta
Castelo
Branco
Proença-a-Nova
Vila de Rei
Tomar
Abrantes
Garrovillas
Brozas
Idanha-a-Nova
Torrejoncillo
Arroyo de
la Luz
Cáceres
Trujillo
Zorita
Logrosán
Madridejos
Herencia
Quintanar
de la Orden
Campo
de Criptana
San Clemente
Tarazona
de la Mancha

Torres Novas
Alpiarça
Santarém
Ponte de Sor
Portalegre
Alter
do Chão
Campo Maior
San Vicente
de Alcántara
Alburquerque
Montijo
Villanueva
de la Serena
Don
Benito
Miajadas
Montánchez
MONTES DE TOLEDO
SA. DE
GUADALUPE
Embalse de
Cijara
Embalse de
Orellana
Piedrabuena
Ciudad
Real
Daimiel
Manzanares
Almagro
La Solana
Valdepeñas
El Bonillo
La Roda
Albacete

Torres Vedras
Cartaxo
Coruche
Alenquer
Villafranca
de Xira
Sintra
Cascais
CABO DA ROCA
LISBON
(Lisboa)
Barreiro
Setúbal
Palmela
CABO ESPICHEL
Ba. de
Setúbal
Alcácer
do Sal
Grândola
Sines
Vila Nova
de Milfontes
Montemor-
o-Novo
Arraiolos
Vila Viçosa
Estremoz
Redondo
Évora
Reguengos
de Monsaraz
Viana do
Alentejo
Ferreira
do Alentejo
Aljustrel
Elvas
Badajoz
Olivenza
Almendralejo
Mérida
Barcarrota
Jerez de los
Caballeros
Los Santos
de Maimona
Zafra
Llerena
Fuente de
Cantos
Fregenal
de la Sierra
Campanario
Castuera
Cabeza del Buey
Belalcázar
Hinojosa del Duque
Peñarroya-
Pueblonuevo
Pozoblanco
Villanueva
de Córdoba
Almadén
Almodóvar
del Campo
Puertollano
La Carolina
Linares
Santisteban
del Puerto
Beas de Segura
Villacarrillo
Úbeda
Cazorla
Quesada
7099
Alcaraz
Tobarra
Hellín
Yeste
Caravaca
Cehegín
Bullas
Mu

Castro Verde
Ourique
Almodôvar
Mértola
Beja
Moura
Serpa
Aracena
Cazalla
de la Sierra
Constantina
Guadalcanal
Azuaga
Fuenteovejuna
Bélmez
Montoro
Andújar
Bailén
Jaén
Martos
Huelma
Pozo
Alcón
Huéscar
Puebla de
Don Fadrique
Alhama
de Murcia
Lorca
Mazarrón

ANDALUCIA
Aljezur
SA. DE
MONCHIQUE
Silves
Portimão
Lagos
CABO DE SÃO VICENTE
Odemira
Valverde
del Camino
Minas de Riotinto
Cortegana
Cañas
Gibraleón
Palma del Río
Fernán Núñez
Castro del Río
Baena
Cabra
Priego
Montefrío
Pinos
Puente
Guadix
SA. DE BAZA
Vélez Rubio
Huércal
Overa
Cuevas del
Almanzora
Vera

ALGARVE
Tavira
Faro
P. Olhão
CABO DE
SANTA MARIA
Vila Real de
Sto. Antonio
Ayamonte
Isla
Cristina
Moguer
Huelva
Almonte
Las Marismas
Utrera
Écija
Aguilar
Lucena
Estepa
Rute
Loja
Santa Fe
Granada
SIERRA NEVADA
Mulhacén
11424
ALPUJARRAS
Berja
Dalías
Gérgal
Almería
CABO DE GATA

Sevilla
Dos
Hermanas
Carmona
Marchena
Morón de la
Frontera
Montellano
Arahal
Puente-
Genil
Antequera
Archidona
Alhama de
Granada
Vélez-Málaga
Motril
Adra
Almuñécar
Golfo
de Almería

Sanlúcar de
Barrameda
Jerez de la Frontera
El Puerto de Sta. María
Cádiz
S. Fernando
Chiclana de la Frontera
Vejer de la Frontera
CABO TRAFALGAR
Lebrija
Arcos de la
Frontera
Villamartín
Ubrique
Olvera
Ronda
Coín
Alora
Álhaurín
Málaga
Medina
Sidonia
Jimena de la
Frontera
San Roque
La Línea
Algeciras
Gibraltar (Br.)
Estepona
Tarifa
PTA. DE TARIFA
Bía. of Gibraltar
Strait of Gibraltar
ISLA DEL ALBORÁN
(Sp.)

C. SPARTEL
PTA. ALMINA
Ceuta
(Sp.)
Tanger
(Tangier)
Tétouan
Asilah
CAP DES TROIS
FOURCHES
Melilla
(Sp.)
Al-Hoceima
Baie d'Alhucemas
ISLAS CHAFARINAS
(Sp.)
Larache
Sebkh
El Ghazaw
Beni Sa
MOROCCO

ATLANTIC OCEAN
ESTREMADURA
PORTUGAL
ALENTEJO
EXTREMADURA
CASTILLA LA NUEVA
CASTILLA LA VIEJA
LEÓN
NAVARRA
SPAIN
SIERRA MORENA
MURCIA

Ebro
Duero
Tajo
Guadiana
Guadalquivir

Relief

Meters		Feet
3050		10000
1525		5000
610		2000
305		1000
152.5		500
0	Sea Level	0
152.5		500
1525		5000
3050		10000

A-552900-76
COPYRIGHT BY
RAND McNALLY & COMPANY
MADE IN U.S.A.

Scale 1:4 000 000, one inch to 64 miles. Conic Projection
Elevations and depressions are given in feet

Longitude West of Greenwich

Continued on pages 170-171

a

SA. DEL HOYO
S. Lorenzo de
El Escorial
4606
El Escorial
El Pardo
Valdemorillo
Las Rozas
de Madrid
Pozuelo de Alarcón
MADRID
Villaviciosa de Odón
Alcorcón
Móstoles
Leganés
Getafe
Scale 1:1 000 000
Navalcarnero
Parla
0 4 8 12 16 Kilometers

Colmenar
Fuente el Saz
Viejo
Galápagar
Algete
S. Sebastián
de los Reyes
Alcobendas
Fuencarral
Barajas
Torrejón
de Madrid
de Ardoz
Alcalá de
Henares
Vicálvaro
S. Fernando de Henares
Loeches
Campo Real
Vallecas
Arganda
Valdilecha
Carabaña
Pinto
Tielmes
S. Martín
de la Vega
Perales
de Tajuña
©RMcN.

b

Mafra
Cheleiros
Alhandra
Alverca
Samora Correia
São João
das Lampas
Montelavar
Almargem
do Bispo
Loures
Sacavém
de Moscavide
Alcochete
Colares
Sintra
Odivelas
Queluz
Amadora
Alcabideche
Barcarena
Carnaxide
Cascais
Estoril
Oeiras
Almada
Costa de Caparica
Barreiro
Seixal
Vedros
Moita
Pinhal Novo
CABO
DA ROCA
Coina
Palmela
**LISBON
(Lisboa)**
Montijo
Alhos
ATLANTIC
OCEAN
Scale 1:1 000 000
0 5 10 Miles
0 4 8 12 16 Kilometers
CABO ESPICHEL
Setúbal
Sesimbra
Ba. de
Setúbal
Comporta
©RMcN.

c

Frattamaggiore
Acerra
Nola
Afragola
Pomigliano d'Arco
Monteforte
Marano di Napoli
Avellino
Somma Vesuviana
Irpino
**NAPLES
(Napoli)**
Portici
Vesuvio
S. Giuseppe
Vesuviano
4190
Pozzuoli
Torre
del Greco
Sarno
Bacoli
Torre Annunziata
Mercato
Severino
C. MISENO
Pompeii Ruins
Angri
Nocera Inf.
I. DI PROCIDA
Castellammare
di Stabia
Gragnano
Cava de'
Tirreni
Forio
2585
Ischia
Golfo di Napoli
Salerno
I. D'ISCHIA
Sorrento
Amalfi
Scale 1:1 000 000
TYRRHENIAN
SEA
0 5 10 Miles
0 4 8 12 16 Kilometers
1932
PUNTA
CAMPANELLA
Capri
I. DI CAPRI
Golfo di Salerno
©RMcN.

d

Pyrgi
Caere
Veio
Monterotondo
Cerveteri
Mentana
Guidonia
Ladispoli
**ROME
(Roma)**
Tivoli
Villa
Adriana
VATICAN CITY
Zagarolo
Fregene
Fiumicino
Frascati
COLLI ALBANI
3114
Ostia Antica
Marino
Genzano di Roma
Lido di Roma
Laurentum
Albano Laziale
Pomezia
Lanúvio
Velletri
TYRRHENIAN
Aprília
Cisterna di
Latina
SEA
Scale 1:1 000 000
0 5 10 Miles
0 4 8 12 16 Kilometers
Nettuno
Anzio
©RMcN.

Pau
Tarbes
Toulouse
Albi
Gaillac
Condom
Verdun
Castres
Lodève
Montpellier
Auch
Muret
Baziège
Castelnaudary
Béziers
Sète
Agde
Carcassonne
Narbonne
Pamiers
Limoux
Foix
Tarascon
Quillan
Perpignan
Prades
Céret
Port Vendres
ANDORRA
Andorra
CAP DE CREUS
CATALUNYA
Golf de Roses
Ripoll
Olot
Berga
Vic
Girona
Manlleu
La Bisbal
Lleida
Manresa
Terrassa
Granollers
Calella
Igualada
Sabadell
Mataró
Sant Feliu
de Guixols
Fraga
Montblanc
BARCELONA
Reus
Tarragona
Vilanova i la Geltrú
CAP DE TORTOSA
Tortosa
Amposta
Morella
Alcanar
Vinaròs
Benicarló
Torreblanca
COLUMBRETES
Castelló de la Plana
Vila-real
Borriana
Golf
Onda
Vall d'Uixó
de
Sagunt
Lliria
Valencia
València
Catarroja
MENORCA
(MINORCA)
Ciutadella
Maó
Es Port
de Pollença
Sóller
Inca
Sa
Pobla
Manacor
BALEARIC
ISLANDS
BALEARS
Palma
Llucmajor
Felanitx
Santanyí
MALLORCA
(MAJORCA)
CAP DE SES SALINES
ILLA DE CABRERA
EIVISSA
(IBIZA)
Sant Antoni de Portmany
Santa Eulària del Riu
Eivissa
FORMENTERA
Sueca
Cullera
Xàtiva
Gandia
Oliva
Ontinyent
Cocentaina
Pego
Dénia
Xàbia
Alcoi
CAP DE LA NAU
Xixona
La Vila Joiosa
Alacant
Elx
Mar Menor
Unión
CABO DE PALOS
Torrevieja
gena
BALEARIC
SEA
ILLES
BALEARS
Valencia
MEDITERRANEAN
SEA
Algiers
(El Djazaïr)
Delles
Boudouaou
Cherchell
Boufarik
El Arba
Bouira
Ténès
El Affroun
El
Boulaida
Meliana
Lemdiyya
Sour el
Echt Cheliff
Carnot
Ghozlane
Mestghanem
ATLAS
MOUNTAINS
Arzew
Sidi Aïssa
CAP FERRAT
Oued Rhiou
Qasr el Boukhari
ALGERIA
El Mohammadia
Ghilizane
Aïn Wessara
Oued Tlelat
Stizef
Bouira-Sahary
mouchent
Mouaskar
Tihert
Ksar
Chellala
Zahrez Chergui

FRANCE
PYRENEES
Golfe du Lion

20 40 60 80 100 120 Miles
20 40 60 80 100 120 140 160 180 200 Kilometers

Continued on pages 168-169

Continued on pages 170-171

Scale 1:4 000 000; one inch to 64 miles. Conic Projection
Elevations and depressions are given in feet

Relief

Meters		Feet
3050		10 000
1525		5000
610		2000
305		1000
152.5		500
0	Sea Level	0
152.5		500
1525		5000
3050		10 000

HUNGARY

Szeged · Makó · Nádlac · Arad · Alba Iulia · Sebeş · Sighişoara · Gheorghe

Bácsalmás · Mohács · Subotica · Senta · Kikinda · Jimbolia · Timişoara · Lugoj · Hunedoara · Deva · Orăştie · Sibiu · Făgăraş · Braşov

Sombor · Apatin · Bačka Topola · Ada · Bečej · Becskerek · BANAT · Caransebeş · Reşiţa · Caransebeş · Petroşani · CARPAŢII MERIDIONALI · (TRANSYLVANIAN ALPS) · Sinaia · Buzău

Osijek · Novi Sad · Vrbas · Srbobran · Čurug · Vršac · Anina · ROMANIA · VALACHIA · Curtea de Argeş · Câmpulung · Mizil

Vukovar · Bačka Palanka · Ruma · Srem. Karlovci · Pančevo · Bela Crkva · Reşiţa · Târgu Jiu · Râmnicu Vâlcea · Piteşti · BUCHAREST (Bucureşti)

Bosanski Šamac · Gradačac · Brčko · Zemun (Semlin) · Belgrade (Beograd) · Smederevo (Semendria) · Požarevac · Orşova IRON GATE · Drobeta-Turnu Severin · Strehaia · Craiova · Drăgăşani · Slatina · Caracal · Alexandria · Roşiori de Vede · Giurgiu · Ruse (Russe) · Vetovo · Dobrich · Balchik

Tuzla · Loznica · Zvornik · Valjevo · Gornji Milanovac · Kragujevac · Svilajnac · Negotin · Bregovo · Vidin · Calafat · Lom · Kozloduy · Selanovtsi · Orekhovo · Corabia · Turnu Măgurele · Zimnicea · Svishtov · Byala · Popovo · Razgrad · Novi Pazar · Provadiya · Varna (Stalin)

Sarajevo · Rogatica · Višegrad · Pribroj · Nova Varoš · Čačak · Kraljevo · Trstenik · Kruševac · Aleksinac · Niš · Pirot · Zaječar · Gramada · Vratsa · Berkovitsa · Knezha · Pleven · Lovech · Gorna Oryakhovitsa · Sevlievo · Veliko Tŭrnovo · Gabrovo · Lyaskovets · Kotel · Smyadovo · Shumen

GOVINA · Foča · Čajniče · Pljevlja · Prijepolje · Sjenica · Raška · Kuršumlija · Leskovac · Vlasotince · Botevgrad · Teteven · STARA PLANINA · Sliven · Straldzha · Karnobat · Aitos · Pomorie

Nevesinje · Gacko · Durmitor 2274 · CRNA GORA (MONTENEGRO) · Nikšić · Bijelo Polje · Novi Pazar · Kos. Mitrovica · Priština · (BALKAN MTS.) · Karlovo · Kazanlŭk · Stara Zagora · Nova Zagora · Yambol · BULGARIA · Burgas · Sozopol

Stolac · Bileća · Trebinje · Podgorica · Cetinje · Peć · Đakovica · Gnjilane · KOSOVO · Vranje · Kyustendil · Breznik · Trŭn · Radomir · Sofia (Sofiya) · Pernik · Samokov · Panagyurishte · Ikhtiman · Golyamo Konare · Plovdiv (Philippopolis) · Chirpan · Topolovgrad · Malko Tŭrnovo · ISTRANCA DAĞLARI

Dubrovnik (Ragusa) · Kotor · Virpazar · Shkodër (Scutari) · Gusinje · ŠAR PLANINA · Prizren · Kumanovo · Kriva Palanka · Kratovo · Kočani · Blagoevgrad (Gorna Dzhumaya) · Razlog · Bansko · Batyak · Peshtera · Asenovgrad · Khaskovo · Svilengrad · Edirne (Adrianople) · Babaeski · Lüleburgaz

Proposed name change from "Yugoslavia" to "Serbia and Montenegro" pending

Lake Scutari · Bar · Ulcinj (Dulcigno) · Lesh (Alessio) · Kruje · YUGOSLAVIA · SERBIA · Tetovo · Skopje · ČAR PLANINA · Radoviš · Štip · Pehčevo · Musala 2925 · RODOPE · Zlatograd · Kŭrdzhali · Dhidhimótikhon · Kárküci · Uzunköprü · Kırklareli · Hayrabolu · Tekirdağ (Rodosto)

Pejg i Drinit · KEP I RODONIT · Gostivar · Kičevo · Debar (Dibra) · Kruševo · Prilep · MACEDONIA · Strumica · Petrich · Sidirókastro · Dráma · Xánthi · Komotiní · Soufli · Enez · THRACE · Malkara · Keşan · Şarköy · GALLIPOLI PENINSULA · Gelibolu (Gallipoli) · Lâpseki · Biga

Durrës · Tiranë · Kavajë · Peqin · Ohrid · Bitola (Monastir) · Florina · Edessa · Kilkís · Lagkadás · Sérres · Kavála · Alexandroúpoli (Dédéagach) · THÁSOS · Theologos · SAMOTHRÁKI · Ecebat (Maidos) · Çanakkale · Troy Ruins · Ezine · Bayramiç

ALBANIA · Elbasan · Lake Ohrid · Lake Prespa · Náousa · Véroia · Giannitsá · Thessaloníki · CHALKIDIKÍ · Polygyros · Kólpos Kassándras · Áthos 2033 · GÖKÇEADA · Kumkale · Bozcaada · BOZCA ADA · Edremit

Fier · Berat · Korçë · Kastoria · Siátista · Katerini · Litókhoro · Olympos 2917 · Thermaïkós Kólpos · Stryminikós Kólpos · Kólpos Aigaíou · LÍMNOS · Myrina · BOZCA ADA · Ayvalık

Brindisi · Mesagne · Lecce · Francavilla · SAZANI · Vlorë (Valona) · Gjirokastër · Grevená · Eláeasón · Tírnavos · THESSALÍA · Lárisa · AGIOS EFSTRATIOS · LÉSVOS · Mytilíni · Agiásos · Plomári · Polichnítos

Manduria · Nardò · Galatina · Delvinë · Kónitsa · Métsovo · Meliovia · PÍNDOS · Tríkala · Kardítsa · Almyrós · Vólos · VOREIOI · SPORADES · Skýros · SKÝROS · PSARÁ

Gallipoli · Maglie · Otranto · OTRANTO · Ioánnina · Kalabáka · ÓROS ÓTHRYS · Famra (Pharsalus) · Fársala · Lamía · SKÓPELOS · SKIATHOS · Chíos · CHÍOS · Çeşme · Urla

S. MARIA DI LEUCA · OTHONOÍ · Kérkyra · KÉRKYRA · PAXOÍ · Árta · Préveza · Lefkáda · Astakós · Agrínio · Amfissa · Delphi Ruins · Leivádia · Thíva (Thebes) · Chalkída · Évvoia · Kými · DODEKÁNISOS (DODECANESE) · CHIOS

IONIAN · Lefkáda · LEFKÁDA · ITHÁKI · Mesolóngi · Aitolikó · Galaxídi · Athens (Athína) · Peiraiás (Piraeus) · ANDROS · Ándros · IKARÍA

Argóstoli · KEFALLONÍA · Aigio · Pátra (Patras) · Korinthiakós Kólpos · Mégara · Salamína · Saronikós Kólpos · Lávrio · TÍNOS · Ermoúpoli · SÝROS · MÝKONOS · DONOUSSA

Amaliáda · Zákynthos · ZÁKYNTHOS · Pýrgos · Kórinthos (Corinth) · Argos · Náfplio · Áigina · AÍGINA · KÉA · KYTHNOS · SÉRIFOS · Sérifos · KIKLÁDES · PÁROS · Páros · NÁXOS · Náxos · AMORGÓS

PELOPONNISOS · Megalópoli · SÍFNOS · SÍKINOS · ÍOS · Kyparissía · Filiatrá · Messíni · Kalamáta · Sparti (Sparta) · KÍMOLOS · MÍLOS

Gargaliánoi · Koróni · Gýtheio · Neápoli · AKRA TAÍNARO · AKRA MALÉAS

IONIAN SEA

AEGEAN SEA

ADRIATIC SEA

Strait of Otranto

Longitude East of Greenwich

0 10 20 30 40 50 60 70 80 90 100 110 120 Miles

0 20 40 60 80 100 120 140 160 180 200 Kilometers

Relief

	Feet	Meters
	5000	1525
	2000	610
	1000	305
	500	152.5
	Sea Level	0
	500	152.5

Continued on pages 166-167

Cities and Towns

0 to 50,000 ·
50,000 to 500,000 ⊙
500,000 to 1,000,000 ⊚
1,000,000 and over

Scale 1:4 000 000; one inch to 64 miles. Conic Projection
Elevations and depressions are given in feet

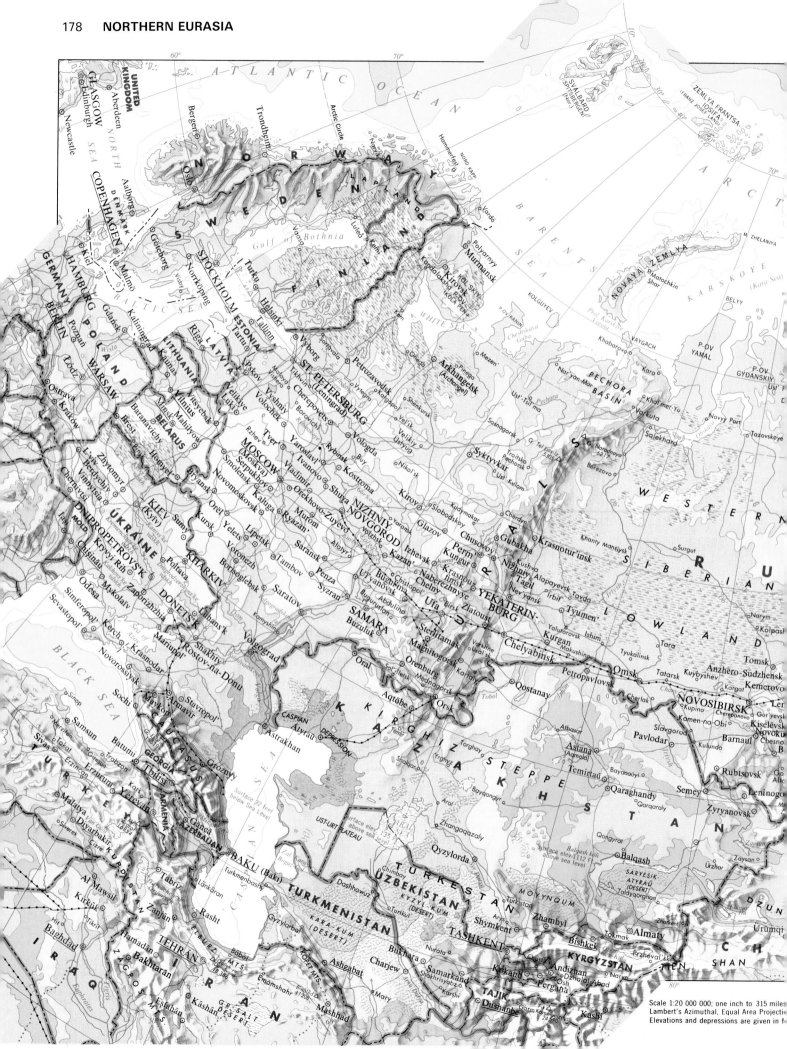

Scale 1:20 000 000; one inch to 315 miles
Lambert's Azimuthal, Equal Area Projection
Elevations and depressions are given in f

Relief

Meters	Feet
3050	10 000
1525	5000
610	2000
305	1000
152.5	500
0 Sea Level	0
152.5	500 Below
1525	5000 Sea Level
3050	10 000

ARCTIC OCEAN

LAPTEV SEA

EAST SIBERIAN SEA

SEVERNAYA ZEMLYA (NORTHERN LAND)

P-OV GORY TAYMYR BYRRANGA

VRANGELYA (WRANGEL I.)

M. SHELAGSKIY

DE LONGA

NOVOSIBIRSKIYE O-VA (NEW SIBERIAN ISLANDS)
FADDEYA
NOVAYA SIBIR
KOTEL'NYY
MALYY LYAKHOVSKIY
M. SVYATOY NOS
LYAKHOVSKIYE

M. CHELYUSKIN
Nordvik
Khatangskiye Zaliv
Taymyr
Bol'shoy Begichev

Ust'-Olenëk
Tiksi
Bulun
Yana
Kazachye
Zashiversk
Nizhne-Kolymsk
Ambarchik
AYON
Srednekolymsk
Markovo
Penzhino

M. Medvezhiy

ARCTIC CIRCLE

CHUKOTSKIY POV

CHUKOTSKOYE NAGOR'YE

Anadyr'
Anadyrskiy Zaliv

KORYAKSKIY KHREBET

Khatanga
GORY PUTORANA
Norilsk
Baykit
Podkamennaya Tunguska
Tura
Nizhnyaya Tunguska
Yartsevo
G. Polkan 3543
Yeniseysk

Olenëk
Zhigansk
Verkhoyansk
Abyy
Gora Chen 3147
Oymyakon
KHREBET CHERSKOGO
Zyryanka
Kolyma

KHREBET GYDAN (KOLYMSKIY)
Magadan
Gizhiga
M. TAYGONOS

Okhotsk
M. ALEVINA

SEA OF OKHOTSK

KAMCHATKA
Ust'-Kamchatsk
Klyuchevskaya 15584
Verkhne-Kamchatsk
Petropavlovsk-Kamchatskiy
Ust'-Bol'sheretsk

KARAGIN

VERKHOYANSKIY KHREBET
Lena
Zhigansk
Suntar
Vilyuy
Vilyuysk
Yakutsk
Aldan
Aldankskaya
Amga
Ust'-Maya
Nelkan
DZHUGDZHUR KHREBET
Ayan
Chumikan
Udskaya Guba
SHANTAR
M. YELIZAVETY
Okha
SAKHALIN
Aleksandrovsk
Poronaysk
Uglegorsk
M. TERPENIYA

Muktuya
Peleduy
Vitim
Bodaybo
G. Golets-Purpula 3377
PATOM PLATEAU
Golets-Skalistyy 9186
Aldan
Tommot
Olëkminsk

Baykit
Ilimsk
Kirensk
Nizhne-Angarsk
Kachuga
Zhigalovo
Vitim
STANOVOY KHREBET
Tyndinskiy
Zeya
Skovorodino
Svobodnyy
Belogorsk
Zeya
KHREBET BUREINSKIY
Ust'-Tyrma
Bureya
Nikolayevsk-na-Amure
Komsomol'sk na-Amure
Sovetskaya Gavan'
Amur
Kholmsk
Yuzhno-Sakhalinsk
Korsakov

TATAR STRAIT
Wakkanai
Sōya Kaikyō
HOKKAIDO
Otaru Sapporo
Goshi

Krasnoyarsk
Kansk
Tayshet
Bratsk
Tulun
Nizhneudinsk
Bratskoye Vdkhr.
Balakhta
Kachuga
SAYAN KHREBET
Pyramida 10801
Minusinsk
Abakan
Cheremkhovo
Angarsk
Munku Sardyk 11457
Irkutsk
Kyren
Kotulik
OZ. Baykal (Lake Baikal)
Surface elev. 1535 ft. above sea level
Barguzin
BAYKAL'SKIY KHREBET
YABLONOVYY KHREBET
VITIM
Ulan-Ude
Chita
Sretensk
Nerchinsk
Nerchinskiy Zavod
NERCHINSKIY KHREBET
Blagoveshchensk
Nenjiang
Goukou
Qiqihar
Hailun
Boli
Dnerechensk
Spassk-Dal'niy
Ussuriysk
Artëm
Partizansk
Nakhodka
Vladivostok
SIKHOTE ALIN

Kyzyl
TANNU-OLA
O Nuur
Khövsgöl Nuur
Petrovsk-Zabaykal'skiy
Gorodok
Kyakhta
Aginskoye
Aksha
Borzya
Onon
Kerulen
Wenquan
Tao an
Jarud Qi
HANGAYN NURUU
KHANGAI MTS.
Uliastay
Hovd
Har Us Nuur
Bast Bogd 13419
Sayr Usa
MONGOLIA
Ulan Bator (Ulaanbaatar)
Ondorhaan
Selenge
GREATER KHINGAN RANGE
LESSER KHINGAN RANGE
Fuyu
Jilin
CHANGCHUN
Shuangliao
Shenyang
Fushun
MANCHURIA
Mudanjiang
HARBIN
Suifenhe
Hunchun
Tumen
Najin
Chŏngjin
SEA OF JAPAN

ALTAY MTS.
Hami
GOBI OR SHAMO (DESERT)
CHINA
Zhangjiakou
Fengzhen
BEIJING
Baoding
TIANJIN
Weichang
Chengde
Chifeng
Lüshun
Dalian
Bo Hai
SHANDONG BANDAO
YELLOW SEA
Korea Bay
Kaesŏng
P'yŏngyang
NORTH KOREA
SEOUL
SOUTH KOREA
Andong
PUSAN
Taegu

HONSHŪ
JAPAN
Kanazawa
Tottori
Matsue
KYOTO
KOBE
OSAKA
Okayama
Hiroshima
Kōchi
Naze Straits

RUSSIA

A-570000-76   -16-16-37
COPYRIGHT BY
RAND MCNALLY & COMPANY
MADE IN U.S.A.

Longitude East of Greenwich

100   200   300   400   500   600 Miles
200   400   600   800   1000 Kilometers

Cities and Towns

0 to 50,000 ○
50,000 to 500,000 ⊙
500,000 to 1,000,000 ◎
1,000,000 and over

Continued on pages 160-161

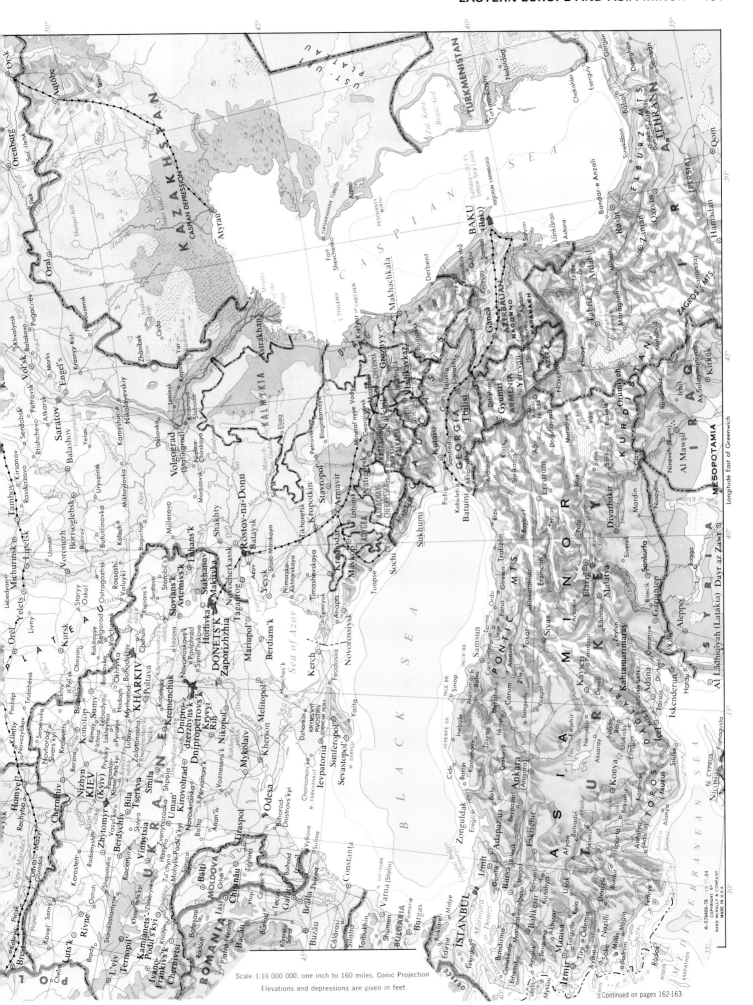

Scale 1:10 000 000; one inch to 160 miles. Conic Projection

Elevations and depressions are given in feet.

Continued on pages 162-163

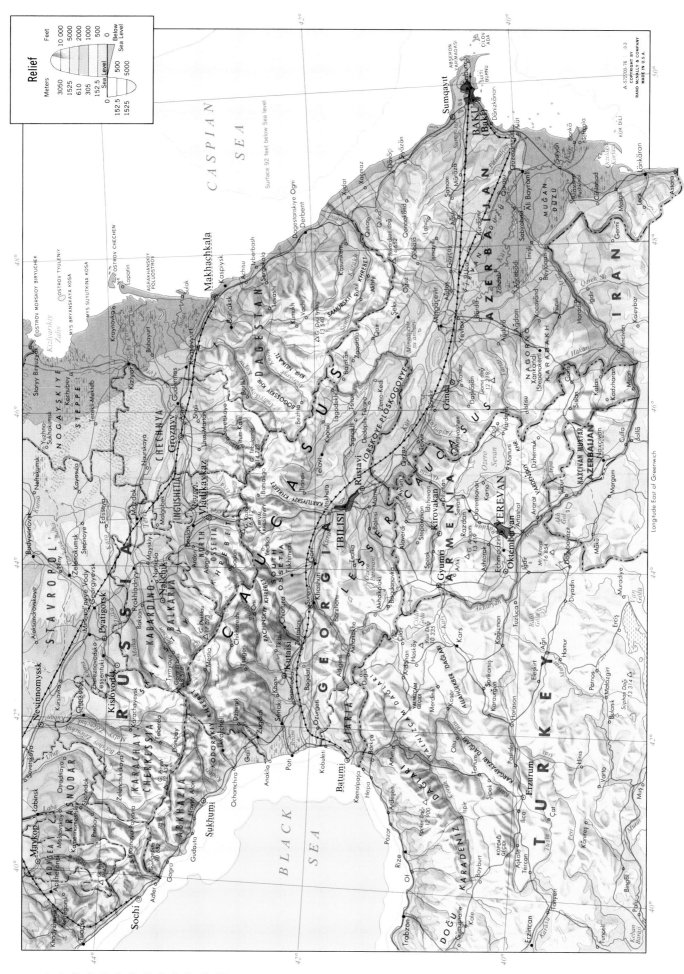

Relief

Meters	Feet	
3050	10 000	
1525	5000	
610	2000	
305	1000	
152.5	500	
0	Sea Level	
152.5	500	Below Sea Level
1525	5000	

CASPIAN SEA

Surface 92 feet below sea level

BLACK SEA

A-572200-76 -3.3
COPYRIGHT BY
RAND M°NALLY & COMPANY
MADE IN U.S.A.

0   10   20   30   40   50   60   70   80   90   100   110   120 Miles
0   20   40   60   80   100   120   140   160   180   200 Kilometers

Scale 1:4 000 000; one inch to 64 miles. Conic Projection
Elevations and depressions are given in feet

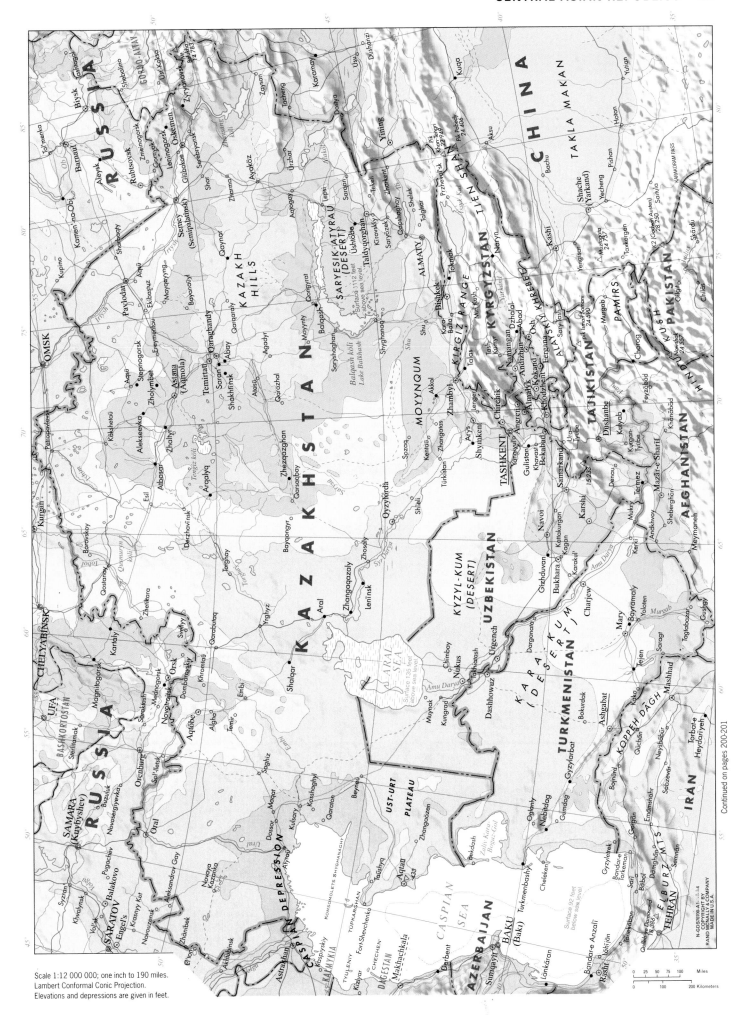

Scale 1:12 000 000; one inch to 190 miles.
Lambert Conformal Conic Projection.
Elevations and depressions are given in feet.

Continued on pages 200-201

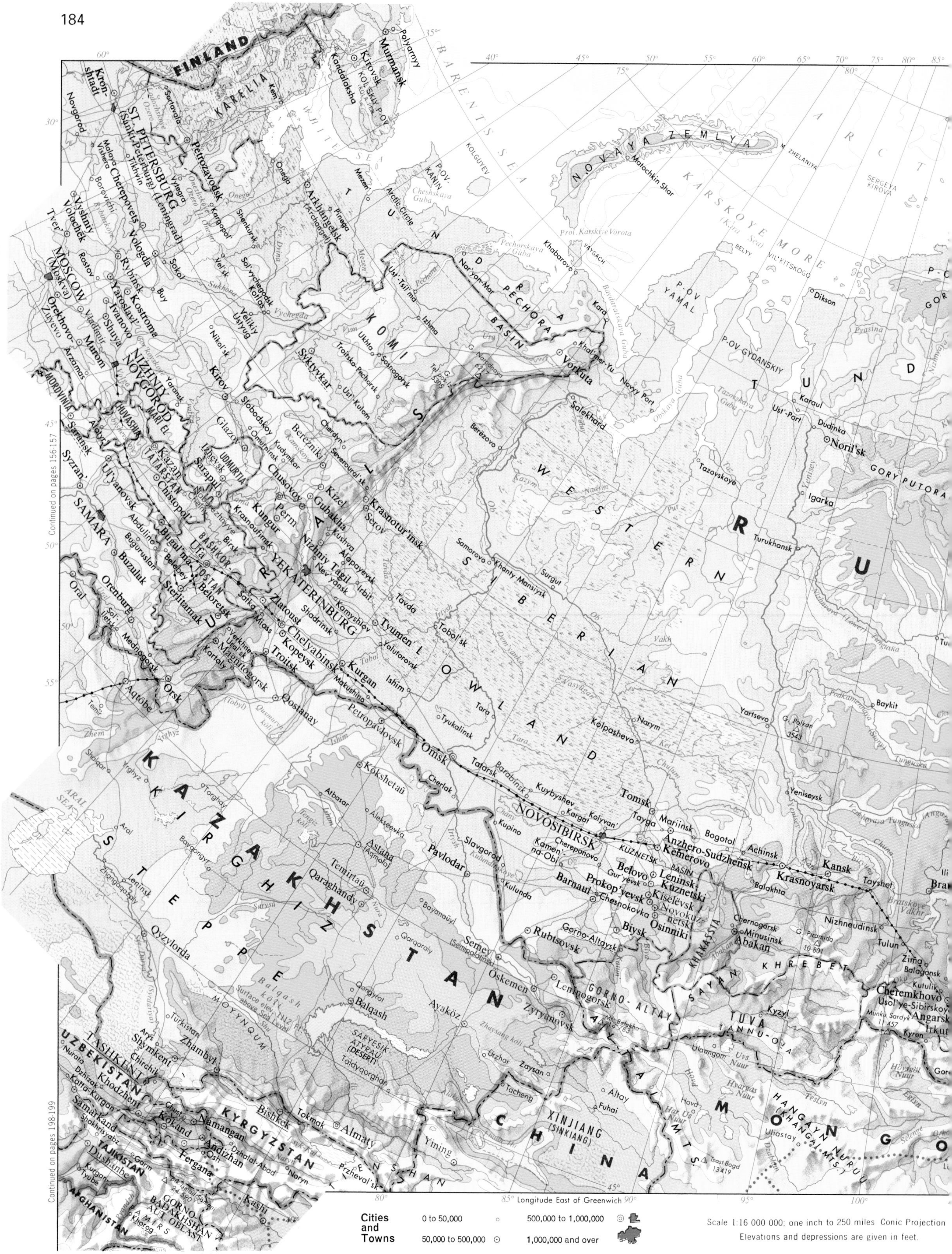

FINLAND

KARELIA

Continued on pages 156-157

Continued on pages 198-199

BARENTS SEA

NOVAYA ZEMLYA

KARSKOYE MORE (Kara Sea)

ARCTIC

SERGEYA KIROVA

ZHELANIYA

Matochkin Shar

BELYY

VILKITSKOGO

Prol. Karskiye Vorota

P-OV YAMAL

P-OV GYDANSKIY

GORY PUTORA

Polyarnyy
Murmansk
Kirovsk
Kandalaksha
KOL'SKY P-OV
Kem'
Kron-shtadt
Novgorod
ST. PETERSBURG (Saint-Petersburg) (Leningrad)
Vyborg
Petrozavodsk
Arkhangel'sk
P-OV KANIN
KOLGUYEV
Khabarovo
VAYGACH
Dikson
Vyshniy Volochëk
Tver'
Cherepovets
Vologda
Onega
Pinega
Mezen'
Cheshskaya Guba
Nar'yan-Mar
Pechorskaya Guba
Karskiye Vorota
Novyy Port
Karaul
Dudinka
Igarka
Nori'sk
MOSCOW (Moskva)
Orekhovo-Zuyevo
Vladimir
Rybinsk
Yaroslavl'
Kostroma
Sokol
Vel'sk
Kotlas
Ukhta
Vorkuta
Salekhard
Berëzovo
Tazovskoye
Noril'sk
Turukhansk
NIZHNIY NOVGOROD
MORDVINIA
Saransk
Murom
Arzamas
Shuya
Ivanovo
Nikol'sk
Syktyvkar
KOMI
Ust'-Tsil'ma
Izhma
Khanty-Mansiysk
Surgut
Yartsevo
Baykit
CHUVASHIA
MARI EL
Cheboksary
Kazan
TATARSTAN
Glazov
UDMURTIA
Izhevsk
Perm
Berezniki
Cherdyn'
WESTERN SIBERIA
LOWLAND
Samarovo
Tobol'sk
Ob'
R U S S I A
Syzran'
SAMARA
Ul'yanovsk
Chistopol'
Bugul'ma
Sarapul
Chusovoy
Kizel
Gubakha
Solikamsk
Krasnoturinsk
Serov
Ishim
Kolpashevo
Narym
Ket'
Yeniseysk
BASHKORTOSTAN
Ufa
Beloretsk
Kungur
Krasnoufimsk
Nizhniy Tagil
Nev'yansk
Alapayevsk
Irbit
Tavda
Kolyvan'
Buzuluk
Sterlitamak
Belebey
Abdulino
Zlatoust
YEKATERINBURG
Kamyshlov
Tyumen'
Yalutorovsk
Tyukalinsk
Tatarsk
Barabinsk
Tomsk
Mariinsk
Bogotol
Achinsk
Kansk
Tayshet
Orenburg
Orsk
Verkhniy Ufaley
Chelyabinsk
Kopeysk
Kurgan
Mokshino
Omsk
Cherlak
Kuybyshev
NOVOSIBIRSK
Anzhero-Sudzhensk
Kemerovo
Krasnoyarsk
Nizhneudinsk
Tulun
Oral
Aqtöbe
Magnitogorsk
Troitsk
Qostanay
Petropavlovsk
Kamen'-na-Obi
Cherepanovo
KUZNETSK BASIN
Belovo
Leninsk-Kuznetskiy
Balakhta
Zima
Balagansk
Temir
ARAL SEA
Aral
Qyzylorda
Kökshetaü
Slavgorod
Kupino
Barnaul
Prokop'yevsk
Kiselëvsk
Novokuznetsk
Chernogorsk
Minusinsk
Abakan
KHAKASSIA
Usol'ye-Sibirskoye
Cheremkhovo
Angarsk
Irkut
KAZAKH STEPPE
Astana (Aqmola)
Pavlodar
Karaganda
Chesnokovka
Biysk
Gorno-Altaysk
Rubtsovsk
Osinniki
SAYAN KHREBET
Kyzyl
TUVA
TANNU-OLA
KAZAKHSTAN
Temirtaü
Qaraghandy
Qarqaraly
Semey (Semipalatinsk)
Öskemen
Leninogorsk
GORNO-ALTAY
ALTAY MTS.
Balqash
Balqash kol
Ayagöz
Zyryanovsk
Zaysan
Orzhar
Tacheng
Altay
Fuhai
MONGOLIA
HANGAYN NURUU (KHANGAI MTS.)
Uliastay
UZBEKISTAN
TASHKENT
Shymkent
Chirchik
Khodzhent
Türkistan
Arys
Zhambyl
Bishkek
Almaty
Yining
XINJIANG (SINKIANG)
CHINA
TIEN SHAN
TAJIKISTAN
Dushanbe
KYRGYZSTAN
Toqmaq
Namangan
Andizhan
Osh
Naryn
Przheval'sk
Kashi
AFGHANISTAN
GORNO-BADAKHSHAN AUTON. OBLAST
Khorog

Cities and Towns

	0 to 50,000	500,000 to 1,000,000
	50,000 to 500,000	1,000,000 and over

Scale 1:16 000 000; one inch to 250 miles Conic Projection
Elevations and depressions are given in feet.

85° Longitude East of Greenwich 90°

Continued on pages 204-205

Relief

Meters	Feet
3050	10 000
1525	5000
610	2000
305	1000
152.5	500
0	Sea Level
152.5	500
1525	5000
3050	10 000

A-579300-76 -11-9-22
COPYRIGHT BY
RAND McNALLY & COMPANY
MADE IN U.S.A.

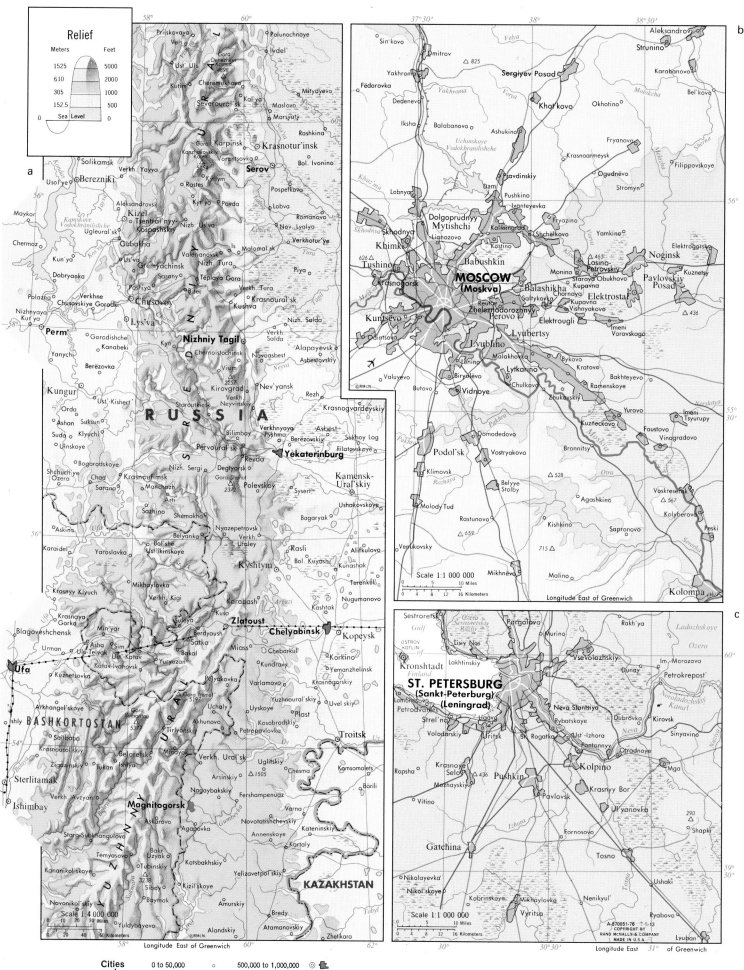

Relief

Meters	Feet
1525	5000
610	2000
305	1000
152.5	500
Sea Level	0

a

RUSSIA

Solikamsk
Berezniki
Usol'ye
Maykor
Chermoz
Kun'ya
Dobryanka
Polazna
Nizhnyaya Kur'ya
Perm'
Yanychi
Kungur
Orda
Ashan
Suda
Klyuchi
Uinskoye
Askino
Karaidel'
Krasnyy Klyuch
Krasnaya Gorka
Blagoveshchensk
Ufa
shly **BASHKORTOSTAN**
Sterlitamak
Ishimbay

Priiskovaya
Vels
Ust' Uls
Gora Denezhkin Kamen 1898
Kutim
Cherëmukhovo
Severoural'sk
Gora Karpinsk
Kanzhakovskiy Kamen 1554
Vorontsovka
Rastes
Kytlym
Verkh. Yayva
Kizel
Tsentral'nyy
Kospashskiy
Ugleural'sk
Gubakha
Us'va
Gremyachinsk
Valerianovsk
Nizh. Us'va
Verkhne Chusovskiye Gorodki
Chusovoy
Lys'va
Gorodishche
Kanabeki
Berëzovka
Nizhniy Tagil
Chernoistochinsk
Visim
2257
Kirovgrad
Verkh. Neyvinskiy
Nov'yansk
Bilimbay
Pervoural'sk
Revda
Degtyarsk
Yekaterinburg
Gora Shunut 2372
Polevskoy
Syosert'
Nizh. Sergi
Krasnoufimsk
Manchazh
Arti
Sazhino
Shemakha
Nyazepetrovsk
Belyanka
Verkh. Ufaley
Bol'she Ust'ikinskoye
Yaroslavka
Mikhaylovka
Verkh. Kigi
Kyshtym
Bol. Kuyash
Kasli
Karabash
Kusa
Argazi
Kashtak
Alifkulovo
Kunashak
Nugumanovo
Terenkul'
Zlatoust
Chelyabinsk
Kopeysk
Min'yar
Krasnaya Gorka
Asha
Sim
Ust'-Katav
Ulu-Telyak
Urman
Katav-Ivanovsk
Kuznetsovka
Satka
Bakal
Berdyaush
Suleya
Miass
Chebarkul'
Korkino
Yemanzhelinsk
Kundravy
Yuryuzan
Gora Iremel' 1592
Polyakovka
Varlamovo
Yuzhnoural'skiy
Uvel skiy
Krasnogorskiy
Akhunovo
Uchaly
Uyskoye
Kosobrodskiy
Plast
Petropavlovka
Tirlyanskiy
Gora Yamantau 1638
Arkhangel'skoye
Beloretsk
Mindyak
Magnitogorsk
Askarovo
Agapovka
Tukan
Ishlya
Verkh. Ural'sk
1505
Chesma
Uglitskiy
Komsomolets
Nagaybakskiy
Arsinskiy
Varna
Fershampenuaz
Novotatishchevskiy
Annenskoye
Kartaly
Kananikol'skoye
Temyasovo
3238
Tubinskiy
Siboy
Yelizavetpol'skiy
Katebakhskiy
Kizil'skoye
Baymak
KAZAKHSTAN
Novonikol'skiy
Bakr Uzyak
Amurskiy
Bredy
Atamanovskiy
Yuldybayevo
Alandskiy
Zhetikara

Scale 1:4 000 000

Longitude East of Greenwich

---

b

Sin'kovo
Dmitrov
Yakhroma
Dedeneva
Iksha
Balabanovo
Fëdorovka
Lobnya
Skhodnya
Skhodnya
Khimki
Tushino
626
Krasnogorsk
Dolgoprudnyy
Mytishchi
Lianozovo
Kaliningrad
Babushkin
MOSCOW (Moskva)
Kuntsevo
Odintsovo
Valuyevo
Butovo
Vidnoye
Strunino
Karabanovo
Aleksandrov
Sergiyev Posad
Khot'kovo
Ashukino
Okhotino
Bel'kovo
Filippovskoye
Pravdinskiy
Krasnoarmeysk
Ogudnëvo
Stromyn
Pushkino
Ivanteyevka
Fryanovo
Yamkino
Shchëlkovo
Fryazino
465
Losino-Petrovskiy
Monino
Staraya Kupavna
Kupavna
Vishnyakovo
Noginsk
Elektrogorsk
Kuznetsy
Pavlovskiy Posad
Elektrostal
436
Balashikha
Saltykovka
Chornaya
Zheleznodorozhnyy
Perovo
Reutov
Lyubertsy
Elektrougli
Imeni Vorovskogo
Lyublino
Malakhovka
Lenino
Birylëvo
Lytkarino
Bykovo
Kratovo
Zhukovskiy
Bakhteyevo
Ramenskoye
Chulkovo
Yurovo
Imeni Tsyurupy
Domodedovo
Vostryakovo
Bronnitsy
Kuzneckovo
Faustovo
Vinogradovo
Podol'sk
Klimovsk
528
Belyye Stolby
Agashkino
Kishkino
Sapronovo
Voskresensk
567
Kolyberovo
Molody Tud
Rastunovo
659
Venukovsky
715
Mikhnëvo
Malino
Peski
Kolomna

Scale 1:1 000 000

0 5 10 Miles
0 4 8 16 Kilometers

Longitude East of Greenwich

---

c

Sestroretsk
Ozero Sestroretskiy Razliv
Pargalovo
Murino
Rakh'ya
Gulf
Lisiy Nos
OSTROV KOTLIN
Kronshtadt
Finland
Lakhtinskiy
Vsevolozhskiy
Im. Morozova
Petrokrepost'
ST. PETERSBURG (Sankt-Peterburg) (Leningrad)
Lomonosov
Petrodvorets
Strel'na
Volodarskiy
Uritsk
Iljovo
Rogatka
Neva Stantsiya
Rybatskoye
Ust'-Izhora
Pontonnyy
Dunay
Otradnoye
Dubrovka
Sinyavino
Kirovsk
Krasnoye Selo
436
Mozhayskiy
Pushkin
Kolpino
Krasnyy Bor
Mga
Ropsha
Pavlovsk
Ul'yanovka
290
Shapki
Vitino
Gatchina
Fornosovo
Tosno
Nikolayevka
Nikol'skoye
Kobrinskoye
Mikhaylovka
Vyritsa
Ushaki
Nenikyul'
Shapki
Ryabovo
Lyuban

Scale 1:1 000 000

0 5 10 Miles
0 4 8 16 Kilometers

A-570051-76 2-5-13
COPYRIGHT BY
RAND MCNALLY & COMPANY
MADE IN U.S.A.

Longitude East 31° *of Greenwich*

Cities and Towns

0 to 50,000	○	500,000 to 1,000,000	◎
50,000 to 500,000	⊙	1,000,000 and over	

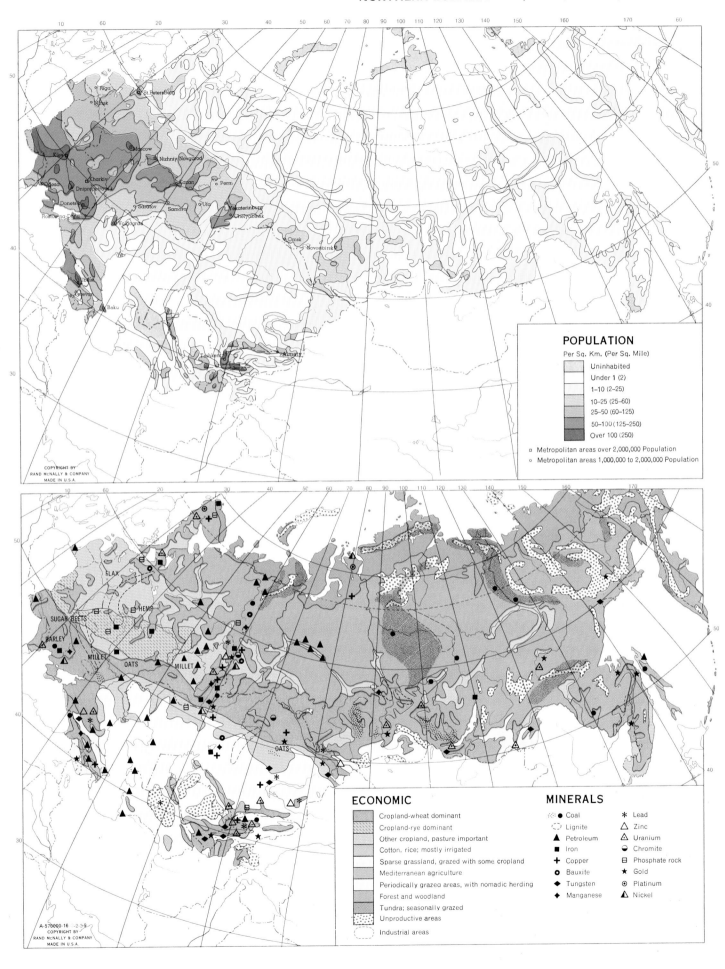

POPULATION

Per Sq. Km. (Per Sq. Mile)

Uninhabited
Under 1 (2)
1–10 (2–25)
10–25 (25–60)
25–50 (60–125)
50–100 (125–250)
Over 100 (250)

□ Metropolitan areas over 2,000,000 Population
○ Metropolitan areas 1,000,000 to 2,000,000 Population

ECONOMIC

Cropland-wheat dominant
Cropland-rye dominant
Other cropland, pasture important
Cotton, rice; mostly irrigated
Sparse grassland, grazed with some cropland
Mediterranean agriculture
Periodically grazed areas, with nomadic herding
Forest and woodland
Tundra; seasonally grazed
Unproductive areas

Industrial areas

MINERALS

● Coal
Lignite
▲ Petroleum
■ Iron
+ Copper
◉ Bauxite
◆ Tungsten
◆ Manganese

* Lead
△ Zinc
△ Uranium
◖ Chromite
⊟ Phosphate rock
★ Gold
⊙ Platinum
△ Nickel

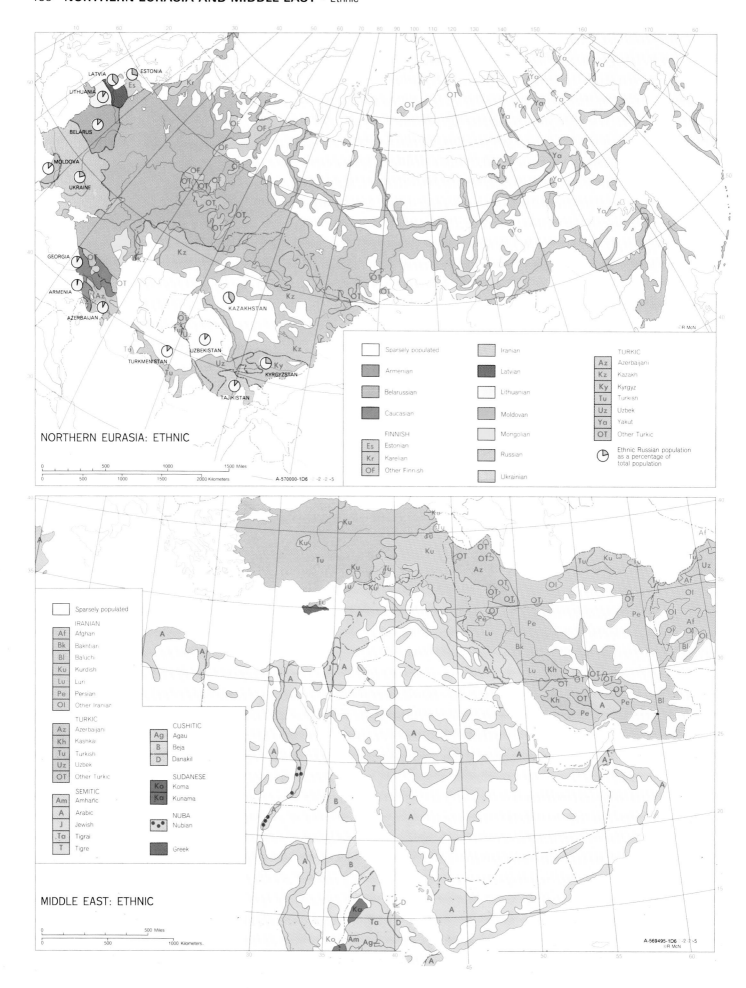

NORTHERN EURASIA: ETHNIC

LATVIA
ESTONIA
LITHUANIA
BELARUS
MOLDOVA
UKRAINE
GEORGIA
ARMENIA
AZERBAIJAN
TURKMENISTAN
UZBEKISTAN
KAZAKHSTAN
KYRGYZSTAN
TAJIKISTAN

	Sparsely populated		Iranian		TURKIC
	Armenian		Latvian	Az	Azerbaijani
	Belarussian		Lithuanian	Kz	Kazakh
	Caucasian		Moldovan	Ky	Kyrgyz
	FINNISH		Mongolian	Tu	Turkish
Es	Estonian		Russian	Uz	Uzbek
Kr	Karelian		Ukrainian	Ya	Yakut
OF	Other Finnish			OT	Other Turkic

Ethnic Russian population as a percentage of total population

0   500   1000   1500 Miles
0   500   1000   1500   2000 Kilometers

A-570000-1D6 -2 -2 -5

MIDDLE EAST: ETHNIC

	Sparsely populated
	IRANIAN
Af	Afghan
Bk	Bakhtiari
Bl	Baluchi
Ku	Kurdish
Lu	Luri
Pe	Persian
OI	Other Iranian

	TURKIC
Az	Azerbaijani
Kh	Kashkai
Tu	Turkish
Uz	Uzbek
OT	Other Turkic

	SEMITIC
Am	Amharic
A	Arabic
J	Jewish
Ta	Tigrai
T	Tigre

	CUSHITIC
Ag	Agau
B	Beja
D	Danakil

	SUDANESE
Ko	Koma
Ka	Kunama

	NUBA
•.•	Nubian

	Greek

0   500 Miles
0   500   1000 Kilometers

A-569495-1D6 -2 -2 -5
©R McN

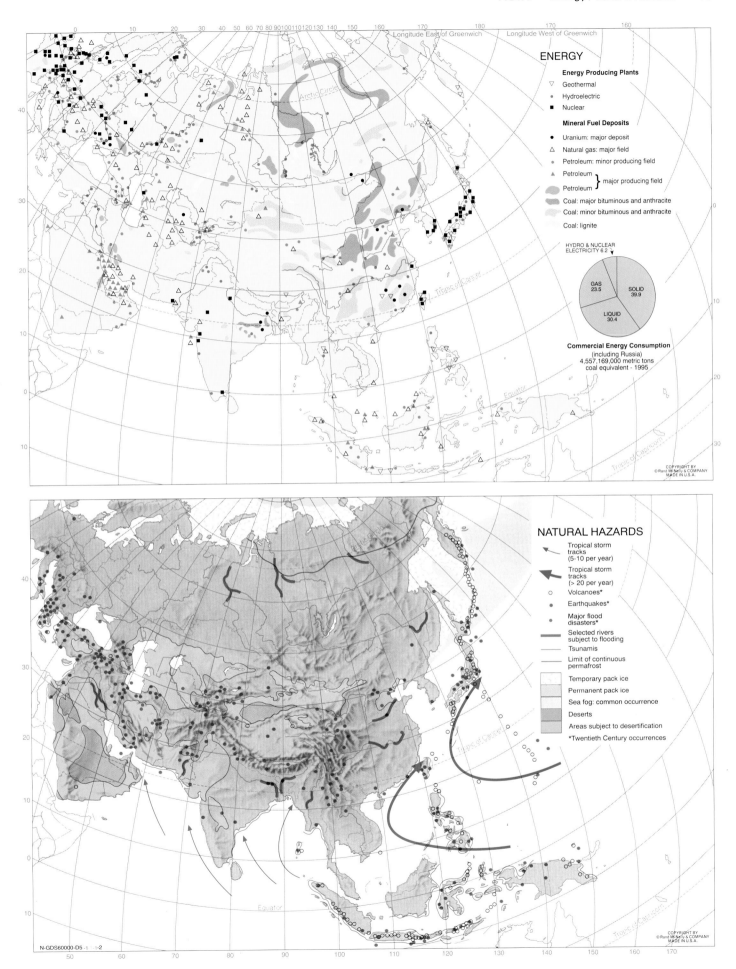

ENERGY

Energy Producing Plants

▽ Geothermal

• Hydroelectric

■ Nuclear

Mineral Fuel Deposits

● Uranium: major deposit

△ Natural gas: major field

• Petroleum: minor producing field

▲ Petroleum ⎫
⎬ major producing field
Petroleum ⎭

Petroleum

Coal: major bituminous and anthracite

Coal: minor bituminous and anthracite

Coal: lignite

HYDRO & NUCLEAR
ELECTRICITY 6.2

GAS
23.5

SOLID
39.9

LIQUID
30.4

Commercial Energy Consumption
(including Russia)
4,557,169,000 metric tons
coal equivalent - 1995

NATURAL HAZARDS

→ Tropical storm
tracks
(5-10 per year)

➤ Tropical storm
tracks
(> 20 per year)

○ Volcanoes*

• Earthquakes*

• Major flood
disasters*

━ Selected rivers
subject to flooding

Tsunamis

Limit of continuous
permafrost

Temporary pack ice

Permanent pack ice

Sea fog: common occurrence

Deserts

Areas subject to desertification

*Twentieth Century occurrences

N-GDS60000-D5 -1 -1-2

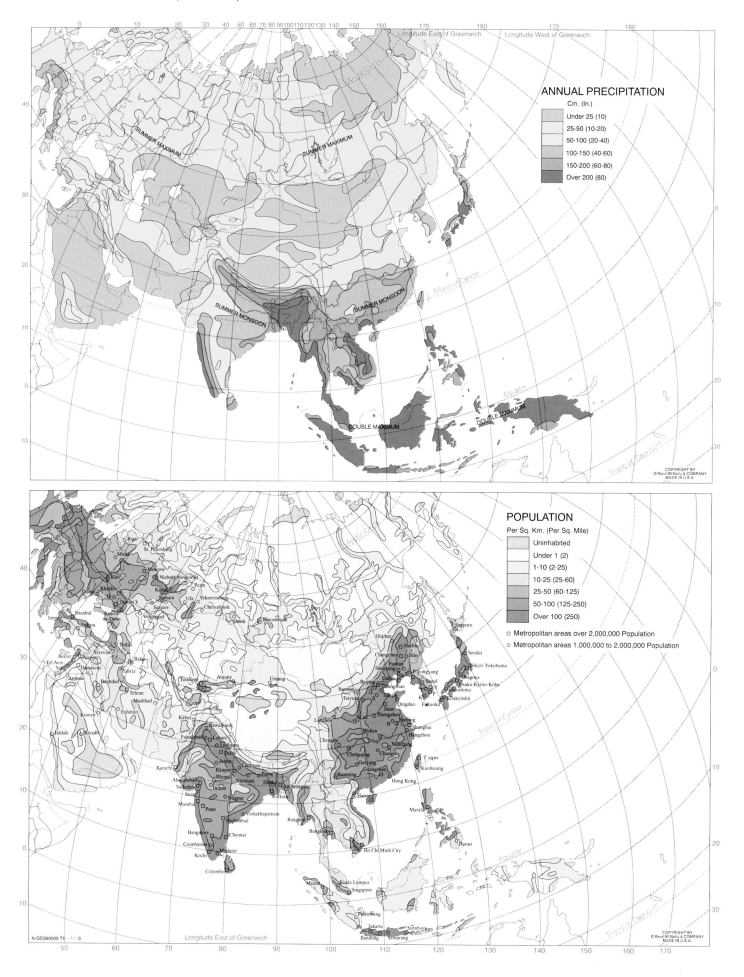

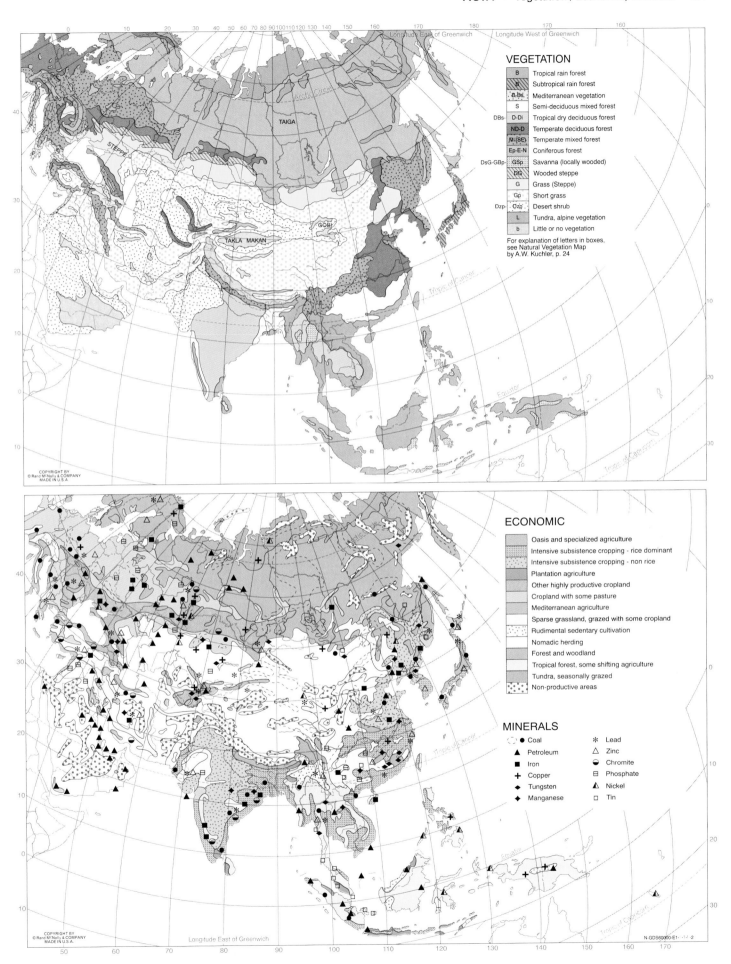

VEGETATION

B	Tropical rain forest
B	Subtropical rain forest
B-Bs	Mediterranean vegetation
S	Semi-deciduous mixed forest
DBs- D-Di	Tropical dry deciduous forest
ND-D	Temperate deciduous forest
M-(SE)	Temperate mixed forest
Ep-E-N	Coniferous forest
DsG-GBp- GSp	Savanna (locally wooded)
DG	Wooded steppe
G	Grass (Steppe)
Gp	Short grass
Dzp- Dzp	Desert shrub
L	Tundra, alpine vegetation
b	Little or no vegetation

For explanation of letters in boxes,
see Natural Vegetation Map
by A.W. Kuchler, p. 24

ECONOMIC

	Oasis and specialized agriculture
	Intensive subsistence cropping - rice dominant
	Intensive subsistence cropping - non rice
	Plantation agriculture
	Other highly productive cropland
	Cropland with some pasture
	Mediterranean agriculture
	Sparse grassland, grazed with some cropland
	Rudimental sedentary cultivation
	Nomadic herding
	Forest and woodland
	Tropical forest, some shifting agriculture
	Tundra, seasonally grazed
	Non-productive areas

MINERALS

●	Coal	✳	Lead
▲	Petroleum	△	Zinc
■	Iron	◠	Chromite
✚	Copper	⊟	Phosphate
◆	Tungsten	◮	Nickel
◆	Manganese	☐	Tin

TAIGA

STEPPE

TAKLA MAKAN

GOBI

N-GDS60000-E1- -1-1 -2

Legend:
- Urban
- Cropland
- Cropland & Woodland
- Cropland & Grazing Land
- Grassland, Grazing Land
- Forest, Woodland
- Swamp, Marshland
- Tundra
- Shrub, Sparse Grass, Wasteland
- Barren Land
- Oasis

Scale 1:36,000,000; one inch to 570 miles. Lambert Azimuthal Equal-Area Projection

ARCTIC OCEAN

ATLANTIC OCEAN

PACIFIC OCEAN

Bering Sea

Sea of Okhotsk

Sea of Japan

East China Sea

Yellow Sea

Philippine Sea

Black Sea

Caspian Sea

Aral Sea

Mediterranean Sea

Baltic Sea

Gulf of Bothnia

Barents Sea

Kara Sea

Laptev Sea

East Siberian Sea

Anadyrskiy Zaliv

Persian Gulf

Red Sea

NOVAYA ZEMLYA

SPITSBERGEN

SAKHALIN

HOKKAIDO

HONSHU

KYUSHU

TAIWAN

KAMCHATKA

POLUOSTROV KAMCHATKA

KHREBET GYDAN

GORY PUTORANA

GREATER KHINGAN RANGE

ALTAI MTS

TIEN SHAN

KUNLUN SHAN

TAKLA MAKAN

PLATEAU OF TIBET

HIMALAYAS

HINDU KUSH

ZAGROS MTS

CAUCASUS

GOBI (DESERT)

URAL

DASHT-E KAVIR

AR RUB AL KHALI

AN NAFUD

SYRIAN DESERT

TOKYO
Sapporo
Vladivostok
Komsomolsk na-Amure
Khabarovsk
Magadan
Tiličiki
Petropavlovsk-Kamchatskiy
Anadyr
Ambarchik
Norilsk
Tura
Yakutsk
SEOUL
SHENYANG
Harbin
BEIJING
SHANGHAI
Zhengzhou
WUHAN
GUANGZHOU
Kunming
Taipei
Ulan Bator
Ürümqi
Irkutsk
Krasnoyarsk
Novosibirsk
YEKATERINBURG
Omsk
Kazan
Arkhangelsk
Murmansk
Narvik
MOSCOW
ST. PETERSBURG
Stockholm
Oslo
BERLIN
Warsaw
BUDAPEST
ISTANBUL
Kiev
VOLGOGRAD
Tashkent
Ashgabat
Kerman
TEHRAN
BAKU
Baghdad
Beirut
CAIRO
Mecca
Riyadh
Muscat
DELHI
KARACHI
Rawalpindi
Kabul
Tabriz

Amur
Argun
Huang
Mekong
Brahmaputra
Ganges
Indus
Lena
Olenek
Ob
Irtysh
Lake Baikal
Lake Balkhash
Volga
Don
Dnieper
Ural
Danube
Sukhona
Tigris
Euphrates

Arctic Circle

Tropic of Cancer

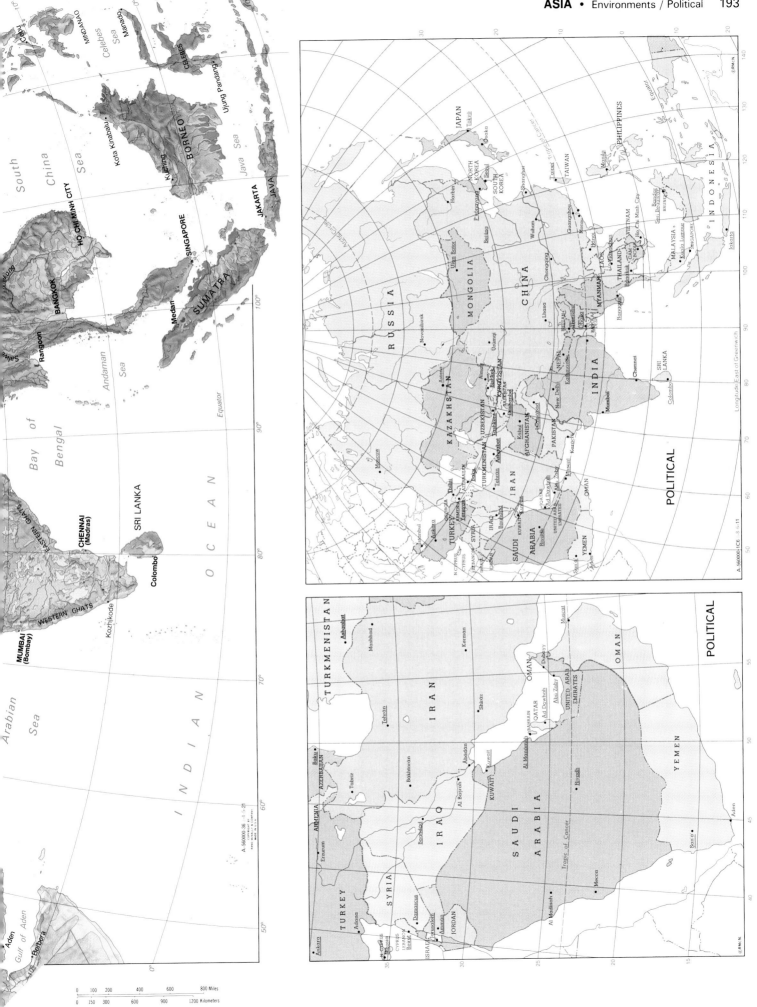

POLITICAL

POLITICAL

Continued on page 228

40,000 SQ MI
AREA

A-519695-26 23-22-45
COPYRIGHT BY
RAND McNALLY & COMPANY
MADE IN U.S.A.

0   300   600
Miles

Scale 1:40 000 000; one inch to 630 miles. Lambert's Azimuthal, Equal Area Projection
Elevations and depressions are given in feet

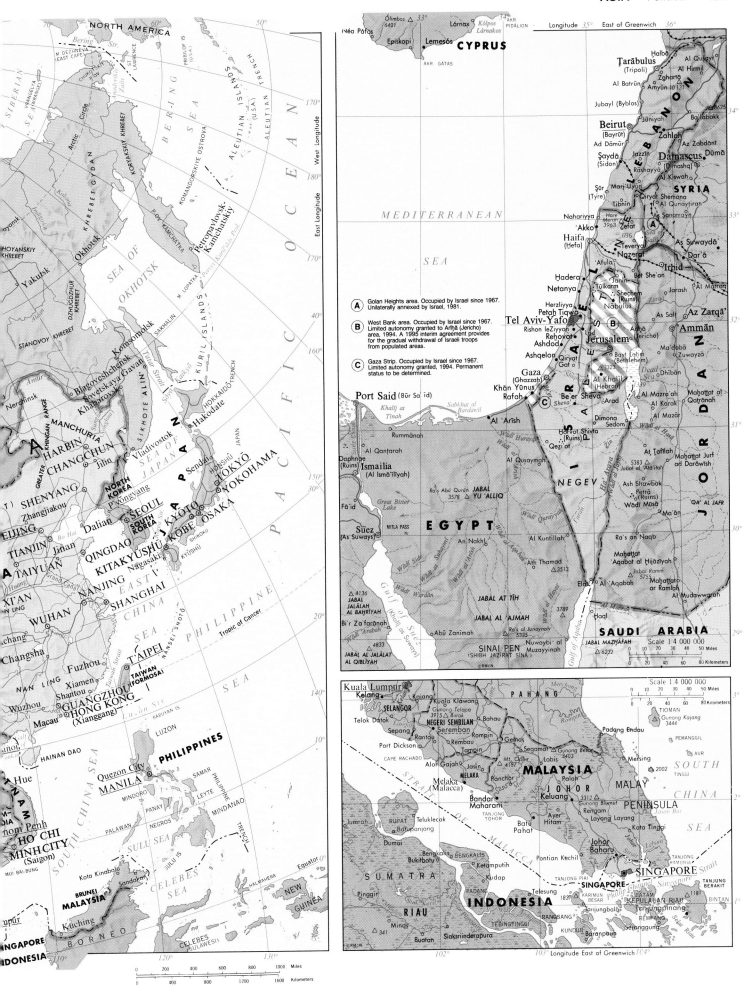

Golan Heights area. Occupied by Israel since 1967. Unilaterally annexed by Israel, 1981.

West Bank area. Occupied by Israel since 1967. Limited autonomy granted to Arīḥā (Jericho) area, 1994. A 1995 interim agreement provides for the gradual withdrawal of Israeli troops from populated areas.

Gaza Strip. Occupied by Israel since 1967. Limited autonomy granted, 1994. Permanent status to be determined.

Continued on pages 229

Relief

Meters		Feet
3050		10 000
1525		5000
610		2000
305		1000
0	Sea Level	0
	Below Sea Level	
152.5		500
1525		5000
3050		10 000
6100		20 000

A-519695-76 A-23-2045
COPYRIGHT BY
RAND McNALLY & COMPANY
MADE IN U.S.A.

Scale 1:40 000 000; one inch to 630 miles. Lambert's Azimuthal, Equal Area Projection
Elevations and depressions are given in feet

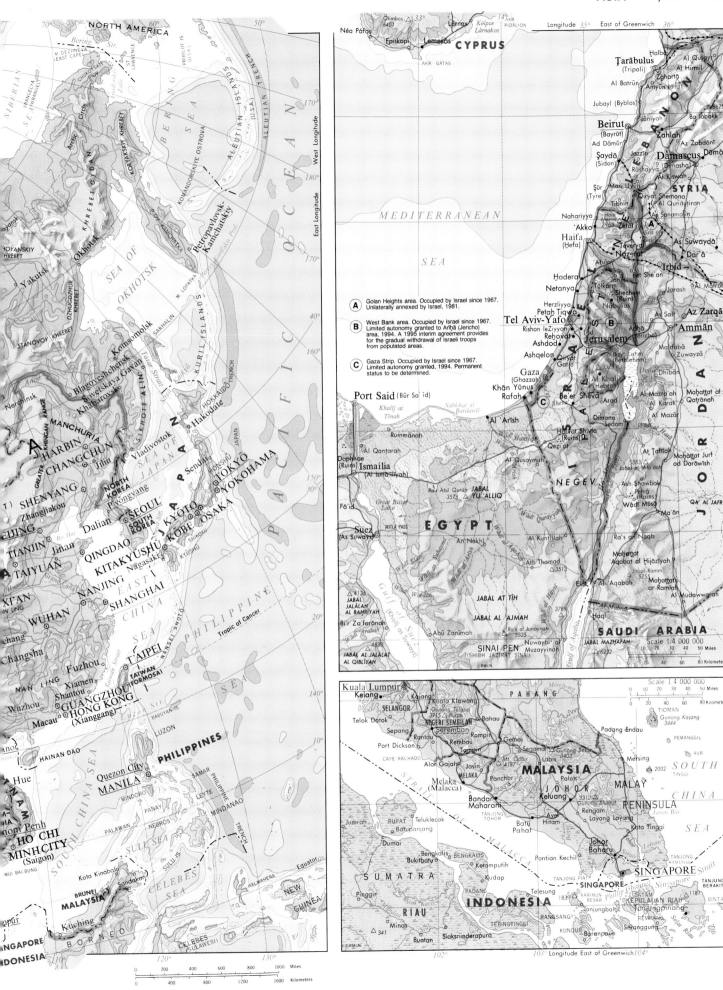

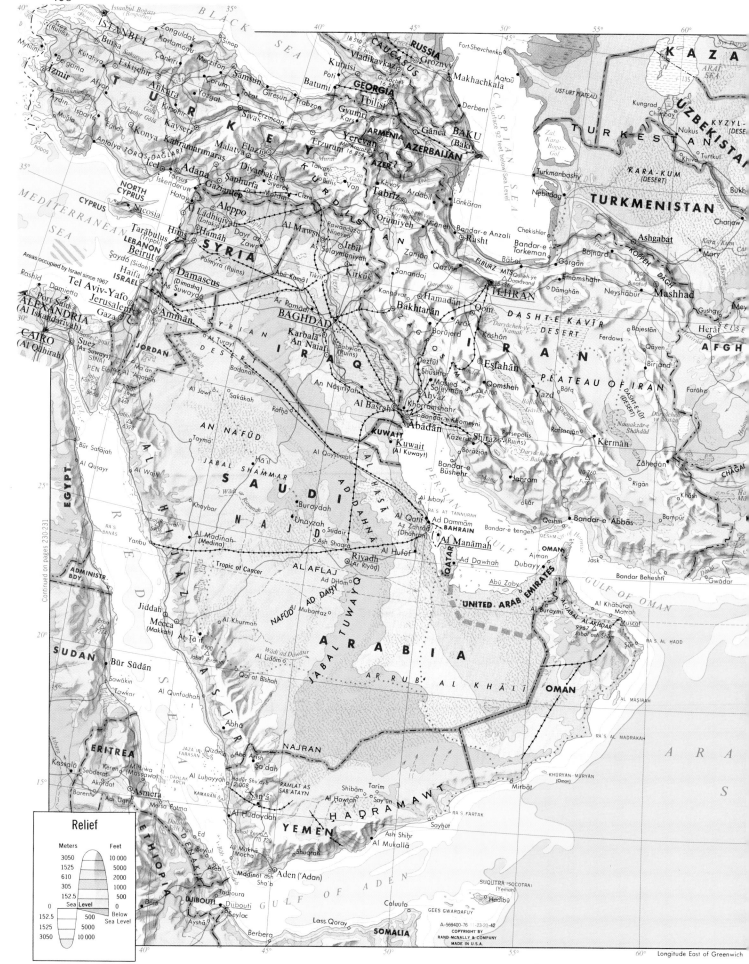

Scale 1:16 000 000; one inch to 250 miles. Polyconic Projection
Elevations and depressions are given in feet

Longitude East of Greenwich

Relief

Meters		Feet
3050		10 000
1525		5000
610		2000
305		1000
152.5		500
0	Sea Level	0
152.5		500
1525		5000
3050		10 000
		Below Sea Level

A-569400-76   23-20-42
COPYRIGHT BY
RAND McNALLY & COMPANY
MADE IN U.S.A.

ued on pages 184-185

a

Balqash köli
+2112

MOYYNQUM

yzylorda

Türkistan   Zhambyl

Shymkent   Bishkek

Arys

TASHKENT   Namangan Dzhalal-
Abad

rata   Kokand   Andizhan

Khudzhand   Fergana   Osh

Dzhizak

tta

arkand   Karshi

Dushanbe

TAJIKISTAN

PAMIRS

Kurgan-Tyube

Khorog

Termez

Mazâr-e Sharif

KUSH

HINDU

Kabul

Peshâwar

TAN

Ghazni

Kandahâr

Ft. Sandeman

Chaman

Quetta

Kalât

Mushki

Shikârpur

Mohenjo-Daro
(Ruins)

Sukkur

RACHI

Hyderâbâd

Inset a (top left)

Jalâlâbâd

AFGHÂNISTAN

MORGA RA

PAKISTAN

Dargai

Chârsadda

KHYBER
PASS

Peshâwar

Scale 1:4 000 000

0   10   20   30   40 Miles

0   20   40   60 Kilometers

Inset b (top right)

AFGHANISTAN   Scale 1:40 000 000

JAMMU
AND
KASHMIR

HIMACHAL
PRADESH

PUNJAB   UTTARANCHAL

PAKISTAN   HARYANA

RÂJASTHÂN   UTTAR
PRADESH

SIKKIM

NEPAL   BHUTAN   ARUNACHAL PRADESH

ÂSSAM   NÂGÂLAND

BIHÂR   MEGHÂLAYA   MIZORAM

Tropic of Cancer

GUJARAT   MADHYA
PRADESH   JHARKHAND   WEST
BENGAL   BANGLADESH

CHHATTISGARH   ORISSA   MYANMAR

7   MAHÂRÂSHTRA

ARABIAN
SEA   ANDHRA PRADESH

KARNATAKA

BAY OF
BENGAL

KERALA   TAMIL
NADU

SRI LANKA
(CEYLON)

INDIA • POLITICAL

1-TRIPURA
2-MANIPUR
3-LAKSHADWEEP
4-DELHI
5-DÂDRA AND NAGAR
 HAVELI
6-PONDICHERRY
7-GOA, DAMÂN, AND DIU

Main map

Kâshi

TAKLA MAKAN

Shache (Yarkand)

XINJIANG UYGUR
(SINKIANG)

Hotan

Garm   pik Ismail Samani

Muztagata   24 757

Murghob

K2   KARAKORAM PASS

Gilgit   KARAKORAM RANGE

Chitral   C

A   B

JAMMU AND KASHMIR

Islâmâbâd   Srînagar

KHYBER PASS   Râwalpindi

Peshâwar   Jammu

Jhelum   HIMACHAL PRADESH

Siâlkot   Amritsar   Simla

PAKISTAN   Gujrânwâla

Dera Ismâil   LAHORE   Jullundur   Ludhiâna

Khân   Faisalabad   Firozpur   Chandîgarh

Dehra Dûn

Multân   PUNJAB   Patiâla   Ambâla   Hardwâr   Almora

Dera Ghâzi   Bhatinda   Sahâranpur   UTTARANCHAL

Khân   HARYANA   Meerut   Morâdâbâd

Bahâwalpur   DELHI   Rampur   Bareilly   Shâhjahânpur

New Delhi   Aligarh   UTTAR   Lucknow   Faizâbâd   Gorakhpur   Darbhanga

Bikâner   Alwar   Mathura   Bhâratpur   PRADESH   Farrukhâbâd

GREAT INDIAN DESERT   Jaipur   Âgra   KÂNPUR   Allahâbâd   Varânâsi   Monghyr   Bhâgalpur

Ajmer   Gwalior   (Benares)   BIHÂR   Patna

Jodhpur   RÂJASTHÂN   Tonk   Jhânsi   Banda   Mirzâpur   Sasarâm   Gaya   Giridih

Kota   Sheopur   Shivpuri   Rewa   Murwâra   JHARKHAND

Udaipur   Sâgar   Jabalpur   CHHATTISGARH   Rânchî   Asansol

Abu Road   Pâlanpur   AHMADÂBÂD   Ujjain   Bhopâl   Bilâspur   Jamshedpur   WEST BENGAL   Burdwân

Jâmnagar   Râjkot   GUJARAT   Indore   MADHYA   PRADESH   Raurkela   Kharagpur   Howrah   KOLKATA

Baroda   VINDHYA RA   Nâgpur   Raipur   Raigarh   (Calcutta)

Bhuj   Bhaunagar   Burhânpur   Amrâvati   Sambalpur   Balasore

Porbandar   Junâgadh   Surat   Dhule   Akola   Wardha   ORISSA   Cuttack

Verâval   Diu   Dâmân   Nâsik   Aurangâbâd   Chandrapur   Bhubaneswar

Bhuj   Ahmadnagar   DECCAN   Puri

MUMBAI   MAHÂRÂSHTRA   Nizâmâbâd   Berhampur

(Bombay)   HYDERÂBÂD   Warangal   Vizianagaram

Pune   Sholâpur   Vishâkhapatnam

HYDERÂBÂD   Rajahmundry

Kolhâpur   Gulbarga   Vijayawâda   Kâkinâda

Sângli   Râichûr   Guntûr   Yanam

Belgaum   Kurnool   Eluru   Machilîpatnam

Panaji   Hubli   Bellary   Nellore

(Panjim)   KARNATAKA   Cuddapah

Mangalore   Kolâr   CHENNAI (Madras)

BANGALORE   Vellore   Kânchipuram

Mysore   Pondicherry

KERALA   Salem   Cuddalore

LAKSHADWEEP   Kozhikode   TAMIL NADU   Kumbakonam

(LACCADIVE IS.)   Coimbatore   Nâgappattinam

(India)   Ernâkulam   Tiruchchirâppalli   Thanjâvûr

Madurai

China / Tibet region (map center-right)

XIZANG (TIBET)   XIZAGN (TIBET)

GANGDISÊ SHAN   Lhasa

Gyangze   Brahmaputra   Yamzo Yumco

Mt. Everest   SIKKIM   Kanchenjunga   Gangtok   BHUTAN   Thimbu   Punakha

Kâthmându   Lalitpur   Darjeeling   ÂSSAM   Sibsâgar

NEPAL   Cooch Behar   Gauhâti   NÂGÂLAND   Kohima

Râjshâhi   Sirâjganj   Shillong   KHASI HILLS   Imphâl

Gorakhpur   BANGLADESH   Dhaka   MANIPUR   Silchar

Rangpur   Mymensingh   MIZORAM   Mogaung

Berhampore   Comilla   Myitkyina

Khulna   Nâkhâli   TRIPURA   Bhamo

Chittagong   Shwebo   Mandalay

BAY OF BENGAL   Mouths of the Ganges   Akyab   Monywa

Sittwe   ARAKAN YOMA   MYANMAR (BURMA)

Kyaukpyu   Yenangyaung   Pyinmana

Sandoway   PEGU YOMA   Prome

PAGODA PT.   Henzada   Pathein   Rangoon (Yangon)

Inset c (bottom right)

Tiruchchirâppalli   Nâgappattinam

Ernâkulam   TAMIL NADU   Thanjâvûr

KERALA   Madurai   Jaffna

Alleppey   Tuticorin   Trincomalee

Quilon   Tirunelveli   Mannar

Thiruvananthapuram   Anuradhapura

CAPE COMORIN   Puttalam

SRI LANKA   Kandy

(CEYLON)

INDIAN   Colombo

OCEAN   DONDRA HEAD   Galle   Matara

Same scale as main map

Legend (bottom left)

A   Area occupied by Pakistan
 and claimed by India.

B   Area claimed and occupied by India;
 status disputed by Pakistan.

C   Area occupied by China
 and claimed by India.

D   Area occupied by India
 and claimed by China.

0   50   100   200   300   400   500 Miles

0   100   200   400   600   800 Kilometers

Continued on pages 204-205

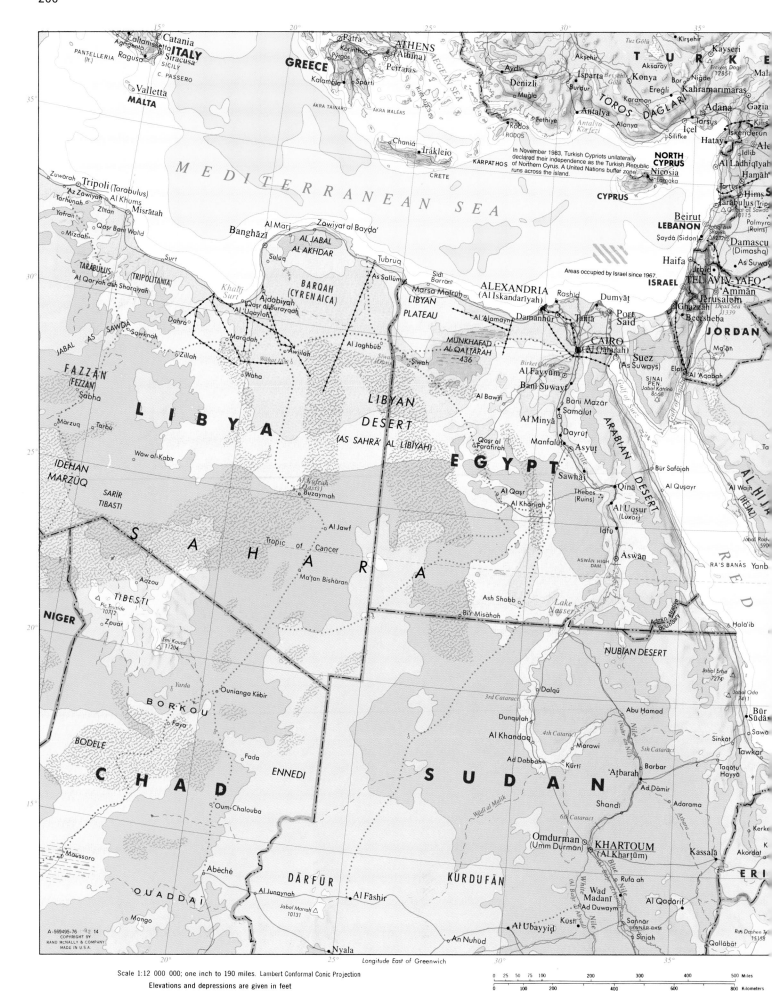

200

MEDITERRANEAN SEA

ITALY
SICILY
Catania
Siracusa
Agrigento
Ragusa
C. PASSERO
PANTELLERIA (It.)
Valletta
MALTA

GREECE
ATHENS (Athína)
Pátra
Pýrgos
Korinthos
Kalamáta
Spárti
Peiraiás
ÁKRA TAÍNARO
ÁKRA MALÉAS
Chaniá
Irákleio
CRETE
KARPATHOS
RODOS
Ródos
AEGEAN SEA

TURKEY
Kırşehir
Kayseri
Erciyes Dagı 12851
Aksaray
Akşehir
Aydın
Denizli
Muğla
Isparta
Bor
Niğde
Konya
Karaman
Ereğli
Burdur
Fethiye
Antalya
Alanya
Silifke
İçel
Tarsus
Antalya Körfezi
TOROS DAĞLARI
Kahramanmaraş
Adana
Gaziantep
Kilis
İskenderun
Hatay
Idlib
Al Lādhiqīyah
Ḩamāh
Ţarţūs
Ḩims

In November 1983, Turkish Cypriots unilaterally declared their independence as the Turkish Republic of Northern Cyrus. A United Nations buffer zone runs across the island.
NORTH CYPRUS
Nicosia
Larnaka
CYPRUS

Beirut
LEBANON
Şaydā (Sidon)
Jabal ash Shaykh 9232
Ţarābulus (Trip...)
Damascus (Dimashq)
As Suwa...
Palmyra (Ruins)
Haifa
Areas occupied by Israel since 1967.
ISRAEL
TEL AVIV-YAFO
Irbid
Ammān
Jerusalem
Dead Sea 1339
Ghazzah
Beersheba
JORDAN
Ma'ān

Zuwārah
Tripoli (Ṭarābulus)
Az Zāwiyah
Al Khums
Misrātah
Tarhūnah
Yafran
Zlītan
Mizdah
Qaşr Bani Walīd

Al Marj
Banghāzī
Zawiyat al Baydā'
Ṭubruq
Sulūq
AL JABAL AL AKHDAR
BARQAH (CYRENAICA)
As Sallūm
Sīdī Barrānī
Marsa Maṭrūḥ
ALEXANDRIA (Al Iskandarīyah)
Rashīd
LIBYAN PLATEAU
Al 'Alamayn
Damanhūr
Dumyāṭ
Port Said
Ṭanṭā
CAIRO (Al Qāhirah)
Suez (As Suways)
Elat
Al 'Aqabah
SINAI PEN.
Jabal Kātrīna 8668
Gulf of Suez

Surt
Khalīj Surt
TARABULUS (TRIPOLITANIA)
Al Qaryah ash Sharqiyah
Ajdabiyah
Qaşr al Burayqah
Al 'Uqaylah
Dāhra
JABAL AS SAWDĀ
Sawknah
Zillah
Marādah
Awjilah
Waha
Wāḥāt Jālū
Al Jaghbūb
Sīwah
Sīwah Oasis
MUNKHAFAD AL QAṬṬĀRAH -436
Birket Qārūn
Al Fayyūm
Banī Suwayf
Al Wāḥāt
Al Minyā

FAZZĀN (FEZZAN)
Sabhā
Mārzūq
Tarbū

Waw al-Kabīr

IDEHAN MARZŪQ
SARĪR TIBASTI

L I B Y A

LIBYAN DESERT (AS SAHRĀ' AL LIBĪYAH)

E G Y P T

Al Bawīṭī
Qaşr al Farāfirah
Manfalūṭ
Samalūṭ
Banī Mazār
Dayrūṭ
Asyūṭ
ARABIAN DESERT
Sawhāj
Al Qaṣr
Al Khārijah
Thebes (Ruins)
Qinā
Al Uqṣur (Luxor)
Idfū
Būr Safājah
Al Quṣayr
Al Wajh
AL HIJĀ [HEJAZ]
Ta

S A H A R A

Tropic of Cancer
Ma'tan Bishāran
Al Kufrah (Oasis)
Buzaymah
Al Jawf

Aswān High Dam
Aswān
RA'S BĀNĀS
Yanb...
RED

NIGER
TIBESTI
Pic Bouside 10712
Zouar
Emi Koussi 11204

Aozou

Ash Shabb
Bi'r Misāhah
Lake Nasser
Jabal Erba 7274
Jabal Oda 7411
Būr Sūdā...
Hala'ib
Admin...
Boundary

NUBIAN DESERT

Yarda
Ounianga Kébir
BORKOU
Faya
BODÉLÉ
Fada
ENNEDI

3rd Cataract
Dalqū
Dunqulah
Abu Hamad
Al Khandaq
4th Cataract
Marawi
Ad Dabbah
Kūrtī
5th Cataract
Nile
Nahr an Nil
Sinkāt
Sawa...
Tawkar

C H A D

S U D A N

Oum-Chalouba
Barbar
Aṭbarah
Ad Dāmir
Shandī
6th Cataract
Adarama

Taqatu Hayyā
Kerke...
ERI...

Moussoro
DĀRFŪR
Abéché
QUADDAÏ
Al Junaynah
Al Fāshir
Jabal Marrah 10131
KURDUFĀN
Wādī al Malik

Omdurman (Umm Durmān)
KHARTOUM (Al Khartūm)
Kassala
Akordat
K...

Mongo
Nyala
Al Ubayyiḍ
An Nuhūd
Küstī
White Nile (Nahr...)
Blue Nile
Wad Madanī
Ad Duwaym
Rufa ah
Al Qadārif
Sannar Dam
Sinjah
Ras Dashen Tr. 15158
Qallābāt

A-569495-76 -92 14
COPYRIGHT BY
RAND McNALLY & COMPANY
MADE IN U.S.A.

Longitude East of Greenwich

Scale 1:12 000 000; one inch to 190 miles. Lambert Conformal Conic Projection
Elevations and depressions are given in feet

0 25 50 75 100   200   300   400   500 Miles
0   100   200   400   600   800 Kilometers

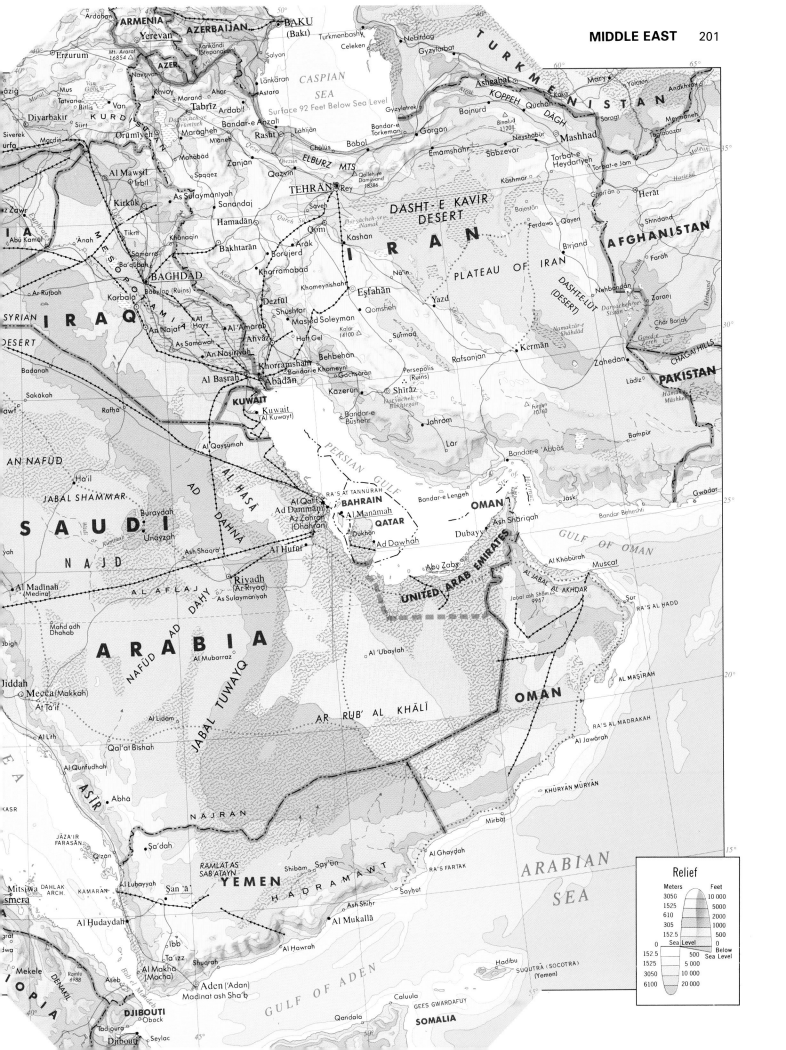

ARMENIA
AZERBAIJAN
BAKU
(Bakı)
Yerevan
Turkmenbashy
Nebitdag
Celeken
Gyzylarbat
TURKMENISTAN
Ashgabat
Mary
Yoloten
Andkhvoy
Ardahan
Erzurum
Mt. Ararat
16854
Xankändi
(Stepanakert)
Salyan
Nakhichevan
AZER.
Salyan
Turkmenbashy
KOPPEH
Quchan
DAGH
Saragt
Tagtabazar
Meymaneh
Mus
Murat
Tatvane
Van Gölü
Khvoy
Marand
Ahar
Astara
CASPIAN
SEA
Surface 92 Feet Below Sea Level
Gzylyretek
Bojnurd
Binalud
11208
Neyshabur
Mashhad
Torbat-e
Heydariyeh
Torbat-e Jam
Ghorian
Herät
Diyarbakir
Bitlis
Van
Orümiyeh
Daryācheh-ye
Orümīyeh
Maragheh
Mianeh
Tabrīz
Ardabil
Bandar-e Anzali
Rasht
Lahijan
Chalus
Babol
Bandar-e
Torkeman
Gorgan
Emamshahr
Sabzevar
Kashmar
Ferdows
Qāyen
Bajestan
Shindand
Farah
Siverek
urfa
Mardin
KURDISTAN
Siirt
Saqqez
Zanjan
Qazvin
Qwzin
ELBURZ MTS
Qalleh-ye
Damävand
18386
Rey
TEHRĀN
Na'in
PLATEAU OF IRAN
Birjand
Nehbandan
Daryācheh-ye
Sistan
Zaranj
AFGHANISTAN
z Zawr
Al Mawşil
Irbil
Kirkūk
'Anah
Abū Kamal
Tikrit
Samarrā
Ba'qubah
BAGHDAD
Khanaqin
Hamadān
Bakhtaran
Borūjerd
Saveh
Qom
Arāk
Kashan
Esfahan
Qomsheh
Yazd
DASHT-E KAVIR
DESERT
IRAN
Qayen
Char Borjak
Gowd-e
Zereh
Hamūn-e
Mashkel
Ládiz
PAKISTAN
SYRIAN
DESERT
IRAQ
MESOPOTAMIA
Karbalā'
Babylon (Ruins)
Al
Ar Rutbah
Al Hayy
Dezfūl
Shūshtar
Khorramabad
Masjed Soleyman
Haft Gel
Kalar
14100
Surmaq
Rafsanjan
Kerman
Zahedan
DASHT-E LUT
(DESERT)
Namakzar-e
Shahdad
Badanah
An Najaf
As Samawah
An Nāşiriyah
Al 'Amārah
Ahvāz
Behbehan
Persepolis
(Ruins)
Shīrāz
Furgun
10760
Bampur
Sakākah
Khorramshahr
Bandar-e Khomeyni
Al Basrah
Abadan
Gachsaran
Kazerūn
Daryācheh-ye
Bakhtegan
Jahrom
Lār
Bandar-e Abbas
Jāsk
Gwadar
awf
KUWAIT
Kuwait
(Al Kuwayt)
Bandar-e
Bushehr
Bandar-e Lengeh
Bandar Beheshti
Rafhā
Al Qayşūmah
AN NAFŪD
Ha'il
JABAL SHAMMAR
Buraydah
'Unayzah
AD DAHNĀ
AL HASA
RA'S AT TANNURAH
Al Qatif
Ad Dammām
Az Zahran
(Dhahran)
BAHRAIN
Al Manāmah
QATAR
Dukhan
Ad Dawhah
Bandar-e Lengeh
OMAN
Ash Shāriqah
GULF OF OMAN
Al Khābūrah
Muscat
yah
SAUDI
NAJD
ar Rumah
Ash Shaqra
Al Hufūf
Al Mubarraz
Abū Zaby
UNITED ARAB EMIRATES
Dubayy
AL JABAL AL AKHDAR
Jabal ash Shām
9957
Sūr
RA'S AL HADD
Al Madīnah
(Medina)
AL AFLAJ
Riyadh
(Ar Riyad)
As Sulaymaniyah
AD DAHY
Al 'Ubaylah
OMAN
RA'S AL MADRAKAH
Mahd adh
Dhahab
abigh
ARABIA
NAFŪD
AD DAHY
Al Lidam
AR RUB' AL KHĀLĪ
RA'S AL MADRAKAH
Al Jawārah
Jiddah
Mecca (Makkah)
At Ta'if
JABAL TUWAYQ
Qal'at Bishah
KHŪRYĀN MŪRYĀN
Al Lith
Al Qunfudhah
NAJRAN
Mirbat
ASIR
Abha
Şa'dah
Al Ghaydah
RA'S AL MADRAKAH
EA
KASR
JĀZA'IR
FARASĀN
Qizan
RAMLAT AS
SAB'ATAYN
Shibam
Say'ūn
YEMEN
HADRAMAWT
RA'S FARTAK
ARABIAN
SEA
Mitsiwa
DAHLAK
ARCH.
smera
KAMARAN
Al Luhayyah
Şan'ā'
Ash Shihr
Sayhut
Al Mukallā
Al Hudaydah
Ibb
Ta'izz
Shuqrah
Al Hawrah
Hadibu
SUQUTRĀ (SOCOTRA)
(Yemen)
Mekele
DENAKIL
Ramlu
6988
Al Makha
(Mocha)
Aseb
IOPIA
Aden ('Adan)
Madinat ash Sha'b
GULF OF ADEN
Caluula
GEES GWARDAFUY
DJIBOUTI
Obock
Tadjoura
Djibouti
Seylac
SOMALIA
Qandala

Relief

Meters	Feet
3050	10 000
1525	5000
610	2000
305	1000
152.5	500
Sea Level	0
	Below Sea Level
152.5	500
1525	5 000
3050	10 000
6100	20 000

202

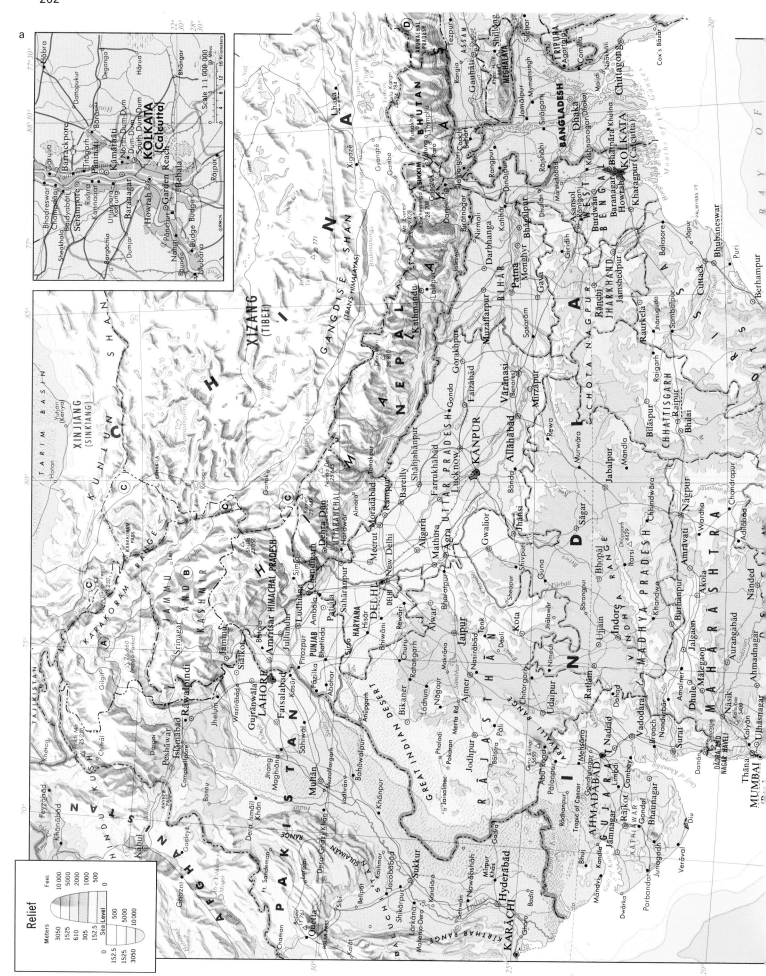

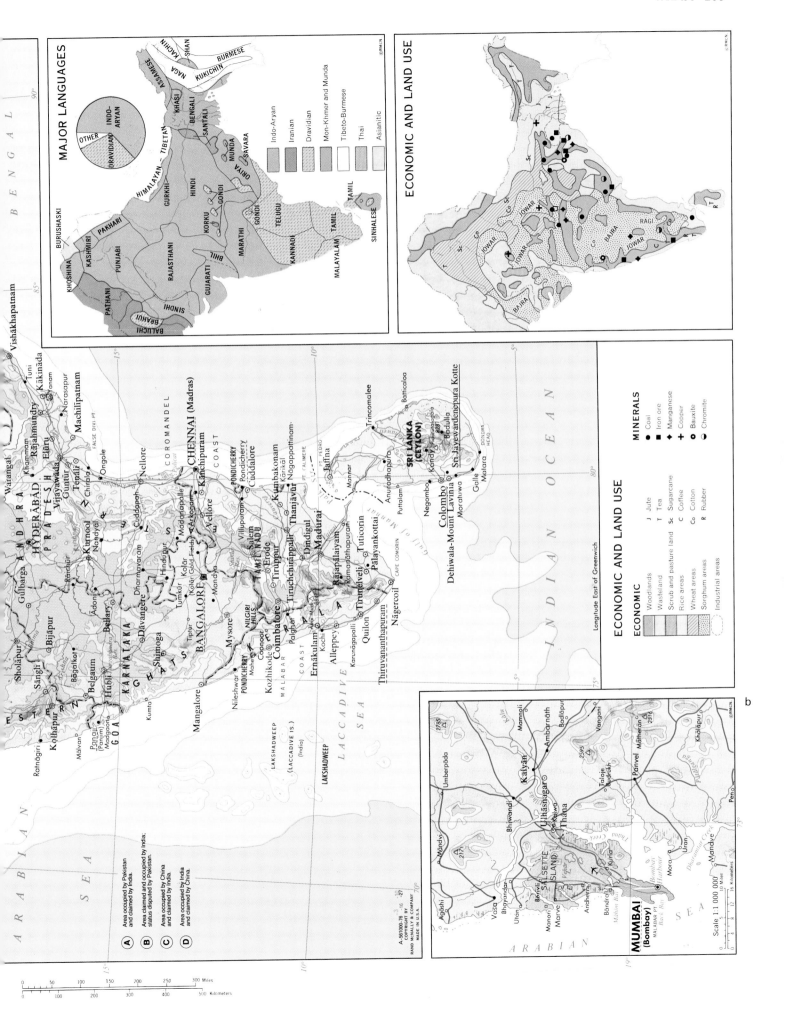

MAJOR LANGUAGES

BURUSHASKI
KHOSHINA
KASHMIRI
PAKHARI
PUNJABI
PATHANI
BALUCHI
BRAHUI
SINDHI
RAJASTHANI
GUJARATI
BHIL
MARATHI
HIMALAYAN – TIBETAN
GURKHI
HINDI
KORKU
GONDI
GONDI
MUNDA
SAVARA
ORIYA
KANNADI
TELUGU
MALAYALAM
TAMIL
TAMIL
SINHALESE

KACHIN
SHAN
BURMESE
KUKICHIN
NAGA
ASSAMESE
KHASI
BENGALI
SANTALI

INDO-ARYAN
OTHER
DRAVIDIAN

Indo-Aryan
Iranian
Dravidian
Mon-Khmer and Munda
Tibeto-Burmese
Thai
Asianitic

ECONOMIC AND LAND USE

ECONOMIC

Woodlands
Wasteland
Scrub and pasture land
Rice areas
Wheat areas
Sorghum areas
Industrial areas

J Jute
Sc Sugarcane
C Coffee
Co Cotton
R Rubber
T Tea

Longitude East of Greenwich

MINERALS

● Coal
■ Iron ore
◆ Copper
+ Manganese
○ Bauxite
◖ Chromite

Vishākhapatnam
Tuni
Kākināda
Yanam
Rājahmundry
Narasapur
Eluru
Machilipatnam
Khammam
Warangal
Vijayawāda
Tenāli
Chirāla
Guntūr
Narsāpur
FALSE DIVI PT.
Ongole
HYDERĀBĀD
ANDHRA PRADESH
Kurnool
Nandyāl
Nellore
Raichūr
Gulbarga
Ādoni
Cuddapah
Madanapalle
Chittoor
CHENNAI (Madras)
COROMANDEL COAST
Sholāpur
Bijāpur
Bāgalkot
Bellary
Hindupur
Kolar (Kolār Gold Fields)
Ārkonam
Kānchipuram
PONDICHERRY
Pondicherry
Cuddalore
Sāngli
Belgaum
Hubli
Dharmavaram
Tumkūr
Tiptūr
BANGALORE
Mandya
Vellore
Villupuram
Kārikāl
Kumbakonam
Thanjāvūr
Nāgappattinam.
Kolhāpur
Dāvangere
Shimoga
Mysore
NILGIRI HILLS
Coonoor
Salem
TAMIL NADU
Erode
Tirupur
Tiruchchirāppalli
Dindigul
Madurai
PT. CALIMERE
Ratnāgiri
KARNĀTAKA
Mangalore
Nileshwar
PONDICHERRY (Māhe)
Kozhikode
Palghāt
Coimbatore
KERALA
Rājapālaiyam
Kambam
Rāmanāthapuram
Tuticorin
Mālvan
Kumta
Ernākulam
Kochi
Alleppey
Quilon
Karunāgapalli
Thiruvananthapuram
Nāgercoil
Tirunelveli
Palayankottai
MALABAR COAST
CAPE COMORIN
EASTERN
Panaji (Panjim)
Madgaon
GOA
WESTERN GHATS
GHATS
GULF OF MANNAR

Trincomalee
Batticaloa
SRI LANKA (CEYLON)
Jaffna
PT. PEDRO
Mannar
Anurādhapura
Puttalam
Negombo
Colombo
Dehiwala-Mount Lavinia
Moratuwa
Galle
Matara
DONDRA HEAD
Kandy
Badulla
Sri Jayewardenepura Kotte
Nuwara Eliya
2524

GULF OF BENGAL
BAY OF BENGAL
ARABIAN SEA
LACCADIVE SEA
INDIAN OCEAN
LACCADIVE IS.
(India)
LAKSHADWEEP
LAKSHADWEEP (LACCADIVE IS.)

Ⓐ Area occupied by Pakistan and occupied by India.
Ⓑ Area claimed and occupied by India: status disputed by Pakistan.
Ⓒ Area occupied by China and claimed by India.
Ⓓ Area occupied by India and claimed by China.

A-561000-76   3   -27
COPYRIGHT BY
RAND MCNALLY & COMPANY
MADE IN U.S.A.

0   50   100   150   200   250   300 Miles
0   100   200   300   400   500 Kilometers

MUMBAI (Bombay)

Scale 1:1 000 000

0   4   8   12   16 Miles
0   4   8   12   16 Kilometers

Umberpāda
Mamnoli
Vangani
Badlāpur
Kalyān
Ambarnath
2785
Mātherān 2595
Panvel
Khopoli
Bhiwandi
Ulhāsnagar
Thāna
Taloje Budrūk
Kalwa
Penn
SALSETTE ISLAND
Borivli
Andheri
Māndvi
Bāndra
Trombay
Uran
Mora
Kurla
Mānori
Marve
Māhim Bay
MALABAR PT.
Bombay Back Bay
Bombay Harbour
Mandve
Vasai
Bhāyandar
Utan
Agāshi
ARABIAN SEA

b

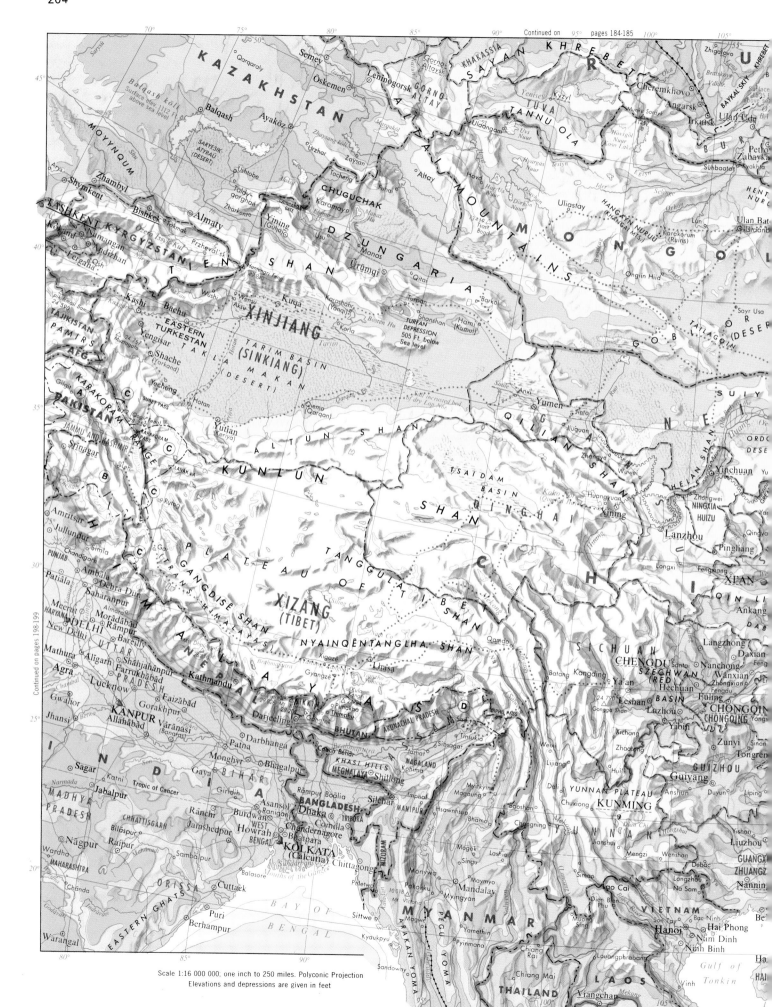

Continued on pages 184-185

Continued on pages 198-199

Scale 1:16 000 000, one inch to 250 miles. Polyconic Projection
Elevations and depressions are given in feet

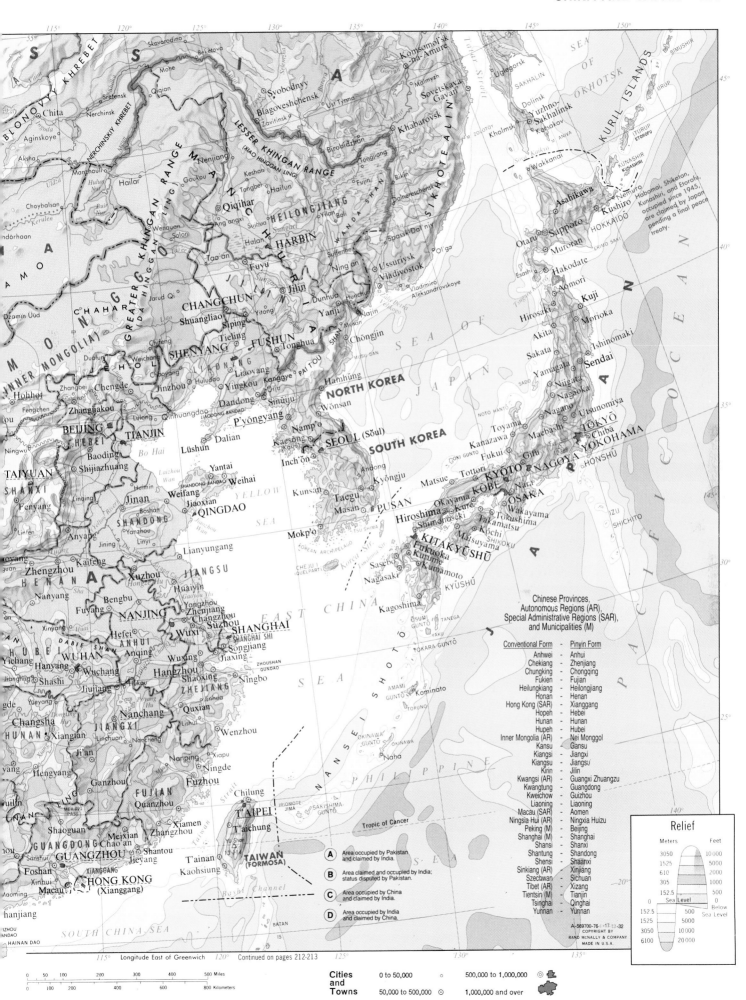

Chinese Provinces,
Autonomous Regions (AR),
Special Administrative Regions (SAR),
and Municipalities (M)

Conventional Form	Pinyin Form
Anhwei	Anhui
Chekiang	Zhejiang
Chungking	Chongqing
Fukien	Fujian
Heilungkiang	Heilongjiang
Honan	Henan
Hong Kong (SAR)	Xianggang
Hopeh	Hebei
Hunan	Hunan
Hupeh	Hubei
Inner Mongolia (AR)	Nei Monggol
Kansu	Gansu
Kiangsi	Jiangxi
Kiangsu	Jiangsu
Kirin	Jilin
Kwangsi (AR)	Guangxi Zhuangzu
Kwangtung	Guangdong
Kweichow	Guizhou
Liaoning	Liaoning
Macau (SAR)	Aomen
Ningsia Hui (AR)	Ningxia Huizu
Peking (M)	Beijing
Shanghai (M)	Shanghai
Shansi	Shanxi
Shantung	Shandong
Shensi	Shaanxi
Sinkiang (AR)	Xinjiang
Szechwan	Sichuan
Tibet (AR)	Xizang
Tientsin (M)	Tianjin
Tsinghai	Qinghai
Yunnan	Yunnan

(A) Area occupied by Pakistan and claimed by India.

(B) Area claimed and occupied by India; status disputed by Pakistan.

(C) Area occupied by China and claimed by India.

(D) Area occupied by India and claimed by China.

A-569700-76-17-13-32
COPYRIGHT BY
RAND McNALLY & COMPANY
MADE IN U.S.A.

Longitude East of Greenwich

Continued on pages 212-213

0 50 100 200 300 400 500 Miles
0 100 200 400 600 800 Kilometers

Relief

Meters	Feet
3050	10 000
1525	5000
610	2000
305	1000
152.5	500
Sea Level	0
	Below Sea Level
152.5	500
1525	5000
3050	10 000
6100	20 000

Cities and Towns

0 to 50,000 ○
50,000 to 500,000 ⊙
500,000 to 1,000,000 ◎
1,000,000 and over

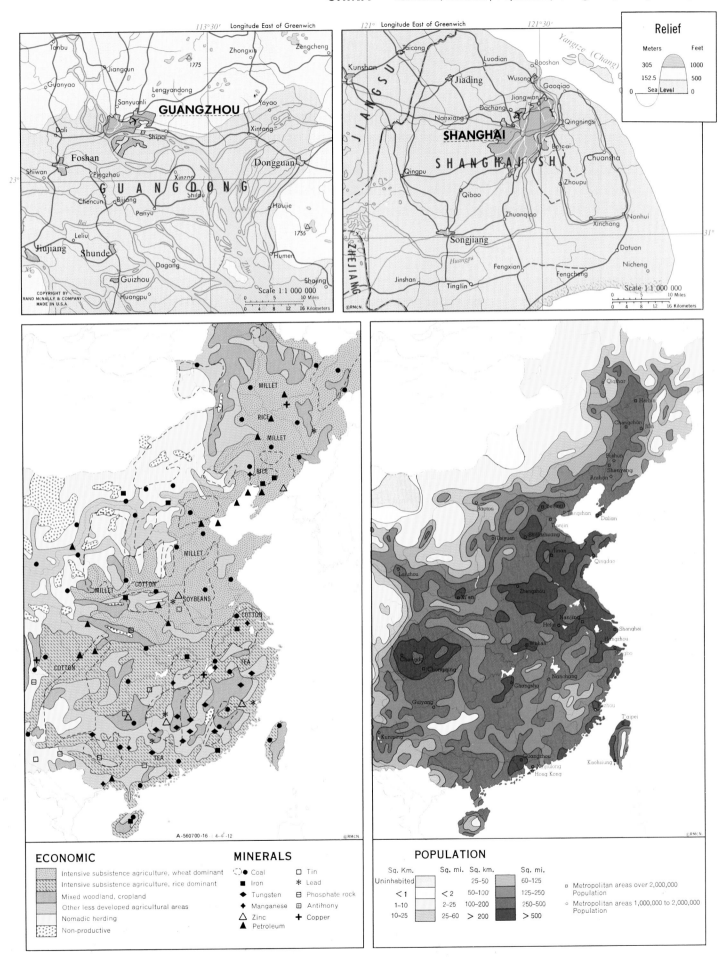

GUANGZHOU

Tanbu, Zhongxin, Zengcheng, Jiangcun, Guanyao, Lengyandong, Yayao, Xinfang, 1775, Sanyuanli, Shipai, Dali, Foshan, Dongguan, Shiwan, Pingzhou, Xinzao, Shilou, Houjie, Chencun, Bijiang, Panyu, Humen, Liuliu, Jiujiang, Shunde, Dagang, 1755, Shajing, Guizhou, Huangpu

113°30', Longitude East of Greenwich, 23°

GUANGDONG, Bei

Scale 1:1 000 000
0 5 10 Miles
0 4 8 12 16 Kilometers

COPYRIGHT BY RAND McNALLY & COMPANY MADE IN U.S.A.

SHANGHAI

121°, Longitude East of Greenwich, 121°30'

Yangtze (Chang), Taicang, Kunshan, Luodian, Baoshan, Jiading, Wusong, Gaoqiao, Jiangwan, Nanxiang, Dachang, Qingningsi, Chuansha, Qingpu, Qibao, Zhoupu, Zhuanqiao, Xinchang, Nanhui, Songjiang, Huangpu, Datuan, Jinshan, Fengxian, Fengcheng, Nicheng, Tinglin

JIANGSU, SHANGHAI SHI, ZHEJIANG, 31°

Scale 1:1 000 000
0 5 10 Miles
0 4 8 12 16 Kilometers
©RMcN.

Relief

Meters		Feet
305		1000
152.5		500
0	Sea Level	0

A-560700-16 4-4-12 ©RMcN ©RMcN

ECONOMIC

- Intensive subsistence agriculture, wheat dominant
- Intensive subsistence agriculture, rice dominant
- Mixed woodland, cropland
- Other less developed agricultural areas
- Nomadic herding
- Non-productive

MINERALS

- ● Coal
- ◼ Iron
- ◆ Tungsten
- ◆ Manganese
- △ Zinc
- ▲ Petroleum
- ☐ Tin
- ✳ Lead
- ⊟ Phosphate rock
- ⊞ Antimony
- + Copper

POPULATION

Sq. Km.	Sq. mi.	Sq. km.	Sq. mi.
Uninhabited		25–50	60–125
<1	<2	50–100	125–250
1–10	2–25	100–200	250–500
10–25	25–60	> 200	> 500

- ▫ Metropolitan areas over 2,000,000 Population
- ○ Metropolitan areas 1,000,000 to 2,000,000 Population

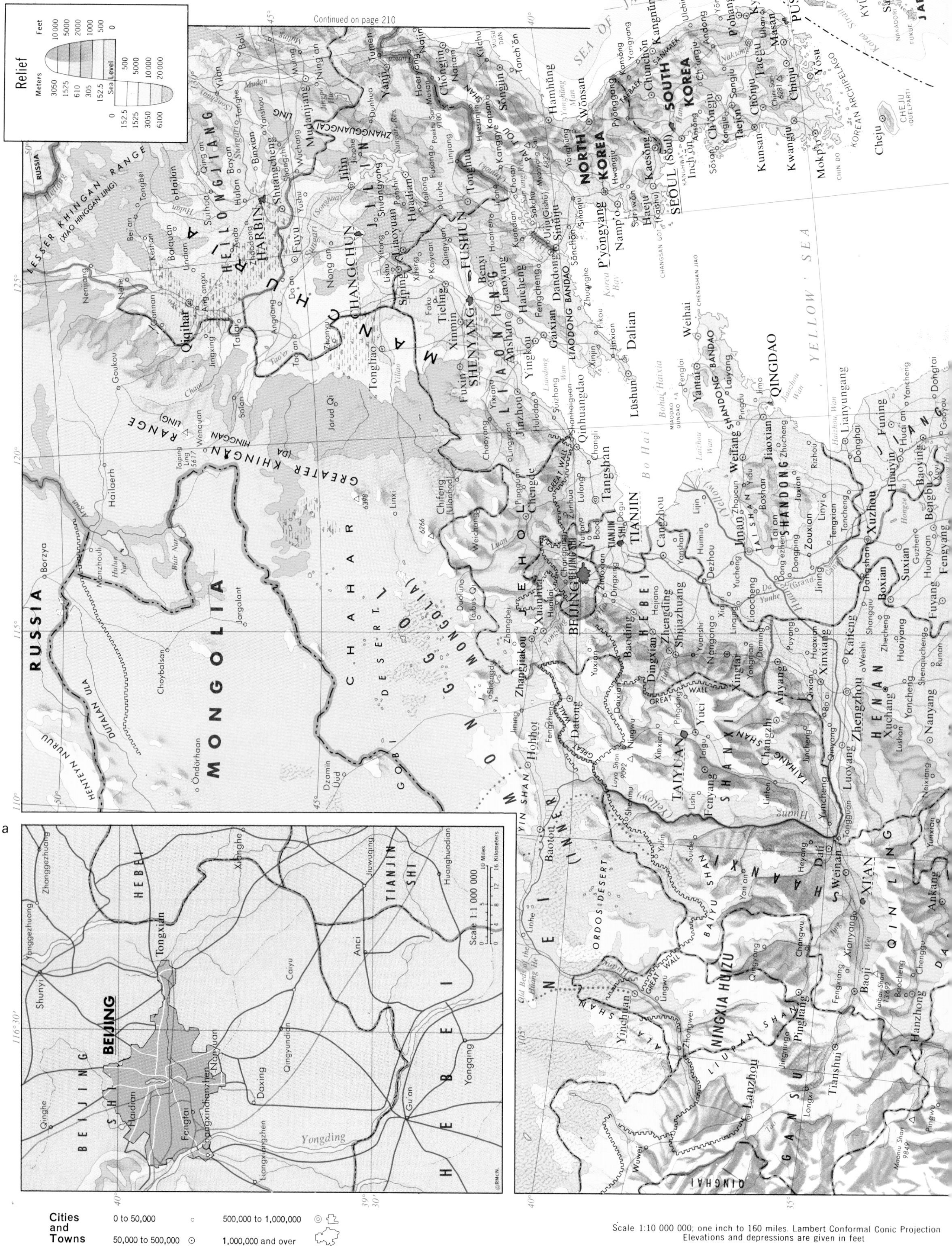

Relief

Meters	Feet
3050	10,000
1525	5000
610	2000
305	1000
152.5	500
0	Sea Level

0	500
152.5	5000
1525	10,000
3050	20,000
6100	

Continued on page 210

SEA OF JAPAN

JAPAN

KYUSHU

PUSAN

SOUTH KOREA

NORTH KOREA

SEOUL (Soul)

RUSSIA

HEILONGJIANG

HARBIN

LESSER KHINGAN RANGE (MIAO HINGGAN LING)

Qiqihar

JILIN

CHANGCHUN

MONGOLIA

GREATER KHINGAN RANGE (DA HINGGAN LING)

GOBI DESERT

CHAHAR

LIAONING

SHENYANG

FUSHUN

BEIJING

TIANJIN

HEBEI

YELLOW SEA

Bo Hai

Dalian

QINGDAO

SHANDONG

HENAN

SHANXI

TAIYUAN

NEI MONGOL (INNER MONGOLIA)

ORDOS DESERT

GREAT WALL

SHAANXI

XIAN

QIN LING

NINGXIA HUIZU

GANSU

QINGHAI

a

HEBEI

BEIJING SHI

BEIJING

TIANJIN SHI

Scale 1:1 000 000

Yongding

Cities and Towns

| 0 to 50,000 | ○ | 500,000 to 1,000,000 | ◎ |
| 50,000 to 500,000 | ⊙ | 1,000,000 and over | |

Scale 1:10 000 000; one inch to 160 miles. Lambert Conformal Conic Projection
Elevations and depressions are given in feet

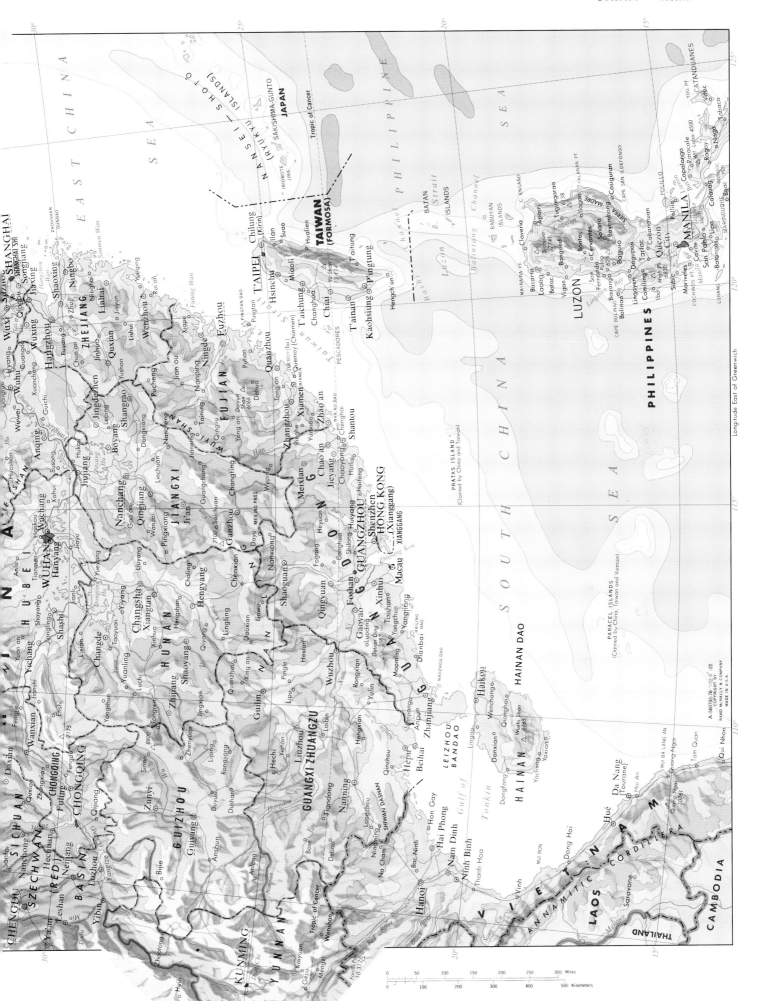

EAST CHINA SEA

NANSEI-SHOTO (RYUKYU ISLANDS)

SAKISHIMA-GUNTO
IRIOMOTE-JIMA

JAPAN

Tropic of Cancer

PHILIPPINE SEA

SHANGHAI
SHANGHAI SHI
Songjiang
Jiaxing
Shaoxing
Ningbo

ZHEJIANG
Hangzhou
Wuxing

Lishui
Wenzhou

FUJIAN
Nanping
Fuzhou
Quanzhou

TAIWAN (FORMOSA)
TAIPEI
Chilung (Kirun)
Ilan
Suao
Hualien
Hsinchu
Miaoli
Taichung
Changhua
Chiai
Taitung
Tainan
Kaohsiung
Pingtung
Heng'un

BATAN ISLANDS
BABUYAN ISLANDS
CAPE ENGAÑO
Aparri
Claveria

LUZON

PHILIPPINES

MANILA
Quezon City
MANILA

PESCADORES

PRATAS ISLAND
(Claimed by China and Taiwan)

Xiamen
Zhangzhou
Zhao'an
Chao'an
Shantou
Jieyang
Haifeng

GUANGDONG
GUANGZHOU
Shenzhen
HONG KONG
(Xianggang)
XIANGGANG
Macau
Foshan
Taishan
Yangjiang

SOUTH CHINA SEA

Changsha
HUNAN
Hengyang
Shaoyang

JIANGXI
Nanchang
Ji'an
Ganzhou

WUYI SHAN
MEILING PASS

Guilin
GUANGXI ZHUANGZU
Liuzhou
Nanning
Zhanjiang
Beihai

LEIZHOU BANDAO

HAINAN DAO
Haikou
HAINAN

PARACEL ISLANDS
(Claimed by China, Taiwan and Vietnam)

Gulf of Tonkin

Hanoi
Hai Phong

VIETNAM

ANNAMITIC CORDILLERA

LAOS

Da Nang (Tourane)
Hué

THAILAND

CAMBODIA

WUHAN
Wuchang
Hanyang

HUBEI

SICHUAN
CHENGDU

SZECHWAN

CHONGQING (RED)
BASIN

GUIZHOU
Guiyang

YUNNAN
KUNMING

Tropic of Cancer

Longitude East of Greenwich

A-560793.76   22
COPYRIGHT BY
RAND M\u0024NALLY & COMPANY
MADE IN U.S.A.

| 0 | 50 | 100 | 150 | 200 | 250 | 300 Miles |

| 0 | 100 | 200 | 300 | 400 | 500 Kilometers |

Continued on pages 208-209

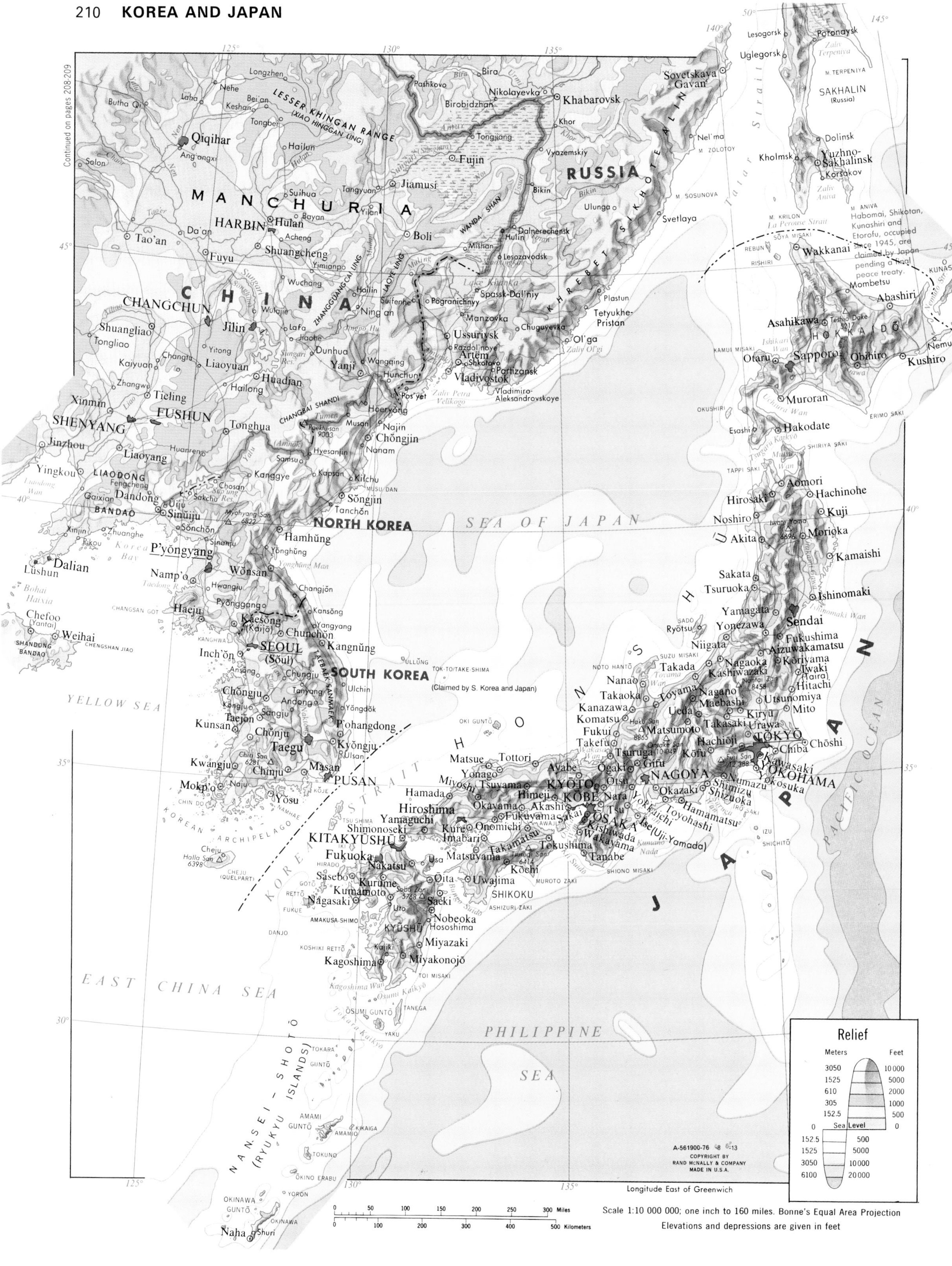

MANCHURIA

RUSSIA

CHINA

SAKHALIN
(Russia)

Qiqihar

Longzhen

Nehe

Laha

Butha Qi

Bei'an

Keshan

Tongbei

Hailun

Salon

Ang'angxi

Tao'an

HARBIN

Hulan

Acheng

Da'an

Fuyu

Shuangcheng

Bira

Bira

Pashkovo

Nikolayevka

Khabarovsk

Birobidzhan

Fujin

Khor

Tongjiang

Vyazemskiy

Jiamusi

Bikin

Bikin

Ilan

Boli

Yilan

Suihua

Tangyuan

Wuchang

Hulin

Dalnerechensk

Mishan

Lesozavodsk

M. SOSUNOVA

Svetlaya

Ulunga

Plastun

Lesogorsk

Uglegorsk

Potonaysk

Zaliv Terpeniya

M. TERPENIYA

Dolinsk

Kholmsk

Yuzhno-Sakhalinsk

Korsakov

M. ANIVA

Zaliv Aniva

CHANGCHUN

Shuangliao

Tongliao

Jilin

Changtu

Yitong

Liaoyuan

Kaiyuan

Zhangwu

Tieling

FUSHUN

Wujie

Lafa

Jiaohe

Dunhua

Yanji

Wangqing

Hunchun

Pos'yet

Suifenhe

Pogranichnyy

Manzovka

Ussuriysk

Razdol'noye

Artëm

Shkotovo

Vladivostok

Zaliv Petra Velikogo

Chuguyevka

Ol'ga

Zaliv Ol'gi

Vladimiro-Aleksandrovskoye

SHENYANG

Jinzhou

Liaoyang

LIAODONG

Xinmin

Tonghua

Huanren

Hailong

Huadian

CHANGBAI SHANDI

Paektu-san 9003

Musan

Hoeryŏng

Najin

Chŏngjin

Nanam

Liaoyang

Yingkou

Gaixian

Zhuanghe

BANDAO

Dandong

Fengcheng

Uiju

Sinŭiju

Sŏnchŏn

Sinanju

Samsu

Hyesanjin

Kanggye

Kapsan

MUSU-DAN

Kilchu

Tanchŏn

Myohyang San 6822

Songjin

Chosan

Sup'ung Res.

Kaishan

Xinjin

Pikou

Dalian

Lüshun

Bohai Haixia

Chefoo (Yantai)

Weihai

SHANDONG BANDAO

Chengshan Jiao

Korea Bay

NORTH KOREA

P'yŏngyang

Namp'o

Hwangju

Pyŏnggang

Haeju

CHANGSAN GOT

Hamhŭng

Yŏnghŭng

Wŏnsan

Changjŏn

Kansŏng

Yangyang

SEA OF JAPAN

Wakkanai

Mombetsu

Rebun

Rishiri

SOYA MISAKI

OKUSHIRI

Otaru

Sapporo

Asahikawa

Teshio Dake 7527

HOKKAIDŌ

Obihiro

Kushiro

Nemuro

Abashiri

Habomai, Shikotan, Kunashiri and Etorofu, occupied since 1945, are claimed by Japan pending a final peace treaty.

KUNASIRI

Muroran

Uchiura Wan

Hakodate

Esashi

ERIMO SAKI

Tsugaru Kaikyo

SHIRIYA SAKI

TAPPI SAKI

Aomori

Hirosaki

Hachinohe

Noshiro

Kuji

Iwate Yama 6696

Morioka

Akita

Kamaishi

Sakata

Tsuruoka

Ishinomaki

Yamagata

Yonezawa

Sendai

Niigata

SADO

Ryōtsu

Aizuwakamatsu

Kōriyama

Iwaki (Taira)

Hitachi

Fukushima

Nagaoka

Nanao

NOTO HANTŌ

Takada

Kashiwazaki

Toyama Wan

SUZU MISAKI

NANSHI

Takaoka

Toyama

Nagano

Maebashi

Utsunomiya

Mito

Kanazawa

Komatsu

Ueda

Takasaki

Kiryū

Fukui

Matsumoto

Takefu

Tsuruga

Kōfu

Fuji San 12388

TOKYO

Chiba

Chōshi

Hachiōji

Urawa

Kawasaki

YOKOHAMA

Yokosuka

YELLOW SEA

Kaesŏng (Kaijō)

Chunchŏn

Inch'ŏn

SEOUL (Sŏul)

Ansong

KANGHWA

Kangnŭng

Ulchin

ULLŬNG

TOK-TO/TAKE-SHIMA (Claimed by S. Korea and Japan)

SOUTH KOREA

Chŏngju

Chungju

Andong

Yŏngdŏk

Taejŏn

Sangju

P'ohangdong

Kunsan

Chŏnju

Kyŏngju

Taegu

Kwangju

Chiri San 6283

Chinju

Masan

Kyŏngju

Mokp'o

Naju

PUSAN

Yŏsu

Chin Do

Cheju (QUELPART)

Halla San 6398

KOREAN ARCHIPELAGO

KŎJE

NAMHAE

KOREA STRAIT

TSU SHIMA

IKI

Fukuoka

KITAKYŪSHŪ

HIRADO

Sasebo

Kurume

GOTŌ RETTŌ

Nakatsu

FUKUE

Kumamoto

Nagasaki

Usa

Ōita

Uto

Saeki

Sobo San 5758

AMAKUSA-SHIMO

DANJO

Nobeoka

Hososhima

KŌSHIKI RETTŌ

KYŪSHŪ

Miyazaki

Kajiki

Kagoshima

Miyakonojō

Kirishima

TOI MISAKI

Kagoshima Wan

ŌSUMI KAIKYŌ

ŌSUMI GUNTŌ

TANEGA

YAKU

Tokara Kaikyo

EAST CHINA SEA

Hamada

Matsue

Yonago

MIYOSHI

Tsuyama

Tottori

OKI GUNTŌ

Ayabe

Maizuru

Ōgaki

Gifu

NAGOYA

Okazaki

Shizuoka

Numazu

Shimizu

Toyohashi

Hamamatsu

IZU

SHICHITŌ

IRŌ SAKI

Hiroshima

Yamaguchi

Kure

Okayama

Fukuyama

Onomichi

Akashi

KYŌTO

Ōtsu

KŌBE

Nara

Tsu

Yokkaichi

Ise (Uji-Yamada)

Shimonoseki

Imabari

Takamatsu

Tokushima

ŌSAKA

Kishiwada

Wakayama

Tanabe

KUMANO NADA

Matsuyama

AWAJI

Tsurugi San 6414

Kōchi

Tombu San 6541

SHIKOKU

Uwajima

ASHIZURI ZAKI

MURO ZAKI

SHIONO MISAKI

MURO TO ZAKI

Kii Suido

KITAN KAIKYO

HARIMA NADA

NANSEI - SHOTŌ (RYUKYU ISLANDS)

TOKARA

GUNTŌ

AMAMI GUNTŌ

AMAMI

KIKAIGA

TOKUNO

ŌKINO ERABU

YORON

OKINAWA GUNTŌ

OKINAWA

Naha

Shuri

PHILIPPINE SEA

PACIFIC OCEAN

J A P A N

Longitude East of Greenwich

A-561900-76

COPYRIGHT BY
RAND McNALLY & COMPANY
MADE IN U.S.A.

Relief		
Meters		Feet
3050		10 000
1525		5000
610		2000
305		1000
152.5		500
0	Sea Level	0
152.5		500
1525		5000
3050		10 000
6100		20 000

| 0 | 50 | 100 | 150 | 200 | 250 | 300 Miles |
| 0 | 100 | 200 | 300 | 400 | 500 Kilometers |

Scale 1:10 000 000; one inch to 160 miles. Bonne's Equal Area Projection

Elevations and depressions are given in feet

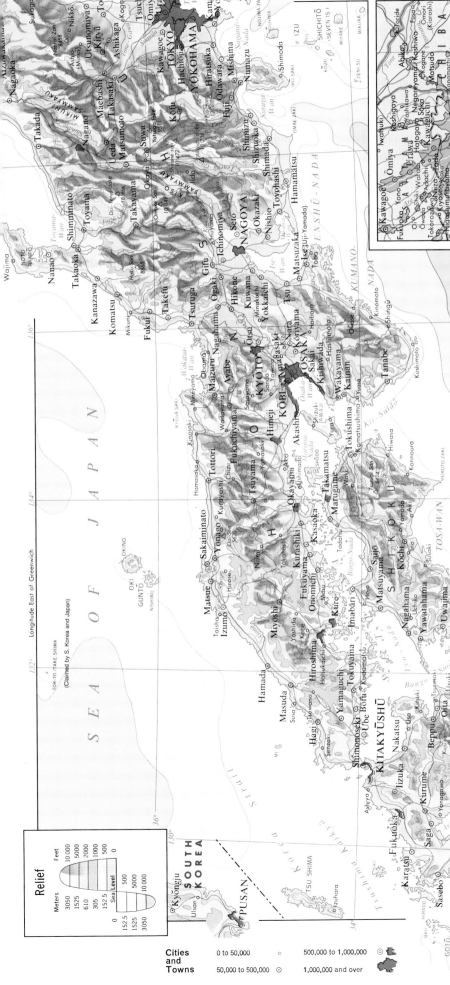

a

b

Scale 1:1 000 000

Scale 1:4 000 000, one inch to 64 miles Conic Projection
Elevations and depressions are given in feet.

Relief

Meters	Feet
3050	10 000
1525	5000
610	2000
305	1000
152.5	500
0	Sea Level
152.5	500
1525	5000
3050	10 000

Cities and Towns
0 to 50,000   500,000 to 1,000,000
50,000 to 500,000   1,000,000 and over

A-561992-76--5-54-10
COPYRIGHT BY
RAND M9NALLY & COMPANY
MADE IN U.S.A.

Relief

Meters		Feet
3050		10 000
1525		5000
610		2000
305		1000
152.5		500
	Sea Level	
152.5		500
1525		5000
3050		10 000
6100		20 000

A-569800-76 · 11-11-33
COPYRIGHT BY
RAND MCNALLY & COMPANY
MADE IN U.S.A.

Scale 1:16 000 000; one inch to 250 miles. Polyconic Projection
Elevations and depressions are given in feet

Continued on pages 204-205

a

PHILIPPINE

PHILIPPINE

ILIPPINES

Catanduanes
Island

3zpi

Sorsogon

Catbalogan

SAMAR

Cebu

Tacloban

LEYTE   DINAGAT ISLAND

PHILIPPINE

BOHOL

3d 578

danao

Butuan

Cagayan

SEA

z

TRENCH

afo

MINDANAO

MT.

Davao

9052

PULAU MIANGAS

KEPULAUAN
TALAUD

PALAU

SONSOROL
ISLANDS

PULAU SANGIHE

PULAU SIAU

nado

Tondano

Ternate

Laut

Maluku

(Molucca Sea)

Halmahera

MOROTAI

KEPULAUAN
MAPIA

Labuha

PULAU BACAN

KEPULAUAN OBI

Laut
Halmahera
(Halmahera Sea)

PULAU
WAIGEO

Selat Dampir

JLAUAN
NGGAI

PULAU
TALIBU

PULAU
MANGOLE

KEPULAUAN
SULA

PULAU SANANA

KEPULAUAN OBI

PULAU
MISOOL

SALAWATI

Sorong

Manokwari

BIAK

PULAU
NUMFOOR

PULAU YAPEN

TG. PERKAM

NINIGO GROUP

MUSSAU
ISLAND

ADMIRALTY ISLANDS

EMIRA
ISLAND

HERMIT IS.

MANUS
ISLAND

NEW HANOVER

Kavieng

JAZIRAH
DOBERAI

Teluk Berau

Teluk
Cenderawasih

PEGUNUNGAN VAN REES

Jayapura
(Sukarnapura)

Aitape

Wewak

BISMARCK

NEW
IRELAND

S I A

Piru

CERAM
(SERAM)

Bula

Fakfak

Kaimana

PULAU ADI

PEGUNUNGAN △ MAOKE

Puncak Jaya △ △ Puncak Trikora
16 503   15 584

Sepik

Namatanai

Rabaul

WITU
ISLANDS

ARCH.

Kokopo

BISMARCK

anui

BURU

Ambon

PULAU AMBON

KEPULAUAN
BANDA

KEPULAUAN
LUCIPARA

PULAU
BANDA

KEPULAUAN KAI

KAI KECIL

Dobo

KEPULAUAN
ARU

PULAU
TRANGAN

NEW GUINEA

Digul

Mt.Gilluwe 14 330 △

Mt. Wilhelm 14 793 △

Mt. Bangeta △
13 524

△ The Father
7546

KARKAR ISLAND

Madang

LONG ISLAND

Talasea

NEW BRITAIN

yowoni

KEPULAUAN
TUKANGBESI

Laut Banda

(BANDA SEA)

KEPULAUAN
TANIMBAR

YAMDENA

PULAU
SELARU

PULAU
YOS
SUDARSA

PAPUA

NEW GUINEA

Lae

Huon Gulf

NEW BRITAIN

NEW BRITAIN TRENCH

PULAU WETAR

N ALOR

De Atauro

Dili

EAST TIMOR

TIMOR

PULAU
DAMAR

PULAU BABAR

PULAU
MOA

TANJUNG VALS

Merauke

Gulf
of Papua

Mt. Albert Edward
13 090 △

Morobe

Buna

TROBRIAND IS.

WOODLARK
ISLAND

D'ENTRECASTEAUX IS.

AU
TAR

pang

TIMOR

SEA

ARAFURA

SEA

Daru

Port Moresby

OWEN STANLEY RA.

Mt. Victoria △
13 238

Samarai

CORAL SEA

Equator

MELVILLE
ISLAND

COBOURG
PEN.   CROKER ISLAND

WESSEL IS.

Torres Strait

C. YORK

CAPE
YORK
PEN.

GREAT
BARRIER
REEF

BATHURST
ISLAND

Van
Diemen Gulf

Gulf of Carpentaria

C. ARNHEM

Darwin

AUSTRALIA

Continued on pages 220-221

0   50 100   200   300   400   500 Miles

0   100   200   400   600   800 Kilometers

Inset map (upper right)

120°

Cabugao

Olquig

Tuguegarao

Bangued

Vigan

Narvacan

Candon

Cervantes

CORDILLERA CENTRAL

Bontoc

Cabagan

Ilagan

Divilacan Bay

S. JUAN

Luna

Mt. Amuyao
8799

Cauayan

Santiago

Echague

Jones

San Fernando

SANTIAGO

Baguio

Bayombong

Bambang

Dupax

Casiguran

Mt. Pulog
9626

Zagabag

Solano

DIJOHAN PT.

Bolinao

Aringay

ABARRUYAN

Lingayen Gulf

Palaman Bay
PALANAN PT.

PHILIPPINE

Bauang

2388

Ban Ilocan

San
Fabian

S. Nicolas

Tayug

S. Quintin

Bani

Alaminos

Dagupan

Urdaneta

Rosales

San Jose

Burgos

Lingayen

San Carlos

CAPE SAN ILDEFONSO

CAIMAN PT.

Infanta

Mangatarem

Bayambang

Muñoz

16°

Santa Cruz

Camiling

Gerona

Victoria

Cabanatuan

SEA

Candelaria

High Pk.
6683

Tarlac

Concepcion

Gapan

Dingalan Bay

PHILIPPINES

Iba

Palaug

LUZON

S. Miguel

Pinatubo
5771 △

Angeles

Arayat

S. Fernando

POLILLO IS.

POLILLO

S. Narciso

Guagua

S. Antonio

Malolos

PATNANONGAN

CALAGUAS ISLAND

Subic

Olongapo

Orani

Sta.
Maria

Infanta

Polillo

Lamon Bay

JOMALIG

Oriani

Balanga

Malabon

Quezon
City

BALESIN

Capalonga

Paracale

Orion

Manila

Pasig

CABALETE

Labo

Talisay

SAMPALOC PT.

Mariveles

Cavite

Daet

Mt. Labo
5068 △

Ragay

CORREGIDOR ISLAND

Naic

Laguna
de Bay

Sta. Cruz

ALABAT

San
Miguel
Bay

Naga △ 6450

Lopez B.

14°

TAAL

Calamba Mauban

Nagcarlan

Gumaca

Pili

Baao

Bahi

Nasugbu

Silang

S. Pablo

177 △ Mt. Banahao

Almonan

Lucena

Macalelon

S. Narciso

Potangui

Moyon
Volcano
8077 △

Tabaco

Balayan

Lemery

Lipa

Rosario

Unisan

Catanauan

Ligao

Legazpi

LUBANG
IS.

Lubang

AMBIL
ISLAND

Balayan
Bay

Batangas

Loba

Tayabas Bay

S. Cruz

Torrijos

GOLD
ISLAND

MARICABAN

Verde I. Passage

VERDE

Calapan

Boac

MARINDUQUE
ISLAND

Gasar

SIBUYAN

CAPE CALAVITE

Paluan

Mt. Halcon
△8471

Naujan

DUMALI PT.

San Pascual

BURIAS

TICAO
ISLAND

Mamburao

MINDORO

Pinamalayan

Jones

Burias Pass

S. JACINTO

Aroroy

Romblon

ROMBLON ISLAND

Sablayan

Mt. Baco
8163 △

Odiongan

Romblon

TABLAS

MASBATE

Masbate

DONGON PT.

Knob Pk.
3037 △

Looc

SIBUYAN

SEA

BUSUANGA

S. Jose

ILIN ISLAND

Bulalacao

Scale 1:4 000 000

0 10 20 30 40 Miles

0 10 20 30 40 50 60 Kilometers

©RMCN

TARA

Mindoro Strait

0°

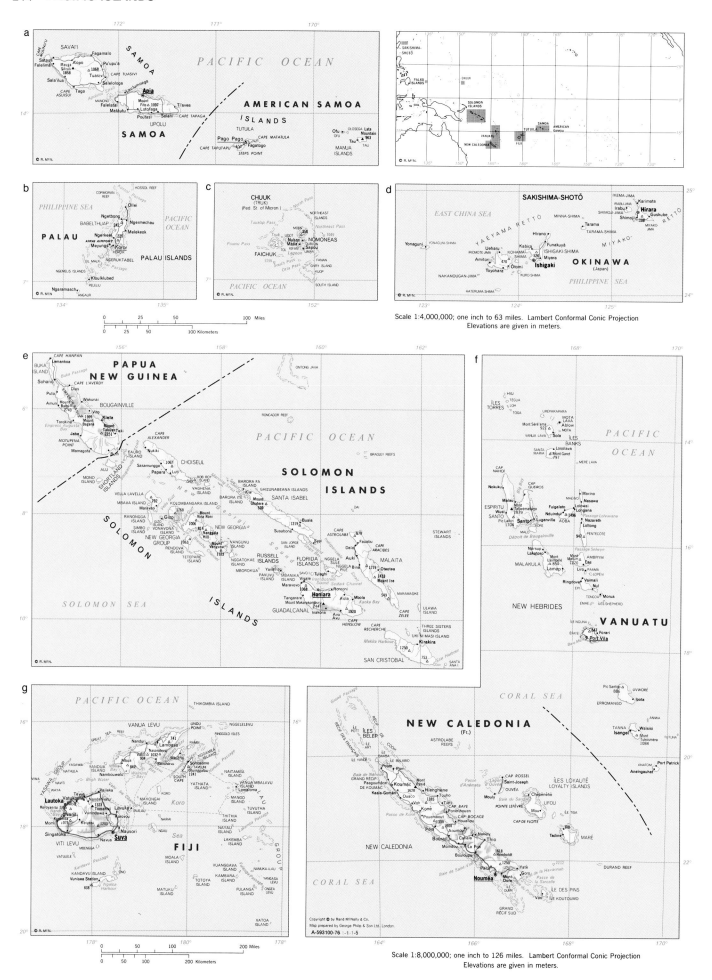

a

SAVAI'I

PACIFIC OCEAN

AMERICAN SAMOA

ISLANDS

SAMOA

Fagamalo
Sataua
Falelima
Masaga
Silisili
1858
Kopo
Pu'upu'a
Tuasivi
CAPE TUASIVI
Sala'ilua
Salelologa
Taga
CAPE
ASUISUI
MANONO
Leulumoega
Apolima Strait
APIA
Mount
Fito 1097
Lotofaga
Falelatai
Matāutu
UPOLU
Poutasi
Salani
CAPE TAPAGA
Ti'avea

SAMOA

TUTUILA

Pago Pago
Fagatogo
CAPE MATATULA
CAPE TAPUTAPU
STEPS POINT

Ofu
OFU
OLOSEGA
OFU
Tau
Lata
Mountain
963
TAU
MANUA
ISLANDS

b

PHILIPPINE SEA

KOSSOL REEF

CORMORAN
REEF

Ollei

PACIFIC
OCEAN

PALAU

Ngetbong
Ngermechau
BABELTHUAP
242
Melekeok
Ngerkeei
225
AIRAI AIRPORT
Meyungs
Koror
KOROR

PALAU ISLANDS

NGEMELIS ISLANDS

EL MALK
NGERUKTABEL

Kloulklubed

PELELIU

Ngaramasch
ANGAUR

c

CHUUK
(TRUK)
(Fed. St. of Micron.)

NORTH PASS

NORTHEAST

Tsuslap Pass

MOEN
UDOT
Nukan
Masa
Sapou
UMAN
1049
DUBLON
FEFAN
NOMONEAS

Pisanu Pass

Truk
Lagoon
FAICHUK
1556
Otta Pass
FANAN

GREY ISLAND
KUOP

SOUTH ISLAND

PACIFIC OCEAN

d

SAKISHIMA-SHOTŌ

IKEMA-JIMA
KARIMATA

EAST CHINA SEA

IRABU-JIMA
SHIMOJI-JIMA
Hirara
Guskube

MINNA-SHIMA
Tarama
SHIMOJI-JIMA
108
MIYAKO-JIMA

YAEYAMA RETTO
TARAMA-SHIMA

Yonaguni
YONAGUNI-SHIMA
Hirano
Kabira
Funakuyá
MIYAKO
IRIOMOTE-JIMA
Ueharu
KOHAMA-
SHIMA
ISHIGAKI-SHIMA
526
Miyara
Amitori
Otomi
Ishigaki
470
OKINAWA
(Japan)
NAKANOUGAN-JIMA
Toyohara
KURO SHIMA

HATERUMA-SHIMA

PHILIPPINE SEA

Scale 1:4,000,000; one inch to 63 miles. Lambert Conformal Conic Projection
Elevations are given in meters.

e

CAPE HANPAN
Lemankoa

PAPUA
NEW GUINEA

ONTONG JAVA

BUKA
ISLAND
Sohano
Buka Passage
CAPE L'AVERDY
Puto
Dios
Amun
Wakunai
Mount
Balbi
2743
Vito
BOUGAINVILLE
Torokina
1999
Mount
Bagana
Kieta
Engress Augusta Bay
Jaba
Takuan
2251
Buin
CAPE
ALEXANDER
Mamagota
MOTUPENA
POINT
Fauro Island
Nukiki
RONCADOR REEF

ALU
SHORTLAND
ISLANDS
Sasamungga
Luti
1067
CHOISEUL
Papara
BRADLEY REEFS

MONO
ISLAND
VELLA LAVELLA
549
ROB ROY
ISLAND
BARORA FA
ISLAND
GHIZUNABEANA ISLANDS
Kia
792
BARORA ITE ISLAND
Ghatere
SANTA ISABEL
DAI

PACIFIC OCEAN

SOLOMON
ISLANDS

MBAVA ISLAND
Maravari
1768
KOLOMBANGARA ISLAND
539
Buala

RANONGGA
ISLAND
Gizo
1006
Mount
Vina Roni
Susubona
1219
Sepi

SIMBO
ISLAND
820
VONAVONA
ISLAND
814
Nanggala
Hill
NEW GEORGIA
1063
SAN JORGE
ISLAND
CAPE
ASTROLABE
879
Fauabu
CAPE
ARACIDES

RENDOVA
ISLAND
1123
Mount
Vangunu
VANGUNU
ISLAND
NGGATOKAE
ISLAND
FLORIDA
ISLANDS
NGGELA
SULE
Dala
1219
Oteotea
Bina
NGGELA
PILE
MALAITA

TETEPARE ISLAND
MBOROKUA
Yaninihu
PAVUVU
ISLAND
RUSSELL
ISLANDS
MBANIKA
SAVO
Visale
Tulaghi
1433
Mount Ire

Maravovo
1068
Tangarare
Mount Makarakomburu
2447
Ronroni
Aola
Mbola
1920
549
Honiara
GUADALCANAL
Inakona
Avu Avu
CAPE
HENSLOW
MARAMASIKE
KokaBay
CAPE
ZELEE
ULAWA
ISLAND

SOLOMON SEA

SOLOMON

ISLANDS

Makira Harbour
UKI NI MASI ISLAND
THREE SISTERS
ISLANDS
1250
Kirakira
753
SAN CRISTOBAL
Star Harbour
SANTA
ANA I.

STEWART
ISLANDS

f

HIU
ÎLES
TORRES
TEGUA
LOH
TOGA

UREPARAPARA
MOTA
LAVA
MOTA
Mont Sére'ama
VANUA LAVA
Sola
ÎLES
BANKS
SANTA
MARIA
Mont Garet
797
MERE LAVA

CAP
NAHOI
Nokuku
PACIFIC
OCEAN

ESPIRITU
SANTO
Malau
Mont Tabwemasana
1879
CAP
QUEIROS
MAEWO
Marino
Nasawa
Wusi
Nduindui
Fulgalato
1496
Longana
AOBA
Loloway
Pic Laluri
1704
Santo
Luganville
Nazareth
Loltong
PENTECOTE
947
MALO
Passage Lolowana

Passage Selwyn
Norsup
Lakatoro
Lambell
Mont
Lambell
854
AMBRYM
Eas
1220
MALAKULA
Liro
Lamap
Ringdove
EPI
CLOPE'I
Vaimali
Nul
TONGOA
EMAE
Morua
ÎLES SHEPHERD
ÎLE NGUNA
547
Forari
ÉRATE
VANUATU
Port Vila

NEW HEBRIDES

Détroit de Bougainville

g

PACIFIC OCEAN

THIKOMBIA ISLAND

VANUA LEVU
UNDU
POINT
NGGELELEVU
RINGGOLD ISLES
RABI
Nandi
741
Lambasa
GREAT
SEA
REEF
Nasorolevu
1032
Mbua
904
Savusavu
842
Somosomo
TAVEUNI
1241
NAITAMBA
ISLAND

YASAWA
YANDUA
ISLAND
Nambouwalu
SOUTH
CAPE
Wainunu Bay
NAIAU
ISLAND

NATHULA
WAYA
VIWA
Vaileka
Tavua
1323
Vatukoula
Vatia
MAKONGAI
ISLAND
Koro
VANUA MBALAVU
ISLAND
LOMALOMA

Lautoka
Vatutu
Koroyandu
1195
MBA
Tomanivi
1323
Mbau
Levuka
OVALAU
THITHIA
ISLAND
TUVUTHA
ISLAND
Nandi
Mba
1075
Viwa
Nausori
NGAU
NAYAU
ISLAND
LAKEMBA
ISLAND
Singatoka
1203
Suva
LAMBEKA
PASSAGE
VITI LEVU
Navua
NAIRAI
Koro
Sea
VUANGGAVA
ISLAND
NAMUKA-I-LAU
KAMBARA
ISLAND
ONGEA
LEVU

VATULELE
MBENGGA
THITHIA
MOALA
ISLAND
TOTOYA
ISLAND
FULANGA
ISLAND
ONGEA
LEVU

KANDAVU ISLAND
Vunisea Station
838
Ngaloa
Harbour

FIJI

VATOA
ISLAND

Kamba
Passage

NEW CALEDONIA

CORAL SEA

Grand Passage
ÎLE POTT
ÎLES
BELEP
RECIF DES FRANÇAIS
ÎLE ART
ASTROLABE
REEFS

Pic Santal
886
UVWORÉ
Ipota
ERROMANGO

LE YANDÉ
Poum
Pam
ÎLE BALABIO
CAP ROSSEL
Passe
d'Anémata
CAP
QUEIROS
TANNA
Isangel
ANIWA
Waisisi
Mont
Tukosméra
1084
FUTUNA

GRAND RECIF
DE KOUMAC
Koumac
Saint-Joseph
Mont
Pané
1628
Hienghéne
Passe
de Ouvéa
ÎLE OUVÉA
Lifou
ÎLES LOYAUTÉ
LOYALTY ISLANDS

Kaala-Gomen
Quaco
Voh
1385
Tiéti
Ponérihouen
Touho
Mouly
Baie du Santal
CHÉPÉNÉHÉ
LIFOU

Pouembout
Poya
Pouembout
1506
1336
Aoumou
CAP BAYE
Houailou
CAP BOCAGE
POINTE LÉFÈVRE
Mou
ÎLE TIGA

Passe de Koné
Boûrail
Nakéty
Canala
Thio
TADINE
Ré
MARÉ

Moindou
La Foa
1618
Mont
Humboldt
1618
Yaté
2012
Goro
DURAND REEF

Bouloupari
Mont
Doré
ÎLE DES PINS
Païta
Mont
Doré
OUEN
ÎLE KOUTOUMO

NEW CALEDONIA

Nouméa

CORAL SEA

GRAND
RÉCIF SUD

Copyright © by Rand McNally & Co.
Map prepared by George Philip & Son Ltd. London.
A-593100-76 -1-1-5

Scale 1:8,000,000; one inch to 126 miles. Lambert Conformal Conic Projection
Elevations are given in meters.

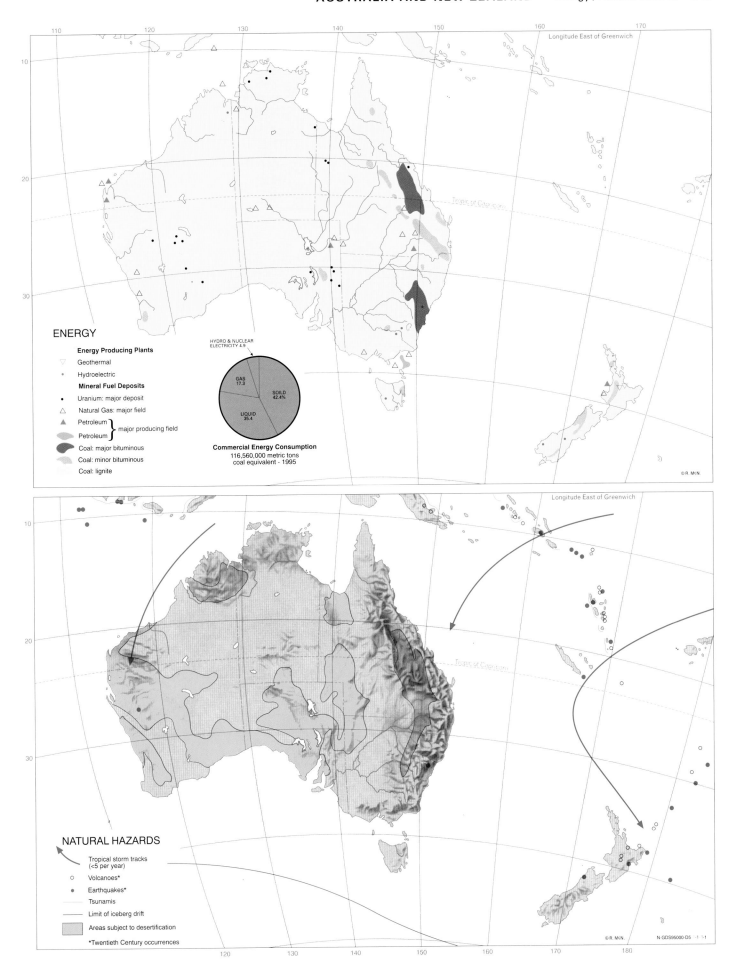

ENERGY

Energy Producing Plants

▽ Geothermal

• Hydroelectric

Mineral Fuel Deposits

• Uranium: major deposit

△ Natural Gas: major field

▲ Petroleum ⎫
⠀⠀⠀⠀⠀⠀⠀⠀⎬ major producing field
Petroleum ⎭

Coal: major bituminous

Coal: minor bituminous

Coal: lignite

HYDRO & NUCLEAR
ELECTRICITY 4.9

GAS
17.3

SOILD
42.4%

LIQUID
35.4

Commercial Energy Consumption
116,560,000 metric tons
coal equivalent - 1995

Longitude East of Greenwich

Tropic of Capricorn

© R. McN.

NATURAL HAZARDS

Tropical storm tracks
(<5 per year)

○ Volcanoes*

• Earthquakes*

Tsunamis

Limit of iceberg drift

Areas subject to desertification

*Twentieth Century occurrences

Longitude East of Greenwich

Tropic of Capricorn

© R. McN.

N-GDS95000-D5 -1 1-1

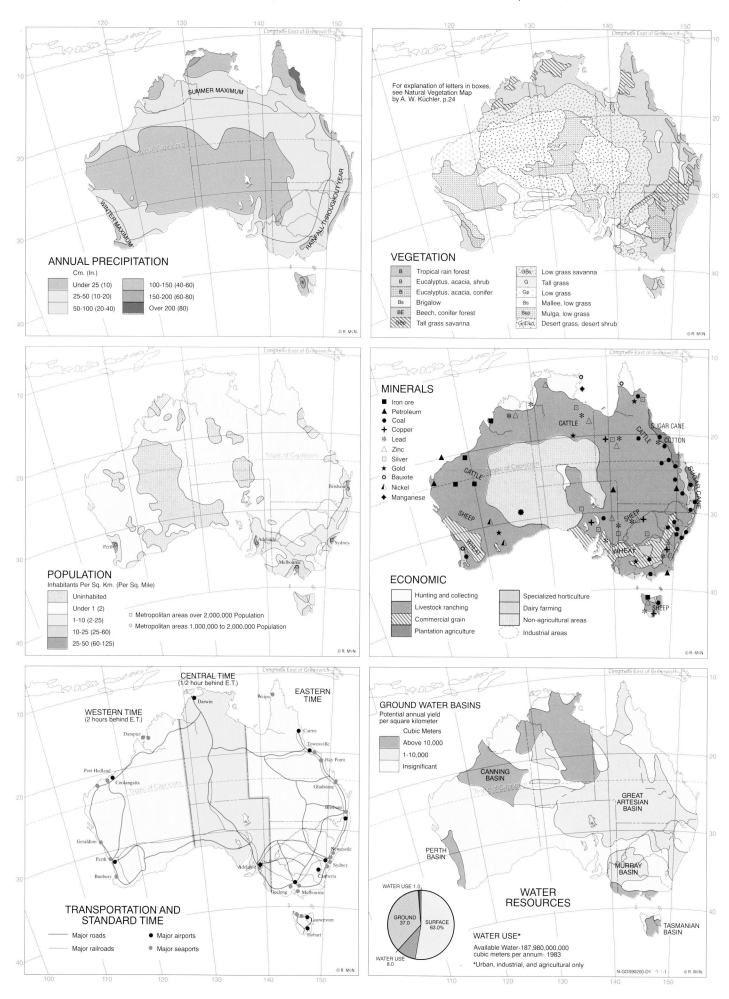

ANNUAL PRECIPITATION

SUMMER MAXIMUM

WINTER MAXIMUM

RAINFALL THROUGHOUT YEAR

Cm. (In.)

- Under 25 (10)
- 25-50 (10-20)
- 50-100 (20-40)
- 100-150 (40-60)
- 150-200 (60-80)
- Over 200 (80)

© R. McN.

VEGETATION

For explanation of letters in boxes,
see Natural Vegetation Map
by A. W. Küchler, p.24

B	Tropical rain forest	GBs	Low grass savanna
B	Eucalyptus, acacia, shrub	G	Tall grass
B	Eucalyptus, acacia, conifer	Gp	Low grass
Bs	Brigalow	Bs	Mallee, low grass
BE	Beech, conifer forest	Bsp	Mulga, low grass
GDp	Tall grass savanna	GpDsp	Desert grass, desert shrub

© R. McN.

POPULATION

Inhabitants Per Sq. Km. (Per Sq. Mile)

- Uninhabited
- Under 1 (2)
- 1-10 (2-25)
- 10-25 (25-60)
- 25-50 (60-125)

□ Metropolitan areas over 2,000,000 Population
○ Metropolitan areas 1,000,000 to 2,000,000 Population

Perth Adelaide Sydney Melbourne Brisbane

© R. McN.

MINERALS

- ■ Iron ore
- ▲ Petroleum
- ● Coal
- + Copper
- ✳ Lead
- △ Zinc
- □ Silver
- ★ Gold
- ○ Bauxite
- ◣ Nickel
- ◆ Manganese

CATTLE SUGAR CANE COTTON SHEEP WHEAT

ECONOMIC

- Hunting and collecting
- Livestock ranching
- Commercial grain
- Plantation agriculture
- Specialized horticulture
- Dairy farming
- Non-agricultural areas
- Industrial areas

© R. McN.

TRANSPORTATION AND STANDARD TIME

WESTERN TIME
(2 hours behind E.T.)

CENTRAL TIME
(1/2 hour behind E.T.)

EASTERN TIME

Darwin Weipa Cairns Townsville Hay Point Gladstone Brisbane Newcastle Sydney Canberra Geelong Melbourne Launceston Hobart Adelaide Bunbury Perth Geraldton Port Hedland Coolangatta Dampier

- —— Major roads
- —— Major railroads
- ● Major airports
- ● Major seaports

© R. McN.

GROUND WATER BASINS

Potential annual yield
per square kilometer

Cubic Meters

- Above 10,000
- 1-10,000
- Insignificant

CANNING BASIN

GREAT ARTESIAN BASIN

PERTH BASIN

MURRAY BASIN

TASMANIAN BASIN

WATER RESOURCES

WATER USE 1.0

GROUND 37.0

SURFACE 63.0%

WATER USE 8.0

WATER USE*

Available Water-187,980,000,000
cubic meters per annum- 1983

*Urban, industrial, and agricultural only

N-GDS90200-D1 -1-1-1   © R. McN.

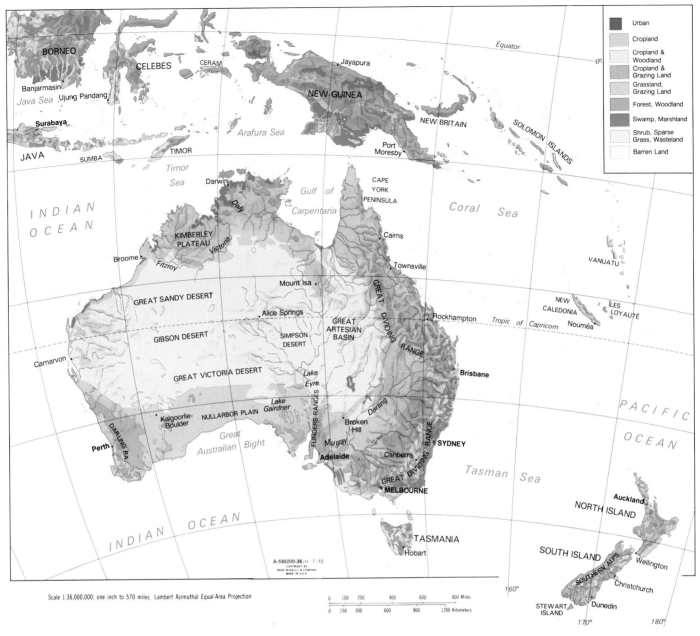

Urban
Cropland
Cropland & Woodland
Cropland & Grazing Land
Grassland, Grazing Land
Forest, Woodland
Swamp, Marshland
Shrub, Sparse Grass, Wasteland
Barren Land

BORNEO

CELEBES

CERAM

Jayapura

Banjarmasin

Ujung Pandang

Java Sea

NEW GUINEA

Surabaya

Arafura Sea

NEW BRITAIN

SOLOMON ISLANDS

JAVA

SUMBA

TIMOR

Port Moresby

Timor Sea

Darwin

Gulf of Carpentaria

CAPE YORK PENINSULA

Coral Sea

INDIAN OCEAN

KIMBERLEY PLATEAU

Victoria

Daly

Cairns

VANUATU

Broome

Fitzroy

Townsville

NEW CALEDONIA

ÎLES LOYAUTÉ

GREAT SANDY DESERT

Mount Isa

Tropic of Capricorn

Rockhampton

Nouméa

Carnarvon

GIBSON DESERT

Alice Springs

SIMPSON DESERT

GREAT ARTESIAN BASIN

GREAT DIVIDING RANGE

GREAT VICTORIA DESERT

Lake Eyre

Brisbane

PACIFIC OCEAN

Kalgoorlie-Boulder

NULLARBOR PLAIN

Lake Gairdner

FLINDERS RANGES

Broken Hill

Darling

SYDNEY

Perth

DARLING RA.

Great Australian Bight

Murray

Adelaide

Canberra

GREAT DIVIDING RANGE

MELBOURNE

Tasman Sea

Auckland

NORTH ISLAND

INDIAN OCEAN

TASMANIA

Hobart

SOUTH ISLAND

SOUTHERN ALPS

Wellington

Christchurch

STEWART ISLAND

Dunedin

A-590200-36
COPYRIGHT BY
RAND M?NALLY & COMPANY
MADE IN U.S.A.

160°

170°

180°

Scale 1:36,000,000; one inch to 570 miles. Lambert Azimuthal Equal-Area Projection

0 100 200 400 600 800 Miles
0 150 300 600 900 1200 Kilometers

---

a

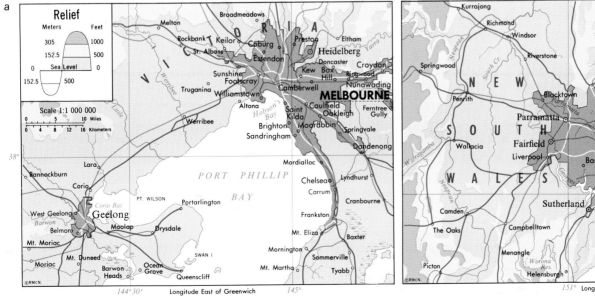

Relief

Meters Feet
305 1000
152.5 500
0 Sea Level 0
152.5 500

Scale 1:1 000 000
0 5 10 Miles
0 4 8 12 16 Kilometers

Broadmeadows
Melton
VICTORIA
Rockbank Keilor Coburg Preston Eltham
St. Albans Essendon Heidelberg
Sunshine Doncaster Croydon
Truganina Footscray Kew Box Hill Ringwood
Williamstown Camberwell Nunawading
Altona MELBOURNE
Werribee Saint Kilda Caulfield Ferntree Gully
Brighton Oakleigh Moorabbin Springvale
Sandringham
Lara Dandenong
Bannockburn Mordialloc
Corio PORT PHILLIP BAY Chelsea Lyndhurst
PT. WILSON Carrum
West Geelong Geelong Portarlington Cranbourne
Belmont Moolap Drysdale Frankston
Mt. Moriac Mt. Eliza
Moriac Mt. Duneed Ocean Grove Mornington Sommerville
Barwon Heads SWAN I. Mt. Martha Tyabb
Queenscliff Baxter

38°

144°30' Longitude East of Greenwich 145°

---

b

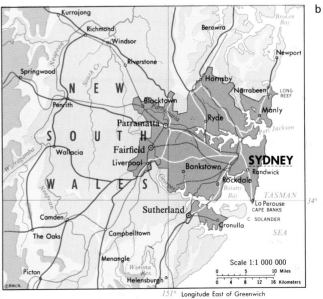

Kurrajong
Richmond
Windsor
Berowra
Broken Bay
Springwood
Riverstone
Newport
NEW
Penrith
Blacktown
Hornsby
Narrabeen
LONG REEF
Parramatta
Ryde
Manly
SOUTH
Wallacia
Fairfield
Port Jackson
Liverpool
Bankstown
SYDNEY
WALES
Randwick
Rockdale
Camden
Sutherland
Botany Bay
La Perouse
CAPE BANKS
C. SOLANDER
The Oaks
Cronulla
TASMAN
Campbelltown
SEA
Menangle
Picton
Helensburgh

Scale 1:1 000 000
0 5 10 Miles
0 4 8 12 16 Kilometers

34°

151° Longitude East of Greenwich

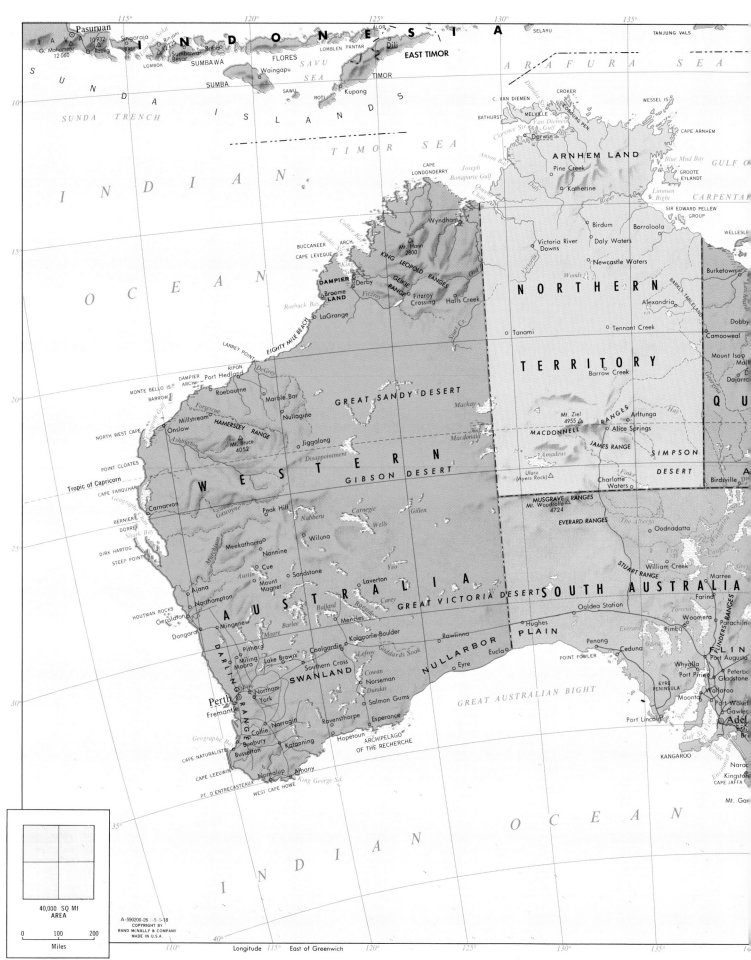

J A V A G. Mahameru 10 932 12 060

Singaraja Rinjani

Pasuruan BALI

LOMBOK Sumbawa Rabio

Besar

SUMBAWA Waingapu FLORES

LOMBOK PANTAR

ALOR LOMBLEN

EAST TIMOR

Dili

I N D O N E S I A

SELARU TANJUNG VALS

SUMBA

SAWU ROTI TIMOR

Kupang

S U N D A I S L A N D S

S

SUNDA TRENCH

SAVU SEA

TIMOR SEA

A R A F U R A   S E A

I N D I A N

O C E A N

CAPE LONDONDERRY

C. VAN DIEMEN CROKER

MELVILLE Van Diemen COBOURG PEN

Dundas Str.

BATHURST Clarence Str.

Darwin

WESSEL IS.

CAPE ARNHEM

GROOTE

EYLANDT

Blue Mud Bay

GULF O

Joseph Bonaparte Gulf

Anson Bay *Daly*

Pine Creek

ARNHEM LAND

Katherine

Limmen Bight

SIR EDWARD PELLEW GROUP

WELLESLE

CARPENTAR

BUCCANEER ARCH.

CAPE LEVEQUE

Wyndham

Mt. Hann 2800

Sunday Str. *Collier Bay*

KING LEOPOLD RANGES

DAMPIER LAND

Broome

Derby

GEIKIE RANGE

Fitzroy Crossing

Halls Creek

Roebuck Bay

Fitzroy

LaGrange

Victoria River Downs

Birdum Daly Waters

Borroloola

Newcastle Waters

N O R T H E R N

Alexandria

Dobby

Barkly Tableland

LARREY POINT

EIGHTY MILE BEACH

Stuart Cr.

Tanami

Tennant Creek

Camooweal

Mount Isa Mall

Dajarra

T E R R I T O R Y

Barrow Creek

Q

RIPON

DAMPIER ARCH. Port Hedland

MONTE BELLO IS.

BARROW

Roebourne

DeGrey

Marble Bar

Nullagine

GREAT SANDY DESERT

Mackay

Mt. Ziel 4955

Arltunga

Hay

NORTH WEST CAPE

Millstream

Onslow

HAMERSLEY RANGE

Mt. Bruce 4052

Jiggalong

Fortescue

Ashburton

Macdonald

MACDONNELL RANGES

Alice Springs

Amadeus

JAMES RANGE

SIMPSON

POINT CLOATES

CAPE FARQUHAR

Tropic of Capricorn

GIBSON DESERT

Disappointment

Uluru (Ayers Rock)

Charlotte Waters

Finke

DESERT

Birdsville

A

Di

CARNARVON

Gascoyne

Peak Hill

Nabberu

Carnegie

Gillen

Wells

Gairdner

MUSGRAVE RANGES

Mt. Woodroffe 4724

EVERARD RANGES

BERNIER I.

DORRE I.

Shark Bay

Meekatharra

Nannine

Murchison

Cue

Wiluna

Yeo

W E S T E R N

Oodnadatta

The Alberga

DIRK HARTOG

STEEP POINT

Ajana

Mount Magnet

Sandstone

Austin

Laverton

Carey

STUART RANGE

William Creek

Marree

Eyre 39

Coopers

HOUTMAN ROCKS

Northampton

Geraldton

Dongara

Mingene

Pithara

Barlee

Moore

Menzies

Kalgoorlie-Boulder

Ballard

Coolgardie

Lefroy

Rawlinna

GREAT VICTORIA DESERT

SOUTH AUSTRALIA

Ooldea Station

Farina

Pimba

Woomera

FLINDERS RANGES

Port Augusta

Peterbo

Gladstone

FLIN

Torrens

Everard

Gairdner

Hughes

NULLARBOR

PLAIN

Penong

Ceduna

Whyalla

Port Pirie

A U S T R A L I A

Miling

Moora

Lake Brown

Southern Cross

Cowan

Norseman

Dundas

Goddard's Soak

Eyre

Eucla

POINT FOWLER

Port Lincoln

EYRE PENINSULA

Moonta

Wallaroo

Gawler

Adel

Br

DARLING RANGE

SWANLAND

Northam York

Perth

Fremantle

Narrogin

Collie

Salmon Gums

GREAT AUSTRALIAN BIGHT

Gulf St

Spencer

Adel

KANGAROO

Narac

Geographe Bay

Bunbury

Busselton

CAPE NATURALISTE

Katanning

Ravensthorpe

Hopetoun

Esperance

ARCHIPELAGO OF THE RECHERCHE

Kingston

CAPE JAFFA

Mt. Gar

CAPE LEEUWIN

Nornalup

Albany

King George Sd.

PT. D'ENTRECASTEAUX WEST CAPE HOWE

I N D I A N   O C E A N

40,000 SQ MI
AREA

0   100   200
Miles

Longitude 115° East of Greenwich

Scale 1:16 000 000; one inch to 250 miles. Lambert's Azimuthal, Equal Area Projection
Elevations and depressions are given in feet

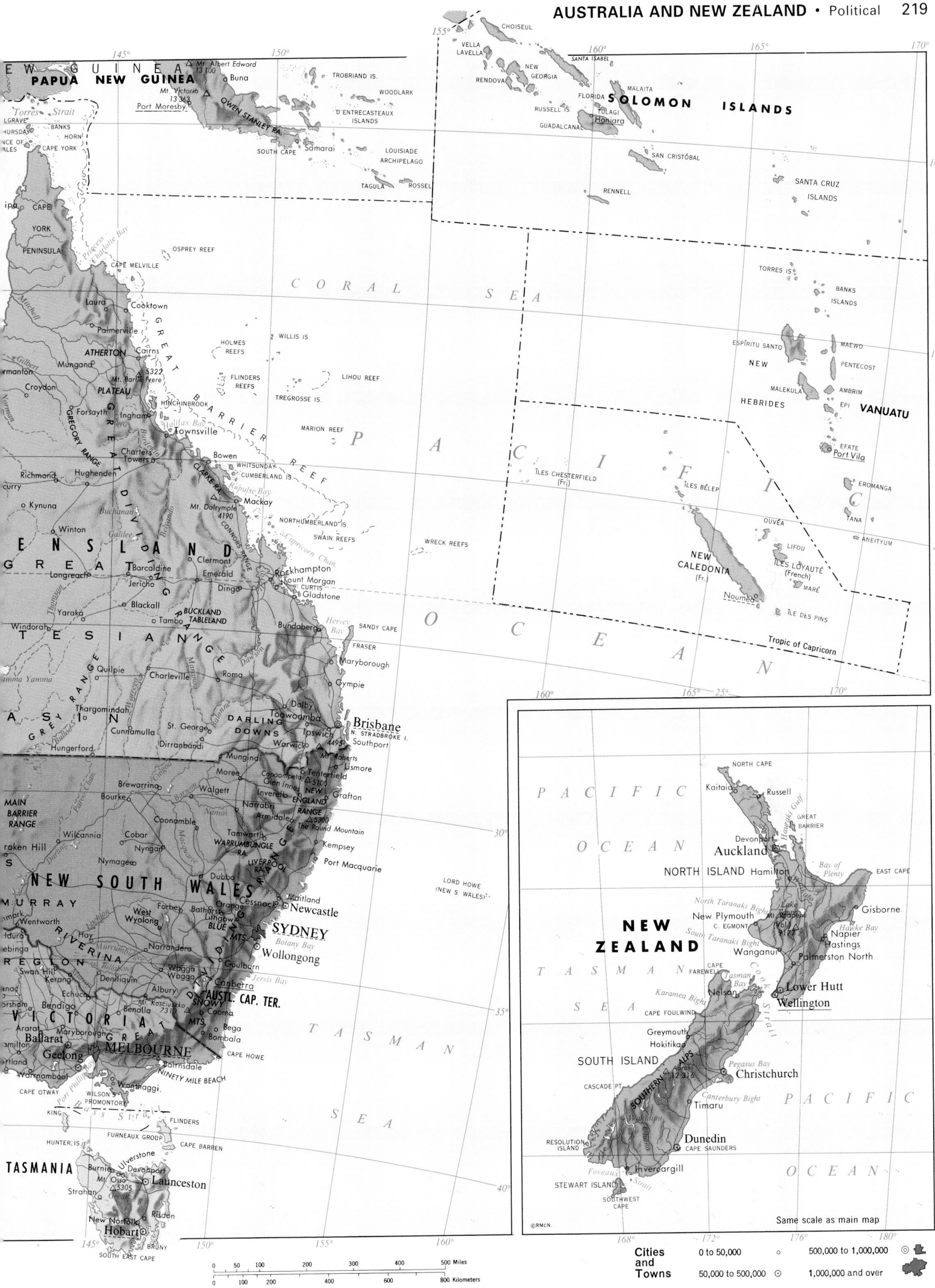

Main Map

CHOISEUL
VELLA LAVELLA
NEW GEORGIA
SANTA ISABEL
RENDOVA
RUSSELL IS.
GUADALCANAL
TULAGI
Honiara
FLORIDA
MALAITA
SOLOMON ISLANDS
SAN CRISTÓBAL
RENNELL
SANTA CRUZ ISLANDS

NEW GUINEA
PAPUA NEW GUINEA
Mt. Albert Edward 13,100
Buna
TROBRIAND IS.
WOODLARK
Mt. Victoria 13,363
Port Moresby
OWEN STANLEY RA.
D'ENTRECASTEAUX ISLANDS
SOUTH CAPE
Samarai
LOUISIADE ARCHIPELAGO
TAGULA
ROSSEL
Torres Strait
BANKS
HORN
CAPE YORK

CAPE YORK PENINSULA

OSPREY REEF

BANKS ISLANDS
TORRES IS.

ESPÍRITU SANTO
MAEWO
NEW HEBRIDES
PENTECOST
MALEKULA
AMBRIM
EPI
VANUATU
EFATE
Port Vila
EROMANGA
TANA
ANEITYUM

CORAL SEA

ATHERTON PLATEAU
Cairns
Mt. Bartle Frere 5322
HINCHINBROOK I.
Halifax Bay
Ingham
Townsville
HOLMES REEFS
WILLIS IS.
FLINDERS REEFS
LIHOU REEF
TREGROSSE IS.
MARION REEF

PACIFIC OCEAN

Charters Towers
Bowen
WHITSUNDAY
CUMBERLAND IS.
Repulse Bay
Mt. Dalrymple 4190
Mackay
NORTHUMBERLAND IS.
SWAIN REEFS
WRECK REEFS

ÎLES CHESTERFIELD (Fr.)
ÎLES BÉLEP
OUVÉA
LIFOU
ÎLES LOYAUTÉ (French)
MARÉ
NEW CALEDONIA (Fr.)
Nouméa
ÎLE DES PINS

Clermont
Emerald
Rockhampton
Mount Morgan
CURTIS
Gladstone
Capricorn Chan.

QUEENSLAND
GREAT DIVIDING RANGE
BUCKLAND TABLELAND

Tropic of Capricorn

Bundaberg
Hervey Bay
SANDY CAPE
FRASER

Maryborough
Gympie

Dalby
Toowoomba
Ipswich
Brisbane
N. STRADBROKE I.
Southport

DARLING DOWNS
Warwick
Lismore
NEW ENGLAND RANGE
Grafton

NEW SOUTH WALES
Moree
Narrabri
Armidale
Tamworth
WARRUMBUNGLE RA.
LIVERPOOL RA.
Kempsey
Port Macquarie

LORD HOWE (NEW S. WALES)

Dubbo
Bathurst
Orange
Lithgow
BLUE MTS.
Cessnock
Maitland
Newcastle
SYDNEY
Botany Bay
Wollongong

Forbes
West Wyalong
Narrandera
Wagga Wagga
Albury
Goulburn
Canberra
Jervis Bay
AUSTL. CAP. TER.

RIVERINA REGION
MURRAY
Swan Hill
Kerang
Echuca
Benalla
Mt. Kosciusko 7316
SNOWY MTS.
Cooma
Bega
Bombala
CAPE HOWE

VICTORIA
Ararat
Maryborough
Bendigo
Ballarat
Geelong
MELBOURNE
Bairnsdale
NINETY MILE BEACH
CAPE OTWAY
Warrnambool
Wonthaggi
WILSON'S PROMONTORY
Port Phillip

KING I.
FURNEAUX GROUP
FLINDERS
HUNTER IS.
CAPE BARREN

TASMANIA
Burnie
Ulverstone
Devonport
Mt. Ossa 5305
Launceston
Strahan
New Norfolk
Risdon
Hobart
SOUTH EAST CAPE
BRUNY

TASMAN SEA

New Zealand Inset

NEW ZEALAND

PACIFIC OCEAN

NORTH CAPE
Kaitaia
Russell
GREAT BARRIER
Hauraki Gulf
Devonport
Auckland
NORTH ISLAND
Hamilton
Bay of Plenty
EAST CAPE

North Taranaki Bight
New Plymouth
C. EGMONT
Mt. Egmont
South Taranaki Bight
Wanganui
Gisborne
Hawke Bay
Napier
Hastings
Palmerston North

CAPE FAREWELL
Tasman Bay
Nelson
Cook Strait
Lower Hutt
Wellington
Karamea Bight
CAPE FOULWIND

TASMAN SEA

Greymouth
Hokitika
SOUTHERN ALPS
Mt. Cook 12,316
SOUTH ISLAND
Pegasus Bay
Christchurch
CASCADE PT.
Canterbury Bight
Timaru

RESOLUTION ISLAND
Lake Wakatipu
Dunedin
CAPE SAUNDERS

Foveaux Strait
Invercargill
STEWART ISLAND
SOUTHWEST CAPE

PACIFIC OCEAN

©RMcN.

Same scale as main map

Cities and Towns	
0 to 50,000 ○	500,000 to 1,000,000
50,000 to 500,000 ⊙	1,000,000 and over

0 50 100 200 300 400 500 Miles
0 200 400 600 800 Kilometers

Continued on pages 212-213

INDONESIA

Pasuruan

Singaraja
BALI
Rinjani
3225
Sumbawa
Besar
LOMBOK
SUMBAWA
FLORES
Waingapu
SUMBA
SAWU
ROTI
LOMBLEN PANTAR
ALOR
TIMOR
Kupang
DILI
EAST TIMOR

SELARU

TANJUNG VALS

A R A F U R A   S E A

S U N D A   I S L A N D S

SAVU
SEA

S U N D A

SUNDA TRENCH

TIMOR   SEA

CAPE
LONDONDERRY

Joseph
Bonaparte Gulf

C. VAN DIEMEN
CROKER
MELVILLE
Van Diemen
Gulf
BATHURST
Clarence Str.
Darwin

COBURG PEN.

WESSEL IS.

CAPE ARNHEM

Blue Mud Bay

GULF O.

Anson Bay
Daly
Pine Creek
Katherine

ARNHEM   LAND

GROOTE
EYLANDT
Limmen
Bight

SIR EDWARD PELLEW
GROUP

CARPENTAR

I N D I A N

O C E A N

BUCCANEER   ARCH.
CAPE LEVEQUE

Sundan
Collier B.

Wyndham

KING
LEOPOLD
RANGES
Mt. Hann
2800
GEIKIE
RANGE
Fitzroy
Crossing
Halls Creek

Queen
Chan.

Victoria River
Downs

Birdum
Borroloola

WELLESLEY

Victoria

Daly Waters

Newcastle Waters

Burketown

BARKLY TABLELAND

N O R T H E R N

DAMPIER
LAND
Broome
Derby
Roebuck Bay
LaGrange

Fitzroy

Tanami

Stuart Cr.

Tennant Creek

Alexandria

Dobby

Camooweal

T E R R I T O R Y

Mount Isa
Malb.

EIGHTY MILE BEACH
LARREY POINT
RIPON
Port Hedland
DeGrey
DAMPIER
ARCH.
MONTE BELLO IS.
BARROW
Roebourne
Marble Bar
Nullagine
Onslow
Millstream
HAMERSLEY   RANGE
Mt. Bruce
4052
Jiggalong

GREAT   SANDY   DESERT

Mackay

Barrow Creek

Macdonald

Mt. Ziel
4955
MACDONNELL   RANGES
Arltunga
Alice Springs
JAMES RANGE

Dajarra

Q U

NORTH WEST CAPE

POINT CLOATES

Disappointment

GIBSON   DESERT

Amadeus

SIMPSON
DESERT

A

Tropic of Capricorn
CAPE FARQUHAR
Carnarvon
Geographe Chan.
Gascoyne
Peak Hill
Nabberu
Carnegie
Wells
Gillen
Uluru
(Ayers Rock)

Finke

Charlotte
Waters

MUSGRAVE   RANGES
Mt. Woodroffe
4724
EVERARD RANGES

Birdsville

Oodnadatta

BERNIER I.
DORRE I.
Shark Bay
DIRK HARTOG
STEEP POINT

W E S T E R N

Meekatharra
Nannine
Cue
Sandstone
Mount
Magnet
Austin

Wiluna

Laverton

Carey
Raeside

The Alberga

STUART RANGE

Eyre Cr.

Coopers Cr.

Greg

William Creek

Marree
Farina

Neale

HOUTMAN ROCKS
Geraldton
Northampton
Ajana
Dongara

A U S T R A L I A

Ballard
Barlee
Moore

Menzies

GREAT   VICTORIA   DESERT

S O U T H   A U S T R A L I A

Woomera
Pimba

Torrens

FLINI

RANGES

Mingenew
Pithara
Milling
Moora
Lake Brown
Southern Cross
SWANLAND

Kalgoorlie-Boulder
Coolgardie
Lefroy
Goddards Soak
Cowan

Rawlinna
Eucla

NULLARBOR   PLAIN

Hughes
Penong
Ooldea Station

Ceduna

Everard

Port Augusta
Whyalla
Port Pirie
Peterbor
Gladstone

Perth
Fremantle
Northam
York
Calfe
Narrogin
Geographe Bay
Bunbury
Busselton
CAPE NATURALISTE

DARLING   RANGE

Dundas
Norseman
Salmon Gums

Esperance
Ravensthorpe
Hopetoun
Katanning

ARCHIPELAGO
OF THE RECHERCHE

Eyre

POINT FOWLER

G R E A T   A U S T R A L I A N   B I G H T

EYRE
PENINSULA

Moonta
Wallaroo
Port Wakefie
Gawler

Adela

CAPE LEEUWIN
Northalup
Albany
King George Sd.
PT. D'ENTRECASTEAUX
WEST CAPE HOWE

Port Lincoln

KANGAROO

Gulf St.

Mur
Brid

Narac
Kingston
CAPE JAFFA

Mt. Gam

I N D I A N   O C E A N

Longitude 115°   East of Greenwich

Scale 1:16 000 000; one inch to 250 miles. Lambert's Azimuthal, Equal Area Projection
Elevations and depressions are given in feet

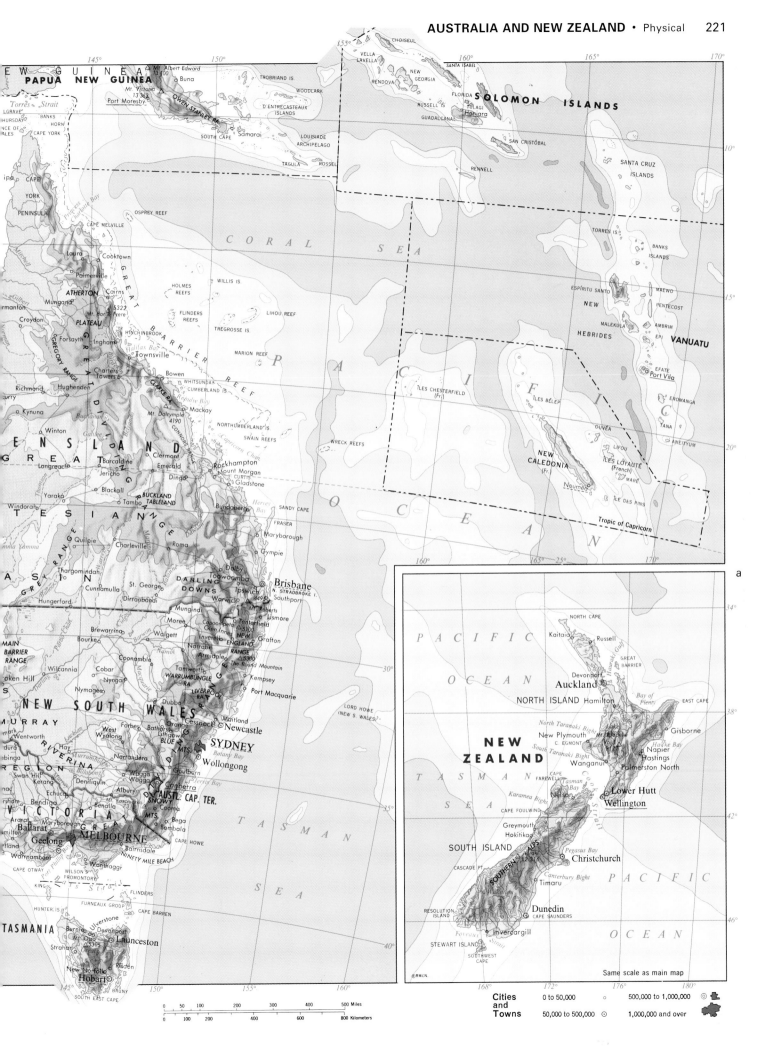

PAPUA NEW GUINEA

EW GUINEA

Mt. Albert Edward
13100

Mt. Victoria
13 363
Port Moresby

Torres Strait

OWEN STANLEY RA.

Buna

TROBRIAND IS.

WOODLARK

D'ENTRECASTEAUX
ISLANDS

SOUTH CAPE

Samarai

LOUISIADE
ARCHIPELAGO

TAGULA

ROSSEL

CHOISEUL

VELLA
LAVELLA

NEW
GEORGIA

SANTA ISABEL

RENDOVA

FLORIDA

RUSSELL IS.

TULAGI
Honiara

GUADALCANAL

SOLOMON ISLANDS

SAN CRISTOBAL

RENNELL

SANTA CRUZ
ISLANDS

ESPIRITU SANTO

NEW

HEBRIDES

MALEKULA

MAEWO

PENTECOST

AMBRIM

EPI

EFATE
Port Vila

VANUATU

EROMANGA

ILES BELEP

TANA

ANEITYUM

ILES CHESTERFIELD
(Fr.)

OUVEA

LIFOU

ILES LOYAUTE
(French)

**NEW
CALEDONIA**
(Fr.)

Noumea

MARE

ILE DES PINS

TORRES IS.

BANKS
ISLANDS

CORAL SEA

PACIFIC

OCEAN

Tropic of Capricorn

OSPREY REEF

CAPE MELVILLE

HOLMES
REEFS

WILLIS IS.

FLINDERS
REEFS

LIHOU REEF

TREGROSSE IS.

MARION REEF

SWAIN REEFS

WRECK REEFS

LORD HOWE I.
(NEW S. WALES)

Laura

Cooktown

Palmerville

ATHERTON

Cairns

Mungana

PLATEAU

Mt. Barth Frere
5322

Croydon

Forsayth

Ingham

HINCHINBROOK I.

Halifax Bay

Townsville

Charters
Towers

CLARKE RA.

Bowen

WHITSUNDAY

Repulse Bay

CUMBERLAND IS.

Mt. Dalrymple
4190

Mackay

NORTHUMBERLAND IS.

CONNORS RANGE

Capricorn Chan.

CURTIS

Gladstone

Mount Morgan

Rockhampton

Dingo

Emerald

Clermont

Barcaldine

Jericho

**BUCKLAND
TABLELAND**

Tambo

Hervey Bay

SANDY CAPE

FRASER

Bundaberg

Maryborough

Gympie

Roma

Dolby

Toowoomba

Ipswich

Brisbane

N. STRADBROKE I.

Southport

Warwick

4495
M. Roberts

Lismore

Tenterfield

**NEW
ENGLAND
RANGE**

5300
The Round Mountain

Grafton

Glen Innes

Inverell

Narrabri

Armidale

Kempsey

Port Macquarie

GREAT

DIVIDING

RANGE

GREGORY RANGE

Richmond

Hughenden

Kynuna

Winton

Longreach

Yaraka

Windorah

Blackall

Quilpie

Charleville

Thargomindah

Cunnamulla

St. George

Dirranbandi

Hungerford

Mungindi

Moree

Walgett

Bourke

Brewarrina

Coonamble

**WARRUMBUNGLE
RA.**

Tamworth

Coonabarabran

**LIVERPOOL
RA.**

Dubbo

Gilgandra

Cobar

Nyngan

Nymagee

Wilcannia

**MAIN
BARRIER
RANGE**

ken Hill

NEW SOUTH WALES

Ballarat

Geelong

Warrnambool

CAPE OTWAY

KING I.

TASMANIA

Burnie

Ulverstone

Devonport

Launceston

Strahan

Mt. Ossa
5305

New Norfolk

Hobart

BRUNY

SOUTH EAST CAPE

FLINDERS

FURNEAUX GROUP

CAPE BARREN

HUNTER IS.

CAPE BARREN

TASMAN

SEA

Orange

Bathurst

**BLUE
MTS.**

Cessnock

Maitland

Newcastle

SYDNEY

Botany Bay

Wollongong

Goulburn

Jervis Bay

Canberra

AUSTL. CAP. TER.

**SNOWY
MTS.**

Cooma

Bega

Bombala

CAPE HOWE

West
Wyalong

Forbes

Narrandera

Wagga
Wagga

Albury

Benalla

Mt. Kosciusko
7316

**GREAT
DIVIDING**

Bendigo

MELBOURNE

Bairnsdale

NINETY MILE BEACH

WILSON'S
PROMONTORY

Wonthaggi

Port Phillip B.

BASS STRAIT

VICTORIA

Ararat

Maryborough

Echuca

Kerang

Swan Hill

Deniliquin

Hay

RIVERINA

REGION

Wentworth

MURRAY

mark

Murrumbidgee

Billabong

Murray

Darling

Paroo

Warrego

Barwon

Namoi

Macquarie

Bogan

Lachlan

Darling

CAPE
YORK
PENINSULA

Thursday I.

BANKS

HORN

CAPE YORK

ENGLAND

GREAT

ARTESIAN

BASIN

PACIFIC

OCEAN

0   50 100   200   300   400   500 Miles

0 100   200   400   600   800 Kilometers

NEW ZEALAND inset

**NEW
ZEALAND**

NORTH CAPE

Kaitaia

Russell

Devonport

Auckland

NORTH ISLAND

Hamilton

Bay of
Plenty

GREAT
BARRIER

EAST CAPE

Gisborne

North Taranaki Bight

New Plymouth

C. EGMONT

Mt. Egmont

South Taranaki Bight

Wanganui

Napier

Hastings

Palmerston North

CAPE
FAREWELL

Karamea Bight

Nelson

Tasman
Bay

Lower Hutt

Wellington

CAPE FOULWIND

Greymouth

Hokitika

SOUTH ISLAND

SOUTHERN ALPS

12349

CASCADE PT.

RESOLUTION
ISLAND

Invercargill

STEWART ISLAND

SOUTHWEST
CAPE

Foveaux Strait

Pegasus Bay

Christchurch

Canterbury Bight

Timaru

Dunedin

CAPE SAUNDERS

PACIFIC

OCEAN

*PACIFIC
OCEAN*

*TASMAN
SEA*

Cook Strait

Hauraki Gulf

©RMcN.

Same scale as main map

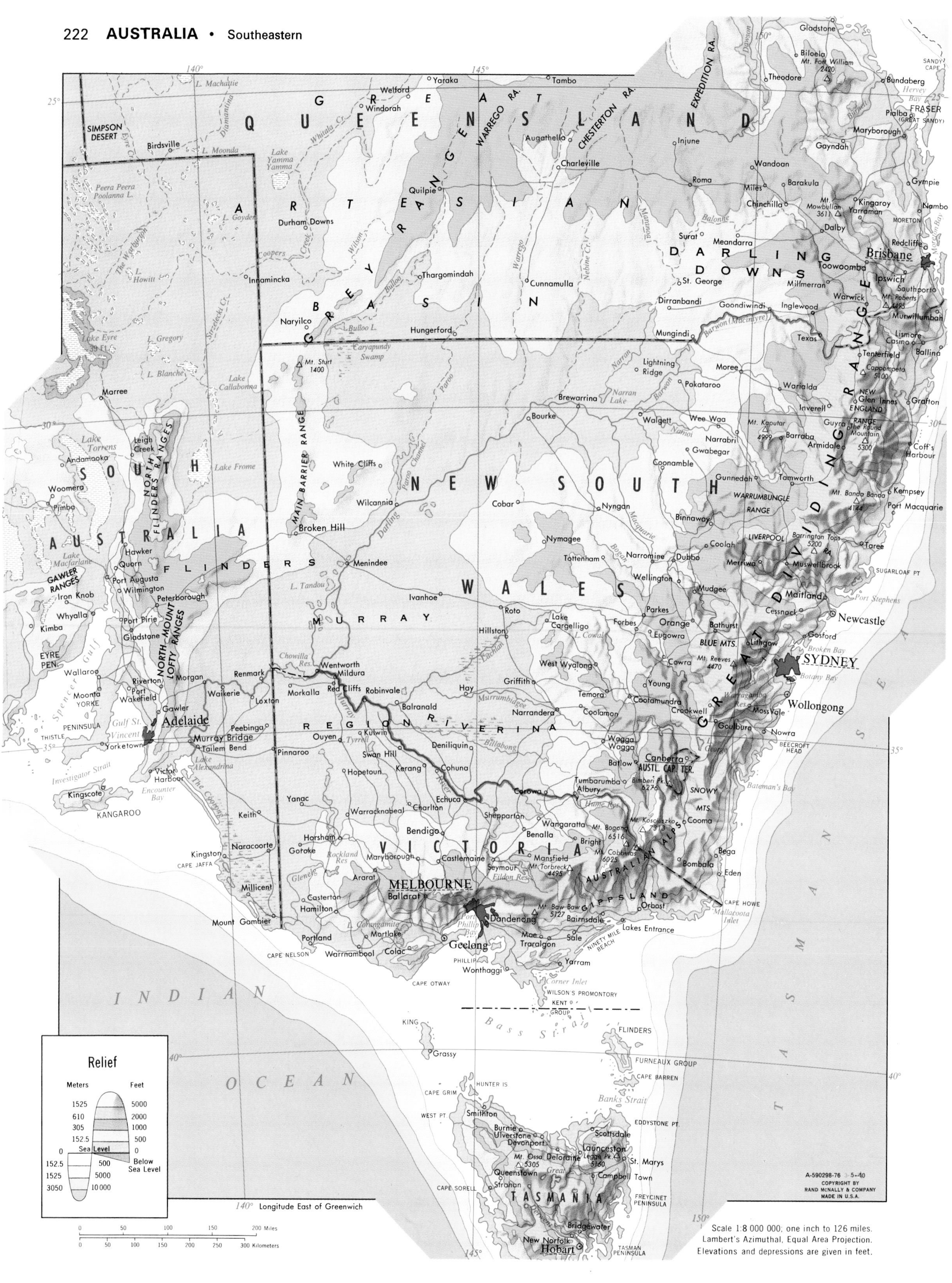

SIMPSON DESERT

QUEENSLAND

GREAT ARTESIAN BASIN

GREY RANGE

WARREGO RA.

CHESTERTON RA.

EXPEDITION RA.

L. Machattie
L. Moonda
Lake Yamma Yamma
Peera Peera Poolanna L.

Welford
Windorah
Yaraka
Tambo
Birdsville
Durham Downs
Quilpie
Augathella
Charleville
Injune
Wandoan
Barakula
Miles
Chinchilla
Roma
Surat
Meandarra
Dalby
Dirranbandi
Millmerran
Thargomindah
Cunnamulla
St. George
Goondiwindi
Inglewood
Warwick
Naryilco
Hungerford
Mungindi
Texas
Lightning Ridge
Pokataroo
Moree
Wee Waa
Warialda
Inverell

Gladstone
Biloela
Mt. Font William 2420
Theodore
Bundaberg
HERVEY BAY
FRASER (GREAT SANDY) I.
Pialba
Maryborough
Gayndah
Gympie
Nambo
MORETON
Redcliffe
Brisbane
Ipswich
Southport
Mt. Roberts 4495
Murwillumbah
Lismore
Casino
Ballina
Tenterfield
Capfompeta 5100
Glen Innes
Grafton
NEW ENGLAND
Guyra
Coff's Harbour

DARLING DOWNS

Mt. Mowbullan 3611
Kingaroy
Yarraman
Toowoomba

SOUTH AUSTRALIA

NORTH FLINDERS RANGES
FLINDERS RANGES
NORTH MOUNT LOFTY RANGES
GAWLER RANGES
EYRE PEN.

Marree
Leigh Creek
Andamooka
Lake Torrens
Lake Frome
Lake Eyre 39 ft.
L. Gregory
L. Blanche
Lake Callabonna
Innamincka
Lake Macfarlane
Woomera
Pimba
Hawker
Quorn
Port Augusta
Wilmington
Iron Knob
Whyalla
Kimba
Peterborough
Gladstone
Port Pirie
Wallaroo
Moonta
Riverton
Port Wakefield
YORKE PENINSULA
Gawler
Adelaide
SPENCER GULF
GULF ST. VINCENT
Kingscote
KANGAROO
Victor Harbour
Encounter Bay
INVESTIGATOR STRAIT
THISTLE I.
Yorketown
Murray Bridge
Tailem Bend
Peebinga
Pinnaroo
Lake Alexandrina

MAIN BARRIER RANGE

White Cliffs
Wilcannia
Broken Hill
Menindee
L. Tandou
Ivanhoe
Balranald
Chowilla Res.
Wentworth
Mildura
Renmark
Morgan
Waikerie
Loxton
Morkalla
Red Cliffs
Robinvale
Kulwin
Ouyen
Swan Hill
Hopetoun
Yanac

NEW SOUTH WALES

Cobar
Nymagee
Tottenham
Narromine
Dubbo
Wellington
Mudgee
Nyngan
Brewarrina
Bourke
Walgett
Narrabri
Gwabegar
Coonamble
Gunnedah
Tamworth
WARRUMBUNGLE RANGE
Coonabarabran
Binnaway
Coolah
Merriwa
Muswellbrook
Mt. Kaputar 4999
Barraba
Armidale
Mt. Banda Banda 4144
Kempsey
Port Macquarie
Taree
LIVERPOOL RANGE
Barrington Tops 5200
Gloucester
SUGARLOAF PT.
Port Stephens
Maitland
Cessnock
Newcastle
The Round Mountain 5300
Guyra

MURRAY

RIVERINA REGION

Narran Lake
Narran
Namoi
Macquarie
Bogan
Lachlan
Murrumbidgee
Billabong

Roto
Hillston
Hay
Deniliquin
Griffith
West Wyalong
Lake Cargelligo
Forbes
Parkes
Orange
Bathurst
Lithgow
BLUE MTS.
Mt. Reeves 4470
Gosford
Broken Bay
SYDNEY
Botany Bay
Wollongong
Moss Vale
BEECROFT HEAD
Nowra
Goulburn
Young
Cootamundra
Crookwell
Temora
Coolamon
Narrandera
Wagga Wagga
Batlow
Canberra
AUSTL. CAP. TER.
Tumbarumba
Albury
Bimberi Pk. 6274
SNOWY MTS.
Cooma
Bega
Eden
CAPE HOWE
Mallacoota Inlet
Bateman's Bay
Bombala
Orbost

VICTORIA

Echuca
Cohuna
Kerang
Charlton
Shepparton
Benalla
Wangaratta
Bright
Mt. Bogong 6516
Mt. Cobbler 6025
Mansfield
Mt. Torbreck 4495
Seymour
Eildon Res.
Bendigo
Castlemaine
Maryborough
Ballarat
MELBOURNE
Dandenong
Mt. Baw Baw 5727
Bairnsdale
Sale
Moe
Traralgon
Yarram
Lakes Entrance
NINETY MILE BEACH
AUSTRALIAN ALPS
GIPPSLAND
Mt. Kosciuszko 7313
Corowa
Cerowa
Hume Res.
Ararat
Horsham
Gotoke
Warracknabeal
Hamilton
Casterton
Portland
Warrnambool
Colac
Martloke
Geelong
PORT PHILLIP BAY
Wonthaggi
PHILLIP I.
CAPE OTWAY
CAPE NELSON
Mount Gambier
Kingston
Naracoorte
Millicent
CAPE JAFFA
Rockland Res.
Glenelg
Corangamite
Keith

Kingston
Grassy
KING I.
WEST PT.
CAPE GRIM
HUNTER IS.
Smithton
Burnie
Ulverstone
Devonport
Mt. Ossa 5305
DeLoraine
Launceston
Scottsdale
EDDYSTONE PT.
St. Marys
FREYCINET PENINSULA
Queenstown
Strahan
Campbell Town
Bridgewater
New Norfolk
Hobart
CAPE SOREL
TASMAN PENINSULA
Legges Pk. 5160
FLINDERS I.
FURNEAUX GROUP
CAPE BARREN
Banks Strait

WILSON'S PROMONTORY
KENT GROUP
Corner Inlet

INDIAN OCEAN

B a s s   S t r a i t

T A S M A N   S E A

TASMANIA

CORAL SEA

SANDY CAPE

Relief

Meters	Feet
1525	5000
610	2000
305	1000
152.5	500
0	Sea Level 0
152.5	500 Below
1525	5000 Sea Level
3050	10 000

0 50 100 150 200 Miles
0 50 100 150 200 250 300 Kilometers

A-590298-76 5-40
COPYRIGHT BY
RAND McNALLY & COMPANY
MADE IN U.S.A.

Scale 1:8 000 000; one inch to 126 miles.
Lambert's Azimuthal, Equal Area Projection.
Elevations and depressions are given in feet.

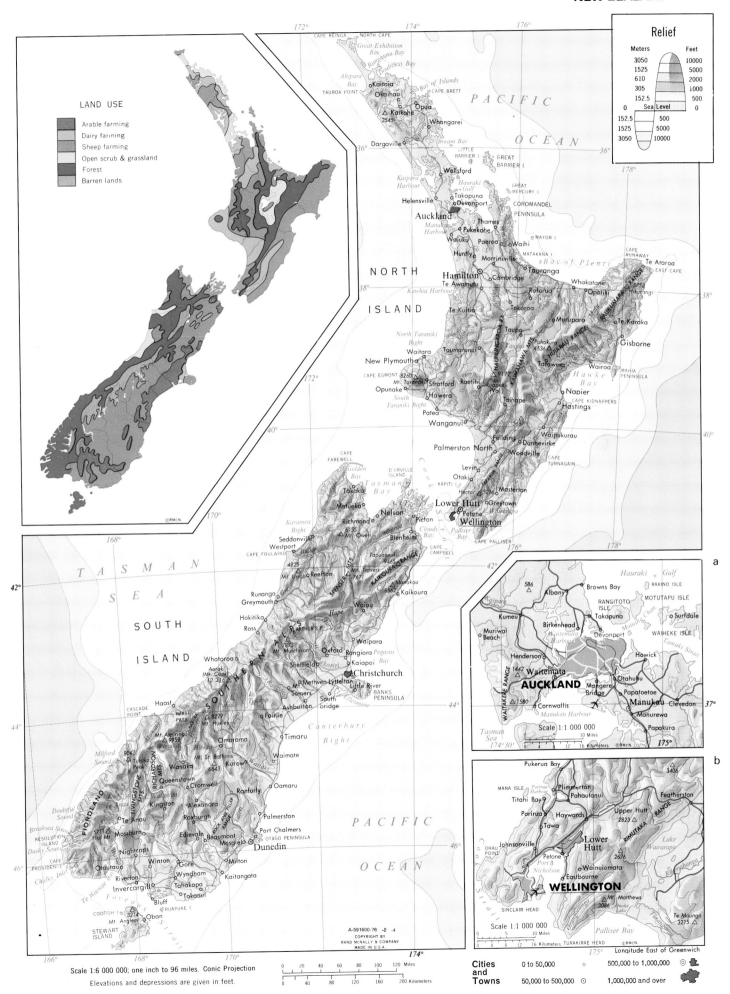

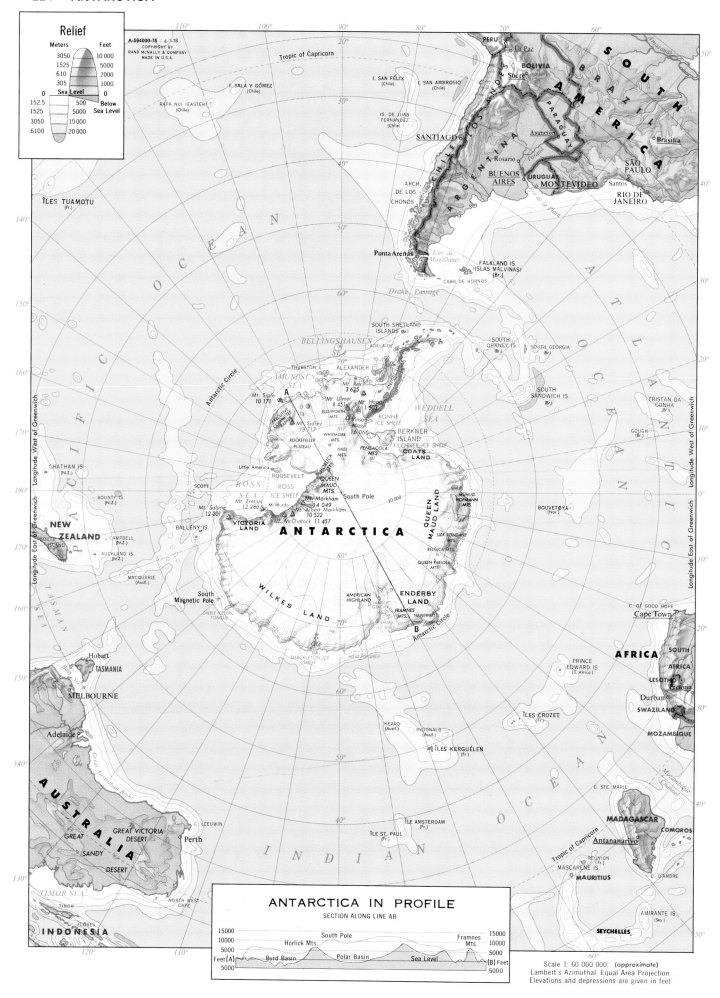

Relief

Meters		Feet
3050		10 000
1525		5000
610		2000
305		1000
	Sea Level	
0		0
152.5		500
		Below
1525		5000	Sea Level
3050		10 000
6100		20 000

A-594000-76   4-7-18
COPYRIGHT BY
RAND McNALLY & COMPANY
MADE IN U.S.A.

Tropic of Capricorn

SOUTH AMERICA

BRAZIL

PERU
La Paz
BOLIVIA
Sucre
PARAGUAY
Asunción
SANTIAGO
Rosario
BUENOS AIRES
URUGUAY
MONTEVIDEO
Santos
SÃO PAULO
RIO DE JANEIRO
Brasília

I. SALA Y GÓMEZ (Chile)
RAPA NUI (EASTER) (Chile)
I. SAN FÉLIX (Chile)
I. SAN AMBROSIO (Chile)
IS. DE JUAN FERNÁNDEZ (Chile)

ÍLES TUAMOTU (Fr.)

ARCH. DE LOS CHONOS

Punta Arenas
Estr. de Magallanes
FALKLAND IS. (ISLAS MALVINAS) (Br.)
CABO DE HORNOS
Drake Passage

PACIFIC OCEAN

ATLANTIC OCEAN

SOUTH SHETLAND ISLANDS (Br.)
Adelaide
SOUTH ORKNEY IS. (Br.)
SOUTH GEORGIA (Br.)

BELLINGSHAUSEN SEA
THURSTON I.
ALEXANDER
Mt. Rex 3 625
AMUNDSEN SEA
Mt. Siple 10 171
Mt. Ulmer 8 451
Mt. Hagg 1 503
ELLSWORTH MTS.
EXECUTIVE COMMITTEE RANGE
Mt. Sidley 13 717
Vinson Massif 16 066
WHITMORE MTS.
WEDDELL SEA
RONNE ICE SHELF
BERKNER ISLAND
FILCHNER ICE SHELF
COATS LAND
SOUTH SANDWICH IS. (Br.)
TRISTAN DA CUNHA (Br.)
GOUGH (Br.)

ROCKEFELLER PLATEAU
THIEL MTS.
PENSACOLA MTS.
Little America
ROOSEVELT I.
HORLICK MTS.
SCOTT
QUEEN MAUD MTS.
South Pole
10 000
QUEEN MAUD LAND
MÜHLIG HOFMANN MTS.
BOUVETØYA (Nor.)

CHATHAM IS. (N.Z.)
BOUNTY IS. (N.Z.)
NEW ZEALAND
CAMPBELL (N.Z.)
AUCKLAND IS. (N.Z.)
MACQUARIE (Austl.)

ROSS SEA
ROSS ICE SHELF
Mt. Erebus 12 280
McMurdo
Mt. Sabine 12 201
BALLENY IS.
VICTORIA LAND
Mt. Markham 4 049
Mt. Albert Markham 10 522
Mt. McClintock 11 457

ANTARCTICA

SØR RONDANE MTS.
BELGICA MTS.
QUEEN FABIOLA MTS.

South Magnetic Pole
WILKES LAND
DIBBLE ICEBERG TONGUE
AMERICAN HIGHLAND
LAMBERT GLACIER
AMERY ICE SHELF
ENDERBY LAND
FRAMNES MTS.
NAPIER MTS.

C. OF GOOD HOPE
Cape Town
AFRICA
SOUTH AFRICA
LESOTHO
Pretoria
Durban
SWAZILAND
MOZAMBIQUE

HOBART
TASMANIA
MELBOURNE
Adelaide

SHACKLETON ICE SHELF
WEST ICE SHELF

PRINCE EDWARD IS. (S. Africa)
ÍLES CROZET (Fr.)

AUSTRALIA
GREAT VICTORIA DESERT
GREAT SANDY DESERT
Perth
C. LEEUWIN

HEARD (Austl.)
McDONALD (Austl.)
ÍLES KERGUÉLEN (Fr.)

MADAGASCAR
COMOROS
Antananarivo

TASMAN SEA
TIMOR SEA
TIMOR
NORTH WEST CAPE
INDONESIA

INDIAN OCEAN

ÍLE AMSTERDAM (Fr.)
ÍLE ST. PAUL (Fr.)
Tropic of Capricorn
RÉUNION (Fr.)
MASCARENE IS.
MAURITIUS

C. STE. MARIE
MOZAMBIQUE CHANNEL
C. D'AMBRE
AMIRANTE IS. (Sey.)
SEYCHELLES

ANTARCTICA IN PROFILE
SECTION ALONG LINE AB

15000		South Pole			15000
10000	Horlick Mts.			Framnes Mts.	10000
5000					5000
Feet (A)	Byrd Basin	Polar Basin	Sea Level		(B) Feet
5000					5000

Scale 1: 60 000 000; (approximate)
Lambert's Azimuthal, Equal Area Projection
Elevations and depressions are given in feet

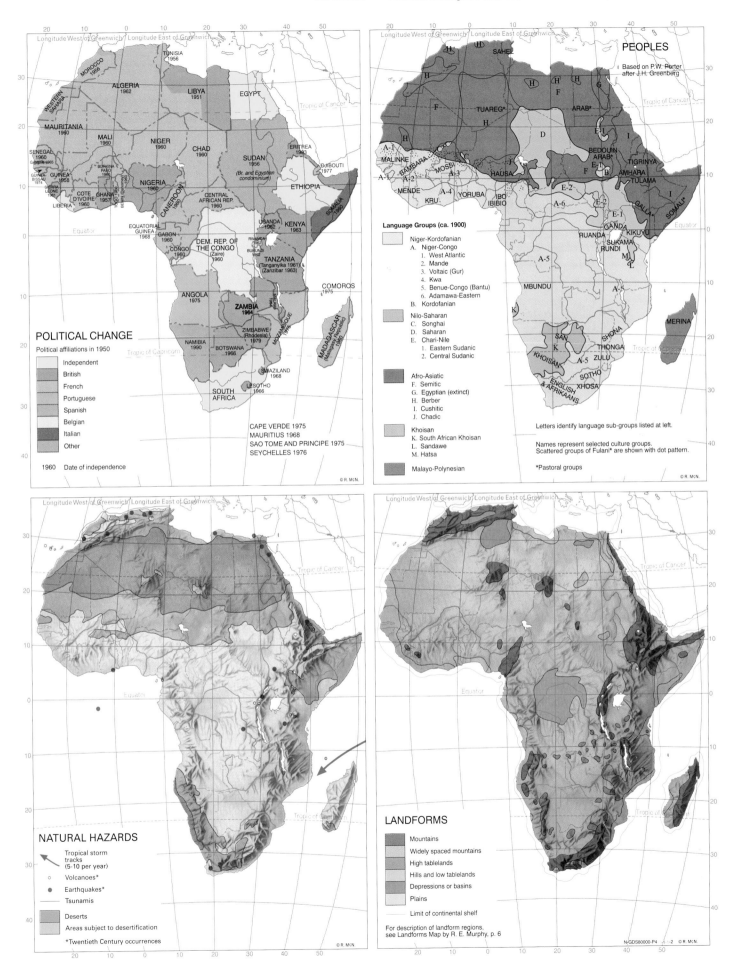

POLITICAL CHANGE

Political affiliations in 1950

- Independent
- British
- French
- Portuguese
- Spanish
- Belgian
- Italian
- Other

1960   Date of independence

CAPE VERDE 1975
MAURITIUS 1968
SAO TOME AND PRINCIPE 1975
SEYCHELLES 1976

© R. McN.

PEOPLES

Based on P.W. Porter
after J.H. Greenberg

Language Groups (ca. 1900)

Niger-Kordofanian
  A. Niger-Congo
    1. West Atlantic
    2. Mande
    3. Voltaic (Gur)
    4. Kwa
    5. Benue-Congo (Bantu)
    6. Adamawa-Eastern
  B. Kordofanian

Nilo-Saharan
  C. Songhai
  D. Saharan
  E. Chari-Nile
    1. Eastern Sudanic
    2. Central Sudanic

Afro-Asiatic
  F. Semitic
  G. Egyptian (extinct)
  H. Berber
  I. Cushitic
  J. Chadic

Khoisan
  K. South African Khoisan
  L. Sandawe
  M. Hatsa

Malayo-Polynesian

Letters identify language sub-groups listed at left.

Names represent selected culture groups.
Scattered groups of Fulani* are shown with dot pattern.

*Pastoral groups

© R. McN.

NATURAL HAZARDS

→ Tropical storm tracks (5-10 per year)
○ Volcanoes*
● Earthquakes*
—— Tsunamis
    Deserts
    Areas subject to desertification

*Twentieth Century occurrences

© R. McN.

LANDFORMS

- Mountains
- Widely spaced mountains
- High tablelands
- Hills and low tablelands
- Depressions or basins
- Plains

—— Limit of continental shelf

For description of landform regions,
see Landforms Map by R. E. Murphy, p. 6

N/GDS80000-P4 · 1-2 © R. McN.

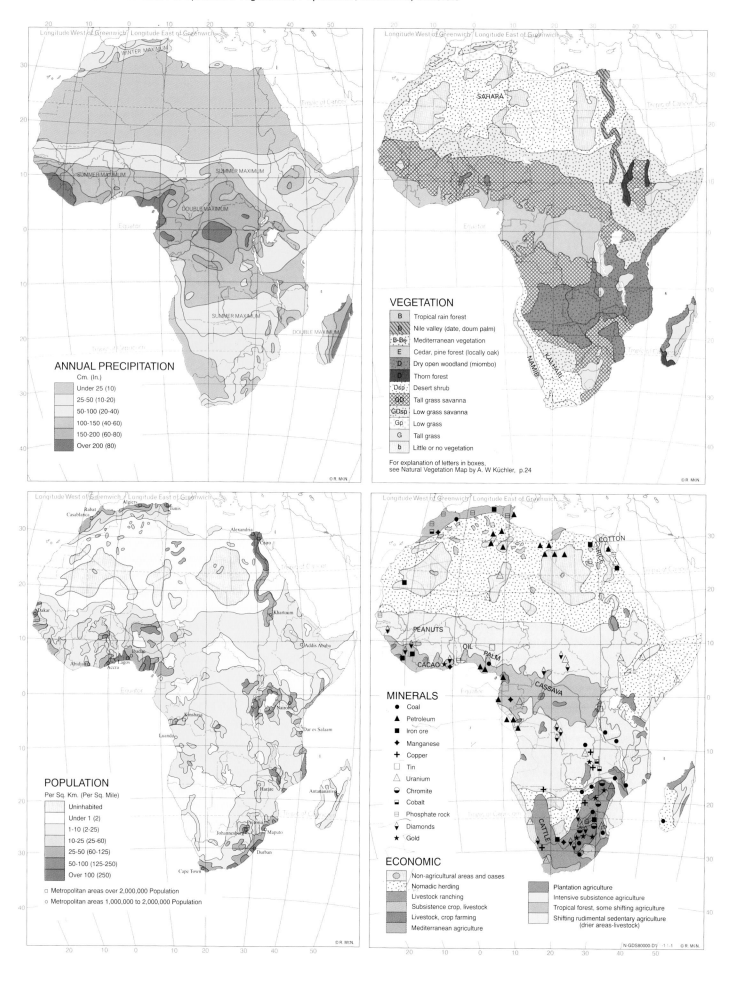

ANNUAL PRECIPITATION

Cm. (In.)

- Under 25 (10)
- 25-50 (10-20)
- 50-100 (20-40)
- 100-150 (40-60)
- 150-200 (60-80)
- Over 200 (80)

VEGETATION

B	Tropical rain forest
B	Nile valley (date, doum palm)
B-Bs	Mediterranean vegetation
E	Cedar, pine forest (locally oak)
D	Dry open woodland (miombo)
D	Thorn forest
Dsp	Desert shrub
GD	Tall grass savanna
GDsp	Low grass savanna
Gp	Low grass
G	Tall grass
b	Little or no vegetation

For explanation of letters in boxes,
see Natural Vegetation Map by A. W Küchler, p.24

POPULATION

Per Sq. Km. (Per Sq. Mile)

- Uninhabited
- Under 1 (2)
- 1-10 (2-25)
- 10-25 (25-60)
- 25-50 (60-125)
- 50-100 (125-250)
- Over 100 (250)

□ Metropolitan areas over 2,000,000 Population

○ Metropolitan areas 1,000,000 to 2,000,000 Population

MINERALS

- ● Coal
- ▲ Petroleum
- ■ Iron ore
- ◆ Manganese
- + Copper
- □ Tin
- △ Uranium
- ◓ Chromite
- ◒ Cobalt
- ▭ Phosphate rock
- ▼ Diamonds
- ★ Gold

ECONOMIC

- Non-agricultural areas and oases
- Nomadic herding
- Livestock ranching
- Subsistence crop, livestock
- Livestock, crop farming
- Mediterranean agriculture
- Plantation agriculture
- Intensive subsistence agriculture
- Tropical forest, some shifting agriculture
- Shifting rudimental sedentary agriculture (drier areas-livestock)

ATLANTIC OCEAN

MADRID
CORSICA
ROME
SARDINIA
İSTANBUL
BAKU
Black Sea
Caspian Sea

SICILY
Athens
CRETE
CYPRUS
TEHRAN

Algiers
Tunis
MALTA
Beirut
Baghdad
Casablanca
Tripoli
Banghāzi
SYRIAN DESERT
Tigris

ATLAS MOUNTAINS
Alexandria
CAIRO
Euphrates

CANARY ISLANDS
Mediterranean Sea
AN NAFŪD

GRAND ERG OCCIDENTAL
GRAND ERG ORIENTAL
LIBYAN DESERT
Riyadh
Mecca

El Aaíun
Tropic of Cancer
AHAGGAR
Lake Nasser
NUBIAN DESERT
Red Sea

S A H A R A
Tamenghest
ARABIAN DESERT
Nile

ADRAR DES IFÓGHAS
TIBESTI

Tombouctou
S U D A N
ENNEDI
Nile
Khartoum
Asmera

Dakar
Niger
Al-Fāshir
White Nile
DANAKIL
Aden
Gulf of Aden

Bamako
Lake Chad
N'Djamena
Blue Nile
Berbera

Kano
Addis Ababa

Freetown
Niger
Mountain Nile

Lagos
Yaoundé
Bangui
Uele
Mogadishu

Abidjan
Ubangi
Congo
Kisangani

Gulf of Guinea

Equator
Kasai
Lake Victoria
Nairobi

INDIAN OCEAN

Congo
Kinshasa
Lake Tanganyika
Dar es Salaam

Luanda

ATLANTIC OCEAN
Lubumbashi
Lake Nyasa
COMORO ISLANDS

Lusaka
Blantyre
Moçambique

Zambezi
Harare
Mozambique Channel

Antananarivo

NAMIB DESERT
MADAGASCAR

Windhoek
KALAHARI DESERT
Limpopo

Tropic of Capricorn

Orange
Johannesburg

Orange
Durban

INDIAN OCEAN

Cape Town

	Urban
	Cropland
	Cropland & Woodland
	Cropland & Grazing Land
	Grassland, Grazing Land
	Forest, Woodland
	Swamp, Marshland
	Shrub, Sparse Grass, Wasteland
	Barren Land
•	Oasis

A-580000-36   -2 3-12
COPYRIGHT BY
RAND McNALLY & COMPANY
MADE IN U.S.A.

Scale 1:36,000,000; one inch to 570 miles.   Lambert Azimuthal Equal-Area Projection

0 100 200   400   600   800 Miles
0 150 300   600   900   1200 Kilometers

Continued on pages 194-195

EUROPE

LONDON
AMSTERDAM
BERLIN
WARSAW
Leipzig
BRUSSELS
PRAGUE
KIEV
PARIS
MUNICH
VIENNA
BUDAPEST
LYON
MILAN
Genoa
Marseille
BARCELONA
ROME
NAPLES
MADRID
LISBON
ISTANBUL
İzmir
TEHRĀN
ATHENS
Damascus
(Dimashq)
Baghdad
Basra
ALEXANDRIA
(Al Iskandarīyah)
Jerusalem
CAIRO (Al Qāhirah)
Suez
Port Said

ATLANTIC OCEAN

MEDITERRANEAN SEA

BLACK SEA

CASPIAN SEA

ALGERIA
LIBYA
EGYPT
MOROCCO
TUNISIA
WESTERN SAHARA
MAURITANIA
MALI
NIGER
CHAD
SUDAN
SENEGAL
THE GAMBIA
GUINEA-BISSAU
GUINEA
SIERRA LEONE
LIBERIA
BURKINA FASO
COTE D'IVOIRE
GHANA
NIGERIA
BENIN
CAMEROON
CENTRAL AFRICAN REPUBLIC
ERITREA
DJIBOUTI
ETHIOPIA
SOMALIA
EQUATORIAL GUINEA
SAO TOME AND PRINCIPE
GABON
CONGO
DEM. REP. OF THE CONGO
UGANDA
RWANDA
BURUNDI
KENYA
TANZANIA
ANGOLA
ZAMBIA
MALAWI
COMOROS
MOZAMBIQUE
ZIMBABWE (RHODESIA)
NAMIBIA
BOTSWANA
MADAGASCAR
SOUTH AFRICA
LESOTHO
SWAZ.

ARABIAN PENINSULA

RED SEA

Mecca (Makkah)

ATLANTIC OCEAN

INDIAN OCEAN

Tropic of Cancer

Equator

Tropic of Capricorn

40,000 SQ MI AREA

0   300   600
Miles

Longitude West of Greenwich   Longitude East of Greenwich

0   200   400   600   800   1000 Miles
0   400   800   1200   1600 Kilometers

Scale 1:40 000 000; one inch to 630 miles. Lambert's Azimuthal, Equal Area Projection
Elevations and depressions are given in feet.

A-580000-26   -14-16-37
COPYRIGHT BY
RAND McNALLY & COMPANY
MADE IN U.S.A.

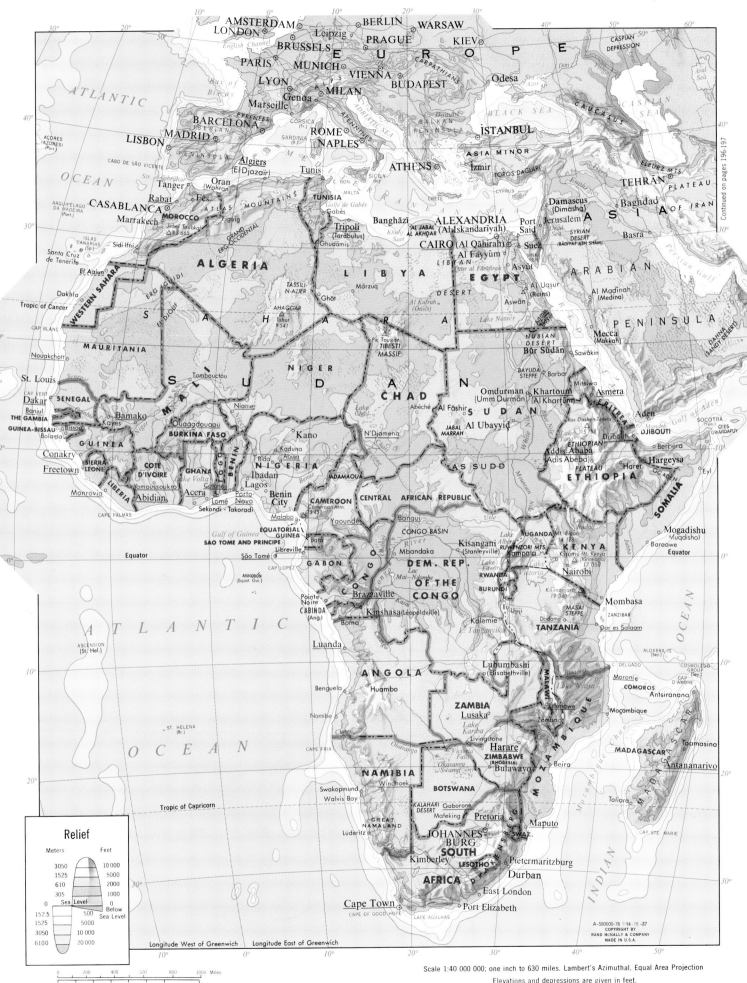

Continued on pages 196-197

Relief

Meters		Feet
3050		10 000
1525		5000
610		2000
305		1000
0	Sea Level	0
		Below
152.5		500
1525		5000
3050		10 000
6100		20 000

Longitude West of Greenwich   Longitude East of Greenwich

A-580000-76 R 14 -16 -37
COPYRIGHT BY
RAND McNALLY & COMPANY
MADE IN U.S.A.

0   200   400   600   800   1000 Miles

0   400   800   1200   1600 Kilometers

Scale 1:40 000 000; one inch to 630 miles. Lambert's Azimuthal, Equal Area Projection
Elevations and depressions are given in feet.

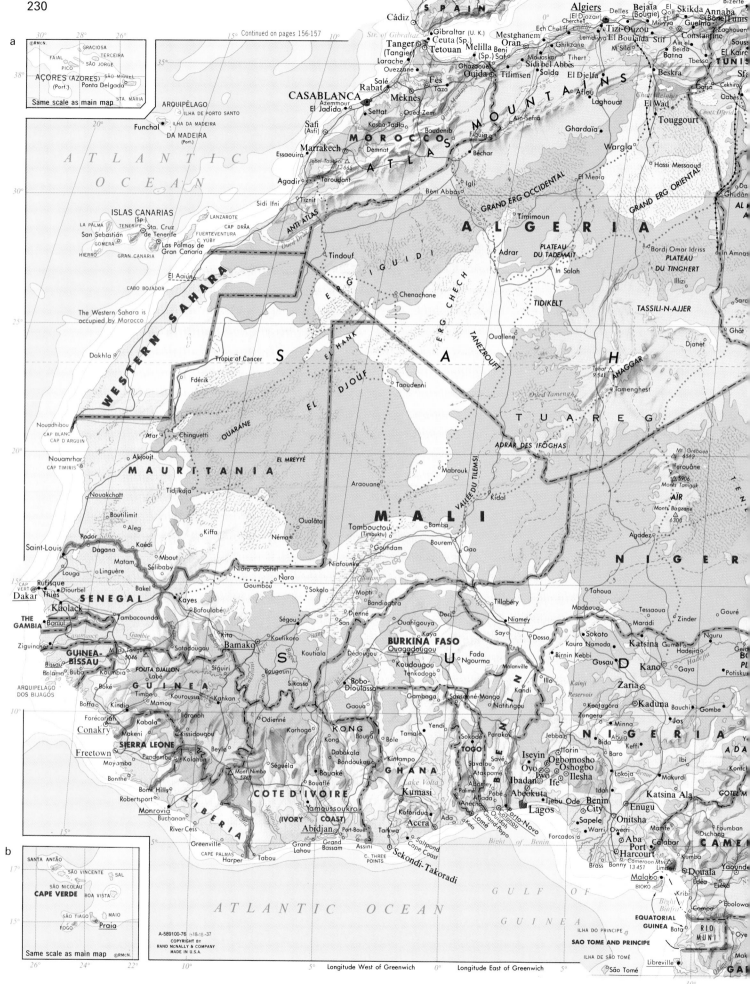

a

©RMCN.

GRACIOSA
FAIAL   TERCEIRA
PICO   SÃO JORGE
AÇORES (AZORES) SÃO MIGUEL
(Port.)   Ponta Delgada
STA. MARIA

Same scale as main map

Continued on pages 156-157

SPAIN

Cádiz

Str. of Gibraltar

Gibraltar (U. K.)
Ceuta (Sp.)
Tanger
(Tangier)
Larache

Tetouan
Melilla
(Sp.)

Algiers
(El Djazair)   Delles
Ech Cheliff   Cherchel
Mestghanem
Oran

Bejaia
(Bougie)   El
Skikda   Annaba
(Bône)
Constantine

Bizerte
Tunis

Ech Cheliff
Ghilizane

Lemdiyya El Boulaida Stif
Ain el   Ain el
M'Sila

Beskra

Zaghouan
El Kairc

TUNIS
Sf

Oujda
Tlemsen
Saïda

El Djelfa

Gafsa
Cehkira
Gabès

Fès
Taza

Salé
Rabat

Meknès

CASABLANCA
El Jadida
Azemmour
Settat

Safi
(Asfi)

Kasba-Tadla
Oued-Zem

Marrakech
Demnat

Essaouira

Boudenib

Béchar

Ghardaïa

Laghouat
El Wad

Touggourt

Hassi Messaoud

Da
Ghudan
AL
A

Agadir
Taroudant

Jebel Toubkal △
13665

Béni Abbas

Igli

Adrar

Ain-Sefra

Figuig

GRAND ERG OCCIDENTAL

Timimoun

El Menia

PLATEAU
DU TADEMAÏT

In Salah

TIDIKELT

Bordj Omar Idriss
PLATEAU
DU TINGHERT

Illizi

In Amnas

GRAND ERG ORIENTAL

MOROCCO

ATLAS MOUNTAINS

ALGERIA

Sidi Ifni

Tiznit

ANTI ATLAS

CAP DRÂA
C. YUBY

Oued Drâa

El Aaiún

CABO BOJADOR

ISLAS CANARIAS
(Sp.)
LANZAROTE
LA PALMA   TENERIFE
Sta. Cruz   FUERTEVENTURA
de Tenerife
San Sebastián
GOMERA   GRAN CANARIA
HIERRO   Las Palmas de
Gran Canaria

WESTERN SAHARA

The Western Sahara is
occupied by Morocco

Tropic of Cancer

Dakhla

Fdérik

Tindouf

ERG IGUIDI

Chenachane

ERG CHECH

TANEZROUFT

Ouallene

TIDIKELT

TASSILI-N-AJJER

Ghât

Djanet

S   A   H

Sara

ARQUIPÉLAGO
ILHA DE PORTO SANTO
DA MADEIRA
(Port.)

Funchal

Chinguetti

OUARÂNE

El Mreyyé

Atar

Taoudenni

EL HANK

EL DJOUF

Araouane

Mabrouk

Tamenghest

AHAGGAR
Tahat
9541 △

Oued Tamengha

ADRAR DES IFOGHAS

TUAREG

Mt Grébour
4562 △

Iferouâne

5906 △
Monts Tamgak

Nouadhibou
CAP BLANC
CAP D'ARGUIN

Nouamrhar
CAP TIMIRIS

Akjoujt

MAURITANIA

Nouakchott

Boutilimit

Aleg

Tidjikdja

Kiffa

Néma

Oualâta

Kidal

VALLÉE DU TILEMSI

AÏR

Monts Bagzane
6300 △

Agadez

M   A   L   I

Tombouctou
(Timbuktu)

Bamba

Goundam
Bourem

Gao

N   I   G   E   R

Saint-Louis

Rosso
Dagana

Kaédi
Mbout

Matam
Sélibaby

Louga

Linguère

Bakel

Nioro du Sahel

Nara

Goumbou

Sokolo

Niafunké

Tahoua

Madaoua

Tessaoua
Zinder

Gouré

CAP
VERT
Dakar
Thies

Rufisque
Diourbel

SENEGAL

Kayes

Bafoulabé

Kita

Koulikoro

Ségou

Djenné

San

Mopti
Bandiagara

Dori

Tillabéry

Niamey

Say

Dosso

Sokoto

Kaura Namoda

Maradi

Katsina   Gumel

Hadejia

Nguru

The Gambia
Banjul

Kaolack
Tambacounda

Ziguinchor
Bissau
GUINEA-
BISSAU
Bolama Buba

ARQUIPÉLAGO
DOS BIJAGÓS

Satadougou

Mt Loma Tongoe
5046 △

FOUTA DJALLON

Labé

Boké

Timbo

Mamou

Koubia

Siguiri

Bougouni

Sikasso

Dédougou

Koutiala

BURKINA FASO
Ouagadougou
Koudougou

Kaya

Fada
N'Gourma

Malanville

Kandi

Illo

Birnin Kebbi

Gusau

Kontagora
Zungeru

SUD

Gambaga
Sansanné-Mango
Natitingou

Kainji
Reservoir

Gaya

Kano

Zaria

Kaduna

Bauchi

Gombe

Potiskum

BO
PL

Geid

Conakry

Freetown
SIERRA LEONE

Kindia
Forécariah
Kabala
Mpkeni

Boffa

Kissidougou
Beyla

GUINEA
Kouroussa
Kankan

Faranah

Odienné

Korhogo

KONG

Bobo-
Dioulasso

Gaoua

Bole

Tenkodogo

Yendi

Tamale

Bouna

Sokodé

Parakou

Jebba
Bida
Baro

Ilorin

Iseyin
Oyo

Jos

Minna

Keffi

Abuja

N   I   G   E   R   I   A

Katsina Ala

GOTEL M

Moyamba
Pandembu
Kolahun

Bonthe

Mont Nimba
5760 △

Séguéla

Bouaké

Bouafle

Dabakala
Bondoukou

Kintampo

Bori Hills

Robertsport

Monrovia

COTE D'IVOIRE
(IVORY   COAST)

Yamoussoukro

Abidjan
Port-Bouet

Tabou

Greenville

CAPE PALMAS
Harper

Grand
Lahou

Grand
Bassam

Assini

C. THREE
POINTS

Sekondi-Takoradi

GHANA

Kumasi

Koforidua

Accra

Ada

Saltpond
Cape Coast

Tarkwa

Keta

Atakpame
Savalou

Palime

Anecho
Lomé

Grand-Popo

Ketou

Abomey

TOGO

Pobé
Porto-Novo
Ouidah

Savé

Ogbomosho
Oshogbo
Ilesha

Ibadan
Iwo
Ife
Abeokuta

Ijebu Ode

Lagos

Benin
City

Sapele

Owerri

Warri

Forcados

Lokoja

Idah

Makurdi

Enugu

Onitsha

Aba
Port
Harcourt

Brass
Bonny

Kumba
Douala

Calabar

Yagua

CAME

Ikom
Mamfe

Dschang

Foumban

ADA
Kontch

Cameroon Mtn.
13451 △

Malabo
BIOKO

EQUATORIAL
GUINEA

Bata

RIO
MUNI

Oye

Mbini

GA

Ebolowa

Campo

Kribi

Edea

Eséka

Yaoundé

LIBERIA

Buchanan

River Cess

GULF   OF
GUINEA

ATLANTIC   OCEAN

SÃO TOMÉ AND PRINCIPE
ILHA DO PRINCIPE
SÃO TOMÉ
ILHA DE SÃO TOMÉ
São Tomé

Libreville

GA

b

SANTA ANTÃO
SÃO VICENTE
SÃO NICOLAU
CAPE VERDE
SÃO TIAGO
FOGO

SAL
BOA VISTA

MAIO

Praia

Same scale as main map

©RMCN.

A-589100-76   (-18-18)-37
COPYRIGHT BY
RAND McNALLY & COMPANY
MADE IN U.S.A.

Longitude West of Greenwich
Longitude East of Greenwich

Scale 1:16 000 000; one inch to 250 miles. Sinusoidal Projection
Elevations and depressions are given in feet

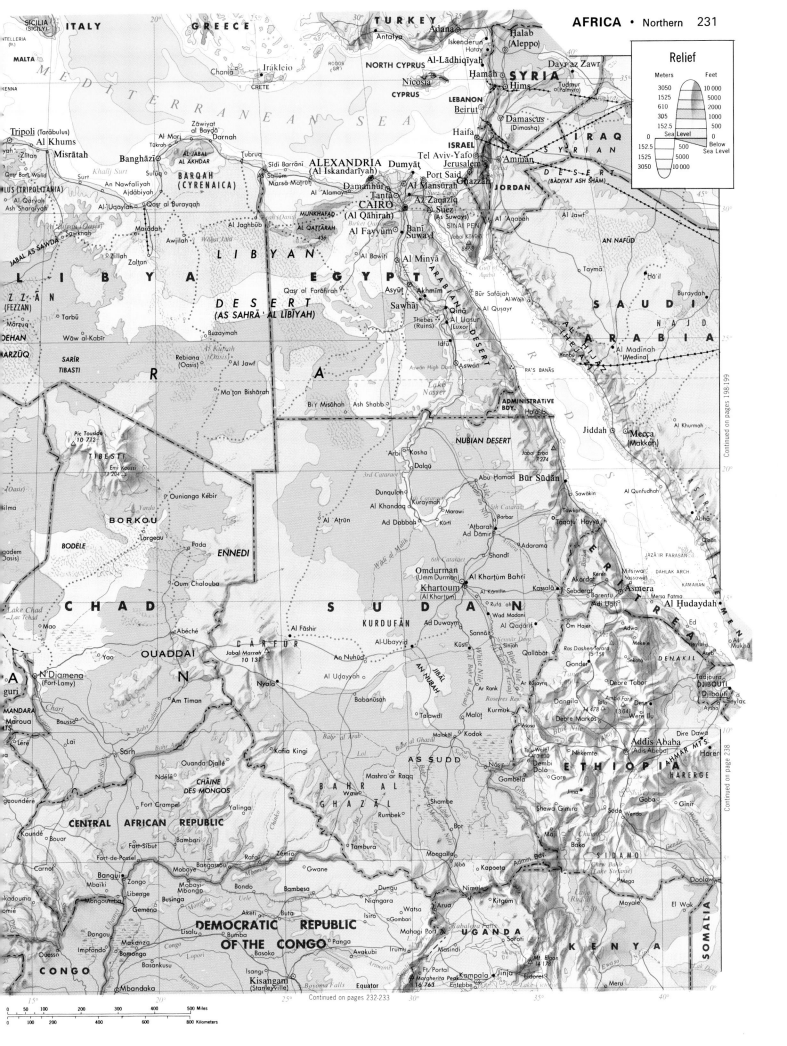

b

SOMALIA

Mt. Kenya
(Kenya)
17 058
Ft. Hall

Nairobi

Kismaayo
Buur Gaabo

Witu
Lamu

Malindi
Takaungu

Mombasa

Vanga

PEMBA ISLAND

ZANZIBAR
Zanzibar

Bagamoyo
Dar es Salaam

Morogoro
Kisaki
Utete

Kilwa Kivinje

Lindi

Mikindani
Masasi

Mocímboa
da Praia
Ibo

Pemba

Lúrio
Memba
Nacala

Moçambique

Angoche
ILHA ANGOCHE

Pebane

I N D I A N

MAFIA

ALDABRA IS
(Sey.)
COSMOLEDO GROUP
(Sey.)

ÎLES GLORIEUSES
(Fr.)

COMOROS
NJAZIDJA   Moroni
MWALI   NZWANI
Dzaoudzi
MAYOTTE
(Fr.)
NOSY BE

CAP D'AMBRE
Antsiranana

Iharana
Maromokotro
2876

Equator

40°   45°   50°

5°

10°

MOZAMBIQUE CHANNEL

CAP SAINT-
ANDRÉ

ÎLE JUAN DE NOVA
(Fr.)

NOSY BARREN

BASSAS DA INDIA
(Fr.)

EUROPA
(Fr.)

Mahajanga
Mandritsara

Maroantsetra

Helodrano
Antongila
NOSY BORAHA

Fenoarivo
Atsinanana

M A D A G A S C A R

m'atond
'azaka

Toamasina

Antananarivo
Tsiafajavona
8671
Vatomandry

Morondava

Antsirabe
Ambositra

Mananjara

Maintirano

Fianarantsoa

Morombe

Ivohibé
Manakara

Farafangana

Toliara

Trafonamby
4417
Faradofay

Betroka

Mahaly

CAP STE. MARIE

c

28°30'

@RMCN.
Wolhuterskop

Jacksonstuin

MAGALIESBERG
Skeerpoort   Hartbeespoort   Swartspruit

4549

Foothills

WITWATERSBERG

Tartton

Krugersdorp

JOHANNESBURG

Randfontein
5725

Roodepoort

Spoortdam
Magalies

Kosmos

Pretoria
North

Hennopsrivier

Olievenhoutpoort

4602

Halfway
House

Modderfontein

Discovery

Florida
Maraisburg

Orlando
Pimville

Turffontein

Pretoria   Cullinan

Silverton
4426   Rayton

Voortrekkerhoogte
Valhalla

Irene

Sesmyl
Rietvlei

Kaalfontein

Alexandra
Primrose

Rosetten-
ville
Alberton

Kempton Park

Putfontein

Boksburg   Benoni

Germiston

Brakpan

Springs

W I T W A T E R S R A N D

Scale 1:1 000 000
0   10 Miles
0 4 8 12 16 Kilometers

Bapsfontein

26°

ORANGE FREE STATE

Arlington

Paul Roux
Senekal

Bethlehem

Fouriesburg

Ficksburg
Clocolan

Butha Buthe
Leribe

Teyateyaneng

Machache
9464

Roma

Kestell

ROYAL NATAL
NAT'L. PK.
Clarens

MALOTI MTS.
10 822
Mt. aux
Sources

Pitseng

Mohale's
Hoek

Zastron

Quthing

Harrismith

Bergville
Winterton
Cathedral Pk.
9856

Cathkin Pk.
10438

Mokhotlong

Thabana
Ntlenyana
11424

L E S O T H O

Qacha's Nek
8820

Dannhauser
Glencoe

Wasbank

Ladysmith

Colenso

Estcourt

Mooirivier

N A T A L

Mt. Gilboa
5903

Impendle

Underberg

Bulwer

8326

Swartberg
7619

Franklin   Matatiele

10159

The Twins

Orange

Dundee

Tugela

Nqutu

Dalton

New
Hanover

Wartburg

Richmond

Donnybrook

Creighton

Mid Illovo

Ntshoni
5851

Pietermaritzburg
Camper-
down

Verulam
Pinetown
Durban
Isipingo

Umkomaas

E A S T E R N

CAP E

Cedarville
Mt. Currie
7297

Kokstad

Mount
Fletcher

Herschel
Witberg
2853
Lady Grey

Ben Macdhui
9846

Rhodes

Mount
Frere

Mount Ayliff

Bizana

Harding

Tabankulu

Flagstaff

Umzinto

Scottburgh

Park Rynie

Sezela

Umtentweni

Port Shepstone

Uvongo Beach
Margate

Port Edward

Lady Frere

Barkly East

Maclear

Qumbu

Tsolo

Libode

Ngqeleni

Port St. Johns

RAME HEAD

Jamestown
8430

Rossouw

Ugie
Elliot

Molteno
STORMBERG
Dordrecht

Indwe
Cala

Sterkstroom

Engcobo

Umtata

Mqanduli

S O U T H

A F R I C A

Waverly

Tarkastad

Cradock

Tylden

Cathcart

Seymour
Stutterheim

Whittlesea

WINTERBERGE
7778

BANKBERG
6606

Pearston

Somerset East
Bedford

Adelaide
Keiskammahoek
Fort
Beaufort
Alice

Kirkwood
Addo

Alexandria

Uitenhage

Port Elizabeth
KAAP RECIFE

SAINT CROIX
ISLAND

BIRD ISLAND

SUURBERGE
Alicedale

Riebeek-Oos

Grahamstown

Salem

Bathurst

Port Alfred (Kowie)

Peddie

Hamburg

Kidd's Beach

Gonubie
East London
Breidbach
Berlin
Bisho
King William's
Town

Kamga
Kei Mouth
Morgan's Bay
Macleantown

Kentani

Butterworth

Willowvale

Ngamakwe

Cofimvaba
Tsomo
Idutywa

Elliotdale

Queenstown

Longitude East of Greenwich

Scale 1:4 000 000
0 10 20 30 40 Miles
0 10 20 30 40 50 60 Kilometers

I N D I A N

O C E A N

5°

10°

15°

20°

25°

30°

30°

32°

34°

35°

40°   45°   26°   28°   30°

Relief

Meters		Feet
3050		10 000
1525		5000
610		2000
305		1000
152.5		500
Sea Level		0
152.5		500
1525		5000
3050		10 000

PUNTILLA NEGRA
CABO BARBAS

WESTERN SAHARA

Fdérik
Kediet Ijill

Tichia

Nouadhibou

CAP BLANC

ÎLE TIDRA

CAP TIMIRIS
Nouamrhar

Sebkha de N'Dhamcha

Nouakchott

MAKTEÏR

OUARANE

EL DJOUF

Taoudenni

SAHARA

TANEZROUFT
N'AHNE

Bordj le Prieur

MAURITANIA

Atar

ADÂFER EL ABIOD

EL MREYYE

Araouane

AZAOUAD

Timétrine Monts

Aguelhok

Akjoujt

TRARZA

Tidjikdja

AOUKÂR

Ayoun el Atrous

Néma

AKLÉ ÂOUÂNA

IRIGUI

MALI

VALLÉE DU TILEMSI

Moudjéria

Aleg

Anefis i-n-Darane

Rosso

Kiffa

Lac Faguibine

Niger

Taoussa

Dagana
Kaédi
Matam

Tombouctou
(Timbuktu)

Gao

Ansongo

Saint-Louis
Louga
Linguère
Ranérou

Balé

Nioro du Sahel

Goumbou
Kogoni

Lac Débo

Macina

Hombori

Douentza

Léré

CAP VERT Thiès
Rufisque
Dakar
Diourbel
Touba

SENEGAL

FERLO

Naye
Kayes

Diéma

Didiéni

Mopti

Koro

Aribinda

Djiba

Dani

Kaolack
Sokona

Tambacounda

Bafoulabé

PARC NATIONAL DE LA BOUCLE DU BAOULE

Banamba
Ségou

San

Ouahigouya

Kaya

Téra

THE GAMBIA
Banjul (Bathurst)

Médina Gonasse
PARC NATIONAL DU NIOKOLO KOBA

Goumbati
1 368

Kita

Koulikoro

Bla

Djibasso

Dédougou

Tougan

Nyou

BURKINA   FASO

Ouagadougou

Pada Ngo

Bignona
Kolda

Koundara

Satadougou

Bamako

Sido

Zangasso

Volta Noire

Kaudougou

Ouarkoye

Boromo

Toécé

Tenkodogo

Madiori

CAP ROXO
Ziguinchor

Mansaba

Massif Du Tamgué 5 046

Sikasso

Bobo Dioulasso

Banfora

Houndé

Lawra

Léo

Pô

Bawku

PARC NAT.

Dapango
Sansanné-Mango

GUINEA-BISSAU

Bissau

Saio
João

Danea

Tombadonkéa

Labé
Dinguiraye

Siguiri

Badogo

Koualé

Tingréla

Niélé

Lokosse

Wa

Walewole

Gushiago

Natitingou

ARQUIPÉLAGO DOS BIJAGÓS

Eticoga

Kabot

Télimélé

Dabola

Kankan

Boundiali

Korhogo

Bouna

Bole

White Volta

Tamale

Niamtougou

Yendi

Bassar

GUINEA

Mamou

Farana

Odienné

PARK NATIONAL DE BOUNA

Kintampo

FORÊT CLASSÉE DU FAZAO

Blitta

Fria

Kindia

Boffa

Kissidougou

Kérouané
Pic De Tio 4 934

Niakaramandougou

Bouaké

Wenchi

Sunyani

GHANA

Mampong

Ejura

Lake Volta

Hohoe

Palimé

TOGO

Conakry

Forécariah

Binliouni Tingi 6 080

Dankanbiriwa

Beyla

Séguéla

Katiola

Bondoukou

Ouellé

Techiman

Agogo

Atakpamé

SIERRA
Makeni
LEONE

Kunsar

Koindu
Vaynoma

Toubo

COTE D'IVOIRE

Bouaflé

Abengourou

Bibiani

Nkawkaw

Akwatia

Begoro

Lomé

Freetown

Moyamba

Bo

Kenema

Pendembu

Nzérékoré
Kamou

MT. NIMBA NAT. PARK

Man

Danané

(IVORY COAST)

Mount Kahoué 3 658

Daloa

Dimbokro

Adzopé

Obuasi

Kumasi

Dunkwa

Oda

Nyakrom

Koforidua
Nsawam

Tema

SAIN

Bonthe

SHERBRO ISLAND

TURNERS PENINSULA

Gbarnga

Samaguélla

Gbanga

Guiglo

Duékoué

Bouaflé

Yamoussoukro

Gagnoa

Agboville

Prested

Tarkwa

Aboso

Winneba

Accra

CAPE MOUNT
Robertsport

Brewerville

Monrovia

LIBERIA

Buchanan

Tchien

Duabo

Divo

Abidjan

Grand-Bassam

Esiama

Cape Coast

Sekondi-Takoradi

Greenville

Sassandra

Mont Niénokoué 2 044

Lagune Tadio

Lagune Ébrié

CAPE THREE POINTS

Harper

CAPE PALMAS

Tabou

GULF OF

ATLANTIC   OCEAN

Relief

Meters	Feet
3050	10 000
1525	5000
610	2000
305	1000
152.5	500
0 Sea Level	0
152.5	500
1525	5000
3050	10 000

Scale 1:10,000,000; one inch to 160 miles. Lambert Azimuthal Equal Area Projection
Elevations and depressions are given in feet.

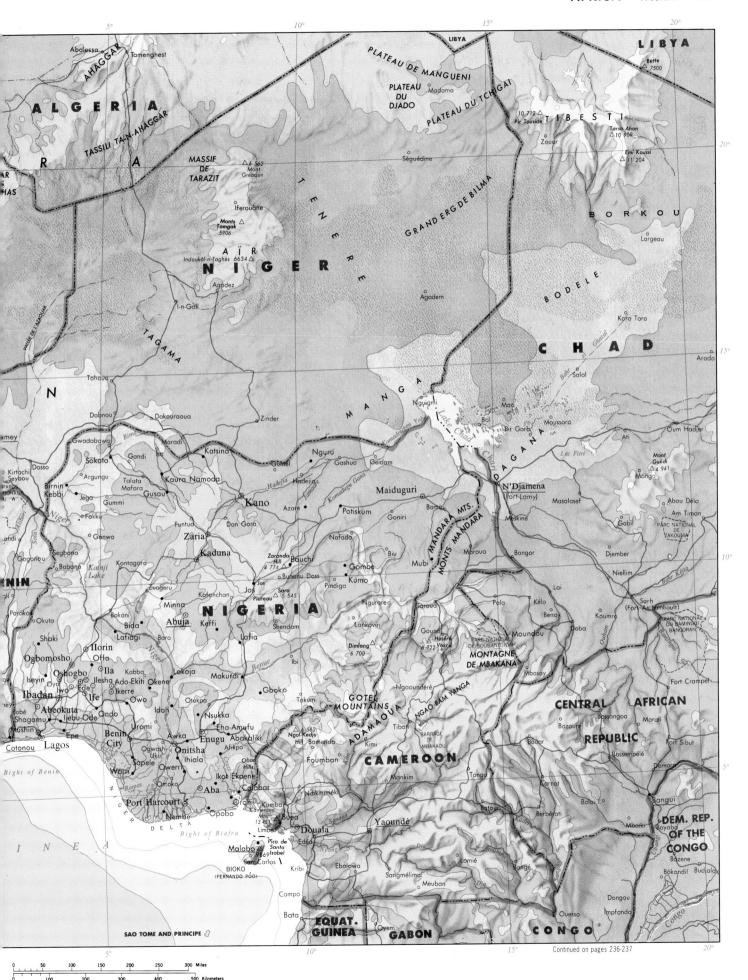

ALGERIA

AHAGGAR

Abalessa   Tamenghest

TASSILI TA-N-AHAGGAR

MASSIF
DE
TARAZIT

△ 6 562
Mont
Grébóun

Iferouàne

Monts
Tamgak △
5906

AïR

Indoukôl-n-Taghès 6634 △

NIGER

Agadez

I-n-Gall

TAGAMA

TENERE

PLATEAU DE MANGUENI

PLATEAU
DU
DJADO

PLATEAU DU TCHIGAI

LIBYA

LIBYA

Madama

Séguédine

TIBESTI

10 712 △
Pic Tousidé

Bette
△ 7500

Tarso Ahon
△ 10 909

Emi Koussi
△ 11 204

Zouar

BORKOU

Largeau

GRAND ERG DE BILMA

BODELE

Agadem

Koro Toro

CHAD

Arada

VALLEE DE L'AZAOUAK

N

Tahoua

Dabnou   Dakouraoua

Zinder

Rima

Gwadabawa

Sokoto   Gandi

Argungu   Maradi

Talata   Kaura Namoda
Mafara

Gusau

Katsina

Gúmel

Nguru

Gashua   Geidam

MANGA

Komadougou Yobé

Nguigmi

Lake Chad

Bir Gara

Mao

Bol

Bahr   Salal

N'Djamena
(Fort-Lamy)

DAGANA

Lac Fitri

Masalasef

Ati

Oum Hadjer

Mont
Guédi
△ 4 941

Mongo

Abou Deïa

Am Timan

Gabil

PARC NATIONAL
DE
ZAKOUMA

mey

Kirtachi
Seybou

Dosso

PARC
NATIO-
NAL
"W"

Birnin
Kebbi

Jega

Gummi

Fokku

G<u>anwo</u>

Funtua

Ganwo

Azare

Kano

Dan Gora

Hadejia   Hadejia

Hadejia

Tomas

Potiskum

Goniri

Maiduguri

Bama

Geidam

MANDARA MTS.

MONTS MANDARA

Maroua

Meskine

Bongor

Kélo

Lai

Niellim

Bahr Kéta

Sarh
(Fort-Archambault)

PARC NATIONAL
DU BAMINGUI
BANGORAN

Zaria

Kaduna

Zaranda
Hill
4 774 △

Bauchi

Jos

Jos
Plateau △ 5 545

Bununu Dass

Pindiga

Gombe

Kumo

Nafada

Biu

Mubi

Garoua

Pala

Benoy

Doba

Koumra

NIGERIA

Kontagora

Zungeru

Kafanchan

Minna

Bokani

Okuta

Bida

Lafiagi

Baro

Abuja

Keffi

Lafia

Shendam

Ngurore

Lankoviri

Dimlang
6 700 △

Hosère
△ 722 Vokré

Goundi

Moundou

MONTAGNE
DE MBAKANA

Mbaya

Bozoum

Bossangoa

Marali

Fort Sibut

Bossembélé

CENTRAL   AFRICAN

REPUBLIC

Ogbomosho

Ilorin

Offa

Ila

Kabba   Okene

Lokoja

Makurdi

Ibi

Benue

Gboko

Takum

GOTEL
MOUNTAINS

ADAMAOUA

Tibati

BARRAGE
DE
MBAKAOU

Bouar

Carnot

Baîbokoum

Berbérati

Bania

Batouri

Mbaïki

Damara

Bangui

DEM. REP.
OF THE
CONGO

Iseyin

Iwo

Ede

Oshogbo

Ilesha

Ife

Ado-Ekiti

Ikerre

Owo

Idah

Otukpa

Nsukka

Eha-Amufu

Enugu

Abakaliki

Afikpo

Ngol
Kedju
Hill △ 5 562

Bamenda

Foumban

Kimi

Mankim

Tongo

Bazene

Bókondil   Budala

Ibadan

Abeokuta

Ijebu-Ode

Ondo

Uromi

Awka

Onitsha

Ihiala

Oban
Hills

Ndikinimék

CAMEROON

NGAO BAM YANGA

Ngaoundéré

Bokondil

Bobé

Shagamu

Mushin

Epe

Benin
City

Ogwashi-
Uku

Sapele

Warri

Owerri

Aba

Calabar

Oron

Kumba

Douala

Yaoundé

Bé

Cotonou

Lagos

Bight of Benin

Port Harcourt

Nembe

DELTA

Opobo

Ikot Ekpene

Cameroon
Mtn.
13 451

Buea

Limbe

Edéa

Eséka

Nyong

Sanaga

Ebolowa

Sangmélima

Lomié

Dja

Meuban

Dja

Bangé

Dongou

Impfondo

Congo

GUINEA

BIOKO
(FERNANDO PÓO)

Malabo

Pico de
Santa
Isabel
△ 9869

San Carlos

Kribi

Campo

Bata

SAO TOME AND PRINCIPE

EQUAT.
GUINEA

Oyem

GABON

Mbalmayo

Ouesso

CONGO

Continued on pages 236-237

0   50   100   150   200   250   300 Miles

0   100   200   300   400   500 Kilometers

Continued on pages 234-235

NIGERIA
Opobo
Douala
Bight of Biafra
Malabo
San Carlos
BIOKO
(FERNANDO PÓO)
EQUATORIAL GUINEA
Buea
Kribi
Campo
Bata
Acalayong
SAO TOME AND PRINCIPE
PRÍNCIPE
CABO SAN JUAN
ISLA DE CORISCO
São Tomé
SÃO TOMÉ
MONTS DE CRISTAL
Libreville
Kango
CAP LOPEZ
Port-Gentil
Omboué
Petit Loango
Tchibanga
Mayumba
Madingo
Pointe-Noire
CABINDA (Ang.)
Cabinda
PONTA DO PADRÃO
Soyo
N'zeto
Ambriz

CAMEROON
Yaoundé
Ebolowa
Sangmélima
Nyong
Eden
Yokadouma
Doumé
Batauri
Meuban
Kom
Moloundou
Souanké
Djoua
Ouesso
Mekambo
Lebango
Makokou
Bifoum
Booué
GABON
Koula-Moutou
St. François de Boundji
Franceville
Mbinda
Mossendjo
Sibiti
Madingou
Kindamba
Brazzaville
Loubomo
Tshela
Matadi
Boma
Nóqui
SERRA DO CONGO
M'banza Congo
Quimbele
Damba

CENTRAL AFRICAN REPUBLIC
Fort de Possel
Boali
Bangui
Mbaiki
Mongoumba
Bozene
Dongou
Impfondo
Mbandaka (Coquilhatville)
Bikoro
Lac Tumba
CONGO
Owando
Gamboma
Djambala
Bandundu
Kinshasa (Léopoldville)
Kisantu
Mbanza-Ngungu
Popokabaka
Kimvula
Masi-Manimba
Kikwit
Kitenda
Kahemba
Kibenga

Kongbo
Bangassou
Bosobolo
Gemena
Budjala
Lisala
Bumba
Basoko
Isangi
Kisanga (Stanleyville)
Simba
Lifanga
Boende
DEMOCRATIC REP. OF THE CONGO (ZAIRE)
Lokolama
Dekese
Ilebo (Port-Francqui)
Domiongo
Kananga (Luluabourg)
Tshikapa
Djokupunda
Demba
Kilembe
Bulunga
Chitata
Marimba
Quimbonge
Caluango
Kapanga
KATANGA
Kangowa
Malanga
Luao
Lucano
Calunda

ATLANTIC OCEAN
Luanda
PONTA DAS PALMEIRINHAS
PARQUE NACIONAL DE QUICAMA
Caxito
Catete
N'dalatando
Dondo
Malanje
Cacóla
Cambundi-Catembo
CABO DAS TRÊS PONTAS
Porto Amboim
Gabela
Sumbe
Lobito
Benguela
SERRA CAMBONDA
Covelo
Waku Kundu
Calucinga
Cuvo
Wama
ANGOLA
Quela
Mussende
Saútar
Coemba
Cangamba
PARQUE NACIONAL DA CAMEIA
Calunda
Curunga
KASHIJI PLAIN
Chitokoloki
LIUWA PLAIN
Mussuma
BAROTSE PLAIN
Mongu
SILOANA PLAINS
Caiundo
Cuando
Mavinga
Ninda

Huambo (Nova Lisboa)
Kuito
Chitembo
Chá Pungana
Lungue-Bungo
CABO DE SANTA MARTA
SERRA DA NEVE
Bentiaba
Caconda
Caluquembe
Cacula
Folgates
PARQUE NACIONAL DO BIKUAR
Cassinga
NAMIBE
Lubango
Chiange
Namibe
Chibemba
PONTA ALBINA
Tombua
PONTA DA MARCA
Baía dos Tigres
PARQUE NACIONAL DO IONA
Foz do Cunene
Oncocua
Cuamato
Melunga
Ruacana Falls
Cuangar
Sambusu
NAMIBIA
Shakawe
CAPRIVI STRIP
BOTS.

Relief
Meters	Feet
3050	10 000
1525	5000
610	2000
305	1000
152.5	500
0 Sea Level	0
152.5	500
1525	5000
3050	10 000

Scale 1:10,000,000; one inch to 160 miles. Lambert Azimuthal Equal Area Projection
Elevations and depressions are given in feet.

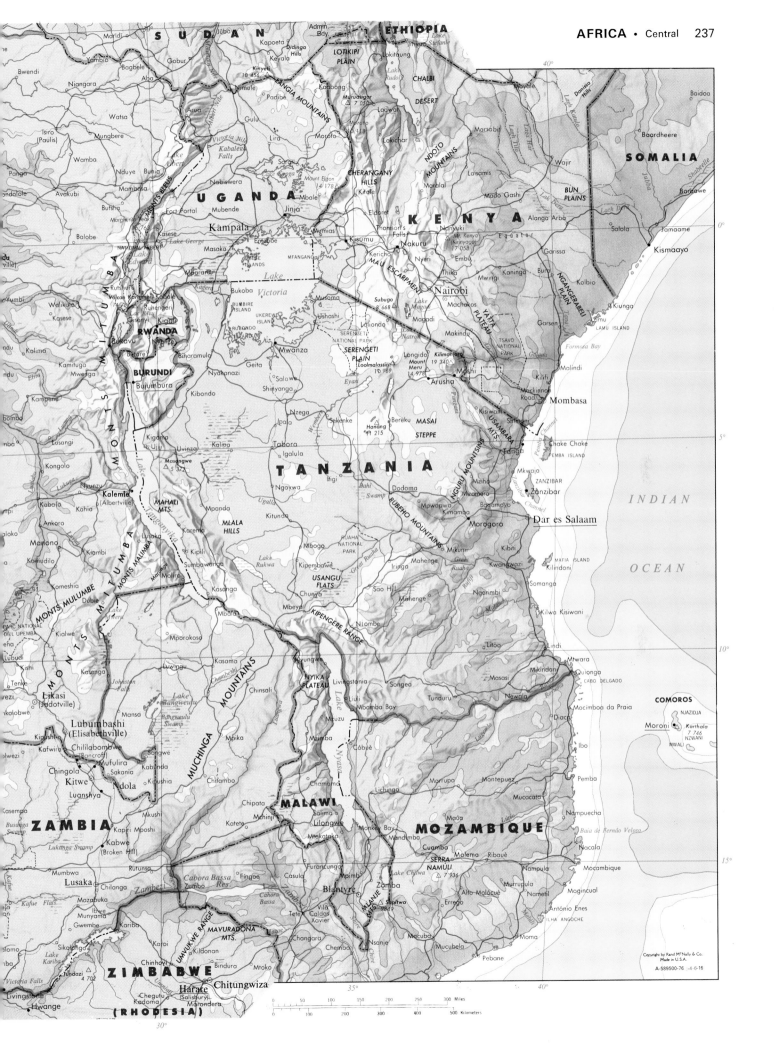

SUDAN
ETHIOPIA

Maridi
Juba
Kapoeta
Admin.
Bdy
Jinja Stefanie
Lake

Yambio
Bagbele
Gobur
Kyala
Didinga
Hills
LOTIKIPI
PLAIN
Lokitaung

Bwendi
Niangara
Aba
Nimule
Kinyeti
10 456
Padibwa
Kaabong
Moroto
LANGIA MOUNTAINS
Lodwar
Lake
Rudolf
CHALBI
DESERT
Mbale

Isiro
(Paulis)
Watsa
Arua
Gulu
Lira
Moroto
8 118
Lokichar
NDOTO
MOUNTAINS
Marsabit
Laisamis
Baidoa

Panga
Wamba
Mungbere
Butsho
Nduye
Bunia
Nabiswera
Soroti
Mount Elgon
14 178
CHERANGANY
HILLS
Kitale
Eldoret
Moralal
Mado Gashi
Wajir
SOMALIA
Baardheere

dandale
Avakubi
Mambasa
Fort Portal
UGANDA
Mbale
Jinja
Thomson's
Falls
Nanyuki
Mt. Kenya
(Kirinyaga)
17 058
Kaninga
Bura
Garissa
BUN
PLAINS
Bardawe

Panga
MONTS BLEUS
Margherita Peak
16 763
Kasese
Mubende
Kampala
Entebbe
Masaka
SESE
ISLANDS
MFANGANO
Kisumu
Kericho
Nakuru
Nyeri
KENYA
Alanga Arba
Mado Gashi
Garissa
Kolbio
Kismaayo

Balobe
PARC
NATIONAL ALBERT
Lake
George
Lake
Edward
Bukoba
Lake
Kagera
Mwanza
Musoma
MAU ESCARPMENT
Thika
Nairobi
Machakos
Embu
YATTA PLATEAU
Garsen
Kiunga
LAMU ISLAND
Lamu

ville
MITUMBA
Rutshuru
Volcan Karisimbi
14 782
Kabale
Biharamulo
BUMBIRE
ISLAND
UKEREWE
ISLAND
Ushashi
Subugo
8 668
Lake
Magadi
Magadi
Makindu
TSAVO
NATIONAL
PARK
Kilifi
Malindi
Formosa Bay

Wumbi
Walikale
Kasese
Gisenyi
Kigali
RWANDA
Bukavu
Bitare
RUBONDO
ISLAND
SERENGETI
NATIONAL PARK
Seronera
Loliondo
SERENGETI
PLAIN
Longido
Mount Meru
14 978
Kilimanjaro
19 340
Moshi
Kisiwani
Shimoni
USAMBARA MTS.
Mackinnon
Road
Mombasa
Chake Chake

ndu
Kalima
Kamituga
Mwenga
BURUNDI
Bujumbura
Nyakanazi
Geita
Salawa
Mwanza
Shinyanga
Loolmalassin
11 969
Arusha
Pangani
Kilwa
Tanga
PEMBA ISLAND
5°

Kampene
MONTS
Kigoma
Ujiji
Lake
Tanganyika
Kibondo
Kigama
Ipala
Nzega
Sekenke
Hanang
11 215
Bereku
MASAI
STEPPE
Mziha
NGURU MOUNTAINS
Mwaja
ZANZIBAR
Zanzibar
Zanzibar Channel
Pemba Channel
INDIAN

mba
Lusangi
Uvinza
Masangwe
5 372
Kaliua
Tabora
Igalula
Bahi
Swamp
Dodoma
Mpwapwa
Kimamba
Bagamoyo
Dar es Salaam

Kalemie
(Albertville)
MAHALI
MTS.
Mpanda
MLALA
HILLS
Karema
Ngoywa
Itigi
Ugalla
RUBEHO MOUNTAINS
Morogoro
Mikumi
Kibiti
OCEAN

Kabalo
Kahia
Ankoro
Kiambi
Kipili
Sumbawanga
Lake
Rukwa
Mbogo
RUAHA
NATIONAL
PARK
Kipembawe
Iringa
Mahenge
Great Ruaha
Kwangwazi
MAFIA ISLAND
Kilindoni

Marono
Kamudilo
Komeshia
Moliro
Kasanga
USANGU
FLATS
Chunya
Sao Hill
Mahenge
Ngarimbi
Somanga
Kilwa Kisiwani

MONTS
MULUMBE
Dubie
Lake
Mweru
Mporokoso
Mbeya
Njombe
KIPENGERE RANGE
Litoo
Lindi
10°

PARC NATIONAL
DE L'UPEMBA
Kialwe
Johnston
Falls
Kasama
Chambeshi
Nyungwe
NYIKA
PLATEAU
Livingstonia
Songea
Tunduru
Masasi
Newala
Mikindani
Mtwara
Quionga
CABO DELGADO

ena
Ludubi
Kishi
Tenke
Kasenga
Luwingu
Chinsali
Mbamba Bay
Mzuzu
Mocimba da Praia
Diaca
Ibo
COMOROS
NJAZIDJA

Likasi
(Jadotville)
Mansa
Lake
Bangweulu
Mpika
Mzimba
Côbuè
Lichinga
Montepuez
Pemba
Moroni
Karthala
7 746
NZWANI

kolobwe
Lubumbashi
(Elisabethville)
Kipushi
Chililabombwe
(Bancroft)
Bangweulu
Swamp
MUCHINGA
MOUNTAINS
Songwe
Chitambo
Chamama
Morrupa
Mucacata
Nampuecha
MWALI

olwezi
Mufulira
Sakania
Kabunda
Kipushia
Chifambo
MALAWI
Salima
Lichinga
Malema
Ribauè
Nacala

Chingola
Kitwe
Ndola
Chipata
Lilongwe
Mtakataka
Mandimba
MOZAMBIQUE
Murrupa
Montepuez
Nampula

Luanshya
Mkushi
Katete
Mchinji
Monkey Bay
Cuamba
SERRA
NAMULI
7 936
Nametil
Mocambique

Busanga
Swamp
ZAMBIA
Kapiri Mposhi
Kabwe
(Broken Hill)
Furancungo
Mpimbe
Lake Chilwa
Zomba
Malema
Murrupula
15°

Mumbwa
Lusaka
Chilanga
Cabora Bassa
Res.
Zumbo
Fingoe
Casula
Mpimbe
Blantyre
SERRA
NAMULI
Alto-Molócuè
Nampula
Mocambique

Kafue
Flats
Mazabuka
Ibwe
Munyama
Gwembe
Kariba
Cahora
Bassa
Vila
Caldas
Xavier
Tete
MLANJE
MTS.
Sapitwa
9849
Erregò
António Enes
ILHA ANGOCHE
Moma

Victoria Falls
Livingstone
Hwange
Sikalongo
Lake
Kariba
Tundazi
4 702
Kariba
Chinhoyi
(Salisbury)
Kadoma
Chitungwiza
Harare
Changara
Chemba
Mucuba
Mucubela
Pebane

ZIMBABWE
(RHODESIA)
UMVUKWE RANGE
Kildonan
MAVURADONA MTS.
Bindura
Mtoko
Nsanje
30°
35°
40°

Copyright by Rand McNally & Co.
Made in U.S.A.
A-589500-76 -4-6-16

0   50   100   150   200   250   300 Miles
0   100   200   300   400   500 Kilometers

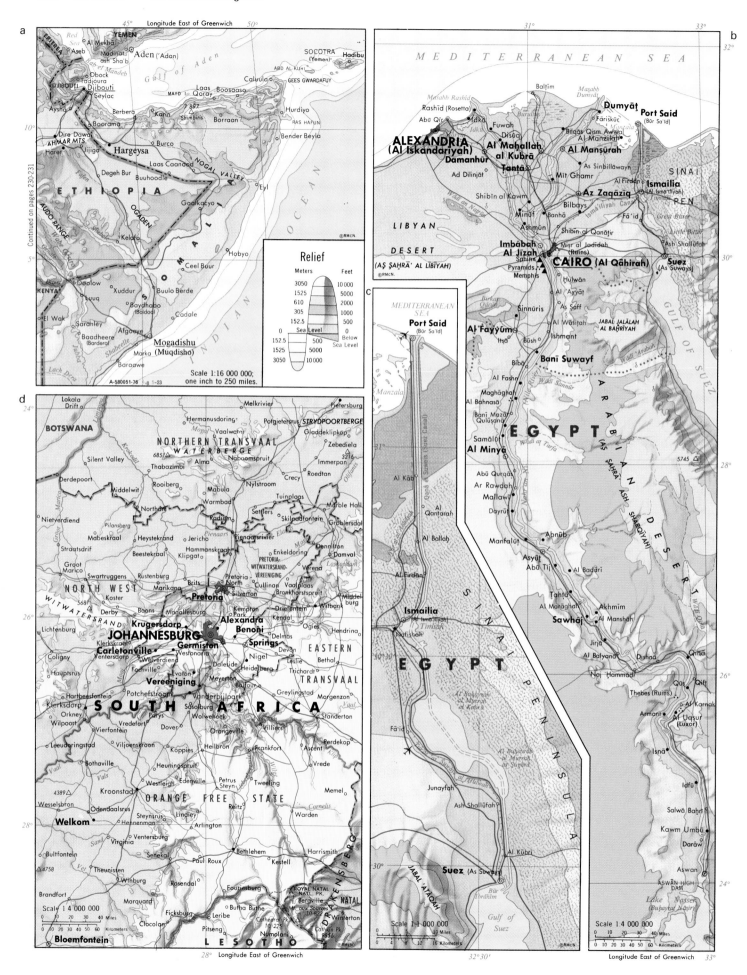

a

Red Sea
Al Mukhā
YEMEN
Aseb
Madīnat ash Sha'b Aden ('Adan)
ERITREA
Obock
Tadjoura
DJIBOUTI
Aysha
Seylac
Berbera
Karin
Shimbiris 7887
Hurdiyo
Borama
Degeh Bur
Dire Dawa
AHMAR MTS.
Harer
Jijiga
Hargeysa
Laas Caanood
NOGAL VALLEY
Buuhoodle
Eyl
AUDO RANGE
E T H I O P I A
OGADEN
Gaalkacyo
Keladē
Xuddur
Dōolow
Luuq
Buulo Berde
Cadale
KENYA
El Wak
Saranley
Baydhabo (Baidoa)
Afgooye
Mogadishu (Muqdisho)
Baraawe
Marka
S O M A L I A
Continued on pages 230-231

Gulf of Aden
Boosaaso
Laas Qoray
Caluula
GEES GWARDAFUY
ABD AL KURI
MAYD I.
HADIBU
SOCOTRA (Yemen)
RAS HAFUN
Bender Beyla
Hobyo
Ceel Buur
INDIAN OCEAN
Shabeelle
Jubba
Lach Dera

45° Longitude East of Greenwich 50°
10°
5°
©RMCN.

Relief

Meters		Feet
3050		10 000
1525		5000
610		2000
305		1000
152.5		500
0	Sea Level	0
152.5		500 Below Sea Level
1525		5000
3050		10 000

Scale 1:16 000 000;
one inch to 250 miles.
A-580051-76   8 5-23

b

M E D I T E R R A N E A N   S E A
Maṣabb Rashīd
Burullus
Maṣabb Dumyāṭ
Balṭīm
Rashīd (Rosetta)
Fāriskūr
Dumyāṭ
Port Said (Būr Saʿīd)
Abū Qīr
Idkū
Fuwah
Bilqās Qism Awwal
Al Manzilah
ALEXANDRIA (Al Iskandarīyah)
Disūq
Al Maḥallah al Kubrā
Al Manṣūrah
SINAI
Damanhūr
Ṭanṭā
As Sinbillāwayn
Mīt Ghamr
Al Firdān
Ismailia (Al Ismāʿīlīyah)
Ad Dilinjāt
Shibīn al Kawm
Az Zaqāzīq
PEN
Ismāʿīlīya Canal
Great Bitter
Fāʾid
LIBYAN
Minūf
Banhā
Bilbays
Ashmūn
Shibīn al Qanāṭir
Ash Shallūfah
Little Bitter
DESERT
(AṢ ṢAḤRĀʾ AL LĪBĪYAH)
Imbābah
Al Jīzah
Misr al Jadīdah (Ruins)
CAIRO (Al Qāhirah)
Suez (As Suways)
©RMCN.
Pyramids
Sphinx
Memphis
Ḥulwān
Al ʿAyyāṭ
GULF OF SUEZ
Birkat Qārūn
Sinnūris
As Ṣaff
Al Wāsiṭah
JABAL JALĀLAH AL BAḤRĪYAH
Al Fayyūm
Itsā
Ishmant
Būsh
Biba
Banī Suwayf
Wādī ʿArabah
Al Fashn
Maghāghah
Al Bahnasā
Banī Mazār
Qulūṣnā
E G Y P T
Samālūṭ
Al Minyā
Abū Qurqāṣ
Ar Rawdah
Mallawī
Dayrūṭ
5745
Manfalūṭ
Abnūb
Al Qūṣīyah
Asyūṭ
Abū Tīj
Al Badārī
AS ṢAḤRĀʾ ASH SHARQĪYAH
Tahtā
Al Marāghah
Akhmīm
Sawhāj
Al Manshāh
Jirjā
Al Balyanā
Dishnā
Naj Ḥammādī
Qinā
Thebes (Ruins)
Qūṣ
Qifṭ
Armant
Al Karnak
Al Uqṣur (Luxor)
Isnā
Idfū
Salwā Baḥrī
Kawm Umbū
Darāw
ASWĀN HIGH DAM
Aswān
Lake Nasser (Buhayrat Nāṣir)
31° 33°
32°
30°
28°
26°
24°
Scale 1:4 000 000
0 10 20 30 40 50 60 Miles
0 10 20 30 40 50 60 Kilometers
Longitude East of Greenwich

c

MEDITERRANEAN SEA
Port Said (Būr Saʿīd)
Manzala
Qanā é Suways (Suez Canal)
Al Kāb
Al Qantarah
SINAI
Al Ballaḥ
Al Firdān
Ismailia (Al Ismāʿīlīyah)
Naftshah
Timsah
Fāʾid
Lake Timsah
E G Y P T
Al Buḥayrah al Murrah al Kubrā
SINAI PENINSULA
Al Buḥayrah al Murrah aṣ Ṣughrā
Al Kūbrī
Junayfah
Ash Shallūfah
Suez (As Suways)
Būr Ibrāhīm
JABAL ʿATAQAH
Gulf of Suez
31°
30°30'
32°30'
Scale 1:4 000 000
0 10 20 30 Miles
0 10 20 30 Kilometers
©RMCN.

d

Lokala Drift
Melkrivier
Pietersburg
BOTSWANA
Hermanusdoring
Potgietersrus
STRYDPOORTBERGE
NORTHERN TRANSVAAL
WATERBERGE
Mogol
Vaalwater
Gladdeklipkop
Silent Valley
6851
Thabazimbi
Alma
Naboomspruit
Zebediela
Immerpan
3216
Derdepoort
Rooiberg
Roedtan
Crecy
Middelwit
Mabula
Nylstroom
Northam
Warmbad
Tuinplaas
Pilansberg
Radium
Settlers
Skilpadfontein
Marble Hall
Groblersdal
Mabeskraal
Heystekrand
Jericho
Hammanskraal
Klipgat
Pienaarsrivier
Enkeldoring
Damval
Straatsdrif
Beestekraal
NORTH WEST
Denniton
Groot Marico
Swartruggens
Rustenburg
Marikana
Brits
Pienaars
PRETORIA-WITWATERSRAND-VEREENIGING
Pretoria North
Cullinan
Verena
5681
Koster
Boons
Magaliesburg
Silverton
Bronkhorstspruit
Middelburg
Derby
Krugersdorp
PRETORIA
Kempton Park
Vaalplaas
Witbank
WITWATERSRAND
Alexandra
Benoni
Driefontein
Kendal
Ogies
Hendrina
Lichtenburg
Coligny
JOHANNESBURG
Germiston
Springs
Nigel
Devon
Bethal
EASTERN
Carletonville
Venterspos
Westonaria
Delmas
Leslie
Trichardt
Hauptrus
Fochville
Evaton
Heidelberg
TRANSVAAL
Klerksdorp
Vereeniging
Meyerton
Balfour
Greylingstad
Morgenzon
Orkney
Vanderbijlpark
Standerton
Wilpoort
Hartbeesfontein
Potchefstroom
Villiers
Perdekop
Leeudoringstad
Vierfontein
Dover
Wolwehoek
Orangeville
Ascent
Vrede
Klerksdorp
4389
S O U T H   A F R I C A
Parys
Frankfort
Wesselsbron
Vredefort
Koppies
Heilbron
Memel
Bothaville
O R A N G E   F R E E   S T A T E
Reitz
Warden
Welkom
Odendaalsrus
Lindley
Arlington
Virginia
Steynsrus
Bultfontein
Ventersburg
Senekal
4758
Theunissen
Paul Roux
Bethlehem
Harrismith
Brandfort
Winburg
Rosendal
Fouriesburg
Bergville
NATAL
Marquard
Ficksburg
Leribe
Winterton
Bloemfontein
Clocolan
Butha Buthe
Ladybrand
ROYAL NATAL NATL. PK.
Mont aux Sources 10 822
Cathedral Pk. 10 225
Cathkin Pk. 9856
DRAKENSBERG
Numolant
Pitseng
LESOTHO
Scale 1:4 000 000
0 10 20 30 40 Miles
0 10 20 30 40 Kilometers
24°
26°
28°
24°
26°
28°
Longitude East of Greenwich
©RMCN.

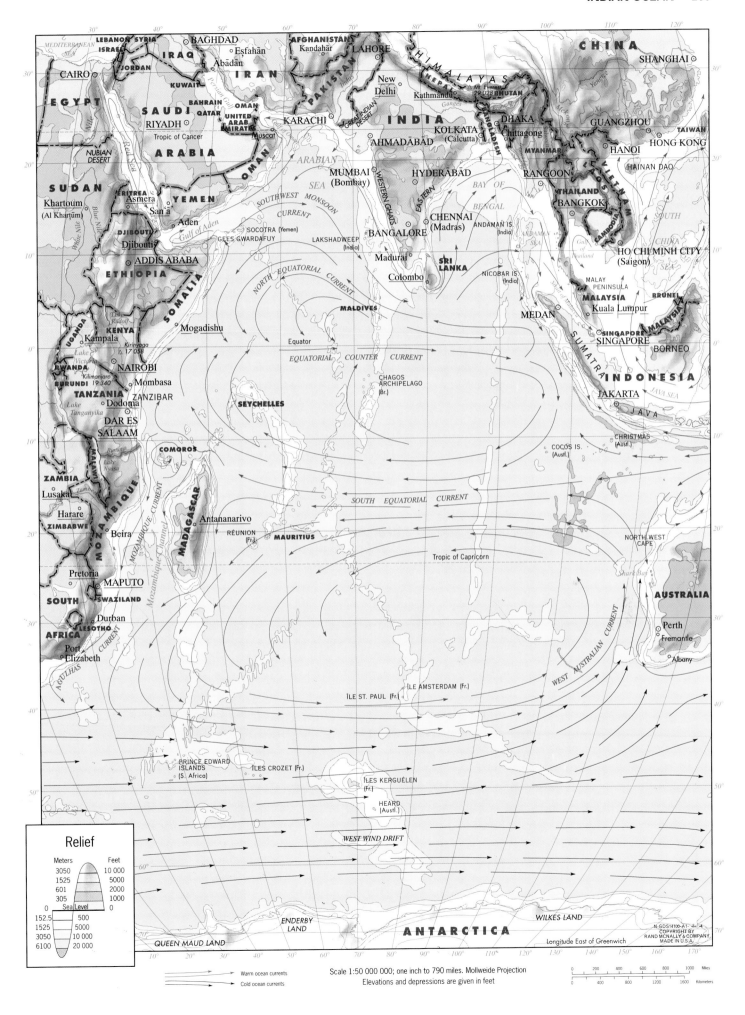

LEBANON SYRIA
ISRAEL
JORDAN
IRAQ
BAGHDAD
Esfahān
Abādān
IRAN
AFGHANISTAN
Kandahār
LAHORE
New
Delhi
CHINA
SHANGHAI

MEDITERRANEAN
SEA
CAIRO
EGYPT
KUWAIT
BAHRAIN
QATAR
SAUDI
RIYADH
UNITED
ARAB
EMIRATES
OMAN
Muscat
Tropic of Cancer
PAKISTAN
KARACHI
HIMALAYAS
NEPAL
Kathmandu
△ Mt. Everest
29,028
BHUTAN
Ganges
DHAKA
KOLKATA
(Calcutta)
Chittagong
GUANGZHOU
TAIWAN
HANOI
HONG KONG

NUBIAN
DESERT
ARABIA
YEMEN
Asmera
San'a
Aden
Gulf of Aden
SOCOTRA (Yemen)
GEES GWARDAFUY
ARABIAN
SEA
SOUTHWEST MONSOON
CURRENT
INDIA
AHMADĀBĀD
MUMBAI
(Bombay)
WESTERN GHATS
HYDERĀBĀD
EASTERN GHATS
CHENNAI
(Madras)
ANDAMAN IS.
(India)
BAY
OF
BENGAL
MYANMAR
RANGOON
THAILAND
BANGKOK
HAINAN DAO
VIETNAM
SOUTH
CHINA
SEA

SUDAN
Khartoum
(Al Khartūm)
ERITREA
DJIBOUTI
Djibouti
ADDIS ABABA
ETHIOPIA
SOMALIA
LAKSHADWEEP
(India)
Madurai
BANGALORE
Colombo
SRI
LANKA
NICOBAR IS.
(India)
ANDAMAN
SEA
Gulf
of
Thailand
CAMBODIA
HO CHI MINH CITY
(Saigon)
MALAY
PENINSULA

Blue Nile
White Nile
Red Sea
Mogadishu
NORTH EQUATORIAL CURRENT
Equator
EQUATORIAL COUNTER CURRENT
MALDIVES
CHAGOS
ARCHIPELAGO
(Br.)
MALAYSIA
Kuala Lumpur
BRUNEI
SINGAPORE
SINGAPORE
BORNEO

UGANDA
Kampala
Lake
Victoria
KENYA
Kiriniyaga
△ 17,058
NAIROBI
Mombasa
Kilimanjaro
△ 19,340
RWANDA
BURUNDI
TANZANIA
ZANZIBAR
Dodoma
Lake
Tanganyika
DAR ES
SALAAM
SEYCHELLES
JAKARTA
JAVA
INDONESIA
JAVA SEA

MALAWI
Lake
Nyasa
ZAMBIA
Lusaka
COMOROS
SOUTH EQUATORIAL CURRENT
COCOS IS.
(Austl.)
CHRISTMAS
(Austl.)
SUMATRA
MEDAN

Zambezi
Harare
ZIMBABWE
Beira
MOZAMBIQUE
MADAGASCAR
Antananarivo
RÉUNION
(Fr.)
MAURITIUS
Tropic of Capricorn
NORTH WEST
CAPE
Shark Bay

MOZAMBIQUE CURRENT
Mozambique Channel
Rufuma
Pretoria
MAPUTO
SWAZILAND
SOUTH
AFRICA
LESOTHO
Durban
AGULHAS
CURRENT
Port
Elizabeth
WEST AUSTRALIAN CURRENT
AUSTRALIA
Perth
Fremantle
Albany

ÎLE AMSTERDAM (Fr.)
ÎLE ST. PAUL (Fr.)

PRINCE EDWARD
ISLANDS
(S. Africa)
ÎLES CROZET (Fr.)
ÎLES KERGUÉLEN
(Fr.)
HEARD
(Austl.)

WEST WIND DRIFT

ENDERBY
LAND
WILKES LAND
ANTARCTICA
QUEEN MAUD LAND
Longitude East of Greenwich
N-GDS14100-A1- 3- 4
COPYRIGHT BY
RAND MCNALLY & COMPANY
MADE IN U.S.A.

Relief

Meters		Feet
3050		10 000
1525		5000
601		2000
305		1000
0	Sea Level	0
152.5		500
1525		5000
3050		10 000
6100		20 000

⟶ Warm ocean currents
⟶ Cold ocean currents

Scale 1:50 000 000; one inch to 790 miles. Mollweide Projection
Elevations and depressions are given in feet

0   200 400 600 800 1000 Miles
0   400   800   1200   1600 Kilometers

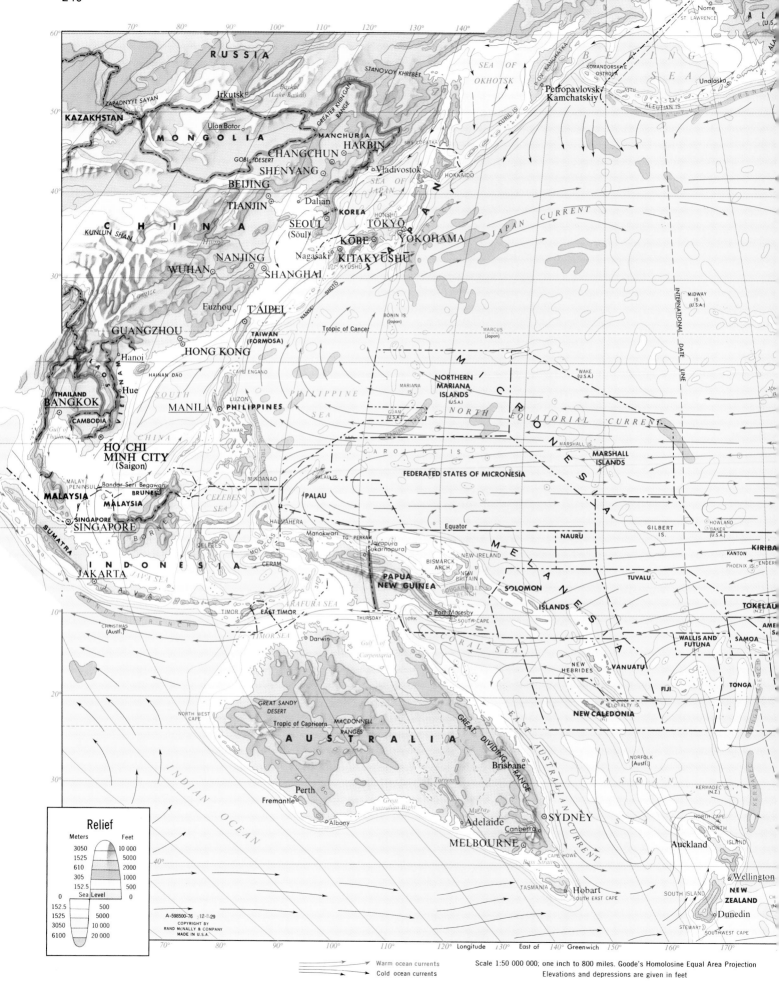

Relief

Meters		Feet
3050		10 000
1525		5000
610		2000
305		1000
152.5		500
0	Sea Level	0
152.5		500
1525		5000
3050		10 000
6100		20 000

A-598500-76   12-8-29
COPYRIGHT BY
RAND McNALLY & COMPANY
MADE IN U.S.A.

→ Warm ocean currents
→ Cold ocean currents

Scale 1:50 000 000; one inch to 800 miles. Goode's Homolosine Equal Area Projection
Elevations and depressions are given in feet

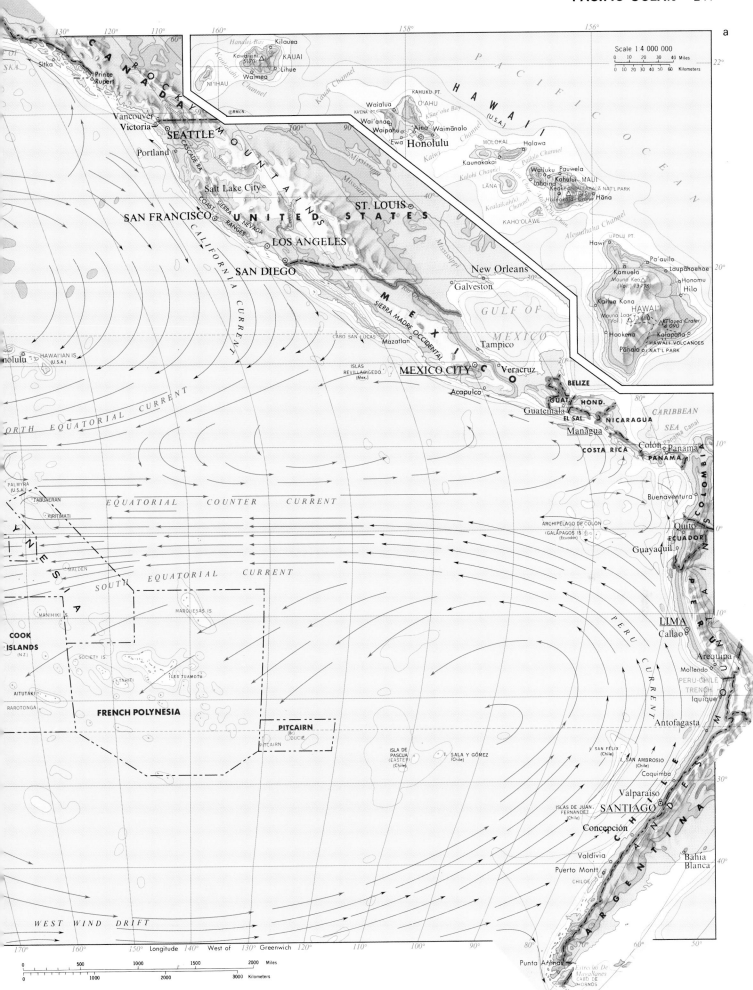

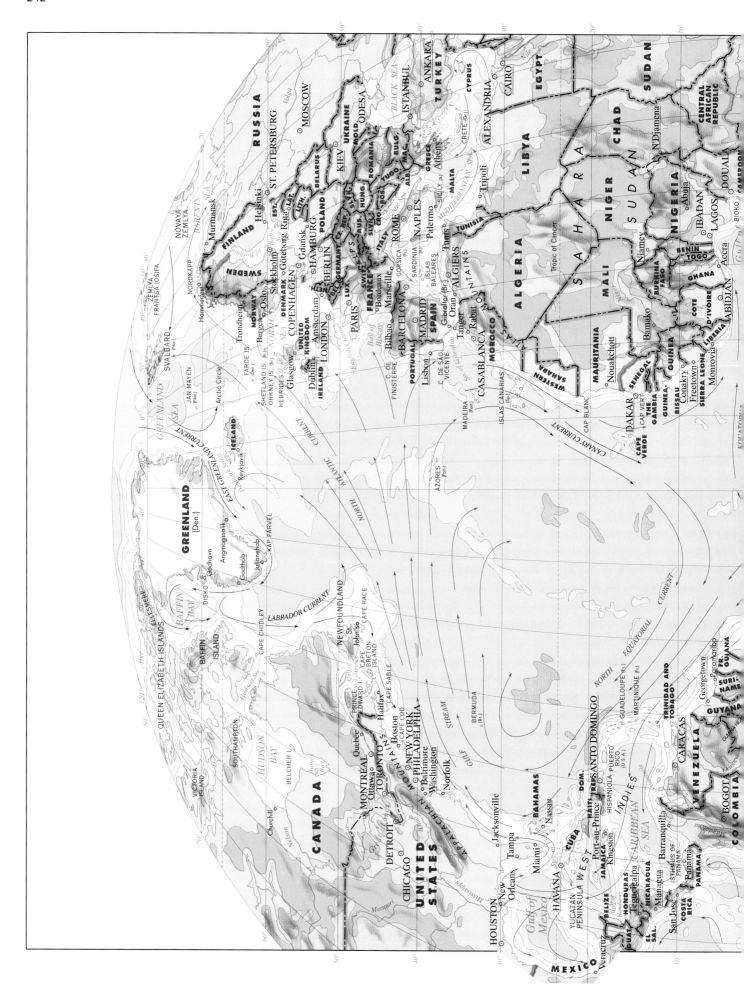

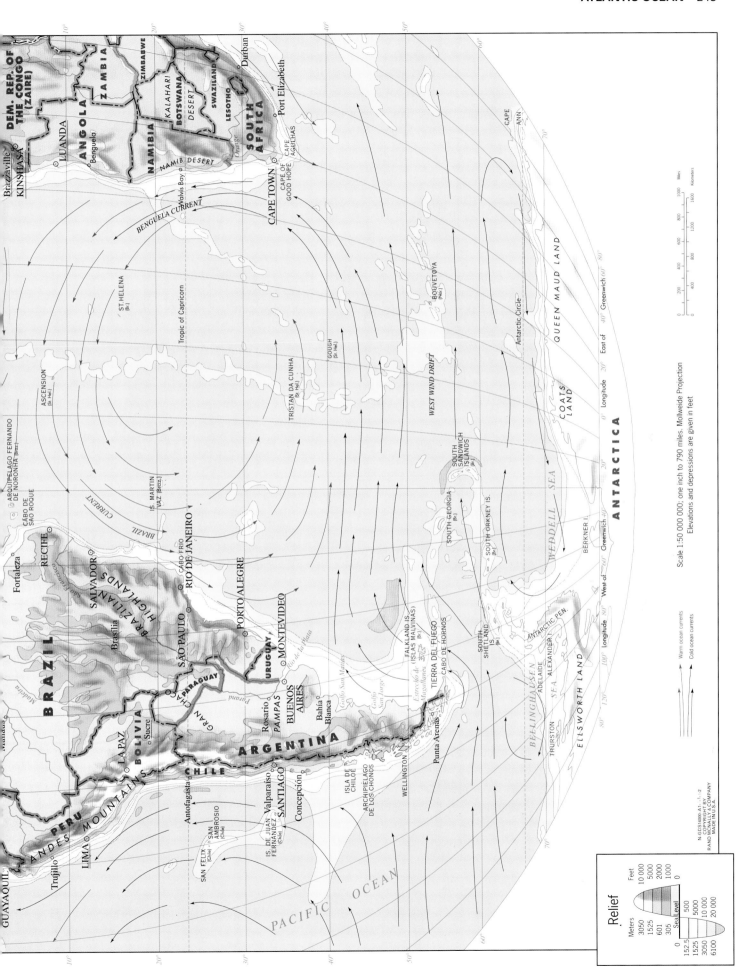

DEM. REP. OF
THE CONGO
(ZAIRE)

Brazzaville
KINSHASA

LUANDA

ANGOLA

ZAMBIA

ZIMBABWE

Benguela

NAMIBIA

KALAHARI
DESERT

BOTSWANA

SWAZILAND

LESOTHO

SOUTH
AFRICA

Durban

Port Elizabeth

NAMIB DESERT

Walvis Bay

Orange

CAPE TOWN

CAPE OF
GOOD HOPE

CAPE
AGULHAS

BENGUELA CURRENT

ST. HELENA
(Br.)

Tropic of Capricorn

ASCENSION
(St. Hel.)

GOUGH
(St. Hel.)

TRISTAN DA CUNHA
(St. Hel.)

BOUVETØYA
(Nor.)

CAPE
ANN

QUEEN MAUD LAND

Antarctic Circle

WEST WIND DRIFT

COATS
LAND

WEDDELL
SEA

BERKNER I.

ANTARCTICA

SOUTH
SANDWICH
ISLANDS
(Br.)

SOUTH GEORGIA
(Br.)

SOUTH ORKNEY IS.
(Br.)

ARQUIPÉLAGO FERNANDO
DE NORONHA (Braz.)

CABO DE
SAO ROQUE

IS. MARTIN
VAZ (Braz.)

BRAZIL
CURRENT

CABO FRIO

RIO DE JANEIRO

PORTO ALEGRE

MONTEVIDEO

URUGUAY

BUENOS
AIRES

PAMPAS

Rosario

Rio de la Plata

Paraná

Gulfo San Matías

Gulfo San Jorge

Bahía
Blanca

FALKLAND IS.
(ISLAS MALVINAS)
(Br.)

SOUTH
SHETLAND
IS.
(Br.)

ANTARCTIC PEN.

ALEXANDER I.

ELLSWORTH LAND

BEELLINGHAUSEN

THURSTON

ADELAIDE

BELLINGHAUSEN
SEA

Fortaleza

RECIFE

SALVADOR

BRAZILIAN
HIGHLANDS

Brasília

BRAZIL

SÃO PAULO

PARAGUAY

GRAN CHACO

BOLIVIA

Sucre

LA PAZ

CHILE

ARGENTINA

TIERRA DEL FUEGO

CABO DE HORNOS

Estrecho de
Magallanes

Punta Arenas

WELLINGTON

ARCHIPIÉLAGO
DE LOS CHONOS

ISLA DE
CHILOÉ

Concepción

Valparaíso
SANTIAGO

IS. DE JUAN
FERNÁNDEZ
(Chile)

SAN
AMBROSIO
(Chile)

SAN FÉLIX
(Chile)

Antofagasta

ANDES MOUNTAINS

PERU

LIMA

Trujillo

GUAYAQUIL

Madeira

São Francisco

PACIFIC
OCEAN

PACIFIC OCEAN

Warm ocean currents

Cold ocean currents

Longitude East of Greenwich

Longitude West of Greenwich

Scale 1:50 000 000; one inch to 790 miles. Mollweide Projection

Elevations and depressions are given in feet

N GDS54000-A1 -- -3--2
COPYRIGHT BY
RAND MCNALLY & COMPANY
MADE IN U.S.A.

Miles
0   200   400   600   800   1000
0 400 800 1200 1600
Kilometers

Relief

Meters	Feet
3050	10 000
1525	5000
601	2000
305	1000
Sea Level	0
152.5	500
1525	5000
3050	10 000
6100	20 000

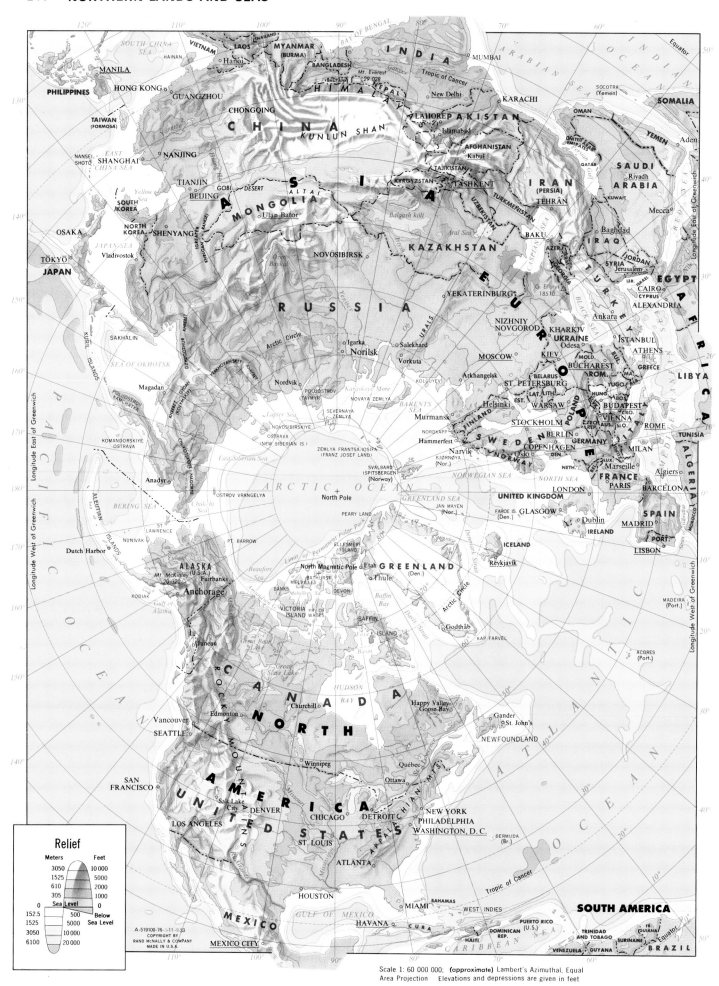

Relief

Meters	Feet
3050	10 000
1525	5000
610	2000
305	1000
0 Sea Level	0
152.5	500
1525	Below
	5000 Sea Level
3050	10 000
6100	20 000

A-519100-76-3-11-9.33
COPYRIGHT BY
RAND M^cNALLY & COMPANY
MADE IN U.S.A.

Scale 1: 60 000 000; (approximate) Lambert's Azimuthal, Equal
Area Projection   Elevations and depressions are given in feet

WORLD POLITICAL INFORMATION TABLE

This table gives the area, population, population density, political status, capital, and predominant languages for every country in the world. The political units listed are categorized by political status in the form of government column of the table, as follows: A—independent countries; B—internally independent political entities which are under the protection of another country in matters of defense and foreign affairs; C—colonies and other dependent political units; and D—the major administrative subdivisions of Australia, Canada, China, the United

Kingdom, and the United States. For comparison, the table also includes the continents and the world. A key to abbreviations of country names appears on page 261. All footnotes to this table appear on page 249.

The populations are estimates for January 1, 1999, made by Rand McNally on the basis of official data, United Nations estimates, and other available information. Area figures include inland water.

REGION OR POLITICAL DIVISION	Area Sq. Mi.	Est. Pop. 1/1/99	Pop. Per. Sq. Mi.	Form of Government and Ruling Power		Capital	Predominant Languages
Afars and Issas, see Djibouti							
† Afghanistan	251,826	25,315,000	101	Islamic council	A	Kābul	Dari, Pashto, Uzbek, Turkmen
Africa	11,700,000	770,300,000	66				
Alabama	52,237	4,344,000	83	State (U.S.)	D	Montgomery	English
Alaska	615,232	625,000	1.0	State (U.S.)	D	Juneau	English, indigenous
† Albania	11,100	3,347,000	302	Republic	A	Tiranë	Albanian, Greek
Alberta	255,287	2,929,000	11	Province (Canada)	D	Edmonton	English
† Algeria	919,595	30,805,000	33	Republic	A	Algiers (El Djazaïr)	Arabic, Berber dialects, French
American Samoa	77	63,000	818	Unincorporated territory (U.S.)	C	Pago Pago	Samoan, English
† Andorra	175	65,000	371	Parliamentary co-principality (Spanish & French)	B	Andorra	Catalan, Spanish (Castilian), French
† Angola	481,354	11,020,000	23	Republic	A	Luanda	Portuguese, indigenous
Anguilla	35	11,000	314	Dependent territory (U.K.)	B	The Valley	English
Anhui	53,668	61,610,000	1,148	Province (China)	D	Hefei	Chinese (Mandarin)
Antarctica	5,400,000	(1)					
† Antigua and Barbuda	171	64,000	374	Parliamentary state	A	St. John's	English, local dialects
† Argentina	1,073,519	36,500,000	34	Republic	A	Buenos Aires and Viedma (4)	Spanish, English, Italian, German, French
Arizona	114,007	4,697,000	41	State (U.S.)	D	Phoenix	English
Arkansas	53,183	2,552,000	48	State (U.S.)	D	Little Rock	English
† Armenia	11,506	3,416,000	297	Republic	A	Yerevan	Armenian, Russian
Aruba	75	68,000	907	Self-governing territory (Netherlands protection)	B	Oranjestad	Dutch, Papiamento, English, Spanish
Ascension	34	1,100	32	Dependency (St. Helena)	C	Georgetown	English
Asia	17,300,000	3,629,100,000	210				
† Australia	2,966,155	18,735,000	6.3	Federal parliamentary state	A	Canberra	English, indigenous
Australian Capital Territory	927	315,000	340	Territory (Australia)	D	Canberra	English
† Austria	32,377	8,136,000	251	Federal republic	A	Vienna (Wien)	German
† Azerbaijan	33,436	7,883,000	236	Republic	A	Baku (Bakı)	Azerbaijani, Russian, Armenian
† Bahamas	5,382	282,000	52	Parliamentary state	A	Nassau	English, Creole
† Bahrain	267	622,000	2,330	Monarchy	A	Al Manāmah	Arabic, English, Farsi, Urdu
† Bangladesh	55,598	126,110,000	2,268	Republic	A	Dhaka (Dacca)	Bangla, English
† Barbados	166	259,000	1,560	Parliamentary state	A	Bridgetown	English, local dialects
Beijing (Peking)	6,486	12,790,000	1,972	Autonomous city (China)	D	Beijing (Peking)	Chinese (Mandarin)
† Belarus	80,155	10,405,000	130	Republic	A	Minsk	Belorussian, Russian
Belau, see Palau							
† Belgium	11,783	10,180,000	864	Constitutional monarchy	A	Brussels (Bruxelles)	Dutch (Flemish), French, German
† Belize	8,866	233,000	26	Parliamentary state	A	Belmopan	English, Spanish, Mayan, Garifuna, Ketchi
† Benin	43,475	6,202,000	143	Republic	A	Porto-Novo and Cotonou	French, Fon, Yoruba, indigenous
Bermuda	21	62,000	2,952	Dependent territory (U.K.)	C	Hamilton	English
† Bhutan	17,954	1,930,000	107	Monarchy (Indian protection)	B	Thimphu	Dzongkha, Tibetan and Nepalese dialects
† Bolivia	424,165	7,904,000	19	Republic	A	La Paz and Sucre	Aymara, Quechua, Spanish
† Bosnia and Herzegovina	19,741	3,427,000	174	Republic	A	Sarajevo	Serbo-Croatian
† Botswana	224,711	1,456,000	6.5	Republic	A	Gaborone	English, Tswana
† Brazil	3,300,172	170,860,000	52	Federal republic	A	Brasília	Portuguese, Spanish, English, French
British Columbia	365,948	4,043,000	11	Province (Canada)	D	Victoria	English
British Indian Ocean Territory	23	(1)		Dependent territory (U.K.)	C		English
British Virgin Islands	59	19,000	322	Dependent territory (U.K.)	C	Road Town	English
† Brunei	2,226	319,000	143	Monarchy	A	Bandar Seri Begawan	Malay, English, Chinese, Tamil
† Bulgaria	42,855	8,215,000	192	Republic	A	Sofia (Sofiya)	Bulgarian, Turkish
† Burkina Faso	105,869	11,420,000	108	Republic	A	Ouagadougou	French, indigenous
Burma, see Myanmar							
† Burundi	10,745	5,634,000	524	Republic	A	Bujumbura	French, Kirundi, Swahili
California	158,869	33,340,000	210	State (U.S.)	D	Sacramento	English
† Cambodia	69,898	11,485,000	164	Constitutional monarchy	A	Phnom Penh (Phnum Pénh)	Khmer, French
† Cameroon	183,568	15,240,000	83	Republic	A	Yaoundé	English, French, indigenous
† Canada	3,849,674	30,450,000	7.9	Federal parliamentary state	A	Ottawa	English, French
† Cape Verde	1,557	403,000	259	Republic	A	Praia	Portuguese, Crioulo
Cayman Islands	100	39,000	390	Dependent territory (U.K.)	C	George Town	English
† Central African Republic	240,535	3,410,000	14	Republic	A	Bangui	French, Sango, Arabic, indigenous
Ceylon, see Sri Lanka							
† Chad	495,755	7,458,000	15	Republic	A	N'Djamena	Arabic, French, indigenous
† Chile	292,135	14,880,000	51	Republic	A	Santiago	Spanish
† China (excl. Taiwan)	3,690,045	1,242,070,000	337	Socialist republic	A	Beijing (Peking)	Chinese dialects
Chongqing	31,815	36,120,000	1,135	Autonomous city (China)	D	Chongqing	Chinese (Mandarin)
Christmas Island	52	2,300	44	External territory (Australia)	C	Settlement	English, Chinese, Malay
Cocos (Keeling) Islands	5.4	600	111	External territory (Australia)	C	West Island	English, Malay
† Colombia	440,831	38,950,000	88	Republic	A	Bogotá	Spanish
Colorado	104,100	3,937,000	38	State (U.S.)	D	Denver	English
† Comoros (excl. Mayotte)	863	554,000	642	Military	A	Moroni	Arabic, French, Comoran
† Congo	132,047	2,688,000	20	Republic	A	Brazzaville	French, Lingala, Kikongo, indigenous
† Congo, Democratic Republic of the	905,446	49,735,000	55	Republic	A	Kinshasa	French, Kikongo, Lingala, Swahili, Tshiluba, Kingwana
Connecticut	5,544	3,260,000	588	State (U.S.)	D	Hartford	English
Cook Islands	91	20,000	220	Self-governing state (New Zealand protection)	B	Avarua	English, Maori
† Costa Rica	19,730	3,639,000	184	Republic	A	San José	Spanish
† Cote d'Ivoire	124,518	15,630,000	126	Republic	A	Abidjan and Yamoussoukro	French, Dioula and other indigenous

REGION OR POLITICAL DIVISION	Area Sq. Mi.	Est. Pop. 1/1/99	Pop. Per. Sq. Mi.	Form of Government and Ruling Power	Capital	Predominant Languages
† Croatia	21,829	4,675,000	214	Republic.......................A	Zagreb	Serbo-Croatian
† Cuba	42,804	11,075,000	259	Socialist republic.................A	Havana (La Habana)	Spanish
† Cyprus	2,277	615,000	270	Republic.......................A	Nicosia (Levkosía)	Greek, English
Cyprus, North (²)	1,295	137,000	106	Republic.......................A	Nicosia (Lefkoşa)	Turkish
† Czech Republic	30,450	10,280,000	338	Republic.......................A	Prague (Praha)	Czech, Slovak
Delaware	2,396	738,000	308	State (U.S.).....................D	Dover	English
† Denmark	16,639	5,347,000	321	Constitutional monarchy ....A	Copenhagen (København)	Danish
District of Columbia	68	516,000	7,588	Federal district (U.S.) ....D	Washington	English
† Djibouti	8,958	444,000	50	Republic.......................A	Djibouti	French, Arabic, Somali, Afar
† Dominica	305	66,000	216	Republic.......................A	Roseau	English, Creole French
† Dominican Republic	18,704	8,064,000	431	Republic.......................A	Santo Domingo	Spanish
East Timor	5,743	922,000	161	Territory under U.N. administration C	Dili	Portuguese, Tetum, Bahasa Indonesia (Malay), indigenous
† Ecuador	105,037	12,450,000	119	Republic.......................A	Quito	Spanish, Quechua, indigenous
† Egypt	386,662	66,660,000	172	Republic.......................A	Cairo (Al Qāhirah)	Arabic
Ellice Islands, see Tuvalu	....	....	....			
† El Salvador	8,124	5,797,000	714	Republic.......................A	San Salvador	Spanish, Nahua
England	50,352	49,240,000	978	Administrative division (U.K.) ....D	London	English
† Equatorial Guinea	10,831	460,000	42	Republic.......................A	Malabo	Spanish, indigenous, English
† Eritrea	36,170	3,907,000	108	Republic.......................A	Asmera	Arabic, Tigrinya, Amharic, Kunama, Tigre, other
† Estonia	17,413	1,414,000	81	Republic.......................A	Tallinn	Estonian, Latvian, Lithuanian, Russian
† Ethiopia	446,953	59,040,000	132	Federal Republic.................A	Addis Ababa	Amharic, Tigrinya, Orominga, Guaraginga, Somali, Arabic
Europe	3,800,000	709,300,000	187			
Falkland Islands (³)	4,700	2,900	0.6	Dependent territory (U.K.) C	Stanley	English
Faroe Islands	540	42,000	78	Self-governing territory (Danish protection) B	Tórshavn	Danish, Faroese
† Fiji	7,056	808,000	115	Republic.......................A	Suva	English, Fijian, Hindustani
† Finland	130,559	5,154,000	39	Republic.......................A	Helsinki (Helsingfors)	Finnish, Swedish, Lapp, Russian
Florida	59,928	15,065,000	251	State (U.S.).....................D	Tallahassee	English
† France (excl. Overseas Departments)	211,208	58,890,000	279	Republic.......................A	Paris	French
French Guiana	32,253	166,000	5.1	Overseas department (France) C	Cayenne	French
French Polynesia	1,360	228,000	168	Overseas territory (France) C	Papeete	French, Tahitian
Fujian	46,332	33,160,000	716	Province (China)..................D	Fuzhou	Chinese dialects
† Gabon	103,347	1,217,000	12	Republic.......................A	Libreville	French, Fang, indigenous
† Gambia, The	4,127	1,314,000	318	Republic.......................A	Banjul	English, Malinke, Wolof, Fula, indigenous
Gansu	173,746	24,970,000	144	Province (China)..................D	Lanzhou	Chinese (Mandarin), Mongolian, Tibetan dialects
Gaza Strip	139	1,094,000	7,871	Israeli occupied territory with limited self-govt.	....	Arabic
Georgia	58,977	7,600,000	129	State (U.S.).....................D	Atlanta	English
† Georgia	26,911	5,085,000	189	Republic.......................A	Tbilisi	Georgian, Russian, Armenian, Azerbaijani
† Germany	137,822	82,700,000	600	Federal republic ....A	Berlin	German
† Ghana	92,098	18,695,000	203	Republic.......................A	Accra	English, Akan and other indigenous
Gibraltar	2.3	29,000	12,609	Dependent territory (U.K.) C	Gibraltar	English, Spanish
Gilbert Islands, see Kiribati	....	....	....			
Golan Heights	454	33,000	73	Occupied by Israel	....	Arabic, Hebrew
Great Britain, see United Kingdom	....					
† Greece	50,949	10,685,000	210	Republic.......................A	Athens (Athína)	Greek, English, French
Greenland	840,004	59,000	0.1	Self-governing territory (Danish protection) B	Godthåb (Nuuk)	Danish, Greenlandic, Inuit dialects
† Grenada	133	96,000	722	Parliamentary state ....A	St. George's	English, French
Guadeloupe (incl. Dependencies)	657	418,000	636	Overseas department (France) C	Basse-Terre	French, Creole
Guam	209	150,000	718	Unincorporated territory (U.S.).........C	Agana	English, Chamorro, Japanese
Guangdong	68,649	70,430,000	1,026	Province (China)..................D	Guangzhou (Canton)	Chinese dialects, Miao-Yao
Guangxi Zhuangzu	91,236	46,580,000	511	Autonomous region (China)...........D	Nanning	Chinese dialects, Thai, Miao-Yao
† Guatemala	42,042	12,170,000	289	Republic.......................A	Guatemala	Spanish, Amerindian
Guernsey (incl. Dependencies)	30	65,000	2,167	Crown dependency (U.K. protection) ....B	St. Peter Port	English, French
† Guinea	94,926	7,508,000	79	Republic.......................A	Conakry	French, indigenous
† Guinea-Bissau	13,948	1,220,000	87	Republic.......................A	Bissau	Portuguese, Crioulo, indigenous
Guizhou	65,637	36,020,000	549	Province (China)..................D	Guiyang	Chinese (Mandarin), Thai, Miao-Yao
† Guyana	83,000	706,000	8.5	Republic.......................A	Georgetown	English, Hindi, Urdu
Hainan	13,205	7,452,000	564	Province (China)..................D	Haikou	Chinese, Min, Tai
† Haiti	10,714	6,833,000	638	Republic.......................A	Port-au-Prince	Creole, French
Hawaii	6,459	1,195,000	185	State (U.S.).....................D	Honolulu	English, Hawaiian, Japanese
Hebei	73,359	65,950,000	899	Province (China)..................D	Shijiazhuang	Chinese (Mandarin)
Heilongjiang	181,082	38,005,000	210	Province (China)..................D	Harbin	Chinese dialects, Mongolian, Tungus
Henan	64,479	93,280,000	1,447	Province (China)..................D	Zhengzhou	Chinese (Mandarin)
Holland, see Netherlands	....	....	....			
† Honduras	43,277	5,931,000	137	Republic.......................A	Tegucigalpa	Spanish, indigenous
Hong Kong	425	6,782,000	15,958	Special Administrative Region (China) ....D	Hong Kong (Xianggang)	Chinese (Cantonese), English, Putonghua
Hubei	72,356	59,250,000	819	Province (China)..................D	Wuhan	Chinese dialects
Hunan	81,081	65,580,000	809	Province (China)..................D	Changsha	Chinese dialects, Miao-Yao
† Hungary	35,919	10,195,000	284	Republic.......................A	Budapest	Hungarian
† Iceland	39,769	272,000	6.8	Republic.......................A	Reykjavík	Icelandic
Idaho	83,574	1,230,000	15	State (U.S.).....................D	Boise	English
Illinois	57,918	12,025,000	208	State (U.S.).....................D	Springfield	English
† India (incl. part of Jammu and Kashmir)	1,237,061	992,470,000	802	Federal republic ....A	New Delhi	English, Hindi, Telugu, Bengali, indigenous
Indiana	36,420	5,919,000	163	State (U.S.).....................D	Indianapolis	English
† Indonesia	752,409	214,530,000	285	Republic.......................A	Jakarta	Bahasa Indonesia (Malay), English, Dutch, indigenous
Iowa	56,276	2,878,000	51	State (U.S.).....................D	Des Moines	English
† Iran	630,578	64,830,000	103	Islamic republic ....A	Tehrān	Farsi, Turkish dialects, Kurdish
† Iraq	169,235	22,070,000	130	Republic.......................A	Baghdād	Arabic, Kurdish, Assyrian, Armenian
† Ireland	27,137	3,626,000	134	Republic.......................A	Dublin (Baile Átha Cliath)	English, Irish Gaelic
Isle of Man	221	75,000	339	Crown dependency (U.K. protection) ....B	Douglas	English, Manx Gaelic
† Israel	8,019	5,353,000	668	Republic.......................A	Jerusalem (Yerushalayim)	Hebrew, Arabic
† Italy	116,336	56,760,000	488	Republic.......................A	Rome (Roma)	Italian, German, French, Slovene
Ivory Coast, see Cote d'Ivoire	....	....	....			
† Jamaica	4,244	2,644,000	623	Parliamentary state ....A	Kingston	English, Creole
† Japan	145,850	126,060,000	864	Constitutional monarchy ....A	Tōkyō	Japanese
Jersey	45	89,000	1,978	Crown dependency (U.K. protection) ....B	St. Helier	English, French
Jiangsu	39,614	72,410,000	1,828	Province (China)..................D	Nanjing (Nanking)	Chinese dialects
Jiangxi	64,325	41,610,000	647	Province (China)..................D	Nanchang	Chinese dialects
Jilin	72,201	26,580,000	368	Province (China)..................D	Changchun	Chinese (Mandarin), Mongolian, Korean

REGION OR POLITICAL DIVISION	Area Sq. Mi.	Est. Pop. 1/1/99	Pop. Per. Sq. Mi.	Form of Government and Ruling Power		Capital	Predominant Languages
† Jordan	35,135	4,491,000	128	Constitutional monarchy	A	ʻAmmān	Arabic
Kansas	82,282	2,606,000	32	State (U.S.)	D	Topeka	English
† Kazakhstan	1,049,155	16,835,000	16	Republic	A	Astana (Aqmola)	Kazakh, Russian
Kentucky	40,411	3,937,000	97	State (U.S.)	D	Frankfort	English
† Kenya	224,961	28,580,000	127	Republic	A	Nairobi	English, Swahili, indigenous
† Kiribati	313	85,000	272	Republic	A	Bairiki	English, I-Kiribati
† Korea, North	46,540	21,230,000	456	Socialist republic	A	P'yŏngyang	Korean
† Korea, South	38,230	46,650,000	1,220	Republic	A	Seoul (Sŏul)	Korean
† Kuwait	6,880	1,952,000	284	Constitutional monarchy	A	Kuwait	Arabic, English
† Kyrgyzstan	76,641	4,531,000	59	Republic	A	Bishkek	Kirghiz, Russian
† Laos	91,429	5,334,000	58	Socialist republic	A	Viangchan (Vientiane)	Lao, French, English
† Latvia	24,595	2,368,000	96	Republic	A	Rīga	Lettish, Lithuanian, Russian, other
† Lebanon	4,016	3,534,000	880	Republic	A	Beirut (Bayrūt)	Arabic, French, Armenian, English
† Lesotho	11,720	2,110,000	180	Constitutional monarchy under military rule	A	Maseru	English, Sesotho
Liaoning	56,255	41,980,000	746	Province (China)	D	Shenyang (Mukden)	Chinese (Mandarin), Mongolian
† Liberia	38,250	2,852,000	75	Republic	A	Monrovia	English, indigenous
† Libya	679,362	4,934,000	7.3	Socialist republic	A	Tripoli (Ṭarābulus)	Arabic
† Liechtenstein	62	32,000	516	Constitutional monarchy	A	Vaduz	German
† Lithuania	25,213	3,592,000	142	Republic	A	Vilnius	Lithuanian, Polish, Russian
Louisiana	49,651	4,371,000	88	State (U.S.)	D	Baton Rouge	English
† Luxembourg	999	427,000	427	Constitutional monarchy	A	Luxembourg	French, Luxembourgish, German
Macau	6.6	433,000	65,606	Special Administrative Region (China)	D	Macau (Aomen)	Chinese (Cantonese), Portuguese
† Macedonia	9,928	2,016,000	203	Republic	A	Skopje	Macedonian, Albanian
† Madagascar	226,658	14,665,000	65	Republic	A	Antananarivo	Malagasy, French
Maine	33,741	1,249,000	37	State (U.S.)	D	Augusta	English
† Malawi	45,747	9,922,000	217	Republic	A	Lilongwe	Chichewa, English
† Malaysia	127,320	21,155,000	166	Federal constitutional monarchy	A	Kuala Lumpur and Putrajaya (4)	Malay, Chinese dialects, English, Tamil
† Maldives	115	295,000	2,565	Republic	A	Male'	Divehi
† Mali	482,077	10,275,000	21	Republic	A	Bamako	French, Bambara, indigenous
† Malta	122	381,000	3,123	Republic	A	Valletta	English, Maltese, Italian
Manitoba	250,947	1,148,000	4.6	Province (Canada)	D	Winnipeg	English
† Marshall Islands	70	64,000	914	Republic (U.S. protection)	A	Majuro (island)	English, indigenous, Japanese
Martinique	436	409,000	938	Overseas department (France)	C	Fort-de-France	French, Creole
Maryland	12,297	5,158,000	419	State (U.S.)	D	Annapolis	English
Massachusetts	9,241	6,163,000	667	State (U.S.)	D	Boston	English
† Mauritania	397,955	2,543,000	6.4	Republic	A	Nouakchott	Arabic, Pular, Soninke, Wolof
† Mauritius (incl. Dependencies)	788	1,175,000	1,491	Republic	A	Port Louis	English, Creole, Bhojpuri, French, Hindi, Tamil, others
Mayotte (5)	144	146,000	1,014	Territorial collectivity (France)	C	Dzaoudzi and Mamoudzou (4)	French, Swahili (Mahorian)
† Mexico	759,533	99,430,000	131	Federal republic	A	Mexico City (Ciudad de México)	Spanish, indigenous
Michigan	96,705	9,882,000	102	State (U.S.)	D	Lansing	English
† Micronesia, Federated States of	271	132,000	487	Republic (U.S. protection)	A	Palikir	English, indigenous
Midway Islands	2.0	100	50	Unincorporated territory (U.S.)	C		English
Minnesota	86,943	4,734,000	54	State (U.S.)	D	St. Paul	English
Mississippi	48,286	2,742,000	57	State (U.S.)	D	Jackson	English
Missouri	69,709	5,457,000	78	State (U.S.)	D	Jefferson City	English
† Moldova	13,012	4,459,000	343	Republic	A	Chişinău (Kishinev)	Romanian (Moldovan), Russian, Gagauz
† Monaco	0.8	32,000	40,000	Constitutional monarchy	A	Monaco	French, English, Italian, Monegasque
† Mongolia	604,829	2,599,000	4.3	Republic	A	Ulan Bator (Ulaanbaatar)	Khalkha Mongol, Turkish, Russian, Chinese
Montana	4,095	896,000	219	State (U.S.)	D	Helena	English
Montserrat	39	13,000	333	Dependent territory (U.K.)	C	Plymouth	English
† Morocco (excl. Western Sahara)	172,414	29,390,000	170	Constitutional monarchy	A	Rabat	Arabic, Berber dialects, French
† Mozambique	308,642	19,895,000	64	Republic	A	Maputo	Portuguese, indigenous
† Myanmar (Burma)	261,228	47,700,000	183	Provisional military government	A	Yangon (Rangoon)	Burmese, indigenous
† Namibia	317,818	1,635,000	5.1	Republic	A	Windhoek	English, Afrikaans, German, indigenous
† Nauru	8.1	11,000	1,358	Republic	A	Yaren District	Nauruan, English
Nebraska	77,359	1,656,000	21	State (U.S.)	D	Lincoln	English
Nei Monggol (Inner Mongolia)	456,759	23,475,000	51	Autonomous region (China)	D	Hohhot	Mongolian
† Nepal	56,827	23,995,000	422	Constitutional monarchy	A	Kathmandu	Nepali, Maithali, Bhojpuri, other indigenous
† Netherlands	16,164	15,770,000	976	Constitutional monarchy	A	Amsterdam and The Hague ('s-Gravenhage)	Dutch
Netherlands Antilles	309	207,000	670	Self-governing territory (Netherlands protection)	B	Willemstad	Dutch, Papiamento, English
Nevada	110,567	1,846,000	17	State (U.S.)	D	Carson City	English
New Brunswick	28,355	752,000	27	Province (Canada)	D	Fredericton	English, French
New Caledonia	7,172	196,000	27	Overseas territory (France)	C	Nouméa	French, indigenous
Newfoundland	156,649	535,000	3.4	Province (Canada)	D	St. John's	English
New Hampshire	9,283	1,195,000	129	State (U.S.)	D	Concord	English
New Hebrides, see Vanuatu							
New Jersey	8,215	8,118,000	988	State (U.S.)	D	Trenton	English
New Mexico	121,599	1,742,000	14	State (U.S.)	D	Santa Fe	English, Spanish
New South Wales	309,499	6,348,000	21	State (Australia)	D	Sydney	English
New York	53,990	18,270,000	338	State (U.S.)	D	Albany	English
† New Zealand	104,454	3,644,000	35	Parliamentary state	A	Wellington	English, Maori
† Nicaragua	50,054	4,650,000	93	Republic	A	Managua	Spanish, English, indigenous
† Niger	489,191	9,815,000	20	Republic	A	Niamey	French, Hausa, Djerma, indigenous
† Nigeria	356,669	112,170,000	314	Provisional military government	A	Abuja	English, Hausa, Fulani, Yoruba, Ibo, indigenous
Ningxia Huizu	25,637	5,216,000	203	Autonomous region (China)	D	Yinchuan	Chinese (Mandarin)
Niue	100	1,600	16	Self-governing state (New Zealand protection)	B	Alofi	English, Niuean
Norfolk Island	14	2,200	157	External territory (Australia)	C	Kingston	English, Tahitian
North America	9,500,000	472,600,000	50				
North Carolina	52,672	7,530,000	143	State (U.S.)	D	Raleigh	English
North Dakota	70,704	652,000	9.2	State (U.S.)	D	Bismarck	English
Northern Ireland	5,467	1,652,000	302	Administrative division (U.K.)	D	Belfast	English
Northern Mariana Islands	184	68,000	370	Commonwealth (U.S. protection)	B	Saipan (island)	English, Chamorro, Carolinian
Northern Territory	519,771	185,000	0.4	Territory (Australia)	D	Darwin	English, indigenous
Northwest Territories	589,315	41,000	0.1	Territory (Canada)	D	Yellowknife	English, indigenous
† Norway (incl. Svalbard and Jan Mayen)	149,405	4,430,000	30	Constitutional monarchy	A	Oslo	Norwegian, Lapp, Finnish
Nova Scotia	21,425	941,000	44	Province (Canada)	D	Halifax	English
Nunavut	733,594	25,000	0.03	Territory (Canada)	D	Iqaluit	English, indigenous

REGION OR POLITICAL DIVISION	Area Sq. Mi.	Est. Pop. 1/1/99	Pop. Per. Sq. Mi.	Form of Government and Ruling Power		Capital	Predominant Languages
Oceania (incl. Australia)	3,300,000	29,900,000	9.1				
Ohio	44,828	11,250,000	251	State (U.S.)	D	Columbus	English
Oklahoma	69,903	3,339,000	48	State (U.S.)	D	Oklahoma City	English
† Oman	82,030	2,405,000	29	Monarchy	A	Muscat	Arabic, English, Baluchi, Urdu, Indian dialects
Ontario	412,581	11,465,000	28	Province (Canada)	D	Toronto	English
Oregon	97,132	3,286,000	34	State (U.S.)	D	Salem	English
† Pakistan (incl. part of Jammu and Kashmir).................	339,732	136,620,000	402	Federal Islamic republic	A	Islāmābād	English, Urdu, Punjabi, Sindhi, Pashto
† Palau (Belau)	196	18,000	92	Republic.........................	A	Koror and Melekeok [4]	Angaur, English, Japanese, Palauan, Sonsorolese, Tobi
† Panama.....................	29,157	2,757,000	95	Republic.........................	A	Panamá	Spanish, English
† Papua New Guinea	178,703	4,652,000	26	Parliamentary state	A	Port Moresby	English, Motu, Pidgin, indigenous
† Paraguay	157,048	5,362,000	34	Republic.........................	A	Asunción	Spanish, Guarani
Pennsylvania.................	46,059	12,110,000	263	State (U.S.)	D	Harrisburg	English
† Peru	496,225	26,365,000	53	Republic.........................	A	Lima	Quechua, Spanish, Aymara
† Philippines	115,831	78,530,000	678	Republic.........................	A	Manila	English, Pilipino, Tagalog
Pitcairn (incl. Dependencies)	19	400	21	Dependent territory (U.K.)	C	Adamstown	English, Tahitian
† Poland	121,196	38,600,000	318	Republic.........................	A	Warsaw (Warszawa)	Polish
† Portugal	35,516	9,925,000	279	Republic.........................	A	Lisbon (Lisboa)	Portuguese
Prince Edward Island	2,185	136,000	62	Province (Canada)	D	Charlottetown	English
Puerto Rico	3,515	3,870,000	1,101	Commonwealth (U.S. protection)	B	San Juan	Spanish, English
† Qatar.....................	4,412	710,000	161	Monarchy	A	Doha (Ad Dawḥah)	Arabic, English
Qinghai	277,993	4,968,000	18	Province (China)	D	Xining	Tibetan dialects, Mongolian, Turkish dialects, Chinese (Mandarin)
Quebec.....................	594,860	7,376,000	12	Province (Canada)	D	Québec	French, English
Queensland	666,875	3,416,000	5.1	State (Australia)	D	Brisbane	English
Reunion	967	711,000	735	Overseas department (France)	C	Saint-Denis	French, Creole
Rhode Island	1,231	970,000	788	State (U.S.)	D	Providence	English
Rhodesia, see Zimbabwe	....	....	....				
† Romania	91,699	22,360,000	244	Republic.........................	A	Bucharest (Bucureşti)	Romanian, Hungarian, German
† Russia	6,592,849	146,630,000	22	Federal republic	A	Moscow (Moskva)	Russian, Tatar, Ukrainian
† Rwanda	10,169	8,055,000	792	Republic.........................	A	Kigali	English, French, Kinyarwanda, Swahili
St. Helena (incl. Dependencies)	121	7,000	58	Dependent territory (U.K.)	C	Jamestown	English
† St. Kitts and Nevis............	104	42,000	404	Parliamentary state	A	Basseterre	English
† St. Lucia	238	153,000	643	Parliamentary state	A	Castries	English, French
St. Pierre and Miquelon	93	7,000	75	Territorial collectivity (France)	C	Saint-Pierre	French
† St. Vincent and the Grenadines	150	120,000	800	Parliamentary state	A	Kingstown	English, French
† Samoa	1,093	228,000	209	Constitutional monarchy	A	Apia	English, Samoan
† San Marino	24	25,000	1,042	Republic.........................	A	San Marino	Italian
† Sao Tome and Principe	372	152,000	409	Republic.........................	A	São Tomé	Portuguese, Fang and other indigenous
Saskatchewan	251,866	1,029,000	4.1	Province (Canada)	D	Regina	English
† Saudi Arabia...............	830,000	21,140,000	25	Monarchy	A	Riyadh (Ar Riyāḍ)	Arabic
Scotland	30,421	5,196,000	171	Administrative division (U.K.)	D	Edinburgh	English, Scots Gaelic
† Senegal...................	75,951	9,885,000	130	Republic.........................	A	Dakar	French, Wolof, Fulani, Serer, indigenous
† Seychelles	175	79,000	451	Republic.........................	A	Victoria	English, French, Creole
Shaanxi	79,151	36,020,000	455	Province (China)	D	Xi'an (Sian)	Chinese (Mandarin)
Shandong	59,074	89,310,000	1,512	Province (China)	D	Jinan	Chinese (Mandarin)
Shanghai	2,394	14,530,000	6,069	Autonomous city (China).........	D	Shanghai	Chinese (Wu)
Shanxi	60,232	31,550,000	524	Province (China)	D	Taiyuan	Chinese (Mandarin)
Sichuan....................	188,263	80,010,000	425	Province (China)	D	Chengdu	Chinese (Mandarin), Tibetan dialects, Miao-Yao
† Sierra Leone	27,925	5,182,000	186	Republic.........................	A	Freetown	English, Krio, Mende, Temne, indigenous
† Singapore	246	3,511,000	14,272	Republic.........................	A	Singapore	Chinese (Mandarin), English, Malay, Tamil
† Slovakia	18,933	5,395,000	285	Republic.........................	A	Bratislava	Slovak, Hungarian
† Slovenia	7,820	1,971,000	252	Republic.........................	A	Ljubljana	Slovenian, Serbo-Croatian
† Solomon Islands	10,954	448,000	41	Parliamentary state	A	Honiara	English, Pidgin
† Somalia	246,201	6,993,000	28	None	A	Mogadishu (Muqdisho)	Arabic, Somali, English, Italian
† South Africa	471,009	43,140,000	92	Republic.........................	A	Pretoria, Cape Town, and Bloemfontein	Afrikaans, English, Sotho, Tswana, Zulu, others
South America	6,900,000	340,800,000	49				
South Australia	379,924	1,510,000	4.0	State (Australia)	D	Adelaide	English
South Carolina	31,189	3,801,000	122	State (U.S.)	D	Columbia	English
South Dakota	77,122	740,000	9.6	State (U.S.)	D	Pierre	English
South Georgia (incl. Dependencies) [3]	1,450	(1)	....	Dependent territory (U.K.)	C	....	English
South West Africa, see Namibia....	....	....	....				
† Spain.....................	194,885	39,150,000	201	Constitutional monarchy	A	Madrid	Spanish (Castilian), Catalan, Galician, Basque
Spanish North Africa [6]..........	12	153,000	12,750	Five possessions (Spain)	C	....	Spanish, Arabic, Berber dialects
Spanish Sahara, see Western Sahara	....	....	....				
† Sri Lanka	24,962	19,040,000	763	Socialist republic................	A	Colombo and Sri Jayawardenapura	English, Sinhala, Tamil
† Sudan	967,499	34,010,000	35	Republic.........................	A	Khartoum (Al Kharṭūm)	Arabic, Nubian and other indigenous, English
† Suriname	63,251	430,000	6.8	Republic.........................	A	Paramaribo	Dutch, Sranan Tongo, English, Hindustani, Javanese
† Swaziland	6,704	975,000	145	Monarchy	A	Mbabane and Lobamba	English, siSwati
† Sweden...................	173,732	8,899,000	51	Constitutional monarchy	A	Stockholm	Swedish, Lapp, Finnish
Switzerland..................	15,943	7,268,000	456	Federal republic	A	Bern (Berne)	German, French, Italian, Romansch
† Syria	71,498	16,955,000	237	Socialist republic................	A	Damascus (Dimashq)	Arabic, Kurdish, Armenian, Aramaic, Circassian
Taiwan	13,900	22,010,000	1,583	Republic.........................	A	T'aipei	Chinese (Mandarin), Taiwanese (Min), Hakka
† Tajikistan.................	55,251	6,059,000	110	Republic.........................	A	Dushanbe	Tajik, Russian
† Tanzania	364,900	30,935,000	85	Republic.........................	A	Dar es Salaam and Dodoma	English, Swahili, indigenous
Tasmania	26,178	485,000	19	State (Australia)	D	Hobart	English
Tennessee	42,146	5,435,000	129	State (U.S.)	D	Nashville	English
Texas	267,278	19,710,000	74	State (U.S.)	D	Austin	English, Spanish
† Thailand	198,115	60,330,000	305	Constitutional monarchy	A	Bangkok (Krung Thep)	Thai, indigenous
Tianjin (Tientsin)	4,363	9,688,000	2,220	Autonomous city (China)..........	D	Tianjin (Tientsin)	Chinese (Mandarin)
† Togo	21,925	4,992,000	228	Republic.........................	A	Lomé	French, Ewe, Mina, Kabye, Dagomba
Tokelau	4.6	1,400	304	Island territory (New Zealand)	C	....	English, Tokelauan

REGION OR POLITICAL DIVISION	Area Sq. Mi.	Est. Pop. 1/1/99	Pop. Per. Sq. Mi.	Form of Government and Ruling Power		Capital	Predominant Languages
† Tonga	288	108,000	375	Constitutional monarchy	A	Nuku'alofa	Tongan, English
† Trinidad and Tobago	1,980	1,110,000	561	Republic	A	Port of Spain	English, Hindi, French, Spanish
Tristan da Cunha	40	300	7.5	Dependency (St. Helena)	C	Edinburgh	English
† Tunisia	63,170	9,448,000	150	Republic	A	Tunis	Arabic, French
† Turkey	300,948	65,090,000	216	Republic	A	Ankara	Turkish, Kurdish, Arabic
† Turkmenistan	188,456	4,332,000	23	Republic	A	Ashkhabad (Ashgabat)	Turkmen, Russian, Uzbek
Turks and Caicos Islands	193	16,000	83	Dependent territory (U.K.)	C	Grand Turk	English
Tuvalu	10	10,000	1,000	Parliamentary state	A	Funafuti	Tuvaluan, English
† Uganda	93,104	22,485,000	242	Republic	A	Kampala	English, Luganda, Swahili, indigenous
† Ukraine	233,090	49,965,000	214	Republic	A	Kiev (Kyïv)	Ukrainian, Russian, Romanian, Polish, Hungarian
† United Arab Emirates	32,278	2,323,000	72	Federation of monarchs	A	Abū Ẓaby (Abu Dhabi)	Arabic, Farsi, English, Hindi, Urdu
† United Kingdom	94,249	59,040,000	626	Parliamentary monarchy	A	London	English, Welsh, Scots Gaelic
† United States	3,787,425	271,490,000	72	Federal republic	A	Washington	English, Spanish
Upper Volta, see Burkina Faso							
† Uruguay	68,500	3,297,000	48	Republic	A	Montevideo	Spanish
Utah	84,905	2,091,000	25	State (U.S.)	D	Salt Lake City	English
† Uzbekistan	172,742	23,940,000	139	Republic	A	Tashkent (Toshkent)	Uzbek, Russian
† Vanuatu	4,707	187,000	40	Republic	A	Port Vila	Bislama, English, French
Vatican City	0.2	1,000	5,000	Monarchical-sacerdotal state	A	Vatican City	Italian, Latin, other
† Venezuela	352,144	23,005,000	65	Federal republic	A	Caracas	Spanish, Amerindian
Vermont	9,615	597,000	62	State (U.S.)	D	Montpelier	English
Victoria	87,877	4,669,000	53	State (Australia)	D	Melbourne	English
† Vietnam	127,428	76,790,000	603	Socialist republic	A	Hanoi	Vietnamese, French, Chinese, English, Khmer, indigenous
Virginia	42,326	6,787,000	160	State (U.S.)	D	Richmond	English
Virgin Islands	133	119,000	895	Unincorporated territory (U.S.)	C	Charlotte Amalie	English, Spanish, Creole
Wake Island	3.0	200	67	Unincorporated territory (U.S.)	C		English
Wales	8,015	2,952,000	368	Administrative division (U.K.)	D	Cardiff	English, Welsh Gaelic
Wallis and Futuna	99	15,000	152	Overseas territory (France)	C	Mata-Utu	French, Wallisian
Washington	70,637	5,701,000	81	State (U.S.)	D	Olympia	English
West Bank	2,262	1,911,000	845	Israeli occupied territory with limited self-govt.			Arabic, Hebrew
Western Australia	975,101	1,807,000	1.9	State (Australia)	D	Perth	English
Western Sahara	102,703	237,000	2.3	Occupied by Morocco	C		Arabic
Western Samoa, see Samoa							
West Virginia	24,231	1,819,000	75	State (U.S.)	D	Charleston	English
Wisconsin	65,500	5,240,000	80	State (U.S.)	D	Madison	English
Wyoming	97,819	489,000	5.0	State (U.S.)	D	Cheyenne	English
Xinjiang Uygur (Sinkiang)	617,763	17,015,000	28	Autonomous region (China)	D	Ürümqi	Turkish dialects, Mongolian, Tungus, English
Xizang (Tibet)	471,044	2,484,000	5.3	Autonomous region (China)	D	Lhasa	Tibetan dialects
† Yemen	203,850	16,660,000	82	Republic	A	Ṣan'ā'	Arabic
† Yugoslavia	39,449	11,205,000	284	Republic	A	Belgrade (Beograd)	Serbo-Croatian, Albanian
Yukon	186,661	30,000	0.2	Territory (Canada)	D	Whitehorse	English, Inuktitut, indigenous
Yunnan	152,124	40,865,000	269	Province (China)	D	Kunming	Chinese (Mandarin), Tibetan dialects, Khmer, Miao-Yao
Zaire, see Congo, Democratic Republic of the							
† Zambia	290,586	9,561,000	33	Republic	A	Lusaka	English, Tonga, Lozi, other indigenous
Zhejiang	39,305	44,340,000	1,128	Province (China)	D	Hangzhou	Chinese dialects
† Zimbabwe	150,873	11,105,000	74	Republic	A	Harare (Salisbury)	English, Shona, Ndebele
WORLD	57,900,000	5,952,000,000	103				

† Member of the United Nations (2000).
. . . None, or not applicable.
(1) No permanent population.
(2) North Cyprus unilaterally declared its independence from Cyprus in 1983.
(3) Claimed by Argentina.
(4) Future capital.
(5) Claimed by Comoros.
(6) Comprises Ceuta, Melilla, and several small islands.

WORLD DEMOGRAPHIC TABLE

CONTINENT / Country	Population Estimate 1/1/99	Pop. Per Sq. Mile	Urban[1] Population Projected 2000	%[1] Urban	Crude Birth[2] Rate per '000 - 1996	Death[2,4] Rate	Natural[2] Increase % - 1996	Infant[2] Mortality 1996	Lifetime Expectance[3] Male 1998	Female 1998
NORTH AMERICA										
Bahamas	282,000	52	267,000	88.5	19	6	1.3	23	70	79
Belize	233,000	26	112,000	46.5	33	6	2.7	34	73	76
Canada	30,450,000	8	23,645,000	77.1	13	7	0.6	6	75	81
Costa Rica	3,639,000	184	1,970,000	51.9	24	4	2.0	14	74	79
Cuba	11,075,000	259	8,727,000	77.9	14	7	0.8	8	74	78
Dominica	66,000	216	50,000	71.0	18	5	1.3	10	74	80
Dominican Republic	8,064,000	431	5,537,000	65.2	24	6	1.8	48	69	73
El Salvador	5,797,000	714	2,947,000	46.6	28	6	2.2	32	66	71
Guatemala	12,170,000	289	4,932,000	40.4	34	7	2.7	51	65	70
Haiti	6,833,000	638	2,727,000	34.9	38	16	2.2	104	57	60
Honduras	5,931,000	137	3,042,000	46.9	33	6	2.8	42	68	72
Jamaica	2,644,000	623	1,451,000	56.1	22	6	1.6	16	72	77
Mexico	99,430,000	131	73,553,000	74.4	26	5	2.2	25	69	75
Nicaragua	4,650,000	93	3,038,000	64.7	34	6	2.8	46	67	70
Panama	2,757,000	95	1,649,000	57.8	23	5	1.8	30	72	76
St. Lucia	153,000	643	57,000	37.8	22	6	1.6	20	66	74
Trinidad and Tobago	1,110,000	561	993,000	74.1	16	7	0.9	18	71	75
United States	271,490,000	72	214,504,000	77.2	15	8	0.7	8	73	80
SOUTH AMERICA										
Argentina	36,500,000	34	33,089,000	89.4	19	9	1.1	28	70	77
Bolivia	7,904,000	19	5,400,000	64.8	32	11	2.2	68	60	63
Brazil	170,860,000	52	137,527,000	81.3	21	9	1.2	55	66	70
Chile	14,880,000	51	12,868,000	84.6	18	6	1.2	14	71	78
Colombia	38,950,000	88	29,154,000	74.9	21	5	1.7	26	67	73
Ecuador	12,450,000	119	7,892,000	62.4	25	6	2.0	35	67	73
Guyana	706,000	9	334,000	38.2	19	10	0.9	51	64	70
Paraguay	5,362,000	34	3,077,000	56.0	31	4	2.7	23	69	73
Peru	26,365,000	53	18,674,000	72.8	24	6	1.8	52	66	69
Suriname	430,000	7	236,000	52.3	24	6	1.8	29	69	74
Uruguay	3,297,000	48	2,990,000	91.3	17	9	0.8	15	70	76
Venezuela	23,005,000	65	21,113,000	87.4	24	5	1.9	30	70	76
EUROPE										
Albania	3,347,000	302	1,367,000	39.1	22	8	1.5	49	70	76
Austria	8,136,000	251	5,361,000	64.7	11	10	0.1	7	74	80
Belarus	10,405,000	130	7,654,000	74.4	12	14	-0.1	13	65	75
Belgium	10,180,000	864	9,985,000	97.4	11	10	0.1	7	74	81
Bosnia and Herzegovina	3,427,000	174	1,872,000	43.1	6	16	-1.0	43	71	76
Bulgaria	8,215,000	192	5,820,000	70.1	8	14	-0.5	16	68	75
Croatia	4,675,000	214	2,589,000	57.7	10	11	-0.2	10	68	77
Czech Republic	10,280,000	338	6,755,000	66.3	10	11	-0.1	8	68	75
Denmark	5,347,000	321	4,522,000	85.7	12	11	0.1	7	73	79
Estonia	1,414,000	81	1,053,000	74.3	11	14	-0.3	17	64	75
Finland	5,154,000	39	3,366,000	65.0	12	10	0.2	5	73	80
France	58,890,000	279	44,630,000	75.6	11	9	0.2	5	74	81
Germany	82,700,000	600	72,386,000	87.5	10	11	-0.2	6	74	80
Greece	10,685,000	210	6,368,000	60.1	11	9	0.1	8	76	81
Hungary	10,195,000	284	6,568,000	67.0	11	15	-0.4	12	65	74
Iceland	272,000	7	260,000	92.3	15	7	0.9	4	76	81
Ireland	3,626,000	134	2,092,000	58.5	14	8	0.5	7	73	79
Italy	56,760,000	488	38,317,000	67.0	10	10	z	7	75	79
Latvia	2,368,000	96	1,781,000	74.3	11	15	-0.4	21	63	75
Lithuania	3,592,000	142	2,755,000	74.7	13	13	z	17	65	76
Luxembourg	427,000	427	391,000	91.1	12	9	0.3	7	73	80
Macedonia	2,016,000	203	1,385,000	62.0	13	8	0.5	30	70	76
Moldova	4,459,000	343	2,460,000	55.2	16	12	0.5	48	64	72
Netherlands	15,770,000	976	14,181,000	89.4	12	8	0.4	6	75	81
Norway	4,430,000	30	3,269,000	74.2	12	10	0.2	6	74	81
Poland	38,600,000	318	25,389,000	65.6	12	10	0.2	12	67	76
Portugal	9,925,000	279	3,719,000	38.0	11	10	z	8	72	79
Romania	22,360,000	244	13,100,000	58.2	10	12	-0.3	23	67	73
Slovakia	5,395,000	285	3,283,000	61.1	13	9	0.3	11	67	75
Slovenia	1,971,000	252	1,007,000	52.6	8	9	-0.1	7	69	78
Spain	39,150,000	201	30,895,000	77.6	8	9	-0.1	7	75	81
Sweden	8,899,000	51	7,414,000	83.3	13	11	0.2	6	76	82
Switzerland	7,268,000	456	4,638,000	62.6	12	9	0.3	6	75	82
Ukraine	49,965,000	214	36,838,000	72.5	11	15	-0.4	23	64	74
United Kingdom	59,040,000	626	52,198,000	89.5	13	11	0.2	6	75	79
Yugoslavia	11,205,000	284	6,286,000	59.9	13	10	0.4	23	70	75
Russia	146,630,000	22	113,567,000	77.7	10	16	-0.6	25	62	74
ASIA										
Afghanistan	25,315,000	101	5,600,000	21.9	43	18	2.5	150	45	46
Armenia	3,416,000	297	2,562,000	70.0	16	8	0.9	39	70	76
Azerbaijan	7,883,000	236	4,483,000	57.3	22	9	1.4	75	68	76
Bahrain	622,000	2,330	570,000	92.2	24	3	2.0	17	71	75
Bangladesh	126,110,000	2,268	27,172,000	21.2	31	11	1.9	102	58	58
Brunei	319,000	143	235,000	72.2	26	5	2.0	24	73	77
Cambodia	11,485,000	164	2,631,000	23.5	44	16	2.8	108	53	55
China	1,242,070,000	337	444,333,000/5	34.3/5	17	7	1.0	39	68	72
Cyprus	615,000	270	n.a.	n.a.	n.a.	n.a.	n.a.	n.a.	76	80
Georgia	5,085,000	189	3,289,000	60.7	13	12	0.1	23	70	78
India	992,470,000	802	286,323,000	28.4	26	10	1.6	71	63	63
Indonesia	214,530,000	285	85,458,000	40.2	24	8	1.5	63	63	67
Iran	64,830,000	103	47,085,000	61.6	34	7	2.7	53	69	70
Iraq	22,070,000	130	17,752,000	76.8	43	7	3.7	60	67	70
Israel	5,353,000	668	5,541,000	91.2	20	6	1.4	8	75	79
Japan	126,060,000	864	99,724,000	78.9	10	8	0.2	4	77	83
Jordan	4,491,000	128	4,697,000	74.2	37	4	3.3	32	68	72
Kazakhstan	16,835,000	16	10,442,000	61.7	19	10	0.9	63	67	75
Korea, North	21,230,000	456	15,021,000	62.8	23	5	1.7	26	69	75
Korea, South	46,650,000	1,220	40,395,000	86.2	16	6	1.1	8	69	76
Kuwait	1,952,000	284	1,919,000	97.6	20	2	1.8	11	74	78
Kyrgyzstan	4,531,000	59	1,821,000	40.1	26	9	1.7	78	67	74
Laos	5,334,000	58	1,336,000	23.5	42	14	2.8	97	52	55
Lebanon	3,534,000	880	2,951,000	89.7	28	6	2.2	37	68	72
Malaysia	21,155,000	166	12,767,000	57.3	26	5	2.1	24	70	74
Mongolia	2,599,000	4	1,738,000	63.5	26	9	1.7	70	64	67

CONTINENT / Country	Population Estimate 1/1/99	Pop. Per Sq. Mile	Urban(1) Population Projected 2000	%(1) Urban	Crude Birth(2) Rate per '000 - 1996	Crude Death(2,4) Rate per '000 - 1996	Natural(2) Increase % - 1996	Infant(2) Mortality 1996	Lifetime Expectancy(3) Male 1998	Lifetime Expectancy(3) Female 1998
Myanmar	47,700,000	183	13,661,000	27.7	30	12	1.8	81	59	62
Nepal	23,995,000	422	2,893,000	11.9	37	13	2.4	79	57	57
Oman	2,405,000	29	2,282,000	84.0	38	4	3.3	27	69	73
Pakistan	136,620,000	402	57,792,000	37.0	36	11	2.5	97	63	65
Philippines	78,530,000	678	43,985,000	58.6	30	7	2.3	36	67	70
Qatar	710,000	161	554,000	92.5	21	4	1.7	20	70	75
Saudi Arabia	21,140,000	25	18,572,000	85.7	38	5	3.3	46	70	73
Singapore	3,511,000	14,272	3,587,000	100.0	16	5	1.2	5	74	79
Sri Lanka	19,040,000	763	4,434,000	23.6	18	6	1.2	21	71	75
Syria	16,955,000	237	8,784,000	54.5	40	6	3.4	40	67	71
Taiwan	22,010,000	1,583	n.a./6	n.a./6	15	6	0.9	7	72	79
Tajikistan	6,059,000	110	2,102,000	32.9	34	8	2.5	113	69	74
Thailand	60,330,000	305	13,057,000	21.6	17	7	1.0	33	65	72
Turkey	65,090,000	216	49,517,000	75.3	22	6	1.7	43	67	71
Turkmenistan	4,332,000	23	2,038,000	45.5	29	9	2.0	82	64	70
United Arab Emirates	2,323,000	72	2,099,000	85.9	26	3	2.3	20	74	77
Uzbekistan	23,940,000	139	10,606,000	42.4	30	8	2.2	80	68	73
Vietnam	76,790,000	603	15,891,000	19.7	23	7	1.6	38	65	70
Yemen	16,660,000	82	6,886,000	38.0	45	10	3.6	72	51	52
AFRICA										
Algeria	30,805,000	33	18,727,000	59.3	29	6	2.3	49	68	70
Angola	11,020,000	23	4,371,000	34.2	45	18	2.7	139	47	51
Benin	6,202,000	143	2,630,000	42.3	47	14	3.3	105	47	51
Botswana	1,456,000	6	1,191,000	73.6	33	17	1.6	54	65	69
Burkina Faso	11,420,000	108	2,226,000	18.5	47	20	2.7	118	45	48
Burundi	5,634,000	524	625,000	9.0	43	15	2.8	102	49	53
Cameroon	15,240,000	83	7,401,000	48.9	42	14	2.9	79	57	60
Cape Verde	403,000	259	272,000	62.2	44	8	3.6	54	66	68
Central African Republic	3,410,000	14	1,499,000	41.2	40	18	2.2	112	48	53
Chad	7,458,000	15	1,729,000	23.8	44	17	2.7	120	48	51
Comoros	554,000	642	237,000	33.2	46	10	3.6	75	58	59
Congo	2,688,000	20	1,865,000	62.5	39	17	2.2	108	48	52
Congo, Democratic Republic of the	49,735,000	55	15,670,000	30.3	48	17	3.1	108	50	53
Cote d'Ivoire	15,630,000	126	7,046,000	46.5	42	16	2.7	82	49	51
Djibouti	444,000	50	572,000	83.3	43	15	2.7	107	49	52
Egypt	66,660,000	172	31,297,000	45.9	28	9	1.9	73	65	67
Equatorial Guinea	460,000	42	218,000	48.2	40	14	2.6	98	48	52
Eritrea	3,907,000	108	714,000	18.7	46	16	3.0	119	51	55
Ethiopia	59,040,000	132	11,679,000	17.7	46	18	2.9	123	48	52
Gabon	1,217,000	12	682,000	55.2	28	14	1.5	90	54	57
Gambia, The	1,314,000	318	404,000	32.5	46	15	3.1	118	45	49
Ghana	18,695,000	203	7,644,000	38.4	35	11	2.4	80	56	60
Guinea	7,508,000	79	2,577,000	32.8	43	19	2.4	134	46	47
Guinea-Bissau	1,220,000	87	280,000	23.7	40	16	2.3	116	44	47
Kenya	28,580,000	127	10,043,000	33.1	33	10	2.3	55	53	55
Lesotho	2,110,000	180	641,000	28.0	33	14	1.9	82	61	66
Liberia	2,852,000	75	1,560,000	47.9	43	12	3.1	108	56	59
Libya	4,934,000	7	5,597,000	87.6	44	8	3.7	60	64	68
Madagascar	14,665,000	65	5,133,000	29.5	43	14	2.8	94	58	61
Malawi	9,922,000	217	1,686,000	15.4	42	24	1.7	140	44	45
Mali	10,275,000	21	3,773,000	30.0	51	19	3.2	103	46	50
Mauritania	2,543,000	6	1,489,000	57.7	47	15	3.2	82	52	55
Mauritius	1,175,000	1,491	487,000	41.3	19	6	1.2	17	68	75
Morocco	29,390,000	170	16,035,000	55.3	27	6	2.2	43	64	68
Mozambique	19,895,000	64	7,869,000	40.2	46	19	2.7	126	45	48
Namibia	1,635,000	5	708,000	40.9	37	8	2.9	47	60	63
Niger	9,815,000	20	2,222,000	20.6	54	25	3.0	118	47	50
Nigeria	112,170,000	314	56,651,000	44.0	43	13	3.0	72	51	54
Rwanda	8,055,000	792	472,000	6.2	39	20	1.9	119	45	48
Sao Tome and Principe	152,000	409	68,000	46.7	34	9	2.6	61	62	66
Senegal	9,885,000	130	4,463,000	47.0	45	12	3.4	64	50	52
Sierra Leone	5,182,000	186	1,783,000	36.6	47	18	2.9	136	39	43
Somalia	6,993,000	28	3,170,000	27.5	44	13	3.1	121	47	51
South Africa	43,140,000	92	23,291,000	50.4	28	10	1.8	49	62	68
Sudan	34,010,000	35	10,772,000	36.1	41	11	2.9	76	54	56
Swaziland	975,000	145	351,000	35.7	43	11	3.2	88	58	62
Tanzania	30,935,000	85	9,376,000	27.8	41	19	2.2	106	50	53
Togo	4,992,000	228	1,556,000	33.3	46	11	3.6	84	55	59
Tunisia	9,448,000	150	6,445,000	65.5	24	5	1.9	35	68	71
Uganda	22,485,000	242	3,180,000	14.2	46	21	2.5	99	42	44
Zambia	9,561,000	33	4,067,000	44.5	45	24	2.1	96	45	47
Zimbabwe	11,105,000	74	4,387,000	35.3	32	18	1.4	73	50	52
OCEANIA										
Australia	18,735,000	6	15,954,000	84.7	14	7	0.7	6	75	81
Fiji	808,000	115	359,000	42.3	23	6	1.7	17	71	75
Kiribati	85,000	272	32,000	37.3	31	12	1.9	98	53	56
Micronesia, Federated States of	132,000	487	42,000	29.7	28	6	2.2	36	66	70
New Zealand	3,644,000	35	3,268,000	86.9	16	8	0.8	7	73	79
Papua New Guinea	4,652,000	26	838,000	17.4	33	10	2.3	60	57	59
Samoa	228,000	209	38,000	21.5	31	6	2.5	34	68	71
Solomon Islands	448,000	41	87,000	19.7	38	4	3.4	26	70	74
Tonga	108,000	375	46,000	46.4	24	7	1.7	20	66	71
Vanuatu	187,000	40	38,000	20.1	31	9	2.2	65	66	70

This table presents data, where available, for most independent nations having an area greater than 200 square miles

n.a. - not available

z - negligible

(1) Source: United Nations *World Urbanization Prospects*

(2) Source: United Nations Bureau of the Census *World Population Profile*

(3) Source: United States Central Intelligence Agency *World Factbook*

(4) Deaths under one year of age per 1,000 live births

(5) Includes data for Taiwan

(6) Data included with China

WORLD AGRICULTURE TABLE

CONTINENT / Country	Area square miles	1994 Area in Agriculture[1]	%	1994-1996 Avg. Production Wheat[1] '000 metric tons	Rice[1] '000 metric tons	Corn[1] '000 metric tons	1994-1996 Avg. Cattle[1] '000	Swine[1] '000	Sheep[1] '000	1994-96 Avg. Agricultural Exports '000,000 of US $	Imports '000,000 of US $
NORTH AMERICA											
Bahamas	5,382	46	0.9%	0	0	z	1	5	6	$7	$2
Belize	8,866	506	5.7%	0	10	30	61	23	3	$2	$1
Canada	3,849,674	287,645	7.5%	25,917	0	7,289	12,712	11,137	633	$15,586	$2,619
Costa Rica	19,730	11,042	56.0%	0	179	29	1,726	317	3	$111	$37
Cuba	42,804	25,815	60.3%	0	277	87	4,633	1,667	310	$4	$94
Dominica	305	69	22.8%	0	0	z	13	5	8	z	$2
Dominican Republic	18,704	15,097	80.7%	0	443	37	2,368	933	133	$3	$62
El Salvador	8,124	6,039	74.3%	0	57	581	1,224	275	5	$8	$66
Guatemala	42,042	17,421	41.4%	25	30	1,099	1,911	774	525	$69	$42
Haiti	10,714	5,425	50.6%	0	100	201	1,243	412	131	$1	$5
Honduras	43,277	13,784	31.9%	1	37	638	2,175	600	13	$30	$12
Jamaica	4,244	1,942	45.8%	0	z	4	437	193	1	$5	$28
Mexico	759,533	411,197	54.1%	3,665	378	18,205	29,678	15,843	5,864	$484	$1,253
Nicaragua	50,054	28,510	57.0%	0	227	298	1,762	387	4	$11	$8
Panama	29,157	8,243	28.3%	0	198	110	1,450	254	0	$3	$19
St. Lucia	238	81	34.1%	0	0	z	12	14	13	$1	$7
Trinidad and Tobago	1,980	514	25.9%	0	13	5	36	32	12	$2	$4
United States	3,787,425	1,622,585	42.8%	61,587	8,210	226,663	102,410	58,719	9,020	$20,308	$14,445
SOUTH AMERICA											
Argentina	1,073,519	653,281	60.9%	12,222	836	10,761	52,222	3,167	20,709	$713	$390
Bolivia	424,165	137,915	32.5%	103	285	557	6,010	2,406	7,870	$93	$22
Brazil	3,300,172	946,717	28.7%	2,329	10,572	33,649	161,490	35,935	18,258	$2,230	$1,058
Chile	292,135	59,652	20.4%	1,294	144	937	3,788	1,461	4,597	$1,523	$220
Colombia	440,831	172,135	39.0%	81	1,729	1,084	25,758	2,510	2,540	$463	$308
Ecuador	105,037	31,386	29.9%	22	1,327	578	5,012	2,595	1,697	$114	$97
Guyana	83,000	6,664	8.0%	0	480	3	253	22	130	$8	$3
Paraguay	157,048	92,567	58.9%	376	101	644	9,551	2,517	386	$276	$4
Peru	496,225	120,695	24.3%	133	1,249	750	4,407	2,459	12,481	$123	$132
Suriname	63,251	344	0.5%	0	227	z	100	26	7	z	$1
Uruguay	68,500	57,235	83.6%	498	799	103	10,535	273	20,394	$281	$106
Venezuela	352,144	84,440	24.0%	z	717	1,098	14,204	3,339	782	$17	$503
EUROPE											
Albania	11,100	4,347	39.2%	365	z	208	837	100	2,460	n.a.	$20
Austria	32,377	13,622	42.1%	1,265	0	1,543	2,309	3,700	363	$1,626	$1,655
Belarus	80,155	36,085	45.0%	423	0	3	5,436	4,027	235	n.a.	n.a.
Belgium	11,783	5,722/2	48.6%/2	1,665/2	0	220/2	3,175/2	7,075/2	163/2	$1,706/2	$2,751/2
Bosnia and Herzegovina	19,741	7,722	39.1%	259	0	552	326	178	279	n.a.	n.a.
Bulgaria	42,855	23,780	55.5%	2,993	6	1,430	673	2,066	3,515	n.a.	n.a.
Croatia	21,829	8,927	40.9%	789	0	1,769	491	1,239	441	$196	$105
Czech Republic	30,450	16,510	54.2%	3,754	0	124	2,060	3,985	165	$606	$477
Denmark	16,639	10,390	62.4%	4,321	0	0	2,096	10,950	153	$1,276	$1,123
Estonia	17,413	5,614	32.2%	78	0	0	418	444	65	n.a.	n.a.
Finland	130,559	9,189	7.0%	392	0	0	1,198	1,330	91	$2,564	$832
France	211,208	115,942	54.9%	32,443	121	13,409	20,428	14,561	10,794	$3,403	$5,893
Germany	137,822	66,826	48.5%	17,741	0	2,584	15,916	24,837	2,368	$4,840	$10,579
Greece	50,949	35,629	69.9%	2,222	209	1,976	579	955	9,154	$377	$552
Hungary	35,919	23,637	65.8%	4,466	12	5,143	946	4,797	1,059	$256	$420
Iceland	39,769	8,803	22.1%	0	0	0	73	42	469	$8	$24
Ireland	27,137	16,954	62.5%	642	0	0	6,417	1,509	5,782	$396	$322
Italy	116,336	60,622	52.1%	8,062	1,368	8,495	7,296	8,144	10,604	$1,375	$9,909
Latvia	24,595	9,807	39.9%	267	0	0	589	512	91	n.a.	n.a.
Lithuania	25,213	13,564	53.8%	708	0	0	1,201	1,242	39	$104	$72
Luxembourg	999	n.a./3	n.a./3	n.a./3	0	n.a./3	n.a./3	n.a./3	n.a./3	n.a./3	n.a./3
Macedonia	9,928	5,004	50.4%	329	12	147	282	177	2,415	n.a.	n.a.
Moldova	13,012	9,873	75.9%	930	0	882	825	1,080	1,360	$9	$15
Netherlands	16,164	7,610	47.1%	1,139	0	78	4,642	14,307	1,705	$6,378	$3,540
Norway	149,405	3,977	2.7%	296	0	0	992	762	2,503	$542	$729
Poland	121,196	72,228	59.6%	8,301	0	259	7,379	19,283	711	$505	$739
Portugal	35,516	15,259	43.0%	410	143	782	1,319	2,387	5,897	$857	$1,003
Romania	91,699	57,135	62.3%	5,649	21	9,625	3,645	8,327	10,926	$229	$169
Slovakia	18,933	9,444	49.9%	1,932	0	622	946	2,098	412	$248	$157
Slovenia	7,820	3,042	38.9%	158	0	288	483	585	22	$127	$358
Spain	194,885	118,981	61.1%	4,494	499	2,895	5,510	18,377	22,466	$1,214	$2,894
Sweden	173,732	12,958	7.5%	1,643	0	0	1,798	2,330	472	$4,204	$1,059
Switzerland	15,943	6,104	38.3%	631	0	228	1,761	1,617	439	$474	$1,319
Ukraine	233,090	161,625	69.3%	14,559	80	2,256	19,596	14,129	4,706	n.a.	n.a.
United Kingdom	94,249	65,815	69.8%	14,575	0	0	11,827	7,609	42,532	$2,092	$5,583
Yugoslavia	39,449	23,946	60.7%	2,568	0	5,306	1,895	4,110	2,654	$116	$205
RUSSIA											
Russia	6,592,849	847,910	12.9%	32,388	458	1,240	43,969	25,349	32,745	n.a.	n.a.
ASIA											
Afghanistan	251,826	146,926	58.3%	2,483	333	310	1,500	0	14,267	$49	$11
Armenia	11,506	4,942	43.0%	156	0	5	501	81	645	n.a.	n.a.
Azerbaijan	33,436	16,486	49.3%	689	4	13	1,645	37	4,580	n.a.	n.a.
Bahrain	267	35	13.0%	0	0	0	12	0	18	z	$30
Bangladesh	55,598	33,680	60.6%	1,248	26,631	2	23,773	0	1,075	$184	$272
Brunei	2,226	50	2.3%	0	1	0	2	5	0	z	$13
Cambodia	69,898	20,483	29.3%	0	2,971	55	2,733	2,071	0	n.a.	n.a.
China	3,690,045	2,059,735	55.8%	104,027	185,459	113,049	96,968	410,203	118,796	$4,011	$8,691
Cyprus	2,277	571	25.1%	11	0	0	65	367	260	$7	$40
Georgia	26,911	11,857	44.1%	120	0	375	966	362	783	n.a.	n.a.
India	1,237,061	699,188	56.5%	62,742	120,994	9,300	207,107	14,389	54,139	$309	$1,234
Indonesia	752,409	162,050	21.5%	0	49,162	8,141	11,578	8,193	7,212	$2,690	$2,092
Iran	630,578	243,085	38.5%	10,704	2,415	652	8,347	0	50,891	$139	$543
Iraq	169,235	36,795	21.7%	1,293	323	114	1,060	0	5,367	z	$12
Israel	8,019	2,243	28.0%	177	0	3	390	136	335	$304	$413
Japan	145,850	19,625	13.5%	496	13,780	z	4,911	10,257	23	$2,405	$15,921
Jordan	35,135	4,529	12.9%	60	0	6	62	0	2,067	$28	$74
Kazakhstan	1,049,155	856,374	81.6%	7,740	231	164	8,093	2,017	25,457	n.a.	n.a.
Korea, North	46,540	7,915	17.0%	117	2,313	1,986	1,200	3,150	363	n.a.	n.a.
Korea, South	38,230	8,197	21.4%	8	6,797	78	3,162	6,311	2	$1,314	$5,890
Kuwait	6,880	552	8.0%	z	0	1	18	0	306	z	$79
Kyrgyzstan	76,641	40,232	52.5%	783	7	154	950	134	5,368	n.a.	n.a.
Laos	91,429	6,371	7.0%	0	1,469	61	1,138	1,723	0	$82	$3
Lebanon	4,016	1,243	31.0%	57	0	5	69	55	244	$18	$95
Malaysia	127,320	30,444	23.9%	0	2,095	43	710	3,260	258	$3,712	$792
Mongolia	604,829	457,413	75.6%	265	0	0	3,018	25	13,761	n.a.	n.a.

CONTINENT / Country	Area square miles	1994 Area in Agriculture[1] square miles	%	1994-1996 Avg. Production '000 metric tons Wheat[1]	Rice[1]	Corn[1]	1994-1996 Avg. '000 Cattle[1]	Swine[1]	Sheep[1]	1994-96 Avg. Agricultural '000,000 of US $ Exports	Imports
Myanmar	261,228	40,235	15.4%	92	17,997	292	9,889	2,967	324	$247	$7
Nepal	56,827	17,475	30.8%	951	3,399	1,317	6,798	639	897	z	$57
Oman	82,030	4,104	5.0%	1	0	0	144	0	149	z	$37
Pakistan	339,732	102,355	30.1%	16,374	5,859	1,287	17,848	0	29,071	$287	$547
Philippines	115,831	41,120	35.5%	0	11,063	4,212	2,028	8,731	30	$182	$511
Qatar	4,412	251	5.7%	z	0	z	13	0	191	z	$14
Saudi Arabia	830,000	477,992	57.6%	1,689	0	6	251	0	7,640	z	$342
Singapore	246	4	1.6%	0	0	0	z	187	0	$1,060	$937
Sri Lanka	24,962	8,969	35.9%	0	2,518	33	1,684	89	17	$115	$88
Syria	71,498	53,228	74.4%	3,989	z	217	769	1	12,150	$160	$90
Taiwan	13,900	4,170/4	30.0%/4	0	2,021	252	6	16,451	0	$1,542	$3,726
Tajikistan	55,251	17,297	31.3%	252	22	42	1,199	28	1,947	n.a.	n.a.
Thailand	198,115	82,027	41.4%	1	21,819	4,217	7,231	4,624	69	$2,491	$2,377
Turkey	300,948	155,015	51.5%	18,015	227	1,917	11,867	16	35,659	$275	$1,646
Turkmenistan	188,456	124,957	66.3%	790	86	92	1,161	123	6,083	n.a.	n.a.
United Arab Emirates	32,278	1,436	4.4%	1	0	4	69	0	357	$262	$188
Uzbekistan	172,742	106,741	61.8%	2,150	425	200	5,373	316	8,922	n.a.	n.a.
Vietnam	127,428	27,359	21.5%	0	24,963	1,286	3,635	16,272	0	$946	$121
Yemen	203,850	67,973	33.3%	164	0	59	1,169	0	3,784	$16	$18
AFRICA											
Algeria	919,595	153,050	16.6%	1,732	2	z	1,255	6	17,570	$9	$300
Angola	481,354	222,008	46.1%	4	23	270	3,103	800	242	z	$14
Benin	43,475	6,629	15.2%	0	18	531	1,282	571	842	$40	$8
Botswana	224,711	100,386	44.7%	1	0	13	2,389	4	243	n.a.	n.a.
Burkina Faso	105,869	36,413	34.4%	0	80	286	403	85	340	$268	$8
Burundi	10,745	8,494	79.1%	9	36	140	4,890	1,407	3,793	$6	$5
Cameroon	183,568	35,367	19.3%	z	65	618	19	472	9	$499	$29
Cape Verde	1,557	259	16.6%	0	0	9	2,798	547	172	z	$4
Central African Republic	240,535	19,382	8.1%	0	11	70	4,642	18	2,293	$61	$1
Chad	495,755	186,316	37.6%	2	89	99	50	0	18	$143	$4
Comoros	863	514	59.5%	0	17	4	70	46	113	z	z
Congo	132,047	39,324	29.8%	0	1	20	134	46	113	$134	$4
Congo, Democratic Republic of the	905,446	88,417	9.8%	9	432	1,170	1,142	1,160	1,052	$11	$6
Cote d'Ivoire	124,518	76,081	61.1%	0	956	546	1,258	369	1,282	$840	$10
Djibouti	8,958	5,019	56.0%	0	0	z	190	0	470	$1	$26
Egypt	386,662	12,606	3.3%	5,298	4,755	4,938	3,030	27	4,171	$187	$715
Equatorial Guinea	10,831	1,290	11.9%	0	0	0	5	5	36	$6	z
Eritrea	36,170	28,595	79.1%	11	0	11	1,307	0	1,527	n.a.	n.a.
Ethiopia	446,953	117,652	26.3%	1,653	0	2,533	29,725	21	21,750	$83	$21
Gabon	103,347	19,923	19.3%	0	1	29	38	207	172	$216	$5
Gambia, The	4,127	1,448	35.1%	0	20	12	315	14	158	z	$2
Ghana	92,098	49,807	54.1%	0	193	994	1,217	363	2,234	$45	$23
Guinea	94,926	46,795	49.3%	0	612	80	2,091	43	572	n.a.	n.a.
Guinea-Bissau	13,948	5,494	39.4%	0	128	13	475	310	255	$1	z
Kenya	224,961	99,691	44.3%	310	60	2,640	13,468	104	5,600	$90	$66
Lesotho	11,720	8,977	76.6%	17	0	133	583	61	1,202	n.a.	n.a.
Liberia	38,250	8,985	23.5%	0	67	0	36	120	210	$55	$1
Libya	679,362	59,517	8.8%	163	0	1	135	0	4,433	$17	$73
Madagascar	226,658	104,652	46.2%	7	2,436	171	10,309	1,593	794	$20	$9
Malawi	45,747	13,699	29.9%	2	55	1,498	690	237	100	$7	$4
Mali	482,077	127,413	26.4%	4	453	286	5,603	63	5,435	$202	$3
Mauritania	397,955	153,398	38.5%	z	57	7	1,179	0	5,589	$3	$3
Mauritius	788	436	55.4%	0	0	1	37	17	7	$10	$58
Morocco	172,414	118,579	68.8%	4,177	42	163	2,378	10	14,322	$137	$481
Mozambique	308,642	182,162	59.0%	2	118	723	1,280	174	121	$16	$12
Namibia	317,818	149,614	47.1%	4	0	25	2,019	19	2,409	n.a.	n.a.
Niger	489,191	57,683	11.8%	4	68	5	1,987	39	3,772	$1	$1
Nigeria	356,669	280,695	78.7%	40	2,823	6,539	16,322	7,159	14,000	$19	$28
Rwanda	10,169	7,124	70.1%	5	5	66	461	83	260	$3	$6
Sao Tome and Principe	372	162	43.6%	0	0	4	4	2	2	z	z
Senegal	75,951	31,139	41.0%	0	155	101	2,808	320	4,800	$20	$19
Sierra Leone	27,925	10,587	37.9%	0	384	8	380	50	328	$1	$2
Somalia	246,201	170,077	69.1%	1	2	146	5,133	9	13,333	$10	$8
South Africa	471,009	382,239	81.2%	2,177	3	9,437	12,996	1,581	28,951	$1,016	$522
Sudan	967,499	483,590	50.0%	479	2	41	22,017	0	23,367	$253	$12
Swaziland	6,704	5,127	76.5%	z	2	108	642	30	26	n.a.	n.a.
Tanzania	364,900	150,309	41.2%	66	690	2,463	13,888	335	3,955	$96	$12
Togo	21,925	10,039	45.8%	0	41	342	246	850	1,145	$36	$3
Tunisia	63,170	34,170	54.1%	1,017	0	0	672	6	6,253	$28	$290
Uganda	93,104	33,205	35.7%	9	79	857	5,213	920	1,890	$8	$4
Zambia	290,586	136,189	46.9%	51	10	1,056	2,633	288	65	$6	$9
Zimbabwe	150,873	77,521	51.4%	201	z	1,925	4,745	263	489	$126	$43
OCEANIA											
Australia	2,966,155	1,782,624	60.1%	16,389	1,008	253	25,955	2,652	124,849	$3,965	$902
Fiji	7,056	1,672	23.7%	0	18	2	349	120	7	$18	$2
Kiribati	313	143	45.6%	0	0	0	0	9	0	$1	$1
Micronesia, Federated States of	271	n.a.	n.a.	0	z	z	9	21	0	n.a.	n.a.
New Zealand	104,454	64,120	61.4%	255	0	171	9,059	426	48,215	$2,261	$142
Papua New Guinea	178,703	2,819	1.6%	0	1	2	107	1,383	4	$231	$6
Samoa	1,093	475	43.4%	0	0	0	26	179	0	z	$2
Solomon Islands	10,954	371	3.4%	0	0	0	10	55	0	$40	z
Tonga	288	201	69.7%	0	0	0	9	85	0	$1	$3
Vanuatu	4,707	560	11.9%	0	0	1	151	60	0	$2	$2

This table presents data, where available, for most independent nations having an area greater than 200 square miles

n.a. - not available

z - negligible

Footnotes:

(1) Source: United Nations Food and Agriculture Organization

(2) Includes data for Luxembourg

(3) Data included with Belgium

(4) Source: United States Central Intelligence Agency *World Factbook*

WORLD ECONOMIC TABLE

CONTINENT / Country	Commercial Energy Production 1995 [1] Total '000 met. tons coal equiv.	Solid Fuels %	Liquid Fuels %	Gas Fuels %	Hydro. & Nuclear %	1994-96 Average Production Coal [3] '000 metric tons	Petroleum [3]	Iron ore [2]	Bauxite [2]	Trade: 1993-95 Average [4] Fuel Exports '000,000 of US $	Fuel Imports	Manufactures Exports	Manufactures Imports
NORTH AMERICA													
Bahamas	n.a.	n.a.	n.a.	n.a.	n.a.	0	0	0	0	$161	$987	$6	$73
Belize	n.a.	n.a.	n.a.	n.a.	n.a.	0	0	0	0	z	$31	$16	$182
Canada	496,012	11.4%	31.3%	42.2%	15.1%	74,556	89,155	23,562	0	$15,251	$5,546	$105,581	$128,329
Costa Rica	1,019	0.0%	0.0%	0.0%	100.0%	0	0	0	0	$19	$275	$560	$2,361
Cuba	1,582	0.0%	95.7%	3.5%	0.8%	0	1,327	0	0	z	$199	$4	$1,445
Dominica	2	0.0%	0.0%	0.0%	100.0%	0	0	0	0	z	$7	$16	$76
Dominican Republic	245	0.0%	0.0%	0.0%	100.0%	0	50	0	0	z	$681	$490	$1,450
El Salvador	926	0.0%	0.0%	0.0%	100.0%	0	0	0	0	$4	$232	$384	$1,737
Guatemala	847	0.0%	66.8%	1.8%	31.4%	0	507	2	0	$35	$354	$472	$2,065
Haiti	20	0.0%	0.0%	0.0%	100.0%	0	0	0	0	z	$55	$58	$262
Honduras	295	0.0%	0.0%	0.0%	100.0%	0	0	0	0	z	$131	$82	$834
Jamaica	15	0.0%	0.0%	0.0%	100.0%	0	0	0	11,428	$18	$463	$838	$1,429
Mexico	282,781	2.2%	78.1%	14.6%	5.2%	8,981	134,984	5,058	0	$3,838	$1,096	$28,950	$41,755
Nicaragua	677	0.0%	0.0%	0.0%	100.0%	0	0	0	0	$2	$154	$79	$539
Panama	297	0.0%	0.0%	0.0%	100.0%	0	50	0	0	$19	$324	$119	$1,738
St. Lucia	n.a.	n.a.	n.a.	n.a.	n.a.	0	0	0	0	z	$23	$30	$200
Trinidad and Tobago	17,530	0.0%	53.2%	46.8%	0.0%	0	6,492	0	0	$955	$7	$511	$847
United States	2,444,217	36.3%	22.9%	28.3%	12.5%	946,597	325,733	38,527	100	$9,894	$56,402	$402,512	$544,765
SOUTH AMERICA													
Argentina	95,425	0.3%	54.9%	38.0%	6.8%	321	35,097	10	0	$1,724	$799	$5,621	$16,751
Bolivia	7,387	0.0%	31.7%	65.4%	2.9%	0	1,336	1	0	$139	$59	$177	$1,043
Brazil	93,543	3.5%	55.1%	7.0%	34.3%	4,300	35,771	110,780	10,398	$386	$4,740	$22,945	$27,891
Chile	6,840	18.1%	13.9%	34.9%	33.1%	1,126	532	5,225	0	$37	$1,166	$1,658	$10,247
Colombia	76,510	31.6%	55.6%	7.3%	5.5%	26,204	27,434	328	0	$2,126	$332	$3,318	$9,200
Ecuador	30,094	0.0%	96.1%	1.2%	2.8%	0	19,075	0	0	$1,320	$205	$287	$2,848
Guyana	1	0.0%	0.0%	0.0%	100.0%	0	0	0	2,082	z	$139	$30	$299
Paraguay	5,110	0.0%	0.0%	0.0%	100.0%	0	0	0	0	$1	$138	$115	$1,546
Peru	11,138	1.3%	81.3%	2.3%	15.2%	144	6,244	3,834	0	$246	$609	$673	$5,187
Suriname	550	0.0%	71.5%	0.0%	28.5%	0	339	0	3,767	$224	$47	$25	$180
Uruguay	921	0.0%	0.0%	0.0%	100.0%	0	0	0	0	$17	$271	$733	$1,973
Venezuela	284,511	1.6%	76.5%	19.5%	2.4%	4,289	138,845	9,615	4,749	$12,884	$101	$2,380	$8,570
EUROPE													
Albania	1,337	4.5%	55.6%	1.2%	38.6%	136	513	0	1	n.a.	$7	n.a.	$404
Austria	8,696	5.5%	17.8%	22.3%	54.3%	1,203	1,088	561	0	$622	$2,511	$42,138	$47,371
Belarus	4,100	24.9%	67.3%	7.7%	0.0%	0	1,898	0	0	n.a.	n.a.	n.a.	n.a.
Belgium	15,761	1.6%	0.0%	0.0%	98.4%	655	596	0	0	$3,696/5	$8,122/5	$108,879/5	$92,485/5
Bosnia and Herzegovina	516	66.1%	0.0%	0.0%	33.7%	2,716	0	57	75	n.a.	n.a.	n.a.	n.a.
Bulgaria	14,449	52.8%	0.4%	0.4%	46.3%	28,636	46	300	0	$367	$676	$3,146	$3,881
Croatia	3,845	2.7%	14.2%	66.3%	16.8%	171	1,679	0	1	$688	$1,377	$13,392	$13,682
Czech Republic	41,234	86.1%	0.5%	0.7%	12.8%	71,831	159	0	0	$1,149	$1,268	$26,294	$27,310
Denmark	20,402	0.0%	64.2%	35.1%	0.7%	0	9,580	0	0	$587	$2,035	$25,764	$17,132
Estonia	3,730	100.0%	0.0%	0.0%	0.0%	12,976	0	0	0	n.a.	n.a.	n.a.	n.a.
Finland	11,630	25.0%	0.0%	0.0%	75.0%	0	0	0	0	$587	$2,035	$25,764	$17,132
France	166,032	4.7%	2.5%	2.7%	90.1%	8,845	2,471	523	0	$5,834	$16,030	$186,918	$180,096
Germany	199,956	56.4%	2.1%	11.4%	30.1%	251,043	2,920	18	0	$4,400	$25,076	$386,350	$287,197
Greece	11,917	90.0%	5.5%	0.6%	3.9%	57,995	451	807	2,283	$996	$2,253	$4,611	$15,837
Hungary	18,307	24.6%	17.3%	29.6%	28.6%	14,314	1,752	0	965	$341	$1,622	$7,235	$10,515
Iceland	931	0.0%	0.0%	0.0%	100.0%	0	0	0	0	z	$111	$187	$1,182
Ireland	5,316	30.2%	0.0%	67.1%	2.7%	1	50	0	0	$144	$887	$25,713	$20,340
Italy	42,928	0.3%	17.4%	60.4%	21.8%	321	4,645	0	11	$2,553	$12,865	$175,169	$117,345
Latvia	473	23.7%	0.0%	0.0%	76.3%	0	0	0	0	n.a.	n.a.	n.a.	n.a.
Lithuania	4,687	0.4%	3.9%	0.0%	95.7%	0	151	0	0	$358	$873	$1,215	$1,464
Luxembourg	102	0.0%	0.0%	0.0%	100.0%	0	0	0	0	n.a./6	n.a./6	n.a./6	n.a./6
Macedonia	2,889	96.6%	0.0%	0.0%	3.4%	4,098	0	9	0	n.a.	n.a.	n.a.	n.a.
Moldova	34	0.0%	0.0%	0.0%	100.0%	60	0	0	0	$4	$257	$111	$233
Netherlands	102,559	0.0%	4.9%	93.6%	1.5%	0	3,317	0	0	$11,447	$11,062	$102,370	$106,491
Norway	258,250	0.1%	76.8%	17.3%	5.8%	279	138,870	1,301	0	$17,100	$814	$9,653	$22,641
Poland	135,480	95.7%	0.3%	3.7%	0.4%	200,175	242	0	0	$1,442	$2,124	$12,816	$17,178
Portugal	1,092	0.0%	0.0%	0.0%	100.0%	143	99	6	0	$559	$2,285	$15,487	$20,122
Romania	43,328	24.7%	23.0%	47.6%	4.7%	40,614	6,747	173	178	$620	$1,821	$4,654	$4,626
Slovakia	6,629	14.8%	1.3%	5.2%	78.7%	2,720	70	232	0	$317	$1,381	$5,632	$4,579
Slovenia	3,214	31.6%	0.1%	0.7%	67.6%	4,851	2	0	0	$85	$513	$6,332	$5,769
Spain	38,977	34.9%	2.9%	1.5%	60.6%	29,336	748	884	0	$1,214	$8,102	$59,352	$68,483
Sweden	34,575	1.0%	0.0%	0.0%	99.0%	0	4	12,591	0	$1,592	$4,025	$54,523	$41,464
Switzerland	13,666	0.0%	0.0%	0.0%	100.0%	0	50	0	0	$135	$1,912	$63,266	$56,311
Ukraine	118,908	58.5%	4.9%	18.7%	17.9%	82,575	3,233	27,367	0	n.a.	n.a.	n.a.	n.a.
United Kingdom	364,154	12.4%	51.4%	26.9%	9.3%	49,059	122,967	0	0	$12,761	$8,141	$170,708	$185,386
Yugoslavia	12,027	69.6%	10.8%	8.1%	11.5%	38,397	1,120	28	128	$59	$726	$2,123	$2,676
Russia	1,512,045	16.1%	28.8%	51.2%	3.9%	281,935	297,509	40,500	3,133	n.a.	n.a.	n.a.	n.a.
ASIA													
Afghanistan	280	1.8%	0.0%	79.6%	18.2%	5	0	0	0	z	$4	$56	$284
Armenia	349	0.0%	0.0%	0.0%	100.0%	0	0	0	0	n.a.	n.a.	n.a.	n.a.
Azerbaijan	21,124	0.0%	63.3%	35.7%	0.9%	0	8,851	92	0	n.a.	n.a.	n.a.	n.a.
Bahrain	12,507	0.0%	28.0%	72.0%	0.0%	0	1,929	0	0	$2,223	$1,242	$609	$1,956
Bangladesh	9,287	0.0%	0.2%	99.4%	0.5%	0	65	0	0	$35	$830	$2,096	$2,813
Brunei	26,531	0.0%	46.5%	53.5%	0.0%	0	8,035	0	0	$2,281	$6	$30	$1,322
Cambodia	9	0.0%	0.0%	0.0%	100.0%	0	0	0	0	n.a.	n.a.	n.a.	n.a.
China/7	1,237,323	78.5%	17.3%	1.9%	2.3%	1,357,825	149,923	74,017	4,967	$8,341	$7,570	$234,342	$236,627
Cyprus	n.a.	n.a.	n.a.	n.a.	n.a.	0	0	0	0	$16	$240	$519	$2,027
Georgia	904	3.7%	31.6%	0.8%	64.0%	59	66	0	0	n.a.	n.a.	n.a.	n.a.
India	310,950	73.1%	15.3%	7.9%	3.7%	273,233	32,173	40,579	5,269	$489	$6,705	$19,618	$14,391
Indonesia	266,739	13.5%	53.9%	31.3%	1.3%	39,724	75,459	195	1,080	$10,354	$2,531	$20,627	$24,599
Iran	323,134	0.3%	81.7%	17.7%	0.3%	993	181,135	4,433	122	$14,418	$76	$743	$9,081
Iraq	58,207	0.0%	92.7%	7.2%	0.1%	0	27,986	0	0	$463	$2	$2	$594
Israel	40	0.0%	17.5%	72.5%	10.0%	0	7	0	0	z	$1,548	$15,065	$21,159
Japan	132,624	3.9%	0.8%	2.3%	93.0%	6,831	553	1	0	$2,405	$45,773	$381,625	$154,377
Jordan	5	0.0%	60.0%	0.0%	40.0%	0	1	0	0	z	$460	$721	$2,159
Kazakhstan	108,856	65.7%	27.1%	6.3%	0.9%	88,048	18,478	7,033	2,879	n.a.	n.a.	n.a.	n.a.
Korea, North	89,425	96.8%	0.0%	0.0%	3.2%	71,587	0	5,033	0	n.a.	n.a.	n.a.	n.a.
Korea, South	29,251	12.6%	0.0%	0.0%	87.4%	6,036	149	111	0	$2,022	$15,314	$94,328	$72,713
Kuwait	162,606	0.0%	92.6%	7.4%	0.0%	0	101,664	0	0	$10,864	$36	$539	$5,815
Kyrgyzstan	2,029	24.4%	6.3%	2.0%	67.3%	1,767	88	0	0	n.a.	n.a.	n.a.	n.a.
Laos	107	0.9%	0.0%	0.0%	99.1%	1	0	0	0	z	$120	$91	$275
Lebanon	90	0.0%	0.0%	0.0%	100.0%	0	0	0	0	$3	$898	$427	$3,710
Malaysia	89,147	0.1%	55.5%	43.3%	1.0%	77	33,466	160	188	$4,191	$1,402	$44,721	$52,235
Mongolia	2,472	100.0%	0.0%	0.0%	0.0%	7,741	0	0	0				

CONTINENT / Country	Total '000 met. tons coal equiv.	Solid Fuels %	Liquid Fuels %	Gas Fuels %	Hydro. & Nuclear %	Coal[3]	Petroleum[3]	Iron ore[2]	Bauxite[2]	Fuel Exports	Fuel Imports	Manuf. Exports	Manuf. Imports
Myanmar	2,866	1.9%	24.0%	67.5%	6.6%	77	766	0	0	$67	$27	$53	$878
Nepal	120	0.0%	0.0%	0.0%	100.0%	12	0	0	0	z	$222	$363	$540
Oman	64,018	0.0%	95.1%	4.9%	0.0%	0	42,106	0	0	$4,343	$65	$767	$2,873
Pakistan	28,997	7.1%	13.6%	69.0%	10.3%	3,224	2,765	0	4	$73	$1,642	$6,099	$5,711
Philippines	9,191	9.7%	2.2%	0.0%	88.1%	1,744	190	0	0	$209	$2,136	$5,795	$13,417
Qatar	48,612	0.0%	62.8%	37.2%	0.0%	0	22,627	0	0	$2,387	$14	$760	$1,590
Saudi Arabia	660,695	0.0%	91.9%	8.1%	0.0%	0	406,540	0	0	$40,702	$53	$3,151	$20,907
Singapore	n.a.	n.a.	n.a.	n.a.	n.a.	0	199	0	0	$6,553	$8,435	$80,851	$86,639
Sri Lanka	554	0.0%	0.0%	0.0%	100.0%	0	0	0	0	$7	$293	$2,382	$3,474
Syria	44,178	0.0%	92.3%	7.0%	0.7%	0	28,771	0	0	$1,607	$142	$1,269	$2,920
Taiwan	n.a.	n.a.	n.a.	n.a.	n.a.	223	62	0	0	$675	$6,300	$89,342	$66,722
Tajikistan	1,903	1.3%	4.8%	2.3%	91.5%	57	55	0	0	n.a.	n.a.	n.a.	n.a.
Thailand	29,662	39.0%	17.7%	40.4%	2.8%	18,206	2,780	46	0	$323	$3,943	$33,721	$46,790
Turkey	26,882	63.9%	18.7%	0.8%	16.6%	55,358	3,426	3,134	407	$239	$3,820	$13,652	$20,070
Turkmenistan	44,210	0.0%	16.2%	83.8%	0.0%	0	3,686	0	0	n.a.	n.a.	n.a.	n.a.
United Arab Emirates	196,363	0.0%	80.7%	19.3%	0.0%	0	110,923	0	0	$1,026	$670	$9,277	$16,040
Uzbekistan	74,513	1.7%	19.2%	78.0%	1.2%	3,342	5,043	0	0	n.a.	n.a.	n.a.	n.a.
Vietnam	20,715	36.0%	53.1%	0.0%	10.9%	7,072	8,096	0	0	$1,322	$299	$551	$3,163
Yemen	24,308	0.0%	100.0%	0.0%	0.0%	0	16,884	0	0	$780	$806	$35	$1,446
AFRICA													
Algeria	170,503	0.0%	51.3%	48.6%	0.0%	21	59,964	1,067	0	$8,911	$94	$349	$6,099
Angola	38,244	0.0%	99.0%	0.6%	0.4%	0	31,286	0	0	$3,034	$54	$3	$1,260
Benin	127	0.0%	100.0%	0.0%	0.0%	0	181	0	0	$7	$49	$5	$369
Botswana	n.a.	n.a.	n.a.	n.a.	n.a.	852	0	0	0	$1	$66	$61	$316
Burkina Faso	9	0.0%	0.0%	0.0%	100.0%	0	0	0	0	z	$41	$3	$134
Burundi	20	30.0%	0.0%	0.0%	70.0%	1	4,972	0	0	$530	$29	$143	$867
Cameroon	7,584	0.0%	95.7%	0.0%	4.3%	0	0	0	0	z	$17	z	$85
Cape Verde	n.a.	n.a.	n.a.	n.a.	n.a.	0	0	0	0	z	$3	$38	$109
Central African Republic	10	0.0%	0.0%	0.0%	100.0%	0	0	0	0	z	$3	$26	$143
Chad	n.a.	n.a.	n.a.	n.a.	n.a.	0	0	0	0	z	$6	$4	$36
Comoros	z	z	z	z	z	0	0	0	0	z	$8	$22	$445
Congo	13,140	0.0%	99.6%	0.0%	0.4%	0	9,560	0	0	$892	$8	$22	$445
Congo, Democratic Republic of the	2,457	3.9%	66.6%	0.0%	29.5%	95	1,423	0	0	$33	$47	$25	$288
Cote d'Ivoire	647	0.0%	79.0%	0.0%	21.0%	0	510	0	0	$69	$327	$141	$1,370
Djibouti	n.a.	n.a.	n.a.	n.a.	n.a.	0	0	0	0	z	$16	$1	$107
Egypt	86,314	0.0%	77.5%	20.9%	1.5%	33	45,294	1,679	0	$1,138	$121	$1,236	$6,099
Equatorial Guinea	357	0.0%	100.0%	0.0%	0.0%	0	496	0	0	z	$3	$2	$28
Eritrea	n.a.	n.a.	n.a.	n.a.	n.a.	0	0	0	0	$21	$110	$18	$647
Ethiopia	228	0.0%	0.0%	0.0%	100.0%	0	0	0	0	$2,125	$20	$27	$666
Gabon	27,248	0.0%	95.6%	4.0%	0.3%	0	17,571	0	0	z	$18	z	$124
Gambia, The	n.a.	n.a.	n.a.	n.a.	n.a.	0	189	0	593	$5	$463	$11	$1,016
Ghana	751	0.0%	0.0%	0.0%	100.0%	0	0	0	15,200	n.a.	n.a.	n.a.	n.a.
Guinea	23	0.0%	0.0%	0.0%	100.0%	0	0	0	0	z	$3	$2	$34
Guinea-Bissau	n.a.	n.a.	n.a.	n.a.	n.a.	0	50	0	0	$211	$456	$471	$1,500
Kenya	739	0.0%	0.0%	0.0%	100.0%	0	0	0	0	n.a.	n.a.	n.a.	n.a.
Lesotho	n.a.	n.a.	n.a.	n.a.	n.a.	0	0	0	0	$2	$62	$4	$109
Liberia	22	0.0%	0.0%	0.0%	100.0%	0	0	0	0	$8,112	$14	$404	$3,377
Libya	106,811	0.0%	92.1%	7.9%	0.0%	0	68,974	0	0	$5	$67	$48	$313
Madagascar	43	0.0%	0.0%	0.0%	100.0%	0	0	0	0	z	$54	$18	$393
Malawi	96	0.0%	0.0%	0.0%	100.0%	54	0	0	0	z	$108	$5	$293
Mali	28	0.0%	0.0%	0.0%	100.0%	0	0	0	0	z	$53	$2	$195
Mauritania	3	0.0%	0.0%	0.0%	100.0%	0	0	7,000	0	z	$131	$979	$1,351
Mauritius	17	0.0%	0.0%	0.0%	100.0%	0	0	0	0	$89	$1,053	$2,073	$4,296
Morocco	764	84.9%	0.9%	4.3%	9.7%	643	13	26	0	$89	$1,053	$2,073	$4,296
Mozambique	44	86.4%	0.0%	0.0%	13.6%	38	0	0	11	$14	$127	$17	$581
Namibia	n.a.	n.a.	n.a.	n.a.	n.a.	0	0	0	0	$2	$86	$4	$180
Niger	173	100.0%	0.0%	0.0%	0.0%	172	0	0	0	$9,443	$476	$29	$5,317
Nigeria	138,317	0.0%	95.1%	4.3%	0.5%	50	101,128	117	0	$9,443	$476	$29	$5,317
Rwanda	20	0.0%	0.0%	0.0%	100.0%	0	0	0	0	z	z	z	$147
Sao Tome and Principe	1	0.0%	0.0%	0.0%	100.0%	0	0	0	0	z	z	z	$15
Senegal	n.a.	n.a.	n.a.	n.a.	n.a.	0	0	0	245	$89	$164	$164	$528
Sierra Leone	n.a.	n.a.	n.a.	n.a.	n.a.	0	0	0	0	z	$3	$34	$102
Somalia	n.a.	n.a.	n.a.	n.a.	n.a.	0	0	0	0	$6	$1	$1	$125
South Africa	168,238	88.8%	7.6%	1.5%	2.2%	202,793	9,432	19,275	0	$2,007	$2,420	$11,151	$18,124
Sudan	116	0.0%	0.0%	0.0%	100.0%	0	205	0	0	$5	$138	$4	$654
Swaziland	n.a.	n.a.	n.a.	n.a.	n.a.	53	0	0	0	n.a.	n.a.	n.a.	n.a.
Tanzania	190	2.6%	0.0%	0.0%	97.4%	5	0	0	0	$26	$328	$78	$983
Togo	1	0.0%	0.0%	0.0%	100.0%	0	0	0	0	z	$22	$15	$175
Tunisia	6,301	0.0%	96.7%	3.3%	0.1%	0	4,432	127	0	$395	$504	$3,688	$5,030
Uganda	96	0.0%	0.0%	0.0%	100.0%	0	0	0	0	$2	$184	$2	$534
Zambia	1,255	24.1%	0.0%	0.0%	75.9%	383	0	0	0	$3	$209	$186	$670
Zimbabwe	2,412	87.9%	0.0%	0.0%	12.1%	3,278	0	108	0	$19	$202	$686	$1,736
OCEANIA													
Australia	261,022	73.7%	13.2%	12.3%	0.8%	238,596	27,597	87,518	42,484	$9,125	$2,707	$14,476	$45,855
Fiji	53	0.0%	0.0%	0.0%	100.0%	0	0	0	0	z	$91	$194	$567
Kiribati	n.a.	n.a.	n.a.	n.a.	n.a.	0	0	0	0	z	$3	z	$16
Micronesia, Federated States of	n.a.	n.a.	n.a.	n.a.	n.a.	0	0	0	0	n.a.	n.a.	n.a.	n.a.
New Zealand	17,264	16.4%	13.9%	35.4%	34.3%	3,211	1,786	767	0	$207	$639	$3,550	$9,859
Papua New Guinea	9,454	0.0%	98.2%	1.2%	0.6%	0	5,185	0	0	$5	$97	$252	$1,035
Samoa	3	0.0%	0.0%	0.0%	100.0%	0	0	0	0	z	$11	z	$55
Solomon Islands	n.a.	n.a.	n.a.	n.a.	n.a.	0	0	0	0	z	$17	z	$74
Tonga	n.a.	n.a.	n.a.	n.a.	n.a.	0	0	0	0	z	$8	$1	$36
Vanuatu	n.a.	n.a.	n.a.	n.a.	n.a.	0	0	0	0	z	$14	$3	$45

This table presents data, where available, for most independent nations having an area greater than 200 square miles

n.a. - not available

z - negligible

Footnotes:

(1) Source: United Nations *Energy Statistics Yearbook*

(2) Source: United States Geological Survey *Minerals Yearbook*

(3) Source: United States Energy Information Administration *International Energy Annual*

(4) Source: Derived from United Nations *Handbook of International Trade and Development Statistics*

(5) Includes data for Luxembourg

(6) Data included with Belgium

(7) Excluding Taiwan

WORLD ENVIRONMENT TABLE

CONTINENT / Country	Area Square Miles	1996 Protected Land[1]		Endangered Species 1996[1] (Critically Endangered, Endangered and Vulnerable) Number of Species						Forest Cover[2]	
		Sq. Miles	%	Mammal	Bird	Reptile	Amphib.	Fish	Invrt.	Total 1995 Sq. Miles	Change: 1990-95 %
NORTH AMERICA											
Bahamas	5,382	563	10.5%	4	4	7	0	1	1	610	-12.2%
Belize	8,866	3,525	39.8%	5	1	5	0	4	1	7,575	-1.7%
Canada	3,849,674	367,995	9.6%	7	5	3	1	13	11	944,294	0.4%
Costa Rica	19,730	4,650	23.6%	14	13	7	1	0	9	4,819	-14.2%
Cuba	42,804	7,370	17.2%	9	13	7	0	4	3	7,112	-6.0%
Dominica	305	66	21.5%	1	2	4	0	0	0	178	0.0%
Dominican Republic	18,704	n.a.	n.a.	4	11	10	1	0	2	6,108	-7.7%
El Salvador	8,124	20	0.2%	2	0	6	0	0	1	405	-15.3%
Guatemala	42,042	8,365	19.9%	8	4	9	0	0	8	14,830	-9.7%
Haiti	10,714	37	0.3%	4	11	6	1	0	2	81	-16.0%
Honduras	43,277	4,366	10.1%	7	4	7	0	0	2	15,888	153.1%
Jamaica	4,244	379	8.9%	4	7	8	4	0	5	676	-31.1%
Mexico	759,533	61,683	8.1%	64	36	18	3	86	40	213,850	-4.4%
Nicaragua	50,054	6,322	12.6%	4	3	7	0	0	2	21,467	-11.9%
Panama	29,157	5,974	20.5%	17	10	7	0	1	2	10,811	-10.2%
St. Lucia	238	37	15.7%	0	3	6	0	0	0	19	-16.7%
Trinidad and Tobago	1,980	81	4.1%	1	3	5	0	0	0	622	-7.5%
United States	3,787,425	767,743	20.3%	35	50	28	24	123	594	820,525	1.4%
SOUTH AMERICA											
Argentina	1,073,519	35,236	3.3%	27	41	5	5	1	11	131,051	-1.3%
Bolivia	424,165	68,798	16.2%	24	27	3	0	0	1	186,526	-5.7%
Brazil	3,300,172	203,367	6.2%	71	103	15	5	12	34	2,127,960	-2.3%
Chile	292,135	54,584	18.7%	16	18	1	3	4	0	30,471	-1.8%
Colombia	440,831	36,159	8.2%	35	64	15	0	5	0	204,588	-2.4%
Ecuador	105,037	60,045	57.2%	28	53	12	0	1	23	43,000	-7.8%
Guyana	83,000	226	0.3%	10	3	8	0	0	1	71,726	-0.2%
Paraguay	157,048	5,410	3.4%	10	26	3	0	0	0	44,506	-12.4%
Peru	496,225	26,102	5.3%	46	64	9	1	0	2	260,858	-1.6%
Suriname	63,251	3,105	4.9%	10	2	6	0	0	0	56,838	-0.4%
Uruguay	68,500	183	0.3%	5	11	0	0	0	1	3,143	-0.2%
Venezuela	352,144	216,373	61.4%	24	22	14	0	5	1	169,866	-5.4%
EUROPE											
Albania	11,100	396	3.6%	2	7	1	0	7	3	4,039	0.0%
Austria	32,377	9,464	29.2%	7	5	1	0	7	41	14,969	0.0%
Belarus	80,155	3,380	4.2%	4	4	0	0	0	6	28,463	4.9%
Belgium	11,783	332	2.8%	6	3	0	0	1	13	2,737/3	0.0%/3
Bosnia and Herzegovina	19,741	103	0.5%	10	2	0	1	6	6	10,463	0.0%
Bulgaria	42,855	1,930	4.5%	13	12	1	0	8	7	12,510	0.1%
Croatia	21,829	1,531	7.0%	10	4	0	1	20	8	10,154	0.0%
Czech Republic	30,450	4,933	16.2%	7	6	0	0	6	17	7,765	5.1%
Denmark	16,639	5,327	32.0%	3	2	0	0	0	10	1,610	0.0%
Estonia	17,413	2,071	11.9%	4	2	0	0	1	3	6,637	2.6%
Finland	130,559	10,968	8.4%	4	4	0	0	1	8	77,332	-0.4%
France	211,208	21,515	10.2%	13	7	3	2	3	61	58,047	5.7%
Germany	137,822	37,140	26.9%	8	5	0	0	7	29	41,467	0.0%
Greece	50,949	1,316	2.6%	13	10	6	1	16	9	25,147	12.1%
Hungary	35,919	2,506	7.0%	8	10	1	0	11	26	11,127	4.5%
Iceland	39,769	3,786	9.5%	1	0	0	0	0	0	42	0.0%
Ireland	27,137	252	0.9%	2	1	0	0	1	2	2,201	14.0%
Italy	116,336	8,509	7.3%	10	7	4	4	9	41	25,081	0.4%
Latvia	24,595	3,173	12.9%	4	6	0	0	1	6	7,046	0.0%
Lithuania	25,213	2,492	9.9%	5	4	0	0	1	5	7,629	2.9%
Luxembourg	999	144	14.4%	3	1	0	0	0	4	n.a./4	n.a./4
Macedonia	9,928	700	7.1%	10	3	1	0	4	2	3,815	-0.1%
Moldova	13,012	195	1.5%	2	7	1	0	9	5	1,378	0.0%
Netherlands	16,164	1,861	11.5%	6	3	0	0	1	9	1,290	0.0%
Norway	149,405	8,056	5.4%	4	3	0	0	1	8	31,170	1.7%
Poland	121,196	11,309	9.3%	10	6	0	0	2	13	33,714	0.7%
Portugal	35,516	2,331	6.6%	13	7	0	1	9	67	11,100	4.4%
Romania	91,699	4,206	4.6%	16	11	2	0	11	21	24,116	-0.1%
Slovakia	18,933	4,095	21.6%	8	4	0	0	7	20	7,680	0.6%
Slovenia	7,820	464	5.9%	10	3	0	1	5	38	4,158	0.0%
Spain	194,885	16,378	8.4%	19	10	6	3	10	57	32,386	0.0%
Sweden	173,732	14,111	8.1%	5	4	0	0	1	13	94,305	0.0%
Switzerland	15,943	2,875	18.0%	6	4	0	0	4	25	4,363	0.0%
Ukraine	233,090	3,469	1.5%	15	10	2	0	12	13	35,676	0.3%
United Kingdom	94,249	19,305	20.5%	4	2	0	0	1	10	9,228	2.8%
Yugoslavia	39,449	1,309	3.3%	12	8	1	0	13	19	6,830	0.0%
Russia	6,592,849	199,494	3.0%	31	38	5	0	13	26	2,947,890	0.0%
ASIA											
Afghanistan	251,826	844	0.3%	11	13	1	1	0	1	5,398	-29.7%
Armenia	11,506	824	7.2%	4	5	3	0	0	6	1,290	14.4%
Azerbaijan	33,436	1,844	5.5%	11	8	3	0	5	6	3,822	0.0%
Bahrain	267	3	1.2%	1	1	0	0	0	0	0	0.0%
Bangladesh	55,598	378	0.7%	18	30	13	0	0	0	3,900	-4.2%
Brunei	2,226	468	21.0%	9	14	4	0	2	0	1,676	-3.1%
Cambodia	69,898	12,614	18.0%	23	18	9	0	5	0	37,954	-7.7%
China	3,690,045	263,657	7.1%	75	90	15	1	28	4	514,763/5	-0.3%/5
Cyprus	2,277	302	13.2%	3	4	3	0	0	1	541	0.0%
Georgia	26,911	754	2.8%	10	5	7	0	3	9	11,537	0.0%
India	1,237,061	55,259	4.5%	75	73	16	3	4	22	250,986	0.1%
Indonesia	752,409	133,251	17.7%	128	104	19	0	60	29	423,905	-4.7%
Iran	630,578	32,058	5.1%	20	14	8	2	7	3	5,961	-8.4%
Iraq	169,235	2	0.0%	7	12	2	0	2	2	320	0.0%
Israel	8,019	1,257	15.7%	13	8	5	0	0	10	394	0.0%
Japan	145,850	9,880	6.8%	29	33	8	10	7	45	97,089	-0.3%
Jordan	35,135	1,151	3.3%	7	4	1	0	0	3	174	-11.8%
Kazakhstan	1,049,155	28,329	2.7%	15	15	1	1	5	4	40,556	10.1%
Korea, North	46,540	1,219	2.6%	7	19	0	0	0	1	23,823	0.0%
Korea, South	38,230	2,640	6.9%	6	19	0	0	0	1	29,444	-0.8%
Kuwait	6,880	105	1.5%	1	3	2	0	0	1	19	0.0%
Kyrgyzstan	76,641	2,679	3.5%	6	5	1	0	0	0	2,819	0.0%
Laos	91,429	10,642	11.6%	30	27	7	0	4	0	48,012	-5.6%
Lebanon	4,016	19	0.5%	5	5	2	0	0	1	201	-33.3%
Malaysia	127,320	5,897	4.6%	42	34	14	0	14	3	59,734	-11.5%
Mongolia	604,829	62,275	10.3%	12	14	0	0	0	3	36,317	0.0%
Myanmar	261,228	670	0.3%	31	44	20	0	1	2	104,831	-6.7%

CONTINENT / Country	Area Square Miles	1996 Protected Land[1] Square Miles	%	Mammal	Bird	Reptile	Amphib.	Fish	Invrt.	Forest Cover[2] Total 1995 Sq. Miles	Change: 1990-95 %
Nepal	56,827	4,905	8.6%	28	27	5	0	0	1	18,618	-5.4%
Oman	82,030	13,236	16.1%	9	5	4	0	3	1	0	0.0%
Pakistan	339,732	14,458	4.3%	13	25	6	0	1	0	6,749	-13.6%
Philippines	115,831	5,614	4.8%	49	86	7	2	26	18	26,124	-16.2%
Qatar	4,412	6	0.1%	0	1	2	0	0	0	0	0.0%
Saudi Arabia	830,000	318,774	38.4%	9	11	2	0	0	1	857	-3.9%
Singapore	246	11	4.6%	6	9	1	0	1	1	15	0.0%
Sri Lanka	24,962	3,357	13.4%	14	11	8	0	8	2	6,934	-5.3%
Syria	71,498	0	0.0%	4	7	3	0	0	3	846	-10.6%
Taiwan	13,900	1,520	10.9%	10	13	3	0	6	1	n.a./6	n.a./6
Tajikistan	55,251	2,266	4.1%	5	9	1	0	1	2	1,583	0.0%
Thailand	198,115	27,325	13.8%	34	45	16	0	14	1	44,904	-12.4%
Turkey	300,948	4,980	1.7%	15	14	12	2	18	9	34,193	0.0%
Turkmenistan	188,456	7,634	4.1%	11	12	2	0	5	3	14,494	0.0%
United Arab Emirates	32,278	0	0.0%	3	4	2	0	1	0	232	0.0%
Uzbekistan	172,742	3,160	1.8%	7	11	0	0	3	1	35,209	14.1%
Vietnam	127,428	3,842	3.0%	38	47	12	1	3	0	35,201	-6.9%
Yemen	203,850	0	0.0%	5	13	2	0	0	2	35	0.0%
AFRICA											
Algeria	919,595	22,745	2.5%	15	8	1	0	1	11	7,185	-5.9%
Angola	481,354	31,588	6.6%	17	13	5	0	0	6	85,715	-5.1%
Benin	43,475	4,875	11.2%	9	1	2	0	0	0	17,857	-6.1%
Botswana	224,711	40,536	18.0%	5	7	0	0	0	0	53,734	-2.5%
Burkina Faso	105,869	11,024	10.4%	6	1	1	0	0	0	16,490	-3.6%
Burundi	10,745	564	5.3%	5	6	0	0	0	3	1,224	-2.2%
Cameroon	183,568	8,099	4.4%	32	14	3	1	26	4	75,668	-3.2%
Cape Verde	1,557	0	0.0%	1	3	3	0	1	0	181	193.8%
Central African Republic	240,535	21,026	8.7%	11	2	1	0	0	0	115,560	-2.1%
Chad	495,755	44,379	9.0%	14	3	1	0	0	1	42,568	-4.1%
Comoros	863	0	0.0%	3	6	2	0	1	4	35	-25.0%
Congo	132,047	6,563	5.0%	10	3	2	0	0	1	75,433	-1.1%
Congo, Democratic Republic of the	905,446	56,515	6.2%	38	26	3	0	1	45	421,797	-3.3%
Cote d'Ivoire	124,518	7,666	6.2%	16	12	4	1	0	1	21,116	-2.7%
Djibouti	8,958	39	0.4%	3	3	2	0	0	0	85	0.0%
Egypt	386,662	3,065	0.8%	15	11	6	0	0	1	131	0.0%
Equatorial Guinea	10,831	0	0.0%	12	4	2	1	0	2	6,876	-2.6%
Eritrea	36,170	1,933	5.3%	6	3	3	0	0	0	1,089	0.0%
Ethiopia	446,953	72,200	16.2%	35	20	1	0	0	4	52,429	-2.2%
Gabon	103,347	2,792	2.7%	12	4	3	0	0	1	68,954	-2.5%
Gambia, The	4,127	87	2.1%	4	1	1	0	0	0	351	-4.2%
Ghana	92,098	4,897	5.3%	13	10	4	0	0	0	34,834	-6.1%
Guinea	94,926	631	0.7%	11	12	3	1	0	3	24,583	-5.5%
Guinea-Bissau	13,948	0	0.0%	4	1	3	0	0	1	8,915	-2.2%
Kenya	224,961	17,522	7.8%	43	24	5	0	20	15	4,988	-1.3%
Lesotho	11,720	26	0.2%	2	5	0	0	1	1	23	0.0%
Liberia	38,250	499	1.3%	11	13	3	1	0	2	17,402	-2.9%
Libya	679,362	668	0.1%	11	2	3	0	0	0	1,544	0.0%
Madagascar	226,658	4,756	2.1%	46	28	17	2	13	14	58,325	-4.1%
Malawi	45,747	4,087	8.9%	7	9	0	0	0	8	12,892	-7.6%
Mali	482,077	17,498	3.6%	13	6	1	0	0	0	44,730	-4.7%
Mauritania	397,955	6,741	1.7%	14	3	3	0	0	0	2,147	0.0%
Mauritius	788	61	7.7%	4	10	6	0	0	32	46	0.0%
Morocco	172,414	1,225	0.7%	18	11	2	0	1	7	14,807	-1.5%
Mozambique	308,642	26,946	8.7%	13	14	5	0	2	7	65,105	-3.3%
Namibia	317,818	43,304	13.6%	11	8	3	1	3	1	47,776	-1.7%
Niger	489,191	37,429	7.7%	11	2	1	0	0	1	9,892	0.0%
Nigeria	356,669	11,666	3.3%	26	9	4	0	0	1	53,205	-4.2%
Rwanda	10,169	1,531	15.1%	9	6	0	0	0	2	965	-0.8%
Sao Tome and Principe	372	0	0.0%	3	9	2	0	0	2	216	0.0%
Senegal	75,951	8,657	11.4%	13	6	7	0	0	0	28,498	-3.3%
Sierra Leone	27,925	592	2.1%	9	12	3	0	0	4	5,054	-14.0%
Somalia	246,201	2,025	0.8%	18	8	2	0	3	1	2,911	-0.8%
South Africa	471,009	25,657	5.4%	33	16	19	9	27	101	32,815	-0.9%
Sudan	967,499	47,294	4.9%	21	9	3	0	0	1	160,669	-4.1%
Swaziland	6,704	232	3.5%	5	6	0	0	0	0	564	0.0%
Tanzania	364,900	101,397	27.8%	33	30	4	0	19	46	125,522	-4.7%
Togo	21,925	1,657	7.6%	8	1	3	0	0	0	4,807	-7.0%
Tunisia	63,170	172	0.3%	11	6	2	0	0	5	2,143	-2.6%
Uganda	93,104	18,978	20.4%	18	10	1	0	28	10	23,568	-4.6%
Zambia	290,586	87,449	30.1%	11	10	0	0	0	6	121,228	-4.0%
Zimbabwe	150,873	19,293	12.8%	9	9	0	0	0	2	33,629	-2.8%
OCEANIA											
Australia	2,966,155	403,742	13.6%	58	45	37	25	37	281	157,947	0.2%
Fiji	7,056	77	1.1%	4	9	6	1	0	2	3,224	-2.1%
Kiribati	313	103	32.9%	0	4	2	0	0	1	0	0.0%
Micronesia, Federated States of	271	0	0.0%	6	6	2	0	0	4	n.a.	n.a.
New Zealand	104,454	24,455	23.4%	3	44	11	1	8	15	30,440	2.8%
Papua New Guinea	178,703	3,993	2.2%	57	31	10	0	13	11	142,622	-1.8%
Samoa	1,093	44	4.1%	2	6	2	0	0	1	525	-5.6%
Solomon Islands	10,954	32	0.3%	20	18	4	0	0	5	9,224	-1.0%
Tonga	288	14	4.8%	0	2	3	0	0	1	0	0.0%
Vanuatu	4,707	13	0.3%	3	6	3	0	0	1	3,475	-4.1%

This table presents data, where available, for most independent nations having an area greater than 200 square miles

Amphib. - Amphibian

Invrt. - Invertebrate

n.a. - not available

Footnotes:

(1) Source: World Conservation Monitoring Centre (WCMC) and World Conservation Union (IUCN); data reprinted by permission

(2) Source: United Nations Food and Agriculture Organization State of the World's Forests

(3) Includes data for Luxembourg

(4) Data included with Belgium

(5) Includes data for Taiwan

(6) Data included with China

WORLD COMPARISONS

General Information

Equatorial diameter of the earth, 7,926.38 miles.
Polar diameter of the earth, 7,899.80 miles.
Mean diameter of the earth, 7,917.52 miles.
Equatorial circumference of the earth, 24,901.46 miles.
Polar circumference of the earth, 24,855.34 miles.
Mean distance from the earth to the sun, 93,020,000 miles.
Mean distance from the earth to the moon, 238,857 miles.
Total area of the earth, 197,000,000 square miles.

Highest elevation on the earth's surface, Mt. Everest, Asia, 29,028 feet.
Lowest elevation on the earth's land surface, shores of the Dead Sea, Asia, 1,339 feet below sea level.
Greatest known depth of the ocean, southwest of Guam, Pacific Ocean, 35,810 feet.
Total land area of the earth (incl. inland water and Antarctica), 57,900,000 square miles.

Area of Africa, 11,700,000 square miles.
Area of Antarctica, 5,400,000 square miles.
Area of Asia, 17,300,000 square miles.
Area of Europe, 3,800,000 square miles.
Area of North America, 9,500,000 square miles.
Area of Oceania (incl. Australia) 3,300,000 square miles.
Area of South America, 6,900,000 square miles.
Population of the earth (est. 1/1/99), 5,952,000,000.

Principal Islands and Their Areas

ISLAND	Area (Sq. Mi.)
Baffin I., Canada	195,928
Banks I., Canada	27,038
Borneo (Kalimantan), Asia	287,298
Bougainville, Papua New Guinea	3,591
Cape Breton I., Canada	3,981
Celebes (Sulawesi), Indonesia	73,057
Ceram (Seram), Indonesia	7,191
Corsica, France	3,367
Crete, Greece	3,190
Cuba, N. America	42,780
Cyprus, Asia	3,572
Devon I., Canada	21,331
Ellesmere I., Canada	75,767
Flores, Indonesia	5,502
Great Britain, U.K.	88,795
Greenland, N. America	840,004
Guadalcanal, Solomon Is.	2,060
Hainan Dao, China	13,127
Hawaii, U.S.	4,021
Hispaniola, N. America	29,300
Hokkaidō, Japan	32,245
Honshū, Japan	89,176
Iceland, Europe	39,769
Ireland, Europe	32,587
Jamaica, N. America	4,247
Java (Jawa), Indonesia	51,038
Kodiak I., U.S.	3,670
Kyūshū, Japan	17,129
Leyte, Philippines	2,785
Long Island, U.S.	1,377
Luzon, Philippines	40,420
Madagascar, Africa	226,642
Melville I., Canada	16,274
Mindanao, Philippines	36,537
Mindoro, Philippines	3,759
Negros, Philippines	4,907
New Britain, Papua New Guinea	14,093
New Caledonia, Oceania	6,467
Newfoundland, Canada	42,031
New Guinea, Asia-Oceania	308,882
New Ireland, Papua New Guinea	3,475
North East Land, Norway	6,350
North I., New Zealand	44,333
Novaya Zemlya, Russia	31,892
Palawan, Philippines	4,550
Panay, Philippines	4,446
Prince of Wales I., Canada	12,872
Puerto Rico, N. America	3,514
Sakhalin, Russia	29,498
Samar, Philippines	5,050
Sardinia, Italy	9,301
Shikoku, Japan	7,258
Sicily, Italy	9,926
Somerset I., Canada	9,570
Southampton I., Canada	15,913
South I., New Zealand	57,708
Spitsbergen, Norway	15,260
Sri Lanka, Asia	24,942
Sumatra (Sumatera), Indonesia	182,860
Taiwan, Asia	13,900
Tasmania, Australia	26,178
Tierra del Fuego, S. America	18,600
Timor, Asia	5,743
Vancouver I., Canada	12,079
Victoria I., Canada	83,897
Vrangelya (Wrangel), Russia	2,819

Principal Lakes, Oceans, Seas, and Their Areas

LAKE Country	Area (Sq. Mi.)
Arabian Sea	1,492,000
Aral Sea, Kazakhstan-Uzbekistan	14,900
Arctic Ocean	5,400,000
Athabasca, L., Canada	3,064
Atlantic Ocean	31,800,000
Balqash kölï (L. Balkhash), Kazakhstan	7,066
Baltic Sea, Europe	163,000
Baykal, Ozero (L. Baikal), Russia	12,162
Bering Sea, Asia-N.A.	876,000
Black Sea, Europe-Asia	178,000
Caribbean Sea, N.A.-S.A.	1,063,000
Caspian Sea, Asia-Europe	143,244
Chad, L., Cameroon-Chad-Nigeria	6,300
Erie, L., Canada-U.S.	9,910
Eyre, L., Australia	3,700
Gairdner, L., Australia	1,660
Great Bear Lake, Canada	12,095
Great Salt Lake, U.S.	1,680
Great Slave Lake, Canada	11,030
Hudson Bay, Canada	475,000
Huron, L., Canada-U.S.	23,000
Indian Ocean	28,900,000
Japan, Sea of, Asia	389,000
Koko Nor (Qinghai Hu), China	1,650
Ladozhskoye Ozero (L. Ladoga), Russia	6,834
Manitoba, L., Canada	1,785
Mediterranean Sea, Europe-Africa-Asia	967,000
Mexico, Gulf of, N. America	596,000
Michigan, L., U.S.	22,300
Nicaragua, Lago de, Nicaragua	3,150
North Sea, Europe	222,000
Nyasa, L., Malawi-Mozambique-Tanzania	11,150
Onezhskoye Ozero (L. Onega), Russia	3,753
Ontario, L., Canada-U.S.	7,540
Pacific Ocean	63,800,000
Red Sea, Africa-Asia	169,000
Rudolf, L., Ethiopia-Kenya	2,473
Superior, L., Canada-U.S.	31,700
Tanganyika. L., Africa	12,350
Titicaca, Lago, Bolivia-Peru	3,200
Torrens, L., Australia	2,278
Vänern (L.), Sweden	2,156
Van Gölü (L.), Turkey	1,420
Victoria, L., Kenya-Tanzania-Uganda	26,820
Winnipeg, L., Canada	9,416
Winnipegosis, L., Canada	2,075
Yellow Sea, China-Korea	480,000

Principal Mountains and Their Heights

MOUNTAIN Country	Elev. (Ft.)
Aconcagua, Cerro, Argentina	22,831
Annapurna, Nepal	26,504
Aoraki, New Zealand	12,316
Api, Nepal	23,399
Apo, Philippines	9,692
Ararat, Mt., Turkey	16,854
Barú, Volcán, Panama	11,401
Bangueta, Mt., Papua New Guinea	13,520
Belukha, Mt., Kazakhstan-Russia	14,783
Bia, Phu, Laos	9,249
Blanc, Mont (Monte Bianco), France-Italy	15,771
Blanca Pk., Colorado, U.S.	14,345
Bolívar, Venezuela	16,427
Bonete, Cerro, Argentina	22,546
Borah Pk., Idaho, U.S.	12,662
Boundary Pk., Nevada, U.S.	13,140
Cameroon Mtn., Cameroon	13,451
Carrauntoohil, Ireland	3,406
Chaltel, Cerro (Monte Fitzroy), Argentina-Chile	10,958
Chimborazo, Ecuador	20,702
Chirripó, Cerro, Costa Rica	12,530
Colima, Nevado de, Mexico	13,911
Cotopaxi, Ecuador	19,347
Cristóbal Colón, Pico, Colombia	19,029
Damāvand, Qolleh-ye, Iran	18,386
Dhawalāgiri, Nepal	26,810
Duarte, Pico, Dominican Rep.	10,417
Dufourspitze (Monte Rosa), Italy-Switzerland	15,203
Elbert, Mt., Colorado, U.S.	14,433
El'brus, Gora, Russia	18,510
Elgon, Mt., Kenya-Uganda	14,178
Erciyeş Dağı, Turkey	12,848
Etna, Mt., Italy	10,902
Everest, Mt., China-Nepal	29,028
Fairweather, Mt., Alaska-Canada	15,300
Folādī, Koh-e, Afghanistan	16,847
Foraker, Mt., Alaska, U.S.	17,400
Fuji-san, Japan	12,388
Galdhøpiggen, Norway	8,100
Gannett Pk., Wyoming, U.S.	13,804
Gasherbrum, China-Pakistan	26,470
Gerlachovský štít, Slovakia	8,711
Giluwe, Mt., Papua New Guinea	14,331
Gongga Shan, China	24,790
Grand Teton, Wyoming, U.S.	13,770
Grossglockner, Austria	12,457
Hadūr Shu'ayb, Yemen	12,008
Haleakala Crater, Hawaii, U.S.	10,023
Hekla, Iceland	4,892
Hood, Mt., Oregon, U.S.	11,239
Huascarán, Nevado, Peru	22,133
Huila, Nevado de, Colombia	18,865
Hvannadalshnúkur, Iceland	6,952
Illampu, Nevado, Bolivia	21,066
Illimani, Nevado, Bolivia	20,741
Iztaccíhuatl, Mexico	17,159
Jaya, Puncak, Indonesia	16,503
Jungfrau, Switzerland	13,642
K2, China-Pakistan	28,250
Kāmet, China-India	25,447
Kānchenjunga, India- Nepal	28,208
Kātrīnā, Jabal, Egypt	8,668
Kebnekaise, Sweden	6,926
Kenya, Mt. (Kirinyaga), Kenya	17,058
Kerinci, Gunung, Indonesia	12,467
Kilimanjaro, Tanzania	19,340
Kinabalu, Gunong, Malaysia	13,455
Klyuchevskaya, Russia	15,584
Kommunizma, Pik, Tajikistan	24,590
Kosciuszko, Mt., Australia	7,313
Koussi, Emi, Chad	11,204
Kula Kangri, Bhutan	24,784
La Selle, Massif de, Haiti	8,793
Lassen Pk., California, U.S.	10,457
Llullaillaco, Volcán, Argentina-Chile	22,110
Logan, Mt., Canada	19,551
Longs Pk., Colorado, U.S.	14,255
Makālu, China-Nepal	27,825
Margherita Peak, Congo, D.R.C.-Uganda	16,763
Markham, Mt., Antarctica	14,049
Maromokotro, Madagascar	9,436
Massive, Mt., Colorado, U.S.	14,421
Matterhorn, Italy-Switzerland	14,692
Mauna Kea, Hawaii, U.S.	13,796
Mauna Loa, Hawaii, U.S.	13,679
Mayon Volcano, Philippines	8,077
McKinley, Mt., Alaska, U.S.	20,320
Meron, Hare, Israel	3,963
Meru, Mt., Tanzania	14,978
Misti, Volcán, Peru	19,101
Mitchell, Mt., North Carolina, U.S.	6,684
Môco, Serra do, Angola	8,596
Moldoveanu, Romania	8,346
Mulhacén, Spain (continental)	11,424
Musala, Bulgaria	9,596
Muztag, China	25,338
Muztagata, China	24,757
Namjagbarwa Feng, China	25,446
Nanda Devi, India	25,645
Nānga Parbat, Pakistan	26,660
Narodnaya, Gora, Russia	6,217
Nevis, Ben, United Kingdom	4,406
Ojos del Salado, Nevado, Argentina-Chile	22,615
Ólimbos, Cyprus	6,401
Ólympos, Greece	9,570
Olympus, Mt., Washington, U.S.	7,965
Orizaba, Pico de, Mexico	18,406
Paektu San, North Korea-China	9,003
Paricutín, Mexico	9,186
Parnassós, Greece	8,061
Pelée, Montagne, Martinique	4,583
Pidurutalagala, Sri Lanka	8,281
Pikes Pk., Colorado, U.S.	14,110
Pobedy, pik, China-Kyrgyzstan	24,406
Popocatépetl, Volcán, Mexico	17,930
Pulog, Mt., Philippines	9,626
Rainier, Mt., Washington, U.S.	14,410
Ramm, Jabal, Jordan	5,755
Ras Dashen Terara, Ethiopia	15,158
Rinjani, Gunung, Indonesia	12,224
Robson, Mt., Canada	12,972
Roraima, Mt., Brazil-Guyana-Venezuela	9,432
Ruapehu, Mt., New Zealand	9,177
St. Elias, Mt., Alaska, U.S.-Canada	18,008
Sajama, Nevado, Bolivia	21,391
Semeru, Gunung, Indonesia	12,060
Shām, Jabal ash, Oman	9,957
Shasta, Mt., California, U.S.	14,162
Snowdon, Wales, U.K.	3,560
Tahat, Algeria	9,541
Tajumulco (Vol.), Guatemala	13,845
Taranaki, Mt., New Zealand	8,260
Tirich Mīr, Pakistan	25,230
Tomanivi (Victoria), Fiji	4,341
Toubkal, Jebel, Morocco	13,665
Triglav, Slovenia	9,396
Trikora, Puncak, Indonesia	15,584
Tupungato, Cerro, Argentina-Chile	21,555
Turquino, Pico, Cuba	6,470
Uluru (Ayers Rock), Australia	2,844
Uncompahgre Pk., Colorado, U.S.	14,309
Vesuvio (Vesuvius), Italy	4,190
Victoria, Mt., Papua New Guinea	13,238
Vinson Massif, Antarctica	16,066
Waddington, Mt., Canada	13,163
Washington, Mt., New Hampshire, U.S.	6,288
Whitney, Mt., California, U.S.	14,494
Wilhelm, Mt., Papua New Guinea	14,793
Wrangell, Mt., Alaska, U.S.	14,163
Xixabangma Feng (Gosainthan), China	26,286
Yü Shan, Taiwan	13,114
Zugspitze, Austria-Germany	9,718

Principal Rivers and Their Lengths

RIVER Continent	Length (Mi.)
Albany, N. America	610
Aldan, Asia	1,412
Amazonas-Ucayali, S. America	4,000
Amu Darya, Asia	1,578
Amur, Asia	2,744
Amur-Argun, Asia	2,761
Araguaia, S. America	1,367
Arkansas, N. America	1,459
Athabasca, N. America	765
Brahmaputra, Asia	1,770
Branco, S. America	580
Brazos, N. America	870
Canadian, N. America	906
Churchill, N. America	1,000
Colorado, N. America (U.S.-Mexico)	1,450
Columbia, N. America	1,243
Congo (Zaïre), Africa	2,880
Cumberland, N. America	720
Danube, Europe	1,776
Darling, Australia	864
Dnepr (Dnieper), Europe	1,367
Dniester, Europe	840
Don, Europe	1,162
Elbe, Europe	720
Euphrates, Asia	1,510
Fraser, N. America	851
Ganges, Asia	1,560
Gila, N. America	630
Godāvari, Asia	930
Green, N. America	730
Huang (Yellow), Asia	3,395
Indus, Asia	1,800
Irrawaddy, Asia	1,300
Juruá, S. America	1,250
Kama, Europe	1,122
Kasai, Africa	1,338
Kolyma, Asia	1,323
Lena, Asia	2,734
Limpopo, Africa	1,100
Loire, Europe	625
Mackenzie, N. America	2,635
Madeira, S. America	2,013
Magdalena, S. America	950
Marañón, S. America	1,000
Mekong, Asia	2,600
Meuse, Europe	575
Mississippi, N. America	2,348
Mississippi-Missouri, N. America	3,740
Missouri, N. America	2,315
Murray, Australia	1,566
Negro, S. America	1,305
Neman, Europe	582
Niger, Africa	2,600
Nile, Africa	4,145
North Platte, N. America	618
Ob'-Irtysh, Asia	3,362
Oder, Europe	565
Ohio, N. America	981
Oka, Europe	932
Orange, Africa	1,300
Orinoco, S. America	1,600
Ottawa, N. America	790
Paraguay, S. America	1,610
Paraná, S. America	2,796
Parnaíba, S. America	850
Peace, N. America	1,195
Pechora, Europe	1,124
Pecos, N. America	735
Pilcomayo, S. America	1,550
Plata-Paraná, S. America	3,030
Purús, S. America	1,860
Red, N. America	1,270
Rhine, Europe	820
Rhône, Europe	505
Rio Grande, N. America	1,885
Roosevelt, S. America	950
St. Lawrence, N. America	800
Salado, S. America	870
Salween (Nu), Asia	1,750
São Francisco, S. America	1,988
Saskatchewan-Bow, N. America	1,205
Sava, Europe	585
Snake, N. America	1,038
Sungari (Songhua), Asia	1,140
Syr Darya, Asia	1,370
Tagus, Europe	625
Tarim, Asia	1,328
Tennessee, N. America	652
Tigris, Asia	1,180
Tisa, Europe	607
Tobol, Asia	989
Tocantins, S. America	1,640
Ucayali, S. America	1,220
Ural, Asia	1,509
Uruguay, S. America	1,025
Verkhnyaya Tunguska (Angara), Asia	1,105
Vilyuy, Asia	1,647
Volga, Europe	2,194
White, N. America (Ark.-Mo.)	720
Wisła (Vistula), Europe	630
Xiang, Asia	930
Xingu, S. America	1,230
Yangtze (Chang), Asia	3,915
Yellowstone, N. America	671
Yenisey, Asia	2,543
Yukon, N. America	1,979
Zambezi, Africa	1,700

PRINCIPAL CITIES OF THE WORLD

City	Population
Abidjan, Cote d'Ivoire	1,929,079
Accra, Ghana (1,390,000)	949,113
Addis Ababa, Ethiopia (1,990,000)	1,912,500
Adelaide, Australia (1,045,854)	16,115
Ahmadābād, India (3,312,216)	2,876,710
Aleppo (Halab), Syria (1,640,000)	1,591,400
Alexandria (Al Iskandarīyah), Egypt (3,350,000)	2,926,859
Algiers (El Djazaïr), Algeria (2,547,983)	1,507,241
Almaty, Kazakhstan (1,190,000)	1,156,200
'Ammān, Jordan (1,500,000)	963,490
Amsterdam, Netherlands (1,104,000)	717,304
Ankara (Angora), Turkey (2,650,000)	2,559,471
Antananarivo, Madagascar	1,250,000
Antwerp (Antwerpen), Belgium (1,140,000)	467,518
Asmera, Eritrea	358,100
Astana (Aqmola), Kazakhstan	286,000
Asunción, Paraguay (700,000)	502,426
Athens (Athína), Greece (3,150,000)	772,072
Atlanta, Georgia, U.S. (2,833,511)	394,017
Auckland, New Zealand (855,571)	315,668
Baghdād, Iraq	3,841,268
Baku (Bakı), Azerbaijan (2,020,000)	1,080,500
Baltimore, Maryland, U.S. (2,382,172)	736,014
Bamako, Mali	658,275
Bandung, Indonesia (2,220,000)	2,058,122
Bangalore, India (4,130,288)	2,660,088
Bangkok (Krung Thep), Thailand (7,060,000)	5,620,591
Barcelona, Spain (4,040,000)	1,714,355
Beijing (Peking), China (7,320,000)	6,690,000
Beirut, Lebanon (1,675,000)	509,000
Belém, Brazil (1,355,000)	765,476
Belfast, N. Ireland, U.K. (685,000)	279,237
Belgrade (Beograd), Yugoslavia (1,554,826)	1,136,786
Belo Horizonte, Brazil (3,340,000)	1,529,566
Berlin, Germany (4,200,000)	3,475,392
Birmingham, England, U.K. (2,705,000)	965,928
Bishkek, Kyrgyzstan	631,300
Bogotá, Colombia (5,290,000)	4,931,796
Bonn, Germany (580,000)	296,859
Boston, Massachusetts, U.S. (4,171,643)	574,283
Brasília, Brazil	1,513,470
Bratislava, Slovakia	441,453
Brazzaville, Congo	693,712
Bremen, Germany (790,000)	551,604
Brisbane, Australia (1,488,883)	806,746
Brussels (Bruxelles), Belgium (2,385,000)	136,424
Bucharest (București), Romania (2,300,000)	2,067,545
Budapest, Hungary (2,450,000)	1,906,798
Buenos Aires, Argentina (11,000,000)	2,960,976
Cairo (Al Qāhirah), Egypt (9,300,000)	6,068,695
Cali, Colombia (1,735,000)	1,641,498
Canberra, Australia (324,536)	298,847
Cape Town, South Africa (1,900,000)	854,616
Caracas, Venezuela (4,000,000)	1,822,465
Casablanca, Morocco (3,400,000)	3,022,000
Changchun, China	2,470,000
Chelyabinsk, Russia (1,325,000)	1,143,000
Chengdu, China	2,760,000
Chennai (Madras), India (5,421,985)	3,841,396
Chicago, Illinois, U.S. (8,065,633)	2,783,726
Chișinău (Kishinev), Moldova	676,700
Chittagong, Bangladesh (2,342,662)	1,566,070
Chongqing (Chungking), China	3,870,000
Cincinnati, Ohio, U.S. (1,744,124)	364,040
Cleveland, Ohio, U.S. (2,759,823)	505,616
Cologne (Köln), Germany (1,820,000)	962,517
Colombo, Sri Lanka (2,050,000)	612,000
Columbus, Ohio, U.S. (1,377,419)	632,910
Conakry, Guinea	950,000
Copenhagen (København), Denmark (1,780,000)	471,300
Cordoba, Argentina (1,260,000)	1,179,067
Curitiba, Brazil (1,815,000)	841,882
Dakar, Senegal	1,490,450
Dalian (Lüda), China	2,400,000
Dallas, Texas, U.S. (3,885,415)	1,006,877
Damascus (Dimashq), Syria (2,230,000)	1,549,932
Dar es Salaam, Tanzania	1,096,000
Delhi, India (8,419,084)	7,206,704
Denver, Colorado, U.S. (1,848,319)	467,610
Detroit, Michigan, U.S. (4,665,236)	1,027,974
Dhaka (Dacca), Bangladesh (6,537,308)	3,637,892
Dnipropetrovs'k, Ukraine (1,615,000)	1,190,000
Donets'k, Ukraine (2,125,000)	1,121,000
Dresden, Germany (870,000)	479,273
Dublin (Baile Átha Cliath), Ireland (1,175,000)	481,854
Durban, South Africa (1,740,000)	715,669
Düsseldorf, Germany (1,225,000)	574,936
Edinburgh, Scotland, U.K. (640,000)	401,910
Essen, Germany (5,050,000)	622,380
Faisalabad, Pakistan	1,104,209
Florence (Firenze), Italy (640,000)	381,762
Fortaleza, Brazil (2,040,000)	743,335
Frankfurt am Main, Germany (1,950,000)	659,803
Fukuoka, Japan (2,000,000)	1,284,795
Gdańsk (Danzig), Poland (892,000)	463,058
Geneva (Génève), Switzerland (470,000)	171,042
Genoa (Genova), Italy (800,000)	655,704
Glasgow, Scotland, U.K. (1,870,000)	662,954
Goiânia, Brazil (1,130,000)	912,136
Guadalajara, Mexico (2,400,000)	1,633,053
Guangzhou (Canton), China	3,750,000
Guatemala, Guatemala (1,500,000)	823,301
Guayaquil, Ecuador	1,508,444
Hamburg, Germany (2,440,000)	1,702,887
Hannover, Germany (1,015,000)	524,823
Hanoi, Vietnam (1,275,000)	905,939
Harare, Zimbabwe (1,470,000)	1,189,103
Harbin, China	3,120,000
Havana (La Habana), Cuba (2,210,000)	2,119,059
Helsinki, Finland (1,075,000)	512,686
Hiroshima, Japan (1,600,000)	1,108,888
Ho Chi Minh City (Saigon), Vietnam (3,300,000)	2,796,229
Hong Kong (Xianggang), China (4,770,000)	1,250,993
Honolulu, Hawaii, U.S. (836,231)	365,272
Houston, Texas, U.S. (3,711,043)	1,630,553
Hyderābād, India (4,344,437)	3,058,093
Ibadan, Nigeria	1,144,000
Indianapolis, Indiana, U.S. (1,249,822)	731,327
İstanbul, Turkey (7,550,000)	6,620,241
İzmir, Turkey (1,900,000)	1,757,414
Jakarta, Indonesia (10,200,000)	8,227,746
Jerusalem, Israel (635,000)	591,400
Jiddah, Saudi Arabia	1,300,000
Jinan, China	2,150,000
Johannesburg, South Africa (4,000,000)	712,507
Kābul, Afghanistan	1,424,400
Kampala, Uganda	773,463
Kānpur, India (2,029,889)	1,874,409
Kansas City, Missouri, U.S. (1,566,280)	435,146
Kaohsiung, Taiwan (1,900,000)	1,401,239
Karāchi, Pakistan (5,300,000)	4,901,627
Katowice, Poland (2,770,000)	359,408
Kazan', Russia (1,165,000)	1,104,000
Kharkiv, Ukraine (2,050,000)	1,622,800
Khartoum (Al Kharṭūm), Sudan (1,450,000)	473,597
Kiev (Kyïv), Ukraine (3,260,000)	2,643,000
Kingston, Jamaica (830,000)	516,500
Kinshasa, Democratic Republic of the Congo	3,000,000
Kitakyūshū, Japan (1,550,000)	1,019,598
Kōbe, Japan (*Ōsaka)	1,423,792
Kolkata (Calcutta), India (11,021,918)	4,399,819
Kuala Lumpur, Malaysia (1,800,000)	1,145,075
Kunming, China	1,500,000
Kuwait (Al Kuwayt), Kuwait (1,126,000)	28,859
Kyōto, Japan (*Ōsaka)	1,463,822
Lagos, Nigeria (3,800,000)	1,213,000
Lahore, Pakistan (3,025,000)	2,707,215
La Paz, Bolivia (1,200,000)	713,378
Leeds, England, U.K. (1,530,000)	424,194
Liège, Belgium (747,000)	194,596
Lille, France (1,050,000)	172,142
Lima, Peru (4,608,010)	371,122
Lisbon (Lisboa), Portugal (2,350,000)	663,394
Liverpool, England, U.K. (1,515,000)	481,786
London, England, U.K. (12,000,000)	7,650,944
Los Angeles, California, U.S. (14,531,529)	3,485,398
Luanda, Angola	1,459,900
Lucknow, India (1,669,204)	1,619,115
Lusaka, Zambia	982,362
Lyon, France (1,335,000)	415,487
Madrid, Spain (4,650,000)	3,102,846
Managua, Nicaragua	864,201
Manaus, Brazil	1,005,634
Manchester, England, U.K. (2,760,000)	402,889
Manila, Philippines (11,200,000)	1,654,761
Mannheim, Germany (1,530,000)	318,025
Maputo, Mozambique	1,069,727
Maracaibo, Venezuela	1,249,670
Marseille, France (1,225,000)	800,550
Mashhad, Iran	1,759,155
Mecca (Makkah), Saudi Arabia	550,000
Medan, Indonesia	1,730,052
Medellín, Colombia (2,290,000)	1,551,160
Melbourne, Australia (3,040,000)	48,650
Memphis, Tennessee, U.S. (981,747)	610,337
Mexico City, Mexico (14,530,000)	8,489,007
Miami, Florida, U.S. (3,192,582)	358,548
Milan (Milano), Italy (3,790,000)	1,305,591
Milwaukee, Wisconsin, U.S. (1,607,183)	628,088
Minneapolis, Minnesota, U.S. (2,464,124)	368,383
Minsk, Belarus (1,722,000)	1,661,000
Mogadishu, Somalia	600,000
Monterrey, Mexico (2,050,000)	1,088,023
Montevideo, Uruguay (1,550,000)	1,251,647
Montréal, Canada (3,326,510)	1,016,376
Moscow (Moskva), Russia (13,170,000)	8,747,000
Mumbai (Bombay), India (12,596,243)	9,925,891
Munich (München), Germany (1,930,000)	1,255,623
Nagoya, Japan (5,250,000)	2,152,184
Nāgpur, India (1,664,006)	1,624,752
Nairobi, Kenya	1,505,000
Nanjing, China	2,490,000
Naples (Napoli), Italy (3,150,000)	1,046,987
Nashville, Tennessee, U.S. (985,026)	487,969
New Delhi, India (*Delhi)	301,297
New Kowloon (Xinjiulong), China (*Hong Kong)	1,526,910
New Orleans, Louisiana, U.S. (1,238,816)	496,938
New York, New York, U.S. (18,087,251)	7,322,564
Nizhniy Novgorod, Russia (2,025,000)	1,441,000
Novosibirsk, Russia (1,600,000)	1,442,000
Nürnberg, Germany (1,070,000)	498,945
Odesa, Ukraine (1,190,000)	1,096,000
Oklahoma City, Oklahoma, U.S. (958,839)	444,719
Omsk, Russia (1,195,000)	1,169,000
Ōsaka, Japan (17,050,000)	2,602,421
Oslo, Norway (703,896)	470,204
Ottawa, Canada (1,010,498)	323,340
Panamá, Panama (770,000)	411,549
Paris, France (10,275,000)	2,152,423
Perm', Russia (1,180,000)	1,099,000
Perth, Australia (1,244,320)	10,095
Philadelphia, Pennsylvania, U.S. (5,899,345)	1,585,577
Phnum Pénh (Phnom Penh), Cambodia	620,000
Phoenix, Arizona, U.S. (2,122,101)	983,403
Pittsburgh, Pennsylvania, U.S. (2,242,798)	369,879
Port-au-Prince, Haiti (1,425,594)	846,247
Portland, Oregon, U.S. (1,477,895)	437,319
Porto Alegre, Brazil (2,850,000)	1,247,352
Prague (Praha), Czech Republic (1,328,000)	1,214,174
Pretoria, South Africa (1,100,000)	525,583
Providence, Rhode Island, U.S. (1,141,510)	160,728
Puebla, Mexico (1,380,000)	1,157,625
Pune, India (2,493,987)	1,566,651
Pusan, South Korea (3,800,000)	3,797,566
P'yŏngyang, North Korea	2,355,000
Qingdao, China	2,300,000
Québec, Canada (671,889)	167,264
Quezon City, Philippines (*Manila)	1,989,419
Quito, Ecuador (1,300,000)	1,100,847
Rabat, Morocco (1,200,000)	717,000
Rangoon (Yangon), Myanmar (2,800,000)	2,705,039
Recife, Brazil (2,880,000)	1,296,995
Rīga, Latvia (1,000,000)	874,200
Rio de Janeiro, Brazil (11,050,000)	5,473,909
Riyadh, Saudi Arabia	1,250,000
Rome (Roma), Italy (3,235,000)	2,649,765
Rosario, Argentina (1,190,000)	894,645
Rostov-na-Donu, Russia (1,165,000)	1,027,000
Rotterdam, Netherlands (1,080,000)	590,436
St. Louis, Missouri, U.S. (2,444,099)	396,685
St. Petersburg (Leningrad), Russia (5,525,000)	4,437,800
Salt Lake City, Utah, U.S. (1,072,227)	159,936
Salvador, Brazil (2,340,000)	2,070,296
Samara, Russia (1,505,000)	1,239,000
San Antonio, Texas, U.S. (1,302,099)	935,933
San Diego, California, U.S. (2,949,000)	1,110,549
San Francisco, California, U.S. (6,253,311)	723,959
San José, Costa Rica (1,549,700)	318,765
San Juan, Puerto Rico (1,877,000)	426,832
San Salvador, El Salvador (1,250,000)	415,346
Santiago, Chile (4,740,000)	4,295,593
Santo Domingo, Dominican Rep.	1,609,966
Santos, Brazil (1,165,000)	415,554
São Paulo, Brazil (16,925,000)	9,393,753
Sapporo, Japan (2,000,000)	1,757,025
Sarajevo, Bosnia and Herzegovina (479,688)	341,200
Saratov, Russia (1,155,000)	909,000
Seattle, Washington, U.S. (2,559,164)	516,259
Seoul (Sŏul), South Korea (15,850,000)	10,627,790
Shanghai, China (11,010,000)	8,930,000
Shenyang (Mukden), China	4,050,000
Singapore, Singapore (3,025,000)	2,690,100
Skopje, Macedonia	440,577
Sofia (Sofiya), Bulgaria (1,280,000)	1,190,126
Stockholm, Sweden (1,491,726)	674,452
Stuttgart, Germany (2,020,000)	594,406
Surabaya, Indonesia	2,473,272
Sydney, Australia (3,741,290)	11,115
Taegu, South Korea	2,228,834
T'aipei, Taiwan (6,200,000)	2,706,453
Taiyuan, China	1,720,000
Tampa, Florida, U.S. (2,067,959)	280,015
Tashkent, Uzbekistan (2,325,000)	2,113,300
Tbilisi, Georgia (1,460,000)	1,279,000
Tegucigalpa, Honduras	576,661
Tehrān, Iran (8,000,000)	6,475,527
Tel Aviv-Yafo, Israel (1,888,000)	355,900
The Hague ('s-Gravenhage), Netherlands (698,000)	441,561
Tianjin (Tientsin), China	5,000,000
Tiranë, Albania	243,000
Tōkyō, Japan (30,300,000)	7,967,614
Toronto, Canada (4,263,757)	2,385,421
Tripoli (Tarābulus), Libya (960,000)	591,062
Tunis, Tunisia (1,300,000)	674,142
Turin (Torino), Italy (1,550,000)	921,485
Ufa, Russia (1,118,000)	1,097,000
Ulan Bator, Mongolia	616,900
València, Spain (1,270,000)	743,933
Vancouver, Canada (1,831,665)	514,008
Venice (Venezia), Italy (420,000)	297,743
Vienna (Wien), Austria (1,900,000)	1,539,848
Vilnius, Lithuania	578,639
Vladivostok, Russia	648,000
Volgograd (Stalingrad), Russia (1,360,000)	1,006,000
Warsaw (Warszawa), Poland (2,312,000)	1,642,694
Washington, D.C., U.S. (3,923,574)	606,900
Wellington, New Zealand (375,000)	150,301
Winnipeg, Canada (667,209)	618,477
Wuhan, China	3,870,000
Xi'an, China	2,410,000
Yekaterinburg, Russia (1,620,000)	1,371,000
Yerevan, Armenia (1,315,000)	1,199,000
Yokohama, Japan (*Tōkyō)	3,307,136
Zagreb, Croatia	867,865
Zurich, Switzerland (870,000)	365,043

Metropolitan area populations are shown in parentheses.
*City is located within the metropolitan area of another city; for example, Kyōto, Japan is located in the Ōsaka metropolitan area.
†Population of entire municipality or district, including rural area.

GLOSSARY OF FOREIGN GEOGRAPHICAL TERMS

Annam . . . Annamese
Arab . . . Arabic
Bantu . . . Bantu
Bur . . . Burmese
Camb . . . Cambodian
Celt . . . Celtic
Chn . . . Chinese
Czech . . . Czech
Dan . . . Danish
Du . . . Dutch
Fin . . . Finnish
Fr . . . French
Ger . . . German
Gr . . . Greek
Hung . . . Hungarian
Ice . . . Icelandic
India . . . India
Indian . . . American Indian
Indon . . . Indonesian
It . . . Italian
Jap . . . Japanese
Kor . . . Korean
Mal . . . Malayan
Mong . . . Mongolian
Nor . . . Norwegian
Per . . . Persian
Pol . . . Polish
Port . . . Portuguese
Rom . . . Romanian
Rus . . . Russian
Siam . . . Siamese
So. Slav . . . Southern Slavonic
Sp . . . Spanish
Swe . . . Swedish
Tib . . . Tibetan
Tur . . . Turkish
Yugo . . . Yugoslav

å, Nor., Swe . . . brook, river
aa, Dan., Nor . . . brook
aas, Dan., Nor . . . ridge
āb, Per . . . water, river
abad, India, Per . . . town, city
ada, Tur . . . island
adrar, Berber . . . mountain
air, Indon . . . stream
akrotírion, Gr . . . cape
älf, Swe . . . river
alp, Ger . . . mountain
altipiano, It . . . plateau
alto, Sp . . . height
archipel, Fr . . . archipelago
archipiélago, Sp . . . archipelago
arquipélago, Port . . . archipelago
arroyo, Sp . . . brook, stream
ås, Nor., Swe . . . ridge
austral, Sp . . . southern
baai, Du . . . bay
bab, Arab . . . gate, port
bach, Ger . . . brook, stream
backe, Swe . . . hill
bad, Ger . . . bath, spa
bahía, Sp . . . bay, gulf
bahr, Arab . . . river, sea, lake
baia, It . . . bay, gulf
baía, Port . . . bay
baie, Fr . . . bay, gulf
bajo, Sp . . . depression
bak, Indon . . . stream
bakke, Dan., Nor . . . hill
balkan, Tur . . . mountain range
bana, Jap . . . point, cape
banco, Sp . . . bank
bandar, Mal., Per. . . . town, port, harbor
bang, Siam . . . village
bassin, Fr . . . basin
batang, Indon., Mal . . . river
ben, Celt . . . mountain, summit
bender, Arab . . . harbor, port
bereg, Rus . . . coast, shore
berg, Du., Ger., Nor., Swe. . . . mountain, hill
bir, Arab . . . well
birkat, Arab . . . lake, pond, pool
bit, Arab . . . house
bjaerg, Dan., Nor . . . mountain
bocche, It . . . mouth
boğazı, Tur . . . strait
bois, Fr . . . forest, wood
boloto, Rus . . . marsh
bolsón, Sp. . . . flat-floored desert valley
boreal, Sp . . . northern
borg, Dan., Nor., Swe . . . castle, town
borgo, It . . . town, suburb
bosch, Du . . . forest, wood
bouche, Fr . . . river mouth
bourg, Fr . . . town, borough
bro, Dan., Nor., Swe . . . bridge
brücke, Ger . . . bridge
bucht, Ger . . . bay, bight
bugt, Dan., Nor., Swe . . . bay, gulf
bulu, Indon . . . mountain
burg, Du., Ger . . . castle, town
buri, Siam . . . town
burun, burnu, Tur . . . cape
by, Dan., Nor., Swe . . . village
caatinga, Port. (Brazil) . . . open brushland
cabezo, Sp . . . summit
cabo, Port., Sp . . . cape
campo, It., Port., Sp . . . plain, field
campos, Port. (Brazil) . . . plains
cañón, Sp . . . canyon
cap, Fr . . . cape
capo, It . . . cape
casa, It., Port., Sp . . . house
castello, It., Port . . . castle, fort
castillo, Sp . . . castle
càte, Fr . . . hill
çay, Tur . . . stream, river
cayo, Sp . . . rock, shoal, islet
cerro, Sp . . . mountain, hill
champ, Fr . . . field
chang, Chn . . . village, middle
château, Fr . . . castle
chen, Chn . . . market town
chiang, Chn . . . river
chott, Arab . . . salt lake
chou, Chn. . . . capital of district; island
chu, Tib . . . water, stream
cidade, Port . . . town, city
cima, Sp . . . summit, peak
città, It . . . town, city
ciudad, Sp . . . town, city
cochilha, Port . . . ridge
col, Fr . . . pass
colina, Sp . . . hill
cordillera, Sp . . . mountain chain
costa, It., Port., Sp . . . coast
côte, Fr . . . coast
cuchilla, Sp . . . mountain ridge
dağ, Tur . . . mountain(s)
dake, Jap . . . peak, summit
dal, Dan., Du., Nor., Swe . . . valley
dan, Kor . . . point, cape
danau, Indon . . . lake
dar, Arab . . . house, abode, country
darya, Per . . . river, sea
dasht, Per . . . plain, desert
deniz, Tur . . . sea
désert, Fr . . . desert
deserto, It . . . desert
desierto, Sp . . . desert
détroit, Fr . . . strait
dijk, Du . . . dam, dike
djebel, Arab . . . mountain
do, Kor . . . island
dorf, Ger . . . village
dorp, Du . . . village
duin, Du . . . dune
dzong, Tib. . . . fort, administrative capital
eau, Fr . . . water
ecuador, Sp . . . equator
eiland, Du . . . island
elv, Dan., Nor . . . river, stream
embalse, Sp . . . reservoir
erg, Arab . . . dune, sandy desert
est, Fr., It . . . east
estado, Sp . . . state
este, Port., Sp . . . east
estrecho, Sp . . . strait
étang, Fr . . . pond, lake
état, Fr . . . state
eyjar, Ice . . . islands
feld, Ger . . . field, plain
festung, Ger . . . fortress
fiume, It . . . river
fjäll, Swe . . . mountain
fjärd, Swe . . . bay, inlet
fjeld, Nor . . . mountain, hill
fjord, Dan., Nor . . . fiord, inlet
fjördur, Ice . . . fiord, inlet
fleuve, Fr . . . river
flod, Dan., Swe . . . river
flói, Ice . . . bay, marshland
fluss, Ger . . . river
foce, It . . . river mouth
fontein, Du . . . a spring
forêt, Fr . . . forest
fors, Swe . . . waterfall
forst, Ger . . . forest
fos, Dan., Nor . . . waterfall
fu, Chn . . . town, residence
fuente, Sp . . . spring, fountain
fuerte, Sp . . . fort
furt, Ger . . . ford
gang, Kor . . . stream, river
gangri, Tib . . . mountain
gat, Dan., Nor . . . channel
gàve, Fr . . . stream
gawa, Jap . . . river
gebergte, Du . . . mountain range
gebiet, Ger . . . district, territory
gebirge, Ger . . . mountains
ghat, India . . . pass, mountain range
gobi, Mong . . . desert
gol, Mong . . . river
göl, gölü, Tur . . . lake
golf, Du., Ger . . . gulf, bay
golfe, Fr . . . gulf, bay
golfo, It., Port., Sp . . . gulf, bay
gomba, gompa, Tib . . . monastery
gora, Rus., So. Slav . . . mountain
góra, Pol . . . mountain
gorod, Rus . . . town
grad, Rus., So. Slav . . . town
guba, Rus . . . bay, gulf
gundung, Indon . . . mountain
guntō, Jap . . . archipelago
gunung, Mal . . . mountain
haf, Swe . . . sea, ocean
hafen, Ger . . . port, harbor
haff, Ger . . . gulf, inland sea
hai, Chn . . . sea, lake
hama, Jap . . . beach, shore
hamada, Arab . . . rocky plateau
hamn, Swe . . . harbor
hāmūn, Per . . . swampy lake, plain
hantō, Jap . . . peninsula
hassi, Arab . . . well, spring
haus, Ger . . . house
haut, Fr . . . summit, top
hav, Dan., Nor . . . sea, ocean
havn, Dan., Nor . . . harbor, port
havre, Fr . . . harbor, port
háza, Hung . . . house, dwelling of
heim, Ger . . . hamlet, home
hem, Swe . . . hamlet, home
higashi, Jap . . . east
hisar, Tur . . . fortress
hissar, Arab . . . fort
ho, Chn . . . river
hoek, Du . . . cape
hof, Ger . . . court, farmhouse
höfn, Ice . . . harbor
hoku, Jap . . . north
holm, Dan., Nor., Swe . . . island
hora, Czech . . . mountain
horn, Ger . . . peak
hoved, Dan., Nor . . . cape
hsien, Chn . . . district, district capital
hu, Chn . . . lake
hügel, Ger . . . hill
huk, Dan., Swe . . . point
hus, Dan., Nor., Swe . . . house
île, Fr . . . island
ilha, Port . . . island
indsö, Dan., Nor . . . lake
insel, Ger . . . island
insjö, Swe . . . lake
irmak, irmagi, Tur . . . river
isla, Sp . . . island
isola, It . . . island
istmo, It., Sp . . . isthmus
järvi, jaur, Fin . . . lake
jebel, Arab . . . mountain
jima, Jap . . . island
jökel, Nor . . . glacier
joki, Fin . . . river
jökull, Ice . . . glacier
kaap, Du . . . cape
kai, Jap . . . bay, gulf, sea
kaikyō, Jap . . . channel, strait
kalat, Per . . . castle, fortress
kale, Tur . . . fort
kali, Mal . . . creek, river
kand, Per . . . village
kang, Chn . . . mountain ridge; village
kap, Dan., Ger . . . cape
kapp, Nor., Swe . . . cape
kasr, Arab . . . fort, castle
kawa, Jap . . . river
kefr, Arab . . . village
kei, Jap . . . creek, river
ken, Jap . . . prefecture
khor, Arab . . . bay, inlet
khrebet, Rus . . . mountain range
kiang, Chn . . . large river
king, Chn . . . capital city, town
kita, Jap . . . north
ko, Jap . . . lake
köbstad, Dan . . . market-town
kol, Mong . . . lake
kólpos, Gr . . . gulf
kong, Chn . . . river
kopf, Ger . . . head, summit, peak
köpstad, Swe . . . market-town
körfezi, Tur . . . gulf
kosa, Rus . . . spit
kou, Chn . . . river mouth
köy, Tur . . . village
kraal, Du. (Africa) . . . native village
ksar, Arab . . . fortified village
kuala, Mal . . . bay, river mouth
kuh, Per . . . mountain
kum, Tur . . . sand
kuppe, Ger . . . summit
küste, Ger . . . coast
kyo, Jap . . . town, capital
la, Tib . . . mountain pass
labuan, Mal . . . anchorage, port
lac, Fr . . . lake
lago, It., Port., Sp . . . lake
lagoa, Port . . . lake, marsh
laguna, It., Port., Sp . . . lagoon, lake
lahti, Fin . . . bay, gulf
län, Swe . . . county
landsby, Dan., Nor . . . village
liehtao, Chn . . . archipelago
liman, Tur . . . bay, port
ling, Chn . . . pass, ridge, mountain
llanos, Sp . . . plains
loch, Celt. (Scotland) . . . lake, bay
loma, Sp . . . long, low hill
lough, Celt. (Ireland) . . . lake, bay
machi, Jap . . . town
man, Kor . . . bay
mar, Port., Sp . . . sea
mare, It., Rom . . . sea
marisma, Sp . . . marsh, swamp
mark, Ger . . . boundary, limit
massif, Fr . . . block of mountains
mato, Port . . . forest, thicket
me, Siam . . . river
meer, Du., Ger . . . lake, sea
mer, Fr . . . sea
mesa, Sp . . . flat-topped mountain
meseta, Sp . . . plateau
mina, Port., Sp . . . mine
minami, Jap . . . south
minato, Jap . . . harbor, haven
misaki, Jap . . . cape, headland
mont, Fr . . . mount, mountain
montagna, It . . . mountain
montagne, Fr . . . mountain
montaña, Sp . . . mountain
monte, It., Port., Sp. . . . mount, mountain
more, Rus., So. Slav . . . sea
morro, Port., Sp . . . hill, bluff
mühle, Ger . . . mill
mund, Ger . . . mouth, opening
mündung, Ger . . . river mouth
mura, Jap . . . township
myit, Bur . . . river
mys, Rus . . . cape
nada, Jap . . . sea
nadi, India . . . river, creek
naes, Dan., Nor . . . cape
nafud, Arab . . . desert of sand dunes
nagar, India . . . town, city
nahr, Arab . . . river
nam, Siam . . . river, water
nan, Chn., Jap . . . south
näs, Nor., Swe . . . cape
nez, Fr . . . point, cape
nishi, nisi, Jap . . . west
njarga, Fin . . . peninsula
nong, Siam . . . marsh
noord, Du . . . north
nor, Mong . . . lake
nord, Dan., Fr., Ger., It., Nor., Swe . . . north
norte, Port., Sp . . . north
nos, Rus . . . cape
nyasa, Bantu . . . lake
ö, Dan., Nor., Swe . . . island
occidental, Sp . . . western
ocna, Rom . . . salt mine
odde, Dan., Nor . . . point, cape
oeste, Port., Sp . . . west
oka, Jap . . . hill
oost, Du . . . east
oriental, Sp . . . eastern
óros, Gr . . . mountain
ost, Ger., Swe . . . east
öster, Dan., Nor., Swe . . . eastern
ostrov, Rus . . . island
oued, Arab . . . river, stream
ouest, Fr . . . west
ozero, Rus . . . lake
pää, Fin . . . mountain
padang, Mal . . . plain, field
pampas, Sp. (Argentina) . . . grassy plains
pará, Indian (Brazil) . . . river
pas, Fr . . . channel, passage
paso, Sp . . . mountain pass, passage
passo, It., Port. mountain pass, passage, strait
patam, India . . . city, town
pei, Chn . . . north
pélagos, Gr . . . open sea
pegunungan, Indon . . . mountains
peña, Sp . . . rock
peresheyek, Rus . . . isthmus
pertuis, Fr . . . strait
peski, Rus . . . desert
pic, Fr . . . mountain peak
pico, Port., Sp . . . mountain peak
piedra, Sp . . . stone, rock
ping, Chn . . . plain, flat
planalto, Port . . . plateau
planina, Yugo . . . mountains
playa, Sp . . . shore, beach
pnom, Camb . . . mountain
pointe, Fr . . . point
polder, Du., Ger . . . reclaimed marsh
polje, So. Slav . . . plain, field
poluostrov, Rus . . . peninsula
pont, Fr . . . bridge
ponta, Port . . . point, headland
ponte, It., Port . . . bridge
pore, India . . . city, town
porthmós, Gr . . . strait
porto, It., Port . . . port, harbor
potamós, Gr . . . river
p'ov, Rus . . . peninsula
prado, Sp . . . field, meadow
presqu'île, Fr . . . peninsula
proliv, Rus . . . strait
pu, Chn . . . commercial village
pueblo, Sp . . . town, village
puerto, Sp . . . port, harbor
pulau, Indon . . . island
punkt, Ger . . . point
punt, Du . . . point
punta, It., Sp . . . point
pur, India . . . city, town
puy, Fr . . . peak
qal'a, qal'at, Arab . . . fort, village
qasr, Arab . . . fort, castle
rann, India . . . wasteland
ra's, Arab . . . cape, head
reka, Rus., So. Slav . . . river
represa, Port . . . reservoir
rettō, Jap . . . island chain
ria, Sp . . . estuary
ribeira, Port . . . stream
riberão, Port . . . river
rio, It., Port . . . stream, river
río, Sp . . . river
rivière, Fr . . . river
roca, Sp . . . rock
rt, Yugo . . . cape
rūd, Per . . . river
saari, Fin . . . island
sable, Fr . . . sand
sahara, Arab . . . desert, plain
saki, Jap . . . cape
sal, Sp . . . salt
salar, Sp . . . salt flat, salt lake
salto, Sp . . . waterfall
san, Jap., Kor . . . mountain, hill
sat, satul, Rom . . . village
schloss, Ger . . . castle
sebkha, Arab . . . salt marsh
see, Ger . . . lake, sea
şehir, Tur . . . town, city
selat, Indon . . . stream
selvas, Port. (Brazil) . . . tropical rain forests
seno, Sp . . . bay
serra, Port . . . mountain chain
serranía, Sp . . . mountain ridge
seto, Jap . . . strait
severnaya, Rus . . . northern
shahr, Per . . . town, city
shan, Chn . . . mountain, hill, island
shatt, Arab . . . river
shi, Jap . . . city
shima, Jap . . . island
shōtō, Jap . . . archipelago
si, Chn . . . west, western
sierra, Sp . . . mountain range
sjö, Nor., Swe . . . lake, sea
sö, Dan., Nor . . . lake, sea
söder, södra, Swe . . . south
song, Annam . . . river
sopka, Rus . . . peak, volcano
source, Fr . . . a spring
spitze, Ger . . . summit, point
staat, Ger . . . state
stad, Dan., Du., Nor., Swe. . . . city, town
stadt, Ger . . . city, town
stato, It . . . state
step', Rus . . . treeless plain, steppe
straat, Du . . . strait
strand, Dan., Du., Ger., Nor., Swe . . . shore, beach
stretto, It . . . strait
strom, Ger . . . river, stream
ström, Dan., Nor., Swe. . . . stream, river
stroom, Du . . . stream, river
su, suyu, Tur . . . water, river
sud, Fr., Sp . . . south
süd, Ger . . . south
suidō, Jap . . . channel
sul, Port . . . south
sund, Dan., Nor., Swe . . . sound
sungai, sungei, Indon., Mal . . . river
sur, Sp . . . south
syd, Dan., Nor., Swe . . . south
tafelland, Ger . . . plateau
take, Jap . . . peak, summit
tal, Ger . . . valley
tanjung, tanjong, Mal . . . cape
tao, Chn . . . island
târg, târgul, Rom . . . market, town
tell, Arab . . . hill
teluk, Indon . . . bay, gulf
terra, It . . . land
terre, Fr . . . earth, land
thal, Ger . . . valley
tierra, Sp . . . earth, land
tō, Jap . . . east; island
tonle, Camb . . . river, lake
top, Du . . . peak
torp, Swe . . . hamlet, cottage
tsangpo, Tib . . . river
tsi, Chn . . . village, borough
tso, Tib . . . lake
tsu, Jap . . . harbor, port
tundra, Rus . . . treeless arctic plains
tung, Chn . . . east
tuz, Tur . . . salt
udde, Swe . . . cape
ufer, Ger . . . shore, riverbank
ujung, Indon . . . point, cape
umi, Jap . . . sea, gulf
ura, Jap . . . bay, coast, creek
ust'ye, Rus . . . river mouth
valle, It., Port., Sp . . . valley
vallée, Fr . . . valley
valli, It . . . lake
vár, Hung . . . fortress
város, Hung . . . town
varoš, So. Slav . . . town
veld, Du . . . open plain, field
verkh, Rus . . . top, summit
ves, Czech . . . village
vest, Dan., Nor., Swe . . . west
vik, Swe . . . cove, bay
vila, Port . . . town
villa, Sp . . . town
villar, Sp . . . village, hamlet
ville, Fr . . . town, city
vostok, Rus . . . east
wad, wādī, Arab. . . . intermittent stream
wald, Ger . . . forest, woodland
wan, Chn., Jap . . . bay, gulf
weiler, Ger . . . hamlet, village
westersch, Du . . . western
wüste, Ger . . . desert
yama, Jap . . . mountain
yarimada, Tur . . . peninsula
yug, Rus . . . south
zaki, Jap . . . cape
zaliv, Rus . . . bay, gulf
zapad, Rus . . . west
zee, Du . . . sea
zemlya, Rus . . . land
zuid, Du . . . south

ABBREVIATIONS OF GEOGRAPHICAL NAMES AND TERMS

Ab., Can.	Alberta, Can.
Afg.	Afghanistan
Afr.	Africa
Ak., U.S.	Alaska, U.S.
Al., U.S.	Alabama, U.S.
Alb.	Albania
Alg.	Algeria
Am. Sam.	American Samoa
And.	Andorra
Ang.	Angola
Ant.	Antarctica
Antig.	Antigua and Barbuda
aq.	Aqueduct
Ar., U.S.	Arkansas, U.S.
Arg.	Argentina
Arm.	Armenia
arpt.	Airport
Aus.	Austria
Austl.	Australia
Az., U.S.	Arizona, U.S.
Azer.	Azerbaijan
b.	Bay, Gulf, Inlet, Lagoon
Bah.	Bahamas
Bahr.	Bahrain
Barb.	Barbados
B.C., Can.	British Columbia, Can.
Bdi.	Burundi
Bel.	Belgium
Bela.	Belarus
Ber.	Bermuda
Bhu.	Bhutan
bk.	Undersea Bank
bldg.	Building
Blg.	Bulgaria
Bngl.	Bangladesh
Bol.	Bolivia
Bos.	Bosnia and Hercegovina
Bots.	Botswana
Braz.	Brazil
Bru.	Brunei
Br. Vir. Is.	British Virgin Islands
bt.	Bight
Burkina	Burkina Faso
c.	Cape, Point
Ca., U.S.	California, U.S.
Cam.	Cameroon
Camb.	Cambodia
can.	Canal
Can.	Canada
C.A.R.	Central African Republic
Cay. Is.	Cayman Islands
C. Iv.	Cote d'Ivoire
clf.	Cliff, Escarpment
co.	County, Parish
Co., U.S.	Colorado, U.S.
Col.	Colombia
Com.	Comoros
cont.	Continent
Cook Is.	Cook Islands
C.R.	Costa Rica
Cro	Croatia
cst.	Coast, Beach
Ct., U.S.	Connecticut, U.S.
C.V.	Cape Verde
Cyp.	Cyprus
Czech Rep.	Czech Republic
d.	Delta
D.C., U.S.	District of Columbia, U.S.
De., U.S.	Delaware, U.S.
Den.	Denmark
dep.	Dependency, Colony
depr.	Depression
dept.	Department, District
des.	Desert
Dji.	Djibouti
Dom.	Dominica
Dom. Rep.	Dominican Republic
D.R.C.	Democratic Republic of the Congo
Ec.	Ecuador
educ.	Educational Facility
El Sal.	El Salvador
Eng., U.K.	England, U.K.
Eq. Gui.	Equatorial Guinea
Erit.	Eritrea
Est.	Estonia
est.	Estuary
Eth.	Ethiopia
E. Timor	East Timor
Eur.	Europe
Falk. Is.	Falkland Islands
Far. Is.	Faroe Islands
Fin.	Finland
fj.	Fjord
Fl., U.S.	Florida, U.S.
for.	Forest, Moor
Fr.	France
Fr. Gu.	French Guiana
Fr. Poly.	French Polynesia
Ga., U.S.	Georgia, U.S.
Gam.	The Gambia
Gaza	Gaza Strip
Geor.	Georgia
Ger.	Germany
Grc.	Greece
Gren.	Grenada
Grnld.	Greenland
Guad.	Guadeloupe
Guat.	Guatemala
Guern.	Guernsey
Gui.	Guinea
Gui.-B.	Guinea-Bissau
Guy.	Guyana
Hi., U.S.	Hawaii, U.S.
hist.	Historic Site, Ruins
hist. reg.	Historic Region
Hond.	Honduras
Hung.	Hungary
i.	Island
Ia., U.S.	Iowa, U.S.
ice	Ice Feature, Glacier
Ice.	Iceland
Id., U.S.	Idaho, U.S.
Il., U.S.	Illinois, U.S.
In., U.S.	Indiana, U.S.
Indon.	Indonesia
I. of Man	Isle of Man
I.R.	Indian Reservation
Ire.	Ireland
is.	Islands
Isr.	Israel
isth.	Isthmus
Jam.	Jamaica
Jord.	Jordan
Kaz.	Kazakhstan
Kir.	Kiribati
Kor., N.	Korea, North
Kor., S.	Korea, South
Ks., U.S.	Kansas, U.S.
Kuw.	Kuwait
Ky., U.S.	Kentucky, U.S.
Kyrg.	Kyrgyzstan
l.	Lake, Pond
La., U.S.	Louisiana, U.S.
Lat.	Latvia
Leb.	Lebanon
Leso.	Lesotho
Lib.	Liberia
Liech.	Liechtenstein
Lith.	Lithuania
Lux.	Luxembourg
Ma., U.S.	Massachusetts, U.S.
Mac.	Macedonia
Madag.	Madagascar
Malay.	Malaysia
Mald.	Maldives
Marsh. Is.	Marshall Islands
Mart.	Martinique
Maur.	Mauritania
May.	Mayotte
Mb., Can.	Manitoba, Canada
Md., U.S.	Maryland, U.S.
Me., U.S.	Maine, U.S.
Mex.	Mexico
Mi., U.S.	Michigan, U.S.
Micron.	Micronesia, Federated States of
Mn., U.S.	Minnesota, U.S.
Mo., U.S.	Missouri, U.S.
Mol.	Moldova
Mong.	Mongolia
Monts.	Montserrat
Mor.	Morocco
Moz.	Mozambique
Ms., U.S.	Mississippi, U.S.
Mt., U.S.	Montana, U.S.
mth.	River Mouth or Channel
mtn.	Mountain
mts.	Mountains
Mwi.	Malawi
Mya.	Myanmar
N.A.	North America
N.B., Can.	New Brunswick, Can.
N.C., U.S.	North Carolina, U.S.
N. Cal.	New Caledonia
N. Cyp.	North Cyprus
N.D., U.S.	North Dakota, U.S.
Ne., U.S.	Nebraska, U.S.
neigh.	Neighborhood
Neth.	Netherlands
Neth. Ant.	Netherlands Antilles
Nf., Can.	Newfoundland, Can.
N.H., U.S.	New Hampshire, U.S.
Nic.	Nicaragua
Nig.	Nigeria
N. Ire., U.K.	Northern Ireland, U.K.
N.J., U.S.	New Jersey, U.S.
N.M., U.S.	New Mexico, U.S.
N. Mar. Is.	Northern Mariana Islands
Nmb.	Namibia
Nor.	Norway
N.S., Can.	Nova Scotia, Can.
N.T., Can.	Northwest Territories, Can.
Nu., Can.	Nunavut, Can.
Nv., U.S.	Nevada, U.S.
N.Y., U.S.	New York, U.S.
N.Z.	New Zealand
o.	Ocean
Oc.	Oceania
Oh., U.S.	Ohio, U.S.
Ok., U.S.	Oklahoma, U.S.
On, Can.	Ontario, Can.
Or., U.S.	Oregon, U.S.
p.	Pass
Pa., U.S.	Pennsylvania, U.S.
Pak.	Pakistan
Pan.	Panama
Pap. N. Gui.	Papua New Guinea
Para.	Paraguay
P.E., Can.	Prince Edward Island, Can.
pen.	Peninsula
Phil.	Philippines
Pit.	Pitcairn
pl.	Plain, Flat
plat.	Plateau, Highland
Pol.	Poland
Port.	Portugal
P.R.	Puerto Rico
prov.	Province, Region
pt. of i.	Point of Interest
Qc., Can.	Quebec, Can.
r.	River, Creek
Reu.	Reunion
rec.	Recreational Site, Park
reg.	Physical Region
rel.	Religious Institution
res.	Reservoir
rf.	Reef, Shoal
R.I., U.S.	Rhode Island, U.S.
Rom.	Romania
Rw.	Rwanda
S.A.	South America
S. Afr.	South Africa
Sau. Ar.	Saudi Arabia
S.C., U.S.	South Carolina, U.S.
sci.	Scientific Station
Scot., U.K.	Scotland, U.K.
S.D., U.S.	South Dakota, U.S.
Sen.	Senegal
sea feat.	Undersea Feature
Sey.	Seychelles
S. Geor.	South Georgia
Sing.	Singapore
Sk., Can.	Saskatchewan, Can.
S.L.	Sierra Leone
Slvk.	Slovakia
Slvn.	Slovenia
S. Mar.	San Marino
Sol. Is.	Solomon Islands
Som.	Somalia
Sp. N. Afr.	Spanish North Africa
Sri L.	Sri Lanka
St. Hel.	St. Helena
St. K./N.	St. Kitts and Nevis
St. Luc.	St. Lucia
St. P./M.	St. Pierre and Miquelon
strt.	Strait, Channel, Sound
S. Tom./P.	Sao Tome and Principe
St. Vin.	St. Vincent and the Grenadines
Sur.	Suriname
Sval.	Svalbard
sw.	Swamp, Marsh
Swaz.	Swaziland
Swe.	Sweden
Switz.	Switzerland
Tai.	Taiwan
Taj.	Tajikistan
Tan.	Tanzania
T./C. Is.	Turks and Caicos Islands
ter.	Territory
Thai.	Thailand
Tn., U.S.	Tennessee, U.S.
trans.	Transportation Facility
Trin.	Trinidad and Tobago
Tun.	Tunisia
Tur.	Turkey
Turkmen.	Turkmenistan
Tx., U.S.	Texas, U.S.
U.A.E.	United Arab Emirates
Ug.	Uganda
U.K.	United Kingdom
Ukr.	Ukraine
Ur.	Uruguay
U.S.	United States
Ut., U.S.	Utah, U.S.
Uzb.	Uzbekistan
Va., U.S.	Virginia, U.S.
val.	Valley, Watercourse
Vat.	Vatican City
Ven.	Venezuela
Viet.	Vietnam
V.I.U.S.	Virgin Islands (U.S.)
vol.	Volcano
Vt., U.S.	Vermont, U.S.
Wa., U.S.	Washington, U.S.
W.B.	West Bank
Wi., U.S.	Wisconsin, U.S.
W. Sah.	Western Sahara
wtfl.	Waterfall
W.V., U.S.	West Virginia, U.S.
Wy., U.S.	Wyoming, U.S.
Yk., Can.	Yukon Territory, Can.
Yugo.	Yugoslavia
Zam.	Zambia
Zimb.	Zimbabwe
Zam.	Zambia

PRONUNCIATION OF GEOGRAPHICAL NAMES

Key to the Sound Values of Letters and Symbols Used in the Index to Indicate Pronunciation

ă-ăt; băttle
ă-fin*ă*l; *ă*ppeal
ā-rāte; elāte
å-senåte; inanimåte
ä-ärm; cälm
à-àsk; bàth
a-sof*a*; m*a*rine (short neutral or indeterminate sound)
â-fâre; prepâre
ch-choose; church
dh-as th in other; either
ē-bē; ēve
ė-ėvent; crėate
ĕ-bĕt; ĕnd
ĕ-rec*ĕ*nt (short neutral or indeterminate sound)
ẽ-cratẽr; cindẽr
g-gō; gāme
gh-guttural g
ĭ-bĭt; wĭll
ĭ-(short neutral or indeterminate sound)
ī-rīde; bīte
ĸ-guttural k as *ch* in German *ich*
ng-sing
ŋ-baŋk; liŋger
ɴ-indicates nasalized
ŏ-nŏd; ŏdd
ŏ-c*ŏ*mmit; c*ŏ*nnect
ō-ōld; bōld
ô-ôbey; hôtel
ô-ôrder; nôrth
oi-boil
o͞o-fo͞od; ro͞ot
ȯ-as oo in foot; wood
ou-out; thou
s-soft; so; sane
sh-dish; finish
th-thin; thick
ū-pūre; cūre
û-ûnite; ûsûrp
û-ûrn; fûr
ŭ-stŭd; ŭp
ŭ-circ*ŭ*s; s*ŭ*bmit
ü-as in French *tu*
zh-as *z* in a*z*ure
'-indeterminate vowel sound

In many cases the spelling of foreign geographic names does not even remotely indicate the pronunciation to an American, i.e., Słupsk in Poland is pronounced swȯpsk; Jujuy in Argentina is pronounced ho͞ohwē′; La Spezia in Italy is lä-spĕ′zyä.

This condition is hardly surprising, however, when we consider that in our own language Worcester, Massachusetts, is pronounced wȯs′tẽr; Sioux City, Iowa, so͞o sĭ′tĭ; Schuylkill Haven, Pennsylvania, sko͞ol′kĭl hā-vĕn; Poughkeepsie, New York, pŏ-kĭp′sė.

The indication of pronunciation of geographic names presents several peculiar problems:

1. Many foreign tongues use sounds that are not present in the English language and which an American cannot normally articulate. Thus, though the nearest English equivalent sound has been indicated, only approximate results are possible.

2. There are several dialects in each foreign tongue which cause variation in the local pronunciation of names. This also occurs in identical names in the various divisions of a great language group, as the Slavic or the Latin.

3. Within the United States there are marked differences in pronunciation, not only of local geographic names, but also of common words, indicating that the sound and tone values for letters as well as the placing of the emphasis vary considerably from one part of the country to another.

4. A number of different letters and diacritical combinations could be used to indicate essentially the same or approximate pronunciations.

Some variation in pronunciation other than that indicated in this index may be encountered, but such a difference does not necessarily indicate that either is in error, and in many cases it is a matter of individual choice as to which is preferred. In fact, an exact indication of pronunciation of many foreign names using English letters and diacritical marks is extremely difficult and sometimes impossible.

PRONOUNCING INDEX

This universal index includes in a single alphabetical list approximately 30,000 names of features that appear on the reference maps. Each name is followed by a page reference and geographical coordinates.

Abbreviation and Capitalization Abbreviations of names on the maps have been standardized as much as possible. Names that are abbreviated on the maps are generally spelled out in full in the index. Periods are used after all abbreviations regardless of local practice. The abbreviation "St." is used only for "Saint". "Sankt" and other forms of this term are spelled out.

Most initial letters of names are capitalized, except for a few Dutch names, such as "s-Gravenhage". Capitalization of noninitial words in a name generally follows local practice.

Alphabetization Names are alphabetized in the order of the letters of the English alphabet. Spanish *ll* and *ch*, for example, are not treated as direct letters. Furthermore, diacritical marks are disregarded in alphabetization — German or Scandinavian *ä* or *ö* are treated as *a* or *o*.

The names of physical features may appear inverted, since they are always alphabetized under the proper, not the generic, part of the name, thus: "Gibraltar, Strait of". Otherwise every entry, whether consisting of one word or more, is alphabetized as a single continuous entity. "Lakeland", for example, appears after "La Crosse" and before "La Salle". Names beginning with articles (Le Harve, Den Helder, Al Manāmah, Ad Dawhah) are not inverted.

In the case of identical names, towns are listed first, then political divisions, then physical features.

Generic Terms Except for cities, the names of all features are followed by terms that represent broad classes of features, for example, Mississippi, r. or Alabama, state. A list of all abbreviations used in the index is on page 261.

Country names and the names of features that extend beyond the boundaries of one county are followed by the name of the continent in which each is located. Country designations follow the names of all other places in the index. The locations of places in the United States and the United Kingdom are further defined by abbreviations that include the state or political division in which each is located.

Pronunciations Pronunciations are included for most names listed. An explanation of the pronunciation system used appears on page 261.

Page References and Geographical Coordinates The geographical coordinates and page references are found in the last columns of each entry.

If a page contains several maps or insets, a lowercase letter identifies the specific map or inset.

Latitude and longitude coordinates for point features, such as cities and mountain peaks, indicate the location of the symbols. For extensive areal features, such as countries or mountain ranges, or linear features, such as canals and rivers, locations are given for the position of the type as it appears on the map.

PLACE (Pronunciation)	PAGE	LAT.	LONG.
A			
Aachen, Ger. (ä´kĕn)	161	50°46′N	6°07′E
Aalborg, Den. (ôl´bôr)	154	57°02′N	9°55′E
Aalen, Ger. (ä´lĕn)	168	48°49′N	10°08′E
Aalsmeer, Neth.	159a	52°16′N	4°44′E
Aalst, Bel.	165	50°58′N	4°00′E
Aarau, Switz. (är′ou)	161	47°22′N	8°03′E
Aarschot, Bel.	159a	50°59′N	4°51′E
Aba, D.R.C.	237	3°52′N	30°14′E
Aba, Nig.	230	5°06′N	7°21′E
Ābādān, Iran (ä-bü-dän′)	198	30°15′N	48°30′E
Abaetetuba, Braz. (ä´bä-ĕ-tĕ-tōō′bá)	143	1°44′S	48°45′W
Abajo Peak, mtn., Ut., U.S. (ä-bá´hŏ)	119	37°51′N	109°28′W
Abakaliki, Nig.	235	6°21′N	8°06′E
Abakan, Russia (ŭ-bá-kän′)	179	53°43′N	91°28′E
Abakan, r., Russia (u-bá-kän′)	184	53°00′N	91°06′E
Abancay, Peru (ä-bän-kä′ĕ)	142	13°44′S	72°46′W
Abashiri, Japan (ä-bä-shē′rĕ)	210	44°00′N	144°13′E
Abasolo, Mex. (ä-bä-sō′lŏ)	130	24°05′N	98°24′W
Abasolo, Mex. (ä-bä-sō′lŏ)	122	27°13′N	101°25′W
Abaya, Lake, l., Eth. (ä-bä′yá)	231	6°24′N	38°22′E
ʻAbbāsah, Turʻat al, can., Egypt	238d	30°45′N	32°15′E
Abbeville, Fr. (ȧb-vēl′)	161	50°08′N	1°49′E
Abbeville, Al., U.S. (ăb′ē-vĭl)	124	31°35′N	85°15′W
Abbeville, Ga., U.S. (ăb′ē-vĭl)	124	31°53′N	83°23′W
Abbeville, La., U.S.	123	29°59′N	92°07′W
Abbeville, S.C., U.S.	125	34°09′N	82°25′W
Abbiategrasso, Italy (äb-byä´tä-gräs′sō)	174	45°23′N	8°52′E
Abbots Bromley, Eng., U.K. (ăb′ŭts brŭm′lė)	158a	52°49′N	1°52′W
Abbotsford, Can. (ăb´ŭts-fĕrd)	116d	49°03′N	122°17′W
ʻAbd al Kūrī, i., Yemen (äbd-ĕl-kó′rē)	238a	12°12′N	51°00′E
Abdulino, Russia (äb-dó-lē′nō)	180	53°42′N	53°40′E
Abengourou, C. Iv.	234	6°44′N	3°29′W
Abeokuta, Nig. (ä-bá-ô-kōō′tä)	230	7°10′N	3°26′E
Abercorn see Mbala, Zam.	232	8°50′S	31°22′E
Aberdare, Wales, U.K. (ăb-ĕr-dâr′)	164	51°45′N	3°35′W
Aberdeen, Scot., U.K. (ăb-ĕr-dēn′)	154	57°10′N	2°05′W
Aberdeen, Md., U.S. (ăb-ĕr-dēn′)	124	33°49′N	88°33′W
Aberdeen, S.D., U.S. (ăb-ĕr-dēn′)	104	45°28′N	98°29′W
Aberdeen, Wa., U.S. (ăb-ĕr-dēn′)	104	46°58′N	123°48′W
Aberford, Eng., U.K. (ăb´ĕr-fĕrd)	158a	53°49′N	1°21′W
Abergavenny, Wales, U.K. (ăb´ĕr-gȧ-vĕn´ĭ)	164	51°45′N	3°05′W
Abert, Lake, l., Or., U.S. (ā´bĕrt)	114	42°39′N	120°24′W
Aberystwyth, Wales, U.K. (ă-bĕr-ĭst′wĭth)	164	52°25′N	4°04′W
Abidjan, C. Iv. (ä-bĕd-zhäN′)	230	5°19′N	4°02′W
Abiko, Japan (ä-bē-kō).	211a	35°53′N	140°01′E
Abilene, Ks., U.S. (ăb´ĭ-lēn)	121	38°54′N	97°12′W
Abilene, Tx., U.S.	104	32°25′N	99°45′W
Abingdon, Eng., U.K.	158b	51°38′N	1°17′W
Abingdon, Il., U.S. (ăb´ĭng-dŭn)	113	40°48′N	90°21′W
Abingdon, Va., U.S.	125	36°42′N	81°57′W
Abington, Ma., U.S. (ăb´ĭng-tŭn)	101a	42°07′N	70°57′W
Abiquiu Reservoir, res., N.M., U.S.	119	36°26′N	106°42′W
Abitibi, l., Can. (ăb-ĭ-tĭb´ĭ)	93	48°27′N	80°20′W
Abitibi, r., Can.	93	49°30′N	81°10′W
Abkhazia, state, Geor.	181	43°10′N	40°45′E
Ablis, Fr. (ȧ-blē´)	171b	48°31′N	1°50′E
Abnûb, Egypt (äb-nōōb′)	238b	27°18′N	31°11′E
Åbo see Turku, Fin.	154	60°28′N	22°12′E
Abohar, India	202	30°12′N	74°13′E
Aboisso, C. Iv.	234	5°28′N	3°12′W
Abomey, Benin (ȧb-ô-mā′)	230	7°11′N	1°59′E
Abony, Hung. (ŏ´bô-ny′)	169	47°12′N	20°00′E
Abou Deïa, Chad	235	11°27′N	19°17′E
Abra, r., Phil. (ä′brä)	213a	17°16′N	120°38′E
Abraão, Braz. (ȧbrȧ-ouN′)	141a	23°10′S	44°10′W
Abraham's Bay, b., Bah.	135	22°20′N	73°50′W
Abram, Eng., U.K. (ā′brȧm)	158a	53°31′N	2°36′W
Abrantes, Port. (ȧ-bränʹtĕs)	172	39°28′N	8°13′W
Abrolhos, Arquipélago dos, is., Braz.	143	17°58′S	38°40′W
Abruka, i., Est. (ä-brô′kȧ)	167	58°09′N	22°30′E
Abruzzi e Molise, hist. reg., Italy	174	42°10′N	13°55′E
Absaroka Range, mts., U.S. (ăb-sä-rō-kä)	106	44°50′N	109°47′W
Abşeron Yarımadası, pen., Azer.	181	40°20′N	50°30′E
Abū Arīsh, Sau. Ar. (ä-bōō ä-rēsh′)	198	16°48′N	43°00′E
Abu Dhabi see Abū Ẕaby, U.A.E.	198	24°15′N	54°28′E
Abū Ḥamad, Sudan (ä´bōō hä´-mĕd)	231	19°37′N	33°21′E
Abuja, Nig.	230	9°12′N	7°11′E
Abū Kamāl, Syria	198	34°45′N	40°46′E
Abunã, r., S.A. (ä-bōō-nä′)	142	10°25′S	67°00′W
Abū Qīr, Egypt (ä´bōō kēr′)	238b	31°18′N	30°06′E
Abū Qurūn, Ra's, mtn., Egypt	197a	30°22′N	33°32′E
Aburatsu, Japan (ä´bo-rät′sōō)	211	31°33′N	131°20′E
Abu Road, India (a′bōō)	199	24°38′N	72°45′E
Abū Tīj, Egypt	238b	27°03′N	31°19′E
Abū Ẕaby, U.A.E.	198	24°15′N	54°28′E
Abū Zanīmah, Egypt	197a	29°03′N	33°08′E
Abyy, Russia	179	68°24′N	134°00′E
Acacias, Col. (ȧ-kä′sēäs)	142a	3°59′N	73°44′W
Acadia National Park, rec., Me., U.S. (ä-kā´dǐ-ȧ)	107	44°19′N	68°01′W
Acajutla, El Sal. (ä-kä-hōōt′lä)	132	13°37′N	89°50′W
Acala, Mex. (ä-kä´lä)	131	16°38′N	92°49′W
Acalayong, Eq. Gui.	236	1°05′N	9°40′E
Acámbaro, Mex. (ä-käm´bä-rō)	130	20°03′N	100°42′W
Acancéh, Mex. (ä-kän-sĕ′)	132a	20°50′N	89°27′W
Acapetlahuaya, Mex. (ä-kä-pĕt´lä-hwä′yä)	130	18°24′N	100°04′W
Acaponeta, Mex. (ä-kä-pŏ-nä´tä)	130	22°31′N	105°25′W
Acaponeta, r., Mex. (ä-kä-pŏ-nä´tä)	130	22°47′N	105°23′W
Acapulco, Mex. (ä-kä-pōōl´kō)	128	16°49′N	99°57′W
Acaraí Mountains, mts., S.A.	143	1°30′N	57°40′W
Acarigua, Ven. (äkä-rē′gwä)	142	9°29′N	69°11′W
Acatlán de Osorio, Mex. (ä-kät-län′dä ô-sô′rē-ō)	130	18°11′N	98°04′W
Acatzingo de Hidalgo, Mex.	131	18°58′N	97°47′W
Acayucan, Mex. (ä-kä-yōō′kän)	131	17°56′N	94°55′W
Accoville, W.V., U.S. (äk´kŏ-vĭl)	108	37°45′N	81°50′W
Accra, Ghana (ä´krä)	230	5°33′N	0°13′W
Accrington, Eng., U.K. (äk´rĭng-tŭn)	158a	53°45′N	2°22′W
Acerra, Italy (ä-chĕ′r-rä)	173c	40°42′N	14°22′E
Achacachi, Bol. (ä-chä-kä′chė)	142	16°11′S	68°32′W
Achelóos, r., Grc.	175	38°45′N	21°26′E
Achill Island, i., Ire. (ä-chĭl′)	160	53°55′N	10°05′W
Achinsk, Russia (ȧ-chĕnsk′)	184	56°13′N	90°32′E
Acireale, Italy (ä-chē-rā-ä′lä)	174	37°37′N	15°12′E
Acklins, i., Bah. (äk´lĭns)	129	22°30′N	73°55′W
Acklins, The Bight of, b., Bah. (äk´lĭns)	135	22°35′N	74°20′W
Acolman, Mex. (ä-kôl-má′n)	131a	19°38′N	98°56′W
Acoma Indian Reservation, I.R., N.M., U.S.	119	34°52′N	107°40′W
Aconcagua, prov., Chile (ä-kôn-kä′gwä)	141b	32°20′S	71°00′W
Aconcagua, r., Chile (ä-kôn-kä′gwä)	141b	32°43′S	70°53′W
Aconcagua, Cerro, mtn., Arg. (ä-kôn-kä′gwä)	144	32°38′S	70°00′W
Açores (Azores), is., Port.	229	37°44′N	29°25′W
A Coruña, Spain	154	43°20′N	8°20′W
Acoyapa, Nic. (ä-kô-yä′pä)	132	11°54′N	85°11′W
Acqui, Italy (äk′kwē)	174	44°41′N	8°22′W
Acre, state, Braz. (ä´krä)	142	8°40′S	70°45′W
Acre, r., S.A.	142	10°33′S	68°34′W
Acton, Can. (äk′tŭn)	102d	43°38′N	80°02′W
Acton, Al., U.S. (äk´tŭn)	110h	33°21′N	86°49′W
Acton, Ma., U.S. (äk´tŭn)	101a	42°29′N	71°26′W
Actopan, Mex. (äk-tô-pän′)	130	20°16′N	98°57′W
Actópan, r., Mex. (äk-tô′pän)	131	19°25′N	96°31′W
Acuitzio del Canje, Mex. (ä-kwēt′zē-ō dĕl kän′hä)	130	19°28′N	101°21′W
Acul, Baie de l', b., Haiti (ä-kōōl′)	135	19°55′N	72°20′W
Ada, Mn., U.S. (ā´dȧ)	112	47°17′N	96°32′W
Ada, Oh., U.S. (ā´dȧ)	108	40°45′N	83°45′W
Ada, Ok., U.S. (ā´dȧ)	121	34°45′N	96°43′W

āt; finᾱl; rāte; senᾱte; ärm; ȧsk; sofᾱ; fâre; ch-choose; dh-as th in other; bē; ėvent; bĕt; recĕnt; cratēr; g-gō; gh-guttural g; bĭt; ī-short neutral; rīde; κ-guttural k as ch in German ich;

PLACE (Pronunciation)	PAGE	LAT.	LONG.
Ada, Yugo. (ä′dä)	175	45°48′N	20°06′E
Adachi, Japan	211a	35°50′N	39°36′E
Adak, Ak., U.S. (ă-dăk′)	103a	56°50′N	176°48′W
Adak, i., Ak., U.S. (ă-dăk′)	103a	51°40′N	176°28′W
Adak Strait, strt., Ak., U.S. (ă-dăk′)	103a	51°42′N	177°16′W
Adamaoua, mts., Afr.	230	6°30′N	11°50′E
Adams, Ma., U.S. (ăd′ămz)	109	42°35′N	73°10′W
Adams, Wi., U.S. (ăd′ămz)	113	43°55′N	89°48′W
Adams, r., Can. (ăd′ămz)	95	51°30′N	119°20′W
Adams, Mount, mtn., Wa., U.S. (ăd′ămz)	106	46°15′N	121°19′W
Adamsville, Al., U.S. (ăd′ămz-vĭl)	110h	33°36′N	86°57′W
Adana, Tur. (ä′dä-nä)	198	37°05′N	35°20′E
Adapazarı, Tur. (ä-dä-pä-zä′rĕ)	163	40°45′N	30°20′E
Adarama, Sudan (ä-dä-rä′mä)	231	17°11′N	34°56′E
Adda, r., Italy (äd′dä)	174	45°43′N	9°31′E
Ad Dabbah, Sudan	231	18°04′N	30°58′E
Ad Dahnā, des., Sau. Ar.	198	26°05′N	47°15′E
Ad-Dāmir, Sudan (ad-dä′mĕr)	231	17°38′N	33°57′E
Ad Dammām, Sau. Ar.	198	26°27′N	49°59′E
Ad Dāmūr, Leb.	197a	33°44′N	35°27′E
Ad Dawhah, Qatar	198	25°02′N	51°28′E
Ad Dilam, Sau. Ar.	198	23°47′N	47°03′E
Ad Dilinjāt, Egypt	238b	30°48′N	30°32′E
Addis Ababa, Eth.	231	9°00′N	38°44′E
Addison, Tx., U.S. (ă′dĭ-sŭn)	117c	32°58′N	96°50′W
Addo, S. Afr. (ădō)	233c	33°33′S	25°43′E
Ad Duwaym, Sudan (ad-dò-ām′)	231	13°56′N	32°22′E
Addyston, Oh., U.S. (ăd′ē-stŭn)	111f	39°09′N	84°42′W
Adel, Ga., U.S. (ā-dĕl′)	124	31°08′N	83°55′W
Adelaide, Austl. (ăd′ē-lād)	218	34°46′S	139°08′E
Adelaide, S. Afr. (ăd-ĕl′ăd)	233c	32°41′S	26°07′E
Adelaide Island, i., Ant. (ăd′ē-lād)	224	67°15′S	68°40′W
Aden ('Adan), Yemen (ä′dĕn)	198	12°48′N	45°00′E
Aden, Gulf of, b.	198	11°45′N	45°45′E
Adi, Pulau, i., Indon. (ä′dē)	213	4°25′S	133°52′E
Adige, r., Italy (ä′dē-jā)	162	46°38′N	10°43′E
Adigrat, Eth.	201	14°17′N	39°28′E
Adilābād, India (ŭ-dĭl-ā-bäd′)	202	19°47′N	78°30′E
Adirondack Mountains, mts., N.Y., U.S. (ăd-ĭ-rŏn′dăk)	107	43°45′N	74°40′W
Adis Abeba *see* Addis Ababa, Eth.	231	9°00′N	38°44′E
Adi Ugri, Erit. (ä-dē ōō′grē)	231	14°54′N	38°52′E
Adjud, Rom. (äd′zhòd)	169	46°05′N	27°12′E
Adkins, Tx., U.S.	117d	29°22′N	98°18′W
Admiralty, i., Ak., U.S. (ăd′mĭ-răl-tē)	103	57°50′N	133°50′W
Admiralty Inlet, Wa., U.S. (ăd′mĭ-răl-tē)	116a	48°10′N	122°45′W
Admiralty Island National Monument, rec., Ak., U.S. (ăd′mĭ-răl-tē)	103	57°50′N	137°30′W
Admiralty Islands, is., Pap. N. Gui. (ăd′mĭ-răl-tē)	213	1°40′S	146°45′E
Ado-Ekiti, Nig.	235	7°38′N	5°12′E
Adolph, Mn., U.S. (ā′dolf)	117h	46°47′N	92°17′W
Ādoni, India	203	15°42′N	77°18′E
Adour, r., Fr. (ä-dōōr′)	161	43°43′N	0°38′W
Adra, Spain (ä′drä)	172	36°45′N	3°02′W
Adrano, Italy (ä-drä′nō)	174	37°42′N	14°52′E
Adrar, Alg.	230	27°53′N	0°15′W
Adria, Italy (ä′drē-ä)	174	45°03′N	12°01′E
Adrian, Mi., U.S. (ā′drĭ-ăn)	108	41°55′N	84°00′W
Adrian, Mn., U.S. (ā′drĭ-ăn)	112	43°39′N	95°56′W
Adrianople *see* Edirne, Tur.	154	41°41′N	26°35′E
Adriatic Sea, sea, Eur.	156	43°30′N	14°27′E
Adwa, Eth.	231	14°02′N	38°58′E
Adwick-le-Street, Eng., U.K. (ăd′wĭk-lē-strēt′)	158a	53°35′N	1°11′W
Adycha, r., Russia (ä′dĭ-chà)	185	66°11′N	136°45′E
Adygea, prov., Russia	180	45°00′N	40°00′E
Adz′va, r., Russia (ädz′vá)	180	67°00′N	59°20′E
Aegean Sea, sea, (ē-jē′ăn)	156	39°04′N	24°56′E
A Estrada, Spain	172	42°42′N	8°29′W
Affton, Mo., U.S.	117e	38°33′N	90°20′W
Afghanistan, nation, Asia (ăf-găn-ĭ-stăn′)	198	33°00′N	63°00′E
Afgooye, Som. (äf-gô′ĭ)	238a	2°08′N	45°08′E
Afikpo, Nig.	235	5°53′N	7°56′E
Aflou, Alg. (ä-flōō′)	230	33°59′N	2°04′E
Afognak, i., Ak., U.S. (ä-fŏg-năk′)	103	58°28′N	151°35′W
A Fonsagrada, Spain	172	43°08′N	7°07′W
Afonso Claudio, Braz. (äl-fōn′sô-klou′dēō)	141a	20°05′S	41°05′W
Afragola, Italy (ä-frà′gō-lä)	173c	40°40′N	14°19′E
Africa, cont.	229	10°00′N	22°00′E
Afton, Mn., U.S. (ăf′tŭn)	117g	44°54′N	92°47′W
Afton, Ok., U.S. (ăf′tŭn)	121	36°42′N	94°56′W
Afton, Wy., U.S. (ăf′tŭn)	115	42°42′N	110°52′W
'Afula, Isr. (ä-fò′là)	197a	32°36′N	35°17′E
Afyon, Tur. (ä-fē-ōn)	198	38°45′N	30°20′E
Agadem, Niger (ä′gá-dĕm)	231	16°50′N	13°17′E
Agadez, Niger (ä′gá-dĕs)	230	16°58′N	7°59′E
Agadir, Mor. (ä-gá-dēr)	230	30°30′N	9°37′W
Agalta, Cordillera de, mts., Hond. (kôr-dēl-yĕ′rä-dĕ-ä-gä′l-tä)	132	15°15′N	85°42′W
Agapovka, Russia (ä-gä-pôv′kä)	186a	53°18′N	59°10′E
Agartala, India	202	23°53′N	91°22′E
Agāshi, India	203b	19°28′N	72°46′E
Agashkino, Russia (á-gäsh′kĭ-nô)	186b	55°18′N	38°13′E
Agattu, i., Ak., U.S. (á′gä-tōō)	103a	52°14′N	173°40′E
Agboville, C. Iv.	234	5°56′N	4°13′W
Ağdam, Azer. (äg′dăm)	181	40°00′N	47°00′E
Agde, Fr. (ägd)	170	43°19′N	3°30′E
Agen, Fr. (á-zhän′)	161	44°13′N	0°31′E
Agiásos, Grc.	175	39°06′N	26°25′E
Aginskoye, Russia (ä-hĭn′skô-yĕ)	179	51°15′N	113°15′E
Ágios Efstrátios, i., Grc.	163	39°30′N	24°58′E
Agíou Órous, Kólpos, b., Grc.	175	40°15′N	24°00′E
Agno, Phil. (äg′nō)	213a	16°07′N	119°49′E
Agno, r., Phil.	213a	15°42′N	120°28′E
Agnone, Italy (än-yō′nā)	174	41°49′N	14°23′E
Agogo, Ghana	234	6°47′N	1°04′W
Agra, India (ä′grä)	199	27°18′N	78°00′E
Ağrı, Tur.	181	39°50′N	43°10′E
Agri, r., Italy (ä′grē)	174	40°15′N	16°21′E
Agrínio, Grc.	163	38°38′N	21°06′E
Agua, vol., Guat. (ä′gwä)	132	14°28′N	90°43′W
Agua Blanca, Río, r., Mex. (rē′ō-ä-gwä-blä′n-kä)	130	21°46′N	102°54′W
Agua Brava, Laguna de, l., Mex.	130	22°04′N	105°40′W
Agua Caliente Indian Reservation, I.R., Ca., U.S. (ä′gwä kal-yĕn′tä)	118	33°50′N	116°24′W
Aguada, Cuba (ä-gwä′dá)	134	22°25′N	80°50′W
Aguada, l., Mex. (ä-gwä′dá)	132a	18°46′N	89°40′W
Aguadas, Col. (ä-gwä′dás)	142	5°37′N	75°27′W
Aguadilla, P.R. (ä-gwä-dēl′yä)	129b	18°27′N	67°10′W
Aguadulce, Pan. (ä-gwä-dōōl′sä)	133	8°15′N	80°33′W
Agua Escondida, Meseta de, plat., Mex.	131	16°54′N	91°35′W
Agua Fria, r., Az., U.S. (ä′gwä frē-ä)	119	33°43′N	112°22′W
Agua Fria National Monument, rec., Az., U.S.	119	34°13′N	112°03′W
Aguai, Braz. (ägwä-ē′)	141a	22°04′S	46°57′W
Agualeguas, Mex. (ä-gwä-lā′gwäs)	122	26°19′N	99°33′W
Aguán, r., Hond. (ä-gwá′n)	132	15°22′N	87°00′W
Aguanaval, r., Mex. (á-guä-nä-väl′)	122	25°12′N	103°28′W
Aguanus, r., Can. (á-gwä′nŭs)	101	50°45′N	62°03′W
Aguascalientes, Mex. (ä′gwäs-käl-yĕn′tās)	128	21°52′N	102°17′W
Aguascalientes, state, Mex. (ä′gwäs-käl-yĕn′tās)	130	22°00′N	102°18′W
Águeda, Port. (ä-gwā′dá)	172	40°36′N	8°26′W
Agueda, r., Eur. (ä-gē-dä)	172	40°50′N	6°44′W
Aguelhok, Mali	234	19°28′N	0°52′E
Aguilar, Spain	172	37°32′N	4°39′W
Aguilar, Co., U.S. (ä-gē-lär′)	120	37°24′N	104°38′W
Aguilas, Spain (ä-gê-läs)	162	37°26′N	1°35′W
Aguililla, Mex. (ä-gē-lēl-yä)	130	18°44′N	102°44′W
Aguililla, r., Mex. (ä-gē-lēl-yä)	130	18°30′N	102°48′W
Aguja, Punta, c., Peru (pŭn′tá á-gōō′ hä)	142	6°00′S	81°15′W
Agulhas, Cape, c., S. Afr. (ä-gōōl′yäs)	232	34°47′S	20°00′E
Agusan, r., Phil. (ä-gōō′sän)	213	8°12′N	126°07′E
Ahaggar, mts., Alg. (á-há-gär′)	230	23°14′N	6°00′E
Ahar, Iran	201	38°28′N	47°04′E
Ahlen, Ger. (ä′lĕn)	168	51°45′N	7°52′E
Ahmadābād, India (ŭ-mĕd-ā-bäd′)	199	23°04′N	72°38′E
Ahmadnagar, India (ä′mŭd-nŭ-gŭr)	199	19°09′N	74°45′E
Ahmar Mountains, mts., Eth.	231	9°22′N	42°00′E
Ahoskie, N.C., U.S. (ā-hŏs′kē)	125	36°15′N	77°00′W
Ahrensburg, Ger. (ä′rĕns-bòrg)	159c	53°40′N	10°14′E
Ahrweiler, Ger. (är′vī-lĕr)	168	50°34′N	7°05′E
Ähtärinjärvi, l., Fin.	167	62°46′N	24°25′E
Ahuacatlán, Mex. (ä-wä-kät-län′)	130	21°05′N	104°28′W
Ahuachapán, El Sal. (ä-wä-chä-pän′)	132	13°57′N	89°53′W
Ahualulco, Mex. (ä-wä-lōōl′kō)	130	20°43′N	103°57′W
Ahuatempan, Mex. (ä-wä-tĕm-pän)	130	18°11′N	98°02′W
Åhus, Swe. (ô′hòs)	166	55°56′N	14°19′E
Ahvāz, Iran	198	31°15′N	48°54′E
Ahvenanmaa (Åland), is., Fin. (ä′vĕ-nán-mô) (ô′länd)	160	60°36′N	19°55′E
'Aiea, Hi., U.S.	126a	21°18′N	157°52′W
Aígina, Grc.	175	37°43′N	23°35′E
Aígina, i., Grc.	175	37°43′N	23°35′E
Aígio, Grc.	175	38°13′N	22°04′E
Aiken, S.C., U.S. (ā′kĕn)	125	33°32′N	81°43′W
Aimorès, Serra dos, mts., Braz. (sĕ′r-rä-dôs-ī-mō-rĕ′s)	143	17°40′S	42°38′W
Aimoto, Japan (ī-mô-tō)	211b	34°59′N	135°09′E
Aincourt, Fr. (ăn-kōō′r)	171b	49°04′N	1°47′E
Aïn el Beïda, Alg.	230	35°57′N	7°25′E
Ainsworth, Ne., U.S. (ānz′wûrth)	112	42°32′N	99°51′W
Aïn Témouchent, Alg. (ä′ĕntĕ-mōō-shăn′)	162	35°20′N	1°23′W
Aïn Wessara, Alg. (ĕn ōō-sā-rà)	173	35°25′N	2°50′E
Aipe, Col. (ī′pĕ)	142a	3°13′N	75°15′W
Aïr, mts., Niger	230	18°00′N	8°30′E
Aire, r., Eng., U.K.	158a	53°42′N	1°00′W
Aire-sur-l'Adour, Fr. (âr)	170	43°42′N	0°17′W
Airhitam, Selat, strt., Indon.	197b	0°58′N	102°38′E
Ai Shan, mts., China (äī′shän)	206	37°27′N	120°35′E
Aisne, r., Fr. (ĕn)	161	49°28′N	3°32′E
Aitape, Pap. N. Gui. (ä-ē-tä′pâ)	213	3°00′S	142°10′E
Aitkin, Mn., U.S. (āt′kĭn)	113	46°32′N	93°43′W
Aitolikó, Grc.	175	38°27′N	21°21′E
Aitos, Blg. (ä-ē′tōs)	175	42°42′N	27°17′E
Aitutaki, i., Cook Is. (ī-tōō-tä′kē)	241	19°00′S	162°00′W
Aiud, Rom. (ä′ē-òd)	163	46°19′N	23°40′E
Aiuruoca, Braz. (äē′ōō-rōōō′-kà)	141a	21°57′S	44°36′W
Aiuruoca, r., Braz.	141a	22°11′S	44°35′W
Aix-en-Provence, Fr. (ĕks-prô-văns)	161	43°32′N	5°27′E
Aix-les-Bains, Fr. (ĕks′-lā-băn′)	171	45°42′N	5°56′E
Aizpute, Lat. (ä′ēz-pōō-tĕ)	167	56°44′N	21°37′E
Aizuwakamatsu, Japan	210	37°27′N	139°51′E
Ajaccio, Fr. (ä-yät′chō)	154	41°55′N	8°42′E
Ajalpan, Mex. (ä-häl′pän)	131	18°21′N	97°14′W
Ajana, Austl. (ăj-ăn′ĕr)	218	28°00′S	114°45′E
Ajaria, state, Geor.	182	41°40′N	42°00′E
Ajdābiyah, Libya	231	30°56′N	20°16′E
Ajjer, Tassili-n-, plat., Alg.	230	25°40′N	6°57′E
Ajmah, Jabal al, mts., Egypt	197a	29°12′N	34°03′E
Ajman, U.A.E.	198	25°15′N	54°30′E
Ajmer, India (ŭj-mēr′)	199	26°26′N	74°42′E
Ajo, Az., U.S. (ä′hô)	119	32°20′N	112°55′W
Ajuchitlán del Progreso, Mex. (ä-hōō-chet-lån)	130	18°11′N	100°32′W
Ajusco, Mex. (ä-hōō′s-kō)	131a	19°13′N	99°12′W
Ajusco, Cerro, mtn., Mex. (sĕ′r-rô-ä-hōō′s-kō)	131a	19°12′N	99°16′W
Akaishi-dake, mtn., Japan (ä-kī-shē dä′kä)	211	35°30′N	138°00′E
Akashi, Japan (ä′kä-shē)	210	34°38′N	134°59′E
Aketi, D.R.C. (ä-kå-tē)	231	2°44′N	23°46′E
Akhaltsikhe, Geor. (äkä′l-tsĭ-kĕ)	181	41°40′N	42°50′E
Akhdar, Al Jabal al, mts., Libya	231	32°00′N	22°00′E
Akhḑar, Al Jabal al, mts., Oman	198	23°30′N	56°43′W
Akhisar, Tur. (äk-hĭs-sär′)	163	38°58′N	27°58′E
Akhtarskaya, Bukhta, b., Russia (bōōk′tä äk-tär′ská-yá)	177	45°53′N	38°22′E
Akhtopol, Blg. (äk′tô-pōl)	175	42°08′N	27°54′E
Akhunovo, Russia (ä-kû′nô-vô)	186a	54°13′N	59°36′E
Aki, Japan (ä′kē)	211	33°31′N	133°51′E
Akiak, Ak., U.S. (äk′yák)	103	61°00′N	161°02′W
Akimiski, i., Can. (ä-kĭ-mĭ′skĭ)	93	52°54′N	80°22′W
Akita, Japan (ä′kē-tä)	205	39°40′N	140°12′E
Akjoujt, Maur.	230	19°45′N	14°23′W
'Akko, Isr.	197a	32°56′N	35°05′E
Aklavik, Can. (äk′lä-vĭk)	90	68°28′N	135°26′W
'Aklé Âouâna, dunes, Afr.	234	18°07′N	6°00′W
Ako, Japan (ä′kô)	211	34°44′N	134°22′E
Akola, India (á-kō′lä)	199	20°47′N	77°00′E
Akordat, Erit.	231	15°34′N	37°54′E
Akpatok, i., Can. (äk′pá-tŏk)	93	60°30′N	67°10′W
Akranes, Ice.	160	64°18′N	21°40′W
Akron, Co., U.S. (ăk′rŭn)	120	40°09′N	103°14′W
Akron, Oh., U.S. (ăk′rŭn)	105	41°05′N	81°30′W
Aksaray, Tur. (äk-sá-rī′)	163	38°30′N	34°05′E
Akşehir, Tur. (äk′shå-hēr)	163	38°20′N	31°20′E
Akşehir Gölü, l., Tur. (äk′shå-hēr)	198	38°40′N	31°30′E
Aksha, Russia (äk′shà)	179	50°28′N	113°00′E
Aksu, China (ä-kŭ-sōō)	204	41°29′N	80°15′E
Akune, Japan (ä′kò-nå)	211	32°03′N	130°16′E
Akureyri, Ice. (ä-kò-rā′rē)	160	65°39′N	18°01′W
Akutan, i., Ak., U.S. (ä-kōō-tän′)	103a	53°58′N	169°54′W
Akwatia, Ghana	234	6°04′N	0°49′W
Alabama, state, U.S. (ăl-á-băm′á)	105	32°50′N	87°30′W
Alabama, r., Al., U.S. (ăl-á-băm′á)	107	31°20′N	87°39′W
Alabat, i., Phil. (ä-lä-bät′)	213a	14°14′N	122°05′E
Alacam, Tur. (ä-lä-chäm′)	181	41°30′N	35°40′E
Alacant, Spain	162	38°20′N	0°30′W
Alacranes, Cuba (ä-lä-krä′nås)	134	22°45′N	81°35′W
Al Aflaj, des., Sau. Ar.	198	24°00′N	44°47′E
Alagôas, state, Braz. (ä-lä-gō′äzh)	143	9°50′S	36°33′W
Alagoinhas, Braz. (ä-lä-gō-ēn′yäzh)	143	12°13′S	38°12′W
Alagón, Spain (ä-lä-gōn′)	172	41°46′N	1°07′W
Alagón, r., Spain (ä-lä-gōn′)	172	39°53′N	6°42′W
Alahuatán, r., Mex. (ä-lä-wä-tá′n)	130	18°30′N	100°00′W
Alajuela, C.R. (ä-lä-hwa′lä)	133	10°01′N	84°14′W
Alajuela, Lago, l., Pan. (ä-lä-hwa′lä)	128a	9°15′N	79°34′W
Alaköl, l., Kaz.	183	45°45′N	81°13′E
'Alalakeiki Channel, strt., Hi., U.S. (ä-lä-lä-kā′kē)	126a	20°40′N	156°30′W
Al 'Alamayn, Egypt	231	30°53′N	28°52′E
Al 'Amārah, Iraq	201	31°50′N	47°09′E
Alameda, Ca., U.S. (ăl-á-mā′dá)	104	37°46′N	122°15′W
Alameda, r., Ca., U.S. (ăl-á-mā′dá)	116b	37°36′N	122°02′W
Alaminos, Phil. (ä-lä-mē′nôs)	213a	16°09′N	119°58′E
Al 'Amirīyah, Egypt	163	31°01′N	29°52′E
Alamo, Mex. (ä′lä-mô)	131	20°55′N	97°41′W
Alamo, Ca., U.S. (ă′lá-mō)	116b	37°51′N	122°02′W
Alamo, Nv., U.S. (ă′lá-mō)	118	37°22′N	115°10′W
Alamo, r., Mex. (ä′lä-mô)	122	26°33′N	99°35′W
Alamogordo, N.M., U.S. (ăl-á-mō-gôr′dō)	119	32°55′N	106°00′W
Alamo Heights, Tx., U.S. (ă′lá-mō)	117d	29°28′N	98°27′W
Alamo Indian Reservation, I.R., N.M., U.S.	119	34°30′N	107°30′W
Alamo Peak, mtn., N.M., U.S. (ă′lá-mō pēk)	122	32°50′N	105°55′W
Alamosa, Co., U.S. (ăl-á-mō′sá)	119	37°25′N	105°50′W
Åland *see* Ahvenanmaa, is., Fin.	160	60°36′N	19°55′E
Alandskiy, Russia (ä-länt′skĭ)	186a	52°14′N	59°48′E
Alanga Arba, Kenya	237	0°07′N	40°25′E
Alanya, Tur.	163	36°40′N	32°10′E
Alaotra, l., Madag. (ä-lä-ō′trá)	233	17°15′S	48°17′E
Alapayevsk, Russia (ä-lä-pä′yĕfsk)	178	57°50′N	61°35′E
Al 'Aqabah, Jord.	198	29°32′N	35°00′E
Alaquines, Mex. (ā-lá-kē′nās)	130	22°07′N	99°35′W
Al 'Arīsh, Egypt (ä-rēsh′)	197a	31°08′N	33°48′E
Alaska, state, U.S. (á-lăs′ká)	106a	64°00′N	150°00′W
Alaska, Gulf of, b., Ak., U.S. (á-lăs′ká)	103	57°42′N	147°40′W
Alaska Highway, Ak., U.S. (á-lăs′ká)	103	63°00′N	142°00′W
Alaska Peninsula, pen., Ak., U.S. (á-lăs′ká)	103	55°50′N	162°10′W
Alaska Range, mts., Ak., U.S. (á-lăs′ká)	103	62°00′N	152°18′W
Al 'Atrūn, Sudan	231	18°13′N	26°44′E
Alatyr′, Russia (ä′lä-tür)	178	54°55′N	46°30′E
Alazani, r., Asia	182	41°05′N	46°40′E
Alba, Italy (äl′bä)	174	44°41′N	8°02′E
Albacete, Spain (äl-bä-thā′tä)	162	39°00′N	1°49′W
Albachten, Ger. (äl-bä′ĸ-tĕn)	171c	51°55′N	7°31′E
Alba de Tormes, Spain (äl-bà dā tôr′mās)	172	40°48′N	5°28′W
Alba Iulia, Rom. (äl-bä yōō′lyà)	163	46°05′N	23°32′E

ng-sing; ŋ-baŋk; ɴ-nasalized n; nŏd; cŏmmit; ōld; ôbey; ôrder; oi-boil; fōōd; ò-as oo in foot; ou-out; s-soft; sh-dish; th-thin; pūre; ûnite; ûrn; stŭd; circŭs; ü-as in French tu; ′-indeterminate vowel.

PLACE (Pronunciation)	PAGE	LAT.	LONG.
Albani, Colli, hills, Italy	173d	41°46'N	12°45'E
Albania, nation, Eur. (ăl-bā'nĭ-ȧ)	154	41°45'N	20°00'E
Albano, Lago, l., Italy (lä'-gō äl-bä'nō)	173d	41°45'N	12°44'E
Albano Laziale, Italy (äl-bä'nō lät-zē-ä'lā)	174	41°44'N	12°43'E
Albany, Austl. (ôl'bȧ-nĭ)	218	35°00'S	118°00'E
Albany, Ca., U.S. (ôl'bȧ-nĭ)	116b	37°54'N	122°18'W
Albany, Ga., U.S. (ôl'bȧ-nĭ)	105	31°35'N	84°10'W
Albany, Mo., U.S. (ôl'bȧ-nĭ)	121	40°14'N	94°18'W
Albany, N.Y., U.S. (ôl'bȧ-nĭ)	105	42°40'N	73°50'W
Albany, Or., U.S. (ôl'bȧ-nĭ)	104	44°38'N	123°06'W
Albany, r., Can. (ôl'bȧ-nĭ)	93	51°45'N	83°30'W
Al Başrah, Iraq	198	30°35'N	47°59'E
Al Batrūn, Leb. (äl-bä-trōōn')	197a	34°16'N	35°39'E
Albemarle, N.C., U.S. (ăl'bê-märl)	125	35°24'N	80°36'W
Albemarle Sound, strt., N.C., U.S. (ăl'bē-märl)	107	36°00'N	76°17'W
Albenga, Italy (äl-bĕŋ'gä)	174	44°04'N	8°13'E
Alberche, r., Spain (äl-bĕr'chå)	172	40°08'N	4°19'W
Alberga, The, r., Austl. (ăl-bŭr'gȧ)	220	27°15'S	135°00'E
Albergaria-a-Velha, Port.	172	40°47'N	8°31'W
Alberhill, Ca., U.S. (ăl'bēr-hĭl)	117a	33°43'N	117°23'W
Albert, Fr. (ȧl-bâr')	170	50°00'N	2°49'E
Albert, l., Afr. (ăl'bērt) (ȧl-bâr')	231	1°50'N	30°40'E
Albert, Parc National, rec., D.R.C.	237	0°05'N	29°30'E
Alberta, prov., Can. (ăl-bûr'tȧ)	90	54°33'N	117°10'W
Alberta, Mount, mtn., Can. (ăl-bûr'tȧ)	95	52°18'N	117°28'W
Albert Edward, Mount, mtn., Pap. N. Gui. (ăl'bērt ĕd'wērd)	213	8°25'S	147°25'E
Alberti, Arg. (ȧl-bĕ'r-tē)	141c	35°01'S	60°16'W
Albert Kanaal, can., Bel.	159a	51°07'N	5°07'E
Albert Lea, Mn., U.S. (ăl'bērt lē')	113	43°38'N	93°24'W
Albert Nile, r., Ug.	237	3°25'N	31°35'E
Alberton, Can. (ăl'bēr-tŭn)	100	46°49'N	64°04'W
Alberton, S. Afr.	233b	26°16'S	28°08'E
Albertville *see* Kalemie, D.R.C.	232	5°56'S	29°12'E
Albertville, Fr. (ȧl-bêr-vēl')	171	45°42'N	6°25'E
Albertville, Al., U.S. (ăl'bērt-vĭl)	124	34°15'N	86°10'W
Albi, Fr. (äl-bē')	161	43°54'N	2°07'E
Albia, Ia., U.S. (ăl-bĭ-ȧ)	113	41°01'N	92°44'W
Albina, Sur. (äl-bē'nä)	143	5°30'N	54°33'W
Albina, Ponta, c., Ang.	236	15°51'S	11°44'E
Albino, Point, c., Can. (äl-bē'nō)	111c	42°50'N	79°05'W
Albion, Mi., U.S. (ăl'bĭ-ŭn)	108	42°15'N	84°50'W
Albion, Ne., U.S. (ăl'bĭ-ŭn)	112	41°42'N	98°00'W
Albion, N.Y., U.S. (ăl'bĭ-ŭn)	109	43°15'N	78°10'W
Alboran, Isla del, i., Spain (ē's-lä-dĕl-äl-bō-rä'n)	156	35°58'N	3°02'W
Albuquerque, N.M., U.S. (ăl-bŭ-kûr'kē)	104	35°05'N	106°40'W
Albuquerque, Cayos de, is., Col.	133	12°12'N	81°24'W
Alburquerque, Spain (äl-bōōr-kĕr'kä)	172	39°13'N	6°58'W
Albury, Austl. (ôl'bēr-ē)	219	36°00'S	147°00'E
Alcabideche, Port. (äl-kȧ-bē-dā'chå)	173b	38°43'N	9°24'W
Alcácer do Sal, Port. (äb'ĭ-lēn)	172	38°24'N	8°33'W
Alcalá de Henares, Spain (äl-kä-lä' dā ā-nä'räs)	173a	40°29'N	3°22'W
Alcalá la Real, Spain (äl-kä-lä'lä rā-äl')	172	37°27'N	3°57'W
Alcamo, Italy (äl'kȧ-mō)	174	37°58'N	13°03'E
Alcanadre, r., Spain (äl-kä-nä'drå)	173	41°41'N	0°18'W
Alcanar, Spain (äl-kä-när')	173	40°35'N	0°27'E
Alcañiz, Spain (äl-kän-yēth')	162	41°03'N	0°08'W
Alcântara, Braz. (äl-kän'tȧ-rȧ)	143	2°17'S	44°29'W
Alcaraz, Spain (äl-kä-räth')	172	38°39'N	2°28'W
Alcaudete, Spain (äb'ĭng-dŭn)	172	37°38'N	4°05'W
Alcázar de San Juan, Spain (äl-kä'thär dā sän hwän')	162	39°22'N	3°12'W
Alcira, Spain (ä-thē'rä)	173	39°09'N	0°26'W
Alcoa, Tn., U.S. (ăl-kō'ȧ)	124	35°45'N	84°00'W
Alcobendas, Spain (äl-kō-bĕn'dås)	173a	40°32'N	3°39'W
Alcochete, Port. (äl-kō-chā'tä)	173b	38°45'N	8°58'W
Alcoi, Spain	162	38°42'N	0°30'W
Alcorcón, Spain	173a	40°22'N	3°50'W
Alcorta, Arg. (äl-kôr'tä)	141c	33°32'S	61°08'W
Alcova Reservoir, res., Wy., U.S. (ăl-kō'vȧ)	115	42°31'N	106°33'W
Alcove, Can. (ăl-kōv')	102c	45°41'N	75°55'W
Alcúdia, Badia d', b., Spain	173	39°48'N	3°20'E
Aldabra Islands, is., Sey. (äl-dä'brä)	233	9°16'S	46°17'E
Aldama, Mex. (äl-dä'mä)	130	22°54'N	98°04'W
Aldama, Mex. (äl-dä'mä)	122	28°50'N	105°54'W
Aldan, Russia	179	58°46'N	125°19'E
Aldan, r., Russia	179	63°00'N	134°00'E
Aldan Plateau, plat., Russia	185	57°42'N	130°28'E
Aldanskaya, Russia	179	61°52'N	135°29'E
Aldenhoven, Ger. (ȧl'dĕn-hō'vĕn)	171c	50°54'N	6°18'E
Aldergrove, Can. (ôl'dēr-grōv)	116d	49°03'N	122°28'W
Alderney, i., Guern. (ôl'dēr-nĭ)	170	49°43'N	2°11'W
Aldershot, Eng., U.K. (ôl'dēr-shŏt)	164	51°14'N	0°46'W
Alderson, W.V., U.S. (ôl-dēr-sŭn)	108	37°40'N	80°40'W
Alderwood Manor, Wa., U.S. (ôl'dēr-wŏod măn'ŏr)	116a	47°49'N	122°18'W
Aldridge-Brownhills, Eng., U.K.	158a	52°38'N	1°55'W
Aledo, Il., U.S. (ȧ-lē'dō)	121	41°12'N	90°47'W
Aleg, Maur.	230	17°03'N	13°55'W
Alegre, Braz. (ȧlĕ'grĕ)	141a	20°41'S	41°32'W
Alegre, r., Braz. (ȧlĕ'grĕ)	144b	22°22'S	43°34'W
Alegrete, Braz. (ä-lå-grā'tā)	144	29°46'S	55°44'W
Aleksandrov, Russia (ä-lyĕk-sän' drôf)	180	56°24'N	38°45'E
Aleksandrovsk, Russia (ä-lyĕk-sän'drôfsk)	186a	59°11'N	57°36'E
Aleksandrovsk, Russia (ä-lyĕk-sän'drôfsk)	179	51°02'N	142°21'E

PLACE (Pronunciation)	PAGE	LAT.	LONG.
Aleksandrów Kujawski, Pol. (ä-lĕk-säh'drōōv kōō-yav'skē)	169	52°54'N	18°45'E
Alekseyevka, Russia (ä-lyĕk-sā-yĕf'kȧ)	177	50°39'N	38°40'E
Aleksin, Russia (äb'ĭng-tŭn)	176	54°31'N	37°07'E
Aleksinac, Yugo. (ȧ-lyĕk-sē-nȧk')	175	43°33'N	21°42'E
Alemán, Presa, res., Mex. (prä'sä-lē-mä'n)	131	18°20'N	96°35'W
Alem Paraíba, Braz. (ä-lĕ'm-pȧ-rāē'bȧ)	141a	21°54'S	42°40'W
Alençon, Fr. (ȧ-län-sôn')	161	48°26'N	0°08'E
Alenquer, Braz. (ä-lĕŋ-kĕr')	143	1°58'S	54°44'W
Alenquer, Port. (ä-lĕŋ-kĕr')	172	39°04'N	9°01'W
Alentejo, hist. reg., Port. (ä-lĕŋ-tā'zhō)	172	38°05'N	7°45'W
Alenuihaha Channel, strt., Hi., U.S. (ä'lå-nōō-ê-hä'hä)	126a	20°20'N	156°05'W
Aleppo, Syria (ȧ-lĕp-ō)	198	36°10'N	37°18'E
Alès, Fr. (ä-lĕs')	161	44°07'N	4°06'E
Alessandria, Italy (ä-lĕs-sän'drê-ä)	162	44°53'N	8°35'E
Ålesund, Nor. (ô'lĕ-sŏn')	166	62°28'N	6°14'E
Aleutian Islands, is., Ak., U.S. (ȧ-lu'shăn)	106b	52°40'N	177°30'W
Aleutian Trench, deep	103a	50°40'N	177°10'E
Alevina, Mys, c., Russia	179	58°49'N	151°44'E
Alexander Archipelago, is., Ak., U.S. (ăl-ĕg-zăn'dēr)	103	57°05'N	138°10'W
Alexander City, Al., U.S.	124	32°55'N	85°55'W
Alexander Indian Reserve, I.R., Can.	102g	53°47'N	114°00'W
Alexander Island, i., Ant.	224	71°00'S	71°00'W
Alexandra, S. Afr. (ȧl-ex-än'drȧ)	238c	26°07'S	28°07'E
Alexandria, Austl. (ăl-ĕg-zăn'drĭ-ȧ)	218	19°00'S	136°56'E
Alexandria, Can. (ăl-ĕg-zăn'drĭ-ȧ)	99	45°50'N	74°35'W
Alexandria, Egypt (ăl-ĕg-zăn'drĭ-ȧ)	231	31°12'N	29°58'E
Alexandria, Rom. (ăl-ĕg-zăn'drĭ-ȧ)	175	43°55'N	25°21'E
Alexandria, S. Afr. (ăl-ĕx-än-drĭ-ȧ)	233c	33°40'S	26°26'E
Alexandria, In., U.S. (ăl-ĕg-zăn'drĭ-ȧ)	108	40°20'N	85°20'W
Alexandria, La., U.S. (ăl-ĕg-zăn'drĭ-ȧ)	105	31°18'N	92°28'W
Alexandria, Mn., U.S. (ăl-ĕg-zăn'drĭ-ȧ)	112	45°53'N	95°23'W
Alexandria, S.D., U.S. (ăl-ĕg-zăn'drĭ-ȧ)	112	43°39'N	97°45'W
Alexandria, Va., U.S. (ăl-ĕg-zăn'drĭ-ȧ)	105	38°50'N	77°05'W
Alexandria Bay, N.Y., U.S. (ăl-ĕg-zăn'drĭ-ȧ)	109	44°20'N	75°55'W
Alexandroúpoli, Grc.	163	40°41'N	25°51'E
Alfaro, Spain (äl-färō)	172	42°08'N	1°43'W
Al-Fāshir, Sudan (äl-fä'shēr)	231	13°38'N	25°21'E
Al Fashn, Egypt	238b	28°47'N	30°53'E
Al Fayyūm, Egypt	231	29°14'N	30°48'E
Alfeiós, r., Grc.	175	37°33'N	21°50'E
Alfenas, Braz. (äl-fĕ'nȧs)	141a	21°26'S	45°55'W
Al Firdān, Egypt (äl-fer-dän')	238b	30°43'N	32°20'E
Alfred, Can. (ăl'frĕd)	102c	45°34'N	74°52'W
Alfreton, Eng., U.K. (ăl'fēr-tŭn)	158a	53°06'N	1°23'W
Algarve, hist. reg., Port. (äl-gär'vĕ)	172	37°15'N	8°12'W
Algeciras, Spain (äl-hä-thē'räs)	172	36°08'N	5°25'W
Algeria, nation, Afr. (ăl-gē'rĭ-ȧ)	230	28°45'N	1°00'E
Algete, Spain (äl-hā'tā)	173a	40°36'N	3°30'W
Al Ghaydah, Yemen	201	16°12'N	52°15'E
Alghero, Italy (äl-gâ'rō)	162	40°32'N	8°22'E
Algiers, Alg. (ăl-jērs)	230	36°51'N	2°56'E
Algoa, Tx., U.S. (ăl-gō'ȧ)	123a	29°24'N	95°11'W
Algoma, Wa., U.S.	116a	47°17'N	122°15'W
Algoma, Wi., U.S.	113	44°38'N	87°29'W
Algona, Ia., U.S.	113	43°04'N	94°11'W
Algonac, Mi., U.S. (ăl'gō-năk)	108	42°35'N	82°30'W
Algonquin, Il., U.S. (ăl-gŏŋ'kwĭn)	111a	42°10'N	88°17'W
Algonquin Provincial Park, rec., Can.	107	45°50'N	78°20'W
Alhama de Granada, Spain (äl-hä'mä-dĕ-grä-nä'dä)	172	37°00'N	3°59'W
Alhama de Murcia, Spain	172	37°50'N	1°24'W
Alhambra, Ca., U.S. (ăl-hăm'brȧ)	117a	34°05'N	118°08'W
Al Ḩammān, Egypt	163	30°46'N	29°42'E
Alhandra, Port. (äl-yän'drȧ)	173b	38°55'N	9°01'W
Alhaurín, Spain (äl-lou-rēn')	172	36°40'N	4°40'W
Al Ḩawrah, Yemen	201	13°49'N	47°37'E
Al Ḩawṭah, Yemen	198	15°58'N	48°26'E
Al Ḩayy, Iraq	201	32°10'N	46°03'E
Al Ḩijāz, reg., Sau. Ar.	198	23°45'N	39°08'E
Al Hirmil, Leb.	197a	34°23'N	36°22'E
Alhos Vedros, Port. (äl'yōs'vā'drōs)	173b	38°39'N	9°02'W
Alhucemas, Baie d', b., Afr.	172	35°18'N	3°50'W
Al Ḩudaydah, Yemen	198	14°43'N	43°03'E
Al Hufūf, Sau. Ar.	198	25°15'N	49°43'E
Al Ḩulwān, Egypt (äl-hĕl'wän)	238b	29°51'N	31°20'E
Aliákmonas, r., Grc.	163	40°26'N	22°17'E
Äli Bayramlı, Azer.	182	39°56'N	48°56'E
Alibori, r., Benin	235	11°40'N	2°55'E
Alice, S. Afr. (ăl-ĭs)	233c	32°47'S	26°51'E
Alice, Tx., U.S. (ăl'ĭs)	122	27°45'N	98°04'W
Alice, Punta, c., Italy (ä-lē'chĕ)	175	39°23'N	17°10'E
Alice Arm, Can.	94	55°29'N	129°29'W
Alicedale, S. Afr. (ăl'ĭs-dāl)	233c	33°18'S	26°04'E
Alice Springs, Austl. (ăl'ĭs)	218	23°38'S	133°56'E
Alicudi, i., Italy (ä-lē-kōō'dē)	174	38°34'N	14°21'E
Alifkulovo, Russia (ä-lĭf-kŭ'lô-vô)	186a	55°57'N	62°06'E
Alīgarh, India (ä-lē-gŭr')	199	27°58'N	78°08'E
Alingsås, Swe. (ȧ'lĭŋ-sôs)	166	57°57'N	12°30'E
Aliquippa, Pa., U.S. (ăl-ĭ-kwĭp'ȧ)	111e	40°37'N	80°15'W
Al Iskandarīyah *see* Alexandria, Egypt	238b	31°12'N	29°58'E
Aliwal North, S. Afr. (ä-lê-wäl')	232	31°09'S	28°26'E
Al Jafr, Qa'al, pl., Jord.	197a	30°15'N	36°24'E
Al Jaghbūb, Libya	231	29°46'N	24°32'E
Al Jawārah, Oman	201	18°55'N	57°17'E

PLACE (Pronunciation)	PAGE	LAT.	LONG.
Al Jawf, Libya	231	24°14'N	23°15'E
Al Jawf, Sau. Ar.	198	29°45'N	39°30'E
Aljezur, Port. (äl-zhā-zōōr')	172	37°18'N	8°52'W
Al Jīzah, Egypt	238b	30°01'N	31°12'E
Al Jubayl, Sau. Ar.	198	27°01'N	49°40'E
Al Jufrah, oasis, Libya	231	29°30'N	15°16'E
Al Junaynah, Sudan	200	13°27'N	22°27'E
Aljustrel, Port. (äl-zhōō-strĕl')	172	37°44'N	8°23'W
Al Kāb, Egypt	238d	30°56'N	32°19'E
Al Kāmilīn, Sudan (käm-lēn')	231	15°09'N	33°06'E
Al Karak, Jord. (kĕ-räk')	197a	31°11'N	35°42'E
Al Karnak, Egypt (kär'nak)	238b	25°42'N	32°43'E
Al Khābūrah, Oman	198	23°45'N	57°30'E
Al Khalīl, W.B.	197a	31°31'N	35°07'E
Al Khandaq, Sudan (kän-däk')	231	18°38'N	30°29'E
Al Khārijah, Egypt	200	25°26'N	30°33'E
Al Khums, Libya	231	32°35'N	14°10'E
Al Khurmah, Sau. Ar.	198	21°37'N	41°44'E
Al Kiswah, Syria	197a	33°31'N	36°13'E
Alkmaar, Neth. (älk-mär')	165	52°39'N	4°42'E
Al Kufrah, oasis, Libya	231	24°45'N	22°45'E
Al Kuntillah, Egypt	197a	29°59'N	34°42'E
Al Kuwayt, Kuw. (äl-kōō-wit)	198	29°04'N	47°59'E
Al Lādhiqīyah, Syria	198	35°32'N	35°51'E
Allagash, r., Me., U.S. (ăl'ȧ-găsh)	100	46°50'N	69°24'W
Allāhābād, India (ŭl-ŭ-hä-bäd')	199	25°32'N	81°53'E
All American Canal, can., Ca., U.S. (ȧl ȧ-mĕr'ĭ-kăn)	118	32°43'N	115°12'W
Alland, Aus.	159e	48°04'N	16°05'E
Allariz, Spain (äl-yä-rēth')	162	42°10'N	7°48'W
Allatoona Lake, res., Ga., U.S. (ăl'ȧ-tōōn'ȧ)	124	34°05'N	84°57'W
Allauch, Fr. (ä-lĕ'ô)	170a	43°21'N	5°30'E
Allaykha, Russia (ä-lī'kȧ)	179	70°32'N	148°53'E
Allegan, Mi., U.S. (ăl'ê-găn)	108	42°30'N	85°55'W
Allegany Indian Reservation, I.R., N.Y., U.S. (ăl-ê-gā'nĭ)	109	42°05'N	78°55'W
Allegheny, r., Pa., U.S. (ăl-ê-gā'nĭ)	109	41°10'N	79°20'W
Allegheny Front, mtn., U.S. (ăl-ê-gā'nĭ)	108	38°12'N	80°03'W
Allegheny Mountains, mts., U.S. (ăl-ê-gā'nĭ)	107	37°35'N	81°55'W
Allegheny Plateau, plat., U.S. (ăl-ê-gā'nĭ)	108	39°00'N	81°15'W
Allegheny Reservoir, res., U.S. (ăl-ê-gā'nĭ)	109	41°50'N	78°55'W
Allen, Ok., U.S. (ăl'ĕn)	121	34°51'N	96°26'W
Allen, Lough, l., Ire. (lŏk ăl'ĕn)	164	54°07'N	8°09'W
Allendale, N.J., U.S. (ăl'ĕn-dāl)	110a	41°02'N	74°08'W
Allendale, S.C., U.S. (ăl'ĕn-dāl)	125	33°00'N	81°19'W
Allende, Mex. (äl-yĕn'då)	131	18°23'N	92°49'W
Allende, Mex.	122	28°20'N	100°50'W
Allentown, Pa., U.S. (ălĕn-toun)	105	40°35'N	75°30'W
Alleppey, India (ȧ-lĕp'ē)	203	9°33'N	76°22'E
Aller, r., Ger. (äl'ĕr)	168	52°43'N	9°50'E
Alliance, Ne., U.S. (ȧ-lī'ăns)	104	42°06'N	102°53'W
Alliance, Oh., U.S. (ȧ-lī'ăns)	108	40°55'N	81°10'W
Al Lidām, Sau. Ar.	198	20°45'N	44°12'E
Allier, r., Fr. (ȧ-lyā')	170	46°43'N	3°03'E
Alligator Point, c., La., U.S. (ăl'ĭ-gā-tēr)	110d	30°57'N	89°41'W
Allinge, Den. (äl'ĭŋ-ĕ)	166	55°16'N	14°48'E
Al Līth, Sau. Ar.	201	20°09'N	40°16'E
All Pines, Belize (ôl pīnz)	132a	16°55'N	88°15'W
Al Luḩayyah, Yemen	198	15°58'N	42°48'E
Alluvial City, La., U.S.	110d	29°51'N	89°42'W
Allyn, Wa., U.S. (ăl'ĭn)	116a	47°23'N	122°51'W
Alma, Can. (ăl'mȧ)	100	45°36'N	64°59'W
Alma, Can.	91	48°29'N	71°42'W
Alma, S. Afr.	238c	24°30'S	28°05'E
Alma, Ga., U.S.	125	31°33'N	82°31'W
Alma, Mi., U.S.	108	43°25'N	84°40'W
Alma, Ne., U.S.	120	40°08'N	99°21'W
Alma, Wi., U.S.	113	44°21'N	91°57'W
Alma-Ata *see* Almaty, Kaz.	183	43°19'N	77°08'E
Almada, Port. (äl-mä'dä)	173b	38°40'N	9°09'W
Almadén, Spain (ȧl-mȧ-dhān')	172	38°47'N	4°50'W
Al Madīnah, Sau. Ar.	198	24°26'N	39°42'E
Al Mafraq, Jord.	197a	32°21'N	36°13'E
Almagre, Laguna, l., Mex. (lä-gô'nä-ȧl-mä'grĕ)	131	23°48'N	97°45'W
Almagro, Spain (äl-mä'grō)	172	38°52'N	3°41'W
Al Maḩallah al Kubrā, Egypt	238b	30°58'N	31°10'E
Al Manāmah, Bahr.	198	26°01'N	50°33'E
Almanor, Lake, l., Ca., U.S. (ăl-măn'ôr)	118	40°11'N	121°20'W
Almansa, Spain (äl-män'sä)	172	38°52'N	1°09'W
Al Manshāh, Egypt	238b	26°31'N	31°46'E
Almansor, r., Port. (äl-män-sôr)	172	38°41'N	8°27'W
Al Manşūrah, Egypt	231	31°02'N	31°25'E
Al Manzilah, Egypt (män'za-la)	238b	31°09'N	32°05'E
Almanzora, r., Spain (äl-män-thō'rä)	172	37°20'N	2°25'W
Al Marāghah, Egypt	238b	26°41'N	31°35'E
Almargem do Bispo, Port. (äl-mär-zhĕn)	173b	38°51'N	9°16'W
Al-Marj, Libya	231	32°44'N	21°08'E
Al Maşīrah, i., Oman	198	20°43'N	58°58'E
Almaty (Alma-Ata), Kaz.	183	43°19'N	77°08'E
Almaty, val., Sau. Ar.	197a	29°16'N	35°12'E
Al Mawşil, Iraq	198	36°00'N	42°53'E
Almazán, Spain (äl-mä-thän')	172	41°30'N	2°33'W
Al Mazār, Jord.	197a	31°04'N	35°41'E
Al Mazra'ah, Jord.	197a	31°17'N	35°33'E
Almeirim, Port. (äl-māĭ-rēɴ')	172	39°13'N	8°31'W
Almelo, Neth. (äl'mĕ-lō)	165	52°20'N	6°42'E

ăt; finăl; rāte; senåte; ärm; åsk; sofȧ; fâre; ch-choose; dh-as th in other; bē; ēvent; bĕt; recĕnt; cratēr; g-gō; gh-guttural g; bĭt; ĭ-short neutral; rīde; ĸ-guttural k as ch in German ich;

PRONOUNCING INDEX

Almendra – Andrelândia 265

PLACE (Pronunciation)	PAGE	LAT.	LONG.
Almendra, Embalse de, res., Spain	172	41°15'N	6°10'W
Almendralejo, Spain (äl-män-drä-lā'hō)	172	38°43'N	6°24'W
Almería, Spain (äl-mā-rē'ä)	154	36°52'N	2°28'W
Almería, Golfo de, b., Spain (gồl-fô-dĕ-äl-mäĭ-reɴ')	172	36°45'N	2°26'W
Älmhult, Swe. (älm'hōōlt)	166	56°35'N	14°08'E
Almina, Punta, c., Mor. (äl-mē'nä)	172	35°58'N	5°17'W
Al Minyā, Egypt	231	28°06'N	30°45'E
Almirante, Pan. (äl-mē-rän'tā)	133	9°18'N	82°24'W
Almirante, Bahía de, b., Pan.	133	9°22'N	82°07'W
Almodóvar del Campo, Spain (äl-mō-dhō'vär)	172	38°43'N	4°10'W
Almoloya, Mex. (äl-mō-lō'yä)	130	19°32'N	99°44'W
Almoloya, Mex. (äl-mō-lō'yä)	131a	19°11'N	99°28'W
Almonte, Can. (ăl-mŏn'tē̇)	99	45°15'N	76°15'W
Almonte, Spain (äl-mōn'tā)	172	37°16'N	6°32'W
Almonte, r., Spain (äl-mōn'tā)	172	39°35'N	5°50'W
Almora, India	199	29°20'N	79°40'E
Al Mubarraz, Sau. Ar.	198	22°31'N	46°27'E
Al Mudawwarah, Jord.	197a	29°20'N	36°01'E
Al Mukhā (Mocha), Yemen	198	13°11'N	43°20'E
Almuñécar, Spain (äl-mōōn-yā'kär)	172	36°44'N	3°43'W
Almyrós, Grc.	175	39°13'N	22°47'E
Alnön, i., Swe.	166	62°20'N	17°39'E
Aloha, Or., U.S. (ä'lồ-hā)	116c	45°29'N	122°52'W
Alor, Pulau, i., Indon. (ä'lồr)	213	8°07'S	125°00'E
Álora, Spain (ä'lồ-rä)	172	36°49'N	4°42'W
Alor Gajah, Malay.	197b	2°23'N	102°13'E
Alor Setar, Malay. (ä'lồr stär)	212	6°10'N	100°16'E
Alouette, r., Can. (ä-lōō-ĕt')	116d	49°16'N	122°32'W
Alpena, Mi., U.S. (ăl-pē'nȧ)	105	45°05'N	83°30'W
Alpes Cotiennes, mts., Eur.	171	44°46'N	7°02'E
Alphen, Neth.	159a	52°07'N	4°38'E
Alpiarça, Port. (äl-pyär'sȧ)	172	39°38'N	8°37'W
Alpine, Tx., U.S. (ăl'pīn)	122	30°21'N	103°41'W
Alps, mts., Eur. (ălps)	156	46°18'N	8°42'E
Alpujarra, Col. (ȧl-pōō-ĸȧ'rȧ)	142a	3°23'N	74°56'W
Al Qaḑārif, Sudan	231	14°03'N	35°11'E
Al Qāhirah *see* Cairo, Egypt	231	30°00'N	31°17'E
Al Qanţarah, Egypt	238d	30°51'N	32°20'E
Al Qaryah Ash Sharqīyah, Libya	231	30°36'N	13°13'E
Al Qaşr, Egypt	200	25°42'N	28°53'E
Al Qaţīf, Sau. Ar.	198	26°30'N	50°00'E
Al Qayşūmah, Sau. Ar.	198	28°15'N	46°20'E
Al Qunaytirah, Syria	197a	33°09'N	35°49'E
Al Qunfudhah, Sau. Ar.	198	19°08'N	41°05'E
Al Quşaymah, Egypt	197a	30°40'N	34°23'E
Al Quşayr, Egypt	231	26°14'N	34°11'E
Al Qusayr, Syria	197a	34°32'N	36°33'E
Als, i., Den. (äls)	166	55°06'N	9°40'E
Alsace, hist. reg., Fr. (äl-sȧ's)	171	48°25'N	7°24'E
Altadena, Ca., U.S. (ăl-tä-dē'nä)	117a	34°12'N	118°08'W
Alta Gracia, Arg. (äl'tä grä'sē̇-a)	144	31°41'S	64°19'W
Altagracia, Ven.	142	10°42'N	71°34'W
Altagracia de Orituco, Ven.	143b	9°53'N	66°22'W
Altai Mountains, mts., Asia (äl'tī')	204	49°11'N	87°15'E
Alta Loma, Ca., U.S. (ăl'tă lō'mä)	117a	34°07'N	117°35'W
Alta Loma, Tx., U.S. (ăl'tȧ lō-mȧ)	123a	29°22'N	95°05'W
Altamaha, r., Ga., U.S. (ôl-tȧ-mȧ-hô')	125	31°50'N	82°00'W
Altamira, Braz. (äl-tä-mē'rä)	143	3°13'S	52°14'W
Altamira, Mex.	131	22°25'N	97°55'W
Altamirano, Arg. (äl-tä-mē̇-rā'nō)	144	35°26'S	58°12'W
Altamura, Italy (äl-tä-mōō'rä)	163	40°40'N	16°35'E
Altavista, Va., U.S. (äl-tä-vĭs'tȧ)	125	37°08'N	79°14'W
Altay, China (äl-tā)	204	47°52'N	86°50'E
Altenburg, Ger. (äl-tĕn-bōōrgh)	168	50°59'N	12°27'E
Altenmarkt an der Triesting, Aus.	159e	48°02'N	16°00'E
Alter do Chão, Port. (äl-tĕr'dȯ shäɴ'ōɴ)	172	39°13'N	7°38'W
Altiplano, pl., Bol. (äl-tē-plȧ'nō)	142	18°38'S	68°20'W
Altlandsberg, Ger. (ält länts'bĕrgh)	159b	52°34'N	13°44'E
Alto, La., U.S. (ăl'tō)	123	32°21'N	91°52'W
Alto Marañón, r., Peru (*ȧ*l'tô-mä-rän-yŏ'n)	142	8°18'S	77°13'W
Altomünster, Ger. (äl'tō-mün'stĕr)	159d	48°24'N	11°16'E
Alton, Can. (ôl'tŭn)	102d	43°52'N	80°05'W
Alton, Il., U.S. (ôl'tŭn)	105	38°53'N	90°11'W
Altona, Austl.	217a	37°52'S	144°50'E
Altona, Can.	97	49°06'N	97°33'W
Altona, Ger. (äl'tō-nȧ)	159c	53°33'N	9°54'E
Altoona, Al., U.S. (ăl-tōō'n*ȧ*)	124	34°01'N	86°15'W
Altoona, Pa., U.S. (ăl-tōō'n*ȧ*)	105	40°25'N	78°25'W
Altoona, Wa., U.S. (ăl-tōō'n*ȧ*)	116c	46°16'N	123°39'W
Alto Rio Doce, Braz. (äl'tồ-rē'ồ-dō'sĕ)	141a	21°02'S	43°23'W
Alto Songo, Cuba (äl-fō-sôŋ'gō)	135	20°10'N	75°45'W
Altotonga, Mex. (ȧl-tō-tôŋ'gä)	131	19°44'N	97°13'W
Alto Velo, i., Dom. Rep. (äl-tồ-vĕ'lō)	135	17°30'N	71°35'W
Altrincham, Eng., U.K. (ôl'trĭng-*ă*m)	158a	53°18'N	2°21'W
Altruppin, Ger. (ält rōō'ppēn)	159b	52°56'N	12°50'E
Altun Shan, mts., China (äl-tȯn shän)	204	36°58'N	85°09'E
Alturas, Ca., U.S. (ăl-tōō'r*ȧ*s)	114	41°29'N	120°33'W
Altus, Ok., U.S. (ăl't*ŭ*s)	120	34°38'N	99°20'W
Al 'Ubaylah, Sau. Ar.	201	21°59'N	50°57'E
Al-Uḑayyah, Sudan	231	12°06'N	28°16'E
Alūksne, Lat. (ä'lȯks-nĕ)	180	57°24'N	27°04'E
Alumette Island, i., Can. (ȧ-lü-mĕt')	99	45°50'N	77°00'W
Alum Rock, Ca., U.S.	116b	37°23'N	121°50'W
Al 'Uqaylah, Libya	231	30°15'N	19°07'E
Al Uqşur, Egypt	231	25°38'N	32°59'E
Alushta, Ukr. (ä'lshȯ-t*ȧ*)	177	44°39'N	34°23'E
Alva, Ok., U.S. (ăl'v*ȧ*)	120	36°46'N	98°41'W

PLACE (Pronunciation)	PAGE	LAT.	LONG.
Alvarado, Mex. (äl-vä-rä'dhō)	131	18°48'N	95°45'W
Alvarado, Luguna de, l., Mex. (lä-gȯ'nä-dĕ-äl-vä-rȧ'dồ)	131	18°44'N	95°45'W
Älvdalen, Swe. (ĕlv'dä-l*ĕ*n)	166	61°14'N	14°04'E
Alverca, Port. (al-vĕr'k*ȧ*)	173b	38°53'N	9°02'W
Alvesta, Swe. (äl-vĕs'tä)	166	56°55'N	14°29'E
Alvin, Tx., U.S. (ăl'vĭn)	123a	29°25'N	95°14'W
Alvinópolis, Braz. (äl-vēnō'pō-lē̇s)	141a	20°07'S	43°03'W
Alviso, Ca., U.S. (ăl-vī'sō)	116b	37°26'N	121°59'W
Al Wajh, Sau. Ar.	198	26°15'N	36°32'E
Alwar, India (ŭl'wŭr)	199	27°39'N	76°39'E
Al Wāsiţah, Egypt	238b	29°21'N	31°15'E
Alytus, Lith. (ä'lē̇-tȯs)	167	54°25'N	24°05'E
Amacuzac, r., Mex. (ä-mä-kōō-zȧk)	130	18°00'N	99°03'W
Amadeus, l., Austl. (ăm-*ȧ*-dē'*ŭ*s)	220	24°30'S	131°25'E
Amadjuak, l., Can. (ä-mädj'wäk)	93	64°50'N	69°20'W
Amadora, Port.	173b	38°45'N	9°14'W
Amagasaki, Japan (ä'mä-gä-sä'kē̇)	211	34°43'N	135°25'E
Amakusa-Shimo, i., Japan (ämä-kōō'sä shē-mō)	210	32°24'N	129°35'E
Åmål, Swe. (ồ'mồl)	166	59°05'N	12°40'E
Amalfi, Col. (ä'mȧ'l-fē)	142a	6°55'N	75°04'W
Amalfi, Italy (ä-mä'l-fē̇)	173c	40°23'N	14°36'E
Amaliáda, Grc.	175	37°48'N	21°23'E
Amalner, India	202	21°07'N	75°06'E
Amambai, Serra de, mts., S.A.	143	20°06'S	57°08'W
Amami, i., Japan	205	28°10'N	129°55'E
Amapala, Hond. (ä-mä-pä'lä)	132	13°16'N	87°39'W
Amarante, Braz. (ä-mä-rän'tā)	143	6°17'S	42°43'W
Amargosa, r., Ca., U.S. (ȧ'mär-gō's*ȧ*)	118	35°55'N	116°45'W
Amarillo, Tx., U.S. (ăm-*ȧ*-rĭl'ō)	104	35°14'N	101°49'W
Amaro, Mount, mtn., Italy (ä-mä'rō)	162	42°07'N	14°07'E
Amasya, Tur. (ä-mä'sē̇-ȧ)	163	40°40'N	35°50'E
Amatenango, Mex. (ä-mä-tā-naŋ'gō)	131	16°30'N	92°29'W
Amatignak, i., Ak., U.S. (ä-mȧ'tē̇-näk)	103a	51°12'N	178°30'W
Amatique, Bahía de, b., N.A. (bä-ē'ä-dĕ-ä-mä-tē'kā)	132	15°58'N	88°50'W
Amatitlán, Guat. (ä-mä-tē̇-tlän')	132	14°27'N	90°39'W
Amatlán de Cañas, Mex. (ä-mät-län'dā kän-yäs)	130	20°50'N	104°22'W
Amazon (Amazonas) (Solimões), r., S.A.	143	2°03'S	53°18'W
Amazonas, state, Braz. (ä-mä-thō'näs)	142	4°15'S	64°30'W
Ambāla, India (ŭm-bä'lŭ)	199	30°31'N	76°48'E
Ambalema, Col. (äm-bä-lā'mä)	142	4°47'N	74°45'W
Ambarchik, Russia (*ŭ*m-bär'chĭk)	179	69°39'N	162°18'E
Ambarnāth, India	203b	19°12'N	73°10'E
Ambato, Ec. (äm-bä'tō)	142	1°15'S	78°30'W
Ambatondrazaka, Madag.	233	17°58'S	48°43'E
Amberg, Ger. (äm'bĕrgh)	168	49°26'N	11°51'E
Ambergris Cay, i., Belize (ăm'bẽr-grēs kāz)	132a	18°04'N	87°43'W
Ambergris Cays, is., T./C. Is.	135	21°20'N	71°40'W
Ambérieu-en-Bugey, Fr. (äɴ-bā-rē̇-u')	171	45°57'N	5°21'E
Ambert, Fr. (äɴ-bĕr')	170	45°32'N	3°41'E
Ambil Island, i., Phil. (äm'bēl)	213a	13°51'N	120°25'E
Ambler, Pa., U.S. (ăm'bl*ĕ*r)	110f	40°09'N	75°13'W
Amboise, Fr. (äɴ-bwăz')	170	47°25'N	0°56'E
Ambon, Indon.	213	3°45'S	128°17'E
Ambon, Pulau, i., Indon.	213	4°50'S	128°45'E
Ambositra, Madag. (äɴ-bồ-sē'trä)	233	20°31'S	47°28'E
Amboy, Il., U.S. (ăm'boi)	108	41°41'N	89°15'W
Amboy, Wa., U.S. (ăm'boi)	116c	45°55'N	122°27'W
Ambre, Cap d', c., Madag.	233	12°06'S	49°15'E
Ambridge, Pa., U.S. (ăm'brĭdj)	111e	40°36'N	80°13'W
Ambrim, i., Vanuatu	221	16°25'S	168°15'E
Ambriz, Ang.	232	7°50'S	13°06'E
Amchitka, i., Ak., U.S. (ăm-chĭt'kȧ)	103a	51°25'N	178°10'E
Amchitka Passage, strt., Ak., U.S. (ăm-chĭt'kȧ)	103a	51°30'N	179°36'W
Amealco, Mex. (ä-mā-äl'kō)	130	20°12'N	100°08'W
Ameca, Mex. (ä-mĕ'kä)	128	20°34'N	104°02'W
Amecameca, Mex. (ä-mȧ-kä-mā'kä)	130	19°06'N	98°46'W
Ameide, Neth.	159a	51°57'N	4°57'E
Ameland, i., Neth.	165	53°29'N	5°54'E
Amelia, Oh., U.S. (ȧ-mēl'yā)	111f	39°01'N	84°12'W
American, South Fork, r., Ca., U.S. (*ȧ*-mĕr'ĭ-k*ă*n)	118	38°43'N	120°45'W
Americana, Braz. (ä-mĕ-rē̇-kȧ'nȧ)	141a	22°46'S	47°19'W
American Falls, Id., U.S. (*ȧ*-mĕr'ĭ-k*ă*n-fāls')	115	42°45'N	112°53'W
American Falls Reservoir, res., Id., U.S. (*ȧ*-mĕr'ĭ-k*ă*n-fāls')	106	42°56'N	113°18'W
American Fork, Ut., U.S.	119	40°20'N	111°50'W
American Highland, plat., Ant.	224	72°00'S	79°00'E
American Samoa, dep., Oc.	2	14°20'S	170°00'W
Americus, Ga., U.S. (*ȧ*-mĕr'ĭ-k*ŭ*s)	105	32°04'N	84°15'W
Amersfoort, Neth. (ä'm*ĕ*rz-fōrt)	159a	52°08'N	5°23'E
Amery, Can. (ā'mẽr-ē̇)	91	56°34'N	94°03'W
Amery, Wi., U.S.	113	45°19'N	92°24'W
Ames, Ia., U.S. (āmz)	113	42°00'N	93°36'W
Amesbury, Ma., U.S. (āmz'bẽr-ē̇)	101a	42°51'N	70°56'W
Amfissa, Grc. (ȧm-fĭ's*ȧ*)	175	38°32'N	22°26'E
Amga, Russia (ŭm-gä')	179	61°08'N	132°09'E
Amga, r., Russia	185	61°41'N	133°11'E
Amgun', r., Russia	185	52°30'N	138°00'E
Amherst, Can. (ăm'hẽrst)	91	45°49'N	64°14'W
Amherst, Oh., U.S.	111d	41°24'N	82°13'W
Amherst, i., Can. (ăm'hẽrst)	99	44°08'N	76°45'W
Amiens, Fr. (ä-myäɴ')	161	49°54'N	2°18'E
Amirante Islands, is., Sey.	5	6°02'S	52°30'E
Amisk Lake, l., Can.	97	54°35'N	102°13'W
Amistad Reservoir, res., N.A.	122	29°20'N	101°00'W
Amite, La., U.S. (ă-mēt')	123	30°43'N	90°32'W

PLACE (Pronunciation)	PAGE	LAT.	LONG.
Amite, r., La., U.S.	123	30°45'N	90°48'W
Amity, Pa., U.S. (ăm'ĭ-tĭ)	111e	40°02'N	80°11'W
Amityville, N.Y., U.S. (ăm'ĭ-tĭ-vĭl)	110a	40°41'N	73°24'W
Amlia, i., Ak., U.S. (ȧ'mlē̇ä)	103a	52°00'N	173°28'W
'Ammān, Jord. (äm'mȧn)	198	31°57'N	35°57'E
Ammersee, l., Ger. (äm'mĕr)	159d	48°00'N	11°08'E
Amnicon, r., Wi., U.S. (ăm'nė-kŏn)	117h	46°35'N	91°56'W
Amorgós, i., Grc. (ä-môr'gōs)	163	36°47'N	25°47'E
Amory, Ms., U.S. (āmồ-rē)	124	33°58'N	88°27'W
Amos, Can. (ā'm*ŭ*s)	91	48°31'N	78°04'W
Amoy *see* Xiamen, China	205	24°30'N	118°10'E
Amparo, Braz. (äm-pȧ'-rô)	141a	22°43'S	46°44'W
Amper, r., Ger. (äm'pĕr)	159d	48°18'N	11°32'E
Amposta, Spain (äm-pōs'tä)	173	40°42'N	0°34'E
Amqui, Can.	100	48°28'N	67°28'W
Amrāvati, India	199	20°58'N	77°47'E
Amritsar, India (ŭm-rĭt's*ŭ*r)	199	31°43'N	74°52'E
Amstelveen, Neth.	159a	52°18'N	4°51'E
Amsterdam, Neth. (äm-stẽr-däm')	154	52°21'N	4°52'E
Amsterdam, N.Y., U.S. (ăm'stĕr-dăm)	109	42°55'N	74°10'W
Amsterdam, Île, i., Afr.	224	37°52'S	77°32'E
Amstetten, Aus. (äm'stĕt-*ĕ*n)	168	48°09'N	14°53'E
Am Timan, Chad (äm'tē̇-män')	231	11°18'N	20°30'E
Amu Darya, r., Asia (ä-mȯ-dä'rēä)	178	38°30'N	64°00'E
Amukta Passage, strt., Ak., U.S. (ä-mōōk'tȧ)	103a	52°30'N	172°00'W
Amundsen Gulf, b., Can. (ä'mŭn-s*ĕ*n-gŭlf')	92	70°17'N	123°28'W
Amundsen Sea, sea, Ant. (ä'mŭn-s*ĕ*n-sē')	224	72°00'S	110°00'W
Amungen, l., Swe.	166	61°07'N	16°00'E
Amur, r., Asia	179	49°00'N	136°00'E
Amurskiy, Russia (ä-mûr'skĭ)	186a	52°35'N	59°36'E
Amurskiy, Zaliv, b., Russia (zä'lĭf ä-mȯr'skĭ)	210	43°20'N	131°40'E
Amusgos, Mex.	130	16°39'N	98°09'W
Amuyao, Mount, mtn., Phil. (ä-mōō-yä'ō)	213a	17°04'N	121°09'E
Amvrakikos Kólpos, b., Grc.	175	39°00'N	21°00'E
Amyun, Leb.	197a	34°18'N	35°48'E
Anabar, r., Russia (ăn-ȧ-bär')	185	71°15'N	113°00'E
Anaco, Ven. (ä-nȧ'kô)	143b	9°29'N	64°27'W
Anaconda, Mt., U.S. (ăn-*ȧ*-kŏn'd*ȧ*)	104	46°07'N	112°55'W
Anacortes, Wa., U.S. (ăn-*ȧ*-kôr'tĕz)	116a	48°30'N	122°37'W
Anadarko, Ok., U.S. (ăn-ȧ-där'kō)	120	35°05'N	98°14'W
Anadyr', Russia (ŭ-n*ȧ*-dĭr')	179	64°47'N	177°01'E
Anadyr, r., Russia	185	65°30'N	172°45'E
Anadyrskiy Zaliv, b., Russia	178	64°10'N	178°00'W
'Ānah, Iraq	201	34°28'N	41°56'E
Anaheim, Ca., U.S. (ăn'ȧ-hīm)	117a	33°50'N	117°55'W
Anahuac, Tx., U.S. (ä-nä'wäk)	123a	29°46'N	94°41'W
Ānai Mudi, mtn., India	203	10°10'N	77°00'E
Anama Bay, Can.	97	51°56'N	98°05'W
Ana María, Cayos, is., Cuba	134	21°25'N	78°50'W
Anambas, Kepulauan, is., Indon. (ä-näm-bäs)	212	2°41'N	106°38'E
Anamosa, Ia., U.S. (ăn-*ȧ*-mō's*ȧ*)	113	42°06'N	91°18'W
Anan'ïv, Ukr.	181	47°43'N	29°59'E
Anapa, Russia (ȧ-nä'pä)	181	44°54'N	37°19'E
Anápolis, Braz. (ä-nȧ'pō-lē̇s)	143	16°17'S	48°47'W
Añatuya, Arg. (ȧ-nyä-tōō'yȧ)	144	28°22'S	62°45'W
Anchieta, Braz. (ȧn-chyĕ'tä)	144b	22°49'S	43°24'W
Ancholme, r., Eng., U.K. (ăn'chŭm)	158a	53°28'N	0°27'W
Anchorage, Ak., U.S. (ăŋ'kẽr-ȧj)	106a	61°12'N	149°48'W
Anchorage, Ky., U.S.	111h	38°16'N	85°32'W
Anci, China (än-tsŭ)	206	39°31'N	116°41'E
Ancienne-Lorette, Can. (äɴ-syĕn' lō-rĕt')	102b	46°48'N	71°21'W
Ancon, Pan. (ăŋ-kōn')	128a	8°55'N	79°32'W
Ancona, Italy (än-kō'nä)	154	43°37'N	13°32'E
Ancud, Chile (äŋ-kōōdh')	144	41°52'S	73°45'W
Ancud, Golfo de, b., Chile (gồl-fô-dĕ-äŋ-kōōdh')	144	41°15'S	73°00'W
Anda, China	208	46°20'N	125°20'E
Åndalsnes, Nor.	166	62°33'N	7°46'E
Andalucia, hist. reg., Spain (än-dä-lōō-sē̇'ă)	172	37°35'N	5°40'W
Andalusia, Al., U.S. (ăn-d*ȧ*-lōō'zhĭ*ȧ*)	124	31°19'N	86°19'W
Andaman Islands, is., India (ăn-dȧ-măn')	212	11°38'N	92°17'E
Andaman Sea, sea, Asia	212	12°44'N	95°45'E
Andarax, r., Spain	172	37°00'N	2°40'W
Anderlecht, Bel. (än'dẽr-lĕkt)	159a	50°49'N	4°16'E
Andernach, Ger. (än'dẽr-näk)	168	50°25'N	7°23'E
Anderson, Arg. (ȧ'n-dĕr-sōn)	141c	35°15'S	60°15'W
Anderson, Ca., U.S. (ăn'dẽr-s*ŭ*n)	114	40°28'N	122°19'W
Anderson, In., U.S. (ăn'dẽr-s*ŭ*n)	108	40°05'N	85°50'W
Anderson, S.C., U.S. (ăn'dẽr-s*ŭ*n)	105	34°30'N	82°40'W
Anderson, r., Can. (ăn'dẽr-s*ŭ*n)	92	68°32'N	125°12'W
Andes Mountains, mts., S.A. (ăn'dēz) (än'dās)	139	13°00'S	75°00'W
Andheri, neigh., India	203b	19°08'N	72°50'E
Andhra Pradesh, state, India	199	16°00'N	79°00'E
Andikýthira, i., Grc.	163	35°50'N	23°20'E
Andizhan, Uzb. (än-dē̇-zhän')	183	40°45'N	72°22'E
Andong, Kor., S. (än'dŭng')	205	36°31'N	128°42'E
Andongwei, China (än-dồŋ-wā)	206	35°08'N	119°19'E
Andorra, And. (än-dồr'rä)	173	42°38'N	1°30'E
Andorra, nation, Eur. (än-dồr'rä)	154	42°30'N	2°00'E
Andover, Ma., U.S. (ăn'dồ-vẽr)	101a	42°39'N	71°08'W
Andover, N.J., U.S. (ăn'dồ-vẽr)	110a	40°59'N	74°45'W
Andøya, i., Nor. (änd-ûē̇)	160	69°12'N	14°58'E
Andreanof Islands, is., Ak., U.S. (än-drȧ-ä'nồf-ī'*ă*ndz)	106b	51°10'N	177°00'W
Andrelândia, Braz. (än-drĕ-lȧ'n-dyȧ)	141a	21°45'S	44°18'W

ng-sing; ŋ-baŋk; ɴ-nasalized n; nŏd; c*ŏ*mmit; ōld; ồbey; ôrder; oi-boil; fōōd; ȯ-as oo in foot; ou-out; s-soft; sh-dish; th-thin; pūre; ůnite; ûrn; stŭd; circ*ŭ*s; ü-as in French tu; '-indeterminate vowel.

266 Andrew Johnson National Historic Site – Archidona PRONOUNCING INDEX

PLACE (Pronunciation)	PAGE	LAT.	LONG.
Andrew Johnson National Historic Site, rec., Tn., U.S. (ăn´drōō jŏn´sŭn)	125	36°15'N	82°55'W
Andrews, N.C., U.S. (ăn´drōōz)	124	35°12'N	83°48'W
Andrews, S.C., U.S. (ăn´drōōz)	125	33°25'N	79°32'W
Andria, Italy (än´drê-ä)	163	41°17'N	15°55'E
Andros, Grc. (àn´dhrôs)	175	37°50'N	24°54'E
Ándros, i., Grc. (àn´drôs)	163	37°59'N	24°55'E
Androscoggin, r., Me., U.S. (ăn-drŭs-kŏg´ĭn)	100	44°25'N	70°45'W
Andros Island, i., Bah. (ăn´drŏs)	129	24°30'N	78°00'W
Anefis i-n-Darane, Mali	234	18°03'N	0°36'E
Anegasaki, Japan (ä´nå-gä-sä´kē)	211a	35°29'N	140°02'E
Aneityum, i., Vanuatu (ä-nå-ē´tê-ŭm)	221	20°15'S	169°49'E
Aneta, N.D., U.S. (ă-nē´tȧ)	112	47°41'N	97°57'W
Aneto, Pico de, mtn., Spain (pē´kō-dĕ-ä-nĕ´tō)	156	42°35'N	0°38'E
Angamacutiro, Mex. (än´gä-mä-kōō-tē´rō)	130	20°08'N	101°44'W
Angangueo, Mex. (än-gän´gwå-ō)	130	19°36'N	100°18'W
Ang'angxi, China (äŋ-äŋ-shyē)	205	47°05'N	123°58'E
Angarsk, Russia	179	52°48'N	104°15'E
Ånge, Swe. (ông´ä)	166	62°31'N	15°39'E
Angel, Salto, wtfl., Ven. (säl´tō-ä´n-hĕl)	142	5°44'N	62°27'W
Ángel de la Guarda, i., Mex. (á´n-hĕl-dĕ-lä-gwä´r-dä)	128	29°30'N	113°00'W
Angeles, Phil. (än´hå-lās)	213a	15°09'N	120°35'E
Ängelholm, Swe. (ĕng´ĕl-hôlm)	166	56°14'N	12°50'E
Angelina, r., Tx., U.S. (ăn-jê lē´nȧ)	123	31°30'N	94°53'W
Angels Camp, Ca., U.S. (ān´jĕls kămp´)	118	38°03'N	120°33'W
Ångermanälven, r., Swe.	160	64°10'N	17°30'E
Angermund, Ger. (än´ngĕr-mŭnd)	171c	51°20'N	6°47'E
Angermünde, Ger. (äng´ĕr-mün-dĕ)	168	53°02'N	14°00'E
Angers, Can. (äN-zhā´)	102c	45°31'N	75°29'W
Angers, Fr.	170	47°29'N	0°36'W
Angkor, hist., Camb. (äng´kôr)	212	13°52'N	103°50'E
Anglesey, i., Wales, U.K. (ăŋ´g'l-sê)	164	53°35'N	4°28'W
Angleton, Tx., U.S. (aŋ´g'l-tŭn)	123a	29°10'N	95°25'W
Angmagssalik, Grnld. (äŋ-mä´sä-lĭk)	89	65°40'N	37°40'W
Angoche, Ilha, i., Moz. (ē´lä-än-gō´chå)	233	16°20'S	40°00'E
Angol, Chile (aŋ-gōl´)	144	37°47'S	72°43'W
Angola, In., U.S. (ăŋ-gō´lȧ)	108	41°35'N	85°00'W
Angola, nation, Afr. (ăŋ-gō´lȧ)	232	14°15'S	16°00'E
Angora *see* Ankara, Tur.	198	39°55'N	32°50'E
Angoulême, Fr. (äŋ´gōō-lâm´)	170	45°40'N	0°09'E
Angra dos Reis, Braz. (aŋ´grä dōs rā´ēs)	141a	23°01'S	44°17'W
Angri, Italy (ä´n-grê)	173c	40°30'N	14°35'E
Anguang, China (än-gůäŋ)	208	45°28'N	123°42'E
Anguilla, dep., N.A.	129	18°15'N	62°54'W
Anguilla Cays, is., Bah. (ăŋ-gwĭl´ȧ)	134	23°30'N	79°35'W
Anguille, Cape, c., Can. (kăp´-äŋ-gē´yē)	101	47°55'N	59°25'W
Anguo, China (än-gwô)	206	38°27'N	115°19'E
Anholt, i., Den. (än´hŏlt)	166	56°43'N	11°34'E
Anhui, prov., China (än-hwā)	205	31°30'N	117°15'E
Aniak, Ak., U.S. (ä-nyà´k)	103	61°32'N	159°35'W
Aniakchak National Monument, rec., Ak., U.S.	104	56°50'N	157°50'W
Animas, r., Co., U.S. (ä´nê-mås)	119	37°03'N	107°50'W
Anina, Rom. (ä-nē´nä)	175	45°03'N	21°50'E
Anita, Pa., U.S. (ȧ-nē´ȧ)	109	41°05'N	79°00'W
Aniva, Mys, c., Russia (mĭs à-nē´và)	210	46°08'N	143°13'E
Aniva, Zaliv, b., Russia (zä´lĭf à-nē´và)	210	46°30'N	143°00'E
Anjou, Can.	102a	45°37'N	73°33'W
Ankang, China (än-käŋ)	204	32°38'N	109°10'E
Ankara, Tur. (än´kȧ-rȧ)	198	39°55'N	32°50'E
Anklam, Ger. (än´kläm)	168	53°52'N	13°43'E
Ankoro, D.R.C. (äŋ-kō´rō)	232	6°45'S	26°57'E
Anloga, Ghana	234	5°47'N	0°50'E
Anlong, China (än-loŋ)	209	25°01'N	105°32'E
Anlu, China (än´lōō´)	209	31°18'N	113°40'E
Ann, Cape, c., Ma., U.S. (kăp´ăn´)	109	42°40'N	70°40'W
Anna, Russia (än´ä)	177	51°31'N	40°27'E
Anna, Il., U.S. (ăn´ȧ)	121	37°28'N	89°15'W
Annaba, Alg.	230	36°57'N	7°39'E
Annaberg-Bucholz, Ger. (än´ä-bĕrgh)	168	50°35'N	13°02'E
An Nafūd, des., Sau. Ar.	198	28°30'N	40°30'E
An Najaf, Iraq (än nä-jäf´)	198	32°00'N	44°25'E
An Nakhl, Egypt	197a	29°55'N	33°45'E
Annamese Cordillera, mts., Asia	212	17°34'N	105°38'E
Annapolis, Md., U.S. (ă-năp´ô-lĭs)	105	39°00'N	76°25'W
Annapolis Royal, Can.	100	44°45'N	65°31'W
Ann Arbor, Mi., U.S. (ăn är´bēr)	105	42°15'N	83°45'W
An Nāşirīyah, Iraq	198	31°08'N	46°15'E
An Nawfalīyah, Libya	231	30°57'N	17°38'E
Annecy, Fr. (àn sē´)	171	45°54'N	6°07'E
Annemasse, Fr. (än´mäs´)	171	46°09'N	6°13'E
Annette Island, i., Ak., U.S.	94	55°13'N	131°30'W
An Nhon, Viet.	212	13°55'N	109°00'E
Annieopsquotch Mountains, mts., Can.	101	48°37'N	57°17'W
Anniston, Al., U.S. (ăn´ĭs-tŭn)	105	33°39'N	85°47'W
Annobón, i., Eq. Gui.	229	2°00'S	3°30'E
Annonay, Fr. (àn´ĭs-tsiŭn)	170	45°16'N	4°36'E
Annotto Bay, Jam. (än-nō´tō)	134	18°15'N	76°45'W
An Nuhūd, Sudan	231	12°39'N	28°18'E
Anoka, Mn., U.S. (ȧ-nō´kȧ)	117g	45°12'N	93°24'W
Anori, Col. (à-nō´rē)	142a	7°01'N	75°09'W
Áno Viánnos, Grc.	174a	35°02'N	25°26'E
Anpu, China (än-pōō)	204	21°28'N	110°00'E
Anqiu, China (än-chyô)	206	36°26'N	119°12'E
Ansbach, Ger. (äns´bäk)	168	49°18'N	10°35'E
Anse à Veau, Haiti (äNs´ ä-vō´)	135	18°30'N	73°25'W
Anse d'Hainault, Haiti (äNs´dĕnō)	135	18°30'N	74°25'W
Anserma, Col. (à´n-sĕ´r-mà)	142a	5°13'N	75°47'W
Ansermanuevo, Col. (à´n-sĕ´r-mà-nwĕ´vō)	142a	4°47'N	75°59'W
Anshan, China	208	41°00'N	123°00'E
Anshun, China (än-shōōn´)	204	26°12'N	105°50'E
Anson, Tx., U.S. (ăn´sŭn)	122	32°45'N	99°52'W
Anson Bay, b., Austl.	220	13°10'S	130°00'E
Ansŏng, Kor., S. (än´sŭng´)	210	37°00'N	127°12'E
Ansongo, Mali	234	15°40'N	0°30'E
Ansonia, Ct., U.S. (ăn-sōnĭ-ȧ)	109	41°20'N	73°05'W
Antalya, Tur. (ä-dä´lê-ä)	163	37°00'N	30°50'E
Antalya Körfezi, b., Tur.	163	36°40'N	31°20'E
Antananarivo, Madag.	233	18°51'S	47°40'E
Antarctica, cont.	224	80°15'S	127°00'E
Antarctic Peninsula, pen., Ant.	224	70°00'S	65°00'W
Antelope Creek, r., Wy., U.S. (ăn´tê-lōp)	115	43°29'N	105°42'W
Antequera, Spain (än-tĕ-kĕ´rä)	162	37°01'N	4°34'W
Anthony, Ks., U.S. (ăn´thô-nê)	120	37°08'N	98°01'W
Anthony Peak, mtn., Ca., U.S.	118	39°51'N	122°58'W
Anti Atlas, mts., Mor.	230	28°45'N	9°30'W
Antibes, Fr. (äN-tēb´)	171	43°36'N	7°12'E
Anticosti, Île d', i., Can. (ăn-tĭ-kŏs´tê)	93	49°30'N	62°00'W
Antigo, Wi., U.S. (ăn´tĭ-gō)	113	45°09'N	89°11'W
Antigonish, Can. (ăn-tĭ-gô-nēsh´)	101	45°35'N	61°55'W
Antigua, Guat. (än-tē´gwä)	128	14°32'N	90°43'W
Antigua, r., Mex.	131	19°16'N	96°36'W
Antigua and Barbuda, nation, N.A.	129	17°15'N	61°15'W
Antigua Veracruz, Mex. (än-tē´gwä vā-rä-krōōz´)	131	19°18'N	96°17'W
Antilla, Cuba (än-tē´lyä)	135	20°50'N	75°50'W
Antioch, Ca., U.S. (ăn´tĭ-ŏk)	116b	38°00'N	121°48'W
Antioch, Il., U.S.	111a	42°29'N	88°06'W
Antioch, Ne., U.S.	112	42°05'N	102°36'W
Antioquia, Col. (än-tê-ō´kēä)	142	6°34'N	75°49'W
Antioquia, dept., Col.	142a	6°48'N	75°42'W
Antlers, Ok., U.S. (ănt´lērz)	121	34°14'N	95°38'W
Antofagasta, Chile (än-tô-fä-gäs´tä)	144	23°32'S	70°21'W
Antofalla, Salar de, pl., Arg. (sà-lár´de àn´tô-fä´lä)	144	26°00'S	67°52'W
Antón, Pan. (än-tōn´)	129	8°24'N	80°15'W
Antongila, Helodrano, b., Madag.	233	16°15'S	50°15'E
Antônio Carlos, Braz. (än-tō´nėō-kà´r-lôs)	141a	21°19'S	43°45'W
António Enes, Moz. (ăn-to´nyō ĕn´ēs)	233	16°14'S	39°58'E
Antonito, Co., U.S. (ăn-tô-nē´tō)	120	37°04'N	106°01'W
Antonopole, Lat. (än´tô-nô-pō lyĕ)	167	56°19'N	27°11'E
Antony, Fr.	171b	48°45'N	2°18'E
Antsirabe, Madag. (änt-sē-rä´bā)	233	19°49'S	47°16'E
Antsiranana, Madag.	233	12°18'S	49°16'E
Antsla, Est. (änt´slȧ)	167	57°49'N	26°29'E
Antuco, vol., S.A. (än-tōō´kō)	144	37°30'S	72°30'W
Antwerp, Bel.	154	51°13'N	4°24'E
Antwerpen *see* Antwerp, Bel.	154	51°13'N	4°24'E
Anūpgarh, India (ŭ-nôp´gŭr)	202	29°22'N	73°20'E
Anuradhapura, Sri L. (ŭ-nōō´rä-dŭ-pōō´rŭ)	203	8°24'N	80°25'E
Anxi, China (än-shyē)	204	40°36'N	95°49'E
Anyang, China (än´yäng)	205	36°05'N	114°22'E
Anykščiai, Lith. (anĭksh-chä´ē)	167	55°34'N	25°04'E
Anzhero-Sudzhensk, Russia (än´zhâ-rô-sod´zhĕnsk)	178	56°08'N	86°08'E
Anzio, Italy (änt´zê-ō)	174	41°28'N	12°39'E
Anzoátegui, dept., Ven. (àn-zôá´tĕ-gê)	143b	9°38'N	64°45'W
Aoba, i., Vanuatu	214f	15°25'S	167°50'E
Aomori, Japan (äô-mō´rê)	205	40°45'N	140°52'E
Aoraki (Cook, Mount), mtn., N.Z.	221a	43°27'S	170°13'E
Aosta, Italy (ä-ôs´tä)	174	45°45'N	7°20'E
Aouk, Bahr, r., Afr. (ä-ōk´)	231	9°30'N	20°45'E
Aoukâr, reg., Maur.	234	18°00'N	9°40'W
Apalachicola, Fl., U.S. (ăp-ȧ-lăch-ĭ-kō´lȧ)	124	29°43'N	84°59'W
Apan, Mex. (ä-pä´n)	130	19°43'N	98°27'W
Apango, Mex. (ä-päŋ´gō)	130	17°41'N	99°22'W
Apaporis, r., S.A. (ä-pä-pô´rĭs)	142	0°48'N	72°32'W
Aparri, Phil. (ä-pär´rē)	212	18°15'N	121°40'E
Apasco, Mex. (ä-pà´s-kō)	130	20°33'N	100°43'W
Apatin, Yugo. (ŏ´pō-tĭn)	175	45°40'N	19°00'E
Apatzingán de la Constitución, Mex.	130	19°07'N	102°21'W
Apeldoorn, Neth. (ä´pĕl-dōōrn)	161	52°14'N	5°55'E
Apennines *see* Appennino, mts., Italy	156	43°48'N	11°06'E
Apía, Col. (à-pē´ä)	142a	5°07'N	75°58'W
Apia, Samoa	214a	13°50'S	171°44'W
Apipilulco, Mex. (ä-pĭ-pĭ-lōōl´kō)	130	18°09'N	99°40'W
Apishapa, r., Co., U.S. (ăp-ĭ-shä´pȧ)	120	37°40'N	104°08'W
Apizaco, Mex. (ä-pê-zä´kō)	130	19°18'N	98°11'W
Apo, Mount, mtn., Phil. (ä´pō)	213	6°56'N	125°05'E
Apopka, Fl., U.S. (ä-pŏp´kȧ)	125a	28°37'N	81°30'W
Apopka, Lake, l., Fl., U.S.	125a	28°38'N	81°50'W
Apostle Islands, is., Wi., U.S. (ȧ-pŏs´l)	113	47°05'N	90°55'W
Appalachia, Va., U.S. (ăpȧ-lăch´ĭ-ȧ)	125	36°54'N	82°49'W
Appalachian Mountains, mts., N.A. (ăp-ȧ-lăch´ĭ-ȧn)	107	37°20'N	82°00'W
Appalachicola, r., Fl., U.S. (ăpȧ-lăch´ĭ-cōlȧ)	107	30°11'N	85°00'W
Äppelbo, Swe. (ĕp-ĕl-bōō)	166	60°30'N	14°02'E
Appelhülsen, Ger. (ä´pĕl-hül´sĕn)	171c	51°55'N	7°26'E
Appennino, mts., Italy (äp-pĕn-nē´nô)	156	43°48'N	11°06'E
Appleton, Mn., U.S. (ăp´l-tŭn)	112	45°10'N	96°01'W
Appleton, Wi., U.S.	105	44°14'N	88°27'W
Appleton City, Mo., U.S.	121	38°10'N	94°02'W
Appomattox, r., Va., U.S. (ăp-ô-măt´ŭks)	125	37°22'N	78°09'W
Aprília, Italy (ȧ-prē´lyȧ)	174	41°36'N	12°40'E
Apsheronsk, Russia	182	44°28'N	39°44'E
Apt, Fr. (äpt)	171	43°54'N	5°19'E
Apure, r., Ven. (ä-pōō´rä)	142	8°08'N	68°46'W
Apurimac, r., Peru (ä-pōō-rê-mäk´)	142	11°39'S	73°48'W
Aqaba, Gulf of, b. (ä´kȧ-bȧ)	198	28°30'N	34°40'E
Aqabah, Wādī al, r., Egypt	197a	29°48'N	34°05'E
Aqmola *see* Astana, Kaz.	183	51°10'N	71°43'E
Aqtaū, Kaz.	183	43°35'N	51°05'E
Aqtöbe, Kaz.	183	50°20'N	57°00'E
Aquasco, Md., U.S. (ȧ´gwă´scō)	110e	38°35'N	76°44'W
Aquidauana, Braz. (ä-kē-däwä´nä)	143	20°24'S	55°46'W
Aquin, Haiti (ä-kăn´)	135	18°20'N	73°25'W
Ara, r., Japan (ä-rä)	211a	35°40'N	139°52'E
Arab, Baḩr al, r., Sudan	231	9°46'N	26°52'E
'Arabah, Wādī, val., Egypt	238b	29°02'N	32°10'E
Arabats'ka Strilka (Tongue of Arabat), spit, Ukr.	177	45°50'N	35°05'E
Arabi, La., U.S.	110d	29°58'N	90°01'W
Arabian Desert, des., Egypt (ȧ-rā´bĭ-ȧn)	231	27°06'N	32°49'E
Arabian Sea, sea, (ȧ-rā´bĭ-ȧn)	196	16°00'N	65°15'E
Aracaju, Braz. (ä-rä´kä-zhōō´)	143	11°00'S	37°01'W
Aracati, Braz. (ä-rä´kä-tē´)	143	4°31'S	37°41'W
Araçatuba, Braz. (ä-rä-sȧ-tōō´bä)	143	21°14'S	50°19'W
Aracena, Spain	172	37°53'N	6°34'W
Arachthos, r., Grc. (är´äk-thôs)	175	39°10'N	21°05'E
Aracruz, Braz. (ä-rä-krōō´s)	143	19°58'S	40°11'W
'Arad, Isr.	197a	31°20'N	35°15'E
Arad, Rom. (ŏ´rŏd)	163	46°10'N	21°18'E
Arafura Sea, sea, (ä-rä-fōō´rä)	213	8°40'S	130°00'E
Aragats, Gora, mtn., Arm.	182	40°32'N	44°14'E
Aragon, hist. reg., Spain (ä-rä-gōn´)	173	40°55'N	0°45'W
Aragón, r., Spain	172	42°35'N	1°10'W
Aragua, dept., Ven. (ä-rä´gwä)	143b	10°00'N	67°05'W
Aragua de Barcelona, Ven.	142	9°29'N	64°48'W
Araguaía, r., Braz. (ä-rä-gwä´yä)	143	8°37'S	49°43'W
Araguari, Braz. (ä-rä-gwä´rē)	143	18°43'S	48°03'W
Araguatins, Braz. (ä-rä-gwä-tēns)	143	5°41'S	48°04'W
Aragüita, Ven. (ärä-gwē´tä)	143b	10°13'N	66°28'W
Araj, oasis, Egypt (ä-räj´)	163	29°05'N	26°51'E
Arāk, Iran	198	34°08'N	49°57'E
Arakan Yoma, mts., Mya. (ŭ-rŭ-kŭn´yō´mä)	199	19°51'N	94°13'E
Aral, Kaz.	183	46°47'N	62°00'E
Aral Sea, sea, Asia	178	45°17'N	60°02'E
Aralsor köli, l., Kaz. (à-räl´sôr´)	181	49°00'N	48°20'E
Aramberri, Mex. (ä-rám-bĕr-rē´)	130	24°05'N	99°47'W
Arana, Sierra, mts., Spain	172	37°17'N	3°28'W
Aranda de Duero, Spain (ä-rän´dä dā dwä´rō)	172	41°43'N	3°45'W
Arandas, Mex. (ä-rän´däs)	130	20°43'N	102°18'W
Aran Island, i., Ire. (ăr´ăn)	164	54°58'N	8°33'W
Aran Islands, is., Ire.	160	53°04'N	9°59'W
Aranjuez, Spain (ä-rän-hwāth´)	162	40°02'N	3°24'W
Aransas Pass, Tx., U.S. (ȧ-răn´sȧs pȧs)	123	27°55'N	97°09'W
Araouane, Mali	230	18°54'N	3°33'W
Arapkir, Tur. (ä-räp-kēr´)	163	39°00'N	38°10'E
Araraquara, Braz. (ä-rä-rä-kwä´rä)	143	21°47'S	48°08'W
Araras, Braz. (ä-rá´räs)	141a	22°21'S	47°22'W
Araras, Serra das, mts., Braz. (sĕ´r-rä-däs-ä-rä´räs)	143	18°03'S	53°23'W
Araras, Serra das, mts., Braz.	144b	22°24'S	43°15'W
Araras, Serra das, mts., Braz. (sĕ´r-rä-däs-ä-rä´räs)	144	23°30'S	53°00'W
Ararat, Austl. (ăr´ȧrăt)	219	37°17'S	142°56'E
Ararat, Mount, mtn., Tur.	198	39°50'N	44°20'E
Arari, l., Braz. (ä-rä´rē)	143	0°30'S	48°50'W
Araripe, Chapada do, hills, Braz. (shä-pä´dä-dô-ä-rä-rē´pĕ)	143	5°55'S	40°42'W
Araruama, Braz. (ä-rä-rōō-ä´mä)	141a	22°53'S	42°19'W
Araruama, Lagoa de, l., Braz.	141a	23°00'S	42°15'W
Aras, r., Asia (á-räs)	198	39°15'N	47°10'E
Aratuípe, Braz. (ä-rä-tōō-ē´pĕ)	143	13°12'S	38°58'W
Arauca, Col. (ä-rou´kä)	142	6°56'N	70°45'W
Arauca, r., S.A.	142	7°13'N	68°43'W
Aravalli Range, mts., India (ä-rä´vŭ-lê)	199	24°15'N	72°40'E
Araya, Punta de, c., Ven. (pŭn´tä-dĕ-ä-rä´yä)	143b	10°40'N	64°15'W
Arayat, Phil. (ä-rä´yät)	213a	15°10'N	120°44'E
'Arbi, Sudan	231	20°36'N	29°57'E
Arboga, Swe. (är-bō´gä)	166	59°26'N	15°50'E
Arborea, Italy (är-bō-rĕ´ä)	174	39°50'N	8°36'E
Arbroath, Scot., U.K. (är-brōth´)	164	56°36'N	2°25'W
Arcachon, Fr. (är-kä-shôN´)	161	44°39'N	1°12'W
Arcachon, Bassin d', Fr. (bä-sĕn´ där-kä-shôn´)	170	44°42'N	1°50'W
Arcadia, Ca., U.S. (är-kā´dĭ-ȧ)	117a	34°08'N	118°02'W
Arcadia, Fl., U.S.	125a	27°12'N	81°51'W
Arcadia, La., U.S.	123	32°33'N	92°56'W
Arcadia, Wi., U.S.	113	44°15'N	91°30'W
Arcata, Ca., U.S. (är-kà´tȧ)	114	40°54'N	124°05'W
Arc Dome Mountain, mtn., Nv., U.S. (ärk dōm)	118	38°51'N	117°21'W
Arcelia, Mex. (är-sä´lê-ä)	130	18°19'N	100°14'W
Archbald, Pa., U.S. (ärch´bôld)	109	41°30'N	75°35'W
Arches National Park, rec., Ut., U.S. (är´ches)	119	38°45'N	109°35'W
Archidona, Ec. (är-chê-dô´nä)	142	1°01'S	77°49'W
Archidona, Spain (är-chē-dô´nä)	172	37°08'N	4°24'W

PRONOUNCING INDEX

Arcis-sur-Aube – Atacama 267

PLACE (Pronunciation)	PAGE	LAT.	LONG.
Arcis-sur-Aube, Fr. (är-sēs′sûr-ōb′)	170	48°31′N	4°04′E
Arco, Id., U.S. (är′kô)	115	43°39′N	113°15′W
Arcola, Tx., U.S.	123a	29°30′N	95°28′W
Arcola, Va., U.S. (är′cōlă)	110e	38°57′N	77°32′W
Arcos de la Frontera, Spain (är′kōs-dĕ-lä-frôn-tĕ′rä)	172	36°44′N	5°48′W
Arctic Ocean, o.	244	85°00′N	170°00′E
Arda, r., Blg. (är′dä)	175	41°36′N	25°18′E
Ardabīl, Iran	198	38°15′N	48°00′E
Ardahan, Tur. (är-dȧ-hän′)	181	41°10′N	42°40′E
Ardatov, Russia (är-dȧ-tôf′)	180	54°58′N	46°10′E
Ardennes, mts., Eur. (ȧr-dĕn′)	161	50°01′N	5°12′E
Ardila, r., Eur. (är-dē′lȧ)	172	38°10′N	7°15′W
Ardmore, Ok., U.S. (ärd′mōr)	104	34°10′N	97°08′W
Ardmore, Pa., U.S.	110f	40°01′N	75°18′W
Ardrossan, Can. (är-dros′ăn)	102g	53°33′N	113°08′W
Ardsley, Eng., U.K. (ärdz′lē)	158a	53°43′N	1°33′W
Åre, Swe.	160	63°12′N	13°12′E
Arecibo, P.R. (ä-rå-sē′bō)	129b	18°28′N	66°45′W
Areia Branca, Braz. (ä-rĕ′yä-brä′n-kä)	143	4°58′S	37°02′W
Arena, Point, c., Ca., U.S. (ä-rā′nȧ)	118	38°57′N	123°40′W
Arenas, Punta, c., Ven. (pōn′tä-rĕ′näs)	143b	10°57′N	64°24′W
Arenas de San Pedro, Spain	172	40°12′N	5°04′W
Arendal, Nor. (ä′rĕn-däl)	166	58°29′N	8°44′E
Arendonk, Bel.	159a	51°19′N	5°07′E
Arequipa, Peru (ä-rå-kē′pä)	142	16°27′S	71°30′W
Arezzo, Italy (ä-rĕt′sō)	162	43°28′N	11°54′E
Arga, r., Spain (är′gä)	172	42°35′N	1°55′W
Arganda, Spain (är-gän′dä)	173a	40°18′N	3°27′W
Argazi, l., Russia (är′gä-zĭ)	186a	55°24′N	60°37′E
Argazi, r., Russia	186a	55°33′N	57°30′E
Argentan, Fr. (ȧr-zhäN-täN′)	170	48°45′N	0°01′W
Argentat, Fr. (ȧr-zhäN-tä′)	170	45°07′N	1°57′E
Argenteuil, Fr. (är-zhäN-tû′y′)	170	48°56′N	2°15′E
Argentina, nation, S.A. (är-jĕn-tē′nȧ)	144	35°30′S	67°00′W
Argentino, l., Arg. (är-Kĕn-tē′nō)	144	50°15′S	72°45′W
Argenton-sur-Creuse, Fr. (är-zhäN′tôN-sür-krûs)	170	46°34′N	1°28′E
Argolikos Kólpos, b., Grc.	175	37°20′N	23°00′E
Argonne, mts., Fr. (ä′r-gôn)	171	49°21′N	5°54′E
Argos, Grc. (är′gŏs)	175	37°38′N	22°45′E
Argostóli, Grc.	175	38°10′N	20°30′E
Arguello, Point, c., Ca., U.S. (är-gwāl′yō)	118	34°35′N	120°40′W
Arguin, Cap d′, c., Maur.	230	20°28′N	17°46′W
Argun′, r., Asia (ȧr-gōōn′)	179	50°00′N	119°00′E
Argungu, Nig.	235	12°45′N	4°31′E
Argyle, Can. (är′gīl)	102f	50°11′N	97°27′W
Argyle, Mn., U.S.	112	48°21′N	96°48′W
Århus, Den. (ôr′hōōs)	160	56°09′N	10°10′E
Ariakeno-Umi, b., Japan (ä-rē′ä-kä′nō ōō′nē)	211	33°03′N	130°18′E
Ariake-Wan, b., Japan (ä′rē-ä′kȧ wän)	211	31°19′N	131°15′E
Ariano, Italy (ä-rē-ä′nō)	174	41°09′N	15°11′E
Ariari, r., Col. (ä-ryá′rē)	142a	3°34′N	73°42′W
Aribinda, Burkina	234	14°14′N	0°52′W
Arica, Chile (ä-rē′kä)	142	18°34′S	70°14′W
Arichat, Can. (ä-rĭ-shät′)	101	45°31′N	61°01′W
Ariège, r., Fr. (ȧ-rê-ĕzh′)	170	43°26′N	1°29′E
Ariel, Wa., U.S. (ā′rĭ-ĕl)	116c	45°57′N	122°34′W
Arieș, r., Rom.	169	46°25′N	23°15′E
Ariguanabo, Lago de, l., Cuba (lä′gô-dĕ-ä-rē-gwä-nä′bô)	135a	22°52′N	82°33′W
Arikaree, r., Co., U.S. (ȧ-rĭ-kȧ-rē′)	120	39°51′N	102°18′W
Arima, Japan (ä′rē-mä′)	211b	34°48′N	135°16′E
Aringay, Phil. (ä-rĭŋ-gä′ê)	213a	16°25′N	120°20′E
Arinos, r., Braz. (ä-rē′nôzh)	143	12°09′S	56°49′W
Aripuanã, r., Braz. (ȧ-rê-pwän-yȧ′)	143	7°06′S	60°29′W
′Arīsh, Wādī al, r., Egypt (ȧ-rēsh′)	197a	30°36′N	34°07′E
Aristazabal Island, i., Can.	94	52°30′N	129°20′W
Arizona, state, U.S. (ăr-ĭ-zō′nȧ)	104	34°00′N	113°00′W
Arjona, Spain (är-hō′nä)	172	37°58′N	4°03′W
Arka, r., Russia	185	60°45′N	142°30′E
Arkabutla Lake, res., Ms., U.S. (är-kȧ-bŭt′lȧ)	124	34°48′N	90°00′W
Arkadelphia, Ar., U.S. (är-kȧ-dĕl′fĭ-ȧ)	121	34°06′N	93°05′W
Arkansas, state, U.S. (är′kăn-sô) (är-kăn′sȧs)	105	34°50′N	93°40′W
Arkansas, r., U.S.	106	37°30′N	97°00′W
Arkansas City, Ks., U.S.	121	37°04′N	97°02′W
Arkhangelsk (Archangel), Russia (ȧr-Kän′gĕlsk)	178	64°30′N	40°25′E
Arkhangel′skoye, Russia (är-Kän-gĕl′skô-yĕ)	186a	54°25′N	56°48′E
Arklow, Ire. (ärk′lō)	164	52°47′N	6°10′W
Arkonam, India (är-kō-näm′)	203	13°05′N	79°43′E
Arlanza, r., Spain (är-län-thä′)	172	42°08′N	3°45′W
Arlanzón, r., Spain (är-län-thōn′)	172	42°12′N	3°58′W
Arlberg Tunnel, trans., Aus. (ärl′bĕrgh)	168	47°05′N	10°15′E
Arles, Fr. (ärl)	170	43°42′N	4°38′E
Arlington, S. Afr.	238c	28°02′S	27°52′E
Arlington, Ga., U.S. (är′lĭng-tun′)	124	31°25′N	84°42′W
Arlington, Ma., U.S.	101a	42°26′N	71°13′W
Arlington, S.D., U.S. (är′lĭng-tŭn)	112	44°23′N	97°09′W
Arlington, Tx., U.S. (ár′lĭng-tŭn)	117c	32°44′N	97°07′W
Arlington, Va., U.S.	110e	38°55′N	77°10′W
Arlington, Vt., U.S.	109	43°05′N	73°05′W
Arlington, Wa., U.S.	116a	48°11′N	122°08′W
Arlington Heights, Il., U.S. (är′lēng-tŭn-hī′ts)	111a	42°05′N	87°59′W
Arltunga, Austl. (ärl-tôŋ′gȧ)	218	23°19′S	134°45′E
Arma, Ks., U.S. (är′mȧ)	121	37°34′N	94°43′W
Armagh, Can. (är-mä′) (är-mäk′)	102b	46°45′N	70°36′W
Armagh, N. Ire., U.K.	160	54°21′N	6°25′W
Armant, Egypt (är-mänt′)	238b	25°37′N	32°32′E
Armaro, Col. (är-mȧ′rō)	142a	4°58′N	74°54′W
Armavir, Russia (ȧr-mȧ-vĭr′)	178	45°00′N	41°00′E
Armenia, Col. (ȧr-mĕ′nēȧ)	142	4°33′N	75°40′W
Armenia, El Sal. (är-mā′nē-ä)	132	13°44′N	89°31′W
Armenia, nation, Asia	178	41°00′N	44°39′E
Armentières, Fr. (ȧr-mäN-tyâr′)	170	50°43′N	2°53′E
Armeria, Río de, r., Mex. (rē′ō-dĕ-är-mȧ-rē′ä)	130	19°36′N	104°10′W
Armherstburg, Can. (ärm′hĕrst-bōōrgh)	98	42°06′N	83°06′W
Armians′k, Ukr.	177	46°06′N	33°42′E
Armidale, Austl. (är′mĭ-dāl)	219	30°27′S	151°50′E
Armour, S.D., U.S. (är′mẽr)	112	43°18′N	98°21′W
Armstrong Station, Can. (ärm′strông)	91	50°21′N	89°00′W
Arnedo, Spain (är-nā′dō)	172	42°12′N	2°03′W
Arnhem, Neth. (ärn′hĕm)	161	51°58′N	5°56′E
Arnhem, Cape, c., Austl.	220	12°15′S	137°00′E
Arnhem Land, reg., Austl. (ärn′hĕm-lănd)	220	13°15′S	133°00′E
Arno, r., Italy (ä′r-nô)	162	43°30′N	11°00′E
Arnold, Eng., U.K. (är′nŭld)	158a	53°00′N	1°08′W
Arnold, Mn., U.S. (ár′nŭld)	117h	46°53′N	92°06′W
Arnold, Pa., U.S.	111e	40°35′N	79°45′W
Arnprior, Can. (ärn-prī′ẽr)	99	45°25′N	76°20′W
Arnsberg, Ger. (ärns′bĕrgh)	171c	51°25′N	8°02′E
Arnstadt, Ger. (ärn′shtät)	168	50°51′N	10°57′E
Aroab, Nmb. (är′ō-ȧb)	232	25°40′S	19°45′E
Aroostook, r., Me., U.S. (ȧ-rōs′tŏŏk)	100	46°44′N	68°15′W
Aroroy, Phil. (ä-rô-rō′ê)	213a	12°30′N	123°24′E
Arpajon, Fr. (ăr-pă-jō′n)	171b	48°35′N	2°15′E
Arpoador, Ponta do, c., Braz. (pô′n-tä-dō-är′pōä-dō′r)	144b	22°59′S	43°11′W
Arraiolos, Port. (är-rī-ō′lōzh)	172	38°47′N	7°59′W
Arran, Island of, Scot., U.K. (ă′răn)	164	55°25′N	5°25′W
Ar Rank, Sudan	231	11°45′N	32°53′E
Arras, Fr. (ȧ-räs′)	161	50°21′N	2°40′E
Ar Rawḑah, Egypt	238b	27°47′N	30°52′E
Arrecifes, Arg. (är-rå-sē′fäs)	141c	34°03′S	60°05′W
Arrecifes, r., Arg.	141c	34°07′S	59°50′W
Arrée, Monts d′, mts., Fr. (är-rā′)	170	48°27′N	4°00′W
Arriaga, Mex. (är-rêä′gä)	131	16°15′N	93°54′W
Arrone, r., Italy	173d	41°57′N	12°17′E
Arrow Creek, r., Mt., U.S. (ăr′ō)	115	47°29′N	109°53′W
Arrowhead, Lake, l., Ca., U.S. (lăk ăr′ōhĕd)	117a	34°17′N	117°13′W
Arrowrock Reservoir, res., Id., U.S. (ăr′ō-rŏk)	114	43°40′N	115°30′W
Arroya Arena, Cuba (är-rô′yä-rĕ′nä)	135a	23°01′N	82°30′W
Arroyo de la Luz, Spain (är-rō′yō-dĕ-lä-lōō′z)	172	39°39′N	6°46′W
Arroyo Seco, Mex. (är-rō′yō sā′kō)	130	21°31′N	99°44′W
Ar Rub′ al Khālī, des., Asia	198	20°00′N	51°00′E
Ar Ruṭbah, Iraq	201	33°02′N	40°17′E
Arsen′yev, Russia	179	44°13′N	133°32′E
Arsinskiy, Russia (är-sĭn′skĭ)	186a	53°46′N	59°54′E
Árta, Grc. (är′tä)	163	39°08′N	21°02′E
Arteaga, Mex. (är-tä-ä′gä)	122	25°28′N	100°50′W
Artëm, Russia (ár-tyôm′)	179	43°28′N	132°29′E
Artemisa, Cuba (är-tå-mē′sä)	134	22°50′N	82°45′W
Artemivs′k, Ukr.	181	48°37′N	38°00′E
Artesia, N.M., U.S. (är-tē′sĭ-ȧ)	120	32°44′N	104°23′W
Arthabaska, Can.	99	46°03′N	71°54′W
Arthur′s Town, Bah.	135	24°40′N	75°40′W
Arti, Russia (är′tĭ)	186a	56°20′N	58°38′E
Artibonite, r., N.A. (är-tê-bô-nē′tä)	135	19°00′N	72°25′W
Aru, Kepulauan, is., Indon.	213	6°20′S	133°00′E
Arua, Ug. (ä′rōō-ä)	231	3°01′N	30°55′E
Aruba, i., Aruba (ä-rōō′bȧ)	129	12°29′N	70°00′W
Arunachal Pradesh, state, India	199	27°35′N	92°56′E
Arusha, Tan. (ȧ-rōō′shä)	232	3°22′S	36°41′E
Arvida, Can.	91	48°26′N	71°11′W
Arvika, Swe. (är-vē′kȧ)	166	59°41′N	12°35′E
Arzamas, Russia (är-zä-mäs′)	180	55°20′N	43°52′E
Arziw, Alg.	162	35°50′N	0°20′W
Arzúa, Spain	172	42°54′N	8°19′W
Aš, Czech Rep. (äsh′)	168	50°12′N	12°13′E
Asahi-Gawa, r., Japan (ȧ-sä′hē-gä′wä)	211	35°01′N	133°40′E
Asahikawa, Japan	205	43°50′N	142°09′E
Asaka, Japan (ä-sä′kä)	211a	35°47′N	139°36′E
Asansol, India	199	23°45′N	86°58′E
Asbest, Russia (äs-bĕst′)	180	57°02′N	61°28′E
Asbestos, Can. (ăs-bĕs′tōs)	99	45°49′N	71°52′W
Asbestovskiy, Russia	186a	57°46′N	61°23′E
Asbury Park, N.J., U.S. (ăz′bĕr-ĭ)	110a	40°13′N	74°01′W
Ascención, Bahía de la, b., Mex.	132a	19°39′N	87°30′W
Ascensión, Mex. (äs-sĕn-sē-ōn′)	130	24°21′N	99°54′W
Ascension, i., St. Hel. (ȧ-sĕn′shŭn)	229	8°00′S	13°00′W
Ascent, S. Afr. (ăs-ĕnt′)	238c	27°14′S	29°06′E
Aschaffenburg, Ger. (ä-shäf′ĕn-bŏrgh)	168	49°58′N	9°12′E
Ascheberg, Ger. (ä′shĕ-bĕrg)	171c	51°47′N	7°38′E
Aschersleben, Ger. (äsh′ĕrs-lā-bĕn)	168	51°46′N	11°28′E
Ascoli Piceno, Italy (äs′kô-lēpê-chä′nō)	174	42°50′N	13°55′E
Aseb, Erit.	231	12°52′N	43°39′E
Asenovgrad, Blg.	175	42°00′N	24°49′E
Aseri, Est. (ä′sĕ-rĭ)	167	59°26′N	26°58′E
Asha, Russia (ä′shä)	186a	55°01′N	57°17′E
Ashabula, l., N.D., U.S. (ăsh′ȧ-bū-lă)	112	47°07′N	97°51′W
Ashan, Russia (ä′shän)	186a	57°08′N	56°25′E
Ashbourne, Eng., U.K. (ăsh′bŭrn)	158a	53°01′N	1°44′W
Ashburn, Ga., U.S. (ăsh′bŭrn)	124	31°42′N	83°42′W
Ashburn, Va., U.S.	110e	39°02′N	77°30′W
Ashburton, r., Austl. (ăsh′bûr-tŭn)	220	22°30′S	115°30′E
Ashby-de-la-Zouch, Eng., U.K. (ăsh′bĭ-dē-lȧ zōōsh′)	158a	52°44′N	1°23′W
Ashdod, Isr.	197a	31°46′N	34°39′E
Ashdown, Ar., U.S. (ăsh′doun)	121	33°41′N	94°07′W
Asheboro, N.C., U.S. (ăsh′bŭr-ô)	125	35°41′N	79°50′W
Asherton, Tx., U.S. (ăsh′ẽr-tŭn)	122	28°26′N	99°45′W
Asheville, N.C., U.S. (ăsh′vĭl)	105	35°35′N	82°35′W
Ash Fork, Az., U.S.	119	35°13′N	112°29′W
Ashgabat, Turkmen.	183	37°57′N	58°23′E
Ashikaga, Japan (ä′shê-kä′gȧ)	211	36°22′N	139°26′E
Ashiya, Japan (ä′shê-yä′)	211	33°54′N	130°40′E
Ashiya, Japan	211b	34°44′N	135°18′E
Ashizuri-Zaki, c., Japan (ä-shē-zō-rē zä-kē)	210	32°43′N	133°04′E
Ashland, Al., U.S. (ăsh′lănd)	124	33°15′N	85°50′W
Ashland, Ks., U.S.	120	37°11′N	99°46′W
Ashland, Ky., U.S.	108	38°25′N	82°40′W
Ashland, Ma., U.S.	101a	42°16′N	71°28′W
Ashland, Me., U.S.	100	46°37′N	68°26′W
Ashland, Ne., U.S.	112	41°02′N	96°23′W
Ashland, Oh., U.S.	108	40°50′N	82°15′W
Ashland, Or., U.S.	114	42°12′N	122°42′W
Ashland, Pa., U.S.	109	40°45′N	76°20′W
Ashland, Wi., U.S.	105	46°34′N	90°55′W
Ashley, N.D., U.S. (ăsh′lē)	112	46°03′N	99°23′W
Ashley, Pa., U.S.	109	41°15′N	75°55′W
Ashmūn, Egypt (ash-mōōn′)	238b	30°19′N	30°57′E
Ashmyany, Bela.	167	54°27′N	25°55′E
Ashqelon, Isr. (äsh′kĕ-lōn)	197a	31°40′N	34°36′E
Ash Shabb, Egypt (shĕb)	231	22°34′N	29°52′E
Ash Shallūfah, Egypt (shäl′lō-fä)	238b	30°09′N	32°33′E
Ash Shaqrā′, Sau. Ar.	198	25°10′N	45°08′E
Ash Shāriqah, U.A.E.	201	25°22′N	55°23′E
Ash Shawbak, Jord.	197a	30°31′N	35°35′E
Ash Shiḥr, Yemen	198	14°45′N	49°32′E
Ashtabula, Oh., U.S. (ăsh-tȧ-bū′lȧ)	105	41°55′N	80°50′W
Ashton, Id., U.S. (ăsh′tŭn)	115	44°04′N	111°28′W
Ashton-in-Makerfield, Eng., U.K. (ăsh′tŭn-ĭn-măk′ẽr-fēld)	158a	53°29′N	2°39′W
Ashton-under-Lyne, Eng., U.K. (ăsh′tŭn-ŭn-dẽr-līn′)	158a	53°29′N	2°04′W
Ashuanipi, l., Can. (ăsh-wȧ-nĭp′ĭ)	93	52°40′N	67°42′W
Ashukino, Russia (ȧ-shōō′kĭnô)	186b	56°10′N	37°57′E
Asia, cont.	196	50°00′N	100°00′E
Asia Minor, reg., Tur. (ā′zhȧ)	157	38°18′N	31°18′E
Asientos, Mex. (ä-sē-ĕn′tōs)	130	22°13′N	102°05′W
Asilah, Mor.	172	35°30′N	6°05′W
Asinara, i., Italy	174	41°02′N	8°22′E
Asinara, Golfo dell′, b., Italy (gôl′fō-dĕl-ä-sē-nä′rä)	174	40°58′N	8°28′E
Asīr, reg., Sau. Ar. (ä-sēr′)	198	19°30′N	42°00′E
Askarovo, Russia (äs-kä-rô′vô)	186a	53°21′N	58°32′E
Askersund, Swe. (äs′kĕr-sŏnd)	166	58°43′N	14°53′E
Askino, Russia (äs′kĭ-nô)	186a	56°06′N	56°29′E
Asmara *see* Asmera, Erit.	230	15°17′N	38°56′E
Asmera, Erit. (äs-mä′rä)	231	15°17′N	38°56′E
Asnieres, Fr. (ä-nyâr′)	171b	48°55′N	2°18′E
Asosa, Eth.	231	10°13′N	34°28′E
Asotin, Wa., U.S. (ȧ-sō′tĭn)	114	46°19′N	117°01′W
Aspen, Co., U.S. (ăs′pĕn)	119	39°15′N	106°55′W
Asperen, Neth.	159a	51°52′N	5°07′E
Aspy Bay, b., Can. (ăs′pē)	101	46°55′N	60°25′W
Aş Şaff, Egypt	238b	29°33′N	31°23′E
As Sallūm, Egypt	231	31°35′N	25°05′E
As Salt, Jord.	197a	32°02′N	35°44′E
Assam, state, India (ăs-săm′)	199	26°00′N	91°00′E
As Samāwah, Iraq	201	31°18′N	45°17′E
Assens, Den. (äs′sĕns)	166	55°16′N	9°54′E
As Sinbillāwayn, Egypt	238b	30°53′N	31°37′E
Assini, C. Iv. (ȧ-sê-nē′)	230	4°52′N	3°16′W
Assiniboia, Can.	90	49°38′N	105°59′W
Assiniboine, r., Can. (ă-sĭn′ĭ-boin)	97	50°03′N	97°57′W
Assiniboine, Mount, mtn., Can.	95	50°52′N	115°39′W
Assis, Braz. (ä-sē′s)	143	22°39′S	50°21′W
Assisi, Italy	162	43°04′N	12°37′E
As-Sudd, reg., Sudan	231	8°45′N	30°45′E
As Sulaymānīyah, Iraq	198	35°47′N	45°23′E
As Sulaymānīyah, Sau. Ar.	201	24°09′N	46°19′E
As Suwaydā′, Syria	198	32°41′N	36°41′E
Astakós, Grc. (äs′tä-kōs)	175	38°42′N	21°00′E
Astana (Aqmola), Kaz.	183	51°10′N	71°43′E
Astara, Azer.	181	38°30′N	48°50′E
Asti, Italy (äs′tē)	162	44°54′N	8°12′E
Astorga, Spain (äs-tôr′gä)	172	42°28′N	6°03′W
Astoria, Or., U.S. (ăs-tō′rĭ-ȧ)	104	46°11′N	123°51′W
Astrakhan′, Russia (äs-trȧ-kän′)	178	46°15′N	48°00′E
Astrida, Rw. (äs-trē′dȧ)	232	2°37′S	29°48′E
Asturias, hist. reg., Spain (äs-tōō′ryäs)	172	43°21′N	6°00′W
Astypalaia, i., Grc.	163	36°31′N	26°19′E
Asunción *see* Ixtaltepec, Mex.	131	16°33′N	95°04′W
Asunción *see* Nochistlán, Mex.	130	21°23′N	102°52′W
Asunción, Para. (ä-sōōn-syōn′)	144	25°25′S	57°30′W
Asunción Mita, Guat. (ä-sōōn-syō′n-mē′tä)	132	14°19′N	89°43′W
Aswān, Egypt (ä-swän′)	231	24°05′N	32°57′E
Aswān High Dam, dam, Egypt	231	23°58′N	32°53′E
Atacama, Desierto de, des., Chile (dĕ-syĕ′r-tô-dĕ-ä-tä-kȧ′mä)	139	23°50′S	69°00′W

268 Atacama – Babylon PRONOUNCING INDEX

PLACE (Pronunciation)	PAGE	LAT.	LONG.
Atacama, Puna de, plat., Bol. (pōō'nä-dĕ-ä-tä-kà'mä)	142	21°35'S	66°58'W
Atacama, Puna de, reg., Chile (pōō'nä-dĕ-ätä-kà'mä)	144	23°15'S	68°45'W
Atacama, Salar de, l., Chile (sà-lär'dĕ-ätä-kà'mä)	144	23°38'S	68°15'W
Ataco, Col. (ä-tà'kō)	142a	3°36'N	75°22'W
Atacora, Chaîne de l', mts., Benin	234	10°15'N	1°15'E
Atā 'itah, Jabal al, mtn., Jord.	197a	30°48'N	35°19'E
Atamanovskiy, Russia (ä-tä-mä'nôv-skĭ)	186a	52°15'N	60°47'E
'Atāqah, Jabal, mts., Egypt	238d	29°59'N	32°20'E
Atar, Maur. (ä-tär')	230	20°45'N	13°16'W
Atascadero, Ca., U.S. (ăt-ăs-kà-dâ'rō)	118	35°29'N	120°40'W
Atascosa, r., Tx., U.S. (ăt-ăs-kō'sà)	122	28°50'N	98°17'W
Atauro, Ilha de, i., E. Timor (dĕ-ä-tä'ōō-rô)	213	8°20'S	126°15'E
Atbara, r., Afr.	231	17°14'N	34°27'E
'Aṭbarah, Sudan (ät'bà-rä)	231	17°45'N	33°15'E
Atbasar, Kaz. (ät'bä-sär')	183	51°42'N	68°28'E
Atchafalaya, r., La., U.S.	123	30°53'N	91°51'W
Atchafalaya Bay, b., La., U.S. (ăch-à-fà-lī'à)	123	29°25'N	91°30'W
Atchison, Ks., U.S. (ăch'ĭ-sŭn)	105	39°33'N	95°08'W
Atco, N.J., U.S. (ăt'kō)	110f	39°46'N	74°53'W
Atempan, Mex. (ä-tĕm-pä'n)	131	19°49'N	97°25'W
Atenguillo, r., Mex. (ä-tĕn-gē'l-yô)	130	20°18'N	104°35'W
Athabasca, Can. (ăth-à-băs'kà)	90	54°43'N	113°17'W
Athabasca, l., Can.	92	59°04'N	109°10'W
Athabasca, r., Can.	92	57°30'N	112°00'W
Athens (Athína), Grc.	175	38°00'N	23°38'E
Athens, Al., U.S. (ăth'ĕnz)	124	34°47'N	86°58'W
Athens, Ga., U.S.	105	33°55'N	83°24'W
Athens, Oh., U.S.	108	39°20'N	82°10'W
Athens, Pa., U.S.	109	42°00'N	76°30'W
Athens, Tn., U.S.	124	35°26'N	84°36'W
Athens, Tx., U.S.	123	32°13'N	95°51'W
Atherstone, Eng., U.K. (ăth'ẽr-stŭn)	158a	52°34'N	1°33'W
Atherton, Eng., U.K. (ăth'ẽr-tŭn)	158a	53°32'N	2°29'W
Atherton Plateau, plat., Austl. (ădh-ẽr-tŏn)	221	17°00'S	144°30'E
Athi, r., Kenya (ä'tē)	233	2°43'S	38°30'E
Athína *see* Athens, Grc.	154	38°00'N	23°38'E
Athlone, Ire. (ăth-lōn')	160	53°24'N	7°30'W
Áthos, mtn., Grc. (ăth'ŏs)	175	40°10'N	24°15'E
Ath Thamad, Egypt	197a	29°41'N	34°17'E
Athy, Ire. (à-thī)	164	52°59'N	7°08'W
Ati, Chad	235	13°13'N	18°20'E
Atibaia, Braz. (ä-tē-bà'yà)	141a	23°08'S	46°32'W
Atikonak, l., Can.	93	52°34'N	63°49'W
Atimonan, Phil. (ä-tē-mō'nän)	213a	13°59'N	121°56'E
Atiquizaya, El Sal. (ä'tē-kē-zä'yä)	132	14°00'N	89°42'W
Atitlan, vol., Guat. (ä-tē-tlän')	132	14°35'N	91°11'W
Atitlan, Lago, l., Guat. (ä-tē-tlän')	132	14°38'N	91°23'W
Atizapán, Mex. (ä'tē-zà-pän')	131a	19°33'N	99°16'W
Atka, Ak., U.S. (ăt'kà)	103a	52°18'N	174°18'W
Atka, i., Ak., U.S.	106b	51°58'N	174°30'W
Atkarsk, Russia (åt-kärsk')	181	51°50'N	45°00'E
Atkinson, Ne., U.S. (ăt'kĭn-sŭn)	112	42°32'N	98°58'W
Atlanta, Ga., U.S. (ăt-lăn'tà)	105	33°45'N	84°23'W
Atlanta, Tx., U.S.	121	33°09'N	94°09'W
Atlantic, Ia., U.S. (ăt-lăn'tĭk)	113	41°23'N	94°58'W
Atlantic, N.C., U.S.	125	34°54'N	76°20'W
Atlantic City, N.J., U.S.	105	39°20'N	74°30'W
Atlantic Highlands, N.J., U.S.	110a	40°25'N	74°04'W
Atlantic Ocean, o.	4	5°00'S	25°00'W
Atlas Mountains, mts., Afr. (ăt'lăs)	230	31°22'N	4°57'W
Atliaca, Mex. (ät-lē-ä'kä)	130	17°38'N	99°24'W
Atlin, l., Can. (ăt'lĭn)	92	59°34'N	133°20'W
Atlixco, Mex. (ät-lēz'kō)	130	18°52'N	98°27'W
Atmore, Al., U.S. (ăt'mōr)	124	31°01'N	87°31'W
Atoka, Ok., U.S. (à-tō'kà)	121	34°23'N	96°07'W
Atoka Reservoir, res., Ok., U.S.	121	34°30'N	96°05'W
Atotonilco el Alto, Mex.	130	20°35'N	102°32'W
Atotonilco el Grande, Mex.	130	20°17'N	98°41'W
Atoui, r., Afr. (à-tōō-ē')	230	21°00'N	15°32'W
Atoyac, Mex. (ä-tô-yäk')	130	20°01'N	103°28'W
Atoyac, r., Mex.	130	18°35'N	98°16'W
Atoyac, r., Mex.	131	16°27'N	97°28'W
Atoyac de Alvarez, Mex. (ä-tô-yäk'dā äl'vä-räz)	130	17°13'N	100°29'W
Atoyatempan, Mex. (ä-tō'yà-tĕm-pän')	131	18°47'N	97°54'W
Atrak, r., Asia	198	37°45'N	56°30'E
Åtran, r., Swe.	166	57°02'N	12°43'E
Atrato, Río, r., Col. (rē'ō-ä-trä'tō)	142	7°15'N	77°18'W
Aṭ Ṭafīlah, Jord. (tä-fē'la)	197a	30°50'N	35°36'E
Aṭ Ṭā'if, Sau. Ar.	198	21°03'N	41°00'E
Attalla, Al., U.S. (à-tăl'yà)	124	34°01'N	86°05'W
Attawapiskat, r., Can. (ăt'à-wà-pĭs'kăt)	93	52°31'N	86°22'W
Attersee, l., Aus.	168	47°57'N	13°25'E
Attica, N.Y., U.S. (ăt'ĭ-kà)	109	42°55'N	78°15'W
Attleboro, Ma., U.S. (ăt''l-bŭr-ô)	110b	41°56'N	71°15'W
Attow, Ben, mtn., Scot., U.K. (bĕn ăt'tô)	164	57°15'N	5°25'W
Attoyac Bay, Tx., U.S. (ă-toi'yăk)	123	31°45'N	94°23'W
Attu, i., Ak., U.S. (ăt-tōō')	106b	53°08'N	173°18'E
Aṭ Ṭūr, Egypt	163	28°09'N	33°47'E
Aṭ Ṭurayf, Sau. Ar.	198	31°32'N	38°30'E
Åtvidaberg, Swe. (ôt-vē'dà-bĕrgh)	166	58°12'N	15°55'E
Atwood, Ks., U.S. (ăt'wŏŏd)	120	39°48'N	101°06'W
Atyraū, Kaz.	183	47°10'N	51°50'E
Atzcapotzalco, Mex. (ät'zkä-pô-tzäl'kō)	130	19°29'N	99°11'W
Atzgersdorf, Aus.	159e	48°10'N	16°17'E
Auau Channel, strt., Hi., U.S. (ä'ō-ä'ōo)	126a	20°55'N	156°50'W
Aubagne, Fr. (ō-bän'y')	171	43°18'N	5°34'E
Aube, r., Fr. (ōb)	170	48°42'N	3°49'E
Aubenas, Fr. (ōb-nä')	170	44°37'N	4°22'E
Aubervilliers, Fr. (ō-bĕr-vē-yā')	171b	48°54'N	2°23'E
Aubin, Fr. (ō-băn')	170	44°29'N	2°12'E
Aubrey, Can. (ô-brē')	102a	45°08'N	73°47'W
Auburn, Al., U.S. (ô'bûrn)	124	32°35'N	85°26'W
Auburn, Ca., U.S.	118	38°52'N	121°05'W
Auburn, Il., U.S.	121	39°36'N	89°46'W
Auburn, In., U.S.	108	41°20'N	85°05'W
Auburn, Ma., U.S.	101a	42°11'N	71°51'W
Auburn, Me., U.S.	105	44°04'N	70°24'W
Auburn, Ne., U.S.	121	40°23'N	95°50'W
Auburn, N.Y., U.S.	109	42°55'N	76°35'W
Auburn, Wa., U.S.	116a	47°18'N	122°14'W
Auburn Heights, Mi., U.S.	111b	42°37'N	83°13'W
Aubusson, Fr. (ō-bü-sôN')	170	45°57'N	2°10'E
Auch, Fr. (ōsh)	161	43°38'N	0°35'E
Aucilla, r., Fl., U.S. (ô-sĭl'à)	124	30°15'N	83°55'W
Auckland, N.Z. (ôk'lănd)	221a	36°53'S	174°45'E
Auckland Islands, is., N.Z.	3	50°30'S	166°30'E
Aude, r., Fr. (ōd)	170	42°55'N	2°08'E
Audierne, Fr. (ō-dyĕrn')	170	48°02'N	4°31'W
Audincourt, Fr. (ō-dăn-kōōr')	171	47°30'N	6°49'E
Audley, Eng., U.K. (ôd'lĭ)	158a	53°03'N	2°18'W
Audo Range, mts., Eth.	238a	6°58'N	41°18'E
Audubon, Ia., U.S. (ô'dŏŏ-bŏn)	113	41°43'N	94°57'W
Audubon, N.J., U.S.	110f	39°54'N	75°04'W
Aue, Ger. (ou'ē)	168	50°35'N	12°44'E
Augathella, Austl. (ôr'gà'thĕ-là)	222	25°49'S	146°40'E
Augrabiesvalle, wtfl., S. Afr.	232	28°30'S	20°00'E
Augsburg, Ger. (ouks'bŏorgh)	161	48°23'N	10°55'E
Augusta, Ar., U.S. (ô-gŭs'tà)	121	35°16'N	91°21'W
Augusta, Ga., U.S.	105	33°26'N	82°00'W
Augusta, Ks., U.S.	121	37°41'N	96°58'W
Augusta, Ky., U.S.	108	38°45'N	84°00'W
Augusta, Me., U.S.	105	44°19'N	69°42'W
Augusta, N.J., U.S.	110a	41°07'N	74°44'W
Augusta, Wi., U.S.	113	44°40'N	91°09'W
Augustow, Pol. (ou-gōōs'tōf)	169	53°52'N	23°00'E
Auki, Sol. Is.	214e	8°46'S	160°42'E
Aulnay-sous-Bois, Fr. (ō-nĕ'sōō-bwä')	171b	48°56'N	2°30'E
Aulne, r., Fr. (ōn)	170	48°08'N	3°53'W
Auneau, Fr. (ō-nēü)	171b	48°28'N	1°45'E
Auob, r., Afr. (ä'wŏb)	232	25°00'S	19°00'E
Aur, i., Malay.	197b	2°27'N	104°51'E
Aura, Fin.	167	60°38'N	22°32'E
Aurangābād, India (ou-rŭŋ-gä-bäd')	199	19°56'N	75°19'E
Aurdal, Nor. (äür-däl)	160	60°54'N	9°24'E
Aurès, Massif de l', mts., Alg.	162	35°16'N	5°53'E
Aurillac, Fr. (ō-rē-yák')	161	44°57'N	2°27'E
Aurora, Can.	99	43°59'N	79°25'W
Aurora, Co., U.S.	120	39°44'N	104°50'W
Aurora, Il., U.S. (ô-rō'rà)	105	41°45'N	88°18'W
Aurora, In., U.S.	111f	39°04'N	84°55'W
Aurora, Mn., U.S.	113	47°31'N	92°17'W
Aurora, Mo., U.S.	121	36°58'N	93°42'W
Aurora, Ne., U.S.	120	40°54'N	98°01'W
Aursunden, l., Nor. (äûr-sŭndĕn)	166	62°42'N	11°10'E
Au Sable, r., Mi., U.S. (ô-sā'b'l)	108	44°40'N	84°25'W
Ausable, r., N.Y., U.S.	109	44°25'N	73°50'W
Austin, Mn., U.S. (ôs'tĭn)	113	43°40'N	92°58'W
Austin, Nv., U.S.	118	39°30'N	117°05'W
Austin, Tx., U.S.	104	30°15'N	97°42'W
Austin, l., Austl.	220	27°45'S	117°30'E
Austin Bayou, Tx., U.S. (ôs'tĭn bī-ōō')	123a	29°17'N	95°21'W
Australia, nation, Oc.	218	25°00'S	135°00'E
Australian Alps, mts., Austl.	222	37°10'S	147°55'E
Australian Capital Territory, ter., Austl. (ôs-trā'lĭ-ăn)	219	35°30'S	148°40'E
Austria, nation, Eur. (ôs'trĭ-à)	154	47°15'N	11°53'E
Authon-la-Plaine, Fr. (ō-tôN-lä-plĕ'n)	171b	48°27'N	1°58'E
Autlán, Mex. (ä-ōōt-län')	128	19°47'N	104°24'W
Autun, Fr. (ō-tŭN')	170	46°58'N	4°14'E
Auvergne, mts., Fr. (ō-vĕrn'y')	170	45°12'N	2°31'E
Auxerre, Fr. (ō-sâr')	161	47°48'N	3°32'E
Ava, Mo., U.S. (ā'và)	121	36°56'N	92°40'W
Avakubi, D.R.C. (ä-vä-kōō'bē)	231	1°20'N	27°34'E
Avallon, Fr. (à-và-lôN')	170	47°30'N	3°58'E
Avalon, Ca., U.S.	118	33°21'N	118°22'W
Avalon, Pa., U.S. (ăv'à-lŏn)	111e	40°31'N	80°05'W
Aveiro, Port. (ä-vā'rô)	162	40°38'N	8°38'W
Avelar, Braz. (ä'vĕ-là'r)	144b	22°20'S	43°25'W
Avellaneda, Arg. (ä-vĕl-yä-nā'dhä)	144	34°40'S	58°23'W
Avellino, Italy (ä-vĕl-lē'nō)	174	40°40'N	14°46'E
Averøya, i., Nor. (ävĕr-ûĕ)	166	63°40'N	7°16'E
Aversa, Italy (ä-vĕr'sä)	174	40°58'N	14°13'E
Avery, Tx., U.S. (ā'vẽr-ĭ)	121	33°34'N	94°46'W
Avesta, Swe. (ä-vĕs'tä)	166	60°16'N	16°09'E
Aveyron, r., Fr. (ä-vâ-rôN)	170	44°07'N	1°45'E
Avezzano, Italy (ä-vât-sä'nō)	174	42°03'N	13°27'E
Avigliano, Italy (ä-vēl-yä'nō)	174	40°45'N	15°44'E
Avignon, Fr. (ä-vē-nyôN')	161	43°55'N	4°50'E
Ávila, Spain (ä'vē-lä)	172	40°39'N	4°42'W
Avilés, Spain (ä-vē-lās')	162	43°33'N	5°55'W
Aviño, Spain	172	43°36'N	8°05'W
Avoca, Ia., U.S. (à-vō'kà)	121	41°29'N	95°16'W
Avon, Ct., U.S. (ā'vŏn)	109	41°40'N	72°50'W
Avon, Ma., U.S. (ā'vŏn)	101a	42°08'N	71°03'W
Avon, Oh., U.S.	111d	41°27'N	82°02'W
Avon, r., Eng., U.K. (ā'vŭn)	164	52°05'N	1°55'W
Avondale, Ga., U.S.	110c	33°47'N	84°16'W
Avon Lake, Oh., U.S.	111d	41°31'N	82°01'W
Avonmore, Can. (ă'vôN-mōr)	102c	45°11'N	74°58'W
Avon Park, Fl., U.S. (ā'vŏn pärk')	125a	27°35'N	81°29'W
Avranches, Fr. (à-vräNsh')	170	48°43'N	1°34'W
Awaji-Shima, i., Japan	210	34°32'N	135°02'E
Awe, Loch, l., Scot., U.K. (lŏκ ôr)	164	56°22'N	5°04'W
Awjilah, Libya	231	29°07'N	21°21'E
Ax-les-Thermes, Fr. (äks'lā tĕrm')	170	42°43'N	1°50'E
Axochiapan, Mex. (äks-ō-chyä'pän)	130	18°29'N	98°49'W
Ay, r., Russia	180	55°55'N	57°55'E
Ayabe, Japan (ä'yä-bĕ)	210	35°16'N	135°17'E
Ayachi, Arin', mtn., Mor.	162	32°29'N	4°57'W
Ayacucho, Arg. (ä-yä-kōō'chō)	144	37°05'S	58°30'W
Ayacucho, Peru	142	13°12'S	74°03'W
Ayaköz, Kaz.	183	48°00'N	80°12'E
Ayamonte, Spain (ä-yä-mô'n-tĕ)	162	37°14'N	7°28'W
Ayan, Russia (à-yän')	179	56°26'N	138°18'E
Ayata, Bol. (ä-yä'tä)	142	15°17'S	68°43'W
Ayaviri, Peru (ä-yä-vē'rē)	142	14°46'S	70°38'W
Aydar, r., Eur. (ī-där')	177	49°15'N	38°48'E
Ayden, N.C., U.S. (ā'dĕn)	125	35°27'N	77°25'W
Aydın, Tur. (āĭy-dĕn)	198	37°40'N	27°40'E
Ayer, Ma., U.S. (âr)	101a	42°33'N	71°36'W
Ayer Hitam, Malay.	197b	1°55'N	103°11'E
Ayers Rock *see* Uluru, mtn., Austl.	220	25°23'S	131°05'E
Aylesbury, Eng., U.K. (âlz'bẽr-ĭ)	164	51°47'N	0°49'W
Aylmer, l., Can. (āl'mẽr)	92	64°27'N	108°22'W
Aylmer, Mount, mtn., Can.	95	51°19'N	115°26'W
Aylmer East, Can. (āl'mẽr)	99	45°24'N	75°50'W
Ayo el Chico, Mex. (ä'yô el chē'kō)	130	20°31'N	102°21'W
Ayon, i., Russia (ī-ôn')	179	69°50'N	168°40'E
Ayorou, Niger	234	14°44'N	0°55'E
Ayotla, Mex. (ä-yōt'lä)	131a	19°18'N	98°55'W
Ayoun el Atrous, Maur.	234	16°40'N	9°37'W
Ayr, Scot., U.K. (âr)	164	55°27'N	4°40'W
Aysha, Eth.	231	10°48'N	42°32'E
Ayutla, Guat. (à-yōōt'lä)	132	14°44'N	92°11'W
Ayutla, Mex.	130	16°50'N	99°16'W
Ayutla, Mex.	130	20°09'N	104°20'W
Ayvalık, Tur. (āĭy-wă-lĭk)	163	39°19'N	26°40'E
Azaouad, reg., Mali	234	18°00'N	3°20'W
Azaouak, Vallée de l', val., Afr.	235	15°50'N	3°10'E
Azare, Nig.	235	11°40'N	10°11'E
Azemmour, Mor. (ä-zē-mōōr')	230	33°20'N	8°21'W
Azerbaijan, nation, Asia	178	40°30'N	47°30'E
Azle, Tx., U.S. (āz'lē)	117c	35°54'N	97°33'W
Azogues, Ec. (ä-sō'gās)	142	2°47'S	78°45'W
Azores *see* Açores, is., Port.	229	37°44'N	29°25'W
Azov, Russia (à-zôf') (ä-zôf)	181	47°07'N	39°19'E
Azov, Sea of, sea, Eur.	178	46°00'N	36°20'E
Aztec, N.M., U.S. (ăz'tĕk)	119	36°40'N	108°00'W
Aztec Ruins National Monument, rec., N.M., U.S.	119	36°50'N	108°00'W
Azua, Dom. Rep. (ä'swä)	135	18°30'N	70°45'W
Azuaga, Spain (ä-thwä'gä)	172	38°15'N	5°42'W
Azucar, Presa de, res., Mex.	122	26°06'N	98°44'W
Azuero, Península de, pen., Pan.	129	7°30'N	80°34'W
Azufre, Cerro (Copiapó), mtn., Chile	144	27°10'S	69°00'W
Azul, Arg. (ä-sōōl')	144	36°46'S	59°51'W
Azul, Cordillera, mts., Peru	142	7°15'S	75°30'W
Azul, Sierra, mts., Mex.	130	23°20'N	98°28'W
Azusa, Ca., U.S. (à-zōō'sà)	117a	34°08'N	117°55'W
Aẓ Ẓahrān (Dhahran), Sau. Ar.	198	26°13'N	50°00'E
Az Zaqāzīq, Egypt	231	30°36'N	31°36'E
Az Zarqā', Jord.	197a	32°03'N	36°07'E
Az Zāwiyah, Libya	230	32°28'N	11°55'E

B

PLACE (Pronunciation)	PAGE	LAT.	LONG.
Baadheere (Bardera), Som.	238a	2°13'N	42°24'E
Baal, Ger. (bäl)	171c	51°02'N	6°17'E
Baao, Phil. (bä'ō)	213a	13°27'N	123°22'E
Baarle-Hertog, Bel.	159a	51°26'N	4°57'E
Baarn, Neth.	159a	52°12'N	5°18'E
Babaeski, Tur. (bä'bä-ĕs'kĭ)	175	41°25'N	27°05'E
Babahoyo, Ec. (bä-bä-ō'yō)	142	1°56'S	79°24'W
Babana, Nig.	235	10°36'N	3°50'E
Babanango, S. Afr.	233c	28°24'S	31°11'E
Babanūsah, Sudan	231	11°30'N	27°55'E
Babar, Pulau, i., Indon. (bä'bär)	213	7°50'S	129°15'E
Bab-el-Mandeb *see* Mandeb, Bab-el-, strt.	198	13°17'N	42°49'E
Babelthuap, i., Palau	214b	7°30'N	134°36'E
Babia, Arroyo de la, r., Mex.	122	28°26'N	101°50'W
Babine, r., Can.	94	55°10'N	127°00'W
Babine Lake, l., Can. (băb'ēn)	92	54°45'N	126°00'W
Bābol, Iran	198	36°30'N	52°48'E
Babruysk, Bela.	180	53°07'N	29°13'E
Babushkin, Russia (bä'bŏsh-kĭn)	184	51°47'N	106°08'W
Babushkin, Russia	176	55°52'N	37°42'E
Babuyan Islands, is., Phil. (bä-bōō-yän')	212	19°30'N	122°38'E
Babyak, Blg. (bäb'zhák)	175	41°59'N	23°42'E
Babylon, N.Y., U.S. (băb'ĭ-lŏn)	110a	40°42'N	73°19'W
Babylon, hist., Iraq	198	32°15'N	45°23'E

ăt; finăl; rāte; senâte; ärm; àsk; sofà; fâre; ch-choose; dh-as th in other; bē; êvent; bĕt; recĕnt; cratẽr; g-gō; gh-guttural g; bĭt; ĭ-short neutral; rīde; κ-guttural k as ch in German ich;

PRONOUNCING INDEX

Bacalar – Bangor 269

PLACE (Pronunciation)	PAGE	LAT.	LONG.
Bacalar, Laguna de, l., Mex. (lä-gōō-nä-dĕ-bä-kä-lär′)	132a	18°50′N	88°31′W
Bacan, Pulau, i., Indon.	213	0°30′S	127°00′E
Bacarra, Phil. (bä-kär′rä)	209	18°22′N	120°40′E
Bacău, Rom.	163	46°34′N	27°00′E
Baccarat, Fr. (bȧ-kȧ-rȧ′)	171	48°29′N	6°42′E
Bacchus, Ut., U.S. (băk′ŭs)	117b	40°40′N	112°06′W
Bachajón, Mex. (bä-chä-hōn′)	131	17°08′N	92°18′W
Bachu, China (bä-chōō)	204	39°50′N	78°23′E
Back, r., Can.	92	65°30′N	104°15′W
Bačka Palanka, Yugo. (bäch′kä pälän-kä)	175	45°14′N	19°24′E
Bačka Topola, Yugo. (bäch′kä tô′pô-lä′)	175	45°48′N	19°38′E
Back Bay, India (băk)	203b	18°55′N	72°45′E
Backstairs Passage, strt., Austl. (băk-stârs′)	220	35°50′S	138°15′E
Bac Lieu, Viet.	212	9°45′N	105°50′E
Bac Ninh, Viet. (bäk′nēn′′)	209	21°10′N	106°02′E
Baco, Mount, mtn., Phil. (bä′kô)	213a	12°50′N	121°11′E
Bacoli, Italy (bä-kō-lē′)	173c	40°33′N	14°05′E
Bacolod, Phil. (bä-kō′lôd)	213	10°42′N	123°03′E
Bácsalmás, Hung. (bäch′ôl-mäs)	169	46°07′N	19°18′E
Bacup, Eng., U.K. (băk′ŭp)	158a	53°42′N	2°12′W
Bad, r., S.D., U.S. (băd)	112	44°04′N	100°58′W
Badajoz, Spain (bä-dhä-hōth′)	162	38°52′N	6°56′W
Badalona, Spain (bä-dhä-lō′nä)	173	41°27′N	2°15′E
Badanah, Sau. Ar.	198	30°49′N	40°45′E
Bad Axe, Mi., U.S. (băd′ ăks)	108	43°50′N	82°55′W
Bad Bramstedt, Ger. (bät bräm′shtĕt)	159c	53°55′N	9°53′E
Baden, Aus. (bä′dĕn)	168	48°00′N	16°14′E
Baden, Switz.	168	47°28′N	8°17′E
Baden-Baden, Ger. (bä′dĕn-bä′dĕn)	161	48°46′N	8°11′E
Bad Freienwalde, Ger. (bät frī′ĕn-väl′dĕ)	168	52°47′N	14°00′E
Bad Hersfeld, Ger. (bät hĕrsh′fĕlt)	168	50°53′N	9°43′E
Badīn, Pak.	202	24°47′N	69°51′E
Bad Ischl, Aus. (bät ĭsh′′l)	168	47°46′N	13°37′E
Bad Kissingen, Ger. (bät kĭs′ĭng-ĕn)	168	50°12′N	10°05′E
Bad Kreuznach, Ger. (bät kroits′näk)	168	49°52′N	7°53′E
Badlands, reg., N.D., U.S. (băd′ lănds)	112	46°43′N	103°22′W
Badlands, reg., S.D., U.S.	112	43°43′N	102°36′W
Badlands National Park, rec., S.D., U.S.	112	43°56′N	102°37′W
Badlāpur, India	203b	19°12′N	73°12′E
Badogo, Mali	234	11°02′N	8°13′W
Bad Oldesloe, Ger. (bät ôl′dĕs-lōĕ)	168	53°48′N	10°21′E
Bad Reichenhall, Ger. (bät rī′kĕn-häl)	168	47°43′N	12°53′E
Bad River Indian Reservation, I.R., Wi., U.S. (băd)	113	46°41′N	90°36′W
Bad Segeberg, Ger. (bät sĕ′gĕ-bōōrgh)	159c	53°56′N	10°18′E
Bad Tölz, Ger. (bät tûltz)	168	47°46′N	11°35′E
Badulla, Sri L.	203	6°55′N	81°07′E
Bad Vöslau, Aus.	159e	47°58′N	16°13′E
Badwater Creek, r., Wy., U.S. (băd′wô-tẽr)	115	43°13′N	107°55′W
Baena, Spain (bä-ā′nä)	162	37°38′N	4°20′W
Baependi, Braz. (bä-å-pĕn′dĭ)	141a	21°57′S	44°51′W
Baffin Bay, b., N.A. (băf′ĭn)	89	72°00′N	65°00′W
Baffin Bay, b., Tx., U.S.	123	27°11′N	97°35′W
Baffin Island, i., Can.	89	67°20′N	71°00′W
Bāfq, Iran (bäfk)	198	31°48′N	55°23′E
Bafra, Tur. (bäf′rä)	163	41°30′N	35°50′E
Bagabag, Phil. (bä-gä-bäg′)	213a	16°38′N	121°16′E
Bāgalkot, India	203	16°14′N	75°40′E
Bagamoyo, Tan. (bä-gä-mō′yō)	233	6°26′S	38°54′E
Bagaryak, Russia (bȧ-gȧr-yäk′)	186a	56°13′N	61°32′E
Bagbele, D.R.C.	237	4°21′N	29°17′E
Bagdad see Baghdād, Iraq	198	33°14′N	44°22′E
Baghdād, Iraq (bȧgh-dȧd′)(băg′dăd)	198	33°14′N	44°22′E
Bagheria, Italy (bä-gå-rē′ä)	174	38°03′N	13°32′E
Bagley, Mn., U.S. (băg′lē)	112	47°31′N	95°24′W
Bagnara, Italy (bän-yä′rä)	174	38°17′N	15°52′E
Bagnell Dam, Mo., U.S. (băg′nĕl)	121	38°13′N	92°40′W
Bagnères-de-Bigorre, Fr. (bän-yâr′dē-bē-gor′)	170	43°04′N	0°09′E
Bagnères-de-Luchon, Fr. (bän-yâr′ dē-lu chôɴ′)	170	42°46′N	0°36′E
Bagnols-sur-Ceze, Fr. (bä-nyôl′)	170	44°09′N	4°37′E
Bago, Mya.	212	17°17′N	96°29′E
Bagoé, r., Mali (bȧ-gô′å)	230	12°22′N	6°34′W
Baguio, Phil. (bä-gē-ō′)	212	16°24′N	120°36′E
Bagzane, Monts, mtn., Niger	230	18°40′N	8°40′E
Bahamas, nation, N.A. (bȧ-hā′mȧs)	129	26°15′N	76°00′W
Bahau, Malay.	197b	2°48′N	102°25′E
Bahāwalpur, Pak. (bŭ-hä′wŭl-pōōr)	199	29°29′N	71°41′E
Bahia, state, Braz.	143	11°05′S	43°00′W
Bahía, Islas de la, i., Hond. (ē′s-läs-dĕ-lä-bä-ē′ä)	128	16°15′N	86°30′W
Bahía Blanca, Arg. (bä-ē′ä blän′kä)	144	38°45′S	62°07′W
Bahía de Caráquez, Ec. (bä-e′ä dā kä-rä′kĕz)	142	0°45′S	80°29′W
Bahía Negra, Para. (bä-ē′ä nā′grä)	143	20°11′S	58°05′W
Bahi Swamp, sw., Tan.	237	6°05′S	35°10′E
Bahoruco, Sierra de, mts., Dom. Rep. (sē-ĕ′r-rä-dĕ-bä-ō-rōō′kô)	135	18°10′N	71°25′W
Bahrain, nation, Asia (bä-rān′)	198	26°15′N	51°17′E
Baḥr al Ghazāl, hist. reg., Sudan (bär ĕl ghä-zäl′)	231	7°56′N	27°15′E
Baḥrīyah, oasis, Egypt (bȧ-hȧ-rē′yä)	163	28°34′N	29°01′E
Baía dos Tigres, Ang.	236	16°36′S	11°43′E
Baia Mare, Rom. (bä′yä mä′rä)	163	47°40′N	23°35′E
Baidyabāti, India	202a	22°47′N	88°21′E
Baie-Comeau, Can.	100	49°13′N	68°10′W
Baie de Wasai, Mi., U.S. (bā dē wä-sä′ē)	117k	46°27′N	84°15′W
Baie-Saint Paul, Can. (bā′sănt-pôl′)	91	47°27′N	70°30′W
Baigou, China (bī-gō)	206	39°08′N	116°02′E
Baihe, China (bī-hŭ)	208	32°30′N	110°15′E
Bai Hu, l., China (bī-hōō)	206	31°22′N	117°38′E
Baiju, China (bī-jyōō)	206	33°04′N	120°17′E
Baikal, Lake see Baykal, Ozero, l., Russia	179	53°00′N	109°28′E
Bailén, Spain (bä-ē-lān′)	172	38°05′N	3°48′W
Băileşti, Rom. (bă-ī-lĕsh′tē)	175	44°01′N	23°21′E
Bainbridge, Ga., U.S. (bān′brĭj)	124	30°52′N	84°35′W
Bainbridge Island, i., Wa., U.S.	116a	47°39′N	122°32′W
Baipu, China (bī-pōō)	206	32°15′N	120°47′E
Baiquan, China (bī-chyuän)	208	47°22′N	126°00′E
Baird, Tx., U.S. (bârd)	122	32°22′N	99°28′W
Bairdford, Pa., U.S. (bârd′fōrd)	111e	40°37′N	79°53′W
Baird Mountains, mts., Ak., U.S.	103	67°35′N	160°10′W
Bairnsdale, Austl. (bârnz′dāl)	219	37°50′S	147°39′E
Baïse, r., Fr. (bä-ēz′)	170	43°52′N	0°23′E
Baiyang Dian, l., China (bī-yäŋ-diĕn)	206	39°00′N	115°45′E
Baiyu Shan, mts., China (bī-yōō shän)	208	37°02′N	108°30′E
Baja, Hung. (bŏ′yŏ)	169	46°11′N	18°55′E
Baja California, state, Mex. (bä-hä)	128	30°15′N	117°25′W
Baja California, pen., Mex.	89	28°00′N	113°30′W
Baja California Sur, state, Mex.	128	26°00′N	113°30′W
Bajo, Canal, can., Spain	173a	40°36′N	3°41′W
Bakal, Russia (bä′kȧl)	186a	54°57′N	58°50′E
Baker, Mt., U.S. (bā′kẽr)	115	46°21′N	104°12′W
Baker, Or., U.S.	104	44°46′N	117°52′W
Baker, i., Oc.	2	1°00′N	176°00′W
Baker, l., Can.	92	63°51′N	96°10′W
Baker, Mount, mtn., Wa., U.S.	106	48°46′N	121°52′W
Baker Creek, r., Il., U.S.	111a	41°13′N	87°47′W
Bakersfield, Ca., U.S. (bā′kẽrz-fēld)	104	35°23′N	119°00′W
Bakerstown, Pa., U.S. (bā′kẽrz-toun)	111e	40°39′N	79°56′W
Bakewell, Eng., U.K. (bāk′wĕl)	158a	53°12′N	1°40′W
Bakhchysarai, Ukr.	177	44°46′N	33°54′E
Bakhmach, Ukr. (bȧk-mäch′)	177	51°09′N	32°47′E
Bakhtarān, Iran	198	34°01′N	47°00′E
Bakhtegan, Daryācheh-ye, l., Iran	198	29°29′N	54°31′E
Bakhteyevo, Russia	186b	55°35′N	38°32′E
Bako, Eth. (bä′kō)	231	5°47′N	36°39′E
Bakony, mts., Hung. (bȧ-kōn′y′)	169	46°57′N	17°30′E
Bakoye, r., Afr. (bȧ-kô′ē)	230	12°47′N	9°35′W
Bakr Uzyak, Russia (bȧkr ōōz′yȧk)	186a	52°59′N	58°43′E
Baku (Bakı), Azer. (bȧ-kōō′)	178	40°28′N	49°45′E
Bakwanga see Mbuji-Mayi, D.R.C.	236	6°09′S	23°28′E
Balabac Island, i., Phil. (bä′lä-bäk)	212	8°00′N	116°28′E
Balabac Strait, strt., Asia	212	7°23′N	116°30′E
Ba′labakk, Leb.	197a	34°00′N	36°13′E
Balabanovo, Russia (bȧ-lȧ-bä′nô-vô)	186b	56°10′N	37°44′E
Balagansk, Russia (bä-lä-gänsk′)	184	53°58′N	103°09′E
Balaguer, Spain (bä-lä-gĕr′)	173	41°48′N	0°50′E
Balakhta, Russia (bȧ′lȧk-tȧ′)	179	55°22′N	91°43′E
Balakliia, Ukr.	177	49°28′N	36°51′E
Balakovo, Russia (bȧ′lȧ-kô′vô)	181	52°00′N	47°40′E
Balancán, Mex. (bä-läŋ-kän′)	131	17°47′N	91°32′W
Balanga, Phil. (bä-läŋ′gä)	213a	14°41′N	120°31′E
Ba Lang An, Mui, c., Viet.	209	15°18′N	109°10′E
Balashikha, Russia (bȧ-lä′shĭ-kȧ)	186b	55°48′N	37°58′E
Balashov, Russia (bȧ′lȧ-shôf)	181	51°30′N	43°00′E
Balasore, India (bä-lȧ-sōr′)	199	21°38′N	86°59′E
Balassagyarmat, Hung. (bô′lôsh-shô-dyôr′môt)	169	48°04′N	19°19′E
Balaton Lake, l., Hung. (bô′lô-tôn)	163	46°47′N	17°55′E
Balayan, Phil. (bä-lä-yän′)	213a	13°56′N	120°44′E
Balayan Bay, b., Phil.	213a	13°46′N	120°46′E
Balboa Heights, Pan. (bäl-bô′ä)	133	8°59′N	79°33′W
Balboa Mountain, mtn., Pan.	128a	9°05′N	79°44′W
Balcarce, Arg. (bäl-kär′sā)	144	37°49′S	58°17′W
Balchik, Blg.	175	43°24′N	28°13′E
Bald Eagle, Mn., U.S. (bôld ē′g′l)	117g	45°06′N	93°01′W
Bald Eagle Lake, l., Mn., U.S.	117g	45°08′N	93°03′W
Baldock Lake, l., Can.	97	56°33′N	97°57′W
Baldwin Park, Ca., U.S. (bôld′wĭn)	117a	34°05′N	117°58′W
Baldwinsville, N.Y., U.S. (bôld′wĭns-vĭl)	109	43°10′N	76°20′W
Baldy Mountain, mtn., Can.	97	51°28′N	100°44′W
Baldy Peak, mtn., Az., U.S. (bôl′dē)	106	33°55′N	109°35′W
Baldy Peak, mtn., Tx., U.S. (bôl′dē pēk)	122	30°38′N	104°11′W
Balearic Islands see Balears, Illes, is., Spain	156	39°25′N	1°28′E
Balearic Sea, sea, Spain (băl-ē-ăr′ĭk)	173	39°40′N	1°05′E
Balears, Illes, is., Spain	156	39°25′N	1°28′E
Baleine, Grande Rivière de la, r., Can.	93	55°00′N	75°30′W
Baler, Phil. (bä-lar′)	213a	15°46′N	121°33′E
Baler Bay, b., Phil.	213a	15°51′N	121°40′E
Balesin, i., Phil.	213a	14°28′N	122°10′E
Baley, Russia (bȧl-yā′)	185	51°29′N	116°12′E
Balfate, Hond. (bäl-fä′tē)	132	15°48′N	86°24′W
Balfour, S. Afr. (băl′fōr)	238c	26°41′S	28°37′E
Bali, i., Indon. (bä′lē)	212	8°00′S	115°22′E
Balıkeşir, Tur. (balĭk′ĕsĭr)	181	39°40′N	27°50′E
Balikpapan, Indon. (bä′lēk-pä′pän)	212	1°13′S	116°52′E
Balintang Channel, strt., Phil. (bā-lĭn-täng′)	212	19°50′N	121°08′E
Balkan Mountains see Stara Planina, mts., Blg.	156	42°50′N	24°45′E
Balkh, Afg. (bälk)	199	36°48′N	66°50′E
Balkhash, Lake see Balqash köli, l., Kaz.	183	45°58′N	72°15′E
Ballancourt, Fr. (bä-äɴ-kòr′)	171b	48°31′N	2°23′E
Ballarat, Austl. (băl′ȧ-răt)	219	37°37′S	144°00′E
Ballard, l., Austl. (băl′ȧrd)	220	29°15′S	120°45′E
Ballater, Scot., U.K. (bäl′ȧ-tẽr)	164	57°05′N	3°06′W
Balleny Islands, is., Ant. (băl′ĕ nē)	224	67°00′S	164°00′E
Ballina, Austl. (băl-ĭ-nä′)	222	28°50′S	153°35′E
Ballina, Ire.	164	54°06′N	9°05′W
Ballinasloe, Ire. (băl′ĭ-nȧ-slō′)	164	53°20′N	8°09′W
Ballinger, Tx., U.S. (băl′ĭn-jẽr)	122	31°45′N	99°58′W
Ballston Spa, N.Y., U.S. (bôls′tŭn spä′)	109	43°05′N	73°50′W
Balmazújváros, Hung. (bŏl′mŏz-ōō′y′vä′rôsh)	169	47°35′N	21°23′E
Balobe, D.R.C.	237	0°05′N	28°00′E
Balonne, r., Austl. (băl-ōn′)	221	27°00′S	149°10′E
Bālotra, India	202	25°56′N	72°12′E
Balqash, Kaz.	183	46°58′N	75°00′E
Balqash köli, l., Kaz.	183	45°58′N	72°15′E
Balranald, Austl. (băl′-rȧn-ăld)	222	34°42′S	143°30′E
Balsam, l., Can. (bôl′sȧm)	99	44°30′N	78°50′W
Balsas, Braz. (bäl′säs)	143	7°09′S	46°04′W
Balsas, r., Mex.	128	18°00′N	101°00′W
Balta, Ukr. (bäl′tȧ)	181	47°57′N	29°38′E
Bălţi, Mol.	181	47°47′N	27°57′E
Baltic Sea, sea, Eur. (bôl′tĭk)	156	55°20′N	16°50′E
Baltīm, Egypt (bál-tēm′)	238b	31°33′N	31°04′E
Baltimore, Md., U.S. (bôl′tĭ-mōr)	105	39°20′N	76°38′W
Baltiysk, Russia (bäl-tēysk′)	167	54°40′N	19°55′E
Baluarte, Río del, Mex. (rē′ō-dĕl-bä-lōō′r-tē)	130	23°09′N	105°42′W
Baluchistān, hist. reg., Asia (bȧ-lò-chĭ-stän′)	199	27°30′N	65°30′E
Balzac, Can. (bôl′zăk)	102e	51°10′N	114°01′W
Bama, Nig.	235	11°30′N	13°41′E
Bamako, Mali (bä-mä-kō′)	230	12°39′N	8°00′W
Bambang, Phil. (bäm-bäng′)	213a	16°24′N	121°08′E
Bambari, C.A.R. (bäm-bȧ-rē)	231	5°44′N	20°40′E
Bamberg, Ger. (bäm′bĕrgh)	161	49°53′N	10°52′E
Bamberg, S.C., U.S. (băm′bûrg)	125	33°17′N	81°04′W
Bamenda, Cam.	235	5°56′N	10°10′E
Bamingui, r., C.A.R.	235	7°35′N	19°45′E
Bampton, Eng., U.K. (băm′tŭn)	158b	51°42′N	1°33′W
Bampūr, Iran (bŭm-pōōr′)	198	27°15′N	60°22′E
Bam Yanga, Ngao, mts., Cam.	235	8°20′N	14°40′E
Banahao, Mount, mtn., Phil. (bä-nä-hä′ô)	213a	14°04′N	121°45′E
Banalia, D.R.C.	237	1°33′N	25°20′E
Banamba, Mali	234	13°33′N	7°27′W
Bananal, Braz. (bä-nä-näl′)	141a	22°42′S	44°17′W
Bananal, Ilha do, i., Braz. (ē′lä-dô-bä-nä-näl′)	143	12°09′S	50°27′W
Banās, r., India (băn-äs′)	199	25°20′N	75°20′E
Banās, Ra′s, c., Egypt	231	23°48′N	36°39′E
Banat, reg., Rom. (bä-nät′)	175	45°35′N	21°05′E
Bancroft, Can. (băn′krŏft)	91	45°05′N	77°55′W
Bancroft see Chililabombwe, Zam.	237	12°18′S	27°43′E
Bānda, India (bän′dȧ)	199	25°36′N	80°21′E
Banda, Kepulauan, is., Indon.	213	4°40′S	129°56′E
Banda, Laut (Banda Sea), sea, Indon.	213	6°05′S	127°28′E
Banda Aceh, Indon.	212	5°10′N	95°10′E
Banda Banda, Mount, mtn., Austl. (băn′dȧ băn′dȧ)	222	31°09′S	152°15′E
Bandama Blanc, r., C. Iv. (bän-dä′mä)	234	6°15′N	5°00′W
Bandar Beheshtī, Iran	198	25°18′N	60°45′E
Bandar-e ′Abbās, Iran (bän-där′ ȧb-bäs′)	198	27°04′N	56°22′E
Bandar-e Būshehr, Iran	198	28°48′N	50°53′E
Bandar-e Lengeh, Iran	198	26°44′N	54°47′E
Bandar-e Torkeman, Iran	198	37°05′N	54°08′E
Bandar Lampung, Indon.	212	5°16′S	105°06′E
Bandar Maharani, Malay. (bän-där′ mä-hä-rä′nē)	197b	2°02′N	102°34′E
Bandar Seri Begawan, Bru.	212	5°00′N	114°59′E
Bande, Spain	172	42°02′N	7°58′W
Bandeira, Pico da, mtn., Braz. (pē′kò dä bän dä′rä)	143	20°27′S	41°47′W
Bandelier National Monument, rec., N.M., U.S. (băn-dĕ-lēr′)	119	35°50′N	106°45′W
Banderas, Bahía de, b., Mex. (bä-ē′ä dē bän-dĕ′räs)	130	20°38′N	105°35′W
Bandirma, Tur. (bän-dĭr′mȧ)	163	40°25′N	27°50′E
Bandon, Or., U.S. (băn′dŭn)	114	43°06′N	124°25′W
Bāndra, India	203b	19°04′N	72°49′E
Bandundu, D.R.C.	232	3°18′S	17°20′E
Bandung, Indon.	212	7°00′S	107°22′E
Banes, Cuba (bä′näs)	135	21°00′N	75°45′W
Banff, Can. (bănf)	90	51°10′N	115°34′W
Banff, Scot., U.K.	164	57°39′N	2°37′W
Banff National Park, rec., Can.	92	51°38′N	116°22′W
Bánfield, Arg. (bá′n-fyĕ′ld)	144a	34°44′S	58°24′W
Banfora, Burkina	234	10°38′N	4°46′W
Bangalore, India (băŋ′gȧ′lôr)	199	13°03′N	77°39′E
Bangassou, C.A.R. (bäɴ-gȧ-sōō′)	231	4°47′N	22°49′E
Bangeta, Mount, mtn., Pap. N. Gui.	213	6°20′S	147°00′E
Banggai, Kepulauan, is., Indon. (bäng-gī′)	213	1°05′S	123°45′E
Banggi, Pulau, i., Malay.	212	7°12′N	117°10′E
Banghāzī, Libya	231	32°07′N	20°04′E
Bangka, i., Indon. (băŋ′kȧ)	212	2°24′S	106°55′E
Bangkalan, Indon. (bäng-kȧ-län′)	212	6°07′S	112°50′E
Bangkok, Thai.	212	13°50′N	100°29′E
Bangladesh, nation, Asia	199	24°15′N	90°00′E
Bangong Co, l., Asia (bäŋ-gôŋ tswo)	202	33°40′N	79°30′E
Bangor, Wales, U.K. (băŋ′ôr)	164	53°13′N	4°05′W
Bangor, Me., U.S. (băn′gẽr)	105	44°47′N	68°47′W

ng-sing; ŋ-baŋk; ɴ-nasalized n; nŏd; cŏmmit; ōld; ôbey; ôrder; oi-boil; fōōd; ò-as oo in foot; ou-out; s-soft; sh-dish; th-thin; pūre; ûnite; ûrn; stŭd; circŭs; ü-as in French tu; ′-indeterminate vowel.

PLACE (Pronunciation)	PAGE	LAT.	LONG.
Bangor, Mi., U.S.	108	42°20'N	86°05'W
Bangor, Pa., U.S.	109	40°55'N	75°10'W
Bangs, Mount, mtn., Az., U.S. (băngs)	119	36°45'N	113°50'W
Bangued, Phil. (bän-gād')	213a	17°36'N	120°38'E
Bangui, C.A.R. (bäɴ-gē')	231	4°22'N	18°35'E
Bangweulu, Lake, l., Zam. (băng-wē-ōō'lōō)	232	10°55'S	30°10'E
Bangweulu Swamp, sw., Zam.	237	11°25'S	30°10'E
Bani, Dom. Rep. (bä'-nē)	135	18°15'N	70°25'W
Bani, Phil. (bä'nē)	213a	16°11'N	119°51'E
Bani, r., Mali	230	13°00'N	5°30'W
Bánica, Dom. Rep. (bä'-nē-kä)	135	19°00'N	71°35'W
Banī Mazār, Egypt	200	28°29'N	30°48'E
Banister, r., Va., U.S. (băn'ĭs-tẽr)	125	36°45'N	79°17'W
Banī Suwayf, Egypt	231	29°05'N	31°06'E
Banja Luka, Bos. (bän-yä-lōō'kȧ)	163	44°45'N	17°11'E
Banjarmasin, Indon. (bän-jẽr-mä'sēn)	212	3°18'S	114°32'E
Banjin, China (bän-jyĭn)	206	32°23'N	120°14'E
Banjul, Gam.	230	13°28'N	16°39'W
Bankberg, mts., S. Afr. (bȧŋk'bûrg)	233c	32°18'S	25°15'E
Banks, Or., U.S. (băŋks)	116c	45°37'N	123°07'W
Banks, i., Austl.	221	10°10'S	143°08'E
Banks, Cape, c., Austl.	217b	34°01'S	151°17'E
Banks Island, i., Can.	89	73°00'N	123°00'W
Banks Island, i., Can.	94	53°25'N	130°10'W
Banks Islands, is., Vanuatu	221	13°38'S	168°23'E
Banks Peninsula, pen., N.Z.	223	43°45'S	172°20'E
Banks Strait, strt., Austl.	222	40°45'S	148°00'E
Bankstown, Austl.	217b	33°55'S	151°02'E
Bann, r., N. Ire., U.K. (băn)	164	54°50'N	6°29'W
Banning, Ca., U.S. (băn'ĭng)	117a	33°56'N	116°53'W
Bannockburn, Austl.	217a	38°03'S	144°11'E
Bannu, Pak.	202	33°03'N	70°39'E
Baños, Ec. (bä'-nyōs)	142	1°30'S	78°22'W
Banská Bystrica, Slvk. (bän'skä bē'strē-tzä)	161	48°46'N	19°10'E
Bansko, Blg. (bän'skō)	175	41°51'N	23°33'E
Banstead, Eng., U.K. (băn'stĕd)	158b	51°18'N	0°09'W
Banton, i., Phil. (bän-tōn')	213a	12°54'N	121°55'E
Bantry, Ire. (băn'trĭ)	164	51°39'N	9°30'W
Bantry Bay, b., Ire.	164	51°25'N	10°09'W
Banyak, Kepulauan, is., Indon.	212	2°08'N	97°15'E
Banyuwangi, Indon. (bän-jō-wän'gē)	212	8°15'S	114°15'E
Baocheng, China (bou-chŭŋ)	208	33°15'N	106°58'E
Baodi, China (bou-dē)	208	39°44'N	117°19'E
Baoding, China (bou-dĭŋ)	208	38°52'N	115°31'E
Baoji, China (bou-jyē)	208	34°10'N	106°58'E
Baoshan, China (bou-shän)	204	25°14'N	99°03'E
Baoshan, China	206	31°25'N	121°29'E
Baotou, China (bou-tō)	205	40°28'N	110°10'E
Baoying, China (bou-yĭŋ)	208	33°14'N	119°20'E
Bapsfontein, S. Afr. (băps-fŏn-tān')	233b	26°01'S	28°26'E
Ba'qūbah, Iraq	201	33°45'N	44°38'E
Baqueroncito, Col. (bä-kĕ-rŏ'n-sē-tô)	142a	3°18'N	74°40'W
Baraawe, Som.	238a	1°20'N	44°00'E
Barabinsk, Russia (bá'rá-bĭnsk)	184	55°18'N	78°00'E
Baraboo, Wi., U.S. (bâr'ȧ-bōō)	113	43°29'N	89°44'W
Baracoa, Cuba (bä-rä-kō'ä)	135	20°20'N	74°25'W
Baracoa, Cuba	135a	23°03'N	82°34'W
Baradères, Baie des, b., Haiti (bä-rä-dâr')	135	18°35'N	73°35'W
Baradero, Arg. (bä-rä-dĕ'ŏ)	141c	33°50'S	59°30'W
Barahona, Dom. Rep. (bä-rä-ō'nä)	135	18°15'N	71°10'W
Barajas de Madrid, Spain (bä-rä'häs dā mä-drēdh')	173a	40°28'N	3°35'W
Baranagar, India	202	22°38'N	88°25'E
Baranavichy, Bela. (bä'rä-nô-vē'chē)	180	53°08'N	25°59'E
Baranco, Belize (bä-räŋ'kō)	132	16°01'N	88°55'W
Baranof, i., Ak., U.S. (bä-rä'nôf)	103	56°48'N	136°08'W
Baranpauh, Indon.	197b	0°40'N	103°28'E
Barão de Melgaço, Braz. (bä-rouɴ-dĕ-mĕl-gä'sô)	143	16°12'S	55°48'W
Bārāsat, India	202a	22°42'N	88°29'E
Barataria Bay, b., La., U.S.	123	29°13'N	89°50'W
Baraya, Col. (bä-rä'yä)	142a	3°10'N	75°04'W
Barbacena, Braz. (bär-bä-sā'nȧ)	143	21°15'S	43°46'W
Barbacoas, Col. (bär-bä-kō'äs)	142	1°39'N	78°12'W
Barbacoas, Ven. (bä-bä-kô'äs)	143b	9°30'N	66°58'W
Barbados, nation, N.A. (bär-bā'dōz)	129	13°30'N	59°00'W
Barbar, Sudan	231	18°11'N	34°00'E
Barbastro, Spain (bär-bäs'trō)	173	42°05'N	0°05'E
Barbeau, Mi., U.S. (bȧr-bō')	117k	46°17'N	84°16'W
Barberton, S. Afr.	232	25°48'S	31°04'E
Barberton, Oh., U.S. (bär'bẽr-tŭn)	111d	41°01'N	81°37'W
Barbezieux, Fr. (bärb'zyû')	170	45°30'N	0°11'W
Barbosa, Col. (bär-bō'-sȧ)	142a	6°26'N	75°19'W
Barboursville, W.V., U.S. (bär'bẽrs-vĭl)	108	38°20'N	82°20'W
Barbourville, Ky., U.S.	124	36°52'N	83°58'W
Barbuda, i., Antig. (bär-bōō'dȧ)	129	17°45'N	61°15'W
Barcaldine, Austl. (bär'kôl-dĭn)	219	23°33'S	145°17'E
Barcarrota, Spain (bär-kär-rō'tä)	172	38°31'N	6°50'W
Barcellona, Italy (bä-chĕl-lō'nä)	174	38°07'N	15°15'E
Barcelona, Spain (bär-thȧ-lō'nä)	154	41°25'N	2°08'E
Barcelona, Ven. (bär-sȧ-lō'nä)	142	10°09'N	64°41'W
Barcelos, Braz. (bär-sĕ'lôs)	142	1°04'S	63°00'W
Barcelos, Port. (bär-thȧ'lōs)	172	41°34'N	8°39'W
Bardawīl, Sabkhat al, b., Egypt	197a	31°20'N	33°24'E
Bardejov, Czech Rep. (bär'dyĕ-yôf)	169	49°18'N	21°18'E
Bardsey Island, i., Wales, U.K. (bärd'sē)	164	52°45'N	4°50'W
Bardstown, Ky., U.S. (bärds'toun)	108	37°50'N	85°30'W
Bardwell, Ky., U.S. (bärd'wĕl)	124	36°51'N	88°57'W
Bareilly, India	199	28°21'N	79°25'E
Barents Sea, sea, Eur. (bä'rĕnts)	178	72°14'N	37°28'E
Barentu, Erit. (bä-rĕn'tōō)	231	15°06'N	37°39'E
Barfleur, Pointe de, c., Fr. (bȧr-flûr')	170	49°43'N	1°17'W
Barguzin, Russia (bär'gōō-zĭn)	179	53°44'N	109°28'E
Bar Harbor, Me., U.S. (bär här'bẽr)	100	44°22'N	68°13'W
Bari, Italy (bä'rē)	154	41°08'N	16°53'E
Barinas, Ven. (bä-rē'näs)	142	8°36'N	70°14'W
Baring, Cape, c., Can. (bâr'ĭng)	92	70°07'N	119°48'W
Barisan, Pegunungan, mts., Indon. (bä-rē-sän')	212	2°38'S	101°45'E
Barito, r., Indon. (bä-rē'tō)	212	2°10'S	114°38'E
Barka, r., Afr.	231	16°44'N	37°34'E
Barkley Sound, strt., Can.	94	48°53'N	125°20'W
Barkly East, S. Afr. (bärk'lē ēst)	233c	30°58'S	27°37'E
Barkly Tableland, plat., Austl. (bär'klē)	220	18°15'S	137°05'E
Barkol, China (bär-kûl)	204	43°43'N	92°50'E
Bârlad, Rom.	163	46°15'N	27°43'E
Bar-le-Duc, Fr. (bär-lē-dük')	171	48°47'N	5°05'E
Barlee, l., Austl. (bär-lē')	220	29°45'S	119°00'E
Barletta, Italy (bär-lĕt'tä)	163	41°19'N	16°20'E
Barmstedt, Ger. (bärm'shtĕt)	159c	53°47'N	9°46'E
Barnaul, Russia (bär-nä-ōl')	178	53°18'N	83°23'E
Barnesboro, Pa., U.S. (bärnz'bẽr-ō)	109	40°45'N	78°50'W
Barnesville, Ga., U.S. (bärnz'vĭl)	124	33°03'N	84°10'W
Barnesville, Mn., U.S.	112	46°38'N	96°25'W
Barnesville, Oh., U.S.	108	39°55'N	81°10'W
Barnet, Vt., U.S. (bär'nĕt)	109	44°20'N	72°00'W
Barnetby le Wold, Eng., U.K. (bär'nĕt-bĭ)	158a	53°34'N	0°26'W
Barnett Harbor, b., Bah.	134	25°40'N	79°20'W
Barnsdall, Ok., U.S. (bärnz'dôl)	121	36°38'N	96°14'W
Barnsley, Eng., U.K. (bärnz'lĭ)	158a	53°33'N	1°29'W
Barnsley, co., Eng., U.K.	158a	53°33'N	1°30'W
Barnstaple, Eng., U.K. (bärn'stā-p'l)	164	51°06'N	4°05'W
Barnwell, S.C., U.S. (bärn'wĕl)	125	33°14'N	81°23'W
Baro, Nig. (bä'rô)	230	8°37'N	6°25'E
Baroda, India (bär-rō'dä)	199	22°21'N	73°12'E
Barotse Plain, pl., Zam.	236	15°50'S	22°55'E
Barqah (Cyrenaica), hist. reg., Libya	231	31°09'N	21°45'E
Barquisimeto, Ven. (bär-kē-sē-mā'tō)	142	10°04'N	69°16'W
Barra, Braz. (bär'rä)	143	11°04'S	43°11'W
Barraba, Austl.	222	30°22'S	150°36'E
Barrackpore, India	202a	22°46'N	88°21'E
Barra do Corda, Braz. (bär'rä dō cōr-dä)	143	5°33'S	45°13'W
Barra Mansa, Braz. (bär'rä män'sä)	141a	22°35'S	44°09'W
Barrancabermeja, Col. (bär-räŋ'kä-bēr-mā'hä)	142	7°06'N	73°49'W
Barranquilla, Col. (bär-rän-kēl'yä)	142	10°57'N	75°00'W
Barras, Braz. (bȧ'r-räs)	143	4°13'S	42°14'W
Barre, Vt., U.S. (băr'ē)	109	44°15'N	72°30'W
Barreiras, Braz. (bär-rā'räs)	143	12°13'S	44°59'W
Barreiro, Port. (bär-rĕ'ē-rò)	162	38°39'N	9°05'W
Barren, r., Ky., U.S.	124	37°00'N	86°20'W
Barren, Cape, c., Austl. (băr'ĕn)	221	40°20'S	149°00'E
Barren, Nosy, is., Madag.	233	18°18'S	43°57'E
Barren River Lake, res., Ky., U.S.	124	36°45'N	86°02'W
Barretos, Braz. (bär-rā'tōs)	143	20°40'S	48°36'W
Barrhead, Can. (băr'hĕd)	90	54°08'N	114°24'W
Barrie, Can. (băr'ĭ)	91	44°25'N	79°45'W
Barrington, Can. (bă-rĕng-tŏn)	102a	45°07'N	73°35'W
Barrington, Il., U.S.	111a	42°09'N	88°08'W
Barrington, R.I., U.S.	110b	41°44'N	71°16'W
Barrington Tops, mtn., Austl.	222	32°00'S	151°25'E
Bar River, Can. (bär)	117k	46°27'N	84°02'W
Barron, Wi., U.S. (băr'ŭn)	113	45°24'N	91°51'W
Barrow, Ak., U.S. (băr'ō)	106a	71°20'N	156°00'W
Barrow, i., Austl.	220	20°50'S	115°00'E
Barrow, r., Ire. (bă-rô)	164	52°35'N	7°05'W
Barrow, Point, c., Ak., U.S.	103	71°20'N	156°00'W
Barrow Creek, Austl.	218	21°23'S	133°55'E
Barrow-in-Furness, Eng., U.K.	160	54°10'N	3°15'W
Barstow, Ca., U.S. (bär'stō)	118	34°53'N	117°03'W
Barstow, Md., U.S.	110e	38°32'N	76°37'W
Barth, Ger. (bärt)	168	54°20'N	12°43'E
Bartholomew Bayou, r., U.S. (bär-thŏl'ō-mū bī-ōō')	121	33°53'N	91°45'W
Barthurst, Can. (bär-thŭrst')	91	47°38'N	65°40'W
Bartica, Guy. (bär'tĭ-kȧ)	143	6°23'N	58°32'W
Bartın, Tur. (bär'tĭn)	163	41°35'N	32°12'E
Bartle Frere, Mount, mtn., Austl. (bärt''l frēr')	221	17°30'S	145°46'E
Bartlesville, Ok., U.S. (bär'tlz-vĭl)	121	36°44'N	95°58'W
Bartlett, Il., U.S. (bärt'lĕt)	111a	41°59'N	88°11'W
Bartlett, Tx., U.S.	123	30°48'N	97°25'W
Barton, Vt., U.S. (bär'tŭn)	109	44°45'N	72°05'W
Barton-upon-Humber, Eng., U.K. (bär'tŭn-ŭp'ŏn-hŭm'bẽr)	158a	53°41'N	0°26'W
Bartoszyce, Pol. (bär-tô-shĭ'tsȧ)	169	54°15'N	20°50'E
Bartow, Fl., U.S. (bär'tō)	125a	27°51'N	81°50'W
Barvinkove, Ukr.	177	48°55'N	36°59'E
Barwon, r., Austl. (bär'wŭn)	221	30°00'S	147°30'E
Barwon Heads, Austl.	217a	38°17'S	144°29'E
Barycz, r., Pol. (bä'rĭch)	168	51°30'N	16°38'E
Barysaw, Bela.	180	54°16'N	28°33'E
Basankusu, D.R.C. (bä-sän-kōō'sōō)	231	1°14'N	19°45'E
Basbeck, Ger. (bäs'bĕk)	159c	53°40'N	9°11'E
Basdahl, Ger. (bäs'däl)	159c	53°27'N	9°00'E
Basehor, Ks., U.S. (bās'hôr)	117f	39°08'N	94°55'W
Basel, Switz. (bä'z'l)	161	47°32'N	7°35'E
Bashee, r., S. Afr. (bă-shē')	233c	31°47'S	28°25'E
Bashi Channel, strt., Asia (bäsh'ē)	205	21°20'N	120°22'E
Bashkortostan, prov., Russia	180	54°12'N	57°15'E
Bashtanka, Ukr. (bȧsh-tän'kȧ)	177	47°32'N	32°31'E
Basilan Island, i., Phil.	212	6°37'N	122°07'E
Basildon, Eng., U.K.	165	51°35'N	0°25'E
Basilicata, hist. reg., Italy (bä-zē-lē-kä'tä)	174	40°30'N	15°55'E
Basin, Wy., U.S. (bā'sĭn)	115	44°22'N	108°02'W
Basingstoke, Eng., U.K. (bă'zĭng-stōk)	158b	51°14'N	1°06'W
Baška, Cro. (bäsh'kȧ)	174	44°58'N	14°44'E
Baskale, Tur. (bäsh-kä'lĕ)	181	38°10'N	44°00'E
Baskatong, Réservoir, res., Can.	99	46°50'N	75°50'W
Baskunchak, l., Russia	181	48°20'N	46°40'E
Basoko, D.R.C. (bȧ-sō'kō)	231	0°52'N	23°50'E
Basque Provinces, hist. reg., Spain	172	43°00'N	2°46'W
Basra *see* Al Başrah, Iraq	198	30°35'N	47°59'E
Bassano, Can. (bäs-sän'ō)	90	50°47'N	112°28'W
Bassano del Grappa, Italy	174	45°46'N	11°44'E
Bassari, Togo	234	9°15'N	0°47'E
Bassas da India, i., Reu. (bäs'säs dä ēn'dē-ȧ)	233	21°23'S	39°42'E
Basse Terre, Guad. (bäs' târ')	129	16°00'N	61°43'W
Basseterre, St. K./N.	133b	17°20'N	62°42'W
Basse Terre, i., Guad.	133b	16°10'N	62°14'W
Bassett, Va., U.S. (băs'sĕt)	125	36°45'N	81°58'W
Bass Islands, is., Oh., U.S. (băs)	108	41°40'N	82°50'W
Bass Strait, strt., Austl.	221	39°40'S	145°40'E
Basswood, l., N.A. (băs'wŏd)	113	48°10'N	91°36'W
Bästad, Swe. (bō'stät)	166	56°26'N	12°46'E
Bastia, Fr. (bäs'tē-ä)	161	42°43'N	9°27'E
Bastogne, Bel. (băs-tôn'y')	165	50°02'N	5°45'E
Bastrop, La., U.S. (băs'trŭp)	123	32°47'N	91°55'W
Bastrop, Tx., U.S.	123	30°08'N	97°18'W
Bastrop Bayou, Tx., U.S.	123a	29°07'N	95°22'W
Bata, Eq. Gui. (bä'tä)	230	1°51'N	9°45'E
Batabano, Golfo de, b., Cuba (gôl-fô-dĕ-bä-tä-bä'nô)	134	22°10'N	83°05'W
Batāla, India	202	31°54'N	75°18'E
Batam, i., Indon. (bä-täm')	197b	1°03'N	104°00'E
Batang, China (bä-täŋ)	204	30°08'N	99°00'E
Batangas, Phil. (bä-tän'gäs)	212	13°45'N	121°04'E
Batan Islands, is., Phil. (bä-tän')	212	20°58'N	122°20'E
Bátaszék, Hung. (bä'tȧ-sĕk)	169	46°07'N	18°40'E
Batavia, Il., U.S. (bȧ-tā'vĭ-ȧ)	111a	41°51'N	88°18'W
Batavia, N.Y., U.S.	109	43°00'N	78°15'W
Batavia, Oh., U.S.	111f	39°05'N	84°10'W
Bataysk, Russia (bȧ-tīsk')	181	47°08'N	39°44'E
Bătdâmbâng, Camb. (bȧt-tȧm-bäng')	212	13°14'N	103°15'E
Batesburg, S.C., U.S. (bāts'bûrg)	125	33°53'N	81°34'W
Batesville, Ar., U.S. (bāts'vĭl)	121	35°46'N	91°39'W
Batesville, In., U.S.	108	39°15'N	85°15'W
Batesville, Ms., U.S.	124	34°17'N	89°55'W
Batetska, Russia (bȧ-tĕ'tskȧ)	176	58°36'N	30°21'E
Bath, Can. (bȧth)	100	46°31'N	67°36'W
Bath, Eng., U.K.	161	51°24'N	2°20'W
Bath, Me., U.S.	100	43°54'N	69°50'W
Bath, N.Y., U.S.	109	42°25'N	77°20'W
Bath, Oh., U.S.	111d	41°11'N	81°38'W
Bathsheba, Barb.	133b	13°13'N	60°30'W
Bathurst, Austl. (băth'ŭrst)	219	33°28'S	149°30'E
Bathurst *see* Banjul, Gam.	230	13°28'N	16°39'W
Bathurst, S. Afr. (băt-hûrst)	233c	33°26'S	26°53'E
Bathurst, i., Austl.	220	11°19'S	130°13'E
Bathurst, Cape, c., Can. (bath'-ûrst)	92	70°33'N	127°55'W
Bathurst Inlet, b., Can.	92	68°10'N	108°00'W
Batia, Benin	234	10°54'N	1°29'E
Batley, Eng., U.K. (băt'lĭ)	158a	53°43'N	1°37'W
Batna, Alg. (bät'nä)	230	35°41'N	6°12'E
Baton Rouge, La., U.S. (băt'ŭn rōōzh')	105	30°28'N	91°10'W
Batticaloa, Sri L.	203	7°40'N	81°10'E
Battle, r., Can.	96	52°20'N	111°59'W
Battle Creek, Mi., U.S. (băt''l krēk')	105	42°20'N	85°15'W
Battle Ground, Wa., U.S. (băt''l ground)	116c	45°47'N	122°32'W
Battle Harbour, Can. (băt''l här'bẽr)	91	52°17'N	55°33'W
Battle Mountain, Nv., U.S.	114	40°40'N	116°56'W
Battonya, Hung. (bät-tô'nyä)	169	46°17'N	21°00'E
Batu, Kepulauan, is., Indon. (bä'tōō)	212	0°10'S	98°00'E
Batumi, Geor. (bŭ-tōō'mē)	178	41°40'N	41°30'E
Batu Pahat, Malay.	212	1°51'N	102°56'E
Batupanjang, Indon.	197b	1°42'N	101°35'E
Bauang, Phil. (bä'wäng)	213a	16°31'N	120°19'E
Bauchi, Nig. (bȧ-ōō'chē)	230	10°19'N	9°50'E
Bauld, Cape, c., Can.	93a	51°38'N	55°25'W
Bāuria, India	202a	22°29'N	88°08'E
Bauru, Braz. (bou-rōō')	143	22°21'S	48°57'W
Bauska, Lat. (bou'skȧ)	167	56°24'N	24°12'E
Bauta, Cuba (bȧ'ōō-tä)	135a	22°59'N	82°33'W
Bautzen, Ger. (bout'sĕn)	161	51°11'N	14°27'E
Bavaria *see* Bayern, hist. reg., Ger.	168	49°00'N	11°16'E
Baw Baw, Mount, mtn., Austl.	222	37°50'S	146°17'E
Bawean, Pulau, i., Indon. (bá'vē-än)	212	5°50'S	112°40'E
Bawtry, Eng., U.K. (bôtrĭ)	158a	53°26'N	1°01'W
Baxley, Ga., U.S. (băks'lĭ)	125	31°47'N	82°22'W
Baxter, Austl.	217a	38°12'S	145°10'E
Baxter Springs, Ks., U.S. (băks'tẽr sprĭngs')	121	37°01'N	94°44'W
Bay, Laguna de, l., Phil. (lä-gōō'nä dä bä'ē)	213a	14°24'N	121°13'E
Bayaguana, Dom. Rep. (bä-yä-gwä'nä)	135	18°45'N	69°40'W
Bay al Kabīr, Wadi, val., Libya	162	29°52'N	14°28'E
Bayambang, Phil. (bä-yäm-bäng')	213a	15°50'N	120°26'E
Bayamo, Cuba (bä-yä'mō)	134	20°25'N	76°35'W
Bayamón, P.R.	129b	18°27'N	66°13'W
Bayan, China (bä-yän)	208	46°00'N	127°20'E
Bayanaūyl, Kaz.	183	50°43'N	75°37'E
Bayard, Ne., U.S. (bā'ẽrd)	112	41°45'N	103°20'W

ăt; finăl; rāte; senāte; ärm; ȧsk; sofȧ; fâre; ch-choose; dh-as th in other; bē; ēvent; bĕt; recĕnt; cratẽr; g-gō; gh-guttural g; bĭt; ĭ-short neutral; rīde; ĸ-guttural k as ch in German ich;

PRONOUNCING INDEX

Bayard – Bengamisa 271

PLACE (Pronunciation)	PAGE	LAT.	LONG.
Bayard, N.M., U.S.	119	32°45'N	108°07'W
Bayard, W.V., U.S.	109	39°15'N	79°20'W
Bayburt, Tur. (bä'ĭ-bòrt)	181	40°15'N	40°10'E
Bay City, Mi., U.S. (bā)	105	43°35'N	83°55'W
Bay City, Tx., U.S.	123	28°59'N	95°58'W
Baydaratskaya Guba, b., Russia	180	69°20'N	66°10'E
Bay de Verde, Can.	101	48°05'N	52°54'W
Baydhabo (Baidoa), Som.	238a	3°19'N	44°20'E
Baydrag, r., Mong.	204	46°09'N	98°52'E
Bayern, state, Ger.	159d	48°05'N	11°30'E
Bayern (Bavaria), hist. reg., Ger. (bī'ērn) (bá-vâ-rĭ-à)	168	49°00'N	11°16'E
Bayeux, Fr. (bá-yû')	161	49°19'N	0°41'W
Bayfield, Wi., U.S. (bā'fēld)	113	46°48'N	90°51'W
Baykal, Ozero (Lake Baikal), l., Russia	179	53°00'N	109°28'E
Baykal'skiy Khrebet, mts., Russia	179	53°30'N	107°30'E
Baykit, Russia (bī-kēt')	179	61°43'N	96°39'E
Baymak, Russia (bäy'mäk)	186a	52°35'N	58°21'E
Bay Mills, Mi., U.S. (bā mĭlls)	117k	46°27'N	84°36'W
Bay Mills Indian Reservation, I.R., Mi., U.S.	113	46°19'N	85°03'W
Bay Minette, Al., U.S. (bā'mĭn-ĕt')	124	30°52'N	87°44'W
Bayombong, Phil. (bä-yôm-bŏng')	213a	16°28'N	121°09'E
Bayonne, Fr. (bá-yôn')	154	43°28'N	1°30'W
Bayonne, N.J., U.S. (bā-yōn')	110a	40°40'N	74°07'W
Bayou Bodcau Reservoir, res., La., U.S. (bī'yōō bŏd'kō)	107	32°49'N	93°22'W
Bayport, Mn., U.S. (bā'pōrt)	117g	45°02'N	92°46'W
Bayqongyr, Kaz.	183	47°46'N	66°11'E
Bayramiç, Tur.	175	39°48'N	26°35'E
Bayreuth, Ger. (bī-roit')	168	49°56'N	11°35'E
Bay Roberts, Can. (bā rŏb'ērts)	101	47°36'N	53°16'W
Bays, Lake of, l., Can. (bās)	99	45°15'N	79°00'W
Bay Saint Louis, Ms., U.S. (bā' sânt lōō'ĭs)	124	30°19'N	89°20'W
Bay Shore, N.Y., U.S. (bā' shôr)	110a	40°44'N	73°15'W
Bayt Lahm, W.B. (bĕth'lē-hĕm)	197a	31°42'N	35°13'E
Baytown, Tx., U.S. (bā'town)	123a	29°44'N	95°01'W
Bayview, Al., U.S. (bā'vū)	110h	33°34'N	86°59'W
Bayview, Wa., U.S.	116a	48°29'N	122°28'W
Bay Village, Oh., U.S. (bā)	111d	41°29'N	81°56'W
Baza, Spain (bä'thä)	162	37°29'N	2°46'W
Baza, Sierra de, mts., Spain	172	37°19'N	2°48'W
Bazar-Dyuzi, mtn., Azer. (bä'zär-dyōōz'ĕ)	181	41°20'N	47°40'E
Bazaruto, Ilha do, i., Moz. (bä-zä-rōō'tō)	232	21°42'S	36°10'E
Bazièges, Fr.	170	43°25'N	1°41'E
Be, Nosy, i., Madag.	233	13°14'S	47°28'E
Beach, N.D., U.S. (bēch)	112	46°55'N	104°00'W
Beachy Head, c., Eng., U.K. (bēchē hĕd)	165	50°40'N	0°25'E
Beacon, N.Y., U.S. (bē'kŭn)	109	41°30'N	73°55'W
Beaconsfield, Can. (bē'kŭnz-fēld)	102a	45°26'N	73°51'W
Beals Creek, r., Tx., U.S. (bēls)	122	32°10'N	101°14'W
Bear, r., Ut., U.S.	117b	41°28'N	112°10'W
Bear, r., U.S.	115	42°17'N	111°42'W
Bear Brook, r., Can.	102c	45°24'N	75°15'W
Bear Creek, Mt., U.S. (bâr krēk)	115	45°11'N	109°07'W
Bear Creek, r., Al., U.S. (bâr)	124	34°27'N	88°00'W
Bear Creek, r., Tx., U.S.	117c	32°56'N	97°09'W
Beardstown, Il., U.S. (bērds'toun)	121	40°01'N	90°26'W
Bearfort Mountain, mtn., N.J., U.S. (bē'fōrt)	110a	41°08'N	74°23'W
Bearhead Mountain, mtn., Wa., U.S. (bâr'hĕd)	116a	47°01'N	121°49'W
Bear Lake, l., Can.	97	55°08'N	96°00'W
Bear Lake, l., Id., U.S.	115	41°56'N	111°10'W
Bear River Range, mts., U.S.	115	41°50'N	111°30'W
Beas de Segura, Spain (bā'äs dā sä-gōō'rä)	172	38°16'N	2°53'W
Beata, i., Dom. Rep. (bĕ-ä'tä)	135	17°40'N	71°40'W
Beata, Cabo, c., Dom. Rep. (kä'bô-bĕ-ä'tä)	135	17°40'N	71°20'W
Beatrice, Ne., U.S. (bē'*à*-trĭs)	104	40°16'N	96°45'W
Beatty, Nv., U.S. (bēt'ê)	118	36°58'N	116°48'W
Beattyville, Ky., U.S. (bēt'ē-vĭl)	108	37°35'N	83°40'W
Beaucaire, Fr. (bō-kâr')	170	43°49'N	4°37'E
Beaucourt, Fr. (bō-kōōr')	171	47°30'N	6°54'E
Beaufort, N.C., U.S. (bō'frt)	125	34°43'N	76°40'W
Beaufort, S.C., U.S.	125	32°25'N	80°40'W
Beaufort Sea, sea, N.A.	103	70°30'N	138°40'W
Beaufort West, S. Afr.	232	32°20'S	22°45'E
Beauharnois, Can. (bō-är-nwä')	99	45°23'N	73°52'W
Beaumont, Can.	102b	46°50'N	71°01'W
Beaumont, Can.	102g	53°22'N	113°18'W
Beaumont, Ca., U.S. (bō'mŏnt)	117a	33°57'N	116°57'W
Beaumont, Tx., U.S.	105	30°05'N	94°06'W
Beaune, Fr. (bōn)	170	47°02'N	4°49'E
Beauport, Can. (bō-pôr')	102b	46°52'N	71°11'W
Beauséjour, Can.	90	50°04'N	96°33'W
Beauvais, Fr. (bō-vĕ')	170	49°25'N	2°05'E
Beaver, Ok., U.S. (bē'vēr)	120	36°46'N	100°31'W
Beaver, Pa., U.S.	111e	40°42'N	80°18'W
Beaver, Ut., U.S.	119	38°15'N	112°40'W
Beaver, i., Mi., U.S.	108	45°40'N	85°30'W
Beaver, r., Can.	92	54°20'N	111°10'W
Beaver City, Ne., U.S.	120	40°08'N	99°52'W
Beaver Creek, r., Co., U.S.	120	39°42'N	103°37'W
Beaver Creek, r., Ks., U.S.	120	39°44'N	101°05'W
Beaver Creek, r., Mt., U.S.	112	46°45'N	104°18'W
Beaver Creek, r., Wy., U.S.	112	43°46'N	104°25'W
Beaver Dam, Wi., U.S.	113	43°29'N	88°50'W
Beaverhead, r., Mt., U.S.	115	45°25'N	112°35'W
Beaverhead Mountains, mts., Mt., U.S. (bē'vēr-hĕd)	115	44°33'N	112°59'W
Beaver Indian Reservation, I.R., Mi., U.S.	108	45°40'N	85°30'W
Beaverton, Or., U.S. (bē'vēr-tŭn)	116c	45°29'N	122°49'W
Bebington, Eng., U.K. (bē'bĭng-tŭn)	158a	53°20'N	2°59'W
Bečej, Yugo. (bĕ'chā)	175	45°36'N	20°03'E
Béchar, Alg.	230	31°39'N	2°14'W
Becharof, l., Ak., U.S. (bĕk-á-rôf)	103	57°58'N	156°58'W
Becher Bay, b., Can. (bēch'ēr)	116a	48°18'N	123°37'W
Beckley, W.V., U.S. (bĕk'lĭ)	108	37°40'N	81°15'W
Bédarieux, Fr. (bā-dá-ryû')	170	43°36'N	3°11'E
Beddington Creek, r., Can. (bĕd'ĕng tŭn)	102e	51°14'N	114°13'W
Bedford, Can. (bĕd'fērd)	99	45°10'N	73°00'W
Bedford, S. Afr.	233c	32°43'S	26°19'E
Bedford, Eng., U.K.	161	52°10'N	0°25'W
Bedford, Ia., U.S.	113	40°40'N	94°41'W
Bedford, In., U.S.	108	38°50'N	86°30'W
Bedford, Ma., U.S.	101a	42°30'N	71°17'W
Bedford, N.Y., U.S.	110a	41°12'N	73°38'W
Bedford, Oh., U.S.	111d	41°23'N	81°32'W
Bedford, Pa., U.S.	109	40°05'N	78°20'W
Bedford, Va., U.S.	125	37°19'N	79°27'W
Bedford Hills, N.Y., U.S.	110a	41°14'N	73°41'W
Beebe, Ar., U.S. (bē'bē)	121	35°04'N	91°54'W
Beecher, Il., U.S. (bē'chûr)	111a	41°20'N	87°38'W
Beechey Head, c., Can. (bē'chĭ hĕd)	116a	48°19'N	123°40'W
Beech Grove, In., U.S. (bēch grōv)	111g	39°43'N	86°05'W
Beecroft Head, c., Austl. (bē'krŭft)	222	35°03'S	151°15'E
Beelitz, Ger. (bĕ'lētz)	159b	52°14'N	12°59'E
Be'er Sheva', Isr. (bēr-shĕ'bá)	197a	31°15'N	34°48'E
Be'er Sheva', r., Isr.	197a	31°23'N	34°30'E
Beestekraal, S. Afr.	238c	25°22'S	27°34'E
Beeston, Eng., U.K. (bēs't'n)	158a	52°55'N	1°11'W
Beetz, r., Ger. (bĕtz)	159b	52°28'N	12°37'E
Beeville, Tx., U.S. (bē'vĭl)	123	28°24'N	97°44'W
Bega, Austl. (bā'g*à*)	219	36°50'S	149°49'E
Beggs, Ok., U.S. (bĕgz)	121	35°46'N	96°06'W
Bègles, Fr. (bĕ'gl')	170	44°47'N	0°34'W
Begoro, Ghana	234	6°23'N	0°23'W
Behala, India	202a	22°31'N	88°19'E
Behbehān, Iran	201	30°35'N	50°14'E
Behm Canal, can., Ak., U.S.	94	55°41'N	131°35'W
Bei, r., China (bā)	207a	22°54'N	113°08'E
Bei'an, China (bā-än)	208	48°05'N	126°26'E
Beicai, China (bā-tsī)	207b	31°12'N	121°33'E
Beifei, r., China (bā-fā)	206	33°14'N	117°03'E
Beihai, China (bā-hī)	204	21°30'N	109°10'E
Beihuangcheng Dao, i., China (bā-hŭäŋ-chŭŋ dou)	206	38°23'N	120°55'E
Beijing, China	205	39°55'N	116°23'E
Beijing Shi, prov., China (bā-jyĭŋ shr)	208	40°07'N	116°00'E
Beira, Moz. (bā'r*à*)	232	19°45'N	34°58'E
Beira, hist. reg., Port. (bĕ'y-rä)	172	40°38'N	8°00'W
Beirut, Leb. (bā-rōōt')	198	33°53'N	35°30'E
Beja, Port. (bā'zhä)	162	38°03'N	7°53'W
Béja, Tun.	162	36°52'N	9°20'E
Bejaïa (Bougie), Alg.	230	36°46'N	5°00'E
Bejar, Spain	172	40°25'N	5°43'W
Bejestān, Iran	198	34°30'N	58°22'E
Bejucal, Cuba (bā-hōō-käl')	134	22°56'N	82°23'W
Bejuco, Pan. (bĕ-κōō'kō)	133	8°37'N	79°54'W
Békés, Hung. (bā'kāsh)	169	46°45'N	21°08'E
Békéscsaba, Hung. (bā'kāsh-chô'bô)	163	46°39'N	21°06'E
Beketova, Russia (bĕkĕ-to'vá)	185	53°23'N	125°21'E
Bela Crkva, Yugo. (bĕ'lä tsĕrk'vä)	175	44°53'N	21°25'E
Belalcázar, Spain (bāl-á-kä'thär)	172	38°35'N	5°12'W
Belarus, nation, Eur.	178	53°30'N	25°33'E
Belau *see* Palau, nation, Oc.	3	7°15'N	134°30'E
Bela Vista de Goiás, Braz.	143	16°57'S	48°47'W
Belawan, Indon. (bå-lä'wán)	212	3°43'N	98°43'E
Belaya, r., Russia (byĕ'lī-yá)	181	52°30'N	56°15'E
Belcher Islands, is., Can. (bĕl'chĕr)	93	56°20'N	80°40'W
Belding, Mi., U.S. (bĕl'dĭng)	108	43°05'N	85°25'W
Belebey, Russia (byĕ'lĕ-bā'ĭ)	180	54°00'N	54°10'E
Belém, Braz. (bå-lĕn')	143	1°18'S	48°27'W
Belén, Para. (bā-lān')	144	23°30'S	57°09'W
Belen, N.M., U.S. (bĕ-lån')	119	34°40'N	106°45'W
Bélep, Îles, is., N. Cal.	221	19°30'S	164°00'E
Belëv, Russia (byĕl'yĕf)	180	53°49'N	36°06'E
Belfair, Wa., U.S. (bĕl'far)	116a	47°27'N	122°50'W
Belfast, N. Ire., U.K.	154	54°36'N	5°45'W
Belfast, Me., U.S. (bĕl'fast)	100	44°25'N	69°01'W
Belfast, Lough, b., N. Ire., U.K. (lŏĸ bĕl'fâst)	164	54°45'N	6°00'W
Belford Roxo, Braz.	144b	22°46'S	43°24'W
Belfort, Fr. (bā-fôr')	161	47°40'N	7°50'E
Belgaum, India	199	15°57'N	74°32'E
Belgium, nation, Eur. (bĕl'jĭ-*ŭ*m)	154	51°00'N	2°52'E
Belgorod, Russia (byĕl'gŭ-r*u*t)	181	50°36'N	36°32'E
Belgorod, prov., Russia	177	50°40'N	36°42'E
Belgrade (Beograd), Yugo.	154	44°48'N	20°32'E
Belhaven, N.C., U.S. (bĕl'hā-v*ĕ*n)	125	35°33'N	76°37'W
Belington, W.V., U.S. (bĕl'ĭng-t*ŭ*n)	109	39°00'N	79°55'W
Belitung, i., Indon.	212	3°30'S	107°30'E
Belize, nation, N.A.	128	17°00'N	88°40'W
Belize, r., Belize	132a	17°16'N	88°56'W
Belize City, Belize (bĕ-lēz')	128	17°31'N	88°10'W
Bel'kovo, Russia (byĕl'kô-vô)	186b	56°15'N	38°49'E
Bel'kovskiy, i., Russia (byĕl-kôf'skĭ)	185	75°45'N	137°00'E
Bell, i., Can. (bĕl)	101	50°45'N	55°35'W
Bell, r., Can.	99	49°25'N	77°15'W
Bella Bella, Can.	94	52°10'N	128°07'W
Bella Coola, Can.	94	52°22'N	126°46'W
Bellaire, Oh., U.S. (bĕl-âr')	108	40°00'N	80°45'W
Bellaire, Tx., U.S.	123a	29°43'N	95°28'W
Bellary, India (bĕl-lä'rē)	199	15°15'N	76°56'E
Bella Union, Ur. (bĕ'l-yá-ōō-nyô'n)	144	30°18'S	57°26'W
Bella Vista, Arg. (bā'lyá vēs'tá)	144	27°07'S	65°14'W
Bella Vista, Arg.	144	28°35'S	58°53'W
Bella Vista, Arg.	144a	34°35'S	58°41'W
Bella Vista, Para.	143	22°16'S	56°14'W
Belle-Anse, Haiti	135	18°15'N	72°00'W
Belle Bay, b., Can. (bĕl)	101	47°35'N	55°15'W
Belle Chasse, La., U.S. (bĕl shäs')	110d	29°52'N	90°00'W
Bellefontaine, Oh., U.S. (bel-fŏn'tån)	108	40°25'N	83°50'W
Bellefontaine Neighbors, Mo., U.S.	117e	38°46'N	90°13'W
Belle Fourche, S.D., U.S. (bĕl' fōōrsh')	112	44°28'N	103°50'W
Belle Fourche, r., Wy., U.S.	112	44°29'N	104°40'W
Belle Fourche Reservoir, res., S.D., U.S.	112	44°51'N	103°44'W
Bellegarde, Fr. (bĕl-gärd')	171	46°06'N	5°50'E
Belle Glade, Fl., U.S. (bĕl glād)	125a	26°39'N	80°37'W
Belle-Île, i., Fr. (bĕlēl')	161	47°15'N	3°30'W
Belle Isle, Strait of, strt., Can.	93	51°35'N	56°30'W
Belle Mead, N.J., U.S. (bĕl mēd)	110a	40°28'N	74°40'W
Belleoram, Can.	101	47°31'N	55°25'W
Belle Plaine, Ia., U.S. (bĕl plān')	113	41°52'N	92°19'W
Belle Vernon, Pa., U.S. (bĕl vûr'n*ŭ*n)	111e	40°08'N	79°52'W
Belleville, Can. (bĕl'vĭl)	99	44°15'N	77°25'W
Belleville, Il., U.S.	117e	38°31'N	89°59'W
Belleville, Ks., U.S.	121	39°49'N	97°37'W
Belleville, Mi., U.S.	111b	42°12'N	83°29'W
Belleville, N.J., U.S.	110a	40°47'N	74°09'W
Bellevue, Ia., U.S. (bĕl'vū)	113	42°14'N	90°26'W
Bellevue, Ky., U.S.	111f	39°06'N	84°29'W
Bellevue, Mi., U.S.	108	42°30'N	85°00'W
Bellevue, Oh., U.S.	108	41°15'N	82°45'W
Bellevue, Pa., U.S.	111e	40°30'N	80°04'W
Bellevue, Wa., U.S.	116a	47°37'N	122°12'W
Belley, Fr. (bĕ-lē')	171	45°46'N	5°41'E
Bellflower, Ca., U.S. (bĕl-flou'ēr)	117a	33°53'N	118°08'W
Bell Gardens, Ca., U.S.	117a	33°59'N	118°11'W
Bellingham, Ma., U.S. (bĕl'ĭng-hăm)	101a	42°05'N	71°28'W
Bellingham, Wa., U.S.	104	48°46'N	122°29'W
Bellingham Bay, b., Wa., U.S.	116d	48°44'N	122°34'W
Bellingshausen Sea, sea, Ant. (bĕl'ĭngz houz'n)	224	72°00'S	80°30'W
Bellinzona, Switz. (bĕl-ĭn-tsō'nä)	168	46°10'N	9°09'E
Bellmore, N.Y., U.S. (bĕl-mōr)	110a	40°40'N	73°31'W
Bello, Col. (bĕ'l-yô)	142	6°20'N	75°33'W
Bellow Falls, Vt., U.S. (bĕl'ōz fôls)	109	43°10'N	72°30'W
Bellpat, Pak.	202	29°08'N	68°00'E
Bell Peninsula, pen., Can.	93	63°50'N	81°16'W
Bells Corners, Can.	102c	45°20'N	75°49'W
Bells Mountain, mtn., Wa., U.S. (bĕls)	116c	45°50'N	122°21'W
Belluno, Italy (bĕl-lōō'nō)	174	46°08'N	12°14'E
Bell Ville, Arg. (bĕl vēl')	144	32°33'S	62°36'W
Bellville, S. Afr.	232a	33°54'S	18°38'E
Bellville, Tx., U.S. (bĕl'vĭl)	123	29°57'N	96°15'W
Bélmez, Spain (bĕl'mĕth)	172	38°17'N	5°17'W
Belmond, Ia., U.S. (bĕl'mŏnd)	113	42°49'N	93°37'W
Belmont, Ca., U.S.	116b	37°34'N	122°18'W
Belmonte, Braz. (bĕl-mōn'tå)	143	15°58'S	38°47'W
Belmopan, Belize	128	17°15'N	88°47'W
Belogorsk, Russia	179	51°09'N	128°32'E
Belo Horizonte, Braz. (bĕ'lôre-sô'n-tĕ)	143	19°54'S	43°56'W
Beloit, Ks., U.S. (bē-loit')	120	39°26'N	98°06'W
Beloit, Wi., U.S.	105	42°31'N	89°04'W
Belomorsk, Russia (byĕl-ô-môrsk')	180	64°30'N	34°42'E
Beloretsk, Russia (byĕ'lō-rĕtsk)	180	53°58'N	58°25'E
Belosarayskaya, Kosa, c., Ukr.	177	46°43'N	37°18'E
Belovo, Russia (bvĕ'l*ŭ*-vû)	184	54°25'N	86°18'E
Beloye, l., Russia	180	60°10'N	38°05'E
Belozersk, Russia (byĕ-l*ŭ*-zyôrsk')	180	60°00'N	38°00'E
Belper, Eng., U.K. (bĕl'pĕr)	158a	53°01'N	1°28'W
Belt, Mt., U.S. (bĕlt)	115	47°11'N	110°58'W
Belt Creek, r., Mt., U.S.	115	47°19'N	110°58'W
Belton, Tx., U.S. (bĕl't*ŭ*n)	123	31°04'N	97°27'W
Belton Lake, l., Tx., U.S.	123	31°15'N	97°35'W
Beltsville, Md., U.S. (belts-vĭl)	110e	39°03'N	76°56'W
Belukha, Mount, mtn., Asia	178	49°47'N	86°23'E
Belvidere, Il., U.S. (bĕl-vē-dēr')	113	42°14'N	88°52'W
Belvidere, N.J., U.S.	109	40°50'N	75°05'W
Belyando, r., Austl. (bĕl-yän'dō)	221	22°09'S	146°48'E
Belyanka, Russia (byĕl'yán-ká)	186a	56°04'N	59°16'E
Belyy, Russia (byĕ'lē)	180	55°52'N	32°58'E
Belyy, i., Russia	178	73°19'N	72°00'E
Belyye Stolby, Russia (byĕ'lĭ-ye stôl'bĭ)	186b	55°20'N	37°52'E
Belzig, Ger. (bĕl'tsēg)	159b	52°08'N	12°35'E
Belzoni, Ms., U.S. (bĕl-zō'nē)	124	33°09'N	90°30'W
Bembe, Ang. (bĕn'bĕ)	232	7°00'S	14°20'E
Bembézar, r., Spain (bĕm-bā-thär')	172	38°00'N	5°18'W
Bemidji, Mn., U.S. (bē-mĭj'ĭ)	113	47°28'N	94°54'W
Bena Dibele, D.R.C. (bĕn'á dē-bĕ'lē)	232	4°00'S	22°49'E
Benalla, Austl. (bĕn-ăl'á)	219	36°30'S	146°00'E
Benares *see* Vārānasi, India	199	25°25'N	83°00'E
Benavente, Spain (bā-nä-vĕn'tä)	162	42°01'N	5°43'W
Benbrook, Tx., U.S. (bĕn'brōōk)	117c	32°41'N	97°27'W
Benbrook Reservoir, res., Tx., U.S.	117c	32°35'N	97°30'W
Bend, Or., U.S. (bĕnd)	104	44°04'N	121°17'W
Bendeleben, Mount, mtn., Ak., U.S. (bĕn-dĕl-bĕn)	103	65°18'N	163°45'W
Bender Beyla, Som.	238a	9°40'N	50°45'E
Bendigo, Austl. (bĕn'dĭ-gō)	219	36°39'S	144°20'E
Benedict, Md., U.S. (bĕnē'dĭct)	110e	38°31'N	76°41'W
Benešov, Czech Rep. (bĕn'ĕ-shôf)	168	49°48'N	14°40'E
Benevento, Italy (bā-nā-vĕn'tō)	162	41°08'N	14°46'E
Bengal, Bay of, b., Asia (bĕn-gôl')	196	17°30'N	87°00'E
Bengamisa, D.R.C.	237	0°57'N	25°10'E

272 Bengbu – Bijou Creek

PRONOUNCING INDEX

PLACE (Pronunciation)	PAGE	LAT.	LONG.
Bengbu, China (bŭŋ-bōō)	205	32°52'N	117°22'E
Benghazi see Banghāzī, Libya	230	32°07'N	20°04'E
Bengkalis, Indon. (bĕng-kä'lĭs)	212	1°29'N	102°06'E
Bengkulu, Indon.	212	3°46'S	102°18'E
Benguela, Ang. (bĕn-gĕl'á)	232	12°35'S	13°25'E
Beni, r., Bol. (bā'nē)	142	13°41'S	67°30'W
Béni-Abbas, Alg. (bā'nē ä-bĕs')	230	30°11'N	2°13'W
Benicia, Ca., U.S. (bē-nĭsh'ĭ-á)	116b	38°03'N	122°09'W
Benin, nation, Afr.	230	8°00'N	2°00'E
Benin, r., Nig. (bĕn-ēn')	235	5°55'N	5°15'E
Benin, Bight of, b., Afr.	230	5°30'N	3°00'E
Benin City, Nig.	230	6°19'N	5°41'E
Beni Saf, Alg. (bā'nē säf')	230	35°23'N	1°20'W
Benito, r., Eq. Gui.	236	1°35'N	10°45'E
Benkelman, Ne., U.S. (bĕn-kĕl-mán)	120	40°05'N	101°35'W
Benkovac, Cro. (bĕn'kō-váts)	174	44°02'N	15°41'E
Bennettsville, S.C., U.S. (bĕn'ĕts vĭl)	125	34°35'N	79°41'W
Bennington, Vt., U.S. (bĕn'ĭng-tŭn)	109	42°55'N	73°15'W
Benns Church, Va., U.S. (bĕnz' chûrch')	110g	36°47'N	76°35'W
Benoni, S. Afr. (bĕ-nō'nī)	232	26°11'S	28°19'E
Benoy, Chad	235	8°59'N	16°19'E
Benque Viejo, Belize (bĕn-kĕ bīĕ'hō)	132a	17°07'N	89°07'W
Bensberg, Ger.	171c	50°58'N	7°09'E
Bensenville, Il., U.S. (bĕn'sĕn-vĭl)	111a	41°57'N	87°56'W
Bensheim, Ger. (bĕns-hīm)	168	49°42'N	8°38'E
Benson, Az., U.S. (bĕn-sŭn)	119	32°00'N	110°20'W
Benson, Mn., U.S.	112	45°18'N	95°36'W
Bentiaba, Ang.	236	14°15'S	12°21'E
Bentleyville, Pa., U.S. (bent'lē vĭl)	111e	40°07'N	80°01'W
Benton, Can.	100	45°59'N	67°36'W
Benton, Ar., U.S. (bĕn'tŭn)	121	34°34'N	92°34'W
Benton, Ca., U.S.	118	37°44'N	118°22'W
Benton, Il., U.S.	108	38°00'N	88°55'W
Benton Harbor, Mi., U.S. (bĕn'tŭn här'bĕr)	108	42°05'N	86°30'W
Bentonville, Ar., U.S. (bĕn'tŭn-vĭl)	121	36°22'N	94°11'W
Benue, r., Afr. (bā'nōō-å)	230	8°00'N	8°00'E
Benut, r., Malay.	197b	1°43'N	103°20'E
Benwood, W.V., U.S. (bĕn-wood)	108	39°55'N	80°45'W
Benxi, China (bŭn-shyē)	208	41°25'N	123°50'E
Beograd see Belgrade, Yugo.	154	44°48'N	20°32'E
Beppu, Japan (bĕ'pōō)	211	33°16'N	131°30'E
Bequia Island, i., St. Vin. (bĕk-ē'ä)	133b	13°00'N	61°08'W
Berakit, Tanjung, c., Indon.	197b	1°16'N	104°44'E
Berat, Alb. (bĕ-rät')	175	40°43'N	19°59'E
Berau, Teluk, b., Indon.	213	2°22'S	131°40'E
Berazategui, Arg. (bĕ-rä-zä'tĕ-gē)	144a	34°46'S	58°14'W
Berbera, Som. (bûr'bûr-á)	238a	10°25'N	45°05'E
Berbérati, C.A.R.	235	4°16'N	15°47'E
Berck, Fr. (bĕrk)	170	50°26'N	1°36'E
Berdians'k, Ukr.	181	46°45'N	36°47'E
Berdians'ka kosa, c., Ukr.	177	46°38'N	36°42'E
Berdyaush, Russia (bĕr'dyå ûsh)	186a	55°10'N	59°12'E
Berdychiv, Ukr.	178	49°53'N	28°32'E
Berea, Ky., U.S. (bē-rē'á)	124	37°30'N	84°19'W
Berea, Oh., U.S.	111d	41°22'N	81°51'W
Berehove, Ukr.	169	48°13'N	22°40'E
Bereku, Tan.	237	4°27'S	35°44'E
Berens, r., Can. (bĕr'ĕnz)	97	52°15'N	96°30'W
Berens Island, i., Can.	97	52°18'N	97°40'W
Berens River, Can.	90	52°22'N	97°02'W
Beresford, S.D., U.S. (bĕr'ĕs-fĕrd)	112	43°05'N	96°46'W
Berettyóújfalu, Hung. (bĕ'rĕt-tyō-ōō'y'fō-lōō)	169	47°14'N	21°33'E
Berezhany, Ukr. (bĕr-yĕ'zhá-nĕ)	169	49°25'N	24°58'E
Berezivka, Ukr.	177	47°12'N	30°56'E
Berezna, Ukr. (bĕr-yôz'ná)	177	51°32'N	31°47'E
Bereznehuvate, Ukr.	177	47°19'N	32°58'E
Berezniki, Russia (bĕr-yôz'nyē-kē)	180	59°25'N	56°46'E
Berëzovka, Russia	186a	57°35'N	57°19'E
Berëzovo, Russia (bĭr-yô'zē-vû)	178	64°10'N	65°10'E
Berëzovskiy, Russia (bĕr-yô'zôf-skĭ)	186a	56°54'N	60°47'E
Berga, Spain (bĕr'gä)	173	42°05'N	1°52'E
Bergama, Tur. (bĕr'gä-mä)	198	39°08'N	27°09'E
Bergamo, Italy (bĕr'gä-mō)	162	45°43'N	9°41'E
Bergantin, Ven. (bĕr-gän-tē'n)	143b	10°04'N	64°23'W
Bergara, Spain	172	43°08'N	2°23'W
Bergedorf, Ger. (bĕr'gĕ-dôrf)	159c	53°29'N	10°12'E
Bergen, Ger. (bĕr'gĕn)	168	54°26'N	13°26'E
Bergen, Nor.	154	60°24'N	5°20'E
Bergenfield, N.J., U.S.	110a	40°55'N	73°59'W
Bergen op Zoom, Neth.	165	51°29'N	4°16'E
Bergerac, Fr. (bĕr-zhĕ-rák')	161	44°49'N	0°28'E
Bergisch Gladbach, Ger. (bĕrg'ĭsh-glät'bäk)	171c	50°59'N	7°08'E
Berglern, Ger. (bĕrgh'lĕrn)	159d	48°24'N	11°55'E
Bergneustadt, Ger.	171c	51°01'N	7°39'E
Bergville, S. Afr. (bĕrg'vĭl)	233c	28°46'S	29°22'E
Berhampur, India	199	19°19'N	84°48'E
Bering Sea, sea, (bē'rĭng)	240	58°00'N	175°00'W
Bering Strait, strt.	106a	64°50'N	169°50'W
Berja, Spain (bĕr'hä)	172	36°50'N	2°56'W
Berkeley, Ca., U.S. (bûrk'lĭ)	104	37°52'N	122°17'W
Berkeley, Mo., U.S.	117e	38°45'N	90°20'W
Berkeley Springs, W.V., U.S. (bûrk'lĭ springz)	109	39°40'N	78°10'W
Berkhamsted, Eng., U.K. (bĕrk'hăm'stĕd)	158b	51°44'N	0°34'W
Berkley, Mi., U.S. (bûrk'lĭ)	111b	42°30'N	83°10'W
Berkovitsa, Blg. (bĕ-kō'vē-tsá)	175	43°14'N	23°08'E
Berkshire, hist. reg., Eng., U.K.	158b	51°23'N	1°07'W
Berland, r., Can.	95	54°00'N	117°10'W
Berlenga, is., Port. (bĕr-lĕn'gäzh)	172	39°25'N	9°33'W
Berlin, Ger. (bĕr-lēn')	154	52°31'N	13°28'E

PLACE (Pronunciation)	PAGE	LAT.	LONG.
Berlin, S. Afr. (bĕr-lĭn)	233c	32°53'S	27°36'E
Berlin, N.H., U.S. (bûr-lĭn)	109	44°25'N	71°10'W
Berlin, N.J., U.S.	110f	39°47'N	74°56'W
Berlin, Wi., U.S. (bûr-lĭn')	113	43°58'N	88°58'W
Bermejo, r., S.A. (bĕr-mā'hō)	144	25°05'S	61°00'W
Bermeo, Spain (bĕr-mā'yō)	172	43°23'N	2°43'W
Bermuda, dep., N.A.	129	32°20'N	65°45'W
Bern, Switz. (bĕrn)	154	46°55'N	7°25'E
Bernal, Arg. (bĕr-näl')	144a	34°43'S	58°17'W
Bernalillo, N.M., U.S. (bĕr-nä-lē'yō)	119	35°20'N	106°30'W
Bernard, l., Can. (bĕr-närd')	109	45°45'N	79°25'W
Bernardsville, N.J., U.S. (bûr nârds' vĭl)	110a	40°43'N	74°34'W
Bernau, Ger. (bĕr'nou)	168	52°40'N	13°35'E
Bernburg, Ger. (bĕrn'bòrgh)	168	51°48'N	11°43'E
Berndorf, Aus. (bĕrn'dôrf)	168	47°57'N	16°05'E
Berne, In., U.S. (bûrn)	108	40°40'N	84°55'W
Berner Alpen, mts., Switz.	168	46°29'N	7°30'E
Bernier, i., Austl. (bĕr-nēr')	220	24°58'S	113°15'E
Bernina, Pizzo, mtn., Eur.	168	46°23'N	9°58'E
Bero, r., Ang.	236	15°10'S	12°20'E
Beroun, Czech Rep. (bā'rōn)	168	49°57'N	14°03'E
Berounka, r., Czech Rep. (bĕ-rōn'ká)	168	49°53'N	13°40'E
Berowra, Austl.	217b	33°36'S	151°10'E
Berre, Étang de, l., Fr. (ā-tôn' dĕ bâr')	170a	43°27'N	5°07'E
Berre-l'Étang, Fr. (bâr'lā-tôn')	170a	43°28'N	5°11'E
Berriozabal, Mex. (bā'rēō-zä-bäl')	131	16°47'N	93°16'W
Berriyyane, Alg.	162	32°50'N	3°49'E
Berry Creek, r., Can.	96	51°15'N	111°40'W
Berryessa, r., Ca., U.S. (bĕ'rĭ ĕs'á)	118	38°35'N	122°33'W
Berry Islands, is., Bah.	134	25°40'N	77°50'W
Berryville, Ar., U.S. (bĕr'ē-vĭl)	121	36°21'N	93°34'W
Bershad', Ukr. (byĕr'shät)	177	48°22'N	29°31'E
Berthier, Can.	102b	46°56'N	70°44'W
Bertrand, r., Wa., U.S. (bûr'trand)	116d	48°58'N	122°31'W
Berwick, Pa., U.S. (bûr'wĭk)	109	41°05'N	76°10'W
Berwick-upon-Tweed, Eng., U.K. (bûr'ĭk)	160	55°45'N	2°01'W
Berwyn, Il., U.S. (bûr'wĭn)	111a	41°49'N	87°47'W
Beryslav, Ukr.	177	46°49'N	33°24'E
Besalampy, Madag. (bĕz-á-lám-pē')	233	16°48'S	44°40'E
Besançon, Fr. (bē-säN-sôn)	161	47°14'N	6°02'E
Besar, Gunong, mtn., Malay.	197b	2°31'N	103°09'E
Besed', r., Eur. (byĕ'syĕt)	176	52°58'N	31°36'E
Beskid Mountains, mts., Eur.	169	49°23'N	19°00'E
Beskra, Alg.	230	34°52'N	5°39'E
Beslan, Russia	182	43°12'N	44°33'E
Bessarabia, hist. reg., Mol.	177	47°00'N	28°30'E
Bességes, Fr. (bĕ-sĕzh')	170	44°20'N	4°07'E
Bessemer, Al., U.S. (bĕs'ē-mĕr)	110h	33°24'N	86°58'W
Bessemer, Mi., U.S.	113	46°29'N	90°04'W
Bessemer City, N.C., U.S.	125	35°16'N	81°17'W
Bestensee, Ger. (bĕs'tĕn-zā)	159b	52°15'N	13°39'E
Betanzos, Spain (bĕ-tän'thōs)	172	43°18'N	8°14'W
Betatakin Ruin, Az., U.S. (bĕt-á-tăk'ĭn)	119	36°40'N	110°29'W
Bethal, S. Afr. (bĕth'ăl)	238c	26°27'S	29°28'E
Bethalto, Il., U.S. (bá-thál'tō)	117e	38°54'N	90°03'W
Bethanien, Nmb.	232	26°20'S	16°10'E
Bethany, Mo., U.S.	121	40°15'N	94°04'W
Bethel, Ak., U.S. (bĕth'ĕl)	106a	60°50'N	161°50'W
Bethel, Ct., U.S.	110a	41°22'N	73°24'W
Bethel, Vt., U.S.	109	43°50'N	72°40'W
Bethel Park, Pa., U.S.	111e	40°19'N	80°02'W
Bethesda, Md., U.S. (bĕ-thĕs'dá)	110e	39°00'N	77°10'W
Bethlehem, S. Afr.	232	28°14'S	28°18'E
Bethlehem, Pa., U.S. (bĕth'lē-hĕm)	109	40°40'N	75°25'W
Bethlehem see Bayt Lahm, W.B.	197a	31°42'N	35°13'E
Béthune, Fr. (bā-tün')	170	50°32'N	2°37'E
Betroka, Madag. (bĕ-trōk'á)	233	23°13'S	46°17'E
Bet She'an, Isr.	197a	32°30'N	35°30'E
Betsiamites, Can.	91	48°57'N	68°36'W
Betsiamites, r., Can.	100	49°11'N	69°20'W
Betsiboka, r., Madag. (bĕt-sĭ-bō'ká)	233	16°47'S	46°45'E
Bettles Field, Ak., U.S. (bĕt'tŭls)	103	66°58'N	151°48'W
Betwa, r., India (bĕt'wá)	199	25°00'N	78°00'E
Betz, Fr. (bĕ)	171b	49°09'N	2°58'E
Beveren, Bel.	159a	51°13'N	4°14'E
B. Everett Jordan Lake, res., N.C., U.S.	115	35°45'N	79°00'W
Beverly, Ma., U.S.	101a	42°34'N	70°53'W
Beverly, N.J., U.S.	110f	40°03'N	74°56'W
Beverly Hills, Ca., U.S.	117a	34°05'N	118°24'W
Bevier, Mo., U.S. (bē-vēr')	121	39°44'N	92°36'W
Bewdley, Eng., U.K. (būd'lĭ)	158a	52°22'N	2°19'W
Bexhill, Eng., U.K. (bĕks'hĭl)	165	50°49'N	0°25'E
Bexley, Eng., U.K. (bĕks'ly)	158b	51°26'N	0°09'E
Beyla, Gui. (bā'lá)	230	8°41'N	8°37'W
Beylul, Erit.	231	13°15'N	42°21'E
Beypazari, Tur. (bā-pá-zä'rĭ)	163	40°10'N	31°40'E
Beyşehir, Tur.	181	38°00'N	31°45'E
Beysugskiy, Liman, b., Russia (lĭ-män' bĕy-sōōg'skĭ)	177	46°07'N	38°35'E
Bezhetsk, Russia (byĕ-zhĕtsk')	180	57°46'N	36°40'E
Bezhitsa, Russia (byĕ-zhĭ'tså)	180	53°19'N	34°18'E
Béziers, Fr. (bā-zyā')	161	43°21'N	3°12'E
Bhadreswar, India	202a	22°49'N	88°22'E
Bhāgalpur, India (bä'gŭl-pòr)	199	25°15'N	86°59'E
Bhamo, Mya. (bŭ-mō')	199	24°00'N	96°15'E
Bhāngar, India	202a	22°30'N	88°36'E
Bharatpur, India (bĕrt'pòr)	199	27°21'N	77°33'E
Bhatinda, India (bŭ-tĭn-då)	199	30°19'N	74°56'E
Bhātpāra, India	199	22°52'N	88°24'E

PLACE (Pronunciation)	PAGE	LAT.	LONG.
Bhaunagar, India (bäv-nŭg'ŭr)	199	21°45'N	72°58'E
Bhayandar, India	203b	19°20'N	72°50'E
Bhilai, India	202	21°14'N	81°23'E
Bhīma, r., India (bē'má)	199	18°00'N	74°45'E
Bhiwandi, India	203b	19°18'N	73°03'E
Bhiwāni, India	202	28°53'N	76°08'E
Bhopāl, India (bô-päl)	199	23°20'N	77°25'E
Bhubaneswar, India (bò-bû-nāsh'vûr)	199	20°21'N	85°53'E
Bhuj, India (bōōj)	199	23°22'N	69°39'E
Bhutan, nation, Asia (bōō-tän')	199	27°15'N	90°30'E
Biafra, Bight of, b., Afr.	230	4°05'N	7°10'E
Biak, i., Indon. (bē'ák)	213	1°00'S	136°00'E
Biała Podlaska, Pol. (byä'wä pōd-läs'kä)	169	52°01'N	23°08'E
Białogard, Pol.	168	54°00'N	16°01'E
Bialystok, Pol. (byä-wĭs'tōk)	154	53°08'N	23°12'E
Biankouma, C. Iv.	234	7°44'N	7°37'W
Biarritz, Fr. (byä-rēts')	161	43°27'N	1°39'W
Bibb City, Ga., U.S. (bĭb' sĭ'tē)	124	32°31'N	84°56'W
Biberach, Ger. (bē'bēräk)	168	48°06'N	9°49'E
Bibiani, Ghana	234	6°28'N	2°20'W
Bic, Can. (bĭk)	100	48°22'N	68°42'W
Bicknell, In., U.S. (bĭk'nĕl)	108	38°45'N	87°20'W
Bicske, Hung. (bĭsh'kē)	169	47°29'N	18°38'E
Bida, Nig. (bē'dä)	230	9°05'N	6°01'E
Biddeford, Me., U.S. (bĭd'ē-fērd)	100	43°29'N	70°29'W
Biddulph, Eng., U.K. (bĭd'ŭlf)	158a	53°07'N	2°10'W
Biebrza, r., Pol. (byĕb'zhá)	169	53°18'N	22°25'E
Biel, Switz. (bēl)	168	47°09'N	7°12'E
Bielefeld, Ger. (bē'lē-fĕlt)	161	52°01'N	8°35'E
Biella, Italy (byĕl'lä)	174	45°34'N	8°05'E
Bielsk Podlaski, Pol. (byĕlsk pūd-lä'skĭ)	161	52°47'N	23°14'E
Bien Hoa, Viet.	212	10°59'N	106°49'E
Bienville, Lac, l., Can.	93	55°32'N	72°45'W
Biesenthal, Ger. (bē'sĕn-täl)	159b	52°46'N	13°38'E
Biferno, r., Italy (bē-fĕr'nō)	174	41°49'N	14°46'E
Bifoum, Gabon	236	0°22'S	10°23'E
Biga, Tur. (bē'ghá)	175	40°13'N	27°14'E
Big Bay de Noc, Mi., U.S. (bĭg bā dē nok')	113	45°48'N	86°41'W
Big Bayou, Ar., U.S. (bĭg'bī'yōō)	121	33°04'N	91°28'W
Big Bear City, Ca., U.S. (bĭg bâr)	117a	34°16'N	116°51'W
Big Belt Mountains, mts., Mt., U.S. (bĭg bĕlt)	106	46°53'N	111°43'W
Big Bend Dam, S.D., U.S. (bĭg bĕnd)	112	44°11'N	99°33'W
Big Bend National Park, rec., Tx., U.S.	106	29°15'N	103°15'W
Big Black, r., Ms., U.S. (bĭg blăk)	124	32°05'N	90°49'W
Big Blue, r., Ne., U.S. (bĭg blōō)	121	40°53'N	97°00'W
Big Canyon, Tx., U.S. (bĭg kăn'yŭn)	122	30°27'N	102°19'W
Big Cypress Indian Reservation, I.R., Fl., U.S.	125a	26°19'N	81°11'W
Big Cypress Swamp, sw., Fl., U.S. (bĭg sī'prĕs)	125a	26°02'N	81°20'W
Big Delta, Ak., U.S. (bĭg dĕl'tá)	103	64°08'N	145°48'W
Big Fork, r., Mn., U.S. (bĭg fôrk)	113	48°08'N	93°47'W
Biggar, Can.	90	52°04'N	108°00'W
Big Hole, r., Mt., U.S. (bĭg hōl)	115	45°53'N	113°15'W
Big Hole National Battlefield, Mt., U.S. (bĭg hōl băt''l-fēld)	115	45°44'N	113°35'W
Bighorn, r., U.S.	106	45°30'N	108°00'W
Bighorn Lake, res., Mt., U.S.	115	45°00'N	108°10'W
Bighorn Mountains, mts., U.S. (bĭg hôrn)	106	44°47'N	107°40'W
Big Island, i., Can.	97	49°10'N	94°40'W
Big Lake, Wa., U.S. (bĭg lāk)	116a	48°24'N	122°14'W
Big Lake, l., Can.	102g	53°35'N	113°47'W
Big Lake, l., Wa., U.S.	116a	48°24'N	122°14'W
Big Lost, r., Id., U.S. (lôst)	115	43°56'N	113°38'W
Big Mossy Point, c., Can.	97	53°45'N	97°50'W
Big Muddy, r., Il., U.S.	108	37°50'N	89°00'W
Big Muddy Creek, r., Mt., U.S. (bĭg mud'ĭ)	115	48°53'N	105°02'W
Bignona, Sen.	234	12°49'N	16°14'W
Big Porcupine Creek, r., Mt., U.S. (pôr'kû-pīn)	115	46°38'N	107°04'W
Big Quill Lake, l., Can.	92	51°55'N	104°22'W
Big Rapids, Mi., U.S. (bĭg răp'ĭdz)	108	43°40'N	85°30'W
Big River, Can.	90	53°50'N	107°01'W
Big Sandy, r., Az., U.S. (bĭg sănd'ē)	119	34°59'N	113°36'W
Big Sandy, r., Ky., U.S.	108	38°15'N	82°35'W
Big Sandy, r., Wy., U.S.	115	42°08'N	109°35'W
Big Sandy Creek, r., Co., U.S.	120	39°08'N	103°36'W
Big Sandy Creek, r., Mt., U.S.	115	48°20'N	110°08'W
Bigsby Island, i., Can.	97	49°04'N	94°35'W
Big Sioux, r., U.S. (bĭg sōō)	112	44°34'N	97°00'W
Big Spring, Tx., U.S. (bĭg sprĭng)	122	32°15'N	101°28'W
Big Stone, l., Mn., U.S. (bĭg stōn)	112	45°29'N	96°40'W
Big Stone Gap, Va., U.S.	125	36°50'N	82°50'W
Big Sunflower, r., Ms., U.S. (sŭn-flou'ēr)	124	32°57'N	90°40'W
Big Timber, Mt., U.S. (bĭg'tĭm-bēr)	115	45°50'N	109°57'W
Big Wood, r., Id., U.S. (bĭg wòd)	115	43°02'N	114°30'W
Bihār, state, India (bē-här')	199	25°30'N	87°00'E
Biharamulo, Tan. (bē-hä-rä-mōō'lō)	232	2°38'S	31°20'E
Bihorului, Munţii, mts., Rom.	169	46°37'N	22°37'E
Bijagós, Arquipélago dos, is., Gui.-B.	230	11°20'N	17°10'W
Bijāpur, India	203	16°53'N	75°42'E
Bijeljina, Bos.	175	44°44'N	19°15'E
Bijelo Polje, Yugo. (bē'yĕ-lô pô'lyĕ)	175	43°02'N	19°48'E
Bijiang, China (bē-jyän)	207a	22°57'N	113°15'E
Bijie, China (bē-jyĕ)	209	27°20'N	105°18'E
Bijou Creek, r., Co., U.S. (bē'zhōō)	120	39°41'N	104°13'W

ăt; finăl; rāte; senåte; ärm; åsk; sofá; fâre; ch-choose; dh-as th in other; bē; ēvent; bĕt; recĕnt; cratẽr; g-gō; gh-guttural g; bĭt; ĭ-short neutral; rīde; K-guttural k as ch in German ich;

PLACE (Pronunciation)	PAGE	LAT.	LONG.
Bīkaner, India (bĭ-kä′nûr)	199	28°07′N	73°19′E
Bikin, Russia (bê-kēn′)	210	46°41′N	134°29′E
Bikin, r., Russia	210	46°37′N	135°55′E
Bikoro, D.R.C. (bê-kō′rō)	232	0°45′S	18°07′E
Bikuar, Parque Nacional do, rec., Ang.	236	15°07′S	14°40′E
Bilāspur, India (bê-läs′po͞or)	199	22°08′N	82°12′E
Bila Tserkva, Ukr.	181	49°48′N	30°09′E
Bilauktaung, mts., Asia	212	14°40′N	98°50′E
Bilbao, Spain (bĭl-bä′ō)	154	43°12′N	2°48′W
Bilbays, Egypt	238b	30°26′N	31°37′E
Bileća, Bos. (bē′lĕ-chä)	175	42°52′N	18°26′E
Bilecik, Tur. (bē-lēd-zhēk′)	163	40°10′N	29°58′E
Bilé Karpaty, mts., Eur.	169	48°53′N	17°35′E
Biłgoraj, Pol. (bēw-gō′rī)	169	50°31′N	22°43′E
Bilhorod-Dnistrovs'kyi, Ukr.	181	46°09′N	30°19′E
Bilimbay, Russia (bē′lĭm-bày)	186a	56°59′N	59°53′E
Billabong, r., Austl. (bĭl′ă-bŏng)	221	35°15′S	145°20′E
Billerica, Ma., U.S. (bĭl′rĭk-ȧ)	101a	42°33′N	71°16′W
Billericay, Eng., U.K.	158b	51°38′N	0°25′E
Billings, Mt., U.S. (bĭl′ĭngz)	104	45°47′N	108°29′W
Bill Williams, r., Az., U.S. (bĭl-wĭl′yumz)	119	34°10′N	113°50′W
Bilma, Niger (bēl′mä)	231	18°41′N	13°20′E
Bilopillia, Ukr.	181	51°10′N	34°19′E
Bilovods'k, Ukr.	177	49°12′N	39°36′E
Biloxi, Ms., U.S. (bĭ-lŏk′sĭ)	105	30°24′N	88°50′W
Bilqās Qism Awwal, Egypt	238b	31°14′N	31°25′E
Bimberi Peak, mtn., Austl. (bĭm′bĕrĭ)	222	35°45′S	148°50′E
Binalonan, Phil. (bē-nä-lô′nän)	213a	16°03′N	120°35′E
Bingen, Ger. (bĭn′gĕn)	168	49°57′N	7°54′E
Bingham, Eng., U.K. (bĭng′ăm)	158a	52°57′N	0°57′W
Bingham, Me., U.S.	100	45°03′N	69°51′W
Bingham Canyon, Ut., U.S.	117b	40°33′N	112°09′W
Binghamton, N.Y., U.S. (bĭng′ăm-tŭn)	105	42°05′N	75°55′W
Bingo-Nada, b., Japan (bĭn′gō nä-dä)	211	34°06′N	133°14′E
Binjai, Indon.	212	3°59′N	108°00′E
Binnaway, Austl. (bĭn′ă-wā)	222	31°42′S	149°22′E
Bintan, i., Indon. (bĭn′tän)	197b	1°09′N	104°43′E
Bintimani, mtn., S.L.	234	9°13′N	11°07′W
Bintulu, Malay. (bēn′to͞o-lo͞o)	212	3°07′N	113°06′E
Binxian, China	208	45°40′N	127°20′E
Binxian, China (bĭn-shyän)	206	37°27′N	117°58′E
Bio Gorge, val., Ghana	234	8°30′N	2°05′W
Bioko (Fernando Póo), i., Eq. Gui.	230	3°35′N	7°45′E
Bira, Russia (bē′rà)	210	49°00′N	133°18′E
Bira, r., Russia	210	48°55′N	132°25′E
Birātnagar, Nepal (bĭ-rät′nŭ-gŭr)	202	26°35′N	87°18′E
Birbka, Ukr.	169	49°36′N	24°18′E
Birch Bay, Wa., U.S. (bûrch)	116d	48°55′N	122°45′W
Birch Bay, b., Wa., U.S.	116d	48°55′N	122°52′W
Birch Island, i., Can.	97	52°25′N	99°55′W
Birch Mountains, mts., Can.	92	57°36′N	113°10′W
Birch Point, c., Wa., U.S.	116d	48°57′N	122°50′W
Bird Island, i., S. Afr. (bērd)	233c	33°51′S	26°21′E
Bird Rock, i., Bah. (bûrd)	135	22°50′N	74°20′W
Birds Hill, Can. (bûrds)	102f	49°58′N	97°00′W
Birdsville, Austl. (bûrdz′vĭl)	218	25°50′S	139°31′E
Birdum, Austl. (bûrd′ŭm)	218	15°45′S	133°25′E
Birecik, Tur. (bē-rĕd-zhĕk′)	163	37°10′N	37°50′E
Bir Gara, Chad	235	13°11′N	15°58′E
Bīrjand, Iran (bēr′jänd)	198	33°07′N	59°16′E
Birkenfeld, Or., U.S.	116c	45°59′N	123°20′W
Birkenhead, Eng., U.K. (bûr′kĕn-hĕd)	164	53°23′N	3°02′W
Birkenwerder, Ger. (bēr′kĕn-vĕr-dĕr)	159b	52°41′N	13°22′E
Birmingham, Eng., U.K.	154	52°29′N	1°53′W
Birmingham, Al., U.S. (bûr′mĭng-häm)	105	33°31′N	86°49′W
Birmingham, Mi., U.S.	111b	42°32′N	83°13′W
Birmingham, Mo., U.S.	117f	39°10′N	94°22′W
Birmingham Canal, can., Eng., U.K.	158a	53°07′N	2°40′W
Bi'r Misāhah, Egypt	231	22°16′N	28°04′E
Birnin Kebbi, Nig.	230	12°32′N	4°12′E
Birobidzhan, Russia (bē′rô-bê-jän′)	179	48°42′N	133°28′E
Birsk, Russia (bĭrsk)	178	55°25′N	55°30′E
Birstall, Eng., U.K. (bûr′stôl)	158a	53°44′N	1°39′W
Biryulëvo, Russia (bēr-yo͞ol′yô-vô)	186b	55°35′N	37°39′E
Biryusa, r., Russia (bēr-yo͞o′sä)	184	56°43′N	97°30′E
Bi'r Za'farānah, Egypt	197a	29°07′N	32°38′E
Biržai, Lith. (bēr-zhä′ē)	167	56°11′N	24°45′E
Bisbee, Az., U.S. (bĭz′bē)	104	31°30′N	109°55′W
Biscay, Bay of, b., Eur. (bĭs′kā′)	156	45°19′N	3°51′W
Biscayne Bay, b., Fl., U.S. (bĭs-kān′)	125a	25°22′N	80°15′W
Bischeim, Fr. (bĭsh′hīm)	171	48°40′N	7°48′E
Biscotasi Lake, l., Can.	98	47°20′N	81°55′W
Biser, Russia (bē′sĕr)	186a	58°24′N	58°54′E
Biševo, is., Yugo. (bē′shĕ-vō)	174	42°58′N	15°50′E
Bishkek, Kyrg.	183	42°49′N	74°42′E
Bisho, S. Afr.	232	32°50′S	27°20′E
Bishop, Ca., U.S. (bĭsh′ŭp)	118	37°22′N	118°25′W
Bishop, Tx., U.S.	123	27°35′N	97°46′W
Bishop's Castle, Eng., U.K. (bĭsh′ŏps käs′l)	158a	52°29′N	2°57′W
Bishopville, S.C., U.S. (bĭsh′ŭp-vĭl)	125	34°11′N	80°13′W
Bismarck, N.D., U.S. (bĭz′märk)	104	46°48′N	100°46′W
Bismarck Archipelago, is., Pap. N. Gui.	213	3°15′S	150°45′E
Bismarck Range, mts., Pap. N. Gui.	213	5°15′S	144°15′E
Bissau, Gui.-B. (bê-sa′o͞o)	234	11°51′N	15°35′W
Bissett, Can.	97	51°01′N	95°45′W
Bistineau, l., La., U.S. (bĭs-tĭ-nō′)	123	32°19′N	93°45′W
Bistrita, Rom. (bĭs-trĭt-sȧ)	163	47°09′N	24°29′E
Bistrita, r., Rom.	169	47°08′N	25°47′E
Bitlis, Tur. (bĭt-lēs′)	198	38°30′N	42°00′E
Bitola, Mac. (bē′tô-lä) (mō′nä-stēr)	174	41°02′N	21°22′E
Bitonto, Italy (bê-tôn′tō)	174	41°08′N	16°42′E
Bitter Creek, r., Wy., U.S. (bĭt′ēr)	115	41°36′N	108°29′W
Bitterfeld, Ger. (bĭt′ēr-fĕlt)	168	51°39′N	12°19′E
Bitterroot, r., Mt., U.S.	115	46°28′N	114°10′W
Bitterroot Range, mts., U.S. (bĭt′ēr-o͞ot)	106	47°15′N	115°13′W
Bityug, r., Russia (bĭt′yo͞og)	177	51°23′N	40°33′E
Biu, Nig.	235	10°35′N	12°13′E
Biwabik, Mn., U.S. (bê-wä′bĭk)	113	47°32′N	92°24′W
Biwa-ko, l., Japan (bê-wä′kō)	211	35°03′N	135°51′E
Biya, r., Russia (bĭ′yȧ)	184	52°22′N	87°28′E
Biysk, Russia (bēsk)	178	52°32′N	85°28′E
Bizana, S. Afr. (bĭz-änä)	233c	30°51′S	29°54′E
Bizerte, Tun. (bê-zĕrt′)	230	37°23′N	9°52′E
Bjelovar, Cro. (byĕ-lō′vär)	174	45°54′N	16°53′E
Bjørnafjorden, b., Nor.	166	60°11′N	5°26′E
Bla, Mali	234	12°57′N	5°46′W
Black, l., Mi., U.S. (blăk)	108	45°25′N	84°15′W
Black, l., N.Y., U.S.	109	44°30′N	75°35′W
Black, r., Asia	212	21°00′N	103°30′E
Black, r., Can.	98	49°20′N	81°15′W
Black, r., Az., U.S.	119	33°35′N	109°35′W
Black, r., N.Y., U.S.	109	43°45′N	75°20′W
Black, r., S.C., U.S.	125	33°55′N	80°10′W
Black, r., Wi., U.S.	113	44°07′N	90°56′W
Black, r., U.S.	121	35°47′N	91°22′W
Blackall, Austl. (blăk′ŭl)	219	24°23′S	145°37′E
Black Bay, b., Can. (blăk)	98	48°36′N	88°32′W
Blackburn, Eng., U.K. (blăk′bûrn)	164	53°45′N	2°28′W
Blackburn Mount, mtn., Ak., U.S.	103	61°50′N	143°12′W
Black Butte Lake, res., Ca., U.S.	118	39°45′N	122°20′W
Black Canyon of the Gunnison National Park, rec., Co., U.S.	119	38°34′N	107°43′W
Black Diamond, Wa., U.S. (dī′mŭnd)	116a	47°19′N	122°00′W
Black Down Hills, hills, Eng., U.K. (blăk′doun)	164	50°58′N	3°19′W
Blackduck, Mn., U.S. (blăk′dŭk)	113	47°41′N	94°33′W
Blackfeet Indian Reservation, I.R., Mt., U.S.	115	48°40′N	113°00′W
Blackfoot, Id., U.S. (blăk′fŏt)	115	43°11′N	112°23′W
Blackfoot, r., Mt., U.S.	115	46°53′N	113°33′W
Blackfoot Indian Reservation, I.R., Mt., U.S.	115	48°49′N	112°53′W
Blackfoot Indian Reserve, I.R., Can.	95	50°45′N	113°00′W
Blackfoot Reservoir, res., Id., U.S.	115	42°53′N	111°23′W
Black Forest *see* Schwarzwald, for., Ger.	168	47°54′N	7°57′E
Black Hills, mts., U.S.	106	44°08′N	103°47′W
Black Island, i., Can.	97	51°10′N	96°30′W
Black Lake, Can.	99	46°02′N	71°24′W
Black Mesa, Az., U.S. (blăk māsȧ)	119	36°33′N	110°40′W
Blackmud Creek, r., Can. (blăk′mŭd)	102g	53°28′N	113°34′W
Blackpool, Eng., U.K. (blăk′po͞ol)	164	53°49′N	3°02′W
Black Range, mts., N.M., U.S.	106	33°15′N	107°55′W
Black River, Jam. (blăk′)	134	18°00′N	77°50′W
Black River Falls, Wi., U.S.	113	44°18′N	90°51′W
Black Rock Desert, des., Nv., U.S. (rŏk)	114	40°55′N	119°00′W
Blacksburg, S.C., U.S. (blăks′bûrg)	125	35°09′N	81°30′W
Black Sea, sea	157	43°01′N	32°16′E
Blackshear, Ga., U.S. (blăk′shĭr)	125	31°20′N	82°15′W
Blackstone, Va., U.S. (blăk′stōn)	125	37°04′N	78°00′W
Black Sturgeon, r., Can. (stû′jŭn)	98	49°12′N	88°41′W
Blacktown, Austl. (blăk′toun)	217b	33°47′S	150°55′E
Blackville, Can. (blăk′vĭl)	100	46°44′N	65°50′W
Blackville, S.C., U.S.	125	33°21′N	81°19′W
Black Volta (Volta Noire), r., Afr.	230	11°30′N	4°00′W
Black Warrior, r., Al., U.S. (blăk wŏr′ĭ-ēr)	124	32°37′N	87°42′W
Blackwater, r., Ire. (blăk-wô′tēr)	164	52°05′N	9°02′W
Blackwater, r., Mo., U.S.	121	38°53′N	93°22′W
Blackwater, r., Va., U.S.	125	37°07′N	77°10′W
Blackwell, Ok., U.S. (blăk′wĕl)	121	36°47′N	97°19′W
Bladel, Neth.	159a	51°22′N	5°15′E
Blagodarnoye, Russia (blä′gô-där-nō′yĕ)	181	45°00′N	43°30′E
Blagoevgrad, Blg.	175	42°01′N	23°06′E
Blagoveshchensk, Russia (blä′gō-vyĕsh′chĕnsk)	179	50°16′N	127°47′E
Blagoveshchensk, Russia	186a	55°03′N	56°00′E
Blaine, Mn., U.S. (blān)	117g	45°11′N	93°14′W
Blaine, Wa., U.S.	116d	48°59′N	122°49′W
Blaine, W.V., U.S.	109	39°25′N	79°10′W
Blair, Ne., U.S. (blâr)	112	41°33′N	96°09′W
Blairmore, Can.	95	49°38′N	114°25′W
Blairsville, Pa., U.S. (blârs′vĭl)	109	40°30′N	79°40′W
Blake, i., Wa., U.S. (blāk)	116a	47°37′N	122°28′W
Blakely, Ga., U.S. (blāk′lē)	124	31°22′N	84°55′W
Blanc, Cap, c., Afr.	230	20°39′N	18°08′W
Blanc, Mont, mtn., Eur. (môn blän)	156	45°50′N	6°53′E
Blanca, Bahía, b., Arg. (bä-ē′ä-blàn′kä)	144	39°30′S	61°00′W
Blanca Peak, mtn., Co., U.S. (blăŋ′kȧ)	106	37°36′N	105°22′W
Blanche, r., Can.	102c	45°34′N	75°38′W
Blanche, Lake, l., Austl. (blănch)	222	29°20′S	139°12′E
Blanchester, Oh., U.S. (blăn′chĕs-tēr)	111f	39°18′N	83°58′W
Blanco, r., Mex.	130	24°05′N	99°21′W
Blanco, r., Mex.	131	18°42′N	96°03′W
Blanco, Cabo, c., Arg. (blăŋ′kō)	144	47°08′S	65°47′W
Blanco, Cabo, c., C.R. (kȧ′bō-blăŋ′kō)	132	9°29′N	85°15′W
Blanco, Cape, c., Or., U.S. (blăn′kō)	114	42°53′N	124°38′W
Blancos, Cayo, i., Cuba (kä′yō-blăŋ′kōs)	134	23°15′N	80°55′W
Blanding, Ut., U.S.	119	37°40′N	109°31′W
Blankenfelde, Ger. (blän′kĕn-fĕl-dĕ)	159b	52°20′N	13°24′E
Blanquefort, Fr.	170	44°53′N	0°38′W
Blanquilla, Arrecife, i., Mex. (är-rĕ-sē′fĕ-blän-kē′l-yä)	131	21°32′N	97°14′W
Blantyre, Mwi. (blăn-tīyr)	232	15°47′S	35°00′E
Blasdell, N.Y., U.S. (blāz′dĕl)	111c	42°48′N	78°51′W
Blato, Cro. (blä′tō)	174	42°55′N	16°47′E
Blaye-et-Sainte Luce, Fr. (blā′ā-săɴt-lüs′)	170	45°08′N	0°40′W
Błażowa, Pol. (bwä-zhō′vȧ)	169	49°51′N	22°05′E
Bleus, Monts, mts., D.R.C.	237	1°10′N	30°10′E
Blind River, Can. (blīnd)	91	46°10′N	83°09′W
Blissfield, Mi., U.S. (blĭs-fēld)	108	41°50′N	83°50′W
Blithe, r., Eng., U.K. (blĭth)	158a	52°22′N	1°49′W
Blitta, Togo	234	8°19′N	0°59′E
Block, i., R.I., U.S. (blŏk)	109	41°05′N	71°35′W
Bloedel, Can.	94	50°07′N	125°23′W
Bloemfontein, S. Afr. (blo͞om′fŏn-tān)	232	29°09′S	26°16′E
Blois, Fr. (blwä)	161	47°36′N	1°21′E
Blood Indian Reserve, I.R., Can.	95	49°30′N	113°10′W
Bloomer, Wi., U.S. (blo͞om′ēr)	113	45°07′N	91°30′W
Bloomfield, Ia., U.S.	113	40°44′N	92°21′W
Bloomfield, In., U.S. (blo͞om′fēld)	108	39°00′N	86°55′W
Bloomfield, Mo., U.S.	121	36°54′N	89°55′W
Bloomfield, Ne., U.S.	112	42°36′N	97°40′W
Bloomfield, N.J., U.S.	110a	40°48′N	74°12′W
Bloomfield Hills, Mi., U.S.	111b	42°35′N	83°15′W
Blooming Prairie, Mn., U.S. (blo͞om′ĭng prā′rĭ)	113	43°52′N	93°04′W
Bloomington, Ca., U.S. (blo͞om′ĭng-tŭn)	117a	34°04′N	117°24′W
Bloomington, Il., U.S.	105	40°30′N	89°00′W
Bloomington, In., U.S.	108	39°10′N	86°35′W
Bloomington, Mn., U.S.	117g	44°50′N	93°18′W
Bloomsburg, Pa., U.S. (blo͞omz′bûrg)	109	41°00′N	76°25′W
Blossburg, Al., U.S. (blŏs′bûrg)	110h	33°38′N	86°57′W
Blossburg, Pa., U.S.	109	41°45′N	77°00′W
Bloubergstrand, S. Afr.	232a	33°48′S	18°28′E
Blountstown, Fl., U.S. (blŭnts′tun)	124	30°24′N	85°02′W
Bludenz, Aus. (blo͞o-dĕnts′)	168	47°09′N	9°50′E
Blue Ash, Oh., U.S. (blo͞o ăsh)	111f	39°14′N	84°23′W
Blue Earth, Mn., U.S. (blo͞o ûrth)	113	43°38′N	94°05′W
Blue Earth, r., Mn., U.S.	113	43°55′N	94°16′W
Bluefield, W.V., U.S. (blo͞o′fēld)	125	37°15′N	81°11′W
Bluefields, Nic. (blo͞o′fēldz)	129	12°03′N	83°45′W
Blue Island, Il., U.S.	111a	41°39′N	87°41′W
Blue Mesa Reservoir, res., Co., U.S.	119	38°25′N	107°00′W
Blue Mountain, mtn., Can.	101	50°28′N	57°11′W
Blue Mountains, mts., Austl.	221	33°35′S	149°00′E
Blue Mountains, mts., Jam.	134	18°05′N	76°35′W
Blue Mountains, mts., U.S.	106	45°15′N	118°50′W
Blue Mud Bay, b., Austl. (bo͞o mŭd)	220	13°20′S	136°45′E
Blue Nile, r., Afr.	231	12°30′N	34°00′E
Blue Rapids, Ks., U.S. (blo͞o răp′ĭdz)	121	39°40′N	96°41′W
Blue Ridge, mtn., U.S. (blo͞o rĭj)	107	35°30′N	82°50′W
Blue River, Can.	90	52°05′N	119°17′W
Blue River, r., Mo., U.S.	117f	38°55′N	94°33′W
Bluff, Ut., U.S.	119	37°18′N	109°34′W
Bluff Park, Al., U.S.	110h	33°24′N	86°52′W
Bluffton, In., U.S. (blŭf-tŭn)	108	40°40′N	85°15′W
Bluffton, Oh., U.S.	108	40°50′N	83°55′W
Blumenau, Braz. (blo͞o′mĕn-ou)	144	26°53′S	48°58′W
Blumut, Gunong, mtn., Malay.	197b	2°03′N	103°34′E
Blyth, Eng., U.K. (blĭth)	164	55°03′N	1°34′W
Blythe, Ca., U.S.	119	33°37′N	114°37′W
Blytheville, Ar., U.S. (blīth′vĭl)	121	35°55′N	89°51′W
Bo, S.L.	234	7°56′N	11°21′W
Boac, Phil.	213a	13°26′N	121°50′E
Boaco, Nic. (bô-ä′kō)	132	12°24′N	85°41′W
Bo'ai, China (bwo-ī)	208	35°10′N	113°08′E
Boa Vista, i., C.V. (bō-ä-vēsh′tȧ)	230b	16°01′N	23°52′W
Boa Vista do Rio Branco, Braz.	143	2°46′N	60°45′W
Bobo Dioulasso, Burkina (bō′bô-dyo͞o-lȧs-sō′)	230	11°12′N	4°18′W
Bobr, Bela. (bô′b'r)	176	54°19′N	29°11′E
Bóbr, r., Pol. (bŭ′br)	168	51°44′N	15°13′E
Bobrov, Russia (bŭb-rôf′)	181	51°07′N	40°01′E
Bobrovyts'a, Ukr.	177	50°43′N	31°27′E
Bobrynets', Ukr.	177	48°04′N	32°10′E
Boca del Pozo, Ven. (bô-kä-dĕl-pô′zō)	143b	11°00′N	64°21′W
Boca de Uchire, Ven. (bô-kä-dĕ-o͞o-chē′rĕ)	143b	10°09′N	65°27′W
Bocaina, Serra da, mtn., Braz. (sĕ′r-rä-dȧ-bô-kä′ē-nä)	141a	22°47′S	44°39′W
Bocas, Mex. (bō′käs)	130	22°29′N	101°03′W
Bocas del Toro, Pan. (bō′käs dĕl tō′rō)	133	9°24′N	82°15′W
Bochnia, Pol. (bōκ′nyä)	169	49°58′N	20°28′E
Bocholt, Ger. (bō′κōlt)	171c	51°50′N	6°37′E
Bochum, Ger.	168	51°29′N	7°13′E
Bockum-Hövel, Ger. (bō′κŏm-hû′fĕl)	171c	51°41′N	7°45′E
Bodalang, D.R.C.	236	3°14′N	22°14′E
Bodaybo, Russia (bō-dī′bō)	179	57°12′N	114°46′E
Bodele, depr., Chad (bō-dȧ-lā′)	231	16°45′N	17°05′E
Boden, Swe.	160	65°51′N	21°29′E
Bodensee, l., Eur. (bō′dĕn zā)	156	47°48′N	9°22′E
Bodmin, Eng., U.K. (bŏd′mĭn)	164	50°29′N	4°45′W
Bodmin Moor, Eng., U.K. (bŏd′mĭn mŏr)	164	50°36′N	4°43′W
Bodrum, Tur.	181	37°10′N	27°07′E
Boende, D.R.C. (bô-ĕn′dȧ)	232	0°13′S	20°52′E
Boerne, Tx., U.S. (bō′ĕrn)	122	29°49′N	98°44′W
Boesmans, r., S. Afr.	233c	33°29′S	26°09′E
Boeuf, r., U.S. (bĕf)	123	32°23′N	91°57′W

ng-sing; ŋ-baŋk; ɴ-nasalized n; nŏd; cŏmmit; ōld; ôbey; ôrder; oi-boil; fo͞od; ŏ-as oo in foot; ou-out; s-soft; sh-dish; th-thin; pūre; ûnite; ûrn; stŭd; circŭs; ü-as in French tu; ′-indeterminate vowel.

274 Boffa – Bowie PRONOUNCING INDEX

PLACE (Pronunciation)	PAGE	LAT.	LONG.
Boffa, Gui. (bôf'à)	230	10°10′N	14°02′W
Bôfu, Japan (bō'fōō)	211	34°03′N	131°35′E
Bogalusa, La., U.S. (bō-gà-lōō'sà)	123	30°48′N	89°52′W
Bogan, r., Austl. (bô'gĕn)	222	32°10′S	147°40′E
Bogense, Den. (bô'gĕn-sĕ)	166	55°34′N	10°09′E
Boggy Peak, mtn., Antig. (bŏg'ĭ-pēk)	133b	17°03′N	61°50′W
Bogong, Mount, mtn., Austl.	222	36°50′S	147°15′E
Bogor, Indon.	212	6°45′S	106°45′E
Bogoroditsk, Russia (bŏ-gŏ'rô-dĭtsk)	176	53°48′N	38°06′E
Bogorodsk, Russia	180	56°02′N	43°40′E
Bogorodskoye, Russia (bô-gô-rôd'skô-yĕ)	186a	56°43′N	56°53′E
Bogotá, Col.	142	4°36′N	74°05′W
Bogotol, Russia (bŏ'gô-tŏl)	179	56°15′N	89°45′E
Boguchar, Russia (bō'gŏ-chär)	181	49°40′N	41°00′E
Bogue Chitto, Ms., U.S. (nôr'fēld)	124	31°26′N	90°25′W
Boguete, Pan. (bŏ-gĕ'tĕ)	133	8°54′N	82°29′W
Bo Hai, b., China	205	38°30′N	120°00′E
Bohai Haixia, strt., China (bwo-hī hī-shyä)	208	38°05′N	121°40′E
Bohain-en-Vermandois, Fr. (bô-ăn-ŏn-vâr-män-dwä')	170	49°58′N	3°22′E
Bohemia *see* Čechy, hist. reg., Czech Rep.	168	49°51′N	13°55′E
Bohemian Forest, mts., Eur. (bô-hē'mĭ-ăn)	156	49°35′N	12°27′E
Bohodukhiv, Ukr.	181	50°10′N	35°31′E
Bohol, i., Phil. (bô-hôl')	213	9°28′N	124°35′E
Bohom, Mex. (bō-ô'm)	131	16°47′N	92°42′W
Bohuslav, Ukr.	177	49°34′N	30°51′W
Boiestown, Can. (boiz'toun)	100	46°27′N	66°25′W
Bois Blanc, i., Mi., U.S. (boi' blăŋk)	108	45°45′N	84°30′W
Boischâtel, Can. (bwä-shä-tĕl')	102b	46°54′N	71°08′W
Bois-des-Filion, Can. (bōō-ä'dĕ-fē-yôn')	102a	45°40′N	73°46′W
Boise, Id., U.S. (boi'zē)	104	43°38′N	116°12′W
Boise, r., Id., U.S.	114	43°43′N	116°30′W
Boise City, Ok., U.S.	120	36°42′N	102°30′W
Boissevain, Can. (bois'vān)	90	49°14′N	100°03′W
Bojador, Cabo, c., W. Sah.	230	26°21′N	16°08′W
Bojnūrd, Iran	198	37°29′N	57°13′E
Bokani, Nig.	235	9°26′N	5°13′E
Boknafjorden, b., Nor.	160	59°12′N	5°37′E
Boksburg, S. Afr. (bŏks'bûrgh)	233b	26°13′N	28°15′E
Bokungu, D.R.C.	236	0°41′S	22°19′E
Bol, Chad	235	13°28′N	14°43′E
Bolai I, C.A.R.	235	4°20′N	17°21′E
Bolama, Gui.-B. (bō-lä'mä)	230	11°34′S	15°41′W
Bolan, mtn., Pak. (bō-län')	202	30°13′N	67°09′E
Bolaños, Mex. (bō-län'yôs)	130	21°40′N	103°48′W
Bolaños, r., Mex.	130	21°26′N	103°54′W
Bolan Pass, p., Pak.	199	29°50′N	67°10′E
Bolbec, Fr. (bôl-bĕk')	170	49°37′N	0°26′E
Bole, Ghana (bō'lå)	230	9°02′N	2°29′W
Bolesławiec, Pol. (bō-lĕ-slä'vyĕts)	168	51°15′N	15°35′E
Bolgatanga, Ghana	230	10°46′N	0°52′W
Bolhrad, Ukr.	181	45°41′N	28°38′E
Boli, China (bwo-lē)	205	45°40′N	130°38′E
Bolinao, Phil. (bō-lē-nä'ô)	213a	16°24′N	119°53′E
Bolívar, Arg. (bô-lē'vär)	144	36°15′S	61°05′W
Bolívar, Col.	142	1°46′N	76°58′W
Bolivar, Mo., U.S. (bŏl'ĭ-vȧr)	121	37°37′N	93°22′W
Bolivar, Tn., U.S.	124	35°14′N	88°56′W
Bolívar, Pico, mtn., Ven.	142	8°44′N	70°54′W
Bolivar Peninsula, pen., Tx., U.S. (bŏl'ĭ-vȧr)	123a	29°25′N	94°40′W
Bolivia, nation, S.A. (bô-lĭv'ĭ-à)	142	17°00′S	64°00′W
Bolkhov, Russia (bŏl-kôf')	180	53°27′N	35°59′E
Bollin, r., Eng., U.K. (bŏl'ĭn)	158a	53°18′N	2°11′W
Bollington, Eng., U.K. (bŏl'ĭng-tŭn)	158a	53°18′N	2°06′W
Bollnäs, Swe. (bôl'nĕs)	166	61°22′N	16°20′E
Bolmen, l., Swe. (bôl'mĕn)	166	56°58′N	13°25′E
Bolobo, D.R.C. (bō'lô-bô)	232	2°14′S	16°18′E
Bologna, Italy (bô-lōn'yä)	154	44°30′N	11°18′E
Bologoye, Russia (bŏ-lŏ-gô'yĕ)	180	57°52′N	34°02′E
Bolonchenticul, Mex. (bô-lôn-chĕn-tē-kōō'l)	132a	20°03′N	89°47′W
Bolondrón, Cuba (bô-lôn-drōn')	134	22°45′N	81°25′W
Bolseno, Lago di, l., Italy (lä'gō-dē-bôl-sā'nô)	174	42°35′N	11°40′E
Bol'shaya Anyuy, r., Russia	185	67°58′N	161°15′E
Bol'shaya Chuya, r., Russia	185	58°15′N	111°40′E
Bol'shaya Kinel', r., Russia	180	53°20′N	52°40′E
Bol'she Ust'ikinskoye, Russia (bôl'she ŏs-tyĭ-kĕn'skô-yĕ)	186a	55°58′N	58°18′E
Bol'shoy Begichëv, i., Russia	179	74°30′N	114°40′E
Bol'shoye Ivonino, Russia (ĭ-vô'nĭ-nô)	186a	59°41′N	61°12′E
Bol'shoy Kuyash, Russia (bôl'-shôy kōō'yásh)	186a	55°52′N	61°07′E
Bolsover, Eng., U.K. (bōl'zō-vẽr)	158a	53°14′N	1°17′W
Boltaña, Spain (bôl-tä'nä)	173	42°28′N	0°03′E
Bolton, Can. (bōl'tŭn)	102d	43°53′N	79°44′W
Bolton, Eng., U.K.	164	53°35′N	2°26′W
Bolton-upon-Dearne, Eng., U.K. (bōl'tŭn-ŭp'ŏn-dûrn)	158a	53°31′N	1°19′W
Bolu, Tur. (bō'lò)	163	40°45′N	31°45′E
Bolva, r., Russia (bôl'vä)	176	53°30′N	34°30′E
Bolvadin, Tur. (bŏl-vä-dēn')	163	38°50′N	30°50′E
Bolzano, Italy (bôl-tsä'nō)	162	46°31′N	11°22′E
Boma, D.R.C. (bō'mä)	232	5°51′S	13°03′E
Bombala, Austl. (bŭm-bä'lȧ)	219	36°55′S	149°07′E
Bombay *see* Mumbai, India	199	18°58′N	72°50′E
Bombay Harbour, b., India	203b	18°55′N	72°52′E
Bomi Hills, Lib.	230	7°00′N	11°00′W
Bom Jardim, Braz. (bôn zhär-dēn')	141a	22°10′S	42°25′W
Bom Jesus do Itabapoana, Braz.	141a	21°08′S	41°51′W
Bømlo, i., Nor. (bûmlô)	166	59°47′N	4°57′E
Bomongo, D.R.C.	231	1°22′N	18°21′E
Bom Sucesso, Braz. (bôn-sōō-sĕ'sō)	141a	21°02′S	44°44′W
Bomu *see* Mbomou, r., Afr.	231	4°50′N	24°00′E
Bon, Cap, c., Tun. (bôn)	162	37°04′N	11°13′E
Bonaire, i., Neth. Ant. (bō-nâr')	142	12°10′N	68°15′W
Bonavista, Can. (bō-nȧ-vĭs'tȧ)	93a	48°39′N	53°07′W
Bonavista Bay, b., Can.	93a	48°45′N	53°20′W
Bond, Co., U.S. (bŏnd)	120	39°53′N	106°40′W
Bondo, D.R.C. (bôn'dô)	184	3°49′N	23°40′E
Bondoc Peninsula, pen., Phil. (bôn-dŏk')	213a	13°24′N	122°30′E
Bondoukou, C. Iv. (bŏn-dōō'kōō)	230	8°02′N	2°48′W
Bonds Cay, i., Bah. (bŏnds kē)	134	25°30′N	77°45′W
Bondy, Fr.	171b	48°54′N	2°28′E
Bône *see* Annaba, Alg.	230	36°57′N	7°39′E
Bone, Teluk, b., Indon.	212	4°09′S	121°00′E
Bonete, Cerro, mtn., Arg. (bô'nĕtĕh çĕrrô)	144	27°50′S	68°35′W
Bonfim, Braz. (bôn-fē'n)	141a	20°20′S	44°15′W
Bongor, Chad	235	10°17′N	15°22′E
Bonham, Tx., U.S. (bŏn'ăm)	121	33°35′N	96°09′W
Bonhomme, Pic, mtn., Haiti	135	19°10′N	72°20′W
Bonifacio, Fr. (bō-nē-fä'chō)	174	41°23′N	9°10′E
Bonifacio, Strait of, strt., Eur.	162	41°14′N	9°02′E
Bonifay, Fl., U.S. (bŏn-ĭ-fā')	124	30°46′N	85°40′W
Bonin Islands, is., Japan (bō'nĭn)	241	26°30′N	141°00′E
Bonn, Ger. (bŏn)	154	50°44′N	7°06′E
Bonne Bay, b., Can. (bŏn)	101	49°33′N	57°55′W
Bonners Ferry, Id., U.S. (bonẽrz fẽr'ĭ)	114	48°41′N	116°19′W
Bonner Springs, Ks., U.S. (bŏn'ẽr sprĭngz)	117f	39°04′N	94°52′W
Bonne Terre, Mo., U.S. (bŏn târ')	121	37°55′N	90°32′W
Bonnet Peak, mtn., Can. (bŏn'ĭt)	95	51°26′N	115°53′W
Bonneville Dam, dam, U.S. (bôn'ē-vĭl)	114	45°37′N	121°57′W
Bonny, Nig. (bŏn'ē)	230	4°29′N	7°13′E
Bonny Lake, Wa., U.S. (bŏn'ē lăk)	116a	47°11′N	122°11′W
Bonnyville, Can. (bônē-vĭl)	95	54°16′N	110°44′W
Bonorva, Italy (bō-nôr'vä)	174	40°26′N	8°46′E
Bonthain, Indon. (bŏn-tīn')	212	5°30′S	119°52′E
Bonthe, S.L.	230	7°32′N	12°30′W
Bontoc, Phil. (bŏn-tŏk')	213a	17°10′N	121°01′E
Booby Rocks, is., Bah. (bōō'bĭ rŏks)	134	23°55′N	77°00′W
Booker T. Washington National Monument, rec., Va., U.S. (bŏŏk'ẽr tē wŏsh'ĭng-tŭn)	125	37°07′N	79°45′W
Boom, Bel.	159a	51°05′N	4°22′E
Boone, Ia., U.S. (bōōn)	113	42°04′N	93°51′W
Booneville, Ar., U.S. (bōōn'vĭl)	121	35°09′N	93°54′W
Booneville, Ky., U.S.	108	37°25′N	83°40′W
Booneville, Ms., U.S.	124	34°37′N	88°35′W
Boons, S. Afr.	238c	25°59′S	27°15′E
Boonton, N.J., U.S. (bōōn'tŭn)	110a	40°54′N	74°24′W
Boonville, In., U.S.	108	38°00′N	87°15′W
Boonville, Mo., U.S.	121	38°57′N	92°44′W
Boorama, Som.	238a	10°05′N	43°08′E
Boosaaso, Som.	238a	11°19′N	49°10′E
Boothbay Harbor, Me., U.S. (bōōth'bā här'bẽr)	100	43°51′N	69°39′W
Boothia, Gulf of, b., Can. (bōō'thĭ-ȧ)	93	69°04′N	86°04′W
Boothia Peninsula, pen., Can.	89	73°30′N	95°00′W
Bootle, Eng., U.K. (bōōt'l)	158a	53°29′N	3°02′W
Bor, Sudan (bôr)	231	6°13′N	31°35′E
Bor, Tur. (bōr)	181	37°50′N	34°40′E
Boraha, Nosy, i., Madag.	233	16°58′S	50°15′E
Borah Peak, mtn., Id., U.S. (bō'rä)	115	44°12′N	113°47′W
Borås, Swe. (bō'rōs)	160	57°43′N	12°55′E
Borāzjān, Iran (bō-räz-jän')	198	29°13′N	51°13′E
Borba, Braz. (bôr'bä)	143	4°23′S	59°31′W
Borborema, Planalto da, plat., Braz. (plä-nàl'tô-dä-bôr-bō-rĕ'mä)	143	7°35′S	36°40′W
Bordeaux, Fr. (bôr-dō')	154	44°50′N	0°37′W
Bordentown, N.J., U.S. (bôr'dĕn-toun)	109	40°05′N	74°40′W
Bordj-bou-Arréridj, Alg. (bôrj-bōō-ȧ-rā-rēj')	162	36°03′N	4°48′E
Bordj Omar Idriss, Alg.	230	28°06′N	6°34′E
Borgarnes, Ice.	160	64°31′N	21°40′W
Borger, Tx., U.S. (bôr'gẽr)	120	35°40′N	101°23′W
Borgholm, Swe. (bôrg-hôlm')	166	56°52′N	16°40′E
Borgne, l., La., U.S. (bôrn'y')	123	30°03′N	89°36′W
Borgomanero, Italy (bôr'gō-mä-nâ'rō)	174	45°40′N	8°28′E
Borgo Val di Taro, Italy (bô'r-zhō-väl-dē-tá'rō)	174	44°29′N	9°44′E
Börili, Kaz.	186a	53°36′N	61°55′E
Boring, Or., U.S. (bōring)	116c	45°26′N	122°22′W
Borisoglebsk, Russia (bŏ-rē sŏ-glyĕpsk')	178	51°20′N	42°00′E
Borisovka, Russia (bŏ-rē-sôf'kȧ)	181	50°38′N	36°00′E
Borivli, India	203b	19°15′N	72°48′E
Borja, Spain (bôr'hä)	172	41°50′N	1°33′W
Borken, Ger. (bōr'kĕn)	171c	51°50′N	6°51′E
Borkou, reg., Chad (bôr-kōō')	231	18°11′N	18°28′E
Borkum, i., Ger. (bōr'kōōm)	168	53°31′N	6°50′E
Borlänge, Swe. (bôr-lĕng'gĕ)	166	60°30′N	15°24′E
Borneo, i., Asia	212	0°25′N	112°39′E
Bornholm, i., Den. (bôrn-hôlm)	156	55°16′N	15°15′E
Boromlia, Ukr.	177	50°36′N	34°58′E
Boromo, Burkina	234	11°45′N	2°56′W
Borovan, Blg. (bō-rō-vän')	175	43°24′N	23°47′E
Borovichi, Russia (bō-rô-vē'chē)	178	58°22′N	33°56′E
Borovsk, Russia (bô'rŏvsk)	176	55°13′N	36°26′E
Borraan, Som.	238a	10°38′N	48°30′E
Borracha, Isla la, i., Ven. (ē's-lä-lä-bôr-rä'chä)	143b	10°18′N	64°44′W
Borriana, Spain	162	39°53′N	0°05′W
Borroloola, Austl. (bŏr-rô-lōō'lȧ)	218	16°15′S	136°19′E
Borshchiv, Ukr.	169	48°47′N	26°04′E
Bort-les-Orgues, Fr. (bôr-lā-zôrg)	170	45°26′N	2°26′E
Borūjerd, Iran	198	33°45′N	48°53′E
Boryslav, Ukr.	169	49°17′N	23°24′E
Boryspil', Ukr.	177	50°17′N	30°54′E
Borzna, Ukr. (bôrz'ná)	181	51°15′N	32°26′E
Borzya, Russia (bôrz'yȧ)	179	50°37′N	116°53′E
Bosa, Italy (bō'sä)	174	40°18′N	8°34′E
Bosanska Dubica, Bos. (bō'sän-skä dōō'bĭt-sä)	174	45°10′N	16°49′E
Bosanska Gradiška, Bos. (bō'sän-skä grä-dĭsh'kä)	175	45°08′N	17°15′E
Bosanski Novi, Bos. (bō's sän-skĭ nō'vē)	174	45°00′N	16°22′E
Bosanski Petrovac, Bos. (bō'sän-skĭ pĕt'rō-väts)	174	44°33′N	16°23′E
Bosanski Šamac, Bos. (bō'sän-skĭ shä'mȧts)	175	45°03′N	18°30′E
Boscobel, Wi., U.S. (bŏs'kô-bĕl)	113	43°08′N	90°44′W
Bose, China (bwo-sŭ)	209	24°00′N	106°38′E
Boshan, China (bwo-shan)	205	36°32′N	117°51′E
Boskoop, Neth.	159a	52°04′N	4°39′E
Boskovice, Czech Rep. (bŏs'kō-vē-tsĕ)	168	49°26′N	16°37′E
Bosna, r., Yugo.	175	44°19′N	17°54′E
Bosnia and Herzegovina, nation, Eur.	175	44°15′N	17°30′E
Bosobolo, D.R.C.	236	4°11′N	19°54′E
Bosporus *see* İstanbul Boğazı, strt., Tur.	198	41°10′N	29°10′E
Bossangoa, C.A.R.	235	6°29′N	17°27′E
Bossier City, La., U.S. (bŏsh'ẽr)	123	32°31′N	93°42′W
Bosten Hu, l., China (bwo-stŭn hōō)	204	42°06′N	88°01′E
Boston, Ga., U.S. (bôs'tŭn)	124	30°47′N	83°47′W
Boston, Ma., U.S.	105	42°15′N	71°07′W
Boston Heights, Oh., U.S.	111d	41°15′N	81°30′W
Boston Mountains, mts., Ar., U.S.	107	35°46′N	93°32′W
Botany Bay, b., Austl. (bŏt'ȧ-nĭ)	221	33°58′S	151°11′E
Botevgrad, Blg.	175	42°54′N	23°41′E
Bothaville, S. Afr. (bō'tȧ-vĭl)	238c	27°24′S	26°38′E
Bothell, Wa., U.S. (bŏth'ĕl)	116a	47°46′N	122°12′W
Bothnia, Gulf of, b., Eur. (bŏth'nĭ-ȧ)	156	63°40′N	21°30′E
Botoşani, Rom. (bô-tô-shän'ĭ)	169	47°46′N	26°40′E
Botswana, nation, Afr. (bŏtswănă)	232	22°10′S	23°13′E
Bottineau, N.D., U.S. (bŏt-ĭ-nō')	112	48°50′N	100°28′W
Bottrop, Ger. (bōt'trōp)	168	51°31′N	6°56′E
Botwood, Can. (bŏt'wŏd)	93a	49°08′N	55°21′W
Bouafle, C. Iv. (bō-ȧ-flā')	230	6°59′N	5°45′W
Bouar, C.A.R. (bōō-är)	231	5°57′N	15°36′E
Bou Areg, Sebkha, Mor.	172	35°09′N	3°02′W
Boubandjidah, Parc National de, rec., Cam.	235	8°20′N	14°40′E
Boucherville, Can. (bōō-shä-vĕl')	102a	45°37′N	73°27′W
Boudenib, Mor. (bōō-dĕ-nĕb')	230	32°14′N	3°04′W
Boudette, Mn., U.S. (bōō-dĕt)	113	48°42′N	94°34′W
Boudouaou, Alg.	173	36°44′N	3°25′E
Boufarik, Alg. (bōō-fȧ-rēk')	173	36°35′N	2°55′E
Bougainville, i., Pap. N. Gui.	214e	6°00′S	155°00′E
Bougainville Trench, deep (bōō-găn-vēl')	241	7°00′S	152°00′E
Bougie *see* Bejaïa, Alg.	230	36°46′N	5°00′E
Bougouni, Mali (bōō-gōō-nē')	230	11°27′N	7°30′W
Bouïra, Alg. (boo-ē'rá)	162	36°25′N	3°55′E
Bouïra-Sahary, Alg. (bwē-rȧ sȧ'ȧ-rē)	173	35°16′N	3°23′E
Bouka, r., Gui.	234	11°05′N	10°40′W
Boulder, Co., U.S.	104	40°02′N	105°19′W
Boulder, r., Mt., U.S.	115	46°10′N	112°07′W
Boulder City, Nv., U.S.	104	35°57′N	114°50′W
Boulder Peak, mtn., Id., U.S.	115	43°53′N	114°33′W
Boulogne-Billancourt, Fr. (bōō-lôn'y'-bē-yän-kōōr')	170	48°50′N	2°14′E
Boulogne-sur-Mer, Fr. (bōō-lôn'y-sür-mâr')	161	50°44′N	1°37′E
Boumba, r., Cam.	235	3°20′N	14°40′E
Bouna, C. Iv. (bōō-nä')	230	9°16′N	3°00′W
Bouna, Parc National de, rec., C. Iv.	234	9°20′N	3°35′W
Boundary Bay, b., N.A. (boun'dȧ-rĭ)	116d	49°03′N	122°59′W
Boundary Peak, mtn., Nv., U.S.	118	37°52′N	118°20′W
Bound Brook, N.J., U.S. (bound brŏŏk)	110a	40°34′N	74°32′W
Bountiful, Ut., U.S. (boun'tĭ-fŏŏl)	117b	40°55′N	111°53′W
Bountiful Peak, mtn., Ut., U.S. (boun'tĭ-fŏŏl)	117b	40°58′N	111°49′W
Bounty Islands, is., N.Z.	5	47°42′S	179°05′E
Bourail, N. Cal.	214f	21°34′S	165°30′E
Bourem, Mali (bōō-rĕm')	230	16°43′N	0°15′W
Bourg-en-Bresse, Fr. (bōōr-gĕn-brĕs')	161	46°12′N	5°13′E
Bourges, Fr. (bōōrzh)	161	47°06′N	2°22′E
Bourget, Can. (bōōr-zhĕ')	102c	45°26′N	75°09′W
Bourgoin, Fr. (bōōr-gwăn')	171	45°46′N	5°17′E
Bourke, Austl. (bŭrk)	219	30°10′S	146°00′E
Bourne, Eng., U.K. (bôrn)	158a	52°46′N	0°22′W
Bournemouth, Eng., U.K. (bôrn'mŭth)	164	50°44′N	1°55′W
Bou Saâda, Alg. (bōō-sä'dä)	162	35°13′N	4°17′E
Bousso, Chad (bōō-sô')	231	10°33′N	16°45′E
Boutilimit, Maur.	230	17°30′N	14°54′W
Bouvetøya, i., Ant.	3	55°00′S	3°00′E
Bow, r., Can. (bō)	92	50°35′N	112°15′W
Bowbells, N.D., U.S. (bō'bĕls)	112	48°50′N	102°16′W
Bowdle, S.D., U.S. (bōd''l)	112	45°28′N	99°42′W
Bowen, Austl. (bō'ĕn)	219	20°02′S	148°14′E
Bowie, Md., U.S. (bōō'ĭ) (bō'ē)	110e	38°59′N	76°47′W
Bowie, Tx., U.S.	121	33°34′N	97°50′W

ăt; finăl; rāte; senāte; ärm; àsk; sofȧ; fâre; ch-choose; dh-as th in other; bē; ēvent; bĕt; recĕnt; cratẽr; g-gō; gh-guttural g; bĭt; ĭ-short neutral; rīde; ĸ-guttural k as ch in German ich;

PRONOUNCING INDEX

Bowling Green – Brownsville 275

PLACE (Pronunciation)	PAGE	LAT.	LONG.
Bowling Green, Ky., U.S. (bōlĭng grēn)	105	37°00'N	86°26'W
Bowling Green, Mo., U.S.	121	39°19'N	91°09'W
Bowling Green, Oh., U.S.	108	41°25'N	83°40'W
Bowman, N.D., U.S. (bō'măn)	112	46°11'N	103°23'W
Bowron, r., Can. (bō'rŭn)	95	53°20'N	121°10'W
Boxelder Creek, r., Mt., U.S. (bŏks'ĕl-dēr)	112	45°35'N	104°28'W
Box Elder Creek, r., Mt., U.S.	115	47°17'N	108°37'W
Box Hill, Austl.	217a	37°49'S	145°08'E
Boxian, China (bwo shyĕn)	208	33°52'N	115°47'E
Boxing, China (bwo-shyĭŋ)	206	37°09'N	118°08'E
Boxtel, Neth.	159a	51°40'N	5°21'E
Boyabo, D.R.C.	236	3°43'N	18°46'E
Boyang, China (bwo-yäŋ)	209	29°00'N	116°42'E
Boyer, r., Can. (boi'ēr)	102b	46°45'N	70°56'W
Boyer, r., Ia., U.S.	112	41°45'N	95°36'W
Boyle, Ire. (boil)	164	53°59'N	8°15'W
Boyne, r., Ire. (boin)	164	53°40'N	6°40'W
Boyne City, Mi., U.S.	108	45°15'N	85°05'W
Boyoma Falls, wtfl., D.R.C.	231	0°30'N	25°12'E
Boysen Reservoir, res., Wy., U.S.	115	43°19'N	108°11'W
Bozcaada, Tur. (bōz-cä'dä)	175	39°50'N	26°05'E
Bozca Ada, i., Tur.	175	39°50'N	26°00'E
Bozeman, Mt., U.S. (bōz'măn)	104	45°41'N	111°00'W
Bozene, D.R.C.	236	2°56'N	19°12'E
Bozhen, China (bwo-jŭn)	206	38°05'N	116°35'E
Bozoum, C.A.R.	235	6°19'N	16°23'E
Bra, Italy (brä)	174	44°41'N	7°52'E
Bracciano, Lago di, l., Italy (lä'gō-dē-brä-chä'nō)	174	42°05'N	12°00'E
Bracebridge, Can. (brās'brĭj)	99	45°05'N	79°20'W
Braceville, Il., U.S. (brās'vĭl)	111a	41°13'N	88°16'W
Bräcke, Swe. (brĕk'kĕ)	160	62°44'N	15°28'E
Brackenridge, Pa., U.S. (brăk'ĕn-rĭj)	111e	40°37'N	79°44'W
Brackettville, Tx., U.S. (brăk'ĕt-vĭl)	122	29°19'N	100°24'W
Braço Maior, mth., Braz.	143	11°00'S	51°00'W
Braço Menor, mth., Braz. (brä'zô-mĕ-nō'r)	143	11°38'S	50°00'W
Bradano, r., Italy (brä-dä'nō)	174	40°43'N	16°22'E
Bradenton, Fl., U.S. (brā'dĕn-tŭn)	125a	27°28'N	82°35'W
Bradfield, Eng., U.K. (brăd'fēld)	158b	51°25'N	1°08'W
Bradford, Eng., U.K. (brăd'fērd)	160	53°47'N	1°44'W
Bradford, Oh., U.S.	108	40°10'N	84°30'W
Bradford, Pa., U.S.	109	42°00'N	78°40'W
Bradley, Il., U.S. (brăd'lĭ)	111a	41°09'N	87°52'W
Bradner, Can. (brăd'nēr)	116d	49°05'N	122°26'W
Brady, Tx., U.S. (brā'dĭ)	122	31°09'N	99°21'W
Braga, Port. (brä'gä)	162	41°20'N	8°25'W
Bragado, Arg. (brä-gä'dō)	144	35°07'S	60°28'W
Bragança, Braz. (brä-gän'sä)	143	1°02'S	46°50'W
Bragança, Port.	172	41°48'N	6°46'W
Bragança Paulista, Braz. (brä-gän'sä-pä'ōō-lē's-tà)	144	22°58'S	46°31'W
Bragg Creek, Can. (brăg)	102e	50°57'N	114°35'W
Brahmaputra, r., Asia (brä'mà-pōō'trà)	199	26°45'N	92°45'E
Brāhui, mts., Pak.	199	28°32'N	66°15'E
Braidwood, Il., U.S. (brād'wŏŏd)	111a	41°16'N	88°13'W
Brăila, Rom. (brē'ēlà)	154	45°15'N	27°58'E
Brainerd, Mn., U.S. (brān'ērd)	113	46°20'N	94°09'W
Braintree, Ma., U.S. (brān'trē)	101a	42°14'N	71°00'W
Braithwaite, La., U.S. (brīth'wīt)	110d	29°52'N	89°57'W
Brakpan, S. Afr. (brăk'păn)	233b	26°15'S	28°22'E
Bralorne, Can. (brā'lôrn)	95	50°47'N	122°49'W
Bramalea, Can.	102d	43°48'N	79°41'W
Brampton, Can. (brămp'tŭn)	99	43°41'N	79°46'W
Branca, Pedra, mtn., Braz. (pĕ'drä-brà'n-kä)	144b	22°55'S	43°28'W
Branchville, N.J., U.S. (brânch'vĭl)	110a	41°09'N	74°44'W
Branchville, S.C., U.S.	125	33°17'N	80°48'W
Branco, r., Braz. (brän'kō)	143	2°21'N	60°38'W
Brandberg, mtn., Nmb.	232	21°15'S	14°15'E
Brandenburg, Ger. (brän'dĕn-bŏŏrgh)	161	52°25'N	12°33'E
Brandenburg, state, Ger.	159b	52°15'N	13°00'E
Brandenburg, hist. reg., Ger.	168	52°12'N	13°31'E
Brandfort, S. Afr. (brăn'd-fôrt)	238c	28°42'S	26°29'E
Brandon, Can. (brăn'dŭn)	90	49°50'N	99°57'W
Brandon, Vt., U.S.	109	43°45'N	73°05'W
Brandon Mountain, mtn., Ire. (brăn-dŏn)	164	52°15'N	10°12'W
Brandywine, Md., U.S. (brăndĭ'wīn)	110e	38°42'N	76°51'W
Branford, Ct., U.S. (brăn'fērd)	109	41°15'N	72°50'W
Braniewo, Pol. (brä-nyĕ'vô)	169	54°23'N	19°50'E
Brańsk, Pol. (brän' sk)	169	52°44'N	22°51'E
Branson, Mo., U.S.	121	36°39'N	93°13'W
Brantford, Can. (brănt'fērd)	99	43°09'N	80°17'W
Bras d'Or Lake, l., Can. (brä-dôr')	101	45°52'N	60°50'W
Brasília, Braz. (brä-sē'lvä)	143	15°49'S	47°39'W
Brasilia Legal, Braz.	143	3°45'S	55°46'W
Brasópolis, Braz. (brä-sô'pô-lēs)	141a	22°30'S	45°36'W
Braşov, Rom.	163	45°39'N	25°35'E
Brass, Nig. (brăs)	230	4°28'N	6°28'E
Brasschaat, Bel. (bräs'kät)	159a	51°19'N	4°30'E
Bratenahl, Oh., U.S. (bră'tĕn-ôl)	111d	41°34'N	81°36'W
Bratislava, Slvk. (brä'tĭs-lä-vä)	154	48°09'N	17°07'E
Bratsk, Russia (brätsk)	179	56°10'N	102°04'E
Bratskoye Vodokhranilishche, res., Russia	179	56°10'N	102°05'E
Bratslav, Ukr. (brät'sláf)	177	48°48'N	28°59'E
Brattleboro, Vt., U.S. (brăt''l-bŭr-ô)	109	42°50'N	72°35'W
Braunau, Aus. (brou'nou)	168	48°15'N	13°05'E
Braunschweig, Ger. (broun'shvīgh)	161	52°16'N	10°32'E
Bråviken, r., Swe.	166	58°40'N	16°40'E
Brawley, Ca., U.S. (brô'lĭ)	104	32°59'N	115°32'W
Bray, Ire. (brā)	164	53°10'N	6°05'W
Braymer, Mo., U.S. (brā'mēr)	121	39°34'N	93°47'W
Brays Bay, Tx., U.S. (brās'bī'yōō)	123a	29°41'N	95°33'W
Brazeau, r., Can.	95	52°55'N	116°10'W
Brazeau, Mount, mtn., Can. (brä-zō')	95	52°33'N	117°21'W
Brazil, In., U.S. (brȧ-zĭl')	108	39°30'N	87°00'W
Brazil, nation, S.A.	143	9°00'S	53°00'W
Brazilian Highlands, mts., Braz. (brȧ zĭl yȧn hī-lăndz)	139	14°00'S	48°00'W
Brazos, r., Tx., U.S. (brä'zōs)	106	33°10'N	98°50'W
Brazos, Clear Fork, r., Tx., U.S.	122	32°56'N	99°14'W
Brazos, Double Mountain Fork, r., Tx., U.S.	120	33°23'N	101°21'W
Brazos, Salt Fork, r., Tx., U.S. (sôlt fôrk)	120	33°20'N	101°57'W
Brazzaville, Congo (brá-zà-vēl')	232	4°16'S	15°17'E
Brčko, Bos. (bērch'kô)	175	44°54'N	18°46'E
Brda, r., Pol. (bēr-dä)	169	53°18'N	17°55'E
Brea, Ca., U.S. (brē'ȧ)	117a	33°55'N	117°54'W
Breakeyville, Can.	102b	46°40'N	71°13'W
Breckenridge, Mn., U.S. (brĕk'ĕn-rĭj)	112	46°17'N	96°35'W
Breckenridge, Tx., U.S.	122	32°46'N	98°53'W
Brecksville, Oh., U.S. (brĕks'vĭl)	111d	41°19'N	81°38'W
Břeclav, Czech Rep. (brzhĕl'läf)	168	48°46'N	16°54'E
Breda, Neth. (brā-dä')	165	51°35'N	4°47'E
Bredasdorp, S. Afr. (brā'das-dôrp)	232	34°15'S	20°00'E
Bredy, Russia (brĕ'dĭ)	186a	52°25'N	60°23'E
Bregenz, Aus. (brā'gĕnts)	168	47°30'N	9°46'E
Bregovo, Blg. (brĕ'gô-vô)	175	44°07'N	22°45'E
Breidafjördur, b., Ice.	160	65°15'N	22°50'W
Breidbach, S. Afr. (brĕd'băk)	233c	32°54'S	27°26'E
Breil-sur-Roya, Fr. (brĕ'y')	171	43°57'N	7°36'E
Brejo, Braz. (brå'zhō)	143	3°33'S	42°46'W
Bremangerlandet, i., Nor.	166	61°51'N	4°25'E
Bremen, Ger. (brā-mĕn)	154	53°05'N	8°50'E
Bremen, In., U.S. (brē'mĕn)	108	41°25'N	86°05'W
Bremerhaven, Ger. (brām-ēr-hä'fĕn)	160	53°33'N	8°38'E
Bremerton, Wa., U.S. (brĕm'ēr-tŭn)	114	47°34'N	122°38'W
Bremervörde, Ger. (brĕ'mĕr-fûr-dĕ)	159c	53°29'N	9°09'E
Bremner, Can. (brĕm'nēr)	102g	53°34'N	113°14'W
Bremond, Tx., U.S. (brĕm'ŭnd)	123	31°11'N	96°40'W
Brenham, Tx., U.S. (brĕn'ăm)	123	30°10'N	96°24'W
Brenner Pass, p., Eur. (brĕn'ēr)	161	47°00'N	11°30'E
Brentwood, Eng., U.K. (brĕnt'wŏŏd)	165	51°37'N	0°18'E
Brentwood, Md., U.S.	109	39°00'N	76°55'W
Brentwood, Mo., U.S.	117e	38°37'N	90°21'W
Brentwood, Pa., U.S.	111e	40°22'N	79°59'W
Brescia, Italy (brā'shä)	162	45°33'N	10°15'E
Bressanone, Italy (brĕs-sä-nō'nā)	174	46°42'N	11°40'E
Bressuire, Fr. (grĕ-swēr')	170	46°49'N	0°14'W
Brest, Bela.	178	52°06'N	23°43'E
Brest, Fr. (brĕst)	154	48°24'N	4°30'W
Brest, prov., Bela.	176	52°30'N	26°50'E
Bretagne, hist. reg., Fr. (brĕ-tän'yĕ)	170	48°00'N	3°00'W
Breton, Pertuis, strt., Fr. (pâr-twē'brĕ-tôN')	170	46°18'N	1°43'W
Breton Sound, strt., La., U.S. (brĕt'ŭn)	124	29°38'N	89°15'W
Breukelen, Neth.	159a	52°09'N	5°00'E
Brevard, N.C., U.S. (brē-värd')	125	35°14'N	82°45'W
Breves, Braz. (brā'vĕzh)	143	1°32'S	50°13'W
Brevik, Nor. (brĕ'vĕk)	166	59°04'N	9°39'E
Brewarrina, Austl. (brōō-ēr-rē'nȧ)	219	29°54'S	146°50'E
Brewer, Me., U.S. (brōō'ēr)	100	44°46'N	68°46'W
Brewerville, Lib.	234	6°26'N	10°47'W
Brewster, N.Y., U.S. (brōō'stēr)	110a	41°23'N	73°38'W
Brewster, Cerro, mtn., Pan. (sĕ'r-rô-brōō'stēr)	133	9°19'N	79°15'W
Brewton, Al., U.S. (brōō'tŭn)	124	31°06'N	87°04'W
Brežice, Slvn. (brĕ'zhē-tsĕ)	174	45°55'N	15°37'E
Breznik, Blg. (brĕs'nĕk)	175	42°44'N	22°55'E
Briancon, Fr. (brē-äN-sôN')	171	44°54'N	6°39'E
Briare, Fr. (brē-är')	170	47°40'N	2°46'E
Bridal Veil, Or., U.S. (brīd'ăl vāl)	116c	45°33'N	122°10'W
Bridge Point, c., Bah. (brĭj)	134	25°35'N	76°40'W
Bridgeport, Al., U.S. (brĭj'pôrt)	124	34°55'N	85°42'W
Bridgeport, Ct., U.S.	105	41°12'N	73°12'W
Bridgeport, Il., U.S.	108	38°40'N	87°45'W
Bridgeport, Ne., U.S.	112	41°40'N	103°06'W
Bridgeport, Oh., U.S.	108	40°00'N	80°45'W
Bridgeport, Pa., U.S.	110f	40°06'N	75°21'W
Bridgeport, Tx., U.S.	121	33°13'N	97°46'W
Bridgeton, Al., U.S. (brĭj'tŭn)	110h	33°27'N	86°39'W
Bridgeton, Mo., U.S.	117e	38°45'N	90°23'W
Bridgeton, N.J., U.S.	109	39°30'N	75°15'W
Bridgetown, Barb. (brĭj' toun)	129	13°08'N	59°37'W
Bridgetown, Can.	100	44°51'N	65°18'W
Bridgeville, Pa., U.S. (brĭj'vĭl)	111e	40°22'N	80°07'W
Bridgewater, Austl. (brĭj'wô-tēr)	222	42°50'S	147°28'E
Bridgewater, Can.	91	44°23'N	64°31'W
Bridgnorth, Eng., U.K. (brĭj'nôrth)	158a	52°32'N	2°25'W
Bridgton, Me., U.S. (brĭj'tŭn)	100	44°04'N	70°45'W
Bridlington, Eng., U.K. (brĭd'lĭng-tŭn)	164	54°06'N	0°10'W
Brie-Comte-Robert, Fr. (brē-kôNt-ĕ-rō-bâr')	171b	48°42'N	2°37'E
Brielle, Neth.	159a	51°54'N	4°08'E
Brierfield, Eng., U.K. (brī'ēr fēld)	158a	53°49'N	2°14'W
Brierfield, Al., U.S. (brī'ēr-fēld)	124	33°01'N	86°55'W
Brier Island, i., Can. (brī'ēr)	100	44°16'N	66°24'W
Brieselang, Ger. (brē'zĕ-läng)	159b	52°36'N	12°59'E
Briey, Fr. (brē-ĕ')	171	49°15'N	5°57'E
Brig, Switz. (brēg)	161	46°17'N	7°59'E
Brigg, Eng., U.K. (brĭg)	158a	53°33'N	0°29'W
Brigham City, Ut., U.S. (brĭg'ăm)	117b	41°31'N	112°01'W
Brighouse, Eng., U.K. (brĭg'hous)	158a	53°42'N	1°47'W
Bright, Austl. (brīt)	222	36°43'S	147°00'E
Bright, In., U.S. (brīt)	111f	39°13'N	84°51'W
Brightlingsea, Eng., U.K. (brī't-lĭng-sē)	158b	51°50'N	1°00'E
Brighton, Austl.	217a	37°55'S	145°00'E
Brighton, Eng., U.K.	161	50°47'N	0°07'W
Brighton, Al., U.S. (brīt'ŭn)	110h	33°27'N	86°56'W
Brighton, Co., U.S.	120	39°58'N	104°49'W
Brighton, Ia., U.S.	113	41°11'N	91°47'W
Brighton, Il., U.S.	117e	39°03'N	90°08'W
Brighton Indian Reservation, I.R., Fl., U.S.	125a	27°05'N	81°25'W
Brihuega, Spain (brē-wā'gä)	172	40°32'N	2°52'W
Brimley, Mi., U.S. (brĭm'lē)	117k	46°24'N	84°34'W
Brindisi, Italy (brēn'dē-zē)	154	40°38'N	17°57'E
Brinje, Cro. (brēn'yĕ)	174	45°00'N	15°08'E
Brinkley, Ar., U.S. (brĭŋk'lĭ)	121	34°52'N	91°12'W
Brinnon, Wa., U.S. (brĭn'ŭn)	116a	47°41'N	122°54'W
Brion, i., Can. (brē-ôN')	101	47°47'N	61°29'W
Brioude, Fr. (brē-ōōd')	170	45°18'N	3°22'E
Brisbane, Austl. (brĭz'bån)	222	27°30'S	153°10'E
Bristol, Eng., U.K.	161	51°29'N	2°39'W
Bristol, Ct., U.S. (brĭs'tŭl)	109	41°40'N	72°55'W
Bristol, Pa., U.S.	110f	40°06'N	74°51'W
Bristol, R.I., U.S.	110b	41°41'N	71°14'W
Bristol, Tn., U.S.	105	36°35'N	82°10'W
Bristol, Va., U.S.	105	36°36'N	82°00'W
Bristol, Vt., U.S.	109	44°10'N	73°00'W
Bristol, Wi., U.S.	111a	42°32'N	88°04'W
Bristol Bay, b., Ak., U.S.	103	58°05'N	158°54'W
Bristol Channel, strt., Eng., U.K.	161	51°20'N	3°47'W
Bristow, Ok., U.S. (brĭs'tō)	121	35°50'N	96°25'W
British Columbia, prov., Can. (brĭt'ĭsh kŏl'ŭm-bĭ-ȧ)	90	56°00'N	124°53'W
British Indian Ocean Territory, dep., Afr.	2	7°00'S	72°00'E
British Isles, is., Eur.	156	54°00'N	4°00'W
Brits, S. Afr.	238c	25°39'S	27°47'E
Britstown, S. Afr. (brĭts'toun)	232	30°30'S	23°40'E
Britt, Ia., U.S. (brĭt)	113	43°05'N	93°47'W
Brittany *see* Bretagne, hist. reg., Fr.	170	48°00'N	3°00'W
Britton, S.D., U.S. (brĭt'ŭn)	112	45°47'N	97°44'W
Brive-la-Gaillarde, Fr. (brēv-lä-gī-yärd'ĕ)	161	45°10'N	1°31'E
Briviesca, Spain (brē-vyās'kȧ)	172	42°34'N	3°21'W
Brno, Czech Rep. (b'r'nô)	154	49°18'N	16°37'E
Broa, Ensenada de la, b., Cuba	134	22°30'N	82°00'W
Broach, India	202	21°47'N	72°58'E
Broad, r., Ga., U.S. (brôd)	124	34°15'N	83°14'W
Broad, r., N.C., U.S.	125	35°38'N	82°40'W
Broadmeadows, Austl. (brôd'mĕd-ōz)	217a	37°40'S	144°53'E
Broadview Heights, Oh., U.S. (brôd'vū)	111d	41°18'N	81°41'W
Brockport, N.Y., U.S. (brŏk'pōrt)	109	43°15'N	77°55'W
Brockton, Ma., U.S. (brŏk'tŭn)	101a	42°04'N	71°01'W
Brockville, Can. (brŏk'vĭl)	91	44°35'N	75°40'W
Brockway, Mt., U.S. (brŏk'wā)	115	47°24'N	105°41'W
Brodnica, Pol. (brôd'nĭt-sȧ)	169	53°16'N	19°26'E
Brody, Ukr. (brô'dĭ)	181	50°05'N	25°10'E
Broken Arrow, Ok., U.S. (brō'kĕn ăr'ō)	121	36°03'N	95°48'W
Broken Bay, b., Austl.	222	33°34'S	151°20'E
Broken Bow, Ne., U.S. (brō'kĕn bō)	112	41°24'N	99°37'W
Broken Bow, Ok., U.S.	121	34°02'N	94°43'W
Broken Hill, Austl. (brōk'ĕn)	219	31°55'S	141°35'E
Broken Hill *see* Kabwe, Zam.	232	14°27'S	28°27'E
Bromley, Eng., U.K. (brŭm'lĭ)	158b	51°23'N	0°01'E
Bromptonville, Can. (brŭmp'tŭn-vĭl)	99	45°30'N	72°00'W
Brønderslev, Den. (brûn'dēr-slĕv)	166	57°15'N	9°56'E
Bronkhorstspruit, S. Afr.	238c	25°50'S	28°48'E
Bronnitsy, Russia (brô-nyĭ'tsĭ)	176	55°26'N	38°16'E
Bronson, Mi., U.S. (brŏn'sŭn)	108	41°55'N	85°15'W
Bronte Creek, r., Can.	102d	43°25'N	79°53'W
Brood, r., S.C., U.S. (brōōd)	125	34°46'N	81°25'W
Brookfield, Il., U.S. (brŏŏk'fēld)	111a	41°49'N	87°51'W
Brookfield, Mo., U.S.	121	39°45'N	93°04'W
Brookhaven, Ga., U.S. (brŏŏk'hāv'n)	110c	33°52'N	84°21'W
Brookhaven, Ms., U.S.	124	31°35'N	90°26'W
Brookings, Or., U.S. (brŏŏk'ĭngs)	114	42°04'N	124°16'W
Brookings, S.D., U.S.	112	44°18'N	96°47'W
Brookline, Ma., U.S. (brŏŏk'lĭn)	101a	42°20'N	71°08'W
Brookline, N.H., U.S.	101a	42°44'N	71°37'W
Brooklyn, Oh., U.S. (brŏŏk'lĭn)	111d	41°26'N	81°44'W
Brooklyn Center, Mn., U.S.	117g	45°05'N	93°21'W
Brook Park, Oh., U.S. (brŏŏk)	111d	41°24'N	81°50'W
Brooks, Can.	95	50°35'N	111°53'W
Brooks Range, mts., Ak., U.S. (brŏŏks)	106a	68°20'N	159°00'W
Brooksville, Fl., U.S. (brŏŏks'vĭl)	125a	28°32'N	82°28'W
Brookville, In., U.S. (brŏŏk'vĭl)	108	39°20'N	85°00'W
Brookville, Pa., U.S.	109	41°10'N	79°00'W
Brookwood, Al., U.S. (brŏŏk'wŏŏd)	124	33°15'N	87°17'W
Broome, Austl. (brōōm)	218	18°00'S	122°15'E
Brossard, Can.	102a	45°26'N	73°28'W
Brothers, is., Bah. (brŭd'hērs)	134	26°05'N	79°00'W
Broumov, Czech Rep. (brōō'môf)	168	50°33'N	15°55'E
Brown Bank, bk.	135	21°30'N	74°35'W
Brownfield, Tx., U.S. (broun'fēld)	120	33°11'N	102°16'W
Browning, Mt., U.S. (broun'ĭng)	115	48°37'N	113°05'W
Brownsboro, Ky., U.S. (brounz'bō-rō)	111h	38°22'N	85°30'W
Brownsburg, Can. (brouns'bûrg)	102a	45°40'N	74°24'W
Brownsburg, In., U.S.	111g	39°51'N	86°23'W
Brownsmead, Or., U.S. (brounz'-mēd)	116c	46°13'N	123°33'W
Brownstown, In., U.S. (brounz'toun)	108	38°50'N	86°00'W
Brownsville, Pa., U.S. (brounz'vĭl)	111e	40°01'N	79°53'W
Brownsville, Tn., U.S.	124	35°35'N	89°15'W

276 Brownsville – Byeshankovichy PRONOUNCING INDEX

PLACE (Pronunciation)	PAGE	LAT.	LONG.
Brownsville, Tx., U.S.	104	25°55'N	97°30'W
Brownville Junction, Me., U.S. (broun'vĭl)	100	45°20'N	69°04'W
Brownwood, Tx., U.S. (broun'wŏŏd)	104	31°44'N	98°58'W
Brownwood, l., Tx., U.S.	122	31°55'N	99°15'W
Brozas, Spain (brō'thäs)	172	39°37'N	6°44'W
Bruce, Mount, mtn., Austl. (brōōs)	220	22°35'S	118°15'E
Bruce Peninsula, pen., Can.	98	44°50'N	81°20'W
Bruceton, Tn., U.S. (brōōs'tŭn)	124	36°02'N	88°14'W
Bruchsal, Ger. (brŏŏk'zäl)	168	49°08'N	8°34'E
Bruck, Aus. (brŏŏk)	168	47°25'N	15°14'E
Bruck, Aus.	168	48°01'N	16°47'E
Brück, Ger. (brük)	159b	52°12'N	12°45'E
Bruderheim, Can. (brōō'dēr-hīm)	102g	53°47'N	112°56'W
Brugge, Bel.	161	51°13'N	3°05'E
Brühl, Ger. (brül)	171c	50°49'N	6°54'E
Bruneau, r., Id., U.S. (brōō-nō')	114	42°47'N	115°43'W
Brunei, nation, Asia (brŏŏ-nī')	212	4°52'N	113°38'E
Brünen, Ger. (brü'nĕn)	171c	51°43'N	6°41'E
Brunete, Spain (brōō-nā'tā)	173a	40°24'N	4°00'W
Brunette, i., Can. (brŏŏ-nĕt')	101	47°16'N	55°54'W
Brunn am Gebirge, Aus. (brōōn'äm gĕ-bĭr'gĕ)	159e	48°07'N	16°18'E
Brunsbüttel, Ger. (brŏŏns'büt-tĕl)	159c	53°58'N	9°10'E
Brunswick, Ga., U.S. (brŭnz'wĭk)	105	31°08'N	81°30'W
Brunswick, Md., U.S.	109	39°20'N	77°35'W
Brunswick, Me., U.S.	100	43°54'N	69°57'W
Brunswick, Mo., U.S.	121	39°25'N	93°07'W
Brunswick, Oh., U.S.	111d	41°14'N	81°50'W
Brunswick, Península de, pen., Chile	144	53°25'S	71°15'W
Bruny, i., Austl. (brōō'nē)	221	43°30'S	147°50'E
Brush, Co., U.S. (brŭsh)	120	40°14'N	103°40'W
Brusque, Braz. (brōō's-kōōĕ)	144	27°15'S	48°45'W
Brussels, Bel.	154	50°51'N	4°21'E
Brussels, Il., U.S. (brŭs'ĕls)	117e	38°57'N	90°36'W
Bruxelles *see* Brussels, Bel.	154	50°51'N	4°21'E
Bryan, Oh., U.S. (brī'ăn)	108	41°25'N	84°30'W
Bryan, Tx., U.S.	123	30°40'N	96°22'W
Bryansk, Russia	178	53°15'N	34°22'E
Bryansk, prov., Russia	176	52°43'N	32°25'E
Bryant, S.D., U.S. (brī'ănt)	112	44°35'N	97°29'W
Bryant, Wa., U.S.	116a	48°14'N	122°10'W
Bryce Canyon National Park, rec., Ut., U.S. (brīs)	106	37°35'N	112°15'W
Bryn Mawr, Pa., U.S. (brĭn mär')	110f	40°02'N	75°20'W
Bryson City, N.C., U.S. (brīs'ŭn)	124	35°25'N	83°25'W
Bryukhovetskaya, Russia (b'ryŭk'ô-vyĕt-skä'yä)	177	45°56'N	38°58'E
Buala, Sol. Is.	214e	8°08'S	159°35'E
Buatan, Indon.	197b	0°45'N	101°49'E
Buba, Gui.-B. (bōō'bȧ)	230	11°39'N	14°58'W
Bucaramanga, Col. (bōō-kä'rä-mäŋ'gä)	142	7°12'N	73°14'W
Buccaneer Archipelago, is., Austl. (bŭk-ȧ-nēr')	220	16°05'S	122°00'E
Buchach, Ukr. (bŏ'chȧch)	169	49°04'N	25°25'E
Buchanan, Lib. (bû-kăn'ăn)	230	5°57'N	10°02'W
Buchanan, Mi., U.S.	108	41°50'N	86°25'W
Buchanan, l., Austl. (bû-kân'nŏn)	221	21°40'S	145°00'E
Buchanan, l., Tx., U.S. (bû-kăn'ăn)	122	30°55'N	98°40'W
Buchans, Can.	101	48°49'N	56°52'W
Bucharest, Rom.	154	44°23'N	26°10'E
Buchholz, Ger. (bōōk'hōltz)	159c	53°19'N	9°53'E
Buck Creek, r., In., U.S. (bŭk)	111g	39°43'N	85°58'W
Buckhannon, W.V., U.S. (bŭk-hăn'ŭn)	108	39°00'N	80°10'W
Buckhaven, Scot., U.K. (bŭk-hā'v'n)	164	56°10'N	3°10'W
Buckie, Scot., U.K. (bŭk'ĭ)	164	57°40'N	2°50'W
Buckingham, Can. (bŭk'ĭng-ăm)	102c	45°35'N	75°25'W
Buckingham, can., India (bŭk'ĭng-ăm)	203	15°18'N	79°50'E
Buckinghamshire, co., Eng., U.K.	158b	51°45'N	0°48'W
Buckland, Can. (bŭk'lănd)	102b	46°37'N	70°33'W
Buckland Tableland, reg., Austl.	221	24°31'S	148°00'E
Buckley, Wa., U.S. (bŭk'lē)	116a	47°10'N	122°02'W
Bucksport, Me., U.S. (bŭks'pôrt)	100	44°35'N	68°47'W
Buctouche, Can. (bŭk-tōōsh')	100	46°28'N	64°43'W
Bucun, China (bōō-tsŏn)	206	36°38'N	117°26'E
Bucureşti *see* Bucharest, Rom.	154	44°23'N	26°10'E
Bucyrus, Oh., U.S. (bû-sī'rŭs)	108	40°50'N	82°55'W
Budapest, Hung. (bōō'dȧ-pĕsht')	154	47°30'N	19°05'E
Budge Budge, India	202a	22°28'N	88°08'E
Budjala, D.R.C.	236	2°39'N	19°42'E
Budyonnovsk, Russia	182	44°46'N	44°09'E
Buea, Cam.	235	4°09'N	9°14'E
Buechel, Ky., U.S. (bē-chûl')	111h	38°12'N	85°38'W
Bueil, Fr. (bwā')	171b	48°55'N	1°27'E
Buena Park, Ca., U.S. (bwā'nȧ pärk)	117a	33°52'N	118°00'W
Buenaventura, Col. (bwā'nä-vĕn-tōō'rȧ)	142	3°46'N	77°09'W
Buenaventura, Cuba	135a	22°53'N	82°22'W
Buenaventura, Bahía de, b., Col.	142	3°45'N	79°23'W
Buena Vista, Co., U.S. (bū'nȧ vĭs'tȧ)	120	38°51'N	106°07'W
Buena Vista, Ga., U.S.	124	32°15'N	84°30'W
Buena Vista, Va., U.S.	109	37°45'N	79°20'W
Buena Vista, Bahía, b., Cuba (bä-ē'ä-bwĕ-nä-vē's-tä)	134	22°30'N	79°10'W
Buena Vista Lake Bed, l., Ca., U.S. (bū'nȧ vĭs'tȧ)	118	35°14'N	119°17'W
Buendia, Embalse de, res., Spain	172	40°30'N	2°45'W
Buenos Aires, Arg. (bwā'nōs ī'rās)	144	34°20'S	58°30'W
Buenos Aires, Col.	142a	3°01'N	76°34'W
Buenos Aires, C.R.	133	9°10'N	83°21'W
Buenos Aires, prov., Arg.	144	36°15'S	61°45'W
Buenos Aires, l., S.A.	144	46°30'S	72°15'W
Buffalo, Mn., U.S. (bŭf'ȧ lō)	113	45°10'N	93°50'W
Buffalo, N.Y., U.S.	105	42°54'N	78°51'W
Buffalo, Tx., U.S.	123	31°28'N	96°04'W
Buffalo, Wy., U.S.	115	44°19'N	106°42'W
Buffalo, r., S. Afr.	233c	28°35'S	30°27'E
Buffalo, r., Ar., U.S.	121	35°56'N	92°58'W
Buffalo, r., Tn., U.S.	124	35°24'N	87°10'W
Buffalo Bayou, Tx., U.S.	123a	29°46'N	95°32'W
Buffalo Creek, r., Mn., U.S.	113	44°46'N	94°28'W
Buffalo Head Hills, hills, Can.	92	57°16'N	116°18'W
Buford, Can. (bū'fŭrd)	102g	53°15'N	113°55'W
Buford, Ga., U.S. (bū'fērd)	124	34°05'N	84°00'W
Bug (Zakhidnyy Buh), r., Eur.	169	52°29'N	21°20'E
Buga, Col. (bōō'gä)	142	3°54'N	76°17'W
Buggenhout, Bel.	159a	51°01'N	4°10'E
Buglandsfjorden, l., Nor.	166	58°53'N	7°55'E
Bugojno, Bos. (bŏ-gō ī nō)	175	44°03'N	17°28'E
Bugul'ma, Russia (bŏ-gŏl'mȧ)	178	54°40'N	52°40'E
Buguruslan, Russia (bŏ-gŏ-rŏs-lȧn')	178	53°30'N	52°32'E
Buhi, Phil. (bōō'ē)	213a	13°26'N	123°31'E
Buhl, Id., U.S. (bŭl)	115	42°36'N	114°45'W
Buhl, Mn., U.S.	113	47°28'N	92°49'W
Buin, Chile (bŏ-ēn')	141b	33°44'S	70°44'W
Buinaksk, Russia (bŏ'ē-näksk)	181	42°40'N	47°20'E
Buir Nur, l., Asia (bōō-ēr nōōr)	205	47°50'N	117°00'E
Bujalance, Spain (bōō-hä-län'thā)	172	37°54'N	4°22'W
Bujumbura, Bdi.	237	3°23'S	29°22'E
Buka Island, i., Pap. N. Gui.	214e	5°15'S	154°35'E
Bukama, D.R.C. (bōō-kä'mä)	232	9°08'S	26°00'E
Bukavu, D.R.C.	232	2°30'S	28°52'E
Bukhara, Uzb. (bŏ-kä'rä)	183	39°31'N	64°22'E
Bukitbatu, Indon.	197b	1°25'N	101°58'E
Bukittinggi, Indon.	212	0°25'S	100°28'E
Bukoba, Tan.	232	1°20'S	31°49'E
Bukovina, hist. reg., Eur. (bŏ-kô'vĭ-nȧ)	169	48°06'N	25°20'E
Bula, Indon. (bōō'lä)	213	3°00'S	130°30'E
Bulalacao, Phil. (bōō-lä-lä'kä-ō)	213a	12°30'N	121°20'E
Bulawayo, Zimb. (bōō-lȧ-wä'yō)	232	20°12'S	28°43'E
Buldir, i., Ak., U.S. (bŭl dĭr)	103a	52°22'N	175°50'E
Bulgaria, nation, Eur. (bŏl-gā'rĭ-ă)	154	42°12'N	24°13'E
Bulkley Ranges, mts., Can. (bŭlk'lē)	94	54°30'N	127°30'W
Bullaque, r., Spain (bōō-lä'kā)	172	39°15'N	4°13'W
Bullas, Spain (bōōl'yäs)	172	38°07'N	1°48'W
Bullfrog Creek, r., Ut., U.S.	119	37°45'N	110°55'W
Bull Harbour, Can. (här'bēr)	94	50°45'N	127°55'W
Bull Head, mtn., Jam.	134	18°10'N	77°15'W
Bull Run, r., Or., U.S. (bŏl)	116c	45°26'N	122°11'W
Bull Run Reservoir, res., Or., U.S.	116c	45°29'N	122°11'W
Bull Shoals Reservoir, res., U.S. (bŏl shōlz)	107	36°35'N	92°57'W
Bulpham, Eng., U.K. (bōōl'făn)	158b	51°33'N	0°21'E
Bultfontein, S. Afr. (bŏlt'fŏn-tān')	238c	28°18'S	26°10'E
Bulun, Russia (bōō-lŏn')	179	70°48'N	127°27'E
Bulungu, D.R.C. (bōō-lŏŋ'gōō)	236	6°04'S	21°54'E
Bulwer, S. Afr. (bŏl-wēr)	233c	29°49'S	29°48'E
Bumba, D.R.C. (bŏm'bȧ)	231	2°11'N	22°28'E
Bumbire Island, i., Tan.	237	1°40'S	32°05'E
Buna, Pap. N. Gui. (bōō'nȧ)	213	8°58'S	148°38'E
Bunbury, Austl. (bŭn'bŭrĭ)	218	33°25'S	115°45'E
Bundaberg, Austl. (bŭn'dȧ-bûrg)	219	24°45'S	152°18'E
Bunguran Utara, Kepulauan, is., Indon.	212	3°22'N	108°00'E
Bunia, D.R.C.	237	1°34'N	30°15'E
Bunker Hill, Il., U.S. (bŭnk'ēr hĭl)	117e	39°03'N	89°57'W
Bunkie, La., U.S. (bŭŋ'kĭ)	123	30°55'N	92°10'W
Bun Plains, pl., Kenya	237	0°55'N	40°35'E
Bununu Dass, Nig.	235	10°00'N	9°31'E
Buor-Khaya, Guba, b., Russia	185	71°45'N	131°00'E
Buor Khaya, Mys, c., Russia	179	71°47'N	133°22'E
Bura, Kenya	237	1°06'S	39°57'E
Buraydah, Sau. Ar.	198	26°23'N	44°14'E
Burbank, Ca., U.S. (bûr'bănk)	117a	34°11'N	118°19'W
Burco, Som.	238a	9°20'N	45°45'E
Burdekin, r., Austl. (bûr'dē-kĭn)	221	19°22'S	145°07'E
Burdur, Tur. (bōōr-dōr')	163	37°50'N	30°15'E
Burdwān, India (bŏd-wän')	199	23°29'N	87°53'E
Bureinskiy, Khrebet, mts., Russia	179	51°15'N	133°30'E
Bureya, Russia (bŏrā'ä)	179	49°55'N	130°00'E
Bureya, r., Russia (bŏ-rā'yä)	185	51°00'N	131°15'E
Burford, Eng., U.K. (bûr-fērd)	158b	51°46'N	1°38'W
Burgas, Blg. (bŏr-gäs')	163	42°29'N	27°30'E
Burgas, Gulf of, b., Blg.	163	42°30'N	27°40'E
Burgaw, N.C., U.S. (bûr'gō)	125	34°31'N	77°56'W
Burgdorf, Switz. (bŏrg'dôrf)	168	47°04'N	7°37'E
Burgenland, state, Aus.	159e	47°58'N	16°57'E
Burgeo, Can.	101	47°36'N	57°34'W
Burgess, Va., U.S.	109	37°53'N	76°21'W
Burgo de Osma, Spain	172	41°35'N	3°02'W
Burgos, Mex. (bŏr'gōs)	122	24°57'N	98°47'W
Burgos, Phil.	213a	16°03'N	119°52'E
Burgos, Spain (bōō'r-gŏs)	162	42°20'N	3°44'W
Burgsvik, Swe. (bŏrgs'vĭk)	166	57°04'N	18°18'E
Burhānpur, India (bŏŏr'hän-pōōr)	199	21°26'N	76°08'E
Burias Island, i., Phil. (bōō'rē-äs)	213a	12°56'N	122°56'E
Burias Pass, strt., Phil. (bōō'rē-äs)	213a	13°04'N	123°11'E
Burica, Punta, c., N.A. (pōō'n-tä-bōō'rē-kä)	133	8°02'N	83°12'W
Burien, Wa., U.S. (bū'rĭ-ĕn)	116a	47°28'N	122°20'W
Burin, Can. (bûr'ĭn)	93a	47°02'N	55°10'W
Burin Peninsula, pen., Can.	101	47°00'N	55°40'W
Burkburnett, Tx., U.S. (bûrk-bûr'nĕt)	120	34°04'N	98°35'W
Burke, Vt., U.S. (bûrk)	109	44°40'N	72°00'W
Burke Channel, strt., Can.	94	52°07'N	127°38'W
Burketown, Austl. (bûrk'toun)	218	17°50'S	139°30'E
Burkina Faso, nation, Afr.	230	13°00'N	2°00'W
Burley, Id., U.S. (bûr'lĭ)	115	42°31'N	113°48'W
Burley, Wa., U.S.	116a	47°25'N	122°38'W
Burlingame, Ca., U.S. (bûr'lĭn-gām)	116b	37°35'N	122°22'W
Burlingame, Ks., U.S.	121	38°45'N	95°49'W
Burlington, Can. (bûr'lĭng-tŭn)	99	43°19'N	79°48'W
Burlington, Co., U.S.	120	39°17'N	102°26'W
Burlington, Ia., U.S.	105	40°48'N	91°05'W
Burlington, Ks., U.S.	121	38°10'N	95°46'W
Burlington, Ky., U.S.	111f	39°01'N	84°44'W
Burlington, Ma., U.S.	101a	42°31'N	71°13'W
Burlington, N.C., U.S.	125	36°05'N	79°26'W
Burlington, N.J., U.S.	110f	40°04'N	74°52'W
Burlington, Vt., U.S.	105	44°30'N	73°15'W
Burlington, Wa., U.S.	116a	48°28'N	122°20'W
Burlington, Wi., U.S.	111a	42°41'N	88°16'W
Burma *see* Myanmar, nation, Asia	194	21°00'N	95°15'E
Burnaby, Can.	90	49°14'N	122°58'W
Burnet, Tx., U.S. (bûrn'ĕt)	122	30°46'N	98°14'W
Burnham on Crouch, Eng., U.K. (bûrn'ăm-ŏn-krouch)	158b	51°38'N	0°48'E
Burnie, Austl. (bûr'nē)	219	41°15'S	146°05'E
Burnley, Eng., U.K. (bûrn'lē)	164	53°47'N	2°19'W
Burns, Or., U.S. (bûrnz)	114	43°35'N	119°05'W
Burnside, Ky., U.S. (bûrn'sīd)	124	36°57'N	84°33'W
Burns Lake, Can. (bûrnz lăk)	90	54°14'N	125°46'W
Burnsville, Can. (bûrnz'vĭl)	100	47°44'N	65°07'W
Burnt, r., Or., U.S. (bûrnt)	114	44°26'N	117°53'W
Burntwood, r., Can.	97	55°53'N	97°30'W
Burrard Inlet, b., Can. (bûr'ărd)	116d	49°19'N	123°15'W
Burr Gaabo, Som.	233	1°14'N	51°47'E
Burro, Serranías del, mts., Mex. (sĕr-rä-nē'äs dĕl bōō'r-rō)	122	29°39'N	102°07'W
Bursa, Tur. (bōōr'sȧ)	198	40°10'N	28°10'E
Būr Safājah, Egypt	231	26°57'N	33°56'E
Burscheid, Ger. (bōōr'shīd)	171c	51°05'N	7°07'E
Būr Sūdān, Sudan (sōō-dán')	231	19°30'N	37°10'E
Burt, N.Y., U.S. (bûrt)	111c	43°19'N	78°45'W
Burt, l., Mi., U.S. (bûrt)	108	45°25'N	84°45'W
Burton, Wa., U.S. (bûr'tŭn)	116a	47°24'N	122°28'W
Burton, Lake, res., Ga., U.S.	124	34°46'N	83°40'W
Burtonsville, Md., U.S. (bûrtŏns-vil)	110e	39°07'N	76°57'W
Burton-upon-Trent, Eng., U.K. (bûr'tŭn-ŭp'-ŏn-trĕnt)	164	52°48'N	1°37'W
Buru, i., Indon.	213	3°30'S	126°30'E
Burullus, l., Egypt	238b	31°20'N	30°58'E
Burundi, nation, Afr.	232	3°00'S	29°30'E
Burwell, Ne., U.S. (bûr'wĕl)	112	41°46'N	99°08'W
Bury, Eng., U.K. (bĕr'ĭ)	158a	53°36'N	2°17'W
Buryatia, prov., Russia	185	55°15'N	112°00'E
Bury Saint Edmunds, Eng., U.K. (bĕr'ĭ-sānt ĕd'mŭndz)	165	52°14'N	0°44'E
Burzaco, Arg. (bōōr-zá'kō)	144a	34°50'S	58°23'W
Busanga Swamp, sw., Zam.	237	14°10'S	25°50'E
Būsh, Egypt (bōōsh)	238b	29°13'N	31°08'E
Bushmanland, hist. reg., S. Afr. (bŏsh-măn lănd)	232	29°15'S	18°45'E
Bushnell, Il., U.S. (bŏsh'nĕl)	121	40°33'N	90°28'W
Businga, D.R.C. (bŏ-sĭŋ'gȧ)	231	3°20'N	20°53'E
Busira, r., D.R.C.	236	0°05'S	19°20'E
Bus'k, Ukr.	169	49°58'N	24°39'E
Busselton, Austl. (bûs'l-tŭn)	218	33°40'S	115°30'E
Bussum, Neth.	159a	52°16'N	5°10'E
Bustamante, Mex. (bōōs-tȧ-män'tā)	122	26°34'N	100°30'W
Busto Arsizio, Italy (bōōs'tō är-sēd'zē-ō)	174	45°47'N	8°51'E
Busuanga, i., Phil. (bōō-swäŋ'gä)	213a	12°20'N	119°43'E
Buta, D.R.C. (bōō'tȧ)	231	2°48'N	24°44'E
Butha Buthe, Leso. (bōō-thȧ-bōō'thȧ)	233c	28°49'S	28°16'E
Butler, Al., U.S. (bŭt'lēr)	124	32°05'N	88°10'W
Butler, In., U.S.	108	41°25'N	84°50'W
Butler, Md., U.S.	110e	39°32'N	76°46'W
Butler, N.J., U.S.	110a	41°00'N	74°20'W
Butler, Pa., U.S.	109	40°50'N	79°55'W
Butovo, Russia (bŏ-tô'vô)	186b	55°33'N	37°36'E
Butsha, D.R.C.	237	0°57'N	29°13'E
Buttahatchee, r., Al., U.S. (bŭt-ȧ-hăch'ē)	124	34°02'N	88°05'W
Butte, Mt., U.S. (būt)	104	46°00'N	112°31'W
Butterworth, S. Afr. (bŭ tēr'wûrth)	233c	32°20'S	28°09'E
Butt of Lewis, c., Scot., U.K. (bŭt ŏv lū'ĭs)	164	58°34'N	6°15'W
Butuan, Phil. (bōō-tōō'än)	213	8°40'N	125°33'E
Buturlinovka, Russia (bōō-tōō-lē-nôf'ka)	181	50°47'N	40°35'E
Buuhoodle, Som.	238a	8°15'N	46°20'E
Buulo Berde, Som.	238a	3°53'N	45°30'E
Buxtehude, Ger.	159c	53°29'N	9°42'E
Buxton, Eng., U.K. (bŭks't'n)	158a	53°15'N	1°55'W
Buxton, Or., U.S.	116c	45°41'N	123°11'W
Buy, Russia (bwē)	178	58°30'N	41°48'E
Büyükmenderes, r., Tur.	198	37°50'N	28°20'E
Buzău, Rom. (bōō-zĕ'ō)	175	45°09'N	26°51'E
Buzău, r., Rom.	177	45°17'N	27°22'E
Buzaymah, Libya	231	25°14'N	22°13'E
Buzi, China (bōō-dz)	206	33°48'N	118°13'E
Buzuluk, Russia (bŏ-zŏ-lŏk')	178	52°50'N	52°10'E
Bwendi, D.R.C.	237	4°01'N	26°41'E
Byala, Blg.	175	43°26'N	25°44'E
Byala Slatina, Blg. (byä'la slä'tēnä)	175	43°26'N	23°56'E
Byalynichy, Bela. (byĕl-ĭ-nĭ'chĭ)	176	54°02'N	29°42'E
Byarezina, r., Bela. (bĕr-yĕ'zē-nȧ)	176	53°20'N	29°05'E
Byaroza, Bela.	169	52°29'N	24°59'E
Byblos *see* Jubayl, Leb.	197a	34°07'N	35°38'E
Bydgoszcz, Pol. (bĭd'gôshch)	160	53°07'N	18°00'E
Byelorussja *see* Belarus, nation, Eur.	178	53°30'N	25°33'E
Byerazino, Bela. (bĕr-yä'zē-nô)	176	53°51'N	28°54'E
Byeshankovichy, Bela.	176	55°04'N	29°29'E

PRONOUNCING INDEX

Byesville – Camp Indian Reservation 277

PLACE (Pronunciation)	PAGE	LAT.	LONG.
Byesville, Oh., U.S. (bīz-vĭl)	108	39°55'N	81°35'W
Bygdin, I., Nor. (bügh-dĕn')	166	61°24'N	8°31'E
Byglandsfjord, Nor. (bügh'länds-fyôr)	166	58°40'N	7°49'E
Bykhaw, Bela.	176	53°32'N	30°15'E
Bykovo, Russia (bĭ-kô'vô)	186b	55°38'N	38°05'E
Byrranga, Gory, mts., Russia	184	74°15'N	94°28'E
Bytantay, r., Russia (byän'täy)	185	68°15'N	132°15'E
Bytom, Pol. (bĭ'tŭm)	161	50°21'N	18°55'E
Bytosh', Russia (bī-tôsh')	176	53°48'N	34°06'E
Bytow, Pol. (bĭ'tŭf)	169	54°10'N	17°30'E

C

PLACE (Pronunciation)	PAGE	LAT.	LONG.
Cabagan, Phil. (kä-bä-gän')	213a	17°27'N	121°50'E
Cabalete, i., Phil. (kä-bä-lā'tå)	213a	14°19'N	122°00'E
Caballones, Canal de, strt., Cuba (kä-nä'l-dĕ-kä-bäl-yô'nĕs)	134	20°45'N	79°20'W
Caballo Reservoir, res., N.M., U.S. (kä-bä-lyō')	119	33°00'N	107°20'W
Cabanatuan, Phil. (kä-bä-nä-twän')	213a	15°30'N	120°56'E
Cabano, Can. (kä-bä-nō')	100	47°41'N	68°54'W
Cabarruyan, i., Phil. (kä-bä-rōō'yän)	213a	16°21'N	120°10'E
Cabedelo, Braz. (kä-bē-dā'lō)	143	6°58'S	34°49'W
Cabeza, Arrecife, i., Mex.	131	19°07'N	95°52'W
Cabeza del Buey, Spain (kå-bā'thä dĕl bwā')	172	38°43'N	5°18'W
Cabimas, Ven. (kä-bē'mäs)	142	10°21'N	71°27'W
Cabinda, Ang.	232	5°33'S	12°12'E
Cabinda, hist. reg., Ang. (kä-bĭn'dà)	232	5°10'S	10°00'E
Cabinet Mountains, mts., Mt., U.S. (kăb'ĭ-nĕt)	114	48°13'N	115°52'W
Cabo Frio, Braz. (kä'bō-frē'ô)	141a	22°53'S	42°02'W
Cabo Frio, Ilha do, Braz. (ē'lä-dô-kä'bō frē'ô)	141a	23°01'S	42°00'W
Cabo Gracias a Dios, Hond. (ká'bō-grä-syäs-ä-dyô's)	133	15°00'N	83°13'W
Cabonga, Réservoir, res., Can.	99	47°25'N	76°35'W
Cabora Bassa Reservoir, res., Moz.	232	15°45'S	32°00'E
Cabot Head, c., Can. (kăb'ŭt)	98	45°15'N	81°20'W
Cabot Strait, strt., Can. (kăb'ŭt)	93a	47°35'N	60°00'W
Cabra, Spain (käb'rä)	172	37°28'N	4°29'W
Cabra, i., Phil.	213a	13°55'N	119°55'E
Cabrera, Illa de, i., Spain	173	39°08'N	2°57'E
Cabrera, Sierra de la, mts., Spain	172	42°15'N	6°45'W
Cabriel, r., Spain (kä-brē-ĕl')	172	39°25'N	1°20'W
Cabrillo National Monument, rec., Ca., U.S. (kä-brēl'yō)	118a	32°41'N	117°03'W
Cabuçu, r., Braz. (kä-bōō'-sōō)	144b	22°57'S	43°36'W
Cabugao, Phil. (kä-bōō'gä-ô)	213a	17°48'N	120°28'E
Čačak, Yugo. (chä'chäk)	175	43°51'N	20°22'E
Caçapava, Braz. (kä'sä-pá'vä)	141a	23°05'S	45°52'W
Cáceres, Braz. (ká'sĕ-rĕs)	143	16°11'S	57°32'W
Cáceres, Spain (ká'thå-rās)	162	39°28'N	6°20'W
Cachapoal, r., Chile (kä-chä-pô-ä'l)	141b	34°23'S	70°19'W
Cache, r., Ar., U.S. (kåsh)	121	35°24'N	91°12'W
Cache Creek, Can.	95	50°48'N	121°19'W
Cache Creek, r., Ca., U.S. (kăsh)	118	38°53'N	122°24'W
Cache la Poudre, r., Co., U.S. (kåsh lá pōōd'r')	120	40°43'N	105°39'W
Cachi, Nevados de, mtn., Arg. (nĕ-vá'dôs-dĕ-ká'chē)	144	25°05'S	66°40'W
Cachinal, Chile (kä-chē-näl')	144	24°57'S	69°33'W
Cachoeira, Braz. (kä-shô-ā'rä)	143	12°32'S	38°47'W
Cachoeirá do Sul, Braz. (kä-shô-ā'rä-dô-sōō'l)	144	30°02'S	52°49'W
Cachoeiras de Macacu, Braz. (kä-shô-ā'räs-dĕ-mä-ká'kōō)	141a	22°28'S	42°39'W
Cachoeiro de Itapemirim, Braz.	143	20°51'S	41°06'W
Cacólo, Ang.	236	10°07'S	19°17'E
Caconda, Ang. (kä-kōn'dä)	232	13°43'S	15°06'E
Cacouna, Can.	100	47°54'N	69°31'W
Cacula, Ang.	236	14°29'S	14°10'E
Cadale, Som.	238a	2°45'N	46°15'E
Caddo, I., La., U.S. (kăd'ō)	123	32°37'N	94°15'W
Cadereyta, Mex. (kä-då-rā'tä)	130	20°42'N	99°47'W
Cadereyta Jimenez, Mex. (kä-dä-rā'tä hĕ-mā'nāz)	122	25°36'N	99°59'W
Cadi, Sierra de, mts., Spain (sē-ĕ'r-rä-dĕ-kä'dē)	173	42°17'N	1°34'E
Cadillac, Mi., U.S. (kăd'ĭ-lăk)	108	44°15'N	85°25'W
Cádiz, Spain (ká'dēz)	154	36°34'N	6°20'W
Cadiz, Ca., U.S. (kā'dĭz)	118	34°33'N	115°30'W
Cadiz, Oh., U.S.	108	40°15'N	81°00'W
Cádiz, Golfo de, b., Spain (gôl-fô-dĕ-ká'dēz)	162	36°50'N	7°00'W
Caen, Fr. (käɴ)	161	49°13'N	0°22'W
Caernarfon, Wales, U.K.	160	53°08'N	4°17'W
Caernarfon Bay, b., Wales, U.K.	164	53°09'N	4°56'W
Cagayan, Phil. (kä-gä-yän')	213	8°13'N	124°30'E
Cagayan, r., Phil.	212	16°45'N	121°55'E
Cagayan Islands, is., Phil.	212	9°40'N	120°30'E
Cagayan Sulu, i., Phil. (kä-gä-yän sōō'lōō)	212	7°00'N	118°30'E
Cagli, Italy (käl'yē)	174	43°35'N	12°40'E
Cagliari, Italy (käl'yä-rē)	154	39°16'N	9°08'E
Cagliari, Golfo di, b., Italy (gôl-fô-dē-käl'yä-rē)	162	39°08'N	9°12'E
Cagnes, Fr. (kän'y')	171	43°40'N	7°14'E
Cagua, Ven. (kä'gwä)	143b	10°12'N	67°27'W
Caguas, P.R. (kä'gwäs)	129b	18°12'N	66°01'W
Cahaba, r., Al., U.S. (kå hä-bä)	124	32°50'N	87°15'W
Cahama, Ang. (kä-á'mä)	232	16°17'S	14°19'E
Cahokia, Il., U.S. (kȧ-hō'kĭ-ȧ)	117e	38°34'N	90°11'W
Cahora-Bassa, wtfl., Moz.	237	15°40'S	32°50'E
Cahors, Fr. (kȧ-ôr')	161	44°27'N	1°27'E
Cahuacán, Mex. (kä-wä-kä'n)	131a	19°38'N	99°25'W
Cahuita, Punta, c., C.R. (pōō'n-tä-kä-wē'tȧ)	133	9°47'N	82°41'W
Cahul, Mol.	177	45°49'N	28°17'E
Caibarién, Cuba (kī-bä-rē-ĕn')	134	22°35'N	79°30'W
Caicedonia, Col. (kī-sĕ-dô-nēä)	142a	4°21'N	75°48'W
Caicos Bank, bk. (kī'kōs)	135	21°35'N	72°00'W
Caicos Islands, is., T./C. Is.	129	21°45'N	71°50'W
Caicos Passage, strt., N.A.	135	21°55'N	72°45'W
Caillou Bay, b., La., U.S. (kȧ-yōō')	123	29°07'N	91°00'W
Caimanera, Cuba (kī-mä-nā'rä)	135	20°00'N	75°10'W
Caiman Point, c., Phil. (kī'mȧn)	213a	15°56'N	119°33'E
Caimito, r., Pan. (kä-ē-mē'tô)	128a	8°50'N	79°45'W
Caimito del Guayabal, Cuba (kä-ē-mē'tō-dĕl-gwä-yä-bä'l)	135a	22°57'N	82°36'W
Cairns, Austl. (kârnz)	219	17°02'S	145°49'E
Cairo, C.R. (kī'rō)	133	10°06'N	83°47'W
Cairo, Egypt	231	30°00'N	31°17'E
Cairo, Ga., U.S. (kā'rō)	124	30°48'N	84°12'W
Cairo, Il., U.S.	105	36°59'N	89°11'W
Caistor, Eng., U.K. (kâs'tēr)	158a	53°30'N	0°20'W
Caiundo, Ang.	236	15°46'S	17°28'E
Caiyu, China (tsī-yōō)	206	39°39'N	116°36'E
Cajamarca, Col. (kä-kä-mä'r-kä)	142a	4°25'N	75°25'W
Cajamarca, Peru (kä-hä-mär'kä)	142	7°16'S	78°30'W
Čajniče, Bos. (chī'nĭ-chĕ)	175	43°32'N	19°04'E
Cajon, Ca., U.S. (kȧ-hōn')	117a	34°18'N	117°28'W
Cajuru, Braz. (kȧ-zhōō'rōō)	141a	21°17'S	47°17'W
Čakovec, Cro. (chá'kō-vĕts)	174	46°23'N	16°27'E
Cala, S. Afr. (cä-lȧ)	233c	31°33'S	27°41'E
Calabar, Nig. (käl-ȧ-bär')	230	4°57'N	8°19'E
Calabazar, Cuba (kä-lä-bä-zä'r)	135a	23°02'N	82°25'W
Calabozo, Ven. (kä-lä-bō'zō)	142	8°48'N	67°27'W
Calabria, hist. reg., Italy (kä-lä'brē-ä)	174	39°26'N	16°23'E
Calafat, Rom. (kȧ-lȧ-fát')	175	43°59'N	22°56'E
Calaguas Islands, is., Phil. (kä-läg'wäs)	213a	14°30'N	123°06'E
Calahoo, Can. (kă-lȧ-hōō')	102g	53°42'N	113°58'W
Calahorra, Spain (kä-lä-ôr'rä)	162	42°18'N	1°58'W
Calais, Fr. (kȧ-lĕ')	154	50°56'N	1°51'E
Calais, Me., U.S.	105	45°11'N	67°15'W
Calama, Chile (kä-lä'mä)	144	22°17'S	68°58'W
Calamar, Col. (kä-lä-mär')	142	10°24'N	75°00'W
Calamar, Col.	142	1°55'N	72°33'W
Calamba, Phil. (kä-läm'bä)	213a	14°12'N	121°10'E
Calamian Group, is., Phil. (kä-lä-myän')	212	12°14'N	118°38'E
Calañas, Spain (kä-län'yäs)	172	37°41'N	6°52'W
Calanda, Spain	173	40°53'N	0°20'W
Calapan, Phil. (kä-lä-pän')	213a	13°25'N	121°11'E
Călăraşi, Rom. (kŭ-lŭ-räsh'ĭ)	163	44°09'N	27°20'E
Calatayud, Spain (kä-lä-tä-yōōdh')	162	41°23'N	1°37'W
Calauag Bay, b., Phil.	213a	14°07'N	122°10'E
Calaveras Reservoir, res., Ca., U.S. (kăl-ȧ-vĕr'ăs)	116b	37°29'N	121°47'W
Calavite, Cape, c., Phil. (kä-lä-vē'tä)	213a	13°29'N	120°00'E
Calcasieu, r., La., U.S. (kăl'kȧ-shū)	123	30°22'N	93°08'W
Calcasieu Lake, I., La., U.S.	123	29°58'N	93°08'W
Calcutta *see* Kolkata, India (kăl-kŭt'ȧ)	199	22°32'N	88°22'E
Caldas, Col. (ká'l-däs)	142a	6°06'N	75°38'W
Caldas, dept., Col.	142a	5°20'N	75°38'W
Caldas da Rainha, Port. (käl'däs dä rīn'yȧ)	172	39°25'N	9°08'W
Calder, r., Eng., U.K. (kôl'dēr)	158a	53°39'N	1°30'W
Caldera, Chile (käl-dā'rä)	144	27°02'S	70°53'W
Calder Canal, can., Eng., U.K.	158a	53°48'N	2°25'W
Caldwell, Id., U.S. (kôld'wĕl)	114	43°40'N	116°43'W
Caldwell, Ks., U.S.	121	37°04'N	97°36'W
Caldwell, Oh., U.S.	108	39°40'N	81°30'W
Caldwell, Tx., U.S.	123	30°30'N	96°40'W
Caledon, Can. (kăl'ē-dŏn)	102d	43°52'N	79°59'W
Caledonia, Mn., U.S. (kăl-ē-dō'nĭ-ȧ)	113	43°38'N	91°31'W
Calella, Spain (kä-lĕl'yä)	173	41°37'N	2°39'E
Calera Victor Rosales, Mex. (kä-lā'rä-vē'k-tôr-rô-sá'lĕs)	130	22°57'N	102°42'W
Calexico, Ca., U.S. (kȧ-lĕk'sĭ-kō)	104	32°41'N	115°30'W
Calgary, Can. (kăl'gȧ-rĭ)	90	51°03'N	114°05'W
Calhoun, Ga., U.S. (kăl-hōōn')	124	34°30'N	84°56'W
Cali, Col. (kä'lē)	142	3°26'N	76°30'W
Caliente, Nv., U.S. (käl-yĕn'tä)	119	37°38'N	114°30'W
California, Mo., U.S. (kăl-ĭ-fôr'nĭ-ȧ)	121	38°38'N	92°38'W
California, Pa., U.S.	111e	40°03'N	79°53'W
California, state, U.S.	104	38°10'N	121°20'W
California, Golfo de, b., Mex. (gôl-fô-dĕ-kä-lē-fôr-nyä)	128	30°30'N	113°45'W
California Aqueduct, aq., Ca., U.S.	118	37°10'N	121°10'W
Călimani, Munţii, mts., Rom.	169	47°05'N	24°47'E
Calimere, Point, c., India	203	10°20'N	80°20'E
Calimesa, Ca., U.S. (kă-lĭ-mā'sȧ)	117a	34°00'N	117°04'W
Calipatria, Ca., U.S. (kăl-ĭ-pát'rĭ-ȧ)	118	33°03'N	115°30'W
Calkini, Mex. (käl-kē-nē')	131	20°21'N	90°06'W
Callabonna, Lake, I., Austl. (călă'bŏnȧ)	222	29°35'S	140°28'E
Callao, Peru (käl-yä'ō)	142	12°02'S	77°07'W
Calling, I., Can. (kôl'ĭng)	95	55°15'N	113°12'W
Calmar, Can. (kăl'mär)	102g	53°16'N	113°49'W
Calmar, Ia., U.S.	113	43°12'N	91°54'W
Calooshatchee, r., Fl., U.S. (kȧ-loo-sȧ-hăch'ē)	125a	26°45'N	81°41'W
Calotmul, Mex. (kä-lôt-mōōl)	132a	20°58'N	88°11'W
Calpulalpan, Mex. (käl-pōō-läl'pän)	130	19°35'N	98°33'W
Caltagirone, Italy (käl-tä-jē-rō'nå)	162	37°14'N	14°32'E
Caltanissetta, Italy (käl-tä-nē-sĕt'tä)	162	37°30'N	14°02'E
Caluango, Ang.	236	8°21'S	19°40'E
Calucinga, Ang.	236	11°18'S	16°12'E
Calumet, Mi., U.S. (kă-lū-mĕt')	113	47°15'N	88°29'W
Calumet, Lake, I., Il., U.S.	111a	41°43'N	87°36'W
Calumet City, Il., U.S.	111a	41°37'N	87°33'W
Calunda, Ang.	236	12°06'S	23°23'E
Caluquembe, Ang.	236	13°47'S	14°44'E
Caluula, Som.	238a	11°53'N	50°40'E
Calvert, Tx., U.S. (kăl'vērt)	123	30°59'N	96°41'W
Calvert Island, i., Can.	92	51°35'N	128°00'W
Calvi, Fr. (käl'vē)	174	42°33'N	8°35'E
Calvillo, Mex. (käl-vēl'yō)	131	21°51'N	102°44'E
Calvinia, S. Afr. (kăl-vĭn'ĭ-ȧ)	232	31°20'S	19°50'E
Cam, r., Eng., U.K. (kăm)	165	52°15'N	0°05'E
Camagüey, Cuba (kä-mä-gwā')	129	21°25'N	78°00'W
Camagüey, prov., Cuba	134	21°30'N	78°10'W
Camajuani, Cuba (kä-mä-hwä'nē)	134	22°25'N	79°50'W
Camano, Wa., U.S. (kä-mä'no)	116a	48°10'N	122°32'W
Camano Island, i., Wa., U.S.	116a	48°11'N	122°29'W
Camargo, Mex. (kä-mär gō)	122	26°19'N	98°49'W
Camarón, Cabo, c., Hond. (ká'bô-kä-mä-rōn')	132	16°06'N	85°05'W
Camas, Wa., U.S. (kăm'ȧs)	116c	45°36'N	122°24'W
Camas Creek, r., Id., U.S.	115	44°10'N	112°09'W
Camatagua, Ven. (kä-mä-tá'gwä)	143b	9°49'N	66°55'W
Ca Mau, Mui, c., Viet.	212	8°36'N	104°43'E
Cambay, India (kăm-bā')	202	22°22'N	72°39'E
Cambodia, nation, Asia	212	12°15'N	104°00'E
Cambonda, Serra, mts., Ang.	236	12°10'S	14°15'E
Camborne, Eng., U.K. (kăm'bôrn)	164	50°15'N	5°28'W
Cambrai, Fr. (käɴ-brĕ')	161	50°10'N	3°15'E
Cambrian Mountains, mts., Wales, U.K. (kăm'brĭ-ăn)	164	52°05'N	4°05'W
Cambridge, Can.	99	43°22'N	80°19'W
Cambridge, Eng., U.K. (kām'brĭj)	161	52°12'N	0°11'E
Cambridge, Ma., U.S.	101a	42°23'N	71°07'W
Cambridge, Md., U.S.	109	38°35'N	76°10'W
Cambridge, Mn., U.S.	113	45°35'N	93°14'W
Cambridge, Ne., U.S.	120	40°17'N	100°10'W
Cambridge, Oh., U.S.	108	40°00'N	81°35'W
Cambridge Bay *see* Kaluktutiak, Can.	92	69°15'N	105°00'W
Cambridge City, In., U.S.	108	39°45'N	85°15'W
Cambridgeshire, co., Eng., U.K.	158a	52°26'N	0°19'W
Cambuci, Braz. (käm-bōō'sē)	141a	21°35'S	41°54'W
Cambundi-Catembo, Ang.	236	10°09'S	17°31'E
Camby, In., U.S. (kăm'bē)	111g	39°40'N	86°19'W
Camden, Austl.	217b	34°03'S	150°42'E
Camden, Al., U.S. (kăm'dĕn)	124	31°58'N	87°15'W
Camden, Ar., U.S.	121	33°36'N	92°49'W
Camden, Me., U.S.	100	44°11'N	69°05'W
Camden, N.J., U.S.	105	39°56'N	75°06'W
Camden, S.C., U.S.	125	34°14'N	80°37'W
Cameia, Parque Nacional da, rec., Ang.	236	11°40'S	21°20'E
Camenca, Mol.	177	48°02'N	28°43'E
Cameron, Mo., U.S. (kăm'ēr-ŭn)	121	39°44'N	94°14'W
Cameron, Tx., U.S.	123	30°52'N	96°57'W
Cameron, W.V., U.S.	108	39°40'N	80°35'W
Cameron Hills, hills, Can.	92	60°13'N	120°20'W
Cameroon, nation, Afr.	230	5°48'N	11°00'E
Cameroon Mountain, mtn., Cam.	230	4°12'N	9°11'E
Camiling, Phil. (kä-mē-lĭng')	213a	15°42'N	120°24'E
Camilla, Ga., U.S. (kȧ-mĭl'ȧ)	124	31°13'N	84°12'W
Caminha, Port. (kä-mĭn'yȧ)	172	41°52'N	8°44'W
Camoçim, Braz. (kä-mô-sēɴ')	143	2°56'S	40°55'W
Camooweal, Austl.	218	20°00'S	138°13'E
Campana, Arg. (käm-pä'nä)	141c	34°10'S	58°58'W
Campana, i., Chile (käm-pän'yä)	144	48°20'S	75°15'W
Campanario, Spain (kä-pä-nä'rē-ō)	172	38°51'N	5°36'W
Campanella, Punta, c., Italy (pô'n-tä-käm-pä-nĕ'lä)	173c	40°20'N	14°21'E
Campanha, Braz. (käm-pän-yäɴ')	141a	21°51'S	45°24'W
Campania, hist. reg., Italy (käm-pän'yä)	174	41°00'N	14°40'E
Campbell, Ca., U.S. (kăm'bĕl)	116b	37°17'N	121°57'W
Campbell, Mo., U.S.	121	36°29'N	90°04'W
Campbell, is., N.Z.	3	52°30'S	169°00'E
Campbellpore, Pak.	202	33°49'N	72°24'E
Campbell River, Can.	90	50°01'N	125°15'W
Campbellsville, Ky., U.S. (kăm'bĕlz-vĭl)	124	37°19'N	85°20'W
Campbellton, Can. (kăm'bĕl-tŭn)	91	48°00'N	66°40'W
Campbelltown, Austl. (kăm'bĕl-toun)	217b	34°04'S	150°49'E
Campbelltown, Scot., U.K. (kăm'b'l-toun)	164	55°25'N	5°50'W
Camp Dennison, Oh., U.S. (dĕ'nĭ-sŏn)	111f	39°12'N	84°17'W
Campeche, Mex. (käm-pā'chå)	128	19°51'N	90°32'W
Campeche, state, Mex.	128	18°55'N	90°20'W
Campeche, Bahía de, b., Mex. (bä-ē'ä-dĕ-käm-pā'chā)	128	19°30'N	93°40'W
Campechuela, Cuba (käm-pȧ-chwā'lä)	134	20°15'N	77°15'W
Camperdown, S. Afr. (kăm'pēr-doun)	233c	29°44'S	30°33'E
Câmpina, Rom.	175	45°08'N	25°47'E
Campina Grande, Braz. (käm-pē'nä grän'dĕ)	143	7°15'S	35°49'W
Campinas, Braz. (käm-pē'nāzh)	143	22°53'S	47°03'W
Camp Indian Reservation, I.R., Ca., U.S. (kămp)	118	32°39'N	116°26'W

ng-sing; ŋ-baŋk; ɴ-nasalized n; nŏd; cŏmmit; ōld; ôbey; ôrder; oi-boil; fōōd; ŏo-as oo in foot; ou-out; s-soft; sh-dish; th-thin; pūre; ûnite; ûrn; stŭd; circŭs; ü-as in French tu; '-indeterminate vowel.

PLACE (Pronunciation)	PAGE	LAT.	LONG.
Campo, Cam. (käm′pō)	230	2°22′N	9°49′E
Campoalegre, Col. (kä′m-pô-ȧlĕ′grĕ)	142	2°34′N	75°20′W
Campobasso, Italy (käm′pô-bäs′sō)	174	41°35′N	14°39′E
Campo Belo, Braz.	141a	20°52′S	45°15′W
Campo de Criptana, Spain (käm′pō dā krēp-tä′nä)	172	39°24′N	3°09′W
Campo Florido, Cuba (kä′m-pō flō-rē′dō)	135a	23°07′N	82°07′W
Campo Grande, Braz. (käm-pò grän′dĕ)	143	20°28′S	54°32′W
Campo Grande, Braz.	144b	22°54′S	43°33′W
Campo Maior, Braz. (käm-pò mä-yôr′)	143	4°48′S	42°12′W
Campo Maior, Port.	172	39°03′N	7°06′W
Campo Real, Spain (käm′pô rå-äl′)	173a	40°21′N	3°23′W
Campos, Braz. (kä′m-pôs)	143	21°46′S	41°19′W
Campos do Jordão, Braz. (kä′m-pôs-dô-zhôr-dou′ɴ)	141a	22°45′S	45°35′W
Campos Gerais, Braz. (kä′m-pôs-zhĕ-ràēs)	141a	21°17′S	45°43′W
Camps Bay, S. Afr. (kămps)	232a	33°57′S	18°22′E
Camp Springs, Md., U.S. (cămp springz)	110e	38°48′N	76°55′W
Câmpulung, Rom.	163	45°15′N	25°03′E
Câmpulung Moldovenesc, Rom.	169	47°31′N	25°36′E
Camp Wood, Tx., U.S. (kămp wòd)	122	29°39′N	100°02′W
Camrose, Can. (kăm-rōz)	90	53°01′N	112°50′W
Camu, r., Dom. Rep. (kä′mōō)	135	19°05′N	70°15′W
Canada, nation, N.A. (kăn′à-dà)	90	50°00′N	100°00′W
Canada Bay, b., Can.	101	50°43′N	56°10′W
Cañada de Gómez, Arg. (kä-nyä′dä-dĕ-gô′mĕz)	144	32°49′S	61°24′W
Canadian, Tx., U.S. (kà-nā′dĭ-ăn)	120	35°54′N	100°24′W
Canadian, r., U.S.	106	35°30′N	102°30′W
Canajoharie, N.Y., U.S. (kăn-à-jô-hăr′ē)	109	42°55′N	74°35′W
Çanakkale, Tur. (chä-näk-kä′lĕ)	163	40°10′N	26°26′E
Çanakkale Boğazi (Dardanelles), strt., Tur.	163	40°05′N	25°50′E
Canandaigua, N.Y., U.S. (kăn-ăn-dā′gwà)	109	42°55′N	77°20′W
Canandaigua, l., N.Y., U.S.	109	42°45′N	77°20′W
Cananea, Mex. (kä-nä-nĕ′ä)	128	31°00′N	110°20′W
Canarias, Islas (Canary Is.), is., Spain (ē′s-läs-kä-nä′ryäs)	229	29°15′N	16°30′W
Canarreos, Archipiélago de los, is., Cuba	134	21°35′N	82°20′W
Canary Islands *see* Canarias, Islas, is., Spain	229	29°15′N	16°30′W
Cañas, C.R. (kä′-nyäs)	132	10°26′N	85°06′W
Cañas, r., C.R.	132	10°20′N	85°21′W
Cañasgordas, Col. (kä′nyäs-gô′r-däs)	142a	6°44′N	76°01′W
Canastota, N.Y., U.S. (kăn-às-tō′tà)	109	43°05′N	75°45′W
Canastra, Serra de, mts., Braz. (sĕ′r-rä-dĕ-kä-nä′s-trä)	143	19°53′S	46°57′W
Canatlán, Mex. (kä-nät-län′)	122	24°30′N	104°45′W
Canaveral, Cape, c., Fl., U.S.	107	28°30′N	80°23′W
Canavieiras, Braz. (kä-nà-vē-ā′räs)	143	15°40′S	38°49′W
Canberra, Austl. (kăn′bĕr-à)	219	35°21′S	149°10′E
Canby, Mn., U.S. (kăn′bĭ)	112	44°43′N	96°15′W
Canchyuaya, Cerros de, mts., Peru (sĕ′r-rôs-dĕ-kän-chōō-ä′iä)	142	7°30′S	74°30′W
Cancuc, Mex. (kän-kōōk)	131	16°58′N	92°17′W
Cancún, Mex.	132a	21°25′N	86°50′W
Candelaria, Cuba (kän-dĕ-lä′ryä)	134	22°45′N	82°55′W
Candelaria, Phil. (kän-då-lä′rē-ä)	213a	15°39′N	119°55′E
Candelaria, r., Mex. (kän-dĕ-lä-ryä)	131	18°25′N	91°21′W
Candeleda, Spain (kän-dhå-lā′dhä)	172	40°09′N	5°18′W
Candia *see* Iráklion, Grc.	154	35°20′N	25°10′E
Candle, Ak., U.S. (kăn′d′l)	103	65°00′N	162°04′W
Cando, N.D., U.S. (kăn′dō)	112	48°27′N	99°13′W
Candon, Phil. (kän-dōn′)	213a	17°13′N	120°26′E
Canelones, Ur. (kä-nĕ-lô-nĕs)	141c	34°32′S	56°19′W
Canelones, dept., Ur.	141c	34°34′S	56°15′W
Cañete, Peru (kän-yā′tå)	142	13°06′S	76°17′W
Caney, Cuba (kä-nā′) (kā′nĭ)	135	20°05′N	75°45′W
Caney, Ks., U.S. (kā′nĭ)	121	37°00′N	95°57′W
Caney Fork, r., Tn., U.S.	124	36°10′N	85°50′W
Cangamba, Ang.	232	13°40′S	19°54′E
Cangas, Spain (kän′gäs)	172	42°15′N	8°43′W
Cangas de Narcea, Spain (kä′n-gäs-dĕ-när-sĕ-ä)	172	43°08′N	6°36′W
Cangzhou, China (tsäŋ-jō)	208	38°21′N	116°53′E
Caniapiscau, l., Can.	93	54°10′N	71°13′E
Caniapiscau, r., Can.	93	57°00′N	68°45′W
Canicatti, Italy (kä-nė-kät′tē)	174	37°18′N	13°58′E
Cañitas, Mex. (kän-yē′täs)	130	23°38′N	102°44′W
Cannell, Can.	102g	53°35′N	113°38′W
Cannelton, In., U.S. (kăn′ĕl-tŭn)	108	37°55′N	86°45′W
Cannes, Fr. (kån)	161	43°34′N	7°05′E
Canning, Can. (kăn′ĭng)	100	45°09′N	64°25′W
Cannock, Eng., U.K. (kăn′ŭk)	158a	52°41′N	2°02′W
Cannock Chase, reg., Eng., U.K. (kăn′ŭk chās)	158a	52°43′N	1°54′W
Cannon, r., Mn., U.S. (kăn′ŭn)	113	44°18′N	93°24′W
Cannonball, r., N.D., U.S. (kăn′ŭn-bäl)	112	46°17′N	101°35′W
Caño, Isla de, i., C.R. (ē′s-lä-dĕ-kä′nō)	133	8°38′N	84°00′W
Canoga Park, Ca., U.S. (kä-nō′gå)	117a	34°07′N	118°36′W
Canoncito Indian Reservation, I.R., N.M., U.S.	119	35°00′N	107°05′W
Canon City, Co., U.S. (kăn′yŭn)	120	38°27′N	105°16′W
Canonsburg, Pa., U.S. (kăn′ŭnz-bûrg)	111e	40°16′N	80°11′W
Canoochee, r., Ga., U.S. (kȧ-nōō′chē)	125	32°25′N	82°11′W
Canora, Can. (kà-nōrà)	90	51°37′N	102°26′W
Canosa, Italy (kä-nō′sä)	174	41°14′N	16°03′E
Canouan, i., St. Vin.	133b	12°44′N	61°10′W
Cansahcab, Mex.	132a	21°11′N	89°05′W
Canso, Can. (kăn′sō)	101	45°20′N	61°00′W
Canso, Cape, c., Can.	101	45°21′N	60°46′W
Canso, Strait of, strt., Can.	101	45°37′N	61°25′W
Cantabrica, Cordillera, mts., Spain	156	43°05′N	6°05′W
Cantagalo, Braz. (kän-tä-gå′lo)	141a	21°59′S	42°22′W
Cantanhede, Port. (kän-täɴ-yā′då)	172	40°22′N	8°35′W
Canterbury, Eng., U.K. (kăn′tĕr-bĕr-ē)	165	51°17′N	1°06′E
Canterbury Bight, b., N.Z.	221a	44°15′S	172°08′E
Cantiles, Cayo, i., Cuba (ky-ō-kän-tē′lås)	134	21°40′N	82°00′W
Canton *see* Guangzhou, China	205	23°07′N	113°15′E
Canton, Ga., U.S.	124	34°13′N	84°29′W
Canton, Il., U.S.	121	40°34′N	90°02′W
Canton, Ma., U.S.	101a	42°09′N	71°09′W
Canton, Mo., U.S.	121	40°08′N	91°33′W
Canton, Ms., U.S.	124	32°36′N	90°01′W
Canton, N.C., U.S.	125	35°32′N	82°50′W
Canton, Oh., U.S.	105	40°50′N	81°25′W
Canton, Pa., U.S.	109	41°50′N	76°45′W
Canton, S.D., U.S.	112	43°17′N	96°37′W
Cantu, Italy (kän-tō′)	174	45°43′N	9°09′E
Cañuelas, Arg. (kä-nyoĕ′-läs)	141c	35°03′S	58°45′W
Canyon, Tx., U.S. (kăn′yŭn)	120	34°59′N	101°57′W
Canyon, r., Wa., U.S.	116a	48°09′N	121°48′W
Canyon de Chelly National Monument, rec., Az., U.S.	119	36°14′N	110°00′W
Canyon Ferry Lake, res., Mt., U.S.	115	46°33′N	111°37′W
Canyonlands National Park, rec., Ut., U.S.	119	38°10′N	110°00′W
Canyons of the Ancients National Monument, rec., Co., U.S.	119	37°30′N	108°50′W
Caoxian, China (tsou shyĕn)	206	34°48′N	115°33′E
Capalonga, Phil. (kä-pä-lôŋ′gä)	213a	14°20′N	122°30′E
Capannori, Italy (kä-pän′nō-rē)	174	43°50′N	10°30′E
Capaya, r., Ven. (kä-pä-iä)	143b	10°28′N	66°15′W
Cap-Chat, Can. (kȧp-shä′)	91	48°02′N	65°20′W
Cap-de-la-Madeleine, Can. (kȧp dē lȧ mȧ-d′lĕn′)	99	46°23′N	72°30′W
Cape Breton, i., Can. (kāp brĕt′ŭn)	101	45°48′N	59°50′W
Cape Breton Highlands National Park, rec., Can.	91	46°45′N	60°45′W
Cape Charles, Va., U.S. (kāp chärlz)	125	37°13′N	76°02′W
Cape Coast, Ghana	230	5°05′N	1°15′W
Cape Fear, r., N.C., U.S. (kāp fēr)	107	35°00′N	79°00′W
Cape Flats, pl., S. Afr. (kāp flăts)	232a	34°01′S	18°37′E
Cape Girardeau, Mo., U.S. (jē-rär-dō′)	105	37°17′N	89°32′W
Cape Krusenstern National Monument, rec., Ak., U.S.	103	67°30′N	163°40′W
Cape May, N.J., U.S. (kāp mā)	109	38°55′N	74°50′W
Cape May Court House, N.J., U.S.	109	39°05′N	75°00′W
Cape Romanzof, Ak., U.S. (rō′ män zôf)	103	61°50′N	165°45′W
Capesterre, Guad.	133b	16°02′N	61°37′W
Cape Tormentine, Can.	100	46°08′N	63°47′W
Cape Town, S. Afr. (kāp toun)	232	33°48′S	18°28′E
Cape Verde, nation, Afr.	230b	15°48′N	26°02′W
Cape York Peninsula, pen., Austl. (kāp yôrk)	221	12°30′S	142°35′E
Cap-Haïtien, Haiti (kȧp ȧ-ē-syăn′)	129	19°45′N	72°15′W
Capilla de Señor, Arg. (kä-pēl′yä dā sān-yôr′)	141c	34°18′S	59°07′W
Capitachouane, r., Can.	99	47°50′N	76°45′W
Capitol Reef National Park, rec., Ut., U.S. (kăp′ĭ-tŏl)	119	38°15′N	111°10′W
Capivari, Braz. (kä-pē-vá′rē)	141a	22°59′S	47°29′W
Capivari, r., Braz.	144b	22°39′S	43°19′W
Capoompeta, mtn., Austl. (kȧ-pōōm-pē′tȧ)	221	29°15′S	152°12′E
Capraia, i., Italy (kä-prä′yä)	162	43°02′N	9°51′E
Caprara Point, c., Italy (kä-prä′rä)	174	41°08′N	8°20′E
Capreol, Can.	99	46°43′N	80°56′W
Caprera, i., Italy (kä-prā′rä)	174	41°12′N	9°28′E
Capri, Italy	173c	40°18′N	14°16′E
Capri, Isola di, i., Italy (ē′-sō-lä-dē-kä′prē)	173c	40°19′N	14°10′E
Capricorn Channel, strt., Austl. (kăp′rĭ-kôrn)	221	22°27′S	151°24′E
Caprivi Strip, hist. reg., Nmb.	232	18°00′S	22°00′E
Cap-Rouge, Can. (kȧp rōōzh′)	102b	46°45′N	71°21′W
Cap-Saint Ignace, Can. (kĭp săɴ-tē-nyás′)	102b	47°02′N	70°27′W
Capua, Italy (kä′pwä)	162	41°07′N	14°14′E
Capulhuac, Mex. (kä-pòl-hwäk′)	130	19°33′N	99°43′W
Capulin Mountain National Monument, rec., N.M., U.S. (kȧ-pū′lĭn)	120	36°15′N	103°58′W
Capultitlán, Mex. (kä-pò′l-tē-tlá′n)	131a	19°15′N	99°40′W
Caquetá (Japurá), r., S.A.	142	0°20′S	73°00′W
Carabaña, Spain (kä-rä-bän′yä)	173a	40°16′N	3°15′W
Carabelle, Fl., U.S. (kăr′á-bĕl)	124	29°50′N	84°40′W
Carabobo, dept., Ven. (kä-rä-bô′-bô)	143b	10°07′N	68°06′W
Caracal, Rom. (kȧ-rȧ-kȧl′)	175	44°06′N	24°22′E
Caracas, Ven. (kä-rä′käs)	142	10°30′N	66°58′W
Carácuaro de Morelos, Mex. (kä-rä′kwä-rō-dĕ-mô-rĕ-lôs)	130	18°44′N	101°04′W
Caraguatatuba, Braz. (kä-rä-gwä-tá-tōō′bä)	141a	23°37′S	45°26′W
Carajás, Serra dos, mts., Braz. (sĕ′r-rä-dôs-kä-rä-zhá′s)	143	5°58′S	51°45′W
Caramanta, Cerro, mtn., Col. (sĕ′r-rô-kä-rä-má′n-tä)	142a	5°29′N	76°01′W
Carangola, Braz. (kä-ràn′gŏ′lä)	141a	20°46′S	42°02′W
Caraquet, Can. (kă-rȧ-kĕt′)	91	47°48′N	64°57′W
Carata, Laguna, l., Nic. (lä-gò′nä-kä-rä′tä)	133	13°59′N	83°41′W
Caratasca, Laguna, l., Hond. (lä-gò′nä-kä-rä-täs′kä)	133	15°20′N	83°45′W
Caravaca, Spain (kä-rä-vä′kä)	172	38°05′N	1°51′W
Caravelas, Braz. (kȧ-rä-vĕl′äzh)	143	17°46′S	39°06′W
Carayaca, Ven. (kȧ-rä-iä′kä)	143b	10°32′N	67°07′W
Caràzinho, Braz. (kä-rȧ′zē-nyŏ)	144	28°22′S	52°33′W
Carballiño, Spain	162	42°26′N	8°04′W
Carballo, Spain (kär-bäl′yō)	172	43°13′N	8°40′W
Carbet, Pitons du, mtn., Mart.	133b	14°40′N	61°05′W
Carbon, r., Wa., U.S. (kär′bŏn)	116a	47°06′N	122°08′W
Carbonado, Wa., U.S. (kȧr-bō-nä′dō)	116a	47°05′N	122°03′W
Carbonara, Cape, c., Italy (kär-bō-nä′rä)	162	39°08′N	9°33′E
Carbondale, Can. (kär′bŏn-dāl)	102g	53°45′N	113°32′W
Carbondale, Il., U.S.	108	37°42′N	89°12′W
Carbondale, Pa., U.S.	109	41°35′N	75°30′W
Carbonear, Can. (kär-bō-nēr′)	101	47°45′N	53°14′W
Carbon Hill, Al., U.S. (kär′bŏn hĭl)	124	33°53′N	87°34′W
Carcaixent, Spain	173	39°09′N	0°29′W
Carcans, Étang de, l., Fr. (ā-taɴ-dĕ-kär-kän)	170	45°12′N	1°00′W
Carcassonne, Fr. (kȧr-kȧ-sôn′)	161	43°12′N	2°23′E
Carcross, Can. (kär′krôs)	90	60°18′N	134°54′W
Cárdenas, Cuba (kär′då-näs)	129	23°00′N	81°10′W
Cárdenas, Mex. (kå′r-dĕ-näs)	131	17°59′N	93°23′W
Cárdenas, Mex.	130	22°01′N	99°38′W
Cárdenas, Bahía de, b., Cuba (bä-ē′ä-dĕ-kär′då-näs)	134	23°10′N	81°10′W
Cardiff, Can. (kär′dĭf)	102g	53°46′N	113°36′W
Cardiff, Wales, U.K.	161	51°30′N	3°18′W
Cardigan, Wales, U.K. (kär′dĭ-găn)	161	52°05′N	4°40′W
Cardigan Bay, b., Wales, U.K.	161	52°35′N	4°40′W
Cardston, Can. (kärds′tŭn)	90	49°12′N	113°18′W
Carei, Rom. (kä-rē′)	169	47°42′N	22°28′E
Carentan, Fr. (kä-rôɴ-täɴ′)	170	49°19′N	1°14′W
Carey, Oh., U.S. (kā′rē)	108	40°55′N	83°25′W
Carey, l., Austl. (kâr′ē)	220	29°20′S	123°35′E
Carhaix-Plouguer, Fr. (kär-ĕ′)	170	48°17′N	3°37′W
Caribbean Sea, sea (kăr-ĭ-bē′ăn)	129	14°30′N	75°30′W
Caribe, Arroyo, r., Mex. (är-ro′i-kä-rē′bĕ)	131	18°18′N	90°38′W
Cariboo Mountains, mts., Can. (kă′rĭ-bōō)	92	53°00′N	121°00′W
Caribou, Me., U.S.	100	46°51′N	68°01′W
Caribou, i., Can.	98	47°22′N	85°42′W
Caribou Lake, l., Mn., U.S.	117h	46°54′N	92°16′W
Caribou Mountains, mts., Can.	92	59°20′N	115°30′W
Carinhanha, Braz. (kä-rĭ-nyän′yä)	143	14°14′S	43°44′W
Carini, Italy (kä-rē′nē)	174	38°09′N	13°10′E
Carleton Place, Can. (kärl′tŭn)	99	45°15′N	76°10′W
Carletonville, S. Afr.	238c	26°20′S	27°23′E
Carlinville, Il., U.S. (kär′lĭn-vĭl)	121	39°16′N	89°52′W
Carlisle, Eng., U.K. (kär-līl′)	154	54°54′N	3°03′W
Carlisle, Ky., U.S.	108	38°20′N	84°00′W
Carlisle, Pa., U.S.	109	40°10′N	77°15′W
Carloforte, Italy (kär′lō-fôr-tå)	174	39°11′N	8°28′E
Carlos Casares, Arg. (kär-lôs-kä-sá′rĕs)	144	35°38′S	61°17′W
Carlow, Ire. (kär′lō)	164	52°50′N	7°00′W
Carlsbad, N.M., U.S. (kärlz′băd)	122	32°24′N	104°12′W
Carlsbad Caverns National Park, rec., N.M., U.S.	122	32°08′N	104°30′W
Carlton, Eng., U.K. (kärl′tŭn)	158a	52°58′N	1°05′W
Carlton, Mn., U.S.	117h	46°40′N	92°26′W
Carlton Center, Mi., U.S. (kärl′tŭn sĕn′tĕr)	108	42°45′N	85°20′W
Carlyle, Il., U.S. (kärlīl′)	121	38°37′N	89°23′W
Carmagnolo, Italy (kär-mä-nyô′lä)	174	44°52′N	7°48′E
Carman, Can. (kär′mȧn)	90	49°32′N	98°00′W
Carmarthen, Wales, U.K. (kär-mär′thĕn)	164	51°50′N	4°20′W
Carmaux, Fr. (kár-mō′)	170	44°05′N	2°09′E
Carmel, N.Y., U.S. (kär′mĕl)	110a	41°25′N	73°42′W
Carmelo, Ur. (kär-mĕ′lo)	141c	33°59′S	58°15′W
Carmen, Isla del, i., Mex. (ē′s-lä-dĕl-kä′r-mĕn)	131	18°43′N	91°40′W
Carmen, Laguna del, l., Mex. (lä-gò′nä-dĕl-kä′r-mĕn)	131	18°15′N	93°26′W
Carmen de Areco, Arg. (kär′mĕn′ dā ä-rā′kō)	141c	34°21′S	59°50′W
Carmen de Patagones, Arg. (kå′r-mĕn-dĕ-pä-tä-gô′nĕs)	144	41°00′S	63°00′W
Carmi, Il., U.S. (kär′mī)	108	38°05′N	88°10′W
Carmo, Braz. (kå′r-mô)	141a	21°57′S	42°45′W
Carmo do Rio Clara, Braz. (kȧ′r-mô-dô-rē′ō-klä′rä)	141a	20°57′S	46°04′W
Carmona, Spain	172	37°28′N	5°38′W
Carnarvon, Austl. (kär-när′vŭn)	218	24°45′S	113°45′E
Carnarvon, S. Afr.	232	31°00′S	22°15′E
Carnation, Wa., U.S. (kär-nā′shŭn)	116a	47°39′N	121°55′W
Carnaxide, Port. (kär-nä-shē′dĕ)	173b	38°44′N	9°15′W
Carndonagh, Ire. (kärn-dō-nä′)	164	55°15′N	7°15′W
Carnegie, Ok., U.S. (kär-nĕg′ĭ)	120	35°06′N	98°38′W
Carnegie, Pa., U.S.	111e	40°24′N	80°06′W
Carneys Point, N.J., U.S. (kär′nēs)	109	39°45′N	75°25′W
Carnic Alps, mts., Eur.	161	46°43′N	12°38′E
Carnot, Alg. (kär nō′)	173	36°15′N	1°40′E
Carnot, C.A.R.	231	5°00′N	15°52′E
Carnsore Point, c., Ire. (kärn′sôr)	164	52°10′N	6°16′W
Caro, Mi., U.S. (kâ′rō)	108	43°30′N	83°25′W
Carolina, Braz. (kä-rô-lē′nä)	143	7°26′S	47°16′W

PRONOUNCING INDEX

Carolina – Celestún 279

PLACE (Pronunciation)	PAGE	LAT.	LONG.
Carolina, S. Afr. (kăr-ō-lī'nȧ)	232	26°07'S	30°09'E
Carolina, I., Mex. (kä-rō-lē'nä)	132a	18°41'N	89°40'W
Caroline Islands, is., Oc.	5	8°00'N	140°00'E
Caroni, r., Ven. (kä-rō'nē)	142	5°49'N	62°57'W
Carora, Ven. (kä-rō'rä)	142	10°09'N	70°12'W
Carpathians, mts., Eur. (kär-pā'thĭ-ăn)	156	49°23'N	20°14'E
Carpaţii Meridionali (Transylvanian Alps), mts., Rom.	156	45°30'N	23°30'E
Carpentaria, Gulf of, b., Austl. (kär-pĕn-târ'ĭȧ)	220	14°45'S	138°50'E
Carpentras, Fr. (kär-päɴ-träs')	171	44°04'N	5°01'E
Carpi, Italy	174	44°48'N	10°54'E
Carrara, Italy (kä-rä'rä)	162	44°05'N	10°05'E
Carrauntoohil, Ire. (kă-răn-to͞o'ĭl)	164	52°01'N	9°48'W
Carretas, Punta, c., Peru (po͞o'n-tä-kär-rĕ'tĕ'räs)	142	14°15'S	76°25'W
Carriacou, i., Gren.	133b	12°28'N	61°20'W
Carrick-on-Sur, Ire. (kăr'-ĭk)	164	52°20'N	7°35'W
Carrier, Can. (kăr'ĭ-ẽr)	102b	46°43'N	71°05'W
Carriere, Ms., U.S. (kȧ-rēr')	124	30°37'N	89°37'W
Carriers Mills, Il., U.S. (kăr'ĭ-ẽrs)	108	37°40'N	88°40'W
Carrington, N.D., U.S. (kăr'ĭng-tŭn)	112	47°26'N	99°06'W
Carr Inlet, Wa., U.S. (kăr ĭn'lĕt)	116a	47°20'N	122°42'W
Carrion Crow Harbor, b., Bah. (kăr'ĭŭn krō)	134	26°35'N	77°55'W
Carrión de los Condes, Spain (kär-rē-ōn' dā los kōn'dås)	172	42°20'N	4°35'W
Carrizo Creek, r., N.M., U.S. (kär-rē'zō)	120	36°22'N	103°39'W
Carrizo Springs, Tx., U.S.	122	28°32'N	99°51'W
Carrizozo, N.M., U.S. (kär-rē-zō'zō)	119	33°40'N	105°55'W
Carroll, Ia., U.S. (kăr'ŭl)	113	42°03'N	94°51'W
Carrollton, Ga., U.S. (kăr-ŭl-tŭn)	124	33°35'N	85°05'W
Carrollton, Il., U.S.	121	39°18'N	90°22'W
Carrollton, Ky., U.S.	108	38°45'N	85°15'W
Carrollton, Mi., U.S.	108	43°30'N	83°55'W
Carrollton, Mo., U.S.	121	39°21'N	93°29'W
Carrollton, Oh., U.S.	108	40°35'N	81°10'W
Carrollton, Tx., U.S.	117c	32°58'N	96°53'W
Carrols, Wa., U.S. (kăr'ŭlz)	116c	46°05'N	122°51'W
Carrot, r., Can.	96	53°12'N	103°50'W
Carry-le-Rouet, Fr. (kä-rē'lẽ-rò-ā')	170a	43°20'N	5°10'E
Carsamba, Tur. (chär-shäm'bä)	163	41°05'N	36°40'E
Carson, r., Nv., U.S. (kär'sŭn)	118	39°15'N	119°25'W
Carson City, Nv., U.S.	104	39°10'N	119°45'W
Carson Sink, Nv., U.S.	118	39°51'N	118°25'W
Cartagena, Col. (kär-tä-hä'nä)	142	10°30'N	75°40'W
Cartagena, Spain (kär-tä-κĕ'nä)	154	37°46'N	1°00'W
Cartago, Col. (kär-tä'gō)	142a	4°44'N	75°54'W
Cartago, C.R.	129	9°52'N	83°56'W
Cartaxo, Port. (kär-tä'shō)	172	39°10'N	8°48'W
Carteret, N.J., U.S. (kär'tē-ret)	110a	40°35'N	74°13'W
Cartersville, Ga., U.S. (kär'tẽrs-vĭl)	124	34°09'N	84°47'W
Carthage, Tun.	230	37°04'N	10°18'E
Carthage, Il., U.S. (kär'thåj)	121	40°27'N	91°09'W
Carthage, Mo., U.S.	121	37°10'N	94°18'W
Carthage, N.C., U.S.	125	35°22'N	79°25'W
Carthage, N.Y., U.S.	109	44°00'N	75°45'W
Carthage, Tx., U.S.	123	32°09'N	94°20'W
Carthcart, S. Afr. (cärth-că't)	233c	32°18'S	27°11'E
Cartwright, Can. (kärt'rĭt)	91	53°36'N	57°00'W
Caruaru, Braz. (kä-rò-ȧ-ro͞o')	143	8°19'S	35°52'W
Carúpano, Ven. (kä-ro͞o'pä-nō)	142	10°45'N	63°21'W
Caruthersville, Mo., U.S. (kȧ-rŭdh'ẽrz-vĭl)	121	36°09'N	89°41'W
Carver, Or., U.S. (kärv'ẽr)	116c	45°24'N	122°30'W
Carvoeiro, Cabo, c., Port. (kȧ'bō-kär-vō-ĕ'y-rō)	172	39°22'N	9°24'W
Cary, Il., U.S. (kă'rē)	111a	42°13'N	88°14'W
Casablanca, Chile (kä-sä-blän'kä)	141b	33°19'S	71°24'W
Casablanca, Mor.	230	33°32'N	7°41'W
Casa Branca, Braz. (kä'sä-brä'ɴ-kä)	141a	21°47'S	47°04'W
Casa Grande, Az., U.S. (kä'sä grän'dā)	119	32°50'N	111°45'W
Casa Grande Ruins National Monument, rec., Az., U.S.	119	33°00'N	111°33'W
Casale Monferrato, Italy (kä-sä'lā)	174	45°08'N	8°26'E
Casalmaggiore, Italy (kä-säl-mäd-jō'rā)	174	45°00'N	10°24'E
Casamance, r., Sen. (kä-sä-mäɴs')	230	12°30'N	15°00'W
Cascade Mountains, mts., N.A.	95	49°10'N	121°00'W
Cascade Point, c., N.Z. (kăs-kād')	221a	43°59'S	168°23'E
Cascade Range, mts., N.A.	106	42°50'N	122°20'W
Cascade-Siskiyou National Monument, rec., Or., U.S.	114	42°05'N	122°30'W
Cascade Tunnel, trans., Wa., U.S.	114	47°41'N	120°53'W
Cascais, Port. (käs-kȧ-ēzh)	172	38°42'N	9°25'W
Case Inlet, Wa., U.S. (kās)	116a	47°22'N	122°47'W
Caseros, Arg. (kä-sā'rōs)	144a	34°35'S	58°34'W
Caserta, Italy (kä-zĕr'tä)	174	41°04'N	14°21'E
Casey, Il., U.S. (kā'sĭ)	108	39°20'N	88°00'W
Cashmere, Wa., U.S. (kăsh'mĭr)	114	47°30'N	120°28'W
Casiguran, Phil. (käs-sē-go͞o'rän)	213a	16°15'N	122°10'E
Casiguran Sound, strt., Phil.	213a	16°02'N	121°51'E
Casilda, Arg. (kä-sē'l-dä)	144	33°02'S	61°11'W
Casilda, Cuba	134	21°50'N	80°00'W
Casimiro de Abreu, Braz. (kä'sē-mē'ro-dĕ-ȧ-brĕ'o͞oo)	141a	22°30'S	42°11'W
Casino, Austl. (kȧ-sē'nō)	222	28°35'S	153°10'E
Casiquiare, r., Ven. (kä-sē-kyä'rā)	142	2°11'N	66°15'W
Caspe, Spain (käs'pā)	173	41°18'N	0°02'W
Casper, Wy., U.S. (kăs'pẽr)	104	42°51'N	106°18'W
Caspian Depression, depr. (kăs'pĭ-ȧn)	178	47°40'N	52°35'E
Caspian Sea, sea	178	40°00'N	52°00'E
Cass, W.V., U.S. (kăs)	109	38°25'N	79°55'W
Cass, I., Mn., U.S.	113	47°23'N	94°28'W
Cassai (Kasai), r., Afr. (kä-sä'ē)	232	11°30'S	21°00'E
Cass City, Mi., U.S. (kăs)	108	43°35'N	83°10'W
Casselman, Can. (kăs''l-mȧn)	102c	45°18'N	75°05'W
Casselton, N.D., U.S. (kăs''l-tŭn)	112	46°53'N	97°14'W
Cássia, Braz. (kȧ'syä)	141a	20°36'S	46°53'W
Cassin, Tx., U.S. (kăs'ĭn)	117d	29°16'N	98°29'W
Cassinga, Ang.	232	15°05'S	16°15'E
Cassino, Italy (käs-sē'nō)	162	41°30'N	13°50'E
Cass Lake, Mn., U.S. (kăs)	113	47°23'N	94°37'W
Cassopolis, Mi., U.S. (kăs-ŏ'pō-lĭs)	108	41°55'N	86°00'W
Cassville, Mo., U.S. (kăs'vĭl)	121	36°41'N	93°52'W
Castanheira de Pêra, Port. (käs-tän-yā'rä-dĕ-pĕ'rä)	172	40°00'N	8°07'W
Castellammare di Stabia, Italy	173c	40°26'N	14°29'E
Castelli, Arg. (kȧs-tĕ'zhē)	141c	36°07'S	57°48'W
Castelló de la Plana, Spain	162	39°59'N	0°05'W
Castelnaudary, Fr. (kȧs'tĕl-nō-dȧ-rē')	170	43°20'N	1°57'E
Castelo, Braz. (käs-tĕ'lō)	141a	20°37'S	41°13'W
Castelo Branco, Port. (käs-tā'lò brän'kò)	162	39°48'N	7°37'W
Castelo de Vide, Port. (käs-tā'lò dĭ vē'dĭ)	172	39°25'N	7°25'W
Castelsarrasin, Fr. (kȧs'tĕl-sȧ-rȧ-zăɴ')	170	44°03'N	1°05'E
Castelvetrano, Italy (käs'tĕl-vē-trä'nō)	174	37°43'N	12°50'E
Castilla, Peru (kȧs-tē'l-yä)	142	5°18'S	80°40'W
Castilla La Nueva, hist. reg., Spain (käs-tē'lyä lä nwā'vȧ)	172	39°15'N	3°55'W
Castilla La Vieja, hist. reg., Spain (käs-tēl'yä lä vyā'hä)	172	40°48'N	4°24'W
Castillo de San Marcos National Monument, rec., Fl., U.S. (käs-tē'lyā de-sän mär-kōs)	125	29°55'N	81°25'W
Castle, i., Bah. (kȧs''l)	135	22°05'N	74°20'W
Castlebar, Ire. (kȧs''l-bär)	164	53°55'N	9°15'W
Castle Dale, Ut., U.S. (kȧs''l dāl)	119	39°15'N	111°00'W
Castle Donington, Eng., U.K. (dŏn'ĭng-tŭn)	158a	52°50'N	1°21'W
Castleford, Eng., U.K. (kȧs'l-fẽrd)	158a	53°43'N	1°21'W
Castlegar, Can. (kȧs''l-gär)	95	49°19'N	117°40'W
Castlemaine, Austl. (kȧs''l-mān)	222	37°05'S	144°10'E
Castle Peak, mtn., Co., U.S.	119	39°00'N	106°50'W
Castle Rock, Wa., U.S. (kȧs''l-rŏk)	114	46°17'N	122°53'W
Castle Rock Flowage, res., Wi., U.S.	113	44°03'N	89°48'W
Castle Shannon, Pa., U.S. (shăn'ŭn)	111e	40°22'N	80°02'W
Castleton, In., U.S. (kȧs''l-tŏn)	111g	39°54'N	86°03'W
Castor, r., Can. (kăs'tôr)	102c	45°16'N	75°14'W
Castor, r., Mo., U.S.	121	36°59'N	89°53'W
Castres, Fr. (kȧs'tr')	170	43°36'N	2°13'E
Castries, St. Luc. (kȧs-trē')	133b	14°01'N	61°00'W
Castro, Braz. (käs'trò)	143	24°56'S	50°00'W
Castro, Chile (käs'trō)	144	42°27'S	73°48'W
Castro Daire, Port. (käs'trò dīr'ĭ)	172	40°56'N	7°57'W
Castro del Río, Spain (käs-trō-dĕl rē'ō)	172	37°42'N	4°28'W
Castrop Rauxel, Ger. (käs'trōp rou'ksĕl)	171c	51°33'N	7°19'E
Castro-Urdiales, Spain	162	43°23'N	3°11'W
Castro Valley, Ca., U.S.	116b	37°42'N	122°05'W
Castro Verde, Port. (käs-trō vĕr'dĕ)	172	37°43'N	8°05'W
Castrovillari, Italy (käs'trō-vēl-lyä'rē)	174	39°48'N	16°11'E
Castuera, Spain (käs-tò-ā'rä)	172	38°43'N	5°33'W
Casula, Moz.	237	15°25'S	33°40'E
Cat, i., Bah.	135	24°30'N	75°30'W
Catacamas, Hond. (kä-tä-kȧ'mäs)	132	14°52'N	85°55'W
Cataguases, Braz. (kä-tä-gwȧ'sĕs)	141a	21°23'S	42°42'W
Catahoula, l., La., U.S. (kăt-ȧ-hò'lȧ)	123	31°35'N	92°20'W
Catalão, Braz. (kä-tä-louɴ')	143	18°09'S	47°42'W
Catalina, i., Dom. Rep. (kä-tä-lē'nä)	135	18°20'N	69°00'W
Catalunya, hist. reg., Spain	173	41°23'N	0°50'E
Catamarca, Arg. (kä-rä-mȧ'r-kä)	144	28°29'S	65°45'W
Catamarca, prov., Arg. (kä-tä-mär'kä)	144	27°15'S	67°15'W
Catanaun, Phil. (kä-tä-nä'wän)	213a	13°36'N	122°20'E
Catanduanes Island, i., Phil. (kä-tän-dwä'nĕs)	213	13°55'N	125°00'E
Catanduva, Braz. (kä-tȧn-do͞o'vä)	143	21°12'S	48°47'W
Catania, Italy (kä-tä'nyä)	154	37°30'N	15°09'E
Catania, Golfo di, b., Italy (gôl-fō-dē-kȧ-tä'nyä)	174	37°24'N	15°28'E
Catanzaro, Italy (kä-tän-dzä'rō)	163	38°53'N	16°34'E
Catarroja, Spain (kä-tär-rō'hä)	173	39°24'N	0°25'W
Catawba, r., N.C., U.S. (kȧ-tô'bȧ)	125	35°25'N	80°55'W
Catbalogan, Phil. (kät-bä-lō'gän)	213	11°45'N	124°52'E
Catemaco, Mex. (kä-tä-mä'kō)	131	18°26'N	95°06'W
Catemaco, Lago, l., Mex. (lä'gô-kä-tä-mä'kō)	131	18°23'N	95°04'W
Caterham, Eng., U.K. (kā'tẽr-ŭm)	158b	51°16'N	0°04'W
Catete, Ang. (kä-tĕ'tĕ)	232	9°06'S	13°43'E
Cathedral Mountain, mtn., Tx., U.S. (kȧ-thē'drȧl)	122	30°09'N	103°46'W
Cathedral Peak, mtn., Afr. (kȧ-thē'drȧl)	233c	28°53'S	29°04'E
Catherine, Lake, l., Ar., U.S. (kȧ-thẽr-ĭn)	121	34°26'N	92°47'W
Cathkin Peak, mtn., Afr. (kăth'kĭn)	232	29°08'S	29°22'E
Cathlamet, Wa., U.S. (kăth-lăm'ĕt)	116c	46°12'N	123°22'W
Catlettsburg, Ky., U.S. (kăt'lĕts-bûrg)	108	38°20'N	82°35'W
Catoche, Cabo, c., Mex. (kä-tô'chĕ)	128	21°30'N	87°15'W
Catonsville, Md., U.S. (kā'tŭnz-vĭl)	110e	39°16'N	76°45'W
Catorce, Mex. (kä-tôr'sā)	130	23°41'N	100°51'W
Catskill, N.Y., U.S. (kăts'kĭl)	109	42°15'N	73°50'W
Catskill Mountains, mts., N.Y., U.S.	107	42°20'N	74°35'W
Cattaraugus Indian Reservation, I.R., N.Y., U.S. (kăt'tȧ-rȧ-gŭs)	109	42°30'N	79°05'W
Catu, Braz. (kȧ-to͞o)	143	12°26'S	38°12'W
Catuala, Ang.	236	16°29'S	19°03'E
Catumbela, r., Ang. (kä'tŏm-bĕl'ȧ)	236	12°40'S	14°10'E
Cauayan, Phil. (kou-ä'yän)	213a	16°56'N	121°46'E
Cauca, r., Col. (kou'kä)	142	7°30'N	75°26'W
Caucagua, Ven. (käò-kȧ'gwä)	143b	10°17'N	66°22'W
Caucasus, mts.	178	43°20'N	42°00'E
Cauchon Lake, l., Can. (kô-shŏn')	97	55°25'N	96°30'W
Caughnawaga, Can.	102a	45°24'N	73°41'W
Caulfield, Austl.	217a	37°53'S	145°03'E
Caulonia, Italy (kou-lō'nyä)	174	38°24'N	16°22'E
Cauquenes, Chile (kou-kā'nās)	144	35°54'S	72°14'W
Caura, r., Ven. (kou'rä)	142	6°48'N	64°40'W
Causapscal, Can.	100	48°22'N	67°14'W
Caution, Cape, c., Can. (kô'shŭn)	94	51°10'N	127°47'W
Cauto, r., Cuba (kou'tō)	134	20°33'N	76°20'W
Cauvery, r., India	199	12°00'N	77°00'E
Cava, Braz. (kȧ'vä)	144b	22°41'S	43°26'W
Cava de' Tirreni, Italy (kä'vä-dĕ-tēr-rĕ'nē)	173c	40°27'N	14°43'E
Cávado, r., Port. (kä-vä'dō)	172	41°43'N	8°08'W
Cavalcante, Braz. (kä-väl-kän'tā)	143	13°45'S	47°33'W
Cavalier, N.D., U.S. (kăv-ȧ-lēr')	112	48°45'N	97°39'W
Cavally, r., Afr.	234	4°40'N	7°30'W
Cavan, Ire. (kăv'ăn)	164	54°01'N	7°00'W
Cavarzere, Italy (kä-vär'dzā-rā)	174	45°08'N	12°06'E
Cavendish, Vt., U.S. (kăv'ĕn-dĭsh)	109	43°25'N	72°35'W
Caviana, Ilha, i., Braz. (kä-vyä'nä)	143	0°45'N	49°33'W
Cavite, Phil. (kä-vē'tā)	213a	14°30'N	120°54'E
Caxambu, Braz. (kä-shä'm-bo͞o)	143	22°00'S	44°45'W
Caxias, Braz. (kä'shē-äzh)	143	4°48'S	43°16'W
Caxias do Sul, Braz. (kä'shē-äzh-dò-so͞o'l)	144	29°13'S	51°03'W
Caxito, Ang. (kä-shē'tò)	232	8°33'S	13°36'E
Cayambe, Ec. (kȧ-īä'm-bĕ)	142	0°03'N	79°09'W
Cayenne, Fr. Gu. (kā-ĕn')	143	4°56'N	52°18'W
Cayetano Rubio, Mex. (kä-yĕ-tȧ-nò-ro͞o'byô)	130	20°37'N	100°21'W
Cayey, P.R.	129b	18°05'N	66°12'W
Cayman Brac, i., Cay. Is. (kī-män' brák)	134	19°45'N	79°50'W
Cayman Islands, dep., N.A.	134	19°30'N	80°30'W
Cay Sal Bank, bk. (kē-săl)	134	23°55'N	80°20'W
Cayuga, l., N.Y., U.S. (kā-yo͞o'gȧ)	109	42°35'N	76°35'W
Cazalla de la Sierra, Spain	172	37°55'N	5°48'W
Cazaux, Étang de, l., Fr. (ā-tăɴ' dẽ kä-zō')	170	44°32'N	0°59'W
Cazenovia, N.Y., U.S. (kăz-ẽ-nō'vĭ-ȧ)	109	42°55'N	75°50'W
Cazenovia Creek, r., N.Y., U.S.	111c	42°49'N	78°45'W
Čazma, Cro. (chäz'mä)	174	45°44'N	16°39'E
Cazombo, Ang. (kä-zō'm-bō)	232	11°54'S	22°52'E
Cazones, r., Mex. (kä-zō'nĕs)	131	20°37'N	97°28'W
Cazones, Ensenada de, b., Cuba (ĕn-sĕ-nä-dä-dĕ-kä-zō'nås)	134	22°05'N	81°30'W
Cazones, Golfo de, b., Cuba (gôl-fō-dĕ-kä-zō'nås)	134	21°55'N	81°15'W
Cazorla, Spain (kä-thôr'lå)	172	37°55'N	2°58'W
Cea, r., Spain (thā'ä)	172	42°18'N	5°10'W
Ceará-Mirim, Braz. (sā-ä-rä'mē-rē'ɴ)	143	6°00'S	35°13'W
Cebaco, Isla, i., Pan. (ē's-lä-sȧ-bä'kō)	133	7°27'N	81°08'W
Cebolla Creek, r., Co., U.S. (sē-bōl'yȧ)	119	38°15'N	107°10'W
Cebreros, Spain (sĕ-brĕ'rōs)	172	40°28'N	4°28'W
Cebu, Phil. (sā-bo͞o')	213	10°22'N	123°49'E
Čechy (Bohemia), hist. reg., Czech Rep.	168	49°51'N	13°55'E
Cecil, Pa., U.S. (sē'sĭl)	111e	40°20'N	80°10'W
Cedar, r., Ia., U.S.	113	42°23'N	92°07'W
Cedar, r., Wa., U.S.	116c	45°56'N	122°32'W
Cedar, West Fork, r., Ia., U.S.	113	42°49'N	93°10'W
Cedar Bayou, Tx., U.S.	123a	29°54'N	94°58'W
Cedar Breaks National Monument, rec., Ut., U.S.	119	37°35'N	112°55'W
Cedarburg, Wi., U.S. (sē'dẽr bûrg)	113	43°23'N	88°00'W
Cedar City, Ut., U.S.	119	37°40'N	113°10'W
Cedar Creek, r., N.D., U.S.	112	46°05'N	102°10'W
Cedar Falls, Ia., U.S.	113	42°31'N	92°29'W
Cedar Keys, Fl., U.S.	124	29°06'N	83°03'W
Cedar Lake, In., U.S.	111a	41°22'N	87°27'W
Cedar Lake, l., In., U.S.	111a	41°23'N	87°25'W
Cedar Lake, res., Can.	92	53°10'N	100°00'W
Cedar Rapids, Ia., U.S.	105	42°00'N	91°43'W
Cedar Springs, Mi., U.S.	108	43°15'N	85°40'W
Cedartown, Ga., U.S. (sē'dẽr-toun)	124	34°00'N	85°15'W
Cedarville, S. Afr. (cēdȧr'vĭl)	233c	30°23'S	29°04'E
Cedral, Mex. (sā-dräl')	130	23°47'N	100°42'W
Cedros, Hond. (sā'drōs)	132	14°36'N	87°07'W
Cedros, i., Mex.	128	28°10'N	115°10'W
Ceduna, Austl. (sē-dò'nȧ)	218	32°15'S	133°55'E
Ceel Buur, Som.	238a	4°35'N	46°40'E
Cega, r., Spain (thā'gä)	172	41°25'N	4°27'W
Cegléd, Hung. (tsā'glād)	169	47°10'N	19°49'E
Ceglie, Italy (chĕ'lyĕ)	175	40°39'N	17°32'E
Cehegín, Spain (thā-ȧ-hēn')	172	38°05'N	1°48'W
Ceiba del Agua, Cuba (sā'bä-dĕl-ȧ'gwä)	135a	22°53'N	82°38'W
Cekhira, Tun.	230	34°17'N	10°00'E
Celaya, Mex. (sā-lä'yä)	128	20°33'N	100°49'W
Celebes (Sulawesi), i., Indon.	212	2°15'S	120°30'E
Celebes Sea, sea, Asia	212	3°45'N	121°52'E
Celestún, Mex. (sĕ-lĕs-to͞o'n)	132a	20°57'N	90°18'W

ăt; finál; rāte; senåte; ärm; ásk; sofá; fãre; ch-choose; dh-as th in other; bē; ĕvent; bĕt; recĕnt; crätēr; g-gō; gh-guttural g; bĭt; ī-short neutral; rīde; ĸ-guttural k as ch in German ich;

PRONOUNCING INDEX

Chautauqua – Chippewa Lake 281

PLACE (Pronunciation)	PAGE	LAT.	LONG.
Chautauqua, l., N.Y., U.S. (shȧ-tô'kwȧ)	109	42°10'N	79°25'W
Chavaniga, Russia	180	66°02'N	37°50'E
Chaves, Port. (chä'vĕzh)	172	41°44'N	7°30'W
Chavinda, Mex. (chä-vē'n-dä)	130	20°01'N	102°27'W
Chavusi, Bela.	176	53°57'N	30°58'E
Chazumba, Mex. (chä-zōm'bä)	131	18°11'N	97°41'W
Cheadle, Eng., U.K. (chē'd'l)	158a	52°59'N	1°59'W
Cheat, W.V., U.S. (chēt)	109	39°35'N	79°40'W
Cheb, Czech Rep. (κĕb)	168	50°05'N	12°23'E
Chebarkul', Russia (chĕ-bàr-kûl')	186a	54°59'N	60°22'E
Cheboksary, Russia (chyĕ-bôk-sä'rĕ)	180	56°00'N	47°20'E
Cheboygan, Mi., U.S. (shē-boi'gȧn)	108	45°40'N	84°30'W
Chech, Erg, des., Alg.	230	24°45'N	2°07'W
Chechen', i., Russia (chyĕch'ĕn)	181	44°00'N	48°10'E
Chechnya, prov., Russia	182	43°30'N	45°50'E
Checotah, Ok., U.S. (chē-kō'tȧ)	121	35°27'N	95°32'W
Chedabucto Bay, b., Can. (chĕd-ȧ-bŭk-tō)	101	45°23'N	61°10'W
Cheduba Island, i., Mya.	212	18°45'N	93°01'E
Cheecham Hills, hills, Can. (chēē'hăm)	96	56°20'N	111°10'W
Cheektowaga, N.Y., U.S. (chēk-tō-wä'gȧ)	111c	42°54'N	78°46'W
Chefoo see Yantai, China	205	37°32'N	121°22'E
Chegutu, Zimb.	232	18°18'S	30°10'E
Chehalis, Wa., U.S. (chē-hā'lĭs)	114	46°39'N	122°58'W
Chehalis, r., Wa., U.S.	114	46°47'N	123°17'W
Cheju, Kor., S. (chĕ'jōō')	210	33°29'N	126°40'E
Cheju (Quelpart), i., Kor., S.	210	33°20'N	126°25'E
Chekalin, Russia (chĕ-kä'lĭn)	176	54°05'N	36°13'E
Chela, Serra da, mts., Ang. (sĕr'rȧ dä shä'lȧ)	232	15°30'S	13°30'E
Chelan, Wa., U.S. (chē-lăn')	114	47°51'N	119°59'W
Chelan, Lake, l., Wa., U.S.	114	48°09'N	120°20'W
Cheleiros, Port. (shĕ-la'rōzh)	173b	38°54'N	9°19'W
Chéliff, r., Alg. (shā-lēf)	230	36°00'N	2°00'E
Chelles, Fr.	171b	48°53'N	2°36'E
Chełm, Pol. (κĕlm)	161	51°08'N	23°30'E
Chełmno, Pol. (κĕlm'nō)	169	53°20'N	18°25'E
Chelmsford, Can.	98	46°35'N	81°12'W
Chelmsford, Eng., U.K. (chĕlm's-fērd)	165	51°44'N	0°28'E
Chelmsford, Ma., U.S.	101a	42°36'N	71°21'W
Chelsea, Austl.	217a	38°05'S	145°08'E
Chelsea, Can.	102c	45°30'N	75°46'W
Chelsea, Al., U.S. (chĕl'sē)	110h	33°20'N	86°38'W
Chelsea, Ma., U.S.	101a	42°23'N	71°02'W
Chelsea, Mi., U.S.	108	42°20'N	84°00'W
Chelsea, Ok., U.S.	121	36°32'N	95°23'W
Cheltenham, Eng., U.K. (chĕlt'nŭm)	164	51°57'N	2°06'W
Cheltenham, Md., U.S. (chĕltĕn-hăm)	110e	38°45'N	76°50'W
Chelyabinsk, Russia (chĕl-yä-bēnsk')	178	55°10'N	61°25'E
Chelyuskin, Mys, c., Russia (chĕl-yōs'-kĭn)	179	77°45'N	104°45'E
Chemba, Moz.	237	17°08'S	34°52'E
Chemnitz, Ger.	161	50°48'N	12°53'E
Chemung, r., N.Y., U.S. (shē-mŭng)	109	42°20'N	77°25'W
Chën, Gora, mtn., Russia	179	65°13'N	142°12'E
Chenāb, r., Asia (chē-näb)	199	30°30'N	71°30'E
Chenachane, Alg. (shē-nȧ-shän')	230	26°14'N	4°14'W
Chencun, China (chŭn-tsòn)	207a	22°58'N	113°14'E
Cheney, Wa., U.S. (chē'nā)	114	47°29'N	117°34'W
Chengde, China (chŭŋ-dŭ)	205	40°50'N	117°50'E
Chengdong Hu, l., China (chŭŋ-dôŋ hōō)	206	32°22'N	116°32'E
Chengdu, China (chŭŋ-dōō)	204	30°30'N	104°10'E
Chenggu, China (chŭŋ-gōō)	208	33°05'N	107°25'E
Chenghai, China (chŭŋ-hī)	209	23°22'N	116°40'E
Chengshan Jiao, c., China (jyou chŭŋ-shän)	208	37°28'N	122°40'E
Chengxi Hu, l., China (chŭŋ-shyē hōō)	206	32°31'N	116°04'E
Chennai (Madras), India	199	13°08'N	80°15'E
Chenxian, China (chŭn-shyĕn)	209	25°40'N	113°00'E
Chepén, Peru (chĕ-pĕ'n)	142	7°17'S	79°24'W
Chepo, Pan. (chā'pō)	133	9°12'N	79°06'W
Chepo, r., Pan.	133	9°10'N	78°36'W
Cher, r., Fr. (shâr)	161	47°14'N	1°34'E
Cherán, Mex. (chā-rän')	130	19°41'N	101°54'W
Cherangany Hills, hills, Kenya	237	1°25'N	35°20'E
Cheraw, S.C., U.S. (chē'rô)	125	34°40'N	79°52'W
Cherbourg, Fr. (shär-bōōr')	154	49°39'N	1°43'W
Cherdyn', Russia (chĕr-dyĕn')	178	60°25'N	56°32'E
Cheremkhovo, Russia (chĕr'yĕm-kô-vō)	179	52°58'N	103°18'E
Cherëmukhovo, Russia (chĕr-yĕ-mû-kô-vô)	186a	60°20'N	60°00'E
Cherepanovo, Russia (chĕr'yĕ pä-nō'vō)	178	54°13'N	83°22'E
Cherepovets, Russia (chĕr-yĕ-pô'vyĕtz)	178	59°08'N	37°59'E
Chereya, Bela. (chĕr-ā'yä)	176	54°38'N	29°16'E
Chergui, i., Tun.	162	34°50'N	11°40'E
Chergui, Chott ech, l., Alg. (chĕr gē)	162	34°12'N	0°10'W
Cherkasy, Ukr.	177	49°26'N	32°03'E
Cherkasy, prov., Ukr.	177	48°58'N	30°55'E
Cherkessk, Russia	182	44°14'N	42°04'E
Cherlak, Russia (chĭr-läk')	178	54°04'N	74°28'E
Chermoz, Russia (chĕr-môz')	180	58°47'N	56°08'E
Chern', Russia (chĕrn)	176	53°28'N	36°49'E
Chërnaya Kalitva, r., Russia (chôr'nȧ yȧ kȧ-lēt'vȧ)	177	50°15'N	39°16'E
Chernihiv, Ukr.	181	51°23'N	31°15'E
Chernihiv, prov., Ukr.	177	51°28'N	31°18'E
Chernihivka, Ukr.	177	47°08'N	36°20'E
Chernivtsi, Ukr.	178	48°18'N	25°56'E

PLACE (Pronunciation)	PAGE	LAT.	LONG.
Chernobyl' see Chornobai, Ukr.	176	51°17'N	30°14'E
Chernogorsk, Russia (chĕr-nŏ-gôrsk')	184	54°01'N	91°07'E
Chernoistochinsk, Russia (chĕr-nôy-stô'chĭnsk)	186a	57°44'N	59°55'E
Chernyanka, Russia (chĕrn-yäŋ'kä)	177	50°56'N	37°48'E
Cherokee, Ia., U.S. (chĕr-ô-kē')	112	42°43'N	95°33'W
Cherokee, Ks., U.S.	121	37°21'N	94°50'W
Cherokee, Ok., U.S.	120	36°44'N	98°22'W
Cherokee Lake, res., Tn., U.S.	124	36°22'N	83°22'W
Cherokees, Lake of the, res., Ok., U.S. (chĕr-ô-kēz')	107	36°32'N	95°14'W
Cherokee Sound, Bah.	134	26°15'N	76°55'W
Cherryfield, Me., U.S. (chĕr'ĭ-fēld)	100	44°37'N	67°56'W
Cherry Grove, Or., U.S.	116c	45°27'N	123°15'W
Cherryvale, Ks., U.S.	121	37°16'N	95°33'W
Cherryville, N.C., U.S. (chĕr'ĭ-vĭl)	125	35°32'N	81°22'W
Cherskogo, Khrebet, mts., Russia	179	67°15'N	140°00'E
Chertsey, Eng., U.K.	158b	51°24'N	0°30'W
Chervonoye, Vozyera, l., Bela. (chĕr-vô'nô-yĕ)	176	52°24'N	28°00'E
Chervyen', Bela. (chĕr'vyĕn)	176	53°43'N	28°26'E
Cherykaw, Bela.	176	53°34'N	31°22'E
Chesaning, Mi., U.S. (chĕs'ȧ-nĭng)	108	43°10'N	84°10'W
Chesapeake, Va., U.S. (chĕs'ȧ-pēk)	110g	36°48'N	76°16'W
Chesapeake Bay, b., U.S.	107	38°20'N	76°15'W
Chesapeake Beach, Md., U.S.	110e	38°42'N	76°33'W
Chesham, Eng., U.K. (chĕsh'ŭm)	158b	51°41'N	0°37'W
Cheshire, Mi., U.S. (chĕsh'ĭr)	108	42°25'N	86°00'W
Cheshire, co., Eng., U.K.	158a	53°16'N	2°30'W
Chëshskaya Guba, b., Russia	178	67°25'N	46°00'E
Cheshunt, Eng., U.K.	158b	51°43'N	0°02'W
Chesma, Russia (chĕs'mȧ)	186a	53°50'N	60°42'E
Chesnokovka, Russia (chĕs-nŏ-kôf'kȧ)	178	53°28'N	83°41'E
Chester, Eng., U.K. (chĕs'tēr)	164	53°12'N	2°53'W
Chester, Il., U.S.	121	37°54'N	89°48'W
Chester, Pa., U.S.	110f	39°51'N	75°22'W
Chester, S.C., U.S.	125	34°42'N	81°11'W
Chester, Va., U.S.	125	37°20'N	77°24'W
Chester, W.V., U.S.	108	40°35'N	80°30'W
Chesterfield, Eng., U.K. (chĕs'tēr-fēld)	164	53°14'N	1°26'W
Chesterfield, Îles, is., N. Cal.	221	19°38'S	160°08'E
Chesterfield Inlet see Igluligaarjuk, Can.	92	63°19'N	91°11'W
Chesterfield Inlet, b., Can.	93	63°59'N	92°09'W
Chestermere Lake, l., Can. (chĕs'tē-mēr)	102e	51°03'N	113°45'W
Chesterton, In., U.S. (chĕs'tēr-tŭn)	108	41°35'N	87°05'W
Chestertown, Md., U.S. (chĕs'tēr-toun)	109	39°15'N	76°05'W
Chesuncook, l., Me., U.S. (chĕs'ŭn-kŏŏk)	100	46°03'N	69°40'W
Chetek, Wi., U.S. (chĕ'tĕk)	113	45°18'N	91°41'W
Chetumal, Bahía de, b., N.A. (bä-ē-ä dĕ chĕt-ōō-mäl')	128	18°07'N	88°05'W
Chevelon Creek, r., Az., U.S. (shĕv'ȧ-lŏn)	119	34°35'N	111°00'W
Cheviot, Oh., U.S. (shĕv'ĭ-ŭt)	111f	39°10'N	84°37'W
Chevreuse, Fr. (shĕ-vrûz')	171b	48°42'N	2°02'E
Chevy Chase, Md., U.S. (shĕvĭ chās)	110e	38°58'N	77°06'W
Chew Bahir, Afr. (stĕf-a-nē)	231	4°46'N	37°31'E
Chewelah, Wa., U.S. (chē-wē'lȧ)	114	48°17'N	117°42'W
Cheyenne, Wy., U.S. (shī-ĕn')	104	41°10'N	104°49'W
Cheyenne, r., U.S.	106	44°20'N	102°15'W
Cheyenne River Indian Reservation, I.R., S.D., U.S.	112	45°07'N	100°46'W
Cheyenne Wells, Co., U.S.	120	38°46'N	102°21'W
Chhattisgarh, state, India	199	23°00'N	83°00'E
Chhindwāra, India	202	22°08'N	78°57'E
Chiai, Tai. (chī'ī')	209	23°28'N	120°28'E
Chiange, Ang.	236	15°45'S	13°48'E
Chiang Mai, Thai.	212	18°38'N	98°44'E
Chiang Rai, Thai.	212	19°53'N	99°48'E
Chiapa, Río de, r., Mex.	132	16°00'N	92°20'W
Chiapa de Corzo, Mex. (chē-ä'pä dā kôr'zō)	131	16°44'N	93°01'W
Chiapas, state, Mex. (chē-ä'päs)	128	17°10'N	93°00'W
Chiapas, Cordilla de, mts., Mex. (kôr-dēl-yĕ'rä-dĕ-chyä'räs)	131	15°55'N	93°15'W
Chiari, Italy (kyä'rē)	174	45°31'N	9°57'E
Chiasso, Switz.	168	45°50'N	8°57'E
Chiatura, Geor.	182	42°17'N	43°17'E
Chiautla, Mex. (chyä-ōōt'lä)	130	18°16'N	98°37'W
Chiavari, Italy (kyä-vä'rē)	174	44°18'N	9°21'E
Chiba, Japan (chē'bä)	205	35°37'N	140°08'E
Chiba, dept., Japan	211a	35°47'N	140°02'E
Chibougamau, Can. (chē-bōō'gä-mou)	91	49°57'N	74°23'W
Chibougamau, l., Can.	99	49°53'N	74°21'W
Chicago, Il., U.S. (shĭ-kô-gō) (chĭ-kä'gō)	105	41°49'N	87°37'W
Chicago Heights, Il., U.S.	111a	41°30'N	87°38'W
Chicapa, r., Afr. (chē-kä'pä)	232	7°45'S	20°25'E
Chicbul, Mex. (chēk-bōō'l)	131	18°45'N	90°56'W
Chic-Chocs, Monts, mts., Can.	93	48°38'N	66°37'W
Chichagof, i., Ak., U.S. (chē-chä'gôf)	103	57°50'N	137°00'W
Chichancanab, Lago de, l., Mex. (lä'gô-dĕ-chē-chän-kä-nä'b)	132a	19°50'N	88°28'W
Chichén Itzá, hist., Mex.	132a	20°40'N	88°35'W
Chichester, Eng., U.K. (chĭch'ĕs-tēr)	164	50°50'N	0°55'W
Chichimilá, Mex. (chē-chē-mē'lä)	132a	20°36'N	88°14'W
Chichiriviche, Ven. (chē-chē-rē-vē-chĕ)	143b	10°56'N	68°17'W
Chickamauga, Ga., U.S. (chĭk-ȧ-mô'gȧ)	124	34°50'N	85°15'W
Chickamauga Lake, res., Tn., U.S.	124	35°18'N	85°22'W

PLACE (Pronunciation)	PAGE	LAT.	LONG.
Chickasawhay, r., Ms., U.S. (chĭk-ȧ-sô'wā)	124	31°45'N	88°45'W
Chickasha, Ok., U.S. (chĭk'ȧ-shā)	104	35°04'N	97°56'W
Chiclana de la Frontera, Spain (chē-klä'nä)	172	36°25'N	6°09'W
Chiclayo, Peru (chē-klä'yō)	142	6°46'S	79°50'W
Chico, Ca., U.S. (chē'kō)	118	39°43'N	121°51'W
Chico, Wa., U.S.	116a	47°37'N	122°43'W
Chico, r., Arg.	144	44°30'S	66°00'W
Chico, r., Arg.	144	49°15'S	69°30'W
Chico, r., Phil.	213a	17°33'N	121°24'E
Chicoloapan, Mex. (chē-kō-lwä'pän)	131a	19°24'N	98°54'W
Chiconautla, Mex.	131a	19°39'N	99°01'W
Chicontepec, Mex. (chē-kōn'tĕ-pĕk')	130	20°58'N	98°08'W
Chicopee, Ma., U.S. (chĭk'ô-pē)	109	42°10'N	72°35'W
Chicoutimi, Can. (shē-kōō'tē-mē')	91	48°26'N	71°04'W
Chicxulub, Mex. (chēk-sōō-lōō'b)	132a	21°10'N	89°30'W
Chiefland, Fl., U.S. (chēf'lȧnd)	125	29°30'N	82°50'W
Chiemsee, l., Ger. (kēm zā)	168	47°58'N	12°20'E
Chieri, Italy (kyâ'rē)	174	45°03'N	7°48'E
Chieti, Italy (kyĕ'tē)	162	42°22'N	14°22'E
Chifeng, China (chr-fŭŋ)	205	42°18'N	118°52'E
Chignanuapan, Mex. (chē'g-nä-nwä-pä'n)	130	19°49'N	98°02'W
Chignecto Bay, b., Can. (shĭg-nĕk'tō)	100	45°33'N	64°50'W
Chignik, Ak., U.S. (chĭg'nĭk)	103	56°14'N	158°12'W
Chignik Bay, b., Ak., U.S.	103	56°18'N	157°22'W
Chigu Co, l., China (chr-gōō tswo)	202	28°55'N	91°47'E
Chigwell, Eng., U.K.	158b	51°38'N	0°05'E
Chihe, China (chr-hŭ)	206	32°32'N	117°57'E
Chihuahua, Mex. (chē-wä'wä)	128	28°37'N	106°06'W
Chihuahua, state, Mex.	128	29°00'N	107°30'W
Chikishlyar, Turkmen. (chē-kēsh-lyär')	183	37°40'N	53°50'E
Chilanga, Zam.	237	15°34'S	28°17'E
Chilapa, Mex. (chē-lä'pä)	130	17°34'N	99°14'W
Chilchota, Mex. (chēl-chō'tä)	130	19°40'N	102°04'W
Chilcotin, r., Can. (chĭl-kō'tĭn)	94	52°20'N	124°15'W
Childress, Tx., U.S. (chīld'rĕs)	120	34°26'N	100°11'W
Chile, nation, S.A. (chē'lā)	144	35°00'S	72°00'W
Chilecito, Arg. (chē-lå-sē'tō)	144	29°06'S	67°25'W
Chilengue, Serra do, mts., Ang.	236	13°20'S	15°00'E
Chilibre, Pan. (chē-lē'brĕ)	128a	9°09'N	79°37'W
Chililabombwe, Zam.	237	12°18'S	27°43'E
Chilka, l., India	202	19°26'N	85°42'E
Chilko, r., Can. (chĭl'kō)	94	51°53'N	123°53'W
Chilko Lake, l., Can.	94	51°20'N	124°05'W
Chillán, Chile (chēl-yän')	144	36°44'S	72°06'W
Chillicothe, Il., U.S. (chĭl-ĭ-kŏth'ē)	108	41°55'N	89°30'W
Chillicothe, Mo., U.S.	121	39°46'N	93°32'W
Chillicothe, Oh., U.S.	108	39°20'N	83°00'W
Chilliwack, Can. (chĭl'ĭ-wăk)	90	49°10'N	121°57'W
Chiloé, Isla de, i., Chile	144	42°30'S	73°55'W
Chilpancingo de los Bravo, Mex.	128	17°32'N	99°30'W
Chilton, Wi., U.S. (chĭl'tŭn)	113	44°00'N	88°12'W
Chilung, Tai. (chī'lung)	205	25°02'N	121°48'E
Chilwa, Lake, l., Afr.	232	15°12'S	36°30'E
Chimacum, Wa., U.S. (chĭm'ă-kŭm)	116a	48°01'N	122°47'W
Chimalpa, Mex. (chē-mäl'pä)	131a	19°26'N	99°22'W
Chimaltenango, Guat. (chē-mäl-tā-näŋ'gō)	132	14°39'N	90°48'W
Chimaltitan, Mex. (chēmäl-tē-tän')	130	21°36'N	103°50'W
Chimbay, Uzb. (chĭm-bī')	183	43°00'N	59°44'E
Chimborazo, mtn., Ec. (chēm-bô-rä'zō)	142	1°35'S	78°45'W
Chimbote, Peru (chēm-bō'tā)	142	9°02'S	78°33'W
China, Mex. (chē'nä)	122	25°43'N	99°13'W
China, nation, Asia (chī'nȧ)	204	36°45'N	93°00'E
Chinameca, El Sal. (Chē-nä-mā'kä)	132	13°31'N	88°18'W
Chinandega, Nic. (chē-nän-dā'gä)	132	12°38'N	87°08'W
Chinati Peak, mtn., Tx., U.S. (chĭ-nä'tē)	122	29°56'N	104°29'W
Chincha Alta, Peru (chĭn'chä äl'tä)	142	13°24'S	76°04'W
Chinchas, Islas, is., Peru (ē's-läs-chē'n-chäs)	142	11°27'S	79°05'W
Chinchilla, Austl. (chĭn-chĭl'ȧ)	222	26°44'S	150°36'E
Chinchorro, Banco, bk., Mex. (bä'n-kô-chēn-chô'r-rō)	132a	18°43'N	87°25'W
Chincilla de Monte Aragon, Spain	172	38°54'N	1°43'W
Chinde, Moz. (shēn'dē)	232	17°39'S	36°34'E
Chin Do, i., Kor., S.	210	34°30'N	125°43'E
Chindwin, r., Mya. (chĭn-dwĭn)	199	23°30'N	94°34'E
Chingola, Zam. (chĭng-gōlä)	232	12°32'S	27°52'E
Chinguar, Ang. (chĭng-gär)	232	12°35'S	16°15'E
Chinguetti, Maur. (chēŋ-gĕt'ē)	230	20°34'N	12°34'W
Chinhoyi, Zimb.	232	17°22'S	30°12'E
Chinju, Kor., S. (chĭn'jōō)	210	35°13'N	128°10'E
Chinko, r., C.A.R. (shĭn'kô)	231	6°37'N	24°31'E
Chinmen see Quemoy, Tai.	209	24°30'N	118°20'E
Chino, Ca., U.S. (chē'nō)	117a	34°01'N	117°42'W
Chinon, Fr. (shē-nôn')	170	47°09'N	0°13'E
Chinook, Mt., U.S. (shĭn-ŏŏk')	115	48°35'N	109°15'W
Chinsali, Zam.	237	10°34'S	32°03'E
Chinteche, Mwi. (chĭn-tĕ'chĕ)	232	11°48'S	34°14'E
Chioggia, Italy (kyôd'jä)	174	45°12'N	12°17'E
Chíos, Grc. (kē'ŏs)	163	38°23'N	26°09'E
Chíos, i., Grc.	163	38°20'N	25°45'E
Chipata, Zam.	232	13°39'S	32°40'E
Chipera, Moz. (zhē-pĕ'rä)	232	15°16'S	32°30'E
Chipley, Fl., U.S. (chĭp'lĭ)	124	30°45'N	85°33'W
Chipman, Can. (chĭp'mȧn)	100	46°11'N	65°53'W
Chipola, r., Fl., U.S. (chĭ-pō'lȧ)	124	30°40'N	85°14'W
Chippawa, Can. (chĭp'ē-wä)	111c	43°03'N	79°03'W
Chippewa, r., Mn., U.S. (chĭp'ē-wä)	112	45°07'N	95°41'W
Chippewa, r., Wi., U.S.	113	45°07'N	91°19'W
Chippewa Falls, Wi., U.S.	113	44°55'N	91°26'W
Chippewa Lake, Oh., U.S.	111d	41°04'N	81°54'W

282 Chiputneticook Lakes – Clearwater

PRONOUNCING INDEX

PLACE (Pronunciation)	PAGE	LAT.	LONG.
Chiputneticook Lakes, l., N.A. (chĭ-pŏt-nĕt'ĭ-kŏŏk)	100	45°47'N	67°45'W
Chiquimula, Guat. (chē-kē-mōō'lä)	132	14°47'N	89°31'W
Chiquimulilla, Guat. (chē-kē-mōō-lē'l-yä)	132	14°08'N	90°23'W
Chiquinquira, Col. (chē-kēŋ'kē-rä')	142	5°33'N	73°49'W
Chirala, India	203	15°52'N	80°22'E
Chirchik, Uzb. (chĭr-chĕk')	183	41°28'N	69°18'E
Chire (Shire), r., Afr.	237	17°15'S	35°25'E
Chiricahua National Monument, rec., Az., U.S. (chĭ-rä-cä'hwä)	119	32°02'N	109°18'W
Chirikof, i., Ak., U.S. (chĭ'rĭ-kôf)	103	55°50'N	155°35'W
Chiriquí, Punta, c., Pan. (pô'n-tä-chē-rē-kē')	133	9°13'N	81°39'W
Chiriquí Grande, Pan. (chē-rē-kē' grän'dā)	133	8°57'N	82°08'W
Chiri San, mtn., Kor., S. (chĭ'rĭ-sän')	210	35°20'N	127°39'E
Chiromo, Mwi.	232	16°34'S	35°13'E
Chirpan, Blg.	163	42°12'N	25°19'E
Chirripó, Río, r., C.R.	133	9°50'N	83°20'W
Chisasibi, Can.	91	53°40'N	78°58'W
Chisholm, Mn., U.S. (chĭz'ŭm)	113	47°28'N	92°53'W
Chişinău, Mol.	178	47°02'N	28°52'E
Chistopol', Russia (chĭs-tô'pôl-y')	178	55°21'N	50°37'E
Chita, Russia (chē-tá')	179	52°09'N	113°39'E
Chitambo, Zam.	237	12°55'S	30°39'E
Chitato, Ang.	236	7°20'S	20°47'E
Chitembo, Ang.	236	13°34'S	16°40'E
Chitina, Ak., U.S. (chĭ-tē'ná)	103	61°28'N	144°35'W
Chitokoloki, Zam.	236	13°50'S	23°13'E
Chitorgarh, India	202	24°59'N	74°42'E
Chitrāl, Pak. (chē-träl')	199	35°58'N	71°48'E
Chittagong, Bngl. (chĭt-á-gông')	199	22°26'N	90°51'E
Chitungwiza, Zimb.	232	17°51'S	31°05'E
Chiumbe, r., Afr. (chê-ŏŏm'bå)	232	9°45'S	21°00'E
Chivasso, Italy (kē-väs'sō)	174	45°13'N	7°52'E
Chivhu, Zimb.	232	18°59'S	30°58'E
Chivilcoy, Arg. (chē-vêl-koi')	144	34°51'S	60°03'W
Chixoy, r., Guat. (chē-ĸoi')	132	15°40'N	90°35'W
Chizu, Japan (chē-zōō')	211	35°16'N	134°15'E
Chloride, Az., U.S. (klō'rīd)	119	35°25'N	114°15'W
Chmielnik, Pol. (ĸmyĕl'nēĸ)	169	50°36'N	20°46'E
Choapa, r., Chile (chô-á'pä)	141b	31°56'S	70°48'W
Choctawhatchee, r., Fl., U.S.	124	30°37'N	85°56'W
Choctawhatchee Bay, b., Fl., U.S. (chôk-tô-hăch'ē)	124	30°15'N	86°32'W
Chodziez, Pol. (ĸōj'yĕsh)	168	52°59'N	16°55'E
Choele Choel, Arg. (chô-ĕ'lĕ-chôĕ'l)	144	39°14'S	65°46'W
Chōfu, Japan (chō'fōō')	211a	35°39'N	139°33'E
Chōgo, Japan (chō-gō)	211a	35°25'N	139°28'E
Choiseul, i., Sol. Is. (shwä-zûl')	221	7°30'S	157°30'E
Choisy-le-Roi, Fr.	171b	48°46'N	2°25'E
Chojnice, Pol. (ĸoi-nē-tsĕ)	169	53°41'N	17°34'E
Cholet, Fr. (shō-lĕ')	161	47°06'N	0°54'W
Cholula, Mex. (chō-lōō'lä)	130	19°04'N	98°19'W
Choluteca, Hond. (chō-lōō-tā'kä)	132	13°18'N	87°12'W
Choluteco, r., Hond.	132	13°34'N	86°59'W
Chomutov, Czech Rep. (kō'mŏŏ-tôf)	168	50°27'N	13°23'E
Chona, r., Russia (chō'nä)	185	60°45'N	109°15'E
Chone, Ec. (chô'nē)	142	0°48'S	80°06'W
Chŏngjin, Kor., N. (chŭng-jĭn')	205	41°48'N	129°46'E
Chŏngju, Kor., S. (chŭng-jōō')	210	36°35'N	127°30'E
Chongming Dao, i., China (chôŋ-mĭŋ dou)	209	31°40'N	122°30'E
Chongqing, China (chôŋ-chyĭŋ)	204	29°38'N	107°30'E
Chongqing, prov., China	204	30°00'N	108°00'E
Chŏnju, Kor., S. (chŭn-jōō')	210	35°48'N	127°08'E
Chonos, Archipiélago de los, is., Chile	144	44°35'N	76°15'W
Chorley, Eng., U.K. (chôr'lĭ)	158a	53°40'N	2°38'W
Chornaya, neigh., Russia	186b	55°45'N	38°04'E
Chornobai, Ukr.	177	51°17'N	30°14'E
Chornobay, Ukr. (chĕr-nō-bī')	177	49°41'N	32°24'E
Chornomors'ke, Ukr.	181	45°29'N	32°43'E
Chorrillos, Peru (chôr-rē'l-yōs)	142	12°17'S	76°55'W
Chortkiv, Ukr.	169	49°01'N	25°48'E
Chosan, Kor., N. (chō-sän')	210	40°44'N	125°48'E
Chosen, Fl., U.S. (chō'z'n)	125a	26°41'N	80°41'W
Chōshi, Japan (chō'shē)	210	35°40'N	140°55'E
Choszczno, Pol. (chôsh'chnô)	168	53°10'N	15°25'E
Chota Nagpur, plat., India	202	23°40'N	82°50'E
Choteau, Mt., U.S. (shō'tō)	115	47°51'N	112°10'W
Chowan, r., N.C., U.S. (chô-wän')	125	36°13'N	76°46'W
Chowilla Reservoir, res., Austl.	222	34°05'S	141°20'E
Chown, Mount, mtn., Can. (choun)	95	53°24'N	119°22'W
Choybalsan, Mong.	205	47°50'N	114°15'E
Christchurch, N.Z. (krīst'chûrch)	221a	43°30'S	172°38'E
Christian, i., Can. (krĭs'chăn)	99	44°50'N	80°00'W
Christiansburg, Va., U.S. (krĭs'chănz-bûrg)	125	37°08'N	80°25'W
Christiansted, V.I.U.S.	129b	17°45'N	64°44'W
Christmas Island, dep., Oc.	212	10°35'S	105°40'E
Christopher, Il., U.S. (krĭs'tô-fẽr)	121	37°58'N	89°04'W
Chrudim, Czech Rep. (ĸrōō'dyĕm)	168	49°57'N	15°46'E
Chrzanów, Pol. (ĸzhä'nôf)	169	50°08'N	19°24'E
Chuansha, China (chůän-shä)	207b	31°12'N	121°41'E
Chubut, prov., Arg. (chŏŏ-bōōt')	144	44°00'S	69°15'W
Chubut, r., Arg. (chŏŏ-bōōt')	144	43°05'S	69°00'W
Chuckatuck, Va., U.S. (chŭck á-tŭck)	110g	36°51'N	76°35'W
Chucunaque, r., Pan. (chōō-kōō-nä'kå)	133	8°36'N	77°48'W
Chudovo, Russia (chŏŏ'dō-vō)	176	59°03'N	31°56'E
Chudskoye Ozero, l., Eur. (chŏŏt'skō-yĕ)	180	58°43'N	26°45'E

PLACE (Pronunciation)	PAGE	LAT.	LONG.
Chuguchak, hist. reg., China (chōō'gōō-chäk')	204	46°09'N	83°58'E
Chuguyevka, Russia (chŏŏ-gōō'yĕf-kå)	210	43°58'N	133°49'E
Chugwater Creek, r., Wy., U.S. (chŭg'wô-tẽr)	112	41°43'N	104°54'W
Chuhuiv, Ukr.	181	49°52'N	36°40'E
Chukotskiy Poluostrov, pen., Russia	179	66°12'N	175°00'W
Chukotskoye Nagor'ye, mts., Russia	179	66°00'N	166°00'E
Chula Vista, Ca., U.S. (chōō'lá vĭs'tá)	118a	32°38'N	117°05'W
Chulkovo, Russia (chōōl-kô vô)	186b	55°33'N	38°04'E
Chulucanas, Peru	142	5°13'S	80°13'W
Chulum, r., Russia	184	57°52'N	84°45'E
Chumikan, Russia (chōō-mē-kän')	179	54°47'N	135°09'E
Chun'an, China (chŏn-än)	209	29°38'N	119°00'E
Chunchŏn, Kor., S. (chŏn-chŭn')	210	37°51'N	127°46'E
Chungju, Kor., S. (chŭng'jōō')	210	37°00'N	128°19'E
Chungking *see* Chongqing, China	204	29°38'N	107°30'E
Chunya, Tan.	237	8°32'S	33°25'E
Chunya, r., Russia (chŏn'yä')	184	61°45'N	101°28'E
Chuquicamata, Chile (chōō-kē-kä-mä'tä)	144	22°08'S	68°57'W
Chur, Switz. (kōōr)	161	46°51'N	9°32'E
Churchill, Can. (chûrch'ĭl)	91	58°50'N	94°10'W
Churchill, r., Can.	92	58°00'N	95°00'W
Churchill, Cape, c., Can.	93	59°07'N	93°50'W
Churchill Falls, wtfl., Can.	93	53°35'N	64°27'W
Churchill Lake, l., Can.	96	56°12'N	108°40'W
Churchill Peak, mtn., Can.	92	58°10'N	125°14'W
Church Stretton, Eng., U.K. (chûrch strĕt'ŭn)	158a	52°32'N	2°49'W
Churchton, Md., U.S.	110e	38°49'N	76°33'W
Churu, India	202	28°22'N	75°00'E
Churumuco, Mex. (chōō-rōō-mōō'kō)	130	18°39'N	101°40'W
Chuska Mountains, mts., Az., U.S. (chŭs-ká)	119	36°21'N	109°11'W
Chusovaya, r., Russia (chōō-sô-vä'yá)	180	58°08'N	58°35'E
Chusovoy, Russia (chōō-sô-vôy')	178	58°18'N	57°50'E
Chust, Uzb. (chōst)	183	41°05'N	71°28'E
Chuuk (Truk), is., Micron.	214c	7°25'N	151°47'E
Chuvashia, prov., Russia	180	55°45'N	46°00'E
Chuviscar, r., Mex. (chōō-vēs-kär')	122	28°34'N	105°36'W
Chuwang, China (chōō-wäŋ)	206	36°08'N	114°53'E
Chuxian, China (chōō shyĕn)	208	32°19'N	118°19'E
Chuxiong, China (chōō-shyôŋ)	204	25°19'N	101°34'E
Chyhyryn, Ukr.	177	49°02'N	32°39'E
Cicero, Il., U.S. (sĭs'ẽr-ō)	111a	41°50'N	87°46'W
Cide, Tur. (jē'dĕ)	163	41°50'N	33°00'E
Ciechanów, Pol. (tsyĕ-kä'nôf)	169	52°52'N	20°39'E
Ciego de Avila, Cuba (syā'gō dā ä'vē-lä)	129	21°50'N	78°45'W
Ciego de Avila, prov., Cuba	134	22°00'N	78°40'W
Ciempozuelos, Spain (thyĕm-pō-thwä'lōs)	172	40°09'N	3°36'W
Ciénaga, Col. (syā'nä-gä)	142	11°01'N	74°15'W
Cienfuegos, Cuba (syĕn-fwā'gōs)	129	22°10'N	80°30'W
Cienfuegos, prov., Cuba	134	22°15'N	80°40'W
Cienfuegos, Bahía, b., Cuba (bä-ē'ä-syĕn-fwā'gōs)	134	22°00'N	80°35'W
Ciervo, Isla de la, i., Nic. (ē's-lä-dĕ-lä-syĕ'r-vō)	133	11°56'N	83°20'W
Cieszyn, Pol. (tsyĕ'shĕn)	169	49°47'N	18°45'E
Cieza, Spain (thyā'thä)	172	38°13'N	1°25'W
Cigüela, r., Spain	172	39°53'N	2°54'W
Cihuatlán, Mex. (sē-wä-tlä'n)	130	19°13'N	104°36'W
Cihuatlán, r., Mex.	130	19°11'N	104°30'W
Cijara, Embalse de, res., Spain	172	39°25'N	5°00'W
Cilician Gates, p., Tur.	181	37°30'N	35°30'E
Cimarron, r., Co., U.S.	120	37°13'N	102°30'W
Cimarron, r., U.S. (sĭm-á-rōn')	106	36°26'N	98°27'W
Cinca, r., Spain (thēŋ'kä)	173	42°09'N	0°08'E
Cincinnati, Oh., U.S. (sĭn-sĭ-nát'ĭ)	105	39°08'N	84°30'W
Cinco Balas, Cayos, is., Cuba (kä'yōs-thēŋ'kō bä'läs)	134	21°05'N	79°25'W
Cintalapa, Mex. (sēn-tä-lä'pä)	131	16°41'N	93°44'W
Cinto, Monte, mtn., Fr. (chēn'tō)	161	42°24'N	8°54'E
Circle, Ak., U.S. (sûr'k'l)	106a	65°49'N	144°22'W
Circleville, Oh., U.S. (sûr'k'lvĭl)	108	39°35'N	83°00'W
Cirebon, Indon.	212	6°50'S	108°33'E
Ciri Grande, r., Pan. (sē'rē-grá'n'dĕ)	128a	8°55'N	80°04'W
Cisco, Tx., U.S. (sĭs'kō)	122	32°23'N	98°57'W
Cisneros, Col. (sēs-nĕ'rōs)	142a	6°33'N	75°05'W
Cisterna di Latina, Italy (chēs-tĕ'r-nä-dē-lä-tē'nä)	173d	41°36'N	12°53'E
Cistierna, Spain (thēs-tyĕr'nä)	172	42°48'N	5°08'W
Citronelle, Al., U.S. (cĭt-rō'nĕl)	124	31°05'N	88°15'W
Cittadella, Italy (chēt-tä-dĕl'lä)	174	45°39'N	11°51'E
Città di Castello, Italy (chĕt-tä'dē käs-tĕl'lō)	174	43°27'N	12°17'E
Ciudad Altamirano, Mex. (syōō-dä'd-äl-tä-mē-rä'nō)	130	18°24'N	100°38'W
Ciudad Bolívar, Ven. (syōō-dhädh' bō-lē'vär)	142	8°07'N	63°41'W
Ciudad Camargo, Mex.	128	27°42'N	105°10'W
Ciudad Chetumal, Mex.	128	18°30'N	88°17'W
Ciudad Darío, Nic. (syōō-dhä'd-dä'rē-ō)	132	12°44'N	86°08'W
Ciudad de la Habana, prov., Cuba	134	23°20'N	82°10'W
Ciudad del Carmen, Mex. (syōō-dä'd-dĕl-kä'r-mĕn)	128	18°39'N	91°49'W
Ciudad del Maíz, Mex. (syōō-dhädh'del mä-ēz')	130	22°24'N	99°37'W
Ciudad Fernández, Mex. (syōō-dhädh'fĕr-nän'dĕz)	130	21°56'N	100°03'W

PLACE (Pronunciation)	PAGE	LAT.	LONG.
Ciudad García, Mex. (syōō-dhädh'gär-sē'ä)	128	22°39'N	103°02'W
Ciudad Guayana, Ven.	142	8°30'N	62°45'W
Ciudad Guzmán, Mex. (syōō-dhädh'gōz-män)	128	19°40'N	103°29'W
Ciudad Hidalgo, Mex. (syōō-dä'd-ē-dä'l-gō)	130	19°41'N	100°35'W
Ciudad Juárez, Mex. (syōō-dhädh hwä'rāz)	128	31°44'N	106°28'W
Ciudad Madero, Mex. (syōō-dä'd-mä-dĕ'rō)	131	22°16'N	97°52'W
Ciudad Mante, Mex. (syōō-dä'd-mán'tĕ)	128	22°34'N	98°58'W
Ciudad Manuel Doblado, Mex. (syōō-dä'd-män-wāl'dō-blä'dō)	130	20°43'N	101°57'W
Ciudad Obregón, Mex. (syōō-dhädh-ô-brĕ-gō'n)	128	27°40'N	109°58'W
Ciudad Real, Spain (thyōō-dhädh'rā-äl')	172	38°59'N	3°55'W
Ciudad Rodrigo, Spain (thyōō-dhädh'rô-drē'gō)	162	40°38'N	6°34'W
Ciudad Serdán, Mex. (syōō-dä'd-sĕr-dá'n)	131	18°58'N	97°26'W
Ciudad Victoria, Mex. (syōō-dhädh'vēk-tō'rē-ä)	128	23°43'N	99°09'W
Ciutadella, Spain	173	40°00'N	3°52'E
Civitavecchia, Italy (chē'vē-tä-vĕk'kyä)	174	42°06'N	11°49'E
Cixian, China (tsē shyĕn)	206	36°22'N	114°23'E
Clackamas, Or., U.S. (klăc-ká'măs)	116c	45°25'N	122°34'W
Claire, l., Can. (klâr)	92	58°33'N	113°16'W
Clair Engle Lake, l., Ca., U.S.	114	40°51'N	122°41'W
Clairton, Pa., U.S. (klârtŭn)	111e	40°17'N	79°53'W
Clanton, Al., U.S. (klăn'tŭn)	124	32°50'N	86°38'W
Clare, Mi., U.S. (klâr)	108	43°50'N	84°45'W
Clare Island, i., Ire.	164	53°46'N	10°00'W
Claremont, Ca., U.S. (klâr'mŏnt)	117a	34°06'N	117°43'W
Claremont, N.H., U.S. (klâr'mŏnt)	109	43°20'N	72°20'W
Claremont, W.V., U.S.	108	37°55'N	81°00'W
Claremore, Ok., U.S. (klâr'mōr)	121	36°16'N	95°37'W
Claremorris, Ire. (klâr-mŏr'ĭs)	164	53°46'N	9°05'W
Clarence Strait, strt., Austl. (klăr'ĕns)	220	12°15'S	130°05'E
Clarence Strait, strt., Ak., U.S.	94	55°25'N	132°00'W
Clarence Town, Bah.	135	23°05'N	75°00'W
Clarendon, Ar., U.S. (klâr'ĕn-dŭn)	121	34°42'N	91°17'W
Clarendon, Tx., U.S.	120	34°55'N	100°52'W
Clarens, S. Afr. (clâ-rĕns)	233c	28°34'S	28°26'E
Claresholm, Can. (klâr'ĕs-hōlm)	90	50°02'N	113°35'W
Clarinda, Ia., U.S. (klá-rĭn'dá)	112	40°42'N	95°00'W
Clarines, Ven. (klä-rē'nĕs)	143b	9°57'N	65°10'W
Clarion, Ia., U.S. (klăr'ĭ-ŭn)	113	42°43'N	93°45'W
Clarion, Pa., U.S.	109	41°10'N	79°25'W
Clark, S.D., U.S. (klärk)	112	44°52'N	97°45'W
Clark, Point, c., Can.	98	44°05'N	81°50'W
Clarkdale, Az., U.S. (klärk-dāl)	119	34°45'N	112°05'W
Clarke City, Can.	91	50°12'N	66°38'W
Clarke Range, mts., Austl.	221	20°30'S	148°00'E
Clark Fork, r., Mt., U.S.	114	47°50'N	115°35'W
Clarksburg, W.V., U.S. (klärkz'bûrg)	105	39°15'N	80°20'W
Clarksdale, Ms., U.S. (klärks-dāl)	124	34°10'N	90°31'W
Clark's Harbour, Can. (klärks)	100	43°26'N	65°38'W
Clarks Hill Lake, res., U.S. (klärk-hĭl)	107	33°50'N	82°35'W
Clarkston, Ga., U.S. (klärks'tŭn)	110c	33°49'N	84°15'W
Clarkston, Wa., U.S.	114	46°24'N	117°01'W
Clarksville, Ar., U.S. (klärks-vĭl)	121	35°28'N	93°26'W
Clarksville, Tn., U.S.	124	36°30'N	87°23'W
Clarksville, Tx., U.S.	121	33°37'N	95°02'W
Clatskanie, Or., U.S.	116c	46°04'N	123°11'W
Clatskanie, r., Or., U.S. (klăt-skā'nē)	116c	46°06'N	123°11'W
Clatsop Spit, Or., U.S. (klăt-sŏp)	116c	46°13'N	124°04'W
Cláudio, Braz. (klou'-dēō)	141a	20°26'S	44°44'W
Claveria, Phil. (klä-vå-rē'ä)	209	18°38'N	121°08'E
Clawson, Mi., U.S. (klô's'n)	111b	42°32'N	83°09'W
Claxton, Ga., U.S. (klăks'tŭn)	125	32°07'N	81°54'W
Clay, Ky., U.S. (klā)	124	37°28'N	87°50'W
Clay Center, Ks., U.S. (klā sĕn'tẽr)	121	39°23'N	97°08'W
Clay City, Ky., U.S. (klā sĭ'tĭ)	108	37°50'N	83°55'W
Claycomo, Mo., U.S. (kla-kō'mo)	117f	39°12'N	94°30'W
Clay Cross, Eng., U.K. (klā krŏs)	158a	53°10'N	1°25'W
Claye-Souilly, Fr. (klĕ-sōō-yē')	171b	48°56'N	2°43'E
Claymont, De., U.S. (klā-mŏnt)	110f	39°48'N	75°28'W
Clayton, Eng., U.K.	158a	53°47'N	1°49'W
Clayton, Al., U.S. (klā'tŭn)	124	31°52'N	85°25'W
Clayton, Ca., U.S.	116b	37°56'N	121°56'W
Clayton, Mo., U.S.	117e	38°39'N	90°20'W
Clayton, N.C., U.S.	125	35°40'N	78°27'W
Clayton, N.M., U.S.	120	36°26'N	103°12'W
Clear, l., Ca., U.S.	118	39°05'N	122°50'W
Clear Boggy Creek, r., Ok., U.S. (klēr bŏg'ĭ krēk)	121	34°21'N	96°22'W
Clear Creek, r., Az., U.S.	119	34°40'N	111°05'W
Clear Creek, r., Tx., U.S.	123a	29°34'N	95°13'W
Clear Creek, r., Wy., U.S.	115	44°35'N	106°20'W
Clearfield, Pa., U.S. (klēr-fēld)	109	41°00'N	78°25'W
Clearfield, Ut., U.S.	117b	41°07'N	112°01'W
Clear Hills, Can.	90	57°11'N	119°20'W
Clear Lake, Ia., U.S.	113	43°09'N	93°23'W
Clear Lake, Wa., U.S.	116a	48°27'N	122°14'W
Clear Lake Reservoir, res., Ca., U.S.	114	41°53'N	121°00'W
Clearwater, Fl., U.S. (klēr-wô'tẽr)	125a	27°43'N	82°45'W
Clearwater, r., Can.	95	52°00'N	114°50'W
Clearwater, r., Can.	96	56°10'N	110°40'W
Clearwater, r., Can.	95	52°00'N	120°10'W
Clearwater, r., Id., U.S.	114	46°27'N	116°33'W

PRONOUNCING INDEX

Clearwater – Comacchio 283

PLACE (Pronunciation)	PAGE	LAT.	LONG.
Clearwater, Middle Fork, r., Id., U.S.	114	46°10'N	115°48'W
Clearwater, North Fork, r., Id., U.S.	114	46°34'N	116°08'W
Clearwater, South Fork, r., Id., U.S.	114	45°46'N	115°53'W
Clearwater Mountains, mts., Id., U.S.	114	45°56'N	115°15'W
Cleburne, Tx., U.S. (klē'bŭrn)	104	32°21'N	97°23'W
Cle Elum, Wa., U.S. (klē ĕl'ŭm)	114	47°12'N	120°55'W
Clementon, N.J., U.S. (klē'mĕn-tŭn)	110f	39°49'N	75°00'W
Cleobury Mortimer, Eng., U.K. (klēō-bĕr'ĭ môr'tĭ-mĕr)	158a	52°22'N	2°29'W
Clermont, Austl. (klēr'mŏnt)	219	23°02'S	147°46'E
Clermont, Can.	99	47°45'N	70°20'W
Clermont-Ferrand, Fr. (klĕr-môn'fĕr-răn')	154	45°47'N	3°03'E
Cleveland, Ms., U.S. (klēv'lănd)	124	33°45'N	90°42'W
Cleveland, Oh., U.S.	105	41°30'N	81°42'W
Cleveland, Ok., U.S.	121	36°18'N	96°28'W
Cleveland, Tn., U.S.	124	35°09'N	84°52'W
Cleveland, Tx., U.S.	123	30°18'N	95°05'W
Cleveland Heights, Oh., U.S.	111d	41°30'N	81°35'W
Cleveland Peninsula, pen., Ak., U.S.	94	55°45'N	132°00'W
Cleves, Oh., U.S. (klē'vĕs)	111f	39°10'N	84°45'W
Clew Bay, b., Ire. (klo͞o)	164	53°47'N	9°45'W
Clewiston, Fl., U.S. (klē'wis-tŭn)	125a	26°44'N	80°55'W
Clichy, Fr. (klē-shē)	170	48°54'N	2°18'E
Clifden, Ire. (klĭf'dĕn)	164	53°31'N	10°04'W
Clifton, Az., U.S. (klĭf'tŭn)	119	33°05'N	109°20'W
Clifton, N.J., U.S.	110a	40°52'N	74°09'W
Clifton, S.C., U.S.	125	35°00'N	81°47'W
Clifton, Tx., U.S.	123	31°45'N	97°31'W
Clifton Forge, Va., U.S.	109	37°50'N	79°50'W
Clinch, r., Tn., U.S. (klĭnch)	124	36°30'N	83°19'W
Clingmans Dome, mtn., U.S. (klĭng'măns dōm)	124	35°37'N	83°26'W
Clinton, Can. (klĭn-'tŭn)	90	51°05'N	121°35'W
Clinton, Ia., U.S.	113	41°50'N	90°13'W
Clinton, Il., U.S.	108	40°10'N	88°55'W
Clinton, In., U.S.	108	39°40'N	87°25'W
Clinton, Ky., U.S.	124	36°39'N	88°56'W
Clinton, Ma., U.S.	101a	42°25'N	71°41'W
Clinton, Md., U.S.	110e	38°46'N	76°54'W
Clinton, Mo., U.S.	121	38°23'N	93°46'W
Clinton, N.C., U.S.	125	34°58'N	78°20'W
Clinton, Ok., U.S.	120	35°31'N	98°56'W
Clinton, S.C., U.S.	125	34°27'N	81°53'W
Clinton, Tn., U.S.	124	36°05'N	84°08'W
Clinton, Wa., U.S.	116a	47°59'N	122°22'W
Clinton, r., Mi., U.S.	111b	42°36'N	83°00'W
Clinton-Colden, l., Can.	92	63°58'N	106°34'W
Clintonville, Wi., U.S. (klĭn'tŭn-vĭl)	113	44°37'N	88°46'W
Clio, Mi., U.S. (klē'ō)	108	43°10'N	83°45'W
Cloates, Point, c., Austl. (klōts)	220	22°47'S	113°45'E
Clocolan, S. Afr.	238c	28°56'S	27°35'E
Clonakilty Bay, b., Ire. (klŏn-á-kĭltē)	164	51°30'N	8°50'W
Cloncurry, Austl. (klŏn-kŭr'ē)	218	20°58'S	140°42'E
Clonmel, Ire. (klŏn-mĕl)	164	52°21'N	7°45'W
Cloquet, Mn., U.S. (klō-kā')	117h	46°42'N	92°28'W
Closter, N.J., U.S. (klōs'tēr)	110a	40°58'N	73°57'W
Cloud Peak, mtn., Wy., U.S. (kloud)	106	44°23'N	107°11'W
Clover, S.C., U.S. (klō'vēr)	125	35°08'N	81°08'W
Clover Bar, Can. (klō'vēr bār)	102g	53°34'N	113°20'W
Cloverdale, Can.	116d	49°06'N	122°44'W
Cloverdale, Ca., U.S. (klō'vēr-dāl)	118	38°47'N	123°03'W
Cloverport, Ky., U.S. (klō'vēr pōrt)	108	37°50'N	86°35'W
Clovis, N.M., U.S. (klō'vĭs)	104	34°24'N	103°11'W
Cluj-Napoca, Rom.	154	46°46'N	23°34'E
Clun, r., Eng., U.K. (klŭn)	158a	52°25'N	2°56'W
Cluny, Fr. (klü-nē')	170	46°27'N	4°40'E
Clutha, r., N.Z. (klo͞o'thá)	221a	45°52'S	169°30'E
Clwyd, hist. reg., Wales, U.K.	158a	53°01'N	2°59'W
Clyde, Ks., U.S.	121	39°34'N	97°23'W
Clyde, Oh., U.S.	108	41°15'N	83°00'W
Clyde, r., Scot., U.K.	164	55°35'N	3°50'W
Clyde, Firth of, b., Scot., U.K. (fûrth ŏv klīd)	164	55°28'N	5°01'W
Côa, r., Port. (kō'ä)	172	40°28'N	6°55'W
Coacalco, Mex. (kō-ä-käl'kō)	131a	19°37'N	99°06'W
Coachella, Canal, can., Ca., U.S. (kō'chĕl-lá)	118	33°15'N	115°25'W
Coahuayana, Río de, r., Mex. (rē'ō-dĕ-kō-ä-wä-yä'nä)	130	19°00'N	103°33'W
Coahuayutla, Mex. (kō'ä-wī-yo͞ot'lä)	130	18°19'N	101°44'W
Coahuila, state, Mex. (kō-ä-wē'lä)	128	27°30'N	103°00'W
Coal City, Il., U.S. (kōl sĭ'tĭ)	111a	41°17'N	88°17'W
Coalcomán, Río de, r., Mex. (rē'ō-dĕ-kō-äl-kō-män')	130	18°45'N	103°15'W
Coalcomán, Sierra de, mts., Mex.	130	18°30'N	102°45'W
Coalcomán de Matamoros, Mex.	130	18°46'N	103°10'W
Coaldale, Can. (kōl'dāl)	95	49°43'N	112°37'W
Coalgate, Ok., U.S. (kōl'gāt)	121	34°44'N	96°13'W
Coal Grove, Oh., U.S. (kōl grōv)	108	38°20'N	82°40'W
Coalinga, Ca., U.S. (kō-á-lĭŋ'gá)	118	36°09'N	120°23'W
Coalville, Eng., U.K. (kōl'vĭl)	158a	52°43'N	1°21'W
Coamo, P.R. (kō-ä'mō)	129b	18°05'N	66°21'W
Coari, Braz. (kō-är'ē)	142	4°06'S	63°10'W
Coast Mountains, mts., N.A. (kōst)	92	54°10'N	128°00'W
Coast Ranges, mts., U.S.	106	41°28'N	123°30'W
Coatepec, Mex. (kō-ä-tā-pĕk)	130	19°23'N	98°44'W
Coatepec, Mex.	131a	19°08'N	99°25'W
Coatepec, Mex.	131	19°26'N	96°56'W
Coatepeque, El Sal.	132	13°56'N	89°30'W
Coatepeque, Guat. (kō-ä-tā-pā'kå)	132	14°40'N	91°52'W
Coatesville, Pa., U.S. (kōts'vĭl)	109	40°00'N	75°50'W
Coatetelco, Mex. (kō-ä-tå-tĕl'kō)	130	18°43'N	99°17'W
Coaticook, Can. (kō'tĭ-ko͝ok)	99	45°10'N	71°55'W
Coatlinchán, Mex. (kô-ä-tlē'n-chä'n)	131a	19°26'N	98°52'W
Coats, i., Can. (kōts)	93	62°23'N	82°11'W
Coats Land, reg., Ant.	224	74°00'S	30°00'W
Coatzacoalcos, Mex.	128	18°09'N	94°26'W
Coatzacoalcos, r., Mex.	131	17°40'N	94°41'W
Coba, hist., Mex. (kô'bä)	132a	20°23'N	87°23'W
Cobalt, Can. (kō'bôlt)	91	47°21'N	79°40'W
Cobán, Guat. (kō-bän')	128	15°28'N	90°19'W
Cobar, Austl.	219	31°28'S	145°50'E
Cobberas, Mount, mtn., Austl. (cō-bĕr-ăs)	222	36°45'S	148°15'E
Cobequid Mountains, mts., Can.	100	45°35'N	64°10'W
Cobh, Ire. (kôv)	154	51°52'N	8°09'W
Cobija, Bol. (kô-bē'hä)	142	11°12'S	68°49'W
Cobourg, Can. (kō'bo͝orgh)	91	43°55'N	78°05'W
Cobre, r., Jam. (kō'brā)	134	18°05'N	77°00'W
Coburg, Austl.	217a	37°45'S	144°58'E
Coburg, Ger. (kō'bo͞org)	168	50°16'N	10°57'E
Cocentaina, Spain (kō-thån-tä-ē'ná)	173	38°44'N	0°27'W
Cochabamba, Bol.	142	17°24'S	66°09'W
Cochinos, Bahía, b., Cuba (bä-ē'ä-kô-chē'nōs)	134	22°05'N	81°10'W
Cochinos Banks, bk.	134	22°20'N	76°15'W
Cochiti Indian Reservation, I.R., N.M., U.S.	119	35°37'N	106°20'W
Cochran, Ga., U.S. (kŏk'răn)	124	32°23'N	83°23'W
Cochrane, Can. (kŏk'răn)	91	49°01'N	81°06'W
Cochrane, Can.	102e	51°11'N	114°28'W
Cockburn, i., Can. (kŏk-bûrn)	98	45°55'N	83°25'W
Cockeysville, Md., U.S. (kŏk'ĭz-vĭl)	110e	39°30'N	76°40'W
Cockrell Hill, Tx., U.S. (kŏk'rĕl)	117c	32°44'N	96°53'W
Coco, r., N.A.	129	14°55'N	83°45'W
Coco, Cayo, i., Cuba (kä'-yō-kô'kô)	134	22°30'N	78°30'W
Coco, Isla del, i., C.R. (ē's-lä-dĕl-kô-kô)	128	5°33'N	87°02'W
Cocoa, Fl., U.S. (kō'kō)	125a	28°21'N	80°44'W
Cocoa Beach, Fl., U.S.	125a	28°20'N	80°35'W
Cocoli, Pan. (kô-kô'lē)	128a	8°58'N	79°36'W
Coconino, Plateau, plat., Az., U.S. (kō kō nē'nō)	119	35°45'N	112°28'W
Cocos (Keeling) Islands, is., Oc. (kō'kōs) (kē'lĭng)	3	11°50'S	90°50'E
Coco Solito, Pan. (kô-kô-sō-lē'tō)	128a	9°21'N	79°53'W
Cocula, Mex. (kō-ko͞o'lä)	130	20°23'N	103°47'W
Cocula, r., Mex.	130	18°17'N	99°45'W
Cod, Cape, pen., Ma., U.S.	107	41°42'N	70°15'W
Codajás, Braz. (kō-dä-häzh')	142	3°44'S	62°09'W
Codera, Cabo, c., Ven. (ká'bô-kô-dĕ'rä)	143b	10°35'N	66°06'W
Codogno, Italy (kô-dō'nyō)	174	45°08'N	9°43'E
Codrington, Antig. (kŏd'rĭng-tŭn)	133b	17°39'N	61°49'W
Cody, Wy., U.S. (kō'dĭ)	115	44°31'N	109°02'W
Coelho da Rocha, Braz.	144b	22°47'S	43°23'W
Coemba, Ang.	236	12°08'S	18°05'E
Coesfeld, Ger. (kûs'fĕld)	171c	51°56'N	7°10'E
Coeur d'Alene, Id., U.S. (kûr dá-lān')	104	47°43'N	116°35'W
Coeur d'Alene, r., Id., U.S.	114	47°26'N	116°35'W
Coeur d'Alene Indian Reservation, I.R., Id., U.S.	114	47°18'N	116°45'W
Coeur d'Alene Lake, l., Id., U.S.	114	47°32'N	116°39'W
Coffeyville, Ks., U.S. (kŏf'ĭ-vĭl)	105	37°01'N	95°38'W
Coff's Harbour, Austl.	222	30°20'S	153°10'E
Cofimvaba, S. Afr. (cäfĭm'vä-bá)	233c	32°01'S	27°37'E
Coghinas, r., Italy (kō'gē-nás)	174	40°31'N	9°00'E
Cognac, Fr. (kôn-yak')	161	45°41'N	0°22'W
Cohasset, Ma., U.S. (kô-hăs'ĕt)	101a	42°14'N	70°48'W
Cohoes, N.Y., U.S. (kô-hōz')	109	42°50'N	73°40'W
Coig, r., Arg. (kô'ēk)	144	51°15'S	71°00'W
Coimbatore, India (kô-ēm-bá-tōr')	199	11°03'N	76°56'E
Coimbra, Port. (kô-ēm'brä)	154	40°14'N	8°23'W
Coín, Spain (kô-ēn')	172	36°40'N	4°45'W
Coina, Port. (kô-ē'ná)	173b	38°35'N	9°03'W
Coina, r., Port. (kô'y-nä)	173b	38°35'N	9°02'W
Coipasa, Salar de, pl., Bol. (sä-lä'r-dĕ-koi-pä'-sä)	142	19°12'S	69°13'W
Coixtlahuaca, Mex. (kō-ēs'tlä-wä'kä)	131	17°42'N	97°17'W
Cojedes, dept., Ven. (kō-kĕ'dĕs)	143b	9°50'N	68°21'W
Cojimar, Cuba (kō-hē-mär')	135a	23°10'N	82°19'W
Cojutepeque, El Sal. (kô-hô-tĕ-pā'kå)	132	13°45'N	88°50'W
Cokato, Mn., U.S. (kô-kā'tō)	113	45°03'N	94°11'W
Cokeburg, Pa., U.S. (kōk bûgh)	111e	40°06'N	80°03'W
Colac, Austl. (kŏ'lăc)	222	38°25'S	143°40'E
Colares, Port. (kō-lä'rĕs)	173b	38°47'N	9°27'W
Colatina, Braz. (kō-lä-tē'nä)	143	19°33'S	40°42'W
Colby, Ks., U.S. (kōl'bĭ)	120	39°23'N	101°04'W
Colchagua, prov., Chile (kôl-chá'gwä)	141b	34°42'S	71°24'W
Colchester, Eng., U.K. (kōl'chĕs-tēr)	165	51°52'N	0°50'E
Cold Lake, l., Can. (kōld)	96	54°33'N	110°05'W
Coldwater, Ks., U.S. (kōld'wô-tēr)	120	37°14'N	99°21'W
Coldwater, Mi., U.S.	108	41°55'N	85°00'W
Coldwater, r., Ms., U.S.	124	34°25'N	90°12'W
Coldwater Creek, r., Tx., U.S.	120	36°10'N	101°45'W
Coleman, Tx., U.S. (kōl'mán)	122	31°50'N	99°25'W
Colenso, S. Afr. (kō-lĕnz'ō)	233c	28°48'S	29°49'E
Coleraine, N. Ire., U.K.	164	55°08'N	6°40'W
Coleraine, Mn., U.S. (kōl-rān')	113	47°16'N	93°29'W
Coleshill, Eng., U.K. (kōlz'hĭl)	158a	52°30'N	1°42'W
Colfax, Ia., U.S. (kōl'făks)	113	41°40'N	93°13'W
Colfax, La., U.S.	123	31°31'N	92°42'W
Colfax, Wa., U.S.	114	46°53'N	117°21'W
Colhué Huapi, l., Arg. (kôl-wā'óá'pē)	144	45°30'S	68°45'W
Coligny, S. Afr.	238c	26°20'S	26°18'E
Colima, Mex. (kōlē'mä)	128	19°13'N	103°45'W
Colima, state, Mex.	130	19°10'N	104°00'W
Colima, Nevado de, mtn., Mex. (nĕ-vä'dô-dĕ-kô-lē'mä)	128	19°30'N	103°38'W
Coll, i., Scot., U.K. (kŏl)	164	56°42'N	6°23'W
College, Ak., U.S.	103	64°43'N	147°50'W
College Park, Ga., U.S. (kŏl'ĕj)	110c	33°39'N	84°27'W
College Park, Md., U.S.	110e	38°59'N	76°58'W
Collegeville, Pa., U.S. (kŏl'ĕj-vĭl)	110f	40°11'N	75°27'W
Collie, Austl. (kŏl'ē)	218	33°20'S	116°20'E
Collier Bay, b., Austl. (kŏl-yēr)	220	15°30'S	123°30'E
Collingswood, N.J., U.S. (kŏl'ĭngz-wo͝od)	110f	39°54'N	75°04'W
Collingwood, Can.	99	44°30'N	80°20'W
Collins, Ms., U.S. (kŏl'ĭns)	124	31°40'N	89°34'W
Collinsville, Il., U.S. (kŏl'ĭnz-vĭl)	117e	38°41'N	89°59'W
Collinsville, Ok., U.S.	121	36°21'N	95°50'W
Colmar, Fr. (kôl'mär)	161	48°03'N	7°25'E
Colmenar de Oreja, Spain (kôl-mā-när' dāōrā'hä)	172	40°06'N	3°25'W
Colmenar Viejo, Spain (kôl-mā-när'vyā'hō)	172	40°40'N	3°46'W
Cologne, Ger.	154	50°56'N	6°57'E
Colombia, Col. (kô-lôm'bē-ä)	142a	3°23'N	74°48'W
Colombia, nation, S.A.	142	3°30'N	72°30'W
Colombo, Sri L. (kô-lôm'bō)	203	6°58'N	79°52'E
Colón, Arg. (kō-lōn')	141c	33°55'S	61°08'W
Colón, Cuba (kô-lô'n)	134	22°45'N	80°55'W
Colón, Mex. (kō-lōn')	130	20°46'N	100°02'W
Colón, Pan. (kô-lô'n)	129	9°22'N	79°54'W
Colón, Archipiélago de, is., Ec.	142	0°10'S	87°45'W
Colón, Montañas de, mts., Hond. (môn-tä'n-yäs-dĕ-kô-lô'n)	133	14°58'N	84°39'W
Colonia, Ur. (kō-lō'nē-ä)	144	34°27'S	57°50'W
Colonia, dept., Ur.	141c	34°08'S	57°50'W
Colonia Suiza, Ur. (kô-lô'nēä-sōē'zä)	141c	34°17'S	57°15'W
Colonna, Capo, c., Italy	175	39°02'N	17°15'E
Colonsay, i., Scot., U.K. (kŏl-ŏn-sā')	165	56°08'N	6°08'E
Coloradas, Lomas, Arg. (lô'mäs-kō-lō-rä'däs)	144	43°30'S	68°00'W
Colorado, state, U.S.	104	39°30'N	106°55'W
Colorado, r., Arg.	144	38°30'S	66°00'W
Colorado, r., N.A.	106	36°00'N	113°30'W
Colorado, r., Tx., U.S.	106	30°08'N	97°33'W
Colorado City, Tx., U.S. (kŏl-ô-rä'dō sĭ'tĭ)	122	32°24'N	100°50'W
Colorado National Monument, rec., Co., U.S.	119	39°00'N	108°40'W
Colorado Plateau, plat., U.S.	106	36°20'N	109°25'W
Colorado River Aqueduct, aq., Ca., U.S.	118	33°38'N	115°43'W
Colorado River Indian Reservation, I.R., Az., U.S.	119	34°03'N	114°02'W
Colorados, Archipiélago de los, is., Cuba	134	22°25'N	84°25'W
Colorado Springs, Co., U.S. (kŏl-ô-rä'dō)	104	38°49'N	104°48'W
Colotepec, r., Mex. (kô-lô'tĕ-pĕk)	131	15°56'N	96°57'W
Colotlán, Mex. (kô-lô-tlän')	130	22°06'N	103°14'W
Colotlán, r., Mex.	130	22°09'N	103°17'W
Colquechaca, Bol. (kôl-kā-chä'kä)	142	18°47'S	66°02'W
Colstrip, Mt., U.S. (kōl'strip)	115	45°54'N	106°38'W
Colton, Ca., U.S. (kōl'tŭn)	117a	34°04'N	117°20'W
Columbia, Il., U.S. (kô-lŭm'bĭ-á)	117e	38°26'N	90°12'W
Columbia, Ky., U.S.	124	37°06'N	85°15'W
Columbia, Md., U.S.	110e	39°15'N	76°51'W
Columbia, Mo., U.S.	105	38°55'N	92°19'W
Columbia, Ms., U.S.	124	31°15'N	89°49'W
Columbia, Pa., U.S.	109	40°00'N	76°25'W
Columbia, S.C., U.S.	105	34°00'N	81°00'W
Columbia, Tn., U.S.	124	35°36'N	87°02'W
Columbia, r., N.A.	92	46°00'N	120°00'W
Columbia, Mount, mtn., Can.	95	52°09'N	117°25'W
Columbia City, In., U.S.	108	41°10'N	85°30'W
Columbia City, Or., U.S.	116c	45°53'N	112°49'W
Columbia Heights, Mn., U.S.	117g	45°03'N	93°15'W
Columbia Icefield, ice, Can.	95	52°08'N	117°26'W
Columbia Mountains, mts., N.A.	95	51°30'N	118°30'W
Columbiana, Al., U.S. (kô-ŭm-bĭ-ă'ná)	124	33°10'N	86°35'W
Columbretes, is., Spain (kô-lo͞om-brē'tĕs)	173	39°54'N	0°54'E
Columbus, Ga., U.S. (kô-lŭm'bŭs)	105	32°29'N	84°56'W
Columbus, In., U.S.	108	39°15'N	85°55'W
Columbus, Ks., U.S.	121	37°10'N	94°50'W
Columbus, Ms., U.S.	124	33°30'N	88°25'W
Columbus, Mt., U.S.	115	45°39'N	109°15'W
Columbus, Ne., U.S.	112	41°25'N	97°25'W
Columbus, N.M., U.S.	119	31°50'N	107°40'W
Columbus, Oh., U.S.	105	40°00'N	83°00'W
Columbus, Tx., U.S.	123	29°44'N	96°34'W
Columbus, Wi., U.S.	113	43°20'N	89°01'W
Columbus Bank, bk. (kô-lŭm'bŭs)	135	22°05'N	75°30'W
Columbus Grove, Oh., U.S.	108	40°55'N	84°05'W
Columbus Point, c., Bah.	135	24°10'N	75°15'W
Colusa, Ca., U.S. (kô-lū'sá)	118	39°12'N	122°01'W
Colville, Wa., U.S. (kōl'vĭl)	114	48°33'N	117°53'W
Colville, r., Ak., U.S.	103	69°00'N	156°25'W
Colville Indian Reservation, I.R., Wa., U.S.	114	48°15'N	119°00'W
Colville R, Wa., U.S.	114	48°25'N	117°58'W
Colvos Passage, strt., Wa., U.S. (kōl'vōs)	116a	47°24'N	122°32'W
Colwood, Can. (kŏl'wo͝od)	116a	48°26'N	123°30'W
Comacchio, Italy (kô-mäk'kyō)	174	44°42'N	12°12'E

ng-sing; ŋ-baŋk; ɴ-nasalized n; nŏd; cŏmmit; ōld; ôbey; ôrder; oi-boil; fo͞od; o͝o-as oo in foot; ou-out; s-soft; sh-dish; th-thin; pūre; ûnite; ûrn; stŭd; circŭs; ü-as in French tu; ʹ-indeterminate vowel.

284 Comala – Cosamaloápan

PRONOUNCING INDEX

PLACE (Pronunciation)	PAGE	LAT.	LONG.
Comala, Mex. (kō-mä-lä')	130	19°22'N	103°47'W
Comalapa, Guat. (kō-mä-lä'-pä)	132	14°43'N	90°56'W
Comalcalco, Mex. (kō-mäl-käl'kō)	131	18°16'N	93°13'W
Comanche, Ok., U.S. (kô-măn'chē)	121	34°20'N	97°58'W
Comanche, Tx., U.S.	122	31°54'N	98°37'W
Comanche Creek, r., Tx., U.S.	122	31°02'N	102°47'W
Comayagua, Hond. (kō-mä-yä'gwä)	128	14°24'N	87°36'W
Combahee, r., S.C., U.S. (kŏm-bȧ-hē')	125	32°42'N	80°40'W
Comer, Ga., U.S. (kŭm'ẽr)	124	34°02'N	83°07'W
Comete, Cape, c., T./C. Is. (kô-mā'tȧ)	135	21°45'N	71°25'W
Comilla, Bngl. (kō-mĭl'ä)	199	23°33'N	91°17'E
Comino, Cape, c., Italy (kô-mē'nō)	174	40°30'N	9°48'E
Comitán, Mex. (kô-mē-tän')	128	16°16'N	92°09'W
Commencement Bay, b., Wa., U.S. (kŏ-mĕns'mĕnt bā)	116a	47°17'N	122°21'W
Commentry, Fr. (kô-mäN-trē')	170	46°16'N	2°44'E
Commerce, Ga., U.S. (kŏm'ẽrs)	124	34°10'N	83°27'W
Commerce, Ok., U.S.	121	36°57'N	94°54'W
Commerce, Tx., U.S.	121	33°15'N	95°52'W
Como, Italy (kō'mō)	162	45°48'N	9°03'E
Como, Lago di, l., Italy (lä'gō-dē-kō'mō)	162	46°00'N	9°30'E
Comodoro Rivadavia, Arg.	144	45°47'S	67°31'W
Como-Est, Can.	102a	45°27'N	74°08'W
Comonfort, Mex. (kô-mōn-fō'rt)	130	20°43'N	100°47'W
Comorin, Cape, c., India (kŏ'mô-rĭn)	203	8°05'N	78°05'E
Comoros, nation, Afr.	233	12°30'S	42°45'E
Comox, Can. (kō'mŏks)	94	49°40'N	124°55'W
Companario, Cerro, mtn., S.A. (sĕ'r-rô-kôm-pä-nä'ryô)	141b	35°54'S	70°23'W
Compiègne, Fr. (kôN-pyĕn'y')	161	49°25'N	2°49'E
Comporta, Port. (kôm-pôr'tȧ)	173b	38°24'N	8°48'W
Compostela, Mex. (kŏm-pô-stä'lä)	130	21°14'N	104°54'W
Compton, Ca., U.S. (kŏmpt'tŭn)	117a	33°54'N	118°14'W
Comrat, Mol. (kôm-rät')	181	46°17'N	28°38'E
Conakry, Gui. (kô-nà-krē')	230	9°31'N	13°43'W
Conanicut, i., R.I., U.S. (kŏn'ȧ-nĭ-kŭt)	110b	41°34'N	71°20'W
Conasauga, r., Ga., U.S. (kô-nà)	124	34°40'N	84°51'W
Concarneau, Fr. (kôN-kär-nō')	170	47°54'N	3°52'W
Concepción, Bol. (kōn-sĕp'syōn')	143	15°47'S	61°08'W
Concepción, Chile	144	36°51'S	72°59'W
Concepción, Pan.	133	8°31'N	82°38'W
Concepción, Para.	144	23°29'S	57°18'W
Concepcion, Phil.	213a	15°19'N	120°40'E
Concepción, vol., Nic.	132	11°36'N	85°43'W
Concepción, r., Mex.	128	30°25'N	112°20'W
Concepción del Mar, Guat. (kōn-sĕp-syōn'dĕl mär')	132	14°07'N	91°23'W
Concepción del Oro, Mex. (kōn-sĕp-syōn' dĕl ō'rō)	128	24°39'N	101°24'W
Concepción del Uruguay, Arg. (kôn-sĕp-syô'n-dĕl-ōō-rōō-gwī')	144	32°31'S	58°10'W
Conception, i., Bah.	135	23°50'N	75°05'W
Conception, Point, c., Ca., U.S.	106	34°27'N	120°28'W
Conception Bay, b., Can. (kŏn-sĕp'shŭn)	101	47°50'N	52°50'W
Concho, r., Tx., U.S. (kŏn'chō)	122	31°34'N	100°00'W
Conchos, r., Mex.	128	29°30'N	105°00'W
Conchos, r., Mex. (kōn'chōs)	122	25°03'N	99°00'W
Concord, Ca., U.S. (kŏŋ'kŏrd)	116b	37°58'N	122°02'W
Concord, Ma., U.S.	101a	42°28'N	71°21'W
Concord, N.C., U.S.	125	35°23'N	80°11'W
Concord, N.H., U.S.	105	43°10'N	71°30'W
Concordia, Arg. (kōn-kôr'dĭ-à)	144	31°18'S	57°59'W
Concordia, Col.	142a	6°04'N	75°54'W
Concordia, Mex. (kôn-kô'r-dyä)	130	23°17'N	106°06'W
Concordia, Ks., U.S.	121	39°32'N	97°39'W
Concrete, Wa., U.S. (kŏn-'krēt)	114	48°33'N	121°44'W
Conde, Fr.	170	48°50'N	0°36'W
Conde, S.D., U.S. (kŏn-dē')	112	45°10'N	98°06'W
Condega, Nic. (kŏn-dĕ'gä)	132	13°20'N	86°27'W
Condeúba, Braz. (kōn-dā-ōō'bä)	143	14°47'S	41°44'W
Condom, Fr.	170	43°58'N	0°22'E
Condon, Or., U.S. (kŏn'dŭn)	114	45°14'N	120°10'W
Conecun, r., Al., U.S. (kô-nē'kū)	124	31°05'N	86°52'W
Conegliano, Italy (kō-nål-yä'nō)	174	45°59'N	12°17'E
Conejos, r., Co., U.S. (kô-nā'hōs)	119	37°07'N	106°19'W
Conemaugh, Pa., U.S. (kŏn'ē-mô)	109	40°25'N	78°50'W
Coney Island, i., N.Y., U.S. (kō'nĭ)	110a	40°34'N	73°27'W
Confolens, Fr. (kôN-fä-läN')	170	46°01'N	0°41'E
Congaree, r., S.C., U.S. (kŏŋ-gȧ-rē')	125	33°53'N	80°55'W
Conghua, China (tsôŋ-hwä)	209	23°30'N	113°40'E
Congleton, Eng., U.K. (kŏŋ'g'l-tŭn)	158a	53°10'N	2°13'W
Congo, nation, Afr. (kŏn'gō)	232	3°00'S	13°48'E
Congo (Zaire), r., Afr. (kŏn'gō)	229	2°00'S	17°00'E
Congo, Democratic Republic of the (Zaire), nation, Afr.	232	1°00'S	22°15'E
Congo, Serra do, mts., Ang.	236	6°25'S	13°30'E
Congo Basin, basin, D.R.C.	229	2°47'N	20°58'E
Conisbrough, Eng., U.K. (kŏn'ĭs-bŭr-ô)	158a	53°29'N	1°13'W
Coniston, Can.	99	46°29'N	80°51'W
Conklin, Can. (kŏŋk'lĭn)	95	55°38'N	111°05'W
Conley, Ga., U.S. (kŏn'lĭ)	110c	33°38'N	84°19'W
Conn, Lough, l., Ire. (lŏk kŏn)	164	53°56'N	9°25'W
Connacht, hist. reg., Ire. (cŏn'åt)	164	53°50'N	8°45'W
Conneaut, Oh., U.S. (kŏn-ē-ôt')	108	41°55'N	80°35'W
Connecticut, state, U.S. (kŏ-nĕt'ĭ-kŭt)	105	41°40'N	73°10'W
Connecticut, r., U.S.	107	43°55'N	72°15'W
Connellsville, Pa., U.S. (kŏn'nĕlz-vĭl)	109	40°00'N	79°40'W
Connemara, mts., Ire. (kŏn-nē-mà'rà)	164	53°30'N	9°54'W
Connersville, In., U.S. (kŏn'ẽrz-vĭl)	108	39°35'N	85°10'W
Connors Range, mts., Austl. (kŏn'nŏrs)	221	22°15'S	149°00'E
Conrad, Mt., U.S. (kŏn'răd)	115	48°11'N	111°56'W
Conrich, Can. (kŏn'rĭch)	102e	51°06'N	113°51'W
Conroe, Tx., U.S. (kŏn'rō)	123	30°18'N	95°23'W
Conselheiro Lafaiete, Braz.	143	20°40'S	43°46'W
Conshohocken, Pa., U.S. (kŏn-shô-hŏk'ĕn)	110f	40°04'N	75°18'W
Consolación del Sur, Cuba (kōn-sô-lä-syōn')	134	22°30'N	83°55'W
Con Son, is., Viet.	212	8°30'N	106°28'E
Constance, Mount, mtn., Wa., U.S. (kŏn'stăns)	116a	47°46'N	123°08'W
Constanţa, Rom. (kōn-stän'tsȧ)	154	44°12'N	28°36'E
Constantina, Spain (kōn-stän-tē'nä)	172	37°52'N	5°39'W
Constantine, Alg. (kôN-stäN'tēn')	230	36°28'N	6°38'E
Constantine, Mi., U.S. (kŏn'stăn-tēn)	108	41°50'N	85°40'W
Constitución, Chile (kōn'stĭ-tōō-syōn')	144	35°24'S	72°25'W
Constitution, Ga., U.S. (kŏn-stĭ-tū'shŭn)	110c	33°41'N	84°20'W
Contagem, Braz. (kōn-tá'zhĕm)	141a	19°54'S	44°05'W
Contepec, Mex. (kōn-tĕ-pĕk')	130	20°04'N	100°07'W
Contreras, Mex. (kôn-trĕ'räs)	131a	19°18'N	99°14'W
Contwoyto, l., Can.	92	65°42'N	110°50'W
Converse, Tx., U.S. (kŏn'vẽrs)	117d	29°31'N	98°17'W
Conway, Ar., U.S. (kŏn'wā)	121	35°06'N	92°27'W
Conway, N.H., U.S.	109	44°00'N	71°10'W
Conway, S.C., U.S.	125	33°49'N	79°01'W
Conway, Wa., U.S.	116a	48°20'N	122°20'W
Conyers, Ga., U.S. (kŏn'yẽrz)	124	33°41'N	84°01'W
Cooch Behār, India (kōōch bē-här')	199	26°25'N	89°34'E
Cook, Cape, c., Can. (kŏŏk)	94	50°08'N	127°55'W
Cook, Mount see Aoraki, mtn., N.Z.	221a	43°27'S	170°13'E
Cookeville, Tn., U.S. (kŏŏk'vĭl)	124	36°07'N	85°30'W
Cooking Lake, Can. (kŏŏk'ĭng)	102g	53°25'N	113°08'W
Cooking Lake, l., Can.	102g	53°25'N	113°02'W
Cook Inlet, b., Ak., U.S.	103	60°50'N	151°38'W
Cook Islands, dep., Oc.	2	20°00'S	158°00'W
Cook Strait, str., N.Z.	221a	40°37'S	174°15'E
Cooktown, Austl. (kŏŏk'toun)	219	15°40'S	145°20'E
Cooleemee, N.C., U.S. (kōō-lē'mē)	125	35°50'N	80°32'W
Coolgardie, Austl. (kōōl-gär'dē)	218	31°00'S	121°25'E
Cooma, Austl. (kōō'mȧ)	219	36°22'S	149°10'E
Coonamble, Austl. (kōō-năm'b'l)	219	31°00'S	148°30'E
Coonoor, India	203	10°22'N	76°15'E
Coon Rapids, Mn., U.S. (kōōn)	117g	45°09'N	93°17'W
Cooper, Tx., U.S. (kōōp'ẽr)	121	33°23'N	95°40'W
Cooper Center, Ak., U.S.	103	61°54'N	15°30'W
Coopers Creek, r., Austl. (kōō'pẽrz)	221	27°32'N	141°19'E
Cooperstown, N.D., U.S.	112	47°26'N	98°07'W
Cooperstown, N.Y., U.S. (kōōp'ẽrs-toun)	109	42°45'N	74°55'W
Coosa, Al., U.S. (kōō'sȧ)	124	32°43'N	86°25'W
Coosa, r., U.S.	107	34°00'N	86°00'W
Coosawattee, r., Ga., U.S.	124	34°37'N	84°45'W
Coos Bay, Or., U.S. (kōōs)	114	43°21'N	124°12'W
Coos Bay, b., Or., U.S.	114	43°19'N	124°40'W
Cootamundra, Austl. (kŏŏtȧ-mŭnd'rȧ)	222	34°25'S	148°00'E
Copacabana, Braz. (kô'pä-kà-bá'nä)	144b	22°57'S	43°11'W
Copalita, r., Mex. (kô-pä-lē'tä)	131	15°55'N	96°06'W
Copán, hist., Hond. (kō-pän')	132	14°50'N	89°10'W
Copano Bay, b., Tx., U.S. (kō-pän'ō)	123	28°08'N	97°25'W
Copenhagen (København), Den.	154	55°43'N	12°27'E
Copiapó, Chile (kō-pyä-pō')	144	27°16'S	70°28'W
Copley, Oh., U.S. (kŏp'lē)	111d	41°06'N	81°38'W
Copparo, Italy (kôp-pä'rō)	174	44°53'N	11°50'E
Coppell, Tx., U.S. (kŏp'pĕl)	117c	32°57'N	97°00'W
Copper, r., Ak., U.S. (kŏp'ẽr)	103	62°38'N	145°00'W
Copper Cliff, Can.	98	46°28'N	81°04'W
Copper Harbor, Mi., U.S.	113	47°27'N	87°53'W
Copperhill, Tn., U.S. (kŏp'ẽr hĭl)	124	35°00'N	84°22'W
Coppermine see Kugluktuk, Can.	92	67°46'N	115°19'W
Coppermine, r., Can.	92	66°48'N	114°59'W
Copper Mountain, mtn., Ak., U.S.	94	55°14'N	132°36'W
Copperton, Ut., U.S. (kŏp'ẽr-tŭn)	117b	40°34'N	112°06'W
Coquilee, Or., U.S. (kô-kēl')	114	43°11'N	124°11'W
Coquilhatville see Mbandaka, D.R.C.	232	0°04'N	18°16'E
Coquimbo, Chile (kô-kēm'bō)	144	29°58'S	71°31'W
Coquimbo, prov., Chile	141b	31°50'S	71°05'W
Coquitlam Lake, l., Can. (kō-kwĭt-lăm)	116d	49°23'N	122°44'W
Corabia, Rom. (kô-rä'bĭ-ȧ)	163	43°45'N	24°29'E
Coracora, Peru (kō'rä-kō'rä)	142	15°12'S	73°42'W
Coral Gables, Fl., U.S.	125a	25°43'N	80°14'W
Coral Rapids, Can. (kŏr'ăl)	91	50°18'N	81°49'W
Coral Sea, sea, Oc. (kŏr'ăl)	221	13°30'S	150°00'E
Coralville Reservoir, res., Ia., U.S.	113	41°45'N	91°50'W
Corangamite, Lake, l., Austl. (cŏr-ăŋ'ä-mīt)	222	38°05'S	142°55'E
Coraopolis, Pa., U.S. (kō-rä-ŏp'ô-lĭs)	111e	40°30'N	80°09'W
Corato, Italy (kô'rä-tô)	174	41°08'N	16°28'E
Corbeil-Essonnes, Fr. (kôr-bā'yĕ-sŏn')	170	48°31'N	2°29'E
Corbett, Or., U.S. (kôr'bĕt)	116c	45°31'N	122°17'W
Corbie, Fr. (kôr-bē')	170	49°55'N	2°27'E
Corbin, Ky., U.S. (kôr'bĭn)	124	36°55'N	84°06'W
Corby, Eng., U.K. (kôr'bĭ)	158a	52°29'N	0°38'W
Corcovado, mtn., Braz. (kôr-kô-vä'dô)	144b	22°57'S	43°13'W
Corcovado, Golfo, b., Chile (kôr-kô-vä'dhō)	144	43°40'S	75°00'W
Cordeiro, Braz. (kôr-dā'rō)	141a	22°03'S	42°22'W
Cordele, Ga., U.S. (kôr-dēl')	124	31°55'N	83°50'W
Cordell, Ok., U.S. (kôr-dĕl')	120	35°19'N	98°58'W
Córdoba, Arg. (kôr'dô-vä)	144	30°20'S	64°03'W
Córdoba, Mex. (kô'r-dô-bä)	128	18°53'N	96°54'W
Córdoba, Spain (kô'r-dô-bä)	172	37°55'N	4°45'W
Córdoba, prov., Arg. (kôr'dô-vä)	144	32°00'S	64°00'W
Córdoba, Sierra de, mts., Arg.	144	31°15'S	64°30'W
Cordova, Ak., U.S. (kôr'dô-vä)	106a	60°34'N	145°38'W
Cordova, Al., U.S. (kôr'dô-ȧ)	124	33°45'N	86°22'W
Cordova Bay, b., Ak., U.S.	94	54°55'N	132°35'W
Corfu see Kérkira, i., Grc.	156	39°33'N	19°36'E
Corigliano, Italy (kō-rē-lyä'nō)	174	39°35'N	16°30'E
Corinth see Kórinthos, Grc.	154	37°56'N	22°54'E
Corinth, Ms., U.S. (kŏr'ĭnth)	124	34°55'N	88°30'W
Corinto, Braz. (kô-rē'n-tō)	143	18°20'S	44°16'W
Corinto, Col.	142a	3°09'N	76°12'W
Corinto, Nic. (kŏr-ĭn'to)	132	12°30'N	87°12'W
Corio, Austl.	217a	38°05'S	144°22'E
Corio Bay, b., Austl.	217a	38°07'S	144°25'E
Corisco, Isla de, i., Eq. Gui.	236	0°50'N	8°40'E
Cork, Ire. (kôrk)	154	51°54'N	8°25'W
Cork Harbour, b., Ire.	164	51°44'N	8°15'W
Corleone, Italy (kôr-lå-ō'nä)	174	37°48'N	13°18'E
Cormorant Lake, l., Can.	97	54°13'N	100°47'W
Cornelia, Ga., U.S. (kôr-nē'lyȧ)	124	34°31'N	83°30'W
Cornelis, r., S. Afr. (kôr-nē'lĭs)	238c	27°48'S	29°15'E
Cornell, Ca., U.S. (kôr-nĕl')	117a	34°06'N	118°46'W
Cornell, Wi., U.S.	113	45°10'N	91°10'W
Corner Brook, Can. (kôr'nẽr)	91	48°57'N	57°57'W
Corner Inlet, b., Austl.	222	38°55'S	146°45'E
Corning, Ar., U.S. (kôr'nĭng)	121	36°26'N	90°35'W
Corning, Ia., U.S.	113	40°58'N	94°40'W
Corning, N.Y., U.S.	109	42°10'N	77°05'W
Corno, Monte, mtn., Italy (kôr'nō)	162	42°28'N	13°37'E
Cornwall, Bah.	134	25°55'N	77°15'W
Cornwall, Can. (kôrn'wôl)	99	45°05'N	74°35'W
Coro, Ven. (kō'rō)	142	11°22'N	69°43'W
Corocoro, Bol. (kō-rō-kō'rō)	142	17°15'S	68°21'W
Coromandel Coast, cst., India (kŏr-ô-man'dĕl)	199	13°30'N	80°30'E
Coromandel Peninsula, pen., N.Z.	223	36°50'S	176°00'E
Corona, Al., U.S. (kō-rō'nȧ)	124	33°42'N	87°28'W
Corona, Ca., U.S.	117a	33°52'N	117°34'W
Coronada, Bahía de, b., C.R. (bä-ē'ä-dĕ-kô-rô-nä'dō)	133	8°47'N	84°04'W
Corona del Mar, Ca., U.S. (kô-rō'nȧ dĕl mär)	117a	33°36'N	117°53'W
Coronado, Ca., U.S. (kŏr-ô-nä'dō)	118a	32°42'N	117°12'W
Coronation Gulf, b., Can. (kŏr-ô-nā'shŭn)	92	68°07'N	112°50'W
Coronel, Chile (kō-rō-nĕl')	144	37°00'S	73°10'W
Coronel Brandsen, Arg. (kô-rô-nĕl-brä'nd-sĕn)	141c	35°09'S	58°15'W
Coronel Dorrego, Arg. (kô-rô-nĕl-dôr-rĕ'gô)	144	38°43'S	61°16'W
Coronel Oviedo, Para. (kô-rô-nĕl-ô-vē'dô)	144	25°28'S	56°22'W
Coronel Pringles, Arg. (kô-rô-nĕl-prēn'glĕs)	144	37°54'S	61°22'W
Coronel Suárez, Arg. (kô-rô-nĕl-swä'rās)	144	37°27'S	61°49'W
Corowa, Austl. (cŏr-ôwȧ)	222	36°02'S	146°23'E
Corozal, Belize (cŏr-ŏth-äl')	132a	18°25'N	88°23'W
Corpus Christi, Tx., U.S. (kôr'pŭs krĭstē)	104	27°48'N	97°24'W
Corpus Christi Bay, b., Tx., U.S.	123	27°47'N	97°14'W
Corpus Christi Lake, l., Tx., U.S.	122	28°08'N	98°20'W
Corral, Chile (kô-räl')	144	39°57'S	73°15'W
Corral de Almaguer, Spain (kô-räl'dā äl-mä-gâr')	172	39°45'N	3°10'W
Corralillo, Cuba (kô-rä-lē-yō)	134	23°00'N	80°40'W
Corregidor Island, i., Phil. (kô-rā-hē-dōr')	213a	14°21'N	120°25'E
Correntina, Braz. (kô-rĕn-tē-nȧ)	143	13°18'S	44°33'W
Corrib, Lough, l., Ire. (lŏk kŏr'ĭb)	164	53°25'N	9°19'W
Corrientes, Arg. (kō-ryĕn'tās)	144	27°25'S	58°39'W
Corrientes, prov., Arg.	144	28°45'S	58°00'W
Corrientes, Cabo, c., Col. (ká'bô-kō-ryĕn'tās)	142	5°34'N	77°35'W
Corrientes, Cabo, c., Cuba (ká'bô-kôr-rē-ĕn'tĕs)	134	21°50'N	84°25'W
Corrientes, Cabo, c., Mex.	128	20°25'N	105°41'W
Corry, Pa., U.S. (kŏr'ĭ)	109	41°55'N	79°40'W
Corse, Cap, c., Fr. (kôrs)	161	42°59'N	9°19'E
Corsica, i., Fr. (kô'r-sē-kä)	156	42°10'N	8°55'E
Corsicana, Tx., U.S. (kôr-sĭ-kăn'ȧ)	104	32°06'N	96°28'W
Cortazar, Mex. (kôr-tä-zär)	130	20°30'N	100°57'W
Corte, Fr. (kôr'tā)	174	42°18'N	9°10'E
Cortegana, Spain (kôr-tå-gä'nä)	172	37°54'N	6°48'W
Cortés, Ensendada de, b., Cuba (ĕn-sĕ-nä-dä-dĕ-kôr-tās')	134	22°05'N	83°45'W
Cortez, Co., U.S.	119	37°21'N	108°35'W
Cortland, N.Y., U.S. (kôrt'lănd)	109	42°35'N	76°10'W
Cortona, Italy (kôr-tō'nä)	174	43°16'N	12°00'E
Corubal, r., Gui.-B.	234	11°43'N	14°40'W
Coruche, Port. (kô-rōō'she)	172	38°58'N	8°34'W
Çoruh, r., Asia (chō-rōōk')	181	40°30'N	41°10'E
Çorum, Tur. (chô-rōōm')	198	40°34'N	34°45'E
Corunna, Mi., U.S. (kô-rŭn'ȧ)	108	43°00'N	84°05'W
Coruripe, Braz. (kō-rô-rē'pĭ)	143	10°09'S	36°13'W
Corvallis, Or., U.S. (kôr-văl'ĭs)	104	44°34'N	123°17'W
Corve, r., Eng., U.K. (kôr'vē)	158a	52°28'N	2°43'W
Corydon, Ia., U.S.	113	40°45'N	93°20'W
Corydon, In., U.S. (kŏr'ĭ-dŭn)	108	38°10'N	86°05'W
Corydon, Ky., U.S.	108	37°45'N	87°40'W
Cosamaloápan, Mex. (kô-sà-mä-lwä'pän)	131	18°21'N	95°48'W

ăt; finăl; rāte; senāte; ärm; åsk; sofȧ; fâre; ch-choose; dh-as th in other; bē; ēvent; bĕt; recĕnt; cratẽr; g-gō; gh-guttural g; bĭt; ĭ-short neutral; rīde; K-guttural k as ch in German ich;

PRONOUNCING INDEX

Coscomatepec – Cuilo 285

PLACE (Pronunciation)	PAGE	LAT.	LONG.
Coscomatepec, Mex. (kôs'kōmä-tě-pěk')	131	19°04'N	97°03'W
Cosenza, Italy (kō-zěnt'sä)	163	39°18'N	16°15'E
Coshocton, Oh., U.S. (kô-shŏk'tŭn)	108	40°15'N	81°55'W
Cosigüina, vol., Nic.	132	12°59'N	87°35'W
Cosmoledo Group, is., Sey. (kŏs-mô-lā'dō)	233	9°42'S	47°45'E
Cosmopolis, Wa., U.S. (kŏz-mŏp'ô-lĭs)	114	46°58'N	123°47'W
Cosne-sur-Loire, Fr. (kōn-sür-lwär')	170	47°25'N	2°57'E
Cosoleacaque, Mex. (kō sō lā-ä-kä'kē)	131	18°01'N	94°38'W
Costa de Caparica, Port.	173b	38°40'N	9°12'W
Costa Mesa, Ca., U.S. (kŏs'tȧ mā'sȧ)	117a	33°39'N	118°54'W
Costa Rica, nation, N.A. (kŏs'tȧ rē'kȧ)	129	10°30'N	84°30'W
Cosumnes, r., Ca., U.S. (kŏ-sŭm'nĕz)	118	38°21'N	121°17'W
Cotabambas, Peru (kō-tä-bàm'bäs)	142	13°49'S	72°17'W
Cotabato, Phil. (kō-tä-bä'tō)	213	7°06'N	124°13'E
Cotaxtla, Mex. (kō-täs'tlä)	131	18°49'N	96°22'W
Cotaxtla, r., Mex.	131	18°54'N	96°21'W
Coteau-du-Lac, Can. (cō-tō'dü-läk)	102a	45°17'N	74°11'W
Coteau-Landing, Can.	102a	45°15'N	74°13'W
Coteaux, Haiti	135	18°15'N	74°05'W
Cote d'Ivoire (Ivory Coast), nation, Afr.	230	7°43'N	6°30'W
Côte d'Or, reg., Fr.	170	47°02'N	4°35'E
Cotija de la Paz, Mex. (kō-tē'-kä-dĕ-lä-pá'z)	130	19°46'N	102°43'W
Cotonou, Benin (kō-tō-nōō')	230	6°21'N	2°26'E
Cotopaxi, mtn., Ec. (kō-tō-păk'sē)	142	0°40'S	78°26'W
Cotorro, Cuba (kō-tôr-rō)	135a	23°03'N	82°17'W
Cotswold Hills, hills, Eng., U.K. (kŏtz'wōld)	164	51°35'N	2°16'W
Cottage Grove, Mn., U.S. (kŏt'āj grōv)	117g	44°50'N	92°52'W
Cottage Grove, Or., U.S.	114	43°48'N	123°04'W
Cottbus, Ger. (kŏtt'bōōs)	161	51°47'N	14°20'E
Cottonwood, r., Mn., U.S. (kŏt'ŭn-wŏd)	112	44°25'N	95°35'W
Cotulla, Tx., U.S. (kō-tŭl'lȧ)	122	28°26'N	99°14'W
Coubert, Fr. (kōō-bâr')	171b	48°40'N	2°43'E
Coudersport, Pa., U.S. (kou'dērz-pōrt)	109	41°45'N	78°00'W
Coudres, Île aux, i., Can.	100	47°17'N	70°12'W
Coulommiers, Fr. (kōō-lô-myā')	171b	48°49'N	3°05'E
Coulto, Serra do, mts., Braz. (sĕ'r-rä-dô-kô-ó'tô)	144b	22°33'S	43°27'W
Council Bluffs, Ia., U.S. (koun'sĭl blŭf)	105	41°16'N	95°53'W
Council Grove, Ks., U.S. (koun'sĭl grōv)	121	38°39'N	96°30'W
Coupeville, Wa., U.S. (kōōp'vĭl)	116a	48°13'N	122°41'W
Courantyne, r., S.A. (kôr'ăntīn)	143	4°28'N	57°42'W
Courtenay, Can. (cōōrt-nā')	90	49°41'N	125°00'W
Coushatta, La., U.S. (kou-shăt'ȧ)	123	32°02'N	93°21'W
Coutras, Fr. (kōō-trá')	170	45°02'N	0°07'W
Covelo, Ang.	236	12°06'S	13°55'E
Coventry, Eng., U.K. (kŭv'ĕn-trĭ)	164	52°25'N	1°29'W
Covina, Ca., U.S. (kô-vē'nȧ)	117a	34°06'N	117°54'W
Covington, Ga., U.S. (kŭv'ĭng-tŭn)	124	33°36'N	83°50'W
Covington, In., U.S.	108	40°10'N	87°15'W
Covington, Ky., U.S.	105	39°05'N	84°31'W
Covington, La., U.S.	123	30°30'N	90°06'W
Covington, Oh., U.S.	108	40°10'N	84°20'W
Covington, Ok., U.S.	121	36°18'N	97°32'W
Covington, Tn., U.S.	124	35°33'N	89°40'W
Covington, Va., U.S.	108	37°50'N	80°00'W
Cowal, Lake, l., Austl. (kou'ăl)	222	33°30'S	147°10'E
Cowan, l., Austl. (kou'ăn)	220	32°00'S	122°30'E
Cowansville, Can.	99	45°13'N	72°47'W
Cow Creek, r., Or., U.S. (kou)	114	42°45'N	123°35'W
Cowes, Eng., U.K. (kouz)	164	50°43'N	1°25'W
Cowichan Lake, l., Can.	94	48°54'N	124°20'W
Cowlitz, r., Wa., U.S. (kou'lĭts)	114	46°30'N	122°45'W
Cowra, Austl. (kou'rȧ)	222	33°50'S	148°33'E
Coxim, Braz. (kō-shēn')	143	18°32'S	54°43'W
Coxquihui, Mex. (kōz-kē-wē')	131	20°10'N	97°34'W
Cox's Bāzār, Bngl.	202	21°32'N	92°00'E
Coyaima, Col. (kō-yàē'mä)	142a	3°48'N	75°11'W
Coyame, Mex. (kō-yä'mā)	122	29°26'N	105°05'W
Coyanosa Draw, Tx., U.S. (kō yà-nō'sä)	122	30°55'N	103°07'W
Coyoacán, Mex. (kô-yô-ä-kän')	130	19°21'N	99°10'W
Coyote, r., Ca., U.S. (kī'ōt)	116b	37°37'N	121°57'W
Coyuca de Benítez, Mex. (kō-yōō'kä dā bā-nē'tāz)	130	17°04'N	100°06'W
Coyuca de Catalán, Mex. (kō-yōō'kä dā kä-tä-län')	130	18°19'N	100°41'W
Coyutla, Mex. (kō-yōō'tlä)	131	20°13'N	97°40'W
Cozad, Ne., U.S. (kō'zăd)	120	40°53'N	99°59'W
Cozaddale, Oh., U.S. (kō-zăd-dāl)	111f	39°16'N	84°09'W
Cozoyoapan, Mex. (kō-zō-yō-ä-pá'n)	130	16°45'N	98°17'W
Cozumel, Mex. (kŏ-zōō-mĕ'l)	132a	20°31'N	86°55'W
Cozumel, Isla de, i., Mex. (ē's-lä-dĕ-kō-zōō-mĕ'l)	128	20°26'N	87°10'W
Crab Creek, r., Wa., U.S. (krăb)	114	46°47'N	119°43'W
Crab Creek, r., Wa., U.S.	114	47°21'N	119°09'W
Cradock, S. Afr. (krä'dŭk)	232	32°12'S	25°38'E
Crafton, Pa., U.S. (krăf'tŭn)	111e	40°26'N	80°04'W
Craig, Co., U.S. (krāg)	115	40°32'N	107°31'W
Craiova, Rom. (krá-yō'vá)	163	44°18'N	23°50'E
Cranberry, l., N.Y., U.S. (krăn'bĕr-ĭ)	109	44°10'N	74°50'W
Cranbourne, Austl.	217a	38°07'S	145°16'E
Cranbrook, Can. (krăn'brŏk)	90	49°31'N	115°46'W
Cranbury, N.J., U.S. (krăn'bē-rĭ)	110a	40°19'N	74°31'W
Crandon, Wi., U.S. (krăn'dŭn)	113	45°35'N	88°55'W
Crane Prairie Reservoir, res., Or., U.S.	114	43°50'N	121°55'W
Cranston, R.I., U.S. (krăns'tŭn)	110b	41°46'N	71°25'W
Crater Lake, l., Or., U.S. (krā'tēr)	114	43°00'N	122°08'W
Crater Lake National Park, rec., Or., U.S.	114	42°58'N	122°40'W
Craters of the Moon National Monument, rec., Id., U.S. (krā'tēr)	115	43°28'N	113°15'W
Crateús, Braz. (krä-tâ-ōōzh')	143	5°09'S	40°35'W
Crato, Braz. (krä'tō)	143	7°19'S	39°13'W
Crawford, Ne., U.S. (krô'fērd)	112	42°41'N	103°25'W
Crawford, Wa., U.S.	116c	45°49'N	122°24'W
Crawfordsville, In., U.S. (krô'fērdz-vĭl)	108	40°00'N	86°55'W
Crazy Mountains, mts., Mt., U.S. (krā'zĭ)	115	46°11'N	110°25'W
Crazy Woman Creek, r., Wy., U.S.	115	44°08'N	106°40'W
Crecy, S. Afr. (krĕ-sē)	238c	24°38'S	28°52'E
Crécy-en-Brie, Fr. (krā-sē'-ĕN-brē')	171b	48°52'N	2°55'E
Crécy-en-Ponthieu, Fr.	170	50°13'N	1°48'E
Credit, r., Can.	102d	43°41'N	79°55'W
Cree, l., Can. (krē)	92	57°35'N	107°52'W
Creighton, S. Afr. (cre-tŏn)	233c	30°02'S	29°52'E
Creighton, Ne., U.S. (krā'tŭn)	112	42°27'N	97°54'W
Creil, Fr. (krĕ'y')	170	49°18'N	2°28'E
Crema, Italy (krā'mä)	174	45°21'N	9°53'E
Cremona, Italy (krā-mō'nä)	162	45°09'N	10°02'E
Crépy-en-Valois, Fr. (krā-pē'ĕN-vä-lwá')	171b	49°14'N	2°53'E
Cres, Cro. (tsrĕs)	174	44°58'N	14°21'E
Crescent Beach, Can.	116d	49°03'N	122°58'W
Crescent City, Ca., U.S. (krĕs'ĕnt)	114	41°46'N	124°13'W
Crescent City, Fl., U.S.	125	29°26'N	81°35'W
Crescent Lake, l., Fl., U.S. (krĕs'ĕnt)	125	29°33'N	81°30'W
Crescent Lake, l., Or., U.S.	114	43°25'N	121°58'W
Cresco, Ia., U.S. (krĕs'kō)	113	43°23'N	92°07'W
Crested Butte, Co., U.S. (krĕst'ĕd būt)	119	38°50'N	107°00'W
Crestline, Ca., U.S. (krĕst-līn)	117a	34°15'N	117°17'W
Crestline, Oh., U.S.	108	40°50'N	82°40'W
Crestmore, Ca., U.S. (krĕst'môr)	117a	34°02'N	117°23'W
Creston, Can. (krĕs'tŭn)	90	49°06'N	116°31'W
Creston, Ia., U.S.	113	41°04'N	94°22'W
Creston, Oh., U.S.	111d	40°59'N	81°54'W
Crestview, Fl., U.S. (krĕst'vū)	124	30°44'N	86°35'W
Crestwood, Ky., U.S. (krĕst'wŏd)	111h	38°20'N	85°28'W
Crestwood, Mo., U.S.	117e	38°33'N	90°23'W
Crete, Il., U.S. (krēt)	111a	41°26'N	87°38'W
Crete, Ne., U.S.	121	40°38'N	96°56'W
Crete, i., Grc.	156	35°15'N	24°30'E
Creus, Cap de, c., Spain	173	42°16'N	3°18'E
Creuse, r., Fr. (krûz)	170	46°51'N	0°49'E
Creve Coeur, Mo., U.S. (krēv kôr)	117e	38°40'N	90°27'W
Crevillent, Spain	173	38°12'N	0°48'W
Crewe, Eng., U.K. (krōō)	164	53°06'N	2°27'W
Crewe, Va., U.S.	125	37°09'N	78°08'W
Crimean Peninsula *see* Kryms'kyi Pivostriv, pen., Ukr.	181	45°18'N	33°30'E
Crimmitschau, Ger. (krĭm'ĭt-shou)	168	50°49'N	12°22'E
Cripple Creek, Co., U.S. (krĭp''l)	120	38°44'N	105°12'W
Crisfield, Md., U.S. (krĭs-fēld)	109	38°00'N	75°50'W
Cristal, Monts de, mts., Gabon	236	0°50'N	10°30'E
Cristina, Braz. (krēs-tē'-nä)	141a	22°13'S	45°15'W
Cristóbal Colón, Pico, mtn., Col. (pē'kō-krēs-tō'bäl-kō-lōn')	142	11°00'N	74°00'W
Crişul Alb, r., Rom. (krē'shōōl älb)	169	46°20'N	22°15'E
Crna, r., Yugo. (ts'r'nȧ)	175	41°03'N	21°46'E
Crna Gora (Montenegro), state, Yugo.	175	42°55'N	18°52'E
Črnomelj, Slvn. (ch'r'nō-māl')	174	45°35'N	15°11'E
Croatia, nation, Eur.	174	45°24'N	15°18'E
Crockett, Ca., U.S. (krŏk'ĕt)	116b	38°03'N	122°14'W
Crockett, Tx., U.S.	123	31°19'N	95°28'W
Crofton, Md., U.S.	110e	39°01'N	76°43'W
Crofton, Ne., U.S.	112	42°44'N	97°32'W
Croix, Lac la, l., N.A. (läk lä krōō-ä')	113	48°19'N	91°53'W
Croker, i., Austl. (krō'kȧ)	220	10°45'S	132°25'E
Cronulla, Austl. (krō-nŭl'ȧ)	217b	34°03'S	151°09'E
Crooked, i., Bah.	135	22°45'N	74°10'W
Crooked, l., Can.	101	48°25'N	56°05'W
Crooked, r., Can.	95	54°30'N	122°55'W
Crooked, r., Or., U.S.	114	44°07'N	120°30'W
Crooked Creek, r., Il., U.S. (krŏŏk'ĕd)	121	40°21'N	90°49'W
Crooked Island Passage, strt., Bah.	135	22°40'N	74°50'W
Crookston, Mn., U.S. (krŏks'tŭn)	112	47°44'N	96°35'W
Crooksville, Oh., U.S. (krŏks'vĭl)	108	39°45'N	82°05'W
Crosby, Eng., U.K.	158a	53°30'N	3°02'W
Crosby, Mn., U.S. (krôz'bĭ)	113	46°29'N	93°58'W
Crosby, N.D., U.S.	112	48°55'N	103°18'W
Crosby, Tx., U.S.	123a	29°55'N	95°04'W
Cross, l., La., U.S.	123	32°33'N	93°58'W
Cross, r., Nig.	235	5°35'N	8°05'E
Cross City, Fl., U.S.	124	29°55'N	83°25'W
Crossett, Ar., U.S. (krôs'ĕt)	121	33°08'N	92°00'W
Cross Lake, l., Can.	92	54°45'N	97°30'W
Cross River Reservoir, res., N.Y., U.S. (krôs)	110a	41°14'N	73°34'W
Cross Sound, strt., Ak., U.S. (krŏs)	103	58°12'N	137°20'W
Crosswell, Mi., U.S. (krŏz'wĕl)	108	43°15'N	82°35'W
Croswell, i., Yugo.	174	44°50'N	14°31'E
Crotch, l., Can.	99	44°55'N	76°55'W
Crotone, Italy (krō-tô'nĕ)	175	39°05'N	17°08'E
Croton Falls Reservoir, res., N.Y., U.S. (krōtŭn)	110a	41°22'N	73°44'W
Croton-on-Hudson, N.Y., U.S. (krō'tŭn-ŏn hŭd'sŭn)	110a	41°12'N	73°53'W
Crow, l., Can.	113	49°13'N	93°29'W
Crow Agency, Mt., U.S.	115	45°36'N	107°27'W
Crow Creek, r., Co., U.S.	120	41°08'N	104°25'W
Crow Creek Indian Reservation, I.R., S.D., U.S.	112	44°17'N	99°17'W
Crow Indian Reservation, I.R., Mt., U.S. (krō)	115	45°26'N	108°12'W
Crowle, Eng., U.K. (kroul)	158a	53°36'N	0°49'W
Crowley, La., U.S. (krou'lē)	123	30°13'N	92°22'W
Crown Mountain, mtn., Can. (kroun)	116d	49°24'N	123°05'W
Crown Mountain, mtn., V.I.U.S.	129c	18°22'N	64°58'W
Crown Point, In., U.S. (kroun point')	111a	41°25'N	87°22'W
Crown Point, N.Y., U.S.	109	44°00'N	73°25'W
Crowsnest Pass, p., Can.	95	49°39'N	114°45'W
Crow Wing, r., Mn., U.S. (krō)	113	44°50'N	94°01'W
Crow Wing, r., Mn., U.S.	113	46°42'N	94°48'W
Crow Wing, North Fork, r., Mn., U.S.	113	45°16'N	94°28'W
Crow Wing, South Fork, r., Mn., U.S.	113	44°59'N	94°42'W
Croydon, Austl. (kroi'dŭn)	219	18°15'S	142°15'E
Croydon, Austl.	217a	37°48'S	145°17'E
Croydon, Eng., U.K.	161	51°22'N	0°06'W
Croydon, Pa., U.S.	110f	40°05'N	74°55'W
Crozet, Îles, is., Afr. (krô-zĕ')	3	46°20'S	51°30'E
Cruces, Cuba (krōō'sås)	134	22°20'N	80°20'W
Cruces, Arroyo de, r., Mex. (är-rō'yô-dĕ-krōō'sĕs)	122	26°17'N	104°32'W
Cruillas, Mex. (krōō-ēl'yäs)	122	24°45'N	98°31'W
Cruz, Cabo, c., Cuba (kä'-bô-krōōz)	129	19°50'N	77°45'W
Cruz, Cayo, i., Cuba (kä'yō-krōōz)	134	22°15'N	77°50'W
Cruz Alta, Braz. (krōōz äl'tä)	144	28°41'S	54°02'W
Cruz del Eje, Arg. (krōō's-dĕl-ĕ-kĕ)	144	30°46'S	64°45'W
Cruzeiro, Braz. (krōō-zā'rô)	141a	22°36'S	44°57'W
Cruzeiro do Sul, Braz. (krōō-zā'rô dô sōōl)	142	7°34'S	72°40'W
Crysler, Can.	102c	45°13'N	75°09'W
Crystal City, Tx., U.S. (krĭs'tăl sĭ'tĭ)	122	28°40'N	99°50'W
Crystal Falls, Mi., U.S. (krĭs'tăl fôls)	113	46°06'N	88°21'W
Crystal Lake, Il., U.S. (krĭs'tăl lăk)	111a	42°15'N	88°18'W
Crystal Springs, Ms., U.S. (krĭs'tăl sprĭngz)	124	31°58'N	90°20'W
Crystal Springs, oasis, Ca., U.S.	116b	37°31'N	122°26'W
Csongrád, Hung. (chôn'gräd)	169	46°42'N	20°09'E
Csorna, Hung. (chôr'nä)	169	47°39'N	17°11'E
Cúa, Ven. (kōō'ä)	143b	10°10'N	66°54'W
Cuajimalpa, Mex. (kwä-hē-mäl'pä)	131a	19°21'N	99°18'W
Cuale, Sierra del, mts., Mex. (sē-ĕ'r-rä-dĕl-kwä'lĕ)	130	20°20'N	104°58'W
Cuamato, Ang. (kwä-mä'tō)	236	17°05'S	15°09'E
Cuamba, Moz.	237	14°49'S	36°33'E
Cuando, Ang. (kwän'dō)	236	16°32'S	22°07'E
Cuando, r., Afr.	232	14°30'S	20°00'E
Cuangar, Ang.	236	17°36'S	18°39'E
Cuango, r., Afr.	232	9°00'S	18°00'E
Cuanza, r., Ang. (kwän'zä)	232	9°45'S	15°00'E
Cuarto, r., Arg.	144	33°00'S	63°25'W
Cuatro Caminos, Cuba (kwä'trô-kä-mē'nôs)	135a	23°01'N	82°13'W
Cuatro Ciénegas, Mex. (kwä'trō syā'nå-gäs)	122	26°59'N	102°03'W
Cuauhtemoc, Mex. (kwä-ōō-tě-mŏk')	131	15°43'N	91°57'W
Cuautepec, Mex. (kwä-ōō-tě-pěk)	130	16°41'N	99°04'W
Cuautepec, Mex.	130	20°01'N	98°19'W
Cuautitlán, Mex. (kwä-ōō-tēt-län')	131a	19°40'N	99°12'W
Cuautla, Mex. (kwä-ōō'tlä)	130	18°47'N	98°57'W
Cuba, Port. (kōō'bȧ)	172	38°10'N	7°55'W
Cuba, nation, N.A. (kū'bȧ)	129	22°00'N	79°00'W
Cubagua, Isla, i., Ven. (ē's-lä-kōō-bä'gwä)	143b	10°48'N	64°10'W
Cubango (Okavango), r., Afr. (kōō-băŋ'gō)	232	17°10'S	18°20'E
Cub Hills, hills, Can. (kŭb)	96	54°20'N	104°30'W
Cucamonga, Ca., U.S. (kōō-kȧ-mŏŋ'gȧ)	117a	34°05'N	117°35'W
Cuchi, Ang.	232	14°40'S	16°50'E
Cuchillo Parado, Mex. (kōō-chē'lyō pä-rä'dō)	122	29°26'N	104°52'W
Cuchumatanes, Sierra de los, mts., Guat.	132	15°35'N	91°10'W
Cúcuta, Col. (kōō'kōō-tä)	142	7°56'N	72°30'W
Cudahy, Wi., U.S. (kŭd'ȧ-hī)	111a	42°57'N	87°52'W
Cuddalore, India (kŭd ȧ-lōr')	199	11°49'N	79°46'E
Cuddapah, India (kŭd'ȧ-pä)	199	14°31'N	78°52'E
Cue, Austl. (kū)	218	27°30'S	118°10'E
Cuéllar, Spain (kwā'lyär')	172	41°24'N	4°15'W
Cuenca, Ec. (kwĕn'kä)	142	2°52'S	78°54'W
Cuenca, Spain	162	40°05'N	2°07'W
Cuenca, Sierra de, mts., Spain (sē-ĕ'r-rä-dě-kwĕ'n-kä)	172	40°02'N	1°50'W
Cuencame, Mex. (kwĕn-kä-mā')	122	24°52'N	103°42'W
Cuerámaro, Mex. (kwā-rä'mä-rō)	130	20°39'N	101°44'W
Cuernavaca, Mex. (kwĕr-nä-vä'kä)	128	18°55'N	99°15'W
Cuero, Tx., U.S. (kwā'rō)	123	29°05'N	97°16'W
Cuetzalá del Progreso, Mex. (kwĕt-zä-lä dĕl prō-grā'sō)	130	18°07'N	99°51'W
Cuetzalan del Progreso, Mex.	131	20°02'N	97°33'W
Cuevas del Almanzora, Spain (kwĕ'väs-dĕl-äl-män-zō-rä)	162	37°19'N	1°54'W
Cuglieri, Italy (kōō-lyâ'rā)	174	40°11'N	8°37'E
Cuicatlán, Mex. (kwē-kä-tlän')	131	17°46'N	96°57'W
Cuilapa, Guat. (kò-ē-lä'pä)	132	14°16'N	90°20'W
Cuilo (Kwilu), r., Afr.	236	9°15'S	19°30'E

ng-sing; ŋ-baŋk; N-nasalized n; nŏd; cŏmmit; ōld; ôbey; ôrder; oi-boil; fōōd; ò-as oo in foot; ou-out; s-soft; sh-dish; th-thin; pūre; ůnite; ûrn; stŭd; circŭs; ü-as in French tu; '-indeterminate vowel.

286 Cuito – Davenport
PRONOUNCING INDEX

PLACE (Pronunciation)	PAGE	LAT.	LONG.
Cuito, r., Ang. (ko͞o-ē-'tō)	232	14°45'S	19°00'E
Cuitzeo, Mex. (kwēt'zā-ō)	130	19°57'N	101°11'W
Cuitzeo, Laguna de, l., Mex. (lä-ō'nä-dĕ-kwēt'zā-ō)	130	19°58'N	101°05'W
Cul de Sac, pl., Haiti (ko͞o'l-dĕ-sä'k)	135	18°35'N	72°05'W
Culebra, i., P.R. (ko͞o-lā'brä)	129b	18°19'N	65°32'W
Culebra, Sierra de la, mts., Spain (sē-ĕ'r-rä-dĕ-lä-ko͞o-lĕ-brä)	172	41°52'N	6°21'W
Culemborg, Neth.	159a	51°57'N	5°14'E
Culfa, Azer.	182	38°58'N	45°38'E
Culgoa, r., Austl. (kŭl-gō'ȧ)	221	29°21'S	147°00'E
Culiacán, Mex. (ko͞o-lyä-kä'n)	128	24°45'N	107°30'W
Culion, Phil. (ko͞o-lē-ōn')	212	11°43'N	119°58'E
Cúllar de Baza, Spain (ko͞o'l-yär-dĕ-bä'zä)	172	37°36'N	2°35'W
Cullera, Spain (ko͞o-lyā'rä)	162	39°12'N	0°15'W
Cullinan, S. Afr. (kŏ'lĭ-năn)	238c	25°41'S	28°32'E
Cullman, Al., U.S. (kŭl'măn)	124	34°10'N	86°50'W
Culpeper, Va., U.S. (kŭl'pĕp-ēr)	109	38°30'N	77°55'W
Culross, Can. (kŭl'rôs)	102f	49°43'N	97°54'W
Culver, In., U.S. (kŭl'vēr)	108	41°15'N	86°25'W
Culver City, Ca., U.S.	117a	34°00'N	118°23'W
Cumaná, Ven.	142	10°28'N	64°10'W
Cumberland, Can. (kŭm'bēr-lănd)	102c	45°31'N	75°25'W
Cumberland, Md., U.S.	105	39°40'N	78°40'W
Cumberland, Wa., U.S.	116a	47°17'N	121°55'W
Cumberland, Wi., U.S.	113	45°31'N	92°01'W
Cumberland, r., U.S.	124	36°45'N	85°33'W
Cumberland, Lake, res., Ky., U.S.	107	36°55'N	85°20'W
Cumberland Islands, is., Austl.	221	20°20'S	149°46'E
Cumberland Peninsula, pen., Can.	93	65°59'N	64°05'W
Cumberland Plateau, plat., U.S.	124	35°25'N	85°30'W
Cumberland Sound, strt., Can.	93	65°27'N	65°44'W
Cundinamarca, dept., Col. (ko͞on-dē-nä-mä'r-kä)	142a	4°57'N	74°27'W
Cunduacán, Mex. (kōn-do͞o-ä-kän')	131	18°04'N	93°23'W
Cunene (Kunene), r., Afr.	232	17°05'S	12°35'E
Cuneo, Italy (ko͞o'nā-ō)	174	44°24'N	7°31'E
Cunha, Braz. (ko͞o'nyä)	141a	23°05'S	44°56'W
Cunnamulla, Austl. (kŭn-ȧ-mŭl-ȧ)	219	28°00'S	145°55'E
Cupula, Pico, mtn., Mex. (pē'kō-ko͞o'po͞o-lä)	128	24°45'N	111°10'W
Cuquío, Mex. (ko͞o-kē'ō)	130	20°55'N	103°03'W
Curaçao, i., Neth. Ant. (ko͞o-rä-sä'ō)	142	12°12'N	68°58'W
Curacautín, Chile (kä-rä-kä͞o-tē'n)	144	38°25'S	71°53'W
Curaumilla, Punta, c., Chile (ko͞o-rou-mē'lyä)	141b	33°05'S	71°44'W
Curepto, Chile (ko͞o-rĕp-tō)	141b	35°06'S	72°02'W
Curitiba, Braz. (ko͞o-rē-tē'bȧ)	143	25°20'S	49°15'W
Curly Cut Cays, is., Bah.	134	23°40'N	77°40'W
Currais Novos, Braz. (ko͞or-rä'ēs nō-vōs)	143	6°02'S	36°39'W
Curran, Can. (kü-răN')	102c	45°30'N	74°59'W
Current, i., Bah. (kŭ-rĕnt)	134	25°20'N	76°50'W
Current, r., Mo., U.S. (kûr'ĕnt)	121	37°18'N	91°21'W
Currie, Mount, mtn., S. Afr. (kŭ-rē)	233c	30°28'S	29°23'E
Currituck Sound, strt., N.C., U.S. (kûr'ĭ-tŭk)	125	36°27'N	75°42'W
Curtis, Ne., U.S. (kûr'tĭs)	120	40°36'N	100°29'W
Curtis, i., Austl.	221	23°38'S	151°43'E
Curtisville, Pa., U.S. (kûr'tĭs-vĭl)	111e	40°38'N	79°50'W
Čurug, Yugo. (cho͞o'rŏg)	175	45°27'N	20°03'E
Curunga, Ang.	236	12°51'S	21°12'E
Curupira, Serra, mts., S.A. (sĕr'rȧ ko͞o-ro͞o-pē'rȧ)	142	1°00'N	65°30'W
Cururupu, Braz. (ko͞o-ro-ro͞o-po͞o')	143	1°40'S	44°56'W
Curvelo, Braz. (kŏr-vĕl'ō)	143	18°47'S	44°14'W
Cusco, Peru	142	13°36'S	71°52'W
Cushing, Ok., U.S. (kŭsh'ĭng)	121	35°58'N	96°46'W
Custer, S.D., U.S. (kŭs'tēr)	112	43°46'N	103°36'W
Custer, Wa., U.S.	116d	48°55'N	122°39'W
Cut Bank, Mt., U.S. (kŭt bănk)	115	48°38'N	112°19'W
Cuthbert, Ga., U.S. (kŭth'bērt)	124	31°47'N	84°48'W
Cuttack, India (kŭ-tăk')	199	20°38'N	85°53'E
Cutzamala, r., Mex. (ko͞o-tzä-mä-lä')	130	18°57'N	100°41'W
Cutzamalá de Pinzón, Mex. (ko͞o-tzä-mä-lä'dĕ-pēn-zô'n)	130	18°28'N	100°36'W
Cuvo, r., Ang. (ko͞o'vō)	232	11°00'S	14°30'E
Cuxhaven, Ger. (kŏks'hä-fĕn)	160	53°51'N	8°43'E
Cuyahoga, r., Oh., U.S. (kī-ȧ-hō'gȧ)	111d	41°22'N	81°38'W
Cuyahoga Falls, Oh., U.S.	111d	41°08'N	81°29'W
Cuyapaire Indian Reservation, I.R., Ca., U.S. (kū-yȧ-pâr)	118	32°46'N	116°20'W
Cuyo Islands, is., Phil. (ko͞o'yō)	212	10°54'N	120°08'E
Cuyotenango, Guat. (ko͞o-yō-tĕ-năŋ'gō)	132	14°30'N	91°35'W
Cuyuni, r., S.A. (ko͞o-yo͞o'nē)	143	6°40'N	60°44'W
Cuyutlán, Mex. (ko͞o-yo͞o-tlän')	130	18°54'N	104°04'W
Cyclades *see* Kikládhes, is., Grc.	156	37°30'N	24°45'E
Cynthiana, Ky., U.S. (sĭn-thĭ-ăn'ȧ)	108	38°20'N	84°20'W
Cypress, Ca., U.S. (sī'prĕs)	117a	33°50'N	118°03'W
Cypress Hills, hills, Can.	96	49°40'N	110°20'W
Cypress Lake, l., Can.	96	49°28'N	109°43'W
Cyprus, nation, Asia (sī'prŭs)	198	35°00'N	31°00'E
Cyprus, North, nation, Asia	198	35°15'N	33°40'E
Cyrenaica *see* Barqah, hist. reg., Libya	231	31°09'N	21°45'E
Czech Republic, nation, Eur.	154	50°00'N	15°00'E
Czersk, Pol. (chĕrsk)	169	53°47'N	17°58'E
Częstochowa, Pol. (chăN-stô kô'vȧ)	161	50°49'N	19°10'E

D

PLACE (Pronunciation)	PAGE	LAT.	LONG.
Da'an, China (dä-än)	208	45°25'N	124°22'E
Dabakala, C. Iv. (dä-bä-kä'lä)	230	8°16'N	4°36'W
Daba Shan, mts., China (dä-bä shän)	204	32°25'N	108°20'E
Dabeiba, Col. (dȧ-bā'bä)	142a	7°01'N	76°16'W
Dabie Shan, mts., China (dä-bĭĕ shän)	205	31°40'N	114°50'E
Dabnou, Niger	235	14°09'N	5°22'E
Dabob Bay, b., Wa., U.S. (dā'bŏb)	116a	47°50'N	122°50'W
Dabola, Gui.	234	10°45'N	11°07'W
Dąbrowa Białostocka, Pol.	169	53°37'N	23°18'E
Dacca *see* Dhaka, Bngl.	198	23°45'N	90°29'E
Dachang, China (dä-chäŋ)	207b	31°18'N	121°25'E
Dachangshan Dao, i., China (dä-chäŋ-shän dou)	206	39°21'N	122°31'E
Dachau, Ger. (dä'κou)	168	48°16'N	11°26'E
Dacotah, Can. (dȧ-kō'tȧ)	102f	49°52'N	97°38'W
Dade City, Fl., U.S. (dād)	125a	28°22'N	82°09'W
Dadeville, Al., U.S. (dād'vĭl)	124	32°48'N	85°44'W
Dādra & Nagar Haveli, India	199	20°00'N	73°00'E
Dadu, r., China (dä-do͞o)	209	29°20'N	103°03'E
Daet, mtn., Phil. (dä'āt)	213a	14°07'N	122°59'E
Dafoe, r., Can.	97	55°50'N	95°50'W
Dafter, Mi., U.S. (dăf'tēr)	117k	46°21'N	84°26'W
Dagana, Sen. (dä-gä'nä)	230	16°31'N	15°30'W
Dagana, reg., Chad	235	12°20'N	15°15'E
Dagang, China (dä-gäŋ)	207a	22°48'N	113°24'E
Dagda, Lat. (dȧg'dȧ)	167	56°04'N	27°30'E
Dagenham, Eng., U.K. (dăg'ĕn-ăm)	158b	51°32'N	0°09'E
Dagestan, prov., Russia (dä-gĕs-tän')	181	43°40'N	46°10'E
Daggett, Ca., U.S. (dăg'ĕt)	118	34°50'N	116°52'W
Dagu, China (dä-go͞o)	208	39°00'N	117°42'E
Dagu, r., China	206	36°29'N	120°06'W
Dagupan, Phil. (dä-go͞o'pän)	213a	16°02'N	120°20'E
Daheishan Dao, i., China (dä-hā-shän dou)	206	37°57'N	120°37'E
Dahl, Ger. (däl)	171c	51°18'N	7°33'E
Dahlak Archipelago, is., Erit.	231	15°45'N	40°30'E
Dahomey *see* Benin, nation, Afr.	230	8°00'N	2°00'E
Dahra, Libya	200	29°34'N	17°50'E
Daibu, China (dī-bo͞o)	206	31°22'N	119°29'E
Daigo, Japan (dī-gō)	211b	34°57'N	135°49'E
Daimiel Manzanares, Spain (dī-myĕl'män-zä-nä'rĕs)	172	39°05'N	3°36'W
Dairen *see* Dalian, China	204	38°54'N	121°35'E
Dairy, r., Or., U.S. (dâr'ĭ)	116c	45°33'N	123°04'W
Dai-Sen, mtn., Japan (dī'sĕn')	211	35°22'N	133°35'E
Dai-Tenjo-dake, mtn., Japan (dī-tĕn'jō dä-kā)	211	36°21'N	137°38'E
Daiyun Shan, mtn., China (dī-yòn shän)	209	25°40'N	118°08'E
Dajabón, Dom. Rep. (dä-κä-bô'n)	135	19°35'N	71°40'W
Dajarra, Austl. (dȧ-jăr'ȧ)	218	21°45'S	139°30'E
Dakar, Sen. (dȧ-kär')	230	14°40'N	17°26'W
Dakhla, W. Sah.	230	23°45'N	16°04'W
Dakouraoua, Niger	235	13°58'N	6°15'E
Dakovica, Yugo.	175	42°33'N	20°28'E
Dalälven, r., Swe.	156	60°26'N	15°50'E
Dalby, Austl. (dôl'bē)	219	27°10'S	151°15'E
Dalcour, La., U.S. (dăl-kour)	110d	29°49'N	89°59'W
Dale, Nor. (dä'lĕ)	166	60°35'N	5°55'E
Dale Hollow Lake, res., Tn., U.S. (dāl hŏl'ō)	107	36°33'N	85°03'W
Dalemead, Can. (dä'lĕ-mēd)	102e	50°53'N	113°38'W
Dalen, Nor. (dä'lĕn)	166	59°28'N	8°01'E
Daleside, S. Afr. (dāl'sīd)	238c	26°30'S	28°03'E
Dalesville, Can. (dālz'vĭl)	102a	45°42'N	74°23'W
Daley Waters, Austl. (dā lē)	218	16°15'N	133°30'E
Dalhart, Tx., U.S. (dăl härt)	120	36°04'N	102°32'W
Dalhousie, Can. (dăl-ho͞o'zē)	100	48°04'N	66°23'W
Dali, China (dä-lē)	207a	23°07'N	113°06'E
Dali, China	204	26°00'N	100°08'E
Dali, China	204	35°00'N	109°38'E
Dalian, China (lü-dä)	205	38°54'N	121°35'E
Dalian Wan, b., China (dä-lĭĕn wän)	206	38°55'N	121°50'E
Dalías, Spain (dä-lē'ăs)	172	36°49'N	2°50'W
Dall, i., Ak., U.S. (dăl)	103	54°50'N	133°10'W
Dallas, Or., U.S. (dăl'lȧs)	114	44°55'N	123°20'W
Dallas, S.D., U.S.	112	43°13'N	99°34'W
Dallas, Tx., U.S.	104	32°45'N	96°48'W
Dalles Dam, Or., U.S.	114	45°36'N	121°08'W
Dall Island, i., Ak., U.S.	94	54°50'N	132°55'W
Dalmacija, hist. reg., Yugo. (däl-mä'tsē-yä)	174	43°25'N	16°37'E
Dalnerechensk, Russia	179	46°07'N	133°21'E
Daloa, C. Iv.	234	6°53'N	6°27'W
Dalroy, Can. (dăl'roi)	102e	51°07'N	113°39'W
Dalrymple, Mount, mtn., Austl. (dăl'rĭm-p'l)	221	21°14'S	148°46'E
Dalton, S. Afr. (dôl'tŏn)	233c	29°21'S	30°41'E
Dalton, Ga., U.S. (dôl'tŭn)	124	34°46'N	84°58'W
Daly, r., Austl. (dā'lĭ)	220	14°15'S	131°15'E
Daly City, Ca., U.S. (dā'lē)	116b	37°42'N	122°27'W
Damān, India	199	20°32'N	72°53'E
Damanhûr, Egypt (dä-män-ho͞or')	231	30°59'N	30°31'E
Damar, Pulau, i., Indon.	213	7°15'S	129°15'E
Damara, C.A.R.	235	4°58'N	18°42'E
Damaraland, hist. reg., Nmb. (dă'nȧ-rȧ-lănd)	232	22°15'S	16°15'E
Damas Cays, is., Bah. (dä'mäs)	134	23°50'N	79°50'W
Damascus, Syria	198	33°30'N	36°18'E
Damāvand, Qolleh-ye, mtn., Iran	198	36°05'N	52°05'E
Damba, Ang. (däm'bä)	232	6°41'S	15°08'E
Dâmboviţa, r., Rom.	175	44°43'N	25°41'E

PLACE (Pronunciation)	PAGE	LAT.	LONG.
Dame Marie, Cap, c., Haiti (dăm mȧrē')	135	18°35'N	74°50'W
Dāmghān, Iran (dăm-gän')	198	35°50'N	54°15'E
Daming, China (dä-mĭŋ)	208	36°15'N	115°09'E
Dammartin-en-Goële, Fr. (däN-mär-tăN-äN-gô-ĕl')	171b	49°03'N	2°40'E
Dampier, Selat, strt., Indon. (däm'pēr)	213	0°40'S	131°15'E
Dampier Archipielago, is., Austl.	220	20°15'S	116°25'E
Dampier Land, reg., Austl.	220	17°30'S	122°25'E
Dan, r., N.C., U.S. (dȧn)	125	36°26'N	79°40'W
Dana, Mount, mtn., Ca., U.S.	118	37°54'N	119°13'W
Da Nang, Viet.	212	16°08'N	108°22'E
Danbury, Eng., U.K.	158b	51°42'N	0°34'E
Danbury, Ct., U.S. (dăn'bēr-ĭ)	110a	41°23'N	73°27'W
Danbury, Tx., U.S.	123a	29°14'N	95°22'W
Dandenong, Austl. (dăn'dē-nông)	222	37°59'S	145°13'E
Dandong, China (dän-dôŋ)	205	40°10'N	124°30'E
Dane, r., Eng., U.K. (dān)	158a	53°11'N	2°14'W
Danea, Gui.	234	11°27'N	13°12'W
Danforth, Me., U.S.	100	45°38'N	67°53'W
Dan Gora, Nig.	235	11°30'N	8°09'E
Dangtu, China (däŋ-to͞o)	209	31°35'N	118°28'E
Dani, Burkina	230	13°43'N	0°10'W
Dania, Fl., U.S. (dā'nĭ-ȧ)	125a	26°01'N	80°10'W
Danilov, Russia (dä'nē-lôf)	180	58°12'N	40°08'E
Danissa Hills, hills, Kenya	237	3°20'N	40°55'E
Dänizkänarı, Azer.	182	40°13'N	49°33'E
Dankov, Russia (däŋ'kôf)	180	53°17'N	39°09'E
Dannemora, N.Y., U.S. (dăn-ē-mō'rȧ)	109	44°45'N	73°45'W
Dannhauser, S. Afr. (dän'hou-zēr)	233c	28°07'S	30°04'E
Dansville, N.Y., U.S. (dănz'vĭl)	109	42°30'N	77°40'W
Danube, r., Eur.	156	43°00'N	24°00'E
Danube, Mouths of the, mth., Rom. (dăn'ub)	177	45°13'N	29°37'E
Danvers, Ma., U.S. (dăn'vērz)	101a	42°34'N	70°57'W
Danville, Ca., U.S. (dăn'vĭl)	116b	37°49'N	122°00'W
Danville, Il., U.S.	108	40°10'N	87°35'W
Danville, In., U.S.	108	39°45'N	86°30'W
Danville, Ky., U.S.	108	37°35'N	84°50'W
Danville, Pa., U.S.	109	41°00'N	76°35'W
Danville, Va., U.S.	105	36°35'N	79°24'W
Danxian, China (dän shyĕn)	209	19°30'N	109°38'E
Danyang, China (dän-yäŋ)	206	32°01'N	119°32'E
Danzig *see* Gdańsk, Pol.	154	54°20'N	18°40'E
Danzig, Gulf of, b., Eur. (dȧn'tsĭk)	160	54°41'N	19°01'E
Daoxian, China (dou shyĕn)	209	25°35'N	111°27'E
Dapango, Togo	234	10°52'N	0°12'E
Daphnae, hist., Egypt	197a	30°43'N	32°12'E
Daqin Dao, i., China (dä-chyĭn dou)	206	38°18'N	120°50'E
Darabani, Rom. (dă-rä-bän'ĭ)	169	48°13'N	26°38'E
Daraj, Libya	230	30°12'N	10°14'E
Darāw, Egypt (dȧ-rä'o͞o)	238b	24°24'N	32°56'E
Darbhanga, India (dŭr-bŭŋ'gä)	199	26°03'N	85°09'E
Darby, Pa., U.S. (där'bĭ)	110f	39°55'N	75°16'W
Darby, i., Bah.	134	23°50'N	76°20'W
Dardanelles *see* Çanakkale Boğazi, strt., Tur.	163	40°05'N	25°50'E
Dar es Salaam, Tan. (där ĕs sȧ-läm')	233	6°48'S	39°17'E
Dārfūr, hist. reg., Sudan (där-fo͞or')	231	13°21'N	23°46'E
Dargai, Pak. (dŭr-gä'ē)	202	34°35'N	72°00'E
Darien, Col. (dä-rĭ-ĕn')	142a	3°56'N	76°30'W
Darien, Ct., U.S. (dâ-rē-ĕn')	110a	41°04'N	73°28'W
Darién, Cordillera de, mts., Nic.	132	13°00'N	85°42'W
Darien, Serranía del, mts.	133	8°13'N	77°28'W
Darjeeling, India (dŭr-jē'lĭng)	199	27°05'N	88°16'E
Darling, r., Austl.	221	31°50'S	143°20'E
Darling Downs, reg., Austl.	221	27°22'S	150°00'E
Darling Range, mts., Austl.	220	30°30'S	115°45'E
Darlington, Eng., U.K. (där'lĭng-tŭn)	164	54°32'N	1°35'W
Darlington, S.C., U.S.	125	34°15'N	79°52'W
Darlington, Wi., U.S.	113	42°41'N	90°06'W
Darłowo, Pol. (där-lô'vô)	168	54°26'N	16°23'E
Darmstadt, Ger. (därm'shtät)	161	49°53'N	8°40'E
Darnah, Libya	231	32°44'N	22°41'E
Darnley Bay, b., Ak., U.S. (därn'lē)	103	70°00'N	124°00'W
Daroca, Spain (dä-rō-kä)	172	41°08'N	1°24'W
Dartford, Eng., U.K.	158b	51°27'N	0°14'E
Dartmoor, for., Eng., U.K. (därt'mo͞or)	164	50°35'N	4°05'W
Dartmouth, Can. (därt'mŭth)	91	44°40'N	63°34'W
Dartmouth, Eng., U.K.	164	50°33'N	3°28'W
Daru, Pap. N. Gui. (dä'ro͞o)	213	9°04'S	143°21'E
Daruvar, Cro. (där'o͞o-vär)	175	45°37'N	17°16'E
Darwen, Eng., U.K. (där'wĕn)	158a	53°42'N	2°28'W
Darwin, Austl. (där'wĭn)	218	12°25'S	131°00'E
Darwin, Cordillera, mts., Chile (kôr-dēl-yĕ'rä-där'wĕn)	144	54°40'S	69°30'W
Dashhowuz, Turkmen.	183	41°50'N	59°45'E
Dash Point, Wa., U.S. (dăsh)	116a	47°19'N	122°25'W
Dasht, r., Pak. (dŭsht)	198	25°30'N	62°30'E
Dasol Bay, b., Phil. (dä-sōl')	213a	15°53'N	119°40'E
Datian Ding, mtn., China (dä-tĭĕn dĭŋ)	209	22°25'N	111°20'E
Datong, China (dä-tôŋ)	208	40°00'N	113°30'E
Dattapukur, India	202a	22°45'N	88°32'E
Datteln, Ger. (dät'tĕln)	171c	51°39'N	7°20'E
Datu, Tandjung, c., Asia	212	2°08'N	110°15'E
Datuan, China (dä-tŭän)	207b	30°57'N	121°43'E
Daugava (Zapadnaya Dvina), r., Eur.	167	56°40'N	24°40'E
Daugavpils, Lat. (dä'ŏ-gäv-pēls)	180	55°52'N	26°32'E
Dauphin, Can. (dô'fĭn)	90	51°09'N	100°00'W
Dauphin Lake, l., Can.	97	51°17'N	99°48'W
Dāvangere, India	203	14°30'N	75°55'E
Davao, Phil. (dä'vä-ô)	213	7°05'N	125°30'E
Davao Gulf, b., Phil.	213	6°30'N	125°45'E
Davenport, Ia., U.S. (dăv'ĕn-pōrt)	105	41°34'N	90°38'W

ăt; finăl; rāte; senāte; ärm; ȧsk; sofȧ; fâre; ch-choose; dh-as th in other; bē; ēvent; bĕt; recĕnt; cratēr; g-gō; gh-guttural g; bĭt; ĭ-short neutral; rīde; κ-guttural k as ch in German ich;

PRONOUNCING INDEX
Davenport – Diablotins 287

PLACE (Pronunciation)	PAGE	LAT.	LONG.
Davenport, Wa., U.S.	114	47°39'N	118°07'W
David, Pan. (då-vēdh′)	129	8°27'N	82°27'W
David City, Ne., U.S. (dā′vĭd)	112	41°15'N	97°10'W
David-Gorodok, Bela. (då-vēt′ gô-rō′dôk)	181	52°02'N	27°14'E
Davis, Ok., U.S. (dā′vĭs)	121	34°34'N	97°08'W
Davis, W.V., U.S.	109	39°15'N	79°25'W
Davis Lake, l., Or., U.S.	114	43°38'N	121°43'W
Davis Mountains, mts., Tx., U.S.	122	30°45'N	104°17'W
Davis Strait, strt., N.A.	89	66°00'N	60°00'W
Davlekanovo, Russia	180	54°15'N	55°05'E
Davos, Switz. (dä′vōs)	168	46°47'N	9°50'E
Dawa, r., Afr.	231	4°30'N	40°30'E
Dawāsir, Wādī ad, val., Sau. Ar.	198	20°48'N	44°07'E
Dawei, Mya.	212	14°04'N	98°19'E
Dawen, r., China (dä-wŭn)	206	35°58'N	116°53'E
Dawley, Eng., U.K. (dô′lĭ)	158a	52°38'N	2°28'W
Dawna Range, mts., Mya. (dô′nȧ)	212	17°02'N	98°01'E
Dawson, Can. (dô′sŭn)	90	64°04'N	139°22'W
Dawson, Ga., U.S.	124	31°45'N	84°29'W
Dawson, Mn., U.S.	112	44°54'N	96°03'W
Dawson, r., Austl.	221	24°20'S	149°45'E
Dawson Bay, b., Can.	97	52°55'N	100°50'W
Dawson Creek, Can.	90	55°46'N	120°14'W
Dawson Range, mts., Can.	103	62°15'N	138°10'W
Dawson Springs, Ky., U.S.	124	37°10'N	87°40'W
Dawu, China (dä-wōō)	206	31°33'N	114°07'E
Dax, Fr. (dȧks)	161	43°42'N	1°06'W
Daxian, China (dä-shyĕn)	204	31°12'N	107°30'E
Daxing, China (dä-shyĭŋ)	208a	39°44'N	116°19'E
Dayiqiao, China (dä-yē-chyou)	206	31°43'N	120°40'E
Dayr az Zawr, Syria (dȧ-ēr̄ēz-zôr′)	198	35°15'N	40°01'E
Dayton, Ky., U.S. (dā′tŭn)	111f	39°07'N	84°28'W
Dayton, N.M., U.S.	120	32°44'N	104°23'W
Dayton, Oh., U.S.	105	39°54'N	84°15'W
Dayton, Tn., U.S.	124	35°30'N	85°00'W
Dayton, Tx., U.S.	123	30°03'N	94°53'W
Dayton, Wa., U.S.	114	46°18'N	117°59'W
Daytona Beach, Fl., U.S. (dā-tō′nȧ)	105	29°11'N	81°02'W
Dayu, China (dä-yōō)	209	25°20'N	114°20'E
Da Yunhe (Grand Canal), can., China (dä yön-hŭ)	205	35°00'N	117°00'E
Dayville, Ct., U.S. (dā′vĭl)	109	41°50'N	71°55'W
De Aar, S. Afr. (dē-är′)	232	30°45'S	24°05'E
Dead, l., Mn., U.S. (dĕd)	112	46°28'N	96°00'W
Dead Sea, l., Asia	198	31°30'N	35°30'E
Deadwood, S.D., U.S. (dĕd′wŏŏd)	104	44°23'N	103°43'W
Deal Island, Md., U.S. (dēl-ī′lănd)	109	38°10'N	75°55'W
Dean, r., Can. (dēn)	94	52°45'N	125°30'W
Dean Channel, strt., Can.	94	52°33'N	127°13'W
Deán Funes, Arg. (dĕ-ȧ′n-fōō-nĕs)	144	30°26'S	64°12'W
Dearborn, Mi., U.S. (dēr′bŭrn)	111b	42°18'N	83°15'W
Dearg, Ben, mtn., Scot., U.K. (bĕn dŭrg)	164	57°48'N	4°59'W
Dease Strait, strt., Can. (dēz)	92	68°50'N	108°20'W
Death Valley, Ca., U.S.	118	36°18'N	116°26'W
Death Valley, val., Ca., U.S.	106	36°30'N	117°00'W
Death Valley National Park, rec., U.S.	118	36°34'N	117°00'W
Debal′tseve, Ukr.	177	48°23'N	38°29'E
Debao, China (dŭ-bou)	204	23°18'N	106°40'E
Debar, Mac. (dĕ′bär) (dā′brä)	175	41°31'N	20°32'E
Dęblin, Pol. (dăN′blĭn)	169	51°34'N	21°49'E
Dębno, Pol. (dĕb-nô′)	168	52°47'N	13°43'E
Debo, Lac, l., Mali	234	15°15'N	4°40'W
Debrecen, Hung. (dĕ′brĕ-tsĕn)	154	47°32'N	21°40'E
Debre Markos, Eth.	231	10°15'N	37°45'E
Debre Tabor, Eth.	231	11°57'N	38°09'E
Decatur, Al., U.S. (dē-kā′tŭr)	124	34°35'N	87°00'W
Decatur, Ga., U.S.	110c	33°47'N	84°18'W
Decatur, Il., U.S.	105	39°50'N	88°59'W
Decatur, In., U.S.	108	40°50'N	84°55'W
Decatur, Mi., U.S.	108	42°10'N	86°00'W
Decatur, Tx., U.S.	121	33°14'N	97°33'W
Decazeville, Fr. (dē-käz′vēl′)	161	44°33'N	2°16'E
Deccan, plat., India (dĕk′ăn)	199	19°05'N	76°40'E
Deception Lake, l., Can.	96	56°33'N	104°15'W
Deception Pass, p., Wa., U.S. (dē-sĕp′shŭn)	116a	48°24'N	122°44'W
Děčín, Czech Rep. (dyĕ′chēn)	168	50°47'N	14°14'E
Decorah, Ia., U.S. (dē-kō′rȧ)	113	43°18'N	91°48'W
Dedenevo, Russia (dyĕ-dyĕ′nyĕ-vô)	186b	56°14'N	37°31'E
Dedham, Ma., U.S. (dĕd′ăm)	101a	42°15'N	71°11'W
Dedo do Deus, mtn., Braz. (dē-dô-dô-dĕ′ōōs)	144b	22°30'S	43°02'W
Dédougou, Burkina (dā-dô-gōō′)	230	12°38'N	3°28'W
Dee, r., Scot., U.K.	164	57°05'N	2°25'W
Dee, r., U.K.	158a	53°15'N	3°05'E
Deep, r., N.C., U.S. (dēp)	125	35°36'N	79°32'W
Deep Fork, r., Ok., U.S.	121	35°35'N	96°42'W
Deep River, Can.	99	46°06'N	77°20'W
Deepwater, Mo., U.S. (dep-wô-tēr)	121	38°15'N	93°46'W
Deer, i., Me., U.S.	100	44°07'N	68°38'W
Deerfield, Il., U.S. (dēr′fēld)	111a	42°10'N	87°51'W
Deer Island, Or., U.S.	116c	45°56'N	122°51'W
Deer Lake, Can.	93a	49°10'N	57°25'W
Deer Lake, l., Can.	97	52°40'N	94°30'W
Deer Lodge, Mt., U.S. (dēr lŏj)	115	46°23'N	112°42'W
Deer Park, Oh., U.S.	111f	39°12'N	84°24'W
Deer Park, Wa., U.S.	114	47°58'N	117°28'W
Deer River, Mn., U.S.	113	47°20'N	93°49'W
Defiance, Oh., U.S. (dē-fī′ăns)	108	41°15'N	84°20'W
DeFuniak Springs, Fl., U.S. (dē fū′nĭ-ăk)	124	30°42'N	86°06'W
Deganga, India	202a	22°41'N	88°41'E
Degeh Bur, Eth.	238a	8°10'N	43°25'E
Deggendorf, Ger. (dĕ′ghĕn-dôrf)	168	48°50'N	12°59'E
Degollado, Mex. (dā-gô-lyä′dō)	130	20°27'N	102°11'W
DeGrey, r., Austl. (dē grā′)	220	20°20'S	119°25'E
Degtyarsk, Russia (dĕg-ty′arsk)	186a	56°42'N	60°05'E
Dehiwala-Mount Lavinia, Sri L.	203	6°47'N	79°55'E
Dehra Dūn, India (dā′rŭ)	199	30°09'N	78°07'E
Dehua, China (dŭ-hwä)	209	25°30'N	118°15'E
Dej, Rom. (dāzh)	163	47°09'N	23°53'E
De Kalb, Il., U.S. (dē kălb′)	108	41°54'N	88°46'W
Dekese, D.R.C.	236	3°27'S	21°24'E
Delacour, Can. (dĕ-lä-kōōr′)	102e	51°09'N	113°45'W
Delagua, Co., U.S. (dĕl-ä′gwä)	120	37°19'N	104°42'W
De Land, Fl., U.S. (dē lănd′)	125	29°00'N	81°19'W
Delano, Ca., U.S. (dĕl′ȧ-nō)	118	35°47'N	119°15'W
Delano Peak, mtn., Ut., U.S.	106	38°25'N	112°25'W
Delavan, Wi., U.S. (dĕl′ȧ-văn)	113	42°39'N	88°38'W
Delaware, Oh., U.S. (dĕl′ȧ-wâr)	108	40°15'N	83°05'W
Delaware, state, U.S.	105	38°40'N	75°30'W
Delaware, r., Ks., U.S.	121	39°45'N	95°47'W
Delaware, r., U.S.	109	41°50'N	75°20'W
Delaware Bay, b., U.S.	107	39°05'N	75°10'W
Delaware Reservoir, res., Oh., U.S.	109	40°30'N	83°05'E
Delémont, Switz. (dē-lā-môN′)	168	47°21'N	7°18'E
De Leon, Tx., U.S. (dē lē-ŏn′)	122	32°06'N	98°33'W
Delft, Neth. (dĕlft)	165	52°01'N	4°20'E
Delfzijl, Neth.	165	53°20'N	6°50'E
Delgada, Punta, c., Arg. (pōō′n-tä-dĕl-gä′dä)	144	43°46'S	63°46'W
Delgado, Cabo, c., Moz. (kȧ′bô-dĕl-gä′dō)	233	10°40'S	40°35'E
Delhi, India	199	28°54'N	77°13'E
Delhi, Il., U.S. (dĕl′hī)	117e	39°03'N	90°16'W
Delhi, La., U.S.	123	32°26'N	91°29'W
Delhi, state, India	199	28°30'N	76°50'E
Delitzsch, Ger. (dā′lĭch)	168	51°32'N	12°18'E
Dellansjöarna, l., Swe.	166	61°57'N	16°25'E
Delles, Alg. (dĕ′lĕs′)	230	36°59'N	3°40'E
Dell Rapids, S.D., U.S. (dĕl)	112	43°50'N	96°43'W
Dellwood, Mn., U.S. (dĕl′wŏŏd)	117g	45°05'N	92°58'W
Del Mar, Ca., U.S. (dĕl mär′)	118a	32°57'N	117°16'W
Delmas, S. Afr. (dĕl′mȧs)	238c	26°08'S	28°43'E
Delmenhorst, Ger. (dĕl′mĕn-hôrst)	168	53°03'N	8°38'E
Del Norte, Co., U.S. (dĕl nôrt′)	119	37°40'N	106°25'W
De-Longa, i., Russia	179	76°21'N	148°56'E
De Long Mountains, mts., Ak., U.S. (dē′lŏng)	103	68°38'N	162°30'W
Deloraine, Austl. (dĕ-lŭ-rān)	222	41°30'S	146°40'E
Delphi, In., U.S. (dĕl′fī)	108	40°35'N	86°40'W
Delphos, Oh., U.S. (dĕl′fŏs)	108	40°50'N	84°20'W
Delray Beach, Fl., U.S. (dĕl-rā′)	125a	26°27'N	80°05'W
Del Rio, Tx., U.S. (dĕl rē′ō)	104	29°21'N	100°52'W
Delson, Can. (dĕl′sŭn)	102a	45°24'N	73°32'W
Delta, Co., U.S.	119	38°45'N	108°05'W
Delta, Ut., U.S.	119	39°20'N	112°35'W
Delta Beach, Can.	102f	50°10'N	98°20'W
Delvine, Alb. (dĕl′vē-nȧ)	175	39°58'N	20°10'E
Dëma, r., Russia (dyĕm′ä)	180	53°40'N	54°30'E
Demba, D.R.C.	236	5°30'S	22°16'E
Dembi Dolo, Eth.	231	8°46'N	34°46'E
Demidov, Russia (dzyĕ′mē-dô′f)	176	55°16'N	31°32'E
Deming, N.M., U.S. (dĕm′ĭng)	104	32°15'N	107°45'W
Demmin, Ger. (dĕm′mēn)	168	53°54'N	13°04'E
Demnat, Mor. (dĕm-nät)	230	31°58'N	7°03'W
Demopolis, Al., U.S. (dē-mŏp′ō-lĭs)	124	32°30'N	87°50'W
Demotte, In., U.S. (dē′mŏt)	111a	41°12'N	87°13'W
Dempo, Gunung, mtn., Indon. (dĕm′pô)	212	4°04'S	103°11'E
Dem'yanka, r., Russia (dyĕm-yän′kä)	184	59°07'N	72°58'E
Demyansk, Russia (dyĕm-yänsk′)	176	57°39'N	32°26'E
Denain, Fr. (dē-năN′)	170	50°23'N	3°21'E
Denakil Plain, pl., Eth.	231	12°45'N	41°01'E
Denali National Park, rec., Ak., U.S.	106a	63°48'N	153°02'W
Denbigh, Wales, U.K. (dĕn′bĭ)	164	53°15'N	3°25'W
Dendermonde, Bel.	159a	51°02'N	4°04'E
Dendron, Va., U.S. (dĕn′drŭn)	125	37°02'N	76°53'W
Denezhkin Kamen, Gora, mtn., Russia (dzyĕ-ŋĕ′zhkĕn kămĭēŋ)	186a	60°26'N	59°35'E
Denham, Mount, mtn., Jam.	129	18°20'N	77°30'W
Den Helder, Neth. (dĕn hĕl′dĕr)	165	52°55'N	5°45'E
Dénia, Spain	173	38°48'N	0°06'E
Deniliquin, Austl. (dĕ-nĭl′ĭ-kwĭn)	219	35°20'S	144°52'E
Denison, Ia., U.S. (dĕn′ĭ-sŭn)	112	42°01'N	95°22'W
Denison, Tx., U.S.	104	33°45'N	97°02'W
Denizli, Tur. (dĕn-ĭz-lē′)	163	37°40'N	29°10'E
Denklingen, Ger. (dĕn′klĕn-gĕn)	171c	50°54'N	7°40'E
Denmark, S.C., U.S. (dĕn′märk)	125	33°18'N	81°09'W
Denmark, nation, Eur.	154	56°14'N	8°30'E
Denmark Strait, strt., Eur.	89	66°30'N	27°00'W
Dennilton, S. Afr. (dĕn-ĭl-tŭn)	238c	25°18'S	29°13'E
Dennison, Oh., U.S. (dĕn′ĭ-sŭn)	108	40°25'N	81°20'W
Denpasar, Indon.	212	8°35'S	115°10'E
Denton, Eng., U.K. (dĕn′tŭn)	158a	53°27'N	2°07'W
Denton, Md., U.S.	109	38°55'N	75°50'W
Denton, Tx., U.S.	121	33°12'N	97°06'W
D'Entrecasteaux, Point, c., Austl. (dăN-tr′-kȧs-tō′)	220	34°50'S	114°45'E
D'Entrecasteaux Islands, is., Pap. N. Gui. (dăN-tr′-kȧs-tō′)	213	9°45'S	152°00'E
Denver, Co., U.S. (dĕn′vēr)	104	39°44'N	104°59'W
Deoli, India	202	25°52'N	75°23'E
De Pere, Wi., U.S. (dē pēr′)	113	44°25'N	88°04'W
Depew, N.Y., U.S. (dē-pū′)	111c	42°55'N	78°43'W
Deping, China (dŭ-pĭŋ)	206	37°28'N	116°57'E
Depue, Il., U.S. (dē pū)	108	41°15'N	89°55'W
De Queen, Ar., U.S. (dē kwēn′)	121	34°02'N	94°21'W
De Quincy, La., U.S. (dē kwĭn′sĭ)	123	30°27'N	93°27'W
Dera, Lach, r., Afr. (läk dä′rä)	238a	0°45'N	41°26'E
Dera, Lak, r., Afr.	231	0°45'N	41°30'E
Dera Ghāzi Khān, Pak. (dā′rŭ gä-zē′ kän′)	199	30°09'N	70°39'E
Dera Ismāīl Khān, Pak. (dā′rŭ ĭs-mä-ēl′ kän′)	202	31°55'N	70°51'E
Derbent, Russia (dĕr-bĕnt′)	181	42°00'N	48°10'E
Derby, Austl. (där′bē) (dûr′bē)	218	17°20'S	123°40'E
Derby, S. Afr. (där′bĭ)	238c	25°55'S	27°02'E
Derby, Eng., U.K. (där′bē)	161	52°55'N	1°29'W
Derby, Ct., U.S. (dûr′bē)	109	41°20'N	73°05'W
Derbyshire, co., Eng., U.K.	158a	53°11'N	1°30'W
Derdepoort, S. Afr.	238c	24°39'S	26°21'E
Derg, Lough, l., Ire. (lŏk dĕrg)	164	53°00'N	8°09'W
De Ridder, La., U.S. (dē rĭd′ēr)	123	30°50'N	93°18'W
Dermott, Ar., U.S. (dûr′mŏt)	121	33°32'N	91°24'W
Derry, N.H., U.S. (dâr′ĭ)	101a	42°53'N	71°22'W
Derventa, Bos. (dĕr′ven-tȧ)	175	44°58'N	17°58'E
Derwent, r., Austl. (dĕr′wĕnt)	222	42°21'S	146°30'E
Derwent, r., Eng., U.K.	158a	52°54'N	1°24'W
Des Arc, Ar., U.S. (dāz ärk′)	121	34°59'N	91°31'W
Descalvado, Braz. (dĕs-käl-vȧ-dô)	141a	21°55'S	47°37'W
Descartes, Fr.	170	46°58'N	0°42'E
Deschambault Lake, l., Can.	96	54°40'N	103°35'W
Deschênes, Can.	102c	45°23'N	75°47'W
Deschenes, Lake, l., Can.	102c	45°25'N	75°53'W
Deschutes, r., Or., U.S. (dā-shōōt′)	114	44°25'N	121°21'W
Desdemona, Tx., U.S. (dĕz-dē-mō′nȧ)	122	32°16'N	98°33'W
Dese, Eth.	231	11°00'N	39°51'E
Deseado, r., Arg. (dā-sā-ä′dhō)	144	46°50'S	67°45'W
Desirade Island, i., Guad. (dā-zē-rȧs′)	133b	16°21'N	60°51'W
De Smet, S.D., U.S. (dē smĕt′)	112	44°23'N	97°33'W
Des Moines, Ia., U.S. (dē moin′)	105	41°35'N	93°37'W
Des Moines, N.M., U.S.	120	36°42'N	103°48'W
Des Moines, Wa., U.S.	116a	46°24'N	122°20'W
Des Moines, r., U.S.	107	42°30'N	94°20'W
Desna, r., Eur. (dyĕs-nȧ′)	181	51°55'N	31°45'E
Desolación, i., Chile (dĕ-sô-lä-syô′n)	144	53°05'S	74°00'W
De Soto, Mo., U.S. (dē sō′tō)	121	38°07'N	90°32'W
Des Peres, Mo., U.S. (dĕs pĕr′ĕs)	117e	38°36'N	90°26'W
Des Plaines, Il., U.S. (dĕs plānz′)	111a	42°02'N	87°54'W
Des Plaines, r., U.S.	111a	41°39'N	87°56'W
Dessau, Ger. (dĕsou)	161	51°50'N	12°15'E
Detmold, Ger. (dĕt′mōld)	168	51°57'N	8°55'E
Detroit, Mi., U.S. (dē-troit′)	105	42°22'N	83°10'W
Detroit, Tx., U.S.	121	33°41'N	95°16'W
Detroit Lake, res., Or., U.S.	114	44°42'N	122°10'W
Detroit Lakes, Mn., U.S. (dē-troit′lăkz)	112	46°48'N	95°51'W
Detva, Slvk. (dyĕt′vȧ)	169	48°32'N	19°21'E
Deurne, Bel.	159a	51°13'N	4°27'E
Deutsch Wagram, Aus.	159e	48°19'N	16°34'E
Deux-Montagnes, Can.	102a	45°33'N	73°53'W
Deux Montagnes, Lac des, l., Can.	102a	45°28'N	74°00'W
Deva, Rom. (dā′vä)	163	45°52'N	22°52'E
Dévaványa, Hung. (dā′vô-vän-yô)	169	47°01'N	20°58'E
Develi, Tur. (dĕ′vȧ-lē)	181	38°20'N	35°10'E
Deventer, Neth. (dĕv′ĕn-tēr)	165	52°14'N	6°07'E
Devils, r., Tx., U.S.	122	29°55'N	101°10'W
Devils Island *see* Diable, Île du, i., Fr. Gu.	143	5°15'N	52°40'W
Devils Lake, N.D., U.S.	104	48°10'N	98°55'W
Devils Lake, l., N.D., U.S. (dĕv′'lz)	112	47°57'N	99°04'W
Devils Lake Indian Reservation, I.R., N.D., U.S.	112	48°08'N	99°40'W
Devils Postpile National Monument, rec., Ca., U.S.	118	37°42'N	119°12'W
Devils Tower National Monument, rec., Wy., U.S.	115	44°38'N	105°07'W
Devoll, r., Alb.	175	40°55'N	20°10'E
Devon, Can.	102g	53°23'N	113°43'W
Devon, S. Afr. (dĕv′ŭn)	238c	26°23'S	28°47'E
Devonport, Austl. (dĕv′ŭn-pôrt)	219	41°20'S	146°30'E
Devonport, N.Z.	221a	36°50'S	174°45'E
Devore, Ca., U.S. (dē-vôr′)	117a	34°13'N	117°24'W
Dewatto, Wa., U.S. (dē-wät′ō)	116a	47°27'N	123°04'W
Dewey, Ok., U.S. (dū′ĭ)	121	36°48'N	95°55'W
De Witt, Ar., U.S. (dē wĭt′)	121	34°17'N	91°22'W
De Witt, Ia., U.S.	113	41°46'N	90°34'W
Dewsbury, Eng., U.K. (dūz′bēr-ĭ)	158a	53°42'N	1°39'W
Dexter, Me., U.S. (dĕks′tēr)	100	45°01'N	69°19'W
Dexter, Mo., U.S.	121	36°46'N	89°56'W
Dezfūl, Iran	198	32°14'N	48°37'E
Dezhnëva, Mys, c., Russia (dyĕzh′nyĭf)	196	68°00'N	172°00'W
Dezhou, China (dŭ-jō)	208	37°28'N	116°17'E
Dhahran *see* Az Zahrān, Sau. Ar.	198	26°13'N	50°00'E
Dhaka, Bngl. (dä′kä) (dăk′ȧ)	199	23°45'N	90°29'E
Dharamtar Creek, r., India	203b	18°49'N	72°54'E
Dharmavaram, India	203	14°32'N	77°43'E
Dhawalāgiri, mtn., Nepal	199	28°42'N	83°31'E
Dhībān, Jord.	197a	31°30'N	35°46'E
Dhidhimótikhon, Grc.	175	41°20'N	26°27'E
Dhule, India	199	20°58'N	74°43'E
Día, i., Grc. (dē′ȧ)	174a	35°27'N	25°17'E
Diable, Île du, i., Fr. Gu.	143	5°15'N	52°40'W
Diablo, Mount, mtn., Ca., U.S. (dyȧ′blō)	116b	37°52'N	121°55'W
Diablo Heights, Pan. (dyȧ′blō)	128a	8°58'N	79°34'W
Diablo Range, mts., Ca., U.S.	116b	37°47'N	121°50'W
Diablotins, Morne, mtn., Dom.	133b	15°31'N	61°24'W

ng-sing; ŋ-baŋk; N-nasalized n; nŏd; cŏmmit; ōld; ôbey; ôrder; oi-boil; fōōd; ŏŏ-as oo in foot; ou-out; s-soft; sh-dish; th-thin; pūre; ûnite; ûrn; stŭd; circŭs; ü-as in French tu; ′-indeterminate vowel.

PLACE (Pronunciation)	PAGE	LAT.	LONG.
Diaca, Moz.	237	11°30'S	39°59'E
Diaka, r., Mali	235	14°40'N	5°00'E
Diamantina, Braz.	143	18°14'S	43°32'W
Diamantina, r., Austl. (dī'man-tē'nà)	220	25°38'S	139°53'E
Diamantino, Braz. (dē-à-män-tē'no)	143	14°22'S	56°23'W
Diamond Peak, mtn., Or., U.S.	114	43°32'N	122°08'W
Diana Bank, bk. (dī'ăn'à)	135	22°30'N	74°45'W
Dianbai, China (dĭĕn-bī)	209	21°30'N	111°20'E
Dian Chi, l., China (dĭĕn chē)	204	24°58'N	103°18'E
Dickinson, N.D., U.S. (dĭk'ĭn-sŭn)	104	46°52'N	102°49'W
Dickinson, Tx., U.S. (dĭk'ĭn-sŭn)	123a	29°28'N	95°02'W
Dickinson Bayou, Tx., U.S.	123a	29°26'N	95°08'W
Dickson, Tn., U.S. (dĭk'sŭn)	124	36°03'N	87°24'W
Dickson City, Pa., U.S.	109	41°25'N	75°40'W
Didcot, Eng., U.K. (dĭd'cŏt)	158b	51°35'N	1°15'W
Didiéni, Mali	234	13°53'N	8°06'W
Die, Fr. (dē)	171	44°45'N	5°22'E
Diefenbaker, res., Can.	92	51°20'N	108°10'W
Diego de Ocampo, Pico, mtn., Dom. Rep. (pē'-kô-dyĕ'gô-dĕ-ō-kä'm-pō)	135	19°40'N	70°45'W
Diego Ramirez, Islas, is., Chile (dē ā'gō rä-mē'räz)	144	56°15'S	70°15'W
Diéma, Mali	234	14°32'N	9°12'W
Dien Bien Phu, Viet.	204	21°38'N	102°49'E
Dieppe, Can. (dē-ĕp')	100	46°06'N	64°45'W
Dieppe, Fr.	161	49°54'N	1°05'E
Dierks, Ar., U.S. (dērks)	121	34°06'N	94°02'W
Diessen, Ger. (dēs'sĕn)	159d	47°57'N	11°06'E
Diest, Bel.	159a	50°59'N	5°05'E
Digby, Can. (dĭg'bĭ)	91	44°37'N	65°46'W
Dighton, Ma., U.S. (dī-tŭn)	110b	41°49'N	71°05'W
Digne, Fr. (dēn'y')	171	44°07'N	6°16'E
Digoin, Fr. (dē-gwăn')	170	46°28'N	4°06'E
Digul, r., Indon.	213	7°00'S	140°27'E
Dijohan Point, c., Phil. (dē-kô-än)	213a	16°24'N	122°25'E
Dijon, Fr. (dē-zhôn')	154	47°21'N	5°02'E
Dikson, Russia (dĭk'sŏn)	178	73°30'N	80°35'E
Dikwa, Nig. (dē'kwà)	231	12°06'N	13°53'E
Dili, E. Timor (dĭl'ē)	213	8°35'S	125°35'E
Di Linosa Island, i., Italy (dē-lē-nō'sä)	162	36°01'N	12°43'E
Dilizhan, Arm.	181	40°45'N	45°00'E
Dillingham, Ak., U.S. (dĭl'ĭng-hăm)	106a	59°10'N	158°38'W
Dillon, Mt., U.S. (dĭl'ŭn)	115	45°12'N	112°40'W
Dillon, S.C., U.S.	125	34°24'N	79°28'W
Dillon Reservoir, res., Oh., U.S.	108	40°05'N	82°05'W
Dilolo, D.R.C. (dē-lō'lō)	232	10°19'S	22°23'E
Dimashq *see* Damascus, Syria	198	33°31'N	36°18'E
Dimbokro, C. Iv.	234	6°39'N	4°42'W
Dimitrovo *see* Pernik, Blg.	163	42°36'N	23°04'E
Dimlang, mtn., Nig.	235	8°24'N	11°47'E
Dimona, Isr.	197a	31°03'N	35°01'E
Dinagat Island, i., Phil.	213	10°15'N	126°15'E
Dinājpur, Bngl.	202	25°38'N	87°39'E
Dinan, Fr. (dē-nän')	170	48°27'N	2°03'W
Dinant, Bel. (dē-nän')	165	50°17'N	4°50'E
Dinara, mts., Yugo. (dē'nä-rä)	163	43°50'N	16°15'E
Dinard, Fr.	170	48°38'N	2°04'W
Dindigul, India	203	10°25'N	78°03'E
Dingalan Bay, b., Phil. (dĭŋ-gä'län)	213a	15°19'N	121°33'E
Dingle, Ire. (dĭng''l)	164	52°10'N	10°13'W
Dingle Bay, b., Ire.	161	52°02'N	10°15'W
Dingo, Austl. (dĭŋ'gō)	219	23°45'S	149°26'E
Dinguiraye, Gui.	234	11°18'N	10°43'W
Dingwall, Scot., U.K. (dĭng'wôl)	164	57°37'N	4°23'W
Dingxian, China (dĭŋ shyĕn)	208	38°30'N	115°00'E
Dingxing, China (dĭŋ-shyĭŋ)	208	39°18'N	115°50'E
Dingyuan, China (dĭŋ-yüän)	206	32°32'N	117°40'E
Dingzi Wan, b., China	206	36°33'N	121°06'E
Dinosaur National Monument, rec., Co., U.S. (dī'nō-sôr)	115	40°45'N	109°17'W
Dinslaken, Ger. (dēns'lä-kĕn)	171c	51°33'N	6°44'E
Dinteloord, Neth.	159a	51°38'N	4°21'E
Dinuba, Ca., U.S. (dĭ-nū'bà)	118	36°33'N	119°29'W
Dios, Cayo de, i., Cuba (kä'yō-dĕ-dē-ōs')	134	22°05'N	83°05'W
Diourbel, Sen. (dē-ōōr-bĕl')	230	14°40'N	16°15'W
Diphu Pass, p., Asia (dĭ-pōō)	204	28°15'N	96°45'E
Diquis, r., C.R. (dē-kēs')	133	8°59'N	83°24'W
Dire Dawa, Eth.	231	9°40'N	41°47'E
Diriamba, Nic. (dēr-yäm'bä)	132	11°52'N	86°15'W
Dirk Hartog, i., Austl.	220	26°25'S	113°15'E
Dirksland, Neth.	159a	51°45'N	4°04'E
Dirranbandi, Austl. (dĭ-rà-băn'dē)	219	28°24'S	148°29'E
Dirty Devil, r., Ut., U.S. (dûr'tĭ dĕv''l)	119	38°20'N	110°30'W
Disappointment, l., Austl.	220	23°20'S	123°00'E
Disappointment, Cape, c., Wa., U.S. (dĭs'à-point'ment)	116c	46°16'N	124°11'W
Discovery, S. Afr. (dĭs-kŭv'ēr-ĭ)	233b	26°10'S	27°53'E
Discovery, is., Can. (dĭs-kŭv'ēr-ē)	116a	48°25'N	123°13'W
Disko, i., Grnld. (dĭs'kō)	89	70°00'N	54°00'W
Disna, Bela. (dēs'nà)	180	55°34'N	28°15'E
Dispur, India	202	26°00'N	91°50'E
Disraëli, Can. (dĭs-rā'lĭ)	99	45°53'N	71°23'W
District of Columbia, dept., U.S.	105	38°50'N	77°00'W
Distrito Federal, dept., Braz. (dēs-trē'tô-fĕ-dĕ-rä'l)	143	15°49'S	47°39'W
Distrito Federal, dept., Mex.	130	19°14'N	99°08'W
Disūq, Egypt (dē-sōōk')	238b	31°07'N	30°41'E
Diu, India (dē'ōō)	199	20°48'N	70°58'E
Divilacan Bay, b., Phil. (dē-vē-lä'kän)	213a	17°26'N	122°25'E
Divinópolis, Braz. (dē-vē-nô'pō-lēs)	143	20°10'S	44°53'W
Divo, C. Iv.	234	5°50'N	5°22'W
Dixon, Il., U.S. (dĭks'ŭn)	113	41°50'N	89°30'W
Dixon Entrance, strt., N.A.	92	54°25'N	132°00'W
Diyarbakir, Tur. (dē-yär-bĕk'ĭr)	198	38°00'N	40°10'E
Dja, r., Afr.	231	2°30'N	14°00'E
Djambala, Congo	236	2°33'S	14°45'E
Djanet, Alg.	230	24°29'N	9°26'E
Djebobo, mtn., Ghana	234	8°20'N	0°37'E
Djedi, Oued, r., Alg.	162	34°18'N	4°39'E
Djember, Chad	235	10°25'N	17°50'E
Djerba, Île de, i., Tun.	162	33°53'N	11°26'E
Djerid, Chott, l., Tun. (jĕr'ĭd)	230	33°15'N	8°29'E
Djibasso, Burkina	234	13°07'N	4°10'W
Djibo, Burkina	234	14°06'N	1°38'W
Djibouti, Dji. (jē-bōō-tē')	238a	11°34'N	43°00'E
Djibouti, nation, Afr.	238a	11°35'N	48°08'E
Djokoumatombi, Congo	236	0°47'N	15°22'E
Djokupunda, D.R.C.	232	5°27'S	20°58'E
Djoua, r., Afr.	236	1°25'N	13°40'E
Djursholm, Swe. (djōōrs'hōlm)	166	59°26'N	18°01'E
Dmitriyev-L'govskiy, Russia (d'mē'trĭ-yĕf l'gôf'skĭ)	176	52°07'N	35°05'E
Dmitrov, Russia (d'mē'trôf)	176	56°21'N	37°32'E
Dmitrovsk, Russia (d'mē'trôfsk)	176	52°30'N	35°10'E
Dmytrivka, Ukr.	177	47°57'N	38°56'E
Dnepropetrovsk *see* Dnipropetrovs'k, Ukr.	178	48°15'N	34°08'E
Dnieper (Dnipro), r., Eur.	181	46°45'N	33°40'E
Dniester, r., Eur.	181	48°21'N	28°10'E
Dniprodzerzhyns'k, Ukr.	181	48°32'N	34°38'E
Dniprodzerzhyns'ke vodoskhovyshche, res., Ukr.	178	49°00'N	34°10'E
Dnipropetrovs'k, Ukr.	178	48°15'N	34°08'E
Dnipropetrovs'k, prov., Ukr.	177	48°15'N	34°10'E
Dniprovs'kyi lyman, b., Ukr.	177	46°33'N	31°45'E
Dnistrovs'kyi lyman, l., Ukr.	177	46°13'N	29°50'E
Dno, Russia (d'nô')	176	57°49'N	29°59'E
Do, Lac, l., Mali	234	15°50'N	2°20'W
Doba, Chad	235	8°39'N	16°51'E
Dobbs Ferry, N.Y., U.S. (dŏbz fĕ'rē)	110a	41°01'N	73°53'W
Dobbyn, Austl. (dôb'ĭn)	218	19°45'S	140°02'E
Dobele, Lat. (dô'bĕ-lē)	167	56°37'N	23°18'E
Doberai, Jazirah, pen., Indon.	213	1°25'S	133°15'E
Dobo, Indon.	213	6°00'S	134°18'E
Doboj, Bos. (dō'boi)	175	44°42'N	18°04'E
Dobrich, Blg.	163	43°33'N	27°52'E
Dobryanka, Russia (dôb-ryän'kà)	186a	58°27'N	56°26'E
Dobšina, Slvk. (dôp'shē-nä)	169	48°48'N	20°25'E
Doce, r., Braz. (dō'sā)	143	19°01'S	42°14'W
Doce, Canal Numero, can., Arg.	141c	36°47'S	59°00'W
Doce Leguas, Cayos de las, is., Cuba	134	20°55'N	79°05'W
Doctor Arroyo, Mex. (dōk-tōr' är-rō'yō)	130	23°41'N	100°10'W
Doddington, Eng., U.K. (dŏd'dĭng-tŏn)	158b	51°17'N	0°47'E
Dodecanese *see* Dodekanisoy, is., Grc.	175	38°00'N	26°10'E
Dodekanisoy (Dodecanese), is., Grc.	175	38°00'N	26°10'E
Dodge City, Ks., U.S. (dŏj)	104	37°44'N	100°01'W
Dodgeville, Wi., U.S. (dŏj'vĭl)	113	42°58'N	90°07'W
Dodoma, Tan. (dō'dô-mà)	232	6°11'S	35°45'E
Dog, l., Can. (dŏg)	98	48°42'N	89°24'W
Dogger Bank, bk. (dŏg'gēr)	165	55°07'N	2°25'E
Dogubayazit, Tur.	181	39°35'N	44°00'E
Doha *see* Ad Dawhah, Qatar	198	25°02'N	51°28'E
Dohad, India	202	22°52'N	74°18'E
Dokshytsy, Bela. (dôk-shētsĕ)	176	54°53'N	27°49'E
Dolbeau, Can.	91	48°52'N	72°16'W
Dole, Fr. (dōl)	161	47°07'N	5°28'E
Dolgaya, Kosa, c., Russia (kô'sà dôl-gä'yä)	177	46°42'N	37°42'E
Dolgeville, N.Y., U.S.	110	43°10'N	74°45'W
Dolgiy, i., Russia	180	69°20'N	59°20'E
Dolgoprudnyy, Russia	186b	55°57'N	37°33'E
Dolinsk, Russia (då-lēnsk')	185	47°29'N	142°31'E
Dollar Harbor, b., Bah.	134	25°30'N	79°15'W
Dolomite, Al., U.S. (dŏl'ô-mīt)	110h	33°28'N	86°57'W
Dolomiti, mts., Italy	174	46°16'N	11°43'E
Dolores, Arg. (dô-lō'rĕs)	144	36°20'S	57°42'W
Dolores, Col.	142a	3°33'N	74°54'W
Dolores, Ur.	141c	33°32'S	58°15'W
Dolores, Tx., U.S. (dô-lō'rĕs)	122	27°42'N	99°47'W
Dolores, r., Co., U.S.	119	38°35'N	108°50'W
Dolores Hidalgo, Mex. (dô-lô'rĕs-ē-dăl'gō)	130	21°09'N	100°56'W
Dolphin and Union Strait, strt., Can. (dŏl'fĭn ūn'yŭn)	92	69°22'N	117°10'W
Dolyna, Ukr.	169	48°57'N	24°01'E
Domažlice, Czech Rep. (dō'mäzh-lē-tsĕ)	168	49°27'N	12°55'E
Dombasle-sur-Meurthe, Fr. (dôn-bäl')	171	48°38'N	6°18'E
Dombóvár, Hung. (dŏm'bō-vär)	169	46°22'N	18°08'E
Domeyko, Cordillera, mts., Chile (kôr-dēl-yĕ'rä-dô-mā'kō)	142	20°50'S	69°02'W
Dominica, nation, N.A. (dŏ-mĭ-nē'kà)	129	15°30'N	60°45'W
Dominica Channel, strt., N.A.	133b	15°00'N	61°30'W
Dominican Republic, nation, N.A. (dô-mĭn'ĭ-kăn)	129	19°00'N	70°45'W
Dominion, Can. (dô-mĭn'yŭn)	101	46°13'N	60°01'W
Domiongo, D.R.C.	236	4°37'S	21°15'E
Domodedovo, Russia (dô-mô-dyĕ'do-vô)	186b	55°27'N	37°45'E
Dom Silvério, Braz. (don-sĕl-vĕ'ryō)	141a	20°09'S	42°57'W
Don, r., Russia	178	49°50'N	41°30'E
Don, r., Eng., U.K.	158a	53°39'N	0°58'W
Don, r., Scot., U.K.	164	57°19'N	2°39'W
Donaldson, Mi., U.S. (dŏn'ăl-sŭn)	117k	46°19'N	84°22'W
Donaldsonville, La., U.S. (dŏn'ăld-sŭn-vĭl)	123	30°05'N	90°58'W
Donalsonville, Ga., U.S.	124	31°02'N	84°50'W
Donawitz, Aus. (dō'nà-vĭts)	168	47°23'N	15°05'E
Don Benito, Spain (dōn'bå-nē'tō)	172	38°55'N	5°52'W
Doncaster, Austl. (doŋ'kăs-tēr)	217a	37°47'S	145°08'E
Doncaster, Eng., U.K. (doŋ'kăs-tēr)	164	53°32'N	1°07'W
Doncaster, co., Eng., U.K.	158a	53°35'N	1°10'W
Dondo, Ang. (dōn'dō)	232	9°38'S	14°25'E
Dondo, Moz.	232	19°33'S	34°47'E
Dondra Head, c., Sri L.	203	5°52'N	80°52'E
Donegal, Ire. (dŏn-ē-gôl')	164	54°44'N	8°05'W
Donegal Bay, Ire. (dŏn-ē-gôl')	160	54°35'N	8°36'W
Donets Coal Basin, reg., Ukr. (dō-nyĕts')	177	48°15'N	38°50'E
Donets'k, Ukr.	178	48°00'N	37°35'E
Donets'k, prov., Ukr.	177	47°55'N	37°40'E
Dong, r., China (dôŋ)	205	24°13'N	115°08'E
Dongara, Austl. (dôn-gă'rà)	218	29°15'S	115°00'E
Dongba, China (dôŋ-bä)	206	31°40'N	119°02'E
Dong'e, China (dôŋ-ŭ)	206	36°21'N	116°14'E
Dong'ezhen, China	208	36°11'N	116°16'E
Dongfang, China (dôŋ-fäŋ)	209	19°08'N	108°42'E
Donggala, Indon. (dôn-gä'lä)	212	0°45'S	119°32'E
Dongguan, China (dôŋ-guän)	207a	23°03'N	113°46'E
Dongguang, China (dôŋ-gůäŋ)	206	37°54'N	116°33'E
Donghai, China (dôŋ-hī)	208	34°35'N	119°05'E
Dong Hoi, Viet. (dông-hô-ē')	212	17°25'N	106°42'E
Dongila, Eth.	231	11°17'N	37°00'E
Dongming, China (dôŋ-mĭŋ)	206	35°16'N	115°06'E
Dongo, Ang. (dôŋ'gō)	232	14°45'S	15°30'E
Dongon Point, c., Phil. (dŏng-ôn')	213a	12°43'N	120°35'E
Dongou, Congo (dôŋ-gōō')	231	2°02'N	18°04'E
Dongping, China (dôŋ-pĭŋ)	208	35°50'N	116°24'E
Dongping Hu, l., China (dôŋ-pĭŋ hōō)	206	36°06'N	116°24'E
Dongshan, China (doŋ-shän)	206	31°05'N	120°24'E
Dongtai, China	206	32°51'N	120°20'E
Dongting Hu, l., China (dôŋ-tĭŋ hōō)	205	29°10'N	112°30'E
Dongxiang, China (dôŋ-shyän)	209	28°18'N	116°38'E
Doniphan, Mo., U.S. (dŏn'ĭ-făn)	121	36°37'N	90°50'W
Donji Vakuf, Bos. (dōn'yĭ väk'ōōf)	175	44°08'N	17°25'E
Don Martin, Presa de, res., Mex. (prĕ'sä-dĕ-dôn-mär-tē'n)	122	27°35'N	100°38'W
Donnacona, Can.	99	46°40'N	71°46'W
Donnemarie-en-Montois, Fr. (dôn-mä-rē'ĕn-môn-twä')	171b	48°29'N	3°09'E
Donner und Blitzen, r., Or., U.S. (dŏn'ēr ŏnt'blĭ'tsĕn)	114	42°45'N	118°57'W
Donnybrook, S. Afr. (dŏ-nĭ-brŏk)	233c	29°56'S	29°54'E
Donora, Pa., U.S. (dŏ-nō'rä)	111e	40°10'N	79°51'W
Donostia-San Sebastián, Spain	154	43°19'N	1°59'W
Donoússa, i., Grc.	175	37°09'N	25°53'E
Doolow, Som.	238a	4°10'N	42°05'E
Doonerak, Mount, mtn., Ak., U.S. (dōō'nē-răk)	103	68°00'N	150°34'W
Doorn, Neth.	159a	52°02'N	5°21'E
Door Peninsula, pen., Wi., U.S. (dōr)	113	44°40'N	87°36'W
Dora Baltea, r., Italy (dō'rä bäl'tā-ä)	174	45°40'N	7°34'E
Doraville, Ga., U.S. (dō'rà-vĭl)	110c	33°54'N	84°17'W
Dorchester, Eng., U.K. (dôr'chĕs-tēr)	164	50°45'N	2°34'W
Dordogne, r., Fr. (dôr-dôn'yĕ)	156	44°53'N	0°16'E
Dordrecht, Neth. (dôr'drĕkt)	165	51°48'N	4°39'E
Dordrecht, S. Afr. (dô'drĕkt)	233c	31°24'S	27°06'E
Doré Lake, l., Can.	96	54°31'N	107°06'W
Dorgali, Italy (dôr'gä-lē)	174	40°18'N	9°37'E
Dörgön Nuur, l., Mong.	204	47°47'N	94°01'E
Dorion-Vaudreuil, Can. (dôr-yō)	102a	45°23'N	74°01'W
Dorking, Eng., U.K. (dôr'kĭng)	158b	51°12'N	0°20'W
Dormont, Pa., U.S. (dôr'mŏnt)	111e	40°24'N	80°02'W
Dornbirn, Aus. (dôrn'bĕrn)	168	47°24'N	9°45'E
Dornoch, Scot., U.K. (dôr'nŏk)	160	57°55'N	4°01'W
Dornoch Firth, b., Scot., U.K. (dôr'nŏk fûrth)	164	57°55'N	3°55'W
Dorogobuzh, Russia (dôrôgô'-bōō'zh)	176	54°57'N	33°18'E
Dorohoi, Rom. (dō-rō-hoi')	169	47°57'N	26°28'E
Dorre Island, i., Austl. (dôr)	220	25°19'S	113°10'E
Dorstsen, Ger.	171c	51°40'N	6°58'E
Dortmund, Ger. (dôrt'mŏŏnt)	161	51°31'N	7°28'E
Dortmund-Ems-Kanal, can., Ger. (dôrt'mōōnd-ĕms'kä-näl')	171c	51°50'N	7°25'E
Dörtyol, Tur. (dûrt'yôl)	163	36°50'N	36°20'E
Dorval, Can. (dôr-vál')	102a	45°26'N	73°44'W
Dos Bahías, Cabo, c., Arg. (kå'bô-dôs-bä-ē'äs)	144	44°55'S	65°35'W
Dos Caminos, Ven. (dôs-kä-mē'nôs)	143b	9°38'N	67°17'W
Dosewallips, r., Wa., U.S. (dō'sē-wăl'lĭps)	116a	47°45'N	123°04'W
Dos Hermanas, Spain (dōsĕr-mä'näs)	172	37°17'N	5°56'W
Dosso, Niger (dôs-ō')	230	13°03'N	3°12'E
Dothan, Al., U.S. (dō'thăn)	105	31°13'N	85°23'W
Douai, Fr. (dōō-ā')	161	50°23'N	3°04'E
Douala, Cam. (dōō-ä'lä)	230	4°03'N	9°42'E
Douarnenez, Fr. (dōō-är nē-nĕs')	170	48°06'N	4°18'W
Double Bayou, Tx., U.S. (dŭb''l bī'yōō)	123a	29°40'N	94°38'W
Doubs, r., Eur.	171	46°15'N	5°50'E
Douentza, Mali	234	15°00'N	2°57'W
Douglas, I. of Man (dŭg'lăs)	164	54°10'N	4°24'W
Douglas, Ak., U.S. (dŭg'lăs)	103	58°18'N	134°35'W
Douglas, Az., U.S.	104	31°20'N	109°30'W
Douglas, Ga., U.S.	125	31°30'N	82°53'W
Douglas, Wy., U.S. (dŭg'lăs)	115	42°45'N	105°21'W
Douglas, r., Eng., U.K. (dŭg'lăs)	158a	53°38'N	2°48'W

PRONOUNCING INDEX

Douglas Channel – East Cleveland 289

PLACE (Pronunciation)	PAGE	LAT.	LONG.
Douglas Channel, strt., Can.	94	53°30'N	129°12'W
Douglas Lake, res., Tn., U.S. (dŭg'lăs)	124	36°00'N	83°35'W
Douglas Lake Indian Reserve, I.R., Can.	95	50°10'N	120°49'W
Douglasville, Ga., U.S. (dŭg'lăs-vĭl)	124	33°45'N	84°47'W
Dourada, Serra, mts., Braz. (sĕ'r-rä-dôōō-rá'dä)	143	15°11'S	49°57'W
Dourdan, Fr. (do͞or-däN')	171b	48°32'N	2°01'E
Douro, r., Port. (dô'ò-rŏ)	172	41°03'N	8°12'W
Dove, r., Eng., U.K. (dŭv)	158a	52°53'N	1°47'W
Dover, S. Afr.	238c	27°05'S	27°44'E
Dover, Eng., U.K.	154	51°08'N	1°19'E
Dover, De., U.S. (dō vẽr)	105	39°10'N	75°30'W
Dover, N.H., U.S.	109	43°15'N	71°00'W
Dover, N.J., U.S.	110a	40°53'N	74°33'W
Dover, Oh., U.S.	108	40°35'N	81°30'W
Dover, Strait of, strt., Eur.	156	50°50'N	1°15'W
Dover-Foxcroft, Me., U.S. (dō'vẽr fŏks'krôft)	100	45°10'N	69°15'W
Dovre Fjell, mts., Nor. (dōv'rĕ fyĕl')	156	62°03'N	8°36'E
Dow, Il., U.S. (dou)	117e	39°01'N	90°20'W
Dowagiac, Mi., U.S. (dô-wô'jăk)	108	42°00'N	86°05'W
Downers Grove, Il., U.S. (dou'nẽrz grōv)	111a	41°48'N	88°00'W
Downey, Ca., U.S. (dou'nĭ)	117a	33°56'N	118°08'W
Downieville, Ca., U.S. (dou'nĭ-nĭl)	118	39°35'N	120°48'W
Downs, Ks., U.S. (dounz)	120	39°29'N	98°32'W
Doylestown, Oh., U.S. (doilz'toun)	111d	40°58'N	81°43'W
Drâa, Cap, c., Mor. (drȧ)	230	28°39'N	12°15'W
Drâa, Oued, r., Afr.	230	28°00'N	9°31'W
Drabiv, Ukr.	177	49°57'N	32°14'E
Drac, r., Fr. (dräk)	171	44°50'N	5°47'E
Dracut, Ma., U.S. (drā'kŭt)	101a	42°40'N	71°19'W
Draganovo, Blg. (drä-gä-nō'vô)	175	43°13'N	25°45'E
Drăgăşani, Rom. (drä-gá-shän'ĭ)	175	44°39'N	24°18'E
Draguignan, Fr. (drä-gēn-yäN')	171	43°35'N	6°28'E
Drahichyn, Bela.	169	52°10'N	25°11'E
Drakensberg, mts., Afr. (drä'kĕnz-bĕrgh)	232	29°15'S	29°07'E
Drake Passage, strt. (drāk păs'ĭj)	139	57°00'S	65°00'W
Dráma, Grc. (drä'mä)	163	41°09'N	24°10'E
Drammen, Nor. (dräm'ĕn)	160	59°45'N	10°15'E
Drau (Drava), r., Eur. (drou)	168	46°44'N	13°45'E
Drava, r., Eur. (drä'vä)	156	45°45'N	17°30'E
Dravograd, Slvn. (drä'vô-gräd')	174	46°37'N	15°01'E
Drawsko Pomorskie, Pol. (dräv'skō pō-mōr'skyĕ)	168	53°31'N	15°50'E
Drayton Harbor, b., Wa., U.S. (drā'tŭn)	116d	48°58'N	122°40'W
Drayton Plains, Mi., U.S.	111b	42°41'N	83°23'W
Drayton Valley, Can.	95	53°13'N	114°59'W
Drensteinfurt, Ger. (drĕn'shtīn-fo͞ort)	171c	51°47'N	7°44'E
Dresden, Ger. (drās'dĕn)	154	51°05'N	13°45'E
Dreux, Fr. (drû)	170	48°44'N	1°24'E
Driefontein, S. Afr.	238c	25°53'S	29°10'E
Drin, r., Alb. (drēn)	175	42°13'N	20°13'E
Drina, r., Yugo. (drē'nä)	163	44°09'N	19°30'E
Drinit, Pellg i, b., Alb.	175	41°42'N	19°17'E
Dr. Ir. W. J. van Blommestein Meer, res., Sur.	143	4°45'N	55°05'W
Drissa, r., Eur.	176	55°44'N	28°58'E
Driver, Va., U.S.	110g	36°50'N	76°30'W
Dröbak, Nor. (drû'bäk)	166	59°40'N	10°35'E
Drobeta-Turnu Severin, Rom.	163	43°54'N	24°49'E
Drogheda, Ire. (drŏ'hē-dȧ)	160	53°43'N	6°15'W
Drohobych, Ukr.	169	49°21'N	23°31'E
Drôme, r., Fr. (drōm)	170	44°42'N	4°53'E
Dronfield, Eng., U.K. (drŏn'fēld)	158a	53°18'N	1°28'W
Drumheller, Can. (drŭm-hĕl-ẽr)	90	51°28'N	112°42'W
Drummond, i., Mi., U.S. (drŭm'ŭnd)	108	46°00'N	83°50'W
Drummondville, Can. (drŭm'ŭnd-vĭl)	91	45°53'N	72°33'W
Drumright, Ok., U.S. (drŭm'rīt)	121	35°59'N	96°37'W
Drunen, Neth.	159a	51°41'N	5°10'E
Drut', r., Bela. (dro͞ot)	176	53°40'N	29°45'E
Druya, Bela. (drò'yȧ)	176	55°45'N	27°26'E
Drwęca, r., Pol. (d'r-vän'tsȧ)	169	53°06'N	19°13'E
Dryden, Can. (drī-dĕn)	91	49°47'N	92°50'W
Drysdale, Austl.	217a	38°11'S	144°34'E
Dry Tortugas, is., Fl., U.S. (tôr-to͞o'gäz)	125a	24°37'N	82°45'W
Dry Tortugas National Park, rec., Fl., U.S.	125a	24°42'N	83°02'W
Dschang, Cam. (dshäng)	230	5°34'N	10°09'E
Duabo, Lib.	234	5°40'N	8°05'W
Duagh, Can.	102g	53°43'N	113°24'W
Duarte, Pico, mtn., Dom. Rep. (dwä'rtĕh pēcô)	129	19°00'N	71°00'W
Duas Barras, Braz. (do͞o'äs-bá'r-räs)	141a	22°03'S	42°30'W
Dubai see Dubayy, U.A.E.	198	25°18'N	55°26'E
Dubăsari, Mol.	177	47°16'N	29°11'E
Dubawnt, l., Can. (do͞o-bônt')	92	63°27'N	103°30'W
Dubawnt, r., Can.	92	61°30'N	103°49'W
Dubayy, U.A.E.	198	25°18'N	55°26'E
Dubbo, Austl. (dŭb'ō)	219	32°20'S	148°42'E
Dubie, D.R.C.	237	8°33'S	28°32'E
Dublin, Ire.	154	53°20'N	6°15'W
Dublin, Ca., U.S. (dŭb'lĭn)	116b	37°42'N	121°56'W
Dublin, Ga., U.S.	125	32°33'N	82°55'W
Dublin, Tx., U.S.	122	32°05'N	98°20'W
Dubna, Russia	176	56°44'N	37°10'E
Dubno, Ukr. (do͞ob'nô)	169	50°24'N	25°44'E
Du Bois, Pa., U.S. (dò-bois')	109	41°10'N	78°45'W
Dubovka, Russia (dò-bôf'kȧ)	181	49°00'N	44°50'E
Dubrovka, Russia (do͞o-brôf'kȧ)	186c	59°51'N	30°56'E
Dubrovnik, Cro. (dò'brôv-nĕk) (rä-go͞o'sä)	154	42°40'N	18°10'E
Dubrowna, Bela.	176	54°39'N	30°54'E
Dubuque, Ia., U.S. (dò-būk')	105	42°30'N	90°43'W
Duchesne, Ut., U.S. (dò-shān')	119	40°12'N	110°23'W
Duchesne, r., Ut., U.S.	119	40°20'N	110°50'W
Duchess, Austl. (dŭch'ĕs)	218	21°30'S	139°55'E
Ducie Island, i., Pit. (dü-sē')	2	25°30'S	126°20'W
Duck, r., Tn., U.S.	124	35°55'N	87°40'W
Duckabush, r., Wa., U.S. (dŭk'á-bŏsh)	116a	47°41'N	123°09'W
Duck Lake, Can.	96	52°47'N	106°13'W
Duck Mountain, mtn., Can.	97	51°35'N	101°00'W
Ducktown, Tn., U.S. (dŭk'toun)	124	35°03'N	84°20'W
Duck Valley Indian Reservation, I.R., Id., U.S.	114	42°02'N	115°49'W
Duckwater Peak, mtn., Nv., U.S. (dŭk-wô-tẽr)	118	39°00'N	115°31'W
Duda, r., Col. (do͞o'dä)	142a	3°25'N	74°23'W
Dudinka, Russia (do͞o-dĭn'kȧ)	178	69°15'N	85°42'E
Dudley, Eng., U.K. (dŭd'lĭ)	161	52°28'N	2°07'E
Duero, r., Eur.	156	41°30'N	4°30'W
Dufourspitze, mtn., Eur.	168	45°55'N	7°52'E
Dugger, In., U.S. (dŭg'ẽr)	108	39°00'N	87°10'W
Dugi Otok, i., Yugo. (do͞o'gē o'tôk)	174	44°03'N	14°40'E
Duisburg, Ger. (do͞o'ĭs-bòrgh)	161	51°26'N	6°46'E
Dukhān, Qatar	201	25°25'N	50°48'E
Dukhovshchina, Russia (do͞o-kôfsh-'chēnȧ)	176	55°13'N	32°26'E
Dukinfield, Eng., U.K. (dŭk'ĭn-fēld)	158a	53°28'N	2°05'W
Dukla Pass, p., Eur. (dò'klä)	161	49°25'N	21°44'E
Dulce, Golfo, b., C.R. (gōl'fô do͞ol'sä)	129	8°25'N	83°13'W
Dülken, Ger. (dül'kĕn)	171c	51°15'N	6°21'E
Dülmen, Ger. (dül'mĕn)	171c	51°50'N	7°17'E
Duluth, Mn., U.S. (dò-lo͞oth')	105	46°50'N	92°07'W
Dumai, Indon.	197b	1°39'N	101°30'E
Dumali Point, c., Phil. (do͞o-mä'lē)	213a	13°07'N	121°42'E
Dumas, Tx., U.S.	120	35°52'N	101°58'W
Dumbarton, Scot., U.K. (dŭm'bár-tŭn)	164	56°00'N	4°35'W
Dum-Dum, India	202a	22°37'N	88°25'E
Dumfries, Scot., U.K. (dŭm-frēs')	164	55°05'N	3°40'W
Dumjor, India	202a	22°37'N	88°14'E
Dumont, N.J., U.S. (do͞o'mŏnt)	110a	40°56'N	74°00'W
Dumyāt, Egypt	231	31°22'N	31°50'E
Dunaföldvár, Hung. (dò'nô-füld'vär)	169	46°48'N	18°55'E
Dunaïvtsi, Ukr.	177	48°52'N	26°51'E
Dunajec, r., Pol. (dò-nä'yĕts)	169	49°52'N	20°53'E
Dunaújváros, Hung.	169	46°57'N	18°55'E
Dunay, Russia (do͞o'nĭ)	186c	59°59'N	30°57'E
Dunbar, W.V., U.S.	108	38°20'N	81°45'W
Duncan, Can. (dŭŋ'kăn)	90	48°47'N	123°42'W
Duncan, Ok., U.S.	121	34°29'N	97°56'W
Duncan, r., Can.	95	50°30'N	116°45'W
Duncan Dam, dam, Can.	95	50°15'N	116°55'W
Duncan Lake, l., Can.	95	50°20'N	117°00'W
Duncansby Head, c., Scot., U.K. (dŭn'kănz-bĭ)	164	58°40'N	3°01'W
Duncanville, Tx., U.S. (dŭn'kăn-vĭl)	117c	32°39'N	96°55'W
Dundalk, Ire. (dŭn'kôk)	160	54°00'N	6°18'W
Dundalk, Md., U.S.	110e	39°16'N	76°31'W
Dundalk Bay, b., Ire. (dŭn'dôk)	164	53°55'N	6°15'W
Dundas, Can. (dŭn-dăs')	99	43°16'N	79°58'W
Dundas, l., Austl. (dŭn-dăs)	220	32°15'S	122°00'E
Dundas Island, i., Can.	94	54°33'N	130°55'W
Dundas Strait, strt., Austl.	220	10°35'S	131°15'E
Dundedin, Fl., U.S. (dŭn-ē'dĭn)	125a	28°00'N	82°43'W
Dundee, S. Afr.	233c	28°14'S	30°16'E
Dundee, Scot., U.K.	154	56°30'N	2°55'W
Dundee, Il., U.S. (dŭn-dē)	111a	42°06'N	88°17'W
Dundrum Bay, b., N. Ire., U.K. (dŭn-drŭm')	164	54°13'N	5°47'W
Dunedin, N.Z.	221a	45°48'S	170°32'E
Dunellen, N.J., U.S. (dŭn-ĕl'ĭ'n)	110a	40°36'N	74°28'W
Dunfermline, Scot., U.K. (dŭn-fĕrm'lĭn)	164	56°05'N	3°30'W
Dungarvan, Ire. (dŭn-gár'văn)	164	52°06'N	7°50'W
Dungeness, Wa., U.S. (dŭnj-nĕs')	116a	48°09'N	123°07'W
Dungeness, r., Wa., U.S.	116a	48°03'N	123°10'W
Dungeness Spit, Wa., U.S.	116a	48°11'N	123°03'W
Dunhua, China (dòn-hwä)	205	43°18'N	128°10'E
Dunkerque, Fr. (dŭN-kĕrk')	161	51°02'N	2°37'E
Dunkirk, In., U.S. (dŭn'kûrk)	108	40°20'N	85°25'W
Dunkwa, Ghana	234	5°22'N	1°12'W
Dun Laoghaire, Ire. (dŭn-lā'rĕ)	160	53°16'N	6°09'W
Dunlap, Ia., U.S. (dŭn'lăp)	112	41°53'N	95°33'W
Dunlap, Tn., U.S.	124	35°23'N	85°23'W
Dunmore, Pa., U.S. (dŭn'mōr)	109	41°25'N	75°30'W
Dunn, N.C., U.S. (dŭn)	125	35°18'N	78°37'W
Dunnellon, Fl., U.S. (dŭn-ĕl'ŏn)	125	29°02'N	82°28'W
Dunnville, Can. (dŭn'vĭl)	99	42°55'N	79°40'W
Dunqulah, Sudan	231	19°21'N	30°19'E
Dunsmuir, Ca., U.S. (dŭnz'mūr)	114	41°08'N	122°17'W
Dunwoody, Ga., U.S. (dŭn-wòd'ĭ)	110c	33°57'N	84°20'W
Duolun, China (dwô-lo͞on)	205	42°12'N	116°15'E
Du Page, r., Il., U.S. (do͞o päj)	111a	41°41'N	88°11'W
Du Page, East Branch, r., Il., U.S.	111a	41°42'N	88°09'W
Du Page, West Branch, r., Il., U.S.	111a	41°42'N	88°09'W
Dupax, Phil. (do͞o'päks)	213a	16°16'N	121°06'E
Dupo, Il., U.S. (dū'pō)	117e	38°31'N	90°12'W
Duque de Caxias, Braz. (do͞o'kĕ-dĕ-kä'shyȧs)	141a	22°46'S	43°18'W
Duquesne, Pa., U.S. (dò-kān')	111e	40°22'N	79°51'W
Du Quoin, Il., U.S. (dò-kwoin')	121	38°01'N	89°14'W
Durance, r., Fr. (dü-räNs')	161	43°46'N	5°52'E
Durand, Mi., U.S. (dů-rănd')	108	42°50'N	84°00'W
Durand, Wi., U.S.	113	44°37'N	91°58'W
Durango, Mex. (do͞o-rä'n-gô)	128	24°02'N	104°42'W
Durango, Co., U.S. (dò-răŋ'gō)	119	37°15'N	107°55'W
Durango, state, Mex.	128	25°00'N	106°00'W
Durant, Ms., U.S. (dů-rănt')	124	33°05'N	89°50'W
Durant, Ok., U.S.	121	33°59'N	96°23'W
Duratón, r., Spain (do͞o-rä-tōn')	172	41°30'N	3°55'W
Durazno, Ur. (do͞o-räz'nō)	144	33°21'S	56°31'W
Durazno, dept., Ur.	141c	33°00'S	56°35'W
Durban, S. Afr. (dûr'băn)	232	29°48'S	31°00'E
Durbanville, S. Afr. (dûr-băn'vĭl)	232a	33°50'S	18°39'E
Durbe, Lat. (do͞or'bĕ)	167	56°36'N	21°24'E
Đurđevac, Cro.	163	46°03'N	17°03'E
Düren, Ger. (dü'rĕn)	171c	50°48'N	6°30'E
Durham, Eng., U.K. (dûr'ăm)	164	54°47'N	1°46'W
Durham, N.C., U.S.	105	36°00'N	78°55'W
Durham Downs, Austl.	222	27°30'S	141°55'E
Durrës, Alb. (dòr'ĕs)	154	41°19'N	19°27'E
Duryea, Pa., U.S. (do͞or-yā')	109	41°20'N	75°50'W
Dushan, China	206	31°38'N	116°16'E
Dushan, China (do͞o-shän)	209	25°50'N	107°42'E
Dushanbe, Taj.	183	38°30'N	68°45'E
Düsseldorf, Ger. (düs'ĕl-dôrf)	161	51°14'N	6°47'E
Dussen, Neth.	159a	51°43'N	4°58'E
Dutalan Ula, mts., Mong.	208	49°25'N	112°40'E
Dutch Harbor, Ak., U.S. (dŭch här'bẽr)	106a	53°58'N	166°30'W
Duvall, Wa., U.S. (do͞o'vâl)	116a	47°44'N	121°59'W
Duwamish, r., Wa., U.S. (do͞o-wăm'ĭsh)	116a	47°24'N	122°18'W
Duyun, China (do͞o-yòn)	204	26°18'N	107°40'E
Dvinskaya Guba, b., Russia	180	65°10'N	38°40'E
Dwārka, India	202	22°18'N	68°59'E
Dwight, Il., U.S. (dwĭt)	108	41°00'N	88°20'W
Dworshak Res, Id., U.S.	114	46°45'N	115°50'W
Dyat'kovo, Russia (dyät'kō-vō)	176	53°36'N	34°19'E
Dyer, In., U.S. (dī'ẽr)	111a	41°30'N	87°31'W
Dyersburg, Tn., U.S. (dī'ẽrz-bûrg)	124	36°02'N	89°23'W
Dyersville, Ia., U.S. (dī'ẽrz-vĭl)	113	42°28'N	91°09'W
Dyes Inlet, Wa., U.S. (dīz)	116a	47°37'N	122°45'W
Dykhtau, Gora, mtn., Russia	182	43°03'N	43°08'E
Dyment, Can. (dī'mĕnt)	97	49°37'N	92°19'W
Dzamïn Üüd, Mong.	205	44°38'N	111°32'E
Dzaoudzi, May. (dzou'dzĭ)	233	12°44'S	45°15'E
Dzavhan, r., Mong.	204	48°19'N	94°08'E
Dzerzhinsk, Russia	180	56°20'N	43°50'E
Dzerzhyns'k, Ukr.	177	48°26'N	37°50'E
Dzhalal-Abad, Kyrg. (jȧ-läl'ȧ-bät')	183	40°56'N	73°00'E
Dzhambul see Zhambyl, Kaz.	183	42°51'N	71°29'E
Dzhankoi, Ukr.	181	45°43'N	34°22'E
Dzhizak, Uzb. (dzhĕ'zäk)	183	40°13'N	67°58'E
Dzhugdzhur Khrebet, mts., Russia (jòg-jo͞or')	179	56°15'N	137°00'E
Działoszyce, Pol. (jyä-wō-shĕ'tsĕ)	169	50°21'N	20°22'E
Dzibalchén, Mex. (zē-bäl-chĕ'n)	132a	19°25'N	89°39'W
Dzidzantún, Mex. (zēd-zän-to͞o'n)	132a	21°18'N	89°00'W
Dzierżoniów, Pol. (dzyĕr-zhôn'yŭf)	168	50°44'N	16°38'E
Dzilam González, Mex. (zē-lä'm-gôn-zä'lĕz)	132a	21°21'N	88°53'W
Dzitás, Mex. (zē-tá's)	132a	20°47'N	88°32'W
Dzungaria, reg., China (dzòŋ-gä'rĭ-ȧ)	204	44°39'N	86°13'E
Dzungarian Gate, p., Asia	204	45°00'N	88°00'E
Dzyarzhynsk, Bela.	176	53°41'N	27°14'E

E

PLACE (Pronunciation)	PAGE	LAT.	LONG.
Eagle, W.V., U.S.	108	38°10'N	81°20'W
Eagle, r., Co., U.S.	119	39°32'N	106°28'W
Eaglecliff, Wa., U.S. (ē'gl-klĭf)	116c	46°10'N	123°13'W
Eagle Creek, r., In., U.S.	111g	39°54'N	86°17'W
Eagle Grove, Ia., U.S.	113	42°39'N	93°55'W
Eagle Lake, Me., U.S.	100	47°03'N	68°38'W
Eagle Lake, Tx., U.S.	123	29°37'N	96°20'W
Eagle Lake, l., Ca., U.S.	114	40°45'N	120°52'W
Eagle Mountain, Ca., U.S.	118	33°49'N	115°27'W
Eagle Mountain L, Tx., U.S.	117c	32°56'N	97°27'W
Eagle Pass, Tx., U.S.	104	28°49'N	100°30'W
Eagle Pk, Ca., U.S.	114	41°18'N	120°11'W
Ealing, Eng., U.K. (ē'lĭng)	158b	51°29'N	0°19'W
Earle, Ar., U.S. (ûrl)	121	35°14'N	90°28'W
Earlington, Ky., U.S. (ûr'lĭng-tŭn)	124	37°15'N	87°31'W
Easley, S.C., U.S. (ēz'lĭ)	125	34°48'N	82°37'W
East, Mount, mtn., Pan.	128a	9°09'N	79°46'W
East Alton, Il., U.S. (ôl'tŭn)	117e	38°53'N	90°08'W
East Angus, Can. (ăŋ'gŭs)	99	45°35'N	71°40'W
East Aurora, N.Y., U.S. (ô-rō'rȧ)	111c	42°46'N	78°38'W
East Bay, b., Tx., U.S.	123a	29°30'N	94°41'W
East Bernstadt, Ky., U.S. (bûrn'stát)	124	37°09'N	84°08'W
Eastbourne, Eng., U.K. (ēst'bôrn)	165	50°48'N	0°16'E
East Caicos, i., T./C. Is. (kī'kōs)	135	21°40'N	71°35'W
East Cape, c., N.Z.	221a	37°37'S	178°33'E
East Cape see Dezhnëva, Mys, c., Russia	196	68°00'N	172°00'W
East Carondelet, Il., U.S. (kȧ-rŏn'dĕ-lĕt)	117e	38°33'N	90°14'W
East Cherokee Indian Reservation, I.R., N.C., U.S.	124	35°33'N	83°12'W
East Chicago, In., U.S. (shĭ-kô'gō)	111a	41°39'N	87°29'W
East China Sea, sea, Asia	205	30°28'N	125°52'E
East Cleveland, Oh., U.S. (klēv'lănd)	111d	41°33'N	81°35'W

290 East Cote Blanche Bay – Ellice Islands

PRONOUNCING INDEX

PLACE (Pronunciation)	PAGE	LAT.	LONG.
East Cote Blanche Bay, b., La., U.S. (kōt blänsh′)	123	29°30′N	92°07′W
East Des Moines, r., Ia., U.S. (dē moin′)	113	42°57′N	94°17′W
East Detroit, Mi., U.S. (dė-troit′)	111b	42°28′N	82°57′W
Easter Island *see* Pascua, Isla de, i., Chile	241	26°50′S	109°00′W
Eastern Ghāts, mts., India	199	13°50′N	78°45′E
Eastern Turkestan, hist. reg., China (tȯr-kĕ-stän′)(tûr-kĕ-stăn′)	204	39°40′N	78°20′E
East Grand Forks, Mn., U.S. (grănd fôrks)	112	47°56′N	97°02′W
East Greenwich, R.I., U.S. (grĭn′ĭj)	110b	41°40′N	71°27′W
Easthampton, Ma., U.S. (ēst-hămp′tŭn)	109	42°15′N	72°45′W
East Hartford, Ct., U.S. (härt′fērd)	109	41°45′N	72°35′W
East Helena, Mt., U.S. (hĕ-hē′nȧ)	115	46°31′N	111°50′W
East Ilsley, Eng., U.K. (ĭl′slē)	158b	51°30′N	1°18′W
East Jordan, Mi., U.S. (jôr′dăn)	108	45°05′N	85°05′W
East Kansas City, Mo., U.S. (kăn′zȧs)	117f	39°09′N	94°30′W
Eastland, Tx., U.S. (ēst′lănd)	122	32°24′N	98°47′W
East Lansing, Mi., U.S. (lăn′sĭng)	108	42°45′N	84°30′W
Eastlawn, Mi., U.S.	111b	42°15′N	83°35′W
East Leavenworth, Mo., U.S. (lĕv′ĕn-wûrth)	117f	39°18′N	94°50′W
East Liverpool, Oh., U.S. (lĭv′ēr-po͞ol)	108	40°40′N	80°35′W
East London, S. Afr. (lŭn′dŭn)	232	33°02′S	27°54′E
East Los Angeles, Ca., U.S. (lōs äŋ′hȧ-lās)	117a	34°01′N	118°09′W
Eastmain, r., Can. (ēst′mān)	93	52°12′N	73°19′W
Eastman, Ga., U.S. (ēst′măn)	124	32°10′N	83°11′W
East Millstone, N.J., U.S. (mĭl′stōn)	110a	40°30′N	74°35′W
East Moline, Il., U.S. (mȯ-lēn′)	113	41°31′N	90°28′W
East Nishnabotna, r., Ia., U.S. (nĭsh-nȧ-bŏt′nȧ)	112	40°53′N	95°23′W
Easton, Md., U.S. (ēs′tŭn)	109	38°45′N	76°05′W
Easton, Pa., U.S.	109	40°45′N	75°15′W
Easton L, Ct., U.S.	110a	41°18′N	73°17′W
East Orange, N.J., U.S. (ŏr′ĕnj)	110a	40°46′N	74°12′W
East Pakistan *see* Bangladesh, nation, Asia	199	24°15′N	90°00′E
East Palo Alto, Ca., U.S.	116b	37°27′N	122°07′W
East Peoria, Il., U.S. (pē-ō′rĭ-ȧ)	108	40°40′N	89°30′W
East Pittsburgh, Pa., U.S. (pĭts′bûrg)	111e	40°24′N	79°50′W
East Point, Ga., U.S.	110c	33°41′N	84°27′W
Eastport, Me., U.S. (ēst′pōrt)	100	44°53′N	67°01′W
East Providence, R.I., U.S. (prŏv′ĭ-dĕns)	110b	41°49′N	71°22′W
East Retford, Eng., U.K. (rĕt′fērd)	158a	53°19′N	0°56′W
East Riding of Yorkshire, co., Eng., U.K.	158a	53°45′N	0°40′W
East Rochester, N.Y., U.S. (rŏch′ĕs-tēr)	109	43°10′N	77°30′W
East Saint Louis, Il., U.S.	105	38°38′N	90°10′W
East Siberian Sea, sea, Russia (sī-bĭr′y′n)	179	73°00′N	153°28′E
Eastsound, Wa., U.S. (ēst-sound)	116d	48°42′N	122°42′W
East Stroudsburg, Pa., U.S. (stroudz′bûrg)	109	41°00′N	75°10′W
East Syracuse, N.Y., U.S. (sĭr′ȧ-kūs)	109	43°05′N	76°00′W
East Tavaputs Plateau, plat., Ut., U.S. (tă-vă′-pŭts)	119	39°25′N	109°45′W
East Tawas, Mi., U.S. (tô′wăs)	108	44°15′N	83°30′W
East Timor, nation, Asia	213	9°00′S	125°30′E
East Walker, r., U.S. (wôk′ẽr)	118	38°36′N	119°02′W
Eaton, Co., U.S. (ē′tŭn)	120	40°31′N	104°42′W
Eaton, Oh., U.S.	108	39°45′N	84°40′W
Eaton Estates, Oh., U.S.	111d	41°19′N	82°01′W
Eaton Rapids, Mi., U.S. (răp′ĭdz)	108	42°30′N	84°40′W
Eatonton, Ga., U.S. (ētŭn-tŭn)	124	33°20′N	83°24′W
Eatontown, N.J., U.S. (ē′tŭn-toun)	110a	40°18′N	74°04′W
Eau Claire, Wi., U.S. (ō klâr′)	105	44°47′N	91°32′W
Ebeltoft, Den. (ĕ′bĕl-tŭft)	166	56°11′N	10°39′E
Ebensburg, Pa., U.S.	109	40°29′N	78°44′W
Ebersberg, Ger. (ĕ′bĕrs-bĕrgh)	159d	48°05′N	11°58′E
Ebingen, Ger. (ā′bĭng-ĕn)	168	48°13′N	9°04′E
Eboli, Italy (ĕb′ô-lē)	174	40°38′N	15°04′E
Ebolowa, Cam.	230	2°54′N	11°09′E
Ebreichsdorf, Aus.	159e	47°58′N	16°24′E
Ebrié, Lagune, b., C. Iv.	234	5°20′N	4°50′W
Ebro, r., Spain (ā′brō)	156	42°00′N	2°00′W
Eccles, Eng., U.K. (ĕk′′lz)	158a	53°29′N	2°20′W
Eccles, W.V., U.S.	108	37°45′N	81°10′W
Eccleshall, Eng., U.K.	158a	52°51′N	2°15′W
Eceabat, Tur.	175	40°10′N	26°21′E
Echague, Phil. (ā-chä′gwā)	213a	16°43′N	121°40′E
Echandi, Cerro, mtn., N.A. (sĕ′r-rô-ĕ-chä′nd)	133	9°05′N	82°51′W
Ech Cheliff, Alg.	230	36°14′N	1°32′E
Echimamish, r., Can.	97	54°15′N	97°30′W
Echmiadzin, Arm.	182	40°10′N	44°18′E
Echo Bay, Can. (ĕk′ō)	117k	46°29′N	84°04′W
Echoing, r., Can. (ĕk′ō-ĭng)	97	55°15′N	91°30′W
Echternach, Lux. (ĕk′tēr-näk)	171	49°48′N	6°25′E
Echuca, Austl. (ė-chȯ′kȧ)	219	36°10′S	144°47′E
Écija, Spain (ā′thė-hä)	162	37°20′N	5°07′W
Eckernförde, Ger.	168	54°27′N	9°51′E
Eclipse, Va., U.S. (ė-klĭps′)	110g	36°55′N	76°29′W
Ecorse, Mi., U.S. (ė-kôrs′)	111b	42°15′N	83°09′W
Ecuador, nation, S.A. (ĕk′wȧ-dôr)	142	0°00′N	78°30′W
Ed, Erit.	231	13°57′N	41°37′E
Eddyville, Ky., U.S. (ĕd′ĭ-vĭl)	124	37°03′N	88°03′W
Ede, Nig.	235	7°44′N	4°27′E
Edéa, Cam. (ĕ-dā′ä)	230	3°48′N	10°08′E

PLACE (Pronunciation)	PAGE	LAT.	LONG.
Eden, Tx., U.S.	122	31°13′N	99°51′W
Eden, Ut., U.S.	117b	41°18′N	111°49′W
Eden, r., Eng., U.K. (ē′dĕn)	164	54°40′N	2°35′W
Edenbridge, Eng., U.K. (ē′dĕn-brĭj)	158b	51°11′N	0°05′E
Edenham, Eng., U.K. (ē′d'n-ăm)	158a	52°46′N	0°25′W
Eden Prairie, Mn., U.S. (prâr′ĭ)	117g	44°51′N	93°29′W
Edenton, N.C., U.S. (ē′dĕn-tŭn)	125	36°02′N	76°37′W
Edenton, Oh., U.S.	111f	39°14′N	84°02′W
Edenvale, S. Afr. (ēd′ĕn-vāl)	233b	26°09′S	28°10′E
Edenville, S. Afr. (ē′d'n-vĭl)	238c	27°33′S	27°42′E
Eder, r., Ger. (ā′dēr)	168	51°05′N	8°52′E
Édessa, Grc.	163	40°48′N	22°04′E
Edgefield, S.C., U.S. (ĕj′fēld)	125	33°52′N	81°55′W
Edgeley, N.D., U.S. (ĕj′lĭ)	112	46°24′N	98°43′W
Edgemont, S.D., U.S. (ĕj′mŏnt)	112	43°19′N	103°50′W
Edgerton, Wi., U.S. (ĕj′ēr-tŭn)	113	42°49′N	89°06′W
Edgewater, Al., U.S. (ĕj-wô-tēr)	110h	33°31′N	86°52′W
Edgewater, Md., U.S.	110e	38°58′N	76°35′W
Edgewood, Can. (ĕj′wȯd)	95	49°47′N	118°08′W
Edina, Mn., U.S. (ė-dī′nȧ)	117g	44°55′N	93°20′W
Edina, Mo., U.S.	121	40°10′N	92°11′W
Edinburg, In., U.S. (ĕd′'n-bûrg)	108	39°20′N	85°55′W
Edinburg, Tx., U.S.	122	26°18′N	98°08′W
Edinburgh, Scot., U.K. (ĕd′'n-bŭr-ȯ)	154	55°57′N	3°10′W
Edirne, Tur.	175	41°41′N	26°35′E
Edisto, r., S.C., U.S. (ĕd′ĭs-tō)	125	33°10′N	80°50′W
Edisto, North Fork, r., S.C., U.S.	125	33°42′N	81°24′W
Edisto, South Fork, r., S.C., U.S.	125	33°43′N	81°35′W
Edisto Island, S.C., U.S.	125	32°32′N	80°20′W
Edmond, Ok., U.S. (ĕd′mŭnd)	121	35°39′N	97°29′W
Edmonds, Wa., U.S. (ĕd′mŭndz)	116a	47°49′N	122°23′W
Edmonton, Can.	90	53°33′N	113°28′W
Edmundston, Can. (ĕd′mŭn-stŭn)	91	47°22′N	68°20′W
Edna, Tx., U.S. (ĕd′nȧ)	123	28°59′N	96°39′W
Edremit, Tur. (ĕd-rĕ-mēt′)	163	39°35′N	27°00′E
Edremit Körfezi, b., Tur.	175	39°28′N	26°35′E
Edson, Can. (ĕd′sŭn)	90	53°35′N	116°26′W
Edward, i., Can. (ĕd′wērd)	98	48°21′N	88°29′W
Edward, l., Afr.	232	0°25′S	29°40′E
Edwardsville, Il., U.S. (ĕd′wērdz-vĭl)	117e	38°49′N	89°58′W
Edwardsville, In., U.S.	111h	38°17′N	85°53′W
Edwardsville, Ks., U.S.	117f	39°04′N	94°49′W
Eel, r., Ca., U.S. (ēl)	114	40°39′N	124°15′W
Eel, r., In., U.S.	108	40°50′N	85°55′W
Efate, i., Vanuatu (å-fä′tā)	221	18°02′S	168°29′E
Effigy Mounds National Monument, rec., Ia., U.S. (ĕf′ĭ-jŭ mounds)	113	43°04′N	91°15′W
Effingham, Il., U.S. (ĕf′ĭng-hăm)	108	39°05′N	88°30′W
Ega, r., Spain (ā′gä)	172	42°40′N	2°20′W
Egadi, Isole, is., Italy (ė′sō-lĕ-ĕ′gä-dē)	162	38°01′N	12°00′E
Egegik, Ak., U.S. (ĕg′ĕ-jĭt)	103	58°10′N	157°22′W
Eger, Hung. (ĕ gĕr)	169	47°53′N	20°24′E
Egersund, Nor. (ĕ′ghĕr-sȯn′)	160	58°29′N	6°01′E
Egg Harbor, N.J., U.S. (ĕg här′bēr)	109	39°30′N	74°35′W
Egham, Eng., U.K. (ĕg′ŭm)	158b	51°24′N	0°33′W
Egiyn, r., Mong.	204	49°41′N	100°40′E
Egmont, Cape, c., N.Z. (ĕg′mŏnt)	221a	39°18′S	173°49′E
Egypt, nation, Afr. (ē′jĭpt)	231	26°58′N	27°01′E
Eha-Amufu, Nig.	235	6°40′N	7°46′E
Eibar, Spain (ā′ė-bär)	172	43°12′N	2°20′W
Eichstätt, Ger. (īk′shtät)	168	48°54′N	11°14′E
Eichwalde, Ger. (īĸ′väl-dĕ)	159b	52°22′N	13°37′E
Eidfjord, Nor. (ĕĭd′fyōr)	166	60°28′N	7°04′E
Eidsvoll, Nor. (īdhs′vôl)	160	60°19′N	11°15′E
Eifel, mts., Ger. (ī′fĕl)	168	50°08′N	6°30′E
Eighty Mile Beach, cst., Austl.	220	19°00′S	121°00′E
Eilenburg, Ger. (ī′lĕn-bȯrgh)	168	51°27′N	12°38′E
Einbeck, Ger. (īn′bĕk)	168	51°49′N	9°52′E
Eindhoven, Neth. (īnd′hō-vĕn)	165	51°29′N	5°20′E
Eisenach, Ger. (ī′zĕn-äĸ)	161	50°58′N	10°18′E
Eisenhüttenstadt, Ger.	168	52°08′N	14°40′E
Eivissa, Spain	173	38°55′N	1°24′E
Eivissa, i., Spain	156	38°55′N	1°24′E
Ejea de los Caballeros, Spain	172	42°07′N	1°05′W
Ejura, Ghana	234	7°23′N	1°22′W
Ejutla de Crespo, Mex. (å-hȯt′lä dā krās′pö)	131	16°34′N	96°44′W
Ekanga, D.R.C.	236	2°23′S	23°14′E
Ekenäs, Fin. (ĕ′kĕ-nâs)	167	59°59′N	23°25′E
Ekeren, Bel.	159a	51°17′N	4°27′E
Ekoli, D.R.C.	236	0°23′S	24°16′E
El Aaiún, W. Sah.	230	26°45′N	13°15′W
El Affroun, Alg. (ĕl ȧf-froun′)	173	36°28′N	2°38′E
Elands, r., S. Afr. (ėlånds)	233c	31°48′S	26°09′E
Elands, r., S. Afr.	238c	25°11′S	28°52′E
El Arahal, Spain (ĕl ä-rä-äl′)	172	37°17′N	5°32′W
El Arba, Alg.	173	36°35′N	3°10′E
Elat, Isr.	198	29°34′N	34°57′E
Elazığ, Tur. (ĕl-ä′zėz)	198	38°40′N	39°00′E
Elba, Al., U.S. (ĕl′bȧ)	124	31°25′N	86°01′W
Elba, Isola d', i., Italy (ė-sō lä-d-ĕl′bȧ)	162	42°42′N	10°25′E
El Banco, Col. (ĕl băn′cȯ)	142	8°58′N	74°01′W
Elbansan, Alb. (ĕl-bä-sän′)	163	41°08′N	20°05′E
Elbe (Labe), r., Eur. (ĕl′bĕ)(lä′bĕ)	156	52°30′N	11°30′E
Elbert, Mount, mtn., Co., U.S. (ĕl′bērt)	106	39°05′N	106°25′W
Elberton, Ga., U.S. (ĕl′bēr-tŭn)	125	34°05′N	82°53′W
Elbeuf, Fr. (ĕl-bûf′)	161	49°16′N	0°59′E
El Beyadh, Alg.	162	33°42′N	1°06′E
Elbistan, Tur. (ēl-bē-stän′)	163	38°20′N	37°10′E
Elblag, Pol. (ĕl′bläŋg)	160	54°11′N	19°25′E
El Bonillo, Spain (ĕl bō-nēl′yȯ)	172	38°56′N	2°31′W
El Boulaïda, Alg.	230	36°33′N	2°45′E
Elbow, r., Can. (ĕl′bō)	102e	51°03′N	114°24′W

PLACE (Pronunciation)	PAGE	LAT.	LONG.
Elbow Cay, i., Bah.	134	26°25′N	76°55′W
Elbow Lake, Mn., U.S.	112	46°00′N	95°59′W
El′brus, Gora, mtn., Russia (ĕl′brȯs′)	178	43°20′N	42°25′E
Elbrus, Mount *see* El′brus, Gora, mtn., Russia	178	43°20′N	42°25′E
Elburz Mountains, mts., Iran (ĕl′bȯrz′)	198	36°30′N	51°00′E
El Cajon, Col. (ĕl-kä-kô′n)	142a	4°50′N	76°35′W
El Cajon, Ca., U.S.	118a	32°48′N	116°58′W
El Cambur, Ven. (käm-bo͞or′)	143b	10°24′N	68°06′W
El Campo, Tx., U.S. (kăm′pō)	123	29°13′N	96°17′W
El Carmen, Chile (kȧ′r-mĕn)	141b	34°14′S	71°23′W
El Carmen, Col. (kȧ′r-mĕn)	142	9°54′N	75°12′W
El Casco, Ca., U.S. (kăs′kȯ)	117a	33°59′N	117°08′W
El Centro, Ca., U.S. (sĕn′trȯ)	118	32°47′N	115°33′W
El Cerrito, Ca., U.S. (sĕr-rē′tō)	116b	37°55′N	122°19′W
El Cuyo, Mex.	132a	21°30′N	87°42′W
Elda, Spain (ĕl′dä)	173	38°28′N	0°44′W
El Djelfa, Alg.	230	34°40′N	3°17′E
El Djouf, des., Afr. (ĕl djo͞of)	230	21°45′N	7°05′W
Eldon, Ia., U.S. (ĕl-dŭn)	113	40°55′N	92°15′W
Eldon, Mo., U.S.	121	38°21′N	92°36′W
Eldora, Ia., U.S. (ĕl-dō′rȧ)	113	42°21′N	93°08′W
El Dorado, Ar., U.S. (ĕl dȯ-rä′dō)	105	33°13′N	92°39′W
Eldorado, Il., U.S.	108	37°50′N	88°30′W
El Dorado, Ks., U.S.	121	37°49′N	96°51′W
Eldorado Springs, Mo., U.S. (sprĭngz)	121	37°51′N	94°02′W
Eldoret, Kenya (ĕl-dȯ-rĕt′)	237	0°31′N	35°17′E
El Ebano, Mex. (ā-bä′nō)	130	22°13′N	98°26′W
Electra, Tx., U.S. (ė-lĕk′trȧ)	120	34°02′N	98°54′W
Electric Peak, mtn., Mt., U.S. (ė-lĕk′trĭk)	115	45°03′N	110°52′W
Elek, r.	181	51°20′N	53°10′E
Elektrogorsk, Russia (ĕl-yĕk′trô-gôrsk)	186b	55°53′N	38°48′E
Elektrostal′, Russia (ĕl-yĕk′trō-stál)	186b	55°47′N	38°27′E
Elektrougli, Russia	186b	55°43′N	38°13′E
Elephant Butte Reservoir, res., N.M., U.S. (ĕl′ė-fănt būt)	106	33°25′N	107°10′W
El Escorial, Spain (ĕl-ĕs-kȯ-ryä′l)	173a	40°38′N	4°08′W
El Espino, Nic. (ĕl-ĕs-pē′nŏ)	132	13°26′N	86°48′W
Eleuthera, i., Bah. (ė-lū′thēr-ȧ)	129	25°05′N	76°10′W
Eleuthera Point, c., Bah.	134	24°35′N	76°05′W
Eleven Point, r., Mo., U.S. (ė-lĕv′ĕn)	121	36°53′N	91°39′W
Elgin, Scot., U.K.	164	57°40′N	3°30′W
Elgin, Il., U.S. (ĕl′jĭn)	111a	42°03′N	88°16′W
Elgin, Ne., U.S.	112	41°58′N	98°04′W
Elgin, Or., U.S.	114	45°34′N	117°58′W
Elgin, Tx., U.S.	123	30°21′N	97°22′W
Elgin, Wa., U.S.	116a	47°23′N	122°42′W
Elgon, Mount, mtn., Afr. (ĕl′gŏn)	231	1°00′N	34°25′E
El Grara, Alg.	162	32°50′N	4°26′E
El Grullo, Mex. (gro͞ol-yȯ)	130	19°46′N	104°10′W
El Guapo, Ven. (gwȧ′pȯ)	143b	10°07′N	66°00′W
El Hank, reg., Afr.	230	23°44′N	6°45′W
El Hatillo, Ven. (ä-tē′l-yȯ)	143b	10°08′N	65°13′W
Elie, Can. (ē′lē)	102f	49°55′N	97°45′W
Elila, r., D.R.C. (ĕ-lē′lȧ)	232	3°30′S	28°00′E
Elisa, i., Wa., U.S. (ė-lĭ′sȧ)	116d	48°43′N	122°37′W
Élisabethville *see* Lubumbashi, D.R.C.	232	11°40′S	27°28′E
Elisenvaara, Russia (ā-lē′sĕn-vä′rȧ)	167	61°25′N	29°46′E
Elizabeth, La., U.S. (ė-lĭz′ȧ-bĕth)	123	30°50′N	92°47′W
Elizabeth, N.J., U.S.	110a	40°40′N	74°13′W
Elizabeth, Pa., U.S.	111e	40°16′N	79°53′W
Elizabeth City, N.C., U.S.	125	36°15′N	76°15′W
Elizabethton, Tn., U.S. (ė-lĭz-ȧ-bĕth′tŭn)	125	36°19′N	82°12′W
Elizabethtown, Ky., U.S. (ė-lĭz′ă-bĕth-toun)	108	37°40′N	85°55′W
El Jadida, Mor.	230	33°14′N	8°34′W
Elk, Pol.	160	53°53′N	22°23′E
Elk, r., Can.	95	50°00′N	115°00′W
Elk, r., Tn., U.S.	124	35°05′N	86°36′W
Elk, r., W.V., U.S.	108	38°30′N	81°05′W
El Kairouan, Tun. (kĕr-ȯ-än)	230	35°46′N	10°04′E
Elk City, Ok., U.S. (ĕlk)	120	35°23′N	99°23′W
El Kef, Tun. (xĕf′)	162	36°14′N	8°42′E
Elkhart, In., U.S. (ĕlk′härt)	108	41°40′N	86°00′W
Elkhart, Ks., U.S.	120	37°00′N	101°54′W
Elkhart, Tx., U.S.	123	31°38′N	95°35′W
Elkhorn, Wi., U.S. (ĕlk′hôrn)	113	42°39′N	88°32′W
Elkhorn, r., Ne., U.S.	112	42°06′N	97°46′W
Elkin, N.C., U.S. (ĕl′kĭn)	125	36°15′N	80°50′W
Elk Island, i., Can.	97	50°45′N	96°32′W
Elk Island National Park, rec., Can. (ĕlk ī′lănd)	92	53°37′N	112°45′W
Elko, Nv., U.S. (ĕl′kō)	104	40°51′N	115°46′W
Elk Point, S.D., U.S.	112	42°41′N	96°41′W
Elk Rapids, Mi., U.S. (răp′ĭdz)	108	44°55′N	85°25′W
Elk River, Id., U.S. (rĭv′ẽr)	114	46°47′N	116°11′W
Elk River, Mn., U.S.	113	45°17′N	93°33′W
Elkton, Ky., U.S. (ĕlk′tŭn)	124	36°47′N	87°08′W
Elkton, Md., U.S.	109	39°35′N	75°50′W
Elkton, S.D., U.S.	112	44°15′N	96°28′W
Elland, Eng., U.K. (el′ănd)	158a	53°41′N	1°50′W
Ellen, Mount, mtn., Ut., U.S. (ĕl′ĕn)	119	38°05′N	110°50′W
Ellendale, N.D., U.S. (ĕl′ĕn-dāl)	112	46°01′N	98°33′W
Ellensburg, Wa., U.S. (ĕl′ĕnz-bûrg)	114	47°00′N	120°31′W
Ellenville, N.Y., U.S. (ĕl′ĕn-vĭl)	109	41°40′N	74°25′W
Ellerslie, Can. (ĕl′ẽrz-lė)	102g	53°25′N	113°30′W
Ellesmere, Eng., U.K. (ĕlz′mēr)	158a	52°55′N	2°54′W
Ellesmere Island, i., Can.	89	81°00′N	80°00′W
Ellesmere Port, Eng., U.K.	158a	53°17′N	2°54′W
Ellice Islands *see* Tuvalu, nation, Oc.	3	5°20′S	174°00′E

ăt; finăl; rāte; senåte; ärm; åsk; sofȧ; fâre; ch-choose; dh-as th in other; bē; ėvent; bĕt; recĕnt; cratẽr; g-gō; gh-guttural g; bĭt; ĭ-short neutral; rīde; ĸ-guttural k as ch in German ich;

PRONOUNCING INDEX

Ellicott City – Estarreja 291

PLACE (Pronunciation)	PAGE	LAT.	LONG.
Ellicott City, is., Md., U.S. (ĕl'ĭ-kŏt sĭ'tē)	110e	39°16'N	76°48'W
Ellicott Creek, r., N.Y., U.S.	111c	43°00'N	78°46'W
Elliot, S. Afr.	233c	31°19'S	27°52'E
Elliot, Wa., U.S. (el'ĭ-ŭt)	116a	47°28'N	122°08'W
Elliotdale, S. Afr. (ĕl-ĭ-ŏt'dāl)	233c	31°58'S	28°42'E
Elliot Lake, Can.	98	46°23'N	82°39'W
Ellis, Ks., U.S. (ĕl'ĭs)	120	38°56'N	99°34'W
Ellisville, Mo., U.S.	117e	38°35'N	90°35'W
Ellisville, Ms., U.S. (ĕl'ĭs-vĭl)	124	31°37'N	89°10'W
Ellsworth, Ks., U.S. (ĕlz'wûrth)	120	38°43'N	98°14'W
Ellsworth, Me., U.S.	100	44°33'N	68°26'W
Ellsworth Mountains, mts., Ant.	224	77°00'S	90°00'W
Ellwangen, Ger. (ĕl'väŋ-gĕn)	168	48°47'N	10°08'E
Elm, Ger. (ĕlm)	159c	53°31'N	9°13'E
Elm, r., S.D., U.S.	112	45°47'N	98°28'W
Elm, r., W.V., U.S.	108	38°30'N	81°05'W
Elma, Wa., U.S. (ĕl'mȧ)	114	47°02'N	123°20'W
El Mahdia, Tun. (mä-dēȧ)(mä'dē-ȧ)	162	35°30'N	11°09'E
Elmendorf, Tx., U.S. (ĕl'mĕn-dôrf)	117d	29°16'N	98°20'W
El Menia, Alg.	230	30°39'N	2°52'E
Elm Fork, Tx., U.S. (ĕlm fôrk)	117c	32°55'N	96°56'W
Elmhurst, Il., U.S. (ĕlm'hûrst)	111a	41°54'N	87°56'W
El Miliyya, Alg. (mē'ä)	230	36°30'N	6°16'E
Elmira, N.Y., U.S. (ĕl-mī'rȧ)	109	42°05'N	76°50'W
Elmira Heights, N.Y., U.S.	109	42°10'N	76°50'W
El Modena, Ca., U.S. (mô-dē'nô)	117a	33°47'N	117°48'W
El Mohammadia, Alg.	173	35°35'N	0°05'E
El Monte, Ca., U.S. (mōn'tȧ)	117a	34°04'N	118°02'W
El Morro National Monument, rec., N.M., U.S.	119	35°05'N	108°20'W
Elmshorn, Ger. (ĕlms'hôrn)	168	53°45'N	9°39'E
Elmwood Place, Oh., U.S. (ĕlm'wŏŏd plās)	111f	39°11'N	84°30'W
Elokomin, r., Wa., U.S. (ē-lō'kō-mĭn)	116c	46°16'N	123°16'W
El Oro, Mex. (ô-rô)	130	19°49'N	100°04'W
El Pao, Ven. (ĕl pá'ō)	142	8°08'N	62°37'W
El Paraíso, Hond. (pä-rä-ē'sō)	132	13°55'N	86°35'W
El Pardo, Spain (pä'r-dô)	173a	40°31'N	3°47'W
El Paso, Tx., U.S. (pas'ō)	104	31°47'N	106°27'W
El Pilar, Ven. (pē-lä'r)	143b	9°56'N	64°48'W
El Porvenir, Pan. (pôr-vä-nēr')	133	9°34'N	78°55'W
El Puerto de Santa María, Spain	172	36°36'N	6°18'W
El Qala, Alg.	162	36°52'N	8°23'E
El Qoll, Alg.	230	37°02'N	6°29'E
El Real, Pan. (rā-äl)	133	8°07'N	77°43'W
El Reno, Ok., U.S. (rē'nō)	121	35°31'N	97°57'W
Elroy, Wi., U.S. (ĕl'roi)	113	43°44'N	90°17'W
Elsa, Can.	103	63°55'N	135°25'W
Elsah, Il., U.S. (ĕl'zȧ)	117e	38°57'N	90°22'W
El Salto, Mex. (säl'tō)	130	23°48'N	105°22'W
El Salvador, nation, N.A.	128	14°00'N	89°30'W
El Sauce, Nic. (ĕl-sá'ō-sĕ)	132	13°00'N	86°40'W
Elsberry, Mo., U.S. (ĕlz'bĕr-ĭ)	121	39°09'N	90°44'W
Elsdorf, Ger. (ĕls'dōrf)	171c	50°56'N	6°35'E
El Segundo, Ca., U.S. (sĕgŭn'dō)	117a	33°55'N	118°24'W
Elsinore, Ca., U.S. (ĕl'sĭ-nôr)	117a	33°40'N	117°19'W
Elsinore Lake, l., Ca., U.S.	117a	33°38'N	117°21'W
Elstorf, Ger. (ĕls'tōrf)	159c	53°25'N	9°48'E
Eltham, Austl. (ĕl'thăm)	217a	37°43'S	145°08'E
El Tigre, Ven. (tē'grĕ)	142	8°49'N	64°15'W
El'ton, l., Russia	181	49°10'N	47°00'E
El Toro, Ca., U.S. (tō'rō)	117a	33°37'N	117°42'W
El Triunfo, El Sal.	132	13°17'N	88°32'W
El Triunfo, Hond. (ĕl-trē-ōō'n-fō)	132	13°06'N	87°00'W
Elūru, India	199	16°44'N	80°09'E
El Vado Res, N.M., U.S.	119	36°37'N	106°30'W
Elvas, Port. (ĕl'väzh)	162	38°53'N	7°11'W
Elverum, Nor. (ĕl'vĕ-rŏŏm)	166	60°53'N	11°33'E
El Viejo, Nic. (ĕl-vyĕ'kŏ)	132	12°10'N	87°10'W
El Viejo, vol., Nic.	132	12°44'N	87°03'W
Elvins, Mo., U.S. (ĕl'vĭnz)	121	37°49'N	90°31'W
El Wad, Alg.	230	33°23'N	6°49'E
El Wak, Kenya (wäk')	231	3°00'N	41°00'E
Elwell, Lake, res., Mt., U.S.	115	48°22'N	111°17'W
Elwood, Il., U.S. (ĕ'wŏŏd)	111a	41°24'N	88°07'W
Elwood, In., U.S.	108	40°15'N	85°50'W
Elx, Spain	173	38°15'N	0°42'W
Ely, Eng., U.K. (ē'lĭ)	165	52°25'N	0°17'E
Ely, Mn., U.S.	113	47°54'N	91°53'W
Ely, Nv., U.S.	104	39°16'N	114°53'W
Elyria, Oh., U.S. (ē-lĭr'ĭ-ȧ)	111d	41°22'N	82°07'W
Ema, r., Est. (ā'mȧ)	167	58°25'N	27°00'E
Emāmshahr, Iran	198	36°25'N	55°01'E
Emån, r., Swe.	166	57°15'N	15°46'E
Embarrass, r., Il., U.S. (ĕm-băr'ăs)	108	39°15'N	88°05'W
Embrun, Can. (ĕm'brŭn)	102c	45°16'N	75°17'W
Embrun, Fr. (äN-brûN')	171	44°35'N	6°32'E
Embu, Kenya	237	0°32'S	37°27'E
Emden, Ger. (ĕm'dĕn)	168	53°21'N	7°15'E
Emerson, Can. (ĕm'ĕr-sŭn)	90	49°00'N	97°12'W
Emeryville, Ca., U.S. (ĕm'ĕr-ĭ-vĭl)	116b	37°50'N	122°17'W
Emi Koussi, mtn., Chad (ā'mē kōō-sē')	231	19°50'N	18°30'E
Emiliano Zapata, Mex. (ĕ-mē-lyá'nō-zä-pá'tä)	131	17°45'N	91°46'W
Emilia-Romagna, hist. reg., Italy (ĕ-mēl'yä rô-mä'n-yä)	174	44°35'N	10°48'E
Eminence, Ky., U.S. (ĕm'ĭ-nĕns)	108	38°25'N	85°15'W
Emira Island, i., Pap. N. Gui. (ā-mē-rä')	213	1°40'S	150°28'E
Emmen, Neth. (ĕm'ĕn)	165	52°48'N	6°55'E
Emmerich, Ger. (ĕm'ĕr-ĭk)	171c	51°51'N	6°16'E
Emmetsburg, Ia., U.S. (ĕm'ĕts-bûrg)	113	43°07'N	94°41'W
Emmett, Id., U.S. (ĕm'ĕt)	114	43°53'N	116°30'W
Emmons, Mount, mtn., Ut., U.S. (ĕm'ŭnz)	106	40°43'N	110°20'W
Emory Peak, mtn., Tx., U.S. (ĕ'mō-rē pēk)	122	29°13'N	103°20'W
Empoli, Italy (ām'pō-lē)	174	43°43'N	10°55'E
Emporia, Ks., U.S. (ĕm-pō'rĭ-ȧ)	104	38°24'N	96°11'W
Emporia, Va., U.S.	125	37°40'N	77°34'W
Emporium, Pa., U.S. (ĕm-pō'rĭ-ŭm)	109	41°30'N	78°15'W
Empty Quarter *see* Ar Rub'al Khālī, des., Asia	198	20°00'N	51°00'E
Ems, r., Ger. (ĕms)	168	52°52'N	7°16'E
Ems-Weser Kanal, can., Ger.	168	52°23'N	8°11'E
Enånger, Swe. (ĕn-ôŋ'gĕr)	166	61°36'N	16°55'E
Encantada, Cerro de la, mtn., Mex. (sĕ'r-rô-dĕ-lä-ĕn-kän-tä'dä)	128	31°58'N	115°15'W
Encanto, Cape, c., Phil. (ĕn-kän'tō)	213a	15°44'N	121°46'E
Encarnación, Para. (ĕn-kär-nä-syōn')	144	27°26'S	55°52'W
Encarnación de Díaz, Mex. (ĕn-kär-nä-syōn dā dē'áz)	130	21°34'N	102°15'W
Encinal, Tx., U.S. (ĕn'sĭ-nôl)	122	28°02'N	99°22'W
Encontrados, Ven. (ĕn-kōn-trä'dōs)	142	9°01'N	72°10'W
Encounter Bay, b., Austl. (ĕn-koun'tĕr)	220	35°50'S	138°45'E
Endako, r., Can.	94	54°05'N	125°30'W
Endau, r., Malay.	197b	2°29'N	103°40'E
Enderbury, i., Kir. (ĕn'dĕr-bûrĭ)	240	2°00'S	171°00'W
Enderby Land, reg., Ant. (ĕn'dĕr bĭ)	224	72°00'S	52°00'E
Enderlin, N.D., U.S. (ĕn'dĕr-lĭn)	112	46°38'N	97°37'W
Endicott, N.Y., U.S. (ĕn'dĭ-kŏt)	109	42°05'N	76°00'W
Endicott Mountains, mts., Ak., U.S.	103	67°30'N	153°45'W
Enez, Tur.	175	40°42'N	26°05'E
Enfer, Pointe d', c., Mart.	133b	14°21'N	60°48'W
Enfield, Eng., U.K.	158b	51°38'N	0°06'W
Enfield, Ct., U.S. (ĕn'fēld)	109	41°55'N	72°35'W
Enfield, N.C., U.S.	125	36°10'N	77°41'W
Engaño, Cabo, c., Dom. Rep. (ká'-bô- ĕn-gä-nô)	129	18°40'N	68°30'W
Engcobo, S. Afr. (ĕŋg-cô-bô)	233c	31°41'S	27°59'E
Engel's, Russia (ĕn'gĕls)	181	51°20'N	45°40'E
Engelskirchen, Ger. (ĕn'gĕls-kĕr'kĕn)	171c	50°59'N	7°25'E
Enggano, Pulau, i., Indon. (ĕng-gä'nō)	212	5°22'S	102°18'E
England, Ar., U.S. (ĭŋ'glănd)	121	34°33'N	91°58'W
England, state, U.K. (ĭŋ'glănd)	154	51°35'N	1°40'W
Englewood, Co., U.S. (ĕn'g'l-wŏŏd)	120	39°39'N	105°00'W
Englewood, N.J., U.S.	110a	40°54'N	73°59'W
English, In., U.S. (ĭn'glĭsh)	108	38°15'N	86°25'W
English, r., Can.	93	50°31'N	94°12'W
English Channel, strt., Eur.	156	49°45'N	3°06'W
Énguera, Spain (ān'gārä)	173	38°58'N	0°42'W
Enid, Ok., U.S. (ē'nĭd)	104	36°25'N	97°52'W
Enid Lake, res., Ms., U.S.	124	34°13'N	89°47'W
Enkeldoring, S. Afr. (ĕŋ'k'l-dôr-ĭng)	238c	25°24'S	28°43'E
Enköping, Swe. (ĕn'kû-pĭng)	166	59°39'N	17°05'E
Ennedi, mts., Chad (ĕn-nĕd'ē)	231	16°45'N	22°45'E
Ennis, Ire. (ĕn'ĭs)	164	52°54'N	9°05'W
Ennis, Tx., U.S.	123	32°20'N	96°38'W
Enniscorthy, Ire. (ĕn-ĭs-kôr'thĭ)	164	52°33'N	6°27'W
Enniskillen, N. Ire., U.K. (ĕn-ĭs-kĭl'ĕn)	164	54°20'N	7°25'W
Ennis Lake, res., Mt., U.S.	115	45°15'N	111°30'W
Enns, r., Aus. (ĕns)	161	47°37'N	14°35'E
Enoree, S.C., U.S. (ē-nō'rē)	125	34°43'N	81°58'W
Enoree, r., S.C., U.S.	125	34°35'N	81°55'W
Enriquillo, Dom. Rep. (ĕn-rē-kē'l-yō)	135	17°55'N	71°15'W
Enriquillo, Lago, l., Dom. Rep. (lä'gô-ĕn-rē-kē'l-yô)	135	18°35'N	71°35'W
Enschede, Neth. (ĕns'kā-dĕ)	161	52°10'N	6°50'E
Enseñada, Arg.	141c	34°50'S	57°55'W
Ensenada, Mex. (ĕn-sĕ-nä'dä)	128	32°00'N	116°30'W
Enshi, China (ŭn-shr)	204	30°18'N	109°25'E
Enshū-Nada, b., Japan (ĕn'shōō nä-dä)	211	34°25'N	137°14'E
Entebbe, Ug.	231	0°04'N	32°28'E
Enterprise, Al., U.S. (ĕn'tĕr-prīz)	124	31°20'N	85°50'W
Enterprise, Or., U.S.	114	45°25'N	117°16'W
Entiat, L, Wa., U.S.	114	45°43'N	120°11'W
Entraygues, Fr. (ĕN-trĕg')	170	44°39'N	2°33'E
Entre Rios, prov., Arg.	144	31°30'S	59°00'W
Enugu, Nig. (ĕ-nōō'gōō)	230	6°27'N	7°27'E
Enumclaw, Wa., U.S. (ĕn'ŭm-klô)	116a	47°12'N	121°59'W
Envigado, Col. (ĕn-vē-gá'dō)	142a	6°10'N	75°34'W
Eolie, Isole, is., Italy (ĕ-ō'-lē-ĕ-ō'lyĕ)	162	38°43'N	14°43'E
Epe, Nig.	235	6°37'N	3°59'E
Épernay, Fr. (ā-pĕr-nĕ')	161	49°02'N	3°54'E
Épernon, Fr. (ā-pĕr-nôN')	171b	48°36'N	1°41'E
Ephraim, Ut., U.S. (ē'frā-ĭm)	119	39°20'N	111°40'W
Ephrata, Wa., U.S. (ĕfrā'tȧ)	114	47°18'N	119°35'W
Epi, Vanuatu (ā'pē)	219	16°59'S	168°29'E
Épila, Spain (ā'pē-lä)	172	41°38'N	1°15'W
Épinal, Fr. (ā-pē-nàl')	161	48°11'N	6°27'E
Episkopi, Cyp.	197a	34°38'N	32°55'E
Epping, Eng., U.K. (ĕp'ĭng)	158b	51°41'N	0°06'E
Epsom, Eng., U.K.	158b	51°20'N	0°16'W
Epupa Falls, wtfl., Afr.	236	17°00'S	13°05'E
Epworth, Eng., U.K. (ĕp'wûrth)	158a	53°31'N	0°50'W
Equatorial Guinea, nation, Afr.	230	2°00'N	7°15'E
Équilles, Fr.	170a	43°34'N	5°21'E
Eramosa, r., Can. (ĕr-ȧ-mō'sȧ)	102d	43°39'N	80°08'W
Erba, Jabal, mtn., Sudan (ĕr-bȧ)	231	20°53'N	36°45'E
Erciyeş Dağı, mtn., Tur.	163	38°30'N	35°36'E
Erding, Ger. (ĕr'dĕng)	159d	48°19'N	11°54'E
Erechim, Braz. (ĕ-rĕ-shē'N)	144	27°43'S	52°11'W
Ereğli, Tur. (ĕ-rå'ĭ-le)	163	37°40'N	34°00'E
Ereğli, Tur.	163	41°15'N	31°25'E
Erfurt, Ger. (ĕr'fŏŏrt)	161	50°59'N	11°04'E
Ergene, r., Tur. (ĕr'gĕ-nĕ)	175	41°17'N	26°50'E
Erges, r., Eur. (ĕr'-zhĕs)	172	39°45'N	7°01'W
Ergli, Lat.	167	56°54'N	25°38'E
Eria, r., Spain (ā-rē'ä)	172	42°10'N	6°08'W
Erick, Ok., U.S. (âr'ĭk)	120	35°14'N	99°51'W
Erie, Ks., U.S. (ē'rĭ)	121	37°35'N	95°17'W
Erie, Pa., U.S.	105	42°05'N	80°05'W
Erie, Lake, l., N.A.	107	42°15'N	81°25'W
Erimo Saki, c., Japan (ā'rē-mō sä-kē)	205	41°53'N	143°20'E
Erin, Can. (ĕ'rĭn)	102d	43°46'N	80°04'W
Eritrea, nation, Afr. (ā-rē-trā'ȧ)	231	16°15'N	38°30'E
Erlangen, Ger. (ĕr'läng-ĕn)	168	49°36'N	11°03'E
Erlanger, Ky., U.S. (ĕr'lăng-ĕr)	111f	39°01'N	84°36'W
Ermoúpoli, Grc.	175	37°30'N	24°56'E
Ernākulam, India	199	9°58'N	76°23'E
Erne, Lower Lough, l., N. Ire., U.K.	164	54°30'N	7°40'W
Erne, Upper Lough, l., N. Ire., U.K. (lŏk ûrn)	164	54°20'N	7°24'W
Erode, India	203	11°20'N	77°45'E
Eromanga, i., Vanuatu	221	18°58'S	169°18'E
Eros, La., U.S. (ē'rōs)	123	32°23'N	92°22'W
Errego, Moz.	237	16°02'S	37°14'E
Errigal, mtn., Ire. (ĕr-ĭ-gôl')	164	55°02'N	8°07'W
Errol Heights, Or., U.S.	116c	45°29'N	122°38'W
Erstein, Fr. (ĕr'shtīn)	171	48°27'N	7°40'E
Erwin, N.C., U.S. (ûr'wĭn)	125	35°16'N	78°40'W
Erwin, Tn., U.S.	125	36°07'N	82°25'W
Erzgebirge, mts., Eur. (ĕrts'gĕ-bē'gĕ)	156	50°29'N	12°40'E
Erzincan, Tur. (ĕr-zĭn-jän')	198	39°50'N	39°30'E
Erzurum, Tur. (ĕrz'rōōm')	198	39°55'N	41°10'E
Esambo, D.R.C.	236	3°40'S	23°24'E
Esashi, Japan (ĕs'ä-shē)	205	41°50'N	140°10'E
Esbjerg, Den. (ĕs'byĕrgh)	160	55°29'N	8°25'E
Escalante, Ut., U.S. (ĕs-kȧ-lăn'tē)	119	37°50'N	111°40'W
Escalante, r., Ut., U.S.	119	37°40'N	111°20'W
Escalón, Mex.	122	26°45'N	104°20'W
Escambia, r., Fl., U.S. (ĕs-kăm'bĭ-ȧ)	124	30°38'N	87°20'W
Escanaba, Mi., U.S. (ĕs-kȧ-nô'bȧ)	105	45°44'N	87°05'W
Escanaba, r., Mi., U.S.	113	46°10'N	87°22'W
Escarpada Point, Phil.	212	18°40'N	122°45'E
Esch-sur-Alzette, Lux.	171	49°32'N	6°21'E
Eschwege, Ger. (ĕsh'vā-gē)	168	51°11'N	10°02'E
Eschweiler, Ger. (ĕsh'vī-lĕr)	171c	50°49'N	6°15'E
Escondido, Ca., U.S. (ĕs-kŏn-dē'dō)	118	33°07'N	117°00'W
Escondido, r., Nic.	133	12°04'N	84°09'W
Escondido, Río, r., Mex. (rē'ō-ĕs-kōn-dē'dô)	122	28°30'N	100°45'W
Escudo de Veraguas, i., Pan. (ĕs-kōō'dä dā vä-rä'gwäs)	133	9°07'N	81°25'W
Escuinapa, Mex. (ĕs-kwē-nä'pä)	128	22°49'N	105°44'W
Escuintla, Guat. (ĕs-kwēn'tlä)	132	14°16'N	90°47'W
Ese, Cayos de, i., Col.	133	12°24'N	81°07'W
Eşfahān, Iran	198	32°38'N	51°30'E
Esgueva, r., Spain (ĕs-gĕ'vä)	172	41°48'N	4°10'W
Esher, Eng., U.K.	158b	51°23'N	0°22'W
Eshowe, S. Afr. (ĕsh'ō-wē)	233c	28°54'S	31°28'E
Esiama, Ghana	234	4°56'N	2°21'W
Eskdale, W.V., U.S. (ĕsk'dāl)	108	38°05'N	81°25'W
Eskifjördur, Ice. (ĕs'kē-fyûr'dōōr)	154	65°04'N	14°01'W
Eskilstuna, Swe. (å'shĕl-stü-na)	160	59°23'N	16°28'E
Eskimo Lakes, l., Can. (es'kĭ-mō)	92	69°40'N	130°10'W
Eskişehir, Tur. (ĕs-kē-shĕ'h'r)	198	39°40'N	30°20'E
Esko, Mn., U.S. (ĕs'kō)	117h	46°27'N	92°22'W
Esla, r., Spain (ĕs-lä)	172	41°50'N	5°48'W
Eslöv, Swe. (ĕs'lûv)	166	55°50'N	13°17'E
Esmeraldas, Ec. (ĕs-mā-räl'däs)	142	0°58'N	79°45'W
Espanola, Can. (ĕs-pȧ-nō'lȧ)	91	46°11'N	81°59'W
Esparta, C.R. (ĕs-pär'tä)	133	9°59'N	84°40'W
Esperance, Austl. (ĕs'pē-răns)	218	33°45'S	122°07'E
Esperanza, Cuba (ĕs-pĕ-rä'n-zä)	134	22°30'N	80°10'W
Espichel, Cabo, c., Port. (ká'bō-ĕs-pē-shĕl')	172	38°25'N	9°13'W
Espinal, Col. (ĕs-pē-näl')	142	4°10'N	74°53'W
Espinhaço, Serra do, mts., Braz. (sĕ'r-rä-dô-ĕs-pē-ná-sŏ)	143	16°00'S	44°00'W
Espinillo, Punta, c., Ur. (pōō'n-tä-ĕs-pē-nē'l-yō)	141c	34°49'S	56°27'W
Espírito Santo, Braz. (ĕs-pē'rē-tô-sän'tō)	143	20°27'S	40°18'W
Espírito Santo, state, Braz.	143	19°57'S	40°58'W
Espiritu Santo, i., Vanuatu (ĕs-pē'rē-tōō sän'tō)	221	15°45'S	166°50'E
Espíritu Santo, Bahía del, b., Mex.	132a	19°25'N	87°28'W
Espita, Mex. (ĕs-pē'tä)	132a	20°57'N	88°22'W
Espoo, Fin.	167	60°13'N	24°41'E
Es Port de Pollença, Spain	173	39°50'N	3°00'E
Esposende, Port. (ĕs-pō-zĕn'dā)	172	41°33'N	8°45'W
Esquel, Arg. (ĕs-kĕ'l)	144	42°47'S	71°22'W
Esquimalt, Can. (ĕs-kwī'mŏlt)	94	48°26'N	123°24'W
Essaouira, Mor.	230	31°34'N	9°44'W
Essen, Bel.	159a	51°28'N	4°27'E
Essen, Ger. (ĕs'sĕn)	154	51°26'N	6°59'E
Essendon, Austl.	217a	37°46'S	144°55'E
Essequibo, r., Guy. (ĕs-ā-kē'bō)	143	4°26'N	58°17'W
Essex, Il., U.S.	111a	41°11'N	88°11'W
Essex, Ma., U.S.	101a	42°38'N	70°47'W
Essex, Md., U.S.	110e	39°19'N	76°29'W
Essex, Vt., U.S.	109	44°30'N	73°05'W
Essex Fells, N.J., U.S. (ĕs'ĕks fĕlz)	110a	40°50'N	74°16'W
Essexville, Mi., U.S. (ĕs'ĕks-vĭl)	108	43°35'N	83°50'W
Esslingen, Ger. (ĕs'slĕn-gĕn)	168	48°45'N	9°19'E
Estacado, Llano, pl., U.S. (yä-nō ĕs-tȧcȧ-dō')	106	33°50'N	103°20'W
Estância, Braz. (ĕs-tän'sĭ-ä)	143	11°17'S	37°18'W
Estarreja, Port. (ĕs-tär-rā'zhä)	172	40°44'N	8°39'W

ng-sing; ŋ-baŋk; N-nasalized n; nŏd; cŏmmit; ōld; ŏbey; ôrder; oi-boil; fōōd; ŏŏ-as oo in foot; ou-out; s-soft; sh-dish; th-thin; pūre; ŭnite; ûrn; stŭd; circŭs; ü-as in French tu; '-indeterminate vowel.

292 Estats – Felipe Carrillo Puerto

PRONOUNCING INDEX

PLACE (Pronunciation)	PAGE	LAT.	LONG.
Estats, Pique d', mtn., Eur.	173	42°43'N	1°30'E
Estcourt, S. Afr. (ĕst-coort)	233c	29°04'S	29°53'E
Este, Italy (ĕs'tā)	174	45°13'N	11°40'E
Estella, Spain (ĕs-tāl'yä)	172	42°40'N	2°01'W
Estepa, Spain (ĕs-tā'pä)	172	37°18'N	4°54'W
Estepona, Spain (ĕs-tå-pō'nä)	172	36°26'N	5°08'W
Esterhazy, Can. (ĕs'tĕr-hä-zē)	97	50°40'N	102°08'W
Estero Bay, b., Ca., U.S. (ĕs-tā'rōs)	118	35°22'N	121°04'W
Estevan, Can. (ĕ-stē'văn)	90	49°07'N	103°05'W
Estevan Group, is., Can.	94	53°05'N	129°40'W
Estherville, Ia., U.S. (ĕs'tĕr-vĭl)	113	43°24'N	94°49'W
Estill, S.C., U.S. (ĕs'tĭl)	125	32°46'N	81°15'W
Eston, Can.	96	51°10'N	108°45'W
Estonia, nation, Eur.	178	59°10'N	25°00'E
Estoril, Port. (ĕs-tô-rēl')	173b	38°45'N	9°24'W
Estrêla, mtn., Port. (mäl-you'n-dä-ĕs-trē'lä)	172	40°20'N	7°38'W
Estrêla, r., Braz. (ĕs-trē'lä)	144b	22°39'S	43°16'W
Estrêla, Serra da, mts., Port. (sĕr'rá dä ĕs-trā'lá)	172	40°25'N	7°45'W
Estremadura, hist. reg., Port. (ĕs-trā-mä-doo'rá)	172	39°00'N	8°36'W
Estremoz, Port. (ĕs-trā-mōzh')	172	38°50'N	7°35'W
Estrondo, Serra do, mts., Braz. (sĕr'-rá dó ĕs-trôn'-dó)	143	9°52'S	48°56'W
Esumba, Île, i., D.R.C.	236	2°00'N	21°12'E
Esztergom, Hung. (ĕs'tĕr-gōm)	169	47°46'N	18°45'E
Etah, Grnld. (ē'tá)	89	78°20'N	72°42'W
Étampes, Fr. (ā-täNp')	170	48°26'N	2°09'E
Étaples, Fr. (ā-täp'l')	170	50°32'N	1°38'E
Etchemin, r., Can. (ĕch'ĕ-mĭn)	102b	46°39'N	71°03'W
Ethiopia, nation, Afr. (ē-thē-ō'pē-à)	231	7°53'N	37°55'E
Eticoga, Gui.-B.	234	11°09'N	16°08'W
Etiwanda, Ca., U.S. (ĕ-tĭ-wän'dá)	117a	34°07'N	117°31'W
Etna, Pa., U.S. (ĕt'ná)	111e	40°30'N	79°55'W
Etna, Mount, vol., Italy	156	37°48'N	15°00'E
Etobicoke Creek, r., Can.	102d	43°44'N	79°48'W
Etolin Strait, strt., Ak., U.S. (ĕt ō lĭn)	103	60°35'S	165°40'W
Etoshapan, pl., Nmb. (ĕtō'shä)	232	19°07'S	15°30'E
Etowah, Tn., U.S. (ĕt'ō-wä)	124	35°18'N	84°31'W
Etowah, r., Ga., U.S.	124	34°23'N	84°19'W
Étréchy, Fr. (ā-trā-shē')	171b	48°29'N	2°12'E
Etten-Leur, Neth.	159a	51°34'N	4°38'E
Etterbeek, Bel. (ĕt'ĕr-bāk)	159a	50°51'N	4°24'E
Etzatlán, Mex. (ĕt-zä-tlän')	130	20°44'N	104°04'W
Eucla, Austl. (ū'klá)	218	31°45'S	128°50'E
Euclid, Oh., U.S. (ū'klĭd)	111d	41°34'N	81°32'W
Eudora, Ar., U.S. (u-dō'rá)	121	33°07'N	91°16'W
Eufaula, Al., U.S. (ů-fô'lá)	124	31°53'N	85°09'W
Eufaula, Ok., U.S.	121	35°16'N	95°35'W
Eufaula Reservoir, res., Ok., U.S.	121	35°00'N	94°45'W
Eugene, Or., U.S. (ů-jēn')	104	44°02'N	123°06'W
Euless, Tx., U.S. (ū'lĕs)	117c	32°50'N	97°05'W
Eunice, La., U.S. (ū'nĭs)	123	30°30'N	92°25'W
Eupen, Bel. (oi'pĕn)	165	50°39'N	6°05'E
Euphrates, r., Asia (ů-frā'tēz)	198	36°00'N	40°00'E
Eure, r., Fr. (ûr)	170	49°03'N	1°22'E
Eureka, Ca., U.S. (û-rē'ká)	104	40°45'N	124°10'W
Eureka, Ks., U.S.	121	37°48'N	96°17'W
Eureka, Mt., U.S.	114	48°53'N	115°07'W
Eureka, Nv., U.S.	118	39°33'N	115°58'W
Eureka, S.D., U.S.	112	45°46'N	99°38'W
Eureka, Ut., U.S.	119	39°55'N	112°10'W
Eureka Springs, Ar., U.S.	121	36°24'N	93°43'W
Europe, cont. (ū'rŭp)	156	50°00'N	15°00'E
Eustis, Fl., U.S. (ūs'tĭs)	125	28°50'N	81°41'W
Eutaw, Al., U.S. (ū-tå)	124	32°48'N	87°50'W
Eutsuk Lake, l., Can. (ōōt'sŭk)	94	53°20'N	126°44'W
Evanston, Il., U.S. (ĕv'ăn-stŭn)	105	42°03'N	87°41'W
Evanston, Wy., U.S.	115	41°17'N	111°02'W
Evansville, In., U.S. (ĕv'ănz-vĭl)	105	38°00'N	87°30'W
Evansville, Wi., U.S.	113	42°46'N	89°19'W
Evart, Mi., U.S. (ĕv'ĕrt)	108	43°55'N	85°10'W
Evaton, S. Afr. (ĕv'á-tŏn)	238c	26°32'S	27°53'E
Eveleth, Mn., U.S. (ĕv'ĕ-lĕth)	113	47°27'N	92°35'W
Everard, l., Austl. (ĕv'ĕr-ård)	220	31°20'S	134°10'E
Everard Ranges, mts., Austl.	220	27°15'S	132°00'E
Everest, Mount, mtn., Asia (ĕv'ĕr-ĕst)	199	28°00'N	86°57'E
Everett, Ma., U.S. (ĕv'ĕr-ĕt)	101a	42°24'N	71°03'W
Everett, Wa., U.S. (ĕv'ĕr-ĕt)	104	47°59'N	122°11'W
Everett Mountains, mts., Can.	93	62°34'N	68°00'W
Everglades, The, sw., Fl., U.S.	125a	25°35'N	80°55'W
Everglades City, Fl., U.S. (ĕv'ĕr-glădz)	125a	25°50'N	81°25'W
Everglades National Park, rec., Fl., U.S.	107	25°39'N	80°57'W
Evergreen, Al., U.S. (ĕv'ĕr-grēn)	124	31°25'N	87°56'W
Evergreen Park, Il., U.S.	111a	41°44'N	87°42'W
Everman, Tx., U.S. (ĕv'ĕr-măn)	117c	32°38'N	97°17'W
Everson, Wa., U.S. (ĕv'ĕr-sŭn)	116d	48°55'N	122°21'W
Évora, Port. (ĕv'ō-rä)	162	38°35'N	7°54'W
Évreux, Fr. (ā-vrû')	161	49°02'N	1°11'E
Evrótas, r., Grc. (ĕv-rō'tås)	175	37°15'N	22°17'E
Évvoia, i., Grc.	163	38°38'N	23°45'E
'Ewa Beach, Hi., U.S. (ē'wä)	126a	21°17'N	158°03'W
Ewaso Ng'iro, r., Kenya	231	0°59'N	37°47'E
Excelsior, Mn., U.S. (ĕk-sel'sĭ-ŏr)	117g	44°54'N	93°35'W
Excelsior Springs, Mo., U.S.	121	39°20'N	94°13'W
Exe, r., Eng., U.K. (ĕks)	164	50°57'N	3°37'W
Exeter, Eng., U.K.	161	50°45'N	3°33'W
Exeter, Ca., U.S. (ĕk'sē-tĕr)	118	36°18'N	119°09'W
Exeter, N.H., U.S.	109	43°00'N	71°00'W
Exmoor, for., Eng., U.K. (ĕks'mōr)	164	51°10'N	3°55'W
Exmouth, Eng., U.K. (ĕks'mŭth)	164	50°40'N	3°20'W
Exmouth Gulf, b., Austl.	220	21°45'S	114°30'E
Exploits, r., Can. (ĕks-ploits')	101	48°50'N	56°15'W
Extórrax, r., Mex. (ĕx-tó'ràx)	130	21°04'N	99°39'W
Extrema, Braz. (ĕsh-trĕ'mä)	141a	22°52'S	46°19'W
Extremadura, hist. reg., Spain (ĕks-trā-mä-doo'rä)	172	38°43'N	6°30'W
Exuma Sound, strt., Bah. (ĕk-sōō'mä)	134	24°20'N	76°20'W
Eyasi, Lake, l., Tan. (å-yä'sē)	232	3°25'S	34°55'E
Eyjafjördur, b., Ice.	160	66°21'N	18°20'W
Eyl, Som.	238a	7°53'N	49°45'E
Eyrarbakki, Ice.	160	63°51'N	20°52'W
Eyre, Austl. (âr)	218	32°15'S	126°20'E
Eyre, l., Austl.	220	28°43'S	137°50'E
Eyre Peninsula, pen., Austl.	220	33°30'S	136°00'E
Ezeiza, Arg. (ĕ-zā'zä)	144a	34°52'S	58°31'W
Ezine, Tur. (å'zĭ-nå)	175	39°47'N	26°18'E

F

PLACE (Pronunciation)	PAGE	LAT.	LONG.
Faaborg, Den. (fō'bôrg)	166	55°06'N	10°19'E
Fabens, Tx., U.S. (fā'bĕnz)	122	31°30'N	106°07'W
Fabriano, Italy (fä-brē-ä'nō)	174	43°20'N	12°55'E
Fada, Chad (fä'dä)	231	17°06'N	21°18'E
Fada Ngourma, Burkina (fä'dä''n gōōr'mä)	230	12°04'N	0°21'E
Faddeya, i., Russia (fád-yā')	179	76°12'N	145°00'E
Faenza, Italy (fä-ĕnd'zä)	174	44°16'N	11°53'E
Fafe, Port. (fä'fā)	172	41°30'N	8°10'W
Fafen, r., Eth.	238a	8°15'N	42°40'E
Făgăras, Rom. (fă-gă'răsh)	175	45°50'N	24°55'E
Fagerness, Nor. (fä'ghĕr-nĕs)	160	61°00'N	9°10'E
Fagnano, l., S.A. (fäk-nä'nō)	144	54°35'S	68°20'W
Faguibine, Lac, l., Mali	234	16°50'N	4°20'W
Faial, i., Port. (fä-yä'l)	230a	38°40'N	29°19'W
Fā'id, Egypt (fä-yēd')	238d	30°19'N	32°18'E
Fairbanks, Ak., U.S. (fâr'bănks)	106a	64°50'N	147°48'W
Fairbury, Il., U.S. (fâr'bĕr-ĭ)	108	40°45'N	88°25'W
Fairbury, Ne., U.S.	121	40°09'N	97°11'W
Fairchild Creek, r., Can. (fâr'chīld)	102d	43°18'N	80°10'W
Fairfax, Mn., U.S. (fâr'făks)	113	44°29'N	94°44'W
Fairfax, S.C., U.S.	125	32°29'N	81°13'W
Fairfax, Va., U.S.	110e	38°51'N	77°20'W
Fairfield, Austl.	217b	33°52'S	150°57'E
Fairfield, Al., U.S. (fâr'fēld)	110h	33°30'N	86°50'W
Fairfield, Ct., U.S.	110a	41°08'N	73°22'W
Fairfield, Ia., U.S.	113	41°00'N	91°59'W
Fairfield, Il., U.S.	108	38°25'N	88°20'W
Fairfield, Me., U.S.	100	44°35'N	69°38'W
Fairhaven, Ma., U.S. (fâr-hā'vĕn)	109	41°35'N	70°55'W
Fair Haven, Vt., U.S.	109	43°35'N	73°15'W
Fair Island, i., Scot., U.K. (fâr)	164a	59°34'N	1°41'W
Fairmont, Mn., U.S. (fâr'mŏnt)	113	43°39'N	94°26'W
Fairmont, W.V., U.S.	108	39°30'N	80°10'W
Fairmont City, Il., U.S.	117e	38°39'N	90°05'W
Fairmount, In., U.S.	108	40°25'N	85°45'W
Fairmount, Ks., U.S.	117f	39°12'N	95°55'W
Fair Oaks, Ga., U.S. (fâr ōks)	110c	33°56'N	84°33'W
Fairport, N.Y., U.S. (fâr'pōrt)	109	43°05'N	77°30'W
Fairport Harbor, Oh., U.S.	108	41°45'N	81°15'W
Fairview, Ok., U.S. (fâr'vū)	120	36°16'N	98°28'W
Fairview, Or., U.S.	116c	45°32'N	112°26'W
Fairview, Ut., U.S.	119	39°35'N	111°30'W
Fairview Park, Oh., U.S.	111d	41°27'N	81°52'W
Fairweather, Mount, mtn., N.A. (fâr-wĕdh'ĕr)	103	59°12'N	137°22'W
Faisalabad, Pak.	199	31°29'N	73°06'E
Faith, S.D., U.S. (fāth)	112	45°02'N	120°02'W
Faizābād, India	199	26°50'N	82°17'E
Fajardo, P.R.	129b	18°20'N	65°40'W
Fakfak, Indon.	213	2°56'S	132°25'E
Faku, China (fä-kōō)	208	42°28'N	123°20'E
Falcón, dept., Ven. (fäl-kō'n)	143b	11°00'N	68°28'W
Falconer, N.Y., U.S. (fô'k'n-ĕr)	109	42°10'N	79°10'W
Falcon Heights, Mn., U.S. (fô'k'n)	117g	44°59'N	93°10'W
Falcon Reservoir, res., N.A. (fôk'n)	122	26°47'N	99°03'W
Făleşti, Mol.	177	47°33'N	27°46'E
Falfurrias, Tx., U.S. (făl'fōō-rē'ás)	122	27°15'N	98°08'W
Falher, Can. (făl'ĕr)	95	55°44'N	117°12'W
Falkenberg, Swe. (făl'kĕn-bĕrgh)	166	56°54'N	12°25'E
Falkensee, Ger. (făl'kĕn-zā)	159b	52°34'N	13°05'E
Falkenthal, Ger. (făl'kĕn-täl)	159b	52°54'N	13°18'E
Falkirk, Scot., U.K. (fôl'kûrk)	164	55°59'N	3°55'W
Falkland Islands, dep., S.A. (fôk'lănd)	144	50°45'S	61°00'W
Falköping, Swe. (făl'chûp-ĭng)	166	58°09'N	13°30'E
Fall City, Wa., U.S.	116a	47°34'N	121°53'W
Fall Creek, r., In., U.S. (fôl)	111g	39°52'N	86°04'W
Fallon, Nv., U.S. (făl'ŭn)	118	39°30'N	118°48'W
Fall River, Ma., U.S.	105	41°42'N	71°07'W
Falls Church, Va., U.S. (fălz chûrch)	110e	38°53'N	77°10'W
Falls City, Ne., U.S.	121	40°04'N	95°37'W
Fallston, Md., U.S. (făls'ton)	110e	39°32'N	76°26'W
Falmouth, Jam.	134	18°30'N	77°40'W
Falmouth, Eng., U.K. (făl'mŭth)	164	50°08'N	5°04'W
Falmouth, Ky., U.S.	108	38°40'N	84°20'W
False Divi Point, c., India	203	15°45'N	80°50'E
Falster, i., Den. (făls'tĕr)	166	54°48'N	11°58'E
Fălticeni, Rom. (fŭl-tē-chān'y')	169	47°27'N	26°17'E
Falun, Swe. (fä-lōōn')	160	60°38'N	15°35'E
Famagusta, N. Cyp. (fä-mä-gōōs'tä)	163	35°08'N	33°59'E
Famatina, Sierra de, mts., Arg.	144	29°00'S	67°50'W
Fangxian, China (fäŋ-shyĕn)	208	32°05'N	110°45'E
Fanning, i., Can.	102f	49°45'N	97°46'W
Fano, Italy (fä'nō)	174	43°49'N	13°01'E
Fanø, i., Den. (fän'û)	166	55°24'N	8°10'E
Fan Si Pan, mtn., Viet.	209	22°25'N	103°50'E
Farafangana, Madag. (fä-rä-fäŋ-gä'nä)	233	23°18'S	47°59'E
Farāh, Afg. (fä-rä')	198	32°15'N	62°13'E
Farallón, Punta, c., Mex. (pō'n-tä-fä-rä-lōn)	130	19°21'N	105°03'W
Faranah, Gui. (fä-rä'nä)	230	10°02'N	10°44'W
Farasān, Jaza'ir, is., Sau. Ar.	198	16°45'N	41°08'E
Faregh, Wadi al, r., Libya (wädē ĕl fä-rĕg')	163	30°10'N	19°34'E
Farewell, Cape, c., N.Z. (fâr-wĕl')	221a	40°37'S	172°40'E
Fargo, N.D., U.S. (fär'gō)	104	46°53'N	96°48'W
Far Hills, N.J., U.S. (fär hĭlz)	110a	40°41'N	74°38'W
Faribault, Mn., U.S. (fâ'rĭ-bō)	113	44°19'N	93°16'W
Farilhões, is., Port. (fä-rē-lyōnzh')	172	39°28'N	9°32'W
Faringdon, Eng., U.K. (fă'rĭng-dŏn)	158b	51°38'N	1°35'W
Färiskūr, Egypt (fä-rēs-kōōr')	238b	31°19'N	31°46'E
Farit, Amba, mtn., Eth.	231	10°51'N	37°52'E
Farley, Mo., U.S. (fär'lē)	117f	39°16'N	94°49'W
Farmers Branch, Tx., U.S.	117c	32°56'N	96°53'W
Farmersburg, In., U.S. (fär'mĕrz-bûrg)	108	39°15'N	87°25'W
Farmersville, Tx., U.S. (fär'mĕrz-vĭl)	121	33°11'N	96°22'W
Farmingdale, N.J., U.S. (färm'ĕng-dāl)	110a	40°11'N	74°10'W
Farmingdale, N.Y., U.S.	110a	40°44'N	73°26'W
Farmingham, Ma., U.S. (färm-ĭng-hăm)	101a	42°17'N	71°25'W
Farmington, Il., U.S. (färm-ĭng-tŭn)	121	40°42'N	90°01'W
Farmington, Me., U.S.	100	44°40'N	70°10'W
Farmington, Mi., U.S.	111b	42°28'N	83°23'W
Farmington, Mo., U.S.	121	37°46'N	90°26'W
Farmington, N.M., U.S.	119	36°40'N	108°10'W
Farmington, Ut., U.S.	117b	40°59'N	111°53'W
Farmville, N.C., U.S. (färm-vĭl)	125	35°35'N	77°35'W
Farmville, Va., U.S.	125	37°15'N	78°23'W
Farnborough, Eng., U.K. (färn'bŭr-ô)	158b	51°15'N	0°45'W
Farne Islands, is., Eng., U.K. (färn)	164	55°40'N	1°32'W
Farnham, Can. (fär'năm)	109	45°15'N	72°55'W
Farningham, Eng., U.K. (fär'nĭng-ŭm)	158b	51°22'N	0°14'E
Farnworth, Eng., U.K. (färn'wŭrth)	158a	53°34'N	2°24'W
Faro, Braz. (fä'rò)	143	2°05'S	56°32'W
Faro, Port.	162	37°01'N	7°57'W
Farodofay, Madag.	233	24°59'S	46°58'E
Faroe Islands, is., Eur.	156	62°00'N	5°45'W
Fårön, i., Swe.	167	57°57'N	19°10'E
Farquhar, Cape, c., Austl. (fär'kwár)	220	23°50'S	112°55'E
Farrell, Pa., U.S. (făr'ĕl)	108	41°10'N	80°30'W
Farrukhābād, India (fŭ-rók-hä-bäd')	199	27°29'N	79°35'E
Fársala, Grc.	175	39°18'N	22°25'E
Farsund, Nor. (fär'sòn)	166	58°05'N	6°47'E
Fartak, Ra's, c., Yemen	198	15°43'N	52°17'E
Fartura, Serra da, mts., Braz. (sĕ'r-rä-dá-fär-tōō'rä)	144	26°40'S	53°15'W
Farvel, Kap, c., Grnld.	89	60°00'N	44°00'W
Farwell, Tx., U.S. (fär'wĕl)	120	34°24'N	103°03'W
Fasano, Italy (fä-zä'nō)	175	40°50'N	17°22'E
Fastiv, Ukr.	177	50°04'N	29°57'E
Fatëzh, Russia	176	52°06'N	35°51'E
Fatima, Port.	173	39°36'N	9°36'E
Fatsa, Tur. (fät'sä)	163	40°50'N	37°30'E
Faucilles, Monts, mts., Fr. (môn' fō-sēl')	171	48°07'N	6°13'E
Fauske, Nor.	160	67°15'N	15°24'E
Faust, Can. (foust)	95	55°19'N	115°38'W
Faustovo, Russia	186b	55°27'N	38°29'E
Faversham, Eng., U.K. (fă'vĕr-sh'm)	158b	51°19'N	0°54'E
Faxaflói, b., Ice.	160	64°33'N	22°40'W
Fayette, Al., U.S. (fā-yĕt')	124	33°40'N	87°54'W
Fayette, Ia., U.S.	113	42°49'N	91°49'W
Fayette, Mo., U.S.	121	39°09'N	92°41'W
Fayette, Ms., U.S.	124	31°43'N	91°00'W
Fayetteville, Ar., U.S. (fā-yĕt'vĭl)	121	36°03'N	94°08'W
Fayetteville, N.C., U.S.	125	35°02'N	78°54'W
Fayetteville, Tn., U.S.	124	35°10'N	86°33'W
Fazao, Forêt Classée du, for., Togo	234	8°50'N	0°40'E
Fazilka, India	202	30°30'N	74°02'E
Fazzān (Fezzan), hist. reg., Libya	231	26°45'N	13°01'E
Fdérik, Maur.	230	22°45'N	12°38'W
Fear, Cape, c., N.C., U.S. (fēr)	125	33°52'N	77°48'W
Feather, r., Ca., U.S. (fĕth'ĕr)	118	38°56'N	121°41'W
Feather, Middle Fork of, r., Ca., U.S.	118	39°49'N	121°10'W
Feather, North Fork of, r., Ca., U.S.	118	40°00'N	121°20'W
Featherstone, Eng., U.K. (fĕdh'ĕr stŭn)	158a	53°39'N	1°21'W
Fécamp, Fr. (fā-käN')	161	49°45'N	0°20'E
Federal, Distrito, dept., Ven. (dēs-trē'tô-fĕ-dĕ-rä'l)	143b	10°34'N	66°55'W
Federal Way, Wa., U.S.	116a	47°20'N	122°20'W
Fëdorovka, Russia (fyô'dô-rôf-kå)	186b	56°15'N	37°14'E
Fehmarn, i., Ger. (fā'märn)	168	54°28'N	11°15'E
Fehrbellin, Ger. (fĕr'bĕl-lēn)	159b	52°49'N	12°46'E
Feia, Logoa, l., Braz. (lô-gôä-fĕ'yä)	141a	21°54'S	41°15'W
Feicheng, China (fā-chŭŋ)	206	36°18'N	116°45'E
Feidong, China (fā-dôŋ)	206	31°53'N	117°28'E
Feira de Santana, Braz. (fĕ'ê-rä dä sänt-än'ä)	143	12°16'S	38°46'W
Feixian, China (fā-shyĕn)	206	35°17'N	117°59'E
Felanitx, Spain (fā-lä-nēch')	162	39°29'N	3°09'E
Feldkirch, Aus. (fĕlt'kĭrk)	168	47°15'N	9°36'E
Feldkirchen, Ger. (fĕld'kĕr-kĕn)	159d	48°09'N	11°44'E
Felipe Carrillo Puerto, Mex.	132a	19°36'N	88°04'W

ăt; finăl; rāte; senāte; ärm; åsk; sofá; fâre; ch-choose; dh-as th in other; bē; êvent; bĕt; recĕnt; cratĕr; g-gō; gh-guttural g; bĭt; ĭ-short neutral; rīde; ĸ-guttural k as ch in German ich;

PRONOUNCING INDEX

Feltre – Fort Bellefontaine 293

PLACE (Pronunciation)	PAGE	LAT.	LONG.
Feltre, Italy (fĕl′trā)	174	46°02′N	11°56′E
Femunden, l., Nor.	160	62°17′N	11°40′E
Fengcheng, China (fŭŋ-chŭŋ)	208	40°28′N	124°03′E
Fengcheng, China	207b	30°55′N	121°38′E
Fengdu, China (fŭŋ-dōō)	204	29°58′N	107°50′E
Fengjie, China (fŭŋ-jyĕ)	204	31°02′N	109°30′E
Fengming Dao, i., China (fŭŋ-mĭŋ dou)	206	39°19′N	121°15′E
Fengrun, China (fŭŋ-ròn)	206	39°51′N	118°06′E
Fengtai, China (fŭŋ-tī)	208a	39°51′N	116°19′E
Fengxian, China (fŭŋ-shyĕn)	207b	30°55′N	121°26′E
Fengxian, China	206	34°41′N	116°36′E
Fengxiang, China (fŭŋ-shyäŋ)	204	34°25′N	107°20′E
Fengyang, China (fŭng′yäng′)	208	32°55′N	117°32′E
Fengzhen, China (fŭŋ-jŭn)	205	40°28′N	113°20′E
Fennimore Pass, strt., Ak., U.S. (fĕn-ĭ-mōr)	103a	51°40′N	175°38′W
Fenoarivo Atsinanana, Madag.	233	17°30′S	49°31′E
Fenton, Mi., U.S. (fĕn-tŭn)	108	42°50′N	83°40′W
Fenton, Mo., U.S.	117e	38°31′N	90°27′W
Fenyang, China	205	37°20′N	111°48′E
Feodosiia, Ukr.	181	45°02′N	35°21′E
Ferdows, Iran	198	34°00′N	58°13′E
Ferentino, Italy (fā-rĕn-tē′nō)	174	41°42′N	13°18′E
Fergana, Uzb.	183	40°23′N	71°46′E
Fergus Falls, Mn., U.S. (fûr′gŭs)	104	46°17′N	96°03′W
Ferguson, Mo., U.S. (fûr-gŭ-sŭn)	117e	38°45′N	90°18′W
Ferkéssédougou, C. Iv.	234	9°36′N	5°12′W
Fermo, Italy (fĕr′mō)	174	43°10′N	13°43′E
Fermoselle, Spain (fĕr-mō-säl′yå)	172	41°20′N	6°23′W
Fermoy, Ire. (fûr-moi′)	164	52°05′N	8°06′W
Fernandina Beach, Fl., U.S. (fûr-năn-dē′nà)	125	30°38′N	81°29′W
Fernando de Noronha, Arquipélago, is., Braz.	143	3°51′S	32°25′W
Fernando Póo see Bioko, i., Eq. Gui.	230	3°35′N	7°45′E
Fernán-Núñez, Spain (fĕr-nän′nōōn′yāth)	172	37°42′N	4°43′W
Fernão Veloso, Baia de, b., Moz.	237	14°20′S	40°55′E
Ferndale, Ca., U.S. (fûrn′dāl)	114	40°34′N	124°18′W
Ferndale, Mi., U.S.	111b	42°27′N	83°08′W
Ferndale, Wa., U.S.	116d	48°51′N	122°36′W
Fernie, Can. (fûr′nĭ)	90	49°30′N	115°03′W
Fern Prairie, Wa., U.S. (fûrn prâr′ĭ)	116c	45°38′N	122°25′W
Ferrara, Italy (fĕr-rä′rä)	162	44°50′N	11°37′E
Ferrat, Cap, c., Alg. (kăp fĕr-rät)	173	35°49′N	0°29′W
Ferreira do Alentejo, Port.	172	38°03′N	8°06′W
Ferreira do Zezere, Port. (fĕr-rĕ′ê-rä dò zå-zā′rĕ)	172	39°49′N	8°17′W
Ferrelview, Mo., U.S. (fĕr′rĕl-vū)	117f	39°18′N	94°40′W
Ferreñafe, Peru (fĕr-rĕn-yå′fĕ)	142	6°38′S	79°48′W
Ferriday, La., U.S. (fĕr′ĭ-dā)	123	31°38′N	91°33′W
Ferrol, Spain	154	43°30′N	8°12′W
Fershampenuaz, Russia (fĕr-shàm′pĕn-wäz)	186a	53°32′N	59°50′E
Fertile, Mn., U.S. (fur′tĭl)	112	47°33′N	96°18′W
Fès, Mor. (fĕs)	230	34°08′N	5°00′W
Fessenden, N.D., U.S. (fĕs′ĕn-dĕn)	112	47°39′N	99°40′W
Festus, Mo., U.S. (fĕst′ŭs)	121	38°12′N	90°22′W
Fethiye, Tur. (fĕt-hē′yĕ)	163	36°40′N	29°05′E
Feuilles, Rivière aux, r., Can.	93	58°30′N	70°50′W
Ffestiniog, Wales, U.K.	164	52°59′N	3°58′W
Fianarantsoa, Madag. (fyà-nä′rān-tsō′à)	233	21°21′S	47°15′E
Ficksburg, S. Afr. (fĭks′bûrg)	238c	28°53′S	27°53′E
Fidalgo Island, i., Wa., U.S. (fĭ-dăl′gō)	116a	48°28′N	122°39′W
Fieldbrook, Ca., U.S. (fēld′bròk)	114	40°59′N	124°02′W
Fier, Alb. (fyĕr)	175	40°43′N	19°34′E
Fife Ness, c., Scot., U.K. (fīf′nes′)	164	56°15′N	2°19′W
Fifth Cataract, wtfl., Sudan	231	18°27′N	33°38′E
Figeac, Fr. (fē-zhàk′)	170	44°37′N	2°02′E
Figeholm, Swe. (fē-ghĕ-hōlm)	166	57°24′N	16°33′E
Figueira da Foz, Port. (fē-gwĕy-rä-dà-fō′z)	172	40°10′N	8°50′W
Figuig, Mor.	230	32°20′N	1°30′W
Fiji, nation, Oc. (fē′jē)	3	18°40′S	175°00′E
Filadelfia, C.R. (fĭl-à-dĕl′fĭ-à)	132	10°26′N	85°37′W
Filatovskoye, Russia (fĭ-lä′tôf-skô-yĕ)	186a	56°49′N	62°20′E
Filchner Ice Shelf, ice, Ant. (fĭlk′nĕr)	224	80°00′S	35°00′W
Filicudi, i., Italy (fē′le-kōō′dē)	174	38°34′N	14°39′E
Filippovskoye, Russia (fĭ-lĭ-pôf′skô-yĕ)	186b	56°06′N	38°38′E
Filipstad, Swe. (fĭl′ĭps-städh)	166	59°44′N	14°09′E
Fillmore, Ut., U.S. (fĭl′môr)	119	39°00′N	112°20′W
Filsa, Nor.	166	60°35′N	12°03′E
Fimi, r., D.R.C.	232	2°43′S	17°50′E
Finch, Can. (fĭnch)	102c	45°09′N	75°06′W
Findlay, Oh., U.S. (fĭnd′lå)	108	41°05′N	83°40′W
Fingoe, Moz.	237	15°12′S	31°50′E
Finke, r., Austl. (fĭŋ′kê)	220	25°25′S	134°30′E
Finland, nation, Eur. (fĭn′lănd)	154	62°45′N	26°13′E
Finland, Gulf of, b., Eur. (fĭn′lănd)	156	59°35′N	23°35′E
Finlandia, Col. (fēn-lä′n-dēä)	142a	4°38′N	75°39′W
Finlay, r., Can. (fĭn′lå)	92	57°45′N	125°30′W
Finow, Ger. (fē′nōv)	159b	52°50′N	13°44′E
Finowfurt, Ger. (fē′nō-fōōrt)	159b	52°50′N	13°41′E
Fircrest, Wa., U.S. (fûr′krĕst)	116a	47°14′N	122°31′W
Firenze see Florence, Italy	154	43°47′N	11°15′E
Firenzuola, Italy (fē-rĕnt-swô′lä)	174	44°08′N	11°21′E
Firozpur, India	199	30°58′N	74°39′E
Fischa, r., Aus.	159e	48°04′N	16°33′E
Fischamend Markt, Aus.	159e	48°07′N	16°37′E
Fish, r., Nmb. (fĭsh)	232	28°00′S	17°30′E
Fish Cay, i., Bah.	135	22°30′N	74°20′W

PLACE (Pronunciation)	PAGE	LAT.	LONG.
Fish Creek, r., Can. (fĭsh)	102e	50°52′N	114°21′W
Fisher, La., U.S. (fĭsh′ẽr)	123	31°28′N	93°30′W
Fisher Bay, b., Can.	97	51°30′N	97°16′W
Fisher Channel, strt., Can.	94	52°10′N	127°42′W
Fisher Strait, strt., Can.	93	62°43′N	84°28′W
Fisterra, Cabo de, c., Spain	156	42°52′N	9°48′W
Fitchburg, Ma., U.S. (fĭch′bûrg)	109	42°35′N	71°48′W
Fitri, Lac, l., Chad	235	12°50′N	17°28′E
Fitzgerald, Ga., U.S. (fĭts-jĕr′ăld)	124	31°42′N	83°17′W
Fitz Hugh Sound, strt., Can. (fĭts hū)	94	51°40′N	127°57′W
Fitzroy, r., Austl. (fĭts-roi′)	220	18°00′S	124°05′E
Fitzroy, r., Austl.	221	23°45′S	150°02′E
Fitzroy, Monte (Cerro Chaltel), mtn., S.A.	144	48°10′S	73°18′W
Fitzroy Crossing, Austl.	218	18°08′S	126°00′E
Fitzwilliam, i., Can. (fĭts-wĭl′yŭm)	98	45°30′N	81°45′W
Fiume see Rijeka, Cro.	162	45°22′N	14°24′E
Fiumicino, Italy (fyōō-mē-chē′nô)	173d	41°47′N	12°19′E
Fjällbacka, Swe. (fyĕl′bĕk-à)	166	58°37′N	11°17′E
Flagstaff, S. Afr. (flăg′stäf)	233c	31°06′S	29°31′E
Flagstaff, Az., U.S. (flăg-stàf)	104	35°15′N	111°40′W
Flagstaff, l., Me., U.S. (flăg-stàf)	109	45°05′N	70°30′W
Flåm, Nor. (flôm)	166	60°50′N	7°00′E
Flambeau, r., Wi., U.S. (flăm-bō′)	113	45°32′N	91°05′W
Flaming Gorge Reservoir, res., U.S.	106	41°13′N	109°30′W
Flamingo, Fl., U.S. (flà-mĭŋ′gô)	125	25°10′N	80°55′W
Flamingo Cay, i., Bah. (flà-mĭŋ′gô)	135	22°50′N	75°50′W
Flamingo Point, c., V.I.U.S.	129c	18°19′N	65°00′W
Flanders, hist. reg., Fr. (flăn′dẽrz)	165	50°53′N	2°29′E
Flandreau, S.D., U.S. (flăn′drō)	112	44°02′N	96°35′W
Flathead, r., N.A.	95	49°30′N	114°30′W
Flathead, Middle Fork, r., Mt., U.S.	115	48°30′N	113°47′W
Flathead, North Fork, r., N.A.	115	48°45′N	114°20′W
Flathead, South Fork, r., Mt., U.S.	115	48°05′N	113°45′W
Flathead Indian Reservation, I.R., Mt., U.S.	115	47°30′N	114°25′W
Flathead Lake, l., Mt., U.S. (flăt′hĕd)	106	47°57′N	114°20′W
Flatow, Ger.	159b	52°44′N	12°58′E
Flat Rock, Mi., U.S. (flăt rŏk)	111b	42°06′N	83°17′W
Flattery, Cape, c., Wa., U.S. (flăt′ẽr-ĭ)	114	48°22′N	124°45′W
Flatwillow Creek, r., Mt., U.S. (flat wĭl′ô)	115	46°45′N	108°47′W
Flekkefjord, Nor. (flăk′kĕ-fyôr)	166	58°19′N	6°38′E
Flemingsburg, Ky., U.S. (flĕm′ĭngz-bûrg)	108	38°25′N	83°45′W
Flensburg, Ger. (flĕns′bòrgh)	160	54°48′N	9°27′E
Flers, Fr. (flĕr)	161	48°43′N	0°37′W
Fletcher, N.C., U.S.	125	35°26′N	82°30′W
Flinders, i., Austl.	221	39°35′S	148°10′E
Flinders, r., Austl.	221	18°48′S	141°07′E
Flinders, reg., Austl. (flĭn′dẽrz)	220	32°15′S	138°45′E
Flinders Reefs, rf., Austl.	221	17°30′S	149°02′E
Flin Flon, Can. (flĭn flŏn)	90	54°46′N	101°53′W
Flint, Wales, U.K.	158a	53°15′N	3°07′W
Flint, Mi., U.S.	105	43°00′N	83°45′W
Flint, r., Ga., U.S. (flĭnt)	107	31°25′N	84°15′W
Flintshire, co., Wales, U.K.	158a	53°13′N	3°00′W
Flora, Il., U.S. (flō′rà)	108	38°40′N	88°25′W
Flora, In., U.S.	108	40°25′N	86°30′W
Florala, Al., U.S. (flŏr-ăl′à)	124	31°01′N	86°19′W
Floral Park, N.Y., U.S. (flôr′ăl pärk)	110a	40°42′N	73°42′W
Florence, Italy	154	43°47′N	11°15′E
Florence, Al., U.S. (flŏr′ĕns)	105	34°46′N	87°40′W
Florence, Az., U.S.	119	33°00′N	111°25′W
Florence, Co., U.S.	120	38°23′N	105°08′W
Florence, Ks., U.S.	121	38°14′N	96°56′W
Florence, S.C., U.S.	125	34°10′N	79°45′W
Florence, Wa., U.S.	116a	48°13′N	122°21′W
Florencia, Col. (flō-rĕn′sê-à)	142	1°31′N	75°13′W
Florencio Sánchez, Ur. (flō-rĕn-sēō-sá′n-chĕz)	141c	33°52′S	57°24′W
Florencio Varela, Arg. (flō-rĕn′sē-o vä-rā′lä)	144a	34°50′S	58°16′W
Flores, Braz. (flō′rĕzh)	143	7°57′S	37°48′W
Flores, Guat.	132a	16°53′N	89°54′W
Flores, dept., Ur.	141c	33°33′S	57°00′W
Flores, i., Indon.	212	8°14′S	121°08′E
Flores, r., Arg.	141c	36°13′S	60°28′W
Flores, Laut (Flores Sea), sea, Indon.	212	7°09′S	120°30′E
Floresville, Tx., U.S. (flō′rĕs-vĭl)	122	29°10′N	98°08′W
Floriano, Braz. (flō-rà-ä′nò)	143	6°17′S	42°58′W
Florianópolis, Braz. (flō-rē-ä-nō′pō-lēs)	144	27°30′S	48°30′W
Florida, Col. (flō-rē′dä)	142a	3°20′N	76°12′W
Florida, Cuba	134	22°10′N	79°50′W
Florida, S. Afr.	233b	26°11′S	27°56′E
Florida, Ur. (flō-rē-dhä)	144	34°06′S	56°14′W
Florida, N.Y., U.S. (flŏr′ĭ-dà)	110a	41°20′N	74°21′W
Florida, state, U.S. (flŏr′ĭ-dà)	105	30°30′N	84°40′W
Florida, dept., Ur. (flō-rē′dhä)	141c	33°48′S	56°15′W
Florida, i., Sol. Is.	221	8°56′S	159°45′E
Florida, Straits of, strt., N.A.	129	24°10′N	81°00′W
Florida Bay, b., Fl., U.S. (flŏr′ĭ-dà)	125a	24°55′N	80°55′W
Florida Keys, is., Fl., U.S.	107	24°33′N	81°20′W
Florida Mountains, mts., N.M., U.S.	119	32°10′N	107°35′W
Florido, Río, r., Mex. (flō-rē′dō)	122	27°21′N	104°48′W
Floridsdorf, Aus. (flō′rĭds-dôrf)	159e	48°16′N	16°25′E
Florina, Grc. (flō-rē′nä)	163	40°48′N	21°24′E
Florissant, Mo., U.S. (flŏr′ĭ-sănt)	117e	38°47′N	90°20′W
Floyd, r., Ia., U.S. (floid)	112	42°38′N	96°15′W
Floydada, Tx., U.S. (floi-dā′dà)	120	33°59′N	101°19′W
Floyds Fork, r., Ky., U.S. (floi-dz)	111h	38°08′N	85°30′W
Flumendosa, r., Italy	174	39°45′N	9°18′E

PLACE (Pronunciation)	PAGE	LAT.	LONG.
Flushing, Mi., U.S. (flûsh′ĭng)	108	43°05′N	83°50′W
Fly, r. (flī)	213	8°00′S	141°45′E
Foča, Bos. (fō′chä)	175	43°29′N	18°48′E
Fochville, S. Afr. (fŏk′vĭl)	238c	26°29′S	27°29′E
Focşani, Rom. (fòk-shä′nē)	169	45°41′N	27°17′E
Fogang, China (fwo-gäŋ)	209	23°50′N	113°35′E
Foggia, Italy (fôd′jä)	163	41°30′N	15°34′E
Fogo, Can. (fō′gō)	101	49°43′N	54°17′W
Fogo, i., Can.	99	49°40′N	54°13′W
Fogo, i., C.V.	230b	14°46′N	24°51′W
Fohnsdorf, Aus. (fōns′dôrf)	168	47°13′N	14°40′E
Föhr, i., Ger. (fûr)	168	54°47′N	8°30′E
Foix, Fr. (fwä)	170	42°58′N	1°34′E
Fokku, Nig.	235	11°40′N	4°31′E
Folādī, Koh-e, mtn., Afg.	199	34°38′N	67°32′E
Folgares, Ang.	236	14°54′S	15°08′E
Foligno, Italy (fō-lēn′yō)	174	42°58′N	12°41′E
Folkestone, Eng., U.K.	165	51°05′N	1°18′E
Folkingham, Eng., U.K. (fō′kĭng-ăm)	158a	52°53′N	0°24′W
Folkston, Ga., U.S.	125	30°50′N	82°01′W
Folsom, Ca., U.S.	118	38°40′N	121°10′W
Folsom, N.M., U.S. (fōl′sŭm)	120	36°47′N	103°56′W
Fomento, Cuba (fō-mĕ′n-tō)	134	21°35′N	78°20′W
Fómeque, Col. (fō′mĕ-kĕ)	142a	4°29′N	73°52′W
Fonda, Ia., U.S. (fŏn′dà)	113	42°33′N	94°51′W
Fond du Lac, Wi., U.S. (fŏn dū lăk′)	105	43°47′N	88°29′W
Fond du Lac Indian Reservation, I.R., Mn., U.S.	113	46°44′N	93°04′W
Fondi, Italy (fōn′dē)	174	41°23′N	13°25′E
Fonseca, Golfo de, b., N.A. (gôl-fô-dĕ-fōn-sā′kä)	128	13°09′N	87°55′W
Fontainebleau, Fr. (fôn-tĕn-blō′)	161	48°24′N	2°42′E
Fontana, Ca., U.S. (fŏn-tă′nà)	117a	34°06′N	117°27′W
Fonte Boa, Braz. (fōn′tå bō′à)	142	2°32′S	66°05′W
Fontenay-le-Comte, Fr. (fônt-nĕ′lē-kônt′)	170	46°28′N	0°53′W
Fontenay-Trésigny, Fr. (fôn-te-nā′ tra-sēn-yē′)	171b	48°43′N	2°53′E
Fontenelle Reservoir, res., Wy., U.S.	115	42°05′N	110°05′W
Fontera, Punta, c., Mex. (pōō′n-tä-fōn-tĕ′rä)	131	18°36′N	92°43′W
Fontibón, Col. (fōn-tē-bôn′)	142a	4°42′N	74°09′W
Fontur, c., Ice.	156	66°21′N	14°02′W
Foothills, S. Afr. (fòt-hĭls)	233b	25°55′S	27°36′E
Footscray, Austl.	217a	37°48′S	144°54′E
Foraker, Mount, mtn., Ak., U.S. (fôr′á-kẽr)	103	62°40′N	152°40′W
Forbach, Fr. (fôr′bäk)	171	49°12′N	6°54′E
Forbes, Austl. (fôrbz)	219	33°24′S	148°05′E
Forbes, Mount, mtn., Can.	95	51°52′N	116°56′W
Forchheim, Ger. (fôrk′hīm)	168	49°43′N	11°05′E
Fordyce, Ar., U.S. (fôr′dīs)	121	33°48′N	92°24′W
Forécariah, Gui. (fōr-kà-rē′ä′)	230	9°26′N	13°06′W
Forel, Mont, mtn., Grnld.	89	65°50′N	37°41′W
Forest, Ms., U.S. (fŏr′ĕst)	124	32°22′N	89°29′W
Forest, r., N.D., U.S.	112	48°08′N	97°45′W
Forest City, Ia., U.S.	113	43°14′N	93°40′W
Forest City, N.C., U.S.	125	35°20′N	81°52′W
Forest City, Pa., U.S.	109	41°35′N	75°30′W
Forest Grove, Or., U.S. (grōv)	116c	45°31′N	123°07′W
Forest Hill, Md., U.S.	110e	39°35′N	76°26′W
Forest Hill, Tx., U.S.	117c	32°40′N	97°16′W
Forestville, Can. (fŏr′ĕst-vĭl)	100	48°45′N	69°06′W
Forestville, Md., U.S.	110e	38°51′N	76°55′W
Forez, Monts du, mts., Fr. (môn dü fō-rā′)	170	44°55′N	3°43′E
Forfar, Scot., U.K. (fôr′fàr)	164	57°10′N	2°55′W
Forillon, Parc National, rec., Can.	100	48°50′N	64°05′W
Forio, mtn., Italy (fô′ryō)	173c	40°29′N	13°55′E
Forked Creek, r., Il., U.S. (fôrk′d)	111a	41°16′N	88°01′W
Forked Deer, r., Tn., U.S.	124	35°53′N	89°29′W
Forli, Italy (fôr-lē′)	162	44°13′N	12°03′E
Formby, Eng., U.K. (fôrm′bē)	158a	53°34′N	3°04′W
Formby Point, c., Eng., U.K.	158a	53°33′N	3°06′W
Formentera, Isla de, i., Spain (ê′s-lä-dĕ-fôr-mĕn-tā′rä)	162	38°43′N	1°25′E
Formiga, Braz. (fôr-mē′gà)	143	20°27′S	45°25′W
Formigas Bank, bk. (fôr-mē′gäs)	135	18°30′N	75°40′W
Formosa, Arg. (fôr-mō′sä)	144	27°25′S	58°12′W
Formosa, Braz.	143	15°32′S	47°10′W
Formosa, prov., Arg.	144	24°30′S	60°45′W
Formosa, Serra, mts., Braz. (sĕ′r-rä)	143	12°59′S	55°11′W
Formosa Bay, b., Kenya	237	2°45′S	40°30′E
Formosa Strait see Taiwan Strait, strt., Asia	205	24°30′N	120°00′E
Fornosovo, Russia (fôr-nô′sô vô)	186c	59°35′N	30°34′E
Forrest City, Ar., U.S. (for′ĕst sĭ′tĭ)	121	35°00′N	90°46′W
Forsayth, Austl. (fôr-sīth′)	219	18°33′S	143°42′E
Forshaga, Swe. (fôrs′hä′gä)	166	59°34′N	13°25′E
Forst, Ger. (fôrst)	161	51°45′N	14°38′E
Forsyth, Ga., U.S. (fôr-sīth′)	124	33°02′N	83°56′W
Forsyth, Mt., U.S.	115	46°15′N	106°41′W
Fort Albany, Can. (fôrt ôl′bà nĭ)	91	52°20′N	81°30′W
Fort Alexander Indian Reserve, I.R., Can.	97	50°27′N	96°15′W
Fortaleza, Braz. (fôr′tä-lā′zà)	143	3°35′S	38°31′W
Fort Apache Indian Reservation, I.R., Az., U.S. (ă-păch′ê)	119	34°02′N	110°27′W
Fort Atkinson, Wi., U.S. (ăt′kĭn-sŭn)	113	42°55′N	88°46′W
Fort Beaufort, S. Afr. (bō′fôrt)	233c	32°47′S	26°39′E
Fort Belknap Indian Reservation, I.R., Mt., U.S.	115	48°16′N	108°38′W
Fort Bellefontaine, Mo., U.S. (bĕl-fōn-tān′)	117f	38°50′N	90°15′W

ng-sing; ŋ-baŋk; ɴ-nasalized n; nŏd; cŏmmit; ōld; ôbey; ôrder; oi-boil; fōōd; ò-as oo in foot; ou-out; s-soft; sh-dish; th-thin; pūre; ûnite; ûrn; stŭd; circŭs; ü-as in French tu; ′-indeterminate vowel.

294 Fort Benton – Fryazino

PRONOUNCING INDEX

PLACE (Pronunciation)	PAGE	LAT.	LONG.
Fort Benton, Mt., U.S. (bĕn´tŭn)	115	47°51′N	110°40′W
Fort Berthold Indian Reservation, I.R., N.D., U.S. (bĕrth´ôld)	112	47°47′N	103°28′W
Fort Bragg, Ca., U.S.	118	39°26′N	123°48′W
Fort Branch, In., U.S. (brănch)	108	38°15′N	87°35′W
Fort Chipewyan, Can.	90	58°46′N	111°15′W
Fort Cobb Reservoir, res., Ok., U.S.	120	35°12′N	98°28′W
Fort Collins, Co., U.S. (kŏl´ĭns)	104	40°36′N	105°04′W
Fort Crampel, C.A.R. (kram-pĕl´)	231	6°59′N	19°11′E
Fort-de-France, Mart. (dē fräns)	129	14°37′N	61°06′W
Fort Deposit, Al., U.S. (dē-pŏz´ĭt)	124	31°58′N	86°35′W
Fort-de-Possel, C.A.R. (dē pô-sĕl´)	231	5°03′N	19°11′E
Fort Dodge, Ia., U.S. (dŏj)	105	42°31′N	94°10′W
Fort Edward, N.Y., U.S. (wẽrd)	109	43°15′N	73°30′W
Fort Erie, Can. (ē´rĭ)	111c	42°55′N	78°56′W
Fortescue, r., Austl. (fôr´tĕs-kū)	220	21°25′S	116°50′E
Fort Fairfield, Me., U.S. (fâr´fēld)	100	46°46′N	67°53′W
Fort Fitzgerald, Can. (fĭts-jĕr´ăld)	90	59°48′N	111°50′W
Fort Frances, Can. (frăn´sĕs)	91	48°36′N	93°24′W
Fort Frederica National Monument, rec., Ga., U.S. (frĕd´ĕ-rī-ka)	124	31°13′N	85°25′W
Fort Gaines, Ga., U.S. (gānz)	124	31°35′N	85°03′W
Fort Gibson, Ok., U.S. (gĭb´sŭn)	121	35°50′N	95°13′W
Fort Good Hope, Can. (go͝od hōp)	90	66°19′N	128°52′W
Forth, Firth of, b., Scot., U.K. (fûrth ôv fōrth)	156	56°04′N	3°03′W
Fort Hall, Kenya (hôl)	233	0°47′S	37°13′E
Fort Hall Indian Reservation, I.R., Id., U.S.	115	43°02′N	112°21′W
Fort Huachuca, Az., U.S. (wä-cho͞o´kä)	119	31°30′N	110°25′W
Fortier, Can. (fôr´tyā´)	102f	49°56′N	97°55′W
Fort Kent, Me., U.S. (kĕnt)	100	47°14′N	68°37′W
Fort Langley, Can. (lăng´lĭ)	116d	49°10′N	122°35′W
Fort Lauderdale, Fl., U.S. (lô´dẽr-dāl)	125a	26°07′N	80°09′W
Fort Lee, N.J., U.S.	110a	40°50′N	73°58′W
Fort Liard, Can.	90	60°16′N	123°34′W
Fort Loudoun Lake, res., Tn., U.S. (fōrt lou´dĕn)	124	35°52′N	84°10′W
Fort Lupton, Co., U.S. (lŭp´tŭn)	120	40°04′N	104°54′W
Fort Macleod, Can. (mȧ-kloud´)	90	49°43′N	113°25′W
Fort Madison, Ia., U.S. (măd´ĭ-sŭn)	113	40°40′N	91°17′W
Fort Matanzas, Fl., U.S. (mä-tän´zäs)	125	29°39′N	81°17′W
Fort McDermitt Indian Reservation, I.R., Or., U.S. (mă̇k dẽr´mĭt)	114	42°04′N	118°07′W
Fort McMurray, Can. (mȧk-mŭr´ĭ)	90	56°44′N	111°23′W
Fort McPherson, Can. (mȧk-fŭr´s´n)	90	67°37′N	134°59′W
Fort Meade, Fl., U.S. (mēd)	125a	27°45′N	81°48′W
Fort Mill, S.C., U.S. (mĭl)	125	35°03′N	80°57′W
Fort Mojave Indian Reservation, I.R., Ca., U.S. (mō-hä´vâ)	118	34°59′N	115°02′W
Fort Morgan, Co., U.S. (môr´gȧn)	120	40°14′N	103°49′W
Fort Myers, Fl., U.S. (mī´ẽrz)	125a	26°36′N	81°45′W
Fort Nelson, Can. (nĕl´sŭn)	90	58°57′N	122°30′W
Fort Nelson, r., Can. (nĕl´sŭn)	92	58°44′N	122°20′W
Fort Payne, Al., U.S. (pān)	124	34°26′N	85°41′W
Fort Peck, Mt., U.S. (pĕk)	115	47°58′N	106°30′W
Fort Peck Indian Reservation, I.R., Mt., U.S.	112	48°22′N	105°40′W
Fort Peck Lake, res., Mt., U.S.	106	47°52′N	106°59′W
Fort Pierce, Fl., U.S. (pērs)	125a	27°25′N	80°20′W
Fort Portal, Ug. (pôr´tàl)	231	0°40′N	30°16′E
Fort Providence, Can. (prŏv´ĭ-dĕns)	90	61°27′N	117°59′W
Fort Pulaski National Monument, rec., Ga., U.S. (pu-läs´kĭ)	125	31°59′N	80°56′W
Fort Qu'Appelle, Can.	96	50°46′N	103°55′W
Fort Randall Dam, dam, S.D., U.S.	112	42°48′N	98°35′W
Fort Resolution, Can. (rĕz´ô-lū´shŭn)	90	61°08′N	113°42′W
Fort Riley, Ks., U.S. (rī´lĭ)	121	39°05′N	96°46′W
Fort Saint James, Can. (fōrt sānt jămz)	90	54°26′N	124°15′W
Fort Saint John, Can. (sānt jŏn)	90	56°15′N	120°51′W
Fort Sandeman, Pak. (săn´da-măn)	199	31°28′N	69°29′E
Fort Saskatchewan, Can. (săs-kăt´cho͞o-ån)	102g	53°43′N	113°13′W
Fort Scott, Ks., U.S. (skŏt)	105	37°50′N	94°43′W
Fort Severn, Can. (sĕv´ẽrn)	91	55°58′N	87°50′W
Fort-Shevchenko, Kaz. (shĕv-chĕn´kô)	183	44°30′N	50°18′E
Fort Sibut, C.A.R. (fôr sē-bü´)	231	5°44′N	19°05′E
Fort Sill, Ok., U.S. (fôrt sĭl)	120	34°41′N	98°25′W
Fort Simpson, Can. (sĭmp´sŭn)	90	61°52′N	121°48′W
Fort Smith, Can.	90	60°09′N	112°08′W
Fort Smith, Ar., U.S. (smĭth)	105	35°23′N	94°24′W
Fort Stockton, Tx., U.S. (stŏk´tŭn)	122	30°54′N	102°51′W
Fort Sumner, N.M., U.S. (sŭm´nẽr)	120	34°30′N	104°17′W
Fort Sumter National Monument, rec., S.C., U.S. (sŭm´tẽr)	125	32°43′N	79°54′W
Fort Thomas, Ky., U.S. (tŏm´ăs)	111f	39°05′N	84°27′W
Fortuna, Ca., U.S. (fôr-tū´nȧ)	114	40°36′N	124°10′W
Fortune, Can. (fôr´tŭn)	101	47°04′N	55°51′W
Fortune, i., Bah.	135	22°35′N	74°20′W
Fortune Bay, b., Can.	93a	47°25′N	55°25′W
Fort Union National Monument, rec., N.M., U.S. (ūn´yŭn)	120	35°51′N	104°57′W
Fort Valley, Ga., U.S. (văl´ĭ)	124	32°33′N	83°53′W
Fort Vermilion, Can. (vẽr-mĭl´yŭn)	90	58°23′N	115°50′W
Fort Victoria *see* Masvingo, Zimb.	232	20°07′S	30°47′E
Fort Wayne, In., U.S. (wān)	105	41°00′N	85°10′W
Fort William, Scot., U.K. (wĭl´yăm)	164	56°50′N	3°00′W
Fort William, Mount, mtn., Austl. (wĭ´ĭ-ăm)	222	24°45′S	151°15′E
Fort Worth, Tx., U.S. (wûrth)	104	32°45′N	97°20′W
Fort Yukon, Ak., U.S. (yo͞o´kŏn)	106a	66°30′N	145°00′W
Fort Yuma Indian Reservation, I.R., Ca., U.S. (yo͞o´mä)	119	32°54′N	114°47′W
Foshan, China	205	23°02′N	113°07′E
Fossano, Italy (fŏs-sä´nō)	174	44°34′N	7°42′E
Fossil Creek, r., Tx., U.S. (fŏs-ĭl)	117c	32°53′N	97°19′W
Fossombrone, Italy (fŏs-sŏm-brō´nā)	174	43°41′N	12°48′E
Foss Res, Ok., U.S.	120	35°38′N	99°11′W
Fosston, Mn., U.S. (fŏs´tŭn)	112	47°34′N	95°44′W
Fosterburg, Il., U.S. (fŏs´tẽr-bûrg)	117e	38°58′N	90°04′W
Fostoria, Oh., U.S. (fŏs-tō´rĭ-ȧ)	108	41°10′N	83°20′W
Fougéres, Fr. (fo͞o-zhâr´)	161	48°23′N	1°14′W
Foula, i., Scot., U.K. (fou´lȧ)	164a	60°08′N	2°04′W
Foulwind, Cape, c., N.Z. (foul´wĭnd)	221a	41°45′S	171°00′E
Foumban, Cam. (fo͞om-bän´)	230	5°43′N	10°55′E
Fountain Creek, r., Co., U.S. (foun´tĭn)	120	38°36′N	104°37′W
Fountain Valley, Ca., U.S.	117a	33°42′N	117°57′W
Fourche la Fave, r., Ar., U.S. (fo͞orsh lä fäv´)	121	34°46′N	93°45′W
Fouriesburg, S. Afr. (fō´rēz-bûrg)	238c	28°38′S	28°13′E
Fourmies, Fr. (fo͞or-mē´)	170	50°01′N	4°01′E
Four Mountains, Islands of the, is., Ak., U.S.	103a	52°58′N	170°40′W
Fourth Cataract, wtfl., Sudan	231	18°52′N	32°07′E
Fouta Djallon, mts., Gui. (fo͞o´tä jä-lôn)	230	11°37′N	12°29′W
Foveaux Strait, strt., N.Z. (fō-vō´)	221a	46°30′S	167°43′E
Fowler, Co., U.S. (foul´ẽr)	120	38°04′N	104°02′W
Fowler, In., U.S.	108	40°35′N	87°20′W
Fowler, Point, c., Austl.	220	32°05′S	132°30′E
Fowlerton, Tx., U.S. (foul´ẽr-tŭn)	122	28°26′N	98°48′W
Fox, i., Wa., U.S. (fŏks)	116a	47°15′N	122°08′W
Fox, r., Il., U.S.	113	41°35′N	88°43′W
Fox, r., Wi., U.S.	113	44°18′N	88°23′W
Foxboro, Ma., U.S. (fŏks´bŭrō)	101a	42°04′N	71°15′W
Foxe Basin, b., Can. (fŏks)	93	67°35′N	79°21′W
Foxe Channel, strt., Can.	93	64°30′N	79°23′W
Foxe Peninsula, pen., Can.	93	64°57′N	77°26′W
Fox Islands, is., Ak., U.S. (fŏks)	103a	53°04′N	167°30′W
Fox Lake, Il., U.S. (lăk)	111a	42°24′N	88°11′W
Fox Lake, l., Il., U.S.	111a	42°24′N	88°07′W
Fox Point, Wi., U.S.	111a	43°10′N	87°54′W
Foyle, Lough, b., Eur. (lŏk foil´)	164	55°07′N	7°08′W
Foz do Cunene, Ang.	236	17°16′S	11°50′E
Fraga, Spain (frä´gä)	173	41°31′N	0°20′E
Fragoso, Cayo, i., Cuba (kä´yō-frä-gō´sō)	134	22°45′N	79°30′W
Framnes Mountains, mts., Ant.	224	67°50′S	62°35′E
Franca, Braz. (frä´n-kä)	143	20°28′S	47°20′W
Francavilla, Italy (fräŋ-kä-vēl´lä)	175	40°32′N	17°37′E
France, nation, Eur. (fråns)	154	46°39′N	0°47′E
Frances, l., Can. (frăn´sĭs)	92	61°27′N	128°28′W
Frances, Cabo, c., Cuba (kä´bō-frän-sĕ´s)	134	21°55′N	84°05′W
Frances, Punta, c., Cuba (po͞o´n-tä-frän-sĕ´s)	134	21°45′N	83°10′W
Francés Viejo, Cabo, c., Dom. Rep. (kå´bō-frän´sås vyā´hō)	135	19°40′N	69°35′W
Franceville, Gabon (fräns-vēl´)	232	1°38′S	13°35′E
Francis Case, Lake, res., S.D., U.S. (från´sĭs)	106	43°15′N	99°00′W
Francisco Sales, Braz. (frän-sē´s-kô-sá´lĕs)	141a	21°42′S	44°26′W
Francistown, Bots. (från´sĭs-toun)	232	21°17′S	27°28′E
Frankfort, S. Afr. (frănk´fŏrt)	233c	32°43′S	27°28′E
Frankfort, S. Afr.	238c	27°17′S	28°30′E
Frankfort, Il., U.S. (frăŋk´fŭrt)	111a	41°30′N	87°51′W
Frankfort, In., U.S.	108	40°15′N	86°30′W
Frankfort, Ks., U.S.	121	39°42′N	96°27′W
Frankfort, Ky., U.S.	105	38°10′N	84°55′W
Frankfort, Mi., U.S.	108	44°40′N	86°15′W
Frankfort, N.Y., U.S.	109	43°05′N	75°05′W
Frankfurt am Main, Ger.	154	50°07′N	8°40′E
Frankfurt an der Oder, Ger.	161	52°20′N	14°31′E
Franklin, S. Afr.	233c	30°19′S	29°28′E
Franklin, In., U.S. (frănk´lĭn)	108	39°25′N	86°00′W
Franklin, Ky., U.S.	124	36°42′N	86°34′W
Franklin, La., U.S.	123	29°47′N	91°31′W
Franklin, Ma., U.S.	101a	42°05′N	71°24′W
Franklin, Ne., U.S.	120	40°06′N	99°01′W
Franklin, N.H., U.S.	109	43°25′N	71°40′W
Franklin, N.J., U.S.	110a	41°08′N	74°35′W
Franklin, Oh., U.S.	108	39°30′N	84°20′W
Franklin, Pa., U.S.	109	41°25′N	79°50′W
Franklin, Tn., U.S.	124	35°54′N	86°54′W
Franklin, Va., U.S.	125	36°41′N	76°57′W
Franklin, l., Nv., U.S.	118	40°23′N	115°10′W
Franklin D. Roosevelt Lake, res., Wa., U.S.	114	48°12′N	118°43′W
Franklin Mountains, mts., Can.	92	65°36′N	125°55′W
Franklin Park, Il., U.S.	111a	41°56′N	87°53′W
Franklin Square, N.Y., U.S.	110a	40°43′N	73°40′W
Franklinton, La., U.S. (frăŋk´lĭn-tŭn)	123	30°49′N	90°09′W
Frankston, Austl.	217a	38°09′S	145°08′E
Franksville, Wi., U.S. (frănkz´vĭl)	111a	42°46′N	87°55′W
Fransta, Swe.	166	62°30′N	16°04′E
Franz Josef Land *see* Zemlya Frantsa-Iosifa, is., Russia	178	81°32′N	40°00′E
Frascati, Italy (fräs-kä´tē)	174	41°49′N	12°45′E
Fraser, Mi., U.S. (frā´zẽr)	111b	42°32′N	82°57′W
Fraser, i., Austl.	221	25°12′S	153°00′E
Fraser, r., Can.	92	51°30′N	122°00′W
Fraserburgh, Scot., U.K. (frā´zẽr-bûrg)	164	57°40′N	2°01′W
Fraser Plateau, plat., Can.	95	51°30′N	122°00′W
Frattamaggiore, Italy (frät-tä-mäg-zhyō´rĕ)	173c	40°41′N	14°16′E
Fray Bentos, Ur. (frī bĕn´tōs)	144	33°10′S	58°19′W
Frazee, Mn., U.S. (frå-zē´)	112	46°42′N	95°43′W
Fraziers Hog Cay, i., Bah.	134	25°25′N	77°55′W
Frechen, Ger. (frĕ´κĕn)	171c	50°54′N	6°49′E
Fredericia, Den. (frĕdh-ĕ-rē´tsē-å)	166	55°35′N	9°45′E
Frederick, Md., U.S. (frĕd´ẽr-ĭk)	105	39°25′N	77°25′W
Frederick, Ok., U.S.	120	34°23′N	99°01′W
Frederick House, r., Can.	98	49°05′N	81°20′W
Fredericksburg, Tx., U.S. (frĕd´ẽr-ĭkz-bûrg)	122	30°16′N	98°52′W
Fredericksburg, Va., U.S.	109	38°20′N	77°30′W
Fredericktown, Mo., U.S. (frĕd´ẽr-ĭk-toun)	121	37°32′N	90°16′W
Fredericton, Can. (frĕd´ẽr-ĭk-tŭn)	91	45°48′N	66°39′W
Frederikshavn, Den. (frĕdh´ĕ-rēks-houn)	160	57°27′N	10°31′E
Frederikssund, Den. (frĕdh´ĕ-rēks-so͝on)	166	55°51′N	12°04′E
Fredonia, Col. (frē-dō´nyȧ)	142a	5°55′N	75°40′W
Fredonia, Ks., U.S. (frē-dō´nĭ-ȧ)	121	36°31′N	95°50′W
Fredonia, N.Y., U.S.	109	42°25′N	79°20′W
Fredrikstad, Nor. (frådh´rēks-ståd)	160	59°14′N	10°58′E
Freeburg, Il., U.S. (frē´bûrg)	117e	38°26′N	89°59′W
Freehold, N.J., U.S. (frē´hōld)	110a	40°15′N	74°16′W
Freeland, Pa., U.S. (frē´lȧnd)	109	41°00′N	75°50′W
Freeland, Wa., U.S.	116a	48°01′N	122°32′W
Freels, Cape, c., Can. (frēlz)	101	46°37′N	53°45′W
Freelton, Can. (frēl´tŭn)	102d	43°24′N	80°02′W
Freeport, Bah.	134	26°30′N	78°45′W
Freeport, Il., U.S. (frē´pōrt)	105	42°19′N	89°30′W
Freeport, N.Y., U.S.	110a	40°39′N	73°35′W
Freeport, Tx., U.S.	123	28°56′N	95°21′W
Freetown, S.L. (frē´toun)	230	8°30′N	13°15′W
Fregenal de la Sierra, Spain (frā-hå-näl´ dā lä syĕr´rä)	172	38°09′N	6°40′W
Fregene, Italy (frĕ-zhĕ´-nĕ)	173d	41°52′N	12°12′E
Freiberg, Ger. (frī´bĕrgh)	161	50°54′N	13°18′E
Freiburg, Ger.	161	48°00′N	7°50′E
Freienried, Ger. (frī´ĕn-rēd)	159d	48°20′N	11°08′E
Freirina, Chile (frå-ī-rē´nä)	144	28°35′S	71°26′W
Freising, Ger. (frī´zĭng)	168	48°25′N	11°45′E
Fréjus, Fr. (frā-zhüs´)	171	43°28′N	6°46′E
Fremantle, Austl. (frē´măn-t'l)	218	32°03′S	116°05′E
Fremont, Ca., U.S. (frē-mŏnt´)	116b	37°33′N	122°00′W
Fremont, Mi., U.S.	108	43°25′N	85°55′W
Fremont, Ne., U.S.	112	41°26′N	96°30′W
Fremont, Oh., U.S.	108	41°20′N	83°05′W
Fremont, r., Ut., U.S.	119	38°20′N	111°30′W
Fremont Peak, mtn., Wy., U.S.	115	43°05′N	109°35′W
French Broad, r., Tn., U.S. (frĕnch brôd)	124	35°59′N	83°01′W
French Frigate Shoals, Hi., U.S.	126b	23°30′N	167°10′W
French Guiana, dep., S.A. (gē-ä´nä)	143	4°20′N	53°00′W
French Lick, In., U.S. (frĕnch lĭk)	108	38°35′N	86°35′W
Frenchman, r., N.A.	96	49°25′N	108°30′W
Frenchman Creek, r., Mt., U.S. (frĕnch-măn)	115	48°51′N	107°20′W
Frenchman Creek, r., Ne., U.S.	120	40°24′N	101°50′W
Frenchman Flat, Nv., U.S.	118	36°55′N	116°11′W
French Polynesia, dep., Oc.	2	15°00′S	140°00′W
French River, Mn., U.S.	117h	46°54′N	91°54′W
Freshfield, Mount, mtn., Can. (frĕsh´fēld)	95	51°44′N	116°57′W
Fresnillo, Mex. (frås-nēl´yō)	128	23°10′N	102°52′W
Fresno, Col. (frĕs´nō)	142a	5°10′N	75°01′W
Fresno, Ca., U.S.	104	36°44′N	119°46′W
Fresno, r., Ca., U.S. (frĕz´nō)	118	37°00′N	120°24′W
Fresno Slough, Ca., U.S.	118	36°39′N	120°12′W
Freudenstadt, Ger. (froi´dĕn-shtät)	168	48°28′N	8°26′E
Freycinet Peninsula, pen., Austl. (frā-sē-nĕ´)	222	42°13′S	148°56′E
Fria, Gui.	234	10°05′N	13°32′W
Fria, r., Az., U.S. (frē-ä)	119	34°03′N	112°12′W
Fria, Cape, c., Nmb. (frĭȧ)	232	18°15′S	12°10′E
Friant-Kern Canal, can., Ca., U.S. (kûrn)	118	36°57′N	119°37′W
Frias, Arg. (frē-äs)	144	28°43′S	65°03′W
Fribourg, Switz. (frē-bo͞or´)	161	46°48′N	7°07′E
Fridley, Mn., U.S. (frĭd´lĭ)	117g	45°05′N	93°16′W
Friedberg, Ger. (frēd´bĕrgh)	159d	48°22′N	11°00′E
Friedland, Ger. (frēt´länt)	168	53°39′N	13°34′E
Friedrichshafen, Ger. (frē-drēks-häf´ĕn)	168	47°39′N	9°28′E
Friend, Ne., U.S. (frĕnd)	121	40°40′N	97°16′W
Friendswood, Tx., U.S. (frĕnds´wo͝od)	123a	29°31′N	95°11′W
Fries, Va., U.S. (frēz)	125	36°42′N	80°59′W
Friesack, Ger. (frē´säk)	159b	52°44′N	12°35′E
Frio, Cabo, c., Braz. (kä´bō-frē´ō)	143	22°58′S	42°08′W
Frio R, Tx., U.S.	122	29°00′N	99°15′W
Frisian Islands, is., Neth. (frē´zhăn)	160	53°30′N	5°20′E
Friuli-Venezia Giulia, hist. reg., Italy	174	46°20′N	13°20′E
Frobisher Bay, b., Can.	93	62°49′N	66°41′W
Frobisher Lake, l., Can. (frŏb´ĭsh´ẽr)	92	56°25′N	108°20′W
Frodsham, Eng., U.K. (frŏdz´ăm)	158a	53°18′N	2°48′W
Frohavet, b., Nor.	160	63°49′N	9°12′E
Frome, Lake, l., Austl. (fro͞om)	220	30°40′S	140°13′E
Frontenac, Ks., U.S. (frŏn´tē-năk)	121	37°27′N	94°41′W
Frontera, Mex. (frôn-tā´rä)	131	18°34′N	92°38′W
Front Range, mts., Co., U.S. (frŭnt)	120	40°59′N	105°29′W
Front Royal, Va., U.S. (frŭnt)	109	38°55′N	78°10′W
Frosinone, Italy (frô-zē-nō´nå)	174	41°38′N	13°22′E
Frostburg, Md., U.S. (frôst´bûrg)	109	39°40′N	78°55′W
Fruita, Co., U.S. (fro͞ot-ȧ)	119	39°10′N	108°45′W
Frunze *see* Bishkek, Kyrg.	183	42°49′N	74°42′E
Fryanovo, Russia (f´ryä´nô-vô)	186b	56°08′N	38°28′E
Fryazino, Russia (f´ryä´zĭ-nô)	186b	55°58′N	38°05′E

ăt; finăl; rāte; senåte; ärm; åsk; sofȧ; fâre; ch-choose; dh-as th in other; bē; ēvent; bĕt; recĕnt; cratẽr; g-gō; gh-guttural g; bĭt; ĭ-short neutral; rīde; κ-guttural k as ch in German ich;

PRONOUNCING INDEX

Frydlant – Gattendorf 295

PLACE (Pronunciation)	PAGE	LAT.	LONG.
Frydlant, Czech Rep. (frēd′länt)	168	50°56′N	15°05′E
Fucheng, China (fōō-chŭŋ)	206	37°53′N	116°08′E
Fuchu, Japan (fōō′chōō)	211a	35°41′N	139°29′E
Fuchun, r., China (fōō-chòn)	209	29°50′N	120°00′E
Fuego, vol., Guat. (fwā′gō)	132	14°29′N	90°52′W
Fuencarral, Spain (fuān-kär-räl′)	173a	40°29′N	3°42′W
Fuensalida, Spain (fwān-sä-lē′dä)	172	40°04′N	4°15′W
Fuente, Mex. (fwĕ′n-tĕ′)	122	28°39′N	100°34′W
Fuente de Cantos, Spain (fwĕn′tä dā kän′tōs)	172	38°15′N	6°18′W
Fuente el Saz, Spain (fwĕn′tä ĕl säth′)	173a	40°39′N	3°30′W
Fuenteobejuna, Spain	172	38°15′N	5°30′W
Fuentesaúco, Spain (fwĕn-tä-sä-ōō′kō)	172	41°18′N	5°25′W
Fuerte, Río del, r., Mex. (rē′ō-dĕl-fōō-ĕ′r-tĕ)	128	26°15′N	108°50′W
Fuerte Olimpo, Para. (fwĕr′tä ō-lēm-pō)	144	21°10′S	57°49′W
Fuerteventura Island, i., Spain (fwĕr′tä-vĕn-tōō′rä)	230	28°24′N	13°21′W
Fuhai, China	204	47°01′N	87°07′E
Fuji, Japan (jōō′jē)	211	35°11′N	138°44′E
Fuji, r., Japan	211	35°20′N	138°23′E
Fujian, prov., China (fōō-jyĕn)	205	25°40′N	117°30′E
Fujidera, Japan	211b	34°34′N	135°37′E
Fujin, China (fōō-jyĭn)	205	47°13′N	132°11′E
Fuji San, mtn., Japan (fōō′jē sän)	205	35°23′N	138°44′E
Fujisawa, Japan (fōō′jē-sä′wa)	211a	35°20′N	139°29′E
Fujiyama *see* Fuji San, mtn., Japan	205	35°23′N	138°44′E
Fukuchiyama, Japan (fō′kò-chē-yä′ma)	211	35°18′N	135°07′E
Fukue, i., Japan (fò-kōō′ä)	210	32°40′N	129°02′E
Fukui, Japan (fōō′kōō-ē)	205	36°05′N	136°14′E
Fukuoka, Japan (fōō′kò-ō′kä)	205	33°35′N	130°23′E
Fukuoka, Japan	211a	35°52′N	139°31′E
Fukushima, Japan (fōō′kò-shē′mä)	210	37°45′N	140°29′E
Fukuyama, Japan (fōō′kò-yä′mä)	210	34°31′N	133°21′E
Fulda, Ger.	161	50°33′N	9°41′E
Fulda, r., Ger. (fòl′dä)	168	51°05′N	9°40′E
Fuling, China (fōō-lĭŋ)	204	29°40′N	107°30′E
Fullerton, Ca., U.S. (fòl′ēr-tŭn)	117a	33°53′N	117°56′W
Fullerton, La., U.S.	123	31°00′N	93°00′W
Fullerton, Ne., U.S.	112	41°21′N	97°59′W
Fulton, Ky., U.S. (fŭl′tŭn)	124	36°30′N	88°53′W
Fulton, Mo., U.S.	121	38°51′N	91°56′W
Fulton, N.Y., U.S.	109	43°20′N	76°25′W
Fultondale, Al., U.S. (fŭl′tŭn-dāl)	110h	33°37′N	86°48′W
Funabashi, Japan (fōō′nà-bä′shē)	211	35°43′N	139°59′E
Funaya, Japan (fōō-nä′yä)	211b	34°45′N	135°52′E
Funchal, Port. (fòn-shäl′)	230	32°41′N	16°15′W
Fundación, Col. (fōōn-dä-syō′n)	142	10°43′N	74°13′W
Fundão, Port. (fòn-douN′)	172	40°08′N	7°32′W
Fundy, Bay of, b., Can. (fŭn′dĭ)	93	45°00′N	66°00′W
Fundy National Park, rec., Can.	93	45°38′N	65°00′W
Funing, China (fōō-nĭŋ)	208	33°55′N	119°54′E
Funing, China	206	39°55′N	119°16′E
Funing Wan, b., China	209	26°48′N	120°35′E
Funtua, Nig.	235	11°31′N	7°17′E
Furancungo, Moz.	237	14°55′S	33°35′E
Furbero, Mex. (fōōr-bĕ′rô)	131	20°21′N	97°32′W
Furgun, mtn., Iran	198	28°47′N	57°00′E
Furmanov, Russia (fûr-mä′nôf)	180	57°14′N	41°11′E
Furnas, Reprêsa de, res., Braz.	143	21°00′S	46°00′W
Furneaux Group, is., Austl. (fûr′nō)	221	40°15′S	146°27′E
Fürstenfeld, Aus. (für′stĕn-fĕlt)	168	47°02′N	16°03′E
Fürstenfeldbruck, Ger. (fur′stĕn-fĕld′brook)	159d	48°11′N	11°16′E
Fürstenwalde, Ger. (für′stĕn-väl-dĕ)	168	52°21′N	14°04′E
Fürth, Ger. (fürt)	161	49°28′N	11°03′E
Furuichi, Japan (fōō′rò-ē′chē)	211b	34°33′N	135°37′E
Fusa, Japan (fōō′sä)	211a	35°52′N	140°08′E
Fuse, Japan	211b	34°40′N	135°33′E
Fushimi, Japan (fōō′shē-mē)	211b	34°57′N	135°47′E
Fushun, China (fōō′shōōn′)	205	41°50′N	124°00′E
Fusong, China (fōō-sòŋ)	208	42°12′N	127°12′E
Futtsu, Japan (fōō′tsōō′)	211a	35°19′N	139°49′E
Futtsu Misaki, c., Japan (fōōt′tsōō′ mē-sä′kē)	211a	35°19′N	139°46′E
Fuwah, Egypt (fōō′wà)	238b	31°13′N	30°35′E
Fuxian, China (fōō shyĕn)	206	39°36′N	121°59′E
Fuxin, China (fōō-shyĭn)	208	42°05′N	121°40′E
Fuyang, China (fōō-yäŋ)	205	32°53′N	115°48′E
Fuyang, China	209	30°10′N	119°58′E
Fuyang, r., China (fōō-yäŋ)	206	36°59′N	114°48′E
Fuyu, China (fōō-yōō)	205	45°20′N	125°00′E
Fuzhou, China (fōō-jō)	205	26°02′N	119°18′E
Fuzhou, r., China	206	39°38′N	121°43′E
Fuzhoucheng, China (fōō-jō-chŭŋ)	206	39°46′N	121°44′E
Fyn, i., Den. (fü′′n)	166	55°24′N	10°33′E
Fyne, Loch, l., Scot., U.K. (fīn)	164	56°14′N	5°10′W
Fyresvatn, l., Nor.	166	59°04′N	7°55′E

G

PLACE (Pronunciation)	PAGE	LAT.	LONG.
Gaalkacyo, Som.	238a	7°00′N	47°30′E
Gabela, Ang.	236	10°48′S	14°20′E
Gabès, Tun. (gä′bĕs)	230	33°51′N	10°04′E
Gabès, Golfe de, b., Tun.	230	32°22′N	10°59′E
Gabil, Chad	235	11°09′N	18°12′E
Gąbin, Pol. (gôN′bĕn)	169	52°23′N	19°47′E
Gabon, nation, Afr. (gȧ-bôN′)	232	0°30′S	10°45′E
Gaborone, Bots.	232	24°28′S	25°59′E
Gabriel, r., Tx., U.S. (gā′brĭ-ĕl)	123	30°38′N	97°15′W
Gabrovo, Blg. (gäb′rô-vō)	175	42°52′N	25°19′E
Gachsārān, Iran	201	30°12′N	50°47′E
Gacko, Bos. (gäts′kô)	175	43°10′N	18°34′E
Gadsden, Al., U.S. (gădz′dĕn)	105	34°00′N	86°00′W
Găeşti, Rom. (gä-yĕsh′tê)	175	44°43′N	25°21′E
Gaeta, Italy (gä-ā′tä)	174	41°18′N	13°34′E
Gaffney, S.C., U.S. (găf′nĭ)	125	35°04′N	81°47′W
Gafsa, Tun. (găf′sä)	230	34°16′N	8°37′E
Gagarin, Russia	176	55°32′N	34°58′E
Gagnoa, C. Iv.	234	6°08′N	5°56′W
Gagra, Geor.	182	43°20′N	40°15′E
Gaillac-sur-Tarn, Fr. (gȧ-yäk′sür-tärn′)	170	43°54′N	1°52′E
Gaillard Cut, reg., Pan. (gä-ĕl-yä′rd)	128a	9°03′N	79°42′W
Gainesville, Fl., U.S. (gānz′vĭl)	105	29°40′N	82°20′W
Gainesville, Ga., U.S.	124	34°16′N	83°48′W
Gainesville, Tx., U.S.	121	33°38′N	97°08′W
Gainsborough, Eng., U.K. (gānz′bŭr-ô)	158a	53°23′N	0°46′W
Gairdner, Lake, l., Austl. (gård′nēr)	220	32°20′S	136°30′E
Gaithersburg, Md., U.S. (gā′thērs′bûrg)	110e	39°08′N	77°13′W
Gaixian, China (gī-shyĕn)	208	40°25′N	122°20′E
Galana, r., Kenya	237	3°00′S	39°30′E
Galapagar, Spain (gä-lä-pä-gär′)	173a	40°36′N	4°00′W
Galapagos Islands *see* Colón, Archipiélago de, is., Ec.	142	0°10′S	87°45′W
Galaria, r., Italy	173d	41°58′N	12°21′E
Galashiels, Scot., U.K. (găl-ȧ-shēlz)	164	55°40′N	2°57′W
Galaţi, Rom.	154	45°25′N	28°05′E
Galatina, Italy (gä-lä-tē′nä)	175	40°10′N	18°12′E
Galaxídi, Grc.	175	38°26′N	22°22′E
Galdhøpiggen, mtn., Nor.	166	61°37′N	8°17′E
Galeana, Mex. (gä-lå-ä′nä)	122	24°50′N	100°04′W
Galena, Il., U.S. (gȧ-lē′nȧ)	113	42°26′N	90°27′W
Galena, In., U.S.	111h	38°21′N	85°55′W
Galena Peak, mtn., Tx., U.S.	123a	29°44′N	95°14′W
Galera, Cerro, mtn., Pan. (sĕ′r-rô-gä-lĕ′rä)	128a	8°55′N	79°38′W
Galeras, vol., Col. (gä-lĕ′räs)	142	0°57′N	77°27′W
Gales, r., Or., U.S. (gālz)	116c	45°33′N	123°11′W
Galesburg, Il., U.S. (gālz′bûrg)	105	40°56′N	90°21′W
Galesville, Wi., U.S. (gālz′vĭl)	113	44°04′N	91°22′W
Galeton, Pa., U.S. (gāl′tŭn)	109	41°45′N	77°40′W
Galich, Russia (gäl′ĭch)	180	58°20′N	42°38′E
Galicia, hist. reg., Pol. (gȧ-lĭsh′ĭ-ȧ)	169	49°48′N	21°05′E
Galicia, hist. reg., Spain (gä-lē′thyä)	172	43°35′N	8°03′W
Galilee, l., Austl. (găl′ĭ-lē)	221	22°23′S	145°09′E
Galilee, Sea of, l., Isr.	197a	32°53′N	35°45′E
Galina Point, c., Jam. (gä-lē′nä)	134	18°25′N	76°50′W
Galion, Oh., U.S. (găl′ĭ-ŭn)	108	40°45′N	82°50′W
Galisteo, N.M., U.S. (gä-lĭs-tā′ō)	120	35°20′N	106°00′W
Gallarate, Italy (gäl-lä-rä′tä)	174	45°37′N	8°48′E
Gallardon, Fr. (gä-lär-dôN′)	171b	48°31′N	1°40′E
Gallatin, Mo., U.S. (găl′ȧ-tĭn)	121	39°55′N	93°58′W
Gallatin, Tn., U.S.	124	36°23′N	86°28′W
Gallatin, r., Mt., U.S.	115	45°12′N	111°10′W
Galle, Sri L. (gäl)	203	6°13′N	80°10′E
Gállego, r., Spain (gäl-yā′gō)	173	42°27′N	0°37′W
Gallinas, Punta de, c., Col. (gä-lyē′näs)	142	12°10′N	72°10′W
Gallipoli, Italy (gäl-lē′pô-lē)	175	40°03′N	17°58′E
Gallipoli *see* Gelibolu, Tur. (gäl-lē′pô-lē)	163	40°25′N	26°40′E
Gallipoli Peninsula, pen., Tur.	175	40°23′N	25°10′E
Gallipolis, Oh., U.S. (găl-ĭ-pô-lēs)	108	38°50′N	82°10′W
Gällivare, Swe. (yĕl-ĭ-vär′ĕ)	160	68°06′N	20°29′E
Gallo, r., Spain (gäl′yō)	172	40°43′N	1°42′W
Gallup, N.M., U.S. (găl′ŭp)	104	35°30′N	108°45′W
Galty Mountains, mts., Ire.	164	52°19′N	8°20′W
Galva, Il., U.S. (găl′vȧ)	121	41°11′N	90°02′W
Galveston, Tx., U.S. (găl′vĕs-tŭn)	105	29°18′N	94°48′W
Galveston Bay, b., Tx., U.S.	107	29°39′N	94°45′W
Galveston I, Tx., U.S.	123a	29°12′N	94°53′W
Galway, Ire.	154	53°16′N	9°05′W
Galway Bay, b., Ire. (gôl′wā)	164	53°10′N	9°47′W
Gamba, China (gäm-bä)	202	28°23′N	89°42′E
Gambaga, Ghana (gäm-bä′gä)	230	10°32′N	0°26′W
Gambela, Eth. (gäm-bā′lȧ)	231	8°15′N	34°33′E
Gambia (Gambie), r., Afr.	234	13°20′N	15°55′W
Gambia, The, nation, Afr.	230	13°38′N	19°38′W
Gambie, r., Afr.	230	12°30′N	13°00′W
Gamboma, Congo (gäm-bō′mä)	232	1°53′S	15°51′E
Gamleby, Swe. (gäm′lĕ-bü)	166	57°54′N	16°20′E
Gan, r., China (gän)	209	26°50′N	115°00′E
Gäncä, Azer.	180	40°40′N	46°22′E
Gandak, r., India	202	26°37′N	84°22′E
Gander, Can. (găn′dēr)	91	48°57′N	54°34′W
Gander, r., Can.	101	49°10′N	54°35′W
Gander Lake, l., Can.	101	48°55′N	55°40′W
Gandhinagar, India	202	23°30′N	72°47′E
Gandi, Nig.	235	12°55′N	5°49′E
Gandía, Spain (gän-dē′ä)	173	38°56′N	0°10′W
Gangdisê Shan (Trans Himalayas), mts., China	204	30°25′N	83°43′E
Ganges, r., Asia (găn′jēz)	199	24°00′N	89°30′E
Ganges, Mouths of the, mth., Asia (găn′jēz)	199	21°18′N	88°40′E
Gangi, Italy (gän′jē)	174	37°48′N	14°15′E
Gangtok, India	199	27°15′N	88°30′E
Gannan, China (gän-nän)	208	47°50′N	123°30′E
Gannett Peak, mtn., Wy., U.S. (găn′ĕt)	106	43°10′N	109°38′W
Gano, Oh., U.S. (ă′nō)	111f	39°18′N	84°24′W
Gänserndorf, Aus.	159e	48°21′N	16°43′E
Gansu, prov., China (gän-sōō)	204	38°50′N	101°10′E
Ganwo, Nig.	235	11°13′N	4°42′E
Ganyu, China (gän-yōō)	206	34°52′N	119°07′E
Ganzhou, China (gän-jō)	205	25°50′N	114°30′E
Gao, Mali (gä′ō)	230	16°16′N	0°03′W
Gao′an, China (gou-än)	209	28°30′N	115°02′E
Gaomi, China (gou-mē)	206	36°23′N	119°46′E
Gaoqiao, China (gou-chyou)	207b	31°21′N	121°35′E
Gaoshun, China (gou-shòn)	206	31°22′N	118°50′E
Gaotang, China (gou-täŋ)	206	36°52′N	116°12′E
Gaoyao, China (gou-you)	209	23°08′N	112°25′E
Gaoyi, China (gou-yē)	206	37°37′N	114°39′E
Gaoyou, China (gou-yō)	208	32°46′N	119°26′E
Gaoyou Hu, l., China (kä′ō-yōō′hōō)	205	32°42′N	118°40′E
Gap, Fr. (gȧp)	161	44°34′N	6°08′E
Gapan, Phil. (gä-pän)	213a	15°18′N	120°56′E
Gar, China	204	31°11′N	80°35′E
Garanhuns, Braz. (gä-rän-yònsh′)	143	8°49′S	36°28′W
Garber, Ok., U.S. (gär′bēr)	121	36°28′N	97°35′W
Garching, Ger. (gär′kĕng)	159d	48°15′N	11°39′E
Garcia, Mex. (gär-sē′ä)	122	25°50′N	100°37′W
García de la Cadena, Mex.	130	21°14′N	103°26′W
Garda, Lago di, l., Italy (lä-gō-dē-gär′dä)	162	45°43′N	10°26′E
Gardanne, Fr. (gȧr-dȧn′)	170a	43°28′N	5°29′E
Gardelegen, Ger. (gär-dē-lå′ghĕn)	168	52°32′N	11°22′E
Garden, i., Mi., U.S. (gär′d′n)	108	45°50′N	85°50′W
Gardena, Ca., U.S. (gär-dē′nȧ)	117a	33°53′N	118°19′W
Garden City, Ks., U.S.	120	37°58′N	100°52′W
Garden City, Mi., U.S.	111b	42°20′N	83°21′W
Garden Grove, Ca., U.S. (gär′d′n grōv)	117a	33°47′N	117°56′W
Garden Reach, India	202a	22°33′N	88°17′E
Garden River, Can.	117k	46°33′N	84°10′W
Gardeyz, Afg.	202	33°43′N	69°09′E
Gardiner, Me., U.S. (gärd′nēr)	100	44°12′N	69°46′W
Gardiner, Mt., U.S.	115	45°03′N	110°43′W
Gardiner, Wa., U.S.	116a	48°03′N	122°55′W
Gardiner Dam, dam, Can.	96	51°17′N	106°51′W
Gardner, Ma., U.S.	109	42°35′N	72°00′W
Gardner Canal, strt., Can.	94	53°28′N	128°15′W
Gardner Pinnacles, Hi., U.S.	126b	25°10′N	167°00′W
Gareloi, i., Ak., U.S. (gär-lōō-ā′)	103a	51°40′N	178°48′W
Garfield, N.J., U.S. (gär′fēld)	110a	40°53′N	74°06′W
Garfield, Ut., U.S.	117b	40°45′N	112°10′W
Garfield Heights, Oh., U.S.	111d	41°25′N	81°36′W
Gargaliánoi, Grc. (gär-gä-lyä′nē)	175	37°07′N	21°50′E
Gargždai, Lith. (gärgzh′dī)	167	55°43′N	20°09′E
Garibaldi, Mount, mtn., Can. (gâr-ĭ-băl′dē)	94	49°51′N	123°01′W
Garin, Arg. (gä-rē′n)	144a	34°25′S	58°44′W
Garissa, Kenya	237	0°28′S	39°38′E
Garland, Tx., U.S. (gär′lănd)	117c	32°55′N	96°39′W
Garland, Ut., U.S.	115	41°45′N	112°10′W
Garm, Taj.	183	39°12′N	70°28′E
Garmisch-Partenkirchen, Ger. (gär′mēsh pär′tĕn-kēr′kĕn)	168	47°38′N	11°10′E
Garnett, Ks., U.S. (gär′nĕt)	121	38°16′N	95°15′W
Garonne, r., Fr. (gȧ-rôn)	156	44°00′N	1°00′E
Garoua, Cam. (gär′wä)	231	9°18′N	13°24′E
Garrett, In., U.S. (găr′ĕt)	108	41°20′N	85°10′W
Garrison, N.D., U.S.	112	47°38′N	101°24′W
Garrison, N.Y., U.S. (găr′ĭ-sŭn)	110a	41°23′N	73°57′W
Garrovillas, Spain (gä-rô-vēl′yäs)	172	39°42′N	6°30′W
Garry, l., Can. (găr′ĭ)	92	66°16′N	99°23′W
Garsen, Kenya	237	2°16′S	40°07′E
Garson, Can.	99	46°34′N	80°52′W
Garstedt, Ger. (gär′shtĕt)	159c	53°40′N	9°58′E
Garulia, India	202a	22°48′N	88°23′E
Garwolin, Pol. (gär-vō′lēn)	169	51°54′N	21°40′E
Gary, In., U.S. (gā′rĭ)	105	41°35′N	87°21′W
Gary, W.V., U.S. (fĭl′bĕrt)	125	37°21′N	81°33′W
Garzón, Col. (gär-thōn′)	142	2°13′N	75°44′W
Gasan, Phil. (gä-sän′)	213a	13°19′N	121°52′E
Gasan-Kuli, Turkmen.	183	37°25′N	53°55′E
Gas City, In., U.S. (găs)	108	40°30′N	85°40′W
Gascogne, reg., Fr. (gäs-kôn′yĕ)	170	43°45′N	1°49′W
Gasconade, r., Mo., U.S. (găs-kô-nād′)	121	37°46′N	92°15′W
Gascoyne, r., Austl. (găs-koin′)	220	25°15′S	117°00′E
Gashland, Mo., U.S. (găsh′-lănd)	117f	39°15′N	94°35′W
Gashua, Nig.	235	12°54′N	11°00′E
Gasny, Fr. (gäs-nē′)	171b	49°05′N	1°36′E
Gaspé, Can.	91	48°50′N	64°29′W
Gaspé, Péninsule de, pen., Can.	93	48°30′N	65°00′W
Gasper Hernández, Dom. Rep. (gäs-pär′ ĕr-nän′dāth)	135	19°40′N	70°15′W
Gassaway, W.V., U.S. (găs′ȧ-wā)	108	38°40′N	80°45′W
Gaston, Or., U.S. (găs′tŭn)	116c	45°26′N	123°08′W
Gastonia, N.C., U.S. (găs-tô′nĭ-ȧ)	125	35°15′N	81°14′W
Gastre, Arg. (gäs-trĕ)	144	42°12′S	68°50′W
Gata, Cabo de, c., Spain (kȧ′bô-dĕ-gä′tä)	162	36°42′N	2°00′W
Gata, Sierra de, mts., Spain (syĕr′rȧ dā gä′tä)	162	40°12′N	6°39′W
Gatchina, Russia (gä-chē′nȧ)	180	59°33′N	30°08′E
Gátes, Akrotírion, c., Cyp.	197a	34°30′N	33°15′E
Gateshead, Eng., U.K. (gāts′hĕd)	164	54°56′N	1°38′W
Gates of the Arctic National Park, rec., Ak., U.S.	103	67°45′N	153°30′W
Gatesville, Tx., U.S. (gāts′vĭl)	123	31°26′N	97°34′W
Gâtine, Hauteurs de, hills, Fr.	170	46°40′N	0°50′W
Gatineau, Can. (gȧ′tē-nō)	102c	45°29′N	75°38′W
Gatineau, r., Can.	99	45°45′N	75°50′W
Gatineau, Parc de la, rec., Can.	99	45°32′N	75°53′W
Gattendorf, Aus.	159e	48°01′N	17°00′E

ng-sing; ŋ-baŋk; N-nasalized n; nŏd; cŏmmit; ōld; ôbey; ôrder; oi-boil; fōōd; ò-as oo in foot; ou-out; s-soft; sh-dish; th-thin; pūre; ûnite; ûrn; stŭd; circŭs; ü-as in French tu; ′-indeterminate vowel.

PLACE (Pronunciation)	PAGE	LAT.	LONG.
Gatun, Pan. (gä-tōōn′)	133	9°16′N	79°25′W
Gatun, r., Pan.	128a	9°21′N	79°40′W
Gatún, Lago, l., Pan.	133	9°13′N	79°24′W
Gatun Locks, trans., Pan.	128a	9°16′N	79°57′W
Gauhāti, India	199	26°09′N	91°51′E
Gauja, r., Lat. (gå′ô-yå)	167	57°10′N	24°30′E
Gaula, r., Nor.	166	62°55′N	10°45′E
Gávdos, i., Grc. (gäv′dôs)	163	34°48′N	24°08′E
Gavins Point Dam, Ne., U.S. (gă′-vĭns)	112	42°47′N	97°47′W
Gāvkhūnī, Bātlāq-e, l., Iran	198	31°40′N	52°48′E
Gävle, Swe. (yĕv′lĕ)	154	60°40′N	17°07′E
Gävlebukten, b., Swe.	166	60°45′N	17°30′E
Gavrilov Posad, Russia (gá′vrĭ-lôf′ka po-sát)	176	56°34′N	40°09′E
Gavrilov-Yam, Russia (gá′vrĭ-lôf yäm′)	176	57°17′N	39°49′E
Gawler, Austl. (gô′lĕr)	218	34°35′S	138°47′E
Gawler Ranges, mts., Austl.	222	32°35′S	136°30′E
Gaya, India (gŭ′yä)(gī′á)	199	24°53′N	85°00′E
Gaya, Nig. (gä′yä)	230	11°58′N	9°05′E
Gaylord, Mi., U.S. (gā′lôrd)	108	45°00′N	84°35′W
Gayndah, Austl. (gān′dāh)	222	25°43′S	151°33′E
Gaza, Gaza	198	31°30′N	34°29′E
Gaziantep, Tur. (gä-zē-än′tĕp)	198	37°10′N	37°30′E
Gbarnga, Lib.	234	7°00′N	9°29′W
Gdańsk, Pol. (g′dänsk)	154	54°20′N	18°40′E
Gdov, Russia (g′dôf′)	180	58°44′N	27°51′E
Gdynia, Pol. (g′dēn′yä)	160	54°29′N	18°30′E
Geary, Ok., U.S. (gē′rĭ)	120	35°36′N	98°19′W
Géba, r., Gui.-B.	234	12°25′N	14°35′W
Gebo, Wy., U.S. (gĕb′ō)	115	43°49′N	108°13′W
Ged, La., U.S. (gĕd)	123	30°07′N	93°36′W
Gediz, r., Tur.	163	38°44′N	28°45′E
Gedney, i., Wa., U.S. (gĕd-nē)	116a	48°01′N	122°18′W
Gedser, Den.	166	54°35′N	12°08′E
Geel, Bel.	159a	51°09′N	5°01′E
Geelong, Austl. (jē-lông′)	219	38°06′S	144°13′E
Gegu, China (gŭ-gōō)	206	39°00′N	117°30′E
Ge Hu, l., China (gŭ hōō)	206	31°37′N	119°57′E
Geidam, Nig.	230	12°57′N	11°57′E
Geikie Range, mts., Austl. (gē′kē)	220	17°35′S	125°32′E
Geislingen, Ger. (gīs′lĭng-ĕn)	168	48°37′N	9°52′E
Geist Reservoir, res., In., U.S. (gēst)	111g	39°57′N	85°59′W
Geita, Tan.	237	2°52′S	32°10′E
Gejiu, China (gŭ-jĭo)	209	23°32′N	102°50′E
Geldermalsen, Neth.	159a	51°53′N	5°18′E
Geldern, Ger. (gĕl′dĕrn)	171c	51°31′N	6°20′E
Gelibolu, Tur. (gĕ-lĭb′ō-lō)	163	40°25′N	26°40′E
Gelsenkirchen, Ger. (gĕl-zĕn-kĭrk-ĕn)	168	51°31′N	7°05′E
Gemas, Malay. (jĕm′ás)	197b	2°35′N	102°37′E
Gemena, D.R.C.	231	3°15′N	19°46′E
Gemlik, Tur. (gĕm′lĭk)	163	40°30′N	29°10′E
Genale (Jubba), r., Afr.	238a	5°15′N	41°00′E
General Alvear, Arg. (gĕ-nĕ-räl′ál-vĕ-á′r)	141c	36°04′S	60°02′W
General Arenales, Arg. (ä-rĕ-nä′lĕs)	141c	34°19′S	61°16′W
General Belgrano, Arg. (bĕl-grá′nô)	141c	35°45′S	58°32′W
General Cepeda, Mex. (sĕ-pĕ′dä)	122	25°24′N	101°29′W
General Conesa, Arg. (kô-nĕ′sä)	141c	36°30′S	57°19′W
General Guido, Arg. (gē′dô)	141c	36°41′S	57°48′W
General Lavalle, Arg. (lá-vá′l-yĕ)	141c	36°25′S	56°55′W
General Madariaga, Arg. (män-dá-rēä′gä)	144	36°59′S	57°14′W
General Paz, Arg. (pá′z)	141c	35°30′S	58°20′W
General Pedro Antonio Santos, Mex.	130	21°37′N	98°58′W
General Pico, Arg. (pē′kô)	144	36°46′S	63°44′W
General Roca, Arg. (rô-kä)	144	39°01′S	67°31′W
General San Martín, Arg. (sän-már-tē′n)	144a	34°35′S	58°32′W
General Sarmiento (San Miguel), Arg.	144a	34°33′S	58°43′W
General Viamonte, Arg. (vēá′môn-tĕ)	141c	35°01′S	60°59′W
General Zuazua, Mex. (zwá′zwä)	122	25°54′N	100°07′W
Genesee, r., N.Y., U.S. (jĕn-ē-sē′)	109	42°25′N	78°10′W
Geneseo, Il., U.S. (jē-nĕsēō)	108	41°28′N	90°11′W
Geneva (Genève), Switz.	154	46°14′N	6°04′E
Geneva, Al., U.S. (jē-nē′vá)	124	31°03′N	85°50′W
Geneva, Il., U.S.	111a	41°53′N	88°18′W
Geneva, Ne., U.S.	121	40°32′N	97°37′W
Geneva, N.Y., U.S.	109	42°50′N	77°00′W
Geneva, Oh., U.S.	108	41°45′N	80°55′W
Geneva, Lake, l., Switz.	161	46°28′N	6°30′E
Genève see Geneva, Switz.	154	46°14′N	6°04′E
Genil, r., Spain (hå-nēl′)	172	37°15′N	4°05′W
Genoa, Italy	154	44°23′N	9°52′E
Genoa, Ne., U.S. (jen′ô-á)	121	41°26′N	97°43′W
Genoa City, Wi., U.S.	111a	42°31′N	88°19′W
Genova, Golfo di, b., Italy (gôl-fô-dē-jĕn′ō-vä)	156	44°10′N	8°45′E
Genovesa, i., Ec. (ĕ′s-lä-gĕ-nō-vĕ-sä)	142	0°08′N	90°15′W
Gent, Bel.	161	51°05′N	3°40′E
Genthin, Ger. (gĕn-tēn′)	168	52°24′N	12°10′E
Genzano di Roma, Italy (gzhĕnt-zá′-nô-dē-rô′mä)	173d	41°43′N	12°49′E
Geographe Bay, b., Austl. (jē-ô-graf′)	220	33°00′S	114°00′E
Geographe Channel, strt., Austl. (jēô′grā-fĭk)	220	24°15′S	112°50′E
George, l., N.Y., U.S. (jôrj)	109	43°40′N	73°30′W
George, Lake, l., N.A. (jôrg)	117k	46°26′N	84°09′W
George, Lake, l., Ug.	237	0°02′N	30°25′E
George, Lake, l., Fl., U.S. (jôr-ĭj)	125	29°10′N	81°50′W
George, Lake, l., In., U.S.	111a	41°31′N	87°17′W
Georges, r., Austl.	217b	33°57′S	151°00′E
George Town, Bah.	135	23°30′N	75°50′W
Georgetown, Can. (jôrg-toun)	102d	43°39′N	79°56′W
Georgetown, Can. (jôr-ĭj-toun)	101	46°11′N	62°32′W
George Town, Cay. Is.	134	19°20′N	81°20′W
Georgetown, Guy. (jôrj′toun)	143	7°45′N	58°04′W
George Town, Malay.	212	5°21′N	100°09′E
Georgetown, Ct., U.S.	110a	41°15′N	73°25′W
Georgetown, De., U.S.	109	38°40′N	75°20′W
Georgetown, Il., U.S.	108	40°00′N	87°40′W
Georgetown, Ky., U.S.	108	38°10′N	84°35′W
Georgetown, Ma., U.S. (jôrg-toun)	101a	42°43′N	71°00′W
Georgetown, Md., U.S.	109	39°25′N	75°55′W
Georgetown, S.C., U.S. (jôr-ĭj-toun)	125	33°22′N	79°17′W
Georgetown, Tx., U.S. (jôrg-toun)	123	30°37′N	97°40′W
George Washington Birthplace National Monument, rec., Va., U.S. (jôrj wŏsh′ĭng-tŭn)	109	38°10′N	77°00′W
George Washington Carver National Monument, rec., Mo., U.S. (jôrg wăsh-ĭng-tŭn kär′vĕr)	121	36°58′N	94°21′W
George West, Tx., U.S.	122	28°20′N	98°07′W
Georgia, nation, Asia	178	42°17′N	43°00′E
Georgia, state, U.S. (jôr′ji-ă)	105	32°40′N	83°50′W
Georgia, Strait of, strt., N.A.	94	49°20′N	124°00′W
Georgiana, Al., U.S. (jôr-jē-ăn′á)	124	31°39′N	86°44′W
Georgian Bay, b., Can.	93	45°15′N	80°50′W
Georgian Bay Islands National Park, rec., Can.	98	45°20′N	81°40′W
Georgina, r., Austl. (jôr-jē′ná)	220	22°00′S	138°15′E
Georgiyevsk, Russia (gyôr-gyĕfsk′)	181	44°05′N	43°30′E
Gera, Ger. (gā′rä)	161	50°52′N	12°06′E
Geral, Serra, mts., Braz. (sĕr′rá zhä-räl′)	144	28°30′S	51°00′W
Geral de Goiás, Serra, mts., Braz. (zhä-räl′-dĕ-gô-yá′s)	143	14°22′S	45°40′W
Geraldton, Austl. (jĕr′ăld-tŭn)	218	28°40′S	114°35′E
Geraldton, Can.	91	49°43′N	87°00′W
Gérgal, Spain (gĕr′gäl)	172	37°08′N	2°29′W
Gering, Ne., U.S. (gē′rĭng)	112	41°49′N	103°41′W
Gerlachovský štít, mtn., Slvk.	169	49°12′N	20°08′E
Germantown, Oh., U.S. (jûr′măn-toun)	108	39°35′N	84°25′W
Germany, nation, Eur. (jûr′mà-nĭ)	154	51°00′N	10°00′E
Germiston, S. Afr. (jûr′mĭs-tŭn)	232	26°19′S	28°11′E
Gerona, Phil. (hā-rō′nä)	213a	15°36′N	120°36′E
Gerrards Cross, Eng., U.K. (jĕrărds krŏs)	158b	51°34′N	0°33′W
Gers, r., Fr. (zhĕr)	173	43°25′N	0°30′E
Gersthofen, Ger. (gĕrst-hō′fĕn)	159d	48°26′N	10°54′E
Getafe, Spain (hā-tä′fā)	172	40°19′N	3°44′W
Gettysburg, Pa., U.S. (gĕt′ĭs-bûrg)	109	39°50′N	77°15′W
Gettysburg, S.D., U.S.	112	45°01′N	99°59′W
Gevelsberg, Ger. (gĕ-fĕls′bĕrgh)	171c	51°18′N	7°20′E
Ghāghra, r., India	199	26°00′N	83°00′E
Ghana, nation, Afr. (gän′ä)	230	8°00′N	2°00′W
Ghanzi, Bots. (gän′zē)	232	21°30′S	22°00′E
Ghardaïa, Alg. (gär-dä′ē-ä)	230	32°29′N	3°38′E
Gharo, Pak.	202	24°50′N	68°35′E
Ghāt, Libya	230	24°52′N	10°16′E
Ghazāl, Bahr al-, r., Sudan	231	9°30′N	30°00′E
Ghazal, Bahr el, r., Chad (bär ĕl ghä-zäl′)	235	14°30′N	17°00′E
Ghazzah see Gaza, Gaza	198	31°30′N	34°29′E
Gheorgheni, Rom.	163	46°48′N	25°30′E
Gherla, Rom. (gĕr′lä)	169	47°01′N	23°55′E
Ghilizane, Alg.	230	35°43′N	0°43′E
Ghorīān, Afg.	201	34°21′N	61°30′E
Ghost Lake, Can.	102e	51°15′N	114°46′W
Ghudāmis, Libya	230	30°07′N	9°26′E
Giannitsá, Grc.	175	40°47′N	22°26′E
Giannutri, Isola di, i., Italy (jän-nōō′trē)	174	42°15′N	11°06′E
Giant Sequoia National Monument, rec., Ca., U.S.	118	36°10′N	118°35′W
Gibara, Cuba (hē-bä′rä)	134	21°05′N	76°10′W
Gibeon, Nmb. (gĭb′ē-ŭn)	232	25°15′S	17°30′E
Gibraleón, Spain (hē-brä-lå-ōn′)	172	37°24′N	7°00′W
Gibraltar, dep., Eur. (gĭ-bräl-tă′r)	154	36°08′N	5°22′W
Gibraltar, Strait of, strt.	156	35°55′N	5°45′W
Gibson City, Il., U.S. (gĭb′sŭn)	108	40°25′N	88°20′W
Gibson Desert, des., Austl.	220	24°45′S	123°15′E
Gibson Island, Md., U.S.	110e	39°05′N	76°26′W
Gibson Reservoir, res., Ok., U.S.	121	36°07′N	95°08′W
Giddings, Tx., U.S. (gĭd′ĭngz)	123	30°11′N	96°55′W
Gideon, Mo., U.S. (gĭd′ē-ŭn)	121	36°27′N	89°56′W
Gien, Fr. (zhē-ăn′)	161	47°43′N	2°37′E
Giessen, Ger. (gēs′sĕn)	168	50°35′N	8°40′E
Gifu, Japan (gē′fōō)	205	35°25′N	136°45′E
Gig Harbor, Wa., U.S. (gĭg)	116a	47°20′N	122°36′W
Giglio, Isola del, i., Italy (jēl′yō)	174	42°23′N	10°55′E
Gijón, Spain (hē-hōn′)	154	43°33′N	5°37′W
Gila, r., U.S. (hē′lá)	106	33°00′N	110°00′W
Gila Bend, Az., U.S.	119	32°59′N	112°41′W
Gila Cliff Dwellings National Monument, rec., N.M., U.S.	119	33°15′N	108°20′W
Gila River Indian Reservation, I.R., Az., U.S.	119	33°11′N	112°38′W
Gilbert, Mn., U.S. (gĭl′bĕrt)	113	47°27′N	92°29′W
Gilbert, r., Austl. (gĭl-bĕrt)	221	17°15′S	142°09′E
Gilbert, Mount, mtn., Can.	94	50°51′N	124°20′W
Gilbert Islands, is., Kir.	241	0°30′S	174°00′E
Gilboa, Mount, mtn., S. Afr. (gĭl-bôá)	233c	29°13′S	30°17′W
Gilford Island, i., Can. (gĭl′fĕrd)	94	50°45′N	126°25′W
Gilgit, Pak. (gĭl′gĭt)	199	35°58′N	73°48′E
Gil Island, i., Can. (gĭl)	94	53°13′N	129°15′W
Gillen, l., Austl. (jĭl′ĕn)	220	26°15′S	125°15′E
Gillett, Ar., U.S. (jĭ-lĕt′)	121	34°07′N	91°22′W
Gillette, Wy., U.S.	115	44°17′N	105°30′W
Gillingham, Eng., U.K. (gĭl′ĭng ăm)	165	51°23′N	0°33′E
Gilman, Il., U.S. (gĭl′măn)	108	40°45′N	87°55′W
Gilman Hot Springs, Ca., U.S.	117a	33°49′N	116°57′W
Gilmer, Tx., U.S. (gĭl′mĕr)	123	32°43′N	94°57′W
Gilmore, Ga., U.S. (gĭl′môr)	110c	33°51′N	84°29′W
Gilo, r., Eth.	231	7°40′N	34°17′E
Gilroy, Ca., U.S. (gĭl-roi′)	118	37°00′N	121°34′W
Giluwe, Mount, mtn., Pap. N. Gui.	213	6°04′S	144°00′E
Gimli, Can. (gĭm′lē)	97	50°39′N	97°00′W
Gimone, r., Fr. (zhē-mōn′)	170	43°26′N	0°36′E
Ginir, Eth.	231	7°13′N	40°44′E
Ginosa, Italy (jē-nō′zä)	174	40°35′N	16°48′E
Gioia del Colle, Italy (jô′yä dĕl kôl′lā)	174	40°48′N	16°55′E
Girard, Ks., U.S. (jĭ-rärd′)	121	37°30′N	94°50′W
Girardot, Col. (hē-rär-dōt′)	142	4°19′N	74°47′W
Giresun, Tur. (ghĕr′ĕ-sŏn′)	198	40°55′N	38°20′E
Giridih, India (jē-rē-dē)	199	24°12′N	86°18′E
Girona, Spain	162	41°55′N	2°48′E
Gironde, r., Fr. (zhē-rônd′)	156	45°31′N	1°00′W
Girvan, Scot., U.K. (gûr′văn)	164	55°15′N	5°01′W
Gisborne, N.Z. (gĭz′bŭrn)	221a	38°40′S	178°08′E
Gisenyi, Rw.	232	1°43′S	29°15′E
Gisors, Fr. (zhē-zôr′)	170	49°19′N	1°47′E
Gitambo, D.R.C.	236	4°21′N	24°45′E
Gitega, Bdi.	232	3°39′S	30°05′E
Giurgiu, Rom. (jŏr′jŏ)	175	43°53′N	25°58′E
Givet, Fr. (zhē-vĕ′)	170	50°08′N	4°47′E
Givors, Fr. (zhē-vôr′)	170	45°35′N	4°46′E
Giza see Al Jīzah, Egypt	238b	30°01′N	31°12′E
Gizhiga, Russia (gē′zhi-gá)	179	61°59′N	160°46′E
Gizo, Sol. Is.	214e	8°06′S	156°51′E
Gizycko, Pol. (gĭ′zhĭ-ko)	160	54°03′N	21°48′E
Gjirokastër, Alb.	163	40°04′N	20°10′E
Gjøvik, Nor. (gyû′vĕk)	160	60°47′N	10°36′E
Glabeek-Zuurbemde, Bel.	159a	50°52′N	4°59′E
Glace Bay, Can. (gläs bā)	101	46°12′N	59°57′W
Glacier Bay National Park, rec., Ak., U.S. (glā′shĕr)	106a	58°40′N	136°50′W
Glacier National Park, rec., Can.	92	51°45′N	117°35′W
Glacier Peak, mtn., Wa., U.S.	114	48°07′N	121°10′W
Glacier Point, c., Can.	116a	48°24′N	123°59′W
Gladbeck, Ger. (gläd′bĕk)	168	51°35′N	6°59′E
Gladdeklipkop, S. Afr.	238c	24°17′S	29°36′E
Gladstone, Austl. (glăd′stōn)	219	23°45′S	152°00′E
Gladstone, Austl.	218	33°15′S	138°20′E
Gladstone, Mi., U.S.	113	45°50′N	87°04′W
Gladstone, N.J., U.S.	110a	40°43′N	74°39′W
Gladstone, Or., U.S.	116c	45°23′N	122°36′W
Gladwin, Mi., U.S. (glăd′wĭn)	108	44°00′N	84°25′W
Glåma, r., Nor.	156	61°30′N	10°30′E
Glarus, Switz. (glä′rŏs)	168	47°02′N	9°03′E
Glasgow, Scot., U.K. (glås′gō)	154	55°54′N	4°25′W
Glasgow, Ky., U.S.	124	37°00′N	85°55′W
Glasgow, Mo., U.S.	121	39°14′N	92°48′W
Glasgow, Mt., U.S.	115	48°14′N	106°39′W
Glassport, Pa., U.S. (glás′pôrt)	111e	40°19′N	79°53′W
Glauchau, Ger. (glou′kou)	168	50°51′N	12°28′E
Glazov, Russia (glä′zôf)	178	58°05′N	52°52′E
Glen, r., Eng., U.K. (glĕn)	158a	52°44′N	0°18′W
Glénan, Îles de, is., Fr. (ĕl-dĕ-glā-nän′)	170	47°43′N	4°42′W
Glen Burnie, Md., U.S. (bûr′nē)	110e	39°10′N	76°38′W
Glen Canyon, p., Ut., U.S.	119	37°10′N	110°50′W
Glen Canyon Dam, dam, Az., U.S. (glĕn kăn′yŭn)	106	36°57′N	111°25′W
Glen Canyon National Recreation Area, rec., U.S.	119	37°00′N	111°20′W
Glen Carbon, Il., U.S. (kär′bŏn)	117e	38°45′N	89°59′W
Glencoe, S. Afr. (glĕn-cō)	233c	28°14′S	30°09′E
Glencoe, Il., U.S.	111a	42°08′N	87°45′W
Glencoe, Mn., U.S. (glĕn′kō)	113	44°44′N	94°07′W
Glen Cove, N.Y., U.S. (kōv)	110a	40°51′N	73°38′W
Glendale, Az., U.S. (glĕn′dāl)	119	33°30′N	112°15′W
Glendale, Ca., U.S.	104	34°09′N	118°15′W
Glendale, Oh., U.S.	111f	31°16′N	84°22′W
Glendive, Mt., U.S. (glĕn′dīv)	104	47°08′N	104°41′W
Glendo, Wy., U.S.	115	42°32′N	104°54′W
Glendora, Ca., U.S. (glĕn-dō′rá)	117a	34°08′N	117°52′W
Glenelg, r., Austl.	222	37°20′S	141°30′E
Glen Ellyn, Il., U.S. (glĕn ĕl′-lĕn)	111a	41°53′N	88°04′W
Glen Innes, Austl. (ĭn′ĕs)	219	29°45′S	152°02′E
Glenns Ferry, Id., U.S. (fĕr′ĭ)	114	42°58′N	115°21′W
Glen Olden, Pa., U.S. (ōl′d′n)	110f	39°54′N	75°17′W
Glenomra, La., U.S. (glĕn-mō′rá)	123	30°58′N	92°36′W
Glenrock, Wy., U.S. (glĕn′rŏk)	115	42°50′N	105°53′W
Glens Falls, N.Y., U.S. (glĕnz fôlz)	109	43°20′N	73°40′W
Glenshaw, Pa., U.S. (glĕn′shô)	111e	40°33′N	79°57′W
Glen Valley, Can.	116d	49°09′N	122°30′W
Glenview, Il., U.S. (glĕn′vū)	111a	42°04′N	87°48′W
Glenville, Ga., U.S. (glĕn′vĭl)	125	31°55′N	81°56′W
Glenwood, Ia., U.S.	112	41°03′N	95°44′W
Glenwood, Mn., U.S.	112	45°39′N	95°23′W
Glenwood, N.M., U.S.	119	33°19′N	108°52′W
Glenwood Springs, Co., U.S.	119	39°35′N	107°20′W
Glienicke, Ger. (glē′nē-kĕ)	159b	52°38′N	13°19′E
Glinde, Ger. (glēn′dĕ)	159c	53°32′N	10°13′E
Glittertinden, mtn., Nor.	166	61°39′N	8°33′E
Gliwice, Pol. (gwĭ-wĭt′sĕ)	161	50°18′N	18°40′E
Globe, Az., U.S. (glōb)	104	33°20′N	110°50′W
Głogów, Pol. (gwō′gōōv)	161	51°40′N	16°04′E
Glommen, r., Nor. (glôm′ĕn)	166	60°03′N	11°15′E
Glonn, Ger. (glônn)	159d	47°59′N	11°52′E

PRONOUNCING INDEX

Glorieuses – Grand Rapids 297

PLACE (Pronunciation)	PAGE	LAT.	LONG.
Glorieuses, Îles, is., Reu.	233	11°28'S	47°50'E
Glossop, Eng., U.K. (glŏs'ŭp)	158a	53°26'N	1°57'W
Gloster, Ms., U.S. (glŏs'tēr)	124	31°10'N	91°00'W
Gloucester, Eng., U.K. (glŏs'tēr)	161	51°54'N	2°11'W
Gloucester, Ma., U.S.	101a	42°37'N	70°40'W
Gloucester City, N.J., U.S.	110f	39°53'N	75°08'W
Glouster, Oh., U.S. (glŏs'tēr)	108	39°35'N	82°05'W
Glover Island, i., Can. (glŭv'ēr)	101	48°44'N	57°45'W
Gloversville, N.Y., U.S. (glŭv'ērz-vĭl)	109	43°05'N	74°20'W
Glovertown, Can. (glŭv'ēr-toun)	101	48°41'N	54°02'W
Glückstadt, Ger. (glük-shtät)	159c	53°47'N	9°25'E
Glushkovo, Russia (glòsh'kô-vō)	177	51°21'N	34°43'E
Gmünden, Aus. (g'mòn'dĕn)	168	47°57'N	13°47'E
Gniezno, Pol. (g'nyāz'nô)	161	52°32'N	17°34'E
Gnjilane, Yugo. (gnyē'là-nĕ)	175	42°28'N	21°27'E
Goa, state, India (gō'á)	199	15°45'N	74°00'E
Goascorán, Hond. (gō-äs'kō-rän')	132	13°37'N	87°43'W
Goba, Eth. (gō'bä)	231	7°17'N	39°58'E
Gobabis, Nmb. (gō-bä'bĭs)	232	22°25'S	18°50'E
Gobi, des., Asia (gō'be)	204	43°29'N	103°15'E
Goble, Or., U.S. (gō'b'l)	116c	46°01'N	122°53'W
Goch, Ger. (gôk)	171c	51°35'N	6°10'E
Godāvari, r., India (gō-dä'vŭ-rē)	199	19°00'N	78°30'E
Goddards Soak, sw., Austl. (gŏd'ȧrdz)	220	31°20'S	123°30'E
Goderich, Can. (gōd'rĭch)	98	43°45'N	81°45'W
Godfrey, Il., U.S. (gŏd'frē)	117e	38°57'N	90°12'W
Godhavn, Grnld. (gōdh'hȧvn)	89	69°15'N	53°30'W
Gods, r., Can. (ŏodz)	97	55°17'N	93°35'W
Gods Lake, Can.	91	54°40'N	94°09'W
Godthåb, Grnld. (gŏt'hŏb)	89	64°10'N	51°32'W
Goéland, Lac au, l., Can.	99	49°47'N	76°41'W
Goffs, Ca., U.S. (gôfs)	118	34°57'N	115°06'W
Gogebic, l., Mi., U.S. (gō-gē'bĭk)	113	46°24'N	89°25'W
Gogebic Range, mts., Mi., U.S.	113	46°37'N	89°48'W
Göggingen, Ger. (gûg'gĕn-gĕn)	159d	48°21'N	10°53'E
Gogland, i., Russia	167	60°04'N	26°55'E
Gogonou, Benin	235	10°50'N	2°50'E
Gogorrón, Mex. (gō-gō-rōn')	130	21°51'N	100°54'W
Goiânia, Braz. (gô-vá'nyä)	143	16°41'S	48°57'W
Goiás, Braz. (gō-yá's)	143	15°57'S	50°10'W
Goiás, state, Braz.	143	16°00'S	48°00'W
Goirle, Neth.	159a	51°31'N	5°06'E
Gökçeada, i., Tur.	175	40°10'N	25°27'E
Göksu, r., Tur. (gûk'sōō')	181	36°40'N	33°30'E
Gol, Nor. (gûl)	166	60°58'N	8°54'E
Golax, Va., U.S. (gō'lăks)	125	36°41'N	80°56'W
Golcar, Eng., U.K. (gŏl'kȧr)	158a	53°38'N	1°52'W
Golconda, Il., U.S. (gŏl-kŏn'dȧ)	121	37°21'N	88°32'W
Gołdap, Pol. (gōl'dăp)	169	54°17'N	22°17'E
Golden, Can.	95	51°18'N	116°58'W
Golden, Co., U.S.	120	39°44'N	105°15'W
Goldendale, Wa., U.S. (gōl'dĕn-dāl)	114	45°49'N	120°48'W
Golden Gate, strt., Ca., U.S. (gōl'dĕn gāt)	116b	37°48'N	122°32'W
Golden Hinde, mtn., Can. (hīnd)	94	49°40'N	125°45'W
Golden's Bridge, N.Y., U.S.	110a	41°17'N	73°41'W
Golden Valley, Mn., U.S.	117g	44°58'N	93°23'W
Goldfield, Nv., U.S. (gōld'fēld)	118	37°42'N	117°15'W
Gold Hill, mtn., Pan.	128a	9°03'N	79°08'W
Gold Mountain, mtn., Wa., U.S. (gōld)	116a	47°33'N	122°48'W
Goldsboro, N.C., U.S. (gōldz-bûr'ô)	125	35°23'N	77°59'W
Goldthwaite, Tx., U.S. (gōld'thwāt)	122	31°27'N	98°34'W
Goleniów, Pol. (gō-lĕ-nyŭf')	168	53°33'N	14°51'E
Golets-Purpula, Gora, mtn., Russia	179	59°08'N	115°22'E
Golfito, C.R. (gōl-fē'tō)	133	8°40'N	83°12'W
Goliad, Tx., U.S. (gō-lĭ-ăd')	123	28°40'N	97°12'W
Golo, r., Fr.	174	42°28'N	9°18'E
Golo Island, i., Phil. (gō'lō)	213a	13°38'N	120°17'E
Golovchino, Russia (gō-lôf'chĕ-nō)	177	50°34'N	35°52'E
Golyamo Konare, Blg. (gō'lâ-mō-kō'nä-rĕ)	175	42°16'N	24°33'E
Golzow, Ger. (gōl'tsōv)	159b	52°17'N	12°36'E
Gombe, Nig.	230	10°19'N	11°02'E
Gomera Island, i., Spain (gō-mā'rä)	230	28°00'N	18°01'W
Gomez Farias, Mex. (gō'māz fä-rē'äs)	122	24°59'N	101°02'W
Gómez Palacio, Mex. (pä-lä'syō)	128	25°35'N	103°30'W
Gonaïves, Haiti (gō-nà-ēv')	129	19°25'N	72°45'W
Gonaïves, Golfe des, b., Haiti (gō-nà-ēv')	135	19°20'N	73°20'W
Gonâve, Île de la, i., Haiti (gō-nàv')	129	18°50'N	73°30'W
Gonda, India	202	27°13'N	82°00'E
Gondal, India	202	22°02'N	70°47'E
Gonder, Eth.	231	12°39'N	37°30'E
Gonesse, Fr. (gō-nĕs')	171b	48°59'N	2°28'E
Gongga Shan, mtn., China (gōŋ-gä shän)	204	29°16'N	101°46'E
Goniri, Nig.	235	11°30'N	12°20'E
Gonō, r., Japan (gō'nō)	211	35°00'N	132°25'E
Gonor, Can. (gō'nōr)	102f	50°04'N	96°57'W
Gonubie, S. Afr. (gŏn'ōō-bē)	233c	32°56'S	28°02'E
Gonzales, Mex. (gōn-zä'lĕs)	130	22°47'N	98°26'W
Gonzales, Tx., U.S. (gŏn-zä'lĕz)	123	29°31'N	97°25'W
González Catán, Arg. (gōn-zá'lĕz-kä-tá'n)	144a	34°47'S	58°39'W
Good Hope, Cape of, c., S. Afr. (kāp ov gŏŏd hōp)	232	34°21'S	18°29'E
Good Hope Mountain, mtn., Can.	94	51°09'N	124°10'W
Gooding, Id., U.S. (gŏŏd'ĭng)	115	42°55'N	114°43'W
Goodland, In., U.S. (gŏŏd'lănd)	108	40°50'N	87°15'W
Goodland, Ks., U.S.	120	39°19'N	101°43'W
Goodwood, S. Afr. (gŏŏd'wŏŏd)	232a	33°54'S	18°33'E
Goole, Eng., U.K. (gōōl)	158a	53°42'N	0°52'W
Goose, r., N.D., U.S.	112	47°40'N	97°41'W

PLACE (Pronunciation)	PAGE	LAT.	LONG.
Gooseberry Creek, r., Wy., U.S. (gōōs-bĕr'ĭ)	115	44°04'N	108°35'W
Goose Creek, r., Id., U.S. (gōōs)	115	42°07'N	113°53'W
Goose Lake, l., Ca., U.S.	114	41°56'N	120°35'W
Gorakhpur, India (gō'rŭk-pōōr)	199	26°45'N	82°39'E
Gorda, Punta, c., Cuba (pōō'n-tä-gôr-dä)	134	22°25'N	82°10'W
Gorda Cay, i., Bah. (gôr'dä)	134	26°05'N	77°30'W
Gordon, Can. (gôr'dŭn)	102f	50°00'N	97°20'W
Gordon, Ne., U.S.	112	42°47'N	102°14'W
Gore, Eth. (gō'rĕ)	231	8°12'N	35°34'E
Gorgān, Iran	198	36°44'N	54°30'E
Gorgona, Isola di, Italy (gôr-gō'nä)	162	43°27'N	9°55'E
Gori, Geor. (gō'rē)	181	42°00'N	44°08'E
Gorinchem, Neth. (gō'rĭn-kĕm)	159a	51°50'N	4°59'E
Goring, Eng., U.K. (gôr'ĭng)	158b	51°30'N	1°08'W
Gorizia, Italy (gō-rē'tsē-yä)	174	45°56'N	13°40'E
Gor'kiy see Nizhniy Novgorod, Russia	178	56°15'N	44°05'E
Gor'kovskoye, res., Russia	178	56°38'N	43°40'E
Gorlice, Pol. (gôr-lē'tsĕ)	169	49°38'N	21°11'E
Görlitz, Ger. (gŭr'lĭts)	161	51°10'N	15°01'E
Gorman, Tx., U.S. (gôr'măn)	122	32°13'N	98°40'W
Gorna Oryakhovitsa, Blg. (gôr'nä-ôr-yĕk'ō-vē-tsá)	175	43°08'N	25°40'E
Gornji Milanovac, Yugo. (gôrn'yē-mē'la-nô-väts)	175	44°02'N	20°29'E
Gorno-Altay, prov., Russia	184	51°00'N	86°00'E
Gorno-Altaysk, Russia (gôr'nŭ'ŭl-tīsk')	178	51°58'N	85°58'E
Gorodishche, Russia (gô-rô'dĭsh-chĕ)	186a	57°57'N	57°03'E
Gorodok, Russia	179	50°30'N	103°58'E
Gorontalo, Indon. (gō-rōn-tä'lō)	213	0°40'N	123°04'E
Gorzów Wielkopolski, Pol. (gō-zhōōv'vyĕl-ko-pōl'skē)	160	53°44'N	15°15'E
Gosely, Eng., U.K.	158a	52°33'N	2°10'W
Goshen, In., U.S. (gō'shĕn)	108	41°35'N	85°50'W
Goshen, Ky., U.S.	111h	38°24'N	85°34'W
Goshen, N.Y., U.S.	110a	41°24'N	74°19'W
Goshen, Oh., U.S.	111f	39°14'N	84°09'W
Goshute Indian Reservation, I.R., Ut., U.S. (gō-shōōt')	119	39°50'N	114°00'W
Goslar, Ger. (gôs'lär)	168	51°55'N	10°25'E
Gospa, r., Ven. (gôs-pä)	143b	9°43'N	64°23'W
Gostivar, Mac. (gos'tē-vär)	175	41°46'N	20°58'E
Gostynin, Pol. (gôs-tē'nĭn)	169	52°24'N	19°30'E
Göta, r., Swe. (gōĕtä)	166	58°11'N	12°03'E
Göta Kanal, can., Swe. (yû'tȧ)	166	58°35'N	15°24'E
Göteborg, Swe. (yû'tĕ-bôrgh)	154	57°39'N	11°56'E
Gotel Mountains, mts., Afr.	235	7°05'N	11°20'E
Gotera, El Sal. (gō-tä'rä)	132	13°41'N	88°06'W
Gotha, Ger. (gō'tȧ)	161	50°47'N	10°43'E
Gothenburg see Göteborg, Swe.	154	57°39'N	11°56'E
Gothenburg, Ne., U.S. (gŏth'ĕn-bûrg)	120	40°57'N	100°08'W
Gotland, i., Swe.	156	57°35'N	17°35'E
Gotska Sandön, i., Swe.	167	58°24'N	19°15'E
Göttingen, Ger. (gŭt'ĭng-ĕn)	168	51°32'N	9°57'E
Gouda, Neth. (gou'dä)	159a	52°00'N	4°42'E
Gough, i., St. Hel. (gŏf)	2	40°00'S	10°00'W
Gouin, Réservoir, res., Can.	93	48°15'N	74°15'W
Goukou, China (gō-kō)	205	48°45'N	121°42'E
Goulais, r., Can.	98	46°45'N	84°10'W
Goulburn, Austl. (gōl'bŭrn)	219	34°47'S	149°40'E
Goumbati, mtn., Sen.	234	13°08'N	12°06'W
Goumbou, Mali (gōōm-bōō')	230	14°59'N	7°27'W
Gouna, Cam.	235	8°32'N	13°34'E
Goundam, Mali (gōōn-dän')	230	16°29'N	3°37'W
Gouverneur, N.Y., U.S. (gŭv-ēr-nōōr')	109	44°20'N	75°25'W
Govenlock, Can. (gŭvĕn-lŏk)	90	49°15'N	109°48'W
Governador, Ilha do, i., Braz. (gô-vĕr-nä-dō-'r-ē-lä'dō)	144b	22°48'S	43°13'W
Governador Portela, Braz. (pōr-tĕ'lá)	144b	22°28'S	43°30'W
Governador Valadares, Braz. (vä-lä-dä'rĕs)	143	18°47'S	41°45'W
Governor's Harbour, Bah.	134	25°15'N	76°15'W
Gowanda, N.Y., U.S. (gô-wŏn'dȧ)	109	42°30'N	78°55'W
Goya, Arg. (gō'yä)	144	29°06'S	59°12'W
Göyçay, Azer. (gē-ŏk'chī)	181	40°40'N	47°40'E
Goyt, r., Eng., U.K. (goit)	158a	53°19'N	2°03'W
Graaff-Reinet, S. Afr. (gräf'rī'nĕt)	232	32°10'S	24°40'E
Gračac, Cro. (grä'chäts)	174	44°16'N	15°50'E
Gračanica, Bos.	175	44°42'N	18°18'E
Graceville, Fl., U.S. (grās'vĭl)	124	30°57'N	85°30'W
Graceville, Mn., U.S.	112	45°33'N	96°25'W
Gracias, Hond. (grä'sē-äs)	132	14°35'N	88°37'W
Graciosa Island, i., Port. (grä-syō'sä)	230a	39°07'N	27°30'W
Gradačac, Bos. (gra-dä'chats)	163	44°50'N	18°28'E
Grado, Spain (grä'dō)	172	43°24'N	6°04'W
Gräfelfing, Ger. (grä'fĕl-fĕng)	159d	48°07'N	11°27'E
Grafing bei München, Ger. (grä'fĕng)	159d	48°03'N	11°58'E
Grafton, Austl. (graf'tŭn)	219	29°38'S	153°05'E
Grafton, Il., U.S.	117e	38°58'N	90°26'W
Grafton, Ma., U.S.	101a	42°13'N	71°41'W
Grafton, N.D., U.S.	112	48°24'N	97°25'W
Grafton, Oh., U.S.	111d	41°16'N	82°04'W
Grafton, W.V., U.S.	108	39°20'N	80°00'W
Gragnano, Italy (grän-yä'nō)	173c	40°27'N	14°32'E
Graham, N.C., U.S. (grā'ăm)	125	36°03'N	79°23'W
Graham, Tx., U.S.	120	33°07'N	98°34'W
Graham, Wa., U.S.	116a	47°03'N	122°18'W
Graham, i., Can.	92	53°50'N	132°40'W
Grahamstown, S. Afr. (grā'ăms'toun)	233c	33°19'S	26°33'E
Grajewo, Pol. (grä-yā'vo)	169	53°38'N	22°28'E

PLACE (Pronunciation)	PAGE	LAT.	LONG.
Grama, Serra de, mtn., Braz. (sĕ'r-rä-dĕ-grā'mà)	141a	20°42'S	42°28'W
Gramada, Blg. (grä'mä-dä)	175	43°46'N	22°41'E
Gramatneusiedl, Aus.	159e	48°02'N	16°29'E
Grampian Mountains, mts., Scot., U.K. (grăm'pĭ-ăn)	156	56°30'N	4°55'W
Granada, Nic. (grä-nä'dhä)	128	11°55'N	85°58'W
Granada, Spain (grä-nä'dä)	162	37°13'N	3°37'W
Gran Bajo, reg., Arg. (grän'bä'kō)	144	47°35'S	68°45'W
Granbury, Tx., U.S. (grăn'bĕr-ĭ)	123	32°26'N	97°45'W
Granby, Can. (grăn'bĭ)	91	45°30'N	72°40'W
Granby, Mo., U.S.	121	36°54'N	94°15'W
Granby, l., Co., U.S.	120	40°07'N	105°40'W
Gran Canaria Island, i., Spain (grän'kä-nä'rē-ä)	230	27°39'N	15°39'W
Gran Chaco, reg., S.A. (grän'chà'kō)	144	25°30'S	62°15'W
Grand, i., Mi., U.S.	113	46°37'N	86°38'W
Grand, l., Can.	100	45°59'N	66°15'W
Grand, l., Me., U.S.	100	45°17'N	67°42'W
Grand, r., Can.	99	43°45'N	80°20'W
Grand, r., Mi., U.S.	108	42°58'N	85°13'W
Grand, r., Mo., U.S.	121	39°50'N	93°52'W
Grand, r., S.D., U.S.	112	45°40'N	101°55'W
Grand, North Fork, r., U.S.	112	45°52'N	102°49'W
Grand, South Fork, r., S.D., U.S.	112	45°38'N	102°56'W
Grand Bahama, i., Bah.	129	26°35'N	78°30'W
Grand Bank, Can. (grănd băngk)	93a	47°06'N	55°47'W
Grand Bassam, C. Iv. (grän bá-säɴ')	230	5°12'N	3°44'W
Grand Bourg, Guad. (gräɴ bōōr')	133b	15°54'N	61°20'W
Grand Caicos, i., T./C. Is. (grănd kä-ē'kōs)	135	21°45'N	71°50'W
Grand Canal see Da Yunhe, can., China	205	35°00'N	117°00'E
Grand Canal, can., Ire.	164	53°21'N	7°15'W
Grand Canyon, Az., U.S.	119	36°05'N	112°10'W
Grand Canyon, p., Az., U.S.	106	35°50'N	113°16'W
Grand Canyon National Park, rec., Az., U.S.	106	36°15'N	112°20'W
Grand Canyon-Parashant National Monument, rec., Az., U.S.	119	36°25'N	113°45'W
Grand Cayman, i., Cay. Is. (kā'măn)	129	19°15'N	81°15'W
Grand Coulee Dam, dam, Wa., U.S. (kōō'lē)	106	47°58'N	119°28'W
Grande, r., Arg.	141b	35°25'S	70°14'W
Grande, r., Bol.	142	16°49'S	63°19'W
Grande, r., Braz.	143	19°48'S	49°54'W
Grande, r., Mex.	131	17°37'N	96°41'W
Grande, r., Nic. (grän'dĕ)	133	13°01'N	84°21'W
Grande, r., Ur.	141c	33°19'S	57°15'W
Grande, Arroyo, r., Mex. (är-rō'yō-grä'n-dĕ)	130	23°30'N	98°45'W
Grande, Bahía, b., Arg. (bä-ē'ä-grán'dĕ)	144	50°45'S	68°00'W
Grande, Boca, mth., Ven. (bō'kä-grä'n-dĕ)	143	8°46'N	60°17'W
Grande, Cuchilla, mts., Ur. (kōō-chē'l-yä)	144	33°00'S	55°15'W
Grande, Ilha, i., Braz. (grän'dĕ)	141a	23°11'S	44°14'W
Grande, Rio, r., N.A. (grän'dä)	106	26°50'N	99°10'W
Grande, Salinas, l., Arg. (sä-lē'näs)	144	29°45'S	65°00'W
Grande, Salto, wtfl., Braz. (säl-tô)	143	16°18'S	39°38'W
Grande Cayemite, Île, i., Haiti	135	18°45'N	73°45'W
Grande de Otoro, r., Hond. (grä'dą dā ô-tō'rô)	132	14°42'N	88°21'W
Grande de Santiago, Río, r., Mex. (rēō-grä'n-dĕ-dĕ-sän-tyá'gô)	128	20°30'N	104°00'W
Grande Pointe, Can. (grănd point')	102f	49°47'N	97°03'W
Grande Prairie, Can. (prâr'ĭ)	90	55°10'N	118°48'W
Grand Erg Occidental, des., Alg.	230	30°00'N	1°00'E
Grand Erg Oriental, des., Alg.	230	30°00'N	7°00'E
Grande Rivière du Nord, Haiti (rē-vyâr' dü nôr')	135	19°35'N	72°10'W
Grande Ronde, r., Or., U.S. (rŏnd')	114	45°32'N	117°52'W
Gran Desierto, des., Mex. (grän-dĕ-syĕ'r-tô)	119	32°14'N	114°28'W
Grande Terre, i., Guad.	133b	16°28'N	61°13'W
Grande Vigie, Pointe de la, c., Guad. (grănd vē-gē')	133b	16°32'N	61°25'W
Grand Falls, Can. (fôlz)	93a	48°56'N	55°40'W
Grandfather Mountain, mtn., N.C., U.S. (grănd-fä-thēr)	125	36°07'N	81°48'W
Grandfield, Ok., U.S. (grănd'fēld)	120	34°13'N	98°39'W
Grand Forks, Can. (fôrks)	90	49°02'N	118°27'W
Grand Forks, N.D., U.S.	104	47°55'N	97°05'W
Grand Haven, Mi., U.S. (hā'v'n)	108	43°05'N	86°15'W
Grand Island, Ne., U.S. (ī'lănd)	104	40°56'N	98°20'W
Grand Island, i., N.Y., U.S.	111c	43°03'N	78°58'W
Grand Junction, Co., U.S. (jŭngk'shŭn)	104	39°05'N	108°35'W
Grand Lake, l., Can. (lāk)	93a	49°00'N	57°10'W
Grand Lake, l., La., U.S.	123	29°57'N	91°25'W
Grand Lake, l., Mn., U.S.	117h	46°54'N	92°26'W
Grand Ledge, Mi., U.S. (lĕj)	108	42°45'N	84°50'W
Grand Lieu, Lac de, l., Fr. (grăn'-lyû)	170	47°00'N	1°45'W
Grand Manan, i., Can. (mȧ-năn)	100	44°40'N	66°50'W
Grand Mère, Can. (gräɴ mâr')	91	46°36'N	72°43'W
Grândola, Port. (grän'dô-lȧ)	172	38°10'N	8°36'W
Grand Portage Indian Reservation, I.R., Mn., U.S. (pōr'tĭj)	113	47°54'N	89°34'W
Grand Portage National Monument, rec., Mi., U.S.	113	47°59'N	89°47'W
Grand Prairie, Tx., U.S. (prĕ'rē)	117c	32°45'N	97°00'W
Grand Rapids, Can.	97	53°08'N	99°20'W
Grand Rapids, Mi., U.S. (răp'ĭdz)	105	43°00'N	85°45'W
Grand Rapids, Mn., U.S.	113	47°16'N	93°33'W

ng-sing; ŋ-baŋk; ɴ-nasalized n; nŏd; cŏmmit; ōld; ôbey; ôrder; oi-boil; fōōd; ŏŏ-as oo in foot; ou-out; s-soft; sh-dish; th-thin; pūre; ůnite; ûrn; stŭd; circŭs; ü-as in French tu; '-indeterminate vowel.

ăt; fināl; rāte; senāte; ärm; àsk; sofá; fâre; ch-choose; dh-as th in other; bē; ĕvent; bĕt; recĕnt; cratēr; g-gō; gh-guttural g; bĭt; ī-short neutral; rīde; ĸ-guttural k as ch in German ich;

PRONOUNCING INDEX
Guadalajara – Haines City 299

PLACE (Pronunciation)	PAGE	LAT.	LONG.
Guadalajara, Spain (gwä-dä-lä-kä′rä)	162	40°37′N	3°10′W
Guadalcanal, Spain (gwä-dhäl-kä-näl′)	172	38°05′N	5°48′W
Guadalcanal, i., Sol. Is.	221	9°48′S	158°43′E
Guadalcázar, Mex. (gwä-dhäl-kä′zär)	130	22°38′N	100°24′W
Guadalete, r., Spain (gwä-dhä-lā′tå)	172	36°53′N	5°38′W
Guadalhorce, r., Spain (gwä-dhäl-ôr′thā)	172	37°05′N	4°50′W
Guadalimar, r., Spain (gwä-dhä-lē-mär′)	172	38°29′N	2°53′W
Guadalope, r., Spain (gwä-dä-lô-pě)	173	40°48′N	0°10′W
Guadalquivir, Río, r., Spain (rē′ō-gwä-dhäl-kē-vēr′)	156	37°30′N	5°00′W
Guadalupe, Mex.	122	31°23′N	106°06′W
Guadalupe, i., Mex.	128	29°00′N	118°45′W
Guadalupe, r., Tx., U.S. (gwä-dhä-lōō′pä)	122	29°54′N	99°03′W
Guadalupe, Sierra de, mts., Spain (syěr′rä dā gwä-dhä-lōō′pä)	162	39°30′N	5°25′W
Guadalupe Mountains, mts., N.M., U.S.	122	32°00′N	104°55′W
Guadalupe Peak, mtn., Tx., U.S.	122	31°55′N	104°55′W
Guadarrama, r., Spain (gwä-dhär-rä′mä)	173a	40°34′N	3°58′W
Guadarrama, Sierra de, mts., Spain (gwä-dhär-rä′mä)	156	41°00′N	3°40′W
Guadatentin, r., Spain	172	37°43′N	1°58′W
Guadeloupe, dep., N.A. (gwä-dē-lōōp)	129	16°40′N	61°10′W
Guadeloupe Passage, strt., N.A.	133b	16°26′N	62°00′W
Guadiana, r., Eur. (gwä-dvä′nä)	156	39°00′N	6°00′W
Guadiana, Bahía de, b., Cuba (bä-ē′ä-dě-gwä-dhě-ä′nä)	134	22°10′N	84°35′W
Guadiana Alto, r., Spain (äl′tō)	172	39°02′N	2°52′W
Guadiana Menor, r., Spain (mā′nôr)	172	37°43′N	2°45′W
Guadiaro, r., Spain (gwä-dhě-ä rō)	172	36°38′N	5°25′W
Guadiela, r., Spain (gwä-dhě-ā′lä)	172	40°27′N	2°05′W
Guadix, Spain (gwä-dēsh′)	172	37°18′N	3°09′W
Guaira, Braz. (gwä-ē-rä)	143	24°03′S	54°02′W
Guaire, r., Ven. (gwī′rě)	143b	10°25′N	66°43′W
Guajaba, Cayo, i., Cuba (kä′yō-gwä-hä′bä)	134	21°50′N	77°35′W
Guajará Mirim, Braz. (gwä-zhä-rä′mē-rēɴ′)	142	10°58′S	65°12′W
Guajira, Península de, pen., S.A.	142	12°35′N	73°00′W
Gualán, Guat. (gwä-län′)	132	15°08′N	89°21′W
Gualeguay, Arg. (gwä-lě-gwä′y)	144	33°10′S	59°20′W
Gualeguay, r., Arg.	144	32°49′S	59°05′W
Gualicho, Salina, l., Arg. (sä-lē′nä-gwä-lē′chō)	144	40°20′S	65°15′W
Guam, i., Oc. (gwäm)	3	14°00′N	143°20′E
Guamo, Col. (gwá′mō)	142a	4°02′N	74°58′W
Gu'an, China (gōō-än)	208a	39°25′N	116°18′E
Guan, r., China (gůän)	206	31°56′N	115°19′E
Guanabacoa, Cuba (gwä-nä-bä-kō′ä)	129	23°08′N	82°19′W
Guanabara, Baía de, b., Braz.	141a	22°44′S	43°09′W
Guanacaste, Cordillera, mts., C.R.	132	10°54′N	85°27′W
Guanacevi, Mex. (gwä-nä-sě-vē′)	128	25°30′N	105°45′W
Guanahacabibes, Península de, pen., Cuba	134	21°55′N	84°35′W
Guanajay, Cuba (gwäṇä-hī′)	134	22°55′N	82°40′W
Guanajuato, Mex. (gwä-nä-hwä′tō)	128	21°01′N	101°16′W
Guanajuato, state, Mex.	128	21°00′N	101°00′W
Guanape, Ven. (gwä-nä′pě)	143b	9°55′N	65°32′W
Guanape, r., Ven.	143b	9°52′N	65°20′W
Guanare, Ven. (gwä-nä′rå)	142	8°57′N	69°47′W
Guanduçu, r., Braz. (gwä′n-dōō′sōō)	144b	22°50′S	43°40′W
Guane, Cuba (gwä′nå)	134	22°10′N	84°05′W
Guangchang, China (gůäŋ-chäŋ)	209	26°50′N	116°18′E
Guangde, China (gůäŋ-dŭ)	209	30°40′N	119°20′E
Guangdong, prov., China (gůäŋ-dôŋ)	205	23°45′N	113°15′E
Guanglu Dao, i., China (gůäŋ-lōō dou)	206	39°13′N	122°21′E
Guangping, China (gůäŋ-pĭŋ)	206	36°30′N	114°57′E
Guangrao, China (gůäŋ-rou)	206	37°04′N	118°24′E
Guangshan, China (gůäŋ-shän)	206	32°02′N	114°53′E
Guangxi Zhuangzu, prov., China (gůäŋ-shyē)	204	24°00′N	108°30′E
Guangzhou, China	204	23°07′N	113°15′W
Guanhu, China (gůän-hōō)	206	34°26′N	117°59′E
Guannan, China (gůän-nän)	206	34°17′N	119°17′E
Guanta, Ven. (gwän′tä)	143b	10°15′N	64°35′W
Guantánamo, Cuba (gwän-tä′nä-mō)	135	20°10′N	75°10′W
Guantánamo, prov., Cuba	135	20°10′N	75°05′W
Guantánamo, Bahía de, b., Cuba	135	19°35′N	75°35′W
Guantao, China (gůän-tou)	206	36°39′N	115°25′E
Guanxian, China (gůän-shyěn)	206	36°30′N	115°28′E
Guanyao, China (gůän-you)	207a	23°13′N	113°04′E
Guanyun, China (gůän-yòn)	206	34°28′N	119°16′E
Guapiles, C.R. (gwä-pē-lěs)	133	10°05′N	83°54′W
Guapimirim, Braz. (gwä-pē-mē-rē′ɴ)	144b	22°31′S	42°59′W
Guaporé, r., S.A. (gwä-pô-rā′)	142	12°11′S	63°47′W
Guaqui, Bol. (guä′kē)	142	16°42′S	68°47′W
Guara, Sierra de, mts., Spain (sē-ě′r-rä-dě-gwä′rä)	173	42°24′N	0°15′W
Guarabira, Braz. (gwä-rä-bē′rå)	143	6°49′S	35°27′W
Guaranda, Ec. (gwä-rån′dä)	142	1°39′S	78°57′W
Guarapari, Braz. (gwä-rä-pä′rè)	143	20°34′S	40°31′W
Guarapiranga, Represa do, res., Braz.	141a	23°45′S	46°44′W
Guarapuava, Braz. (gwä-rä-pwä′vå)	144	25°29′S	51°26′W
Guarda, Port. (gwär′dä)	172	40°32′N	7°17′W
Guardiato, r., Spain	172	38°10′N	5°05′W
Guarena, Spain (gwä-rā′nyä)	172	38°52′N	6°08′W
Guaribe, r., Ven. (gwä-rě′bě)	143b	9°48′N	65°17′W
Guárico, dept., Ven.	143b	9°42′N	67°25′W
Guarulhos, Braz. (gwå-rò′l-yôs)	141a	23°28′S	46°30′W
Guarus, Braz. (gwå′rōōs)	141a	21°44′S	41°19′W
Guasca, Col. (gwäs′kä)	142a	4°52′N	73°52′W
Guasipati, Ven. (gwä-sē-pä′tē)	143	7°26′N	61°57′W
Guastalla, Italy (gwäs-täl′lä)	174	44°53′N	10°39′E
Guasti, Ca., U.S. (gwäs′tĭ)	117a	34°04′N	117°35′W
Guatemala, Guat. (guä-tå-mä′lä)	128	14°37′N	90°32′W
Guatemala, nation, N.A.	128	15°45′N	91°45′W
Guatire, Ven. (gwä-tē′rě)	143b	10°28′N	66°34′W
Guaviare, r., Col.	142	3°35′N	69°28′W
Guayabal, Cuba (gwä-yä-bä′l)	134	20°40′N	77°40′W
Guayalejo, r., Mex. (gwä-yä-lě′hô)	130	23°24′N	99°09′W
Guayama, P.R. (gwä-yä′mä)	129b	18°00′N	66°08′W
Guayamouc, r., Haiti	135	19°05′N	72°00′W
Guayaquil, Ec. (gwī-ä-kēl′)	142	2°16′S	79°53′W
Guayaquil, Golfo de, b., Ec. (gôl-fô-dě)	142	3°03′S	82°12′W
Guaymas, Mex. (gwá′y-mäs)	128	27°49′N	110°58′W
Guayubin, Dom. Rep. (gwá-yōō-bē′n)	135	19°40′N	71°25′W
Guazacapán, Guat. (gwä-zä-kä-pän′)	132	14°04′N	90°26′W
Gubakha, Russia (gōō-bä′kå)	178	58°53′N	57°35′E
Gubbio, Italy (gōōb′byô)	174	43°23′N	12°36′E
Guben, Ger.	168	51°57′N	14°43′E
Gucheng, China (gōō-chŭŋ)	206	39°09′N	115°43′E
Gúdar, Sierra de, mts., Spain	173	40°28′N	0°47′W
Gudena, r., Den.	166	56°20′N	9°47′E
Gudermes, Russia	182	43°20′N	46°08′E
Gudvangen, Nor. (gōōdh′väŋ-gěn)	166	60°52′N	6°45′E
Guebwiller, Fr. (gěb-vē-lâr′)	171	47°53′N	7°10′E
Guédi, Mont, mtn., Chad	235	12°14′N	18°58′E
Guelma, Alg. (gwěl′mä)	230	36°32′N	7°17′E
Guelph, Can. (gwělf)	99	43°33′N	80°15′W
Güere, r., Ven. (gwě′rě)	143b	9°39′N	65°00′W
Guéret, Fr. (gā-rě′)	170	46°09′N	1°52′E
Guernsey, dep., Eur.	170	49°28′N	2°35′W
Guernsey, i., Guern. (gûrn′zĭ)	161	49°27′N	2°36′W
Guerrero, Mex. (gěr-rā′rō)	122	26°47′N	99°20′W
Guerrero, Mex.	122	28°20′N	100°24′W
Guerrero, state, Mex.	128	17°45′N	100°15′W
Gueydan, La., U.S. (gā′dăn)	123	30°01′N	92°31′W
Guia de Pacobaíba, Braz. (gwě′ä-dě-pä′kō-bī′bä)	144b	22°42′S	43°10′W
Guiana Highlands, mts., S.A.	139	3°20′N	60°00′W
Guichi, China (gwā-chr)	209	30°35′N	117°28′E
Guichicovi, Mex. (gwē-chē-kō′vē)	131	16°58′N	95°10′W
Guidonia, Italy (gwē-dō′nyä)	174	42°00′N	12°45′E
Guiglo, C. Iv.	234	6°33′N	7°29′W
Guignes-Rabutin, Fr. (gēɴ′yě)	171b	48°38′N	2°48′E
Güigüe, Ven. (gwě′gwě)	143b	10°05′N	67°48′W
Guija, Lago, l., N.A. (gē′hä)	132	14°16′N	89°21′W
Guildford, Eng., U.K. (gĭl′fērd)	164	51°13′N	0°34′W
Guilford, In., U.S. (gĭl′fērd)	111f	39°10′N	84°55′W
Guilin, China (gwā-lĭn)	205	25°18′N	110°22′E
Guimarães, Port. (gē-mä-rănsh′)	172	41°27′N	8°22′W
Guinea, nation, Afr. (gĭn′ē)	230	10°48′N	12°28′W
Guinea, Gulf of, b., Afr.	230	2°00′N	1°00′E
Guinea-Bissau, nation, Afr. (gĭn′ē)	230	12°00′N	20°00′W
Guingamp, Fr. (găn-gän′)	170	48°35′N	3°10′W
Guir, r., Mor.	162	31°55′N	2°48′W
Güira de Melena, Cuba (gwē′rä dā må-lā′nä)	134	22°45′N	82°30′W
Güiria, Ven. (gwê-rē′ä)	142	10°43′N	62°16′W
Guise, Fr. (guēz)	170	49°54′N	3°37′E
Guisisil, vol., Nic. (gē-sē-sēl′)	132	12°40′N	86°11′W
Guiyang, China (gwā-yäŋ)	204	26°45′N	107°00′E
Guizhou, China (gwā-jō)	207a	22°46′N	113°15′E
Guizhou, prov., China	204	27°00′N	106°10′E
Gujānwāla, Pak. (gòj-rän′va-lå)	199	32°08′N	74°14′E
Gujarat, India	199	22°54′N	72°00′E
Gulbarga, India (gòl-bûr′gå)	199	17°25′N	76°52′E
Gulbene, Lat. (gòl-bă′ně)	167	57°09′N	26°49′E
Gulfport, Ms., U.S. (gŭlf′pōrt)	124	30°24′N	89°05′W
Gulja *see* Yining, China	204	43°58′N	80°40′E
Gull Lake, Can.	96	50°10′N	108°25′W
Gull Lake, l., Can.	95	52°35′N	114°00′W
Gulu, Ug.	237	2°47′N	32°18′E
Gumaca, Phil. (gōō-mä-kä′)	213a	13°55′N	122°06′E
Gumbeyka, r., Russia (gòm-běy′kå)	186a	53°20′N	59°42′E
Gumel, Nig.	230	12°39′N	9°22′E
Gummersbach, Ger. (gòm′ěrs-bäk)	168	51°02′N	7°34′E
Gummi, Nig.	235	12°09′N	5°09′E
Gumpoldskirchen, Aus.	159e	48°04′N	16°15′E
Guna, India	202	24°44′N	77°17′E
Gunisao, r., Can. (gŭn-ĭ-sä′ō)	97	53°40′N	97°35′W
Gunisao Lake, l., Can.	97	53°35′N	96°10′W
Gunnedah, Austl. (gŭ′nē-dä)	222	31°00′S	150°10′E
Gunnison, Co., U.S. (gŭn′ĭ-sŭn)	119	38°33′N	106°56′W
Gunnison, Ut., U.S.	119	39°10′N	111°50′W
Gunnison, r., Co., U.S.	119	38°45′N	108°20′W
Guntersville, Al., U.S. (gŭn′tērz-vĭl)	124	34°20′N	86°19′W
Guntersville Lake, res., Al., U.S.	124	34°30′N	86°20′W
Guntramsdorf, Aus.	159e	48°04′N	16°19′E
Guntūr, India (gòn′tōōr)	199	16°22′N	80°29′E
Guoyang, China (gwô-yän)	206	33°32′N	116°10′E
Gurdon, Ar., U.S. (gûr′dŭn)	121	33°56′N	93°10′W
Gurgueia, r., Braz.	143	8°12′S	43°49′W
Guri, Embalse, res., Ven.	142	7°30′N	63°00′W
Gurnee, Il., U.S. (gûr′nē)	111a	42°22′N	87°55′W
Gurskøy, i., Nor. (gōōrskûē)	166	62°18′N	5°20′E
Gurupi, Serra do, mts., Braz. (sě′r-rä-dô-gōō-rōō-pē′)	143	5°32′S	47°02′W
Guru Sikhar, mtn., India	202	29°42′N	72°50′E
Gur'yevsk, Russia (gōōr-yĭfsk′)	178	54°17′N	85°56′E
Gusau, Nig. (gōō-zä′ōō)	230	12°12′N	6°40′E
Gusev, Russia (gōō′sěf)	167	54°35′N	22°15′E
Gushi, China (gōō-shr)	206	32°11′N	115°39′E
Gushiago, Ghana	234	9°55′N	0°12′W
Gusinje, Yugo. (gōō-sēn′yě)	175	42°34′N	19°54′E
Gus'-Khrustal'nyy, Russia (gōōs-krōō-stäl′ny′)	180	55°39′N	40°41′E
Gustavo A. Madero, Mex. (gōōs-tä′vô-ä-mä-dě′rô)	130	19°29′N	99°07′W
Güstrow, Ger. (güs′trō)	168	53°48′N	12°12′E
Gütersloh, Ger. (gü′těrs-lo)	168	51°54′N	8°22′E
Guthrie, Ok., U.S. (gŭth′rĭ)	121	35°52′N	97°26′W
Guthrie Center, Ia., U.S.	113	41°41′N	94°33′W
Gutiérrez Zamora, Mex. (gōō-tĭ-âr′rāz zä-mō′rä)	131	20°27′N	97°17′W
Guttenberg, Ia., U.S. (gŭt′ĕn-bûrg)	113	42°48′N	91°09′W
Guyana, nation, S.A. (gŭy′ănă)	143	7°45′N	59°00′W
Guyang, China (gōō-yäŋ)	206	34°56′N	114°57′E
Guye, China (gōō-yŭ)	206	39°46′N	118°23′E
Guymon, Ok., U.S. (gī′mŏn)	120	36°41′N	101°29′W
Guysborough, Can. (gīz′bŭr-ô)	101	45°23′N	61°30′W
Guzhen, China (gōō-jŭn)	208	33°20′N	117°18′E
Gvardeysk, Russia (gvår-děysk′)	167	54°39′N	21°11′E
Gwadabawa, Nig.	235	13°20′N	5°15′E
Gwādar, Pak. (gwä′dŭr)	198	25°15′N	62°29′E
Gwalior, India	199	26°13′N	78°10′E
Gwane, D.R.C. (gwän)	231	4°43′N	25°50′E
Gwardafuy, Gees, c., Som.	238a	11°55′N	51°30′E
Gwda, r., Pol.	168	53°27′N	16°52′E
Gwembe, Zam.	237	16°30′S	27°35′E
Gweru, Zimb.	232	19°15′S	29°48′E
Gwinn, Mi., U.S. (gwĭn)	113	46°15′N	87°30′W
Gyaring Co, l., China	202	30°37′N	88°33′E
Gydan, Khrebet (Kolymskiy), mts., Russia	179	61°45′N	155°00′E
Gydanskiy Poluostrov, pen., Russia	178	70°42′N	76°03′E
Gympie, Austl. (gĭm′pē)	219	26°20′S	152°50′E
Gyöngyös, Hung. (dyûn′dyûsh)	163	47°47′N	19°55′E
Györ, Hung. (dyûr)	163	47°40′N	17°37′E
Gyōtoku, Japan (gyō′tô-kōō′)	211a	35°42′N	139°56′E
Gypsumville, Can. (jĭp′sŭm′vĭl)	90	51°45′N	98°35′W
Gýtheio, Grc.	175	36°50′N	22°37′E
Gyula, Hung. (dyô′lä)	169	46°38′N	21°18′E
Gyumri, Arm.	181	40°40′N	43°50′E
Gyzylarbat, Turkmen.	183	38°55′N	56°33′E

H

PLACE (Pronunciation)	PAGE	LAT.	LONG.
Haan, Ger. (hän)	171c	51°12′N	7°00′E
Haapamäki, Fin. (häp′ä-mě-kē)	167	62°16′N	24°20′E
Haapsalu, Est. (häp′sä-lò)	167	58°56′N	23°33′E
Haar, Ger. (här)	159d	48°06′N	11°44′E
Ha'Arava (Wādī al Jayb), val., Asia	197a	30°33′N	35°10′E
Haarlem, Neth. (här′lěm)	165	52°22′N	4°37′E
Habana, prov., Cuba (hä-vä′nä)	134	22°45′N	82°25′W
Hābra, India	202a	22°49′N	88°38′E
Hachinohe, Japan (hä′chē-nō′hå)	210	40°29′N	141°40′E
Hachiōji, Japan (hä′chē-ō′jē)	210	35°39′N	139°18′E
Hackensack, N.J., U.S. (hăk′ĕn-săk)	110a	40°54′N	74°03′W
Ḩadd, Ra's al, c., Oman	198	22°29′N	59°46′E
Haddonfield, N.J., U.S. (hăd′ŭn-fēld)	110f	39°53′N	75°02′W
Haddon Heights, N.J., U.S. (hăd′ŭn hīts)	110f	39°53′N	75°03′W
Hadejia, Nig. (hä-dā′jä)	230	12°30′N	9°59′E
Hadejia, r., Nig.	230	12°15′N	10°00′E
Ḩadera, Isr. (κå-dě′rå)	197a	32°26′N	34°55′E
Haderslev, Den. (hä′dhěrs-lěv)	166	55°17′N	9°28′E
Hadiach, Ukr.	181	50°22′N	33°59′E
Ḩadīdū, Yemen	198	12°40′N	53°50′E
Hadlock, Wa., U.S. (hăd′lŏk)	116a	48°02′N	122°46′W
Ḩaḑramawt, reg., Yemen	198	15°22′N	48°40′E
Hadūr Shu'ayb, mtn., Yemen	198	15°45′N	43°45′E
Haeju, Kor., N. (hä′ĕ-jŭ)	210	38°03′N	125°42′E
Hafnarfjördur, Ice.	160	64°02′N	21°32′W
Haft Gel, Iran	201	31°27′N	49°27′E
Hafun, Ras, c., Som. (hä-fōōn′)	238a	10°15′N	51°35′E
Hageland, Mt., U.S. (hăge′lånd)	115	48°53′N	108°43′W
Hagen, Ger. (hä′gěn)	168	51°21′N	7°29′E
Hagerstown, In., U.S. (hā′gērz-toun)	108	39°55′N	85°10′W
Hagerstown, Md., U.S.	105	39°40′N	77°45′W
Hagi, Japan (hä′gĭ)	211	34°25′N	131°25′E
Hague, Cap de la, c., Fr. (dē lá ág′)	170	49°44′N	1°55′W
Haguenau, Fr. (ág′nō′)	171	48°47′N	7°48′E
Hai'an, China (hī-än)	206	32°35′N	120°25′E
Haibara, Japan (hä′ē-bä′rä)	211	34°29′N	135°57′E
Haicheng, China (hī-chŭŋ)	208	40°58′N	122°45′E
Haidian, China (hī-dĭěn)	206	39°59′N	116°17′E
Haifa, Isr. (hä′ē-få)	198	32°48′N	35°00′E
Haifeng, China (hä′ē-fěng′)	209	23°00′N	115°20′E
Haifuzhen, China (hī-fōō-jŭn)	206	31°57′N	121°48′E
Haikou, China (hī-kō)	209	20°00′N	110°20′E
Ḩā'il, Sau. Ar.	198	27°30′N	41°47′E
Hailar, China	205	49°10′N	118°40′E
Hailey, Id., U.S. (hā′lĭ)	115	43°31′N	114°19′W
Haileybury, Can.	99	47°27′N	79°38′W
Haileyville, Ok., U.S. (hā′lĭ-vĭl)	121	34°51′N	95°34′W
Hailing Dao, i., China (hī-lĭŋ dou)	209	21°30′N	112°15′E
Hailong, China (hī-loŋ)	208	42°32′N	125°52′E
Hailun, China (hä′ē-lōōn′)	205	47°18′N	126°50′E
Hainan, prov., China	204	19°00′N	109°30′E
Hainan Dao, i., China (hī-nän dou)	205	19°00′N	111°10′E
Hainburg, Aus.	168	48°09′N	16°57′E
Haines, Ak., U.S. (hānz)	103	59°10′N	135°38′W
Haines City, Fl., U.S.	125a	28°05′N	81°38′W

PLACE (Pronunciation)	PAGE	LAT.	LONG.
Hai Phong, Viet. (hī'fông')(hä'ĕp-hŏng)	212	20°52'N	106°40'E
Haisyn, Ukr.	181	48°46'N	29°22'E
Haiti, nation, N.A. (hā'tĭ)	129	19°00'N	72°15'W
Haizhou, China	206	34°34'N	119°11'E
Haizhou Wan, b., China	208	34°49'N	120°35'E
Hajdúböszormény, Hung. (hôl'dō-bû'sûr-män')	169	47°41'N	21°30'E
Hajdúhadház, Hung. (hô'ĭ-dō-hôd'häz)	169	47°32'N	21°32'E
Hajdúnánás, Hung. (hô'ĭ-dō-nä'näsh)	169	47°52'N	21°27'E
Hakodate, Japan (hä-kō-dä'tå)	205	41°46'N	140°42'E
Haku-San, mtn., Japan (hä'kōō-sän')	210	36°11'N	136°45'E
Halā'ib, Egypt (hä-lä'ēb)	231	22°10'N	36°40'E
Halbe, Ger. (häl'bĕ)	159b	52°07'N	13°43'E
Halberstadt, Ger. (häl'bĕr-shtät)	168	51°54'N	11°07'E
Halcon, Mount, mtn., Phil. (häl-kōn')	213a	13°19'N	120°55'E
Halden, Nor. (häl'dĕn)	160	59°10'N	11°21'E
Haldensleben, Ger.	168	52°18'N	11°23'E
Hale, Eng., U.K. (hāl)	158a	53°22'N	2°20'W
Haleakalā Crater, depr., Hi., U.S. (hä'lå-ä'kä-lä)	126a	20°44'N	156°15'W
Haleakalā National Park, rec., Hi., U.S.	126a	20°46'N	156°00'W
Hales Corners, Wi., U.S. (hālz kŏr'nĕrz)	111a	42°56'N	88°03'W
Halesowen, Eng., U.K. (hālz'ō-wĕn)	158a	52°26'N	2°03'W
Halethorpe, Md., U.S. (hāl-thôrp)	110e	39°15'N	76°40'W
Haleyville, Al., U.S. (hā'lĭ-vĭl)	124	34°11'N	87°36'W
Half Moon Bay, Ca., U.S. (hăf'mōōn)	116b	37°28'N	122°26'W
Halfway House, S. Afr. (häf-wā hous)	233b	26°00'S	28°08'E
Halfweg, Neth.	159a	52°23'N	4°45'E
Halifax, Can. (hăl'ĭ-făks)	91	44°39'N	63°36'W
Halifax, Eng., U.K.	164	53°44'N	1°52'W
Halifax Bay, b., Austl. (hăl'ĭ-făx)	221	18°56'S	147°07'E
Halifax Harbour, b., Can.	100	44°35'N	63°31'W
Halkett, Cape, c., Ak., U.S.	103	70°50'N	151°15'W
Hallam Peak, mtn., Can.	95	52°11'N	118°46'E
Halla San, mtn., Kor., S. (häl'lä-sän)	210	33°20'N	126°37'E
Halle, Bel. (häl'lĕ)	159a	50°45'N	4°13'E
Halle, Ger.	161	51°30'N	11°59'E
Hallettsville, Tx., U.S. (hăl'ĕts-vĭl)	123	29°26'N	96°55'W
Hallock, Mn., U.S. (hăl'ŭk)	112	48°46'N	96°57'W
Hall Peninsula, pen., Can. (hôl)	93	63°14'N	65°40'W
Halls Bayou, Tx., U.S.	123a	29°55'N	95°23'W
Hallsberg, Swe. (häls'bĕrgh)	166	59°04'N	15°04'E
Halls Creek, Austl. (hôlz)	218	18°15'S	127°45'E
Halmahera, i., Indon. (häl-mä-hä'rä)	213	0°45'N	128°45'E
Halmahera, Laut, Indon.	213	1°00'S	129°00'E
Halmstad, Swe. (hälm'städ)	160	56°40'N	12°46'E
Halsafjorden, b., Nor. (häl'sĕ fyôrd)	166	63°03'N	8°23'E
Halstead, Ks., U.S. (hôl'stĕd)	121	38°02'N	97°36'W
Haltern, Ger. (häl'tĕrn)	171c	51°45'N	7°10'E
Haltom City, Tx., U.S. (hôl'tŏm)	117c	32°48'N	97°13'W
Halver, Ger.	171c	51°11'N	7°30'E
Hamada, Japan	210	34°53'N	132°05'E
Hamadān, Iran (hŭ-mŭ-dän')	198	34°45'N	48°07'E
Ḥamāh, Syria (hä'mä)	198	35°08'N	36°53'E
Hamamatsu, Japan (hä'mä-mät'sō)	210	34°41'N	137°43'E
Hamar, Nor. (hä'mär)	160	60°49'N	11°05'E
Hamasaka, Japan (hä'mä-sä'kä)	211	35°57'N	134°27'E
Hamborn, Ger. (häm'bōrn)	171c	51°30'N	6°43'E
Hamburg, Ger. (häm'bōōrgh)	154	53°34'N	10°02'E
Hamburg, S. Afr. (hăm'bûrg)	233c	33°18'S	27°28'E
Hamburg, Ar., U.S. (hăm'bûrg)	121	33°15'N	91°49'W
Hamburg, N.J., U.S.	110a	41°09'N	74°35'W
Hamburg, N.Y., U.S.	111c	42°44'N	78°51'W
Hamden, Ct., U.S. (hăm'dĕn)	109	41°20'N	72°55'W
Hämeenlinna, Fin. (hĕ'mân-lĭn-nå)	160	61°00'N	24°29'E
Hameln, Ger. (hä'mĕln)	168	52°06'N	9°23'E
Hamelwörden, Ger. (hä'mĕl-vûr-dĕn)	159c	53°47'N	9°19'E
Hamersley Range, mts., Austl. (hăm'ĕrz-lē)	220	22°15'S	117°50'E
Hamhŭng, Kor., N. (häm'hòng')	205	39°57'N	127°35'E
Hami, China (hä-mē)	204	42°58'N	93°14'E
Hamilton, Austl. (hăm'ĭl-tŭn)	219	37°50'S	142°10'E
Hamilton, Can.	91	43°15'N	79°52'W
Hamilton, N.Z.	221a	37°45'S	175°28'E
Hamilton, Al., U.S.	124	34°09'N	88°01'W
Hamilton, Ma., U.S.	101a	42°37'N	70°52'W
Hamilton, Mo., U.S.	121	39°43'N	93°59'W
Hamilton, Mt., U.S.	115	46°15'N	114°09'W
Hamilton, Oh., U.S.	105	39°22'N	84°33'W
Hamilton, Tx., U.S.	122	31°42'N	98°07'W
Hamilton, Lake, l., Ar., U.S.	121	34°25'N	93°32'W
Hamilton Harbour, b., Can.	102d	43°17'N	79°50'W
Hamilton Inlet, b., Can.	93	54°20'N	56°57'W
Hamina, Fin. (hä'mē-nå)	167	60°34'N	27°15'E
Hamlet, N.C., U.S. (hăm'lĕt)	125	34°53'N	79°42'W
Hamlin, Tx., U.S. (hăm'lĭn)	120	32°54'N	100°08'W
Hamm, Ger. (häm)	168	51°40'N	7°48'E
Hammanskraal, S. Afr. (hä-mäns-kräl')	238c	25°24'S	28°17'E
Hamme, Bel.	159a	51°06'N	4°07'E
Hamme-Oste Kanal, can., Ger. (hä'mĕ-ōs'tĕ kä-näl)	159c	53°20'N	8°59'E
Hammerfest, Nor. (häm'mĕr-fĕst)	154	70°38'N	23°59'E
Hammond, In., U.S. (hăm'ŭnd)	105	41°37'N	87°31'W
Hammond, La., U.S.	123	30°30'N	90°28'W
Hammond, Or., U.S.	116c	46°12'N	123°57'W
Hammonton, N.J., U.S. (hăm'ŭn-tŭn)	109	39°40'N	74°45'W
Hampden, Me., U.S. (hăm'dĕn)	100	44°44'N	68°51'W
Hampstead, Md., U.S.	110e	39°36'N	76°54'W
Hampstead Norris, Eng., U.K. (hămp-stĕd nŏ'rĭs)	158b	51°27'N	1°14'W
Hampton, Can. (hămp'tŭn)	100	45°32'N	65°51'W
Hampton, Ia., U.S.	113	42°43'N	93°15'W
Hampton, Va., U.S.	109	37°02'N	76°21'W
Hampton Roads, b., Va., U.S.	110g	36°56'N	76°23'W
Hams Fork, r., Wy., U.S.	115	41°55'N	110°40'W
Hamtramck, Mi., U.S. (hăm-trăm'ĭk)	111b	42°24'N	83°03'W
Han, r., China (hän)	209	25°00'N	116°35'E
Han, r., China	205	31°40'N	112°04'E
Han, r., Kor., S.	210	37°10'N	127°40'E
Hāna, Hi., U.S. (hä'nä)	126a	20°43'N	155°59'W
Hanábana, r., Cuba (hä-nä-bä'nä)	134	22°30'N	80°55'W
Hanalei Bay, b., Hi., U.S. (hä-nä-lā'ē)	126a	22°15'N	159°40'W
Hanang, mtn., Tan.	237	4°26'S	35°24'E
Hanau, Ger. (hä'nou)	168	50°08'N	8°56'E
Hancock, Mi., U.S. (hăn'kŏk)	105	47°08'N	88°37'W
Handan, China (hän-dän)	206	36°37'N	114°30'E
Haney, Can. (hā-nē)	95	49°13'N	122°36'W
Hanford, Ca., U.S. (hăn'fĕrd)	118	36°20'N	119°38'W
Hangayn Nuruu, mts., Mong.	204	48°03'N	99°45'E
Hango, Fin. (häŋ'gû)	154	59°49'N	22°56'E
Hangzhou, China (häng'chō')	205	30°17'N	120°12'E
Hangzhou Wan, b., China (häŋ-jō wän)	209	30°20'N	121°25'E
Hankamer, Tx., U.S. (hăn'kå-mĕr)	123a	29°52'N	94°42'W
Hankinson, N.D., U.S. (häŋ'kĭn-sŭn)	112	46°04'N	96°54'W
Hankou, China (hän-kō)	209	30°42'N	114°22'E
Hann, Mount, mtn., Austl. (hän)	220	16°05'S	126°07'E
Hanna, Can. (hăn'å)	90	51°38'N	111°54'W
Hanna, Wy., U.S.	115	41°51'N	106°34'W
Hannah, N.D., U.S.	112	48°58'N	98°42'W
Hannibal, Mo., U.S. (hăn'ĭ băl)	105	39°42'N	91°22'W
Hannover, Ger. (hän-ō'vĕr)	154	52°22'N	9°45'E
Hannover, hist. reg., Ger.	168	52°52'N	8°27'E
Hanöbukten, b., Swe.	166	55°54'N	14°55'E
Hanoi, Viet. (hä-noi')	212	21°04'N	105°50'E
Hanover, Can. (hăn'ō-vĕr)	98	44°10'N	81°05'W
Hanover, Ma., U.S.	101a	42°07'N	70°49'W
Hanover, N.H., U.S.	109	43°45'N	72°15'W
Hanover, Pa., U.S.	109	39°50'N	77°00'W
Hanover, i., Chile	144	51°00'S	74°45'W
Hanshan, China (hän'shän')	206	31°43'N	118°06'E
Hans Lollick, i., V.I.U.S. (häns'lôl'ĭk)	129c	18°24'N	64°55'W
Hanson, Ma., U.S. (hăn'sŭn)	101a	42°04'N	70°53'W
Hansville, Wa., U.S. (hăns'-vĭl)	116a	47°55'N	122°33'W
Hantengri Feng, mtn., Asia (hän-tüŋ-rē fŭŋ)	204	42°10'N	80°20'E
Hantsport, Can. (hănts'pōrt)	100	45°04'N	64°11'W
Hanyang, China (han'yäng')	205	30°30'N	114°10'E
Hanzhong, China (hän-jōŋ)	208	33°02'N	107°00'E
Haocheng, China (hou-chŭŋ)	206	33°19'N	117°33'E
Haparanda, Swe. (hä-pa-rän'dä)	160	65°54'N	23°57'E
Hapeville, Ga., U.S. (hāp'vĭl)	110c	33°39'N	84°25'W
Happy Camp, Ca., U.S.	114	41°47'N	123°22'W
Happy Valley-Goose Bay, Can.	91	53°19'N	60°33'W
Ḥaql, Sau. Ar.	197a	29°15'N	34°57'E
Har, Laga, r., Kenya	237	2°15'N	39°30'E
Haradok, Bela.	176	55°27'N	29°58'E
Harare, Zimb.	232	17°50'S	31°03'E
Harbin, China	205	45°40'N	126°30'E
Harbor Beach, Mi., U.S. (här'bĕr bēch)	108	43°50'N	82°40'W
Harbor Springs, Mi., U.S.	108	45°25'N	85°05'W
Harbour Breton, Can. (brĕt'ŭn) (brē-tôN')	101	47°29'N	55°48'W
Harbour Grace, Can. (grās)	101	47°32'N	53°13'W
Harburg, Ger. (här-bōrgh)	159c	53°28'N	9°58'E
Hardangerfjorden, Nor. (här-däng'ĕr fyôrd)	160	59°58'N	6°30'E
Hardin, Mt., U.S. (här'dĭn)	115	45°44'N	107°36'W
Harding, S. Afr. (här'dĭng)	232	30°34'S	29°54'E
Harding, Lake, res., U.S.	124	32°43'N	85°00'W
Hardwār, India (hŭr'dvär)	199	29°56'N	78°06'E
Hardy, r., Mex. (här'dĭ)	118	32°04'N	115°10'W
Hare Bay, b., Can. (hâr)	101	51°18'N	55°50'W
Harer, Eth.	231	9°43'N	42°10'E
Harerge, hist. reg., Eth.	231	8°15'N	41°00'E
Hargeysa, Som. (här-gā'ē-så)	238a	9°20'N	43°57'E
Harghita, Munţii, mts., Rom.	169	46°25'N	25°40'E
Harima-Nada, b., Japan (hä'rē-mä nä-dä)	211	34°34'N	134°37'E
Haringvliet, r., Neth.	159a	51°49'N	4°03'E
Harīrūd, r., Asia	198	34°29'N	61°16'E
Harlan, Ia., U.S. (här'lăn)	121	41°40'N	95°10'W
Harlan, Ky., U.S.	124	36°50'N	83°19'W
Harlan County Reservoir, res., Ne., U.S.	120	40°03'N	99°51'W
Harlem, Mt., U.S. (hár'lĕm)	115	48°33'N	108°50'W
Harlingen, Neth. (här'lĭng-ĕn)	165	53°10'N	5°24'E
Harlingen, Tx., U.S.	104	26°12'N	97°42'W
Harlow, Eng., U.K. (här'lō)	158b	51°46'N	0°08'E
Harlowton, Mt., U.S. (här'lō-tun)	115	46°26'N	109°50'W
Harmony, In., U.S. (här'mō-nĭ)	108	39°35'N	87°00'W
Harney Basin, Or., U.S. (här'nĭ)	114	43°26'N	120°19'W
Harney Lake, l., Or., U.S.	114	43°11'N	119°23'W
Harney Peak, mtn., S.D., U.S.	106	43°52'N	103°32'W
Härnosand, Swe. (hĕr-nû-sänd)	160	62°37'N	17°54'E
Haro, Spain (ä'rō)	172	42°35'N	2°49'W
Haro Strait, strt., N.A. (hă'rō)	116a	48°27'N	123°11'W
Harpenden, Eng., U.K. (här'pĕn-d'n)	158b	51°48'N	0°22'W
Harper, Lib.	230	4°25'N	7°43'W
Harper, Ks., U.S. (här'pĕr)	120	37°17'N	98°02'W
Harper, Wa., U.S.	116a	47°31'N	122°32'W
Harpers Ferry, W.V., U.S. (här'pĕrz)	109	39°20'N	77°45'W
Harricana, r., Can.	99	50°10'N	78°50'W
Harriman, Tn., U.S. (hăr'ĭ-măn)	124	35°55'N	84°34'W
Harrington, De., U.S. (hăr'ĭng-tŭn)	109	38°55'N	75°35'W
Harris, i., Scot., U.K. (hăr'ĭs)	164	57°55'N	6°40'W
Harris, Lake, l., Fl., U.S.	125a	28°43'N	81°40'W
Harrisburg, Il., U.S. (hăr'ĭs-bûrg)	108	37°45'N	88°35'W
Harrisburg, Pa., U.S.	105	40°15'N	76°50'W
Harrismith, S. Afr. (hă-rĭs'mĭth)	238c	28°17'S	29°08'E
Harrison, Ar., U.S. (hăr'ĭ-sŭn)	121	36°13'N	93°06'W
Harrison, Oh., U.S.	111f	39°16'N	84°45'W
Harrisonburg, Va., U.S. (hăr'ĭ-sŭn-bûrg)	109	38°30'N	78°50'W
Harrison Lake, l., Can.	95	49°31'N	121°59'W
Harrisonville, Mo., U.S. (hăr-ĭ-sŭn-vĭl)	121	38°39'N	94°21'W
Harrisville, Ut., U.S. (hăr'ĭs-vĭl)	117b	41°17'N	112°00'W
Harrisville, W.V., U.S.	108	39°10'N	81°05'W
Harrodsburg, Ky., U.S. (hăr'ŭdz-bûrg)	108	37°45'N	84°50'W
Harrods Creek, r., Ky., U.S. (hăr'ŭdz)	111h	38°24'N	35°33'W
Harrow, Eng., U.K. (hăr'ō)	158b	51°34'N	0°21'W
Harsefeld, Ger. (här'zĕ-fĕld')	159c	53°27'N	9°30'E
Harstad, Nor. (här'städh)	160	68°49'N	16°10'E
Hart, Mi., U.S. (härt)	108	43°40'N	86°25'W
Hartbeesfontein, S. Afr.	238c	26°46'S	26°25'E
Hartbeespoortdam, res., S. Afr.	233b	25°47'S	27°43'E
Hartford, Al., U.S. (härt'fĕrd)	124	31°05'N	85°42'W
Hartford, Ar., U.S.	121	35°01'N	94°21'W
Hartford, Ct., U.S.	105	41°45'N	72°40'W
Hartford, Il., U.S.	117e	38°50'N	90°06'W
Hartford, Ky., U.S.	124	37°25'N	86°50'W
Hartford, Mi., U.S.	108	42°15'N	86°15'W
Hartford, Wi., U.S.	113	43°19'N	88°25'W
Hartford City, In., U.S.	108	40°35'N	85°25'W
Hartington, Eng., U.K. (härt'ĭng-tŭn)	158a	53°08'N	1°48'W
Hartington, Ne., U.S.	112	42°37'N	97°18'W
Hartland Point, c., Eng., U.K.	164	51°03'N	4°40'W
Hartlepool, Eng., U.K. (här't'l-pōōl)	160	54°40'N	1°12'W
Hartley, Ia., U.S. (härt'lĭ)	112	43°12'N	95°29'W
Hartley Bay, Can.	94	53°25'N	129°15'W
Hart Mountain, mtn., Can. (härt)	97	52°25'N	101°30'W
Hartsbeespoort, S. Afr.	233b	25°44'S	27°51'E
Hartselle, Al., U.S. (härt'sĕl)	124	34°24'N	86°55'W
Hartshorne, Ok., U.S. (härts'hôrn)	121	34°49'N	95°34'W
Hartsville, S.C., U.S. (härts'vĭl)	125	34°20'N	80°04'W
Hartwell, Ga., U.S. (härt'wĕl)	125	34°21'N	82°56'W
Hartwell Lake, res., U.S.	107	34°30'N	83°00'W
Hārua, India	202a	22°36'N	88°40'E
Harvard, Il., U.S. (här'vȧrd)	113	42°25'N	88°39'W
Harvard, Ma., U.S.	101a	42°30'N	71°35'W
Harvard, Ne., U.S.	120	40°36'N	98°08'W
Harvard, Mount, mtn., Co., U.S.	119	38°55'N	106°20'W
Harvey, Can.	100	45°44'N	64°46'W
Harvey, Il., U.S.	111a	41°37'N	87°39'W
Harvey, La., U.S.	110d	29°54'N	90°05'W
Harvey, N.D., U.S.	112	47°46'N	99°55'W
Harwich, Eng., U.K. (här'wĭch)	165	51°53'N	1°13'E
Haryana, state, India	199	29°00'N	75°45'E
Harz Mountains, mts., Ger. (härts)	168	51°42'N	10°50'E
Hashimoto, Japan (hä'shē-mō'tō)	211	34°19'N	135°37'E
Haskell, Ok., U.S. (hăs'kĕl)	121	35°49'N	95°41'W
Haskell, Tx., U.S.	120	33°09'N	99°43'W
Haslingden, Eng., U.K. (hăz'lĭng dĕn)	158a	53°43'N	2°19'W
Hassi Messaoud, Alg.	230	31°17'N	6°13'E
Hässleholm, Swe. (hĕs'lĕ-hōlm)	166	56°10'N	13°44'E
Hastings, N.Z.	221a	39°33'S	176°53'E
Hastings, Eng., U.K. (hās'tĭngz)	161	50°52'N	0°28'E
Hastings, Mi., U.S.	108	42°40'N	85°20'W
Hastings, Mn., U.S.	117g	44°44'N	92°51'W
Hastings, Ne., U.S.	104	40°34'N	98°42'W
Hastings-on-Hudson, N.Y., U.S. (ŏn-hŭd'sŭn)	110a	40°59'N	75°53'W
Hatay, Tur.	198	36°20'N	36°10'E
Hatchie, r., Tn., U.S. (hăch'ē)	124	35°28'N	89°14'W
Haţeg, Rom. (kät-säg')	175	45°35'N	22°57'E
Hatfield Broad Oak, Eng., U.K. (hăt-fēld brôd ōk)	158b	51°50'N	0°14'E
Hatogaya, Japan (hä'tō-gä-yä)	211a	35°50'N	139°45'E
Hatsukaichi, Japan (hät'sōō-kä'ē-chē)	211	34°22'N	132°19'E
Hatteras, Cape, c., N.C., U.S. (hăt'ēr-ȧs)	107	35°15'N	75°24'W
Hattiesburg, Ms., U.S. (hăt'ĭz-bûrg)	105	31°20'N	89°18'W
Hattingen, Ger. (hä'tĕn-gĕn)	171c	51°24'N	7°11'E
Hatvan, Hung. (hôt'vôn)	169	47°39'N	19°44'E
Hat Yai, Thai.	212	7°01'N	100°29'E
Haugesund, Nor. (hou'gĕ-soon')	160	59°26'N	5°20'E
Haukivesi, l., Fin. (hou'kē-vĕ'sē)	167	62°02'N	29°02'E
Haultain, r., Can.	96	56°15'N	106°35'W
Hauptsrus, S. Afr.	238c	26°35'S	26°16'E
Hauraki Gulf, b., N.Z. (hä-ōō-rä'kē)	221a	36°30'S	175°00'E
Haut, Isle au, Me., U.S. (hō)	100	44°03'N	68°13'W
Haut Atlas, mts., Mor.	162	32°10'N	5°49'W
Hauterive, Can.	100	49°11'N	68°16'W
Hau'ula, Hi., U.S.	126a	21°37'N	157°45'W
Havana, Cuba	129	23°08'N	82°23'W
Havana, Il., U.S. (hȧ-vă'nȧ)	121	40°17'N	90°02'W
Havasu, Lake, res., U.S. (hăv'ȧ-sōō)	119	34°26'N	114°09'W
Havel, r., Ger. (hä'fĕl)	168	53°09'N	13°10'E
Havel-Kanal, can., Ger.	159b	52°36'N	13°12'E
Haverhill, Ma., U.S. (hā'vĕr-hĭl)	101a	42°46'N	71°05'W
Haverhill, N.H., U.S.	109	44°00'N	72°05'W
Haverstraw, N.Y., U.S. (hă'vĕr-strô)	110a	41°11'N	73°58'W
Havlíčkův Brod, Czech Rep.	161	49°38'N	15°34'E
Havre, Mt., U.S. (hăv'ĕr)	104	48°34'N	109°42'W
Havre-Boucher, Can. (häv'rȧ-bōō-shā')	101	45°42'N	61°30'W
Havre de Grace, Md., U.S. (hăv'ēr dē grȧs')	109	39°35'N	76°05'W
Havre-Saint Pierre, Can.	100	50°15'N	63°36'W
Haw, r., N.C., U.S. (hô)	125	36°17'N	79°46'W

ăt; finȧl; rāte; senåte; ärm; ȧsk; sofȧ; fâre; ch-choose; dh-as th in other; bē; ēvent; bĕt; recĕnt; cratĕr; g-gō; gh-guttural g; bĭt; ĭ-short neutral; rīde; κ-guttural k as ch in German ich;

PRONOUNCING INDEX

Hawaii – Hindupur 301

PLACE (Pronunciation)	PAGE	LAT.	LONG.
Hawaii, state, U.S.	106c	20°00'N	157°40'W
Hawai'i, i., Hi., U.S. (häw wī'ē)	106c	19°30'N	155°30'W
Hawai'ian Islands, is., Hi., U.S. (hä-wī'án)	106c	22°00'N	158°00'W
Hawai'i Volcanoes National Park, rec., Hi., U.S.	106c	19°30'N	155°25'W
Hawarden, Ia., U.S. (hā'wàr-dĕn)	112	43°00'N	96°28'W
Hawi, Hi., U.S. (hä'wē)	126a	20°16'N	155°48'W
Hawick, Scot., U.K. (hô'ĭk)	164	55°25'N	2°55'W
Hawke Bay, b., N.Z. (hôk)	221a	39°17'S	177°20'E
Hawker, Austl. (hô'kẽr)	222	31°58'S	138°12'E
Hawkesbury, Can. (hôks'bẽr-ĭ)	99	45°35'N	74°35'W
Hawkinsville, Ga., U.S. (hô'kĭnz-vĭl)	124	32°15'N	83°30'W
Hawks Nest Point, c., Bah.	135	24°05'N	75°30'W
Hawley, Mn., U.S. (hô'lĭ)	112	46°52'N	96°18'W
Haworth, Eng., U.K. (hä'wûrth)	158a	53°50'N	1°57'W
Hawthorne, Ca., U.S. (hô'thôrn)	117a	33°55'N	118°22'W
Hawthorne, Nv., U.S.	118	38°33'N	118°39'W
Haxtun, Co., U.S. (hăks'tŭn)	120	40°39'N	102°38'W
Hay, r., Austl. (hā)	220	23°00'S	136°45'E
Hay, r., Can.	92	60°21'N	117°14'W
Hayama, Japan (hä-yä'mä)	211a	35°16'N	139°35'E
Hayashi, Japan (hä-yä'shē)	211a	35°13'N	139°38'E
Hayden, Az., U.S. (hā'dĕn)	119	33°00'N	110°50'W
Hayes, r., Can.	93	55°25'N	93°55'W
Hayes, Mount, mtn., Ak., U.S. (hāz)	103	63°32'N	146°40'W
Haynesville, La., U.S. (hānz'vĭl)	123	32°55'N	93°08'W
Hayrabolu, Tur.	175	41°14'N	27°05'E
Hay River, Can.	90	60°50'N	115°53'W
Hays, Ks., U.S. (hāz)	120	38°51'N	99°20'W
Haystack Mountain, mtn., Wa., U.S. (hā-stăk')	116a	48°26'N	122°07'W
Hayward, Ca., U.S. (hā'wẽrd)	116b	37°40'N	122°06'W
Hayward, Wi., U.S.	113	46°01'N	91°31'W
Hazard, Ky., U.S. (hăz'árd)	124	37°13'N	83°10'W
Hazelhurst, Ga., U.S. (hā'z'l-hûrst)	125	31°50'N	82°36'W
Hazelhurst, Ms., U.S.	124	31°52'N	90°23'W
Hazel Park, Mi., U.S.	111b	42°28'N	83°06'W
Hazelton, Can. (hā'z'l-tŭn)	90	55°15'N	127°40'W
Hazelton Mountains, mts., Can.	94	55°00'N	128°00'W
Hazleton, Pa., U.S.	109	41°00'N	76°00'W
Headland, Al., U.S. (hĕd'lănd)	124	31°22'N	85°20'W
Healdsburg, Ca., U.S. (hēldz'bûrg)	118	38°37'N	122°52'W
Healdton, Ok., U.S. (hēld'tŭn)	121	34°13'N	97°28'W
Heanor, Eng., U.K. (hēn'ŏr)	158a	53°01'N	1°22'W
Heard Island, i., Austl. (hûrd)	3	53°10'S	74°35'E
Hearne, Tx., U.S. (hûrn)	123	30°53'N	96°35'W
Hearst, Can. (hûrst)	91	49°36'N	83°40'W
Heart, r., N.D., U.S. (härt)	112	46°46'N	102°34'W
Heart Lake Indian Reserve, I.R., Can.	95	55°02'N	111°30'W
Heart's Content, Can. (härts kŏn'tĕnt)	101	47°52'N	53°22'W
Heavener, Ok., U.S. (hēv'nẽr)	121	34°52'N	94°36'W
Hebbronville, Tx., U.S. (hē'brŭn-vĭl)	122	27°18'N	98°40'W
Hebei, prov., China (hŭ-bā)	205	39°15'N	115°40'E
Heber City, Ut., U.S. (hē'bẽr)	119	40°30'N	111°25'W
Heber Springs, Ar., U.S.	121	35°28'N	91°59'W
Hebgen Lake, res., Mt., U.S. (hĕb'gĕn)	115	44°47'N	111°38'W
Hebrides, is., Scot., U.K.	156	57°00'N	6°30'W
Hebrides, Sea of the, sea, Scot., U.K.	164	57°00'N	7°00'W
Hebron, Can. (hēb'rŭn)	91	58°11'N	62°56'W
Hebron, In., U.S.	111a	41°19'N	87°13'W
Hebron, Ky., U.S.	111f	39°04'N	84°43'W
Hebron, N.D., U.S.	112	46°54'N	102°04'W
Hebron, Ne., U.S.	121	40°11'N	97°36'W
Hebron *see* Al Khalīl, W.B.	197a	31°31'N	35°07'E
Heby, Swe. (hĭ'bü)	166	59°56'N	16°48'E
Hecate Strait, strt., Can. (hĕk'á-tē)	92	53°00'N	131°00'W
Hecelchakán, Mex. (ā-sĕl-chä-kän')	131	20°10'N	90°09'W
Hechi, China (hŭ-chr)	209	24°50'N	108°18'E
Hechuan, China (hŭ-chyuän)	204	30°00'N	106°20'E
Hecla Island, i., Can.	97	51°08'N	96°45'W
Hedemora, Swe. (hĭ-dĕ-mō'rä)	166	60°16'N	15°55'E
Hedon, Eng., U.K. (hĕ-dŭn)	158a	53°44'N	0°12'W
Heemstede, Neth.	159a	52°20'N	4°36'E
Heerlen, Neth.	165	50°55'N	5°58'E
Hefei, China (hŭ-fā)	205	31°51'N	117°15'E
Heflin, Al., U.S. (hĕf'lĭn)	124	33°40'N	85°33'W
Heide, Ger. (hī'dē)	168	54°13'N	9°06'E
Heidelberg, Austl. (hī'dĕl-bûrg)	217a	37°45'S	145°04'E
Heidelberg, Ger. (hīdĕl-bĕrgh)	161	49°24'N	8°43'E
Heidelberg, S. Afr.	238c	26°32'S	28°22'E
Heidenheim, Ger. (hī'dĕn-hīm)	168	48°41'N	10°09'E
Heilbron, S. Afr. (hīl'brōn)	238c	27°17'S	27°58'E
Heilbronn, Ger. (hīl'brōn)	161	49°09'N	9°16'E
Heiligenhaus, Ger. (hī'lē-gĕn-houz)	171c	51°19'N	6°58'E
Heiligenstadt, Ger. (hī'lē-gĕn-shtät)	168	51°21'N	10°10'E
Heilongjiang, prov., China (hā-lôŋ-jyäŋ)	205	46°36'N	128°07'E
Heinola, Fin. (hå-nō'lä)	167	61°13'N	26°03'E
Heinsberg, Ger. (hīnz'bĕrgh)	171c	51°04'N	6°07'E
Heist-op-den-Berg, Bel.	159a	51°05'N	4°14'E
Hejaz *see* Al Ḩijāz, reg., Sau. Ar.	198	23°45'N	39°08'E
Hejian, China (hŭ-jyĕn)	208	38°28'N	116°05'E
Hekla, vol., Ice.	156	63°53'N	19°37'W
Hel, Pol. (hāl)	169	54°37'N	18°53'E
Helagsfjället, mtn., Swe.	160	62°54'N	12°24'E
Helan Shan, mts., China (hŭ-län shän)	204	38°02'N	105°20'E
Helena, Ar., U.S. (hē-lē'ná)	105	34°33'N	90°35'W
Helena, Mt., U.S. (hĕ-lē'ná)	104	46°35'N	112°01'W
Helensburgh, Austl. (hĕl'ĕnz-bŭr-ō)	217b	34°11'S	150°59'E
Helensburgh, Scot., U.K.	164	56°01'N	4°53'W
Helgoland, i., Ger. (hĕl'gô-länd)	168	54°13'N	7°30'E
Hellier, Ky., U.S. (hĕl'yẽr)	125	37°16'N	82°27'W
Hellín, Spain (ĕl-yén')	162	38°30'N	1°40'W
Hells Canyon, p., U.S.	114	45°20'N	116°45'W
Helmand, r., Afg. (hĕl'mŭnd)	198	31°00'N	63°48'E
Hel'miaziv, Ukr.	177	49°49'N	31°54'E
Helmond, Neth. (hĕl'mŏnt) (ĕl'môɴ')	165	51°35'N	5°04'E
Helmstedt, Ger. (hĕlm'shtĕt)	168	52°14'N	11°03'E
Helotes, Tx., U.S. (hē'lōts)	117d	29°35'N	98°41'W
Helper, Ut., U.S. (hĕlp'ẽr)	119	39°40'N	110°55'W
Helsingborg, Swe. (hĕl'sĭng-bôrgh)	160	56°04'N	12°40'E
Helsingfors *see* Helsinki, Fin.	154	60°10'N	24°53'E
Helsingør, Den. (hĕl-sĭng-ŭr')	160	56°03'N	12°33'E
Helsinki, Fin. (hĕl'sĕn-kĕ)	154	60°10'N	24°53'E
Hemel Hempstead, Eng., U.K. (hĕm'ĕl hĕmp'stĕd)	158b	51°43'N	0°29'W
Hemer, Ger.	171c	51°22'N	7°46'E
Hemet, Ca., U.S. (hĕm'ĕt)	117a	33°45'N	116°57'W
Hemingford, Ne., U.S. (hĕm'ĭng-fērd)	112	42°21'N	103°30'W
Hemphill, Tx., U.S. (hĕmp'hĭl)	123	31°20'N	93°48'W
Hempstead, N.Y., U.S. (hĕmp'stĕd)	110a	40°42'N	73°37'W
Hempstead, Tx., U.S.	123	30°07'N	96°05'W
Hemse, Swe. (hĕm'sē)	166	57°15'N	18°25'E
Hemsön, i., Swe.	166	62°43'N	18°22'E
Henan, prov., China (hŭ-nän)	205	33°58'N	112°33'E
Henares, r., Spain (å-nä'rås)	172	40°50'N	2°55'W
Henderson, Ky., U.S. (hĕn'dẽr-sŭn)	108	37°50'N	87°30'W
Henderson, N.C., U.S.	125	36°18'N	78°24'W
Henderson, Nv., U.S.	118	36°09'N	115°04'W
Henderson, Tn., U.S.	124	35°25'N	88°40'W
Henderson, Tx., U.S.	123	32°09'N	94°48'W
Hendersonville, N.C., U.S. (hĕn'dẽr-sŭn-vĭl)	125	35°17'N	82°28'W
Hendersonville, Tn., U.S.	124	36°18'N	86°37'W
Hendon, Eng., U.K. (hĕn'dŭn)	158b	51°34'N	0°13'W
Hendrina, S. Afr. (hĕn-drē'ná)	238c	26°10'S	29°44'E
Hengch'un, Tai. (hĕng'chŭn')	209	22°00'N	120°42'E
Hengelo, Neth. (hĕngĕ-lō)	165	52°20'N	6°45'E
Hengshan, China (hĕng'shän')	209	27°20'N	112°40'E
Hengshui, China (hĕng'shōō-ē')	206	37°43'N	115°42'E
Hengxian, China (hŭŋ shyĕn)	209	22°40'N	109°20'E
Hengyang, China	205	26°58'N	112°30'E
Heniches'k, Ukr.	181	46°11'N	34°47'E
Henley on Thames, Eng., U.K. (hĕn'lē ŏn tĕmz)	158b	51°31'N	0°54'W
Henlopen, Cape, c., De., U.S. (hĕn-lō'pĕn)	109	38°45'N	75°05'W
Hennebont, Fr. (ĕn-bôɴ')	170	47°47'N	3°16'W
Hennenman, S. Afr.	238c	27°59'S	27°03'E
Hennessey, Ok., U.S. (hĕn'ĕ-sĭ)	121	36°04'N	97°53'W
Hennigsdorf, Ger. (hĕ'nēngz-dōrf)	159b	52°39'N	13°12'E
Hennops, r., S. Afr. (hĕn'ŏps)	233b	25°51'S	27°57'E
Hennopsrivier, S. Afr.	233b	25°50'S	27°59'E
Henrietta, Ok., U.S. (hĕn-rĭ-ĕt'á)	121	35°25'N	95°58'W
Henrietta, Tx., U.S. (hen-rĭ-ĕ'tá)	120	33°47'N	98°11'W
Henrietta Maria, Cape, c., Can. (hĕn-rĭ-ĕt'á)	93	55°10'N	82°20'W
Henry Mountains, mts., Ut., U.S. (hĕn'rĭ)	106	37°55'N	110°45'W
Henrys Fork, r., Id., U.S.	115	43°52'N	111°55'W
Henteyn Nuruu, mtn., Russia	208	49°40'N	111°00'E
Hentiyn Nuruu, mts., Mong.	204	49°25'N	107°51'E
Henzada, Mya.	199	17°38'N	95°28'E
Heppner, Or., U.S. (hĕp'nẽr)	114	45°21'N	119°33'W
Hepu, China (hŭ-pōō)	209	21°28'N	109°10'E
Herāt, Afg. (hĕ-rät')	198	34°28'N	62°13'E
Hercules, Can.	102g	53°27'N	113°20'W
Herdecke, Ger. (hĕr'dĕ-kĕ)	171c	51°24'N	7°26'E
Heredia, C.R. (ā-rā'dhē-ä)	133	10°04'N	84°06'W
Hereford, Eng., U.K. (hĕrĕ'fērd)	164	52°05'N	2°44'W
Hereford, Md., U.S.	110e	39°35'N	76°42'W
Hereford, Tx., U.S. (hĕr'ĕ-fērd)	120	34°47'N	102°25'W
Hereford and Worcester, co., Eng., U.K.	158a	52°24'N	2°15'W
Herencia, Spain (å-rān'thē-ä)	172	39°23'N	3°22'W
Herentals, Bel.	159a	51°10'N	4°51'E
Herford, Ger. (hĕr'fôrt)	168	52°06'N	8°42'E
Herington, Ks., U.S. (hĕr'ĭng-tŭn)	121	38°41'N	96°57'W
Herisau, Switz. (hā'rē-zou)	168	47°23'N	9°18'E
Herk-de-Stad, Bel.	159a	50°56'N	5°13'E
Herkimer, N.Y., U.S. (hûr'kĭ-mẽr)	109	43°05'N	75°00'W
Hermansville, Mi., U.S. (hûr'măns-vĭl)	108	45°40'N	87°35'W
Hermantown, Mn., U.S. (hẽr'mán-toun)	117h	46°46'N	92°12'W
Hermanusdorings, S. Afr.	238c	24°08'S	27°46'E
Herminie, Pa., U.S. (hûr-mī'nē)	111e	40°16'N	79°45'W
Hermitage Bay, b., Can. (hûr'mĭ-tĕj)	101	47°35'N	56°05'W
Hermit Islands, is., Pap. N. Gui. (hûr'mĭt)	213	1°48'S	144°55'E
Hermosa Beach, Ca., U.S. (hĕr-mō'sá)	117a	33°51'N	118°24'W
Hermosillo, Mex. (ĕr-mô-sē'l-yō)	128	29°00'N	110°57'W
Herndon, Va., U.S. (hĕrn'don)	110e	38°58'N	77°22'W
Herne, Ger. (hĕr'nĕ)	171c	51°32'N	7°13'E
Herning, Den. (hĕr'nĭng)	160	56°08'N	8°55'E
Heron, l., Mn., U.S. (hĕr'ŭn)	112	43°42'N	95°23'W
Heron Lake, Mn., U.S.	112	43°48'N	95°20'W
Herrero, Punta, Mex. (pô'n-tä-ĕr-rĕ'rō)	132a	19°18'N	87°24'W
Herrin, Il., U.S. (hĕr'ĭn)	108	37°50'N	89°00'W
Herschel, S. Afr. (hĕr'-shĕl)	233c	30°37'S	27°12'E
Herscher, Il., U.S. (hĕr'shẽr)	111a	41°03'N	88°06'W
Herstal, Bel. (hĕr'stäl)	165	50°42'N	5°32'E
Hertford, Eng., U.K.	164	51°48'N	0°05'W
Hertford, N.C., U.S. (hûrt'fẽrd)	125	36°10'N	76°30'W
Hertfordshire, co., Eng., U.K.	158b	51°46'N	0°05'W
Hertzberg, Ger. (hĕrtz'bĕrgh)	159b	52°54'N	12°58'E
Hervás, Spain	172	40°16'N	5°51'W
Herzliyya, Isr.	197a	32°10'N	34°49'E
Hessen, hist. reg., Ger. (hĕs'ĕn)	168	50°42'N	9°00'E
Hetch Hetchy Aqueduct, Ca., U.S. (hĕtch hĕt'chĭ ăk'wē-dŭkt)	118	37°27'N	120°54'W
Hettinger, N.D., U.S. (hĕt'ĭn-jẽr)	112	45°58'N	102°36'W
Heuningspruit, S. Afr.	238c	27°28'S	27°26'E
Hexian, China (hŭ shyĕn)	209	24°20'N	111°28'E
Hexian, China	206	31°44'N	118°20'E
Heyang, China (hŭ-yäŋ)	208	35°18'N	110°18'E
Heystekrand, S. Afr.	238c	25°16'S	27°14'E
Heyuan, China (hŭ-yůän)	209	23°48'N	114°45'E
Heywood, Eng., U.K. (hā'wŏŏd)	158a	53°36'N	2°12'W
Heze, China (hŭ-dzŭ)	206	35°13'N	115°28'E
Hialeah, Fl., U.S. (hī-á-lē'äh)	125a	25°49'N	80°18'W
Hiawatha, Ks., U.S. (hī-á-wô'thá)	121	39°50'N	95°33'W
Hiawatha, Ut., U.S.	119	39°25'N	111°05'W
Hibbing, Mn., U.S. (hĭb'ĭng)	105	47°26'N	92°58'W
Hickman, Ky., U.S. (hĭk'mán)	124	34°33'N	89°10'W
Hickory, N.C., U.S. (hĭk'ō-rĭ)	125	35°43'N	81°21'W
Hicksville, N.Y., U.S.	108	41°15'N	84°45'W
Hicksville, N.Y., U.S. (hĭks'vĭl)	110a	40°47'N	73°25'W
Hico, Tx., U.S. (hī'kō)	122	32°00'N	98°02'W
Hidalgo, Mex. (ē-dhäl'gō)	130	24°14'N	99°25'W
Hidalgo, Mex.	122	27°49'N	99°53'W
Hidalgo, state, Mex.	128	20°45'N	99°30'W
Hidalgo del Parral, Mex. (ē-dä'l-gō-dĕl-pär-rá'l)	128	26°55'N	105°40'W
Hidalgo Yalalag, Mex. (ē-dhäl'gō-yä-lä-läg)	131	17°12'N	96°11'W
Hierro Island, i., Spain (yĕ'r-rō)	230	27°37'N	18°29'W
Higashimurayama, Japan	211a	35°46'N	139°28'E
Higashiōsaka, Japan	211b	34°40'N	135°44'E
Higgins, l., Mi., U.S. (hĭg'ĭnz)	108	44°20'N	84°45'W
Higginsville, Mo., U.S. (hĭg'ĭnz-vĭl)	121	39°05'N	93°44'W
High, i., Mi., U.S.	108	45°45'N	85°45'W
High Bluff, Can.	102f	50°01'N	98°08'W
Highborne Cay, i., Bah. (hībôrn kē)	134	24°45'N	76°50'W
Highgrove, Ca., U.S. (hī'grōv)	117a	34°01'N	117°20'W
High Island, Tx., U.S.	123a	29°34'N	94°24'W
Highland, Ca., U.S. (hī'lănd)	117a	34°08'N	117°13'W
Highland, Il., U.S.	121	38°44'N	89°41'W
Highland, In., U.S.	111a	41°33'N	87°28'W
Highland, Mi., U.S.	111b	42°38'N	83°37'W
Highland Park, Il., U.S.	111a	42°11'N	87°47'W
Highland Park, Mi., U.S.	111b	42°24'N	83°06'W
Highland Park, N.J., U.S.	110a	40°30'N	74°25'W
Highland Park, Tx., U.S.	117c	32°49'N	96°48'W
Highlands, N.J., U.S. (hī-lăndz)	110a	40°24'N	73°59'W
Highlands, Tx., U.S.	123a	29°49'N	95°01'W
Highmore, S.D., U.S. (hī'mōr)	112	44°30'N	99°26'W
High Ongar, Eng., U.K. (ŏn'gẽr)	158b	51°43'N	0°15'E
High Peak, mtn., Phil.	213a	15°38'N	120°05'E
High Point, N.C., U.S.	125	35°55'N	80°00'W
High Prairie, Can.	90	55°26'N	116°29'W
High Ridge, Mo., U.S.	117e	38°27'N	90°32'W
High River, Can.	90	50°35'N	113°52'W
High Rock Lake, res., N.C., U.S. (hī'-rŏk)	125	35°40'N	80°15'W
High Springs, Fl., U.S.	125	29°48'N	82°38'W
High Tatra Mountains, mts., Eur.	169	49°15'N	19°40'E
Hightstown, N.J., U.S. (hīts-toun)	110a	40°16'N	74°32'W
High Wycombe, Eng., U.K. (wĭ-kŭm)	164	51°36'N	0°45'W
Higuero, Punta, c., P.R.	129b	18°21'N	67°11'W
Higuerote, Ven. (ē-gē-rô'tĕ)	143b	10°29'N	66°06'W
Higüey, Dom. Rep. (ē-gwĕ'y)	135	18°40'N	68°45'W
Hiiumaa, i., Est. (hē'ŏŏm-ô)	180	58°47'N	22°05'E
Hikone, Japan (hē'kō-nĕ)	211	35°15'N	136°15'E
Hildburghausen, Ger. (hĭld'bŏŏrg hou-zĕn)	168	50°26'N	10°45'E
Hilden, Ger. (hēl'dĕn)	171c	51°10'N	6°56'E
Hildesheim, Ger. (hĭl'dĕs-hīm)	161	52°08'N	9°56'E
Hillaby, Mount, mtn., Barb. (hĭl'á-bĭ)	133b	13°15'N	59°35'W
Hill City, Ks., U.S. (hĭl)	120	39°22'N	99°54'W
Hill City, Mn., U.S.	113	46°58'N	93°38'W
Hillegersberg, Neth.	159a	51°57'N	4°29'E
Hillerød, Den. (hē'lĕ-rûdh)	166	55°56'N	12°17'E
Hillsboro, Il., U.S. (hĭlz'bŭr-ō)	121	39°09'N	89°28'W
Hillsboro, Ks., U.S.	121	38°22'N	97°11'W
Hillsboro, N.D., U.S.	112	47°23'N	97°05'W
Hillsboro, N.H., U.S.	109	43°05'N	71°55'W
Hillsboro, Oh., U.S.	108	39°10'N	83°40'W
Hillsboro, Or., U.S.	116c	45°31'N	122°59'W
Hillsboro, Tx., U.S.	123	32°01'N	97°06'W
Hillsboro, Wi., U.S.	113	43°39'N	90°20'W
Hillsburgh, Can. (hĭlz'bûrg)	102d	43°48'N	80°09'W
Hills Creek Lake, res., Or., U.S.	114	43°41'N	122°26'W
Hillsdale, Mi., U.S. (hĭls-dāl)	119	41°55'N	84°35'W
Hilo, Hi., U.S. (hē'lō)	106c	19°44'N	155°01'W
Hilvarenbeek, Neth.	159a	51°29'N	5°10'E
Hilversum, Neth. (hĭl'vẽr-sŭm)	159a	52°13'N	5°10'E
Himachal Pradesh, India	199	32°00'N	77°30'E
Himalayas, mts., Asia	199	29°30'N	85°02'E
Himeji, Japan (hē'mâ-jē)	210	34°50'N	134°42'E
Himmelpforten, Ger. (hē'mĕl-pfōr-tĕn)	159c	53°37'N	9°19'E
Ḩimş, Syria	198	34°44'N	36°43'E
Hinche, Haiti (hēn'chå) (ăɴsh)	135	19°10'N	72°05'W
Hinchinbrook, i., Austl. (hĭn-chĭn-brŏŏk)	220	18°23'S	146°57'W
Hinckley, Eng., U.K. (hĭnk'lĭ)	158a	52°32'N	1°21'W
Hindley, Eng., U.K. (hĭnd'lĭ)	158a	53°32'N	2°35'W
Hindu Kush, mts., Asia (hĭn'dōō kōōsh')	199	35°15'N	68°44'E
Hindupur, India (hĭn'dōō-pŏŏr)	203	13°52'N	77°34'E

302 Hingham – Hualapai Mountains PRONOUNCING INDEX

PLACE (Pronunciation)	PAGE	LAT.	LONG.
Hingham, Ma., U.S. (hĭng′ăm)	101a	42°14′N	70°53′W
Hinkley, Oh., U.S. (hĭnk′-lĭ)	111d	41°14′N	81°45′W
Hinojosa del Duque, Spain (ê-nô-kô′sä)	172	38°30′N	5°09′W
Hinsdale, Il., U.S. (hĭnz′dāl)	111a	41°48′N	87°56′W
Hinton, Can. (hĭn′tŭn)	95	53°25′N	117°34′W
Hinton, W.V., U.S. (hĭn′tŭn)	108	37°40′N	80°55′W
Hirado, i., Japan (hē′rä-dō)	210	33°19′N	129°18′E
Hirakata, Japan (hē′rä-kä′tä)	211b	34°49′N	135°40′E
Hirara, Japan	214d	24°48′N	125°17′E
Hiratsuka, Japan (hē-rät-sōō′kà)	211	35°20′N	139°19′E
Hirosaki, Japan (hē′rô-sä′kē)	205	40°31′N	140°38′E
Hirose, Japan (hē′rô-sä)	211	35°20′N	133°11′E
Hiroshima, Japan (hē-rô-shē′mà)	205	34°22′N	132°25′E
Hirson, Fr. (ēr-sôɴ′)	170	49°54′N	4°00′E
Hisar, India	202	29°15′N	75°47′E
Hispaniola, i., N.A. (hĭ′spăn-ĭ-ō-là)	129	17°30′N	73°15′W
Hitachi, Japan (hē-tä′chē)	210	36°42′N	140°47′E
Hitchcock, Tx., U.S. (hĭch′kŏk)	123a	29°21′N	95°01′W
Hitoyoshi, Japan (hē′tô-yō′shē)	211	32°13′N	130°45′E
Hitra, i., Nor. (hĭträ)	160	63°34′N	7°37′E
Hittefeld, Ger. (hē′tĕ-fĕld)	159c	53°23′N	9°59′E
Hiwasa, Japan (hē′wà-sä)	211	33°44′N	134°31′E
Hiwassee, r., Tn., U.S. (hī-wôs′sē)	124	35°10′N	84°35′W
Hjälmaren, l., Swe.	160	59°07′N	16°05′E
Hjo, Swe. (yō)	166	58°19′N	14°11′E
Hjørring, Den. (jûr′ĭng)	160	57°27′N	9°59′E
Hlobyne, Ukr.	177	49°22′N	33°17′E
Hlohovec, Slvk. (hlō′ho-vĕts)	169	48°24′N	17°49′E
Hlukhiv, Ukr.	181	51°42′N	33°52′E
Hlybokaye, Bela.	180	55°08′N	27°44′E
Hobart, Austl. (hō′bȧrt)	219	43°00′S	147°30′E
Hobart, In., U.S.	111a	41°31′N	87°15′W
Hobart, Ok., U.S.	120	35°02′N	99°06′W
Hobart, Wa., U.S.	116a	47°25′N	121°58′W
Hobbs, N.M., U.S. (hŏbs)	120	32°41′N	103°15′W
Hoboken, Bel. (hō′bō-kĕn)	159a	51°11′N	4°20′E
Hoboken, N.J., U.S.	110a	40°43′N	74°03′W
Hobro, Den. (hô-brō′)	166	56°38′N	9°47′E
Hobson, Va., U.S. (hŏb′sŭn)	110g	36°54′N	76°31′W
Hobson's Bay, b., Austl. (hŏb′sŭnz)	217a	37°54′S	144°45′E
Hobyo, Som.	238a	5°24′N	48°28′E
Ho Chi Minh City, Viet.	212	10°46′N	106°34′E
Hockinson, Wa., U.S. (hŏk′ĭn-sŭn)	116c	45°44′N	122°29′W
Hoctún, Mex. (ôk-tōō′n)	132a	20°52′N	89°10′W
Hodgenville, Ky., U.S. (hŏj′ĕn-vĭl)	108	37°35′N	85°45′W
Hodges Hill, mtn., Can. (hŏj′ĕz)	101	49°04′N	55°53′W
Hódmezővásárhely, Hung. (hōd′mĕ-zû-vô′shôr-hĕl-y′)	169	46°24′N	20°21′E
Hodna, Chott el, l., Alg.	162	35°20′N	3°27′E
Hodonín, Czech Rep. (hē′dô-nén)	169	48°50′N	17°06′E
Hoegaarden, Bel.	159a	50°46′N	4°55′E
Hoek van Holland, Neth.	159a	51°59′N	4°05′E
Hoeryŏng, Kor., N. (hwĕr′yŭng)	210	42°28′N	129°39′E
Hof, Ger. (hōf)	168	50°19′N	11°55′E
Hofsjökull, ice, Ice. (hôfs′yü′kōōl)	160	64°55′N	18°40′W
Hog, i., Mi., U.S.	108	45°50′N	85°20′W
Hogansville, Ga., U.S. (hō′gănz-vĭl)	124	33°10′N	84°54′W
Hog Cay, i., Bah.	135	23°35′N	75°30′W
Hogsty Reef, rf., Bah.	135	21°45′N	73°50′W
Hohenbrunn, Ger. (hō′hĕn-brōōn)	159d	48°03′N	11°42′E
Hohenlimburg, Ger. (hō′hĕn lĕm′bōōrg)	171c	51°20′N	7°35′E
Hohen Neuendorf, Ger. (hō′hĕn noi′ĕn-dōrf)	159b	52°40′N	13°22′E
Hohe Tauern, mts., Aus. (hō′ĕ tou′ĕrn)	168	47°11′N	12°12′E
Hohhot, China (hŭ-hōō-tŭ)	205	41°05′N	111°50′E
Hohoe, Ghana	234	7°09′N	0°28′E
Hohokus, N.J., U.S. (hō-hō-kŭs)	110a	41°01′N	74°08′W
Hoi An, Viet.	209	15°48′N	108°30′E
Hoisington, Ks., U.S. (hoi′zĭng-tŭn)	120	38°30′N	98°46′W
Hojo, Japan (hō′jō)	211	33°58′N	132°50′E
Hokitika, N.Z. (hō-kĭ-tē′kä)	221a	42°43′S	170°59′E
Hokkaidō, i., Japan (hôk′kĭ-dō)	210	43°30′N	142°45′E
Holbæk, Den. (hôl′bĕk)	166	55°42′N	11°40′E
Holbox, Mex. (ôl-bō′x)	132a	21°33′N	87°19′W
Holbox, Isla, i., Mex. (ē′s-lä-ôl-bō′x)	132a	21°40′N	87°21′W
Holbrook, Az., U.S. (hōl′brŏŏk)	119	34°55′N	110°15′W
Holbrook, Ma., U.S.	101a	42°10′N	71°01′W
Holden, Ma., U.S. (hōl′dĕn)	101a	42°21′N	71°51′W
Holden, Mo., U.S.	121	38°42′N	94°00′W
Holden, W.V., U.S.	108	37°45′N	82°05′W
Holdenville, Ok., U.S. (hōl′dĕn-vĭl)	121	35°05′N	96°25′W
Holdrege, Ne., U.S. (hōl′drĕj)	120	40°25′N	99°28′W
Holguín, Cuba (ôl-gēn′)	129	20°55′N	76°15′W
Holguín, prov., Cuba	134	20°40′N	76°15′W
Holidaysburg, Pa., U.S. (hŏl′ĭ-dāz-bûrg)	109	40°30′N	78°30′W
Hollabrunn, Aus.	168	48°33′N	16°04′E
Holland, Mi., U.S. (hŏl′ănd)	108	42°45′N	86°10′W
Hollands Diep, strt., Neth.	159a	51°43′N	4°25′E
Hollenstedt, Ger. (hō′lĕn-shtĕt)	159c	53°22′N	9°43′E
Hollis, N.H., U.S. (hŏl′ĭs)	101a	42°30′N	71°29′W
Hollis, Ok., U.S.	120	34°39′N	99°56′W
Hollister, Ca., U.S. (hŏl′ĭs-tĕr)	118	36°50′N	121°25′W
Holliston, Ma., U.S. (hŏl′ĭs-tŭn)	101a	42°12′N	71°25′W
Holly, Mi., U.S. (hŏl′ĭ)	108	42°45′N	83°30′W
Holly, Wa., U.S.	116a	47°34′N	122°58′W
Holly Springs, Ms., U.S. (hŏl′ĭ sprĭngz)	124	34°45′N	89°28′W
Hollywood, Ca., U.S. (hŏl′ē-wŏŏd)	117a	34°06′N	118°20′W
Hollywood, Fl., U.S.	125a	26°00′N	80°11′W
Holmes Reefs, rf., Austl. (hōmz)	221	16°33′S	148°43′E
Holmestrand, Nor. (hôl′mĕ-strän)	166	59°29′N	10°17′E
Holmsbu, Nor. (hôlms′bōō)	166	59°36′N	10°26′E
Holmsjön, l., Swe.	166	62°23′N	15°43′E
Holstebro, Den. (hôl′stĕ-brô)	160	56°22′N	8°39′E
Holstein, hist. reg., Ger.	168	54°10′N	9°40′E
Holston, r., Tn., U.S. (hōl′stŭn)	124	36°02′N	83°42′W
Holt, Eng., U.K. (hōlt)	158a	53°05′N	2°53′W
Holton, Ks., U.S. (hōl′tŭn)	121	39°27′N	95°43′W
Holy Cross, Ak., U.S. (hō′lĭ krôs)	103	62°10′N	159°40′W
Holyhead, Wales, U.K. (hŏl′ē-hĕd)	164	53°18′N	4°45′W
Holy Island, i., Eng., U.K.	164	55°43′N	1°48′W
Holy Island, i., Wales, U.K. (hō′lĭ)	164	53°15′N	4°45′W
Holyoke, Co., U.S. (hōl′yōk)	120	40°36′N	102°18′W
Holyoke, Ma., U.S.	109	42°10′N	72°40′W
Homano, Japan (hō-mä′nō)	211a	35°33′N	140°08′E
Homberg, Ger. (hōm′bĕrgh)	171c	51°27′N	6°42′E
Hombori, Mali	234	15°17′N	1°42′W
Home Gardens, Ca., U.S. (hōm gär′d′nz)	117a	33°53′N	117°32′W
Homeland, Ca., U.S. (hōm′lănd)	117a	33°44′N	117°07′W
Homer, Ak., U.S. (hō′mēr)	103	59°42′N	151°30′W
Homer, La., U.S.	123	32°46′N	93°05′W
Homer Youngs Peak, mtn., Mt., U.S.	115	45°19′N	113°41′W
Homestead, Fl., U.S. (hōm′stĕd)	125a	25°27′N	80°28′W
Homestead, Mi., U.S.	117k	46°20′N	84°07′W
Homestead, Pa., U.S.	111e	40°29′N	79°55′W
Homestead National Monument of America, rec., Ne., U.S.	121	40°16′N	96°51′W
Homewood, Al., U.S. (hōm′wŏŏd)	110h	33°28′N	86°48′W
Homewood, Il., U.S.	111a	41°34′N	87°40′W
Hominy, Ok., U.S. (hŏm′ĭ-nĭ)	121	36°25′N	96°24′W
Homochitto, r., Ms., U.S. (hō-mō-chĭt′ō)	124	31°23′N	91°15′W
Homyel', Bela.	180	52°20′N	31°03′E
Homyel', prov., Bela.	176	52°18′N	29°00′E
Honda, Col. (hōn′dà)	142	5°13′N	74°45′W
Honda, Bahía, b., Cuba (bä-ē′ä-ô′n-dä)	134	23°10′N	83°20′W
Hondo, Tx., U.S.	122	29°20′N	99°08′W
Hondo, r., N.M., U.S.	120	33°22′N	105°06′W
Hondo, Río, r., N.A. (hon-dō′)	132a	18°16′N	88°32′W
Honduras, nation, N.A. (hŏn-dōō′ràs)	128	14°30′N	88°00′W
Honduras, Gulf of, b., N.A.	128	16°30′N	87°30′W
Honea Path, S.C., U.S. (hŭn′ĭ păth)	125	34°25′N	82°16′W
Hønefoss, Nor. (hē′nē-fōs)	160	60°10′N	10°15′E
Honesdale, Pa., U.S. (hōnz′dāl)	109	41°30′N	75°15′W
Honey Grove, Tx., U.S. (hŭn′ĭ grōv)	121	33°35′N	95°54′W
Honey Lake, l., Ca., U.S. (hŭn′ĭ)	118	40°11′N	120°34′W
Honfleur, Can. (ôɴ-flûr′)	102b	46°39′N	70°53′W
Honfleur, Fr. (ôɴ-flûr′)	170	49°26′N	0°13′E
Hon Gay, Viet.	209	20°58′N	107°10′E
Hong Kong (Xianggang), China	205	21°45′N	115°00′E
Hongshui, r., China (hôŋ-shwä)	204	24°30′N	105°00′E
Honguedo, Détroit d', strt., Can.	100	49°08′N	63°45′W
Hongze Hu, l., China	205	33°17′N	118°37′E
Honiara, Sol. Is.	219	9°26′S	159°57′E
Honiton, Eng., U.K. (hŏn′ĭ-tŏn)	164	50°49′N	3°10′W
Honolulu, Hi., U.S. (hŏn-ô-lōō′lōō)	106c	21°18′N	157°50′W
Honomu, Hi., U.S. (hŏn′ô-mōō)	126a	19°50′N	155°04′W
Honshū, i., Japan	205	36°00′N	138°00′E
Hood, Mount, mtn., Or., U.S.	106	45°20′N	121°43′W
Hood Canal, b., Wa., U.S. (hŏŏd)	116a	47°45′N	122°45′W
Hood River, Or., U.S.	104	45°42′N	121°30′W
Hoodsport, Wa., U.S. (hŏŏdz′pōrt)	116a	47°25′N	123°09′W
Hoogly, r., India (hōōg′lĭ)	199	21°35′N	87°50′E
Hoogstraten, Bel.	159a	51°24′N	4°46′E
Hooker, Ok., U.S. (hŏŏk′ēr)	120	36°49′N	101°13′W
Hool, Mex. (ōō′l)	132a	19°32′N	90°22′W
Hoonah, Ak., U.S. (hōō′nā)	103	58°05′N	135°25′W
Hoopa Valley Indian Reservation, I.R., Ca., U.S.	114	41°18′N	123°35′W
Hooper, Ne., U.S. (hŏŏp′ēr)	121	41°37′N	96°31′W
Hooper, Ut., U.S.	117b	41°10′N	112°08′W
Hooper Bay, Ak., U.S.	103	61°32′N	166°02′W
Hoopeston, Il., U.S. (hōōps′tŭn)	108	40°35′N	87°40′W
Hoosick Falls, N.Y., U.S. (hōō′sĭk)	109	42°55′N	73°15′W
Hoover Dam, Nv., U.S. (hōō′vēr)	118	36°00′N	115°06′W
Hoover Dam, dam, U.S.	106	36°00′N	114°27′W
Hopatcong, Lake, l., N.J., U.S. (hō-păt′kong)	110a	40°57′N	74°38′W
Hope, Ak., U.S. (hōp)	103	60°54′N	149°48′W
Hope, Ar., U.S.	121	33°41′N	93°35′W
Hope, N.D., U.S.	112	47°17′N	97°45′W
Hope, Ben, mtn., Scot., U.K. (bĕn hōp)	164	58°25′N	4°25′W
Hopedale, Can. (hōp′dāl)	91	55°26′N	60°11′W
Hopedale, Ma., U.S. (hōp′dāl)	101a	42°08′N	71°33′W
Hopelchén, Mex. (o-pĕl-chĕ′n)	132a	19°47′N	89°51′W
Hopes Advance, Cap, c., Can. (hōps ăd-vans′)	93	61°05′N	69°35′W
Hopetoun, Austl. (hōp′toun)	218	33°50′S	120°15′E
Hopetown, S. Afr. (hōp′toun)	232	29°35′S	24°10′E
Hopewell, Va., U.S. (hōp′wĕl)	125	37°14′N	77°15′W
Hopewell Culture National Historical Park, rec., Oh., U.S.	108	39°25′N	83°00′W
Hopi Indian Reservation, I.R., Az., U.S. (hō′pē)	119	36°20′N	110°30′W
Hopkins, Mn., U.S. (hŏp′kĭns)	117g	44°55′N	93°24′W
Hopkinsville, Ky., U.S. (hŏp′kĭns-vĭl)	105	36°50′N	87°28′W
Hopkinton, Ma., U.S. (hŏp′kĭn-tŭn)	101a	42°14′N	71°31′W
Hoquiam, Wa., U.S. (hō′kwĭ-ăm)	104	47°00′N	123°53′W
Horconcitos, Pan. (ŏr-kôn-sē′-tôs)	133	8°18′N	82°11′W
Horgen, Switz. (hôr′gĕn)	168	47°16′N	8°35′E
Horicon, Wi., U.S. (hŏr′ĭ-kŏn)	113	43°26′N	88°40′W
Horlivka, Ukr.	181	48°17′N	38°03′E
Hormuz, Strait of, strt., Asia (hôr′mŭz′)	198	26°30′N	56°30′E
Horn, i., Austl. (hôrn)	221	10°30′S	143°30′E
Horn, Cape *see* Hornos, Cabo de, c., Chile	144	56°00′S	67°00′W
Hornavan, l., Swe.	160	65°54′N	16°17′E
Horneburg, Ger. (hŏr′nĕ-bŏrgh)	159c	53°30′N	9°35′E
Hornell, N.Y., U.S. (hŏr-nĕl′)	109	42°20′N	77°40′W
Hornos, Cabo de, c., Chile	144	56°00′S	67°00′W
Horn Plateau, plat., Can.	92	62°12′N	120°29′W
Hornsby, Austl. (hôrnz′bĭ)	217b	33°43′S	151°06′E
Horodenka, Ukr.	169	48°40′N	25°30′E
Horodnia, Ukr.	177	51°54′N	31°31′E
Horodok, Ukr.	169	49°47′N	23°39′E
Horqueta, Para. (ŏr-kĕ′tä)	144	23°20′S	57°00′W
Horse Creek, r., Co., U.S. (hôrs)	120	38°49′N	103°48′W
Horse Creek, r., Wy., U.S.	112	41°33′N	104°39′W
Horse Islands, is., Can.	101	50°11′N	55°45′W
Horsens, Den. (hôrs′ĕns)	166	55°50′N	9°49′E
Horseshoe Bay, Can. (hôrs-shōō)	116d	49°23′N	123°16′W
Horsforth, Eng., U.K. (hôrs′fŭrth)	158a	53°50′N	1°38′W
Horsham, Austl. (hôr′shăm) (hôrs′ăm)	219	36°42′S	142°17′E
Horst, Ger. (hôrst)	159c	53°49′N	9°37′E
Horten, Nor. (hŏr′tĕn)	166	59°26′N	10°27′E
Horton, Ks., U.S. (hôr′tŭn)	121	39°38′N	95°32′W
Horton, r., Ak., U.S. (hôr′tŭn)	103	68°38′N	122°00′W
Horwich, Eng., U.K. (hŏr′ĭch)	158a	53°36′N	2°33′W
Horyn', r., Eur. (gō′rĕn′)	169	50°55′N	26°07′E
Hososhima, Japan (hō′sô-shē′mä)	210	32°26′N	131°40′E
Hoste, i., Chile (ôs′tā)	144	55°20′S	70°45′W
Hostotipaquillo, Mex. (ôs-tō′tĭ-pä-kēl′yô)	130	21°09′N	104°05′W
Hota, Japan (hō′tä)	211a	35°08′N	139°50′E
Hotan, China (hwô-tän)	204	37°11′N	79°50′E
Hotan, r., China	204	39°09′N	81°08′E
Hoto Mayor, Dom. Rep. (ô-tô-mä-yô′r)	135	18°45′N	69°10′W
Hot Springs, Ak., U.S. (hŏt sprĭngs)	103	65°00′N	150°20′W
Hot Springs, Ar., U.S.	105	34°29′N	93°02′W
Hot Springs, S.D., U.S.	112	43°28′N	103°32′W
Hot Springs, Va., U.S.	109	38°00′N	79°55′W
Hot Springs National Park, rec., Ar., U.S.	107	34°30′N	93°00′W
Hotte, Massif de la, mts., Haiti	135	18°25′N	74°00′W
Hotville, Ca., U.S. (hŏt′vĭl)	118	32°50′N	115°24′W
Houdan, Fr. (ōō-däɴ′)	171b	48°47′N	1°36′E
Houghton, Mi., U.S. (hō′tŭn)	113	47°06′N	88°36′W
Houghton, l., Mi., U.S.	108	44°20′N	84°45′W
Houilles, Fr. (ōō-yĕs′)	171b	48°55′N	2°11′E
Houjie, China (hwô-jyĕ)	207a	22°58′N	113°39′E
Houlton, Me., U.S. (hōl′tŭn)	100	46°07′N	67°50′W
Houma, La., U.S. (hōō′mà)	123	29°36′N	90°43′W
Housatonic, r., U.S. (hōō-sȧ-tŏn′ĭk)	109	41°50′N	73°25′W
House Springs, Mo., U.S. (hous sprĭngs)	117e	38°24′N	90°34′W
Houston, Ms., U.S. (hūs′tŭn)	124	33°53′N	89°00′W
Houston, Tx., U.S.	105	29°46′N	95°21′W
Houston Ship Channel, strt., Tx., U.S.	123a	29°38′N	94°57′W
Houtbaai, S. Afr.	232a	34°03′S	18°22′E
Houtman Rocks, is., Austl. (hout′män)	220	28°15′S	112°45′E
Houzhen, China (hwô-jŭn)	206	36°59′N	118°59′E
Hovd, Mong.	204	48°08′N	91°40′E
Hovd Gol, r., Mong.	204	49°06′N	91°16′E
Hove, Eng., U.K. (hōv)	164	50°50′N	0°09′W
Hövsgöl Nuur, l., Mong.	204	51°11′N	99°11′E
Howard, Ks., U.S. (hou′ărd)	121	37°27′N	96°10′W
Howard, S.D., U.S.	112	44°01′N	97°31′W
Howden, Eng., U.K. (hou′dĕn)	158a	53°44′N	0°52′W
Howe, Cape, c., Austl. (hou)	221	37°30′S	150°40′E
Howell, Mi., U.S. (hou′ĕl)	108	42°40′N	84°00′W
Howe Sound, strt., Can.	94	49°22′N	123°18′W
Howick, Can. (hou′ĭk)	102a	45°11′N	73°51′W
Howick, S. Afr.	233c	29°29′S	30°16′E
Howland, i., Oc. (hou′lănd)	2	1°00′N	176°00′W
Howrah, India (hou′rä)	199	22°33′N	88°20′E
Howse Peak, mtn., Can.	95	51°30′N	116°40′W
Howson Peak, mtn., Can.	94	54°25′N	127°45′W
Hoxie, Ar., U.S. (hŏk′sĭ)	121	36°03′N	91°00′W
Hoy, i., Scot., U.K. (hoi)	164a	58°53′N	3°10′W
Hōya, Japan	211a	35°45′N	139°35′E
Hoylake, Eng., U.K. (hoi-lāk′)	158a	53°23′N	3°11′W
Hoyo, Sierra del, mts., Spain (sē-ĕ′r-rä-dĕl-ō′yō)	173a	40°39′N	3°56′W
Hradec Králové, Czech Rep.	161	50°12′N	15°50′E
Hradyz'k, Ukr.	177	49°12′N	33°06′E
Hranice, Czech Rep. (hrän′yĕ-tsĕ)	169	49°33′N	17°45′E
Hröby, Swe. (hûr′bü)	166	55°50′N	13°41′E
Hrodna, Bela.	180	53°40′N	23°49′E
Hron, r., Slvk.	169	48°22′N	18°42′E
Hrubieszów, Pol. (hrōō-byä′shōōf)	169	50°48′N	23°54′E
Hsawnhsup, Mya.	204	24°29′N	94°45′E
Hsinchu, Tai. (hsĭn′chōō′)	209	24°48′N	121°00′E
Huadian, China (hwä-dĭĕn)	208	42°38′N	126°45′E
Huai, r., China (hwī)	205	32°07′N	114°38′E
Huai'an, China (hwī-än)	208	33°31′N	119°11′E
Huailai, China	208	40°20′N	115°45′E
Huailin, China (hwī-lĭn)	206	31°27′N	117°36′E
Huainan, China	206	32°38′N	117°02′E
Huaiyang, China (hōōāī′yang)	208	33°45′N	114°54′E
Huaiyuan, China (hwī-yüän)	208	32°53′N	117°13′E
Huajicori, Mex. (wä-jē-kō′rē)	130	22°41′N	105°24′W
Huajuapan de León, Mex. (wäj-wä′pām dā lā-ón′)	131	17°46′N	97°45′W
Hualapai Indian Reservation, I.R., Az., U.S. (wälăpī)	119	35°41′N	113°38′W
Hualapai Mountains, mts., Az., U.S.	119	34°53′N	113°54′W

ăt; fināl; rāte; senāte; ärm; åsk; sofȧ; fâre; ch-choose; dh-as th in other; bē; ēvent; bĕt; recĕnt; cratēr; g-gō; gh-guttural g; bĭt; ĭ-short neutral; rīde; ĸ-guttural k as ch in German ich;

PLACE (Pronunciation)	PAGE	LAT.	LONG.
Hualien, Tai. (hwä′lyĕn′)	209	23°58′N	121°58′E
Huallaga, r., Peru (wäl-yä′gä)	142	8°12′S	76°34′W
Huamachuco, Peru (wä-mä-chōō′kō)	142	7°52′S	78°11′W
Huamantla, Mex. (wä-män′tlȧ)	131	19°18′N	97°54′W
Huambo, Ang.	232	12°44′S	15°47′E
Huamuxtitlán, Mex. (wä-mōōs-tē-tlän′)	130	17°49′N	98°38′W
Huancavelica, Peru (wän′kä-vā-lē′kä)	142	12°47′S	75°02′W
Huancayo, Peru (wän-kä′yô)	142	12°09′S	75°04′W
Huanchaca, Bol. (wän-chä′kä)	142	20°09′S	66°40′W
Huang (Yellow), r., China (hůäŋ)	205	35°06′N	113°39′E
Huang, Old Beds of the, mth., China	204	40°28′N	106°34′E
Huang, Old Course of the, r., China	206	34°28′N	116°59′E
Huangchuan, China (hůäŋ-chůän)	208	32°07′N	115°01′E
Huanghua, China (hůäŋ-hwä)	206	38°28′N	117°18′E
Huanghuadian, China (hůäŋ-hwä-dĭĕn)	206	39°22′N	116°53′E
Huangli, China (hōōäng′lē)	206	31°39′N	119°42′E
Huangpu, China (hůäŋ-pōō)	207a	22°44′N	113°20′E
Huangpu, r., China	207b	30°56′N	121°16′E
Huangqiao, China (hůän-chyou)	206	32°15′N	120°13′E
Huangxian, China (hůäŋ shyĕn)	206	37°39′N	120°32′E
Huangyuan, China (hůäŋ-yůän)	204	37°00′N	101°01′E
Huanren, China (hůän-rŭn)	208	41°10′N	125°30′E
Huánuco, Peru (wä-nōō′kô)	142	9°50′S	76°17′W
Huánuni, Bol. (wä-nōō′nē)	142	18°11′S	66°43′W
Huaquechula, Mex. (wä-kĕ-chōō′lä)	130	18°44′N	98°37′W
Huaral, Peru (wä-rä′l)	142	11°28′S	77°11′W
Huarás, Peru (öä′rà′s)	142	9°32′S	77°29′W
Huascarán, Nevados, mts., Peru (wäs-kä-rän′)	142	9°05′S	77°50′W
Huasco, Chile (wäs′kō)	144	28°32′S	71°16′W
Huatla de Jiménez, Mex. (wá′tlä-dĕ-kē-mĕ′nĕz)	131	18°08′N	96°49′W
Huatlatlauch, Mex. (wä′tlä-tlä-ōō′ch)	130	18°40′N	98°04′W
Huatusco, Mex. (wä-tōōs′kô)	131	19°09′N	96°57′W
Huauchinango, Mex. (wä-ōō-chē-näŋ′gô)	130	20°09′N	98°03′W
Huaunta, Nic. (wä-ô′n-tä)	133	13°30′N	83°32′W
Huaunta, Laguna, l., Nic. (lä-gô′nä-wä-ô′n-tä)	133	13°35′N	83°46′W
Huautla, Mex. (wä-ōō′tlä)	130	21°04′N	98°13′W
Huaxian, China (hwä shyĕn)	208	35°34′N	114°32′E
Huaynamota, Río de, r., Mex. (rē′ō-dĕ-wäy-nä-mō′tä)	130	22°10′N	104°36′W
Huazolotitlán, Mex. (wäzô-lô-tlē-tlän′)	131	16°18′N	97°55′W
Hubbard, N.H., U.S. (hŭb′ẽrd)	101a	42°53′N	71°12′W
Hubbard, Tx., U.S.	123	31°53′N	96°46′W
Hubbard, l., Mi., U.S.	108	44°45′N	83°30′W
Hubbard Creek Reservoir, res., Tx., U.S.	122	32°50′N	98°55′W
Hubei, prov., China (hōō-bā)	205	31°20′N	111°58′E
Hubli, India (hŏ′blē)	199	15°25′N	75°09′E
Hückeswagen, Ger. (hü′kĕs-vä′gĕn)	171c	51°09′N	7°20′E
Hucknall, Eng., U.K. (hŭk′năl)	158a	53°02′N	1°12′W
Huddersfield, Eng., U.K. (hŭd′ẽrz-fēld)	164	53°39′N	1°47′W
Hudiksvall, Swe. (hōō′dĭks-väl)	160	61°44′N	17°05′E
Hudson, Can. (hŭd′sŭn)	102a	45°26′N	74°08′W
Hudson, Ma., U.S.	101a	42°24′N	71°34′W
Hudson, Mi., U.S.	108	41°50′N	84°15′W
Hudson, N.Y., U.S.	109	42°15′N	73°45′W
Hudson, Oh., U.S.	111d	41°15′N	81°27′W
Hudson, Wi., U.S.	117g	44°59′N	92°45′W
Hudson, r., U.S.	107	42°30′N	73°55′W
Hudson Bay, Can.	97	52°52′N	102°25′W
Hudson Bay, b., Can.	93	60°15′N	85°30′W
Hudson Falls, N.Y., U.S.	109	43°20′N	73°30′W
Hudson Heights, Can.	102a	45°28′N	74°09′W
Hudson Strait, strt., Can.	93	63°25′N	74°05′W
Hue, Viet. (ü-ā′)	212	16°28′N	107°42′E
Huebra, r., Spain (wĕ′brä)	172	40°44′N	6°17′W
Huehuetenango, Guat. (wā-wå-tå-näŋ′gô)	132	15°19′N	91°26′W
Huejotzingo, Mex. (wā-hô-tzĭŋ′gō)	130	19°09′N	98°24′W
Huejúcar, Mex. (wā-hōō′kär)	130	22°26′N	103°12′W
Huejuquilla el Alto, Mex. (wā-hōō-kēl′yä ĕl äl′tō)	130	22°42′N	103°54′W
Huejutla, Mex. (wā-hōō′tlä)	130	21°08′N	98°26′W
Huelma, Spain (wĕl′mä)	172	37°39′N	3°36′W
Huelva, Spain (wĕl′vä)	162	37°16′N	6°58′W
Huércal-Overa, Spain (wĕr-käl′ ō-vä′rä)	172	37°12′N	1°58′W
Huerfano, r., Co., U.S. (wâr′fȧ-nō)	120	37°41′N	105°13′W
Huésca, Spain (wĕs-kä)	162	42°07′N	0°25′W
Huéscar, Spain (wās′kär)	172	37°50′N	2°34′W
Huetamo de Núñez, Mex.	130	18°34′N	100°53′W
Huete, Spain (wā′tå)	172	40°09′N	2°42′W
Hueycatenango, Mex. (wĕy-kȧ-tĕ-nä′n-gô)	130	17°31′N	99°10′W
Hueytlalpan, Mex. (wā′ĭ-tläl′păn)	131	20°03′N	97°41′W
Hueytown, Al., U.S.	110h	33°28′N	86°59′W
Huffman, Al., U.S. (hŭf′măn)	110h	33°36′N	86°42′W
Hugh Butler, l., Ne., U.S.	120	40°21′N	100°40′W
Hughenden, Austl. (hū′ĕn-dĕn)	219	20°58′S	144°13′E
Hughes, Austl. (hūz)	218	30°45′S	129°30′E
Hughesville, Md., U.S.	110e	38°32′N	76°48′W
Hugo, Mn., U.S. (hū′gō)	117g	45°10′N	93°00′W
Hugo, Ok., U.S.	121	34°01′N	95°32′W
Hugoton, Ks., U.S. (hū′gō-tŭn)	120	37°10′N	101°28′W
Hugou, China (hōō-gō)	206	33°22′N	117°07′E
Huichapan, Mex. (wē-chä-păn′)	130	20°22′N	99°39′W
Huila, dept., Col. (wē′lä)	142a	3°10′N	75°20′W
Huila, Nevado de, mtn., Col. (nĕ-vä-dô-de-wē′lä)	142a	2°59′N	76°01′W
Huilai, China	209	23°02′N	116°18′E
Huili, China	204	26°48′N	102°20′E
Huimanguillo, Mex. (wē-män-gēl′yō)	131	17°50′N	93°16′W
Huimin, China (hōōĭ mĭn)	205	37°29′N	117°32′E
Huitzilac, Mex. (ōē′t-zē-lä′k)	131a	19°01′N	99°16′W
Huitzitzilingo, Mex. (wē-tzē-tzē-lē′n-go)	130	21°11′N	98°42′W
Huitzuco, Mex. (wē-tzōō′kō)	130	18°16′N	99°20′W
Huixquilucan, Mex. (ōē′x-kē-lōō-kä′n)	131a	19°21′N	99°22′W
Huiyang, China	209	23°05′N	114°25′E
Hukou, China (hōō-kō)	205	29°58′N	116°20′E
Hulan, China (hōō′län′)	205	45°58′N	126°32′E
Hulan, r., China	208	47°20′N	126°30′E
Huliaipole, Ukr.	177	47°39′N	36°12′E
Hulin, China (hōō′lĭn′)	210	45°45′N	133°25′E
Hull, Can. (hŭl)	91	45°26′N	75°43′W
Hull, Ma., U.S.	101a	42°18′N	70°54′W
Hull, r., Eng., U.K.	158a	53°47′N	0°20′W
Hulst, Neth. (hôlst)	159a	51°17′N	4°01′E
Huludao, China (hōō-lōō-dou)	205	40°40′N	120°55′E
Hulun Nur, l., China (hōō-lôn nôr)	205	48°50′N	116°45′E
Humacao, P.R. (ōō-mä-kä′ō)	129b	18°09′N	65°49′W
Humansdorp, S. Afr. (hōō′mäns-dôrp)	232	33°57′S	24°45′E
Humbe, Ang. (hòm′bā)	232	16°50′S	14°55′E
Humber, r., Can.	102d	43°53′N	79°40′W
Humber, r., Eng., U.K. (hŭm′bẽr)	160	53°30′N	0°30′E
Humbermouth, Can. (hŭm′bẽr-mŭth)	101	48°58′N	57°55′W
Humberside, hist. reg., Eng., U.K.	158a	53°47′N	0°36′W
Humble, Tx., U.S. (hŭm′b′l)	123	29°58′N	95°15′W
Humboldt, Can. (hŭm′bōlt)	90	52°12′N	105°07′W
Humboldt, Ia., U.S.	113	42°43′N	94°11′W
Humboldt, Ks., U.S.	121	37°48′N	95°26′W
Humboldt, Ne., U.S.	121	40°10′N	95°57′W
Humboldt, r., Nv., U.S.	106	40°30′N	116°50′W
Humboldt, East Fork, r., Nv., U.S.	114	40°59′N	115°21′W
Humboldt, North Fork, r., Nv., U.S.	114	41°25′N	115°45′W
Humboldt Bay, b., Ca., U.S.	114	40°48′N	124°25′W
Humboldt Range, mts., Nv., U.S.	118	40°12′N	118°16′W
Humbolt, Tn., U.S.	124	35°47′N	88°55′W
Humbolt Salt Marsh, Nv., U.S.	118	39°49′N	117°41′W
Humbolt Sink, Nv., U.S.	118	39°58′N	118°54′W
Humen, China (hōō-mŭn)	207a	22°49′N	113°39′E
Humphreys Peak, mtn., Az., U.S. (hŭm′frĭs)	106	35°20′N	111°40′W
Humpolec, Czech Rep. (hòm′pō-lĕts)	168	49°33′N	15°21′E
Humuya, r., Hond. (ōō-mōō′yä)	132	14°38′N	87°36′W
Hunaflói, b., Ice. (hōō′nä-flō′ĭ)	160	65°41′N	20°44′W
Hunan, prov., China (hōō′nän′)	205	28°08′N	111°25′E
Hunchun, China (hòn-chůn)	205	42°53′N	130°34′E
Hunedoara, Rom. (kōō′nĕd-wä′rȧ)	175	45°45′N	22°54′E
Hungary, nation, Eur. (hŭŋ′gȧ-rĭ)	154	46°44′N	17°55′E
Hungerford, Austl. (hŭn′gẽr-fẽrd)	219	28°50′S	144°32′E
Hungry Horse Reservoir, res., Mt., U.S. (hŭŋ′gá-rĭ hôrs)	115	48°11′N	113°30′W
Hunsrück, mts., Ger. (hōōns′rûk)	168	49°43′N	7°12′E
Hunte, r., Ger. (hòn′tē)	168	52°45′N	8°26′E
Hunter Islands, is., Austl. (hŭn-tẽr)	221	40°33′S	143°36′E
Huntingburg, In., U.S. (hŭnt′ĭng-bûrg)	108	38°15′N	86°55′W
Huntingdon, Can. (hŭnt′ĭng-dŭn)	99	45°10′N	74°05′W
Huntingdon, Can.	116d	49°00′N	122°16′W
Huntingdon, Tn., U.S.	124	36°00′N	88°23′W
Huntington, In., U.S.	108	40°55′N	85°30′W
Huntington, Pa., U.S.	109	40°30′N	78°00′W
Huntington, W.V., U.S.	105	38°25′N	82°25′W
Huntington Beach, Ca., U.S.	117a	33°39′N	118°00′W
Huntington Park, Ca., U.S.	117a	33°59′N	118°14′W
Huntington Station, N.Y., U.S.	110a	40°51′N	73°25′W
Huntley, Mt., U.S.	115	45°54′N	108°01′W
Huntsville, Can.	91	45°20′N	79°15′W
Huntsville, Al., U.S. (hŭnts′vĭl)	124	34°44′N	86°36′W
Huntsville, Mo., U.S.	121	39°24′N	92°32′W
Huntsville, Tx., U.S.	123	30°44′N	95°34′W
Huntsville, Ut., U.S.	117b	41°16′N	111°46′W
Huolu, China (hòŭ lōō)	206	38°05′N	114°20′E
Huon Gulf, b., Pap. N. Gui.	213	7°15′S	147°45′E
Huoqiu, China (hwô-chyō)	206	32°19′N	116°17′E
Huoshan, China (hwô-shän)	209	31°30′N	116°25′E
Ḩuraydin, Wādī, r., Egypt	197a	30°55′N	34°12′E
Hurd, Cape, c., Can. (hûrd)	98	45°15′N	81°45′W
Hurdiyo, Som.	238a	10°43′N	51°05′E
Hurley, Wi., U.S. (hûr′lĭ)	113	46°26′N	90°11′W
Hurlingham, Arg. (ōō′r-lēn-gäm)	144a	34°36′S	58°38′W
Huron, Oh., U.S. (hū′rŏn)	108	41°20′N	82°35′W
Huron, S.D., U.S.	104	44°22′N	98°15′W
Huron, r., Mi., U.S.	111b	42°12′N	83°26′W
Huron, Lake, l., N.A. (hū′rŏn)	107	45°15′N	82°40′W
Huron Mountains, mts., Mi., U.S. (hū′rŏn)	113	46°47′N	87°52′W
Hurricane, Ak., U.S. (hŭr′ĭ-kān)	103	63°00′N	149°30′W
Hurricane, Ut., U.S.	119	37°10′N	113°20′W
Hurricane Flats, bk. (hŭ-rĭ-kăn flăts)	134	23°35′N	78°30′W
Hurst, Tx., U.S.	117c	32°48′N	97°12′W
Húsavik, Ice.	160	66°00′N	17°10′W
Huşi, Rom. (kòsh′)	177	46°52′N	28°04′E
Huskvarna, Swe. (hòsk-vär′nȧ)	166	57°48′N	14°16′E
Husum, Ger. (hōō′zòm)	168	54°29′N	9°04′E
Hutchins, Tx., U.S. (hŭch′ĭnz)	117c	32°38′N	96°43′W
Hutchinson, Ks., U.S. (hŭch′ĭn-sŭn)	104	38°02′N	97°56′W
Hutchinson, Mn., U.S.	113	44°53′N	94°23′W
Hutuo, r., China	208	38°10′N	114°00′E
Huy, Bel. (ū-ē′) (hû′ē)	165	50°33′N	5°14′E
Hvannadalshnúkur, mtn., Ice.	160	64°09′N	16°46′W
Hvar, i., Yugo. (кhvär)	174	43°08′N	16°28′E
Hwange, Zimb.	232	18°22′S	26°29′E
Hwangju, Kor., N. (hwäng′jōō′)	210	38°39′N	125°49′E
Hyargas Nuur, l., Mong.	204	48°00′N	92°32′E
Hyattsville, Md., U.S. (hī′ăt′s-vil)	110e	38°57′N	76°58′W
Hyco Lake, res., N.C., U.S. (rŏks′ bŭr-ô)	125	36°22′N	78°58′W
Hydaburg, Ak., U.S. (hī-dă′bûrg)	103	55°12′N	132°49′W
Hyde, Eng., U.K. (hīd)	158a	53°27′N	2°05′W
Hyderābād, India (hī-dẽr-å-băd′)	199	17°29′N	78°28′E
Hyderabad, India	199	18°30′N	76°50′E
Hyderābād, Pak.	199	25°29′N	68°28′E
Hyéres, Fr. (ē-âr′)	161	43°09′N	6°08′E
Hyéres, Îles d′, is., Fr. (ēl′dyâr′)	161	42°57′N	6°17′E
Hyesanjin, Kor., N. (hyĕ′sän-jĭn′)	210	41°11′N	128°12′E
Hymera, In., U.S. (hī-mē′rȧ)	108	39°10′N	87°20′W
Hyndman Peak, mtn., Id., U.S. (hīnd′măn)	106	43°38′N	114°04′W
Hyōgo, dept., Japan (hĭyō′gō)	211b	34°54′N	135°15′E
I			
Ia, r., Japan (ē′ä)	211b	34°54′N	135°34′E
Iahotyn, Ukr.	177	50°18′N	31°46′E
Ialomiţa, r., Rom.	175	44°37′N	26°42′E
Iaşi, Rom. (yä′shē)	154	47°10′N	27°40′E
Iasinia, Ukr.	169	48°17′N	24°21′E
Iavoriv, Ukr.	169	49°56′N	23°24′E
Iba, Phil. (ē′bä)	213a	15°20′N	119°59′E
Ibadan, Nig. (ē-bä′dän)	230	7°17′N	3°30′E
Ibagué, Col.	142	4°27′N	75°14′W
Ibar, r., Yugo. (ē′bär)	175	43°22′N	20°35′E
Ibaraki, Japan (ē-bä′rä-gē)	211b	34°49′N	135°35′E
Ibarra, Ec. (ē-bär′rä)	142	0°19′N	78°08′W
Ibb, Yemen	201	14°01′N	44°10′E
Iberville, Can. (ē-bår-vēl′)(ī′bẽr-vĭl)	99	45°14′N	73°01′W
Ibi, Nig. (ē′bē)	230	8°12′N	9°45′E
Ibiapaba, Serra da, mts., Braz. (sĕ′r-rä-dä-ē-byä-pá′bä)	143	3°30′S	40°55′W
Ibiza *see* Eivissa, i., Spain	156	38°55′N	1°24′E
Ibo, Moz. (ē′bō)	233	12°20′S	40°35′E
Ibrāhīm, Būr, b., Egypt	238d	29°57′N	32°33′E
Ibrahim, Jabal, mtn., Sau. Ar.	198	20°31′N	41°17′E
Ibwe Munyama, Zam.	237	16°09′S	28°34′E
Ica, Peru (ē′kȧ)	142	14°09′S	75°42′W
Icá (Putumayo), r., S.A.	142	3°00′S	69°00′W
Içana, Braz. (ē-sä′nä)	142	0°15′N	67°19′W
Ice Harbor Dam, Wa., U.S.	114	46°15′N	118°54′W
İçel, Tur.	198	37°00′N	34°40′E
Iceland, nation, Eur. (īs′lănd)	154	65°12′N	19°45′W
Ichibusayama, mtn., Japan (ē′chē-bōō′sá-yä′mä)	211	32°19′N	131°08′E
Ichihara, Japan	211a	35°31′N	140°05′E
Ichikawa, Japan (ē′chē-kä′wä)	211a	35°44′N	139°54′E
Ichinomiya, Japan (ē′chē-nō-mē′yȧ)	211	35°19′N	136°49′E
Ichinomoto, Japan (ē-chē′nō-mō-tō)	211b	34°37′N	135°50′E
Ichnia, Ukr.	181	50°47′N	32°23′E
Icy Cape, c., Ak., U.S. (ī′sĭ)	103	70°20′N	161°40′W
Idabel, Ok., U.S. (ī′dȧ-bĕl)	121	33°52′N	94°47′W
Idagrove, Ia., U.S. (ī′dȧ-grōv)	112	42°22′N	95°29′W
Idah, Nig. (ē′dä)	230	7°07′N	6°43′E
Idaho, state, U.S. (ī′dȧ-hō)	104	44°00′N	115°10′W
Idaho Falls, Id., U.S.	104	43°30′N	112°01′W
Idaho Springs, Co., U.S.	120	39°43′N	105°32′W
Idanha-a-Nova, Port. (ē-dän′yȧ-ä-nō′vȧ)	172	39°58′N	7°13′W
Ider, r., Mong.	204	48°58′N	98°38′E
Idi, Indon. (ē′dē)	212	4°58′N	97°47′E
Idkū Lake, l., Egypt	238b	31°13′N	30°22′E
Idle, r., Eng., U.K. (īd″l)	158a	53°22′N	0°56′W
Idlib, Syria	200	35°55′N	36°38′E
Idriaj, Slvn. (ē′drē-ä)	174	46°01′N	14°01′E
Idutywa, S. Afr. (ē-dò-tī′wȧ)	233c	32°06′S	28°18′E
Ienakiieve, Ukr.	177	48°14′N	38°12′E
Ieper, Bel.	165	50°50′N	2°53′E
Ierápetra, Grc.	174a	35°01′N	25°48′E
Iesi, Italy (yā′sē)	174	43°37′N	13°20′E
Ievpatoriia, Ukr.	181	45°13′N	33°22′E
Ife, Nig.	230	7°30′N	4°30′E
Iferouâne, Niger (ēf′rōō-än′)	230	19°04′N	8°24′E
Ifôghas, Adrar des, plat., Afr.	230	19°55′N	2°00′E
Igalula, Tan.	237	5°14′S	33°00′E
Igarka, Russia (ē-gär′kȧ)	178	67°22′N	86°16′E
Iglesias, Italy (ē-lĕ′syôs)	162	39°20′N	8°34′E
Igli, Alg. (ē-glē′)	230	30°32′N	2°15′W
Igluligaarjuk (Chesterfield Inlet), Can.	91	63°19′N	91°11′W
Iglulik, Can.	91	69°33′N	81°18′W
Ignacio, Ca., U.S. (ĭg-nä′cĭ-ō)	116b	38°05′N	122°32′W
Iguaçu, r., Braz. (ē-gwä-sōō′)	144b	22°42′S	43°19′W
Iguala, Mex. (ē-gwä′lä)	130	18°18′N	99°34′W
Igualada, Spain (ē-gwä-lä′dä)	173	41°35′N	1°38′E
Iguassu, r., S.A. (ē-gwä-sōō′)	144	25°45′S	52°30′W
Iguassu Falls, wtfl., S.A.	143	25°40′S	54°16′W
Iguatama, Braz. (ē-gwä-tá′mä)	141a	20°13′S	45°40′W
Iguatu, Braz. (ē-gwä-tōō′)	143	6°22′S	39°17′W
Iguidi, Erg, Afr.	230	26°22′N	6°53′W
Iguig, Phil. (ē-gēg′)	213a	17°46′N	121°44′E
Iharana, Madag.	233	13°35′S	50°05′E
Ihiala, Nig.	235	5°51′N	6°51′E
Iida, Japan (ē′ē-dȧ)	211	35°39′N	137°53′E

304 Iijoki – Isla-Cristina PRONOUNCING INDEX

PLACE (Pronunciation)	PAGE	LAT.	LONG.
Iijoki, r., Fin. (ē´yō´kĭ)	180	65°28'N	27°00'E
Iizuka, Japan (ē´ē-zò-kȧ)	211	33°39'N	130°39'E
Ijebu-Ode, Nig. (ê-jĕ´bōō ōdȧ)	230	6°50'N	3°56'E
IJmuiden, Neth.	159a	52°27'N	4°36'E
IJsselmeer, l., Neth. (ī´sĕl-mär)	165	52°46'N	5°14'E
Ikaalinen, Fin. (ē´kä-lĭ-nĕn)	167	61°47'N	22°55'E
Ikaría, i., Grc. (ē-kä´ryȧ)	175	37°43'N	26°07'E
Ikeda, Japan (ē´kȧ-dä)	211b	34°49'N	135°26'E
Ikerre, Nig.	235	7°31'N	5°14'E
Ikhtiman, Blg. (ĕk´tê-män)	175	42°26'N	23°49'E
Iki, i., Japan (ē´kê)	210	33°46'N	129°44'E
Ikoma, Japan	211b	34°41'N	135°43'E
Ikoma, Tan. (ê-kō´mä)	232	2°08'S	34°47'E
Iksha, Russia (ĭk´shȧ)	186b	56°10'N	37°30'E
Ila, Nig.	235	8°01'N	4°55'E
Ilagan, Phil.	213a	17°09'N	121°52'E
Ilan, Tai. (ē´län´)	209	24°50'N	121°42'E
Iława, Pol. (ê-lä´vȧ)	169	53°35'N	19°36'E
Île-á-la-Crosse, Can.	96	55°34'N	108°00'W
Ilebo, D.R.C.	232	4°19'S	20°35'E
Ilek, Russia (ē´lyĕk)	181	51°30'N	53°10'E
Île-Perrot, Can. (yl-pĕ-rōt´)	102a	45°21'N	73°54'W
Ilesha, Nig.	230	7°38'N	4°45'E
Ilford, Eng., U.K. (ĭl´fẽrd)	158b	51°33'N	0°06'E
Ilfracombe, Eng., U.K. (ĭl-frȧ-kōōm´)	164	51°13'N	4°08'W
Ilhabela, Braz. (ē´lä-bĕ´lä)	141a	23°47'S	45°21'W
Ilha Grande, Baía de, b., Braz. (ēl´yȧ grän´dĕ)	141a	23°17'S	44°25'W
Ílhavo, Port. (ēl´yȧ-vō)	162	40°36'N	8°41'W
Ilhéus, Braz. (ē-lĕ´ōōs)	143	14°52'S	39°00'W
Ili, r., Asia	184	44°30'N	76°45'E
Iliamna, Ak., U.S. (ē-lê-äm´nȧ)	103	59°45'N	155°05'W
Iliamna, Ak., U.S.	103	60°18'N	153°25'W
Iliamna, l., Ak., U.S.	103	59°25'N	155°30'W
Ilim, r., Russia (ê-lyĕm´)	184	57°28'N	103°00'E
Ilimsk, Russia (ê-lyĕmsk´)	179	56°47'N	103°43'E
Ilin Island, i., Phil. (ê-lyĕn´)	213a	12°16'N	120°57'E
Ilion, N.Y., U.S. (ĭl´ĭ-ŭn)	109	43°00'N	75°05'W
Ilkeston, Eng., U.K. (ĭl´kĕs-tŭn)	158a	52°58'N	1°19'W
Illampu, Nevado, mtn., Bol. (nĕ-vá´dô-ēl-yäm-pōō´)	142	15°50'S	68°15'W
Illapel, Chile (ē-zhä-pĕ´l)	144	31°37'S	71°10'W
Iller, r., Ger. (ĭlẽr)	168	47°52'N	10°06'E
Illimani, Nevado, mtn., Bol. (nĕ-vá´dô-ēl-yê-mä´nĕ)	142	16°50'S	67°38'W
Illinois, state, U.S. (ĭl-ĭ-noi´) (ĭl-ĭ-noiz´)	105	40°25'N	90°40'W
Illinois, r., Il., U.S.	107	39°00'N	90°30'W
Illintsi, Ukr.	177	49°07'N	29°13'E
Illizi, Alg.	230	26°35'N	8°24'E
Il'men, l., Russia (ô´zĕ-rô el´´men´´) (ĭl´mĕn)	180	58°18'N	32°00'E
Ilo, Peru	142	17°46'S	71°13'W
Ilobasco, El Sal. (ê-lô-bäs´kô)	132	13°57'N	88°46'W
Iloilo, Phil. (ē-lô-ē´lō)	212	10°49'N	122°33'E
Ilopango, Lago, l., El Sal. (ē-lô-päŋ´gō)	132	13°48'N	88°50'W
Ilorin, Nig. (ē-lô-rēn´)	230	8°30'N	4°32'E
Ilūkste, Lat.	167	55°59'N	26°20'E
Ilwaco, Wa., U.S. (ĭl-wā´kô)	116c	46°19'N	124°02'W
Ilych, r., Russia (ê´l´ĭch)	180	62°30'N	57°30'E
Imabari, Japan (ē´mä-bä´rê)	210	34°05'N	132°58'E
Imai, Japan (ê-mī´)	211b	34°30'N	135°47'E
Iman, r., Russia (ê-män´)	210	45°40'N	134°31'E
Imandra, l., Russia (ē-män´drȧ)	180	67°40'N	32°30'E
Imbābah, Egypt (ēm-bä´bȧ)	238b	30°06'N	31°09'E
Imeni Morozova, Russia (ĭm-yĕ´nyĭ mô rô´zô vȧ)	186c	59°58'N	31°02'E
Imeni Moskvy, Kanal (Moscow Canal), can., Russia (kȧ-näl´ĭm-yä´nĭ mŏs-kvĭ)	176	56°33'N	37°15'E
Imeni Tsyurupy, Russia	186b	55°30'N	38°39'E
Imeni Vorovskogo, Russia	186b	55°43'N	38°21'E
Imlay City, Mi., U.S. (ĭm´lā)	108	43°00'N	83°15'W
Immenstadt, Ger. (ĭm´ĕn-shtät)	168	47°34'N	10°12'E
Immerpan, S. Afr. (ĭmẽr-pän)	238c	24°29'S	29°14'E
Imola, Italy (ē´mô-lä)	174	44°19'N	11°43'E
Imotski, Cro. (ē-môts´kê)	175	43°25'N	17°15'E
Impameri, Braz.	143	17°44'S	48°03'W
Impendle, S. Afr. (ĭm-pĕnd´lȧ)	233c	29°38'S	29°54'E
Imperia, Italy (ēm-pä´rê-ä)	162	43°52'N	8°00'E
Imperial, Pa., U.S. (ĭm-pē´rĭ-ăl)	111e	40°27'N	80°15'W
Imperial Beach, Ca., U.S.	118a	32°34'N	117°08'W
Imperial Valley, Ca., U.S.	118	33°00'N	115°22'W
Impfondo, Congo (ĭmp-fōn´dô)	231	1°37'N	18°04'E
Imphāl, India (ĭmp´hŭl)	199	24°42'N	94°00'E
Ina, r., Japan (ê-nä´)	211b	34°56'N	135°21'E
Inaja Indian Reservation, I.R., Ca., U.S. (ê-nä´hä)	118	32°56'N	116°37'W
Inari, l., Fin.	160	69°02'N	26°22'E
Inca, Spain (ēŋ´kä)	173	39°43'N	2°53'E
Ince Burun, c., Tur. (ĭn´jȧ)	163	42°00'N	35°00'E
Inch'ŏn, Kor., S. (ĭn´chŭn)	205	37°26'N	126°46'E
Incudine, Monte, mtn., Fr. (ēn-kōō-dē´nȧ) (äɴ-kü-dēn´)	174	41°53'N	9°17'E
Indalsälven, r., Swe.	160	62°50'N	16°50'E
Independence, Ks., U.S. (ĭn-dê-pĕn´dĕns)	121	37°14'N	95°42'W
Independence, Mo., U.S.	117f	39°06'N	94°26'W
Independence, Oh., U.S.	111d	41°23'N	81°39'W
Independence, Or., U.S.	114	44°49'N	123°13'W
Independence Mountains, mts., Nv., U.S.	114	41°15'N	116°02'W
Inder köli, l., Kaz.	181	48°20'N	52°10'E
India, nation, Asia (ĭn´dĭ-ȧ)	199	23°00'N	77°30'E
Indian, l., Mi., U.S. (ĭn´dĭ-ăn)	113	46°04'N	86°34'W
Indian, r., N.Y., U.S.	109	44°05'N	75°45'W
Indiana, Pa., U.S. (ĭn-dĭ-ăn´ȧ)	109	40°40'N	79°10'W
Indiana, state, U.S.	105	39°50'N	86°45'W
Indianapolis, In., U.S. (ĭn-dĭ-ăn-ăp´ô-lĭs)	105	39°45'N	86°08'W
Indian Arm, b., Can. (ĭn´dĭ-ăn ärm)	116d	49°21'N	122°55'W
Indian Head, Can.	90	50°29'N	103°44'W
Indian Lake, l., Can.	98	47°00'N	82°00'W
Indian Ocean, o.	5	10°00'S	70°00'E
Indianola, Ia., U.S. (ĭn-dĭ-ăn-ō´lȧ)	113	41°22'N	93°33'W
Indianola, Ms., U.S.	124	33°29'N	90°35'W
Indigirka, r., Russia (ēn-dê-gēr´kȧ)	185	67°45'N	145°45'E
Indio, r., Pan. (ē´n-dyô)	128a	9°13'N	79°28'W
Indochina, reg., Asia (ĭn-dô-chī´nȧ)	212	17°22'N	105°18'E
Indonesia, nation, Asia (ĭn´dô-nē-zhȧ)	212	4°38'S	118°45'E
Indore, India (ĭn-dōr´)	199	22°48'N	76°51'E
Indragiri, r., Indon. (ĭn-drȧ-jē´rê)	212	0°27'S	102°05'E
Indrāvati, r., India (ĭn-drŭ-vä´tê)	199	19°00'N	82°00'E
Indre, r., Fr. (ăɴ´dr´)	170	47°13'N	0°29'E
Indus, Can. (ĭn´dŭs)	102e	50°55'N	113°45'W
Indus, r., Asia	199	26°43'N	67°41'E
Indwe, S. Afr. (ĭnd´wȧ)	233c	31°30'S	27°21'E
Inebolu, Tur. (ê-nȧ-bō´lōō)	163	41°50'N	33°40'E
Inego, Tur. (ē´nȧ-gŭ)	181	40°05'N	29°20'E
Infanta, Phil. (ēn-fän´tä)	213a	14°44'N	121°39'E
Infanta, Phil.	213a	15°50'N	119°53'E
Inferror, Laguna, l., Mex. (lä-gò´nä-ēn-fĕr-rôr)	131	16°18'N	94°40'W
Infiernillo, Presa de, res., Mex.	130	18°50'N	101°50'W
Infiesto, Spain (ēn-fyĕ´s-tô)	172	43°21'N	5°24'W
I-n-Gall, Niger	235	16°47'N	6°56'E
Ingersoll, Can. (ĭn´gẽr-sŏl)	98	43°05'N	81°00'W
Ingham, Austl. (ĭng´ăm)	219	18°45'S	146°14'E
Ingles, Cayos, is., Cuba (kä-yōs-ē´n-glĕ´s)	134	21°55'N	82°35'W
Inglewood, Can.	102d	43°48'N	79°56'W
Inglewood, Ca., U.S. (ĭn´g´l-wòd)	117a	33°57'N	118°22'W
Ingoda, r., Russia (ēn-gō´dȧ)	185	51°29'N	112°32'E
Ingolstadt, Ger. (ĭŋ´gôl-shtät)	168	48°46'N	11°27'E
Ingur, r., Geor. (ēn-gòr´)	181	42°30'N	42°00'E
Ingushetia, prov., Russia	182	43°15'N	45°00'E
Inhambane, Moz. (ēn-äm-bä´-nĕ)	232	23°47'S	35°28'E
Inhambupe, Braz. (ēn-yäm-bōō´pä)	143	11°47'S	38°13'W
Inharrime, Moz. (ēn-yär-rē´mä)	232	24°17'S	35°07'E
Inhomirim, Braz. (ē-nô-mê-rē´ɴ)	144b	22°34'S	43°11'W
Inhul, r., Ukr.	177	47°22'N	32°52'E
Inhulets', r., Ukr.	177	47°12'N	33°12'E
Inírida, r., Col. (ē-nê-rē´dä)	142	2°25'N	70°38'W
Injune, Austl. (ĭn´jòn)	222	25°52'S	148°30'E
Inkeroinem, Fin. (ĭn´kĕr-oi-nĕn)	167	60°42'N	26°50'E
Inkster, Mi., U.S. (ĭngk´stẽr)	111b	42°18'N	83°19'W
Inn, r., Eur. (ĭn)	161	48°00'N	12°00'E
Innamincka, Austl. (ĭnn-ȧ´mĭn-kȧ)	222	27°50'S	140°48'E
Inner Brass, i., V.I.U.S. (bräs)	129c	18°23'N	64°58'W
Inner Hebrides, is., Scot., U.K.	164	57°20'N	6°20'W
Inner Mongolia *see* Nei Monggol, prov., China	204	40°15'N	105°00'E
Innisfail, Can.	90	52°02'N	113°57'W
Innsbruck, Aus. (ĭns´bròk)	161	47°15'N	11°25'E
Ino, Japan (ē´nô)	211	33°34'N	133°23'E
Inongo, D.R.C. (ē-nôŋ´gō)	232	1°57'S	18°16'E
Inowrocław, Pol. (ē-nô-vrôts´läf)	169	52°48'N	18°16'E
In Salah, Alg.	230	27°13'N	2°22'E
Inscription House Ruin, Az., U.S. (ĭn´skrĭp-shŭn hous rōō´ĭn)	119	36°45'N	110°47'W
International Falls, Mn., U.S. (ĭn´tẽr-năsh´ŭn-ăl fôlz)	105	48°34'N	93°26'W
Inuvik, Can.	90	68°40'N	134°10'W
Inuyama, Japan (ē´nōō-yä´mä)	211	35°24'N	137°01'E
Invercargil, N.Z. (ĭn-vẽr-kär´gĭl)	223	46°25'S	168°27'E
Inverel, Austl. (ĭn-vẽr-el´)	219	29°50'S	151°32'E
Invergrove Heights, Mn., U.S. (ĭn´vẽr-grōv)	117g	44°51'N	93°01'W
Inverness, Can. (ĭn-vẽr-nĕs´)	101	46°14'N	61°18'W
Inverness, Scot., U.K.	160	57°30'N	4°07'W
Inverness, Fl., U.S.	125	28°48'N	82°22'W
Investigator Strait, strt., Austl. (ĭn-vĕst´ĭ´gā-tôr)	222	35°33'S	137°00'E
Inyangani, mtn., Zimb. (ēn-yän-gä´nê)	232	18°06'S	32°37'E
Inyokern, Ca., U.S.	118	35°39'N	117°51'W
Inyo Mountains, mts., Ca., U.S. (ĭn´yō)	106	36°55'N	118°04'W
Inzer, r., Russia (ĭn´zẽr)	186a	54°24'N	57°17'E
Inzia, r., D.R.C.	236	5°55'S	17°50'E
Ioánnina, Grc. (yô-ä´nê-nȧ)	163	39°39'N	20°52'E
Ioco, Can.	116d	49°18'N	122°53'W
Iola, Ks., U.S. (ī-ō´lȧ)	121	37°55'N	95°23'W
Iôna, Parque Nacional do, rec., Ang.	236	16°35'S	12°00'E
Ionia, Mi., U.S. (ī-ō´nĭ-ȧ)	108	43°00'N	85°10'W
Ionian Islands, is., Grc. (ī-ō´nĭ-ăn)	163	39°10'N	20°05'E
Ionian Sea, sea, Eur.	156	38°59'N	18°48'E
Iori, r., Asia	182	41°03'N	46°17'E
Íos, i., Grc. (ī´ŏs)	175	36°48'N	25°25'E
Iowa, state, U.S. (ī´ô-wȧ)	105	42°05'N	94°20'W
Iowa, r., Ia., U.S.	113	41°55'N	92°20'W
Iowa City, Ia., U.S.	105	41°39'N	91°31'W
Iowa Falls, Ia., U.S.	113	42°32'N	93°16'W
Iowa Park, Tx., U.S.	120	33°57'N	98°39'W
Ipala, Tan.	237	4°30'S	32°53'E
Ipeirus, hist. reg., Grc.	175	39°35'N	20°45'E
Ipel', r., Eur. (ē´pĕl)	169	48°08'N	19°00'E
Ipiales, Col. (ē-pê-ä´lȧs)	142	0°48'N	77°45'W
Ipoh, Malay.	212	4°45'N	101°05'E
Ipswich, Austl. (ĭps´wĭch)	219	27°40'S	152°50'E
Ipswich, Eng., U.K.	161	52°05'N	1°05'E
Ipswich, Ma., U.S.	101a	42°41'N	70°50'W
Ipswich, S.D., U.S.	112	45°26'N	99°01'W
Ipu, Braz. (ē-pōō)	143	4°11'S	40°45'W
Iput', r., Eur. (ê-pòt´)	181	52°53'N	31°57'E
Iqaluit, Can.	91	63°48'N	68°31'W
Iquique, Chile (ē-kē´kĕ)	142	20°16'S	70°07'W
Iquitos, Peru (ê-kē´tōs)	142	3°39'S	73°18'W
Irákleio, Grc.	154	35°20'N	25°10'E
Iran, nation, Asia (ē-rän´)	198	31°15'N	53°30'E
Iran, Plateau of, plat., Iran	198	32°28'N	58°00'E
Iran Mountains, mts., Asia	212	2°30'N	114°30'E
Irapuato, Mex. (ē-rä-pwä´tō)	130	20°41'N	101°24'W
Iraq, nation, Asia (ē-räk´)	198	32°00'N	42°30'E
Irazú, vol., C.R. (ē-rä-zōō´)	133	9°58'N	83°54'W
Irbid, Jord. (ẽr-bēd´)	200	32°33'N	35°51'E
Irbīl, Iraq	198	36°10'N	44°00'E
Irbit, Russia (ẽr-bêt´)	178	57°40'N	63°10'E
Irébou, D.R.C. (ē-rā´bōō)	232	0°40'S	17°48'E
Ireland, nation, Eur. (īr-lănd)	154	53°33'N	8°00'W
Iremel', Gora, mtn., Russia (gá-rä´ĭ-rĕ´mĕl)	186a	54°32'N	58°52'E
Irene, S. Afr. (ĭ-rē-nē)	233b	25°53'S	28°13'E
Irîgui, reg., Mali	234	16°45'N	5°35'W
Iriklinskoye Vodokhranilishche, res., Russia	181	52°20'N	58°50'E
Iringa, Tan. (ē-rĭŋ´gä)	232	7°46'S	35°42'E
Iriomote Jima, i., Japan (ērē´-ō-mō-tā)	205	24°20'N	123°30'E
Iriona, Hond. (ê-rê-ō´nä)	132	15°53'N	85°12'W
Irish Sea, sea, Eur. (ī´rĭsh)	156	53°55'N	5°25'W
Irkutsk, Russia (ĭr-kòtsk´)	179	52°16'N	104°00'E
Irlam, Eng., U.K. (ûr´lăm)	158a	53°26'N	2°26'W
Irois, Cap des, c., Haiti	135	18°25'N	74°50'W
Iron Bottom Sound, strt., Sol. Is.	214e	9°15'S	160°00'E
Irondale, Al., U.S. (ī´ẽrn-dāl)	110h	33°32'N	86°43'W
Iron Gate, val., Eur.	175	44°43'N	22°32'E
Iron Knob, Austl. (ī-ăn nŏb)	222	32°47'S	137°10'E
Iron Mountain, Mi., U.S. (ī´ẽrn)	113	45°49'N	88°04'W
Iron River, Mi., U.S.	113	46°09'N	88°39'W
Ironton, Oh., U.S. (ī´ẽrn-tŭn)	108	38°30'N	82°45'W
Ironwood, Mi., U.S. (ī´ẽrn-wòd)	113	46°28'N	90°10'W
Ironwood Forest National Monument, rec., Az., U.S.	119	32°30'N	111°25'W
Iroquois, r., Il., U.S. (ĭr´ô-kwoi)	108	40°55'N	87°20'W
Iroquois Falls, Can.	91	48°41'N	80°39'W
Irō-Saki, c., Japan (ē´rō sä´kê)	210	34°35'N	138°54'E
Irpin, r., Ukr.	177	50°13'N	29°55'E
Irrawaddy, r., Mya. (ĭr-ȧ-wäd´ê)	199	23°27'N	96°25'E
Irtysh, r., Asia (ĭr-tĭsh´)	178	59°00'N	69°00'E
Irumu, D.R.C. (ê-rò´mōō)	231	1°30'N	29°52'E
Irun, Spain (ê-rōōn´)	172	43°20'N	1°47'W
Irvine, Scot., U.K.	164	55°39'N	4°40'W
Irvine, Ca., U.S. (ûr´vĭn)	117a	33°40'N	117°45'W
Irvine, Ky., U.S.	108	37°40'N	84°00'W
Irving, Tx., U.S. (ûr´vĕng)	117c	32°49'N	96°57'W
Irvington, N.J., U.S. (ûr´vĕng-tŭn)	110a	40°43'N	74°15'W
Irwin, Pa., U.S. (ûr´wĭn)	111e	40°19'N	79°42'W
Is, Russia (ēs)	186a	58°48'N	59°44'E
Isa, Nig.	235	13°14'N	6°24'E
Isaacs, Mount, mtn., Pan. (ē-sä-á´ks)	128a	9°22'N	79°31'W
Isabela, i., Ec. (ē-sä-bä´lä)	142	0°47'S	91°35'W
Isabela, Cabo, c., Dom. Rep. (ká´bô-ê-sä-bĕ´lä)	135	20°00'N	71°00'W
Isabella, Cordillera, mts., Nic. (kôr-dēl-yĕ´rä-ē-sä-bĕlä)	132	13°20'N	85°37'W
Isabella Indian Reservation, I.R., Mi., U.S. (ĭs-á-bĕl´-lȧ)	108	43°35'N	84°55'W
Isaccea, Rom. (ê-säk´chä)	177	45°16'N	28°26'E
Ísafjördur, Ice. (ēs´á-fÿr-dòr)	160	66°09'N	22°39'W
Isangi, D.R.C. (ē-säŋ´gê)	204	0°46'N	24°15'E
Isar, r., Ger. (ē´zär)	161	48°30'N	12°30'E
Isarco, r., Italy (ê-sär´kō)	174	46°37'N	11°25'E
Isarog, Mount, mtn., Phil. (ê-sä-rô-g)	213a	13°40'N	123°23'E
Ischia, Italy (ēs´kyä)	173c	40°29'N	13°58'E
Ischia, Isola d', i., Italy (dĕ´sh-kyä)	162	40°26'N	13°55'E
Ise, Japan (ĭs´hĕ) (ū´gē-yä´mä´dȧ)	210	34°30'N	136°43'E
Iseo, Lago d', l., Italy (lä-´gō-dē-ê-zĕ´ō)	174	45°50'N	9°55'E
Isére, r., Fr. (ê-zâr´)	161	45°15'N	5°15'E
Iserlohn, Ger. (ē´zĕr-lōn)	171c	51°22'N	7°42'E
Isernia, Italy (ê-zĕr´nyä)	174	41°35'N	14°14'E
Ise-Wan, b., Japan (ē´sĕ wän)	210	34°49'N	136°44'E
Iseyin, Nig.	230	7°58'N	3°36'E
Ishigaki, Japan	214d	24°20'N	124°09'E
Ishikari Wan, b., Japan (ē´shē-kä-rē wän)	210	43°30'N	141°05'E
Ishim, Russia (ĭsh-ĕm´)	178	56°07'N	69°13'E
Ishim, r., Asia	178	53°17'N	67°45'E
Ishimbay, Russia (ē-shēm-bī´)	186a	53°28'N	56°02'E
Ishinomaki, Japan (ĭsh-nō-mä´kē)	205	38°22'N	141°22'E
Ishinomaki Wan, b., Japan (ē-shē-nō-mä´kē wän)	210	38°10'N	141°40'E
Ishly, Russia (ĭsh´lĭ)	186a	54°13'N	55°55'E
Ishlya, Russia (ĭsh´lyȧ)	186a	53°54'N	57°48'E
Ishmant, Egypt	238b	29°17'N	31°15'E
Ishpeming, Mi., U.S. (ĭsh´pê-mĭng)	113	46°28'N	87°42'W
Isipingo, S. Afr. (ĭs-ĭ-pĭŋ-gô)	233c	29°59'S	30°58'E
Isiro, D.R.C.	231	2°47'N	27°37'E
İskenderun, Tur. (ĭs-kĕn´dĕr-ōōn)	198	36°45'N	36°15'E
İskenderun Körfezi, b., Tur.	163	36°22'N	35°25'E
İskilip, Tur. (ĕs´kĭ-lêp´)	163	40°40'N	34°30'E
Iskŭr, r., Blg. (ĭs´k'r)	175	43°05'N	23°37'E
Isla-Cristina, Spain (ī´lä-krê-stē´nä)	172	37°13'N	7°20'W

ăt; finăl; rāte; senåte; ärm; åsk; sofȧ; fâre; ch-choose; dh-as th in other; bē; êvent; bĕt; recĕnt; cratẽr; g-gō; gh-guttural g; bĭt; ĭ-short neutral; rīde; ĸ-guttural k as ch in German ich;

PLACE (Pronunciation)	PAGE	LAT.	LONG.
Islāmābād, Pak.	199	33°55'N	73°05'E
Isla Mujeres, Mex. (ē's-lä-mōō-kĕ'rĕs)	132a	21°25'N	86°53'W
Island Lake, l., Can.	93	53°47'N	94°25'W
Islands, Bay of, b., Can. (ī'lăndz)	101	49°10'N	58°15'W
Islay, i., Scot., U.K. (ī'lā)	160	55°55'N	6°35'W
Isle, r., Fr. (ēl)	170	45°02'N	0°29'E
Isle of Axholme, reg., Eng., U.K. (ăks'-hōm)	158a	53°33'N	0°48'W
Isle of Man, dep., Eur. (măn)	164	54°26'N	4°21'W
Isle Royale National Park, rec., Mi., U.S. (īl'roi-ăl')	107	47°57'N	88°37'W
Isleta, N.M., U.S. (ēs-lā'tȧ) (ī-lē'tȧ)	119	34°55'N	106°45'W
Isleta Indian Reservation, I.R., N.M., U.S.	119	34°55'N	106°45'W
Ismailia, Egypt (ēs-mä-ēl'ēȧ)	238b	30°35'N	32°17'E
Ismā'īlīyah Canal, can., Egypt	238b	30°25'N	31°45'E
Ismail Samani, pik, mtn., Taj.	183	38°57'N	72°01'E
Ismaning, Ger. (ēz'mä-nēng)	159d	48°14'N	11°41'E
Isparta, Tur. (ē-spär'tȧ)	198	37°50'N	30°40'E
Israel, nation, Asia	198	32°40'N	34°00'E
Issaquah, Wa., U.S. (ĭz'să-kwăh)	116a	47°32'N	122°02'W
Isselburg, Ger. (ē'sĕl-bōōrg)	171c	51°50'N	6°28'E
Issoire, Fr. (ē-swȧr')	170	45°32'N	3°13'E
Issoudun, Fr. (ē-sōō-däN')	170	46°56'N	2°00'E
Issum, Ger. (ē'sōōm)	171c	51°32'N	6°24'E
Issyk-Kul, Ozero, l., Kyrg.	183	42°13'N	76°12'E
İstanbul, Tur. (ē-stän-bōōl')	198	41°02'N	29°00'E
İstanbul Boğazı (Bosporus), strt., Tur.	198	41°10'N	29°10'E
Istiaía, Grc. (ĭs-tyī'yä)	175	38°58'N	23°11'E
Istmina, Col. (ēst-mē'nä)	142a	5°10'N	76°40'W
Istokpoga, Lake, l., Fl., U.S. (īs-tŏk-pō'gȧ)	125a	27°20'N	81°33'W
Istra, pen., Yugo. (ē-strä)	174	45°18'N	13°48'E
Istranca Dağlari, mts., Eur. (ī-strän'jȧ)	175	41°50'N	27°25'E
Istres, Fr. (ēs'tr')	170a	43°30'N	5°00'E
Itabaiana, Braz. (ē-tä-bä-yȧ-nä)	143	10°42'S	37°17'W
Itabapoana, Braz. (ē-tä'-bä-pôȧ'nä)	141a	21°19'S	40°58'W
Itabapoana, r., Braz.	141a	21°11'S	41°18'W
Itabirito, Braz. (ē-tä-bē-rē'tô)	141a	20°15'S	43°46'W
Itabuna, Braz. (ē-tä-bōō'nȧ)	143	14°47'S	39°17'W
Itacoara, Braz. (ē-tä-kō'ä-rä)	141a	21°41'S	42°04'W
Itacoatiara, Braz. (ē-tȧ-kwȧ-tyä'rȧ)	143	3°03'S	58°18'W
Itagüí, Col. (ē-tä'gwē)	142a	6°11'N	75°36'W
Itagui, r., Braz.	144b	22°53'S	43°43'W
Itaipava, Braz. (ē-tī-pȧ'-vä)	144b	22°23'S	43°09'W
Itaipu, Braz. (ē-tī'pōō)	144b	22°58'S	43°02'W
Itaituba, Braz. (ē-tä'ī-tōō'bȧ)	143	4°12'S	56°00'W
Itajái, Braz. (ē-tä-zhī')	144	26°52'S	48°39'W
Italy, Tx., U.S.	123	32°11'N	96°51'W
Italy, nation, Eur. (ĭt'ȧ-lē)	154	43°58'N	11°14'E
Itambi, Braz. (ē-tä'm-bē)	144b	22°44'S	42°57'W
Itami, Japan (ē'tä'mē')	211b	34°47'N	135°25'E
Itapecerica, Braz. (ē-tä-pĕ-sĕ-rē'kȧ)	141a	20°29'S	45°08'W
Itapecuru-Mirim, Braz. (ē-tä-pĕ'kōō-rōō-mē-rēN')	143	3°17'S	44°15'W
Itaperuna, Braz. (ē-tȧ'pâ-rōō'nä)	143	21°12'S	41°53'W
Itapetininga, Braz. (ē-tä-pĕ-tē-nē'N-gä)	143	23°37'S	48°03'W
Itapira, Braz. (ē-tä-pē'rȧ)	143	20°42'S	51°19'W
Itapira, Braz.	141a	22°27'S	46°47'W
Itarsi, India	202	22°43'N	77°45'E
Itasca, Tx., U.S. (ī-tăs'kȧ)	123	32°09'N	97°08'W
Itasca, l., Mn., U.S.	112	47°13'N	95°14'W
Itatiaia, Pico da, mtn., Braz. (pē'-kô-dȧ-ē-tä-tyȧ'ēä)	143	22°18'S	44°41'W
Itatiba, Braz. (ē-tä-tē'bä)	141a	23°01'S	46°48'W
Itaúna, Braz. (ē-tä-ōō'nä)	141a	20°05'S	44°35'W
Ithaca, Mi., U.S. (ĭth'ȧ-kȧ)	108	43°20'N	84°35'W
Ithaca, N.Y., U.S.	105	42°25'N	76°30'W
Itháka, i., Grc. (ē'thä-kĕ)	175	38°27'N	20°48'E
Itigi, Tan.	237	5°42'S	34°29'E
Itimbiri, r., D.R.C.	236	2°40'N	23°30'E
Itoko, D.R.C. (ē-tō'kō)	232	1°13'S	22°07'E
Itu, Braz. (ē-tōō')	141a	23°16'S	47°16'W
Ituango, Col. (ē-twäṅ'gō)	142	7°07'N	75°44'W
Ituiutaba, Braz. (ē-tōō-ēōō-tä'bä)	143	18°56'S	49°17'W
Itumirim, Braz. (ē-tōō-mē-rē'N)	141a	21°20'S	44°51'W
Itundujia Santa Cruz, Mex. (ē-tōōn-dōō-hē'ȧ sä'n-tä krōō'z)	131	16°50'N	97°43'W
Iturbide, Mex. (ē'tōōr-bē'dhȧ)	132a	19°38'N	89°31'W
Iturup, i., Russia (ē-tōō-rōōp')	185	45°35'N	147°15'E
Ituzaingo, Arg. (ē-tōō-zä-ē'n-gô)	144a	34°40'S	58°40'W
Itzehoe, Ger. (ē'tzĕ-hō)	168	53°55'N	9°31'E
Iuka, Ms., U.S. (ī-ū'kȧ)	124	34°47'N	88°10'W
Iúna, Braz. (ē-ōō'-nä)	141a	20°22'S	41°32'W
Ivanhoe, Austl. (ĭv'ăn-hō)	222	32°53'S	144°10'E
Ivanivka, Ukr.	176	46°43'N	34°33'E
Ivano-Frankivs'k, Ukr.	181	48°53'N	24°46'E
Ivanopil', Ukr.	177	49°51'N	28°11'E
Ivanovo, Russia (ē-vä'nô-vō)	178	57°02'N	41°54'E
Ivanovo, prov., Russia	176	56°55'N	40°30'E
Ivanteyevka, Russia (ē-vȧn-tyĕ'yĕf-kȧ)	186b	55°58'N	37°56'E
Ivdel', Russia (ĭv'dyĕl)	186a	60°42'N	60°27'E
Iviza *see* Eivissa, i., Spain	156	38°55'N	1°24'E
Ivohibé, Madag. (ē-vô-hē-bā')	233	22°28'S	46°59'E
Ivory Coast *see* Cote d'Ivoire, nation, Afr.	230	7°43'N	6°30'W
Ivrea, Italy (ē-vrĕ'ä)	162	45°25'N	7°54'E
Ivry-sur-Seine, Fr.	171b	48°49'N	2°23'E
Ivujivik, Can.	91	62°17'N	77°52'W
Ivvavik National Park, rec., Can.	103	69°10'N	139°30'W
Iwaki, Japan	210	37°03'N	140°57'E
Iwate Yama, mtn., Japan (ē-wä-tĕ-yä'mä)	210	39°50'N	140°56'E
Iwatsuki, Japan	211a	35°48'N	139°43'E
Iwaya, Japan (ē'wȧ-yȧ)	211b	34°35'N	135°01'E
Iwo, Nig.	230	7°38'N	4°11'E
Ixcateopán, Mex. (ēs-kä-tä-ō-pän')	130	18°29'N	99°49'W
Ixelles, Bel.	159a	50°49'N	4°23'E
Ixhautlán, Mex. (ēs-wȧt-län')	130	20°41'N	98°01'W
Ixhuatán, Mex. (ēs-hwä-tän')	131	16°19'N	94°30'W
Ixmiquilpan, Mex. (ēs-mē-kēl'pän)	130	20°30'N	99°12'W
Ixopo, S. Afr.	233c	30°10'S	30°04'E
Ixtacalco, Mex. (ēs-tȧ-käl'kō)	131a	19°23'N	99°07'W
Ixtaltepec, Mex. (ēs-täl-tĕ-pĕk')	131	16°33'N	95°04'W
Ixtapalapa, Mex. (ēs'tä-pä-lä'pä)	131a	19°21'N	99°06'W
Ixtapaluca, Mex. (ēs'tä-pä-lōō'kä)	131a	19°18'N	98°53'W
Ixtepec, Mex. (ēks-tĕ'pĕk)	131	16°37'N	95°09'W
Ixtlahuaca, Mex. (ēs-tlä-wä'kä)	130	19°34'N	99°46'W
Ixtlán de Juárez, Mex. (ēs-tlän' dā hwä'răz)	131	17°20'N	96°29'W
Ixtlán del Río, Mex. (ēs-tlän'dĕl rē'ō)	130	21°05'N	104°22'W
Iya, r., Russia	184	53°45'N	99°30'E
Iyo-Nada, b., Japan (ē'yō nä-dä)	211	33°33'N	132°07'E
Izabal, Guat. (ē'zä-bäl')	132	15°23'N	89°10'W
Izabal, Lago, l., Guat.	132	15°30'N	89°04'W
Izalco, El Sal. (ē-zäl'kō)	132	13°50'N	89°40'W
Izamal, Mex. (ē-zä-mä'l)	132a	20°55'N	89°00'W
Izberbash, Russia	182	42°33'N	47°52'E
Izhevsk, Russia (ē-zhyĕfsk')	178	56°50'N	53°15'E
Izhma, Russia (ĭzh'mȧ)	180	65°00'N	54°05'E
Izhma, r., Russia	180	64°00'N	53°00'E
Izhora, r., Russia (ēz'hô-rȧ)	186c	59°36'N	30°20'E
Izmaïl, Ukr.	181	45°00'N	28°49'E
İzmir, Tur. (ĭz-mēr')	198	38°25'N	27°05'E
İzmit, Tur. (ĭz-mĕt')	163	40°45'N	29°45'E
Iznajar, Embalse de, res., Spain	172	37°15'N	4°30'W
Iztaccíhuatl, mtn., Mex.	130	19°10'N	98°38'W
Izuhara, Japan (ē'zōō-hä'rä)	211	34°11'N	129°18'E
Izumi-Ōtsu, Japan (ē'zōō-mōō ō'tsōō)	211b	34°30'N	135°24'E
Izumo, Japan (ē'zōō-mō)	211	35°22'N	132°45'E
Izu Shichitō, is., Japan	205	34°32'N	139°25'E
J			
Jabal, Bahr al, r., Sudan	231	7°30'N	31°00'E
Jabalpur, India	199	23°18'N	79°59'E
Jablonec nad Nisou, Czech Rep. (yäb'lô-nyĕts)	168	50°43'N	15°12'E
Jablunkov Pass, p., Eur. (yäb'lòn-kôf)	169	49°31'N	18°35'E
Jaboatão, Braz. (zhä-bô-ȧ-touN)	143	8°14'S	35°08'W
Jaca, Spain (hä'kä)	173	42°35'N	0°30'W
Jacala, Mex. (hä-kȧ'lä)	130	21°01'N	99°11'W
Jacaltenango, Guat. (hä-kȧl-tĕ-näṅ'gō)	132	15°39'N	91°41'W
Jacarézinho, Braz. (zhä-kä-rĕ'zē-nyō)	143	23°13'S	49°58'W
Jachymov, Czech Rep. (yä'chĭ-môf)	168	50°22'N	12°51'E
Jacinto City, Tx., U.S. (hä-sēn'tō) (jȧ-sĭn'tō)	123a	29°45'N	95°14'W
Jacksboro, Tx., U.S. (jăks'bŭr-ō)	120	33°13'N	98°11'W
Jackson, Al., U.S. (jăk'sŭn)	124	31°31'N	87°52'W
Jackson, Ca., U.S.	118	38°22'N	120°47'W
Jackson, Ga., U.S.	124	33°19'N	83°55'W
Jackson, Ky., U.S.	124	37°32'N	83°17'W
Jackson, La., U.S.	123	30°50'N	91°13'W
Jackson, Mi., U.S.	105	42°15'N	84°25'W
Jackson, Mn., U.S.	112	43°37'N	95°00'W
Jackson, Mo., U.S.	121	37°23'N	89°40'W
Jackson, Ms., U.S.	105	32°17'N	90°10'W
Jackson, Oh., U.S.	108	39°00'N	82°40'W
Jackson, Tn., U.S.	105	35°37'N	88°49'W
Jackson, Port, b., Austl.	217b	33°50'S	151°18'E
Jackson Lake, l., Wy., U.S.	115	43°57'N	110°28'W
Jacksonville, Al., U.S. (jăk'sŭn-vĭl)	124	33°52'N	85°45'W
Jacksonville, Fl., U.S.	105	30°20'N	81°40'W
Jacksonville, Il., U.S.	105	39°43'N	90°12'W
Jacksonville, Tx., U.S.	123	31°58'N	95°18'W
Jacksonville Beach, Fl., U.S.	125	31°18'N	81°25'W
Jacmel, Haiti (zhȧk-mĕl')	135	18°15'N	72°30'W
Jaco, l., Mex. (hä'kō)	122	27°51'N	103°50'W
Jacobābād, Pak.	202	28°22'N	68°30'E
Jacobina, Braz. (zhä-kō-bē'nȧ)	143	11°13'S	40°30'W
Jacques-Cartier, r., Can.	102b	47°04'N	71°28'W
Jacques Cartier, Détroit de, strt., Can.	100	50°07'S	63°58'W
Jacques-Cartier, Mont, mtn., Can.	100	48°59'N	66°00'W
Jacquet River, Can. (zhȧ-kĕ')(jăk'ĕt)	100	47°55'N	66°00'W
Jacutinga, Braz. (zhȧ-kōō-tēn'gä)	141a	22°17'S	46°36'W
Jadebusen, b., Ger.	168	53°28'N	8°17'E
Jadotville *see* Likasi, D.R.C.	232	10°59'S	26°44'E
Jaén, Peru (kä-ĕ'n)	142	5°38'S	78°49'W
Jaen, Spain	162	37°45'N	3°48'W
Jaffa, Cape, c., Austl. (jăf'ȧ)	220	36°58'S	139°29'E
Jaffna, Sri L. (jäf'nȧ)	203	9°44'N	80°09'E
Jagüey Grande, Cuba (hä'gwā grän'dā)	134	22°35'N	81°05'W
Jahore Strait, strt., Asia	197b	1°22'N	103°37'E
Jahrom, Iran	198	28°30'N	53°28'E
Jaibo, r., Cuba (hä-ē'bō)	135	20°10'N	75°20'W
Jaipur, India	199	27°00'N	75°50'E
Jaisalmer, India	202	27°00'N	70°54'E
Jajce, Bos. (yī'tsĕ)	175	44°20'N	17°19'E
Jajpur, India	199	20°49'N	86°37'E
Jakarta, Indon. (yä-kär'tä)	212	6°17'S	106°45'E
Jakobstad, Fin. (yȧ'kôb-städh)	160	63°33'N	22°31'E
Jalacingo, Mex. (hä-lä-sĭṅ'gō)	131	19°47'N	97°16'W
Jalālābād, Afg. (jŭ-lä-lȧ-bäd)	199a	34°25'N	70°27'E
Jalālah al Baḩrīyah, Jabal, mts., Egypt	238b	29°20'N	32°00'E
Jalapa, Guat. (hä-lä'pȧ)	132	14°38'N	89°58'W
Jalapa de Díaz, Mex.	131	18°06'N	96°33'W
Jalapa del Marqués, Mex. (dĕl mär-kās')	131	16°30'N	95°29'W
Jaleswar, Nepal	202	26°50'N	85°55'E
Jalgaon, India	202	21°08'N	75°33'E
Jalisco, Mex. (hä-lēs'kō)	130	21°27'N	104°54'W
Jalisco, state, Mex.	128	20°07'N	104°45'W
Jalón, r., Spain (hä-lōn')	172	41°22'N	1°46'W
Jalostotitlán, Mex. (hä-lōs-tē-tlȧn')	130	21°09'N	102°30'W
Jalpa, Mex. (häl'pä)	131	18°12'N	93°06'W
Jalpa, Mex. (häl'pä)	130	21°40'N	103°04'W
Jalpan, Mex. (häl'pän)	130	21°13'N	99°31'W
Jaltepec, Mex. (häl-tȧ-pĕk')	131	17°20'N	95°15'W
Jaltipan, Mex. (häl-tȧ-pän')	131	17°59'N	94°42'W
Jaltocan, Mex. (häl-tô-kän')	130	21°08'N	98°32'W
Jamaare, r., Nig.	235	11°50'N	10°10'E
Jamaica, nation, N.A.	129	17°45'N	78°00'W
Jamaica Cay, i., Bah.	135	22°45'N	75°55'W
Jamālpur, Bngl.	202	24°56'N	89°58'E
Jamay, Mex. (hä-mī')	130	20°16'N	102°43'W
Jambi, Indon. (mäm'bē)	212	1°45'S	103°28'E
James, r., Mo., U.S.	121	36°51'N	93°22'W
James, r., Va., U.S.	107	37°35'N	77°50'W
James, r., U.S.	106	46°25'N	98°55'W
James, Lake, res., N.C., U.S.	125	36°07'N	81°48'W
James Bay, b., Can. (jāmz)	93	53°53'N	80°40'W
Jamesburg, N.J., U.S. (jāmz'bûrg)	110a	40°21'N	74°26'W
James Point, c., Bah.	134	25°20'N	76°30'W
James Range, mts., Austl.	220	24°15'S	133°30'E
James Ross, i., Ant.	139	64°20'S	58°20'W
Jamestown, S. Afr.	233c	31°07'S	26°49'E
Jamestown, N.D., U.S.	104	46°54'N	98°42'W
Jamestown, N.Y., U.S. (jāmz'toun)	105	42°05'N	79°15'W
Jamestown, R.I., U.S.	110b	41°30'N	71°21'W
Jamestown Reservoir, res., N.D., U.S.	112	47°16'N	98°40'W
Jamiltepec, Mex. (hä-mēl-tȧ-pĕk)	131	16°16'N	97°54'W
Jammerbugten, b., Den.	166	57°20'N	9°28'E
Jammu, India	199	32°50'N	74°52'E
Jammu and Kashmir, state, India (kȧsh-mēr')	199	34°30'N	76°00'E
Jammu and Kashmīr, hist. reg., Asia (kȧsh-mēr')	199	39°10'N	75°05'E
Jāmnagar, India (jäm-nŭ'gŭr)	199	22°33'N	70°03'E
Jamshedpur, India (jäm'shĕd-pōōr)	199	22°52'N	86°11'E
Jándula, r., Spain (hän'dōō-lȧ)	172	38°28'N	3°52'W
Janesville, Wi., U.S. (jānz'vĭl)	113	42°41'N	89°03'W
Janin, W.B.	197a	32°27'N	35°19'E
Jan Mayen, i., Nor. (yän mī'ĕn)	160	70°59'N	8°05'W
Jánoshalma, Hung. (yä'nôsh-hôl-mô)	169	46°17'N	19°18'E
Janów Lubelski, Pol. (yä'nōōf lū-bĕl'skĭ)	169	50°40'N	22°25'E
Januária, Braz. (zhä-nwä'rē-ä)	143	15°31'S	44°17'W
Japan, nation, Asia (jȧ-păn')	205	36°30'N	133°30'E
Japan, Sea of, sea, Asia (jȧ-păn')	205	40°08'N	132°55'E
Japeri, Braz. (zhȧ-pĕ'rē)	144b	22°38'S	43°40'W
Japurá (Caquetá), r., S.A.	142	2°00'S	68°00'W
Jarabacoa, Dom. Rep. (kä-rä-bä-kō'ä)	135	19°05'N	70°40'W
Jaral del Progreso, Mex. (hä-räl dĕl prō-grā'sō)	130	20°21'N	101°05'W
Jarama, r., Spain (hä-rä'mä)	172	40°33'N	3°30'W
Jarash, Jord.	197a	32°17'N	35°53'E
Jardines, Banco, bk., Cuba (bä'n-kō-här-dē'nȧs)	134	21°45'N	81°40'W
Jargalant, Mong.	208	46°28'N	115°10'E
Jari, r., Braz. (zhä-rē)	143	0°28'N	53°00'W
Jarocin, Pol. (yȧ-rō'tsyēn)	169	51°58'N	17°31'E
Jarosław, Pol. (yȧ-rôs-wȧf)	161	50°01'N	22°41'E
Jarud Qi, China (jya-lōō-tū shyē)	205	44°35'N	120°40'E
Jasin, Malay.	197b	2°19'N	102°26'E
Jašiūnai, Lith. (dzȧ-shōō-nȧ'yĕ)	167	54°27'N	25°25'E
Jāsk, Iran (jäsk)	198	25°46'N	57°48'E
Jasło, Pol. (yäs'wō)	169	49°44'N	21°28'E
Jason Bay, b., Malay.	197b	1°53'N	104°14'E
Jasonville, In., U.S. (jā'sŭn-vĭl)	108	39°10'N	87°15'W
Jasper, Can.	90	52°53'N	118°05'W
Jasper, Al., U.S. (jăs'pēr)	124	33°50'N	87°17'W
Jasper, Fl., U.S.	125	30°30'N	82°56'W
Jasper, In., U.S.	108	38°20'N	86°55'W
Jasper, Mn., U.S.	112	43°51'N	96°22'W
Jasper, Tx., U.S.	123	30°55'N	93°59'W
Jasper National Park, rec., Can.	92	53°09'N	117°45'W
Jászapáti, Hung. (yäs'ô-pä-tē)	169	47°29'N	20°10'E
Jászberény, Hung.	169	47°30'N	19°56'E
Jatibonico, Cuba (hä-tē-bō-nē'kō)	134	22°00'N	79°15'W
Jauja, Peru (kä-ō'ĸ)	142	11°43'S	75°32'W
Jaumave, Mex. (hou-mä'vȧ)	130	23°23'N	99°24'W
Jaunjelgava, Lat. (youn'yĕl'gȧ-vȧ)	180	56°37'N	25°06'E
Java (Jawa), i., Indon.	212	8°35'S	111°11'E
Javari, r., S.A. (kȧ-vä-rē)	142	4°25'S	72°07'W
Java Trench, deep	212	9°45'S	107°30'E
Jawa, Laut (Java Sea), sea, Indon.	212	5°10'S	110°30'E
Jawor, Pol. (yä'vôr)	168	51°04'N	16°12'E
Jaworzno, Pol. (yä-vôzh'nô)	169	50°11'N	19°18'E
Jaya, Puncak, mtn., Indon.	213	4°00'S	137°00'E
Jayapura, Indon.	212	2°30'S	140°45'W
Jayb, Wādī al (Ha'Arava), val., Asia	197a	30°33'N	35°10'E

ng-sing; ŋ-baŋk; N-nasalized n; nŏd; cŏmmit; ōld; ōbey; ôrder; oi-boil; fōōd; ȯ-as oo in foot; ou-out; s-soft; sh-dish; th-thin; pūre; ûnite; ûrn; stŭd; circŭs; ü-as in French tu; '-indeterminate vowel.

PLACE (Pronunciation)	PAGE	LAT.	LONG.
Jazzīn, Leb.	197a	33°34'N	35°37'E
Jeanerette, La., U.S. (jĕn-ēr-et') (zhän-rĕt')	123	29°54'N	91°41'W
Jebba, Nig. (jĕb'ä)	230	9°07'N	4°46'E
Jeddore Lake, l., Can.	101	48°07'N	55°35'W
Jędrzejów, Pol. (yăɴ-dzhă'yòf)	169	50°38'N	20°18'E
Jefferson, Ga., U.S. (jĕf'ēr-sŭn)	124	34°05'N	83°35'W
Jefferson, Ia., U.S.	113	42°10'N	94°22'W
Jefferson, La., U.S.	110d	29°57'N	90°04'W
Jefferson, Tx., U.S.	123	32°47'N	94°21'W
Jefferson, Wi., U.S.	113	42°59'N	88°45'W
Jefferson, r., Mt., U.S.	115	45°37'N	112°22'W
Jefferson, Mount, mtn., Or., U.S.	114	44°41'N	121°50'W
Jefferson City, Mo., U.S.	105	38°34'N	92°10'W
Jeffersontown, Ky., U.S. (jĕf'ēr-sŭn-toun)	111h	38°11'N	85°34'W
Jeffersonville, In., U.S. (jĕf'ēr-sŭn-vĭl)	111h	38°17'N	85°44'W
Jega, Nig.	235	12°15'N	4°23'E
Jehol, hist. reg., China (jĕ-hŏl)	205	42°31'N	118°12'E
Jēkabpils, Lat. (yĕk'ab-pĭls)	180	56°29'N	25°50'E
Jelenia Góra, Pol. (yĕ-lĕn'yà gò'rà)	168	50°53'N	15°43'E
Jelgava, Lat.	167	56°39'N	23°42'E
Jellico, Tn., U.S. (jĕl'ĭ-kō)	124	36°34'N	84°06'W
Jemez Indian Reservation, I.R., N.M., U.S.	119	35°35'N	106°45'W
Jena, Ger. (yā'nä)	161	50°55'N	11°37'E
Jenkins, Ky., U.S. (jĕŋ'kĭnz)	125	37°09'N	82°38'W
Jenkintown, Pa., U.S. (jĕŋ'kĭn-toun)	110f	40°06'N	75°08'W
Jennings, La., U.S. (jĕn'ĭngz)	123	30°14'N	92°40'W
Jennings, Mi., U.S.	108	44°20'N	85°20'W
Jennings, Mo., U.S.	117e	38°43'N	90°16'W
Jequitinhonha, r., Braz. (zhĕ-kē-tĕŋ-ō'n-yä)	143	16°47'S	41°19'W
Jérémie, Haiti (zhā-rā-mē')	135	18°40'N	74°10'W
Jeremoabo, Braz. (zhĕ-rä-mō-ä'bō)	143	10°03'S	38°13'W
Jerez, Punta, c., Mex. (pōō'n-tä-ĸĕ-räz')	131	23°04'N	97°44'W
Jerez de la Frontera, Spain	162	36°42'N	6°09'W
Jerez de los Caballeros, Spain	172	38°20'N	6°45'W
Jericho, Austl. (jĕr'ĭ-kō)	219	23°38'S	146°24'E
Jericho, S. Afr. (jĕr-ĭkô)	238c	25°16'N	27°47'E
Jericho see Arīḥā, W.B.	197a	31°51'N	35°28'E
Jerome, Az., U.S. (jē-rōm')	104	34°45'N	112°10'W
Jerome, Id., U.S.	115	42°44'N	114°31'W
Jersey, dep., Eur.	170	49°15'N	2°10'W
Jersey, i., Jersey (jûr'zĭ)	161	49°13'N	2°07'W
Jersey City, N.J., U.S.	105	40°43'N	74°05'W
Jersey Shore, Pa., U.S.	109	41°10'N	77°15'W
Jerseyville, Il., U.S. (jēr'zē-vĭl)	121	39°07'N	90°18'W
Jerusalem, Isr. (jē-rōō'sá-lĕm)	198	31°46'N	35°14'E
Jesup, Ga., U.S. (jĕs'ŭp)	125	31°36'N	81°53'W
Jesús Carranza, Mex. (hē-sōō's-kär-rá'n-zä)	131	17°26'N	95°01'W
Jewel, Or., U.S. (jū'ĕl)	116c	45°56'N	123°30'W
Jewel Cave National Monument, rec., S.D., U.S.	112	43°44'N	103°52'W
Jhālawār, India	199	24°30'N	76°00'E
Jhang Maghiāna, Pak.	202	31°21'N	72°19'E
Jhānsi, India (jän'sē)	199	25°29'N	78°32'E
Jharkhand, state, India	199	23°30'N	85°00'E
Jhārsuguda, India	202	22°51'N	84°13'E
Jhelum, Pak.	199	32°59'N	73°43'E
Jhelum, r., Asia (jā'lŭm)	199	31°40'N	71°51'E
Jiading, China (jyä-dĭŋ)	206	31°23'N	121°15'E
Jialing, r., China (jyä-lĭŋ)	204	32°30'N	105°30'E
Jiamusi, China	210	46°50'N	130°21'E
Ji'an, China (jyē-än)	205	27°15'N	115°10'E
Ji'an, China	208	41°00'N	126°04'E
Jianchangying, China (jyĕn-chäŋ-yĭŋ)	206	40°09'N	118°47'E
Jiangcun, China (jyän-tsòn)	207a	23°16'N	113°14'E
Jiangling, China (jyäŋ-lĭŋ)	205	30°30'N	112°10'E
Jiangshanzhen, China (jyäŋ-shän-jŭn)	206	36°39'N	120°31'E
Jiangsu, prov., China (jyäŋ-sōō)	205	33°45'N	120°30'E
Jiangwan, China (jyäŋ-wän)	207b	31°18'N	121°29'E
Jiangxi, prov., China (jyäŋ-shyē)	205	28°15'N	116°00'E
Jiangyin, China (jyäŋ-yĭn)	209	31°54'N	120°15'E
Jianli, China (jyĕn-lē)	209	29°50'N	112°52'E
Jianning, China (jyĕn-nĭŋ)	209	26°50'N	116°55'E
Jian'ou, China (jyĕn-ō)	209	27°10'N	118°18'E
Jianshi, China (jyĕn-shr)	209	30°40'N	109°45'E
Jiaohe, China	206	38°03'N	116°18'E
Jiaohe, China (jyou-hŭ)	208	43°40'N	127°20'E
Jiaoxian, China (jyou shyĕn)	205	36°18'N	120°01'E
Jiaozuo, China (jyou-dzwô)	206	35°15'N	113°18'E
Jiashan, China (jyä-shän)	206	32°41'N	118°00'E
Jiaxing, China (jyä-shyĭŋ)	205	30°45'N	120°50'E
Jiayu, China (jyä-yōō)	209	30°00'N	114°00'E
Jiazhou Wan, b., China (jyä-jō wän)	205	36°10'N	119°55'E
Jicarilla Apache Indian Reservation, I.R., N.M., U.S. (ĸē-kä-rēl'yà)	119	36°45'N	107°00'W
Jicarón, Isla, i., Pan. (ĸē-kä-rōn')	133	7°14'N	81°41'W
Jiddah, Sau. Ar.	198	21°30'N	39°15'E
Jieshou, China	206	33°17'N	115°20'E
Jieyang, China (jyĕ-yäŋ)	205	23°38'N	116°20'E
Jiggalong, Austl. (jĭg'ä-lông)	218	23°20'S	120°45'E
Jiguani, Cuba (ĸē-gwä-nē')	134	20°20'N	76°30'W
Jigüey, Bahía, b., Cuba (bä-ē'ä-ĸē'gwā)	134	22°15'N	78°10'W
Jihlava, Czech Rep. (yē'hlà-và)	161	49°23'N	15°33'E
Jijel, Alg.	161	36°49'N	5°47'E
Jijia, r., Rom.	169	47°35'N	27°02'E
Jijiashi, China (jyē-jyä-shr)	206	32°10'N	120°17'E
Jijiga, Eth.	238a	9°15'N	42°48'E
Jilin, China (jyē-lĭn)	205	43°58'N	126°40'E

PLACE (Pronunciation)	PAGE	LAT.	LONG.
Jilin, prov., China	205	44°20'N	124°50'E
Jiloca, r., Spain (ĸē-lō'kà)	172	41°13'N	1°30'W
Jilotepeque, Guat. (ĸē-lô-tĕ-pĕ'kĕ)	132	14°39'N	89°36'W
Jima, Eth.	231	7°41'N	36°52'E
Jimbolia, Rom. (zhĭm-bô'lyä)	175	45°45'N	20°44'E
Jiménez, Mex. (ĸē-mā'nâz)	130	24°12'N	98°29'W
Jiménez, Mex.	122	27°09'N	104°55'W
Jiménez, Mex.	122	29°03'N	100°42'W
Jiménez del Téul, Mex. (tĕ-ōō'l)	130	21°28'N	103°51'W
Jimo, China (jyē-mwo)	208	36°22'N	120°28'E
Jim Thorpe, Pa., U.S. (jĭm' thôrp')	109	40°50'N	75°45'W
Jinan, China (jyē-nän)	205	36°40'N	117°01'E
Jincheng, China (jyĭn-chŭŋ)	208	35°30'N	112°50'E
Jindřichův Hradec, Czech Rep. (yĕn'd'r-zhĭ-kōōf hrä'dĕts)	168	49°09'N	15°02'E
Jing, r., China (jyĭŋ)	208	34°40'N	108°20'E
Jing'anji, China (jyĭŋ-än-jē)	206	34°30'N	116°55'E
Jingdezhen, China (jyĭŋ-dŭ-jŭn)	209	29°18'N	117°18'E
Jingjiang, China (jyĭŋ-jyäŋ)	206	32°02'N	120°15'E
Jingning, China (jyĭŋ-nĭŋ)	208	35°28'N	105°50'E
Jingpo Hu, l., China (jyĭŋ-pwo hōō)	208	44°10'N	129°00'E
Jingxian, China (jyĭŋ shyĕn)	209	26°32'N	109°45'E
Jingxian, China	206	37°43'N	116°17'E
Jingxing, China (jyĭŋ-shyĭŋ)	208	47°00'N	123°00'E
Jingzhi, China (jyĭŋ-jr)	206	36°19'N	119°23'E
Jinhua, China (jyĭn-hwä)	205	29°10'N	119°42'E
Jining, China (jyē-nĭŋ)	205	35°26'N	116°34'E
Jining, China	208	41°00'N	113°10'E
Jinja, Ug. (jĭn'jä)	231	0°26'N	33°12'E
Jinotega, Nic. (kē-nô-tā'gä)	132	13°07'N	86°00'W
Jinotepe, Nic. (kē-nô-tā'pā)	132	11°52'N	86°12'W
Jinqiao, China (jyĭn-chyou)	206	31°46'N	116°46'E
Jinshan, China (jyĭn-shän)	207b	30°53'N	121°09'E
Jinta, China (jyĭn-tä)	204	40°11'N	98°45'E
Jintan, China (jyĭn-tän)	206	31°47'N	119°34'E
Jin Xian, China (jyĭn shyĕn)	208	39°04'N	121°40'E
Jinxiang, China (jyĭn-shyäŋ)	206	35°03'N	116°20'E
Jinyun, China (jyĭn-yòn)	209	28°40'N	120°08'E
Jinzhai, China (jyĭn-jī)	206	31°41'N	115°51'E
Jinzhou, China (jyĭn-jō)	205	41°00'N	121°00'E
Jinzhou Wan, b., China (jyĭn-jō wän)	206	39°07'N	121°17'E
Jinzū-Gawa, r., Japan (jēn'zōō gä'wä)	211	36°26'N	137°18'E
Jipijapa, Ec. (ĸē-pē-hä'pä)	142	1°36'S	80°52'W
Jiquilisco, El Sal. (ĸē-kē-lē's-kô)	132	13°18'N	88°32'W
Jiquilpan de Juárez, Mex. (ĸē-kēl'pän dā hwä'rāz)	130	20°00'N	102°43'W
Jiquipilco, Mex. (hē-kē-pē'l-kô)	131a	19°32'N	99°37'W
Jitotol, Mex. (ĸē-tô-tōl')	131	17°03'N	92°54'W
Jiu, r., Rom.	175	44°45'N	23°17'E
Jiujiang, China (jyô-jyän)	207a	22°50'N	113°02'E
Jiujiang, China	205	29°43'N	116°00'E
Jiuquan, China (jyô-chyän)	204	39°46'N	98°26'E
Jiurongcheng, China (jyô-rôŋ-chŭŋ)	206	37°23'N	122°31'E
Jiushouzhang, China (jyô-shō-jäŋ)	206	35°59'N	115°52'E
Jiuwuqing, China (jyô-wōō-chyĭŋ)	208a	32°31'N	116°51'E
Jiuyongnian, China (jyô-yôŋ-nĭĕn)	206	36°41'N	114°46'E
Jixian, China (jyē shyĕn)	206	35°25'N	114°03'E
Jixian, China	206	37°37'N	115°33'E
Jixian, China	206	40°03'N	117°25'E
Jiyun, r., China (jyē-yōōm)	206	39°35'N	117°34'E
Joachimsthal, Ger.	159b	52°58'N	13°45'E
João Pessoa, Braz.	143	7°09'S	34°45'W
João Ribeiro, Braz. (zhô-uɴ-rē-bā'rō)	141a	20°42'S	44°03'W
Jobabo, r., Cuba (hō-bä'bä)	134	20°50'N	77°15'W
Jock, r., Can. (jŏk)	102c	45°08'N	75°51'W
Jocotepec, Mex. (jô-kō-tå-pĕk')	130	20°17'N	103°26'W
Jodar, Spain (hō'där)	172	37°54'N	3°20'W
Jodhpur, India (hōd'pōōr)	199	26°23'N	73°00'E
Joensuu, Fin. (yô-ĕn'sōō)	167	62°35'N	29°46'E
Joffre, Mount, mtn., Can. (jŏ'f'r)	95	50°32'N	115°13'W
Jõgeva, Est. (yû'gĕ-và)	167	58°45'N	26°23'E
Joggins, Can. (jŏ'gĭnz)	100	45°42'N	64°27'W
Johannesburg, S. Afr. (yô-hän'ĕs-bòrgh)	232	26°08'S	27°54'E
John Day, r., Or., U.S. (jŏn'dā)	114	44°46'N	120°15'W
John Day, Middle Fork, r., Or., U.S.	114	44°53'N	119°04'W
John Day, North Fork, r., Or., U.S.	114	45°03'N	118°50'W
John Day Dam, Or., U.S.	114	45°40'N	120°15'W
John H. Kerr Reservoir, res., U.S.	107	36°30'N	78°38'W
John Martin Reservoir, res., Co., U.S. (jŏn mär'tĭn)	120	37°57'N	103°04'W
Johnson, r., Or., U.S. (jŏn'sŭn)	116c	45°27'N	122°20'W
Johnsonburg, Pa., U.S. (jŏn'sŭn-bûrg)	109	41°30'N	78°40'W
Johnson City, Il., U.S. (jŏn'sŭn)	108	37°50'N	88°55'W
Johnson City, N.Y., U.S.	109	42°10'N	76°00'W
Johnson City, Tn., U.S.	105	36°17'N	82°23'W
Johnston, i., Oc. (jŏn'stŭn)	2	17°00'N	168°00'W
Johnstone Strait, strt., Can.	94	50°25'N	126°00'W
Johnston Falls, wtfl., Afr.	237	10°35'S	28°50'E
Johnstown, N.Y., U.S. (jonz'toun)	109	43°00'N	74°20'W
Johnstown, Pa., U.S.	105	40°20'N	78°50'W
Johor, r., Malay. (jü-hōr')	197b	1°39'N	103°52'E
Johor Baharu, Malay.	212	1°28'N	103°46'E
Jõhvi, Est. (yû'vĭ)	167	59°21'N	27°21'E
Joigny, Fr. (zhwän-yē')	170	47°58'N	3°26'E
Joinville, Braz. (zhwăn-vēl')	144	26°18'S	48°47'W
Joinville, Fr.	171	48°28'N	5°05'E
Joinville, i., Ant.	139	63°00'S	53°30'W
Jojutla, Mex. (hō-hōō'tlà)	130	18°39'N	99°11'W
Jola, Mex. (kô'lä)	130	21°08'N	104°26'W
Joliet, Il., U.S. (jō-lĭ-ĕt')	111a	41°32'N	88°05'W
Joliette, Can. (zhô-lyĕt')	91	46°01'N	73°30'W
Jolo, Phil. (hō-lō)	212	5°59'N	121°05'E
Jolo Island, i., Phil.	212	5°55'N	121°15'E

PLACE (Pronunciation)	PAGE	LAT.	LONG.
Jomalig, i., Phil. (hô-mä'lēg)	213a	14°44'N	122°34'E
Jomulco, Mex. (hô-mōōl'kô)	130	21°08'N	104°24'W
Jonacatepec, Mex.	130	18°39'N	98°46'W
Jonava, Lith. (yō-nä'vá)	167	55°05'N	24°15'E
Jones, Phil. (jōnz)	213a	12°56'N	122°05'E
Jones, Phil.	213a	16°35'N	121°39'E
Jonesboro, Ar., U.S. (jōnz'bûro)	105	35°49'N	90°42'W
Jonesboro, La., U.S.	123	32°14'N	92°43'W
Jonesville, La., U.S. (jōnz'vĭl)	123	31°35'N	91°50'W
Jonesville, Mi., U.S.	108	42°00'N	84°45'W
Jong, r., S.L.	234	8°10'N	12°10'W
Joniškis, Lith. (yô'nĭsh-kĭs)	167	56°14'N	23°36'E
Jönköping, Swe. (yûn'chû-pĭng)	160	57°47'N	14°10'E
Jonquiere, Can. (zhôn-kyâr')	91	48°25'N	71°15'W
Jonuta, Mex. (hô-nōō'tä)	131	18°07'N	92°09'W
Jonzac, Fr. (zhôn-zák')	170	45°27'N	0°27'W
Joplin, Mo., U.S. (jŏp'lĭn)	105	37°05'N	94°31'W
Jordan, nation, Asia (jôr'dăn)	198	30°15'N	38°00'E
Jordan, r., Asia	197a	32°05'N	35°35'E
Jordan, r., Ut., U.S.	117b	40°42'N	111°56'W
Jorhāt, India (jôr-hät')	199	26°43'N	94°16'E
Jorullo, Volcán de, vol., Mex. (vôl-kä'n-dĕ-hô-rōōl'yō)	130	18°54'N	101°38'W
José C. Paz, Arg.	144a	34°32'S	58°44'W
Joseph Bonaparte Gulf, b., Austl. (jô'sĕf bō'ná-pärt)	220	13°30'S	128°40'E
Josephburg, Can.	102g	53°45'N	113°06'W
Joseph Lake, l., Can. (jô'sĕf lāk)	102g	53°18'N	113°06'W
Joshua Tree National Park, rec., Ca., U.S. (jô'shū-á trē)	118	34°02'N	115°53'W
Jos Plateau, plat., Nig. (jŏs)	235	9°53'N	9°05'E
Jostedalsbreen, ice, Nor. (yôstĕ-däls-brĕĕn)	160	61°40'N	6°55'E
Jotunheimen, mts., Nor.	160	61°44'N	8°11'E
Joulter's Cays, is., Bah. (jōl'tērz)	134	25°20'N	78°10'W
Jouy-le-Chatel, Fr. (zhwē-lē-shä-tĕl')	171b	48°40'N	3°07'E
Jovellanos, Cuba (hō-vĕl-yä'nōs)	134	22°50'N	81°10'W
J. Percy Priest Lake, res., Tn., U.S.	124	36°00'N	86°45'W
Juan Aldama, Mex. (kôá'n-äl-dá'mä)	130	24°16'N	103°21'W
Juan de Fuca, Strait of, strt., N.A. (hwän' dā fōō'kä)	92	48°25'N	124°37'W
Juan de Nova, Île, i., Reu.	233	17°18'S	43°07'E
Juan Diaz, r., Pan. (ĸōōá'n-dē'äz)	128a	9°05'N	79°30'W
Juan Fernández, Islas de, is., Chile	139	33°30'S	79°00'W
Juan L. Lacaze, Ur. (hōōá'n-ĕ'lĕ-lä-kä'zĕ)	141c	34°25'S	57°28'W
Juan Luis, Cayos de, is., Cuba (ka-yōs-dĕ-hwän lōō-ēs')	134	22°15'N	82°00'W
Juárez, Arg. (hōōä'rĕz)	144	37°42'S	59°46'W
Juázeiro, Braz. (zhōōá'zā'rō)	143	9°27'S	40°28'W
Juazeiro do Norte, Braz. (zhōōá'zā'rō-dô-nôr-tĕ)	143	7°16'S	38°57'W
Jubayl, Leb. (jōō-bīl')	197a	34°07'N	35°38'E
Jubba (Genale), r., Afr.	238a	1°30'N	42°25'E
Juby, Cap, c., Mor. (yōō'bē)	230	28°01'N	13°21'W
Júcar, r., Spain (hōō'kär)	162	39°10'N	1°22'W
Júcaro, Cuba (hōō'kä-rô)	134	21°40'N	78°50'W
Juchipila, Mex. (hōō-chē-pē'lä)	130	21°26'N	103°09'W
Juchitán, Mex. (hōō-chē-tän')	128	16°15'N	95°00'W
Juchitlán, Mex. (hōō-chē-tlän)	130	20°05'N	104°07'W
Jucuapa, El Sal. (ĸōō-kwä'pä)	132	13°30'N	88°24'W
Judenburg, Aus. (jōō'dĕn-bûrg)	168	47°10'N	14°40'E
Judith, r., Mt., U.S. (jōō'dĭth)	115	47°20'N	109°36'W
Juhua Dao, i., China (jyōō-hwä dou)	206	40°30'N	120°47'E
Juigalpa, Nic. (hwē-gäl'pä)	132	12°02'N	85°24'W
Juiz de Fora, Braz. (zhò-ēzh' dā fō'rä)	143	21°47'S	43°20'W
Jujuy, Arg. (hōō-hwē')	144	24°14'S	65°15'W
Jujuy, prov., Arg. (hōō-hwē')	144	23°00'S	65°45'W
Jukskei, r., S. Afr.	233b	25°58'S	27°58'E
Julesburg, Co., U.S. (jōōlz'bûrg)	120	40°59'N	102°16'W
Juliaca, Peru (hōō-lē-ä'kä)	142	15°26'S	70°12'W
Julian Alps, mts., Yugo.	162	46°05'N	14°05'E
Julianehåb, Grnld.	89	60°07'N	46°20'W
Jülich, Ger. (yü'lĕk)	171c	50°55'N	6°22'E
Jullundur, India	199	31°29'N	75°39'E
Julpaiguri, India	202	26°35'N	88°48'E
Jumento Cays, is., Bah. (hōō-mĕn'tō)	135	23°05'N	75°40'W
Jumilla, Spain (hōō-mēl'yä)	172	38°28'N	1°20'W
Jump, r., Wi., U.S. (jŭmp)	113	45°18'N	90°53'W
Jumpingpound Creek, r., Can. (jŭmp-ĭng-pound)	102e	51°01'N	114°34'W
Jumrah, Indon.	197b	1°48'N	101°04'E
Junagādh, India (jò-nä'gŭd)	199	21°33'N	70°25'E
Junayfah, Egypt	238d	30°11'N	32°26'E
Junaynah, Ra's al; mtn., Egypt	197a	29°02'N	33°58'E
Junction, Tx., U.S. (jŭŋk'shŭn)	122	30°29'N	99°48'W
Junction City, Ks., U.S.	121	39°01'N	96°49'W
Jundiaí, Braz.	143	23°11'S	46°52'W
Juneau, Ak., U.S. (jōō'nō)	106a	58°25'N	134°30'W
Jungfrau, mtn., Switz. (yòng'frou)	168	46°30'N	7°59'E
Junín, Arg. (hōō-nē'n)	144	34°35'S	60°56'W
Junín, Col.	142a	4°47'N	73°39'W
Juniyah, Leb. (jōō-nē'ĕ)	197a	33°59'N	35°38'E
Jupiter, r., Can.	100	49°40'N	63°20'W
Jupiter, Mount, mtn., Wa., U.S.	116a	47°42'N	123°04'W
Jur, r., Sudan (jòr)	231	6°38'N	27°52'E
Jura, mts., Eur. (zhü-rá')	161	46°55'N	6°49'E
Jura, i., Scot., U.K. (jōō'rà)	164	56°09'N	6°45'W
Jura, Sound of, strt., Scot., U.K. (jōō'rá)	164	55°45'N	5°55'W
Jurbarkas, Lith. (yōōr-bär'käs)	167	55°06'N	22°50'E
Jūrmala, Lat.	167	56°57'N	23°37'E
Jurong, China (jyōō-roŋ)	206	31°58'N	119°12'E
Juruá, r., S.A.	142	5°30'S	67°30'W
Juruena, r., Braz. (zhōō-rōōĕ'nä)	143	12°22'S	58°34'W

PRONOUNCING INDEX

Jutiapa – Kara-Kum 307

PLACE (Pronunciation)	PAGE	LAT.	LONG.
Jutiapa, Guat. (hōō-tē-ä'pä)	132	14°16'N	89°55'W
Juticalpa, Hond. (hōō-tē-käl'pä)	128	14°35'N	86°17'W
Jutland see Jylland, reg., Den.	160	56°04'N	9°00'E
Juventino Rosas, Mex.	130	20°38'N	101°02'W
Juventud, Isla de la, i., Cuba	129	21°40'N	82°45'W
Juxian, China (jyōō shyĕn)	208	35°35'N	118°50'E
Juxtlahuaca, Mex. (hōōs-tlä-hwä'kä)	130	17°20'N	98°02'W
Juye, China (jyōō-yŭ)	206	35°25'N	116°05'E
Južna Morava, r., Yugo. (ŭ'zhnä mô'rä-vä)	175	42°30'N	22°00'E
Jylland, reg., Den.	160	56°04'N	9°00'E
K			
K2(Qogir Feng), mtn., Asia	199	36°06'N	76°38'E
Kaabong, Ug.	237	3°31'N	34°08'E
Kaalfontein, S. Afr. (kärl-fōn-tān)	233b	26°02'S	28°16'E
Kaappunt, c., S. Afr.	232a	34°21'S	18°30'E
Kabaena, Pulau, i., Indon. (kä-bá-ā'ná)	212	5°35'S	121°07'E
Kabala, S.L. (ká-bá'lá)	230	9°43'N	11°39'W
Kabale, Ug.	237	1°15'S	29°59'E
Kabalega Falls, wtfl., Ug.	231	2°15'N	31°41'E
Kabalo, D.R.C. (kä-bä'lō)	232	6°03'S	26°55'E
Kabambare, D.R.C. (kä-bäm-bä'rá)	232	4°47'S	27°45'E
Kabardino-Balkaria, prov., Russia	180	43°30'N	43°30'E
Kabba, Nig.	235	7°50'N	6°03'E
Kabe, Japan (kä'bā)	211	34°32'N	132°30'E
Kabinakagami, r., Can.	98	49°00'N	84°15'W
Kabinda, D.R.C. (kä-bēn'dä)	232	6°08'S	24°29'E
Kabompo, r., Zam. (ká-bôm'pō)	232	14°00'S	23°40'E
Kabongo, D.R.C. (ká-bông'ō)	232	7°58'S	25°10'E
Kabot, Gui.	234	10°48'N	14°57'W
Kaboudia, Ra's, c., Tun.	162	35°17'N	11°28'E
Kābul, Afg. (kä'bo͝ol)	199	34°39'N	69°14'E
Kabul, r., Asia (kä'bo͝ol)	199	34°44'N	69°43'E
Kabunda, D.R.C.	237	12°25'S	29°22'E
Kabwe, Zam.	232	14°27'S	28°27'E
Kachuga, Russia (kå-chōō-gå)	179	54°09'N	105°43'E
Kadei, r., Afr.	235	4°00'N	15°10'E
Kadnikov, Russia (käd'nē-kôf)	180	59°30'N	40°10'E
Kadoma, Japan	211b	34°43'N	135°36'E
Kadoma, Zimb.	232	18°21'S	29°55'E
Kaduna, Nig. (kä-dōō'nä)	230	10°33'N	7°27'E
Kaduna, r., Nig.	235	9°30'N	6°00'E
Kaédi, Maur. (kä-ā-dē')	230	16°09'N	13°30'W
Ka'ena Point, c., Hi., U.S. (kä'ā-nä)	106d	21°33'N	158°19'W
Kaesŏng, Kor., N. (kä'ĕ-sŭng) (kī'jō)	205	38°00'N	126°35'E
Kafanchan, Nig.	235	9°36'N	8°17'E
Kafia Kingi, Sudan (kä'fē-á kiŋ'gē)	231	9°17'N	24°28'E
Kafue, Zam. (kä'fōō)	232	15°45'S	28°17'E
Kafue, r., Zam.	232	15°45'S	26°30'E
Kafue Flats, sw., Zam.	237	16°15'S	26°30'E
Kafue National Park, rec., Zam.	237	15°00'S	25°35'E
Kafwira, D.R.C.	237	12°10'S	27°33'E
Kagal'nik, r., Russia (kä-gäl''nēk)	177	46°58'N	39°25'E
Kagera, r., Afr. (kä-gā'rá)	232	1°10'S	31°10'E
Kagoshima, Japan (kä'gô-shē'má)	205	31°35'N	130°31'E
Kagoshima-Wan, b., Japan (kä'gô-shē'mä wän)	210	31°24'N	130°39'E
Kahayan, r., Indon.	212	1°45'S	113°40'E
Kahemba, D.R.C.	236	7°17'S	19°00'E
Kahia, D.R.C.	237	6°21'S	28°24'E
Kahoka, Mo., U.S. (ká-hō'ká)	121	40°26'N	91°42'W
Kaho'olawe, i., Hi., U.S. (kä-hōō-lä'wē)	106c	20°28'N	156°48'W
Kahramanmaraş, Tur.	198	37°40'N	36°50'E
Kahshahpiwi, r., Can.	113	48°24'N	90°56'W
Kahuku Point, c., Hi., U.S. (kä-hōō'kōō)	106d	21°50'N	157°50'W
Kahului, Hi., U.S.	106c	20°53'N	156°28'W
Kai, Kepulauan, is., Indon.	213	5°35'S	132°45'E
Kaiang, Malay.	197b	3°00'N	101°47'E
Kaiashk, r., Can.	98	49°40'N	89°30'W
Kaibab Indian Reservation, I.R., Az., U.S. (kä'ē-băb)	119	36°55'N	112°45'W
Kaibab Plat, Az., U.S.	119	36°30'N	112°10'W
Kaidu, r., China (kī-dōō)	204	42°35'N	84°04'E
Kaieteur Fall, wtfl., Guy. (kī-ĕ-tōōr')	143	4°48'N	59°24'W
Kaifeng, China (kī-fŭŋ)	205	34°48'N	114°22'E
Kai Kecil, i., Indon.	213	5°45'S	132°40'E
Kailua, Hi., U.S. (kä'ē-lōō'ä)	106c	21°18'N	157°43'W
Kailua Kona, Hi., U.S.	126a	19°49'N	155°59'W
Kaimana, Indon.	213	3°32'S	133°47'E
Kaimanawa Mountains, mts., N.Z.	223	39°10'S	176°00'E
Kainan, Japan (kä'ē-nän')	211	34°09'N	135°14'E
Kainji Lake, res., Nig.	230	10°25'N	4°50'E
Kaiserslautern, Ger. (kī-zĕrs-lou'tĕrn)	161	49°26'N	7°46'E
Kaitaia, N.Z. (kä-ē-tä'ē-á)	221a	35°30'S	173°28'E
Kaiwi Channel, strt., Hi., U.S. (kä'ē-wē)	106c	21°10'N	157°38'W
Kaiyuan, China (kī-yuän)	209	23°42'N	103°20'E
Kaiyuan, China	208	42°30'N	124°00'E
Kaiyuh Mountains, mts., Ak., U.S. (kī-yōō')	103	64°25'N	157°38'W
Kajaani, Fin. (kä'yá-nē)	160	64°15'N	27°16'E
Kajang, Gunong, mtn., Malay.	197b	2°47'N	104°05'E
Kajiki, Japan (kä'jē-kē)	210	31°44'N	130°41'E
Kakhovka, Ukr. (kä-kôf'ká)	177	46°46'N	33°32'E
Kakhovs'ke vodoskhovyshche, res., Ukr.	178	47°21'N	33°33'E
Kākināda, India	199	16°58'N	82°18'E
Kaktovik, Ak., U.S. (käk-tō'vĭk)	103	70°08'N	143°51'W
Kakwa, r., Can. (käk'wá)	95	54°00'N	118°55'W
Kalach, Russia (ká-lách')	181	50°15'N	40°55'E
Kaladan, r., Asia	204	21°07'N	93°04'E
Kalae, c., Hi., U.S.	126a	18°55'N	155°41'W
Kalahari Desert, des., Afr. (kä-lä-hä'rē)	232	23°00'S	22°03'E
Kalama, Wa., U.S. (ká-lăm'á)	116c	46°01'N	122°50'W
Kalama, r., Wa., U.S.	116c	46°03'N	122°47'W
Kalamáta, Grc.	154	37°04'N	22°08'E
Kalamazoo, Mi., U.S. (kăl-á-má-zōō')	105	42°20'N	85°40'W
Kalamazoo, r., Mi., U.S.	108	42°35'N	86°00'W
Kalanchak, Ukr. (kä-län-chäk')	177	46°17'N	33°14'E
Kalandula, Ang. (dōō'kā dá brä-gäN'sä)	232	9°06'S	15°57'E
Kalaotoa, Pulau, i., Indon.	212	7°22'S	122°30'E
Kalapana, Hi., U.S. (kä-lä-pá'nä)	126a	19°25'N	155°00'W
Kalar, mtn., Iran	198	31°43'N	51°41'E
Kalāt, Pak. (kŭ-lät')	199	29°05'N	66°36'E
Kalemie, D.R.C.	232	5°56'S	29°12'E
Kalgan see Zhangjiakou, China	205	40°45'N	114°58'E
Kalgoorlie-Boulder, Austl. (kăl-gōōr'lē)	218	30°45'S	121°35'E
Kaliakra, Nos, c., Blg.	163	43°25'N	28°42'E
Kalima, D.R.C.	237	2°34'S	26°37'E
Kaliningrad, Russia	178	54°42'N	20°32'E
Kaliningrad, Russia (kä-lē-nēn'grät)	186b	55°55'N	37°49'E
Kalinkavichy, Bela.	176	52°07'N	29°19'E
Kalispel Indian Reservation, I.R., Wa., U.S. (kăl-ĭ-spĕl')	114	48°25'N	117°30'W
Kalispell, Mt., U.S. (kăl'ĭ-spĕl)	104	48°12'N	114°18'W
Kalisz, Pol. (kä'lēsh)	161	51°45'N	18°05'E
Kaliua, Tan.	237	5°04'S	31°48'E
Kalixälven, r., Swe.	160	67°12'N	22°00'E
Kalmar, Swe. (käl'mär)	160	56°40'N	16°19'E
Kalmarsund, strt., Swe. (käl'mär)	166	56°30'N	16°17'E
Kal'mius, r., Ukr. (käl''myōōs)	177	47°15'N	37°38'E
Kalmykia, prov., Russia	181	46°56'N	46°00'E
Kalocsa, Hung. (kä'lô-chä)	169	46°32'N	19°00'E
Kalohi Channel, strt., Hi., U.S. (kä-lō'hĭ)	126a	20°55'N	157°15'W
Kaloko, D.R.C.	237	6°47'S	25°48'E
Kalomo, Zam. (kä-lō'mō)	232	17°02'S	26°30'E
Kalsubai Mount, mtn., India	202	19°43'N	73°47'E
Kaltenkirchen, Ger. (käl'tĕn-kēr-kĕn)	159c	53°50'N	9°57'E
Kālu, r., India	203b	19°18'N	73°14'E
Kaluga, Russia (ká-lō'gä)	178	54°29'N	36°12'E
Kaluga, prov., Russia	176	54°10'N	35°00'E
Kaluktutiak (Cambridge Bay), Can.	90	69°15'N	105°00'W
Kalundborg, Den. (ká-lòn'bôr')	166	55°42'N	11°07'E
Kalush, Ukr. (kä'lòsh)	169	49°02'N	24°24'E
Kalvarija, Lith. (käl-vä-rē'yá)	167	54°24'N	23°17'E
Kalwa, India	203b	19°12'N	72°59'E
Kal'ya, Russia (käl'yá)	186a	60°17'N	59°58'E
Kalyān, India	202	19°16'N	73°07'E
Kalyazin, Russia (käl-yá'zēn)	176	57°13'N	37°55'E
Kama, r., Russia (kä'mä)	178	56°10'N	53°50'E
Kamaishi, Japan (kä'mä-ē'shē)	210	39°16'N	142°03'E
Kamakura, Japan (kä'mä-kōō'rä)	211	35°19'N	139°33'E
Kamarān, i., Yemen	198	15°19'N	41°47'E
Kāmārhāti, India	202a	22°41'N	88°23'E
Kambove, D.R.C. (käm-bō'vĕ)	232	10°58'S	26°43'E
Kamchatka, r., Russia	185	54°15'N	158°38'E
Kamchatka, Poluostrov, pen., Russia	185	55°19'N	157°45'E
Kamen, Ger. (kä'mĕn)	171c	51°35'N	7°40'E
Kamenjak, Rt, c., Cro. (kä'mĕ-nyäk)	174	44°45'N	13°57'E
Kamen'-na-Obi, Russia (kä-mĭny'nŭ ô'bē)	178	53°43'N	81°28'E
Kamensk-Shakhtinskiy, Russia (kä'mĕnsk shäk'tĭn-skĭ)	177	48°17'N	40°16'E
Kamensk-Ural'skiy, Russia (kä'mĕnsk ōō-räl'skĭ)	180	56°27'N	61°55'E
Kamenz, Ger. (kä'mĕnts)	168	51°16'N	14°05'E
Kameoka, Japan (kä'mā-ōkä)	211b	35°01'N	135°35'E
Kāmet, mtn., Asia	202	30°50'N	79°42'E
Kamianets'-Podil's'kyi, Ukr.	181	48°41'N	26°34'E
Kamianka-Buz'ka, Ukr.	169	50°06'N	24°20'E
Kamień Pomorski, Pol.	168	53°57'N	14°48'E
Kamikoma, Japan (kä'mē-kō'mä)	211b	34°45'N	135°50'E
Kamina, D.R.C.	232	8°44'S	25°00'E
Kaministikwia, r., Can. (ká-mĭ-nĭ-stĭk'wĭ-á)	113	48°40'N	89°41'W
Kamituga, D.R.C.	237	3°04'S	28°11'E
Kamloops, Can. (kăm'lōōps)	90	50°40'N	120°20'W
Kamp, r., Aus. (kämp)	168	48°30'N	15°45'E
Kampala, Ug. (käm-pä'lä)	231	0°19'N	32°25'E
Kampar, r., Indon. (käm'pär)	212	0°30'N	101°30'E
Kampene, D.R.C.	237	3°36'S	26°40'E
Kampenhout, Bel.	159a	50°56'N	4°33'E
Kamp-Lintfort, Ger. (kämp-lēnt'fōrt)	171c	51°30'N	6°34'E
Kâmpóng Saôm, Camb.	212	10°40'N	103°50'E
Kâmpóng Thum, Camb. (kŏm'pŏng-tŏm)	212	12°41'N	104°29'E
Kâmpôt, Camb. (käm'pōt)	212	10°41'N	104°07'E
Kampuchea see Cambodia, nation, Asia	212	12°15'N	104°00'E
Kamsack, Can. (kăm'săk)	90	51°34'N	101°54'W
Kamskoye, res., Russia	178	59°08'N	56°30'E
Kamudilo, D.R.C.	237	7°42'S	27°18'E
Kamuela, Hi., U.S.	126a	20°01'N	155°40'W
Kamui Misaki, c., Japan	210	43°25'N	139°35'E
Kámuk, Cerro, mtn., C.R. (sĕ'r-rô-kä-mōō'k)	133	9°18'N	83°02'W
Kamyshevatskaya, Russia	177	46°24'N	37°58'E
Kamyshin, Russia (kä-mwēsh'ĭn)	178	50°08'N	45°20'E
Kamyshlov, Russia (kä-mēsh'lôf)	178	56°50'N	62°32'E
Kan, r., Russia (kän)	184	56°30'N	94°17'E
Kanab, Ut., U.S. (kăn'ăb)	119	37°00'N	112°30'W
Kanabeki, Russia (ká-nä'byĕ-kĭ)	186a	57°48'N	57°16'E
Kanab Plateau, plat., Az., U.S.	119	36°31'N	112°55'W
Kanaga, i., Ak., U.S. (kă-nä'gă)	103a	52°02'N	177°38'W
Kanagawa, dept., Japan (kä'nä-gä'wä)	211a	35°29'N	139°32'E
Kanā'is, Ra's al, c., Egypt	163	31°14'N	28°08'E
Kanamachi, Japan (kä-nä-mä'chē)	211a	35°46'N	139°52'E
Kananga, D.R.C.	232	6°14'S	22°17'E
Kananikol'skoye, Russia	186a	52°48'N	57°29'E
Kanasín, Mex. (kä-nä-sē'n)	132a	20°54'N	89°31'W
Kanatak, Ak., U.S. (kă-nă'tŏk)	103	57°35'N	155°48'W
Kanawha, r., W.V., U.S. (ká-nô'wá)	107	37°55'N	81°50'W
Kanaya, Japan (kä-nä'yä)	211a	35°10'N	139°49'E
Kanazawa, Japan (kä'ná-zä'wá)	205	36°34'N	136°38'E
Kānchenjunga, mtn., Asia (kĭn-chĭn-jòn'gá)	199	27°30'N	88°18'E
Kānchipuram, India	199	12°55'N	79°43'E
Kandahār, Afg.	199	31°43'N	65°58'E
Kanda Kanda, D.R.C. (kän'dá kän'dá)	232	6°56'S	23°36'E
Kandalaksha, Russia (kán-dá-lák'shá)	178	67°10'N	33°05'E
Kandalakshskiy Zaliv, b., Russia	180	66°20'N	35°00'E
Kandava, Lat. (kän'dá-vá)	167	57°03'N	22°45'E
Kandi, Benin (käN-dē')	230	11°08'N	2°56'E
Kandiāro, Pak.	202	27°09'N	68°12'E
Kandla, India (kŭnd'lŭ)	202	23°00'N	70°20'E
Kandy, Sri L. (kän'dē)	203	7°18'N	80°42'E
Kane, Pa., U.S. (kān)	109	41°40'N	78°50'W
Kāne'ohe, Hi., U.S. (kä-nā-ō'hā)	126a	21°25'N	157°47'W
Kāne'ohe Bay, b., Hi., U.S.	106d	21°32'N	157°40'W
Kanevskaya, Russia (ká-nyĕf'ská)	177	46°07'N	38°58'E
Kangaroo, i., Austl. (kăŋ-gá-rō')	220	36°05'S	137°05'E
Kangāvar, Iran (kŭŋ'gŭ-vär)	198	34°37'N	46°45'E
Kangean, Kepulauan, is., Indon. (käŋ'gē-än)	212	6°50'S	116°22'E
Kanggye, Kor., N. (käng'gyĕ)	205	40°55'N	126°40'E
Kanghwa, i., Kor., S. (käng'hwä)	210	37°38'N	126°00'E
Kangnŭng, Kor., S. (käng'nò ng)	210	37°42'N	128°50'E
Kango, Gabon (käN-gō)	232	0°09'N	10°08'E
Kangowa, D.R.C.	236	9°55'S	22°48'E
Kanin, Poluostrov, pen., Russia	178	68°00'N	45°00'E
Kaningo, Kenya	237	0°49'S	38°32'E
Kanin Nos, Mys, c., Russia	180	68°40'N	44°00'E
Kaniv, Ukr.	177	49°46'N	31°27'E
Kanivs'ke vodoskhovyshche, res., Ukr.	178	50°10'N	30°40'E
Kanjiža, Yugo. (kä'nyē-zhä)	175	46°05'N	20°02'E
Kankakee, Il., U.S. (kăŋ-ká-kē')	108	41°07'N	87°53'W
Kankakee, r., Il., U.S.	108	41°15'N	88°15'W
Kankan, Gui. (käN-käN) (kän-kän')	230	10°23'N	9°18'W
Kannapolis, N.C., U.S. (kăn-ăp'ō-lĭs)	125	35°30'N	80°38'W
Kannoura, Japan (kä'nō-ōō'rä)	211	33°34'N	134°18'E
Kano, Nig. (kä'nō)	230	12°00'N	8°30'E
Kanonkop, mtn., S. Afr.	232a	33°49'S	18°37'E
Kanopolis Reservoir, res., Ks., U.S. (kăn-ŏp'ō-lĭs)	120	38°44'N	98°01'W
Kānpur, India (kän'pûr)	202	26°30'N	80°10'E
Kansas, state, U.S. (kăn'zás)	104	38°30'N	99°40'W
Kansas, r., Ks., U.S.	121	39°08'N	95°52'W
Kansas City, Ks., U.S.	105	39°06'N	94°39'W
Kansas City, Mo., U.S.	105	39°05'N	94°35'W
Kansk, Russia	179	56°14'N	95°43'E
Kansŏng, Kor., S.	210	38°09'N	128°29'E
Kantang, Thai. (kän'täng')	212	7°26'N	99°28'E
Kantchari, Burkina	234	12°29'N	1°31'E
Kanton, i., Kir.	240	3°50'S	174°00'W
Kantunilkin, Mex. (kän-tōō-nēl-kē'n)	132a	21°07'N	87°30'W
Kanzhakovskiy Kamen, Gora, mtn., Russia (kán-zhä'kôvs-kēē kămĭen)	186a	59°38'N	59°12'E
Kaohsiung, Tai. (kä-ô-syòng')	205	22°35'N	120°25'E
Kaolack, Sen.	230	14°09'N	16°04'W
Kaouar, oasis, Niger	231	19°16'N	13°09'E
Kapaa, Hi., U.S.	126a	22°06'N	159°20'W
Kapanga, D.R.C.	236	8°21'S	22°35'E
Kapfenberg, Aus. (käp'fĕn-bĕrgh)	168	47°27'N	15°16'E
Kapiri Mposhi, Zam.	237	13°58'S	28°41'E
Kapoeta, Sudan	231	4°45'N	33°35'E
Kaposvár, Hung. (kô'pôsh-vär)	169	46°21'N	17°45'E
Kapsan, Kor., N. (käp'sän')	210	40°59'N	128°22'E
Kapuskasing, Can.	91	49°28'N	82°22'W
Kapuskasing, r., Can.	98	48°55'N	82°55'W
Kapustin Yar, Russia (kä'pòs-tēn yär')	181	48°30'N	45°40'E
Kaputar, Mount, mtn., Austl. (kă-pû-tăr)	222	30°11'S	150°11'E
Kapuvár, Hung. (kô'pōō-vär)	169	47°35'N	17°02'E
Kara, Russia (kärá)	178	68°42'N	65°30'E
Kara, r., Russia	180	68°30'N	65°20'E
Karabalā', Iraq (kŭr'bá-lä)	198	32°31'N	43°58'E
Karabanovo, Russia (kä'rá-bá-nō-vô)	176	56°19'N	38°43'E
Karabash, Russia (kó-rá-bäsh')	186a	55°27'N	60°14'E
Kara-Bogaz-Gol, Zaliv, b., Turkmen. (ká-rä' bŭ-gäs')	183	41°30'N	53°40'E
Karachay-Cherkessia, prov., Russia	182	44°00'N	42°00'E
Karachev, Russia (ká-rá-chôf')	180	53°08'N	34°54'E
Karāchi, Pak.	199	24°59'N	68°56'E
Karaganda see Qaraghandy, Kaz.	183	49°42'N	73°18'E
Karaidel', Russia (kä'rī-dĕl)	186a	55°52'N	56°54'E
Karakoram Pass, p., Asia	199	35°35'N	77°45'E
Karakoram Range, mts., India (kä'rä kō'rōm)	199	35°24'N	76°38'E
Karakorum, hist., Mong.	204	47°25'N	102°22'E
Kara-Kum, des., Turkmen.	183	40°00'N	57°00'E

ng-sing; ŋ-baŋk; N-nasalized n; nŏd; cŏmmit; ōld; ôbey; ôrder; oi-boil; fōōd; ò-as oo in foot; ou-out; s-soft; sh-dish; th-thin; pūre; ûnite; ûrn; stŭd; circŭs; ü-as in French tu; '-indeterminate vowel.

308 Kara Kum Canal – Keshan PRONOUNCING INDEX

PLACE (Pronunciation)	PAGE	LAT.	LONG.
Kara Kum Canal, can., Turkmen.	183	37°35'N	61°50'E
Karaman, Tur. (kä-rä-män')	163	37°10'N	33°00'E
Karamay, China (kär-äm-ā)	204	45°37'N	84°53'E
Karamea Bight, b., N.Z. (kà-rà-mē'à bīt)	221a	41°20'S	171°30'E
Kara Sea *see* Karskoye More, sea, Russia	178	74°00'N	68°00'E
Karashahr (Yanqui), China (kä-rä-shä-är) (yän-chyē)	204	42°14'N	86°28'E
Karatsu, Japan (kä'rà-tsōō)	211	33°28'N	129°59'E
Karaul, Russia (kä-rä-ōl')	184	70°13'N	83°46'E
Karawanken, mts., Eur.	168	46°32'N	14°07'E
Karcag, Hung. (kär'tsäg)	169	47°18'N	20°58'E
Kárditsa, Grc.	175	39°23'N	21°57'E
Kärdla, Est. (kĕrd'là)	167	58°59'N	22°44'E
Karelia, prov., Russia	184	62°30'N	32°35'E
Karema, Tan.	232	6°49'S	30°26'E
Kargat, Russia (kär-gät')	178	55°17'N	80°07'E
Karghalik *see* Yecheng, China	204	37°54'N	77°25'E
Kargopol', Russia (kär-gō-pōl'')	178	61°30'N	38°50'E
Kariba, Lake, res., Afr.	232	17°15'S	27°55'E
Karibib, Nmb. (kär'á-bīb)	232	21°55'S	15°50'E
Kārikāl, India (kä-rē-käl')	203	10°58'N	79°49'E
Karimata, Kepulauan, is., Indon. (kä-rē-mä'tà)	212	1°08'S	108°10'E
Karimata, Selat, strt., Indon.	212	1°00'S	107°10'E
Karimun Besar, i., Indon.	197b	1°10'N	103°28'E
Karimunjawa, Kepulauan, is., Indon. (kä'rē-mōōn-yä'vä)	212	5°36'S	110°15'E
Karin, Som. (kär'ĭn)	238a	10°43'N	45°50'E
Karkar Island, i., Pap. N. Gui. (kär'kär)	213	4°50'S	146°45'E
Karkheh, r., Iran	198	32°45'N	47°50'E
Karkinits'ka zatoka, b., Ukr.	177	45°50'N	32°45'E
Karlivka, Ukr.	177	49°26'N	35°08'E
Karlobag, Cro. (kär-lō-bäg')	174	44°30'N	15°03'E
Karlovac, Cro. (kär'lô-váts)	163	45°29'N	15°16'E
Karlovo, Blg. (kär'lô-vō)	175	42°39'N	24°48'E
Karlovy Vary, Czech Rep. (kär'lô-vē vä'rē)	161	50°13'N	12°53'E
Karlshamn, Swe. (kärls'häm)	166	56°11'N	14°50'E
Karlskrona, Swe. (kärls'krō-nä)	160	56°10'N	15°33'E
Karlsruhe, Ger. (kärls'rōō-ĕ)	161	49°00'N	8°23'E
Karlstad, Swe. (kärl'städ)	154	59°25'N	13°28'E
Karluk, Ak., U.S. (kär'lŭk)	103	57°30'N	154°22'W
Karmøy, i., Nor. (kärm-ûe)	166	59°14'N	5°00'E
Karnataka, state, India	199	14°55'N	75°00'E
Karnobat, Blg. (kär-nô'bät)	175	42°39'N	26°59'E
Karonga, Mwi. (kà-rōŋ'gà)	232	9°52'S	33°57'E
Kárpathos, i., Grc.	163	35°34'N	27°26'E
Karpinsk, Russia (kär'pĭnsk)	186a	59°46'N	60°00'E
Kars, Tur. (kärs)	198	40°35'N	43°00'E
Kārsava, Lat. (kär'sä-vä)	167	56°46'N	27°39'E
Karshi, Uzb. (kär'shē)	183	38°30'N	66°08'E
Karskiye Vorota, Proliv, strt., Russia	178	70°30'N	58°07'E
Karskoye More (Kara Sea), sea, Russia	178	74°00'N	68°00'E
Kartaly, Russia (kár'tá lê)	178	53°05'N	60°40'E
Karunagapalli, India	203	9°09'N	76°34'E
Karvina, Czech Rep.	169	49°50'N	18°30'E
Kasai (Cassai), r., Afr.	232	3°45'S	19°10'E
Kasama, Zam. (kà-sä'mà)	232	10°13'S	31°12'E
Kasanga, Tan. (kà-säŋ'gà)	232	8°28'S	31°09'E
Kasaoka, Japan (kä'sà-ō'kà)	211	34°33'N	133°29'E
Kasba-Tadla, Mor. (käs'bà-täd'là)	230	32°37'N	5°57'W
Kasempa, Zam. (kà-sĕm'pà)	232	13°27'S	25°50'E
Kasenga, D.R.C. (kà-seŋ'gà)	232	10°22'S	28°38'E
Kasese, D.R.C.	237	1°38'S	27°07'E
Kasese, Ug.	237	0°10'N	30°05'E
Kāshān, Iran (kä-shän')	198	33°52'N	51°15'E
Kashgar *see* Kashi, China	204	39°29'N	76°00'E
Kashi (Kashgar), China (kä-shr) (käsh-gär)	204	39°29'N	76°00'E
Kashihara, Japan (kä'shē-hä'rä)	211b	34°31'N	135°48'E
Kashiji Plain, pl., Zam.	236	13°25'S	22°30'E
Kashin, Russia (kä-shēn')	176	57°20'N	37°38'E
Kashira, Russia (kä-shē'rà)	176	54°49'N	38°11'E
Kashiwa, Japan (kä'shē-wä)	211a	35°51'N	139°58'E
Kashiwara, Japan	211b	34°35'N	135°38'E
Kashiwazaki, Japan (kä'shē-wä-zä'kē)	210	37°06'N	138°17'E
Kāshmar, Iran	201	35°12'N	58°27'E
Kashmir *see* Jammu and Kashmir, state, India	199	34°30'N	76°00'E
Kashmor, Pak.	202	28°33'N	69°34'E
Kashtak, Russia (käsh'ták)	186a	55°18'N	61°25'E
Kasimov, Russia (kà-sē'môf)	180	54°56'N	41°23'E
Kaskanak, Ak., U.S. (kăs-kă'năk)	103	60°00'N	158°00'W
Kaskaskia, r., Il., U.S. (kăs-kăs'kĭ-à)	108	39°10'N	88°50'W
Kaskattama, r., Can. (kăs-kă-tä'mà)	97	56°28'N	90°55'W
Kaskö (Kaskinen), Fin. (käs'kû) (käs'kē-nĕn)	167	62°24'N	21°18'E
Kasli, Russia (käs'lĭ)	180	55°53'N	60°46'E
Kasongo, D.R.C. (kä-sōŋ'gō)	232	4°31'S	26°42'E
Kásos, i., Grc.	163	35°20'N	26°55'E
Kaspiysk, Russia	182	42°52'N	47°38'E
Kassándras, Kólpos, b., Grc.	175	40°10'N	23°35'E
Kassel, Ger. (käs'ĕl)	161	51°19'N	9°30'E
Kasson, Mn., U.S. (kăs'ŭn)	113	44°01'N	92°45'W
Kastamonu, Tur. (kä-stá-mō'nōō)	198	41°20'N	33°50'E
Kastoría, Grc. (kás-tō'rĭ-à)	163	40°28'N	21°17'E
Kasūr, Pak.	202	31°10'N	74°29'E
Kataba, Zam.	237	16°05'S	25°10'E
Katahdin, Mount, mtn., Me., U.S. (kà-tä'dĭn)	100	45°56'N	68°57'W
Katanga, hist. reg., D.R.C. (kà-täŋ'gà)	232	8°30'S	25°00'E
Katanning, Austl. (kà-tăn'ĭng)	218	33°45'S	117°45'E
Katav-Ivanovsk, Russia (kä'tăf ĭ-vä'nôfsk)	186a	54°46'N	58°13'E
Kateninskiy, Russia (kátyĕ'nĭs-kĭ)	186a	53°12'N	61°05'E
Kateríni, Grc.	175	40°18'N	22°36'E
Katete, Zam.	237	14°05'S	32°07'E
Katherine, Austl. (kăth'ĕr-ĭn)	218	14°15'S	132°20'E
Kāthiāwār, pen., India (kä'tyà-wär')	199	22°10'N	70°20'E
Kathmandu, Nepal (kät-män-dōō')	199	27°49'N	85°21'E
Kathryn, Can. (kăth'rĭn)	102e	51°13'N	113°42'W
Kathryn, Ca., U.S.	117a	33°42'N	117°45'W
Katihār, India	202	25°39'N	87°39'E
Katiola, C. Iv.	234	8°08'N	5°06'W
Katmai National Park, rec., Ak., U.S. (kăt'mī)	106a	58°38'N	155°00'W
Katompi, D.R.C.	237	6°11'S	26°20'E
Katopa, D.R.C.	237	2°45'S	25°06'E
Katowice, Pol.	154	50°15'N	19°00'E
Katrineholm, Swe. (kà-trē'nĕ-hōlm)	166	59°01'N	16°10'E
Katsbakhskiy, Russia (kàts-bäk'skĭ)	186a	52°57'N	59°37'E
Katsina, Nig. (kät'sē-nà)	230	13°00'N	7°32'E
Katsina Ala, Nig.	230	7°10'N	9°17'E
Katsura, r., Japan (kä'tsō-rä)	211b	34°55'N	135°43'E
Katta-Kurgan, Uzb. (kà-tà-kòr-gän')	183	39°45'N	66°42'E
Kattegat, strt., Eur. (kăt'ĕ-gät)	156	56°57'N	11°25'E
Katumba, D.R.C.	237	7°45'S	25°18'E
Katun', r., Russia (kà-tōn')	184	51°30'N	86°18'E
Katwijk aan Zee, Neth.	159a	52°12'N	4°23'E
Kauai, i., Hi., U.S.	106c	22°09'N	159°15'W
Kauai Channel, strt., Hi., U.S. (kä-ōō-ä'ē)	106c	21°35'N	158°52'W
Kaufbeuren, Ger. (kouf'boi-rĕn)	168	47°52'N	10°38'E
Kaufman, Tx., U.S. (kôf'măn)	123	32°36'N	96°18'W
Kaukauna, Wi., U.S. (kô-kô'nă)	113	44°17'N	88°15'W
Kaulakahi Channel, strt., Hi., U.S. (kä'ōō-lá-kä'hē)	126a	22°00'N	159°55'W
Kaunakakai, Hi., U.S. (kä'ōō-nà-kä'kĭ)	126a	21°06'N	156°59'W
Kaunas, Lith. (kou'nàs) (kôv'nô)	178	54°42'N	23°54'E
Kaura Namoda, Nig.	230	12°35'N	6°35'E
Kavála, Grc. (kä-vä'lä)	163	40°55'N	24°24'E
Kavieng, Pap. N. Gui. (kä-vē-ĕng')	213	2°44'S	151°02'E
Kavīr, Dasht-e, des., Iran (dŭsht-ē-ka-vēr')	198	34°41'N	53°30'E
Kawagoe, Japan (kä-wä-gō'å)	211	35°55'N	139°29'E
Kawaguchi, Japan (kä-wä-gōō-chē)	211a	35°48'N	139°44'E
Kawaikini, mtn., Hi., U.S. (kä-wä'ē-kĭ-nĭ)	126a	22°05'N	159°33'W
Kawanishi, Japan (kä-wä'nē-shē)	211b	34°49'N	135°26'E
Kawasaki, Japan (kä-wä-sä'kē)	210	35°32'N	139°43'E
Kaxgar, r., China	204	39°30'N	75°00'E
Kaya, Burkina (kä'yä)	230	13°05'N	1°05'W
Kayan, r., Indon.	212	1°45'N	115°38'E
Kaycee, Wy., U.S. (kā-sē')	115	43°43'N	106°38'W
Kayes, Mali (kāz)	230	14°27'N	11°26'W
Kayseri, Tur. (kī'sĕ-rē)	198	38°45'N	35°20'E
Kazach'ye, Russia	179	70°46'N	135°47'E
Kazakhstan, nation, Asia	178	48°45'N	59°00'E
Kazan', Russia (kà-zän')	178	55°50'N	49°18'E
Kazanka, Ukr. (kà-zän'kà)	177	47°49'N	32°50'E
Kazanlŭk, Blg. (kà'zàn-lĕk)	175	42°47'N	25°23'E
Kazbek, Gora, mtn. (káz-bĕk')	181	42°42'N	44°31'E
Kāzerūn, Iran	198	29°37'N	51°44'E
Kazincbarcika, Hung. (kô'zĭnts-bôr-tsĭ-ko)	169	48°15'N	20°39'E
Kazungula, Zam.	237	17°45'S	25°20'E
Kazusa Kameyama, Japan (kä-zōō-sä kä-mā'yä-mä)	211a	35°14'N	140°06'E
Kazym, r., Russia (kä-zēm')	184	63°30'N	67°41'E
Kéa, i., Grc.	175	37°36'N	24°13'E
Kealaikahiki Channel, strt., Hi., U.S. (kä-ä'lä-ē-kä-hē'kē)	126a	20°38'N	157°00'W
Keansburg, N.J., U.S. (kēnz'bûrg)	110a	40°26'N	74°08'W
Kearney, Ne., U.S. (kär'nĭ)	112	40°42'N	99°05'W
Kearny, N.J., U.S.	110a	40°46'N	74°09'W
Keasey, Or., U.S. (kēz'ĭ)	116c	45°51'N	123°20'W
Kebnekaise, mtn., Swe. (kĕp'nĕ-kà-ēs'ĕ)	156	67°53'N	18°10'E
Kecskemét, Hung. (kĕch'kĕ-māt)	163	46°52'N	19°42'E
Kedah, hist. reg., Malay. (kä'dä)	212	6°00'N	100°31'E
Kédainiai, Lith. (kē-dī'nĭ-ī)	167	55°16'N	23°58'E
Kedgwick, Can. (kĕdj'wĭk)	100	47°39'N	67°21'W
Keenbrook, Ca., U.S. (kēn'brŏk)	117a	34°16'N	117°29'W
Keene, N.H., U.S. (kēn)	109	42°55'N	72°15'W
Keetmanshoop, Nmb. (kāt'mans-hōp)	232	26°30'S	18°05'E
Keet Seel Ruin, Az., U.S. (kēt sēl)	119	36°46'N	110°32'W
Keewatin, Mn., U.S. (kē-wä'tĭn)	113	47°24'N	93°03'W
Kefallonía, i., Grc.	163	38°08'N	20°58'E
Keffi, Nig. (kĕf'ē)	230	8°51'N	7°52'E
Ke Ga, Mui, c., Viet.	212	12°58'N	109°50'E
Kei, r., Afr. (kā)	233c	32°57'S	26°50'E
Keila, Est. (kā'là)	167	59°19'N	24°25'E
Keilor, Austl.	217a	37°43'S	144°50'E
Kei Mouth, S. Afr.	233c	32°40'S	28°23'E
Keiskammahoek, S. Afr. (kās'kämä-hōōk')	233c	32°42'S	27°11'E
Kéita, Bahr, r., Chad	235	9°30'N	19°17'E
Keitele, l., Fin. (kā'tĕ-lĕ)	167	62°50'N	25°40'E
Kekaha, Hi., U.S.	126a	21°57'N	159°42'W
Kelafo, Eth.	238a	5°40'N	44°00'E
Kelang, Malay.	212	3°20'N	101°27'E
Kelang, r., Malay.	197b	3°00'N	101°40'E
Kelkit, r., Tur.	163	40°38'N	37°03'E
Keller, Tx., U.S. (kĕl'ĕr)	117c	32°56'N	97°15'W
Kellinghusen, Ger. (kĕ'lĕng-hōō-zĕn)	159c	53°57'N	9°43'E
Kellogg, Id., U.S. (kĕl'ŏg)	114	47°32'N	116°07'W
Kelme', Lith. (kĕl-må)	167	55°36'N	22°53'E
Kélo, Chad	235	9°19'N	15°48'E
Kelowna, Can.	90	49°53'N	119°29'W
Kelsey Bay, Can. (kĕl'sē)	94	50°24'N	125°57'W
Kelso, Wa., U.S.	116c	46°09'N	122°54'W
Keluang, Malay.	197b	2°01'N	103°19'E
Kem', Russia (kĕm)	178	65°00'N	34°48'E
Kemah, Tx., U.S. (kē'mà)	123a	29°32'N	95°01'W
Kemerovo, Russia	178	55°31'N	86°05'E
Kemi, Fin. (kā'mē)	160	65°48'N	24°38'E
Kemi, r., Fin.	160	67°02'N	27°50'E
Kemigawa, Japan (kĕ'mē-gä'wä)	211a	35°38'N	140°07'E
Kemijarvi, Fin. (kā'mē-yĕr-vē)	160	66°48'N	27°21'E
Kemi-joki, l., Fin.	160	66°37'N	28°13'E
Kemmerer, Wy., U.S. (kĕm'ĕr-ĕr)	115	41°48'N	110°36'W
Kemp, l., Tx., U.S. (kĕmp)	120	33°55'N	99°22'W
Kempen, Ger. (kĕm'pĕn)	171c	51°22'N	6°25'E
Kempsey, Austl. (kĕmp'sē)	219	30°59'S	152°50'E
Kempt, l., Can. (kĕmpt)	99	47°28'N	74°00'W
Kempten, Ger. (kĕmp'tĕn)	161	47°44'N	10°17'E
Kempton Park, S. Afr. (kĕmp'tŏn pärk)	238c	26°07'S	28°29'E
Ken, r., India	202	25°00'N	79°55'E
Kenai, Ak., U.S. (kĕ-nī')	103	60°38'N	151°18'W
Kenai Fjords National Park, rec., Ak., U.S.	103	59°45'N	150°00'W
Kenai Mountains, mts., Ak., U.S.	103	60°00'N	150°00'W
Kenai Pen, Ak., U.S.	103	64°40'N	150°18'W
Kendal, S. Afr.	238c	26°03'S	28°58'E
Kendal, Eng., U.K. (kĕn'dăl)	164	54°20'N	1°48'W
Kendallville, In., U.S. (kĕn'dăl-vĭl)	108	41°25'N	85°20'W
Kenedy, Tx., U.S. (kĕn'ĕ-dĭ)	123	28°49'N	97°50'W
Kenema, S.L.	234	7°52'N	11°12'W
Kenitra, Mor. (kĕ-nē'trà)	162	34°21'N	6°34'W
Kenmare, N.D., U.S. (kĕn-mâr')	112	48°41'N	102°05'W
Kenmore, N.Y., U.S. (kĕn'mōr)	111c	42°58'N	78°53'W
Kennebec, r., Me., U.S. (kĕn-ē-bĕk')	100	44°23'N	69°48'W
Kennebunk, Me., U.S. (kĕn-ē-buŋk')	100	43°24'N	70°33'W
Kennedale, Tx., U.S. (kĕn'-ē-dāl)	117c	32°38'N	97°13'W
Kennedy, Cape *see* Canaveral, Cape, c., Fl., U.S.	107	28°30'N	80°23'W
Kennedy, Mount, mtn., Can.	103	60°25'N	138°50'W
Kenner, La., U.S. (kĕn'ĕr)	123	29°58'N	90°15'W
Kennett, Mo., U.S. (kĕn'ĕt)	121	36°14'N	90°01'W
Kennewick, Wa., U.S. (kĕn'ē-wĭk)	114	46°12'N	119°06'W
Kenney Dam, dam, Can.	94	53°37'N	124°58'W
Kennydale, Wa., U.S. (kĕn-nē'dāl)	116a	47°31'N	122°12'W
Kénogami, Can. (kĕn-ŏ'gä-mē)	91	48°26'N	71°14'W
Kenogamissi Lake, l., Can.	98	48°15'N	81°31'W
Keno Hill, Can.	103	63°58'N	135°18'W
Kenora, Can. (kē-nō'rà)	91	49°47'N	94°29'W
Kenosha, Wi., U.S. (kē-nō'shà)	105	42°34'N	87°50'W
Kenova, W.V., U.S. (kē-nō'và)	108	38°20'N	82°35'W
Kensico Reservoir, res., N.Y., U.S. (kĕn'sĭ-kō)	110a	41°08'N	73°45'W
Kent, Oh., U.S. (kĕnt)	108	41°05'N	81°20'W
Kent, Wa., U.S.	116a	47°23'N	122°14'W
Kentani, S. Afr. (kĕnt-änĭ')	233c	32°31'S	28°19'E
Kentland, In., U.S. (kĕnt'lănd)	108	40°50'N	87°25'W
Kenton, Oh., U.S. (kĕn'tŭn)	108	40°40'N	83°35'W
Kent Peninsula, pen., Can.	92	68°28'N	108°10'W
Kentucky, state, U.S. (kĕn-tŭk'ĭ)	105	37°30'N	87°35'W
Kentucky, res., U.S.	107	36°20'N	88°50'W
Kentucky, r., Ky., U.S.	107	38°15'N	85°01'W
Kentwood, La., U.S. (kĕnt'wŏd)	123	30°56'N	90°31'W
Kenya, nation, Afr. (kēn'yà)	232	1°00'N	36°53'E
Kenya, Mount (Kirinyaga), mtn., Kenya	233	0°10'S	37°20'E
Kenyon, Mn., U.S. (kĕn'yŭn)	113	44°15'N	92°58'W
Keokuk, Ia., U.S. (kē'ō-kŭk)	105	40°24'N	91°34'W
Keoma, Can. (kē-ō'mà)	102e	51°13'N	113°39'W
Kepenkeck Lake, l., Can.	101	48°13'N	54°45'W
Kępno, Pol. (kăŋ'pnō)	169	51°17'N	17°59'E
Kerala, state, India	199	16°38'N	76°00'E
Kerang, Austl. (kē-răng')	219	35°32'S	143°58'E
Kerch, Ukr.	178	45°20'N	36°26'E
Kerchenskiy Proliv, strt., Eur. (kĕr-chĕn'skĭ prô'lĭf)	177	45°08'N	36°35'E
Kerempe Burun, c., Tur.	163	42°00'N	33°20'E
Keren, Erit.	231	15°46'N	38°28'E
Kerguélen, Îles, is., Afr. (kĕr'gå-lĕn)	3	49°50'S	69°30'E
Kericho, Kenya	237	0°22'S	35°17'E
Kerinci, Gunung, mtn., Indon.	212	1°45'S	101°18'E
Keriya *see* Yutian, China	204	36°55'N	81°39'E
Keriya, r., China (kē'rē-yä)	204	37°13'N	81°59'E
Kerkebet, Erit.	200	16°18'N	37°24'E
Kerkenna, Îles, i., Tun. (kĕr'kĕn-nä)	230	34°49'N	11°37'E
Kerki, Turkmen. (kĕr'kē)	183	37°52'N	65°15'E
Kérkyra, Grc.	163	39°36'N	19°56'E
Kérkyra, i., Grc.	162	39°33'N	19°36'E
Kermadec Islands, is., N.Z. (kĕr-măd'ĕk)	3	30°30'S	177°00'E
Kermān, Iran (kĕr-män')	198	30°23'N	57°08'E
Kermānshāh *see* Bakhtarān, Iran	198	34°01'N	47°00'E
Kern, r., Ca., U.S.	118	35°31'N	118°37'W
Kern, South Fork, r., Ca., U.S.	118	35°40'N	118°15'W
Kerpen, Ger. (kĕr'pĕn)	171c	50°52'N	6°42'E
Kerrobert, Can.	96	51°53'N	109°13'W
Kerrville, Tx., U.S. (kûr'vĭl)	122	30°02'N	99°07'W
Kerulen, r., Asia (kĕr'ōō-lĕn)	205	47°52'N	113°22'E
Kesagami Lake, l., Can.	99	50°23'N	80°15'W
Keşan, Tur. (kĕ'shàn)	175	40°50'N	26°37'E
Keshan, China (kŭ-shän)	205	48°00'N	126°30'E

ăt; fĭnăl; rāte; senåte; ärm; åsk; sofá; fâre; ch-choose; dh-as th in other; bē; ēvent; bĕt; recĕnt; cratĕr; g-gō; gh-guttural g; bĭt; ĭ-short neutral; rīde; κ-guttural k as ch in German ich;

PRONOUNCING INDEX

Kesour – Kitgum 309

PLACE (Pronunciation)	PAGE	LAT.	LONG.
Kesour, Monts des, mts., Alg.	162	32°51'N	0°30'W
Kestell, S. Afr. (kĕs'tĕl)	238c	28°19'S	28°43'E
Keszthely, Hung. (kĕst'hĕl-lĭ)	169	46°46'N	17°12'E
Ket', r., Russia (kyĕt)	184	58°30'N	84°15'E
Keta, Ghana	230	6°00'N	1°00'E
Ketamputih, Indon.	197b	1°25'N	102°19'E
Ketapang, Indon. (kĕ-tȧ-päng')	212	2°00'S	109°57'E
Ketchikan, Ak., U.S. (kĕch-ĭ-kăn')	106a	55°21'N	131°35'W
Kętrzyn, Pol. (käŋ't'r-zĭn)	169	54°04'N	21°24'E
Kettering, Eng., U.K. (kĕt'ẽr-ĭng)	158a	52°23'N	0°43'W
Kettering, Oh., U.S.	108	39°40'N	84°15'W
Kettle, r., Can.	95	49°40'N	119°00'W
Kettle, r., Mn., U.S. (kĕt''l)	113	46°20'N	92°57'W
Kettwig, Ger. (kĕt'vēg)	171c	51°22'N	6°56'E
Kęty, Pol. (kän tĭ)	169	49°54'N	19°16'E
Ketzin, Ger. (kĕ'tzēn)	159b	52°29'N	12°51'E
Keuka, l., N.Y., U.S. (kē-ū'kȧ)	109	42°30'N	77°10'W
Kevelaer, Ger. (kĕ'fĕ-lär)	171c	51°35'N	6°15'E
Kew, Austl.	217a	37°49'S	145°02'E
Kewanee, Il., U.S. (kē-wä'nē)	113	41°15'N	89°55'W
Kewaunee, Wi., U.S. (kē-wô'nē)	113	44°27'N	87°33'W
Keweenaw Bay, b., Mi., U.S. (kē'wē-nô)	113	46°59'N	88°15'W
Keweenaw Peninsula, pen., Mi., U.S.	113	47°28'N	88°12'W
Keya Paha, r., S.D., U.S. (kē-yȧ pä'hä)	112	43°11'N	100°10'W
Key Largo, i., Fl., U.S.	125a	25°11'N	80°15'W
Keyport, N.J., U.S. (kē'pōrt)	110a	40°26'N	74°12'W
Keyport, Wa., U.S.	116a	47°42'N	122°38'W
Keyser, W.V., U.S. (kī'sẽr)	109	39°25'N	79°00'W
Key West, Fl., U.S. (kē wĕst')	105	24°31'N	81°47'W
Kežmarok, Slvk. (kĕzh'mȧ-rôk)	169	49°10'N	20°27'E
Khabarovo, Russia (kŭ-bär-ôvô)	178	69°31'N	60°41'E
Khabarovsk, Russia (kä-bä'rôfsk)	179	48°35'N	135°12'E
Khakassia, prov., Russia	184	52°32'N	89°33'E
Khālāpur, India	203b	18°48'N	73°17'E
Khalkidhiki, pen., Grc.	175	40°30'N	23°18'E
Khal'mer-Yu, Russia (kŭl-myĕr'-yōō')	178	67°52'N	64°25'E
Khalturin, Russia (käl'tōō-rēn)	180	58°28'N	49°00'E
Khambhāt, Gulf of, b., India	199	21°20'N	72°27'E
Khammam, India	203	17°09'N	80°13'E
Khānābād, Afg.	202	36°43'N	69°11'E
Khānaqīn, Iraq	201	34°21'N	45°22'E
Khandwa, India	202	21°53'N	76°22'E
Khaníon, Kólpos, b., Grc.	174a	35°35'N	23°55'E
Khanka, l., Asia (kän'kȧ)	179	45°09'N	133°28'E
Khānpur, Pak.	202	28°42'N	70°42'E
Khanty-Mansiysk, Russia (kŭn-te'mŭn-sēsk')	178	61°02'N	69°01'E
Khān Yūnus, Gaza	197a	31°21'N	34°19'E
Kharagpur, India (kŭ-rŭg'pòr)	199	22°26'N	87°21'E
Kharkiv, Ukr.	178	50°00'N	36°10'E
Kharkiv, prov., Ukr.	177	49°33'N	35°55'E
Kharkov see Kharkiv, Ukr.	178	50°00'N	36°10'E
Kharlovka, Russia	180	68°47'N	37°20'E
Kharmanli, Blg. (kȧr-män'lē)	175	41°54'N	25°55'E
Khartoum, Sudan	231	15°34'N	32°36'E
Khasavyurt, Russia	182	43°15'N	46°37'E
Khāsh, Iran	198	28°08'N	61°08'E
Khāsh, r., Afg.	198	32°30'N	64°27'E
Khasi Hills, hills, India	199	25°38'N	91°55'E
Khaskovo, Blg. (kȧs'kō-vō)	163	41°56'N	25°32'E
Khatanga, Russia (kȧ-tän'gȧ)	179	71°48'N	101°47'E
Khatangskiy Zaliv, b., Russia (kä-täŋ'g-skē)	179	73°45'N	108°30'E
Khaybār, Sau. Ar.	198	25°45'N	39°28'E
Kherson, Ukr. (kĕr-sôn')	181	46°38'N	32°34'E
Kherson, prov., Ukr.	177	46°32'N	32°55'E
Khiitola, Russia (khē'tō-lȧ)	167	61°14'N	29°40'E
Khimki, Russia (kēm'kĭ)	186b	55°54'N	37°27'E
Khmel'nyts'kyi, Ukr.	181	49°29'N	26°54'E
Khmel'nyts'kyy, prov., Ukr.	177	49°27'N	26°30'E
Khmil'nyk, Ukr.	177	49°34'N	27°58'E
Kholm, Russia (kôlm)	176	57°09'N	31°07'E
Kholmsk, Russia (kŭlmsk)	179	47°09'N	142°33'E
Khomeynīshahr, Iran	201	32°41'N	51°31'E
Khon Kaen, Thai.	212	16°37'N	102°41'E
Khopër, r., Russia (kô'pẽr)	181	52°00'N	43°00'E
Khor, Russia (kôr')	210	47°50'N	134°52'E
Khor, r., Russia	210	47°23'N	135°20'E
Khóra Sfakión, Grc.	174a	35°12'N	24°10'E
Khorog, Taj.	183	37°30'N	71°36'E
Khorol, Ukr. (kô'rôl)	177	49°48'N	33°17'E
Khorol, r., Ukr.	177	49°50'N	33°21'E
Khorramābād, Iran	201	33°30'N	48°20'E
Khorramshahr, Iran (kô-ram'shär)	198	30°36'N	48°15'E
Khot'kovo, Russia	186b	56°15'N	38°00'E
Khotyn, Ukr.	181	48°29'N	26°32'E
Khoyniki, Bela.	177	51°54'N	30°00'E
Khudzhand, Taj.	183	40°17'N	69°37'E
Khulna, Bngl.	199	22°50'N	89°38'E
Khūryān Mūryān, is., Oman	198	17°27'N	56°02'E
Khust, Ukr. (kōst)	169	48°10'N	23°18'E
Khvalynsk, Russia (kvȧ-lĭnsk')	181	52°30'N	48°00'E
Khvoy, Iran	198	38°32'N	45°01'E
Khyber Pass, p., Asia (kī'bẽr)	199	34°28'N	71°18'E
Kialwe, D.R.C.	237	9°22'S	27°08'E
Kiambi, D.R.C. (kyäm'bē)	232	7°20'S	28°01'E
Kiamichi, r., Ok., U.S. (kyȧ-mē'chē)	121	34°31'N	95°34'W
Kianta, l., Fin. (kyän'tȧ)	180	65°00'N	28°15'E
Kibenga, D.R.C.	236	7°55'S	17°35'E
Kibiti, Tan.	237	7°44'S	38°57'E
Kibombo, D.R.C.	232	3°54'S	25°55'E
Kibondo, Tan.	237	3°35'S	30°42'E
Kičevo, Mac. (kē'chĕ-vô)	175	41°30'N	20°59'E

PLACE (Pronunciation)	PAGE	LAT.	LONG.
Kickapoo, r., Wi., U.S. (kĭk'ȧ-pōō)	113	43°20'N	90°55'W
Kicking Horse Pass, p., Can.	95	51°25'N	116°10'W
Kidal, Mali (kē-dȧl')	230	18°33'N	1°00'E
Kidderminster, Eng., U.K. (kĭd'ẽr-mĭn-stẽr)	158a	52°23'N	2°14'W
Kidd's Beach, S. Afr. (kĭdz)	233c	33°09'S	27°43'E
Kidsgrove, Eng., U.K. (kĭdz'grōv)	158a	53°05'N	2°15'W
Kiel, Ger. (kēl)	154	54°19'N	10°08'E
Kiel, Wi., U.S.	113	43°52'N	88°04'W
Kiel Bay, b., Ger.	168	54°33'N	10°19'E
Kiel Canal see Nord-Ostsee Kanal, can., Ger.	168	54°03'N	9°23'E
Kielce, Pol. (kyĕl'tsĕ)	169	50°50'N	20°41'E
Kieldrecht, Bel. (kēl'drĕkt)	159a	51°17'N	4°09'E
Kiev (Kyïv), Ukr.	178	50°27'N	30°30'E
Kiffa, Maur. (kēf'ȧ)	230	16°37'N	11°24'W
Kigali, Rw. (kē-gä'lē)	232	1°59'S	30°05'E
Kigoma, Tan. (kē-gō'mä)	232	4°57'S	29°38'E
Kii-Suido, strt., Japan (kē sōō-ē'dō)	210	33°53'N	134°55'E
Kikaiga, i., Japan	210	28°25'N	130°10'E
Kikinda, Yugo. (kē'kēn-dä)	175	45°49'N	20°30'E
Kikládes, is., Grc.	162	37°30'N	24°45'E
Kikwit, D.R.C. (kē'kwēt)	232	5°02'S	18°49'E
Kil, Swe. (kēl)	166	59°30'N	13°15'E
Kilauea, Hi., U.S. (kē-lä-ōō-ā'ä)	126a	22°12'N	159°25'W
Kilauea Crater, depr., Hi., U.S.	126a	19°28'N	155°18'W
Kilbuck Mountains, mts., Ak., U.S. (kĭl-bŭk)	103	60°05'N	160°00'W
Kilchu, Kor., N. (kĭl'chò)	210	40°59'N	129°23'E
Kildare, Ire. (kĭl-dâr')	164	53°09'N	7°05'W
Kilembe, D.R.C.	236	5°42'S	19°55'E
Kilgore, Tx., U.S.	123	32°23'N	94°53'W
Kilia, Ukr.	177	45°28'N	29°17'E
Kilifi, Kenya	237	3°38'S	39°51'E
Kilimanjaro, mtn., Tan. (kyl-ē-măn-jä'rō)	233	3°09'S	37°19'E
Kilimatinde, Tan. (kĭl-ē-mä-tĭn'dȧ)	232	5°48'S	34°58'E
Kilindoni, Tan.	237	7°55'S	39°39'E
Kilingi-Nõmme, Est. (kē'lĭn-gē-nôm'mĕ)	167	58°08'N	25°03'E
Kilis, Tur. (kē'lĭs)	163	36°50'N	37°20'E
Kilkenny, Ire. (kĭl-kĕn-ĭ)	161	52°40'N	7°30'W
Kilkis, Grc. (kĭl'kĭs)	175	40°59'N	22°51'E
Killala, Ire. (kĭ-lä'lȧ)	164	54°11'N	9°10'W
Killarney, Ire.	164	52°03'N	9°05'W
Killdeer, N.D., U.S. (kĭl'dẽr)	112	47°22'N	102°45'W
Killiniq Island, i., Can.	93	60°32'N	63°56'W
Kilmarnock, Scot., U.K. (kĭl-mär'nŭk)	164	55°38'N	4°25'W
Kilrush, Ire. (kĭl'rŭsh)	164	52°40'N	9°16'W
Kilwa Kisiwani, Tan.	237	8°58'S	39°30'E
Kilwa Kivinje, Tan.	233	8°43'S	39°18'E
Kim, r., Cam.	235	5°40'N	11°17'E
Kimamba, Tan.	237	6°47'S	37°08'E
Kimba, Austl. (kĭm'bȧ)	222	33°08'S	136°25'E
Kimball, Ne., U.S. (kĭm-bál)	112	41°14'N	103°41'W
Kimball, S.D., U.S.	112	43°44'N	98°58'W
Kimberley, Can. (kĭm'bẽr-lĭ)	90	49°41'N	115°59'W
Kimberley, S. Afr.	232	28°40'S	24°50'E
Kimi, Cam.	235	6°05'N	11°30'E
Kimmirut (Lake Harbour), Can.	91	62°43'N	69°40'W
Kímolos, i., Grc. (kē'mō-lôs)	175	36°52'N	24°20'E
Kimry, Russia (kĭm'rē)	180	56°53'N	37°24'E
Kimvula, D.R.C.	236	5°44'S	15°58'E
Kinabalu, Gunong, mtn., Malay.	212	5°45'N	115°26'E
Kincardine, Can. (kĭn-kär'dĭn)	91	44°10'N	81°15'W
Kinda, D.R.C.	237	9°18'S	25°04'E
Kindanba, Congo	236	3°44'S	14°31'E
Kinder, La., U.S. (kĭn'dẽr)	123	30°30'N	92°50'W
Kindersley, Can. (kĭn'dẽrz-lē)	90	51°27'N	109°10'W
Kindia, Gui. (kĭn'dē-ȧ)	230	10°04'N	12°51'W
Kindu, D.R.C.	232	2°57'S	25°56'E
Kinel'-Cherkassy, Russia	180	53°32'N	51°32'E
Kineshma, Russia (kē-nĕsh'mȧ)	180	57°27'N	41°02'E
King, i., Austl. (kĭng)	221	39°35'S	143°40'E
Kingaroy, Austl. (kĭŋ'gă-roi)	222	26°37'S	151°50'E
King City, Can.	102d	43°56'N	79°32'W
King City, Ca., U.S. (kĭng sĭ'tĭ)	118	36°12'N	121°08'W
Kingcome Inlet, b., Can. (kĭng'kŭm)	94	50°50'N	126°10'W
Kingfisher, Ok., U.S. (kĭng'fĭsh-ẽr)	121	35°51'N	97°55'W
King George Sound, strt., Austl. (jôrj)	220	35°17'S	118°30'E
Kingisepp, Russia (kĭŋ-gē-sep')	180	59°22'N	28°38'E
King Leopold Ranges, mts., Austl. (lē'ô-pōld)	220	16°25'S	125°00'E
Kingman, Az., U.S. (kĭng'măn)	119	35°10'N	114°05'W
Kingman, Ks., U.S. (kĭng'măn)	120	37°38'N	98°07'W
Kings, r., Ca., U.S.	118	36°28'N	119°43'W
Kings Canyon National Park, rec., Ca., U.S. (kăn'yŭn)	106	36°52'N	118°53'W
Kingsclere, Eng., U.K. (kĭngs-clẽr)	158b	51°18'N	1°15'W
Kingscote, Austl. (kĭngz'kŭt)	222	35°45'S	137°32'E
King's Lynn, Eng., U.K. (kĭngz lĭn')	165	52°45'N	0°20'E
Kings Mountain, N.C., U.S.	125	35°13'N	81°30'W
Kings Norton, Eng., U.K. (nôr'tŭn)	158a	52°25'N	1°54'W
King Sound, strt., Austl.	220	16°50'S	123°35'E
Kings Park, N.Y., U.S. (kĭngz pärk)	110a	40°53'N	73°16'W
Kings Peak, mtn., Ut., U.S.	106	40°46'N	110°20'W
Kingsport, Tn., U.S. (kĭngz'pōrt)	125	36°33'N	82°36'W
Kingston, Austl. (kĭngz'tŭn)	218	37°52'S	139°52'E
Kingston, Can.	91	44°15'N	76°30'W
Kingston, Jam.	129	18°00'N	76°45'W
Kingston, N.Y., U.S.	105	42°00'N	74°00'W
Kingston, Pa., U.S.	109	41°15'N	75°50'W
Kingston, Wa., U.S.	116a	47°04'N	122°29'W
Kingston upon Hull, Eng., U.K.	154	53°45'N	0°25'W

PLACE (Pronunciation)	PAGE	LAT.	LONG.
Kingstown, St. Vin. (kĭngz'toun)	129	13°10'N	61°14'W
Kingstree, S.C., U.S. (kĭngz'trē)	125	33°30'N	79°50'W
Kingsville, Tx., U.S. (kĭngz'vĭl)	123	27°32'N	97°52'W
King William Island, i., Can. (kĭng wĭl'yăm)	92	69°25'N	97°00'W
King William's Town, S. Afr. (kĭng-wĭl'-yŭmz-toun)	233c	32°53'S	27°24'E
Kinira, r., S. Afr.	233c	30°37'S	28°52'E
Kinloch, Mo., U.S. (kĭn-lŏk)	117e	38°44'N	90°19'W
Kinnaird, Can. (kĭn-ârd')	95	49°17'N	117°39'W
Kinnairds Head, c., Scot., U.K. (kĭn-ârds'hĕd)	160	57°42'N	3°55'W
Kinomoto, Japan (kē'nō-mō'tō)	211	33°53'N	136°07'E
Kinosaki, Japan (kē'nō-sä'kē)	211	35°38'N	134°47'E
Kinshasa, D.R.C.	232	4°18'S	15°18'E
Kinsley, Ks., U.S. (kĭnz'lĭ)	120	37°55'N	99°24'W
Kinston, N.C., U.S. (kĭnz'tŭn)	125	35°15'N	77°35'W
Kintampo, Ghana (kēn-täm'pō)	230	8°03'N	1°43'W
Kintyre, pen., Scot., U.K.	164	55°50'N	5°40'W
Kiowa, Ks., U.S. (kī'ō-wȧ)	120	37°01'N	98°30'W
Kiowa, Ok., U.S.	121	34°42'N	95°53'W
Kipawa, Lac, l., Can.	99	46°55'N	79°00'W
Kipembawe, Tan. (kē-pĕm-bä'wȧ)	232	7°39'S	33°24'E
Kipengere Range, mts., Tan.	237	9°10'S	34°00'E
Kipili, Tan.	237	7°26'S	30°36'E
Kipushi, D.R.C.	237	11°46'S	27°14'E
Kirakira, Sol. Is.	214e	10°27'S	161°55'E
Kirby, Tx., U.S. (kŭr'bĭ)	117d	29°29'N	98°23'W
Kirbyville, Tx., U.S. (kŭr'bĭ-vĭl)	123	30°39'N	93°54'W
Kirenga, r., Russia (kē-rĕŋ'gȧ)	185	56°30'N	108°18'E
Kirensk, Russia (kē-rĕnsk')	179	57°47'N	108°22'E
Kirgiz Range, mts., Asia	183	42°30'N	74°00'E
Kiri, D.R.C.	236	1°27'S	19°00'E
Kiribati, nation, Oc.	3	1°30'S	173°00'E
Kirin see Chilung, Tai.	205	25°02'N	121°48'E
Kiritimati, i., Kir.	2	2°20'N	157°40'W
Kirkby, Eng., U.K.	158a	53°29'N	2°54'W
Kirkby-in-Ashfield, Eng., U.K. (kûrk'bē-ĭn-ăsh'fēld)	158a	53°06'N	1°16'W
Kirkcaldy, Scot., U.K. (kẽr-kô'dĭ)	164	56°06'N	3°15'W
Kirkenes, Nor.	160	69°40'N	30°03'E
Kirkham, Eng., U.K. (kûrk'ăm)	158a	53°47'N	2°53'W
Kirkland, Wa., U.S. (kûrk'lănd)	116a	47°41'N	122°12'W
Kirklareli, Tur. (kẽrk'lär-ĕ'lē)	163	41°44'N	27°15'E
Kirksville, Mo., U.S. (kûrks'vĭl)	105	40°12'N	92°35'W
Kirkūk, Iraq (kĭr-kōōk')	198	35°28'N	44°22'E
Kirkwall, Scot., U.K. (kûrk'wôl)	160	58°58'N	2°59'W
Kirkwood, S. Afr.	233c	33°26'S	25°24'E
Kirkwood, Mo., U.S. (kûrk'wòd)	117e	38°35'N	90°24'W
Kirn, Ger. (kērn)	168	49°47'N	7°23'E
Kirov, Russia	176	54°04'N	34°19'E
Kirov, Russia	178	58°35'N	49°35'E
Kirovakan, Arm.	182	40°48'N	44°30'E
Kirovgrad, Russia (kē-rŭ-vŭ-grad)	186a	57°26'N	60°03'E
Kirovohrad, Ukr.	181	48°33'N	32°17'E
Kirovohrad, prov., Ukr.	177	48°23'N	31°10'E
Kirovsk, Russia (kē-rôfsk')	186c	59°52'N	30°59'E
Kirovsk, Russia	178	67°40'N	33°58'E
Kirsanov, Russia (kẽr-sȧ'nôf)	181	52°40'N	42°40'E
Kırşehir, Tur. (kẽr-shĕ'hẽr)	198	39°10'N	34°00'E
Kirtachi Seybou, Niger	235	12°48'N	2°29'E
Kīrthar Range, mts., Pak. (kĭr-tŭr)	199	27°00'N	67°10'E
Kirton, Eng., U.K. (kûr'tŭn)	158a	53°29'N	0°35'W
Kiruna, Swe. (kē-rōō'nä)	160	67°49'N	20°08'E
Kirundu, D.R.C.	237	0°44'S	25°32'E
Kirwin Reservoir, res., Ks., U.S. (kûr'wĭn)	120	39°34'N	99°04'W
Kiryū, Japan	210	36°24'N	139°20'E
Kirzhach, Russia (kĕr-zhák')	176	56°08'N	38°53'E
Kisaki, Tan. (kē-sá'kē)	233	7°37'S	37°43'E
Kisangani, D.R.C.	231	0°30'N	25°12'E
Kisarazu, Japan (kē'sȧ-rȧ'zōō)	211a	35°23'N	139°55'E
Kiselëvsk, Russia (kē-sĭ-lyôfsk')	178	54°00'N	86°39'E
Kishinev see Chişinău, Mol.	178	47°02'N	28°52'E
Kishiwada, Japan (kē'shē-wä'dä)	210	34°25'N	135°18'E
Kishkino, Russia (kēsh'kĭ-nô)	186b	55°15'N	38°04'E
Kisiwani, Tan.	237	4°08'S	37°57'E
Kiska, i., Ak., U.S. (kĭs'kä)	106b	52°08'N	177°10'E
Kiskatinaw, r., Can.	95	55°10'N	120°20'W
Kiskittogisu Lake, l., Can.	97	54°05'N	99°00'W
Kiskitto Lake, l., Can. (kĭs-kĭ'tō)	97	54°16'N	98°34'W
Kiskunfélegyháza, Hung. (kĭsh'kòn-fā'lĕd-y'hä'zô)	169	46°42'N	19°52'E
Kiskunhalas, Hung. (kĭsh'kòn-hô'lôsh)	169	46°24'N	19°26'E
Kiskunmajsa, Hung. (kĭsh'kòn-mī'shô)	169	46°29'N	19°42'E
Kislovodsk, Russia	182	43°55'N	42°44'E
Kismaayo, Som.	233	0°18'S	42°30'E
Kiso-Gawa, r., Japan (kē'sō-gä'wä)	211	35°29'N	137°12'E
Kiso-Sammyaku, mts., Japan (kē'sō säm'myȧ-kōō)	211	35°47'N	137°39'E
Kíssamos, Grc.	174a	35°13'N	23°35'E
Kissidougou, Gui. (kē'sē-dōō'gōō)	230	9°11'N	10°06'W
Kissimmee, Fl., U.S. (kĭ-sĭm'ē)	125a	28°17'N	81°25'W
Kissimmee, r., Fl., U.S.	125a	27°45'N	81°07'W
Kissimmee, Lake, l., Fl., U.S.	125a	27°58'N	81°17'W
Kisujszállás, Hung.	169	47°12'N	20°47'E
Kisumu, Kenya (kē'sōō-mōō)	232	0°06'S	34°45'E
Kita, Mali (kē'tȧ)	230	13°03'N	9°29'W
Kitakami Gawa, r., Japan	210	39°20'N	141°10'E
Kitakyūshū, Japan	205	33°53'N	130°50'E
Kitale, Kenya	237	1°01'N	35°00'E
Kit Carson, Co., U.S.	120	38°46'N	102°48'W
Kitchener, Can. (kĭch'ĕ-nẽr)	91	43°25'N	80°35'W
Kitenda, D.R.C.	236	6°53'S	17°21'E
Kitgum, Ug. (kĭt'gòm)	231	3°29'N	33°04'E

310 Kitimat – Kozhikode

PRONOUNCING INDEX

PLACE (Pronunciation)	PAGE	LAT.	LONG.
Kitimat, Can. (kĭ′tĭ-măt)	90	54°03′N	128°33′W
Kitimat, r., Can.	94	53°50′N	129°00′W
Kitimat Ranges, mts., Can.	94	53°30′N	128°50′W
Kitlope, r., Can. (kĭt′lōp)	94	53°00′N	128°00′W
Kitsuki, Japan (kět′sò-kė)	211	33°24′N	131°35′E
Kittanning, Pa., U.S. (kĭ-tăn′ĭng)	109	40°50′N	79°30′W
Kittatinny Mountains, mts., N.J., U.S. (kĭ-tŭ-tĭ′nė)	110a	41°16′N	74°44′W
Kittery, Me., U.S. (kĭt′ẽr-ĭ)	100	43°07′N	70°45′W
Kittsee, Aus.	159e	48°05′N	17°05′E
Kitty Hawk, N.C., U.S. (kĭt′tė hôk)	125	36°04′N	75°42′W
Kitunda, Tan.	237	6°48′S	33°13′E
Kitwe, Zam.	237	12°49′S	28°13′E
Kitzingen, Ger. (kĭt′zĭng-ĕn)	168	49°44′N	10°08′E
Kiunga, Kenya	237	1°45′S	41°29′E
Kivu, Lac, l., Afr.	232	1°45′S	28°55′E
Kīyose, Japan	211a	35°47′N	139°32′E
Kizel, Russia (kē′zĕl)	180	59°05′N	57°42′E
Kızıl, r., Tur.	198	40°00′N	34°00′E
Kizil′skoye, Russia (kĭz′ĭl-skô-yĕ)	186a	52°43′N	58°53′E
Kizlyar, Russia (kĭz-lyär′)	181	44°00′N	46°50′E
Kizlyarskiy Zaliv, b., Russia	182	44°33′N	46°55′E
Kizu, Japan (kē′zōō)	211	34°43′N	135°49′E
Klaas Smits, r., S. Afr.	233c	31°45′S	26°33′E
Klaaswaal, Neth.	159a	51°46′N	4°25′E
Kladno, Czech Rep. (kläd′nō)	168	50°10′N	14°05′E
Klagenfurt, Aus. (klä′gĕn-fòrt)	161	46°38′N	14°19′E
Klaipéda, Lith. (klī′på-då)	180	55°43′N	21°10′E
Klamath, r., U.S.	114	41°40′N	123°25′W
Klamath Falls, Or., U.S.	104	42°13′N	121°49′W
Klamath Mountains, mts., Ca., U.S.	114	42°00′N	123°25′W
Klarälven, r., Swe.	160	60°40′N	13°00′E
Klaskanine, r., Or., U.S. (klăs′kå-nīn)	116c	46°02′N	123°43′W
Klatovy, Czech Rep. (klå′tỏ-vė)	161	49°23′N	13°18′E
Klawock, Ak., U.S. (klā′wăk)	103	55°32′N	133°10′W
Kleinmachnow, Ger. (klīn-mäκ′nō)	159b	52°22′N	13°12′E
Klerksdorp, S. Afr. (klẽrks′dôrp)	238c	26°52′S	26°40′E
Klerksraal, S. Afr. (klẽrks′kräl)	238c	26°15′N	27°10′E
Kletnya, Russia (klyĕt′nyå)	176	53°19′N	33°14′E
Kleve, Ger. (klĕ′fĕ)	168	51°47′N	6°09′E
Klickitat, r., Wa., U.S.	114	46°01′N	121°07′W
Klimovichi, Bela. (klē-mỏ-vē′chė)	176	53°37′N	31°21′E
Klimovsk, Russia (klĭ′môfsk)	186b	55°21′N	37°32′E
Klin, Russia (klĕn)	176	56°18′N	36°43′E
Klintehamn, Swe. (klēn′tē-häm)	166	57°24′N	18°14′E
Klintsy, Russia (klĭn′tsĭ)	181	52°46′N	32°14′E
Klip, r., S. Afr. (klĭp)	238c	27°18′N	29°25′E
Klipgat, S. Afr.	238c	25°26′S	27°57′E
Klippan, Swe. (klyp′pån)	166	56°08′N	13°09′E
Kłodzko, Pol. (klôd′skỏ)	168	50°26′N	16°38′E
Klondike Region, hist. reg., N.A. (klŏn′dīk)	90	64°12′N	142°38′W
Klosterfelde, Ger. (klōs′tĕr-fĕl-dĕ)	159b	52°47′N	13°29′E
Klosterneuburg, Aus. (klōs-tẽr-noi′bo͝orgh)	159e	48°19′N	16°20′E
Kluane, l., Can.	92	61°15′N	138°40′W
Kluane National Park, rec., Can.	92	60°25′N	137°53′W
Kluczbork, Pol. (klo͞och′bōrk)	169	50°59′N	18°15′E
Klyaz′ma, r., Russia (klyäz′må)	176	55°49′N	39°19′E
Klyetsk, Bela. (klĕtsk)	176	53°04′N	26°43′E
Klyuchevskaya, vol., Russia (klyo͞o-chĕfskä′yä)	179	56°13′N	160°00′E
Klyuchi, Russia (klyo͞o′chĭ)	186a	57°03′N	57°20′E
Knezha, Blg. (knyā′zhå)	163	43°27′N	24°03′E
Knife, r., N.D., U.S. (nīf)	112	47°06′N	102°33′W
Knight Inlet, b., Can. (nīt)	94	50°41′N	125°40′W
Knightstown, In., U.S. (nīts′toun)	108	39°45′N	85°30′W
Knin, Cro. (knēn)	174	44°02′N	16°14′E
Knittelfeld, Aus.	161	47°13′N	14°50′E
Knob Peak, mtn., Phil. (nŏb)	213a	12°30′N	121°20′E
Knottingley, Eng., U.K. (nŏt′ĭng-lĭ)	158a	53°42′N	1°14′W
Knox, In., U.S. (nŏks)	108	41°15′N	86°40′W
Knox, Cape, c., Can.	94	54°12′N	133°20′W
Knoxville, Ia., U.S. (nŏks′vĭl)	113	41°19′N	93°05′W
Knoxville, Tn., U.S.	105	35°58′N	83°55′W
Knutsford, Eng., U.K. (nŭts′fẽrd)	158a	53°18′N	2°22′W
Knyszyn, Pol. (knĭ′shĭn)	169	53°16′N	22°59′E
Kobayashi, Japan (kō′bå-yä′shė)	211	31°58′N	130°59′E
Kōbe, Japan (kō′bĕ)	205	34°30′N	135°10′E
Kobeliaky, Ukr.	181	49°11′N	34°12′E
København *see* Copenhagen, Den.	154	55°43′N	12°27′E
Koblenz, Ger. (kō′blĕntz)	161	50°18′N	7°36′E
Kobozha, r., Russia (kỏ-bō′zhå)	176	58°55′N	35°18′E
Kobrinskoye, Russia (kô-brĭn′skô-yĕ)	186c	59°25′N	30°07′E
Kobryn, Bela. (kō′brĕn′)	181	52°13′N	24°23′E
Kobuk, r., Ak., U.S. (kō′bŭk)	103	66°58′N	158°48′W
Kobuk Valley National Park, rec., Ak., U.S.	103	67°20′N	159°00′W
Kobuleti, Geor. (kỏ-bỏ-lyā′tė)	181	41°50′N	41°40′E
Kočani, Mac. (kô′chä-nĕ)	175	41°54′N	22°25′E
Kočevje, Slvn. (kô′chāv-ye)	174	45°38′N	14°51′E
Kocher, r., Ger. (kỏκ′ĕr)	168	49°00′N	9°52′E
Kochi, India	203	9°58′N	76°19′E
Kōchi, Japan (kō′chė)	205	33°35′N	133°32′E
Kodaira, Japan	211a	35°43′N	139°29′E
Kodiak, Ak., U.S. (kō′dyăk)	106a	57°50′N	152°30′W
Kodiak Island, i., Ak., U.S.	103	57°24′N	153°32′W
Kodok, Sudan (ko′dŏk)	231	9°57′N	32°08′E
Koforidua, Ghana (kō fỏ-rĭ-do͞o′å)	230	6°03′N	0°17′W
Kōfu, Japan (kō′fo͞o′)	210	35°41′N	138°34′E
Koga, Japan (kō′gå)	211	36°13′N	139°40′E
Kogan, r., Gui.	234	11°30′N	14°05′W
Kogane, Japan (kō′gä-nå)	211a	35°50′N	139°56′E
Koganei, Japan (kō′gä-nā)	211a	35°42′N	139°31′E
Køge, Den. (kû′gĕ)	166	55°27′N	12°09′E
Køge Bugt, b., Den.	166	55°30′N	12°25′E
Kogoni, Mali	234	14°44′N	6°02′W
Kohīma, India (kỏ-ē′må)	199	25°45′N	94°41′E
Kohyl′nyk, r., Eur.	177	46°08′N	29°10′E
Koito, r., Japan (kỏ′ė-tō)	211a	35°19′N	139°58′E
Kŏje, i., Kor., S. (kû′jĕ)	210	34°53′N	129°00′E
Kokand, Uzb. (kỏ-känt′)	183	40°27′N	71°07′E
Kokemäenjoki, r., Fin.	167	61°23′N	22°03′E
Kokhma, Russia (kôκ′må)	176	56°57′N	41°08′E
Kokkola, Fin. (kô′kỏ-lå)	160	63°47′N	22°58′E
Kokomo, In., U.S. (kō′kỏ-mỏ)	108	40°30′N	86°20′W
Koko Nor (Qinghai Hu), l., China (kō′kỏ nor) (chyĭŋ-hī ho͞o)	204	37°26′N	98°30′E
Kokopo, Pap. N. Gui. (kỏ-kỏ′pō)	213	4°25′S	152°27′E
Kökshetaū, Kaz.	183	53°15′N	69°13′E
Koksoak, r., Can. (kỏk′sỏ-ăk)	93	57°42′N	69°50′W
Kokstad, S. Afr. (kỏk′shtät)	233c	30°33′S	29°27′E
Kokubu, Japan (kō′ko͞o-bo͞o)	211	31°42′N	130°46′E
Kokuou, Japan (kỏ′ko͞o-ỏ′o͞oo)	211b	34°34′N	135°39′E
Kola Peninsula *see* Kol′skiy Poluostrov, pen., Russia	178	67°15′N	37°40′E
Kolār (Kolār Gold Fields), India (kỏl-är′)	199	13°39′N	78°33′E
Kolárvo, Slvk. (kōl-árōvō)	169	47°54′N	17°59′E
Kolbio, Kenya	237	1°10′S	41°15′E
Kol′chugino, Russia (kỏl-chò′gė-nô)	176	56°19′N	39°29′E
Kolda, Sen.	234	12°53′N	14°57′W
Kolding, Den. (kŭl′dĭng)	166	55°29′N	9°24′E
Kole, D.R.C. (kō′lå)	232	3°19′S	22°46′E
Kolguyev, i., Russia (kỏl-gò′yĕf)	178	69°00′N	49°00′E
Kolhāpur, India	203	16°48′N	74°15′E
Kolin, Czech Rep. (kō′lēn)	168	50°01′N	15°11′E
Kolkasrags, c., Lat. (kôl-käs′rågz)	167	57°46′N	22°39′E
Kolkata (Calcutta), India	199	22°32′N	88°22′E
Köln *see* Cologne, Ger.	171c	50°56′N	6°57′E
Kolno, Pol. (kôw′nỏ)	169	53°23′N	21°56′E
Koło, Pol. (kô′wỏ)	169	52°11′N	18°37′E
Kołobrzeg, Pol. (kỏ-lôb′zhĕk)	160	54°10′N	15°35′E
Kolomna, Russia (kål-ỏm′nå)	180	55°06′N	38°47′E
Kolomyia, Ukr.	169	48°32′N	25°04′E
Kolp′, r., Russia (kôlp)	176	59°18′N	35°32′E
Kolpashevo, Russia (kŭl pȧ shô′vȧ)	178	58°16′N	82°43′E
Kolpino, Russia (kôl′pė-nỏ)	180	59°45′N	30°37′E
Kolpny, Russia (kôlp′nyė)	176	52°14′N	36°54′E
Kol′skiy Poluostrov, pen., Russia	178	67°15′N	37°40′E
Kolva, r., Russia	180	61°00′N	57°00′E
Kolwezi, D.R.C. (kōl-wĕ′zē)	232	10°43′S	25°28′E
Kolyberovo, Russia (kỏ-lĭ-byâ′rô-vô)	186b	55°16′N	38°45′E
Kolyma, r., Russia	179	66°30′N	151°45′E
Kolymskiy Mountains *see* Gydan, Khrebet, mts., Russia	179	61°45′N	155°00′E
Kom, r., Afr.	236	2°15′N	12°05′E
Komadugu Gana, r., Nig.	235	12°15′N	11°10′E
Komae, Japan	211a	35°37′N	139°35′E
Komandorskiye Ostrova, is., Russia	197	55°40′N	167°13′E
Komárno, Slvk. (kỏ′mär-nỏ)	169	47°46′N	18°08′E
Komarno, Ukr.	169	49°38′N	23°42′E
Komárom, Hung. (kỏ′mä-rỏm)	169	47°45′N	18°06′E
Komatipoort, S. Afr. (kō-mä′tė-pōrt)	232	25°21′S	32°00′E
Komatsu, Japan (kō-mät′so͞o)	210	36°23′N	136°26′E
Komatsushima, Japan (kō-mät′so͞o-shė′mä)	211	34°04′N	134°32′E
Komeshia, D.R.C.	237	8°01′S	27°07′E
Komga, S. Afr. (kōm′gå)	233c	32°36′S	27°54′E
Komi, prov., Russia (kỏmė)	184	63°00′N	55°00′E
Kommetijie, S. Afr.	232a	34°09′S	18°19′E
Komoé, r., C. Iv.	234	5°40′N	3°40′W
Komsomolets, Kaz.	186a	53°45′N	62°04′E
Komsomol′sk-na-Amure, Russia	179	50°46′N	137°14′E
Kona, Mali	234	14°57′N	3°53′W
Konda, r., Russia (kỏn′då)	180	60°50′N	64°00′E
Kondas, r., Russia (kỏn′dås)	186a	59°30′N	56°28′E
Kondoa, Tan. (kỏn-dō′å)	232	4°52′S	36°00′E
Kondolole, D.R.C.	237	1°20′N	25°58′E
Koné, N. Cal.	214f	21°04′S	164°52′E
Kong, C. Iv. (kông)	230	9°05′N	4°41′W
Kongbo, C.A.R.	236	4°44′N	21°23′E
Kongolo, D.R.C. (kôŋ′gō′lō)	232	5°23′S	27°00′E
Kongsberg, Nor. (kŭngs′bĕrg)	166	59°40′N	9°36′E
Kongsvinger, Nor. (kŭngs′vĭŋ-gẽr)	166	60°12′N	12°00′E
Koni, D.R.C. (kō′nē)	232	10°32′S	27°27′E
Königsberg *see* Kaliningrad, Russia	178	54°42′N	20°32′E
Königsbrunn, Ger. (kû′nēgs-bro͞on)	159d	48°16′N	10°53′E
Königs Wusterhausen, Ger. (kû′nēgs vo͞os′tĕr-hou-zĕn)	159b	52°18′N	13°38′E
Konin, Pol. (kô′nyĕn)	161	52°11′N	18°17′E
Kónitsa, Grc. (kỏ′nyē′tså)	175	40°03′N	20°46′E
Konjic, Bos. (kôn′yēts)	175	43°38′N	17°59′E
Konju, Kor., S.	210	36°21′N	127°05′E
Konnagar, India	202a	22°41′N	88°22′E
Konotop, Ukr. (kỏ-nỏ-tôp′)	181	51°13′N	33°14′E
Konpienga, r., Burkina	234	11°15′N	0°35′E
Konqi, r., China (kỏn-chyē)	204	41°09′N	87°46′E
Końskie, Pol. (koin′′skyĕ)	169	51°12′N	20°26′E
Konstanz, Ger. (kỏn′shtänts)	168	47°39′N	9°10′E
Kontagora, Nig. (kōn-tå-gō′rä)	230	10°24′N	5°28′E
Konya, Tur. (kōn′yå)	198	36°55′N	32°25′E
Koocanusa, Lake, res., N.A.	114	49°00′N	115°10′W
Kootenay (Kootenai), r., N.A.	95	49°45′N	117°05′W
Kootenay Lake, l., Can.	95	49°35′N	116°50′W
Kootenay National Park, rec., Can. (ko͞o′tė-nå)	90	51°06′N	117°02′W
Kōō-zan, mtn., Japan (ko͞o′zän)	211b	34°53′N	135°32′E
Kopervik, Nor. (kô′pĕr-vėk)	166	59°18′N	5°20′E
Kopeysk, Russia (kỏ-pāsk′)	184	55°07′N	61°37′E
Köping, Swe. (chû′pĭng)	166	59°32′N	15°58′E
Kopparberg, Swe. (kŏp′pår-bĕrgh)	166	59°53′N	15°00′E
Koppeh Dāgh, mts., Asia	198	37°28′N	58°29′E
Koppies, S. Afr.	238c	27°15′S	27°35′E
Koprivnica, Cro. (kô′prēv-nė′tså)	174	46°10′N	16°48′E
Kopychyntsi, Ukr.	169	49°06′N	25°55′E
Korčula, i., Yugo. (kỏr′cho͞o-lå)	175	42°50′N	17°05′E
Korea, North, nation, Asia	205	40°00′N	127°00′E
Korea, South, nation, Asia	205	36°30′N	128°00′E
Korea Bay, b., Asia	208	39°18′N	123°50′E
Korean Archipelago, is., Kor., S.	205	34°05′N	125°35′E
Korea Strait, strt., Asia	205	33°30′N	128°30′E
Korets′, Ukr.	169	50°35′N	27°13′E
Korhogo, C. Iv. (kỏr-hō′gō)	230	9°27′N	5°38′W
Korinthiakós Kólpos, b., Grc.	163	38°15′N	22°33′E
Kórinthos, Grc. (kỏ-rĕn′thỏs) (kŏr′ĭnth)	154	37°56′N	22°54′E
Koriukivka, Ukr.	177	51°44′N	32°24′E
Kōriyama, Japan (kō′rė-yä′mä)	210	37°18′N	140°25′E
Korkino, Russia (kôr′kē-nŭ)	186a	54°53′N	61°25′E
Korla, China (kōr-lä)	204	41°37′N	86°03′E
Körmend, Hung. (kûr′mĕnt)	168	47°02′N	16°36′E
Kornat, i., Yugo. (kỏr-nät′)	174	43°46′N	15°10′E
Korneuburg, Aus. (kỏr′noi-bòrgh)	159e	48°22′N	16°21′E
Koro, Mali	234	14°04′N	3°05′W
Korocha, Russia (kỏ-rō′chå)	177	50°50′N	37°13′E
Korop, Ukr. (kō′rôp)	177	51°33′N	32°54′E
Koro Sea, sea, Fiji	214g	18°00′S	179°50′E
Korosten′, Ukr. (kô′rỏs-tĕn)	181	50°51′N	28°39′E
Korostyshiv, Ukr.	177	50°19′N	29°05′E
Koro Toro, Chad	235	16°05′N	18°30′E
Korotoyak, Russia (kỏ′rỏ-tỏ-yåk′)	177	51°00′N	39°06′E
Korsakov, Russia (kôr′så-kôf′)	179	46°42′N	143°16′E
Korsnäs, Fin. (kôrs′nĕs)	167	62°51′N	21°17′E
Korsør, Den. (kôrs′ûr′)	166	55°19′N	11°08′E
Kortrijk, Bel.	165	50°49′N	3°10′E
Koryakskiy Khrebet, mts., Russia	179	62°00′N	168°45′E
Kosa Byriuchyi ostriv, i., Ukr.	177	46°07′N	35°12′E
Kościan, Pol. (kŭsh′tsyån)	168	52°05′N	16°38′E
Kościerzyna, Pol. (kŭsh-tsyĕ-zhē′nå)	169	54°08′N	17°59′E
Kosciusko, Ms., U.S. (kŏs-ĭ-ŭs′kō)	124	33°04′N	89°35′W
Kosciuszko, Mount, mtn., Austl.	221	36°26′S	148°20′E
Kosha, Sudan	231	20°49′N	30°27′E
Koshigaya, Japan (kỏ′shė-gä′yä)	211a	35°53′N	139°48′E
Köshim, r., Kaz.	181	50°30′N	50°40′E
Kosi, r., India (kỏ′sē)	202	26°00′N	86°20′E
Košice, Slvk. (kō′shė-tsĕ′)	161	48°43′N	21°17′E
Kosmos, S. Afr. (kŏz′mŏs)	233b	25°45′S	27°51′E
Kosobrodskiy, Russia (kä-sô′brỏd-skĭ)	186a	54°14′N	60°53′E
Kosovo, hist. reg., Yugo.	175	42°35′N	21°00′E
Kosovska Mitrovica, Yugo. (kỏ′sỏv-skä′ mė′trỏ-vė-tsä′)	175	42°51′N	20°50′E
Kostajnica, Cro. (kôs′tä-ė-nē′tså)	174	45°14′N	16°32′E
Koster, S. Afr.	238c	25°52′S	26°52′E
Kostiantynivka, Ukr.	177	48°33′N	37°42′E
Kostino, Russia (kôs′tĭ-nô)	186b	55°54′N	37°51′E
Kostroma, Russia (kỏs-trỏ-må′)	178	57°46′N	40°55′E
Kostroma, prov., Russia	176	57°50′N	41°10′E
Kostrzyn, Pol. (kôst′chĕn)	161	52°35′N	14°38′E
Kos′va, r., Russia (kôs′vå)	186a	58°44′N	57°08′E
Koszalin, Pol. (kô-shä′lĭn)	160	54°12′N	16°10′E
Köszeg, Hung. (kû′sĕg)	168	47°21′N	16°32′E
Kota, India	199	25°17′N	75°49′E
Kota Baharu, Malay. (kō′tä bä′ro͞o)	212	6°15′N	102°23′E
Kotabaru, Indon.	212	3°22′S	116°15′E
Kota Kinabalu, Malay.	212	5°55′N	116°05′E
Kota Tinggi, Malay.	197b	1°43′N	103°54′E
Kotel, Blg. (kō-tĕl′)	175	42°54′N	26°28′E
Kotel′nich, Russia (kỏ-tyĕl′nĕch)	180	58°15′N	48°20′E
Kotel′nyy, i., Russia (kỏ-tyĕl′nė)	179	74°51′N	134°09′E
Kotka, Fin. (kŏt′kå)	160	60°28′N	26°56′E
Kotlas, Russia (kôt′lås)	180	61°10′N	46°50′E
Kotlin, Ostrov, i., Russia (ỏs-trôf′ kôt′lĭn)	186c	60°02′N	29°49′E
Kotor, Yugo.	175	42°25′N	18°46′E
Kotorosl′, r., Russia (kỏ-tô′rỏsl)	176	57°18′N	39°08′E
Kotovs′k, Ukr.	177	47°49′N	29°31′E
Kotto, r., C.A.R.	231	5°17′N	22°04′E
Kotuy, r., Russia (kô-to͞o′)	184	71°00′N	103°15′E
Kotzebue, Ak., U.S. (kỏt′sē-bo͞o)	106a	66°48′N	162°42′W
Kotzebue Sound, strt., Ak., U.S.	103	67°00′N	164°28′W
Kouchibouguac National Park, rec., Can.	100	46°53′N	65°35′W
Koudougou, Burkina (ko͞o-do͞o′go͞o)	230	12°15′N	2°22′W
Kouilou, r., Congo	232	4°30′S	12°00′E
Koula-Moutou, Gabon	236	1°08′S	12°29′E
Koulikoro, Mali (ko͞o-lė-kō′rỏ)	230	12°53′N	7°33′W
Koulouguidi, Mali	235	13°27′N	17°33′E
Koumac, N. Cal.	214f	20°33′S	164°17′E
Koumra, Chad	235	8°55′N	17°33′E
Koundara, Gui.	234	12°29′N	13°18′W
Kouroussa, Gui. (ko͞o-ro͞o′sä)	230	10°39′N	9°53′W
Koutiala, Mali (ko͞o-tė-ä′lä)	230	12°29′N	5°29′W
Kouvola, Fin. (kō′ỏ-vỏ-lä)	167	60°51′N	26°40′E
Kouzhen, China (kō-jŭn)	206	36°19′N	117°37′E
Kovda, l., Russia (kôv′då)	180	66°45′N	32°00′E
Kovel′, Ukr. (kō′vĕl)	181	51°13′N	24°45′E
Kovno *see* Kaunas, Lith.	178	54°42′N	23°54′E
Kovrov, Russia (kỏv-rôf′)	180	56°23′N	41°21′E
Koyuk, Ak., U.S. (kỏ-yo͞ok′)	103	65°00′N	161°18′W
Koyukuk, r., Ak., U.S. (kỏ-yo͞o′kòk)	103	66°25′N	153°50′W
Kozáni, Grc.	163	40°16′N	21°51′E
Kozelets′, Ukr. (kỏzĕ-lyĕts)	177	50°53′N	31°07′E
Kozel′sk, Russia (kỏ-zĕlsk′)	176	54°01′N	35°49′E
Kozhikode, India	199	11°19′N	75°49′E

ăt; finăl; rāte; senåte; ärm; åsk; sofȧ; fâre; ch-choose; dh-as th in other; bē; ėvent; bĕt; recĕnt; cratẽr; g-gō; gh-guttural g; bĭt; ĭ-short neutral; rīde; κ-guttural k as ch in German ich;

PRONOUNCING INDEX Koziatyn – Lábrea 311

PLACE (Pronunciation)	PAGE	LAT.	LONG.
Koziatyn, Ukr.	181	49°43'N	28°50'E
Kozienice, Pol. (kō-zyĕ-nē'tsĕ)	169	51°34'N	21°35'E
Koźle, Pol. (kôzh'lĕ)	169	50°19'N	18°10'E
Kozloduy, Blg. (kŭz'lô-dwē)	175	43°45'N	23°42'E
Kōzu, i., Japan (kō'zōō)	211	34°16'N	139°03'E
Kra, Isthmus of, isth., Asia	212	9°30'S	99°45'E
Kraai, r., S. Afr. (krā'ē)	233c	30°50'S	27°03'E
Krabbendijke, Neth.	159a	51°26'N	4°05'E
Krâchéh, Camb.	212	12°28'N	106°06'E
Kragujevac, Yugo. (krä'gōō'yĕ-vats)	163	44°01'N	20°55'E
Kraków, Pol. (krä'kof)	154	50°05'N	20°00'E
Kraljevo, Yugo. (kräl'ye-vô)	163	43°39'N	20°48'E
Kramators'k, Ukr.	177	48°43'N	37°32'E
Kramfors, Swe. (kräm'fôrs)	166	62°54'N	17°49'E
Kranj, Slvn. (krän')	162	46°16'N	14°23'E
Kranskop, S. Afr. (kränz'kŏp)	233c	28°57'S	30°54'E
Krāslava, Lat. (kräs'lä-vä)	167	55°53'N	27°12'E
Kraslice, Czech Rep. (kräs'lê-tsĕ)	168	50°19'N	12°30'E
Krasnaya Gorka, Russia	186a	55°12'N	56°40'E
Krasnaya Sloboda, Russia	181	48°25'N	44°35'E
Kraśnik, Pol. (kräsh'nĭk)	169	50°53'N	22°15'E
Krasnoarmeysk, Russia (kräs'nô-ár-maśk')	186b	56°06'N	38°09'E
Krasnoarmiis'k, Ukr.	177	48°19'N	37°04'E
Krasnodar, Russia (kräs'nô-dár)	178	45°03'N	38°55'E
Krasnodarskiy, prov., Russia (kras-nô-där'skĭ ôb'làst)	177	45°25'N	38°10'E
Krasnogorsk, Russia	186b	55°49'N	37°20'E
Krasnogorskiy, Russia (kräs-nô-gôr'skĭ)	186a	54°36'N	61°15'E
Krasnogvardeyskiy, Russia (krå'sno-gvár-dzyē ĕs-kēē)	186a	57°17'N	62°05'E
Krasnohrad, Ukr.	177	49°23'N	35°26'E
Krasnokamsk, Russia (kräs-nô-kämsk')	180	58°00'N	55°45'E
Krasnokuts'k, Ukr.	177	50°03'N	35°05'E
Krasnoslobodsk, Russia (kräs'nô-slôbôtsk')	180	54°20'N	43°50'E
Krasnotur'insk, Russia (krŭs-nŭ-tōō-rensk')	178	59°47'N	60°15'E
Krasnoufimsk, Russia (krŭs-nŭ-ōō-fēmsk')	178	56°38'N	57°46'E
Krasnoural'sk, Russia (kräs'nô-ōō-rälsk')	180	58°21'N	60°05'E
Krasnousol'skiy, Russia (kräs-nô-ô-sôl'skĭ)	186a	53°54'N	56°27'E
Krasnovishersk, Russia (kräs-nô-vêshersk')	180	60°22'N	57°20'E
Krasnoyarsk, Russia (kräs-nô-yársk')	179	56°13'N	93°12'E
Krasnoye Selo, Russia (kräs'nŭ-yŭ sâ'lō)	186c	59°44'N	30°06'E
Krasny Kholm, Russia (kräs'nē kōlm)	176	58°03'N	37°11'E
Krasnystaw, Pol. (kräs-nē-stáf')	169	50°59'N	23°11'E
Krasnyy Bor, Russia (kräs'nê bôr)	186c	59°41'N	30°40'E
Krasnyy Klyuch, Russia (kräs'nê'klyûch')	186a	55°24'N	56°43'E
Krasnyy Kut, Russia (kras-nê kōōt')	181	50°50'N	47°00'E
Kratovo, Mac. (krä'tô-vô)	175	42°04'N	22°12'E
Kratovo, Russia (krä'tô-vô)	186b	55°35'N	38°10'E
Krefeld, Ger. (krā'fĕlt)	171c	51°20'N	6°34'E
Kremenchuk, Ukr.	181	49°04'N	33°26'E
Kremenchuts'ke vodoskhovyshche, res., Ukr.	181	49°20'N	32°45'E
Kremenets', Ukr.	169	50°06'N	25°43'E
Kremmen, Ger. (krĕ'mĕn)	159b	52°45'N	13°02'E
Krempe, Ger. (krĕm'pĕ)	159c	53°50'N	9°29'E
Krems, Aus. (krĕms)	168	48°25'N	15°36'E
Krestovyy, Pereval, p., Geor.	182	42°32'N	44°28'E
Kresttsy, Russia (krâst'sê)	176	58°16'N	32°25'E
Kretinga, Lith. (krĕ-tĭŋ'gà)	167	55°55'N	21°17'E
Kribi, Cam. (krē'bê)	230	2°57'N	9°55'E
Krilon, Mys, c., Russia (mĭs krĭl'ôn)	210	45°58'N	142°00'E
Krimpen aan de IJssel, Neth.	159a	51°55'N	4°34'E
Krishna, r., India	199	16°00'N	79°00'E
Krishnanagar, India	202	23°29'N	88°33'E
Kristiansand, Nor. (krĭs-tyán-sän'')	154	58°09'N	7°59'E
Kristianstad, Swe. (krĭs-tyán-städ')	160	56°02'N	14°09'E
Kristiansund, Nor. (krĭs-tyán-sòn'')	160	63°07'N	7°49'E
Kristinehamn, Swe. (krēs-tē'nĕ-häm')	160	59°20'N	14°05'E
Kristinestad, Fin. (krĭs-tē'nĕ-städh)	167	62°16'N	21°28'E
Kriva-Palanka, Mac. (krē-và-pà-läŋ'kà)	175	42°12'N	22°21'E
Krivoy Rog *see* Kryvyi Rih, Ukr.	178	47°54'N	33°22'E
Križevci, Cro. (krē'zhĕv-tsĭ)	174	46°02'N	16°30'E
Krk, i., Yugo. (k'rk)	174	45°06'N	14°33'E
Krnov, Czech Rep. (k'r'nôf)	169	50°05'N	17°41'E
Krokodil, r., S. Afr. (krŏ'kō-dĭl)	238c	24°25'S	27°08'E
Krolevets', Ukr.	181	51°33'N	33°21'E
Kromy, Russia (krô'mê)	176	52°44'N	35°41'E
Kronshtadt, Russia (krōn'shtät)	180	59°59'N	29°47'E
Kroonstad, S. Afr. (krōn'shtät)	232	27°40'S	27°15'E
Kropotkin, Russia (krá-pôt'kĭn)	181	45°25'N	40°30'E
Krosno, Pol. (krôs'nô)	169	49°41'N	21°46'E
Krotoszyn, Pol. (krô-tō'shĭn)	169	51°41'N	17°25'E
Krško, Slvn. (k'rsh'kô)	174	45°58'N	15°30'E
Kruger National Park, rec., S. Afr. (krōō'gĕr) (krü'gĕr)	232	23°22'S	30°18'E
Krugersdorp, S. Afr. (krōō'gĕrz-dôrp)	232	26°06'S	27°46'E
Krung Thep *see* Bangkok, Thai.	212	13°50'N	100°29'E
Kruševac, Yugo. (krò'shĕ-vats)	175	43°34'N	21°21'E
Kruševo, Mac.	175	41°20'N	21°15'E
Krychaw, Bela.	176	53°44'N	31°39'E
Krylbo, Swe. (krül'bô)	166	60°07'N	16°14'E
Krym, Respublika, prov., Ukr.	177	45°08'N	34°05'E
Krymskaya, Russia (krĭm'skà-yà)	177	44°58'N	38°01'E
Kryms'kyi Pivostriv (Crimean Peninsula), pen., Ukr.	181	45°18'N	33°30'E
Krynki, Pol. (krĭn'kê)	169	53°15'N	23°47'E
Kryve Ozero, Ukr.	177	47°57'N	30°21'E
Kryvyi Rih, Ukr.	178	47°54'N	33°22'E
Ksar Chellala, Alg.	173	35°12'N	2°20'E
Ksar-el-Kebir, Mor.	162	35°01'N	5°48'W
Ksar-es-Souk, Mor.	162	31°58'N	4°25'W
Kuai, r., China (kōō-ī)	206	33°30'N	116°56'E
Kuala Klawang, Malay.	197b	2°57'N	102°04'E
Kuala Lumpur, Malay. (kwä'lä lòm-pōōr')	212	3°08'N	101°42'E
Kuandian, China (kůän-dĭĕn)	208	40°40'N	124°50'E
Kuban, r., Russia	181	45°20'N	40°05'E
Kubenskoye, l., Russia	180	59°40'N	39°40'E
Kuching, Malay. (kōō'chĭng)	212	1°30'N	110°26'E
Kuchinoerabo, i., Japan (kōō'chē nō ĕr'á-bō)	211	30°31'N	129°53'E
Kudamatsu, Japan (kōō'dá-mä'tsōō)	211	34°00'N	131°51'E
Kudap, Indon.	197b	1°14'N	102°30'E
Kudat, Malay. (kōō-dät')	212	6°56'N	116°48'E
Kudirkos Naumietis, Lith. (kōōdĭr-kôs nå'ô-mĕ'tĭs)	167	54°51'N	23°00'E
Kudymkar, Russia (kōō-dĭm-kär')	178	58°43'N	54°52'E
Kufstein, Aus. (kōōf'shtīn)	168	47°34'N	12°11'E
Kugluktuk (Coppermine), Can.	90	67°46'N	115°19'W
Kuhstedt, Ger. (kōō'shtĕ)	159c	53°23'N	8°58'E
Kuibyshev *see* Kuybyshev, Russia	178	53°10'N	50°05'E
Kuilsrivier, S. Afr.	232a	33°56'S	18°41'E
Kuito, Ang.	232	12°22'S	16°56'E
Kuji, Japan	205	40°11'N	141°46'E
Kujū-san, mtn., Japan (kōō'jò-sän')	211	33°07'N	131°14'E
Kukës, Alb. (kōō'kĕs)	175	42°03'N	20°25'E
Kula, Blg. (kōō'là)	175	43°52'N	23°13'E
Kula, Tur.	163	38°32'N	28°30'E
Kula Kangri, mtn., Bhu.	199	33°11'N	90°36'E
Kular, Khrebet, mts., Russia (kò-lär')	185	69°00'N	131°45'E
Kuldīga, Lat. (kòl'dē-gà)	167	56°59'N	21°59'E
Kulebaki, Russia (kōō-lĕ-bäk'ĭ)	180	55°22'N	42°30'E
Kulmbach, Ger. (klòlm'bäk)	168	50°07'N	11°28'E
Kulunda, Russia (kò-lòn'dá)	178	52°38'N	79°00'E
Kulundinskoye, l., Russia	184	52°45'N	77°18'E
Kum, r., Kor., S. (kòm)	210	36°50'N	127°30'E
Kuma, r., Russia (kōō'mä)	181	44°50'N	45°10'E
Kumamoto, Japan (kōō'mä-mō'tô)	205	32°49'N	130°40'E
Kumano-Nada, b., Japan (kōō-mä'nō nä-dä)	211	34°03'N	136°36'E
Kumanovo, Mac. (kò-mä'nô-vô)	175	42°10'N	21°41'E
Kumasi, Ghana (kōō-mä'sê)	230	6°41'N	1°35'W
Kumba, Cam. (kòm'bà)	230	4°38'N	9°25'E
Kumbakonam, India (kòm'bŭ-kō'nŭm)	199	10°59'N	79°25'E
Kumkale, Tur.	175	39°59'N	26°10'E
Kumo, Nig.	235	10°03'N	11°13'E
Kumta, India	203	14°19'N	75°28'E
Kumul *see* Hami, China	204	42°58'N	93°14'E
Kunashak, Russia (kû-nä'shák)	186a	55°43'N	61°35'E
Kunashir (Kunashiri), i., Russia (kōō-nŭ-shēr')	205	44°00'N	145°45'E
Kunda, Est.	167	59°30'N	26°28'E
Kundravy, Russia (kōōn'drá-vĭ)	186a	54°50'N	60°14'E
Kundur, i., Indon.	197b	0°49'N	103°20'E
Kunene (Cunene), r., Afr.	232	17°05'S	12°35'E
Kungälv, Swe. (kŭng'ĕlf)	166	57°53'N	12°01'E
Kungsbacka, Swe. (kŭngs'bä-kà)	166	57°31'N	12°04'E
Kungur, Russia (kòn-gōōr')	178	57°27'N	56°53'E
Kunlun Shan, mts., China (kōōn-lōōn shän)	204	35°26'N	83°09'E
Kunming, China (kōōn-mĭŋ)	204	25°10'N	102°50'E
Kunsan, Kor., S. (kòn'sän')	205	35°54'N	126°46'E
Kunshan, China (kōōnshän)	207b	31°23'N	120°57'E
Kuntsëvo, Russia (kòn-tsyô'vô)	176	55°43'N	37°27'E
Kun'ya, Russia	186a	58°42'N	56°47'E
Kun'ya, r., Russia (kòn'yá)	176	56°45'N	30°53'E
Kuopio, Fin. (kò-ô'pê-ŏ)	160	62°48'N	28°30'E
Kupa, r., Yugo.	174	45°32'N	14°50'E
Kupang, Indon.	213	10°14'S	123°37'E
Kupavna, Russia	186b	55°49'N	38°11'E
Kupians'k, Ukr.	181	49°44'N	37°38'E
Kupino, Russia (kōō-pĭ'nô)	178	54°00'N	77°47'E
Kupiškis, Lith. (kò-pĭsh'kĭs)	167	55°50'N	24°55'E
Kuqa, China (kōō-chyä)	204	41°34'N	82°44'E
Kür, r., Asia	181	41°10'N	45°40'E
Kurashiki, Japan (kōō'rä-shē'kê)	211	34°37'N	133°44'E
Kuraymah, Sudan	231	18°34'N	31°49'E
Kurayoshi, Japan (kōō'rá-yō'shê)	211	35°25'N	133°49'E
Kurdistan, hist. reg., Asia (kûrd'ĭ-stăn)	198	37°40'N	43°30'E
Kurdufān, hist. reg., Sudan (kôr-dô-făn')	231	14°08'N	28°39'E
Kŭrdzhali, Blg.	175	41°39'N	25°21'E
Kure, Japan (kōō'rĕ)	205	34°17'N	132°35'E
Kuressaare, Est. (kó'rĕ-sä'rĕ)	167	58°15'N	22°26'E
Kurgan, Russia (kòr-gän')	178	55°28'N	65°14'E
Kurgan-Tyube, Taj. (kòr-gän' tyō'bĕ)	183	38°00'N	68°49'E
Kurihama, Japan (kōō-rē-hä'mä)	211a	35°14'N	139°42'E
Kuril Islands, is., Russia (kōō'rĭl)	185	46°20'N	149°30'E
Kurisches Haff, b., Eur.	167	55°10'N	21°08'E
Kurla, neigh., India	203b	19°03'N	72°53'E
Kurmuk, Sudan (kòr'mōōk)	231	10°40'N	34°13'E
Kurnool, India (kòr-nōōl')	199	16°00'N	78°04'E
Kurrajong, Austl.	217b	33°33'S	150°40'E
Kuršenai, Lith. (kòr'shâ-nĭ)	167	56°01'N	22°56'E
Kursk, Russia (kòrsk)	178	51°44'N	36°08'E
Kuršumlija, Yugo. (kòr'shòm'lĭ-yá)	175	43°08'N	21°18'E
Kuruman, S. Afr. (kōō-rōō-män')	232	27°25'S	23°30'E
Kurume, Japan (kōō'rò-mĕ)	205	33°10'N	130°30'E
Kururi, Japan (kōō'rò-rē)	211a	35°17'N	140°05'E
Kusa, Russia (kōō'sá)	186a	55°19'N	59°27'E
Kushchëvskaya, Russia	177	46°34'N	39°40'E
Kushikino, Japan (kōō'shĭ-kē'nō)	211	31°44'N	130°19'E
Kushimoto, Japan (kōō'shĭ-mō'tō)	211	33°29'N	135°47'E
Kushiro, Japan (kōō'shē-rō)	205	43°00'N	144°22'E
Kushva, Russia (kōōsh'vá)	178	58°18'N	59°51'E
Kuskokwim, r., Ak., U.S.	103	61°32'N	160°36'W
Kuskokwim Bay, b., Ak., U.S. (kŭs'kô-kwĭm)	103	59°25'N	163°14'W
Kuskokwim Mountains, mts., Ak., U.S.	103	62°08'N	158°00'W
Kuskovak, Ak., U.S. (kŭs-kō'văk)	103	60°10'N	162°50'W
Kütahya, Tur. (kû-tä'hyà)	198	39°20'N	29°50'E
Kutaisi, Geor. (kōō-tŭ-ē'sē)	181	42°15'N	42°40'E
Kutch, Gulf of, b., India	199	22°45'N	68°33'E
Kutch, Rann of, sw., Asia	199	23°59'N	69°13'E
Kutenholz, Ger. (kōō'tĕn-hōlts)	159c	53°29'N	9°20'E
Kutim, Russia (kōō'tĭm)	186a	60°22'N	58°51'E
Kutina, Cro. (kōō'tê-nà)	174	45°29'N	16°48'E
Kutno, Pol. (kòt'nô)	161	52°14'N	19°22'E
Kutno, l., Russia	180	65°15'N	31°30'E
Kutulik, Russia (kò tōō'lyĭk)	179	53°12'N	102°51'E
Kuujjuaq, Can.	91	58°06'N	68°25'W
Kuusamo, Fin. (kōō'sá-mô)	160	65°59'N	29°10'E
Kuvshinovo, Russia (kòv-shē'nô-vô)	176	57°01'N	34°09'E
Kuwait *see* Al Kuwait, Kuw.	198	29°04'N	47°59'E
Kuwait, nation, Asia	198	29°00'N	48°45'E
Kuwana, Japan (kōō'wá-ná)	211	35°02'N	136°40'E
Kuybyshev *see* Samara, Russia	180	53°10'N	50°05'E
Kuybyshevskoye, res., Russia	178	53°40'N	49°00'E
Kuzneckovo, Russia	186b	55°29'N	38°22'E
Kuznetsk, Russia (kōōz-nyĕtsk')	180	53°00'N	46°30'E
Kuznetsk Basin, basin, Russia	178	56°30'N	86°15'E
Kuznetsovka, Russia (kòz-nyĕt'sôf-kȧ)	186a	54°41'N	56°40'E
Kuznetsovo, Russia (kòz-nyĕt-sô'vô)	176	56°39'N	36°55'E
Kuznetsy, Russia	186b	55°50'N	38°39'E
Kvarner Zaliv, b., Yugo. (kvär'nĕr)	174	44°41'N	14°05'E
Kwa, r., D.R.C.	236	3°00'S	16°45'E
Kwahu Plateau, plat., Ghana	234	7°00'N	1°35'W
Kwando (Cuando), r., Afr.	236	16°50'S	22°40'E
Kwangju, Kor., S.	210	35°09'N	126°54'E
Kwango (Cuango), r., Afr. (kwäng'ō')	236	6°35'S	16°50'E
Kwangwazi, Tan.	237	7°47'S	38°15'E
Kwekwe, Zimb.	232	18°49'S	29°45'E
Kwenge, r., Afr. (kwĕŋ'gĕ)	232	6°45'S	18°23'E
Kwilu, r., Afr. (kwē'lōō)	232	4°00'S	18°00'E
Kyakhta, Russia (kyäk'tà)	179	51°00'N	107°30'E
Kyaukpyu, Mya. (chouk'pyoo')	199	19°19'N	93°33'E
Kybartai, Lith. (kē'bär-tī')	167	54°40'N	22°46'E
Kyïv *see* Kiev, Ukr.	178	50°27'N	30°30'E
Kyïvs'ke vodoskhovyshche, res., Ukr.	178	51°00'N	30°20'E
Kými, Grc.	175	38°38'N	24°05'E
Kyn, Russia (kĭn')	186a	57°52'N	58°42'E
Kynuna, Austl. (kī-nōō'ná)	219	21°30'S	142°12'E
Kyoga, Lake, l., Ug.	231	1°30'N	32°45'E
Kyōga-Saki, c., Japan (kyō'gä sa'kê)	211	35°46'N	135°14'E
Kyŏngju, Kor., S. (kyŭng'yōō)	205	35°48'N	129°12'E
Kyōto, Japan (kyō'tō')	205	35°00'N	135°46'E
Kyōto, dept., Japan	211b	34°56'N	135°42'E
Kyparissía, Grc.	163	37°17'N	21°43'E
Kyparissiakós Kólpos, b., Grc.	175	37°28'N	21°15'E
Kyren, Russia (kĭ-rĕn')	179	51°46'N	102°13'E
Kyrgyzstan, nation, Asia	178	41°45'N	74°38'E
Kyrönjoki, r., Fin.	167	63°03'N	22°20'E
Kyrya, Russia (kēr'yá)	186a	59°18'N	59°03'E
Kyshtym, Russia (kĭsh-tĭm')	180	55°42'N	60°34'E
Kýthira, i., Grc.	163	36°15'N	22°56'E
Kýthnos, i., Grc.	175	37°24'N	24°10'E
Kytlym, Russia (kĭt'lĭm)	186a	59°30'N	59°15'E
Kyūshū, i., Japan	205	33°00'N	131°00'E
Kyustendil, Blg. (kyòs-tĕn-dĭl')	163	42°16'N	22°39'E
Kyyiv, prov., Ukr.	177	50°05'N	30°40'E
Kyzyl, Russia (kĭ zĭl)	179	51°37'N	93°38'E
Kyzyl-Kum, des., Asia	178	42°47'N	64°45'E

L

PLACE (Pronunciation)	PAGE	LAT.	LONG.
Laa, Aus.	168	48°42'N	16°23'E
La Almunia de Doña Godina, Spain	172	41°29'N	1°22'W
Laas Caanood, Som.	238a	8°24'N	47°20'E
La Asunción, Ven. (lä ä-sōōn-syōn')	142	11°02'N	63°57'W
La Baie, Can.	99	48°21'N	70°53'W
La Banda, Arg. (lä bän'dä)	144	27°48'S	64°12'W
La Barca, Mex. (lä bär'ká)	130	20°17'N	102°33'W
Laberge, Lake, l., Can. (lå-bĕrzh')	92	61°08'N	136°42'W
Laberinto de las Doce Leguas, is., Cuba	134	20°40'N	78°35'W
Labinsk, Russia	181	44°30'N	40°40'E
Labis, Malay. (läb'ĭs)	197b	2°23'N	103°01'E
La Bisbal, Spain (lä bēs-bäl')	173	41°55'N	3°00'E
Labo, Phil. (lä'bô)	213a	14°11'N	122°49'E
Labo, Mount, mtn., Phil.	213a	14°00'N	122°47'E
Labouheyre, Fr. (là-bōō-âr')	170	44°14'N	0°58'W
Laboulaye, Arg. (lä-bô'ōō-lä-yĕ)	144	34°01'S	63°10'W
Labrador, reg., Can. (lăb'rȧ-dôr)	93	53°05'N	63°30'W
Labrador Sea, sea, Can.	101	50°38'N	55°00'W
Lábrea, Braz. (lä-brā'ä)	142	7°28'S	64°39'W

ng-sing; ŋ-baŋk; ɴ-nasalized n; nŏd; cŏmmit; ōld; ôbey; ôrder; oi-boil; fōōd; ò-as oo in foot; ou-out; s-soft; sh-dish; th-thin; pūre; ûnite; ûrn; stŭd; circŭs; ü-as in French tu; '-indeterminate vowel.

312 Labuan – L'Anse

PRONOUNCING INDEX

PLACE (Pronunciation)	PAGE	LAT.	LONG.
Labuan, Pulau, i., Malay. (lä-bö-än′)	212	5°28′N	115°11′E
Labuha, Indon.	213	0°43′S	127°35′E
L'Acadie, Can. (lä-kä-dē′)	102a	45°18′N	73°22′W
L'Acadie, r., Can.	102a	45°24′N	73°21′W
La Calera, Chile (lä-kä-lĕ-rä)	141b	32°47′S	71°11′W
La Calera, Col.	142a	4°43′N	73°58′W
Lac Allard, Can.	100	50°38′N	63°28′W
La Canada, Ca., U.S. (lä kän-yä′dä)	117a	34°13′N	118°12′W
Lacantum, r., Mex. (lä-kän-tōō′m)	131	16°13′N	90°52′W
La Carolina, Spain (lä kä-rō-lē′nä)	172	38°16′N	3°48′W
La Catedral, Cerro, mtn., Mex. (sĕ′r-rō-lä-kä-tĕ-drà′l)	131a	19°32′N	99°31′W
Lac-Beauport, Can. (läk-bō-pōr′)	102b	46°58′N	71°17′W
Laccadive Islands *see* Lakshadweep, is., India	199	11°00′N	73°02′E
Laccadive Sea, sea, Asia	203	9°10′N	75°17′E
Lac Court Oreille Indian Reservation, I.R., Wi., U.S.	113	46°04′N	91°18′W
Lac du Flambeau Indian Reservation, I.R., Wi., U.S.	113	46°12′N	89°50′W
La Ceiba, Hond. (lå sēbä)	128	15°45′N	86°52′W
La Ceja, Col. (lä-sĕ-ĸä)	142a	6°02′N	75°25′W
Lac-Frontière, Can.	91	46°42′N	70°00′W
Lacha, l., Russia (là′chä)	180	61°15′N	39°05′E
La Chaux de Fonds, Switz. (lå shō dē-fôN′)	168	47°07′N	6°47′E
L'Achigan, r., Can. (lä-shē-gäN)	102a	45°49′N	73°48′W
Lachine, Can. (lȧ-shēn′)	102a	45°26′N	73°40′W
Lachlan, r., Austl. (läk′lăn)	221	34°00′S	145°00′E
La Chorrera, Pan. (làchôr-rā′rä)	133	8°54′N	79°47′W
Lachute, Can. (lå-shōōt′)	99	45°39′N	74°20′W
La Ciotat, Fr. (lå syō-tå′)	171	43°13′N	5°35′E
Lackawanna, N.Y., U.S. (lak-å-wŏn′á)	111c	42°49′N	78°50′W
Lac La Biche, Can.	90	54°46′N	112°58′W
Lacombe, Can.	90	52°28′N	113°44′W
Laconia, N.H., U.S. (lȧ-kō′nĭ-ȧ)	109	43°30′N	71°30′W
La Conner, Wa., U.S. (lå kŏn′ēr)	116a	48°23′N	122°30′W
Lacreek, l., S.D., U.S. (lă′krēk)	112	43°04′N	101°46′W
La Cresenta, Ca., U.S. (lȧ krĕs′ĕnt-å)	117a	34°14′N	118°13′W
La Cross, Ks., U.S. (lȧ-krôs′)	120	38°30′N	99°20′W
La Crosse, Wi., U.S.	105	43°48′N	91°14′W
La Cruz, Col. (lȧ krōōz′)	142	1°37′N	77°00′W
La Cruz, C.R. (lä-krōō′z)	132	11°05′N	85°37′W
Lacs, Riviere des, r., N.D., U.S. (rē-vyĕr′ de läk)	112	48°30′N	101°45′W
La Cuesta, C.R. (lä-kwĕ′s-tä)	133	8°32′N	82°51′W
La Cygne, Ks., U.S. (là-sēn′y′) (lå-sēn′)	121	38°20′N	94°45′W
Ladd, Il., U.S. (lăd)	108	41°25′N	89°25′W
Ladíspoli, Italy (lä-dē′s-pô-lē)	173d	41°57′N	12°05′E
Lādīz, Iran	201	28°56′N	61°19′E
Ladner, Can. (lăd′nēr)	94	49°05′N	123°05′W
Lādnun, India (läd′nōn)	202	27°45′N	74°20′E
Ladoga, Lake *see* Ladozhskoye Ozero, l., Russia	178	60°59′N	31°30′E
La Dorado, Col. (lä dô-rä′då)	142	5°28′N	74°42′W
Ladozhskoye Ozero, Russia (lá-dôsh′skô-yē ô′zē-rô)	178	60°59′N	31°30′E
La Durantaye, Can. (lä dü-räN-tā′)	102b	46°51′N	70°51′W
Lady Frere, S. Afr. (lā-dē frâ′r′)	233c	31°48′S	27°16′E
Lady Grey, S. Afr.	233c	30°44′S	27°17′E
Ladysmith, Can. (lā′dĭ-smĭth)	94	48°58′N	123°49′W
Ladysmith, S. Afr.	232	28°38′S	29°48′E
Ladysmith, Wi., U.S.	113	45°27′N	91°07′W
Lae, Pap. N. Gui. (lä′å)	213	6°15′S	146°57′E
Laerdalsøyri, Nor.	166	61°08′N	7°26′E
La Esperanza, Hond. (lä ĕs-på-rän′zä)	132	14°20′N	88°21′W
Lafayette, Al., U.S.	124	32°52′N	85°25′W
Lafayette, Ca., U.S.	116b	37°53′N	122°07′W
Lafayette, Ga., U.S. (lă-fā-yĕt′)	124	34°41′N	85°19′W
Lafayette, In., U.S.	105	40°25′N	86°55′W
Lafayette, La., U.S.	105	30°15′N	92°02′W
La Fayette, R.I., U.S.	110b	41°34′N	71°29′W
La Ferté-Alais, Fr. (lä-fĕr-tā′ā-lā′)	171b	48°29′N	2°19′E
La Ferté-sous-Jouarre, Fr. (lå fĕr-tā′sōō-zhōō-är′)	171b	48°56′N	3°07′E
Lafia, Nig.	235	8°30′N	8°30′E
Lafiagi, Nig.	235	8°52′N	5°25′E
La Flèche, Fr. (lå flāsh′)	170	47°43′N	0°03′W
La Follete, Tn., U.S. (lă-fŏl′ĕt)	124	36°23′N	84°07′W
Lafourche, Bayou, r., La., U.S. (bă-yōō′lȧ-fōōrsh′)	123	29°25′N	90°15′W
La Gaiba, Braz. (lä-gī′bä)	143	17°54′S	57°32′W
La Galite, i., Tun. (gä-lēt)	162	37°36′N	8°03′E
Lågan, r., Nor. (lô′ghĕn)	156	61°00′N	10°00′E
Lagan, r., Swe.	166	56°34′N	13°25′E
Lagan, r., N. Ire., U.K. (lā′găn)	164	54°30′N	6°00′W
Lagarto, r., Pan. (lä-gä′r-tō)	128a	9°08′N	80°05′W
Lagartos, l., Mex. (lä-gä′r-tôs)	132a	21°32′N	88°15′W
Laghouat, Alg. (lä-gwät′)	230	33°45′N	2°49′E
Lagkadás, Grc.	175	40°44′N	23°10′E
Lagny, Fr. (län-yē′)	171b	48°53′N	2°41′E
Lagoa da Prata, Braz. (lä-gô′ä-dä-prā′tä)	141a	20°04′S	45°33′W
Lagoa Dourada, Braz. (lä-gô′ä-dō-rä′dä)	141a	20°55′S	44°03′W
Lagogne, Fr. (laN-gōn′y′)	170	44°43′N	3°50′E
Lagonay, Phil.	213a	13°44′N	123°31′E
Lagos, Nig. (lä′gōs)	230	6°27′N	3°24′E
Lagos, Port. (lä′gōzh)	172	37°08′N	8°43′W
Lagos de Moreno, Mex. (lä′gōs dā mō-rā′nō)	128	21°21′N	101°55′W
La Grand' Combe, Fr. (lå gräN kaNb′)	170	44°12′N	4°03′E
La Grande, Or., U.S. (lȧ grănd′)	104	45°20′N	118°06′W

PLACE (Pronunciation)	PAGE	LAT.	LONG.
La Grande, r., Can.	93	53°55′N	77°30′W
La Grange, Austl. (lä grānj)	218	18°40′S	122°00′E
La Grange, Ga., U.S. (lȧ-grānj′)	105	33°01′N	85°00′W
La Grange, Il., U.S.	111a	41°49′N	87°53′W
Lagrange, In., U.S.	108	41°40′N	85°25′W
La Grange, Ky., U.S.	108	38°20′N	85°25′W
La Grange, Mo., U.S.	121	40°04′N	91°30′W
Lagrange, Oh., U.S.	111d	41°14′N	82°07′W
Lagrange, Tx., U.S.	123	29°55′N	96°50′W
La Grita, Ven. (lä grē′tå)	142	8°02′N	71°59′W
La Guaira, Ven. (lä gwä′ē-rä)	142	10°36′N	66°54′W
La Guardia, Spain (lä gwär′dē-å)	172	41°55′N	8°48′W
Laguna, Braz. (lä-gōō′nä)	144	28°19′S	48°42′W
Laguna, Cayos, is., Cuba (kä′yōs-lä-gōō′nä)	134	22°15′N	82°45′W
Laguna Indian Reservation, I.R., N.M., U.S.	119	35°00′N	107°30′W
Lagunillas, Bol. (lä-gōō-nēl′yäs)	142	19°42′S	63°38′W
Lagunillas, Mex. (lä-gōō-nē′l-yäs)	130	21°34′N	99°41′W
La Habana *see* Havana, Cuba	129	23°08′N	82°23′W
La Habra, Ca., U.S. (lȧ háb′rȧ)	117a	34°56′N	117°57′W
Lahaina, Hi., U.S. (lä-hä′ē-nä)	126a	20°52′N	156°39′W
Lāhījān, Iran	201	37°12′N	50°01′E
Laholm, Swe. (lä′hôlm)	166	56°30′N	13°00′E
La Honda, Ca., U.S. (lā hôn′dă)	116b	37°20′N	122°16′W
Lahore, Pak. (lä-hōr′)	199	32°00′N	74°18′E
Lahr, Ger. (lär)	168	48°19′N	7°52′E
Lahti, Fin. (lä′tē)	160	60°59′N	27°39′E
Lai, Chad	231	9°29′N	16°18′E
Lai'an, China (lī-än)	206	32°27′N	118°25′E
Laibin, China (lī-bĭn)	209	23°42′N	109°20′E
L'Aigle, Fr. (lĕ′gl′)	170	48°45′N	0°37′E
Laisamis, Kenya	237	1°36′N	37°48′E
Laiyang, China (läī′yäng)	208	36°59′N	120°42′E
Laizhou Wan, b., China (lī-jō wän)	205	37°22′N	119°19′E
Laja, Río de la, r., Mex. (rē′ō-dĕ-lä-lä′ĸä)	130	21°17′N	100°57′W
Lajas, Cuba (lä′häs)	134	22°25′N	80°20′W
Lajeado, Braz. (lä-zhĕă′dô)	144	29°24′S	51°46′W
Lajes, Braz. (lä′zhĕs)	144	27°47′S	50°17′W
Lajinha, Braz. (lä-zhē′nyä)	141a	20°08′S	41°36′W
La Jolla, Ca., U.S. (lȧ hoi′yȧ)	118a	32°51′N	117°16′W
La Jolla Indian Reservation, I.R., Ca., U.S.	118	33°19′N	116°21′W
La Junta, Co., U.S. (lȧ hōōn′tȧ)	120	37°59′N	103°35′W
Lake Arthur, La., U.S. (är′thŭr)	123	30°06′N	92°40′W
Lake Barkley, res., U.S.	124	36°45′N	88°00′W
Lake Benton, Mn., U.S. (bĕn′tŭn)	112	44°15′N	96°17′W
Lake Bluff, Il., U.S. (blŭf)	111a	42°17′N	87°50′W
Lake Brown, Austl. (broun)	218	31°03′S	118°30′E
Lake Charles, La., U.S. (chärlz′)	105	30°15′N	93°14′W
Lake City, Fl., U.S.	125	30°09′N	82°40′W
Lake City, Ia., U.S.	113	42°14′N	94°43′W
Lake City, Mn., U.S.	113	44°28′N	92°19′W
Lake City, S.C., U.S.	125	33°57′N	79°45′W
Lake Clark National Park, rec., Ak., U.S.	103	60°30′N	153°15′W
Lake Cowichan, Can. (kou′ĭ-chăn)	94	48°50′N	124°03′W
Lake Crystal, Mn., U.S. (krĭs′tăl)	113	44°05′N	94°12′W
Lake District, reg., Eng., U.K. (lāk)	164	54°25′N	3°20′W
Lake Elmo, Mn., U.S. (ĕlmō)	117g	45°00′N	92°53′W
Lake Forest, Il., U.S. (fŏr′ĕst)	111a	42°16′N	87°50′W
Lake Fork, r., Ut., U.S.	119	40°30′N	110°25′W
Lake Geneva, Wi., U.S. (jĕ-nē′vȧ)	113	42°36′N	88°28′W
Lake Havasu City, Az., U.S.	119	34°27′N	114°22′W
Lake June, Tx., U.S. (jōōn)	117c	32°43′N	96°45′W
Lakeland, Fl., U.S. (lāk′lănd)	105	28°02′N	81°58′W
Lakeland, Ga., U.S.	124	31°02′N	83°02′W
Lakeland, Mn., U.S.	117g	44°57′N	92°47′W
Lake Linden, Mi., U.S. (lĭn′dĕn)	113	47°11′N	88°26′W
Lake Louise, Can. (lōō-ēz′)	95	51°26′N	116°11′W
Lake Mead National Recreation Area, rec., U.S.	119	36°00′N	114°30′W
Lake Mills, Ia., U.S. (mĭlz′)	113	43°25′N	93°32′W
Lakemore, Oh., U.S. (lāk-mōr)	111d	41°01′N	81°24′W
Lake Odessa, Mi., U.S.	108	42°50′N	85°15′W
Lake Oswego, Or., U.S. (ŏs-wē′gō)	116c	45°25′N	122°40′W
Lake Placid, N.Y., U.S.	109	44°17′N	73°59′W
Lake Point, Ut., U.S.	117b	40°41′N	112°16′W
Lakeport, Ca., U.S. (lāk′pōrt)	118	39°03′N	122°54′W
Lake Preston, S.D., U.S. (prĕs′tŭn)	112	44°21′N	97°23′W
Lake Providence, La., U.S. (prŏv′ĭ-dĕns)	123	32°48′N	91°12′W
Lake Red Rock, res., Ia., U.S.	113	41°30′N	93°15′W
Lake Sharpe, res., S.D., U.S.	112	44°30′N	100°00′W
Lakeside, Ca., U.S. (lāk′sīd)	118a	32°52′N	116°55′W
Lake Station, In., U.S.	111a	41°34′N	87°15′W
Lake Stevens, Wa., U.S.	116a	48°01′N	122°04′W
Lake Success, N.Y., U.S. (sŭk-sĕs′)	110a	40°46′N	73°43′W
Lakeview, Or., U.S.	114	42°11′N	120°21′W
Lake Village, Ar., U.S.	121	33°20′N	91°17′W
Lake Wales, Fl., U.S. (wālz′)	125a	27°54′N	81°35′W
Lakewood, Ca., U.S. (lāk′wŏŏd)	117a	33°50′N	118°09′W
Lakewood, Co., U.S.	120	39°44′N	105°06′W
Lakewood, Oh., U.S.	105	41°29′N	81°48′W
Lakewood, Pa., U.S.	109	40°05′N	74°10′W
Lakewood, Wa., U.S.	116a	48°09′N	122°13′W
Lakewood Center, Wa., U.S.	116a	47°10′N	122°31′W
Lake Worth, Fl., U.S. (wûrth′)	125a	26°37′N	80°04′W
Lake Worth Village, Tx., U.S.	117c	32°49′N	97°26′W
Lake Zurich, Il., U.S. (tsü′rĭk)	111a	42°11′N	88°05′W
Lakhdenpokh'ya, Russia (l′äk-dĭe′npōkyä)	167	61°33′N	30°10′E
Lakhtinskiy, Russia (lák-tĭn′skĭ)	186c	59°59′N	30°10′E
Lakota, N.D., U.S. (lȧ-kō′tȧ)	112	48°04′N	98°21′W

PLACE (Pronunciation)	PAGE	LAT.	LONG.
Lakshadweep, state, India	199	10°10′N	72°50′E
Lakshadweep, is., India	199	11°00′N	73°02′E
La Libertad, El Sal.	132	13°29′N	89°20′W
La Libertad, Guat. (lä lē-bĕr-tädh′)	132	15°31′N	91°44′W
La Libertad, Guat.	132a	16°46′N	90°12′W
La Ligua, Chile (lä lē′gwä)	141b	32°21′S	71°13′W
Lalín, Spain (lä-lē′n)	172	42°40′N	8°05′W
La Línea, Spain (lä lē′nå-ä)	162	36°11′N	5°22′W
Lalitpur, Nepal	199	27°23′N	85°24′E
La Louviere, Bel. (lå lōō-vyâr′)	165	50°30′N	4°10′E
La Luz, Mex. (lä lōōz′)	130	21°04′N	101°19′W
Lama-Kara, Togo	234	9°33′N	1°12′E
La Malbaie, Can. (lå mäl-bå′)	91	47°39′N	70°10′W
La Mancha, reg., Spain (lä män′chä)	172	38°55′N	4°20′W
Lamar, Co., U.S. (lȧ-mär′)	120	38°04′N	102°44′W
Lamar, Mo., U.S.	121	37°28′N	94°15′W
La Marmora, Punta, mtn., Italy (lä-mä′r-mô-rä)	162	40°00′N	9°28′E
La Marque, Tx., U.S. (lå-märk)	123a	29°23′N	94°58′W
Lamas, Peru (lä′mås)	142	6°24′S	76°41′W
Lamballe, Fr. (läN-bäl′)	170	48°29′N	2°36′W
Lambari, Braz. (läm-bá′rē)	141a	21°58′S	45°22′W
Lambasa, Fiji	214g	16°26′S	179°24′E
Lambayeque, Peru (läm-bä-yā′kå)	142	6°41′S	79°58′W
Lambert, Ms., U.S. (lăm′bērt)	124	34°10′N	90°16′W
Lambertville, N.J., U.S. (lăm′bērt-vĭl)	109	40°20′N	75°00′W
Lame Deer, Mt., U.S. (lām dēr′)	115	45°36′N	106°40′W
Lamego, Port. (lä-mā′gō)	172	41°07′N	7°47′W
La Mesa, Col.	142a	4°38′N	74°27′W
La Mesa, Ca., U.S. (lä mā′sä)	118a	32°46′N	117°01′W
Lamesa, Tx., U.S.	120	32°44′N	101°54′W
Lamía, Grc. (lå-mē′å)	163	38°54′N	22°25′E
Lamon Bay, b., Phil. (lä-mōn′)	212	14°35′N	121°52′E
La Mora, Chile (lä-mō′rä)	141b	32°28′S	70°56′W
La Moure, N.D., U.S. (lȧ mōōr′)	112	46°23′N	98°17′W
Lampa, r., Chile (lá′m-pä)	141b	33°15′S	70°55′W
Lampasas, Tx., U.S. (lăm-păs′ăs)	122	31°06′N	98°10′W
Lampasas, r., Tx., U.S.	122	31°18′N	98°08′W
Lampazos, Mex. (läm-pä′zōs)	128	27°03′N	100°30′W
Lampedusa, i., Italy (läm-på-dōō′sä)	162	35°29′N	12°58′E
Lamstedt, Ger. (läm′shtĕt)	159c	53°38′N	9°06′E
Lamu, Kenya (lä′mōō)	233	2°16′S	40°54′E
Lamu Island, i., Kenya	237	2°25′S	40°50′E
La Mure, Fr. (lå mür′)	171	44°55′N	5°50′E
Lan', r., Bela. (làn′)	176	52°38′N	27°05′E
Lāna'i, i., Hi., U.S. (lä-nä′ē)	106c	20°48′N	157°06′W
Lanai City, Hi., U.S.	126a	20°50′N	156°56′W
Lanak La, p., China	204	34°40′N	79°50′E
Lanark, Scot., U.K. (lăn′ȧrk)	164	55°40′N	3°50′W
Lancashire, co., Eng., U.K. (lăŋ′kȧ-shĭr)	158a	53°49′N	2°42′W
Lancaster, Eng., U.K.	160	54°04′N	2°55′W
Lancaster, Ky., U.S.	108	37°35′N	84°30′W
Lancaster, Ma., U.S.	101a	42°28′N	71°40′W
Lancaster, N.H., U.S.	109	44°25′N	71°30′W
Lancaster, N.Y., U.S.	111c	42°54′N	78°42′W
Lancaster, Oh., U.S.	108	39°40′N	82°35′W
Lancaster, Pa., U.S.	105	40°05′N	76°20′W
Lancaster, Tx., U.S.	117c	32°36′N	96°45′W
Lancaster, Wi., U.S.	113	42°51′N	90°44′W
Lândana, Ang. (län-dä′nä)	232	5°15′S	12°07′E
Landau, Ger. (län′dou)	168	49°13′N	8°07′E
Lander, Wy., U.S. (lăn′dēr)	115	42°49′N	108°24′W
Landerneau, Fr. (läN-dĕr-nō′)	170	48°28′N	4°14′W
Landes, reg., Fr. (länd)	170	44°22′N	0°52′W
Landsberg, Ger. (länds′bōōrgh)	168	48°03′N	10°53′E
Lands End, c., Eng., U.K.	156	50°03′N	5°45′W
Landshut, Ger. (länts′hōōt)	161	48°32′N	12°09′E
Landskrona, Swe. (làns-krō′nà)	166	55°51′N	12°47′E
Lanett, Al., U.S. (lȧ-nĕt′)	124	32°52′N	85°13′W
Langat, r., Malay.	197b	2°46′N	101°33′E
Langdon, Can. (lăng′dŭn)	102e	50°58′N	113°40′W
Langdon, Mn., U.S.	117g	44°49′N	92°56′W
L'Ange-Gardien, Can. (läNzh gàr-dyăN′)	102b	46°55′N	71°06′W
Langeland, i., Den.	166	54°52′N	10°46′E
Langenzersdorf, Aus.	159e	48°30′N	16°22′E
Langesund, Nor. (läng′ĕ-sōn′)	166	58°59′N	9°38′E
Langfjorden, b., Nor.	166	62°40′N	7°45′E
Langhorne, Pa., U.S. (lăng′hôrn)	110f	40°10′N	74°55′W
Langia Mountains, mts., Ug.	237	3°35′N	33°35′E
Langjökoll, ice, Ice. (läng-yû′kōōl)	160	64°40′N	20°31′W
Langla Co, l., China (läŋ-lä tswo)	202	30°42′N	80°40′E
Langley, Can. (lăng′lĭ)	95	49°06′N	122°39′W
Langley, S.C., U.S.	125	33°32′N	81°52′W
Langley, Wa., U.S.	116a	48°02′N	122°25′W
Langley Indian Reserve, I.R., Can.	116d	49°12′N	122°31′W
Langnau, Switz. (läng′nou)	168	46°56′N	7°46′E
Langon, Fr. (läN-gôN′)	170	44°34′N	0°16′W
Langres, Fr. (läN′gr′)	171	47°53′N	5°20′E
Langres, Plateau de, plat., Fr. (plä-tō′dĕ-läN′grĕ)	170	47°39′N	5°00′E
Langsa, Indon. (läng′sà)	212	4°33′N	97°52′E
Lang Son, Viet. (lăng′sŏn′)	212	21°52′N	106°42′E
L'Anguille, r., Ar., U.S. (läN-gē′y′)	121	35°23′N	90°52′W
Langxi, China (läŋ-shyē)	206	31°10′N	119°09′E
Langzhong, China (läŋ-jôŋ)	204	31°40′N	106°05′E
Lanham, Md., U.S. (lăn′ăm)	110e	38°58′N	76°54′W
Lanigan, Can. (lăn′ĭ-găn)	90	51°52′N	105°02′W
Länkäran, Azer. (lĕn-kō-rän′)	178	38°52′N	48°58′E
Lankoviri, Nig.	235	9°00′N	11°25′E
Lansdale, Pa., U.S. (lănz′dāl)	109	40°20′N	75°15′W
Lansdowne, Pa., U.S.	110f	39°57′N	75°17′W
L'Anse, Mi., U.S. (läns)	113	46°43′N	88°28′W

ăt; finăl; rāte; senåte; ärm; åsk; sofȧ; fâre; ch-choose; dh-as th in other; bē; ėvent; bĕt; recĕnt; cratēr; g-gō; gh-guttural g; bĭt; ĭ-short neutral; rīde; ĸ-guttural k as ch in German ich;

PRONOUNCING INDEX
L'Anse and Vieux Desert – Leivádia 313

PLACE (Pronunciation)	PAGE	LAT.	LONG.
L'Anse and Vieux Desert Indian Reservation, I.R., Mi., U.S.	113	46°41′N	88°12′W
Lansford, Pa., U.S. (lănz′fērd)	109	40°50′N	75°50′W
Lansing, Ia., U.S.	113	43°22′N	91°16′W
Lansing, Il., U.S.	111a	41°34′N	87°33′W
Lansing, Ks., U.S.	117f	39°15′N	94°53′W
Lansing, Mi., U.S.	105	42°45′N	84°35′W
Lanús, Arg. (lä-nōōs′)	144a	34°42′S	58°24′W
Lanusei, Italy (lä-nōō-sĕ′y)	174	39°51′N	9°34′E
Lanúvio, Italy (lä-nōō′vyô)	173d	41°41′N	12°42′E
Lanzarote Island, i., Spain (län-zá-rō′tä)	230	29°04′N	13°03′W
Lanzhou, China (län-jō)	204	35°55′N	103°55′E
Laoag, Phil. (lä-wäg′)	212	18°13′N	120°38′E
Laon, Fr. (läɴ)	170	49°36′N	3°35′E
La Oroya, Peru (lä-ô-rō′yä)	142	11°30′S	76°00′W
Laos, nation, Asia (lä-ōs) (lá-ōs′)	212	20°15′N	102°00′E
Laoshan Wan, b., China (lou-shän wän)	206	36°21′N	120°48′E
La Palma, Pan. (lä-päl′mä)	133	8°25′N	78°07′W
La Palma, Spain	172	37°24′N	6°36′W
La Palma Island, i., Spain	230	28°42′N	19°03′W
La Pampa, prov., Arg.	144	37°25′S	67°00′W
Lapa Rio Negro, Braz. (lä-pä-rē′ō-nĕ′grô)	144	26°12′S	49°56′W
La Paz, Arg. (lä päz′)	144	30°48′S	59°47′W
La Paz, Bol.	142	16°31′S	68°03′W
La Paz, Hond.	132	14°15′N	87°40′W
La Paz, Mex. (lä-pá′z)	130	23°39′N	100°44′W
La Paz, Mex.	128	24°00′N	110°15′W
Lapeer, Mi., U.S. (lá-pēr′)	108	43°05′N	83°15′W
La-Penne-sur-Huveaune, Fr. (la-pĕn′sür-ü-vōn′)	170a	43°18′N	5°33′E
La Perouse, Austl.	217b	33°59′S	151°14′E
La Piedad Cabadas, Mex. (lä pyå-dhädh′ kä-bä′dhäs)	130	20°20′N	102°04′W
Lapland, hist. reg., Eur. (lăp′lănd)	154	68°20′N	22°00′E
La Plata, Arg. (lä plä′tä)	144	34°54′S	57°57′W
La Plata, Mo., U.S. (lá plā′tá)	121	40°03′N	92°28′W
La Plata Peak, mtn., Co., U.S.	119	39°00′N	106°25′W
La Pocatière, Can. (lá pô-ká-tyâr′)	99	47°24′N	70°01′W
La Poile Bay, b., Can. (lá pwäl′)	101	47°38′N	58°20′W
La Porte, In., U.S. (lá pōrt′)	108	41°35′N	86°45′W
Laporte, Oh., U.S.	111d	41°19′N	82°05′W
La Porte, Tx., U.S.	123a	29°40′N	95°01′W
La Porte City, Ia., U.S.	113	42°20′N	92°10′W
Lappeenranta, Fin. (lä′pēn-rän′tä)	167	61°04′N	28°08′E
La Prairie, Can. (lá-prâ-rē′)	102a	45°24′N	73°30′W
Lâpseki, Tur. (läp′sá-kē)	175	40°20′N	26°41′E
Laptev Sea, sea, Russia (läp′tyĭf)	179	75°39′N	120°00′E
La Puebla de Montalbán, Spain	172	39°54′N	4°21′W
La Puente, Ca., U.S. (pwĕn′tē)	117a	34°01′N	117°57′W
Lapuşul, r., Rom. (lä′pōō-shōōl)	169	47°29′N	23°46′E
La Quiaca, Arg. (lä kē-ä′kä)	144	22°15′S	65°44′W
L'Aquila, Italy (lá′kē-lä)	162	42°22′N	13°24′E
Lār, Iran (lär)	198	27°31′N	54°12′E
Lara, Austl.	217a	38°02′S	144°24′E
Larache, Mor. (lä-räsh′)	230	35°15′N	6°09′W
Laramie, Wy., U.S. (lăr′á-mĭ)	104	41°20′N	105°40′W
Laramie, r., Co., U.S.	120	40°56′N	105°55′W
Larchmont, N.Y., U.S. (lärch′mŏnt)	110a	40°56′N	73°46′W
Larch Mountain, mtn., Or., U.S. (lärch)	116c	45°32′N	122°06′W
Laredo, Spain (lá-rā′dhō)	172	43°24′N	3°24′W
Laredo, Tx., U.S.	104	27°31′N	99°29′W
La Réole, Fr. (lá rå-ōl′)	170	44°37′N	0°03′W
Largeau, Chad (lär-zhō′)	231	17°55′N	19°07′E
Largo, Cayo, Cuba (kä′yō-lär′gō)	134	21°40′N	81°30′W
Larimore, N.D., U.S. (lăr′ĭ-môr)	112	47°53′N	97°38′W
Larino, Italy (lä-rē′nô)	174	41°48′N	14°54′E
La Rioja, Arg. (lä rê-ōhä)	144	29°18′S	67°42′W
La Rioja, prov., Arg. (lä-rê-ô′kä)	144	28°45′S	68°00′W
Lárisa, Grc. (lä′rê-sá)	163	39°38′N	22°25′E
Lārkāna, Pak.	202	27°40′N	68°12′E
Larnaka, Cyp.	163	34°55′N	33°37′E
Lárnakos, Kólpos, b., Cyp.	197a	36°50′N	33°45′E
Larned, Ks., U.S. (lär′nĕd)	120	38°09′N	99°07′W
La Robla, Spain (lä rōb′lä)	172	42°48′N	5°36′W
La Rochelle, Fr. (lá rô-shĕl′)	154	46°10′N	1°09′W
La Roche-sur-Yon, Fr. (lá rôsh′sûr-yôɴ′)	161	46°39′N	1°27′W
La Roda, Spain (lä rō′dä)	172	39°13′N	2°08′W
La Romona, Dom. Rep. (lä-rä-mô′nä)	135	18°25′N	69°00′W
Larrey Point, c., Austl. (lăr′ē)	220	19°15′S	118°15′E
Laruns, Fr. (lá-răɴs′)	170	42°58′N	0°28′W
Larvik, Nor. (lär′vĕk)	160	59°06′N	10°03′E
La Sabana, Ven. (lä-sä-bá′nä)	143b	10°38′N	66°24′W
La Sabina, Cuba (lä-sä-bē′nä)	135a	22°51′N	82°05′W
La Sagra, mtn., Spain (lä sä′grä)	162	37°56′N	2°35′W
La Sal, Ut., U.S. (lá sál′)	119	38°10′N	109°20′W
La Salle, Can. (lá sál′)	111b	42°14′N	83°06′W
La Salle, Can.	102a	45°26′N	73°39′W
La Salle, Can.	102f	49°41′N	97°16′W
La Salle, Il., U.S.	108	41°20′N	89°05′W
Las Animas, Co., U.S. (lás ă′nĭ-mås)	120	38°03′N	103°16′W
La Sarre, Can.	91	48°43′N	79°12′W
Lascahobas, Haiti (läs-kä-ō′bås)	135	19°00′N	71°55′W
Las Cruces, Mex. (läs-krōō′sĕs)	131	16°37′N	93°54′W
Las Cruces, N.M., U.S.	104	32°20′N	106°50′W
La Selle, Massif de, mtn., Haiti (lä′sĕl′)	135	18°25′N	72°05′W
La Serena, Chile (lä-sĕ-rĕ′nä)	144	29°55′S	71°24′W
La Seyne, Fr. (lä-sån′)	161	43°07′N	5°52′E
Las Flores, Arg. (läs flō′rĕs)	144	36°01′S	59°07′W
Lashio, Mya. (lăsh′ē-ō)	204	22°58′N	98°03′E
Las Juntas, C.R. (läs-кōō′n-täs)	132	10°15′N	85°00′W
Las Maismas, sw., Spain (läs-mī′s-mäs)	172	37°05′N	6°25′W
La Solana, Spain (lä-sô-lä-nä)	172	38°56′N	3°13′W
Las Palmas, Pan.	133	8°08′N	81°30′W
Las Palmas de Gran Canaria, Spain (läs päl′mäs)	230	28°07′N	15°28′W
La Spezia, Italy (lä-spě′zyä)	154	44°07′N	9°48′E
Las Piedras, Ur. (läs-pyĕ′drås)	141c	34°42′S	56°08′W
Las Pilas, vol., Nic. (läs-pē′läs)	132	12°32′N	86°43′W
Las Rosas, Mex. (läs rō′thäs)	131	16°24′N	92°23′W
Las Rozas de Madrid, Spain (läs rō′thas dā mä-dhrēd′)	173a	40°29′N	3°53′W
Lassee, Aus.	159e	48°14′N	16°50′E
Lassen Peak, mtn., Ca., U.S. (lăs′ĕn)	106	40°30′N	121°32′W
Lassen Volcanic National Park, rec., Ca., U.S.	106	40°43′N	121°35′W
L'Assomption, Can. (lás-sôm-syôɴ)	102a	45°50′N	73°25′W
Lass Qoray, Som.	238a	11°13′N	48°19′E
Las Tablas, Pan. (läs tä′bläs)	133	7°48′N	80°16′W
Last Mountain, l., Can. (lást moun′tĭn)	92	51°05′N	105°10′W
Lastoursville, Gabon (lás-tōōr-vēl′)	232	1°00′S	12°49′E
Las Tres Vírgenes, Volcán, vol., Mex. (vē′r-hĕ-nĕs)	128	26°00′N	111°45′W
Las Tunas, prov., Cuba	134	21°05′N	77°00′W
Las Vacas, Mex. (läs-vá′käs)	131	16°24′N	95°48′W
Las Vegas, Chile (läs-vĕ′gäs)	141b	32°50′S	70°59′W
Las Vegas, N.M., U.S.	104	35°36′N	105°13′W
Las Vegas, Nv., U.S. (läs vā′gäs)	104	36°12′N	115°10′W
Las Vegas, Ven. (läs-vĕ′gäs)	143b	10°26′N	64°08′W
Las Vigas, Mex.	131	19°38′N	97°03′W
Las Vizcachas, Meseta de, plat., Arg.	144	49°35′S	71°00′W
Latacunga, Ec. (lä-tä-kòŋ′gä)	142	1°02′S	78°33′W
Latakia *see* Al Lādhiqīyah, Syria	198	35°32′N	35°51′E
La Teste-de-Buch, Fr. (lä-tĕst-dĕ-büsh)	170	44°38′N	1°11′W
Lathrop, Mo., U.S. (lā′thrŭp)	121	39°32′N	94°21′W
La Tortuga, Isla, i., Ven. (ē′s-lä-lä-tôr-tōō′gä)	142	10°55′N	65°18′W
Latorytsia, r., Eur.	169	48°27′N	22°30′E
Latourell, Or., U.S. (lá-tou′rĕl)	116c	45°32′N	122°13′W
La Tremblade, Fr. (lä-trĕɴ-bläd′)	170	45°45′N	1°12′W
Latrobe, Pa., U.S. (lá-trōb′)	109	40°25′N	79°15′W
La Tuque, Can. (lá′tük′)	91	47°27′N	72°49′W
Lātūr, India (lä-tōōr′)	202	18°20′N	76°35′E
Latvia, nation, Eur.	178	57°28′N	24°29′E
Lau Group, is., Fiji	214g	18°20′S	178°30′W
Launceston, Austl. (lôn′sĕs-tŭn)	219	41°35′S	147°22′E
Launceston, Eng., U.K. (lôrn′stŏn)	164	50°38′N	4°26′W
La Unión, Chile (lä-ōō-nyô′n)	144	40°15′S	73°04′W
La Unión, El Sal.	132	13°18′N	87°51′W
La Unión, Mex. (lä ōōn-nyōn′)	130	17°59′N	101°48′W
La Unión, Spain	162	37°38′N	0°50′W
Laura, Austl. (lôrá)	219	15°40′S	144°45′E
Laurel, De., U.S. (lô′rĕl)	109	38°30′N	75°40′W
Laurel, Md., U.S.	110e	39°06′N	76°51′W
Laurel, Ms., U.S.	105	31°42′N	89°07′W
Laurel, Mt., U.S.	115	45°41′N	108°45′W
Laurel, Wa., U.S.	116d	48°52′N	122°29′W
Laurelwood, Or., U.S. (lô′rĕl-wòd)	116c	45°25′N	123°05′W
Laurens, S.C., U.S. (lô′rĕnz)	125	34°29′N	82°03′W
Laurentian Highlands, hills, Can. (lô′rĕn-tĭ-ăn)	89	49°00′N	74°50′W
Laurentides, Can. (lô′rĕn-tīdz)	102a	45°51′N	73°46′W
Lauria, Italy (lou′rē-ä)	163	40°03′N	15°02′E
Laurinburg, N.C., U.S. (lô′rĭn-bûrg)	125	34°45′N	79°27′W
Laurium, Mi., U.S. (lô′rĭ-ŭm)	113	47°13′N	88°28′W
Lausanne, Switz. (lō-zán′)	154	46°32′N	6°35′E
Laut, Pulau, i., Indon.	212	3°39′S	116°07′E
Lautaro, Chile (lou-tä′rô)	144	38°40′S	72°24′W
Laut Kecil, Kepulauan, is., Indon.	212	4°44′S	115°43′E
Lautoka, Fiji	214g	17°37′S	177°27′E
Lauzon, Can. (lō-zōɴ′)	102b	46°50′N	71°10′W
Lava Beds National Monument, rec., Ca., U.S. (lä′vá bĕds)	114	41°38′N	121°44′W
Lavaca, r., Tx., U.S. (lá-vák′á)	123	29°05′N	96°50′W
Lava Hot Springs, Id., U.S.	115	42°37′N	111°58′W
Laval, Can.	91	45°31′N	73°44′W
Laval, Fr. (lä-väl′)	161	48°05′N	0°47′W
La Vecilla de Curueño, Spain	172	42°53′N	5°18′W
La Vega, Dom. Rep. (lä-vĕ′gä)	135	19°15′N	70°35′W
Lavello, Italy (lä-vĕl′lô)	174	41°05′N	15°50′E
La Verne, Ca., U.S. (lá vûrn′)	117a	34°06′N	117°46′W
Laverton, Austl. (lā′vēr-tŭn)	218	28°45′S	122°30′E
La Victoria, Ven. (lä vēk-tō′rē-ä)	142	10°14′N	67°20′W
La Vila Joiosa, Spain	173	38°30′N	0°14′W
Lavonia, Ga., U.S. (lá-vō′nĭ-á)	124	34°26′N	83°05′W
Lavon Reservoir, res., Tx., U.S.	123	33°06′N	96°20′W
Lavras, Braz. (lä′vräzh)	141a	21°15′S	44°59′W
Lávrio, Grc.	175	37°44′N	24°05′E
Lavry, Russia (lou′rá)	176	57°35′N	27°28′E
Lawndale, Ca., U.S. (lôn′dāl)	117a	33°54′N	118°22′W
Lawra, Ghana	234	10°39′N	2°52′W
Lawrence, In., U.S. (lô′rĕns)	111g	39°59′N	86°01′W
Lawrence, Ks., U.S.	105	38°57′N	95°13′W
Lawrence, Ma., U.S.	101a	42°42′N	71°09′W
Lawrence, Pa., U.S.	111e	40°18′N	80°07′W
Lawrenceburg, In., U.S. (lô′rĕns-bûrg)	111f	39°06′N	84°47′W
Lawrenceburg, Ky., U.S.	108	38°00′N	85°00′W
Lawrenceburg, Tn., U.S.	124	35°13′N	87°20′W
Lawrenceville, Ga., U.S. (lô-rĕns-vĭl)	124	33°56′N	83°57′W
Lawrenceville, Il., U.S.	108	38°45′N	87°45′W
Lawrenceville, N.J., U.S.	110a	40°17′N	74°44′W
Lawrenceville, Va., U.S.	125	36°43′N	77°52′W
Lawsonia, Md., U.S. (lô-sō′nĭ-á)	109	38°00′N	75°50′W
Lawton, Ok., U.S. (lô′tŭn)	104	34°36′N	98°25′W
Lawz, Jabal al, mtn., Sau. Ar.	198	28°46′N	35°37′E
Layang Layang, Malay. (lä-yäng′ lä-yäng′)	197b	1°49′N	103°28′E
Laysan, i., Hi., U.S.	126b	26°00′N	171°00′W
Layton, Ut., U.S. (lā′tŭn)	117b	41°04′N	111°58′W
Lazdijai, Lith. (läzh′dē-yī′)	167	54°12′N	23°35′E
Lazio (Latium), hist. reg., Italy	174	42°05′N	12°25′E
Lead, S.D., U.S. (lēd)	104	44°22′N	103°47′W
Leader, Can.	96	50°55′N	109°32′W
Leadville, Co., U.S. (lĕd′vĭl)	120	39°14′N	106°18′W
Leaf, r., Ms., U.S. (lēf)	124	31°43′N	89°20′W
League City, Tx., U.S. (lēg)	123a	29°31′N	95°05′W
Leamington, Can. (lĕm′ĭng-tŭn)	98	42°05′N	82°35′W
Leamington, Eng., U.K. (lĕ′mĭng-tŭn)	164	52°17′N	1°25′W
Leatherhead, Eng., U.K. (lĕdh′ēr-hĕd′)	158b	51°17′N	0°20′W
Leavenworth, Ks., U.S. (lĕv′ĕn-wûrth)	105	39°19′N	94°54′W
Leavenworth, Wa., U.S.	114	47°35′N	120°39′W
Leawood, Ks., U.S. (lē′wòd)	117f	38°58′N	94°37′W
Łeba, Pol. (lā′bä)	169	54°45′N	17°34′E
Lebam, r., Malay.	197b	1°35′N	104°09′E
Lebango, Congo	236	0°22′N	14°49′E
Lebanon, Il., U.S. (lĕb′á-nŭn)	117e	38°36′N	89°49′W
Lebanon, In., U.S.	108	40°00′N	86°30′W
Lebanon, Ky., U.S.	124	37°32′N	85°15′W
Lebanon, Mo., U.S.	121	37°40′N	92°43′W
Lebanon, N.H., U.S.	109	43°40′N	72°15′W
Lebanon, Oh., U.S.	108	39°25′N	84°10′W
Lebanon, Or., U.S.	114	44°31′N	122°53′W
Lebanon, Pa., U.S.	109	40°20′N	76°20′W
Lebanon, Tn., U.S.	124	36°10′N	86°16′W
Lebanon, nation, Asia	198	34°00′N	34°00′E
Lebedyan′, Russia (lyĕ′bĕ-dyän′)	180	53°03′N	39°08′E
Lebedyn, Ukr.	181	50°34′N	34°27′E
Le Blanc, Fr. (lĕ-bläɴ′)	170	46°38′N	0°59′E
Le Borgne, Haiti (lĕ bōrn′y′)	135	19°50′N	72°30′W
Lębork, Pol. (lăɴ-bòrk′)	169	54°33′N	17°46′E
Lebrija, Spain (lå-brē′hä)	172	36°55′N	6°06′W
Lecce, Italy (lĕt′chä)	163	40°22′N	18°11′E
Lecco, Italy (lĕk′kō)	174	45°52′N	9°28′E
Lech, r., Ger. (lĕk)	168	47°41′N	10°52′E
Le Châtelet-en-Brie, Fr. (lĕ-shä-tĕ-lā′ĕɴ-brē′)	171b	48°29′N	2°50′E
Leche, Laguna de, l., Cuba (lä-gò′nä-dĕ-lĕ′chĕ)	134	22°10′N	78°30′W
Leche, Laguna de la, l., Mex.	122	27°16′N	102°45′W
Lecompte, La., U.S.	123	31°06′N	92°25′W
Le Creusot, Fr. (lĕkrû-zô)	161	46°48′N	4°23′E
Ledesma, Spain (lå-dĕs′mä)	172	41°05′N	5°59′W
Leduc, Can. (lĕ-dōōk′)	95	53°16′N	113°33′W
Leech, l., Mn., U.S. (lēch)	113	47°06′N	94°16′W
Leeds, Eng., U.K.	154	53°48′N	1°33′W
Leeds, Al., U.S. (lēdz)	110h	33°33′N	86°33′W
Leeds, N.D., U.S.	112	48°18′N	99°24′W
Leeds, co., Eng., U.K.	158a	53°50′N	1°30′W
Leeds and Liverpool Canal, can., Eng., U.K. (lĭv′ēr-pōōl)	158a	53°36′N	2°38′W
Leegebruch, Ger. (lĕh′gĕn-brōōк)	159b	52°43′N	13°12′E
Leek, Eng., U.K. (lēk)	158a	53°06′N	2°01′W
Leer, Ger. (lār)	168	53°14′N	7°27′E
Leesburg, Fl., U.S. (lēz′bûrg)	125	28°49′N	81°53′W
Leesburg, Va., U.S.	109	39°10′N	77°30′W
Lees Summit, Mo., U.S.	117f	38°55′N	94°23′W
Lee Stocking, i., Bah.	134	23°45′N	76°05′W
Leesville, La., U.S. (lēz′vĭl)	123	31°09′N	93°17′W
Leetonia, Oh., U.S. (lē-tō′nĭ-á)	108	40°50′N	80°45′W
Leeuwarden, Neth. (lā′wär-dĕn)	161	52°12′N	5°50′E
Leeuwin, Cape, c., Austl. (lōō′wĭn)	220	34°15′S	114°30′E
Leeward Islands, is., N.A. (lē′wērd)	123	17°00′N	62°15′W
Lefkáda, Grc.	175	38°49′N	20°43′E
Lefkáda, i., Grc.	163	38°42′N	20°22′E
Le François, Mart.	133b	14°37′N	60°55′W
Lefroy, l., Austl. (lē-froi′)	220	31°30′S	122°00′E
Leganés, Spain (lå-gä′nås)	173a	40°20′N	3°46′W
Legazpi, Phil. (lå-gäs′pē)	213	13°09′N	123°44′E
Legge Peak, mtn., Austl. (lĕg)	222	41°33′S	148°10′E
Leggett, Ca., U.S.	118	39°51′N	123°42′W
Leghorn *see* Livorno, Italy	154	43°32′N	11°18′E
Legnano, Italy (lå-nyä′nō)	174	45°35′N	8°53′E
Legnica, Pol. (lĕk-nĭt′sá)	161	51°13′N	16°10′E
Leh, India (lā)	202	34°10′N	77°40′E
Le Havre, Fr. (lē ȧv′r′)	154	49°31′N	0°07′E
Lehi, Ut., U.S. (lē′hī)	119	40°25′N	111°55′W
Lehman Caves National Monument, rec., Nv., U.S. (lē′măn)	119	38°54′N	114°08′W
Lehnin, Ger. (lĕh′nēn)	159b	52°19′N	12°45′E
Leicester, Eng., U.K. (lĕs′tēr)	154	52°37′N	1°08′W
Leicestershire, co., Eng., U.K.	158a	52°40′N	1°12′W
Leichhardt, r., Austl. (līk′härt)	220	18°30′S	139°45′E
Leiden, Neth. (lī′dĕn)	165	52°09′N	4°29′E
Leigh Creek, Austl. (lē krēk)	222	30°33′S	138°30′E
Leikanger, Nor. (lī′käŋ′gēr)	166	61°11′N	6°51′E
Leimuiden, Neth.	159a	52°13′N	4°40′E
Leine, r., Ger. (lī′nĕ)	168	51°58′N	9°56′E
Leinster, hist. reg., Ire. (lĕn-stēr)	164	52°45′N	7°19′W
Leipsic, Oh., U.S. (līp′sĭk)	108	41°05′N	84°00′W
Leipzig, Ger. (līp′tsĭk)	154	51°20′N	12°24′E
Leiria, Port. (lā-rē′ä)	172	39°45′N	8°50′W
Leitchfield, Ky., U.S. (lēch′fēld)	124	37°28′N	86°20′W
Leitha, r., Aus.	159e	48°04′N	16°57′E
Leitrim, Can.	102c	45°20′N	75°36′W
Leivádia, Grc.	175	38°25′N	22°51′E

314 Leizhou Bandao – Lincoln Park PRONOUNCING INDEX

PLACE (Pronunciation)	PAGE	LAT.	LONG.
Leizhou Bandao, pen., China (lā-jō bän-dou)	204	20°42'N	109°10'E
Leksand, Swe. (lĕk'sänd)	166	60°45'N	14°56'E
Leland, Wa., U.S. (lē'lǎnd)	116a	47°54'N	122°53'W
Leliu, China (lŭ-lĭō)	207a	22°52'N	113°09'E
Le Locle, Switz. (lē lô'kl')	168	47°03'N	6°43'E
Le Maire, Estrecho de, strt., Arg. (ĕs-trĕ'chô-dĕ-lĕ-mī'rĕ)	144	55°15'S	65°30'W
Le Mans, Fr. (lē mäN')	161	48°01'N	0°12'E
Le Marin, Mart.	133b	14°28'N	60°55'W
Le Mars, Ia., U.S. (lē märz')	112	42°46'N	96°09'W
Lemay, Mo., U.S.	117e	38°32'N	90°17'W
Lemdiyya, Alg.	230	36°18'N	2°40'E
Lemery, Phil. (lā-mā-rē')	213a	13°51'S	120°55'E
Lemhi, r., Id., U.S.	115	44°40'N	113°27'W
Lemhi Range, mts., Id., U.S. (lĕm'hī)	115	44°35'N	113°33'W
Lemmon, S.D., U.S. (lĕm'ŭn)	112	45°55'N	102°10'W
Le Môle, Haiti (lē mōl')	135	19°50'N	73°20'W
Lemon Grove, Ca., U.S. (lĕm'ŭn-grōv)	118a	32°44'N	117°02'W
Le Moule, Guad. (lē mōōl')	133b	16°19'N	61°22'W
Lempa, r., N.A. (lĕm'pä)	132	13°20'N	88°46'W
Lemvig, Den. (lĕm'vēgh)	166	56°33'N	8°16'E
Lena, r., Russia	179	68°00'N	123°00'E
Lençóes Paulista, Braz. (lĕn-sôNs' pou-lēs'tà)	144	22°30'S	48°45'W
Lençóis, Braz. (lĕn-sóis)	143	12°38'S	41°28'W
Lenexa, Ks., U.S. (lē'nĕx-ǎ)	117f	38°58'N	99°44'W
Lengyandong, China (lŭŋ-yän-dôŋ)	207a	23°12'N	113°21'E
Lenik, r., Malay.	197b	1°59'N	102°51'E
Leningrad *see* Saint Petersburg, Russia	178	59°57'N	30°20'E
Leningrad, prov., Russia	176	59°15'N	30°30'E
Leningradskaya, Russia (lyĕ-nĭn-gräd'skà-yà)	177	46°19'N	39°23'E
Lenino, Russia (lyĕ'nĭ-nô)	186b	55°37'N	37°41'E
Leninogorsk, Kaz.	183	50°29'N	83°25'E
Lenīnsk, Kaz.	183	45°39'N	63°19'E
Leninsk, Russia (lyĕ-nēnsk')	181	48°40'N	45°10'E
Leninsk-Kuznetski, Russia (lyĕ-nênsk'kōōz-nyĕt'skĭ)	178	54°28'N	86°48'E
Lennox, S.D., U.S. (lĕn'ŭks)	112	43°22'N	96°53'W
Lenoir, N.C., U.S. (lē-nōr')	125	35°54'N	81°35'W
Lenoir City, Tn., U.S.	124	35°47'N	84°16'W
Lenox, Ia., U.S.	113	40°51'N	94°29'W
Léo, Burkina	234	11°06'N	2°06'W
Leoben, Aus. (lå-ō'bĕn)	168	47°22'N	15°09'E
Léogane, Haiti (lā-ô-gan')	135	18°30'N	72°35'W
Leola, S.D., U.S. (lē-ō'là)	112	45°43'N	99°55'W
Leominster, Ma., U.S. (lĕm'ĭn-stēr)	109	42°32'N	71°45'W
León, Mex. (lå-ōn')	128	21°08'N	101°41'W
León, Nic. (lĕ-ō'n)	128	12°28'N	86°53'W
León, Spain (lĕ-ō'n)	162	42°38'N	5°33'W
Leon, Ia., U.S. (lē'ŏn)	113	40°43'N	93°44'W
León, hist. reg., Spain	172	41°18'N	5°50'W
Leon, r., Tx., U.S. (lē'ŏn)	122	31°54'N	98°20'W
Leonforte, Italy (lā-ôn-fôr'tā)	174	37°40'N	14°27'E
Leopold II, Lac *see* Mai-Ndombe, Lac, l., D.R.C.	232	2°16'S	19°00'E
Leopoldina, Braz. (lā-ô-pôl-dē'nä)	141a	21°32'S	42°38'W
Leopoldsburg, Bel.	159a	51°07'N	5°18'E
Leopoldsdorf im Marchfelde, Aus. (lā'ô-pôlts-dôrf')	159e	48°14'N	16°42'E
Léopoldville *see* Kinshasa, D.R.C.	232	4°18'S	15°18'E
Leova, Mol.	177	46°30'N	28°16'E
Lepe, Spain (lā'pā)	172	37°15'N	7°12'W
Leping, China (lŭ-pĭŋ)	209	29°02'N	117°12'E
L'Epiphanie, Can. (lā-pē-fä-nē')	102a	45°51'N	73°29'W
Le Plessis-Belleville, Fr. (lĕ-plĕ-sē'bĕl-vēl')	171b	49°05'N	2°46'E
Lepreau, Can. (lē-prō')	100	45°10'N	66°28'W
Le Puy, Fr. (lē pwē')	161	45°02'N	3°54'E
Lercara Friddi, Italy (lĕr-kä'rä)	174	37°47'N	13°36'E
Lerdo, Mex. (lĕr'dō)	128	25°31'N	103°30'W
Leribe, Leso.	233c	28°53'S	28°02'E
Lerma, Mex. (lĕr'mä)	131	19°49'N	90°34'W
Lerma, Mex.	131a	19°17'N	99°30'W
Lerma, Spain (lĕ'r-mä)	172	42°03'N	3°45'W
Lerma, r., Mex.	130	20°14'N	101°50'W
Le Roy, N.Y., U.S. (lē roi')	109	43°00'N	78°00'W
Lerwick, Scot., U.K. (lĕr'ĭk) (lûr'wĭk)	154	60°08'N	1°27'W
Léry, Can. (lā-rī')	102a	45°21'N	73°49'W
Léry, Lake, l., La., U.S. (lĕ'rē)	110d	29°48'N	89°45'W
Les Andelys, Fr. (lā-zäN-dē-lē')	171b	49°15'N	1°25'E
Les Borges Blanques, Spain	173	41°29'N	0°53'E
Lesbos *see* Lésvos, i., Grc.	156	39°15'N	25°40'E
Les Cayes, Haiti	135	18°15'N	73°45'W
Les Cèdres, Can. (lā-sĕdr')	102a	45°18'N	74°03'W
Lesh, Alb. (lĕshĕ) (ä-lā'sē-ō)	175	41°47'N	19°40'E
Leshan, China (lŭ-shän)	204	29°40'N	103°40'E
Lésina, Lago di, l., Italy (lä'gō dē lā'zē-nä)	174	41°48'N	15°12'E
Leskovac, Yugo. (lĕs'kô-vàts)	163	43°00'N	21°58'E
Leslie, S. Afr.	238c	26°23'S	28°57'E
Leslie, Ar., U.S. (lĕz'lĭ)	121	35°49'N	92°32'W
Lesnoy, Russia (lĕs'noi)	180	66°45'N	34°45'E
Lesogorsk, Russia (lyĕs'ô-gôrsk)	210	49°28'N	141°59'E
Lesotho, nation, Afr. (lĕsō'thō)	232	29°45'S	28°07'E
Lesozavodsk, Russia (lyĕ-sô-zà-vôdsk')	210	45°21'N	133°19'E
Les Sables-d'Olonne, Fr. (lā sà'bl'dō-lŭn')	161	46°30'N	1°47'W
Les Saintes Islands, is., Guad. (lā-săNt')	133b	15°50'N	61°40'W

PLACE (Pronunciation)	PAGE	LAT.	LONG.
Lesser Antilles, is.	129	12°15'N	65°00'W
Lesser Caucasus, mts., Asia	182	41°00'N	44°35'E
Lesser Khingan Range, mts., China	205	49°50'N	129°26'E
Lesser Slave, r., Can.	95	55°15'N	114°30'W
Lesser Slave Lake, l., Can. (lĕs'ēr slāv)	92	55°25'N	115°30'W
Lesser Sunda Islands, is., Indon.	212	9°00'S	120°00'E
L'Estaque, Fr. (lĕs-täl)	170a	43°22'N	5°20'E
Les Thilliers-en-Vexin, Fr. (lā-tē-yā'ĕN-vĕ-săN')	171b	49°19'N	1°36'E
Le Sueur, Mn., U.S. (lē sōōr')	113	44°27'N	93°53'W
Lésvos, i., Grc.	156	39°15'N	25°40'E
Leszno, Pol. (lĕsh'nô)	161	51°51'N	16°35'E
Le Teil, Fr. (lē tā'y')	170	44°34'N	4°39'E
Lethbridge, Can. (lĕth'brĭj)	90	49°42'N	112°50'W
Leticia, Col. (lĕ-tē'syà)	142	4°04'S	69°57'W
Leting, China (lŭ-tĭŋ)	206	39°26'N	118°53'E
Le Tréport, Fr. (lē-trā'pôr')	170	50°03'N	1°21'E
Letychiv, Ukr.	177	49°22'N	27°29'E
Leuven, Bel.	165	50°53'N	4°42'E
Levack, Can.	98	46°38'N	81°23'W
Levallois-Perret, Fr. (lē-vàl-wä'pĕ-rĕ')	171b	48°53'N	2°17'E
Levanger, Nor. (lĕ-väng'ĕr)	160	63°42'N	11°01'E
Levanna, mtn., Eur. (lå-vä'nä)	174	45°25'N	7°14'E
Leveque, Cape, c., Austl. (lē-vĕk')	220	16°26'S	123°08'E
Leverkusen, Ger. (lĕ'fĕr-kōō-zĕn)	171c	51°01'N	6°59'E
Levice, Slvk. (lā'vĕt-sĕ)	169	48°13'N	18°37'E
Levico, Italy (lā'vē-kō)	174	46°02'N	11°20'E
Le Vigan, Fr. (lē vē-gäN')	170	43°59'N	3°36'E
Lévis, Can. (lā-vē') (lē'vĭs)	91	46°49'N	71°11'W
Levittown, Pa., U.S. (lĕ'vĭt-toun)	110f	40°08'N	74°50'W
Levoča, Slvk. (lā'vô-chà)	169	49°03'N	20°38'E
Levuka, Fiji	214g	17°41'S	178°50'E
Lewes, Eng., U.K.	165	50°51'N	0°01'E
Lewes, De., U.S. (lōō'ĭs)	109	38°45'N	75°10'W
Lewis, r., Wa., U.S.	114	46°05'N	122°09'W
Lewis, East Fork, r., Wa., U.S.	116c	45°52'N	122°40'W
Lewis, Island of, i., Scot., U.K. (lōō'ĭs)	164	58°05'N	6°07'W
Lewisburg, Tn., U.S. (lū'ĭs-bûrg)	124	35°27'N	86°47'W
Lewisburg, W.V., U.S.	108	37°50'N	80°20'W
Lewis Hills, hills, Can.	101	48°48'N	58°30'W
Lewisporte, Can. (lū'ĭs-pōrt)	101	49°15'N	55°04'W
Lewis Range, mts., Mt., U.S. (lū'ĭs)	115	48°15'N	113°20'W
Lewis Smith Lake, res., Al., U.S.	124	34°05'N	87°07'W
Lewiston, Id., U.S. (lū'ĭs-tŭn)	104	46°24'N	116°59'W
Lewiston, Me., U.S.	105	44°05'N	70°14'W
Lewiston, N.Y., U.S.	111c	43°11'N	79°02'W
Lewiston, Ut., U.S.	115	41°58'N	111°51'W
Lewistown, Il., U.S. (lū'ĭs-toun)	121	40°23'N	90°06'W
Lewistown, Mt., U.S.	104	47°05'N	109°25'W
Lewistown, Pa., U.S.	109	40°35'N	77°30'W
Lexington, Ky., U.S. (lĕk'sĭng-tŭn)	105	38°05'N	84°30'W
Lexington, Ma., U.S.	101a	42°27'N	71°14'W
Lexington, Mo., U.S.	121	39°11'N	93°52'W
Lexington, Ms., U.S.	124	33°08'N	90°02'W
Lexington, N.C., U.S.	125	35°47'N	80°15'W
Lexington, Ne., U.S.	120	40°46'N	99°44'W
Lexington, Tn., U.S.	124	35°37'N	88°24'W
Lexington, Va., U.S.	109	37°45'N	79°20'W
Leyte, i., Phil. (lā'tā)	213	10°35'N	125°35'E
Leżajsk, Pol. (lĕ'zhä-ĭsk)	169	50°14'N	22°25'E
Lezha, r., Russia (lĕ-zhä')	176	58°59'N	40°27'E
L'gov, Russia (lgôf)	177	51°42'N	35°15'E
Lhasa, China (läs'ä)	204	29°41'N	91°12'E
Liangxiangzhen, China (lĭäŋ-shyäŋ-jŭn)	208a	39°43'N	116°08'E
Lianjiang, China (lĭĕn-jyäŋ)	209	21°38'N	110°15'E
Lianozovo, Russia (lĭ-a-nô'zô-vô)	186b	55°54'N	37°36'E
Lianshui, China (lĭĕn-shwā)	206	33°46'N	119°15'E
Lianyungang, China (lĭĕn-yòn-gäŋ)	205	34°35'N	119°09'E
Liao, r., China	208	41°40'N	122°40'E
Liao, r., China	205	43°37'N	120°05'E
Liaocheng, China (lĭou-chŭŋ)	208	36°27'N	115°56'E
Liaodong Bandao, pen., China (lĭou-dôŋ bän-dou)	205	39°45'N	122°22'E
Liaodong Wan, b., China (lĭou-dôŋ wäŋ)	208	40°25'N	121°15'E
Liaoning, prov., China	205	41°31'N	122°11'E
Liaoyang, China (lyä'ō-yäng')	205	41°18'N	123°10'E
Liaoyuan, China (lĭou-yüän)	208	43°00'N	124°59'E
Liard, r., Can. (lē-är')	92	59°43'N	126°42'W
Libano, Col. (lē'bà-nō)	142a	4°55'N	75°05'W
Libby, Mt., U.S. (lĭb'ē)	114	48°27'N	115°35'W
Libenge, D.R.C. (lē-bĕŋ'gā)	231	3°39'N	18°40'E
Liberal, Ks., U.S. (lĭb'ēr-ǎl)	120	37°01'N	100°56'W
Liberec, Czech Rep. (lē'bĕr-ĕts)	161	50°45'N	15°06'E
Liberia, C.R.	132	10°38'N	85°28'W
Liberia, nation, Afr. (lī-bē'rĭ-ǎ)	230	6°30'N	9°55'W
Libertad, Arg.	144a	34°42'S	58°42'W
Libertad de Orituco, Ven. (lē-bĕr-tä'd-dĕ-ō-rē-tōō'kô)	143b	9°32'N	66°24'W
Liberty, In., U.S. (lĭb'ēr-tĭ)	108	39°35'N	84°55'W
Liberty, Mo., U.S.	117f	39°15'N	94°25'W
Liberty, S.C., U.S.	125	34°47'N	82°41'W
Liberty, Tx., U.S.	123	30°03'N	94°46'W
Liberty, Ut., U.S.	117b	41°20'N	111°52'W
Liberty Bay, b., Wa., U.S.	116a	47°43'N	122°41'W
Liberty Lake, l., Md., U.S.	110e	39°25'N	76°56'W
Libertyville, Il., U.S. (lĭb'ēr-tĭ-vĭl)	111a	42°17'N	87°57'W
Libode, S. Afr. (lĭ-bō'dĕ)	233c	31°33'S	29°03'E
Libón, r., N.A.	135	19°30'N	71°45'W
Libourne, Fr. (lē-bōōrn')	161	44°55'N	0°12'W
Libres, Mex. (lē'brās)	131	19°26'N	97°41'W
Libreville, Gabon (lē-br'vēl')	232	0°23'N	9°27'E

PLACE (Pronunciation)	PAGE	LAT.	LONG.
Liburn, Ga., U.S. (lĭb'ûrn)	110c	33°53'N	84°09'W
Libya, nation, Afr. (lĭb'ē-ä)	231	27°38'N	15°00'E
Libyan Desert, des., Afr. (lĭb'ē-ǎn)	231	28°23'N	23°34'E
Libyan Plateau, plat., Afr.	200	30°58'N	26°20'E
Licancábur, Cerro, mtn., S.A. (sĕ'r-rô-lē-kàn-kà'bōōr)	144	22°45'S	67°45'W
Licanten, Chile (lē-kän-tĕ'n)	141b	34°58'S	72°00'W
Lichfield, Eng., U.K. (lĭch'fēld)	158a	52°41'N	1°49'W
Lichinga, Moz.	237	13°18'S	35°14'E
Lichtenburg, S. Afr. (lĭk'tĕn-bĕrgh)	238c	26°09'S	26°10'E
Lick Creek, r., In., U.S. (lĭk)	111g	39°43'N	86°06'W
Licking, r., Ky., U.S. (lĭk'ĭng)	108	38°30'N	84°10'W
Lida, Bela. (lē'dà)	169	53°53'N	25°19'E
Lidgerwood, N.D., U.S. (lĭj'ēr-wood)	112	46°04'N	97°10'W
Lidköping, Swe. (lēt'chû-pĭng)	166	58°31'N	13°06'E
Lido di Roma, Italy (lē'dô-dē-rô'mä)	173d	41°19'N	12°17'E
Lidzbark, Pol. (lĭts'bärk)	169	54°07'N	20°36'E
Liebenbergsvlei, r., S. Afr.	238c	27°35'S	28°25'E
Liebenwalde, Ger. (lē'bĕn-väl-dĕ)	159b	52°52'N	13°24'E
Liechtenstein, nation, Eur. (lĕk'tĕn-shtīn)	161	47°10'N	10°00'E
Liège, Bel.	161	50°38'N	5°34'E
Lienz, Aus. (lē-ĕnts')	168	46°49'N	12°45'E
Liepāja, Lat. (lĕ'pä-yä')	180	56°31'N	20°59'E
Lier, Bel.	159a	51°08'N	4°34'E
Liesing, Aus. (lē'sĭng)	159e	48°09'N	16°17'E
Liestal, Switz. (lēs'täl)	168	47°28'N	7°44'E
Lifanga, D.R.C.	236	0°19'N	21°57'E
Lifou, i., N. Cal.	221	21°15'S	167°32'E
Ligao, Phil. (lē-gä'ô)	213a	13°14'N	123°33'E
Lightning Ridge, Austl.	222	29°23'S	147°50'E
Ligonha, r., Moz. (lē-gō'nyǎ)	233	16°14'S	39°00'E
Ligonier, In., U.S. (lĭg-ô-nēr)	108	41°30'N	85°35'W
Ligovo, Russia (lē'gô-vô)	186c	59°51'N	30°13'E
Liguria, hist. reg., Italy (lē-gōō-rē-ä)	174	44°24'N	8°27'E
Ligurian Sea, sea, Eur. (lĭ-gū'rĭ-ǎn)	162	43°42'N	8°32'E
Lihou Reef, rf., Austl. (lē-hōō')	221	17°23'S	152°43'E
Lihuang, China (lē'hōōäng)	206	31°32'N	115°46'E
Lihue, Hi., U.S. (lē-hōō'ā)	106c	21°59'N	159°23'W
Lihula, Est. (lē'hò-là)	167	58°41'N	23°50'E
Liji, China (lē-jyē)	206	33°47'N	117°47'E
Lijiang, China (lē-jyäŋ)	204	27°00'N	100°08'E
Lijin, China (lē-jyĭn)	208	37°30'N	118°15'E
Likasi, D.R.C.	232	10°59'S	26°44'E
Likhoslavl', Russia (lyē-kôslävl'l)	176	57°07'N	35°27'E
Likouala, r., Congo	236	0°10'S	16°30'E
Lille, Fr. (lēl)	154	50°38'N	3°01'E
Lille Baelt, strt., Den.	166	55°09'N	9°53'E
Lillehammer, Nor. (lēl'ĕ-häm'mĕr)	160	61°07'N	10°25'E
Lillesand, Nor. (lēl'ĕ-sän')	166	58°16'N	8°19'E
Lilleström, Nor. (lēl'ĕ-strûm)	166	59°56'N	11°04'E
Lilliwaup, Wa., U.S. (lĭl'ĭ-wŏp)	116a	47°28'N	123°07'W
Lillooet, Can. (lĭ'lōō-ĕt)	90	50°30'N	121°55'W
Lillooet, r., Can.	95	49°50'N	122°10'W
Lilongwe, Mwi. (lē-lô-än)	232	13°59'S	33°44'E
Lima, Peru (lē'mä)	142	12°06'S	76°55'W
Lima, Swe.	166	60°54'N	13°24'E
Lima, Oh., U.S. (lī'mǎ)	105	40°40'N	84°05'W
Lima, r., Eur.	172	41°45'N	8°22'W
Lima Duarte, Braz. (dwä'r-tĕ)	141a	21°52'S	43°47'W
Lima Reservoir, res., Mt., U.S.	115	44°45'N	112°15'W
Limassol, Cyp.	163	34°39'N	33°02'E
Limay, r., Arg. (lē-mä'ē)	144	39°50'S	69°15'W
Limbazi, Lat. (lĕm'bä-zĭ)	167	57°32'N	24°44'E
Limbdi, India	202	22°37'N	71°52'E
Limbe, Cam.	230	4°01'N	9°12'E
Limburg an der Lahn, Ger. (lem-bòrg')	168	50°22'N	8°03'E
Limeira, Braz. (lē-mā'rä)	141a	22°34'S	47°24'W
Limerick, Ire. (lĭm'nák)	161	52°39'N	8°35'W
Limestone Bay, b., Can. (lĭm'stōn)	97	53°50'N	98°50'W
Limfjorden, Den.	160	56°55'N	8°56'E
Limmen Bight, b., Austl. (lĭm'ĕn)	220	14°45'S	136°00'E
Limnos, i., Grc.	163	39°58'N	24°48'E
Limoges, Can. (lē-môzh')	102c	45°20'N	75°15'W
Limoges, Fr.	161	45°50'N	1°15'E
Limón, C.R. (lē-mōn')	129	10°01'N	83°02'W
Limón, Hond. (lē-mō-n)	132	15°53'N	85°34'W
Limon, Co., U.S. (lī'mǒn)	120	39°15'N	103°41'W
Limon, r., Dom. Rep.	135	18°20'N	71°40'W
Limón, Bahía, b., Pan.	128a	9°21'N	79°58'W
Limours, Fr. (lē-mōōr')	171b	48°39'N	2°05'E
Limousin, Plateaus du, plat., Fr. (plä-tō' dü lē-mōō-zăN')	170	45°44'N	1°09'E
Limoux, Fr. (lē-mōō')	170	43°03'N	2°14'E
Limpopo, r., Afr. (lĭm-pō'pō)	232	23°15'S	27°46'E
Linares, Chile (lē-nä'rās)	144	35°51'S	71°35'W
Linares, Mex.	128	24°53'N	99°34'W
Linares, Spain (lē-nä'rĕs)	162	38°07'N	3°38'W
Linares, prov., Chile	141b	35°53'S	71°30'W
Linaro, Cape, c., Italy (lē-nä'rä)	174	42°02'N	11°53'E
Linchuan, China (lĭn-chůän)	205	27°58'N	116°18'E
Lincoln, Arg. (lĭn'kŭn)	144	34°51'S	61°29'W
Lincoln, Can.	102d	43°10'N	79°29'W
Lincoln, Eng., U.K.	160	53°14'N	0°33'W
Lincoln, Ca., U.S.	118	38°51'N	121°19'W
Lincoln, Il., U.S.	121	40°09'N	89°21'W
Lincoln, Ks., U.S.	120	39°02'N	98°08'W
Lincoln, Ma., U.S.	101a	42°25'N	71°19'W
Lincoln, Me., U.S.	100	45°23'N	68°31'W
Lincoln, Ne., U.S.	104	40°49'N	96°43'W
Lincoln, Mount, mtn., Co., U.S.	120	39°20'N	106°19'W
Lincoln Heath, reg., Eng., U.K.	158a	53°23'N	0°39'W
Lincoln Park, Mi., U.S.	111b	42°14'N	83°11'W
Lincoln Park, N.J., U.S.	110a	40°56'N	74°18'W

ăt; finǎl; rāte; senåte; ärm; åsk; sofǎ; fâre; ch-choose; dh-as th in other; bē; ēvent; bĕt; recĕnt; cratēr; g-gō; gh-guttural g; bĭt; ĭ-short neutral; rīde; K-guttural k as ch in German ich;

PLACE (Pronunciation)	PAGE	LAT.	LONG.
Lincolnshire, co., Eng., U.K.	158a	53°12'N	0°29'W
Lincolnshire Wolds, Eng., U.K. (woldz′)	164	53°25'N	0°23'W
Lincolnton, N.C., U.S. (lĭŋ′kŭn-tŭn)	125	35°27'N	81°15'W
Lindale, Ga., U.S. (lĭn′dāl)	124	34°10'N	85°10'W
Lindau, Ger. (lĭn′dou)	168	47°33'N	9°40'E
Linden, Al., U.S. (lĭn′dĕn)	124	32°16'N	87°47'W
Linden, Mo., U.S.	117f	39°13'N	94°35'W
Linden, N.J., U.S.	110a	40°39'N	74°14'W
Lindenhurst, N.Y., U.S. (lĭn′dĕn-hûrst)	110a	40°41'N	73°23'W
Lindenwold, N.J., U.S. (lĭn′dĕn-wōld)	110f	39°50'N	75°00'W
Lindesberg, Swe. (lĭn′dĕs-bĕrgh)	166	59°37'N	15°14'E
Lindesnes, c., Nor. (lĭn′ĕs-nĕs)	156	58°00'N	7°05'E
Lindi, Tan. (lĭn′dē)	233	10°00'S	39°43'E
Lindi, r., D.R.C.	231	1°00'N	27°13'E
Lindian, China (lĭn-dĭĕn)	208	47°08'N	124°59'E
Lindley, S. Afr. (lĭnd′lē)	238c	27°52'S	27°55'E
Lindow, Ger. (lēn′dōv)	159b	52°58'N	12°59'E
Lindsay, Can. (lĭn′zē)	99	44°20'N	78°45'W
Lindsay, Ok., U.S.	121	34°50'N	97°38'W
Lindsborg, Ks., U.S. (lĭnz′bôrg)	121	38°34'N	97°42'W
Lineville, Al., U.S. (līn′vĭl)	124	33°18'N	85°45'W
Linfen, China	205	36°00'N	111°38'E
Linga, Kepulauan, is., Indon.	212	0°35'S	105°05'E
Lingao, China (lĭn-gou)	209	19°58'N	109°40'E
Lingayen, Phil. (lĭŋ′gä-yän′)	212	16°01'N	120°13'E
Lingayen Gulf, b., Phil.	213a	16°18'N	120°11'E
Lingdianzhen, China	206	31°52'N	121°28'E
Lingen, Ger. (lĭŋ′gĕn)	168	52°32'N	7°20'E
Lingling, China (lĭŋ-lĭŋ)	209	26°10'N	111°40'E
Lingshou, China (lĭŋ-shō)	206	38°21'N	114°41'E
Linguère, Sen. (lĭŋ-gĕr′)	230	15°24'N	15°07'W
Lingwu, China	208	38°05'N	106°18'E
Lingyuan, China (lĭŋ-yůän)	208	41°12'N	119°20'E
Linhai, China	209	28°52'N	121°08'E
Linhe, China (lĭn-hŭ)	208	40°49'N	107°45'E
Linhuaiguan, China (lĭn-hwī-gůän)	206	32°55'N	117°38'E
Linhuanji, China	206	33°42'N	116°33'E
Linjiang, China (lĭn-jyäŋ)	208	41°45'N	127°00'E
Linköping, Swe. (lĭn′chû-pĭng)	160	58°25'N	15°35'E
Linnhe, Loch, b., Scot., U.K. (lĭn′ē)	164	56°35'N	4°30'W
Linqing, China (lĭn-chyĭŋ)	205	36°49'N	115°42'E
Linqu, China (lĭn-chyōō)	206	36°31'N	118°33'E
Lins, Braz. (lē′ɴs)	143	21°42'S	49°41'W
Linthicum Heights, Md., U.S. (lĭn′thĭ-kŭm)	110e	39°12'N	76°39'W
Linton, In., U.S. (lĭn′tŭn)	108	39°05'N	87°15'W
Linton, N.D., U.S.	112	46°16'N	100°15'W
Linwu, China (lĭn′wōō′)	209	25°20'N	112°30'E
Linxi, China (lĭn-shyē)	208	43°30'N	118°02'E
Linyi, China (lĭn-yē)	205	35°04'N	118°21'E
Linying, China (lĭn′yĭng′)	206	33°48'N	113°56'E
Linz, Aus. (lĭnts)	161	48°18'N	14°18'E
Linzhang, China (lĭn-jäŋ)	206	36°19'N	114°40'E
Lion, Golfe du, b., Fin.	156	43°00'N	4°00'E
Lipa, Phil. (lē-pä′)	212	13°55'N	121°10'E
Lipari, Italy (lē′pä-rē)	174	38°29'N	15°00'E
Lipari, i., Italy	174	38°32'N	15°04'E
Lipetsk, Russia (lyē′pĕtsk)	178	52°26'N	39°34'E
Lipetsk, prov., Russia	176	52°18'N	38°30'E
Liping, China (lē-pĭŋ)	204	26°18'N	109°00'E
Lipno, Pol. (lēp′nō)	169	52°50'N	19°12'E
Lippe, r., Ger. (lĭp′ĕ)	171b	51°36'N	6°45'E
Lippstadt, Ger. (lĭp′shtät)	168	51°39'N	8°20'E
Lipscomb, Al., U.S. (lĭp′skŭm)	110h	33°26'N	86°56'W
Lipu, China (lē-pōō)	209	24°38'N	110°35'E
Lira, Ug.	237	2°15'N	32°54'E
Liri, r., Italy (lē′rē)	174	41°49'N	13°30'E
Lisala, D.R.C. (lē-sä′lä)	231	2°09'N	21°31'E
Lisboa *see* Lisbon, Port.	154	38°42'N	9°05'W
Lisbon (Lisboa), Port.	154	38°42'N	9°05'W
Lisbon, N.D., U.S.	112	46°21'N	97°43'W
Lisbon, Oh., U.S.	108	40°45'N	80°50'W
Lisbon Falls, Me., U.S.	100	43°59'N	70°03'W
Lisburn, N. Ire., U.K. (lĭs′bŭrn)	164	54°35'N	6°05'W
Lisburne, Cape, c., Ak., U.S.	106a	68°20'N	165°40'W
Lishi, China (lē-shr)	208	37°32'N	111°12'E
Lishu, China	208	43°12'N	124°18'E
Lishui, China (lĭ′shwĭ′)	206	31°41'N	119°01'E
Lishui, China	205	28°28'N	120°00'E
Lisianski Island, i., Hi., U.S.	126b	25°30'N	174°00'W
Lisieux, Fr. (lē-zyû′)	170	49°10'N	0°13'E
Lisiy Nos, Russia (lĭ′sĭy-nôs)	186c	60°01'N	30°00'E
Liski, Russia (lyēs′kē)	177	50°56'N	39°28'E
Lisle, Il., U.S. (līl)	111a	41°48'N	88°04'W
L'Isle-Adam, Fr. (lēl-ädäɴ′)	171b	49°05'N	2°13'E
Lismore, Austl. (lĭz′môr)	219	28°48'S	153°18'E
Litani, r., Leb.	197a	33°28'N	35°42'E
Litchfield, Il., U.S. (lĭch′fēld)	121	39°10'N	89°38'W
Litchfield, Mn., U.S.	113	45°08'N	94°34'W
Litchfield, Oh., U.S.	111d	41°10'N	82°01'W
Lithgow, Austl. (lĭth′gō)	219	33°23'S	149°31'E
Lithinon, Akra, c., Grc.	174a	34°59'N	24°35'E
Lithonia, Ga., U.S. (lĭ-thō′nĭ-ȧ)	110c	33°43'N	84°07'W
Lithuania, nation, Eur. (lĭth-û-ā′nĭ-ȧ)	178	55°42'N	23°30'E
Litóchoro, Grc.	175	40°05'N	22°29'E
Litoko, D.R.C.	236	1°13'S	24°47'E
Litoměřice, Czech Rep. (lē′tô-myĕr′zhĭ-tsĕ)	168	50°33'N	14°10'E
Litomyšl, Czech Rep. (lē′tô-mêsh′l)	168	49°52'N	16°14'E
Litoo, Tan.	237	9°45'S	38°24'E
Little, r., Austl.	217a	37°54'S	144°27'E
Little, r., Tn., U.S.	124	36°28'N	89°39'W

PLACE (Pronunciation)	PAGE	LAT.	LONG.
Little, r., Tx., U.S.	123	30°48'N	96°50'W
Little Abaco, i., Bah. (ä′bä-kō)	134	26°55'N	77°45'W
Little Abitibi, r., Can.	98	50°15'N	81°30'W
Little America, sci., Ant.	224	78°30'S	161°30'W
Little Andaman, i., India (ăn-dȧ-măn′)	212	10°39'N	93°08'E
Little Bahama Bank, bk. (bȧ-hā′mȧ)	134	26°55'N	78°40'W
Little Belt Mountains, mts., Mt., U.S. (bĕlt)	106	47°00'N	110°50'W
Little Bighorn, r., Mt., U.S. (bĭg-hôrn)	115	45°08'N	107°30'W
Little Bighorn Battlefield National Monument, rec., Mt., U.S. (bĭg-hôrn băt′′l-fēld)	115	45°44'N	107°15'W
Little Bitter Lake, l., Egypt	238b	30°10'N	32°36'E
Little Bitterroot, r., Mt., U.S. (bĭt′ēr-ōōt)	115	47°45'N	114°45'W
Little Blue, r., Ia., U.S. (blōō)	117f	38°52'N	94°25'W
Little Blue, r., Ne., U.S.	120	40°15'N	98°01'W
Littleborough, Eng., U.K. (lĭt′′l-bŭr-ō)	158a	53°39'N	2°06'W
Little Calumet, r., Il., U.S. (kăl-û-mĕt′)	111a	41°38'N	87°38'W
Little Cayman, i., Cay. Is. (kā′mȧn)	134	19°40'N	80°05'W
Little Colorado, r., Az., U.S. (kŏl-ō-rä′dō)	106	36°05'N	111°35'W
Little Compton, R.I., U.S. (kŏmp′tŏn)	110b	41°31'N	71°07'W
Little Corn Island, i., Nic.	133	12°19'N	82°50'W
Little Exuma, i., Bah. (ĕk-sōō′mä)	135	23°25'N	75°40'W
Little Falls, Mn., U.S. (fôlz)	113	45°58'N	94°23'W
Little Falls, N.Y., U.S.	109	43°05'N	74°55'W
Littlefield, Tx., U.S. (lĭt′′l-fēld)	120	33°55'N	102°17'W
Little Fork, r., Mn., U.S. (fôrk)	113	48°24'N	93°30'W
Little Goose Dam, dam, Wa., U.S.	114	46°35'N	118°02'W
Little Hans Lollick, i., V.I.U.S. (häns lôl′lĭk)	129c	18°25'N	64°54'W
Little Humboldt, r., Nv., U.S. (hŭm′bōlt)	114	41°10'N	117°40'W
Little Inagua, i., Bah. (ē-nä′gwä)	135	21°30'N	73°00'W
Little Isaac, i., Bah. (ī′zȧk)	134	25°55'N	79°00'W
Little Kanawha, r., W.V., U.S. (kȧ-nô′wȧ)	108	39°05'N	81°30'W
Little Karroo, plat., S. Afr. (kä-rōō)	232	33°50'S	21°02'E
Little Mecatina, r., Can. (mĕ cȧ tĭ nå)	93	52°40'N	62°21'W
Little Miami, r., Oh., U.S. (mī-ăm′ĭ)	111f	39°19'N	84°15'W
Little Minch, strt., Scot., U.K.	164	57°35'N	6°45'W
Little Missouri, r., Ar., U.S. (mĭ-sōō′rĭ)	121	34°15'N	93°54'W
Little Missouri, r., U.S.	106	46°00'N	104°00'W
Little Pee Dee, r., S.C., U.S. (pē-dē′)	125	34°35'N	79°21'W
Little Powder, r., Wy., U.S. (pou′dēr)	115	44°51'N	105°20'W
Little Red, r., Ar., U.S. (rĕd)	121	35°25'N	91°55'W
Little Red, r., Ok., U.S.	121	33°53'N	94°38'W
Little Rock, Ar., U.S. (rôk)	105	34°42'N	92°16'W
Little Sachigo Lake, l., Can. (să′chĭ-gō)	97	54°09'N	92°11'W
Little Salt Lake, l., Ut., U.S.	119	37°55'N	112°53'W
Little San Salvador, i., Bah. (săn săl′vȧ-dôr)	135	24°35'N	75°55'W
Little Satilla, r., Ga., U.S. (sȧ-tĭl′ȧ)	125	31°43'N	82°47'W
Little Sioux, r., Ia., U.S. (sōō)	112	42°22'N	95°47'W
Little Smoky, r., Can. (smōk′ĭ)	95	55°10'N	116°55'W
Little Snake, r., Co., U.S. (snāk)	115	40°40'N	108°21'W
Little Tallapoosa, r., Al., U.S. (tăl-ȧ-pōō′sȧ)	124	32°25'N	85°28'W
Little Tennessee, r., Tn., U.S. (tĕn-ĕ-sē′)	124	35°36'N	84°05'W
Littleton, Co., U.S. (lĭt′′l-tŭn)	120	39°34'N	105°01'W
Littleton, Ma., U.S.	101a	42°32'N	71°29'W
Littleton, N.H., U.S.	109	44°15'N	71°45'W
Little Wabash, r., Il., U.S. (wô′băsh)	108	38°50'N	88°30'W
Little Wood, r., Id., U.S. (wŏŏd)	115	43°00'N	114°08'W
Lityn, Ukr.	177	49°16'N	28°11'E
Liubar, Ukr.	177	49°56'N	27°44'E
Liuhe, China	208	42°10'N	125°38'E
Liuli, Tan.	237	11°05'S	34°38'E
Liupan Shan, mts., China	208	36°20'N	105°30'E
Liuwa Plain, pl., Zam.	236	14°30'S	22°40'E
Liuyang, China (lyōō′yäng′)	209	28°10'N	113°35'E
Liuyuan, China (lĭō-yůän)	206	36°09'N	114°37'E
Liuzhou, China (lĭō-jō)	204	24°25'N	109°30'E
Līvāni, Lat. (lē′vȧ-nē)	167	56°24'N	26°12'E
Lively, Can.	98	46°26'N	81°09'W
Livengood, Ak., U.S. (lĭv′ĕn-gŏŏd)	103	65°30'N	148°35'W
Live Oak, Fl., U.S. (lĭv′ōk)	124	30°15'N	83°00'W
Livermore, Ca., U.S. (lĭv′ēr-mōr)	116b	37°41'N	121°46'W
Livermore, Ky., U.S.	108	37°30'N	87°05'W
Liverpool, Austl. (lĭv′ēr-pōōl)	217b	33°55'S	150°56'E
Liverpool, Can.	91	44°02'N	64°41'W
Liverpool, Eng., U.K.	154	53°25'N	2°52'W
Liverpool, Tx., U.S.	123a	29°18'N	95°17'W
Liverpool Bay, b., Can.	103	69°45'N	130°00'W
Liverpool Range, mts., Austl.	221	31°47'S	151°00'E
Livindo, r., Afr.	231	1°09'N	13°30'E
Livingston, Guat.	132	15°50'N	88°45'W
Livingston, Al., U.S. (lĭv′ĭng-stŭn)	124	32°35'N	88°09'W
Livingston, Il., U.S.	117e	38°58'N	89°51'W
Livingston, Mt., U.S.	104	45°40'N	110°35'W
Livingston, N.J., U.S.	110a	40°47'N	74°20'W
Livingston, Tn., U.S.	124	36°23'N	85°20'W
Livingstone, Zam. (lĭv-ĭng-stŏn)	232	17°50'S	25°53'E
Livingstone, Chutes de, wtfl., Afr.	236	4°50'S	14°30'E
Livingstonia, Mwi. (lĭv-ĭng-stō′nĭ-ȧ)	232	10°36'S	34°07'E
Livno, Bos. (lēv′nō)	163	43°50'N	17°03'E
Livny, Russia (lēv′nē)	181	52°28'N	37°36'E

PLACE (Pronunciation)	PAGE	LAT.	LONG.
Livonia, Mi., U.S. (lĭ-vō-nĭ-ȧ)	111b	42°25'N	83°23'W
Livorno, Italy (lē-vôr′nō) (lĕg′hôrn)	154	43°32'N	11°18'E
Livramento, Braz. (lē-vrä-mĕ′n-tô)	144	30°46'S	55°21'W
Lixian, China (lē shyĕn)	209	29°42'N	111°40'E
Lixian, China	206	38°30'N	115°38'E
Liyang, China (lē′yäng′)	209	31°30'N	119°29'E
Lizard Point, c., Eng., U.K. (lĭz′ȧrd)	161	49°55'N	5°09'W
Lizy-sur-Ourcq, Fr. (lēk-sē′sür-ōōrk′)	171b	49°01'N	3°02'E
Ljubljana, Slvn. (lyōō′blyȧ′na)	154	46°04'N	14°29'E
Ljubuški, Bos. (lyōō′bōsh-kē)	175	43°11'N	17°29'E
Ljungan, r., Swe.	166	62°50'N	13°45'E
Ljungby, Swe. (lyŭng′bü)	166	56°49'N	13°56'E
Ljusdal, Swe. (lyōōs′däl)	166	61°50'N	16°11'E
Ljusnan, r., Swe.	160	61°55'N	15°33'E
Llandudno, Wales, U.K. (lăn-düd′nō)	164	53°20'N	3°46'W
Llanelli, Wales, U.K. (lȧ-nĕl′ĭ)	161	51°44'N	4°09'W
Llanes, Spain (lyä′nås)	162	43°25'N	4°41'W
Llano, Tx., U.S. (lä′nō) (lyä′nō)	122	30°45'N	98°41'W
Llano, r., Tx., U.S.	122	30°38'N	99°04'W
Llanos, reg., S.A. (lyá′nōs)	142	4°00'N	71°15'W
Lleida, Spain	162	41°38'N	0°37'E
Llera, Mex. (lyā′rä)	130	23°16'N	99°03'W
Llerena, Spain (lyā-rā′nä)	172	38°14'N	6°02'W
Lliria, Spain	173	39°35'N	0°34'W
Llobregat, r., Spain (lyō-brĕ-gät′)	173	41°55'N	1°55'E
Lloyd Lake, l., Can. (loid)	102e	50°52'N	114°13'W
Lloydminster, Can.	90	53°17'N	110°00'W
Llucena, Spain	173	40°08'N	0°18'W
Llucmajor, Spain	173	39°28'N	2°53'E
Llullaillaco, Volcán, vol., S.A. (lyōō-lyī-lyä′kō)	144	24°50'S	68°30'W
Loange, r., Afr. (lō-äŋ′gā)	232	5°00'S	20°15'E
Lobamba, Swaz.	232	26°27'S	31°12'E
Lobatse, Bots. (lō-bä′tsē)	232	25°13'S	25°35'E
Lobería, Arg. (lō-bĕ′rē′ä)	144	38°13'S	58°48'W
Lobito, Ang. (lō-bē′tō)	232	12°30'S	13°34'E
Lobnya, Russia (lôb′nyȧ)	186b	56°01'N	37°29'E
Lobo, Phil.	213a	13°39'N	121°14'E
Lobos, Arg. (lō′bōs)	141c	35°10'S	59°08'W
Lobos, Cayo, i., Bah. (lō′bōs)	134	22°25'N	77°40'W
Lobos, Isla de, i., Mex. (ē′s-lä-dĕ-lō′bōs)	131	21°24'N	97°11'W
Lobos de Tierra, i., Peru (lō′bō-dĕ-tyĕ′r-rä)	142	6°29'S	80°55'W
Lobva, Russia (lôb′vȧ)	186a	59°12'N	60°28'E
Lobva, r., Russia	186a	59°14'N	60°17'E
Locarno, Switz. (lō-kär′nō)	168	46°10'N	8°43'E
Loches, Fr. (lōsh)	170	47°08'N	0°56'E
Loch Raven Reservoir, res., Md., U.S.	110e	39°28'N	76°38'W
Lockeport, Can.	100	43°42'N	65°07'W
Lockhart, S.C., U.S. (lŏk′härt)	125	34°47'N	81°30'W
Lockhart, Tx., U.S.	123	29°54'N	97°40'W
Lock Haven, Pa., U.S. (lŏk′hā-vĕn)	109	41°05'N	77°30'W
Lockland, Oh., U.S. (lŏk′lănd)	111f	39°14'N	84°27'W
Lockport, Il., U.S.	111a	41°35'N	88°04'W
Lockport, N.Y., U.S.	109	43°11'N	78°43'W
Loc Ninh, Viet. (lōk′nĭng′)	212	12°00'N	106°30'E
Lod, Isr. (lōd)	197a	31°57'N	34°55'E
Lodève, Fr. (lō-dĕv′)	170	43°43'N	3°18'E
Lodeynoye Pole, Russia (lō-dĕy-nō′yĕ)	180	60°43'N	33°24'E
Lodge Creek, r., N.A. (lŏj)	115	49°20'N	110°20'W
Lodge Creek, r., Mt., U.S.	115	48°51'N	109°30'W
Lodgepole Creek, r., Wy., U.S. (lŏj′pōl)	112	41°22'N	104°48'W
Lodhran, Pak.	202	29°40'N	71°39'E
Lodi, Italy (lō′dē)	174	45°18'N	9°30'E
Lodi, Ca., U.S. (lō′dī)	118	38°07'N	121°17'W
Lodi, Oh., U.S. (lō′dī)	111d	41°02'N	82°01'W
Lodosa, Spain (lō-dō′sä)	172	42°27'N	2°04'W
Lodwar, Kenya	237	3°07'N	35°36'E
Łódź, Pol.	154	51°46'N	19°30'E
Loeches, Spain (lō-āch′ĕs)	173a	40°22'N	3°25'W
Loffa, r., Afr.	234	7°10'N	10°35'W
Lofoten, is., Nor. (lō′fō-tĕn)	156	68°26'N	13°42'E
Logăn, Oh., U.S. (lō′gȧn)	108	39°35'N	82°25'W
Logan, Ut., U.S.	104	41°46'N	111°51'W
Logan, W.V., U.S.	108	37°50'N	82°00'W
Logan, Mount, mtn., Can.	92	60°54'N	140°33'W
Logansport, In., U.S. (lō′gănz-pōrt)	105	40°45'N	86°25'W
Logone, r., Afr. (lō-gō′nä) (lō-gōn′)	231	10°20'N	15°30'E
Logroño, Spain (lō-grō′nyō)	162	42°28'N	2°25'W
Logrosán, Spain (lō-grō-sän′)	172	39°22'N	5°29'W
Løgstør, Den. (lügh-stûr′)	166	56°56'N	9°15'E
Loir, r., Fr. (lwär)	170	47°40'N	0°07'E
Loire, r., Fr.	156	47°30'N	2°00'E
Loja, Ec. (lō′hä)	142	3°49'S	79°13'W
Loja, Spain (lō′-kä)	172	37°10'N	4°11'W
Loka, D.R.C.	236	0°20'N	17°57'E
Lokala Drift, Bots. (lō′kä-lȧ drĭft)	238c	24°00'S	26°38'E
Lokandu, D.R.C.	237	2°31'S	25°47'E
Lokhvytsia, Ukr.	181	50°21'N	33°16'E
Lokichar, Kenya	237	2°23'N	35°39'E
Lokitaung, Kenya	237	4°16'N	35°45'E
Lokofa-Bokolongo, D.R.C.	236	0°12'N	19°22'E
Lokoja, Nig. (lō-kō′yä)	230	7°47'N	6°45'E
Lokolama, D.R.C.	236	2°34'S	19°53'E
Lokosso, Burkina	234	10°19'N	3°40'W
Lol, r., Sudan (lōl)	231	9°06'N	28°09'E
Loliondo, Tan.	237	2°03'S	35°37'E
Lolland, i., Den. (lôl′än′)	166	54°41'N	11°00'E
Lolo, Mt., U.S.	115	46°45'N	114°05'W
Lom, Blg. (lōm)	163	43°48'N	23°15'E

316 Loma Linda – Łuków PRONOUNCING INDEX

PLACE (Pronunciation)	PAGE	LAT.	LONG.
Loma Linda, Ca., U.S. (lō′mȧ lĭn′dȧ)	117a	34°04′N	117°16′W
Lomami, r., D.R.C.	232	0°50′S	24°40′E
Lomas de Zamora, Arg. (lō′mäs dā zä-mō′rä)	141c	34°46′S	58°24′W
Lombard, Il., U.S. (lŏm-bärd)	111a	41°53′N	88°01′W
Lombardia, hist. reg., Italy (lôm-bär-dē′ä)	174	45°20′N	9°30′E
Lomblen, Pulau, i., Indon. (lŏm-blĕn′)	213	8°08′S	123°45′E
Lombok, i., Indon. (lŏm-bŏk′)	212	9°15′S	116°15′E
Lomé, Togo	230	6°08′N	1°13′E
Lomela, D.R.C. (lō-mā′lȧ)	232	2°19′S	23°33′E
Lomela, r., D.R.C.	232	0°35′S	21°20′E
Lometa, Tx., U.S. (lō-mē′tȧ)	122	31°10′N	98°25′W
Lomié, Cam. (lō-mē-ā′)	235	3°10′N	13°37′E
Lomita, Ca., U.S. (lō-mē′tȧ)	117a	33°48′N	118°20′W
Lommel, Bel.	159a	51°14′N	5°21′E
Lommond, Loch, l., Scot., U.K. (lŏk lō′mŭnd)	164	56°15′N	4°40′W
Lomonosov, Russia (lô-mô′nô-sof)	186c	59°54′N	29°47′E
Lompoc, Ca., U.S. (lŏm-pŏk′)	118	34°39′N	120°30′W
Łomża, Pol. (lôm′zhȧ)	169	53°11′N	22°04′E
Lonaconing, Md., U.S. (lō-nȧ-kō′nĭng)	109	39°35′N	78°55′W
London, Can. (lŭn′dŭn)	91	43°00′N	81°20′W
London, Eng., U.K.	154	51°30′N	0°07′W
London, Ky., U.S.	124	37°07′N	84°06′W
London, Oh., U.S.	108	39°50′N	83°30′W
Londonderry, Can. (lŭn′dŭn-dĕr-ĭ)	100	45°29′N	63°36′W
Londonderry, N. Ire., U.K.	160	55°00′N	7°19′W
Londonderry, Cape, c., Austl.	220	13°30′S	127°00′E
Londrina, Braz. (lôn-drē′nä)	143	21°53′S	51°17′W
Lonely, i., Can. (lōn′lĭ)	93	45°35′N	81°30′W
Lone Pine, Ca., U.S.	118	36°36′N	118°03′W
Lone Star, Nic.	133	13°58′N	84°25′W
Long, i., Bah.	129	23°25′N	75°10′W
Long, i., Can.	100	44°21′S	66°25′W
Long, l., N.D., U.S.	112	46°47′N	100°14′W
Long, l., Wa., U.S.	116a	47°29′N	122°36′W
Longa, r., Ang. (lôŋ′gȧ)	232	10°20′S	15°15′E
Long Bay, b., S.C., U.S.	125	33°30′N	78°54′W
Long Beach, Ca., U.S. (lông bēch)	104	33°46′N	118°12′W
Long Beach, N.Y., U.S.	110a	40°35′N	73°38′W
Long Branch, N.J., U.S. (lông brȧnch)	110a	40°18′N	73°59′W
Longdon, N.D., U.S. (lông′-dŭn)	112	48°45′N	98°23′W
Long Eaton, Eng., U.K. (ē′tŭn)	158a	52°54′N	1°16′W
Longford, Ire. (lŏng′fērd)	164	53°43′N	7°40′W
Longgu, China (lôŋ-gōō)	206	34°52′N	116°48′E
Longhorn, Tx., U.S. (lông-hôrn)	117d	29°33′N	98°23′W
Longido, Tan.	237	2°44′S	36°41′E
Long Island, i., Pap. N. Gui.	213	5°10′S	147°30′E
Long Island, i., Ak., U.S.	94	54°54′N	132°45′W
Long Island, i., N.Y., U.S. (lông)	107	40°50′N	72°50′W
Long Island Sound, strt., U.S. (lông ī′lănd)	107	41°05′N	72°45′W
Longjumeau, Fr. (lôN-zhü-mō′)	171b	48°42′N	2°17′E
Longkou, China (lôŋ-kō)	206	37°39′N	120°21′E
Longlac, Can. (lông′lák)	91	49°41′N	86°28′W
Longlake, S.D., U.S. (lông-lāk)	112	45°52′N	99°06′W
Long Lake, l., Can.	98	49°10′N	86°45′W
Longmont, Co., U.S. (lông′mŏnt)	120	40°11′N	105°07′W
Longnor, Eng., U.K. (lông′nôr)	158a	53°11′N	1°52′W
Long Pine, Ne., U.S. (lông pīn)	112	42°31′N	99°42′W
Long Point, c., Can.	97	53°02′N	98°40′W
Long Point, c., Can.	101	48°48′N	58°46′W
Long Point, c., Can.	99	42°35′N	80°05′W
Long Point Bay, b., Can.	99	42°40′N	80°10′W
Long Range Mountains, mts., Can.	93a	48°00′N	58°30′W
Longreach, Austl. (lông′rēch)	219	23°32′S	144°17′E
Long Reach, r., Can.	100	45°26′N	66°05′W
Long Reef, c., Austl.	217b	33°45′S	151°22′E
Longridge, Eng., U.K. (lông′rĭj)	158a	53°51′N	2°37′W
Longs Peak, mtn., Co., U.S. (lôngz)	106	40°17′N	105°37′W
Longtansi, China (lôŋ-tä-sz)	206	32°12′N	115°53′E
Longton, Eng., U.K. (lông′tŭn)	158a	52°59′N	2°08′W
Longueuil, Can. (lôN-gû′y′)	99	45°32′N	73°30′W
Longview, Tx., U.S.	123	32°29′N	94°44′W
Longview, Wa., U.S. (lông-vū)	114	46°06′N	123°02′W
Longville, La., U.S. (lông′vĭl)	123	30°36′N	93°14′W
Longwy, Fr. (lôN-wē′)	171	49°32′N	6°14′E
Longxi, China (lôŋ-shyē)	204	35°00′N	104°40′E
Long Xuyen, Viet. (loung′ sōō′yĕn)	212	10°31′N	105°28′E
Longzhou, China (lôŋ-jō)	204	22°20′N	107°02′E
Lonoke, Ar., U.S. (lō′nōk)	121	34°48′N	91°52′W
Lons-le-Saunier, Fr. (lôN-lē-sō-nyā′)	171	46°40′N	5°33′E
Lontue, r., Chile (lôn-tòĕ′)	141b	35°20′S	70°45′W
Looc, Phil. (lō-ōk′)	213a	12°16′N	121°59′E
Loogootee, In., U.S.	108	38°40′N	86°55′W
Lookout, Cape, c., N.C., U.S. (lòkōut)	125	34°34′N	76°38′W
Lookout Point Lake, res., Or., U.S.	114	43°51′N	122°38′W
Loolmalasin, mtn., Tan.	237	3°03′S	35°46′E
Looma, Can. (ō′mȧ)	102g	53°22′N	113°15′W
Loop Head, c., Ire. (lōōp)	164	52°32′N	9°59′W
Loosahatchie, r., Tn., U.S. (lōz-ȧ-hă′chē)	124	35°20′N	89°45′W
Loosdrechtsche Plassen, l., Neth.	159a	52°11′N	5°09′E
Lopatka, Mys, c., Russia (lō-pät′kȧ)	197	51°00′N	156°52′E
Lopez, Cap, c., Gabon	236	0°37′N	8°43′E
Lopez Bay, b., Phil. (lō′pāz)	213a	14°04′N	122°00′E
Lopez I, Wa., U.S.	116a	48°25′N	122°53′W
Lopori, r., D.R.C. (lō-pō′rē)	231	1°35′N	20°43′E
Lora, Spain (lō′rä)	172	37°40′N	5°31′W
Lorain, Oh., U.S. (lō-rān′)	111d	41°28′N	82°10′W
Loralai, Pak. (lō-rŭ-lī′)	199	30°31′N	68°35′E
Lorca, Spain (lôr′kä)	162	37°39′N	1°40′W
Lord Howe, i., Austl. (lôrd hou)	220	31°44′S	157°56′W
Lordsburg, N.M., U.S. (lôrdz′bûrg)	119	32°20′N	108°45′W
Lorena, Braz. (lō-rā′nȧ)	141a	22°45′S	45°07′W
Loreto, Braz. (lō-rā′tō)	143	7°09′S	45°10′W
Loretteville, Can. (lō-rĕt-vēl′)	102b	46°51′N	71°21′W
Lorica, Col. (lō-rē′kä)	142	9°14′N	75°54′W
Lorient, Fr. (lō-rē-äN′)	161	47°45′N	3°22′W
Lorn, Firth of, b., Scot., U.K. (fûrth ōv lôrn′)	164	56°10′N	6°09′W
Lörrach, Ger. (lûr′äk)	168	47°36′N	7°38′E
Lorraine, hist. reg., Fr.	171	49°00′N	6°00′E
Los Alamitos, Ca., U.S. (lōs ăl-ȧ-mē′tōs)	117a	33°48′N	118°04′W
Los Alamos, N.M., U.S. (ăl-ȧ-mōs′)	119	35°53′N	106°20′W
Los Altos, Ca., U.S. (ăl-tōs′)	116b	37°23′N	122°06′W
Los Andes, Chile (ăn′dĕs)	141b	32°44′S	70°36′W
Los Angeles, Chile (äŋ′hā-lās)	144	37°27′S	72°15′W
Los Angeles, Ca., U.S.	104	34°03′N	118°14′W
Los Angeles, Ca., U.S.	118	34°03′N	118°14′W
Los Angeles, r., Ca., U.S.	117a	33°50′N	118°13′W
Los Angeles Aqueduct, Ca., U.S.	118	35°12′N	118°02′W
Los Bronces, Chile (lōs brō′n-sĕs)	141b	33°09′S	70°18′W
Loscha, r., Id., U.S. (lŏs′chă)	114	46°20′N	115°11′W
Los Estados, Isla de, i., Arg. (ē′s-lä dĕ lōs ĕs-dŏs)	144	54°45′S	64°25′W
Los Gatos, Ca., U.S. (gä′tōs)	118	37°13′N	121°59′W
Los Herreras, Mex. (ĕr-rā-räs)	122	25°55′N	99°23′W
Los llanos, Dom. Rep. (lōs ē-lä′nōs)	135	18°35′N	69°30′W
Los Indios, Cayos de, is., Cuba (kä′vōs dĕ lōs ē′n-dvō′s)	134	21°50′N	83°10′W
Lošinj, i., Yugo.	174	44°35′N	14°34′E
Losino Petrovskiy, Russia	186b	55°52′N	38°12′E
Los Nietos, Ca., U.S. (nyā′tōs)	117a	33°57′N	118°05′W
Los Palacios, Cuba	134	22°35′N	83°15′W
Los Pinos, r., Co., U.S. (pē′nōs)	119	36°58′N	107°35′W
Los Reyes, Mex.	128	19°35′N	102°29′W
Los Reyes, Mex.	131a	19°21′N	98°58′W
Los Santos, Pan. (săn′tōs)	133	7°57′N	80°24′W
Los Santos de Maimona, Spain (săn′tōs)	172	38°38′N	6°30′W
Lost, r., Or., U.S.	114	42°07′N	121°30′W
Los Teques, Ven. (tĕ′kĕs)	142	10°22′N	67°04′W
Lost River Range, mts., Id., U.S. (rĭ′vēr)	115	44°23′N	113°48′W
Los Vilos, Chile (vē′lōs)	144	31°56′S	71°29′W
Lot, r., Fr. (lôt)	161	44°30′N	1°30′E
Lota, Chile (lō′tä)	144	37°11′S	73°14′W
Lothian, Md., U.S. (lōth′ĭăn)	110e	38°50′N	76°38′W
Lotikipi Plain, pl., Afr.	237	4°25′N	34°55′E
Lötschberg Tunnel, trans., Switz.	168	46°26′N	7°54′E
Louangphrabang, Laos (lōō-ang′prä-bäng′)	212	19°47′N	102°15′E
Loudon, Tn., U.S. (lou′dŭn)	124	35°43′N	84°20′W
Loudonville, Oh., U.S. (lou′dŭn-vĭl)	108	40°40′N	82°15′W
Loudun, Fr.	170	47°03′N	0°00′
Loughborough, Eng., U.K. (lŭf′bŭr-ō)	158a	52°46′N	1°12′W
Louisa, Ky., U.S. (lōō′ēz-ȧ)	108	38°05′N	82°40′W
Louisade Archipelago, is., Pap. N. Gui.	221	10°44′S	153°58′E
Louisberg, N.C., U.S. (lōō′ĭs-bûrg)	125	36°05′N	79°19′W
Louisburg, Can. (lōō′ĭs-bourg)	101	45°55′N	59°58′W
Louiseville, Can.	99	46°17′N	72°58′W
Louisiana, Mo., U.S. (lōō-ē-zē-ăn′ȧ)	121	39°24′N	91°03′W
Louisiana, state, U.S.	105	30°50′N	92°50′W
Louis Trichardt, S. Afr. (lōō′ĭs trĭchărt)	232	22°52′S	29°53′E
Louisville, Co., U.S. (lōō′ĭs-vĭl) (lōō′ē-vĭl)	120	39°58′N	105°08′W
Louisville, Ga., U.S.	125	33°00′N	82°25′W
Louisville, Ky., U.S.	105	38°15′N	85°45′W
Louisville, Ms., U.S.	124	33°07′N	89°02′W
Louis XIV, Pointe, c., Can.	93	54°35′N	79°51′W
Louny, Czech Rep. (lō′nē)	168	50°20′N	13°47′E
Loup, r., Ne., U.S. (lōōp)	112	41°17′N	97°58′W
Loup City, Ne., U.S.	112	41°15′N	98°59′W
Lourdes, Fr. (lōōrd)	161	43°06′N	0°03′W
Lourenço Marques *see* Maputo, Moz.	232	26°50′S	32°30′E
Loures, Port. (lō′rĕzh)	173b	38°49′N	9°10′W
Lousa, Port. (lō′zȧ)	172	40°05′N	8°12′W
Louth, Eng., U.K. (louth)	164	53°27′N	0°02′W
Louvain *see* Leuven, Bel.	165	50°53′N	4°42′E
Louviers, Fr. (lōō-vyā′)	170	49°13′N	1°11′E
Lovech, Blg. (lō′vĕts)	175	43°10′N	24°40′E
Loveland, Co., U.S. (lŭv′lănd)	120	40°24′N	105°04′W
Loveland, Oh., U.S.	111f	39°16′N	84°15′W
Lovell, Wy., U.S. (lŭv′ĕl)	115	44°50′N	108°23′W
Lovelock, Nv., U.S. (lŭv′lŏk)	118	40°10′N	118°37′W
Lovick, Al., U.S. (lŭ′vĭk)	110h	33°34′N	86°38′W
Loviisa, Fin. (lô′vē-sȧ)	167	60°28′N	26°10′E
Low, Cape, c., Can. (lō)	93	62°58′N	86°50′W
Lowa, r., D.R.C. (lō′wȧ)	232	1°30′S	27°18′E
Lowell, In., U.S.	111a	41°17′N	87°26′W
Lowell, Ma., U.S.	105	42°38′N	71°18′W
Lowell, Mi., U.S.	108	42°55′N	85°20′W
Löwenberg, Ger. (lû′vĕn-bĕrgh)	159b	52°53′N	13°09′E
Lower Brule Indian Reservation, I.R., S.D., U.S. (brü′lā)	112	44°15′N	100°21′W
Lower California *see* Baja California, pen., Mex.	89	28°00′N	113°30′W
Lower Granite Dam, dam, Wa., U.S.	114	46°40′N	117°26′W
Lower Hutt, N.Z. (hŭt)	221a	41°10′S	174°55′E
Lower Klamath Lake, l., Ca., U.S. (klăm′ăth)	114	41°55′N	121°50′W
Lower Lake, l., Ca., U.S.	114	41°21′N	119°53′W
Lower Marlboro, Md., U.S. (lō′ēr märl′bōrō)	110e	38°40′N	76°42′W
Lower Monumental Dam, dam, Wa., U.S.	114	46°34′N	118°32′W
Lower Otay Lake, res., Ca., U.S. (ō′tā)	118a	32°37′N	116°46′W
Lower Red Lake, l., Mn., U.S.	113	47°58′N	94°31′W
Lower Saxony *see* Niedersachsen, state, Ger.	159c	53°30′N	9°30′E
Lowestoft, Eng., U.K. (lō′stŏf)	165	52°31′N	1°45′E
Łowicz, Pol. (lō′vĭch)	169	52°06′N	19°57′E
Lowville, N.Y., U.S. (lou′vĭl)	109	43°45′N	75°30′W
Loxicha, Mex.	131	16°03′N	96°46′W
Loxton, Austl. (lŏks′tŭn)	222	34°25′S	140°38′E
Loyauté, Îles, is., N. Cal.	221	21°00′S	167°00′E
Loznica, Yugo. (lōz′nē-tsȧ)	163	44°31′N	19°16′E
Lozova, Ukr.	181	48°53′N	36°23′E
Luama, r., D.R.C. (lōō′ä-mȧ)	232	4°17′S	27°45′E
Lu′an, China (lōō-än)	209	31°45′N	116°29′E
Luan, r., China	205	41°25′N	117°15′E
Luanda, Ang. (lōō-än′dä)	232	8°48′S	13°14′E
Luanguinga, r., Afr. (lōō-ä-gĭŋ′gȧ)	232	14°00′S	20°45′E
Luanshya, Zam.	237	13°08′S	28°24′E
Luanxian, China (luăn shyĕn)	206	39°47′N	118°40′E
Luao, Ang.	236	10°42′S	22°12′E
Luarca, Spain (lwä′kä)	162	43°33′N	6°30′W
Lubaczów, Pol. (lōō-bä′chòf)	169	50°08′N	23°10′E
Lubán, Pol. (lōō′bän′)	168	51°08′N	15°17′E
Lubānas Ezers, l., Lat. (lōō-bä′nȧs ä′zĕrs)	167	56°48′N	26°30′E
Lubang, Phil. (lōō-bäng′)	213a	13°49′N	120°07′E
Lubang Islands, is., Phil.	212	13°47′N	119°56′E
Lubango, Ang.	232	14°55′S	13°30′E
Lubartów, Pol. (lōō-bär′tòf)	169	51°27′N	22°37′E
Lubawa, Pol. (lōō-bä′vä)	169	53°31′N	19°47′E
Lübben, Ger. (lüb′ĕn)	168	51°56′N	13°53′E
Lubbock, Tx., U.S.	105	33°35′N	101°50′E
Lubec, Me., U.S. (lū′bĕk)	100	44°49′N	67°01′W
Lübeck, Ger. (lü′bĕk)	154	53°53′N	10°42′E
Lübecker Bucht, b., Ger. (lü′bĕ-kĕr bōōĸt)	160	54°10′N	11°20′E
Lubilash, r., D.R.C. (lōō-bē-làsh′)	232	7°35′S	23°55′E
Lubin, Pol. (lyō′bĭn)	168	51°24′N	16°14′E
Lublin, Pol. (lyò′blĕn′)	154	51°14′N	22°33′E
Lubny, Ukr. (lòb′nē)	181	50°01′N	33°02′E
Lubuagan, Phil. (lò-bwä-gä′n)	213a	17°24′N	121°11′E
Lubudi, D.R.C.	237	9°57′S	25°58′E
Lubudi, r., D.R.C. (lò-bò′dē)	232	10°00′S	24°30′E
Lubumbashi, D.R.C.	232	11°40′S	27°28′E
Lucano, Ang.	236	11°16′S	21°38′E
Lucca, Italy (lōōk′kä)	162	43°51′N	10°29′E
Lucea, Jam.	134	18°25′N	78°10′W
Luce Bay, b., Scot., U.K. (lūs)	164	54°45′N	4°45′W
Lucena, Phil. (lōō-sā′nä)	213a	13°55′N	121°36′E
Lucena, Spain (lōō-thā′nä)	162	37°25′N	4°28′W
Lučenec, Slvk. (lōō′châ-nyĕts)	161	48°19′N	19°41′E
Lucera, Italy (lōō-châ′rä)	174	41°31′N	15°22′E
Luchi, China	209	28°18′N	110°10′E
Lucin, Ut., U.S. (lů-sĕn′)	115	41°23′N	113°59′W
Lucipara, Kepulauan, is., Indon.	213	5°45′S	128°15′E
Luckenwalde, Ger.	168	52°05′N	13°10′E
Lucknow, India (lŭk′nou)	199	26°54′N	80°58′E
Lucky Peak Lake, res., Id., U.S.	114	43°33′N	116°00′W
Luçon, Fr. (lü-sôN′)	170	46°27′N	1°12′W
Lucrecia, Cabo, c., Cuba	135	21°05′N	75°30′W
Luda Kamchiya, r., Blg.	175	42°46′N	27°13′E
Lüdenscheid, Ger. (lü′dĕn-shĭt)	171c	51°13′N	7°38′E
Lüderitz, Nmb. (lü′dĕr-ĭts) (lü′dĕ-rĭts)	232	26°35′S	15°15′E
Lüderitz Bucht, b., Nmb.	232	26°35′S	14°30′E
Ludhiāna, India	199	31°00′N	75°52′E
Lüdinghausen, Ger.	171c	51°46′N	7°27′E
Ludington, Mi., U.S. (lŭd′ĭng-tŭn)	108	44°00′N	86°25′W
Ludlow, Eng., U.K. (lŭd′lō)	158a	52°22′N	2°43′W
Ludlow, Ky., U.S.	111f	39°05′N	84°33′W
Ludvika, Swe. (loodh-vē′kȧ)	166	60°10′N	15°09′E
Ludwigsburg, Ger.	168	48°53′N	9°14′E
Ludwigsfelde, Ger.	159b	52°18′N	13°16′E
Ludwigshafen, Ger.	168	49°29′N	8°26′E
Ludwigslust, Ger.	168	53°18′N	11°31′E
Ludza, Lat. (lōōd′zȧ)	167	56°33′N	27°45′E
Luebo, D.R.C. (lōō-ā′bò)	232	5°15′S	21°22′E
Luena, Ang.	232	11°45′S	19°55′E
Luena, D.R.C.	237	9°27′S	25°47′E
Lufira, r., D.R.C. (lōō-fē′rȧ)	232	9°32′S	27°15′E
Lufkin, Tx., U.S. (lŭf′kĭn)	123	31°21′N	94°43′W
Luga, Russia (lōō′gȧ)	180	58°43′N	29°52′E
Luga, r., Russia	176	59°00′N	29°25′E
Lugano, Switz. (lōō-gä′nō)	168	46°01′N	8°52′E
Lugenda, r., Moz.	233	12°05′S	38°15′E
Lugo, Italy (lōō′gò)	174	44°28′N	11°57′E
Lugo, Spain (lōō′gō)	162	43°01′N	7°32′W
Lugoj, Rom.	163	45°51′N	21°56′E
Luhans′k, Ukr.	178	48°34′N	39°18′E
Luhans′k, prov., Ukr.	177	49°30′N	38°35′E
Luhe, China (lōō-hŭ)	206	32°22′N	118°50′E
Luiana, Ang.	236	17°23′S	23°03′E
Luilaka, r., D.R.C. (lōō-ē-lä′kȧ)	232	2°18′S	21°15′E
Luis Moya, Mex. (lōōē′s-mô-yä)	130	22°26′N	102°14′W
Luján, Arg. (lōō-hän′)	141c	34°36′S	59°07′W
Luján, r., Arg.	141c	34°33′S	58°59′W
Lujia, China (lōō-jyä)	206	31°17′N	120°54′W
Lukanga Swamp, sw., Zam. (lōō-kän′gȧ)	232	14°30′S	27°25′E
Lukenie, r., D.R.C. (lōō-kā′ynȧ)	232	3°10′S	19°05′E
Lukolela, D.R.C.	232	1°03′S	17°01′E
Lukovit, Blg. (lōō′kō-vēt′)	175	43°13′N	24°07′E
Łuków, Pol. (wò′kòf)	169	51°57′N	22°25′E

ăt; finăl; rāte; senāte; ärm; ȧsk; sofȧ; fâre; ch-choose; dh-as th in other; bē; ēvent; bĕt; recĕnt; cratēr; g-gō; gh-guttural g; bĭt; ĭ-short neutral; rīde; ĸ-guttural k as ch in German ich;

PRONOUNCING INDEX

Lukuga – Maḩaţţat Jurf ad Darāwīsh 317

PLACE (Pronunciation)	PAGE	LAT.	LONG.
Lukuga, r., D.R.C. (lōō-kōō'gȧ)	232	5°50'S	27°35'E
Lüleburgaz, Tur. (lü'lĕ-bòr-gäs')	175	41°25'N	27°23'E
Luling, Tx., U.S. (lū'lĭng)	123	29°41'N	97°38'W
Lulong, China (lōō-lôŋ)	205	39°54'N	118°53'E
Lulonga, r., D.R.C.	236	1°00'N	18°37'E
Luluabourg see Kananga, D.R.C.	232	6°14'S	22°17'E
Lulu Island, i., Can.	116d	49°09'N	123°05'W
Lulu Island, i., Ak., U.S.	94	55°28'N	133°30'W
Lumajangdong Co, l., China	202	34°00'N	81°47'E
Lumber, r., N.C., U.S. (lŭm'bẽr)	125	34°45'N	79°10'W
Lumberton, Ms., U.S. (lŭm'bẽr-tŭn)	124	31°00'N	89°25'W
Lumberton, N.C., U.S.	125	34°47'N	79°00'W
Luminárias, Braz. (lōō-mē-nä'ryäs)	141a	21°32'S	44°53'W
Lummi, i., Wa., U.S.	116d	48°42'N	122°43'W
Lummi Bay, b., Wa., U.S. (lŭm'ĭ)	116d	48°47'N	122°44'W
Lummi Island, Wa., U.S.	116d	48°44'N	122°42'W
Lumwana, Zam.	237	11°50'S	25°10'E
Lün, Mong.	204	47°58'N	104°52'E
Luna, Phil. (lōō'nä)	213a	16°51'N	120°22'E
Lund, Swe. (lŭnd)	160	55°42'N	13°10'E
Lundy, i., Eng., U.K. (lŭn'dē)	164	51°12'N	4°50'W
Lüneburg, Ger. (lü'nĕ-bòrgh)	168	53°16'N	10°25'E
Lunel, Fr. (lü-nĕl')	170	43°41'N	4°07'E
Lünen, Ger. (lü'nĕn)	171c	51°36'N	7°30'E
Lunenburg, Can. (lōō'nĕn-bûrg)	91	44°23'N	64°19'W
Lunenburg, Ma., U.S.	101a	42°36'N	71°44'W
Lunéville, Fr. (lü-nā-vel')	171	48°37'N	6°29'E
Lunga, Ang.	236	14°42'S	18°32'E
Lungué-Bungo, r., Afr.	232	13°00'S	20°30'E
Lunsar, S.L.	234	8°41'N	12°32'W
Luodian, China (lwô-dĭĕn)	206	31°25'N	121°20'E
Luoding, China (lwô-dĭŋ)	209	23°42'N	111°35'E
Luohe, China (lwô-hŭ)	206	33°35'N	114°02'E
Luoyang, China (lwô-yäŋ)	205	34°45'N	112°32'E
Luozhen, China (lwô-jŭn)	206	37°45'N	118°29'E
Luque, Para. (loo'kā)	144	25°18'S	57°17'W
Luray, Va., U.S. (lū-rā')	109	38°40'N	78°25'W
Lurgan, N. Ire., U.K. (lûr'găn)	160	54°27'N	6°28'W
Lúrio, Moz. (lōō'rē-ō)	233	13°17'S	40°29'E
Lúrio, Moz.	233	14°00'S	38°45'E
Lusaka, D.R.C.	237	7°10'S	29°27'E
Lusaka, Zam. (lò-sä'kȧ)	237	15°25'S	28°17'E
Lusambo, D.R.C. (lōō-säm'bō)	232	4°58'S	23°27'E
Lusanga, D.R.C.	232	5°13'S	18°43'E
Lusangi, D.R.C.	237	4°37'S	27°08'E
Lushan, China	208	33°45'N	113°00'E
Lushiko, r., Afr.	236	6°35'S	19°45'E
Lushoto, Tan. (lōō-shō'tō)	233	4°47'S	38°17'E
Lüshun, China (lü-shŭn)	205	38°49'N	121°15'E
Lusikisiki, S. Afr. (lōō-sē-kē-sē'kē)	233c	31°22'S	29°37'E
Lusk, Wy., U.S. (lŭsk)	112	42°46'N	104°27'W
Lūt, Dasht-e, des., Iran (dä'sht-ē-lōōt)	198	31°47'N	58°38'E
Lutcher, La., U.S. (lŭch'ẽr)	123	30°03'N	90°43'W
Luton, Eng., U.K. (lū'tŭn)	164	51°55'N	0°28'W
Luts'k, Ukr.	181	50°45'N	25°20'E
Luuq, Som.	238a	3°38'N	42°35'E
Luverne, Al., U.S. (lū-vûn')	124	31°42'N	86°15'W
Luverne, Mn., U.S.	112	43°40'N	96°13'W
Luwingu, Zam.	237	10°15'S	29°55'E
Luxapallila Creek, r., U.S. (lŭk-sȧ-pôl'ĭ-lȧ)	124	33°36'N	88°08'W
Luxembourg, Lux.	154	49°38'N	6°30'E
Luxembourg, nation, Eur.	154	49°30'N	6°22'E
Luxeuil-les-Baines, Fr.	171	47°49'N	6°19'E
Luxomni, Ga., U.S. (lŭx'ôm-nī)	110c	33°54'N	84°07'W
Luxor see Al Uqşur, Egypt	231	25°38'N	32°59'E
Luya Shan, mtn., China	208	38°50'N	111°40'E
Luyi, China (lōō-yē)	206	33°52'N	115°32'E
Luzern, Switz. (lò-tsĕrn)	161	47°03'N	8°18'E
Luzhou, China (lōō-jō)	204	28°58'N	105°25'E
Luziânia, Braz. (lōō-zyà'nēȧ)	143	16°17'S	47°44'W
Luzon, i., Phil. (lōō-zŏn')	212	17°10'N	119°45'E
Luzon Strait, strt., Asia	209	20°40'N	121°00'E
L'viv, Ukr.	178	49°50'N	24°00'E
L'vov see L'viv, Ukr.	178	49°50'N	24°00'E
Lyalta, Can.	102e	51°07'N	113°36'W
Lyalya, r., Russia (lyá'lyȧ)	186a	58°58'N	60°17'E
Lyaskovets, Blg.	175	43°07'N	25°41'E
Lydenburg, S. Afr. (lī'dĕn-bûrg)	232	25°06'S	30°21'E
Lyell, Mount, mtn., Ca., U.S. (lī'ĕl)	118	37°44'N	119°22'W
Lyepye', Bela. (lyĕ-pĕl')	176	54°52'N	28°41'E
Lykens, Pa., U.S. (lī'kĕnz)	109	40°35'N	76°45'W
Lykhivka, Ukr.	177	48°52'N	33°57'E
Lyna, r., Eur. (lĭn'ȧ)	169	53°56'N	20°30'E
Lynch, Ky., U.S. (lĭnch)	125	36°56'N	82°55'W
Lynchburg, Va., U.S. (lĭnch'bûrg)	105	37°23'N	79°08'W
Lynch Cove, Wa., U.S. (lĭnch)	116a	47°26'N	122°54'W
Lynden, Can. (lĭn'dĕn)	102d	43°14'N	80°08'W
Lynden, Wa., U.S.	116d	48°56'N	122°27'W
Lyndhurst, Austl.	217a	38°03'S	145°14'E
Lyndon, Ky., U.S. (lĭn'dŭn)	111h	38°15'N	85°36'W
Lyndonville, Vt., U.S. (lĭn'dŭn-vĭl)	109	44°35'N	72°00'W
Lynn, Ma., U.S. (lĭn)	105	42°28'N	70°57'W
Lynn Lake, Can. (lăk)	90	56°51'N	101°05'W
Lynwood, Ca., U.S. (lĭn'wòd)	117a	33°56'N	118°13'W
Lyon, Fr. (lē-ôN')	154	45°44'N	4°52'E
Lyons, Ga., U.S. (lī'ŭnz)	125	32°08'N	82°19'W
Lyons, Ks., U.S.	120	38°20'N	98°11'W
Lyons, Ne., U.S.	112	41°57'N	96°28'W
Lyons, N.J., U.S.	110a	40°41'N	74°33'W
Lyons, N.Y., U.S.	109	43°05'N	77°00'W
Lyptsi, Ukr.	177	50°11'N	36°25'E
Lysefjorden, b., Nor.	166	58°59'N	6°35'E
Lysekil, Swe. (lü'sĕ-kĕl)	166	58°17'N	11°22'E
Lys'va, Russia (lĭs'vȧ)	180	58°07'N	57°47'E
Lytham, Eng., U.K. (lĭth'ăm)	158a	53°44'N	2°58'W
Lytkarino, Russia	186b	55°35'N	37°55'E
Lyttelton, S. Afr. (lĭt'l'tŏn)	233b	25°51'S	28°13'E
Lyuban', Russia (lyōō'bȧn)	176	59°21'N	31°15'E
Lyubertsy, Russia (lyōō'bĕr-tsĕ)	176	55°40'N	37°55'E
Lyubim, Russia (lyōō-bēm')	176	58°24'N	40°39'E
Lyublino, Russia (lyōōb'lĭ-nô)	186b	55°41'N	37°45'E
Lyudinovo, Russia (lū-dē'novō)	176	53°52'N	34°28'E

M

PLACE (Pronunciation)	PAGE	LAT.	LONG.
Ma'ān, Jord. (mä-än')	198	30°12'N	35°45'E
Maartensdijk, Neth.	159a	52°09'N	5°10'E
Maas (Meuse), r., Eur.	165	51°50'N	5°40'E
Maastricht, Neth. (mäs'trĭkt)	165	50°51'N	5°35'E
Mabaia, Ang.	236	7°13'S	14°03'E
Mabana, Wa., U.S. (mä-bä-nä)	116a	48°06'N	122°25'W
Mabank, Tx., U.S. (mā'bănk)	123	32°21'N	96°05'W
Mabeskraal, S. Afr.	238c	25°12'S	26°47'E
Mableton, Ga., U.S. (mā'b'l-tŭn)	110c	33°49'N	84°34'W
Mabrouk, Mali	230	19°27'N	1°16'W
Mabula, S. Afr. (mȧ'bōō-la)	238c	24°49'S	27°59'E
Macalelon, Phil. (mä-kä-lā-lōn')	213a	13°46'N	122°09'E
Macau, Braz. (mä-kà'ò)	143	5°12'S	36°34'W
Macau, China	205	22°00'N	113°00'E
Macaya, Pico de, mtn., Haiti	135	18°25'N	74°00'W
Macclesfield, Eng., U.K. (măk''lz-fēld)	158a	53°15'N	2°07'W
Macclesfield Canal, can., Eng., U.K. (măk''lz-fēld)	158a	53°14'N	2°07'W
Macdona, Tx., U.S. (măk-dō'nȧ)	117d	29°20'N	98°42'W
Macdonald, l., Austl. (măk-dŏn'ăld)	220	23°40'S	127°40'E
Macdonnell Ranges, mts., Austl. (măk-dŏn'ĕl)	220	23°40'S	131°30'E
MacDowell Lake, l., Can. (măk-dou ĕl)	97	52°15'N	92°45'W
Macdui, Ben, mtn., Scot., U.K. (bĕn măk-dōō'ē)	160	57°06'N	3°45'W
Macedonia, Oh., U.S. (măs-ē-dō'nĭ-ȧ)	111d	41°19'N	81°30'E
Macedonia, nation, Eur.	175	41°50'N	22°00'E
Macedonia, hist. reg., Eur. (măs-ē-dō'nĭ-ȧ)	163	41°05'N	22°15'E
Maceió, Braz.	143	9°40'S	35°43'W
Macerata, Italy (mä-chå-rä'tä)	174	43°18'N	13°28'E
Macfarlane, Lake, l., Austl. (mȧc'fär-lān)	222	32°10'S	137°00'E
Machache, mtn., Leso.	233c	29°22'S	27°53'E
Machado, Braz. (mä-shà-dô)	141a	21°42'S	45°55'W
Machakos, Kenya	237	1°31'S	37°16'E
Machala, Ec. (mä-chá'lä)	142	3°18'S	78°54'W
Machens, Mo., U.S. (măk'ĕns)	117e	38°54'N	90°20'W
Machias, Me., U.S. (mȧ-chī'ȧs)	100	44°22'N	67°29'W
Machida, Japan (mä-chē'dä)	211a	35°32'N	139°28'E
Machilipatnam, India	199	16°22'N	81°10'E
Machu Picchu, Peru (mä'chò-pē'k-chò)	142	13°07'S	72°34'W
Măcin, Rom. (mä-chēn')	177	45°15'N	28°09'E
Macina, reg., Mali	234	14°50'N	4°40'W
Mackay, Austl. (mȧ-kī')	219	21°15'S	149°08'E
Mackay, Id., U.S. (măk-kā')	115	43°55'N	113°38'W
Mackay, l., Austl. (mȧ-kī')	220	22°30'S	127°45'E
MacKay, l., Can. (măk-kā')	92	64°10'N	112°35'W
Mackenzie, r., Can.	92	63°38'N	124°23'W
Mackenzie Bay, b., Can.	103	69°20'N	137°10'W
Mackenzie Mountains, mts., Can. (mȧ-kĕn'zĭ)	92	63°41'N	129°27'W
Mackinaw, r., Il., U.S.	108	40°35'N	89°25'W
Mackinaw City, Mi., U.S. (măk'ĭ-nô)	108	45°45'N	84°45'W
Mackinnon Road, Kenya	237	3°44'S	39°03'E
Macleantown, S. Afr. (măk-lăn'toun)	233c	32°48'S	27°48'E
Maclear, S. Afr. (mȧ-klēr')	232	31°06'S	28°23'E
Macomb, Il., U.S. (mȧ-kōōm')	121	40°27'N	90°40'W
Mâcon, Fr. (mä-kôN)	161	46°19'N	4°51'E
Macon, Ga., U.S. (mā'kŏn)	105	32°49'N	83°39'W
Macon, Mo., U.S.	121	39°42'N	92°29'W
Macon, Ms., U.S.	124	32°07'N	88°31'W
Macquarie, r., Austl.	221	31°43'S	148°04'E
Macquarie Islands, is., Austl. (mȧ-kwŏr'ē)	3	54°36'S	158°45'E
Macuelizo, Hond. (mä-kwĕ-lē'zō)	132	15°22'N	88°32'W
Mad, r., Ca., U.S. (măd)	114	40°38'N	123°37'W
Madagascar, nation, Afr. (măd-ȧ-găs'kȧr)	233	18°05'S	43°12'E
Madame, i., Can. (mȧ-dȧm')	101	45°33'N	61°02'W
Madanapalle, India	203	13°06'N	78°09'E
Madang, Pap. N. Gui. (mä-däng')	213	5°15'S	145°45'E
Madaoua, Niger (mȧ-dou'ȧ)	230	14°04'N	6°03'E
Madawaska, r., Can. (măd-ȧ-wôs'kȧ)	99	45°20'N	77°25'W
Madeira, r., S.A.	142	6°48'S	62°43'W
Madeira, Arquipélago da, is., Port.	229	33°26'N	16°44'W
Madeira, Ilha da, i., Port. (mä-dā'rä)	230	32°41'N	16°15'W
Madeleine, Îles de la, is., Can.	93	47°30'N	61°45'W
Madelia, Mn., U.S. (mȧ-dē'lĭ-ȧ)	113	44°03'N	94°23'W
Madeline, i., Wi., U.S. (măd'ĕ-lĭn)	113	46°47'N	91°30'W
Madera, Ca., U.S. (mȧ-dā'rȧ)	118	36°57'N	120°04'W
Madera, vol., Nic.	132	11°27'N	85°30'W
Madgaon, India	203	15°09'N	73°58'E
Madhya Pradesh, state, India (mŭd'vŭ prŭ-dāsh')	199	22°04'N	77°48'E
Madill, Ok., U.S. (mȧ-dĭl')	121	34°04'N	96°45'W
Madīnat ash Sha'b, Yemen	198	12°45'N	44°00'E
Madingo, Congo	236	4°07'S	11°22'E
Madingou, Congo	236	4°09'S	13°34'E
Madison, Fl., U.S. (măd'ĭ-sŭn)	124	30°28'N	83°25'W
Madison, Ga., U.S.	124	33°34'N	83°29'W
Madison, Il., U.S.	117e	38°40'N	90°09'W
Madison, In., U.S.	108	38°45'N	85°25'W
Madison, Ks., U.S.	121	38°08'N	96°07'W
Madison, Me., U.S.	100	44°47'N	69°52'W
Madison, Mn., U.S.	112	44°59'N	96°13'W
Madison, N.C., U.S.	125	36°22'N	79°59'W
Madison, Ne., U.S.	112	41°49'N	97°27'W
Madison, N.J., U.S.	110a	40°46'N	74°25'W
Madison, S.D., U.S.	112	44°01'N	97°08'W
Madison, Wi., U.S.	105	43°05'N	89°23'W
Madison Res, Mt., U.S.	115	45°25'N	111°28'W
Madisonville, Ky., U.S. (măd'ĭ-sŭn-vĭl)	108	37°20'N	87°30'W
Madisonville, La., U.S.	123	30°22'N	90°10'W
Madisonville, Tx., U.S.	123	30°57'N	95°55'W
Madjori, Burkina	234	11°26'N	1°15'E
Mado Gashi, Kenya	237	0°44'N	39°10'E
Madona, Lat. (mä'dō'nȧ)	167	56°50'N	26°14'E
Madrakah, Ra's al, c., Oman	198	18°53'N	57°48'E
Madras see Chennai, India	199	13°08'N	80°15'E
Madre, Laguna, l., Mex. (lä-gōō'nä mä'drå)	123	25°08'N	97°41'W
Madre, Sierra, mts., N.A. (sē-ĕ'r-rä-mä'drĕ)	131	15°55'N	92°40'W
Madre, Sierra, mts., Phil.	213a	16°40'N	122°10'E
Madre de Dios, r., S.A. (mä'drå dā dē-ōs')	142	12°07'S	68°02'W
Madre de Dios, Archipiélago, is., Chile (mä'drå dā dē-ōs')	144	50°40'S	76°30'W
Madre del Sur, Sierra, mts., Mex. (sē-ĕ'r-rä-mä'drå dĕlsōōr')	128	17°35'N	100°35'W
Madre Occidental, Sierra, mts., Mex.	128	29°30'N	107°30'W
Madre Oriental, Sierra, mts., Mex.	128	25°30'N	100°45'W
Madrid, Spain (mä-drē'd)	154	40°26'N	3°42'W
Madrid, Ia., U.S. (măd'rĭd)	113	41°51'N	93°48'W
Madridejos, Spain (mä-dhrē-dhä'hōs)	172	39°29'N	3°32'W
Madura, i., Indon. (mȧ-dōō'rä)	212	6°45'S	113°30'E
Madurai, India (mä-dōō'rä)	199	9°57'N	78°04'E
Madureira, Serra do, mts., Braz. (sĕ'r-rä-dô-mä-dōō-rā'rȧ)	144b	22°49'S	43°30'W
Maebashi, Japan (mä-ĕ-bä'shē)	205	36°26'N	139°04'E
Maestra, Sierra, mts., Cuba (sē-ĕ'r-rȧ-mä-ās'trä)	129	20°05'N	77°05'W
Maewo, i., Vanuatu	221	15°17'S	168°16'E
Mafeking, S. Afr. (măf'ē-kĭng)	232	25°46'S	24°45'E
Mafra, Braz. (mä'frä)	144	26°21'N	49°59'W
Mafra, Port. (măf'rȧ)	173b	38°56'N	9°20'W
Magadan, Russia (mȧ-gȧ-dän')	179	59°39'N	150°43'E
Magadan Oblast, Russia	185	65°00'N	160°00'E
Magadi, Kenya	237	1°54'S	36°17'E
Magalies, r., S. Afr. (mä-gä'lyĕs)	233b	25°51'S	27°42'E
Magaliesberg, mts., S. Afr.	233b	25°45'S	27°43'E
Magaliesburg, S. Afr.	238c	26°01'S	27°32'E
Magallanes, Estrecho de, strt., S.A.	144	52°30'S	68°45'W
Magat, r., Phil. (mä-gät')	213a	16°45'N	121°16'E
Magdalena, Arg. (măg-dä-lā'nä)	141c	35°05'S	57°32'W
Magdalena, Bol.	142	13°17'S	63°57'W
Magdalena, Mex.	104	30°34'N	110°50'W
Magdalena, N.M., U.S.	119	34°10'N	107°45'W
Magdalena, i., Chile	144	44°45'S	73°15'W
Magdalena, r., Col.	142	7°45'N	74°04'W
Magdalena, Bahía, b., Mex. (bä-ē'ä-mäg-dä-lā'nä)	128	24°30'N	114°00'W
Magdeburg, Ger. (mäg'dĕ-bòrgh)	154	52°07'N	11°39'E
Magellan, Strait of see Magallanes, Estrecho de, strt., S.A.	144	52°30'S	68°45'W
Magenta, Italy (mȧ-jĕn'tȧ)	174	45°26'N	8°53'E
Magerøya, i., Nor.	160	71°10'N	24°11'E
Maggiore, Lago, l., Italy	162	46°03'N	8°25'E
Maghāghah, Egypt	238b	28°38'N	30°50'W
Maghniyya, Alg.	162	34°52'N	1°40'W
Magiscatzin, Mex. (mä-kēs-kät-zēn')	130	22°48'N	98°42'W
Maglaj, Bos. (mä'glä-ē)	175	44°34'N	18°12'E
Maglie, Italy (mäl'yā)	175	40°06'N	18°20'E
Magna, Ut., U.S. (măg'nȧ)	117b	40°43'N	112°06'W
Magnitogorsk, Russia (mág-nyĕ'tô-gôrsk)	178	53°26'N	59°05'E
Magnolia, Ar., U.S. (măg-nō'lĭ-ȧ)	121	33°16'N	93°13'W
Magnolia, Ms., U.S.	124	31°08'N	90°27'W
Magny-en-Vexin, Fr. (mä-nyē'ĕN-vĕ-sàN')	171b	49°09'N	1°45'E
Magog, Can. (mȧ-gŏg')	99	45°15'N	72°10'W
Magpie, r., Can.	100	50°40'N	64°30'W
Magpie, r., Can.	98	48°13'N	84°50'W
Magpie, Lac, l., Can.	100	50°55'N	64°39'W
Magrath, Can.	90	49°25'N	112°52'W
Magude, Moz. (mä-gōō'dȧ)	232	24°58'S	32°39'E
Magwe, Mya. (mŭg-wā')	199	20°19'N	94°57'E
Mahābād, Iran	201	36°55'N	45°50'E
Mahahi Port, D.R.C. (mä-hä'gē)	231	2°14'N	31°12'E
Mahajanga, Madag.	233	15°12'S	46°26'E
Mahakam, r., Indon.	212	0°30'S	116°15'E
Mahali Mountains, mts., Tan.	237	6°20'S	30°00'E
Mahaly, Madag. (mȧ-hȧl-ē')	233	24°09'S	46°20'E
Mahanoro, Madag. (mȧ-hȧ-nô'rō)	233	19°57'S	48°47'E
Mahanoy City, Pa., U.S. (mä-hȧ-noi')	109	40°50'N	76°10'W
Maḩaţţat al Qaţrānah, Jord.	197a	31°15'N	36°04'E
Maḩaţţat 'Aqabat al Ḩijāzīyah, Jord.	197a	29°45'N	35°55'E
Maḩaţţat ar Ramlah, Jord.	197a	29°31'N	35°57'E
Maḩaţţat Jurf ad Darāwīsh, Jord.	197a	30°41'N	35°51'E

ng-sing; ŋ-baŋk; N-nasalized n; nŏd; cŏmmit; ōld; ôbey; ôrder; oi-boil; fōōd; ò-as oo in foot; ou-out; s-soft; sh-dish; th-thin; pūre; ûnite; ûrn; stŭd; circŭs; ü-as in French tu; '-indeterminate vowel.

318 Mahd adh-Dhahab – Mansfield PRONOUNCING INDEX

PLACE (Pronunciation)	PAGE	LAT.	LONG.
Mahd adh-Dhahab, Sau. Ar.	201	23°30'N	40°52'E
Mahe, India (mä-ā')	199	11°42'N	75°39'E
Mahenge, Tan. (mä-hĕŋ'gȧ)	232	7°38'S	36°16'E
Mahi, r., India	202	23°16'N	73°20'E
Mahilyow, Bela.	180	53°53'N	30°22'E
Mahilyow, prov., Bela.	176	53°28'N	30°15'E
Māhīm Bay, b., India	203b	19°03'N	72°45'E
Mahlabatini, S. Afr. (mä'lȧ-bȧ-tē'nė)	233c	28°15'S	31°29'E
Mahlow, Ger. (mä'lōv)	159b	52°23'N	13°24'E
Mahnomen, Mn., U.S. (mô-nō'mĕn)	112	47°18'N	95°58'W
Mahone Bay, Can. (mȧ-hōn')	100	44°27'N	64°23'W
Mahone Bay, b., Can.	100	44°30'N	64°15'W
Mahopac, Lake, l., N.Y., U.S. (mā-hō'păk)	110a	41°24'N	73°45'W
Mahwah, N.J., U.S. (mȧ-wä')	110a	41°05'N	74°09'W
Maidenhead, Eng., U.K. (mād'ĕn-hĕd)	158b	51°30'N	0°44'W
Maidstone, Eng., U.K.	165	51°17'N	0°32'E
Maiduguri, Nig. (mä'ē-dȧ-gōō'rē)	231	11°51'N	13°10'E
Maigualida, Sierra, mts., Ven. (sē-ĕ'r-rȧ-mī-gwä'lē-dĕ)	142	6°30'N	65°50'W
Maijdi, Bngl.	202	22°59'N	91°08'E
Maikop *see* Maykop, Russia	178	44°35'N	40°07'E
Main, r., Ger. (mīn)	168	49°49'N	9°20'E
Main Barrier Range, mts., Austl. (băr''ēr)	221	31°25'S	141°40'E
Mai-Ndombe, Lac, l., D.R.C.	232	2°16'S	19°00'E
Maine, state, U.S. (mān)	105	45°25'N	69°50'W
Mainland, i., Scot., U.K. (măn-lănd)	160	60°19'N	2°40'W
Maintenon, Fr. (măN-tĕ-nôN')	171b	48°35'N	1°35'E
Maintirano, Madag. (mä'ēn-tē-rä'nō)	233	18°05'S	44°08'E
Mainz, Ger. (mīnts)	154	49°59'N	8°16'E
Maio, i., C.V. (mä'yo)	230b	15°15'N	22°50'W
Maipo, S.A.	144	34°08'S	69°51'W
Maipo, r., Chile (mī'pō)	141b	33°45'S	71°08'W
Maiquetía, Ven. (mī-kĕ-tē'ä)	142	10°37'N	66°56'W
Maison-Rouge, Fr. (mā-zôN-rōōzh')	171b	48°34'N	3°09'E
Maisons-Laffitte, Fr.	171b	48°57'N	2°09'E
Maitland, Austl. (māt'lănd)	219	32°45'S	151°40'E
Maizuru, Japan (mä-ī'zōō-rōō)	211	35°26'N	135°15'E
Majene, Indon.	212	3°34'S	119°00'E
Maji, Eth.	231	6°14'N	35°34'E
Majorca *see* Mallorca, i., Spain	156	39°18'N	2°22'E
Makah Indian Reservation, I.R., Wa., U.S.	114	48°17'N	124°52'W
Makanya, Tan. (mä-kän'yä)	233	4°15'S	37°49'E
Makanza, D.R.C.	231	1°42'N	19°08'E
Makarakomburu, Mount, mtn., Sol. Is.	214e	9°43'S	160°02'E
Makarska, Cro. (mä'kär-skȧ)	175	43°17'N	17°05'E
Makar'yev, Russia	180	57°50'N	43°48'E
Makasar *see* Ujung Pandang, Indon.	212	5°08'S	119°28'E
Makasar, Selat (Makassar Strait), strt., Indon.	212	2°00'S	118°07'E
Makaw, D.R.C.	236	3°29'S	18°19'E
Make, i., Japan (mä'kȧ)	211	30°43'N	130°49'E
Makeni, S.L.	230	8°53'N	12°03'W
Makgadikgadi Pans, pl., Bots.	236	20°38'S	21°31'E
Makhachkala, Russia (mäk'äch-kä'lä)	181	43°00'N	47°40'E
Makhaleng, r., Leso.	233c	29°53'S	27°33'E
Makiïvka, Ukr.	181	48°03'N	38°00'E
Makindu, Kenya	237	2°17'S	37°49'E
Makkah *see* Mecca, Sau. Ar.	198	21°27'N	39°45'E
Makkovik, Can.	91	55°01'N	59°10'W
Makokou, Gabon (mȧ-kȯ-kōō')	230	0°34'N	12°52'E
Maków Mazowiecki, Pol. (mä'kōov mä-zō-vyĕts'kē)	169	52°51'N	21°07'E
Makuhari, Japan (mä-kōō-hä'rē)	211a	35°39'N	140°04'E
Makurazaki, Japan (mä'kȯ-rä-zä'kē)	211	31°16'N	130°18'E
Makurdi, Nig.	230	7°45'N	8°32'E
Makushin, Ak., U.S. (mȧ-kōō'shĭn)	103	53°57'N	166°28'W
Makushino, Russia (mȧ-kȯ-shēn'ō)	178	55°03'N	67°43'E
Mala, Punta, c., Pan. (pō'n-tä-mä'lä)	133	7°32'N	79°44'W
Malabar Coast, cst., India (măl'ȧ-bär)	203	11°19'N	75°33'E
Malabar Point, c., India	203b	18°57'N	72°47'E
Malabo, Eq. Gui.	230	3°45'N	8°47'E
Malabon, Phil.	213a	14°39'N	120°57'E
Malacca, Strait of, strt., Asia (mȧ-lăk'ȧ)	212	4°15'N	99°44'E
Malad City, Id., U.S. (mȧ-lăd')	115	42°11'N	112°15'W
Maladzyecha, Bela.	180	54°18'N	26°57'E
Málaga, Col. (mä'lä-gȧ)	142	6°41'N	72°46'W
Málaga, Spain	154	36°45'N	4°25'W
Malagón, Spain (mä-lä-gōn')	172	39°12'N	3°52'W
Malaita, i., Sol. Is. (mȧ-lä'ē-tȧ)	221	8°38'S	161°15'E
Malakāl, Sudan (mȧ-lȧ-käl')	231	9°46'N	31°54'E
Malakhovka, Russia (mȧ-läk'ôf-kȧ)	186b	55°38'N	38°01'E
Malang, Indon.	212	8°06'S	112°50'E
Malanje, Ang. (mä-läŋ-gȧ)	232	9°32'S	16°20'E
Malanville, Benin	230	12°04'N	3°09'E
Mälaren, l., Swe.	160	59°38'N	16°55'E
Malartic, Can.	91	48°07'N	78°11'W
Malatya, Tur. (mȧ-lä'tyȧ)	198	38°30'N	38°15'E
Malawi, nation, Afr.	232	11°15'S	33°45'E
Malawi, Lake *see* Nyasa, Lake, l., Afr.	232	10°45'S	34°30'E
Malaya Vishera, Russia (vē-shä'rä)	178	58°51'N	32°13'E
Malay Peninsula, pen., Asia (mȧ-lā') (mā'lā)	212	6°00'N	101°00'E
Malaysia, nation, Asia (mȧ-lā'zhȧ)	212	4°10'N	101°22'E
Malbon, Austl. (măl'bŭn)	218	21°15'S	140°30'E
Malbork, Pol. (mäl'bȯrk)	160	54°02'N	19°04'E
Malcabran, r., Port. (mäl-kä-brän')	173b	38°47'N	8°46'W
Malden, Ma., U.S. (môl'dĕn)	101a	42°26'N	71°04'W
Malden, Mo., U.S.	121	36°32'N	89°56'W
Malden, i., Kir.	2	4°20'S	154°30'W
Maldives, nation, Asia	194	4°30'N	71°30'E
Maldon, Eng., U.K. (môrl'dŏn)	158b	51°44'N	0°39'E
Maldonado, Ur. (mäl-dō-nȧ'dȯ)	144	34°54'S	54°57'W
Maldonado, Punta, c., Mex. (pōō'n-tä)	130	16°18'N	98°34'W
Maléas, Ákra, c., Grc.	163	36°31'N	23°13'E
Mālegaon, India	202	20°35'N	74°30'E
Malé Karpaty, mts., Slvk.	169	48°31'N	17°15'E
Malekula, i., Vanuatu (mä-lā-kōō'lä)	221	16°44'S	167°45'E
Malema, Moz.	237	14°57'S	37°20'E
Malheur, r., Or., U.S. (mȧ-lōōr')	114	43°45'N	117°41'W
Malheur Lake, l., Or., U.S. (mȧ-lōōr')	114	43°16'N	118°37'W
Mali, nation, Afr.	230	15°45'N	0°15'W
Malibu, Ca., U.S. (măl'ĭ-bōō)	117a	34°03'N	118°38'W
Malik, Wādī al, r., Sudan	231	16°48'N	29°30'E
Malimba, Monts, mts., D.R.C.	237	7°45'S	29°15'E
Malinalco, Mex. (mä-lē-näl'kō)	130	18°54'N	99°31'W
Malinaltepec, Mex. (mä-lē-näl-tȧ-pĕk')	130	17°01'N	98°41'W
Malindi, Kenya (mä-lēn'dē)	233	3°14'S	40°04'E
Malin Head, c., Ire.	160	55°23'N	7°24'W
Malino, Russia (mä'lĭ-nô)	186b	55°07'N	38°12'E
Malkara, Tur. (mäl'kȧ-rȧ)	175	40°51'N	26°52'E
Malko Tŭrnovo, Blg. (mäl'kō-t'r'nō-vȧ)	175	41°59'N	27°28'E
Mallaig, Scot., U.K.	164	56°59'N	5°55'W
Mallet Creek, Oh., U.S. (măl'ĕt)	111d	41°10'N	81°55'W
Mallorca, i., Spain	156	39°30'N	3°00'E
Mallow, Ire. (măl'ō)	164	52°07'N	9°04'W
Malmédy, Bel. (mál-mā-dē')	165	50°25'N	6°01'E
Malmesbury, S. Afr. (mämz'bēr-ĭ)	232	33°30'S	18°35'E
Malmköping, Swe. (mälm'chû'pĭng)	166	59°09'N	16°39'E
Malmö, Swe.	154	55°36'N	13°00'E
Malmyzh, Russia (mȧl-mēzh')	179	49°58'N	137°07'E
Malmyzh, Russia	180	56°30'N	50°48'E
Maloarkhangelsk, Russia (mä'lô-ár-kän'gĕlsk)	176	52°26'N	36°29'E
Malolos, Phil. (mä-lô'lôs)	213a	14°51'N	120°49'E
Malomal'sk, Russia (mȧ-lō-mälsk'')	186a	58°47'N	59°55'E
Malone, N.Y., U.S. (mȧ-lōn')	109	44°50'N	74°20'W
Malonga, D.R.C.	236	10°24'S	23°10'E
Maloti Mountains, mts., Leso.	233c	29°00'S	28°29'E
Maloyaroslavets, Russia (mä'lô-yä-rô-slä-vyĕts)	176	55°01'N	36°25'E
Malozemel'skaya Tundra, reg., Russia	180	67°30'N	50°00'E
Malpas, Eng., U.K. (măl'pȧz)	158a	53°01'N	2°46'W
Malpelo, Isla de, i., Col. (mäl-pā'lō)	142	3°55'N	81°30'W
Malpeque Bay, b., Can. (môl-pĕk')	100	46°30'N	63°47'W
Malta, Mt., U.S. (môl'tȧ)	115	48°20'N	107°50'W
Malta, nation, Eur.	154	35°52'N	13°30'E
Maltahöhe, Nmb. (mäl'tä-hō'ē)	232	24°45'S	16°45'E
Maltrata, Mex. (mäl-trä'tä)	131	18°48'N	97°16'W
Maluku (Moluccas), is., Indon.	213	2°22'S	128°25'E
Maluku, Laut (Molucca Sea), sea, Indon.	213	0°15'N	125°41'E
Malūţ, Sudan	231	10°30'N	32°17'E
Mālvan, India	203	16°08'N	73°32'E
Malvern, Ar., U.S. (măl'vērn)	121	34°21'N	92°47'W
Malyn, Ukr.	177	50°44'N	29°15'E
Malynivka, Ukr.	177	49°50'N	36°43'E
Malyy Anyuy, r., Russia	185	67°52'N	164°30'E
Malyy Tamir, i., Russia	185	78°10'N	107°30'E
Mamantel, Mex. (mä-mȧn-tĕl')	131	18°36'N	91°06'W
Mamaroneck, N.Y., U.S. (măm'ȧ-rō-nĕk)	110a	40°57'N	73°44'W
Mambasa, D.R.C.	237	1°21'N	29°03'E
Mamburao, Phil. (mäm-bōō'rä-ō)	213a	13°14'N	120°35'E
Mamfe, Cam. (mäm'fĕ)	230	5°46'N	9°17'E
Mamihara, Japan (mä'mē-hä-rä)	211	32°41'N	131°12'E
Mammoth Cave, Ky., U.S. (măm'ŏth)	124	37°10'N	86°04'W
Mammoth Cave National Park, rec., Ky., U.S.	107	37°20'N	86°21'W
Mammoth Hot Springs, Wy., U.S. (măm'ŭth hôt sprĭngz)	115	44°55'N	110°50'W
Mamnoli, India	203b	19°17'N	73°15'E
Mamoré, r., S.A.	142	13°00'S	65°20'W
Mamou, Gui.	230	10°26'N	12°07'W
Mampong, Ghana	234	7°04'N	1°24'W
Mamry, Jezioro, l., Pol. (mäm'rĭ)	169	54°10'N	21°28'E
Man, C. Iv.	234	7°24'N	7°33'W
Manacor, Spain (mä-nä-kôr')	173	39°35'N	3°15'E
Manado, Indon.	213	1°29'N	124°50'E
Managua, Cuba (mä-nä'gwä)	135a	22°58'N	82°17'W
Managua, Nic.	128	12°10'N	86°16'W
Managua, Lago de, l., Nic. (lä'gô-dĕ)	132	12°28'N	86°10'W
Manakara, Madag. (mä-nä-kä'rŭ)	233	22°17'S	48°06'E
Manama *see* Al Manāmah, Bahr.	198	26°01'N	50°33'E
Mananara, r., Madag. (mä-nä-nä'rŭ)	233	23°15'S	48°15'E
Mananjary, Madag. (mä-nän-zhä'rē)	233	20°16'S	48°13'E
Manas, China	204	44°30'N	86°00'E
Manassas, Va., U.S. (mȧ-năs'ȧs)	109	38°45'N	77°30'W
Manaus, Braz. (mä-nä'ōōzh)	143	3°01'S	60°00'W
Mancelona, Mi., U.S. (măn-sē-lō'nȧ)	108	44°50'N	85°05'W
Mancha Real, Spain (män'chä rā-äl')	172	37°48'N	3°37'W
Manchazh, Russia (män'chȧsh)	186a	56°30'N	58°10'E
Manchester, Eng., U.K.	154	53°28'N	2°14'W
Manchester, Ct., U.S. (măn'chĕs-tēr)	109	41°45'N	72°30'W
Manchester, Ga., U.S.	124	32°50'N	84°37'W
Manchester, Ia., U.S.	113	42°30'N	91°30'W
Manchester, Ma., U.S.	101a	42°35'N	70°47'W
Manchester, Mo., U.S.	117e	38°36'N	90°31'W
Manchester, N.H., U.S.	105	43°00'N	71°30'W
Manchester, Oh., U.S.	108	38°40'N	83°35'W
Manchester Ship Canal, Eng., U.K.	158a	53°20'N	2°40'W
Manchuria, hist. reg., China (măn-chōō'rē-ȧ)	205	48°00'N	124°58'E
Mandal, Nor. (män'däl)	166	58°03'N	7°28'E
Mandalay, Mya. (măn'dȧ-lā)	199	22°00'N	96°08'E
Mandalselva, r., Nor.	166	58°25'N	7°30'E
Mandan, N.D., U.S. (măn'dăn)	104	46°49'N	100°54'W
Mandara Mountains, mts., Afr. (män-dä'rä)	231	10°15'N	13°23'E
Mandau Siak, r., Indon.	197b	1°03'N	101°25'E
Mandeb, Bab-el-, strt. (băb'ĕl män-dĕb')	198	13°17'N	42°49'E
Mandimba, Moz.	237	14°21'S	35°39'E
Mandinga, Pan. (män-dĭŋ'gä)	133	9°32'N	79°04'W
Mandla, India	202	22°43'N	80°23'E
Mándra, Grc. (män'drä)	175	38°06'N	23°32'E
Mandritsara, Madag. (mȧn-drēt-sä'rȧ)	233	15°49'S	48°47'E
Manduria, Italy (män-dōō'rē-ä)	175	40°23'N	17°41'E
Mandve, India	203b	18°47'N	72°52'E
Māndvi, India (mŭnd'vē)	203b	19°29'N	72°53'E
Māndvi, India (mŭnd'vē)	199	22°54'N	69°23'E
Mandya, India	203	12°40'N	77°00'E
Manfredonia, Italy (män-frȧ-dô'nyä)	174	41°39'N	15°55'E
Manfredónia, Golfo di, b., Italy (gôl-fō-dē)	174	41°34'N	16°05'E
Mangabeiras, Chapada das, pl., Braz.	143	8°05'S	47°32'W
Mangalore, India (mŭŋ-gŭ-lōr')	199	12°53'N	74°52'E
Mangaratiba, Braz. (män-gä-rä-tē'bȧ)	141a	22°56'S	44°03'W
Mangatarem, Phil. (män'gȧ-tä'rĕm)	213a	15°48'N	120°18'E
Mange, D.R.C.	236	0°54'N	20°30'E
Mangkalihat, Tanjung, c., Indon.	212	1°25'N	119°55'E
Mangles, Islas de, Cuba (ē's-läs-dĕ-mäŋ'glās) (măn'g'lz)	134	22°05'N	82°50'W
Mangoche, Mwi.	232	14°16'S	35°14'E
Mangoky, r., Madag. (män-gō'kē)	233	22°02'S	44°11'E
Mangole, Pulau, i., Indon.	213	1°35'S	126°22'E
Mangualde, Port. (män-gwäl'dĕ)	172	40°38'N	7°44'W
Mangueira, Lagoa da, l., Braz.	144	33°15'S	52°45'W
Mangum, Ok., U.S. (măŋ'gŭm)	120	34°52'N	99°31'W
Mangzhangdian, China (mäŋ-jäŋ-dĭĕn)	206	32°07'N	114°44'E
Manhattan, Il., U.S.	111a	41°25'N	87°29'W
Manhattan, Ks., U.S. (măn-hăt'ăn)	104	39°11'N	96°34'W
Manhattan Beach, Ca., U.S.	117a	33°53'N	118°24'W
Manhuaçu, Braz. (män-ōȧ'sōō)	141a	20°17'S	42°01'W
Manhumirim, Braz. (män-ōō-mē-rē'N)	141a	22°30'S	41°57'W
Manicouagane, r., Can.	93	50°00'N	68°35'W
Manicouagane, Lac, res., Can.	93	51°30'N	68°19'W
Manicuare, Ven. (mä-nē-kwä'rē)	143b	10°35'N	64°10'W
Manihiki Islands, is., Cook Is. (mä'nē-hē'kē)	241	9°40'S	158°00'W
Manila, Phil.	212	14°37'N	121°00'E
Manila Bay, b., Phil. (mȧ-nĭl'ȧ)	213a	14°38'N	120°46'E
Manisa, Tur. (mä'nē-sä)	163	38°40'N	27°30'E
Manistee, Mi., U.S. (măn-ĭs-tē')	108	44°15'N	86°20'W
Manistee, r., Mi., U.S.	108	44°25'N	85°45'W
Manistique, Mi., U.S. (măn-ĭs-tēk')	113	45°58'N	86°16'W
Manistique, l., Mi., U.S.	113	46°14'N	85°30'W
Manistique, r., Mi., U.S.	113	46°05'N	86°09'W
Manitoba, prov., Can. (măn-ĭ-tō'bȧ)	90	55°12'N	97°29'W
Manitoba, Lake, l., Can.	92	51°00'N	98°45'W
Manito Lake, l., Can. (măn'ĭ-tō)	96	52°45'N	109°45'W
Manitou, i., Mi., U.S. (măn'ĭ-tōō)	113	47°21'N	87°33'W
Manitou, l., Can.	113	49°21'N	93°01'W
Manitou Islands, is., Mi., U.S.	108	45°05'N	86°00'W
Manitoulin Island, i., Can. (măn-ĭ-tōō'lĭn)	93	45°45'N	81°30'W
Manitou Springs, Co., U.S.	120	38°51'N	104°58'W
Manitowoc, Wi., U.S. (măn-ĭ-tô-wŏk')	113	44°05'N	87°42'W
Manitqueira, Serra da, mts., Braz.	141a	22°40'S	45°12'W
Maniwaki, Can.	99	46°23'N	76°00'W
Manizales, Col. (mä-nē-zä'lås)	142	5°05'N	75°31'W
Manjacaze, Moz. (man'yä-kä'zĕ)	232	24°37'S	33°49'E
Mankato, Ks., U.S. (măn-kā'tō)	120	39°45'N	98°12'W
Mankato, Mn., U.S.	105	44°10'N	93°59'W
Mankim, Cam.	235	5°01'N	12°00'E
Manlléu, Spain (män-lyā'ōō)	173	42°00'N	2°16'E
Mannar, Sri L. (mȧ-när')	203	9°48'N	80°03'E
Mannar, Gulf of, b., Asia	199	8°47'N	78°33'E
Mannheim, Ger. (män'hīm)	161	49°30'N	8°31'E
Manning, Ia., U.S. (măn'ĭng)	112	41°53'N	95°04'W
Manning, S.C., U.S.	125	33°41'N	80°12'W
Mannington, W.V., U.S. (măn'ĭng-tŭn)	108	39°30'N	80°55'W
Mano, r., Afr.	234	7°00'N	11°25'W
Man of War Bay, b., Bah.	135	21°05'N	74°05'W
Man of War Channel, strt., Bah.	134	22°45'N	76°10'W
Manokwari, Indon. (mȧ-nōk-wä'rē)	213	0°56'S	134°10'E
Manono, D.R.C.	237	7°18'S	27°25'E
Manor, Can. (măn'ēr)	97	49°36'N	102°05'W
Manor, Wa., U.S.	116c	45°45'N	122°36'W
Manori, neigh., India	203b	19°13'N	72°43'E
Manosque, Fr. (mȧ-nōsh')	171	43°51'N	5°48'E
Manotick, Can.	102c	45°13'N	75°41'W
Manouane, r., Can.	99	50°15'N	70°30'W
Manouane, Lac, l., Can. (mȧ-nōō'ȧn)	100	50°36'N	70°50'W
Manresa, Spain (män-rā'sä)	162	41°44'N	1°52'E
Mansa, Zam.	232	11°12'S	28°53'E
Mansel, i., Can. (măn'sĕl)	93	61°56'N	81°10'W
Manseriche, Pongo de, reg., Peru (pō'n-gō-dĕ-män-sĕ-rē'chĕ)	142	4°15'S	77°45'W
Mansfield, Eng., U.K. (mănz'fēld)	158a	53°08'N	1°12'W
Mansfield, La., U.S.	123	32°02'N	93°43'W
Mansfield, Oh., U.S.	108	40°45'N	82°30'W
Mansfield, Wa., U.S.	114	47°48'N	119°39'W
Mansfield, Mount, mtn., Vt., U.S.	109	44°30'N	72°45'W

PRONOUNCING INDEX

Mansfield Woodhouse – Marystown 319

PLACE (Pronunciation)	PAGE	LAT.	LONG.
Mansfield Woodhouse, Eng., U.K. (wŏd-hous)	158a	53°08'N	1°12'W
Manta, Ec. (män'tä)	142	1°03'S	80°16'W
Manteno, Il., U.S. (măn-tē-nō)	111a	41°15'N	87°50'W
Manteo, N.C., U.S.	125	35°55'N	75°40'W
Mantes-la-Jolie, Fr. (mänt-ĕ-lä-zhō-lē')	170	48°59'N	1°42'E
Manti, Ut., U.S. (măn'tī)	119	39°15'N	11°40'W
Mantova, Italy (män'tô-vä) (măn'tů-ȧ)	162	45°09'N	10°47'E
Mantua, Cuba (män-tōō'ä)	134	22°20'N	84°15'W
Mantua *see* Mantova, Italy	162	45°09'N	10°47'E
Mantua, Ut., U.S. (măn'tů-ȧ)	117b	41°30'N	111°57'W
Manua Islands, is., Am. Sam.	214a	14°13'S	169°35'W
Manui, Pulau, i., Indon. (mä-nōō'ē)	213	3°35'S	123°38'E
Manus Island, i., Pap. N. Gui. (mä'nōōs)	213	2°22'S	146°22'E
Manvel, Tx., U.S. (măn'vel)	123a	29°28'N	95°22'W
Manville, N.J., U.S. (măn'vĭl)	110a	40°33'N	74°36'W
Manville, R.I., U.S.	110b	41°57'N	71°27'W
Manzala Lake, l., Egypt	238b	31°14'N	32°04'E
Manzanares, Col. (män-sä-nä'rĕs)	142a	5°15'N	75°09'W
Manzanares, r., Spain (mänz-nä'rĕs)	173a	40°36'N	3°48'W
Manzanares, Canal del, Spain (kä-nä'l-dĕl-män-thä-nä'rĕs)	173a	40°20'N	3°38'W
Manzanillo, Cuba (män'zä-nēl'yō)	129	20°20'N	77°05'W
Manzanillo, Mex.	128	19°02'N	104°21'W
Manzanillo, Bahía de, b., Mex. (bä-ē'ä-dĕ-män-zä-nē'l-yō)	130	19°00'N	104°38'W
Manzanillo, Bahía de, b., N.A.	135	19°55'N	71°50'W
Manzanillo, Punta, c., Pan.	133	9°40'N	79°33'W
Manzhouli, China (män-jō-lē)	205	49°25'N	117°15'E
Manzovka, Russia (mȧn-zhô'f-kȧ)	210	44°16'N	132°13'E
Mao, Chad (mä'ô)	231	14°07'N	15°19'E
Mao, Dom. Rep.	135	19°35'N	71°10'W
Maó, Spain	162	39°52'N	4°15'E
Maoke, Pegunungan, mts., Indon.	213	4°00'S	138°00'E
Maoming, China	205	21°55'N	110°40'E
Maoniu Shan, mtn., China (mou-nĭō shän)	208	32°45'N	104°09'E
Mapastepec, Mex. (ma-päs-tå-pĕk')	131	15°24'N	92°52'W
Mapia, Kepulauan, i., Indon.	213	0°57'N	134°22'E
Mapimí, Mex. (mä-pē-mē')	122	25°50'N	103°50'W
Mapimí, Bolsón de, des., Mex. (bôl-sô'n-dĕ-mä-pē'mē)	122	27°27'N	103°20'W
Maple Creek, Can. (mā'p'l) (crēk)	90	49°55'N	109°27'W
Maple Grove, Can. (grōv)	102a	45°19'N	73°51'W
Maple Heights, Oh., U.S.	111d	41°25'N	81°34'W
Maple Shade, N.J., U.S. (shād)	110f	39°57'N	75°01'W
Maple Valley, Wa., U.S. (văl'ê)	116a	47°24'N	122°02'W
Maplewood, Mn., U.S. (wŏd)	117g	45°00'N	93°03'W
Maplewood, Mo., U.S.	117e	38°37'N	90°20'W
Mapumulo, S. Afr. (mä-pä-mōō'lō)	233c	29°12'S	31°05'E
Maputo, Moz.	232	26°50'S	32°30'E
Maquela do Zombo, Ang. (mȧ-kā'lȧ dò zôm'bò)	232	6°08'S	15°15'E
Maquoketa, Ia., U.S. (mȧ-kō-kē-tȧ)	113	42°04'N	90°42'W
Maquoketa, r., Ia., U.S.	113	42°08'N	90°40'W
Mar, Serra do, mts., Braz. (sĕr'rȧ dò mär')	144	26°30'S	49°15'W
Maracaibo, Ven. (mä-rä-kī'bō)	142	10°38'N	71°45'W
Maracaibo, Lago de, l., Ven. (lä'gô-dĕ-mä-rä-kī'bō)	142	9°55'N	72°13'W
Maracay, Ven. (mä-rä-käy')	142	10°15'N	67°35'W
Marādah, Libya	231	29°10'N	19°07'E
Maradi, Niger (mȧ-rȧ-dē')	230	13°29'N	7°06'E
Marāgheh, Iran	201	37°20'N	46°10'E
Maraisburg, S. Afr.	233b	26°12'S	27°57'E
Marais des Cygnes, r., Ks., U.S.	121	38°30'N	95°30'W
Marajó, Ilha de, i., Braz.	143	1°00'S	49°30'W
Maralal, Kenya	237	1°06'N	36°42'E
Marali, C.A.R.	235	6°01'N	18°24'E
Marand, Iran	201	38°26'N	45°46'E
Maranguape, Braz. (mä-räŋ-gwä'pĕ)	143	3°48'S	38°38'W
Maranhão, state, Braz. (mä-rän-youn)	143	5°15'S	45°52'W
Maranoa, r., Austl. (mä-rä-nō'ä)	221	27°01'S	148°03'E
Marano di Napoli, Italy (mä-rä'nô-dē-nȧ'pô-lē)	173c	40°39'N	14°12'E
Marañón, r., Peru (mä-rä-nyōn')	142	4°26'S	75°08'W
Marapanim, Braz. (mä-rä-pä-nē'n)	143	0°45'S	47°42'W
Marathon, Can.	91	48°50'N	86°10'W
Marathon, Fl., U.S. (măr'ȧ-thŏn)	125a	24°41'N	81°06'W
Marathon, Oh., U.S.	111f	39°09'N	83°59'W
Maravatio, Mex. (mä-rȧ-vä'tē-ō)	130	19°54'N	100°25'W
Marawi, Sudan	231	18°07'N	31°57'E
Marble Bar, Austl. (märb''l bär)	218	21°15'S	119°15'E
Marble Canal, can., Az., U.S. (mär'b'l)	119	36°21'N	111°48'W
Marblehead, Ma., U.S. (mär'b'l-hĕd)	101a	42°30'N	70°51'W
Marburg an der Lahn, Ger.	168	50°49'N	8°46'E
Marca, Ponta da, c., Ang.	236	16°31'S	11°42'E
Marcala, Hond. (mär-kä-lä)	132	14°08'N	88°01'W
Marceline, Mo., U.S. (mär-sė-lēn')	121	39°42'N	92°56'W
Marche, hist. reg., Italy (mär'kā)	174	43°35'N	12°33'E
Marchegg, Aus.	159e	48°18'N	16°55'E
Marchena, Spain (mär-chā'nä)	162	37°20'N	5°25'W
Marchena, i., Ec. (ĕ's-lä-mär-chĕ'nä)	142	0°29'N	90°31'W
Marchfeld, reg., Aus.	159e	48°14'N	16°37'E
Mar Chiquita, Laguna, l., Arg. (lä-gōō'nä-mȧr-chē-kē'tä)	141c	34°25'S	61°10'W
Marcos Paz, Arg. (mär-kōs' päz)	141c	34°49'S	58°51'W
Marcus, i., Japan (mär'kŭs)	241	24°00'N	155°00'E
Marcus Hook, Pa., U.S. (mär'kŭs hŏk)	110f	39°49'N	75°25'W
Marcy, Mount, mtn., N.Y., U.S. (mär'sė)	109	44°10'N	73°55'W
Mar de Espanha, Braz. (mär-dĕ-ĕs-pȧ'nyȧ)	141a	21°53'S	43°00'W
Mar del Plata, Arg. (mär dĕl- plä'ta)	144	37°59'S	57°35'W
Mardin, Tur. (mär-dēn')	198	37°25'N	40°40'E
Maré, i., N. Cal. (mȧ-rā')	221	21°53'S	168°30'E
Maree, Loch, b., Scot., U.K. (mä-rē')	164	57°40'N	5°44'W
Marengo, Ia., U.S. (mȧ-rĕŋ'gō)	113	41°47'N	92°04'W
Marennes, Fr. (mȧ-rĕn')	170	45°49'N	1°08'W
Marfa, Tx., U.S. (mär'fȧ)	122	30°19'N	104°01'W
Margarita, Pan. (mär-gōō-rē'tä)	128a	9°20'N	79°55'W
Margarita, Isla de, i., Ven. (mä-gȧ-rē'tȧ)	142	11°00'N	64°15'W
Margate, S. Afr. (mä-gāt')	233c	30°52'S	30°21'E
Margate, Eng., U.K. (mär'gāt)	165	51°21'N	1°17'E
Margherita Peak, mtn., Afr.	231	0°22'N	29°51'E
Marguerite, r., Can.	100	50°39'N	66°42'W
Marhanets', Ukr.	177	47°41'N	34°33'E
Maria, Can. (mȧ-rē'ȧ)	100	48°10'N	66°04'W
Mariager, Den. (mä-rė-ägh'ĕr)	166	56°38'N	10°00'E
Mariana, Braz. (mä-ryä'nä)	141a	20°23'S	43°24'W
Mariana Islands, is., Oc.	5	16°00'N	145°30'E
Marianao, Cuba (mä-rē-ä-nä'ō)	129	23°05'N	82°26'W
Mariana Trench, deep	241	12°00'N	144°00'E
Marianna, Ar., U.S. (mā-rĭ-ăn'ȧ)	121	34°45'N	90°45'W
Marianna, Fl., U.S.	124	30°46'N	85°14'W
Marianna, Pa., U.S.	111e	40°01'N	80°05'W
Mariano Acosta, Arg. (mä-rėä'nô-ä-kōs'tä)	144a	34°28'S	58°48'W
Mariánské Lázně, Czech Rep. (mär'yȧn-skĕ'läz'nyĕ)	168	49°58'N	12°42'E
Marias, r., Mt., U.S. (mȧ-rī'ȧz)	115	48°15'N	110°50'W
Marías, Islas, is., Mex. (mä-rē'äs)	128	21°30'N	106°40'W
Mariato, Punta, c., Pan.	133	7°17'N	81°09'W
Maribo, Den. (mä'rė-bô)	166	54°46'N	11°29'E
Maribor, Slvn. (mä're-bôr)	154	46°33'N	15°37'E
Maricaban, i., Phil. (mä-rė-kä-bän')	213a	13°40'N	120°44'E
Mariefred, Swe. (mä-rē'ĕ-frĭd)	166	59°17'N	17°09'E
Marie Galante, i., Guad. (mȧ-rē' gȧ-länt')	133b	15°58'N	61°05'W
Mariehamn, Fin. (mȧ-rē'ĕ-häm''n)	167	60°07'N	19°57'E
Mari El, prov., Russia	180	56°30'N	48°00'E
Mariestad, Swe. (mä-rē'ĕ-städ')	166	58°43'N	13°45'E
Marietta, Ga., U.S. (mā-rĭ-ĕt'ȧ)	110c	33°57'N	84°33'W
Marietta, Oh., U.S.	108	39°25'N	81°30'W
Marietta, Ok., U.S.	121	33°53'N	97°07'W
Marietta, Wa., U.S.	116d	48°48'N	122°35'W
Mariinsk, Russia (mȧ-re'ĭnsk)	184	56°15'N	87°28'E
Marijampole, Lith. (mä-rē-yäm-pô'lĕ)	167	54°33'N	23°26'E
Marikana, S. Afr. (mă'-rĭ-kä-nă)	238c	25°40'S	27°28'E
Marília, Braz. (mä-rē'lyȧ)	143	22°02'S	49°48'W
Marimba, Ang.	236	8°28'S	17°08'E
Marín, Spain	172	42°24'N	8°40'W
Marinduque Island, i., Phil. (mä-rēn-dōō'kä)	213a	13°14'N	121°45'E
Marine, Il., U.S. (mȧ-rēn')	117e	38°48'N	89°47'W
Marine City, Mi., U.S.	108	42°45'N	82°30'W
Marine Lake, l., Mn., U.S.	117g	45°13'N	92°55'W
Marine on Saint Croix, Mn., U.S.	117g	45°11'N	92°47'W
Marinette, Wi., U.S. (măr-ĭ-nĕt')	105	45°04'N	87°40'W
Maringa, r., D.R.C. (mä-riŋ'gä)	231	0°30'N	21°00'E
Marinha Grande, Port. (mä-rēn'yȧ grän'dĕ)	172	39°49'N	8°53'W
Marion, Al., U.S. (măr'ĭ-ŭn)	124	32°36'N	87°19'W
Marion, Ia., U.S.	113	42°01'N	91°39'W
Marion, Il., U.S.	108	37°40'N	88°55'W
Marion, In., U.S.	105	40°35'N	85°45'W
Marion, Ks., U.S.	121	38°21'N	97°02'W
Marion, Ky., U.S.	124	37°19'N	88°05'W
Marion, N.C., U.S.	125	35°40'N	82°00'W
Marion, N.D., U.S.	112	46°37'N	98°20'W
Marion, Oh., U.S.	108	40°35'N	83°10'W
Marion, S.C., U.S.	125	34°08'N	79°23'W
Marion, Va., U.S.	125	36°48'N	81°33'W
Marion, Lake, res., S.C., U.S.	125	33°25'N	80°35'W
Marion Reef, rf., Austl.	221	18°57'S	151°31'E
Mariposa, Chile (mä-rē-pô'sä)	141b	35°33'S	71°21'W
Mariposa Creek, r., Ca., U.S.	118	37°14'N	120°30'W
Mariquita, Col. (mä-rē-kē'tä)	142a	5°13'N	74°52'W
Mariscal Estigarribia, Para.	144	22°03'S	60°28'W
Marisco, Ponta do, c., Braz. (pô'n-tä-dô-mä-rē's-kö)	144b	23°01'S	43°17'W
Maritime Alps, mts., Eur. (mă'rĭ-tīm ălps)	161	44°20'N	7°02'E
Mariupol', Ukr.	178	47°07'N	37°32'E
Mariveles, Phil.	213a	14°27'N	120°29'E
Marj Uyan, Leb.	197a	33°21'N	35°36'E
Marka, Som.	238a	1°45'N	44°47'E
Markaryd, Swe. (mär'kä-rüd)	166	56°30'N	13°34'E
Marked Tree, Ar., U.S. (märkt trē)	121	35°31'N	90°26'W
Marken, i., Neth.	159a	52°26'N	5°08'E
Market Bosworth, Eng., U.K. (bŏz'wûrth)	158a	52°37'N	1°23'W
Market Deeping, Eng., U.K. (dēp'ĭng)	158a	52°40'N	0°19'W
Market Drayton, Eng., U.K. (drā'tŭn)	158a	52°54'N	2°29'W
Market Harborough, Eng., U.K. (här'bŭr-ô)	158a	52°28'N	0°55'W
Market Rasen, Eng., U.K. (rā'zĕn)	158a	53°23'N	0°21'W
Markham, Can. (märk'ȧm)	99	43°53'N	79°15'W
Markham, Mount, mtn., Ant.	224	82°59'S	159°30'E
Markivka, Ukr.	177	49°32'N	39°34'E
Markovo, Russia (mär'kô-vô)	179	64°46'N	170°48'E
Markrāna, India	202	27°08'N	74°43'E
Marks, Russia	181	51°42'N	46°46'E
Marksville, La., U.S. (märks'vĭl)	123	31°09'N	92°05'W
Markt Indersdorf, Ger. (märkt ēn'dĕrs-dōrf)	159d	48°22'N	11°23'E
Marktredwitz, Ger. (märk-rĕd'vĭts)	168	50°02'N	12°05'E
Markt Schwaben, Ger. (märkt shvä'bĕn)	159d	48°12'N	11°52'E
Marl, Ger. (märl)	171c	51°40'N	7°05'E
Marlboro, N.J., U.S.	110a	40°18'N	74°15'W
Marlborough, Ma., U.S.	101a	42°21'N	71°33'W
Marlette, Mi., U.S. (mär-lĕt')	108	43°25'N	83°05'W
Marlin, Tx., U.S. (mär'lĭn)	123	31°18'N	96°52'W
Marlinton, W.V., U.S. (mär'lĭn-tŭn)	108	38°15'N	80°10'W
Marlow, Eng., U.K. (mär'lō)	158b	51°33'N	0°46'W
Marlow, Ok., U.S.	121	34°38'N	97°56'W
Marls, The, b., Bah. (märls)	134	26°30'N	77°15'W
Marmande, Fr. (mȧr-mäNd')	170	44°30'N	0°10'E
Marmara Denizi, sea, Tur.	198	40°40'N	28°00'E
Marmarth, N.D., U.S. (mär'mȧrth)	112	46°19'N	103°57'W
Mar Muerto, l., Mex. (mär-mòĕ'r-tô)	131	16°13'N	94°22'W
Marne, Ger. (mär'nĕ)	159c	53°57'N	9°01'E
Marne, r., Fr. (märn)	161	49°00'N	4°30'E
Maroa, Ven. (mä-rō'ä)	142	2°43'N	67°37'W
Maroantsetra, Madag. (mȧ-rō-äŋ-tsä'trȧ)	233	15°18'S	49°48'E
Maro Jarapeto, mtn., Col. (mä-rô-hä-rä-pĕ'tô)	142a	6°29'N	76°39'W
Maromokotro, mtn., Madag.	233	14°00'S	49°11'E
Marondera, Zimb.	232	18°10'S	31°36'E
Maroni, r., S.A. (mȧ-rō'nė)	143	3°02'N	53°54'W
Maro Reef, rf., Hi., U.S.	126b	25°15'N	170°00'W
Maroua, Cam. (mär'wä)	231	10°36'N	14°20'E
Marple, Eng., U.K. (mär'p'l)	158a	53°24'N	2°04'W
Marquard, S. Afr.	238c	28°41'S	27°26'E
Marquesas Islands, is., Fr. Poly. (mär-kĕ'säs)	2	8°50'S	141°00'W
Marquesas Keys, is., Fl., U.S. (mȧr-kē'zȧs)	125a	24°37'N	82°15'W
Marquês de Valença, Braz. (mȧr-kĕ's-dĕ-vä-lĕ'n-sȧ)	141a	22°16'S	43°42'W
Marquette, Can. (mȧr-kĕt')	102f	50°04'N	97°43'W
Marquette, Mi., U.S.	105	46°32'N	87°25'W
Marquez, Tx., U.S. (mär-kāz')	123	31°14'N	96°15'W
Marra, Jabal, mtn., Sudan (jĕb'ĕl mär'ä)	231	13°00'N	23°47'E
Marrakech, Mor. (mär-rä'kĕsh)	230	31°38'N	8°00'W
Marree, Austl. (măr'rē)	218	29°38'S	137°55'E
Marrero, La., U.S.	110d	29°55'N	90°06'W
Marrupa, Moz.	237	13°08'S	37°30'E
Mars, Pa., U.S. (märz)	111e	40°42'N	80°01'W
Marsabit, Kenya	237	2°20'N	37°59'E
Marsala, Italy (mär-sä'lä)	162	37°48'N	12°28'E
Marsden, Eng., U.K. (märz'dĕn)	158a	53°36'N	1°55'W
Marseille, Fr. (mȧr-så'y')	154	43°18'N	5°25'E
Marseilles, Il., U.S. (mär-sĕlz')	108	41°20'N	88°40'W
Marshall, Il., U.S. (mär'shăl)	108	39°20'N	87°40'W
Marshall, Mi., U.S.	108	42°20'N	84°55'W
Marshall, Mn., U.S.	112	44°28'N	95°49'W
Marshall, Mo., U.S.	121	39°07'N	93°12'W
Marshall, Tx., U.S.	105	32°33'N	94°22'W
Marshall Islands, nation, Oc.	3	10°00'N	165°00'E
Marshalltown, Ia., U.S. (mär'shȧl-toun)	113	42°02'N	92°55'W
Marshallville, Ga., U.S. (mär'shȧl-vĭl)	124	32°29'N	83°55'W
Marshfield, Ma., U.S. (märsh'fēld)	101a	42°06'N	70°43'W
Marshfield, Mo., U.S.	121	37°20'N	92°53'W
Marshfield, Wi., U.S.	113	44°40'N	90°10'W
Marsh Harbour, Bah.	134	26°30'N	77°00'W
Mars Hill, In., U.S. (märz'hĭl')	111g	39°43'N	86°15'W
Mars Hill, Me., U.S.	100	46°34'N	67°54'W
Marstrand, Swe. (mär'stränd)	166	57°54'N	11°33'E
Marsyaty, Russia (märs'yȧ-tĭ)	186a	60°03'N	60°28'E
Mart, Tx., U.S. (märt)	123	31°32'N	96°49'W
Martaban, Gulf of, b., Mya. (mär-tŭ-bän')	212	16°34'N	96°58'E
Martapura, Indon.	212	3°19'S	114°45'E
Martha's Vineyard, i., Ma., U.S. (mär'thȧz vĭn'yȧrd)	109	41°25'N	70°35'W
Martigny, Switz. (mȧr-tē-nyē')	168	46°06'N	7°00'E
Martigues, Fr.	171	43°24'N	5°05'E
Martin, Tn., U.S. (mär'tĭn)	124	36°20'N	88°45'W
Martina Franca, Italy (mär-tē'nä fräŋ'kä)	175	40°43'N	17°21'E
Martinez, Ca., U.S. (mär-tē'nĕz)	116b	38°01'N	122°08'W
Martinez, Tx., U.S.	117d	29°25'N	98°20'W
Martinique, dep., N.A. (mȧr-tė-nēk')	129	14°50'N	60°40'W
Martin Lake, res., Al., U.S.	124	32°40'N	86°05'W
Martin Point, c., Ak., U.S.	103	70°10'N	142°00'W
Martinsburg, W.V., U.S. (mär'tĭnz-bûrg)	109	39°30'N	78°00'W
Martins Ferry, Oh., U.S. (mär'tĭnz)	108	40°05'N	80°45'W
Martinsville, In., U.S. (mär'tĭnz-vĭl)	108	39°25'N	86°25'W
Martinsville, Va., U.S.	125	36°40'N	79°53'W
Martos, Spain (mär'tōs)	172	37°43'N	3°58'W
Martre, Lac la, l., Can. (läk la märtr)	92	63°24'N	119°58'W
Marugame, Japan (mä'rōō-gä'mä)	211	34°19'N	133°48'E
Marungu, mts., D.R.C.	237	7°50'S	29°50'E
Marve, neigh., India	203b	19°12'N	72°43'E
Mary, Turkmen. (mä'rė)	183	37°45'N	61°47'E
Mar'yanskaya, Russia (mȧr-yän'skȧ-yȧ)	177	45°04'N	38°39'E
Maryborough, Austl. (mā'rĭ-bŭr-ô)	219	25°35'S	152°40'E
Maryborough, Austl.	219	37°00'S	143°50'E
Maryland, state, U.S. (mĕr'ĭ-lănd)	105	39°10'N	76°25'W
Marys, r., Nv., U.S. (mā'rĭz)	114	41°25'N	115°10'W
Marystown, Can. (mâr'ĭz-toun)	101	47°11'N	55°10'W

320 Marysville – Medan PRONOUNCING INDEX

PLACE (Pronunciation)	PAGE	LAT.	LONG.
Marysville, Can.	100	45°59'N	66°35'W
Marysville, Ca., U.S.	118	39°09'N	121°37'W
Marysville, Oh., U.S.	108	40°15'N	83°25'W
Marysville, Wa., U.S.	116a	48°03'N	122°11'W
Maryville, Il., U.S. (mā'rĭ-vĭl)	117e	38°44'N	89°57'W
Maryville, Mo., U.S.	121	40°21'N	94°51'W
Maryville, Tn., U.S.	124	35°44'N	83°59'W
Mārzuq, Libya	231	26°00'N	14°09'E
Marzūq, Idehan, des., Libya	230	24°30'N	13°00'E
Masai Steppe, plat., Tan.	237	4°30'S	36°40'E
Masaka, Ug.	237	0°20'S	31°44'E
Masalasef, Chad	235	11°43'N	17°08'E
Masalembo-Besar, i., Indon.	212	5°40'S	114°28'E
Masan, Kor., S. (mä-sän')	205	35°10'N	128°31'E
Masangwe, Tan.	237	5°28'S	30°05'E
Masasi, Tan. (mä-sä'sē)	233	10°43'S	38°48'E
Masatepe, Nic. (mä-sä-tĕ'pĕ)	132	11°57'N	86°10'W
Masaya, Nic. (mä-sä'yä)	132	11°58'N	86°05'W
Masbate, Phil. (mäs-bä'tä)	213a	12°21'N	123°38'E
Masbate, i., Phil.	213	12°19'N	123°03'E
Mascarene Islands, is., Afr.	5	20°20'S	56°40'E
Mascot, Tn., U.S. (măs'kŏt)	124	36°04'N	83°45'W
Mascota, Mex. (mäs-kō'tä)	130	20°33'N	104°45'W
Mascota, r., Mex.	130	20°33'N	104°52'W
Mascouche, Can. (màs-kōōsh')	102a	45°45'N	73°36'W
Mascouche, r., Can.	102a	45°44'N	73°45'W
Mascoutah, Il., U.S. (măs-kū'tā)	117e	38°29'N	89°48'W
Maseru, Leso. (măz'ēr-ōō)	232	29°09'S	27°11'E
Mashhad, Iran	198	36°17'N	59°30'E
Māshkel, Hāmūn-i-, l., Asia (hä-mōōn'ē māsh-kĕl')	198	28°28'N	64°13'E
Mashra'ar Raqq, Sudan	231	8°28'N	29°15'E
Masi-Manimba, D.R.C.	236	4°46'S	17°55'E
Masindi, Ug. (mä-sēn'dē)	231	1°44'N	31°43'E
Masjed Soleymān, Iran	198	31°45'N	49°17'E
Mask, Lough, b., Ire. (lŏk másk)	164	53°35'N	9°23'W
Maslovo, Russia (mäs'lô-vô)	186a	60°08'N	60°28'E
Mason, Mi., U.S. (mā'sŭn)	108	42°35'N	84°25'W
Mason, Oh., U.S.	111f	39°22'N	84°18'W
Mason, Tx., U.S.	122	30°46'N	99°14'W
Mason City, Ia., U.S.	105	43°08'N	93°14'W
Massa, Italy (mäs'sä)	174	44°02'N	10°08'E
Massachusetts, state, U.S. (măs-ȧ-chōō'sĕts)	105	42°20'N	72°30'W
Massachusetts Bay, b., Ma., U.S.	100	42°26'N	70°20'W
Massafra, Italy (mäs-sä'frä)	175	40°35'N	17°05'E
Massa Marittima, Italy	174	43°03'N	10°55'E
Massapequa, N.Y., U.S.	110a	40°41'N	73°28'W
Massaua *see* Mitsiwa, Erit.	231	15°40'N	39°19'E
Massena, N.Y., U.S. (mă-sē'nȧ)	109	44°55'N	74°55'W
Masset, Can. (măs'ĕt)	90	54°02'N	132°09'W
Masset Inlet, b., Can.	95	53°42'N	132°20'E
Massif Central, Fr. (mà-sēf' säɴ-tràl')	154	45°12'N	3°02'E
Massillon, Oh., U.S. (măs'ĭ-lŏn)	108	40°50'N	81°35'W
Massinga, Moz. (mä-sĭn'gä)	232	23°18'S	35°18'E
Massive, Mount, mtn., Co., U.S. (măs'ĭv)	106	39°05'N	106°30'W
Masson, Can. (mäs-sŭn)	102c	45°33'N	75°25'W
Masuda, Japan (mä-sōō'dä)	211	34°42'N	131°53'E
Masuria, reg., Pol.	169	53°40'N	21°10'E
Masvingo, Zimb.	232	20°07'S	30°47'E
Matadi, D.R.C. (mà-tä'dē)	232	5°49'S	13°27'E
Matagalpa, Nic. (mä-tä-gäl'pä)	128	12°52'N	85°57'W
Matagami, l., Can. (mȧ-tä-gä'mē)	93	50°10'N	78°28'W
Matagorda Bay, b., Tx., U.S. (măt-ȧ-gôr'dȧ)	123	28°32'N	96°13'W
Matagorda Island, i., Tx., U.S.	123	28°13'N	96°27'W
Matam, Sen. (mä-täm')	230	15°40'N	13°15'W
Matamoros, Mex. (mä-tä-mō'rôs)	122	25°32'N	103°13'W
Matamoros, Mex.	128	25°52'N	97°30'W
Matane, Can. (mȧ-tăn')	91	48°51'N	67°32'W
Matanzas, Cuba (mä-tän'zäs)	129	23°05'N	81°35'W
Matanzas, prov., Cuba	134	22°45'N	81°20'W
Matanzas, Bahía, b., Cuba (bä-ē'ä)	134	23°10'N	81°30'W
Matapalo, Cabo, c., C.R. (kà'bô-mä-tä-pä'lō)	133	8°22'N	83°25'W
Matapédia, Can. (mă-tȧ-pā'dē-ȧ)	100	47°58'N	66°56'W
Matapédia, l., Can.	100	48°33'N	67°32'W
Matapédia, r., Can.	100	48°10'N	67°10'W
Mataquito, r., Chile (mä-tä-kē'tō)	141b	35°08'S	71°35'W
Matara, Sri L. (mä-tä'rä)	203	5°59'N	80°35'E
Mataram, Indon.	212	8°45'S	116°15'E
Matatiele, S. Afr. (mä-tä-tyā'lä)	233c	30°21'S	28°49'E
Matawan, N.J., U.S.	110a	40°24'N	74°13'W
Matehuala, Mex. (mä-tå-wä'lä)	128	23°38'N	100°39'W
Matera, Italy (mä-tå'rä)	174	40°42'N	16°37'E
Mateur, Tun. (mȧ-tûr')	162	37°09'N	9°43'E
Mātherān, India	203b	18°58'N	73°16'E
Matheson, Can.	99	48°35'N	80°33'W
Mathews, Lake, l., Ca., U.S. (măth ūz)	117a	33°50'N	117°24'W
Mathura, India (mu-tŏ'rŭ)	199	27°39'N	77°39'E
Matias Barbosa, Braz. (mä-tē'äs-bár-bô-sä)	141a	21°53'S	43°19'W
Matillas, Laguna, l., Mex. (lä-gŏ'nä-mä-tē'l-yäs)	131	18°02'N	92°36'W
Matina, C.R. (mä-tē'nä)	133	10°06'N	83°20'W
Matiši, Lat. (mä'tē-sē)	167	57°43'N	25°09'E
Matlalcueyetl, Cerro, mtn., Mex. (sĕ'r-rä-mä-tläl-kwĕ'yĕtl)	130	19°13'N	98°02'W
Matlock, Eng., U.K. (măt'lŏk)	158a	53°08'N	1°33'W
Matochkin Shar, Russia (mä'tŏch-kĭn)	178	73°57'N	56°16'E
Mato Grosso, Braz. (mät'ŏ grōs'ŏo)	143	15°04'S	59°58'W
Mato Grosso, state, Braz.	143	14°38'S	55°36'W
Mato Grosso, Chapada de, hills, Braz. (shä-pä'dä-dĕ)	143	13°39'S	55°42'W
Mato Grosso do Sul, state, Braz.	143	20°00'S	56°00'W
Matosinhos, Port.	172	41°10'N	8°48'W
Maṭraḥ, Oman (mȧ-trä')	198	23°36'N	58°27'E
Matsubara, Japan	211b	34°34'N	135°34'E
Matsudo, Japan (mät'sō-dō)	211a	35°48'N	139°55'E
Matsue, Japan (mät'sō-ĕ)	205	35°29'N	133°04'E
Matsumoto, Japan (mät'sō-mō'tō)	210	36°15'N	137°59'E
Matsuyama, Japan (mät'sō-yä'mä)	205	33°48'N	132°45'E
Matsuzaka, Japan (mät'sō-zä'kä)	211	34°35'N	136°34'E
Mattamuskeet, Lake, l., N.C., U.S. (măt-tȧ-mŭs'kēt)	125	35°34'N	76°03'W
Mattaponi, r., Va., U.S. (măt'ȧ-poni')	109	37°45'N	77°00'W
Mattawa, Can. (măt'ȧ-wȧ)	91	46°15'N	78°49'W
Matterhorn, mtn., Eur. (mät'ēr-hôrn)	168	45°57'N	7°36'E
Matteson, Il., U.S. (mătt'ē-sŭn)	111a	41°30'N	87°42'W
Matthew Town, Bah. (măth'ū toun)	135	21°00'N	73°40'W
Mattoon, Il., U.S. (mă-tōōn')	105	39°30'N	88°20'W
Maturín, Ven. (mä-tōō-rēn')	142	9°48'N	63°16'W
Maúa, Moz.	237	13°51'S	37°10'E
Mauban, Phil. (mä'ōō-bän')	213a	14°11'N	121°44'E
Maubeuge, Fr. (mō-bûzh')	170	50°18'N	3°57'E
Maud, Oh., U.S. (môd)	111f	39°21'N	84°23'W
Mauer, Aus. (mou'ēr)	159e	48°09'N	16°16'E
Maués, Braz. (mà-wĕ's)	143	3°34'S	57°30'W
Mau Escarpment, cliff, Kenya	237	0°45'S	35°50'E
Maui, i., Hi., U.S. (mä'ōō-ē)	106c	20°52'N	156°02'W
Maule, r., Chile (mà'ō-lĕ)	141b	35°45'S	70°50'W
Maumee, Oh., U.S. (mô-mē')	108	41°30'N	83°40'W
Maumee, r., In., U.S.	108	41°10'N	84°50'W
Maumee Bay, b., Oh., U.S.	108	41°50'N	83°20'W
Maun, Bots. (mä-ōn')	232	19°52'S	23°40'E
Mauna Kea, mtn., Hi., U.S. (mä'ō-näkä'ä)	106c	19°52'N	155°30'W
Mauna Loa, mtn., Hi., U.S. (mä'ō-nälō'ä)	106c	19°28'N	155°38'W
Maurepas Lake, l., La., U.S. (mō-rē-pä')	123	30°18'N	90°40'W
Mauricie, Parc National de la, rec., Can.	99	46°46'N	73°00'W
Mauritania, nation, Afr. (mô-rē-tā'nĭ-ȧ)	230	19°38'N	13°30'W
Mauritius, nation, Afr. (mô-rĭsh'ĭ-ŭs)	3	20°18'S	57°36'E
Maury, Wa., U.S. (mô'rĭ)	116a	47°22'N	122°23'W
Mauston, Wi., U.S. (môs'tŭn)	113	43°46'N	90°05'W
Maverick, r., Az., U.S. (mā-vûr'ĭk)	119	33°40'N	109°30'W
Mavinga, Ang.	236	15°50'S	20°21'E
Mawlamyine, Mya.	212	16°30'N	97°39'E
Maxville, Can. (măks'vĭl)	102c	45°17'N	74°52'W
Maxville, Mo., U.S.	117e	38°26'N	90°24'W
Maya, r., Russia (mä'yä)	185	58°00'N	135°45'E
Mayaguana, i., Bah.	135	22°25'N	73°00'W
Mayaguana Passage, strt., Bah.	135	22°20'N	73°25'W
Mayagüez, P.R. (mä-yä-gwāz')	129	18°12'N	67°10'W
Mayari, r., Cuba	135	20°25'N	75°35'W
Mayas, Montañas, mts., N.A. (môntăn'ăs mä'ăs)	132a	16°43'N	89°00'W
Mayd, i., Som.	238a	11°24'N	46°38'E
Mayen, Ger. (mī'ĕn)	168	50°19'N	7°14'E
Mayenne, r., Fr. (mȧ-yĕn)	170	48°14'N	0°45'W
Mayfield, Ky., U.S. (mā'fēld)	124	36°44'N	88°19'W
Mayfield Creek, r., Ky., U.S.	124	36°54'N	88°47'W
Mayfield Heights, Oh., U.S.	111d	41°31'N	81°26'W
Mayfield Lake, res., Wa., U.S.	114	46°31'N	122°34'W
Maykop, Russia	178	44°35'N	40°07'E
Maykor, Russia (mī-kôr')	186a	59°01'N	55°52'E
Maymyo, Mya. (mī'myō)	204	22°14'N	96°32'E
Maynard, Ma., U.S. (mā'nȧrd)	101a	42°25'N	71°27'W
Mayne, Can. (mān)	116d	48°51'N	123°18'W
Mayne, i., Can.	116d	48°52'N	123°14'W
Mayo, Can. (mä-yō')	90	63°40'N	135°51'W
Mayo, Fl., U.S.	124	30°02'N	83°08'W
Mayo, Md., U.S.	110e	38°54'N	76°31'W
Mayodan, N.C., U.S. (mā-yō'dăn)	125	36°25'N	79°59'W
Mayon Volcano, vol., Phil. (mä-yōn')	213a	13°21'N	123°43'E
Mayotte, dep., Afr. (mȧ-yŏt')	233	13°07'S	45°32'E
May Pen, Jam.	134	18°00'N	77°25'W
Mayraira Point, c., Phil.	209	18°40'N	120°45'E
Mayran, Laguna de, l., Mex. (lä-ō'nä-dĕ-mī-rän')	128	25°40'N	102°35'W
Mayskiy, Russia	182	43°38'N	44°04'E
Maysville, Ky., U.S. (māz'vĭl)	108	38°35'N	83°45'W
Mayumba, Gabon	232	3°25'S	10°39'E
Mayville, N.D., U.S.	112	47°30'N	97°20'W
Mayville, N.Y., U.S. (mā'vĭl)	109	42°15'N	79°30'W
Mayville, Wi., U.S.	113	43°30'N	88°45'W
Maywood, Ca., U.S. (mā'wŏd)	117a	33°59'N	118°11'W
Maywood, Il., U.S.	111a	41°53'N	87°51'W
Mazabuka, Zam. (mä-zä-bōō'kä)	232	15°51'S	27°46'E
Mazagão, Braz. (mä-zȧ-gou'n)	143	0°05'S	51°27'W
Mazapil, Mex. (mä-zä-pēl')	122	24°40'N	101°30'W
Mazara del Vallo, Italy (mät-sä'rä dĕl väl'lō)	174	37°40'N	12°37'E
Mazār-i-Sharīf, Afg. (mȧ-zär'-ē-shȧ-rēf')	199	36°48'N	67°12'E
Mazarrón, Spain (mä-zär-rō'n)	172	37°37'N	1°29'W
Mazatenango, Guat. (mä-zä-tä-näŋ'gō)	128	14°30'N	91°30'W
Mazatla, Mex.	131a	19°30'N	99°24'W
Mazatlán, Mex.	128	23°14'N	106°27'W
Mazatlán (San Juan), Mex. (mä-zä-tlän') (saZ hwän')	131	17°05'N	95°26'W
Mažeikiai, Lith. (mà-zhā'kē-ī)	167	56°19'N	22°24'E
Mazhafah, Jabal, mtn., Sau. Ar.	197a	28°56'N	35°05'E
Mazyr, Bela.	181	52°03'N	29°14'E
Mbabane, Swaz. (m'bä-bä'nĕ)	232	26°18'S	31°14'E
Mbaiki, C.A.R. (m'bȧ-ē'kē)	231	3°53'N	18°00'E
Mbakana, Montagne de, mts., Cam.	235	7°55'N	14°40'E
Mbakaou, Barrage de, dam, Cam.	235	6°10'N	12°55'E
Mbala, Zam.	232	8°50'S	31°22'E
Mbale, Ug.	237	1°05'N	34°10'E
Mbamba Bay, Tan.	237	11°17'S	34°46'E
Mbandaka, D.R.C.	232	0°04'N	18°16'E
M'banza Congo, Ang.	232	6°30'S	14°10'E
Mbanza-Ngungu, D.R.C.	232	5°20'S	10°55'E
Mbarara, Ug.	237	0°37'S	30°39'E
Mbasay, Chad	235	7°39'N	15°40'E
Mbigou, Gabon (m-bē-gōō')	232	2°07'S	11°30'E
Mbinda, Congo	236	2°00'S	12°55'E
Mbogo, Tan.	237	7°26'S	33°26'E
Mbomou (Bomu), r., Afr. (m'bō'mōō)	231	4°50'N	24°00'E
Mbout, Maur. (m'bōō')	230	16°03'N	12°31'W
Mbuji-Mayi, D.R.C.	236	6°09'S	23°38'E
McAdam, Can. (măk-ăd'ăm)	100	45°36'N	67°20'W
McAfee, N.J., U.S. (măk-ȧ'fē)	110a	41°10'N	74°32'W
McAlester, Ok., U.S. (măk ăl'ĕs-tēr)	105	34°55'N	95°45'W
McAllen, Tx., U.S. (măk-ăl'ĕn)	122	26°12'N	98°14'W
McBride, Can. (măk-brīd')	90	53°18'N	120°10'W
McCalla, Al., U.S. (măk-kăl'lā)	110h	33°20'N	87°00'W
McCamey, Tx., U.S. (mȧ-kā'mĭ)	122	31°08'N	102°13'W
McColl, S.C., U.S. (mȧ-kōl')	125	34°40'N	79°34'W
McComb, Ms., U.S. (mȧ-kōm')	124	31°14'N	90°27'W
McConaughy, Lake, l., Ne., U.S. (măk kō'nō ĭ')	112	41°24'N	101°40'W
McCook, Ne., U.S. (mȧ-kŏok')	120	40°13'N	100°37'W
McCormick, S.C., U.S. (mȧ-kôr'mĭk)	125	33°56'N	82°20'W
McDonald, Pa., U.S. (măk-dŏn'ăid)	111e	40°22'N	80°13'W
McDonald Island, i., Austl.	224	53°00'S	72°45'E
McDonald Lake, l., Can. (măk-dŏn-ăld)	102e	51°12'N	113°53'W
McGehee, Ar., U.S. (mȧ-gē')	121	33°39'N	91°22'W
McGill, Nv., U.S. (mȧ-gĭl')	119	39°25'N	114°47'W
McGowan, Wa., U.S. (măk-gou'ăn)	116c	46°15'N	123°55'W
McGrath, Ak., U.S. (măk'gràth)	106a	62°58'N	155°20'W
McGregor, Can. (măk-grĕg'ēr)	111b	42°08'N	82°58'W
McGregor, Ia., U.S.	113	42°58'N	91°12'W
McGregor, Tx., U.S.	123	31°26'N	97°23'W
McGregor, r., Can.	95	54°10'N	121°00'W
McGregor Lake, l., Can. (măk-grĕg'ēr)	102c	45°38'N	75°44'W
McHenry, Il., U.S. (măk-hĕn'rĭ)	111a	42°21'N	88°16'W
Mchinji, Mwi.	232	13°42'S	32°50'E
McIntosh, S.D., U.S. (măk'ĭn-tŏsh)	112	45°54'N	101°22'W
McKay, r., Or., U.S.	116c	45°43'N	123°00'W
McKeesport, Pa., U.S. (mȧ-kez'pōrt)	111e	40°21'N	79°51'W
McKees Rocks, Pa., U.S. (mȧ-kēz' rŏks)	111e	40°29'N	80°05'W
McKenzie, Tn., U.S. (mȧ-kĕn'zĭ)	124	36°07'N	88°30'W
McKenzie, r., Or., U.S.	114	44°07'N	122°20'W
McKinley, Mount, mtn., Ak., U.S. (mȧ-kĭn'lĭ)	106a	63°00'N	151°02'W
McKinney, Tx., U.S. (mȧ-kĭn'ĭ)	121	33°12'N	96°35'W
McLaughlin, S.D., U.S. (măk-lŏf'lĭn)	112	45°48'N	100°45'W
McLean, Va., U.S. (măc'lān)	110e	38°56'N	77°11'W
McLeansboro, Il., U.S. (mȧ-klānz'bŭr-ō)	108	38°10'N	88°35'W
McLennan, Can. (măk-lĭn'nán)	90	55°42'N	116°54'W
McLeod, r., Can.	95	53°45'N	115°55'W
McLeod Lake, Can.	94	54°59'N	123°02'W
McLoughlin, Mount, mtn., Or., U.S. (măk-lŏk'lĭn)	114	42°27'N	122°20'W
McMillan Lake, l., Tx., U.S. (măk-mĭl'ăn)	122	32°40'N	104°09'W
McMillin, Wa., U.S. (măk-mĭl'ĭn)	116a	47°08'N	122°14'W
McMinnville, Or., U.S. (măk-mĭn'vĭl)	114	45°13'N	123°13'W
McMinnville, Tn., U.S.	124	35°41'N	85°47'W
McMurray, Wa., U.S. (măk-mŭr'ĭ)	116a	48°19'N	122°15'W
McNary, Az., U.S. (măk-nâr'ē)	119	34°10'N	109°55'W
McNary, La., U.S.	123	30°58'N	92°32'W
McNary Dam, Or., U.S.	114	45°57'N	119°15'W
McPherson, Ks., U.S. (măk-fŭr's'n)	121	38°21'N	97°41'W
McRae, Ga., U.S. (mȧk-rā')	125	32°02'N	82°55'W
McRoberts, Ky., U.S. (măk-rŏb'ērts)	125	37°12'N	82°40'W
Mead, Ks., U.S. (mēd)	120	37°17'N	100°21'W
Mead, Lake, l., U.S.	106	36°20'N	114°14'W
Meade Peak, mtn., Id., U.S.	115	42°19'N	111°16'W
Meadow Lake, Can. (mĕd'ō lāk)	90	54°08'N	108°26'W
Meadows, Can. (mĕd'ōz)	102f	50°02'N	97°35'W
Meadville, Pa., U.S. (mēd'vĭl)	108	41°40'N	80°10'W
Meaford, Can. (mĕ'fērd)	99	44°35'N	80°40'W
Mealy Mountains, mts., Can. (mē'lē)	93	53°32'N	57°58'W
Meandarra, Austl. (mē-ăn-dă'rȧ)	222	27°47'S	149°40'E
Meaux, Fr. (mō)	170	48°58'N	2°53'E
Mecapalapa, Mex. (mā-kä-pä-lä'pä)	131	20°32'N	97°52'W
Mecatina, r., Can. (mā-kȧ-tē'nȧ)	101	50°50'N	59°45'W
Mecca (Makkah), Sau. Ar. (mĕk'ȧ)	198	21°27'N	39°45'E
Mechanic Falls, Me., U.S. (mē-kăn'ĭk)	100	44°05'N	70°23'W
Mechanicsburg, Pa., U.S. (mē-kăn'ĭks-bûrg)	109	40°15'N	77°00'W
Mechanicsville, Md., U.S. (mē-kăn'ĭks-vĭl)	110e	38°27'N	76°45'W
Mechanicville, N.Y., U.S. (mēkăn'ĭk-vĭl)	109	42°55'N	73°45'W
Mechelen, Bel.	165	51°01'N	4°28'E
Mechriyya, Alg.	162	33°30'N	0°13'W
Medicine Bow Range, mts., Co., U.S. (mĕd'ĭ-sĭn bō)	120	40°55'N	106°02'W
Mecklenburg, hist. reg., Ger.	168	53°30'N	13°00'E
Medan, Indon. (må-dän')	212	3°35'N	98°35'E

ăt; finăl; rāte; senāte; ärm; åsk; sofȧ; fâre; ch-choose; dh-as th in other; bē; ēvent; bĕt; recĕnt; cratēr; g-gō; gh-guttural g; bĭt; ĭ-short neutral; rīde; ĸ-guttural k as ch in German ich;

PRONOUNCING INDEX

Medanosa – Mezquitic 321

PLACE (Pronunciation)	PAGE	LAT.	LONG.
Medanosa, Punta, c., Arg. (po͞o′n-tä-mĕ-dä-nô′sä)	144	47°50′S	65°53′W
Medden, r., Eng., U.K. (mĕd′ĕn)	158a	53°14′N	1°05′W
Medellín, Col. (må-dhĕl-yēn′)	142	6°15′N	75°34′W
Medellin, Mex. (mĕ-dĕl-yė′n)	131	19°03′N	96°08′W
Medenine, Tun. (mā-dẽ-nēn′)	162	33°22′N	10°33′E
Medfeld, Ma., U.S. (mĕd′fēld)	101a	42°11′N	71°19′W
Medford, Ma., U.S. (mĕd′fẽrd)	101a	42°25′N	71°07′W
Medford, N.J., U.S.	110f	39°54′N	74°50′W
Medford, Ok., U.S.	121	36°47′N	97°44′W
Medford, Or., U.S.	104	42°19′N	122°52′W
Medford, Wi., U.S.	113	45°09′N	90°22′W
Media, Pa., U.S. (mē′dĭ-ȧ)	110f	39°55′N	75°24′W
Mediaş, Rom. (mĕd-yäsh′)	169	46°09′N	24°21′E
Medical Lake, Wa., U.S. (mĕd′ĭ-kăl)	114	47°34′N	117°40′W
Medicine Bow, r., Wy., U.S.	115	41°58′N	106°30′W
Medicine Hat, Can. (mĕd′ĭ-sĭn hăt)	90	50°03′N	110°40′W
Medicine Lake, l., Mt., U.S. (mĕd′ĭ-sĭn)	115	48°24′N	104°15′W
Medicine Lodge, Ks., U.S.	120	37°17′N	98°37′W
Medicine Lodge, r., Ks., U.S.	120	37°20′N	98°57′W
Medina *see* Al Madīnah, Sau. Ar.	198	24°26′N	39°42′E
Medina, N.Y., U.S. (mė-dī′nȧ)	109	43°15′N	78°20′W
Medina, Oh., U.S.	111d	41°08′N	81°52′W
Medina, r., Tx., U.S.	122	29°45′N	99°13′W
Medina del Campo, Spain (må-dē′nä dĕl käm′pō)	162	41°18′N	4°54′W
Medina de Ríoseco, Spain (må-dē′nä dā rė-ô-sā′kô)	172	41°53′N	5°05′W
Medina Lake, l., Tx., U.S.	122	29°36′N	98°47′W
Medina Sidonia, Spain	172	36°28′N	5°58′W
Mediterranean Sea, sea (mĕd-ĭ-tẽr-ā′nė-ăn)	162	36°22′N	13°25′E
Medjerda, Oued, r., Afr.	162	36°43′N	9°54′E
Mednogorsk, Russia	178	51°27′N	57°22′E
Medveditsa, r., Russia (mĕd-vyĕ′dė tsȧ)	181	50°10′N	43°40′E
Medvezhegorsk, Russia (mĕd-vyĕzh′yĕ-gôrsk′)	180	63°00′N	34°20′E
Medway, Ma., U.S. (mĕd′wā)	101a	42°08′N	71°23′W
Medway Towns, co., Eng., U.K.	158b	51°27′N	0°30′E
Medyn′, Russia (mĕ-dēn′)	176	54°58′N	35°53′E
Medzhybizh, Ukr.	177	49°23′N	27°29′E
Meekatharra, Austl. (mē-kȧ-thăr′ȧ)	218	26°30′S	118°38′E
Meeker, Co., U.S. (mēk′ẽr)	119	40°00′N	107°55′W
Meelpaeg Lake, l., Can. (mēl′pȧ-ĕg)	101	48°22′N	56°52′W
Meerane, Ger. (mā-rä′nẽ)	168	50°51′N	12°27′E
Meerbusch, Ger.	171c	51°15′N	6°41′E
Meerut, India (mē′rŏt)	199	28°59′N	77°43′E
Megalópoli, Grc.	175	37°22′N	22°08′E
Mégara, Grc. (mĕg′ȧ-rȧ)	175	37°59′N	23°21′E
Megget, S.C., U.S. (mĕg′ĕt)	125	32°44′N	80°15′W
Megler, Wa., U.S. (mĕg′lẽr)	116c	46°15′N	123°52′W
Mehanom, Mys, c., Ukr.	177	44°48′N	35°17′E
Meherrin, r., Va., U.S. (mė-hĕr′ĭn)	125	36°40′N	77°49′W
Mehlville, Mo., U.S.	117e	38°30′N	90°19′W
Mehsāna, India	202	23°42′N	72°23′E
Mehun-sur-Yévre, Fr. (mē-ŭɴ-sür-yĕvr′)	170	47°11′N	2°14′E
Meiling Pass, p., China (mā′lĭng′)	205	25°22′N	115°00′E
Meinerzhagen, Ger. (mī′nĕrts-hä-gĕn)	171c	51°06′N	7°39′E
Meiningen, Ger. (mī′nĭng-ĕn)	168	50°35′N	10°25′E
Meiringen, Switz.	168	46°45′N	8°11′E
Meissen, Ger.	168	51°11′N	13°28′E
Meizhu, China (mā-jo͞o)	206	31°17′N	119°12′E
Mejillones, Chile (må-ĸė-lyō′nås)	144	23°07′S	70°31′W
Mekambo, Gabon	236	1°01′N	13°56′E
Mekele, Eth.	231	13°31′N	39°19′E
Meknés, Mor. (mĕk′nĕs) (mĕk-nĕs′)	230	33°56′N	5°44′W
Mekong, r., Asia	212	18°00′N	104°30′E
Melaka, Malay.	212	2°11′N	102°15′E
Melaka, state, Malay.	197b	2°19′N	102°09′E
Melanesia, is., Oc.	240	13°00′S	164°00′E
Melbourne, Austl. (mĕl′bŭrn)	219	37°52′S	145°08′E
Melbourne, Eng., U.K.	158a	52°49′N	1°26′W
Melbourne, Fl., U.S.	125a	28°05′N	80°37′W
Melbourne, Ky., U.S.	111f	39°02′N	84°22′W
Melcher, Ia., U.S. (mĕl′chẽr)	113	41°13′N	93°11′W
Melekess, Russia (mĕl-yĕk-ĕs)	180	54°14′N	49°39′E
Melenki, Russia (mĕ-lyĕŋ′kė)	180	55°25′N	41°34′E
Melfort, Can. (mĕl′fôrt)	90	52°52′N	104°36′W
Melghir, Chott, l., Alg.	230	33°52′N	5°22′E
Melilla, Sp. N. Afr. (mā-lēl′yä)	230	35°24′N	3°30′W
Melipilla, Chile (må-lė-pē′lyä)	144	33°40′S	71°12′W
Melita, Can.	97	49°11′N	101°09′W
Melitopol′, Ukr. (mā-lė-tô′pôl-y′)	181	46°49′N	35°19′E
Melívoia, Grc.	175	39°42′N	22°47′E
Melkrivier, S. Afr.	238c	24°01′S	28°23′E
Mellen, Wi., U.S. (mĕl′ĕn)	113	46°20′N	90°40′W
Mellerud, Swe. (mål′ĕ-ro͞odh)	166	58°43′N	12°25′E
Melmoth, S. Afr.	233c	28°38′S	31°26′E
Melo, Ur. (mā′lō)	144	32°18′S	54°07′W
Melocheville, Can. (mĕ-lôsh-vēl′)	102a	45°24′N	73°56′W
Melozha, r., Russia (myĕ′lô-zhȧ)	186b	56°06′N	38°34′E
Melrose, Ma., U.S. (mĕl′rōz)	101a	42°29′N	71°06′W
Melrose, Mn., U.S.	113	45°39′N	94°49′W
Melrose Park, Il., U.S.	111a	41°54′N	87°52′W
Meltham, Eng., U.K. (mĕl′thăm)	158a	53°35′N	1°51′W
Melton, Austl. (mĕl′tŭn)	217a	37°41′S	144°35′E
Melton Mowbray, Eng., U.K. (mō′brâ)	158a	52°45′N	0°52′W
Melúli, r., Moz.	237	16°10′S	39°30′E
Melun, Fr. (mẽ-lŭɴ′)	161	48°32′N	2°40′E
Melunga, Ang.	236	17°16′S	16°24′E
Melville, Can. (mĕl′vĭl)	90	50°55′N	102°48′W
Melville, La., U.S.	123	30°39′N	91°45′W
Melville, i., Austl.	220	11°30′S	131°12′E
Melville, l., Can.	93	53°46′N	59°31′W
Melville, Cape, c., Austl.	221	14°15′S	145°50′E
Melville Hills, hills, Can.	92	69°18′N	124°57′W
Melville Peninsula, pen., Can.	93	67°44′N	84°09′W
Melvindale, Mi., U.S. (mĕl′vĭn-dāl)	111b	42°17′N	83°11′W
Melyana, Alg.	161	36°19′N	1°56′E
Mélykút, Hung. (mā′l′ko͞ot)	169	46°14′N	19°21′E
Memba, Moz. (mĕm′bȧ)	233	14°12′N	40°35′E
Memel *see* Klaipėda, Lith.	180	55°43′N	21°10′E
Memel, S. Afr. (mĕ′mĕl)	238c	27°42′S	29°35′E
Memmingen, Ger. (mĕm′ĭng-ĕn)	168	47°59′N	10°10′E
Memo, r., Ven. (mĕ′mō)	143b	9°32′N	66°30′W
Memphis, Mo., U.S. (mĕm′fĭs)	121	40°27′N	92°11′W
Memphis, Tn., U.S. (mĕm′fĭs)	105	35°07′N	90°03′W
Memphis, Tx., U.S.	120	34°42′N	100°33′W
Memphis, hist., Egypt	238b	29°50′N	31°12′E
Mena, Ukr. (mē-nȧ′)	177	51°31′N	32°14′E
Mena, Ar., U.S. (mē′nȧ)	121	34°35′N	94°09′W
Menangle, Austl.	217b	34°08′S	150°48′E
Menard, Tx., U.S. (mė-närd′)	122	30°56′N	99°48′W
Menasha, Wi., U.S. (mė-năsh′ȧ)	113	44°12′N	88°29′W
Mende, Fr. (mäɴd)	170	44°31′N	3°30′E
Menden, Ger. (mĕn′dĕn)	171c	51°26′N	7°47′E
Mendes, Braz. (mĕ′n-dĕs)	144b	22°32′S	43°44′W
Mendocino, Ca., U.S.	118	39°18′N	123°47′W
Mendocino, Cape, c., Ca., U.S. (mĕn′dô-sē′nō)	107	40°25′N	12°42′W
Mendota, Il., U.S. (mĕn-dō′tȧ)	113	41°34′N	89°06′W
Mendota, l., Wi., U.S.	113	43°09′N	89°41′W
Mendoza, Arg. (mĕn-dō′sä)	144	32°48′S	68°45′W
Mendoza, prov., Arg.	144	35°10′S	69°00′W
Mengcheng, China (mŭŋ-chŭŋ)	206	33°15′N	116°34′E
Meng Shan, mts., China (mŭŋ shän)	206	35°47′N	117°23′E
Mengzi, China	204	23°22′N	103°20′E
Menindee, Austl. (mĕ-nĭn-dē)	222	32°23′S	142°30′E
Menlo Park, Ca., U.S. (mĕn′lō pärk)	116b	37°27′N	122°11′W
Menno, S.D., U.S. (mĕn′ô)	112	43°14′N	97°34′W
Menominee, Mi., U.S. (mė-nŏm′ĭ-nē)	113	45°08′N	87°40′W
Menominee, r., Mi., U.S.	113	45°37′N	87°54′W
Menominee Falls, Wi., U.S. (fôls)	111a	43°11′N	88°06′W
Menominee Ra, Mi., U.S.	113	46°07′N	88°53′W
Menomonee, r., Wi., U.S.	111a	43°09′N	88°06′W
Menomonie, Wi., U.S.	113	44°53′N	91°55′W
Menongue, Ang.	236	14°36′S	17°48′E
Menorca (Minorca), i., Spain (mĕ-nô′r-kä)	156	40°05′N	3°58′E
Mentana, Italy (mĕn-tȧ′nä)	173d	42°02′N	12°40′E
Mentawai, Kepulauan, is., Indon. (mĕn-tä-vī′)	212	1°08′S	98°10′E
Menton, Fr. (mäɴ-tôɴ′)	171	43°46′N	7°37′E
Mentone, Ca., U.S. (mĕn′tŏne)	117a	34°05′N	117°08′W
Mentz, l., S. Afr. (mĕnts)	233c	33°13′S	25°15′E
Menzel Bourguiba, Tun.	162	37°12′N	9°51′E
Menzelinsk, Russia (mĕn′zyĕ-lėnsk′)	180	55°40′N	53°15′E
Menzies, Austl. (mĕn′zēz)	218	29°45′S	122°15′E
Meogui, Mex. (må-ō′gē)	122	28°17′N	105°28′W
Meppel, Neth. (mĕp′ĕl)	165	52°41′N	6°08′E
Meppen, Ger. (mĕp′ĕn)	168	52°40′N	7°18′E
Merabéllou, Kólpos, b., Grc.	174a	35°16′N	25°55′E
Meramec, r., Mo., U.S. (mĕr′ȧ-mĕk)	121	38°06′N	91°06′W
Merano, Italy (må-rä′nō)	162	46°39′N	11°10′E
Merasheen, i., Can. (mē′rȧ-shēn)	101	47°30′N	54°15′W
Merauke, Indon. (må-rou′kā)	213	8°32′S	140°17′E
Meraux, La., U.S. (mẽ-ro′)	110d	29°56′N	89°56′W
Mercato San Severino, Italy	173c	40°34′N	14°38′E
Merced, Ca., U.S. (mẽr-sĕd′)	118	37°17′N	120°30′W
Merced, r., Ca., U.S.	118	37°25′N	120°31′W
Mercedario, Cerro, mtn., Arg. (mĕr-så-dhä′rė-ō)	144	31°58′S	70°07′W
Mercedes, Arg.	141c	34°41′S	59°26′W
Mercedes, Arg. (mĕr-sā′dhās)	144	29°04′S	58°01′W
Mercedes, Ur.	144	33°17′S	58°04′W
Mercedes, Tx., U.S.	123	26°09′N	97°55′W
Mercedita, Chile (mĕr-sĕ-dė′tä)	141b	33°51′S	71°10′W
Mercer Island, Wa., U.S. (mûr′sẽr)	116a	47°35′N	122°15′W
Mercês, Braz. (mĕ-sĕ′s)	141a	21°13′S	43°20′W
Merchtem, Bel.	159a	50°57′N	4°13′E
Mercier, Can.	102a	45°19′N	73°45′W
Mercy, Cape, c., Can.	93	64°48′N	63°22′W
Meredith, N.H., U.S. (mĕr′ė-dĭth)	109	43°35′N	71°35′W
Merefa, Ukr. (må-rĕf′ȧ)	177	49°49′N	36°04′E
Merendón, Serranía de, mts., Hond.	132	15°01′N	89°05′W
Mereworth, Eng., U.K. (mĕ-rĕ wûrth)	158b	51°15′N	0°23′E
Mergui, Mya. (mĕr-gē′)	212	12°29′N	98°39′E
Mergui Archipelago, is., Mya.	212	12°04′N	97°02′E
Meric (Maritsa), r., Eur.	167	40°43′N	26°19′E
Mérida, Mex.	128	20°58′N	89°37′W
Mérida, Ven.	142	8°30′N	71°15′W
Mérida, Cordillera de, mts., Ven. (mĕ′rė-dhä)	142	8°30′N	70°45′W
Meriden, Ct., U.S. (mĕr′ĭ-dĕn)	109	41°30′N	72°50′W
Meridian, Ms., U.S. (mė-rĭd-ĭ-ăn)	105	32°21′N	88°41′W
Meridian, Tx., U.S.	123	31°56′N	97°37′W
Mérignac, Fr.	170	44°50′N	0°40′W
Merikarvia, Fin. (mā′rē-kȧr′vė-ȧ)	167	61°51′N	21°30′E
Mering, Ger. (mĕ′rēng)	159d	48°16′N	11°00′E
Merkel, Tx., U.S. (mûr′kĕl)	122	32°26′N	100°02′W
Merkinė, Lith.	167	54°10′N	24°10′E
Merksem, Bel.	159a	51°15′N	4°27′E
Merkys, r., Lith. (măr′kĭs)	169	54°23′N	25°00′E
Merlo, Arg. (mĕr-lô)	144a	34°40′S	58°44′W
Meron, Hare, mtn., Isr.	197a	32°58′N	35°25′E
Merriam, Ks., U.S. (mĕr-rĭ-yȧm)	117f	39°01′N	94°42′W
Merriam, Mn., U.S.	117g	44°44′N	93°36′W
Merrick, N.Y., U.S. (mĕr′ĭk)	110a	40°40′N	73°33′W
Merrifield, Va., U.S. (mĕr′ĭ-fēld)	110e	38°50′N	77°12′W
Merrill, Wi., U.S. (mĕr′ĭl)	113	45°11′N	89°42′W
Merrimac, Ma., U.S. (mĕr′ĭ-măk)	101a	45°20′N	71°00′W
Merrimack, N.H., U.S.	101a	42°51′N	71°25′W
Merrimack, r., Ma., U.S. (mĕr′ĭ-măk)	109	43°10′N	71°30′W
Merritt, Can. (mĕr′ĭt)	90	50°07′N	120°47′W
Merryville, La., U.S. (mĕr′ĭ-vĭl)	123	30°46′N	93°34′W
Mersa Fatma, Erit.	231	14°54′N	40°14′E
Merseburg, Ger. (mĕr′zĕ-bo͞orgh)	168	51°21′N	11°59′E
Mersey, r., Eng., U.K. (mûr′zė)	158a	53°20′N	2°55′W
Merseyside, hist. reg., Eng., U.K.	158a	53°29′N	2°59′W
Mersing, Malay.	197b	2°25′N	103°51′E
Merta Road, India (măr′tŭ rōd)	202	26°50′N	73°54′E
Merthyr Tydfil, Wales, U.K. (mûr′thẽr tĭd′vĭl)	164	51°46′N	3°30′W
Mértola Almodóvar, Port. (mĕr-tô-lȧ-äl-mô-dô′vär)	172	37°39′N	8°04′W
Méru, Fr. (mā-rü′)	170	49°14′N	2°08′E
Meru, Kenya (mā′ro͞o)	231	0°01′N	37°45′E
Meru, Mount, mtn., Tan.	237	3°15′S	36°43′E
Merume Mountains, mts., Guy. (mĕr-ü′mĕ)	143	5°45′N	60°15′W
Merwede Kanaal, can., Neth.	159a	52°15′N	5°01′E
Merwin, l., Wa., U.S. (mĕr′wĭn)	116c	45°58′N	122°27′W
Merzifon, Tur. (mĕr′ze-fōn)	198	40°50′N	35°30′E
Mesa, Az., U.S. (mā′sȧ)	119	33°25′N	111°50′W
Mesabi Range, mts., Mn., U.S. (mā-sŏb′bē)	113	47°17′N	93°04′W
Mesagne, Italy (mā-sān′yå)	175	40°34′N	17°51′E
Mesa Verde National Park, rec., Co., U.S. (vĕr′dē)	106	37°22′N	108°27′W
Mescalero Apache Indian Reservation, I.R., N.M., U.S. (mĕs-kä-lā′rō)	119	33°10′N	105°45′W
Meshchovsk, Russia (myĕsh′chĕfsk)	176	54°17′N	35°19′E
Mesilla, N.M., U.S. (må-sē′yä)	119	32°15′N	106°45′W
Meskine, Chad	235	11°25′N	15°21′E
Mesolóngi, Grc.	175	38°23′N	21°28′E
Mesopotamia, hist. reg., Asia	201	34°00′N	44°00′E
Mesquita, Braz.	144b	22°48′S	43°26′W
Messina, Italy (mĕ-sē′nȧ)	154	38°11′N	15°34′E
Messina, S. Afr.	232	22°17′S	30°13′E
Messina, Stretto di, strt., Italy (stĕ′t-tô dē)	163	38°10′N	15°34′E
Messíni, Grc.	175	37°05′N	22°00′E
Mestaganem, Alg.	230	36°04′N	0°11′E
Mestre, Italy (mĕs′trā)	174	45°29′N	12°15′E
Meta, dept., Col. (mĕ′tä)	142a	3°28′N	74°07′W
Meta, r., S.A.	142	4°33′N	72°09′W
Métabetchouane, r., Can. (mĕ-tȧ-bĕt-cho͞o-än′)	99	47°45′N	72°00′W
Metairie, La., U.S.	123	30°00′N	90°11′W
Metán, Arg. (mĕ-tȧ′n)	144	25°32′S	64°51′W
Metangula, Moz.	232	12°42′S	34°48′E
Metapán, El Sal. (må-täpän′)	132	14°21′N	89°26′W
Metcalfe, Can. (mĕt-käf)	102c	45°14′N	75°27′W
Metchosin, Can.	116a	48°22′N	123°33′W
Metepec, Mex. (må-tĕ-pĕk′)	130	18°56′N	98°31′W
Metepec, Mex.	130	19°15′N	99°36′W
Methow, r., Wa., U.S. (mĕt′hou) (mĕt hou′)	114	48°26′N	120°15′W
Methuen, Ma., U.S. (mė-thū′ĕn)	101a	42°44′N	71°11′W
Metković, Cro. (mĕt′kô-vĭch)	175	43°02′N	17°40′E
Metlakatla, Ak., U.S. (mĕt-lȧ-kăt′lȧ)	103	55°08′N	131°35′W
Metropolis, Il., U.S. (mė-trŏp′ô-lĭs)	121	37°09′N	88°46′W
Metter, Ga., U.S. (mĕt′ẽr)	125	32°21′N	82°05′W
Mettmann, Ger. (mĕt′män)	171c	51°15′N	6°58′E
Metuchen, N.J., U.S. (mĕ-tŭ′chĕn)	110a	40°32′N	74°21′W
Metz, Fr. (mĕtz)	161	49°08′N	6°10′E
Metztitlán, Mex. (mĕtz-tėt-län)	130	20°36′N	98°45′W
Meuban, Cam.	235	2°27′N	12°41′E
Meuse (Maas), r., Eur. (mûz) (müz)	165	50°32′N	5°22′E
Mexborough, Eng., U.K. (mĕks′bŭr-ô)	158a	53°30′N	1°17′W
Mexia, Tx., U.S. (må-hē′ä)	123	31°32′N	96°29′W
Mexian, China	205	24°20′N	116°10′E
Mexicalcingo, Mex. (mĕ-kē-käl-sēn′go)	131a	19°13′N	99°34′W
Mexicali, Mex. (måk-sė-kä′lė)	128	32°28′N	115°29′W
Mexicana, Altiplanicie, plat., Mex.	130	22°38′N	102°33′W
Mexican Hat, Ut., U.S. (mĕk′sĭ-kăn hăt)	119	37°10′N	109°55′W
Mexico, Me., U.S. (mĕk′sĭ-kō)	100	44°34′N	70°33′W
Mexico, Mo., U.S.	121	39°09′N	91°51′W
Mexico, nation, N.A.	128	23°45′N	104°00′W
Mexico, Gulf of, b., N.A.	128	25°15′N	93°45′W
Mexico City, Mex. (mĕk′sĭ-kō)	128	19°28′N	99°09′W
Mexticacán, Mex. (mĕs′tė-kä-kän′)	130	21°12′N	102°43′W
Meyers Chuck, Ak., U.S.	94	55°44′N	132°15′W
Meyersdale, Pa., U.S. (mī′ẽrz-dāl)	109	39°55′N	79°00′W
Meyerton, S. Afr. (mī′ẽr-tŭn)	238c	26°35′S	28°01′E
Meymaneh, Afg.	198	35°53′N	64°38′E
Mezen′, Russia	178	65°50′N	44°05′E
Mezen′, r., Russia	180	65°20′N	44°45′E
Mézenc, Mont, mtn., Fr. (mŏɴ-mā-zĕɴ′)	170	44°55′N	4°12′E
Mezha, r., Eur. (myā′zhȧ)	176	55°53′N	31°44′E
Mézieres-sur-Seine, Fr. (mā-zyâr′sür-sån′)	171b	48°58′N	1°49′E
Mezökövesd, Hung. (mĕ′zû-kû′vĕsht)	169	47°49′N	20°36′E
Mezötur, Hung. (mĕ′zû-to͞or)	169	47°00′N	20°36′E
Mezquital, Mex. (måz-kė-täl′)	130	23°30′N	104°20′W
Mezquitic, Mex. (måz-kė-tēk′)	130	22°25′N	103°43′W
Mezquitic, r., Mex.	130	22°25′N	103°45′W

ng-sing; ŋ-baŋk; ɴ-nasalized n; nŏd; cŏmmit; ōld; ôbey; ôrder; oi-boil; fo͞od; o̊-as oo in foot; ou-out; s-soft; sh-dish; th-thin; pūre; ůnite; ûrn; stŭd; circŭs; ü-as in French tu; ′-indeterminate vowel.

322 Mfangano Island – Mississippi PRONOUNCING INDEX

PLACE (Pronunciation)	PAGE	LAT.	LONG.
Mfangano Island, i., Kenya	237	0°28′S	33°35′E
Mga, Russia (m'gȧ)	186c	59°45′N	31°04′E
Mglin, Russia (m'glĕn′)	176	53°03′N	32°52′W
Mia, Oued, r., Alg.	162	29°26′N	3°15′E
Miacatlán, Mex. (mē′ä-kä-tlän′)	130	18°42′N	99°17′W
Miahuatlán, Mex. (mē′ä-wä-tlän′)	131	16°20′N	96°38′W
Miajadas, Spain (mē-ä-hä′däs)	172	39°10′N	5°53′W
Miami, Az., U.S.	104	33°20′N	110°55′W
Miami, Fl., U.S.	105	25°45′N	80°11′W
Miami, Ok., U.S.	121	36°51′N	94°51′W
Miami, Tx., U.S.	120	35°41′N	100°39′W
Miami Beach, Fl., U.S.	125a	25°47′N	80°07′W
Miamisburg, Oh., U.S. (mī-ăm′iz-bûrg)	108	39°40′N	84°20′W
Miamitown, Oh., U.S. (mī-ăm′ĭ-toun)	111f	39°13′N	84°43′W
Mīāneh, Iran	198	37°15′N	47°13′E
Miangas, Pulau, i., Indon.	213	5°30′N	127°00′E
Miaoli, Tai. (mē-ou′lĭ)	209	24°30′N	120°48′E
Miaozhen, China (mi̇ou-jŭn)	206	31°44′N	121°28′E
Miass, Russia (mī-äs′)	184	54°59′N	60°06′E
Miastko, Pol. (myäst′kô)	168	54°01′N	17°00′E
Miccosukee Indian Reservation, I.R., Fl., U.S.	125a	26°10′N	80°50′W
Michalovce, Slvk. (mē′kä-lôf′tsĕ)	169	48°44′N	21°56′E
Michel Peak, mtn., Can.	94	53°35′N	126°25′W
Michelson, Mount, mtn., Ak., U.S. (mĭch′ĕl-sŭn)	103	69°11′N	144°12′W
Michendorf, Ger. (mē′kĕn-dōrf)	159b	52°19′N	13°02′E
Miches, Dom. Rep. (mē′chĕs)	135	19°00′N	69°05′W
Michigan, state, U.S. (mĭsh-′ĭ-găn)	105	45°55′N	87°00′W
Michigan, Lake, l., U.S.	107	43°20′N	87°10′W
Michigan City, In., U.S.	108	41°40′N	86°55′W
Michipicoten, r., Can.	113	47°56′N	84°42′W
Michipicoten Harbour, Can.	113	47°58′N	84°58′W
Michurinsk, Russia (mĭ-chōō-rĭnsk′)	181	52°53′N	40°32′E
Mico, Punta, c., Nic. (pōō′n-tä-mē′kô)	133	11°38′N	83°24′W
Micronesia, is., Oc.	240	11°00′N	159°00′E
Micronesia, Federated States of, nation, Oc.	3	5°00′N	152°00′E
Midas, Nv., U.S. (mī′dȧs)	114	41°15′N	116°50′W
Middelfart, Den. (mēd′′l-färt)	166	55°30′N	9°45′E
Middle, r., Can.	94	55°00′N	125°50′W
Middle Andaman, i., India (ăn-dȧ-măn′)	212	12°44′N	93°21′E
Middle Bayou, Tx., U.S.	123a	29°38′N	95°06′W
Middleburg, S. Afr. (mĭd′ĕl-bûrg)	232	31°30′S	25°00′E
Middleburg, S. Afr.	238c	25°47′S	29°30′E
Middlebury, Vt., U.S. (mĭd′′l-bĕr-ĭ)	109	44°00′N	73°10′W
Middle Concho, Tx., U.S. (kŏn′chō)	122	31°21′N	100°50′W
Middle River, Md., U.S.	110e	39°20′N	76°27′W
Middlesboro, Ky., U.S. (mĭd′′lz-bŭr-ô)	124	36°36′N	83°42′W
Middlesbrough, Eng., U.K. (mĭd′′lz-brŭ)	160	54°35′N	1°18′W
Middlesex, N.J., U.S. (mĭd′′l-sĕks)	110a	40°34′N	74°30′W
Middleton, Can. (mĭd′′l-tŭn)	100	44°57′N	65°04′W
Middleton, Eng., U.K.	158a	53°34′N	2°12′W
Middletown, Ct., U.S.	109	41°35′N	72°40′W
Middletown, De., U.S.	109	39°30′N	75°40′W
Middletown, Ma., U.S.	101a	42°35′N	71°01′W
Middletown, N.Y., U.S.	109	41°26′N	74°25′W
Middletown, Oh., U.S.	108	39°30′N	84°25′W
Middlewich, Eng., U.K. (mĭd′′l-wĭch)	158a	53°11′N	2°27′W
Middlewit, S. Afr. (mĭd′l′wĭt)	238c	24°50′S	27°00′E
Midfield, Al., U.S.	110h	33°28′N	86°54′W
Midi, Canal du, Fr. (kä-näl-dü-mē-dē′)	161	43°22′N	1°35′E
Mid Illovo, S. Afr. (mĭd ĭl′ô-vō)	233c	29°59′S	30°32′E
Midland, Can. (mĭd′lănd)	91	44°45′N	79°50′W
Midland, Mi., U.S.	108	43°40′N	84°20′W
Midland, Tx., U.S.	122	32°05′N	102°05′W
Midvale, Ut., U.S. (mĭd′vāl)	117b	40°37′N	111°54′W
Midway, Al., U.S. (mĭd′wā)	124	32°03′N	85°30′W
Midway Islands, is., Oc.	2	28°00′N	179°00′W
Midwest, Wy., U.S. (mĭd-wĕst′)	115	43°25′N	106°15′W
Midye, Tur. (mēd′yĕ)	181	41°35′N	28°10′E
Międzyrzecz, Pol. (myăn-dzŭ′zhĕch)	168	52°26′N	15°35′E
Mielec, Pol. (myĕ′lĕts)	169	50°17′N	21°27′E
Mier, Mex. (myâr)	122	26°26′N	99°08′W
Mieres, Spain (myā′rās)	172	43°14′N	5°45′W
Mier y Noriega, Mex. (myâr′ē nô-rē-ā′gä)	130	23°28′N	100°08′W
Miguel Auza, Mex.	130	24°17′N	103°27′W
Miguel Pereira, Braz.	144b	22°27′S	43°28′W
Mijares, r., Spain	173	39°55′N	0°01′W
Mikage, Japan (mē′kȧ-gȧ)	211b	34°42′N	135°15′E
Mikawa-Wan, b., Japan (mē′kä-wä wän)	211	34°43′N	137°09′E
Mikhaylov, Russia (mē-kāy′lôf)	180	54°14′N	39°03′E
Mikhaylovka, Russia	186a	55°35′N	57°57′E
Mikhaylovka, Russia	186c	59°20′N	30°21′E
Mikhaylovka, Russia	181	50°05′N	43°10′E
Mikhnëvo, Russia (mĭk-nyô′vô)	186b	55°08′N	37°57′E
Miki, Japan (mē′kē)	211b	34°47′N	134°59′E
Mikindani, Tan. (mē-kēn-dä′nē)	233	10°17′S	40°07′E
Mikkeli, Fin. (mĕk′ĕ-lĭ)	160	61°42′N	27°14′E
Mikulov, Czech Rep. (mĭ′kōō-lôf)	168	48°47′N	16°39′E
Mikumi, Tan.	237	7°24′S	36°59′E
Mikuni, Japan (mē′kōō-nē)	211	36°09′N	136°14′E
Mikuni-Sammyaku, mts., Japan (säm′myä-kōō)	211	36°51′N	138°38′E
Mikura, i., Japan (mē′kōō-rä)	211	33°53′N	139°26′E
Milaca, Milaca, Mn., U.S. (mē-lăk′ȧ)	113	45°45′N	93°41′W
Milan (Milano), Italy (mē-lä′nō)	174	45°29′N	9°12′E
Milan, Mi., U.S. (mī′lăn)	108	42°05′N	83°40′W
Milan, Mo., U.S.	121	40°13′N	93°07′W
Milan, Tn., U.S.	124	35°54′N	88°47′W
Milâs, Tur. (mē′läs)	163	37°10′N	27°25′E
Milazzo, Italy	174	38°13′N	15°17′E
Milbank, S.D., U.S. (mĭl′băŋk)	112	45°13′N	96°38′W
Mildura, Austl. (mĭl-dū′rȧ)	219	34°10′S	142°18′E
Miles City, Mt., U.S. (mīlz)	104	46°24′N	105°50′W
Milford, Ct., U.S. (mĭl′fērd)	109	41°15′N	73°05′W
Milford, De., U.S.	109	38°55′N	75°25′W
Milford, Ma., U.S.	101a	42°09′N	71°31′W
Milford, Mi., U.S.	111b	42°35′N	83°36′W
Milford, N.H., U.S.	109	42°50′N	71°40′W
Milford, Oh., U.S.	111f	39°11′N	84°18′W
Milford, Ut., U.S.	119	38°20′N	113°05′W
Milford Sound, strt., N.Z.	223	44°35′S	167°47′E
Miling, Austl. (mĭl′′ng)	218	30°30′S	116°25′E
Milipitas, Ca., U.S. (mĭl-ĭ-pĭ′tăs)	116b	37°26′N	121°54′W
Milk, r., N.A.	106	48°30′N	107°00′W
Millau, Fr. (mē-yō′)	161	44°06′N	3°04′E
Millbrae, Ca., U.S. (mĭl′brā)	116b	37°36′N	122°23′W
Millbury, Ma., U.S. (mĭl′bĕr-ĭ)	101a	42°12′N	71°46′W
Mill Creek, r., Can. (mĭl)	102g	53°28′N	113°25′W
Mill Creek, r., Ca., U.S.	118	40°07′N	121°55′W
Milledgeville, Ga., U.S. (mĭl′ĕj-vĭl)	124	33°05′N	83°15′W
Mille Îles, Rivière des, r., Can. (rē-vyâr′ dā mēl′ēl′)	102a	45°41′N	73°40′W
Mille Lac Indian Reservation, I.R., Mn., U.S. (mĭl lăk′)	113	46°14′N	94°13′W
Mille Lacs, l., Mn., U.S.	113	46°25′N	93°22′W
Mille Lacs, Lac des, l., Can. (läk dĕ mēl läks)	98	48°52′N	90°53′W
Millen, Ga., U.S. (mĭl′ĕn)	125	32°47′N	81°55′W
Miller, S.D., U.S. (mĭl′ēr)	112	44°31′N	99°00′W
Millerovo, Russia (mĭl′ĕ-rô-vô)	181	48°58′N	40°27′E
Millersburg, Ky., U.S. (mĭl′ērz-bûrg)	108	38°15′N	84°10′W
Millersburg, Oh., U.S.	108	40°35′N	81°55′W
Millersburg, Pa., U.S.	109	40°35′N	76°55′W
Millerton, Can. (mĭl′ēr-tŭn)	100	46°56′N	65°40′W
Millertown, Can. (mĭl′ēr-toun)	101	48°49′N	56°32′W
Millicent, Austl. (mĭl-ĭ-sĕnt)	222	37°30′S	140°20′E
Millinocket, Me., U.S. (mĭl-ĭ-nŏk′ĕt)	100	45°40′N	68°44′W
Millis, Ma., U.S. (mĭl-ĭs)	101a	42°10′N	71°22′W
Millstadt, Il., U.S. (mĭl′stăt)	117e	38°27′N	90°06′W
Millstone, r., N.J., U.S. (mĭl′stōn)	110a	40°27′N	74°38′W
Millstream, Austl. (mĭl′strēm)	218	21°45′S	117°10′E
Milltown, Can. (mĭl′toun)	100	45°13′N	67°19′W
Mill Valley, Ca., U.S. (mĭl)	116b	37°54′N	122°32′W
Millwood Reservoir, res., Ar., U.S.	121	33°00′N	94°00′W
Milly-la-Forêt, Fr. (mē-yē′-la-fō-rĕ′)	171b	48°24′N	2°28′E
Milnerton, S. Afr. (mĭl′nēr-tŭn)	232a	33°52′S	18°30′E
Milnor, N.D., U.S. (mĭl′nēr)	112	46°17′N	97°29′W
Milo, Me., U.S.	100	44°16′N	69°01′W
Milos, i., Grc. (mē′lŏs)	163	36°45′N	24°35′E
Milpa Alta, Mex. (mē′l-pä-ȧ′l-tä)	131a	19°11′N	99°01′W
Milton, Can.	102d	43°31′N	79°53′W
Milton, Fl., U.S. (mĭl′tŭn)	124	30°37′N	87°02′W
Milton, Pa., U.S.	109	41°00′N	76°50′W
Milton, Ut., U.S.	117b	41°04′N	111°44′W
Milton, Wa., U.S.	116a	47°15′N	122°20′W
Milton, Wi., U.S.	113	42°45′N	89°00′W
Milton-Freewater, Or., U.S.	114	45°57′N	118°25′W
Milvale, Pa., U.S. (mĭl′vāl)	111e	40°29′N	79°58′W
Milville, N.J., U.S. (mĭl′vĭl)	109	39°25′N	75°00′W
Milwaukee, Wi., U.S.	105	43°03′N	87°55′W
Milwaukee, r., Wi., U.S.	111a	43°10′N	87°56′W
Milwaukie, Or., U.S. (mĭl-wô′kē)	114	45°27′N	122°38′W
Mimiapan, Mex. (mē-myä-pän′)	131a	19°26′N	99°28′W
Mimoso do Sul, Braz. (mē-mō′sō-dô-sōō′l)	141a	21°03′S	41°21′W
Min, r., China (mĭn)	205	26°03′N	118°30′E
Min, r., China	209	29°30′N	104°00′E
Mina, r., Alg. (mē′nȧ)	173	35°24′N	0°51′E
Minago, r., Can. (mĭ-nä′gō)	97	54°25′N	98°45′W
Minakuchi, Japan (mē′nȧ-kōō′chē)	211	34°59′N	136°06′E
Minas, Cuba (mē′näs)	134	21°30′N	77°35′W
Minas, Indon.	197b	0°52′N	101°29′E
Minas, Ur. (mē′näs)	144	34°18′S	55°12′W
Minas, Sierra de las, mts., Guat. (syĕr′rȧ dā läs mē′näs)	132	15°08′N	90°25′W
Minas Basin, b., Can. (mī′nȧs)	100	45°20′N	64°00′W
Minas Channel, strt., Can.	100	45°15′N	64°45′W
Minas de Oro, Hond. (mē′näs-dĕ-dĕ-ō-rô)	132	14°52′N	87°19′W
Minas de Riotinto, Spain (mē′näs dā rē-ô-tēn′tō)	172	37°43′N	6°35′W
Minas Novas, Braz. (mē′näzh nō′väzh)	143	17°20′S	42°19′W
Minatare, I., Ne., U.S. (mĭn′ȧ-târ)	112	41°56′N	103°07′W
Minatitlán, Mex. (mē-nä-tē-tlän′)	128	17°59′N	94°33′W
Minatitlán, Mex.	130	19°21′N	104°02′W
Minato, Japan (mē′nȧ-tô)	211	35°13′N	139°52′E
Minch, The, strt., Scot., U.K.	156	58°04′N	6°04′W
Mindanao, i., Phil.	213	8°00′N	125°00′E
Mindanao Sea, sea, Phil.	213	8°55′N	124°00′E
Minden, Ger. (mĭn′dĕn)	168	52°17′N	8°58′E
Minden, La., U.S.	123	32°36′N	93°19′W
Minden, Ne., U.S.	120	40°30′N	98°54′W
Mindoro, i., Phil.	212	12°50′N	121°05′E
Mindoro Strait, strt., Phil.	213a	12°28′N	120°33′E
Mindyak, Russia (mēn′dyȧk)	186a	54°01′N	58°48′E
Mineola, N.Y., U.S. (mĭn-ē-ō′lȧ)	110a	40°43′N	73°38′W
Mineola, Tx., U.S.	123	32°39′N	95°31′W
Mineral del Chico, Mex. (mē-nå-räl′dĕl chē′kô)	130	20°13′N	98°46′W
Mineral del Monte, Mex. (mē-nå-räl dĕl mōn′tå)	130	20°18′N	98°39′W
Mineral'nyye Vody, Russia	181	44°10′N	43°15′E
Mineral Point, Wi., U.S. (mĭn′ēr-ăl)	113	42°50′N	90°10′W
Mineral Wells, Tx., U.S. (mĭn′ēr-ăl wĕlz)	122	32°48′N	98°06′W
Minerva, Oh., U.S. (mĭ-nur′vȧ)	108	40°45′N	81°10′W
Minervino, Italy (mē-nĕr-vē′nô)	174	41°07′N	16°05′E
Mineyama, Japan (mē-nĕ-yä′mä)	211	35°38′N	135°05′E
Mingäçevir, Azer.	182	40°45′N	47°03′E
Mingäçevir su anbarı, res., Azer.	182	40°50′N	46°50′E
Mingan, Can.	91	50°18′N	64°02′W
Mingenew, Austl. (mĭn′gĕ-nū)	218	29°15′S	115°45′E
Mingo Junction, Oh., U.S. (mĭŋ′gō)	108	40°15′N	80°40′W
Minho, hist. reg., Port. (mēn yō)	172	41°32′N	8°13′W
Minho (Miño), r., Eur. (mē′n-yō)	172	41°28′N	9°05′W
Ministik Lake, l., Can. (mĭ-nĭs′tĭk)	102g	53°23′N	113°05′W
Minna, Nig. (mĭn′ȧ)	230	9°37′N	6°33′E
Minneapolis, Ks., U.S. (mĭn-ē-ăp′ô-lĭs)	121	39°07′N	97°41′W
Minneapolis, Mn., U.S.	105	44°58′N	93°15′W
Minnedosa, Can. (mĭn-ē-dō′sȧ)	90	50°14′N	99°51′W
Minneota, Mn., U.S. (mĭn-ē-ō′tȧ)	112	44°34′N	95°59′W
Minnesota, state, U.S. (mĭn-ē-sō′tȧ)	105	46°10′N	90°20′W
Minnesota, r., Mn., U.S.	107	44°30′N	95°00′W
Minnetonka, l., Mn., U.S. (mĭn-ē-tôŋ′kȧ)	113	44°52′N	93°34′W
Minnitaki Lake, l., Can. (mĭ′nĭ-tä′kē)	97	49°58′N	92°00′W
Mino, r., Japan	211b	34°56′N	135°06′E
Minonk, Il., U.S. (mī′nŏnk)	108	40°55′N	89°00′W
Minooka, Il., U.S. (mĭ-nōō′kȧ)	111a	41°27′N	88°15′W
Minot, N.D., U.S.	104	48°13′N	101°17′W
Minsk, Bela. (mēnsk)	178	53°54′N	27°35′E
Minsk, prov., Bela.	176	53°50′N	27°43′E
Mińsk Mazowiecki, Pol. (mēn′sk mä-zô-vyĕt′skĭ)	169	52°10′N	21°35′E
Minsterley, Eng., U.K. (mĭnstēr-lē)	158a	52°38′N	2°55′W
Minto, Can.	100	46°05′N	66°05′W
Minto, l., Can.	93	57°18′N	75°50′W
Minturno, Italy (mēn-tōōr′nō)	174	41°17′N	13°44′E
Minūf, Egypt (mē-nōōf′)	238b	30°26′N	30°55′E
Minusinsk, Russia (mē-nô-sēnsk′)	179	53°47′N	91°45′E
Min'yar, Russia	186a	55°06′N	57°33′E
Miquelon Lake, l., Can. (mĭ′kē-lôn)	102g	53°16′N	112°55′W
Miquihuana, Mex. (mē-kē-wä′nä)	130	23°36′N	99°45′W
Mir, Bela. (mēr)	169	53°27′N	26°25′E
Miracema, Braz. (mē-rä-sĕ′mä)	141a	21°24′S	42°10′W
Miracema do Tocantins, Braz.	143	9°34′S	48°24′W
Mirador, Braz. (mē-rȧ-dōr′)	143	6°19′S	44°12′W
Miraflores, Col. (mē-rä-flō′räs)	142	5°10′N	73°13′W
Miraflores, Peru	142	16°19′S	71°20′W
Miraflores Locks, trans., Pan.	128a	9°00′N	79°35′W
Miragoâne, Haiti (mē-rȧ-gwän′)	135	18°25′N	73°05′W
Mira Loma, Ca., U.S. (mĭ′rȧ lō′mȧ)	117a	34°01′N	117°32′W
Miramar, Ca., U.S. (mĭr′ă-mär)	118a	32°53′N	117°08′W
Miramas, Fr.	170	43°35′N	5°00′E
Miramichi Bay, b., Can. (mĭr′ȧ-mē′shē)	100	47°08′N	65°08′W
Miranda, Col. (mē-rä′n-dä)	142a	3°14′N	76°11′W
Miranda, Ca., U.S.	118	40°14′N	123°49′W
Miranda, Ven.	143b	10°09′N	68°24′W
Miranda, dept., Ven.	143b	10°17′N	66°41′W
Miranda de Ebro, Spain (mē-rä′n-dä-dĕ-ĕ′brô)	172	42°42′N	2°59′W
Miranda do Douro, Port. (mē-rän′dä dô-dwĕ′rô)	172	41°30′N	6°17′W
Mirandela, Port. (mē-rän-dā′lȧ)	172	41°28′N	7°10′W
Mirando City, Tx., U.S. (mĭr-ăn′dō)	122	27°25′N	99°03′W
Mira Por Vos Islets, is., Bah. (mē′rä pôr vōs)	135	22°05′N	74°30′W
Mira Por Vos Pass, strt., Bah.	135	22°10′N	74°35′W
Mirbāṭ, Oman	198	16°58′N	54°42′E
Mirebalais, Haiti (mēr-bȧ-lĕ′)	135	18°50′N	72°05′W
Mirecourt, Fr. (mēr-kōōr′)	171	48°20′N	6°08′E
Mirfield, Eng., U.K. (mûr′fēld)	158a	53°41′N	1°42′W
Miri, Malay. (mē′rē)	212	4°13′N	113°56′E
Mirim, Lagoa, l., S.A. (mē-rēn′)	144	33°00′S	53°15′W
Miropol'ye, Ukr. (mē-rô-pôl′yĕ)	177	51°02′N	35°13′E
Mirpur Khās, Pak. (mēr′pōōr kȧs)	202	25°36′N	69°10′E
Mirzāpur, India (mēr′zä-pōōr)	199	25°12′N	82°38′E
Misantla, Mex. (mē-sän′tlä)	131	19°55′N	96°49′W
Miscou, i., Can. (mĭs′kō)	100	47°58′N	64°35′W
Miscou Point, c., Can.	100	48°04′N	64°32′W
Miseno, Cape, c., Italy (mē-zĕ′nō)	173c	40°33′N	14°12′E
Misery, Mount, mtn., St. K./N. (mĭz′rē-ĭ)	133b	17°28′N	62°47′W
Mishan, China (mĭ′shän)	210	45°32′N	132°19′E
Mishawaka, In., U.S. (mĭsh-ȧ-wôk′ȧ)	108	41°45′N	86°15′W
Mishima, Japan (mē′shē-mä)	211	35°09′N	138°56′E
Misiones, prov., Arg. (mē-syō′nās)	144	27°00′S	54°30′W
Miskito, Cayos, is., Nic.	133	14°34′N	82°30′W
Miskolc, Hung. (mĭsh′kōlts)	154	48°07′N	20°50′E
Misool, Pulau, i., Indon. (mē-sōl′)	213	2°00′S	130°05′E
Misquah Hills, Mn., U.S. (mĭs-kwä′ hĭlz)	113	47°50′N	90°30′W
Miṣr al Jadīdah, Egypt	238b	30°06′N	31°35′E
Misrātah, Libya	231	32°23′N	14°58′E
Missinaibi, r., Can. (mĭs′ĭn-ä′ē-bē)	93	50°27′N	83°01′W
Missinaibi Lake, l., Can.	98	48°23′N	83°40′W
Mission, Ks., U.S. (mĭsh′ŭn)	117f	39°02′N	94°39′W
Mission, Tx., U.S.	122	26°14′N	98°19′W
Mission City, Can. (sĭ′tĭ)	95	49°08′N	112°18′W
Mississagi, r., Can.	98	46°35′N	83°30′W
Mississauga, Can.	99	43°34′N	79°37′W
Mississippi, state, U.S. (mĭs-ĭ-sĭp′ē)	105	32°30′N	89°45′W
Mississippi, l., Can.	99	45°05′N	76°15′W
Mississippi, r., U.S.	107	32°00′N	91°30′W

PRONOUNCING INDEX

Mississippi Sound – Monterotondo 323

PLACE (Pronunciation)	PAGE	LAT.	LONG.
Mississippi Sound, strt., Ms., U.S.	124	34°16'N	89°10'W
Missoula, Mt., U.S. (mĭ-zo͞o'lá)	104	46°55'N	114°00'W
Missouri, state, U.S. (mĭ-so͞o'rē)	105	38°00'N	93°40'W
Missouri, r., U.S.	106	40°40'N	96°00'W
Missouri City, Tx., U.S.	123a	29°37'N	95°32'W
Missouri Coteau, hills, U.S.	106	47°30'N	101°00'W
Missouri Valley, Ia., U.S.	112	41°35'N	95°53'W
Mist, Or., U.S. (mĭst)	116c	46°00'N	123°15'W
Mistassini, Can. (mĭs-tá-sĭ'nē)	99	48°56'N	71°55'W
Mistassini, l., Can. (mĭs-tá-sĭ'nē)	93	50°48'N	73°30'W
Mistelbach, Aus. (mĭs'tĕl-bäk)	168	48°34'N	16°33'E
Misteriosa, Lago, l., Mex. (mēs-tē-ryō'sä)	132a	18°05'N	90°15'W
Misti, Volcán, vol., Peru	142	16°04'S	71°20'W
Mistretta, Italy (mē-strĕt'tä)	174	37°54'N	14°22'E
Misty Fjords National Monument, rec., Ak., U.S.	103	51°00'N	131°00'W
Mita, Punta de, c., Mex. (po͞o'n-tä-dĕ-mē'tä)	130	20°44'N	105°34'W
Mitaka, Japan (mē'tä-kä)	211a	35°42'N	139°34'E
Mitchell, Il., U.S. (mĭch'ĕl)	117e	38°46'N	90°05'W
Mitchell, In., U.S.	108	38°45'N	86°25'W
Mitchell, Ne., U.S.	112	41°56'N	103°49'W
Mitchell, S.D., U.S.	104	43°42'N	98°01'W
Mitchell, Mount, mtn., N.C., U.S.	107	35°47'N	82°15'W
Mit Ghamr, Egypt	238b	30°43'N	31°20'E
Mitla Pass, p., Egypt	197a	30°03'N	32°40'E
Mito, Japan (mē'tō)	210	36°20'N	140°23'E
Mitsiwa, Erit.	231	15°40'N	39°19'E
Mitsu, Japan (mēt'sōō)	211	34°21'N	132°49'E
Mittelland Kanal, can., Ger. (mĭt'ĕl-länd)	168	52°18'N	10°42'E
Mittenwalde, Ger. (mē'tĕn-väl-dĕ)	159b	52°16'N	13°33'E
Mittweida, Ger. (mĭt-vī'dä)	168	50°59'N	12°58'E
Mitumba, Monts, mts., D.R.C.	237	10°50'S	27°00'E
Mityayevo, Russia (mĭt-yä'yĕ-vô)	186a	60°17'N	61°02'E
Miura, Japan	211a	35°08'N	139°37'E
Miwa, Japan (mē'wä)	211b	34°32'N	135°51'E
Mixico, Guat. (mēs'kō)	132	14°37'N	90°37'W
Mixquiahuala, Mex. (mēs-kē-wä'lä)	130	20°12'N	99°13'W
Mixteco, r., Mex. (mēs-tā'kō)	130	17°45'N	98°10'W
Miyake, Japan (mē'yä-kå)	211b	34°35'N	135°34'E
Miyake, i., Japan (mē'yä-kå)	211	34°06'N	139°21'E
Miyakonojō, Japan	210	31°44'N	131°04'E
Miyazaki, Japan (mē'yä-zä'kē)	210	31°55'N	131°27'E
Miyoshi, Japan (mē-yō'shē')	210	34°48'N	132°49'E
Mizdah, Libya (mēz'dä)	200	31°29'N	13°09'E
Mizil, Rom. (mē'zēl)	175	45°01'N	26°30'E
Mizoram, state, India	199	23°25'N	92°45'E
Mjölby, Swe. (myûl'bü)	166	58°20'N	15°09'E
Mjörn, l., Swe.	166	57°55'N	12°22'E
Mjösa, l., Nor. (myûsä)	160	60°41'N	11°25'E
Mkalama, Tan.	232	4°07'S	34°38'E
Mkushi, Zam.	237	13°40'S	29°20'E
Mkwaja, Tan.	237	5°47'S	38°51'E
Mladá Boleslav, Czech Rep. (mlä'dä bô'lĕ-slåf)	168	50°26'N	14°52'E
Mlala Hills, hills, Tan.	237	6°47'S	31°45'E
Mlanje Mountains, mts., Mwi.	237	15°55'S	35°30'E
Mława, Pol. (mwä'vá)	160	53°07'N	20°25'E
Mmabatho, S. Afr.	232	25°42'S	25°43'E
Moa, r., Afr.	234	7°40'N	11°15'W
Moa, Pulau, i., Indon.	213	8°30'S	128°30'E
Moab, Ut., U.S. (mō'ăb)	119	38°35'N	109°35'W
Moanda, Gabon	232	1°37'S	13°09'E
Moar Lake, l., Can. (môr)	97	52°00'N	95°09'W
Moba, D.R.C.	232	7°12'S	29°39'E
Mobaye, C.A.R. (mô-bä'y')	231	4°19'N	21°11'E
Mobayi-Mbongo, D.R.C.	231	4°14'N	21°11'E
Moberly, Mo., U.S. (mō'bēr-lĭ)	105	39°24'N	92°25'W
Mobile, Al., U.S. (mô-bēl')	105	30°42'N	88°03'W
Mobile, r., Al., U.S.	124	31°15'N	88°00'W
Mobile Bay, b., Al., U.S.	107	30°26'N	87°56'W
Mobridge, S.D., U.S. (mō'brĭj)	112	45°32'N	100°26'W
Moca, Dom. Rep. (mô'kä)	135	19°25'N	70°35'W
Moçambique, Moz. (mō-sän-bē'kĕ)	237	15°03'S	40°42'E
Moçâmedes, Ang. (mô-zá-mĕ-dĕs)	232	15°10'S	12°09'E
Moçâmedes, hist. reg., Ang.	232	16°00'S	12°15'E
Mochitlán, Mex. (mō-chē-tlän')	130	17°10'N	99°19'W
Mochudi, Bots. (mō-cho͞o'dē)	232	24°13'S	26°07'E
Mocímboa da Praia, Moz. (mô-sē'ēm-bô-á prä'ēá)	233	11°20'S	40°21'E
Moclips, Wa., U.S.	114	47°14'N	124°13'W
Môco, Serra do, mtn., Ang.	236	12°25'S	15°10'E
Mococa, Braz. (mô-kô'ká)	141a	21°29'S	46°58'W
Moctezuma, Mex. (mŏk'tā-zo͞o'mä)	130	22°44'N	101°06'W
Mocuba, Moz.	237	16°50'S	36°59'E
Modderfontein, S. Afr.	233b	26°06'S	28°10'E
Modena, Italy (mô'dĕ-nä)	162	44°38'N	10°54'E
Modesto, Ca., U.S. (mô-dĕs'tō)	118	37°39'N	121°00'W
Mödling, Aus. (mûd'lĭng)	159e	48°06'N	16°17'E
Moelv, Nor.	166	60°55'N	10°40'E
Moengo, Sur.	143	5°43'N	54°19'W
Moenkopi, Az., U.S.	119	36°07'N	111°13'W
Moers, Ger. (mûrs)	171c	51°27'N	6°38'E
Moffat Tunnel, trans., Co., U.S. (môf'ăt)	120	39°52'N	106°20'W
Mogadishu (Muqdisho), Som.	238a	2°08'N	45°22'E
Mogadore, Oh., U.S. (mŏg-á-dōr')	111d	41°04'N	81°23'E
Mogaung, Mya. (mô-gä'ông)	199	25°30'N	96°52'E
Mogi das Cruzes, Braz. (mô-gē-däs-kro͞o'sĕs)	143	23°33'S	46°10'W
Mogi-Guaçu, r., Braz. (mô-gē-gwá'so͞o)	141a	22°06'S	47°12'W
Mogilno, Pol. (mô-gēl'nô)	168	52°38'N	17°58'E
Mogi-Mirim, Braz. (mô-gē-mē-rē'n)	141a	22°26'S	46°57'W
Mogok, Mya. (mô-gōk')	199	23°14'N	96°38'E
Mogol, r., S. Afr. (mô-gŏl)	238c	24°12'S	27°55'E
Mogollon Plateau, plat., Az., U.S.	106	34°15'N	110°45'W
Mogollon Rim, cliff, Az., U.S. (mō-gō-yōn')	119	34°26'N	111°17'W
Moguer, Spain (mô-gĕr')	172	37°15'N	6°50'W
Mohács, Hung. (mô'häch)	169	45°59'N	18°38'E
Mohale's Hoek, Leso.	233c	30°09'S	27°28'E
Mohall, N.D., U.S. (mō'hôl)	112	48°46'N	101°29'W
Mohave, l., Nv., U.S. (mô-hä'vä)	119	35°23'N	114°40'W
Mohe, China (mwo-hŭ)	205	53°33'N	122°30'E
Mohenjo-Dero, hist., Pak.	199	27°20'N	68°10'E
Mohyliv-Podil's'kyi, Ukr.	181	48°27'N	27°51'E
Mõisaküla, Est. (mē'ē'sá-kü'lä)	167	58°07'N	25°12'E
Moissac, Fr. (mwä-såk')	170	44°07'N	1°05'E
Moita, Port. (mō-ē'tá)	173b	38°39'N	9°00'W
Mojave, Ca., U.S.	118	35°06'N	118°09'W
Mojave, r., Ca., U.S. (mô-hä'vä)	118	34°46'N	117°24'W
Mojave Desert, Ca., U.S.	118	35°05'N	117°30'W
Mojave Desert, des., Ca., U.S.	106	35°00'N	117°00'W
Mokhotlong, Leso.	233c	29°18'S	29°06'E
Mokp'o, Kor., S. (môk'pō')	205	34°50'N	126°30'E
Mol, Bel.	159a	51°21'N	5°09'E
Moldavia *see* Moldova, nation, Eur.	178	48°00'N	28°00'E
Moldavia, hist. reg., Rom.	169	47°20'N	27°12'E
Molde, Nor. (môl'dĕ)	160	62°44'N	7°15'E
Moldova, nation, Eur.	178	48°00'N	28°00'E
Moldova, r., Rom.	169	47°17'N	26°27'E
Moldoveanu, Vârful, mtn., Rom.	175	45°33'N	24°38'E
Molepolole, Bots. (mō-lå-pō-lō'lå)	232	24°15'S	25°33'W
Molfetta, Italy (môl-fĕt'tä)	163	41°11'N	16°38'E
Molina, Chile (mŏ-lē'nä)	141b	35°07'S	71°17'W
Molina de Aragón, Spain (mô-lē'nä dĕ ä-rä-gô'n)	172	40°40'N	1°54'W
Molína de Segura, Spain (mô-lē'nä dĕ sĕ-go͞o'rä)	172	38°03'N	1°07'W
Moline, Il., U.S. (mô-lēn')	121	41°31'N	90°34'W
Moliro, D.R.C.	232	8°13'S	30°34'E
Moliterno, Italy (môl-ē-tĕr'nō)	174	40°13'N	15°54'W
Mollendo, Peru (mô-lyĕn'dō)	142	17°02'S	71°59'W
Moller, Port, Ak., U.S. (pōrt mōl'ēr)	103	56°18'N	161°30'W
Mölndal, Swe. (mûln'däl)	166	57°39'N	12°01'E
Molochna, r., Ukr.	177	47°05'N	35°22'E
Molochnyĭ lyman, l., Ukr.	177	46°35'N	35°32'E
Molody Tud, Russia (mō-lō-dô'ē to͞o'd)	186b	55°17'N	37°31'E
Molokai, i., Hi., U.S. (mō-lô kä'ē)	106c	21°15'N	157°05'E
Molokcha, r., Russia (mô'lôk-chä)	186b	56°15'N	38°29'E
Molopo, r., Afr. (mō-lō-pô)	232	27°45'S	20°45'E
Molson Lake, l., Can. (mōl'sŭn)	97	54°12'N	96°45'W
Molteno, S. Afr. (môl-tā'nô)	233c	31°24'S	26°23'E
Moluccas *see* Maluku, is., Indon.	213	2°22'S	128°25'E
Moma, Moz.	237	16°44'S	39°14'E
Mombasa, Kenya (mōm-bä'sä)	233	4°03'S	39°40'E
Mombetsu, Japan (môm'bĕt-so͞o')	210	44°21'N	142°48'E
Momence, Il., U.S. (mô-mĕns')	111a	41°09'N	87°40'W
Momostenango, Guat. (mô-môs-tā-näŋ'gô)	132	15°02'N	91°25'W
Momotombo, Nic.	132	12°25'N	86°43'W
Mompog Pass, strt., Phil. (mŏm-pŏg')	213a	13°35'N	122°09'E
Mompos, Col. (mōm-pōs')	142	9°05'N	74°30'W
Momtblanc, Spain	173	41°20'N	1°08'E
Møn, i., Den. (mûn)	166	54°54'N	12°30'E
Monaca, Pa., U.S. (mō-ná'kō)	111e	40°41'N	80°17'W
Monaco, nation, Eur. (mŏn'á-kō)	154	43°43'N	7°47'E
Monaghan, Ire. (mŏ'á-găn)	164	54°16'N	7°20'W
Mona Passage, strt., N.A. (mō'nä)	129	18°00'N	68°10'W
Monarch Mountain, mtn., Can. (mŏn'ērk)	94	51°41'N	125°53'W
Monashee Mountains, mts., Can. (mŏ-nă'shē)	95	50°30'N	118°30'W
Monastir *see* Bitola, Mac.	174	41°02'N	21°22'E
Monastir, Tun. (mōn-ás-tēr')	162	35°49'N	10°56'E
Monastyrshchina, Russia (mô-nás-tērsh'chĭ-ná)	176	54°19'N	31°49'E
Monastyryshche, Ukr.	177	48°57'N	29°53'E
Monção, Braz. (mon-soun')	143	3°39'S	45°23'W
Moncayo, mtn., Spain (mōn-kä'yō)	172	41°44'N	1°48'W
Monchegorsk, Russia (mōn'chĕ-gôrsk)	180	69°00'N	33°35'E
Mönchengladbach, Ger. (mûn'kĕn gläd'bäk)	168	51°12'N	6°28'E
Moncique, Serra de, mts., Port. (sĕr'rä dä mōn-chē'kĕ)	172	37°22'N	8°37'W
Monclova, Mex. (mōn-klō'vä)	128	26°53'N	101°25'W
Moncton, Can. (mŭŋk'tŭn)	91	46°06'N	64°47'W
Mondêgo, r., Port. (mōn-dĕ'gō)	172	40°10'N	8°36'W
Mondego, Cabo, c., Port. (ká'bō mōn-dā'gō)	172	40°12'N	8°55'W
Mondombe, D.R.C. (mōn-dôm'bå)	232	0°45'S	23°06'E
Mondoñedo, Spain (mōn-dô-nyā'dō)	172	43°35'N	7°18'W
Mondovi, Wi., U.S. (mŏn-dō'vĭ)	113	44°35'N	91°42'W
Monee, Il., U.S. (mō-nĭ)	111a	41°25'N	87°45'W
Monessen, Pa., U.S. (mō-nĕs'sĕn)	111e	40°09'N	79°53'W
Monett, Mo., U.S. (mō-nĕt')	121	36°55'N	93°55'W
Monfalcone, Italy	174	45°49'N	13°30'E
Monforte de Lemos, Spain (môn-fôr'tä dĕ lĕ'môs)	172	42°30'N	7°30'W
Mongala, r., D.R.C. (mōŋ-gäl'á)	231	3°20'N	21°30'E
Mongalla, Sudan	231	5°11'N	31°46'E
Monghyr, India (mŏn-gēr')	199	25°23'N	86°34'E
Mongo, r., Afr.	234	9°50'N	11°50'W
Mongolia, nation, Asia (mŏŋ-gō'lĭ-á)	204	46°00'N	100°00'E
Mongos, Chaîne des, mts., C.A.R.	231	8°04'N	21°59'E
Mongoumba, C.A.R. (mŏŋ-go͞om'bá)	231	3°38'N	18°36'E
Mongu, Zam. (mŏŋ-go͞o')	232	15°15'S	23°09'E
Monkey Bay, Mwi.	237	14°05'S	34°55'E
Monkey River, Belize (mŭŋ'kĭ)	132a	16°22'N	88°33'W
Monkland, Can. (mŭngk-lănd)	102c	45°12'N	74°52'W
Monkoto, D.R.C. (mōn-kō'tō)	232	1°38'S	20°39'E
Monmouth, Il., U.S. (mŏn'mŭth) (mŏn'mouth)	121	40°54'N	90°38'W
Monmouth Junction, N.J., U.S. (mŏn'mouth jŭngk'shŭn)	110a	40°23'N	74°33'W
Monmouth Mountain, mtn., Can. (mŏn'mŭth)	94	51°00'N	123°47'W
Mono, r., Afr.	234	7°20'N	1°25'E
Mono Lake, l., Ca., U.S. (mō'nō)	118	38°04'N	119°00'W
Monon, In., U.S. (mō'nŏn)	108	40°55'N	86°55'W
Monongah, W.V., U.S. (mô-nŏŋ'gá)	108	39°25'N	80°10'W
Monongahela, Pa., U.S. (mô-nŏn-gá-hē'lá)	111a	40°11'N	79°55'W
Monongahela, r., W.V., U.S.	108	39°30'N	80°10'W
Monopoli, Italy (mô-nô'pô-lē)	175	40°55'N	17°17'E
Monóvar, Spain (mô-nō'vär)	173	38°26'N	0°50'W
Monreale, Italy (mōn-rå-ä'lä)	174	38°04'N	13°15'E
Monroe, Ga., U.S. (mŭn-rō')	124	33°47'N	83°43'W
Monroe, La., U.S.	105	32°30'N	92°06'W
Monroe, Mi., U.S.	108	41°55'N	83°25'W
Monroe, N.C., U.S.	125	34°58'N	80°34'W
Monroe, N.Y., U.S.	110a	41°19'N	74°11'W
Monroe, Ut., U.S.	119	38°35'N	112°10'W
Monroe, Wa., U.S.	116a	47°52'N	121°58'W
Monroe, Wi., U.S.	113	42°35'N	89°40'W
Monroe, Lake, l., Fl., U.S.	125	28°50'N	81°15'W
Monroe City, Mo., U.S.	121	39°38'N	91°41'W
Monroeville, Al., U.S. (mŭn-rō'vĭl)	124	31°33'N	87°19'W
Monroeville, Pa., U.S.	111e	40°26'N	79°46'W
Monrovia, Lib.	230	6°18'N	10°47'W
Monrovia, Ca., U.S. (mŏn-rō'vĭ-á)	117a	34°09'N	118°00'W
Mons, Bel. (môn')	161	50°29'N	3°55'E
Monson, Me., U.S. (mŏn'sŭn)	100	45°17'N	69°28'W
Mönsterås, Swe. (mŭn'stĕr-ōs)	166	57°04'N	16°24'E
Montagne Tremblant Provincial Park, rec., Can.	107	46°30'N	75°51'W
Montague, Can. (mŏn'tá-gū)	101	46°10'N	62°39'W
Montague, Mi., U.S.	108	43°30'N	86°25'W
Montague, i., Ak., U.S.	103	60°10'N	147°00'W
Montalbán, Ven. (mōnt-äl-bän)	143b	10°14'N	68°19'W
Montalegre, Port. (mōn-tä-lā'grĕ)	172	41°49'N	7°48'W
Montana, state, U.S. (mŏn-tăn'á)	104	47°10'N	111°50'W
Montánchez, Spain (mōn-tän'chāth)	172	39°18'N	6°09'W
Montargis, Fr. (môn-tár-zhē')	161	47°59'N	2°42'E
Montataire, Fr. (môn-tá-târ)	171b	49°15'N	2°26'E
Montauban, Fr. (môn-tō-bän')	161	44°01'N	1°22'E
Montauk, N.Y., U.S.	109	41°03'N	71°57'W
Montauk Point, c., N.Y., U.S. (mŏn-tôk')	109	41°05'N	71°55'W
Montbard, Fr. (môn-bár')	170	47°40'N	4°19'E
Montbéliard, Fr. (môn-bā-lyár')	171	47°32'N	6°45'E
Mont Belvieu, Tx., U.S. (mŏnt bĕl'vū)	123a	29°51'N	94°53'W
Montbrison, Fr. (môn-brē-zon')	170	45°38'N	4°06'E
Montceau, Fr. (môn-sō')	170	46°39'N	4°22'E
Montclair, N.J., U.S. (mŏnt-klâr')	110a	40°49'N	74°13'W
Mont-de-Marsan, Fr. (môn-dē-már-sän')	161	43°54'N	0°32'W
Montdidier, Fr. (mōn-dē-dyā')	170	49°42'N	2°33'E
Monte, Arg. (mŏ'n-tĕ)	141c	35°25'S	58°49'W
Monteagudo, Bol. (mōn'tā-ä-go͞o'dhō)	142	19°49'S	63°48'W
Montebello, Can.	102c	45°40'N	74°56'W
Montebello, Ca., U.S. (mŏn-tē-bĕl'ō)	117a	34°01'N	118°06'W
Monte Bello Islands, is., Austl.	220	20°30'S	114°10'E
Monte Caseros, Arg. (mŏ'n-tĕ-kä-sĕ'rôs)	144	30°16'S	57°39'W
Montecillos, Cordillera de, mts., Hond.	132	14°19'N	87°52'W
Monte Cristi, Dom. Rep. (mŏ'n-tĕ-krē's-tē)	135	19°50'N	71°40'W
Montecristo, Isola di, i., Italy (mōn'tā-krēs'tō)	174	42°20'N	10°19'E
Monte Escobedo, Mex. (mōn'tā ĕs-kô-bā'dhō)	130	22°18'N	103°34'W
Monteforte Irpino, Italy (mōn-tĕ-fō'r-tĕ ē'r-pē'nō)	173c	40°39'N	14°42'E
Montefrío, Spain (mōn-tå-frē'ō)	172	37°20'N	4°02'W
Montego Bay, Jam. (mŏn-tē'gō)	129	18°30'N	77°55'W
Montelavar, Port. (mōn-tĕ-lá-vär')	173b	38°51'N	9°20'W
Montélimar, Fr. (môn-tā-lē-mär')	161	44°33'N	4°47'E
Montellano, Spain (mōn-tå-lyä'nō)	172	37°00'N	5°34'W
Montello, Wi., U.S. (mŏn-tĕl'ō)	113	43°47'N	89°20'W
Montemorelos, Mex. (mōn'tå-mō-rā'lōs)	128	25°14'N	99°50'W
Montemor-o-Novo, Port. (mōn-tĕ-mŏr'ò-nô'vò)	172	38°39'N	8°11'W
Montenegro *see* Crna Gora, state, Yugo.	175	42°55'N	18°52'E
Montenegro, reg., Moz.	237	13°07'S	39°00'E
Montepulciano, Italy (mōn'tå-po͞ol-chä'nō)	174	43°05'N	11°48'E
Montereau-faut-Yonne, Fr. (môn-t'rō'fō-yōn')	170	48°24'N	2°57'E
Monterey, Ca., U.S. (mŏn-tĕ-rā')	104	36°36'N	121°53'W
Monterey, Tn., U.S.	124	36°06'N	85°15'W
Monterey Bay, b., Ca., U.S.	106	36°48'N	122°01'W
Monterey Park, Ca., U.S.	117a	34°04'N	118°08'W
Montería, Col. (mōn-tā-rē'ä)	142	8°47'N	75°57'W
Monteros, Arg. (mōn-tĕ'rôs)	144	27°14'S	65°29'W
Monterotondo, Italy (mōn-tĕ-rô-tô'n-dō)	173d	42°03'N	12°39'E

ng-sing; ŋ-baŋk; n-nasalized n; nŏd; cŏmmit; ōld; ôbey; ôrder; oi-boil; fo͞od; ò-as oo in foot; ou-out; s-soft; sh-dish; th-thin; pūre; ûnite; ûrn; stŭd; circŭs; ü-as in French tu; '-indeterminate vowel.

PLACE (Pronunciation)	PAGE	LAT.	LONG.
Monterrey, Mex. (mōn-tĕr-rā′)	128	25°43′N	100°19′W
Montesano, Wa., U.S. (mŏn-tē-sä′nō)	114	46°59′N	123°35′W
Monte Sant'Angelo, Italy (mô′n-tĕ sän ä′n-gzhĕ-lô)	163	41°43′N	15°59′E
Montes Claros, Braz. (môn-tĕs-klä′rôs)	143	16°44′S	43°41′W
Montevallo, Al., U.S. (mŏn-tē-văl′ō)	124	33°05′N	86°49′W
Montevarchi, Italy (mōn-tā-vär′kē)	174	43°30′N	11°45′E
Montevideo, Ur. (mōn′tā-vē-dhā′ō)	144	34°50′S	56°10′W
Montevideo, Mn., U.S. (mŏn′tā-vē-dhā′ō)	112	44°56′N	95°42′W
Monte Vista, Co., U.S. (mŏn′tē vĭs′tȧ)	119	37°35′N	106°10′W
Montezuma, Ga., U.S. (mŏn-tē-zōō′mȧ)	124	32°17′N	84°00′W
Montezuma Castle National Monument, rec., Az., U.S.	119	34°38′N	111°50′W
Montfoort, Neth.	159a	52°02′N	4°56′E
Montfor-l'Amaury, Fr. (mŏn-fōr′lä-mō-rē′)	171b	48°47′N	1°49′E
Montfort, Fr. (mŏn-fōr)	170	48°09′N	1°58′W
Montgomery, Al., U.S. (mŏnt-gŭm′ẽr-ĭ)	105	32°23′N	86°17′W
Montgomery, W.V., U.S.	108	38°10′N	81°25′W
Montgomery City, Mo., U.S.	121	38°58′N	91°29′W
Monticello, Ar., U.S. (mŏn-tĭ-sĕl′ō)	121	33°38′N	91°47′W
Monticello, Fl., U.S.	124	30°32′N	83°53′W
Monticello, Ga., U.S.	124	33°00′N	83°11′W
Monticello, Ia., U.S.	113	42°14′N	91°13′W
Monticello, Il., U.S.	108	40°05′N	88°35′W
Monticello, In., U.S.	108	40°40′N	86°50′W
Monticello, Ky., U.S.	124	36°47′N	84°50′W
Monticello, Me., U.S.	100	46°19′N	67°53′W
Monticello, Mn., U.S.	113	45°18′N	93°48′W
Monticello, N.Y., U.S.	109	41°35′N	74°40′W
Monticello, Ut., U.S.	119	37°55′N	109°25′W
Montijo, Port. (mōn-tē′zhō)	173b	38°42′N	8°58′W
Montijo, Spain (mōn-tē′hō)	172	38°55′N	6°35′W
Montijo, Bahía, b., Pan. (bä-ē′ä mōn-tē′hō)	129	7°36′N	81°11′W
Mont-Joli, Can. (môn zhō-lē′)	91	48°35′N	68°11′W
Montluçon, Fr. (môn-lü-sôn′)	161	46°20′N	2°35′E
Montmagny, Can. (môn-mȧn-yē′)	99	46°59′N	70°33′W
Montmorency, Fr. (môn′mō-rän-sē′)	171b	48°59′N	2°19′E
Montmorency, r., Can. (mŏnt-mō-rĕn′sĭ)	102b	47°03′N	71°10′W
Montmorillon, Fr. (môn′mō-rē-yôn′)	170	46°26′N	0°50′E
Montone, r., Italy (mōn-tō′nĕ)	174	44°03′N	11°45′E
Montoro, Spain (mōn-tō′rō)	172	38°01′N	4°22′W
Montpelier, Id., U.S.	115	42°19′N	111°19′W
Montpelier, In., U.S. (mŏnt-pēl′yẽr)	108	40°35′N	85°20′W
Montpelier, Oh., U.S.	108	41°35′N	84°35′W
Montpelier, Vt., U.S.	105	44°20′N	72°35′W
Montpellier, Fr. (môn-pĕ-lyā′)	161	43°38′N	3°53′E
Montréal, Can. (mŏn-trē-ôl′)	91	45°30′N	73°35′W
Montreal, r., Can.	99	47°50′N	80°30′W
Montreal, r., Can.	98	47°15′N	84°20′W
Montreal Lake, l., Can.	96	54°20′N	105°40′W
Montréal-Nord, Can.	102a	45°36′N	73°38′W
Montreuil, Fr.	171b	48°52′N	2°27′E
Montreux, Switz. (môn-trû′)	168	46°26′N	6°52′E
Montrose, Scot., U.K.	164	56°45′N	2°25′W
Montrose, Ca., U.S. (mŏnt-rōz)	117a	34°13′N	118°13′W
Montrose, Co., U.S. (mŏn-trōz′)	119	38°30′N	107°55′W
Montrose, Oh., U.S.	111d	41°08′N	81°38′W
Montrose, Pa., U.S. (mŏnt-rōz′)	109	41°50′N	75°50′W
Montrouge, Fr.	171b	48°49′N	2°19′E
Mont-Royal, Can.	102a	47°31′N	73°39′W
Monts, Pointe des, c., Can. (pwănt′ dā môn′)	100	49°19′N	67°22′W
Mont Saint Martin, Fr. (môn sân mär-tăn′)	171	49°34′N	6°13′E
Montserrat, dep., N.A. (mŏnt-sĕ-răt′)	129	16°48′N	63°15′W
Montvale, N.J., U.S. (mŏnt-vāl′)	110a	41°02′N	74°01′W
Monywa, Mya. (mŏn′yōō-wȧ)	199	22°02′N	95°16′E
Monza, Italy (mōn′tsä)	174	45°34′N	9°17′E
Monzón, Spain (mōn-thōn′)	173	41°54′N	0°09′E
Moody, Tx., U.S. (mōō′dĭ)	123	31°18′N	97°20′W
Mooi, r., S. Afr. (mōō′ĭ)	238c	26°34′S	27°03′E
Mooi, r., S. Afr.	233c	29°00′S	30°15′E
Mooirivier, S. Afr.	233c	29°14′S	29°59′E
Moolap, Austl.	217a	38°11′S	144°26′E
Moonta, Austl. (mōōn′tȧ)	218	34°05′S	137°42′E
Moora, Austl. (mōr′ȧ)	218	30°35′S	116°12′E
Moorabbin, Austl.	217a	37°56′S	145°02′E
Moore, l., Austl. (mōr)	220	29°50′S	118°12′E
Moorenweis, Ger. (mō′rĕn-vīz)	159d	48°10′N	11°05′E
Moore Reservoir, res., Vt., U.S.	109	44°20′N	72°10′W
Moorestown, N.J., U.S. (morz′toun)	110f	39°58′N	74°56′W
Mooresville, In., U.S. (mōrz′vĭl)	111g	39°37′N	86°22′W
Mooresville, N.C., U.S.	125	35°34′N	80°48′W
Moorhead, Mn., U.S. (mōr′hĕd)	112	46°52′N	96°44′W
Moorhead, Ms., U.S.	124	33°25′N	90°30′W
Moose, r., Can.	93	51°01′N	80°42′W
Moose Creek, Can.	102c	45°16′N	74°58′W
Moosehead, Me., U.S. (mōōs′hĕd)	100	45°37′N	69°15′W
Moose Island, i., Can.	97	51°50′N	97°09′W
Moose Jaw, Can. (mōōs jô)	90	50°23′N	105°32′W
Moose Jaw, r., Can.	96	50°34′N	105°17′W
Moose Lake, Can.	97	53°40′N	100°28′W
Moose Mountain, mtn., Can.	97	49°45′N	102°37′W
Moose Mountain Creek, r., Can.	97	49°12′N	102°10′W
Moosilauke, mtn., N.H., U.S. (mōō-sĭ-lä′kē)	109	44°00′N	71°50′W
Moosinning, Ger. (mō′zē-nēng)	159d	48°17′N	11°51′E
Moosomin, Can. (mōō′sô-mĭn)	97	50°07′N	101°40′W
Moosonee, Can. (mōō′sô-nē)	91	51°20′N	80°44′W
Mopti, Mali (mŏp′tē)	230	14°30′N	4°12′W
Moquegua, Peru (mô-kā′gwä)	142	17°15′S	70°54′W
Mór, Hung. (mōr)	169	47°25′N	18°14′E
Mora, India	203b	18°54′N	72°56′E
Mora, Spain (mō-rä)	172	39°42′N	3°45′W
Mora, Swe. (mō′rä)	166	61°00′N	14°29′E
Mora, Mn., U.S. (mō′rȧ)	113	45°52′N	93°18′W
Mora, N.M., U.S.	120	35°58′N	105°17′W
Morādābād, India (mō-rä-dä-bäd′)	199	28°57′N	78°48′E
Morales, Guat. (mô-rä′lĕs)	132	15°29′N	88°46′W
Moramanga, Madag. (mō-rä-mäŋ′gä)	233	18°48′S	48°09′E
Morant Point, c., Jam. (mō-rănt′)	134	17°55′N	76°10′W
Morata de Tajuña, Spain (mō-rä′tä dā tä-hōō′nyä)	173a	40°14′N	3°27′W
Moratuwa, Sri L.	203	6°35′N	79°59′E
Morava (Moravia), hist. reg., Czech Rep.	168	49°21′N	16°57′E
Morava, r., Eur.	161	49°00′N	17°30′E
Moravia *see* Morava, hist. reg., Czech Rep.	168	49°21′N	16°57′E
Morawhanna, Guy. (mō-rȧ-hwä′nȧ)	143	8°12′N	59°33′W
Moray Firth, b., Scot., U.K. (mŭr′ā)	156	57°41′N	3°55′W
Mörbylånga, Swe. (mûr′bü-lôŋ′gȧ)	166	56°32′N	16°23′E
Morden, Can. (môr′dĕn)	90	49°11′N	98°05′W
Mordialloc, Austl. (môr-dĭ-ăl′ŏk)	217a	38°00′S	145°05′E
Mordvinia, prov., Russia	180	54°18′N	43°50′E
More, Ben, mtn., Scot., U.K. (bĕn môr)	164	58°09′N	5°01′W
Moreau, r., S.D., U.S. (mô-rō′)	112	45°13′N	102°22′W
Moree, Austl. (mō′rē)	219	29°20′S	149°50′E
Morehead, Ky., U.S.	108	38°10′N	83°25′W
Morehead City, N.C., U.S. (mōr′hĕd)	125	34°43′N	76°43′W
Morehouse, Mo., U.S. (mōr′hous)	121	36°49′N	89°41′W
Morelia, Mex. (mô-rā′lyä)	128	19°43′N	101°12′W
Morella, Spain (mô-rāl′yä)	173	40°38′N	0°07′W
Morelos, Mex. (mô-rā′lōs)	130	22°46′N	102°36′W
Morelos, Mex.	131a	19°41′N	99°29′W
Morelos, Mex.	122	28°24′N	100°51′W
Morelos, r., Mex.	122	25°27′N	99°35′W
Morena, Sierra, mtn., Ca., U.S. (syĕr′rä mô-rā′nä)	116b	37°24′N	122°19′W
Morena, Sierra, mts., Spain (syĕr′rä mô-rā′nä)	156	38°15′N	5°45′W
Morenci, Az., U.S. (mō-rĕn′sĭ)	119	33°05′N	109°25′W
Morenci, Mi., U.S.	108	41°50′N	84°50′W
Moreno, Arg. (mō-rĕ′nō)	144a	34°39′S	58°47′W
Moreno, Ca., U.S.	117a	33°55′N	117°09′W
Mores, i., Bah. (mōrz)	134	26°20′N	77°35′W
Moresby, i., Can. (mōrz′bĭ)	116d	48°43′N	123°15′W
Moresby Island, i., Can.	92	52°50′N	131°55′W
Moreton, i., Austl. (môr′tŭn)	222	26°53′S	152°42′E
Moreton Bay, b., Austl. (môr′tŭn)	222	27°12′S	153°10′E
Morewood, Can. (mōr′wŏŏd)	102c	45°11′N	75°17′W
Morgan, Mt., U.S. (môr′găn)	115	48°55′N	107°56′W
Morgan, Ut., U.S.	115	41°04′N	111°42′W
Morgan City, La., U.S.	123	29°41′N	91°11′W
Morganfield, Ky., U.S. (môr′găn-fēld)	108	37°40′N	87°55′W
Morgan's Bay, S. Afr.	233c	32°42′S	28°19′E
Morganton, N.C., U.S. (môr′găn-tŭn)	125	35°44′N	81°42′W
Morgantown, W.V., U.S. (môr′găn-toun)	109	39°40′N	79°55′W
Morga Range, mts., Afg.	199a	34°02′N	70°38′E
Morgenzon, S. Afr. (môr′gănt-sŏn)	238c	26°44′S	29°39′E
Moriac, Austl.	217a	38°15′S	144°20′E
Morice Lake, l., Can.	94	54°00′N	127°37′W
Moriguchi, Japan (mō′rē-gōō′chē)	211b	34°44′N	135°34′E
Morinville, Can. (mō′rĭn-vĭl)	102g	53°48′N	113°39′W
Morioka, Japan (mō′rē-ō′kȧ)	205	39°40′N	141°21′E
Morkoka, r., Russia (môr-kô′kȧ)	185	65°35′N	111°00′E
Morlaix, Fr. (môr-lĕ′)	161	48°36′N	3°48′W
Morley, Can. (mŏr′lē)	102e	51°10′N	114°51′W
Mormant, Fr.	171b	48°35′N	2°54′E
Morne Gimie, St. Luc. (mōrn′ zhē-mē′)	133b	13°53′N	61°03′W
Mornington, Austl.	217a	38°13′S	145°02′E
Morobe, Pap. N. Gui.	213	8°03′S	147°45′E
Morocco, nation, Afr. (mô-rŏk′ō)	230	32°00′N	7°00′W
Morogoro, Tan. (mō-rō-gō′rō)	233	6°49′S	37°40′E
Moroleón, Mex. (mô-rō-lā-ōn′)	130	20°07′N	101°15′W
Morombe, Madag. (mōō-rōōm′bā)	233	21°39′S	43°34′E
Morón, Arg. (mo-rō′n)	141c	34°39′S	58°37′W
Morón, Cuba (mô-rōn′)	134	22°05′N	78°35′W
Morón, Ven. (mô-rō′n)	143b	10°29′N	68°11′W
Morondava, Madag. (mō-rōn-dȧ′vȧ)	233	20°17′S	44°18′E
Morón de la Frontera, Spain (mô-rōn′dā läf rōn-tā′rä)	172	37°08′N	5°20′W
Morongo Indian Reservation, I.R., Ca., U.S. (mō-rôŋ′gō)	118	33°54′N	116°47′W
Moroni, Com.	233	11°41′S	43°16′E
Moroni, Ut., U.S. (mô-rō′nĭ)	119	39°30′N	111°40′W
Morotai, i., Indon. (mō-rô-tä′ē)	213	2°12′N	128°30′E
Moroto, Ug.	237	2°32′N	34°39′E
Morozovsk, Russia	181	48°20′N	41°50′E
Morrill, Ne., U.S. (mŏr′ĭl)	112	41°59′N	103°54′W
Morrilton, Ar., U.S. (mŏr′ĭl-tŭn)	121	35°09′N	92°42′W
Morrinhos, Braz. (mô-rēn′yōzh)	143	17°45′S	48°56′W
Morris, Can. (mŏr′ĭs)	90	49°21′N	97°22′W
Morris, Il., U.S.	108	41°20′N	88°25′W
Morris, Mn., U.S.	112	45°35′N	95°53′W
Morris, r., Can.	97	49°30′N	97°30′W
Morrison, Il., U.S. (mŏr′ĭ-sŭn)	113	41°48′N	89°58′W
Morris Reservoir, res., Ca., U.S.	117a	34°11′N	117°49′W
Morristown, N.J., U.S. (mŏr′ĭs-toun)	110a	40°48′N	74°29′W
Morristown, Tn., U.S.	124	36°10′N	83°18′W
Morrisville, Pa., U.S. (mŏr′ĭs-vĭl)	110f	40°12′N	74°46′W
Morro do Chapéu, Braz. (môr-ō dô-shä-pĕ′ōō)	143	11°34′S	41°03′W
Morrow, Oh., U.S. (mŏr′ō)	111f	39°21′N	84°07′W
Mors, i., Den.	166	56°46′N	8°38′E
Morshansk, Russia (môr-shänsk′)	180	53°25′N	41°35′E
Mortara, Italy (môr-tä′rä)	174	45°13′N	8°47′E
Morteros, Arg. (mŏr-tĕ′tôs)	144	30°47′S	62°00′W
Mortes, Rio das, r., Braz. (rēō-däs-mô′r-tĕs)	141a	21°04′S	44°29′W
Morton Indian Reservation, I.R., Mn., U.S. (mŏr′tŭn)	113	44°35′N	94°48′W
Mortsel, Bel. (môr-sĕl′)	159a	51°10′N	4°28′E
Morvan, mts., Fr. (mōr-vän′)	170	47°11′N	4°10′E
Morzhovets, i., Russia (mōr′zhô-vyĕts′)	180	66°40′N	42°30′E
Mosal'sk, Russia (mō-zálsk′)	176	54°27′N	34°57′E
Moscavide, Port.	173b	38°47′N	9°06′W
Moscow (Moskva), Russia	178	55°45′N	37°37′E
Moscow, Id., U.S. (mŏs′kō)	104	46°44′N	116°57′W
Mosel (Moselle), r., Eur. (mō′sĕl) (mô-zĕl)	168	49°49′N	7°00′E
Moses, r., S. Afr.	238c	25°17′S	29°04′E
Moses Lake, Wa., U.S.	114	47°08′N	119°15′W
Moses Lake, l., Wa., U.S. (mō′zĕz)	114	47°09′N	119°30′W
Moshchnyy, is., Russia (môsh′chnĭ)	167	59°56′N	28°07′E
Moshi, Tan. (mō′shē)	233	3°21′S	37°20′E
Mosjøen, Nor.	160	65°50′N	13°10′E
Moskva *see* Moscow, Russia	178	55°45′N	37°37′E
Moskva, prov., Russia	176	55°38′N	36°48′E
Moskva, r., Russia	180	55°30′N	37°05′E
Mosonmagyaróvár, Hung.	169	47°51′N	17°16′E
Mosquitos, Costa de, cst., Nic. (kŏs-tä-dĕ-mōs-kē′tō)	133	12°05′N	83°49′W
Mosquitos, Gulfo de los, b., Pan. (gōō′l-fō-dĕ-lôs-mōs-kē′tōs)	129	9°17′N	80°59′W
Moss, Nor. (môs)	160	59°29′N	10°39′E
Moss Beach, Ca., U.S. (môs bēch)	116b	37°32′N	122°31′W
Mosselbaai, S. Afr. (mô′sul bā)	232	34°06′S	22°23′E
Mossendjo, Congo	236	2°57′S	12°44′E
Mossley, Eng., U.K. (môs′lĭ)	158a	53°31′N	2°02′W
Moss Point, Ms., U.S. (môs)	124	30°25′N	88°32′W
Most, Czech Rep. (môst)	168	50°32′N	13°37′E
Mostar, Bos. (môs′tär)	163	43°20′N	17°51′E
Móstoles, Spain (mōs-tō′lās)	173a	40°19′N	3°52′W
Mostoos Hills, hills, Can. (mŏs′tōōs)	96	54°50′N	108°45′W
Mosvatnet, l., Nor.	166	59°55′N	7°50′E
Motagua, r., N.A. (mō-tä′gwä)	132	15°29′N	88°39′W
Motala, Swe. (mō-tō′lä)	166	58°34′N	15°00′E
Motherwell, Scot., U.K. (mŭdh′ẽr-wĕl)	160	55°45′N	4°05′W
Motril, Spain (mō-trēl′)	162	36°44′N	3°32′W
Motul, Mex. (mō-tōō′l)	132a	21°07′N	89°14′W
Mouaskar, Alg.	230	35°25′N	0°08′E
Mouchoir Bank, bk. (mōō-shwȧr′)	135	21°35′N	70°40′W
Mouchoir Passage, strt., T./C. Is.	135	21°05′N	71°05′W
Moudjéria, Maur.	234	17°53′N	12°20′W
Mouila, Gabon	236	1°52′S	11°01′E
Mouille Point, c., S. Afr.	232a	33°54′S	18°19′E
Moulins, Fr. (mōō-lăn′)	161	46°34′N	3°19′E
Moulouya, Oued, r., Mor. (mōō-lōō′yȧ)	230	34°00′N	4°00′W
Moultrie, Ga., U.S. (mōl′trĭ)	124	31°10′N	83°48′W
Moultrie, Lake, l., S.C., U.S.	125	33°12′N	80°00′W
Mound City, Il., U.S.	121	37°06′N	89°13′W
Mound City, Mo., U.S.	121	40°08′N	95°13′W
Moundou, Chad	235	8°34′N	16°05′E
Moundsville, W.V., U.S. (moundz′vĭl)	108	39°50′N	80°50′W
Mount, Cape, c., Lib.	234	6°47′N	11°20′W
Mountain Brook, Al., U.S. (moun′tĭn brŏŏk)	110h	33°30′N	86°45′W
Mountain Creek Lake, l., Tx., U.S.	117c	32°43′N	97°03′W
Mountain Grove, Mo., U.S. (grōv)	121	37°07′N	92°16′W
Mountain Home, Id., U.S. (hōm)	114	43°08′N	115°43′W
Mountain Park, Can. (pärk)	90	52°55′N	117°14′W
Mountain View, Ca., U.S. (moun′tĭn vū)	116b	37°25′N	122°07′W
Mountain View, Mo., U.S.	121	36°59′N	91°46′W
Mount Airy, N.C., U.S. (âr′ĭ)	125	36°28′N	80°37′W
Mount Ayliff, S. Afr. (ā′lĭf)	233c	30°48′S	29°24′E
Mount Ayr, Ia., U.S. (âr)	113	40°43′N	94°06′W
Mount Carmel, Il., U.S. (kär′mĕl)	108	38°25′N	87°45′W
Mount Carmel, Pa., U.S.	109	40°50′N	76°25′W
Mount Carooll, Il., U.S.	113	42°05′N	89°55′W
Mount Clemens, Mi., U.S. (klĕm′ĕnz)	111b	42°36′N	82°52′W
Mount Desert, i., Me., U.S. (dē-zûrt′)	100	44°15′N	68°08′W
Mount Dora, Fl., U.S. (dō′rȧ)	125a	28°45′N	81°38′W
Mount Duneed, Austl.	217a	38°15′S	144°20′E
Mount Eliza, Austl.	217a	38°11′S	145°05′E
Mount Fletcher, S. Afr. (flĕ′chẽr)	233c	30°42′S	28°32′E
Mount Forest, Can. (fŏr′ĕst)	99	44°00′N	80°45′W
Mount Frere, S. Afr. (frâr′)	233c	30°54′S	29°02′E
Mount Gambier, Austl. (găm′bēr)	218	37°30′S	140°53′E
Mount Gilead, Oh., U.S. (gĭl′ēăd)	108	40°30′N	82°50′W
Mount Healthy, Oh., U.S. (hĕlth′ē)	111f	39°14′N	84°32′W
Mount Holly, N.J., U.S. (hŏl′ĭ)	110f	39°59′N	74°47′W
Mount Hope, Can.	102d	43°09′N	79°55′W
Mount Hope, N.J., U.S. (hōp)	110a	40°55′N	74°32′W
Mount Hope, W.V., U.S.	108	37°55′N	81°10′W
Mount Isa, Austl. (ī′zȧ)	218	21°00′S	139°45′E
Mount Kisco, N.Y., U.S. (kĭs′kō)	110a	41°12′N	73°44′W
Mountlake Terrace, Wa., U.S. (mount lāk tĕr′ĭs)	116a	47°48′N	122°19′W
Mount Lebanon, Pa., U.S. (lĕb′ȧ-nŭn)	111e	40°22′N	80°03′W
Mount Magnet, Austl. (măg-nĕt)	218	28°00′S	118°00′E
Mount Martha, Austl.	217a	38°17′S	145°01′E
Mount Morgan, Austl. (môr-găn)	219	23°42′S	150°45′E

PRONOUNCING INDEX

Mount Moriac – Nabberu 325

PLACE (Pronunciation)	PAGE	LAT.	LONG.
Mount Moriac, Austl.	217a	38°13'S	144°12'E
Mount Morris, Mi., U.S. (mŏr'ĭs)	108	43°10'N	83°45'W
Mount Morris, N.Y., U.S.	109	42°45'N	77°50'W
Mount Nimba National Park, rec., C. Iv.	234	7°35'N	8°10'W
Mount Olive, N.C., U.S. (ŏl'ĭv)	125	35°11'N	78°05'W
Mount Peale, Ut., U.S.	119	38°26'N	109°16'W
Mount Pleasant, Ia., U.S. (plĕz'ănt)	113	40°59'N	91°34'W
Mount Pleasant, Mi., U.S.	108	43°35'N	84°45'W
Mount Pleasant, S.C., U.S.	125	32°46'N	79°51'W
Mount Pleasant, Tn., U.S.	124	35°31'N	87°12'W
Mount Pleasant, Tx., U.S.	123	33°10'N	94°56'W
Mount Pleasant, Ut., U.S.	119	39°35'N	111°20'W
Mount Prospect, Il., U.S. (prŏs'pĕkt)	111a	42°03'N	87°56'W
Mount Rainier National Park, rec., Wa., U.S. (rå-nēr')	106	46°47'N	121°17'W
Mount Revelstoke National Park, rec., Can. (rĕv'ĕl-stōk)	90	51°22'N	120°15'W
Mount Savage, Md., U.S. (săv'āj)	109	39°45'N	78°55'W
Mount Shasta, Ca., U.S. (shăs'tȧ)	114	41°18'N	122°17'W
Mount Sterling, Il., U.S. (stûr'lĭng)	121	39°59'N	90°44'W
Mount Sterling, Ky., U.S.	108	38°05'N	84°00'W
Mount Stewart, Can. (stū'ărt)	101	46°22'N	62°52'W
Mount Union, Pa., U.S. (ūn'yŭn)	109	40°25'N	77°50'W
Mount Vernon, Il., U.S. (vûr'nŭn)	108	38°20'N	88°50'W
Mount Vernon, In., U.S.	108	37°55'N	87°50'W
Mount Vernon, Mo., U.S.	121	37°09'N	93°48'W
Mount Vernon, N.Y., U.S.	110a	40°55'N	73°51'W
Mount Vernon, Oh., U.S.	108	40°25'N	82°30'W
Mount Vernon, Va., U.S.	110e	38°43'N	77°06'W
Mount Vernon, Wa., U.S.	114	48°25'N	122°20'W
Moura, Braz. (mō'rȧ)	143	1°33'S	61°38'W
Moura, Port.	172	38°08'N	7°28'W
Mourne Mountains, mts., N. Ire., U.K. (môrn)	164	54°10'N	6°09'W
Moussoro, Chad	235	13°39'N	16°29'E
Moûtiers, Fr. (mo͞o-tyâr')	171	45°31'N	6°34'E
Mowbullan, Mount, mtn., Austl.	222	26°50'S	151°34'E
Moyahua, Mex. (mô-yä'wä)	130	21°16'N	103°10'W
Moyale, Kenya (mô-yä'lä)	231	3°28'N	39°04'E
Moyamba, S.L. (mô-yäm'bä)	230	8°10'N	12°26'W
Moyen Atlas, mts., Mor.	162	32°49'N	5°28'W
Moyeuvre-Grande, Fr.	171	49°15'N	6°26'E
Moyie, r., Id., U.S. (moi'yê)	114	38°50'N	116°10'W
Moyobamba, Peru (mō-yô-bäm'bä)	142	6°12'S	76°56'W
Moyuta, Guat. (mô-ē-o͞o'tä)	132	14°01'N	90°05'W
Moyyero, r., Russia	184	67°15'N	104°10'E
Moyynqum, des., Kaz.	183	44°30'N	70°00'E
Mozambique, nation, Afr. (mō-zăm-bēk')	232	20°15'S	33°53'E
Mozambique Channel, strt., Afr. (mō-zăm-bek')	233	24°00'S	38°00'E
Mozdok, Russia (môz-dôk')	181	43°45'N	44°35'E
Mozhaysk, Russia (mô-zhäysk')	176	55°31'N	36°02'E
Mozhayskiy, Russia (mô-zháy'skĭ)	186c	59°42'N	30°08'E
Mpanda, Tan.	237	6°22'S	31°02'E
Mpika, Zam.	237	11°54'S	31°26'E
Mpimbe, Mwi.	237	15°18'S	35°04'E
Mporokoso, Zam. ('m-pō-rô-kō'sō)	232	9°23'S	30°05'E
Mpwapwa, Tan. ('m-pwä'pwä)	232	6°21'S	36°29'E
Mqanduli, S. Afr. ('m-kän'do͞o-lê)	233c	31°50'S	28°42'E
Mrągowo, Pol. (mrăŋ'gô-vô)	169	53°52'N	21°18'E
M'Sila, Alg. (m'sē'lȧ)	230	35°47'N	4°34'E
Msta, r., Russia (m'stá')	180	58°30'N	33°00'E
Mstsislaw, Bela.	176	54°01'N	31°42'E
Mtakataka, Mwi.	237	14°12'S	34°32'E
Mtamvuna, r., Afr.	233c	30°43'S	29°53'E
Mtata, r., S. Afr.	233c	31°48'S	29°03'E
Mtsensk, Russia (m'tsĕnsk)	180	53°17'N	36°33'E
Mtwara, Tan.	237	10°16'S	40°11'E
Muar, r., Malay.	197b	2°18'N	102°43'E
Mubende, Ug.	237	0°35'N	31°23'E
Mubi, Nig.	235	10°18'N	13°20'E
Mucacata, Moz.	237	13°20'S	39°59'E
Much, Ger. (mo͝ok)	171c	50°54'N	7°24'E
Muchinga Mountains, mts., Zam.	237	12°40'S	30°50'E
Much Wenlock, Eng., U.K. (mŭch wĕn'lŏk)	158a	52°35'N	2°33'W
Muckalee Creek, r., Ga., U.S. (mŭk'ă lē)	124	31°55'N	84°10'W
Muckleshoot Indian Reservation, I.R., Wa., U.S. (mŭck''l-sho͞ot)	116a	47°21'N	122°04'W
Mucubela, Moz.	237	16°55'S	37°52'E
Mud, l., Mi., U.S. (mŭd)	113	46°12'N	84°32'W
Mudan, r., China (mo͞o-dän)	208	45°30'N	129°40'E
Mudanjiang, China (mo͞o-dän-jyäŋ)	208	44°28'N	129°38'E
Muddy, r., Nv., U.S. (mŭd'ĭ)	119	36°56'N	114°42'W
Muddy Boggy Creek, r., Ok., U.S. (mud'ĭ bôg'ĭ)	121	34°42'N	96°11'W
Muddy Creek, r., Ut., U.S. (mŭd'ĭ)	119	38°45'N	111°10'W
Mudgee, Austl. (mŭ-jē)	222	32°47'S	149°10'E
Mudjatik, r., Can.	96	56°23'N	107°40'W
Mufulira, Zam.	237	12°33'S	28°14'E
Muğla, Tur. (mo͞og'lä)	198	37°10'N	28°20'E
Mühldorf, Ger. (mül-dôrf)	168	48°15'N	12°33'E
Mühlhausen, Ger. (mül'hou-zĕn)	168	51°13'N	10°25'E
Muhu, i., Est. (mo͞o'ho͞o)	167	58°41'N	22°55'E
Muir Woods National Monument, rec., Ca., U.S. (mūr)	118	37°54'N	123°22'W
Muizenberg, S. Afr. (mwĭz-ĕn-bûrg')	232a	34°07'S	18°28'E
Mukacheve, Ukr.	169	48°25'N	22°43'E
Mukden *see* Shenyang, China	204	41°45'N	123°22'E
Mukhtuya, Russia (mòk-to͞o'yȧ)	179	61°00'N	113°00'E
Mukilteo, Wa., U.S. (mū-kĭl-tā'ō)	116a	47°57'N	122°18'W
Muko, Japan (mo͞o'kô)	211b	34°57'N	135°43'E
Muko, r., Japan (mo͞o'kô)	211b	34°52'N	135°17'E
Mukutawa, r., Can.	97	53°10'N	97°28'W
Mukwonago, Wi., U.S. (mū-kwō-nȧ'gō)	111a	42°52'N	88°19'W
Mula, Spain (mo͞o'lä)	172	38°05'N	1°12'W
Mula, Al., U.S. (mŭl'gȧ)	110h	33°33'N	86°59'W
Mulde, r., Ger. (mòl'dĕ)	168	50°30'N	12°30'E
Muleros, Mex. (mo͞o-lā'rōs)	130	23°44'N	104°00'W
Muleshoe, Tx., U.S.	120	34°13'N	102°43'W
Mulgrave, Can. (mŭl'grāv)	101	45°37'N	61°23'W
Mulhacén, mtn., Spain	162	37°04'N	3°18'W
Mülheim, Ger. (mül'hīm)	171c	51°25'N	6°53'E
Mulhouse, Fr. (mü-lo͞oz')	161	47°46'N	7°20'E
Muling, China (mo͞o-lĭŋ)	208	44°32'N	130°18'E
Muling, r., China	208	44°40'N	130°30'E
Mull, Island of, i., Scot., U.K. (mŭl)	164	56°40'N	6°19'W
Mullan, Id., U.S. (mŭl'ăn)	114	47°26'N	115°50'W
Müller, Pegunungan, mts., Indon. (mül'ĕr)	212	0°22'N	113°05'E
Mullingar, Ire. (mŭl-ĭn-gär)	164	53°31'N	7°26'W
Mullins, S.C., U.S. (mŭl'ĭnz)	125	34°11'N	79°13'W
Mullins River, Belize	132a	17°08'N	88°18'W
Multān, Pak. (mò-tän')	199	30°17'N	71°13'E
Multnomah Channel, strt., Or., U.S. (mŭl nō mȧ)	116c	45°41'N	122°53'W
Mulumbe, Monts, mts., D.R.C.	237	8°47'S	27°20'E
Mulvane, Ks., U.S. (mŭl-vān')	121	37°30'N	97°13'W
Mumbai (Bombay), India	199	18°58'N	72°50'E
Mumbwa, Zam. (mòm'bwä)	232	14°59'S	27°04'E
Mumias, Kenya	237	0°20'N	34°29'E
Muna, Mex. (mo͞o'nȧ)	132a	20°28'N	89°42'W
München *see* Munich, Ger.	154	48°08'N	11°35'E
Muncie, In., U.S. (mŭn'sĭ)	105	40°10'N	85°30'W
Mundelein, Il., U.S. (mŭn-dê-lĭn')	111a	42°16'N	88°00'W
Mundonueva, Pico de, mtn., Col. (pē'kô-dĕ-mo͞o'n-dô-nwĕ'vä)	142a	4°18'N	74°12'W
Muneco, Cerro, mtn., Mex. (sĕ'r-rô-mo͞o-nĕ'kō)	131a	19°13'N	99°20'W
Mungana, Austl. (mŭn-găn'ȧ)	219	17°15'S	144°18'E
Mungbere, D.R.C.	237	2°38'N	28°30'E
Munger, Mn., U.S. (mŭn'gẽr)	117h	46°48'N	92°20'W
Mungindi, Austl. (mŭn-gĭn'dē)	219	29°00'S	148°45'E
Munhall, Pa., U.S. (mŭn'hôl)	111e	40°24'N	79°53'W
Munhango, Ang. (mòn-hän'gȧ)	232	12°15'S	18°55'E
Munich, Ger.	154	48°08'N	11°35'E
Munising, Mi., U.S. (mū'nĭ-sĭng)	113	46°24'N	86°41'W
Muniz Freire, Braz.	141a	20°29'S	41°25'W
Munku Sardyk, mtn., Asia (mòn'kò sär-dĭk')	179	51°45'N	100°30'E
Muñoz, Phil. (mo͞on-nyōth')	213a	15°44'N	120°53'E
Münster, Ger. (mün'stĕr)	161	51°57'N	7°38'E
Munster, In., U.S. (mŭn'stẽr)	111a	41°34'N	87°31'W
Munster, hist. reg., Ire. (mŭn-stẽr)	164	52°30'N	9°24'W
Muntok, Indon. (mòn-tŏk')	212	2°05'S	105°11'E
Muong Sing, Laos (mo͞o'ông-sĭng')	212	21°06'N	101°17'E
Muping, China (mo͞o-pĭŋ)	206	37°23'N	121°36'E
Muqui, Braz. (mo͞o-kòê)	141a	20°56'S	41°20'W
Mur, r., Eur. (mo͞or)	161	47°00'N	15°00'E
Muradiye, Tur. (mo͞o-rä'dê-yĕ)	181	39°00'N	43°40'E
Murat, Fr. (mü-rä')	170	45°05'N	2°56'E
Murat, r., Tur. (mo͞o-rát')	198	39°00'N	42°00'E
Murchison, r., Austl. (mûr'chĭ-sŭn)	220	26°45'S	116°15'E
Murcia, Spain (mo͞or'thyä)	154	38°00'N	1°10'W
Murcia, hist. reg., Spain	172	38°35'N	1°51'W
Murdo, S.D., U.S. (mûr'dô)	112	43°53'N	100°42'W
Mureş, r., Rom. (mo͞o'rĕsh)	163	46°02'N	21°50'E
Muret, Fr. (mü-rĕ')	170	43°28'N	1°17'E
Murfreesboro, Tn., U.S. (mûr'frēz-bŭr-ô)	124	35°50'N	86°19'W
Murgab, Taj.	183	38°10'N	73°59'E
Murgab, r., Asia (mo͞or-gäb')	198	37°07'N	62°32'E
Muriaé, r., Braz.	141a	21°20'S	41°40'W
Murino, Russia (mo͞o'rĭ-nô)	186c	60°03'N	30°28'E
Müritz, l., Ger. (mür'its)	168	53°20'N	12°33'E
Murmansk, Russia (mo͞or-mänsk')	178	69°00'N	33°20'E
Murom, Russia (mo͞o'rôm)	178	55°30'N	42°00'E
Muroran, Japan (mo͞o'rô-rán)	205	42°21'N	141°05'E
Muros, Spain (mo͞o'rōs)	172	42°48'N	9°00'W
Muroto-Zaki, c., Japan (mo͞o'rô-tō zä'kê)	210	33°14'N	134°12'E
Murphy, Mo., U.S. (mŭr'fĭ)	117e	38°29'N	90°29'W
Murphy, N.C., U.S.	124	35°05'N	84°00'W
Murphysboro, Il., U.S. (mŭr'fĭz-bŭr-ô)	121	37°46'N	89°21'W
Murray, Ky., U.S. (mŭr'ĭ)	124	36°39'N	88°17'W
Murray, Ut., U.S.	117b	40°40'N	111°53'W
Murray, r., Austl.	220	34°20'S	140°00'E
Murray, r., Can.	95	55°00'N	121°00'W
Murray, Lake, res., S.C., U.S. (mŭr'ĭ)	125	34°07'N	81°18'W
Murray Bridge, Austl.	218	35°10'S	139°35'E
Murray Harbour, Can.	101	46°00'N	62°31'W
Murray Region, reg., Austl. (mŭ'rē)	221	33°20'S	142°30'E
Murrumbidgee, r., Austl. (mŭr-ŭm-bĭd'jē)	221	34°30'S	145°20'E
Murrupula, Moz.	237	15°27'S	38°47'E
Murshidābād, India (mòr'shê-dä-bäd')	202	24°08'N	88°11'E
Murska Sobota, Slvn. (mo͞or'skä sô'bô-tä)	174	46°40'N	16°14'E
Muruasigar, mtn., Kenya	237	3°08'N	35°02'E
Murwāra, India	199	23°54'N	80°23'E
Murwillumbah, Austl. (mŭr-wĭl'lŭm-bŭ)	222	28°15'S	153°30'E
Mürz, r., Aus. (mürts)	168	47°30'N	15°21'E
Mürzzuschlag, Aus. (mürts'tso͞o-shlägh)	168	47°37'N	15°41'E
Mus, Tur. (mo͞osh)	181	38°55'N	41°30'E
Musala, mtn., Blg.	175	42°05'N	23°24'E
Musan, Kor., N. (mò'sän)	205	41°11'N	129°10'E
Musashino, Japan (mo͞o-sä'shē-nō)	211a	35°43'N	139°35'E
Muscat, Oman (mŭs-kăt')	198	23°23'N	58°30'E
Muscat and Oman *see* Oman, nation, Asia	198	20°00'N	57°45'E
Muscatine, Ia., U.S. (mŭs-kȧ-tēn)	113	41°26'N	91°00'W
Muscle Shoals, Al., U.S. (mŭs''l shōlz)	124	34°44'N	87°38'W
Musgrave Ranges, mts., Austl. (mŭs'grāv)	220	26°15'S	131°15'E
Mushie, D.R.C. (mŭsh'ê)	232	3°04'S	16°50'E
Mushin, Nig.	235	6°32'N	3°22'E
Musi, r., Indon. (mo͞o'sê)	212	2°40'S	103°42'E
Musinga, Alto, mtn., Col. (ä'l-tô-mo͞o-sĕ'n-gä)	142a	6°40'N	76°13'W
Muskego Lake, l., Wi., U.S. (mŭs-kē'gō)	111a	42°53'N	88°10'W
Muskegon, Mi., U.S. (mŭs-kē'gŭn)	105	43°15'N	86°20'W
Muskegon, r., Mi., U.S.	108	43°20'N	85°55'W
Muskegon Heights, Mi., U.S.	108	43°10'N	86°20'W
Muskingum, r., Oh., U.S. (mŭs-kĭŋ'gŭm)	108	39°45'N	81°55'W
Muskogee, Ok., U.S. (mŭs-kō'gê)	105	35°44'N	95°21'W
Muskoka, l., Can. (mŭs-kō'kȧ)	99	45°00'N	79°30'W
Musoma, Tan.	237	1°30'S	33°48'E
Mussau Island, i., Pap. N. Gui. (mo͞o-sä'o͞o)	213	1°30'S	149°32'E
Musselshell, r., Mt., U.S. (mŭs''l-shĕl)	115	46°25'N	108°20'W
Mussende, Ang.	236	10°32'S	16°05'E
Mussuma, Ang.	236	14°14'S	21°59'E
Mustafakemalpaşa, Tur.	163	40°05'N	28°30'E
Mustang Bayou, Tx., U.S.	123a	29°22'N	95°12'W
Mustang Creek, r., Tx., U.S. (mŭs'tăng)	120	36°22'N	102°46'W
Mustang Island, i., Tx., U.S.	123	27°43'N	97°00'W
Mustique, i., St. Vin. (mŭs-tēk')	133b	12°53'N	61°03'W
Mustvee, Est. (mo͞ost'vĕ-ĕ)	167	58°50'N	26°54'E
Musu Dan, c., Kor., N. (mò'sò dán)	205	40°51'N	130°00'E
Muswellbrook, Austl. (mŭs'wŭnl-bròk)	222	32°15'S	150°50'E
Mutare, Zimb.	232	18°49'S	32°39'E
Mutombo Mukulu, D.R.C. (mo͞o-tôm'bō mo͞o-ko͞o'lo͞o)	232	8°12'S	23°56'E
Mutsu Wan, b., Japan (mo͞ot'so͞o wän)	210	41°20'N	140°55'E
Mutton Bay, Can. (mŭt''n)	101	50°48'N	59°02'W
Mutum, Braz. (mo͞o-to͞o'm)	141a	19°48'S	41°24'W
Muzaffargarh, Pak.	202	30°09'N	71°15'E
Muzaffarpur, India	202	26°13'N	85°20'E
Muzon, Cape, c., Ak., U.S.	94	54°41'N	132°44'W
Múzquiz, Mex. (mo͞oz'kēz)	122	27°53'N	101°31'W
Muztagata, mtn., China	204	38°20'N	75°28'E
Mvomero, Tan.	237	6°20'S	37°25'E
Mvoti, r., S. Afr.	233c	29°18'S	30°52'E
Mwali, i., Com.	233	12°15'S	43°45'E
Mwanza, Tan. (mwän'zä)	232	2°31'S	32°54'E
Mwaya, Tan. (mwä'yä)	232	9°19'S	33°51'E
Mwenga, D.R.C.	237	3°02'S	28°26'E
Mweru, l., Afr.	232	8°50'S	28°50'E
Mwingi, Kenya	237	0°56'S	38°04'E
Myanmar (Burma), nation, Asia	194	21°00'N	95°15'E
Myingyan, Mya. (myĭng-yŭn')	199	21°37'N	95°26'E
Myitkyina, Mya. (myĭ'chē-nȧ)	199	25°33'N	97°25'E
Myjava, Slvk. (mû'yȧ-vä)	169	48°45'N	17°33'E
Mykhailivka, Ukr.	177	47°16'N	35°12'E
Mykolaïv, Ukr.	178	46°58'N	32°02'E
Mykolaïv, prov., Ukr.	177	47°27'N	31°25'E
Mýkonos, i., Grc.	175	37°26'N	25°30'E
Mymensingh, Bngl.	199	24°48'N	90°28'E
Mynämäki, Fin.	167	60°41'N	21°58'E
Myohyang San, mtn., Kor., N. (myō'hyang)	210	40°00'N	126°12'E
Mýrdalsjökull, ice, Ice. (mür'däls-yû'kòl)	160	63°34'N	18°04'W
Myrhorod, Ukr.	181	49°56'N	33°36'E
Mýrina, Grc.	175	39°52'N	25°01'E
Myrtle Beach, S.C., U.S. (mûr't'l)	125	33°42'N	78°53'W
Myrtle Point, Or., U.S.	114	43°04'N	124°08'W
Mysen, Nor.	166	59°32'N	11°16'E
Myshikino, Russia (mêsh'kê-nô)	176	57°48'N	38°21'E
Mysore, India (mī-sōr')	199	12°31'N	76°42'E
Mysovka, Russia (mê' sôf-kȧ)	167	55°11'N	21°17'E
Mystic, Ia., U.S. (mĭs'tĭk)	113	40°47'N	92°54'W
Mytilíni, Grc.	163	39°09'N	26°35'E
Mytishchi, Russia (mê-tēsh'chi)	186b	55°55'N	37°46'E
Mziha, Tan.	237	5°54'S	37°47'E
Mzimba, Mwi. ('m-zĭm'bä)	232	11°52'S	33°34'E
Mzimkulu, r., Afr.	233c	30°12'S	29°57'E
Mzimvubu, r., S. Afr.	233c	31°22'S	29°20'E
Mzuzu, Mwi.	237	11°30'S	34°10'E

N

PLACE (Pronunciation)	PAGE	LAT.	LONG.
Naab, r., Ger. (näp)	168	49°38'N	12°15'E
Naaldwijk, Neth.	159a	52°00'N	4°11'E
Nā'ālehu, Hi., U.S.	126a	19°00'N	155°35'W
Naantali, Fin. (nän'tȧ-lê)	167	60°29'N	22°03'E
Nabberu, l., Austl. (năb'ẽr-o͞o)	220	26°05'S	120°35'E

ng-sing; ŋ-baŋk; ɴ-nasalized n; nŏd; cŏmmit; ōld; ōbey; ôrder; oi-boil; fo͞od; ò-as oo in foot; ou-out; s-soft; sh-dish; th-thin; pūre; ûnite; ûrn; stŭd; circŭs; ü-as in French tu; '-indeterminate vowel.

326 Naberezhnyye Chelny – Nduye PRONOUNCING INDEX

PLACE (Pronunciation)	PAGE	LAT.	LONG.
Naberezhnyye Chelny, Russia	178	55°42'N	52°19'E
Nabeul, Tun. (nā-bûl')	230	36°34'N	10°45'E
Nabiswera, Ug.	237	1°28'N	32°16'E
Naboomspruit, S. Afr.	238c	24°32'S	28°43'E
Nābulus, W.B.	197a	32°13'N	35°16'E
Nacala, Moz. (nä-kä'lä)	233	14°34'S	40°41'E
Nacaome, Hond. (nä-kä-ō'mā)	132	13°32'N	87°28'W
Na Cham, Viet. (nä chäm')	209	22°02'N	106°30'E
Naches, r., Wa., U.S. (năch'ĕz)	114	46°51'N	121°03'W
Náchod, Czech Rep. (näk'ôt)	168	50°25'N	16°08'E
Nacimiento, Lake, res., Ca., U.S. (nå-sĭ-myĕn'tō)	118	35°50'N	121°00'W
Nacogdoches, Tx., U.S. (năk'ō-dō'chĕz)	123	31°36'N	94°40'W
Nadadores, Mex. (nä-dä-dō'räs)	122	27°04'N	101°36'W
Nadiād, India	202	22°45'N	72°51'E
Nadir, V.I.U.S.	129c	18°19'N	64°53'W
Nădlac, Rom.	175	46°09'N	20°52'E
Nadvirna, Ukr.	169	48°37'N	24°35'E
Nadym, r., Russia (nå'dĭm)	184	64°30'N	72°48'E
Naestved, Den. (nĕst'vĭdh)	160	55°14'N	11°46'E
Nafada, Nig.	235	11°08'N	11°20'E
Nafishah, Egypt	238d	30°34'N	32°15'E
Náfplio, Grc.	175	37°33'N	22°46'E
Nafūd ad Daḩy, des., Sau. Ar.	198	22°15'N	44°15'E
Nag, Co, l., China	202	31°38'N	91°18'E
Naga, Phil. (nä'gä)	213	13°37'N	123°12'E
Naga, i., Japan	211	32°09'N	130°16'E
Nagahama, Japan (nä'gä-hä'mä)	211	33°32'N	132°29'E
Nagahama, Japan	211	35°23'N	136°16'E
Nagaland, India	199	25°47'N	94°15'E
Nagano, Japan (nä'gä-nō)	205	36°42'N	138°12'E
Nagaoka, Japan (nä'gå-ō'kå)	205	37°22'N	138°49'E
Nagaoka, Japan	211b	34°54'N	135°42'E
Nāgappattinam, India	199	10°48'N	79°51'E
Nagarote, Nic. (nä-gä-rō'tĕ)	132	12°17'N	86°35'W
Nagasaki, Japan (nä'gå-sä'kē)	205	32°48'N	129°53'E
Nāgaur, India	202	27°19'N	73°41'E
Nagaybakskiy, Russia (nå-gày-bäk'skĭ)	186a	53°33'N	59°33'E
Nagcarlan, Phil. (näg-kär-län')	213a	14°07'N	121°24'E
Nāgercoil, India	203	8°15'N	77°29'E
Nagorno Karabakh, hist. reg., Azer. (nu-gôr'nŭ-kŭ-rŭ-bäk')	181	40°10'N	46°50'E
Nagoya, Japan	205	35°09'N	136°53'E
Nāgpur, India (näg'pōōr)	199	21°12'N	79°09'E
Nagua, Dom. Rep. (nå'gwä)	135	19°20'N	69°40'W
Nagykanizsa, Hung. (nôd'y'kô'nē-shô)	163	46°27'N	17°00'E
Nagykőrös, Hung. (nôd'y'kŭ-rūsh)	169	47°02'N	19°46'E
Naha, Japan (nä'hä)	205	26°02'N	127°43'E
Nahanni National Park, rec., Can.	92	62°10'N	125°15'W
Nahant, Ma., U.S. (nå-hănt)	101a	42°26'N	70°55'W
Nahariyya, Isr.	197a	33°01'N	35°06'E
Nahuel Huapi, l., Arg. (nä'wĭl wä'pē)	144	41°00'S	71°30'W
Nahuizalco, El Sal. (nä-wē-zäl'kō)	132	13°50'N	89°43'W
Naic, Phil. (nä-ēk)	213a	14°20'N	120°46'E
Naica, Mex. (nä-ē'kä)	122	27°53'N	105°30'W
Naiguata, Pico, mtn., Ven. (pē'kō)	143b	10°32'N	66°44'W
Nain, Can. (nīn)	91	56°29'N	61°52'W
Nā'īn, Iran	201	32°52'N	53°05'E
Nairn, Scot., U.K. (nârn)	164	57°35'N	3°54'W
Nairobi, Kenya (nī-rō'bē)	232	1°17'S	36°49'E
Naivasha, Kenya (nī-vä'shȧ)	232	0°47'S	36°29'E
Najd, hist. reg., Sau. Ar.	198	25°18'N	42°38'E
Najin, Kor., N. (nä'jĭn)	205	42°04'N	130°35'E
Najran, des., Sau. Ar. (nŭj-rän')	198	17°29'N	45°30'E
Naju, Kor., S. (nä'jōō')	210	35°02'N	126°42'E
Najusa, r., Cuba (nä-hōō'sä)	134	20°55'N	77°55'W
Nakatsu, Japan (nä'käts-ōō)	210	33°34'N	131°10'E
Nakhodka, Russia (nŭ-κôt'kŭ)	179	43°03'N	133°08'E
Nakhon Ratchasima, Thai.	212	14°56'N	102°14'E
Nakhon Sawan, Thai.	212	15°42'N	100°06'E
Nakhon Si Thammarat, Thai.	212	8°27'N	99°58'E
Nakło nad Notecia, Pol.	169	53°10'N	17°35'E
Nakskov, Den. (näk'skou)	160	54°51'N	11°06'E
Naktong, r., Kor., S. (näk'tŭng)	210	36°10'N	128°30'E
Nal'chik, Russia (nål-chēk')	181	43°30'N	43°35'E
Nalón, r., Spain (nä-lōn')	172	43°15'N	5°38'W
Nālūt, Libya (nä-lōōt')	230	31°51'N	10°49'E
Namak, Daryacheh-ye, l., Iran	198	34°58'N	51°33'E
Namakan, l., Mn., U.S. (nă'mȧ-kăn)	113	48°20'N	92°43'W
Namangan, Uzb. (nå-mån-gän')	183	41°08'N	71°59'E
Namao, Can.	102g	53°43'N	113°30'W
Namatanai, Pap. N. Gui. (nä'mä-tå-nä'ē)	213	3°43'S	152°26'E
Nambour, Austl. (năm'bŏŏr)	222	26°48'S	153°00'E
Nam Co, l., China (näm tswo)	204	30°30'N	91°10'E
Nam Dinh, Viet. (näm dĕnκ')	212	20°30'N	106°10'E
Nametil, Moz.	237	15°43'S	39°21'E
Namhae, i., Kor., S. (näm'hī')	210	34°23'N	128°05'E
Namib Desert, des., Nmb. (nä-mēb')	232	18°45'S	12°45'E
Namibia, nation, Afr.	232	19°30'S	16°13'E
Namoi, r., Austl. (nămoi)	221	30°10'S	148°43'E
Namous, Oued en, r., Alg. (nå-mōōs')	162	31°48'N	0°19'W
Nampa, Id., U.S. (năm'pȧ)	104	43°35'N	116°35'W
Namp'o, Kor., N.	205	38°47'N	125°28'E
Nampuecha, Moz.	237	13°59'S	40°18'E
Nampula, Moz.	237	15°07'S	39°15'E
Namsos, Nor. (näm'sōs)	160	64°28'N	11°14'E
Namu, Can.	94	51°53'N	127°50'W
Namuli, Serra, mts., Moz.	237	15°05'S	37°05'E
Namur, Bel. (nå-mür')	161	50°29'N	4°55'E
Namutoni, Nmb. (nå-mōō-tō'nē)	232	18°45'S	17°00'E
Nan, r., Thai.	212	18°11'N	100°29'E
Nanacamilpa, Mex. (nä-nä-kä-mē'l-pä)	131a	19°30'N	98°33'W
Nanaimo, Can. (nȧ-nī'mō)	90	49°10'N	123°56'W
Nanam, Kor., N. (nä'nän')	210	41°38'N	129°37'E
Nanao, Japan (nä'nä-ō)	210	37°03'N	136°59'E
Nan'ao Dao, i., China (nän-ou dou)	209	23°30'N	117°30'E
Nanchang, China (nän'chäng')	205	28°38'N	115°48'E
Nanchangshan Dao, i., China (nän-chäŋ-shän dou)	206	37°56'N	120°42'E
Nancheng, China (nän-chäŋ)	205	26°50'N	116°40'E
Nanchong, China (nän-chôŋ)	204	30°45'N	106°05'E
Nancy, Fr. (näɴ-sē')	161	48°42'N	6°11'E
Nancy Creek, r., Ga., U.S. (năn'cē)	110c	33°51'N	84°25'W
Nanda Devi, mtn., India (nän'dä dā'vē)	199	30°30'N	80°25'E
Nānded, India	202	19°13'N	77°21'E
Nandurbār, India	202	21°29'N	74°13'E
Nandyāl, India	203	15°54'N	78°09'E
Nanga Parbat, mtn., Pak.	202	35°20'N	74°35'E
Nangi, India	202a	22°30'N	88°14'E
Nangis, Fr. (näɴ-zhē')	171b	48°33'N	3°01'E
Nangong, China (nän-gôŋ)	208	37°22'N	115°22'E
Nangweshi, Zam.	236	16°26'S	23°17'E
Nanhuangcheng Dao, i., China (nän-hûäŋ-chŭŋ dou)	206	38°22'N	120°54'E
Nanhui, China	206	31°03'N	121°45'E
Nanjing, China (nän-jyĭŋ)	205	32°04'N	118°46'E
Nanjuma, r., China (nän-jyōō-mä)	206	39°37'N	115°45'E
Nanking *see* Nanjing, China	204	32°04'N	118°46'E
Nanle, China (nän-lŭ)	206	36°03'N	115°13'E
Nan Ling, mts., China	205	25°15'N	111°40'E
Nanliu, r., China (nän-lĭō)	209	22°00'N	109°18'E
Nannine, Austl. (nă-nēn')	218	25°50'S	118°30'E
Nanning, China (nän'nĭng')	204	22°56'N	108°10'E
Nanpan, r., China (nän-pän)	209	24°50'N	105°30'E
Nanping, China (nän-pĭŋ)	205	26°40'N	118°05'E
Nansei-shotō, is., Japan	205	27°30'N	127°00'E
Nansemond, Va., U.S. (năn'sē-mŭnd)	110g	36°46'N	76°32'W
Nantai Zan, mtn., Japan (nän-täē zän)	210	36°47'N	139°28'E
Nantes, Fr. (näɴt')	154	47°13'N	1°37'W
Nanteuil-le-Haudouin, Fr. (näɴ-tû-lē-ō-dwăɴ')	171b	49°08'N	2°49'E
Nanticoke, Pa., U.S. (năn'tĭ-kōk)	109	41°10'N	76°00'W
Nantong, China (nän-tôŋ)	206	32°02'N	120°51'E
Nantong, China	206	32°08'N	121°06'E
Nantucket, i., Ma., U.S. (năn-tŭk'ĕt)	107	41°15'N	70°05'W
Nantwich, Eng., U.K. (nănt'wĭch)	158a	53°04'N	2°31'W
Nanxiang, China (nän-shyäŋ)	206	31°17'N	121°17'E
Nanxiong, China (nän-shôŋ)	209	25°10'N	114°20'E
Nanyang, China	205	33°00'N	112°42'E
Nanyang Hu, l., China (nän-yäŋ hōō)	206	35°14'N	116°24'E
Nanyuan, China (nän-yůän)	208a	39°48'N	116°24'E
Naolinco, Mex. (nä-ō-lēŋ'kō)	131	19°39'N	96°50'W
Náousa, Grc. (nä'ōō-sä)	175	40°38'N	22°05'E
Naozhou Dao, i., China (nou-jō dou)	209	20°58'N	110°58'E
Napa, Ca., U.S. (năp'ȧ)	104	38°20'N	122°17'W
Napanee, Can. (năp'ȧ-nē)	99	44°15'N	77°00'W
Naperville, Il., U.S. (nā'pēr-vĭl)	111a	41°46'N	88°09'W
Napier, N.Z. (nā'pĭ-ēr)	221a	39°30'S	177°00'E
Napierville, Can. (nā'pĭ-ē-vĭl)	102a	45°11'N	73°24'W
Naples (Napoli), Italy	154	40°37'N	14°12'E
Naples, Fl., U.S. (nā'p'lz)	125a	26°07'N	81°46'W
Napo, r., S.A. (nä'pō)	142	1°49'S	74°20'W
Napoleon, Oh., U.S. (nȧ-pō'lē-ŭn)	108	41°20'N	84°10'W
Napoleonville, La., U.S. (nȧ-pō'lē-ŭn-vĭl)	123	29°56'N	91°03'W
Napoli *see* Naples, Italy	154	40°37'N	14°12'E
Napoli, Golfo di, b., Italy	162	40°29'N	14°08'E
Nappanee, In., U.S. (năp'ȧ-nē)	108	41°30'N	86°00'W
Nara, Japan (nä'rä)	205	34°41'N	135°50'E
Nara, Mali	230	15°09'N	7°27'W
Nara, dept., Japan	211b	34°36'N	135°49'E
Nara, r., Russia	176	55°05'N	37°16'E
Narach, Vozyera, l., Bela.	176	54°51'N	27°00'E
Naracoorte, Austl. (nå-rå-kōōn'tē)	218	36°50'S	140°50'E
Narashino, Japan	211a	35°41'N	140°01'E
Naraspur, India	203	16°32'N	81°43'E
Narberth, Pa., U.S. (när'bûrth)	110f	40°01'N	75°17'W
Narbonne, Fr. (når-bôn')	161	43°12'N	3°00'E
Nare, Col. (nä'rē)	142a	6°12'N	74°37'W
Narew, r., Pol. (när'ĕf)	169	52°43'N	21°19'E
Narmada, r., India	199	22°30'N	75°30'E
Narodnaya, Gora, mtn., Russia (nå-rôd'nå-yå)	178	65°10'N	60°10'E
Naro-Fominsk, Russia (nä'rō-mēnsk')	180	55°23'N	36°43'E
Narrabeen, Austl. (năr-ȧ-bĭn)	217b	33°44'S	151°18'E
Narragansett, R.I., U.S. (năr-ȧ-găn'sĕt)	110b	41°26'N	71°27'W
Narragansett Bay, b., R.I., U.S.	109	41°20'N	71°15'W
Narrandera, Austl. (nå-rån-dē'rå)	219	34°40'S	146°40'E
Narrogin, Austl. (năr'ō-gĭn)	218	33°00'S	117°15'E
Narva, Est. (når'vå)	180	59°24'N	28°12'E
Narvacan, Phil. (när-vä-kän')	213a	17°27'N	120°29'E
Narva Jõesuu, Est. (når'vå ô-ô-ā'sōō-ô)	167	59°26'N	28°02'E
Narvik, Nor. (när'vĕk)	154	68°21'N	17°18'E
Narvskiy Zaliv, b., Eur. (når'vskĭ zä'lĭf)	167	59°35'N	27°25'E
Narvskoye, res., Eur.	167	59°18'N	28°14'E
Nar'yan-Mar, Russia (när'yan mär')	178	67°42'N	53°30'E
Naryilco, Austl. (năr-ĭl'kō)	222	28°40'S	141°50'E
Narym, Russia (nä-rēm')	178	58°47'N	82°05'E
Naryn, r., Asia (nŭ-rĭn')	184	41°20'N	76°00'E
Naseby, Eng., U.K. (nāz'bĭ)	158a	52°23'N	0°59'W
Nashua, Mo., U.S. (năsh'ŭ-ȧ)	117f	39°18'N	94°34'W
Nashua, N.H., U.S.	105	42°47'N	71°23'W
Nashville, Ar., U.S. (năsh'vĭl)	121	33°56'N	93°50'W
Nashville, Ga., U.S.	124	31°12'N	83°15'W
Nashville, Il., U.S.	121	38°21'N	89°42'W
Nashville, Mi., U.S.	108	42°35'N	85°50'W
Nashville, Tn., U.S.	105	36°10'N	86°48'W
Nashwauk, Mn., U.S. (năsh'wôk)	113	47°21'N	93°12'W
Näsi, l., Fin.	160	61°42'N	24°05'E
Našice, Cro. (nä'shē-tsĕ)	163	45°29'N	18°06'E
Nasielsk, Pol. (nä'syĕlsk)	169	52°35'N	20°50'E
Nāsik, India (nä'sĭk)	199	20°02'N	73°49'E
Nāşir, Sudan (nä-zēr')	231	8°30'N	33°06'E
Nasirabād, India	202	26°13'N	74°48'E
Naskaupi, r., Can. (năs'kô-pĭ)	93	53°59'N	61°10'W
Nasondoye, D.R.C.	237	10°22'S	25°06'E
Nass, r., Can. (năs)	94	55°00'N	129°30'W
Nassau, Bah. (năs'ô)	129	25°05'N	77°20'W
Nassenheide, Ger. (nä'sĕn-hī-dĕ)	159b	52°49'N	13°13'E
Nasser, Lake, res., Egypt	231	23°50'N	32°50'E
Nasugbu, Phil. (nȧ-sŏg-bōō')	213a	14°05'N	120°37'E
Nasworthy Lake, l., Tx., U.S. (năz'wûr-thē)	122	31°17'N	100°30'W
Natagaima, Col. (nä-tä-gī'mä)	142a	3°38'N	75°07'W
Natal, Braz. (nä-täl')	143	6°00'S	35°13'W
Natashquan, Can. (nä-täsh'kwän)	91	50°11'N	61°49'W
Natashquan, r., Can.	101	50°35'N	61°35'W
Natchez, Ms., U.S. (năch'ĕz)	105	31°35'N	91°20'W
Natchitoches, La., U.S. (năk'ĭ-tŏsh) (nách-ĭ-tŏsh')	123	31°46'N	93°06'W
Natick, Ma., U.S. (nā'tĭk)	101a	42°17'N	71°21'W
National Bison Range, I.R., Mt., U.S. (năsh'ŭn-ăl bī's'n)	115	47°18'N	113°58'W
National City, Ca., U.S.	118a	32°38'N	117°01'W
Natitingou, Benin	230	10°19'N	1°22'E
Natividade, Braz. (nä-tē-vē-dä'dĕ)	143	11°43'S	47°34'W
Natron, Lake, l., Tan. (nā'trŏn)	232	2°17'S	36°10'E
Natrona Heights, Pa., U.S. (nā'trō nă)	111e	40°38'N	79°43'W
Naţrūn, Wādī an, val., Egypt	238b	30°33'N	30°12'E
Natuna Besar, is., Indon.	212	4°00'N	106°50'E
Natural Bridges National Monument, rec., Ut., U.S. (năt'ū-răl brĭj'ĕs)	119	37°20'N	110°20'W
Naturaliste, Cape, c., Austl. (năt-ů-rȧ-lĭst')	220	33°30'S	115°10'E
Nau, Cap de la, c., Spain	156	38°43'N	0°14'E
Naucalpan de Juárez, Mex.	131a	19°28'N	99°14'W
Nauchampatepetl, mtn., Mex. (näōō-chäm-pä-tĕ'pĕtl)	131	19°32'N	97°09'W
Nauen, Ger. (nou'ĕn)	159b	52°36'N	12°53'E
Naugatuck, Ct., U.S. (nô'gȧ-tŭk)	109	41°25'N	73°05'W
Naujan, Phil. (nä-ō-hän')	213a	13°19'N	121°17'E
Naumburg, Ger. (noum'bŏŏrgh)	168	51°10'N	11°50'E
Nauru, nation, Oc.	3	0°30'S	167°00'E
Nautla, Mex. (nä-ōōt'lä)	128	20°14'N	96°44'W
Nava, Mex. (nä'vä)	122	28°25'N	100°44'W
Nava del Rey, Spain (nä-vä dĕl rā'ē)	172	41°22'N	5°04'W
Navahermosa, Spain (nä-vä-ĕr-mō'sä)	172	39°39'N	4°28'W
Navajas, Cuba (nä-vä-häs')	134	22°40'N	81°20'W
Navajo Hopi Joint Use Area, I.R., Az., U.S.	119	36°15'N	110°30'W
Navajo Indian Reservation, I.R., U.S. (năv'ȧ-hō)	119	36°31'N	109°24'W
Navajo National Monument, rec., Az., U.S.	119	36°43'N	110°39'W
Navajo Reservoir, res., N.M., U.S.	119	36°57'N	107°26'W
Navalcarnero, Spain (nä-väl'kär-nä'rō)	173a	40°17'N	4°05'W
Navalmoral de la Mata, Spain	172	39°53'N	5°32'W
Navan, Can. (nă'vån)	102c	45°25'N	75°26'W
Navarino, l., Chile (nä-vä-rē'nō)	144	55°30'S	68°15'W
Navarra, hist. reg., Spain (nä-vär'rä)	172	42°40'N	1°35'W
Navarro, Arg. (nä-vå'r-rō)	141c	35°00'S	59°16'W
Navasota, Tx., U.S. (năv-ȧ-sō'tȧ)	123	30°24'N	96°05'W
Navasota, r., Tx., U.S.	123	31°03'N	96°11'W
Navassa, i., N.A. (nȧ-văs'ȧ)	135	18°25'N	75°15'W
Navia, r., Spain (nä-vē'ä)	172	43°10'N	6°45'W
Navidad, Chile (nä-vē-dä'd)	141b	33°57'S	71°51'W
Navidad Bank, bk. (nä-vē-dädh')	135	20°05'N	69°00'W
Navidade do Carangola, Braz. (nå-vē-dä'dô-kå-rän-gô'la)	141a	21°04'S	41°58'W
Navojoa, Mex. (nä-vô-kō'ä)	128	27°00'N	109°40'W
Nawābshāh, Pak. (nȧ-wäb'shä)	202	26°20'N	68°30'E
Naxçıvan, Azer.	181	39°10'N	45°30'E
Naxçıvan Muxtar, state, Azer.	182	39°20'N	45°30'E
Náxos, i., Grc. (nák'sôs)	163	37°15'N	25°20'E
Nayarit, state, Mex. (nä-yä-rēt')	128	22°00'N	105°15'W
Nayarit, Sierra de, mts., Mex. (sē-ĕ'r-rä-dĕ)	130	23°20'N	105°07'W
Naye, Sen.	234	14°25'N	12°12'W
Naylor, Md., U.S. (nā'lōr)	110e	38°43'N	76°46'W
Nazaré da Mata, Braz. (dä-mä-tä)	143	7°46'S	35°13'W
Nazas, Mex. (nä'zäs)	122	25°14'N	104°08'W
Nazas, r., Mex.	128	25°30'N	104°40'W
Nazerat, Isr.	197a	32°43'N	35°19'E
Nazilli, Tur. (nä-zĭ-lē')	181	37°40'N	28°10'E
Naziya, r., Russia (nå-zē'yå)	186c	59°48'N	31°18'E
Nazko, r., Can.	94	52°35'N	123°10'W
N'dalatando, Ang.	236	9°18'S	14°54'E
Ndali, Benin	235	9°51'N	2°43'E
Ndikiniméki, Cam.	235	4°46'N	10°50'E
N'Djamena, Chad	231	12°07'N	15°03'E
Ndola, Zam. (n'dō'lä)	232	12°58'S	28°38'E
Ndoto Mountains, mts., Kenya	237	1°55'N	37°05'E
Ndrhamcha, Sebkha de, l., Maur.	234	18°50'N	15°15'W
Nduye, D.R.C.	237	1°50'N	29°01'E

PRONOUNCING INDEX

Neagh – New Providence 327

PLACE (Pronunciation)	PAGE	LAT.	LONG.
Neagh, Lough, l., N. Ire., U.K. (lŏk nā)	160	54°40'N	6°47'W
Néa Páfos, Cyp.	197a	34°46'N	32°27'E
Neapean, r., Austl.	217b	33°40'S	150°39'E
Neápoli, Grc.	175	36°35'N	23°08'E
Neápolis, Grc.	174a	35°17'N	25°37'E
Near Islands, is., Ak., U.S. (nēr)	103a	52°20'N	172°40'E
Neath, Wales, U.K. (nēth)	164	51°41'N	3°50'W
Nebine Creek, r., Austl. (nĕ-bēne')	222	27°50'S	147°00'E
Nebitdag, Turkmen.	183	39°30'N	54°20'E
Nebraska, state, U.S. (nē-brăs'kȧ)	104	41°45'N	101°30'W
Nebraska City, Ne., U.S.	121	40°40'N	95°50'W
Nechako, r., Can.	94	53°45'N	124°55'W
Nechako Plateau, plat., Can. (nĭ-chă'kō)	94	54°00'N	124°30'W
Nechako Range, mts., Can.	94	53°20'N	124°30'W
Nechako Reservoir, res., Can.	94	53°25'N	125°10'W
Neches, r., Tx., U.S. (nĕch'ĕz)	123	31°03'N	94°40'W
Neckar, r., Ger. (nĕk'är)	168	49°16'N	9°06'E
Necker Island, i., Hi., U.S.	126b	24°00'N	164°00'W
Necochea, Arg. (nā-kô-chā'ä)	144	38°30'S	58°45'W
Nedryhailiv, Ukr.	177	50°49'N	33°52'E
Needham, Ma., U.S. (nēd'ăm)	101a	42°17'N	71°14'W
Needles, Ca., U.S. (nē'd'lz)	119	34°51'N	114°39'W
Neenah, Wi., U.S. (nē'nȧ)	113	44°10'N	88°30'W
Neepawa, Can.	90	50°13'N	99°29'W
Nee Reservoir, res., Co., U.S. (nee)	120	38°26'N	102°56'W
Negareyama, Japan (nā'gä-rȧ-yä'mä)	211a	35°52'N	139°54'E
Negaunee, Mi., U.S. (nē-gô'nē)	113	46°30'N	87°37'W
Negeri Sembilan, state, Malay. (nā'grē-sĕm-bē-län')	197b	2°46'N	101°54'E
Negev, des., Isr. (nĕ'gĕv)	197a	30°34'N	34°43'E
Negombo, Sri L.	203	7°39'N	79°49'E
Negotin, Yugo. (nĕ'gô-tēn)	175	44°13'N	22°33'E
Negro, r., Arg.	144	39°50'S	65°00'W
Negro, r., N.A.	132	13°01'N	87°10'W
Negro, r., S.A.	141c	33°17'S	58°18'W
Negro, r., S.A. (nā'grō)	142	0°18'S	63°21'W
Negro, Cerro, mtn., Pan. (sĕ'-rrō-nā'grō)	133	8°44'N	80°37'W
Negros, i., Phil. (nā'grōs)	212	9°50'N	121°45'E
Nehalem, r., Or., U.S. (nē-hăl'ĕm)	114	45°52'N	123°37'W
Nehaus an der Oste, Ger. (noi'houz) (ōz'tĕ)	159c	53°48'N	9°02'E
Nehbandān, Iran	201	31°32'N	60°02'E
Nehe, China (nŭ-hŭ)	208	48°23'N	124°58'E
Neheim-Hüsten, Ger. (nĕ'hīm)	171c	51°28'N	7°58'E
Neiba, Dom. Rep. (nå-ē'bä)	135	18°30'N	71°20'W
Neiba, Bahía de, b., Dom. Rep.	135	18°10'N	71°00'W
Neiba, Sierra de, mts., Dom. Rep. (sē-ĕr'rä-dĕ)	135	18°40'N	71°40'W
Neihart, Mt., U.S. (nī'hărt)	115	46°54'N	110°39'W
Neijiang, China (nā-jyäŋ)	209	29°38'N	105°01'E
Neillsville, Wi., U.S. (nēlz'vĭl)	113	44°35'N	90°37'W
Nei Monggol (Inner Mongolia), state, China	204	40°15'N	105°00'E
Neiqiu, China (nā-chyō)	206	37°17'N	114°32'E
Neira, Col. (nā'rä)	142a	5°10'N	75°32'W
Neisse, r., Eur. (nēs)	168	51°30'N	15°00'E
Neiva, Col. (nå-ē'vä)(nā'vä)	142	2°55'N	75°16'W
Neixiang, China (nā-shyäŋ)	208	33°00'N	111°38'E
Nekemte, Eth.	231	9°09'N	36°29'E
Nekoosa, Wi., U.S. (nē-kōō'sȧ)	113	44°19'N	89°54'W
Neligh, Ne., U.S. (nē'-lē)	112	42°06'N	98°02'W
Nel'kan, Russia (nĕl-kän')	179	57°45'N	136°36'E
Nellore, India (nĕl-lōr')	199	14°28'N	79°59'E
Nel'ma, Russia (nĕl-mä')	210	47°34'N	139°05'E
Nelson, Can. (nĕl'sŭn)	90	49°29'N	117°17'W
Nelson, N.Z.	221a	41°15'S	173°22'E
Nelson, Eng., U.K.	158a	53°50'N	2°13'W
Nelson, i., Ak., U.S.	103	60°38'N	164°42'W
Nelson, r., Can.	97	56°50'N	93°40'W
Nelson, Cape, c., Austl.	222	38°29'S	141°20'E
Nelsonville, Oh., U.S. (nĕl'sŭn-vĭl)	108	39°30'N	82°15'W
Néma, Maur. (nā'mä)	230	16°37'N	7°15'W
Nemadji, r., Wi., U.S. (nĕ-măd'jē)	117h	46°33'N	92°16'W
Neman, Russia (ŋĕ'-män)	167	55°02'N	22°01'E
Neman, r., Eur.	180	53°28'N	24°45'E
Nembe, Nig.	235	4°35'N	6°26'E
Nemeiben Lake, l., Can. (nĕ-mē'bȧn)	96	55°20'N	105°20'W
Nemours, Fr.	170	48°16'N	2°41'E
Nemuro, Japan (nā'mô-rō)	205	43°13'N	145°10'E
Nemuro Strait, strt., Asia	210	43°07'N	145°10'E
Nemyriv, Ukr.	177	48°56'N	28°51'E
Nen, r., China (nŭn)	205	47°07'N	123°28'E
Nen, r., Eng., U.K. (nĕn)	158a	52°32'N	0°19'W
Nenagh, Ire. (nē'nȧ)	164	52°50'N	8°05'W
Nenana, Ak., U.S. (nå-nä'nȧ)	103	64°28'N	149°18'W
Nenikyul', Russia (nĕ-nyē'kyûl)	186c	59°26'N	30°40'E
Nenjiang, China (nŭn-jyäŋ)	205	49°02'N	125°15'E
Neodesha, Ks., U.S. (nē-ô-dĕ-shô')	121	37°24'N	95°41'W
Neosho, Mo., U.S.	121	36°51'N	94°22'W
Neosho, r., Ks., U.S. (nē-ō'shō)	121	38°07'N	95°40'W
Nepal, nation, Asia (nĕ-pôl')	199	28°45'N	83°00'E
Nephi, Ut., U.S. (nē'fī)	119	39°40'N	111°50'W
Nepomuceno, Braz. (nĕ-pô-mōō-sĕ'no)	141a	21°15'S	45°13'W
Nera, r., Italy (nā'rä)	174	42°45'N	12°54'E
Nérac, Fr. (nā-rák')	170	44°08'N	0°19'E
Nerchinsk, Russia (nyĕr' chĕnsk)	179	51°47'N	116°17'E
Nerchinskiy Khrebet, mts., Russia	179	50°30'N	118°30'E
Nerchinskiy Zavod, Russia (nyĕr'chĕn-skĭzȧ-vôt')	179	51°35'N	119°46'E
Nerekhta, Russia (nyĕ-rĕk'tȧ)	176	57°29'N	40°34'E
Neretva, r., Yugo. (nĕ'rĕt-vȧ)	175	43°08'N	17°50'E
Nerja, Spain (nĕr'hä)	172	36°45'N	3°53'W
Nerl', r., Russia (nyĕrl)	176	56°59'N	37°57'E
Nerskaya, r., Russia (nyĕr'skȧ-yȧ)	186b	55°31'N	38°46'E
Nerussa, r., Russia (nyå-rōō'sȧ)	176	52°24'N	34°20'E
Ness, Loch, l., Scot., U.K. (lŏĸ nĕs)	164	57°23'N	4°20'W
Ness City, Ks., U.S. (nĕs)	120	38°27'N	99°55'W
Nesterov, Russia (nyĕs-tă'rôf)	167	54°39'N	22°38'E
Néstos (Mesta), r., Eur. (nās'tōs)	175	41°25'N	24°12'E
Netanya, Isr.	197a	32°19'N	34°52'E
Netcong, N.J., U.S. (nĕt'cŏnj)	110a	40°54'N	74°42'W
Netherlands, nation, Eur. (nĕdh'ĕr-lăndz)	154	53°01'N	3°57'E
Netherlands Guiana see Suriname, nation, S.A.	143	4°00'N	56°00'W
Nettilling, l., Can.	93	66°30'N	70°40'W
Nett Lake Indian Reservation, I.R., Mn., U.S. (nĕt lăk)	113	48°23'N	93°19'W
Nettuno, Italy (nĕt-tōō'nô)	173d	41°28'N	12°40'E
Neubeckum, Ger. (noi'bĕ-kōōm)	171c	51°48'N	8°01'E
Neubrandenburg, Ger. (noi-brän'dĕn-bòrgh)	168	53°33'N	13°16'E
Neuburg, Ger. (noi'bòrgh)	168	48°43'N	11°12'E
Neuchâtel, Switz. (nû-shȧ-tĕl')	161	47°00'N	6°52'E
Neuchâtel, Lac de, l., Switz.	168	46°48'N	6°53'E
Neuenhagen, Ger. (noi'ĕn-hä-gĕn)	159b	52°31'N	13°41'E
Neuenrade, Ger. (noi'ĕn-rä-dĕ)	171c	51°17'N	7°47'E
Neufchâtel-en-Bray, Fr. (nû-shä-tĕl'ĕɴ-brā')	170	49°43'N	1°25'E
Neulengbach, Aus.	159e	48°13'N	15°55'E
Neumarkt, Ger. (noi'märkt)	168	49°17'N	11°30'E
Neumünster, Ger. (noi'münstĕr)	160	54°04'N	10°00'E
Neunkirchen, Aus. (noin'kĭrĸ-ĕn)	168	47°43'N	16°05'E
Neuquén, Arg. (nĕ-ô-kān')	144	38°52'S	68°12'W
Neuquén, prov., Arg.	144	39°40'S	70°45'W
Neuquén, r., Arg.	144	38°45'S	69°00'W
Neuruppin, Ger. (noi'rōō-pēn)	168	52°55'N	12°48'E
Neuse, r., N.C., U.S. (nūz)	125	36°12'N	78°50'W
Neusiedler See, l., Eur. (noi-zēd'lĕr)	168	47°54'N	16°31'E
Neuss, Ger. (nois)	171c	51°12'N	6°41'E
Neustadt, Ger. (noi'shtät)	168	49°21'N	8°08'E
Neustadt bei Coburg, Ger. (bī kō'bōōrgh)	168	50°20'N	11°09'E
Neustadt in Holstein, Ger.	168	54°06'N	10°50'E
Neustrelitz, Ger. (noi-strā'lĭts)	168	53°21'N	13°05'E
Neutral Hills, hills, Can. (nū'trăl)	96	52°10'N	110°50'W
Neu Ulm, Ger. (noi ò lm')	168	48°23'N	10°01'E
Neuville, Can. (nū'vĭl)	102b	46°39'N	71°35'W
Neuwied, Ger. (noi'vēdt)	168	50°26'N	7°28'E
Neva, r., Russia (nyĕ-vä')	176	59°49'N	30°54'E
Nevada, Ia., U.S. (nē-vä'dȧ)	113	42°01'N	93°27'W
Nevada, Mo., U.S.	121	37°49'N	94°21'W
Nevada, state, U.S. (nĕ vä'dȧ)	104	39°30'N	117°00'W
Nevada, Sierra, mts., Spain (syĕr'rä nā-vä'dhä)	156	37°01'N	3°28'W
Nevada, Sierra, mts., U.S. (sē-ĕ'r-rä nĕ-vă'dȧ)	106	39°20'N	120°05'W
Nevado, Cerro el, mtn., Col. (sĕ'r-rô-ĕl-nĕ-vä'dô)	142a	4°02'N	74°08'W
Neva Stantsiya, Russia (nyĕ-vä' stän'tsĭ-yȧ)	186c	59°53'N	30°30'E
Neve, Serra da, mts., Ang.	236	13°40'S	13°20'E
Nevel', Russia (nyĕ'vĕl)	180	56°03'N	29°57'E
Neveri, r., Ven. (nĕ-vĕ-rē)	143b	10°13'N	64°18'W
Nevers, Fr. (nĕ-vår')	161	46°59'N	3°10'E
Neves, Braz.	144b	22°51'S	43°06'W
Nevesinje, Bos. (nĕ-vĕ'sēn-yĕ)	175	43°15'N	18°08'E
Nevinnomyssk, Russia	182	44°38'N	41°56'E
Nevis, i., St. K./N. (nē'vĭs)	129	17°05'N	62°38'W
Nevis, Ben, mtn., Scot., U.K. (bĕn)	160	56°47'N	5°00'W
Nevis Peak, mtn., St. K./N.	133b	17°11'N	62°33'W
Nevşehir, Tur. (nĕv-shĕ'hĕr)	163	38°40'N	34°35'E
Nev'yansk, Russia (nĕv-yänsk')	178	57°29'N	60°14'E
New, r., Va., U.S. (nū)	125	37°20'N	80°35'W
Newala, Tan.	237	10°56'S	39°18'E
New Albany, In., U.S. (nû ôl'bȧ-nĭ)	111h	38°17'N	85°49'W
New Albany, Ms., U.S.	125	34°28'N	39°00'W
New Amsterdam, Guy. (ăm'stĕr-dăm)	143	6°14'N	57°30'W
Newark, Eng., U.K. (nū'ẽrk)	158a	53°04'N	0°49'W
Newark, Ca., U.S. (nū'ẽrk)	116b	37°32'N	122°02'W
Newark, De., U.S. (nōō'ärk)	109	39°40'N	75°45'W
Newark, N.J., U.S. (nōō'ûrk)	105	40°44'N	74°10'W
Newark, N.Y., U.S. (nū'ẽrk)	109	43°05'N	77°10'W
Newark, Oh., U.S.	108	40°05'N	82°25'W
Newaygo, Mi., U.S. (nū'wā-go)	108	43°25'N	85°50'W
New Bedford, Ma., U.S. (bĕd'fẽrd)	105	41°35'N	70°55'W
Newberg, Or., U.S. (nū'bûrg)	108	45°17'N	122°58'W
New Bern, N.C., U.S. (bûrn)	105	35°05'N	77°05'W
Newbern, Tn., U.S.	124	36°05'N	89°12'W
Newberry, Mi., U.S. (nū'bĕr-ĭ)	113	46°22'N	85°31'W
Newberry, S.C., U.S.	125	34°15'N	81°40'W
New Boston, Mi., U.S. (bôs'tŭn)	111b	42°10'N	83°24'W
New Boston, Oh., U.S.	108	38°45'N	82°55'W
New Braunfels, Tx., U.S. (nū broun'fĕls)	122	29°43'N	98°07'W
New Brighton, Mn., U.S. (brī'tŭn)	117g	45°04'N	93°12'W
New Brighton, Pa., U.S.	111e	40°34'N	80°18'W
New Britain, Ct., U.S. (brĭt''n)	109	41°40'N	72°45'W
New Britain, i., Pap. N. Gui.	213	6°45'S	149°38'E
New Brunswick, N.J., U.S. (brŭnz'wĭk)	110a	40°29'N	74°27'W
New Brunswick, prov., Can.	91	47°14'N	66°30'W
Newburg, In., U.S.	108	38°00'N	87°25'W
Newburg, Mo., U.S.	121	37°54'N	91°53'W
Newburgh, N.Y., U.S.	109	41°30'N	74°00'W
Newburgh Heights, Oh., U.S.	111d	41°27'N	81°40'W
Newbury, Eng., U.K. (nū'bĕr-ĭ)	164	51°24'N	1°26'W
Newbury, Ma., U.S.	101a	42°48'N	70°52'W
Newbury, co., Eng., U.K.	158b	51°25'N	1°15'W
Newburyport, Ma., U.S. (nū'bĕr-ĭ-pōrt)	101a	42°48'N	70°53'W
New Caledonia, dep., Oc.	219	21°28'S	164°40'E
New Canaan, Ct., U.S. (kā-nȧn)	110a	41°06'N	73°30'W
New Carlisle, Can. (kär-līl')	91	48°01'N	65°20'W
Newcastle, Austl. (nū-kȧs''l)	222	33°00'S	151°55'E
Newcastle, Can.	91	47°00'N	65°34'W
New Castle, De., U.S.	109	39°40'N	75°35'W
New Castle, In., U.S.	108	39°55'N	85°25'W
New Castle, Oh., U.S.	108	40°20'N	82°10'W
New Castle, Pa., U.S.	108	41°00'N	80°25'W
Newcastle, Tx., U.S.	120	33°13'N	98°44'W
Newcastle, Wy., U.S.	112	43°51'N	104°11'W
Newcastle under Lyme, Eng., U.K. (nů-kȧs''l) (nū-käs''l)	158a	53°01'N	2°14'W
Newcastle upon Tyne, Eng., U.K.	154	55°00'N	1°45'W
Newcastle Waters, Austl. (wô'tẽrz)	218	17°10'S	133°25'E
Newcomerstown, Oh., U.S. (nū'kŭm-ẽrz-toun)	108	40°15'N	81°40'W
New Croton Reservoir, res., N.Y., U.S. (krō'tŏn)	110a	41°15'N	73°47'W
New Delhi, India (dĕl'hī)	199	28°43'N	77°18'E
Newell, S.D., U.S. (nū'ĕl)	112	44°43'N	103°26'W
New England Range, mts., Austl. (nů ĭŋ'glănd)	221	29°32'S	152°30'E
Newenham, Cape, c., Ak., U.S. (nū-ĕn-hăm)	103	58°40'N	162°32'W
Newfane, N.Y., U.S. (nū-fān)	111c	43°17'N	78°44'W
Newfoundland, i., Can.	93a	48°30'N	56°00'W
Newfoundland and Labrador, prov., Can.	91	48°15'N	56°53'W
Newgate, Can. (nū'gāt)	95	49°01'N	115°10'W
New Georgia, i., Sol. Is. (jôr'jĭ-ȧ)	221	8°08'S	158°00'E
New Georgia Group, is., Sol. Is.	214e	8°30'S	157°20'E
New Georgia Sound, strt., Sol. Is.	214e	8°00'S	158°10'E
New Glasgow, Can. (glȧs'gō)	91	45°35'N	62°36'W
New Guinea, i. (gĭne)	213	5°45'S	140°00'E
Newhalem, Wa., U.S. (nū hā'lŭm)	114	48°44'N	121°11'W
New Hampshire, state, U.S. (hămp'shĭr)	105	43°55'N	71°40'W
New Hampton, Ia., U.S. (hămp'tŭn)	113	43°03'N	92°20'W
New Hanover, S. Afr. (hăn'ôvẽr)	233c	29°23'S	30°32'E
New Hanover, i., Pap. N. Gui.	213	2°37'S	150°15'E
New Harmony, In., U.S. (nū här'mô-nĭ)	108	38°10'N	87°55'W
New Haven, Ct., U.S. (hā'vĕn)	105	41°20'N	72°55'W
New Haven, In., U.S. (nū hāv''n)	108	41°05'N	85°00'W
New Hebrides, is., Vanuatu	221	16°00'S	167°00'E
New Holland, Eng., U.K. (hŏl'ănd)	158a	53°42'N	0°21'W
New Holland, N.C., U.S.	125	35°27'N	76°14'W
New Hope Mountain, mtn., Al., U.S. (hōp)	110h	33°23'N	86°45'W
New Hudson, Mi., U.S. (hŭd'sŭn)	111b	42°30'N	83°36'W
New Iberia, La., U.S. (ī-bē'rĭ-ȧ)	123	30°00'N	91°50'W
Newington, Can. (nū'ĕng-tŏn)	102c	45°07'N	75°00'W
New Ireland, i., Pap. N. Gui. (īr'lănd)	213	3°15'S	152°30'E
New Jersey, state, U.S. (jûr'zĭ)	105	40°30'N	74°50'W
New Kensington, Pa., U.S. (kĕn'zĭng-tŭn)	111e	40°34'N	79°35'W
Newkirk, Ok., U.S. (nū'kûrk)	121	36°52'N	97°03'W
New Lenox, Il., U.S. (lĕn'ŭk)	111a	41°31'N	87°58'W
New Lexington, Oh., U.S. (lĕk'sĭng-tŭn)	108	39°40'N	82°10'W
New Lisbon, Wi., U.S. (lĭz'bŭn)	113	43°52'N	90°11'W
New Liskeard, Can.	99	47°30'N	79°40'W
New London, Ct., U.S. (lŭn'dŭn)	109	41°20'N	72°05'W
New London, Wi., U.S.	113	44°24'N	88°45'W
New Madrid, Mo., U.S. (măd'rĭd)	121	36°34'N	89°31'W
Newman's Grove, Ne., U.S. (nū'măn grōv)	112	41°46'N	97°44'W
Newmarket, Can. (nū'mär-kĕt)	99	44°00'N	79°30'W
New Martinsville, W.V., U.S. (mär'tĭnz-vĭl)	108	39°35'N	80°50'W
New Meadows, Id., U.S.	114	44°58'N	116°20'W
New Mexico, state, U.S. (mĕk'sĭ-kō)	104	34°30'N	107°10'W
New Mills, Eng., U.K. (mĭlz)	158a	53°22'N	2°00'W
New Munster, Wi., U.S. (mŭn'stẽr)	111a	42°35'N	88°13'W
Newnan, Ga., U.S. (nū'năn)	124	33°22'N	84°47'W
New Norfolk, Austl. (nôr'fŏk)	219	42°50'S	147°17'E
New Orleans, La., U.S. (ôr'lê-ănz)	105	30°00'N	90°05'W
New Philadelphia, Oh., U.S. (fĭl-ȧ-dĕl'fĭ-ȧ)	108	40°30'N	81°30'W
New Plymouth, N.Z. (plĭm'ŭth)	221a	39°04'S	174°13'E
Newport, Austl.	217b	33°39'S	151°19'E
Newport, Eng., U.K. (nū-pôrt)	164	50°41'N	1°25'W
Newport, Eng., U.K.	158a	52°46'N	2°22'W
Newport, Wales, U.K.	161	51°36'N	3°05'W
Newport, Ar., U.S. (nū'pôrt)	121	35°35'N	91°16'W
Newport, Ky., U.S.	105	39°05'N	84°30'W
Newport, Me., U.S.	100	44°49'N	69°20'W
Newport, Mn., U.S.	117g	44°52'N	92°59'W
Newport, N.H., U.S.	109	43°20'N	72°10'W
Newport, Or., U.S.	114	44°39'N	124°02'W
Newport, R.I., U.S.	109	41°29'N	71°16'W
Newport, Tn., U.S.	124	35°55'N	83°12'W
Newport, Vt., U.S.	109	44°55'N	72°15'W
Newport, Wa., U.S.	114	48°12'N	117°01'W
Newport Beach, Ca., U.S. (bēch)	117a	33°36'N	117°55'W
Newport News, Va., U.S.	105	36°59'N	76°24'W
New Prague, Mn., U.S. (nū prāg)	113	44°33'N	93°35'W
New Providence, i., Bah. (prŏv'ĭ-dĕns)	134	25°00'N	77°25'W

ng-sing; ŋ-baŋk; ɴ-nasalized n; nŏd; cŏmmit; ōld; ôbey; ôrder; oi-boil; fōōd; ò-as oo in foot; ou-out; s-soft; sh-dish; th-thin; pūre; ůnite; ûrn; stŭd; circŭs; ü-as in French tu; '-indeterminate vowel.

328 New Richmond – Norman

PRONOUNCING INDEX

PLACE (Pronunciation)	PAGE	LAT.	LONG.
New Richmond, Oh., U.S. (rĭch′mŭnd)	108	38°55′N	84°15′W
New Richmond, Wi., U.S.	113	45°07′N	92°34′W
New Roads, La., U.S. (rōds)	123	30°42′N	91°26′W
New Rochelle, N.Y., U.S. (rū-shĕl′)	110a	40°55′N	73°47′W
New Rockford, N.D., U.S. (rŏk′fẽrd)	112	47°40′N	99°08′W
New Ross, Ire. (rôs)	164	52°25′N	6°55′W
New Sarepta, Can.	102g	53°17′N	113°09′W
New Siberian Islands *see* Novosibirskiye Ostrova, is., Russia	179	74°00′N	140°30′E
New Smyrna Beach, Fl., U.S. (smûr′nȧ)	125	29°00′N	80°57′W
New South Wales, state, Austl. (wālz)	219	32°45′S	146°14′E
Newton, Can. (nū′tŭn)	102f	49°56′N	98°04′W
Newton, Eng., U.K.	158a	53°27′N	2°37′W
Newton, Ia., U.S.	113	41°42′N	93°04′W
Newton, Il., U.S.	108	39°00′N	88°10′W
Newton, Ks., U.S.	121	38°03′N	97°22′W
Newton, Ma., U.S.	101a	42°21′N	71°13′W
Newton, Ms., U.S.	124	32°18′N	89°10′W
Newton, N.C., U.S.	125	35°40′N	81°19′W
Newton, N.J., U.S.	110a	41°03′N	74°45′W
Newton, Tx., U.S.	123	30°47′N	93°45′W
Newtonsville, Oh., U.S. (nū′tŭnz-vĭl)	111f	39°11′N	84°04′W
Newtown, N.D., U.S. (nū′toun)	112	47°57′N	102°25′W
Newtown, Oh., U.S.	111f	39°08′N	84°22′W
Newtown, Pa., U.S.	110f	40°13′N	74°56′W
Newtownards, N. Ire., U.K. (nu-t′n-ardz′)	164	54°35′N	5°39′W
New Ulm, Mn., U.S. (ŭlm)	113	44°18′N	94°27′W
New Waterford, Can. (wô′tẽr-fẽrd)	91	46°15′N	60°05′W
New Westminster, Can. (wĕst′mĭn-stẽr)	95	49°12′N	122°55′W
New York, N.Y., U.S. (yôrk)	105	40°40′N	73°58′W
New York, state, U.S.	105	42°45′N	78°05′W
New Zealand, nation, Oc. (zē′lȧnd)	221a	42°00′S	175°00′E
Nexapa, r., Mex. (nĕks-ä′pä)	130	18°32′N	98°29′W
Neya-gawa, Japan (nā′yä gä′wä)	211b	34°47′N	135°38′E
Neyshābūr, Iran	198	36°06′N	58°45′E
Neyva, r., Russia (nĕy′vȧ)	186a	57°39′N	60°37′E
Nezahualcóyotl, Mex.	131a	19°27′N	99°03′W
Nez Perce, Id., U.S. (nĕz′ pûrs′)	114	46°16′N	116°15′W
Nez Perce Indian Reservation, I.R., Id., U.S.	114	46°20′N	116°30′W
Ngami, l., Bots. (n′gä′mē)	232	20°56′S	22°31′E
Ngangerabeli Plain, pl., Kenya	237	1°20′S	40°10′E
Ngangla Ringco, l., China (ŋäŋ-lä rĭŋ-tswo)	202	31°42′N	82°53′E
Ngarimbi, Tan.	237	8°28′S	38°36′E
Ngoko, r., Afr.	236	1°55′N	15°53′E
Ngol-Kedju Hill, mtn., Cam.	235	6°20′N	9°45′E
Ngong, Kenya (′n-gông)	232	1°27′S	36°39′E
Ngounié, r., Gabon	236	1°15′S	10°43′E
Ngoywa, Tan.	237	5°56′S	32°48′E
Ngqeleni, S. Afr. (′ng-kĕ-lā′nē)	233c	31°41′S	29°04′E
Nguigmi, Niger (′n-gēg′mē)	231	14°15′N	13°07′E
Ngurore, Nig.	235	9°18′N	12°14′E
Nguru, Nig. (′n-gōō′rōō)	230	12°53′N	10°26′E
Nguru Mountains, mts., Tan.	237	6°10′S	37°35′E
Nha Trang, Viet. (nyä-träng′)	212	12°08′N	108°56′E
Niafounke, Mali	230	16°03′N	4°17′W
Niagara, Wi., U.S. (nī-ăg′ȧ-rȧ)	113	45°45′N	88°05′W
Niagara, r., N.A.	111c	43°12′N	79°03′W
Niagara Falls, Can.	111c	43°05′N	79°05′W
Niagara Falls, N.Y., U.S.	105	43°06′N	79°02′W
Niagara-on-the-Lake, Can.	102d	43°16′N	79°05′W
Niakaramandougou, C. Iv.	234	8°40′N	5°17′W
Niamey, Niger (nē-ä-mā′)	230	13°31′N	2°07′E
Niamtougou, Togo	234	9°46′N	1°06′E
Niangara, D.R.C. (nē-äŋ-gä′rȧ)	231	3°42′N	27°52′E
Niangua, r., Mo., U.S. (nī-ăŋ′gwȧ)	121	37°30′N	93°05′W
Nias, Pulau, i., Indon. (nē′äs′)	212	0°58′N	97°43′E
Nibe, Den. (nē′bĕ)	166	56°57′N	9°36′E
Nicaragua, nation, N.A. (nĭk-ȧ-rä′gwȧ)	128	12°45′N	86°15′W
Nicaragua, Lago de, l., Nic. (lä′gô dĕ)	128	11°45′N	85°28′W
Nicastro, Italy (nē-käs′trō)	163	38°39′N	16°15′E
Nicchehabin, Punta, c., Mex. (pōō′n-tä-nĕ-chĕ-ä-bē′n)	132a	19°50′N	87°20′W
Nice, Fr. (nēs)	154	43°42′N	7°21′E
Nicheng, China (nē-chŭŋ)	207b	30°54′N	121°48′E
Nichicun, l., Can. (nĭch′ĭ-kŭn)	93	53°07′N	72°10′W
Nicholas Channel, strt., N.A. (nĭk′ô-lȧs)	134	23°30′N	80°20′W
Nicholasville, Ky., U.S. (nĭk′ô-lȧs-vĭl)	108	37°55′N	84°35′W
Nicobar Islands, is., India (nĭk-ô-bär′)	212	8°28′N	94°04′E
Nicolai Mountain, mtn., Or., U.S. (nē-cō lī′)	116c	46°05′N	123°27′W
Nicolás Romero, Mex. (nē-kô-lä′s rô-mĕ′rô)	131a	19°38′N	99°20′W
Nicolet, Lake, l., Mi., U.S. (nĭ′kô-lĕt)	117k	46°22′N	84°14′W
Nicolls Town, Bah.	134	25°10′N	78°00′W
Nicols, Mn., U.S. (nĭk′ĕls)	117g	44°50′N	93°12′W
Nicomeki, r., Can.	116d	49°04′N	122°47′W
Nicosia, Cyp. (nē-kô-sē′ȧ)	198	35°10′N	33°22′E
Nicoya, C.R. (nē-kō′yä)	132	10°08′N	85°27′W
Nicoya, Golfo de, b., C.R. (gôl-fô-dĕ)	132	10°03′N	85°04′W
Nicoya, Península de, pen., C.R.	132	10°05′N	86°00′W
Nidzica, Pol. (nē-jēt′sȧ)	169	53°21′N	20°30′E
Niedere Tauern, mts., Aus.	168	47°15′N	13°41′E
Niederkrüchten, Ger. (nē′dĕr-krük-tĕn)	171c	51°12′N	6°14′E
Niederösterreich, state, Aus.	159e	48°24′N	16°20′E
Niedersachsen (Lower Saxony), state, Ger. (nē′dĕr-zäk-sĕn)	159c	53°30′N	9°30′E
Niellim, Chad	235	9°42′N	17°49′E
Nienburg, Ger. (nē′ĕn-bōrgh)	168	52°40′N	9°15′E
Nietverdiend, S. Afr.	238c	25°02′S	26°10′E
Nieuw Nickerie, Sur. (nē-nē′kĕ-rē′)	143	5°51′N	57°00′W
Nieves, Mex. (nyā′vās)	130	24°00′N	102°57′W
Niğde, Tur. (nĭg′dĕ)	163	37°55′N	34°40′E
Nigel, S. Afr. (nī′jĕl)	238c	26°26′S	28°27′E
Niger, nation, Afr. (nī′jẽr)	230	18°02′N	8°30′E
Niger, r., Afr.	230	8°00′N	6°00′E
Niger Delta, d., Nig.	235	4°45′N	5°20′E
Nigeria, nation, Afr. (nī-jē′rĭ-ȧ)	230	8°57′N	6°30′E
Nihoa, i., Hi., U.S.	126b	23°15′N	161°30′W
Nii, i., Japan (nē)	211	34°26′N	139°23′E
Niigata, Japan (nē′ē-gä′tȧ)	205	37°47′N	139°04′E
Ni′ihau, i., Hi., U.S. (nē′ē-ha′ōō)	106c	21°50′N	160°05′W
Niimi, Japan (nē′mē)	211	34°59′N	133°28′E
Niiza, Japan	211a	35°48′N	139°34′E
Nijmegen, Neth. (nī′mā-gĕn)	165	51°50′N	5°52′E
Nikitinka, Russia (nē-kĭ′tĭn-kȧ)	176	55°33′N	33°19′E
Nikolayevka, Russia (nē-kô-lä′yĕf-kȧ)	186c	59°29′N	29°48′E
Nikolayevka, Russia	210	48°37′N	134°09′E
Nikolayevskiy, Russia	181	50°00′N	45°30′E
Nikolayevsk-na-Amure, Russia	179	53°18′N	140°49′E
Nikol′sk, Russia (nē-kôlsk′)	178	59°30′N	45°40′E
Nikol′skoye, Russia (nē-kôl′skô-yĕ)	186c	59°27′N	30°00′E
Nikopol, Blg. (nē′kô-pōl′)	163	43°41′N	24°52′E
Nikopol′, Ukr.	181	47°36′N	34°24′E
Nilahue, r., Chile (nē-lä′wĕ)	141b	34°36′S	71°50′W
Nile, r., Afr. (nīl)	231	27°30′N	31°00′E
Niles, Mi., U.S. (nīlz)	108	41°50′N	86°15′W
Niles, Oh., U.S.	108	41°15′N	80°45′W
Nileshwar, India	203	12°08′N	74°14′E
Nilgiri Hills, hills, India	203	12°05′N	76°22′E
Nilópolis, Braz. (nē-lô′pō-lēs)	141a	22°48′S	43°25′W
Nīmach, India	202	24°32′N	74°51′E
Nimba, Mont, mtn., Afr. (nĭm′bȧ)	230	7°40′N	8°33′W
Nimba Mountains, mts., Afr.	234	7°30′N	8°35′W
Nîmes, Fr. (nēm)	154	43°49′N	4°22′E
Nimrod Reservoir, res., Ar., U.S. (nĭm′rŏd)	121	34°58′N	93°46′W
Nimule, Sudan (nē-mōō′lā)	231	3°38′N	32°12′E
Ninda, Ang.	236	14°47′S	21°24′E
Nine Mile Creek, r., Ut., U.S. (mīn′ĭmôd′)	119	39°50′N	110°30′W
Ninety Mile Beach, cst., Austl.	221	38°20′S	147°30′E
Nineveh, Iraq (nĭn′ē-vȧ)	198	36°30′N	43°10′E
Ning′an, China (nĭŋ-än)	205	44°20′N	129°20′E
Ningbo, China (nĭŋ-bwo)	205	29°56′N	121°30′E
Ningde, China (nĭŋ-dŭ)	205	26°38′N	119°33′E
Ninghai, China (nĭng′hī′)	209	29°20′N	121°20′E
Ninghe, China (nĭŋ-hŭ)	206	39°20′N	117°50′E
Ningjin, China (nĭŋ-jyĭn)	206	37°39′N	116°47′E
Ningjin, China	206	37°37′N	114°55′E
Ningming, China	209	22°22′N	107°06′E
Ningwu, China (nĭng′wōō′)	205	39°00′N	112°12′E
Ningxia Huizu, prov., China (nĭŋ-shyä)	204	37°10′N	106°00′E
Ningyang, China (nĭng′yäng′)	206	35°46′N	116°48′E
Ninh Binh, Viet. (nēn bĕnk′)	212	20°22′N	106°00′E
Ninigo Group, is., Pap. N. Gui.	213	1°15′S	143°30′E
Ninnescah, r., Ks., U.S. (nĭn′ĕs-kä)	120	37°37′N	98°31′W
Nioaque, Braz. (nēô-ä′-kĕ)	143	21°14′S	55°41′W
Niobrara, r., U.S. (nī-ô-brâr′ȧ)	106	42°46′N	98°46′W
Niokolo Koba, Parc National du, rec., Sen.	234	13°05′N	13°00′W
Nioro du Sahel, Mali (nē-ō′rō)	230	15°15′N	9°35′W
Nipawin, Can.	90	53°22′N	104°00′W
Nipe, Bahía de, b., Cuba (bä-ē′ä-dĕ-nē′pä)	135	20°50′N	75°30′W
Nipe, Sierra de, mts., Cuba (sē-ĕ′r-rȧ-dĕ)	135	20°20′N	75°50′W
Nipigon, Can. (nĭp′ĭ-gŏn)	91	48°58′N	88°17′W
Nipigon, l., Can.	93	49°37′N	89°55′W
Nipigon Bay, b., Can.	98	48°56′N	88°00′W
Nipisiguit, r., Can. (nĭ-pĭ′sĭ-kwĭt)	100	47°26′N	66°15′W
Nipissing, l., Can. (nĭp′ĭ-sĭng)	93	45°59′N	80°19′W
Niquero, Cuba (nē-kā′rō)	134	20°00′N	77°35′W
Nirmali, India	202	26°30′N	86°43′E
Niš, Yugo.	154	43°19′N	21°54′E
Nisa, Port. (nē′sȧ)	172	39°32′N	7°41′W
Nišava, r., Eur. (nē′shȧ-vȧ)	175	43°17′N	22°17′E
Nishino, i., Japan (nēsh′ē-nô)	211	36°06′N	132°49′E
Nishinomiya, Japan (nēsh′ē-nô-mē′yȧ)	211b	34°44′N	135°21′E
Nishio, Japan (nēsh′ē-ô)	211	34°50′N	137°01′E
Niska Lake, l., Can. (nĭs′kȧ)	96	55°35′N	108°38′W
Nisko, Pol. (nēs′kô)	169	50°30′N	22°07′E
Nisku, Can. (nĭs-kū′)	102g	53°21′N	113°33′W
Nisqually, r., Wa., U.S. (nĭs-kwôl′ĭ)	114	46°51′N	122°33′W
Nissan, r., Swe.	166	57°06′N	13°22′E
Nisser, l., Nor. (nĭs′ẽr)	166	59°14′N	8°35′E
Nissum Fjord, b., Den.	166	56°24′N	7°35′E
Niterói, Braz. (nē-tĕ-rô′ĭ)	143	22°53′S	43°07′W
Nith, r., Scot., U.K. (nĭth)	164	55°13′N	3°55′W
Nitra, Slvk. (nē′trȧ)	169	48°18′N	18°04′E
Nitra, r., Slvk.	169	48°13′N	18°14′E
Nitro, W.V., U.S. (nī′trō)	108	38°25′N	81°50′W
Niue, dep., Oc. (nĭ′ō)	241	19°50′S	167°00′W
Nivelles, Bel. (nē′vĕl′)	165	50°33′N	4°17′E
Nixon, Tx., U.S. (nĭk′sŭn)	123	29°16′N	97°48′W
Nizāmābād, India	199	18°48′N	78°07′E
Nizhne-Angarsk, Russia (nyēzh′nyĭ-ŭngärsk′)	179	55°49′N	108°46′E
Nizhne-Chirskaya, Russia	181	48°20′N	42°50′E
Nizhne-Kolymsk, Russia (kô-lėmsk′)	179	68°32′N	160°56′E
Nizhneudinsk, Russia (nĕzh′nyĭ-ōōdĕnsk′)	179	54°58′N	99°15′E
Nizhniye Sergi, Russia (nyēzh′ nyē sĕr′gē)	180	56°41′N	59°19′E
Nizhniy Novgorod (Gor′kiy), Russia	178	56°15′N	44°05′E
Nizhniy Tagil, Russia (tŭgēl′)	178	57°54′N	59°59′E
Nizhnyaya Kur′ya, Russia (nyē′zhnyȧ-yȧ koor′yȧ)	186a	58°01′N	56°00′E
Nizhnyaya Salda, Russia (nyē′zhnya′ya säl′da′)	186a	58°05′N	60°43′E
Nizhnyaya Taymyra, r., Russia	184	72°30′N	95°18′E
Nizhnyaya Tunguska, r., Russia	179	64°13′N	91°30′E
Nizhnyaya Tura, Russia (tōō′rȧ)	186a	58°38′N	59°50′E
Nizhnyaya Us′va, Russia (ò′vȧ)	186a	59°05′N	58°53′E
Nizhyn, Ukr.	181	51°03′N	31°52′E
Nízke Tatry, mts., Slvk.	169	48°57′N	19°18′E
Njazidja, i., Com.	233	11°44′S	42°38′E
Njombe, Tan.	237	9°20′S	34°46′E
Njurunda, Swe. (nyōō-rōn′dȧ)	166	62°15′N	17°24′E
Nkala Mission, Zam.	237	15°55′S	26°00′E
Nkandla, S. Afr. (′n-känd′lä)	233c	28°40′S	31°06′E
Nkawkaw, Ghana	234	6°33′N	0°47′W
Nkhota, Mwi. (kō-tȧ kō-tȧ)	232	12°52′S	34°16′E
Noākhāli, Bngl.	199	22°52′N	91°08′E
Noatak, Ak., U.S. (nô-ȧ′tȧk)	103	67°22′N	163°28′W
Noatak, r., Ak., U.S.	103	67°58′N	162°15′W
Nobeoka, Japan (nō-bȧ-ō′kȧ)	210	32°36′N	131°41′E
Noblesville, In., U.S. (nō′bl′z-vĭl)	108	40°00′N	86°00′W
Nobleton, Can. (nō′bl′tŭn)	102d	43°54′N	79°39′W
Nocera Inferiore, Italy (ĕn-fĕ-ryō′rĕ)	173c	40°30′N	14°38′E
Nochistlán, Mex. (nô-chēs-tlän′)	130	21°23′N	102°52′W
Nochixtlón, Mex. (ä-sòn-syōn′)	131	17°28′N	97°12′W
Nogales, Mex. (nō-gä′lĕs)	131	18°49′N	97°09′W
Nogales, Mex.	128	31°15′N	111°00′W
Nogales, Az., U.S. (nô-gä′lĕs)	104	31°20′N	110°55′W
Nogal Valley, val., Som. (nô′gäl)	238a	8°30′N	47°50′E
Nogent-le-Roi, Fr. (nŏ-zhŏn-lĕ-rwä′)	171b	48°39′N	1°32′E
Nogent-le-Rotrou, Fr. (rō-trōō′)	170	48°22′N	0°47′E
Noginsk, Russia (nô-gēnsk′)	180	55°52′N	38°28′E
Noguera Pallaresa, r., Spain	173	42°18′N	1°03′E
Noia, Spain	172	42°46′N	8°50′W
Noirmoutier, Île de, i., Fr. (nwȧr-mōō-tyā′)	161	47°03′N	3°08′W
Nojima-Zaki, c., Japan (nō′jē-mä zä-kē)	211	34°54′N	139°48′E
Nokomis, Il., U.S. (nô-kō′mĭs)	108	39°15′N	89°10′W
Nola, Italy (nô′lä)	174	40°41′N	14°32′E
Nolinsk, Russia (nô-lēnsk′)	180	57°32′N	49°50′E
Noma Misaki, c., Japan (nô′mä mē′sä-kē)	211	31°25′N	130°09′E
Nombre de Dios, Mex. (nôm-brĕ-dĕ-dyō′s)	130	23°50′N	104°14′W
Nombre de Dios, Pan. (nô′m-brĕ)	133	9°34′N	79°28′W
Nome, Ak., U.S. (nōm)	106a	64°30′N	165°20′W
Nonacho, l., Can.	92	61°48′N	111°20′W
Nong′an, China (nôŋ-än)	208	44°25′N	125°10′E
Nongoma, S. Afr. (nōn-gō′mȧ)	232	27°48′S	31°45′E
Nooksack, Wa., U.S. (nòk′săk)	116d	48°55′N	122°19′W
Nooksack, r., Wa., U.S.	116d	48°54′N	122°31′W
Noordwijk aan Zee, Neth.	159a	52°14′N	4°25′E
Noordzee Kanaal, can., Neth.	159a	52°27′N	4°42′E
Nootka, i., Can. (nōōt′kȧ)	92	49°32′N	126°42′W
Nootka Sound, strt., Can.	94	49°33′N	126°38′W
Nóqui, Ang. (nô-kē′)	232	5°51′S	13°25′E
Nor, r., China (nou′)	210	46°55′N	132°45′E
Nora, Swe.	166	59°32′N	14°56′E
Nora, In., U.S. (nō′rȧ)	111g	39°54′N	86°08′W
Noranda, Can.	99	48°15′N	79°01′W
Norbeck, Md., U.S. (nôr′bĕk)	110e	39°06′N	77°05′W
Norborne, Mo., U.S. (nôr′bôrn)	121	39°17′N	93°39′W
Norco, Ca., U.S. (nôr′kô)	117a	33°57′N	117°33′W
Norcross, Ga., U.S. (nôr′krôs)	110c	33°56′N	84°13′W
Nord, Riviere du, Can. (rēv-yĕr′ dü nōr)	102a	45°45′N	74°02′W
Nordegg, Can. (nûr′dĕg)	95	52°28′N	116°04′W
Norden, Ger. (nôr′dĕn)	168	53°35′N	7°14′E
Norderney, i., Ger. (nōr′dĕr-nĕy)	168	53°45′N	6°58′E
Nordfjord, b., Nor. (nô′fyôr)	166	61°50′N	5°35′E
Nordhausen, Ger. (nôrt′hau-zĕn)	161	51°30′N	10°48′E
Nordhorn, Ger. (nôrt′hôrn)	168	52°26′N	7°05′E
Nord Kapp, c., Nor.	180	71°11′N	25°48′E
Nordland, Wa., U.S. (nôrd′lȧnd)	116a	48°03′N	122°41′W
Nördlingen, Ger. (nûrt′lĭng-ĕn)	168	48°51′N	10°30′E
Nord-Ostsee Kanal (Kiel Canal), can., Ger. (nōrd-ōzt-zā) (kēl)	168	54°03′N	9°23′E
Nordrhein-Westfalen (North Rhine-Westphalia), state, Ger. (nōrd′hīn-vĕst-fä-lĕn)	171c	51°40′N	7°00′E
Nordvik, Russia (nôrd′vēk)	179	73°57′N	111°15′E
Nore, r., Ire. (nōr)	164	52°34′N	7°15′W
Norfolk, Ma., U.S. (nôr′fŏk)	101a	42°07′N	71°19′W
Norfolk, Ne., U.S.	104	42°10′N	97°25′W
Norfolk, Va., U.S.	105	36°55′N	76°15′W
Norfolk, i., Oc.	241	27°10′S	166°50′E
Norfork, Lake, l., Ar., U.S.	121	36°25′N	92°09′W
Noril′sk, Russia (nô rēlsk′)	178	69°00′N	87°11′E
Normal, Il., U.S. (nôr′mȧl)	108	40°35′N	89°00′W
Norman, r., Austl.	221	18°27′S	141°29′E
Norman, Lake, res., N.C., U.S.	107	35°30′N	80°53′W

PRONOUNCING INDEX

Normandie – Nowa Sól 329

PLACE (Pronunciation)	PAGE	LAT.	LONG.
Normandie, hist. reg., Fr. (nôr-mäɴ-dē′)	170	49°02′N	0°17′E
Normandie, Collines de, hills, Fr. (kō-lēn′ dē-nôr-män-dē′)	170	48°46′N	0°50′W
Normandy see Normandie, hist. reg., Fr.	170	49°02′N	0°17′E
Normanton, Austl. (nôr′mán-tŭn)	219	17°45′S	141°10′E
Normanton, Eng., U.K.	158a	53°40′N	1°21′W
Norman Wells, Can.	90	65°26′N	127°00′W
Nornalup, Austl. (nôr-năl′ŭp)	218	35°00′S	117°00′E
Nørresundby, Den. (nû-rĕ-sôn′bü)	166	57°04′N	9°55′E
Norris, Tn., U.S. (nŏr′ĭs)	124	36°09′N	84°05′W
Norris Lake, res., Tn., U.S.	107	36°17′N	84°10′W
Norristown, Pa., U.S. (nŏr′ĭs-town)	110f	40°07′N	75°21′W
Norrköping, Swe. (nôr′chûp′ĭng)	154	58°37′N	16°10′E
Norrtälje, Swe. (nôr-tĕl′yĕ)	160	59°47′N	18°39′E
Norseman, Austl. (nôrs′măn)	218	32°15′S	122°00′E
Norte, Punta, c., Arg. (po͞o′n-tä-nŏr′tĕ)	141c	36°17′S	56°46′W
Norte, Serra do, mts., Braz. (sĕ′r-rä-dô-nôr′te)	143	12°04′S	59°08′W
North, Cape, c., Can.	101	47°02′N	60°25′W
North Adams, Ma., U.S. (ăd′ămz)	109	42°40′N	73°05′W
Northam, Austl. (nôr-dhăm)	218	31°50′S	116°45′E
Northam, S. Afr. (nôr′thăm)	238c	24°52′S	27°16′E
North America, cont.	89	45°00′N	100°00′W
North American Basin, deep (á-mĕr′ĭ-kăn)	4	23°45′N	62°45′W
Northampton, Austl. (nôr-thămp′tŭn)	218	28°22′S	114°45′E
Northampton, Eng., U.K. (nôrth-ămp′tŭn)	161	52°14′N	0°56′W
Northampton, Ma., U.S.	109	42°20′N	72°45′W
Northampton, Pa., U.S.	109	40°45′N	75°30′W
Northamptonshire, co., Eng., U.K.	158a	52°25′N	0°47′W
North Andaman Island, i., India (ăn-dá-măn′)	212	13°15′N	93°30′E
North Andover, Ma., U.S. (ăn′dô-vēr)	101a	42°42′N	71°07′W
North Arm, mth., Can. (ärm)	116d	49°13′N	123°01′W
North Atlanta, Ga., U.S. (ăt-lăn′tá)	110c	33°52′N	84°20′W
North Attleboro, Ma., U.S. (ăt′′l-bŭr-ô)	110b	41°59′N	71°18′W
North Baltimore, Oh., U.S. (bôl′tĭ-môr)	108	41°10′N	83°40′W
North Basque, Tx., U.S. (băsk)	122	31°56′N	98°01′W
North Battleford, Can. (băt′′l-fērd)	90	52°47′N	108°17′W
North Bay, Can.	91	46°13′N	79°26′W
North Bend, Or., U.S. (bĕnd)	114	43°23′N	124°13′W
North Berwick, Me., U.S. (bûr′wĭk)	100	43°18′N	70°46′W
North Bight, b., Bah. (bīt)	134	24°30′N	77°40′W
North Bimini, i., Bah. (bĭ′mĭ-nē)	134	25°45′N	79°20′W
North Borneo see Sabah, hist. reg., Malay.	212	5°10′N	116°25′E
Northborough, Ma., U.S.	101a	42°19′N	71°39′W
Northbridge, Ma., U.S. (nôrth′brĭj)	101a	42°09′N	71°39′W
North Caicos, i., T./C. Is. (kī′kōs)	135	21°55′N	72°00′W
North Cape, c., N.Z.	221a	34°31′S	173°02′E
North Carolina, state, U.S. (kăr-ô-lī′ná)	105	35°40′N	81°30′W
North Cascades National Park, rec., Wa., U.S.	114	48°50′N	120°50′W
North Cat Cay, i., Bah.	134	25°35′N	79°20′W
North Channel, strt., Can.	98	46°10′N	83°20′W
North Channel, strt., U.K.	156	55°15′N	7°56′W
North Charleston, S.C., U.S. (chärlz′tŭn)	125	32°49′N	79°57′W
North Chicago, Il., U.S. (shĭ-kô′gō)	111a	42°19′N	87°51′W
North College Hill, Oh., U.S. (kŏl′ĕj hĭl)	111f	39°13′N	84°33′W
North Concho, Tx., U.S. (kŏn′chō)	122	31°40′N	100°48′W
North Cooking Lake, Can. (kŏk′ĭng lăk)	102g	53°28′N	112°57′W
North Cyprus, nation, Asia	198	35°15′N	33°40′E
North Dakota, state, U.S. (dá-kō′tá)	104	47°20′N	101°55′W
North Downs, Eng., U.K. (dounz)	164	51°11′N	0°01′W
North Dum-Dum, India	202a	22°38′N	88°23′E
Northeast Cape, c., Ak., U.S. (nôrth-ēst)	103	63°15′N	169°04′W
Northeast Point, c., Bah.	135	21°25′N	73°00′W
Northeast Point, c., Bah.	135	22°45′N	73°50′W
Northeast Providence Channel, strt., Bah. (prŏv′ĭ-dĕns)	134	25°45′N	77°00′W
Northeim, Ger. (nôrt′hīm)	168	51°42′N	9°59′E
North Elbow Cays, is., Bah.	134	23°55′N	80°30′W
Northern Cheyenne Indian Reservation, I.R., Mt., U.S.	115	45°32′N	106°43′W
Northern Dvina see Severnaya Dvina, r., Russia	178	63°00′N	42°40′E
Northern Ireland, state, U.K. (ĭr′lănd)	154	54°48′N	7°00′W
Northern Land see Severnaya Zemlya, is., Russia	179	79°33′N	101°15′E
Northern Mariana Islands, dep., Oc. (mä-rē-ä′nä)	3	17°20′N	145°00′E
Northern Territory, ter., Austl.	218	18°15′S	133°00′E
Northern Yukon National Park, rec., Can.	103	69°00′N	140°00′W
Northfield, Mn., U.S. (nôrth′fēld)	113	44°28′N	93°11′W
North Flinders Ranges, mts., Austl. (flĭn′dērz)	222	31°55′S	138°45′E
North Foreland, Eng., U.K. (nôrth-fōr′lănd)	165	51°20′N	1°30′E
North Franklin Mountain, mtn., Tx., U.S. (frăn′klĭn)	122	31°55′N	106°30′W
North Frisian Islands, is., Eur.	160	55°16′N	8°15′E
North Gamboa, Pan. (găm-bô′ä)	133	9°07′N	79°40′W
North Gower, Can. (gŏw′ĕr)	102c	45°08′N	75°43′W
North Hollywood, Ca., U.S. (hŏl′ē-wŏd)	117a	34°10′N	118°23′W
North Island, i., N.Z.	221a	37°20′S	173°30′E
North Island, i., Ca., U.S.	118a	32°39′N	117°14′W
North Judson, In., U.S. (jŭd′sŭn)	108	41°15′N	86°50′W
North Kansas City, Mo., U.S. (kăn′zás)	117f	39°08′N	94°34′W
North Kingstown, R.I., U.S.	110b	41°34′N	71°26′W
North Lincolnshire, co., Eng., U.K.	158a	53°40′N	0°35′W
North Little Rock, Ar., U.S. (lĭt′′l rŏk)	121	34°46′N	92°13′W
North Loup, r., Ne., U.S. (lo͞op)	112	42°05′N	100°10′W
North Magnetic Pole, pt. of i.	244	77°19′N	101°49′W
North Manchester, In., U.S. (măn′chĕs-tēr)	108	41°00′N	85°45′W
Northmoor, Mo., U.S. (nôth′mo͝or)	117f	39°10′N	94°37′W
North Moose Lake, l., Can.	97	54°09′N	100°20′W
North Mount Lofty Ranges, mts., Austl.	222	33°50′S	138°30′E
North Ogden, Ut., U.S. (ŏg′dĕn)	117b	41°18′N	111°58′W
North Ogden Peak, mtn., Ut., U.S.	117b	41°23′N	111°59′W
North Olmsted, Oh., U.S. (ōlm-stĕd)	111d	41°25′N	81°55′W
North Ossetia, prov., Russia	180	43°00′N	44°15′E
North Pease, r., Tx., U.S. (pēz)	120	34°19′N	100°58′W
North Pender, i., Can. (pĕn′dēr)	116d	48°48′N	123°16′W
North Plains, Or., U.S. (plānz)	116c	45°36′N	123°00′W
North Platte, Ne., U.S. (plăt)	104	41°08′N	100°45′W
North Platte, r., U.S.	106	41°20′N	102°40′W
North Point, c., Barb.	133b	13°22′N	59°36′W
North Point, c., Mi., U.S.	108	45°00′N	83°20′W
North Pole, pt. of i.	244	90°00′N	0°00′
Northport, Al., U.S. (nôrth′pōrt)	124	33°12′N	87°35′W
Northport, N.Y., U.S.	110a	40°53′N	73°20′W
Northport, Wa., U.S.	114	48°53′N	117°47′W
North Reading, Ma., U.S. (rĕd′ĭng)	101a	42°34′N	71°04′W
North Richland Hills, Tx., U.S.	117c	32°50′N	97°13′W
Northridge, Ca., U.S. (nôrth′ridj)	117a	34°14′N	118°32′W
North Ridgeville, Oh., U.S. (rĭj-vĭl)	111d	41°23′N	82°01′W
North Ronaldsay, i., Scot., U.K.	164a	59°21′N	2°23′W
North Royalton, Oh., U.S. (roi′ăl-tŭn)	111d	41°19′N	81°44′W
North Saint Paul, Mn., U.S. (sânt pôl′)	113	45°01′N	92°59′W
North Santiam, r., Or., U.S. (săn′tyăm)	114	44°42′N	122°50′W
North Saskatchewan, r., Can. (săn-kăch′ē-wän)	92	54°00′N	111°30′W
North Sea, Eur.	154	56°09′N	3°16′E
North Skunk, r., Ia., U.S. (skŭnk)	113	41°39′N	92°46′W
North Stradbroke Island, i., Austl. (străd′brōk)	221	27°45′S	154°18′E
North Sydney, Can. (sĭd′nē)	101	46°13′N	60°15′W
North Taranaki Bight, N.Z. (tá-rá-nä′kĭ bīt)	221a	38°40′S	174°00′E
North Tarrytown, N.Y., U.S. (tăr′ĭ-toun)	110a	41°05′N	73°52′W
North Thompson, r., Can.	95	50°50′N	120°10′W
North Tonawanda, N.Y., U.S. (tŏn-á-wŏn′dá)	111c	43°02′N	78°53′W
North Truchas Peaks, mtn., N.M., U.S. (tro͞o′chäs)	106	35°58′N	105°40′W
North Twillingate, i., Can. (twĭl′ĭn-gāt)	100	35°58′N	105°37′W
North Uist, i., Scot., U.K. (û′ĭst)	164	57°37′N	7°22′W
Northumberland, N.H., U.S.	109	44°30′N	71°30′W
Northumberland Islands, is., Austl.	221	21°42′S	151°30′E
Northumberland Strait, strt., Can. (nôr thŭm′bēr-lánd)	100	46°25′N	64°20′W
North Umpqua, r., Or., U.S. (ŭmp′kwá)	114	43°20′N	122°50′W
North Vancouver, Can. (văn-ko͞o′vēr)	90	49°19′N	123°04′W
North Vernon, In., U.S. (vûr′nŭn)	108	39°05′N	85°45′W
Northville, Mi., U.S. (nôrth-vĭl)	111b	42°26′N	83°28′W
North Wales, Pa., U.S. (wālz)	110f	40°12′N	75°16′W
North West Cape, c., Austl. (nôrth′wĕst)	220	21°50′S	112°25′E
Northwest Cape Fear, r., N.C., U.S. (căp fēr)	125	34°34′N	79°46′W
North West Gander, r., Can. (găn′dēr)	101	48°40′N	55°15′W
Northwest Providence Channel, strt., Bah. (prŏv′ĭ-dĕns)	134	26°15′N	78°45′W
Northwest Territories, ter., Can. (tĕr′ĭ-tō′rĭs)	90	65°00′N	120°00′W
Northwich, Eng., U.K. (nôrth′wĭch)	158a	53°15′N	2°31′W
North Wilkesboro, N.C., U.S. (wĭlks′bûrô)	125	36°08′N	81°10′W
Northwood, Ia., U.S. (nôrth′wŏd)	113	43°26′N	93°13′W
Northwood, N.D., U.S.	112	47°44′N	97°36′W
North Yamhill, r., Or., U.S. (yăm′ hĭl)	116c	45°22′N	123°21′W
North York, Can.	99	43°47′N	79°25′W
North York Moors, for., Eng., U.K. (yôrk mo͝orz′)	164	54°20′N	0°40′W
North Yorkshire, co., Eng., U.K.	158a	53°50′N	1°10′W
Norton, Ks., U.S. (nôr′tŭn)	120	39°40′N	99°54′W
Norton, Ma., U.S.	110b	41°58′N	71°08′W
Norton, Va., U.S.	125	36°54′N	82°36′W
Norton Bay, b., Ak., U.S.	103	64°22′N	162°18′W
Norton Reservoir, res., Ma., U.S.	110b	42°01′N	71°07′W
Norton Sound, strt., Ak., U.S.	103	63°48′N	164°50′W
Norval, Can. (nôr′văl)	102d	43°39′N	79°52′W
Norwalk, Ca., U.S. (nôr′wôk)	117a	33°54′N	118°05′W
Norwalk, Ct., U.S.	110a	41°06′N	73°25′W
Norwalk, Oh., U.S.	108	41°15′N	82°35′W
Norway, Me., U.S.	100	44°11′N	70°35′W
Norway, Mi., U.S.	113	45°47′N	87°55′W
Norway, nation, Eur. (nôr′wā)	154	63°48′N	11°17′E
Norway House, Can.	90	53°59′N	97°50′W
Norwegian Sea, sea, Eur. (nôr-wē′jăn)	160	66°54′N	1°43′E
Norwell, Ma., U.S. (nôr′wĕl)	101a	42°10′N	70°47′W
Norwich, Eng., U.K.	161	52°40′N	1°15′E
Norwich, Ct., U.S. (nôr′wĭch)	109	41°20′N	72°00′W
Norwich, N.Y., U.S.	109	42°35′N	75°30′W
Norwood, Ma., U.S. (nôr′wo͝od)	101a	42°11′N	71°13′W
Norwood, N.C., U.S.	125	35°15′N	80°08′W
Norwood, Oh., U.S.	111f	39°10′N	84°27′W
Nose Creek, r., Can. (nōz)	102e	51°09′N	114°02′W
Noshiro, Japan (nō′shê-rô)	210	40°09′N	140°02′E
Nosivka, Ukr. (nō′sôf-ká)	177	50°54′N	31°35′E
Nossob, r., Afr. (nō′sŏb)	232	24°15′S	19°10′E
Noteć, r., Pol. (nō′tĕcn)	168	52°50′N	16°19′E
Notodden, Nor. (nōt′ôd′n)	166	59°35′N	9°15′E
Notre Dame, Monts, mts., Can.	100	46°35′N	70°35′W
Notre Dame Bay, b., Can. (nô′t’r dām′)	93a	49°45′N	55°15′W
Notre-Dame-du-Lac, Can.	100	47°37′N	68°51′W
Nottawasaga Bay, b., Can. (nŏt′á-wá-sä′gá)	99	44°45′N	80°35′W
Nottaway, r., Can. (nôt′á-wā)	93	50°58′N	78°02′W
Nottingham, Eng., U.K. (nŏt′ĭng-ăm)	161	52°58′N	1°09′W
Nottingham Island, i., Can.	93	62°58′N	78°53′W
Nottinghamshire, co., Eng., U.K.	158a	53°03′N	1°05′W
Nottoway, r., Va., U.S. (nôt′á-wā)	125	36°53′N	77°47′W
Notukeu Creek, r., Can.	96	49°55′N	106°30′W
Nouadhibou, Maur.	230	21°02′N	17°09′W
Nouakchott, Maur.	230	18°06′N	15°57′W
Nouamrhar, Maur.	230	19°22′N	16°31′W
Nouméa, N. Cal. (no͞o-mā′ä)	219	22°16′S	166°27′E
Nouvelle, Can. (no͞o-vĕl′)	100	48°09′N	66°22′W
Nouvelle-France, Cap de, c., Can.	93	62°03′N	74°00′W
Nouzonville, Fr. (no͞o-zôɴ-vēl′)	170	49°51′N	4°43′E
Nova Cruz, Braz. (nō′vá-kro͞o′z)	143	6°22′S	35°20′W
Nova Friburgo, Braz. (frê-bo͞or′gô)	143	22°18′S	42°31′W
Nova Iguaçu, Braz. (nō′vä-ē-gwä-so͞o′)	143	22°45′S	43°27′W
Nova Lima, Braz. (lē′mä)	141a	19°59′S	43°51′W
Nova Lisboa see Huambo, Ang.	232	12°44′S	15°47′E
Nova Mambone, Moz. (nō′vá-mám-bō′nĕ)	232	21°04′S	35°13′E
Nova Odesa, Ukr.	177	47°18′N	31°48′E
Nova Praha, Ukr.	177	48°34′N	32°54′E
Novara, Italy (nô-vä′rä)	162	45°24′N	8°38′E
Nova Resende, Braz.	141a	21°12′S	46°25′W
Nova Scotia, prov., Can. (skō′shá)	91	44°28′N	65°00′W
Nova Vodolaha, Ukr.	177	49°43′N	35°51′E
Novaya Ladoga, Russia (nô′vá-ya lá-dô-gá)	167	60°06′N	32°16′E
Novaya Lyalya, Russia (lyá′lyá)	186a	59°03′N	60°36′E
Novaya Sibir, i., Russia (sê-bēr′)	179	75°00′N	149°00′E
Novaya Zemlya, i., Russia (zĕm-lyá′)	178	72°00′N	54°46′E
Nova Zagora, Blg. (zä′gô-rá)	175	42°30′N	26°01′E
Novelda, Spain (nō-vĕl′dá)	173	38°22′N	0°46′W
Nové Mesto nad Váhom, Slvk. (nô′vĕ myĕs′tô)	169	48°44′N	17°47′E
Nové Zámky, Slvk. (zám′kĕ)	161	47°58′N	18°10′E
Novgorod, Russia (nôv′gô-rŏt)	180	58°32′N	31°16′E
Novgorod, prov., Russia	176	58°27′N	31°55′E
Novhorod-Sivers′kyi, Ukr.	181	52°01′N	33°14′E
Novi, Mi., U.S. (nō′vĭ)	111b	42°29′N	83°28′W
Novigrad, Cro. (nō′vĭ gràd)	174	44°09′N	15°34′E
Novi Ligure, Italy (nô′vê)	174	44°43′N	8°48′E
Novinger, Mo., U.S. (nŏv′ĭn-jēr)	121	40°14′N	92°43′W
Novi Pazar, Blg. (pä-zär′)	175	43°22′N	27°26′E
Novi Pazar, Yugo. (pá-zär′)	163	43°08′N	20°30′E
Novi Sad, Yugo. (săd′)	154	45°15′N	19°53′E
Novoaidar, Ukr.	177	48°57′N	39°01′E
Novoasbest, Russia (nô-vô-äs-bĕst′)	186a	57°43′N	60°14′E
Novocherkassk, Russia (nô′vô-chĕr-kásk′)	181	47°25′N	40°04′E
Novokuznetsk, Russia (nō′vô-kô′z-nyĕ′tsk) (stá′lênsk)	178	53°43′N	86°59′E
Novo-Ladozhskiy Kanal, can., Russia (nô-vô-lä′dôzh-skĭ ká-näl′)	167	59°54′N	31°19′E
Novo Mesto, Slvn. (nôvô mās′tô)	174	45°48′N	15°13′E
Novomoskovsk, Russia (nô′vô-môs-kôfsk′)	178	54°06′N	38°08′E
Novomoskovs′k, Ukr.	181	48°37′N	35°12′E
Novomyrhorod, Ukr.	177	48°46′N	31°44′E
Novonikol′skiy, Russia (nô′vô-nyĭ-kôl′skĭ)	186a	52°28′N	57°12′E
Novorossiysk, Russia (nô′vô-rô-sēsk′)	178	44°43′N	37°48′E
Novorzhev, Russia (nô′vô-rzhêv′)	176	57°01′N	29°17′E
Novo-Selo, Blg. (nō′vô-sĕ′lô)	175	44°09′N	22°46′E
Novosibirsk, Russia (nô′vô-sê-bērsk′)	178	55°09′N	82°58′E
Novosibirskiye Ostrova (New Siberian Islands), is., Russia	179	74°00′N	140°30′E
Novosil′, Russia (nô′vô-sĭl)	176	52°58′N	37°03′E
Novosokol′niki, Russia (nô′vô-sô-kôl′nē-kē)	176	56°18′N	30°07′E
Novotatishchevskiy, Russia (nô′vô-tá-tyĭsh′chĕv-skĭ)	186a	53°22′N	60°24′E
Novoukraïnka, Ukr.	181	48°18′N	31°33′E
Novouzensk, Russia (nô-vô-ô-zĕnsk′)	181	50°40′N	48°08′E
Novozybkov, Russia (nô′vô-zĕp′kôf)	181	52°31′N	31°54′E
Novyi Buh, Ukr.	177	47°43′N	32°33′E
Nový Jičín, Czech Rep. (nô′vē yē′chĕn)	169	49°36′N	18°02′E
Novyy Oskol, Russia (ôs-kôl′)	177	50°46′N	37°53′E
Novyy Port, Russia (nô′vē)	178	67°19′N	72°28′E
Nowa Sól, Pol. (nô′vá sül′)	168	51°49′N	15°41′E

ng-sing; ŋ-baŋk; ɴ-nasalized n; nŏd; cŏmmit; ōld; ôbey; ôrder; oi-boil; fo͞od; ŏ-as oo in foot; ou-out; s-soft; sh-dish; th-thin; pūre; ûnite; ûrn; stŭd; circŭs; ü-as in French tu; ′-indeterminate vowel.

āt; finǎl; rāte; senáte; ärm; ásk; sofá; fâre;   ch-choose;   dh-as th in other;   bē; ěvent; bět; recěnt; cratēr;   g-gō; gh-guttural g;   bǐt; ī-short neutral; rīde;   κ-guttural k as ch in German ich;

PRONOUNCING INDEX

Ojo Caliente – Orikhiv 331

PLACE (Pronunciation)	PAGE	LAT.	LONG.
Ojo Caliente, Mex. (ŏкō käl-yĕn′tå)	130	21°50′N	100°43′W
Ojocaliente, Mex. (ô-kō-kä-lyĕ′n-tĕ)	130	22°39′N	102°15′W
Ojo del Toro, Pico, mtn., Cuba (pē′kō-ô-kō-dĕl-tô′rô)	134	19°55′N	77°25′W
Oka, Can. (ō-kä)	102a	45°28′N	74°05′W
Oka, r., Russia (ô-kå′)	180	55°10′N	42°10′E
Oka, r., Russia (ō-kä′)	184	53°28′N	101°09′E
Oka, r., Russia (ô-kä′)	181	52°10′N	35°20′E
Okahandja, Nmb.	232	21°50′S	16°45′E
Okanagan (Okanogan), r., N.A. (ō′ká-näg′án)	95	49°06′N	119°43′W
Okanagan Lake, l., Can.	92	50°00′N	119°28′W
Okano, r., Gabon (ō′kä′nō)	230	0°15′N	11°08′E
Okanogan, Wa., U.S.	114	48°20′N	119°34′W
Okanogan, r., Wa., U.S.	114	48°36′N	119°33′W
Okatibbee, r., Ms., U.S. (ō′kä-tĭb′ē)	124	32°37′N	88°54′W
Okatoma Creek, r., Ms., U.S. (ō-kȧ-tō′mȧ)	124	31°43′N	89°34′W
Okavango (Cubango), r., Afr.	232	18°00′S	20°00′E
Okavango Swamp, sw., Bots.	232	19°30′S	23°02′E
Okaya, Japan (ō′kȧ-yȧ)	211	36°04′N	138°01′E
Okayama, Japan (ō′kȧ-yä′mȧ)	205	34°39′N	133°54′E
Okazaki, Japan (ō′kȧ-zä′kē)	210	34°58′N	137°09′E
Okeechobee, Fl., U.S. (ō-kē-chō′bē)	125	27°15′N	80°50′W
Okeechobee, Lake, l., Fl., U.S.	107	27°00′N	80°49′W
Okeene, Ok., U.S. (ō-kēn′)	120	36°06′N	98°19′W
Okefenokee Swamp, sw., U.S. (ō′kē-fē-nō′kē)	125	30°54′N	82°20′W
Okemah, Ok., U.S. (ô-kē′mä)	121	35°26′N	96°18′W
Okene, Nig.	235	7°33′N	6°15′E
Okha, Russia (ŭ-кä′)	179	53°44′N	143°12′E
Okhotino, Russia (ô-кô′tĭ-nô)	186b	56°14′N	38°24′E
Okhotsk, Russia (ô-кôtsk′)	179	59°28′N	143°32′E
Okhotsk, Sea of, sea, Asia (ô-kôtsk′)	179	56°45′N	146°00′E
Okhtyrka, Ukr.	181	50°18′N	34°53′E
Okinawa, i., Japan	205	26°30′N	128°00′E
Okino, i., Japan (ō′kē-nô)	211	36°22′N	133°27′E
Ōkino Erabu, i., Japan (ō-kē′nô-å-rä′bōō)	210	27°18′N	129°00′E
Oklahoma, state, U.S. (ō-klå-hō′må)	104	36°00′N	98°20′W
Oklahoma City, Ok., U.S.	104	35°27′N	97°32′W
Oklawaha, r., Fl., U.S. (ŏk-lȧ-wô′hô)	125	29°13′N	82°00′W
Okmulgee, Ok., U.S. (ôk-mŭl′gē)	121	35°37′N	95°58′W
Okolona, Ky., U.S. (ō-kô-lō′nȧ)	111h	38°08′N	85°41′W
Okolona, Ms., U.S.	124	33°59′N	88°43′W
Oktemberyan, Arm.	182	40°09′N	44°02′E
Okushiri, i., Japan (ō′koo-shē′rē)	210	42°12′N	139°30′E
Okuta, Nig.	235	9°14′N	3°15′E
Olalla, Wa., U.S. (ō-lä′lȧ)	116a	47°26′N	122°33′W
Olanchito, Hond. (ō′län-chē′tô)	132	15°28′N	86°35′W
Öland, i., Swe. (û-länd′)	156	57°03′N	17°15′E
Olathe, Ks., U.S. (ō-lā′thē)	117f	38°53′N	94°49′W
Olavarría, Arg. (ō-lä-vär-rē′ä)	144	36°49′N	60°15′W
Oława, Pol. (ô-lä′vȧ)	169	50°57′N	17°18′E
Olazoago, Arg. (ô-läz-kōä′gô)	141c	35°14′S	60°37′W
Olbia, Italy (ô′l-byä)	174	40°55′N	9°28′E
Olching, Ger. (ōl′kĕng)	159d	48°13′N	11°21′E
Old Bahama Channel, strt., N.A. (bȧ-hā′mȧ)	134	22°45′N	78°30′W
Old Bight, Bah.	135	24°15′N	75°20′W
Old Bridge, N.J., U.S. (brĭj)	110a	40°24′N	74°22′W
Old Crow, Can. (crō)	90	67°51′N	139°58′W
Oldenburg, Ger. (ôl′dĕn-bòrgh)	160	53°09′N	8°13′E
Old Forge, Pa., U.S. (fôrj)	109	41°20′N	75°50′W
Oldham, Eng., U.K. (ōld′ăm)	164	53°32′N	2°07′W
Oldham, co., Eng., U.K.	158a	53°35′N	2°05′W
Old Harbor, Ak., U.S. (här′bẽr)	103	57°18′N	153°20′W
Old Head of Kinsale, c., Ire. (ōld hĕd ŏv kĭn-sāl)	164	51°35′N	8°35′W
Old R, Tx., U.S.	123a	29°54′N	94°52′W
Olds, Can. (ōldz)	90	51°47′N	114°06′W
Old Tate, Bots.	232	21°18′S	27°43′E
Old Town, Me., U.S. (toun)	100	44°55′N	68°42′W
Old Wives Lake, l., Can. (wīvz)	96	50°05′N	106°00′W
Olean, N.Y., U.S. (ō-lē-ăn′)	105	42°05′N	78°25′W
Olecko, Pol. (ô-lĕt′skô)	169	54°02′N	22°29′E
Olekma, r., Russia (ô-lyĕk-mȧ′)	185	55°41′N	120°33′E
Olëkminsk, Russia (ô-lyĕk-mĕnsk′)	179	60°39′N	120°40′E
Oleksandriia, Ukr.	176	48°40′N	33°07′E
Olenëk, r., Russia (ô-lyĕ-nyôk′)	179	68°00′N	113°00′E
Oléron Île, d′, i., Fr. (ēl′ dō lā-rôɴ′)	161	45°52′N	1°58′W
Oleśnica, Pol. (ô-lĕsh-nĭ′tsȧ)	161	51°13′N	17°24′E
Olfen, Ger. (ōl′fĕn)	171c	51°43′N	7°22′E
Ol′ga, Russia (ôl′gȧ)	179	43°48′N	135°44′E
Ol′gi, Zaliv, b., Russia (zä′lĭf ôl′gĭ)	210	43°43′N	135°25′E
Olhão, Port. (ôl-youɴ′)	162	37°02′N	7°54′W
Ol′hopil′, Ukr.	177	48°11′N	29°28′E
Olievenhoutpoort, S. Afr.	233b	25°58′S	27°55′E
Ólimbos, mtn., Cyp.	197a	34°56′N	32°52′E
Olinda, Braz. (ô-lē′n-dä)	143	8°00′S	34°58′W
Olinda, Braz.	144b	22°49′S	43°25′W
Oliva, Spain (ô-lē′vä)	173	38°54′N	0°07′W
Oliva de la Frontera, Spain (ô-lē′vä dā)	172	38°33′N	6°55′W
Olive Hill, Ky., U.S. (ŏl′ĭv)	108	38°15′N	83°10′W
Oliveira, Braz. (ô-lē-vā′rä)	141a	20°42′S	44°49′W
Olivenza, Spain (ô-lē-vĕn′thä)	172	38°42′N	7°06′W
Oliver, Can. (ŏ′lĭ-vẽr)	90	49°11′N	119°33′W
Oliver, Can.	102g	53°38′N	113°21′W
Oliver, Wi., U.S. (ŏ′lĭvẽr)	117h	46°39′N	92°12′W
Oliver Lake, l., Can.	102g	53°19′N	113°00′W
Olivia, Mn., U.S. (ō-lĭv′ē-ȧ)	112	44°46′N	95°00′W
Olivos, Arg. (ōlē′vōs)	144a	34°30′S	58°29′W
Ollagüe, Chile (ô-lyä′gā)	142	21°17′S	68°17′W
Ollerton, Eng., U.K. (ôl′ẽr-tŭn)	158a	53°12′N	1°02′W
Olmos Park, Tx., U.S. (ōl′mŭs pärk′)	117d	29°27′N	98°32′W
Olney, Il., U.S. (ŏl′nĭ)	108	38°45′N	88°05′W
Olney, Or., U.S. (ŏl′nē)	116c	46°06′N	123°45′W
Olney, Tx., U.S.	120	33°24′N	98°43′W
Olomane, r., Can. (ō′lō mȧ′nĕ)	101	51°05′N	60°50′W
Olomouc, Czech Rep. (ô′lô-mōts)	161	49°37′N	17°15′E
Olonets, Russia (ô-lô′nĕts)	167	60°58′N	32°54′E
Olongapo, Phil.	212	14°49′S	120°17′E
Oloron, Gave d′, r., Fr. (gäv-dō-lō-rôɴ′)	170	43°21′N	0°44′W
Oloron-Sainte Marie, Fr. (ō-lō-rônt′săɴt mȧ-rē′)	170	43°11′N	1°37′W
Olot, Spain (ô-lōt′)	162	42°09′N	2°30′E
Olpe, Ger. (ōl′pĕ)	171c	51°02′N	7°51′E
Olsnitz, Ger. (ōlz′nĕtz)	168	50°25′N	12°11′E
Olsztyn, Pol. (ôl′shtĭn)	160	53°47′N	20°28′E
Olt, r., Rom.	163	44°09′N	24°40′E
Olten, Switz. (ôl′tĕn)	168	47°20′N	7°53′E
Olteniţa, Rom. (ôl-tā′nĭ-tsȧ)	175	44°05′N	26°39′E
Olvera, Spain (ôl-vĕ′rä)	172	36°55′N	5°16′W
Olympia, Wa., U.S. (ô-lĭm′pĭ-ȧ)	104	47°02′N	122°52′W
Olympic Mountains, mts., Wa., U.S.	114	47°54′N	123°58′W
Olympic National Park, rec., Wa., U.S. (ô-lĭm′pĭk)	106	47°54′N	123°00′W
Ólympos, mtn., Grc.	162	40°05′N	22°21′E
Olympus, Mount, mtn., Wa., U.S. (ô-lĭm′pŭs)	114	47°43′N	123°30′W
Olyphant, Pa., U.S. (ŏl′ĭ-fănt)	109	41°30′N	75°40′W
Olyutorskiy, Mys, c., Russia (ŭl-yōō′tŏr-skē)	179	59°49′N	167°16′E
Omae-Zaki, c., Japan (ō′mä-å zä′kē)	211	34°37′N	138°15′E
Omagh, N. Ire., U.K. (ō′mä)	164	54°35′N	7°25′W
Omaha, Ne., U.S. (ō′mȧ-hä)	105	41°18′N	95°57′W
Omaha Indian Reservation, I.R., Ne., U.S.	112	42°09′N	96°08′W
Oman, nation, Asia	198	20°00′N	57°45′E
Oman, Gulf of, b., Asia	198	24°24′N	58°58′E
Omaruru, Nmb. (ō-mä-rōō′rōō)	232	21°25′S	16°50′E
Ombrone, r., Italy (ôm-brō′nä)	174	42°48′N	11°18′E
Omdurman, Sudan	231	15°45′N	32°30′E
Omealca, Mex. (ōmā-äl′kō)	131	18°44′N	96°45′W
Ometepec, Mex. (ô-mā-tȧ-pĕk′)	130	16°41′N	98°27′W
Om Hajer, Eth.	231	14°06′N	36°46′E
Omineca, r., Can. (ō-mĭ-nĕk′ȧ)	94	55°50′N	125°45′W
Omineca Mountains, mts., Can.	94	56°00′N	125°00′W
Ōmiya, Japan (ō′mē-yȧ)	211	35°54′S	139°38′E
Omo, r., Eth. (ō′mō)	231	5°54′N	36°09′E
Omoa, Hond. (ô-mō′rä)	132	15°43′N	88°03′W
Omoko, Nig.	235	5°20′N	6°39′E
Omolon, r., Russia (ō′mō)	185	67°43′N	159°15′E
Ōmori, Japan (ō′mô-rē)	211a	35°50′N	140°09′E
Omotepe, Isla de, i., Nic. (ē′s-lä-dĕ-ō-mō-tā′pȧ)	132	11°32′N	85°30′W
Omro, Wi., U.S. (ŏm′rō)	113	44°01′N	89°46′W
Omsk, Russia (ômsk)	178	55°12′N	73°19′E
Ōmura, Japan (ō′mōō-rȧ)	211	32°56′N	129°57′E
Ōmuta, Japan (ō-mò-tȧ)	211	33°02′N	130°28′E
Omutninsk, Russia (ō′mōō-tnēnsk)	180	58°38′N	52°10′E
Onawa, Ia., U.S. (ŏn-ȧ-wȧ)	112	42°02′N	96°05′W
Onaway, Mi., U.S.	108	45°25′N	84°10′W
Oncócua, Ang.	236	16°34′S	13°28′E
Onda, Spain (ōn′dä)	173	39°58′N	0°13′W
Ondava, r., Slvk. (ōn′dȧ-vȧ)	169	48°51′N	21°40′E
Ondo, Nig.	235	7°04′N	4°47′E
Öndörhaan, Mong.	205	47°20′N	110°40′E
Onega, Russia (ô-nyĕ′gȧ)	178	63°50′N	38°08′E
Onega, r., Russia	180	63°20′N	39°20′E
Onega, Lake *see* Onezhskoye Ozero, l., Russia	180	62°02′N	34°35′E
Oneida, N.Y., U.S. (ô-nī′dȧ)	109	43°05′N	75°40′W
Oneida, l., N.Y., U.S.	109	43°10′N	76°00′W
O′Neill, Ne., U.S. (ō-nēl′)	112	42°28′N	98°38′W
Oneonta, N.Y., U.S. (ō-nē-ŏn′tȧ)	109	42°25′N	75°05′W
Onezhskaja Guba, b., Russia	180	64°30′N	36°00′E
Onezhskiy, Poluostrov, pen., Russia	180	64°30′N	37°40′E
Onezhskoye Ozero, Russia (ô-năsh′skô-yĕ ô′zĕ-rô)	180	62°02′N	34°35′E
Ongiin Hiid, Mong.	204	46°00′N	102°46′E
Ongole, India	203	15°36′N	80°03′E
Onilahy, r., Madag.	233	23°41′S	45°00′E
Onitsha, Nig. (ô-nĭt′shȧ)	230	6°09′N	6°47′W
Onomichi, Japan (ō′nô-mē′chē)	210	34°27′N	133°12′E
Onon, r., Asia (ō′nôn)	179	49°00′N	112°00′E
Onoto, Ven. (ô-nō′tô)	143b	9°38′N	65°03′W
Onslow, Austl. (ŏnz′lō)	218	21°53′S	115°00′E
Onslow B, N.C., U.S. (ônz′lō)	125	34°22′N	77°35′W
Ontake San, mtn., Japan (ôn′tä-kå sän)	210	35°55′N	137°29′E
Ontario, Ca., U.S. (ŏn-tā′rĭ-ō)	117a	34°04′N	117°39′E
Ontario, Or., U.S.	114	44°02′N	116°57′W
Ontario, prov., Can.	91	50°47′N	88°50′W
Ontario, Lake, l., N.A.	107	43°35′N	79°05′W
Ontinyent, Spain	173	38°48′N	0°35′W
Ontonagon, Mi., U.S. (ŏn-tô-năg′ŏn)	113	46°50′N	89°20′W
Ōnuki, Japan (ō′nōō-kē)	211a	35°17′N	139°51′E
Oodnadatta, Austl. (ōōd′nȧ-dȧ′tȧ)	218	27°38′S	135°40′E
Ooldea Station, Austl. (ōōl-dā′ä)	218	30°35′S	132°08′E
Oologah Reservoir, res., Ok., U.S.	107	36°43′N	95°32′W
Ooltgensplaat, Neth.	159a	51°41′N	4°19′E
Oostanaula, r., Ga., U.S. (ōō-stȧ-nô′lȧ)	124	34°25′N	85°10′W
Oostende, Bel. (ōst-ĕn′dĕ)	161	51°14′N	2°55′E
Oosterhout, Neth.	159a	51°38′N	4°52′E
Ooster Schelde, r., Neth.	159a	51°40′N	3°40′E
Ootsa Lake, l., Can.	94	53°49′N	126°18′W
Opalaca, Sierra de, mts., Hond. (sē-sĕ′r-rä-dĕ-ō-pä-lä′kä)	132	14°30′N	88°29′W
Opasquia, Can. (ō-păs′kwē-ȧ)	97	53°16′N	93°53′W
Opatów, Pol. (ô-pä′tòf)	169	50°47′N	21°25′E
Opava, Czech Rep. (ō′pä-vä)	169	49°56′N	17°52′E
Opelika, Al., U.S. (ŏp-ê-lī′kȧ)	124	32°39′N	85°23′W
Opelousas, La., U.S. (ŏp-ē-lōō′sȧs)	123	30°33′N	92°04′W
Opeongo, l., Can. (ŏp-ê-ôŋ′gō)	99	45°40′N	78°20′W
Opheim, Mt., U.S. (ô-fīm′)	115	48°51′N	106°19′W
Ophir, Ak., U.S. (ō′fẽr)	103	63°10′N	156°28′W
Ophir, Mount, mtn., Malay.	197b	2°22′N	102°37′E
Opico, El Sal. (ô-pē′kō)	132	13°50′N	89°23′W
Opinaca, r., Can. (ŏp-ĭ-nä′kȧ)	93	52°28′N	77°40′W
Opishnia, Ukr.	177	49°57′N	34°34′E
Opladen, Ger. (ōp′lä-dĕn)	171c	51°04′N	7°00′E
Opobo, Nig.	235	4°34′N	7°27′E
Opochka, Russia (ô-pôch′kȧ)	180	56°43′N	28°39′E
Opoczno, Pol. (ô-pôch′nô)	169	51°22′N	20°18′E
Opole, Pol. (ô-pôl′ä)	161	50°42′N	17°55′E
Opole Lubelskie, Pol. (ō-pō′lā lōō-bĕl′skyĕ)	169	51°09′N	21°58′E
Opp, Al., U.S. (ŏp)	124	31°18′N	86°15′W
Oppdal, Nor. (ôp′däl)	166	62°37′N	9°41′E
Opportunity, Wa., U.S. (ŏp-ŏr tū′nĭ tĭ)	114	47°37′N	117°20′W
Oquirrh Mountains, mts., Ut., U.S. (ō′kwẽr)	117b	40°38′N	112°11′W
Oradea, Rom. (ô-räd′yä)	154	47°02′N	21°55′E
Oral, Kaz.	183	51°14′N	51°22′E
Oran, Alg. (ō-rän) (ô-rän′)	230	35°46′N	0°45′W
Orán, Arg. (ô-rá′n)	144	23°13′S	64°17′W
Oran, Mo., U.S. (ôr′ăn)	121	37°05′N	89°39′W
Oran, Sebkha d′, l., Alg.	173	35°28′N	0°28′W
Orange, Austl. (ŏr′ĕnj)	219	33°15′S	149°08′E
Orange, Fr. (ô-ranzh′)	161	44°08′N	4°48′E
Orange, Ca., U.S.	117a	33°48′N	117°51′W
Orange, Ct., U.S.	109	41°15′N	73°00′W
Orange, N.J., U.S.	110a	40°46′N	74°14′W
Orange, Tx., U.S.	121	30°07′N	93°44′W
Orange, r., Afr.	232	29°15′S	17°30′E
Orange, Cabo, c., Braz. (kȧ-bô-rȧ′n-zhĕ)	143	4°25′N	51°30′W
Orangeburg, S.C., U.S. (ŏr′ĕnj-bûrg)	125	33°30′N	80°50′W
Orange Cay, i., Bah. (ŏr-ĕnj kē)	134	24°55′N	79°05′W
Orange City, Ia., U.S.	112	43°01′N	96°06′W
Orange Lake, l., Fl., U.S.	125	29°30′N	82°12′W
Orangeville, Can. (ŏr′ĕnj-vĭl)	99	43°55′N	80°06′W
Orangeville, S. Afr.	238c	27°05′S	28°13′E
Orange Walk, Belize (wôl′′k)	132a	18°09′N	88°32′W
Orani, Phil. (ō-rä′nē)	213a	14°47′N	120°32′E
Oranienburg, Ger. (ō-rä′nē-ĕn-bòrgh)	168	52°45′N	13°14′E
Oranjemund, Nmb.	232	28°33′S	16°20′E
Orăştie, Rom. (ô-rûsh′tyå)	175	45°50′N	23°14′E
Orbetello, Italy (ôr-bȧ-tĕl′lō)	174	42°27′N	11°15′E
Orbigo, r., Spain (ôr-bē′gō)	172	42°30′N	5°55′W
Orbost, Austl. (ôr′bŭst)	222	37°43′S	148°20′E
Orcas, i., Wa., U.S. (ôr′kȧs)	116d	48°43′N	122°52′W
Orchard Farm, Mo., U.S. (ôr′chẽrd färm)	117e	38°53′N	90°27′W
Orchard Park, N.Y., U.S.	111c	42°46′N	78°46′W
Orchards, Wa., U.S. (ôr′chĕdz)	116c	45°40′N	122°33′W
Orchila, Isla, i., Ven.	142	11°47′N	66°34′W
Ord, Ne., U.S. (ôrd)	112	41°35′N	98°57′W
Ord, r., Austl.	220	17°30′S	128°40′E
Ord, Mount, mtn., Az., U.S.	119	33°55′N	109°40′W
Orda, Kaz. (ôr′dȧ)	181	48°50′N	47°30′E
Orda, Russia (ôr′dȧ)	186a	57°10′N	57°12′E
Ordes, Spain	172	43°00′N	8°24′W
Ordos Desert, des., China	204	39°12′N	108°10′E
Ordu, Tur. (ôr′dò)	163	41°00′N	37°50′E
Ordway, Co., U.S. (ôrd′wā)	120	38°11′N	103°46′W
Örebro, Swe. (û′rē-brō)	160	59°16′N	15°11′E
Oredezh, r., Russia (ô′rĕ-dĕzh)	186c	59°23′N	30°21′E
Oregon, Il., U.S.	113	42°01′N	89°21′W
Oregon, state, U.S.	104	43°40′N	121°50′W
Oregon Caves National Monument, rec., Or., U.S. (cāvz)	114	42°05′N	123°13′W
Oregon City, Or., U.S.	116c	45°21′N	122°36′W
Öregrund, Swe. (û-rĕ-grònd)	166	60°20′N	18°26′E
Orekhovo, Blg.	175	43°43′N	23°59′E
Orekhovo-Zuyevo, Russia (ôr-yĕ′kô-vô zô′yĕ-vô)	178	55°46′N	39°00′E
Orël, Russia (ôr-yôl′)	178	52°59′N	36°05′E
Orël, prov., Russia	176	52°35′N	36°08′E
Orem, Ut., U.S. (ō′rĕm)	119	40°15′N	111°50′W
Ore Mountains *see* Erzgebirge, mts., Eur.	156	50°29′N	12°40′E
Orenburg, Russia (ō′rĕn-bōōrg)	178	51°50′N	55°05′E
Øresund, strt., Eur.	166	55°50′N	12°40′E
Órganos, Sierra de los, mts., Cuba (sē-ĕ′r-rȧ-dĕ-lôs-ŏ′r-gä-nôs)	134	22°20′N	84°10′W
Organ Pipe Cactus National Monument, rec., Az., U.S. (ôr′găn pīp kăk′tŭs)	119	32°14′N	113°05′W
Orgãos, Serra das, mts., Braz. (sĕ′r-rä-däs-ôr-gouɴ′s)	141a	22°30′S	43°01′W
Orhei, Mol.	181	47°27′N	28°49′E
Orhon, r., Mong.	204	48°33′N	103°07′E
Oriental, Cordillera, mts., Col. (kôr-dēl-yĕ′rä)	142a	3°30′N	74°27′W
Oriental, Cordillera, mts., Dom. Rep. (kôr-dēl-yĕ′rä-ô-ryĕ′n-täl)	135	18°55′N	69°40′W
Oriental, Cordillera, mts., S.A. (kôr-dēl-yĕ′rä ō-rē-ĕn-täl′)	142	14°00′S	68°33′W
Orikhiv, Ukr.	177	47°34′N	35°51′E

PLACE (Pronunciation)	PAGE	LAT.	LONG.
Oril', r., Ukr.	177	49°08'N	34°55'E
Orillia, Can. (ô-rĭl'ĭ-*á*)	91	44°35'N	79°25'W
Orin, Wy., U.S.	115	42°40'N	105°10'W
Orinda, Ca., U.S.	116b	37°53'N	122°11'W
Orinoco, r., Ven. (ō-rĭ-nō'kô)	142	8°32'N	63°13'W
Oriola, Spain	173	38°04'N	0°55'W
Orion, Phil. (ō-rē-ōn')	213a	14°37'N	120°34'E
Orissa, state, India (ŏ-rĭs'á)	199	25°09'N	83°50'E
Oristano, Italy (ô-rēs-tä'nō)	162	39°53'N	8°38'E
Oristano, Golfo di, b., Italy (gôl-fô-dē-ô-rēs-tä'nō)	174	39°53'N	8°12'E
Orituco, r., Ven. (ô-rē-tōō'kō)	143b	9°37'N	66°25'W
Oriuco, r., Ven. (ô-rēōō'kō)	143b	9°36'N	66°25'W
Orivesi, l., Fin.	167	62°15'N	29°55'E
Orizaba, Mex. (ô-rē-zä'bä)	129	18°52'N	97°05'E
Orizaba, Pico de, vol., Mex.	128	19°04'N	97°14'W
Orkanger, Nor.	166	63°19'N	9°54'W
Orkla, r., Nor. (ôr'klå)	166	62°55'N	9°50'E
Orkney, S. Afr. (ôrk'nĭ)	238c	26°58'S	26°39'E
Orkney Islands, is., Scot., U.K.	156	59°01'N	2°08'W
Orlando, S. Afr. (ôr-lăn-dô)	233b	26°15'S	27°56'E
Orlando, Fl., U.S. (ôr-lăn'dō)	105	28°32'N	81°22'W
Orland Park, Il., U.S. (ôr-lănd')	111a	41°38'N	87°52'W
Orleans, Can. (ôr-lå-än')	102c	45°28'N	75°31'W
Orléans, Fr. (ôr-lā-än')	154	47°55'N	1°56'E
Orleans, In., U.S. (ôr-lēnz')	108	38°40'N	86°25'W
Orléans, Île d', i., Can.	99	46°56'N	70°57'W
Orly, Fr.	171b	48°45'N	2°24'E
Ormond Beach, Fl., U.S. (ôr'm*ŏ*nd)	125	29°15'N	81°05'W
Ormskirk, Eng., U.K. (ôrms'kĕrk)	158a	53°34'N	2°53'W
Ormstown, Can. (ôrms'toun)	102a	45°07'N	74°00'W
Orneta, Pol. (ôr-nyĕ'tä)	169	54°07'N	20°10'E
Örnsköldsvik, Swe. (ûrn'skôlts-vēk)	160	63°10'N	18°32'E
Oro, Río del, r., Mex. (rē'ō dĕl ō'rō)	130	18°04'N	100°59'W
Oro, Río del, r., Mex.	119	26°04'N	105°40'W
Orobie, Alpi, mts., Italy (äl'pē-ô-rō'byĕ)	174	46°05'N	9°47'E
Oron, Nig.	235	4°48'N	8°14'E
Orosei, Golfo di, b., Italy (gôl-fô-dē-ō-rô-sā'ē)	174	40°12'N	9°45'E
Orosháza, Hung. (ô-rôsh-hä'sô)	169	46°33'N	20°31'E
Orosi, vol., C.R. (ō-rō'sē)	132	11°00'N	85°30'W
Oroville, Ca., U.S. (ōr'ô-vĭl)	118	39°29'N	121°34'W
Oroville, Wa., U.S.	114	48°55'N	119°25'W
Oroville, Lake, res., Ca., U.S.	118	39°32'N	121°25'W
Orreagal, Spain	172	43°00'N	1°17'W
Orrville, Oh., U.S. (ôr'vĭl)	108	40°45'N	81°50'W
Orsa, Swe. (ōr'sä)	166	61°08'N	14°35'E
Orsha, Bela. (ôr'shá)	180	54°29'N	30°28'E
Orsk, Russia (ôrsk)	178	51°15'N	58°50'E
Orşova, Rom. (ôr'shô-vä)	175	44°43'N	22°26'E
Ortega, Col. (ôr-tĕ'gä)	142a	3°56'N	75°12'W
Ortegal, Cabo, c., Spain (kå'bô-ôr-tå-gäl')	162	43°46'N	8°15'W
Orth, Aus.	159e	48°09'N	16°42'E
Orthez, Fr. (ôr-tĕz')	171	43°29'N	0°43'W
Órthrys, Óros, mtn., Grc.	175	39°00'N	22°15'E
Ortigueira, Spain (ôr-tē-gā'ê-rä)	162	43°40'N	7°50'W
Orting, Wa., U.S. (ôrt'ĭng)	116a	47°06'N	122°12'W
Ortona, Italy (ôr-tō'nä)	174	42°22'N	14°22'E
Ortonville, Mn., U.S. (ôr-t*ŭ*n-vĭl)	112	45°18'N	96°26'W
Orūmīyeh, Iran	198	37°30'N	45°15'E
Orūmīyeh, Daryacheh-ye, l., Iran	198	38°01'N	45°17'E
Oruro, Bol. (ō-rōō'rō)	142	17°57'S	66°59'W
Orvieto, Italy (ôr-vyå'tō)	174	42°43'N	12°08'E
Osa, Russia (ō'sä)	180	57°18'N	55°25'E
Osa, Península de, pen., C.R. (ō'sä)	133	8°30'N	83°25'W
Osage, Ia., U.S. (ō'sāj)	113	43°16'N	92°49'W
Osage, r., Mo., U.S.	121	38°10'N	93°12'W
Osage City, Ks., U.S. (ō'sāj sĭ'tĭ)	121	38°28'N	95°53'W
Ōsaka, Japan (ō'sä-kä)	205	34°40'N	135°27'E
Ōsaka, dept., Japan	211b	34°45'N	135°36'E
Ōsaka-Wan, b., Japan (wän)	210	34°34'N	135°16'E
Osakis, Mn., U.S. (ô-sā'kĭs)	112	45°51'N	95°09'W
Osakis, l., Mn., U.S.	113	45°55'N	94°55'W
Osawatomie, Ks., U.S. (ŏs-*á*-wät'ō-mē)	121	38°29'N	94°57'W
Osborne, Ks., U.S. (ŏz'b*ŭ*rn)	120	39°25'N	98°42'W
Osceola, Ar., U.S. (ŏs-ê-ō'lå)	121	35°42'N	89°58'W
Osceola, Ia., U.S.	113	41°04'N	93°45'W
Osceola, Mo., U.S.	121	38°02'N	93°41'W
Osceola, Ne., U.S.	112	41°11'N	97°34'W
Oscoda, Mi., U.S. (ŏs-kō'd*á*)	108	44°25'N	83°20'W
Osëtr, r., Russia (ō'sĕt'r)	176	54°27'N	38°15'E
Osgood, In., U.S. (ŏz'gŏŏd)	108	39°10'N	85°20'W
Osgoode, Can.	102c	45°09'N	75°37'W
Osh, Kyrg. (ōsh)	183	40°33'N	72°48'E
Oshawa, Can. (ŏsh'*á*-w*á*)	91	43°50'N	78°50'W
Ōshima, i., Japan (ō'shē'mä)	211	34°47'N	139°35'E
Oshkosh, Ne., U.S. (ŏsh'kŏsh)	112	41°24'N	102°22'W
Oshkosh, Wi., U.S.	105	44°01'N	88°35'W
Oshogbo, Nig.	230	7°47'N	4°34'E
Osijek, Cro. (ôs'ĭ-yĕk)	163	45°33'N	18°48'E
Osinniki, Russia (ŭ-sē'nyĭ-kē)	184	53°37'N	87°21'E
Oskaloosa, Ia., U.S. (ŏs-k*á*-lōō's*á*)	113	41°16'N	92°40'W
Oskarshamn, Swe. (ôs'kärs-häm'n)	166	57°16'N	16°24'E
Oskarström, Swe. (ôs'kärs-strûm)	166	56°48'N	12°55'E
Öskemen, Kaz.	183	49°58'N	82°38'E
Oskil, r., Eur.	181	51°00'N	37°41'E
Oslo, Nor. (ŏs'lō)	154	59°56'N	10°41'E
Oslofjorden, b., Nor.	166	59°03'N	10°35'E
Osmaniye, Tur.	163	37°10'N	36°30'E
Osnabrück, Ger. (ôs-nä-brük')	168	52°16'N	8°05'E
Osorno, Chile (ô-sŏ'r-nō)	144	40°42'S	73°13'W
Osøyra, Nor.	166	60°24'N	5°22'E
Osprey Reef, rf., Austl. (ŏs'prå)	221	14°00'S	146°45'E
Ossa, Mount, mtn., Austl. (ŏs*á*)	221	41°45'S	146°05'E
Osseo, Mn., U.S. (ŏs'sē-ō)	117g	45°07'N	93°24'W
Ossining, N.Y., U.S. (ŏs'ĭ-nĭng)	110a	41°09'N	73°51'W
Ossipee, N.H., U.S. (ŏs'ĭ-pē)	100	43°42'N	71°08'W
Ossjøen, l., Nor. (ôs-syûĕn)	166	61°20'N	12°00'E
Ostashkov, Russia (ôs-täsh'kôf)	180	57°07'N	33°04'E
Oster, Ukr. (ōs'tĕr)	177	50°55'N	30°52'E
Osterdalälven, r., Swe.	160	61°40'N	13°00'E
Østerfjord, b., Nor. (ûs'tĕr fyôr')	166	60°40'N	5°25'E
Östersund, Swe. (ûs'tĕr-sōōnd)	160	63°09'N	14°49'E
Östhammar, Swe. (ûst'häm'är)	166	60°16'N	18°21'E
Ostrava, Czech Rep.	154	49°51'N	18°18'E
Ostróda, Pol. (ôs'trōt-à)	169	53°41'N	19°58'E
Ostrogozhsk, Russia (ôs-tr-gôzhk')	181	50°53'N	39°03'E
Ostroh, Ukr.	181	50°21'N	26°40'E
Ostrołęka, Pol. (ôs-trô-wôɴ'kà)	169	53°04'N	21°35'E
Ostrov, Russia (ôs-trôf')	180	57°21'N	28°22'E
Ostrowiec Świętokrzyski, Pol. (ôs-trō'vyĕts shvyĕɴ-tō-kzhĭ'ske)	161	50°55'N	21°24'E
Ostrów Lubelski, Pol. (ôs'trôf lōō'bĕl-skĭ)	169	51°32'N	22°49'E
Ostrów Mazowiecka, Pol. (mä-zô-vyĕt'skä)	161	52°47'N	21°54'E
Ostrów Wielkopolski, Pol. (ôs'trōōf vyĕl-kō-pōl'skē)	161	51°38'N	17°49'E
Ostrzeszów, Pol. (ôs-tzhä'shôf)	169	51°26'N	17°56'E
Ostuni, Italy (ôs-tōō'nē)	175	40°44'N	17°35'E
Osum, r., Alb. (ō'sòm)	175	40°37'N	20°00'E
Osuna, Spain (ô-sōō'nä)	172	37°18'N	5°05'W
Osveya, Bela. (ôs'vĕ-yá)	176	56°00'N	28°08'E
Oswaldtwistle, Eng., U.K. (ŏz-w*ŭ*ld-twĭs''l)	158a	53°44'N	2°23'W
Oswegatchie, r., N.Y., U.S. (ŏs-wê-găch'ĭ)	109	44°15'N	75°20'W
Oswego, Ks., U.S. (ŏs-wē'gō)	121	37°10'N	95°08'W
Oswego, N.Y., U.S.	105	43°25'N	76°30'W
Oświęcim, Pol. (ôsh-vyăɴ'tsyĭm)	169	50°02'N	19°17'E
Otaru, Japan (ô'tá-rò)	205	43°07'N	141°00'E
Otavalo, Ec. (ōtä-vä'lō)	142	0°14'N	78°16'W
Otavi, Nmb. (ô-tä'vê)	232	19°35'S	17°20'E
Otay, Ca., U.S. (ō'tā)	118a	32°36'N	117°04'W
Otepää, Est.	167	58°03'N	26°30'E
Oti, r., Afr.	234	9°00'N	0°10'E
Otish, Monts, mts., Can. (ô-tĭsh')	93	52°15'N	70°20'W
Otjiwarongo, Nmb. (ŏt-jê-wá-rôn'gō)	232	20°20'S	16°25'E
Otočac, Cro. (ō'tô-chàts)	174	44°53'N	15°15'E
Otra, r., Nor.	166	59°13'N	7°20'E
Otra, r., Russia (ôt'rá)	186b	55°22'N	38°20'E
Otradnoye, Russia (ô-trå'd-nôyĕ)	186c	59°46'N	30°50'E
Otranto, Italy (ô'trän-tō) (ô-trän'tō)	175	40°07'N	18°30'E
Otranto, Strait of, strt., Eur.	156	40°30'N	18°45'E
Otsego, Mi., U.S. (ŏt-sē'gō)	108	42°25'N	85°45'W
Otsu, Japan (ō'tsò)	210	35°00'N	135°54'E
Otta, l., Nor. (ôt'tà)	166	61°53'N	8°40'E
Ottawa, Can. (ŏt'*á*-w*á*)	91	45°25'N	75°43'W
Ottawa, Il., U.S.	108	41°20'N	88°50'W
Ottawa, Ks., U.S.	121	38°37'N	95°16'W
Ottawa, Oh., U.S.	108	41°00'N	84°00'W
Ottawa, r., Can.	93	46°05'N	77°20'W
Otter Creek, r., Ut., U.S. (ŏt'ĕr)	119	38°20'N	111°55'W
Otter Creek, r., Vt., U.S.	109	44°05'N	73°15'W
Otter Point, c., Can.	116a	48°21'N	123°50'W
Otter Tail, l., Mn., U.S.	112	46°21'N	95°52'W
Otterville, Il., U.S. (ŏt'ĕr-vĭl)	117e	39°03'N	90°24'W
Ottery, S. Afr. (ŏt'ĕr-ĭ)	232a	34°02'S	18°31'E
Ottumwa, Ia., U.S. (ô-tŭm'w*á*)	105	41°00'N	92°26'W
Otukpa, Nig.	235	7°09'N	7°41'E
Otumba, Mex. (ô-tŭm'bä)	130	19°41'N	98°46'W
Otway, Cape, c., Austl. (ŏt'wā)	221	38°55'S	153°40'E
Otway, Seno, b., Chile (sĕ'nō-ô't-wä'y)	144	53°00'S	73°00'W
Otwock, Pol. (ôt'vôtsk)	169	52°05'N	21°18'E
Ouachita, r., U.S.	107	33°25'N	92°30'W
Ouachita Mountains, mts., U.S. (wŏsh'ĭ-tô)	107	34°29'N	95°01'W
Ouagadougou, Burkina (wä'gä-dōō'gōō)	230	12°22'N	1°31'W
Ouahigouya, Burkina (wä-ê-gōō'yä)	230	13°35'N	2°25'W
Oualâta, Maur. (wä-lä'tä)	230	17°11'N	6°50'W
Ouallene, Alg. (wäl-lân')	230	24°43'N	1°15'E
Ouanaminthe, Haiti	135	19°35'N	71°45'W
Ouarane, reg., Maur.	230	20°44'N	10°27'W
Ouarkoye, Burkina	234	12°05'N	3°40'W
Ouassel, r., Alg.	173	35°30'N	1°55'E
Oubangui (Ubangi), r., Afr. (ōō-bäŋ'gē)	236	4°30'N	20°35'E
Oude Rijn, r., Neth.	159a	52°09'N	4°33'E
Oudewater, Neth.	159a	52°01'N	4°52'E
Oud-Gastel, Neth.	159a	51°35'N	4°27'E
Oudtshoorn, S. Afr. (outs'hōrn)	232	33°33'S	23°36'E
Oued Rhiou, Alg.	173	35°55'N	0°57'E
Oued Tlelat, Alg.	173	35°33'N	0°28'W
Oued-Zem, Mor. (wĕd-zĕm')	230	33°05'N	5°49'W
Ouessant, Island d', i., Fr. (ēl-dwĕ-säɴ')	161	48°28'N	5°00'W
Ouesso, Congo	231	1°37'N	16°04'E
Ouest, Point, c., Haiti	135	19°00'N	73°25'W
Ouezzane, Mor. (wĕ-zan')	230	34°48'N	5°40'W
Ouham, r., Afr.	235	8°38'N	17°50'E
Ouidah, Benin (wē-dä')	230	6°25'N	2°05'E
Oujda, Mor.	230	34°41'N	1°45'W
Oulins, Fr. (ōō-làɴ')	171b	48°52'N	1°27'E
Oullins, Fr. (ōō-lăɴ')	170	45°44'N	4°46'E
Oulu, Fin. (ō'lò)	154	64°58'N	25°43'E
Oulujärvi, l., Fin.	160	64°20'N	25°48'E
Oum Chalouba, Chad (ōōm shä-lōō'bä)	231	15°48'N	20°30'E
Oum Hadjer, Chad	235	13°18'N	19°41'E
Ounas, r., Fin. (ō'nás)	160	67°46'N	24°40'E
Oundle, Eng., U.K. (ôn'd'l)	158a	52°28'N	0°28'W
Ounianga Kébir, Chad (ōō-nē-äŋ'gá kē-bēr')	231	19°04'N	20°22'E
Ouray, Co., U.S. (ōō-rā')	120	38°00'N	107°40'W
Ourense, Spain	172	42°20'N	7°52'W
Ourinhos, Braz. (ôò-rē'nyôs)	143	23°04'S	49°45'W
Ourique, Port. (ō-rē'*kĕ*)	172	37°39'N	8°10'W
Ouro Fino, Braz. (ōŭ-rô-fē'nō)	141a	22°18'S	46°21'W
Ouro Prêto, Braz. (ō'rò prā'tò)	144	20°24'S	43°30'W
Outardes, Rivière aux, r., Can.	93	50°53'N	68°50'W
Outer, i., Wi., U.S. (out'ĕr)	113	47°03'N	90°20'W
Outer Brass, i., V.I.U.S. (bräs)	129c	18°24'N	64°58'W
Outer Hebrides, is., Scot., U.K.	164	57°20'N	7°50'W
Outjo, Nmb. (ōt'yō)	232	20°05'S	17°10'E
Outlook, Can.	96	51°31'N	107°05'W
Outremont, Can. (ōō-trē-môɴ')	102a	45°31'N	73°36'W
Ouvéa, i., N. Cal.	221	20°43'S	166°48'E
Ouyen, Austl. (ōō-*ĕ*n)	222	35°05'S	142°10'E
Ovalle, Chile (ō-väl'yä)	144	30°43'S	71°16'W
Ovando, Bahía de, b., Cuba (bä-ē'ä-dĕ-ô-vä'n-dō)	135	20°10'N	74°05'W
Ovar, Port. (ô-vär')	172	40°52'N	8°38'W
Overijse, Bel.	159a	50°46'N	4°32'E
Overland, Mo., U.S. (ō-vēr-l*ă*nd)	117e	38°42'N	90°22'W
Overland Park, Ks., U.S.	117f	38°59'N	94°40'W
Overlea, Md., U.S. (ō'vĕr-lā)(ō'vĕr-lē)	110e	39°21'N	76°31'W
Övertornea, Swe.	160	66°19'N	23°31'E
Ovidiopol', Ukr.	177	46°15'N	30°28'E
Oviedo, Dom. Rep. (ô-vyĕ'dō)	135	17°50'N	71°25'W
Oviedo, Spain (ō-vê-ā'dhō)	154	43°22'N	5°50'W
Ovruch, Ukr.	177	51°19'N	28°51'E
Owada, Japan (ō'wä-dá)	211a	35°49'N	139°33'E
Owambo, hist. reg., Nmb.	232	18°10'S	15°00'E
Owando, Congo	232	0°29'S	15°55'E
Owasco, l., N.Y., U.S. (ō-wăsk'kō)	109	42°50'N	76°30'W
Owase, Japan (ō'wä-shē)	211	34°03'N	136°12'E
Owego, N.Y., U.S. (ō-wē'gō)	109	42°05'N	76°15'W
Owen, Wi., U.S. (ō'ĕn)	113	44°56'N	90°35'W
Owensboro, Ky., U.S. (ō'ĕnz-bŭr-ô)	105	37°45'N	87°05'W
Owens Lake, l., Ca., U.S.	118	37°13'N	118°20'W
Owen Sound, Can. (ō'ĕn)	91	44°30'N	80°55'W
Owen Stanley Range, mts., Pap. N. Gui. (stăn'lē)	213	9°00'S	147°30'E
Owensville, In., U.S. (ō'ĕnz-vĭl)	108	38°15'N	87°40'W
Owensville, Mo., U.S.	121	38°20'N	91°29'W
Owensville, Oh., U.S.	111f	39°08'N	84°07'W
Owenton, Ky., U.S. (ō'ĕn-t*ŭ*n)	108	38°35'N	84°55'W
Owerri, Nig. (ô-wĕr'ê)	230	5°26'N	7°04'E
Owings Mill, Md., U.S. (ōwĭngz mĭl)	110e	39°25'N	76°50'W
Owl Creek, r., Wy., U.S. (oul)	115	43°45'N	108°46'W
Owo, Nig.	235	7°15'N	5°37'E
Owosso, Mi., U.S. (ô-wŏs'ō)	108	43°00'N	84°15'W
Owyhee, r., U.S.	106	43°04'N	117°45'W
Owyhee, Lake, res., Or., U.S.	106	43°27'N	117°30'W
Owyhee, South Fork, r., Id., U.S.	114	42°07'N	116°43'W
Owyhee Mountains, mts., Id., U.S. (ô-wĭ'hê)	106	43°15'N	116°48'W
Oxbow, Can.	97	49°12'N	102°11'W
Oxchuc, Mex. (ôs-chōōk')	131	16°47'N	92°24'W
Oxford, Can. (ŏks'fērd)	100	45°44'N	63°52'W
Oxford, Eng., U.K.	161	51°43'N	1°16'W
Oxford, Al., U.S. (ŏks'fērd)	125	33°38'N	80°46'W
Oxford, Ma., U.S.	101a	42°07'N	71°52'W
Oxford, Mi., U.S.	108	42°50'N	83°15'W
Oxford, Ms., U.S.	124	34°22'N	89°30'W
Oxford, N.C., U.S.	125	36°17'N	78°35'W
Oxford, Oh., U.S.	108	39°30'N	84°45'W
Oxford Lake, l., Can.	97	54°51'N	95°37'W
Oxfordshire, co., Eng., U.K.	158b	51°36'N	1°30'W
Oxkutzcab, Mex. (ôx-kōō'tz-käb)	132a	20°18'N	89°22'W
Oxmoor, Al., U.S. (ŏks'mór)	110h	33°25'N	86°52'W
Oxnard, Ca., U.S. (ŏks'närd)	118	34°08'N	119°12'W
Oxon Hill, Md., U.S. (ōks'ōn hĭl)	110e	38°48'N	77°00'W
Oyapock, r., S.A. (ō-yä-pŏk')	143	2°45'N	52°15'W
Oyem, Gabon	230	1°37'N	11°35'E
Øyeren, l., Nor. (ûĭĕrĕn)	166	59°50'N	11°25'E
Oymyakon, Russia (oi-myŭ-kôn')	179	63°14'N	142°58'E
Oyo, Nig. (ō'yō)	230	7°51'N	3°56'E
Oyonnax, Fr. (ô-yô-náks')	171	46°16'N	5°40'E
Oyster Bay, N.Y., U.S.	110a	40°52'N	73°32'W
Oyster Bayou, Tx., U.S.	123a	29°41'N	94°33'W
Oyster Creek, r., Tx., U.S. (ois'tēr)	123a	29°13'N	95°29'W
Oyyl, r., Kaz.	181	49°30'N	55°10'E
Ozama, r., Dom. Rep. (ō-zä'mä)	135	18°45'N	69°55'W
Ozamiz, Phil. (ô-zä'mēz)	213	8°06'N	123°43'E
Ozark, Al., U.S. (ō'zärk)	124	31°28'N	85°28'W
Ozark, Ar., U.S.	121	35°29'N	93°49'W
Ozark Plateau, plat., U.S.	107	36°37'N	93°56'W
Ozarks, Lake of the, l., Mo., U.S. (ō'zärksz)	107	38°06'N	93°26'W
Ozëry, Russia (ô-zyô'rê)	176	54°53'N	38°31'E
Ozieri, Italy	162	40°38'N	8°53'E
Ozorków, Pol. (ô-zôr'kôf)	169	51°58'N	19°20'E
Ozuluama, Mex.	131	21°34'N	97°52'W
Ozumba, Mex.	131a	19°02'N	98°48'W
Ozurgeti, Geor.	182	41°56'N	42°00'E

ăt; finăl; rāte; senåte; ärm; åsk; sofá; fâre; ch-choose; dh-as th in other; bē; ēvent; bĕt; recĕnt; cratēr; g-gō; gh-guttural g; bĭt; ĭ-short neutral; rīde; ĸ-guttural k as ch in German ich;

PRONOUNCING INDEX

Paarl – Paris 333

P

PLACE (Pronunciation)	PAGE	LAT.	LONG.
Paarl, S. Afr. (pärl)	232	33°45'S	18°55'E
Pa'auilo, Hi., U.S. (pä-ä-ōō'ē-lō)	126a	20°03'N	155°25'W
Pabianice, Pol. (pä-byå-nē'tsĕ)	169	51°40'N	19°29'E
Pacaás Novos, Massiço de, mts., Braz.	142	11°03'S	64°02'W
Pacaraima, Serra, mts., S.A. (sĕr'rá pä-kä-rä-ē'mä)	142	3°45'N	62°30'W
Pacasmayo, Peru (pä-käs-mä'yō)	142	7°24'S	79°30'W
Pachuca, Mex. (pä-chōō'kä)	128	20°07'N	98°43'W
Pacific, Wa., U.S. (pá-sĭf'ĭk)	116a	47°16'N	122°15'W
Pacifica, Ca., U.S. (pá-sĭf'ĭ-kä)	116b	37°38'N	122°29'W
Pacific Beach, Ca., U.S.	118a	32°47'N	117°22'W
Pacific Grove, Ca., U.S.	118	36°37'N	121°54'W
Pacific Islands, Trust Territory of the *see* Palau, nation, Oc.	3	7°15'N	134°30'E
Pacific Ocean, o.	2	0°00'	170°00'W
Pacific Ranges, mts., Can.	94	51°00'N	125°30'W
Pacific Rim National Park, rec., Can.	94	49°00'N	126°00'W
Pacolet, r., S.C., U.S. (pă'cō-lĕt)	125	34°55'N	81°49'W
Pacy-sur-Eure, Fr. (pä-sē-sür-ûr')	171b	49°01'N	1°24'E
Padang, Indon. (pä-däng')	212	1°01'S	100°28'E
Padang, i., Indon.	197b	1°12'N	102°21'E
Padang Endau, Malay.	197b	2°39'N	103°38'E
Paden City, W.V., U.S. (pā'dĕn)	108	39°30'N	80°55'W
Paderborn, Ger. (pä-dĕr-bôrn')	168	51°43'N	8°46'E
Padibe, Ug.	237	3°28'N	32°50'E
Padiham, Eng., U.K. (păd'ĭ-hăm)	158a	53°48'N	2°19'W
Padilla, Mex. (pä-dēl'yä)	130	24°00'N	98°45'W
Padilla Bay, b., Wa., U.S. (pä-dĭl'là)	116a	48°31'N	122°34'W
Padova, Italy (pä'dô-vä)(păd'û-á)	162	45°24'N	11°53'E
Padre Island, i., Tx., U.S. (pä'drā)	123	27°09'N	97°15'W
Padua *see* Padova, Italy	162	45°24'N	11°53'E
Paducah, Ky., U.S.	105	37°05'N	88°36'W
Paducah, Tx., U.S.	120	34°01'N	100°18'W
Paektu-san, mtn., Asia (pâk'tōō-sän')	210	42°00'N	128°03'E
Pag, i., Yugo. (päg)	174	44°30'N	14°48'E
Pagai Selatan, Pulau, i., Indon.	212	2°48'S	100°22'E
Pagai Utara, Pulau, i., Indon.	212	2°45'S	100°02'E
Pagasitikós Kólpos, b., Grc.	175	39°15'N	23°00'E
Page, Az., U.S.	119	36°57'N	111°27'W
Pago Pago, Am. Sam.	214a	14°16'S	170°42'W
Pagosa Springs, Co., U.S. (pá-gō'sá)	120	37°15'N	107°05'W
Pāhala, Hi., U.S. (pä-hä'lä)	126a	19°11'N	155°28'W
Pahang, state, Malay.	197b	3°02'N	102°57'E
Pahang, r., Malay.	212	3°39'N	102°41'E
Pahokee, Fl., U.S. (pá-hō'kē)	125a	26°45'N	80°40'W
Paide, Est. (pī'dĕ)	167	58°54'N	25°30'E
Päijänne, l., Fin. (pĕ'ē-yĕn-nĕ)	160	61°38'N	25°05'E
Pailolo Channel, strt., Hi., U.S. (pä-ē-lō'lō)	126a	21°05'N	156°41'W
Paine, Chile (pī'nĕ)	141b	33°49'S	70°44'W
Painesville, Oh., U.S. (pānz'vĭl)	108	41°40'N	81°15'W
Painted Desert, des., Az., U.S. (pānt'ĕd)	120	36°15'N	111°35'W
Painted Rock Reservoir, res., Az., U.S.	119	33°00'N	113°05'W
Paintsville, Ky., U.S. (pānts'vĭl)	108	37°50'N	82°50'W
Paisley, Scot., U.K. (pāz'lĭ)	160	55°50'N	4°30'W
Paita, Peru (pä-ē'tä)	142	5°11'S	81°12'W
Pai T'ou Shan, mts., Kor., N.	205	40°30'N	127°20'E
Paiute Indian Reservation, I.R., Ut., U.S.	119	38°17'N	113°50'W
Pajápan, Mex. (pä-hä'pän)	131	18°16'N	94°41'W
Pakanbaru, Indon.	212	0°43'N	101°15'E
Pakhra, r., Russia (päk'rá)	186b	55°29'N	37°51'E
Pakistan, nation, Asia	199	28°00'N	67°30'E
Pakokku, Mya. (pá-kŏk'kò)	204	21°29'N	95°00'E
Paks, Hung. (pôksh)	169	46°38'N	18°53'E
Pala, Chad	235	9°22'N	14°54'E
Palacios, Tx., U.S. (pä-lä'syōs)	123	28°42'N	96°12'W
Palagruža, Otoci, is., Cro.	174	42°20'N	16°23'E
Palaiseau, Fr. (pá-lĕ-zō')	171b	48°44'N	2°16'E
Palana, Russia	179	59°07'N	159°58'E
Palanan Bay, b., Phil. (pä-lä'nän)	213a	17°14'N	122°35'E
Palanan Point, c., Phil.	213a	17°12'N	122°40'E
Pālanpur, India (pä'lŭn-pōōr)	199	24°08'N	73°29'E
Palapye, Bots. (pá-läp'yĕ)	232	22°34'S	27°28'E
Palatine, Il., U.S. (păl'á-tīn)	111a	42°07'N	88°03'W
Palatka, Fl., U.S. (pá-lăt'ká)	125	29°39'N	81°40'W
Palau (Belau), nation, Oc. (pä-lä'ò)	3	7°15'N	134°30'E
Palauig, Phil. (pá-lou'ĕg)	213a	15°27'N	119°54'E
Palawan, i., Phil. (pä-lä'wán)	212	9°50'N	117°38'E
Pālayankottai, India	203	8°50'N	77°50'E
Paldiski, Est. (päl'dĭ-skĭ)	167	59°22'N	24°04'E
Palembang, Indon. (pä-lĕm-băng')	212	2°57'S	104°40'E
Palencia, Guat. (pä-lĕn'sē-á)	132	14°40'N	90°22'W
Palencia, Spain (pä-lĕ'n-syä)	162	42°02'N	4°32'W
Palenque, Mex. (pä-lĕŋ'kā)	131	17°34'N	91°58'W
Palenque, Punta, c., Dom. Rep. (pōō'n-tä)	135	18°10'N	70°10'W
Palermo, Col. (pä-lĕr'mô)	142a	2°53'N	75°26'W
Palermo, Italy	154	38°08'N	13°24'E
Palestine, Tx., U.S.	105	31°46'N	95°38'W
Palestine, hist. reg., Asia (păl'ĕs-tīn)	197a	31°33'N	35°00'E
Paletwa, Mya. (pŭ-lĕt'wä)	199	21°19'N	92°52'E
Palghāt, India	203	10°49'N	76°40'E
Pāli, India	202	25°53'N	73°18'E
Palín, Guat. (pä-lēn')	132	14°42'N	90°42'W
Palizada, Mex. (pä-lē-zä'dä)	131	18°17'N	92°04'W
Palk Strait, strt., Asia (pôk)	199	10°00'N	79°23'E
Palma, Braz. (päl'mä)	141a	21°23'S	42°18'W
Palma, Spain	154	39°35'N	2°38'E
Palma, Bahía de, b., Spain	173	39°24'N	2°37'E
Palma del Río, Spain	172	37°43'N	5°19'W
Palmares, Braz. (päl-má'rĕs)	143	8°46'S	35°28'W
Palmas, Braz. (päl'mäs)	144	26°20'S	51°56'W
Palmas, Braz.	143	10°08'S	48°18'W
Palmas, Cape, c., Lib.	230	4°22'N	7°44'W
Palma Soriano, Cuba (sò-rē-ä'nō)	134	20°15'N	76°00'W
Palm Beach, Fl., U.S. (päm bēch')	125a	26°43'N	80°03'W
Palmeira dos Índios, Braz. (pä-mā'rä-dôs-ē'n-dyôs)	143	9°26'S	36°33'W
Palmeirinhas, Ponta das, c., Ang.	236	9°05'S	13°00'E
Palmela, Port. (päl-mā'lä)	172	38°34'N	8°54'W
Palmer, Ak., U.S. (päm'ĕr)	103	61°38'N	149°15'W
Palmer, Wa., U.S.	116a	47°19'N	121°53'W
Palmerston North, N.Z. (päm'ĕr-stŭn)	221a	40°20'S	175°35'E
Palmerville, Austl. (päm'ĕr-vĭl)	219	16°08'S	144°15'E
Palmetto, Fl., U.S. (pál-mĕt'ō)	125a	27°32'N	82°34'W
Palmetto Point, c., Bah.	135	21°15'N	73°25'W
Palmi, Italy (päl'mē)	174	38°21'N	15°54'E
Palmira, Col. (päl-mē'rä)	142	3°33'N	76°17'W
Palmira, Cuba	134	22°15'N	80°25'W
Palmyra, Mo., U.S. (păl-mī'rá)	121	39°45'N	91°32'W
Palmyra, N.J., U.S.	110f	40°01'N	75°00'W
Palmyra, i., Oc.	2	6°00'N	162°20'W
Palmyra, hist., Syria	198	34°25'N	38°28'E
Palmyras Point, c., India	202	20°42'N	87°45'E
Palo Alto, Ca., U.S. (pă'lō ăl'tō)	116b	37°27'N	122°09'W
Paloduro Creek, r., Tx., U.S. (pă-lô-dōō'rô)	120	36°16'N	101°12'W
Paloh, Malay.	197b	2°11'N	103°12'E
Paloma, l., Mex. (pä-lō'mä)	122	26°53'N	104°02'W
Palomo, Cerro el, mtn., Chile (sĕ'r-rô-ĕl-pä-lô'mô)	141b	34°36'S	70°20'W
Palos, Cabo de, c., Spain (kä'bô-dĕ-pä'lôs)	162	39°38'N	0°43'W
Palos Verdes Estates, Ca., U.S. (pă'lŭs vûr'dĭs)	117a	33°48'N	118°24'W
Palouse, Wa., U.S. (pá-lōōz')	114	46°54'N	117°04'W
Palouse, r., Wa., U.S.	114	47°02'N	117°35'W
Palu, Tur. (pä-loo')	181	38°55'N	40°10'E
Paluan, Phil. (pä-lōō'än)	213a	13°25'N	120°29'E
Pamiers, Fr. (pá-myā')	161	43°07'N	1°34'E
Pamirs, mts., Asia	199	38°14'N	72°27'E
Pamlico, r., N.C., U.S. (păm'lĭ-kō)	125	35°25'N	76°59'W
Pamlico Sound, strt., N.C., U.S.	107	35°10'N	76°10'W
Pampa, Tx., U.S. (păm'pá)	104	35°32'N	100°56'W
Pampa de Castillo, pl., Arg. (pä'm-pä-dĕ-käs-tē'l-yô)	144	45°30'S	67°30'W
Pampana, r., S.L.	234	8°35'N	11°55'W
Pampanga, r., Phil. (päm-päŋ'gä)	213a	15°20'N	120°48'E
Pampas, reg., Arg. (päm'päs)	144	37°00'S	64°30'W
Pampilhosa do Botão, Port. (päm-pē-lyō'sá-dô-bō-touN)	172	40°21'N	8°32'W
Pamplona, Col. (päm-plō'nä)	142	7°19'N	72°41'W
Pamplona, Spain (päm-plô'nä)	162	42°49'N	1°39'W
Pamunkey, r., Va., U.S. (pá-mŭŋ'kĭ)	109	37°40'N	77°20'W
Pana, Il., U.S. (pā'ná)	108	39°25'N	89°05'W
Panagyurishte, Blg. (pá-ná-gyōō'rĕsh-tĕ)	175	42°30'N	24°11'E
Panaji (Panjim), India	199	15°33'N	73°52'E
Panamá, Pan.	129	8°58'N	79°32'W
Panama, nation, N.A.	129	9°00'N	80°00'W
Panamá, Istmo de, isth., Pan.	129	9°00'N	80°00'W
Panama Canal, can., Pan.	128a	9°20'N	79°55'W
Panama City, Fl., U.S. (păn-á mä' sĭ'tĭ)	124	30°08'N	85°39'W
Panamint Range, mts., Ca., U.S. (păn-á-mĭnt')	118	36°40'N	117°30'W
Panarea, i., Italy (pä-nä'rĕ-a)	174	38°37'N	15°05'E
Panaro, r., Italy (pä-nä'rô)	174	44°47'N	11°06'E
Panay, i., Phil. (pä-nī')	212	11°15'N	121°38'E
Pančevo, Yugo. (pán'chĕ-vô)	163	44°52'N	20°42'E
Panchor, Malay.	197b	2°11'N	102°43'E
Pānchur, India	202a	22°31'N	88°17'E
Panda, D.R.C. (pän'dä')	232	10°59'S	27°24'E
Pan de Guajaibon, mtn., Cuba (pän dā gwä-já-bōn')	134	22°50'N	83°20'W
Panevėžys, Lith. (pä'nyĕ-vāzh'ēs)	180	55°44'N	24°21'E
Panga, D.R.C. (päŋ'gá)	231	1°51'N	26°25'E
Pangani, Tan. (pän-gä'nē)	233	5°28'S	38°58'E
Pangani, r., Tan.	237	4°40'S	37°45'E
Pangkalpinang, Indon. (päng-käl'pē-näng')	212	2°11'S	106°04'E
Pangnirtung, Can.	91	66°08'N	65°26'W
Panguitch, Ut., U.S. (păn'gwĭch)	119	37°50'N	112°30'W
Panié, Mont, mtn., N. Cal.	214f	20°36'S	164°46'E
Pānihāti, India	202a	22°42'N	88°23'E
Panimávida, Chile (pä-nē-má'vē-dä)	141b	35°44'S	71°26'W
Panshi, China (pän-shē)	208	42°50'N	126°48'E
Pantar, Pulau, i., Indon. (pän'tär)	213	8°40'N	123°45'E
Pantelleria, i., Italy (pän-tĕl-lå-rē'ä)	162	36°43'N	11°59'E
Pantepec, Mex. (pän-tå-pĕk')	131	17°11'N	93°04'W
Panuco, Mex. (pä'nōō-kô)	130	22°04'N	98°11'W
Pánuco, Mex. (pä'nōō-kô)	130	23°25'N	105°55'W
Panuco, r., Mex.	128	21°59'N	98°20'W
Pánuco de Coronado, Mex. (pä'nōō-kô dā kō-rô-nä'dhō)	122	24°33'N	104°20'W
Panvel, India	203b	18°59'N	73°06'E
Panyu, China (pä-yōō)	207a	22°56'N	113°22'E
Panzós, Guat. (pän-zós')	132	15°26'N	89°40'W
Pao, r., Ven. (pä'ō)	143b	9°52'N	67°57'W
Paola, Ks., U.S. (på-ō'lá)	121	38°34'N	94°51'W
Paoli, In., U.S. (på-ō'lĭ)	108	38°35'N	86°30'W
Paoli, Pa., U.S.	110f	40°03'N	75°29'W
Paonia, Co., U.S. (pā-ō'nyá)	119	38°50'N	107°40'W
Pápa, Hung. (pä'pô)	163	47°18'N	17°27'E
Papagayo, r., Mex. (pä-pä-gä'yō)	130	16°52'N	99°41'W
Papagayo, Golfo del, b., C.R. (gôl-fô-dĕl-pä-pä-gá'yō)	132	10°44'N	85°56'W
Papagayo, Laguna, l., Mex. (lä-ò-nä)	130	16°44'N	99°44'W
Papantla de Olarte, Mex. (pä-pän'tlä dä-ô-lä'r-tĕ)	128	20°30'N	97°15'W
Papatoapan, r., Mex. (pä-pä-tô-ä-pá'n)	131	18°00'N	96°22'W
Papenburg, Ger. (päp'ĕn-bôrgh)	168	53°05'N	7°23'E
Papinas, Arg. (pä-pē'näs)	141c	35°30'S	57°19'W
Papineauville, Can. (pä-pē-nō'vĕl)	102c	45°38'N	75°01'W
Papua, Gulf of, b., Pap. N. Gui. (păp-ōō-á)	213	8°20'S	144°45'E
Papua New Guinea, nation, Oc. (păp-ōō-á)(gĭne)	213	7°00'S	142°15'E
Papudo, Chile (pä-pōō'dô)	141b	32°30'S	71°25'W
Paquequer Pequeno, Braz. (pä-kĕ-kĕ'r-pĕ-kĕ'nô)	144b	22°19'S	43°02'W
Para, r., Russia	176	53°45'N	40°58'E
Paracale, Phil. (pä-rä-kä'lå)	213a	14°17'N	122°47'E
Paracambi, Braz.	144b	22°36'S	43°43'W
Paracatu, Braz. (pä-rä-kä-tōō')	143	17°17'S	46°43'W
Paracel Islands, is., Asia	212	16°40'N	113°00'E
Paraćin, Yugo. (pá'rä-chĕn)	163	43°51'N	21°26'E
Para de Minas, Braz. (pä-rä-dĕ-mē'näs)	143	19°52'S	44°37'W
Paradise, i., Bah.	134	25°05'N	77°20'W
Paradise Valley, Nv., U.S. (păr'á-dīs)	114	41°28'N	117°32'W
Parados, Cerro de los, mtn., Col. (sĕ'r-rô-dĕ-lôs-pä-rä'dōs)	142a	5°44'N	75°13'W
Paragould, Ar., U.S. (păr'á-gōōld)	121	36°03'N	90°29'W
Paraguaçu, r., Braz. (pä-rä-gwä-zōō')	143	12°25'S	39°46'W
Paraguay, nation, S.A. (păr'á-gwā)	144	24°00'S	57°00'W
Paraguay, r., S.A. (pä-rä-gwä'y)	144	21°12'S	57°31'W
Paraíba, state, Braz. (pä-rä-ē'bä)	143	7°11'S	37°05'W
Paraíba, r., Braz.	141a	23°02'S	45°43'W
Paraíba do Sul, Braz. (dô-sōō'l)	141a	22°10'S	43°18'W
Paraibuna, Braz. (pä-räē-bōō'nä)	141a	23°23'S	45°38'W
Paraíso, C.R.	133	9°50'N	83°53'W
Paraíso, Mex.	131	18°24'N	93°11'W
Paraiso, Pan. (pä-rä-ē'sō)	128a	9°02'N	79°38'W
Paraisópolis, Braz. (pä-räē-sô'pô-lēs)	141a	22°35'S	45°45'W
Paraitinga, r., Braz. (pä-rä-ē-tē'n-gä)	141a	23°15'S	45°24'W
Parakou, Benin (pá-rà-kōō')	230	9°21'N	2°37'E
Paramaribo, Sur. (pá-rá-mä'rē-bô)	143	5°50'N	55°15'W
Paramatta, Austl. (păr-á-măt'á)	217b	33°49'S	150°59'E
Paramillo, mtn., Col. (pä-rä-mē'l-yô)	142a	7°06'N	75°55'W
Paramus, N.J., U.S.	110a	40°56'N	74°04'W
Paran, r., Asia	197a	30°05'N	34°50'E
Paraná, Arg.	144	31°44'S	60°32'W
Paraná, r., S.A.	144	24°00'S	54°00'W
Paranaíba, Braz. (pä-rä-ná-ē'bá)	143	19°43'S	51°13'W
Paranaíba, r., Braz.	143	18°58'S	50°44'W
Paraná Ibicuy, r., Arg.	141c	33°27'S	59°26'W
Paranam, Sur.	143	5°39'N	55°13'W
Paranápanema, r., Braz. (pä-rä'ná'pä-nĕ-mä)	143	22°28'S	52°15'W
Paraopeda, r., Braz. (pä-rä-o-pĕ'dä)	141a	20°09'S	44°14'W
Parapara, Ven. (pä-rä-pä-rä)	143b	9°44'N	67°17'W
Parati, Braz. (pä-rätē)	141a	23°14'S	44°43'W
Paray-le-Monial, Fr. (pá-rĕ'lē-mô-nyäl')	170	46°27'N	4°14'E
Pārbati, r., India	202	24°50'N	76°44'E
Parchim, Ger. (par'kĭm)	168	53°25'N	11°52'E
Parczew, Pol. (pär'chĕf)	169	51°38'N	22°53'E
Pardo, r., Braz. (pär'dō)	143	15°25'S	39°40'W
Pardo, r., Braz.	141a	21°32'S	46°40'W
Pardubice, Czech Rep. (pär'dò-bĭt-sĕ)	168	50°02'N	15°47'E
Parecis, Serra dos, mts., Braz. (sĕr'rá dōs pä-rå-sēzh')	143	13°45'S	59°28'W
Paredes de Nava, Spain (pä-rā'dås dä nä'vä)	172	42°10'N	4°41'W
Paredón, Mex.	122	25°56'N	100°58'W
Parent, Can.	91	47°59'N	74°30'W
Parent, Lac, l., Can.	99	48°40'N	77°00'W
Parepare, Indon.	212	4°01'S	119°38'E
Pargolovo, Russia (pár-gô'lô vô)	186c	60°04'N	30°18'E
Paria, r., Az., U.S.	119	37°07'N	111°51'W
Paria, Golfo de, b. (gôl-fô-dĕ-br-pä-rē-ä)	142	10°33'N	62°14'W
Paricutín, Volcán, vol., Mex.	130	19°27'N	102°14'W
Parida, Río de la, r., Mex. (rē'ō-dĕ-lä-pä-rē'dä)	122	26°23'N	104°40'W
Parima, Serra, mts., S.A. (sĕr'rá pä-rē'mä)	142	3°45'N	64°00'W
Pariñas, Punta, c., Peru (pōō'n-tä-pä-rē'n-yäs)	142	4°30'S	81°23'W
Parintins, Braz. (pä-rĭn-tĭNzh')	143	2°34'S	56°30'W
Paris, Can.	99	43°15'N	80°23'W
Paris, Fr. (pá-rē')	154	48°51'N	2°20'E
Paris, Ar., U.S. (păr'ĭs)	121	35°17'N	93°43'W
Paris, Il., U.S.	108	39°35'N	87°40'W
Paris, Ky., U.S.	108	38°15'N	84°15'W
Paris, Mo., U.S.	121	39°27'N	91°59'W
Paris, Tn., U.S.	124	36°16'N	88°20'W
Paris, Tx., U.S.	105	33°39'N	95°33'W

ng-sing; ŋ-baŋk; N-nasalized n; nŏd; cŏmmit; ōld; ōbey; ôrder; oi-boil; fōōd; ò-as oo in foot; ou-out; s-soft; sh-dish; th-thin; pūre; ûnite; ûrn; stŭd; circŭs; ü-as in French tu; '-indeterminate vowel.

334 Parita – Penistone
PRONOUNCING INDEX

PLACE (Pronunciation)	PAGE	LAT.	LONG.
Parita, Golfo de, b., Pan. (gôl-fō-dĕ-pä-rē'tä)	133	8°06'N	80°10'W
Park City, Ut., U.S.	115	40°39'N	111°33'W
Parker, S.D., U.S. (pär'kẽr)	112	43°24'N	97°10'W
Parker Dam, dam, U.S.	106	34°20'N	114°00'W
Parkersburg, W.V., U.S. (pär'kẽrz-bûrg)	105	39°15'N	81°35'W
Parkes, Austl. (pärks)	222	33°10'S	148°10'E
Park Falls, Wi., U.S. (pärk)	113	45°55'N	90°29'W
Park Forest, Il., U.S.	111a	41°29'N	87°41'W
Parkland, Wa., U.S. (pärk'lănd)	116a	47°09'N	122°26'W
Park Range, mts., Co., U.S.	115	40°54'N	106°40'W
Park Rapids, Mn., U.S.	112	46°53'N	95°05'W
Park Ridge, Il., U.S.	111a	42°00'N	87°50'W
Park River, N.D., U.S.	112	48°22'N	97°43'W
Parkrose, Or., U.S. (pärk'rōz)	116c	45°33'N	122°33'W
Park Rynie, S. Afr.	233c	30°22'S	30°43'E
Parkston, S.D., U.S. (pärks'tŭn)	112	43°22'N	97°59'W
Parkville, Md., U.S.	110e	39°22'N	76°32'W
Parkville, Mo., U.S.	117f	39°12'N	94°41'W
Parla, Spain (pär'lä)	173a	40°14'N	3°46'W
Parma, Italy (pär'mä)	162	44°48'N	10°20'E
Parma, Oh., U.S.	111d	41°23'N	81°44'W
Parma Heights, Oh., U.S.	111d	41°23'N	81°36'W
Parnaíba, Braz. (pär-nä-ē'bä)	143	3°00'S	41°42'W
Parnaiba, r., Braz.	143	3°57'S	42°30'W
Parnassós, mtn., Grc.	175	38°36'N	22°35'E
Parndorf, Aus.	159e	48°00'N	16°52'E
Pärnu, Est. (pĕr'nōō)	180	58°24'N	24°29'E
Pärnu, r., Est.	167	58°40'N	25°05'E
Pärnu Laht, b., Est. (läкt)	167	58°15'N	24°17'E
Paro, Bhu. (pä'rô)	202	27°30'N	89°30'E
Paroo, r., Austl. (pä'rōō)	221	30°00'S	144°00'E
Páros, Grc. (pä'rôs) (pā'rŏs)	175	37°05'N	25°14'E
Páros, i., Grc.	163	37°11'N	25°00'E
Parow, S. Afr. (pă'rô)	232a	33°54'S	18°36'E
Parowan, Ut., U.S. (păr'ô-wăn)	119	37°50'N	112°50'W
Parral, Chile (pär-rä'l)	144	36°07'S	71°47'W
Parral, r., Mex.	122	27°25'N	105°08'W
Parramatta, r., Austl. (păr-ȧ-măt'ȧ)	217b	33°42'S	150°58'E
Parras, Mex. (pär-räs')	122	25°28'N	102°08'W
Parrita, C.R. (pär-rē'tä)	133	9°32'N	84°17'W
Parrsboro, Can. (pärz'bŭr-ô)	100	45°24'N	64°20'W
Parry, i., Can. (păr'ĭ)	99	45°15'N	80°00'W
Parry, Mount, mtn., Can.	94	52°53'N	128°45'W
Parry Islands, is., Can.	89	75°30'N	110°00'W
Parry Sound, Can.	91	45°20'N	80°00'W
Parsnip, r., Can. (pärs'nĭp)	95	54°45'N	122°20'W
Parsons, Ks., U.S. (pär's'nz)	105	37°20'N	95°16'W
Parsons, W.V., U.S.	109	39°05'N	79°40'W
Parthenay, Fr. (pȧr-t'nĕ')	170	46°39'N	0°16'W
Partinico, Italy (pär-tē'nê-kô)	174	38°02'N	13°11'E
Partizansk, Russia	179	43°15'N	133°19'E
Parys, S. Afr. (pȧ-rīs')	238c	26°53'S	27°28'E
Pasadena, Ca., U.S. (păs-ȧ-dē'nȧ)	104	34°09'N	118°09'W
Pasadena, Md., U.S.	110e	39°06'N	76°35'W
Pasadena, Tx., U.S.	123a	29°43'N	95°13'W
Pascagoula, Ms., U.S. (păs-kȧ-gōō'lȧ)	124	30°22'N	88°33'W
Pascagoula, r., Ms., U.S.	124	30°52'N	88°48'W
Paşcani, Rom. (päsh-kän')	169	47°46'N	26°42'E
Pasco, Wa., U.S. (păs'kō)	114	46°13'N	119°04'W
Pascua, Isla de (Easter Island), i., Chile	241	26°50'S	109°00'W
Pasewalk, Ger. (pä'zĕ-välk)	168	53°31'N	14°01'E
Pashiya, Russia (pä'shĭ-yȧ)	186a	58°27'N	58°17'E
Pashkovo, Russia (pȧsh-kô'vô)	210	48°52'N	131°09'E
Pashkovskaya, Russia (pȧsh-kôf'skȧ-yȧ)	177	45°00'N	39°04'E
Pasig, Phil.	213a	14°34'N	121°05'E
Pasión, Río de la, r., Guat. (rē'ō-dĕ-lä-pä-syōn')	132a	16°31'N	90°11'W
Paso de los Libres, Arg. (pä-sô-dĕ-lôs-lē'brĕs)	144	29°33'S	57°05'W
Paso de los Toros, Ur. (tŏ'rôs)	141c	32°43'S	56°33'W
Paso Robles, Ca., U.S. (pă'sō rō'blĕs)	118	35°38'N	120°44'W
Pasquia Hills, hills, Can. (păs'kwē-ȧ)	97	53°13'N	102°37'W
Passaic, N.J., U.S. (pă-sā'ĭk)	110a	40°52'N	74°08'W
Passaic, r., N.J., U.S.	110a	40°42'N	74°26'W
Passamaquoddy Bay, b., N.A. (păs'ȧ-mȧ-kwŏd'ĭ)	100	45°06'N	66°59'W
Passa Tempo, Braz. (pä's-sä-tĕ'm-pô)	141a	20°40'S	44°29'W
Passau, Ger. (päs'ou)	161	48°34'N	13°27'E
Pass Christian, Ms., U.S. (pȧs krĭs'tyĕn)	124	30°20'N	89°15'W
Passero, Cape, c., Italy (päs-sĕ'rô)	156	36°34'N	15°13'E
Passo Fundo, Braz. (pä'sō fōōn'dô)	144	28°16'S	52°13'W
Passos, Braz. (pä's-sōs)	143	20°45'S	46°37'W
Pastaza, r., S.A. (päs-tä'zä)	142	3°05'S	76°18'W
Pasto, Col. (päs'tô)	142	1°15'N	77°19'W
Pastora, Mex. (päs-tô-rä)	130	22°08'N	100°04'W
Pasuruan, Indon.	212	7°45'S	112°50'E
Pasvalys, Lith. (päs-vä-lēs')	167	56°04'N	24°23'E
Patagonia, reg., Arg. (păt-ȧ-gō'nĭ-ȧ)	144	46°45'S	69°30'W
Pātālganga, r., India	203b	18°52'N	73°08'E
Patapsco, r., Md., U.S. (pȧ-tăps'kō)	110e	39°12'N	76°30'W
Pateros, Lake, res., Wa., U.S.	114	48°05'N	119°45'W
Paterson, N.J., U.S. (păt'ẽr-sŭn)	110a	40°55'N	74°10'W
Pathein, Mya.	199	16°46'N	94°47'E
Pathfinder Reservoir, res., Wy., U.S. (păth'fīn-dẽr)	115	42°22'N	107°10'W
Patiāla, India (pŭt-ē-ä'lŭ)	199	30°25'N	76°28'E
Pati do Alferes, Braz. (pä-tē-dô-ȧl-fĕ'rĕs)	144b	22°25'S	43°25'W
Patna, India (pŭt'nŭ)	199	25°33'N	85°18'E
Patnanongan, i., Phil. (pät-nä-nŏn'gän)	213a	14°50'N	122°25'E
Patoka, r., In., U.S. (pȧ-tō'kȧ)	108	38°25'N	87°25'W
Patom Plateau, plat., Russia	179	59°30'N	115°00'E
Patos, Braz. (pä'tōzh)	143	7°03'S	37°14'W
Patos, Wa., U.S. (pă'tŏs)	116d	48°47'N	122°57'W
Patos, Lagoa dos, l., Braz. (lä'gō-ȧ dozh pä'tōzh)	144	31°15'S	51°30'W
Patos de Minas, Braz. (dĕ-mē'năzh)	143	18°39'S	46°31'W
Pátra, Grc.	163	38°15'N	21°48'E
Patraïkós Kólpos, b., Grc.	175	38°16'N	21°19'E
Patras *see* Pátrai, Grc.	163	38°15'N	21°48'E
Patrocínio, Braz. (pä-trō-sē'nē-ŏ)	143	18°48'S	46°47'W
Pattani, Thai. (pät'ȧ-nē)	212	6°56'N	101°13'E
Patten, Me., U.S. (păt''n)	100	45°59'N	68°27'W
Patterson, La., U.S. (păt'ẽr-sŭn)	123	29°41'N	91°20'W
Patterson, i., Can.	98	48°38'N	87°14'W
Patton, Pa., U.S.	109	40°40'N	78°45'W
Patuca, r., Hond.	133	15°22'N	84°31'W
Patuca, Punta, c., Hond. (pōō'n-tä-pä-tōō'kä)	133	15°55'N	84°05'W
Patuxent, r., Md., U.S. (pȧ-tŭk'sĕnt)	109	39°10'N	77°10'W
Pátzcuaro, Mex. (päts'kwä-rô)	130	19°30'N	101°36'W
Pátzcuaro, Lago de, l., Mex. (lä'gô-dĕ)	130	19°36'N	101°38'W
Patzicia, Guat. (pät-zē'syä)	132	14°36'N	90°57'W
Patzún, Guat. (pät-zōōn')	132	14°40'N	91°00'W
Pau, Fr. (pō)	161	43°18'N	0°23'W
Pau, Gave de, r., Fr. (gäv-dē)	170	43°33'N	0°51'W
Paulding, Oh., U.S. (pôl'dĭng)	108	41°05'N	84°35'W
Paulinenaue, Ger. (pou'lē-nĕ-nou-ĕ)	159b	52°40'N	12°43'E
Paulistano, Braz. (pá'ô-lēs-tä-nä)	143	8°13'S	41°06'W
Paulo Afonso, Salto, wtfl., Braz. (säl-tô-pou'lô äf-fôn'sô)	143	9°33'S	38°32'W
Paul Roux, S. Afr. (pôrl rōō)	238c	28°18'S	27°57'E
Paulsboro, N.J., U.S. (pôlz'bẽ-rô)	110f	39°50'N	75°16'W
Pauls Valley, Ok., U.S. (pôlz văl'ē)	121	34°43'N	97°13'W
Pavarandocito, Col. (pä-vä-rän-dô-sē'tô)	142a	7°18'N	76°32'W
Pavda, Russia (päv'da)	186a	59°16'N	59°32'E
Pavia, Italy (pä-vē'ä)	162	45°12'N	9°11'E
Pavlodar, Kaz. (pȧv-lô-dȧr')	183	52°17'N	77°23'E
Pavlof Bay, b., Ak., U.S. (păv-lōf)	103	55°20'N	161°20'W
Pavlohrad, Ukr.	181	48°32'N	35°52'E
Pavlovsk, Russia (páv-lôfsk')	177	50°28'N	40°05'E
Pavlovsk, Russia	186c	59°41'N	30°27'E
Pavlovskiy Posad, Russia (pȧv-lôf'skĭ pô-sȧt')	180	55°47'N	38°39'E
Pavuna, Braz. (pä-vōō'nȧ)	144b	22°48'S	43°21'W
Päwesin, Ger. (pȧ'vĕ-zēn)	159b	52°31'N	12°44'E
Pawhuska, Ok., U.S. (pô-hŭs'kȧ)	121	36°41'N	96°20'W
Pawnee, Ok., U.S. (pô-nē')	121	36°20'N	96°47'W
Pawnee, r., Ks., U.S.	120	38°18'N	99°42'W
Pawnee City, Ne., U.S.	121	40°08'N	96°09'W
Paw Paw, Mi., U.S. (pô'pô)	108	42°15'N	85°55'W
Paw Paw, r., Mi., U.S.	113	42°14'N	86°21'W
Pawtucket, R.I., U.S. (pô-tŭk'ĕt)	109	41°53'N	71°23'W
Paxoi, i., Grc.	175	39°14'N	20°15'E
Paxton, Il., U.S. (păks'tŭn)	108	40°35'N	88°00'W
Payette, Id., U.S. (pȧ-ĕt')	114	44°05'N	116°55'W
Payette, r., Id., U.S.	114	43°57'N	116°26'W
Payette, North Fork, r., Id., U.S.	114	44°10'N	116°10'W
Payette, South Fork, r., Id., U.S.	114	44°07'N	115°43'W
Pay-Khoy, Khrebet, mts., Russia	180	68°08'N	63°04'E
Payne, l., Can. (pān)	93	59°22'N	73°16'W
Paynesville, Mn., U.S. (pānz'vĭl)	113	45°23'N	94°43'W
Paysandú, Ur. (pī-sän-dōō')	144	32°16'S	57°55'W
Payson, Ut., U.S. (pā's'n)	119	40°05'N	111°45'W
Pazardzhik, Blg. (pä-zȧr-dzhek')	163	42°10'N	24°22'E
Pazin, Cro. (pä'zēn)	174	45°14'N	13°57'E
Peabody, Ks., U.S. (pē'bŏd-ĭ)	121	38°09'N	97°09'W
Peabody, Ma., U.S.	101a	42°32'N	70°56'W
Peace, r., Can.	92	57°30'N	117°30'W
Peace Creek, r., Fl., U.S. (pēs)	125a	27°16'N	81°53'W
Peace Dale, R.I., U.S. (dāl)	110b	41°27'N	71°30'W
Peace River, Can. (rĭv'ẽr)	90	56°14'N	117°17'W
Peacock Hills, hills, Can. (pē-kŏk' hĭlz)	92	66°08'N	109°55'W
Peak Hill, Austl.	218	25°38'S	118°50'E
Pearl, r., U.S. (pûrl)	107	30°30'N	89°45'W
Pearland, Tx., U.S. (pûrl'ănd)	123a	29°34'N	95°17'W
Pearl Harbor, Hi., U.S.	126a	21°20'N	157°53'W
Pearl Harbor, b., Hi., U.S.	106d	21°22'N	157°58'W
Pearsall, Tx., U.S. (pēr'sôl)	122	28°53'N	99°06'W
Pearse Island, i., Can. (pērs)	94	54°51'N	130°21'W
Pearston, S. Afr. (pē'ērstŏn)	233c	32°36'S	25°09'E
Peary Land, reg., Grnld. (pēr'ĭ)	244	82°00'N	40°00'W
Pease, r., Tx., U.S. (pēz)	120	34°07'N	99°53'W
Peason, La., U.S. (pēz''n)	123	31°25'N	93°19'W
Pebane, Moz. (pĕ-bá'nē)	233	17°10'S	38°08'E
Pecan Bay, Tx., U.S. (pē-kăn')	122	32°04'N	99°15'W
Peçanha, Braz. (på-kän'yȧ)	143	18°37'S	42°26'W
Pecatonica, r., Il., U.S. (pĕk-ȧ-tŏn-ĭ-kȧ)	113	42°21'N	89°28'W
Pechenga, Russia (pyĕ'chĕŋ-gȧ)	180	69°30'N	31°10'E
Pechora, r., Russia	178	66°00'N	54°00'E
Pechora Basin, Russia (pyĕ-chô'rȧ)	178	67°55'N	58°37'E
Pechori, Russia (pĕt'sĕ-rĕ)	176	57°48'N	27°33'E
Pecos, N.M., U.S. (pā'kôs)	119	35°29'N	105°41'W
Pecos, Tx., U.S.	122	31°26'N	103°30'W
Pecos, r., U.S.	106	31°10'N	103°10'W
Pécs, Hung. (pāch)	163	46°04'N	18°15'E
Peddie, S. Afr.	233c	33°13'S	27°09'E
Pedley, Ca., U.S. (pĕd'lē)	117a	33°59'N	117°29'W
Pedra Azul, Braz. (pā'drä-zōō'l)	143	16°03'S	41°13'W
Pedreiras, Braz. (pĕ-drā'räs)	143	4°30'S	44°31'W
Pedro, Point, c., Sri L. (pē'drô)	203	9°50'N	80°14'E
Pedro Antonio Santos, Mex.	132a	18°55'N	88°13'W
Pedro Betancourt, Cuba (bā-tāŋ-kōrt')	134	22°40'N	81°15'W
Pedro de Valdivia, Chile (pĕ'drô-dĕ-väl-dē'vē-ä)	144	22°32'S	69°55'W
Pedro do Rio, Braz. (dô-rē'rô)	144b	22°20'S	43°09'W
Pedro II, Braz. (pā'drô sâ-gŏn'dô)	143	4°20'S	41°27'W
Pedro Juan Caballero, Para. (hòá'n-kä-bäl-yĕ'rō)	144	22°40'S	55°42'W
Pedro Miguel, Pan. (mē-gāl')	128a	9°01'N	79°36'W
Pedro Miguel Locks, trans., Pan. (mē-gāl')	128a	9°01'N	79°36'W
Peebinga, Austl. (pē-bĭng'ȧ)	218	34°43'S	140°55'E
Peebles, Scot., U.K. (pē'b'lz)	164	55°40'N	3°15'W
Peekskill, N.Y., U.S. (pēks'kĭl)	110a	41°17'N	73°55'W
Pegasus Bay, b., N.Z. (pĕg'ȧ-sŭs)	221a	43°18'S	173°25'E
Pegnitz, r., Ger. (pĕgh-nēts)	168	49°38'N	11°40'E
Pego, Spain (pā'gō)	173	38°50'N	0°09'W
Peguis Indian Reserve, I.R., Can.	97	51°20'N	97°35'W
Pegu Yoma, mts., Mya. (pĕ-gōō'yō'mä)	199	19°16'N	95°59'E
Pehčevo, Mac. (pĕк'chĕ-vô)	175	41°42'N	22°57'E
Peigan Indian Reserve, I.R., Can.	95	49°35'N	113°40'W
Peipus, Lake *see* Chudskoye Ozero, l., Eur.	180	58°43'N	26°45'E
Peiraiás, Grc.	163	37°57'N	23°38'E
Pekin, Il., U.S. (pē'kĭn)	108	40°35'N	89°30'W
Peking *see* Beijing, China	205	39°55'N	116°23'E
Pelagie, Isole, is., Italy	162	35°46'N	12°32'E
Pélagos, i., Grc.	175	39°17'N	24°05'E
Pelahatchie, Ms., U.S. (pĕl-ȧ-hăch'ē)	124	32°17'N	89°48'W
Pelat, Mont, mtn., Fr. (pē-lá')	161	44°16'N	6°43'E
Peleduy, Russia (pyĕl-yĭ-dōō'ē)	179	59°50'N	112°47'E
Pelée, Mont, mtn., Mart. (pē-lā')	133b	14°49'N	61°10'W
Pelee, Point, c., Can.	98	41°55'N	82°30'W
Pelee Island, i., Can. (pē'lē)	98	41°45'N	82°30'W
Pelequén, Chile (pĕ-lĕ-kĕ'n)	141b	34°26'S	71°52'W
Pelham, Ga., U.S. (pĕl'hăm)	124	31°07'N	84°10'W
Pelham, N.H., U.S.	101a	42°43'N	71°22'W
Pelican, l., Mn., U.S.	113	46°36'N	94°00'W
Pelican Bay, b., Can.	97	52°45'N	100°20'W
Pelican Harbor, b., Bah. (pĕl'ĭ-kăn)	134	26°20'N	76°45'W
Pelican Rapids, Mn., U.S. (pĕl'ĭ-kăn)	112	46°34'N	96°05'W
Pella, Ia., U.S. (pĕl'ȧ)	113	41°25'N	92°50'W
Pellworm, i., Ger. (pĕl'vôrm)	168	54°33'N	8°25'E
Pelly, l., Can.	92	66°08'N	102°57'W
Pelly, r., Can.	92	62°20'N	133°00'W
Pelly Bay, b., Can. (pĕl'ĭ)	93	68°57'N	91°05'W
Pelly Crossing, Can.	103	62°50'N	136°50'W
Pelly Mountains, mts., Can.	92	61°50'N	133°05'W
Peloncillo Mountains, mts., Az., U.S. (pĕl-ôn-sĭl'lō)	119	32°40'N	109°20'W
Peloponnisos, pen., Grc.	175	37°28'N	22°14'E
Pelotas, Braz. (på-lō'tăzh)	144	31°45'S	52°18'W
Pelton, Can. (pĕl'tŭn)	111b	42°15'N	82°57'W
Pelym, r., Russia	180	60°20'N	63°05'E
Pelzer, S.C., U.S. (pĕl'zẽr)	125	34°38'N	82°30'W
Pemanggil, i., Malay.	197b	2°37'N	104°41'E
Pematangsiantar, Indon.	212	2°58'N	99°03'E
Pemba, Moz. (pĕm'bá)	233	12°58'S	40°30'E
Pemba, Zam.	232	15°29'S	27°22'E
Pemba Channel, strt., Afr.	237	5°10'S	39°30'E
Pemba Island, i., Tan.	237	5°20'S	39°57'E
Pembina, N.D., U.S. (pĕm'bĭ-nȧ)	112	48°58'N	97°15'W
Pembina, r., Can.	95	53°05'N	114°30'W
Pembina, r., N.A.	97	49°08'N	98°20'W
Pembroke, Can. (pĕm' brōk)	91	45°50'N	77°00'W
Pembroke, Wales, U.K.	164	51°40'N	5°00'W
Pembroke, Ma., U.S. (pĕm'brōk)	101a	42°05'N	70°49'W
Pen, India	203b	18°44'N	73°06'E
Penafiel, Port. (pā-nȧ-fyĕl')	172	41°12'N	8°19'W
Peñafiel, Spain (pā-nyȧ-fyĕl')	172	41°38'N	4°08'W
Peñalara, mtn., Spain (pä-nyä-lä'rä)	162	40°52'N	3°57'W
Pena Nevada, Cerro, Mex.	130	23°47'N	99°52'W
Peñaranda de Bracamonte, Spain	172	40°54'N	5°11'W
Peñarroya-Pueblonuevo, Spain (pĕn-yär-rô'yä-pwĕ'blô-nwĕ'vô)	172	38°18'N	5°18'W
Peñas, Cabo de, c., Spain (kȧ'bô-dĕ-pā'nyäs)	172	43°42'N	6°12'W
Penas, Golfo de, b., Chile (gôl-fô-dĕ-pĕ'n-äs)	144	47°15'S	77°30'W
Penasco, r., Tx., U.S. (pā-nás'kō)	122	32°50'N	104°45'W
Pendembu, S.L. (pĕn-dĕm'bōō)	230	8°06'N	10°42'W
Pender, Ne., U.S. (pĕn'dẽr)	112	42°08'N	96°43'W
Penderisco, r., Col. (pĕn-dĕ-rē's-kô)	142a	6°30'N	76°21'W
Pendjari, Parc National de la, rec., Benin	234	11°25'N	1°30'E
Pendleton, Or., U.S. (pĕn'd'l-tŭn)	104	45°41'N	118°47'W
Pend Oreille, r., Wa., U.S.	114	48°44'N	117°20'W
Pend Oreille, Lake, l., Id., U.S. (pŏn-dô-rā') (pĕn-dô-rĕl')	106	48°09'N	116°38'W
Penedo, Braz. (pȧ-nā'dô)	143	10°17'S	36°28'W
Penetanguishene, Can. (pĕn'ē-tăŋ-gĭ-shēn')	99	44°45'N	79°55'W
Pengcheng, China (pŭŋ-chŭŋ)	206	36°24'N	114°11'E
Penglai, China (pŭŋ-lī)	208	37°49'N	120°45'E
Peniche, Port. (pĕ-nē'chȧ)	172	39°22'N	9°24'W
Peninsula, Oh., U.S. (pĕn-ĭn'sū-lȧ)	111d	41°14'N	81°32'W
Penistone, Eng., U.K. (pĕn'ĭ-stŭn)	158a	53°31'N	1°38'W

ăt; finăl; rāte; senâte; ärm; ȧsk; sofȧ; fâre; ch-choose; dh-as th in other; bē; ēvent; bĕt; recĕnt; cratẽr; g-gō; gh-guttural g; bĭt; ĭ-short neutral; rīde; к-guttural k as ch in German ich;

PRONOUNCING INDEX

Penjamillo – Pillar Rocks 335

PLACE (Pronunciation)	PAGE	LAT.	LONG.
Penjamillo, Mex. (pĕn-hä-mēl′yō)	130	20°06′N	101°56′W
Pénjamo, Mex. (pān′hä-mō)	130	20°27′N	101°43′W
Penk, r., Eng., U.K. (pĕnk)	158a	52°41′N	2°10′W
Penkridge, Eng., U.K. (pĕnk′rĭj)	158a	52°43′N	2°07′W
Penne, Italy (pĕn′nā)	174	42°28′N	13°57′E
Penner, r., India (pĕn′ẽr)	199	14°43′N	79°09′E
Pennines, hills, Eng., U.K. (pĕn-īn′)	164	54°30′N	2°10′W
Pennines, Alpes, mts., Eur.	168	46°02′N	7°07′E
Pennsboro, W.V., U.S. (pĕnz′bŭr-ô)	108	39°10′N	81°00′W
Penns Grove, N.J., U.S. (pĕnz grōv)	110f	39°44′N	75°28′W
Pennsylvania, state, U.S. (pĕn-sĭl-vā′nĭ-*á*)	105	41°00′N	78°10′W
Penn Yan, N.Y., U.S. (pĕn yăn′)	109	42°40′N	77°00′W
Pennycutaway, r., Can.	97	56°10′N	93°25′W
Peno, l., Russia (pā′nô)	176	56°55′N	32°28′E
Penobscot, r., Me., U.S.	107	45°00′N	68°36′W
Penobscot Bay, b., Me., U.S. (pē-nŏb′skŏt)	100	44°20′N	69°00′W
Penong, Austl. (pē-nông′)	218	32°00′S	133°00′E
Penrith, Austl.	217b	33°45′S	150°42′E
Pensacola, Fl., U.S. (pĕn-s*á*-kō′l*á*)	105	30°25′N	87°13′W
Pensacola Dam, Ok., U.S.	121	36°27′N	95°02′W
Pensilvania, Col. (pĕn-sêl-vä′nyä)	142a	5°31′N	75°05′W
Pentecost, i., Vanuatu (pĕn′tē-kŏst)	221	16°05′S	168°28′E
Penticton, Can.	90	49°30′N	119°35′W
Pentland Firth, strt., Scot., U.K. (pĕnt′l*ă*nd)	164	58°44′N	3°25′W
Penza, Russia (pĕn′zá)	178	53°10′N	45°00′E
Penzance, Eng., U.K. (pĕn-zăns′)	164	50°07′N	5°40′W
Penzberg, Ger. (pĕnts′bĕrgh)	168	47°43′N	11°21′E
Penzhina, r., Russia (pyĭn-zē-nŭ)	185	62°15′N	166°30′E
Penzhino, Russia	179	63°42′N	168°00′E
Penzhinskaya Guba, b., Russia	185	60°30′N	161°30′E
Peoria, Il., U.S. (pē-ō′rĭ-*á*)	105	40°45′N	89°35′W
Peotillos, Mex. (på-ō-tel′yōs)	130	22°30′N	100°39′W
Peotone, Il., U.S. (pē′ō-tŏn)	111a	41°20′N	87°47′W
Pepacton Reservoir, res., N.Y., U.S. (pĕp-ăc′t*ŭ*n)	109	42°05′N	74°40′W
Pepe, Cabo, c., Cuba (kä′bô-pĕ′pĕ)	134	21°30′N	83°10′W
Pepperell, Ma., U.S. (pĕp′ẽr-ĕl)	101a	42°40′N	71°36′W
Peqin, Alb. (pĕ-kēn′)	175	41°03′N	19°48′E
Perales, r., Spain (pā-rä′lās)	173a	40°24′N	4°07′W
Perales de Tajuña, Spain (dā tä-hōō′nyä)	173a	40°14′N	3°22′W
Perche, Collines du, hills, Fr.	170	48°25′N	0°40′E
Perchtoldsdorf, Aus. (pĕrk′tōlts-dôrf)	159e	48°07′N	16°17′E
Perdekop, S. Afr.	238c	27°11′S	29°38′E
Perdido, r., Al., U.S. (pĕr-dī′dō)	124	30°45′N	87°38′W
Perdido, Monte, mtn., Spain (pĕr-dē′dō)	173	42°40′N	0°00′
Perdões, Braz. (pĕr-dô′ĕs)	141a	21°05′S	45°05′W
Pereiaslav-Khmel′nyts′kyi, Ukr.	181	50°05′N	31°25′E
Pereira, Col. (på-rā′rä)	142	4°49′N	75°42′W
Pere Marquette, Mi., U.S.	108	43°55′N	86°10′W
Pereshchepyne, Ukr.	177	49°02′N	35°19′E
Pereslavl′-Zalesskiy, Russia (på-rå-sláv′′l zá-lyĕs′kĭ)	180	56°43′N	38°52′E
Pergamino, Arg. (pĕr-gä-mē′nō)	144	33°53′S	60°36′W
Perham, Mn., U.S. (pẽr′h*ă*m)	112	46°37′N	95°35′W
Peribonca, r., Can. (pĕr-ĭ-bŏŋ′kȧ)	93	50°30′N	71°00′W
Périgueux, Fr. (pā-rē-gû′)	161	45°12′N	0°43′E
Perija, Sierra de, mts., Col. (sē-ĕ′r-rä-dĕ-pĕ-rē′kä)	142	9°25′N	73°30′W
Perkam, Tanjung, c., Indon.	213	1°20′S	138°45′E
Perkins, Can. (pẽr′k*ĕ*ns)	102c	45°37′N	75°37′W
Perlas, Archipiélago de las, is., Pan.	133	8°29′N	79°15′W
Perlas, Laguna las, l., Nic. (lä-gō′nä-dĕ-läs)	133	12°34′N	83°19′W
Perleberg, Ger. (pĕr′lē-bĕrg)	168	53°06′N	11°51′E
Perm′, Russia (pĕrm)	178	58°00′N	56°15′E
Pernambuco *see* Recife, Braz.	143	8°09′S	34°59′W
Pernambuco, state, Braz. (pĕr-näm-bōō′kō)	143	8°08′S	38°54′W
Pernik, Blg. (pĕr-nēk′)	163	42°36′N	23°04′E
Péronne, Fr. (pā-rŏn′)	170	49°57′N	2°49′E
Perote, Mex. (pĕ-rō′tĕ)	131	19°33′N	97°13′W
Perovo, Russia (pâ′rô-vô)	186b	55°43′N	37°47′E
Perpignan, Fr. (pĕr-pē-nyäɴ′)	161	42°42′N	2°48′E
Perris, Ca., U.S. (pĕr′ĭs)	117a	33°46′N	117°14′W
Perros, Bahía, b., Cuba (bä-ē′ä-pā′rōs)	134	22°25′N	78°35′W
Perrot, Île, i., Can.	102a	45°23′N	73°57′W
Perry, Fl., U.S. (pĕr′ĭ)	124	30°06′N	83°35′W
Perry, Ga., U.S.	124	32°27′N	83°44′W
Perry, Ia., U.S.	113	41°49′N	94°40′W
Perry, N.Y., U.S.	109	42°45′N	78°00′W
Perry, Ok., U.S.	121	36°17′N	97°18′W
Perry, Ut., U.S.	117b	41°27′N	112°02′W
Perry Hall, Md., U.S.	110e	39°24′N	76°29′W
Perryopolis, Pa., U.S. (pĕ-rē-ŏ′pō-lĭs)	111e	40°05′N	79°45′W
Perrysburg, Oh., U.S. (pĕr ĭz-bûrg)	108	41°35′N	83°35′W
Perryton, Tx., U.S. (pĕr′ĭ-t*ŭ*n)	120	36°23′N	100°48′W
Perryville, Ak., U.S. (pĕr-ĭ-vĭl)	103	55°58′N	159°28′W
Perryville, Mo., U.S.	121	37°41′N	89°52′W
Persan, Fr. (pĕr-säɴ′)	171b	49°09′N	2°15′E
Persepolis, hist., Iran (pẽr-sĕpō-lĭs)	198	30°15′N	53°08′E
Persian Gulf, b., Asia (pûr′zh*ă*n)	198	27°38′N	50°30′E
Perth, Austl. (pûrth)	218	31°50′S	116°10′E
Perth, Can.	99	44°40′N	76°15′W
Perth, Scot., U.K.	160	56°24′N	3°25′W
Perth Amboy, N.J., U.S. (ăm′boi)	110a	40°31′N	74°16′W
Pertuis, Fr. (pĕr-tüē′)	171	43°43′N	5°29′E
Peru, Il., U.S. (pē-rōō′)	108	41°20′N	89°10′W
Peru, In., U.S.	108	40°45′N	86°00′W
Peru, nation, S.A.	142	10°00′S	75°00′W
Peru-Chile Trench, deep	139	25°00′S	71°30′W
Perugia, Italy (pā-rōō′jä)	162	43°08′N	12°24′E
Peruque, Mo., U.S. (pē rō′kĕ)	117e	38°52′N	90°36′W
Pervomais′k, Ukr.	181	48°04′N	30°52′E
Pervoural′sk, Russia (pĕr-vô-ô-rálsk′)	186a	56°54′N	59°58′E
Pesaro, Italy (pā′zä-rō)	162	43°54′N	12°55′E
Pescado, r., Ven. (pĕs-kä′dō)	143b	9°33′N	65°32′W
Pescara, Italy (pās-kä′rä)	174	42°26′N	14°15′E
Pescara, r., Italy	174	42°18′N	13°22′E
Peschanyy müyisi, c., Kaz.	181	43°10′N	51°20′E
Pescia, Italy (pā′shä)	174	43°53′N	11°42′E
Peshāwar, Pak. (pĕ-shä′w*ŭ*r)	199	34°01′N	71°34′E
Peshtera, Blg.	175	42°03′N	24°19′E
Peshtigo, Wi., U.S. (pĕsh′tē-gō)	113	45°03′N	87°46′W
Peshtigo, r., Wi., U.S.	113	45°15′N	88°14′W
Peski, Russia (pyâs′kĭ)	186b	55°13′N	38°48′E
Pêso da Régua, Port. (pā-sò-dä-rā′gwä)	172	41°09′N	7°47′W
Pespire, Hond. (pås-pē′rå)	132	13°35′N	87°20′W
Pesqueria, r., Mex. (pås-kå-rē′*á*)	122	25°55′N	100°25′W
Pessac, Fr.	170	44°48′N	0°38′W
Petacalco, Bahía de, b., Mex. (bä-ē′ä-dĕ-pĕ-tä-käl′kô)	130	17°55′N	102°00′W
Petah Tiqwa, Isr.	197a	32°05′N	34°53′E
Petaluma, Ca., U.S. (pét-*á*-lō′m*á*)	118	38°15′N	122°38′W
Petare, Ven. (pĕ-tä′rĕ)	143b	10°28′N	66°48′W
Petatlán, Mex. (pā-tä-tlän′)	130	17°31′N	101°17′W
Petawawa, Can.	99	45°54′N	77°17′W
Petén, Laguna de, l., Guat. (lä-gō′nä-dĕ-pâ-tān′)	132a	17°05′N	89°54′W
Petenwell Reservoir, res., Wi., U.S.	113	44°10′N	89°55′W
Peterborough, Austl.	218	32°53′S	138°58′E
Peterborough, Can. (pē′tẽr-bŭr-ô)	91	44°20′N	78°20′W
Peterborough, Eng., U.K.	164	52°35′N	0°14′W
Peterhead, Scot., U.K. (pē-tẽr-hĕd′)	164	57°36′N	3°47′W
Peter Pond Lake, l., Can. (pŏnd)	92	55°55′N	108°44′W
Petersburg, Ak., U.S. (pē′tẽrz-bûrg)	103	56°52′N	133°10′W
Petersburg, Il., U.S.	121	40°01′N	89°51′W
Petersburg, In., U.S.	108	38°30′N	87°15′W
Petersburg, Ky., U.S.	111f	39°04′N	84°52′W
Petersburg, Va., U.S.	105	37°12′N	77°30′W
Petershagen, Ger. (pĕ′tĕrs-hä-gĕn)	159b	52°32′N	13°46′E
Petershausen, Ger. (pĕ′tĕrs-hou-zĕn)	159d	48°25′N	11°29′E
Pétionville, Haiti	135	18°30′N	72°20′W
Petitcodiac, Can. (pē-tē-kô-dyàk′)	100	45°56′N	65°10′W
Petite Terre, i., Guad. (pē-tēt′târ′)	133b	16°12′N	61°00′W
Petit Goâve, Haiti (pē-tē′ gô-àv′)	135	18°25′N	72°50′W
Petit Jean Creek, r., Ar., U.S. (pē-tē′zhäɴ′)	121	35°05′N	93°55′W
Petit Loango, Gabon	236	2°16′S	9°35′E
Petlalcingo, Mex. (pĕ-tläl-sĕŋ′gô)	131	18°05′N	97°53′W
Peto, Mex. (pĕ′tô)	132a	20°07′N	88°49′W
Petorca, Chile (pā-tōr′kȧ)	141b	32°14′S	70°55′W
Petoskey, Mi., U.S. (pē-tŏs-kĭ)	108	45°25′N	84°55′W
Petra, hist., Jord.	197a	30°21′N	35°25′E
Petra Velikogo, Zaliv, b., Russia	210	42°40′N	131°50′E
Petre, Point, c., Can.	99	43°50′N	77°00′W
Petrich, Blg. (pā′trĭch)	163	41°24′N	23°13′E
Petrified Forest National Park, rec., Az., U.S. (pĕt′rĭ-fīd fŏr′ĕst)	119	34°58′N	109°35′W
Petrinja, Cro. (pā′trēn-yȧ)	174	45°25′N	16°17′E
Petrodvorets, Russia (pyĕ-trô-dvô-ryĕts′)	186c	59°53′N	29°55′E
Petrokrepost′, Russia (pyĕ′trô-krĕ-pôst)	180	59°56′N	31°03′E
Petrolia, Can. (pē-trō′lĭ-*á*)	98	42°50′N	82°10′W
Petrolina, Braz. (pĕ-trō-lē′n*á*)	143	9°18′S	40°28′W
Petronell, Aus.	159e	48°07′N	16°52′E
Petropavlivka, Ukr.	177	48°24′N	36°23′E
Petropavlovka, Russia	186a	54°10′N	59°50′E
Petropavlovsk, Kaz.	183	54°44′N	69°07′E
Petropavlovsk-Kamchatskiy, Russia (käm-chät′skĭ)	179	53°13′N	158°56′E
Petrópolis, Braz. (på-trō-pô-lēzh′)	143	22°31′S	43°10′W
Petroşani, Rom.	175	45°24′N	23°24′E
Petrovsk, Russia (pyĕ-trôfsk′)	181	52°20′N	45°15′E
Petrovskaya, Russia (pyĕ-trôf′skȧ-yȧ)	177	45°25′N	37°50′E
Petrovskoye, Russia	181	45°20′N	43°00′E
Petrovsk-Zabaykal′skiy, Russia (pyĕ-trôfskzä-bī-käl′skĭ)	179	51°13′N	109°08′E
Petrozavodsk, Russia (pyā′trô-zȧ-vôtsk′)	178	61°46′N	34°25′E
Petrus Steyn, S. Afr.	238c	27°40′S	28°09′E
Petrykivka, Ukr.	177	48°43′N	34°29′E
Pewaukee, Wi., U.S. (pĭ-wô′kē)	111a	43°05′N	88°15′W
Pewaukee Lake, l., Wi., U.S.	111a	43°03′N	88°18′W
Pewee Valley, Ky., U.S. (pe wē)	111h	38°19′N	85°29′W
Peza, r., Russia (pyâ′zá)	180	65°35′N	46°50′E
Pézenas, Fr. (pā-zē-nä′)	170	43°26′N	3°24′E
Pforzheim, Ger. (pfōrts′hīm)	161	48°52′N	8°43′E
Phalodi, India	202	27°13′N	72°22′E
Phan Thiet, Viet. (p′hän′)	212	11°30′N	108°43′E
Phelps Lake, l., N.C., U.S.	125	35°46′N	76°27′W
Phenix City, Al., U.S. (fē′nĭks)	124	32°29′N	85°00′W
Philadelphia, Ms., U.S. (fĭl-*á*-dĕl′phĭ-*á*)	124	32°45′N	89°07′W
Philadelphia, Pa., U.S.	105	40°00′N	75°13′W
Philip, S.D., U.S. (fĭl′ĭp)	112	44°03′N	101°35′W
Philippeville *see* Skikda, Alg.	230	36°58′N	6°51′E
Philippines, nation, Asia (fĭl′ĭ-pēnz)	213	14°25′N	125°00′E
Philippine Sea, sea (fĭl′ĭ-pēn)	241	16°00′N	133°00′E
Philippine Trench, deep	213	10°30′N	127°15′E
Philipsburg, Pa., U.S. (fĭl′lĭps-bẽrg)	109	40°55′N	78°10′W
Philipsburg, Wy., U.S.	115	46°19′N	113°19′W
Phillip, i., Austl. (fĭl′ĭp)	222	38°32′S	145°10′E
Phillip Channel, strt., Indon.	197b	1°04′N	103°40′E
Phillipi, W.V., U.S. (fĭ-lĭp′ĭ)	108	39°10′N	80°00′W
Phillips, Wi., U.S. (fĭl′ĭps)	113	45°41′N	90°24′W
Phillipsburg, Ks., U.S. (fĭl′lĭps-bẽrg)	120	39°44′N	99°19′W
Phillipsburg, N.J., U.S.	109	40°45′N	75°10′W
Phitsanulok, Thai.	212	16°51′N	100°15′E
Phnom Penh (Phnum Pénh), Camb. (nŏm′pĕn′)	212	11°39′N	104°53′E
Phnum Pénh *see* Phnom Penh, Camb.	212	11°39′N	104°53′E
Phoenix, Az., U.S. (fē′nĭks)	104	33°30′N	112°00′W
Phoenix, Md., U.S.	110e	39°31′N	76°40′W
Phoenix Islands, is., Kir.	2	4°00′S	174°00′W
Phoenixville, Pa., U.S. (fē′nĭks-vĭl)	110f	40°08′N	75°31′W
Phou Bia, mtn., Laos	212	19°36′N	103°00′E
Phra Nakhon Si Ayutthaya, Thai.	212	14°16′N	100°37′E
Phuket, Thai.	212	7°57′N	98°19′E
Phu Quoc, Dao, i., Viet.	212	10°13′N	104°00′E
Pi, r., China (bē)	206	32°06′N	116°31′E
Piacenza, Italy (pyä-chĕnt′sä)	162	45°02′N	9°42′E
Pianosa, i., Italy (pyä-nō′sä)	174	42°13′N	15°45′E
Piave, r., Italy (pyä′vā)	174	45°45′N	12°15′E
Piazza Armerina, Italy (pyät′sä är-må-rē′nä)	174	37°23′N	14°26′E
Pibor, r., Sudan (pē′bôr)	231	7°21′N	32°54′E
Pic, r., Can. (pĕk)	98	48°48′N	86°28′W
Picara Point, c., V.I.U.S. (pē-kä′rä)	129c	18°23′N	64°57′W
Picayune, Ms., U.S. (pĭk′á yōōn)	124	30°32′N	89°41′W
Picher, Ok., U.S. (pĭch′ẽr)	121	36°58′N	94°49′W
Pichilemu, Chile (pē-chē-lĕ′mōō)	141b	34°22′S	72°01′W
Pichucalco, Mex. (pē-chōō-käl′kô)	131	17°34′N	93°06′W
Pickerel, l., Can. (pĭk′ẽr-ĕl)	98	48°35′N	91°10′W
Pickwick Lake, res., U.S. (pĭk′wĭck)	124	35°04′N	88°05′W
Pico, Ca., U.S. (pē′kô)	117a	34°01′N	118°05′W
Pico Island, i., Port. (pē′kò)	230a	38°16′N	28°49′W
Pico Rivera, Ca., U.S.	117a	34°01′N	118°05′W
Picos, Braz. (pē′kōzh)	143	7°13′S	41°23′W
Picton, Austl. (pĭk′tŭn)	217b	34°11′S	150°37′E
Picton, Can.	99	44°00′N	77°15′W
Pictou, Can. (pĭk-tōō′)	101	45°41′N	62°43′W
Pidálion, Akrotírion, c., Cyp.	197a	34°50′N	34°05′E
Pidurutalagala, mtn., Sri L. (pē′dò-rò-tä′lȧ-gä′lȧ)	203	7°00′N	80°46′E
Pidvolochys′k, Ukr.	177	49°32′N	26°16′E
Pie, i., Can. (pī)	98	48°10′N	89°07′W
Piedade, Braz. (pyā-dä′dĕ)	141a	23°42′S	47°25′W
Piedmont, Al., U.S. (pēd′mŏnt)	124	33°54′N	85°36′W
Piedmont, Ca., U.S.	116b	37°50′N	122°14′W
Piedmont, Mo., U.S.	121	37°09′N	90°42′W
Piedmont, S.C., U.S.	125	34°40′N	82°27′W
Piedmont, W.V., U.S.	109	39°30′N	79°05′W
Piedrabuena, Spain (pyā-drä-bwā′nä)	172	39°01′N	4°10′W
Piedras, Punta, c., Arg. (pōō′n-tä-pyĕ′dräs)	141c	35°25′S	57°10′W
Piedras Negras, Mex. (pyā′dräs nā′gräs)	128	28°41′N	100°33′W
Pieksämäki, Fin. (pyĕk′sĕ-mĕ-kē)	167	62°18′N	27°14′E
Piemonte, hist. reg., Italy (pyĕ-mô′n-tĕ)	174	44°30′N	7°42′E
Pienaars, r., S. Afr.	238c	25°13′S	28°05′E
Pienaarsrivier, S. Afr.	238c	25°12′S	28°18′E
Pierce, Ne., U.S. (pērs)	112	42°11′N	97°33′W
Pierce, W.V., U.S.	109	39°15′N	79°30′W
Piermont, N.Y., U.S. (pēr′mŏnt)	110a	41°03′N	73°55′W
Pierre, S.D., U.S. (pēr)	104	44°22′N	100°20′W
Pierrefonds, Can.	102a	45°29′N	73°52′W
Piešt′any, Slvk.	169	48°36′N	17°48′E
Pietermaritzburg, S. Afr. (pē-tēr-mȧ-rĭts-bûrg)	232	29°36′S	30°23′E
Pietersburg, S. Afr. (pē′tẽrz-bûrg)	232	23°56′S	29°30′E
Piet Retief, S. Afr. (pēt rĕ-tēf′)	232	27°00′S	30°58′E
Pietrosu, Vârful, mtn., Rom.	169	47°35′N	24°49′E
Pieve di Cadore, Italy (pyā′vå dē kä-dō′rå)	162	46°26′N	12°22′E
Pigeon, r., N.A. (pĭj′*ŭ*n)	113	48°05′N	90°13′W
Pigeon Lake, Can.	102f	49°57′N	97°36′W
Pigeon Lake, l., Can.	95	53°00′N	114°00′W
Piggott, Ar., U.S. (pĭg-ŭt)	121	36°22′N	90°10′W
Pijijiapan, Mex. (pēkē-kē-ä′pän)	131	15°40′N	93°12′W
Pijnacker, Neth.	159a	52°01′N	4°25′E
Pikes Peak, mtn., Co., U.S. (pīks)	106	38°49′N	105°03′W
Pikeville, Ky., U.S. (pĭk′vĭl)	108	37°28′N	82°31′W
Pikou, China (pē-kō)	208	39°25′N	122°19′E
Pikwitonei, Can. (pĭk′wĭ-tōn)	97	55°35′N	97°09′W
Piła, Pol. (pē′lȧ)	168	53°09′N	16°44′E
Pilansberg, mtn., S. Afr. (pĕ′ăns′bûrg)	238c	25°08′S	26°55′E
Pilar, Arg. (pē′lär)	141c	34°27′S	58°55′W
Pilar, Para.	144	27°00′S	58°15′W
Pilar de Goiás, Braz. (dĕ-gô′yá′s)	143	14°47′S	49°33′W
Pilchuck, r., Wa., U.S.	116a	48°03′N	121°58′W
Pilchuck Creek, r., Wa., U.S. (pĭl′chŭck)	116a	48°19′N	122°11′W
Pilchuck Mountain, mtn., Wa., U.S.	116a	48°03′N	121°48′W
Pilcomayo, r., S.A. (pēl-cō-mī′ō)	144	24°45′S	59°15′W
Pili, Phil. (pē′lē)	213a	13°34′N	123°17′E
Pilica, r., Pol. (pē-lēt′sä)	169	51°00′N	19°48′E
Pillar Point, c., Wa., U.S. (pĭl′*á*r)	116a	48°14′N	124°06′W
Pillar Rocks, Wa., U.S.	116c	46°16′N	123°35′W

ng-sing; ŋ-baŋk; ɴ-nasalized n; nŏd; c*ŏ*mmit; ōld; ôbey; ôrder; oi-boil; fōōd; ò-as oo in foot; ou-out; s-soft; sh-dish; th-thin; pūre; ûnite; ûrn; stŭd; circ*ŭ*s; ü-as in French tu; ′-indeterminate vowel.

PLACE (Pronunciation)	PAGE	LAT.	LONG.
Pilón, r., Mex. (pē-lōn′)	130	24°13′N	99°03′W
Pilot Point, Tx., U.S. (pī′lŭt)	121	33°24′N	97°00′W
Pilsen see Plzeň, Czech Rep.	154	49°46′N	13°25′E
Piltene, Lat. (pĭl′tē-nĕ)	167	57°17′N	21°40′E
Pimal, Cerra, mtn., Mex. (sĕ′r-rä-pē-mäl′)	130	22°58′N	104°19′W
Pimba, Austl. (pĭm′bȧ)	218	31°15′S	137°50′E
Pimville, neigh., S. Afr. (pĭm′vĭl)	233b	26°17′S	27°54′E
Pinacate, Cerro, mtn., Mex. (sĕ′r-rô-pē-nä-kä′tĕ)	128	31°45′N	113°30′W
Pinamalayan, Phil. (pē-nä-mä-lä′yän)	213a	13°04′N	121°31′E
Pinang see George Town, Malay.	212	5°21′N	100°09′E
Pinarbaşi, Tur. (pē′när-bä′shĭ)	163	38°50′N	36°10′E
Pinar del Río, Cuba (pē-när′ dĕl rē′ô)	129	22°25′N	83°35′W
Pinar del Río, prov., Cuba	134	22°45′N	83°25′W
Pinatubo, mtn., Phil. (pē-nä-tōō′bô)	213a	15°09′N	120°19′E
Pincher Creek, Can. (pĭn′chĕr krēk)	95	49°29′N	113°57′W
Pinckneyville, Il., U.S. (pĭnk′nĭ-vĭl)	121	38°06′N	89°22′W
Pińczów, Pol. (pēn′′chôf)	169	50°32′N	20°33′E
Pindamonhangaba, Braz. (pē′n-dä-mōnyä′n-gä-bä)	141a	22°56′S	45°26′W
Pinder Point, c., Bah.	134	26°35′N	78°35′W
Pindiga, Nig.	235	9°59′N	10°54′E
Píndos Óros, mts., Grc.	156	39°48′N	21°19′E
Pine, r., Can. (pīn)	95	55°30′N	122°20′W
Pine, r., Wi., U.S.	113	45°50′N	88°37′W
Pine Bluff, Ar., U.S. (pīn blŭf)	105	34°13′N	92°01′W
Pine City, Mn., U.S. (pīn)	113	45°50′N	93°01′W
Pine Creek, Austl.	218	13°45′S	132°00′E
Pine Creek, r., Nv., U.S.	118	40°15′N	116°17′W
Pine Falls, Can.	97	50°35′N	96°15′W
Pine Flat Lake, res., Ca., U.S.	118	36°52′N	119°18′W
Pine Forest Range, mts., Nv., U.S.	114	41°35′N	118°45′W
Pinega, Russia (pē-nyĕ′gȧ)	178	64°40′N	43°30′E
Pinega, r., Russia	180	64°10′N	42°30′E
Pine Hill, N.J., U.S. (pīn hĭl)	110f	39°47′N	74°59′W
Pineiós, r., Grc.	175	39°30′N	21°40′E
Pine Island Sound, strt., Fl., U.S.	125a	26°32′N	82°30′W
Pine Lake Estates, Ga., U.S. (lāk ĕs-tāts′)	110c	33°47′N	84°13′W
Pinelands, S. Afr. (pīn′lănds)	232a	33°57′S	18°30′E
Pine Lawn, Mo., U.S. (lôn)	117e	38°42′N	90°17′W
Pine Pass, p., Can.	95	55°22′N	122°40′W
Pinerolo, Italy (pē-nā-rô′lō)	174	44°47′N	7°18′E
Pines, Lake o' the, Tx., U.S.	123	32°50′N	94°40′W
Pinetown, S. Afr. (pīn′toun)	233c	29°47′S	30°52′E
Pine View Reservoir, res., Ut., U.S. (vū)	117b	41°17′N	111°54′W
Pineville, Ky., U.S. (pīn′vĭl)	124	36°48′N	83°43′W
Pineville, La., U.S.	123	31°20′N	92°25′W
Ping, r., Thai.	212	17°54′N	98°29′E
Pingding, China (pĭŋ-dĭŋ)	208	37°50′N	113°30′E
Pingdu, China (pĭŋ-dōō)	208	36°46′N	119°57′E
Pinggir, Indon.	197b	1°05′N	101°12′E
Pinghe, China (pĭŋ-hŭ)	209	24°30′N	117°02′E
Pingle, China (pĭŋ-lŭ)	209	24°30′N	110°22′E
Pingliang, China (pĭng′lyäng′)	204	35°12′N	106°50′E
Pingquan, China (pĭŋ-chyůän)	208	40°58′N	118°40′E
Pingtan, China (pĭŋ-tän)	209	25°30′N	119°45′E
Pingtan Dao, i., China (pĭŋ-tän dou)	209	25°40′N	119°45′E
P'ingtung, Tai.	209	22°40′N	120°35′E
Pingwu, China (pĭŋ-wōō)	208	32°20′N	104°40′E
Pingxiang, China (pĭŋ-shyäŋ)	209	27°40′N	113°50′E
Pingyi, China (pĭŋ-yē)	206	35°30′N	117°38′E
Pingyuan, China (pĭŋ-yůän)	206	37°11′N	116°26′E
Pingzhou, China (pĭŋ-jō)	207a	23°01′N	113°11′E
Pinhal, Braz. (pē-nyá′l)	141a	22°11′S	46°43′W
Pinhal Novo, Port. (nô vô)	173b	38°38′N	8°54′W
Pinhel, Port. (pēn-yĕl′)	172	40°45′N	7°03′W
Pini, Pulau, i., Indon.	212	0°07′S	98°38′E
Pinnacles National Monument, rec., Ca., U.S. (pĭn′ȧ-k'lz)	118	36°30′N	121°00′W
Pinneberg, Ger. (pĭn′ĕ-bĕrg)	159c	53°40′N	9°48′E
Pinole, Ca., U.S. (pĭ-nō′lē)	116b	38°01′N	122°17′W
Pinos-Puente, Spain (pwān′tā)	172	37°15′N	3°43′W
Pinotepa Nacional, Mex. (pē-nô-tā′pä nä-syô-näl′)	130	16°21′N	98°04′W
Pins, Île des, i., N. Cal.	221	22°44′S	167°44′E
Pinsk, Bela. (pēn′sk)	178	52°07′N	26°05′E
Pinta, i., Ec.	142	0°41′N	90°47′W
Pintendre, Can. (pĕN-täNdr′)	102b	46°45′N	71°07′W
Pinto, Spain (pēn′tō)	173a	40°14′N	3°42′W
Pinto Butte, Can. (pĭn′tō)	96	49°22′N	107°25′W
Pioche, Nv., U.S. (pī-ō′chē)	119	37°56′N	114°28′W
Piombino, Italy (pyôm-bē′nō)	162	42°56′N	10°33′E
Pioneer Mountains, mts., Mt., U.S. (pī′ô-nēr′)	115	45°23′N	112°51′W
Piotrków Trybunalski, Pol. (pyōtr′kōōv trĭ-bōō-nal′skē)	161	51°23′N	19°44′E
Piper, Al., U.S. (pī′pēr)	124	33°04′N	87°00′W
Piper, Ks., U.S.	117f	39°09′N	94°51′W
Pipe Spring National Monument, rec., Az., U.S. (pīp spring)	119	36°50′N	112°45′W
Pipestone, Mn., U.S. (pīp′stōn)	112	44°00′N	96°19′W
Pipestone National Monument, rec., Mn., U.S.	112	44°03′N	96°24′W
Pipmuacan, Réservoir, res., Can. (pĭp-mä-kän′)	99	49°45′N	70°00′W
Piqua, Oh., U.S. (pĭk′wȧ)	108	40°10′N	84°15′W
Piracaia, Braz. (pē-rä-kà′yä)	141a	23°04′S	46°20′W
Piracicaba, Braz. (pē-rä-sē-kä′bä)	143	22°43′S	47°39′W
Piraíba, r., Braz. (pä-rä-ē′bȧ)	141a	21°38′S	41°29′W
Piramida, mtn., Russia	179	54°00′N	96°00′E
Piran, Slvn. (pē-rá′n)	174	45°31′N	13°34′E
Piranga, Braz. (pē-rä′n-gä)	141a	20°41′S	43°17′W
Pirapetinga, Braz. (pē-rä-pĕ-tē′n-gä)	141a	21°40′S	42°20′W
Pirapora, Braz. (pē-rȧ-pō′rȧ)	143	17°39′S	44°54′W
Pirassununga, Braz. (pē-rä-sōō-nōō′n-gä)	141a	22°00′S	47°24′W
Pirenópolis, Braz. (pē-rĕ-nô′pō-lēs)	143	15°56′S	48°49′W
Piritu, Laguna de, l., Ven. (lä-gô′nä-dĕ-pē-rē′tōō)	143b	10°00′N	64°57′W
Pirmasens, Ger. (pĭr-mä-zĕns′)	168	49°12′N	7°34′E
Pirna, Ger. (pĭr′nä)	168	50°57′N	13°56′E
Pirot, Yugo. (pē′rōt)	163	43°09′N	22°35′E
Pirtleville, Az., U.S. (pûr′t'l-vĭl)	119	31°25′N	109°35′W
Piru, Indon. (pē-rōō′)	213	3°15′S	128°25′E
Pisa, Italy (pē′sä)	162	43°52′N	10°24′E
Pisagua, Chile (pē-sä′gwä)	142	19°43′S	70°12′W
Piscataway, Md., U.S. (pĭs-kă-tă-wā)	110e	38°42′N	76°59′W
Piscataway, N.J., U.S.	110a	40°35′N	74°27′W
Pisco, Peru (pēs′kō)	142	13°43′S	76°07′W
Pisco, Bahía de, b., Peru	142	13°43′S	77°48′W
Piseco, l., N.Y., U.S. (pĭ-sā′kô)	109	43°25′N	74°35′W
Pisek, Czech Rep. (pē′sĕk)	161	49°18′N	14°08′E
Pisticci, Italy (pēs-tē′chē)	174	40°24′N	16°34′E
Pistoia, Italy (pēs-tô′yä)	162	43°57′N	11°54′E
Pisuerga, r., Spain (pē-swĕr′gä)	172	41°48′N	4°28′W
Pit, r., Ca., U.S. (pĭt)	114	40°58′N	121°42′W
Pitalito, Col. (pē-tä-lē′tō)	142	1°45′N	75°09′W
Pitcairn, dep., Oc.	2	25°04′S	130°05′W
Piteälven, r., Swe.	160	66°08′N	18°51′E
Piteşti, Rom. (pē-tĕsht′′)	175	44°51′N	24°51′E
Pithara, Austl. (pĭt′ărȧ)	218	30°27′S	116°45′E
Pithiviers, Fr. (pē-tē-vyā′)	170	48°12′N	2°14′E
Pitman, N.J., U.S. (pĭt′mȧn)	110f	39°44′N	75°08′W
Pitseng, Leso.	233c	29°03′S	28°13′E
Pitt, r., Can.	116d	49°19′N	122°39′W
Pitt Island, i., Can.	94	53°35′N	129°45′W
Pittsburg, Ca., U.S. (pĭts′bûrg)	116b	38°01′N	121°52′W
Pittsburg, Ks., U.S.	105	37°25′N	94°43′W
Pittsburg, Tx., U.S.	121	32°00′N	94°57′W
Pittsburgh, Pa., U.S.	105	40°26′N	80°01′W
Pittsfield, Il., U.S. (pĭts′fēld)	121	39°37′N	90°47′W
Pittsfield, Ma., U.S.	109	42°25′N	73°15′W
Pittsfield, Me., U.S.	100	44°45′N	69°44′W
Pittston, Pa., U.S. (pĭts′tŭn)	109	41°20′N	75°50′W
Piúi, Braz. (pē-ōō′ē)	141a	20°27′S	45°57′W
Piura, Peru (pē-ōō′rä)	142	5°13′S	80°46′W
Pivdennyi Buh, r., Ukr.	181	48°12′N	30°13′E
Piya, Russia (pē′yȧ)	186a	58°34′N	61°12′E
Placentia, Can.	101	47°15′N	53°58′W
Placentia, Ca., U.S. (plă-sĕn′shĭ-ȧ)	117a	33°52′N	117°50′W
Placentia Bay, b., Can.	93a	47°14′N	54°30′W
Placerville, Ca., U.S. (plăs′ēr-vĭl)	118	38°43′N	120°47′W
Placetas, Cuba (plä-thā′täs)	134	22°10′N	79°40′W
Placid, l., N.Y., U.S. (plăs′ĭd)	109	44°20′N	74°00′W
Plain City, Ut., U.S. (plān)	117b	41°18′N	112°06′W
Plainfield, Il., U.S. (plān′fēld)	111a	41°37′N	88°12′W
Plainfield, In., U.S.	111g	39°42′N	86°23′W
Plainfield, N.J., U.S.	110a	40°38′N	74°25′W
Plainview, Ar., U.S. (plān′vū)	121	34°59′N	93°15′W
Plainview, Mn., U.S.	113	44°09′N	93°12′W
Plainview, Ne., U.S.	112	42°20′N	97°47′W
Plainview, Tx., U.S.	120	34°11′N	101°42′W
Plainwell, Mi., U.S. (plan′wĕl)	108	42°25′N	85°40′W
Plaisance, Can. (plĕ-zäNs′)	102c	45°37′N	75°07′W
Plana or Flat Cays, is., Bah. (plä′nä)	135	22°35′N	73°35′W
Planegg, Ger. (plä′nĕg)	159d	48°06′N	11°27′E
Plano, Tx., U.S. (plā′nō)	121	33°01′N	96°42′W
Plantagenet, Can. (pläN-täzh-nĕ′)	102c	45°33′N	75°00′W
Plant City, Fl., U.S. (plȧnt sĭ′tĭ)	125a	28°00′N	82°07′W
Plaquemine, La., U.S. (pläk′mēn′)	123	30°17′N	91°14′W
Plasencia, Spain (plä-sĕn′thē-ä)	172	40°02′N	6°07′W
Plast, Russia (plȧst)	180	54°22′N	60°48′E
Plaster Rock, Can. (plȧs′tēr rŏk)	100	46°54′N	67°24′W
Plastun, Russia (plȧs-tōōn′)	210	44°41′N	136°08′E
Plata, Río de la, est., S.A. (dălä plä′tä)	144	34°35′S	58°15′W
Platani, r., Italy (plä-tä′nē)	174	37°26′N	13°28′E
Plateforme, Pointe, c., Haiti	135	19°35′N	73°50′W
Platinum, Ak., U.S. (plăt′ĭ-nŭm)	103	59°00′N	161°27′W
Plato, Col. (plä′tō)	142	9°49′N	74°48′W
Platón Sánchez, Mex. (plä-tōn′ sän′chĕz)	130	21°14′N	98°20′W
Platte, S.D., U.S. (plăt)	112	43°22′N	98°51′W
Platte, r., Mo., U.S.	121	40°09′N	94°40′W
Platte, r., Ne., U.S.	106	40°50′N	100°40′W
Platteville, Wi., U.S. (plăt′vĭl)	113	42°44′N	90°31′W
Plattsburg, Mo., U.S. (plăts′bûrg)	121	39°33′N	94°26′W
Plattsburg, N.Y., U.S.	109	44°40′N	73°30′W
Plattsmouth, Ne., U.S. (plăts′mŭth)	112	41°00′N	95°53′W
Plauen, Ger. (plou′ĕn)	161	50°30′N	12°08′E
Playa de Guanabo, Cuba (plä-yä-dĕ-gwä-nä′bô)	135a	23°10′N	82°07′W
Playa de Santa Fé, Cuba	135a	23°05′N	82°31′W
Playas Lake, l., N.M., U.S. (plä′yȧs)	119	31°50′N	108°30′W
Playa Vicente, Mex. (vē-sĕn′tā)	131	17°49′N	95°49′W
Playa Vicente, r., Mex.	131	17°36′N	96°13′W
Playgreen Lake, l., Can. (plā′grēn)	97	54°00′N	98°10′W
Pleasant, l., N.Y., U.S. (plĕz′ănt)	109	43°25′N	74°25′W
Pleasant Grove, Al., U.S.	110h	33°29′N	86°57′W
Pleasant Hill, Ca., U.S.	116b	37°57′N	122°04′W
Pleasant Hill, Mo., U.S.	121	38°46′N	94°18′W
Pleasanton, Ca., U.S. (plĕz′ăn-tŭn)	116b	37°40′N	121°53′W
Pleasanton, Ks., U.S.	121	38°10′N	94°41′W
Pleasanton, Tx., U.S.	122	28°58′N	98°30′W
Pleasant Plain, Oh., U.S. (plĕz′ănt)	111f	39°17′N	84°06′W
Pleasant Ridge, Mi., U.S.	111b	42°28′N	83°09′W
Pleasant View, Ut., U.S. (plĕz′ănt vū)	117b	41°20′N	112°02′W
Pleasantville, N.Y., U.S. (plĕz′ănt-vĭl)	110a	41°08′N	73°47′W
Pleasure Ridge Park, Ky., U.S. (plĕzh′ēr rĭj)	111h	38°09′N	85°49′W
Plenty, Bay of, b., N.Z. (plĕn′tē)	221a	37°30′S	177°10′E
Plentywood, Mt., U.S. (plĕn′tē-wŏŏd)	115	48°47′N	104°38′W
Ples, Russia (plyĕs)	176	57°26′N	41°29′E
Pleshcheyevo, l., Russia (plĕsh-chā′yĕ-vô)	176	56°50′N	38°22′E
Plessisville, Can. (plĕ-sē′vēl′)	99	46°12′N	71°47′W
Pleszew, Pol. (plĕ′zhĕf)	169	51°54′N	17°48′E
Plettenberg, Ger. (plĕ′tĕn-bĕrgh)	171c	51°13′N	7°53′E
Pleven, Blg. (plĕ′vĕn)	163	43°24′N	24°26′E
Pljevlja, Yugo. (plĕv′lyä)	163	43°20′N	19°21′E
Płock, Pol. (pwôtsk)	161	52°32′N	19°44′E
Ploërmel, Fr. (plô-ĕr-mĕl′)	170	47°56′N	2°25′W
Ploieşti, Rom. (plô-yĕsht′′)	154	44°56′N	26°01′E
Plomári, Grc.	175	38°51′N	26°24′E
Plomb du Cantal, mtn., Fr. (plôN′dükäN-täl′)	161	45°30′N	2°49′E
Plonge, Lac la, l., Can. (plōNzh)	96	55°08′N	107°25′W
Plovdiv, Blg. (plôv′dĭf) (fĭl-ĭp-ŏp′ô-lĭs)	154	42°09′N	24°43′E
Pluma Hidalgo, Mex. (plōō′mä ē-däl′gō)	131	15°54′N	96°23′W
Plunge, Lith. (plōn′gā)	167	55°56′N	21°45′E
Plymouth, Monts.	133b	16°43′N	62°12′W
Plymouth, Eng., U.K. (plĭm′ŭth)	161	50°25′N	4°14′W
Plymouth, In., U.S.	108	41°20′N	86°20′W
Plymouth, Ma., U.S.	109	42°00′N	70°45′W
Plymouth, Mi., U.S.	111b	42°23′N	83°27′W
Plymouth, N.C., U.S.	125	35°50′N	76°44′W
Plymouth, N.H., U.S.	109	43°50′N	71°40′W
Plymouth, Pa., U.S.	109	41°15′N	75°55′W
Plymouth, Wi., U.S.	113	43°45′N	87°59′W
Plyussa, r., Russia (plyōō′sȧ)	176	58°33′N	28°30′E
Plzeň, Czech Rep.	154	49°45′N	13°23′E
Po, r., Italy	156	45°10′N	11°00′E
Pocahontas, Ar., U.S. (pō-kȧ-hŏn′tȧs)	121	36°15′N	91°01′W
Pocahontas, Ia., U.S.	113	42°43′N	94°41′W
Pocatello, Id., U.S. (pō-kȧ-tĕl′ō)	104	42°54′N	112°30′W
Pochëp, Russia (pô-chĕp′)	181	52°56′N	33°27′E
Pochinok, Russia (pô-chē′nôk)	176	54°14′N	32°27′E
Pochinski, Russia	180	54°40′N	44°50′E
Pochotitán, Mex. (pô-chô-tē-tá′n)	130	21°37′N	104°33′W
Pochutla, Mex.	131	15°46′N	96°28′W
Pocomoke City, Md., U.S. (pō-kō-mōk′)	109	38°05′N	75°35′W
Pocono Mountains, mts., Pa., U.S. (pō-cō′nō)	109	41°10′N	75°30′W
Poços de Caldas, Braz. (pō-sôs-dĕ-käl′dȧs)	143	21°48′S	46°34′W
Poder, Sen. (pô-dôr′)	230	16°35′N	15°04′W
Podgorica, Yugo.	175	42°25′N	19°15′E
Podkamennaya Tunguska, r., Russia	179	61°43′N	93°45′E
Podol'sk, Russia (pô-dôl′′sk)	180	55°26′N	37°33′E
Poggibonsi, Italy (pôd-jē-bôn′sē)	174	43°27′N	11°12′E
Pogodino, Bela. (pô-gô′dē-nô)	180	54°17′N	31°00′E
P'ohangdong, Kor., S.	210	35°57′N	129°23′E
Pointe-à-Pitre, Guad. (pwăNt′ á pē-tr′)	129	16°15′N	61°32′W
Pointe-aux-Trembles, Can. (pōō-ăNt′ ō-träNbl)	102a	45°39′N	73°30′W
Pointe Claire, Can. (pōō-ăNt′ klĕr)	102a	45°27′N	73°48′W
Pointe-des-Cascades, Can. (kăs-kădz′)	102a	45°19′N	73°58′W
Pointe Fortune, Can. (fôr′tŭn)	102a	45°34′N	74°23′W
Pointe-Gatineau, Can. (pōō-ănt′gä-tē-nō′)	102c	45°28′N	75°42′W
Pointe Noire, Congo	232	4°48′S	11°51′E
Point Hope, Ak., U.S. (hōp)	103	68°18′N	166°38′W
Point Pleasant, W.V., U.S. (plĕz′ănt)	108	38°50′N	82°10′W
Point Roberts, Wa., U.S. (rŏb′ērts)	116d	48°59′N	123°04′W
Poissy, Fr. (pwȧ-sē′)	171b	48°55′N	2°02′E
Poitiers, Fr. (pwȧ-tyā′)	161	46°35′N	0°18′E
Pokaran, India (pō′kŭr-ŭn)	202	27°00′N	72°05′E
Pokrov, Russia (pô-krôf)	176	55°56′N	39°09′E
Pokrovskoye, Russia (pô-krôf′skô-yĕ)	177	47°27′N	38°54′E
Pola, r., Russia (pō′lä)	176	57°44′N	31°53′E
Pola de Laviana, Spain (dĕ-lä-vyä′nä)	172	43°15′N	5°29′W
Pola de Siero, Spain	172	43°24′N	5°39′W
Poland, nation, Eur. (pō′lănd)	154	52°37′N	17°01′E
Polangui, Phil. (pō-län′gē)	213a	13°18′N	123°29′E
Polatsk, Bela.	180	55°30′N	28°48′E
Polazna, Russia (pô′láz-nȧ)	186a	58°18′N	56°25′E
Polessk, Russia (pô′lĕsk)	167	54°50′N	21°14′E
Polevskoy, Russia (pô-lĕ′vs-kô′ē)	186a	56°28′N	60°14′E
Polgár, Hung. (pôl′gär)	169	47°54′N	21°10′E
Policastro, Golfo di, b., Italy	174	40°00′N	13°23′E
Polichnítos, Grc.	175	39°05′N	26°11′E
Poligny, Fr. (pō-lē-nyē′)	171	46°48′N	5°42′E
Polillo, Phil. (pō-lēl′yō)	213a	14°42′N	121°56′E
Polillo Islands, is., Phil.	199	15°05′N	122°15′E
Polillo Strait, strt., Phil.	213a	15°02′N	121°40′E
Polist', r., Russia (pô′lĭst)	176	57°42′N	31°02′E
Polistena, Italy (pō-lēs-tā′nä)	174	38°25′N	16°05′E
Polkan, Gora, mtn., Russia	179	60°18′N	92°08′E
Polochic, r., Guat. (pō-lô-chēk′)	132	15°19′N	89°45′W
Polonne, Ukr.	177	50°07′N	27°31′E
Polpaico, Chile (pōl-pá′y-kô)	141b	33°10′S	70°53′W
Polson, Mt., U.S. (pōl′sŭn)	115	47°40′N	114°10′W

ăt; finăl; rāte; senāte; ärm; åsk; sofȧ; fâre; ch-choose; dh-as th in other; bē; ēvent; bĕt; recĕnt; cratēr; g-gō; gh-guttural g; bĭt; ĭ-short neutral; rīde; K-guttural k as ch in German ich;

PRONOUNCING INDEX

Poltava – Pratas Island 337

PLACE (Pronunciation)	PAGE	LAT.	LONG.
Poltava, Ukr. (pôl-tä′vä)	178	49°35′N	34°33′E
Poltava, prov., Ukr.	177	49°53′N	32°58′E
Põltsamaa, Est. (põlt′sà-mä)	167	58°39′N	26°00′E
Polunochnoye, Russia (pô-lōō-nô′ch-nô′yĕ)	186a	60°52′N	60°27′E
Poluy, r., Russia (pôl′wê)	184	65°45′N	68°15′E
Polyakovka, Russia (pŭl-yä′kôv-kà)	186a	54°38′N	59°42′E
Polyarnyy, Russia (pŭl-yär′nē)	178	69°10′N	33°30′E
Polygyros, Grc.	175	40°23′N	23°27′E
Polynesia, is., Oc.	240	4°00′S	156°00′W
Pomba, r., Braz. (pô′m-bà)	141a	21°28′S	42°28′W
Pomerania, hist. reg., Pol. (pŏm-ê-rā′nĭ-à)	168	53°50′N	15°20′E
Pomeroy, S. Afr. (pŏm′ẽr-roi)	233c	28°36′S	30°26′E
Pomeroy, Wa., U.S. (pŏm′ẽr-oi)	114	46°28′N	117°35′W
Pomezia, Italy (pô-mĕ′t-zyä)	173d	41°41′N	12°31′E
Pomigliano d'Arco, Italy (pô-mē-lyà′nô-d-ä′r-kô)	173c	40°39′N	14°23′E
Pomme de Terre, Mn., U.S. (pŏm dē tĕr′)	112	45°22′N	95°52′W
Pomona, Ca., U.S. (pô-mō′nà)	104	34°04′N	117°45′W
Pomorie, Blg.	163	42°24′N	27°41′E
Pompano Beach, Fl., U.S. (pŏm′pà-nô)	125a	26°12′N	80°07′W
Pompeii Ruins, hist., Italy	173c	40°31′N	14°29′E
Pompton Lakes, N.J., U.S. (pŏmp′tŏn)	110a	41°01′N	74°16′W
Pomuch, Mex. (pô-mōō′ch)	132a	20°12′N	90°10′W
Ponca, Ne., U.S. (pŏn′kà)	112	42°34′N	96°43′W
Ponca City, Ok., U.S.	121	36°42′N	97°07′W
Ponce, P.R. (pōn′sā)	129	18°01′N	66°43′W
Pondicherry, India	199	11°58′N	79°48′E
Pondicherry, state, India	199	11°50′N	74°50′E
Ponferrada, Spain (pôn-fĕr-rä′dhä)	162	42°33′N	6°38′W
Ponoka, Can. (pŏ-nō′kà)	90	52°42′N	113°35′W
Ponoy, Russia	180	66°58′N	41°00′E
Ponoy, r., Russia	180	67°00′N	39°00′E
Ponta Delgada, Port. (pôn′tà dĕl-gä′dà)	230a	37°40′N	25°45′W
Ponta Grossa, Braz. (grō′sà)	143	25°09′S	50°05′W
Pont-à-Mousson, Fr. (pôn′tà-mōōsôn′)	171	48°55′N	6°02′E
Pontarlier, Fr. (pôn′tár-lyā′)	171	46°53′N	6°22′E
Pont-Audemer, Fr. (pôn′tōd′mâr′)	170	49°23′N	0°28′E
Pontchartrain Lake, l., La., U.S. (pôn-shàr-trăn′)	123	30°10′N	90°10′W
Ponteareas, Spain	172	42°09′N	8°23′W
Pontedera, Italy (pōn-tå-dā′rä)	174	43°37′N	10°37′E
Ponte de Sor, Port.	172	39°14′N	8°03′W
Pontefract, Eng., U.K. (pŏn′tē-frăkt)	158a	53°41′N	1°18′W
Ponte Nova, Braz. (pô′n-tĕ-nô′và)	143	20°26′S	42°52′W
Pontevedra, Spain (pôn-tĕ-vĕ-drä)	162	42°28′N	8°38′W
Ponthierville *see* Ubundi, D.R.C.	232	0°21′S	25°29′E
Pontiac, Il., U.S. (pŏn′tĭ-ăk)	108	40°55′N	88°35′W
Pontiac, Mi., U.S.	105	42°37′N	83°17′W
Pontianak, Indon. (pôn-tē-ä′nàk)	212	0°04′S	109°20′E
Pontian Kechil, Malay.	197b	1°29′N	103°24′E
Pontic Mountains, mts., Tur.	181	41°20′N	34°30′E
Pontivy, Fr. (pôn-tē-vē′)	170	48°05′N	2°57′W
Pontoise, Fr. (pôn-twáz′)	170	49°03′N	2°05′E
Pontonnyy, Russia (pôn′tôn-nyĭ)	186c	59°47′N	30°39′E
Pontotoc, Ms., U.S. (pŏn-tô-tŏk′)	124	34°11′N	88°59′W
Pontremoli, Italy (pôn-trĕm′ô-lē)	174	44°21′N	9°50′E
Ponziane, Isole, i., Italy (ē′sō-lĕ)	162	40°55′N	12°58′E
Poole, Eng., U.K. (pōōl)	164	50°43′N	2°00′W
Poolesville, Md., U.S. (poolēs-vĭl)	110e	39°08′N	77°26′W
Pooley Island, i., Can. (pōō′lē)	94	52°44′N	128°16′W
Poopó, Lago de, l., Bol.	142	18°45′S	67°07′W
Popayán, Col. (pō-pä-yän′)	142	2°21′N	76°43′W
Poplar, Mt., U.S. (pŏp′lẽr)	115	48°08′N	105°10′W
Poplar, r., Mt., U.S.	115	48°34′N	105°20′W
Poplar, West Fork, r., Mt., U.S.	115	48°59′N	106°06′W
Poplar Bluff, Mo., U.S. (blŭf)	121	36°43′N	90°22′W
Poplar Plains, Ky., U.S. (plāns)	108	38°20′N	83°40′W
Poplar Point, Can.	102f	50°04′N	97°57′W
Poplarville, Ms., U.S. (pŏp′lẽr-vĭl)	124	30°50′N	89°33′W
Popocatépetl Volcán, Mex. (pô-pô-kä-tā′pĕ′t'l)	128	19°01′N	98°38′W
Popokabaka, D.R.C. (pō′pô-kà-bä′kà)	232	5°42′S	16°35′E
Popovo, Blg. (pô′pô-vō)	175	43°23′N	26°17′E
Porbandar, India (pōr-bŭn′dŭr)	199	21°44′N	69°40′E
Porce, r., Col. (pôr-sĕ)	142a	7°11′N	74°55′W
Porcher Island, i., Can. (pôr′kẽr)	94	53°57′N	130°30′W
Porcuna, Spain (pôr-kōō′nä)	172	37°54′N	4°10′W
Porcupine, r., N.A.	103	67°38′N	140°07′W
Porcupine Creek, r., Mt., U.S.	115	48°27′N	106°24′W
Porcupine Hills, hills, Can.	97	52°30′N	101°45′W
Pordenone, Italy (pōr-då-nō′nå)	174	45°58′N	12°38′E
Pori, Fin. (pô′rê)	160	61°29′N	21°45′E
Poriúncula, Braz.	141a	20°58′S	42°02′W
Porkhov, Russia (pôr′kôf)	180	57°46′N	29°33′E
Porlamar, Ven. (pōr-lä-mär′)	142	11°00′N	63°55′W
Pornic, Fr. (pôr-nēk′)	170	47°08′N	2°07′W
Poronaysk, Russia (pô′rô-nīsk)	179	49°21′N	143°23′E
Porrentruy, Switz. (pô-rän-trüē′)	166	47°25′N	7°02′E
Porsgrunn, Nor. (pŏrs′grŏn′)	166	59°09′N	9°36′E
Portachuelo, Bol. (pôrt-ä-chwā′lô)	142	17°20′S	63°12′W
Portage, Pa., U.S. (pôr′tāj)	109	40°25′N	78°35′W
Portage, Wi., U.S.	113	43°33′N	89°29′W
Portage Des Sioux, Mo., U.S. (dē sōō)	117e	38°56′N	90°21′W
Portage la Prairie, Can. (lä-prā′rĭ)	90	49°57′N	98°25′W
Port Alberni, Can. (pōr äl-bẽr-nē′)	90	49°14′N	124°48′W
Portalegre, Port. (pôr-tä-lā′grĕ)	162	39°18′N	7°26′W
Portales, N.M., U.S. (pôr-tä′lĕs)	120	34°10′N	103°11′W
Port Alfred, S. Afr.	232	33°36′S	26°55′E
Port Alice, Can. (ăl′ĭs)	90	50°23′N	127°27′W
Port Allegany, Pa., U.S. (ăl-ê-gā′nĭ)	109	41°50′N	78°10′W
Port Angeles, Wa., U.S. (ăn′jē-lĕs)	104	48°07′N	123°26′W
Port Antonio, Jam.	129	18°10′N	76°25′W
Portarlington, Austl.	217a	38°07′S	144°39′E
Port Arthur, Tx., U.S.	105	29°52′N	93°59′W
Port Augusta, Austl. (ô-gŭs′tă)	222	32°28′S	137°50′E
Port au Port Bay, b., Can. (pôr′tō pōr′)	101	48°41′N	58°45′W
Port-au-Prince, Haiti (prăns′)	129	18°35′N	72°20′W
Port Austin, Mi., U.S. (ôs′tĭn)	108	44°00′N	83°00′W
Port Blair, India (blâr)	212	12°07′N	92°45′E
Port Bolivar, Tx., U.S. (bŏl′ĭ-vár)	123a	29°22′N	94°46′W
Port Borden, Can. (bôr′dĕn)	100	46°15′N	63°42′W
Port-Bouët, C. Iv.	230	5°24′N	3°56′W
Port-Cartier, Can.	100	50°01′N	66°53′W
Port Chester, N.Y., U.S. (chĕs′tẽr)	110a	40°59′N	73°40′W
Port Chicago, Ca., U.S. (shĭ-kô′gō)	116b	38°03′N	122°01′W
Port Clinton, Oh., U.S. (klĭn′tŭn)	108	41°30′N	83°00′W
Port Colborne, Can.	99	42°53′N	79°13′W
Port Coquitlam, Can. (kô-kwĭt′lăm)	95	49°16′N	122°46′W
Port Credit, Can. (krĕd′ĭt)	102d	43°33′N	79°35′W
Port-de-Bouc, Fr. (pōr-dē-bōōk′)	170a	43°24′N	5°00′E
Port de Paix, Haiti (pē)	135	19°55′N	72°50′W
Port Dickson, Malay. (dĭk′sŭn)	197b	2°33′N	101°49′E
Port Discovery, b., Wa., U.S. (dĭs-kŭv′ẽr-ĭ)	116a	48°05′N	122°55′W
Port Edward, S. Afr. (ĕd′wẽrd)	233c	31°04′S	30°14′E
Port Elgin, Can. (ĕl′jĭn)	100	46°03′N	64°05′W
Port Elizabeth, S. Afr. (ê-lĭz′à-bĕth)	232	33°57′S	25°37′E
Porterdale, Ga., U.S. (pōr′tẽr-dāl)	124	33°34′N	83°53′W
Porterville, Ca., U.S. (pōr′tẽr-vĭl)	118	36°03′N	119°05′W
Port Francqui *see* Ilebo, D.R.C.	232	4°19′S	20°35′E
Port Gamble, Wa., U.S. (găm′bŭl)	116a	47°52′N	122°36′W
Port Gamble Indian Reservation, I.R., Wa., U.S.	116a	47°54′N	122°33′W
Port-Gentil, Gabon (zhän-tē′)	232	0°43′S	8°47′E
Port Gibson, Ms., U.S.	124	31°56′N	90°57′W
Port Harcourt, Nig. (här′kŭrt)	230	4°43′N	7°05′E
Port Hardy, Can. (här′dĭ)	94	50°43′N	127°29′W
Port Hawkesbury, Can.	101	45°37′N	61°21′W
Port Hedland, Austl. (hĕd′lănd)	218	20°30′S	118°30′E
Porthill, Id., U.S.	114	49°00′N	116°30′W
Port Hood, Can. (hŏd)	101	46°01′N	61°32′W
Port Hope, Can. (hōp)	99	43°55′N	78°10′W
Port Huron, Mi., U.S. (hū′rŏn)	105	43°00′N	82°30′W
Portici, Italy (pôr′tē-chē)	173c	40°34′N	14°20′E
Portillo, Chile (pôr-tē′l-yô)	141b	32°51′S	70°09′W
Portimão, Port. (pôr-tē-moun)	172	37°09′N	8°34′W
Port Jervis, N.Y., U.S. (jûr′vĭs)	110a	41°22′N	74°41′W
Portland, Austl. (pōrt′lănd)	219	38°20′S	142°40′E
Portland, In., U.S.	108	40°25′N	85°00′W
Portland, Me., U.S.	105	43°40′N	70°16′W
Portland, Mi., U.S.	108	42°50′N	85°00′W
Portland, Or., U.S.	104	45°31′N	122°41′W
Portland, Tx., U.S.	123	27°53′N	97°20′W
Portland Bight, b., Jam.	134	17°45′N	77°05′W
Portland Canal, can., Ak., U.S.	94	55°10′N	130°08′W
Portland Inlet, b., Can.	94	54°50′N	130°15′W
Portland Point, c., Jam.	134	17°40′N	77°20′W
Port Lavaca, Tx., U.S. (lȧ-vä′kȧ)	123	28°36′N	96°38′W
Port Lincoln, Austl. (lĭŋ-kŭn)	218	34°39′S	135°50′E
Port Ludlow, Wa., U.S. (lŭd′lō)	116a	47°26′N	122°41′W
Port Macquarie, Austl. (mȧ-kwŏ′rĭ)	219	31°25′S	152°45′E
Port Madison Indian Reservation, I.R., Wa., U.S. (măd′ĭ-sŭn)	116a	47°46′N	122°38′W
Port Maria, Jam. (mȧ-rī′ȧ)	134	18°20′N	76°55′W
Port Moody, Can. (mōōd′ĭ)	95	49°17′N	122°51′W
Port Moresby, Pap. N. Gui. (mōrz′bē)	213	9°34′S	147°20′E
Port Neches, Tx., U.S. (nĕch′ĕz)	123	29°59′N	93°57′W
Port Nelson, Can. (nĕl′sŭn)	97	57°03′N	92°36′W
Portneuf-Sur-Mer, Can. (pôr-nûf′sür mĕr)	100	48°36′N	69°06′W
Port Nolloth, S. Afr. (nŏl′ŏth)	232	29°10′S	17°00′E
Porto (Oporto), Port. (pōr′tò)	154	41°10′N	8°38′W
Porto Acre, Braz. (ä′krĕ)	142	9°38′S	67°34′W
Porto Alegre, Braz. (ä-lā′grĕ)	144	29°58′S	51°11′W
Porto Amboim, Ang.	232	11°01′S	13°45′E
Portobelo, Pan. (pôr′tô-bā′lô)	129	9°32′N	79°40′W
Pôrto de Pedras, Braz. (pā′drázh)	143	9°09′S	35°20′W
Pôrto Feliz, Braz. (fĕ-lē′s)	141a	23°12′S	47°30′W
Portoferraio, Italy (pōr′tô-fĕr-rä′yō)	174	42°47′N	10°20′E
Port of Spain, Trin. (spān)	143	10°44′N	61°24′W
Portogruaro, Italy (pōr′tô-grŏŏ-ä′rō)	174	45°48′N	12°49′E
Portola, Ca., U.S. (pôr′tō-lȧ)	118	39°47′N	120°29′W
Porto Mendes, Braz. (mĕ′n-dĕs)	143	24°41′S	54°13′W
Porto Murtinho, Braz. (mòr-tēn′yò)	143	21°43′S	57°43′W
Porto Nacional, Braz. (nä-syô-näl′)	143	10°43′S	48°14′W
Porto Novo, Benin (pōr′tô-nō′vō)	230	6°29′N	2°37′E
Port Orchard, Wa., U.S. (ôr′chẽrd)	116a	47°32′N	122°38′W
Port Orchard, b., Wa., U.S.	116a	47°40′N	122°39′W
Porto Santo, Ilha de, i., Port. (sän′tò)	230	32°41′N	16°15′W
Porto Seguro, Braz. (sā-gōō′rò)	143	16°26′S	38°59′W
Porto Torres, Italy (tôr′rĕs)	174	40°49′N	8°25′E
Porto-Vecchio, Fr. (vĕk′ē-ô)	174	41°36′N	9°17′E
Porto Velho, Braz. (vāl′yò)	142	8°45′S	63°43′W
Portoviejo, Ec. (pôr-tō-vyā′hō)	142	1°11′S	80°28′W
Port Phillip Bay, b., Austl. (fĭl′ĭp)	221	37°57′S	144°50′E
Port Pirie, Austl. (pĭ′rē)	218	33°10′S	138°00′E
Port Royal, b., Jam. (roi′ăl)	134	17°50′N	76°45′W
Port Said, Egypt	238d	31°15′N	32°19′E
Port Saint Johns, S. Afr. (sănt jŏnz)	232	31°37′S	29°32′E
Port Saint Lucie, Fl., U.S.	125a	27°20′N	80°20′W
Port Shepstone, S. Afr. (shĕps′tŭn)	232	30°45′S	30°23′E
Portsmouth, Dom.	133b	15°33′N	61°28′W
Portsmouth, Eng., U.K. (pôrts′mŭth)	154	50°45′N	1°03′W
Portsmouth, N.H., U.S.	105	43°05′N	70°50′W
Portsmouth, Oh., U.S.	105	38°45′N	83°00′W
Portsmouth, Va., U.S.	105	36°50′N	76°19′W
Port Sulphur, La., U.S. (sŭl′fẽr)	124	29°28′N	89°41′W
Port Susan, b., Wa., U.S. (sū-zán′)	116a	48°11′N	122°25′W
Port Townsend, Wa., U.S. (tounz′ĕnd)	116a	48°07′N	122°46′W
Port Townsend, b., Wa., U.S.	116a	48°05′N	122°47′W
Portugal, nation, Eur. (pōr′tu-găl)	154	38°15′N	8°08′W
Portugalete, Spain (pōr-tōō-gä-lā′tā)	172	43°18′N	3°05′W
Portuguese West Africa *see* Angola, nation, Ang.	232	14°15′S	16°00′E
Port Vendres, Fr.	170	42°32′N	3°07′E
Port Vila, Vanuatu	219	17°44′S	168°19′E
Port Wakefield, Austl. (wāk′fēld)	218	34°12′S	138°10′E
Port Washington, N.Y., U.S. (wôsh′ĭng-tŭn)	110a	40°49′N	73°42′W
Port Washington, Wi., U.S.	113	43°24′N	87°52′W
Posadas, Arg. (pō-sä′dhäs)	144	27°32′S	55°56′W
Posadas, Spain (pô-sä-däs)	172	37°48′N	5°09′W
Poshekhon'ye Volodarsk, Russia (pô-shyĕ′kôn-yĕ vôl′ô-dàrsk)	176	58°31′N	39°07′E
Poso, Danau, l., Indon. (pō′sō)	212	2°00′S	119°40′E
Pospelokova, Russia (pôs-pyĕl′kô-và)	186a	59°25′N	60°50′E
Possession Sound, strt., Wa., U.S. (pŏ-zĕsh-ŭn)	116a	47°59′N	122°17′W
Possum Kingdom Reservoir, res., Tx., U.S. (pŏs′ŭm kĭng′dŭm)	122	32°58′N	98°12′W
Post, Tx., U.S. (pōst)	120	33°12′N	101°21′W
Postojna, Slvn. (pōs-tōynȧ)	174	45°45′N	14°13′E
Pos'yet, Russia (pos-yĕt′)	210	42°27′N	130°47′E
Potawatomi Indian Reservation, I.R., Ks., U.S. (pŏt-ȧ-wä′tō mē)	121	39°30′N	96°11′W
Potchefstroom, S. Afr. (pŏch′ĕf-strōm)	232	26°42′S	27°06′E
Poteau, Ok., U.S. (pô-tō′)	121	35°03′N	94°37′W
Poteet, Tx., U.S. (pô-tēt)	122	29°05′N	98°35′W
Potenza, Italy (pô-tĕnt′sä)	163	40°39′N	15°49′E
Potenza, r., Italy	174	43°09′N	13°00′E
Potgietersrus, S. Afr. (pôt-kē′tẽrs-rûs)	232	24°09′S	29°04′E
Potholes Reservoir, res., Wa., U.S.	114	47°00′N	119°20′W
Poti, Geor. (pô′tê)	181	42°10′N	41°40′E
Potiskum, Nig.	230	11°43′N	11°05′E
Potomac, Md., U.S. (pô-tō′măk)	110e	39°01′N	77°13′W
Potomac, r., U.S. (pô-tō′măk)	107	38°15′N	76°55′W
Potosí, Bol.	142	19°35′S	65°45′W
Potosi, Mo., U.S. (pŏ-tō′sĭ)	121	37°56′N	90°46′W
Potosi, r., Mex. (pō-tô-sē′)	122	25°04′N	99°36′W
Potrerillos, Hond. (pō-trȧ-rēl′yōs)	132	15°13′N	87°58′W
Potsdam, Ger. (pôts′däm)	161	52°24′N	13°04′E
Potsdam, N.Y., U.S. (pŏts′dăm)	109	44°40′N	75°00′W
Pottenstein, Aus.	159e	47°58′N	16°06′E
Potters Bar, Eng., U.K. (pŏt′ĕz bär)	158b	51°41′N	0°12′W
Pottstown, Pa., U.S. (pŏts′toun)	109	40°15′N	75°40′W
Pottsville, Pa., U.S. (pôts′vĭl)	109	40°40′N	76°15′W
Poughkeepsie, N.Y., U.S. (pŏ-kĭp′sē)	105	41°45′N	73°55′W
Poulsbo, Wa., U.S. (pōlz′bò)	116a	47°44′N	122°38′W
Poulton-le-Fylde, Eng., U.K. (pōl′tŭn-lē-fīld′)	158a	53°52′N	2°59′W
Pouso Alegre, Braz. (pō′zò ä-lā′grĕ)	143	22°13′S	45°56′W
Póvoa de Varzim, Port. (pō-vō′á dā vär′zēn)	162	41°23′N	8°44′W
Powder, r., Or., U.S.	114	44°55′N	117°35′W
Powder, r., U.S. (pou′dẽr)	106	45°18′N	105°37′W
Powder, South Fork, r., Wy., U.S.	115	43°13′N	106°54′W
Powder River, Wy., U.S.	115	43°06′N	106°55′W
Powell, Wy., U.S. (pou′ĕl)	115	44°44′N	108°44′W
Powell, Lake, res., U.S.	106	37°26′N	110°25′W
Powell Lake, l., Can.	94	50°10′N	124°13′W
Powell Point, c., Bah.	134	24°50′N	76°20′W
Powell Reservoir, res., Ky., U.S.	124	36°30′N	83°35′W
Powell River, Can.	90	49°52′N	124°33′W
Poyang Hu, l., China	205	29°20′N	116°28′E
Poygan, r., Wi., U.S. (poi′găn)	113	44°10′N	89°05′W
Požarevac, Yugo. (pô′zhá-rĕ-váts)	175	44°38′N	21°12′E
Poza Rica, Mex. (pô-zô-rē′kä)	131	20°32′N	97°25′W
Poznań, Pol.	154	52°25′N	16°55′E
Pozoblanco, Spain (pô-thō-blän′kō)	172	38°23′N	4°50′W
Pozos, Mex. (pô′zōs)	130	22°05′N	100°50′W
Pozuelo de Alarcón, Spain (pô-thwā′lō dā ä-lär-kōn′)	173a	40°27′N	3°49′W
Pozzuoli, Italy (pôt-swô′lē)	174	40°34′N	14°08′E
Pra, r., Ghana (prȧ)	234	5°45′N	1°35′W
Pra, r., Russia	176	55°00′N	40°13′E
Prachin Buri, Thai. (prä′chēn)	212	13°59′N	101°15′E
Pradera, Col. (prä-dĕ′rä)	142a	3°24′N	76°13′W
Prades, Fr. (pråd)	170	42°37′N	2°23′E
Prado, Col. (prädō)	142a	3°44′N	74°55′W
Prado Reservoir, res., Ca., U.S. (prä′dō)	117a	33°45′N	117°40′W
Prados, Braz. (prá′dôs)	141a	21°05′S	44°04′W
Prague, Czech Rep.	168	50°05′N	14°26′E
Praha *see* Prague, Czech Rep.	154	50°05′N	14°26′E
Praia, C.V. (prä′yȧ)	230b	15°00′N	23°30′W
Praia Funda, Ponta da, c., Braz. (pôn′tä-dȧ-prä′yȧ-fōō′n-dä)	144b	23°04′S	43°34′W
Prairie du Chien, Wi., U.S. (prâ′rĭ dò shēn′)	113	43°02′N	91°10′W
Prairie Grove, Can. (prâ′rĭ grōv)	102f	49°48′N	96°57′W
Prairie Island Indian Reservation, I.R., Mn., U.S.	113	44°42′N	92°32′W
Prairies, Rivière des, r., Can. (rē-vyâr′ dā prâ-rē′)	102a	45°40′N	73°34′W
Pratas Island, i., Asia	209	20°40′N	116°30′E

338 Prato – Purkersdorf

PRONOUNCING INDEX

PLACE (Pronunciation)	PAGE	LAT.	LONG.
Prato, Italy (prä'tō)	174	43°53'N	11°03'E
Pratt, Ks., U.S. (prăt)	120	37°37'N	98°43'W
Prattville, Al., U.S. (prăt'vĭl)	124	32°28'N	86°27'W
Pravdinsk, Russia	167	54°26'N	21°00'E
Pravdinskiy, Russia (práv-dĕn'skĭ)	186b	56°03'N	37°52'E
Pravia, Spain (prä'vē-ä)	172	43°30'N	6°08'W
Pregolya, r., Russia (prĕ-gô'lă)	167	54°37'N	20°50'E
Premont, Tx., U.S. (prē-mŏnt')	122	27°20'N	98°07'W
Prenzlau, Ger. (prĕnts'lou)	168	53°19'N	13°52'E
Přerov, Czech Rep. (przhĕ'rôf)	161	49°28'N	17°28'E
Prescot, Eng., U.K. (prĕs'kŭt)	158a	53°25'N	2°48'W
Prescott, Can. (prĕs'kŭt)	109	44°45'N	75°35'W
Prescott, Ar., U.S.	121	33°47'N	93°23'W
Prescott, Az., U.S. (prĕs'kŏt)	104	34°30'N	112°30'W
Prescott, Wi., U.S. (prĕs'kŏt)	117g	44°45'N	92°48'W
Presho, S.D., U.S. (prĕsh'ō)	112	43°56'N	100°04'W
Presidencia Roque Sáenz Peña, Arg.	144	26°52'S	60°15'W
Presidente Epitácio, Braz. (prā-sē-dĕn'tĕ å-pē-tä'syò)	143	21°56'S	52°01'W
Presidio, Tx., U.S. (prĕ-sĭ'dĭ-ō)	122	29°33'N	104°23'W
Presidio, Río del, r., Mex. (rē'ō-dĕl-prĕ-sē'dyô)	130	23°54'N	105°44'W
Prešov, Slvk. (prĕ'shôf)	161	49°00'N	21°18'E
Prespa, Lake, l., Eur. (prĕs'pä)	175	40°49'N	20°50'E
Prespuntal, r., Ven.	143b	9°55'N	64°32'W
Presque Isle, Me., U.S. (prĕsk'ēl')	100	46°41'N	68°03'W
Pressbaum, Aus.	159e	48°12'N	16°06'E
Prestea, Ghana	234	5°27'N	2°08'W
Preston, Austl.	217a	37°45'S	145°01'E
Preston, Eng., U.K. (prĕs'tŭn)	164	53°46'N	2°42'W
Preston, Id., U.S. (pres'tŭn)	115	42°05'N	111°54'W
Preston, Mn., U.S. (prĕs'tŭn)	113	43°42'N	92°06'W
Preston, Wa., U.S.	116a	47°31'N	121°56'W
Prestonburg, Ky., U.S. (prĕs'tŭn-bûrg)	108	37°35'N	82°50'W
Prestwich, Eng., U.K. (prĕst'wĭch)	158a	53°32'N	2°17'W
Pretoria, S. Afr. (prĕ-tō'rĭ-ȧ)	232	25°43'S	28°16'E
Pretoria North, S. Afr. (prĕ-tō'rĭ-ȧ nōōrd)	238c	25°41'S	28°11'E
Préveza, Grc. (prĕ'vå-zä)	175	38°58'N	20°44'E
Pribilof Islands, is., Ak., U.S. (prĭ'bĭ-lof)	103	57°00'N	169°20'W
Priboj, Yugo. (prē'boi)	175	43°33'N	19°33'E
Price, Ut., U.S. (prīs)	119	39°35'N	110°50'W
Price, r., Ut., U.S.	119	39°21'N	110°35'W
Prichard, Al., U.S. (prĭt'chârd)	124	30°44'N	88°04'W
Priddis, Can. (prĭd'dĭs)	102e	50°53'N	114°20'W
Priddis Creek, r., Can.	102e	50°56'N	114°32'W
Priego, Spain (prē-ā'gō)	172	37°27'N	4°13'W
Prienai, Lith. (prē-ĕn'ī)	167	54°38'N	23°56'E
Prieska, S. Afr. (prē-ĕs'kȧ)	232	29°40'S	22°50'E
Priest Lake, l., Id., U.S. (prēst)	114	48°30'N	116°43'W
Priest Rapids Dam, Wa., U.S.	114	46°39'N	119°55'W
Priest Rapids Lake, res., Wa., U.S.	114	46°42'N	119°58'W
Priiskovaya, Russia (prĭ-ēs'kô-vá-yá)	186a	60°50'N	58°55'E
Prijedor, Bos. (prē'yĕ-dôr)	174	44°58'N	16°43'E
Prijepolje, Yugo. (prē'yĕ-pô'lyĕ)	175	43°22'N	19°41'E
Prilep, Mac. (prē'lĕp)	163	41°20'N	21°35'E
Primorsk, Russia (prē-môrsk')	167	60°24'N	28°35'E
Primorsko-Akhtarskaya, Russia (prē-môr'skô äk-tär'skĭ-ê)	181	46°03'N	38°09'E
Primrose, S. Afr.	233b	26°11'S	28°11'E
Primrose Lake, l., Can.	96	54°55'N	109°45'W
Prince Albert, Can. (prĭns ăl'bērt)	90	53°12'N	105°46'W
Prince Albert National Park, rec., Can.	92	54°10'N	105°25'W
Prince Albert Sound, strt., Can.	92	70°23'N	116°57'W
Prince Charles Island, i., Can. (chärlz)	93	67°41'N	74°10'W
Prince Edward Island, prov., Can.	91	46°45'N	63°10'W
Prince Edward Islands, is., S. Afr.	224	46°36'S	37°57'E
Prince Edward National Park, rec., Can. (ĕd'wērd)	93	46°33'N	63°35'W
Prince Edward Peninsula, pen., Can.	109	44°00'N	77°15'W
Prince Frederick, Md., U.S. (prĭnce frĕdĕrĭk)	110e	38°33'N	76°35'W
Prince George, Can. (jôrj)	90	53°51'N	122°57'W
Prince of Wales, i., Austl.	221	10°47'S	142°15'E
Prince of Wales, i., Ak., U.S.	103	55°47'N	132°50'W
Prince of Wales, Cape, c., Ak., U.S. (wālz)	103	65°48'N	169°08'W
Prince Rupert, Can. (roo'pērt)	90	54°19'N	130°19'W
Princes Risborough, Eng., U.K. (prĭns'ĕz rĭz'brŭ)	158b	51°41'N	0°51'W
Princess Charlotte Bay, b., Austl. (shär'lŏt)	221	13°45'S	144°15'E
Princess Royal Channel, strt., Can. (roi'ăl)	94	53°10'N	128°37'W
Princess Royal Island, i., Can.	94	52°57'N	128°49'W
Princeton, Can. (prĭns'tŭn)	90	49°27'N	120°31'W
Princeton, Il., U.S.	108	41°20'N	89°25'W
Princeton, In., U.S.	108	38°20'N	87°35'W
Princeton, Ky., U.S.	124	37°07'N	87°52'W
Princeton, Mi., U.S.	113	46°16'N	87°33'W
Princeton, Mn., U.S.	113	45°34'N	93°36'W
Princeton, Mo., U.S.	121	40°23'N	93°34'W
Princeton, N.J., U.S.	109	40°21'N	74°40'W
Princeton, Wi., U.S.	113	43°50'N	89°09'W
Princeton, W.V., U.S.	125	37°21'N	81°05'W
Prince William Sound, strt., Ak., U.S. (wĭl'yăm)	103	60°40'N	147°10'W
Príncipe, i., S. Tom./P. (prēn'sē-pĕ)	230	1°37'N	7°25'E
Principe Channel, strt., Can. (prĭn'sĭ-pē)	94	53°28'N	129°45'W
Prineville, Or., U.S. (prīn'vĭl)	114	44°17'N	120°48'W
Prineville Reservoir, res., Or., U.S.	114	44°07'N	120°45'W
Prinzapolca, Nic. (prēn-zä-pōl'kä)	133	13°18'N	83°35'W
Prinzapolca, r., Nic.	133	13°23'N	84°23'W
Prior Lake, Mn., U.S. (prī'ēr)	117g	44°43'N	93°26'W
Priozërsk, Russia (prĭ-ô'zĕrsk)	167	61°03'N	30°08'E
Pripet, r., Eur.	181	51°50'N	29°45'E
Pripet Marshes, sw., Eur.	181	52°10'N	27°30'E
Priština, Yugo. (prēsh'tĭ-nä)	163	42°39'N	21°12'E
Pritzwalk, Ger. (prēts'välk)	168	53°09'N	12°12'E
Privas, Fr. (prē-väs')	170	44°44'N	4°37'E
Prizren, Yugo. (prē'zrĕn)	163	42°11'N	20°45'E
Procida, Italy (prô'chē-dä)	173c	40°31'N	14°02'E
Procida, Isola di, i., Italy	173c	40°32'N	13°57'E
Proctor, Mn., U.S. (prŏk'tēr)	117h	46°45'N	92°14'W
Proctor, Vt., U.S.	109	43°40'N	73°00'W
Proebstel, Wa., U.S. (prōb'stĕl)	116c	45°40'N	122°29'W
Proenca-a-Nova, Port. (prô-ān'sȧ-ä-nō'vȧ)	172	39°44'N	7°55'W
Progreso, Hond. (prô-grĕ'sô)	132	15°28'N	87°49'W
Progreso, Mex. (prô-grā'sō)	128	21°14'N	89°39'W
Progreso, Mex.	122	27°29'N	101°05'W
Prokhladnyy, Russia	182	43°46'N	44°00'E
Prokop'yevsk, Russia	184	53°53'N	86°45'E
Prokuplje, Yugo. (prô'kōp'l-yĕ)	175	43°16'N	21°40'E
Prome, Mya.	212	18°46'N	95°15'E
Pronya, r., Bela. (prô'nyä)	176	54°08'N	30°58'E
Pronya, r., Russia	176	54°08'N	39°30'E
Prospect, Ky., U.S. (prŏs'pĕkt)	111h	38°21'N	85°36'W
Prospect Park, Pa., U.S. (prŏs'pĕkt pärk)	110f	39°53'N	75°18'W
Prosser, Wa., U.S. (prŏs'ēr)	114	46°10'N	119°46'W
Prostějov, Czech Rep. (prôs'tyĕ-yôf)	169	49°28'N	17°08'E
Protection, i., Wa., U.S. (prô-tĕk'shŭn)	116a	48°07'N	122°56'W
Protoka, r., Russia (prôt'ō-kȧ)	176	55°00'N	36°42'E
Provadiya, Blg. (prō-väd'ē-yȧ)	175	43°13'N	27°28'E
Providence, Ky., U.S. (prŏv'ĭ-dĕns)	108	37°25'N	87°45'W
Providence, R.I., U.S.	105	41°50'N	71°23'W
Providence, Ut., U.S.	115	41°42'N	111°50'W
Providencia, Isla de, i., Col.	133	13°21'N	80°55'W
Providenciales, i., T./C. Is.	135	21°50'N	72°15'W
Provideniya, Russia (prô-vĭ-dă'nĭ-yá)	103	64°30'N	172°54'W
Provincetown, Ma., U.S.	109	42°03'N	70°11'W
Provo, Ut., U.S. (prō'vō)	104	40°15'N	111°40'W
Prozor, Bos. (prō'zôr)	175	43°48'N	17°59'E
Prudence Island, i., R.I., U.S. (prōō'dĕns)	110b	41°38'N	71°20'W
Prudhoe Bay, b., Ak., U.S.	103	70°40'N	147°25'W
Prudnik, Pol. (prŏd'nĭk)	169	50°19'N	17°34'E
Prussia, hist. reg., Eur. (prŭsh'ȧ)	168	50°43'N	8°35'E
Pruszków, Pol. (prōsh'kôf)	169	52°09'N	20°50'E
Prut, r., Eur. (prōōt)	156	48°05'N	27°07'E
Pryluky, Ukr.	181	50°36'N	32°21'E
Prymors'k, Ukr.	177	46°43'N	36°21'E
Pryor, Ok., U.S. (prī'ēr)	121	36°16'N	95°19'W
Pryvil'ne, Ukr.	177	47°30'N	32°21'E
Przedbórz, Pol.	169	51°05'N	19°53'E
Przemyśl, Pol. (pzhĕ'mĭsh'l)	154	49°47'N	22°45'E
Przheval'sk, Kyrg. (p'r-zhĭ-välsk')	183	42°29'N	78°24'E
Psel, r., Eur.	181	49°45'N	33°42'E
Pskov, Russia (pskôf)	178	57°48'N	28°19'E
Pskov, prov., Russia	176	57°33'N	29°05'E
Pskovskoye Ozero, l., Eur. (p'skôv'skô'yĕ ôzē-rô)	180	58°05'N	28°15'E
Ptich', r., Bela. (p'tēch)	180	53°17'N	28°16'E
Ptuj, Slvn. (ptōō'ē)	174	46°24'N	15°54'E
Pucheng, China (pōō'chĕng')	209	28°02'N	118°25'E
Pucheng, China (pōō-chŭŋ)	206	35°43'N	115°22'E
Puck, Pol. (pòtsk)	169	54°43'N	18°23'E
Pudozh, Russia (pōō'dôzh)	180	61°50'N	36°50'E
Puebla, Mex. (pwā'blä)	128	19°02'N	98°11'W
Puebla, state, Mex.	131	19°00'N	97°45'W
Puebla de Don Fadrique, Spain	172	37°55'N	2°55'W
Pueblo, Co., U.S. (pwā'blō)	104	38°15'N	104°36'W
Pueblo Nuevo, Mex. (nwā'vô)	130	23°23'N	105°21'W
Pueblo Viejo, Mex. (vyā'hô)	131	17°23'N	93°46'W
Puente Alto, Chile (pwĕ'n-tĕ äl'tô)	141b	33°36'S	70°34'W
Puentedeume, Spain (pwĕn-tå-dhå-ōō'må)	172	43°28'N	8°09'W
Puente-Genil, Spain (pwĕn'tå-hå-nēl')	172	37°25'N	4°18'W
Puerco, Rio, r., N.M., U.S. (pwĕr'kō)	119	35°15'N	107°05'W
Puerto Aisén, Chile (pwĕ'r-tō ä'y-sĕ'n)	144	45°28'S	72°44'W
Puerto Angel, Mex. (pwĕ'r-tō äŋ'hâl)	131	15°42'N	96°32'W
Puerto Armuelles, Pan. (pwe'r-tô är-mōō-ā'lyās)	133	8°18'N	82°52'W
Puerto Barrios, Guat. (pwĕ'r-tô bär'rê-ôs)	128	15°43'N	88°36'W
Puerto Bermúdez, Peru (pwĕ'r-tō bĕr-mōō'dāz)	142	10°17'S	74°57'W
Puerto Berrío, Col. (pwĕ'r-tō bĕr-rē'ō)	142	6°29'N	74°27'W
Puerto Cabello, Ven. (pwĕ'r-tō kä-bĕl'yō)	142	10°28'N	68°01'W
Puerto Cabezas, Nic. (pwĕ'r-tō kä-bā'zäs)	133	14°01'N	83°26'W
Puerto Casado, Para. (pwĕ'r-tō kä-sä'dō)	144	22°16'S	57°57'W
Puerto Castilla, Hond. (pwĕ'r-tō käs-tēl'yō)	132	16°01'N	86°01'W
Puerto Chicama, Peru (pwĕ'r-tō chē-kä'mä)	142	7°46'S	79°18'W
Puerto Colombia, Col. (pwĕr'tô kô-lôm'bē-ä)	142	11°08'N	75°09'W
Puerto Cortés, C.R. (pwĕ'r-tō kôr-tās')	133	9°00'N	83°37'W
Puerto Cortés, Hond. (pwĕ'r-tō kôr-tās')	128	15°48'N	87°57'W
Puerto Cumarebo, Ven. (pwĕ'r-tō kōō-mä-rĕ'bô)	142	11°25'N	69°17'W
Puerto de Luna, N.M., U.S. (pwĕr'tô dā lōō'nä)	120	34°49'N	104°36'W
Puerto de Nutrias, Ven. (pwĕ'r-tō dĕ nōō-trē-äs')	142	8°02'N	69°19'W
Puerto Deseado, Arg. (pwĕ'r-tō dā-sä-ä'dhō)	144	47°38'S	66°00'W
Puerto de Somport, p., Eur.	173	42°51'N	0°25'W
Puerto Eten, Peru (pwĕ'r-tō ĕ-tĕ'n)	142	6°59'S	79°51'W
Puerto Jiménez, C.R. (pwĕ'r-tō ĸē-mĕ'nĕz)	133	8°35'N	83°23'W
Puerto La Cruz, Ven. (pwĕ'r-tō lä krōō'z)	142	10°14'N	64°38'W
Puertollano, Spain (pwĕ-tôl-yä'nō)	162	38°41'N	4°05'W
Puerto Madryn, Arg. (pwĕ'r-tō mä-drĕn')	144	42°45'S	65°01'W
Puerto Maldonado, Peru (pwĕ'r-tō mäl-dō-nä'dô)	142	12°43'S	69°01'W
Puerto Miniso, Mex. (pwĕ'r-tō mē-nē'sô)	130	16°06'N	98°02'W
Puerto Montt, Chile (pwĕ'r-tō mô'nt)	144	41°29'S	73°00'W
Puerto Natales, Chile (pwĕ'r-tō nä-tá'lĕs)	144	51°48'S	72°01'W
Puerto Niño, Col. (pwĕ'r-tō nē'n-yô)	142a	5°57'N	74°36'W
Puerto Padre, Cuba (pwĕ'r-tō pä'drā)	134	21°10'N	76°40'W
Puerto Peñasco, Mex. (pwĕ'r-tō pĕn-yä's-kô)	128	31°39'N	113°15'W
Puerto Pinasco, Para. (pwĕ'r-tō pē-ná's-kô)	144	22°31'S	57°50'W
Puerto Píritu, Ven. (pwĕ'r-tō pē'rē-tōō)	143b	10°05'N	65°04'W
Puerto Plata, Dom. Rep. (pwĕ'r-tō plä'tä)	129	19°50'N	70°40'W
Puerto Princesa, Phil. (pwĕr-tô prēn-sä'sä)	212	9°45'N	118°41'E
Puerto Rico, dep., N.A. (pwĕr'tô rē'kō)	129	18°16'N	66°50'W
Puerto Rico Trench, deep	129	19°45'N	66°30'W
Puerto Salgar, Col. (pwĕ'r-tō säl-gär')	142a	5°30'N	74°39'W
Puerto Santa Cruz, Arg. (pwĕ'r-tō sän'tä krōōz')	144	50°04'S	68°32'W
Puerto Suárez, Bol. (pwĕ'r-tō swä'rāz)	143	18°55'S	57°39'W
Puerto Tejada, Col. (pwĕ'r-tō tĕ-kä'dä)	142	3°13'N	76°23'W
Puerto Vallarta, Mex. (pwĕ'r-tō väl-yär'tä)	130	20°36'N	105°13'W
Puerto Varas, Chile (pwĕ'r-tō vä'räs)	144	41°16'S	73°03'W
Puerto Wilches, Col. (pwĕ'r-tō vēl'c-hĕs)	142	7°19'N	73°54'W
Pugachëv, Russia (pōō'gá-chyôf)	181	52°00'N	48°40'E
Puget, Wa., U.S. (pū'jĕt)	116c	46°10'N	123°23'W
Puget Sound, strt., Wa., U.S.	114	47°49'N	122°26'W
Puglia (Apulia), hist. reg., Italy (pōō'lyä) (ä-pōō'lyä)	174	41°13'N	16°10'E
Pukaskwa National Park, rec., Can.	93	48°22'N	85°55'W
Pukeashun Mountain, mtn., Can.	95	51°12'N	119°14'W
Pukin, r., Malay.	197b	2°53'N	102°54'E
Pula, Cro. (pōō'lä)	162	44°52'N	13°55'E
Pulacayo, Bol. (pōō-lä-kä'yō)	142	20°12'N	66°33'W
Pulaski, Tn., U.S. (pŭ-lăs'kĭ)	124	35°11'N	87°03'W
Pulaski, Va., U.S.	125	37°00'N	81°45'W
Puławy, Pol. (pò-wä'vĕ)	169	51°24'N	21°59'E
Pulicat, r., India	203	13°58'N	79°52'E
Pullman, Wa., U.S. (pòl'măn)	114	46°44'N	117°10'W
Pulog, Mount, mtn., Phil. (pōō'lōg)	213a	16°38'N	120°53'E
Puma Yumco, l., China (pōō-mä yōōm-tswo)	202	28°30'N	90°10'E
Pumpkin Creek, r., Mt., U.S. (pŭmp'kĭn)	115	45°47'N	105°35'W
Punakha, Bhu. (pōō-nŭk'ŭ)	199	27°45'N	89°59'E
Punata, Bol. (pōō-nä'tä)	142	17°43'S	65°43'W
Pune, India	199	18°38'N	73°53'E
Punjab, state, India (pŭn'jäb')	199	31°00'N	75°30'E
Puno, Peru (pōō'nô)	142	15°58'S	70°02'W
Punta Arenas, Chile (pōō'n-tä-rĕ'näs)	144	53°09'S	70°48'W
Punta de Piedras, Ven. (pōō'n-tä dĕ pyĕ'dräs)	143b	10°54'N	64°06'W
Punta Gorda, Belize (pòn'tä gôr'dä)	132	16°07'N	88°50'W
Punta Gorda, Fl., U.S. (pŭn'tȧ gôr'dȧ)	125a	26°55'N	82°02'W
Punta Gorda, Río, r., Nic. (pōō'n-tä gô'r-dä)	133	11°34'N	84°13'W
Punta Indio, Canal, strt., Arg. (pōō'n-tä-ē'n-dyô)	141c	34°56'S	57°20'W
Puntarenas, C.R. (pònt-ä-rā'näs)	129	9°59'N	84°49'W
Punto Fijo, Ven. (pōō'n-tô fē'kô)	142	11°48'N	70°14'W
Punxsutawney, Pa., U.S. (pŭnk-sŭ-tô'nē)	109	40°55'N	79°00'W
Puquio, Peru (pōō'kyô)	142	14°43'S	74°02'W
Pur, r., Russia	184	65°30'N	77°30'E
Purcell, Ok., U.S. (pûr-sĕl')	121	35°01'N	97°22'W
Purcell Mountains, mts., N.A. (pûr-sĕl')	95	50°00'N	116°30'W
Purdy, Wa., U.S. (pûr'dē)	116a	47°23'N	122°37'W
Purépero, Mex. (pōō-rā'pā-rō)	130	19°56'N	102°02'W
Purgatoire, r., Co., U.S. (pûr-gá-twär')	120	37°25'N	103°53'W
Puri, India (pò'rē)	199	19°52'N	85°51'E
Purial, Sierra de, mts., Cuba (sē-ĕ'r-rá-dĕ-pōō-rē-äl')	135	20°15'N	74°40'W
Purificación, Col. (pōō-rē-fē-kä-syōn')	142	3°52'N	74°54'W
Purificación, Mex. (pōō-rē-fē-kä-syō'n)	130	19°44'N	104°38'W
Purificación, r., Mex.	130	19°30'N	104°54'W
Purkersdorf, Aus.	159e	48°13'N	16°11'E

PRONOUNCING INDEX

Puruandiro – Ramanāthapuram 339

PLACE (Pronunciation)	PAGE	LAT.	LONG.
Puruandiro, Mex. (pò-rōō-än'dė-rō)	130	20°04'N	101°33'W
Purús, r., S.A. (pōō-rōō's)	142	6°45'S	64°34'W
Pusan, Kor., S.	205	35°08'N	129°05'E
Pushkin, Russia (pòsh'kĭn)	180	59°43'N	30°25'E
Pushkino, Russia (pōōsh'kė-nô)	176	56°01'N	37°51'E
Pustoshka, Russia (pûs-tôsh'kȧ)	176	56°20'N	29°33'E
Pustunich, Mex. (pōōs-tōō'nēch)	131	19°10'N	90°29'W
Putaendo, Chile (pōō-tä-ĕn-dô)	141b	32°37'S	70°42'W
Puteaux, Fr. (pü-tō')	171b	48°52'N	2°12'E
Putfontein, S. Afr. (pòt'fŏn-tān)	233b	26°08'S	28°24'E
Putian, China (pōō-tĭĕn)	209	25°40'N	119°02'E
Putla de Guerrero, Mex. (pōō'tlä-dĕ-gĕr-rĕ'rō)	131	17°03'N	97°55'W
Putnam, Ct., U.S. (pŭt'nȧm)	109	41°55'N	71°55'W
Putorana, Gory, mts., Russia	179	68°45'N	93°15'E
Puttalam, Sri L.	203	8°02'N	79°44'E
Putumayo, r., S.A. (pò-tōō-mä'yō)	142	1°02'S	73°50'W
Putung, Tanjung, c., Indon.	212	3°35'S	111°50'E
Putyvl', Ukr.	177	51°21'N	33°52'E
Puulavesi, I., Fin.	167	61°49'N	27°10'E
Puyallup, Wa., U.S. (pū-ăl'ŭp)	116a	47°12'N	122°18'W
Puyang, China (pōō-yäŋ)	208	35°42'N	114°58'E
Pweto, D.R.C. (pwā'tō)	232	8°29'S	28°58'E
Pyasina, r., Russia (pyä-sē'nȧ)	184	72°45'N	87°37'E
Pyatigorsk, Russia (pyȧ-tė-gôrsk')	181	44°00'N	43°00'E
Pyetrykaw, Bela.	176	52°09'N	28°30'E
Pyhäjärvi, I., Fin.	167	60°57'N	21°50'E
Pyinmana, Mya. (pyēn-mä'nŭ)	199	19°47'N	96°15'E
Pymatuning Reservoir, res., Pa., U.S. (pī-mȧ-tûn'ĭng)	108	41°40'N	80°30'W
Pyŏnggang, Kor., N. (pyŭng'gäng')	210	38°21'N	127°18'E
P'yŏngyang, Kor., N.	205	39°03'N	125°48'E
Pyramid, I., Nv., U.S. (pĭ'rȧ-mĭd)	118	40°02'N	119°50'W
Pyramid Lake Indian Reservation, I.R., Nv., U.S.	118	40°17'N	119°52'W
Pyramids, hist., Egypt	238b	29°53'N	31°10'E
Pyrenees, mts., Eur. (pĭr-e-nēz')	156	43°00'N	0°05'E
Pýrgos, Grc.	163	37°51'N	21°28'E
Pyriatyn, Ukr.	181	50°13'N	32°31'E
Pyrzyce, Pol. (pĕzhĭ'tsĕ)	168	53°09'N	14°53'E

Q

PLACE (Pronunciation)	PAGE	LAT.	LONG.
Qal'at Bishah, Sau. Ar.	198	20°01'N	42°30'E
Qamdo, China (chyäm-dwō)	204	31°06'N	96°30'E
Qandala, Som.	201	11°28'N	49°52'E
Qaraghandy (Karaganda), Kaz.	183	49°42'N	73°18'E
Qaraözen, r.	181	49°50'N	49°35'E
Qarqan *see* Qiemo, China	204	38°02'N	85°16'E
Qarqan, r., China	204	38°55'N	87°15'E
Qarqaraly, Kaz.	183	49°18'N	75°28'E
Qārūn, Birket, I., Egypt	231	29°34'N	30°34'E
Qaṣr al Burayqah, Libya	231	30°25'N	19°20'E
Qasr al-Farāfirah, Egypt	231	27°04'N	28°13'E
Qaṣr Banī Walīd, Libya	231	31°45'N	14°04'E
Qasr el Boukhari, Alg.	162	35°50'N	2°48'E
Qatar, nation, Asia (kä'tar)	198	25°00'N	52°45'E
Qaṭārah, Munkhafaḍ al, depr., Egypt	231	30°07'N	27°30'E
Qausuittuq (Resolute), Can.	89	74°41'N	95°00'W
Qāyen, Iran	198	33°45'N	59°08'E
Qazvīn, Iran	198	36°10'N	49°59'E
Qeshm, Iran	198	26°51'N	56°10'E
Qeshm, i., Iran	198	26°52'N	56°15'E
Qezel Owzan, r., Iran	198	36°30'N	49°00'E
Qezi'ot, Isr.	197a	30°53'N	34°28'E
Qianwei, China (chyĕn-wā)	206	40°11'N	120°05'E
Qi'anzhen, China (chyē-än-jŭn)	206	32°16'N	120°59'E
Qibao, China (chyē-bou)	207b	31°06'N	121°16'E
Qiblīyah, Jabal al Jalālat al, mts., Egypt	197a	28°49'N	32°21'E
Qijiang, China (chyē-jyäŋ)	209	29°05'N	106°40'E
Qikou, China (chyē-kō)	206	38°37'N	117°33'E
Qilian Shan, mts., China (chyē-lĭĕn shän)	204	38°43'N	98°00'E
Qiliping, China (chyē-lē-pĭŋ)	206	31°28'N	114°41'E
Qindao, China (chyĭn-dou)	205	36°05'N	120°10'E
Qing'an, China (chyĭŋ-än)	208	46°50'N	127°30'E
Qingcheng, China (chyĭŋ-chŭŋ)	206	37°12'N	117°43'E
Qingfeng, China (chyĭŋ-fŭŋ)	206	35°52'N	115°05'E
Qinghai, prov., China (chyĭŋ-hī)	204	36°14'N	95°30'E
Qinghai Hu *see* Koko Nor, I., China	204	37°26'N	98°30'E
Qinghe, China (chyĭŋ-hŭ)	208a	40°08'N	116°16'E
Qingjiang, China (chyĭŋ-jyäŋ)	209	28°00'N	115°30'E
Qingjiang, China	206	33°34'N	118°58'E
Qingliu, China (chyĭŋ-lĭō)	209	26°15'N	116°50'E
Qingningsi, China (chyĭŋ-nĭŋ-sz)	207b	31°16'N	121°33'E
Qingping, China (chyĭŋ-pĭŋ)	206	36°46'N	116°03'E
Qingpu, China (chyĭŋ-pōō)	209	31°08'N	121°06'E
Qingxian, China (chyĭŋ shyĕn)	206	38°37'N	116°48'E
Qingyang, China (chyĭŋ-yäŋ)	204	36°02'N	107°42'E
Qingyuan, China (chyĭŋ-yòän)	209	23°43'N	113°10'E
Qingyuan, China	208	42°05'N	125°00'E
Qingyun, China (chyĭŋ-yòn)	206	37°52'N	117°26'E
Qingyundian, China (chĭŋ-yòn-dĭĕn)	208a	39°41'N	116°31'E
Qinhuangdao, China (chyĭn-huaŋ-dou)	205	39°57'N	119°34'E
Qin Ling, mts., China (chyĭn lĭŋ)	204	33°25'N	108°58'E
Qinyang, China (chyĭn-yäŋ)	208	35°00'N	112°55'E
Qinzhou, China (chyĭn-jō)	209	22°00'N	108°35'E
Qionghai, China (chyôŋ-hī)	209	19°10'N	110°28'E
Qiqian, China (chyē-chyĕn)	205	52°23'N	121°04'E
Qiqihar, China	205	47°18'N	124°00'E
Qiryat Gat, Isr.	197a	31°38'N	34°36'E
Qiryat Shemona, Isr.	197a	33°12'N	35°34'E
Qitai, China (chyē-tī)	204	44°07'N	89°04'E
Qiuxian, China (chyô shyĕn)	206	36°43'N	115°13'E
Qixian, China (chyē-shyĕn)	206	34°33'N	114°47'E
Qixian, China	208	35°36'N	114°13'E
Qiyang, China (chyē-yäŋ)	209	26°40'N	112°00'E
Qobda, r., Kaz. (kä-rȧ kôb'dȧ)	181	50°40'N	55°00'E
Qogir Feng *see* K2, mtn., Asia	199	36°06'N	76°38'E
Qom, Iran	198	34°28'N	50°53'E
Qongyrat, Kaz.	183	47°25'N	75°10'E
Qostanay, Kaz.	183	53°10'N	63°39'E
Quabbin Reservoir, res., Ma., U.S. (kwā'bĭn)	109	42°20'N	72°10'W
Quachita, Lake, I., Ar., U.S. (kwä shĭ'tô)	121	34°47'N	93°37'W
Quadra Island, i., Can.	94	50°08'N	125°16'W
Quakertown, Pa., U.S. (kwā'kēr-toun)	109	40°30'N	75°20'W
Quanah, Tx., U.S. (kwä'nȧ)	120	34°19'N	99°43'W
Quang Ngai, Viet. (kwäng n'gä'ė)	212	15°05'N	108°58'E
Quang Ngai, mtn., Viet.	209	15°10'N	108°20'E
Quanjiao, China (chyuän-jyou)	206	32°06'N	118°17'E
Quanzhou, China (chyuän-jō)	205	24°58'N	118°40'E
Quanzhou, China	209	25°58'N	111°02'E
Qu'Appelle, r., Can.	92	50°30'N	104°00'W
Qu'Appelle Dam, dam, Can.	96	51°00'N	106°25'W
Quartu Sant'Elena, Italy (kwär-tōō' sänt a'lå-nä)	174	39°16'N	9°12'E
Quartzsite, Az., U.S.	119	33°40'N	114°13'W
Quatsino Sound, strt., Can. (kwŏt-sē'nō)	94	50°25'N	128°10'W
Quba, Azer. (kōō'bā)	181	41°05'N	48°30'E
Qūchān, Iran	201	37°06'N	58°30'E
Qudi, China	206	37°06'N	117°15'E
Québec, Can. (kwė-bĕk') (kā-bĕk')	102b	46°49'N	71°13'W
Quebec, prov., Can.	91	51°07'N	70°25'W
Quedlinburg, Ger. (kvĕd'lĭn-bōōrgh)	168	51°45'N	11°10'E
Queen Bess, Can.	94	51°16'N	124°34'W
Queen Charlotte Islands, is., Can. (kwēn shär'lŏt)	92	53°30'N	132°25'W
Queen Charlotte Ranges, mts., Can.	94	53°00'N	132°00'W
Queen Charlotte Sound, strt., Can.	94	51°30'N	129°30'W
Queen Charlotte Strait, strt., Can. (strāt)	92	50°40'N	127°25'W
Queen Elizabeth Islands, is., Can. (ė-lĭz'á-bĕth)	89	78°20'N	110°00'W
Queen Maud Gulf, b., Can. (mäd)	92	68°27'N	102°55'W
Queen Maud Land, reg., Ant.	224	75°00'S	10°00'E
Queen Maud Mountains, mts., Ant.	224	85°00'S	179°00'W
Queens Channel, strt., Austl. (kwēnz)	220	14°25'S	129°10'E
Queenscliff, Austl.	217a	38°16'S	144°39'E
Queensland, state, Austl. (kwēnz'lănd)	219	22°45'S	141°01'E
Queenstown, Austl. (kwēnz'toun)	222	42°00'S	145°40'E
Queenstown, S. Afr.	233c	31°54'S	26°53'E
Queimados, Braz. (kā-mȧ'dôs)	144b	22°42'S	43°34'W
Quela, Ang.	236	9°16'S	17°02'E
Quelimane, Moz. (kā-lė-mä'nĕ)	233	17°48'S	37°05'E
Queluz, Port.	173b	38°45'N	9°15'W
Quemado de Güines, Cuba (kā-mä'dhä-dĕ-gwē'nĕs)	134	22°45'N	80°20'W
Quemoy, Tai.	209	24°30'N	118°20'E
Quemoy, i., Tai.	209	24°27'N	118°23'E
Quepos, C.R. (kā'pôs)	133	9°26'N	84°10'W
Quepos, Punta, c., C.R. (pōō'n-tä)	133	9°23'N	84°20'W
Querétaro, Mex. (kå-rā'tä-rō)	128	20°37'N	100°25'W
Querétaro, state, Mex.	130	21°00'N	100°00'W
Quesada, Spain (kā-sä'dhä)	172	37°51'N	3°04'W
Quesnel, Can. (kā-nĕl')	90	52°59'N	122°30'W
Quesnel, r., Can.	95	52°15'N	122°00'W
Quesnel Lake, I., Can.	92	52°32'N	121°05'W
Quetame, Col. (kĕ-tä'mĕ)	142a	4°20'N	73°50'W
Quetta, Pak. (kwĕt'ä)	199	30°19'N	67°01'E
Quezaltenango, Guat. (kå-zäl'tå-näŋ'gō)	128	14°50'N	91°30'W
Quezaltepeque, El Sal. (kĕ-zäl'tĕ'pĕ-kĕ)	132	13°50'N	89°17'W
Quezaltepeque, Guat. (kå-zäl'tå-pā'kå)	132	14°39'N	89°26'W
Quezon City, Phil. (kā-zōn)	212	14°40'N	121°02'E
Qufu, China (chyōō-fōō)	206	35°37'N	116°54'E
Quibdo, Col. (kēb'dō)	142	5°42'N	76°41'W
Quiberon, Fr. (kė-bē-rôn')	170	47°29'N	3°08'W
Quiçama, Parque Nacional de, rec., Ang.	236	10°00'S	13°25'E
Quicksborn, Ger. (kvēks'bōrn)	159c	53°44'N	9°54'E
Quilcene, Wa., U.S. (kwĭl-sēn')	116a	47°50'N	122°53'W
Quilimari, Chile (kē-lē-mä'rē)	141b	32°06'S	71°28'W
Quillan, Fr. (kė-yän')	170	42°53'N	2°13'E
Quillota, Chile (kėl-yō'tä)	144	32°52'S	71°14'W
Quilmes, Arg. (kēl'mās)	141c	34°43'S	58°16'W
Quilon, India (kwė-lōn')	203	8°58'N	76°16'E
Quilpie, Austl. (kwĭl'pė)	219	26°34'S	149°20'E
Quimbaya, Col. (kēm-bä'yä)	142a	4°38'N	75°46'W
Quimbele, Ang.	236	6°28'S	16°13'E
Quimbonge, Ang.	236	8°36'S	18°30'E
Quimper, Fr. (kăn-pĕr')	161	47°59'N	4°04'W
Quinalt, r., Wa., U.S.	114	47°23'N	124°10'W
Quinault Indian Reservation, I.R., Wa., U.S.	114	47°27'N	124°34'W
Quincy, Fl., U.S. (kwĭn'sė)	124	30°35'N	84°35'W
Quincy, Il., U.S.	105	39°55'N	91°23'W
Quincy, Ma., U.S.	101a	42°15'N	71°00'W
Quincy, Mi., U.S.	108	42°00'N	84°50'W
Quincy, Or., U.S.	116c	46°08'N	123°10'W
Qui Nhon, Viet. (kwĭnyŏn)	212	13°51'N	109°03'E
Quinn, r., Nv., U.S. (kwĭn)	114	41°42'N	117°45'W
Quintanar de la Orden, Spain (kēn-tä-när')	172	39°36'N	3°02'W
Quintana Roo, state, Mex. (rô'ô)	128	19°30'N	88°30'W
Quintero, Chile (kēn-tĕ'rô)	141b	32°48'S	71°30'W
Quionga, Moz.	237	10°37'S	40°30'E
Quiroga, Mex. (kē-rô'gä)	130	19°39'N	101°30'W
Quiroga, Spain (kē-rô'gä)	172	42°28'N	7°18'W
Quitman, Ga., U.S. (kwĭt'măn)	124	30°46'N	83°35'W
Quitman, Ms., U.S.	124	33°02'N	88°43'W
Quito, Ec. (kē'tō)	142	0°17'S	78°32'W
Qumbu, S. Afr. (kòm'bōō)	233c	31°10'S	28°48'E
Quorn, Austl. (kwôrn)	222	32°20'S	138°00'E
Qurayyah, Wādī, r., Egypt	197a	30°08'N	34°27'E
Qusmuryn köli, I., Kaz.	183	52°30'N	64°15'E
Qutang, China (chyōō-täŋ)	206	32°33'N	120°07'E
Quthing, Leso.	233c	30°35'S	27°42'E
Quxian, China (chyōō-shyĕn)	205	28°58'N	118°58'E
Quxian, China	209	30°40'N	106°48'E
Quzhou, China (chyoŏ-jō)	206	36°47'N	114°58'E
Qyzylorda, Kaz.	183	44°58'N	65°45'E

R

PLACE (Pronunciation)	PAGE	LAT.	LONG.
Raab (Raba), r., Eur. (räp)	168	46°55'N	15°55'E
Raahe, Fin. (rä'ĕ)	160	64°39'N	24°22'E
Rab, i., Yugo. (räb)	174	44°45'N	14°40'E
Raba, Indon.	212	8°32'S	118°49'E
Raba (Raab), r., Eur.	169	47°28'N	17°12'E
Rabat, Mor. (rȧ-bät')	230	33°59'N	6°47'W
Rabaul, Pap. N. Gui. (rä'boul)	213	4°15'S	152°19'E
Rābigh, Sau. Ar.	201	22°48'N	39°01'E
Raccoon, r., Ia., U.S. (ră-kōōn')	113	42°07'N	94°45'W
Raccoon Cay, i., Bah.	135	22°25'N	75°50'W
Race, Cape, c., Can. (rās)	101	46°40'N	53°10'W
Rachado, Cape, c., Malay.	197b	2°26'N	101°29'E
Racibórz, Pol. (rä-chē'bōōzh)	169	50°06'N	18°14'E
Racine, Wi., U.S. (rȧ-sēn')	105	42°43'N	87°49'W
Raco, Mi., U.S. (rȧ cō)	117k	46°22'N	84°43'W
Rădăuţi, Rom.	163	47°53'N	25°55'E
Radcliffe, Eng., U.K. (răd'klĭf)	158a	53°34'N	2°20'W
Radevormwald, Ger. (rä'dĕ-fōrm-väld)	171c	51°12'N	7°22'E
Radford, Va., U.S. (răd'fērd)	125	37°06'N	81°33'W
Rādhanpur, India	202	23°57'N	71°38'E
Radium, S. Afr. (rā'dĭ-ŭm)	238c	25°06'S	28°18'E
Radom, Pol. (rä'dôm)	161	51°24'N	21°11'E
Radomir, Blg. (rä'dô-mēr)	175	42°33'N	22°58'E
Radomsko, Pol. (rä-dôm'skô)	161	51°04'N	19°27'E
Radomyshl, Ukr. (rä-dô-mēsh''l)	181	50°30'N	29°13'E
Radul', Ukr. (rȧ'dōōl)	177	51°52'N	30°46'E
Radviliškis, Lith. (räd'vė-lēsh'kēs)	167	55°49'N	23°31'E
Radwah, Jabal, mtn., Sau. Ar.	198	24°44'N	38°14'E
Radzyń Podlaski, Pol. (räd'zēn-y' pŭd-lä'skĭ)	169	51°49'N	22°40'E
Raeford, N.C., U.S. (rā'fērd)	125	34°57'N	79°15'W
Raesfeld, Ger. (răz'fĕld)	171c	51°46'N	6°50'E
Raeside, I., Austl. (rā'sīd)	220	29°20'S	122°30'E
Rae Strait, strt., Can. (rā)	92	68°40'N	95°03'W
Rafaela, Arg. (rä-fä-ā'lä)	144	31°15'S	61°21'W
Rafah, Pak. (rä'fä)	197a	31°14'N	34°12'E
Rafsanjān, Iran	198	30°45'N	56°30'E
Raft, r., Id., U.S. (răft)	115	42°20'N	113°17'W
Ragay, Phil. (rä-gī')	213a	13°49'N	122°45'E
Ragay Gulf, b., Phil.	213a	13°44'N	122°38'E
Ragunda, Swe. (rä-gòn'dä)	166	63°07'N	16°24'E
Ragusa, Italy (rä-gōō'sä)	162	36°58'N	14°41'E
Rahachow, Bela.	180	53°07'N	30°04'E
Rahway, N.J., U.S. (rô'wā)	110a	40°37'N	74°16'W
Rāichūr, India (rä'ė-chōōr')	199	16°23'N	77°18'E
Raigarh, India (rī'gŭr)	199	21°57'N	83°32'E
Rainbow Bridge National Monument, rec., Ut., U.S. (rān'bō)	119	37°05'N	111°00'W
Rainbow City, Pan.	128a	9°20'N	79°53'W
Rainier, Or., U.S.	116c	46°05'N	122°56'W
Rainier, Mount, mtn., Wa., U.S. (rā-nēr')	106	46°52'N	121°46'W
Rainy, r., N.A.	107	48°50'N	94°41'W
Rainy Lake, I., N.A. (rān'ė)	93	48°43'N	94°29'W
Rainy River, Can.	91	48°43'N	94°29'W
Raipur, India (rä'jŭ-bōō-rė')	202	21°25'N	81°37'E
Raisin, r., Mi., U.S. (rā'zĭn)	108	42°00'N	83°35'W
Raitan, N.J., U.S. (rā-tăn)	110a	40°34'N	74°40'W
Rājahmundry, India (räj-ŭ-mŭn'drė)	199	17°03'N	81°51'E
Rajang, r., Malay.	212	2°10'N	113°30'E
Rājapālaiyam, India	203	9°30'N	77°33'E
Rājasthān, state, India (rä'jŭs-tän)	199	26°00'N	72°00'E
Rājkot, India (räj'kōt)	199	22°20'N	70°48'E
Rājpur, India	202a	22°24'N	88°25'E
Rājshāhi, Bngl.	199	24°26'S	88°39'E
Rakhiv, Ukr.	169	48°02'N	24°13'E
Rakh'oya, Russia (räk'yȧ)	186c	60°06'N	30°50'E
Rakitnoye, Russia (rȧ-kĕt'nô-yĕ)	181	50°51'N	35°53'E
Rakovník, Czech Rep.	168	50°07'N	13°45'E
Rakvere, Est. (räk'vĕ-rĕ)	180	59°22'N	26°14'E
Raleigh, N.C., U.S.	105	35°45'N	78°39'W
Rama, r., Can.	95	52°10'N	115°05'W
Rama, Nic. (rä'mä)	133	12°11'N	84°14'W
Ramallo, Arg. (rä-mä'l-yô)	141c	33°28'S	60°02'W
Ramanāthapuram, India	203	9°13'N	78°52'E

340 Rambouillet – Revda PRONOUNCING INDEX

PLACE (Pronunciation)	PAGE	LAT.	LONG.
Rambouillet, Fr. (räN-bōō-yĕ')	170	48°39'N	1°49'E
Rame Head, c., S. Afr.	233c	31°48'S	29°22'E
Ramenskoye, Russia (rá'mĕn-skô-yĕ)	176	55°34'N	38°15'E
Ramlat as Sab'atayn, reg., Asia	198	16°08'N	45°15'E
Ramm, Jabal, mtn., Jord.	197a	29°37'N	35°32'E
Râmnicu Sărat, Rom.	163	45°24'N	27°06'E
Râmnicu Vâlcea, Rom.	175	45°07'N	24°22'E
Ramos, Mex. (rä'mōs)	130	22°46'N	101°52'W
Ramos, r., Nig.	235	5°10'N	5°40'E
Ramos Arizpe, Mex. (ä-rēz'pā)	122	25°33'N	100°57'W
Rampart, Ak., U.S. (răm'pärt)	103	65°28'N	150°18'W
Rampo Mountains, mts., N.J., U.S. (răm'pō)	110a	41°06'N	72°12'W
Rāmpur, India (räm'pōōr)	199	28°53'N	79°03'E
Ramree Island, i., Mya. (räm'rē')	212	19°01'N	93°23'E
Ramsayville, Can. (răm'zē vĭl)	102c	45°23'N	75°34'W
Ramsbottom, Eng., U.K. (rămz'bŏt-ŭm)	158a	53°39'N	2°20'W
Ramsey, I. of Man (răm'zē)	164	54°20'N	4°25'W
Ramsey, N.J., U.S.	110a	41°03'N	74°09'W
Ramsey Lake, l., Can.	98	47°15'N	82°16'W
Ramsgate, Eng., U.K. (rămz''gāt)	165	51°19'N	1°20'E
Ramu, r., Pap. N. Gui. (rä'mōō)	213	5°35'S	145°16'E
Rancagua, Chile (rän-kä'gwä)	144	34°10'S	70°43'W
Rance, r., Fr. (räNs)	170	48°17'N	2°30'W
Rānchī, India	199	23°21'N	85°20'E
Rancho Boyeros, Cuba (rä'n-chô-bô-yĕ'rôs)	135a	23°00'N	82°23'W
Randallstown, Md., U.S. (răn'dălz-toun)	110e	39°22'N	76°48'W
Randers, Den. (rän'ĕrs)	160	56°28'N	10°03'E
Randfontein, S. Afr. (rănt'fŏn-tān)	233b	26°10'S	27°42'E
Randleman, N.C., U.S. (răn'd'l-măn)	125	35°49'N	79°50'W
Randolph, Ma., U.S. (răn'dŏlf)	101a	42°10'N	71°03'W
Randolph, Ne., U.S.	112	42°22'N	97°22'W
Randolph, Vt., U.S.	109	43°55'N	72°40'W
Random Island, i., Can. (răn'dŭm)	101	48°12'N	53°25'W
Randsfjorden, Nor.	166	60°35'N	10°10'E
Randwick, Austl.	217b	33°55'S	151°15'E
Ranérou, Sen.	234	15°18'N	13°58'W
Rangeley, Me., U.S. (rānj'lē)	100	44°56'N	70°38'W
Rangeley, l., Me., U.S.	100	45°00'N	70°25'W
Ranger, Tx., U.S. (rān'jēr)	104	32°26'N	98°41'W
Rangia, India	202	26°32'N	91°39'E
Rangoon (Yangon), Mya. (răŋ-gōōn')	199	16°46'N	96°09'E
Rangpur, Bngl. (rŭng'pōōr)	199	25°48'N	89°19'E
Rangsang, i., Indon. (räng'säng')	197b	0°53'N	103°05'E
Rangsdorf, Ger. (rängs'dōrf)	159b	52°17'N	13°25'E
Rānīganj, India (rä-nē-gŭnj')	202	23°40'N	87°08'E
Rankin Inlet, b., Can. (răŋ'kĕn)	93	62°45'N	94°27'W
Ranova, r., Russia (rä'nô-vá)	176	53°55'N	40°03'E
Rantau, Malay.	197b	2°35'N	101°58'E
Rantekombola, Bulu, mtn., Indon.	212	3°22'S	119°50'E
Rantoul, Il., U.S. (răn-tōōl')	108	40°25'N	88°05'W
Raoyang, China (rou-yäŋ)	206	38°16'N	115°45'E
Rapallo, Italy (rä-päl'lō)	174	44°21'N	9°14'E
Rapel, r., Chile (rä-pål')	141b	34°05'S	71°30'W
Rapid, r., Mn., U.S. (răp'ĭd)	113	48°21'N	94°50'W
Rapid City, S.D., U.S.	104	44°06'N	103°14'W
Rapla, Est. (räp'lå)	167	59°02'N	24°46'E
Rappahannock, r., Va., U.S. (răp'ă-hăn'ŭk)	109	38°20'N	75°25'W
Raquette, l., N.Y., U.S. (răk'ĕt)	109	43°50'N	74°35'W
Raritan, r., N.J., U.S. (răr'ĭ-tăn)	110a	40°32'N	74°27'W
Rarotonga, Cook Is. (rä'rô-tŏŋ'gá)	2	20°40'S	163°00'W
Ra's an Naqb, Jord.	197a	30°00'N	35°29'E
Raşcov, Mol.	177	47°55'N	28°51'E
Ras Dashen Terara, mtn., Eth. (räs dä-shän')	231	12°49'N	38°14'E
Raseiniai, Lith. (rä-syā'nyī)	167	55°23'N	23°04'E
Rashayya, Leb.	197a	33°30'N	35°50'E
Rashīd, Egypt (rå-shēd') (rô-zĕt'á)	200	31°22'N	30°25'E
Rashīd, Masabb, mth., Egypt	238b	31°30'N	29°58'E
Rashkina, Russia (răsh'kĭ-nå)	186a	59°57'N	61°30'E
Rasht, Iran	198	37°13'N	49°45'E
Raška, Yugo. (răsh'kå)	175	43°16'N	20°40'E
Rasskazovo, Russia (räs-kä'sô-vô)	181	52°40'N	41°40'E
Rastatt, Ger. (rä-shtät)	168	48°51'N	8°12'E
Rastes, Russia (rås'tĕs)	186a	59°24'N	58°49'E
Rastunovo, Russia (rås-tōō'nô-vô)	186b	55°15'N	37°50'E
Ratangarh, India (rŭ-tŭn'gŭr)	202	28°10'N	74°30'E
Ratcliff, Tx., U.S. (răt'klĭf)	123	31°22'N	95°09'W
Rathenow, Ger. (rä'tĕ-nō)	168	52°36'N	12°20'E
Rathlin Island, i., N. Ire., U.K. (răth-lĭn)	164	55°18'N	6°13'W
Ratingen, Ger. (rä'tēn-gĕn)	171c	51°18'N	6°51'E
Rat Islands, is., Ak., U.S. (răt)	103a	51°35'N	176°48'E
Ratlām, India	202	23°19'N	75°05'E
Ratnāgiri, India	203	17°04'N	73°24'E
Raton, N.M., U.S. (rá-tōn')	104	36°52'N	104°26'W
Rattlesnake Creek, r., Or., U.S. (răt''l snāk)	114	42°38'N	117°39'W
Rättvik, Swe. (rĕt'vēk)	166	60°54'N	15°07'E
Rauch, Arg. (rá'ōōch)	144	36°47'S	59°05'W
Raufoss, Nor. (rou'fôs)	166	60°44'N	10°30'E
Raúl Soares, Braz. (rä-ōō'l-sôá'rĕs)	141a	20°05'S	42°28'W
Rauma, Fin. (rä'ô-mä)	160	61°07'N	21°31'E
Rauna, Lat. (råŭ'nå)	167	57°21'N	25°31'E
Raurkela, India	199	22°15'N	84°53'E
Rautalampi, Fin. (rä'ōō-tĕ-läm'pô)	167	62°39'N	26°25'E
Rava-Rus'ka, Ukr.	169	50°14'N	23°40'E
Ravenna, Italy (rä-vĕn'nä)	162	44°27'N	12°13'E
Ravenna, Ne., U.S. (rá-vĕn'á)	112	41°20'N	98°50'W
Ravenna, Oh., U.S.	108	41°10'N	81°20'W
Ravensburg, Ger. (rä'vĕns-bōōrgh)	168	47°48'N	9°35'E

PLACE (Pronunciation)	PAGE	LAT.	LONG.
Ravensdale, Wa., U.S. (rā'vĕnz-dāl)	116a	47°22'N	121°58'W
Ravensthorpe, Austl. (rā'vĕns-thôrp)	218	33°30'S	120°20'E
Ravenswood, W.V., U.S. (rā'vĕnz-wŏŏd)	108	38°55'N	81°50'W
Rāwalpindi, Pak. (rä-wŭl-pēn'dē)	199	33°40'N	73°10'E
Rawa Mazowiecka, Pol.	169	51°46'N	20°17'E
Rawāndūz, Iraq	198	36°37'N	44°30'E
Rawicz, Pol. (rä'vēch)	168	51°36'N	16°51'E
Rawlina, Austl. (rôr-lēnă)	218	31°13'S	125°45'E
Rawlins, Wy., U.S. (rô'lĭnz)	104	41°46'N	107°15'W
Rawson, Arg. (rô'sŭn)	144	43°16'S	65°09'W
Rawson, Arg.	141c	34°36'S	60°03'W
Rawtenstall, Eng., U.K. (rô'tĕn-stôl)	158a	53°42'N	2°17'W
Ray, Cape, c., Can. (rā)	93a	47°40'N	59°18'W
Raya, Bukit, mtn., Indon.	212	0°45'S	112°11'E
Raychikinsk, Russia (rī'chĭ-kēnsk)	185	49°52'N	129°17'E
Rayleigh, Eng., U.K. (rā'lē)	158b	51°35'N	0°36'E
Raymond, Can. (rā'mŭnd)	95	49°27'N	112°39'W
Raymond, Wa., U.S.	114	46°41'N	123°42'W
Raymondville, Tx., U.S. (rā'mŭnd-vĭl)	121	26°30'N	97°46'W
Ray Mountains, mts., Ak., U.S.	103	65°40'N	151°45'W
Rayne, La., U.S. (rān)	123	30°12'N	92°15'W
Rayón, Mex. (rä-yōn')	130	21°49'N	99°39'W
Rayton, S. Afr. (rā'tŭn)	233b	25°45'S	28°33'E
Raytown, Mo., U.S. (rā'toun)	117f	39°01'N	94°48'W
Rayville, La., U.S. (rā-vĭl)	123	32°28'N	91°46'W
Raz, Pointe du, c., Fr. (pwănt dü rä)	161	48°02'N	4°43'W
Razdan, Arm.	182	40°30'N	44°46'E
Razdol'noye, Russia (räz-dôl'nô-yĕ)	210	43°38'N	131°58'E
Razgrad, Blg.	163	43°32'N	26°32'E
Razlog, Blg. (räz'lôk)	175	41°54'N	23°32'E
Razorback Mountain, mtn., Can. (rā'zēr-băk)	94	51°35'N	124°42'W
Rea, r., Eng., U.K. (rē)	158a	52°25'N	2°31'W
Reaburn, Can. (rā'bûrn)	102f	50°06'N	97°53'W
Reading, Eng., U.K. (rĕd'ĭng)	161	51°25'N	0°58'W
Reading, Ma., U.S.	101a	42°32'N	71°07'W
Reading, Mi., U.S.	108	41°45'N	84°45'W
Reading, Oh., U.S.	111f	39°14'N	84°26'W
Reading, Pa., U.S.	105	40°20'N	75°55'W
Reading, co., Eng., U.K.	158a	52°37'N	0°40'W
Realengo, Braz. (rĕ-ä-lān-gô)	141a	23°50'S	43°25'W
Rebiana, Libya	231	24°10'N	22°03'E
Rebun, i., Japan (rē'bōōn)	210	45°25'N	140°54'E
Recanati, Italy (rā-kä-nä'tē)	174	43°25'N	13°35'E
Recherche, Archipelago of the, is., Austl. (rē-shârsh')	220	34°17'S	122°30'E
Rechytsa, Bela. (ryĕ'chĕt-så)	181	52°22'N	30°24'E
Recife, Braz. (rå-sē'fĕ)	143	8°09'S	34°59'W
Recife, Kapp, c., S. Afr. (rå-sē'fĕ)	233c	34°03'S	25°43'E
Recklinghausen, Ger. (rĕk'lĭng-hou-zĕn)	171c	51°36'N	7°13'E
Reconquista, Arg. (rā-kôn-kēs'tä)	144	29°01'S	59°41'W
Rector, Ar., U.S. (rĕk'tēr)	121	36°16'N	90°21'W
Red, r., Asia	212	21°00'N	103°00'E
Red, r., N.A. (rĕd)	106	48°00'N	97°00'W
Red, r., Tn., U.S.	124	36°35'N	86°55'W
Red, r., U.S.	107	31°40'N	92°55'W
Red, North Fork, r., U.S.	120	35°20'N	100°08'W
Red, Prairie Dog Town Fork, r., U.S. (prâ'rĭ)	120	34°54'N	101°31'W
Red, Salt Fork, r., U.S.	120	35°04'N	100°31'W
Redan, Ga., U.S. (rē-dăn') (rĕd'ăn)	110c	33°44'N	84°09'W
Red Bank, N.J., U.S. (băngk)	110a	40°21'N	74°06'W
Red Bluff Reservoir, res., Tx., U.S.	122	32°03'N	103°52'W
Redby, Mn., Mn., U.S. (rĕd'bē)	113	47°52'N	94°55'W
Red Cedar, r., Wi., U.S. (sē'dēr)	113	45°03'N	91°48'W
Redcliff, Can. (rĕd'clĭf)	90	50°05'N	110°47'W
Redcliffe, Austl. (rĕd'clĭf)	222	27°20'S	153°12'E
Red Cliff Indian Reservation, I.R., Wi., U.S.	113	46°48'N	91°22'W
Red Cloud, Ne., U.S. (kloud)	120	40°06'N	98°32'W
Red Deer, Can. (dēr)	90	52°16'N	113°48'W
Red Deer, r., Can.	92	51°00'N	111°00'W
Red Deer, r., Can.	97	52°55'N	102°10'W
Red Deer Lake, l., Can.	97	52°58'N	101°28'W
Reddick, Il., U.S. (rĕd'dĭk)	111a	41°06'N	88°16'W
Redding, Ca., U.S. (rĕd'ĭng)	114	40°36'N	122°25'W
Redenção da Serra, Braz. (rĕ-dĕn-soun-dä-sĕ'r-rä)	141a	23°17'S	45°31'W
Redfield, S.D., U.S. (rĕd'fēld)	112	44°53'N	98°30'W
Red Fish Bar, Tx., U.S.	123a	29°29'N	94°53'W
Red Indian Lake, l., Can. (ĭn'dĭ-ăn)	93a	48°40'N	56°50'W
Red Lake, Can. (lāk)	91	51°02'N	93°49'W
Red Lake, r., Mn., U.S.	112	48°02'N	96°04'W
Red Lake Falls, Mn., U.S. (lāk fôls)	112	47°52'N	96°17'W
Red Lake Indian Reservation, I.R., Mn., U.S.	112	48°09'N	95°55'W
Redlands, Ca., U.S. (rĕd'lăndz)	117a	34°04'N	117°11'W
Red Lion, Pa., U.S. (lī'ŭn)	109	39°55'N	76°30'W
Red Lodge, Mt., U.S.	115	45°13'N	107°16'W
Redmond, Wa., U.S. (rĕd'mŭnd)	116a	47°40'N	122°07'W
Rednitz, r., Ger. (rĕd'nētz)	168	49°10'N	11°00'E
Red Oak, Ia., U.S. (ōk)	112	41°00'N	95°12'W
Redon, Fr. (rē-dôN')	170	47°42'N	2°03'W
Redonda, Isla, i., Braz. (ē's-lä-rĕ-dô'n-dä)	144b	23°05'S	43°11'W
Redonda Island, i., Antig. (rĕ-dŏn'dá)	133b	16°55'N	62°28'W
Redondela, Spain (rā-dhôn-dā'lä)	172	42°16'N	8°34'W
Redondo, Port. (rå-dôn'dô)	172	38°40'N	7°32'W
Redondo, Wa., U.S. (rē-dŏn'dō)	116a	47°21'N	122°19'W
Redondo Beach, Ca., U.S.	117a	33°50'N	118°23'W
Red Pass, Can. (pås)	95	52°59'N	118°59'W
Red Rock, r., Mt., U.S.	115	44°54'N	112°44'W
Red Sea, sea	198	23°15'N	37°00'E

PLACE (Pronunciation)	PAGE	LAT.	LONG.
Redstone, Can. (rĕd'stōn)	94	52°08'N	123°42'W
Red Sucker Lake, l., Can. (sŭk'ēr)	97	54°09'N	93°40'W
Redwater, r., Mt., U.S.	115	47°37'N	105°25'W
Red Willow Creek, r., Ne., U.S.	120	40°34'N	100°48'W
Red Wing, Mn., U.S.	113	44°34'N	92°35'W
Redwood City, Ca., U.S. (rĕd' wŏŏd)	116b	37°29'N	122°13'W
Redwood Falls, Mn., U.S.	112	44°32'N	95°06'W
Redwood National Park, rec., Ca., U.S.	114	41°20'N	124°00'W
Redwood Valley, Ca., U.S.	118	39°15'N	123°12'W
Ree, Lough, l., Ire. (lŏk'rē')	160	53°30'N	7°45'W
Reed City, Mi., U.S. (rēd)	108	43°50'N	85°35'W
Reed Lake, l., Can.	97	54°37'N	100°30'W
Reedley, Ca., U.S. (rēd'lē)	118	36°37'N	119°27'W
Reedsburg, Wi., U.S. (rēdz'bûrg)	113	43°32'N	90°01'W
Reedsport, Or., U.S. (rēdz'pôrt)	114	43°42'N	124°08'W
Reelfoot Lake, res., Tn., U.S. (rēl'fŏŏt)	124	36°18'N	89°20'W
Rees, Ger. (rĕz)	171c	51°46'N	6°25'E
Reeves, Mount, mtn., Austl. (rēv's)	222	33°50'S	149°56'E
Reform, Al., U.S. (rē-fôrm')	124	33°23'N	88°00'W
Refugio, Tx., U.S. (rå-fōō'hyô) (rĕ-fū'jō)	123	28°18'N	97°15'W
Rega, r., Pol. (rĕ-gä)	168	53°48'N	15°30'E
Regen, r., Ger. (rā'ghĕn)	168	49°09'N	12°21'E
Regensburg, Ger. (rā'ghĕns-bōrgh)	161	49°02'N	12°06'E
Reggio, La., U.S. (rĕg'jĭ-ō)	110d	29°50'N	89°46'W
Reggio di Calabria, Italy (rĕ'jô dē kä-lä'brē-ä)	163	38°07'N	15°42'E
Reggio nell' Emilia, Italy	162	44°43'N	10°34'E
Reghin, Rom. (rå-gēn')	169	46°47'N	24°44'E
Regina, Can. (rē-jī'nå)	96	50°25'N	104°39'W
Regla, Cuba (rāg'lä)	134	23°08'N	82°20'W
Regnitz, r., Ger. (rĕg'nētz)	168	49°50'N	10°55'E
Reguengos de Monsaraz, Port.	172	38°26'N	7°30'W
Rehoboth, Nmb.	232	23°10'S	17°15'E
Reḥovot, Isr.	197a	31°53'N	34°49'E
Reichenbach, Ger. (rī'kĕn-bäk)	168	50°36'N	12°18'E
Reidsville, N.C., U.S. (rēdz'vĭl)	125	36°20'N	79°37'W
Reigate, Eng., U.K. (rī'gāt)	164	51°12'N	0°12'W
Reims, Fr. (răNs)	154	49°16'N	4°00'E
Reina Adelaida, Archipiélago, is., Chile	144	52°00'S	74°15'W
Reinbeck, Ia., U.S. (rīn'bĕk)	113	42°22'N	92°34'W
Reindeer, l., Can. (rān'dēr)	92	57°36'N	101°23'W
Reindeer, r., Can.	96	55°45'N	103°30'W
Reindeer Island, i., Can.	97	52°25'N	98°00'W
Reinosa, Spain (rå-ē-nō'sä)	172	43°01'N	4°08'W
Reistertown, Md., U.S. (rēs'tēr-toun)	110e	39°28'N	76°50'W
Reitz, S. Afr.	238c	27°48'S	28°25'E
Rema, Jabal, mtn., Yemen	198	14°13'N	44°38'E
Rembau, Malay.	197b	2°36'N	102°06'E
Remedios, Col. (rĕ-mĕ'dyôs)	142a	7°03'N	74°42'W
Remedios, Cuba (rā-mā'dhē-ōs)	134	22°30'N	79°35'W
Remedios, Pan. (rĕ-mĕ'dyōs)	133	8°14'N	81°46'W
Remiremont, Fr. (rē-mēr-môN')	171	48°01'N	6°35'E
Rempang, i., Indon.	197b	0°51'N	104°04'E
Remscheid, Ger. (rĕm'shīt)	171c	51°10'N	7°11'E
Rena, Nor.	166	61°08'N	11°17'E
Rendova, i., Sol. Is. (rĕn'dô-vá)	221	8°38'S	156°26'E
Rendsburg, Ger. (rĕnts'bōrgh)	168	54°19'N	9°39'E
Renfrew, Can. (rĕn'frōō)	91	45°30'N	76°30'W
Rengam, Malay. (rĕn'gäm')	197b	1°53'N	103°24'E
Rengo, Chile (rĕn'gō)	141b	34°22'S	70°50'W
Reni, Ukr. (rān')	177	45°26'N	28°18'E
Renmark, Austl. (rĕn'märk)	218	34°10'S	140°50'E
Rennel, i., Sol. Is. (rĕn-nĕl')	221	11°50'S	160°38'E
Rennes, Fr. (rĕn)	154	48°07'N	1°02'W
Reno, Nv., U.S. (rē'nō)	104	39°32'N	119°49'W
Reno, r., Italy (rā'nô)	174	44°10'N	10°55'E
Renovo, Pa., U.S. (rē-nō'vō)	109	41°20'N	77°50'W
Renqiu, China (rŭn-chyô)	206	38°44'N	116°05'E
Rensselaer, In., U.S. (rĕn'sē-lâr)	108	41°00'N	87°10'W
Rensselaer, N.Y., U.S. (rĕn'sē-lâr)	109	42°40'N	73°45'W
Rentchler, Il., U.S. (rĕnt'chlĕr)	117e	38°30'N	89°52'W
Renton, Wa., U.S. (rĕn'tŭn)	116a	47°29'N	122°13'W
Repentigny, Can.	102a	45°47'N	73°26'W
Republic, Al., U.S. (rē-pŭb'lĭk)	110h	33°37'N	86°54'W
Republic, Wa., U.S.	114	48°38'N	118°44'W
Republican, r., U.S.	106	40°15'N	100°00'W
Republican, South Fork, r., Co., U.S. (rē-pŭb'lĭ-kăn)	120	39°35'N	102°28'W
Repulse Bay, b., Austl. (rē-pŭls')	221	20°56'S	149°22'E
Requena, Spain (rå-kā'nä)	162	39°29'N	1°03'W
Resende, Braz. (rĕ-sĕ'n-dĕ)	141a	22°30'S	44°26'W
Resende Costa, Braz. (kôs-tä)	141a	20°55'S	44°12'W
Reshetylivka, Ukr.	177	49°34'N	34°04'E
Resistencia, Arg. (rā-sēs-tĕn'syä)	144	27°24'S	58°54'W
Reşiţa, Rom. (rā'shē-tá)	175	45°18'N	21°56'E
Resolute *see* Qausuittuq, Can.	89	74°41'N	95°00'W
Resolution, i., Can. (rĕz-ô-lū'shŭn)	93	61°30'N	63°58'W
Resolution Island, i., N.Z. (rĕz-ŏl-ûshŭn)	221a	45°43'S	166°20'E
Restigouche, r., Can.	100	47°35'N	67°35'W
Restrepo, Col. (rĕs-trĕ'pô)	142a	3°49'N	76°31'W
Restrepo, Col.	142a	4°16'N	73°32'W
Retalhuleu, Guat. (rā-täl-ōō-lān')	132	14°31'N	91°41'W
Rethel, Fr. (r-tĕl')	170	49°34'N	4°20'E
Réthimnon, Grc.	174a	35°21'N	24°30'E
Retie, Bel.	159a	51°16'N	5°08'E
Retsil, Wa., U.S. (rĕt'sĭl)	116a	47°33'N	122°37'W
Reunion, dep., Afr. (rā-ü-nyôn')	3	21°06'S	55°36'E
Reus, Spain (rā'ōōs)	162	41°08'N	1°05'E
Reutlingen, Ger. (roit'lĭng-ĕn)	168	48°29'N	9°13'E
Reutov, Russia (rĕ-ōō'ôf)	186b	55°45'N	37°52'E
Revda, Russia (ryâv'dá)	186a	56°48'N	59°57'E

ăt; finăl; rāte; senåte; ärm; åsk; sofá; fâre; ch-choose; dh-as th in other; bē; ėvent; bĕt; recĕnt; cratẽr; g-gō; gh-guttural g; bĭt; ĭ-short neutral; rīde; K-guttural k as ch in German ich;

PRONOUNCING INDEX

Revelstoke – Rockingham Forest 341

PLACE (Pronunciation)	PAGE	LAT.	LONG.
Revelstoke, Can. (rĕv'ĕl-stōk)	90	51°00'N	118°12'W
Reventazón, Río, r., C.R. (rå-vĕn-tä-zōn')	133	10°10'N	83°30'W
Revere, Ma., U.S. (rê-vēr')	101a	42°24'N	71°01'W
Revillagigedo, Islas, is., Mex. (ê's-läs-rĕ-vêl-yä-hê'gĕ-dô)	128	18°45'N	111°00'W
Revillagigedo Chan, Ak., U.S. (rĕ-vĭl'ȧ-gĭ-gē'dō)	94	55°10'N	131°13'W
Revillagigedo Island, i., Ak., U.S.	94	55°35'N	131°23'W
Revin, Fr. (rĕ-văɴ)	170	49°56'N	4°34'E
Rewa, India (rā'wä)	199	24°41'N	81°11'E
Rewāri, India	202	28°19'N	76°39'E
Rexburg, Id., U.S. (rĕks'bûrg)	115	43°50'N	111°48'W
Rey, Iran	201	35°35'N	51°25'E
Rey, l., Mex. (rā)	122	27°00'N	103°33'W
Rey, Isla del, i., Pan. (ê's-lä-dĕl-rā'ê)	133	8°20'N	78°40'W
Reyes, Bol. (rā'yĕs)	142	14°19'S	67°16'W
Reyes, Point, c., Ca., U.S.	118	38°00'N	123°00'W
Reykjanes, c., Ice. (rā'kyȧ-nĕs)	156	63°37'N	24°33'W
Reykjavík, Ice. (rā'kyȧ-vēk)	154	64°09'N	21°39'W
Reynosa, Mex. (rā-ê-nō'sä)	122	26°05'N	98°21'W
Rēzekne, Lat. (rā'zĕk-nĕ)	180	56°31'N	27°19'E
Rezh, Russia (rĕzh')	186a	57°22'N	61°23'E
Rezina, Mol. (ryĕzh'ĕ-nĭ)	177	47°44'N	28°56'E
Rhaetian Alps, mts., Eur.	168	46°30'N	10°00'E
Rhaetien Alps, mts., Eur.	174	46°22'N	10°33'E
Rheinberg, Ger. (rīn'bĕrgh)	171c	51°33'N	6°37'E
Rheine, Ger. (rī'nĕ)	168	52°16'N	7°26'E
Rheinkamp, Ger.	171c	51°30'N	6°37'E
Rheinland, hist. reg., Ger.	168	50°05'N	6°40'E
Rheydt, Ger. (rĕ'yt)	171c	51°10'N	6°28'E
Rhin, r., Ger. (rēn)	159b	52°52'N	12°49'E
Rhine, r., Eur.	156	50°34'N	7°21'E
Rhinelander, Wi., U.S. (rīn'lăn-dēr)	113	45°39'N	89°25'W
Rhin Kanal, can., Ger. (rēn kä-näl')	159b	52°47'N	12°40'E
Rhiou, r., Alg.	173	35°45'N	1°18'E
Rhode Island, state, U.S. (rōd ī'lănd)	105	41°35'N	71°40'W
Rhode Island, i., R.I., U.S.	110b	41°31'N	71°14'W
Rhodes, S. Afr. (rôdz)	233c	30°48'S	27°56'E
Rhodes *see* Ródhos, i., Grc.	156	36°00'N	28°29'E
Rhodesia *see* Zimbabwe, nation, Afr.	232	17°50'S	29°30'E
Rhodope Mountains, mts., Eur. (rô'dô-pĕ)	156	42°00'N	24°08'E
Rhondda, Wales, U.K. (rŏn'dhȧ)	164	51°40'N	3°40'W
Rhône, r., Fr. (rōn)	156	44°30'N	4°45'E
Rhoon, Neth.	159a	51°52'N	4°24'E
Rhum, i., Scot., U.K. (rŭm)	164	57°00'N	6°20'W
Riachão, Braz. (rê-ä-chouɴ')	143	7°15'S	46°30'W
Rialto, Ca., U.S. (rē-äl'tō)	117a	34°06'N	117°23'W
Riau, prov., Indon.	197b	0°56'N	101°25'E
Riau, Kepulauan, i., Indon.	212	0°30'N	104°55'E
Riau, Selat, strt., Indon.	197b	0°40'N	104°27'E
Riaza, r., Spain (rê-ä'thä)	172	41°25'N	3°25'W
Ribadavia, Spain (rē-bä-dhä'vê-ä)	172	42°18'N	8°06'W
Ribadeo, Spain (rē-bä-dhā'ō)	172	43°32'N	7°05'W
Ribadesella, Spain (rē'bä-dā-säl'yä)	172	43°30'N	5°02'W
Ribe, Den. (rē'bĕ)	166	55°20'N	8°45'E
Ribeirão Prêto, Braz. (rê-bā-rouɴ-prĕ'tô)	143	21°11'S	47°47'W
Ribera, N.M., U.S. (rē-bĕ'rä)	120	35°23'N	105°27'W
Riberalta, Bol. (rē-bå-räl'tä)	142	11°06'S	66°02'W
Rib Lake, Wi., U.S. (rĭb lāk)	113	45°20'N	90°11'W
Rîbniţa, Mol.	177	47°45'N	29°02'E
Rice, l., Can.	99	44°05'N	78°10'W
Rice Lake, Wi., U.S.	113	45°30'N	91°44'W
Rice Lake, l., Mn., U.S.	117g	45°10'N	93°09'W
Richards Island, i., Can. (rĭch'ērds)	103	69°45'N	135°30'W
Richards Landing, Can. (lănd'ĭng)	117k	46°18'N	84°02'W
Richardson, Tx., U.S. (rĭch'ērd-sŭn)	117c	32°56'N	96°44'W
Richardson, Wa., U.S.	116a	48°27'N	122°54'W
Richardson Mountains, mts., Can.	92	66°58'N	136°19'W
Richardson Mountains, mts., N.Z.	223	44°50'S	168°30'E
Richardson Park, De., U.S. (pärk)	109	39°45'N	75°35'W
Richelieu, r., Can. (rēsh'lyû')	99	45°05'N	73°25'W
Richfield, Mn., U.S.	117g	44°53'N	93°17'W
Richfield, Oh., U.S.	111d	41°14'N	81°38'W
Richfield, Ut., U.S.	119	38°45'N	112°05'W
Richford, Vt., U.S. (rĭch'fērd)	109	45°00'N	72°35'W
Rich Hill, Mo., U.S. (rĭch hĭl)	121	38°05'N	94°21'W
Richibucto, Can. (rĭ-chĭ-bŭk'tō)	91	46°41'N	64°52'W
Richland, Ga., U.S. (rĭch'lănd)	124	32°05'N	84°40'W
Richland, Wa., U.S.	114	46°17'N	119°19'W
Richland Center, Wi., U.S. (sĕn'tēr)	113	43°20'N	90°25'W
Richmond, Austl. (rĭch'mŭnd)	219	20°47'S	143°14'E
Richmond, Austl.	217b	33°36'S	150°45'E
Richmond, Can.	102c	45°12'N	75°49'W
Richmond, Can.	99	45°40'N	72°07'W
Richmond, S. Afr.	233c	29°52'S	30°17'E
Richmond, Il., U.S.	111a	42°29'N	88°18'W
Richmond, In., U.S.	108	39°50'N	85°00'W
Richmond, Ky., U.S.	108	37°45'N	84°20'W
Richmond, Mo., U.S.	121	39°16'N	93°58'W
Richmond, Tx., U.S.	123	29°35'N	95°45'W
Richmond, Ut., U.S.	115	41°55'N	111°50'W
Richmond, Va., U.S.	105	37°35'N	77°30'W
Richmond Beach, Wa., U.S.	116a	47°47'N	122°23'W
Richmond Heights, Mo., U.S.	117e	38°38'N	90°20'W
Richmond Highlands, Wa., U.S.	116a	47°46'N	122°22'W
Richmond Hill, Can. (hĭl)	99	43°53'N	79°26'W
Richton, Ms., U.S. (rĭch'tŭn)	124	31°20'N	89°54'W
Richwood, W.V., U.S. (rĭch'wŏod)	108	38°10'N	80°30'W
Ridderkerk, Neth.	159a	51°52'N	4°35'E
Rideau, r., Can.	102c	45°17'N	75°41'W
Rideau Lake, l., Can. (rē-dō')	99	44°40'N	76°20'W

PLACE (Pronunciation)	PAGE	LAT.	LONG.
Ridgefield, Ct., U.S. (rĭj'fēld)	110a	41°16'N	73°30'W
Ridgefield, Wa., U.S.	116c	45°49'N	122°40'W
Ridgeway, Can. (rĭj'wā)	111c	42°53'N	79°02'W
Ridgewood, N.J., U.S. (rĭdj'wŏod)	110a	40°59'N	74°08'W
Ridgway, Pa., U.S.	109	41°25'N	78°40'W
Riding Mountain, mtn., Can. (rīd'ĭng)	97	50°37'N	99°37'W
Riding Mountain National Park, rec., Can. (rīd'ĭng)	92	50°59'N	99°19'W
Riding Rocks, is., Bah.	134	25°20'N	79°10'W
Riebeek-Oos, S. Afr.	233c	33°14'S	26°09'E
Ried, Aus. (rēd)	168	48°13'N	13°30'E
Riesa, Ger. (rē'zȧ)	168	51°17'N	13°17'E
Rieti, Italy (rê-ā'tē)	162	42°25'N	12°51'E
Rievleidam, res., S. Afr.	233b	25°52'S	28°18'E
Riffe Lake, res., Wa., U.S.	114	46°20'N	122°10'W
Rifle, Co., U.S. (rī'f'l)	119	39°35'N	107°50'W
Rīga, Lat. (rē'gȧ)	178	56°55'N	24°05'E
Riga, Gulf of, b., Eur.	180	57°56'N	23°05'E
Rīgān, Iran	198	28°45'N	58°55'E
Rigaud, Can. (rê-gō')	102a	45°29'N	74°18'W
Rigby, Id., U.S. (rĭg'bê)	115	43°40'N	111°55'W
Rigeley, W.V., U.S. (rĭj'lê)	109	39°40'N	78°45'W
Rīgestān, des., Afg.	198	30°53'N	64°42'E
Rigolet, Can. (rĭg-ō-lā')	91	54°10'N	58°40'W
Riihimäki, Fin.	167	60°44'N	24°44'E
Rijeka, Cro. (rĭ-yĕ'kä)	162	45°22'N	14°24'E
Rijkevorsel, Bel.	159a	51°21'N	4°46'E
Rijswijk, Neth.	159a	52°03'N	4°19'E
Rika, r., Ukr. (rê'kȧ)	169	48°21'N	23°37'E
Rima, r., Nig.	235	13°30'N	5°50'E
Rimavska Sobota, Slvk. (rē'máf-ská sô'bô-tȧ)	169	48°25'N	20°01'E
Rimbo, Swe. (rēm'bô)	166	59°45'N	18°22'E
Rimini, Italy (rē'mê-nē)	162	44°03'N	12°33'E
Rimouski, Can. (rê-mōōs'kê)	91	48°27'N	68°32'W
Rincón de Romos, Mex. (rēn-kōn dā rô-mōs')	130	22°13'N	102°21'W
Ringkøbing, Den. (rĭng'kûb-ĭng)	160	56°06'N	8°14'E
Ringkøbing Fjord, b., Den.	166	55°55'N	8°04'E
Ringsted, Den. (rĭng'stĕdh)	166	55°27'N	11°49'E
Ringvassøya, i., Nor. (rĭng'väs-ûê)	160	69°58'N	16°43'E
Ringwood, Austl.	217a	37°49'S	145°14'E
Rinjani, Gunung, mtn., Indon.	212	8°39'S	116°22'E
Río Abajo, Pan. (rē'ō-ä-bä'κô)	128a	9°01'N	78°30'W
Río Balsas, Mex. (rē'ō-bäl-säs)	130	17°59'N	99°45'W
Riobamba, Ec. (rē'ō-bäm-bä)	142	1°45'S	78°37'W
Rio Bonito, Braz. (rē'ōō bō-nē'tô)	141a	22°44'S	42°38'W
Rio Branco, Braz. (rē'ŏ brän'kô)	142	9°57'S	67°50'W
Río Branco, Ur. (rĭō brăncō)	144	32°33'S	53°29'W
Rio Casca, Braz. (rē'ō-kå's-kä)	141a	20°15'S	42°39'W
Río Chico, Ven. (rē'ō chē'kŏ)	143b	10°20'N	65°58'W
Rio Claro, Braz. (rē'ŏ klä'rō)	143	22°25'S	47°33'W
Río Cuarto, Arg. (rē'ō kwär'tō)	144	33°05'S	64°15'W
Rio das Flores, Braz. (rē'ō-däs-flô-rĕs)	141a	22°10'S	43°35'W
Rio de Janeiro, Braz. (rē'ō dā zhä-nå'ê-rô)	144b	22°50'S	43°20'W
Rio de Janeiro, state, Braz.	143	22°27'S	42°43'W
Río de Jesús, Pan.	133	7°54'N	80°59'W
Río Frío, Mex. (rē'ō-frē'ô)	131a	19°21'N	98°40'W
Río Gallegos, Arg. (rē'ō gä-lā'gōs)	144	51°43'S	69°15'W
Rio Grande, Braz. (rē'ŏ grän'dĕ)	144	31°04'S	52°14'W
Río Grande, Mex. (rē'ō grän'dā)	130	23°51'N	102°59'W
Riogrande, Tx., U.S. (rē'ō grän-dā)	122	26°23'N	98°48'W
Rio Grande do Norte, state, Braz.	143	5°26'S	37°20'W
Rio Grande do Sul, state, Braz. (rē'ŏ grän'dĕ-dô-sōōl)	144	29°00'S	54°00'W
Ríohacha, Col. (rē'ō-ä'chä)	142	11°30'N	72°54'W
Río Hato, Pan. (rē'ō-ä'tô)	133	8°19'N	80°11'W
Riom, Fr. (rê-ôɴ')	170	45°54'N	3°08'E
Rio Muni, hist. reg., Eq. Gui. (rē'ō mōō'nê)	230	1°47'N	8°33'E
Ríonegro, Col. (rê'ō-nĕ'grō)	142a	6°09'N	75°22'W
Río Negro, prov., Arg. (rē'ō nā'grō)	144	40°15'S	68°15'W
Río Negro, dept., Ur. (rē'ō-nĕ'grō)	141c	32°48'S	57°45'W
Río Negro, Embalse del, res., Ur.	144	32°45'S	55°50'W
Rionero, Italy (rē-ō-nā'rô)	174	40°55'N	15°42'E
Rioni, r., Geor.	182	42°08'N	41°39'E
Rio Novo, Braz. (rē'ō-nô'vô)	141a	21°30'S	43°08'W
Rio Pardo de Minas, Braz. (rē'ō pär'dō-dĕ-mē'näs)	143	15°43'S	42°24'W
Rio Pombo, Braz. (rē'ō pôm'bä)	141a	21°17'S	43°09'W
Rio Sorocaba, Represa do, res., Braz.	141a	23°37'S	47°19'W
Ríosucio, Col. (rē'ō-sōō'syô)	142a	5°25'N	75°41'W
Río Tercero, Arg. (rê'ō dĕr-sĕ'rô)	144	32°12'S	63°59'W
Rio Verde, Braz. (vĕr'dĕ)	143	17°47'S	50°49'W
Ríoverde, Mex. (rē'ō-vĕr'dȧ)	128	21°54'N	99°59'W
Ripley, Eng., U.K. (rĭp'lê)	158a	53°03'N	1°24'W
Ripley, Ms., U.S.	124	34°44'N	88°55'W
Ripley, Tn., U.S.	124	35°44'N	89°34'W
Ripoll, Spain (rê-pōl'')	173	42°10'N	2°10'E
Ripon, Wi., U.S. (rĭp'ŏn)	113	43°49'N	88°50'W
Ripon, i., Austl.	220	20°05'S	118°10'E
Ripon Falls, wtfl., Ug.	232	0°38'N	33°02'E
Risaralda, dept., Col.	142a	5°15'N	76°00'W
Risdon, Austl. (rĭz'dŭn)	219	42°37'S	147°32'E
Rishiri, i., Japan (rē-shē'rē)	210	45°10'N	141°08'E
Rishon le Ziyyon, Isr.	197a	31°57'N	34°48'E
Rishra, India	202a	22°42'N	88°22'E
Rising Sun, In., U.S. (rīz'ĭng sŭn)	108	38°55'N	84°55'W
Risor, Nor. (rēs'ûr)	160	58°44'N	9°10'E
Ritacuva, Alto, mtn., Col. (ä'l-tô-rē-tä-kōō'vä)	142	6°22'N	72°13'W
Rittman, Oh., U.S. (rĭt'năn)	111d	40°58'N	81°47'W
Ritzville, Wa., U.S. (rĭts'vĭl)	114	47°08'N	118°23'W

PLACE (Pronunciation)	PAGE	LAT.	LONG.
Riva, Dom. Rep. (rē'vä)	135	19°10'N	69°55'W
Riva, Italy (rē'vä)	174	45°54'N	10°49'E
Riva, Md., U.S. (rĭ'vȧ)	110e	38°57'N	76°36'W
Rivas, Nic. (rē'väs)	132	11°25'N	85°51'W
Rive-de-Gier, Fr. (rēv-dē-zhē-ā')	170	45°32'N	4°37'E
Rivera, Ur. (rê-vā'rä)	144	30°52'S	55°32'W
River Cess, Lib. (rĭv'ēr sĕs)	230	5°46'N	9°52'W
Riverdale, Il., U.S. (rĭv'ēr dāl)	111a	41°38'N	87°36'W
Riverdale, Ut., U.S.	117b	41°11'N	112°00'W
River Falls, Al., U.S.	124	31°20'N	86°25'W
River Falls, Wi., U.S.	113	44°48'N	92°38'W
Riverhead, N.Y., U.S. (rĭv'ēr hĕd)	109	40°55'N	72°40'W
Riverina, reg., Austl. (rĭv-ēr-ē'nä)	221	34°55'S	144°30'E
River Jordan, Can. (jôr'dăn)	116a	48°25'N	124°03'W
River Oaks, Tx., U.S. (ōkz)	117c	32°47'N	97°24'W
River Rouge, Mi., U.S. (rōōzh)	111b	42°16'N	83°09'W
Rivers, Can.	97	50°01'N	100°15'W
Riverside, Ca., U.S. (rĭv'ēr-sīd)	104	33°59'N	117°21'W
Riverside, N.J., U.S.	110f	40°02'N	74°58'W
Rivers Inlet, Can.	94	51°45'N	127°15'W
Riverstone, Austl.	217b	33°41'S	150°52'E
Riverton, Va., U.S.	109	39°00'N	78°15'W
Riverton, Wy., U.S.	115	43°02'N	108°24'W
Rivesaltes, Fr. (rēv'zält')	170	42°48'N	2°48'E
Riviera Beach, Fl., U.S. (rĭv-ĭ-ĕr'ȧ bēch)	125a	26°46'N	80°04'W
Riviera Beach, Md., U.S.	110e	39°10'N	76°32'W
Rivière-Beaudette, Can.	102a	45°14'N	74°20'W
Rivière-du-Loup, Can. (rê-vyâr' dü lōō')	91	47°50'N	69°32'W
Rivière Qui Barre, Can. (rēv-yĕr' kē-bär)	102g	53°47'N	113°51'W
Rivière-Trois-Pistoles, Can. (trwä'pēs-tôl')	100	48°07'N	69°10'W
Rivne, Ukr.	177	48°11'N	31°46'E
Rivne, Ukr.	181	50°37'N	26°17'E
Rivne, prov., Ukr.	177	50°55'N	27°00'E
Riyadh, Sau. Ar.	198	24°31'N	46°47'E
Rize, Tur. (rē'zĕ)	163	41°00'N	40°30'E
Rizhao, China (rē-jou)	208	35°27'N	119°28'E
Rizzuto, Cape, c., Italy (rēt-sōō'tô)	175	38°53'N	17°05'E
Rjukan, Nor. (ryōō'kän)	160	59°53'N	8°30'E
Roanne, Fr. (rō-än')	161	46°02'N	4°04'E
Roanoke, Al., U.S. (rō'ȧ-nōk)	124	33°08'N	85°21'W
Roanoke, Va., U.S.	105	37°16'N	79°55'W
Roanoke, r., U.S.	107	36°17'N	77°22'W
Roanoke Rapids, N.C., U.S.	125	36°25'N	77°40'W
Roanoke Rapids Lake, res., N.C., U.S.	125	36°28'N	77°37'W
Roan Plateau, plat., Co., U.S. (rōn)	119	39°25'N	110°00'W
Roatan, Hond. (rō-ä-tän')	132	16°18'N	86°33'W
Roatán, i., Hond.	132	16°19'N	86°46'W
Robbeneiland, i., S. Afr.	232a	33°48'S	18°22'E
Robbins, Il., U.S. (rŏb'ĭnz)	111a	41°39'N	87°42'W
Robbinsdale, Mn., U.S. (rŏb'ĭnz-dāl)	117g	45°03'N	93°22'W
Robe, Wa., U.S. (rōb)	116a	48°06'N	121°50'W
Roberts, Mount, mtn., Austl. (rŏb'ērts)	221	28°05'S	152°30'E
Roberts, Point, c., Wa., U.S. (rŏb'ērts)	116d	48°58'N	123°05'W
Robertson, Lac, l., Can.	101	51°00'N	59°10'W
Robertsport, Lib. (rŏb'ērts-pōrt)	230	6°45'N	11°22'W
Roberval, Can. (rŏb'ēr-văl) (rô-bĕr-vål')	91	48°32'N	72°15'W
Robinson, Can.	101	48°16'N	58°50'W
Robinson, Il., U.S. (rŏb'ĭn-sŭn)	108	39°00'N	87°45'W
Robinvale, Austl. (rŏb-ĭn'vāl)	222	34°45'S	142°45'E
Roblin, Can.	97	51°15'N	101°25'W
Robson, Mount, mtn., Can. (rŏb'sŭn)	95	53°07'N	119°09'W
Robstown, Tx., U.S. (rŏbz'toun)	123	27°46'N	97°41'W
Roca, Cabo da, c., Port. (kå'bō-dä-rô'kȧ)	172	38°47'N	9°30'W
Rocas, Atol das, atoll, Braz. (ä-tôl-däs-rō'kȧs)	143	3°50'S	33°46'W
Rocha, Ur. (rō'chȧs)	144	34°26'S	54°14'W
Rochdale, Eng., U.K. (rŏch'dāl)	164	53°37'N	2°09'W
Roche à Bateau, Haiti (rôsh á bȧ-tō')	135	18°10'N	74°00'W
Rochefort, Fr. (rôsh-fŏr')	161	45°55'N	0°57'W
Rochelle, Il., U.S. (rô-shĕl')	113	41°53'N	89°06'W
Rochester, Eng., U.K.	158a	51°24'N	0°30'E
Rochester, In., U.S. (rŏch'ĕs-tēr)	108	41°05'N	86°20'W
Rochester, Mi., U.S.	111b	42°41'N	83°09'W
Rochester, Mn., U.S.	105	44°01'N	92°30'W
Rochester, N.H., U.S.	109	43°20'N	71°00'W
Rochester, N.Y., U.S.	105	43°15'N	77°35'W
Rochester, Pa., U.S.	111e	40°42'N	80°16'W
Rock, r., Ia., U.S.	112	43°17'N	96°13'W
Rock, r., Or., U.S.	116c	45°34'N	122°52'W
Rock, r., Or., U.S.	116c	45°52'N	123°14'W
Rock, r., U.S.	107	41°40'N	90°00'W
Rockaway, N.J., U.S. (rŏck'ȧ-wā)	110a	40°54'N	74°30'W
Rockbank, Austl.	217a	37°44'S	144°40'E
Rockcliffe Park, Can. (rok'klĭf pärk)	102c	45°27'N	75°40'W
Rock Creek, r., Can. (rŏk)	115	49°01'N	107°00'W
Rock Creek, r., Il., U.S.	111a	41°16'N	87°54'W
Rock Creek, r., Mt., U.S.	115	46°25'N	113°40'W
Rock Creek, r., Or., U.S.	114	45°30'N	120°06'W
Rock Creek, r., Wa., U.S.	114	47°09'N	117°50'W
Rockdale, Austl.	217b	33°57'S	151°08'E
Rockdale, Md., U.S.	110e	39°22'N	76°49'W
Rockdale, Tx., U.S. (rŏk'dāl)	123	30°39'N	97°00'W
Rock Falls, Il., U.S. (rŏk fôlz)	113	41°45'N	89°42'W
Rockford, Il., U.S. (rŏk'fērd)	105	42°16'N	89°07'W
Rockhampton, Austl. (rŏk-hămp'tŭn)	219	23°26'S	150°29'E
Rock Hill, S.C., U.S. (rŏk'hĭl)	105	34°55'N	81°01'W
Rockingham, N.C., U.S. (rŏk'ĭng-hăm)	125	34°54'N	79°45'W
Rockingham Forest, for., Eng., U.K. (rok'ĭng-hăm)	158a	52°29'N	0°43'W

ng-sing; ŋ-baŋk; ɴ-nasalized n; nŏd; cŏmmit; ōld; ôbey; ôrder; oi-boil; fōōd; ŏo-as oo in foot; ou-out; s-soft; sh-dish; th-thin; pūre; ûnite; ûrn; stŭd; circŭs; ü-as in French tu; '-indeterminate vowel.

342 Rock Island – Rumbek

PRONOUNCING INDEX

PLACE (Pronunciation)	PAGE	LAT.	LONG.
Rock Island, Il., U.S.	105	41°31'N	90°37'W
Rock Island Dam, Wa., U.S. (ī lănd)	114	47°17'N	120°33'W
Rockland, Can. (rŏk'lănd)	102c	45°33'N	75°17'W
Rockland, Ma., U.S.	101a	42°07'N	70°55'W
Rockland, Me., U.S.	100	44°06'N	69°09'W
Rockland Reservoir, res., Austl.	222	36°55'S	142°20'E
Rockmart, Ga., U.S. (rŏk'märt)	124	33°58'N	85°00'W
Rockmont, Wi., U.S. (rŏk'mŏnt)	117h	46°34'N	91°54'W
Rockport, In., U.S. (rŏk'pōrt)	108	38°20'N	87°00'W
Rockport, Ma., U.S.	101a	42°39'N	70°37'W
Rockport, Mo., U.S.	121	40°25'N	95°30'W
Rockport, Tx., U.S.	123	28°03'N	97°03'W
Rock Rapids, Ia., U.S. (răp'ĭdz)	112	43°26'N	96°10'W
Rock Sound, strt., Bah.	134	24°50'N	76°05'W
Rocksprings, Tx., U.S. (rŏk sprĭngs)	122	30°02'N	100°12'W
Rock Springs, Wy., U.S.	104	41°35'N	109°13'W
Rockstone, Guy. (rŏk'stōn)	143	5°55'N	57°27'W
Rock Valley, Ia., U.S. (văl'ĭ)	112	43°13'N	96°17'W
Rockville, In., U.S. (rŏk'vĭl)	108	39°45'N	87°15'W
Rockville, Md., U.S.	110e	39°05'N	77°11'W
Rockville Centre, N.Y., U.S. (sĕn'tēr)	110a	40°39'N	73°39'W
Rockwall, Tx., U.S. (rŏk'wôl)	121	32°55'N	96°23'W
Rockwell City, Ia., U.S. (rŏk'wĕl)	113	42°22'N	94°37'W
Rockwood, Can. (rŏk-wood)	102d	43°37'N	80°08'W
Rockwood, Me., U.S.	100	45°39'N	69°45'W
Rockwood, Tn., U.S.	124	35°51'N	84°41'W
Rocky, East Branch, r., Oh., U.S.	111d	41°13'N	81°43'W
Rocky, West Branch, r., Oh., U.S.	111d	41°17'N	81°54'W
Rocky Boys Indian Reservation, I.R., Mt., U.S.	115	48°08'N	109°34'W
Rocky Ford, Co., U.S.	120	38°02'N	103°43'W
Rocky Hill, N.J., U.S. (hĭl)	110a	40°24'N	74°38'W
Rocky Island Lake, l., Can.	98	46°56'N	83°04'W
Rocky Mount, N.C., U.S.	125	35°55'N	77°47'W
Rocky Mountain House, Can.	95	52°22'N	114°55'W
Rocky Mountain National Park, rec., Co., U.S.	106	40°29'N	106°06'W
Rocky Mountains, mts., N.A.	89	50°00'N	114°00'W
Rocky River, Oh., U.S.	111d	41°29'N	81°51'W
Rodas, Cuba (rō'dhäs)	134	22°20'N	80°35'W
Roden, r., Eng., U.K. (rō'dĕn)	158a	52°49'N	2°38'W
Rodeo, Mex. (rô-dā'ō)	122	25°12'N	104°34'W
Rodeo, Ca., U.S. (rō'dēō)	116b	38°02'N	122°16'W
Roderick Island, i., Can. (rŏd'ē-rĭk)	94	52°40'N	128°22'W
Rodez, Fr. (rô-dĕz')	161	44°22'N	2°34'E
Rodnei, Munţii, mts., Rom.	169	47°41'N	24°05'E
Rodniki, Russia (rôd'nê-kê)	180	57°08'N	41°48'E
Rodonit, Kep I, c., Alb.	175	41°38'N	19°01'E
Ródos, Grc.	163	36°24'N	28°15'E
Ródos, i., Grc.	162	36°00'N	28°29'E
Roebling, N.J., U.S. (rōb'lĭng)	110f	40°07'N	74°48'W
Roebourne, Austl. (rō'bŭrn)	218	20°50'S	117°15'E
Roebuck Bay, b., Austl. (rō'bŭck)	220	18°15'S	121°10'E
Roedtan, S. Afr.	238c	24°37'S	29°08'E
Roeselare, Bel.	165	50°55'N	3°05'E
Roesiger, l., Wa., U.S. (rōz'ĭ-gēr)	116a	47°59'N	121°56'W
Roes Welcome Sound, strt., Can. (rōz)	93	64°10'N	87°23'W
Rogatica, Bos. (rô-gä'tê-tsä)	175	43°46'N	19°00'E
Rogers, Ar., U.S. (rŏj-ērz)	121	36°19'N	94°07'W
Rogers City, Mi., U.S.	108	45°30'N	83°50'W
Rogersville, Tn., U.S.	124	36°21'N	83°00'W
Rognac, Fr. (rŏn-yäk')	170a	43°29'N	5°15'E
Rogoaguado, l., Bol. (rō'gō-ä-gwä-dō)	142	12°42'S	66°46'W
Rogovskaya, Russia (rô-gôf'skȧ-yȧ)	177	45°43'N	38°42'E
Rogózno, Pol. (rô'gôzh-nô)	168	52°44'N	16°53'E
Rogue, r., Or., U.S. (rōg)	114	42°32'N	124°13'W
Rohatyn, Ukr.	169	49°22'N	24°37'E
Rojas, Arg. (rō'häs)	141c	34°11'S	60°42'W
Rojo, Cabo, c., Mex. (rō'hō)	131	21°35'N	97°16'W
Rojo, Cabo, c., P.R. (rō'hō)	129b	17°55'N	67°14'W
Rokel, r., S.L.	234	9°00'N	11°55'W
Rokkō-Zan, mtn., Japan (rôk'kō zän)	211b	34°46'N	135°16'E
Rokycany, Czech Rep. (rô'kĭ'tsȧ-nĭ)	168	49°44'N	13°37'E
Roldanillo, Col. (rôl-dä-nē'l-yō)	142a	4°24'N	76°09'W
Rolla, Mo., U.S.	121	37°56'N	91°45'W
Rolla, N.D., U.S.	112	48°52'N	99°32'W
Rolleville, Bah.	134	23°40'N	76°00'W
Roma, Austl. (rō'mȧ)	219	26°30'S	148°48'E
Roma *see* Rome, Italy	154	41°52'N	12°37'E
Roma, Leso.	233c	29°28'S	27°43'E
Romaine, r., Can. (rô-mĕn')	93	51°22'N	63°23'W
Roman, Rom. (rō'män)	169	46°56'N	26°57'E
Romania, nation, Eur. (rō-mā'nê-ȧ)	154	46°18'N	22°53'E
Romano, Cape, c., Fl., U.S. (rō-mä'nō)	125a	25°48'N	82°00'W
Romano, Cayo, i., Cuba (kä'yō-rô-mä'nô)	134	22°15'N	78°00'W
Romanovo, Russia (rô-mä'nô-vô)	186a	59°09'N	61°24'E
Romans, Fr. (rô-mäN')	170	45°04'N	4°49'E
Romblon, Phil. (rōm-blōn')	213a	12°34'N	122°16'E
Romblon Island, i., Phil.	213a	12°33'N	122°17'E
Rome (Roma), Italy	154	41°52'N	12°37'E
Rome, Ga., U.S. (rōm)	105	34°14'N	85°10'W
Rome, N.Y., U.S.	109	43°15'N	75°25'W
Romeo, Mi., U.S. (rō'mê-ō)	108	42°50'N	83°00'W
Romford, Eng., U.K. (rŭm'fērd)	158b	51°35'N	0°11'E
Romilly-sur-Seine, Fr. (rô-mê-yē'sür-sān')	170	48°32'N	3°41'E
Romita, Mex. (rō-mē'tä)	130	20°53'N	101°32'W
Romny, Ukr. (rôm'nĭ)	181	50°46'N	33°31'E
Rømø, i., Den. (rûm'û)	166	55°08'N	8°17'E
Romoland, Ca., U.S. (rō'mō'lănd)	117a	33°44'N	117°11'W
Romorantin-Lanthenay, Fr. (rô-mô-rän-tăN')	170	47°24'N	1°46'E
Rompin, Malay.	197b	2°42'N	102°30'E

PLACE (Pronunciation)	PAGE	LAT.	LONG.
Rompin, r., Malay.	197b	2°54'N	103°10'E
Romsdalsfjorden, Nor.	166	62°40'N	7°05'W
Romulus, Mi., U.S. (rom'ū lŭs)	111b	42°14'N	83°24'W
Ron, Mui, c., Viet.	209	18°05'N	106°45'E
Ronan, Mt., U.S. (rō'nȧn)	115	47°28'N	114°03'W
Roncador, Serra do, mts., Braz. (sĕr'rȧ dô rôn-kä-dôr')	143	12°44'S	52°19'W
Ronceverte, W.V., U.S. (rŏn'sê-vûrt)	108	37°45'N	80°30'W
Ronda, Spain (rōn'dä)	181	36°45'N	5°10'W
Ronda, Sierra de, mts., Spain	172	36°35'N	5°03'W
Rondônia, state, Braz.	142	10°15'S	63°07'W
Ronge, Lac la, l., Can. (rōnzh)	92	55°10'N	105°00'W
Rongjiang, China (rôŋ-jyäŋ)	209	25°52'N	108°45'E
Rongxian, China	209	22°50'N	110°32'E
Rønne, Den. (rûn'ĕ)	160	55°08'N	14°46'E
Ronneby, Swe. (rōn'ĕ-bü)	166	56°13'N	15°17'E
Ronne Ice Shelf, ice, Ant.	224	77°30'S	38°00'W
Roodepoort, S. Afr. (rō'dĕ-pōrt)	233b	26°10'S	27°52'E
Roodhouse, Il., U.S. (ro͞od'hous)	121	39°29'N	90°21'W
Rooiberg, S. Afr.	238c	24°46'S	27°42'E
Roosendaal, Neth. (rō'zĕn-däl)	159a	51°32'N	4°27'E
Roosevelt, Ut., U.S. (rōz''vĕlt)	119	40°20'N	110°00'W
Roosevelt, r., Braz. (rô'sĕ-vĕlt)	143	9°22'S	60°28'W
Roosevelt Island, i., Ant.	224	79°30'S	168°00'W
Root, r., Wi., U.S.	111a	42°49'N	87°54'W
Roper, r., Austl. (rōp'ēr)	220	14°50'S	134°00'E
Ropsha, Russia (rôp'shȧ)	186c	59°44'N	29°53'E
Roque Pérez, Arg. (rô'kĕ-pĕ'rĕz)	141c	35°23'S	59°22'W
Roques, Islas los, is., Ven.	142	12°25'N	67°40'W
Roraima, state, Braz. (rô'rī-mȧ)	142	2°00'N	62°15'W
Roraima, Mount, mtn., S.A. (rô-rä-ē'mä)	143	5°12'N	60°52'W
Røros, Nor. (rûr'ôs)	160	62°36'N	11°25'E
Ros', r., Ukr. (rôs)	177	49°40'N	30°22'E
Rosa, Monte, mtn., Italy (mōn'tä rō'zä)	162	45°56'N	7°51'E
Rosales, Mex. (rō-zä'läs)	122	28°15'N	100°43'W
Rosales, Phil. (rô-sä'lĕs)	213a	15°54'N	120°38'E
Rosamorada, Mex. (rō'zä-mō-rä'dhä)	130	22°06'N	105°16'W
Rosaria, Laguna, l., Mex. (lä-gō'nä-rô-sȧ'ryä)	131	17°50'N	93°51'W
Rosario, Arg. (rô-zä'rê-ō)	144	32°58'S	60°42'W
Rosario, Braz. (rô-zä'rê-ò)	143	2°49'S	44°15'W
Rosario, Mex.	122	26°31'N	105°40'W
Rosario, Mex.	130	22°58'N	105°54'W
Rosario, Phil.	213a	13°49'N	121°13'W
Rosario, Ur.	141c	34°19'S	57°24'E
Rosario, Cayo, i., Cuba (kä'yō-rô-sä'ryō)	134	21°40'N	81°55'W
Rosário do Sul, Braz. (rô-zä'rê-ò-dô-so͞o'l)	144	30°17'S	54°52'W
Rosário Oeste, Braz. (ō'ĕst'ē)	143	14°47'S	56°20'W
Rosario Strait, strt., Wa., U.S.	116a	48°27'N	122°45'W
Rosbach, Ger. (rōz'bäk)	171c	50°47'N	7°38'E
Roscoe, Tx., U.S. (rôs'kō)	122	32°26'N	100°38'W
Roseau, Dom.	133b	15°17'N	61°23'W
Roseau, Mn., U.S. (rô-zō')	112	48°52'N	95°47'W
Roseau, r., Mn., U.S.	112	48°52'N	96°11'W
Roseberg, Or., U.S. (rōz'bûrg)	104	43°13'N	123°30'W
Rosebud, r., Can. (rōz'bŭd)	95	51°20'N	112°20'W
Rosebud Creek, r., Mt., U.S.	115	45°48'N	106°34'W
Rosebud Indian Reservation, I.R., S.D., U.S.	112	43°13'N	100°42'W
Rosedale, Ms., U.S.	124	33°49'N	90°56'W
Rosedale, Wa., U.S.	116a	47°20'N	122°39'W
Roseires Reservoir, res., Sudan	231	11°15'N	34°45'E
Roselle, Il., U.S. (rō-zĕl')	111a	41°59'N	88°05'W
Rosemère, Can. (rōz'mĕr)	102a	45°38'N	73°48'W
Rosemount, Mn., U.S. (rōz'mount)	117g	44°44'N	93°08'W
Rosendal, S. Afr. (rō-sĕn'täl)	238c	28°32'S	27°56'E
Rosenheim, Ger. (rō'zĕn-hīm)	161	47°52'N	12°06'E
Roses, Golf de, b., Spain	173	42°10'N	3°20'E
Rosetown, Can. (rōz'toun)	90	51°33'N	108°00'W
Rosetta *see* Rashīd, Egypt	200	31°22'N	30°25'E
Rosettenville, neigh., S. Afr.	233b	26°15'S	28°04'E
Roseville, Ca., U.S. (rōz'vĭl)	118	38°44'N	121°19'W
Roseville, Mi., U.S.	111b	42°30'N	82°55'W
Roseville, Mn., U.S.	117g	45°01'N	93°10'W
Rosiclare, Il., U.S. (rōz'ĭ-klâr)	108	37°30'N	88°15'W
Rosignol, Guy. (rŏs-ĭg-nŏl)	143	6°16'N	57°37'W
Roşiori de Vede, Rom. (rô-shôr'ê dĕ vĕ-dĕ)	175	44°06'N	25°00'E
Roskilde, Den. (rôs'kēl-dĕ)	166	55°39'N	12°04'E
Roslavl', Russia (rôs'läv'l)	180	53°56'N	32°52'E
Roslyn, Wa., U.S. (rŏz'lĭn)	114	47°14'N	121°00'W
Rösrath, Ger. (rûz'rät)	171c	50°53'N	7°11'E
Ross, Oh., U.S. (rôs)	111f	39°19'N	84°39'W
Rossano, Italy (rô-sä'nō)	163	39°34'N	16°38'E
Rossan Point, c., Ire.	164	54°45'N	8°30'W
Ross Creek, r., Can.	102g	53°40'N	113°08'W
Rosseau, l., Can. (rôs-sō')	99	45°15'N	79°30'W
Rossel, i., Pap. N. Gui. (rô-sĕl')	221	11°31'S	154°00'E
Rosser, Can. (rôs'sēr)	102f	49°59'N	97°27'W
Ross Ice Shelf, ice, Ant.	224	81°30'S	175°00'W
Rossignol, Lake, l., Can.	100	44°10'N	65°10'W
Ross Island, i., Can.	97	54°14'N	97°45'W
Ross Lake, res., Wa., U.S.	114	48°40'N	121°07'W
Rossland, Can. (rôs'lȧnd)	90	49°05'N	118°48'W
Rossosh', Russia (rôs'sŭsh)	181	50°12'N	39°32'E
Rossouw, S. Afr.	233c	31°12'S	27°18'E
Ross Sea, sea, Ant.	224	76°00'S	178°00'W
Rossvatnet, l., Nor.	160	65°36'N	13°08'E
Rossville, Ga., U.S. (rôs'vĭl)	124	34°57'N	85°22'W
Rosthern, Can.	96	52°41'N	106°25'W
Rostock, Ger. (rôs'tŭk)	160	54°04'N	12°06'E

PLACE (Pronunciation)	PAGE	LAT.	LONG.
Rostov, Russia	180	57°13'N	39°23'E
Rostov, prov., Russia	177	47°38'N	39°15'E
Rostov-na-Donu, Russia (rôstôv-nȧ-dô-no͞o)	178	47°16'N	39°47'E
Roswell, Ga., U.S. (rŏz'wĕl)	124	34°02'N	84°21'W
Roswell, N.M., U.S.	104	33°23'N	104°32'W
Rotan, Tx., U.S. (rô-tăn')	120	32°51'N	100°27'W
Rothenburg, Ger.	168	49°20'N	10°10'E
Rotherham, Eng., U.K. (rŏdh'ēr-ăm)	158a	53°26'N	1°21'W
Rotherham, co., Eng., U.K.	158a	53°52'N	1°45'W
Rothesay, Can. (rôth'sȧ)	100	45°23'N	66°00'W
Rothesay, Scot., U.K.	164	55°50'N	3°14'W
Rothwell, Eng., U.K.	158a	53°44'N	1°30'W
Roti, Pulau, i., Indon. (rō'tê)	212	10°30'S	122°52'E
Roto, Austl. (rō'tô)	222	33°07'S	145°30'E
Rotorua, N.Z.	223	38°07'S	176°17'E
Rotterdam, Neth. (rôt'ĕr-däm')	154	51°55'N	4°27'E
Rottweil, Ger. (rōt'vīl)	168	48°10'N	8°36'E
Roubaix, Fr. (ro͞o-bĕ')	170	50°42'N	3°10'E
Rouen, Fr. (ro͞o-äN')	154	49°25'N	1°05'E
Rouge, r., Can. (ro͞ozh)	102d	43°53'N	79°21'W
Rouge, r., Can.	99	46°40'N	74°50'W
Rouge, r., Mi., U.S.	111b	42°30'N	83°15'W
Rough River Reservoir, res., Ky., U.S.	108	37°45'N	86°10'W
Round Lake, Il., U.S.	111a	42°21'N	88°05'W
Round Pond, l., Can.	101	48°15'N	55°57'W
Round Rock, Tx., U.S.	123	30°31'N	97°41'W
Round Top, mtn., Or., U.S. (tŏp)	116c	45°41'N	123°22'W
Roundup, Mt., U.S. (round'ŭp)	115	46°25'N	108°35'W
Rousay, i., Scot., U.K. (ro͞o'zȧ)	164a	59°10'N	3°04'W
Rouyn, Can. (ro͞on)	91	48°22'N	79°03'W
Rovaniemi, Fin. (rô'vȧ-nyĕ'mĭ)	160	66°29'N	25°45'E
Rovato, Italy (rô-vä'tō)	174	45°33'N	10°00'E
Roven'ki, Russia	177	49°54'N	38°54'E
Roven'ky, Ukr.	177	48°06'N	39°44'E
Rovereto, Italy (rō-vå-rā'tô)	174	45°53'N	11°05'E
Rovigo, Italy (rô-vē'gô)	174	45°05'N	11°48'E
Rovinj, Cro. (rô'ēn')	174	45°05'N	13°40'E
Rovira, Col. (rô-vē'rä)	142a	4°14'N	75°13'W
Rovuma (Ruvuma), r., Afr.	237	10°50'S	39°50'E
Rowley, Ma., U.S. (rou'lē)	101a	42°43'N	70°53'W
Roxana, Il., U.S. (rŏks'ăn-nȧ)	117e	38°51'N	90°05'W
Roxas, Phil. (rô-xäs)	212	11°30'N	122°47'E
Roxo, Cap, c., Sen.	234	12°20'N	16°43'W
Roy, N.M., U.S. (roi)	120	35°54'N	104°09'W
Roy, Ut., U.S.	117b	41°10'N	112°02'W
Royal, i., Bah.	134	25°30'N	76°50'W
Royal Canal, can., Ire. (roi-ăl)	164	53°28'N	6°45'W
Royal Natal National Park, rec., S. Afr.	233c	28°35'S	28°54'E
Royal Oak, Can. (roi'ăl ōk)	116a	48°30'N	123°24'W
Royal Oak, Mi., U.S.	111b	42°29'N	83°09'W
Royalton, Mi., U.S. (roi'ăl-tŭn)	108	42°00'N	86°25'W
Royan, Fr. (rwä-yäN')	170	45°40'N	1°02'W
Roye, Fr. (rwä)	170	49°43'N	2°40'E
Royersford, Pa., U.S. (roi'yērz-fērd)	110f	40°11'N	75°32'W
Royston, Ga., U.S. (roiz'tŭn)	124	34°15'N	83°06'W
Royton, Eng., U.K. (roi'tŭn)	158a	53°34'N	2°07'W
Rozay-en-Brie, Fr. (rô-zā-ĕN-brē')	171b	48°41'N	2°57'E
Rozdil'na, Ukr.	177	46°47'N	30°08'E
Rozhaya, r., Russia (rô'zhȧ-yȧ)	186b	55°20'N	37°37'E
Rozivka, Ukr.	177	47°14'N	36°35'E
Rožňava, Slvk. (rôzh'nyȧ-vȧ)	169	48°39'N	20°32'E
Rtishchevo, Russia ('r-tĭsh'chĕ-vô)	181	52°15'N	43°40'E
Ru, r., China (ro͞o)	206	33°07'N	114°18'E
Ruacana Falls, wtfl., Afr.	232	17°15'S	14°45'E
Ruaha National Park, rec., Tan.	237	7°15'S	34°50'E
Ruapehu, vol., N.Z. (rô-ȧ-pā'ho͞o)	221a	39°15'S	175°37'E
Rub' al Khali *see* Ar Rub' al Khālī, des., Asia	198	20°00'N	51°00'E
Rubeho Mountains, mts., Tan.	237	6°45'S	36°15'E
Rubidoux, Ca., U.S.	117a	33°59'N	117°24'W
Rubizhne, Ukr.	177	48°53'N	38°29'E
Rubondo Island, i., Tan.	237	2°10'S	31°55'E
Rubtsovsk, Russia	178	51°31'N	81°17'E
Ruby, Ak., U.S. (ro͞o'bê)	106a	64°38'N	155°22'W
Ruby, l., Nv., U.S.	118	40°11'N	115°20'W
Ruby, r., Mt., U.S.	115	45°06'N	112°10'W
Ruby Mountains, mts., Nv., U.S.	118	40°11'N	115°36'W
Rudkøbing, Den. (ro͞odh'kûb-ĭng)	166	54°56'N	10°44'E
Rüdnitz, Ger. (rüd'nētz)	159b	52°44'N	13°38'E
Rudolf, Lake, l., Afr. (ro͞o'dŏlf)	231	3°30'N	36°05'E
Rufā'ah, Sudan (ro͞o-fä'ä)	231	14°52'N	33°30'E
Ruffec, Fr. (rü-fĕk')	170	46°03'N	0°11'E
Rufiji, r., Tan. (ro͞o-fē'jê)	233	8°00'S	38°00'E
Rufisque, Sen. (rü-fēsk')	230	14°43'N	17°17'W
Rufunsa, Zam.	237	15°05'S	29°40'E
Rufus Woods, Wa., U.S.	114	48°02'N	119°33'W
Rugao, China (ro͞o-gou)	208	32°24'N	120°33'E
Rugby, Eng., U.K. (rŭg'bê)	158a	52°22'N	1°15'W
Rugby, N.D., U.S.	112	48°22'N	100°00'W
Rugeley, Eng., U.K. (ro͞oj'lē)	158a	52°46'N	1°56'W
Rügen, i., Ger. (rü'ghĕn)	156	54°28'N	13°47'E
Ruhnu-Saar, i., Est. (ro͞onô-sȧ'ȧr)	167	57°46'N	23°15'E
Ruhr, r., Ger. (ro͞or)	168	51°18'N	8°17'E
Rui'an, China (rwā-än)	209	27°48'N	120°40'E
Ruiz, Mex. (roē'z)	130	21°55'N	105°09'W
Ruiz, Nevado del, vol., Col. (nĕ-vä'dō-dĕl-ro͞oē'z)	142a	4°52'N	75°20'W
Rūjiena, Lat. (ro͞o'yĭ-ă-nȧ)	167	57°54'N	25°19'E
Ruki, r., D.R.C.	236	0°05'S	18°55'E
Rukwa, Lake, l., Tan. (ro͞ok-wä')	232	8°00'S	32°25'E
Rum, r., Mn., U.S. (rŭm)	113	45°52'N	93°45'W
Ruma, Yugo. (ro͞o'mȧ)	175	45°00'N	19°53'E
Rumbek, Sudan (rŭm'bĕk)	231	6°52'N	29°43'E

PRONOUNCING INDEX Rum Cay – Saint George 343

PLACE (Pronunciation)	PAGE	LAT.	LONG.
Rum Cay, i., Bah.	135	23°40'N	74°50'W
Rumford, Me., U.S. (rŭm'fẽrd)	100	44°32'N	70°35'W
Rummah, Wādī ar, val., Sau. Ar.	198	26°17'N	41°45'E
Rummānah, Egypt	197a	31°01'N	32°39'E
Runan, China (ro͞o-nän)	208	32°59'N	114°22'E
Runcorn, Eng., U.K. (rŭŋ'kôrn)	158a	53°20'N	2°44'W
Ruo, r., China (rwô)	204	41°15'N	100°46'E
Rupat, i., Indon. (ro͞o'pät)	197b	1°55'N	101°35'E
Rupat, Selat, strt., Indon.	197b	1°55'N	101°17'E
Rupert, Id., U.S. (ro͞o'pẽrt)	115	42°36'N	113°41'W
Rupert, Rivière de, r., Can.	93	51°35'N	76°30'W
Ruse, Blg. (ro͞o'sĕ) (rö'sĕ)	154	43°50'N	25°59'E
Rushan, China (ro͞o-shän)	206	36°54'N	121°31'E
Rush City, Mn., U.S.	113	45°40'N	92°59'W
Rushville, Il., U.S. (rŭsh'vĭl)	121	40°08'N	90°34'W
Rushville, In., U.S.	108	39°35'N	85°30'W
Rushville, Ne., U.S.	112	42°43'N	102°27'W
Rusizi, r., Afr.	237	3°00'S	29°05'E
Rusk, Tx., U.S. (rŭsk)	123	31°49'N	95°09'W
Ruskin, Can. (rŭs'kĭn)	116d	49°10'N	122°25'W
Russ, r., Aus.	159e	48°12'N	16°55'E
Russas, Braz. (ro͞o's-säs)	143	4°48'S	37°50'W
Russell, Can. (rŭs'ĕl)	90	50°47'N	101°15'W
Russell, Can.	102c	45°15'N	75°22'W
Russell, Ca., U.S.	116b	37°39'N	122°08'W
Russell, Ks., U.S.	120	38°51'N	98°51'W
Russell, Ky., U.S.	108	38°30'N	82°45'W
Russel Lake, l., Can.	97	56°15'N	101°30'W
Russell Islands, is., Sol. Is.	221	9°16'S	158°30'E
Russellville, Al., U.S. (rŭs'ĕl-vĭl)	124	34°29'N	87°44'W
Russellville, Ar., U.S.	121	35°16'N	93°08'W
Russellville, Ky., U.S.	124	36°48'N	86°51'W
Russia, nation, Russia	178	61°00'N	60°00'E
Russian, r., Ca., U.S. (rŭsh'ăn)	118	38°59'N	123°10'W
Rustavi, Geor.	182	41°33'N	45°02'E
Rustenburg, S. Afr. (rŭs'tĕn-bûrg)	238c	25°40'S	27°15'E
Ruston, La., U.S. (rŭs'tŭn)	123	32°32'N	92°39'W
Ruston, Wa., U.S.	116a	47°18'N	122°30'W
Rute, Spain (ro͞o'tā)	172	38°20'N	4°34'W
Ruth, Nv., U.S. (ro͞oth)	118	39°17'N	115°00'W
Ruthenia, hist. reg., Ukr.	169	48°25'N	23°00'E
Rutherfordton, N.C., U.S. (rŭdh'ẽr-fẽrd-tŭn)	125	35°23'N	81°58'W
Rutland, Vt., U.S.	109	43°35'N	72°55'W
Rutledge, Md., U.S. (rŭt'lĕdj)	110e	39°34'N	76°33'W
Rutog, China	204	33°29'N	79°26'E
Rutshuru, D.R.C. (ro͞ot-sho͞o'ro͞o)	232	1°11'S	29°27'E
Ruvo, Italy (ro͞o'vô)	174	41°07'N	16°32'E
Ruvuma, r., Afr.	232	11°30'S	37°00'E
Ruza, Russia (ro͞o'zá)	176	55°42'N	36°12'E
Ruzhany, Bela. (rö-zhän'ĭ)	169	52°49'N	24°54'E
Rwanda, nation, Afr.	232	2°10'S	29°37'E
Ryabovo, Russia (ryä'bô-vô)	186c	59°24'N	31°08'E
Ryazan', Russia (ryä-zän'')	178	54°37'N	39°43'E
Ryazan', prov., Russia	176	54°10'N	39°37'E
Ryazhsk, Russia (ryäzh'sk')	180	53°43'N	40°04'E
Rybachiy, Poluostrov, pen., Russia	180	69°50'N	33°20'E
Rybatskoye, Russia	186c	59°50'N	30°31'E
Rybinsk, Russia	178	58°02'N	38°52'E
Rybinskoye, res., Russia	178	58°23'N	38°15'E
Rybnik, Pol. (rĭb'nĕk)	169	50°06'N	18°37'E
Ryde, Eng., U.K. (rīd)	164	50°43'N	1°16'W
Rye, N.Y., U.S. (rī)	110a	40°58'N	73°42'W
Ryl'sk, Russia (rēl''sk)	181	51°33'N	34°42'E
Ryōtsu, Japan (ryōt'so͞o)	210	38°02'N	138°23'E
Rypin, Pol. (rĭ'pēn)	169	53°04'N	19°25'E
Rysy, mtn., Eur.	169	49°12'N	20°04'E
Ryukyu Islands see Nansei-shotō, is., Japan	205	27°30'N	127°00'E
Rzeszów, Pol. (zhå-shòf)	161	50°02'N	22°00'E
Rzhev, Russia ('r-zhĕf)	178	56°16'N	34°17'E
Rzhyshchiv, Ukr.	177	49°58'N	31°05'E

S

PLACE (Pronunciation)	PAGE	LAT.	LONG.
Saale, r., Ger. (sä-lĕ)	168	51°14'N	11°52'E
Saalfeld, Ger. (säl'fĕlt)	168	50°38'N	11°20'E
Saarbrücken, Ger. (zähr'brü-kĕn)	161	49°15'N	7°01'E
Saaremaa, i., Est.	180	58°25'N	22°30'E
Saavedra, Arg. (sä-ä-vā'drä)	144	37°45'S	62°23'W
Saba, i., Neth. Ant. (sä'bä)	133b	17°39'N	63°20'W
Šabac, Yugo. (shä'bats)	163	44°45'N	19°49'E
Sabadell, Spain (sä-bä-dhāl')	162	41°32'N	2°07'E
Sabah, hist. reg., Malay.	212	5°10'N	116°25'E
Sabana, Archipiélago de, is., Cuba	134	23°05'N	80°00'W
Sabana, Río, r., Pan. (sä-bä'nä)	133	8°40'N	78°02'W
Sabana de la Mar, Dom. Rep. (sä-bä'nä dā lä mär')	135	19°05'N	69°30'W
Sabana de Uchire, Ven. (sä-bá'nä dĕ o͞o-chē'rĕ)	143b	10°02'N	65°32'W
Sabanagrande, Hond. (sä-bä'nä-grä'n-dĕ)	132	13°47'N	87°16'W
Sabanalarga, Col. (sä-bá'nä-lär'gä)	142	10°38'N	75°02'W
Sabanas Páramo, mtn., Col. (sä-bá'näs pá'rä-mô)	142a	6°28'N	76°08'W
Sabancuy, Mex. (sä-bäŋ-kwē')	131	18°58'N	91°09'W
Sabang, Indon. (sä'bäng)	212	5°52'N	95°26'E
Sabaudia, Italy (sá-bou'dē-ä)	174	41°19'N	13°00'E
Sabetha, Ks., U.S. (sá-bĕth'á)	121	39°54'N	95°49'W
Sabi (Rio Save), r., Afr. (sä'bē)	232	20°18'S	32°07'E
Sabile, Lat. (sá'bē-lĕ)	167	57°03'N	22°34'E
Sabinal, Tx., U.S. (sá-bī'nál)	122	29°19'N	99°27'W
Sabinal, Cayo, i., Cuba (kä'yō sä-bē-näl')	134	21°40'N	77°20'W
Sabinas, Mex.	128	28°05'N	101°30'W
Sabinas, r., Mex. (sä-bē'näs)	122	26°37'N	99°52'W
Sabinas, Río, r., Mex. (rē'ō sä-bē'näs)	122	27°25'N	100°33'W
Sabinas Hidalgo, Mex. (ē-däl'gō)	122	26°30'N	100°10'W
Sabine, Tx., U.S. (sá-bēn')	123	29°44'N	93°54'W
Sabine, r., U.S.	107	32°00'N	94°30'W
Sabine, Mount, mtn., Ant.	224	72°05'S	169°10'E
Sabine Lake, l., La., U.S.	123	29°53'N	93°41'W
Sablayan, Phil. (säb-lä-yän')	213a	12°49'N	120°47'E
Sable, Cape, c., Can. (sā'b'l)	93	43°25'N	65°24'W
Sable, Cape, c., Fl., U.S.	107	25°12'N	81°10'W
Sables, Rivière aux, r., Can.	99	49°00'N	70°20'W
Sablé-sur-Sarthe, Fr. (säb-lā-sür-särt')	170	47°50'N	0°17'W
Sablya, Gora, mtn., Russia	180	64°50'N	59°00'E
Sàbor, r., Port. (sä-bōr')	172	41°18'N	6°54'W
Sabunchu, Azer.	182	40°26'N	49°56'E
Sabzevār, Iran	201	36°13'N	57°42'E
Sac, r., Mo., U.S. (sôk)	121	38°11'N	93°45'W
Sacandaga Reservoir, res., N.Y., U.S. (să-kăn-dâ'gá)	109	43°10'N	74°15'W
Sacavém, Port. (sä-kä-vĕɴ')	173b	38°47'N	9°06'W
Sacavém, r., Port.	173b	38°52'N	9°06'W
Sac City, Ia., U.S. (sŏk)	112	42°25'N	95°00'W
Sachigo Lake, l., Can. (săch'ĭ-gō)	97	53°49'N	92°08'W
Sachsen, hist. reg., Ger. (zäĸ'sĕn)	168	50°45'N	12°17'E
Sacketts Harbor, N.Y., U.S. (săk'ĕts)	109	43°55'N	76°05'W
Sackville, Can. (săk'vĭl)	100	45°54'N	64°22'W
Saco, Me., U.S. (sô'kō)	100	43°30'N	70°28'W
Saco, r., Braz. (sä'kô)	144b	22°20'S	43°26'W
Saco, r., Me., U.S.	100	43°53'N	70°46'W
Sacramento, Mex.	122	25°45'N	103°22'W
Sacramento, Mex.	122	27°05'N	101°45'W
Sacramento, Ca., U.S. (săk-rá-mĕn'tō)	104	38°35'N	121°30'W
Sacramento, r., Ca., U.S.	118	40°20'N	122°07'W
Şa'dah, Yemen	198	16°50'N	43°45'E
Saddle Lake Indian Reserve, I.R., Can.	95	54°00'N	111°40'W
Saddle Mountain, mtn., Or., U.S. (săd''l)	116c	45°58'N	123°40'W
Sadiya, India (sŭ-dē'yä)	199	27°53'N	95°35'E
Sado, i., Japan (sä'dō)	205	38°05'N	138°26'E
Sado, r., Port. (sä'dò)	172	38°15'N	8°20'W
Saeby, Den. (sĕ'bü)	166	57°21'N	10°29'E
Saeki, Japan (sä'å-kĕ)	210	32°56'N	131°51'E
Säffle, Swe.	166	59°10'N	12°55'E
Safford, Az., U.S. (săf'fẽrd)	119	32°50'N	109°45'W
Safi, Mor. (sä'fē) (ăs'fē)	230	32°24'N	9°09'W
Safīd Koh, Selseleh-ye, mts., Afg.	198	34°45'N	63°58'E
Saga, Japan (sä'gä)	211	33°15'N	130°18'E
Sagami-Nada, b., Japan (sä'gä'mē nä-dä)	211	35°06'N	139°24'E
Sagamore Hills, Oh., U.S. (săg'á-môr hĭlz)	111d	41°19'N	81°34'W
Saganaga, l., N.A. (să-gá-nä'gá)	113	48°13'N	91°17'W
Sāgar, India	199	23°55'N	78°45'E
Saghyz, r., Kaz.	181	48°30'N	56°10'E
Saginaw, Mi., U.S. (săg'ĭ-nô)	105	43°25'N	84°00'W
Saginaw, Mn., U.S.	117h	46°51'N	92°26'W
Saginaw, Tx., U.S.	117c	32°52'N	97°22'W
Saginaw Bay, b., Mi., U.S.	107	43°50'N	83°40'W
Saguache, Co., U.S. (sá-wăch') (sá-gwä'chē)	119	38°05'N	106°10'W
Saguache Creek, r., Co., U.S.	108	38°05'N	106°40'W
Sagua de Tánamo, Cuba (sä-gwä dĕ tä'nä-mō)	135	20°40'N	75°15'W
Sagua la Grande, Cuba (sä-gwä lä grä'n-dĕ)	134	22°45'N	80°05'W
Saguaro National Park, rec., Az., U.S. (säg-wä'rō)	119	32°12'N	110°40'W
Saguenay, r., Can. (săg-ē-nā')	93	48°20'N	70°15'W
Sagunt, Spain	173	38°58'N	1°29'E
Sagunto, Spain (sä-gōn'tō)	162	39°40'N	0°17'W
Sahara, des., Afr. (sá-hä'rá)	230	23°44'N	1°40'W
Saharan Atlas, mts., Afr.	162	32°51'N	1°02'W
Sahāranpur, India (sŭ-hä'rŭn-po͞or')	199	29°58'N	77°41'E
Sahara Village, Ut., U.S. (sá-hä'rá)	117b	41°06'N	111°58'W
Sahel see Sudan, reg., Afr.	230	15°00'N	7°00'E
Sāhīwal, Pak.	202	30°43'N	73°04'E
Sahuayo de Dias, Mex.	130	20°03'N	102°43'W
Saigon see Ho Chi Minh City, Viet.	212	10°46'N	106°34'E
Saijō, Japan (sä'ē-jō)	211	33°55'N	133°13'E
Saimaa, l., Fin. (sä'ĭ-mä)	160	61°24'N	28°45'E
Sain Alto, Mex. (sä-ēn' äl'tō)	130	23°35'N	103°13'W
Saint Adolphe, Can. (sânt a'dôlf) (săɴ' tá-dôlf')	102f	49°40'N	97°07'W
Saint Afrique, Fr. (săɴ' tá-frēk')	170	43°58'N	2°52'E
Saint Albans, Austl. (sânt ôl'bănz)	217a	37°44'S	144°47'E
Saint Albans, Eng., U.K.	164	51°44'N	0°20'W
Saint Albans, Vt., U.S.	109	44°50'N	73°05'W
Saint Albans, W.V., U.S.	108	38°20'N	81°50'W
Saint Albert, Can. (sânt ăl'bẽrt)	95	53°38'N	113°38'W
Saint Amand-Mont Rond, Fr. (săɴ't á-mäɴ' môɴ-rôɴ')	170	46°44'N	2°28'E
Saint André-Est, Can.	102a	45°33'N	74°19'W
Saint Andrews, Can.	91	45°05'N	67°03'W
Saint Andrews, Scot., U.K.	164	56°20'N	2°40'W
Saint Andrew's Channel, strt., Can.	101	46°06'N	60°28'W
Saint Anicet, Can. (sĕɴt ä-nē-sĕ')	102a	45°07'N	74°23'W
Saint Ann, Mo., U.S. (sânt ăn')	117e	38°44'N	90°23'W
Sainte Anne, Guad.	133b	16°15'N	61°23'W
Saint Anne, Il., U.S.	111a	41°01'N	87°44'W
Sainte Anne, r., Can. (sănt ăn') (sânt ăn')	99	46°55'N	71°46'W
Sainte-Anne, r., Can.	102b	47°07'N	70°50'W
Sainte Anne-des-Plaines, Can. (dā plĕɴ)	102a	45°46'N	73°49'W
Saint Ann's Bay, Jam.	134	18°25'N	77°15'W
Saint Anns Bay, b., Can. (ănz)	101	46°20'N	60°30'W
Saint Anselme, Can. (săɴ' tăɴ-sĕlm')	102b	46°37'N	70°58'W
Saint Anthony, Can. (săn ăn'thô-nē)	91	51°24'N	55°35'W
Saint Anthony, Id., U.S. (sânt ăn'thô-nē)	115	43°59'N	111°42'W
Saint Antoine-de-Tilly, Can.	102b	46°40'N	71°31'W
Saint Apollinaire, Can. (săɴ' tá-pôl-ē-nâr')	102b	46°36'N	71°30'W
Saint Arnoult-en-Yvelines, Fr. (sáɴ-tär-no͞o'ĕɴ-nēv-lēn')	171b	48°33'N	1°55'E
Saint Augustin-de-Québec, Can. (sĕn tō-güs-tēn')	102b	46°45'N	71°27'W
Saint Augustin-Deux-Montagnes, Can.	102a	45°38'N	73°59'W
Saint Augustine, Fl., U.S. (sânt ô'gŭs-tēn)	105	29°53'N	81°21'W
Sainte Barbe, Can. (sânt bärb')	102a	45°14'N	74°12'W
Saint Barthélemy, i., Guad.	133b	17°55'N	62°32'W
Saint Bees Head, c., Eng., U.K. (sânt bēz' hĕd)	164	54°30'N	3°40'W
Saint Benoit, Can. (sĕn bĕ-no͞o-ä')	102a	45°34'N	74°05'W
Saint Bernard, La., U.S. (bẽr-närd')	110d	29°52'N	89°52'W
Saint Bernard, Oh., U.S.	111f	39°10'N	84°30'W
Saint Bride, Mount, mtn., Can. (sânt brīd)	95	51°30'N	115°57'W
Saint Brieuc, Fr. (săɴ' brēs')	161	48°32'N	2°47'W
Saint Bruno, Can. (brū'nō)	102a	45°31'N	73°20'W
Saint Canut, Can. (săɴ' ká-nū')	102a	45°43'N	74°04'W
Saint Casimir, Can. (ká-zē-mēr')	99	46°45'N	72°34'W
Saint Catharines, Can. (kăth'á-rĭnz)	91	43°10'N	79°14'W
Saint Catherine, Mount, mtn., Gren.	133b	12°10'N	61°42'W
Saint Chamas, Fr. (sáɴ-shä-mä')	170a	43°32'N	5°03'E
Saint Chamond, Fr. (săɴ' shá-môɴ')	161	45°30'N	4°17'E
Saint Charles, Can. (săɴ' shärlz')	102b	46°47'N	70°57'W
Saint Charles, Il., U.S. (sânt chärlz')	111a	41°55'N	88°19'W
Saint Charles, Mi., U.S.	108	43°20'N	84°10'W
Saint Charles, Mn., U.S.	113	43°56'N	92°05'W
Saint Charles, Mo., U.S.	117e	38°47'N	90°29'W
Saint Charles, Lac, l., Can.	102b	46°56'N	71°21'W
Saint Christopher-Nevis see Saint Kitts and Nevis, nation, N.A.	128	17°24'N	63°30'W
Saint Clair, Mi., U.S. (sânt klâr)	108	42°55'N	82°30'W
Saint Clair, l., Can.	107	42°25'N	82°30'W
Saint Clair, r., Can.	98	42°45'N	82°25'W
Sainte Claire, Can.	102b	46°36'N	70°52'W
Saint Clair Shores, Mi., U.S.	111b	42°30'N	82°54'W
Saint Claude, Fr. (săɴ' klōd')	171	46°24'N	5°53'E
Saint Clet, Can. (săɴt' klā')	102a	45°22'N	74°21'W
Saint Cloud, Fl., U.S. (sânt kloud')	125a	28°13'N	81°17'W
Saint Cloud, Mn., U.S.	105	45°33'N	94°08'W
Saint Constant, Can. (kōn'stănt)	102a	45°23'N	73°34'W
Saint Croix, i., V.I.U.S. (sânt kroi')	129	17°40'N	64°43'W
Saint Croix, r., N.A. (kroi')	100	45°28'N	67°32'W
Saint Croix, r., U.S. (sânt kroi')	107	45°45'N	93°00'W
Saint Croix Indian Reservation, I.R., Wi., U.S.	113	45°40'N	92°21'W
Saint Croix Island, i., S. Afr. (săɴ krwä)	233c	33°48'S	25°45'E
Saint Damien-de-Buckland, Can. (sânt dā'mē-ĕn)	102b	46°37'N	70°39'W
Saint David, Can. (dā'vĭd)	102b	46°47'N	71°11'W
Saint David's Head, c., Wales, U.K.	164	51°54'N	5°25'W
Saint-Denis, Fr. (săɴ'dē-nē')	161	48°26'N	2°22'E
Saint Dizier, Fr. (dē-zyā')	161	48°49'N	4°55'E
Saint Dominique, Can. (sĕɴ dō-mē-nēk')	102a	45°19'N	74°09'W
Saint Edouard-de-Napierville, Can. (sĕɴ-tĕ-do͞o-är')	102a	45°14'N	73°31'W
Saint Elias, Mount, mtn., N.A. (sânt ē-lī'ăs)	92	60°25'N	141°00'W
Saint Étienne, Fr.	161	45°26'N	4°22'E
Saint Etienne-de-Lauzon, Can. (săɴ' tā-tyĕn')	102b	46°39'N	71°19'W
Sainte Euphémie, Can. (sĕɴt û-fē-mē')	102b	46°47'N	70°27'W
Saint Eustache, Can. (săɴ' tû-stásh')	102a	45°34'N	73°54'W
Saint Eustache, Can.	102f	49°58'N	97°47'W
Sainte Famille, Can. (săɴt fá-mē'y')	102b	46°58'N	70°58'W
Saint Félicíen, Can. (săɴ fā-lē-syăɴ')	91	48°39'N	72°28'W
Sainte Felicite, Can.	100	48°54'N	67°20'W
Saint Féréol, Can. (fa-rā-ôl')	102b	47°07'N	70°52'W
Saint Florent-sur-Cher, Fr. (săɴ' flô-räɴ'sür-shâr')	170	46°58'N	2°15'E
Saint Flour, Fr. (săɴ flo͞or')	170	45°02'N	3°09'E
Sainte Foy, Can. (săɴt fwä)	99	46°47'N	71°18'W
Saint Francis, r., Ar., U.S.	121	35°56'N	90°27'W
Saint Francis Lake, l., Can. (săɴ frăɴ'sĭs)	99	45°00'N	74°20'W
Saint François, Can. (săɴ'frăɴ-swä')	102b	47°01'N	70°49'W
Saint François de Boundji, Congo	236	1°03'S	15°22'E
Saint Francois Xavier, Can.	102f	49°55'N	97°32'W
Saint Gaudens, Fr. (gō-dăɴs')	170	43°07'N	0°43'E
Sainte Genevieve, Mo., U.S. (sânt jĕn'ĕ-vēv)	121	37°58'N	90°02'W
Saint George, Austl. (sânt jôrj')	219	28°02'S	148°40'E

ng-sing; ŋ-baŋk; ɴ-nasalized n; nŏd; cŏmmit; ōld; ôbey; ôrder; oi-boil; fo͞od; ò-as oo in foot; ou-out; s-soft; sh-dish; th-thin; pūre; ûnite; ûrn; stŭd; circŭs; ü-as in French tu; '-indeterminate vowel.

344 Saint George – Salem PRONOUNCING INDEX

PLACE (Pronunciation)	PAGE	LAT.	LONG.
Saint George, Can. (sǎn jôrj′)	91	45°08′N	66°49′W
Saint George, Can. (sǎn′zhôrzh′)	102d	43°14′N	80°15′W
Saint George, S.C., U.S. (sånt jôrj′)	125	33°11′N	80°35′W
Saint George, Ut., U.S.	119	37°05′N	113°40′W
Saint George, i., Ak., U.S.	103	56°30′N	169°40′W
Saint George, Cape, c., Can.	93a	48°28′N	59°15′W
Saint George, Cape, c., Fl., U.S.	124	29°30′N	85°20′W
Saint George's, Can. (jôrj′ĕs)	91	48°26′N	58°29′W
Saint Georges, Fr. Gu.	143	3°48′N	51°47′W
Saint George's, Gren.	133b	12°02′N	61°57′W
Saint George's Bay, b., Can.	93a	48°20′N	59°00′W
Saint Georges Bay, b., Can.	101	45°49′N	61°45′W
Saint George's Channel, strt., Eur. (jôr-jĕz)	156	51°45′N	6°30′W
Saint Germain-en-Laye, Fr. (sǎn′ zhĕr-mǎn-äN-lā′)	170	48°53′N	2°05′E
Saint Gervais, Can. (zhĕr-vĕ′)	102b	46°43′N	70°53′W
Saint Girons, Fr. (zhē-rôn′)	170	42°58′N	1°08′E
Saint Gotthard Pass, p., Switz.	168	46°33′N	8°34′E
Saint Gregory, Mount, mtn., Can. (sånt grĕg′ĕr-ė)	101	49°19′N	58°13′W
Saint Helena, i., St. Hel.	229	16°01′S	5°16′W
Saint Helenabaai, b., S. Afr.	232	32°25′S	17°15′E
Saint Helens, Eng., U.K. (sånt hĕl′ĕnz)	158a	53°27′N	2°44′W
Saint Helens, Or., U.S. (hĕl′ĕnz)	116c	45°52′N	122°49′W
Saint Helens, Mount, vol., Wa., U.S.	114	46°13′N	122°10′W
Saint Helier, Jersey (hyĕl′yĕr)	170	49°12′N	2°06′W
Saint Henri, Can. (sǎn′ hĕn′rē)	102b	46°41′N	71°04′W
Saint Hubert, Can.	102a	45°29′N	73°24′W
Saint Hyacinthe, Can.	91	45°35′N	72°55′W
Saint Ignace, Mi., U.S. (sånt ĭg′nås)	113	45°51′N	84°39′W
Saint Ignace, i., Can. (sǎn′ ĭg′nås)	98	48°47′N	88°14′W
Saint Irenee, Can. (sǎn′ tē-rā-nā′)	99	47°34′N	70°15′W
Saint Isidore-de-Laprairie, Can.	102a	45°18′N	73°41′W
Saint Isidore-de-Prescott, Can. (sǎn′ ĭz′ĭ-dôr-prĕs-kŏt)	102c	45°23′N	74°54′W
Saint Isidore-Dorchester, Can. (dŏr-chĕs′tĕr)	102b	46°35′N	71°05′W
Saint Jacob, Il., U.S. (jā-kŏb)	117e	38°43′N	89°46′W
Saint James, Mn., U.S. (sånt jāmz′)	113	43°58′N	94°37′W
Saint James, Mo., U.S.	121	37°59′N	91°37′W
Saint James, Cape, c., Can.	94	51°58′N	131°00′W
Saint Janvier, Can. (sǎn′ zhän-vyā′)	102a	45°43′N	73°56′W
Saint Jean, Can. (sǎn′ zhäN′)	91	45°20′N	73°15′W
Saint Jean, Can.	102b	46°55′N	70°54′W
Saint Jean, Lac, l., Can.	93	48°35′N	72°00′W
Saint Jean-Chrysostome, Can. (krĭ-zōs-tōm′)	102b	46°43′N	71°12′W
Saint Jean-d'Angely, Fr. (däN-zhå-lē′)	170	45°56′N	0°33′W
Saint Jean-de-Luz, Fr. (dē lüz′)	170	43°23′N	1°40′W
Saint Jérôme, Can. (sånt jĕ-rōm′) (sǎn zhā-rōm′)	102a	45°47′N	74°00′W
Saint Joachim-de-Montmorency, Can. (sånt jō′ȧ-kĭm)	102b	47°04′N	70°51′W
Saint John, Can. (sånt jŏn)	91	45°16′N	66°03′W
Saint John, In., U.S.	111a	41°27′N	87°29′W
Saint John, Ks., U.S.	120	37°59′N	98°44′W
Saint John, N.D., U.S.	112	48°57′N	99°42′W
Saint John, i., V.I.U.S.	129b	18°16′N	64°48′W
Saint John, r., N.A.	93	47°00′N	68°00′W
Saint John, Cape, c., Can.	101	50°00′N	55°32′W
Saint Johns, Antig.	133b	17°07′N	61°50′W
Saint John's, Can. (jŏns)	93a	47°34′N	52°43′W
Saint Johns, Az., U.S. (jŏnz)	119	34°30′N	109°25′W
Saint Johns, Mi., U.S.	108	43°05′N	84°35′W
Saint Johns, r., Fl., U.S.	107	29°54′N	81°32′W
Saint Johnsbury, Vt., U.S. (jŏnz′bĕr-ė)	109	44°25′N	72°00′W
Saint Joseph, Dom.	133b	15°25′N	61°26′W
Saint Joseph, Mi., U.S.	108	42°05′N	86°30′W
Saint Joseph, Mo., U.S. (sånt jō-sĕf)	105	39°44′N	94°49′W
Saint Joseph, i., Can.	108	46°15′N	83°55′W
Saint Joseph, l., Can. (jō′zhûf)	93	51°31′N	90°40′W
Saint Joseph, r., Mi., U.S. (sånt jō′sĕf)	108	41°45′N	85°50′W
Saint Joseph Bay, b., Fl., U.S. (jō′zhûf)	124	29°48′N	85°26′W
Saint Joseph-de-Beauce, Can. (sĕN zhō-zĕf′dē bōs)	99	46°18′N	70°52′W
Saint Joseph-du-Lac, Can. (sĕN zhō-zĕf′ dü läk)	102a	45°32′N	74°00′W
Saint Joseph Island, i., Tx., U.S. (sånt jō-sĕf)	123	27°58′N	96°50′W
Saint Junien, Fr. (sǎn′zhü-nyǎN′)	170	45°53′N	0°54′E
Sainte Justine-de-Newton, Can. (sånt jŭs-tēn′)	102a	45°22′N	74°22′W
Saint Kilda, Austl.	217a	37°52′S	144°59′E
Saint Kilda, i., Scot., U.K. (kĭl′dȧ)	164	57°50′N	8°32′W
Saint Kitts, i., St. K./N. (sånt kĭtts)	129	17°24′N	63°30′W
Saint Kitts and Nevis, nation, N.A.	129	17°24′N	63°30′W
Saint Lambert, Can.	109	45°29′N	73°29′W
Saint Lambert-de-Lévis, Can.	102b	46°35′N	71°12′W
Saint Laurent, Can. (sǎN′lō-rän)	102a	45°31′N	73°41′W
Saint Laurent, Fr. Gu.	143	5°27′N	53°56′W
Saint Laurent-d'Orleans, Can.	102b	46°52′N	71°00′W
Saint Lawrence, Can. (sånt lô′rĕns)	101	46°55′N	55°23′W
Saint Lawrence, i., Ak., U.S. (sånt lô′rĕns)	106a	63°10′N	172°12′W
Saint Lawrence, r., N.A.	93	48°24′N	69°30′W
Saint Lawrence, Gulf of, b., Can.	93	48°00′N	62°00′W
Saint Lazare, Can. (sǎN′lá-zár′)	102b	46°39′N	70°48′W
Saint Lazare-de-Vaudreuil, Can.	102a	45°24′N	74°08′W
Saint Léger-en-Yvelines, Fr. (sǎn-lā-zhĕ′ĕN-nēv-lēn′)	171b	48°43′N	1°45′E
Saint Leonard, Can. (sånt lĕn′ȧrd)	100	47°10′N	67°56′W
Saint Léonard, Can.	102a	45°36′N	73°35′W
Saint Leonard, Md., U.S.	110e	38°29′N	76°31′W
Saint Lô, Fr.	161	49°07′N	1°05′W
Saint-Louis, Sen.	230	16°02′N	16°30′W
Saint Louis, Mi., U.S. (sånt lo͞o′ĭs)	108	43°25′N	84°35′W
Saint Louis, Mo., U.S. (sånt lo͞o′ĭs) (lo͞o′ė)	105	38°39′N	90°15′W
Saint Louis, r., Mn., U.S. (sånt lo͞o′ĭs)	113	46°57′N	92°58′W
Saint Louis, Lac, l., Can. (sǎN′ lo͞o-ē′)	102a	45°24′N	73°51′W
Saint Louis-de-Gonzague, Can. (sǎN′ lo͞o ē′)	102a	45°13′N	74°00′W
Saint Louis Park, Mn., U.S.	117g	44°56′N	93°21′W
Saint Lucia, nation, N.A.	129	13°54′N	60°40′W
Saint Lucia Channel, strt., N.A. (lū′shĭ-ȧ)	133b	14°15′N	61°00′W
Saint Lucie Canal, can., Fl., U.S. (lū′sė)	125a	26°57′N	80°25′W
Saint Magnus Bay, b., Scot., U.K. (măg′nŭs)	164a	60°25′N	2°09′W
Saint Malo, Fr. (sǎN′ mȧ-lō′)	161	48°40′N	2°02′W
Saint Malo, Golfe de, b., Fr. (gôlf-dē-sǎN-mä-lō′)	161	48°50′N	2°49′W
Saint Marc, Haiti (sǎN′ mȧrk′)	135	19°10′N	72°40′W
Saint-Marc, Canal de, strt., Haiti	135	19°05′N	73°15′W
Saint Marcellin, Fr. (mär-sē-lǎN′)	171	45°08′N	5°15′E
Saint Margarets, Md., U.S.	110e	39°02′N	76°30′W
Sainte Marie, Cap, c., Madag.	233	25°31′S	45°00′E
Sainte-Marie-aux-Mines, Fr. (sǎN′tē-mä-rē′ō-mēn′)	171	48°14′N	7°08′E
Sainte Marie-Beauce, Can. (sǎnt′mȧ-rē′)	99	46°27′N	71°03′W
Saint Maries, Id., U.S. (sånt mā′rēs)	114	47°18′N	116°34′W
Saint Martin, i., N.A. (mär′tĭn)	133b	18°06′N	62°54′W
Sainte Martine, Can.	102a	45°14′N	73°37′W
Saint Martins, Can. (mär′tĭnz)	100	45°21′N	65°32′W
Saint Martinville, La., U.S. (mär′tĭn-vĭl)	123	30°08′N	91°50′W
Saint Mary, r., Can. (mā′rė)	95	49°25′N	113°00′W
Saint Mary, Cape, c., Gam.	234	13°28′N	16°40′W
Saint Mary Reservoir, res., Can.	95	49°30′N	113°00′W
Saint Marys, Austl. (mā′rėz)	222	41°40′S	148°10′E
Saint Marys, Can.	98	43°15′N	81°10′W
Saint Marys, Ga., U.S.	125	30°43′N	81°35′W
Saint Mary's, Ks., U.S.	121	39°12′N	96°03′W
Saint Mary's, Oh., U.S.	108	40°30′N	84°25′W
Saint Marys, Pa., U.S.	109	41°25′N	78°30′W
Saint Marys, W.V., U.S.	108	39°20′N	81°15′W
Saint Marys, r., N.A.	117k	46°27′N	84°33′W
Saint Marys, r., U.S.	125	30°37′N	82°05′W
Saint Mary's Bay, b., Can.	101	46°50′N	53°47′W
Saint Marys Bay, b., Can.	100	44°20′N	66°10′W
Saint Mathew, S.C., U.S. (măth′ū)	125	33°40′N	80°46′W
Saint Matthew, i., Ak., U.S.	103	60°25′N	172°10′W
Saint Matthews, Ky., U.S. (măth′ūz)	111h	38°15′N	85°39′W
Saint Maur-des-Fossés, Fr.	171b	48°48′N	2°29′E
Saint Maurice, r., Can. (sǎN′ mô-rēs′) (sånt mô′rĭs)	93	47°20′N	72°55′W
Saint Michael, Ak., U.S. (sånt mī′kĕl)	103	63°22′N	162°20′W
Saint Michel, Can. (sǎN′mē-shĕl′)	102b	46°52′N	70°54′W
Saint Michel, Bras, r., Can.	102b	46°47′N	70°51′W
Saint Michel-de-l'Atalaye, Haiti	135	19°25′N	72°20′W
Saint Michel-de-Napierville, Can.	102a	45°14′N	73°34′W
Saint Mihiel, Fr. (sǎN′ mē-yĕl′)	171	48°53′N	5°30′E
Saint Nazaire, Fr. (sǎN′nȧ-zâr′)	154	47°18′N	2°13′W
Saint Nérée, Can. (nā-rā′)	102b	46°43′N	70°43′W
Saint Nicolas, Can. (ne-kô-lä′)	102b	46°42′N	71°22′W
Saint Nicolas, Cap, c., Haiti	135	19°45′N	73°35′W
Saint Omer, Fr. (sǎN′tô-mâr′)	170	50°44′N	2°16′E
Saint Pascal, Can. (sĕN pȧ-skȧl′)	100	47°32′N	69°48′W
Saint Paul, Can. (sånt pôl′)	90	53°59′N	111°17′W
Saint Paul, Mn., U.S.	105	44°57′N	93°05′W
Saint Paul, Ne., U.S.	112	41°13′N	98°28′W
Saint Paul, i., Can.	101	47°15′N	60°10′W
Saint Paul, i., Ak., U.S.	103	57°10′N	170°20′W
Saint Paul, r., Lib.	234	7°10′N	10°00′W
Saint Paul, Île, i., Afr.	3	38°43′S	77°31′E
Saint Paul Park, Mn., U.S. (pärk)	117g	44°51′N	93°00′W
Saint Pauls, N.C., U.S. (pôls)	125	34°47′N	78°57′W
Saint Peter, Mn., U.S. (pē tĕr)	113	44°20′N	93°56′W
Saint Peter Port, Guern.	170	49°27′N	2°35′W
Saint Petersburg (Sankt-Peterburg) (Leningrad), Russia	178	59°57′N	30°20′E
Saint Petersburg, Fl., U.S. (pē′tērz-bûrg)	105	27°47′N	82°38′W
Sainte Pétronille, Can. (sĕNt pĕt-rō-nēl′)	102b	46°51′N	71°08′W
Saint Philémon, Can. (sĕN fēl-mōN′)	102b	46°41′N	70°28′W
Saint Philippe-d'Argenteuil, Can. (sǎN′fe-lēp′)	102a	45°38′N	74°25′W
Saint Philippe-de-Lapairie, Can.	102a	45°20′N	73°28′W
Saint Pierre, Mart. (sǎN′pyâr′)	133b	14°45′N	61°12′W
Saint Pierre, St. P./M.	101	46°47′N	56°11′W
Saint Pierre, i., St. P./M.	101	46°47′N	56°11′W
Saint Pierre, Lac, l., Can.	99	46°07′N	72°45′W
Saint Pierre and Miquelon, dep., N.A.	93a	46°53′N	56°40′W
Saint Pierre-d'Orléans, Can.	102b	46°53′N	71°04′W
Saint Pierre-Montmagny, Can.	102b	46°55′N	70°37′W
Saint Placide, Can. (plăs′ĭd)	102a	45°32′N	74°11′W
Saint Pol-de-Léon, Fr. (sǎN-pô′dē-lā-ôN′)	170	48°41′N	4°00′W
Saint Quentin, Fr. (sǎN′kän-tǎN′)	161	49°52′N	3°16′E
Saint Raphaël, Can. (rä-fā-ĕl′)	102b	46°48′N	70°46′W
Saint Raymond, Can.	99	46°50′N	71°51′W
Saint Rédempteur, Can. (sǎN rā-dǎnp-tûr′)	102b	46°42′N	71°18′W
Saint Rémi, Can. (sĕN rē-mē′)	102a	45°15′N	73°36′W
Saint Romuald-d'Etchemin, Can. (sĕN rō′mo͞o-äl)	99	46°45′N	71°14′W
Sainte Rose, Guad.	133b	16°19′N	61°45′W
Saintes, Fr.	170	45°44′N	0°41′W
Sainte Scholastique, Can. (skō-lȧs-tēk′)	102a	45°39′N	74°05′W
Saint Siméon, Can.	99	47°51′N	69°55′W
Saint Stanislas-de-Kostka, Can.	102a	45°11′N	74°08′W
Saint Stephen, Can. (stē′vĕn)	91	45°12′N	66°17′W
Saint Sulpice, Can.	102a	45°50′N	73°21′W
Saint Thérèse-de-Blainville, Can. (tē-rĕz′ dē blĕN-vēl′)	99	45°38′N	73°51′W
Saint Thomas, Can. (tŏm′ȧs)	91	42°45′N	81°15′W
Saint Thomas, i., V.I.U.S.	129	18°22′N	64°57′W
Saint Thomas Harbor, b., V.I.U.S. (tŏm′ȧs)	129c	18°19′N	64°56′W
Saint Timothée, Can. (tē-mô-tā′)	102a	45°17′N	74°03′W
Saint Tropez, Fr. (trô-pĕ′)	171	43°15′N	6°42′E
Saint Valentin, Can. (väl-ĕn-tĭn)	102a	45°07′N	73°19′W
Saint Valéry-sur-Somme, Fr. (vȧ-lā-rē′)	170	50°10′N	1°39′E
Saint Vallier, Can. (väl-yā′)	102b	46°54′N	70°49′W
Saint Victor, Can. (vĭk′tĕr)	99	46°09′N	70°56′W
Saint Vincent, Gulf, b., Austl. (vĭn′sĕnt)	222	34°55′S	138°00′E
Saint Vincent and the Grenadines, nation, N.A.	129	13°20′N	60°50′W
Saint Vincent Passage, strt., N.A.	133b	13°35′N	61°10′W
Saint Walburg, Can.	90	53°39′N	109°12′W
Saint Yrieix-la-Perche, Fr. (ē-rē-ĕ)	170	45°30′N	1°08′E
Saitama, dept., Japan (sī′tä-mä)	211a	35°52′N	139°40′E
Saitbaba, Russia (sá-ĕt′bá-bȧ)	186a	54°06′N	56°42′E
Sajama, Nevada, mtn., Bol. (nĕ-vȧ′dä-sä-hȧ′mä)	142	18°13′S	68°53′W
Sakai, Japan (sä′kä-ė)	210	34°34′N	135°28′E
Sakaiminato, Japan	211	35°33′N	133°15′E
Sakākah, Sau. Ar.	198	29°58′N	40°03′E
Sakakawea, Lake, res., N.D., U.S.	106	47°49′N	101°58′W
Sakania, D.R.C. (sȧ-kä′nĭ-ȧ)	232	12°45′S	28°34′E
Sakarya, r., Tur. (sȧ-kär′yȧ)	198	40°10′N	31°00′E
Sakata, Japan (sä′kä-tä)	205	38°56′N	139°57′E
Sakchu, Kor., N. (säk′chō)	210	40°29′N	125°09′E
Sakha (Yakutia), prov., Russia	185	65°21′N	117°13′E
Sakhalin, i., Russia (sȧ-kȧ-lēn′)	179	52°00′N	143°00′E
Šakiai, Lith. (shä′kĭ-ī)	167	54°59′N	23°05′E
Sakishima-guntō, is., Japan (sä′kē-shē′ma gòn′tō′)	205	24°25′N	125°00′E
Sakmara, r., Russia	181	52°00′N	56°10′E
Sakomet, r., R.I., U.S. (sä-kō′mĕt)	110b	41°32′N	71°11′W
Sakurai, Japan	211b	34°31′N	135°51′E
Sakwaso Lake, l., Can. (sȧ-kwȧ′sō)	97	53°01′N	91°55′W
Sal, i., C.V. (säal)	230b	16°45′N	22°39′W
Sal, r., Russia (sál)	181	47°30′N	43°00′E
Sal, Cay, i., Bah. (kē säl)	134	23°45′N	80°25′W
Sala, Swe. (sô′lä)	166	59°56′N	16°34′E
Sala Consilina, Italy (sä′lä kōn-sē-lē′nä)	174	40°24′N	15°38′E
Salada, Laguna, l., Mex. (lä-gò′nä-sä-lä′dä)	118	32°34′N	115°45′W
Saladillo, Arg. (sä-lä-dēl′yō)	144	35°38′S	59°48′W
Salado, Hond. (sä-lä′dhō)	132	15°44′N	87°03′W
Salado, r., Arg.	141c	35°53′S	58°12′W
Salado, r., Arg.	144	37°00′S	67°00′W
Salado, r., Arg. (sä-lä′dō)	144	26°05′S	63°35′W
Salado, r., Mex.	128	28°00′N	102°00′W
Salado, r., Mex. (sä-lä′dō)	131	18°30′N	97°29′W
Salado Creek, r., Tx., U.S.	117d	29°23′N	98°25′W
Salado de los Nadadores, Rio, r., Mex. (dĕ-lōs-nä-dä-dō′rĕs)	122	27°26′N	101°35′W
Salal, Chad	235	14°51′N	17°13′E
Salamanca, Chile (sä-lä-mä′n-kä)	141b	31°48′S	70°57′W
Salamanca, Mex.	128	20°36′N	101°10′W
Salamanca, Spain (sä-lä-mä′n-kȧ)	154	40°54′N	5°42′W
Salamanca, N.Y., U.S. (sál-ȧ-măŋ′kȧ)	109	42°10′N	78°45′W
Salamat, Bahr, r., Chad (bär sä-lä-mät′)	231	10°06′N	19°16′E
Salamina, Col. (sä-lä-mē′-nä)	142a	5°25′N	75°29′W
Salamína, Grc.	175	37°58′N	23°30′E
Salat-la-Canada, Fr.	170	44°52′N	1°13′E
Salaverry, Peru (sä-lä-vā′rē)	142	8°16′S	78°54′W
Salawati, i., Indon. (sä-lä-wä′tē)	213	1°07′S	130°52′E
Salawe, Tan.	237	3°19′S	32°52′E
Sala y Gómez, Isla, i., Chile	241	26°50′S	105°50′W
Salcedo, Dom. Rep. (säl-sā′dō)	135	19°25′N	70°30′W
Saldaña, r., Col. (säl-dȧ′n-yä)	142a	3°42′N	75°16′W
Saldanha, S. Afr.	232	32°55′S	18°05′E
Saldus, Lat. (sál′dòs)	167	56°39′N	22°30′E
Sale, Austl. (sāl)	222	38°10′S	147°07′E
Sale, Eng., U.K.	158a	53°24′N	2°20′W
Sale, r., Can. (sál′rē-vyâr′)	102f	49°44′N	97°11′W
Salekhard, Russia (sŭ-lyĭ-kärt)	180	66°35′N	66°50′E
Salem, India	199	11°39′N	78°11′E
Salem, S. Afr.	233c	33°29′S	26°30′E
Salem, Il., U.S. (sā′lĕm)	108	38°40′N	89°00′W
Salem, In., U.S.	108	38°35′N	86°00′W
Salem, Ma., U.S.	101a	42°31′N	70°54′W
Salem, Mo., U.S.	121	37°36′N	91°33′W
Salem, N.H., U.S.	101a	42°46′N	71°16′W
Salem, N.J., U.S.	109	39°35′N	75°30′W
Salem, Oh., U.S.	108	40°55′N	80°50′W
Salem, Or., U.S.	104	44°55′N	123°03′W

ăt; finȧl; rāte; senåte; ärm; ȧsk; sofȧ; fâre; ch-choose; dh-as th in other; bē; ėvent; bĕt; recĕnt; cratẽr; g-gō; gh-guttural g; bĭt; ĭ-short neutral; rīde; ᴋ-guttural k as ch in German ich;

PRONOUNCING INDEX

Salem – San Felipe 345

PLACE (Pronunciation)	PAGE	LAT.	LONG.
Salem, S.D., U.S.	112	43°43'N	97°23'W
Salem, Va., U.S.	125	37°16'N	80°05'W
Salem, W.V., U.S.	108	39°15'N	80°35'W
Salemi, Italy (sä-lă'mē)	174	37°49'N	12°48'E
Salerno, Italy (sä-lĕr'nô)	162	40°27'N	14°46'E
Salerno, Golfo di, b., Italy (gôl-fô-dē)	162	40°30'N	14°40'E
Salford, Eng., U.K. (săl'fẽrd)	164	53°26'N	2°19'W
Salgótarján, Hung. (shôl'gō-tôr-yän)	169	48°06'N	19°50'E
Salhyr, r., Ukr.	177	45°25'N	34°22'E
Salida, Co., U.S. (sȧ-lī'dȧ)	120	38°31'N	106°01'W
Salies-de-Béan, Fr.	170	43°27'N	0°58'W
Salima, Mwi.	237	13°47'S	34°26'E
Salina, Ks., U.S. (sȧ-lī'nȧ)	104	38°50'N	97°37'W
Salina, Ut., U.S.	119	39°00'N	111°55'W
Salina, i., Italy (sä-lē'nä)	174	38°35'N	14°48'E
Salina Cruz, Mex. (sä-lē'nä krōōz')	128	16°10'N	95°12'W
Salina Point, c., Bah.	135	22°10'N	74°20'W
Salinas, Mex.	128	22°38'N	101°42'W
Salinas, P.R.	129b	17°58'N	66°16'W
Salinas, Ca., U.S. (sȧ-lē'nȧs)	118	36°41'N	121°40'W
Salinas, r., Mex. (sä-lē'näs)	131	16°15'N	90°31'W
Salinas, r., Ca., U.S.	118	36°33'N	121°29'W
Salinas, Bahía de, b., N.A. (bä-ē'ä-dĕ-sȧ-lē'nȧs)	132	11°05'N	85°55'W
Salinas National Monument, rec., N.M., U.S.	119	34°10'N	106°05'W
Salinas Victoria, Mex. (sä-lē'näs vēk-tō'rē-ä)	122	25°59'N	100°19'W
Saline, r., Ar., U.S. (sȧ-lēn')	121	34°06'N	92°30'W
Saline, r., Ks., U.S.	120	39°05'N	99°43'W
Salins-les-Bains, Fr. (sȧ-lăn'-lā-băN')	171	46°55'N	5°54'E
Salisbury, Can.	100	46°03'N	65°05'W
Salisbury, Eng., U.K. (sôlz'bē-rē)	161	50°35'N	1°51'W
Salisbury, Md., U.S.	109	38°20'N	75°40'W
Salisbury, Mo., U.S.	121	39°24'N	92°47'W
Salisbury, N.C., U.S.	125	35°40'N	80°29'W
Salisbury *see* Harare, Zimb.	232	17°50'S	31°03'E
Salisbury Island, i., Can.	93	63°36'N	76°20'W
Salisbury Plain, pl., Eng., U.K.	164	51°15'N	1°52'W
Salkehatchie, r., S.C., U.S. (sô-kē-hăch'ē)	125	33°09'N	81°10'W
Sallisaw, Ok., U.S. (săl'ĭ-sô)	121	35°27'N	94°48'W
Salmon, Id., U.S. (săm'ŭn)	115	45°11'N	113°54'W
Salmon, r., Can.	94	54°00'N	123°50'W
Salmon, r., Can.	100	46°19'N	65°36'W
Salmon, r., Id., U.S.	106	45°30'N	115°45'W
Salmon, r., N.Y., U.S.	109	44°35'N	74°15'W
Salmon, r., Wa., U.S.	116c	45°44'N	122°36'W
Salmon, Middle Fork, r., Id., U.S.	114	44°50'N	114°52'W
Salmon Arm, Can.	95	50°42'N	119°16'W
Salmon Falls Creek, r., Id., U.S.	115	42°22'N	114°53'W
Salmon Gums, Austl. (gŭmz)	218	33°00'S	122°00'E
Salmon River Mountains, mts., Id., U.S.	106	44°15'N	115°44'W
Salon-de-Provence, Fr. (sȧ-lôN-dē-prō-văNs')	171	43°48'N	5°09'E
Salonika *see* Thessaloníki, Grc.	154	40°38'N	22°59'E
Salonta, Rom. (sä-lôn'tä)	169	46°46'N	21°38'E
Saloum, r., Sen.	234	14°10'N	15°45'W
Salsette Island, i., India	203b	19°12'N	72°52'E
Sal'sk, Russia (sälsk)	181	46°30'N	41°20'E
Salt, r., Az., U.S. (sôlt)	106	33°28'N	111°35'W
Salt, r., Mo., U.S.	121	39°54'N	92°11'W
Salta, Arg. (säl'tä)	144	24°50'S	65°16'W
Salta, prov., Arg.	144	25°15'S	65°00'W
Saltair, Ut., U.S. (sôlt'âr)	117b	40°46'N	112°09'W
Salt Cay, i., T./C. Is.	135	21°20'N	71°15'W
Salt Creek, r., Il., U.S. (sôlt)	111a	42°01'N	88°01'W
Saltillo, Mex. (säl-tēl'yō)	128	25°24'N	100°59'W
Salt Lake City, Ut., U.S. (sôlt lāk sĭ'tĭ)	104	40°45'N	111°52'W
Salto, Arg. (säl'tō)	141c	34°17'S	60°15'W
Salto, Ur.	144	31°18'S	57°45'W
Salto, r., Mex.	130	22°16'N	99°18'W
Salto, Serra do, mtn., Braz. (sĕ'r-rä-dō)	141a	20°26'S	43°28'W
Salto Grande, Braz. (grän'dä)	143	22°57'S	49°58'W
Salton Sea, Ca., U.S. (sôlt'ŭn)	118	33°28'N	115°43'W
Salton Sea, I., Ca., U.S.	106	33°19'N	115°50'W
Saltpond, Ghana	230	5°16'N	1°07'W
Salt River Indian Reservation, I.R., Az., U.S. (sôlt rĭv'ẽr)	119	33°40'N	112°01'W
Saltsjöbaden, Swe. (sält'shû-bäd'ĕn)	166	59°15'N	18°20'E
Saltspring Island, i., Can. (sält'sprĭng)	94	48°47'N	123°30'W
Saltville, Va., U.S. (sôlt'vĭl)	125	36°50'N	81°45'W
Saltykovka, Russia (sȧl-tē'kôf-kȧ)	186b	55°45'N	37°56'E
Salud, Mount, mtn., Pan. (sä-lōō'th)	128a	9°14'N	79°42'W
Saluda, S.C., U.S. (sȧ-lōō'dȧ)	125	34°02'N	81°46'W
Saluda, r., S.C., U.S.	125	34°07'N	81°48'W
Saluzzo, Italy (sä-lōōt'sō)	174	44°39'N	7°31'E
Salvador, Braz. (säl-vä-dōr') (bä-ē'ȧ)	143	12°59'S	38°27'W
Salvador Lake, I., La., U.S.	123	29°45'N	90°20'W
Salvador Point, c., Bah.	134	24°30'N	77°45'W
Salvatierra, Mex. (säl-vä-tyĕr'rä)	130	20°13'N	100°52'W
Salween, r., Asia	196	21°00'N	98°00'E
Salyan, Azer.	181	39°40'N	49°10'E
Salzburg, Aus. (sälts'bŏŏrgh)	161	47°48'N	13°04'E
Salzwedel, Ger. (sälts-vä'dĕl)	168	52°51'N	11°10'E
Samālūt, Egypt (sä-mä-lōōt')	200	28°17'N	30°43'E
Samana, Cabo, c., Dom. Rep.	129	19°20'N	69°00'W
Samana or Atwood Cay, i., Bah.	135	23°05'N	73°45'W
Samar, i., Phil. (sä'mär)	213	11°30'N	126°07'E
Samara (Kuybyshev), Russia	180	53°10'N	50°05'E
Samara, r., Russia	181	52°50'N	50°35'E
Samara, r., Ukr. (sȧ-mä'rȧ)	177	48°47'N	35°30'E
Samarai, Pap. N. Gui. (sä-mä-rä'ē)	213	10°45'S	150°49'E
Samarinda, Indon.	212	0°30'S	117°10'E
Samarkand, Uzb. (sȧ-mȧr-känt')	183	39°42'N	67°00'E
Şamaxı, Azer.	181	40°35'N	48°40'E
Samba, D.R.C.	237	4°38'S	26°22'E
Sambalpur, India (sŭm'bŭl-pŏŏr)	199	21°30'N	84°05'E
Sāmbhar, r., India	202	27°00'N	74°58'E
Sambir, Ukr.	169	49°31'N	23°12'E
Samborombón, r., Arg.	141c	35°20'S	57°52'W
Samborombón, Bahía, b., Arg. (bä-ē'ä-säm-bô-rôm-bô'n)	141c	35°57'S	57°05'W
Sambre, r., Eur. (säN'br')	165	50°20'N	4°15'E
Sambungo, Ang.	236	8°39'S	20°43'E
Sammamish, r., Wa., U.S.	116a	47°43'N	122°08'W
Sammamish, Lake, I., Wa., U.S. (sȧ-măm'ĭsh)	116a	47°35'N	122°02'W
Samoa, nation, Oc.	2	14°30'S	172°00'W
Samoa Islands, is., Oc.	214a	14°00'S	171°00'W
Samokov, Blg. (sä'mô-kôf)	175	42°20'N	23°33'E
Samora Correia, Port. (sä-mō'rä-kôr-rĕ'yä)	173b	38°55'N	8°52'W
Samorovo, Russia (sȧ-mȧ-rô'vô)	184	60°47'N	69°13'E
Sámos, i., Grc. (să'mŏs)	163	37°53'N	26°35'E
Samothráki, i., Grc.	163	40°23'N	25°10'E
Sampaloc Point, c., Phil. (säm-pä'lŏk)	213a	14°43'N	119°56'E
Sam Rayburn Reservoir, res., Tx., U.S.	123	31°10'N	94°15'W
Samson, Al., U.S. (săm'sŭn)	124	31°06'N	86°02'W
Samsu, Kor., N. (säm'sōō')	210	41°12'N	128°00'E
Samsun, Tur. (sȧm'sōōn')	198	41°20'N	36°05'E
Samtredia, Geor. (sȧm'trĕ-dē)	181	42°18'N	42°25'E
Samuel, i., Can. (săm'ū-ĕl)	116d	48°50'N	123°10'W
Samur, r. (sä-mōōr')	181	41°40'N	47°20'E
San, Mali (sän)	230	13°18'N	4°54'W
San, r., Eur.	161	50°33'N	22°12'E
Şan'ā', Yemen (sän'ä)	198	15°17'N	44°05'E
Sanaga, r., Cam. (sä-nä'gä)	230	4°30'N	12°00'E
San Ambrosio, Isla, i., Chile (ē's-lä-dĕ-săn äm-brō'zē-ō)	139	26°40'S	80°00'W
Sanana, Pulau, i., Indon.	213	2°15'S	126°38'E
Sanandaj, Iran	198	36°44'N	46°43'E
San Andreas, Ca., U.S. (săn ăn'drē-ăs)	118	38°10'N	120°42'W
San Andreas, I., Ca., U.S.	116b	37°36'N	122°26'W
San Andrés, Col. (sän-än-drĕ's)	142a	6°57'N	75°41'W
San Andrés, Mex. (sän än-drās')	131a	19°15'N	99°10'W
San Andrés, i., Col.	133	12°32'N	81°34'W
San Andres, Laguna de, I., Mex.	131	22°40'N	97°50'W
San Andres Mountains, mts., N.M., U.S. (săn ăn'drē-ăs)	106	33°00'N	106°40'W
San Andrés Tuxtla, Mex. (sän-än-drā's-tōōs'tlä)	128	18°27'N	95°12'W
San Angelo, Tx., U.S. (săn ăn-jĕ-lō)	104	31°28'N	100°22'W
San Antioco, Isola di, i., Italy (ē'sō-lä-dē-sän-än-tyô'kō)	174	39°00'N	8°25'E
San Antonio, Chile (sän-ån-tô'nyō)	144	33°34'S	71°36'W
San Antonio, Col.	142a	2°57'N	75°06'W
San Antonio, Col.	142a	3°55'N	75°28'W
San Antonio, Phil.	213a	14°57'N	120°05'E
San Antonio, Tx., U.S. (săn ăn-tō'nē-ō)	104	29°25'N	98°30'W
San Antonio, r., Tx., U.S.	123	29°00'N	97°58'W
San Antonio, Cabo, c., Cuba (kȧ'bô-sän-än-tô'nyô)	129	21°55'N	84°55'W
San Antonio, Lake, res., Ca., U.S.	118	36°00'N	121°13'W
San Antonio Bay, b., Tx., U.S.	123	28°20'N	97°08'W
San Antonio de Areco, Arg. (dā ä-rā'kō)	141c	34°16'S	59°30'W
San Antonio de las Vegas, Cuba	135a	22°51'N	82°23'W
San Antonio de los Baños, Cuba (då lōs bän'yōs)	134	22°54'N	82°30'W
San Antonio de los Cobres, Arg. (då lōs kō'brås)	144	24°15'S	66°29'W
San Antônio de Pádua, Braz. (dĕ-pá'dwä)	141a	21°32'S	42°09'W
San Antonio de Tamanaco, Ven.	143b	9°42'N	66°03'W
San Antonio Oeste, Arg. (sän-nä-tō'nyō ô-ĕs'tå)	144	40°49'S	64°56'W
San Antonio Peak, mtn., Ca., U.S. (săn ăn-tō'nĭ-ō)	117a	34°17'N	117°39'W
Sanarate, Guat. (sä-nä-rä'tĕ)	132	14°47'N	90°12'W
San Augustine, Tx., U.S. (săn ô'gŭs-tēn)	123	31°33'N	94°08'W
San Bartolo, Mex. (sän bär-tō'lō)	131a	19°36'N	99°43'W
San Bartolo, Mex.	122	24°43'N	103°12'W
San Bartolomeo, Italy (bär-tô-lô-mā'ō)	174	41°25'N	15°04'E
San Benedetto del Tronto, Italy (bā'nå-dĕt'tō dĕl trōn'tō)	174	42°58'N	13°54'E
San Benito, Tx., U.S. (săn bĕ-nē'tō)	123	26°07'N	97°37'W
San Benito, r., Ca., U.S.	118	36°40'N	121°20'W
San Bernardino, Ca., U.S. (bûr-när-dē'nō)	104	34°07'N	117°19'W
San Bernardino Mountains, mts., Ca., U.S.	118	34°05'N	116°23'W
San Bernardo, Chile (sän bĕr-när'dō)	141b	33°35'S	70°42'W
San Blas, Mex. (sän bläs')	128	21°33'N	105°19'W
San Blas, Cape, c., Fl., U.S.	107	29°38'N	85°38'W
San Blas, Cordillera de, mts., Pan.	133	9°17'N	78°20'W
San Blas, Golfo de, b., Pan.	133	9°33'N	78°42'W
San Blas, Punta, c., Pan.	133	9°35'N	78°55'W
San Bruno, Ca., U.S. (săn brū-nô)	116b	37°38'N	122°25'W
San Buenaventura, Mex. (bwā'nȧ-vĕn-tōō'rȧ)	122	27°07'N	101°30'W
San Carlos, Chile (sän-kȧ'r-lŏs)	144	36°23'S	71°58'W
San Carlos, Col.	142a	6°11'N	74°58'W
San Carlos, Eq. Gui.	236	3°27'N	8°33'E
San Carlos, Mex. (sän kär'lōs)	131	17°49'N	92°33'W
San Carlos, Mex.	122	24°36'N	98°52'W
San Carlos, Nic. (sän-kä'r-lŏs)	133	11°08'N	84°48'W
San Carlos, Phil.	213a	15°56'N	120°20'E
San Carlos, Ca., U.S. (săn kär'lŏs)	116b	37°30'N	122°15'W
San Carlos, Ven.	142	9°36'N	68°35'W
San Carlos, r., C.R.	133	10°36'N	84°18'W
San Carlos de Bariloche, Arg.	144	41°15'S	71°26'W
San Carlos Indian Reservation, I.R., Az., U.S. (săn kär'lōs)	119	33°27'N	110°15'W
San Carlos Lake, res., Az., U.S.	119	33°05'N	110°29'W
San Casimiro, Ven. (kä-sē-mē'rō)	143b	10°01'N	67°02'W
San Cataldo, Italy (kä-täl'dō)	174	37°30'N	13°59'E
Sánchez, Dom. Rep. (sän'chĕz)	129	19°15'N	69°40'W
Sanchez, Río de los, r., Mex. (rē'ō-dĕ-lŏs)	130	20°31'N	102°29'W
Sánchez Román, Mex. (rô-mà'n)	130	21°48'N	103°20'W
San Clemente, Spain (sän klå-mĕn'tå)	172	39°25'N	2°24'W
San Clemente Island, i., Ca., U.S.	106	32°54'N	118°29'W
San Cristóbal, Dom. Rep. (krēs-tô'bäl)	135	18°25'N	70°05'W
San Cristóbal, Guat.	132	15°22'N	90°26'W
San Cristóbal, Ven.	142	7°43'N	72°15'W
San Cristobal, i., Sol. Is.	221	10°47'S	162°17'E
San Cristóbal de las Casas, Mex.	128	16°44'N	92°39'W
Sancti Spíritus, Cuba (säŋk'tē spē'rē-tōōs)	129	21°55'N	79°25'W
Sancti Spiritus, prov., Cuba	134	22°05'N	79°20'W
Sancy, Puy de, mtn., Fr. (pwē-dĕ-säN-sē')	161	45°30'N	2°53'E
Sand, i., Or., U.S. (sănd)	116c	46°16'N	124°01'W
Sand, i., Wi., U.S.	113	46°03'N	91°09'W
Sand, r., S. Afr.	233c	28°30'S	29°30'E
Sand, r., S. Afr.	238c	28°09'S	26°46'E
Sanda, Japan (sän'dä)	211	34°53'N	135°14'E
Sandakan, Malay. (sȧn-dä'kȧn)	212	5°51'N	118°03'E
Sanday, i., Scot., U.K. (sănd'ā)	164a	59°17'N	2°25'W
Sandbach, Eng., U.K. (sănd'băch)	158a	53°08'N	2°22'W
Sandefjord, Nor. (sän'dĕ-fyôr')	166	59°09'N	10°14'E
San de Fuca, Wa., U.S. (de-fōō-cä)	116a	48°14'N	122°44'W
Sanders, Az., U.S.	119	35°13'N	109°20'W
Sanderson, Tx., U.S. (săn'dẽr-sŭn)	122	30°09'N	102°24'W
Sandersville, Ga., U.S. (săn'dẽrz-vĭl)	125	32°57'N	82°50'W
Sandhammaren, c., Swe. (sänt'häm-mȧr)	160	55°24'N	14°37'E
Sand Hills, reg., Ne., U.S. (sănd)	112	41°57'N	101°29'W
Sand Hook, N.J., U.S. (sănd hŏŏk)	110a	40°29'N	74°05'W
Sandhurst, Eng., U.K. (sănd'hûrst)	158b	51°20'N	0°48'W
Sandia Indian Reservation, I.R., N.M., U.S.	119	35°15'N	106°30'W
San Diego, Ca., U.S. (săn dē-ā'gō)	104	32°43'N	117°10'W
San Diego, Tx., U.S.	120	27°47'N	98°13'W
San Diego, r., Ca., U.S.	118	32°53'N	116°57'W
San Diego de la Unión, Mex. (sän dĕ-å-gô då lä ōō-nyōn')	130	21°27'N	100°52'W
Sandies Creek, r., Tx., U.S. (sănd'ēz)	123	29°13'N	97°34'W
San Dimas, Mex. (dē-mäs')	130	24°08'N	105°57'W
San Dimas, Ca., U.S. (săn dē-mȧs)	117a	34°07'N	117°49'W
Sandnes, Nor. (sänd'nĕs)	166	58°52'N	5°44'E
Sandoa, D.R.C. (sän-dō'ȧ)	232	9°39'S	23°00'E
Sandomierz, Pol. (sän-dô'myĕzh)	169	50°39'N	21°45'E
San Doná di Piave, Italy (sän dô nà' dē pyä'vĕ)	174	45°38'N	12°34'E
Sandoway, Mya. (sän-dô-wī')	199	18°24'N	94°28'E
Sandpoint, Id., U.S. (sănd point)	114	48°17'N	116°34'W
Sandringham, Austl. (săn'drĭng-ăm)	217a	37°57'S	145°01'E
Sandrio, Italy (sä'n-dryô)	174	46°11'N	9°53'E
Sand Springs, Ok., U.S. (sănd sprĭnz)	121	36°08'N	96°06'W
Sandstone, Austl. (sănd'stōn)	218	28°00'S	119°25'E
Sandstone, Mn., U.S.	113	46°08'N	92°53'W
Sanduo, China (sän-dwô)	206	32°49'N	119°39'E
Sandusky, Al., U.S. (săn-dŭs'kē)	110h	33°32'N	86°50'W
Sandusky, Mi., U.S.	108	43°25'N	82°50'W
Sandusky, Oh., U.S.	105	41°25'N	82°45'W
Sandusky, r., Oh., U.S.	108	41°10'N	83°20'W
Sandwich, Il., U.S. (sănd'wĭch)	108	42°35'N	88°53'W
Sandy, Or., U.S. (sănd'ē)	116c	45°24'N	122°16'W
Sandy, Ut., U.S.	117b	40°36'N	111°53'W
Sandy, r., Or., U.S.	116c	45°28'N	122°17'W
Sandy Cape, c., Austl.	221	24°25'S	153°10'E
Sandy Hook, Ct., U.S. (hŏŏk)	110a	41°25'N	73°17'W
Sandy Lake, I., Can.	102g	53°46'N	113°58'W
Sandy Lake, I., Can.	101	49°16'N	57°00'W
Sandy Lake, I., Can.	97	53°00'N	93°07'W
Sandy Point, Tx., U.S.	123a	29°22'N	95°27'W
Sandy Point, c., Wa., U.S.	116d	48°48'N	122°42'W
Sandy Springs, Ga., U.S. (springz)	110c	33°55'N	84°23'W
San Estanislao, Para. (ĕs-tä-nēs-lä'ō)	144	24°38'S	56°20'W
San Esteban, Hond. (ĕs-tĕ'bän)	132	15°13'N	85°53'W
San Fabian, Phil. (fä-byä'n)	213a	16°14'N	120°28'E
San Felipe, Chile (få-lē'på)	144	32°45'S	70°43'W
San Felipe, Mex. (fē-lē'pĕ)	130	21°29'N	101°13'W
San Felipe, Mex.	130	22°21'N	105°26'W
San Felipe, Ven. (fĕ-lē'pĕ)	142	10°13'N	68°45'W
San Felipe, Cayos de, is., Cuba (kä'yōs-dĕ-sän-fĕ-lē'pĕ)	134	22°00'N	83°30'W

ng-sing; ŋ-baŋk; N-nasalized n; nŏd; cŏmmit; ōld; ôbey; ôrder; oi-boil; fōōd; ŏŏ-as oo in foot; ou-out; s-soft; sh-dish; th-thin; pūre; ûnite; ûrn; stŭd; circŭs; ü-as in French tu; '-indeterminate vowel.

346 San Felipe Creek – San Sebastian
PRONOUNCING INDEX

PLACE (Pronunciation)	PAGE	LAT.	LONG.
San Felipe Creek, r., Ca., U.S. (săn fē-lēp′á)	118	33°10′N	116°03′W
San Felipe Indian Reservation, I.R., N.M., U.S.	119	35°26′N	106°26′W
San Félix, Isla, i., Chile (ē′s-lä-dĕ-săn fā-lēks′)	139	26°20′S	80°10′W
San Fernanda, Spain (fĕr-nä′n-dä)	172	36°28′N	6°13′W
San Fernando, Arg. (fĕr-ná′n-dô)	144a	34°26′S	58°34′W
San Fernando, Chile	141b	35°36′S	70°58′W
San Fernando, Mex. (fĕr-nän′dô)	122	24°52′N	98°10′W
San Fernando, Phil. (sän fĕr-nä′n-dô)	212	16°38′N	120°19′E
San Fernando, Ca., U.S. (fĕr-nän′dô)	117a	34°17′N	118°27′W
San Fernando, r., Mex. (săn fĕr-nän′dô)	122	25°07′N	98°25′W
San Fernando de Apure, Ven. (sän-fĕr-nä′n-dō-dĕ-ä-pōō′rå)	142	7°46′N	67°29′W
San Fernando de Atabapo, Ven. (dĕ-ä-tä-bä′pô)	142	3°58′N	67°41′W
San Fernando de Henares, Spain (dĕ-ā-nä′rås)	173a	40°23′N	3°31′W
Sånfjället, mtn., Swe.	160	62°19′N	13°30′E
Sanford, Can. (săn′fērd)	102f	49°41′N	97°27′W
Sanford, Fl., U.S. (săn′fôrd)	105	28°46′N	81°18′W
Sanford, Me., U.S. (săn′fērd)	100	43°26′N	70°47′W
Sanford, N.C., U.S.	125	35°26′N	79°10′W
San Francisco, Arg. (săn frăn′sĭs′kô)	144	31°23′S	62°09′W
San Francisco, El Sal.	132	13°48′N	88°11′W
San Francisco, Ca., U.S.	104	37°45′N	122°26′W
San Francisco, r., N.M., U.S.	119	33°35′N	108°55′W
San Francisco Bay, b., Ca., U.S. (săn frăn′sĭs′kô)	118	37°45′N	122°21′W
San Francisco del Oro, Mex. (dĕl ō′rō)	128	27°00′N	106°37′W
San Francisco del Rincón, Mex. (dĕl rēn-kōn′)	130	21°01′N	101°51′W
San Francisco de Macaira, Ven. (dĕ-mä-kī′rä)	143b	9°58′N	66°17′W
San Francisco de Macoris, Dom. Rep. (dā-mä-kō′rēs)	135	19°20′N	70°15′W
San Francisco de Paula, Cuba (dā pou′lä)	135a	23°04′N	82°18′W
San Gabriel, Ca., U.S. (săn gä-brē-ĕl′) (gā′brē-ĕl)	117a	34°06′N	118°06′W
San Gabriel, r., Ca., U.S.	117a	33°47′N	118°06′W
San Gabriel Chilac, Mex. (sän-gä-brē-ĕl-chē-läk′)	131	18°19′N	97°22′W
San Gabriel Mts, Ca., U.S.	117a	34°17′N	118°03′W
San Gabriel Reservoir, res., Ca., U.S.	117a	34°14′N	117°48′W
Sangamon, r., Il., U.S. (săn′gá-mŭn)	121	40°08′N	90°08′W
Sanger, Ca., U.S. (săng′ēr)	118	36°42′N	119°33′W
Sangerhausen, Ger. (säng′ĕr-hou-zĕn)	168	51°28′N	11°17′E
Sangha, r., Afr.	231	2°40′N	16°10′E
Sangihe, Pulau, i., Indon.	213	3°30′N	125°30′E
San Gil, Col. (sän-кē′l)	142	6°32′N	73°13′W
San Giovanni in Fiore, Italy (sän jô-vän′nē ēn fyō′rå)	174	39°15′N	16°40′E
San Giuseppe Vesuviano, Italy	173c	40°36′N	14°31′E
Sangju, Kor., S. (säng′jōō′)	210	36°20′N	128°07′E
Sāngli, India	199	16°56′N	74°38′E
Sangmélima, Cam.	235	2°56′N	11°59′E
San Gorgonio Mountain, mtn., Ca., U.S. (săn gôr-gō′nĭ-ō)	117a	34°06′N	116°50′W
Sangre de Cristo Mountains, mts., U.S.	106	37°45′N	105°50′W
San Gregoria, Ca., U.S. (săn grĕ-gôr′ä)	116b	37°20′N	122°23′W
Sangro, r., Italy (säŋ′grô)	174	41°38′N	13°56′E
Sangüesa, Spain (sän-gwĕ′sä)	172	42°36′N	1°15′W
Sanhe, China (sän-hŭ)	206	39°59′N	117°06′E
Sanibel Island, i., Fl., U.S. (săn′ĭ-bĕl)	125a	26°26′N	82°15′W
San Ignacio, Belize	132a	17°11′N	89°04′W
San Ildefonso, Cape, c., Phil. (sän-ēl-dĕ-fōn-sō)	213a	16°03′N	122°10′E
San Ildefonso o la Granja, Spain (ō lä grän′khä)	172	40°54′N	4°02′W
San Isidro, Arg. (ē-sē′drō)	141c	34°28′S	58°31′W
San Isidro, C.R.	133	9°24′N	83°43′W
San Jacinto, Phil. (sän hä-sēn′tō)	213a	12°33′N	123°43′E
San Jacinto, Ca., U.S. (săn já-sĭn′tō)	117a	33°47′N	116°57′W
San Jacinto, r., Ca., U.S. (săn já-sĭn′tō)	117a	33°44′N	117°14′W
San Jacinto, r., Tx., U.S.	123	30°25′N	95°05′W
San Jacinto, West Fork, r., Tx., U.S.	123	30°35′N	95°37′W
San Javier, Chile (sän-hä-vē′ĕr)	141b	35°35′S	71°43′W
San Jerónimo, Mex.	131a	19°31′N	98°46′W
San Jerónimo de Juárez, Mex. (hå-rō′nē-mô dā hwä′râz)	130	17°08′N	100°30′W
San Joaquin, Ven.	143b	10°16′N	67°47′W
San Joaquin, r., Ca., U.S. (săn hwä-kēn′)	118	37°10′N	120°51′W
San Joaquin Valley, Ca., U.S.	118	36°45′N	120°30′W
San Jorge, Golfo, b., Arg. (gôl-fô-săn-кô′r-кĕ)	144	46°15′S	66°45′W
San José, C.R. (săn hô-sā′)	129	9°57′N	84°05′W
San Jose, Phil.	213a	12°22′N	121°04′E
San Jose, Phil.	213a	15°49′N	120°57′E
San Jose, Ca., U.S. (săn hô-zā′)	104	37°20′N	121°54′W
San José, i., Mex. (кô-sĕ′)	128	25°00′N	110°35′W
San José, Isla de, i., Pan. (ē′s-lä-dĕ-săn hô-sā′)	133	8°17′N	79°20′W
San Jose, Rio, r., N.M., U.S. (săn hô-zā′)	119	35°15′N	108°10′W
San José de Feliciano, Arg. (då lä ĕs-kē′nä)	144	30°26′S	58°44′W
San José de Gauribe, Ven. (sän-hô-sĕ′dĕ-gàōō-rē′bĕ)	143b	9°51′N	65°49′W
San José de las Lajas, Cuba (sän-кô-sĕ′dĕ-läs-lá′käs)	135a	22°58′N	82°10′W
San José Iturbide, Mex. (ē-tōōr-bē′dĕ)	130	21°00′N	100°24′W
San Juan, Arg. (hwän′)	144	31°36′S	68°29′W
San Juan, Col. (hòá′n)	142a	3°23′N	73°48′W
San Juan, Dom. Rep. (săn hwän′)	135	18°50′N	71°15′W
San Juan, Phil.	213a	16°41′N	120°20′E
San Juan, P.R. (săn hwän′)	129	18°30′N	66°10′W
San Juan, prov., Arg.	144	31°00′S	69°30′W
San Juan, r., Mex. (sän-hōō-än′)	131	18°10′N	95°23′W
San Juan, r., N.A.	129	10°58′N	84°18′W
San Juan, r., U.S.	106	36°30′N	109°00′W
San Juan, Cabezas de, c., P.R.	129b	18°29′N	65°30′W
San Juan, Cabo, c., Eq. Gui.	236	1°08′N	9°23′E
San Juan, Pico, mtn., Cuba (pē′kô-sän-kòá′n)	134	21°55′N	80°00′W
San Juan, Río, r., Mex. (rē′ō-sän-hwän)	122	25°35′N	99°15′W
San Juan Bautista, Para. (sän hwän′ bou-tēs′tä)	144	26°48′S	57°09′W
San Juan Capistrano, Mex. (sän-hōō-än′ kä-pēs-trä′nô)	130	22°41′N	104°07′W
San Juan Creek, r., Ca., U.S. (săn hwän′)	118	35°24′N	120°12′W
San Juan de Guadalupe, Mex. (sän hwan dā gwä-dhä-lōō′pā)	122	24°37′N	102°43′W
San Juan del Norte, Nic.	133	10°55′N	83°44′W
San Juan del Norte, Bahía de, b., Nic.	133	11°12′N	83°40′W
San Juan de los Lagos, Mex. (sän-hōō-än′dā los lä′gôs)	130	21°15′N	102°18′W
San Juan de los Lagos, r., Mex. (dā lōs lä′gôs)	130	21°13′N	102°12′W
San Juan de los Morros, Ven. (dĕ-lôs-mô′r-rôs)	143b	9°54′N	67°22′W
San Juan del Río, Mex.	130	20°21′N	99°59′W
San Juan del Río, Mex. (săn hwän del rē′ō)	122	24°47′N	104°29′W
San Juan del Sur, Nic. (dĕl sōōr)	128	11°15′N	85°53′W
San Juan Evangelista, Mex. (sän-hōō-ä′n-å-väŋ-kå-lēs′ta′)	131	17°57′N	95°08′W
San Juan Island, i., Wa., U.S.	116a	48°28′N	123°08′W
San Juan Islands, is., Can. (săn hwän)	94	48°49′N	123°14′W
San Juan Islands, is., Wa., U.S.	186a	48°36′N	122°50′W
San Juan Ixtenco, Mex. (ēx-tĕ′n-kô)	131	19°14′N	97°52′W
San Juan Martínez, Cuba	134	22°15′N	83°50′W
San Juan Mountains, mts., Co., U.S. (san hwán′)	106	37°50′N	107°30′W
San Julián, Arg. (sän hōō-lyá′n)	144	49°17′S	68°02′W
San Justo, Arg. (hōōs′tō)	144a	34°40′S	58°33′W
Sankanbiriwa, mtn., S.L.	234	8°56′N	10°48′W
Sankarani, r., Afr. (sän′kä-rä′nē)	230	11°10′N	8°35′W
Sankt Gallen, Switz.	161	47°25′N	9°22′E
Sankt Moritz, Switz. (zäŋkt mō′rĭts) (sănt mō′rēts)	168	46°31′N	9°50′E
Sankt Pölten, Aus. (zäŋkt-pûl′tĕn)	168	48°12′N	15°38′E
Sankt Veit, Aus. (zäŋкт vīt′)	168	46°46′N	14°20′E
Sankuru, r., D.R.C. (săn-kōō′rōō)	232	4°00′S	22°35′E
San Lázaro, Cabo, c., Mex. (sän-lá′zä-rō)	128	24°58′N	113°30′W
San Leandro, Ca., U.S. (săn lē-ăn′drō)	116b	37°43′N	122°10′W
Şanlıurfa, Tur.	198	37°20′N	38°45′E
San Lorenzo, Arg. (sän lô-rĕn′zô)	144	32°46′S	60°44′W
San Lorenzo, Hond. (sän lô-rĕn′zô)	132	13°24′N	87°24′W
San Lorenzo, Ca., U.S. (săn lô-rĕn′zô)	116b	37°41′N	122°08′W
San Lorenzo de El Escorial, Spain	172	40°36′N	4°09′W
Sanlúcar de Barrameda, Spain (sän-lōō′kär)	162	36°46′N	6°21′W
San Lucas, Bol. (lōō′kás)	142	20°12′S	65°06′W
San Lucas, Cabo, c., Mex.	128	22°45′N	109°45′W
San Luis, Arg. (lô-ēs′)	144	33°16′S	66°15′W
San Luis, Col. (lòē′s)	142a	6°03′N	74°57′W
San Luis, Cuba	135	20°15′N	75°50′W
San Luis, Guat.	132	14°38′N	89°42′W
San Luis, prov., Arg.	144	32°45′S	66°00′W
San Luis de la Paz, Mex. (dā lä päz′)	130	21°17′N	100°32′W
San Luis del Cordero, Mex. (dĕl kôr-dā′rō)	122	25°25′N	104°20′W
San Luis Obispo, Ca., U.S. (ô-bĭs′pō)	104	35°18′N	120°40′W
San Luis Obispo Bay, b., Ca., U.S.	118	35°07′N	121°05′W
San Luis Potosí, Mex.	128	22°08′N	100°58′W
San Luis Potosí, state, Mex.	128	22°45′N	101°45′W
San Luis Rey, r., Ca., U.S. (rā′ē)	118	33°22′N	117°06′W
San Manuel, Az., U.S. (săn măn′ū-ĕl)	119	32°30′N	110°45′W
San Marcial, N.M., U.S. (săn mar-shäl′)	119	33°40′N	107°00′W
San Marco, Italy (sän mär′kô)	174	41°53′N	15°50′E
San Marcos, Guat. (mär′kôs)	132	14°57′N	91°49′W
San Marcos, Mex.	130	16°46′N	99°23′W
San Marcos, Tx., U.S. (săn mär′kôs)	123	29°53′N	97°56′W
San Marcos, r., Tx., U.S.	122	30°08′N	98°15′W
San Marcos de Colón, Hond. (sän-má′r-kōs-dĕ-kô-lô′n)	132	13°17′N	86°50′W
San Maria di Léuca, Cape, c., Italy (dē-lĕ′ōō-kä)	163	39°47′N	18°20′E
San Marino, S. Mar. (sän mä-rē′nô)	174	44°55′N	12°26′E
San Marino, Ca., U.S. (săn mẽr-ē′nô)	117a	34°07′N	118°06′W
San Marino, nation, Eur.	154	43°40′N	13°00′E
San Martín, Col. (sän mär-tē′n)	142a	3°42′N	73°44′W
San Martín, vol., Mex. (mär-tē′n)	131	18°36′N	95°11′W
San Martín, l., S.A.	144	48°15′S	72°30′W
San Martín Chalchicuautla, Mex.	130	21°22′N	98°39′W
San Martin de la Vega, Spain (sän mär ten′ dā lä vā′gä)	173a	40°12′N	3°34′W
San Martín Hidalgo, Mex. (sän mär-tē′n-ē-dä′l-gô)	130	20°27′N	103°55′W
San Mateo, Mex.	131	16°59′N	97°04′W
San Mateo, Ca., U.S. (săn mä-tā′ô)	116b	37°34′N	122°20′W
San Mateo, Ven. (sän má-tĕ′ô)	143b	9°45′N	64°34′W
San Matías, Golfo, b., Arg. (sän mä-tē′äs)	144	41°30′S	63°45′W
Sanmen Wan, b., China	209	29°00′N	122°15′E
San Miguel, El Sal. (sän mē-gāl′)	128	13°28′N	88°11′W
San Miguel, Mex. (sän mē-gāl′)	131	18°18′N	97°09′W
San Miguel, Pan.	133	8°26′N	78°55′W
San Miguel, Phil. (sän mē-gĕ′l)	213a	15°09′N	120°56′E
San Miguel, Ven. (sän mē-gĕ′l)	143b	9°56′N	64°58′W
San Miguel, vol., El Sal.	132	13°27′N	88°17′W
San Miguel, i., Ca., U.S.	118	34°03′N	120°23′W
San Miguel, r., Bol. (sän-mē-gĕl′)	142	13°34′S	63°58′W
San Miguel, r., N.A. (săn mē-gāl′)	131	15°27′N	92°00′W
San Miguel, r., Co., U.S. (săn mē-gĕl′)	119	38°15′N	108°40′W
San Miguel, Bahía, b., Pan. (bä-ē′ä-sän mē-gāl′)	133	8°17′N	78°26′W
San Miguel Bay, b., Phil.	213a	13°55′N	123°12′E
San Miguel de Allende, Mex. (dā ä-lyĕn′dā)	130	20°54′N	100°44′W
San Miguel el Alto, Mex. (ĕl äl′tô)	130	21°03′N	102°26′W
Sannār, Sudan	231	14°25′N	33°30′E
San Narcisco, Phil. (sän när-sē′sô)	213a	15°01′N	120°05′E
San Narcisco, Phil.	213a	13°34′N	122°33′E
San Nicolás, Arg. (sän nē-kô-lá′s)	144	33°20′S	60°14′W
San Nicolas, Phil. (nē-kô-läs′)	213a	16°05′N	120°45′E
San Nicolas, i., Ca., U.S. (săn nĭ′kô-lá)	118	33°14′N	119°10′W
San Nicolás, r., Mex.	130	19°40′N	105°08′W
Sanniquellie, Lib.	234	7°22′N	8°43′W
Sannūr, Wādī, Egypt	238b	28°48′N	31°12′E
Sanok, Pol. (sä′nôk)	169	49°31′N	22°13′E
San Pablo, Phil. (sän-pä-blô)	213a	14°05′N	121°20′E
San Pablo, Ca., U.S. (săn păb′lō)	116b	37°58′N	122°21′W
San Pablo, Ven. (sän-pá′blô)	143b	9°46′N	65°04′W
San Pablo, r., Pan. (sän päb′lô)	133	8°12′N	81°12′W
San Pablo Bay, b., Ca., U.S. (săn păb′lō)	116b	38°04′N	122°25′W
San Pablo Res, Ca., U.S.	116b	37°55′N	122°12′W
San Pascual, Phil. (päs-kwäl′)	213a	13°08′N	122°59′E
San Pedro, Arg. (sän pā′drô)	144	24°15′S	64°15′W
San Pedro, Arg.	141c	33°41′S	59°42′W
San Pedro, Chile (sän pĕ′drô)	141b	33°54′S	71°27′W
San Pedro, El Sal. (sän pā′drô)	132	13°49′N	88°58′W
San Pedro, Mex. (sän pā′drô)	131	18°38′N	92°25′W
San Pedro, Para. (sän-pĕ′drô)	144	24°13′S	57°00′W
San Pedro, Ca., U.S. (săn pē′drô)	117a	33°44′N	118°17′W
San Pedro, r., Cuba (sän-pĕ′drô)	134	21°05′N	78°15′W
San Pedro, r., Mex. (sän pā′drô)	130	22°08′N	104°59′W
San Pedro, r., Mex.	122	27°56′N	105°50′W
San Pedro, r., Az., U.S.	119	32°48′N	110°37′W
San Pedro, Río de, r., Mex.	130	21°51′N	102°24′W
San Pedro, Río de, r., N.A.	131	18°23′N	92°13′W
San Pedro Bay, b., Ca., U.S. (săn pē′drô)	117a	33°42′N	118°12′W
San Pedro de las Colonias, Mex. (dĕ-läs-kô-lô′nyäs)	122	25°47′N	102°58′W
San Pedro de Macorís, Dom. Rep. (sän-pĕ′drō-dā mä-kô-rēs′)	135	18°30′N	69°30′W
San Pedro Lagunillas, Mex. (sän pā′drô lä-gōō-nēl′yäs)	130	21°12′N	104°47′W
San Pedro Sula, Hond. (sän pā′drô sōō′lä)	132	15°29′N	88°01′W
San Pietro, Isola di, i., Italy (ē′sō-lä-dē-sän pyā′trô)	174	39°09′N	8°15′E
San Quentin, Ca., U.S. (săn kwĕn-tēn′)	116b	37°57′N	122°29′W
San Quintin, Phil. (sän kēn-tēn′)	213a	15°59′N	120°47′E
San Rafael, Arg. (sän rä-fä-ĕl′)	144	34°30′S	68°13′W
San Rafael, Col. (sän-rä-fä-ĕ′l)	142a	6°18′N	75°02′W
San Rafael, Ca., U.S. (săn rá-fĕl)	116b	37°58′N	122°31′W
San Rafael, r., Ut., U.S. (săn rá-fĕl′)	119	39°05′N	110°50′W
San Rafael, Cabo, c., Dom. Rep. (ká′bô)	135	19°00′N	68°50′W
San Ramón, C.R.	133	10°07′N	84°30′W
San Ramon, Ca., U.S. (săn rä-mōn′)	116b	37°47′N	122°59′W
San Remo, Italy (sän rā′mô)	174	43°48′N	7°46′E
San Roque, Col. (sän-rô′kĕ)	142a	6°29′N	75°00′W
San Roque, Spain	172	36°13′N	5°23′W
San Saba, Tx., U.S. (săn sä′bá)	122	31°12′N	98°43′W
San Saba, r., Tx., U.S.	122	30°58′N	99°12′W
San Salvador, El Sal. (săn säl-vä-dōr′)	128	13°45′N	89°11′W
San Salvador (Watling), i., Bah. (săn săl′vá-dôr)	135	24°05′N	74°30′W
San Salvador, i., Ec.	142	0°14′S	90°50′W
San Salvador, r., Ur. (sän-säl-vä-dô′r)	141c	33°42′S	58°04′W
Sansanné-Mango, Togo (sän-sá-nā′ mäɴ′gō)	230	10°21′N	0°28′E
San Sebastian, Spain (sän sá-bås-tyän′)	230	28°09′N	17°11′W

ăt; finăl; rāte; senåte; ärm; åsk; sofá; fâre; ch-choose; dh-as th in other; bē; ēvent; bĕt; recĕnt; cratẽr; g-gō; gh-guttural g; bĭt; ĭ-short neutral; rīde; к-guttural k as ch in German ich;

PRONOUNCING INDEX

San Sebastián – Sapitwa 347

PLACE (Pronunciation)	PAGE	LAT.	LONG.
San Sebastián *see* Donostia-San Sebastián, Spain	154	43°19'N	1°59'W
San Sebastián, Ven. (sän-sĕ-bäs-tyä'n)	143b	9°58'N	67°11'W
San Sebastiàn de los Reyes, Spain	173a	40°33'N	3°38'W
San Severo, Italy (sän sĕ-vâ'rō)	163	41°43'N	15°24'E
Sanshui, China (sän-shwā)	205	23°14'N	112°51'E
San Simon Creek, r., Az., U.S. (sån sī-mōn')	119	32°45'N	109°30'W
Santa Ana, El Sal.	128	14°02'N	89°35'W
Santa Ana, Mex. (sän'tä ä'nä)	130	19°18'N	98°10'W
Santa Ana, Ca., U.S. (săn'tȧ ăn'ȧ)	104	33°45'N	117°52'W
Santa Ana, r., Ca., U.S.	117a	33°41'N	117°57'W
Santa Ana Mountains, mts., Ca., U.S.	117a	33°44'N	117°36'W
Santa Anna, Tx., U.S.	122	31°44'N	99°18'W
Santa Antão, i., C.V. (sä-tä-ä'n-zhĕ-lō)	230b	17°20'N	26°05'W
Santa Bárbara, Braz. (sän-tä-bá'r-bä-rä)	143	19°57'S	43°25'W
Santa Bárbara, Hond.	132	14°52'N	88°20'W
Santa Barbara, Mex.	122	26°48'N	105°50'W
Santa Barbara, Ca., U.S.	104	34°26'N	119°43'W
Santa Barbara, i., Ca., U.S.	118	33°30'N	118°44'W
Santa Barbara Channel, strt., Ca., U.S.	118	34°15'N	120°00'W
Santa Branca, Braz. (sän-tä-brä'n-kä)	141a	23°25'S	45°52'W
Santa Catalina, i., Ca., U.S.	106	33°29'N	118°37'W
Santa Catalina, Cerro de, mtn., Pan.	133	8°39'N	81°36'W
Santa Catalina, Gulf of, b., Ca., U.S. (săn'tȧ kă-tȧ-lē'nȧ)	118	33°00'N	117°58'W
Santa Catarina, Mex. (sän'tä kä-tä-rē'nä)	122	25°41'N	100°27'W
Santa Catarina, state, Braz. (sän-tä-kä-tä-rē'nä)	144	27°15'S	50°30'W
Santa Catarina, r., Mex.	130	16°31'N	98°39'W
Santa Clara, Cuba (sän't klä'rá)	129	22°25'N	80°00'W
Santa Clara, Mex.	122	24°29'N	103°22'W
Santa Clara, Ur.	144	32°46'S	54°51'W
Santa Clara, Ca., U.S. (săn'tȧ klârȧ)	114	37°21'N	121°56'W
Santa Clara, vol., Nic.	132	12°44'N	87°00'W
Santa Clara, r., Ca., U.S. (săn'tȧ klă'rȧ)	118	34°22'N	118°53'W
Santa Clara, Bahía de, b., Cuba (bä-ē'ä-dĕ-sän-tä-klä-rä)	134	23°05'N	80°50'W
Santa Clara, Sierra, mts., Mex. (sē-ĕ'r-rä-sän'tä klä'rä)	128	27°30'N	113°50'W
Santa Clara Indian Reservation, I.R., N.M., U.S.	119	35°59'N	106°10'W
Santa Cruz, Bol. (sän'tá krōōz')	142	17°45'S	63°03'W
Santa Cruz, Braz. (sän-tä-krōō's)	144	29°43'S	52°15'W
Santa Cruz, Braz.	144b	22°55'S	43°41'W
Santa Cruz, Chile	141b	34°38'S	71°21'W
Santa Cruz, C.R.	132	10°16'N	85°37'W
Santa Cruz, Mex.	122	25°50'N	105°25'W
Santa Cruz, Phil.	213a	13°28'N	122°02'E
Santa Cruz, Phil.	213a	15°46'N	119°53'E
Santa Cruz, Phil.	213a	14°17'N	121°25'E
Santa Cruz, Ca., U.S.	104	36°59'N	122°02'W
Santa Cruz, prov., Arg.	144	48°00'S	70°00'W
Santa Cruz, i., Ec. (sän-tä-krōō'z)	142	0°38'S	90°20'W
Santa Cruz, r., Arg. (sän'tä krōōz')	144	50°05'S	71°00'W
Santa Cruz, r., Az., U.S. (săn'tȧ krōōz')	119	32°30'N	111°30'W
Santa Cruz Barillas, Guat. (sän-tä-krōō'z-bä-rē'l-yäs)	132	15°47'N	91°22'W
Santa Cruz del Sur, Cuba (sän-tä-krōō's-dĕl-sōō'r)	134	20°45'N	78°00'W
Santa Cruz de Tenerife, Spain (sän'tä krōōz dā tā-nå-rē'fā)	228	28°07'N	15°27'W
Santa Cruz Islands, is., Sol. Is.	221	10°58'S	166°47'E
Santa Cruz Mountains, mts., Ca., U.S. (săn'tȧ krōōz')	116b	37°30'N	122°19'W
Santa Domingo, Cay, i., Bah.	135	21°50'N	75°45'W
Santa Fe, Arg. (sän'tä fā')	144	31°33'S	60°45'W
Santa Fé, Cuba (sän-tä-fē')	134	21°45'N	82°40'W
Santa Fe, Spain (sän'tä-fā')	172	37°12'N	3°43'W
Santa Fe, N.M., U.S. (săn'tȧ fā')	104	35°40'N	106°00'W
Santa Fe, prov., Arg. (sän'tä fā')	144	32°00'S	61°15'W
Santa Fe de Bogotá *see* Bogotá, Col.	142	4°36'N	74°05'W
Santa Filomena, Braz. (sän-tä-fē-lō-mĕ'nä)	143	9°09'S	44°45'W
Santa Genoveva, mtn., Mex. (sän-tä-hĕ-nō-vĕ'vä)	128	23°30'N	110°00'W
Santai, China (san-tī)	204	31°02'N	105°02'E
Santa Inés, Ven. (sän'tä ē-nĕ's)	143b	9°54'N	64°21'W
Santa Inés, i., Chile (sän'tä ē-nās')	144	53°45'S	74°15'W
Santa Isabel, i., Sol. Is.	221	7°57'S	159°28'E
Santa Isabel, Pico de, mtn., Eq. Gui.	235	3°35'N	8°46'E
Santa Lucia, Cuba (sän'tä lōō-sē'ä)	134	21°15'N	77°30'W
Santa Lucia, Ur. (sän-tä-lōō-sē'ä)	144	34°27'S	56°23'W
Santa Lucia, Ven.	143b	10°18'N	66°40'W
Santa Lucia, r., Ur.	141c	34°19'S	56°13'W
Santa Lucia Bay, b., Cuba (sän'tä lōō-sē'ä)	134	22°55'N	84°20'W
Santa Margarita, i., Mex. (sän'tä mär-gä-rē'tä)	128	24°15'N	112°00'W
Santa Maria, Braz. (sän'tä mä-rē'ä)	144	29°40'S	54°00'W
Santa Maria, Italy (sän-tä mä-rē'ä)	174	41°05'N	14°15'E
Santa Maria, Phil. (sän-tä-mä-rē'ä)	213a	14°48'N	120°57'E
Santa Maria, Ca., U.S. (săn-tȧ mȧ-rē'ȧ)	118	34°57'N	120°28'W
Santa María, vol., Guat.	132	14°45'N	91°33'W
Santa Maria, r., Mex. (sän'tä mä-rē'ä)	130	21°33'N	100°17'W
Santa Maria, Cabo de, c., Port. (ká'bō-dĕ-sän-tä-mä-rē'ä)	172	36°58'N	7°54'W
Santa Maria, Cape, c., Bah.	135	23°45'N	75°30'W
Santa Maria, Cayo, i., Cuba	134	22°40'N	79°00'W
Santa María del Oro, Mex. (sän'tä-mä-rē'ä-dĕl-ô-rō)	130	21°21'N	104°35'W
Santa Maria de los Angeles, Mex. (dĕ-lôs-á'n-hĕ-lĕs)	130	22°10'N	103°34'W
Santa María del Río, Mex.	130	21°46'N	100°43'W
Santa María de Ocotán, Mex.	130	22°56'N	104°30'W
Santa Maria Island, i., Port. (sän-tä-mä-rē'ä)	230a	37°09'N	26°02'W
Santa Maria Madalena, Braz.	141a	22°00'S	42°00'W
Santa Marta, Col. (sän'tá mär'tá)	142	11°15'N	74°13'W
Santa Marta, Cabo de, c., Ang.	236	13°52'S	12°25'E
Santa Monica, Ca., U.S. (săn'tȧ mŏn'ĭ-kȧ)	104	34°01'N	118°29'W
Santa Monica Mountains, mts., Ca., U.S.	117a	34°08'N	118°38'W
Santana, r., Braz. (sän-tä'nä)	144b	22°33'S	43°37'W
Santander, Col. (sän-tän-dĕr')	142a	3°00'N	76°25'W
Santander, Spain (sän-tän-dâr')	154	43°27'N	3°50'W
Sant Antoni de Portmany, Spain	173	38°59'N	1°17'E
Santa Paula, Ca., U.S. (săn'tȧ pô'lȧ)	118	34°24'N	119°05'W
Santarém, Braz. (sän-tä-rĕn')	143	2°28'S	54°37'W
Santarém, Port.	172	39°18'N	8°48'W
Santaren Channel, strt., Bah. (săn-tȧ-rĕn')	134	24°15'N	79°30'W
Santa Rita do Sapucai, Braz. (sä-pò-kä'ē)	141a	22°15'S	45°41'W
Santa Rosa, Arg. (sän-tä-rô-sä)	144	36°45'S	64°10'W
Santa Rosa, Col. (sän-tä-rô-sä)	142a	6°38'N	75°26'W
Santa Rosa, Ec.	142	3°29'S	79°55'W
Santa Rosa, Guat. (sän'tä rō'sä)	132	14°21'N	90°16'W
Santa Rosa, Hond.	132	14°45'N	88°51'W
Santa Rosa, Ca., U.S. (săn'tȧ rō'zȧ)	104	38°27'N	122°42'W
Santa Rosa, N.M., U.S. (săn'tȧ rō'sȧ)	120	34°55'N	104°41'W
Santa Rosa, Ven. (sän-tä-rô-sä)	143b	9°37'N	64°10'W
Santa Rosa de Cabal, Col. (sän-tä-rô-sä-dĕ-kä-bä'l)	142a	4°53'N	75°38'W
Santa Rosa de Viterbo, Braz. (sän-tä-rô-sá-dĕ-vē-tĕr'-bô)	141a	21°30'S	47°21'W
Santa Rosa Indian Reservation, I.R., Ca., U.S. (săn'tȧ rō'zȧ')	118	33°28'N	116°50'W
Santa Rosalía, Mex. (sän'tä rō-zä'lē-ä)	128	27°13'N	112°15'W
Santa Rosa Range, mts., Nv., U.S. (săn'tȧ rō'zȧ)	114	41°33'N	117°50'W
Santa Susana, Ca., U.S. (săn'tȧ sōō-zä'nȧ)	117a	34°16'N	118°42'W
Santa Teresa, Arg. (sän-tä-tĕ-rĕ'sä)	141c	33°27'S	60°47'W
Santa Teresa, Ven.	143b	10°14'N	66°40'W
Santa Uxia, Spain	172	42°34'N	8°55'W
Santa Vitória do Palmar, Braz. (sän-tä-vē-tō'ryä-dô-päl-màr)	144	33°30'S	53°16'W
Santa Ynez, r., Ca., U.S. (săn'tȧ ē-nĕz')	118	34°40'N	120°20'W
Santa Ysabel Indian Reservation, I.R., Ca., U.S. (săn-tȧ ĭ-zȧ-bĕl')	118	33°05'N	116°46'W
Santee, Ca., U.S. (săn tē')	118a	32°50'N	116°58'W
Santee, r., S.C., U.S.	107	33°00'N	79°45'W
Sant' Eufemia, Golfo di, b., Italy (gôl-fô-dē-sän-tĕ'ò-fĕ'myä)	174	38°53'N	15°53'E
Sant Feliu de Guixols, Spain	173	41°45'N	3°01'E
Santiago, Braz. (sän-tyä'gô)	144	29°05'S	54°46'W
Santiago, Chile (sän-tē-ä'gô)	144	33°26'S	70°40'W
Santiago, Pan.	129	8°07'N	80°58'W
Santiago, Phil. (sän-tyä'gō)	213a	16°42'N	121°33'E
Santiago, prov., Chile (sän-tyá'gō)	141b	33°28'S	70°55'W
Santiago, i., Phil.	213a	16°29'N	120°03'E
Santiago de Compostela, Spain	162	42°52'N	8°32'W
Santiago de Cuba, Cuba (sän-tyá'gô-dā kōō'bä)	129	20°00'N	75°50'W
Santiago de Cuba, prov., Cuba	134	20°20'N	76°05'W
Santiago de las Vegas, Cuba (sän-tyá'gô-dĕ-läs-vĕ'gäs)	135a	22°58'N	82°23'W
Santiago del Estero, Arg.	144	27°50'S	64°14'W
Santiago del Estero, prov., Arg. (sän-tē-á'gō-dĕl ĕs-tā-rō)	144	27°15'S	63°30'W
Santiago de los Cabelleros, Dom. Rep.	129	19°30'N	70°45'W
Santiago Mountains, mts., Tx., U.S. (sän-tē-ä'gō)	106	30°00'N	103°30'W
Santiago Reservoir, res., Ca., U.S.	117a	33°47'N	117°42'W
Santiago Rodriguez, Dom. Rep. (sän-tyá'gô-rô-drē'gĕz)	135	19°30'N	71°25'W
Santiago Tuxtla, Mex. (sän-tyá'gô-tōō'x-tlä)	131	18°28'N	95°18'W
Santiaguillo, Laguna de, l., Mex. (lä-oō'nä-dĕ-sän-tē-a-gēl'yō)	122	24°51'N	104°43'W
Santisteban del Puerto, Spain (sän'tē stå-bän'dĕl pwĕr'tō)	172	38°15'N	3°12'W
Sant Mateu, Spain	173	40°26'N	0°09'E
Santo Amaro, Braz. (sän'tò ä-mä'rò)	143	12°32'S	38°33'W
Santo Amaro de Campos, Braz.	141a	22°01'S	41°05'W
Santo André, Braz.	141a	23°40'S	46°31'W
Santo Angelo, Braz. (sän-tô-á'n-zhĕ-lô)	144	28°16'S	53°59'W
Santo Antônio do Monte, Braz. (sän-tô-än-tô'nyô-dô-môn'tĕ)	141a	20°06'S	45°18'W
Santo Domingo, Cuba (sän'tô-dōmĭn'gô)	134	22°35'N	80°20'W
Santo Domingo, Dom. Rep. (săn'tô dô-mĭn'gô)	129	18°30'N	69°55'W
Santo Domingo, Nic. (sän-tô-dô-mē'n-gō)	133	12°15'N	84°56'W
Santo Domingo de la Caizada, Spain (dā lä käl-thä'dä)	172	42°27'N	2°55'W
Santoña, Spain (sän-tō'nyä)	172	43°25'N	3°27'W
Santos, Braz. (sän'tozh)	143	23°58'S	46°20'W
Santos Dumont, Braz. (sän'tôs-dô-mô'nt)	143	21°28'S	43°33'W
Sanuki, Japan (sä'nōō-kē)	211a	35°16'N	139°53'E
San Urbano, Arg. (sän-ōr-bä'nō)	141c	33°39'S	61°28'W
San Valentin, Monte, mtn., Chile (sän-vä-lĕn-tē'n)	144	46°41'S	73°30'W
San Vicente, Arg. (sän-vē-sĕn'tĕ)	141c	35°00'S	58°26'W
San Vicente, Chile	141b	34°25'S	71°06'W
San Vicente, El Sal. (sän vē-sĕn'tå)	132	13°41'N	88°43'W
San Vicente de Alcántara, Spain	172	39°24'N	7°08'W
San Vito al Tagliamento, Italy (san vē'tô)	174	45°53'N	12°52'E
San Xavier Indian Reservation, I.R., Az., U.S. (x-ä'vĭēr)	119	32°07'N	111°12'W
San Ysidro, Ca., U.S. (săn ysĭ-drō')	118a	32°33'N	117°02'W
Sanyuanli, China (sän-yüän-lē)	207a	23°11'N	113°16'E
São Bernardo do Campo, Braz. (soun-bĕr-nàr'dô-dô-kà'm-pô)	141a	23°44'S	46°33'W
São Borja, Braz. (soun-bôr-zhä)	144	28°44'S	55°59'W
São Carlos, Braz. (soun kär'lōzh)	143	22°02'S	47°54'W
São Cristovão, Braz. (soun-krĕs-tō-voun)	143	11°04'S	37°11'W
São Fidélis, Braz. (soun-fē-dĕ'lēs)	141a	21°41'S	41°45'W
São Francisco, Braz. (soun frän-sēsh'kō)	143	15°59'S	44°42'W
São Francisco, r., Braz. (sän-frän-sē's-kō)	143	8°56'S	40°20'W
São Francisco do Sul, Braz. (soun frän-sēsh'kō-dô-sōō'l)	144	26°15'S	48°42'W
São Gabriel, Braz. (soun'gä-brē-ĕl')	144	30°28'S	54°11'W
São Geraldo, Braz. (soun-zhĕ-rä'l-dô)	141a	21°01'S	42°49'W
São Gonçalo, Braz. (soun'gŏn-sä'lò)	141a	22°55'S	43°04'W
Sao Hill, Tan.	237	8°20'S	35°12'E
São João, Gui.-B.	234	11°32'N	15°26'W
São João da Barra, Braz. (soun-zhôun-dä-bà'rä)	141a	21°40'S	41°03'W
São João da Boa Vista, Braz. (soun-zhôun-dä-bôä-vē's-tä)	141a	21°58'S	46°45'W
São João del Rei, Braz. (soun zhô-oun'dĕl-rā)	144	21°08'S	44°14'W
São João de Meriti, Braz. (soun-zhôun-dĕ-mĕ-rē-tē)	144b	22°47'S	43°22'W
São João do Araguaia, Braz. (soun zhô-oun'dô-ä-rä-gwä'yä)	143	5°29'S	48°44'W
São João dos Lampas, Port. (soun' zhô-oun' dôzh län-pàzh')	173b	38°52'N	9°24'W
São João Nepomuceno, Braz. (soun-zhôun-nĕ-pô-mōō-sĕ-nō)	141a	21°33'S	43°00'W
São Jorge Island, i., Port. (soun zhôr'zhĕ)	230a	38°28'N	27°34'W
São José do Rio Pardo, Braz. (soun-zhô-sĕ'dô-rē'ō-pà'r-dō)	141a	21°36'S	46°50'W
São José do Rio Prêto, Braz. (soun zhô-zĕ'dô-re'ō-prĕ-tō)	143	20°57'S	49°12'W
São José dos Campos, Braz. (soun zhô-zā'dōzh kän pōzh')	141a	23°12'S	45°53'W
São Leopoldo, Braz. (soun-lĕ-ō-pôl'dô)	144	29°46'S	51°09'W
São Luis, Braz.	143	2°31'S	43°14'W
São Luis do Paraitinga, Braz. (soun-lōōē's-dô-pä-rä-ē-tē'n-gä)	141a	23°15'S	45°18'W
São Manuel, r., Braz.	143	8°28'S	57°07'E
São Mateus, Braz. (soun mä-tā'ōzh)	143	18°44'S	39°45'W
São Mateus, Braz.	144b	22°49'S	43°23'W
São Miguel Arcanjo, Braz. (soun-mē-gĕ'l-ár-kän-zhō)	141a	23°54'S	47°59'W
São Miguel Island, i., Port.	230a	37°59'N	26°38'W
Saona, i., Dom. Rep. (sä-ō'nä)	135	18°10'N	68°55'W
Saône, r., Fr. (sōn)	156	47°00'N	5°30'E
São Nicolau, i., C.V. (soun' nē-kō-loun')	230b	16°19'N	25°19'W
São Paulo, Braz. (soun' pou'lò)	143	23°34'S	46°38'W
São Paulo, state, Braz. (soun pou'lò)	143	21°45'S	50°47'W
São Paulo de Olivença, Braz. (soun'pou'lòdå ô-lē-vĕn'sȧ)	142	3°32'S	68°46'W
São Pedro, Braz. (soun-pĕ'drô)	141a	22°34'S	47°54'W
São Pedro de Aldeia, Braz. (soun-pĕ'drô-dĕ-äl-dĕ'yä)	141a	22°50'S	42°04'W
São Pedro e São Paulo, Rocedos, rocks, Braz.	139	1°50'N	30°00'W
São Raimundo Nonato, Braz. (soun' rī-mò'n-do nō-nä'tō)	143	9°09'S	42°32'W
São Roque, Braz. (soun' rō'kĕ)	141a	23°32'S	47°08'W
São Roque, Cabo de, c., Braz. (kä'bo-dĕ-soun' rō'kĕ)	143	5°06'S	35°11'W
São Sebastião, Braz. (soun sȧ-bäs-tē-oun')	141a	23°48'S	45°25'W
São Sebastião, Ilha de, i., Braz.	141a	23°52'S	45°22'W
São Sebastião do Paraíso, Braz.	141a	20°54'S	46°58'W
São Simão, Braz. (soun-sē-moun)	141a	21°30'S	47°33'W
São Tiago, i., C.V. (soun tē-ä'gô)	230b	15°09'N	24°45'W
São Tomé, S. Tom./P.	230	0°20'N	6°44'E
Sao Tome and Principe, nation, Afr. (prēn'sē-pĕ)	230	1°00'N	6°00'E
Saoura, Oued, r., Alg.	230	29°39'N	1°42'W
São Vicente, Braz. (soun ve-se'n-tĕ)	143	23°57'S	46°25'W
São Vicente, i., C.V. (soun vē-sĕn'tä)	230b	16°51'N	24°35'W
São Vicente, Cabo de, c., Port. (ká'bō-dĕ-sän-vē-sĕ'n-tĕ)	156	37°03'N	9°31'W
Sapele, Nig. (sä-pā'lā)	230	5°54'N	5°41'E
Sapitwa, mtn., Mwi.	237	15°58'S	35°38'E

ng-sing; ŋ-baŋk; ɴ-nasalized n; nŏd; cŏmmit; ōld; ôbey; ôrder; oi-boil; fōōd; ò-as oo in foot; ou-out; s-soft; sh-dish; th-thin; pūre; ûnite; ûrn; stŭd; circŭs; ü-as in French tu; '-indeterminate vowel.

348 Sa Pobla – Segura

PRONOUNCING INDEX

PLACE (Pronunciation)	PAGE	LAT.	LONG.
Sa Pobla, Spain	173	39°46´N	3°02´E
Sapozhok, Russia (sä-pô-zhôk´)	176	53°58´N	40°44´E
Sapporo, Japan (säp-pô´rō)	205	43°02´N	141°29´E
Sapronovo, Russia (såp-rô´nô-vô)	186b	55°13´N	38°25´E
Sapucaí, r., Braz. (sä-pōō-kå-ē´)	141a	22°20´S	45°53´W
Sapucaia, Braz. (sä-pōō-kä´yá)	141a	22°01´S	42°54´W
Sapucaí Mirim, r., Braz. (sä-pōō-kå-ē´mē-rēɴ)	141a	21°06´S	47°03´W
Sapulpa, Ok., U.S. (sá-pŭl´pá)	121	36°01´N	96°05´W
Saqqez, Iran	201	36°14´N	46°16´E
Saquarema, Braz. (sä-kwä-rĕ-mä)	141a	22°56´S	42°32´W
Sara, Wa., U.S. (sä´rä)	116c	45°45´N	122°42´W
Sara, Bahr, r., Chad (bär)	231	8°19´N	17°44´E
Sarajevo, Bos. (sä-rä-yĕv´ō) (så-rä´ya-vô)	154	43°50´N	18°26´E
Sarakhs, Iran	201	36°32´N	61°11´E
Sarana, Russia (sá-rä´ná)	186a	56°31´N	57°44´E
Saranac Lake, N.Y., U.S.	109	44°20´N	74°05´W
Saranac Lake, l., N.Y., U.S. (săr´á-năk)	109	44°15´N	74°20´W
Sarandi, Arg. (sä-rän´dê)	144a	34°41´S	58°21´W
Sarandi Grande, Ur. (sä-rän´dē-grän´dĕ)	141c	33°42´S	56°21´W
Saranley, Som.	238a	2°28´N	42°15´E
Saransk, Russia (sá-ränsk´)	178	54°10´N	45°10´E
Sarany, Russia (sá-rá´nĭ)	186a	58°33´N	58°48´E
Sara Peak, mtn., Nig.	235	9°37´N	9°25´E
Sarapul, Russia (sä-räpòl´)	180	56°28´N	53°50´E
Sarasota, Fl., U.S. (săr-á-sōtá)	125a	27°27´N	82°30´W
Saratoga, Tx., U.S. (săr-á-tō´gá)	123	30°17´N	94°31´W
Saratoga, Wa., U.S.	116a	48°04´N	122°29´W
Saratoga Pass, Wa., U.S.	116a	48°09´N	122°33´W
Saratoga Springs, N.Y., U.S. (sprĭngz)	109	43°05´N	74°50´W
Saratov, Russia (sá rä´tôf)	178	51°30´N	45°30´E
Saravane, Laos	209	15°48´N	106°40´E
Sarawak, hist. reg., Malay. (sá-rä´wäk)	212	2°30´N	112°45´E
Sárbogárd, Hung. (shär´bô-gärd)	169	46°53´N	18°38´E
Sarcee Indian Reserve, I.R., Can. (sär´sê)	102e	50°58´N	114°23´W
Sarcelles, Fr.	171b	49°00´N	2°23´E
Sardalas, Libya	230	25°59´N	10°33´E
Sardinia, i., Italy (sär-dĭn´ĭá)	156	40°08´N	9°05´E
Sardis, Ms., U.S. (sär´dĭs)	124	34°26´N	89°55´W
Sardis Lake, res., Ms., U.S.	124	34°27´N	89°43´W
Sargent, Ne., U.S. (sär´jĕnt)	112	41°40´N	99°38´W
Sarh, Chad (är-chan-bō´)	231	9°09´N	18°23´E
Sarikamis, Tur.	181	40°30´N	42°40´E
Sariñena, Spain (sä-rēn-yĕ´nä)	173	41°46´N	0°11´W
Sark, i., Guern. (särk)	170	49°28´N	2°22´W
Şarköy, Tur. (shär´kû-ê)	175	40°39´N	27°07´E
Sarmiento, Monte, mtn., Chile (mô´n-tĕ-sär-myĕn´tō)	144	54°28´S	70°40´W
Sarnia, Can. (sär´nê-á)	91	43°00´N	82°25´W
Sarno, Italy (sä´r-nô)	173c	40°35´N	14°38´E
Sarny, Ukr. (sär´nê)	181	51°17´N	26°39´E
Saronikós Kólpos, b., Grc.	175	37°51´N	23°30´E
Saros Körfezi, b., Tur. (sä´rôs)	175	40°30´N	26°20´E
Sárospatak, Hung. (shä´rôsh-pô´tôk)	169	48°19´N	21°35´E
Šar Planina, mts., Yugo. (shär plä´nê-na)	175	42°07´N	21°54´E
Sarpsborg, Nor. (särps´bôrg)	166	59°17´N	11°07´E
Sarrebourg, Fr. (sär-bōōr´)	171	48°44´N	7°02´E
Sarreguemines, Fr. (sär-gē-mēn´)	161	49°06´N	7°05´E
Sarria, Spain (sär´ê-ä)	162	42°14´N	7°17´W
Sarstun, r., N.A. (särs-tōō´n)	132	15°50´N	89°26´W
Sartène, Fr. (sär-tĕn´)	174	41°36´N	8°59´E
Sarthe, r., Fr. (särt)	161	47°44´N	0°32´W
Şärur, Azer.	182	39°33´N	44°58´E
Sárvár, Hung. (shär´vär)	168	47°14´N	16°55´E
Sarych, Mys, c., Ukr. (mĭs sá-rēch´)	181	44°25´N	33°00´E
Saryesik-Atyraū, des., Kaz.	183	45°30´N	76°00´E
Sary-Ishikotrau, Peski, des., Kyrg. (sä´rê ē´ shēk-ō´trou)	183	46°12´N	75°30´E
Sarysū, r., Kaz. (sä´rē-sōō)	183	47°47´N	69°14´E
Sasarām, India (sŭs-ŭ-räm´)	199	25°00´N	84°00´E
Sasayama, Japan (sä´sä-yä´mä)	211	35°05´N	135°14´E
Sasebo, Japan (sä´så-bô)	205	33°12´N	129°43´E
Saskatchewan, prov., Can.	90	54°46´N	107°40´W
Saskatchewan, r., Can. (săs-kăch´ê-wän)	92	53°45´N	103°20´W
Saskatoon, Can. (săs-ká-tōōn´)	90	52°07´N	106°38´W
Sasolburg, S. Afr.	238c	26°52´S	27°47´E
Sasovo, Russia (sás´ô-vô)	180	54°20´N	42°00´E
Saspamco, Tx., U.S. (săs-păm´cō)	117d	29°13´N	98°18´W
Sassandra, C. Iv.	234	4°58´N	6°05´W
Sassandra, r., C. Iv. (sás-sän´drá)	230	5°35´N	6°25´W
Sassari, Italy (säs´sä-rê)	162	40°44´N	8°33´E
Sassnitz, Ger. (säs´nêts)	168	54°31´N	13°37´E
Satadougou, Mali (sä-tá-dōō-gōō´)	234	12°21´N	12°07´W
Säter, Swe. (sĕ´tĕr)	166	60°21´N	15°50´E
Satilla, r., Ga., U.S. (sá-tĭl´á)	125	31°15´N	82°13´W
Satka, Russia (sät´kå)	180	55°03´N	59°02´E
Sátoraljaujhely, Hung. (shä´tô-rô-lyô-ōō´yĕl´)	169	48°24´N	21°40´E
Satu Mare, Rom. (sá´tōō-má´rĕ)	163	47°50´N	22°53´E
Saturna, Can. (să-tûr´ná)	116d	48°48´N	123°12´W
Saturna, i., Can.	116d	48°47´N	123°03´W
Sauda, Nor.	160	59°40´N	6°21´E
Saudárkrókur, Ice.	154	65°41´N	19°38´W
Saudi Arabia, nation, Asia (sá-ō´dĭ á-rä´bĭ-á)	198	22°40´N	46°00´E
Sauerlach, Ger. (zou´ĕr-läк)	159d	47°58´N	11°39´E
Saugatuck, Mi., U.S. (sô´gá-tŭk)	108	42°40´N	86°10´W
Saugeen, r., Can.	98	44°20´N	81°20´W
Saugerties, N.Y., U.S. (sô´gēr-tēz)	109	42°05´N	73°55´W
Saugus, Ma., U.S. (sô´gŭs)	101a	42°28´N	71°01´W
Sauk, r., Mn., U.S. (sôk)	113	45°30´N	94°45´W
Sauk Centre, Mn., U.S.	113	45°43´N	94°58´W
Sauk City, Wi., U.S.	113	43°16´N	89°45´W
Sauk Rapids, Mn., U.S. (răp´ĭd)	113	45°35´N	94°08´W
Sault Sainte Marie, Can.	91	46°31´N	84°20´W
Sault Sainte Marie, Mi., U.S. (sōō sānt má-rē´)	105	46°29´N	84°21´W
Saumatre, Etang, l., Haiti	135	18°40´N	72°10´W
Saunders Lake, l., Can. (sän´dērs)	102g	53°18´N	113°25´W
Saurimo, Ang.	232	9°39´S	20°24´E
Sausalito, Ca., U.S. (sô-sá-lē´tô)	116b	37°51´N	122°29´W
Sausset-les-Pins, Fr. (sō-sĕ´lā-päɴ´)	170a	43°20´N	5°08´E
Saútar, Ang.	236	11°06´S	18°27´E
Sauvie Island, i., Or., U.S. (sô´vē)	116c	45°43´N	123°49´W
Sava, r., Yugo. (sä´vä)	156	44°50´N	18°30´E
Savage, Md., U.S. (să´vĕj)	110e	39°07´N	76°49´W
Savage, Mn., U.S.	117g	44°47´N	93°20´W
Savai'i, i., Samoa	214a	13°35´S	172°25´W
Savalen, l., Nor.	166	62°19´N	10°15´E
Savalou, Benin	230	7°56´N	1°58´E
Savanna, Il., U.S. (sá-văn´á)	113	42°05´N	90°09´W
Savannah, Ga., U.S. (sá-văn´á)	105	32°04´N	81°07´W
Savannah, Mo., U.S.	121	39°58´N	94°49´W
Savannah, Tn., U.S.	124	35°13´N	88°14´W
Savannah, r., U.S.	107	33°11´N	81°51´W
Savannakhét, Laos	212	16°33´N	104°45´E
Savanna la Mar, Jam. (sá-vän´á lá mär´)	134	18°10´N	78°10´W
Save, r., Fr.	170	43°32´N	0°50´E
Save, Rio (Sabi), r., Afr. (rē´ō-sä´vē)	232	21°28´S	34°14´E
Sāveh, Iran	201	35°01´N	50°20´E
Saverne, Fr. (sá-vĕrn´)	171	48°40´N	7°22´E
Savigliano, Italy (sä-vēl-yä´nô)	174	44°38´N	7°42´E
Savigny-sur-Orge, Fr.	171b	48°41´N	2°22´E
Savona, Italy (sä-nō´nä)	162	44°19´N	8°28´E
Savonlinna, Fin. (sá´vôn-lēn´ná)	167	61°53´N	28°49´E
Savran', Ukr. (säv-rän´)	177	48°07´N	30°09´E
Sawahlunto, Indon.	212	0°37´S	100°50´E
Sawākin, Sudan	231	19°02´N	37°19´E
Sawda, Jabal as, mts., Libya	231	28°14´N	13°46´E
Sawhāj, Egypt	231	26°34´N	31°40´E
Sawknah, Libya	231	29°04´N	15°53´E
Sawu, Laut (Savu Sea), sea, Asia	212	9°15´S	122°15´E
Sawyer, l., Wa., U.S. (sô´yēr)	116a	47°20´N	122°02´W
Saxony *see* Sachsen, hist. reg., Ger.	168	50°45´N	12°17´E
Say, Niger (sä´ē)	230	13°09´N	2°16´E
Sayan Khrebet, mts., Russia (sŭ-yän´)	179	51°30´N	90°00´E
Sayḥūt, Yemen	198	15°23´N	51°28´E
Sayre, Ok., U.S. (sā´ēr)	120	35°19´N	99°40´W
Sayre, Pa., U.S.	109	41°55´N	76°30´W
Sayreton, Al., U.S. (sā´ēr-tŭn)	110h	33°34´N	86°51´W
Sayreville, N.J., U.S. (sâr´vĭl)	110a	40°28´N	74°21´W
Sayr Usa, Mong.	204	44°15´N	107°00´E
Sayula, Mex. (sä-yōō´lä)	131	17°51´N	94°56´W
Sayula, Mex.	130	19°50´N	103°33´W
Sayula, Luguna de, l., Mex. (lä-gô´nä-dĕ)	130	20°00´N	103°33´W
Say'un, Yemen	198	16°00´N	48°59´E
Sayville, N.Y., U.S. (sā´vĭl)	109	40°45´N	73°10´W
Sazanit, i., Alb.	163	40°30´N	19°17´E
Sázava, r., Czech Rep.	168	49°36´N	15°24´E
Sazhino, Russia (sáz-hē´nô)	186a	56°20´N	58°15´E
Scandinavian Peninsula, pen., Eur.	196	62°00´N	14°00´E
Scanlon, Mn., U.S. (skăn´lôn)	117h	46°27´N	92°26´W
Scappoose, Or., U.S. (skă-pōōs´)	116c	45°46´N	122°53´W
Scappoose, r., Or., U.S.	116c	45°47´N	122°57´W
Scarborough, Eng., U.K. (skär´bŭr-ô)	164	54°16´N	0°19´W
Scarsdale, N.Y., U.S. (skärz´dāl)	110a	41°01´N	73°47´W
Scatari I, Can. (skăt´á-rē)	101	46°00´N	59°44´W
Schaerbeek, Bel. (skär´bāk)	159a	50°50´N	4°23´E
Schaffhausen, Switz. (shäf´hou-zĕn)	161	47°42´N	8°38´E
Schefferville, Can.	91	54°52´N	67°01´W
Schelde,, r., Eur.	165	51°04´N	3°55´E
Schenectady, N.Y., U.S. (skĕ-nĕk´tá-dê)	105	42°50´N	73°55´W
Scheveningen, Neth.	159a	52°06´N	4°15´E
Schiedam, Neth.	159a	51°55´N	4°23´E
Schiltigheim, Fr. (shēl´tegh-hīm)	171	48°48´N	7°47´E
Schio, Italy (skē´ô)	174	45°43´N	11°23´E
Schleswig, Ger. (shlĕs´vēgh)	160	54°32´N	9°32´E
Schleswig , hist. reg., Ger. (shĕls´vēgh)	168	54°40´N	9°10´E
Schleswig-Holstein, state, Ger. (shlĕs´vēgh-hōl´shtīn)	159c	53°40´N	9°45´E
Schmalkalden, Ger. (shmäl´käl-dĕn)	168	50°41´N	10°25´E
Schneider, In., U.S. (schnīd´ēr)	111a	41°12´N	87°26´W
Schofield, Wi., U.S. (skō´fēld)	113	44°52´N	89°37´W
Schönebeck, Ger. (shû´nĕ-bergh)	168	52°01´N	11°44´E
Schoonhoven, Neth.	159a	51°56´N	4°51´E
Schramberg, Ger. (shräm´bĕrgh)	168	48°14´N	8°24´E
Schreiber, Can.	98	48°50´N	87°10´W
Schroon, l., N.Y., U.S. (skrōōn)	109	43°50´N	73°50´W
Schultzendorf, Ger. (shōōl´tzĕn-dōrf)	159b	52°21´N	13°55´E
Schumacher, Can.	98	48°30´N	81°30´W
Schuyler, Ne., U.S. (slī´ler)	112	41°28´N	97°05´W
Schuylkill, r., Pa., U.S. (skōōl´kĭl)	110f	40°10´N	75°31´W
Schuylkill-Haven, Pa., U.S. (skōōl´kĭl hā-vĕn)	109	40°35´N	76°10´W
Schwabach, Ger. (shvä´bäk)	168	49°19´N	11°02´E
Schwäbische Alb, mts., Ger. (shvă´bē-shĕ älb)	168	48°11´N	9°09´E
Schwäbisch Gmünd, Ger. (shvă´bēsh gmünd)	168	48°47´N	9°49´E
Schwäbisch Hall, Ger. (häl)	168	49°08´N	9°44´E
Schwandorf, Ger. (shvän´dôrf)	168	49°19´N	12°08´E
Schwaner, Pegunungan, mts., Indon. (sкvän´ēr)	212	1°05´S	112°30´E
Schwarzwald, for., Ger. (shvärts´väld)	168	47°54´N	7°57´E
Schwaz, Aus.	168	47°20´N	11°45´E
Schwechat, Aus. (shvĕk´át)	168	48°09´N	16°29´E
Schwedt, Ger. (shvĕt)	168	53°04´N	14°17´E
Schweinfurt, Ger. (shvīn´fŏrt)	168	50°03´N	10°14´E
Schwelm, Ger. (shvĕlm)	171c	51°17´N	7°18´E
Schwerin, Ger. (shvĕ-rēn´)	168	53°36´N	11°25´E
Schweriner See, l., Ger. (shvĕ´rē-nĕr zā)	168	53°40´N	11°06´E
Schwerte, Ger. (shvĕr´tĕ)	171c	51°26´N	7°34´E
Schwielowsee, l., Ger. (shvē´lōv zā)	159b	52°20´N	12°52´E
Schwyz, Switz. (schēts)	168	47°01´N	8°38´E
Sciacca, Italy (shē-äk´kä)	174	37°30´N	13°09´E
Scilly, Isles of, is., Eng., U.K. (sĭl´ê)	156	49°56´N	6°50´W
Scioto, r., Oh., U.S. (sī-ō´tō)	107	39°10´N	82°55´W
Scituate, Ma., U.S. (sĭt´ū-āt)	101a	42°12´N	70°45´W
Scobey, Mt., U.S. (skō´bê)	115	48°48´N	105°29´W
Scoggin, Or., U.S. (skŏ´gĭn)	116c	45°28´N	123°14´W
Scotch, r., Can. (skŏch)	102c	45°21´N	74°56´W
Scotia, Ca., U.S. (skō´shá)	114	40°29´N	124°06´W
Scotland, S.D., U.S.	112	43°08´N	97°43´W
Scotland, state, U.K. (skŏt´lánd)	154	57°05´N	5°10´W
Scotland Neck, N.C., U.S. (nĕk)	125	36°06´N	77°25´W
Scotstown, Can. (skŏts´toun)	109	45°35´N	71°15´W
Scott, r., Ca., U.S.	114	41°20´N	122°55´W
Scott, Cape, c., Can. (skŏt)	92	50°47´N	128°26´W
Scott, Mount, mtn., Or., U.S.	116c	45°27´N	122°33´W
Scott, Mount, mtn., Or., U.S.	114	42°55´N	122°00´W
Scott Air Force Base, Il., U.S.	117e	38°33´N	89°52´W
Scottburgh, S. Afr. (skŏt´bŭr-ô)	232	30°18´S	30°42´E
Scott City, Ks., U.S.	120	38°28´N	100°54´W
Scottdale, Ga., U.S. (skŏt´dāl)	110c	33°47´N	84°16´W
Scott Islands, is., Ant.	224	67°00´S	178°00´E
Scottsbluff, Ne., U.S. (skŏts´blŭf)	112	41°52´N	103°40´W
Scottsboro, Al., U.S. (skŏts´bŭro)	124	34°40´N	86°03´W
Scottsburg, In., U.S. (skŏts´bûrg)	108	38°40´N	85°50´W
Scottsdale, Austl. (skŏts´dāl)	222	41°12´S	147°37´E
Scottsville, Ky., U.S. (skŏts´vĭl)	124	36°45´N	86°10´W
Scottville, Mi., U.S.	108	44°00´N	86°20´W
Scranton, Pa., U.S. (skrăn´tŭn)	105	41°15´N	75°45´W
Scugog, l., Can. (skū´gôg)	99	44°05´N	78°55´W
Scunthorpe, Eng., U.K. (skŭn´thôrp)	158a	53°36´N	0°38´W
Scutari *see* Shkodër, Alb.	154	42°04´N	19°30´E
Scutari, Lake, l., Eur. (skōō´tä-rê)	163	42°14´N	19°33´E
Seabeck, Wa., U.S. (sē´bĕck)	116a	47°38´N	122°50´W
Sea Bright, N.J., U.S. (sē brīt)	110a	40°22´N	73°58´W
Seabrook, Tx., U.S. (sē´brŏok)	123	29°34´N	95°01´W
Seaford, De., U.S. (sē´fērd)	109	38°35´N	75°40´W
Seagraves, Tx., U.S. (sē´grāvs)	120	32°51´N	102°38´W
Sea Islands, is., Ga., U.S. (sē)	125	31°21´N	81°05´W
Seal, r., Can.	92	59°08´N	96°37´W
Seal Beach, Ca., U.S.	117a	33°44´N	118°06´W
Seal Cays, is., Bah.	135	22°40´N	75°55´W
Seal Cays, is., T./C. Is.	135	21°10´N	71°45´W
Seal Island, i., S. Afr. (sēl)	232a	34°07´S	18°36´E
Sealy, Tx., U.S. (sē´lê)	123	29°46´N	96°10´W
Searcy, Ar., U.S. (sûr´sê)	121	35°13´N	91°43´W
Searles, l., Ca., U.S. (sûrl´s)	118	35°44´N	117°22´W
Searsport, Me., U.S. (sērz´pōrt)	100	44°28´N	68°55´W
Seaside, Or., U.S. (sē´sīd)	114	45°59´N	123°55´W
Seattle, Wa., U.S. (sê-ăt´'l)	104	47°36´N	122°20´W
Sebaco, Nic. (sĕ-bä´kô)	132	12°50´N	86°03´W
Sebago, Me., U.S. (sê-bā´gō)	100	43°52´N	70°20´W
Sebastián Vizcaíno, Bahía, b., Mex.	128	28°45´N	115°15´W
Sebastopol, Ca., U.S. (sê-bás´tô-pôl)	118	38°27´N	122°50´W
Sebderat, Erit.	231	15°30´N	36°45´E
Sebewaing, Mi., U.S. (se´bê-wăng)	108	43°45´N	83°25´W
Sebezh, Russia (syĕ´bĕzh)	176	56°16´N	28°29´E
Sebinkarahisar, Tur.	163	40°15´N	38°10´E
Sebnitz, Ger. (zĕb´nēts)	168	51°01´N	14°16´E
Sebou, Oued, r., Mor.	230	34°23´N	5°18´W
Sebree, Ky., U.S. (sê-brē´)	108	37°35´N	87°30´W
Sebring, Fl., U.S. (sē´brĭng)	125a	27°30´N	81°26´W
Sebring, Oh., U.S.	108	40°55´N	81°05´W
Secchia, r., Italy (sĕ´kyä)	174	44°25´N	10°25´E
Seco, r., Mex. (sĕ´kô)	131	18°11´N	93°18´W
Sedalia, Mo., U.S.	105	38°42´N	93°12´W
Sedan, Fr. (sē-däɴ)	161	49°49´N	4°55´E
Sedan, Ks., U.S. (sê-dăn´)	121	37°07´N	96°08´W
Sedom, Isr.	197a	31°04´N	35°24´E
Sedro Woolley, Wa., U.S. (sē´drô-wŏol´ê)	116a	48°30´N	122°14´W
Šeduva, Lith. (shĕ´dŏo-vá)	167	55°46´N	23°45´E
Seestall, Ger. (zā´shtäl)	159d	47°58´N	10°52´E
Sefrou, Mor. (sē-frōō´)	162	33°49´N	4°46´W
Seg, l., Russia (syĕgh)	180	63°20´N	33°30´E
Segamat, Malay. (sā´gá-mát)	197b	2°30´N	102°49´E
Segang, China (sŭ-gäŋ)	206	31°59´N	114°13´E
Segbana, Benin	235	10°56´N	3°42´E
Segorbe, Spain (sĕ-gôr-bĕ)	173	39°50´N	0°30´W
Ségou, Mali (sā-gōō´)	230	13°27´N	6°16´W
Segovia, Col. (sĕ-gô´vēä)	142a	7°08´N	74°42´W
Segovia, Spain (så-gō´vê-ä)	162	40°58´N	4°05´W
Segre, r., Spain (så´grä)	173	41°54´N	1°10´E
Seguam, i., Ak., U.S. (sē´gwäm)	103a	52°16´N	172°10´W
Seguam Passage, strt., Ak., U.S.	103a	52°20´N	173°00´W
Séguédine, Niger	235	20°12´N	12°59´E
Séguéla, C. Iv. (sā-gā-lä´)	230	7°57´N	6°40´W
Seguin, Tx., U.S. (sē-gēn´)	123	29°35´N	97°58´W
Segula, i., Ak., U.S. (sē-gū´lá)	103a	52°08´N	178°35´E
Segura, r., Spain	162	38°24´N	2°12´W

ăt; finăl; rāte; senåte; ärm; åsk; sofá; fâre; ch-choose; dh-as th in other; bē; êvent; bĕt; recĕnt; cratēr; g-gō; gh-guttural g; bĭt; ĭ-short neutral; rīde; ĸ-guttural k as ch in German ich;

PRONOUNCING INDEX

Segura – Sheksna 349

PLACE (Pronunciation)	PAGE	LAT.	LONG.
Segura, Sierra de, mts., Spain (sē-ĕ´r-rä-dĕ)	172	38°05'N	2°45'W
Sehwān, Pak.	202	26°33'N	67°51'E
Seibo, Dom. Rep. (sĕ´y-bō)	135	18°45'N	69°05'W
Seiling, Ok., U.S.	120	36°09'N	98°56'W
Seim, r., Eur.	181	51°23'N	33°22'E
Seinäjoki, Fin. (så´e̊-nĕ-yo̊´ke̊)	167	62°47'N	22°50'E
Seine, r., Can. (sån)	102f	49°48'N	97°03'W
Seine, r., Can. (sån)	98	49°04'N	91°00'W
Seine, r., Fr.	156	48°00'N	4°30'E
Seine, Baie de la, b., Fr. (bī dĕ lä sån)	170	49°37'N	0°53'W
Seio do Venus, mtn., Braz. (sĕ-yo̊-do̊-vĕ´no͞os)	144b	22°28'S	43°12'W
Seixal, Port. (så-e̊-shäl´)	173b	38°38'N	9°06'W
Sekenke, Tan.	237	4°16'S	34°10'E
Şeki, Azer.	182	41°12'N	47°12'E
Sekondi-Takoradi, Ghana (sĕ-kôn´de̊ tä-ko̊-rä´de̊)	230	4°59'N	1°43'W
Sekota, Eth.	231	12°47'N	38°59'E
Selangor, state, Malay. (så-län´gōr)	197b	2°53'N	101°29'E
Selanovtsi, Blg. (sål´å-nôv-tsĭ)	175	43°42'N	24°05'E
Selaru, Pulau, i., Indon.	213	8°30'S	130°30'E
Selatan, Tanjung, c., Indon. (så-lä´tän)	212	4°09'S	114°40'E
Selawik, Ak., U.S. (sē-lå-wĭk)	103	66°30'N	160°09'W
Selayar, Pulau, i., Indon.	212	6°15'S	121°15'E
Selbusjøen, l., Nor. (sĕl´bo͞o)	166	63°18'N	11°55'E
Selby, Eng., U.K. (sĕl´be̊)	158a	53°47'N	1°03'W
Seldovia, Ak., U.S. (sĕl-dō´ve̊-ȧ)	103	59°26'N	151°42'W
Selemdzha, r., Russia (sâ-lĕmt-zhä´)	185	52°28'N	131°50'E
Selenga (Selenge), r., Asia (sĕ lĕŋ gä´)	179	49°00'N	102°00'E
Selenge, r., Asia	204	49°04'N	102°23'E
Selennyakh, r., Russia (sĕl-yĭn-yäk)	185	67°42'N	141°45'E
Sélestat, Fr. (sẽ-lẽ-stä´)	171	48°16'N	7°27'E
Sélibaby, Maur. (så-le̊-bå-bē´)	230	15°21'N	12°11'W
Seliger, l., Russia (sĕl´le̊-gĕr)	180	57°14'N	33°18'E
Selizharovo, Russia (så´le̊-zhä´ro̊-vo̊)	176	56°51'N	33°28'E
Selkirk, Can. (sĕl´kûrk)	90	50°09'N	96°52'W
Selkirk Mountains, mts., Can.	92	51°00'N	117°40'W
Selleck, Wa., U.S. (sĕl´ĕck)	116a	47°22'N	121°52'W
Sellersburg, In., U.S. (sĕl´ĕrs-bûrg)	111h	38°25'N	85°45'W
Sellya Khskaya, Guba, b., Russia (sĕl-yäk´skå-yå)	185	72°30'N	136°00'E
Selma, Al., U.S. (sĕl´mȧ)	105	32°25'N	87°00'W
Selma, Ca., U.S.	118	36°34'N	119°37'W
Selma, N.C., U.S.	125	35°33'N	78°16'W
Selma, Tx., U.S.	117d	29°33'N	98°19'W
Selmer, Tn., U.S.	124	35°11'N	88°36'W
Selsingen, Ger. (zĕl´zēn-gĕn)	159c	53°22'N	9°13'E
Selway, r., Id., U.S. (sĕl´wå)	114	46°07'N	115°12'W
Selwyn, l., Can. (sĕl´wĭn)	92	59°41'N	104°30'W
Seman, r., Alb.	175	40°48'N	19°53'E
Semarang, Indon. (sĕ-mä´räng)	212	7°03'S	110°27'E
Semenivka, Ukr.	181	52°10'N	32°34'E
Semeru, Gunung, mtn., Indon.	212	8°06'S	112°55'E
Semey (Semipalatinsk), Kaz.	183	50°28'N	80°29'E
Semiahmoo Indian Reserve, I.R., Can.	116d	49°01'N	122°43'W
Semiahmoo Spit, Wa., U.S. (sĕm´ĭ-å-mo͞o)	116d	48°59'N	122°52'W
Semichi Islands, is., Ak., U.S. (sē-mē´chī)	103a	52°40'N	174°50'E
Seminoe Reservoir, res., Wy., U.S. (sĕm´ĭ no̊)	115	42°08'N	107°10'W
Seminole, Ok., U.S. (sĕm´ĭ-nōl)	121	35°13'N	96°41'W
Seminole, Tx., U.S.	122	32°43'N	102°39'W
Seminole, Lake, res., U.S.	124	30°57'N	84°46'W
Semipalatinsk *see* Semey, Kaz.	183	50°28'N	80°29'E
Semisopochnoi, i., Ak., U.S. (sĕ-mē-så-pōsh´ noi)	103a	51°45'N	179°25'E
Semliki, r., Afr. (sĕm´le̊-kē)	231	0°45'N	29°36'E
Semmering Pass, p., Aus. (sĕm´ĕr-ĭng)	168	47°39'N	15°50'E
Senador Pompeu, Braz. (sĕ-nä-dōr-pôm-pĕ´o̊)	143	5°34'S	39°18'W
Senaki, Geor.	182	42°17'N	42°04'E
Senatobia, Ms., U.S. (sĕ-nå-tō´be̊-ȧ)	124	34°36'N	89°56'W
Sendai, Japan (sĕn-dī´)	205	38°18'N	141°02'E
Seneca, Ks., U.S. (sĕn´ĕ-kȧ)	121	39°49'N	96°03'W
Seneca, Md., U.S.	110e	39°04'N	77°20'W
Seneca, S.C., U.S.	125	34°40'N	82°58'W
Seneca, l., N.Y., U.S.	109	42°30'N	76°55'W
Seneca Falls, N.Y., U.S.	109	42°55'N	76°55'W
Senegal, nation, Afr. (sĕn-ĕ-gôl´)	230	14°53'N	14°58'W
Sénégal, r., Afr.	230	16°00'N	14°00'W
Senekal, S. Afr. (sĕn´e̊-kȧl)	238c	28°20'S	27°37'E
Senftenberg, Ger. (zĕnf´tĕn-bĕrgh)	168	51°32'N	14°00'E
Sengunyane, r., Leso.	233c	29°35'S	28°08'E
Senhor do Bonfim, Braz. (sĕn-yo̊r do̊ bôn-fē´n)	143	10°21'S	40°09'W
Senigallia, Italy (så-ne̊-gäl´lyä)	174	43°42'N	13°16'E
Senj, Cro. (sĕn´)	174	44°58'N	14°55'E
Senja, i., Nor. (sĕnyä)	160	69°28'N	16°10'E
Senlis, Fr. (sän-lēs´)	171b	49°13'N	2°35'E
Sennar Dam, dam, Sudan	231	13°38'N	33°38'E
Senneterre, Can.	91	48°20'N	77°22'W
Sens, Fr. (säns)	170	48°05'N	3°18'E
Sensuntepeque, El Sal. (sĕn-so͞on-tå-pā´kå)	132	13°53'N	88°34'W
Senta, Yugo. (sĕn´tä)	163	45°54'N	20°05'E
Senzaki, Japan (sĕn´zä-kē)	211	34°22'N	131°09'E
Seoul (Sŏul), Kor., S.	205	37°35'N	127°03'E
Sepang, Malay.	197b	2°43'N	101°45'E
Sepetiba, Baía de, b., Braz. (bäē´ä dĕ så-på-tē´bȧ)	144b	23°01'S	43°42'W
Sepik, r. (sĕp-ēk´)	213	4°07'S	142°40'E
Septentrional, Cordillera, mts., Dom. Rep.	135	19°50'N	71°15'W
Septeuil, Fr. (sĕ-tû´)	171b	48°53'N	1°40'E
Sept-Îles, Can. (sĕ-tēl´)	100	50°12'N	66°23'W
Sequatchie, r., Tn., U.S. (se̊-kwăch´e̊)	124	35°33'N	85°14'W
Sequim, Wa., U.S. (sē´kwĭm)	116a	48°05'N	123°07'W
Sequim Bay, b., Wa., U.S.	116a	48°04'N	122°58'W
Sequoia National Park, rec., Ca., U.S. (se̊-kwoi´ȧ)	106	36°34'N	118°37'W
Seraing, Bel. (sẽ-răn´)	165	50°38'N	5°28'E
Serāmpore, India	202a	22°44'N	88°21'E
Serang, Indon. (så-räng´)	212	6°13'S	106°10'E
Seranggung, Indon.	197b	0°49'N	104°11'E
Serbia *see* Srbija, hist. reg., Yugo.	175	44°05'N	20°35'E
Serdobsk, Russia (sĕr-dôpsk´)	181	52°30'N	44°20'E
Sered', Slvk.	169	48°17'N	17°43'E
Seredyna-Buda, Ukr.	176	52°11'N	34°03'E
Seremban, Malay. (sĕr-ĕm-bän´)	197b	2°44'N	101°57'E
Serengeti National Park, rec., Tan.	237	2°20'S	34°50'E
Serengeti Plain, pl., Tan.	237	2°40'S	34°55'E
Serenje, Zam. (sē-rĕn´ye̊)	232	13°12'S	30°49'E
Seret, r., Ukr. (sĕr´ĕt)	169	49°45'N	25°30'E
Sergeya Kirova, i., Russia (sēr-gyē´yå ke̊´ro̊-vå)	184	77°30'N	86°10'E
Sergipe, state, Braz. (sĕr-zhē´pĕ)	143	10°27'S	37°04'W
Sergiyev Posad, Russia	186b	56°18'N	38°08'E
Sergiyevsk, Russia	180	53°58'N	51°00'E
Sérifos, Grc.	175	37°10'N	24°32'E
Sérifos, i., Grc.	175	37°42'N	24°17'E
Serodino, Arg. (sĕ-ro̊-de̊´nō)	141c	32°36'S	60°56'W
Seropédica, Braz. (sĕ-ro̊-pĕ´dē-kä)	144b	22°44'S	43°43'W
Serov, Russia (syĕ-rôf´)	184	59°36'N	60°30'E
Serowe, Bots. (sĕ-rō´wĕ)	232	22°18'S	26°39'E
Serpa, Port. (sĕr-pä)	172	37°56'N	7°38'W
Serpukhov, Russia (syĕr´po̊-kôf)	178	54°53'N	37°27'E
Sérres, Grc. (sĕr´rĕ) (sĕr´ĕs)	163	41°06'N	23°36'E
Serrinha, Braz. (sĕr-rēn´yå)	143	11°43'S	38°49'W
Serta, Port. (sĕr´tå)	172	39°48'N	8°01'W
Sertânia, Braz. (sĕr-tå´nyä)	143	8°28'S	37°13'W
Sertãozinho, Braz. (sĕr-toun-ze̊´n-yo̊)	141a	21°10'S	47°58'W
Serting, r., Malay.	197b	3°01'N	102°32'E
Sese Islands, is., Ug.	237	0°30'S	32°30'E
Sesia, r., Italy (såz´yä)	174	45°33'N	8°25'E
Sesimbra, Port. (sĕ-se̊´m-brä)	173b	38°27'N	9°06'W
Sesmyl, r., S. Afr.	233b	25°51'S	28°06'E
Ses Salines, Cap de, c., Spain	173	39°16'N	3°03'E
Sestri Levante, Italy (sĕs´tre̊ lå-vän´tå)	174	44°15'N	9°24'E
Sestroretsk, Russia (sĕs-trô-rĕtsk)	180	60°06'N	29°58'E
Sestroretskiy Razliv, Ozero, l., Russia	186c	60°05'N	30°07'E
Seta, Japan (sĕ´tä)	211b	34°58'N	135°56'W
Séte, Fr. (sĕt)	161	43°24'N	3°42'E
Sete Lagoas, Braz. (sĕ-tĕ lä-gô´äs)	143	19°23'S	43°58'W
Sete Pontes, Braz.	144b	22°51'S	43°05'W
Seto, Japan (sē´tō)	211	35°11'N	137°07'E
Seto-Naikai, sea, Japan (sĕ´to̊ nī´kī)	211	33°50'N	132°25'E
Settat, Mor. (sĕt-ät´) (sē-tå´)	230	33°02'N	7°30'W
Sette-Cama, Gabon (sĕ-tĕ-kä-mä´)	232	2°29'S	9°40'E
Settlement Point, c., Bah. (sĕt´l-mĕnt)	134	26°40'N	79°00'W
Settlers, S. Afr. (sĕt´lẽrs)	238c	24°57'S	28°33'E
Settsu, Japan	211b	34°46'N	135°33'E
Setúbal, Port. (så-to͞o´bäl)	162	30°32'N	8°54'W
Setúbal, Baía de, b., Port.	172	38°27'N	9°08'W
Seul, Lac, l., Can. (låk sûl)	93	50°20'N	92°30'W
Sevan, l., Arm. (syĭ-vän´)	181	40°10'N	45°20'E
Sevastopol', Ukr. (syĕ-vås-tô´po̊l´´)	178	44°34'N	33°34'E
Sevenoaks, Eng., U.K. (sĕ-vĕn-o̊ks´)	158b	51°16'N	0°12'E
Severka, r., Russia (sâ´vĕr-kå)	186b	55°11'N	38°41'E
Severn, r., Can. (sĕv´ẽrn)	93	55°21'N	88°42'W
Severn, r., U.K.	164	51°50'N	2°25'W
Severna Park, Md., U.S. (sĕv´ẽrn-å)	110e	39°04'N	76°33'W
Severnaya Dvina, r., Russia	178	63°00'N	42°40'E
Severnaya Zemlya (Northern Land), is., Russia (sĕ-vyĭr-nīů zĭ-m'lyä´)	179	79°33'N	101°15'E
Severoural'sk, Russia (sĕ-vyĭ-rŭ-o͞o-rälsk´)	184	60°08'N	59°53'E
Sevier, r., Ut., U.S.	106	39°25'N	112°20'W
Sevier, East Fork, r., Ut., U.S.	119	37°45'N	112°10'W
Sevier Lake, l., Ut., U.S. (se̊-vēr´)	119	38°55'N	113°10'W
Sevilla, Col. (sĕ-ve̊´l-yä)	142a	4°16'N	75°56'W
Sevilla, Spain (så-vēl´yä)	154	37°29'N	5°58'W
Seville, Oh., U.S. (sĕ´vĭl)	111d	41°01'N	81°45'W
Sevlievo, Blg. (sĕv´lyĕ-vo̊)	163	43°02'N	25°05'E
Sevsk, Russia (syĕfsk)	176	52°08'N	34°28'E
Seward, Ak., U.S. (sū´ård)	106a	60°18'N	149°28'W
Seward, Ne., U.S.	121	40°55'N	97°06'W
Seward Peninsula, pen., Ak., U.S.	103	65°40'N	164°00'W
Sewell, Chile (sĕ´o̊-ĕl)	144	34°01'S	70°18'W
Sewickley, Pa., U.S. (se̊-wĭk´le̊)	111e	40°33'N	80°11'W
Seybaplaya, Mex. (sā-e̊-bä-plä´yä)	131	19°38'N	90°40'W
Seychelles, nation, Afr. (sā-shĕl´)	3	5°20'S	55°10'E
Seydisfjördur, Ice. (sā´de̊s-fyûr-do̊r)	160	65°21'N	14°08'W
Seyhan, r., Tur.	163	37°28'N	35°40'E
Seylac, Som.	238a	11°19'N	43°20'E
Seymour, S. Afr. (sē´môr)	233c	32°33'S	26°48'E
Seymour, Ia., U.S.	113	40°41'N	93°03'W
Seymour, In., U.S. (sē´mōr)	108	38°55'N	85°55'W
Seymour, Tx., U.S.	120	33°35'N	99°16'W
Sezela, S. Afr.	233c	30°33'S	30°37'W
Sezze, Italy (sĕt´så)	174	41°32'N	13°00'E
Sfântu Gheorghe, Rom.	163	45°53'N	25°49'E
Sfax, Tun. (sfäks)	230	34°51'N	10°45'E
's-Gravenhage *see* The Hague, Neth. ('s krä´vĕn-hä´kĕ) (hāg)	154	52°05'N	4°16'E
Sha, r., China (shä)	205	33°33'N	114°30'E
Shaanxi, prov., China (shän-shyē)	204	35°30'N	109°10'E
Shabeelle (Shebele), r., Afr.	238a	1°38'N	43°50'E
Shache, China (shä-chŭ)	204	38°15'N	77°15'E
Shackleton Ice Shelf, ice, Ant. (shăk´'l-tŭn)	224	65°00'S	100°00'E
Shades Creek, r., Al., U.S. (shādz)	110h	33°20'N	86°55'W
Shades Mountain, mtn., Al., U.S.	110h	33°22'N	86°51'W
Shagamu, Nig.	235	6°51'N	3°39'E
Shāhdād, Namakzār-e, l., Iran (nŭ-mŭk-zär´)	198	31°00'N	58°30'E
Shāhjahānpur, India (shä-jŭ-hän´po͞or)	199	27°58'N	79°58'E
Shajing, China (shä-jyĭŋ)	207a	22°44'N	113°48'E
Shaker Heights, Oh., U.S. (shā´kẽr)	111d	41°28'N	81°34'W
Shakhty, Russia (shäk´te̊)	178	47°41'N	40°11'E
Shaki, Nig.	235	8°39'N	3°25'E
Shakopee, Mn., U.S. (shăk´ô-pe)	117g	44°48'N	93°31'W
Shala Lake, l., Eth. (shä´lå)	231	7°34'N	39°00'E
Shalqar, Kaz.	183	47°52'N	59°41'E
Shalqar köli, l., Kaz.	181	50°30'N	51°30'E
Shām, Jabal ash, mtn., Oman	198	23°01'N	57°45'E
Shambe, Sudan (shäm´bå)	231	7°08'N	30°46'E
Shammar, Jabal, mts., Sau. Ar. (jĕb´ĕl shŭm´år)	198	27°13'N	40°16'E
Shamokin, Pa., U.S. (shȧ-mō´kĭn)	109	40°45'N	76°30'W
Shamrock, Tx., U.S. (shăm´rŏk)	120	35°14'N	100°12'W
Shamva, Zimb. (shäm´vå)	232	17°18'S	31°35'E
Shandon, Oh., U.S. (shăn-dŭn)	111f	39°20'N	84°13'W
Shandong, prov., China (shän-do̊ŋ)	205	36°08'N	117°09'E
Shandong Bandao, pen., China (shän-do̊ŋ bän-dou)	205	37°00'N	120°10'E
Shangcai, China (shäŋ-tsī)	206	33°16'N	114°16'E
Shangcheng, China (shäŋ-chŭŋ)	206	31°47'N	115°22'E
Shangdu, China (shäŋ-do͞o)	208	41°38'N	113°22'E
Shanghai, China (shäng´hī´)	205	31°14'N	121°27'E
Shanghai Shi, prov., China (shäŋ-hī shr)	205	31°30'N	121°45'E
Shanghe, China (shäŋ-hŭ)	206	37°18'N	117°10'E
Shanglin, China (shäŋ-lĭn)	206	38°20'N	116°05'E
Shangqiu, China (shäŋ-chyo̊)	208	34°24'N	115°39'E
Shangrao, China (shäŋ-rou)	209	28°25'N	117°58'E
Shangzhi, China (shäŋ-jr)	208	45°18'N	127°52'E
Shanhaiguan, China	208	40°01'N	119°45'E
Shannon, Al., U.S. (shăn´ŭn)	110h	33°23'N	86°52'W
Shannon, r., Ire. (shăn´ŏn)	161	52°30'N	10°15'W
Shanshan, China (shän´shän´)	204	42°51'N	89°53'E
Shantar, i., Russia (shän´tär)	185	55°13'N	138°42'E
Shantou, China (shän-tō)	205	23°20'N	116°40'E
Shanxi, prov., China (shän-shyē)	205	37°30'N	112°00'E
Shan Xian, China (shän shyĕn)	206	34°47'N	116°04'E
Shaobo, China (shou-bwo)	208	32°33'N	119°30'E
Shaobo Hu, l., China (shou-bwo ho͞o)	206	32°47'N	119°13'E
Shaoguan, China (shou-gůän)	205	24°58'N	113°42'E
Shaoxing, China (shou-shyĭŋ)	205	30°00'N	120°40'E
Shaoyang, China	205	27°15'N	111°28'E
Shapki, Russia (shäp´kĭ)	186c	59°36'N	31°11'E
Shark Bay, b., Austl. (shärk)	220	25°30'S	113°00'E
Sharon, Ma., U.S. (shăr´ŏn)	101a	42°07'N	71°11'W
Sharon, Pa., U.S.	108	41°15'N	80°30'W
Sharon Springs, Ks., U.S.	120	38°51'N	101°45'W
Sharonville, Oh., U.S. (shăr´ŏn vĭl)	111f	39°16'N	84°24'W
Sharpsburg, Pa., U.S. (shărps´bûrg)	111e	40°30'N	79°54'W
Sharr, Jabal, mtn., Sau. Ar.	198	28°00'N	36°07'E
Shashi, China (shä-shē)	205	30°20'N	112°18'E
Shasta, Mount, mtn., Ca., U.S.	106	41°35'N	122°12'W
Shasta Lake, res., Ca., U.S. (shăs´tȧ)	106	40°51'N	122°32'W
Shatsk, Russia (shȧtsk)	180	54°00'N	41°40'E
Shattuck, Ok., U.S. (shăt´ŭk)	120	36°16'N	99°53'W
Shaunavon, Can.	90	49°40'N	108°25'W
Shaw, Ms., U.S. (shô)	124	33°36'N	90°44'W
Shawano, Wi., U.S. (shȧ-wô´no̊)	113	44°41'N	88°13'W
Shawinigan, Can.	91	46°32'N	72°46'W
Shawnee, Ks., U.S. (shô-nē´)	117f	39°01'N	94°43'W
Shawnee, Ok., U.S.	104	35°20'N	96°54'W
Shawneetown, Il., U.S. (shô´nē-toun)	108	37°40'N	88°05'W
Shayang, China	209	31°00'N	112°38'E
Shchara, r., Bela. (sh-chå´rå)	169	53°17'N	25°12'E
Shchëlkovo, Russia (shchĕl´ko̊-vo̊)	176	55°55'N	38°00'E
Shchigry, Russia (shchē´gre̊)	177	51°52'N	36°54'E
Shchors, Ukr. (shchôrs)	177	51°38'N	31°58'E
Shchuch'ye Ozero, Russia (shcho͞och´yĕ ô´zĕ-rō)	186a	56°31'N	56°35'E
Sheakhala, India	202a	22°47'N	88°10'E
Shebele (Shabeelle), r., Afr. (shā´bå-lē)	238a	6°07'N	43°10'E
Sheboygan, Wi., U.S. (she̊-boi´găn)	105	43°45'N	87°44'W
Sheboygan Falls, Wi., U.S.	113	43°43'N	87°51'W
Shechem, hist., W.B.	197a	32°15'N	35°22'E
Shedandoah, Pa., U.S.	109	40°50'N	76°15'W
Shediac, Can. (shĕ´de̊-ăk)	100	46°13'N	64°32'W
Shedin Peak, mtn., Can. (shĕd´ĭn)	94	55°55'N	127°32'W
Sheerness, Eng., U.K. (shēr´nĕs)	158b	51°26'N	0°46'E
Sheffield, Can.	102d	43°20'N	80°13'W
Sheffield, Eng., U.K.	160	53°23'N	1°28'W
Sheffield, Al., U.S. (shĕf´fēld)	124	35°42'N	87°42'W
Sheffield, Oh., U.S.	111d	41°26'N	82°05'W
Sheffield, co., Eng., U.K.	158a	53°52'N	1°35'W
Sheffield Lake, Oh., U.S.	111d	41°30'N	82°03'W
Sheksna, r., Russia (shĕks´nå)	180	59°50'N	38°40'E

ng-sing; ŋ-baŋk; n-nasalized n; nŏd; cŏmmit; ōld; ôbey; ôrder; oi-boil; fo͞od; o̊-as oo in foot; ou-out; s-soft; sh-dish; th-thin; pūre; ůnite; ûrn; stŭd; circŭs; ü-as in French tu; ´-indeterminate vowel.

350 Shelagskiy – Silverdale PRONOUNCING INDEX

PLACE (Pronunciation)	PAGE	LAT.	LONG.
Shelagskiy, Mys, c., Russia (shĭ-läg′skē)	179	70°08′N	170°52′E
Shelbina, Ar., U.S. (shĕl-bī′nȧ)	121	39°41′N	92°03′W
Shelburn, In., U.S. (shĕl′bûrn)	108	39°10′N	87°30′W
Shelburne, Can.	91	43°46′N	65°19′W
Shelburne, Can.	99	44°04′N	80°12′W
Shelby, In., U.S. (shĕl′bē)	111a	41°12′N	87°21′W
Shelby, Mi., U.S.	108	43°35′N	86°20′W
Shelby, Ms., U.S.	124	33°56′N	90°44′W
Shelby, Mt., U.S.	115	48°35′N	111°55′W
Shelby, N.C., U.S.	125	35°16′N	81°35′W
Shelby, Oh., U.S.	108	40°50′N	82°40′W
Shelbyville, Il., U.S. (shĕl′bē-vĭl)	108	39°20′N	88°45′W
Shelbyville, In., U.S.	108	39°30′N	85°45′W
Shelbyville, Ky., U.S.	108	38°10′N	85°15′W
Shelbyville, Tn., U.S.	124	35°30′N	86°28′W
Shelbyville Reservoir, res., Il., U.S.	108	39°30′N	88°45′W
Sheldon, Ia., U.S. (shĕl′dŭn)	112	43°10′N	95°50′W
Sheldon, Tx., U.S.	123a	29°52′N	95°07′W
Shelekhova, Zaliv, b., Russia	179	60°00′N	156°00′E
Shelikof Strait, strt., Ak., U.S. (shĕ′lē-kôf)	103	57°56′N	154°20′W
Shellbrook, Can.	96	53°15′N	106°22′W
Shelley, Id., U.S. (shĕl′lē)	115	43°24′N	112°06′W
Shellrock, r., Ia., U.S. (shĕl′rŏk)	113	43°25′N	93°19′W
Shelon′, r., Russia (shå′lôn)	176	57°50′N	29°40′E
Shelton, Ct., U.S. (shĕl′tŭn)	109	41°15′N	73°05′W
Shelton, Ne., U.S.	120	40°46′N	98°41′W
Shelton, Wa., U.S.	114	47°14′N	123°05′W
Shemakha, Russia (shĕ-mȧ-kä′)	186a	56°16′N	59°19′E
Shenandoah, Ia., U.S. (shĕn-ăn-dō′ȧ)	121	40°46′N	95°23′W
Shenandoah, Va., U.S.	109	38°30′N	78°30′W
Shenandoah, r., Va., U.S.	109	38°55′N	78°05′W
Shenandoah National Park, rec., Va., U.S.	107	38°35′N	78°25′W
Shendam, Nig.	235	8°53′N	9°32′E
Shengfang, China (shengfäng)	206	39°05′N	116°40′E
Shenkursk, Russia (shĕn-ko͞orsk′)	178	62°10′N	43°08′E
Shenmu, China	208	38°55′N	110°35′E
Shenqiu, China	208	33°11′N	115°06′E
Shenxian, China (shŭn shyän)	206	38°02′N	115°33′E
Shenxian, China (shŭn shyĕn)	206	36°14′N	115°38′E
Shenyang, China (shŭn-yäŋ)	205	41°45′N	123°22′E
Shenze, China (shŭn-dzŭ)	206	38°12′N	115°12′E
Shenzhen, China	209	22°32′N	114°08′E
Sheopur, India	199	25°37′N	77°10′E
Shepard, Can. (shĕ′pärd)	102e	50°57′N	113°55′W
Shepetivka, Ukr.	181	50°10′N	27°01′E
Shepparton, Austl. (shĕp′ăr-tŭn)	222	36°15′S	145°25′E
Sherborn, Ma., U.S. (shûr′bŭrn)	101a	42°15′N	71°22′W
Sherbrooke, Can.	91	45°24′N	71°54′W
Sherburn, Eng., U.K. (shûr′bûrn)	158a	53°47′N	1°15′W
Shereshevo, Bela. (shĕ-rĕ-shĕ-vô)	169	52°31′N	24°08′E
Sheridan, Ar., U.S. (shĕr′ĭ-dăn)	121	34°19′N	92°21′W
Sheridan, Or., U.S.	114	45°06′N	123°22′W
Sheridan, Wy., U.S.	104	44°48′N	106°56′W
Sherman, Tx., U.S. (shĕr′măn)	104	33°39′N	96°37′W
Sherna, r., Russia (shĕr′nȧ)	186b	56°08′N	38°45′E
Sherridon, Can.	97	55°10′N	101°10′W
′s Hertogenbosch, Neth. (sĕr-tō′ghĕn-bôs)	165	51°41′N	5°19′E
Sherwood, Or., U.S.	116c	45°21′N	122°50′W
Sherwood Forest, for., Eng., U.K.	158a	53°11′N	1°07′W
Sherwood Park, Can.	95	53°31′N	113°19′W
Shetland Islands, is., Scot., U.K. (shĕt′lănd)	156	60°35′N	2°10′W
Shewa Gimira, Eth.	231	7°13′N	35°49′E
Shexian, China (shŭ shyĕn)	206	36°34′N	113°42′E
Sheyang, r., China (she-yäŋ)	206	33°42′N	119°40′E
Sheyenne, r., N.D., U.S. (shī-ĕn′)	112	46°42′N	97°52′W
Shi, r., China (shr)	206	31°58′N	115°50′E
Shi, r., China	206	32°09′N	114°11′E
Shiawassee, r., Mi., U.S. (shī-ȧ-wôs′ē)	108	43°15′N	84°05′W
Shibām, Yemen (shē′bäm)	198	16°02′N	48°40′E
Shibīn al Kawn, Egypt (shė-bēn′ĕl kōm′)	238b	30°31′N	31°01′E
Shibīn al Qanāţir, Egypt (kȧ-nä′tĕr)	238b	30°18′N	31°21′E
Shicun, China (shr-tsòn)	206	33°47′N	117°18′E
Shields, r., Mt., U.S. (shēldz)	115	45°54′N	110°40′W
Shifnal, Eng., U.K. (shĭf′năl)	158a	52°40′N	2°22′W
Shijian, China (shr-jyĕn)	206	31°27′N	117°51′E
Shijiazhuang, China (shr-jyä-jůäŋ)	205	38°04′N	114°31′E
Shijiu Hu, I., China (shr-jyȯ ho͞o)	206	31°29′N	119°07′E
Shikārpur, Pak.	199	27°51′N	68°52′E
Shiki, Japan (shē′kē)	211a	35°50′N	139°35′E
Shikoku, i., Japan (shē′kō′ko͞o)	205	33°43′N	133°33′E
Shilka, r., Russia (shĭl′kȧ)	185	53°00′N	118°45′E
Shilla, mtn., India	202	32°18′N	78°17′E
Shillong, India (shėl-lông′)	199	25°39′N	91°58′E
Shiloh, Il., U.S. (shī′lō)	117e	38°34′N	89°54′W
Shilong, China (shr-lôŋ)	209	23°05′N	113°58′E
Shilou, China	207a	22°58′N	113°29′E
Shimabara, Japan (shē′mä-bä′rä)	211	32°46′N	130°22′E
Shimada, Japan (shē′mä-dä)	211	34°49′N	138°13′E
Shimbiris, mtn., Som.	238a	10°40′N	47°23′E
Shimizu, Japan (shē′mė-zo͞o)	210	35°00′N	138°29′E
Shimminato, Japan (shĕm′mė′nä-tô)	211	36°47′N	137°05′E
Shimoda, Japan (shē′mô-dȧ)	211	34°41′N	138°58′E
Shimoga, India	203	13°59′N	75°38′E
Shimoni, Kenya	237	4°39′S	39°23′E
Shimonoseki, Japan	205	33°58′N	130°55′E
Shimo-Saga, Japan (shē′mô sä′gä)	211b	35°01′N	135°41′E
Shin, Loch, I., Scot., U.K. (lŏĸ shĭn)	164	58°08′N	4°02′W
Shinagawa-Wan, b., Japan (shē′nä-gä′wä wän)	211a	35°37′N	139°49′E
Shinano-Gawa, r., Japan (shė-nä′nô gä′wä)	211	36°43′N	138°22′E
Shīndand, Afg.	201	33°18′N	62°08′E
Shinji, I., Japan (shĭn′jē)	211	35°23′N	133°05′E
Shinkolobwe, D.R.C.	237	11°02′S	26°35′E
Shinyanga, Tan. (shĭn-yäŋ′gä)	232	3°40′S	33°26′E
Shiono Misaki, c., Japan (shė-ō′nô mē′sä-kė)	210	33°20′N	136°10′E
Shipai, China (shr-pī)	207a	23°07′N	113°23′E
Ship Channel Cay, i., Bah. (shĭp chă-nĕl kē)	134	24°50′N	76°50′W
Shipley, Eng., U.K. (shĭp′lē)	158a	53°50′N	1°47′W
Shippegan, Can. (shĭ′pė-găn)	100	47°45′N	64°42′W
Shippegan Island, i., Can.	100	47°50′N	64°38′W
Shippenburg, Pa., U.S. (shĭp′ĕn bûrg)	109	40°00′N	77°30′W
Shipshaw, r., Can. (shĭp′shô)	99	48°50′N	71°03′W
Shiqma, r., Isr.	197a	31°31′N	34°40′E
Shirane-san, mtn., Japan (shē′rä′nå-sän′)	211	35°44′N	138°14′E
Shirati, Tan. (shė-rä′tē)	232	1°15′S	34°02′E
Shīrāz, Iran (shē-räz′)	198	29°32′N	52°27′E
Shire, r., Afr. (shē′rȧ)	232	15°00′S	35°00′E
Shiriya Saki, c., Japan (shē′rä sä′kė)	210	41°25′N	142°10′E
Shirley, Ma., U.S. (shûr′lē)	101a	42°33′N	71°39′W
Shishaldin Volcano, vol., Ak., U.S. (shī-shăl′dĭn)	103a	54°48′N	164°00′W
Shively, Ky., U.S. (shīv′lē)	111h	38°11′N	85°47′W
Shivpuri, India	199	25°31′N	77°46′E
Shivta, Horvot, hist., Isr.	197a	30°54′N	34°36′E
Shivwits Plateau, plat., Az., U.S.	119	36°13′N	113°42′W
Shiwan, China (shr-wän)	207a	23°01′N	113°04′E
Shiwan Dashan, mts., China (shr-wän dä-shän)	209	22°10′N	107°30′E
Shizuki, Japan (shĭ′zo͞o-kė)	211	34°29′N	134°51′E
Shizuoka, Japan (shē′zo͞o′ōkȧ)	210	34°58′N	138°24′E
Shklow, Bela.	176	54°11′N	30°23′E
Shkodër, Alb. (shkô′dûr) (sko͞o′tarē)	154	42°04′N	19°30′E
Shkotovo, Russia (shkô′tô-vô)	210	43°15′N	132°21′E
Shoal Creek, r., Il., U.S. (shōl)	121	38°37′N	89°25′W
Shoal Lake, I., Can.	97	49°32′N	95°00′W
Shoals, In., U.S. (shōlz)	108	38°40′N	86°45′W
Shōdo, i., Japan (shō′dō)	211	34°27′N	134°27′E
Sholāpur, India (shō′lä-po͞or)	199	17°42′N	75°51′E
Shorewood, Wi., U.S. (shōr′wo͝od)	111a	43°05′N	87°54′W
Shoshone, Id., U.S. (shō-shōn′tė)	115	42°56′N	114°24′W
Shoshone, r., Wy., U.S.	115	44°35′N	108°50′W
Shoshone Lake, I., Wy., U.S.	115	44°17′N	110°50′W
Shoshoni, Wy., U.S.	115	43°14′N	108°05′W
Shostka, Ukr. (shôst′kȧ)	177	51°51′N	33°31′E
Shouguang, China (shō-gůäŋ)	206	36°53′N	118°45′E
Shouxian, China (shō shyĕn)	206	32°36′N	116°45′E
Shpola, Ukr. (shpô′lȧ)	181	49°01′N	31°36′E
Shreveport, La., U.S. (shrēv′pōrt)	105	32°30′N	93°46′W
Shrewsbury, Eng., U.K. (shro͞oz′bĕr-ĭ)	164	52°43′N	2°44′W
Shrewsbury, Ma., U.S.	101a	42°18′N	71°43′W
Shropshire, co., Eng., U.K.	158a	52°36′N	2°45′W
Shroud Cay, i., Bah.	134	24°20′N	76°40′W
Shuangcheng, China (shůäŋ-chŭŋ)	208	45°18′N	126°18′E
Shuanghe, China (shůäŋ-hŭ)	206	31°33′N	116°48′E
Shuangliao, China	205	43°37′N	123°30′E
Shuangyang, China	208	43°28′N	125°45′E
Shuhedun, China (sho͞o-hŭ-dòn)	206	31°33′N	117°01′E
Shuiye, China (shwā-yŭ)	206	36°08′N	114°07′E
Shule, r., China (sho͞o-lŭ)	204	40°53′N	94°55′E
Shullsburg, Wi., U.S. (shŭlz′bûrg)	113	42°35′N	90°16′W
Shumagin, is., Ak., U.S. (sho͞o′mȧ-gėn)	103	55°22′N	159°20′W
Shumen, Blg.	163	43°15′N	26°54′E
Shunde, China (shòn-dŭ)	207a	22°50′N	113°15′E
Shungnak, Ak., U.S. (shŭng′nȧk)	103	66°55′N	157°20′W
Shunut, Gora, mtn., Russia (gȧ-rä sho͞o′nòt)	186a	56°33′N	59°45′E
Shunyi, China (shòn-yē)	206	40°09′N	116°38′E
Shuqrah, Yemen	198	13°32′N	46°02′E
Shūrāb, r., Iran (sho͞o räb)	198	31°08′N	55°30′E
Shuri, Japan (sho͞o′rē)	210	26°10′N	127°48′E
Shurugwi, Zimb.	232	19°34′S	30°03′E
Shūshtar, Iran (sho͞osh′tŭr)	198	31°50′N	48°46′E
Shuswap Lake, I., Can. (sho͞os′wŏp)	95	50°57′N	119°15′W
Shuya, Russia (sho͞o′yȧ)	178	56°52′N	41°23′E
Shuyang, China (sho͞o yäng)	206	34°09′N	118°47′E
Shweba, Mya.	199	22°23′N	96°13′E
Shymkent, Kaz.	183	42°17′N	69°42′E
Shyroke, Ukr.	177	47°40′N	33°18′E
Siak Kecil, r., Indon.	197b	1°01′N	101°45′E
Siaksriinderapura, Indon. (sė-äks′rĭ ĕn′drȧ-po͞o′rä)	197b	0°48′N	102°05′E
Siālkot, Pak. (sė-äl′kōt)	199	32°39′N	74°30′E
Siátista, Grc. (syä′tĭs-ta)	175	40°15′N	21°32′E
Siau, Pulau, i., Indon.	213	2°40′N	126°00′E
Šiauliai, Lith. (shė-ou′lė-ī)	180	55°57′N	23°19′E
Sibay, Russia (sē′bȧy)	186a	52°41′N	58°40′E
Šibenik, Cro. (shė-bā′nēk)	163	43°44′N	15°55′E
Siberia, reg., Russia	196	57°00′N	97°00′E
Siberut, Pulau, i., Indon. (sē′bȧ-ro͞ot)	212	1°22′S	99°45′E
Sibiti, Congo (sė-bė-tē′)	232	3°41′S	13°21′E
Sibiu, Rom. (sė-bĭ-o͞o′)	163	45°47′N	24°09′E
Sibley, Ia., U.S. (sĭb′lē)	112	43°24′N	95°33′W
Sibolga, Indon. (sė-bō′gȧ)	212	1°45′N	98°45′E
Sibsāgar, India (sĕb-sŭ′gŭr)	199	26°47′N	94°45′E
Sibutu Island, i., Phil.	212	4°40′N	119°30′E
Sibuyan, i., Phil. (sē-bo͞o-yän′)	213a	12°19′N	122°25′E
Sibuyan Sea, sea, Phil.	212	12°43′N	122°38′E
Sichuan, prov., China (sz-chůän)	204	31°20′N	103°00′E
Sicily, i., Italy (sĭs′ĭ-lē)	156	37°38′N	13°30′E
Sico, r., Hond. (sē-kô)	132	15°32′N	85°42′W
Sidamo, hist. reg., Eth. (sē-dä′mô)	231	5°08′N	37°45′E
Siderno Marina, Italy (sė-dĕr′nô mä-rē′nä)	174	38°18′N	16°19′E
Sídheros, Ákra, c., Grc.	174a	35°19′N	26°20′E
Sidi Aïssa, Alg.	173	35°53′N	3°44′E
Sidi bel Abbès, Alg. (sē′dē-bĕl ȧ-bĕs′)	230	35°15′N	0°43′W
Sidi Ifni, Mor. (ēf′nē)	230	29°22′N	10°15′W
Sidirókastro, Grc.	175	41°13′N	23°27′E
Sidley, Mount, mtn., Ant. (sĭd′lē)	224	77°25′S	129°00′W
Sidney, Can.	94	48°39′N	123°24′W
Sidney, Mt., U.S. (sĭd′nē)	115	47°43′N	104°07′W
Sidney, Ne., U.S.	112	41°10′N	103°00′W
Sidney, Oh., U.S.	108	40°20′N	84°10′W
Sidney Lanier, Lake, res., Ga., U.S. (lăn′yẽr)	107	34°27′N	83°56′W
Sido, Mali	234	11°40′N	7°36′W
Sidon see Saydā, Leb.	198	33°34′N	35°23′E
Sidr, Wādī, r., Egypt	197a	29°43′N	32°58′E
Sidra, Gulf of see Surt, Khalīj, b., Libya	231	31°30′N	18°28′E
Siedlce, Pol. (syĕd′l-tsĕ)	169	52°09′N	22°20′E
Siegburg, Ger. (zēg′bo͞orgh)	168	50°48′N	7°13′E
Siegen, Ger. (zē′ghĕn)	168	50°52′N	8°01′E
Sieghartskirchen, Aus.	159e	48°16′N	16°00′E
Siemiatycze, Pol. (syĕm′yä′tė-chĕ)	169	52°26′N	22°52′E
Siemionówka, Pol. (sĕĕ-mēō′nôf-kä)	169	52°53′N	23°50′E
Siem Reap, Camb. (syĕm′rä′äp)	212	13°32′N	103°54′E
Siena, Italy (sė-ĕn′ä)	162	43°19′N	11°21′E
Sieradz, Pol. (syĕ′rädz)	169	51°35′N	18°45′E
Sierpc, Pol. (syĕrpts)	169	52°51′N	19°42′E
Sierra Blanca, Tx., U.S. (sē-ĕ′rȧ blaŋ-kä)	122	31°10′N	105°20′W
Sierra Blanca Peak, mtn., N.M., U.S. (blăn′kȧ)	106	33°25′N	105°50′W
Sierra Leone, nation, Afr. (sė-ĕr′rä lå-ō′nä)	230	8°48′N	12°30′W
Sierra Madre, Ca., U.S. (mä′drē)	117a	34°10′N	118°03′W
Sierra Mojada, Mex. (sē-ĕ′r-rä-mô-ĸä′dä)	122	27°22′N	103°42′W
Sífnos, i., Grc.	175	36°58′N	24°30′E
Sigean, Fr. (sē-zhôɴ′)	170	43°02′N	2°56′E
Sigeurney, Ia., U.S. (sē-gûr-nĭ)	113	41°16′N	92°10′W
Sighetu Marmaţiei, Rom.	169	47°57′N	23°55′E
Sighişoara, Rom. (sē-gė-shwä′rȧ)	169	46°11′N	24°48′E
Siglufjördur, Ice.	160	66°06′N	18°45′W
Signakhi, Geor.	181	41°45′N	45°50′E
Signal Hill, Ca., U.S. (sĭg′năl hĭl)	117a	33°48′N	118°11′W
Sigsig, Ec. (sēg-sēg′)	142	3°04′S	78°44′W
Sigtuna, Swe. (sēgh-to͞o′nȧ)	166	59°40′N	17°39′E
Siguanea, Ensenada de la, b., Cuba	134	21°45′N	83°15′W
Siguatepeque, Hond. (sē-gwä′tĕ-pĕ-kĕ)	132	14°33′N	87°51′W
Sigüenza, Spain (sē-gwĕ′n-zä)	162	41°03′N	2°38′W
Siguiri, Gui. (sē-gė-rē′)	230	11°25′N	9°10′W
Sihong, China (sz-hôŋ)	206	33°25′N	118°13′E
Siirt, Tur. (sĭ-ērt′)	181	38°00′N	42°00′E
Sikalongo, Zam.	237	16°46′S	27°07′E
Sikasso, Mali (sė-käs′sō)	230	11°19′N	5°40′W
Sikeston, Mo., U.S. (sīks′tŭn)	121	36°50′N	89°35′W
Sikhote Alin′, Khrebet, mts., Russia (se-ĸô′ta a-lēn′)	179	45°00′N	135°45′E
Síkinos, i., Grc. (sĭ′kĭ-nōs)	175	36°45′N	24°55′E
Sikkim, state, India	199	27°42′N	88°25′E
Siklós, Hung. (sĭ′klōsh)	169	45°51′N	18°18′E
Sil, r., Spain (sē′l)	172	42°20′N	7°13′W
Silang, Phil. (sė-läng′)	213a	14°14′N	120°58′E
Silao, Mex. (sē-lä′ō)	130	20°56′N	101°25′W
Silchar, India (sĭl-chär′)	199	24°52′N	92°50′E
Silent Valley, S. Afr. (sī′lĕnt vă′lē)	238c	24°32′S	26°40′E
Siler City, N.C., U.S. (sī′lẽr)	125	35°45′N	79°29′W
Silesia, hist. reg., Pol. (sĭ-lē′shȧ)	168	50°58′N	16°53′E
Silifke, Tur.	163	36°20′N	34°00′E
Siling Co, I., China	204	32°05′N	89°10′E
Silistra, Blg. (sė-lēs′trȧ)	163	44°01′N	27°13′E
Siljan, I., Swe. (sēl′yän)	160	60°48′N	14°28′E
Silkeborg, Den. (sĭl′kĕ-bôr′)	166	56°10′N	9°33′E
Sillery, Can. (sēl′-re′)	102b	46°46′N	71°15′W
Siloam Springs, Ar., U.S. (sĭ-lōm)	121	36°10′N	94°32′W
Siloana Plains, pl., Zam.	236	16°55′S	23°10′E
Silocayoápan, Mex. (sē-lô-kä-yô-ȧ′pän)	130	17°29′N	98°09′W
Silsbee, Tx., U.S. (sĭlz′ bē)	123	30°19′N	94°09′W
Šilutė, Lith.	167	55°21′N	21°29′E
Silva Jardim, Braz. (sē′l-vä-zhär-dēn)	141a	22°40′N	42°24′W
Silvana, Wa., U.S. (sĭ-vän′ȧ)	116a	48°12′N	122°16′W
Silvânia, Braz. (sēl-vá′nyä)	143	16°43′S	48°33′W
Silvassa, India	202	20°10′N	73°00′E
Silver, I., Mo., U.S.	121	39°38′N	93°12′W
Silverado, Ca., U.S. (sĭl-vĕr-ä′dō)	117a	33°45′N	117°40′W
Silver Bank, bk.	135	20°40′N	69°40′W
Silver Bank Passage, strt., N.A.	135	20°40′N	70°20′W
Silver Bay, Mn., U.S.	113	47°24′N	91°07′W
Silver City, Pan.	133	9°20′N	79°54′W
Silver City, N.M., U.S. (sĭl′vẽr sĭ′tĭ)	119	32°45′N	108°20′W
Silver Creek, N.Y., U.S. (crēk)	109	42°35′N	79°10′W
Silver Creek, r., Az., U.S.	119	34°30′N	110°05′W
Silver Creek, r., In., U.S.	111h	38°20′N	85°45′W
Silver Creek, Muddy Fork, r., In., U.S.	111h	38°26′N	85°52′W
Silverdale, Wa., U.S. (sĭl′vẽr-dāl)	116a	49°39′N	122°42′W

PRONOUNCING INDEX

Silver Lake – Soest 351

PLACE (Pronunciation)	PAGE	LAT.	LONG.
Silver Lake, Wi., U.S. (lăk)	111a	42°33'N	88°10'W
Silver Lake, l., Wi., U.S.	111a	42°35'N	88°08'W
Silver Spring, Md., U.S. (spring)	110e	39°00'N	77°00'W
Silver Star Mountain, mtn., Wa., U.S.	116c	45°45'N	122°15'W
Silverthrone Mountain, mtn., Can. (sĭl'vĕr-thrōn)	94	51°31'N	126°06'W
Silverton, S. Afr.	238c	25°45'S	28°13'E
Silverton, Co., U.S. (sĭl'vĕr-tŭn)	119	37°50'N	107°40'W
Silverton, Oh., U.S.	111f	39°12'N	84°24'W
Silverton, Or., U.S.	114	45°02'N	122°46'W
Silves, Port. (sēl'vĕzh)	162	37°15'N	8°24'W
Silvies, r., Or., U.S. (sĭl'vēz)	114	43°44'N	119°15'W
Sim, Russia (sĭm)	186a	55°00'N	57°42'E
Sim, r., Russia	186a	54°50'N	56°50'E
Simao, China (sz-mou)	204	22°56'N	101°07'E
Simard, Lac, l., Can.	99	47°38'N	78°40'W
Simba, D.R.C.	236	0°36'N	22°55'E
Simcoe, Can. (sĭm'kō)	164	42°50'N	80°20'W
Simcoe, l., Can.	93	44°30'N	79°20'W
Simeulue, Pulau, i., Indon.	212	2°27'N	95°30'E
Simferopol', Ukr.	178	44°58'N	34°04'E
Similk Beach, Wa., U.S. (sē'mĭlk)	116a	48°27'N	122°35'W
Simla, India (sĭm'là)	199	31°09'N	77°15'E
Şimleu Silvaniei, Rom.	163	47°14'N	22°46'E
Simms Point, c., Bah.	134	25°00'N	77°40'W
Simojovel, Mex. (sē-mō-hō-vĕl')	131	17°12'N	92°43'W
Simonésia, Braz. (sē-mō-nĕ'syä)	141a	20°04'S	41°53'W
Simonette, r., Can. (sī-mŏn-ĕt')	95	54°15'N	118°00'W
Simonstad, S. Afr.	232a	34°11'S	18°25'E
Simood Sound, Can.	94	50°45'N	126°25'W
Simplon Pass, p., Switz. (sĭm'plŏn) (săn-plôN')	168	46°13'N	7°53'E
Simpson, i., Can.	113	48°43'N	87°44'W
Simpson Desert, des., Austl. (sĭmp-sŭn)	220	24°40'S	136°40'E
Simrishamn, Swe. (sēm'rēs-häm'n)	166	55°35'N	14°19'E
Sims Bayou, Tx., U.S. (sĭmz bī-yōō')	123a	29°37'N	95°23'W
Simushir, i., Russia (se-mōō'shēr)	205	47°15'N	150°47'E
Sinaia, Rom. (sĭ-nä'yȧ)	175	45°20'N	25°30'E
Sinai Peninsula, pen., Egypt (sī'nī)	231	29°24'N	33°29'E
Sinaloa, state, Mex. (sē-nä-lô-ä)	128	25°15'N	107°45'W
Sinan, China (sz-nän)	204	27°50'N	108°30'E
Sinanju, Kor., N. (sĭ'nän-jŏ')	210	39°39'N	125°41'E
Sincelejo, Col. (sēn-så-lā'hō)	142	9°12'N	75°30'W
Sinclair Inlet, Wa., U.S. (sĭn-klâr')	116a	47°31'N	122°41'W
Sinclair Mills, Can.	95	54°02'N	121°41'W
Sindi, Est. (sēn'dē)	167	58°20'N	24°40'E
Sines, Port. (sē'nāzh)	172	37°57'N	8°50'W
Singapore, Sing. (sĭn'gȧ-pōr')	212	1°18'N	103°52'E
Singapore, nation, Asia	212	1°22'N	103°45'E
Singapore Strait, strt., Asia	197b	1°14'N	104°20'E
Singu, Mya. (sĭn'gŭ)	204	22°37'N	96°04'E
Siniye Lipyagi, Russia (sēn'ê lēp'yä-gê)	177	51°24'N	38°29'E
Sinj, Cro. (sēn')	174	43°42'N	16°39'E
Sinjah, Sudan	231	13°09'N	33°52'E
Sinkāt, Sudan	200	18°50'N	36°50'E
Sinkiang see Xinjiang, prov., China	204	40°15'N	82°15'E
Sin'kovo, Russia (sĭn-kô'vô)	186b	56°23'N	37°19'E
Sinnamary, Fr. Gu.	143	5°15'N	52°52'W
Sinni, r., Italy (sēn'nē)	174	40°05'N	16°15'E
Sinnūris, Egypt	238b	29°25'N	30°52'E
Sino, Pedra de, mtn., Braz. (pĕ'drä-dô-sē'nō)	144b	22°27'S	43°02'W
Sinop, Tur.	198	42°00'N	35°05'E
Sint Eustatius, i., Neth. Ant.	133b	17°32'N	62°45'W
Sint Niklaas, Bel.	159a	51°10'N	4°07'E
Sinton, Tx., U.S. (sĭn'tŭn)	123	28°03'N	97°30'W
Sintra, Port. (sēn'trȧ)	172	38°48'N	9°23'W
Sint Truiden, Bel.	159a	50°49'N	5°14'E
Sinŭiju, Kor., N. (sĭ'nŏĭ-jōō)	205	40°04'N	124°33'E
Sinyavino, Russia (sĭn-yä'vĭ-nô)	186c	59°50'N	31°07'E
Sinyaya, r., Eur. (sēn'yȧ-yȧ)	176	56°40'N	28°20'E
Sion, Switz. (sē'ôN')	168	46°15'N	7°17'E
Sioux City, Ia., U.S. (sōō sĭ'tĭ)	104	42°30'N	96°25'W
Sioux Falls, S.D., U.S. (fôlz)	104	43°33'N	96°43'W
Sioux Lookout, Can.	91	50°06'N	91°55'W
Siping, China (sz-pĭŋ)	205	43°05'N	124°24'E
Sipiwesk, Can.	90	55°27'N	97°24'W
Sipsey, r., Al., U.S. (sĭp'sē)	124	33°26'N	87°42'W
Sipura, Pulau, i., Indon.	212	2°15'S	99°33'E
Siqueros, Mex. (sē-kā'rōs)	130	23°19'N	106°14'W
Siquia, Río, r., Nic. (sē-kē'ä)	133	12°23'N	84°36'W
Siracusa, Italy (sē-rä-koo'sä)	163	37°02'N	15°19'E
Sirājganj, Bngl. (sĭ-räj'gŭnj)	199	24°23'N	89°43'E
Sirama, El Sal. (Sē-rä-mä)	132	13°23'N	87°55'W
Sir Douglas, Mount, mtn., Can. (sûr dŭg'lăs)	95	50°44'N	115°20'W
Sir Edward Pellew Group, is., Austl. (pĕl'ū)	220	15°15'S	137°15'E
Siret, Rom.	169	47°58'N	26°01'E
Siret, r., Eur.	163	47°00'N	27°00'E
Sirhān, Wadi, depr., Sau. Ar.	198	31°02'N	37°16'E
Sirsa, India	202	29°39'N	75°02'E
Sir Sandford, Mount, mtn., Can. (sûr sănd'fērd)	95	51°40'N	117°52'W
Sirvintos, Lith. (shēr'vĭn-tôs)	167	55°02'N	24°59'E
Sir Wilfrid Laurier, Mount, mtn., Can. (sûr wĭl'frĭd lôr'yēr)	95	52°47'N	119°45'W
Sisak, Cro. (sē'sȧk)	163	45°29'N	16°20'E
Sisal, Mex. (sē-säl')	128	21°09'N	90°03'W
Sishui, China (sz-shwā)	206	35°40'N	117°17'E
Sisquoc, r., Ca., U.S. (sĭs'kwŏk)	118	34°47'N	120°13'W
Sisseton, S.D., U.S. (sĭs'tŭn)	112	45°39'N	97°04'W
Sistān, Daryacheh-ye, l., Asia	198	31°45'N	61°15'E
Sisteron, Fr. (sēst'rôN')	171	44°10'N	5°55'E
Sisterville, W.V., U.S. (sĭs'tēr-vĭl)	108	39°30'N	81°00'W
Sitia, Grc. (sē'tĭ-ȧ)	174a	35°09'N	26°10'E
Sitka, Ak., U.S. (sĭt'kȧ)	106a	57°08'N	135°18'W
Sittingbourne, Eng., U.K. (sĭt-ĭng-bôrn)	158b	51°20'N	0°44'E
Sittwe, Mya.	199	20°09'N	92°54'E
Sivas, Tur. (sē'väs)	198	39°50'N	36°50'E
Siverek, Tur. (sē'vĕ-rĕk)	198	37°50'N	39°20'E
Siverskaya, Russia (sē'vĕr-skȧ-yȧ)	167	59°17'N	30°03'E
Sivers'kyi Donets', r., Eur.	177	48°48'N	38°42'E
Sīwah, Egypt	200	29°12'N	25°31'E
Siwah, oasis, Egypt (sē'wä)	231	29°33'N	25°11'E
Sixaola, r., C.R.	133	9°31'N	83°07'W
Sixian, China (sz shyĕn)	206	33°37'N	117°51'E
Sixth Cataract, wtfl., Sudan	231	16°26'N	32°44'E
Siyang, China (sz-yäŋ)	206	33°43'N	118°42'E
Sjaelland, i., Den. (shĕl'lăn')	166	55°34'N	11°35'E
Sjenica, Yugo. (syĕ'nĕ-tsȧ)	175	43°15'N	20°02'E
Skadovs'k, Ukr.	177	46°08'N	32°54'E
Skagen, Den. (skä'ghĕn)	166	57°43'N	10°32'E
Skagerrak, strt., Eur. (skä-ghĕ-räk')	156	57°43'N	8°28'E
Skagit, r., Wa., U.S.	114	48°29'N	121°52'W
Skagit Bay, b., Wa., U.S. (skăg'ĭt)	116a	48°20'N	122°32'W
Skagway, Ak., U.S. (skăg-wā)	106a	59°30'N	135°28'W
Skälderviken, b., Swe.	166	56°20'N	12°25'E
Skalistyy, Golets, mtn., Russia	179	57°28'N	119°48'E
Skalistyy Khrebet, mts., Russia	182	43°15'N	43°00'E
Skamania, Wa., U.S. (skȧ-mā'nĭ-ȧ)	116c	45°37'N	112°03'W
Skamokawa, Wa., U.S.	116c	46°16'N	123°27'W
Skanderborg, Den. (skän-ĕr-bôr')	166	56°04'N	9°55'E
Skaneateles, N.Y., U.S. (skăn-ĕ-ăt'lĕs)	109	42°55'N	76°25'W
Skaneateles, l., N.Y., U.S.	109	42°50'N	76°20'W
Skänninge, Swe. (shĕn'ĭng-ĕ)	166	58°24'N	15°02'E
Skanör-Falsterbo, Swe. (skän'ûr)	166	55°24'N	12°49'E
Skara, Swe. (skä'rȧ)	166	58°25'N	13°24'E
Skeena, r., Can. (skē'nȧ)	92	54°30'N	129°00'W
Skeena Mountains, mts., Can.	94	56°00'N	128°00'W
Skeerpoort, S. Afr.	233b	25°49'S	27°45'E
Skeerpoort, r., S. Afr.	233b	25°58'S	27°41'E
Skeldon, Guy. (skĕl'dŭn)	143	5°49'N	57°15'W
Skellefteå, Swe. (shĕl'ĕf-tĕ-ȧ')	160	64°47'N	20°48'E
Skellefteälven, r., Swe.	160	65°15'N	19°30'E
Skhodnya, Russia (skôd'nyȧ)	186b	55°57'N	37°21'E
Skhodnya, r., Russia	186b	55°55'N	37°16'E
Skíathos, i., Grc. (skē'á-thôs)	175	39°15'N	23°25'E
Skibbereen, Ire. (skĭb'ēr-ēn)	164	51°32'N	9°25'W
Skidegate, b., Can. (skĭ'-dē-gāt')	94	53°15'N	132°00'W
Skidmore, Tx., U.S. (skĭd'mōr)	123	28°16'N	97°40'W
Skien, Nor. (skē'ĕn)	160	59°13'N	9°35'E
Skierniewice, Pol. (skyĕr-nyĕ-vēt'sĕ)	169	51°58'N	20°13'E
Skihist Mountain, mtn., Can.	95	50°11'N	121°54'W
Skikda, Alg.	230	36°58'N	6°51'E
Skilpadfontein, S. Afr.	238c	25°02'S	28°50'E
Skive, Den. (skē'vĕ)	166	56°34'N	8°56'E
Skjálfandafljót, r., Ice. (skyäl'fänd-ô)	160	65°24'N	16°40'W
Skjerstad, Nor. (skyĕr-städ)	160	67°12'N	15°37'E
Škofja Loka, Slvn. (shkôf'yȧ lō'kȧ)	174	46°10'N	14°20'E
Skokie, Il., U.S. (skō'kē)	111a	42°02'N	87°45'W
Skokomish Indian Reservation, I.R., Wa., U.S. (Skō-kō'mĭsh)	116a	47°22'N	123°07'W
Skole, Ukr. (skô'lĕ)	169	49°03'N	23°32'E
Skópelos, i., Grc. (skô'pȧ-lôs)	175	39°04'N	23°31'E
Skopin, Russia (skô-pĕn)	180	53°49'N	39°35'E
Skopje, Mac. (skôp'yĕ)	174	42°02'N	21°26'E
Skövde, Swe. (shûv'dĕ)	160	58°25'N	13°48'E
Skovorodino, Russia (skô'vô-rô'dĭ-nô)	179	53°53'N	123°56'E
Skowhegan, Me., U.S. (skou-hē'găn)	100	44°45'N	69°27'W
Skradin, Cro. (skrä'dĕn)	175	43°49'N	17°58'E
Skreia, Nor. (skrā'ȧ)	166	60°40'N	10°55'E
Skudeneshavn, Nor. (skōō'dĕ-nes-houn')	166	59°10'N	5°19'E
Skull Valley Indian Reservation, I.R., Ut., U.S. (skŭl)	119	40°25'N	112°50'W
Skuna, r., Ms., U.S. (skû'nȧ)	124	33°57'N	89°36'W
Skunk, r., Ia., U.S. (skŭnk)	113	41°12'N	92°14'W
Skuodas, Lith. (skwô'dȧs)	167	56°16'N	21°32'E
Skurup, Swe. (skû'rŏŏp)	166	55°29'N	13°27'E
Skvyra, Ukr.	181	49°43'N	29°41'E
Skwierzyna, Pol. (skvē-ĕr'zhĭ-nȧ)	168	52°35'N	15°30'E
Skye, Island of, i., Scot., U.K. (skī)	160	57°25'N	6°17'W
Skykomish, r., Wa., U.S. (skī'kō-mĭsh)	116a	47°50'N	121°55'W
Skyring, Seno de, b., Chile (sĕ'nô-s-krĕ'ng)	144	52°35'S	72°30'W
Skýros, Grc.	175	38°53'N	24°32'E
Skýros, i., Grc.	163	38°50'N	24°43'E
Slagese, Den.	166	55°25'N	11°19'E
Slamet, Gunung, mtn., Indon. (slä'mĕt)	212	7°15'S	109°15'E
Slănic, Rom. (slŭ'nĕk)	175	45°13'N	25°56'E
Slater, Mo., U.S. (slāt'ēr)	121	39°13'N	93°03'W
Slatina, Rom. (slä'tē-nä)	175	44°26'N	24°21'E
Slaton, Tx., U.S. (slā'tŭn)	120	33°26'N	101°38'W
Slave, r., Can. (slāv)	92	59°40'N	111°21'W
Slavgorod, Russia (slåf'gō-rôt)	178	52°58'N	78°43'E
Slavonija, hist. reg., Yugo. (slä-vô'nē-yä)	175	45°29'N	17°31'E
Slavonska Požega, Cro. (slä-vôn'skä pô'zhĕ-gä)	175	45°18'N	17°42'E
Slavonski Brod, Cro. (skä-vôn'skĕ brôd)	163	45°10'N	18°01'E
Slavuta, Ukr. (slå-vōō'tȧ)	177	50°18'N	27°01'E
Slavyanskaya, Russia (slåv-yȧn'skȧ-yȧ)	177	45°14'N	38°09'E
Sławno, Pol. (swav'nō)	168	54°21'N	16°38'E
Slayton, Mn., U.S. (slā'tŭn)	112	44°00'N	95°44'W
Sleaford, Eng., U.K. (slē'fērd)	158a	53°00'N	0°25'W
Sleepy Eye, Mn., U.S. (slēp'ĭ ī)	113	44°17'N	94°44'W
Slidell, La., U.S. (slī-dĕl')	123	30°17'N	89°47'W
Sliedrecht, Neth.	159a	51°49'N	4°46'E
Sligo, Ire. (slī'gō)	160	54°17'N	8°19'W
Slite, Swe. (slē'tĕ)	166	57°41'N	18°47'E
Sliven, Blg. (slē'vĕn)	163	42°41'N	26°20'E
Sloatsburg, N.Y., U.S. (slōts'bûrg)	110a	41°09'N	74°11'W
Slonim, Bela. (swō'nĕm)	169	53°05'N	25°19'E
Slough, Eng., U.K. (slou)	158b	51°29'N	0°36'W
Slovakia, nation, Eur.	169	48°50'N	20°00'E
Slovenia, nation, Eur.	174	45°58'N	14°43'E
Slovians'k, Ukr.	181	48°52'N	37°34'E
Sluch, r., Ukr.	181	50°56'N	26°48'E
Slunj, Cro. (slōn')	174	45°08'N	15°46'E
Słupsk, Pol. (swōpsk)	160	54°28'N	17°02'E
Slutsk, Bela. (slōtsk)	180	53°02'N	27°34'E
Slyne Head, c., Ire. (slīn)	160	53°25'N	10°05'W
Smackover, Ar., U.S. (smăk'ō-vēr)	121	33°22'N	92°42'W
Smederevo, Yugo.	175	44°39'N	20°54'E
Smederevska Palanka, Yugo. (smĕ-dĕ-rĕv'skä pä-län'kä)	175	44°21'N	21°00'E
Smedjebacken, Swe. (smĭ'tyĕ-bä-kĕn)	166	60°09'N	15°19'E
Smethport, Pa., U.S. (smĕth'pōrt)	109	41°50'N	78°25'W
Smethwick, Eng., U.K.	164	52°31'N	2°04'W
Smila, Ukr.	181	49°14'N	31°52'E
Smile, Ukr.	177	50°55'N	33°36'E
Smiltene, Lat. (smēl'tĕ-nĕ)	167	57°26'N	25°57'E
Smith, Can. (smĭth)	90	55°10'N	114°02'W
Smith, i., Wa., U.S.	116a	48°20'N	122°53'W
Smith, r., Mt., U.S.	115	47°00'N	111°20'W
Smith Center, Ks., U.S. (sĕn'tēr)	120	39°45'N	98°46'W
Smithers, Can. (smĭth'ērs)	90	54°47'N	127°10'W
Smithfield, N.C., U.S. (smĭth'fēld)	125	35°30'N	78°21'W
Smithfield, Ut., U.S.	115	41°50'N	111°49'W
Smithland, Ky., U.S. (smĭth'lănd)	108	37°10'N	88°25'W
Smith Mountain Lake, res., Va., U.S.	125	37°00'N	79°45'W
Smith Point, Tx., U.S.	123a	29°32'N	94°45'W
Smiths Falls, Can. (smĭths)	91	44°55'N	76°05'W
Smithton, Austl. (smĭth'tŭn)	222	40°55'S	145°12'E
Smithton, Il., U.S.	117e	38°24'N	89°59'W
Smithville, Tx., U.S. (smĭth'vĭl)	123	30°00'N	97°08'W
Smitswinkelvlakte, pl., S. Afr.	232a	34°16'S	18°25'E
Smoke Creek Desert, des., Nv., U.S. (smōk crēk)	118	40°28'N	119°40'W
Smoky, r., Can. (smōk'ĭ)	95	55°30'N	117°30'W
Smoky Hill, r., U.S. (smōk'ĭ hĭl)	106	38°40'N	100°00'W
Smøla, i., Nor. (smûlä)	160	63°16'N	7°40'E
Smolensk, Russia (smô-lyĕnsk')	178	54°46'N	32°03'E
Smolensk, prov., Russia	176	55°00'N	32°18'E
Smyadovo, Blg.	175	43°04'N	27°00'E
Smyrna see İzmir, Tur.	198	38°25'N	27°05'E
Smyrna, De., U.S. (smûr'nȧ)	109	39°20'N	75°35'W
Smyrna, Ga., U.S.	110c	33°53'N	84°31'W
Snag, Can. (snăg)	103	62°18'N	140°30'W
Snake, r., Mn., U.S. (snāk)	113	45°58'N	93°20'W
Snake, r., U.S.	106	45°30'N	117°00'W
Snake Range, mts., Nv., U.S.	119	39°20'N	114°15'W
Snake River Plain, pl., Id., U.S.	115	43°08'N	114°46'W
Snap Point, c., Bah.	134	23°45'N	77°30'W
Sneffels, Mount, mtn., Co., U.S. (snĕf'ĕlz)	119	38°00'N	107°50'W
Snelgrove, Can. (snĕl'grōv)	102d	43°44'N	79°50'W
Śniardwy, Jezioro, l., Pol. (snyärt'vĭ)	169	53°46'N	21°59'E
Snöhetta, mtn., Nor. (snû-hĕttä)	160	62°18'N	9°12'E
Snohomish, Wa., U.S. (snô-hō'mĭsh)	116a	47°55'N	122°05'W
Snohomish, r., Wa., U.S.	116a	47°53'N	122°04'W
Snoqualmie, Wa., U.S. (snō qwäl'mē)	116a	47°32'N	121°50'W
Snoqualmie, r., Wa., U.S.	114	47°32'N	121°53'W
Snov, r., Eur. (snôf)	177	51°38'N	31°38'E
Snowdon, mtn., Wales, U.K.	164	53°05'N	4°04'W
Snow Hill, Md., U.S. (hĭl)	109	38°15'N	75°20'W
Snow Lake, Can.	97	54°50'N	100°10'W
Snowy Mountains, mts., Austl. (snō'ē)	221	36°17'S	148°30'E
Snyder, Ok., U.S. (snī'dēr)	120	34°40'N	98°57'W
Snyder, Tx., U.S.	122	32°48'N	100°53'W
Soar, r., Eng., U.K. (sōr)	158a	52°44'N	1°09'W
Sobat, r., Sudan (sō'bȧt)	231	9°04'N	32°02'E
Sobinka, Russia (sô-bĭŋ'kȧ)	176	55°59'N	40°02'E
Sobo Zan, mtn., Japan (sô'bô zän)	210	32°47'N	131°27'E
Sobral, Braz. (sô-brä'l)	143	3°39'S	40°16'W
Sochaczew, Pol. (sô-kä'chĕf)	169	52°14'N	20°18'E
Sochi, Russia (sôch'ĭ)	178	43°35'N	39°50'E
Society Islands, is., Fr. Poly. (sô-sī'ĕ-tē)	241	15°00'S	157°30'W
Socoltenango, Mex. (sô-kôl-tĕ-näŋ'gō)	131	16°17'N	92°20'W
Socorro, Braz. (sô-kô'r-rō)	141a	22°35'S	46°32'W
Socorro, Col. (sô-kôr'rō)	142	6°23'N	73°19'W
Socorro, N.M., U.S.	119	34°05'N	106°55'W
Socúellamos, Spain (sô-kōō-āl'yä-mōs)	172	39°18'N	2°48'W
Soda, l., Ca., U.S. (sō'dȧ)	118	35°12'N	116°25'W
Soda Peak, mtn., Wa., U.S.	116c	45°53'N	122°04'W
Soda Springs, Id., U.S. (sprĭngz)	115	42°39'N	111°37'W
Söderhamn, Swe. (sû-dĕr-häm''n)	160	61°20'N	17°00'E
Söderköping, Swe.	166	58°30'N	16°14'E
Södertälje, Swe. (sû-dĕr-tĕl'yĕ)	160	59°12'N	17°35'E
Sodo, Eth.	231	7°03'N	37°46'E
Soest, Ger. (zōst)	168	51°35'N	8°05'E

ng-sing; ŋ-baŋk; N-nasalized n; nŏd; cŏmmit; ōld; ôbey; ôrder; oi-boil; fōōd; ò-as oo in foot; ou-out; s-soft; sh-dish; th-thin; pūre; ûnite; ûrn; stŭd; circŭs; ü-as in French tu; '-indeterminate vowel.

352 Sofia – Spas-Klepiki

PRONOUNCING INDEX

PLACE (Pronunciation)	PAGE	LAT.	LONG.
Sofia (Sofiya), Blg. (sô'fê-yà) (sô'fê-ä)	154	42°43'N	23°20'E
Sofiïvka, Ukr.	177	48°03'N	33°53'E
Sofiya *see* Sofia, Blg.	154	42°43'N	23°20'E
Soga, Japan (sō'gä)	211a	35°35'N	140°08'E
Sogamoso, Col. (sô-gä-mō'sō)	142	5°42'N	72°51'W
Sognafjorden, b., Nor.	156	61°09'N	5°30'E
Sogozha, r., Russia (sô'gô-zhà)	176	58°35'N	39°08'E
Sohano, Pap. N. Gui.	214e	5°27'S	154°40'E
Soissons, Fr. (swä-sôN')	170	49°23'N	3°17'E
Sōka, Japan (sō'kä)	211a	35°50'N	139°49'E
Sokal', Ukr. (sô'käl')	169	50°28'N	24°20'E
Söke, Tur. (sû'kĕ)	163	37°40'N	27°10'E
Sokółka, Pol. (sô-kòl'kà)	169	53°23'N	23°30'E
Sokolo, Mali (sô-kô-lō')	230	14°51'N	6°09'W
Sokołów Podlaski, Pol. (sô-kô-wòf' pŭd-lä'skĭ)	169	52°24'N	22°15'E
Sokone, Sen.	234	13°53'N	16°22'W
Sokoto, Nig. (sō'kô-tō)	230	13°04'N	5°16'E
Sola de Vega, Mex.	131	16°31'N	96°58'W
Solander, Cape, c., Austl.	217b	34°03'S	151°16'E
Solano, Phil. (sō-lä'nō)	213a	16°31'N	121°11'E
Soledad, Col. (sō-lĕ-dä'd)	142	10°47'N	75°00'W
Soledad Díez Gutiérrez, Mex.	130	22°19'N	100°54'W
Soleduck, r., Wa., U.S. (sōl'dŭk)	114	47°59'N	124°28'W
Solentiname, Islas de, is., Nic. (ē's-läs-dĕ-sô-lĕn-tē-nä'mà)	132	11°15'N	85°16'W
Solihull, Eng., U.K. (sō'lĭ-hŭl)	158a	52°25'N	1°46'W
Solihull, co., Eng., U.K.	158a	52°25'N	1°42'W
Solikamsk, Russia (sô-lē-kàmsk')	180	59°38'N	56°48'E
Sol'-Iletsk, Russia	178	51°10'N	55°05'E
Solimões *see* Amazon, r., Braz.	142	2°45'S	67°44'W
Solingen, Ger. (zō'lĭng-ĕn)	168	51°10'N	7°05'E
Sóller, Spain (sō'lyĕr)	173	39°45'N	2°40'E
Sologne, reg., Fr. (sō-lōn'yĕ)	170	47°36'N	1°53'E
Solola, Guat. (sô-lō'lä)	132	14°45'N	91°12'W
Solomon, r., Ks., U.S.	120	39°24'N	98°19'W
Solomon, North Fork, r., Ks., U.S.	120	39°34'N	99°52'W
Solomon, South Fork, r., Ks., U.S.	120	39°19'N	99°52'W
Solomon Islands, nation, Oc. (sŏ'lō-mūn)	3	7°00'S	160°00'E
Solon, China (swo-lo͞on)	205	46°32'N	121°18'E
Solon, Oh., U.S. (sō'lŭn)	111d	41°23'N	81°26'W
Solothurn, Switz. (zō'lō-tho͞orn)	168	47°13'N	7°30'E
Solovetskiye Ostrova, is., Russia	180	65°10'N	35°40'E
Šolta, i., Yugo. (shôl'tä)	174	43°20'N	16°15'E
Soltau, Ger. (sōl'tou)	168	53°00'N	9°50'E
Sol'tsy, Russia (sôl'tsē)	176	58°04'N	30°13'E
Solvay, N.Y., U.S. (sŏl'vā)	109	43°05'N	76°10'W
Sölvesborg, Swe. (sûl'vĕs-bôrg)	166	56°04'N	14°35'E
Sol'vychegodsk, Russia (sôl'vê-chĕ-gôtsk')	180	61°18'N	46°58'E
Solway Firth, b., U.K. (sŏl'wā fûrth')	154	54°42'N	3°55'W
Solwezi, Zam.	237	12°11'S	26°25'E
Soly, Bela.	166	54°31'N	26°11'E
Somalia, nation, Afr. (sō-mä'lē-ä)	238a	3°28'N	44°47'E
Somanga, Tan.	237	8°24'S	39°17'E
Sombor, Yugo. (sôm'bôr)	163	45°45'N	19°10'E
Sombrerete, Mex. (sōm-brå-rā'tå)	130	23°38'N	103°37'W
Sombrero, Cayo, i., Ven. (kä-yô-sôm-brĕ'rô)	143b	10°52'N	68°12'W
Somerset, Ky., U.S. (sŭm'ēr-sĕt)	124	37°05'N	84°35'W
Somerset, Ma., U.S.	110b	41°46'N	71°05'W
Somerset, Pa., U.S.	109	40°00'N	79°05'W
Somerset, Tx., U.S.	117d	29°13'N	98°39'W
Somerset East, S. Afr.	233c	32°44'S	25°36'E
Somersworth, N.H., U.S. (sŭm'ērz-wûrth)	100	43°16'N	70°53'W
Somerton, Az., U.S. (sŭm'ēr-tŭn)	119	32°36'N	114°43'W
Somerville, Ma., U.S. (sŭm'ēr-vĭl)	101a	42°23'N	71°06'W
Somerville, N.J., U.S.	110a	40°34'N	74°37'W
Somerville, Tn., U.S.	124	35°14'N	89°21'W
Somerville, Tx., U.S.	123	30°21'N	96°31'W
Someş, r., Eur.	169	47°43'N	23°09'E
Somma Vesuviana, Italy (sôm'mä vā-zo͞o-vē-ä'nä)	173c	40°38'N	14°27'E
Somme, r., Fr. (sŏm)	170	50°02'N	2°04'E
Sommerfeld, Ger. (zō'mĕr-fĕld)	159b	52°48'N	13°02'E
Sommerville, Austl.	217a	38°14'S	145°10'E
Somoto, Nic. (sô-mō'tō)	132	13°28'N	86°37'W
Son, r., India (sōn)	199	24°40'N	82°35'E
Sŏnchŏn, Kor., N. (sŭn'shŭn)	210	39°49'N	124°56'E
Sondags, r., S. Afr.	233c	33°17'S	25°14'E
Sønderborg, Den. (sûn''er-bôrgh)	160	54°55'N	9°47'E
Sondershausen, Ger. (zōn'dērz-hou'zĕn)	168	51°17'N	10°45'E
Song Ca, r., Viet.	209	19°15'N	105°00'E
Songea, Tan. (sôn-gā'ä)	232	10°41'S	35°39'E
Songjiang, China	205	31°01'N	121°14'E
Sŏngjin, Kor., N. (sŭng'jĭn')	210	40°38'N	129°10'E
Songkhla, Thai. (sông'κlä')	212	7°09'N	100°34'E
Songwe, D.R.C.	237	12°25'S	29°40'E
Sonneberg, Ger. (sôn'ē-bĕrgh)	168	50°20'N	11°14'E
Sonora, Ca., U.S. (sō-nō'rá)	118	37°58'N	120°22'W
Sonora, Tx., U.S.	122	30°33'N	100°38'W
Sonora, state, Mex.	128	29°45'N	111°15'W
Sonora, r., Mex.	128	28°45'N	111°35'W
Sonora Peak, mtn., Ca., U.S.	106	38°22'N	119°39'W
Sonseca, Spain (sôn-sā'kä)	172	39°41'N	3°56'W
Sonsón, Col. (sôn-sôn')	142	5°42'N	75°28'W
Sonsonate, El Sal. (sōn-sō-nä'tå)	132	13°46'N	89°43'W
Sonsorol Islands, is., Palau (sŏn-sō-rōl')	213	5°03'N	132°33'E
Sooke Basin, b., Can. (so͝ok)	116a	48°21'N	123°47'W
Soo Locks, trans., Mi., U.S. (so͞o lŏks)	117a	46°30'N	84°30'W
Sopetrán, Col. (sō-pĕ-trä'n)	142a	6°30'N	75°44'W
Sopot, Pol. (sô'pôt)	169	54°26'N	18°25'E
Sopron, Hung. (shŏp'rôn)	163	47°41'N	16°36'E
Sora, Italy (sō'rä)	174	41°43'N	13°37'E
Sorbas, Spain (sôr'bäs)	172	37°05'N	2°07'W
Sordo, r., Mex. (sō'r-dō)	131	16°39'N	97°33'W
Sorel, Can. (sô-rĕl')	91	46°01'N	73°07'W
Sorell, Cape, c., Austl.	222	42°10'S	144°50'E
Soresina, Italy (sō-rå-zē'nä)	174	45°17'N	9°51'E
Soria, Spain (sō'rē-ä)	162	41°46'N	2°28'W
Soriano, dept., Ur. (sō-rēä'nō)	141c	33°25'S	58°00'W
Soroca, Mol.	181	48°09'N	28°17'E
Sorocaba, Braz. (sō-rō-kä'bå)	143	23°29'S	47°27'W
Sorong, Indon. (sō-rông')	213	1°00'S	131°20'E
Sorot', r., Russia (sō-rō'tzh)	176	57°08'N	29°23'E
Soroti, Ug. (sō-rō'tē)	231	1°43'N	33°37'E
Sørøya, i., Nor.	160	70°37'N	20°58'E
Sorraia, r., Port. (sôr-rī'à)	172	38°55'N	8°42'W
Sorrento, Italy (sôr-rĕn'tō)	174	40°23'N	14°23'E
Sorsogon, Phil. (sôr-sōgōn')	213	12°51'N	124°02'E
Sortavala, Russia (sôr'tä-vä-lä)	178	61°43'N	30°40'E
Sosna, r., Russia (sôs'nà)	177	50°33'N	38°15'E
Sosnogorsk, Russia	178	63°13'N	54°09'E
Sosnowiec, Pol. (sôs-nô'vyĕts)	169	50°17'N	19°10'E
Sosnytsia, Ukr.	177	51°30'N	32°29'E
Sosunova, Mys, c., Russia (mĭs sô'sò-nôf'á)	210	46°28'N	138°06'E
Sos'va, r., Russia (sôs'vá)	186a	59°55'N	60°40'E
Sos'va, r., Russia (sôs'vá)	180	63°10'N	63°30'E
Sota, r., Benin	235	11°10'N	3°20'E
Sota la Marina, Mex. (sô-tä-lä-mä-rē'nä)	130	23°45'N	98°11'W
Soteapan, Mex. (sō-tā-ä'pän)	131	18°14'N	94°51'W
Soto la Marina, Río, r., Mex. (rē'ō-so'tō lä mä-rē'nä)	130	23°55'N	98°30'W
Sotuta, Mex. (sô-to͞o'tä)	132a	20°35'N	89°00'W
Soublette, Ven. (sō-o͞o-blĕ'tĕ)	143b	9°55'N	66°06'W
Souflí, Grc.	175	41°12'N	26°17'E
Soufrière, St. Luc. (so͞o-frē-âr')	133b	13°50'N	61°03'W
Soufrière, mtn., St. Vin.	133b	13°19'N	61°12'W
Soufrière, vol., Guad. (so͞o-frē-ăr')	133b	16°06'N	61°42'W
Sŏul *see* Seoul, Kor., S.	205	37°35'N	127°03'E
Sounding Creek, r., Can. (soun'dĭng)	96	51°35'N	111°00'W
Souq Ahras, Alg.	161	36°23'N	8°00'E
Sources, Mount aux, mtn., Afr. (môN'tō sòrs')	232	28°47'S	29°04'E
Soure, Port. (sōr-ĕ)	172	40°04'N	8°37'W
Souris, Can. (so͞o'rē')	101	46°20'N	62°17'W
Souris, Can.	90	49°38'N	100°15'W
Souris, r., N.A.	92	48°30'N	101°30'W
Sourlake, Tx., U.S. (sour'lāk)	123	30°09'N	94°24'W
Sousse, Tun. (so͞os)	230	36°00'N	10°39'E
South, r., Ga., U.S.	110c	33°40'N	84°15'W
South, r., N.C., U.S.	125	34°49'N	78°33'W
South Africa, nation, Afr.	232	28°00'S	24°50'E
South Amboy, N.J., U.S. (south'ăm'boi)	110a	40°28'N	74°17'W
South America, cont.	139	15°00'S	60°00'W
Southampton, Eng., U.K. (south-ămp'tŭn)	154	50°54'N	1°30'W
Southampton, N.Y., U.S.	109	40°53'N	72°24'W
Southampton Island, i., Can.	93	64°38'N	84°00'W
South Andaman Island, i., India (ăn-dá-măn')	212	11°57'N	93°24'E
South Australia, state, Austl. (ôs-trā'lĭ-á)	218	29°45'S	132°00'E
South Bay, b., Bah.	135	20°55'N	73°35'W
South Bend, In., U.S. (bĕnd)	105	41°40'N	86°20'W
South Bend, Wa., U.S. (bĕnd)	114	46°39'N	123°48'W
South Bight, b., Bah.	134	24°20'N	77°35'W
South Bimini, i., Bah. (bē'mē-nē)	134	25°40'N	79°20'W
Southborough, Ma., U.S. (south'bŭr-ō)	101a	42°18'N	71°33'W
South Boston, Va., U.S. (bôs'tŭn)	125	36°41'N	78°55'W
Southbridge, Ma., U.S. (south'brĭj)	109	42°05'N	72°00'W
South Caicos, i., T./C. Is. (kī'kōs)	135	21°30'N	71°35'W
South Carolina, state, U.S. (kăr-ō-lī'ná)	105	34°15'N	81°10'W
South Cave, Eng., U.K. (cāv)	158a	53°45'N	0°35'W
South Charleston, W.V., U.S.	108	38°20'N	81°40'W
South China Sea, sea, Asia (chī'ná)	212	15°23'N	114°12'E
South Creek, r., Austl.	217b	33°43'S	150°50'E
South Dakota, state, U.S. (dá-kō'tá)	104	44°20'N	101°55'W
South Downs, Eng., U.K. (dounz)	164	50°55'N	1°13'W
South Dum-Dum, India	202a	22°36'N	88°25'E
South East Cape, c., Austl.	221	43°47'S	146°03'E
Southend-on-Sea, Eng., U.K. (south-ĕnd')	165	51°33'N	0°41'E
Southern Alps, mts., N.Z. (sŭ-thûrn ălps)	221a	43°35'S	170°00'E
Southern Cross, Austl.	218	31°13'S	119°30'E
Southern Indian, l., Can. (sŭth'ērn ĭn'dĭ-ăn)	92	56°46'N	98°57'W
Southern Pines, N.C., U.S. (sŭth'ērn pīnz)	125	35°10'N	79°23'W
Southern Ute Indian Reservation, I.R., Co., U.S. (ūt)	119	37°05'N	108°23'W
South Euclid, Oh., U.S. (ū'klĭd)	111d	41°30'N	81°34'W
South Fox, i., Mi., U.S. (fŏks)	108	45°25'N	85°55'W
South Gate, Ca., U.S. (gāt)	117a	33°57'N	118°13'W
South Georgia, i., S. Geor. (jôr'jā)	139	54°00'S	37°00'W
South Haven, Mi., U.S. (hāv''n)	108	42°25'N	86°15'W
South Hill, Va., U.S.	125	36°44'N	78°08'W
South Holston Lake, res., U.S.	125	36°35'N	82°00'W
South Indian Lake, Can.	97	56°50'N	99°00'W
Southington, Ct., U.S. (sŭdh'ĭng-tŭn)	109	41°35'N	72°55'W
South Island, i., N.Z.	221a	42°40'S	169°00'E
South Loup, r., Ne., U.S. (lo͞op)	112	41°21'N	100°08'W
South Magnetic Pole, pt. of i.	224	65°18'S	139°30'E
South Merrimack, N.H., U.S. (mĕr'ĭ-măk)	101a	42°47'N	71°36'W
South Milwaukee, Wi., U.S. (mĭl-wô'kē)	111a	42°55'N	87°52'W
South Moose Lake, l., Can.	97	53°51'N	100°20'W
South Nation, r., Can.	99	45°00'N	75°25'W
South Negril Point, c., Jam. (nå-grēl')	134	18°15'N	78°25'W
South Ogden, Ut., U.S. (ŏg'dĕn)	117b	41°12'N	111°58'W
South Orkney Islands, is., Ant.	139	57°00'S	45°00'W
South Ossetia, hist. reg., Geor.	182	42°20'N	44°00'E
South Paris, Me., U.S. (păr'ĭs)	100	44°13'N	70°32'W
South Park, Ky., U.S. (pärk)	111h	38°06'N	85°43'W
South Pasadena, Ca., U.S. (păs-à-dē'ná)	117a	34°06'N	118°08'W
South Pease, r., Tx., U.S. (pēz)	120	33°54'N	100°45'W
South Pender, i., Can. (pĕn'dēr)	116d	48°45'N	123°09'W
South Pittsburg, Tn., U.S. (pĭs'bûrg)	124	35°00'N	85°42'W
South Platte, r., U.S. (plăt)	106	40°40'N	102°40'W
South Point, c., Barb.	133b	13°00'N	59°43'W
South Point, c., Mi., U.S.	108	44°50'N	83°20'W
South Pole, pt. of i., Ant.	224	90°00'S	0°00'
South Porcupine, Can.	98	48°28'N	81°13'W
Southport, Austl. (south'pōrt)	219	27°57'S	153°27'E
Southport, Eng., U.K. (south'pôrt)	164	53°38'N	3°00'W
Southport, In., U.S.	111g	39°40'N	86°07'W
Southport, N.C., U.S.	125	35°55'N	78°02'W
South Portland, Me., U.S. (pōrt-lănd)	100	43°37'N	70°15'W
South Prairie, Wa., U.S. (prâ'rĭ)	116a	47°08'N	122°06'W
South Range, Wi., U.S. (rānj)	117h	46°37'N	91°59'W
South River, N.J., U.S. (rĭv'ēr)	110a	40°27'N	74°23'W
South Ronaldsay, i., Scot., U.K. (rŏn'ăld-s'ā)	164a	58°48'N	2°55'W
South Saint Paul, Mn., U.S.	117g	44°54'N	93°02'W
South Salt Lake, Ut., U.S. (sôlt lāk)	117b	40°44'N	111°53'W
South Sandwich Islands, is., S. Geor. (sănd'wĭch)	139	58°00'S	27°00'W
South Sandwich Trench, deep	139	55°00'S	27°00'W
South San Francisco, Ca., U.S. (săn frăn-sĭs'kô)	116b	37°39'N	122°24'W
South Saskatchewan, r., Can. (sás-kach'ĕ-wän)	92	50°30'N	110°30'W
South Shetland Islands, is., Ant.	139	62°00'S	70°00'W
South Shields, Eng., U.K. (shēldz)	160	55°00'N	1°22'W
South Sioux City, Ne., U.S. (so͞o sĭt'ē)	112	42°48'N	96°26'W
South Taranaki Bight, b., N.Z. (tä-rä-nä'kē)	221a	39°35'S	173°50'E
South Thompson, r., Can. (tŏmp'sŭn)	95	50°41'N	120°21'W
Southton, Tx., U.S. (south'tŭn)	117d	29°18'N	98°26'W
South Uist, i., Scot., U.K. (ū'ĭst)	164	57°15'N	7°24'W
South Umpqua, r., Or., U.S. (ŭmp'kwå)	114	43°00'N	122°54'W
Southwell, Eng., U.K. (south'wĕl)	158a	53°04'N	0°56'W
South West Africa *see* Namibia, nation, Afr.	232	19°30'S	16°13'E
Southwest Miramichi, r., Can. (mĭr á-mē'shē)	100	46°35'N	66°17'W
Southwest Point, c., Bah.	134	25°50'N	77°10'W
Southwest Point, c., Bah.	135	23°55'N	74°30'W
South Yorkshire, hist. reg., Eng., U.K.	158a	53°29'N	1°35'W
Sovetsk, Russia (sô-vyĕtsk')	180	55°04'N	21°54'E
Sovetskaya Gavan', Russia (sŭ-vyĕt'skī-u gä'vŭn')	179	48°59'N	140°14'E
Sow, r., Eng., U.K. (sou)	158a	52°45'N	2°12'W
Soya Kaikyō, strt., Asia	210	45°45'N	141°38'E
Sōya Misaki, c., Japan (sō'yä mē'sä-kē)	210	45°35'N	141°25'E
Soyo, Ang.	232	6°10'S	12°25'E
Sozh, r., Eur. (sôzh)	181	52°50'N	31°00'E
Sozopol, Blg. (sôz'ô-pôl')	175	42°18'N	27°50'E
Spa, Bel. (spä)	165	50°30'N	5°50'E
Spain, nation, Eur. (spān)	154	40°15'N	4°30'W
Spalding, Ne., U.S. (spôl'dĭng)	112	41°43'N	98°23'W
Spanaway, Wa., U.S. (spăn'á-wā)	116a	47°06'N	122°26'W
Spangler, Pa., U.S. (spăng'lēr)	109	40°40'N	78°50'W
Spanish Fork, Ut., U.S. (spăn'ĭsh fôrk)	119	40°10'N	111°40'W
Spanish Town, Jam.	129	18°00'N	76°55'W
Sparks, Nv., U.S. (spärks)	118	39°34'N	119°45'W
Sparrows Point, Md., U.S. (spăr'ōz)	110e	39°13'N	76°29'W
Sparta *see* Spárti, Grc.	175	37°07'N	22°28'E
Sparta, Ga., U.S. (spär'tá)	125	33°16'N	82°59'W
Sparta, Il., U.S.	121	38°07'N	89°42'W
Sparta, Mi., U.S.	108	43°10'N	85°45'W
Sparta, Tn., U.S.	124	35°54'N	85°26'W
Sparta, Wi., U.S.	113	43°56'N	90°50'W
Sparta Mountains, mts., N.J., U.S.	110a	41°00'N	74°38'W
Spartanburg, S.C., U.S. (spär'tăn-bûrg)	105	34°57'N	82°13'W
Spartel, Cap, c., Mor. (spär-tĕl')	172	35°48'N	5°50'W
Spárti (Sparta), Grc.	175	37°07'N	22°28'E
Spartivento, Cape, c., Italy (spär-tē-vĕn'tô)	174	37°55'N	16°09'E
Spartivento, Capo, c., Italy	156	38°54'N	8°52'E
Spas-Demensk, Russia (spàs dyĕ-mĕnsk')	176	54°24'N	34°02'E
Spas-Klepiki, Russia (spàs klĕp'ĕ-kê)	176	55°09'N	40°11'E

ăt; finăl; rāte; senåte; ärm; àsk; sofá; fâre; ch-choose; dh-as th in other; bē; ėvent; bĕt; recĕnt; cratĕr; g-gō; gh-guttural g; bĭt; ĭ-short neutral; rīde; κ-guttural k as ch in German ich;

PRONOUNCING INDEX

Spassik-Ryazanskiy – Strängnäs 353

PLACE (Pronunciation)	PAGE	LAT.	LONG.
Spassik-Ryazanskiy, Russia (ryä-zän'skĭ)	176	54°24'N	40°21'E
Spassk-Dal'niy, Russia (spŭsk'däl'nyē)	179	44°30'N	133°00'E
Spátha, Ákra, c., Grc.	174a	35°42'N	23°45'E
Spaulding, Al., U.S. (spôl'dĭng)	110h	33°27'N	86°50'W
Spear, Cape, c., Can. (spēr)	101	47°32'N	52°32'W
Spearfish, S.D., U.S. (spēr'fĭsh)	112	44°28'N	103°52'W
Speed, In., U.S. (spēd)	111h	38°25'N	85°45'W
Speedway, In., U.S. (spēd'wā)	111g	39°47'N	86°14'W
Speichersee, l., Ger.	159d	48°12'N	11°47'E
Spencer, Ia., U.S.	112	43°09'N	95°08'W
Spencer, In., U.S. (spĕn'sẽr)	108	39°15'N	86°45'W
Spencer, N.C., U.S.	125	35°43'N	80°25'W
Spencer, W.V., U.S.	108	38°55'N	81°20'W
Spencer Gulf, b., Austl. (spĕn'sẽr)	220	34°20'S	136°55'E
Sperenberg, Ger. (shpĕ'rĕn-bĕrgh)	159b	52°09'N	13°22'E
Spey, l., Scot., U.K. (spā)	164	57°25'N	3°29'W
Speyer, Ger. (shpī'ẽr)	168	49°18'N	8°26'E
Sphinx, hist., Egypt (sfĭnks)	238b	29°57'N	31°08'E
Spijkenisse, Neth.	159a	51°51'N	4°18'E
Spinazzola, Italy (spē-nät'zō-lä)	174	40°58'N	16°05'E
Spirit Lake, Ia., U.S. (lăk)	112	43°25'N	95°08'W
Spirit Lake, Id., U.S. (spĭr'ĭt)	114	47°58'N	116°51'W
Spišská Nová Ves, Slvk. (spēsh'skä nō'vä vĕs)	161	48°56'N	20°35'E
Spitsbergen *see* Svalbard, dep., Nor.	178	77°00'N	20°00'E
Split, Cro. (splēt)	154	43°30'N	16°28'E
Split Lake, l., Can.	97	56°08'N	96°15'W
Spokane, Wa., U.S. (spōkăn')	104	47°39'N	117°25'W
Spokane, r., Wa., U.S.	114	47°47'N	118°00'W
Spokane Indian Reservation, I.R., Wa., U.S.	114	47°55'N	118°00'W
Spoleto, Italy (spō-lā'tō)	174	42°44'N	12°44'E
Spoon, r., Il., U.S. (spōōn)	121	40°36'N	90°22'W
Spooner, Wi., U.S. (spōōn'ẽr)	113	45°50'N	91°53'W
Spotswood, N.J., U.S. (spŏtz'wŏŏd)	110a	40°23'N	74°22'W
Sprague, r., Or., U.S. (sprāg)	114	42°30'N	121°42'W
Spratly, i., Asia (sprăt'lē)	212	8°38'N	111°54'E
Spray, N.C., U.S. (sprā)	125	36°30'N	79°44'W
Spree, r., Ger. (shprā)	168	51°53'N	14°08'E
Spremberg, Ger. (shprĕm'bĕrgh)	168	51°35'N	14°23'E
Spring, r., Ar., U.S.	121	36°25'N	91°35'W
Springbok, S. Afr. (spring'bŏk)	232	29°35'S	17°55'E
Spring Creek, r., Nv., U.S. (sprĭng)	118	40°18'N	117°45'W
Spring Creek, r., Tx., U.S.	123	30°03'N	95°43'W
Spring Creek, r., Tx., U.S.	122	31°08'N	100°50'W
Springdale, Can.	101	49°30'N	56°05'W
Springdale, Ar., U.S. (sprĭng'dāl)	121	36°10'N	94°07'W
Springdale, Pa., U.S.	111e	40°33'N	79°46'W
Springer, N.M., U.S. (spring'ẽr)	120	36°21'N	104°37'W
Springerville, Az., U.S.	119	34°08'N	109°17'W
Springfield, Co., U.S. (spring'fēld)	120	37°24'N	102°04'W
Springfield, Il., U.S.	105	39°46'N	89°37'W
Springfield, Ky., U.S.	108	37°35'N	85°10'W
Springfield, Ma., U.S.	105	42°05'N	72°35'W
Springfield, Mn., U.S.	113	44°14'N	94°59'W
Springfield, Mo., U.S.	105	37°13'N	93°17'W
Springfield, Oh., U.S.	105	39°55'N	83°50'W
Springfield, Or., U.S.	114	44°01'N	123°02'W
Springfield, Tn., U.S.	124	36°30'N	86°53'W
Springfield, Vt., U.S.	109	43°20'N	72°35'W
Springfontein, S. Afr. (spring'fōn-tīn)	232	30°16'S	25°45'E
Springhill, Can. (spring-hĭl')	91	45°39'N	64°03'W
Spring Mountains, mts., Nv., U.S.	118	36°18'N	115°49'W
Springs, S. Afr. (springs)	238c	26°16'S	28°27'E
Springstein, Can. (spring'stīn)	102f	49°49'N	97°29'W
Springton Reservoir, res., Pa., U.S. (spring-tŭn)	110f	39°57'N	75°26'W
Springvale, Austl.	217a	37°57'N	145°09'E
Spring Valley, Ca., U.S.	118a	32°46'N	117°01'W
Springvalley, Il., U.S. (spring-văl'ĭ)	108	41°20'N	89°15'W
Spring Valley, Mn., U.S.	113	43°41'N	92°26'W
Spring Valley, N.Y., U.S.	110a	41°07'N	74°03'W
Springville, Ut., U.S. (spring-vĭl)	119	40°10'N	111°40'W
Springwood, Austl.	217b	33°42'S	150°34'E
Spruce Grove, Can. (sprōōs grōv)	102g	53°32'N	113°55'W
Spur, Tx., U.S. (spûr)	120	33°29'N	100°51'W
Squam, l., N.H., U.S. (skwŏm)	109	43°45'N	71°30'W
Squamish, Can. (skwŏ'mĭsh)	94	49°42'N	123°09'W
Squamish, r., Can.	94	50°10'N	123°30'W
Squillace, Golfo di, b., Italy (gōō'l-fō-dē skwēl-lä'chā)	174	38°44'N	16°47'E
Srbija (Serbia), hist. reg., Yugo. (sr bē-yä) (sĕr'bē-ä)	175	44°05'N	20°35'E
Srbobran, Yugo. (s'r'bō-brän')	175	45°32'N	19°50'E
Sredne-Kolymsk, Russia (s'rĕd'nyĕ kō-lēmsk')	179	67°49'N	154°55'E
Sredne Rogatka, Russia (s'red'ná-ya) (rô gär'tkà)	186c	59°49'N	30°20'E
Sredniy Ik, r., Russia (srĕd'nĭ ĭk)	186a	55°46'N	58°50'E
Sredniy Ural, mts., Russia (ŏ'rál)	186a	57°47'N	59°00'E
Śrem, Pol. (shrĕm)	169	52°06'N	17°01'E
Sremska Karlovci, Yugo. (srĕm'skĕ kär'lov-tsĕ)	175	45°10'N	19°57'E
Sremska Mitrovica, Yugo. (srĕm'skä mē'trō-vē-tsä')	175	44°59'N	19°39'E
Sretensk, Russia (s'rĕ'tĕnsk)	179	52°13'N	117°39'E
Sri Jayewardenepura Kotte, Sri L.	203	6°50'N	80°05'E
Sri Lanka, nation, Asia	203	8°45'N	82°30'E
Srīnagar, India (srē-nŭg'ŭr)	199	34°11'N	74°49'E
Środa, Pol. (shrō'dà)	169	52°14'N	17°17'E
Stabroek, Bel.	159a	51°20'N	4°21'E
Stade, Ger. (shtä'dĕ)	168	53°36'N	9°28'E
Städjan, mtn., Swe. (stĕd'yän)	166	61°53'N	12°50'E
Stafford, Eng., U.K. (stăf'fẽrd)	164	52°48'N	2°06'W
Stafford, Ks., U.S.	120	37°58'N	98°37'W
Staffordshire, co., Eng., U.K.	158a	52°45'N	2°00'W
Stahnsdorf, Ger. (shtäns'dōrf)	159b	52°22'N	13°10'E
Staines, Eng., U.K.	158b	51°26'N	0°13'W
Stakhanov, Ukr.	181	48°34'N	38°37'E
Stalingrad *see* Volgograd, Russia	178	48°40'N	42°20'E
Stalybridge, Eng., U.K.	158a	53°29'N	2°03'W
Stambaugh, Mi., U.S. (stăm'bô)	113	46°03'N	88°38'W
Stamford, Eng., U.K.	158a	52°39'N	0°28'W
Stamford, Ct., U.S. (stăm'fẽrd)	110a	41°03'N	73°32'W
Stamford, Tx., U.S.	120	32°57'N	99°48'W
Stammersdorf, Aus. (shtäm'ĕrs-dôrf)	159e	48°19'N	16°25'E
Stamps, Ar., U.S. (stămps)	121	33°22'N	93°31'W
Stanberry, Mo., U.S. (stan'bĕr-ē)	121	40°12'N	94°34'W
Standerton, S. Afr. (stăn'dẽr-tŭn)	232	26°57'S	29°17'E
Standing Rock Indian Reservation, I.R., N.D., U.S. (stănd'ĭng rŏk)	112	47°07'N	101°05'W
Standish, Eng., U.K. (stăn'dĭsh)	158a	53°36'N	2°39'W
Stanford, Ky., U.S. (stăn'fẽrd)	124	37°29'N	84°40'W
Stanger, S. Afr. (stăŋ-ger)	233c	29°22'S	31°18'E
Staniard Creek, Bah.	134	24°50'N	77°55'W
Stanislaus, r., Ca., U.S. (stăn'ĭs-lô)	118	38°10'N	120°16'W
Stanley, Can. (stăn'lē)	100	46°17'N	66°44'W
Stanley, Falk. Is.	144	51°46'S	57°59'W
Stanley, N.D., U.S.	112	48°20'N	102°25'W
Stanley, Wi., U.S.	113	44°56'N	90°56'W
Stanley Pool, l., Afr.	232	4°07'S	15°40'E
Stanley Reservoir, res., India (stăn'lē)	203	12°07'N	77°27'E
Stanleyville *see* Kisangani, D.R.C.	231	0°30'S	25°12'E
Stann Creek, Belize (stăn krēk)	132a	17°01'N	88°14'W
Stanovoy Khrebet, mts., Russia (stŭn-à-voi')	179	56°12'N	127°12'E
Stanton, Ca., U.S. (stăn'tŭn)	117a	33°48'N	118°00'W
Stanton, Ne., U.S.	112	41°57'N	97°15'W
Stanton, Tx., U.S.	122	32°08'N	101°46'W
Stanwood, Wa., U.S. (stăn'wŏŏd)	116a	48°14'N	122°23'W
Staples, Mn., U.S. (stā'p'lz)	113	46°21'N	94°48'W
Stapleton, Al., U.S.	124	30°45'N	87°48'W
Stara Planina, mts., Blg.	156	42°50'N	24°45'E
Staraya Kupavna, Russia (stä'rà-yà kû-päf'nà)	186b	55°48'N	38°10'E
Staraya Russa, Russia (stä'rà-yà rōōsà)	180	57°58'N	31°21'E
Stara Zagora, Blg. (zä'gô-rà)	163	42°26'N	25°37'E
Starbuck, Can. (stär'bŭk)	102f	49°46'N	97°36'W
Stargard Szczeciński, Pol. (shtär'gärt shchĕ-chyn'skē)	160	53°19'N	15°03'E
Staritsa, Russia (stä'rē-tsà)	176	56°29'N	34°58'E
Starke, Fl., U.S. (stärk)	125	29°55'N	82°07'W
Starkville, Co., U.S. (stärk'vĭl)	120	37°06'N	104°34'W
Starkville, Ms., U.S.	124	33°27'N	88°47'W
Starnberg, Ger. (shtärn-bĕrgh)	159d	47°59'N	11°20'E
Starnberger See, l., Ger.	168	47°58'N	11°30'E
Starobil's'k, Ukr.	181	49°19'N	38°57'E
Starodub, Russia (stä-rô-drōp')	176	52°25'N	32°49'E
Starogard Gdański, Pol. (stä'rō-grad gdĕn'skē)	160	53°58'N	18°33'E
Starokostiantyniv, Ukr.	181	49°45'N	27°12'E
Staro-Minskaya, Russia (stä'rô mĭn'skà-yà)	181	46°19'N	38°51'E
Staro-Shcherbinovskaya, Russia	177	46°38'N	38°38'E
Staro-Subkhangulovo, Russia (stäro-sōōb-kan-gōō'lōvō)	186a	53°08'N	57°24'E
Staroutkinsk, Russia (stá-rô-ōōt'kĭnsk)	186a	57°14'N	59°21'E
Starovirivka, Ukr.	177	49°31'N	35°48'E
Start Point, c., Eng., U.K. (stärt)	161	50°14'N	3°34'W
Staryi Ostropil', Ukr.	177	49°48'N	27°32'E
Stary Sącz, Pol. (stä-rē sôṇch')	169	49°32'N	20°36'E
Staryy Oskol, Russia (stä'rē ôs-kôl')	181	51°18'N	37°51'E
Stassfurt, Ger. (shtäs'fōōrt)	168	51°52'N	11°35'E
Staszów, Pol. (stä'shŏf)	169	50°32'N	21°13'E
State College, Pa., U.S. (stāt kŏl'ĕj)	109	40°50'N	77°55'W
State Line, Mn., U.S. (līn)	117h	46°36'N	92°18'W
Staten Island, i., N.Y., U.S. (stăt'ĕn)	110a	40°35'N	74°10'W
Statesboro, Ga., U.S. (stāts'bŭr-ô)	125	32°26'N	81°47'W
Statesville, N.C., U.S. (stās'vĭl)	125	34°45'N	80°54'W
Staunton, Il., U.S. (stôn'tŭn)	117e	39°01'N	89°47'W
Staunton, Va., U.S.	109	38°10'N	79°05'W
Stavanger, Nor. (stä'väng'ẽr)	154	58°59'N	5°44'E
Stave, r., Can. (stāv)	116d	49°12'N	122°24'W
Staveley, Eng., U.K. (stāv'lē)	158a	53°17'N	1°21'W
Stavenisse, Neth.	159a	51°35'N	3°59'E
Stavropol', Russia	178	45°05'N	41°50'E
Steamboat Springs, Co., U.S. (stēm'bōt')	120	40°30'N	106°48'W
Stebliv, Ukr.	177	49°23'N	31°03'E
Steel, r., Can. (stēl)	98	49°08'N	86°55'W
Steelton, Pa., U.S. (stēl'tŭn)	109	40°15'N	76°45'W
Steenbergen, Neth.	159a	51°35'N	4°18'E
Steens Mountain, mts., Or., U.S. (stēnz)	114	42°15'N	118°52'W
Steep Point, c., Austl. (stēp)	220	26°15'N	112°05'E
Stefanie, Lake *see* Chew Bahir, l., Afr.	231	4°46'N	37°31'E
Steinbach, Can.	90	49°32'N	96°41'W
Steinkjer, Nor. (stēin-kyĕr)	160	64°00'N	11°19'E
Stella, Wa., U.S. (stĕl'á)	116c	46°11'N	123°12'W
Stellarton, Can. (stĕl'ár-tŭn)	91	45°34'N	62°40'W
Stendal, Ger. (shtĕn'däl)	168	52°37'N	11°51'E
Stepanakert *see* Xankändi, Azer.	180	39°50'N	46°40'E
Stephens, Port, b., Austl. (stē'fĕns)	222	32°43'N	152°55'E
Stephenville, Can. (stē'vĕn-vĭl)	93a	48°33'N	58°35'W
Stepnogorsk, Kaz.	183	52°20'N	72°05'E
Sterkrade, Ger. (shtĕr'krädĕ)	171c	51°31'N	6°51'E
Sterkstroom, S. Afr.	233c	31°33'S	26°36'E
Sterling, Co., U.S. (stûr'lĭng)	104	40°38'N	103°14'W
Sterling, Il., U.S.	108	41°48'N	89°42'W
Sterling, Ks., U.S.	120	38°11'N	98°11'W
Sterling, Ma., U.S.	101a	42°26'N	71°41'W
Sterling, Tx., U.S.	122	31°53'N	100°58'W
Sterlitamak, Russia (styĕr'lē-ta-mák')	178	53°38'N	55°56'E
Šternberk, Czech Rep. (shtĕrn'bĕrk)	169	49°44'N	17°18'E
Stettin *see* Szczecin, Pol.	154	53°25'N	14°35'E
Stettler, Can.	90	52°19'N	112°43'W
Steubenville, Oh., U.S. (stū'bĕn-vĭl)	108	40°20'N	80°40'W
Stevens, l., Wa., U.S. (stē'vĕnz)	116a	47°59'N	122°06'W
Stevens Point, Wi., U.S.	113	44°30'N	89°35'W
Stevensville, Mt., U.S. (stē'vĕnz-vĭl)	115	46°31'N	114°03'E
Stewart, r., Can. (stū'ẽrt)	92	63°27'N	138°48'W
Stewart Island, i., N.Z.	221a	46°56'S	167°40'E
Stewiacke, Can. (stū'wê-ăk)	100	45°08'N	63°21'W
Steynsrus, S. Afr. (stīns'rōōs)	238c	27°58'S	27°33'E
Steyr, Aus. (shtīr)	161	48°03'N	14°24'E
Stif, Alg.	230	36°18'N	5°21'E
Stikine, r., Can. (stĭ-kēn')	92	58°17'N	130°10'W
Stikine Ranges, Can.	90	59°05'N	130°00'W
Stillaguamish, r., Wa., U.S.	116a	48°11'N	122°18'W
Stillaguamish, South Fork, r., Wa., U.S. (stĭl-á-gwä'mĭsh)	116a	48°05'N	121°59'W
Stillwater, Mn., U.S. (stĭl'wô-tẽr)	117g	45°04'N	92°48'W
Stillwater, Mt., U.S.	115	45°23'N	109°45'W
Stillwater, Ok., U.S.	121	36°06'N	97°03'W
Stillwater, r., Mt., U.S.	115	48°47'N	114°40'W
Stillwater Range, mts., Nv., U.S.	118	39°43'N	118°11'W
Štip, Mac. (shtĭp)	175	41°43'N	22°07'E
Stirling, Scot., U.K. (stûr'lĭng)	164	56°05'N	3°59'W
Stittsville, Can. (stĭts'vĭl)	102c	45°15'N	75°54'W
Stizef, Alg. (mĕr-syā' lá-kôɴb)	173	35°18'N	0°11'W
Stjördalshalsen, Nor. (styûr-däls-hälsĕn)	166	63°26'N	11°00'E
Stockbridge Munsee Indian Reservation, I.R., Wi., U.S. (stŏk'brĭdj mŭn-sē)	113	44°49'N	89°00'W
Stockerau, Aus. (shtŏ'kĕ-rou)	168	48°24'N	16°13'E
Stockholm, Swe. (stôk'hôlm)	154	59°23'N	18°00'E
Stockholm, Me., U.S. (stŏk'hōlm)	100	47°05'N	68°08'W
Stockport, Eng., U.K. (stŏk'pôrt)	164	53°24'N	2°09'W
Stockton, Eng., U.K.	164	54°35'N	1°25'W
Stockton, Ca., U.S. (stŏk'tŭn)	104	37°56'N	121°16'W
Stockton, Ks., U.S.	120	39°26'N	99°16'W
Stockton, i., Wi., U.S.	113	46°56'N	90°25'W
Stockton Plateau, plat., Tx., U.S.	106	30°34'N	102°35'W
Stockton Reservoir, res., Mo., U.S.	121	37°40'N	93°45'W
Stöde, Swe. (stû'dĕ)	166	62°26'N	16°35'E
Stoeng Trêng, Camb. (stông'trĕng')	212	13°36'N	106°00'E
Stoke-on-Trent, Eng., U.K. (stōk-ŏn-trĕnt)	160	53°01'N	2°12'W
Stokhid, r., Ukr.	169	51°24'N	25°20'E
Stolac, Bos. (stô'láts)	175	43°03'N	17°59'E
Stolbovoy, is., Russia (stôl-bô-voi')	185	74°05'N	136°00'E
Stolin, Bela. (stô'lĕn)	169	51°54'N	26°52'E
Stömstad, Swe.	166	58°58'N	11°09'E
Stone, Eng., U.K.	158a	52°54'N	2°09'W
Stoneham, Can. (stōn'ám)	102b	46°59'N	71°22'W
Stoneham, Ma., U.S.	101a	42°30'N	71°05'W
Stonehaven, Scot., U.K. (stōn'hā-v'n)	164	56°57'N	2°09'W
Stone Mountain, Ga., U.S. (stōn)	110c	33°49'N	84°10'W
Stonewall, Can. (stōn'wôl)	102f	50°09'N	97°21'W
Stonewall, Ms., U.S.	124	32°08'N	88°44'W
Stoney Creek, Can. (stō'nē)	102d	43°13'N	79°45'W
Stonington, Ct., U.S. (stōn'ĭng-tŭn)	109	41°20'N	71°55'W
Stony Indian Reserve, I.R., Can.	102e	51°10'N	114°45'W
Stony Mountain, Can.	102f	50°05'N	97°13'W
Stony Plain, Can. (stō'nē plān)	102g	53°32'N	114°00'W
Stony Plain Indian Reserve, I.R., Can.	102g	53°29'N	113°48'W
Stony Point, N.Y., U.S.	110a	41°13'N	73°58'W
Stora Sotra, i., Nor.	166	60°24'N	4°35'E
Stord, i., Nor. (stōrd)	166	59°54'N	5°15'E
Store Baelt, strt., Den.	166	55°25'N	10°50'E
Storfjorden, b., Nor.	166	62°17'N	6°19'E
Stormberg, mts., S. Afr. (stôrm'bûrg)	233c	31°28'S	26°35'E
Storm Lake, Ia., U.S.	112	42°39'N	95°12'W
Stormy Point, c., V.I.U.S. (stôr'mē)	129c	18°22'N	65°01'W
Stornoway, Scot., U.K. (stôr'nō-wā)	160	58°13'N	6°21'W
Storozhynets', Ukr.	169	48°10'N	25°44'E
Storsjo, Swe. (stôr'shû)	166	62°49'N	13°08'E
Storsjoen, l., Nor. (stôr-syûĕn)	166	61°32'N	11°30'E
Storsjön, l., Swe.	166	63°06'N	14°00'E
Storvik, Swe.	166	60°37'N	16°31'E
Stoughton, Wi., U.S.	113	42°54'N	89°15'W
Stour, r., Eng., U.K. (stour)	165	52°09'N	0°29'E
Stourbridge, Eng., U.K. (stour'brĭj)	158a	52°27'N	2°08'W
Stow, Ma., U.S. (stō)	101a	42°56'N	71°31'W
Stow, Oh., U.S.	111d	41°09'N	81°26'W
Straatsdrif, S. Afr.	238c	25°19'S	26°22'E
Strabane, N. Ire., U.K. (stră-băn')	164	54°59'N	7°27'W
Straelen, Ger. (shtrā'lĕn)	171c	51°26'N	6°16'E
Strahan, Austl. (strā'ăn)	219	42°08'S	145°28'E
Strakonice, Czech Rep. (strä'kō-nyē-tsĕ)	168	49°18'N	13°52'E
Straldzha, Blg. (sträl'dzhà)	175	42°37'N	26°44'E
Stralsund, Ger. (shträl'sŏnt)	160	54°18'N	13°04'E
Strangford Lough, l., N. Ire., U.K.	164	54°30'N	5°34'W
Strängnäs, Swe. (strĕng'nĕs)	166	59°23'N	16°59'E

PLACE (Pronunciation)	PAGE	LAT.	LONG.
Stranraer, Scot., U.K. (străn-rär´)	164	54°55´N	5°05´W
Strasbourg, Fr. (străs-bōōr´)	154	48°36´N	7°49´E
Stratford, Can. (străt´fĕrd)	98	43°20´N	81°05´W
Stratford, Ct., U.S.	109	41°10´N	73°05´W
Stratford, Wi., U.S.	113	44°16´N	90°02´W
Stratford-upon-Avon, Eng., U.K.	164	52°13´N	1°41´W
Straubing, Ger. (strou´bĭng)	168	48°52´N	12°36´E
Strausberg, Ger. (strous´bĕrgh)	168	52°35´N	13°50´E
Strawberry, r., Ut., U.S.	119	40°05´N	110°55´W
Strawn, Tx., U.S. (strŏn)	122	32°38´N	98°28´W
Streator, Il., U.S. (strē´tĕr)	108	41°05´N	88°50´W
Streeter, N.D., U.S.	112	46°40´N	99°22´W
Streetsville, Can. (strētz´vĭl)	102d	43°34´N	79°43´W
Strehaia, Rom. (strĕ-kä´ya)	175	44°37´N	23°13´E
Strel´na, Russia (strĕl´na)	186c	59°52´N	30°01´E
Stretford, Eng., U.K. (strĕt´fĕrd)	158a	53°25´N	2°19´W
Strickland, r., Pap. N. Gui. (strĭk´lănd)	213	6°15´S	142°00´E
Strijen, Neth.	159a	51°44´N	4°32´E
Stromboli, Italy (strŏm´bô-lē)	163	38°46´N	15°16´E
Stromyn, Russia (strô´mĭn)	186b	56°02´N	38°29´E
Strong, r., Ms., U.S. (strŏng)	124	32°03´N	89°42´W
Strongsville, Oh., U.S. (strŏngz´vĭl)	111d	41°19´N	81°50´W
Stronsay, i., Scot., U.K. (strŏn´sā)	164a	59°09´N	2°35´W
Stroudsburg, Pa., U.S. (stroudz´bŭrg)	109	41°00´N	75°15´W
Struer, Den.	166	56°29´N	8°34´E
Strugi Krasnyye, Russia (strōō´gĭ krä´s-ny´yĕ)	176	58°14´N	29°10´E
Struma, r., Eur. (strōō´má)	175	41°55´N	23°05´E
Strumica, Mac. (strōō´mĭ-tsä)	175	41°26´N	22°38´E
Strunino, Russia	186b	56°23´N	38°34´E
Struthers, Oh., U.S. (strŭdh´ērz)	108	41°00´N	80°35´W
Struvenhütten, Ger. (shtrōō´vĕn-hü-tĕn)	159c	53°52´N	10°04´E
Strydpoortberge, mts., S. Afr.	238c	24°08´N	29°18´E
Stryi, Ukr.	169	49°16´N	23°51´E
Strzelce Opolskie, Pol. (stzhĕl´tsĕ o-pŏl´skyĕ)	169	50°31´N	18°20´E
Strzelin, Pol. (stzhĕ-lĭn)	169	50°48´N	17°06´E
Strzelno, Pol. (stzhál´nô)	169	52°37´N	18°10´E
Stuart, Fl., U.S. (stū´ērt)	125a	27°10´N	80°14´W
Stuart, Ia., U.S.	113	41°31´N	94°20´W
Stuart, i., Ak., U.S.	103	63°25´N	162°45´W
Stuart, i., Wa., U.S.	116d	48°42´N	123°10´W
Stuart Lake, l., Can.	94	54°32´N	124°35´W
Stuart Range, mts., Austl.	220	29°00´S	134°30´E
Sturgeon, r., Can.	102g	53°41´N	113°46´W
Sturgeon, r., Mi., U.S.	113	46°43´N	88°43´W
Sturgeon Bay, Wi., U.S.	113	44°50´N	87°22´W
Sturgeon Bay, b., Can.	97	52°00´N	98°00´W
Sturgeon Falls, Can.	91	46°19´N	79°49´W
Sturgis, Ky., U.S.	108	37°35´N	88°00´W
Sturgis, Mi., U.S.	108	41°45´N	85°25´W
Sturgis, S.D., U.S.	112	44°25´N	103°31´W
Sturt Creek, r., Austl.	220	19°40´S	127°40´E
Sturtevant, Wi., U.S. (stŭr´tĕ-vănt)	111a	42°42´N	87°54´W
Stutterheim, S. Afr. (stŭrt´ĕr-hĭm)	233c	32°33´N	27°27´E
Stuttgart, Ger. (shtōōt´gärt)	154	48°48´N	9°15´E
Stuttgart, Ar., U.S. (stŭt´gärt)	121	34°30´N	91°33´W
Stykkishólmur, Ice.	160	65°00´N	21°48´W
Styr´, r., Eur. (stēr)	169	51°44´N	26°07´E
Suao, Tai. (sōōōu)	209	24°35´N	121°45´E
Subarnarekha, r., India	202	22°38´N	86°26´E
Subata, Lat. (sô´bá-tä)	167	56°02´N	25°54´E
Subic, Phil. (sōō´bĭk)	213a	14°52´N	120°15´E
Subic Bay, b., Phil.	213a	14°41´N	120°11´E
Subotica, Yugo. (sōō´bô´tĕ-tsä)	154	46°06´N	19°41´E
Subugo, mtn., Kenya	237	1°40´S	35°49´E
Succasunna, N.J., U.S. (sŭk´ká-sŭn´ná)	110a	40°52´N	74°37´W
Suceava, Rom. (sōō-chä-ä´vá)	169	47°39´N	26°17´E
Suceava, r., Rom.	169	47°45´N	26°10´E
Sucha, Pol. (sōō´ká)	169	49°44´N	19°40´E
Suchiapa, Mex. (sōō-chē-ä´pä)	131	16°38´N	93°08´W
Suchiapa, r., Mex.	131	16°27´N	93°26´W
Suchitoto, El Sal. (sōō-chē-tō´tô)	132	13°58´N	89°03´W
Sucio, r., Col. (sōō´syô)	142a	6°55´N	76°15´W
Sucre, Bol. (sōō´krā)	142	19°06´S	65°16´W
Sucre, dept., Ven. (sōō´krĕ)	143b	10°18´N	64°12´W
Sud, Canal du, strt., Haiti	135	18°40´N	73°15´W
Sud, Rivière du, r., Can. (rē-vyär´dü süd´)	102b	46°56´N	70°35´W
Suda, Russia (sô´dá)	186a	56°58´N	56°45´E
Suda, r., Russia	176	59°24´N	36°40´E
Sudair, Sau. Ar. (sū-dä´ēr)	198	25°48´N	46°28´E
Sudalsvatnet, l., Nor.	166	59°35´N	6°59´E
Sudan, nation, Afr.	231	14°00´N	28°00´E
Sudan, reg., Afr. (sōō-dăn´)	230	15°00´N	7°00´E
Sudbury, Can. (sŭd´bĕr-ĕ)	91	46°28´N	81°00´W
Sudbury, Ma., U.S.	101a	42°23´N	71°25´W
Sudetes, mts., Eur.	156	50°41´N	15°37´E
Sudogda, Russia (sô´dôk-dä)	176	55°57´N	40°29´E
Sudost´, r., Eur. (sô-dôst´)	176	52°43´N	33°13´E
Sudzha, Russia (sōō´zhá)	177	51°14´N	35°11´E
Sueca, Spain (swā´kä)	173	39°12´N	0°18´W
Suez, Egypt	231	29°58´N	32°34´E
Suez, Gulf of, b., Egypt (sōō-ēz´)	231	29°53´N	32°33´E
Suez Canal, can., Egypt	231	30°53´N	32°21´E
Suffern, N.Y., U.S. (sŭf´fĕrn)	110a	41°07´N	74°09´W
Suffolk, Va., U.S. (sŭf´ŭk)	110g	36°43´N	76°35´W
Sugar City, Co., U.S.	120	38°12´N	103°42´W
Sugar Creek, Mo., U.S.	117f	39°06´N	94°27´W
Sugar Creek, r., Il., U.S. (shŏg´ēr)	121	40°14´N	89°28´W
Sugar Creek, r., In., U.S.	108	39°55´N	87°10´W

PLACE (Pronunciation)	PAGE	LAT.	LONG.
Sugar Island, i., Mi., U.S.	117k	46°31´N	84°12´W
Sugarloaf Point, c., Austl. (sōgēr´lôf)	222	32°19´S	153°04´E
Suggi Lake, l., Can.	97	54°22´N	102°47´W
Sühbaatar, Mong.	204	50°18´N	106°31´E
Suhl, Ger. (zōōl)	168	50°37´N	10°41´E
Suichuan, mtn., China	209	26°25´N	114°10´E
Suide, China (swä-dŭ)	208	37°32´N	110°12´E
Suifenhe, China (swä-fŭn-hŭ)	205	44°47´N	131°13´E
Suihua, China	205	46°38´N	126°50´E
Suining, China (sōō´ē-nĭng´)	206	33°54´N	117°57´E
Suipacha, Arg. (swĕ-pä´chä)	141c	34°45´S	59°43´W
Suiping, China (swä-pĭn)	206	33°09´N	113°58´E
Suir, r., Ire. (sūr)	164	52°20´N	7°32´W
Suisun Bay, b., Ca., U.S. (sōōĕ-sōōn´)	116b	38°07´N	122°02´W
Suita, Japan (só´ē-tä)	211b	34°45´N	135°32´E
Suitland, Md., U.S. (sót´lănd)	110e	38°51´N	76°57´W
Suixian, China (swä shyĕn)	209	31°42´N	113°20´E
Suiyüan, hist. reg., China (swä-yüĕn)	204	41°31´N	107°04´E
Suizhong, China (swä-jŏn)	208	40°22´N	120°20´E
Sukabumi, Indon.	212	6°52´S	106°56´E
Sukadana, Indon.	212	1°15´S	110°30´E
Sukagawa, Japan (sōō´kä-gä´wä)	211	37°08´N	140°07´E
Sukhinichi, Russia (sōō´κĕ´nĕ-chĕ)	180	54°07´N	35°18´E
Sukhona, r., Russia (sô-κô´ná)	180	59°30´N	42°20´E
Sukhoy Log, Russia (sōō´κôy lôg)	186a	56°55´N	62°03´E
Sukhumi, Geor. (sô-kóm´)	181	43°00´N	41°00´E
Sukkur, Pak. (sŭk´ŭr)	199	27°49´N	68°50´E
Sukkwan Island, i., Ak., U.S.	94	55°05´N	132°45´W
Suksun, Russia (sôk´sôn)	186a	57°08´N	57°22´E
Sukumo, Japan (sōō´kó-mô)	211	32°58´N	132°45´E
Sukunka, r., Can.	95	55°00´N	121°50´W
Sula, r., Ukr. (sōō-lä´)	177	50°36´N	33°13´E
Sula, Kepulauan, is., Indon.	213	2°20´S	125°20´E
Sulaco, r., Hond. (sōō-lä´kô)	132	14°55´N	87°31´W
Sulaimān Range, mts., Pak. (sô-lä-ē-män´)	199	29°47´N	69°10´E
Sulak, r., Russia (sōō-läk´)	181	43°30´N	47°00´E
Sulfeld, Ger. (zōō´fĕld)	159c	53°48´N	10°13´E
Sulina, Rom. (sōō-lē´ná)	163	45°08´N	29°38´E
Sulitelma, mtn., Eur. (sōō-lē-tyĕl´má)	160	67°03´N	16°35´E
Sullana, Peru (sōō-lyä´ná)	142	4°57´S	80°47´W
Sulligent, Al., U.S. (sŭl´ĭ-jĕnt)	124	33°52´N	88°06´W
Sullivan, In., U.S. (sŭl´ĭ-văn)	108	41°35´N	88°35´W
Sullivan, Il., U.S.	108	39°05´N	87°20´W
Sullivan, Mo., U.S.	121	38°13´N	91°09´W
Sulmona, Italy (sōōl-mō´ná)	174	42°02´N	13°58´E
Sulphur, Ok., U.S. (sŭl´fŭr)	121	34°31´N	96°58´W
Sulphur, r., Tx., U.S.	121	33°26´N	95°06´W
Sulphur Springs, Tx., U.S. (springz)	121	33°09´N	95°36´W
Sultan, Wa., U.S. (sŭl´tăn)	116a	47°52´N	121°49´W
Sultan, r., Wa., U.S.	116a	47°55´N	121°49´W
Sultepec, Mex. (sōōl-tā-pĕk´)	130	18°50´N	99°51´W
Sulu Archipelago, is., Phil. (sōō´lōō)	212	5°52´N	122°00´E
Suluntah, Libya	163	32°39´N	21°49´E
Sulūq, Libya	231	31°39´N	20°15´E
Sulu Sea, sea, Asia	212	8°25´N	119°00´E
Suma, Japan (sōō´mä)	211b	34°39´N	135°08´E
Sumas, Wa., U.S. (sū´más)	116d	49°00´N	122°16´W
Sumatera, i., Indon.	212	2°06´N	99°40´E
Sumatra see Sumatera, i., Indon.	212	2°06´N	99°40´E
Sumba, i., Indon. (sŭm´bá)	212	9°52´S	119°00´E
Sumba, Île, i., D.R.C.	236	1°44´N	19°32´E
Sumbawa, i., Indon. (sóm-bä´wä)	212	9°00´S	118°18´E
Sumbawa-Besar, Indon.	212	8°32´S	117°20´E
Sumbawanga, Tan.	237	7°58´S	31°37´E
Sumbe, Ang.	232	11°13´S	13°50´E
Sümeg, Hung. (shü´mĕg)	169	46°59´N	17°19´E
Sumida, r., Japan (sōō´mē-dä)	211	36°01´N	139°24´E
Sumidouro, Braz. (sōō-mē-dó´ró)	141a	22°04´S	42°41´W
Sumiyoshi, Japan (sōō´mē-yō´shĕ)	211b	34°43´N	135°16´E
Summer Lake, l., Or., U.S. (sŭm´ēr)	114	42°50´N	120°35´W
Summerland, Can. (sŭ´mĕr-lănd)	95	49°39´N	119°40´W
Summerside, Can. (sŭm´ēr-sīd)	91	46°25´N	63°47´W
Summerton, S.C., U.S. (sŭm´ĕr-tŭn)	125	33°37´N	80°22´W
Summerville, S.C., U.S. (sŭm´ĕr-vĭl)	125	33°00´N	80°10´W
Summit, Il., U.S. (sŭm´mĭt)	111a	41°47´N	87°48´W
Summit, N.J., U.S.	110a	40°43´N	74°21´W
Summit Lake Indian Reservation, I.R., Nv., U.S.	114	41°35´N	119°30´W
Summit Peak, mtn., Co., U.S.	119	37°20´N	106°40´W
Sumner, Wa., U.S.	116a	47°12´N	122°14´W
Šumperk, Czech Rep. (shòm´pĕrk)	169	49°57´N	17°02´E
Sumqayit, Azer.	182	40°36´N	49°38´E
Sumrall, Ms., U.S. (sŭm´rôl)	124	31°25´N	89°34´W
Sumter, S.C., U.S. (sŭm´tĕr)	125	33°55´N	80°21´W
Sumy, Ukr. (sōō´mĭ)	178	50°54´N	34°47´E
Sumy, prov., Ukr.	177	51°02´N	34°05´E
Sun, r., Mt., U.S. (sŭn)	115	47°34´N	111°53´W
Sunburst, Mt., U.S.	115	48°53´N	111°55´W
Sunda, Selat, strt., Indon.	212	5°45´S	106°15´E
Sundance, Wy., U.S. (sŭn´dăns)	115	44°24´N	104°27´W
Sundarbans, sw., Asia (sŏn´dēr-bŭns)	199	21°50´N	89°00´E
Sunday Strait, strt., Austl. (sŭn´dā)	220	15°50´S	122°45´E
Sundbyberg, Swe. (sŏn´bü-bĕrgh)	166	59°24´N	17°56´E
Sunderland, Eng., U.K. (sŭn´dĕr-lănd)	160	54°55´N	1°25´W
Sunderland, Md., U.S.	110e	38°41´N	76°36´W
Sundsvall, Swe. (sŏnds´väl)	154	62°24´N	19°19´E
Sungari (Songhua), r., China	205	46°09´N	127°53´E
Sungari Reservoir, res., China	208	42°55´N	127°50´E
Sungurlu, Tur. (sŏn´gór-ló´)	163	40°08´N	34°20´E
Sun Kosi, r., Nepal	202	27°13´N	85°52´E
Sunland, Ca., U.S. (sŭn-lănd)	117a	34°16´N	118°18´W
Sunne, Swe. (sōōn´ĕ)	166	59°51´N	13°07´E
Sunninghill, Eng., U.K. (sŭnĭng´hĭl)	158b	51°23´N	0°40´W

PLACE (Pronunciation)	PAGE	LAT.	LONG.
Sunnymead, Ca., U.S. (sŭn´ĭ-mĕd)	117a	33°56´N	117°15´W
Sunnyside, Ut., U.S.	119	39°35´N	110°20´W
Sunnyside, Wa., U.S.	114	46°19´N	120°00´W
Sunnyvale, Ca., U.S. (sŭn-nĕ-vāl)	116b	37°23´N	122°02´W
Sunol, Ca., U.S. (sōō´nŭl)	116b	37°36´N	122°53´W
Sunset, Ut., U.S. (sŭn-sĕt)	117b	41°08´N	112°02´W
Sunset Crater National Monument, rec., Az., U.S. (krā´tĕr)	119	35°20´N	111°30´W
Sunshine, Austl.	217a	37°47´S	144°50´E
Suntar, Russia (sôn-tár´)	179	62°14´N	117°49´E
Sunyani, Ghana	234	7°20´N	2°20´W
Suoyarvi, Russia (sōō´ó-yĕr´vĕ)	180	62°12´N	32°29´E
Superior, Az., U.S. (su-pē´rĭ-ēr)	119	33°15´N	111°10´W
Superior, Ne., U.S.	120	40°04´N	98°05´W
Superior, Wi., U.S.	105	46°44´N	92°06´W
Superior, Wy., U.S.	115	41°45´N	108°57´W
Superior, Laguna, l., Mex. (lä-gōō´ná sōō-pä-rĕ-ōr´)	131	16°20´N	94°55´W
Superior, Lake, l., N.A.	107	47°38´N	89°20´W
Superior Village, Wi., U.S.	117h	46°38´N	92°07´W
Sup´ung Reservoir, res., Asia (sōō´pōong)	210	40°35´N	126°00´E
Suqian, China (sōō-chyĕn)	206	33°57´N	118°17´E
Suquamish, Wa., U.S. (sōō-gwä´mĭsh)	116a	47°44´N	122°34´W
Suquţrā (Socotra), i., Yemen (sô-kō´trä)	198	13°00´N	52°30´E
Şūr, Leb. (sōōr) (tīr)	197a	33°16´N	35°13´E
Şūr, Oman	198	22°23´N	59°28´E
Surabaya, Indon.	212	7°23´S	112°45´E
Surakarta, Indon.	212	7°35´S	110°45´E
Šurany, Slvk. (shōō´rä-nû´)	169	48°05´N	18°11´E
Surat, Austl. (sū-rät)	222	27°18´S	149°00´E
Surat, India (sō´rŭt)	199	21°08´N	73°22´E
Surat Thani, Thai.	212	8°59´N	99°14´E
Surazh, Bela.	155	55°24´N	30°46´E
Surazh, Russia (sōō-räzh´)	176	53°02´N	32°27´E
Surgères, Fr. (sür-zhâr´)	170	46°06´N	0°51´W
Surgut, Russia (sôr-gót´).	178	61°18´N	73°38´E
Suriname, nation, S.A. (sōō-rĕ-näm´)	143	4°00´N	56°00´W
Sürmaq, Iran	201	31°03´N	52°48´E
Surt, Libya	231	31°14´N	16°37´E
Surt, Khalīj, b., Libya	231	31°30´N	18°28´E
Suruga-Wan, b., Japan (sōō´rōō-gä wän)	210	34°52´N	138°36´E
Susa, Japan	211	34°40´N	131°39´E
Sušak, i., Yugo.	174	42°45´N	16°30´E
Susak, Otok, i., Yugo.	174	44°31´N	14°15´E
Susaki, Japan (sōō´sä-kĕ)	211	33°23´N	133°16´E
Sušice, Czech Rep.	168	49°14´N	13°31´E
Susitna, Ak., U.S. (sōō-sīt´ná)	103	61°28´N	150°28´W
Susitna, r., Ak., U.S.	103	62°00´N	150°28´W
Susong, China (sōō-sòŋ)	209	30°18´N	116°08´E
Susquehanna, Pa., U.S. (sŭs´kwĕ-hăn´á)	109	41°55´N	73°55´W
Susquehanna, r., U.S.	109	39°50´N	76°20´W
Sussex, Can. (sŭs´ĕks)	91	45°43´N	65°31´W
Sussex, N.J., U.S.	110a	41°12´N	74°36´W
Sussex, Wi., U.S.	111a	43°08´N	88°12´W
Sutherland, Austl.	217b	34°02´S	151°04´E
Sutherland, S. Afr. (sŭ´thĕr-lănd)	232	32°25´S	20°40´E
Sutlej, r., Asia (sŭt´lĕj)	199	30°15´N	73°00´E
Sutton, Eng., U.K. (sŭt´'n)	158b	51°21´N	0°12´W
Sutton, Ma., U.S.	101a	42°09´N	71°46´W
Sutton Coldfield, Eng., U.K. (kōld´fĕld)	158a	52°34´N	1°49´W
Sutton-in-Ashfield, Eng., U.K. (ĭn-ăsh´fĕld)	158a	53°07´N	1°15´W
Suurberge, mts., S. Afr.	233c	33°15´S	25°32´E
Suva, Fiji	214g	18°08´S	178°25´E
Suwa, Japan (sōō´wä)	211	36°03´N	138°08´E
Suwałki, Pol. (sô-vou´kĕ)	169	54°05´N	22°58´E
Suwanee Lake, l., Can.	97	56°08´N	100°10´W
Suwannee, r., U.S. (sô-wô´nĕ)	107	29°42´N	83°00´W
Suways al Hulwah, Tur´ at as, can., Egypt	238d	30°15´N	32°20´E
Suxian, China (sōō shyĕn)	208	33°29´N	117°51´E
Suzdal´, Russia (sōōz´dál)	176	56°26´N	40°29´E
Suzhou, China (sōō-jō)	205	31°19´N	120°37´E
Suzu Misaki, c., Japan (sōō´zōō mē´sä-kĕ)	210	37°30´N	137°35´E
Svalbard (Spitsbergen), dep., Nor. (sväl´bärt) (spĭts´bŭr-gĕn)	178	77°00´N	20°00´E
Svaneke, Den. (svä´nĕ-kĕ)	166	55°08´N	15°07´E
Svatove, Ukr.	181	49°23´N	38°10´E
Svedala, Swe. (svĕ´dä-lä)	166	55°29´N	13°11´E
Sveg, Swe.	166	62°03´N	14°22´E
Svelvik, Nor. (svĕl´vĕk)	166	59°37´N	10°18´E
Svenčionys, Lith.	167	55°09´N	26°09´E
Svendborg, Den. (svĕn-bôrgh)	166	55°05´N	10°35´E
Svensen, Or., U.S. (svĕn´sĕn)	116c	46°10´N	123°39´W
Sverdlovsk see Yekaterinburg, Russia	178	56°51´N	60°36´E
Svetlaya, Russia (svĕt´lä-yä)	210	46°09´N	137°53´E
Svicha, r., Ukr.	169	49°09´N	24°10´E
Svilajnac, Yugo. (svē´lä-ē-näts)	175	44°12´N	21°14´E
Svilengrad, Blg. (svĕl´ĕn-grät)	175	41°44´N	26°11´E
Svir´, r., Russia	180	60°15´N	33°40´E
Svir Kanal, can., Russia (kä-näl´)	167	60°10´N	32°40´E
Svishtov, Blg. (svēsh bôf)	163	43°38´N	25°21´E
Svisloch´, r., Bela. (svēs´lôk)	155	53°38´N	28°10´E
Svitavy, Czech Rep.	168	49°46´N	16°28´E
Svobodnyy, Russia (svô-bôd´nĭ)	179	51°28´N	128°28´E
Svolvaer, Nor. (svôl´vĕr)	160	68°15´N	14°29´E
Svyatoy Nos, Mys, c., Russia (svyū´toi nôs)	179	72°18´N	139°28´E

PRONOUNCING INDEX

Swadlincote – Tamiahua 355

PLACE (Pronunciation)	PAGE	LAT.	LONG.
Swadlincote, Eng., U.K. (swōd′lĭn-kōt)	158a	52°46′N	1°33′W
Swain Reefs, rf., Austl. (swān)	221	22°12′S	152°08′E
Swainsboro, Ga., U.S. (swānz′bŭr-ō)	125	32°37′N	82°21′W
Swakopmund, Nmb. (svä′kôp-mònt) (swȧ′kôp-mònd)	232	22°40′S	14°30′E
Swallowfield, Eng., U.K. (swŏl′ō-fēld)	158b	51°21′N	0°58′W
Swampscott, Ma., U.S. (swômp′skŏt)	101a	42°28′N	70°55′W
Swan, r., Austl.	220	31°30′S	116°30′E
Swan, r., Can.	97	51°58′N	101°45′W
Swan, r., Mt., U.S.	115	47°50′N	113°40′W
Swan Hill, Austl.	219	35°20′S	143°30′E
Swan Hills, Can. (hĭlz)	90	54°52′N	115°45′W
Swan Island, i., Austl. (swŏn)	217a	38°15′S	144°41′E
Swan Lake, l., Can.	97	52°30′N	100°45′W
Swanland, reg., Austl. (swŏn′lănd)	220	31°45′S	119°15′E
Swan Range, mts., Mt., U.S.	115	47°50′N	113°40′W
Swan River, Can. (swŏn rĭv′ẽr)	90	52°06′N	101°16′W
Swansea, Wales, U.K.	161	51°37′N	3°59′W
Swansea, Il., U.S. (swŏn′sē)	117e	38°32′N	89°59′W
Swansea, Ma., U.S.	110b	41°45′N	71°09′W
Swanson Reservoir, res., Ne., U.S. (swŏn′sŭn)	120	40°13′N	101°30′W
Swartberg, mtn., Afr.	233c	30°08′S	29°34′E
Swartkop, mtn., S. Afr.	232a	34°13′S	18°27′E
Swartruggens, S. Afr.	238c	25°40′S	26°40′E
Swartspruit, S. Afr.	233b	25°44′S	28°01′E
Swatow *see* Shantou, China	205	23°20′N	116°40′E
Swaziland, nation, Afr. (Swä′zē-lănd)	232	26°45′S	31°30′E
Sweden, nation, Eur. (swē′dĕn)	154	60°10′N	14°10′E
Swedesboro, N.J., U.S. (swēdz′bē-rô)	110f	39°45′N	75°22′W
Sweetwater, Tn., U.S. (swēt′wô-tẽr)	124	35°36′N	84°29′W
Sweetwater, Tx., U.S.	104	32°28′N	100°25′W
Sweetwater, l., N.D., U.S.	112	48°15′N	98°35′W
Sweetwater, r., Wy., U.S.	115	42°19′N	108°35′W
Sweetwater Reservoir, res., Ca., U.S.	118a	32°42′N	116°54′W
Świdnica, Pol. (shvĭd-nē′tsä)	168	50°50′N	16°30′E
Świdwin, Pol. (shvĭd′vĭn)	168	53°46′N	15°48′E
Świebodzice, Pol.	168	50°51′N	16°17′E
Świebodzin, Pol. (shvyĕn-bo′jĕts)	168	52°16′N	15°36′E
Świecie, Pol. (shvyän′tsyĕ)	169	53°23′N	18°26′E
Świętokrzyskie, Góry, mts., Pol. (shvyĕn-tō-kzhĭ′skyĕ gōō′rĭ)	169	50°57′N	21°02′E
Swift, r., Eng., U.K.	158a	52°26′N	1°08′W
Swift, r., Me., U.S. (swĭft)	101	44°42′N	70°40′E
Swift Creek Reservoir, res., Wa., U.S.	114	46°03′N	122°10′W
Swift Current, Can. (swĭft kûr′ĕnt)	90	50°17′N	107°50′W
Swindle Island, i., Can.	94	52°32′N	128°35′W
Swindon, Eng., U.K. (swĭn′dŭn)	164	51°35′N	1°55′W
Swinomish Indian Reservation, I.R., Wa., U.S. (swĭ-nō′mĭsh)	116a	48°25′N	122°27′W
Świnoujście, Pol. (shvĭ-nĭ-ō-wēsh′chyĕ)	168	53°56′N	14°14′E
Swinton, Eng., U.K. (swĭn′tŭn)	158a	53°30′N	1°19′W
Swissvale, Pa., U.S. (swĭs′văl)	111e	40°25′N	79°53′W
Switzerland, nation, Eur. (swĭt′zẽr-lănd)	154	46°30′N	7°43′E
Syanno, Bela. (syĕ′nô)	176	54°48′N	29°43′E
Syas′, r., Russia (syäs)	176	59°28′N	33°24′E
Sycamore, Il., U.S. (sĭk′á-mōr)	113	42°00′N	88°42′W
Sycan, r., Or., U.S.	114	42°45′N	121°00′W
Sychëvka, Russia (sē-chôf′kȧ)	176	55°52′N	34°18′E
Sydney, Austl. (sĭd′nē)	219	33°55′S	151°17′E
Sydney, Can.	91	46°09′N	60°11′W
Sydney Mines, Can.	91	46°14′N	60°14′W
Syktyvkar, Russia (sük-tüf′kär)	178	61°35′N	50°40′E
Sylacauga, Al., U.S. (sĭl-á-kô′gá)	124	33°10′N	86°15′W
Sylarna, mtn., Eur.	166	63°00′N	12°10′E
Sylt, i., Ger. (sĭlt)	168	54°55′N	8°30′E
Sylvania, Ga., U.S. (sĭl-vā′nĭ-á)	125	32°44′N	81°40′W
Sylvester, Ga., U.S. (sĭl-vĕs′tẽr)	124	31°32′N	83°50′W
Sými, i., Grc.	163	36°27′N	27°41′E
Synel′nykove, Ukr.	181	48°19′N	35°33′E
Syracuse, Ks., U.S. (sĭr′á-kūs)	120	37°59′N	101°44′W
Syracuse, N.Y., U.S.	105	43°05′N	76°10′W
Syracuse, Ut., U.S.	117b	41°06′N	112°04′W
Syr Darya, r., Asia	178	44°15′N	65°45′E
Syria, nation, Asia (sĭr′ĭ-á)	198	35°00′N	37°15′E
Syrian Desert, des., Asia	198	32°00′N	40°00′E
Sýros, i., Grc.	163	37°23′N	24°55′E
Sysert′, Russia (sĕ′sẽrt)	186a	56°30′N	60°48′E
Sysola, r., Russia	180	60°50′N	50°40′E
Syvash, zatoka, b., Ukr.	177	45°55′N	34°42′E
Syzran′, Russia (sĕz-rän′)	178	53°09′N	48°27′E
Szamotuły, Pol. (shȧ-mô-tōō′wĕ)	168	52°36′N	16°34′E
Szarvas, Hung. (sôr′vôsh)	169	46°51′N	20°36′E
Szczebrzeszyn, Pol. (shchĕ-bzhā′shĕn)	169	50°41′N	22°58′E
Szczecin, Pol. (shchĕ′tsĭn)	154	53°25′N	14°35′E
Szczecinek, Pol. (shchĕ′tsĭ-nĕk)	160	53°41′N	16°42′E
Szczuczyn, Pol. (shchōō′chĭn)	169	53°32′N	22°17′E
Szczytno, Pol. (shchĭt′nô)	169	53°33′N	21°00′E
Szechwan Basin, basin, China	204	30°45′N	104°40′E
Szeged, Hung. (sĕ′gĕd)	154	46°15′N	20°12′E
Székesfehérvár, Hung. (sā′kĕsh-fĕ′hār-vär)	163	47°12′N	18°26′E
Szekszárd, Hung. (sĕk′särd)	163	46°19′N	18°42′E
Szentendre, Hung. (sĕnt′ĕn-drĕ)	169	47°40′N	19°07′E
Szentes, Hung. (sĕn′tĕsh)	169	46°38′N	20°18′E
Szigetvar, Hung. (sĭ′gĕt-vär)	169	46°05′N	17°50′E
Szolnok, Hung.	169	47°11′N	20°12′E
Szombathely, Hung. (sôm′bôt-hĕl′)	163	47°13′N	16°35′E
Szprotawa, Pol. (shprō-tä′vä)	168	51°34′N	15°29′E
Szydłowiec, Pol. (shid-wô′vyets)	169	51°13′N	20°53′E
T			
Taal, l., Phil. (tä-äl′)	213a	13°58′N	121°06′E
Tabaco, Phil. (tä-bä′kō)	213a	13°27′N	123°40′E
Tabankulu, S. Afr. (tā-băn-kōō′la)	233c	30°56′S	29°19′E
Tabasará, Serranía de, mts., Pan.	133	8°29′N	81°22′W
Tabasco, Mex. (tä-bäs′kō)	130	21°47′N	103°04′W
Tabasco, state, Mex.	128	18°10′N	93°00′W
Taber, Can.	90	49°47′N	112°08′W
Tablas, i., Phil. (tä′bläs)	213a	12°26′N	122°00′E
Tablas Strait, strt., Phil.	213a	12°17′N	121°41′E
Table Bay, b., S. Afr. (tā′b′l)	232a	33°41′S	18°27′E
Table Mountain, mtn., S. Afr.	232a	33°58′S	18°26′E
Table Rock Lake, Mo., U.S.	121	36°37′N	93°29′W
Tabligbo, Togo	234	6°35′N	1°30′E
Taboga, i., Pan. (tä-bō′gä)	128a	8°48′N	79°35′W
Taboguilla, i., Pan. (tä-bô-gē′l-yä)	128a	8°48′N	79°31′W
Tábor, Czech Rep. (tä′bôr)	168	49°25′N	14°40′E
Tabora, Tan. (tä-bō′rä)	232	5°01′S	32°48′E
Tabou, C. Iv. (tȧ-bōō′)	230	4°25′N	7°21′W
Tabrīz, Iran (tȧ-brēz′)	198	38°00′N	46°13′E
Tabuaeran, i., Kir.	2	3°52′N	159°20′W
Tabwémasana, Mont, mtn., Vanuatu	214f	15°20′S	166°44′E
Tacámbaro, r., Mex. (tä-käm′bä-rō)	130	18°55′N	101°25′W
Tacámbaro de Codallos, Mex.	130	19°12′N	101°28′W
Tacarigua, Laguna de la, l., Ven.	143b	10°18′N	65°43′W
Tacheng, China (tä-chŭŋ)	204	46°50′N	83°24′E
Tachie, r., Can.	94	54°30′N	125°00′W
Tacloban, Phil. (tä-klō′bän)	213	11°06′N	124°58′E
Tacna, Peru (täk′nä)	142	18°34′S	70°16′W
Tacoma, Wa., U.S. (tȧ-kō′mȧ)	104	47°14′N	122°27′W
Taconic Range, mts., N.Y., U.S. (tȧ-kŏn′ĭk)	109	41°55′N	73°40′W
Tacotalpa, Mex. (tä-kô-täl′pä)	131	17°37′N	92°51′W
Tacotalpa, r., Mex.	131	17°24′N	92°38′W
Tademaït, Plateau du, plat., Alg. (tä-dē-mä′ēt)	230	28°00′N	2°15′E
Tadio, Lagune, b., C. Iv.	234	5°20′N	5°25′W
Tadjoura, Dji. (tȧd-zhōō′rȧ)	238a	11°48′N	42°54′E
Tadley, Eng., U.K. (tăd′lē)	158b	51°19′N	1°08′W
Tadotsu, Japan (tä′dô-tsō)	211	34°14′N	133°43′E
Tadoussac, Can. (tȧ-dōō-sȧk′)	99	48°09′N	69°43′W
Tadzhikistan *see* Tajikistan, nation, Asia	178	39°22′N	69°30′E
Taebaek Sanmaek, mts., Asia (tī-bĭk′ sän-mĭk′)	210	37°20′N	128°50′E
Taedong, r., Kor., N. (tī-dŏng)	210	38°38′N	124°32′E
Taegu, Kor., S. (tī′gōō′)	205	35°49′N	128°41′E
Taejŏn, Kor., S.	210	36°20′N	127°26′E
Tafalla, Spain (tä-fäl′yä)	172	42°30′N	1°42′W
Tafna, r., Alg. (täf′nä)	172	35°28′N	1°00′W
Taft, Ca., U.S. (tȧft)	118	35°09′N	119°27′W
Tagama, reg., Niger	235	15°50′N	6°30′E
Taganrog, Russia (tȧ-gȧn-rôk′)	181	47°12′N	38°56′E
Taganrogskiy Zaliv, b., Eur. (tȧ-gȧn-rôk′skĭ zä′lĭf)	181	46°55′N	38°17′E
Tagula, i., Pap. N. Gui. (tä′gōō-lȧ)	221	11°45′S	153°46′E
Tagus (Tajo), r., Eur. (tā′gŭs)	156	39°40′N	5°07′W
Tahan, Gunong, mtn., Malay.	212	4°33′N	101°52′E
Tahat, mtn., Alg. (tä-hät′)	230	23°22′N	5°21′E
Tahiti, i., Fr. Poly. (tä-hē′tē) (tȧ′ē-tē′)	2	17°30′S	149°30′W
Tahkuna Nina, c., Est. (tȧh-kōō′nȧ nē′nȧ)	167	59°08′N	22°03′E
Tahlequah, Ok., U.S. (tă-lĕ-kwä′)	121	35°54′N	94°58′W
Tahoe, l., U.S. (tä′hō)	106	39°09′N	120°18′W
Tahoua, Niger (tä′ōō-ä)	230	14°54′N	5°16′E
Tahtsa Lake, l., Can.	94	53°33′N	127°47′W
Tahuya, Wa., U.S. (tȧ-hū-yā′)	116a	47°23′N	123°03′W
Tahuya, r., Wa., U.S.	116a	47°28′N	122°55′W
Tai′an, China (tī-än)	208	36°13′N	117°08′E
Taibai Shan, mtn., China (tī-bī shän)	208	33°42′N	107°25′E
Taibus Qi, China (tī-bōō-sz chyē)	208	41°52′N	115°25′E
Taicang, China (tī-tsäŋ)	206	31°26′N	121°06′E
T′aichung, Tai. (tī′chŏng)	205	24°10′N	120°42′E
Tai′erzhuang, China (tī-är-jûäŋ)	206	34°34′N	117°44′E
Taigu, China (tī-gōō)	208	37°25′N	112°35′E
Taihang Shan, mts., China (tī-häŋ shän)	208	35°45′N	112°00′E
Taihe, China (tī-hŭ)	206	33°10′N	115°38′E
Tai Hu, l., China (tī hōō)	205	31°13′N	120°00′E
Tailagoin, reg., Mong. (tī′lȧ-gän′ kä′rä)	204	43°39′N	105°54′E
Tailai, China (tī-lī)	208	46°20′N	123°10′E
Tailem Bend, Austl. (tā-lĕm)	222	35°15′S	139°30′E
T′ainan, Tai. (tī′nan′)	205	23°08′N	120°18′E
Taínaro, c., Grc.	162	37°45′N	22°00′E
Taining, China (tī′nĭng′)	209	26°58′N	117°15′E
T′aipei, Tai. (tī′pā′)	205	25°02′N	121°38′E
Taiping, pt. of i., Malay.	212	4°56′N	100°39′E
Taiping Ling, mtn., China	208	47°03′N	120°30′E
Taisha, Japan (tī′shä)	211	35°23′N	132°40′E
Taishan, China (tī-shän)	209	22°15′N	112°50′E
Tai Shan, mts., China (tī shän)	208	36°16′N	117°05′E
Taitao, Península de, pen., Chile	144	46°20′S	77°15′W
T′aitung, Tai. (tī′tōōng′)	209	22°45′N	121°02′E
Taiwan, nation, Asia (tī-wän) (fôr-mō′sȧ)	205	23°30′N	122°20′E
Taiwan Strait, strt., Asia	205	24°30′N	120°00′E
Taixian, China (tī shyĕn)	206	32°31′N	119°54′E
Taixing, China (tī-shyĭŋ)	206	32°12′N	119°58′E
Taiyuan, China (tī-yûän)	205	37°32′N	112°38′E
Taizhou, China (tī-jō)	206	32°23′N	119°41′E
Ta′Izz, Yemen	201	13°38′N	44°04′E
Tajano de Morais, Braz. (tĕ-zhä′nô-dĕ-mō-rä′ēs)	141a	22°05′S	42°04′W
Tajikistan, nation, Asia	178	39°22′N	69°30′E
Tajumulco, vol., Guat. (tä-hōō-mōōl′kō)	132	15°03′N	91°53′W
Tajuña, r., Spain (tä-kōō′n-yä)	172	40°23′N	2°36′W
Tājūrā′, Libya	162	32°56′N	13°24′W
Tak, Thai.	212	16°57′N	99°12′E
Taka, i., Japan (tä′kä)	211	30°47′N	130°23′E
Takada, Japan (tä′kȧ-dä)	210	37°08′N	138°30′E
Takahashi, Japan (tä′kä′hä-shĭ)	211	34°47′N	133°35′E
Takaishi, Japan	211b	34°32′N	135°27′E
Takamatsu, Japan (tä′kä′mä-tsōō′)	205	34°20′N	134°02′E
Takamori, Japan (tä′kä′mô-rē′)	211	32°50′N	131°08′E
Takaoka, Japan (tä′kä′ō-kä′)	210	36°45′N	136°59′E
Takapuna, N.Z.	223	36°48′S	174°47′E
Takarazuka, Japan (tä′kä-rä-zōō′kä)	211b	34°48′N	135°22′E
Takasaki, Japan (tä′kät′sōō-kē′)	210	36°20′N	139°00′E
Takatsu, Japan (tä-kät′sōō) (mĕ′zō-nô-kō′chĕ)	211a	35°36′N	139°37′E
Takatsuki, Japan (tä′kät′sōō-kē′)	211b	34°51′N	135°38′E
Takayama, Japan (tä′kä′yä′mä)	211	36°11′N	137°16′E
Takefu, Japan (tä′kĕ-fōō)	210	35°57′N	136°09′E
Take-shima, is., Asia	210	37°15′N	131°51′E
Takla Lake, l., Can.	92	55°25′N	125°53′W
Takla Makan, des., China (mä-kän′)	204	39°22′N	82°34′E
Takoma Park, Md., U.S. (tȧ′kōmȧ pärk)	110e	38°59′N	77°00′W
Takum, Nig.	235	7°17′N	9°59′E
Tala, Mex. (tä′lä)	130	20°39′N	103°42′W
Talagante, Chile (tä-lä-gä′n-tĕ)	141b	33°39′S	70°54′W
Talamanca, Cordillera de, mts., C.R.	133	9°37′N	83°55′W
Talanga, Hond. (tä-lä′n-gä)	132	14°21′N	87°09′W
Talara, Peru (tä-lä′rä)	142	4°32′S	81°17′W
Talasea, Pap. N. Gui. (tä-lä-sā′ä)	213	5°20′S	150°00′E
Talata Mafara, Nig.	235	12°35′N	6°04′E
Talaud, Kepulauan, is., Indon. (tä-lout′)	213	4°17′N	127°30′E
Talavera de la Reina, Spain	162	39°58′N	4°51′W
Talca, Chile (täl′kä)	144	35°25′S	71°39′W
Talca, prov., Chile	141b	35°23′S	71°15′W
Talca, Punta, c., Chile (pōō′n-tä-täl′kä)	141b	33°25′S	71°42′W
Talcahuano, Chile (täl-kä-wä′nō)	144	36°41′S	73°05′W
Taldom, Russia (täl-dôm)	176	56°44′N	37°33′E
Taldyqorghan, Kaz.	183	45°03′N	77°18′E
Talea de Castro, Mex. (tä′lā-ä dā käs′trō)	131	17°22′N	96°14′W
Talibu, Pulau, i., Indon.	213	1°30′S	125°00′E
Talim, i., Phil. (tä-lēm′)	213a	14°21′N	121°14′E
Talisay, Phil. (tä-lē′sī)	213a	14°08′N	122°56′E
Talkeetna, Ak., U.S. (tál-kēt′nȧ)	103	62°18′N	150°02′W
Talladega, Al., U.S. (tăl-á-dē′gá)	124	33°25′N	86°06′W
Tallahassee, Fl., U.S. (tăl-á-hăs′ē)	105	30°25′N	84°17′W
Tallahatchie, r., Ms., U.S. (tal-á hăch′ē)	124	34°21′N	90°03′W
Tallapoosa, Ga., U.S. (tăl-á-pōō′sá)	124	33°44′N	85°15′W
Tallapoosa, r., Al., U.S.	124	32°22′N	86°08′W
Tallassee, Al., U.S. (tăl′á-sē)	124	32°30′N	85°54′W
Tallinn, Est. (tál′lĕn) (rá′väl)	178	59°26′N	24°44′E
Tallmadge, Oh., U.S. (tăl′mĭj)	111d	41°06′N	81°26′W
Tallulah, La., U.S. (tă-lōō′lȧ)	123	32°25′N	91°13′W
Tal′ne, Ukr.	177	48°52′N	30°43′E
Talo, mtn., Eth.	231	10°45′N	37°55′E
Taloje Budrukh, India	203b	19°05′N	73°05′E
Talpa de Allende, Mex. (täl′pä dā äl-yĕn′dā)	130	20°25′N	104°48′W
Talquin, Lake, res., Fl., U.S.	124	30°26′N	84°33′W
Talsi, Lat. (tal′sĭ)	167	57°16′N	22°35′E
Taltal, Chile (täl-täl′)	144	25°26′S	70°32′W
Taly, Russia (täl′ĭ)	177	49°51′N	40°07′E
Tama, Ia., U.S. (tā′mȧ)	113	41°57′N	92°36′W
Tama, r., Japan	211a	35°38′N	139°35′E
Tamale, Ghana (tä-mä′lå)	230	9°25′N	0°50′W
Taman′, Russia (tȧ-män′)	177	45°13′N	36°46′E
Tamanaco, r., Ven. (tä-mä-nä′kō)	143b	9°32′N	66°00′W
Tamaqua, Pa., U.S. (tȧ-mô′kwȧ)	109	40°45′N	75°50′W
Tamar, r., Eng., U.K. (tā′mär)	164	50°35′N	4°15′W
Tamarite de Litera, Spain (tä-mä-rē′tā)	173	41°52′N	0°24′E
Tamaulipas, state, Mex. (tä-mä-ōō-lē′päs′)	128	23°45′N	98°30′W
Tamazula de Gordiano, Mex.	130	19°44′N	103°09′W
Tamazulapan del Progreso, Mex.	131	17°41′N	97°34′W
Tamazunchale, Mex. (tä-mä-zōn-chä′lå)	130	21°16′N	98°46′W
Tambacounda, Sen. (täm-bä-kōōn′dä)	230	13°47′N	13°40′W
Tambador, Serra do, mts., Braz. (sĕ′r-rä-dô-täm′bä-dōr)	143	10°33′S	41°16′W
Tambelan, Kepulauan, is., Indon. (täm-bå-län′)	212	0°38′N	107°38′E
Tambo, Austl. (tăm′bō)	219	24°50′S	146°15′E
Tambov, Russia (tȧm-bôf′)	178	52°45′N	41°10′E
Tambov, prov., Russia	176	52°50′N	40°42′E
Tambre, r., Spain (täm′brā)	172	42°59′N	8°33′W
Tambura, Sudan (täm-bōō′rä)	231	5°34′N	27°30′E
Tame, r., Eng., U.K. (tām)	158a	52°41′N	1°42′W
Tâmega, r., Port. (tȧ-mā′gȧ)	172	41°30′N	7°45′W
Tamenghest, Alg.	230	22°34′N	5°34′E
Tamenghest, Oued, r., Alg.	230	22°15′N	2°51′E
Tamgak, Monts, mtn., Niger (tam-gäk′)	230	18°40′N	8°40′E
Tamgué, Massif du, mtn., Gui.	230	12°15′N	12°35′W
Tamiahua, Mex. (tä-myä-wä)	131	21°17′N	97°26′W

356 Tamiahua – Temoaya

PRONOUNCING INDEX

PLACE (Pronunciation)	PAGE	LAT.	LONG.
Tamiahua, Laguna, l., Mex. (lä-gö'nä-tä-myä-wä)	131	21°38'N	97°33'W
Tamiami Canal, can., Fl., U.S. (tă-mī-ăm'ĭ)	125a	25°52'N	80°08'W
Tamil Nadu, state, India	199	11°30'N	78°00'E
Tampa, Fl., U.S. (tăm'pȧ)	105	27°57'N	82°25'W
Tampa Bay, b., Fl., U.S.	107	27°35'N	82°38'W
Tampere, Fin. (tȧm'pĕ-rĕ)	160	61°21'N	23°39'E
Tampico, Mex. (täm-pē'kō)	128	22°14'N	97°51'W
Tampico Alto, Mex. (täm-pē'kō äl'tō)	131	22°07'N	97°48'W
Tampin, Malay.	197b	2°28'N	102°15'E
Tam Quan, Viet.	209	14°20'N	109°10'E
Tamuín, Mex. (tä-mōō-ē'n)	130	22°04'N	98°47'W
Tamworth, Austl. (tăm'wûrth)	219	31°01'S	151°00'E
Tamworth, Eng., U.K.	158a	52°38'N	1°41'W
Tana, i., Vanuatu	221	19°32'S	169°27'E
Tana, r., Kenya (tä'nä)	233	0°30'S	39°30'E
Tanabe, Japan (tä-nä'bā)	210	33°45'N	135°21'E
Tanabe, Japan	211b	34°49'N	135°46'E
Tanacross, Ak., U.S. (tă'nȧ-crôs)	103	63°20'N	143°30'W
Tanaga, i., Ak., U.S. (tä-nä'gä)	103a	51°28'N	178°10'W
Tanahbala, Pulau, i., Indon. (tȧ-nä-bä'lä)	212	0°30'S	98°22'E
Tanahmasa, Pulau, i., Indon. (tȧ-nä-mä'sä)	212	0°03'S	97°30'E
Tanakpur, India (tăn'ăk-pòr)	202	29°10'N	80°07'E
Tana Lake, l., Eth.	231	12°09'N	36°41'E
Tanami, Austl. (tȧ-nä'mē)	218	19°45'S	129°50'E
Tanana, Ak., U.S. (tă'nȧ-nô)	103	65°18'N	152°20'W
Tanana, r., Ak., U.S.	103	64°26'N	148°40'W
Tanaro, r., Italy (tä-nä'rô)	174	44°45'N	8°02'E
Tanashi, Japan	211a	35°44'N	139°34'E
Tanbu, China (tän-bōō)	207a	23°20'N	113°06'E
Tancheng, China (tän-chŭŋ)	208	34°37'N	118°22'E
Tanchŏn, Kor., N. (tän'chŭn)	210	40°29'N	128°50'E
Tancítaro, Mex. (tän-sē'tä-rō)	130	19°16'N	102°24'W
Tancítaro, Cerro de, mtn., Mex. (sĕ'r-rō-dĕ)	130	19°24'N	102°19'W
Tancoco, Mex. (tän-kō'kō)	131	21°16'N	97°45'W
Tandil, Arg. (tän-dēl')	144	36°16'S	59°01'W
Tandil, Sierra del, mts., Arg.	144	38°40'S	59°40'W
Tanega, i., Japan (tä'nȧ-gä')	205	30°36'N	131°11'E
Tanezrouft, reg., Alg. (tä'nĕz-rȯft)	230	24°17'N	0°30'W
Tang, r., China (täŋ)	206	33°38'N	117°29'E
Tang, r., China	206	39°13'N	114°45'E
Tanga, Tan. (tăŋ'gȧ)	233	5°04'S	39°06'E
Tangancícuaro, Mex. (täŋ-gän-sē'kwa-rô)	130	19°52'N	102°13'W
Tanganyika, Lake, l., Afr.	232	5°15'S	29°40'E
Tanger, Mor. (tăn-jĕr')	230	35°52'N	5°55'W
Tangermünde, Ger. (täŋ'ĕr-mün'de)	168	52°33'N	11°58'E
Tanggu, China (täŋ-gōō)	206	39°04'N	117°41'E
Tanggula Shan, mts., China (täŋ-gōō-lä shän)	204	33°15'N	89°07'E
Tanghe, China	208	32°40'N	112°50'E
Tangier *see* Tanger, Mor.	230	35°52'N	5°55'W
Tangipahoa, r., La., U.S. (tăn'jē-pȧ-hō'ȧ)	123	30°48'N	90°28'W
Tangra Yumco, l., China (täŋ-rä yōōm-tswo)	202	30°50'N	85°40'E
T'angshan, China	208	39°38'N	118°11'E
Tangxian, China (täŋ shyĕn)	206	38°49'N	115°00'E
Tangzha, China (täŋ-jä)	206	32°06'N	120°48'E
Tanimbar, Kepulauan, is., Indon.	213	8°00'S	132°00'E
Tanjong Piai, c., Malay.	197b	1°16'N	103°11'E
Tanjong Ramunia, c., Malay.	197b	1°27'N	104°44'E
Tanjungbalai, Indon. (tän'jông-bä'lå)	197b	1°00'N	103°26'E
Tanjungpandan, Indon.	212	2°47'S	107°51'E
Tanjungpinang, Indon. (tän'jŏng-pē'näng)	197b	0°55'N	104°29'E
Tannu-Ola, mts., Asia	179	51°00'N	94°00'E
Tannūrah, Ra's at, c., Sau. Ar.	198	26°45'N	49°59'E
Tano, r., Afr.	234	5°40'N	2°30'W
Tanquijo, Arrecife, i., Mex. (är-rĕ-sē'fē-tän-kē'kô)	131	21°07'N	97°16'W
Ţanţā, Egypt	231	30°47'N	31°00'E
Tantoyuca, Mex. (tän-tō-yōō'kä)	130	21°22'N	98°13'W
Tanyang, Kor., S.	210	36°53'N	128°20'E
Tanzania, nation, Afr.	232	6°48'S	33°58'E
Tao, r., China (tou)	208	35°30'N	103°40'E
Tao'an, China (tou-än)	205	45°15'N	122°45'E
Tao'er, r., China (tou-är)	205	45°40'N	122°00'E
Taormina, Italy (tä-ôr-mē'nä)	174	37°53'N	15°18'E
Taos, N.M., U.S. (tä'ôs)	119	36°25'N	105°35'W
Taoudenni, Mali (tä'ōō-dĕ-nē')	230	22°57'N	3°37'W
Taoussa, Mali	234	16°55'N	0°35'W
Taoyuan, China (tou-yůän)	209	29°00'N	111°15'E
Tapa, Est. (tá'pȧ)	167	59°16'N	25°56'E
Tapachula, Mex.	132	14°55'N	92°20'W
Tapajós, r., Braz. (tä-pä-zhô's)	143	3°27'S	55°33'W
Tapalque, Arg. (tä-päl-kĕ')	141c	36°22'S	60°05'W
Tapanatepec, Mex. (tä-pä-nä-tĕ-pĕk)	131	16°22'N	94°19'W
Tāpi, r., India	199	21°00'N	76°30'E
Tappi Saki, c., Japan (täp'pē sä'kē)	210	41°05'N	139°40'E
Tapps, l., Wa., U.S. (täpz)	116a	47°20'N	122°12'W
Taquara, Serra de, mts., Braz. (sĕ'r-rä-dĕ-tä-kwä'rä)	143	15°28'S	54°33'W
Taquari, r., Braz. (tä-kwä'rī)	143	18°35'S	56°50'W
Tar, r., N.C., U.S. (tär)	125	35°58'N	78°06'W
Tara, Russia (tä'rȧ)	178	56°58'N	74°13'E
Tara, i., Phil. (tä'rä)	213a	12°18'N	120°28'E
Tara, r., Russia (tä'rȧ)	184	56°32'N	76°13'E
Ţarābulus, Leb. (tȧ-rä'bō-lōōs)	198	34°25'N	35°50'E
Ţarābulus (Tripolitania), hist. reg., Libya	230	31°00'N	12°26'E

PLACE (Pronunciation)	PAGE	LAT.	LONG.
Tarakan, Indon.	212	3°17'N	118°04'E
Taranaki, Mount, vol., N.Z.	223	39°18'S	174°04'E
Tarancón, Spain (tä-rän-kōn')	172	40°01'N	3°00'W
Taranto, Italy (tä'rän-tô)	163	40°30'N	17°15'E
Taranto, Golfo di, b., Italy (gôl-fō-dē tä'rän-tô)	156	40°03'N	17°10'E
Tarapoto, Peru (tä-rä-pô'tō)	142	6°29'S	76°26'W
Tarare, Fr. (tȧ-rär')	170	45°55'N	4°23'E
Tarascon, Fr. (tȧ-rás-kôN')	170	42°53'N	1°35'E
Tarascon, Fr. (tä-räs-kôN)	170	43°47'N	4°41'E
Tarashcha, Ukr. (tä'rȧsh-chȧ)	177	49°34'N	30°52'E
Tarata, Bol. (tä-rä'tä)	142	17°43'S	66°00'W
Taravo, r., Fr.	174	41°54'N	8°58'E
Tarazit, Massif de, mts., Niger	235	20°05'N	7°35'E
Tarazona, Spain (tä-rä-thō'nä)	172	41°54'N	1°45'W
Tarazona de la Mancha, Spain (tä-rä-zô'nä-dĕ-lä-mä'n-chä)	172	39°13'N	1°50'W
Tarbes, Fr. (tȧrb)	161	43°04'N	0°05'E
Tarboro, N.C., U.S. (tär'bŭr-ô)	125	35°53'N	77°34'W
Taree, Austl. (tă-rē')	222	31°52'S	152°21'E
Tarentum, Pa., U.S. (tȧ-rĕn'tŭm)	111e	40°36'N	79°44'W
Tarfa, Wādī at, val., Egypt	238b	28°14'N	31°00'E
Târgovişte, Rom.	163	44°54'N	25°29'E
Târgu Jiu, Rom.	163	45°02'N	23°17'E
Târgu Mureş, Rom.	163	46°33'N	24°33'E
Târgu Neamţ, Rom.	169	47°14'N	26°23'E
Târgu Ocna, Rom.	169	46°18'N	26°38'E
Târgu Secuiesc, Rom.	169	46°04'N	26°06'E
Tarhūnah, Libya	200	32°26'N	13°38'E
Tarija, Bol. (tär-rē'hä)	142	21°42'S	64°52'W
Tarīm, Yemen (tȧ-rĭm')	198	16°13'N	49°08'E
Tarim, r., China (tȧ-rĭm')	204	40°45'N	85°39'E
Tarim Basin, basin, China (tȧ-rĭm')	204	39°52'N	82°34'E
Tarka, r., S. Afr. (tä'kȧ)	233c	32°15'S	26°00'E
Tarkastad, S. Afr.	233c	32°01'S	26°18'E
Tarkhankut, Mys, c., Ukr. (mĭs tär-kän'kòt)	181	45°21'N	32°30'E
Tarkio, Mo., U.S. (tär'kĭ-ō)	121	40°27'N	95°22'W
Tarkwa, Ghana (tärk'wä)	230	5°19'N	1°59'W
Tarlac, Phil. (tär'läk)	212	15°29'N	120°36'E
Tarlton, S. Afr. (tärl'tŭn)	233b	26°05'S	27°38'E
Tarma, Peru (tär'mä)	142	11°26'S	75°40'W
Tarn, r., Fr. (tärn)	161	43°45'N	2°00'E
Târnăveni, Rom.	169	46°19'N	24°18'E
Tarnów, Pol. (tär'nòf)	161	50°02'N	21°00'E
Taro, r., Italy (tä'rō)	174	44°41'N	10°03'E
Taroudant, Mor. (tȧ-rōō-dänt')	230	30°39'N	8°52'W
Tarpon Springs, Fl., U.S. (tär'pŏn)	125a	28°07'N	82°44'W
Tarporley, Eng., U.K. (tär'pĕr-lē)	158a	53°09'N	2°40'W
Tarpum Bay, b., Bah. (tär'pŭm)	134	25°05'N	76°20'W
Tarquinia, Italy (tär-kwē'nē-ä)	174	42°16'N	11°46'E
Tarragona, Spain (tär-rä-gō'nä)	154	41°05'N	1°15'E
Tarrant, Al., U.S. (tăr'ănt)	110h	33°35'N	86°46'W
Tárrega, Spain (tä rå-gä)	173	41°40'N	1°09'E
Tarrejón de Ardoz, Spain (tär-rĕ-κô'n-dĕ-är-dôz)	173a	40°28'N	3°29'W
Tarrytown, N.Y., U.S. (tăr'ĭ-toun)	110a	41°04'N	73°52'W
Tarsus, Tur. (tär'sòs) (tär'sŭs)	198	37°00'N	34°50'E
Tartagal, Arg. (tär-tä-gá'l)	144	23°31'S	63°47'W
Tartu, Est. (tär'tōō) (dôr'pät)	178	58°23'N	26°44'E
Ţarţūs, Syria	200	34°54'N	35°59'E
Tarumi, Japan (tä'rōō-mē)	211b	34°38'N	135°04'E
Tarusa, Russia (tä-rōōs'ȧ)	176	54°43'N	37°11'E
Tarzana, Ca., U.S. (tär-ză'ȧ)	117a	34°10'N	118°32'W
Tashkent, Uzb. (tȧsh'kĕnt)	183	41°23'N	69°04'E
Tasman Bay, b., N.Z. (tăz'măn)	221a	40°50'S	173°20'E
Tasmania, state, Austl.	219	41°28'S	142°30'E
Tasman Peninsula, pen., Austl.	222	43°00'S	148°30'E
Tasman Sea, sea, Oc.	241	29°30'S	155°00'E
Tasquillo, Mex. (täs-kē'lyō)	130	20°34'N	99°21'W
Tatarsk, Russia (tȧ-tärsk')	178	55°13'N	75°58'E
Tatarstan, prov., Russia	180	55°00'N	51°00'E
Tatar Strait, strt., Russia	179	51°00'N	141°45'E
Tater Hill, mtn., Or., U.S. (tāt'ẽr hĭl)	116c	45°47'N	123°02'W
Tateyama, Japan (tä'tē-yä'mä)	211	35°04'N	139°52'E
Tatlow, Mount, mtn., Can.	94	51°23'N	123°52'W
Tau, Nor.	166	59°05'N	5°59'E
Tauern Tunnel, trans., Aus.	168	47°12'N	13°17'E
Taung, S. Afr. (tä'ŏng)	232	27°25'S	24°47'E
Taunton, Ma., U.S. (tän'tŭn)	109	41°54'N	71°03'W
Taunton, r., R.I., U.S.	110b	41°50'N	71°02'W
Taupo, Lake, l., N.Z. (tä'ōō-pō)	221a	38°42'S	175°55'E
Taurage, Lith. (tou'rȧ-gä)	167	55°15'N	22°18'E
Taurus Mountains *see* Toros Dağları, mts., Tur.	198	37°00'N	32°40'E
Tauste, Spain (tä-ōōs'tå)	172	41°55'N	1°15'W
Tavda, Russia (tàv-dá')	178	58°00'N	64°44'E
Tavda, r., Russia	184	58°30'N	64°15'E
Taverny, Fr. (tȧ-vĕr-nē')	171b	49°02'N	2°13'E
Taviche, Mex. (tä-vē'chĕ)	131	16°43'N	96°35'W
Tavira, Port. (tä-vē'rȧ)	172	37°09'N	7°42'W
Tavşanlı, Tur. (tàv'shän-lĭ)	181	39°30'N	29°30'E
Tawakoni, l., Tx., U.S.	123	32°51'N	95°59'W
Tawaramoto, Japan (tä'wä-rä-mô-tô)	211b	34°33'N	135°48'E
Tawas City, Mi., U.S.	108	44°15'N	83°30'W
Tawas Point, c., Mi., U.S. (tô'wȧs)	108	44°15'N	83°25'W
Tawitawi Group, is., Phil. (tä'wē-tä'wē)	212	4°52'N	120°35'E
Tawkar, Sudan	231	18°28'N	37°46'E
Taxco de Alarcón, Mex. (täs'kō dĕ ä-lär-kō'n)	130	18°34'N	99°37'W
Tay, r., Scot., U.K.	164	56°35'N	3°37'W
Tay, Loch, l., Scot., U.K.	164	56°25'N	4°07'W
Tayabas Bay, b., Phil. (tä-yä'bäs)	213a	13°44'N	121°40'E
Tayga, Russia (tī'gä)	184	56°12'N	85°47'E

PLACE (Pronunciation)	PAGE	LAT.	LONG.
Taygonos, Mys, c., Russia	179	60°37'N	160°17'E
Taylor, Tx., U.S.	123	30°35'N	97°25'W
Taylor, Mount, mtn., N.M., U.S.	106	35°20'N	107°40'W
Taylorville, Il., U.S. (tā'lẽr-vĭl)	108	39°30'N	89°20'W
Taymyr, l., Russia (tī-mĭr')	179	74°13'N	100°45'E
Taymyr, Poluostrov, pen., Russia	179	75°15'N	95°00'E
Tayshet, Russia (tī-shĕt')	179	56°09'N	97°49'E
Tayug, Phil.	213a	16°01'N	120°45'E
Taz, r., Russia (táz)	184	67°15'N	80°45'E
Taza, Mor. (tä'zä)	230	34°08'N	4°00'W
Tazovskoye, Russia	178	66°58'N	78°28'E
Tbessa, Alg.	230	35°27'N	8°13'E
Tbilisi, Geor. ('tbĭl-yē'sē)	181	41°40'N	44°45'E
Tchentlo Lake, l., Can.	94	55°11'N	125°00'W
Tchibanga, Gabon (chē-bäŋ'gä)	232	2°51'S	11°02'E
Tchien, Lib.	234	6°04'N	8°08'W
Tchigai, Plateau du, plat., Afr.	235	21°20'N	14°50'E
Tczew, Pol. (t'chĕf')	160	54°06'N	18°48'E
Teabo, Mex. (tĕ-ä'bô)	132a	20°25'N	89°14'W
Teague, Tx., U.S.	123	31°39'N	96°16'W
Teapa, Mex. (tā-ä'pä)	131	17°35'N	92°56'W
Tebing Tinggi, i., Indon. (teb'ing-tĭng'gä)	197b	0°54'N	102°39'E
Tecalitlán, Mex. (tā-kä-lē-tlän')	130	19°28'N	103°17'W
Techiman, Ghana	234	7°35'N	1°56'W
Tecoanapa, Mex. (tāk-wä-nä-pä')	130	16°33'N	98°46'W
Tecoh, Mex. (tĕ-kô)	132a	20°46'N	89°27'W
Tecolotlán, Mex. (tā-kô-lô-tlän')	130	20°13'N	103°57'W
Tecolutla, Mex. (tā-kô-lōō'tlä)	131	20°33'N	97°00'W
Tecolutla, r., Mex.	131	20°16'N	97°14'W
Tecomán, Mex. (tā-kô-män')	130	18°53'N	103°53'W
Tecómitl, Mex. (tĕ-kō'mētl)	131a	19°13'N	98°59'W
Tecozautla, Mex. (tā'kō-zä-ōō'tlä)	130	20°33'N	99°38'W
Tecpan de Galeana, Mex. (tĕk-pän' dā gä-lā-ä'nä)	130	17°13'N	100°41'W
Tecpatán, Mex. (tĕk-pä-tá'n)	131	17°08'N	93°18'W
Tecuala, Mex. (tĕ-kwä-lä)	130	22°24'N	105°29'W
Tecuci, Rom. (ta-kōch')	163	45°51'N	27°30'E
Tecumseh, Can. (tē-kŭm'sĕ)	111b	42°19'N	82°53'W
Tecumseh, Mi., U.S.	108	42°00'N	84°00'W
Tecumseh, Ne., U.S.	121	40°21'N	96°09'W
Tecumseh, Ok., U.S.	121	35°18'N	96°55'W
Tees, r., Eng., U.K. (tēz)	164	54°40'N	2°10'W
Teganuna, l., Japan (tā'gä-nōō'nä)	211a	35°50'N	140°02'E
Tegucigalpa, Hond. (tå-gōō-sē-gäl'pä)	128	14°08'N	87°15'W
Tehachapi Mountains, mts., Ca., U.S. (tĕ-hă-shă'pĭ)	118	34°50'N	118°55'W
Tehrān, Iran (tĕ-hrän')	198	35°45'N	51°30'E
Tehuacan, Mex. (tā-wä-kän')	128	18°27'N	97°23'W
Tehuantepec, Mex.	128	16°20'N	95°14'W
Tehuantepec, r., Mex.	131	16°30'N	95°23'W
Tehuantepec, Golfo de, b., Mex. (gôl-fô dĕ)	128	15°45'N	95°00'W
Tehuantepec, Istmo de, isth., Mex. (ē'st-mô dĕ)	131	17°55'N	94°35'W
Tehuehuetla, Arroyo, r., Mex. (tĕ-wĕ-wĕ'tlä är-rō-yō)	130	17°54'N	100°26'W
Tehuitzingo, Mex. (tā-wē-tzĭŋ'gō)	130	18°21'N	98°16'W
Tejeda, Sierra de, mts., Spain (sē-ĕ'r-rä dĕ tĕ-kĕ'dä)	172	36°55'N	4°00'W
Tejúpan, Mex. (tĕ-kōō-pä'n) (sän-tyá'gô)	131	17°39'N	97°34'W
Tejúpan, Punta, c., Mex.	130	18°19'N	103°30'W
Tejupilco de Hidalgo, Mex. (tå-hōō-pēl'kô dä ē-dhäl'gō)	130	18°52'N	100°07'W
Tekamah, Ne., U.S. (tē-kā'mȧ)	112	41°46'N	96°13'W
Tekax de Alvaro Obregon, Mex.	132a	20°12'N	89°11'W
Tekeze, r., Afr.	231	13°38'N	38°00'E
Tekit, Mex. (tĕ-kē't)	132a	20°35'N	89°18'W
Tekoa, Wa., U.S. (tē-kō'ȧ)	114	47°15'N	117°03'W
Tela, Hond. (tā'lä)	128	15°45'N	87°25'W
Tela, Bahía de, b., Hond.	132	15°53'N	87°29'W
Telapa Burok, Gunong, mtn., Malay.	197b	2°51'N	102°04'E
Telavi, Geor.	181	42°00'N	45°20'E
Tel Aviv-Yafo, Isr. (tĕl-ä-vēv'jä'fȧ)	198	32°03'N	34°46'E
Telegraph Creek, Can. (tĕl'ē-gráf)	90	57°59'N	131°22'W
Teleneşti, Mol.	177	47°31'N	28°22'E
Telescope Peak, mtn., Ca., U.S. (tĕl'ē skōp)	106	36°12'N	117°05'W
Telesung, Indon.	197b	1°07'N	102°53'E
Telica, vol., Nic. (tå-lē'kä)	132	12°38'N	86°52'W
Tell City, In., U.S. (tĕl)	108	38°00'N	86°45'W
Teller, Ak., U.S. (tĕl'ẽr)	103	65°17'N	166°28'W
Tello, Col. (tĕ'l-yō)	142a	3°05'N	75°08'W
Telluride, Co., U.S. (tĕl'ū-rīd)	119	37°55'N	107°50'W
Telok Datok, Malay.	197b	2°51'N	101°33'E
Teloloapan, Mex. (tā'lô-lô-ä'pän)	130	18°19'N	99°54'W
Tel'pos-Iz, Gora, mtn., Russia (tyĕl'pôs-ēz')	178	63°50'N	59°20'E
Telšiai, Lith. (tĕl'sha'ē)	167	55°59'N	22°17'E
Teltow, Ger. (tĕl'tō)	159b	52°24'N	13°12'E
Teluklecak, Indon.	197b	1°53'N	101°45'E
Tema, Ghana	234	5°38'N	0°01'E
Temascalcingo, Mex. (tā'mäs-käl-sĭŋ'gō)	130	19°55'N	100°00'W
Temascaltepec, Mex. (tā'mäs-käl-tå pĕk)	130	19°00'N	100°03'W
Temax, Mex. (tĕ'mäx)	128	21°10'N	88°51'W
Temir, Kaz.	183	49°10'N	57°15'E
Temirtaū, Kaz.	183	50°08'N	73°13'E
Temiscouata, l., Can. (tĕ'mĭs-kō-ä'tä)	100	47°40'N	68°50'W
Témiskaming, Can. (tē-mĭs'kȧ-mĭng)	91	46°41'N	79°01'W
Temoaya, Mex. (tĕ-mô-a-um-yä)	131a	19°28'N	99°36'W

ăt; finăl; rāte; senåte; ärm; ȧsk; sofȧ; fâre; ch-choose; dh-as th in other; bē; ēvent; bĕt; recĕnt; cratẽr; g-gō; gh-guttural g; bĭt; ĭ-short neutral; rīde; κ-guttural k as ch in German ich;

PRONOUNCING INDEX
Tempe – Tidjikdja 357

PLACE (Pronunciation)	PAGE	LAT.	LONG.
Tempe, Az., U.S.	119	33°24'N	111°54'W
Temperley, Arg. (tĕ'm-pĕr-lā)	144a	34°47'S	58°24'W
Tempio Pausania, Italy (tĕm'pē-ō pou-sä'nē-ä)	174	40°55'N	9°05'E
Temple, Tx., U.S. (tĕm'p'l)	123	31°06'N	97°20'W
Temple City, Ca., U.S.	117a	34°07'N	118°02'W
Templeton, Can. (tĕm'p'l-tŭn)	102c	45°29'N	75°37'W
Templin, Ger. (tĕm-plēn')	168	53°08'N	13°30'E
Tempoal, r., Mex. (tĕm-pô-ä'l)	130	21°38'N	98°23'W
Temryuk, Russia (tyĕm-ryŏok')	181	45°17'N	37°21'E
Temuco, Chile (tå-mōō'kō)	144	38°46'S	72°38'W
Temyasovo, Russia (tĕm-yä'sô-vô)	186a	53°00'N	58°06'E
Tenāli, India	203	16°10'N	80°32'E
Tenamaxtlán, Mex. (tā'nä-mäs-tlän')	130	20°13'N	104°06'W
Tenancingo, Mex. (tå-nän-sēŋ'gō)	130	18°54'N	99°36'W
Tenango, Mex. (tå-näŋ'gō)	131a	19°09'N	98°51'W
Tenasserim, Mya. (tĕn-ăs'ēr-ĭm)	212	12°09'N	99°01'E
Tendrivs'ka Kosa, ostriv, i., Ukr.	177	46°12'N	31°17'E
Tenerife Island, i., Spain (tå-nå-rē'fä) (tĕn-ēr-ĭf')	230	28°41'N	17°02'W
Tènès, Alg. (tā-nĕs')	161	36°28'N	1°22'E
Tengiz köli, l., Kaz.	183	50°45'N	68°39'E
Tengxian, China (tŭŋ shyĕn)	208	35°07'N	117°08'E
Tenjin, Japan (tĕn'jĕn)	211b	34°54'N	135°04'E
Tenke, D.R.C. (tĕŋ'kå)	232	11°26'S	26°45'E
Tenkiller Ferry Reservoir, res., Ok., U.S. (tĕn-kĭl'ēr)	121	35°42'N	94°47'W
Tenkodogo, Burkina (tĕŋ-kô-dō'gō)	230	11°47'N	0°22'W
Tenmile, r., Wa., U.S. (tĕn mīl)	116d	48°52'N	122°32'W
Tennant Creek, Austl. (tĕn'ănt)	218	19°45'S	134°00'E
Tennessee, state, U.S. (tĕn-ĕ-sē')	105	35°50'N	88°00'W
Tennessee, r., U.S.	107	35°35'N	88°20'W
Tennille, Ga., U.S. (tĕn'ĭl)	124	32°55'N	86°50'W
Teno, r., Chile (tĕ'nô)	141b	34°55'S	71°00'W
Tenora, Austl. (tĕn-ôră)	222	34°23'S	147°33'E
Tenosique, Mex. (tā-nô-sē'kå)	131	17°27'N	91°25'W
Tenri, Japan	211b	34°36'N	135°50'E
Tenryū-Gawa, r., Japan (tĕn'ryōō'gä'wä)	211	35°16'N	137°54'E
Tensas, r., La., U.S. (tĕn'sô)	123	31°54'N	91°30'W
Tensaw, r., Al., U.S. (tĕn'sô)	124	30°45'N	87°52'W
Tenterfield, Austl. (tĕn'tēr-fēld)	219	29°00'S	152°06'E
Ten Thousand, Islands, is., Fl., U.S. (tĕn thou'zănd)	125a	25°45'N	81°35'W
Teocaltiche, Mex. (tā'ō-käl-tē'chå)	130	21°27'N	102°38'W
Teocelo, Mex. (tā-ō-sā'lō)	131	19°22'N	96°57'W
Teocuitatlán de Corona, Mex.	130	20°06'N	103°22'W
Teófilo Otoni, Braz. (tĕ-ô'fē-lō-tô'nē)	143	17°49'S	41°18'W
Teoloyucan, Mex. (tā'ō-lô-yōō'kän)	130	19°43'N	99°12'W
Teopisca, Mex. (tā-ô-pēs'kä)	131	16°30'N	92°33'W
Teotihuacán, Mex. (tĕ-ô-tē-wä-kä'n)	131a	19°40'N	98°52'W
Teotitlán del Camino, Mex. (tā-ô-tē-tlän' dĕl kä-mē'nō)	131	18°07'N	97°04'W
Tepalcatepec, Mex. (tā'päl-kä-tå'pĕk)	130	19°11'N	102°51'W
Tepalcatepec, r., Mex.	130	18°54'N	102°25'W
Tepalcingo, Mex. (tā-päl-sēŋ'gō)	130	18°34'N	98°49'W
Tepatitlán de Morelos, Mex. (tā-pä-tē-tlän' dā mō-rā'los)	128	20°55'N	102°47'W
Tepeaca, Mex. (tā-på-ä'kä)	131	18°57'N	97°54'W
Tepecoacuilco de Trujano, Mex.	130	18°15'N	99°29'W
Tepeji del Río, Mex. (tā-på-ke' dĕl rē'ō)	130	19°55'N	99°22'W
Tepelmeme, Mex. (tā'pĕl-mā'må)	131	17°51'N	97°23'W
Tepetlaoxtoc, Mex. (tā'på-tlä'ôs-tōk')	130	19°34'N	98°49'W
Tepezala, Mex. (tā-på-zä-lä')	130	22°12'N	102°12'W
Tepic, Mex. (tā-pēk')	128	21°32'N	104°53'W
Tëplaya Gora, Russia (tyôp'lå-yå gô-rå)	186a	58°32'N	59°08'W
Teplice, Czech Rep.	161	50°39'N	13°50'E
Teposcolula, Mex.	131	17°33'N	97°29'W
Tequendama, Salto de, wtfl., Col. (sä'l-tô dĕ tĕ-kĕn-dä'mä)	142	4°34'N	74°18'W
Tequila, Mex. (tå-kē'lä)	130	20°53'N	103°48'W
Tequisistlán, r., Mex. (tĕ-kē-sēs-tlá'n)	131	16°20'N	95°40'W
Tequisquiapan, Mex. (tå-kēs-kē-ä'pän)	130	20°33'N	99°57'W
Ter, r., Spain (tĕr)	173	42°04'N	2°52'E
Téra, Niger	234	14°01'N	0°45'E
Tera, r., Spain (tā'rä)	172	42°05'N	6°24'W
Teramo, Italy (tā'rä-mô)	174	42°40'N	13°41'E
Terborg, Neth. (tĕr-bōrg)	171c	51°55'N	6°23'E
Tercan, Tur. (tĕr'jän)	181	39°40'N	40°12'E
Terceira Island, i., Port. (tĕr-sā'rä)	230a	38°49'N	26°36'W
Terebovlia, Ukr.	169	49°18'N	25°43'E
Terek, r., Russia	181	43°30'N	45°10'E
Terenkul', Russia (tĕ-rĕn'kōl)	186a	55°38'N	62°18'E
Teresina, Braz. (tĕr-å-sē'nă)	143	5°04'S	42°42'W
Teresópolis, Braz. (tĕr-ā-sŏ'pô-lēzh)	141a	22°25'S	42°59'W
Teriberka, Russia (tyĕr-ê-byôr'kå)	180	69°00'N	35°15'E
Terme, Tur. (tĕr'mĕ)	181	41°05'N	37°00'E
Termez, Uzb. (tyĕr'mĕz)	183	37°19'N	67°20'E
Termini, Italy (tĕr'mē-nē)	174	37°58'N	13°39'E
Términos, Laguna de, l., Mex. (lä-gô'nä dĕ tĕ'r-mē-nôs)	128	18°37'N	91°32'W
Termoli, Italy (tĕr'mô-lē)	174	42°00'N	15°01'E
Tern, r., Eng., U.K. (tûrn)	158a	52°49'N	2°31'W
Ternate, Indon. (tĕr-nä'tä)	213	0°52'N	127°25'E
Terni, Italy (tĕr'nē)	162	42°38'N	12°41'E
Ternopil', Ukr.	181	49°32'N	25°36'E
Terpeniya, Mys, c., Russia	179	48°44'N	144°42'E
Terpeniya, Zaliv, b., Russia (zä'lĭf tĕr-pă'nĭ-yå)	210	49°10'N	143°05'E
Terrace, Can. (tĕr'ĭs)	90	54°31'N	128°35'W

PLACE (Pronunciation)	PAGE	LAT.	LONG.
Terracina, Italy (tĕr-rä-chē'nä)	162	41°18'N	13°14'E
Terra Nova National Park, rec., Can.	93a	48°37'N	54°15'W
Terrassa, Spain	173	41°34'N	2°01'E
Terrebonne, Can. (tĕr-bŏn')	109	45°42'N	73°38'W
Terrebonne Bay, b., La., U.S.	123	28°55'N	90°30'W
Terre Haute, In., U.S. (tĕr-ê hōt')	105	39°25'N	87°25'W
Terrell, Tx., U.S. (tĕr'ĕl)	123	32°44'N	96°15'W
Terrell, Wa., U.S.	116d	48°53'N	122°44'W
Terrell Hills, Tx., U.S. (tĕr'ĕl hĭlz)	117d	29°28'N	98°27'W
Terschelling, i., Neth. (tĕr-skĕl'ĭng)	165	53°25'N	5°12'E
Teruel, Spain (tå-rōō-ĕl')	162	40°20'N	1°05'W
Tešanj, Bos. (tĕ'shän')	175	44°36'N	17°59'E
Teschendorf, Ger. (tĕ'shĕn-dōrf)	159b	52°51'N	13°10'E
Tesecheacan, Mex. (tĕ-sĕ-chĕ-ä-kà'n)	131	18°10'N	95°41'W
Teshekpuk, l., Ak., U.S. (tē-shĕk'pŭk)	103	70°18'N	152°36'W
Teshio Dake, mtn., Japan (tĕsh'ê-ō-dä'kā)	210	44°00'N	142°50'E
Teshio Gawa, r., Japan (tĕsh'ê-ō gä'wä)	210	44°53'N	144°55'E
Tesiyn, r., Asia	204	49°45'N	96°00'E
Teslin, Can. (tĕs-lĭn)	103	60°10'N	132°30'W
Teslin, l., Can.	92	60°12'N	132°08'W
Teslin, r., Can.	92	61°18'N	134°14'W
Tessaoua, Niger (tĕs-sä'ô-ä)	230	13°53'N	7°53'E
Tessenderlo, Bel.	159a	51°04'N	5°08'E
Test, r., Eng., U.K. (tĕst)	164	51°10'N	1°30'W
Testa del Gargano, c., Italy (tās'tä dĕl gär-gä'nō)	174	41°48'N	16°13'E
Tetachuck Lake, l., Can.	94	53°20'N	125°50'W
Tete, Moz. (tā'tĕ)	232	16°13'S	33°35'E
Tête Jaune Cache, Can. (tĕt'zhōn-kăsh)	95	52°57'N	119°26'W
Teteriv, r., Ukr.	181	51°05'N	29°30'E
Teterow, Ger. (tā'tĕ-rō)	168	53°46'N	12°33'E
Teteven, Blg. (tĕt'ĕ-ven')	175	42°57'N	24°15'E
Teton, r., Mt., U.S. (tē'tŏn)	115	47°54'N	111°37'W
Tétouan, Mor.	230	35°42'N	5°34'W
Tetovo, Mac. (tā'tô-vô)	175	42°01'N	21°00'E
Tetyukhe-Pristan, Russia (tĕt-yōō'kĕ prī-stän')	210	44°21'N	135°44'E
Tetyushi, Russia (tĕt-yŏ'shĭ)	180	54°57'N	48°50'E
Teupitz, Ger. (toi'pētz)	159b	52°08'N	13°37'E
Tevere, r., Italy	162	42°30'N	12°14'E
Teverya, Isr.	197a	32°48'N	35°32'E
Tewksbury, Ma., U.S. (tūks'bēr-ĭ)	101a	42°37'N	71°14'W
Texada Island, i., Can.	94	49°40'N	124°24'W
Texarkana, Ar., U.S. (tĕk-sär-kăn'ă)	105	33°26'N	94°02'W
Texarkana, Tx., U.S.	105	33°26'N	94°04'W
Texas, state, U.S.	104	31°00'N	101°00'W
Texas City, Tx., U.S.	123	29°23'N	94°54'W
Texcaltitlán, Mex. (tās-käl'tē-tlän')	130	18°54'N	99°51'W
Texcoco, Mex. (tās-kō'kō)	130	19°31'N	98°53'W
Texcoco, Lago de, l., Mex.	131a	19°30'N	99°00'W
Texel, i., Neth. (tĕk'sĕl)	165	53°10'N	4°45'E
Texistepec, Mex. (tĕk-sēs-tā-pĕk')	131	17°51'N	94°46'W
Texmelucan, Mex.	130	19°17'N	98°26'W
Texoma, Lake, res., U.S. (tĕk'ō-mă)	106	34°03'N	96°28'W
Texontepec, Mex. (tå-zōn-tå-pĕk')	130	19°52'N	98°48'W
Texontepec de Aldama, Mex. (dā äl-dä'mä)	130	20°19'N	99°19'W
Teyateyaneng, Leso.	233c	29°11'S	27°43'E
Teykovo, Russia (tĕy-kô-vô)	180	56°52'N	40°34'E
Teziutlán, Mex. (tå-zê-ōō-tlän')	131	19°48'N	97°21'W
Tezpur, India	202	26°42'N	92°52'E
Tha-anne, r., Can.	92	60°50'N	96°56'W
Thabana Ntlenyana, mtn., Leso.	233c	29°28'S	29°17'E
Thabazimbi, S. Afr.	238c	24°36'S	27°22'E
Thailand, nation, Asia	212	16°30'N	101°00'E
Thailand, Gulf of, b., Asia	212	11°37'N	100°46'E
Thale Luang, l., Thai.	212	7°51'N	99°39'E
Thame, Eng., U.K. (tām)	158b	51°43'N	0°59'W
Thames, r., Can. (tĕmz)	98	42°40'N	81°45'W
Thames, r., Eng., U.K.	156	51°30'N	1°30'W
Thāmit, Wadi, r., Libya	163	30°39'N	16°23'E
Thāna, India (thä'nŭ)	202	19°13'N	72°58'E
Thāna Creek, r., India	203b	19°03'N	72°58'E
Thanh Hoa, Viet. (tän'hō'ä)	212	19°46'N	105°42'E
Thanjāvūr, India	199	10°51'N	79°11'E
Thann, Fr. (tän)	171	47°49'N	7°05'E
Thaon-les-Vosges, Fr. (tä-ŏn-lā-vōzh')	171	48°16'N	6°24'E
Thargomindah, Austl. (thär'gō-mĭn'dȧ)	219	27°58'S	143°57'E
Thásos, i., Grc. (thă'sôs)	163	40°41'N	24°53'E
Thatch Cay, i., V.I.U.S. (thăch)	129c	18°22'N	64°53'W
Thaya, r., Eur. (tä'yȧ)	168	48°48'N	15°40'E
Thayer, Mo., U.S. (thâ'ēr)	121	36°30'N	91°34'W
Thebes *see* Thíva, Grc.	163	38°20'N	23°18'E
Thebes, hist., Egypt (thēbz)	231	25°47'N	32°39'E
The Brothers, mtn., Wa., U.S.	116a	47°39'N	123°08'W
The Coorong, l., Austl. (kŏ'rŏng)	222	36°07'S	139°45'E
The Coteau, hills, Can.	96	51°10'N	107°30'W
The Dalles, Or., U.S. (dălz)	104	45°36'N	121°10'W
The Father, mtn., Pap. N. Gui.	213	5°05'S	151°30'E
The Hague ('s-Gravenhage), Neth.	154	52°05'N	4°16'E
The Oaks, Austl.	217b	34°04'S	150°36'E
Theodore, Austl. (thē'ō'dôr)	222	24°51'S	150°09'E
Theodore Roosevelt Dam, dam, Az., U.S. (thē-ô-doř rōō-sȧ-vĕlt)	119	33°46'N	111°25'W
Theodore Roosevelt Lake, res., Az., U.S.	119	33°45'N	111°00'W
Theodore Roosevelt National Park, rec., N.D., U.S.	112	47°20'N	103°42'W

PLACE (Pronunciation)	PAGE	LAT.	LONG.
Theológos, Grc.	175	40°37'N	24°41'E
The Pas, Can. (pä)	90	53°50'N	101°15'W
Thermopolis, Wy., U.S. (thēr-mŏp'ô-lĭs)	115	43°38'N	108°11'W
The Round Mountain, mtn., Austl.	222	30°17'S	152°19'E
Thessalía, hist. reg., Grc.	175	39°50'N	22°09'E
Thessalon, Can.	91	46°11'N	83°37'W
Thessaloníki, Grc. (thĕs-sȧ-lô-nē'kē)	154	40°38'N	22°59'E
Thetford Mines, Can. (thĕt'fērd mīns)	99	46°05'N	71°20'W
The Twins, mtn., Afr. (twĭnz)	233c	30°09'S	28°29'E
Theunissen, S. Afr.	238c	28°25'S	26°44'E
The Wrekin, co., Eng., U.K.	158a	53°43'N	2°30'W
Thibaudeau, Can. (tĭ'bō-dō')	97	57°05'N	94°08'W
Thibodaux, La., U.S. (tē-bō-dō')	123	29°48'N	90°48'W
Thief, l., Mn., U.S. (thēf)	112	48°32'N	95°46'W
Thief, r., Mn., U.S.	113	48°18'N	96°07'E
Thief Rivers Falls, Mn., U.S. (thēf rĭv'ēr fôlz)	112	48°07'N	96°11'W
Thiers, Fr. (tyâr)	170	45°51'N	3°32'E
Thiès, Sen. (tē-ĕs')	230	14°48'N	16°56'W
Thika, Kenya	237	1°03'S	37°05'E
Thimphu, Bhu.	199	27°33'N	89°42'E
Thingvallavatn, l., Ice.	160	64°12'N	20°22'W
Thio, N. Cal.	214f	21°37'S	166°14'E
Thionville, Fr. (tyôn-vēl')	161	49°23'N	6°31'E
Third Cataract, wtfl., Sudan	231	19°53'N	30°11'E
Thiruvananthapuram, India	203	8°34'N	76°58'E
Thisted, Den. (tēs'tĕdh)	166	56°57'N	8°38'E
Thistilfjördur, b., Ice.	160	66°29'N	14°59'W
Thistle, i., Austl. (thĭs''l)	222	34°55'S	136°11'E
Thíva (Thebes), Grc.	162	38°20'N	23°18'E
Thjörsá, r., Ice. (tyûr'sȧ)	160	64°23'N	19°18'W
Thohoyandou, S. Afr.	232	23°00'S	30°29'E
Tholen, Neth.	159a	51°32'N	4°11'E
Thomas, Ok., U.S. (tŏm'ăs)	120	35°44'N	98°43'W
Thomas, W.V., U.S.	109	39°15'N	79°30'W
Thomaston, Ga., U.S. (tŏm'ăs-tŭn)	124	32°51'N	84°17'W
Thomasville, Al., U.S. (tŏm'ăs-vĭl)	124	31°55'N	87°43'W
Thomasville, N.C., U.S.	125	35°52'N	80°05'W
Thomlinson, Mount, mtn., Can.	94	55°33'N	127°29'W
Thompson, Can.	90	55°48'N	97°59'W
Thompson, r., Can.	95	50°15'N	121°20'W
Thompson, r., Mo., U.S.	121	40°32'N	93°49'W
Thompson Falls, Mt., U.S.	114	47°35'N	115°20'W
Thomson, r., Austl. (tŏm-sŏn)	221	24°30'S	143°07'E
Thomson's Falls, Kenya	237	0°02'N	36°22'E
Thonon-les-Bains, Fr. (tô-nôn'lȧ-băn')	171	46°22'N	6°27'E
Thorne, Eng., U.K. (thôrn)	158a	53°37'N	0°58'W
Thorntown, In., U.S. (thôrn'tŭn)	108	40°05'N	86°35'W
Thorold, Can. (thō'rōld)	99	43°13'N	79°12'W
Thouars, Fr. (tōō-är')	170	47°00'N	0°17'W
Thousand Islands, is., N.Y., U.S. (thou'zănd)	109	44°15'N	76°10'W
Thrace, hist. reg. (thrās)	175	41°20'N	26°07'E
Thrapston, Eng., U.K. (thrăp'stŭn)	158a	52°23'N	0°32'W
Three Forks, Mt., U.S. (thrē fôrks)	115	45°56'N	111°35'W
Three Oaks, Mi., U.S. (thrē ōks)	108	41°50'N	86°40'W
Three Points, Cape, c., Ghana	230	4°45'N	2°06'W
Three Rivers, Mi., U.S.	108	42°00'N	83°40'W
Thule, Grnld.	89	76°34'N	68°47'W
Thun, Switz. (tōōn)	168	46°46'N	7°34'E
Thunder Bay, Can.	98	48°28'N	89°12'W
Thunder Bay, b., Can. (thŭn'dēr)	98	48°29'N	88°52'W
Thunder Hills, hills, Can.	96	54°30'N	106°00'W
Thunersee, l., Switz.	168	46°40'N	7°30'E
Thurber, Tx., U.S. (thûr'bēr)	122	32°30'N	98°23'W
Thüringen (Thuringia), hist. reg., Ger. (tü'rĭng-ĕn)	168	51°07'N	10°45'E
Thurles, Ire. (thûrlz)	164	52°44'N	7°45'W
Thurrock, co., Eng., U.K.	158b	51°30'N	0°22'E
Thursday, i., Austl. (thûrz-dā)	221	10°17'S	142°23'E
Thurso, Can. (thŭn'sô)	102c	45°36'N	75°15'W
Thurso, Scot., U.K.	164	58°35'N	3°40'W
Thurston Island, i., Ant. (thûrs'tŭn)	224	71°20'S	98°00'W
Tiachiv, Ukr.	169	48°01'N	23°42'E
Tiandong, China (tĭĕn-dôŋ)	209	23°32'N	107°10'E
Tianjin, China	205	39°08'N	117°14'E
Tianjin Shi, prov., China (tĭĕn-jyĭn shr)	208	39°30'N	117°13'E
Tianmen, China (tĭĕn-mŭn)	209	30°40'N	113°10'E
Tianshui, China (tĭĕn-shwā)	208	34°25'N	105°40'E
Tiasmyn, r., Ukr.	177	49°14'N	32°23'E
Tibagi, Braz. (tē'bȧ-zhē)	143	24°40'S	50°35'W
Tibasti, Sarir, des., Libya	231	24°00'N	16°30'E
Tibati, Cam.	235	6°27'N	12°38'E
Tiber *see* Tevere, r., Italy	162	42°30'N	12°14'E
Tibesti, mts., Chad	231	20°40'N	17°48'E
Tibet *see* Xizang, prov., China (tĭ-bĕt')	204	32°22'N	83°30'E
Tibnīn, Leb.	197a	33°12'N	35°23'E
Tiburon, Haiti	135	18°35'N	74°25'W
Tiburon, Ca., U.S. (tē-bōō-rōn')	116b	37°53'N	122°27'W
Tiburón, i., Mex.	128	28°45'N	113°10'W
Tiburón, Cabo, c. (kà'bô)	133	8°42'N	77°19'W
Tiburon Island, i., Ca., U.S.	116b	37°52'N	122°26'W
Ticao Island, i., Phil. (tē-kä'ō)	213a	12°40'N	123°30'E
Tickhill, Eng., U.K. (tĭk'ĭl)	158a	53°26'N	1°06'W
Ticonderoga, N.Y., U.S. (tī-kŏn-dēr-ō'gȧ)	109	43°50'N	73°30'W
Ticul, Mex. (tē-kōō'l)	132a	20°22'N	89°32'W
Tidaholm, Swe. (tē'dä-hōlm)	166	58°11'N	13°53'E
Tideswell, Eng., U.K. (tīdz'wĕl)	158a	53°17'N	1°47'W
Tidikelt, reg., Alg. (tē-dē-kĕlt')	230	25°53'N	2°11'E
Tidjikdja, Maur. (tē-jĭk'jä)	230	18°33'N	11°25'W

ng-sing; ŋ-baŋk; ɴ-nasalized n; nŏd; cŏmmit; ōld; ôbey; ôrder; oi-boil; fōōd; ŏ-as oo in foot; ou-out; s-soft; sh-dish; th-thin; pūre; ûnite; ûrn; stŭd; circŭs; ü-as in French tu; '-indeterminate vowel.

358 Tidra – Topol'čany

PRONOUNCING INDEX

PLACE (Pronunciation)	PAGE	LAT.	LONG.
Tidra, Île, i., Maur.	234	19°50'N	16°45'W
Tieling, China (tĭĕ-liŋ)	205	42°18'N	123°50'E
Tielmes, Spain (tyâl-màs')	173a	40°15'N	3°20'W
Tienen, Bel.	159a	50°49'N	4°58'E
Tien Shan, mts., Asia	204	42°00'N	78°46'E
Tientsin see Tianjin, China	205	39°08'N	117°14'E
Tierp, Swe. (tyĕrp)	166	60°21'N	17°28'E
Tierpoort, S. Afr.	233b	25°53'S	28°26'E
Tierra Blanca, Mex. (tyĕ'r-rä-blä'n-kä)	131	18°28'N	96°19'W
Tierra del Fuego, i., S.A. (tyĕr'rä dĕl fwā'gō)	144	53°50'S	68°45'W
Tiétar, r., Spain (tê-ā'tär)	172	39°56'N	5°44'W
Tiffin, Oh., U.S. (tĭf'ĭn)	108	41°10'N	83°15'W
Tifton, Ga., U.S. (tĭf'tŭn)	124	31°25'N	83°34'W
Tigard, Or., U.S. (tī'gärd)	116c	45°25'N	122°46'W
Tighina, Mol.	181	46°49'N	29°29'E
Tignish, Can. (tĭg'nĭsh)	100	46°57'N	64°02'W
Tigoda, r., Russia (tē'gô-dà)	186c	59°29'N	31°15'E
Tigre, r., Peru	142	2°20'S	75°41'W
Tigres, Península dos, pen., Ang. (pĕ-nê'n-sōō-lä-dôs-tê'grĕs)	232	16°30'S	11°45'E
Tigris, r., Asia	198	34°45'N	44°10'E
Tīh, Jabal at, mts., Egypt	197a	29°23'N	34°05'E
Tihert, Alg.	230	35°28'N	1°15'E
Tihuatlán, Mex. (tê-wä-tlän')	131	20°43'N	97°34'W
Tijuana, Mex. (tê-hwä'nä)	128	32°32'N	117°02'W
Tijuca, Pico da, mtn., Braz. (pē'kō-dä-tē-zhōō'kà)	144b	22°56'S	43°17'W
Tikal, hist., Guat. (tê-käl')	132a	17°16'N	89°49'W
Tikhoretsk, Russia (tê-kôr-yĕtsk')	181	45°55'N	40°05'E
Tikhvin, Russia (têk-vēn')	178	59°36'N	33°38'E
Tikrīt, Iraq	198	34°36'N	43°31'E
Tiksi, Russia (têk-sē')	179	71°42'N	128°32'E
Tilburg, Neth. (tĭl'bûrg)	161	51°33'N	5°05'E
Tilbury, Eng., U.K.	158b	51°28'N	0°23'E
Tilemsi, Vallée du, val., Mali	234	17°50'N	0°25'E
Tilichiki, Russia (tyĭ-le-chĭ-kê)	179	60°49'N	166°14'E
Tilimsen, Alg.	230	34°53'N	1°21'W
Tillabéry, Niger (tē-yà-bā-rē')	230	14°14'N	1°30'E
Tillamook, Or., U.S. (tĭl'ȧ-mŏk)	114	45°27'N	123°50'W
Tillamook Bay, b., Or., U.S.	114	45°32'N	124°26'W
Tillberga, Swe. (tēl-bĕr'ghȧ)	166	59°40'N	16°34'E
Tillsonburg, Can. (tĭl'sŭn-bûrg)	99	42°50'N	80°50'W
Tim, Russia (têm)	177	51°39'N	37°07'E
Timaru, N.Z. (tĭm'ȧ-rōō)	221a	44°26'S	171°17'E
Timashevskaya, Russia (tēmä-shĕfs-kä'yä)	181	45°47'N	38°57'E
Timbalier Bay, b., La., U.S. (tĭm'bȧ-lēr)	123	28°55'N	90°14'W
Timber, Or., U.S. (tĭm'bēr)	116c	45°43'N	123°17'W
Timbo, Gui. (tĭm'bō)	230	10°41'N	11°51'W
Timbuktu see Tombouctou, Mali	230	16°46'N	3°01'W
Timétrine Monts, mts., Mali	234	19°50'N	0°30'W
Timimoun, Alg. (tē-mê-mōōn')	230	29°14'N	0°22'E
Timiris, Cap, c., Maur.	230	19°23'N	16°32'W
Timiş, r., Eur.	175	45°28'N	21°06'E
Timişoara, Rom.	163	45°44'N	21°21'E
Timmins, Can. (tĭm'ĭnz)	91	48°25'N	81°22'W
Timmonsville, S.C., U.S. (tĭm'ŭnz-vĭl)	125	34°09'N	79°55'W
Timok, r., Eur.	175	43°35'N	22°13'E
Timor, i., Asia (tê-mōr')	213	10°08'S	125°00'E
Timor Sea, sea	220	12°40'S	125°00'E
Timpanogos Cave National Monument, rec., Ut., U.S. (tĭ-măn'ō-gŏz)	119	40°25'N	111°45'W
Timpson, Tx., U.S. (tĭmp'sŭn)	123	31°55'N	94°24'W
Timsāh, l., Egypt (tĭm'sä)	238b	30°34'N	32°22'E
Tina, r., S. Afr. (tē'nȧ)	233c	30°50'S	28°44'E
Tina, Monte, mtn., Dom. Rep. (mô'n-tĕ-tē'nä)	135	18°50'N	70°40'W
Tinaguillo, Ven. (tē-nä-gē'l-yō)	143b	9°55'N	68°18'W
Tīnah, Khalīj at, b., Egypt	197a	31°06'N	32°42'E
Tindouf, Alg. (tên-dōōf')	230	27°43'N	7°44'W
Tinggi, i., Malay.	197b	2°16'N	104°16'E
Tinghert, Plateau du, plat., Alg.	230	27°30'N	7°30'E
Tingi Mountains, mts., S.L.	234	9°00'N	10°50'W
Tinglin, China	207b	30°53'N	121°18'E
Tingo María, Peru (tē'ngô-mä-rē'ä)	142	9°15'S	76°04'W
Tingréla, C. Iv.	234	10°29'N	6°24'W
Tingsryd, Swe. (tĭngs'rüd)	166	56°32'N	14°58'E
Tinguindio, Mex.	130	19°38'N	102°02'W
Tinguiririca, r., Chile (tē'n-gē-rē-rē'kä)	141b	34°48'S	70°45'W
Tinley Park, Il., U.S. (tĭn'lē)	111a	41°34'N	87°47'W
Tinnoset, Nor. (tĕn'nôs'sĕt)	166	59°44'N	9°00'E
Tinogasta, Arg. (tē-nō-gäs'tä)	144	28°07'S	67°30'W
Tínos, i., Grc.	163	37°45'N	25°12'E
Tinsukia, India (tin-sōō''kĭ-ȧ)	198	27°18'N	95°29'W
Tintic, Ut., U.S. (tĭn'tĭk)	119	39°55'N	112°15'W
Tio, Pic de, mtn., Gui.	234	8°55'N	8°55'W
Tioman, i., Malay.	197b	2°50'N	104°15'E
Tipitapa, Nic. (tē-pē-tä'pä)	132	12°14'N	86°05'W
Tipitapa, r., Nic.	132	12°13'N	85°57'W
Tippah Creek, r., Ms., U.S. (tĭp'pȧ)	124	34°43'N	88°15'W
Tippecanoe, r., In., U.S. (tĭp-ē-kȧ-nōō')	108	40°55'N	86°45'W
Tipperary, Ire. (tĭ-pē-râ'rē)	161	52°28'N	8°13'W
Tippo Bay, Ms., U.S. (tĭp'ō bīōō')	121	33°35'N	90°06'W
Tipton, Ia., U.S.	113	41°46'N	91°10'W
Tipton, In., U.S.	108	40°15'N	86°00'W
Tiranë, Alb. (tê-rä'nä)	154	41°48'N	19°50'E
Tirano, Italy (tê-rä'nō)	174	46°12'N	10°09'E
Tiraspol, Mol.	181	46°52'N	29°38'E
Tire, Tur. (tē'rĕ)	163	38°05'N	27°48'E
Tiree, i., Scot., U.K. (tī-rē')	160	56°34'N	6°30'W
Tirlyanskiy, Russia (tĭr-lyän'skĭ)	186a	54°13'N	58°37'E
Tiruchchirāppalli, India (tĭr'ŏ-chĭ-rä'pà-lĭ)	199	10°49'N	78°48'E
Tirunelveli, India	203	8°53'N	77°43'E
Tiruppur, India	203	11°11'N	77°08'E
Tisdale, Can. (tĭz'dāl)	90	52°51'N	104°04'W
Tista, r., Asia	202	26°00'N	89°30'E
Tisza, r., Eur. (tĭ'sä)	156	47°30'N	21°00'E
Titāgarh, India	202a	22°44'N	88°23'E
Titicaca, Lago, l., S.A. (lä'gô-tē-tē-kä'kä)	142	16°12'S	70°33'W
Titiribi, Col. (tē-tē-rē-bē')	142a	6°05'N	75°47'W
Tito, Lagh, r., Kenya	237	2°25'N	39°05'E
Titov Veles, Mac. (tê'tôv vĕ'lĕs)	175	41°42'N	21°50'E
Titterstone Clee Hill, hill, Eng., U.K. (klê)	158a	52°24'N	2°37'W
Titule, D.R.C.	237	3°17'N	25°32'E
Titusville, Fl., U.S. (tĭ'tŭs-vĭl)	125a	28°37'N	80°44'W
Titusville, Pa., U.S.	109	40°40'N	79°40'W
Titz, Ger. (tētz)	171c	51°00'N	6°26'E
Tiverton, R.I., U.S. (tĭv'ēr-tun)	110b	41°38'N	71°11'W
Tivoli, Italy (tē'vô-lê)	162	41°38'N	12°48'E
Tixkokob, Mex. (tēx-kō-kō'b)	132a	21°01'N	89°23'W
Tixtla de Guerrero, Mex. (tē'x-tlä-dĕ-gĕr-rĕ'rô)	130	17°36'N	99°24'W
Tizard Bank and Reef, rf., Asia (tĭz'ård)	212	10°51'N	113°20'E
Tizimín, Mex. (tē-zē-mē'n)	132a	21°08'N	88°10'W
Tizi-Ouzou, Alg. (tē'zē-ōō-zōō')	230	36°44'N	4°04'E
Tiznados, r., Ven. (tēz-nä'dôs)	143b	9°53'N	67°49'W
Tiznit, Mor. (tēz-nēt)	230	29°52'N	9°39'W
Tkvarcheli, Geor.	182	42°15'N	41°41'E
Tlacolula de Matamoros, Mex.	131	16°56'N	96°29'W
Tlacotálpan, Mex. (tlä-kō-täl'pän)	131	18°39'N	95°40'W
Tlacotepec, Mex. (tlä-kô-tå-pĕ'k)	131	17°46'N	99°57'W
Tlacotepec, Mex.	130	19°11'N	99°41'W
Tlacotepec, Mex.	131	18°41'N	97°40'W
Tláhuac, Mex. (tlä-wäk')	131a	19°16'N	99°00'W
Tlajomulco de Zúñiga, Mex. (tlä-hô-mōō'l-ko-dĕ-zōō'n-yē-gä)	130	20°30'N	103°27'W
Tlalchapa, Mex. (tläl-chä'pä)	130	18°26'N	100°29'W
Tlalixcoyan, Mex. (tlä-lēs'kō-yän')	131	18°53'N	96°04'W
Tlalmanalco, Mex. (tläl-mä-nä'l-kô)	131a	19°12'N	98°48'W
Tlalnepantla, Mex.	131a	19°32'N	99°13'W
Tlalnepantla, Mex. (tläl-nå-pän'tlä)	131a	18°59'N	99°01'W
Tlalpan, Mex. (tläl-pä'n)	130	19°17'N	99°10'W
Tlalpujahua, Mex. (tläl-pōō-kä'wä)	130	19°50'N	100°10'W
Tlapa, Mex. (tlä'pä)	130	17°30'N	98°30'W
Tlapacoyan, Mex. (tlä-pä-kô-yä'n)	131	19°57'N	97°11'W
Tlapehuala, Mex. (tlä-på-wä'lä)	130	18°17'N	100°30'W
Tlaquepaque, Mex. (tlä-kĕ-pä'kĕ)	130	20°39'N	103°17'W
Tlatlaya, Mex. (tlä-tlä'yä)	130	18°36'N	100°14'W
Tlaxcala, Mex. (tläs-kä'lä)	128	19°16'N	98°14'W
Tlaxcala, state, Mex.	130	19°30'N	98°15'W
Tlaxco, Mex. (tläs'kō)	130	19°37'N	98°06'W
Tlaxiaco Santa María Asunción, Mex.	131	17°16'N	97°41'W
Tlayacapan, Mex. (tlä-yä-kä-pä'n)	131a	18°57'N	99°00'W
Tlevak Strait, strt., Ak., U.S.	94	53°03'N	132°58'W
Tlumach, Ukr. (t'lû-mäch')	169	48°47'N	25°00'E
Toa, r., Cuba (tō'ä)	135	20°25'N	74°35'W
Toamasina, Madag.	233	18°14'S	49°25'E
Toar, Cuchillas de, mts., Cuba (kōō-chê'l-lyäs-dĕ-tô-ä'r)	135	20°20'N	74°50'W
Tobago, i., Trin. (tō-bā'gō)	129	11°15'N	60°30'W
Toba Inlet, b., Can.	94	50°20'N	124°50'W
Tobarra, Spain (tō-bär'rä)	172	38°37'N	1°42'W
Tobol (Tobyl), r., Asia	184	52°00'N	62°00'E
Tobol'sk, Russia (tō-bôlsk')	184	58°09'N	68°28'E
Tobyl see Tobol, r., Asia	184	52°00'N	62°00'E
Tocaima, Col. (tō-kä'y-mä)	142a	4°28'N	74°38'W
Tocantinópolis, Braz. (tō-kän-tē-nō'pō-lês)	143	6°27'S	47°18'W
Tocantins, state, Braz.	143	10°00'S	48°00'W
Tocantins, r., Braz. (tō-kän-tēns')	143	3°28'S	49°22'W
Toccoa, Ga., U.S. (tŏk'ō-ȧ)	124	34°35'N	83°20'W
Toccoa, r., Ga., U.S.	124	34°53'N	84°24'W
Tochigi, Japan (tō'chē-gĭ)	211	36°25'N	139°45'E
Tocoa, Hond. (tō-kō'ä)	132	15°37'N	86°01'W
Tocopilla, Chile (tō-kō-pēl'yä)	144	22°03'S	70°08'W
Tocuyo de la Costa, Ven. (tô-kōō'yō-dĕ-lä-kôs'tä)	143b	11°03'N	68°24'W
Toda, Japan	211a	35°48'N	139°42'E
Todmorden, Eng., U.K. (tŏd'môr-dĕn)	158a	53°43'N	2°05'W
Tofino, Can. (tō-fē'nō)	94	49°09'N	125°54'W
Töfsingdalens National Park, rec., Swe.	166	62°09'N	13°05'E
Tōgane, Japan (tō'gä-nä)	211	35°29'N	140°16'E
Togian, Kepulauan, is., Indon.	212	0°20'S	122°00'E
Togo, nation, Afr. (tō'gō)	230	8°00'N	0°52'E
Toguzak, r., Russia (tô'gō-zák)	186a	53°40'N	61°42'E
Tohono O'odham Indian Reservation, I.R., Az., U.S.	119	32°33'N	112°12'W
Tohopekaliga, Lake, l., Fl., U.S. (tō'hō-pē'kȧ-lī'gȧ)	125a	28°16'N	81°09'W
Tohor, Tanjong, c., Malay.	197b	1°53'N	102°29'E
Toijala, Fin. (toi'yȧ-lȧ)	167	61°11'N	23°46'E
Toi-Misaki, c., Japan (toi mĕ'sä-kê)	210	31°20'N	131°20'E
Toiyabe, Nv., U.S. (toi'yȧ-bē)	118	38°59'N	117°22'W
Tokachi Gawa, r., Japan (tō-kä'chē gä'wä)	210	43°10'N	142°30'E
Tokaj, Hung. (tô'kô-ê)	169	48°06'N	21°24'E
Tokat, Tur. (tô-kät')	198	40°20'N	36°30'E
Tokelau, dep., Oc. (tō-kê-lä'ō)	2	8°00'S	176°00'W
Tokmak, Kyrg. (tôk'mák)	183	42°44'N	75°41'E
Tokmak, Ukr.	177	47°17'N	35°48'E
Tokorozawa, Japan (tô'kô-rô-zä'wä)	211a	35°47'N	139°29'E
Tok-to, atoll, Asia	210	37°15'N	131°51'E
Tokuno, i., Japan (tô-kōō'nō)	205	27°42'N	129°25'E
Tokushima, Japan (tō'kŏ'shē-mä)	205	34°06'N	134°31'E
Tokuyama, Japan (tō'kŏ'yä-mä)	211	34°04'N	131°49'E
Tōkyō, Japan	205	35°42'N	139°46'E
Tōkyō-Wan, b., Japan (tō'kyō wän)	211	35°56'N	139°56'E
Tolcayuca, Mex. (tôl-kä-yōō'kä)	130	19°55'N	98°54'W
Toledo, Spain (tō-lē'dō)	162	39°53'N	4°02'W
Toledo, Ia., U.S. (tô-lē'dō)	113	41°59'N	92°35'W
Toledo, Oh., U.S.	105	41°40'N	83°35'W
Toledo, Or., U.S.	114	44°37'N	123°58'W
Toledo, Montes de, mts., Spain (mô'n-tĕs-dĕ-tô-lĕ'dô)	172	39°33'N	4°40'W
Toledo Bend Reservoir, res., U.S.	107	31°30'N	93°30'W
Toliara, Madag.	233	23°16'S	43°44'E
Tolima, dept., Col. (tô-lē'mä)	142a	4°07'N	75°20'W
Tolima, Nevado del, mtn., Col. (nĕ-vä-dô-dĕl-tô-lē'mä)	142a	4°40'N	75°20'W
Tolimán, Mex. (tô-lê-män')	130	20°54'N	99°54'W
Tollesbury, Eng., U.K. (tōl'z-bĕrĭ)	158b	51°46'N	0°49'E
Tolmezzo, Italy (tôl-mĕt'zô)	174	46°25'N	13°03'E
Tolmin, Slvn. (tôl'mēn)	174	46°12'N	13°45'E
Tolna, Hung. (tôl'nô)	169	46°25'N	18°47'E
Tolo, Teluk, b., Indon. (tō'lō)	212	2°00'S	122°06'E
Tolosa, Spain (tô-lō'sä)	162	43°10'N	2°05'W
Tolt, r., Wa., U.S. (tōlt)	116a	47°13'N	121°49'W
Toluca, Mex. (tô-lōō'kà)	128	19°17'N	99°40'W
Toluca, Il., U.S. (tō-lōō'kȧ)	108	41°00'N	89°10'W
Toluca, Nevado de, mtn., Mex. (nĕ-vä-dô-dĕ-tô-lōō'kä)	128	19°09'N	99°42'W
Tolyatti, Russia	180	53°30'N	49°10'E
Tom', r., Russia	184	55°33'N	85°00'E
Tomah, Wi., U.S. (tō'mȧ)	113	43°58'N	90°31'W
Tomahawk, Wi., U.S. (tŏm'ȧ-hôk)	113	45°27'N	89°44'W
Tomakivka, Ukr.	177	47°49'N	34°43'E
Tomanivi, mtn., Fiji	214g	17°37'S	178°01'E
Tomar, Port. (tō-mär')	172	39°36'N	8°26'W
Tomashovka, Bela.	169	51°34'N	23°37'E
Tomaszów Lubelski, Pol. (tô-mä'shŏf lōō-bĕl'skĭ)	169	50°20'N	23°27'E
Tomaszów Mazowiecki, Pol. (tô-mä'shŏf mä-zō'vyĕt-skĭ)	169	51°33'N	20°00'E
Tomatlán, Mex. (tô-mä-tlà'n)	130	19°54'N	105°14'W
Tombadonkéa, Gui.	234	11°00'N	14°23'W
Tombador, Serra do, mts., Braz. (sĕr'rȧ dō tōm-bä-dōr')	143	11°31'S	57°33'W
Tombigbee, r., U.S. (tŏm-bĭg'bê)	107	33°00'N	88°30'W
Tombos, Braz. (tô'm-bōs)	141a	20°53'S	42°00'W
Tombouctou, Mali	230	16°46'N	3°01'W
Tombstone, Az., U.S. (tōōm'stōn)	119	31°40'N	110°00'W
Tombua, Ang. (à-lĕ-zhän'drĕ)	232	15°49'S	11°53'E
Tomelilla, Swe. (tô'mĕ-lēl-lä)	166	55°34'N	13°55'E
Tomelloso, Spain (tō-mål-lyō'sō)	172	39°09'N	3°02'W
Tommot, Russia (tŏm-mŏt')	179	59°13'N	126°22'E
Tomsk, Russia (tŏmsk)	178	56°29'N	84°57'E
Tonala, Mex.	130	20°38'N	103°14'W
Tonalá, r., Mex.	131	18°05'N	94°08'W
Tonawanda, N.Y., U.S. (tôn-ȧ-wŏn'dȧ)	111c	43°01'N	78°53'W
Tonawanda Creek, r., N.Y., U.S.	111c	43°05'N	78°43'W
Tonbridge, Eng., U.K. (tŭn-brij)	158b	51°11'N	0°17'E
Tonda, Japan (tôn'dä)	211b	34°51'N	135°38'E
Tondabayashi, Japan (tôn-dä-bä'yä-shê)	211b	34°29'N	135°36'E
Tondano, Indon. (tôn-dä'nō)	213	1°15'N	124°50'E
Tønder, Den. (tûn'nēr)	166	54°47'N	8°49'E
Tone-Gawa, r., Japan (tō'nĕ gä'wa)	211	36°12'N	139°19'E
Tonga, nation, Oc. (tŏŋ'gȧ)	240	18°50'S	175°20'W
Tong'an, China (tôŋ-än)	209	24°48'N	118°02'E
Tonga Trench, deep	240	23°00'S	172°30'W
Tongbei, China (tôŋ-bā)	205	48°00'N	126°48'E
Tongguan, China (tôŋ-gūän)	205	34°48'N	110°25'E
Tonghe, China (tôŋ-hŭ)	208	45°58'N	128°40'E
Tonghua, China (tôŋ-hwä)	205	41°43'N	125°50'E
Tongjiang, China (tôŋ-jyäŋ)	205	47°38'N	132°54'E
Tongliao, China (tôŋ-lĭou)	208	43°30'N	122°15'E
Tongo, Cam.	235	5°11'N	14°00'E
Tongoy, Chile (tōn-goi')	144	30°16'S	71°29'W
Tongren, China (tôŋ-rŭn)	204	27°45'N	109°12'E
Tongshan, China (tôŋ-shän)	206	34°27'N	116°27'E
Tongtian, r., China (tôŋ-tĭĕn)	204	33°00'N	97°00'E
Tongue, r., Mt., U.S. (tŭng)	115	45°08'N	106°40'W
Tongxian, China (tôŋ shyĕn)	206	39°55'N	116°40'E
Tonj, r., Sudan (tônj)	231	6°18'N	28°33'E
Tonk, India (Tŏŋk)	199	26°13'N	75°45'E
Tonkawa, Ok., U.S. (tŏŋ kȧ-wô)	121	36°42'N	97°19'W
Tonkin, Gulf of, b., Asia (tôn-kăn')	212	20°30'N	108°10'E
Tonle Sap, l., Camb. (tôn'lā säp')	212	13°03'N	102°49'E
Tonneins, Fr. (tô-năn')	170	44°24'N	0°18'E
Tönning, Ger. (tû'nēng)	168	54°20'N	8°55'E
Tonopah, Nv., U.S. (tō-nō-pä')	104	38°04'N	117°15'W
Tönsberg, Nor. (tûns'bĕrgh)	160	59°19'N	10°25'E
Tonto, r., Mex. (tôn'tō)	131	18°15'N	96°13'W
Tonto Creek, r., Az., U.S.	119	34°05'N	111°15'W
Tonto National Monument, rec., Az., U.S. (tôn'tô)	119	33°33'N	111°08'W
Tooele, Ut., U.S. (tŏ-ĕl ê)	117b	40°33'N	112°17'W
Toowoomba, Austl. (tó wōōm'bȧ)	219	27°32'S	152°10'E
Topanga, Ca., U.S. (tō'păn-gȧ)	117a	34°05'N	118°36'W
Topeka, Ks., U.S. (tô-pē'kȧ)	105	39°02'N	95°41'W
Topilejo, Mex. (tō-pē-lĕ'hô)	131a	19°12'N	99°09'W
Topock, Az., U.S.	119	34°40'N	114°20'W
Topol'čany, Slvk. (tô-pôl'chä-nü)	169	48°38'N	18°10'E

ăt; finăl; rāte; senåte; ärm; åsk; sofȧ; fâre; ch-choose; dh-as th in other; bē; ėvent; bĕt; recĕnt; cratēr; g-gō; gh-guttural g; bĭt; ĭ-short neutral; rīde; κ-guttural k as ch in German ich;

PRONOUNCING INDEX

Topolobampo – Tsiafajovona 359

PLACE (Pronunciation)	PAGE	LAT.	LONG.
Topolobampo, Mex. (tō-pō-lō-bä'm-pô)	128	25°45'N	109°00'W
Topolovgrad, Blg.	175	42°05'N	26°19'E
Toppenish, Wa., U.S. (tôp'ĕn-ĭsh)	114	46°22'N	120°00'W
Torbat-e Ḩeydarīyeh, Iran	201	35°16'N	59°13'E
Torbat-e Jām, Iran	201	35°14'N	60°36'E
Torbay, Can. (tôr-bā')	101	47°40'N	52°43'W
Torbay *see* Torquay, Eng., U.K.	164	50°30'N	3°26'W
Torbreck, Mount, mtn., Austl. (tōr-brĕk)	222	37°05'S	146°55'E
Torch, l., Mi., U.S. (tôrch)	108	45°00'N	85°30'W
Töreboda, Swe. (tū'rĕ-bō'dä)	166	58°44'N	14°04'E
Torhout, Bel.	165	51°01'N	3°04'E
Toribío, Col. (tō-rē-bē'ō)	142a	2°58'N	76°14'W
Toride, Japan (tō'rē-dā)	211a	35°54'N	104°04'E
Torino *see* Turin, Italy	154	45°05'N	7°44'E
Tormes, r., Spain (tōr'mās)	172	41°12'N	6°15'W
Torneälven, r., Eur.	156	67°00'N	22°30'E
Torneträsk, l., Swe. (tôr'nĕ trĕsk)	160	68°10'N	20°36'E
Torngat Mountains, mts., Can.	93	59°18'N	64°35'W
Tornio, Fin. (tôr'nĭ-ô)	154	65°55'N	24°09'E
Toro, Lac, l., Can.	99	46°53'N	73°46'W
Toronto, Can. (tō-rŏn'tō)	91	43°40'N	79°23'W
Toronto, Oh., U.S.	108	40°30'N	80°35'W
Toronto, res., Mex.	122	27°35'N	105°37'W
Toropets, Russia (tô'rô-pyĕts)	180	56°31'N	31°37'E
Toros Dağları, mts., Tur. (tô'rŭs)	198	37°00'N	32°40'E
Torote, r., Spain (tō-rō'tā)	173a	40°36'N	3°24'W
Torquay, Eng., U.K. (tôr-kē')	164	50°30'N	3°26'W
Torra, Cerro, mtn., Col. (sĕ'r-rô-tô'r-rä)	142a	4°41'N	76°22'W
Torrance, Ca., U.S. (tŏr'rănc)	117a	33°50'N	118°20'W
Torre Annunziata, Italy (tôr'rā ä-nōōn-tsē-ä'tä)	173c	40°31'N	14°27'E
Torreblanca, Spain	173	40°18'N	0°12'E
Torre del Greco, Italy (tôr'rå dĕl grā'kô)	174	40°32'N	14°23'E
Torrejoncillo, Spain (tôr'rā-hōn-thē'lyō)	172	39°54'N	6°26'W
Torrelavega, Spain (tôr-rā'lä-vā'gä)	172	43°22'N	4°02'W
Torre Maggiore, Italy (tôr'rā mäd-jō'rā)	174	41°41'N	15°18'E
Torrens, Lake, l., Austl. (tŏr-ĕns)	220	30°07'S	137°40'E
Torrent, Spain	173	39°25'N	0°28'W
Torreón, Mex. (tôr-rå-ōn')	128	25°32'N	103°26'W
Torres Islands, is., Vanuatu (tôr'rĕs) (tŏr'ĕz)	221	13°18'N	165°59'E
Torres Martinez Indian Reservation, I.R., Ca., U.S. (tôr'ĕz mär-tē'nĕz)	118	33°33'N	116°21'W
Torres Novas, Port. (tôr'rĕzh nō'väzh)	172	39°28'N	8°37'W
Torres Strait, strt., Austl. (tôr'rĕs)	221	10°30'S	141°30'E
Torres Vedras, Port. (tôr'rĕsh vă'dräzh)	172	39°08'N	9°18'W
Torrevieja, Spain (tôr-rā-vyā'hä)	173	37°58'N	0°40'W
Torrijos, Phil. (tôr-rē'hōs)	213a	13°19'N	122°06'E
Torrington, Ct., U.S. (tŏr'ĭng-tŭn)	109	41°50'N	73°10'W
Torrington, Wy., U.S.	112	42°04'N	104°11'W
Torro, Spain (tô'r-rō)	172	41°27'N	5°23'W
Torsby, Swe. (tôrs'bü)	166	60°07'N	12°56'E
Torshälla, Swe. (tôrs'hĕl-ä)	166	59°26'N	16°21'E
Tórshavn, Far. Is. (tôrs-houn')	154	62°00'N	6°55'W
Tortola, i., Br. Vir. Is. (tôr-tō'lä)	129b	18°34'N	64°40'W
Tortona, Italy (tôr-tō'nä)	174	44°52'N	8°52'W
Tortosa, Spain (tôr-tō'sä)	154	40°59'N	0°33'E
Tortosa, Cap de, c., Spain	173	40°42'N	0°55'E
Tortue, Canal de la, strt., Haiti (tôr-tü')	135	20°05'N	73°20'W
Tortue, Île de la, i., Haiti	135	20°10'N	73°00'W
Tortue, Rivière de la, r., Can. (lä tōr-tü')	102a	45°12'N	73°32'W
Toruń, Pol.	154	53°02'N	18°35'E
Tõrva, Est. (t'r'vȧ)	167	58°02'N	25°56'E
Torzhok, Russia (tôr'zhôk)	180	57°03'N	34°53'E
Toscana, hist. reg., Italy (tôs-kä'nä)	174	43°23'N	11°08'E
Tosna, r., Russia	186c	59°28'N	30°53'E
Tosno, Russia (tôs'nô)	176	59°32'N	30°52'E
Tostado, Arg. (tôs-tä'dô)	144	29°10'S	61°43'W
Tosya, Tur. (tôz'yȧ)	163	41°00'N	34°00'E
Totana, Spain (tō-tä-nä)	172	37°45'N	1°28'W
Tot'ma, Russia (tôt'mȧ)	180	60°00'N	42°20'E
Totness, Sur.	143	5°51'N	56°17'W
Totonicapán, Guat. (tōtō-nē-kä'pän)	128	14°55'N	91°20'W
Totoras, Arg. (tō-tō'räs)	141c	32°33'S	61°13'W
Totsuka, Japan (tōt'sōō-kä)	211a	35°24'N	139°32'E
Tottenham, Eng., U.K. (tŏt'ĕn-ȧm)	158b	51°35'N	0°06'W
Tottori, Japan (tō'tō-rē)	205	35°30'N	134°15'E
Touba, C. Iv.	234	8°17'N	7°41'W
Touba, Sen.	234	14°51'N	15°53'W
Toubkal, Jebel, mtn., Mor.	230	31°15'N	7°46'W
Tougan, Burkina	234	13°04'N	3°04'W
Touggourt, Alg. (tōō-gōōrt') (tōō-gōōr')	230	33°09'N	6°07'E
Touil, Oued, r., Alg. (tōō-ēl')	162	34°42'N	2°16'E
Toul, Fr. (tōōl)	161	48°39'N	5°51'E
Toulon, Fr. (tōō-lôn')	154	43°09'N	5°54'E
Toulouse, Fr. (tōō-lōōz')	154	43°37'N	1°27'E
Toungoo, Mya. (tō-ŏŋ-gōō')	212	19°00'N	96°29'E
Tourcoing, Fr. (tōr-kwăn')	161	50°44'N	3°06'E
Tournan-en-Brie, Fr. (tōōr-näɴ-ĕɴ-brē')	171b	48°45'N	2°47'E
Tours, Fr. (tōōr)	154	47°23'N	0°39'E
Touside, Pic, mtn., Chad (tōō-sē-dā')	231	21°10'N	16°30'E
Tovdalselva, r., Nor. (tôv-däls-ĕlvȧ)	166	58°23'N	8°16'E
Towanda, Pa., U.S. (tō-wän'dȧ)	109	41°45'N	76°30'W
Town Bluff Lake, l., Tx., U.S.	123	30°52'N	94°30'W
Towner, N.D., U.S. (tou'nẽr)	112	48°21'N	100°24'W
Townsend, Ma., U.S. (toun'zĕnd)	101a	42°41'N	71°42'W
Townsend, Mt., U.S.	115	46°19'N	111°35'W
Townsend, Mount, mtn., Wa., U.S.	116a	47°52'N	123°03'W
Townsville, Austl. (tounz'vĭl)	219	19°18'S	146°50'E
Towson, Md., U.S. (tou'sŭn)	110e	39°24'N	76°36'W
Towuti, Danau, l., Indon. (tō-wōō'tē)	212	3°00'S	121°45'E
Toxkan, r., China	204	40°34'N	77°15'E
Toyah, Tx., U.S. (tô'yȧ)	122	31°19'N	103°46'W
Toyama, Japan (tō'yä-mä)	205	36°42'N	137°14'E
Toyama-Wan, b., Japan	211	36°58'N	137°16'E
Toyohashi, Japan (tō'yō-hä'shē)	210	34°44'N	137°21'E
Toyonaka, Japan (tō'yō-nä'kȧ)	211b	34°47'N	135°28'E
Tozeur, Tun. (tō-zûr')	162	33°59'N	8°11'E
Trabzon, Tur. (tråb'zôn)	198	41°00'N	39°45'E
Tracy, Can.	99	46°00'N	73°13'W
Tracy, Ca., U.S. (trā'sē)	118	37°45'N	121°27'W
Tracy, Mn., U.S.	112	44°13'N	95°37'W
Tracy City, Tn., U.S.	124	35°15'N	85°44'W
Trafalgar, Cabo, c., Spain (kå'bô-trä-fäl-gä'r)	172	36°10'N	6°02'W
Trafonomby, mtn., Madag.	233	24°32'S	46°35'E
Trail, Can. (trāl)	90	49°06'N	117°42'W
Traisen, r., Aus.	159e	48°15'N	15°55'E
Traiskirchen, Aus.	159e	48°01'N	16°18'E
Trakai, Lith. (trá-kāy)	167	54°38'N	24°59'E
Trakiszki, Pol. (trá-kē'-sh-kē)	169	54°16'N	23°07'E
Tralee, Ire. (trȧ-lē')	161	52°16'N	9°20'W
Tranås, Swe. (trän'ôs)	166	58°03'N	14°56'E
Trancoso, Port. (träŋ-kō'sō)	172	40°46'N	7°23'W
Trangan, Pulau, i., Indon. (träŋ'gän)	213	6°52'S	133°30'E
Trani, Italy (trä'nē)	174	41°15'N	16°25'E
Transylvania, hist. reg., Rom. (trăn-sĭl-vā'nĭ-ȧ)	169	46°30'N	22°35'E
Trapani, Italy	162	38°01'N	12°31'E
Trappes, Fr. (tråp)	171b	48°47'N	2°01'E
Traralgon, Austl. (tră'răl-gŏn)	222	38°15'S	146°33'E
Trarza, reg., Maur.	234	17°35'N	15°15'W
Trasimeno, Lago, l., Italy (lä'gō trä-sē-mā'nō)	174	43°00'N	12°12'E
Trás-os-Montes, hist. reg., Port. (träzh'ōzh mōn'tāzh)	162	41°33'N	7°13'W
Traun, r., Aus. (troun)	168	48°10'N	14°15'E
Traunstein, Ger. (troun'stīn)	168	47°52'N	12°38'E
Traverse, Lake, l., Mn., U.S. (trăv'ẽrs)	112	45°46'N	96°53'W
Traverse City, Mi., U.S.	108	44°45'N	85°40'W
Travnik, Bos. (träv'nēk)	175	44°13'N	17°43'E
Treasure Island, i., Ca., U.S. (trĕzh'ẽr)	116b	37°49'N	122°22'W
Trebbin, Ger. (trĕ'bēn)	159b	52°13'N	13°13'E
Trebinje, Bos. (trå'bēn-yĕ)	175	42°43'N	18°21'E
Trebišov, Slvk. (trĕ'bē-shôf)	169	48°36'N	21°32'E
Tregrosse Islands, is., Austl. (trē-grōs')	221	18°08'S	150°53'E
Treinta y Tres, Ur. (trå-ēn'tā ē trās')	144	33°14'S	54°17'W
Trelew, Arg. (trē'lū)	144	43°15'S	65°25'W
Trelleborg, Swe.	166	55°24'N	13°07'E
Tremiti, Isole, is., Italy (ē'sō-lĕ trā-mē'tē)	174	42°07'N	16°33'E
Trenčín, Czech Rep. (trĕn'chēn)	161	48°52'N	18°02'E
Trenque Lauquén, Arg. (trĕn'kĕ-lä'ōō-kĕ'n)	144	35°50'S	62°44'W
Trent, r., Can. (trĕnt)	99	44°15'N	77°55'W
Trent, r., Eng., U.K.	158a	53°25'N	0°45'W
Trent and Mersey Canal, can., Eng., U.K. (trĕnt) (mûr zē)	158a	53°11'N	2°24'W
Trentino-Alto Adige, hist. reg., Italy	174	46°16'N	10°47'E
Trento, Italy (trĕn'tô)	162	46°04'N	11°07'E
Trenton, Can. (trĕn'tŭn)	91	44°05'N	77°35'W
Trenton, Can.	101	45°37'N	62°38'W
Trenton, Mi., U.S.	111b	42°08'N	83°12'W
Trenton, Mo., U.S.	121	40°05'N	93°36'W
Trenton, N.J., U.S.	105	40°13'N	74°46'W
Trenton, Tn., U.S.	124	35°57'N	88°55'W
Trepassey, Can. (trē-păs'ē)	101	46°44'N	53°22'W
Trepassey Bay, b., Can.	101	46°40'N	53°20'W
Tres Arroyos, Arg. (trās'är-rō'yōs)	144	38°18'S	60°16'W
Três Corações, Braz. (trĕ's kō-rä-zô'ĕs)	141a	21°41'S	45°14'W
Tres Cumbres, Mex. (trĕ's kōō'm-brĕs)	131a	19°03'N	99°14'W
Três Lagoas, Braz. (trĕ's lä-gô'ás)	143	20°48'S	51°42'W
Três Marias, Reprêsa, res., Braz.	143	18°15'S	45°30'W
Tres Morros, Alto de, mtn., Col. (ȧ'l-tō dĕ trĕ's mô'r-rôs)	142a	7°08'N	76°10'W
Três Pontas, Braz. (trĕ'pô'n-täs)	141a	21°22'S	45°30'W
Três Pontas, Cabo das, c., Ang.	236	10°23'S	13°32'E
Três Rios, Braz. (trĕ's rē'ōs)	141a	22°07'S	43°13'W
Très-Saint Rédempteur, Can. (săɴ rā-dāɴp-tûr')	102a	45°26'N	74°23'W
Treuenbrietzen, Ger. (troi'ĕn-brē-tzĕn)	159b	52°06'N	12°52'E
Treviglio, Italy (trā-vē'lyô)	174	45°30'N	9°34'E
Treviso, Italy (trĕ-vē'sō)	162	45°39'N	12°15'E
Trichardt, S. Afr. (trĭ-kärt')	238c	26°32'N	29°16'E
Trier, Ger.	161	49°45'N	6°38'E
Trieste, Italy (trē-ĕs'tā)	154	45°39'N	13°48'E
Triglav, mtn., Slvn.	174	46°23'N	13°50'E
Trigueros, Spain (trē-gā'rōs)	172	37°23'N	6°50'W
Tríkala, Grc.	163	39°33'N	21°49'E
Trikora, Puncak, mtn., Indon.	213	4°15'S	138°45'E
Trim Creek, r., Il., U.S. (trĭm)	111a	41°19'N	87°39'W
Trincomalee, Sri L. (trĭŋ-kō-mȧ-lē')	203	8°39'N	81°12'E
Tring, Eng., U.K. (trĭng)	158b	51°46'N	0°40'W
Trinidad, Bol. (trē-nē-dhädh')	142	14°48'S	64°43'W
Trinidad, Cuba (trē-nē-dhädh')	129	21°50'N	80°00'W
Trinidad, Ur.	144	33°29'S	56°55'W
Trinidad, Co., U.S. (trĭn'ĭdăd)	104	37°11'N	104°31'W
Trinidad, i., Trin. (trĭn'ĭ-dăd)	143	10°00'N	61°00'W
Trinidad, r., Pan.	128a	8°55'N	80°01'W
Trinidad, Sierra de, mts., Cuba (sē-ĕ'r-rä dĕ trē-nē-dä'd)	134	21°50'N	79°55'W
Trinidad and Tobago, nation, N.A. (trĭn'ĭ-dăd) (tō-bā'gō)	129	11°00'N	61°00'W
Trinitaria, Mex. (trē-nē-tä'ryä)	131	16°09'N	92°04'W
Trinity, Can. (trĭn'ĭ-tē)	101	48°59'N	53°55'W
Trinity, Tx., U.S.	123	30°52'N	95°27'W
Trinity, is., Ak., U.S.	103	56°25'N	153°15'W
Trinity, r., Ca., U.S.	114	40°50'N	123°20'W
Trinity, r., Tx., U.S.	107	30°50'N	95°09'W
Trinity, East Fork, r., Tx., U.S.	121	33°24'N	96°42'W
Trinity, West Fork, r., Tx., U.S.	120	33°22'N	98°26'W
Trinity Bay, b., Can.	93	48°00'N	53°40'W
Trino, Italy (trē'nô)	174	45°11'N	8°16'E
Trion, Ga., U.S. (trī'ŏn)	124	34°32'N	85°18'W
Tripoli, Grc.	163	37°32'N	22°32'E
Tripoli (Tarābulus), Libya	231	32°50'N	13°13'E
Tripolitania *see* Tarābulus, hist. reg., Libya	230	31°00'N	12°26'E
Tripura, state, India	199	24°00'N	92°00'E
Tristan da Cunha Islands, is., St. Hel. (três-tän'dä kōōn'yä)	2	35°30'S	12°15'W
Triste, Golfo, b., Ven. (gôl-fô trĕ's-tĕ)	143b	10°40'N	68°05'W
Triticus Reservoir, res., N.Y., U.S. (trī tĭ-cŭs)	110a	41°20'N	73°36'W
Trnava, Slvk. (t'r'nȧ-vȧ)	169	48°22'N	17°34'E
Trobriand Islands, is., Pap. N. Gui. (trō-brē-ănd')	213	8°25'S	151°45'E
Trogir, Cro. (trô'gēr)	174	43°32'N	16°17'E
Trois Fourches, Cap des, c., Mor.	172	35°28'N	2°58'W
Trois-Rivières, Can. (trwä'rē-vyâ')	91	46°21'N	72°35'W
Troitsk, Russia (trô'ētsk)	184	54°06'N	61°35'E
Troits'ke, Ukr.	177	47°39'N	30°16'E
Troitsko-Pechorsk, Russia (trô'ĭtsk-ô-pyĕ-chôrsk')	178	62°18'N	56°07'E
Trollhättan, Swe. (trôl'hĕt-ĕn)	160	58°17'N	12°17'E
Trollheimen, mts., Nor. (trôll-hĕĭm)	166	62°48'N	9°05'E
Trona, Ca., U.S. (trō'nȧ)	118	35°49'N	117°20'W
Tronador, Cerro, mtn., S.A. (sĕ'r-rô trō-nä-dôr)	144	41°17'S	71°56'W
Troncoso, Mex. (trôn-kô'sō)	130	22°43'N	102°22'W
Trondheim, Nor. (trôn'hâm)	154	63°25'N	11°35'E
Trosa, Swe. (trô'sä)	166	58°54'N	17°25'E
Trout, l., Can.	93	51°16'N	92°46'W
Trout, l., Can.	92	61°10'N	121°30'W
Trout Creek, r., Or., U.S.	114	42°18'N	118°31'W
Troutdale, Or., U.S. (trout'dāl)	116c	45°32'N	122°23'W
Trout Lake, Mi., U.S.	113	46°20'N	85°02'W
Trouville, Fr. (trōō-vēl')	170	49°23'N	0°05'E
Troy, Al., U.S. (troi)	124	31°47'N	85°46'W
Troy, Il., U.S.	117e	38°44'N	89°53'W
Troy, Ks., U.S.	121	39°46'N	95°07'W
Troy, Mo., U.S.	120	38°56'N	99°57'W
Troy, Mt., U.S.	114	48°28'N	115°56'W
Troy, N.C., U.S.	125	35°21'N	79°58'W
Troy, N.Y., U.S.	105	42°45'N	73°45'W
Troy, Oh., U.S.	108	40°00'N	84°10'W
Troy, hist., Tur.	198	39°59'N	26°14'E
Troyes, Fr. (trwä)	161	48°18'N	4°03'E
Trstenik, Yugo. (t'r'stĕ-nēk)	163	43°36'N	21°00'E
Trubchëvsk, Russia (trōp'chĕfsk)	181	52°36'N	33°46'E
Trucial States *see* United Arab Emirates, nation, Asia	198	24°00'N	54°00'E
Truckee, Ca., U.S. (trŭk'ē)	118	39°20'N	120°12'W
Truckee, r., Ca., U.S.	118	39°25'N	120°07'W
Truganina, Austl.	217a	37°49'N	144°44'E
Trujillo, Col. (trō-кē'l-yō)	142a	4°10'N	76°20'W
Trujillo, Peru	142	8°08'S	79°00'W
Trujillo, Spain (trōō-кē'l-yō)	162	39°27'N	5°50'W
Trujillo, Ven.	142	9°15'N	70°28'W
Trujillo, r., Mex.	130	23°12'N	103°10'W
Trujin, Lago, l., Dom. Rep. (trōō-кēn')	135	17°45'N	71°25'W
Truk *see* Chuuk, is., Micron.	214c	7°25'N	151°47'E
Trumann, Ar., U.S. (trōō'măn)	121	35°41'N	90°31'W
Trŭn, Blg. (trŭn)	175	42°49'N	22°39'E
Truro, Can. (trōō'rō)	91	45°22'N	63°16'W
Truro, Eng., U.K.	164	50°17'N	5°05'W
Trussville, Al., U.S. (trŭs'vĭl)	110h	33°37'N	86°37'W
Truth or Consequences, N.M., U.S. (trōōth ŏr kŏn'sē-kwĕn-sĭs)	119	33°10'N	107°20'W
Trutnov, Czech Rep. (trōt'nôf)	168	50°36'N	15°36'E
Trzcianka, Pol. (tchyän'kȧ)	168	53°02'N	16°27'E
Trzebiatów, Pol. (tchĕ-byä'tō-v)	168	54°03'N	15°16'E
Tsaidam Basin, basin, China (tsī-däm)	204	37°19'N	94°08'E
Tsala Apopka Lake, r., Fl., U.S. (tsä'lȧ ă-pŏp'kȧ)	125	28°57'N	82°11'W
Tsast Bogd, mtn., Mong.	204	46°44'N	92°34'E
Tsavo National Park, rec., Kenya	237	2°35'S	38°45'E
Tsawwassen Indian Reserve, I.R., Can.	116d	49°03'N	123°11'W
Tsentral'nyy-Kospashskiy, Russia (tsĕn-träl'nyĭ-kôs-pásh'skĭ)	186a	59°03'N	57°48'E
Tshela, D.R.C. (tshā'lȧ)	232	4°59'S	12°56'E
Tshikapa, D.R.C. (tshē-kä'pä)	232	6°25'S	20°48'E
Tshofa, D.R.C.	237	5°14'S	25°15'E
Tshuapa, r., D.R.C.	232	0°30'S	22°00'E
Tsiafajovona, mtn., Madag.	233	19°17'S	47°27'E

ng-sing; ŋ-baŋk; ɴ-nasalized n; nŏd; cŏmmit; ōld; ôbey; ôrder; oi-boil; fōōd; ȯ-as oo in foot; ou-out; s-soft; sh-dish; th-thin; pūre; ûnite; ûrn; stŭd; circŭs; ü-as in French tu; '-indeterminate vowel.

360 Tsiribihina – Uglegorsk PRONOUNCING INDEX

PLACE (Pronunciation)	PAGE	LAT.	LONG.
Tsiribihina, r., Madag. (tsē′rê-bē-hê-nä′)	233	19°45′S	43°30′E
Tsitsa, r., S. Afr. (tsē′tsȧ)	233c	31°28′S	28°53′E
Tskhinvali, Geor.	182	42°13′N	43°56′E
Tsolo, S. Afr. (tsō′lō)	233c	31°19′S	28°47′E
Tsomo, S. Afr.	233c	32°03′S	27°49′E
Tsomo, r., S. Afr.	233c	31°53′S	27°48′E
Tsu, Japan (tsōō)	210	34°42′N	136°31′E
Tsuchiura, Japan (tsōō′chê-ōō-rä)	211	36°04′N	140°09′E
Tsuda, Japan (tsōō′dä)	211b	34°48′N	135°43′E
Tsugaru Kaikyō, strt., Japan	205	41°25′N	140°20′E
Tsumeb, Nmb. (tsōō′mĕb)	232	19°10′S	17°45′E
Tsunashima, Japan (tsōō′nä-shê′mä)	211a	35°32′N	139°37′E
Tsuruga, Japan (tsōō′rö-gä)	210	35°39′N	136°04′E
Tsurugi San, mtn., Japan (tsōō′rö-gê sän)	210	33°52′N	134°07′E
Tsuruoka, Japan (tsōō′rö-ō′kä)	210	38°43′N	139°51′E
Tsurusaki, Japan (tsōō′rö-sä′kê)	211	33°15′N	131°42′E
Tsu Shima, is., Japan (tsōō shê′mä)	205	34°28′N	129°30′E
Tsushima Strait, strt., Asia	205	34°00′N	129°00′E
Tsuwano, Japan (tsōō′wȧ-nō′)	211	34°28′N	131°47′E
Tsuyama, Japan (tsōō′yä-mä′)	210	35°05′N	134°00′E
Tua, r., Port. (tōō′ä)	172	41°23′N	7°18′W
Tualatin, r., Or., U.S. (tōō′ȧ-lā-tĭn)	116c	45°25′N	122°54′W
Tuamoto, Îles, Fr. Poly. (tōō-ä-mō′tōō)	241	19°00′S	141°20′W
Tuapse, Russia (tö′äp-sĕ)	181	44°00′N	39°10′E
Tuareg, hist. reg., Alg.	230	21°26′N	2°51′E
Tubarão, Braz. (tōō-bä-rouɴ′)	144	28°23′N	48°56′W
Tübingen, Ger. (tü′bĭng-ĕn)	168	48°33′N	9°05′E
Tubinskiy, Russia (tû bĭn′skĭ)	186a	52°53′N	58°15′E
Tubruq, Libya	231	32°03′N	24°04′E
Tucacas, Ven. (tōō-kä′käs)	142	10°48′N	68°20′W
Tucker, Ga., U.S. (tŭk′ẽr)	110c	33°51′N	84°13′W
Tucson, Az., U.S. (tōō-sŏn′)	104	32°15′N	111°00′W
Tucumán, Arg. (tōō-kōō-män′)	144	26°52′S	65°08′W
Tucumán, prov., Arg.	144	26°30′S	65°30′W
Tucumcari, N.M., U.S. (tōō′kŭm-kâr-ê)	120	35°11′N	103°43′W
Tucupita, Ven. (tōō-kōō-pē′tä)	142	9°00′N	62°09′W
Tudela, Spain (tōō-dhä′lä)	162	42°03′N	1°37′W
Tugaloo, r., Ga., U.S. (tŭg′ȧ-lōō)	124	34°35′N	83°05′W
Tugela, r., S. Afr. (tōō-gel′ȧ)	233c	28°50′S	30°52′E
Tugela Ferry, S. Afr.	233c	28°44′S	30°27′E
Tug Fork, r., U.S. (tŭg)	108	37°50′N	82°30′W
Tuguegarao, Phil. (tōō-gā-gȧ-rä′ō)	212	17°37′N	121°44′E
Tuhai, r., China (tōō-hī)	206	37°05′N	116°56′E
Tui, Slvn.	172	42°03′N	8°38′W
Tuinplaas, S. Afr.	238c	24°54′S	28°46′E
Tujunga, Ca., U.S. (tōō-jŭŋ′gȧ)	117a	34°15′N	118°16′W
Tukan, Russia (tōō′kȧn)	186a	53°52′N	57°25′E
Tukangbesi, Kepulauan, is., Indon.	213	6°00′S	124°15′E
Tūkrah, Libya	231	32°34′N	20°47′E
Tuktoyaktuk, Can.	90	69°32′N	132°37′W
Tuktut Nogait National Park, rec., Can.	92	69°00′N	122°00′W
Tukums, Lat. (tö′kōms)	180	56°57′N	23°09′E
Tukuyu, Tan. (tōō-kōō′yȧ)	232	9°13′S	33°43′E
Tukwila, Wa., U.S. (tŭk′wĭ-lȧ)	116a	47°28′N	122°16′W
Tula, Mex. (tōō′lä)	130	20°04′N	99°22′W
Tula, Russia (tōō′lȧ)	180	54°12′N	37°37′E
Tula, prov., Russia	176	53°45′N	37°19′E
Tula, r., Mex. (tōō′lä)	130	20°40′N	99°27′W
Tulagai, i., Sol. Is. (tōō-lä′gē)	221	9°15′S	160°17′E
Tulaghi, Sol. Is.	214e	9°06′S	160°09′E
Tulalip, Wa., U.S. (tū-lă′lĭp)	116a	48°04′N	122°18′W
Tulalip Indian Reservation, I.R., Wa., U.S.	116a	48°06′N	122°16′W
Tulancingo, Mex. (tōō-län-sĭŋ′gō)	128	20°04′N	98°24′W
Tulangbawang, r., Indon.	212	4°17′S	105°00′E
Tulare, Ca., U.S. (tōō-lä′rā) (tul-âr′)	118	36°12′N	119°22′W
Tulare Lake Bed, l., Ca., U.S.	118	35°57′N	120°18′W
Tularosa, N.M., U.S. (tŭl-ȧ-rō′zȧ)	119	33°05′N	106°05′W
Tulcán, Ec. (tōōl-kän′)	142	0°44′N	77°52′W
Tulcea, Rom. (tōōl′chȧ)	163	45°10′N	28°47′E
Tul′chyn, Ukr.	181	48°42′N	28°53′E
Tulcingo, Mex. (tōōl-sĭŋ′gō)	130	18°03′N	98°27′W
Tule, r., Ca., U.S. (tōōl′lȧ)	118	36°08′N	118°50′W
Tule River Indian Reservation, I.R., Ca., U.S. (tōō′lȧ)	118	36°00′N	118°40′W
Tuli, Zimb. (tōō′lê)	232	20°58′S	29°12′E
Tulia, Tx., U.S. (tōō′lĭ-ȧ)	120	34°32′N	101°46′W
Tulik Volcano, vol., Ak., U.S. (tö′lĭk)	103a	53°28′N	168°10′W
Tūlkarm, W.B. (tōōl kärm)	197a	32°19′N	35°02′E
Tullahoma, Tn., U.S. (tŭl-ȧ-hō′mȧ)	124	35°21′N	86°12′W
Tullamore, Ire. (tŭl-ȧ-mōr′)	164	53°15′N	7°29′W
Tulle, Fr. (tül)	170	45°15′N	1°45′E
Tulln, Aus. (töln)	168	48°21′N	16°04′E
Tullner Feld, reg., Aus.	159e	48°20′N	15°59′E
Tulpetlac, Mex. (tōōl-pȧ-tlȧk′)	131a	19°33′N	99°04′W
Tulsa, Ok., U.S. (tŭl′sȧ)	105	36°08′N	95°58′W
Tulum, Mex. (tōō-lō′m)	132a	20°17′N	87°26′W
Tulun, Russia (tö-lōōn′)	179	54°29′N	100°43′E
Tuma, r., Nic. (tōō′mä)	132	13°07′N	85°32′W
Tumba, Lac, l., D.R.C. (tŏm′bä)	232	0°50′S	17°45′E
Tumbes, Peru (tōō′m-bĕs)	142	3°39′S	80°27′W
Tumbiscatío, Mex. (tōōm-bê-skä-tē′ō)	130	18°32′N	102°23′W
Tumbo, i., Can.	116d	48°49′N	123°04′W
Tumen, China (tōō-mün)	208	43°00′N	129°50′E
Tumen, r., Asia	210	42°08′N	128°40′E
Tumeremo, Ven. (tōō-må-rä′mō)	143	7°15′N	61°28′W
Tumkūr, India	203	13°22′N	77°05′E
Tumuacacori National Monument, rec., Az., U.S. (tōō-mä-kä′kȧ-rē)	119	31°36′N	110°20′W
Tumuc-Humac Mountains, mts., S.A. (tōō-mök′ōō-mäk′)	143	2°15′N	54°50′W
Tunas de Zaza, Cuba (tōō′näs dā zä′zä)	134	21°40′N	79°35′W
Tunbridge Wells, Eng., U.K. (tŭn′brĭj welz′)	165	51°05′N	0°09′E
Tunduru, Tan.	237	11°07′S	37°21′E
Tungabhadra Reservoir, res., India	203	15°26′N	75°57′E
Tuni, India	203	17°29′N	82°38′E
Tunica, Ms., U.S. (tū′nĭ-kȧ)	124	34°41′N	90°23′W
Tunis, Tun. (tū′nĭs)	230	36°59′N	10°06′E
Tunis, Golfe de, b., Tun.	162	37°06′N	10°43′E
Tunisia, nation, Afr. (tu-nĭzh′ê-ȧ)	230	35°00′N	10°11′E
Tunja, Col. (tōō′n-hȧ)	142	5°32′N	73°19′W
Tunkhannock, Pa., U.S. (tŭnk-hăn′ŭk)	109	41°35′N	75°55′W
Tunnel, r., Wa., U.S. (tŭn′ĕl)	116a	47°48′N	123°04′W
Tuoji Dao, i., China (twô-jyē dou)	206	38°11′N	120°45′E
Tuolumne, r., Ca., U.S. (twô-lŭm′nê)	118	37°35′N	120°37′W
Tuostakh, r., Russia	185	67°09′N	137°30′E
Tupelo, Ms., U.S. (tū′pê-lō)	124	34°14′N	88°43′W
Tupinambaranas, Ilha, i., Braz.	143	3°04′S	58°09′W
Tupiza, Bol. (tōō-pē′zä)	142	21°26′S	65°43′W
Tupper Lake, N.Y., U.S. (tŭp′ẽr)	109	44°15′N	74°25′W
Tüpqaraghan tübegi, pen., Kaz.	181	44°30′N	50°40′E
Tupungato, Cerro, vol., S.A.	144	33°30′S	69°52′W
Tuquerres, Col. (tōō-kĕ′r-rĕs)	142	1°12′N	77°44′W
Tura, Russia (tör′ȧ)	179	64°08′N	99°58′E
Turbio, r., Mex. (tōōr-byô)	130	20°28′N	101°40′W
Turbo, Col. (tōō′bō)	142	8°02′N	76°43′W
Turda, Rom. (tör′dȧ)	169	46°35′N	23°47′E
Turfan Depression, depr., China	204	42°16′N	90°00′E
Turffontein, neigh., S. Afr.	233b	26°15′S	28°02′E
Tŭrgovishte, Blg.	175	43°14′N	26°36′E
Turgutlu, Tur.	181	38°30′N	27°20′E
Türi, Est. (tü′rĭ)	167	58°49′N	25°29′E
Turia, r., Spain (tōō′ryä)	172	40°12′N	1°18′W
Turicato, Mex. (tōō-rê-kä′tō)	130	19°03′N	101°24′W
Turiguano, i., Cuba (tōō-rê-gwä′nō)	134	22°20′N	78°35′W
Turin, Italy	154	45°05′N	7°44′E
Turiya, r., Ukr.	169	51°18′N	24°55′E
Turka, Ukr. (tōōr′kȧ)	169	49°10′N	23°02′E
Turkestan, hist. reg., Asia	178	43°27′N	62°14′E
Turkey, nation, Asia	155	38°45′N	32°00′E
Turkey, r., Ia., U.S. (tûrk′ê)	113	43°20′N	92°16′W
Türkistan, Kaz.	183	44°00′N	68°00′E
Turkmenbashy, Turkmen.	183	40°00′N	52°50′E
Turkmenistan, nation, Asia	178	40°46′N	56°01′E
Turks, is., T./C. Is. (tûrks)	129	21°40′N	71°45′W
Turks Island Passage, strt., T./C. Is.	135	21°15′N	71°25′W
Turku, Fin. (törgökö)	154	60°28′N	22°12′E
Turlock, Ca., U.S. (tûr′lŏk)	118	37°30′N	120°51′W
Turneffe, i., Belize	128	17°25′N	87°43′W
Turner, Ks., U.S. (tûr′nẽr)	117f	39°05′N	94°42′W
Turner Sound, strt., Bah.	134	24°20′N	78°05′W
Turners Peninsula, pen., S.L.	234	7°20′N	12°40′W
Turnhout, Bel. (tŭrn-hout′)	165	51°19′N	4°58′E
Turnov, Czech Rep. (tör′nôf)	168	50°36′N	15°12′E
Turnu Măgurele, Rom.	163	43°54′N	24°49′E
Turpan, China (tōō-är-pän)	204	43°06′N	88°41′E
Turquino, Pico, mtn., Cuba (pē′kō dā tōōr-kē′nō)	134	20°00′N	76°50′W
Turrialba, C.R. (tōōr-ryä′l-bä)	133	9°54′N	83°41′W
Turtkul′, Uzb. (tört-kōl′)	183	41°28′N	61°02′E
Turtle, r., Can.	97	49°20′N	92°30′W
Turtle Bay, b., Tx., U.S.	123a	29°48′N	94°38′W
Turtle Creek, r., S.D., U.S.	112	44°40′N	98°53′W
Turtle Mountain Indian Reservation, I.R., N.D., U.S.	112	48°45′N	99°57′W
Turtle Mountains, mts., N.D., U.S.	112	48°57′N	100°11′W
Turukhansk, Russia (tōō-rōō-känsk′)	178	66°03′N	88°39′E
Tuscaloosa, Al., U.S. (tŭs-kȧ-lōō′sȧ)	105	33°10′N	87°35′W
Tuscarora, Nv., U.S. (tŭs-kȧ-rō′rȧ)	114	41°18′N	116°15′W
Tuscarora Indian Reservation, I.R., N.Y., U.S.	111c	43°10′N	78°51′W
Tuscola, Il., U.S. (tŭs-kō-lȧ)	108	39°50′N	88°20′W
Tuscumbia, Al., U.S. (tŭs-kŭm′bĭ-ȧ)	124	34°41′N	87°42′W
Tushino, Russia (tōō′shĭ-nô)	186b	55°51′N	37°24′E
Tuskegee, Al., U.S. (tŭs-kē′gê)	124	32°25′N	85°40′W
Tustin, Ca., U.S. (tŭs′tĭn)	117a	33°44′N	117°49′W
Tutayev, Russia (tōō-tȧ-yĕf′)	180	57°53′N	39°34′E
Tutbury, Eng., U.K. (tŭt′bẽr-ê)	158a	52°52′N	1°51′W
Tuticorin, India (tōō-tê-kô-rĭn′)	203	8°51′N	78°09′E
Tutitlan, Mex. (tōō-tê-tlä′n)	131a	19°38′N	99°10′W
Tutóia, Braz. (tōō-tō′yȧ)	143	2°42′S	42°21′W
Tutrakan, Blg.	163	44°02′N	26°36′E
Tuttle Creek Reservoir, res., Ks., U.S.	121	39°30′N	96°38′W
Tuttlingen, Ger. (töt′ lĭng-ĕn)	168	47°58′N	8°50′E
Tutuila, i., Am. Sam.	214a	14°18′S	170°42′W
Tutwiler, Ms., U.S. (tŭt′wĭ-lẽr)	124	34°01′N	90°25′W
Tuva, prov., Russia	184	51°15′N	90°45′E
Tuvalu, nation, Oc.	3	5°20′S	174°00′E
Tuwayq, Jabal, mts., Sau. Ar.	198	20°45′N	46°30′E
Tuxedo Park, N.Y., U.S. (tŭk-sē′dō pärk)	110a	41°11′N	74°11′W
Tuxford, Eng., U.K. (tŭks′fẽrd)	158a	53°14′N	0°54′W
Tuxpan, Mex. (tōōs′pän)	130	19°34′N	103°22′W
Túxpan, Mex.	128	20°57′N	97°26′W
Túxpan, r., Mex. (tōōs′pän)	131	20°55′N	97°52′W
Túxpan, Arrecife, i., Mex. (är-rĕ-sē′fê-tōō′x-pä′n)	131	21°01′N	97°12′W
Tuxtepec, Mex. (tōs-tå-pĕk′)	131	18°06′N	96°09′W
Tuxtla Gutiérrez, Mex. (tōs′tlä gōō-tyâr′rĕs)	128	16°44′N	93°08′W
Tuy, r., Ven. (tōō′ê)	143b	10°15′N	66°03′W
Tuyra, r., Pan. (tōō-ē′rȧ)	133	7°55′N	77°37′W
Tuz Gölü, l., Tur.	180	38°45′N	33°25′E
Tuzigoot National Monument, rec., Az., U.S.	119	34°40′N	111°52′W
Tuzla, Bos. (tōz′lȧ)	163	44°33′N	18°46′E
Tvedestrand, Nor. (tvĭ′dhĕ-stränd)	166	58°39′N	8°54′E
Tveitsund, Nor. (tvåt′sōnd)	166	59°03′N	8°29′E
Tver′, Russia	178	56°52′N	35°57′E
Tver′, prov., Russia	176	56°50′N	33°08′E
Tvertsa, r., Russia (tvĕr′tsȧ)	176	56°58′N	35°22′E
Tweed, r., U.K. (twēd)	164	55°32′N	2°35′W
Tweeling, S. Afr. (twē′lĭng)	238c	27°34′S	28°31′E
Twenty Mile Creek, r., Can. (twĕn′tĭ mīl)	102d	43°09′N	79°49′W
Twickenham, Eng., U.K. (twĭk′′n-ăm)	158b	51°26′N	0°20′W
Twillingate, Can. (twĭl′ĭn-gāt)	93a	49°39′N	54°46′W
Twin Bridges, Mt., U.S. (twĭn brĭ-jĕz)	115	45°34′N	112°17′W
Twin Falls, Id., U.S. (fôls)	104	42°33′N	114°29′W
Twinsburg, Oh., U.S. (twĭnz′bûrg)	111d	41°19′N	81°26′W
Twitchell Reservoir, res., Ca., U.S.	118	34°50′N	120°10′W
Two Butte Creek, r., Co., U.S. (tōō būt)	120	37°39′N	102°45′W
Two Harbors, Mn., U.S.	113	47°00′N	91°42′W
Two Prairie Bay, Ar., U.S. (prâ′rĭ bī ōō′)	121	34°48′N	92°07′W
Two Rivers, Wi., U.S. (rĭv′ẽrz)	113	44°09′N	87°36′W
Tyabb, Austl.	217a	38°16′S	145°11′E
Tylden, S. Afr. (tĭl-dĕn)	233c	32°08′S	27°06′E
Tyldesley, Eng., U.K. (tĭldz′lê)	158a	53°32′N	2°28′W
Tyler, Mn., U.S. (tī′lẽr)	112	44°18′N	96°08′W
Tyler, Tx., U.S.	105	32°21′N	95°19′W
Tylertown, Ms., U.S. (tī′lẽr-toun)	124	31°08′N	90°06′W
Tylihul, r., Ukr.	177	47°25′N	30°27′E
Tyndall, S.D., U.S. (tĭn′dȧl)	112	42°58′N	97°52′W
Tyndinskiy, Russia	179	55°22′N	124°45′E
Tyne, r., Eng., U.K. (tīn)	164	54°59′N	1°56′W
Tynemouth, Eng., U.K. (tīn′mŭth)	160	55°04′N	1°39′W
Tyngsboro, Ma., U.S. (tĭnj-bûr′ô)	101a	42°40′N	71°27′W
Tynset, Nor. (tün′sĕt)	160	62°17′N	10°45′E
Tyre see Şūr, Leb.	197a	33°16′N	35°13′E
Tyrifjorden, l., Nor.	166	60°03′N	10°25′E
Tyrnavos, Grc.	175	39°50′N	22°14′E
Tyrone, Pa., U.S.	109	40°40′N	78°15′W
Tyrrell, Lake, l., Austl. (tĭr′ĕll)	222	35°12′S	143°00′E
Tyrrhenian Sea, sea, Italy (tĭr-rē′nĭ-ăn)	156	40°10′N	12°15′E
Tyukalinsk, Russia (työ-kȧ-lĭnsk′)	178	56°03′N	71°43′E
Tyukyan, r., Russia (työk′yȧn)	185	65°42′N	116°09′E
Tyuleniy, i., Russia	181	44°30′N	48°00′E
Tyumen′, Russia (työō-mĕn′)	178	57°02′N	65°28′E
Tzucacab, Mex. (tzōō-kä-kä′b)	132a	20°06′N	89°03′W

U

PLACE (Pronunciation)	PAGE	LAT.	LONG.
Uaupés, Braz. (wä-ōō′pās)	142	0°02′S	67°03′W
Ubangi, r., Afr. (ōō-bäŋ′gê)	231	3°00′N	18°00′E
Ubatuba, Braz. (ōō-bȧ-tōō′bȧ)	141a	23°25′S	45°06′W
Ubeda, Spain (ōō′bå-dä)	172	38°01′N	3°23′W
Uberaba, Braz. (ōō-bå-rä′bȧ)	143	19°47′S	47°47′W
Uberlândia, Braz. (ōō-bĕr-lá′n-dyä)	143	18°54′S	48°11′W
Ubombo, S. Afr. (ōō-bôm′bô)	232	27°33′S	32°13′E
Ubon Ratchathani, Thai. (ōō′bŭn rä′chätá-nē)	212	15°15′N	104°52′E
Ubort′, r., Eur. (ōō-bôrt′)	177	51°18′N	27°43′E
Ubrique, Spain (ōō-brē′kå)	172	36°43′N	5°36′W
Ubundu, D.R.C.	232	0°21′S	25°29′E
Ucayali, r., Peru (ōō′kä-yä′lē)	142	8°58′S	74°13′W
Uccle, Bel. (ü′kl′)	159a	50°48′N	4°17′E
Uchaly, Russia (û-chä′lĭ)	186a	54°22′N	59°28′E
Uchiko, Japan (ōō′chê-kō)	211	33°30′N	132°39′E
Uchinoura, Japan (ōō′chê-nô-ōō′rȧ)	211	31°16′N	131°03′E
Uchinskoye Vodokhranilishche, res., Russia	186b	56°08′N	37°44′E
Uchiura-Wan, b., Japan (ōō′chê-ōō′rä wän)	210	42°20′N	140°44′E
Uchur, r., Russia (ö-chōr′)	185	57°25′N	130°35′E
Uda, r., Russia	185	53°54′N	131°29′E
Uda, r., Russia (ö′dȧ)	185	52°28′N	110°51′E
Udai, r., Ukr.	177	50°45′N	32°13′E
Udaipur, India (ö-dŭ′ê-pōōr)	202	24°41′N	73°41′E
Uddevalla, Swe. (ōōd′dĕ-väl-ȧ)	160	58°21′N	11°55′E
Udine, Italy (ōō′dê-nå)	162	46°05′N	13°14′E
Udmurtia, prov., Russia	180	57°00′N	53°00′E
Udon Thani, Thai.	212	17°31′N	102°51′E
Udskaya Guba, b., Russia	179	55°00′N	136°30′E
Ueckermünde, Ger.	168	53°43′N	14°01′E
Ueda, Japan (wä′dä)	210	36°26′N	138°16′E
Uele, r., D.R.C. (wä′lȧ)	231	3°55′N	23°30′E
Uelzen, Ger. (ült′sĕn)	168	52°58′N	10°34′E
Ufa, Russia (ö′fȧ)	178	54°45′N	55°57′E
Ufa, r., Russia	180	56°00′N	57°05′E
Ugab, r., Nmb. (ōō′gäb)	232	21°10′S	14°00′E
Ugalla, r., Tan. (ōō-gä′lä)	232	6°15′S	32°30′E
Uganda, nation, Afr. (ōō-găn′dä) (û-găn′dȧ)	231	2°00′N	32°28′E
Ugashik Lake, l., Ak., U.S. (ōō′gȧ-shêk)	103	57°36′N	157°10′W
Ugie, S. Afr. (ö′jē)	233c	31°13′S	28°14′E
Uglegorsk, Russia (ōō-glĕ-gôrsk)	179	49°00′N	142°31′E

PRONOUNCING INDEX Ugleural'sk – Valdecañas 361

PLACE (Pronunciation)	PAGE	LAT.	LONG.
Ugleural'sk, Russia (òg-lĕ-ò-rálsk′)	186a	58°58′N	57°35′E
Uglich, Russia (ōōg-lĕch′)	176	57°33′N	38°19′E
Uglitskiy, Russia (òg-lĭt′skĭ)	186a	53°50′N	60°18′E
Uglovka, Russia (ōōg-lôf′kà)	176	58°14′N	33°24′E
Ugra, r., Russia (ōōg′rà)	180	54°43′N	34°20′E
Ugŭrchin, Blg.	175	43°06′N	24°23′E
Uhrichsville, Oh., U.S. (ū′rĭks-vĭl)	108	40°25′N	81°20′W
Uíge, Ang.	232	7°37′S	15°03′E
Uiju, Kor., N. (ò′ējōō)	205	40°09′N	124°33′E
Uinkaret Plateau, plat., Az., U.S. (û-ĭn′kâr-ēt)	119	36°43′N	113°15′W
Uinskoye, Russia (ò-ĭn′skô-yĕ)	186a	56°53′N	56°25′E
Uinta, r., Ut., U.S. (û-ĭn′tà)	119	40°25′N	109°55′W
Uintah and Ouray Indian Reservation, I.R., Ut., U.S.	119	40°20′N	110°20′W
Uinta Mountains, mts., Ut., U.S.	106	40°35′N	111°00′W
Uitenhage, S. Afr.	232	33°46′S	25°26′E
Uithoorn, Neth.	159a	52°13′N	4°49′E
Uji, Japan (ōō′jē)	211b	34°53′N	135°49′E
Ujiji, Tan. (ōō-jē′jē)	232	4°55′S	29°41′E
Ujjain, India (ōō-jŭēn)	199	23°18′N	75°37′E
Ujungpandang, Indon.	212	5°08′S	119°28′E
Ukerewe Island, i., Tan.	237	2°00′S	32°40′E
Ukhta, Russia (ōōk′tà)	180	65°22′N	31°30′E
Ukhta, Russia	180	63°08′N	53°42′E
Ukiah, Ca., U.S. (ū-kī′à)	118	39°09′N	122°12′W
Ukmerge, Lith. (òk′mĕr-ghå)	180	55°16′N	24°45′E
Ukraine, nation, Eur.	178	49°15′N	30°15′E
Uku, i., Japan (ōōk′ōō)	211	33°18′N	129°02′E
Ulaangom, Mong.	204	50°23′N	92°14′E
Ulan Bator (Ulaanbaatar), Mong.	204	47°56′N	107°00′E
Ulan-Ude, Russia (ōō′län ōō′dâ)	179	51°59′N	107°41′E
Ulchin, Kor., S. (ōōl′chĕn′)	210	36°57′N	129°26′E
Ulcinj, Yugo. (ōōl′tsĕn′)	163	41°56′N	19°15′E
Ulhās, r., India	203b	19°13′N	73°03′E
Ulhāsnagar, India	202	19°10′N	73°07′E
Uliastay, Mong.	204	47°49′N	97°00′E
Ulindi, r., D.R.C. (ōō-lĭn′dē)	232	1°55′S	26°17′E
Ulla, Bela. (òl′à)	176	55°14′N	29°15′E
Ulla, r., Bela.	176	54°58′N	29°03′E
Ulla, r., Spain (ōō′lä)	172	42°45′N	8°33′W
Ullŭng, i., Kor., S. (ōōl′lòng′)	210	37°29′N	130°50′E
Ulm, Ger. (òlm)	161	48°24′N	9°59′E
Ulmer, Mount, mtn., Ant. (ŭl′mûr′)	224	77°30′S	86°00′W
Ulricehamn, Swe. (òl-rē′sĕ-häm)	166	57°49′N	13°23′E
Ulsan, Kor., S. (ōōl′sän′)	210	35°35′N	129°22′E
Ulster, hist. reg., Eur. (ŭl′stẽr)	164	54°41′N	7°10′W
Ulua, r., Hond. (ōō-lōō′à)	132	15°49′N	87°45′W
Ulubāria, India	202a	22°27′N	88°09′E
Ulukişla, Tur. (ōō-lōō-kēsh′lå)	163	36°40′N	34°30′E
Ulunga, Russia (ò-lōōn′gà)	210	46°16′N	136°29′E
Ulungur, r., China (ōō-lōōn-gûr)	204	46°31′N	88°00′E
Uluru (Ayers Rock), mtn., Austl.	220	25°23′S	131°05′E
Ulu-Telyak, Russia (ōō lò′tĕlyăk)	186a	54°54′N	57°01′E
Ulverstone, Austl. (ŭl′vẽr-stŭn)	219	41°20′S	146°22′E
Ul'yanovka, Russia	186c	59°38′N	30°47′E
Ul'yanovsk, Russia (ōō-lyä′nôfsk)	178	54°20′N	48°24′E
Ulysses, Ks., U.S. (ū-lĭs′ēz)	120	37°34′N	101°25′W
Umán, Mex. (ōō-män′)	132a	20°52′N	89°44′W
Uman', Ukr. (ò-man′)	181	48°44′N	30°13′E
Umatilla Indian Reservation, I.R., Or., U.S. (ū-mà-tĭl′à)	114	45°38′N	118°35′W
Umberpāda, India	203b	19°28′N	73°04′E
Umbria, hist. reg., Italy (ŭm′brĭ-à)	174	42°53′N	12°22′E
Umeälven, r., Swe.	156	64°57′N	18°51′E
Umhlatuzi, r., S. Afr. (òm′hlà-tōō′zĭ)	233c	28°47′S	31°17′E
Umiat, Ak., U.S. (ōō′mĭ-ăt)	106a	69°20′N	152°28′W
Umkomaas, S. Afr. (òm-kō′mäs)	233c	30°12′S	30°48′E
Umnak, i., Ak., U.S. (ōōm′nák)	106b	53°10′N	169°08′W
Umnak Pass, Ak., U.S.	103a	53°10′N	168°04′W
Umniati, r., Zimb.	232	17°08′S	29°11′E
Umpqua, r., Or., U.S. (ŭmp′kwå)	114	43°42′N	123°50′W
Umtata, S. Afr. (òm-tä′tä)	232	31°36′S	28°47′E
Umtentweni, S. Afr.	233c	30°41′S	30°29′E
Umzimkulu, S. Afr. (òm-zēm-kōō′lōō)	233c	30°12′S	29°53′E
Umzinto, S. Afr. (òm-zĭn′tō)	233c	30°19′S	30°41′E
Una, r., Yugo. (ōō′nà)	174	44°38′N	16°10′E
Unalakleet, Ak., U.S. (ū-nà-lăk′lēt)	103	63°50′N	160°42′W
Unalaska, Ak., U.S. (ū-nà-lås′kå)	103a	53°30′N	166°20′W
Unare, r., Ven.	143b	9°45′N	65°12′W
Unare, Laguna de, l., Ven. (lä-gò′nä-de-ōō-nà′rĕ)	143b	10°07′N	65°23′W
Unayzah, Sau. Ar.	198	25°50′N	44°02′E
Uncas, Can. (ŭŋ′kȧs)	102g	53°30′N	113°02′W
Uncia, Bol. (ōōn′sē-ä)	142	18°28′S	66°32′W
Uncompahgre, r., Co., U.S.	119	38°20′N	107°45′W
Uncompahgre Peak, mtn., Co., U.S. (ŭn-kŭm-pä′grē)	119	38°00′N	107°30′W
Uncompahgre Plateau, plat., Co., U.S.	119	38°40′N	108°40′W
Underberg, S. Afr. (ŭn′dẽr-bûrg)	233c	29°51′S	29°32′E
Unecha, Russia (ò-nĕ′chá)	176	52°51′N	32°44′E
Ungava, Péninsule d', pen., Can.	93	59°55′N	74°00′W
Ungava Bay, b., Can. (ŭŋ-gä′và)	93	59°46′N	67°18′W
União da Vitória, Braz. (ōō-nē-ouN′ dä vē-tô′ryä)	144	26°17′S	51°13′W
Unije, i., Yugo. (ōō′nē-yĕ)	174	44°39′N	14°10′E
Unimak, i., Ak., U.S. (ōō-nē-mák′)	103	54°30′N	163°35′W
Unimak Pass, Ak., U.S.	103a	54°22′N	165°22′W
Union, Mo., U.S.	121	38°28′N	90°59′W
Union, Ms., U.S. (ūn′yŭn)	124	32°35′N	89°07′W
Union, N.C., U.S.	125	34°42′N	81°40′W
Union, Or., U.S.	114	45°13′N	117°52′W
Union City, Ca., U.S.	116b	37°36′N	122°01′W
Union City, In., U.S.	108	40°10′N	85°00′W
Union City, Mi., U.S.	108	42°00′N	85°10′W
Union City, Pa., U.S.	109	41°50′N	79°50′W
Union City, Tn., U.S.	124	36°25′N	89°04′W
Unión de Reyes, Cuba	134	22°45′N	81°30′W
Unión de San Antonio, Mex.	130	21°07′N	101°56′W
Unión de Tula, Mex.	130	19°57′N	104°14′W
Union Grove, Wi., U.S. (ūn-yŭn grōv)	111a	42°41′N	88°03′W
Unión Hidalgo, Mex. (ē-dä′lgô)	131	16°29′N	94°51′W
Union Point, Ga., U.S.	124	33°37′N	83°08′W
Union Springs, Al., U.S. (sprĭngz)	124	32°08′N	85°43′W
Uniontown, Al., U.S. (ūn′yŭn-toun)	124	32°26′N	87°30′W
Uniontown, Oh., U.S.	111d	40°58′N	81°25′W
Uniontown, Pa., U.S.	109	39°55′N	79°45′W
Unionville, Mo., U.S. (ūn′yŭn-vĭl)	121	40°28′N	92°58′W
Unisan, Phil. (ōō-nē′sän)	213a	13°50′N	121°59′E
United Arab Emirates, nation, Asia	198	24°00′N	54°00′E
United Kingdom, nation, Eur.	154	56°30′N	1°40′W
United States, nation, N.A.	104	38°00′N	110°00′W
Unity, Can.	96	52°27′N	109°10′W
Universal, In., U.S. (ū-nĭ-vûr′sál)	108	39°35′N	87°30′W
University City, Mo., U.S. (ū′nĭ-vûr′sĭ-tĭ)	117e	38°40′N	90°19′W
University Park, Tx., U.S.	117c	32°51′N	96°48′W
Unna, Ger. (ōō′nä)	171c	51°32′N	7°41′E
Uno, Canal Numero, can., Arg.	141c	36°43′S	58°14′W
Unterhaching, Ger. (ōōn′tĕr-hä-kĕng)	159d	48°03′N	11°38′E
Ünye, Tur. (ün′yĕ)	163	41°00′N	37°10′E
Unzha, r., Russia (òn′zhå)	180	57°45′N	44°10′E
Upa, r., Russia (ò′pá)	176	53°54′N	36°48′E
Upata, Ven. (ōō-pä′tä)	142	7°58′N	62°27′W
Upemba, Parc National de l', rec., D.R.C.	237	9°10′S	26°15′E
Upington, S. Afr. (ŭp′ĭng-tŭn)	232	28°25′S	21°15′E
Upland, Ca., U.S. (ŭp′lănd)	117a	34°06′N	117°38′W
Upolu, i., Samoa	214a	13°55′S	171°45′W
Upolu Point, c., Hi., U.S. (ōō-pô′lōō)	126a	20°15′N	155°48′W
Upper Arrow Lake, l., Can. (ăr′ō)	95	50°30′N	117°55′W
Upper Darby, Pa., U.S. (där′bĭ)	110f	39°58′N	75°16′W
Upper des Lacs, l., N.A. (dĕ läk)	112	48°58′N	101°55′W
Upper Kapuas Mountains, mts., Asia	212	1°45′N	112°06′E
Upper Klamath Lake, l., Or., U.S.	114	42°23′N	122°55′W
Upper Lake, l., Nv., U.S. (ŭp′ẽr)	114	41°42′N	119°59′W
Upper Marlboro, Md., U.S. (ûpẽr märl′bōrō)	110e	38°49′N	76°46′W
Upper Mill, Wa., U.S. (mĭl)	116a	47°11′N	121°55′W
Upper Red Lake, l., Mn., U.S. (rĕd)	113	48°14′N	94°53′W
Upper Sandusky, Oh., U.S. (săn-dŭs′kē)	108	40°50′N	83°20′W
Upper San Leandro Reservoir, res., Ca., U.S. (ŭp′ẽr săn lē-ăn′drō)	116b	37°47′N	122°04′W
Upper Volta see Burkina Faso, nation, Afr.	230	13°00′N	2°00′W
Uppingham, Eng., U.K. (ŭp′ĭng-ăm)	158a	52°35′N	0°43′W
Uppsala, Swe. (ōōp′sà-lä)	154	59°53′N	17°39′E
Uptown, Ma., U.S. (ŭp′toun)	101a	42°10′N	71°36′W
Uraga, Japan (ōō′rà-gá′)	211a	35°15′N	139°43′E
Ural, r. (ò-räl′′) (ū-rôl)	178	48°00′N	51°00′E
Urals, mts., Russia	178	56°28′N	58°13′E
Uran, India (ōō-rän′)	203b	18°53′N	72°46′E
Uranium City, Can.	90	59°34′N	108°59′W
Urawa, Japan (ōō′rä-wä′)	210	35°52′N	139°39′E
Urayasu, Japan (ōō′rä-yä′sōō)	211a	35°40′N	139°54′W
Urazovo, Russia (ò-rà′zô-vô)	177	50°08′N	38°03′E
Urbana, Il., U.S. (ûr-băn′à)	108	40°10′N	88°15′W
Urbana, Oh., U.S.	108	40°05′N	83°50′W
Urbino, Italy (ōōr-bē′nō)	174	43°43′N	12°37′E
Urdaneta, Phil. (ōōr-dä-nä′tä)	213a	15°59′N	120°34′E
Urdinarrain, Arg. (ōōr-dē-när-räē′n)	141c	32°43′S	58°53′W
Uritsk, Russia (ōō′rĭtsk)	186c	59°50′N	30°11′E
Urla, Tur. (òr′là)	175	38°20′N	26°44′E
Urman, Russia (òr′mán)	186a	54°53′N	56°52′E
Urmi, r., Russia (òr′mē)	210	48°50′N	134°00′E
Uromi, Nig.	235	6°44′N	6°18′E
Urrao, Col. (ōōr-rà′ō)	142	6°19′N	76°11′W
Urshel'skiy, Russia (ōōr-shĕl′skēē)	176	55°50′N	40°11′E
Ursus, Pol.	169	52°12′N	20°53′E
Urubamba, r., Peru (ōō-rōō-bäm′bä)	142	11°48′S	72°34′W
Uruguaiana, Braz.	144	29°45′S	57°00′W
Uruguay, nation, S.A. (ōō-rōō-gwī′) (ū′rōō-gwā)	144	32°45′S	56°00′W
Uruguay, r., S.A. (ōō-rōō-gwī′)	144	27°05′S	55°15′W
Ürümqi, China (ů-rŭm-chyē)	204	43°49′N	87°43′E
Urup, i., Russia (ò′ròp′)	205	46°00′N	150°00′E
Uryupinsk, Russia (òr′yò-pēn-sk′)	181	50°50′N	42°00′E
Ürzhar, Kaz.	183	47°28′N	82°00′E
Urziceni, Rom. (ò-zē-chĕn′′)	175	44°45′N	26°42′E
Usa, Japan	210	33°31′N	131°22′E
Usa, r., Russia (ò′sà)	180	66°00′N	58°20′E
Uşak, Tur. (ōō′shák)	163	38°45′N	29°15′E
Usakos, Nmb. (ōō-sä′kōs)	232	22°00′S	15°40′E
Usambara Mountains, mts., Tan.	237	4°40′S	38°25′E
Usangu Flats, sw., Tan.	237	8°10′S	34°00′E
Ushaki, Russia (ōō′shá-kĭ)	186c	59°28′N	31°00′E
Ushakovskoye, Russia (ò-shá-kôv′skô-yĕ)	186a	56°18′N	62°23′E
Ushashi, Tan.	237	2°00′S	33°57′E
Ushiku, Japan (ōō′shē-kōō)	211a	35°24′N	140°09′E
Ushimado, Japan (ōō′shē-mä′dō)	211	34°37′N	134°09′E
Ushuaia, Arg. (ōō-shōō-ī′ä)	144	54°46′S	68°24′W
Usman', Russia (ōōs-mán′)	181	52°03′N	39°40′E
Usol'ye, Russia (ò-sô′lyĕ)	186a	59°24′N	56°40′E
Usol'ye-Sibirskoye, Russia (ò-sô′lyĕsĭ′ bēr′skô-yĕ)	184	52°44′N	103°46′E
Uspallata Pass, p., S.A. (ōōs-pä-lyä′tä)	144	32°47′S	70°08′W
Uspanapa, r., Mex. (ōōs-pä-nä′pä)	131	17°43′N	94°14′W
Ussel, Fr. (üs′ĕl)	170	45°33′N	2°17′E
Ussuri, r., Asia (ōō-sōō′rē)	185	47°30′N	134°00′E
Ussuriysk, Russia	179	43°48′N	132°09′E
Ust'-Bol'sheretsk, Russia	179	52°41′N	157°00′E
Ustica, Isola di, i., Italy	174	38°43′N	12°11′E
Ústí nad Labem, Czech Rep.	168	50°40′N	14°02′E
Ust'-Izhora, Russia (òst-ēz′hô-rà)	186c	59°49′N	30°35′E
Ustka, Pol. (ōōst′kà)	168	54°34′N	16°52′E
Ust'-Kamchatsk, Russia	179	56°13′N	162°18′E
Ust'-Katav, Russia (òst kà′táf)	186a	54°55′N	58°12′E
Ust'-Kishert', Russia (òst kē′shĕrt)	186a	57°21′N	57°13′E
Ust'-Kulom, Russia (kò′lŭm)	178	61°38′N	54°00′E
Ust'-Maya, Russia (má′yȧ)	179	60°33′N	134°43′E
Ust' Olenëk, Russia	179	72°52′N	120°15′E
Ust-Ordynskiy, Russia (òst-ôr-dyēnsk′ĭ)	184	52°47′N	104°39′E
Ust' Penzhino, Russia	185	63°00′N	165°10′E
Ust' Port, Russia (òst′pôrt′)	178	69°20′N	83°41′E
Ust'-Tsil'ma, Russia (tsĭl′má)	178	65°25′N	52°10′E
Ust'-Tyrma, Russia (tur′má)	179	50°27′N	131°17′E
Ust' Uls, Russia	186a	60°35′N	58°32′E
Ust-Urt, Plateau, plat., Asia	178	44°03′N	54°58′E
Ustynivka, Ukr.	177	47°59′N	32°31′E
Ustyuzhna, Russia (yōōzh′ná)	180	58°49′N	36°19′E
Usu, China (ů-sōō)	204	44°28′N	84°07′E
Usuki, Japan (ōō′sōō-kē′)	211	33°06′N	131°47′E
Usulutan, El Sal. (ōō-sōō-lä-tän′)	132	13°22′N	88°25′W
Usumacinta, r., N.A. (ōō′sōō-mä-sēn′tō)	131	18°24′N	92°30′W
Us'va, Russia (ōōs′vá)	186a	58°41′N	57°38′E
Utah, state, U.S. (ū′tô)	104	39°25′N	112°40′W
Utah Lake, l., Ut., U.S.	119	40°10′N	111°55′W
Utan, India	203b	19°17′N	72°43′E
Ute Mountain Indian Reservation, I.R., N.M., U.S.	119	36°57′N	108°34′W
Utena, Lith. (ōō′tā-nä)	167	55°32′N	25°40′E
Utete, Tan. (ōō-tā′tå)	233	8°05′S	38°47′E
Utica, In., U.S. (ū′tĭ-kȧ)	111h	38°20′N	85°39′W
Utica, N.Y., U.S.	105	43°05′N	75°10′W
Utiel, Spain (ōō-tyâl′)	172	39°34′N	1°13′W
Utika, Mi., U.S. (ū′tĭ-kȧ)	111b	42°37′N	83°02′W
Utik Lake, l., Can.	97	55°16′N	96°00′W
Utikuma Lake, l., Can.	95	55°50′N	115°25′W
Utila, i., Hond. (ōō-tē′lä)	132	16°07′N	87°05′W
Uto, Japan (ōō′tō′)	210	32°43′N	130°39′E
Utrecht, Neth. (ü′trĕkt) (ū′trĕkt)	161	52°05′N	5°06′E
Utrera, Spain (ōō-trā′rä)	162	37°12′N	5°48′W
Utsunomiya, Japan (ōōt′sò-nô-mē-yá′)	205	36°35′N	139°52′E
Uttaradit, Thai.	212	17°47′N	100°10′E
Uttaranchal, state, India	199	29°30′N	78°30′E
Uttarpara-Kotrung, India	202a	22°40′N	88°21′E
Uttar Pradesh, state, India (òt-tär-prä-dĕsh)	199	27°00′N	80°00′E
Uttoxeter, Eng., U.K. (ŭt-tôk′sē-tẽr)	158a	52°54′N	1°52′W
Utuado, P.R. (ōō-tōō-ä′dhō)	129b	18°16′N	66°40′W
Uusikaupunki, Fin.	167	60°48′N	21°24′E
Uvalde, Tx., U.S. (ū-văl′dē)	122	29°14′N	99°47′W
Uvel'skiy, Russia (ò-vyĕl′skĭ)	186a	54°27′N	61°22′E
Uvinza, Tan.	237	5°06′S	30°22′E
Uvira, D.R.C. (ōō-vē′rä)	232	3°28′S	29°03′E
Uvod', r., Russia (ò-vôd′)	176	56°40′N	41°10′E
Uvongo Beach, S. Afr.	233c	30°49′S	30°23′E
Uvs Nuur, l., Asia	204	50°29′N	93°32′E
Uwajima, Japan (ōō-wä′jē-mä)	210	33°12′N	132°35′E
Uxbridge, Ma., U.S. (ŭks′brĭj)	101a	42°05′N	71°38′W
Uxmal, hist., Mex. (ōō′x-mä′l)	132a	20°22′N	89°44′W
Uy, r., Russia (ōōy)	186a	54°05′N	62°11′E
Uyskoye, Russia (ûy′skô-yĕ)	186a	54°22′N	60°01′E
Uyuni, Bol. (ōō-yōō′nē)	142	20°28′S	66°45′W
Uyuni, Salar de, pl., Bol. (sä-lär-dĕ)	142	20°58′S	67°09′W
Uzbekistan, nation, Asia	178	42°42′N	60°00′E
Uzh, r., Ukr. (òzh)	177	51°07′N	29°05′E
Uzhhorod, Ukr.	169	48°38′N	22°18′E
Užice, Yugo. ōō′zhĕ-tsĕ	175	43°51′N	19°53′E
Uzunköprü, Tur.	175	41°17′N	26°42′E

V

PLACE (Pronunciation)	PAGE	LAT.	LONG.
Vaal, r., S. Afr. (väl)	232	28°15′S	24°30′E
Vaaldam, res., S. Afr.	238c	26°58′S	28°37′E
Vaalplaas, S. Afr.	238c	25°39′S	28°56′E
Vaalwater, S. Afr.	238c	24°17′S	28°08′E
Vaasa, Fin. (vä′sà)	154	63°06′N	21°39′E
Vác, Hung. (väts)	169	47°46′N	19°10′E
Vache, Île à, i., Haiti	135	18°05′N	73°40′W
Vadstena, Swe. (väd′stĭ′nà)	166	58°27′N	14°53′E
Vaduz, Liech. (vä′dòts)	168	47°10′N	9°32′E
Vaga, r., Russia (va′gà)	180	61°55′N	42°30′E
Vah, r., Slvk. (väk)	161	48°07′N	17°52′E
Vaigai, r., India	203	10°20′N	78°13′E
Vakh, r., Russia (vák)	184	61°30′N	81°33′E
Valachia, hist. reg., Rom.	175	44°45′N	24°17′E
Valcartier-Village, Can. (väl-kärt-yĕ′vē-läzh′)	102b	46°56′N	71°28′W
Valdai Hills, hills, Russia (vál-dī′ gô′rĭ)	180	57°50′N	32°35′E
Valday, Russia (vál-dī′)	180	57°58′N	33°13′E
Valdecañas, Embalse de, res., Spain	172	39°45′N	5°30′W

ng-sing; ŋ-baŋk; N-nasalized n; nŏd; cŏmmit; ōld; ôbey; ôrder; oi-boil; fōōd; ò-as oo in foot; ou-out; s-soft; sh-dish; th-thin; pūre; ûnite; ûrn; stŭd; circŭs; ü-as in French tu; ′-indeterminate vowel.

362 Valdemārpils – Vernon

PRONOUNCING INDEX

PLACE (Pronunciation)	PAGE	LAT.	LONG.
Valdemārpils, Lat.	167	57°22'N	22°34'E
Valdemorillo, Spain (väl-dā-mô-rēl'yō)	173a	40°30'N	4°04'W
Valdepeñas, Spain (väl-då-pān'yäs)	162	38°46'N	3°22'W
Valderaduey, r., Spain (väl-dĕ-rä-dwĕ'y)	172	41°39'N	5°35'W
Valdés, Península, pen., Arg. (väl-dĕ's)	144	42°15'S	63°15'W
Valdez, Ak., U.S. (văl'dĕz)	103	61°10'N	146°18'W
Valdilecha, Spain (väl-dê-lā'chä)	173a	40°17'N	3°19'W
Valdivia, Chile (väl-dē'vä)	144	39°47'S	73°13'W
Valdivia, Col. (väl-dē'vēä)	142a	7°10'N	75°26'W
Val-d'Or, Can.	91	48°03'N	77°50'W
Valdosta, Ga., U.S. (văl-dŏs'tá)	105	30°50'N	83°18'W
Vale, Or., U.S. (vāl)	114	43°59'N	117°14'W
Valença, Braz. (vä-lĕn'sá)	143	13°43'S	38°58'W
Valença, Port.	172	42°03'N	8°36'W
Valence, Fr. (vä-lĕnns)	161	44°56'N	4°54'E
València, Spain	154	39°26'N	0°23'W
Valencia, Ven. (vä-lĕn'syä)	142	10°11'N	68°00'W
València, hist. reg., Spain	173	39°08'N	0°43'W
València, Golf de, b., Spain	173	39°50'N	0°30'E
Valencia, Lago de, l., Ven.	143b	10°11'N	67°45'W
Valencia de Alcántara, Spain	172	39°34'N	7°13'W
Valenciennes, Fr. (vá-läN-syĕn')	170	50°24'N	3°36'E
Valentine, Ne., U.S. (vá lăN-tê-nyĕ')	104	42°52'N	100°34'W
Valera, Ven. (vä-lĕ'rä)	142	9°12'N	70°45'W
Valerianovsk, Russia (vá-lĕ-rĭ-ä'nôvsk)	186a	58°47'N	59°34'E
Valga, Est. (väl'gá)	180	57°47'N	26°03'E
Valhalla, S. Afr. (vál-hăl-á)	233b	25°49'S	28°09'E
Valier, Mt., U.S. (vă-lēr')	115	48°17'N	112°14'W
Valjevo, Yugo. (väl'yå-vô)	175	44°17'N	19°57'E
Valky, Ukr.	177	49°49'N	35°40'E
Valladolid, Mex. (väl-yä-dhô-lēdh')	128	20°39'N	88°13'W
Valladolid, Spain (väl-yä-dhô-lēdh')	154	41°41'N	4°41'W
Valle, Arroyo del, Ca., U.S. (ä-rō'yō dĕl väl'yå)	118	37°36'N	121°43'W
Vallecas, Spain (väl-yā'käs)	173a	40°23'N	3°37'W
Valle de Allende, Mex. (väl'yā dā äl-yĕn'då)	122	26°55'N	105°25'W
Valle de Bravo, Mex. (brä'vô)	130	19°12'N	100°07'W
Valle de Guanape, Ven. (vä'l-yĕ-dĕ-gwä-nä'pĕ)	143b	9°54'N	65°41'W
Valle de la Pascua, Ven. (lä-pä's-kōōä)	142	9°12'N	65°08'W
Valle del Cauca, dept., Col. (vä'l-yĕ del kou'kä)	142a	4°03'N	76°13'W
Valle de Santiago, Mex. (sän-tē-ä'gô)	130	20°23'N	101°11'W
Valledupar, Col. (dōō-pär')	142	10°13'N	73°39'W
Valle Grande, Bol. (grän'dā)	142	18°27'S	64°03'W
Vallejo, Ca., U.S. (vä-yā'hō) (vă-lā'hō)	104	38°06'N	122°15'W
Vallejo, Sierra de, mts., Mex. (sē-ĕ'r-rä-dĕ-väl-yĕ'kô)	130	21°00'N	105°10'W
Vallenar, Chile (väl-yå-när')	144	28°39'S	70°52'W
Valles, Mex.	128	21°59'N	99°02'W
Valletta, Malta (väl-lĕt'ä)	162	35°50'N	14°29'E
Valle Vista, Ca., U.S. (väl'yā vĭs'tá)	117a	33°45'N	116°53'W
Valley City, N.D., U.S.	104	46°55'N	97°59'W
Valley City, Oh., U.S. (văl'ĭ)	111d	41°14'N	81°56'W
Valley Falls, Ks., U.S.	121	39°25'N	95°26'W
Valleyfield, Can. (văl'ē-fēld)	91	45°16'N	74°09'W
Valley Park, Mo., U.S. (văl'ē pärk)	117e	38°33'N	90°30'W
Valley Stream, N.Y., U.S. (văl'ĭ strēm)	110a	40°39'N	73°42'W
Valli di Comácchio, l., Italy (vä'lē-dē-kô-má'chyô)	174	44°38'N	12°15'E
Vallière, Haiti (väl-yâr')	135	19°30'N	71°55'W
Vallimanca, r., Arg. (väl-yē-mä'n-kä)	141c	36°21'S	60°55'W
Valls, Spain (väls)	162	41°15'N	1°15'E
Valmiera, Lat. (vál'myĕ-rá)	180	57°34'N	25°54'E
Valognes, Fr. (vá-lôn'y')	170	49°32'N	1°30'W
Valona *see* Vlorë, Alb.	163	40°28'N	19°31'E
Valozhyn, Bela.	176	54°04'N	26°38'E
Valparaíso, Chile (väl'pä-rä-ē'sô)	144	33°02'S	71°32'W
Valparaíso, Mex.	130	22°49'N	103°33'W
Valparaiso, In., U.S. (văl-pá-rā'zō)	108	41°25'N	87°05'W
Valpariso, prov., Chile	141b	32°58'S	71°23'W
Valréas, Fr. (vål-rā-ä')	170	44°25'N	4°56'E
Vals, r., S. Afr.	238c	27°32'S	26°51'E
Vals, Tanjung, c., Indon.	213	8°30'S	137°15'E
Valsbaai, b., S. Afr.	232a	34°14'S	18°35'E
Valuyevo, Russia (vá-lōō'yĕ-vô)	186b	55°34'N	37°21'E
Valuyki, Russia (vá-lò-ē'kē)	181	50°14'N	38°04'E
Valverde del Camino, Spain (väl-vĕr-dĕ-dĕl-kä-mē'nō)	172	37°34'N	6°44'W
Vammala, Fin.	167	61°19'N	22°51'E
Van, Tur. (vän)	198	38°04'N	43°10'E
Van Buren, Ar., U.S. (văn bū'rĕn)	121	35°26'N	94°20'W
Van Buren, Me., U.S.	100	47°09'N	67°58'W
Vanceburg, Ky., U.S. (văns'bûrg)	108	38°35'N	83°20'W
Vancouver, Can. (văn-kōō'vĕr)	90	49°16'N	123°06'W
Vancouver, Wa., U.S.	104	45°37'N	122°40'W
Vancouver Island, i., Can.	92	49°50'N	125°05'W
Vancouver Island Ranges, mts., Can.	94	49°25'N	125°25'W
Vandalia, Il., U.S. (văn-dā'lĭ-á)	108	39°00'N	89°00'W
Vandalia, Mo., U.S.	121	39°19'N	91°30'W
Vanderbijlpark, S. Afr.	238c	26°43'S	27°50'E
Vanderhoof, Can.	90	54°01'N	124°01'W
Van Diemen, Cape, c., Austl. (văndē'mĕn)	220	11°05'S	130°15'E
Van Diemen Gulf, b., Austl.	220	11°50'S	131°30'E
Vanegas, Mex. (vä-nĕ'gäs)	128	23°54'N	100°54'W
Vänern, l., Swe.	156	58°52'N	13°17'E
Vänersborg, Swe. (vĕ'nĕrs-bôr')	160	58°24'N	12°15'E
Vanga, Kenya (väŋ'gä)	233	4°38'S	39°10'E
Vangani, India	203b	19°07'N	73°15'E
Van Gölü, l., Tur.	180	38°33'N	42°46'E
Van Horn, Tx., U.S.	122	31°03'N	104°50'W
Vanier, Can.	102c	45°27'N	75°39'W
Van Lear, Ky., U.S. (văn lēr')	108	37°45'N	82°50'W
Vannes, Fr. (vån)	161	47°42'N	2°46'W
Van Nuys, Ca., U.S. (văn nīz')	117a	34°11'N	118°27'W
Van Rees, Pegunungan, mts., Indon.	213	2°30'S	138°45'E
Vantaan, r., Fin.	167	60°25'N	24°43'E
Vanua Levu, i., Fiji	214g	16°33'S	179°15'E
Vanuatu, nation, Oc.	219	16°02'S	169°15'E
Van Wert, Oh., U.S. (văn wûrt')	108	40°50'N	84°35'W
Vara, Swe. (vä'rä)	166	58°17'N	12°55'E
Varaklāni, Lat.	167	56°38'N	26°46'E
Varallo, Italy (vä-räl'lô)	174	45°44'N	8°14'E
Vārānasi (Benares), India	199	25°25'N	83°00'E
Varangerfjorden, b., Nor.	157	70°05'N	30°20'E
Varano, Lago di, l., Italy (lä'gō-dē-vä-rä'nô)	174	41°52'N	15°55'E
Varaždin, Cro. (vä'räzh'dēn)	163	46°17'N	16°20'E
Varazze, Italy (vä-rät'sā)	174	44°23'N	8°34'E
Varberg, Swe. (vär'bĕrg)	166	57°06'N	12°16'E
Vardar, r., Yugo. (vär'där)	175	41°40'N	21°50'E
Varėna, Lith. (vä-rä'ná)	167	54°16'N	24°35'E
Varennes, Can. (vá-rĕn')	102a	45°41'N	73°27'W
Vareš, Bos. (vä'rĕsh)	175	44°10'N	18°20'E
Varese, Italy (vä-rā'så)	174	45°45'N	8°49'E
Varginha, Braz. (vär-zhē'n-yä)	143	21°33'S	45°25'W
Varkaus, Fin. (vär'kous)	167	62°19'N	27°51'E
Varlamovo, Russia (vár-lá'mô-vô)	186a	54°37'N	60°41'E
Varna, Blg. (vär'ná)	154	43°14'N	27°58'E
Varna, Russia	186a	53°22'N	60°59'E
Värnamo, Swe. (vĕr'ná-mô)	166	57°11'N	13°45'E
Varnsdorf, Czech Rep. (värns'dôrf)	168	50°54'N	14°36'E
Varnville, S.C., U.S. (värn'vĭl)	125	32°49'N	81°05'W
Vasa, India	203b	19°20'N	72°47'E
Vascongadas *see* Basque Provinces, hist. reg., Spain	172	43°00'N	2°46'W
Vashka, r., Russia	180	64°00'N	48°00'E
Vashon, Wa., U.S. (văsh'ŭn)	116a	47°27'N	122°28'W
Vashon Heights, Wa., U.S. (hītz)	116a	47°30'N	122°28'W
Vashon Island, i., Wa., U.S.	116a	47°27'N	122°27'W
Vaslui, Rom. (vás-lōō'ē)	169	46°39'N	27°49'E
Vassar, Mi., U.S. (văs'ẽr)	108	43°25'N	83°35'W
Vassouras, Braz. (väs-sō'räzh)	141a	22°25'S	43°40'W
Västerås, Swe. (vĕs'tĕr-ôs)	160	59°39'N	16°30'E
Västerdalälven, r., Swe.	160	61°06'N	13°10'E
Västervik, Swe. (vĕs'tĕr-vēk)	160	57°45'N	16°35'E
Vasto, Italy (väs'tô)	162	42°06'N	12°42'E
Vasyl'kiv, Ukr.	181	50°10'N	30°22'E
Vasyugan, r., Russia (vás-yōō-gán')	184	58°52'N	77°30'E
Vatican City, nation, Eur.	174	41°54'N	12°22'E
Vaticano, Cape, c., Italy (vä-tê-kä'nô)	174	38°38'N	15°52'E
Vatnajökull, ice, Ice. (vät'ná-yû-kôl)	160	64°34'N	16°41'W
Vatomandry, Madag.	233	18°53'S	48°13'E
Vatra Dornei, Rom. (vát'rá dôr'nā')	169	47°22'N	25°20'E
Vättern, l., Swe.	156	58°15'N	14°24'E
Vattholma, Swe.	166	60°01'N	17°40'E
Vaudreuil, Can. (vô-drû'y')	102a	45°24'N	74°02'W
Vaugh, Wa., U.S. (vôn)	116a	47°21'N	122°47'W
Vaughan, Can.	102d	43°47'N	79°36'W
Vaughn, N.M., U.S.	120	34°37'N	105°13'W
Vaupés, r., S.A. (vá'ōō-pĕ's)	142	1°18'N	71°14'W
Vawkavysk, Bela. (vôl-kô-vêsk')	169	53°11'N	24°29'E
Vaxholm, Swe. (väks'hôlm)	166	59°26'N	18°19'E
Växjo, Swe. (vĕks'shû)	160	56°53'N	14°46'E
Vaygach, i., Russia (vī-gách')	178	70°00'N	59°00'E
Veadeiros, Chapadas dos, hills, Braz. (shä-pä'däs-dôs-vĕ-á-dā'rōs)	143	14°00'S	47°00'W
Vedea, r., Rom. (vĕ'dyá)	175	44°25'N	24°45'E
Vedia, Arg. (vĕ'dyä)	141c	34°29'S	61°30'W
Veedersburg, In., U.S. (vē'dẽrz-bûrg)	108	40°05'N	87°15'W
Vega, i., Nor.	160	65°38'N	10°51'E
Vega de Alatorre, Mex. (vā'gä dā ä-lä-tōr'rå)	131	20°02'N	96°39'W
Vega Real, reg., Dom. Rep. (vĕ'gä-rĕ-ä'l)	135	19°30'N	71°05'W
Vegreville, Can.	90	53°30'N	112°03'W
Vehār Lake, l., India	203b	19°11'N	72°52'E
Veinticinco de Mayo, Arg.	141c	35°26'S	60°09'W
Vejer de la Frontera, Spain	172	36°15'N	5°58'W
Vejle, Den. (vī'lĕ)	160	55°41'N	9°29'E
Velbert, Ger. (fĕl'bĕrt)	171c	51°20'N	7°03'E
Velebit, mts., Yugo. (vā'lĕ-bēt)	163	44°25'N	15°23'E
Velen, Ger. (fĕ'lĕn)	171c	51°54'N	7°00'E
Vélez-Málaga, Spain (vā'lāth-mä'lä-gä)	172	36°48'N	4°05'W
Vélez-Rubio, Spain (rōō'bē-ô)	172	37°38'N	2°05'W
Velika Kapela, mts., Yugo. (vĕ'lē-kä kä-pĕ'lä)	163	45°03'N	15°20'E
Velika Morava, r., Yugo. (mô'rä-vä)	163	44°00'N	21°30'E
Velikaya, r., Russia (vå-lē'ká-yá)	176	57°25'N	28°07'E
Velikiye Luki, Russia (vyē-lē'-kyē lōō'ke)	178	56°19'N	30°32'E
Velikiy Ustyug, Russia (vå-lē'kĭ ōōs-tyòg')	178	60°45'N	46°38'E
Veliko Tŭrnovo, Blg.	163	43°06'N	25°38'E
Velikoye, Russia (vå-lē'kô-yĕ)	176	57°21'N	39°45'E
Velikoye, l., Russia	176	57°00'N	36°53'E
Veli Lošinj, Cro. (lō'shēn')	174	44°30'N	14°29'E
Velizh, Russia (vå'lēzh)	180	55°37'N	31°11'E
Vella Lavella, i., Sol. Is.	221	8°00'S	156°42'E
Velletri, Italy (vĕl-lā'trē)	174	41°42'N	12°48'E
Vellore, India (vĕl-lōr')	199	12°57'N	79°09'E
Vels, Russia (vĕls)	186a	60°35'N	58°47'E
Vel'sk, Russia (vĕlsk)	178	61°00'N	42°18'E
Velten, Ger. (fel'tĕn)	159b	52°41'N	13°11'E
Velya, r., Russia (vĕl'yá)	186b	56°23'N	37°54'E
Velyka Lepetykha, Ukr.	177	47°11'N	33°58'E
Velykyi Bychkiv, Ukr.	169	47°59'N	24°01'E
Venadillo, Col. (vĕ-nä-dē'l-yō)	142a	4°43'N	74°55'W
Venado, Mex. (vå-mä'dō)	130	22°54'N	101°07'W
Venado Tuerto, Arg. (vĕ-nä'dô-tōōĕ'r-tô)	144	33°28'S	61°47'W
Vendôme, Fr. (väN-dōm')	170	47°46'N	1°05'E
Veneto, hist. reg., Italy (vĕ-nĕ'tô)	174	45°58'N	11°24'E
Venëv, Russia (vĕn-ĕf')	180	54°19'N	38°14'E
Venezia *see* Venice, Italy	154	45°25'N	12°18'E
Venezuela, nation, S.A. (vĕn-ĕ-zwē'lá)	142	8°00'N	65°00'W
Venezuela, Golfo de, b., S.A. (gôl-fô-dĕ)	142	11°34'N	71°02'W
Veniaminof, Mount, mtn., Ak., U.S.	103	56°12'N	159°20'W
Venice, Italy	154	45°25'N	12°18'E
Venice, Ca., U.S. (vĕn'ĭs)	117a	33°59'N	118°28'W
Venice, Il., U.S.	117e	38°40'N	90°10'W
Venice, Gulf of, b., Italy	162	45°23'N	13°00'E
Venlo, Neth.	171c	51°22'N	6°11'E
Venta, r., Eur. (vĕn'tá)	167	57°05'N	21°45'E
Ventana, Sierra de la, mts., Arg. (sē-ĕ-rá-dĕ-lä-vĕn-tá'nä)	144	38°00'S	63°00'W
Ventersburg, S. Afr. (vĕn-tĕrs'bûrg)	238c	28°06'S	27°10'E
Ventersdorp, S. Afr. (vĕn-tĕrs'dôrp)	238c	26°20'S	26°48'E
Ventimiglia, Italy (vĕn-tê-mēl'yä)	174	43°46'N	7°37'E
Ventnor, N.J., U.S. (vĕnt'nẽr)	109	39°20'N	74°25'W
Ventspils, Lat. (vĕnt'spêls)	180	57°24'N	21°41'E
Ventuari, r., Ven. (vĕn-tōōá'rē)	142	4°47'N	65°56'W
Ventura, Ca., U.S. (vĕn-tōō'rá)	118	34°18'N	119°18'W
Venukovsky, Russia (vĕ-nōō'kôv-skĭ)	186b	55°10'N	37°26'E
Venustiano Carranza, Mex. (vĕ-nōōs-tyä'nō-kär-rä'n-zä)	130	19°44'N	103°48'W
Venustiano Carranzo, Mex. (kär-rä'n-zô)	131	16°21'N	92°36'W
Vera, Arg. (vĕ-rä)	144	29°22'S	60°09'W
Vera, Spain (vā'rä)	172	37°18'N	1°53'W
Veracruz, Mex.	128	19°13'N	96°07'W
Vera Cruz, state, Mex. (vā-rä-krōōz')	128	20°30'N	97°15'W
Verāval, India (vĕr'vŭ-väl)	199	20°59'N	70°49'E
Vercelli, Italy (vĕr-chĕl'lē)	174	45°18'N	8°27'E
Verchères, Can. (vĕr-shâr')	102a	45°46'N	73°21'W
Verde, i., Phil. (vĕr'då)	213a	13°34'N	121°11'E
Verde, r., Mex.	130	21°48'N	99°50'W
Verde, r., Mex.	130	20°50'N	103°00'W
Verde, r., Mex.	131	16°05'N	97°44'W
Verde, r., Az., U.S. (vûrd)	119	34°04'N	111°40'W
Verde, Cap, c., Bah.	135	22°50'N	75°00'W
Verde, Cay, i., Bah.	135	22°00'N	75°05'W
Verde Island Passage, strt., Phil. (vĕr'dē)	213a	13°36'N	120°39'E
Verdemont, Ca., U.S. (vûr'dē-mŏnt)	117a	34°12'N	117°22'W
Verden, Ger. (fĕr'dĕn)	168	52°55'N	9°15'E
Verdigris, r., Ok., U.S. (vûr'dē-grēs)	121	36°50'N	95°29'W
Verdun, Can. (vĕr'dŭn')	99	45°27'N	73°34'W
Verdun, Fr. (vâr-dûN')	161	49°09'N	5°21'E
Verdun, Fr.	171	43°48'N	1°10'E
Vereeniging, S. Afr. (vĕ-rä'nĭ-gĭng)	238c	26°40'S	27°56'E
Verena, S. Afr. (vĕr-ĕn á)	238c	25°30'S	29°02'E
Vereya, Russia (vĕ-rā'yá)	176	55°21'N	36°08'E
Verín, Spain (vå-rēn')	172	41°56'N	7°26'W
Verkhne-Kamchatsk, Russia (vyĕrk'nyĕ kám-chatsk')	179	54°42'N	158°41'E
Verkhne Neyvinskiy, Russia (nā-vĭn'skĭ)	186a	57°17'N	60°10'E
Verkhne Ural'sk, Russia (ò-ralsk')	178	53°53'N	59°13'E
Verkhniy Avzyan, Russia (vyĕrk'nyē áv-zyán')	186a	53°32'N	57°30'E
Verkhniye Kigi, Russia (vyĕrk'nĭ-yĕ kĭ'gĭ)	186a	55°23'N	58°37'E
Verkhniy Ufaley, Russia (ò-fá'lā)	186a	56°04'N	60°15'E
Verkhnyaya Pyshma, Russia (vyĕrk'nyä-yä pōōsh'má)	186a	56°57'N	60°37'E
Verkhnyaya Salda, Russia (säl'dá)	186a	58°03'N	60°33'E
Verkhnyaya Tunguska (Angara), r., Russia (tòn-gōs'ká)	184	58°13'N	97°00'E
Verkhnyaya Tura, Russia (tò'rá)	186a	58°22'N	59°51'E
Verkhnyaya Yayva, Russia (yäy'vá)	186a	59°28'N	57°38'E
Verkhotur'ye, Russia (vyĕr-kô-tōōr'yĕ)	186a	58°52'N	60°47'E
Verkhoyansk, Russia (vyĕr-kô-yänsk')	179	67°43'N	133°33'E
Verkhoyanskiy Khrebet, mts., Russia (vyĕr-kô-yänskĭ)	179	67°45'N	128°00'E
Vermilion, Can. (vẽr-mĭl'yŭn)	90	53°22'N	110°51'W
Vermilion, l., Mn., U.S.	113	47°49'N	92°35'W
Vermilion, r., Can.	99	47°30'N	73°15'W
Vermilion, r., Can.	96	53°30'N	111°00'W
Vermilion, r., Il., U.S.	108	41°05'N	89°00'W
Vermilion, r., Mn., U.S.	113	48°09'N	92°31'W
Vermilion Hills, hills, Can.	96	50°43'N	106°50'W
Vermilion Range, mts., Mn., U.S.	113	47°55'N	91°59'W
Vermillion, S.D., U.S.	112	42°46'N	96°56'W
Vermillion, r., S.D., U.S.	112	43°54'N	97°14'W
Vermillion Bay, b., La., U.S.	123	29°47'N	92°00'W
Vermont, state, U.S. (vẽr-mŏnt')	105	43°50'N	72°50'W
Vernal, Ut., U.S. (vûr'năl)	115	40°29'N	109°40'W
Verneuk Pan, pl., S. Afr. (vĕr-nŭk')	232	30°10'S	21°46'E
Vernon, Can. (vĕr-nôN')	90	50°18'N	119°15'W
Vernon, Can.	102c	45°10'N	75°27'W
Vernon, Ca., U.S. (vûr'nŭn)	117a	34°01'N	118°12'W

ăt; finăl; rāte; senåte; ärm; àsk; sofá; fâre; ch-choose; dh-as th in other; bē; ēvent; bĕt; recĕnt; cratẽr; g-gō; gh-guttural g; bĭt; ĭ-short neutral; rīde; ĸ-guttural k as ch in German ich;

PLACE (Pronunciation)	PAGE	LAT.	LONG.
Vernon, In., U.S. (vûr′nŭn)	108	39°00′N	85°40′W
Vernon, N.J., U.S.	110a	39°00′N	85°40′W
Vernon, Tx., U.S.	120	34°09′N	99°16′W
Vernonia, Or., U.S. (vûr-nō′nyȧ)	116c	45°52′N	123°12′W
Vero Beach, Fl., U.S. (vē′rō̇)	125a	27°36′N	80°25′W
Véroia, Grc.	175	40°30′N	22°13′E
Verona, Italy (vā-rō′nä)	162	45°28′N	11°02′E
Versailles, Fr. (vĕr-sī′y′)	161	48°48′N	2°07′E
Versailles, Ky., U.S. (vēr-sālz′)	108	38°05′N	84°45′W
Versailles, Mo., U.S.	121	38°27′N	92°52′W
Vert, Cap, c., Sen.	230	14°43′N	17°30′W
Verulam, S. Afr. (vĕ-ro͞o-lăm)	233c	29°39′S	31°08′E
Verviers, Bel. (vĕr-vyā′)	165	50°35′N	5°57′E
Vesele, Ukr.	177	46°59′N	34°56′E
Vesijärvi, l., Fin.	167	61°09′N	25°10′E
Vesoul, Fr. (vē-so͞ol′)	171	47°38′N	6°11′E
Vestavia Hills, Al., U.S.	110h	33°26′N	86°46′W
Vesterålen, is., Nor. (vĕs′tẽr ô′lĕn)	160	68°54′N	14°03′E
Vestfjord, b., Nor.	156	67°33′N	12°59′E
Vestmannaeyjar, Ice. (vĕst′män-ä-ā′yär)	160	63°12′N	20°17′W
Vesuvio, vol., Italy (vĕ-so͞o′vyä)	156	40°35′N	14°26′E
Ves′yegonsk, Russia (vĕ-syĕ-gônsk′)	176	58°42′N	37°09′E
Veszprem, Hung. (vĕs′prām)	169	47°05′N	17°53′E
Vészto, Hung. (vĕs′tû)	169	46°55′N	21°18′E
Vet, r., S. Afr. (vĕt)	238c	28°25′S	26°37′E
Vetlanda, Swe. (vĕt-län′dä)	166	57°26′N	15°05′E
Vetluga, Russia (vyĕt-lo͞o′gȧ)	180	57°50′N	45°42′E
Vetluga, r., Russia	180	56°50′N	45°50′E
Vetovo, Blg. (vā′tô-vô)	175	43°42′N	26°18′E
Vetren, Blg. (vĕt′rĕn′)	175	42°16′N	24°04′E
Vevay, In., U.S. (vē′vā)	108	38°45′N	85°05′W
Veynes, Fr. (vān′′)	171	44°31′N	5°47′E
Vézère, r., Fr. (vā-zer′)	170	45°01′N	1°00′E
Viacha, Bol. (vēȧ′chȧ)	142	16°43′S	68°16′W
Viadana, Italy (vē̇-ä-dä′nä)	174	44°55′N	10°30′E
Vian, Ok., U.S. (vī′ăn)	121	35°30′N	95°00′W
Viana, Braz. (vē-ä′nä)	143	3°09′S	44°44′W
Viana do Alentejo, Port. (vē̇-ä′nȧ dȯ ä-lĕɴ-tā′hȯ)	172	38°20′N	8°02′W
Viana do Bolo, Spain	172	42°10′N	7°07′W
Viana do Castelo, Port. (dȯ käs-tā′lȯ)	162	41°41′N	8°45′W
Viangchan, Laos	212	18°07′N	102°33′E
Viar, r., Spain (vē̇-ä′rä)	172	38°15′N	6°08′W
Viareggio, Italy (vē̇-ä-rĕd′jô)	174	43°52′N	10°14′E
Viborg, Den. (vē′bôr)	166	56°27′N	9°22′E
Vibo Valentia, Italy (vē̇′bô-vä-lĕ′n-tyä)	174	38°47′N	16°06′E
Vic, Spain	173	41°55′N	2°14′E
Vicálvaro, Spain	173a	40°25′N	3°37′W
Vicente López, Arg. (vē-sĕ′n-tĕ-lŏ′pĕz)	144a	34°31′S	58°29′W
Vicenza, Italy (vē̇-chĕnt′sä)	162	45°33′N	11°33′E
Vichuga, Russia (vē-cho͞o′gȧ)	180	57°13′N	41°58′E
Vichy, Fr. (vē̇-shē′)	161	46°06′N	3°28′E
Vickersund, Nor.	166	60°00′N	9°59′E
Vicksburg, Mi., U.S. (vĭks′bûrg)	108	42°10′N	85°30′W
Vicksburg, Ms., U.S.	105	32°20′N	90°50′W
Viçosa, Braz. (vē-sô′sä)	141a	20°46′S	42°51′W
Victoria, Arg. (vēk-tô′rē̇ä)	144	32°36′S	60°09′W
Victoria, Can. (vĭk-tō′rĭ-ȧ)	90	48°26′N	123°23′W
Victoria, Chile (vēk-tô-rē̇ä)	144	38°15′S	72°16′W
Victoria, Col. (vēk-tô′rē̇ä)	142a	5°19′N	74°54′W
Victoria, Phil. (vē̇k-tô-ryä)	213a	15°34′N	120°41′E
Victoria, Tx., U.S. (vĭk-tō′rĭ-ȧ)	123	28°48′N	97°00′W
Victoria, Va., U.S.	125	36°57′N	78°13′W
Victoria, state, Austl.	219	36°46′S	143°15′E
Victoria, l., Afr.	232	0°50′S	32°50′E
Victoria, r., Austl.	220	17°25′S	130°50′E
Victoria, Mount, mtn., Mya.	199	21°26′N	93°59′E
Victoria, Mount, mtn., Pap. N. Gui.	213	9°35′S	147°45′E
Victoria de las Tunas, Cuba (vē̇k-tō′rē̇-ä dā läs to͞o′näs)	134	20°55′N	77°05′W
Victoria Falls, wtfl., Afr.	232	17°55′S	25°51′E
Victoria Island, i., Can.	89	70°13′N	107°45′W
Victoria Lake, l., Can.	101	48°20′N	57°40′W
Victoria Land, reg., Ant.	224	75°00′S	160°00′E
Victoria Nile, r., Ug.	237	2°20′N	31°35′E
Victoria Peak, mtn., Belize (vē̇k-tōrĭ′ȧ)	132a	16°47′N	88°40′W
Victoria Peak, mtn., Can.	94	50°03′N	126°06′W
Victoria River Downs, Austl. (vĭc-tô̇r′ĭȧ)	218	16°30′S	131°10′E
Victoria Strait, strt., Can. (vĭk-tō′rĭ-ȧ)	92	69°10′N	100°58′W
Victoriaville, Can. (vĭk-tō′rĭ-ȧ-vĭl)	91	46°04′N	71°59′W
Victoria West, S. Afr. (wĕst)	232	31°25′S	23°10′E
Vidalia, Ga., U.S. (vĭ-dā′lĭ-ȧ)	125	32°10′N	82°26′W
Vidalia, La., U.S.	123	31°33′N	91°28′W
Vidin, Blg. (vĭ′dē̇n)	163	44°00′N	22°53′E
Vidnoye, Russia	186b	55°33′N	37°41′E
Vidzy, Bela. (vē̇′dzĭ)	176	55°23′N	26°46′E
Viedma, Arg. (vyād′mä)	144	40°55′S	63°03′W
Viedma, l., Arg.	144	49°40′S	72°35′W
Viejo, r., Nic. (vyā′hō)	132	12°45′N	86°19′W
Vienna (Wien), Aus.	154	48°13′N	16°22′E
Vienna, Ga., U.S. (vē̇-ĕn′ȧ)	124	32°03′N	83°50′W
Vienna, Il., U.S.	121	37°24′N	88°50′W
Vienna, Va., U.S.	110e	38°54′N	77°16′W
Vienne, Fr. (vyĕn′)	161	45°31′N	4°54′E
Vienne, r., Fr.	170	47°06′N	0°20′E
Vientiane *see* Viangchan, Laos	212	18°07′N	102°33′E
Vieques, P.R. (vyā′kås)	129b	18°09′N	65°27′W
Vieques, i., P.R. (vyā′kås)	129b	18°05′N	65°28′W
Vierfontein, S. Afr. (vēr′fôn-tān)	238c	27°06′S	26°45′E
Viersen, Ger. (fēr′zĕn)	171c	51°15′N	6°24′E
Vierwaldstätter See, l., Switz.	168	46°54′N	8°36′E
Vierzon, Fr. (vyâr-zôɴ′)	161	47°14′N	2°04′E
Viesca, Mex. (vē̇-ās′kä)	122	25°21′N	102°47′W
Viesca, Laguna de, l., Mex. (lä-ȯ′nä-dĕ)	122	25°30′N	102°40′W
Vieste, Italy (vyĕs′tå)	174	41°52′N	16°10′E
Vietnam, nation, Asia (vyĕt′näm′)	212	18°00′N	107°00′E
Vigan, Phil. (vēgän)	212	17°36′N	120°22′E
Vigevano, Italy (vē̇-jå-vä′nô)	174	45°18′N	8°52′E
Vigny, Fr. (vē̇n-y′ē′)	171b	49°05′N	1°54′E
Vigo, Spain (vē′gō)	154	42°18′N	8°42′W
Vihti, Fin. (vē′tĭ)	167	60°27′N	24°18′E
Vijayawāda, India	199	16°31′N	80°37′E
Viksøyri, Nor.	166	61°06′N	6°35′E
Vila Caldas Xavier, Moz.	237	15°59′S	34°12′E
Vila de Manica, Moz. (vē′lä dā mä-nē′kȧ)	232	18°48′S	32°49′E
Vila de Rei, Port. (vē′lȧ dā rā′ĭ)	172	39°42′N	8°03′W
Vila do Conde, Port. (vē′lȧ dȯ kôn′dĕ)	172	41°21′N	8°44′W
Vilafranca del Penedès, Spain	173	41°20′N	1°40′E
Vilafranca de Xira, Port. (fräŋ′kȧ dā shē′rȧ)	172	38°58′N	8°59′W
Vilaine, r., Fr. (vē-lȧn′)	170	47°34′N	2°15′W
Vilalba, Spain	172	43°18′N	7°43′W
Vilanculos, Moz. (vē̇-län-ko͞o′lô̇s)	232	22°03′S	35°13′E
Vilāni, Lat. (vē′lȧ-nĭ)	167	56°31′N	27°00′E
Vila Nova de Foz Côa, Port. (nō′vȧ dā fôz-kō′ȧ)	172	41°08′N	7°11′W
Vila Nova de Gaia, Port. (vē′lȧ nō′vȧ dā gä′yä)	172	41°08′N	8°40′W
Vila Nova de Milfontes, Port. (nō′vȧ dā mē̇l-fôn′tāzh)	172	37°44′N	8°48′W
Vila Real, Port. (rā-äl′)	162	41°18′N	7°48′W
Vila-real, Spain	173	39°55′N	0°07′W
Vila Real de Santo Antonio, Port.	172	37°14′N	7°25′W
Vila Viçosa, Port. (vē̇-sō′zȧ)	172	38°47′N	7°24′W
Vileyka, Bela. (vē̇-lā′ē̇-kȧ)	176	54°19′N	26°58′E
Vilhelmina, Swe.	160	64°37′N	16°30′E
Viljandi, Est. (vēl′yän-dē̇)	180	58°24′N	25°34′E
Viljoenskroon, S. Afr.	238c	27°13′S	26°58′E
Vilkaviškis, Lith. (vē̇l-kȧ-vēsh′kē̇s)	167	54°40′N	23°08′E
Vil′kitskogo, i., Russia (vyl-kēts-kōgō)	184	73°25′N	76°00′E
Villa Acuña, Mex. (vē̇l′yä-ko͞o′n-yä)	122	29°20′N	100°56′W
Villa Ahumada, Mex. (ä-o͞o-mä′dä)	122	30°43′N	106°30′W
Villa Alta, Mex. (äl′tä)(sän ēl-då-fōn′sō)	131	17°20′N	96°08′W
Villa Angela, Arg. (vē̇′l-yä ȧ′n-ĸĕ-lä)	144	27°31′S	60°42′W
Villa Ballester, Arg. (vē̇′l-yä-bȧl-yĕs-tĕr)	144a	34°33′S	58°33′W
Villa Bella, Bol. (bĕ′l-yä)	142	10°25′S	65°22′W
Villablino, Spain (vē̇l-yä-blē′nō̇)	172	42°58′N	6°18′W
Villacañas, Spain (vē̇l-yä-kän′yäs)	172	39°39′N	3°20′W
Villacarrillo, Spain (vē̇l-yä-kä-rēl′yō̇)	172	38°09′N	3°07′W
Villach, Aus. (fē̇′läĸ)	161	46°38′N	13°50′E
Villacidro, Italy (vē-lä-chē′drō̇)	174	39°28′N	8°41′E
Villa Clara, prov., Cuba	134	22°40′N	80°10′W
Villa Constitución, Arg. (kōn-stē̇-to͞o-syōn′)	141c	33°15′S	60°19′W
Villa Coronado, Mex. (kō-rō-nä′dhō̇)	122	26°45′N	105°10′W
Villa Cuauhtémoc, Mex. (vē̇l′yä-ko͞o-äȯ-tĕ′mō̇k)	131	22°11′N	97°50′W
Villa de Allende, Mex. (vēl′yä′dā äl-yĕn′då)	122	25°18′N	100°01′W
Villa de Alvarez, Mex. (vē̇l′yä-dĕ-ä′l-vä-rĕz)	130	19°17′N	103°44′W
Villa de Cura, Ven. (dĕ-ko͞o′rä)	143b	10°03′N	67°29′W
Villa de Guadalupe, Mex. (dĕ-gwä-dhä-lo͞o′på)	130	23°22′N	100°44′W
Villa de Mayo, Arg.	144a	34°31′S	58°41′W
Villa Dolores, Arg. (vēl′yä dō̇-lō′rās)	144	31°50′S	65°05′W
Villa Escalante, Mex. (vē̇l′yä-ĕs-kä-lȧn′tĕ)	130	19°24′N	101°36′W
Villa Flores, Mex. (vē̇l′yä-flō′rās)	131	16°13′N	93°17′W
Villafranca, Italy (vēl-lä-fräŋ′kä)	174	45°22′N	10°53′E
Villafranca del Bierzo, Spain	172	42°37′N	6°49′W
Villafranca de los Barros, Spain	172	38°34′N	6°22′W
Villafranche-de-Rouergue, Fr. (dē-ro͞o-ĕrg′)	170	44°21′N	2°02′E
Villa García, Mex. (gär-sē′ä)	130	22°07′N	101°55′W
Villagarcía, Spain	172	42°38′N	8°43′W
Villagrán, Mex.	122	24°28′N	99°30′W
Villa Grove, Il., U.S. (vĭl′ȧ grōv′)	108	39°55′N	88°15′W
Villaguay, Arg. (vē̇′l-yä-gwī)	144	31°47′S	58°53′W
Villa Hayes, Para. (vēl′yä äyås)(hāz)	144	25°07′S	57°31′W
Villahermosa, Mex. (vēl′yä-ĕr-mō′sä)	128	17°59′N	92°56′W
Villa Hidalgo, Mex. (vēl′yäē-däl′gō)	130	21°39′N	102°41′W
Villaldama, Mex. (vēl-yäl-dä′mä)	128	26°30′N	100°26′W
Villa Lopez, Mex. (vēl′yä lō′pĕz)	122	27°00′N	105°02′W
Villalpando, Spain (vēl-yäl-pän′dō)	172	41°54′N	5°24′W
Villa María, Arg. (vē̇′l-yä-mä-rē′ä)	144	32°17′S	63°08′W
Villamatín, Spain (vēl-yä-mä-tē̇′n)	172	36°50′N	5°38′W
Villa Mercedes, Arg. (mĕr-sā′dås)	144	33°38′S	65°16′W
Villa Montes, Bol. (vē̇′l-yä-mô′n-tĕs)	142	21°13′S	63°26′W
Villa Morelos, Mex. (mō̇-rĕ′lomcs)	130	20°01′N	101°24′W
Villanueva, Col. (vē̇′l-yä-nȯĕ′vä)	142	10°44′N	73°08′W
Villanueva, Hond. (vēl′yä-nwā′vä)	132	15°19′N	88°02′W
Villanueva, Mex. (vē̇l′yä-nȯĕ′vä)	130	22°25′N	102°53′W
Villanueva de Córdoba, Spain (vē̇l-yä-nwĕ′vä-dā kô̇r′dō̇-bä)	172	38°18′N	4°38′W
Villanueva de la Serena, Spain (lä sā-rā′nä)	172	38°59′N	5°56′W
Villa Obregón, Mex. (vē′l-yä-ô-brĕ-gô′n)	131a	19°21′N	99°11′W
Villa Ocampo, Mex. (ô̇-käm′pō)	122	26°26′N	105°30′W
Villa Pedro Montoya, Mex. (vē̇l′yä-pĕ′drō̇-mō̇n-tô′yȧ)	130	21°38′N	99°51′W
Villard-Bonnot, Fr. (vēl-yär′bô̇n-nō̇′)	171	45°15′N	5°53′E
Villarrica, Para. (vēl-yä-rē′kä)	144	25°55′S	56°23′W
Villarrobledo, Spain (vēl-yär-rō̇-blā′dhō)	162	39°15′N	2°37′W
Villa Unión, Mex. (vē̇l′yä-o͞o-nyōn′)	130	23°10′N	106°14′W
Villavicencio, Col. (vē̇′l-yä-vē-sĕ′n-syō)	142	4°09′N	73°38′W
Villaviciosa de Odón, Spain	173a	40°22′N	3°38′W
Villavieja, Col. (vē̇′l-yä-vē-ĕ′ĸȧ)	142a	3°13′N	75°13′W
Villazón, Bol. (vē̇′l-yä-zô′n)	142	22°02′S	65°42′W
Villefranche, Fr.	161	45°59′N	4°43′E
Villejuif, Fr. (vēl′zhüst′)	171b	48°48′N	2°22′E
Ville-Maríe, Can.	91	47°18′N	79°22′W
Villena, Spain (vē-lyā′nȧ)	162	38°37′N	0°52′W
Villeneuve, Can. (vēl′nûv′)	102g	53°40′N	113°49′W
Villeneuve-Saint Georges, Fr. (săɴ-zhôrzh′)	171b	48°43′N	2°27′E
Villeneuve-sur-Lot, Fr. (sür-lō′)	170	44°25′N	0°41′E
Ville Platte, La., U.S. (vēl plȧt′)	123	30°41′N	92°17′W
Villers Cotterêts, Fr. (vē-ār′kō̇-trā′)	171b	49°15′N	3°05′E
Villerupt, Fr. (vēl′rüp′)	171	49°28′N	6°16′E
Ville-Saint Georges, Can. (vĭl-sĕɴ-zhôrzh′)	99	46°07′N	70°40′W
Villeta, Col. (vē′l-yĕ′tȧ)	142a	5°02′N	74°29′W
Villeurbanne, Fr. (vēl-ûr-bän′)	161	45°43′N	4°55′E
Villiers, S. Afr. (vĭl′ĭ-ērs)	238c	27°03′S	28°38′E
Villingen-Schwenningen, Ger.	168	48°04′N	8°33′E
Villisca, Ia., U.S. (vĭ′lĭs′kȧ)	113	40°56′N	94°56′W
Villupuram, India	203	11°59′N	79°33′E
Vilnius, Lith. (vĭl′nē̇-ȯs)	178	54°40′N	25°26′E
Vilppula, Fin. (vĭl′pŭ-lȧ)	167	62°01′N	24°24′E
Vil′shanka, Ukr.	177	48°14′N	30°52′E
Vil′shany, Ukr.	177	50°02′N	35°54′E
Vilvoorde, Bel.	159a	50°56′N	4°25′E
Vilyuy, r., Russia (vēl′yĭ)	179	63°00′N	121°00′E
Vilyuysk, Russia (vē̇-lyo͞o′ĭsk′)	179	63°41′N	121°47′E
Vimmerby, Swe. (vĭm′ēr-bü)	166	57°41′N	15°51′E
Vimperk, Czech Rep. (vĭm-pĕrk′)	168	49°04′N	13°41′E
Viña del Mar, Chile (vē′nyä dĕl mär′)	144	33°00′S	71°33′W
Vinalhaven, Me., U.S. (vī-năl-hā′vĕn)	100	44°03′N	68°49′W
Vinaròs, Spain	173	40°29′N	0°27′E
Vincennes, Fr. (văɴ-sĕn′)	171b	48°51′N	2°27′E
Vincennes, In., U.S. (vĭn-zĕnz′)	105	38°40′N	87°30′W
Vincent, Al., U.S. (vĭn′sĕnt)	124	33°21′N	86°25′W
Vindelälven, r., Swe.	160	65°02′N	18°30′E
Vindeln, Swe. (vĭn′dĕln)	160	64°10′N	19°52′E
Vindhya Range, mts., India (vĭnd′yä)	199	22°30′N	75°50′E
Vineland, N.J., U.S. (vīn′lănd)	109	39°30′N	75°00′W
Vinh, Viet. (vē̇n′y′)	212	18°38′N	105°42′E
Vinhais, Port. (vē̇n-yä′ēzh)	172	41°51′N	7°00′W
Vinings, Ga., U.S. (vī′nĭngz)	110c	33°52′N	84°28′W
Vinita, Ok., U.S. (vĭ-nē′tȧ)	121	36°38′N	95°09′W
Vinkovci, Cro. (vēn′kō̇v-tsē̇)	175	45°17′N	18°47′E
Vinnytsia, Ukr.	178	49°13′N	28°31′E
Vinnytsya, prov., Ukr.	177	48°45′N	28°01′E
Vinogradovo, Russia (vĭ-nō̇-grä′do-vô)	186b	55°25′N	38°33′E
Vinson Massif, mtn., Ant.	224	77°40′S	87°00′W
Vinton, Ia., U.S. (vĭn′tŭn)	113	42°08′N	92°01′W
Vinton, La., U.S.	123	30°12′N	93°35′W
Violet, La., U.S. (vī′ō̇-lĕt)	110d	29°54′N	89°54′W
Virac, Phil. (vē̇-räk′)	209	13°38′N	124°20′E
Virbalis, Lith. (vē̇r′bȧ-lē̇s)	167	54°38′N	22°55′E
Virden, Can. (vûr′dĕn)	90	49°51′N	101°55′W
Virden, Il., U.S.	121	39°28′N	89°46′W
Virgin, r., U.S.	119	36°51′N	113°50′W
Virginia, S. Afr.	238c	28°07′S	26°54′E
Virginia, Mn., U.S. (vẽr-jĭn′yȧ)	105	47°32′N	92°36′W
Virginia, state, U.S.	105	37°00′N	80°45′W
Virginia Beach, Va., U.S.	109	36°50′N	75°58′W
Virginia City, Nv., U.S.	118	39°18′N	119°40′W
Virgin Islands, is., N.A. (vûr′jĭn)	129	18°15′N	64°00′W
Viroqua, Wi., U.S. (vĭ-rō′kwȧ)	113	43°33′N	90°54′W
Virovitica, Cro. (vē̇-rō̇-vē′tē̇-tsȧ)	175	45°50′N	17°24′E
Virpazar, Yugo. (vē̇r′pä-zär′)	175	42°16′N	19°06′E
Virrat, Fin. (vĭr′ät)	167	62°15′N	23°45′E
Virserum, Swe. (vĭr′sĕ-rȯm)	166	57°22′N	15°35′E
Vis, Cro. (vē̇s)	174	43°03′N	16°11′E
Vis, i., Yugo.	163	43°00′N	16°10′E
Visalia, Ca., U.S. (vĭ-sā′lĭ-ȧ)	118	36°20′N	119°18′W
Visby, Swe. (vĭs′bü)	154	57°39′N	18°19′E
Viscount Melville Sound, strt., Can.	89	74°00′N	110°00′W
Višegrad, Bos. (vē′shĕ-gräd)	175	43°48′N	19°17′E
Vishākhapatnam, India	199	17°48′N	83°21′E
Vishera, r., Russia (vĭ′shĕ-rȧ)	186a	60°40′N	58°46′E
Vishnyakovo, Russia	186b	55°44′N	38°10′E
Vishoek, S. Afr.	232a	34°13′S	18°26′E
Visim, Russia (vē′sĭm)	186a	57°38′N	59°32′E
Viskan, r., Swe.	166	57°20′N	12°25′E
Viški, Lat. (vēs′kĭ)	167	56°02′N	26°47′E
Visoko, Bos. (vē′sō̇-kō̇)	175	43°59′N	18°10′E
Vistula *see* Wisła, r., Pol.	156	52°30′N	20°00′E
Vitebsk, prov., Bela.	176	55°05′N	29°18′E
Viterbo, Italy (vē̇-tĕr′bō)	162	42°24′N	12°08′E
Viti Levu, i., Fiji	214g	18°00′S	178°00′E
Vitim, Russia (vē′tē̇m)	179	59°22′N	112°43′E
Vitim, r., Russia (vē′tē̇m)	179	54°00′N	115°00′E
Vitino, Russia (vē′tĭ-nō̇)	186c	59°40′N	29°51′E
Vitória, Braz. (vē̇-tō′rē̇-ä)	143	20°09′S	40°17′W
Vitoria, Spain (vē-tô-ryä)	162	42°43′N	2°43′W

ng-sing; ŋ-baŋk; ɴ-nasalized n; nŏd; cŏmmit; ōld; ôbey; ôrder; oi-boil; fo͞od; ȯ-as oo in foot; ou-out; s-soft; sh-dish; th-thin; pūre; ûnite; ûrn; stŭd; circŭs; ü-as in French tu; ′-indeterminate vowel.

364 Vitória de Conquista – Wanzhi

PRONOUNCING INDEX

PLACE (Pronunciation)	PAGE	LAT.	LONG.
Vitória de Conquista, Braz. (vê-tō′rē-ä-dä-kōn-kwē′s-tä)	143	14°51′S	40°44′W
Vitry-le-François, Fr. (vē-trē′lē-fräN-swȧ′)	170	48°44′N	4°34′E
Vitsyebsk, Bela. (vē′tyěpsk)	180	55°12′N	30°16′E
Vittorio, Italy (vē-tô′rē-ô)	174	45°59′N	12°17′E
Viveiro, Spain	172	43°39′N	7°37′W
Vivian, La., U.S. (vĭv′ĭ-ȧn)	123	32°51′N	93°59′W
Vizianagaram, India	199	18°10′N	83°29′E
Vlaardingen, Neth. (vlär′dĭng-ěn)	165	51°54′N	4°20′E
Vladikavkaz, Russia	181	43°05′N	44°35′E
Vladimir, Russia (vlȧ-dyē′mēr)	178	56°08′N	40°24′E
Vladimir, prov., Russia (vlä-dyē′mēr)	176	56°08′N	39°53′E
Vladimiro-Aleksandrovskoye, Russia	210	42°50′N	133°00′E
Vladivostok, Russia (vlȧ-dē-vôs-tôk′)	179	43°06′N	131°47′E
Vlasenica, Bos. (vlä′sě-nět′sȧ)	175	44°11′N	18°58′E
Vlasotince, Yugo. (vlä′sô-tēn-tsě)	175	42°58′N	22°08′E
Vlieland, i., Neth. (vlē′länt)	165	53°19′N	4°55′E
Vlissingen, Neth. (vlĭs′sĭng-ěn)	165	51°30′N	3°34′E
Vlorë, Alb.	163	40°27′N	19°30′E
Vltava, r., Czech Rep.	168	49°24′N	14°18′E
Vodl, l., Russia (vôd′′l)	180	62°20′N	37°20′E
Voerde, Ger.	171c	51°35′N	6°41′E
Voghera, Italy (vô-gā′rä)	174	44°58′N	9°02′E
Voight, r., Wa., U.S.	116a	47°03′N	122°08′W
Voinjama, Lib.	234	8°25′N	9°45′W
Voiron, Fr. (vwȧ-rôN′)	171	45°23′N	5°48′E
Voisin, Lac, l., Can. (vwŏ′-zĭn)	96	54°13′N	107°15′W
Volchansk, Ukr. (vôl-chänsk′)	181	50°18′N	36°56′E
Volga, r., Russia (vôl′gä)	178	47°30′N	46°20′E
Volga, Mouths of the, mth.	181	46°00′N	49°10′E
Volgograd, Russia (vŏl-gō-grȧ′t)	178	48°40′N	42°20′E
Volgogradskoye, res., Russia (vôl-gô-grad′skô-yě)	178	51°10′N	45°10′E
Volkhov, Russia (vôl′kôf)	167	59°54′N	32°21′E
Volkhov, r., Russia	180	58°45′N	31°40′E
Volodarskiy, Russia (vô-lô-där′skĭ)	186c	59°49′N	30°06′E
Volodymyr-Volyns′kyi, Ukr.	169	50°50′N	24°20′E
Vologda, Russia (vô′lôg-dȧ)	178	59°12′N	39°52′E
Vologda, prov., Russia	176	59°00′N	37°26′E
Volokolamsk, Russia (vô-lô-kôlȧmsk)	176	56°02′N	35°58′E
Volokonovka, Russia (vô-lô-kô′nôf-kȧ)	177	50°28′N	37°52′E
Vol′sk, Russia (vôl′sk)	181	52°02′N	47°23′E
Volta, r., Ghana	234	6°05′N	0°30′E
Volta, Lake, res., Ghana (vôl′tȧ)	230	7°10′N	0°30′W
Volta Blanche (White Volta), r., Afr.	234	11°30′N	0°40′W
Volta Noire *see* Black Volta, r., Afr.	230	11°30′N	4°00′W
Volta Redonda, Braz. (vôl′tä-rä-dôn′dä)	143	22°32′S	44°05′W
Volterra, Italy (vôl-těr′rä)	174	43°22′N	10°51′E
Voltri, Italy (vōl′trē)	174	44°25′N	8°45′E
Volturno, r., Italy (vôl-tōōr′nô)	174	41°12′N	14°20′E
Vólvi, Límni, l., Grc.	175	40°41′N	23°23′E
Volzhskoye, l., Russia (vôl′sh-skô-yě)	176	56°43′N	36°18′E
Von Ormy, Tx., U.S. (vŏn ôr′mē)	117d	29°18′N	98°36′W
Võõpsu, Est. (vōōp′sŏ)	167	58°06′N	27°30′E
Voorburg, Neth.	159a	52°04′N	4°21′E
Voortrekkerhoogte, S. Afr.	233b	25°48′S	28°10′E
Vop′, r., Russia (vôp)	176	55°20′N	32°55′E
Vopnafjördur, Ice.	160	65°43′N	14°58′W
Vordingborg, Den. (vôr′dĭng-bôr)	166	55°10′N	11°55′E
Vóreioi Sporades, is., Grc.	175	38°55′N	24°05′E
Vóreios Evvoïkós Kólpos, b., Grc.	175	38°48′N	23°02′E
Vorkuta, Russia (vôr-kōō′tȧ)	178	67°28′N	63°40′E
Vormsi, i., Est. (vôrm′sĭ)	167	59°06′N	23°05′E
Vorona, r., Russia (vô-rô′nȧ)	181	51°50′N	42°00′E
Voronava, Bela.	169	54°07′N	25°16′E
Voronezh, Russia (vô-rô′nyězh)	178	51°39′N	39°11′E
Voronezh, prov., Russia	177	51°10′N	39°13′E
Voronezh, r., Russia	181	52°17′N	39°32′E
Vorontsovka, Russia (vô-rônt′sôv-kȧ)	186a	59°40′N	60°14′E
Voron′ya, r., Russia (vô-rônyȧ)	180	68°20′N	35°20′E
Võrts-Järv, l., Est. (vôrts yärv)	167	58°15′N	26°12′E
Võru, Est. (vô′rû)	180	57°50′N	26°58′E
Vorya, r., Russia (vôr′yȧ)	186b	55°55′N	38°15′E
Vosges, mts., Fr. (vōzh)	161	48°09′N	6°57′E
Voskresensk, Russia (vôs-krě-sěnsk′)	186b	55°20′N	38°42′E
Voss, Nor. (vôs)	160	60°40′N	6°24′E
Vostryakovo, Russia	186b	55°23′N	37°49′E
Votkinsk, Russia (vôt-kēnsk′)	180	57°00′N	54°00′E
Votkinskoye Vodokhranilishche, res., Russia	180	57°30′N	55°00′E
Vouga, r., Port. (vō′gȧ)	172	40°43′N	7°51′W
Vouziers, Fr. (vōō-zyā′)	170	49°25′N	4°40′E
Voxnan, r., Swe.	166	61°30′N	15°24′E
Voyageurs National Park, rec., Mn., U.S.	113	48°30′N	92°40′W
Vozhe, l., Russia (vôzh′yě)	180	60°40′N	39°00′E
Voznesens′k, Ukr.	181	47°34′N	31°22′E
Vradiïvka, Ukr.	177	47°51′N	30°38′E
Vrangelya (Wrangel), i., Russia	178	71°25′N	178°30′W
Vranje, Yugo. (vrän′yě)	175	42°33′N	21°55′E
Vratsa, Blg. (vrät′sȧ)	163	43°12′N	23°31′E
Vrbas, Yugo. (v′r′bäs)	175	45°34′N	19°43′E
Vrbas, r., Yugo.	175	44°25′N	17°17′E
Vrchlabí, Czech Rep. (v′r′chlä-bē)	168	50°32′N	15°51′E
Vrede, S. Afr. (vrĭ′dě)(vrēd)	238c	27°25′S	29°11′E
Vredefort, S. Afr. (vrĭ′dě-fôrt)(vrēd′fōrt)	238c	27°00′S	27°21′E
Vreeswijk, Neth.	159a	52°00′N	5°06′E
Vršac, Yugo. (v′r′shàts)	163	45°08′N	21°18′E
Vrutky, Slvk. (vrōōt′kē)	169	49°09′N	18°55′E
Vryburg, S. Afr. (vrī′bûrg)	232	26°55′S	24°45′E
Vryheid, S. Afr. (vrī′hīt)	232	27°43′S	30°58′E
Vsetín, Czech Rep. (fsět′yēn)	169	49°21′N	18°01′E
Vsevolozhskiy, Russia (vsyě′vôlô′zh-skēē)	186c	60°01′N	30°41′E
Vuelta Abajo, reg., Cuba (vwěl′tä ä-bä′hō)	134	22°20′N	83°45′W
Vught, Neth.	159a	51°38′N	5°18′E
Vukovar, Cro. (vō′kô-vär)	175	45°20′N	19°00′E
Vulcan, Mi., U.S. (vŭl′kȧn)	108	45°45′N	87°50′W
Vulcano, i., Italy (vōōl-kä′nô)	174	38°23′N	15°00′E
Vŭlchedrŭma, Blg.	175	43°43′N	23°29′E
Vuntut National Park, rec., Can.	92	68°27′N	139°58′W
Vyartsilya, Russia (vyȧr-tsē′lyȧ)	167	62°10′N	30°40′E
Vyatka, r., Russia (vyát′kȧ)	180	59°20′N	51°25′E
Vyazemskiy, Russia (vyȧ-zěm′skĭ)	210	47°29′N	134°39′E
Vyaz′ma, Russia (vyȧz′mȧ)	180	55°12′N	34°17′E
Vyazniki, Russia (vyȧz′nē-kē)	180	56°10′N	42°10′E
Vyborg, Russia (vwē′bôrk)	178	60°43′N	28°46′E
Vychegda, r., Russia (vē′chěg-dȧ)	180	61°40′N	48°00′E
Vyerkhnyadzvinsk, Bela.	176	55°48′N	27°59′E
Vyetka, Bela. (vyět′kȧ)	176	52°36′N	31°05′E
Vylkove, Ukr.	181	45°24′N	29°36′E
Vym, r., Russia (vwēm)	180	63°15′N	51°20′E
Vyritsa, Russia (vē′rĭ-tsȧ)	186c	59°24′N	30°20′E
Vyshnevolotskoye, l., Russia (vŭy′sh-ŋě′vôlôt′s-kô′yě)	176	57°30′N	34°27′E
Vyshniy Volochëk, Russia (vêsh′nyĭ vôl-ô-chěk′)	178	57°34′N	34°35′E
Vyškov, Czech Rep. (vêsh′kôf)	168	49°17′N	16°58′E
Vysoké Mýto, Czech Rep. (vû′sô-kā mû′tô)	168	49°58′N	16°07′E
Vysokovsk, Russia (vĭ-sô′kôfsk)	176	56°16′N	36°32′E
Vytegra, Russia (vû′těg-rȧ)	178	61°00′N	36°20′E
Vyzhnytsia, Ukr.	169	48°16′N	25°12′E

W

PLACE (Pronunciation)	PAGE	LAT.	LONG.
W, Parcs Nationaux du, rec., Niger	235	12°20′N	2°40′E
Waal, r., Neth. (väl)	165	51°46′N	5°00′E
Waalwijk, Neth.	159a	51°41′N	5°05′E
Wabamun, Grc.	163	39°23′N	22°56′E
Wabamuno, Can. (wŏ′bă-mŭn)	95	53°33′N	114°28′W
Wabasca, Can. (wŏ-bȧs′kă)	95	56°00′N	113°53′W
Wabash, In., U.S. (wô′băsh)	108	40°45′N	85°50′W
Wabash, r., U.S.	107	38°00′N	88°00′W
Wabasha, Mn., U.S. (wä′bȧ-shô)	113	44°24′N	92°04′W
Wabe Gestro, r., Eth.	231	6°25′N	41°21′E
Wabowden, Can. (wä-bō′d′n)	97	54°55′N	98°38′W
Wąbrzeźno, Pol. (vôŋ-bzězh′nô)	169	53°17′N	18°59′E
Wabu Hu, l., China (wä-bōō hōō)	206	32°25′N	116°35′E
W. A. C. Bennett Dam, dam, Can.	95	56°01′N	122°10′W
Waccamaw, r., S.C., U.S. (wăk′ȧ-mô)	125	33°47′N	78°55′W
Waccasassa Bay, b., Fl., U.S. (wă-kȧ-să′sȧ)	124	29°02′N	83°10′W
Wachow, Ger. (vä′kōv)	159b	52°32′N	12°46′E
Waco, Tx., U.S. (wā′kō)	104	31°35′N	97°06′W
Waconda Lake, res., Ks., U.S.	120	39°45′N	98°15′W
Wadayama, Japan (wä′dä′yä-mä)	211	35°19′N	134°49′E
Waddenzee, sea, Neth.	165	53°00′N	4°50′E
Waddington, Mount, mtn., Can. (wŏd′dĭng-tŭn)	92	51°23′N	125°15′W
Wadena, Can.	96	51°57′N	103°50′W
Wadena, Mn., U.S. (wŏ-dē′nȧ)	112	46°26′N	95°09′W
Wadesboro, N.C., U.S. (wādz′bŭr-ô)	125	34°57′N	80°05′W
Wadley, Ga., U.S. (wŭd′lē)	125	32°54′N	82°25′W
Wad Madani, Sudan (wäd mē-dä′nē)	231	14°27′N	33°31′E
Wadowice, Pol. (vȧ-dô′vēt-sě)	169	49°53′N	19°31′E
Wadsworth, Oh., U.S. (wŏdz′wûrth)	111d	41°01′N	81°44′W
Wager Bay, b., Can. (wā′jēr)	93	65°48′N	88°19′W
Wagga Wagga, Austl. (wŏg′ȧ wôg′ä)	219	35°10′S	147°30′E
Wagoner, Ok., U.S. (wăg′ŭn-ēr)	121	35°58′N	95°22′W
Wagon Mound, N.M., U.S. (wăg′ŭn mound)	120	35°59′N	104°45′W
Wągrowiec, Pol. (vôŋ-grô′vyěts)	169	52°47′N	17°14′E
Waha, Libya	200	28°16′N	19°54′E
Wahiawā, Hi., U.S.	106d	21°30′N	158°03′W
Wahoo, Ne., U.S. (wä-hōō′)	112	41°14′N	96°39′W
Wahpeton, N.D., U.S. (wô′pē-tŭn)	112	46°17′N	96°38′W
Waialua, Hi., U.S. (wä′ē-ä-lōō′ä)	126a	21°33′N	158°08′W
Wai′anae, Hi., U.S. (vä′ē-ȧ-nä′ä)	126a	21°25′N	158°11′W
Waidhofen, Aus. (vīd′hôf-ěn)	168	47°58′N	14°46′E
Waigeo, Pulau, i., Indon. (wä-ē-gā′ô)	213	0°07′N	131°00′E
Waikato, r., N.Z. (wä′ē-kä′to)	221a	38°10′S	175°35′E
Waikerie, Austl. (wā′kēr-ē)	222	34°15′S	140°00′E
Wailuku, Hi., U.S. (wä′ē-lōō′kōō)	106c	20°55′N	156°30′W
Waimānalo, Hi., U.S. (wä-ē-mä′nä-lo)	126a	21°19′N	157°43′W
Waimea, Hi., U.S. (wä-ē-mā′ä)	126a	21°56′N	159°38′W
Wainganga, r., India (wä-ēn-gŭŋ′gä)	199	20°30′N	80°15′E
Waingapu, Indon.	212	9°32′S	120°00′E
Wainwright, Can.	90	52°49′N	110°52′W
Wainwright, Ak., U.S. (wān-rīt)	103	74°40′N	159°00′W
Waipahu, Hi., U.S. (wä′ē-pä′hōō)	106d	21°20′N	158°02′W
Waiska, r., Mi., U.S. (wā-ĭz-kȧ)	117k	46°20′N	84°38′W
Waitsburg, Wa., U.S. (wāts′bûrg)	114	46°17′N	118°08′W
Wajima, Japan (wä′jē-mȧ)	211	37°23′N	136°56′E
Wajir, Kenya	237	1°45′N	40°04′E
Wakami, r., Can.	98	47°43′N	82°22′W
Wakasa-Wan, b., Japan (wä′kä-sä wän)	210	35°43′N	135°39′E
Wakatipu, l., N.Z. (wä-kä-tē′pōō)	221a	45°04′S	168°30′E
Wakayama, Japan (wä-kä′yä-mä)	205	34°14′N	135°11′E
Wake, i., Oc. (wāk)	3	19°25′N	167°00′E
Wa Keeney, Ks., U.S. (wô-kē′nē)	120	39°01′N	99°53′W
Wakefield, Can. (wāk-fēld)	102c	45°39′N	75°55′W
Wakefield, Eng., U.K.	164	53°41′N	1°25′W
Wakefield, Ma., U.S.	101a	42°31′N	71°05′W
Wakefield, Mi., U.S.	113	46°28′N	89°55′W
Wakefield, Ne., U.S.	112	42°15′N	96°52′W
Wakefield, R.I., U.S.	110b	41°26′N	71°30′W
Wakefield, co., Eng., U.K.	158a	53°12′N	1°25′W
Wake Forest, N.C., U.S. (wāk fŏr′ěst)	125	35°58′N	78°31′W
Waki, Japan (wä′kē)	211	34°05′N	134°10′E
Wakkanai, Japan (wä′kä-nä′ē)	205	45°19′N	141°43′E
Wakkerstroom, S. Afr. (vák′ēr-strōm)(wăk′ēr-strōōm)	232	27°19′S	30°04′E
Wakonassin, r., Can.	98	46°35′N	82°10′W
Waku Kundo, Ang.	232	11°25′S	15°07′E
Wałbrzych, Pol. (väl′bzhûk)	168	50°46′N	16°16′E
Walcott, Lake, res., Id., U.S.	115	42°40′N	113°23′W
Wałcz, Pol. (välch)	168	53°11′N	16°30′E
Waldoboro, Me., U.S. (wôl′dô-bŭr-ô)	100	44°06′N	69°22′W
Waldo Lake, l., Or., U.S. (wôl′dō)	114	43°46′N	122°10′W
Waldorf, Md., U.S. (wăl′dôrf)	110e	38°37′N	76°57′W
Waldron, Mo., U.S.	117f	39°14′N	94°47′W
Waldron, i., Wa., U.S.	116d	48°42′N	123°02′W
Wales, Ak., U.S. (wālz)	103	65°35′N	168°14′W
Wales, state, U.K.	154	52°12′N	3°40′W
Walewale, Ghana	234	10°21′N	0°48′W
Walgett, Austl. (wôl′gět)	219	30°00′S	148°10′E
Walhalla, S.C., U.S. (wŭl-hăl′ȧ)	124	34°45′N	83°04′W
Walikale, D.R.C.	237	1°25′S	28°03′E
Walkden, Eng., U.K.	158a	53°32′N	2°24′W
Walker, Mn., U.S. (wôk′ēr)	113	47°06′N	94°37′W
Walker, r., Nv., U.S.	118	39°07′N	119°10′W
Walker, Mount, mtn., Wa., U.S.	116a	47°47′N	122°54′W
Walker Lake, l., Can.	97	54°42′N	96°57′W
Walker Lake, l., Nv., U.S.	118	38°46′N	118°30′W
Walker River Indian Reservation, I.R., Nv., U.S.	118	39°06′N	118°20′W
Walkerville, Mt., U.S. (wôk′ēr-vĭl)	115	46°20′N	112°32′W
Wallace, Id., U.S. (wŏl′ȧs)	114	47°27′N	115°55′W
Wallaceburg, Can.	98	42°39′N	82°25′W
Wallacia, Austl.	217b	33°52′S	150°40′E
Wallaroo, Austl. (wŏl-ȧ-rōō)	218	33°52′S	137°45′E
Wallasey, Eng., U.K. (wŏl′ȧ-sē)	158a	53°25′N	3°03′W
Walla Walla, Wa., U.S. (wŏl′ȧ wŏl′ȧ)	104	46°03′N	118°20′W
Walled Lake, Mi., U.S. (wôl′d lāk)	111b	42°32′N	83°29′W
Wallel, Tulu, mtn., Eth.	231	9°00′N	34°52′E
Wallingford, Eng., U.K. (wŏl′ĭng-fērd)	158b	51°34′N	1°08′W
Wallingford, Vt., U.S.	109	43°30′N	72°55′W
Wallis and Futuna Islands, dep., Oc.	241	13°00′S	176°10′E
Wallisville, Tx., U.S. (wŏl′ĭs-vĭl)	123a	29°50′N	94°44′W
Wallowa, Or., U.S. (wôl′ô-wȧ)	114	45°34′N	117°32′W
Wallowa, r., Or., U.S.	114	45°28′N	117°28′W
Wallowa Mountains, mts., Or., U.S.	114	45°10′N	117°22′W
Wallula, Wa., U.S.	114	46°08′N	118°55′W
Walnut, Ca., U.S. (wôl′nŭt)	117a	34°00′N	117°51′W
Walnut, r., Ks., U.S.	121	37°28′N	97°06′W
Walnut Canyon National Mon, rec., Az., U.S.	119	35°10′N	111°30′W
Walnut Creek, Ca., U.S.	116b	37°54′N	122°04′W
Walnut Creek, r., Tx., U.S.	117c	32°37′N	97°03′W
Walnut Ridge, Ar., U.S. (rĭj)	121	36°04′N	90°56′W
Walpole, Ma., U.S. (wôl′pōl)	101a	42°09′N	71°15′W
Walpole, N.H., U.S.	109	43°05′N	72°25′W
Walsall, Eng., U.K. (wôl-sôl)	164	52°35′N	1°58′W
Walsenburg, Co., U.S. (wôl′sěn-bûrg)	120	37°38′N	104°46′W
Walsum, Ger.	171c	51°32′N	6°41′E
Walter F. George Reservoir, res., U.S.	124	32°00′N	85°00′W
Walters, Ok., U.S. (wôl′tērz)	120	34°21′N	98°19′W
Waltham, Ma., U.S. (wôl′thȧm)	101a	42°22′N	71°14′W
Walthamstow, Eng., U.K. (wôl′tȧm-stō)	158b	51°34′N	0°01′W
Walton, N.Y., U.S.	109	42°10′N	75°05′W
Walton-le-Dale, Eng., U.K. (lē-dāl′)	158a	53°44′N	2°40′W
Walvis Bay, Nmb. (wôl′vĭs)	232	22°50′S	14°30′E
Walworth, Wi., U.S. (wôl′wûrth)	113	42°33′N	88°39′W
Wama, Ang.	236	12°14′S	15°33′E
Wamba, r., D.R.C.	232	7°00′S	18°00′E
Wamego, Ks., U.S. (wŏ-mē′gō)	121	39°13′N	96°17′W
Wami, r., Tan. (wä′mē)	233	6°31′S	37°17′E
Wanapitei Lake, l., Can.	99	46°45′N	80°45′W
Wanaque, N.J., U.S. (wŏn′ȧ-kē)	110a	41°03′N	74°16′W
Wanaque Reservoir, res., N.J., U.S.	110a	41°06′N	74°20′W
Wanda Shan, mts., China (wän-dä shän)	205	45°54′N	131°45′E
Wandoan, Austl.	222	26°09′S	149°51′E
Wandsbek, Ger. (vänds′běk)	159c	53°34′N	10°07′E
Wandsworth, Eng., U.K. (wôndz′wûrth)	158b	51°26′N	0°12′W
Wanganui, N.Z. (wôŋ′gȧ-nōō′ē)	221a	39°53′S	175°01′E
Wangaratta, Austl. (wŏŋ′gȧ-răt′ȧ)	222	36°23′S	146°18′E
Wangeroog, i., Ger. (vän′gě-rōg)	168	53°49′N	7°57′E
Wangqingtuo, China (wäŋ-chyĭŋ-twô)	206	39°14′N	116°56′E
Wangsi, China (wäŋ-sē)	206	37°59′N	116°57′E
Wantage, Eng., U.K. (wŏn′tȧj)	158b	51°33′N	1°26′W
Wantagh, N.Y., U.S.	110a	40°41′N	73°30′W
Wanxian, China (wän shyěn)	206	38°51′N	115°10′E
Wanxian, China (wän-shyěn)	204	30°48′N	108°22′E
Wanzai, China (wän-dzī)	209	28°05′N	114°25′E
Wanzhi, China (wän-jr)	206	31°11′N	118°31′E

ăt; finȧl; rāte; senȧte; ärm; ȧsk; sofȧ; fâre; ch-choose; dh-as th in other; bē; ėvent; bět; recěnt; cratẽr; g-gō; gh-guttural g; bĭt; ĭ-short neutral; rīde; K-guttural k as ch in German ich;

PRONOUNCING INDEX

Wapakoneta – Wessel Islands 365

PLACE (Pronunciation)	PAGE	LAT.	LONG.
Wapakoneta, Oh., U.S. (wä'pȧ-kô-nĕt'ȧ)	108	40°35'N	84°10'W
Wapawekka Hills, hills, Can. (wô'pă-wĕ'kă-hĭlz)	96	54°45'N	104°20'W
Wapawekka Lake, l., Can.	96	54°55'N	104°40'W
Wapello, Ia., U.S. (wŏ-pĕl'ō)	113	41°10'N	91°11'W
Wappapello Reservoir, res., Mo., U.S. (wă'pȧ-pĕl-lō)	107	37°07'N	90°10'W
Wappingers Falls, N.Y., U.S. (wŏp'ĭn-jẽrz)	109	41°35'N	73°55'W
Wapsipinicon, r., Ia., U.S. (wŏp'sĭ-pĭn'ĭ-kŏn)	113	42°16'N	91°35'W
Wapusk National Park, rec., Can.	92	58°00'N	94°15'W
Warabi, Japan (wä'rä-bê)	211a	35°50'N	139°41'E
Warangal, India (wŭ'ráŋ-gal)	199	18°03'N	79°45'E
Warburton, The, r., Austl. (wŏr'bûr-tŭn)	220	27°30'S	138°45'E
Wardān, Wādī, r., Egypt	197a	29°22'N	33°00'E
Ward Cove, Ak., U.S.	94	55°24'N	131°43'W
Warden, S. Afr. (wôr'dĕn)	238c	27°52'S	28°59'E
Wardha, India (wŭr'dä)	199	20°46'N	78°42'E
War Eagle, W.V., U.S. (wôr ē'g'l)	108	37°30'N	81°50'W
Waren, Ger. (vä'rĕn)	168	53°32'N	12°43'E
Warendorf, Ger. (vä'rĕn-dōrf)	171c	51°57'N	7°59'E
Wargla, Alg.	230	32°00'N	5°18'E
Warialda, Austl.	222	29°32'S	150°34'E
Warmbad, Nmb. (värm'bäd) (wôrm'băd)	232	28°25'S	18°45'E
Warmbad, S. Afr.	238c	24°52'S	28°18'E
Warm Beach, Wa., U.S. (wôrm)	116a	48°10'N	122°22'W
Warm Springs Indian Reservation, I.R., Or., U.S. (wôrm sprĭnz)	114	44°55'N	121°30'W
Warm Springs Reservoir, res., Or., U.S.	114	43°42'N	118°40'W
Warner Mountains, mts., Ca., U.S.	106	41°30'N	120°17'W
Warner Robins, Ga., U.S.	124	32°37'N	83°36'W
Warnow, r., Ger. (vär'nō)	168	53°51'N	11°55'E
Warracknabeal, Austl.	222	36°20'S	142°28'E
Warragamba Reservoir, res., Austl.	222	33°40'S	150°00'E
Warrego, r., Austl. (wôr'ê-gô)	221	27°13'S	145°58'E
Warren, Can.	102f	50°08'N	97°32'W
Warren, Ar., U.S. (wŏr'ĕn)	121	33°37'N	92°03'W
Warren, In., U.S.	108	40°40'N	85°25'W
Warren, Mi., U.S.	111b	42°33'N	83°03'W
Warren, Mn., U.S.	112	48°11'N	96°44'W
Warren, Oh., U.S.	108	41°15'N	80°50'W
Warren, Or., U.S.	116c	45°49'N	122°51'W
Warren, Pa., U.S.	109	41°50'N	79°10'W
Warren, R.I., U.S.	110b	41°44'N	71°14'W
Warrendale, Pa., U.S. (wŏr'ĕn-dāl)	111e	40°39'N	80°04'W
Warrensburg, Mo., U.S. (wŏr'ĕnz-bûrg)	121	38°45'N	93°42'W
Warrenton, Ga., U.S. (wŏr'ĕn-tŭn)	125	33°26'N	82°37'W
Warrenton, Or., U.S.	116c	46°10'N	123°56'W
Warrenton, Va., U.S.	109	38°45'N	77°50'W
Warri, Nig. (wär'ê)	230	5°33'N	5°43'E
Warrington, Eng., U.K.	158a	53°22'N	2°30'W
Warrington, Fl., U.S. (wŏ'ĭng-tŭn)	124	30°21'N	87°15'W
Warrnambool, Austl. (wôr'năm-bōōl)	219	38°20'S	142°28'E
Warroad, Mn., U.S. (wôr'rōd)	112	48°55'N	95°20'W
Warrumbungle Range, mts., Austl. (wôr'ŭm-bŭŋ-g'l)	221	31°18'S	150°00'E
Warsaw, Pol.	154	52°15'N	21°05'E
Warsaw, Il., U.S. (wôr'sô)	121	40°21'N	91°26'W
Warsaw, In., U.S.	108	41°15'N	85°50'W
Warsaw, N.Y., U.S.	109	42°45'N	78°10'W
Warsaw, NC, N.C., U.S.	125	35°00'N	78°07'W
Warsop, Eng., U.K. (wôr'sŭp)	158a	53°13'N	1°05'W
Warszawa *see* Warsaw, Pol.	154	52°15'N	21°05'E
Warta, r., Pol. (vär'tà)	161	52°30'N	16°00'E
Wartburg, S. Afr.	233c	29°26'S	30°39'E
Warwick, Austl. (wŏr'ĭk)	219	28°05'S	152°10'E
Warwick, Can.	99	45°58'N	71°57'W
Warwick, Eng., U.K.	164	52°19'N	1°46'W
Warwick, N.Y., U.S.	110a	41°15'N	74°22'W
Warwick, R.I., U.S.	109	41°42'N	71°27'W
Warwickshire, co., Eng., U.K.	158a	52°30'N	1°35'W
Wasatch Mountains, mts., Ut., U.S. (wô'săch)	117b	40°45'N	111°46'W
Wasatch Plateau, plat., Ut., U.S.	119	38°55'N	111°40'W
Wasatch Range, mts., U.S.	106	39°10'N	111°30'W
Wasbank, S. Afr.	233c	28°27'S	30°09'E
Wasco, Or., U.S. (wăs'kō)	114	45°36'N	120°42'W
Waseca, Mn., U.S. (wô-sē'kȧ)	113	44°04'N	93°31'W
Wash, The, Eng., U.K. (wŏsh)	160	53°00'N	0°20'E
Washburn, Me., U.S. (wŏsh'bŭrn)	100	46°46'N	68°10'W
Washburn, Wi., U.S.	113	46°41'N	90°55'W
Washburn, Mount, mtn., Wy., U.S.	115	44°55'N	110°10'W
Washington, D.C., U.S. (wŏsh'ĭng-tŭn)	105	38°50'N	77°00'W
Washington, Ga., U.S.	125	33°43'N	82°46'W
Washington, Ia., U.S.	113	41°17'N	91°42'W
Washington, In., U.S.	108	38°40'N	87°10'W
Washington, Ks., U.S.	121	39°48'N	97°04'W
Washington, Mo., U.S.	121	38°33'N	91°00'W
Washington, N.C., U.S.	125	35°32'N	77°01'W
Washington, Pa., U.S.	108	40°10'N	80°14'W
Washington, state, U.S.	104	47°30'N	121°10'W
Washington, i., Wi., U.S.	113	45°18'N	86°42'W
Washington, Lake, l., Wa., U.S.	116a	47°34'N	122°12'W
Washington, Mount, mtn., N.H., U.S.	107	44°15'N	71°15'W
Washington Court House, Oh., U.S.	108	39°30'N	83°25'W
Washington Park, Il., U.S.	117e	38°38'N	90°06'W
Washita, r., Ok., U.S. (wŏsh'ĭ-tô)	120	35°33'N	99°16'W
Washougal, Wa., U.S. (wŏ-shōō'gál)	116c	45°35'N	122°21'W
Washougal, r., Wa., U.S.	116c	45°38'N	122°17'W

PLACE (Pronunciation)	PAGE	LAT.	LONG.
Wasilków, Pol. (vá-sēl'kòf)	169	53°12'N	23°13'E
Waskaiowaka Lake, l., Can. (wŏ'skă-yō'wŏ-kă)	97	56°30'N	96°20'W
Wassenberg, Ger. (vä'sĕn-bĕrgh)	171c	51°06'N	6°07'E
Wassuk Range, mts., Nv., U.S. (wàs'sŭk)	118	38°58'N	119°00'W
Waswanipi, Lac, l., Can.	99	49°35'N	76°15'W
Water, i., V.I.U.S. (wô'tẽr)	129c	18°20'N	64°57'W
Waterberge, mts., S. Afr. (wôrtẽr'bûrg)	238c	24°25'S	27°53'E
Waterboro, S.C., U.S. (wô'tẽr-bûr-ō)	125	32°50'N	80°40'W
Waterbury, Ct., U.S. (wô'tẽr-bĕr-ê)	109	41°30'N	73°00'W
Water Cay, i., Bah.	135	22°55'N	75°50'W
Waterdown, Can. (wô'tẽr-doun)	102d	43°20'N	79°54'W
Wateree Lake, res., S.C., U.S. (wô'tẽr-ē)	125	34°40'N	80°48'W
Waterford, Ire. (wô'tẽr-fẽrd)	161	52°20'N	7°03'W
Waterford, Wi., U.S.	111a	42°46'N	88°13'W
Waterloo, Bel.	159a	50°44'N	4°24'E
Waterloo, Can. (wô-tẽr-lōō')	99	43°30'N	80°40'W
Waterloo, Can.	99	45°25'N	72°30'W
Waterloo, Ia., U.S.	105	42°30'N	92°22'W
Waterloo, Il., U.S.	121	38°19'N	90°08'W
Waterloo, Md., U.S.	110e	39°11'N	76°50'W
Waterloo, N.Y., U.S.	109	42°55'N	76°50'W
Waterton-Glacier International Peace Park, rec., N.A. (wô'ter-tŭn-glā'shûr)	106	48°55'N	114°10'W
Waterton Lakes National Park, rec., Can.	95	49°05'N	113°50'W
Watertown, Ma., U.S. (wô'tẽr-toun)	101a	42°22'N	71°11'W
Watertown, N.Y., U.S.	105	44°00'N	75°55'W
Watertown, S.D., U.S.	104	44°53'N	97°07'W
Watertown, Wi., U.S.	113	43°13'N	88°40'W
Water Valley, Ms., U.S. (văl'ê)	124	34°08'N	89°38'W
Waterville, Me., U.S.	100	44°34'N	69°37'W
Waterville, Mn., U.S.	113	44°10'N	93°35'W
Waterville, Wa., U.S.	114	47°38'N	120°04'W
Watervliet, N.Y., U.S. (wô'tẽr-vlēt')	109	42°45'N	73°54'W
Watford, Eng., U.K. (wŏt'fŏrd)	164	51°38'N	0°24'W
Wathaman Lake, l., Can.	96	56°55'N	103°43'W
Watlington, Eng., U.K.	158b	51°37'N	1°01'W
Watonga, Ok., U.S. (wŏ-tôŋ'gȧ)	121	35°50'N	98°26'E
Watsa, D.R.C. (wät'sä)	231	3°03'N	29°32'E
Watseka, Il., U.S. (wŏt-sē'kȧ)	108	40°45'N	87°45'W
Watson, In., U.S. (wŏt'sŭn)	111h	38°21'N	85°42'W
Watson Lake, Can.	90	60°18'N	128°50'W
Watsonville, Ca., U.S. (wŏt'sŭn-vĭl)	118	36°55'N	121°46'W
Wattenscheid, Ger. (vä'tĕn-shīd)	171c	51°30'N	7°07'E
Watts, Ca., U.S. (wŏts)	117a	33°56'N	118°15'W
Watts Bar Lake, res., Tn., U.S. (bär)	124	35°45'N	84°49'W
Waubay, S.D., U.S. (wô'bā)	112	45°19'N	97°18'W
Wauchula, Fl., U.S. (wô-chōō'lȧ)	125a	27°32'N	81°48'W
Wauconda, Il., U.S. (wô-kŏn'dȧ)	111a	42°15'N	88°08'W
Waukegan, Il., U.S. (wô-kē'găn)	105	42°22'N	87°51'W
Waukesha, Wi., U.S. (wô'kê-shô)	111a	43°01'N	88°13'W
Waukon, Ia., U.S. (wô kŏn)	113	43°15'N	91°30'W
Waupaca, Wi., U.S. (wô-păk'ȧ)	113	44°22'N	89°06'W
Waupun, Wi., U.S. (wô-pŭn')	113	43°37'N	88°45'W
Waurika, Ok., U.S. (wô-rē'kȧ)	121	34°09'N	97°59'W
Wausau, Wi., U.S. (wô'sô)	105	44°58'N	89°40'W
Wausaukee, Wi., U.S. (wô-sô'kê)	113	45°22'N	87°58'W
Wauseon, Oh., U.S. (wô'sê-ŏn)	108	41°30'N	84°10'W
Wautoma, Wi., U.S. (wô-tō'mȧ)	113	44°04'N	89°11'W
Wauwatosa, Wi., U.S. (wô-wȧ-t'ō'sȧ)	111a	43°03'N	88°00'W
Waveney, r., Eng., U.K. (wāv'nê)	165	52°27'N	1°17'E
Waverly, S. Afr.	233c	31°54'S	26°29'E
Waverly, Ia., U.S. (wā'vẽr-lê)	113	42°43'N	92°29'W
Waverly, Tn., U.S.	124	36°04'N	87°46'W
Wāw, Sudan	231	7°41'N	28°00'E
Wawa, Can.	98	47°59'N	84°47'W
Wāw al-Kabir, Libya	231	25°23'N	16°52'E
Wawanesa, Can. (wŏ'wŏ-nē'sä)	97	49°36'N	99°41'W
Wawasee, l., In., U.S. (wô-wô-sē')	108	41°25'N	85°45'W
Waxahachie, Tx., U.S. (wăk-sȧ-hăch'ê)	123	32°23'N	96°50'W
Wayland, Ky., U.S. (wā'lănd)	125	37°25'N	82°47'W
Wayland, Ma., U.S.	101a	42°23'N	71°22'W
Wayne, Mi., U.S.	111b	42°17'N	83°23'W
Wayne, Ne., U.S.	112	42°13'N	97°03'W
Wayne, N.J., U.S.	110a	40°56'N	74°16'W
Wayne, Pa., U.S.	110f	40°03'N	75°22'W
Waynesboro, Ga., U.S. (wānz'bŭr-ô)	125	33°05'N	82°02'W
Waynesboro, Pa., U.S.	109	39°45'N	77°35'W
Waynesboro, Va., U.S.	109	38°05'N	78°50'W
Waynesburg, Pa., U.S. (wānz'bûrg)	108	39°55'N	80°10'W
Waynesville, N.C., U.S. (wānz'vĭl)	125	35°28'N	82°58'W
Waynoka, Ok., U.S. (wā-nō'kȧ)	120	36°34'N	98°52'W
Wayzata, Mn., U.S. (wā-zä-tà)	117g	44°58'N	93°31'W
Wazīrbad, Pak.	202	32°39'N	74°11'E
Weagamow Lake, l., Can. (wē'ăg-ă-mou)	97	52°53'N	91°22'W
Weald, The, reg., Eng., U.K. (wēld)	164	50°58'N	0°15'W
Weatherford, Ok., U.S. (wĕ-dhẽr-fẽrd)	120	85°32'N	98°41'W
Weatherford, Tx., U.S.	123	32°45'N	97°46'W
Weaver, r., Eng., U.K. (wē'vẽr)	158a	53°09'N	2°31'W
Weaverville, Ca., U.S. (wē'vẽr-vĭl)	114	40°44'N	122°55'W
Webb City, Mo., U.S.	121	37°10'N	94°26'W
Weber, r., Ut., U.S.	117b	41°13'N	112°07'W
Webster, Ma., U.S.	101a	42°04'N	71°52'W
Webster, S.D., U.S.	112	45°19'N	97°30'W
Webster City, Ia., U.S.	113	42°28'N	93°49'W
Webster Groves, Mo., U.S. (grōvz)	117e	38°36'N	90°22'W
Webster Springs, W.V., U.S. (sprĭngz)	108	38°30'N	80°20'W
Weddell Sea, sea, Ant. (wĕd'ĕl)	224	73°00'S	45°00'W

PLACE (Pronunciation)	PAGE	LAT.	LONG.
Wedel, Ger. (vā'dĕl)	159c	53°35'N	9°42'E
Wedge Mountain, mtn., Can. (wĕj)	95	50°10'N	122°50'W
Wedgeport, Can. (wĕj'pōrt)	100	43°44'N	65°59'W
Wednesfield, Eng., U.K. (wĕd''nz-fēld)	158a	52°36'N	2°04'W
Weed, Ca., U.S. (wēd)	114	41°35'N	122°21'W
Weenen, S. Afr. (vā'nĕn)	233c	28°52'S	30°05'E
Weert, Neth.	165	51°16'N	5°39'E
Weesp, Neth.	159a	52°18'N	5°01'E
Węgorzewo, Pol. (vôŋ-gô'zhĕ-vô)	169	54°14'N	21°46'E
Węgrow, Pol. (vôŋ'gròf)	169	52°23'N	22°02'E
Wei, r., China (wā)	206	35°47'N	114°27'E
Wei, r., China (wā)	204	34°00'N	108°10'E
Weichang, China (wā-chăŋ)	205	41°50'N	118°00'E
Weiden, Ger.	168	49°41'N	12°09'E
Weifang, China	205	36°43'N	119°08'E
Weihai, China (wa'hăī')	205	37°30'N	122°05'E
Weilheim, Ger. (vīl'hīm')	168	47°50'N	11°06'E
Weimar, Ger. (vī'mär)	161	50°59'N	11°20'E
Weinan, China	208	34°32'N	109°40'E
Weipa, Austl.	219	12°25'S	141°54'E
Weir, r., Can. (wēr-rĭv-ẽr)	97	56°49'N	94°04'W
Weirton, W.V., U.S.	108	40°25'N	80°35'W
Weiser, Id., U.S. (wē'zẽr)	114	44°15'N	116°58'W
Weiser, r., Id., U.S.	114	44°26'N	116°40'W
Weishi, China (wā-shr)	208	34°23'N	114°12'E
Weissenburg, Ger.	168	49°04'N	11°20'E
Weissenfels, Ger. (vī'sĕn-fĕlz)	168	51°13'N	11°58'E
Weiss Lake, res., Al., U.S.	124	34°15'N	85°35'W
Weixi, China (wā-shyē)	204	27°27'N	99°30'E
Weixian, China (wā shyĕn)	206	36°59'N	115°17'E
Wejherowo, Pol. (vā-hĕ-rô'vô)	169	54°36'N	18°15'E
Welch, W.V., U.S. (wĕlch)	125	37°24'N	81°28'W
Weldon, N.C., U.S. (wĕl'dŭn)	125	36°24'N	77°36'W
Weldon, r., Mo., U.S.	121	40°22'N	93°39'W
Weleetka, Ok., U.S. (wê-lēt'kȧ)	121	35°19'N	96°08'W
Welford, Austl. (wĕl'fẽrd)	222	25°08'S	144°43'E
Welkom, S. Afr. (wĕl'kŏm)	232	27°57'S	26°45'E
Welland, Can. (wĕl'ănd)	99	42°59'N	79°13'W
Wellesley, Ma., U.S. (wĕlz'lê)	101a	42°18'N	71°17'W
Wellesley Islands, is., Austl.	220	16°15'S	139°25'E
Wellington, Austl. (wĕl'lĭng-tŭn)	222	32°40'S	148°50'E
Wellington, N.Z.	221a	41°15'S	174°45'E
Wellington, Eng., U.K.	158a	52°42'N	2°30'W
Wellington, Ks., U.S.	121	37°16'N	97°24'W
Wellington, Oh., U.S.	108	41°10'N	82°10'W
Wellington, Tx., U.S.	120	34°51'N	100°12'W
Wellington, i., Chile (òĕ'lĕng-tŏn)	144	49°30'S	76°30'W
Wells, Can.	90	53°06'N	121°34'W
Wells, Mi., U.S.	108	45°50'N	87°00'W
Wells, Mn., U.S.	113	43°44'N	93°43'W
Wells, Nv., U.S.	114	41°07'N	115°04'W
Wells, l., Austl. (wĕlz)	220	26°35'S	123°40'E
Wellsboro, Pa., U.S. (wĕlz'bŭ-rô)	109	41°45'N	77°15'W
Wellsburg, W.V., U.S. (wĕlz'bûrg)	108	40°10'N	80°40'W
Wells Dam, dam, Wa., U.S.	114	48°00'N	119°39'W
Wellston, Oh., U.S. (wĕlz'tŭn)	108	39°05'N	82°30'W
Wellsville, Mo., U.S. (wĕlz'vĭl)	121	39°04'N	91°33'W
Wellsville, N.Y., U.S.	109	42°10'N	78°00'W
Wellsville, Oh., U.S.	108	40°35'N	80°40'W
Wellsville, Ut., U.S.	115	41°38'N	111°57'W
Wels, Aus. (vĕls)	161	48°10'N	14°01'E
Welshpool, Wales, U.K. (wĕlsh'pōōl)	164	52°44'N	3°10'W
Welverdiend, S. Afr. (vĕl-vẽr-dēnd')	238c	26°23'S	27°16'E
Welwyn Garden City, Eng., U.K. (wĕlĭn)	158b	51°46'N	0°17'W
Wem, Eng., U.K. (wĕm)	158a	52°51'N	2°44'W
Wembere, r., Tan.	237	4°35'S	33°55'E
Wen, r., China (wŭn)	206	36°24'N	119°00'E
Wenan Wa, sw., China (wĕn'än' wä)	206	38°56'N	116°29'E
Wenatchee, Wa., U.S. (wê-năch'ê)	114	47°24'N	120°18'W
Wenatchee Mountains, mts., Wa., U.S.	114	47°28'N	121°10'W
Wenchang, China (wŭn-chăŋ)	209	19°32'N	110°42'E
Wenchi, Ghana	234	7°42'N	2°07'W
Wendeng, China (wŭn-dŭŋ)	206	37°14'N	122°03'E
Wendo, Eth.	231	6°37'N	38°29'E
Wendorer, Ut., U.S.	115	40°47'N	114°01'W
Wendover, Can. (wĕn-dōv'ẽr)	102c	45°34'N	75°07'W
Wendover, Eng., U.K.	158b	51°44'N	0°45'W
Wenham, Ma., U.S. (wĕn'ăm)	101a	42°36'N	70°53'W
Wenquan, China (wŭn-chyůän)	205	47°10'N	120°00'E
Wenshan, China	204	23°20'N	104°15'E
Wenshang, China (wŭn'shăng)	206	35°43'N	116°31'E
Wensu, China (wĕn-sò)	204	41°45'N	80°30'E
Wentworth, Austl. (wĕnt'wûrth)	219	34°03'S	141°53'E
Wenzhou, China (wŭn-jō)	205	28°00'N	120°40'E
Wepener, S. Afr. (wē'pĕn-ẽr) (vā'pĕn-ẽr)	232	29°43'S	27°04'E
Werder, Ger. (vĕr'dẽr)	159b	52°23'N	12°56'E
Were Ilu, Eth.	231	10°39'N	39°21'E
Werl, Ger. (vĕrl)	171c	51°33'N	7°55'E
Wermelskirchen, Ger.	171c	51°08'N	7°13'E
Werneuchen, Ger. (vĕr'hoi-kĕn)	159b	52°38'N	13°44'E
Werra, r., Ger. (vĕr'ä)	168	51°16'N	9°54'E
Werribee, Austl.	217a	37°54'S	144°40'E
Werribee, r., Austl.	217a	37°40'S	144°37'E
Wertach, r., Ger. (vĕr'täk)	168	48°12'N	10°40'E
Weseke, Ger. (vĕ'zĕ-kĕ)	171c	51°54'N	6°51'E
Wesel, Ger. (vā'zĕl)	171c	51°39'N	6°37'E
Weser, r., Ger. (vā'zẽr)	156	51°00'N	10°30'E
Weslaco, Tx., U.S. (wĕs-lā'kō)	123	26°10'N	97°59'W
Weslemkoon, l., Can.	99	45°02'N	77°25'W
Wesleyville, Can. (wĕs'lē-vĭl)	101	49°09'N	53°34'W
Wessel Islands, is., Austl. (wĕs'ĕl)	220	11°45'S	136°25'E

ng-sing; ŋ-baŋk; ɴ-nasalized n; nŏd; cŏmmit; ōld; ôbey; ôrder; oi-boil; fōōd; ò-as oo in foot; ou-out; s-soft; sh-dish; th-thin; pūre; ûnite; ûrn; stŭd; circŭs; ü-as in French tu; '-indeterminate vowel.

366 Wesselsbron – William Creek PRONOUNCING INDEX

PLACE (Pronunciation)	PAGE	LAT.	LONG.
Wesselsbron, S. Afr. (wĕs´ĕl-brŏn)	238c	27°51′S	26°22′E
Wessington Springs, S.D., U.S. (wĕs´ĭng-tŭn)	112	44°06′N	98°35′W
West, Mount, mtn., Pan.	128a	9°10′N	79°52′W
West Allis, Wi., U.S. (wĕst-ăl´ĭs)	111a	43°01′N	88°01′W
West Alton, Mo., U.S. (ôl´tŭn)	117e	38°52′N	90°13′W
West Bay, b., Fl., U.S.	124	30°20′N	85°45′W
West Bay, b., Tx., U.S.	123a	29°11′N	95°03′W
West Bend, Wi., U.S. (wĕst bĕnd)	113	43°25′N	88°13′W
West Bengal, state, India (bĕn-gôl´)	199	23°30′N	87°30′E
West Blocton, Al., U.S. (blŏk´tŭn)	124	33°05′N	87°05′W
Westborough, Ma., U.S. (wĕst´bŭr-ô)	101a	42°17′N	71°37′W
West Boylston, Ma., U.S. (boil´stŭn)	101a	42°22′N	71°46′W
West Branch, Mi., U.S. (wĕst brȧnch)	108	44°15′N	84°10′W
West Bridgford, Eng., U.K. (brĭj´fẽrd)	158a	52°55′N	1°08′W
West Bromwich, Eng., U.K. (wĕst brŭm´ĭj)	158a	52°32′N	1°59′W
Westbrook, Me., U.S. (wĕst´brŏok)	100	43°41′N	70°23′W
Westby, Wi., U.S. (wĕst´bē)	113	43°40′N	90°52′W
West Caicos, i., T./C. Is. (kăē´kō) (kī´kōs)	135	21°40′N	72°30′W
West Cape Howe, c., Austl.	220	35°15′S	117°30′E
West Chester, Oh., U.S. (chĕs´tẽr)	111f	39°20′N	84°24′W
West Chester, Pa., U.S.	110f	39°57′N	75°36′W
West Chicago, Il., U.S. (chĭ-kȧ´gō)	111a	41°53′N	88°12′W
West Columbia, S.C., U.S. (cŏl´ŭm-bē-ȧ)	125	33°58′N	81°05′W
West Columbia, Tx., U.S.	123	29°08′N	95°39′W
West Cote Blanche Bay, b., La., U.S.	123	29°30′N	92°17′W
West Covina, Ca., U.S. (wĕst kō-vē´nȧ)	117a	34°04′N	117°55′W
West Des Moines, Ia., U.S. (dē moin´)	113	41°35′N	93°42′W
West Des Moines, r., Ia., U.S.	113	42°52′N	94°32′W
West End, Bah.	134	26°40′N	78°55′W
Westerham, Eng., U.K. (wĕ´stẽr´ŭm)	158b	51°15′N	0°05′E
Westerhörn, Ger. (vĕs´tĕr-hōrn)	159c	53°52′N	9°41′E
Westerlo, Bel.	159a	51°05′N	4°57′E
Westerly, R.I., U.S. (wĕs´tẽr-lē)	109	41°25′N	71°50′W
Western Australia, state, Austl. (ôs-trā´lĭ-ȧ)	218	24°15′S	121°30′E
Western Dvina, r., Eur.	167	55°30′N	28°27′E
Western Ghāts, mts., India	199	17°35′N	74°00′E
Western Port, Md., U.S. (wĕs´tẽrn pōrt)	109	39°30′N	79°00′W
Western Sahara, dep., Afr. (sȧ-hä´rȧ)	230	23°05′N	15°33′W
Western Samoa *see* Samoa, nation, Oc.	2	14°30′S	172°00′W
Western Siberian Lowland, depr., Russia	178	63°37′N	72°45′E
Westerville, Oh., U.S. (wĕs´tẽr-vĭl)	108	40°10′N	83°00′W
Westerwald, for., Ger. (vĕs´tĕr-väld)	168	50°35′N	7°45′E
Westfalen, hist. reg., Ger. (vĕst-fä-lĕn)	168	51°20′N	8°30′E
Westfield, Ma., U.S. (wĕst´fēld)	109	42°05′N	72°45′W
Westfield, N.J., U.S.	110a	40°39′N	74°21′W
Westfield, N.Y., U.S. (wĕst´fēld)	110a	42°20′N	79°40′W
Westford, Ma., U.S. (wĕst´fẽrd)	101a	42°35′N	71°26′W
West Frankfort, Il., U.S. (frăŋk´fŭrt)	108	37°55′N	88°55′W
West Ham, Eng., U.K.	158b	51°30′N	0°00′W
West Hartford, Ct., U.S. (härt´fẽrd)	109	41°45′N	72°45′W
West Helena, Ar., U.S. (hĕl´ĕn-ȧ)	121	34°32′N	90°39′W
West Indies, is. (ĭn´dēz)	129	19°00′N	78°30′W
West Jordon, Ut., U.S. (jôr´dăn)	117b	40°37′N	111°56′W
West Kirby, Eng., U.K. (kûr´bē)	158a	53°22′N	3°11′W
West Lafayette, In., U.S. (lä-fā-yĕt´)	108	40°25′N	86°55′W
Westlake, Oh., U.S.	111d	41°27′N	81°55′W
Westleigh, S. Afr. (wĕst-lē)	238c	27°39′S	27°18′E
West Liberty, Ia., U.S. (wĕst lĭb´ẽr-tĭ)	113	41°34′N	91°15′W
West Linn, Or., U.S. (lĭn)	116c	45°22′N	122°37′W
Westlock, Can. (wĕst´lŏk)	95	54°09′N	113°52′W
West Memphis, Ar., U.S.	121	35°08′N	90°11′W
West Midlands, hist. reg., Eng., U.K.	158a	52°26′N	1°50′W
Westminster, Ca., U.S. (wĕst´mĭn-stẽr)	117a	33°45′N	117°59′W
Westminster, Md., U.S.	109	39°40′N	76°55′W
Westminster, S.C., U.S.	124	34°38′N	83°10′W
Westmount, Can. (wĕst´mount)	102a	45°29′N	73°36′W
West Newbury, Ma., U.S. (nū´bẽr-ē)	101a	42°47′N	70°57′W
West Newton, Pa., U.S. (nū´tŭn)	111e	40°12′N	79°45′W
West New York, N.J., U.S. (nû yŏrk)	110a	40°47′N	74°01′W
West Nishnabotna, r., Ia., U.S. (nĭsh-nȧ-bŏt´nȧ)	112	40°56′N	95°37′W
Weston, Ma., U.S. (wĕs´tŭn)	101a	42°22′N	71°18′W
Weston, W.V., U.S.	108	39°00′N	80°30′W
Westonaria, S. Afr.	238c	26°19′S	27°38′E
Weston-super-Mare, Eng., U.K. (wĕs´tŭn sū´pẽr-mā´rē)	164	51°23′N	3°00′W
West Orange, N.J., U.S. (wĕst ŏr´ĕnj)	110a	40°46′N	74°14′W
West Palm Beach, Fl., U.S. (päm bēch)	105	26°44′N	80°04′W
West Pensacola, Fl., U.S. (pĕn-sȧ-kō´lȧ)	124	30°24′N	87°18′W
West Pittsburg, Ca., U.S. (pĭts´bûrg)	116b	38°02′N	121°56′W
Westplains, Mo., U.S. (wĕst-plānz´)	121	36°42′N	91°51′W
West Point, Ga., U.S.	124	32°52′N	85°10′W
West Point, Ms., U.S.	124	33°36′N	88°39′W
Westpoint, Ne., U.S.	112	41°50′N	96°00′W
West Point, N.Y., U.S.	110a	41°23′N	73°58′W
West Point, Ut., U.S.	117b	41°07′N	112°05′W
West Point, Va., U.S.	109	37°25′N	76°50′W
West Point Lake, res., U.S.	124	33°00′N	85°10′W
Westport, Ire.	164	53°44′N	9°36′W
Westport, Ct., U.S. (wĕst´pōrt)	110a	41°07′N	73°22′W
Westport, Or., U.S. (wĕst´pôrt)	116c	46°08′N	123°22′W
Westray, i., Scot., U.K. (wĕs´trā)	164a	59°19′N	3°05′W
West Road, r., Can. (rōd)	94	53°00′N	124°00′W
West Saint Paul, Mn., U.S. (sȧnt pôl´)	117g	44°55′N	93°05′W
West Sand Spit, i., T./C. Is.	135	21°25′N	72°10′W
West Slope, Or., U.S.	116c	45°30′N	122°46′W
West Tavaputs Plateau, plat., Ut., U.S. (wĕst tăv´ȧ-pŏts)	119	39°45′N	110°35′W
West Terre Haute, In., U.S. (tĕr-ê hōt´)	108	39°30′N	87°30′W
West Union, Ia., U.S. (ūn´yŭn)	113	42°58′N	91°48′W
West University Place, Tx., U.S.	123a	29°43′N	95°26′W
Westview, Oh., U.S. (wĕst´vū)	111d	41°21′N	81°54′W
West View, Pa., U.S.	111e	40°31′N	80°02′W
Westville, Can. (wĕst´vĭl)	101	45°35′N	62°43′W
Westville, Il., U.S.	108	40°00′N	87°40′W
West Virginia, state, U.S. (wĕst vẽr-jĭn´ĭ-ȧ)	105	39°00′N	80°50′W
West Walker, r., Ca., U.S. (wôk´ẽr)	118	38°25′N	119°25′W
West Warwick, R.I., U.S. (wŏr´ĭk)	110b	41°42′N	71°31′W
Westwego, La., U.S. (wĕst-wē´gō)	110d	29°55′N	90°09′W
Westwood, Ca., U.S. (wĕst´wŏod)	118	40°18′N	121°00′W
Westwood, Ks., U.S.	117f	39°03′N	94°37′W
Westwood, Ma., U.S.	101a	42°13′N	71°14′W
Westwood, N.J., U.S.	110a	40°59′N	74°02′W
West Wyalong, Austl. (wī´ȧlông)	219	34°00′S	147°20′E
West Yorkshire, hist. reg., Eng., U.K.	158a	53°37′N	1°48′W
Wetar, Pulau, i., Indon. (wĕt´ȧr)	213	7°34′S	126°00′E
Wetaskiwin, Can. (wĕ-tăs´kē-wŏn)	90	52°58′N	113°22′W
Wetmore, Tx., U.S. (wĕt´mōr)	117d	29°34′N	98°25′W
Wetter, Ger.	171c	51°23′N	7°23′E
Wetumpka, Al., U.S. (wê-tŭmp´kȧ)	124	32°33′N	86°12′W
Wetzlar, Ger. (vets´lär)	168	50°35′N	8°30′E
Wewak, Pap. N. Gui. (wȧ-wäk´)	213	3°19′S	143°30′E
Wewoka, Ok., U.S. (wê-wō´kȧ)	121	35°09′N	96°30′W
Wexford, Ire. (wĕks´fẽrd)	161	52°20′N	6°30′W
Weybridge, Eng., U.K. (wā´brĭj)	158b	51°20′N	0°26′W
Weyburn, Can. (wā´bûrn)	90	49°41′N	103°52′W
Weymouth, Eng., U.K. (wā´mŭth)	164	50°37′N	2°34′W
Weymouth, Ma., U.S.	101a	42°44′N	70°57′W
Weymouth, Oh., U.S.	111d	41°11′N	81°48′W
Whale Cay, i., Bah.	134	25°20′N	77°45′W
Whale Cay Channels, strt., Bah.	134	26°45′N	77°10′W
Wharton, N.J., U.S. (hwôr´tŭn)	110a	40°54′N	74°35′W
Wharton, Tx., U.S.	123	29°19′N	96°06′W
What Cheer, Ia., U.S. (hwŏt chēr)	113	41°23′N	92°24′W
Whatcom, Lake, l., Wa., U.S. (hwät´kŭm)	116c	48°44′N	123°34′W
Whatshan Lake, l., Can. (wŏt´shăn)	95	50°00′N	118°03′W
Wheatland, Wy., U.S. (hwēt´lănd)	115	42°04′N	104°52′W
Wheatland Reservoir Number 2, res., Wy., U.S.	115	41°52′N	105°36′W
Wheaton, Il., U.S. (hwē´tŭn)	111a	41°52′N	88°06′W
Wheaton, Md., U.S.	110e	39°05′N	77°05′W
Wheaton, Mn., U.S.	112	45°48′N	96°29′W
Wheeler Peak, mtn., N.M., U.S.	120	36°34′N	105°25′W
Wheeler Peak, mtn., Nv., U.S.	106	38°58′N	114°15′W
Wheeling, Il., U.S. (hwēl´ĭng)	111a	42°08′N	87°54′W
Wheeling, W.V., U.S.	108	40°05′N	80°45′W
Wheelwright, Arg. (ōē´l-rē´gt)	141c	33°46′S	61°14′W
Whidbey Island, i., Wa., U.S. (hwĭd´bē)	116a	48°13′N	122°50′W
Whippany, N.J., U.S. (hwĭp´ȧ-nē)	110a	40°49′N	74°25′W
Whitby, Can. (hwĭt´bē)	91	43°50′N	79°00′W
Whitchurch, Eng., U.K. (hwĭt´chûrch)	158a	52°58′N	2°49′W
White, l., Can.	98	48°47′N	85°50′W
White, l., Can.	99	45°15′N	76°35′W
White, r., Can.	98	48°34′N	85°46′W
White, r., In., U.S.	108	39°15′N	86°45′W
White, r., S.D., U.S.	112	43°13′N	101°04′W
White, r., Tx., U.S.	120	36°25′N	102°20′W
White, r., Vt., U.S.	109	43°45′N	72°35′W
White, r., Wa., U.S.	114	47°07′N	121°48′W
White, r., U.S.	107	35°30′N	92°00′W
White, r., U.S.	112	43°41′N	99°48′W
White, r., U.S.	119	40°10′N	108°55′W
White, East Fork, r., In., U.S.	108	38°45′N	86°20′W
White Bay, b., Can.	93a	50°00′N	56°30′W
White Bear Indian Reserve, I.R., Can.	97	49°50′N	102°15′W
White Bear Lake, l., Mn., U.S.	117g	45°04′N	92°58′W
White Castle, La., U.S.	123	30°10′N	91°09′W
White Center, Wa., U.S.	116a	47°31′N	122°21′W
White Cloud, Mi., U.S.	108	43°35′N	85°45′W
Whitecourt, Can. (wĭt´côrt)	90	54°09′N	115°41′W
White Earth, r., N.D., U.S.	112	48°30′N	102°44′W
White Earth Indian Reservation, I.R., Mn., U.S.	112	47°18′N	95°42′W
Whiteface, r., Mn., U.S. (whīt´fās)	113	47°12′N	92°13′W
Whitefield, N.H., U.S. (hwĭt´fēld)	109	44°20′N	71°35′W
Whitefish Bay, Wi., U.S.	111a	43°07′N	77°54′W
Whitefish Bay, b., Can.	97	49°26′N	94°14′W
Whitefish Bay, b., N.A.	113	46°36′N	84°50′W
White Hall, Il., U.S.	121	39°26′N	90°23′W
Whitehall, Mi., U.S. (hwĭt´hôl)	108	43°20′N	86°20′W
Whitehall, N.Y., U.S.	109	43°30′N	73°25′W
Whitehaven, Eng., U.K. (hwĭt´hā-vĕn)	164	54°35′N	3°30′W
Whitehorn, Point, c., Wa., U.S. (hwĭt´hôrn)	116d	48°54′N	122°48′W
Whitehorse, Can. (whĭt´hôrs)	90	60°39′N	135°01′W
White Lake, l., La., U.S.	123	29°40′N	92°35′W
White Mountain Peak, mtn., Ca., U.S.	118	37°38′N	118°13′W
White Mountains, mts., Me., U.S.	100	44°22′N	71°15′W
White Mountains, mts., N.H., U.S.	109	42°20′N	71°05′W
Whitemouth, l., Can.	97	49°14′N	95°40′W
White Nile (Al Bahr al Abyad), r., Sudan	231	12°30′N	32°30′E
White Otter, l., Can.	98	49°15′N	91°48′W
White Pass, p., N.A.	103	59°35′N	135°03′W
White Plains, N.Y., U.S.	110a	41°02′N	73°47′W
White River, Can.	98	48°38′N	85°23′W
White Rock, Can.	95	49°01′N	122°49′W
Whiterock Reservoir, res., Tx., U.S. (hwĭt´rŏk)	117c	32°51′N	96°40′W
White Russia *see* Belarus, nation, Eur.	178	53°30′N	25°33′E
Whitesail Lake, l., Can. (whīt´sāl)	94	53°30′N	127°00′W
White Sands National Monument, rec., N.M., U.S.	119	32°50′N	106°20′W
White Sea, sea, Russia	178	66°00′N	40°00′E
White Settlement, Tx., U.S.	117c	32°45′N	97°28′W
White Sulphur Springs, Mt., U.S.	115	46°32′N	110°49′W
White Umfolzi, r., S. Afr. (ŭm-fō-lō´zē)	233c	28°12′S	30°55′E
Whiteville, N.C., U.S. (hwĭt´vĭl)	125	34°18′N	78°45′W
White Volta (Volta Blanche), r., Afr.	234	9°40′N	1°10′W
Whitewater, Wi., U.S. (whĭt-wŏt´ẽr)	113	42°49′N	88°40′W
Whitewater, l., Can.	97	49°14′N	100°39′W
Whitewater, r., In., U.S.	111f	39°19′N	84°55′W
Whitewater Bay, b., Fl., U.S.	125a	25°16′N	80°21′W
Whitewater Creek, r., Mt., U.S.	115	48°50′N	107°50′W
Whitewell, Tn., U.S. (hwĭt´wĕl)	124	35°11′N	85°31′W
Whitewright, Tx., U.S. (hwĭt´rīt)	121	33°33′N	96°25′W
Whitham, r., Eng., U.K. (wĭth´ŭm)	158a	53°08′N	0°15′W
Whiting, In., U.S. (hwīt´ĭng)	111a	41°41′N	87°30′W
Whitinsville, Ma., U.S. (hwīt´ĕns-vĭl)	101a	42°06′N	71°40′W
Whitman, Ma., U.S. (hwĭt´măn)	101a	42°05′N	70°57′W
Whitmire, S.C., U.S. (hwĭt´mīr)	125	34°30′N	81°40′W
Whitney, Mount, mtn., Ca., U.S.	106	36°34′N	118°18′W
Whitney Lake, l., Tx., U.S. (hwĭt´nē)	123	32°02′N	97°36′W
Whitstable, Eng., U.K. (wĭt´stăb´l)	158b	51°22′N	1°03′E
Whitsunday, i., Austl. (hwĭt´s´n-dā)	221	20°16′S	149°00′E
Whittier, Ca., U.S. (hwĭt´ĭ-ẽr)	117a	33°58′N	118°02′W
Whittlesea, S. Afr. (wĭt´l´sē)	233c	32°11′S	26°51′E
Whitworth, Eng., U.K. (hwĭt´wŭrth)	158a	53°40′N	2°10′W
Whyalla, Austl. (hwī-ăl´ȧ)	218	33°00′S	137°32′E
Whymper, Mount, mtn., Can. (wĭm´pẽr)	94	48°57′N	124°10′W
Wiarton, Can. (wī´ȧr-tŭn)	91	44°45′N	80°45′W
Wichita, Ks., U.S. (wĭch´ĭ-tô)	104	37°42′N	97°21′W
Wichita, r., Tx., U.S.	120	33°50′N	99°38′W
Wichita Falls, Tx., U.S. (fôls)	104	33°54′N	98°29′W
Wichita Mountains, mts., Ok., U.S.	106	34°48′N	98°43′W
Wick, Scot., U.K. (wĭk)	160	58°25′N	3°05′W
Wickatunk, N.J., U.S. (wĭk´á-tŭnk)	110a	40°21′N	74°15′W
Wickenburg, Az., U.S.	119	33°58′N	112°44′W
Wickiup Reservoir, res., Or., U.S.	114	43°40′N	121°43′W
Wickliffe, Oh., U.S. (wĭk´klĭf)	111d	41°37′N	81°29′W
Wicklow, Ire.	164	52°59′N	6°06′W
Wicklow Mountains, mts., Ire. (wĭk´lō)	164	52°49′N	6°20′W
Wickup Mountain, mtn., Or., U.S. (wĭk´ŭp)	116c	46°06′N	123°35′W
Wiconisco, Pa., U.S. (wĭ-kŏn´ĭs-kō)	109	43°35′N	76°45′W
Widen, W.V., U.S. (wī´dĕn)	108	38°25′N	80°55′W
Widnes, Eng., U.K. (wĭd´nĕs)	158a	53°21′N	2°44′W
Wieliczka, Pol. (vyĕ-lēch´kȧ)	169	49°58′N	20°06′E
Wien *see* Vienna, Aus.	154	48°13′N	16°22′E
Wien, state, Aus.	159e	48°11′N	16°23′E
Wiener Neustadt, Aus. (vē´nẽr noi´shtät)	161	47°48′N	16°15′E
Wiener Wald, for., Aus.	159e	48°09′N	16°05′E
Wieprz, r., Pol. (vyĕpzh)	169	51°25′N	22°45′E
Wiergate, Tx., U.S. (wẽr´gāt)	123	31°00′N	93°42′W
Wiesbaden, Ger. (vēs´bä-dĕn)	161	50°05′N	8°15′E
Wigan, Eng., U.K. (wĭg´ăn)	164	53°33′N	2°37′W
Wiggins, Ms., U.S. (wĭg´ĭnz)	124	30°51′N	89°05′W
Wight, Isle of, i., Eng., U.K. (wīt)	164	50°44′N	1°17′W
Wilber, Ne., U.S. (wĭl´bẽr)	121	40°29′N	96°57′W
Wilburton, Ok., U.S. (wĭl´bẽr-tŭn)	121	34°54′N	95°18′W
Wilcannia, Austl. (wĭl-căn-ĭȧ)	219	31°30′S	143°30′E
Wildau, Ger. (vēl´dou)	159b	52°20′N	13°39′E
Wildberg, Ger. (vēl´bĕrgh)	159b	52°52′N	12°39′E
Wildcat Hill, hill, Can. (wīld´kăt)	97	53°17′N	102°30′W
Wildhay, r., Can. (wīld´hā)	95	53°15′N	117°20′W
Wildomar, Ca., U.S. (wĭl´dô-mär)	117a	33°35′N	117°17′W
Wild Rice, r., Mn., U.S.	112	47°10′N	96°40′W
Wild Rice, r., N.D., U.S.	112	46°10′N	97°12′W
Wild Rice Lake, l., Mn., U.S.	117h	46°54′N	92°10′W
Wildspitze, mtn., Aus.	168	46°55′N	10°50′E
Wildwood, N.J., U.S.	109	39°00′N	74°50′W
Wiley, Co., U.S. (wī´lē)	120	38°08′N	102°41′W
Wilge, r., S. Afr. (wĭl´jē)	238c	25°38′S	29°09′E
Wilge, r., S. Afr.	238c	27°27′S	28°46′E
Wilhelm, Mount, mtn., Pap. N. Gui.	213	5°58′S	144°58′E
Wilhelmina Gebergte, mts., Sur.	143	4°30′N	57°00′W
Wilhelmina Kanaal, can., Neth.	159a	51°37′N	4°55′E
Wilhelmshaven, Ger. (vēl-hĕlms-hä´fĕn)	160	53°30′N	8°10′E
Wilkes-Barre, Pa., U.S. (wĭlks´băr-ē)	105	41°15′N	75°50′W
Wilkes Land, reg., Ant.	224	71°00′S	126°00′E
Wilkeson, Wa., U.S. (wĭl-kē´sŭn)	116a	47°06′N	122°03′W
Wilkie, Can. (wĭlk´ē)	90	52°25′N	108°43′W
Wilkinsburg, Pa., U.S. (wĭl´kĭnz-bûrg)	111e	40°26′N	79°53′W
Willamette, r., Or., U.S.	106	45°00′N	123°00′W
Willapa Bay, b., Wa., U.S.	114	46°37′N	124°00′W
Willard, Oh., U.S. (wĭl´ȧrd)	108	41°00′N	82°50′W
Willard, Ut., U.S.	117b	41°24′N	112°02′W
Willcox, Az., U.S. (wĭl´kŏks)	119	32°15′N	109°50′W
Willcox Playa, l., Az., U.S.	119	32°08′N	109°51′W
Willemstad, Neth. Ant.	142	12°12′N	68°58′W
Willesden, Eng., U.K. (wĭlz´dĕn)	158b	51°31′N	0°17′W
William "Bill" Dannelly Reservoir, res., Al., U.S.	124	32°10′N	87°15′W
William Creek, Austl. (wĭl´yăm)	218	28°45′S	136°20′E

PLACE (Pronunciation)	PAGE	LAT.	LONG.
Williams, Az., U.S. (wĭl′yămz)	119	35°15′N	112°15′W
Williams, i., Bah.	134	24°30′N	78°30′W
Williamsburg, Ky., U.S. (wĭl′yămz-bûrg)	124	36°42′N	84°09′W
Williamsburg, Oh., U.S.	111f	39°04′N	84°02′W
Williamsburg, Va., U.S.	125	37°15′N	76°41′W
Williams Lake, Can.	95	52°08′N	122°09′W
Williamson, W.V., U.S. (wĭl′yăm-sŭn)	108	37°40′N	82°15′W
Williamsport, Md., U.S.	109	39°35′N	77°45′W
Williamsport, Pa., U.S.	109	41°15′N	77°05′W
Williamston, N.C., U.S. (wĭl′yămz-tŭn)	125	35°50′N	77°04′W
Williamston, S.C., U.S.	125	34°36′N	82°30′W
Williamstown, Austl.	217a	37°52′S	144°54′E
Williamstown, W.V., U.S. (wĭl′yămz-toun)	108	39°20′N	81°30′W
Williamsville, N.Y., U.S. (wĭl′yăm-vĭl)	111c	42°58′N	78°46′W
Willimantic, Ct., U.S. (wĭl-ĭ-măn′tĭk)	109	41°40′N	72°10′W
Willis, Tx., U.S. (wĭl′ĭs)	123	30°24′N	95°29′W
Willis Islands, is., Austl.	221	16°15′S	150°30′E
Williston, N.D., U.S. (wĭl′ĭs-tŭn)	104	48°08′N	103°38′W
Williston, Lake, l., Can.	92	55°40′N	123°40′W
Willmar, Mn., U.S. (wĭl′mär)	112	45°07′N	95°05′W
Willoughby, Oh., U.S. (wĭl′ô-bê)	111d	41°39′N	81°25′W
Willow, Ak., U.S.	103	61°50′N	150°00′W
Willow Creek, r., Or., U.S.	114	44°21′N	117°34′W
Willow Grove, Pa., U.S.	110f	40°07′N	75°07′W
Willowick, Oh., U.S. (wĭl′ô-wĭk)	111d	41°39′N	81°28′W
Willowmore, S. Afr. (wĭl′ô-môr)	232	33°15′S	23°37′E
Willow Run, Mi., U.S. (wĭl′ô rŭn)	111b	42°16′N	83°34′W
Willows, Ca., U.S. (wĭl′ōz)	118	39°32′N	122°11′W
Willow Springs, Mo., U.S. (sprĭngz)	121	36°59′N	91°56′W
Willowvale, S. Afr. (wĭ-lô′văl)	233c	32°17′S	28°32′E
Wills Point, Tx., U.S. (wĭlz point)	123	32°42′N	96°02′W
Wilmer, Tx., U.S. (wĭl′mẽr)	117c	32°35′N	96°40′W
Wilmette, Il., U.S. (wĭl-mĕt′)	111a	42°04′N	87°42′W
Wilmington, Austl.	222	32°39′S	138°07′E
Wilmington, Ca., U.S. (wĭl′mĭng-tŭn)	117a	33°46′N	118°16′W
Wilmington, De., U.S.	105	39°45′N	75°33′W
Wilmington, Il., U.S.	111a	41°19′N	88°09′W
Wilmington, Ma., U.S.	101a	42°34′N	71°10′W
Wilmington, N.C., U.S.	105	34°12′N	77°56′W
Wilmington, Oh., U.S.	108	39°20′N	83°50′W
Wilmore, Ky., U.S. (wĭl′môr)	108	37°50′N	84°35′W
Wilmslow, Eng., U.K. (wĭlmz′lō)	158a	53°19′N	2°14′W
Wilno see Vilnius, Lith.	178	54°40′N	25°26′E
Wilpoort, S. Afr.	238c	26°57′S	26°17′E
Wilson, Ar., U.S. (wĭl′sŭn)	121	35°35′N	90°02′W
Wilson, N.C., U.S.	125	35°42′N	77°55′W
Wilson, Ok., U.S.	121	34°09′N	97°27′W
Wilson, r., Al., U.S.	124	34°53′N	87°28′W
Wilson, Mount, mtn., Ca., U.S.	117a	34°15′N	118°06′W
Wilson, Point, c., Austl.	217a	38°05′S	144°31′E
Wilson Lake, res., Al., U.S.	107	34°45′N	87°30′W
Wilson's Promontory, pen., Austl. (wĭl′sŭnz)	221	39°05′S	146°50′E
Wilsonville, Il., U.S. (wĭl′sŭn-vĭl)	117e	39°04′N	89°52′W
Wilstedt, Ger. (vēl′shtĕt)	159c	53°45′N	10°04′E
Wilster, Ger. (vēl′stĕr)	159c	53°55′N	9°23′E
Wilton, Ct., U.S. (wĭl′tŭn)	110a	41°11′N	73°25′W
Wilton, N.D., U.S.	112	47°09′N	100°47′W
Wiluna, Austl. (wĭ-lōō′nȧ)	218	26°35′S	120°25′E
Winamac, In., U.S. (wĭn′ȧ măk)	108	41°05′N	86°40′W
Winburg, S. Afr. (wĭm-bûrg)	238c	28°31′S	27°02′E
Winchester, Eng., U.K.	164	51°04′N	1°20′W
Winchester, Ca., U.S. (wĭn′chĕs-tẽr)	117a	33°41′N	117°06′W
Winchester, Id., U.S.	114	46°14′N	116°39′W
Winchester, In., U.S.	108	40°10′N	84°50′W
Winchester, Ky., U.S.	108	38°00′N	84°15′W
Winchester, Ma., U.S.	101a	42°28′N	71°09′W
Winchester, N.H., U.S.	109	42°45′N	72°25′W
Winchester, Tn., U.S.	124	35°11′N	86°06′W
Winchester, Va., U.S.	109	39°10′N	78°10′W
Wind, r., Wy., U.S.	115	43°17′N	109°02′W
Windber, Pa., U.S. (wĭnd′bẽr)	109	40°15′N	78°45′W
Wind Cave National Park, rec., S.D., U.S.	112	43°36′N	103°53′W
Winder, Ga., U.S. (wīn′dẽr)	124	33°58′N	83°43′W
Windermere, Eng., U.K. (wĭn′dẽr-mẽr)	164	54°25′N	2°59′W
Windham, Ct., U.S. (wĭnd′ăm)	109	41°45′N	72°05′W
Windham, N.H., U.S.	101a	42°49′N	71°21′W
Windhoek, Nmb. (vĭnt′hŏŏk)	232	22°05′S	17°10′E
Wind Lake, l., Wi., U.S.	111a	42°49′N	88°06′W
Wind Mountain, mtn., N.M., U.S.	122	32°02′N	105°30′W
Windom, Mn., U.S. (wĭn′dŭm)	112	43°50′N	95°04′W
Windora, Austl. (wĭn-dō′rȧ)	219	25°15′S	142°50′E
Wind River Indian Reservation, I.R., Wy., U.S.	115	43°26′N	109°00′W
Wind River Range, mts., Wy., U.S.	106	43°19′N	109°47′W
Windsor, Austl. (wĭn′zẽr)	217b	33°37′S	150°49′E
Windsor, Can.	91	42°19′N	83°00′W
Windsor, Can.	93a	48°57′N	55°40′W
Windsor, Can.	91	44°59′N	64°08′W
Windsor, Eng., U.K.	164	51°27′N	0°37′W
Windsor, Co., U.S.	120	40°27′N	104°51′W
Windsor, Mo., U.S.	121	38°32′N	93°31′W
Windsor, N.C., U.S.	125	35°58′N	76°57′W
Windsor, Vt., U.S.	109	43°30′N	72°25′W
Windward Islands, is., N.A. (wĭnd′wẽrd)	129	12°45′N	61°40′W
Windward Passage, strt., N.A.	129	19°30′N	74°20′W
Winefred Lake, l., Can.	96	55°30′N	110°35′W
Winfield, Ks., U.S.	121	37°14′N	97°00′W
Winifred, Mt., U.S. (wĭn ĭ frĕd)	115	47°35′N	109°20′W
Winisk, r., Can.	93	54°30′N	86°30′W
Wink, Tx., U.S. (wĭŋk)	122	31°48′N	103°06′W
Winkler, Can. (wĭnk′lẽr)	97	49°11′N	97°56′W
Winneba, Ghana (wĭn′ê-bȧ)	234	5°25′N	0°36′W
Winnebago, Mn., U.S. (wĭn′ê-bā′gō)	113	43°45′N	94°08′W
Winnebago, Lake, l., Wi., U.S.	113	44°09′N	88°10′W
Winnebago Indian Reservation, I.R., Ne., U.S.	112	42°15′N	96°06′W
Winnemucca, Nv., U.S. (wĭn-ê-mŭk′ȧ)	104	40°59′N	117°43′W
Winnemucca, l., Nv., U.S.	118	40°06′N	119°07′W
Winner, S.D., U.S. (wĭn′ẽr)	112	43°22′N	99°50′W
Winnetka, Il., U.S. (wĭ-nĕt′kȧ)	111a	42°07′N	87°44′W
Winnett, Mt., U.S. (wĭn′ĕt)	115	47°01′N	108°20′W
Winnfield, La., U.S. (wĭn′fēld)	123	31°56′N	92°39′W
Winnibigoshish, l., Mn., U.S. (wĭn′ĭ-bĭ-gō′shĭsh)	113	47°30′N	93°45′W
Winnipeg, Can. (wĭn′ĭ-pĕg)	90	49°53′N	97°09′W
Winnipeg, r., Can.	92	50°30′N	95°00′W
Winnipeg, Lake, l., Can.	92	52°00′N	97°00′W
Winnipegosis, Can. (wĭn′ĭ-pê-gō′sĭs)	90	51°39′N	99°56′W
Winnipegosis, l., Can.	92	52°30′N	100°00′W
Winnipesaukee, l., N.H., U.S. (wĭn′ê-pê-sô′kê)	109	43°40′N	71°20′W
Winnsboro, La., U.S. (wĭnz′bŭr′ô)	123	32°09′N	91°42′W
Winnsboro, S.C., U.S.	125	34°29′N	81°05′W
Winnsboro, Tx., U.S.	121	32°56′N	95°15′W
Winona, Can. (wĭ-nō′nȧ)	102d	43°13′N	79°39′W
Winona, Mn., U.S.	105	44°03′N	91°40′W
Winona, Ms., U.S.	124	33°29′N	89°43′W
Winooski, Vt., U.S. (wĭ-nōōs′kê)	109	44°30′N	73°10′W
Winsen, Ger. (vēn′zĕn)	159c	53°22′N	10°13′E
Winsford, Eng., U.K. (wĭnz′fẽrd)	158a	53°11′N	2°30′W
Winslow, Az., U.S. (wĭnz′lō)	119	35°00′N	110°45′W
Winslow, Wa., U.S.	116a	47°38′N	122°31′W
Winsted, Ct., U.S. (wĭn′stĕd)	109	41°55′N	73°05′W
Winster, Eng., U.K. (wĭn′stẽr)	158a	53°08′N	1°38′W
Winston-Salem, N.C., U.S. (wĭn stŭn-sā′lĕm)	105	36°05′N	80°15′W
Winterberge, mts., Afr.	233c	32°18′S	26°25′E
Winter Garden, Fl., U.S. (wĭn′tẽr gär′d′n)	125a	28°32′N	81°35′W
Winter Haven, Fl., U.S. (hā′vĕn)	125a	28°01′N	81°38′W
Winter Park, Fl., U.S. (pärk)	125a	28°35′N	81°21′W
Winters, Tx., U.S. (wĭn′tẽrz)	122	31°59′N	99°58′W
Winterset, Ia., U.S. (wĭn′tẽr-sĕt)	113	41°19′N	94°03′W
Winterswijk, Neth.	171c	51°58′N	6°44′E
Winterthur, Switz. (vĭn′tẽr-tōōr)	168	47°30′N	8°32′E
Winterton, S. Afr.	233c	28°51′S	29°33′E
Winthrop, Ma., U.S.	101a	42°23′N	70°59′W
Winthrop, Me., U.S. (wĭn′thrŭp)	100	44°19′N	70°00′W
Winthrop, Mn., U.S.	113	44°31′N	94°20′W
Winton, Austl. (wĭn-tŭn)	219	22°17′S	143°08′E
Wipperfürth, Ger. (vē′pẽr-fürt)	171c	51°07′N	7°23′E
Wirksworth, Eng., U.K. (wûrks′wûrth)	158a	53°05′N	1°35′W
Wisconsin, state, U.S. (wĭs-kŏn′sĭn)	105	44°30′N	91°00′W
Wisconsin, r., Wi., U.S.	107	43°14′N	90°34′W
Wisconsin Dells, Wi., U.S.	113	43°38′N	89°46′W
Wisconsin Rapids, Wi., U.S.	113	44°24′N	89°50′W
Wishek, N.D., U.S. (wĭsh′ĕk)	112	46°15′N	99°34′W
Wisła, r., Pol. (vēs′wȧ)	156	52°30′N	20°00′E
Wisłoka, r., Pol. (vēs-wô′kȧ)	169	49°55′N	21°26′E
Wismar, Ger. (vĭs′mär)	160	53°53′N	11°28′E
Wismar, Guy. (wĭs′mȧr)	143	5°58′N	58°15′W
Wisner, Ne., U.S. (wĭz′nẽr)	112	42°00′N	96°55′W
Wissembourg, Fr. (vê-sän-bōōr′)	171	49°03′N	7°58′E
Wister, Lake, l., Ok., U.S. (vĭs′tẽr)	121	35°02′N	94°52′W
Witbank, S. Afr. (wĭt-băŋk)	238c	25°53′S	29°14′E
Witberg, mtn., Afr.	233c	30°32′S	27°18′E
Witham, Eng., U.K. (wĭdh′ăm)	158b	51°48′N	0°37′E
Witham, r., Eng., U.K.	158a	53°11′N	0°20′W
Withamsville, Oh., U.S. (wĭdh′ămz-vĭl)	111f	39°04′N	84°16′W
Withlacoochee, r., Fl., U.S. (wĭth-lȧ-kōō′chê)	125a	28°58′N	82°30′W
Withlacoochee, r., Ga., U.S.	124	31°15′N	83°30′W
Withrow, Mn., U.S. (wĭth′rō)	117g	45°08′N	92°54′W
Witney, Eng., U.K. (wĭt′nê)	158b	51°45′N	1°30′W
Witt, Il., U.S. (vĭt)	108	39°10′N	89°15′W
Witten, Ger. (vē′tĕn)	171c	51°26′N	7°19′E
Wittenberg, Ger. (vē′tĕn-bĕrgh)	168	51°53′N	12°40′E
Wittenberge, Ger. (vĭt-ĕn-bĕr′gĕ)	168	52°59′N	11°45′E
Wittlich, Ger. (vĭt′lĭk)	168	49°58′N	6°54′E
Witu, Kenya (wē′tōō)	233	2°18′S	40°28′E
Witu Islands, is., Pap. N. Gui.	213	4°45′S	149°50′E
Witwatersberg, mts., S. Afr. (wĭt-wôr-tẽrz-bûrg)	233b	25°58′S	27°53′E
Witwatersrand, mtn., S. Afr. (wĭt-wôr′tẽrs-rănd)	238c	25°55′S	26°27′E
Wkra, r., Pol. (f′krȧ)	169	52°40′N	20°35′E
Włocławek, Pol. (vwô-tswä′vĕk)	169	52°38′N	19°08′E
Włodawa, Pol. (vwô-dä′vä)	169	51°33′N	23°33′E
Włoszczowa, Pol. (vwôsh-chô′vä)	169	50°51′N	19°58′E
Woburn, Ma., U.S. (wō′bŭrn) (wô′bŭrn)	101a	42°29′N	71°10′W
Woerden, Neth.	159a	52°05′N	4°52′E
Woking, Eng., U.K.	158b	51°18′N	0°33′W
Wokingham, Eng., U.K. (wô′kĭng-hăm)	158b	51°23′N	0°50′W
Wolcott, Ks., U.S. (wōl′kŏt)	117f	39°12′N	94°47′W
Wolf, i., Can. (wŏlf)	99	44°10′N	76°25′W
Wolf, r., Ms., U.S.	124	30°45′N	89°36′W
Wolf, r., Wi., U.S.	113	45°14′N	88°45′W
Wolfenbüttel, Ger. (vôl′fĕn-büt-ĕl)	168	52°10′N	10°32′E
Wolf Lake, l., Il., U.S.	111a	41°39′N	87°33′W
Wolf Point, Mt., U.S. (wŏlf point)	115	48°07′N	105°40′W
Wolfratshausen, Ger. (vōlf′räts-hou-zĕn)	159d	47°55′N	11°25′E
Wolfsburg, Ger. (vōlfs′bōōrgh)	168	52°30′N	10°37′E
Wolfville, Can. (wŏlf′vĭl)	100	45°05′N	64°22′W
Wolgast, Ger. (vôl′gäst)	168	54°04′N	13°46′E
Wolhuterskop, S. Afr.	233b	25°41′S	27°40′E
Wolkersdorf, Aus.	159e	48°24′N	16°31′E
Wollaston, l., Can. (wŏl′ăs-tŭn)	92	58°15′N	103°20′W
Wollaston Peninsula, pen., Can.	92	70°00′N	115°00′W
Wollongong, Austl. (wŏl′ŭn-gŏng)	219	34°26′S	151°05′E
Wołomin, Pol. (vō-wō′mēn)	169	52°19′N	21°17′E
Wolseley, Can.	96	50°25′N	103°15′W
Woltersdorf, Ger. (vōl′tĕs-dōrf)	159b	52°07′N	13°13′E
Wolverhampton, Eng., U.K. (wŏl′vẽr-hămp-tŭn)	161	52°35′N	2°07′W
Wolwehoek, S. Afr.	238c	26°55′S	27°50′E
Wŏnsan, Kor., N. (wŭn′sän′)	205	39°08′N	127°24′E
Wonthaggi, Austl. (wŏnt-hăg′ê)	219	38°45′S	145°42′E
Wood, S.D., U.S. (wŏd)	112	43°26′N	100°25′W
Woodbine, Ia., U.S. (wŏd′bīn)	112	41°44′N	95°42′W
Woodbridge, N.J., U.S. (wŏd′brĭj′)	110a	40°33′N	74°18′W
Wood Buffalo National Park, rec., Can.	92	59°50′N	118°53′W
Woodburn, Il., U.S. (wŏd′bûrn)	117e	39°03′N	90°01′W
Woodburn, Or., U.S.	114	45°10′N	122°51′W
Woodbury, N.J., U.S. (wŏd′bĕr-ê)	110f	39°50′N	75°14′W
Woodcrest, Ca., U.S. (wŏd′krĕst)	117a	33°53′N	117°18′W
Woodinville, Wa., U.S. (wŏd′ĭn-vĭl)	116a	47°46′N	122°09′W
Woodland, Ca., U.S. (wŏd′lănd)	118	38°41′N	121°47′W
Woodland, Wa., U.S.	116c	45°54′N	122°45′W
Woodland Hills, Ca., U.S.	117a	34°10′N	118°36′W
Woodlark Island, i., Pap. N. Gui. (wŏd′lärk)	213	9°07′S	152°00′E
Woodlawn Beach, N.Y., U.S. (wŏd′lôn bēch)	111c	42°48′N	78°51′W
Wood Mountain, mtn., Can.	96	49°14′N	106°20′W
Wood River, Il., U.S.	117e	38°52′N	90°06′W
Woodroffe, Mount, mtn., Austl. (wŏd′rŭf)	220	26°05′S	132°00′E
Woodruff, S.C., U.S. (wŏd′rŭf)	125	34°43′N	82°03′W
Woods, l., Austl. (wŏdz)	220	18°00′S	133°18′E
Woods, Lake of the, l., N.A.	93	49°25′N	93°25′W
Woods Cross, Ut., U.S. (krôs)	117b	40°53′N	111°54′W
Woodsfield, Oh., U.S. (wŏdz-fēld)	108	39°45′N	81°10′W
Woodson, Or., U.S. (wŏdsŭn)	116c	46°07′N	123°20′W
Woodstock, Can. (wŏd′stŏk)	99	43°10′N	80°50′W
Woodstock, Can.	91	46°09′N	67°34′W
Woodstock, Eng., U.K.	158b	51°48′N	1°22′W
Woodstock, Il., U.S.	113	42°20′N	88°29′W
Woodstock, Va., U.S.	109	38°55′N	78°25′W
Woodsville, N.H., U.S. (wŏdz′vĭl)	109	44°10′N	72°00′W
Woodville, Ms., U.S. (wŏd′vĭl)	124	31°06′N	91°11′W
Woodville, Tx., U.S.	123	30°48′N	94°25′W
Woodward, Ok., U.S. (wŏd′wôrd)	120	36°25′N	99°24′W
Woolwich, Eng., U.K. (wŏŏl′ĭj)	158b	51°28′N	0°05′E
Woomera, Austl. (wōōm′ẽrȧ)	218	31°15′S	136°43′E
Woonsocket, R.I., U.S. (wōōn-sŏk′ĕt)	110b	42°00′N	71°30′W
Woonsocket, S.D., U.S.	112	44°03′N	98°17′W
Wooster, Oh., U.S. (wŏs′tẽr)	108	40°50′N	81°55′W
Worcester, S. Afr. (wōōs′tẽr)	232	33°35′S	19°31′E
Worcester, Eng., U.K. (wŏ′stẽr)	161	52°09′N	2°14′W
Worcester, Ma., U.S. (wŏs′tẽr)	105	42°16′N	71°49′W
Worcestershire, co., Eng., U.K.	158a	52°25′N	2°10′W
Worden, Il., U.S. (wôr′dĕn)	117e	38°56′N	89°50′W
Workington, Eng., U.K. (wûr′kĭng-tŭn)	164	54°40′N	3°30′W
Worksop, Eng., U.K. (wûrk′sŏp) (wûr′sŭp)	158a	53°18′N	1°07′W
Worland, Wy., U.S. (wûr′lănd)	115	44°02′N	107°56′W
Worms, Ger. (vōrms)	161	49°37′N	8°22′E
Worona Reservoir, res., Austl.	217b	34°12′S	150°55′E
Worth, Il., U.S. (wûrth)	111a	41°42′N	87°47′W
Wortham, Tx., U.S. (wûr′dhăm)	123	31°46′N	96°22′W
Worthing, Eng., U.K. (wûr′dhĭng)	164	50°48′N	0°29′W
Worthington, In., U.S. (wûr′dhĭng-tŭn)	108	39°05′N	87°00′W
Worthington, Mn., U.S.	112	43°38′N	95°36′W
Worth Lake, l., Tx., U.S.	117c	32°48′N	97°32′W
Wowoni, Pulau, i., Indon. (wō-wō′nê)	213	4°05′S	123°45′E
Wragby, Eng., U.K. (răg′bê)	158a	53°17′N	0°19′W
Wrangell, Ak., U.S. (răn′gĕl)	106a	56°28′N	132°25′W
Wrangell, Cape, c., Ak., U.S.	103a	52°55′N	172°30′E
Wrangell, Mount, mtn., Ak., U.S.	103	61°58′N	143°50′W
Wrangell Mountains, mts., Ak., U.S.	103	62°28′N	142°40′W
Wrangell-Saint Elias National Park, rec., Ak., U.S.	103	61°00′N	142°00′W
Wrath, Cape, c., Scot., U.K. (răth)	164	58°34′N	5°01′W
Wray, Co., U.S. (rā)	120	40°06′N	102°14′W
Wreak, r., Eng., U.K. (rĕk)	158a	52°45′N	0°59′W
Wreck Reefs, rf., Austl. (rĕk)	221	22°00′S	155°52′E
Wrekin, The, mtn., Eng., U.K. (rĕk′ĭn)	158a	52°40′N	2°33′W
Wrens, Ga., U.S. (rĕnz)	125	33°15′N	82°25′W
Wrentham, Ma., U.S.	101a	42°04′N	71°20′W
Wrexham, Wales, U.K. (rĕk′săm)	164	53°03′N	3°00′W
Wrexham, co., Wales, U.K.	158a	53°00′N	2°57′W
Wrights Corners, N.Y., U.S. (rītz kôr′nẽrz)	111c	43°14′N	78°42′W
Wrightsville, Ga., U.S. (rīts′vĭl)	125	32°44′N	82°44′W
Wrocław, Pol. (vrôtsläv) (brĕs′lou)	169	51°07′N	17°10′E
Wrotham, Eng., U.K. (rōōt′ŭm)	158b	51°18′N	0°19′E
Września, Pol. (vzhăsh′nyȧ)	169	52°19′N	17°33′E
Wu, r., China (wōō′)	204	27°30′N	107°00′E
Wuchang, China	208	44°59′N	127°00′E
Wuchang, China (wōō-chăn)	205	30°32′N	114°25′E
Wucheng, China (wōō-chŭŋ)	206	37°14′N	116°03′E
Wuhan, China	205	30°30′N	114°15′E

ng-sing; ŋ-baŋk; ɴ-nasalized n; nŏd; cŏmmit; ōld; ôbey; ôrder; oi-boil; fōōd; ŏ-as oo in foot; ou-out; s-soft; sh-dish; th-thin; pūre; ûnite; ûrn; stŭd; circŭs; ü-as in French tu; ′-indeterminate vowel.

368 Wuhu – Yellowstone Lake
PRONOUNCING INDEX

PLACE (Pronunciation)	PAGE	LAT.	LONG.
Wuhu, China (wo͞o′ho͞o)	209	31°22′N	118°22′E
Wuji, China (wo͞o-jyĭ)	206	38°12′N	114°57′E
Wujiang, China (wo͞o-jyäŋ)	206	31°10′N	120°38′E
Wuleidao Wan, b., China (wo͞o-lā-dou wän)	206	36°55′N	122°00′E
Wulidian, China (wo͞o-lē-dĭĕn)	206	32°09′N	114°17′E
Wünsdorf, Ger. (vüns′dorf)	159b	52°10′N	13°29′E
Wupatki National Monument, rec., Az., U.S.	119	35°35′N	111°45′W
Wuping, China (wo͞o-pĭŋ)	209	25°05′N	116°01′E
Wuppertal, Ger. (vòp′ĕr-täl)	161	51°16′N	7°14′E
Wuqiao, China (wo͞o-chyou)	206	37°37′N	116°29′E
Würm, r., Ger. (vürm)	159d	48°07′N	11°20′E
Würselen, Ger. (vür′zĕ-lĕn)	171c	50°49′N	6°09′E
Würzburg, Ger. (vürts′bòrgh)	161	49°48′N	9°57′E
Wurzen, Ger. (vòrt′sĕn)	161	51°22′N	12°45′E
Wushi, China (wo͞o-shr)	204	41°13′N	79°08′E
Wusong, China (wo͞o-sôŋ)	206	31°23′N	121°29′E
Wustermark, Ger. (vo͞os′tĕr-märk)	159b	52°33′N	12°57′E
Wustrau, Ger. (vōost′rou)	159b	52°40′N	12°51′E
Wuustwezel, Bel.	159a	51°23′N	4°36′E
Wuwei, China (wo͞o′wā′)	209	31°19′N	117°53′E
Wuxi, China (wo͞o-shyē)	205	31°36′N	120°17′E
Wuxing, China (wo͞o-shyĭŋ)	205	30°38′N	120°10′E
Wuyi Shan, mts., China (wo͞o-yē shän)	209	26°38′N	116°35′E
Wuyou, China (wo͞o-yō)	206	33°18′N	120°15′E
Wuzhi Shan, mtn., China (wo͞o-jr shän)	209	18°48′N	109°30′E
Wuzhou, China (wo͞o-jō)	205	23°32′N	111°25′E
Wyandotte, Mi., U.S. (wī′ăn-dŏt)	111b	42°12′N	83°10′W
Wye, Eng., U.K. (wī)	158b	51°12′N	0°57′E
Wye, r., Eng., U.K.	158a	53°14′N	1°46′W
Wylie, Lake, res., S.C., U.S.	125	35°02′N	81°21′W
Wymore, Ne., U.S. (wī′mōr)	121	40°09′N	96°41′W
Wynberg, S. Afr. (wĭn′bĕrg)	232a	34°00′S	18°28′E
Wyndham, Austl. (wĭnd′ăm)	218	15°30′S	128°15′E
Wynne, Ar., U.S. (wĭn)	121	35°12′N	90°46′W
Wynnewood, Ok., U.S. (wĭn′wòd)	121	34°39′N	97°10′W
Wynona, Ok., U.S. (wī-nō′nȧ)	121	36°33′N	96°19′W
Wynyard, Can. (wĭn′yērd)	90	51°47′N	104°10′W
Wyoming, Oh., U.S. (wī-ō′mĭng)	111f	39°14′N	84°28′W
Wyoming, state, U.S.	104	42°50′N	108°30′W
Wyoming Range, mts., Wy., U.S.	106	42°43′N	110°35′W
Wyre Forest, for., Eng., U.K. (wīr)	158a	52°24′N	2°24′W
Wysokie Mazowieckie, Pol. (vẻ-sô′kyĕ mä-zô-vyĕts′kyĕ)	169	52°55′N	22°42′E
Wyszków, Pol. (vẻsh′kòf)	169	52°35′N	21°29′E
Wytheville, Va., U.S. (wĭth′vĭl)	125	36°55′N	81°06′W

X

PLACE (Pronunciation)	PAGE	LAT.	LONG.
Xàbia, Spain	173	38°45′N	0°07′E
Xagua, Banco, bk., Cuba (bä′n-kō-sä′gwä)	134	21°35′N	80°50′W
Xai Xai, Moz.	232	25°00′S	33°45′E
Xalapa, Mex.	128	19°32′N	96°53′W
Xangongo, Ang.	232	16°50′S	15°05′E
Xankändi (Stepanakert), Azer. (styĕ′pän-ȧ-kĕrt)	181	39°50′N	46°40′E
Xanten, Ger. (ksän′tĕn)	171c	51°40′N	6°28′E
Xánthi, Grc.	163	41°08′N	24°53′E
Xàtiva, Spain	162	38°58′N	0°31′W
Xau, Lake, l., Bots.	232	21°15′S	24°38′E
Xcalak, Mex. (sä-lä′k)	132a	18°15′N	87°50′W
Xelva, Spain	172	39°43′N	1°00′W
Xenia, Oh., U.S. (zē′nĭ-ȧ)	108	39°40′N	83°55′W
Xi, r., China (shyē)	209	23°15′N	112°10′E
Xiajin, China (shyä-jyĭn)	208	36°58′N	115°59′E
Xiamen, China	205	24°30′N	118°10′E
Xiamen, i., Tai. (shyä-mŭn)	209	24°28′N	118°20′E
Xi′an, China (shyē-än)	204	34°20′N	109°00′E
Xiang, r., China (shyäŋ)	205	27°30′N	112°30′E
Xianghe, China (shyäŋ-hŭ)	206	39°46′N	116°59′E
Xiangtan, China (shyäŋ-tän)	205	27°55′N	112°45′E
Xianyang, China (shyĕn-yäŋ)	208	34°20′N	108°40′E
Xiaoxingkai Hu, l., China (shyou-shyĭŋ-kī ho͞o)	210	42°25′N	132°45′E
Xiapu, China (shyä-po͞o)	205	27°00′N	120°00′E
Xiayi, China (shyä-yē)	206	34°15′N	116°07′E
Xicotencatl, Mex. (sē-kô-tĕn-kät′′l)	130	23°00′N	98°58′W
Xifeng, China (shyē-fŭŋ)	208	42°40′N	124°40′E
Xiheying, China (shyē-hŭ-yĭŋ)	206	39°58′N	114°50′E
Xiliao, r., China (shyē-lĭou)	208	43°23′N	121°40′E
Xilitla, Mex. (sẻ-lē′tlä)	130	21°24′N	98°59′W
Xinchang, China (shyn-chäŋ)	207b	31°02′N	121°38′E
Xing′an, China (shyĭŋ-än)	209	25°44′N	110°32′E
Xingcheng, China (shyĭŋ-chŭŋ)	206	40°38′N	120°41′E
Xinghua, China (shyĭŋ-hwä)	206	32°58′N	119°48′E
Xingjiawan, China (shyĭŋ-jyä-wän)	206	37°16′N	114°54′E
Xingtai, China (shyĭŋ-tī)	208	37°04′N	114°33′E
Xingu, r., Braz. (zhẻŋ-gò′)	143	6°20′S	52°34′W
Xinhai, China (shyĭn-hī)	206	36°59′N	117°33′E
Xinhua, China (shyĭn-hwä)	209	27°45′N	111°20′E
Xinhuai, r., China (shyĭn-hwī)	206	33°48′N	119°39′E
Xinhui, China (shyn-hwā)	209	22°40′N	113°08′E
Xining, China (shyē-nĭŋ)	204	36°52′N	101°36′E
Xinjiang (Sinkiang), prov., China (shyĭn-jyäŋ)	204	40°15′N	82°15′E
Xinjin, China (shyĭn-jyĭn)	208	39°23′N	121°57′E
Xinmin, China (shyĭn-mĭn)	208	42°00′N	122°42′E
Xintai, China (shyĭn-tī)	206	35°55′N	117°44′E
Xintang, China (shyĭn-täŋ)	207a	23°08′N	113°36′E
Xinxian, China (shyĭn shyĕn)	206	31°47′N	114°50′E
Xinxian, China	208	38°20′N	112°45′E
Xinxiang, China (shyĭn-shyäŋ)	208	35°17′N	113°49′E
Xinyang, China (shyĭn-yäŋ)	205	32°08′N	114°04′E
Xinye, China (shyĭn-yŭ)	208	32°40′N	112°20′E
Xinzao, China (shyĭn-dzou)	207a	23°01′N	113°25′E
Xinzheng, China (shyĭn-jŭŋ)	206	34°24′N	113°43′E
Xinzo de Limia, Spain	172	42°03′N	7°43′W
Xiongyuecheng, China (shyôŋ-yůĕ-chŭŋ)	206	40°10′N	122°08′E
Xiping, China (shyē-pĭŋ)	206	33°21′N	114°01′E
Xishui, China (shyē-shwā)	209	30°30′N	115°10′E
Xixian, China (shyē shyĕn)	206	32°20′N	114°42′E
Xixona, Spain	173	38°31′N	0°29′W
Xiyang, China (shyē-yäŋ)	206	37°37′N	113°42′E
Xiyou, China (shyē-yō)	206	37°21′N	119°59′E
Xizang (Tibet), prov., China (shyē-dzäŋ)	204	31°15′N	87°30′E
Xizhong Dao, i., China (shyē-jôŋ dou)	206	39°27′N	121°06′E
Xochihuehuetlán, Mex. (sô-chē-wĕ-wĕ-tlá′n)	131	17°53′N	98°29′E
Xochimilco, Mex. (sō-chẻ-mēl′kô)	131a	19°15′N	99°06′W
Xuancheng, China (shyůän-chŭŋ)	209	30°52′N	118°48′E
Xuanhua, China (shyůän-hwä)	208	40°35′N	115°05′E
Xuanhuadian, China (shyůän-hwä-dĭĕn)	206	31°42′N	114°29′E
Xuchang, China (shyo͞o-chäŋ)	208	34°02′N	113°49′E
Xudat, Azer.	182	41°38′N	48°42′E
Xuddur, Som.	238a	3°55′N	43°45′E
Xun, r., China (shyòn)	209	23°28′N	110°30′E
Xuzhou, China	205	34°17′N	117°10′E

Y

PLACE (Pronunciation)	PAGE	LAT.	LONG.
Ya′an, China (yä-än)	204	30°00′N	103°20′E
Yablonovyy Khrebet, mts., Russia (yȧ-blô-nô-vẻ′)	179	51°15′N	111°30′E
Yablunivsikyi, Pereval, p., Ukr.	169	48°20′N	24°25′E
Yacheng, China (yä-chŭŋ)	209	18°20′N	109°10′E
Yachiyo, Japan	211a	35°43′N	140°07′E
Yacolt, Wa., U.S. (yă′kôlt)	116c	45°52′N	122°24′W
Yacolt Mountain, mtn., Wa., U.S.	116c	45°52′N	122°27′W
Yacona, r., Ms., U.S. (yȧ′cō nă)	124	34°13′N	89°30′W
Yacuiba, Bol. (yȧ-ko͞o-ē′bȧ)	142	22°02′S	63°44′W
Yadkin, r., N.C., U.S. (yăd′kĭn)	125	36°12′N	80°40′W
Yafran, Libya	230	31°57′N	12°04′E
Yaguajay, Cuba (yä-guä-hä′ẻ)	134	22°20′N	79°20′W
Yahagi-Gawa, r., Japan (yä′hä-gẻ gä′wä)	211	35°16′N	137°22′E
Yahongqiao, China (yä-hôŋ-chyou)	206	39°45′N	117°52′E
Yahualica, Mex. (yä-wä-lē′kä)	130	21°08′N	102°53′W
Yajalón, Mex. (yä-hä-lōn′)	131	17°16′N	92°20′W
Yakhroma, Russia (yäl′rô-ma)	186b	56°17′N	37°30′E
Yakhroma, r., Russia	186b	56°15′N	37°38′E
Yakima, Wa., U.S. (yăk′ĭmȧ)	104	46°35′N	120°30′W
Yakima, r., Wa., U.S. (yăk′ĭ-mȧ)	114	46°48′N	120°22′W
Yakima Indian Reservation, I.R., Wa., U.S.	114	46°16′N	121°03′W
Yakoma, D.R.C.	236	4°05′N	22°27′E
Yaku, i., Japan (yä′ko͞o)	205	30°15′N	130°41′E
Yakutat, Ak., U.S. (yȧk′ò-tȧt)	103	59°32′N	139°35′W
Yakutsk, Russia (yȧ-kòtsk′)	179	62°13′N	129°49′E
Yale, Mi., U.S.	108	43°05′N	82°45′W
Yale, Ok., U.S.	121	36°07′N	96°42′W
Yale Lake, res., Wa., U.S.	114	46°00′N	122°20′W
Yalinga, C.A.R. (yȧ-lĭŋ′gȧ)	231	6°56′N	23°22′E
Yalobusha, r., Ms., U.S. (yȧ-lô-bòsh′ȧ)	124	33°48′N	90°02′W
Yalong, r., China (yä-lôŋ)	204	32°29′N	98°41′E
Yalta, Ukr. (yäl′tȧ)	181	44°29′N	34°12′E
Yalu, r., Asia	205	41°20′N	126°35′E
Yalutorovsk, Russia (yä-lo͞o-tô′rôfsk)	178	56°42′N	66°32′E
Yamada, Japan (yä′mȧ-dȧ)	211	33°37′N	133°39′E
Yamagata, Japan (yä-mȧ′gä-tȧ)	205	38°12′N	140°24′E
Yamaguchi, Japan (yä-mȧ′go͞o-chẻ)	210	34°10′N	131°30′E
Yamal, Poluostrov, pen., Russia (yä-mäl′)	178	71°15′N	70°00′E
Yamantau, Gora, mtn., Russia (gȧ-rä′ yä′man-tȧw)	186a	54°16′N	58°08′E
Yamasaki, Japan (yä′mȧ′sä-kẻ)	211	35°01′N	134°33′E
Yamasaki, Japan	211b	34°53′N	135°41′E
Yamashina, Japan (yä′mä-shẻ′nä)	211b	34°59′N	135°50′E
Yamashita, Japan (yä′mä-shẻ′tä)	211b	34°53′N	135°25′E
Yamato, Japan	211a	35°28′N	139°28′E
Yamato-Kōriyama, Japan	211b	34°39′N	135°48′E
Yamato-takada, Japan (yä′mä-tô tä′kä-dä)	211b	34°31′N	135°45′E
Yambi, Mesa de, mtn., Col. (mĕ′sä-dĕ-yȧ′m-bē)	142	1°55′N	71°45′W
Yambol, Blg. (yȧm′bôl)	163	42°28′N	26°31′E
Yamdena, i., Indon.	213	7°23′S	130°30′E
Yamethin, Mya. (yŭ-mē′thẻn)	199	20°14′N	96°27′E
Yamhill, Or., U.S. (yäm′hĭl)	116c	45°20′N	123°11′W
Yamkino, Russia (yäm′kĭ-nô)	186b	55°56′N	38°25′E
Yamma Yamma, Lake, l., Austl. (yäm′ȧ yäm′ȧ)	221	26°15′S	141°30′E
Yamoussoukro, C. Iv.	230	6°49′N	5°17′W
Yamsk, Russia (yämsk)	179	59°41′N	154°09′E
Yamuna, r., India	199	25°30′N	80°30′E
Yamzho Yumco, l., China (yäm-jwo yo͞om-tswo)	204	29°11′N	91°26′E
Yana, r., Russia (yä′nȧ)	179	71°00′N	136°00′E
Yanac, Austl. (yăn′ăk)	219	36°10′S	141°30′E
Yanagawa, Japan (yä-nä′gä-wä)	211	33°11′N	130°24′E
Yanam, India (yŭnŭm′)	199	16°48′N	82°15′E
Yan′an, China (yän-än)	204	36°46′N	109°15′E
Yanbu′, Sau. Ar.	198	23°57′N	38°02′E
Yancheng, China (yän-chŭŋ)	208	33°23′N	120°11′E
Yancheng, China	208	33°38′N	113°59′E
Yandongi, D.R.C.	236	2°51′N	22°16′E
Yangcheng Hu, l., China (yäŋ-chŭŋ ho͞o)	206	31°30′N	120°31′E
Yangchun, China (yäŋ-chòn)	209	22°08′N	111°48′E
Yang′erzhuang, China (yäŋ-är-jůäŋ)	206	38°18′N	117°31′E
Yanggezhuang, China (yäŋ-gŭ-jůäŋ)	208a	40°10′N	116°48′E
Yanggu, China (yäŋ-go͞o)	206	36°06′N	115°46′E
Yanghe, China (yäŋ-hŭ)	206	33°48′N	118°23′E
Yangjiang, China (yäŋ-jyäŋ)	209	21°52′N	111°58′E
Yangjiaogou, China (yäŋ-jyou-gō)	206	37°17′N	118°53′E
Yangon *see* Rangoon, Mya.	199	16°46′N	96°09′E
Yangquan, China (yäŋ-chyůän)	206	37°52′N	113°36′E
Yangtze (Chang), r., China (yäng′tse) (chäŋ)	205	30°30′N	117°25′E
Yangxin, China (yäŋ-shyĭn)	206	37°39′N	117°34′E
Yangyang, Kor., S. (yäng′yäng′)	210	38°02′N	128°38′E
Yangzhou, China (yäŋ-jō)	205	32°24′N	119°24′E
Yanji, China (yän-jyē)	205	42°55′N	129°35′E
Yanjiahe, China (yän-jyä-hŭ)	206	31°55′N	114°47′E
Yanjin, China (yän-jyĭn)	206	35°09′N	114°13′E
Yankton, S.D., U.S. (yănk′tŭn)	104	42°51′N	97°24′W
Yanling, China (yän-lĭŋ)	206	34°07′N	114°12′E
Yanshan, China (yän-shän)	208	38°05′N	117°15′E
Yanshou, China (yän-shō)	208	45°25′N	128°43′E
Yantai, China	205	37°32′N	121°22′E
Yanychi, Russia (yä′nĭ-chĭ)	186a	57°42′N	56°24′E
Yanzhou, China (yäŋ-jō)	205	35°35′N	116°50′E
Yanzhuang, China (yän-jůäŋ)	206	36°08′N	117°47′E
Yao, Chad (yä′ō)	218	13°00′N	17°38′E
Yao, Japan	211b	34°37′N	135°37′E
Yaoundé, Cam.	230	3°52′N	11°31′E
Yap, i., Micron. (yăp)	3	11°00′N	138°00′E
Yapen, Pulau, i., Indon.	213	1°30′S	136°15′E
Yaque del Norte, r., Dom. Rep. (yä′kå dĕl nôr′tå)	129	19°40′N	71°25′W
Yaque del Sur, r., Dom. Rep. (yä-kĕ-dĕl-so͞o′r)	135	18°35′N	71°05′W
Yaqui, r., Mex. (yä′kē)	128	28°15′N	109°40′W
Yaracuy, dept., Ven. (yä-rä-ko͞o′ē)	143b	10°10′N	68°31′W
Yaraka, Austl. (yȧ-răk′ȧ)	219	24°50′S	144°08′E
Yaransk, Russia (yä-ränsk′)	178	57°18′N	48°05′E
Yarda, oasis, Chad (yär′dȧ)	231	18°29′N	19°13′E
Yare, r., Eng., U.K.	165	52°40′N	1°32′E
Yarkand *see* Shache, China	204	38°15′N	77°15′E
Yarmouth, Can. (yär′mŭth)	100	43°50′N	66°07′W
Yaroslavka, Russia (yȧ-rô-släv′kȧ)	186a	55°52′N	57°59′E
Yaroslavl′, Russia (yȧ-rô-släv′′l)	178	57°37′N	39°54′E
Yaroslavl′, prov., Russia	176	58°05′N	38°05′E
Yarra, r., Austl.	217a	37°51′S	144°54′E
Yarro-to, l., Russia (yȧ′rô-tô′)	180	67°55′N	71°35′E
Yartsevo, Russia (yär′tsyẻ-vô)	180	55°04′N	32°38′E
Yartsevo, Russia	179	60°13′N	89°52′E
Yarumal, Col. (yä-ro͞o-mäl′)	142	6°57′N	75°24′W
Yasawa Group, is., Fiji	214g	17°00′S	177°23′E
Yasel′da, r., Bela. (yä-syŭl′dȧ)	169	52°13′N	25°53′E
Yateras, Cuba (yä-tā′räs)	135	20°00′N	75°00′W
Yates Center, Ks., U.S. (yāts)	121	37°53′N	95°44′W
Yathkyed, l., Can. (yȧth-kī-ĕd′)	92	62°41′N	98°00′W
Yatsuga-take, mtn., Japan (yät′so͞o-gä dä′kā)	211	36°01′N	138°21′W
Yatsushiro, Japan (yät′so͞o′shẻ-rô)	211	32°30′N	130°35′E
Yatta Plateau, plat., Kenya	237	1°55′S	38°10′E
Yautepec, Mex. (yä-ōō-tå-pĕk′)	130	18°53′N	99°04′W
Yawata, Japan (yä′wä-tä)	211	34°52′N	135°43′E
Yawatahama, Japan (yä′wä′tä′hä-mä)	211	33°24′N	132°25′E
Yaxian, China (yä shyĕn)	209	18°10′N	109°32′E
Yayama, D.R.C.	236	1°16′S	23°07′E
Yayao, China (yä-you)	207a	23°10′N	113°40′E
Yazd, Iran	198	31°59′N	54°03′E
Yazoo, r., Ms., U.S. (yă′zo͞o)	107	32°32′N	90°40′W
Yazoo City, Ms., U.S.	124	32°50′N	90°18′W
Ýdra, i., Grc.	175	37°20′N	23°30′E
Ye, Mya. (yā)	212	15°13′N	97°52′E
Yeadon, Pa., U.S. (yē′dŭn)	110f	39°56′N	75°16′W
Yecla, Spain (yā′klä)	172	38°35′N	1°09′W
Yefremov, Russia (yĕ-frä′môf)	176	53°08′N	38°04′E
Yegor′yevsk, Russia (yĕ-gôr′yĕfsk)	180	55°23′N	38°59′E
Yeji, China (yŭ-jyē)	206	31°52′N	115°57′E
Yekaterinburg, Russia	178	56°51′N	60°36′E
Yelabuga, Russia (yĕ-lä′bò-gȧ)	180	55°50′N	52°18′E
Yelan, Russia	181	50°50′N	44°00′E
Yelets, Russia (yĕ-lyĕts′)	178	52°35′N	38°28′E
Yelizavetpol′skiy, Russia (yĕ′lĭ-za-vĕt-pôl-skĭ)	186a	52°51′N	60°38′E
Yelizavety, Mys, c., Russia (yĕ-lyē-sȧ-vyĕ′tĭ)	179	54°28′N	142°59′E
Yell, i., Scot., U.K. (yĕl)	164a	60°35′N	1°27′W
Yellow *see* Huang, r., China	205	35°06′N	113°39′E
Yellow, r., Fl., U.S. (yĕl′ô)	124	30°33′N	86°53′W
Yellowhead Pass, p., Can. (yĕl′ô-hĕd)	95	52°52′N	118°35′W
Yellowknife, Can. (yĕl′ô-nīf)	90	62°29′N	114°38′W
Yellow Sea, sea, Asia	205	35°20′N	122°15′E
Yellowstone, r., U.S.	106	46°00′N	108°00′W
Yellowstone, Clarks Fork, r., U.S.	115	44°55′N	109°05′W
Yellowstone Lake, l., Wy., U.S.	106	44°27′N	110°03′W

ăt; finăl; rāte; senåte; ärm; ȧsk; sofȧ; fâre; ch-choose; dh-as th in other; bē; ẻvent; bĕt; recĕnt; cratẽr; g-gō; gh-guttural g; bĭt; ĭ-short neutral; rīde; ĸ-guttural k as ch in German ich;

PRONOUNCING INDEX

Yellowstone National Park – Zeya 369

PLACE (Pronunciation)	PAGE	LAT.	LONG.
Yellowstone National Park, rec., U.S. (yĕl'ō-stōn)	106	44°45'N	110°35'W
Yel'nya, Russia (yĕl'nyȧ)	176	54°34'N	33°12'E
Yemanzhelinsk, Russia (yĕ-mȧn-zhâ'lĭnsk)	186a	54°47'N	61°24'E
Yemen, nation, Asia (yĕm'ĕn)	198	15°00'N	47°00'E
Yemetsk, Russia	180	63°28'N	41°28'E
Yenangyaung, Mya. (yā'nän-d oung)	199	20°27'N	94°59'E
Yencheng, China	204	37°30'N	79°26'E
Yendi, Ghana (yĕn'dē)	230	9°26'N	0°01'W
Yengisar, China (yŭn-gē-sär)	204	39°01'N	75°29'E
Yenice, r., Tur.	181	41°10'N	33°00'E
Yenisey, r., Russia (yĕ-nē-sĕ'ē)	178	71°00'N	82°00'E
Yeniseysk, Russia (yĕ-nĭĕsā'ĭsk)	179	58°27'N	90°28'E
Yeo, l., Austl. (yō)	220	28°15'S	124°00'E
Yerevan, Arm. (yĕ-rĕ-vän')	181	40°10'N	44°30'E
Yerington, Nv., U.S. (yē'rĭng-tŭn)	118	38°59'N	119°10'W
Yermak, i., Russia	180	66°45'N	71°30'E
Yeste, Spain (yĕs'tā)	172	38°23'N	2°19'W
Yeu, Île d', i., Fr. (ēl dyû)	161	46°43'N	2°45'W
Yevlax, Azer.	182	40°36'N	47°09'E
Yexian, China (yŭ-shyĕn)	206	37°09'N	119°57'E
Yeya, r., Russia (yä'yȧ)	177	46°25'N	39°17'E
Yeysk, Russia (yĕysk)	181	46°41'N	38°13'E
Yi, r., China	206	34°38'N	118°07'E
Yibin, China (yē-bĭn)	204	28°50'N	104°40'E
Yichang, China (yē-chäŋ)	205	30°38'N	111°22'E
Yidu, China (yē-do͞o)	208	36°42'N	118°30'E
Yilan, China (yē-län)	205	46°10'N	129°40'E
Yinchuan, China (yĭn-chůän)	204	38°22'N	106°22'E
Yingkou, China (yĭŋ-kō)	205	40°35'N	122°10'E
Yining, China (yē-nĭŋ)	204	43°58'N	80°40'E
Yin Shan, mts., China (yĭng'shän')	208	40°50'N	110°30'E
Yishan, China (yē-shän)	204	24°32'N	108°42'E
Yishui, China (yē-shwā)	206	35°49'N	118°40'E
Yitong, China (yē-tôŋ)	205	43°15'N	125°10'E
Yixian, China (yē shyĕn)	208	41°30'N	121°15'E
Yixing, China	206	31°26'N	119°57'E
Yiyang, China (yē-yäŋ)	209	28°52'N	112°12'E
Yoakum, Tx., U.S. (yō'kŭm)	123	29°18'N	97°09'W
Yockanookany, r., Ms., U.S. (yŏk'á-no͞o-kă-nĭ)	124	32°47'N	89°38'W
Yodo-Gawa, strt., Japan (yō'dō'gä-wä)	211b	34°46'N	135°35'E
Yog Point, c., Phil. (yōg)	209	14°00'N	124°30'E
Yogyakarta, Indon. (yŏg-yá-kär'tá)	212	7°50'S	110°20'E
Yoho National Park, rec., Can. (yō'hō)	90	51°26'N	116°30'W
Yojoa, Lago de, l., Hond. (lä'gô dĕ yô-hō'ä)	132	14°49'N	87°53'W
Yokkaichi, Japan (yō'kä'ē-chē)	210	34°58'N	136°35'E
Yokohama, Japan (yō'kô-hä'mạ)	205	35°37'N	139°40'E
Yokosuka, Japan (yô-kō'sò-kä)	210	35°17'N	139°40'E
Yokota, Japan (yō-kō'tä)	211a	35°23'N	140°02'E
Yola, Nig. (yō'lä)	230	9°13'N	12°27'E
Yolaina, Cordillera de, mts., Nic.	133	11°34'N	84°34'W
Yomou, Gui.	234	7°34'N	9°16'W
Yonago, Japan (yō'nä-gō)	210	35°27'N	133°19'E
Yonezawa, Japan (yō'nĕ'zá-wä)	210	37°50'N	140°07'E
Yong'an, China (yôŋ-än)	209	26°00'N	117°22'E
Yongding, r., China (yôŋ-dĭŋ)	208	40°25'N	115°00'E
Yŏngdŏk, Kor., S. (yŭng'dŭk')	210	36°28'N	129°25'E
Yŏnghŭng, Kor., N. (yŭng'hoong')	210	39°31'N	127°11'E
Yonghŭng Man, b., Kor., N.	210	39°10'N	128°00'E
Yongnian, China (yôŋ-nĭĕn)	208	36°47'N	114°32'E
Yongqing, China (yôŋ-chyĭŋ)	208a	39°18'N	116°27'E
Yongshun, China (yôŋ-shòn)	204	29°05'N	109°58'E
Yonkers, N.Y., U.S. (yŏŋ'kĕrz)	110a	40°57'N	73°54'W
Yonne, r., Fr. (yôn)	170	48°18'N	3°15'E
Yono, Japan (yō'nō)	211a	35°53'N	139°36'E
Yorba Linda, Ca., U.S. (yôr'bă lĭn'dȧ)	117a	33°55'N	117°51'W
York, Austl.	218	32°00'S	117°00'E
York, Eng., U.K.	160	53°58'N	1°10'W
York, Al., U.S. (yôrk)	124	32°33'N	88°16'W
York, Ne., U.S.	121	40°52'N	97°36'W
York, Pa., U.S.	105	40°00'N	76°40'W
York, S.C., U.S.	125	34°59'N	81°14'W
York, Cape, c., Austl.	221	10°45'S	142°35'E
York, Kap, c., Grnld.	89	75°30'N	73°00'W
Yorke Peninsula, pen., Austl.	222	34°24'S	137°20'E
Yorketown, Austl.	222	35°00'S	137°28'E
York Factory, Can.	97	57°05'N	92°18'W
Yorkshire Wolds, Eng., U.K. (yôrk'shĭr)	164	54°00'N	0°35'W
Yorkton, Can. (yôrk'tŭn)	90	51°13'N	102°28'W
Yorktown, Tx., U.S. (yôrk'toun)	123	28°57'N	97°30'W
Yorktown, Va., U.S.	125	37°12'N	76°31'W
Yoro, Hond. (yō'rō)	132	15°09'N	87°05'W
Yoron, i., Japan	210	26°48'N	128°40'E
Yosemite National Park, rec., Ca., U.S. (yô-sĕm'ĭ-tē)	106	38°03'N	119°36'W
Yoshida, Japan (yō'shē-dȧ)	211	34°39'N	132°41'E
Yoshikawa, Japan (yō-shē'kä'wä')	211a	35°53'N	139°51'E
Yoshino, r., Japan (yō'shē-nō)	211	34°04'N	133°57'E
Yoshkar-Ola, Russia (yôsh-kär'ô-lä')	180	56°35'N	48°05'E
Yos Sudarsa, Pulau, i., Indon.	213	7°20'S	138°30'E
Yŏsu, Kor., S. (yŭ'so͞o')	210	34°42'N	127°42'W
You, r., China (yō)	209	23°55'N	106°50'E
Youghal, Ire. (yo͞o'ôl) (yôl)	165	51°58'N	7°57'E
Youghal Bay, b., Ire.	164	51°52'N	7°46'W
Young, Austl. (yŭng)	222	34°15'S	148°18'E
Young, Ur. (yô-o͞o'ng)	141c	32°42'S	57°38'W
Youngs, l., Wa., U.S. (yŭngz)	116a	47°25'N	122°08'W
Youngstown, N.Y., U.S.	111c	43°15'N	79°02'W
Youngstown, Oh., U.S.	108	41°05'N	80°40'W
Yozgat, Tur. (yôz'gȧd)	198	39°50'N	34°50'E
Ypsilanti, Mi., U.S. (ĭp-sĭ-lăn'tĭ)	111b	42°15'N	83°37'W
Yreka, Ca., U.S. (wī-rē'kȧ)	114	41°43'N	122°36'W
Yrghyz, Kaz.	183	48°30'N	61°17'E
Yrghyz, r., Kaz.	156	49°30'N	60°32'E
Ysleta, Tx., U.S. (ēz-lĕ'tȧ)	122	31°42'N	106°18'W
Yssingeaux, Fr. (ē-săN-zhō)	170	45°09'N	4°08'E
Ystad, Swe.	160	55°25'N	13°49'E
Ystādeh-ye Moqor, Āb-e, l., Afg.	202	32°35'N	68°00'E
Yu'alliq, Jabal, mts., Egypt	197a	30°12'N	33°42'E
Yuan, r., China (yůän)	205	28°50'N	110°50'E
Yuan'an, China (yůän-än)	209	31°08'N	111°28'E
Yuanling, China (yůän-lĭŋ)	209	28°30'N	110°18'E
Yuanshi, China (yůän-shr)	208	37°45'N	114°32'E
Yuasa, Japan	211	34°02'N	135°10'E
Yuba City, Ca., U.S. (yo͞o'bȧ)	118	39°08'N	121°38'W
Yucaipa, Ca., U.S. (yŭ-kȧ-ē'pȧ)	117a	34°02'N	117°02'W
Yucatán, state, Mex. (yo͞o-kä-tän')	128	20°45'N	89°00'W
Yucatan Channel, strt., N.A.	128	22°30'N	87°00'W
Yucatan Peninsula, pen., N.A.	132	19°30'N	89°00'W
Yucheng, China (yo͞o-chŭŋ)	206	34°31'N	115°54'E
Yucheng, China	208	36°55'N	116°39'E
Yuci, China (yo͞o-tsz)	208	37°32'N	112°40'E
Yudoma, r., Russia (yo͞o-dō'mȧ)	185	59°13'N	137°00'E
Yueqing, China (yůĕ-chyĭn)	209	28°02'N	120°40'E
Yueyang, China (yůĕ-yäŋ)	205	29°25'N	113°05'E
Yuezhuang, China (yůĕ-jůäŋ)	206	36°13'N	118°17'E
Yug, r., Russia (yòg)	180	59°50'N	45°55'E
Yugoslavia, nation, Eur. (yo͞o-gô-slä-vĭ-ȧ)	154	44°00'N	21°00'E
Yukhnov, Russia (yòk'nof)	176	54°44'N	35°15'E
Yukon, ter., Can. (yo͞o'kŏn)	90	63°16'N	135°30'W
Yukon, r., N.A.	106a	64°00'N	159°30'W
Yukutat Bay, b., Ak., U.S. (yo͞o-kū tăt')	103	59°34'N	140°50'W
Yuldybayevo, Russia (yòld'bä'yĕ-vô)	186a	52°20'N	57°52'E
Yulin, China (yo͞o-lĭn)	209	22°38'N	110°10'E
Yulin, China	204	38°18'N	109°45'E
Yuma, Az., U.S. (yo͞o'mä)	104	32°40'N	114°40'W
Yuma, Co., U.S.	120	40°08'N	102°50'W
Yuma, r., Dom. Rep.	135	19°05'N	70°05'W
Yumbi, D.R.C.	237	1°14'S	26°14'E
Yumen, China (yo͞o-mŭn)	204	40°14'N	96°56'E
Yuncheng, China (yòn-chŭŋ)	208	35°00'N	110°40'E
Yunnan, prov., China (yun'nän')	204	24°23'N	101°03'E
Yunnan Plat, plat., China (yò-nän)	204	26°03'N	101°26'E
Yunxian, China (yòn shyĕn)	205	32°50'N	110°55'E
Yunxiao, China (yòn-shyou)	209	24°00'N	117°20'E
Yura, Japan (yo͞o'rä)	211	34°18'N	134°54'E
Yurécuaro, Mex. (yo͞o-rā'kwä-rō)	130	20°21'N	102°16'W
Yurimaguas, Peru (yo͞o-rē-mä'gwäs)	142	5°59'S	76°12'W
Yuriria, Mex. (yo͞o'rē-rē'ä)	130	20°11'N	101°08'W
Yurovo, Russia	186b	55°30'N	38°24'E
Yur'yevets, Russia	180	57°15'N	43°08'E
Yuscarán, Hond. (yo͞os-kä-rän')	132	13°57'N	86°48'W
Yushan, China (yo͞o-shän)	209	28°42'N	118°20'E
Yü Shan, mtn., Tai.	205	23°38'N	121°05'E
Yushu, China (yo͞o-sho͞o)	208	44°58'N	126°32'E
Yutian, China (yo͞o-tĭĕn)	208	39°54'N	117°45'E
Yutian, China (yo͞o-tĭĕn) (kŭ-r-yä)	204	36°55'N	81°39'E
Yuty, Para. (yo͞o-tē')	144	26°45'S	56°13'W
Yuwangcheng, China (yü'wäng'chĕng)	206	31°32'N	114°26'E
Yuxian, China (yo͞o shyĕn)	208	39°40'N	114°38'E
Yuzha, Russia (yo͞o'zhȧ)	180	56°38'N	42°20'E
Yuzhno-Sakhalinsk, Russia (yo͞ozh'nô-sä-kä-lĭnsk')	179	47°11'N	143°04'E
Yuzhnoural'skiy, Russia (yo͞ozh-nô-ô-rál'skĭ)	186a	54°26'N	61°17'E
Yuzhnyy Ural, mts., Russia (yo͞o'zhnĭ ò-räl')	186a	52°51'N	57°48'E
Yverdon, Switz. (ē-vĕr-dôn)	168	46°46'N	6°35'E
Yvetot, Fr. (ēv-tō')	170	49°39'N	0°45'E

Z

PLACE (Pronunciation)	PAGE	LAT.	LONG.
Za, r., Mor.	162	34°19'N	2°23'W
Zaachila, Mex. (sä-ä-chē'lȧ)	131	16°56'N	96°45'W
Zaandam, Neth. (zän'dȧm)	165	52°25'N	4°49'E
Ząbkowice Śląskie, Pol.	168	50°35'N	16°48'E
Zabrze, Pol. (zäb'zhĕ)	161	50°18'N	18°48'E
Zacapa, Guat. (sä-kä'pä)	132	14°56'N	89°30'W
Zacapoaxtla, Mex. (sä-kä-pō-äs'tlä)	131	19°51'N	97°34'W
Zacatecas, Mex. (sä-kä-tā'käs)	128	22°44'N	102°32'W
Zacatecas, state, Mex.	128	24°00'N	102°45'W
Zacatecoluca, El Sal. (sä-kä-tå-kô-lo͞o'kä)	132	13°31'N	88°50'W
Zacatelco, Mex.	130	19°12'N	98°12'W
Zacatepec, Mex. (sä-kä-tå-pĕk') (sän-tē-ä'gō)	131	17°10'N	95°53'W
Zacatlán, Mex. (sä-kä-tlän')	131	19°55'N	97°57'W
Zacoalco de Torres, Mex. (sä-kô-äl'kō dā tôr'rĕs)	130	20°12'N	103°33'W
Zacualpan, Mex. (sä-kô-äl-pän')	130	18°43'N	99°46'W
Zacualtipan, Mex. (sá-kò-äl-tē-pän')	130	20°38'N	98°39'W
Zadar, Cro. (zä'där)	154	44°08'N	15°16'E
Zadonsk, Russia (zä-dônsk')	176	52°22'N	38°55'E
Žagare, Lat. (zhágarĕ)	167	56°21'N	23°14'E
Zagarolo, Italy (tzä-gä-rô'lô)	173d	41°51'N	12°53'E
Zaghouan, Tun. (zá-gwäN')	230	36°30'N	10°04'E
Zagreb, Cro. (zä'grĕb)	154	45°50'N	15°58'E
Zagros Mountains, mts., Iran	198	33°30'N	46°30'E
Zāhedān, Iran (zä'hȧ-dän)	198	29°37'N	60°31'E
Zahlah, Leb. (zä'lä')	197a	33°50'N	35°54'E
Zaire *see* Congo, Democratic Republic of the , nation, Afr.	232	1°00'S	22°15'E
Zaječar, Yugo. (zä'yĕ-chär')	175	43°54'N	22°16'E
Zakhidnyi Buh (Bug), r., Eur.	168	52°29'N	21°20'E
Zakopane, Pol. (zȧ-kô-pä'nĕ)	169	49°18'N	19°57'E
Zakouma, Parc National de, rec., Chad	235	10°50'N	19°20'E
Zákynthos, Grc.	175	37°48'N	20°55'E
Zákynthos, i., Grc.	163	37°45'N	20°32'E
Zalaegerszeg, Hung. (zŏ'lô-ĕ'gĕr-sĕg)	168	46°50'N	16°50'E
Zalău, Rom. (zȧ-lŭ'ò)	169	47°11'N	23°06'E
Zaltan, Libya	231	28°20'N	19°40'E
Zaltbommel, Neth.	159a	51°48'N	5°15'E
Zambezi, r., Afr. (zȧm-bā'zē)	232	16°00'S	29°45'E
Zambia, nation, Afr. (zăm'bē-ȧ)	232	14°23'S	24°15'E
Zamboanga, Phil. (säm-bô-aŋ'gä)	212	6°58'N	122°02'E
Zambrów, Pol. (zäm'bròf)	169	52°29'N	22°17'E
Zamora, Mex. (sä-mō'rä)	128	19°59'N	102°16'W
Zamora, Spain (thä-mō'rä)	162	41°32'N	5°43'W
Zanatepec, Mex.	131	16°30'N	94°22'W
Zandvoort, Neth.	159a	52°22'N	4°30'E
Zanesville, Oh., U.S. (zānz'vĭl)	108	39°55'N	82°00'W
Zangasso, Mali	234	12°09'N	5°37'W
Zanjān, Iran	198	36°26'N	48°24'E
Zanzibar, Tan. (zăn'zĭ-bär)	233	6°10'S	39°11'E
Zanzibar, i., Tan.	233	6°20'S	39°37'E
Zanzibar Channel, strt., Tan.	237	6°05'S	39°00'E
Zaozhuang, China (dzou-jůäŋ)	206	34°51'N	117°34'E
Zapadnaya Dvina *see* Western Dvina, r., Eur.	167	55°30'N	28°27'E
Zapala, Arg. (zä-pä'lä)	144	38°53'S	70°02'W
Zapata, Tx., U.S. (sä-pä'tä)	122	26°52'N	99°18'W
Zapata, Ciénaga de, sw., Cuba (syĕ'nä-gä-dĕ-zä-pá'tä)	134	22°30'N	81°20'W
Zapata, Península de, pen., Cuba (pĕ-nĕ'n-so͞o-lä-dĕ-zä-pá'tä)	134	22°20'N	81°30'W
Zapatera, Isla, i., Nic. (ē's-lä-sä-pä-tā'rō)	132	11°45'N	85°45'W
Zapopan, Mex. (sä-pō'pän)	130	20°42'N	103°23'W
Zaporizhzhia, Ukr.	178	47°50'N	35°10'E
Zaporizhzhia, prov., Ukr.	177	47°20'N	35°05'E
Zaporoshskoye, Russia (zȧ-pô-rôsh'skô-yĕ)	167	60°36'N	30°31'E
Zapotiltic, Mex. (sä-pô-tēl-tēk')	130	19°37'N	103°25'W
Zapotitlán, Mex. (sä-pô-tē-tlän')	130	17°13'N	98°58'W
Zapotitlán, Punta, c., Mex.	131	18°34'N	94°48'W
Zapotlanejo, Mex. (sä-pô-tlä-nā'hô)	130	20°38'N	103°05'W
Zaragoza, Mex. (sä-rä-gō'sä)	130	23°59'N	99°45'W
Zaragoza, Mex.	130	22°02'N	100°45'W
Zaragoza, Spain (thä-rä-gō'thä)	154	41°39'N	0°53'W
Zarand, Munţii, mts., Rom.	169	46°07'N	22°21'E
Zaranda Hill, mtn., Nig.	235	10°15'N	9°35'E
Zaranj, Afg.	201	31°06'N	61°53'E
Zarasai, Lith. (zä-rä-sī')	167	55°45'N	26°18'E
Zárate, Arg. (zä-rä'tā)	144	34°05'S	59°05'W
Zaraysk, Russia (zä-rä'ĕsk)	180	54°46'N	38°53'E
Zaria, Nig. (zä'rē-ä)	230	11°07'N	7°44'E
Zarqā', r., Jord.	197a	32°13'N	35°43'E
Zarzal, Col. (zär-zá'l)	142a	4°23'N	76°04'W
Zashiversk, Russia (zá'shĭ-vĕrsk')	179	67°08'N	144°02'E
Zastavna, Ukr. (zás-täf'nȧ)	169	48°32'N	25°50'E
Zastron, S. Afr. (zás'trŭn)	233c	30°19'S	27°07'E
Žatec, Czech Rep. (zhä'tĕts)	168	50°19'N	13°32'E
Zavitinsk, Russia	185	50°12'N	129°44'E
Zawiercie, Pol. (zȧ-vyĕr'tsyĕ)	169	50°28'N	19°25'E
Zāwiyat al-Baydā', Libya	231	32°49'N	21°46'E
Zāyandeh, r., Iran	198	32°15'N	51°00'E
Zaysan, Kaz. (zī'sȧn)	183	47°43'N	84°44'E
Zaza, r., Cuba (zá'zá)	134	21°40'N	79°25'W
Zbarazh, Ukr. (zbä-räzh')	169	49°39'N	25°48'E
Zbruch, r., Ukr. (zbròch)	169	48°56'N	26°18'E
Zdolbuniv, Ukr.	169	50°31'N	26°17'E
Zduńska Wola, Pol. (zdo͞on''skä vō'lä)	169	51°36'N	18°27'E
Zebediela, S. Afr.	238c	24°19'S	29°21'E
Zeeland, Mi., U.S. (zē'lănd)	108	42°50'N	86°00'W
Zefat, Isr.	197a	32°58'N	35°30'E
Zehdenick, Ger. (tsā'dē-nēk)	168	52°59'N	13°20'E
Zehlendorf, Ger. (tsā'lĕn-dôrf)	159b	52°47'N	13°23'E
Zeist, Neth.	159a	52°05'N	5°14'E
Zelenogorsk, Russia (zĕ-lă'nô-gôrsk)	167	60°13'N	29°39'E
Zella-Mehlis, Ger. (tsål'á-mā'lēs)	168	50°40'N	10°38'E
Zémio, C.A.R. (za-myō')	231	5°03'N	25°11'E
Zemlya Frantsa-Iosifa (Franz Josef Land), is., Russia	178	81°32'N	40°00'E
Zempoala, Punta, c., Mex. (po͞o'n-tä-sĕm-pô-ä'lä)	131	19°30'N	96°18'W
Zempoatlépetl, mtn., Mex. (sĕm-pô-ä-tlā'pĕt'l)	131	17°13'N	95°59'W
Zemun, Yugo. (zĕ'mo͞on) (sĕm'lĭn)	163	44°50'N	20°25'E
Zengcheng, China (dzŭŋ-chŭŋ)	207a	23°18'N	113°49'E
Zenica, Bos. (zĕ'nēt-sä)	175	44°10'N	17°54'E
Zeni-Su, is., Japan (zĕ'nē so͞o)	211	33°55'N	138°55'E
Žepče, Bos. (zhĕp'chĕ)	177	44°26'N	18°01'E
Zepernick, Ger. (tsĕ'pĕr-nēk)	159b	52°39'N	13°32'E
Zerbst, Ger. (tsĕrbst)	168	51°58'N	12°03'E
Zerpenschleuse, Ger. (tsĕr'pĕn-shloi-zē)	159b	52°51'N	13°30'E
Zeuthen, Ger. (tsoi'tĕn)	159b	52°21'N	13°38'E
Zevenaar, Neth.	171c	51°56'N	6°06'E
Zevenbergen, Neth.	159a	51°38'N	4°36'E
Zeya, Russia (zâ'yȧ)	179	53°43'N	127°29'E

ng-sing; ŋ-baŋk; N-nasalized n; nŏd; cŏmmit; ōld; ôbey; ôrder; oi-boil; fo͞od; ò-as oo in foot; ou-out; s-soft; sh-dish; th-thin; pūre; ůnite; ûrn; stŭd; circŭs; ü-as in French tu; '-indeterminate vowel.

SUBJECT INDEX

Listed below are major topics covered by the thematic maps, graphs and/or statistics.
Page citations are for world, continent and country maps and for world tables.

SOURCES

The sources listed below have been consulted during the process of creating and updating the thematic maps and statistics for the 20th Edition.

AAMA Motor Vehicle Facts and Figures, American Automobile Manufacturers Association

Agricultural Atlas of the United States, U.S. Dept. of Commerce, Bureau of the Census

Agricultural Statistics, U.S. Dept. of Agriculture

Anuario Estatistico do Brasil, Fundacao Instituto Brasileiro de Geografia e Estatistica

Atlas of African Agriculture, United Nations, Food and Agriculture Organization

Atlas of India, TT Maps and Publications, Government of India

Atlas of the Middle East, U.S. Dept. of State, Central Intelligence Agency

Canada Year Book, Statistics Canada, Minister of Industry, Science and Technology

Census of Agriculture, U.S. Dept. of Commerce, Bureau of the Census

Census of Canada, Statistics Canada, Minister of Supplies and Services

Census of Population Characteristics: United States, U.S. Dept. of Commerce, Economics and Statistics Administration

Census of Population, U.S. Dept. of Commerce, Bureau of the Census

China Statistical Yearbook, State Statistical Bureau of the People's Republic of China

City and County Data Book, U.S. Dept. of Commerce, Bureau of the Census

Coal Production, U.S. Dept. of Energy, Energy Information Administration

Compendium of Social Statistics and Indicators, United Nations, Department of International Economic and Social Affairs

Contemporary Conflicts, Canadian Forces College Information Resource Centre, Dept. of National Defence

The Defense Monitor, Center for Defense Information

Demographic Yearbook, United Nations, Department of International Economic and Social Affairs

Earthquakes and Volcanoes, U.S. Dept. of the Interior, U.S. Geological Survey

Ecoregions of the Continents, U.S. Dept. of the Agriculture, Forest Service

Energy Information Administration Country Analysis Briefs, U.S. Dept. of Energy, Energy Information Administration

Energy Map of Central Asia, The Petroleum Economist, Ltd.

Energy Map of the World, The Petroleum Economist, Ltd.

Energy Statistics Yearbook (UN), United Nations, Department of International Economic and Social Affairs

Estimated Use of Water in the United States, U.S. Dept of the Interior, U.S. Geological Survey

FAA Statistical Handbook of Aviation, U.S. Dept. of Transportation, Federal Aviation Administration

FAO Atlas of the Living Resources of the Seas, United Nations, Food and Agriculture Organization

FAO Production Yearbook, United Nations, Food and Agriculture Organization

FAO Trade Yearbook, United Nations, Food and Agriculture Organization

FAOSTAT, United Nations, Food and Agriculture Organization

FAS Online, U.S. Dept. of Agriculture, Foreign Agriculture Service

Fiber Organon World Man-made Fiber Survey, Fiber Economics Bureau, Inc.

Geothermal Energy Worldwide, Geothermal Education Office

Global Volcanism Program, Smithsonian Institution, National Museum of Natural History

A Guide to Your National Forests, U.S. Dept. of Agriculture, Forest Service

Handbook of International Economic Statistics, U.S. Dept. of State, Central Intelligence Agency

Handbook of International Trade and Development Statistics, United Nations, Conference on Trade and Development

ILO Yearbook of Labour Statistics, International Labour Organisation

International Data Base, U.S. Dept. of Commerce, Bureau of the Census

International Energy Annual, U.S. Dept. of Energy, Energy Information Administration

International Petroleum Encyclopedia, PennWell Publishing Co.

International Trade Statistics Yearbook, United Nations, Dept. of Economic and Social Development

International Water Power and Dam Construction Handbook, Reed Business Publishing Ltd.

IUCN Red List of Threatened Animals, World Conservation Union / World Conservation Monitoring Centre

Maritime Transport, Organization for Economic and Social Co-operation and Development

Merchant Fleets of the World, United States Maritime Administration, Office of Trade Analysis and Insurance

Mineral Industries of Africa and Middle East, U.S. Dept of the Interior, U.S. Geological Survey

Mineral Industries of Latin America and Canada, U.S. Dept of the Interior, U.S. Geological Survey

Mineral Industries of the Asia and the Pacific, U.S. Dept of the Interior, U.S. Geological Survey

Mineral Industry Surveys, U.S. Dept of the Interior, U.S. Geological Survey

Minerals Yearbook, U.S. Dept of the Interior, U.S. Geological Survey

Monthly Bulletin of Statistics, United Nations, Dept. of Economic and Social Development

National Atlas - Canada, Dept. of Energy, Mines, and Resources

National Atlas - Chile, Instituto Geografico Militar

National Atlas - China, Cartographic Publishing House

National Atlas - Japan, Geographical Survey Institute

National Atlas - United States, U.S. Dept of the Interior, U.S. Geological Survey

National Priorities List, U.S. Environmental Protection Agency

Natural Gas Annual, U.S. Dept. of Energy, Energy Information Administration

Nuclear Power Reactors in the World, International Atomic Energy Agency

Oxford Economic Atlas of the World, Oxford University Press

Petroleum Supply Annual, U.S. Dept. of Energy, Energy Information Administration

Population and Dwelling Counts: A National Overview, Minister of Industry, Science and Technology, Statistics Canada

Population and Vital Statistics Reports, United Nations, Dept. for Economic and Social Information and Policy Analysis

Populations of Concern to UNHCR, United Nations, United Nations High Commissioner for Refugees (UNHCR)

Post-Soviet Geography, V.H. Winston and Son, Inc.

Public Land Surveys, U.S. Dept of the Interior, U.S. Geological Survey

Rail in Canada, Statistics Canada, Transport Division, Surface and Marine Transport Section

Rand McNally Road Atlas, Rand McNally

Rubber Statistical Bulletin, International Rubber Study Group

Significant Earthquake Database, National Oceanic and Atmospheric Administration, National Geophysical Data Center

Statistical Abstract of India, Central Statistical Organisation

Statistical Abstract of the United States, U.S. Dept. of Commerce, Bureau of the Census

Statistical Pocket-Book of Yugoslavia, Federal Statistical Office

Statistical Yearbook, United Nations, Department of International Economic and Social Affairs

Statistical Yearbook, United Nations, Educational, Scientific and Cultural Organization (UNESCO)

Status of Armed Conflicts, International Institute for Strategic Studies

Sugar Yearbook, International Sugar Organization

Survey of Energy Resources, World Energy Council

United Nations List of Protected Areas, World Conservation Monitoring Centre

Uranium Resources, Production and Demand, United Nations, Organization for Economic Co-operation and Development

This Dynamic Planet: World Map of Volcanoes, Earthquakes and Plate Tectonics, Smithsonian Institution / U.S. Geological Survey

Volcanoes of the World, Geoscience Press

WHO Estimates of Health Personnel, United Nations, World Health Organization

World Atlas of Agriculture, Instituto Geografico De Agostini

World Atlas of Geology and Mineral Deposits, Mining Journal Books, Ltd.

The World's Busiest Airport, Airports Council International

World Coal Resources and Major Trade Routes, Miller Freeman Publications, Inc.

World Conflict List, National Defense Council Foundation

World Development Report, World Bank

World Directory of Manufactured Fiber Producers, Fiber Economics Bureau, Inc.

World Factbook, U.S. Dept. of State, Central Intelligence Agency

World Gas Map, The Petroleum Economist, Ltd.

World Mineral Statistics, British Geological Survey

World Oil International Outlook, Gulf Publishing Company

World Population Profile, U.S. Dept. of Commerce, Bureau of the Census

World Population Prospects, United Nations, Department of International Economic and Social Affairs

World Transport Statistics, International Road Transport Union, Dept. of Economic Affairs

World Urbanization Prospects, United Nations, Department of International Economic and Social Affairs

Year Book Australia, Australian Bureau of Statistics